Walford's Guide to Reference Material

WALFORD'S GUIDE TO REFERENCE MATERIAL

SIXTH EDITION • VOLUME 2

Social and Historical Sciences, Philosophy and Religion

EDITED BY

ALAN DAY

MA, MPhil, PhD, DipLib FRGS, FLA

and

JOAN M. HARVEY

MA, FLA

LIBRARY ASSOCIATION PUBLISHING
LONDON

Published by
Library Association Publishing Ltd
7 Ridgmount Street
London WC1E 7AE

First published 1959
Supplement 1963
Second edition 1968
Third edition 1975
Fourth edition 1982
Fifth edition 1990
This sixth revised edition 1994

British Library Cataloguing in Publication Data
A catalogue record for this book is available from The
British Library

ISBN 1-85604-044-5

Computer production software and typesetting by LIBPAC
(Computer Services) Ltd, Whittle le Woods, Lancs.
Printed and made in Great Britain by Bookcraft (Bath) Ltd.

Contents

Introduction

From its first edition the purpose of *Walford* has been to identify and evaluate the widest possible range of reference materials. In addition to the expected bibliographies, indexes, dictionaries, encyclopedias, directories, etc., a number of important textbooks and manuals of general practice are included. While the majority of items are reference 'books', *Walford* is a guide to reference 'material'. Thus periodical articles, microforms, online and CD-ROM sources are all represented and there is an index of online and database services. The objective is for *Walford* to become a 'one-stop' source of information on all types of reference material, regardless of form. Targeted users include librarians developing and revising reference collections, staff on enquiry desks needing advice on further sources when local stock has been checked, research workers in the preliminary stages of projects, and students of library and information studies.

To be of manageable proportions a guide such as this must inevitably be selective. Most major reference tools are included, whenever originally published, provided they remain useful. Geographic scope is international, but with an emphasis on English-language material. A special effort has been made to ensure that the output of small and specialist publishers is not neglected.

Entries in *Walford* follow a subject arrangement based on the Universal Decimal Classification International Medium Edition of 1985 (BS1000M). Subject access for users unfamiliar with UDC can be gained either by checking the contents page to find the relevant section and then browsing through the entries, which are subdivided by form, place etc., or by using the subject index. The first level of subheading within each broad subject class is typographically highlighted by the use of rules (see sample entry overleaf).

Terms in the subject index are generated by the classification numbers given to the entries. Each entry has been allocated a running serial number in the text to provide easy access from both the subject and author/title indexes. Full instruction on the structure and use of the indexes can be found in their introductions.

Individual entries in *Walford* are nearly always based on examination of the actual item and include full bibliographical detail, ISBN and, if in print, the price when it can be ascertained. Brief critical annotations are provided in most cases, giving summary publishing history, outline of contents, comparison with other works, especially notable features and a brief general assessment of overall value, often illustrated by quotations from or references to reviews. The example below shows the general layout of entries.

912 Maps & Atlases

Broad subject class

First level subheading

World Atlases

Running number used for index reference

[5495]

The Times atlas of the world. Comprehensive ed. 9th ed. London, Times books, 1992. xlvii,122 double + 1 single plates, 237p. illus., col. maps, diagrs., index. ISBN: 0723004927.

Comprehensive edition first published 1967. Preceded by *The Times atlas* (1895); *The Times survey atlas of the world* (2v., 1920-22); and *The Times atlas of the world* (Mid-century ed. 5v., 1955-59). Foreign language editions: 1. München, Droemersche Verlagsantalt, *Knaurs Grosser Weltatlas*(German) - 2. Ede, Kluwer Algemene Boeken, *De Grote Times Wereldatlas* (Dutch) - 3. Paris, Sélection du Readers Digest, *L'Atlas Universel* (French).

Full publishing history

Foreign language editions

123 plates of maps (nearly all double page spread) include 8 thematic maps *e.g.* 'World climatology and food potential; and 'World mankind', the rest physico - political printed in 8 colours. Various scales: most European countries at scales ranging from 1:500,000 to 1:250,000; most cities and islands inset maps are at 1:250,000. 15 different styles of Times Roman lettering ensures high standards of legibility. Spelling of place names corresponds to the principles and practices of the British Permanent Committee on Geographical names. English conventional names of important places added where space permits. Chinese names in Pinyin style. Preliminaries include 'States and Territories of the World' Geographical comparisons (areas of continents, oceans and seas *etc.*); Star charts; Solar system; Space flight, map projection. Glossary and abbreviations p.1-3. Index-gazetteer *c.*210,000 place names. Includes the new states formed from USSR and Yugoslavia. Map detail updated includes over 2000 name revisions. Maps prepared by John Bartholomew & Son, Edinburgh. 'It will stand for many years to come as one of the leading cartographic sources of reference for the major topographic, social and economic features of our planet in the mid-1980's' (*New Scientist*, 2 January 1986, p.46).
Class No: 912.01

Explanatory detail of contents

Updated information

Authoritative comment from review

Subject arrangement by UDC

Source of review

[5496]

The Times atlas of the world. Family edition. 2nd ed. London, Times Books; 1992. 68+156p. maps, tables, index. £17. ISBN: 0723004900, UK.

Introductory section includes states and territories of the world (col. flag, area, population, capital, currency *etc.*), physical maps, solar system, earthquakes and volcanoes, annual rainfall, population and geographic dictionary (p.94-9). Index of 30,000 entries. New nations of Croatia and Slovenia included but not Bosnia. For home, school and office use. 'Excellent value, although obviously less comprehensive than the main edition' (*Good Book Guide*, no.44, September/October 1989, p.18). *Class No:* 912.01

Secondary entry

Work on this volume was completed in early 1994. Although no cut-off date for new material was specified, the aim has been to include as many 1993 publications as possible, together with some items published early in 1994. Intimation of planned new and revised editions is also given where possible.

Something in the region of 500 new entries have been added to the first half of this volume, mainly in the sections on Economics and Business & Management. Other entries have been updated as necessary and some considered to be out-of-date or superseded by newer titles have been deleted. However, several indexing or abstracting services which have recently ceased publication have been retained in this edition for retrospective searching.

Approximately 800 new entries have been included in the Historical Sciences section and over 500 have been updated. A thorough revision of the 930.25 Archive section has been effected with the result that almost all publications relating to archives, with very few considered exceptions, are now to be found there. Major world events and anniversaries reflected in this edition include the breakup of the communist regimes in Eastern Europe and the former Soviet Union, the quincentenary of Columbus' voyages of discovery in 1492, and the fiftieth anniversary of D-Day, 6th June 1944.

This volume is the work of two compilers: Alan Day was responsible for Class 9. Joan Harvey was responsible for Classes 1, 2, 3 and 65. The whole project was overseen by Kathryn Beecroft of Library Association Publishing. Joan Bibby ably constructed a thesaurus based on the UDC classification scheme. Martin Harrison of LIBPAC Computer Services automated the data capture, indexing and typesetting.

The compilers are indebted to John Walford for his continuing interest in this work and his contributions in the form of advice and notes on new material.

Libraries consulted
(a) *General libraries*
The British Library (British Library Information Sciences Service; Document Supply Centre; Humanities & Social Sciences; India Office Library; The Map Library; Oriental Collections; Official Publications and Social Sciences Service; Science Reference and Information Service (Business Information Service).

(b) *Academic libraries*
Cambridge; Leeds; London (Institute of Classical Studies; Institute of Commonwealth Studies; Institute of Historical Research; School of Oriental and African Studies; School of Slavonic Studies; University of London Library (Senate House); British Library of Political and Economic Science; Institute of Advanced Legal Studies; Institute of Education; Heythrop College; University College London (Institute of Archaeology); Manchester Metropolitan University; John Rylands, University of Manchester; Southampton University; University of Queensland.

(c) *Public libraries*
Auckland; Birmingham; Brisbane (Indooroopilly); City of London (Bishopsgate Library;

Guildhall; City Business Library); Clwyd (Colwyn Bay); Edinburgh; Hampshire (Portsmouth); Kent (Maidstone); Lancashire (Preston); Leeds; Liverpool; Manchester; North Conway (New Hampshire); Queensland State; Sefton (Southport); Stockport; Trafford; Warwickshire (Stratford-upon-Avon); Westminster; West Sussex (Chichester; Worthing); Whistler (British Columbia).

(d) *Special libraries*

Australia House; Canada House; Central Statistical Office; Department of Education; Department of Health; Department of Trade and Industry (Export Market Information Centre); Institute of International Affairs; Imperial War Museum; National Register of Archives; Royal Commonwealth Society; Office of Population Censuses and Surveys; Royal Geographical Society; Society of Genealogists

Abbreviations

Listed below are the chief bibliographical abbreviations used in the *Guide*. Generally accepted abbreviations such as Co., Corpn. *e.g.*, *i.e.*, Inc., Ltd. and *q.v.* are not included.

AG [German] – Aktiengesellschaft: Co.
ALA – American Library Association
Abt. [German] – Abteiling: part
ampl. [Italian] – ampliata: enlarged
    [Spanish] – ampliado: enlarged
Aufl. [German] – Auflage: edition
augm. [French] – augmenté: enlarged
aum. [Portuguese] – aumentada: enlarged
    [Spanish] – aumentado: enlarged
Ausg. [German] – Ausgabe: printing, edition

BS – British Standard
Bd [German] – Band: volume
BFr – Belgian francs
bearb. [German] – bearbeitet: compiled, edited
Belg. – Belgian

c – copyright date
C. Cd. Cmd. Cmnd. – Command papers
ch. – chapter(s)
chron. – chronology
col. – colour, coloured
cols. – columns
comp. – compiler
corr. – corrected
    [French] – corrigé: corrected
    [Spanish] – corregido: corrected
    [Portuguese] – corrigida: corrected

DFI – Dutch florins
Dan. – Danish
diagrs. – diagrams
distr. – distributed
DM [German] – Deutsche Mark
druk [Dutch] – edition

ea. – each

ed. – edition, editor(s)
    [Italian] – edizione
    [Spanish] – edición
    [French] – édition
    [Portuguese] – ediçáo: edition
enl. – enlarged
erw., erweit. [German] – erweiterte: enlarged
exp. – expanded

FID – Fédération Internationale de Documentation
facsim(s) – facsimile(s)
fasc(s) – fascicule(s)
fig. – figures
fldg. – folding
FFr – French francs
front. – frontispiece

ganz. [German] – gänzlich: complete
glav.red. [Russian] – glavnyi redaktor: editor-in-chief
Gld. [Dutch] – guilders
GmbH [German] – Gesellschaft mit beschränkter Haftung: Ltd
Gosud. [Russian] – Gosudarstvo: State

HMSO – Her Majesty's Stationery Office
Hft [German] – Heft: part number
hrsg. [German] – herausgegeben: edited, published

illus. – illustrations, illustrated
imp. [French] – imprimé, imprimerie: printed, printing firm
izd. [Russian] – izdanie: edition
    [Serbo-Croat] – izdanje: edition
Izdat. [Russian] – Izdatel': publisher

Jahrg. [German] – Jahrgang: annual publication

kiad. [Hungarian] – kiadás: edition
Kr [Danish, Norwegian, Swedish] – kroner

L. [Italian] – lire
l. – leaves
Lfg. [German] – Lieferung: number, part

m. fl. [Danish] – med flere: and others

n.d. – no date
neubearb. [German]: – neubearbeitet: revised
no. – number
Nor. – Norwegian
nouv. [French] – nouvelle: new (edition)
n.p. – no place of publication
Nr [Danish, German] – Nummer: number
n.s. – new series
NV [Dutch] – naamloze vennootschap: limited
   company

o.p. – out of print
omarb. [Swedish] – omarbetad: revised
opl. [Danish] – oplag: edition

p. – page(s)
pl. – plate(s)
port. – portrait(s)
pt(s) – part(s)
pub. – publisher
pubn. – publication

réd. [French] – rédigé: edited, compiled
repr. – reprinted
rev. – revised, revision
   [French] – révisé: revised
   [Portuguese] – revistada: revised

riv. [Italian] – riveduto: revised
R. [South Africa] – rands
Rs – rupees

Sch – Schillings
ser. – series
sér. [French] – série: series
SFr – Swiss francs
supp. – supplementary, supplement(s)
Sw. – Swiss
Swed. – Swedish

t. [French] – tome(s): volume(s)
T. [German] – Teil(e): part(s)

u. [German] – und: and
UDC – Universal Decimal Classification
udg. [Danish] – udgave: edition
uit. [Dutch] – uitgaaf: publication
uitg. [Dutch] – uitgegeven: published
umgearb. [German] – umbearbeitete: revised
Univ. – University
unveränd. [German] – unverändert: unaltered
uppl. [Swedish] – upplaga: edition
utg. [Norwegian] – utgave: edition

v. – volume(s)
v. p. – various pagings
VEB [German] – Volkseigener Betrieb: People's
   Concern
verand. [German] – verandert: revised
verb. [German] – verbesserte: improved
verm [German] – vermehrte: enlarged
vyd. [Czech] – vydání: edition
   [Slovak] – vydanie: edition

wyd. [Polish] – wydanie: edition

1 Philosophy & Psychology

Philosophy

[1]

SPARKES, A.W. **Talking philosophy: a wordbook.** London, Routledge, 1991. [v],307p. £40. ISBN: 0415042224.

Attempts to give an account of the more important components of the vocabulary of philosophy in 10 chapters: 1. Saying things - 2. Meaning - 3. Nonsense, necessity, and possibility - 4. Inferring, implying, arguing, and 'if' - 5. Investigating - 6. Symbols: basic propositional forms; basic argumental forms - 7. of isms, ists, and ologies - 8. Arguing and investigating again - 9. Doing - 10. Relations. Notes (p.262-3). Bibliography (p.264-291). Index (p.292-307). 'A wonderful book to read' (*Choice,* v.28(10), June 1991, p.1624). *Class No:* 101

Bibliographies of Bibliographies

[2]

A Bibliography of philosophical bibliographies, edited and compiled by H. Guerry. Westport, Conn. & London, Greenwood Press, 1977. xiii, [1], 332p. $46.95; £45. ISBN: 083719542x.

2,353 numbered entries, covering the period *c.*1450-1974. Two main sections: 1. Bibliographies of individual philosophers (1-1395); 2. Subject bibliographies (subjects, A-Z; items 1396-2353). Some entries have brief annotations. 'J.J. Rousseau': entries 1120-35, including articles. 'Logic': entries 1994-2025. Author index. Interprets the scope of philosophy in a wide sense. *Class No:* 101(009)

Bibliographies

[3]

BAXTER, P.M. **Psychology:** a guide to reference and information sources. Littleton, Col.,Libraries Unlimited, 1993. 219p. $36.50. (*(Reference sources in the social sciences).)* ISBN: 0872877086.

In 4 parts: part 1 lists general social science reference sources; pt 2 'Social science disciplines', covers materials relative to psychology; pt 3 has general psychology reference sources (guides, bibliographies, indexing and abstracting tools, online databases, handbooks and yearbooks, dictionaries and encyclopedias, biographies, journals, organizations, publishers, and directories); and pt 4, with well over half the entries, is divided among 24 subtopics (history, theory, test construction, intelligence, personality, etc.). Entries are annotated. Author, title and subject indexes. *Class No:* 101(01)

[4]

Bibliographie de la philosophie/Bibliography of philosophy. Paris, Librairie Philosophique, 1937-. Quarterly. $131; F 570. ISSN: 00061352.

Published by Institut International de Philosophie with the aid of Unesco.

Each issue has *c.*250 entries for books, arranged in 10 subject sections (1. Philosophy in general. Metaphysics. Phenomenology - 2. Logic. Semantics. Philosophy of science - 3. Philosophical psychology - 4. Philosophy of art. Aesthetics - 5. Ethics. Philosophy of values - 6. Social philosophy, Philosophy of law and politics - 7. Philosophy of history, of culture, of education - 8. Philosophy of religion - 9. History of philosophy - 10. Annuals. Reference books, Miscellanea. Annotations in language of the original for books in English, French, German, Italian and Spanish; in English or French for books in other languages. Annual indexes of books, names, and publishers. *Class No:* 101(01)

[5]

Bibliographie Philosophie. Berlin, Zentralstelle für philosophische Information und Dokumentation, Institute für Marxistisch-leninistische Philosophie, 1967-87. v.1-21. Quarterly.

Jg.21(1) has 673 references in classified order. Author and subject indexes per issue. East German origin. *Class No:* 101(01)

[6]

BYNAGLE, H.E. **Philosophy,** a guide to the reference literature. Littleton, Col., Libraries Unlimited, 1986. x, 170p. $35. ISBN: 0872874648.

An annotated listing of general and specialized, mainly English-language, reference works in philosophy and related areas. Arranged in 14 numbered sections by type of reference work (indexing, abstracting and reviewing publications; directories and biographical sources; concordances; indexes; works of individual philosophers; computer databases), with general sources preceding specialized works. Author/title and subject indexes. '... detailed and judicious guide ...' (*Bulletin of the ABTPL,* no. 40, November 1987, p.2). DeGeorge's *'The philosophers' guide'* Lawrence, Kans, Regents Press of Kansas, 1980 (qv), is more comprehensive but less up-to-date. *Class No:* 101(01)

[7]

D'ANGELO, E. **Developing a basic philosophy collection** - for reference and research. In *The Reference librarian,*v.40, 1993, p.169-188.

Recommendations for philosophy collections. In 6 sections: 1. General bibliographies - 2. Bibliographies of fields, schools or traditions - 3. Bibliographies of writings by and about philosophers - 4. Indexes and abstracts - 5. Journals for reviews - 6. General review media. Most entries have short annotations. *Class No:* 101(01)

[8]
DEGEORGE, R.T. A Guide to philosophical bibliography and research. New York, Appleton-Century-Crofts: Meredith Corporation, 1971. vii,141p.

About 1500 entries, briefly annotated, for sources, bibliographies and other reference tools, both general and special. 9 sections: 1. Dictionaries - 2. Encyclopedias - 3. Histories of philosophy - 4. Sources: bibliographies, standard editions and collected works of individual philosophers - 5. Bibliographies - 6. Library catalogues, trade bibliographies and American doctoral dissertations - 7. Philosophical serials - 8. Philosophical research, reports and publishing - 9. Biographies - 10. Philosophical professional life. Detailed subject, author and anonymous title index. Graduate and research level. *Class No:* 101(01)

[9]
—**DEGEORGE, R.T. The Philosopher's guide to sources, research tools, professional life, and related fields.** Lawrence, Kans., Regents Press of Kansas, 1980. 242p.

A 10-year supplement to the above. About 1600 annotated entries, plus 400 citations to reference works in other disciplines. 4 parts: general histories and reference works; sources for the history of philosophy; divisions of the field, movements and national/regional trends; serials, publishing, and professional trends. 40p. index. 'Superb' (*RQ*, Winter 1980, p.214, on which this annotation is based). *Class No:* 101(01)

[10]
LUCAS, G.R. The Genesis of modern process thought: historical outline, with bibliography. Metuchen, N.J., Scarecrow Press, 1983. 245p. $18.50, £16.50. (*ATLA bibliography series, 7.*) ISBN: 0810815893.

Essays precede annotated lists of articles and monographs. Arranged in 6 sections: Process rationalism - The Whiteheadian School - Evolutionary cosmology - Hegelian idealism - Pragmatism and realism - Bridge movements (personalism and English Hegelianism) - Concluding comments: The 'Heuristic Fallacy' in process metaphysics. Each section is subdivided by sub-topics. Bibliography of sources. Author index. '... balanced and much-needed volume ...' (*Choice*, October 1983. p.253). *Class No:* 101(01)

[11]
Philosophical books. 1960- Quarterly. Ellis, A., *ed.* Oxford, Basil Blackwell (previously Leicester University Press), 1960-. Institutions: £51. $107. Individuals: £22. $43 pa. ISSN: 00318051.

Aims to provide prompt scholarly reviews to assist both the librarian and individuals in the choice of professional works of philosophy, with both short one-page reviews to lengthy critical notices and regular subject surveys. Arranged in subject sections, including History of philosophy, General philosophy, Metaphysics, Philosophy of mind, Ethics, Philosophy of religion, Aesthetics, Philosophy of science, Political philosophy, Philosophy of social science, and Legal philosophy, preceded by sections of new journals and critical notices. *Class No:* 101(01)

[12]
—**The Philosophical quarterly.** Fife, University of St. Andrews, for the Scots Philosophical Club, 1950-. £33pa. ISSN: 00318094.

Each issue carries several articles and a number of lengthy book reviews of 1-2 pages. Also lists books received. *Class No:* 101(01)

[13]
—**Philosophischer Literaturanzeiger.** Meisenheim, Hein (previously Munich, Reinhardt), 1945/50-. Quarterly (previously 8pa). DM85pa. ISSN: 00318175.

A reviewing journal on an international scale, reviewing *c.*100 items pa and listing others. Author index. *Class No:* 101(01)

[14]
Répertoire bibliographique de la philosophie. Louvain, Editions de l'Institut Supérieur de Philosophie (de l'Université Catholique de Louvain), 1949-. v.1-. Quarterly. F.1750pa. ISSN: 00344567.

Over 10,000 references a year. Issues 1-3 cover books and periodical articles; issue 4 includes list of review articles and a general index of names. Arranged in subject sections. Claims to have complete coverage of monographs in Western languages. *Class No:* 101(01)

[15]
TICE, T.N. *and* **SLAVENS, T.P. Research guide to philosophy.** Chicago, American Library Association, 1983. xii, 608p. $40. £39.95. (*Sources of information in the humanities, no.3.*) ISBN: 0838903339.

In 3 parts: a historical survey (p.3-301): 17 areas of philosophy p.305-500; reference works, classified, annotated (p.503-519). Author/title and subject indexes (p.517-608). 'An excellent work; the best in the field. It does not exactly replace R.T. DeGeorge's *The philosophers' guide* but it will be of greater help to reference librarians assisting advanced students in philosophy ...' (*RQ*, Summer 1984, p.479). *Class No:* 101(01)

Ancient Greece & Rome

[16]
'The Classical world' bibliography of philosophy, religion and rhetoric. New York & London, Garland Publishing Inc., 1978. 396p. (Garland reference library of the humanities, v.95). $51. ISBN: 0824098781.

19 bibliographical essays (some with critical comments) on Greek and Roman philosophy, Roman religion and ancient rhetoric (*e.g.* 'A bibliography of works on Lucretius, 1945-1972', p.139-226 (822 items in 15 sections); 'Early Roman religion, 1945-1972', p.227-42. Reprinted from the monthly *Classical world* (Classical Association of the Atlantic States. Duquesne University, Department of Classics, Pittsburgh, Pa.). 'This book will be of great use to the researcher as well as the teacher and students' (*American reference books annual*, v.10, 1979, item 1080). *Class No:* 101(01)(37/38)

Aristotle

[17]
ARISTOTELIAN SOCIETY. A Synoptic index to the 'Proceedings of the Aristotelian Society... Scott, J.W., *ed.* V.1 Oxford, Blackwell, 1954. v.2-3. London, Methuen, 1961, 1975. 3v.

V.1: 1900-1949; v.2: 1950-1959; v.3: 1960-1969.

.... *(contd.)*

Pt.1 of the 1900-1949 volume consists of entries, arranged by authors of papers, A-Z. Synopses of arguments for all the papers listed. Synopses are asterisked if the contributor has not collaborated in making them. Pt.2 is an index of subjects, with cross-references to pt.1. An appendix gives contents lists of separate volumes of the 'Proceedings' for the pre-1900 period (*i.e.* 1887-96), for 1900-49, and for 1950-53. Covers a wide range of aspects of philosophy. Considered 'a major new tool for the subject, an indexing and abstracting service' (Stavely, R. *Notes on subject bibliography* (1959), p.34). *Class No:* 101(01)ARI

[18]

—BARNES, J., *and others*. Aristotle: a bibliography. Rev. ed. Oxford, University of Oxford, Sub-Faculty of Philosophy, 1981. [vii], 88p. *(Study aids, v.7.)*

10 sections: 1. Introductory (tests, etc.; biography; Aristotle; general studies; collections) - 2. Juvenilia - 3. Logic - 4. Metaphysics - 5. Philosophy of science - 6. Science - 7. Psychology - 8. Ethics - 9. Politics - 10. Poetics. About 1000 references. No index. 'Designed primarily to suit the interests of English-speaking philosophers' *(Preface)*. *Class No:* 101(01)ARI

Augustine

[19]

INSTITUT DES ÉTUDES AUGUSTINIENNES, PARIS. Fichier Augustinien/Augustine bibliography. Boston, Mass., G.K. Hall, 1972. 4v. (2,675p.). $355 the set. ISBN: 0816109478.

60,000 photolithographed cards. Author and subject catalogues. Based on the bibliographies appearing in the quarterly *Augustiniana*. A supplement was published in 1981 ($125. 0816103658).

T.J. van Bavei's *Répertoire bibliographique de Saint Augustin, 1950-1960* (Steenbergen, Abbatia Santi Petri, 1963. 991p.) has author and name indexes.
Class No: 101(01)AUG

[20]

MIETHE, T.L. Augustinian bibliography, 1970-1980, with essays on the fundamentals of Augustinian scholarship. Westport, CT., Greenwood Press, 1982. 218p. $35. ISBN: 0313226295.

A listing of 1400 (mostly secondary) books, parts of books, and periodical articles published worldwide during the 1970s and of American dissertations from the 1890s to the present. An elaborate subject arrangement within 4 main chapters covering the life and works, philosophical issues, and historical and doctrinal relations. Name index but no subject index. 'Need time to use the bibliography - not for rapid access' (*Bulletin of ABTAPL*, no.28, November 1983, p.6-7). *Class No:* 101(01)AUG

Buber

[21]

MOONAN, W. Martin Buber and his critics: an annotated bibliography of writings in English through 1978. New York, Garland, 1981. 240p. $39.50.

Compiled as a retrospective contribution to Buber's 1978 centenary. Over 1000 items noted, including 378 of Buber's in their English version. Many entries substantially annotated. Comprehensive subject index, index of translated

.... *(contd.)*

titles, index of translators, and index of authors of secondary works. ' ... a model of reliable and cogent presentation'. (*Bulletin* of ABTAPL, No.28. November 1983. p.6). *Class No:* 101(01)BUB

Descartes

[22]

The Cambridge companion to Descartes. Cottingham, J., *ed.* Cambridge, Cambridge University Press, 1992. 624p. £35. (*Cambridge companions to philosophy.*) ISBN: 0521366232.

An account of his life, development of his thought, intellectual background and reception of his work. A central section is on Cartesian metaphysics. *Class No:* 101(01)DES

[23]

SEBBA, G. Bibliographia Cartesiana: a critical guide to the Descartes literature, 1800-1960. The Hague, Nijhoff, 1964.

3612 numbered entries. In 3 pts.: (1) bibliographical and biographical studies of Descartes (11 subheadings); (2) an exhaustive bibliography of Descartes's writings; (3) a bibliography of all works devoted to Descartes (excluding items in (1), published 1800-1960, classified and A-Z subect indexes. *Class No:* 101(01)DES

Freud

[24]

The Cambridge companion to Freud. Neu, J., *ed.* Cambridge, Cambridge University Press, 1992. 368p. £40. (*Cambridge companions to philosophy.*) ISBN: 0521374243.

Approaches Freud from the philosophical, historical, psychoanalytical, anthropological and sociological perspectives, showing how he gave new and powerful way to think about human thought and action. 14 contributors. *Class No:* 101(01)FRE

Hegel

[25]

INWOOD, M. A Hegel dictionary. Oxford, Blackwell, 1992. 260p. £37.50. ISBN: 0631175326.

Two chapters (*Hegel and his language; Introducing Hegel*) precede the dictionary of *c.*100 key terms used by Hegel, covering German words and their English, Greek and Latin equivalents. Annotated bibliography of *c.*300 items. Index of foreign-language terms. General index, p.251-60. '... helpfully arranged, thorough, beautifully produced ...' (*Choice*, v.30(6), February 1993, p.941). *Class No:* 101(01)HEG

[26]

STEINHAUER, K., *comp*. Hegel bibliography: background material on the international recognition of Hegel within the context of the history of philosophy/Hegel Bibliographie... Munich, K.G. Saur, 1980. xvi,894p. DM248. ISBN: 059803184x.

Over 13,000 entries. Sections: Bibliographies (complete works; selected works; single editions & correspondence) - Bibliography of secondary sources (including disserations, theses and articles) on Hegel's philosophy and the philosophy of his period, arranged chronologically. 1802-1975 (18 periods; items 871-12,032). Annex: Index of articles on Hegel, p.669-76. List of most significant periodicals and series. Index of authors, editors and

....*(contd.)*
translators. 'This work replaces all other Hegel bibliographies' (*Choice,* v.18, no.10, June 1981, p.1394).
Class No: 101(01)HEG

Hume

[27]
HALL, R. Fifty years of Hume scholarship: a bibliographical guide. Edinburgh, Edinburgh University Press, 1978. 166p.
Aims at completeness for the 50 years, 1925-76, and also lists titles of main contributions, 1900-24. Author and subject indexes. 'An extremely useful book' (*Library journal,* v.104(6), 15 March 1979, p.717). *Class No:* 101(01)HUM

[28]
—JESSOP, T.E. A Bibliography of David Hume, and of Scottish philosophy, from Francis Hutcheson to Lord Balfour. London, Brown, 1938. xiv,201p.
Hume (p.3-71): Collected works - Works published by Hume and translations of these - Posthumously published works - Spuria - Works on Hume.
Scottish philosophy: chronological list of authors; general; philosophers, A-Z. An appendix on the Gifford Lectures gives a complete list of the lectures published. Index of names. *Class No:* 101(01)HUM

Kant

[29]
The Cambridge companion to Kant. Guyer, P., *ed.* Cambridge, Cambridge University Press, 1992. 496p. £40. (*Cambridge companions to philosophy.*) ISBN: 0521365872.
A systematic and comprehensive account of the full range of Kant's writings available. 14 contributors.
Class No: 101(01)KAN

[30]
WALKER, R.C.S. A Selective bibliography on Kant. 2nd. ed. Oxford, Sub-Faculty of Philosophy, 1978. vi, 68p. Mimeographed. (*Study aids, v.5.*)
9 sections: 1. Works by Kant and their English translations - 2. Books - 3. Development up to 1781 - 4. *Critique of pure reason* and *Prolegomena* - 5. *Critique of practical reason* and *Grundlegung* - 6. *Critique of judgement* - 7. *Metaphysical foundations of natural science* - 8. *Metaphysics of morals* - 9. Opus postumum. List A: 'Compulsory reading'; B; 'Slightly less compulsory reading'. Aims at being 'a bibliography which may be of some use to graduate students'. *Class No:* 101(01)KAN

[31]
—EISLER, R. Kant-Lexikon. Nachschlagewerk zu Kants sämlichen Schriften, Briefen und handschriftlichen Nachlass. Berlin, Mittler, 1930 (reprinted 1964). viii,642 p.
Compiled with the co-operation of the Kangessellschaft.
A dictionary-index to keywords in Kant's writings, with numerous cross-references. List of Kant's works, p.640-2.
Class No: 101KAN(01)

Kierkegaard

[32]
EVANS, C.D. Søren Kierkegaard bibliographies: remnants, 1944-80, and multi-media, 1929-1991. Montreal, Quebec, McGill University Library, 1993. 185p. $25. ((*Fontanus monograph series, ll).*)
475 unique items, supplementing and continuing J. Himmelstrup's *Søren Kierkegaard: international bibliography* (1962) and F.H.Lapointe's *Søren Kierkegaard and his critics* (1981) (*qv*). Entries arranged A-Z under each grouping. No annotations or index. All items included in the International Kierkegaard Bibliographic Database at the University of Toronto. *Class No:* 101(01)KIE

[33]
HIMMELSTRUP, J. *and* **BIRKET-SMITH, K.,** *eds.* **Søren Kierkegaard:** international bibliografi. København, Nyt Nordisk Forlag, 1962. 216p.
6,995 entries, in 2 sections: 1. Works by Kierkegaard; 2. Literature on Kierkegaard, citing important reviews.
Class No: 101(01)KIE

[34]
—JØRGENSEN, A. Søren Kierkegaard-Literatur, 1961-1970. Aarhus, Akademisk Boghandel, 1971. 99p.
Class No: 101(01)KIE

[35]
—JØRGENSEN, R. Søren Kierkegaard-Literatur, 1971-1980: en bibliografi. Aarhus, Akademisk Boghandel, 1983, 112p. ISBN: 9798017209.
Both Jørgensen's volumes update the earlier title. Introductions and notes are in Danish.
Class No: 101(01)KIE

[36]
LAPOINTE, F.H., *comp.* **Søren Kierkegaard and his critics:** an international bibliography of criticism. Westport, CT., Greenwood Press, 1980. viii,430p.
In 2 parts: Bibliography of Søren Kierkegaard - Bibliography on Søren Kierkegaard. Part 2 has 8 chapters: 1. Books and reviews - 2. Dissertations - 3. General discussion of ... work and life - 4. Studies of individual works - 5. Entries arranged by proper names - 6. Entries arranged by subject - 7. Memoirs, portraits, personal - 8. Anniversary and commemoration. Items are numbered. No annotations. Appendix: Kierkegaard bibliographies. Index of authors and editors, p.389-430. *Class No:* 101(01)KIE

Leibniz

[37]
MÜLLER, K. Leibniz-Bibliographie: der Literatur über Leibniz bis 1980. Neue Aufl. Frankfurt am Main, Klostermann, 1982 [?].
First published 1967.
6796 items on Leibniz. 7 main sections: 1. General - 2. Leibniz' life - 3. General characteristics - 4. Special characteristics - 5. Leibniz' work (p.83-208) - 6. Philosophy - 7. Connections, activities. *Class No:* 101(01)LEI

[38]
—RAVIER, E. Bibliographie des oeuvres de Leibniz. Paris, Alcan, 1937 (facsimile reprint, Hildesheim, G. Olms Verlagsbuchhandlung, 1966). v.703p.
Complementary to the above. *Class No:* 101(01)LEI

Locke

[39]

YOLTON, J.S. *and* YOLTON, J.W. **John Locke: a reference guide.** Boston, Mass., G.K. Hall, 1985. 294p. $49.50. £49. (*A reference guide to literature*.) ISBN: 0816182361.

Over 1800 entries, with resumés, of secondary works published from 1689 to 1982. Arranged chronologically by publication date subdivided by author, A-Z. Name and subject indexes. Supercedes Christopherson's *Bibliographical notes to the study of John Locke* (1930). Some large blocks of numbers in the index under one heading (*e.g.* 140 under 'Education, some thoughts concerning') 'but despite flaws, high recommended' (*Choice*, v.22(11/12), July/August 1985, p.1622).
Class No: 101(01)LOC

Marx

[40]

The Cambridge companion to Marx. Carver, T., *ed.* Cambridge, Cambridge University Press, 1992. 373p. £40. (*Cambridge companions to philosophy*.) ISBN: 0521366259.

Aims to place Marx's writings in their historical context and to separate what he actually said from what others (Engels, etc.) interpreted him as saying. Covers all the major areas in which he made significant contributions. 13 contributors. *Class No:* 101(01)MAR

Mill

[41]

LAINE, M. **Bibliography of works on John Stuart Mill.** Toronto, University of Toronto Press, 1981. 173p. $31.25; £26.50. ISBN: 0802024149. *Class No:* 101(01)MIL

Nietzsche

[42]

REICHERT, H.W. *and* SCHLECTA, K., *comps. & eds.* **International Nietzsche bibliography.** Rev. & expanded ed. Chapel Hill, University of North Carolina Press, 1969. 162p.

First published 1960.

Updated to 1967, identifying some 566 new publications. 4566 numbered entries, 'omitting most of the purely popular accounts' (*Library journal,* v.94(22), 15 December 1969, p.4514). *Class No:* 101(01)NIE

Plato

[43]

McKIRAHAN, R.D. **Plato and Socrates:** a comprehensive bibliography, 1958-1973. New York, Garland, 1978. 592p. (Garland reference library of the humanities, v.78). $75. ISBN: 0824098951.

Continues 'Plato (1950-1957)' by Harold Cherniss, in *Lustrum*, v.4 (1959) & 5 (1960). Over 4,600 unannotated entries under detailed topics, with full cross-references. Lists book reviews. Author index. ' ... an essential tool in graduate and advanced undergraduate collections'. (*Choice*, September 1978, p.843). *Class No:* 101(01)PLA

Rousseau

[44]

DENT, N.J.H. **The Rousseau dictionary** Oxford, Blackwell, 1992. 260p. £37.50. (*(Blackwell philosopher dictionaries)*.) ISBN: 0631175687.

Over 100 entries A-Z on the principal philosophical, social and political works of Rousseau, and his life.
Class No: 101(01)ROU

Russell

[45]

MARTIN, W., *comp.* **Bertrand Russell:** a bibliography of his writings ... 1895-1976. New York, K.G. Saur, 1981. xlv, 332p. $27. ISBN: 3598103484.

The bibliography is arranged chronologically, and supported by several indexes (p.261-332), a chronological index of main works; a synopsis; secondary literature; index of works; and list of sources. In English and German.
Class No: 101(01)RUS

Sartre

[46]

BELKIND, A. **Jean-Paul Sartre:** Sartre and existentialism in English; a bibliographical guide. Kent, Ohio, Kent State University Press, 1970 (available from Books on Demand UMI). 234p. $63.50. ISBN: 0835793672.

Lists English translations of Sartre's works, English books on Sartre, periodical reviews of Sartre's works, etc. List of sources; index, p.217-34. *Library journal* (v.95(12), 15 June 1970, p.2247) praises tracing of pamphlets, periodical material, unpublished theses and dissertations.
Class No: 101(01)SAR

[47]

—Les Écrits de Sartre. Chronologie, bibliographie commentée. Contat, M. *and* Rybalka, M., *comps.* Paris Gallimard, 1970. 788p.

An annotated bibliography (7 sections, p.45-482), preceded by a detailed chronology. Index of titles; index of periodicals; index of names and subjects.
Class No: 101(01)SAR

[48]

The Cambridge companion to Sartre. Howells, C., *ed.* Cambridge, Cambridge University Press, 1992. 400p. £35. (*Cambridge companions to philosophy*.) ISBN: 0521381142.

Essays cover Sartre's writings on ontology, phenomenology, psychology, ethics, and aesthetics, as well as his work on history, commitment and progress. Special feature is the treatment of recently published posthumous works. 11 contributors. *Class No:* 101(01)SAR

[49]

LAPOINTE, F.H. *and* LAPOINTE, C., *comps.* **Jean-Paul Sartre and his critics:** an international bibliography (1938-1980): annotated and revised. 2nd ed. Bowling Green, Ohio, Philosophy Documentation Centre, 1981. 697p. $39.25.
Class No: 101(01)SAR

Schopenhauer

[50]

HÜBSCHER, A. **Schopenhauer-Bibliographie.** Stuttgart-Bad Cannstatt, Frommann-Holzhoog, 1981. 331p. DM.98.

Includes both primary and secondary sources, in German and in the other languages. Detailed subject arrangement includes sections on philosophers and their contemporaries. Author index and detailed list of contents, but no subject index. *Class No:* 101(01)SCH

Spinoza

[51]

OKO, A.S., *comp.* **The Spinoza bibliography.** Boston, Mass., G.K. Hall, under the auspices of the Columbia University Libraries, 1970. xxiii,700p. $85. ISBN: 0816106991.

A photolithographed reproduction of about 7000 cards (10 per page). Classified arrangement in main sections A-M. No index. *Class No:* 101(01)SPI

St. Thomas

[52]

MIETHE, T.L. *and* BOURKE, V.J. **Thomastic bibliography, 1940-1978.** Westport, CT., Greenwood Press, 1980. 318p. $46.95; £23.95. ISBN: 0313219915.

Continues V.J. Bourke's *Thomastic bibliography, 1920-1940,* listing 4746 titles, which appeared as a supplement to v.21 (1945) of *The Modern schoolman* (St. Louis, Missouri, 1945, viii,312p. (Reprinted by Hackett Publishers)).

Includes 4097 entries for editions and translations of St. Thomas's writings, and books and periodical articles on his life, teachings and influence. *Class No:* 101(01)THO

Teilhard de Chardin

[53]

JARQUE, J.E. **Bibliographie générale des oeuvres et articles sur Pierre Teilhard de Chardin.** Fribourg, Éditions Universitaires Fribourg, 1970. 206p.

2228 unannotated entries (with many interpolations) on Teilhard de Chardin, under authors, A-Z. Appended list of items not in French, of reviews and publishers. Subject and name indexes. *Class No:* 101(01)TEI

[54]

—BAUDRY, G.-H. Pierre Teilhard de Chardin: bibliographie (1881-1972). Lille, Facultés Catholiques, 1972. 113,[1]p. (*Mémoires et travaux, fasc.61.*)

Devotes part 1 to listing editions of works and corespondence, and part 2 to works and articles on Teilhard de Chardin (p.25-100; 1855 entries). Appendix of theses in French. Index of authors, persons cited and subjects. *Class No:* 101(01)TEI

[55]

—McCARTHY, J.M. Pierre Teilhard de Chardin: a comprehensive bibliography. New York, Garland, 1981. 438p. $40. (*Garland reference library of the humanities, v.158.*) *Class No:* 101(01)TEI

Wittgenstein

[56]

LAPOINTE, F.H. **Ludwig Wittgenstein:** a comprehensive bibliography. Westport, CT., Greenwood Press, 1980. ix,297p. $46.95; £22.95. ISBN: 0313221278.

An unannotated bibliography of Wittgenstein's writings and writings on Wittgenstein, the second section including books and review, dissertations, studies of individual works, and a general discussion of the works of Wittgenstein. Entries arranged by proper names, p.134-158; entries arranged by subjects, p.159-258. Index, p.269-297. *Class No:* 101(01)WIT

Encyclopaedias

[57]

Enciclopedia filosofica. Centro di Studi Filosofici di Gallarate. 2nd ed. Novara, Edipem, 1979. 8v.

First published 1957 (4v).

A scholarly encyclopedia, with signed and well documented articles. Range extends to literary, scientific and legal concepts. Features biographical articles (*eg.* on Coleridge), emphasizing philosophical thinking or contributions. V.8 includes two classified indexes, one arranged by branches of philosophy, the other by periods and regions. 'For layman and scholar alike'. (Entry based on Swidan, F.A. *Reference courses* (6th ed., 1988, p.63) and Sheehy's *Guide to reference books* (10th ed. 1986), entry BA 73). *Class No:* 101(031)

English

[58]

Dictionary of the history of ideas: studies of selected pivotal ideas. Wiener, P.P., *ed.* New York, Scribner's, 1968-73. 4v. & index. (3066p.). 5v. boxed set issued 1980, $67.50. ISBN: 0684164183.

V.1: Abstraction in the form of concepts - design argument; v.2: Despotism - Law, Common; v.3: Law, Concept of - Protest movements; v.4: Psychological ideas - Zeitgeist; v.5: Index.

About 250 contributors . Preface outlines 'domains and disciplines' involved in the history of ideas: the external order of nature, anthropology, psychology, religion and philosophy, literature and the arts; historical criticism; economics, law and politics; mathematics, logic, linguistics. Articles A-Z on 311 selected 'pivotal ideas' ('Cosmology from antiquity to 1850': v.1. p.535-54, with 1 col. of bibliography). Other articles, at random, on 'Baroque in literature'. 'Buddhism', 'China on Western thought and culture'. 'Faith, hope and charity', 'Welfare state', 'Space', 'Balance of power', 'Moral sense', 'Relativity', 'Game theory'. Index ([lx], 479p.) is fully analytical (*e.g.* 'Evil'; over 5 columns). *Class No:* 101(031)=20

[59]

The Encyclopedia of philosophy. Edwards, P., *ed.* New York, Collier-Macmillan, 1973. 4v. (2400p.). $200. £250. ISBN: 0028949501.

First published in 1967 in 8v.

1450 comprehensive signed articles (over 900 on individual thinkers). 500 contributors from 24 countries; international editorial board of 153. Some Western slant. Systematic bibliographical coverage is a feature. Copious cross-references. Detailed subject index with 38,000 entries.

....(contd.)

Articles are scholarly but readable. 'A valuable, definitive encyclopedia' (*ARBA*, 1975, item 1287).

Class No: 101(031)=20

[60]
PARKINSON, G.H.R., ed. An Encyclopaedia of philosophy. London, Routledge, 1990.$bxi, 950p.$c£90. ISBN: 0415603237.

Designed to provide a survey of current philosophical thought which will not merely provide information but will also help the reader to understand the nature of the subject (*Preface*). 37 self-contained articles are grouped in 6 sections (A: Meaning and truth - B: Theory of knowledge - C: Metaphysics - D: Philosophy of mind - E: Moral philosophy - F. Society, art and religion). Each section includes notes and a bibliography for further reading. The work is prefaced by a survey of various views of the nature of philosophy, and completed by a glossary of philosophical terms (p.885-908); a chronological survey, 1600-1960; an index of names (p.921-925); and an analytical subject index (p.926-935). *Class No:* 101(031)=20

[61]
REESE, W.L. Dictionary of philosophy and religion: Eastern and Western thought. Atlantic Highlands, N.J., Humanities Press; Hassocks, West Sussex, Harvester Press, 1980. iv, 644p. diagrs. $29.95; £80. ISBN: 0855271477.

'Has many encyclopedic features, including analysis of the thought of all major philosophers and religious leaders' (*Preface*). A key feature; numerous cross-references from concepts to the thinkers concerned. Major emphasis is on explication of terms. 'Santayana'; 2½ cols. (11 sections), listing principal writings and noting concepts. Sometimes there is main entry under the term (*e.g.* 'Ontology': 2 cols., 13 sections - 1 per philosopher's concept). Expensive. 'Not an essential purchase for most reference collections. It could be very useful for personal collections or for a small library'. (*Choice*, v.17, no 5/6, July/August 1980, p.656). *Class No:* 101(031)=20

German

[62]
RITTER, J., ed. Historisches Wörterbuch der Philosophie, unter Mitwirkung von mehr als 700 Fachgelehrten in Verbindung mit Guenther Bien [and others]. Völlig neubearb. Basel & Stuttgart, Schwabe & Co., AG., 1971- v.1-8 (1971-92) A-Sc.

Revision of Rudolf Eisler's *Wörterbuch der philosphischen Begriffe* (4. Aufl. 1927-30, 3v.).

Planned to be in 10v. (*c.*5500 articles), plus an index volume. Almost 1000 contributors. Unsigned articles, often lengthy. Appended to each volume are a list of articles in that volume, a list of contributors, and abbreviations for sources and for periodicals. No biographies, but 'isms' are included. *Class No:* 101(031)=30

Handbooks & Manuals

[63]
FLEW, A. An Introduction to Western philosophy: ideas and arguments from Plato to Popper. New rev. ed. London, Thames & Hudson, 1989. 512p. £10.95. ISBN: 0500275475.

First published 1971, subtitled 'ideas and arguments from

....(contd.)

Plato to Sartre'.

An introduction and textbook. Begins with Plato's Theory of Forms and ends with existentialism, linguistic philosophy and Karl Popper's radical integration of philosophy with the scientific method. Analytical index. *Class No:* 101(035)

[64]
PARKINSON, G.H.R., and others, eds. The Handbook of Western philosophy. New York, Macmillan, 1988. 935p. $90. ISBN: 0029495938.

Aims to give an account of the present state of philosophical thinking, mainly in British philosophy, European philosophy being treated only as necessary. 37 scholarly articles are grouped in 6 sections (Meaning and truth - Theory of knowledge - Metaphysics - Philosophy of mind - Moral philosophy - Society, art and religion). Each section has an introduction; each article has endnotes and an annotated bibliography. Several appendices, including a glossary of philosophical terms and a chronological chart. Subject and name indexes. 'The handbook will become a standard source of reference ... complementing the bibliographic essays in Tice and Slaven's *Research guide to philosophy* (1984)' (*Choice*, v.26(5), January 1989, p.782). *Class No:* 101(035)

Dictionaries

[65]
Dictionary of the history of ideas: studies of selected pivotal ideas. P.P. Weiner, editor-in-chief. New York, Scribner's, 1968-73. 4v. & index. (3066p.) 5v. boxed set issued 1980, $67.50. ISBN: 0684164183.

V.1. Abstraction in the form of concepts - Design argument; 2. Despotism - Law, Common; 3. Law, Concept of - Protest movements; 4. Psychological ideas - Zeitgeist; 5. Index. About 250 contributors. Preface outlines 'domains and disciplines' involved in the history of ideas: the external order of nature, anthropology, psychology, religion and philosophy; literature and the arts; historical criticism; economics, law and politics; mathematics, logic, linguistics. Articles A-Z on 311 selected 'pivotal ideas' (*e.g.* 'Baroque in literature', 'Buddhism', 'Cosmology from antiquity to 1850', 'Faith, hope and charity', 'Welfare state', 'Relativity', 'Game theory'). Index ([lx], 479p.) is fully analytical (*e.g.* 'Evil'; over 5 columns). *Class No:* 101(038)

[66]
DURBIN, P.T. Dictionary of concepts in the philosophy of science. Westport, CT., Greenwood Press, 1988. 362p. $59.95. (*Reference sources for the social sciences and humanities*, 6.) ISBN: 0313229791.

About 100 terms from the natural and social sciences are included. Entries average about 4 pages in length and contain extended definitions and discussions of related philosophic issues, followed by a bibliography of up to 12 sources. Good index of subjects and persons. '... an excellent source for an entree to scholarly literature on basic topics (*e.g.* chance, gender, history, indeterminism, instrumentalism, paradigm, vitalism)' (*Choice*, v.26(6), February 1989, p.918). *Class No:* 101(038)

[67]
GRASSL, W., *ed*. **Dictionary of conservative thought.**
London, Routledge & Kegan Paul, 1988. 300p. £27.50.
ISBN: 0415003024.

About 100 lengthy articles arranged A-Z by topic, the aim
being to map the range of the philosophic, economic and
political ideas developed under general heading of
conservatism. (Anarchism, Aristocracy, Art ... Democracy,
Deviance, Duty ... Marxism ... War, Welfare).
Class No: 101(038)

English
[68]
ANGELES, P.A. **A Dictionary of philosophy.** 2nd ed.
London, HarperCollins, 1992. ix, 326p. £7.99. ISBN:
0064610268.

First published 1981.
Intended for students,laypersons and teachers, 'the
emphasis is on areas most commonly covered by philosophy
courses, including epistemology, metaphysics, logic, ethics,
aesthetics and the philosophies of religion and politics'
(*Preface*). Entries vary in length from *c*.20 to *c*.200 words.
Cross-references. Index of philosophers, referring to page
numbers of entries in which they are mentioned.
Class No: 101(038)=20

[69]
BALDWIN, J.M., *ed*. **Dictionary of philosophy and
psychology,** including many of the principal conceptions of
ethics, logic, aesthetics, philosophy of religion, mental
pathology, anthropology, political and social philosophy,
philology, physical science and education, and giving a
terminology in English, French, German and Italian. New
York, Macmillan, 1901-05 (Reprinted New York, Gordon
Press, 1977). 3v. in 4. $395 the set. ISBN: 0849017211.

The editor was assisted by 17 consulting editors from
various countries and 50 contributing subject-specialists.
Mainly concerned with philosophical subjects; articles on
psychology are hopelessly dated and biography is treated
very summarily. 'Antiquated' (*Times literary supplement*
no.3, 420, 14 September 1967. p.809). Signed articles by
experts, chiefly American and British. Thus the 3-column
article 'Scepticism', by John Dewey, states etymology and
discusses philosophical, ethical and religious aspects, with
ten references. But the article on 'Plato' is 20 lines only,
with cross-references. Appended to v.2 are indexes of
Greek, Latin, German, French and Italian terms.
Class No: 101(038)=20

[70]
BULLOCK, A., *and others*. **The Fontana dictionary of
modern thought.** 2nd ed. completely rev., expanded &
updated. London, Fontana Press, 1988. xxvi,917p. £9.95.
ISBN: 0006861296.

First published 1977, ed. by A. Bullock & O. Stallybrass.
Published in New York, by Harper & Row as *The Harper
dictionary of modern thought*.
About 230 contributors. A dictionary-encyclopedia, it
assembles some 5000 key terms from across the whole range
of modern thought, sets them within their context, and offers
short explanatory accounts (anything from ten to a thousand
words), written by experts, but in language as simple as can
be used without over-simplification or distortion (according

....(contd.)
to the preface to the 1st ed.). Cross-references. Companion
volume to *The Fontana biographical companion to modern
thought*. *Class No:* 101(038)=20

[71]
LACEY, A.R. **A Dictionary of philosophy.** 2nd ed. London,
Routledge & Kegan Paul, 1986. viii, 266p. £14.95; $21.95.
ISBN: 0710209916.

First published 1976.
Aims 'to give the layman or student a pocket
encyclopaedia of philosophy, one with a bias towards
explaining terminology' (*Preface*). 'Epistemology and logic
occupy far more space than, say, either politics or aesthetics'
(*Preface*). Longer articles have briefly annotated references
(*e.g.* 'Naturalism': 3p., including 1p. of bibliography,
'Ought, obligation, duty': 2½p. 14 references). Potted
biographies. Entries well-written, but too small to be useful
and 'can in no way compete with Paul Edwards' 'The
Encyclopaedia of philosophy' (8v. 1967). (*Choice,* October
1987, p.286). *Class No:* 101(038)=20

[72]
LAWRENCE URDANG ASSOCIATES LTD. **A Dictionary
of philosophy,** prepared by Lawrence Urdang Associates
Ltd. (Antony Flew, editorial consultant; Jennifer Speake,
editor). 2nd rev. ed. London, Macmillan; New York, St.
Martin's Press, 1984. xiii, 380p. £25; $22.50. ISBN:
0333369777.

1st ed. 1979.
Majority of items are accounts of keywords and phrases,
but also includes some biographical entries (as much as
3000/4000 words for the greatest philosophers). Double
column. Heavily cross-referenced. *Class No:* 101(038)=20

Russian
[73]
BALLESTREM, K.G. **Russian philosophical terminology.**
Dordrecht, Netherlands, D. Reidel Publishing Company,
1964. viii, 117p. $18.50. (*Sovietica series no. 19.*) ISBN:
9027700362.

Glossary of *c*.1000 Russian philosophical terms, arranged
in Russian alphabetical order, numbered, and followed by
English, German and French equivalents. English, German
and French indexes. *Class No:* 101(038)=82

Theses
[74]
BECHTLE, T.C. *and* RILEY, M.F. **Dissertations in
philosophy accepted at American Universities, 1861-1975.**
New York & London, Garland Publishing Inc., 1978. xix,
537p. (Garland reference library in the humanities, v.112).
$73. ISBN: 0824098358.

Lists 7,503 Ph.D. dissertations under authors, A-Z. Partly
analytical subject index. *Class No:* 101(043)

Reviews & Abstracts
[75]
FRANCIS. 519. **Bulletin signalétique. 519. Philosophie.**
Paris, Centre National de la Recherche Scientifique, 1947-.
Quarterly. F.520pa. ISSN: 11573694.

Formerly *Bulletin analytique, Philosophie* (v.1-9, 1947-
55), then *Bulletin signalétique. 519. Philosophie*

....*(contd.)*

1989 (v.43): 4974 indicative abstracts and references. Sections: 01. Études historiques - 02. Philosophie générale. Metaphysique - 03. Théorie des valeurs et philosophie morale. Philosophie de l'action - 04. Philosophie de l'histoire. Philosophie politique et sociale. Philosophie du droit - 05. Philosophie de la religion - 06. Philosophie de l'art. Esthétique - 07. Esprit et corps. Identité personnelle - 08. Philosophie de la culture. Anthropologie philosophique - 09. Économie. Civilization. Éducation - 10. Logique philosophie. Philosophie du langage - 11. Épistemologic. Philosophie des sciences. Théorie de la connaissance - 12. Dictionnaires. Encyclopédies. Bibliographies. Sociétés. Divers. Each issue has a list of periodicals processed. Index of concepts (analytical); index of authors. Available online (Telesystems, Questel). *Class No:* 101(048)

[76]

The Philosopher's index: an international index to philosophical periodicals and books. Bowling Green, Ohio, Bowling Green University, 1967-.v.1,no.1-, Quarterly. $155. ISSN: 00317993.

*c.*2000 indicative and informative abstracts each year of articles in *c.*300 major journals in English, French, German, Spanish and Italian. Subject index. Arrangement is under authors. Includes books and dissertations as well as journal articles. *The philosopher's index: a retrospective index to US publications from 1940* (1978. 3v.) includes entries for *c.*15,000 articles and *c.*6000 books, 1940-76. 'Philosopher's index' database covers international philosophical periodicals, 1967-, and US philosophical periodicals, 1940-. Also available online (DIALOG) and CD-ROM. *Class No:* 101(048)

[77]

World philosophy: essay reviews of 225 major works. Magill, F.N. *and* McGreal, I.P., *eds.* Englewood Cliffs, N.J., Salem Press, 1982. 5v.

An expansion of *Master pieces of world philosophy in summary form* (1961. 2v.).

A chronological series of essay-digests of major philosophical treatises, explaining basic themes. Each essay carries further readings (briefly annotated). Western philosophical works preponderate. *Class No:* 101(048)

Periodicals & Progress Reports

[78]

RUBEN, D.H., *comp*. Philosophy journals and serials: an analytical guide. Westport, CT., Greenwood Press, 1985. 147p. $35; £40.95. (*Annotated bibliographies of serials, no.2.*) ISBN: 0313239584.

An evaluative guide to 335 English-language serials, 38 of which are British, arranged A-Z by title. Each entry includes detailed information about publisher, price, circulation, MS selection, indexes and abstracts, target audience, acceptance rates, and critical annotation. 'This will be a valuable research tool for scholars and a selection tool for librarians' (*Journal of academic librarianship*, v.11(5), November 1985, p.321). *Class No:* 101(05)

Yearbooks & Directories

[79]

International directory of philosophy and philosophers, 1993-1994. 8th ed. Bowling Green, Ohio, Philosophy Documentation Centre, Bowling Green State University, 1993. 336p. $89. ISBN: 0912632941.

First published 1965; 4th ed. 1978.

3 parts: 1. International organizations - 2. Alphabetical listing of *c.*100 countries (Afghanistan ... Zimbabwe) - 3. Indexes (philosophers; societies; universities; centers and institutions; journals; publishers). *Class No:* 101(058)

Quotations

[80]

ADLER, M.J. *and* VAN DORAN, C., *eds*. Great treasury of Western thought: comments on man and his institutions by the great thinkers in Western history. New York, Bowker, 1977. 1771p. $49.50. £41. ISBN: 0835208338.

Nearly 50,000 entries, arranged chronologically in 20 chapters (127 subdivisions). Coverage extends to political as well as philosophical, ethical and religious topics. Author and subject indexes. Very favourably reviewed in *RQ*, v.17(3), September 1978, p.268-9. *Class No:* 101(082.2)

Histories

[81]

BALES, E.F. A Ready reference to philosophy East and West. Lanham, MD., University Press of America, 1988. 289p. $24.50. ISBN: 0819166404.

A concise manual of the history of Western, Indian and Chinese philosophy. A summary chapter compares Western, Indian and Chinese thought, and bibliographies of selected works are appended to each entry. Index of philosophers. *Choice* (v.25(9), May 1988, p.1378) considers it surpasses recent philosophy reference books. *Class No:* 101(091)

[82]

BRÉHIER, É. The History of philosophy. Translated from French by W. Baskin. Chicago & London, University of Chicago Press, 1963-69. 7v.

Translated from *Histoire de la philosophie* (Paris, Presses Universitaires de France. 1st ed. 1928-38. 6v.: 9th ed. 1967-68. 1: *The Hellenic age.* 1963. 2.: *The Hellenistic and Roman age.* 1965. 3: *The Middle Ages and the Renaissance.* New ed. 1966. 4: *The seventeenth century.* 1966. New ed. 1969. 5: *The eighteenth century.* 1967. New ed,. 1971. 6: *The nineteenth century: period of systems.* 1800-50. 1968. 7.: *Contemporary philosophy since 1850.* 1969.

A clear and comprehensive study of the development of philosophical thought, with chapter bibliographies. The author, Professor of Philosophy of the Sorbonne.

The French original has two supplementary fascicules: *La Philosophie en Orient*, by P. Masson-Oursel (1948), and *La philosophie byzantine*, by B. Tatakis (1949). *Class No:* 101(091)

[83]

CAVALIER, R., *and others*. Ethics in the history of Western philosophy. London, Macmillan Press, 1989. 336p. £35. ISBN: 0333452437.

A series of 13 studies of selected ethical theories of major figures in the history of philosophy, seeking to uncover their original context. 16 contributors. A basic work in the field. *Class No:* 101(091)

[84]

COPLESTON, F.C. **A History of philosophy.** Tunbridge Wells, Kent, Search Press Ltd. (previously Burns & Oates), 1947-1975. 9v. £12.50 each vol. £105 for 9 vols. ISBN: 0855324384, the set.

A lucid, scholarly work, written from the standpoint of the scholastic philosopher. Volume titles are: 1. Greece and Rome - 2. Augustine to Scotus - 3. Ockham to Suárez - 4. Descartes to Leibniz - 5. Hobbes to Hume - 6. Wolff to Kant - 7. Fichte to Nietzsche - 8. Bentham to Russell - 9. Maine de Biran to Sartre. Each volume has a substantial bibliography (*e.g.* v.9: p.419-68), many footnote references and a detailed, partly analytical index. Father Copleston, S.J., was Professor of the History of Philosophy at Heythrop College, Oxford, 1939-70. *Class No:* 101(091)

[85]

—COPLESTON, F.C. Philosophy in Russia: from Herzen to Lenin and Berdyaev. Tunbridge Wells, Kent, Search Press Ltd. 1986. 480p. £25. ISBN: 0855325771.

Complements the above, covering the subject broadly and in detail from the eighteenth century to Lenin and into post-Stalin period. *Class No:* 101(091)

[86]

GUTHRIE, W. K. C. **A History of Greek philosophy.** Cambridge, Cambridge University Press, 1962-81. 6v. £60.00 each vol. ISBN: 0521051592 V.1; 0521051606 V.2; 0521075661 V.3; 0521200024 V.4; 0521200032 V.5; 0521235731 V.6.

V.1: *The earlier Presocratics and the Pythagoreans*(1962); V.2: *The Presocratic tradition, from Parmenides to Democritus*(1965); V.3: *The fifth-century enlightenment*(1969); 4: *Plato. The man and his Dialogues: earlier period* (1975); 5: *The later Plato and the Academy*(1978); 6: *Aristotle: an encounter*(1981). The study of Anaxagoras in v.2.(p.266-344) provides a detailed analysis of his writings, with citations and footnote references. Each volume has an index of passages quoted or referred to, and a general, analytical index, plus a bibliography (unhelpfully arranged A-Z by authors; *e.g.* v.5,p.493-514). The section on Plato's *Apology* (v.5. p.70-93) gives date, historicity, summary and comment, with 30 footnotes. V.3. deals fully with the Sophists, their contemporaries, and Socrates. One reviewer (*Philosophy* v.39.no.148, April 1964, p.184-5) notes the paucity of Greek quotations, confined to footnotes and appendices. A scholarly survey, by the Professor of Ancient Philosophy in Cambridge University. 'Indispensable' (*British book news,* December 1976, p.892). *Class No:* 101(091)

[87]

A History of Western philosophy. Oxford, Oxford University Press, 1985-.

A comprehensive and up-to-date survey of philosophical ideas from earliest times to the present day, for students of philosophy and the general reader. 8 volumes are planned: No.1. Classical thought, by T. Irwin (1989 ISBN 0192191969). No.2. Medieval philosophy, by D. Luscombe. No.3. Renaissance philosophy, by C. Schmitt. (1988. ISBN 0521251044). No.4. The Rationalists, by J. Coningham (1988. ISBN 0192192094). No.5. The Empiricists, by R.S. Woolhouse (1988. ISBN 0192192075). No.6. English-language philosophy, 1750 - 1945, by J. Skorwski 1993 (ISBN 0192192116). No.7. Continental philosophy since

....(contd.)

1750, by R. Solomon (1985. ISBN 0192192167) No.8. English-language philosophy since 1945, by D. Stroud. *Class No:* 101(091)

[88]

MARENBON, J. Later medieval philosophy (1150-1350): an introduction. London, Routledge & Kegan Paul, 1987. xi, 230p. £18.95. ISBN: 0710202865.

Aims to provide some of the important information without which medieval philosophical texts tend to baffle or mislead, and to give some detailed examples of how later medieval thinkers argued. 11 chapters in 2 parts: pt.1 examines the organization of studies in medieval universities; pt.2 examines in detail the way in which some important later medieval thinkers discussed a difficult and central question, the nature of intellectual knowledge. Bibliography, by chapter, p.194-224. Index, p.225-230. *Class No:* 101(091)

[89]

—MARENBON, J. Early medieval philosophy (480-1150): an introduction. Rev. ed. London, Routledge & Kegan Paul, 1988. xiv,197p. £8.95. ISBN: 041500070x.

First published 1983.

A companion volume to the above. *Class No:* 101(091)

[90]

PASSMORE, J.A. A Hundred years of philosophy. 2nd ed. London, Duckworth, 1966 (Reprinted Harmondsworth, Penguin Books, 1970). 574p. £5.95. ISBN: 0140209271.

First published 1957.

Author was Professor of Philosophy at the Australian National University. An excellent survey of 19th century and contemporary philosophers (starting with J.S. Mill and ending with Nagel and Feyerabend). The 2nd ed. adds considerably to accounts of Ayer, Popper, Wittgenstein and Sartre, completely rewritten and much enlarged sections on Austin, Jaspers and Heidegger, and a new section on Merleu-Ponty, etc. Extensive footnote references and notes; 'Further reading', p.147-9. Index of names; index (non-analytical) of subjects. 'One of the best handbooks on modern thought, as it is certainly one of the most readable' (*British book news,* no.338, October 1968, p.731). *Class No:* 101(091)

[91]

—PASSMORE, J.A. Recent philosophers: a supplement to *A Hundred years of philosophy.* London, Duckworth, 1985. 173p. £19.50; $21.95. ISBN: 0715618962.

Sketches recent happenings in the field and supplies a print of entry for those who wish to explore more deeply. 5 chapters (1. Introduction; change and continuity - 2. Structure and syntax - 3. From syntax to semantics - 4. Davidson and Dummett - 5. Realism and relativism). Notes, p.123-164. Index, p.165-173. *Class No:* 101(091)

[92]

RUSSELL, B. **History of Western philosophy** and its connection with political and social circumstances from the earliest times to the present day. 2nd ed., 1960, new impression of 2nd ed. 1992. London, Allen and Unwin, 1992. 916p. £30. ISBN: 0415090733.

First published 1946.

In 3 sections, each subdivided: Book 1. Ancient philosophy (part 1. The Pre-Socratics; pt.2. Socrates, Plato and Aristotle; pt.3. Ancient philosophy after Aristotle); Book 2. Catholic philosophy (pt.1. The fathers; pt.2. The schoolmen); Book 3. Modern philosophy (pt.1. From the

....(contd.)

Renaissance to Hume; 2. From Rousseau to the present day). Detailed index. ' ... brilliantly written exposé of changing philosophical doctrines ... ' (*Sir Julian Huxley*). ' ... monument of learning ... flashes of humour ... touches of malicious wit ... (C.E.M. Joad). *Class No:* 101(091)

[93]
WEDBERG, A. **A History of philosophy.** Oxford, Oxford University Press, 1982-84. 3v. illus., fig. v.1: £10.50;v.2: £12.50; v.3: £17.50. ISBN: 0198246390, v.1; 0198246404, v.2; 0198246412, v.3.

Originally published in Swedish in 1958 under the title 'Filosofins historia' and translated into English by Wedberg himself.

V.1. Antiquity and the Middle Ages; v.2 The Modern Age to Romanticism; v.3. From Bolzano to Wittgenstein. Aims to give an insight into the nature of problems, themes, and theories which are of present day, and possibly permanent, philosophical interest. Emphasis is on intellectual problems, and the content of theories, rather than on the personalities of the philosophers. Separate indexes to each volume.
Class No: 101(091)

Ancient Greece & Rome

[94]
The Cambridge history of later Greek and early medieval philosophy, ed. by A.H. Armstrong. Cambridge, University Press, 1967. xiv, 710 [1]p. £80; ISBN: 0521226058.

'Originally planned in connection with W.K.C. Guthrie's *History of Greek philosophy*, but has developed on rather different lines ... It is an independent survey designed to show how Greek philosophy took the form which it was known to and influenced the Jews, the Christians of East and West and the Moslems, and what these inheritors of Greek thought did with their heritage during, especially the first millennium' (*Preface*). Coverage: from the Old Academy (4th century B.C.) to St. Anselm (beginning of 12th century A.D.). Final chapter 8: 'Early Islamic philosophy'. Select bibliography, by chapters, p.670-91. Index of ancient and medieval books referred to in the text; general, analytical index; index of Greek terms. *Class No:* 101(091)(37/38)

[95]
GOULET, R., *ed*. **Dictionnaire des philosophies antiques.** Paris, Centre National de la Recherche Scientifique, 1989-.

V.1: Abam(m)on à Axiothá. 838p. F.425. ISBN 2222040426.

Concerned primarily with Greek philosophers from earliest times to about the 6th century. 'Aristotle': over 150p. Citation to articles in Pauly-Wissowa. Well documented, with lists of standard editions, translations. Outline form for longer articles. Lengthy appendix on the Academy in Athens, plus maps and illustrations. Name, keyword and Greek keyword indexes. 'Recommended for all libraries with extensive collections in classics or philosophy.'(*College and research libraries*, v.52(2), March 1991, p.177). *Class No:* 101(091)(37/38)

Middle Ages

[96]
The Cambridge history of later medieval philosophy, from the rediscovery of Aristotle to the disintegration of Scholasticism, 1100-1600. Kretzmann, Norman, *and others, eds*. Cambridge, Cambridge University Press, 1982. xiv, 1035p. (New ed. in paperback, 1988. .£32.50. ISBN: 0521369339.

11 sections, each subdivided (1. Medieval philosophical literature; 2. Aristotle in the Middle Ages; 3. The old logic; 4. Logic in the Middle Ages: semantic theory; 5. Logic in the Middle Ages: propositions and modalities; 6. Metaphysics & epistemology; 7. Natural philosophy; 8. Philosophy of mind and action; 9. Ethics; 10. Politics; 11. The defeat, neglect and revival of Scholasticism). 41 academic contributors. Brief biographies, arranged A-Z by first name, p.853-892. Bibliography, p.893-975. Index nominum (name index with 'see' references), p.979-994. Index regum (subject index), p.995-1035.
Class No: 101(091)"01/14"

[97]
GILSON, É. **History of Christian philosophy in the Middle Ages.** 2nd ed. London, Sheed & Ward, 1972 (reprinted 1980). xvii,829p. £27.50. ISBN: 0722041144.

Based on the French *La philosophie au moyen âge, des origines patristiques à la fin du XIVe siècle* (Paris, Payot, 1922; 2nd ed. 1944), being not a translation but a 'reworking' of the material.

Arranged in 11 parts, covering 14 centuries. Bibliographical and other notes (p.549-804) on each of the leading philosophers. Indexes of authors and historians. The work of a leading expert in the field. Roman Catholic viewpoint. *Class No:* 101(091)"01/14"

[98]
—STEENBERGHEN, F. van. Histoire de la philosophie. Périod chrétienne. Louvain, Publications Universitaires, 1964. 196p.

Period covered ranges from the end of the 5th century to the end of the 12th; pt.3 deals with Arabic philosophy. The bibliography (p.181-6) notes both sources for research work and items for further reading. *Class No:* 101(091)"01/14"

[99]
—WEINBERG, J.R. A Short history of medieval philosophy. Princeton, N.J., Princeton University Press, 1964. ix,304p.

Considered by *Philosophical review* (v.75(3), July 1966, p.407-9) to be a work of first-rate scholarship and something of a classic. Selective bibliography, p.295-300.
Class No: 101(091)"01/14"

Renaissance

[100]
The Cambridge history of renaissance philosophy. Schmitt, C.B., *and others*. Cambridge, Cambridge University Press, 1988. xiii,968p. £50. ISBN: 0521251044.

Aims to offer a balanced and comprehensive account of philosophical thought from the middle of the 14th century to the emergence of modern philosophy at the turn of the 17th century. 23 chapters arranged in 13 sections in 3 parts: Part 1 (I. Conditions of enquiry - II. The renaissance concept of philosophy - III. Translations, terminology and style in philosophical discourse - IV. Humanism). Part 2. (V. Logic and language - VI. Natural philosophy - VII. Moral philosophy - VIII. Political philosophy - IX. Psychology - X.

....(contd.)

Metaphysics - XI. Problems of knowledge and action - XII. Philosophy and humanistic disciplines). Part 3 (XIII. Appendices: The availability of ancient works. The rise of the philosophical textbook). Footnotes throughout. Biobibliographies, p.805-941. Bibliography, p.842-930, divided into primary and secondary sources, each A-Z. Index nominum, p.931-947. Index rerum, p.948-968.

Class No: 101(091)"1095-1300"

Modern Times

[101]

SCRUTON, R. From Descartes to Wittgenstein: a short history of modern philosophy. London, Routledge & Kegan Paul, 1981. vi, 298p. £25. ISBN: 0710007981.

A survey of modern philosophy in 5 chapters (1. Rationalism - 2. Empiricism - 3. Kant and idealism - 4. The political transformation - 5. Recent philosophy). Bibliography (p.285-293). Index (p.294-298).

Class No: 101(091)"15/19"

20th Century

[102]

AYER, A.J. Philosophy in the twentieth century. London, Weidenfeld & Nicolson, 1982. x, 283p. £12.50. ISBN: 0297781790.

Conceived as a sequel to B. Russell's *History of Western philosophy,* the major part of the book is devoted to representatives of two major schools, the American pragmatists and the analytic movement, dealing in depth with a relatively small number of outstanding individuals. Chapter I. Philosophical inheritance; II. The revolt from Hegel; III. Pragmatism; IV. Wittgenstein, Popper and the Vienna Circle; V. Wittgenstein, Carnap and Ryle; VI. Physicalism; VII. The philosophy of R.G. Collingwood; VIII. Phenomenology and Existentialism; IX. Later developments. Index p.271-83 in double column. *Class No:* 101(091)"19"

Biographies

[103]

BULLOCK, A. *and* **WOODINGS, R.B.,** *eds.* **The Fontana biographical companion to modern thought.** London, Collins, 1983. xxv,867p. ISBN: 0002163292.

Cover title: *The Fontana dictionary of modern thinkers.*

Over 1500 entries, each by an authority on the subject, giving biographical details and an assessment of career and work. A list of contributors precedes the biography (AALTO ... ZWICKY); entries include subject, details of birth and death, subject's category, publications, bibliography (restricted to critical studies relating to subject's life and work and limited to 2 titles. Details of the subject's own publications are included in the entry itself. Entries average about a column in length. Cross-references.

Class No: 101(092)

[104]

COLLINSON, D. Fifty major philosophers: a reference guide. London, Croom Helm, 1987. [4],170p. £22.50; $29.50. ISBN: 0709934661.

The philosophers included are all Western, all deceased, and range from Thrale to Sartre, in chronological order. Easy-to-read essays, describing the main thrust of the philosopher's thinking, information about his life, and

....(contd.)

concise expositions of one or two aspects of his thought, along with mention, where appropriate, of its connection with the thought of other philosophers. Notes and lists for further reading attached to each entry. Cross-references. Glossary of philosophical terms, p.164-170.

Class No: 101(092)

[105]

Thinkers of the twentieth century: a biographical, bibliographical and critical dictionary. Turner, R.W. 2nd ed. New York, St. James' Press, 1987. 977p. $85; £64. ISBN: 091228983x.

First published in 1983.

A selection of 500 individuals representing a wide range of thinkers in the fields of philosophy, theology, social thought, psychology, economics, law, mathematics, and the biological and physical sciences. Entries include a biographical sketch, an extensive bibliography, a reading list, and a critical essay (of up to 3000 words) written by a noted expert on the individual. *Class No:* 101(092)

[106]

VESEY, G., *ed.* **Philosophers ancient and modern.** Cambridge, Cambridge University Press, 1986. v.313p. £8.95. ISBN: 0521337992.

Royal Institute of Philosophy lecture series 20. Published as a supplement to *Philosophy* (1986).

Chapters on Plato, Aristotle, Descartes, Hume, Marx, J.S. Mill, Nietzsche, Russell, Ayer and Sartre. Name index, p.309-312; subject index, p.313. Intended for examinations. *Class No:* 101(092)

Europe

Encyclopaedias

[107]

Great thinkers of the Western world the major ideas and classic works of more then 100 outstanding Western philosophers, physical and social scientists, psychologists, religious writers and theologians. McGreal, I.P., *ed.* New York, HarperCollins, 1992. 592p. $40. ISBN: 006270026x.

116 essays by 35 contributors, each with a brief annotated bibliography. Non-political expositions. Wider in range than Urmson's *Concise encyclopedia.* *Class No:* 101(4)(031)

[108]

URMSON, J.O. *and* **RÉE, J.,** *eds.* **The Concise encyclopedia of Western philosophy and philosophers.** New ed. [3rd], completely revised. London, Unwin Hyman, 1989. xiii,331p. £25. ISBN: 0044453795.

First published 1960, by Hutchinson.

79 contributors. Signed articles (Hobbes: 6½ columns). Cross-references indicated in bold in the text. 80 new articles added to this edition, but bibliography omitted. *Class No:* 101(4)(031)

Histories

[109]

HIRSCHBERGER, J. A Short history of Western philosophy. Guildford, Lutterworth Press, 1976. xi,218p. £4.50. ISBN: 071882279x.

A translation from the German by Jeremy Moiser of *Geschichte der Philosophie* (9th ed., Freiburg, Herder, 1971).

....(contd.)

In 4 parts, each subdivided: 1. The philosophy of antiquity - 2. The philosophy of the Middle Ages - 3. The philosophy of modern times - 4. The philosophy of the 19th and 20th centuries. No bibliography but works are referred to in the text. Indexes of names and subjects. *Class No:* 101(4)(091)

[110]
O'CONNOR, D.J., *ed*. **A Critical history of Western philosophy.** 2nd ed. London, Macmillan Educational, 1985. viii,600p. £12.95. ISBN: 033339366x.

First published 1964.

'... designed for use of undergraduate students of philosophy and for the intelligent general reader ...' (*Preface*). 21 chapters, most of which are devoted to one particular philosopher: (1. Early Greek philosophy - 2. Socrates and Plato ... 18. Bertrand Russell - 19. Logical positivism - 20. Existentialism - 21. Contemporary British philosophers). Notes, p 557-575, by chapter and page. Bibliography, p.576-789, by chapter, updated and simplified with this edition. Analytical index, p.591-600.
Class No: 101(4)(091)

Renaissance
[111]
DRONKE, P., *ed*. **A History of twelfth-century Western philosophy.** Cambridge, Cambridge University Press, 1988. xi,495p. £37.50. ISBN: 0521258960.

'15 scholars from 8 different countries have collaborated to make the first detailed survey of the subject' (Book jacket). 16 chapters arranged in 4 parts: 1. Background - 2. New perspectives - 3. Innovations - 4. The entry of the 'new' Aristotle. Biobibliographies of important persons, p.443-457. General bibliography, p.459-486, arranged A-Z. Index of manuscripts, p.487. General analytical index, p.488-495. *Class No:* 101(4)(091)"1095-1300"

Contemporary
[112]
BOCHÉNSKI, I.M. **Contemporary European philosophy.** Translated from the German by Donald Nicholl and Karl Aschenbrennen. Berkeley, Los Angeles & London, University of California Press, 1956. (Reprinted by Greenwood, 1982). xviii, 326p. $38.50; £26.75. ISBN: 0313234906.

7 chapters, 26 sections (separate sections for Croce, Bergson, Heidegger, etc.). Appendix: Mathematical logic. International organizations. Bibliography, p.265-321 (by chapters and sections). Index. *Class No:* 101(4)"312"

Great Britain
[113]
SORLEY, W.R. **A History of British philosophy, to 1900.** Cambridge, University Press, 1965 (Reprinted Westport, Conn., Greenwood Press, 1973. xx, 386p. $35; £22.95. ISBN: 0837167183.

First published 1920.

The text is based upon a series of chapters contributed to *The Cambridge history of English literature* and is ably written. The lengthy chapter-bibliographies in the 1st ed. (p.323-73) have been revised and brought up to date.
Class No: 101(410)

Germany
[114]
BUBNER, R. **Modern German philosophy.** Cambridge, Cambridge Univesity Press, 1981. xi,223p. £25. ISBN: 0521229081.

Translated from the German by E. Matthews.

Structured thematically to demonstrate the different active strains of philosophy. Deals with individual philosophers as well as the schools of the period. Introduction, 'On the historicity of philosophy' is followed by 3 sections, all subdivided: (1. Phenomenology and hermeneutics - 2. Philosophy of language and theory of science - 3. Dialectic and philosophy of practice) and concluding remarks. Index of names, p.221-223. *Class No:* 101(430)

[115]
Contemporary German philosophy, v.1-6, 1982-87. Christensen, D.E., *and others*. University Park, PA., Pennsylvania University Press, 1982-87. 6v. $26.50 each vol.

Each volume contains several articles, book reviews and review articles. Devoted principally to making available in English, contributions to philosophical comprehension originally published in German. *Class No:* 101(430)

[116]
SCHNÄDELBACH, H. **Philosophy in Germany, 1831-1933.** Cambridge, Cambridge University Press, 1984. x,265p. £25. ISBN: 0521227933.

Translated from the German by E. Matthews.

'... an attempt to give an account of the history of German philosophy between the end of the Idealist period and the first stirrings of the philosophy of our own time' (*Introduction*). 8 chapters: 1. Sketch of an age - 2. History - 3. Science - 4. Understanding - 5. Life - 6. Values - 7. Being - 8. Epilogue: Man. Notes, by chapter, p.235-256. Select bibliography, by chapter, p.257-259. Index, p.260-65.
Class No: 101(430)

France
[117]
DESCOMBES, V. **Modern French philosophy.** Cambridge, Cambridge University Press, 1981. xii,192p. £22.50. ISBN: 0521228379.

Translated from the French original, *Le Même de l'autre*, by L. Scott-Fox and J.M. Harding.

An introduction, *Philosophy in France*, is followed by 6 sections, all subdivided: 1. The humanisation of nothingness - 2. The human origin of truth - 3. Semiology - 4. The critique of history - 5. Difference - 6. The end of time. Footnotes throughout. Index, p.191-192. *Class No:* 101(44)

Asia
[118]
NAUMANN, St. E., *jr*. **Dictionary of Asian philosophies.** New ed. London, Routledge & Kegan Paul, 1990. xxi,394p. tables. £17.99. ISBN: 0415039711.

Abhidharma ... Zoroastrianism. Entries for terms (giving pronunciation), philosophies and thinkers. Sufism: p.316-21; Mao Tse-tung: p.248-59; Indian philosophy (p.171-93: 7 sections). Text interspersed with quotations. Cross-references. Preliminaries include 'Chronology of Asian philosophers', p.xiii-xvii. 'No doubt it could be better, but in any case, it is the best there is' (*American reference books*

....(contd.)

annual, v.10, 1979, item 1082). 'The best source [for Eastern philosophers] is still the *Encyclopedia of philosophy*, edited by Paul Edwards' (*Choice*, v.16, no.1, March 1979, p.57). *Class No:* 101(5)

China

[119]

ADELMANN, F.J., *ed.* **Contemporary Chinese philosophy.** The Hague, Martinus Nijhoff, 1982. xx,219p. £44.75. (*Martinus Nijhoff philosophy library, v.9. Boston College studies in philosophy, VI.*) ISBN: 9024730570.

An introduction by the editor is followed by 8 chapters by 8 contributors. 76 references are given at the end of the book. *Class No:* 101(510)

[120]

CHAN, W.-T. **An Outline and an annotated bibliography of Chinese philosophy.** Rev. ed. New Haven, CT., Far Eastern Publications, Yale University, 1969. vii,220p. $7.50. ISBN: 0887100554.

Previous editions as *An outline and bibliography of Chinese philosophy*.

The same author's *A source book in Chinese philosophy*, (Princeton, N.J., Princeton University Press, 1963) has chapter bibliographies and a list of works in European languages referred to, p.793-811. *Class No:* 101(510)

[121]

FU, C.W. *and* CHANG, W. **Guide to Chinese philosophy.** London, C. Prior; Boston, Mass., G.K. Hall, 1978. xxxi,362p. (*The Asian philosophies and religious resources guides.*)

About 1500 entries, with evaluative annotations. 16 closely divided chapters (*e.g.* 1. Confucius and Lao-Tza; 14. Companion with Western philosophy; 16. Authoritative texts and their philosophical significance). English translations of original Chinese classics, plus secondary books and articles about Chinese philosophy, with some important French and German items. Numerous cross-references. 'An indispensible guide' (*RQ*, v.18(3), Spring 1979, p.306). *Class No:* 101(510)

[122]

FUNG, Y.L. **A History of Chinese philosophy.** London, Allen & Unwin, 1937-53. 2v.

Translated by D. Bodde.

1. *The period of the philosophers* (from the beginnings to *c.*100 B.C.); 2. *The period of classical learning* (from the 2nd century B.C. to the 20th century A.D.). A thorough and scholarly presentation of a subject hardly covered (especially as regards the period of v.2.) in Western writings. Well translated. Detailed chronological tables, bibliographies, (v.1. p.xxiii-xxvi, 410-22; v.2. p.726-54) and indexes at the end of each volume. A shortened version, titled *A short history of Chinese philosophy* was published in 1966 (Free Press, £13.95). *Class No:* 101(510)

India

[123]

DASGUPTA, S. **A History of Indian philosophy.** Cambridge, Cambridge University Press, 1922-25. (Available from Oriental Bk. Dist.). 5v. $56 the set. ISBN: 0842609636.

Mainly intended as an exposition of Indian thought, strictly

....(contd.)

on the basis of the original texts and commentaries. Often the ground covered is wholly new and the materials have been obtained by a direct and first-hand study of all available texts and manusicripts. No attempt has been made to draw any comparison or contrasts with Western philosophy (*Preface to v.2*). Each volume has footnotes and an analytical index. *Class No:* 101(540)

[124]

GRIMES, J. **A Concise dictionary of Indian philosophy:** Sanscrit terms defined in English. New York, State University of New York, 1989. 440p. $39.50. ISBN: 0791401006.

'It is basic in that (i) it includes virtually all the words basic to the various Indian philosophical systems, and (ii) it defines those terms, in their dictionary or common and literal meanings. The book is comprehensive in that it defines many of its terms with the specific meaning that a word has for a specific school' (*Preface*). Sanscrit terms are given in Devanagari script and transliterated. '... a kind of "ready reference" which will be found useful both by scholars and generalists' (*Choice*, v.27(5), January 1990, p.768). *Class No:* 101(540)

[125]

LAL, B.K. **Contemporary Indian philosophy.** New ed. Delhi, Motilal Banarsidass, India, 1987. xxi,346p. Rs.50; £9. ISBN: 8120802608.

First published 1973.

An introduction, 'Characteristics of contemporary Indian philosophy' precedes 7 chapters devoted to Indian philosophers (1. Swami Vivekanande - 2. Rabindranath Tagore - 3. Mahatma Gandhi... 7. Sir Mohammad Iqbal. Footnotes. Bibliography, p.335-341, arranged by chapters. Index, p.342-345. *Class No:* 101(540)

[126]

POTTER, K.H., *and others.* **Guide to Indian philosophy.** Boston, Mass., G.K. Hall & Co., 1988. xviii,159p. $37.50. (*The Asian philosophies and religions resource guides.*) ISBN: 0816179042.

'Indian philosophy' defined as thought originating in India and concerning the subject of bondage and liberation. 884 books and journal articles are listed and briefly annotated. Material selected was published between 1975 and 1985 and covers standard philosophical topics such as epistemology; logic; metaphysics and ethics; plus aesthetics; philosophy of religion; social, legal and political philosophy; philosophy of history; and philosophy of education. Name index, p.133-146; subject index, p.147-159. *Class No:* 101(540)

Islamic World

[127]

FAKHRY, M. **A History of Islamic philosophy.** 2nd ed. New York, Columbia University Press; Harlow, Essex, Longman Group, 1983. xxx,394p. $29.50; £23. (*Columbia studies in oriental culture.*) ISBN: 0231055323, US; 0582783240, UK.

First published 1970.

A detailed survey, in chronological order, from the 7th century to the present. 'Fakhry's book should now be considered the best comprehensive book ever written on the history of Arabic philosophy' (*Journal of the history of philosophy*, v.10(2), April 1972, p.223, of the first edition). *Class No:* 101(5.297)

[128]
LEAMAN, O. **An Introduction to medieval Islamic philosophy.** Cambridge, Cambridge University Press, 1985. xii,208p. £20. ISBN: 0521247071.

An introduction to debates on philosophy within the medieval Islamic world. 6 chapters in 2 parts: 1. Ghazali's attack on philosophy - 2. Reason v. revelation in practical reasoning. Further reading, p.202-203. Glossary, p.204. Index of passages, p.205-206. General index, p.207-208. *Class No:* 101(5.297)

USA

[129]
Directory of American philosophers, 1994-95. 17th ed. Bowling Green, OH., Philosophy Documentation Center, Bowling Green State University, 1994. Biennial. 500p. tables. $99. ISBN: 091263295x.

First published 1970 for 1970-71.

Arrangement is by universities, A-Z for US and separately for Canada. Information on faculties of philosophy, with names and addresses; specialities of philosophers; data on colleges and universities; philosophical societies; philosophical centres and institutes; philosophical journals; publishers of philosophical works; data on fellowships, etc., available in philosophy. Indexes of philosophers (names and addresses); universities, centres and institutes; societies; journals; and publishers. . *Class No:* 101(73)

Jews

[130]
SIRAT, C. **A History of Jewish philosophy in the Middle Ages.** Cambridge, Cambridge University Press; Paris, Editions de la Maison des Sciences de l'Homme, 1985. x, 477p. £45. ISBN: 0521260876, UK; 2735101037, France.

An introduction to the study of Jewish medieval philosophy, based on the texts themselves, printed or in manuscript. 9 chapters: 1. Introduction - 2. The Mutakallimŭn and other Jewish thinkers inspired by Muslim theological movements - 3. The Neoplatonists - 4. Judah Halevi and Abu-l-Barakăt - 5. Aristotelianism - 6. Maimonides - 7. The thirteenth century - 8. The fourteenth century - 9. The fifteenth century. Bibliography, p.413-457, relates to pages of text. Analytical index, p.459-475. Index of ancient works quoted in the text, p.476-477. *Class No:* 101(=924)

Conferences

[131]
GELDSETZER, L. **Bibliography of the international congresses of philosophy/Bibliographie der internationalen Philosophie Kongress, 1900-1978...** Munich, etc., K.G. Saur, 1981. 209p. DM.98.

Full listing of papers presented at 16 international philosophy congresses (arranged chronologically). Detailed name and subject indexes, p.158-208. *Class No:* 101:061:061.3

Wittgenstein

[132]
FRONGIA, G. *and* McGUINNESS, B. **Wittgenstein: a bibliographic guide.** Oxford, Blackwell, 1990. x,438p. £65. ISBN: 0631137653.

Part I: History of the reception of Wittgenstein's work; Pt.II: Lists and indexes. Publications of writings by Wittgenstein. Writings *on* Wittgenstein. Reviews of Wittgenstein's own writings. Entries are annotated and numbered. Indexes of subjects, of thinkers referred to in the literature, and of authors of items. *Class No:* 101WIT

Metaphysics

Death

Bibliographies

[133]
FULTON, R., *and others*. **Death, grief and bereavement II:** a bibliography, 1975-1980. ARNO, 1981. 230p. $25. ISBN: 0405142129.

Continues the author's *Death, grief and bereavement: a bibliography, 1845-1975* (Ayer Co. Publications, 1976, $27.50. 0405095708), which had 3800 entries.

2300 entries arranged A-Z by author and numbered. Broad subject index of terms refers to the numbered entries. An addendum, J.C. Santora's *Guide to doctoral dissertations on death and dying, 1970-1978* duplicates some of the entries in the main section. *Class No:* 128(01)

[134]
SIMPSON, M.A. **Dying, death and grief:** a critical bibliography. Pittsburgh, Pa., University of Pittsburgh (distributed by Harper), 1987. xv, 259p. $27.95. (*Contemporary community health series.*) ISBN: 0822935619.

First published in 1979 by Plenum Press.

1,700 non-fiction and fiction books published, mainly, since 1979, on subjects such as grief, suicide, murder, war, counselling, loneliness, death customs of different peoples, hospices, genocide, and the death penalty. Arranged A-Z by title, most entries having an evaluative annotation. Ratings given for recommendation, 1-5. Subject and author indexes. *Class No:* 128(01)

Handbooks & Manuals

[135]
RAPHAEL, B. **When disaster strikes:** a handbook for the caring professions. London, Hutchinson Ltd., 1986. x,342p. £19.95. ISBN: 009165470x.

In two parts: the 1st part, 'The disaster experience', has 7 chapters on reactions to disasters; the 2nd part has 5 chapters on psychosocial care, mental health and adjustment, victims and helpers. Each part has substantial reference, subject and name indexes. Presentation is excellent. *Class No:* 128(035)

Occultism & Parapsychology

[136]
GORDON, S. **The Paranormal:** an illustrated encyclopedia. Headland, Cleveland, Headline, 1992. 736p. 40 illus. £18.99. ISBN: 0747203563.

'Looks at every conceivable phenomenon and idea that strays outside what is perceived as 'normal''. (*British book news*, April 1992, p.298). *Class No:* 133

Bibliographies

[137]
CLARIE, T.C. **Occult/paranormal bibliography:** an annotated list of books published in English, 1976 through 1981. Metuchen, N.J., Scarecrow Press, 1984. 579p. $37.50; £29.65. ISBN: 0810816741.

Continues the same author's '*Occult bibliography: an annotated list of books published in English, 1971 through 1975*' (482p. $32.50. £24.35. ISBN 0810811529). *Class No:* 133(01)

[138]
KIES, C. **The Occult in the Western world:** an annotated bibliography. Hamden, C.T., Shoe String Press, 1986. 233p. $29.50. ISBN: 0208021132.

Intended to be a source book for beginners and casual readers needing a general overview of occult topics, the bibliography contains nearly 900 important English-language monographs on witchcraft, magic, mysticism, parapsychology, U.F.O.'s, mythical creatures, prophesy and astrology. Emphasis is given to books useful as reference works. Includes a glossary, name and title indexes. 'Excellent and well-written introductory material ... entries well organized' (*Choice*, January 1987, p.744). *Class No:* 133(01)

[139]
SOCIETY FOR PSYCHICAL RESEARCH. **Catalogue of the Library of the Society for Psychical Research.** Boston, Mass., G.K. Hall, 1976. 341p. $75. ISBN: 081610008x.

Author-title catalogue; 7,100 photolithographically reproduced cards. Coverage includes telepathy, paranormal cognition, mediumship, psychology, philosophy, mysticism, hypnotism. *Class No:* 133(01)

Encyclopaedias

[140]
CAVENDISH, R., *ed*. **Encyclopedia of the unexplained:** the ultimate guide to the unknown, the esoteric and the unproven. 2nd ed. London, Penguin Books, 1990. 304p. illus. ISBN: 0140191909.

First published 1974.

Highly readable entries, A-Z, covering terms, persons, organizations and movements. Longer articles are signed and documented. Embraces spiritualism, astrology, ESP, the mystery religions, Eastern beliefs, divinations and the like. Updates significantly Fodor's *Encyclopaedia of psychic science* (1933) and Spence's *Encyclopaedia of occultism* (1920), states *Library journal* (August 1974, p.1925). *Class No:* 133(031)

[141]
CAVENDISH, R., *ed*. **Man, myth and magic:** the illustrated encyclopaedia of mythology, religion and the unknown. 2nd ed. Freeport, N.Y., Marshall Cavendish, 1983. 12v. (3268p.). $399.95; £313.50. ISBN: 0863070418.

First published 1970 in 24 vols.

Heavily illustrated articles, treating their subjects in an objective, reportorial manner, Nearly all the revision is in the bibliographies (appended to articles) and subject bibliographies. 'For a popular audience. Libraries lacking the 1970 ed. should fill that void'. (*Wilson library bulletin*, November 1983, p.228-9). *Class No:* 133(031)

[142]
Harper's encyclopedia of mystical & paranormal experiences. Guiley, R.E., *ed*. New York & London, HarperCollins, 1991. 666p. illus. 35.95. £15.99. ISBN: 0062503659.

500 entries, arranged A-Z and cross-referenced. Emphasis is on major personalities, mystical techniques and traditions, locations of interest, original and paranormal phenomena. All articles list bibliographical references. *Class No:* 133(031)

[143]
SHEPARD, L.A., *ed*. **Encyclopedia of occultism and parapsychology.** 3rd ed. Detroit, Mich., Gale Research Co., 1991. 2v. (2008p.). ISBN: 0810349078.

First published in 1978, 2nd ed. 1984-85. Adapted from L. Spence's *Encyclopaedia of the occult* (1920) and N. Fodor's *Encyclopaedia of psychic science* (1934).

Over 5000 entries, varying from 1 sentence to many pages in length in one A-Z sequence. Scope includes the occult, magic, miracles and witchcraft, as well as numerous paranormal events previously regarded as supernatural. Prominent individuals in the field are covered. Many entries include a wide range of bibliographical references. Comprehensive general index and 9 topical indexes. 'Can be faulted in many cases by its ignoring of evidence and conclusions ... Would be a valuable resource if supplemented by the use of critical studies' (*Choice*, v.28(10), June 1991, p.1615). *Class No:* 133(031)

Handbooks & Manuals

[144]
LITVINOFF, S., *ed*. **The Illustrated guide to the supernatural.** Boston, Mass., G.K. Hall, 1986. iv,156p. illus. $25. (*Hall reference*.) ISBN: 0816189048.

145 articles, arranged A-Z by subject, covering popular occult areas such as magical beliefs, fortune-telling and divination, psychic phenomena, and biographies from ancient times to the present. Introductory level, not for the specialist. Entries vary in length from a paragraph to 3 pages, with references to other entries at the end of each article. Table of contents. Bibliography. '... entertaining, profusely illustrated guide...' (*Reference books bulletin*, 1986/87, p.50). *Class No:* 133(035)

[145]
WILSON, D. *and* WILSON, C. **Unsolved mysteries past and present.** London, Headline, 1993. 448p. £19.99. ISBN: 0747208379.

Attempts to explain historical enigma, voices from the grave, and psychic and supernatural occurrences. *Class No:* 133(035)

Dictionaries

[146]

DRURY, N. **Dictionary of mysticism and the esoteric traditions.** Rev. ed. New York, ABC-Clio, 1992. 328p. $49.50. ISBN: 0874366992.

First published 1985 by Harper & Row as Dictionary of mysticism and the occult

Nearly 3000 names and terms from the fields of magic, mysticism, parapsychology and spiritualism. Includes brief biographies of prominent occult figures. Entries are short, but clear. 'No substitute for Shepard's *Encyclopedia of occultism and parapsychology'* (*qv*) but a good, inexpensive ready-reference tool (*Choice,* v.23(2), October 1985, p.270) of the lst ed. *Class No:* 133(038)

[147]

GETTINGS, F. **Dictionary of occult, hermetic and alchemical sigils.** London, Routledge & Kegan Paul, 1981. 410p. £15.95. ISBN: 0710000952.

Designed as a reference, guide and sourcebook for those involved in general occult studies. 1500 headings. Meanings of over 9000 sigils (line patterns with magical significance) which appear in European alchemical, astrological, geomatic and related hermetic sources, plus a unique graphic index of sigils by number of strokes, p.323-410. Bibliography, p.293-312. Dating of sigils, p.239-291. 7 appendices (7, 'standard' sigils in modern astrology from Deutsche [*Die Deutsche Ephemeride,* 1980). *Class No:* 133(038)

[148]

PICKNETT, L. **The Encyclopedia of the paranormal:** a complete guide to the unexplained. London, Macmillan, 1990. [5],296p. 196 illus (16 col). £19.95. ISBN: 0333491009.

Deals comprehensively and objectively with all the main documented instances of phenomena that cannot be explained. Claims to be about the paranormal, not the "occult". 8 chapters: 1. The power of belief - 2. Secrets of the mind - 3. Extraordinary people - 4. The unpredictable world - 5. The UFO enigma - 6. Psi research - 7. Frontiers of science - 8. Life after death. Index, p.288-296. *Class No:* 133(038)

[149]

WATSON, D., *ed.* **A Dictionary of mind and spirit.** London, Deutsch, 1991. 406p. £15.99. ISBN: 0233986715.

Over 500 terms related to paranormal phenomena. esoteric and parapsychology. 'An instructive and entertaining attempt to draw together science and the spiritual tradition.'*(The good book guide,* v.56, March/April 1992, p.11). *Class No:* 133(038)

Histories

[150]

HAYNES, R. **The Society for Psychical Research, 1882-1982:** a history. London, Macdonald & Co., 1982. 256p. £7.95. ISBN: 0356078752.

'Any serious research into "the unknown", whether it be apparitions or mediumship, precognition or electro-voice phenomena, out-of-body experiences or poltergeists, would not only find this work of considerable value but also, because of the "behind-the-scenes" detail, of great interest' (*British book news,* November 1982, p.667). *Class No:* 133(091)

[151]

INGLIS, B. **Natural and supernatural:** a history of the paranormal. Bridport, Dorset, Prism Press, 1992. 508p. £9.95. ISBN: 1853270741.

First published 1977.

A history of the paranormal from early times to 1944, together with the careers of people associated with such phenomena. Sources, p.454-72. Bibliography, p.473-94. Index, p.495-500. *Class No:* 133(091)

Research Projects

[152]

OPPENHEIM, J. **The Other world:** spiritualism and psychical research in England, 1850-1914. Cambridge, Cambridge University Press, 1985. xii, 503p. plus 16 unnumbered pages of illustrations. £40. ISBN: 0521265053.

Examines the public fascination with spiritualism in Britain from the mid-19th to early 20th century. Based on extensive research of manuscripts, pamphlets, newspapers and books by and about Victorian spiritualists and psychical researchers. 8 chapters in 3 parts: Part I. The setting (1. Mediums - 2. Membership); II. A surrogate faith (3. Spiritualism and Christianity - 4. Psychical research and agnosticism - 5. Theosophy and the occult); III. A pseudoscience (6. Concepts of mind - 7. The problem of evolution - 8. Physics and psychic phenomena). A conclusion is followed by section of notes relating to the various chapters (1162 references, p.399-486) and a detailed index (p.487-503) with cross-references. 'An altogether superior study' (*Nature,* 4 July 1985, p.25). *Class No:* 133:061:061.62.005

Occultism

Encyclopaedias

[153]

GUILEY, R.E. **The Encyclopedia of ghosts and spirits.** New York, Facts on File, 1992. 374p. illus. $40. £21.95. ISBN: 0816021406.

Aims to present both sceptical and believing viewpoints. Very thorough coverage, with concise, clear entries. Includes sources for further reading. 'A useful addition to reference shelves'(*Library journal,* 1 September 1992, p.168). *Class No:* 133.2(031)

[154]

—SPENCER, J *and* SPENCER, A. The Encyclopedia of ghosts and spirits. London, Headline, 1992. 416p. 16 illus. £18.99. $39.95. ISBN: 0747205086. *Class No:* 133.2(031)

Dictionaries

[155]

BLETZER, J.G. **The Donning international encyclopedic psychic dictionary.** Norfolk, VA., Donning, 1986. 888p. $29.95. ISBN: 089865372x.

Includes over 9000 terms taken from popular occultism. Entries are brief, with no etymology. Extensive cross-references. *Class No:* 133.2(038)

[156]

HAINING, P. A Dictionary of ghosts. London, Robert Hale, 1982. 271p. 136 illus. £9.50. ISBN: 0709196229.

'... does not claim to be exhaustive ... but it *is* representative and does ... give a very fair coverage of the topic ...' (Foreword). Entries vary in length from 5 or 6 lines to a page and cover the various different types of ghosts throughout the world, detailing the most famous hauntings, and including information on all the people and phenomena associated with the topic. *Class No:* 133.2(038)

[157]

SPENCE, L. An Encyclopaedia of occultism: a compendium of information on the occult sciences, occult personalities, psychic science, magic, demonology, spiritualism and mysticism. London, Routledge, 1920 (Reprinted Citadel Press, 1985). 464p. illus. $12.95; £11.95. ISBN: 0806509058.

'This is perhaps the finest source book on the subject' (*RQ,* v.11(1), Fall, 1971, p.12). Articles, A-Z, are supported by references. 'Banshee' : 1¾ cols.; 'Paracelsus': 5½ cols. Select bibliography. Index. *Class No:* 133.2(038)

Histories

[158]

BARROW, L. Independent spirits: spiritualism and English plebeians, 1850-1910. London, Routledge & Kegan Paul, 1986. xiii, 338p. 21 illus. £20. (*History workshop series.*) ISBN: 0710098839.

'Concerning the intellectual world of the humbly-born in late 19th and early 20th century Britain, focusing on plebeian, or working- and lower middle-class spiritualists. Chapter 1. Germination - 2. Owenism and the millennium - 3. Nottingham and cabala - 4. The problematic and imponderables - 5. Plebeians and others - 6. Presence and problems of democratic epistemology - 7. Healing - 8. Bridging the great divide. Notes (p.281-329) are arranged by chapter. Index (p.300-332). *Class No:* 133.2(091)

Parapsychology

[159]

BERGER, A.S. *and* **BERGER, J. The Encyclopedia of parapsychology and psychical research.** New York, Paragon House, 1991. 554p. $45. ISBN: 1557780439.

1400 entries, A-Z, relating to both areas of the paranormal - concepts, methods, phenomena, research organizations, publications and biographies. Short bibliographies after each entry. Cross-references. 3 appendices, including a country index and a 39-page bibliography. Intended for the general public, science writers and journalists. '... an authoritative and unbiased reference source...'(*Booklist*, v.87(12), 15 February 1991, p.1248). *Class No:* 133.3

[160]

WOLMAN, B.B., *ed.* **Handbook of parapsychology.** New York, Van Nostrand, Reinhold, 1977 (reprinted by McFarland & Co., 1986). xxiv, 1007p. illus. $49.95. ISBN: 0899501869.

31 contributors. 11 parts: 1. History of parapsychology - 2. Research methods - 3. Perception, communication, and parapsychology - 4. Parapsychology and physical systems - 5. Parapsychology and altered states of consciousness - 6. Parapsychology and healing - 7. Survival of bodily death - 8. Parapsychology and other fields (*e.g.* anthropology) - 9.

....(contd.)

Parapsychologic models and theories - 10. Social research in parapsychology - 11. Suggested readings (annotated bibliography, p.907-20). Glossary, p.921-36. Parts 1-10 each have appended bibliogaphies. Name and subject indexes. *Class No:* 133.3

Bibliographies

[161]

WHITE, R.A. *and* **DALE, L.A. Parapsychology:** sources of information. Compiled under the auspices of the American Society of Psychical Research. Metuchen, N.J. Scarecrow Press, 1973. 303p. $19. ISBN: 0810806177.

Annotated bibliography of 282 books, under 24 subject headings. Short introduction to each subject section. Annotations indicate level of readership; type of library; notes inclusion of glossaries, illustrations and bibliographies; and gives citations to book reviews. 'The authors have produced the "Winchell" of parapsychology' (*Library journal*, v.99(2), 15 January 1974, p.126). *Class No:* 133.3(01)

[162]

—**WHITE, R.** New sources of information, 1973-1989. Metuchen, NJ, Scarecrow Press, 1990. 699p. $67.50. ISBN: 0810823853.

Chronological continuation of the above, with *c.*480 books, with descriptive annotations, arranged in 27 topical categories, each category prefaced by a brief bibliographical essay. Also includes chapters on the field's journals, organizations and graduate theses: '... a carefully crafted guide to the recent literature.'(*Wilson library bulletin*, v.65(9), p.141). *Class No:* 133.3(01)

Reviews & Abstracts

[163]

Exceptional human experience: studies of the psychic-spontaneous -intangible, 1983- 2pa. Dix Hills, N.Y., Parapsychology Sources of Information, 1983-. $50 pa. ISSN: 07407629.

Prior to 1990 title was *Parapsychology abstracts international*

*c.*250 abstracts in each issue, each abstract containing 200-300 words or more, arranged in 9 subject sections. About 100 current parapsychological journals are analysed, together with material of interest found in non-parapsychological journals, books, etc., mainly in English although some non-English material is included. Author and detailed subject index in each issue. '... a model of its kind ...' (*Library journal,* v.109(20), December 1984, p.2252). Also available online. *Class No:* 133.3(048)

USA

[164]

BERGER, A.S. Lives and letters in American parapsychology: a biographical history, 1850-1987. Jefferson, N.C., McFarland, 1988. 381p. illus. $39.95; £29.95. ISBN: 0899503454.

An overview, outlining significant events in American parapsychology and providing biographies of predominant figures. Divided into 5 periods, each with short introduction followed by highlights of the history of parapsychology, chronologically arranged, and with emphasis on the persons

....(contd.)

who contributed. Many quotations included. Footnotes. 54 pages of references but no comprehensive bibliography. Index of persons, topics and titles. *Class No:* 133.3(73)

Witchcraft & Magic

[165]
Early modern European witchcraft: centres and peripheries. Ankarloo, B. *and* Henningsen, G., *eds.* Oxford, Clarendon Press, 1990. [9],477p. 5 figs., maps. £45. ISBN: 019821989x.

First published by Olin Foundation in Swedish.

18 chapters in 4 sections: 1. Witchcraft, law and theology; 2. Origins of the witch's sabbath; 3. Witch-hunting in Scandinavia and other peripheries; 4. Conclusions. 19 contributors. Footnotes. Bibliography of secondary works, p.446. Index. *Class No:* 133.4

[166]
GUILEY, R.E. The Encyclopedia of witches and witchcraft. New York, Facts on File, 1989. 421p. illus. $45. ISBN: 081601793x.

Arranged A-Z by subjects and covering the history of witchhunts, beliefs of witches, their organizations, folk magic, pagan deities, sorcery, occultism, shamanism, etc. Includes biographies. The length of citations varies from a paragraph to several pages. 100 black-and-white illus. Bibliography of 355 items, and also a list of works mentioned in the text. Cross-references. '... comprehensive coverage of terminology, biography and history make this work an important addition to the reference works available on the topic' (*Reference books bulletin,* November 1989, p.604). '... fills a unique niche. While covering the history of witchcraft in a serviceable and accurate way, it also includes a large amount of material, mostly biographical, on modern witches' (*Choice,* v.27(5), January 1990, p.768). *Class No:* 133.4

Histories

[167]
RUSSELL, J.B. A History of witchcraft throughout the ages. London, Thames and Hudson, 1981. 192p. illus. £5.95. ISBN: 0580272425.

A critical study of witchcraft throughout the ages. Following an introduction ('What is a witch?'), 10 chapters are arranged in 2 parts: 1. Sorcery and historical witchcraft (Sorcery - The roots of European witchcraft - Witchcraft, heresy, and inquisition - The witch-craze on the continent of Europe - Witchcraft in Britain and America - Witchcraft and society - The decline of Witchcraft) and 2. Modern witchcraft (Survivals and revivals - The religion of the witches - The role of witchcraft). The study concludes with a section of 74 reference notes on the text, a bibliography (p.180-183) arranged A-Z by author, and a detailed subject index (p.188-192). *Class No:* 133.4(091)

[168]
THORNDIKE, L. History of magic and experimental science. New York, Columbia University Press, 1923-58. 8v.

V.1-2: First 13 centuries; 3-4; 14 & 15 centuries; 5-6: 16 century; 7-8: 17 century.

'Based on an examination of the original MSS and documents of the early writers, scientists and historians in

....(contd.)

library collections all over the world'. The word 'magic' as used in the title 'is understood in its broadest sense as including all occult arts and sciences, superstitions and folklore' (Hawkins, R.R. *Scientific, medical and technical books ... 1930-44,* p.4). Well documented. V.1-2 include a general index, bibliographical index, and index of MSS; v.3-4 & 5-6, general index, index of MSS and index of incipits; v.7-8, general index and index of MSS. A monumental survey. *Class No:* 133.4(091)

Alchemy

[169]
Alchemy: a comprehensive bibliography of the Manly P. Hall Collection of books and manuscripts. Hogart, R.C., *ed.* Los Angeles, CA., Philos Research, 1985. xiv,[1],314p. illus. (incl.pl.), facsims. $125. ISBN: 0893145424. *Class No:* 133.5

[170]
PRITCHARD, A. Alchemy; a bibliography of English-language writings. London, Routledge & Kegan Paul, jointly with The Library Association, 1980. [vii], 439p. ISBN: 0710004729.

Originally as a bibliography approved for the L.A. diploma. 3,188 entries for items written 1597-1978: A. Alchemical texts (16 sections: Greek and hermetic texts) - B. Works about alchemy: countries (19 sections: Ancient Middle East ... U.S.A.) - C. Works about alchemy: subjects (Alchemy, general - Bibliography and libraries ... Symbols and yearbooks ... Science - Chemistry - Art - Literature and fiction - Biographies - Unclassified). Section A items are often annotated. Items not examined are asterisked. Appendix: 'Major sources searched', p.402-6. Index of 'all personal names occurring in the bibliography, together with subjects', p.407-39. Preface: 'On alchemy and its bibliography', p.1-9. Includes theses. 'An outstanding contribution to works on alchemy in English ...' (*British book news,* October 1980, p.588-9). Awarded the Library Association's Besterman Medal for 1980. *Class No:* 133.5

[171]
—**HAEFFNER, M. The Dictionary of alchemy:** from Maria Prophetinsa to Isaac Newton. London, Aquarium Press, 1991. 272p. illus. £12.99. ISBN: 1855380854.

A glossary of alchemical terms, concepts and symbols, and main practitioners. Includes Western, Indo-Tibetan and Chinese Taoist traditions. *Class No:* 133.5

Astrology

[172]
FILBY, J. *and* **FILBY, P. Astronomy for astrologers.** Wellingborough, Northants., The Aquarian Press, 1984. 255p. tables, charts. £6.55. ISBN: 0850303931.

An introduction to the astronomical basis of astrology. 11 chapters: 1. An outline of the history of astronomy - 2. The development of modern astronomy ... 4. The calendar - 5. Time - 6. The astrological ephemeris ... 10. The universe: stars and galaxies - 11. Cosmic cycles and mundane events. Glossary, p.193-202. 5 appendices: 3. Calculation tables; 5. Star charts. Bibliography, p.246-250. Index, p.251-255. *Class No:* 133.52

[173]

PARKER, D. *and* **PARKER, J. Parker's astrology.** London, Dorling Kindersley, 1991. 415p. illus. charts. £19.95. ISBN: 0863186017.

A practical guide to astrology. A foreword on the craft of the astrologer and 'How to use this book' are followed by 5 chapters: 1. Astrological techniques; 2. Understanding the Sun signs; 3. Astrology in action; 4. The planets at work; 5. Astrological tables. Profusely illustrated. 'Coffee table' size. Analytical index, p.412-6. *Class No:* 133.52

[174]

WHITE, S. The New astrology. London, Macmillan, 1986. [2], 682, [5]p. £10.95. ISBN: 0333434919.

First published in France by Editions Robert Laffont, S.A., under the title *La double astrologie.*

Claims to be a unique synthesis of the world's two great astrological systems: The Chinese and Western.
Class No: 133.52

Bibliographies

[175]

GARDNER, F.L. Bibliotheca astrologica: catalog of astrological publications of the 15th through the 19th centuries ... with a sketch of the history of astrology by Dr. William Wynn Westcott. North Hollywood, CA., Symbols and Signs, 1977. xx, 164p. $12.50. ISBN: 0912504382.

Reprint of the 1911 edition.

1340 items arranged A-Z by author (or title in some cases) subdivided chronologically. Some entries annotated. Items 944-1003 are periodical titles indexed A-Z and inserted in the main sequence between P and Q. Some cross-references. Index, which includes important persons (*e.g.* William Lilly). *Class No:* 133.52(01)

[176]

PARA RESEARCH INC. Astrology books in print, 1981. New York, Para Research Inc., 1981. 128p. $3.95. ISBN: 0914918257.

900 titles divided by form (textbooks, general works, ephemerides, tables and atlases, dictionaries, tools and charts, magazines, annuals, calendars. Each entry includes title, author, price, type of binding. ISBN, pagination, publisher, and brief description. Guide to 140 publishers with addresses. Brief author index. Publisher promised to revise and expand the work eventually.
Class No: 133.52(01)

[177]

PATTIE, T.S. Astrology, as illustrated in the collections of the British Library and the British Museum: an historical account of the subject which includes the author's 'Horoscope for the British Library'. London, British Library, Reference Division, 1981. 36p. illus. £1.95. ISBN: 0904654494.

Includes 4 plates and 16 black-and-white illus.
Class No: 133.52(01)

Handbooks & Manuals

[178]

FREEMAN, M. How to interpret a birth chart: a guide to the analysis and synthesis of astrological charts. Wellingborough, Northants, Aquarian Press, 1981. [128]p. illus. £3.99. ISBN: 0850302498. *Class No:* 133.52(035)

[179]

LYNDOE, E. Everyman's astrology. Rev. ed. Sudbury, Suffolk, Neville Spearman Ltd., 1970 (reprinted 1972 and 1977). xi, 236p. illus. £3.95. ISBN: 0854352848.

First published 1959.

A simple how-to-do-it guide to making astrological maps and reading them. In 5 parts: Drawing the map - Meaning in the map - Judgement of the map - Tertiary directions - Tabulations (p.101-236) include planetary tables 1900-1999 inclusive. *Class No:* 133.52(035)

[180]

SAKOIAN, F. *and* **ACKER, L.S. Astrologer's handbook.** New ed. Harmondsworth, Herts., Penguin Books Ltd., 1981. xiv,461p. £7.99. ISBN: 0140053360.

Originally published by Harper & Row, 1973, and P. Davies, 1984.

16 chapters in two parts: I. Basic astrology; II. Interpreting the aspects. '... designed to provide the layman, the astrological student, and the practitioner of astrology with the information necessary for interpreting horoscopes'. (Section on 'How to read this book'). Glossary, p.441-442. General index, p.443-449. Cross index of aspects, p.450-461. *Class No:* 133.52(035)

Dictionaries

[181]

GETTINGS, F. Dictionary of astrology. London, Routledge & Kegan Paul, 1985. x, 365p. £25. ISBN: 0710096720.

Aimed at the non-specialist and the practical astrologer, and 'designed to form a reference guide and sourcebook' (*Introduction*). Over 3000 headings, including terms derived from the major post-medieval sources up to the present. Entries vary in length from one or two lines to 2 pages. Many 'see' references. Bibliography (p.359-365) A-Z by author. '... a fit companion for *Larousse encyclopedia of astrology* (1980) (*Choice*, v.23 (10), June 1986, p.1520). *Class No:* 133.52(038)

Histories

[182]

PARKER, D. *and* **PARKER, J. A History of astrology.** London, André Deutsch Ltd., 1983. 192p. 111 illus. (36 col.). ISBN: 0233975764.

Following an introduction, the work is divided into 11 chapters (1. Distant beginnings - 2. The prestigious planets - 3. Through the doors of Greece - 4. The imperial planets - 5. The pervasive planets - 6. The coming of Christianity - 7. Astrology in medieval Europe - 8. 'First cause of motion, cruel firmament' - 9. Success - and the beginning of failure - 10. Towards the dark - 11. Into the twentieth century). A brief glossary (p.189) and bibliography (p.190) are followed by an index (p.191-2). *Class No:* 133.52(091)

[183]

TESTER, J. A History of Western astrology. Woodbridge, Suffolk, Boydell Press, 1987. 256p. illus. £19.95. ISBN: 0851154468.

A history of astrological ideas and practices from their shadowy beginnings in Mesopotamia and subsequent scientific establishment in Greece in about the 5th century, up to today's surviving popular almanacs and astrological magazines, showing how little has changed. Lucid and concise. *Class No:* 133.52(091)

Palmistry

[184]
BROEKMAN, M. **Complete encyclopaedia of practical palmistry.** London, Souvenir Press, 1986. [6], 187p. illus. £6.95. ISBN: 0285627767.

Reissue of the 1st, 1972 ed.

Aims to be a comprehensive straightforward introduction to the ancient art of palmistry. In 4 sections: 1. Event markings - 2. Character markings - 3. Analysis - 4. Sample readings. *Class No:* 133.6

[185]
FITZHERBERT, A. **The Palmist's companion:** a history and bibliography of palmistry. Metuchen, NJ, Scarecrow Press, 1992. 236p. $27.60. ISBN: 0810825244.

Choice (December 1992) considers it to be haphazard, with errors, and that it succeeds only because information is difficult to find elsewhere. Partly a bibliography, partly a history of palmistry, and partly biographies of palmists. Title index. *Class No:* 133.6

Philosophical Systems

[186]
DUNN, J., *and others*. **The British Empiricists:** Locke, Berkeley, Hume. Oxford, Oxford University Press, 1992. 304p. £8.99. ISBN: 0192830686.

Concise introductions to Locke's theory of knowledge, Berkeley's philosophy in relation to the thought of Newton, and Hume's ideas on perception and self-identity. *Class No:* 14

[187]
EBENSTEIN, W. **Today's isms: Communism, Fascism, Capitalism, Socialism.** 9th ed. Englewood Cliffs, N.J., Prentice-Hall, 1985. x,229p. illus. $29. ISBN: 0139244735.

Arranged in 4 sections, each subdivided. 1. Communism - 2. Fascism - 3. Capitalism - 4. Socialism. A discussion of the main representations on each side. Lists of further reading are appended to each section. Index, p.221-229.

A 10th rev. ed. by A.O.Ebenstein and others was issued in 1993 (ISBN 013138595x). *Class No:* 14

Mysticism

Bibliographies

[188]
GRANT, P. **Literature of mysticism in Western tradition.** London, Macmillan Press, 1983. x,179p. £35. ISBN: 0333287983.

7 essays claiming that mysticism cannot be well discussed separately from a framework of faith: 1. Mysticism, faith and culture - 2. Imagination and mystery - 3. Historical crises: from incarnation to imagination - 4. Self and ego - 5. The Cross - 6. The Way - 7. Conclusion. Notes, p.156-167, by chapter. Bibliographical guide to texts, without comment, p.168-174, by chapter. Index, p.175-179. *Class No:* 141.33(01)

Socialist Systems

[189]
SCRUTON, R. **Thinkers of the new Left.** Harlow, Essex, Longman Group UK Ltd., 1985. [5],227p. £15. ISBN: 0582902738.

An analysis of 14 of the thinkers most influential on the attitudes of the post-1960 new Left. Chapter 1. What is Left?; ch.2-15 on individuals; ch.16 What is right?. Appendix: Biographical and bibliographical data (p.212-233) summarizes their careers and most important writings. Index of names (p.225-227). Originally appeared as separate essays in *The Salisbury review*. *Class No:* 141.8

Histories

[190]
COLE, G.D.H. **A History of Socialist thought.** London, Macmillan, 1953-60 (Reprinted 1961-63). 5v. (7v. in reprint).

1. *Socialist thought: the forerunners. 1789-1850.*
2. *Socialist thought: Marxism and Anarchism, 1850-1890.*
3. *The Second International, 1889-1914* (forms v.3-4 of reprint).
4. *Communism and social democracy, 1914-1931* (v.5-6 of reprint).
5. *Socialism and Fascism, 1931-1939* (v.7 of reprint).

Not a history of Socialism but of Socialist thought. Cole originally intended his history to go up to 1945, but he died in 1959 with this objective uncompleted. V.1 has 26 chapters, a select bibliography (p.317-32: chapter bibliographies preceded by general references), index of names and subject index. *Class No:* 141.8(091)

[191]
DROZ, J., *ed*. **Histoire générale du socialisme.** Paris, Presses Universitaires de France, 1972-78. 4v. illus.

V.1. From the origins to 1875 (1972. 600p.); v.2. From 1875 to 1919 (1974. 676p.); v.3. From 1919 to 1945 (1977. 762p.); v.4. From 1945 to the present (1978. 705,48p.). A comprehensive study of the general history of socialism in the French language. Includes notes, bibliographies and indexes in all 4v. *Class No:* 141.8(091)

[192]
YOUNG, J.D. **Socialism since 1889:** a biographical history. London, Pinter Publishers, 1988. viii,269p. £29.50. ISBN: 0861879856.

Describes the history of the labour movement, 1889-1986, through portraits of 18 men and women, varying from Hyndman and De Leon, through Lenin and Zetkin to Kolakowski and Fanon. 11 chapters: 1. The history of socialism; an overview, 1889-1939; 2-10. devotes each chapter to two socialists; 11. Contemporary socialism: tragedies and crises, 1939-86. Includes many quotations. 768 notes, p.237-262. Index, p.263-269. *Class No:* 141.8(091)

Great Britain

[193]
BEER, M. **History of British Socialism.** Nottingham, Spokesman Books, 1984. xiii,271p. illus., ports. £11.95. ISBN: 0851244084.

First published 1919.

Introduction to this ed. by R.H. Tawney. 18 chapters, each subdivded, in two parts: 1. Primitive Christian influences - 2. The English Schoolmen - 3. Early English

....(contd.)

Communism ... 7. The economic revolution ... 11. The economists - 12. Robert Owen - 13. The Co-operative Socialists ... 16. The birth of Chartism - 17. The alliance between the working class and the middle class - 18. Separation of the middle and working classes. Includes 300 illus. *Class No:* 141.8(091)(410)

USSR

[194]

WALICKI, A. A History of Russian thought: from the enlightenment to Marxism. Oxford, Clarendon Press, 1980 (reprinted as a paperback, 1988). xvii,456p. £14.95. ISBN: 0198277040.

First published in Polish in 1973 as *Rosyjska filozofia i myśl społeczna od oświecenia do marksizmu.* First published in English, translated by H. Andrews-Rusiecka, by Oxford University Press in 1980.

18 chapters (1. Trends in enlightenment thought ... 6. The Slavophiles - 7. The Russian Hegelians ... 10. The origins of Russian socialism ... 12. Populist ideologies - 13. Anarchism ... 18. From populism to Marxism). Footnotes. Index of names, p.449-456. '... excellent and brilliant work' (*Political studies,* September 1989, p.476-7). *Class No:* 141.8 (091)(47)

Utopian Socialism

[195]

CLARK, I.F., *Comp.* **The Tale of the future,** from the beginning to the present day: an annotated bibliography of those satires, ideal states, imaginary wars and invasions, coming catastrophies and end-of-the-world stories, political warnings and forecasts, inter-planetary voyages and scientific romances - all located in an imaginary future period - that have been published in the United Kingdon between 1644-1976. 3rd ed. London, Library Association, 1978. xvii, 357p.

First published 1961.

Over 4000 concisely annotated entries. 5 parts: 1. Chronological list, with annotations - 2. Short-title index - 3. Author index - 4. Notes - 5. Bibliography (p.356-7). Annotations 'now include the date of publication for American and British titles that were first published in the United States and the original titles of foreign works published in English translation ...' (*The arrangement of this bibliography*). Fills a gap. *Class No:* 141.81

[196]

FOGARTY, R.S. Dictionary of American communal and utopian history. Westport, CT., Greenwood Press, 1980. 320p. $40.95. ISBN: 031321347x.

Over 140 short biographies of major figures, 'biographies' of 59 communities, and a chronological list of 270 settlements founded before 1919 compiled by O. Okugawa. A review in *Library journal* (1 June 1980) deplores the lack of volume and page numbers for articles cited but 'even so, in a field of great interest and few general references, this would be an essential tool in most libraries'.

An update of the author's bibliographical essay published in *Choice* in 1973. *Class No:* 141.81

[197]

NEGLEY, G.R. Utopian literature: a bibliography. Lawrence, University Press of Kansas, 1978. 288p. $25. ISBN: 0700601643.

A list of utopias and dystopias, mostly European and American, ranging from Thomas More's to the present, arranged under authors, A-Z. Major locations given. Short titles and chronological indexes. *Class No:* 141.81

Chartism. Owenism

Chartism

[198]

HAMBRICK, M. A Chartist's library. London, Mansell Publishing Ltd., 1986. [iii], 266p. £30.00. ISBN: 072011831x.

A catalogue of some 1634 titles, of which *c.*1400 were owned by the Chartist, George Julian Harney. Arranged A-Z by author (anonymous works by title). Cross-references for editors, pseudonyms and some translators. Each entry includes name of author, complete title, place and year of publication, pagination, and the Vanderbilt University library accession number. Also includes descriptive notes about the book; full text of annotations, enclosures, dedications, autographs and inscriptions; and bibliographic information about the newspaper clippings found in the books. The introduction includes a short biography of Harney. *Class No:* 141.814CHA

[199]

HARRISON, J.F.C. *and* **THOMPSON, D. Bibliography of the Chartist movement, 1837-1976.** Hassocks, Sussex, Harvester Press; Atlantic Highlands, N.J., Humanities Press Inc., 1978. xvi, 214p.

'Intended as a modest tool for working scholars and a survey of the state of Chartist scholarship to date' (*Introduction*). Lists the major manuscript collections; pamphlets, serials and other printed materials by Chartists and their contemporaries: relevant parliamentary papers; and secondary source books and articles on the movement, the aim being to include all known items in local and national libraries and archives, including certain libraries abroad. Contains about 2,000 items. Index principally of names and titles, but includes some topical entries. Very favourably reviewed when first published. *Class No:* 141.814CHA

Communism. Marxism. Leninism

[200]

A Dictionary of Marxist thought. Bottomore, T., *ed.* 2nd ed. Oxford, Basil Blackwell Publishers Ltd.; Cambridge, Mass., Harvard University Press, 1992. 672p. £50; $64.95. ISBN: 0631164812, UK.

lst ed. 1983.

Provides clear accounts of concepts, schools of thought and individual Thinkers by *c.*80 eminent scholars of Marxism, taking account of different interpretations and criticisms. Each entry is a short essay, followed by a short bibliography or guide to further reading. Includes an editorial article on critics of Marxism. Also includes a list of contributors, with affiliations; a consolidated bibliography, A-Z by author (p.593-633); a chronological list of writings by Marx and Engels; and a subject index (p.567-87). Lists 49 entries new to the 2nd ed. '... an excellent guide'. (*College and research libraries,* v.45(4), July 1984, p.293).

....(contd.)

'Definitely supersedes Russell's *Marx-Engel's dictionary'* (1981) (*Library journal,* 15 October 1983, p.1955). *Class No:* 141.82

Bibliographies

[201]

HAYNES, J.E. **Communism and anti-Communism in the United States:** an annotated guide to historical writings. New York, Garland, 1987. 321p. $47. ISBN: 0824085205.

Author is editor of the Newsletter of the Historians of American Communism and entries are drawn from the newsletter's annual bibliography. Includes books, journal articles and dissertations. Concerned with the period from the Bolshevik Revolution through McCarthyism of the 1950s, the emphasis is on scholarly examinations of the history and influence of Communism in American life, and includes some primary materials. Structured into 37 time-periods and issues (labour, literature, women, etc.). Author index but no subject index (table of contents) '... otherwise a unique and useful volume' (*College and research libraries,* January 1988, p.62). *Class No:* 141.82(01)

[202]

KINNELL, S.K., *ed.* **Communism in the world since 1945:** an annotated bibliography. Santa Barbara, CA., ABC-Clio, 1987. 415p. $85. (*Clio bibliography series, 25.*) ISBN: 0874361699.

4151 entries, half of them on the Soviet Union and Eastern Europe, published between 1974 and 1985. Non-English-language titles are given English sub-titles. Cross-references. Author and subject indexes. Scholarly. Complements Charles Hobday's *Communist and Marxist parties of the world* (1986). *Class No:* 141.82(01)

[203]

LUBITZ, W. **Trotsky bibliography:** a classified list of published items about Leon Trotsky and Trotskyism. 2nd ed. rev. & expanded. New York, K.G. Saur, 1988. 581p. $120. ISBN: 3598107544.

First published 1982.

A classified bibliography of 5009 items, including monographs, journal articles, symposia, masters' theses and doctoral dissertations, published speeches, review articles, introductions and prefaces to Trotsky's works, etc. Arranged in 8 topical sections, each section subdivided. Several indexes. Complements Louis Sinclair's *Leon Trotsky* (1972; supplements 1977 & 1980). *Class No:* 141.82(01)

[204]

NARKIEWICZ, O. **Eurocommunism, 1968-1986:** a select bibliography. London, Mansell Publishing Ltd.; New York, H.W. Wilson, 1987. xxi,188p. £25; $56. ISBN: 0720118018.

1425 items arranged in 2 parts: 1. Bibliography of monographs, studies and selected essays - 2. Bibliography of published sources (journals and newspapers). Entries listed A-Z in each part, with very brief annotations. Includes a lengthy introductory essay on the subject, p.vii-xxi, which states that the volume was compiled with a view to documenting new and interesting political phenomenon, both for the specialist and for the student of politics. No indexes. *Class No:* 141.82(01)

[205]

SINCLAIR, L. **Trotsky: a bibliography.** Aldershot, Hanst, Scolar Press, 1989. 2v.(1384p). £95. ISBN: 0859678202.

Earlier ed. published 1972 as *Leon Trotsky: a bibliography.*

*c.*5200 items listed chronologically, with references to later reprints, translations, etc. Also lists a further *c.*7200 unpublished items. '... a valuable and useful approach ...'(*International review of social history,* v.36(1), 1991,p.113). *Class No:* 141.82(01)

Dictionaries

French

[206]

LABICA, G. *and* BENSUSSAN, G., *eds.* **Dictionnaire critique du Marxisme.** 2e. refondue et augmentée. Paris, Presses Universitaire de Paris, 1985. xvi,1240p. ISBN: 213038739x.

First published 1982.

Lengthy entries of between 2 to 10 pages each, followed by bibliographies and lists of alternative or related terms. Cross-references. Notes. A list of contributors precedes. *Class No:* 141.82(038)=40

Chinese

[207]

DOOLIN, D. *and* RIDLEY, C. A **Chinese-English dictionary of Communist Chinese terminology.** Stanford, CA., Hoover Institution Press, 1973. 569p. $30. ISBN: 0817962417. *Class No:* 141.82(038)=951

Periodicals

[208]

The Left index: a quarterly index to periodicals of the Left. Santa Cruz, CA., The Left Index, 1982-. Quarterly. $60 pa (institutions); $30 pa (individuals). ISSN: 07332998.

Covers journals representing a Marxist, radical, or Left perspective, and includes topics on anthropology, black studies, economics, education, philosophy, political science, psychology, science, sociology, and women's studies. *c.*80 journals are indexed regularly, including 22 foreign titles. *c.*500 numbered entries in each issue, arranged A-Z by author. Cross-references. Book review index (arranged A-Z by author); cumulated subject index (based on Library of Congress subject headings); journal index (analysing contents). '... some overlap with *Alternative press index'.* (*Reference books bulletin,* August 1988). *Class No:* 141.82(051)

Quotations

[209]

WEEKS, A.L., *comp.* & *ed.* **Brassey's Soviet and communist quotations.** Washington, D.C., Pergamon-Brassey's; International Defence Publishers, 1987. xxii,387p. $50. ISBN: 0080344887.

Statements rather than mere quotations. 2117 numbered items arranged by subject in 17 chapters: 1. Capitalism and socialism - 2. Class and class warfare - 3. Communism - 4. Communist party ... 9. Marxist-Leninist ideologies ... 12. Religion and ethics - 13. Revolution ... 15. Terrorism/

....*(contd.)*

guerrilla warfare ... 17. War preparation. Quotations are followed by the source (person, and where published). Index, by chapter, p.369-386. 'A useful and unique reference source, it would be vastly improved by a more utilitarian index' (*College & research libraries*, v.49(1), January 1988, p.62). *Class No:* 141.82(082.2)

Histories

[210]

STERN, G. **Atlas of Communism.** New York, Macmillan, 1991. 256p. illus. 48 maps. $95. ISBN: 0028972651.

A descriptive, historical essay, with maps, on the origins, development and recent decline of Communism, and some movements that had viewpoints in common with Communism. 5 main sections, each subdivided: The roots of Communism, 1848-1917 - The Soviet experience, 1917-1945 - Cold War Communism, 1945-62 - New perspectives, 1962-85 - Reform and revolution, 1985 to the present. Index. 'The book's main strength is that it is comprehensive ... coverage, combined with an excellent index, gives it considerable value as a reference tool.'(*Choice*, v.29(1), September 1991, p.51). *Class No:* 141.82(091)

Biographies

[211]

GORMAN, R.A., *ed.* **Biographical dictionary of Marxism.** London, Mansell Publishing; Westport, CT., Greenwood Press, 1986. x, 389p. £45. $55. ISBN: 0720118190, UK; 0313248516, US.

Focuses on materialist or orthodox Marxism. Selective biographies of over 210 major twentieth-century philosophers throughout the world. Each entry, ranging from ½-page to 3 pages in length, has biographical data on the individual, a summary of his/her significant contributions to Marxist theory and practice, and a bibliography of primary and secondary sources for research. Appendix: Entrants by nationality contribution. Index (p.371-388, double-column).' ... eminently readable ...' (*Library journal*, 1 February 1986, p.73). '... clearly written and concise entries ...' (*Choice*, July/August 1986, p.1651). *Class No:* 141.82(092)

[212]

GORMAN, R.A., *ed.* **Biographical dictionary of Neo-Marxism.** London, Mansell Publishing Ltd.; Westport, CT., Greenwood Press, 1986. x, 464p. £45. $55. ISBN: 0720118204, UK; 0313235139, US.

Companion volume to the author's *'Biographical dictionary of Marxism'* (qv).

A useful introduction, outlining the origins and several key components of Neo-Marxist thought and action, precedes more than 205 biographical entries and 10 entries describing important groups, movements and journals. Cross-references. Selective bibliography of primary and secondary sources. Two appendices: Entrants by nationality; List of contributors. Good subject index (p.447-463 double-column). '... a valuable reference for the study of Neo-Marxism'. (*Choice*, v.23(9), May 1986, p.1368). *Class No:* 141.82(092)

Official Records

[213]

Documents on Communist affairs, 1985. Szajkowski, B., *ed.* 5th in series. Brighton, Sussex, Wheatsheaf; New York, St. Martin's, 1986. xi,340p. £50. ISBN: 0745002528, UK; 0312004281, US.

The series was commenced in 1977; later issues 1978, 1979 & 1980.

An introduction is followed by the documents, in English translation, grouped by region (Africa, Arab world, Asia, International meetings, Latin America & Caribbean, North America, Soviet Union and Eastern Europe, Western Europe). Material included is from original sources which became available between 1981 and 1985. Includes Chronology of 15 US-Soviet Summits held between 1943 and 1985. Index, p.334-340. *Class No:* 141.82(093.2)

Psychology

---

[214]

The Blackwell dictionary of cognitive psychology. Eysenck, M.W. Oxford, Blackwell, 1991. xvi,390p. £60. ISBN: 0651156828.

One of the main aims of the book is to 'provide the reader with the scope and diversity of contemporary cognitive psychology' (*Introduction*). Arranged A-Z, 140 terms are defined at length. Each essay-length entry includes a well-balanced bibliography with details of the key publications relating to the particular topic. 'an outstanding publication of high quality content matched by thoughtful editing, arrangement and indexing ... good value ...'(*Reference reviews*, v.5(2), 1991, p.8. *Class No:* 159.9

[215]

BORCHARDT, D.H. *and* FRANCIS, R.D. **How to find out in psychology:** a guide to the literature and methods of research. Oxford, Pergamon Press, 1986. xi,189p. 17 illus. £14.75. ISBN: 0080312802.

First published in 1968 as *How to find out in philosophy and psychology*, by D.H. Borchardt.

'... eleven chapters. The first two deal with what psychology is about and its major theories, and chapters III-VI deal with the bibliographic aids used by psychologists ... How one gathers and presents such material is the subject of chapters VIII-X ... Chapter XI is concerned with professional matters and includes information on psychological organizations ...' (*Preface*). 5 appendices A. A guide to library searches ... E. Psychological societies). Bibliography, p.175-186. A-Z by author; journals A-Z by title. Subject index, p.187-189. *Class No:* 159.9

[216]

GRATTAN-GUINNESS, I., *ed.* **Psychical research:** a guide to its history, principles and practice. Wellingborough, Northants, The Aquarian Press, 1982. 424p. ISBN: 0850303168.

Published to celebrate the centenary of the Society for Psychical Research, 1882-1982.

34 chapters in 5 parts: 1. Introduction (including a chapter on 'History of psychical research') - 2. The range of psychical phenomena - 3. Aspects of psychical research - 4. Psychical research and other subjects - 5. Information (ch.31. Short glossary of terms; 32. Organizations and

.... *(contd.)*

education in psychical research: a selected list; 33. Notes on contributors; 34. Indexes of persons and entities, and of subjects). *Class No:* 159.9

[217]
MAITAL, S., *ed.* **Applied behavioural economics:** based on the International Conference of Economics and Psychology. Brighton, Sussex, Harvester/Wheatsheaf, 1988. 2v. (xvii,831,[7]p.). £95; $168.15 the set. ISBN: 074500511x.

Aims to represent the best in current applied work by researchers in economic psychology (tax evasion, entrepreneurship, social security, expectations, the family, values, labour relations, managerial behaviour, etc.). 17 chapters in the two volumes, each subdivided, and with references appended. 66 contributors. V.2 has subject index, p.825-831, and 7-page name index. *Class No:* 159.9

[218]
STRATTON, P. *and* **HAYES, N. A Student's dictionary of psychology.** 2nd ed. London, Edward Arnold; New York, Routledge, Chapman & Hall, 1993. 240p. illus. £10.99. ISBN: 0340569263.

First published in 1988.

An explaining, rather than a defining dictionary. Includes definitions of basic terms used in contemporary psychology; brief notes on famous psychologists; explanations of statistical and methodological terms; and longer entries on topics representing significant areas within modern psychology. Uses illustrations to clarify difficult points. *Class No:* 159.9

Databases

[219]
BRAND, A.A. *and* **KINZIE, L.A. 'A Comparison of online access to psychoanalytic literature'.** In *Database,* v.7(1), February 1984, p.54-55, 58-63.

Includes evaluation of PSYCINFO, MEDLINE, and NIMH. 6 appendices: 1. Major mental health databases - 2. Comparison of psychoanalytic journal coverage by selected databases - 3-6. other comparisons. *Class No:* 159.9(003.4)

[220]
PsycINFO database. Arlington, VA., American Psychological Association, 1974 -. Quarterly.

Includes references to all relevant original research and other significant published material drawn from over 1400 periodicals, dissertations, technical reports, etc. Includes over 340,000 citations.

See *The Reference librarian,* v.40, 1993, p.144-5, for a discussion on search differences between PsycINFO and Silverplatter's PsycLIT. *Class No:* 159.9(003.4)

Bibliographies

[221]
Bibliographic guide to psychology. The Research Libraries of the New York Public Library and the Library of Congress. Boston, Mass., G.K. Hall, 1974-. Annual. prices vary; *c.*$175. ISSN: 0360277x.

Formerly *Psychology book guide.*

Each annual volume lists all materials catalogued during the previous year by the N.Y.P.L. Research Libraries, with additions from Library of Congress MARC tapes. Covers all aspects of psychology, as well as parapsychology and the occult sciences. *Class No:* 159.9(01)

[222]
COHEN, D. Psychology exposed. In *British book news,* July 1990, p.436-9.

'Psychology books cover everything from detailed studies of how biochemistry and neurology affect thinking to what often seems rather obvious advice on how to have a better sex life.'(Opening sentence of the article). Surveys 54 books. *Class No:* 159.9(01)

[223]
Current contents: social and behavioral sciences. Philadelphia, Pa., Institute for Scientific Information, 1969-, v.1. no.1-. Weekly. $390 pa. ISSN: 00926361.

Originally as *Current contents: behavioral, social and management sciences* and *Current contents: education.*

Reproduces tables of contents of several hundred domestic and foreign journals *c.* 150 journal issues covered in each weekly part. Coverage includes Anthropology, Psychology, Psychiatry, etc. Also available online (BRS, DIALOG) *Class No:* 159.9(01)

[224]
Female psychology: a partially annotated bibliography, edited by C. Dilling and B.L. Claster. New York, New York City Coalition for Women's Mental Health, 1985. 326p. $25. ISBN: 0961602805.

Lists recent and historically important articles and books in areas of female developmental theory, psychoanalytic theory and practice, psychopathology, gender and sex roles, and special issues relevant to women and their mental health needs in a psychological, sociological and political context. *Class No:* 159.9(01)

[225]
GILMORE, W.J. Psychological enquiry: a comprehensive research bibliography. New York, Garland, 1984. 317p. $40. (*Garland reference library of social science, 156.*) ISBN: 0824091671.

*c.*5000 entries arranged in two parts: the first part methodology; the second part studies arranged by geographical area and subject, concentrating on Europe and the US. About 20% of the entries are annotated. 'Informative introduction and helpful author index' (*Choice,* v.22(2), October 1984, p.248). *Class No:* 159.9(01)

[226]
HOWELLS, J.G. *and* **OSBORN, M.L. A Reference companion to the history of abnormal psychology.** Westport, CT., Greenwood Press, 1984. 2v. (1141p.) illus. $95 the set. ISBN: 0313221839.

4000 entries, arranged A-Z, referring to persons, institutions, beliefs, terminology, groups, books, etc. that have figured in the history of psychopathology from antiquity to the present time. References are connected by the use of 'q.v.'. General index. '... serves a need not apparently met by any existing library resource for a combined biographical dictionary and brief encyclopedia for the field ...' (*RQ,* Fall 1984, p.109). 'A unique contribution' (*Library journal,* 15 December 1983, p.2324). *Class No:* 159.9(01)

[227]

KIELL, N. **Psychoanalysis, psychology and literature:** a bibliography. 2nd ed. Metuchen, N.J., Scarecrow Press, 1982. 2v. (1269p.). $65. £58.10. ISBN: 0810814218.

First published 1963.

19,764 unannotated entries for books, journal articles and dissertations published between 1900 and 1980, arranged in 14 categories. Author, title and subject indexes. A supplement was issued in l990 ($67.50. ISBN 0810821788

Class No: 159.9(01)

[228]

McINNIS, R.G. **Research guide for psychology.** Westport, CT., Greenwood Press, 1982. xxvi, 604p. illus. $50.95. (*Reference sources for social science and humanities, 1.*) ISBN: 0313213992.

17 chapters are each bibliographic essays on a different sub-division of psychology, with general commentary and annotations about specific sources. Covers indexes and abstracts, literature reviews, current and retrospective bibliographies, encyclopedias and handbooks, etc. Combined author, subject and title index. 'An ambitious guide of slightly uneven quality' (*RQ,* Winter 1982, p.205-6). 'Arrangement is logical and analytical, enhanced by ... index' (*Choice,* v.20(4), December 1982, p.562).

Class No: 159.9(01)

[229]

NATOLI, J. *and* RUSCH, F.L. **Psychocriticism:** an annotated bibliography. Westport, CT, Greenwood Press, [1984]. 267p. (Bibliographies and indexes in world literature, 1). $35. ISBN: 0313236410.

Long introductory essay, followed by entries for 1435 English-language books, articles and essays selected from critical and scholarly secondary works published between 1969 and 1982. Each chapter begins with a list of general items, followed by items by specific authors. Annotations of one or two sentences. Subject and author indexes.

Class No: 159.9(01)

[230]

NORTH EAST LONDON POLYTECHNIC. **The Psychology readings catalogue of the North East London Polytechnic.** Boston, Mass., G.K. Hall, 1976. 2v. (1308p.). $155 the set. ISBN: 0816111790.

27,400 photolithographically reproduced catalogue cards, - analytical entries, filed under authors, A-Z. Covers books of readings, symposia, conference proceedings, annual meetings, festschriften and the like. Entries show original sources as well as locations of other reprints, thus collecting together all details of an author's separate papers. Selective topic index. *Class No:* 159.9(01)

[231]

Psychological index: an annual bibliography of the literature of psychology and cognate subjects, 1894-1935, v.1-42. Princeton, N.J., Psychological Review Co., 1895-1936. 42v.

Continued Section G of v.3 ('*Bibliography of philosophy*'), by B. Rand (1905), of J.M. Baldwin's Dictionary of philosophy and psychology. A classified index to 150,844 books and periodical articles published during the period. Author indexes but no subject index. *Cumulative author index to 'Psychological index,' 1894 to 1935, and 'Psychological abstracts,' 1927 to 1958,* compiled by Columbia University, New York (Boston, Mass., G.K. Hall, 1960. 5v. (4286p.)) has *c.*320,000 entries.

Class No: 159.9(01)

[232]

TAVISTOCK JOINT LIBRARY. London. **Catalogue of the Tavistock Joint Library.** Boston, Mass., G.K. Hall, 1975. 2v.(1085p.). $145. ISBN: 0816111677.

Covers the combined holdings of the Tavistock Clinic and the Tavistock Institute of Human Relations - *c.*15,000 books and pamphlets. Extensive analyticals. A list of the Library's periodical holdings (230 periodicals in psychology are currently received) is appended. Main strength: psychology, psychiatry, psychoanalysis and the study of organizations.

Class No: 159.9(01)

[233]

—TAVISTOCK JOINT LIBRARY. London. Annotated list of publications, 1947-1987. London, the Library, 1988. [ii],112p. £3.

915 entries, mostly annotated, for books, pamphlets, periodical articles and conference papers on psychosocial subjects. Under authors, A-Z, with detailed, partly analytical,. subject index. Supplement: *Annotated list of publications, 1975-1980* ([1980]. [i],25p.).

Class No: 159.9(01)

[234]

VANDE KEMP, H. **Psychology and theology in Western thought, 1672-1965:** a historical and annotated bibliography. Millwood, N.Y., Kraus International Publications, [1984]. 367p. (Bibliographies in the history of psychology and psychiatry). $65. ISBN: 0527927791.

Concerned with the movement leading towards 'psychotheological integration', hence the dates 1672-1965. Covers books, monographs, pamphlets and journal titles. Arranged by topic, then chronological by date of publication. Particular attention given to 'schools' or traditions. Final section on major journals, institutions, and special book series. Separate name, institution, title and subject indexes.

Class No: 159.9(01)

[235]

WERTHEIMER, M.L. 'Psychology'. In Webb, W.H. *Sources of information in the social sciences* (3rd ed. American Library Association, 1986, p.403-54).

The late Robert I. Wilson, Sr., who completed his draft of this chapter shortly before he died, provided an overview of the most significant literature in psychology as a social science up to the middle of 1980. M.L. Wertheimer has appended a small number of more recent works in each of the subdivisions. In two parts, survey of the field and survey of the reference works (guides to the literature, reviews, abstracts and summaries, bibliographies of bibliographies, current bibliographies, retrospective bibliographies, periodicals, directories and biographical information, dictionaries, encyclopedias, handbooks, audiovisual materials, sources of scholarly contributions, sources of current information, and computerized databases. *c.*300 references. *Class No:* 159.9(01)

Encyclopaedias

[236]

CORSINI, R.J., *ed.* **Encyclopedia of psychology.** New York, John Wiley & Sons, 1984. 4v. (1988p.). tables, charts. $399.95; £189.95 the set. ISBN: 047186594x.

V.1. A - Eysenck, Hans; v.2. Fabre, Jean Maris - Perception; v.3. Perceptual - Zubin, Joseph; v.4. Bibliography. Name index. Subject index (analytical). Includes 1500 signed topical articles and 650 biographical

....(contd.)

articles, with references at the end of some entries. Cross-references. Length of entries varies (*e.g.* 'Chomsky': 28 lines; 'Chromosome disorders': 2½ cols.; 'Comparative psychology': 6½ cols., in sections including 2 references and 9 cross-references to other subject entries). *RQ* (v.24(3), Spring 1985, p.356-7) complains that bibliographical references give inadequate detail and that biographical entries are sparse. A skillful abridgement, cutting out many of the biographical entries is *Concise encyclopedica of psychology* (Wiley, 1987. xxi,1242p. £71. $89.95. ISBN 0471010685). *Class No:* 159.9(031)

[237]

Dictionnaire encyclopédique de psychologie. Sillamy, N. Paris, Bordas, 1980. 2v. (1287p.). illus. ISBN: 2040080406, v.1; 2040080503, v.2.

1680 entries arranged A-Z (v.1: A-K; v.2: L-Z) by 150 contributors from 25 countries. All articles are signed and some include short bibliographies. Index, p.1251-1287. *Class No:* 159.9(031)

[238]

Encyclopedia of learning and memory. Squire, L.R., *ed.* London, Macmillan, 1992. 678p. illus. $105. ISBN: 0028974085.

A compendium of psychological and biological research on learning and memory. 185 essays, A-Z, signed and with lists of references, 500-2000 word in length. Illustrations include diagrams and photographs. Cross-references. Detailed index. '... an authoritative and scholarly work ...' (*Booklist*, April 15, 1993, p.1992). 'A welcome addition ... well-designed and easy to use ...'(*Choice*, v.30(8), April 1993, p.1294). *Class No:* 159.9(031)

[239]

EYSENCK, H.J., *and others.* **Encyclopedia of psychology.** 2nd ed. London, Search Press, 1979. 3v. illus. ISBN: 0855324392.

First published 1972.

Covers all aspects of modern psychology. *c.*5000 entries; 300 major articles, some attaining 4000 words, with bibliographies. Some biographies are included. *Class No:* 159.9(031)

[240]

WOLMAN, B.B., *ed.* **International encyclopedia of psychiatry, psychology, psychoanalysis & neurology.** New York, Van Nostrand Reinhold, for Aesculapius Publishers Inc., 1977. 12v. diagrs. $675 the set. ISBN: 0918228018.

1500 authors: nearly 300 editors and consultants. Nearly 2000 survey-articles, each documented. 305 biographies (*e.g.* Adler: v.1, p.235-40; ½ column of biography); 1605 articles on concepts and issues (*e.g.* 'Aggression in children': v.1, p.348-53; 11/3 cols. of bibliography); v.12 (410p.): Author and subject indexes. (The non-analytical subject index has *c.*200 unspecified entries under 'Transference'). 'This eminently readable and impressive encyclopedia' (*Library journal,* 15 April 1978, p.817).

Progress volume 1 (New York, Aesculapius Publishers Inc., 1983. xxxiv, 599p. $89. ISBN 091822828x) is the first supplement to the basic 12 volumes. *Class No:* 159.9(031)

Handbooks & Manuals

[241]

GROTH-MARNAT, G. **Handbook of psychological assessments.** 2nd ed. Chichester, New York, Wiley-Interscience, 1990. xiii,594p. tables, diagrs. £36. ISBN: 0471510343.

lst published 1984.

12 chapters: 1. Introduction; 2. The context of clinical assessments; 3. The assessment interview; 4. Behavioral assessment; 5. Wechsler intelligence scales ... 11. Projective drawings; 12. The psychological report. Includes appendices A to T. Bibliography, p.499-563. Author and subject indexes. *Class No:* 159.9(035)

[242]

Handbook of developmental psychology. Wolman, J.B., *ed.* Englewood Cliffs, NJ., Prentice Hall, 1987. xv,953p. $132. ISBN: 0133725995.

In 6 parts, each subdivided: 1. Research methods and theories - 2. Infancy - 3. Childhood - 4. Adolescence - 5. Adulthood - 6. Aging. *c.*75 contributors. Deals with fundamental concepts and research findings. Author index, p.937-953 (*c.*7000 entries). *Class No:* 159.9(035)

[243]

International handbook of psychology. Gilgen, A.R. *and* Gilgen, C.K., *eds.* Westport, CT., Greenwood Press, 1987. 629p. $75; £44.50. ISBN: 0313238324.

A collection of status reports in the field of psychology for 29 countries and 'black Africa'. Introduction presents a historical overview of the discipline from the 1st International Congress in Paris in 1889 to the present. Reports focus on the nature and scope of the discipline, major programmes, funding, curriculum, major journals and textbooks, trends, etc. Suggested readings. Name and subject indexes. *Class No:* 159.9(035)

[244]

LINDZEY, G. *and* **ARONSON, E.,** *eds.* **Handbook of social psychology.** 3rd ed. New York, Newbery Award Records/ Random House, 1985. 2v. v.1: $50. v.2: $45. set: $95. ISBN: 0394350499, v.1; 0394350502, v.2.

First published 1954.

V.1: *Theory and method;* v.2: *Special fields and applications.* 30 chapters in all. The authors hoped to provide an affordable compendium that would be widely read by professionals and graduate students and not treated merely as a reference work. Each volume has a list of references and a subject and name index. *Class No:* 159.9(035)

[245]

The Oxford companion to the mind. Gregory, R.L. *and* Zangwill, O.L. Oxford, Oxford University Press, 1987. xvii,856p. illus (200 half-tone & line-drawings). £25; $49.95. ISBN: 019866124x.

Wide-ranging reference book written for a non-specialist readership, with 1001 articles in the fields of psychology, philosophy of mind, and physiology of the brain and nervous system, by a team of over 100 authorities and scholars. Entries range from brief definitions to substantial essays. Predominantly, but not exclusively, Anglo-American. Cross-references. Includes biographies of deceased persons. '... fun to browse through ...' (*Choice*, v.25(7), March 1988, p.1068). '... overanxious to avoid being stuffy ...' (*Philosophy*, April 1988, p.289-90). *Class No:* 159.9(035)

Dictionaries

[246]

GOLDENSON, Robert M., *editor-in-chief.* **Longman dictionary of psychology and psychiatry.** New York & London, Longman, 1984. xvi, 816p. $39.95; £29.50. ISBN: 0582282578.

Aims were to present a comprehensive lexicon on all phases of the two vast areas; to place heavy emphasis on current terms the reader is likely to encounter in the professional literature and professional practice today, without overlooking older terms that have special historical value; and to avoid the limitations of a one-dimensional glossary by giving a maximum amount of information in a minimum number of words. Comprises 21,164 entries, including 488 kinds of tests, 216 therapy entries, 70 entries treating Piaget's work and ideas, 100 treating Jung's etc. *Class No:* 159.9(038)

[247]

HARRÉ, R. *and* **LAMB, R., eds.** **The Encyclopedic dictionary of psychology.** Cambridge, Mass., MIT Press; Oxford, Basil Blackwell, 1983. 718p. $80; £55. ISBN: 0262081350, US; 0631126635, UK.

1300 entries covering all established areas of human and animal psychology, and ranging in length from concise definitions to substantial articles, some with bibliographies. Schools of psychology, important practitioners, fundamental concepts and empirical techniques are treated in depth. Cross-references. Index. '... hard work but endlesssly useful and suggestive' (*The Times educational supplement,* 18th May 1984, p.36). 'A major tool combining the features of a dictionary and an encyclopedia' (*Library journal,* 15th April, 1984, p.785). *Class No:* 159.9(038)

[248]

JUNG, C.G. Dictionary of analytical psychology. London, Routledge, 1987. [4], 183p. £4.50. ISBN: 0744800773.

Sums up Jung's ideas (types) in his own words, providing an introduction for anyone who wants to understand his typology and his ideas about human personality. General descriptions of introverted and extroverted types precede the dictionary proper. Bibliography, p.167-172. Index, p.173-180. *Class No:* 159.9(038)

[249]

KRISTAL, L., ed. **ABC of psychology.** New ed. London, Michael Joseph; New York, Facts on File, 1982. 250p. 60 illus. £7.95; $16.95. ISBN: 0871968444.

First published 1981 by Murray.

A layman's encyclopedia of concepts in modern psychology. *Class No:* 159.9(038)

[250]

POPPLESTONE, J.A. *and* **McPHERSON, M.W. Dictionary of concepts in general psychology.** Westport, CT., Greenwood Press, 1988. xi,380p. $65. (*Reference sources for the social sciences and humanities, 7.*) ISBN: 0313231907.

Includes *c.*50 concepts and *c.*50 cross-references. Entries all lengthy and include references and sources of additional information (*e.g.* 'Anger': 3½ pages of definition; 12 references and sources - nearly 5p. in all; 'Intelligence': 4 definitions in 4½ pages of text; 18 references and sources - nearly 6p. in all). Author index, p.357-372;p analytical subject index, p.373-380. *Class No:* 159.9(038)

[251]

Psychoanalytic terms and concepts. Moore, B.E. *and* Fine, B.D., eds. 3rd ed. New Haven, Co., American Psychoanalytic Association/Yale University Press, 1990. xxv,210p. £35. ISBN: 0300045778.

First published 1967; revised ed. 1968 as *A glossary of psychological terms and concepts.*

Nearly 300 concepts defined, the long definitions containing both historical and current aspects of many of the terms. Includes references to cited works. 'See' references. *c.*200 experts contributed. 'This is a fine reference tool' (*Choice,* v.27(11/12), July/August 1990, p.1810). *Class No:* 159.9(038)

[252]

SUTHERLAND, S. Macmillan dictionary of psychology. London, Macmillan Press, 1989. [7],491p. diagrs. £29.95. ISBN: 0333388291.

Published in the US by Crossroad/Continuum in 1989 with the title *The International dictionary of psychology* (ISBN 0826404405).

Intended as a dictionary for psychologists, including terms from neurology, linguistics, artificial intelligence, sociology, anthropology, statistics and philosophy. Includes *c.*10,000 terms, A-Z, with entries varying in length from *c.*5-120 words (averaging 20-50 words). Liberal cross-references. Examples are given in many cases. The 5 appendices are maps of the brain. Author is Professor of Experimental Psychology at the University of Sussex. '... for the most part, definitions succeed in fulfilling the book's purpose' (*Reference books bulletin,* v.81(21), July 1989, p.1884). *Class No:* 159.9(038)

[253]

WOLMAN, B.B., *comp. and ed*. Dictionary of behavioral science. 2nd ed. London, Academic Press; New York, Van Nostrand Reinhold, 1989. 720p. $59. ISBN: 0127624554.

First ed. published 1973.

*c.*10,000 terms in all areas of theoretical, experimental and applied psychology and psychiatry. Includes biographical notes. *Class No:* 159.9(038)

[254]

ZUSNE, L. Eponyms in psychology: a dictionary and biographical sourcebook. Westport, CT., Greenwood Press, 1987. 339p. $85. ISBN: 0313257507.

*c.*850 terms in the field of psychology and selected related fields are defined, their origins discussed, and short bibliographies included. *Class No:* 159.9(038)

Polyglot

[255]

DUIJKER, H.C.J. *and* **RIJSWIJK, M.J. van, eds.** **Trilingual psychological dictionary.** International Union of Psychological Science. Bern, Huber, 1978. 3v. £30 each vol.

V.1. English-French-German (xiv,355p.); V.2. Français-Allemand-Anglais (xiii,342p.); v.3. Deutsch - Englisch - Französisch (xiv.400p.). V.1. has 3-column text and *c.*20,000 headwords. Different applications of terms are numbered; genders given 'Books used in preparing the present version', p.x-xii. *Class No:* 159.9(038)=00

English

[256]

BRUNO, F.J. **Dictionary of key words in psychology.** London, Routledge & Kegan Paul, 1986. xi, 275p. £16.95. ISBN: 0710201907.

'This book does not seek to present an exhaustive catalogue of psychological terms, but a selective list of key terms - terms that are used with very high levels of frequency' (*Preface*). A tripartite form of presentation (Abnormal behaviour - Zen): 1. Definition; 2. Example; 3. Connections. Bibliography (p.259-262) is a selective listing, A-Z by author. Analytical topical index, name index and subject index (p.263-275). *Class No:* 159.9(038)=20

[257]

ENGLISH, H.B. *and* ENGLISH, A.C. **A Comprehensive dictionary of psychological and psychoanalytical terms:** a guide to usage. New York, Longmans Green, 1958 (reprinted by Mackay). xiv. 594p. diagrs. ISBN: 0679300333.

More than 13,000 terms and abbreviations are explained. The aim (*Preface*) is to include all terms frequently used in a special or technical sense by psychologists, with one set of definitions for the comparative layman and another set for the person working in the field of psychology. Pronunciation is given for unusual or difficult words. The inclusion of compound-word terms is a feature (*e.g.* 'Reinforcement' and its compounds occupy 5 pages). Extensive cross-references. *Class No:* 159.9(038)=20

[258]

HARRÉ, R. *and* LAMB, R., *eds*. **The Dictionary of personality and social psychology.** Oxford, Basil Blackwell, 1986. 416p. illus. £29.50. ISBN: 0631146016.

Over 300 entries on the theories of personality development and organization, and the topics and approaches which make up social psychology. *Class No:* 159.9(038)=20

[259]

REBER, R.S. **The Penguin dictionary of psychology.** Harmondsworth, Mddx., Penguin Books; New York, Viking/Penguin Inc., 1985. xiii, 848p. £9.99. $8.98. ISBN: 0140510796, UK; 0670801364, US.

*c.*17,000 terms from psychology, psychiatry and related fields. Entries vary in length from one line to 2 columns (*e.g.* Dream: ½ col.; Dream symbolism: ½ col; Hysteria: 1 col.; Mind: 2 cols.; Mysticism: ½ col.). Excludes biographies except for those who have given their names to a subject (*e.g.* Freudian, Pavlovian, Adlerian). Cross-references. The dictionary proper is preceded by a list of terms which are given extensive coverage, and ends with a list of authorities cited (p.839-848). *Class No:* 159.9(038)=20

Reviews & Abstracts

[260]

L'Année psychologique. 1894-. Paris, Presses Universitaire de France, 1895-. v.1-. Quarterly (previously 2pa., annual until 1951 (1952). F.485pa. ISSN: 00035033.

Published with the assistance of the Centre National des Lettres, previously the Centre National de la Recherche Scientifique.

Each issue has 3 main sections: Memoires originaux' (original contributions, in French but with abstracts in

.... (contd.)

English) - 'Revues critiques' - 'Analyses bibliographiques' (signed abstracts of periodical articles, and book reviews). International coverage. *Class No:* 159.9(048)

[261]

The Annual review of psychology. Stanford, CA., Annual Reviews Inc., 1950-.v.1-. Annual. $31. ISSN: 00664308.

A systematic critical, well-documented review of developments in various fields of psychology, so arranged that the fields are surveyed at regular intervals. Author and subject indexes; cumulative indexes of authors and chapter titles. *Class No:* 159.9(048)

[262]

Contemporary psychology: a journal of reviews. Washington, D.C., American Psychological Association, 1956-. v.1, no.1-. Monthly. $110pa. ISSN: 00107549.

Each issue consists of some 23 sections, with *c.*55 extended critical reviews of books and films; short notices; and a list of books received. Apparently confined to English-language material published in the US. A feature is the inclusion in longer reviews of the detailed qualifications of both reviewer and author/editor. Coverage extends to psychiatry, public opinion and animal behaviour. Annual author and reviewer index. *Class No:* 159.9(048)

[263]

PsycBooks: books and chapters in psychology, 1987-. Arlington, VA., American Psychological Association, 1989-91. Annual. 5v. each year. ISSN: 10441514.

Psychological abstracts ceased to include books in 1980. In 1984 an effort was made to rectify this deficiency, resulting in this title.

Gives access to the latest books and chapters in psychology. V.I. Experimental psychology: basic and applied - II. Developmental, personality, social psychology - III. Professional psychology, disorders and treatment - IV. Educational psychology and health psychology - V. Author and subject indexes. *Class No:* 159.9(048)

[264]

Psychological abstracts: non-evaluative summaries of the serial literature in psychology and related disciplines. Arlington, VA., The American Psychological Association Inc., 1927-. Monthly. $1245pa. ISSN: 00332887.

Over 3000 entries in each issue, from over 1400 journals, arranged in a classified order: General psychology - Psychometrics - Human experimental psychology - Animal experimental and comparative psychology - Psychological psychology - Psychological intervention - Communication systems - Developmental psychology - Social processes and social issues - Social psychology - Personality - Physical and psychological disorders - Treatment and prevention - Professional personnel and professional issues - Educational psychology - Applied psychology - Sport psychology and leisure. Brief subject index; author index. Available online. Vendors: BRS, DIMDI, Data-Star (PSYC), DIALOG, Orbit Information Technologies. Also on CD-ROM (American Psychological Association, Silver Platter (PsyclLIT). *Class No:* 159.9(048)

[265]

Psychological bulletin. Washington DC., American Psychological Association, 1904-. v.1-. Bi-monthly. $126pa.

Features review articles (*e.g.* March 1989 issue (v.105(2)) has 4 review articles, including 'Socioeconomic status and obesity: a review of the literature' with bibliography, p.270-285). An important aid to bibliographical research. *Class No:* 159.9(048)

Periodicals & Progress Reports

[266]

MARKLE, A. and RINN, R. Author's guide to journals in psychology, psychiatry & social work. New York, Haworth Press, 1977. 256p. $29.95; £25.90. ISBN: 0917724003.

Profiles of more than 400 journals, based on replies to questionnaires. Data include topic coverage, time lag in publishing, style requirements, circulation, price and coverage by indexing/abstracting services. Subject, title and keyword index. *Class No:* 159.9(05)

[267]

OSIER, D.V. and WOZNIAK, R.H. A Century of serial publications in psychology, 1850-1950; an international bibliography. Millwood, N.Y., Kraus International, 1984. 805p. $100. (*Bibliographies in the history of psychology and psychiatry.*) ISBN: 0527981966.

1107 serial titles arranged chronologically by inaugural year of publication, with titles published in the same year arranged A-Z. Also included are 41 entries for titles that first appeared between 1783 and 1849. Titles that began since 1950 are excluded. Each entry contains title, name of sponsoring organization, variations of title, publication date, frequency, numbering variations, publisher, primary editors, associated editors, and editorial board members. Title and name indexes, with cross-references. An appendix lists titles, with dates of publication, of serials in allied fields. *Class No:* 159.9(05)

Yearbooks & Directories

[268]

International directory of psychologists, exclusive of the USA. Pawlik, K., *ed.* 4th ed. Amsterdam, North Holland, 1985. viii,1182p. Dfl.180; $94.75; £49.72. ISBN: 0444877746.

First published 1958.

Lists over 32,000 psychologists from 43 countries outside the US. Information includes name and title, sex, date and place of birth, mailing address, highest academic degree, present position, membership of psychological associations and primary fields of interest or research in psychology. *Class No:* 159.9(058)

[269]

WOLMAN, B.B. International directory of psychology: a guide to people, places and policies. New York & London, Plenum Press, 1979. xxxiv, 279p. tables. $45. ISBN: 0306402092.

Describes the structure and functions of nearly 70 national psychological organizations. Under countries, A-Z, data on educational and research facilities, legal status and occupations of psychologists, and the major publications (journals and books) in the field. *Class No:* 159.9(058)

Histories

[270]

GAULD, A. A History of hypnotism. Cambridge, Cambridge University Press, 1992. xvii,738p. illus. £60. ISBN: 0521306752.

A detailed and scholarly history of the practice and theory of mesmerism, hypnotism and multiple personality disorder. Prologue on Mesmer is followed by 25 chapters in 2 parts: 1. The successors of Mesmer; 2. The heyday of hypnotism. Notes after each chapter. References on animal magnetism and hypnotism, p.631-722, each A-Z by author. Index of names. Analytical index of subjects, p.733-38. *Class No:* 159.9(091)

[271]

SCHULTZ, D.P. and SCHULTZ, S.E. History of modern psychology. 4th ed. New York, Academic Press, 1987. xii,403p. $27. ISBN: 0155374656.

First published 1969. A 5th ed. was published in 1992 (xv,416p. $45.25. ISBN 0155374672).

Arranged in 15 sections, all subdivided: 1. The study of the history of psychology - 2. Philosophical influences on psychology - 3. Physiological influences on psychology - 4. The new psychology - 5. Structuralism - 6.7.8. Functionalism - 9.10.11. Behaviorism - 12. Gestalt psychology - 13.14. Psychoanalysis - 14. Beyond the schools of thought: more recent developments. Suggested readings are given at the end of each section. References, p.381-394, A-Z. Index, p.395-403. *Class No:* 159.9(091)

[272]

WERTHEIMER, M. A Brief history of psychology. 3rd ed. New York, Holt, Rinehart & Winston, 1987. 175p. $19. ISBN: 0030095042.

Previous ed. 1979.

An encapsulated overview of a select set of individuals and ideas, from Plato to major psychologists of the 20th century, who have played a significant role in psychology's history. 'A clear exposition...' (*Contemporary psychology.* v.33(5), May 1988, p.419). *Class No:* 159.9(091)

Bibliographies

[273]

PEETERS, H., and others. Historical behavioural sciences. A guide to the literature. Tilburg, Netherlands, Tilburg University Press, 1988. xx.311p. Dfl.49.50. ISBN: 9036195225.

In 2 parts. Pt.1 discusses 40 journals relevant to the study of the historical sciences. Pt.2 has *c.*5500 bibliographical entries for articles, books, collections, essays, all thematically arranged (Theory - Methods and techniques - Psychological functions - Psychological development - Personality - Ecology - Mentalities and culture - Family and kinship - Deviant behaviour and social control - Women's history. Author index. *Class No:* 159.9(091)(01)

Biographies

[274]

BREITHART, B.R., ed. Who's who in the behavioral sciences. 2nd ed. New York, Research Institute of Psychopathology, 1987. 292p. $87.50. ISBN: 0914709011.

First published 1984.

Includes information on over 1100 active professionals in physiopsychology, biopsychiatry, psychometrics,

.... (contd.)

behavioural medicine, health psychology, etc. International in scope. Entries include biographical information, areas of speciality, positions past and present, concurrent positions, current activities, professional membership, and honours and awards. No references to publications are given in this edition. Discipline index; geographical index.
Class No: 159.9(092)

[275]
ZUSNE, L. **Biographical dictionary of psychology.** Westport, CT., Greenwood Press; London, Aldwych Press, 1984. xxi,563p. $49.95; £47.50. ISBN: 0313240272.

544 brief biographies of deceased psychologists, A-Z. 3 appendices: A. Chronological list; B: List by degree of eminence; C: Academic and research institutions by country.
Class No: 159.9(092)

Great Britain

Histories

[276]
HEARNSHAW, L.S. **A Short history of British psychology, 1804-1940.** London, Methuen, 1964 (reprinted by Greenwood Press, 1986). 344p. £59.40 $62.50. *(Methuen's manuals of modern psychology series.)* ISBN: 0313252785.

'Likely to be a standard work on its subject for many years to come. It will encourage students to attain what is necessary in a human science - a sense of historical and social process ... ' (*The British journal of psychology*, v.56 pts.2 & 3, August 1965. p.321-2). 'Select bibliography', p.298-316 (arranged by chapters).
Class No: 159.9(410)(091)

Counselling

[277]
DRYDEN, W., *and others.* **Handbook of counselling in Britain.** London, Tavistock/Routledge, in association with the British Association for Counselling, 1989. xvi,454p. tables. £30. ISBN: 0415013275.

A review of the main fields of counselling activity in Britain, a source of information for professional counsellors, students, and voluntary organisers. 25 chapters in 5 parts: 1. Introduction - 2. Areas - 3. Settings - 4. Themes - 5. Issues. Appendices on codes of ethics. Author and subject indexes.
Class No: 159.9(410)COU

USSR

[278]
JORAVSKY, D. **Russian psychology:** a critical history. Oxford. Basil Blackwell Ltd., 1989. 624p. £45. ISBN: 0631163379.

Assesses the familiar and less familiar, the political and the cultural expressions of Russian psychology.
Class No: 159.9(47)

America—North & Central

Libraries

[279]
EPSTEIN, B.A. *and* DETLEFSEN, E.G., *eds.* **Directory of mental health libraries and information centers.** Washington, D.C., American Psychiatric Press Inc., 1984. vii,297,[4]p. $20. ISBN: 0880480475.

Compiled under the auspices of the Association of Mental Health Libraries.

Geographical arrangement, A-Z by State for the US, then Canada. Information includes name and address, telephone number, parent institute, funding, staff, specialized services, stock of publications, access, and publications of the organization. 1 page per library or information centre. Personnel, institution and subject indexes.
Class No: 159.9(71/73):061:026/027

USA

[280]
BENJAMIN, L.T., *and others.* **A History of American psychology in notes and news, 1883-1945:** an index to journal sources. White Plains, NY, Kraus International Publications, 1988. 896p. $125. ISBN: 0527066265.

Indexes the 'notes and news' sections from the six major journals in the development time period of American psychology in one cross-referenced A-Z listing. Over 50,000 citations to individuals, institutions, awards, special meetings, apparatus, etc., relating to psychology and associated fields. *Class No:* 159.9(73)

[281]
Directory of the American Psychological Association. 1989 ed. Washington, DC., the Association, 1989. 1792p. $70. ISBN: 1557980586. ISSN: 01966545.

First published 1918. Quadrennial. Early title was *Biographical directory.*

Lists *c.*47,000 members, with geographical index.
Class No: 159.9(73)

Thesauri

[282]
AMERICAN PSYCHOLOGICAL ASSOCIATION. **Thesaurus of psychological index terms.** Staff of the Retrieval Service Unit, Psycinfo Dept.,. 6th ed. Arlington, Va., the Association, 1991. 332p. $65. ISBN: 1557981116.

First published 1974.

*c.*7000 terms, A-Z ('Abdomen' ... 'Zungs self rating depression scale'). Relationships noted are use/used for/ broader/narrower/related. Rotated alphabetical terms section (preferred *Thesaurus* terms are listed in alphabetical order by each word contained in them. Generated from file of *Psychological abstracts. Class No:* 159.9:025.43

Experimental Psychology

[283]
BORING, E.G. **A History of experimental psychology.** 2nd ed. New York, Appleton-Century-Crofts, 1950. xxi, 771p. $48. ISBN: 0133900398.

First published 1929.

Ranges from the time of Copernicus up to 1950. Particularly valuable for its bio-bibliographical data (*e.g.*

....*(contd.)*

Wundt, p.316-27). 26 chapters, each with notes and references appended. Chapter 27: 'Retrospect'. Index of names and analytical index of subjects. *Class No:* 159.9.07

Child Psychology

[284]
BRUNO, F.J. The Family encyclopedia of child psychology and child development: an easy to understand parents' guide. New York, Wiley, 1992. 432p. $30. ISBN: 0477827939. *Class No:* 159.922.7

[285]
Child development abstracts and bibliography. 1927-. 3pa. Chicago, Ill., University of Chicago Press, for the Society for Research in Child Development, 1927-. $58 pa. ISSN: 00093939.

Over 2000 abstracts and references a year. Main sections: Biology, health medicine - Cognition, learning, perception - Social, psychological, cultural and personality studies - Educational processes - Psychiatry, clinical psychology - History, theory and methodology. Book notices. Books received. Author and subject indexes per issue, cumulated annually. List of journals regularly searched. *Class No:* 159.922.7

[286]
JOHNSON, R.C. and MEDINNUS, G.R. Child psychology: behavior and development. 3rd ed. New York, London, etc., Wiley, 1974. xiv, 562p. illus, tables. $26.95. ISBN: 0471446246.

First published 1965.

17 chapters, in 5 sections: 1. Introduction - 2. Basic factors in development - 3. The family and its influence on development - 4. Societal influence on socialization - 5. The emerging self. Extensive chapter references (*e.g.* 15: Personality development: 9½p. of references). Author and subject indexes. Data are 'directed towards presenting a solid body of information rather than defending a specific theoretical position' (*Preface to the second edition*. 1968). *Class No:* 159.922.7

[287]
SATTLER, J.M. Assessment of children's intelligence and special abilities. 2nd ed. Boston, Mass., Allyn & Bacon, 1981. xxiv,722,[2]p. ISBN: 020507362x.

First published 1974 as *Assessment of children's intelligence.*

'Designed to teach clinical assessment skills to students in clinical, school, and counselling psychology and to enable students in special education to understand the assessment process. It also serves as a reference book for practicing professionals in these areas'(*Preface*). Arranged in 25 chapters, all subdivided. Notes, p.534-540, include references; 5 appendices (A. Publishers of tests reviewed; C. Miscellaneous tables); extensive glossary (p.630-646); over 1800 references, A-Z (647-699); name index (p.700-712); subject index (p.713-722). *Class No:* 159.922.7

Personality

[288]
BUROS, O.K., ed. Personality tests and reviews... Highland Park, N.J., Gryphon Press, University of Nebraska Press, 1970-1975. 2v. (xxxi,1659p. 841p.). v.I. $50; v.II. $55. ISBN: 0910674108, v.1; 0910674191, v.2.

....*(contd.)*

Sub-title to v.I is 'including an index to *The mental measurement yearbooks*'.

V.I has Personality test index, p.1-241; Personality test reviews, p.242-1345; a classified index to 'TIMMY', p.1346-1427; 'MMY' book review index, p.1428-77. Index of titles; index of names; scanning index to tests. 'Invaluable for users who want published names, prices, descriptions and a critical evaluation of these testing instruments' (*Wilson library bulletin*, v. 44(8), April 1970. p.879). *Class No:* 159.923

[289]
HARGREAVES, G. *and* **WILSON, P. Dictionary of graphology:** the A-Z of your personality. London, Peter Owen, 1983. 215p. £10.95. ISBN: 0720605938.

A-Z listing of the various ways of writing, capitals and small letters - descriptions - character qualities revealed; Character traits - type of writing described; Glossary - Recommended reading (1p.). *Class No:* 159.923

[290]
MOSAK, H.H. *and* **MOSAK, B. A Bibliography of Adlerian psychology.** New York, Halstead Press: Wiley, 1975 (for v.1.); New York, Hemisphere Publishing Corp., 1985 (for v.2). 2v. ([xv],320p.; 403p.). V.2: $49.95. ISBN: 0891162968, v.2:.

Sponsored by The International Association of Individual Psychology and The North American Society of Adlerian Psychology.

V.1 has nearly 10,000 references under authors, A-Z (Adler: nos.125-579), and covers books, chapters of books, dissertations, journal and newspaper articles, with a non-analytical subject index (p.283-320). In v.2 the listings are expanded from 1973 through 1977, adding 3635 references and numerous corrections to the original volume. Entries are unannotated, arranged A-Z by author, and numbered. *Choice,* (v.24(1), September 1986, p.90) says '... numbering system ... can be confusing in utilization'. It is necessary to use both volumes together. *Class No:* 159.923

Intelligence

[291]
BOFF, K.R., and others, eds. Handbook of perception and human performance. New York, Wiley, 1986. 2v. (xxi,1568p.;xxi,1358p.). v.1 $125; v.2 $145.95. ISBN: 0471885444, v.1; 0471829579, v.2; 0471829560, set.

V.1. *Sensory processes and perception;* v.2. *Cognitive processes and performance.* 45 essays by 166 contributors and arranged in 7 sections in the 2 vols. (Sections 1-4 in v.1, 5-7 in v.2): 1. Theory and method - 2.-3. Basic sensory processes - 4. Space and motion perception - 5. Information processing - 6. Perceptual organization and cognition - 7. Human performance. Author index. Cumulative subject index of 99p. *Class No:* 159.928

Dreams

[292]
JUNG, C.G. Dreams. London, Routledge/Ark paperback, 1985. xix,337p. illus. £5.50. ISBN: 0744800323.

First published in the UK 1982. Translated by R.F.C. Hull.

....*(contd.)*

8 chapters in 4 parts: 1. Dreams and psychoanalysis - 2. Dreams and psychic energy - 3. The practical use of dream-analysis - 4. Individual dream symbolism in relation to alchemy. A bibliography (p.299-311) is in 2 sections: A. Volumes containing collections of alchemical works by various authors; B. General bibliography. Analytical index, p.313-337. *Class No:* 159.963.3

[293]

The Oxford book of dreams. Brook, S., *comp.* Oxford, Oxford University Press, 1983. xii,268p. £8.95. ISBN: 0192141309.

An anthology, mostly of instances of the literary exploitation of the dream experience, with some examples of dream interpretation. Arranged in 3 sections: I. From birth to death - II. Earthly things - III. The dream world. Index (of names), p.266-268. *Class No:* 159.963.3

[294]

WHITMORE, E.C. *and* **PERERA, S.B. Dreams: a portal to the source:** a guide to dream interpretation. London, Routledge, 1989. 200p. £19.95. ISBN: 0415010705.

An introductory guidebook to the interpretation of dreams. *Class No:* 159.963.3

Encyclopaedias

[295]

Encyclopedia of sleep and dreaming. Carskadon, M.A., *ed.* New York, Macmillan, 1993. 704p. illus. diagrs, tables, graphs. $105. ISBN: 0028970853.

Summarizes the findings on the medical, biological and psychological facets of sleep and dreaming. Aimed at the public, the student and the researcher. Entries are half to a page in length, signed, and most have current bibliographies attached. Detailed analytical index. *Class No:* 159.963.3(031)

[296]

FORARI, A.M. Illustrated encyclopedia of dreams. London, Hamlyn Publishing Group, 1989. 192p. 282 col.illus. £12.95. ISBN: 0600567060.

An introduction, 'sleep: the pattern of your dreams' precedes the dictionary, which has short descriptions of dreams and what they mean, arranged A-Z (Abandonment ... Zebra). A dictionary rather than an encyclopedia. *Class No:* 159.963.3(031)

[297]

GUILEY, R.E. The Encyclopedia of dreams: symbols and interpretations. New York, Crossroad, 1993. 176p. $27.50. ISBN: 0824512405.

Essays on the science of dreams, cross-cultural beliefs, nightmares, dreams and the paranormnal, dreams and alchemy, working with dreams. Lists *c.*1000 entries, A-Z, of dream symbols and their interpretations. Cross-references. Bibliography of 125 titles. 'The result is a do-it-yourself dream manual anchored in symbols primarily from the Western tradition.'(*Booklist*, v.90(4), 15 October 1993, p.470). *Class No:* 159.963.3(031)

Psychoanalysis

[298]

BADCOCK, C. Essential Freud. 2nd ed. Oxford, Blackwell, 1991. 192p. £12.95 ISBN: 0631177744.

An introduction to the topics that most crucially characterize the contribution Freud's thinking has made. This edition takes account of recent developments in evolutionary science and examines fresh evidence. *Class No:* 159.964.2

[299]

Feminism and psychoanalysis: a critical dictionary. Wright, E., *ed.* Oxford, Blackwell, 1992. xix,485p. £40. ISBN: 0631173129.

'... not a dictionary in the conventional sense, for it does not merely define terms, but explores, historizes and politicizes them ...'(Introduction). Entries are signed by the 73 contributors, and include phrases as well as words, and also people. They are often lengthy and subdivided (Sigmond Freud: 6p.; Freud's female patients: 6p.). Each entry ends with a substantial bibliography. Cross-references. Analytical index, p.462-85. *Class No:* 159.964.2

[300]

HINSHELWOOD, R.D. A Dictionary of Kleinian thought. Free Association Books (distributed by Columbia University Press), 1989. [6],482p. $47. ISBN: 0946960828.

In 2 main parts: A. Main entries, p.1-208, with 13 lengthy entries for fundamentals of Kleinian thought, in chronological order; B. General entries, of words, phrases and proper names associated with Kleinian thought, arranged A-Z, a paragraph to 6 pages in length. Finally a bibliography of Kleinian publications (p.455-482), published from 1920 to 1987 in chronological order of publication. Lacks a subject index. *Class No:* 159.964.2

[301]

HOPCKE, R.H. A Guided tour of the collected works of Jung. Shambala, 1992. 208p. £8.99. ISBN: 0877735824.

A guide to Jung's 19-volume *Collected works.* *Class No:* 159.964.2

Bibliographies

[302]

GRINSTEIN, A., *comp.* *and* *ed*. **The Index of psychoanalytic writings.** New York, International Universities Press Inc. (distributed by Academic Press), 1956-75. 14v. v.1-5, 6-9, v.10-14, $150 each of the 3 sets. ISBN: 0823684008, v.1-5; 0823684016, v.6-9.

A revision and updating of J. Rickman's *Index psychoanalyticus* (covering 1893-1926).

Covers psychoanalytic literature up to the end of 1969, well over 100,000 items. V.1-5 set (1956-60) indexes the literature to the end of 1952 - 37,121 numbered items under authors A-Z, followed by anonymous items and reports. All of Freud's writings that are known or currently available are listed at nos. 10,350-10,714. V.5, the subject index to v.1-4, covers *c.*25,000 conceptual categories and notes additions and corrections. The v.6-9 and v.10-14 sets, similarly arranged, list supplementary items. *Class No:* 159.964.2(01)

[303]
—GRINSTEIN, A., *comp and ed*. Sigmund Freud's writings: a comprehensive bibliography. New York, International Universities Press Inc., 1977. 181p. $22.50. ISBN: 0823660761.

Includes Freud's early non-psychological writings not included in the Standard edition, and also a bibliography of Freud's letters. *Class No:* 159.964.2(01)

[304]
—GUTTMAN, S.A., *ed*. The Concordance to the Standard edition of the complete psychological works of Sigmund Freud. Boston, Mass., G.K. Hall, 1980. 6v. (5512p.). $800. ISBN: 0823610756.

Based on the 24v. English translation by James Strachey. *Class No:* 159.964.2(01)

[305]
VINCIE, J.F. and RATHBAUER-VINCIE, M. C.G. Jung and analytical psychology: a comprehensive bibliography. New York, Garland Publishing Co., 1977. xiv,[1],297p.

'Works on Jung and analytical psychology', p.1-236 (3687 entries, arranged chronologically by years, pre 1916 to 1976). Book reviews of works by Jung (1942-75). Subject and author indexes. *Class No:* 159.964.2(01)

[306]
—General bibliography of C.G. Jung's writings. Ress, L., *comp*. London, Routledge & Kegan Paul, 1979. x,263p.

Translated from the German by R.F.C. Hull. Forms v.19 of *The collected works*, v.20 being the *General index*.

3 sections: 1. The published works of C.G. Jung: original works and translations - 2. The collected works - 3. Seminar notes. Indexes of titles; personal names; congresses, organizations, societies, etc.; periodicals. Addenda, p.259-63. *Class No:* 159.964.2(01)

Dictionaries

[307]
LAPLANCHE, J. and PONTALIS, J.-B. The Language of psychoanalysis. Translated by Donald Nicholas-Smith. London, Hogarth Press and the Institute of Psychoanalysis, 1973. xv, 510p. £17.50. ISBN: 0701203439.

Originally as *Vocabulaire de la psychoanalyse* (Paris, Presses Universitaires de France, 1967; 5 éd. 1976). Paperback published in 1988 (London, Karnac House. 510p. ISBN 0946439494).

Entries (Abreaction ... Working-through) give German, Spanish, French, Italian and Portuguese equivalents of terms, plus definitions, discussion and references. 'Unconscious': 3p.: 3 main definitions, plus sub-entries: 4 references: 4 cross-references. Bibliography, p.491-7 (works by Freud cited: other authors: journals). Indexes of German and English terms. Intended for readers of Freud's writings. *Class No:* 159.964.2(038)

[308]
RYCROFT, C. A Critical dictionary of psychoanalysis. London, Harmondsworth, Middlesex, Penguin Books, 1972. xxvi, 189p. £6.99. ISBN: 0140510524.

About 500 entries, Abreaction-Zoophilia. 'Hysteria': 1p.; 'Depression': 1p.; references, cross-references. Introductory reading list and a comprehensive bibliography (p.183-9). Clear definitions. *Class No:* 159.964.2(038)

[309]
SAMUELS, A., *and others*. A Critical dictionary of Jungian analysis. London, Routledge & Kegan Paul, 1986. [4],171p. £18.95; $36. ISBN: 0710204108.

In A-Z dictionary format, consisting of 'Jargon' words usually associated with Jung, words and concepts originated by him, and terms that have a special meaning in the context of Jung's understanding of the nature of psychic life. References, p.163-168, A-Z. List of entries, p.169-171. '... a useful, practical reference to Jungian terminology and ideas ...' (*Contemporary psychology*, v.33(2), February 1988, p.166). *Class No:* 159.964.2(038)

Histories

[310]
FINE, R. A History of psychoanalysis. New York, Columbia University Press, 1979. xii, [1], 686p. (Reprinted 1990. 784p. $50.) ISBN: 0876687915.

20 chapters: 1. The need for historical perspective ... 4/5. Organizational vicissitudes ... 9/10. The unconscious - 11/12. Ego psychology ... 19. The advance of psychoanalysis to a unifying theory of human behaviour - 20. Observations, hopes and dreams. Notes, p.581-600. Bibliography (A-Z authors), p.601-49. Analytical index (p.651-86). *Class No:* 159.964.2(091)

Mental Disorders & Deficiencies

[311]
GREENBERT, B. How to find out in psychiatry: a guide to sources of mental health information. Oxford, Pergamon Press, 1978. . xii[1],112,[1]p. facsims., tables. £16. ISBN: 0080218601.

12 chapters: 1. Introduction to the literature of psychiatry - 2. Guides to libraries & the psychiatric literature - 3. Primary sources of information; periodicals and books - 4. Secondary sources of information: bibliographies, indexes, abstracts & reviews - 5. Dictionaries, glossaries, encyclopedias & handbooks - 6. Directories - 7. Nomenclature & classification - 8. Education - 9. Mental health statistics - 10. Drugs and drug therapy - 11. Tests and measurements - 12. Nonprint materials. References (9). p.83. Appendix A: Classics in psychiatric literature (chronologically arranged, p.87-97). Index of titles, authors. 'Highly recommended' (*Choice* v.16. no.5/6, July/August 1979. p.648). *Class No:* 159.972/.973

[312]
THAKURDAS, H. and THAKURDAS, L. Dictionary of psychiatry. Revised by Betty Thakurdas. Lancaster, MTP., 1979. vii, 111p. diagrs. £13.75. ISBN: 0852002351.

About 900 definitions, designed as a ready reference for doctors, medical-students, psychiatric nurses, social workers 'or anybody involved with psychiatric patients' (*Introductory note*). Appendix A: International Standard classification of mental disorders - B. List of abbreviations - C. A guide to prefixes and suffixes - D. Common phobias - E. Normal values in the body - F. Essential statistical formulae - H. Symbols of the Mental Health Act, 1959. *Class No:* 159.972/.973

Mental Tests

[313]
HERSEN, M. *and* BELLACK, A.S., *eds*. **Dictionary of behavioral assessment techniques.** London & New York, Pergamon Press, 1988. 519p. $85; £67. ISBN: 0080319750.

Surveys *c.*300 behavioural assessment techniques used by psychiatrists and counsellors to deal with psychological problems ranging from depression and marital distress to eating disorders and unassertiveness. Arranged A-Z by name of technique, experts examine their purpose, reliability and usefulness. References to the reviews from the literature follow each entry. '... users guide is an inadequate substitute for a detailed subject index'. (*Choice*, v.26(7), March 1989, p.1120). *Class No:* 159.98

[314]
KRUG, Samuel E., *comp. and ed*. **Psychware sourcebook.** 2nd., 1987-88. Test Corporation of America (distributed by Gale Research Co., Detroit), 1987. xiv, 457p. $97.75. ISBN: 093370111x.

First published 1984 as *Psychware*.

A guide to computer-based products for assessment in psychology, education, and business. Lists about 400 products in numeric order by product code and also in alphabetical order by title. Information given includes product number, name, supplier, category, application, sale restrictions, pricing, and product description. 5 indexes (product title, product category, product application, service, and supplier). *Class No:* 159.98

Tables & Data Books

[315]
ANASTASI, A. **Psychological testing.** 6th ed. London, Collin Macmillan, 1988. xiv,817p. tables. £16.95. ISBN: 0029775108.

First published 1954.

20 chapters in 5 parts: 1. Context of psychological testing - 2. Technical and methodological principles - 3. Tests of general intellectual level - 4. Tests of separate abilities - 5. Personality tests. 4 appendices (A. Ethical principles of psychologists; B. A suggested outline for test evaluation; C. Test publishers; D. Classified list of representative tests). Name and subject indexes. *Class No:* 159.98(083)

[316]
Test critiques. Keyser, D.J. *and* Sweetland, R. C., *eds*. Kansas City, Test Corporation of America, 1985-. $97.75 each vol.

A continuing project.

In each volume noted experts evaluate the validity of more than 100 tests for psychology, education and business. These in-depth analyses range from 5-15 pages each. *Class No:* 159.98(083)

[317]
Tests: a comprehensive reference... Sweetland, R. C. *and* Keyser, D.J., *eds*. 3rd ed. Kansas City, Test Corporation of America, 1991. 1251p. $89.00. ISBN: 0890792550.

First published, 1983.

Descriptive entries for more than 4000 tests of 437 publishers. Arranged in 3 broad categories: (Psychology, Education, Business) and more than 70 specific subject subheadings. Cross-references. Entries provide statements of

....(contd.)
test's purpose, description of test, relevant cost and availability information, a set of coded visual keys, intended age level, and name of publisher. 8 indexes. *Class No:* 159.98(083)

[318]
Tests in print III: an index to tests, test reviews and the literature on specific tests. Mitchell, J.V., *ed*. Lincoln, NE., Buros Institute of Mental Measurement, 1983. xxxiii,714p. $85. ISBN: 0910674523.

A companion volume to *Mental measurements yearbooks, Test I* and *Test II* and other Buros publications.

A bibliography of 2672 tests, arranged A-Z by test name/ use of specific tests, test title index, classified subject index, a publishers directory and index that includes addresses, and a name index of all test authors and reviewers. *Class No:* 159.98(083)

Logic

[319]
GREENSTEIN, C.H., *ed*. **Dictionary of logical terms and symbols.** Rev. ed. New York, Van Nostrand Reinhold, 1982. 188p. $9.95; £8.45. ISBN: 0442228341.

First published 1978.

Aims 'to present compactly, concisely and side by side a variety of alternative notational systems currently used by logicians, computer scientists, and engineers' (*Preface*). Glossary of logical terms, p.111-177. Bibliography, p.179-188. *Class No:* 164

Bibliographies

[320]
PEACOCKE, C.A.B. *and* SCOTT, D., *eds*. **A Selective bibliography of philosophical logic.** 3rd ed. rev. by M. Davies and G. Forbes. Oxford, Sub-Faculty at Philosophy, 1978. [v],125p. mimeographed. (*Study aids, v.1.*)

First published 1975.

6 main sections: 0. Books (collected works; monographs) - 1. References (proper names; definitive descriptions; pronouns and relative pronouns; demonstratives; eliminability of singular terms; ontological commitment; abstract objects) - 2. Predication - 3. Composition - 4. Interference - 5. Meaning. Further subdivisions; final chronological order. No index. *Class No:* 164(01)

[321]
RISSE, W. **Bibliographia logica.** Hildesheim, G. Olms Verlagsbuchhandlung, 1965-79. 4v.

V.1. 1472 - 1800 (1965); 2. 1800 bis zu Gegenwart (1973); 3. Zeitschriftenartikel (1979); 4. Handschriften zur logic (1979) V.1. contains *c.*6000 entries, arranged chronologically by year, locations in 171 libraries (65 of them German). Four indexes of authors, anonymous works and commentators, and a systematic index. *Class No:* 164(01)

[322]

—Notre Dame journal of formal logic: devoted to symbolic logic. Notre Dame, Indiana, University of Notre Dame Press, 1960-. Quarterly. $40pa. ISSN: 00294527.

Focuses on foundations of mathematical logic. *Class No:* 164(01)

Handbooks & Manuals

[323]

BASTABLE, P.K. **Logic: depth grammar of rationality.** A textbook of the science and history of logic. Dublin, Gill and Macmillan, 1975. [vii],429p.

Sections A-F: A. Preparatory section - B. Formal logic - C. Metalogic - D. Philosophy of logic - E. Applied logic - F. A bibliography of logic (p.389-420). Indexes of proper names and subjects. *Class No:* 164(035)

[324]

Handbook of philosophical logic. Gabbay, D. *and* Guenthner, F., *eds*. Dordrecht, D. Reidel Publishing Co., 1983-86. 4v. v.1 £77.50; v.2 £95.50; v.3 £71.75; v.4 £112.00. ISBN: 9027715424, v.1; 9027716048, v.2; 9027716056, v.3; 9027716064, v.4.

V.1: Elements of classical logic (6 essays); v.2: Extensions of classical logic (12 essays); v.3: Alternatives to classical logic (8 essays); v.4: Topics in the philosophy of language (14 essays). References are appended to each essay. Name and subject indexes in each volume. *Class No:* 164(035)

Histories

[325]

DUMITRIU, A. **History of logic.** New York, Abacus Press, 1977. 4v. ISBN: 0856261394, set; 0856261408, v.1; 0856261416, v.2; 0856261424, v.3; 0856261432, v.4.

A summary by the author of his *Istoria logicii.*

Attempts to deal exhaustively with the whole range of the discipline, covering methodology of science, the problem of categories, the dialectics, the philosophy of logic, etc. Includes many quotations to supplement and explain his argument. *Class No:* 164(091)

[326]

KNEALE, W. *and* KNEALE, M. **The Development of logic.** Oxford, Clarendon Press, 1975 (reprinted by Oxford University Press, 1984). 790p. £12.95. ISBN: 0198247737.

The 1975 ed. was a corrected reprint of the first ed., 1962.

Development of formal logic from its origin with the Greeks to the present day. 12 chapters: 2. Aristotle's *Organon* - 3. The Megarians and the Stoics - 4. Roman and medieval logic - 5. Logic after the Renaissance - 6. Mathematical abstraction - 7. Numbers, sets and series - 8. Frege's general logic - 9. Formal developments after Frege - 10. The philosophy of logic after Frege - 11. The philosophy of mathematics after Frege - 12. The theory of deductive systems. Appendix (translations from Latin quotations in chapter 4). Selective bibliography, p.765-73 (A-Z authors). Analytical index. *Class No:* 164(091)

Knowledge Theories & Beliefs

[327]

A Companion to epistemology. Dancy, J. *and* Sosa, E., *eds*. Oxford, Blackwell, 1992. xv,541p. £65. $74.95. (*(Blackwell companions to philosophy)*.) ISBN: 0631172041.

*c.*250 original articles on topics of Anglo-American epistemology, by 130 scholars. Articles are 250-3500 words in length, often with selected bibliographies, on subjects which includes people, terms and phrases. Cross-references. Detailed index. *Class No:* 165

Utopias

[328]

SARGENT, L.T. **British and American utopian literature, 1516-1985:** an annotated, chronological bibliography. New edition. New York, Garland, 1988. 559p. $75. (*Garland reference library in the humanities.*) ISBN: 0824006941.

First published 1979, by G.K. Hall.

Lists science fiction works with utopian dimensions, arranged chronologically. Annotations are brief. US library locations indicated for every book title. ' ... magisterial bibliography ... Introduction is a model of clarity as to intention, definition of terms, and rationale for inclusion or exclusion (*Choice,* October 1988, p.296). *Class No:* 167.5

Ethics

[329]

A Companion to ethics. Singer, P., *ed*. Oxford, Blackwell, 1991. xxii,565p. (*Blackwell companion to philosophy.*) ISBN: 0631162119.

47 original essays, arranged in 7 parts, dealing 'with the origins of ethics, with the great ethical traditions, with theories about how we ought to live, with arguments about specific ethical issues, and with the nature of ethics itself' (*Intro.*). Detailed analytical index, p.547-565. *Class No:* 17

Bibliographies

[330]

BAKER, J. **A Select bibliography of moral philosophy.** Oxford, Sub-Faculty of Philosophy, 1977. xviii,144p. Mimeographed. (*Study aids, v.9.*)

8 main sections (closely subdivided): 1. Introductory - 2. Some metaethical theories - 3. Practical reasoning and rationality - 4. Morality and moral reasoning - 5. Morality and the moral concepts - 6. Normative ethical views - 7. Responsibility, blame, punishment - 8. Moral problems. Finally, chronological order. Cross-references. No index. *Class No:* 17(01)

[331]

A Bibliographic guide to the comparative study of ethics. Carman, J. *and* Juergensmeyer, M., *eds*. Cambridge, Mass., Harvard University Press, 1991. 811p. $100. ISBN: 0521344484.

15 bibliographical essays by scholars who participated in

....(contd.)
the Berkeley-Harvard Program in Comparative Religion. Essays follow a standard format and each is devoted to a particular tradition (*e.g.*,Islam, Taoism). *Class No:* 17(01)

[332]
HERRING, M.Y. Ethics and the professor: an annotated bibliography, 1970-1985. New York, Garland, 1988. 576p. $77. (*Garland reference library of the humanities, 742.*) ISBN: 0824084919.

1905 informative, sometimes also evaluative, entries dealing with professional ethics, ethics and government, personal values, moral and religious education, professional moral conduct, justice, science and ethics, etc. Brief introductory essays precede subject sections. Name, title and brief subject indexes. *Class No:* 17(01)

Encyclopaedias

[333]
Encyclopedia of ethics. Becker, L. *and* Becker, C., *eds.* Hamden, CT, Garland; London, St. James Press, 1992. 2v.(1462p). $150. £140. ((*Garland reference library of the humanities, v.925.*).) ISBN: 081530403x, US; 1558621539, UK.

435 signed articles, of 1000-3000 words each, on concepts, issues, principles, theories, major figures and history of philosophical ethics. Each article carries its own bibliography. Analytical index of names and subjects. Some omissions, but generally well-written and well-edited, according to *Library journal*, 15 June 1992, p.88. '... a well-organized, scholarly achievement.'(*Choice*, v.30(3), November 1992, p.440). *Class No:* 17(031)

[334]
Encyclopedia of religion and ethics. Hastings, J, *and others.* Edinburgh, T & T. Clarke Ltd.; New York, Scribner, 1908-26. 12v. and index. £450; $650 for 13v. set. ISBN: 0567094898 UK; 0567065146 US.

Aims to include articles on every religious belief or custom, every ethical movement, every philosophical idea, and every moral practice. Includes persons and places famous in history of religion and morals. Particularly valuable for its comparative approach. Extensive articles by leading experts on philosophers and ethical and philosophical subjects are included, with bibliographical references. Thus, the article 'Ethics and morality' (v.5. p.436-522) has 18 sections ('American', 'Australian', 'Babylonian' ...), each by a specialist; 'Drunkenness': 6 sections (11 columns), with 54½ lines of bibliography. Extensive quotations, in very small type. Analytical subject index in v.13.
Class No: 17(031)

[335]
—The Encyclopedia of philosophy. Edwards, P., *ed.* New York, Collier-Macmillan, 1973. 4v. (2400p). $425.00. £250. ISBN: 0028949501.

Carries articles on ethics (v.3. p.87-134) and various aspects of it. *Class No:* 17(031)

Histories

[336]
BOURNE, V.I. History of ethics. Garden City, N.Y., Doubleday, 1968. 432p.

5 parts (18 chapters): 1. Graeco-Roman ethics - 2. Patristic and medieval theories - 3. Early modern ethics,

....(contd.)
1450-1750 - 4. Modern theories - 5. Contemporary ethics. Notes (by chapters), p.311-51; bibliography (by chapters), p.353-417). Detailed index, p.419-32. *Class No:* 17(091)

Social Ethics

[337]
LENDER, H.E. Dictionary of American temperance biography: from temperance reform to alcohol research, the 1600s to the 1980s. Westport, CT., Greenwood Press, 1984. 572p. $95. ISBN: 0313223351.

Short biographies of 373 men and women who have attempted to understand and 'come to grips' with the human and social problems associated with alcohol abuse. Each entry includes basic biography and career information of about 2 paragraphs in length, followed by up to a dozen bibliographical references by or about the person. Somewhat arbitrary selection of names for inclusion, but 'on the whole there is much accurate and useful information presented ...' (*Choice*, v.22(2), October 1984, p.250). *Class No:* 172

Business Ethics

[338]
Business ethics. Drummond, J., *ed.* London, Butterworth-Heinemann, 1993. 200p. £16.95. ISBN: 0750606630.

Essays and extracts contributed by leading figures in business ethics worldwide. Covers marketing, advertising, investment, strategic business and ethics. *Class No:* 174.4

[339]
McHUGH, F.P. Keyguide to information sources in business ethics. London, Mansell Publishing Ltd.; New York, Nichols Publishing, 1988. viii,173p. £28; $34.50. ISBN: 0720118492, UK; 0893973270, US.

An overview and survey in 3 parts: 1. Review of business ethics and its literature - 2. Bibliographical listing of sources - 3. Directory of selected organizations. Part 1 is a narrative account of the historical development of the subject in 5 chapters. Part 2 has 685 items, unannotated, of books and journal articles in a classified arrangement, and with an emphasis on contemporary literature. Part 3 (items 686-922) lists academic centres, business organizations, centres and organizations for professional ethics, and libraries, all subdivided by country, A-Z. Index, p.151-173.
Class No: 174.4

Bibliographies

[340]
Bibliography of business ethics. Jones, D.G., *and others, eds.* University of Virginia, 1977-86. 3v.

The bibliography covering 1971-75 was published in 1977 (207p. $14.95. ISBN 081390711x); that for 1976-80 in 1982 (220p. $14.95. ISBN 081390921x); and the latest for 1981-85 (304p. $69.95. ISBN 0889461546) in 1986.
Class No: 174.4(01)

[341]

BICK, P.A. Business ethics and responsibility an information sourcebook. Phoenix, AZ., Oryx, 1988. 204p. $32.50. (*Oryx series in business and management, 11.*) ISBN: 0897742966.

1018 annotated entries arranged in 13 subject sections, each section including a core collection. Journal articles selected from business publications and dissertations published between 1980 and 1986. '... a solid work ...' (*Choice,* October 1988, p.284). *Class No:* 174.4(01)

Recreational Ethics

Bibliographies

[342]

COOPER, T.W., *and others, eds*. **Television and ethics:** a bibliography. Boston, Mass., G.K. Hall, 1988. 203p. $45. ISBN: 0816189668.

Includes over 1000 items, nearly half of which are annotated, of books, journal articles, conference papers and dissertations. The first part contains items on classical ethics; professional ethics; business, legal, medical, governmental, science and engineering, communications and mass media ethics. The second part deals with advertising, children and T.V., T.V. news, politics and government, law and court-room coverage, public T.V., etc. Author and subject indexes. *Class No:* 175(01)

2 Religion

Religion

[343]
ELIADE, M. **A History of religious ideas.** Translated from the French. Chicago, Ill., 1979-83. 3v. (c.1500p.). $27.50 each vol. ISBN: 0226204006, v.1; 0226204022, v.2; 0226204049, v.3.

Translated from *Histoire des croyances et des idéas religieuses* (Paris, Payot).

V.1. *From the Stone Age to the Eleusinian mysteries* (1979) 15 footnoted chapters on Sumerian, ancient Egyptian, Hittite and Canaanite, Vedic and Indian religions before Buddha, with several chapters on Greek religion. 125 sections, each with bibliography. V.2. *From Gautama Buddha to the triumph of Christianity* (1985) progresses through the history of religious ideas, covering the religions of ancient China, Brahminism and Hinduism, Buddha and his contemporaries, Roman religion, Celtic and German religion, Judaism, the Hellenistic period, the Iranian syntheses, and the birth of Christianity. V.3 *From Muhammed to the age of reforms* (1986) examines the movement of Jewish thought out of ancient Eurasia, the Christian transformation to the Mediterranean area and Europe, and the rise and diffusion of Islam from approximately the sixth century through the 17th century. Each volume has a bibliography and index. *Class No: 20*

[344]
PETERS, F.E. **Judaism, Christianity and Islam:** the classical texts and their interpretation. Princeton, NJ, Princeton University Press, 1990. 3v.(1216p.). $85. ISBN: 0691020442, v.1; 069102054x, v.2; 0691020558, v.3; 0691073562, set.

Selects and compiles quotations from the religions' classical period plus connective commentary with explanatory and factual data. V.1: From covenant to community; v.2: The word and the law and the people of God; v.3: The works of the spirit. Short titles index at the end of each volume. *Class No: 20*

[345]
SUTHERLAND, S., *ed*. **The World's religions.** London, Routledge & Kegan Paul; Boston, Mass., G.K. Hall, 1988. 995p. £50; $75. ISBN: 0413003245, UK; 0816189781, US.

An introduction, giving an account of the history, the theological basis and the practice of religion and religions, and also of the current state of the study of religion and religions. The chapters are organized into 6 parts: 1. Religion and the study of religions - 2. Judaism and Christianity - 3. Islam - 4. The religions of Asia - 5. Traditional religions - 6. New religious movements. Each chapter includes a select bibliography. 'This volume is clearly a major contribution to the field, forming an invaluable one-volume reference work for students studying comparative and world religions' (*Bulletin of the ABTPL*, v.2(10), March 1991, p.21). *Class No: 20*

[346]
WHALING, F., *ed*. **Religion in today's world:** the religious situation of the world from 1945 to the present day. Edinburgh, T. & T. Clark, 1987. viii,383p. £16.95. ISBN: 0567094529.

13 essays by 11 experts from 10 different universities around the world. Attempts to look in breadth and in depth at the religious situation of the world as a whole in the latter part of the 20th century. In addition to focusing on the 5 major religious traditions (Buddhist, Christian, Hindu, Jewish and Muslim) and the present religious situations in China and Japan, the authors also look at civil religion, cults and new religious movements, secular world-views, spirituality, and the study of religion in today's world. Analytical index, p.370-383. *Class No: 20*

Abbreviations & Symbols

[347]
Internationales Abkürzungsverzeichnis für Theologie und Grenzgebiete/International glossary of abbreviations for theology and related subjects. Berlin & New York, de Gruyter, 1974. 348p. $55. ISBN: 3110040271.

About 8000 entries (A ... ZYGON). Main section has entries under full name of periodical, etc., plus place of publication and date of starting; preceded by a list of abbreviations plus fullnames. 'It offers suggestions for standard abbreviations of periodicals, serials, dictionaries and source works for standard abbreviations of periodicals'. 'Marred by the paucity - and uncertainty - of the information given' (*Heythrop journal*, v.17, 1976, p.108). *Class No: 20(003)*

Bibliographies

[348]
ADAMS, C.J., *ed*. **A Reader's guide to the great religions.** 2nd ed. New York, Collier Macmillan, 1977. xvii, 521p. $24.95. ISBN: 0029002400.

First published 1965.

14 contributors (13 of them North American). 13 chapters: 1. Primitive religion - 2. The ancient world - 3. The religions of Mexico and of Central and South America - 4. The religions of China - 5. Hinduism - 6. Buddhism - 7. The Sikhs - 8. The Jainas - 9. The religions of Japan - 10. Early and Classical Judaism - 11. Medieval and modern Judaism - 12. Christianity (p.345-406) - 13. Islam. Appendix: 'The history of religions'. Running commentary. Chapter 9 (p.247-82) has appended lists: 1. Reference books relevant to religions of Japan - 2. Published bibliographies (5 sections) - 3. Periodicals relevant to religions of Japan. Author index; analytical subject index (p.494-521). 'It is hard to fault such an excellent work' (*American reference books annual.* 1978, v.9, entry no.969). *Class No: 20(01)*

[349]

'A Basic stock of religious books' In *The bookseller*, October 20th, 1984, p.1701-2.

50 titles, arrranged in four sections: General guides to world religions and their texts - Books of synthesis and dialogue - Books on individual world religions - Philosophical, scientific and psychological approaches. *Class No:* 20(01)

[350]

Bibliographies of books printed before 1800. Careless, G.C. and Morris, P., eds. Deeside, Clwyd, St Deniol's Library, 1980 - 81. 9v. £1.20 to £2.60 each vol.

V.1. Biblical studies and patristics; v.2. Philosophy and Christian doctrine; v.3. Life in the Church - spirituality, morality, and homiletics; v.4. Liturgical studies; v. 5-6. Church history; v.7. European history; v.8. Language and literature; v.9. Miscellaneous. A complete listing of the library's main pre-1800 collection. *Class No:* 20(01)

[351]

DR. WILLIAMS'S LIBRARY, London. **Catalogue ...** the Library, 1841-.

Volumes so far are: *Catalogue of the Library* (1841. 2v. (v.2: Tracts and pamphlet material)); *Catalogue of the Library.* v.3 [1842-1885] (1885. 3 pts); *Author catalogue of additions,* 1900-1932 [with supplement of publications of learned societies, connected series, etc.]. (1933. 3 pts.); *Catalogue of accessions,* 1900-1950; being a catalogue of books published and added to the Library during that period [with supplement of titles of periodicals, publications of learned societies, connected series, etc.]. (1955. viii,776,cxlvp.); *Catalogue of accessions,* v.2; being a catalogue of books published in the twentieth century and added to the Library, 1951-1960 (1961. xi,181,xxxvp.); *Catalogue of accessions,* v.3: being a catalogue of books published in the twentieth century and added to the Library, 1961-1970 (1973. x,261,xlvp.); *Catalogue of accessions,* v.4; books added 1971-1980 (1983. ix,165,xxxviiip.).

A catalogue, by authors, of a library founded in 1715 and now possessing some 100,000v. covering all aspects of religion, philosophy and kindred subjects; especially strong in early Nonconformist material. Each volume has a supplement listing serials, periodicals and other regularly taken titles. No printed catalogue exits for the years 1886-99. *Class No:* 20(01)

[352]

FRANCIS. 527. Bulletin signalétique. 527. Histoire et sciences des religions. Paris, Centre National de la Recherche Scientifique, Centre de Documentation. Sciences Humaines, 1947-. Quarterly. F.565 pa. ISSN: 01809296.

Formerly part of *Bulletin signalétique. Philosophie* (v.1-9, 1947-55), then of *Bulletin signalétique. 19. Philosophie. Sciences humaines* (1956-60), later *Bulletin signalétique. 527* . V.31(1), 1989 has 2379 indicative abstracts and references. 9 main sections: 01. Studies in religion - 02. Ancient religions - 03. Israel - 04. Christianity - 05. Exegisis and Biblical criticism - 06. Islam - 07. African religions - 08. Religions in America, Arctic and Oceania - 09. Asian religions. List of periodicals scanned. Subject indexes (01 ... 09) and author index per issue. '04. Christianity' occupies entries 337-1957 of the 2379 total. Available online (Telesystems, Questel) and on CD-ROM. *Class No:* 20(01)

[353]

GORMAN, G.E. *and* **GORMAN, L. Theological and religious reference materials.** Westport, CT., Greenwood Press, 1984-. To be in 4 vols. v.1 $58.95; v.2 $59.95; v.3 $50.95. (*Bibliographies and indexes in religious studies, 1, 2, & 7.*) ISBN: 0313209243, v.1; 031324779x, v.2; 0313253978, v.3.

Aim was to provide a work introducing students to the full range of reference materials likely to be required in theological or religious studies and available in academic libraries. 5845 titles have been listed in the 3 vols. published, almost all titles having evaluative annotations and references to related titles. Volumes are: 1. General resources and biblical studies - 2. Systematic theology and church history - 3. Practical theology. V.4 will deal with comparative and non-Christian religions. There is a tentative promise of a supplement to incorporate new material. Scope is both international and interdenominational. Periodical articles are omitted. Each volume is self-contained with author, title and subject indexes. 'Will not replace Kepple ... but a must for all academic and theological libraries (*Journal of academic librarianship,* July, 1985, p.4873). 'Planned work greatly exceeds scope of Kepple or McCabe, tho' less convenient to use' (*Wilson library bulletin,* November 1984, p.228-9). 'A new standard work' (*Bulletin of ABTAPL,* no.39, June 1987, p.4). *Class No:* 20(01)

[354]

HOLM, J. 'Recent books on world religions'. In *British book news,* December 1985, p.706-709.

110 references, arranged A-Z by author. Covers the comparative study of religions, individual religions, religion in the modern world, aspects of religions, founders and reformers, sacred writings, etc. *Class No:* 20(01)

[355]

HOMAN, R., *comp.* **The Sociology of religion:** a bibliographical survey. Westport, CT., Greenwood Press, 1986. 309p. $45. £39.95. (*Bibliographies and indexes in religious studies, 9.*) ISBN: 0313247102.

Introductory essay examines the foundations of the sociology of religion, and is followed by 1013 annotated entries to books on the subject. Annotations are clearly written and often evaluative as well as descriptive. Mainly material in English published in the last 20 years. Arranged in 20 subject areas. Author, title and subject indexes. 'A well-realized bibliography of lasting value' (*Choice,* March 1987, p.1032), but *RQ* (v.26(4) p.524) considers Blasi and Cuneo's *Issue in sociology ...* better. *Class No:* 20(01)

[356]

International bibliography of social and cultural anthropology. London, Tavistock Publications, 1955-, v.1-. Annual. (*International bibliography of the social sciences.*) ISSN: 00852074.

V.38: 1992 (1993. lxxix,215p.) has *c.*1700 numbered entries, arranged in 10 subject sections (*e.g.* F. Religion, magic, witchcraft). *Class No:* 20(01)

[357]

KARPINSKI, L.M., *comp.* **The Religious life of man:** guide to basic literature. Metuchen, N.J., & London, Scarecrow Press, 1978. xx,399p. $27.50; £18.95. ISBN: 0810811103.

2032 numbered, unannotated entries for books and periodical articles. 6 parts (further divided): 1. Religions of mankind (general) - 2. Religions of the past - 3. Judaism, Christianity, Islam - 4. Asian religions (Hinduism,

....(contd.)
Buddhism, Confucianism, Taoism, etc.; items 1199-1688) - 5. The beliefs of native peoples - 6. The occult. Author title and subject index. *Class No:* 20(01)

[358]
LAMBE, D. Reference works on world religions. In *Bulletin of the Association of British theological and philosophical libraries,* v.2(10), March 1991, p.20-24.
10 major reference works are given comparative evaluation. *Class No:* 20(01)

[359]
Library research guide to religion and theology: illustrated search strategy and sources. Kennedy, J.R. 2nd rev. ed. Ann Arbor, Mich., Pierian Press, 1984. $25. ISBN: 0876501854.
First published 1974.
Aims to instruct students in religious studies how to use books and libraries as part of the research process. 'A reliable technique and an adequate resource guide for research in the general area of religious studies' (*RQ,* v.14(4), Summer 1975, p.356-7, of the 1st ed.). *Class No:* 20(01)

[360]
MITROS, J.F. Religions: a select, classified bibliography. New York, Learned Publications, 1973. 435p. $45. (*Philosophical questions, 8.*) ISBN: 0912116080.
Aims 'to provide a student of religion with a handy guide in his research while he is preparing a paper, an examination, a lecture, a course, writing a book or conducting a seminar' (*Introduction*). Annotated entries in 7 sections, including general reference books and relevant journals, Christianity (with special reference to Patristic studies), the Scriptures, and non-Christian religions. 'An excellent bibliography ... for the advanced student in Western religious history' (*College & research libraries,* v.30, January 1975, p.64). *Class No:* 20(01)

[361]
Religion and theology, 1989: a book guide. Editorial Department of SCM Press, *comps.* London, SCM Press, 1989. [iv], 117p. £2.95. ISBN: 033402322x.
First published 1976. Annual.
Selective descriptive catalogue of religious and theological books currently available which have proved their worth. *c.*2000 entries in 8 main subject sections, subdivided A-Z by author. Very brief annotations of 2 lines or less. Index, p.111-117. *Class No:* 20(01)

[362]
Religion index one: periodicals: a subject index to periodical literature, including an author/editor index and Scripture index. Evanston, Ill., American Theological Library Association, v.13(1977-78)-. Irregular. $285 pa. ISSN: 01498428.
Previously as *Index to religious periodical literature,* v.1-12, 1949-76. V.22 (1990) has a list of periodicals indexed; a subject index of 407 double-column pages; an author and editor index; and a Scripture index. ATLA religion database includes this title, and is available through BRS Information Technologies; DIALOG; and WILSONLINE; also a CD-ROM through H.W. Wilson Co. *Class No:* 20(01)

[363]
—Religion index two: multi-author works, 1976-. Evanston, Ill., American Theological Library Association, 1978-. Annual. $335 pa. ISSN: 01498436.
The 1987 v. indexes 412 books and the 6113 articles/parts they contained. In addition 32 festschriften and collections of conference proceedings are indexed at book level. Contents: List of titles indexed; Subject index; Author/editor index; Scripture index.
Both series are online in the ATLA Religion database; RIO v.1-4 (1949-1959) & v.2 (1975)-; RIT from 1960. Available online (BRS, DIALOG) and on CD-ROM. *Class No:* 20(01)

[364]
Religious and inspirational books and serials in print. 5th ed. New York, R.R. Bowker Company, 1987. xxxvi, 1826p. $79.95. ISSN: 00000868.
First published 1978 and issued biennially thereafter. Early title was *Religious books and serials in print: a reference catalog.*
Finding and ordering information for current books and serials. Covers all the world's religions and a range of such allied subjects as the religious implications of abortion, homosexuality, business ethics, ecology, or any human experience. In two sections: Books, by subject, author and title, and Serials, by subject and title. Produced from records stored on magnetic tape, this edition has 61204 entries for titles available from 3000 publishers. Subject index follows Library of Congress subject headings. Key to publishers' and distributors' abbreviations, including address, telephone no., etc. Also available online. *Class No:* 20(01)

[365]
Religious books in print: a reference catalogue, 1993. London, J. Whitaker, 1993. 796p. £37. ISBN: 0850212340. ISSN: 0305960x.
First published 1974. Annual.
Lists over 27,000 in-print titles plus a directory of their 1400 publishers and distributors. Author, title and keyword index. Classified index of 18 principal subjects and 127 subsidiaries. *Class No:* 20(01)

[366]
Religious information sources: a worldwide guide. Melton, J.G. *and* Köszegi, M.A., *comps.* New York, Garland, 1992. xxiii,569p. $75. ((*Garland reference library of the humanities, v.1593*). (*Religious information systems series, v.2*).) ISBN: 0815308590.
A comprehensive guide to the many sources of information in the broad field of religion. An introduction to non-print sources in religion is followed by 7 sections: 1. Religion: general and theoretical considerations; 2. The religions of the world (General - Eastern - Africa and the Middle East - The Americas, Europe and Oceania); 3. Issues in comparative religion; 4. Christianity; 5. Christianity: issues in Christian studies; 6. Christian historical studies; 7. Christian denominational family traditions. Indexes of titles, authors, organizations and subjects. *Class No:* 20(01)

[367]
SHERMIS, M. Jewish-Christian relations: an annotated bibliography and resource guide. Indiana University Press, 1988. 291p. $29.95. ISBN: 0253331536.
Includes entries, many annotated, for books, pamphlets, journal articles, journal issues and special publications, and non-print media, arranged by broad subject areas. Includes

....*(contd.)*

examples of syllabi for study of Jewish-Christian relations, and lists organizations and speakers on the subject. '...valuable addition to the growing body of literature ...' (*Choice,* v.26(6), February 1989, p.926). *Class No:* 20(01)

[368]

Theological and religious bibliographies. Harrogate, North Yorks., Theological Abstracting and Bibliographical Services, (T.A.B.S), 1979-81. Irregular.

Continued *Theological and religious index,* 1972-1978. (ISSN 0306087x).

About 1000 index entries per issue, arranged in subject sections. *Class No:* 20(01)

Encyclopaedias

[369]

ELIADE, M. and COULLARDO, A.P. The Eliade guide to world religions: the authoritative compendium of the 33 major religious traditions. New York, HarperCollins, 1991. 301p. $22.95. ISBN: 0060621481.

A one-volume compendium. Brief and unbiassed. Scholarly, but accessible to the informed lay reader. (Eliade died in May, 1991). *Class No:* 20(031)

[370]

FISHER, M.P. and LUYSTER, R.W. Living religions: an encyclopedia of the world's faiths. London, I.B.Taurus, 1990. 367p. 200 illus. £19.95. ISBN: 1850432996.

13 chapters, all subdivided: 1. The religious response; 2. Indigenous sacred ways; 3. Hinduism; 4. Jainism; 5. Buddhism; 6. Taoism and Confucianism; 7. Shinto; 8. Zoroastrianism; 9. Judaism; 10. Christianity; 11. Islam; 12. Sikhism; 13. New religious movements. A feature is interviews with believers. 'Suggested reading' after each subdivision. Notes (by chapters), p.349-56. Glossary, p.357-61. Index, p.362-67. '... this is the best for the general reader who wants a clear, attractive and accurate introduction to world religions ...' (*Bulletin of the Association of British Theological and Philosophical Libraries,* v.2(10), March 1991, p.22). *Class No:* 20(031)

[371]

MELTON, J.G. Encyclopedia of American religions. 4th ed. Detroit, Mich., Gale Research Co., 1993. 3v. $175. ISBN: 089243497x.

First published 1980.

Detailed information on individual churches, religious bodies and spiritual groups, ranging from Adventists to Zen Buddhism, organized into religious families of churches related to one another through similarities of creed. Includes essays on the historical development of the American religions and on each religious group, including information on beliefs and practices of the religion, publications produced, headquarters or contact address, number of congregations and membership, and list of sources for further information. There are various indexes. 'Especially valuable for its exhaustive coverage of religious bodies outside the main stream' (*Reference books bulletin,* 1986/87, p.53-4). Complemented by the author's *Encyclopedia of American religions: religious creeds. (qv).*
Class No: 20(031)

[372]

MELTON, J.G. Encyclopedia of American religions: religious creeds. Detroit, Mich., Gale Research Co., 1988. 838p. $125. ISBN: 0810321327.

A collection of over 450 creeds, confessions, and statements of belief of America's religious groups (not only Christian, but also Jewish, Islamic, Scientology, Wiccan (witches), etc., and even 'Flying saucer' groups), arranged in 23 chapters, representing religious families, each sub-divided by names of religious groups. Information for each group includes historical notes and comments as well as the texts of the creeds, etc. Detailed table of contents, name and keyword index. Complements the author's *Encyclopedia of American religions (q.v.).*

A new ed. was issued in 1993 ($135. ISBN 0810354918). *Class No:* 20(031)

English

[373]

ELIADE, M., ed. The Encyclopedia of religion. New York, Collier Macmillan, 1987. 16v. (8000p.). £950.00; $1400.00 the set. ISBN: 0029094801.

*c.*2750 signed articles, plus a further 150 articles featuring biographies of scholars of religion, arranged A-Z through vols. 1-15, written by 1400 international scholars. Articles vary in length from *c.*300 to *c.*15000 words, and each article is followed by a bibliography. Covers 'the history of religious traditions past and present, large and small, Western and non-Western; cross-cultural themes, symbols, legends, rituals and motifs; religious beliefs, doctrines, literature and practices; religious institutions, organizations and communities; the major figures in religion; the history, theories, terms, concepts, methods and leading authorities in the study of religion; the place of religion in culture and society, including the arts, philosophy, science, politics, law and social organizations' (*Publicity document no. 19*). V.16, *Index* (352p.), includes a directory of contributors; an alphabetical list of entries; and synoptic outline of contents (p.97-127), as well as a detailed index (p.129-470) and corrigenda. 'Major event in encyclopaedia publishing ... two strengths ... are its organization and its bibliographies'. (*Choice,* v.25(10), June 1988, p.1517-8). 'Improvements could doubtless have been made in the selection of topics, the balance of the articles, the correspondence between theory and practice, and the accessibility of relevance of the data to the "nonspecialist educated reader". With all its defects and inbalances ... remains a good achievement'. (*Bulletin of ABTPL* (no. 40, November 1987, p.13). *Class No:* 20(031)=20

[374]

Encyclopaedia of religion and ethics: edited by J. Hastings, with the assistance of J.A. Selbie and other scholars. Edinburgh, T. & T. Clark Ltd; New York, Scribner, 1908-26. 12v. & index. £450; $650 for 13v. set. ISBN: 0567094898, UK; 0567065146, US.

Aims to include articles on every religious belief or custom, every ethical movement, every philosophical idea, and every moral practice. Includes persons and places famous in history of religion and morals. Particularly valuable for its comparative approach (*e.g.* the series of articles: Faith, Buddhist; Faith, Christian; Faith, Greek; Faith, Hindu; Faith, Muslim ...). Articles are signed and well documented; systematic treatment of major subjects (*e.g.* 'Architecture' (v.1. p.677-733) has 24 sections., from

....(contd.)

'Aegean' to 'Shinto'). The index volume comprises a general, analytical index (p.1-660), an index to foreign words, an index to Scripture passages, and an index to authors or articles. Diacritical markings are given. *Class No:* 20(031)=20

[375]
The Encyclopedia of world faiths: an illustrated survey of the world's living religions. Bishop, P. *and* Darton, M., *eds.* New York, Facts on File, 1988; London, Macdonald & Co. (Publishers) Ltd., 1987. 352p. illus, maps (some col.), charts, diagrs. $40. £19.95. ISBN: 081601860x, US; 0356140628, UK.

Introduction on the nature of religion is followed by information on 12 major religions, covering the history, beliefs, writings, ethics, rituals and worship, subgroups, and present day organization. The religions are Judaism, Zoroastrianism, Christianity, Islam, Baha'i, Hinduism, Jainism, Buddhism, Sikhism, Confucianism, Taoism, and Shinto. Concluding chapters are on new religious movements in modern Western society, new religious movements among pastoral peoples, and conclusions. Further reading (p.324-326) is arranged by chapter, subdivided by authors. Glossary, p.327-345. Index, p.346-352. *Class No:* 20(031)=20

German

[376]
Die Religion in Geschicht und Gegenwart. Handwörterbuch für Theologie und Religionswissenschaft. 3.völlig. neu bearb. Aufl. in Gemeinschaft mit Hans Freiherr v. Campenhausen u.a.; hrsg. von Kurt Galling. Tübingen, Mohr, 1957-65. 7v. illus., maps.

First published 1909-13. 5v.; 2nd ed. 1927-32. 5v.

A scholarly work; all articles signed, with bibliographies. A feature is the lengthy systematic treatment of subjects. 'Kirchenbau' (v.3) covers columns 1347-1411, including 58 plans, 16 pages of plates, and treats the subject in terms of its major periods. 10p. on Buddhism; 18p. on Islam. Valuable, too, for its articles on marginal topics and appropriate men of letters (*e.g.* articles on the ikon, Existentialism, the film, and Franz Kafka). V.7, the index, comprises bibliographical notes on the *c.*3000 contributors, a subject index (p.272-1102); and errata. German Protestant standpoint. *Class No:* 20(031)=30

Dictionaries

English

[377]
Abingdon dictionary of living religions. Crim, K., *ed.* Nashville, Tenn., Abingdon Press, 1981. 864p. illus. $39.95. £25. ISBN: 0687004098.

1600 keywords and phrases. Concentrates on religions currently practiced in the world today. Over 150 American scholars contributed, providing comprehensive articles on the historical development and current status of the religions, describing the doctrines, sects, movements, significant personalities, sacred writings, religious practices, and holy sites and objects. Pronunciations given where not in general English usage. Complements Brandon's *Dictionary of*

....(contd.)

comparative religion (1970), which has fewer non-Christian religion entries. 'A good buy' (*RQ*, v.21(3), Spring 1982, p.296). *Class No:* 20(038)=20

[378]
BRANDON, S.G.F., *ed*. A Dictionary of comparative religion. London, Weidenfeld & Nicolson; New York, Scribner, 1978. viii, 704p. $60. ISBN: 0684155613.

4 section editors; 28 contributors. About 4000 concise signed articles (*e.g.* 'Scandinavian religion': p.159-64; 25 lines of bibliography. 'Buddhism. General survey', p.157-60). Adequate cross-references. General index, p.680-704. List of main sources, p.9-15. A standard dictionary to update Hastings' *Encyclopaedia of religion and ethics* (Edinburgh, T.& T. Clark Ltd; New York, Scribner, 1908-26) in this field. *Class No:* 20(038)=20

[379]
—GASKELL, G.A. Dictionary of all Scriptures and myths. New York, Julian Press, 1960 (Reprinted Dorset Press, 1989). 842p. $29.95. ISBN: 0880292695.

Over 5000 entries, stressing symbolism of religious terms and how symbols vary from religion to religion. Many quotations and cross references. *Class No:* 20(038)=20

[380]
Chambers dictionary of beliefs and religions. Goring, R., *ed.* London, Chambers, 1992. 672p. 100 illus. £25. ISBN: 0550150005.

Over 3000 entries, A-Z. Subject coverage is wide-ranging and includes scientology, pantheism and witchcraft. *Class No:* 20(038)=20

[381]
HINNELLS, J.R., *ed*. The Penguin dictionary of religions. London, Allan Lane/Penguin Books; New York, Facts on File, 1984. 550p. illus., diagrs., maps. £14.75. $27.95. ISBN: 0713915145, UK; 0871968622, US.

Mainly concerned with 'living' religions, including new religious movements, astrology, magic, the occult, as well as secular alternatives to religion, such as Marxism and humanism. A-Z arrangement and ample cross-references. The 29 international contributors have written entries ranging from *c.*40 to *c.*1500 words in length. Valuable scholarly bibliography is arranged under 30 broad subject headings and keyed to the dictionary entries (p.382-446). Also includes maps (p.366-381); a general index (p.465-550); and a synoptic index (p.447-464). Flowing, readable text, and the work's strength is in its coverage of Eastern religions and concepts. *Class No:* 20(038)=20

[382]
PYE, M. Macmillan dictionary of religion. London, Macmillan, 1993. 500p. £29.50. ISBN: 033345409x.

Based on 'concepts drawn partly from the various religious traditions and partly from the historical and reflective study of religion as a modern academic discipline'. Gives concise explanations of nearly 6000 terms covering all aspects of the subject, and distinguishing between religious and theological terminology. Subject arrangement (Extinct and ancient religions - Israelite religion and Judaism - Islam - Christianity - Indian religions ... Sociology of religion - Psychology of religion ... Religions in various cultural disciplines). *Class No:* 20(038)=20

[383]

REESE, W.L. **Dictionary of philosophy and religion:**
Eastern and Western thought. Atlantic Highlands, N.J.,
Humanities Press; Hassocks, West Sussex, Harvester Press,
1980. iv, 644p. diagrs. $29.95; £80.00. ISBN: 0855271477.

'Has many encyclopedic features, including analysis of the
thought of all major philosophers and religious leaders'
(*Preface*). A key feature is numerous cross-references from
concepts to the thinkers concerned. Major emphasis is on
explication terms. Expensive. *Class No:* 20(038)=20

Reviews & Abstracts

[384]

Religious and theological abstracts. 1958-. v.1-. 4pa.
Myerstown, Pa., Religious and Theological Abstracts Inc.,
1958-. $85. (institutions); $42.50. (individuals). CD-ROM
$595; renewals $5295. ISSN: 00344044.

Abstracts of articles from more than 300 scholarly
periodicals in religion, including Christian, Jewish and other
world religions. Four main classes: 1. Biblical - 2.
Theological - 3. Historical - 4. Practical. Subject index and
author index. Addresses of journals. Annual subject, author
and Scripture indexes in 4th volume each year.
Class No: 20(048)

[385]

Religious studies review: a quarterly review of publications in
the field of religion and related disciplines. 1975-. Macon,
Georgia, Council of Societies for the Study of Religion,
1975-. $36 (institutions); $30 (individuals) pa. ISSN:
0319485x.

Each issue contains *c.* 12 reviews of 3-4 double column
pages; *c.* 250 notices of recent publications (*c.*1/3 col. each);
and notices of recent dissertations in religion.
Class No: 20(048)

[386]

—WALSH, M.J., *and others*. Religious bibliographies in serial
literature: a guide. London, Mansell, 1981. 240p. £20.
ISBN: 0720115930.

Describes *c.175* current serials that include bibliographical
coverage of religious study. *Class No:* 20(048)

Periodicals

[387]

BURNS, E. **Religious periodicals:** a recommended collection.
In *Serials review*, v.7 January-March 1981, p.9-32.

Reviews of 77 English-language serial titles, mostly
published in US. Separate sections, each with an
introduction, on charismatic Christianity (2 entries);
bibliographic aids (3); 36 best known titles selected from
many religious traditions, academic disciplines and
ecclesiastical slants; Catholic periodicals (12); Judaic
theological journals (6); and Mormon periodicals (18); the
last three sections being by other contributors. Some
duplication of titles. *Class No:* 20(051)

[388]

CORNISH, G.P., *ed*. **Religious periodicals directory.** Santa
Barbara, CA., ABC-Clio, 1986. xii, 330p. $89. £77.95.
ISBN: 0874363659.

Claims to be a 'comprehensive source of information
about periodicals and other serials in the field of religion and
theology in the broadest sense of those terms' (*Preface*), and
coverage extends to journals in the fields of anthropology,

....(contd.)

linguistics, sociology, archeology, art and literature. 1800
periodicals are listed by title within country sections, that are
arranged A-Z within broad geographical regions. Entries
include information on frequency, publisher with address,
sponsoring body, statement of purpose or subject content,
language of publication, sources in which indexed, variant
titles, and special features. Title and subject/geographic
indexes. *Class No:* 20(051)

[389]

FIEG, E.C., *comp*. **Religion journals and serials:** an
analytical guide. Westport, CT., Greenwood Press, 1988.
218p. $45. (*Annotated bibliographies of serials: a subject
approach, 13.*) ISBN: 0313245134.

Primary aim is to help libraries in the selection of
scholarly journals, and 328 titles have been selected from
about 2000 English-language serials in religion. Titles
arranged under broad subject headings. Entries include title,
date founded, frequency, publisher, etc., and descriptive
annotations. *Class No:* 20(051)

[390]

KASTEN, S. 'Religion periodical indexes': a basic list. in
RSR, v.9(1); January-March 1981, p.53-55.

One reference librarian's selection of significant titles
among the currently-published religion periodical indexes.
Brief descriptions included suggest how the tools might be
useful. *Class No:* 20(051)

[391]

LIPPY, C.H., *ed*. **Religious periodicals of the United States:**
academic and scholarly journals. London, Greenwood Press,
1986. xxi,607p. £46.95; $67.95. (*Historical guides to the
world's periodicals and newspapers.*) ISBN: 0313234205.

A selection of *c.*100 American academic religious and
theological journals. Represents academic, scholarly and
professional societies; religious groups and denominations;
institutions such as theological seminaries and universities.
Articles on each title are 3-4 pages in length. 2 appendices
(A. Chronological capsule; B. Listing by sponsoring
organization or religious orientation). Index, p.563-600.
Class No: 20(051)

[392]

REGAZZI, J.J. *and* HINES, T.C. **A Guide to indexed
periodicals in religion.** Metuchen, N.J., Scarecrow Press,
1975. 328p. $22.50. £15. ISBN: 0810808684.

Lists over 2700 periodicals (A-Z by title and also by
keyword in context), indicating which of 17 indexing or
abstracting services cover them. The 17 services are then
listed (no details), sub-arranged by titles of periodicals
served. 'A significant addition to the bibliographic control in
the fields of religion and theology' (*Library journal*,
v.101(3), 1 March 1976,. p.705). *Class No:* 20(051)

Quotations

[393]

MEAD, F.S., *ed. & comp*. **Encyclopaedia of religious
quotations.** London, Peter Davies, 1965. [vii],534p.

More than 10,000 quotations, arranged A-Z by topics,
from 'Advertising' (19 entries, authors A-Z, anonymous
preceding) to 'Zeal' (16 entries). 170 subject headings.
Covers verse and prose, and draws on non-Christian as well
as Christian (including Biblical) sources. Quotations are

....(contd.)

sometimes lengthy, but there are obvious omissions. Indexes of authors and topics, but no first-line index. *Class No:* 20(082.2)

[394]

—NEIL, W., *comp.* Concise dictionary of religious quotations. London, Mowbrays, 1975. vii,214p.

Includes *c.* 2500 quotations, many from the Bible. Source index; keyword subject index. Prefers the 'eminently forgettable New English Bible every time to the King James Version' (*TLS*, no.3821, 30 May 1975, p.604). *Class No:* 20(082.2)

[395]

—WOODS, R.L., *comp. & ed.* The World treasury of religious quotations. New York, Hawthorn, 1966. 1106p.

10,000 quotations, chronologically under 1500 subject headings. Universal coverage; no poetry and only 2 Bible verses. Author, title and date of publication for each quotation. Author index, but no keyword index. *Class No:* 20(082.2)

[396]

PARRINDER, E.G., *comp.* **A Dictionary of religious and spiritual quotations.** London, Routledge; New York, Simon & Schuster, 1990. xi,218p. £14.99; $40. ISBN: 0132101211, US; 0415041287, UK.

Over 3000 quotations, arranged under 18 broad headings, with 177 subdivisions. Author and title index. Subject index. Eastern religions are well represented. Wider in scope than Pepper. *Class No:* 20(082.2)

[397]

PEPPER, M., *comp.* **Dictionary of religious quotations.** London, André Deutsch, 1989. 496p. ISBN: 0233983732.

Paperback ed. as *The Pan dictionary of religious quotations* (London, Pan Books, 1991. ISBN 0330315005). American ed. as *The Harper religious and inspirational quotation companion* (Harper, 1989. ISBN 0060161795).

Over 4000 quotations under topics, A-Z, with two or more quotations for each subject, spanning the world's major religions from classical times to the present. Includes unusual and entertaining quotations. Subject index, p.461-468. Index of authors and major works, p.469-496. *Class No:* 20(082.2)

Tables & Data Books

[398]

Reviews of United Kingdom statistical sources: v.20: Religion. Oxford, Pergamon Press for the Royal Statistical Society and the Economic and Social Research Council, 1987. 635p. £97. ISBN: 0080347789.

Four reviews (nos. 33, 34, 35, & 36), each review standing alone: Recurrent Christian sources - Non-recurrent Christian data - Judaism - Other religions. *c.*500 pages of the 635p. given to Christian sources. Each review starts with a general introductory section of background information, specific problems and topics. This is followed by the 'Quick reference list', arranged by subject or denomination, including types of data, geographical area covered, date, publications details, etc. The 'Key' to sources listed has full bibliographical details. There is then a second bibliography listing workings of wider scope, and a subject index. *Class No:* 20(083)

Histories

[399]

BLEEKER, C.J. *and* **WIDENGREN, G. Historia religionum:** handbook for the history of religions. Leiden, E.J. Brill, 1969-71. 2v. (viii, 691 & vi, 715p.). V.1 Gld.144. $72. V.2 Gld.166. $83. ISBN: 9004089284, v.1; 9004025987, v.2.

A second impression of v.1 was made in 1988; v.2 is still the 1971 edition.

V.1: *Religions of the past,* includes a section on prehistoric religion, and on Israelite-Jewish religion (p.222-317); bibliography (p.313-7). V.2: *Religions of the present,* has sections on Christianity (p.49-124), with bibliography) and Buddhism (p.372-464; bibliography of 91 items). It also has indexes of authors and subjects. *Class No:* 20(091)

[400]

International bibliography of the history of religions/ Bibliographie internationale de l'histoire des religions ... 1952-73. Leiden, E.J. Brill, 1954-1979. ISSN: 05385105.

The 1973 volume (the last to be published) has *c.*3000 unannotated entries for books, periodical articles and reviews. 11 sections: 1. General works - 2. Prehistorical and primitive religions - 3. Religions of antiquity - 4. Judaism - 5. Christianity - 6. Islam - 7. Hinduism - 8. Buddhism - 9. Chinese religions - 10. Japanese religions - 11. Minor religions. About 500 journals in theory, archaeology and antiquities were scanned. Name index. *Class No:* 20(091)

[401]

SMART, N. The World's religions: old traditions and modern transformations. Cambridge, Cambridge University Press, 1989. 576p. illus., maps. £25. ISBN: 0521340055.

Looks at the world's religions in terms of world history and as constantly developing systems of belief, each religion being analysed in its main aspects - practical or ritual, emotional, narrative or mythic, doctrinal, ethical or legal, social or institutional. Part I traces the development of religions, region by region, as they evolved; Part II examines the changes to faiths and cultures. Richly illustrated with 200 half-tones and maps, 48 col.photos. *Class No:* 20(091)

Biographies

[402]

HINNELLS, J.R. Who's who of religions. London, Macmillan; New York, Simon & Schuster, 1991. 450p. illus. £29.95. $75. ISBN: 0333440994, UK; 0139529462, US.

Biographical studies of *c.*1500 prominent religious leaders throughout the world. *c.*60 contributors. The longer entries are for lesser-known people. 'Objective and authoritative information, some of which is difficult to obtain elsewhere.' (*Library journal,* 1 February 1992, p.82). *Class No:* 20(092)

[403]

LIPPY, C.H., *ed.* **Twentieth-century shapers of American popular religion.** Westport CT., Greenwood Press, 1989. 494p. $65. ISBN: 0313253560.

Biographical and bibliographical information on more than 60 individuals who have influenced popular religion in North America during the 20th century. Arranged A-Z by name (William Aberhart ... Wovoka). Supplements Peter. W.

....(contd.)
Williams' *Popular religion in America* (1980) ' ... this engaging volume' (*Choice* v.27(1) September 1989, p.96). *Class No:* 20(092)

USSR
[404]
The Modern encyclopedia of religions in Russia and the Soviet Union. Steeves, P.D., *ed.* Gulf Breeze, Fl., Academic International, 1989-. V1: $37.50. Expected to be in 35 vols. ISBN: 0875691064, v.1.

V.1. Aaron ... annunciation (241p.).An ambitious project which is to take 15 years to complete, providing detailed information on the religious culture of the peoples inhabiting the Soviet Union. Entries are essay-length, with extensive bibliographies appended. Many entries are original, but reprints and translations from other sources are also included. 'Highly commended' (*Choice*, v.26(11/12), July/August 1989, p.1815). *Class No:* 20(47)

USA
[405]
PITTS, W.L. 'Religious cults in the United States'. In *Choice*, v.21(8), April 1984, p.1094-1102.
Includes 119 references. *Class No:* 20(73)

Libraries
[406]
Guide to the theological libraries of Great Britain and Ireland. Lea, E.R.M., *Comp and* Jesson, A.F., *ed.*. Westcliffe-on-Sea, Essex, ABTAPL Publishing, 1986. xxv, 321p. with loose insert. £10. $15. ISBN: 0948945001.

Aim was a comprehensive survey of library resources in the field. Substantial introduction is followed by a bibliographical essay with 91 references scanning the British and Irish religious-library field under two headings: A. Christian theological collections - B. Non-Christian theological collections. Lists 397 'significant' collections, A-Z by place, subdivided by library, A-Z. Information includes name and address, function, coverage, special collections, librarian, governing body, history, stock, catalogues, access, staff, publications (except for 77 of the libraries, which did not reply to the questionnaire). Reduced typescript. Based on a dissertation for a Master's degree.
Class No: 20:061:026/027

Psychology of Religion
[407]
CAPPS, D., *and others*. **Psychology of religion:** a guide to information sources. Detroit, Mich., Gale Research Co., 1976. xii, 352p. $68. (*Philosophy and religion information guide series.*) ISBN: 0810313561.

About 4000 briefly annotated entries. Sections A-G (A: General works on psychology of religion; B-G: mythological, ritual, experimental, dispositional, social and directional dimensions of religion). Author, title and subject indexes. Limited to material published 1950-74.
Class No: 20:159.9

[408]
SALIBA, J.A. Psychiatry and the cults: an annotated bibliography. New York, Garland, 1987. 601p. $60.00. (*Sects and cults in America. Bibliographical guides, 10. Garland reference library of social sciences, 349.*) ISBN: 0824085868.

1916 annotated entries, with author and subject indexes. '... balanced bibliography ... reflects all professional and academic viewpoints, including those with which [the author] disagrees'. (*Choice*, v.25 (7), March 1988, p.1070.

Complements D. Capp's *Psychology of religion: a guide to information sources* (q.v.). *Class No:* 20:159.9

Rationalism

Bibliographies
[409]
STEIN, G. Freethought in the United Kingdom and the Commonwealth: a descriptive bibliography. Westport, CT., Greenwood Press, [1981]. xxiii, 193p. $76.95. ISBN: 0313208697.

Arranged by historical periods (1624-1760, 1760-1860, 1860-1915, 1915 to the present). Each section has a detailed essay, followed by a bibliography of the publications cited. Appendices on the freethought movement in New Zealand, Canada, Australia and India, giving brief information on the same lines as the main text. Other appendices indicate libraries with major holdings in the field, and a list of master's theses and dissertations. Glossary of terms. Author, title and subject indexes. *Class No:* 211.5(01)

[410]
STEIN, G. God pro and con: a bibliography of Atheism. New York, Garland, 1990. xv,531p. $65. ((*Garland reference library of social science, 588).*) ISBN: 0824070410.

Pseudonyms of Atheist/Freethought authors precedes the main 3 sections: I.A. Atheist books and pamphlets; B. Historical/philosophical studies of Atheism. II.A. Atheist periodicals; B. Important articles about Atheism (pro & con). III. Anti-Atheist books and pamphlets. Title index, p.393-531. *Class No:* 211.5(01)

Encyclopaedias
[411]
STEIN, G., *ed*. **The Encyclopedia of unbelief.** Buffalo, NY, Prometheus Books, 1986. 2v. (819p.). $99.95 the set. ISBN: 0879753072.

Over 100 articles, including short bibliographies, covering philosophy, history and biography of the various branches of unbelief from scepticism to atheism. Cross-references. 5 appendices include 'Periodicals of unbelief' with nearly 500 periodical and newspaper titles. 'There is no comparable work' (*Library journal*, 1 November 1985, p.87). *Class No:* 211.5 (031)

Histories
[412]
BERMAN, D. A History of atheism in Britain: from Hobbes to Russell. London, Croom Helm, 1987. 242p. £30. ISBN: 0709932715.

10 chapters: 1. The repression of atheism - 2. Restoration atheists: founding followers of Hobbes ... 5. The birth of

.... *(contd.)*

avowed atheism, 1782-1979... 9. The atheists: 1822-1842 - 10. Militant and academic atheism. Epilogue: The ethics of unbelief. Index. *Class No:* 211.5(091)

[413]

POSPIELOVSKY, D.V. **A History of Soviet atheism in theory and practice,** and the believer. London, Macmillan Press, 1987-88. 3v. (856p.). V.1: £29.50; v.2: £29.50; v.3: £35. ISBN: 0333423267, v.1; 0333423275, v.2; 0333423283, v.3.

Outlines the theoretical and ideological foundations of Soviet atheism from Feuerbach and Marx to Khrushchev and Adropov. V.1: *A history of the Marxist-Leninist atheism and Soviet anti-religious policies,* deals with the theory of Marxism and with the offical Soviet policy declarations regarding 'the struggle' against religion through history. V.2: *Soviet anti-religious campaigns and persecutions,* exposes and analyses the strategy and tactics of the anti-religious propaganda and persecutions in day-to-day practice, from 1917 to 1986. V.3: *Soviet studies on the Church and the believer's response to atheism,* presents a picture of how the Church and believers actually live in a society of militant atheism. Each volume has appendices ('Annotated texts of Soviet laws on religion' is in v.1.), bibliographies, and indexes. (*Theology,* v.42, no.747, May 1989, p.225-227) remarks that it is expensive and has too many misprints 'but brings together an immense quantity of detailed information about policies and events which is relevant to any attempt to evaluate the changes now taking place'. *Class No:* 211.5(091)

Science & Religion

[414]

EISEN, S. *and* LIGHTMAN, B.V. **Victorian science and religion:** bibliography of works and ideas and institutions with emphasis on revolution, belief and unbelief, comprised of works published from *c.*1900-1975. Santa Barbara, CA., ABC-Clio, 1985. xix, 696p. $55. ISBN: 0208020101.

6267 items of work about science, religion and their interrelationship during the Victorian era (*c.*1830 to 1900). Includes articles, books and dissertations, focusing mainly on England and almost exclusively on the Christian religion. Organized topically in 3 sections: Main currents - National theology, geology and evolution - Religion: ideas and institutions. Each section subdivided by subjects or persons. Unannotated. Author and subject indexes. 'Citations clear and consistant' (*Choice,* v.22(9), May 1985, p.1304). *Class No:* 215

[415]

McIVOR, T. **Anti-evolution:** an annotated bibliography. 385p. $39.95. ISBN: 0899503135.

Entries are arranged A-Z by author, with descriptive annotations varying from one line to ½-page in length. Focuses on books, tracts and pamphlets, and includes Islamic and Jewish as well as Protestant sources; also anti-Darwinian material. Name, title and subject indexes keyed to numbered entries, the name index including both authors and important individuals mentioned in the annotations. Comparable publications are E. Lazar's *The creation/evolution bibliography & directory* (privately printed. 3rd. ed. 1987) and the CREVO/IMS database, maintained since

.... *(contd.)*

1982 by creationist students. 'This unique bibliography provides an invaluable tool for scholars ...' (*Choice,* v.26(7), March 1989, p.1126). *Class No:* 215

Worship & Meditation

[416]

WHITAKER, S. **The Good retreat guide.** 2nd ed. London, Rider, 1994. 224p. £11.99. ISBN: 071266047x.

1st published 1991.

Explains the nature of retreats and lists more than 300 places 'to find peace and spiritual renewal' in Britain, Ireland, France and Spain. *Class No:* 217

Bible

Databases

[417]

The Bible on-line. Austin, Texas, Bible Research System, 1981. 8 floppy disks. $159.95.

The full text of the King James Version of the Bible for Apple computer users. *Class No:* 22(003.4)

Bibliographies

[418]

Elenchus of biblica. Rome, Pontificio Istituto Biblico. 1985-. v.1-. Annual. L.150000; $140.

Continues *Elenchus bibliographieus biblicus* (1920-1984, v.1-65), issued as part of the periodical *Biblica* from 1920 to 1967.

A bibliography covering all areas of the investigation which involves the scientific study of the Bible. V.1, 1985 (1988. 1048p.) has data for 1985 arranged in 20 sections, with subdivisions (I. Bibliographia ... V. Exegesis totius VT vel cum NT ... IX. NT exegesis generalis ... XII. Actus Apostolorum ... XVI. Philologia biblica ... XX. Historia scientiae biblicae). Index. Mainly in Latin. Roman Catholic viewpoint. *Class No:* 22(01)

Encyclopaedias

[419]

BAUER, J.B., *ed*. **Encyclopedia of Biblical theology.** London & Sydney, Sheed & Ward, 1970 (reprinted 1982). 3v. (xxxiii, 1141p.). illus. £22.50 the set. ISBN: 0722034202.

Originally as *Bibeltheologie Wörterbuch* (Graz, Verlag Styria, 1959). Translated from the 1967. 3rd. rev. and enl. German ed.

53 contributors. Signed and documented articles (*e.g.* 'Eucharist': v.1, p.227-41: ½col. of bibliography). V.3 (p.797-1141) carries a supplementary bibliography (subjects A-Z, p.1015-25) and appendices: analytical index of articles and cross-references: index of Biblical references; index of Hebrew and Greek words. 'An outstanding example of the renewal of Catholic biblical scholarship' (*Library journal,* v.96 no.2, 15 January 1971, p.102). *Class No:* 22(031)

[420]

The International standard Bible encyclopedia.
Bromiley, G.W., *ed*. 3rd ed. Grand Rapids, Mich.,
Eerdmans, 1984-1988. 4v. illus., maps. $159.80 the set.
ISBN: 0802881610, v.1; 0802881629, v.2; 0802881637,
v.3; 0802881645, v.4; 0802881602, set.

First published 1915. 2nd ed. 1929.

Presents the Protestant evangelical viewpoint, as before,
but with some literalisation. RSV texts used. Original
Hebrew, Aramaic and Greek words are transliterated.
Includes entries for every person, or place mentioned in the
Bible, and also articles treating of the Bible itself. Longer
articles are signed and include bibliographies. High
recommended by *Choice,* (v.16(12), February 1980,
p.1562). *Class No:* 22(031)

[421]

MILLER, M.S. *and* **MILLER, J.L. Harper's encyclopedia
of Bible life.** Bennett, B.M. *and* Scott, D.H., *eds*. 3rd rev.
ed. London, A. & C. Black , 1979. xviii,423p. illus., maps.
ISBN: 0713619139.

First published 1944.

4 contributors. 3 main sections (closely subdivided): 1.
The world of the Bible - 2. How the people of the Bible lived
- 3. How the people of the Bible worked. 'Suggestions for
further reading' (p.390-5; subdivided). Index of scriptural
references, p.397-410; Index of names and subjects, p.411-
23. 150 illus., with descriptive captions. 'A recently-revised
work that should prove very useful' (Rogers, A.R. *The
humanities.* 2nd ed., 1979. entry 176). *Class No:* 22(031)

[422]

The Zondervan pictorial encyclopedia of the Bible.
Tenney, M. *and* Barabas, S., *eds*. New York, Zondervan
Press, 1977. 5v. illus (some col.). $149.95 the set. ISBN:
0310331889.

7500 signed articles, contributed by 238 scholars - an
international team. 32p. of full-colour maps (with index in
v.5); 48p. of colour plates, unfortunately unnumbered and
lacking text cross-references. Truly pictorial. Conservative
standpoint. Compared with *The interpreter's dictionary of
the Bible (qv)* in *American reference books annual 1976*
(entry 1104) and considered 'particularly valuable for its
supplementary information and alternative viewpoints.'
Class No: 22(031)

Handbooks & Manuals

[423]

ALTER, R. *and* **KERMODE, F.,** *eds*. **The Literary guide to
the Bible.** London, Collins, 1987. [6], 678p. £20. ISBN:
0002174391.

International team of contributors. Includes a general
introduction and introductions to the Old and New
Testaments. The main part of the publication is a book-by-
book discussion from Genesis to Revelation, followed by
essays on various aspects of Biblical literature, including one
on English translations of the Bible. Glossary of Biblical and
literary terms (p.668-670). Analytical index (p.673-678).
Class No: 22(035)

[424]

Marshall's Bible handbook. Packer, J.I., *and others*.
London, Marshall, Morgan & Scott, 1980. 765p. illus.
ISBN: 0551008342.

Arranged in 46 chapters: 1. The ancient world - 2. Bible
history - 3. Bible chronology - 4. Text and translations - 5.
Archaeology - 6. Pagan religions and cultures ... 14.
Minerals and gems ... 17. Agriculture ... 44. Outline of the
books of the Bible - 45. All the people of the Bible (p.602-
677, A-Z) - 46. All the places of the Bible (p.678-726, A-Z).
Index to proper names and other significant topics, p.729-
765. *Class No:* 22(035)

Dictionaries

[425]

BLAIKLOCK, E.M. *and* **HARRISON, R.K.,** *eds*. **The New
international dictionary of Biblical archaeology.** Grand
Rapids, Mich., Regency Reference Library, Zondervan
Publishing House, 1983. 485p. illus. 33 col. maps. $30.95.
ISBN: 0310212502.

Brief definitions of terms and concise signed articles on
persons, places, deities relevant to the study of Biblical
archaeology. Most articles are followed by bibliographies.
Citations to the Bible, classical sources, etc. are frequently
included in the text. Pronunciations given for entry words
other than English. Cross-references from alternative terms
and variant spellings. *Class No:* 22(038)

[426]

The Eerdmans Bible dictionary. Myers, Allen C., *and
others, eds*. Grand Rapids, Missouri, W. Eerdmans, 1987.
1094p. maps. $29.85. ISBN: 0802824021.

Based on the highly respected Dutch *Bijbelse encyclopedie*
(rev. ed. 1975).

About 5,000 entries and many cross-references. Uses the
Revised Standard Version of the Bible as authority for
quoted passages and forms of names. This American edition
adds about 300 new articles and revises many others, but
retains the Protestant evangelical flavour of the earlier work.
Includes basic information concerning people, places and
things of the Bible; surveys all the books of the Bible;
includes articles on the animals, jewels, birds, etc.,
mentioned; and investigates the chief themes and ideas.
Bibliographies are somewhat sketchy. 'Entries reflect
modern biblical scholarship and archaeological research. An
excellent and inexpensive study aid ...' (*Library journal,*
August 1987, p.115). *Class No:* 22(038)

[427]

GEHMAN, H.S., *ed*. **The New Westminster dictionary of
the Bible.** 1982 thumb-indexed ed. Philadelphia, Pa.,
Westminster Press, 1982. 1064p. illus. $25.95. ISBN:
066421388x.

First published 1944 as *The Westminster dictionary of the
Bible,* revised ed. by J.D. Davis, 1970.

*c.*4000 entries, with brief biographies of Biblical
characters, outlines of Biblical books and entries for flora,
fauna, etc., mentioned in the Bible. Pronunciations shown;
numerous references to the Revised Standard Version.
'Nineveh': 3 columns, 1 illus.; 'Romans, the Epistle ...': 3½
cols. 16 full-colour maps, taken from *Westminster historical
atlas to the Bible.* Incorporates results of recent
archaeological finds. 'One of the best and most useful 1-

....*(contd.)*

volume Bible dictionaries' (*Library journal,* v.95, no.15, 1 April 1970, p.2758). Protestant viewpoint.
Class No: 22(038)

[428]

Harper's Bible dictionary. Achtermeier, P.J., *ed and* Society of Biblical Literature. New ed. New York, Harper & Row, 1985. 1178p. illus (some col.), maps. $29.95. £23.95. ISBN: 0060698624.

First published 1952. Published in the UK as *Black's Bible dictionary,* 1st ed., 1954; 8th ed. 1973, compiled by M.S. & J.L. Miller.

A one-volume dictionary intended to embody recent discoveries in archaeology, geography, chronology, textual criticism and other fields of contemporary Biblical investigation. Over 3700 commissioned articles by 179 Christian and Jewish scholars are included in this non-sectarian source which can be used with any Bible translation. A-Z arrangement of entries which deal with all important persons and places in the Bible, together with theological terms. Written in non-technical language. 92 maps (76 in black & white, 16 in colour). '... this splendid volume presents a balanced summary of current Biblical scholarship accessible to the general reader ...' (*Library journal,* v.111(1), January 1986, p.72). 'It is likely to become an indispensable vade-mecum for serious students of the Bible' (*Church times,* 10 October 1986, p.7).
Class No: 22(038)

[429]

HASTINGS, J., *ed.* **A Dictionary of the Bible,** dealing with its language, literature, and contents, including Biblical theology. Edinburgh, T. & T. Clark Ltd., 1898-1904. 5v.

The standard dictionary, containing articles, some of considerable length and sectionalized, by Biblical scholars, on persons, places, antiquities, archaeology, ethnology, geology, natural history, Biblical theology and ethnics. Etymology given. The article 'Jerusalem' (34½ large columns; 1 plan) has 8 sections, the last, 'Literature' (34 lines), being an evaluative survey. The fifth, 'extra' volume contains supplementary articles, with maps and indexes. Protestant standpoint.

The one-volume *Dictionary of the Bible,* edited by J. Hastings, with the co-operation of J.A. Selbie (Edinburgh, T. & T. Clark Ltd., 1909) is an independent work. A 2nd ed., revised by F.C. Grant and H.H. Rowley (1963. xvi, 1059, 16p. £14.95. ISBN 0567062015) is a thorough overhaul, based on the Revised Standard Version, with cross-references from both A.V. and R.V. forms; 148 contributions; sectionalized longer articles. No appended bibliographies, but abbreviated references in text. 16 coloured maps. For clergy. Protestant standpoint.
Class No: 22(038)

[430]

HILLYER, N., *ed.* **The New Bible dictionary.** 2nd ed. Leicester, Inter-Varsity Press; Wheaton, Ill., Tyndale House, 1982. xviii, 1326p. 43 illus., 52 diagr., 76 maps. £21.95. ISBN: 0851106307.

First published in 1962, edited by J.D. Douglas.

'... a major product of the Tyndale Fellowship for Biblical Research' (*Preface*). *c.*2300 signed articles, with short bibliographies, by more than 150 contributors. Longer articles (*e.g.* 'Messiah', over 12 column's, bibliography of 11 items) are sectionalized. Each book of the Bible is analysed; Biblical references. Strong in archaeology (*e.g.*

....*(contd.)*

'Palestine': p.865-71; 3 maps; 3 diagrams; bibliography of 9 items). Better layout than McKenzie (*q.v.*). Protestant viewpoint. *Class No:* 22(038)

[431]

The Interpreter's dictionary of the Bible: an illustrated encyclopedia, identifying and explaining all proper names and significant terms and subjects in the Holy Scriptures, including the Apocrypha, with attention to archaeological discussions and researches into the life and faith of ancient times. New York, Abingdon Press, 1962 (Supplement 1977). (Reprinted 1979). 4v. & supplement. illus (inc. col. plates). maps. $119 the set of 4 vols; $24.95 for supplement. ISBN: 0687192684.

About 250 contributors, mostly American. Signed longer articles with brief bibliographies (*e.g.* 'Daniel': I. The man - II. The book; nearly 8p.; bibliography of 26 lines; 'Jerusalem': p.843-66; 4 illus., 5 maps; 6 references). V.1 has 24p. of coloured maps. In all nearly 1000 illus. and 32 col. plates. Scholarly; gives etymology. Intended as companion to the 12v. *Interpreter's Bible.* Protestant approach. *Class No:* 22(038)

[432]

—Anchor Bible dictionary. Freedman, D.N., *ed.* New York, Bantam Doubleday,1992. 6v. $60 each vol. ISBN: 0385193513, v.1(A-C); 0385193602, v.2(D-G); 0385193610, v.3(H-J); 0385193629, v.4(K-N); 0385193637, v.5(O-Sh); 038526190x, v.6(Si-Z).

Supersedes the 'Interpreter's dictionary of the Bible', but that should be kept for more complete coverage of Biblical words.

More than 6000 entries from nearly 1000 contributors. A virtual encyclopedia, most articles having substantial bibliographies. Cross-references. *Class No:* 22(038)

[433]

—DOUGLAS, J.D., *ed.* The Illustrated Bible dictionary. Leicester, Inter-Varsity Press, 1980. 3v. (each 592p.).

An extensive revision of *The new Bible dictionary* (1962).

More than 160 contributors. Over 2000 articles, *c.*1600 illus., mostly in colour, 200 maps and 250 charts. Quotations use the Revised Standard Version. 'It will be invaluable to every minister, teacher or student fortunate enough to own it' (*British book news,* April 1981, p.264).
Class No: 22(038)

[434]

LÉON-DUFOUR, K., *ed.* **Dictionary of Biblical theology.** 2nd ed. London & Dublin, Geoffrey Chapman, 1973 (Reprinted 1982). xxxii,712p. £17.95. ISBN: 0225660083.

Translated by P.J. Cahill from *Vocabulaire de théologie biblique* (Paris, Les Éditions du Cerf, 1962, 2 éd., 1970). First English edition 1969.

70 contributions. Arranged under broad subject headings (*e.g.* Creation; Faith; Salvation), with extended discussion based closely on Biblical teaching, plus appropriate Bible references. Numerous cross-references. Analytical table of subject headings. Intended primarily for Roman Catholic Clergy and laity. 'A first-rate work of Roman Catholic scholarship (*The Church times,* 14 December 1973, p.7).
Class No: 22(038)

[435]

ODELAIN, O. *and* **SÉGUINEAU, R. Dictionary of proper names and places in the Bible.** New ed. London, Robert Hale, 1991. 528p. 12p. of maps. £10.95. ISBN: 0709044003.

First published 1982.

Over 3500 proper names and places found in the Old and New Testaments arranged A-Z. Each entry cites the number of times a name occurs in the Bible, provides a transcription of the name from the original language or one of the other ancient languages, gives its meaning and its etymological kinship with other names. Cross-references. An appendix gathers together the most-used information from the Bible into one section for handy reference (*e.g.* the Tribes of Israel; the sons of David; the descendents of Levi). Also a general chronology, dynastic chart, and 12 pages of full-colour maps. *Class No:* 22(038)

[436]

RICHARDSON, A., *ed.* **A Theological word book of the Bible.** London, S.C.M. Press, 1950 (14th impression 1977). 288p. £12.50. ISBN: 0334016207.

A work on the lines of Kittel's *Theologisches Wörterbuch* (*qv*), by a team of English-speaking scholars, elucidating the distinctly theological meanings of the main Bible keywords, and based on the Revised Version. All Hebrew and Greek words are transliterated and historical details are included where necessary for theological understanding.

Class No: 22(038)

[437]

TURNER, N. Handbook for Biblical studies. Oxford, Basil Blackwell Ltd.; Philadelphia, Pa., Westminster Press, 1982. 156p. maps. £6.95. $6.95. ISBN: 063113025x, UK; 066424436x, US.

Contains short definitions from the jargon of the scholar in religious and Biblical studies. Primarily aimed as an introduction to unfamiliar words for the seminary students, but is also useful to laypeople. Includes a *Theological who's who* of scholars, past and present. 'Most definitions too brief to be more than cursory explanations of words ... Handy source for quick answers to questions' (*Choice*, v.20(9), May 1983, p.1272). *Class No:* 22(038)

[438]

WIGODER, G., *and others, eds.* **Illustrated dictionary and concordance of the Bible.** New York, Collier-Macmillan, 1987. 1970p. illus (some col.), maps. $100. £90. ISBN: 0029163803.

More than 4000 entries, ranging from one-line definitions to long articles on major figures, places and concepts. Based on the new King James Version English translation. Identifies and describes all the persons and places mentioned in the Bible; also fundamental concepts; tribes; civilizations; plants, animals and food; and objects such as coins and glass. Outstanding illustrations. 'Although some may prefer a plain concordance ... the dictionary portion by itself is excellent enough to recommend the work' (*Choice*, April 1987, p.1200). *Reference books bulletin* (1986/87, p.51-52) prefers Harper's Bible dictionary but 'outstanding illustrations and reliable scholarship make this a desirable secondary purchase ...'. *Class No:* 22(038)

Periodicals

[439]

HUPPER, W.G., *comp. and ed.* **An Index to English periodical literature on the Old Testament and ancient Near Eastern studies. V.I.** Metuchen, N.J., American Theological Library Association and Scarecrow Press, 1987. 516p. $47.50. (*ATLA bibliography series, 21.*) ISBN: 0810819848.

An analytical index to periodical literature on the Old Testament and ancient Near Eastern studies, this volume is the first of a series. Over 600 journals of archaeology, history, language, science and theology, covering English-language articles from 1793 to 1969/70 have been indexed. Articles arranged chronologically under specific sections, this first volume containing 138 sections on bibliographical, biographical and historical material, etc. (V.II was published in 1988 (544p. $45. ISBN 0810821265); V.III in 1990 (823p. $79.50. ISBN 0810823195); V.IV in 1990 (594p. $62.50. ISBN 0810823934); V.V in 1992 (797p. $72.50. ISBN 0810826186). *Class No:* 22(051)

Quotations

[440]

CASTAGNO, A.J., *ed.* **Book of Biblical quotations.** London & Glasgow, Pickering & Inglis, 1981. 271p. £3.95. ISBN: 072080485x.

Published in the US by Lawrence Urdang Inc., as *A Treasury of Biblical quotations.*

4000 Scripture quotations arranged A-Z under 1150 topic headings. Several quotations are given for each topic (*e.g.* 'Friendship' has 11; 'Scorn' has 8). Sources are given. '... a topical anthology of better-known verses designed for use by Bible students, pastors, Bible teachers, professional speakers and writers and lay persons ...' (*Introduction*). *Class No:* 22(082.2)

[441]

LEVINE, M.L. *and* **RACHLIS, E.,** *eds.* **The Complete book of Bible quotations.** New York, Peter Bedrick Books, 1986; London, Robert Hale Ltd., 1987. xxi,568p. $12.95. £14.95. ISBN: 0671498649, US; 0709031610, UK.

*c.*5000 quotations from the Old and New Testaments in the King James version of the Bible, arranged under about 800 subject headings. Cross-references. An appendix has reprints from famous Bible passages. Full keyword index to significant words. 'Judiciously selected quotations' (*Reference books bulletin*, 1986/87, p.51). *Class No:* 22(082.2)

[442]

McLEISH, K. *and* **McLEISH, V. Longman guide to Bible quotations.** Harlow, Essex, Longman Group, 1986. vi,415p. £11.95. ISBN: 0582555736.

Arranged in 3 sections (Old Testament - Apocrypha - New Testament) each subdivided by the Books (Genesis ... Revelation). *c.*2000 quotations, each identified by verse-numbers in the Authorized Version. Keyword index, p.371-415. *Class No:* 22(082.2)

[443]

SPEAKE, J. **Biblical quotations.** New York, Facts on File, 1983. 203p. $22.95. ISBN: 0871962411.

Arranged by the books of the Old and New Testaments and the Apocrypha, and employing the text of the King James Version of 1611, except for the Book of Psalms, which employs Coverdale's translation. '... may be regarded more as a highly selective miniconcordance ...' '... a very useful addition to any reference collection'. (*RQ*, v.24(1), Fall 1984, p.99). *Class No:* 22(082.2)

[444]

—VICHAS, B.P. Annotated handbook of biblical quotations, verses and parables. Englewood Cliffs, N.J., Prentice-Hall, 1986. xviii,411p. $29.95. ISBN: 0130378704.

Cites *c*.1600 verses, grouped in 200 contemporary topics, reflecting a conservative point of view. Extensive cross-references. Does not claim to be a theological work or a concordance. *Class No:* 22(082.2)

Gazetteers

[445]

ROWLEY, H.H. **Dictionary of Bible place names.** London, Oliphants, 1970. [vii],173p. maps.

About 2000 concise entries for every place name mentioned in the Revised Standard Version, including the Apocrypha. States meaning of place name and modern name (if any), plus Biblical references. 8p. of black-and-white maps. *Class No:* 22(083.86)

Maps & Atlases

[446]

GROLLENBERG, L.H. **Atlas of the Bible.** Reid, J.M.H. *and* Rowley, H.H., *trans. and eds.* London, Nelson, 1956. 166p. illus., maps.

First published as *Atlas van den Bijbel* (Amsterdam, 1954).

Contains 37 excellent maps in colour and 408 photogravure illus. The three media (maps, photographs & text) are independent. The illus., which include aerial views, cover ancient monuments and sites, landscapes and localities in the Holy Land. 26-page index of places and persons aims 'to catalogue and describe all the "Geographical indications" provided by the Bible ... Non-Biblical place-names and personal names are included where their mention on the maps or in the text appear to require further elucidation'. Index entries give etymology, map reference and Biblical reference. 'Absolutely essential to any intelligent study of the Bible ...' (*Times literary supplement*, no.2859, 14 December 1956, p.753). Page size: 35 x 26cm. *Class No:* 22(084.3)

[447]

—GROLLENBERG, L.H. Penguin shorter atlas of the Bible. Hudland, M.F., *trans.* Harmondsworth, Mddx., Penguin Books, 1978. 284p. illus., maps. £4.50. ISBN: 0140510567.

A popular edition of the atlas, in smaller format. Over 100 plates and maps. Page size: 19.8 x 12.9cm. *Class No:* 22(084.3)

[448]

MAY, H.G., *with others, eds.* **Oxford Bible atlas.** Day, J., *ed.* 3rd ed. rev. New York & Toronto, Oxford University Press, 1984. 144p. illus. $18.95. £8.50. ISBN: 0191434523.

First published 1962. 3rd ed. revised by John Day.

The 26 coloured maps and plans well reflect archaeological advances since the earlier editions. Illus. are admirably diverse, and some new ones have been inserted in the 3rd ed. Also map colours changed or shadings intensified to provide greater clarity, but not redrawn. Textual changes have not involved resetting. Combined gazetteer and index. 'It can form an exciting and valuable starting point for more detailed study by the student of Bible history and of the supporting evidence for modern archaeological work' (*Geographical journal*, v.140, 1974, p.515, of the 2nd ed.). *Class No:* 22(084.3)

[449]

Reader's Digest atlas of the Bible: an illustrated guide to the Holy Land. Gardner, J.L., *ed.* Rev.ed. New York, Rand McNally, 1992. 239p. illus., maps. $39.95. ISBN: 0528835394.

Profusely illustrated, some in colour. A popular guide. Sections: 'In the beginning... ' - People of the Bible - Animals of the Bible - Plants of the Bible - Weights and measures, currency - History of the Bible ... Historical atlas of Biblical times, with text. Gazetteer of the Bible world. Chronology of Biblical times. Biblical citations. Detailed index. *Class No:* 22(084.3)

[450]

RHYMER, J. **Atlas of the Biblical world.** London, Hamlyn, 1983. 224p. illus. (incl. col.), maps, charts. £8.95. ISBN: 0600384861.

Aims to provide a bridge between the world of the Bible and the world of the present day and, as such, is not really an atlas - includes small maps but mainly text and pictures. In 5 parts: 1. God's chosen people - 2. The birth of Palestine - 3. The fall of the kingdom - 4. Rebuilding the Hebrew nation - 5. The origins of Christianity. Appendices include a chronology, a glossary (p.218-219), and an index (p.220-224). *Class No:* 22(084.3)

[451]

ROGERSON, J. **The New atlas of the Bible.** London, Macdonald; New York, Facts on File, 1985. 240p. 400 illus (300 col.). £14.95. $35. ISBN: 035610706x.

Arranged in 12 geographical sections (as opposed to the more usual historical orientation). Clear, detailed and colourful maps and also many aerial photographs, Gazetteer and index. '... collection of Biblical art is superfluous and picture captions include redundancies between picture captions and text ... On the whole, though, enthusiastically recommended' (*Wilson library bulletin*, November 1985, p.59). *Class No:* 22(084.3)

[452]

The Times atlas of the Bible. Pritchard, J.B., *ed.* London, Times Books, 1987; New York, Harper & Row, 1988. 254p. illus. maps. £25; $49.95. ISBN: 0723002959, UK; 0061818836, US.

Published in the US as *The Harper atlas of the Bible*.

Based on the latest archaeological research. Arranged chronologically: Old Testament (In the beginning - Emergence of Israel: patriarchal traditions - Between Genesis and Exodus: 400 years of Egyptian supremacy -

....(contd.)

From Egyptian bondage to settlement in Canaan - The institution of the monarchy - The imperial age of Solomon - The divided kingdom: Israel - The divided kingdom; Judah - Judah under Babylon); Inter-Testamental period (The Persian period - Judah in the Hellenistic era); New Testament (Palestine under the Romans - The Christian era). Chronology, p.15-23. People of the Bible, p.195-208. Gazetteer. Over 600 coloured maps and illustrations. '... a visually stunning and almost perfectly integrated work combining text, illustrations and maps with such clarity and scholarly weight as to make this a standard reference work ...' (*Bulletin of ABTPL*, v.2(2), June 1988).
Class No: 22(084.3)

[453]

—The Times concise atlas of the Bible. Pritchard, J.B., *ed.* London, Times Books, 1991. 151p. col. illus., col. maps, bibliog., indexes. £14.99. ISBN: 0723003459.

A revised text and some new maps are included in this compact version of *The Times atlas of the Bible (q.v.)*. 68 theme spreads *e.g.* Writing and its users (including The libraries of the Ancient Near East); Mapping Biblical narratives; Historical geography and archaeology. Bibliography p.140-1. Glossary p.141. 'Eminently successful as a reference work the atlas will be indispensable to teachers and students of biblical studies' (*Geographical Journal*, v.159, no.1, March 1993, p.83-84).
Class No: 22(084.3)

Histories

[454]

The Cambridge history of the Bible. new ed. Cambridge, Cambridge University Press, 1963-70. 3v. £27.50 each vol,: £50 the set. ISBN: 0521099730, v.1; 0521290171, v.2; 0521290163, v.3; 052129018x, Set.

First published 1963-70 in 3v.

Contents: V.1. *From the beginnings to Jerome* (xv,649p. illus.); v.2 *The West, from the Fathers to the Reformation* (x,566p. 48 illus.); v.3. *The West, from the Reformation to the present day* (x,590p.). 'Deals with the history of the Bible in the West, that is, in Western Europe and America' (*Preface* to 1st ed.), *i.e.*, 'accounts of the texts and versions of the Bible used in the West, of its multiplication of manuscripts and exegesis; and of its place in the life of Western Church'. *Class No:* 22(091)

Biographies

[455]

CALVOCORESSI, P. Who's who in the Bible. New York, Viking, 1987. 269p. maps. $19.95. £10.95. ISBN: 0670811882.

Biographies of *c.*450 major and minor Biblical characters (Aaron ... Zophar) from Old and New Testaments and Apocrypha with, in addition lists of art and literature where these characters have appeared. Cross-references and bibliographical references for most entries. Genealogical appendix (p.241-247). Index (mainly names) (p.249-269). '... not an essential reference work, but it may appeal to browsers searching for an entertaining perspective on Bible figures' (*Reference books bulletin*, 1 April 1988, p.1327).
Class No: 22(092)

[456]

LOCKYER, H. All the men of the Bible: a portrait gallery and reference library of more than 3000 Biblical characters. Grand Rapids, MI., Zondervan, 1983. 381p. $14.95. ISBN: 031028080x.

First published in London by Pickering & Inglis, 1958.

Most entries are short; longer ones appear to be somewhat imaginatively extended. Occasionally supplements Hastings' *Dictionary of the Bible*. *Class No:* 22(092)

[457]

—LOCKYER, H. All the women of the Bible. Grand Rapids, MI., Zondervan, 1983. 321p. $12.95; £10.25. ISBN: 0310281504.

Supercedes Edith Deen's *All the women of the Bible* (1959).

Complementary to the above. *Class No:* 22(092)

Natural History

[458]

MOLLER-CHRISTENSEN, V. *and* JORGENSEN, K.E.J. Encyclopedia of Bible creatures. Heinecken, M.T., *ed.* Philadelphia, Pa., Fortress Press, 1965. 302p. illus.

Translated from the Danish by Carol Wilde.

Gives scientific and popular names, dictionary definition, Greek and Hebrew names, and habitat of every known creature in the Bible; explanations of Bible references. Editor has added footnotes based on the Revised Standard Version and current Biblical research. 3 indexes: Latin and common names; Biblical names and places; Scriptural index. *Class No:* 22:59

[459]

—MOLDENKE, H.N. *and* MOLDENKE, A.L. Plants of the Bible. Waltham, Mass., Chronica Botanica, 1952 (reprinted Dover, 1986). xix,328p. illus., facsims. $8.95. ISBN: 0486250695.

Includes a bibliography, p.259-74. *Class No:* 22:59

[460]

ZOHARY, M. Plants of the Bible: a complete handbook to all the plants, with 200 full-colour plates taken in the natural habitat. Cambridge, Cambridge University Press, 1982. 224p. illus.(col.), maps. £12.95. ISBN: 0521249260.

Bibliography, p.211-212. Index. *Class No:* 22:59

Introductions

[461]

MANSON, T.W. A Companion to the Bible. Rowley, H.H., *ed.* New ed. Edinburgh, T. & T. Clark Ltd., 1963. xii, 628p. 6 maps. £9.95. ISBN: 0567021971.

First published in 1959.

Main parts: 1. The book (chapters 1-7) - 2. The land and its people (8-11) - 3. The religion of the Bible (12-18). Each chapter has an appended bibliography. Six folding maps and plans. Four indexes: Scripture references; authors; general; Latin, Greek and Oriental works. Retains the original high level of scholarship. 'Invaluable for systematic accounts of the revelation against the historical and geographical background'. (*British book news*, no.283, March 1964, p.176). *Class No:* 22.01

Dictionaries

[462]

COGGINS, R.J. **A Dictionary of Biblical interpretation.** London, SCM Press; Philadelphia, PA, Trinity Press International, 1990. 848p. £30. (*TPI New Testament commentaries.*) ISBN: 033400294x.

Articles devoted to each book of the Bible, showing the history of its interpretation, and discussions of the various techniques and methods employed in its interpretation. Generous cross-references. Suggestions for further reading. *Class No:* 22.01(038)

Versions

[463]

The New Jerusalem Bible: standard edition. London, Darton, Longman & Todd; New York, Doubleday & Company, 1985. xv,2108p. 7 maps, plus index to maps 8p.). £25. ISBN: 0232516502.

First published 1966. This ed. is translation of *Bible de Jerusalem,* 1973 revision, translated by the staff of the École Biblique, Jerusalem, the originators.

One-volume Bible, together with the means of studying it. 'A comprehensive revision of text, notes and other materials; (Dust jacket). Old and New Testaments are followed by supplementary tables - Chronological table; Geneological table; Calendar; Table of measures and money; Alphabetical table of the major footnotes; Index of persons; Index of original collaborators. Cross-references. On Indian paper. *Class No:* 22.014

Prophecies

[464]

PAYNE, J.B. **Encyclopedia of Biblical prophecy:** the complete guide to Scriptural predictions and their fulfillment. New York, Harper & Row, 1973 (Reprinted Grand Rapids, Mich., Baker Books, 1980). xxv, 753p. $21.95. ISBN: 0801070511.

Lengthy introduction, p.3-150 (356 footnotes). Entries are arranged in the order of the books of Old and New Testaments. Summaries are appended. Bibliography, p.685-92. 5 indexes, including 1. 'The Biblical predictions'; 3. 'subjects'. Evangelical Christian viewpoint. *Class No:* 22.016

Concordances

[465]

A Concordance to the Apocrypha/Deuterocanonical books of the Revised Standard Version, derived from the Bible Data Bank of the Centre Informatique et Bible (Abbey of Maredsous). New York, Eerdmans, 1983. 479p. $35. ISBN: 0802823122.

Includes all the words in the 1977 edition of the Revised Standard Version Apocrypha, except 77 words of very high frequency, along with the exact frequency count. All different forms of the same word are grouped in one entry (*e.g.* men, man, etc., under Man). Easy-to-read double column pages. 'Clearly a must for any library aspiring to maintain a decent collection in Biblical studies' (*Choice,* v.21(1), September 1983, p.60). *Class No:* 22.03

[466]

CRUDEN, A.A. **A Complete concordance to the Old and New Testament ... with ... a concordance to the Apocrypha.** 3rd ed. London, Warne, 1769 (frequently reprinted: *e.g.* Lutterworth Press. £25; Warne. £16.95; Zondervan. $10.95. 9441p. ISBN: 0718802055, UK; 0723202605, UK; 0310229219, US.

First published 1737, forming the basis for modern concordances.

*c.*250,000 entries in all, A-Z by English word (Authorized Version), with appendices of proper names and the Apocrypha concordance. 'Cruden's work is accurate and full, and later concordances only supersede him by combining an English with a Greek and Hebrew concordance' (*Encyclopaedia Britannica,* 11th ed., v.6, p.832). Particularly valuable for inclusion of the Apocrypha. *Class No:* 22.03

[467]

GOODRICK, E.W. and KOHLENBERGER, J.P. **The NIV complete concordance.** Grand Rapids, MI., Zondervan, 1981. 1056p. $29.95. ISBN: 0310436508.

This concordance of the New International Version of the Bible has 250,000 entries, the index words arranged in dictionary format and in bold type. Cross-references are given in parentheses. The contexts of the key words are comparatively long and useful. Small print, but easy to read. *Class No:* 22.03

[468]

JOY, C.R., *comp.* **Harper's topical concordance.** Rev. & enl. ed., 1961 (Reprinted 1976). New York, Harper & Row, 1976. 640p. $10.95. ISBN: 0060642297.

First published as *Harper's topical concordance* (1940); reprinted as *A concordance of subjects* (London, Black, 1952); and *Lutterworth's topical concordance* (2nd ed. London, Lutterworth, 1961).

A new type of Bible concordance, enabling texts and quotations to be easily found. Verses are arranged under 2775 topics, and a fairly complete list of texts specifically connected with these topics is given. Appended list of cross-references. *Class No:* 22.03

[469]

STRONG, J. **Abingdon's Strong's exhaustive concordance of the Bible,** with exclusive key-word comparison: words of Jesus in red. Nashville, Tenn., Abingdon Press; London, S.P.C.K., 1986 (44th printing of the 1894 edition). 2336p. $26.95. £26.95. ISBN: 0687400325.

Originally published by Hodder in London, 1894., with various printings since then.

About 400,000 entries. Contains key-words and phrases from the Authorized Version, set out for comparison with the five leading translations. Easy-to-read print. The most complete Bible concordance. *Class No:* 22.03

[470]

—YOUNG, R. **Analytical concordance to the Holy Bible:** about 311,000 references, subdivided under the Hebrew and Greek originals, with the literal meaning and pronunciation of each. 8th ed. London, Lutterworth Press, 1879. (Various reprints). 1220p. £29. ISBN: 0718860214.

Based on the Authorised Version. Appended index lexicons to the Old and New Testaments, and a complete list of Scripture proper names. *Class No:* 22.03

[471]

THOMPSON, N.W. *and* STOCK, R. **Complete concordance to the Bible (Douay Version).** 4th rev. and enl. ed. St. Louis, Mo., Herder, 1945. 2, [1], 1914p.

First published 1942.

Uses the text of the Roman Catholic Bible, which differes in several ways from the AV, in being translated from the Latin Vulgate. The Old Testament in this version has 46 books, as opposed to 39 in the AV, although the additional books appear in the Protestant Apocrypha. *Class No:* 22.03

[472]

WHITAKER, R.E., *comp.* **The Eerdmans analytical concordance to the Revised Standard Version of the Bible.** New York, Wm. B. Eerdmans Publishing Co., 1988. 1548p. $49.95. ISBN: 080282403x.

Claims to be the only analytical concordance to the RSV of the entire Bible and the Apocrypha. Entries are listed in dictionary form (A-Z), followed by every context in which any form of the word is found, and all forms of the word are under the same heading. All uses of each word are given in one list, not separated by language (Hebrew, Greek, Latin, etc.). Proper names and numbers are listed separately. Indexes of all Hebrew, Aramaic, Latin and Greek words translated in the RSV, with their English equivalents. Highly recommended by *Choice* (v.26(5), January 1989, p.790). *Class No:* 22.03

Commentaries

[473]

The Abingdon Bible commentary. Eiselen, F.C., *ed. and others.* London, Epworth Press, 1932. (Nashville, Tenn., Abingdon Press; London, S.P.C.K., 1981. Doubleday, $17.95). xvi, 1452p. ISBN: 0385148771, US.

First published 1929 by Abingdon Press.

Probably the best of the single-volume Bible commentaries. 66 scholarly contributors. Chapter-by-chapter commentary on the various books, plus more general treatment. Includes bibliogaphies. *Class No:* 22.07

[474]

—FULLER, R.C., *ed.* A New Catholic commentary on Holy Scripture. New & fully rev. ed. London, Nelson, 1969. xix, 1377p. £50. ISBN: 0840750170.

First published in 1953 as *A Catholic commentary on Holy Scripture.*

Based on the Douai version, it has *c.*65 contributors and reflects international scholarship. Commentary is paragraph by paragraph, according to the sense, rather than verse by verse. *Class No:* 22.07

[475]

—The New Jerome Biblical commentary. Poole, Dorset, Cassell; Englewood Cliffs, Prentice-Hall, l989. l478p. £60. $69.95. ISBN: 0225665883, UK; 0136149340, US.

First published in l968 as =2 The Jerome Biblical commentary.

The work of Roman Catholic scholars. In addition to book-by-book commentary, topical articles take up about a third of the text, many of which present other points of view in addition to the RC interpretation. Bibliographies are appended to each chapter and for major divisions within chapters. Analytical index. *Class No:* 22.07

[476]

—Peake's commentary on the Bible. Black, M. *and* Rowley, H.H., *eds.* New ed. London, Nelson, 1962. xv, 1162p. illus., maps. $39.95. ISBN: 0840750196.

First published 1919.

Based on the Revised Standard Version, with 62 distinguished contributors; bibliographies; detailed index. *Class No:* 22.07

[477]

The Cambridge Bible commentary on the New English Bible. London, Cambridge University Press, 1963-1977.

Old Testament (including *Making of the Old Testament* (1972), *Old Testament illustrations* (1971) and *Understanding the Old Testament* (1971-77. 31v.).

Apocrypha (1972-74. 4v.).

New Testament (including *New Testament illustrations* (1966) and *Understanding the New Testament* (1965). (1963-67. 17v.).

Full text of the New English Bible, with simple and brief commentary, dispensing with Hebrew or Greek words and strings of biblical references. Aimed at school user. *Class No:* 22.07

[478]

Harper's Bible commentary. Mays, J.L., *ed.* New York, Harper & Row, 1988. xviii,1328p. illus. (mostly coloured). $37.95. ISBN: 0060655410.

Introductory matter (p.1-84) is followed by the Books of the Bible, Genesis ... Revelations, including the Apocrypha, each with an introduction, commentary and bibliography. 4p. index precedes an appendix of coloured maps (16p.) *c.*70 contributors. *Class No:* 22.07

[479]

International critical commentary on the Holy Scriptures. Driver, S.R., *ed. and others.* 2nd ed. Edinburgh, T. & T. Clark Ltd., 1930 (1963 reprint). 43v. in 46.

A scholarly series of commentaries on individual books of the Bible, contributed by specialists and bringing modern research and criticism to bear on questions of authorship, etc. Each volume, which is complete in itself, carries a bibliography.

The series is being extended and renewed. Under the editorship of Professors J.A. Emerton, C.E.B. Cranfield, and the editor-elect, G.N. Stanton, commentaries on books of the Bible which have not appeared in the I.C.C. before are now in preparation and new editions of all existing volumes are being commissioned. (T. & T. Clark Ltd., 1989). *Class No:* 22.07

[480]

The Interpreter's Bible: the Holy Scriptures in the King James and Revised Standard Versions, with general articles and introduction, exegesis, exposition for each book of the Bible. Harmon, N.B., *ed.* New York, Abingdon-Cokesbury Press, 1952-57. (Reprinted by Abingdon Press, 1984). Originally in 12 vols. Reprint in 8 vols. £45 the set; £5.95 each vol. ISBN: 0687192315, set.

V.1. The Pentateuch ... - 2. Old Testament history ... - 3. Wisdom, literature and poetry - 4. The major prophets - 5. The minor prophets and the Apocrypha ... 6. The Gospels - 7. Acts and Paul's letters ... - 8. Revelation and the general Epistles. Contributors (including eminent British theologians and Biblical scholars) represent almost every branch of the Christian Church: consulting editors, from larger Protestant groups. Each page has text of A.V. and R.S.V. in parallel

.... *(contd.)*

columns, with exegesis and exposition below. Aimed at the general reader, teacher and preacher of the Bible. Indispensible, although some volumes are now dated. *Class No:* 22.07

[481]
—The Interpreter's one-volume commentary on the Bible, including all the books of the Old and New Testament and the Apochrypha, together with forty-three general articles. Layamon, C.M., *ed.* Nashville, Tenn., Abingdon Press, 1983,. 1412p. illus., diagrs., 16 maps. $24.95; £30. ISBN: 0687192994.

First published 1971.

Provides a verse-by-verse commentary aimed at layman and teacher. The work of *c.*70 contributors (mostly American; Protestant, Catholic and Jewish). Analytical subject index. *Class No:* 22.07

Bible. Old Testament

Bibliographies

[482]
FITZMYER, J.A. **The Dead Sea scrolls:** major publications and tools for study. Missoula, Montana, Society of Biblical Literature (distributed by Scholars' Press, Roanoke, Va.,), 1975. xiv, 171p. $14.95.

Records lists of surveys, bibliographies of scrolls, and aids (*e.g.* dictionaries and concordances) as well as unpublished reports. Biblical cross-indexes. 'This authoritative guide supersedes earlier efforts' [*e.g.* C. Burchard's *Bibliographie zu den Handschriften vom Toten Meer* (Berlin, Topelmann, 1957. xv, 118p.), updated in *Revue de Qumran*] (Rogers, A.R. *The humanities* (1979), item 81, on which this annotation is partly based). *Class No:* 222(01)

Encyclopaedias

[483]
BOTTERWECK, G.J. *and* RINGGREN, H., *eds.* **Theologisches Wörterbuch zum Alten Testament.** Stuttgart, Kohlhammer, 1970-,v.1-. To be in 12v. (6v. published so far).

Will provide for the Old Testament a counterpart to Kittel's Theologisches Wörterbuch zum Neuen Testament (*q.v.,*).

V.1-3: A-HARAS. V.2 (xc p., 574 cols.) has *c.*130 entries for Hebrew words, by 64 contributors. Appended list of German catchwords, bibliography of sources, and journal, etc. sources. *Class No:* 222(031)

[484]
—BOTTERWECK, G.J. *and* RINGGREN, H., *eds.* Theological dictionary of the Old Testament. Grand Rapids, Mich., Eerdmans; London, S.C.M. Press, 1974-.v.1-. To be in 12v. £27.50 each vol. (5v. published so far). ISBN: 0802823300.

Translated from the German edition (above) by J.T. Willis.

The intention is to concentrate on meaning, starting from narrower everyday senses of the words and building to an understanding of theologically significant concepts. Articles are by international scholars of various traditions. *Class No:* 222(031)

Reviews & Abstracts

[485]
Old Testament abstracts, 1978-. Cambridge, Mass., Weston School of Theology, 1978-. 3pa. $14pa. ISSN: 03648591.

Abstracts of books and also of articles from about 350 Catholic, Protestant and Jewish periodicals. V.12(3), October 1989 has *c.*300 abstracts and also over 20 pages of book notices and 'books received'. Author index; index of scripture texts; index of words in Hebrew, etc.; and List of periodicals abstracted. Intended for the lay persons as well as the scholar. *Class No:* 222(048)

Biographies

[486]
COMAY, J. **Who's Who in the Old Testament,** together with the Apocrypha. London, Weidenfeld & Nicolson, 1971. 448p. illus. £8.95. ISBN: 0297004093.

Over 3,000 entries, covering all characters in the O.T. and Apocrypha - the history of the Jewish people up to the end of the First Book of Maccabees, *i.e.,* 135 B.C. The chief feature - the profusion and variety of illustrations. (450 black-and-white, plus 16 in colour). Favourably reviewed, with minor reservations, in T.L.S., 25 February, 1972. p.225. *Class No:* 222(092)

Bible. New Testament

Bibliographies

[487]
ELLIOTT, J.K. **A Bibliography of Greek New Testament manuscripts.** Cambridge, Cambridge University Press, 1989. 168p. £30. (*Society for New Testament Studies monograph series v.62.*) ISBN: 052135479x.

Includes references to every recognised Greek New Testament manuscript for which there exists an *editio princeps,* printed editions, facsimiles, photographic plates, collations, and major studies, *c.*5000 in all. Intended to assist those who wish to investigate the readings in a manuscript by directing them to primary sources. *Class No:* 225(01)

[488]
FRANCE, R.T., *ed.* **A Bibliographical guide to New Testament research.** 3rd ed. Sheffield, Journal for the Study of the Old Testament/JSOT Press, 1979. 56p. £2.25. ISBN: 0905774191.

First published in 1968 by the Tyndale Fellowship for Biblical Research.

Briefly annotated entries in 27 sections (1. Library facilities - 2. Bibliographical aids - 3. Periodicals - 4. Texts of the New Testament ... 10. Dictionaries and encyclopaedias ... 14. New Testament archaeology ... 24. Judaism and Rabbinical literature - 25. Early Christian and Gnostic literature ... 27. Modern languages. *Class No:* 225(01)

[489]

HULTGREN, A.J., *comp*. **New Testament Christology:** a critical assessment and annotated bibliography. Westport, CT., Greenwood Press, 1988. 485p. $65. (*Bibliographies and indexes in religious studies, 12*.) ISBN: 0313251886.

The introductory critical assessment is followed by the bibliography of 1917 items, arranged in 4 sections (Orientation and Christological foundations; Christological titles; Christologies of New Testament writers; Christological themes), each section subdivided and arranged A-Z by author within each subdivision. Includes books and periodical articles. The clear and concise annotations are descriptive rather than evaluative. Material included mainly published from the 1950s onwards. Author, editor and compiler index; title index; and subject index. 'The strength and particular value of this bibliography is that Hultgren keeps his focus on the doctrine of Christology and does not introduce extraneous material ...' (*Choice*,v.26(9), May 1989, p.1494). *Class No:* 225(01)

[490]

WAGNER, G. **An Exegetical bibliography of the New Testament.** Macon, GA., Mercer University, 1983. 667p. $35. ISBN: 0865540136.

A bibliography of critical books and journal articles on the Gospels of Matthew and Mark, arranged by verse of scripture. Includes foreign language works. No subject or author indexes. 'This work would nicely supplement any theological or university religion reference section' (*Choice*, v.21(1), September 1983, p.60). *Class No:* 225(01)

Encyclopaedias

[491]

BALZ, H. **Exegetical dictionary of the New Testament. V.1: A-E.** Schneider, G., *eds*. Grand Rapids, Mich., Eerdmans Publishing, 1990. 463p. $49.95. ISBN: 0802824099.

To be in 3v.

Attempts to provide definitions of every significant word in the New Testament. Over 100 contributors, primarily from Germany, Austria and Switzerland. Arranged A-Z by Greek word, with transliteration and English translation. For major concepts, a bibliography of scholarly references. V.3 is to include an English index. *Theological dictionary of the New Testament* (Eerdman, 1964-76) is more comprehensive, but is more dated and less accessible to readers without Greek. *Class No:* 225(031)

[492]

KITTEL, G. *and* FRIEDRICH, G., *eds*. **Theologisches Wörterbuch zum Neuen Testament.** Stuttgart, Kohlhammer, 1932-79. 10v.

V.1-9: ALPHA-OMEGA, v.10: Index & literature supplement (1978-79). An important work, planned by a distinguished Rabbinist with special collaborators, on a scale comparable with the new Liddell and Scott. It defines specific meanings which Greek terms have come to possess within Christian thought as a whole, and many articles amount to complete monographs. *Class No:* 225(031)

[493]

—Theological dictionary of the New Testament. Bromiley, G.W., *ed*. Grand Rapids, Mich., Eerdmans; Exeter, Devon, Paternoster Press, 1964-77. 10v. $399.50. ISBN: 0802823246.

Fully authorized English translation of G. Kittel's *Theologisches Wörterbuch zum Neuen Testament* (above) 'Indispensable for those seeking to do depth study in New Testament literature' (*Choice*, v.10(1), March 1973, p.62).

A one-volume abridgement, by G.W. Bromiley has been published by Paternoster Press (1985. £44.95. xxxvi,1356p.). *Class No:* 225(031)

Dictionaries

[494]

BROWN, C. **The New international dictionary of New Testament theology.** Exeter, Devon, Paternoster Press, 1975-86. 4v. & addenda. v.1: £24.95; v.2: £26.95; v.3: £39.95; v.4: £29.95; Addenda: £0.80. ISBN: 085364425x, v.1; 0853644268, v.2; 0853641803, v.3; 0853644284, v.4; 0853643601, Addenda.

Translated, with additions and revisions, from the German *Theologisches Begriffslexikon zum neuen Testament*. edited by Luther Coenen and others.

V.1 has 88 contributors, 'Bishop, Presbyter, Elder' (p.188-201), with Greek word boxed, has 2/3 column of bibliography. 'Word' (v.3, p.1081-1146) has 3p. of bibliography. Cross-references. Index of Hebrew and Aramaic words; index of Greek words; general index. Protestant standpoint. 'Expressly theologian in intension' (*Introduction*, v.1). *Class No:* 225(038)

Reviews & Abstracts

[495]

New Testament abstracts: a record of current literature. 1956-. v.10. no.1-. 3pa. Cambridge, Mass., Weston School of Theology, in co-operation with The Catholic Biblical Association of America, 1956-. $30 pa. ISSN: 00286877.

Each issue has *c.*500 concise and readable signed, 150-word abstracts of articles from more than 200 periodicals in ten languages. Sections: New Testament general - Gospels - Acts - Epistles - Revelation - Biblical theology - New Testament world. 'Book notices' is a *c.*50-page list of recent publications with short descriptions of contents, and is followed by a short list of 'Additional books received'. Annual indexes to principal Scriptural texts; authors; 'Book notices'. Annual list of journals abstracted. A cumulative index to v.1-15 (1956-11970) has been issued. *Class No:* 225(048)

[496]

—Zeitschrift für die neutestamentliche Wissenschaft. Berlin, Töpelmann (later Walter de Gruyter und Co), 1900- 2pa. $86pa. ISSN: 00442615.

Has a systematically arranged bibliography of periodical articles ('Zeitschrift - Bibliographie'), citing *c.*50 journals in each issue. *Class No:* 225(01)

Histories

[497]

FINEGAN, J. The Archaeology of the New Testament: the Mediterranean world of the early Christian Apostles. Boulder, Col., Westview Press; London, Croom Helm, 1981. xxxii,250p. illus., 13 maps, 22 plans. £19.95.

Alphabetical list of ancient sources (p.xxi-xxx) precedes the 8 chapters: 1. Sources - 2. Chronological history - 3. Beginnings... 8. In Rome; which trace the 15,000 mile travels of Paul. Lavishly illustrated with photographs of archaeological sites and museum artifices, plus maps and site places. Notes, p.235-244. Index of Biblical references, p.245-246. General index, p.247-250. Companion volume to the author's *The archaeology of the New Testament: the life of Jesus and the beginnings of the early Church* (Princeton University Press, 1972). *Class No:* 225(091)

Biographies

[498]

BROWNRIGG, R. Who's who in the New Testament. London, Weidenfeld & Nicolson, 1971. 448p. illus., facsims.

Companion volume to Joan Comay's *Who's who in the Old Testament, together with the Apocrypha* and, similarly, noted for its profusion and variety of illus. Favourably reviewed, with minor reservations, in *T.L.S.,* 25 February 1972, p.225. *Class No:* 225(092)

Concordances

[499]

BULLINGER, E.W. A Critical lexicon and concordance to the English and Greek New Testament, together with an index of Greek words, and several appendices. 9th ed. London, Bagster, Grand Rapids, MI., Zondervan, 1975. 1040p. £10.95; $30.95. ISBN: 0851501222, UK; 0310203104, US.

First published 1877.

Gives every word in alphabetical order, and under each the Greek word or words so translated, with variants; thus a Greek word with its literal and derivative meanings may be found for every word in the English N.T. The index is of Greek words in A-Z order, with the English translation following. A helpful and handy work. *Class No:* 225.03

[500]

—ARNDT, W.F. *and* GINGRICH, F.W. A Greek-English lexikon of the New Testament and other early Christian literature. 2nd ed. Chicago University Press, 1979. xl,900p. $47.50.

A translation and adaptation of Walter Bauer's *Griechisch-deutsches Wörterbuch zu den Schriften des Neuen Testaments* ... (5th rev. ed. 1981 reprint. $43.20. De Gruyter. ISBN 3110020734). The English work was first published by Oxford University Press in 1964.

A comparable work to the above, but with wider scope. 'The results cannot be praised too highly' (*Heythrop journal,* July, 1980, p.329). A condensed version is F.W. Gingrich's *Shorter lexicon of the Greek New Testament* (Chicago, University of Chicago Press, 1965, 304p.). *Class No:* 225.03

[501]

GORMAN, G.E. 'Concordances for Biblical studies'. In *Bulletin of ABTAPL,* no. 28, November 1983, p.12-16.

Introduction is followed by a bibliographical list of 7 concordances (General - Latin - Hebrew - Greek - English). *Class No:* 225.03

[502]

MORRISON, C. An Analytical concordance to the Revised Standard Version of the New Testament. Philadelphia, Pa., 1979. xxv, 770p. $19.95. ISBN: 0664207731.

About 100,000 entries, 'Based on an analysis of the RSV New Testament that relates the RSV English to the original Greek' (*Explanatory notes*). Omits the most common Greek words in the New Testament for 'the', 'and', 'self', etc. 'Index-lexicon' (p.661-754) is an index to the analytical concordance and a lexicon of New Testament Greek. 2 appendices (1. Notes on the analysis of RSV New Testament). 'Will be an important tool for New Testament studies' (*Library journal,* v.104, no.14, August 1979, p.1551-2). *Class No:* 225.03

[503]

MOULTON, W.F. *and* **GEDEN, A.S.,** *eds.* **A Concordance to the Greek Testament.** 5th ed. Edinburgh, T. & T. Clark Ltd., New York, Attic Press, 1978. 1120p. £28.95; $59.95. ISBN: 056701021x.

First published 1897.

The standard and complete concordance, following the text of Westcott and Hort, but equally available for Tischendorf and the 'revisers' text. Marginal readings are included in all cases, and Hebrew text is given beneath the Greek in all direct quotations from the Old Testament. *Class No:* 225.03

Bible. New Testament. Acts of the Apostles

---

[504]

MATTILL, A.J. *and* **MATTILL, M.B. A Classified bibliography of literature on the Acts of the Apostles.** Leiden, E.J. Brill, 1966. xviii, 513p. Gld.97. (*New Testament tools and studies, v.7.*) ISBN: 9004015531.

6646 numbered items, drawn from *c.*200 journals. 9 main sections: 1. Bibliographical studies - 2. General studies - 3. Textual studies - 4. Philological studies - 5. Literary studies - 6. Form-critical studies - 7. Historical studies (p.181-265) - 8. Theological studies - 9. Exegetical studies of individual passages. Entries date from the period of the Church Fathers up to 1961. Index of authors ('Anonymous' at end) only. A.J. Mattill was Professor of New Testament Language and Literature, Winebrenner Theological Seminary. *Class No:* 226.6

Bible. Apocrypha

---

[505]

CHARLES, R.H., *ed.* **The Apocrypha and Pseudepigrapha of the Old Testament in English ...,** edited, in conjunction with many scholars, by R.H. Charles. Oxford, Clarendon Press, 1913, Reissued by Oxford University Press, 1963. 2v. (696 + 886p.). v.1: £50; v.2 £45. ISBN: 0198261551,

....*(contd.)*
v.1; 0198261527, v.2.

The most important collection in English of all the non-canonical Jewish literature from 200 B.C.-A.D.. 100. Each book is translated from the best critical text, with an introduction giving detailed textual and bibliographical information, plus critical and explanatory notes. General index in v.2 (*The Pseudepigrapha*). *Class No:* 229

[506]
CHARLESWORTH, J.H. The New Testament Apocrypha and Pseudepigrapha: a guide to publications, with excursuses on Apocalypses. Metuchen, NY, Scarecrow Press, 1987. 450p. $42.50; £31.85. (*ATLA bibliography series, no. 17.*) ISBN: 0810818450.

More than 5000 citations to the primary and secondary literature concerning the extracanonical writings, being a companion volume to Charlesworth's '*The Pseudepigrapha and modern research with a supplement*'. Arranged in five broad sections: General studies (562 citations; apocalyptic literature (77); apocryphical acts (84); canon (168); agrapha, fragments of unknown works (284), followed by a list of citations under names of 99 major writings or cycles of writings. Entries arranged A-Z giving basic information, with occasional brief annotations. 3 introductory chapters report research and give overviews. Author index. '... an indispensible bibliography for anyone doing research on the Christian literature of the first few centuries of the Common Era' (*College and research libraries,* v.49(4), July 1988, p.344). *Class No:* 229

[507]
CHARLESWORTH, J.H. The Pseudepigraphia and modern research, with a supplement. Chicago, CA., Scholars Press, 1981. 344p. $13.95; £11.95. (*Society biblical literature septuagint and cognate studies.*) ISBN: 0891304404.

Covers writings related to Hebrew scriptures.
Class No: 229

23/28 Christianity

Christianity

[508]

MACQUARRIE, J. **Twentieth-century religious thoughts:** the frontiers of philosophy and theology, 1900-80. 3rd ed. London, S.C.M. Press, 1988. 468p. £15. ISBN: 0334017092.

First published 1963.

Written as a guide to students 'through the tangled maze of religious thought in the modern period' (Publisher's advertisement). In 121 sections in 24 chapters: 1. Introductory comments ... 23 has most new material - 24. Concluding comments. Footnotes. Analytical index, p.453-468. *Class No:* 230

Bibliographies

[509]

BRANSON, M.L. **The Reader's guide to the best evangelical books.** New York, Harper & Row, 1982. 208p. $5.95. ISBN: 0060610468.

Focuses on books written by and for evangelicals within the parameters of classical orthodox thought. Arranged in subject areas: Popular treatments of the broad area of Christian life - Biblical materials - Church history - Christian ethics - The Church - The Christian in the world. Brief introductory essays to each area broadly evaluating the available literature, followed by the bibliographical entries with one-line annotations. Only includes books published between 1950 and 1980. '... invaluable for its intended audience' (*Library journal,* 13 September 1982, p.743). *Class No:* 230(01)

[510]

GENTZ, W.H. **The Religious writer's marketplace.** Rev. ed. Philadelphia, Pa., Abingdon, 1993. 224p. $16.95. ISBN: 0087360528.

Earlier editions were published in 1981, 1985 and 1989.

A religiously oriented *Writer's market,* listing Christian periodicals, Christian publishing houses, and general presses that also offer religious titles. *Class No:* 230(01)

[511]

NICHOLS, A. **'Bibliography of current books on Christianity and politics, Christianity and the social order'.** In *Bulletin of the Association of British Theological and Philosophical Libraries,* v.2(3), November 1988, p.8-10.

21 items listed with brief descriptive annotations. *Class No:* 230(01)

Encyclopaedias

[512]

BARRETT, D.B., *ed.* **World Christian encyclopedia:** a comparative survey of churches and religions in the modern world, AD 1900-2000. Nairobi, Oxford University Press, 1982. [12], 1010p. illus., maps., tables. £110. ISBN: 0195724356.

Covers 20800 denominations. 14 parts (1. Status - 2. Chronology - 3. Methodology - 4. Culture - 5. Evangelization - 6. Codebook - 7. Survey (a survey of Christianity and religions in 223 countries, A-Z by country, p.131-771) - 8. Statistics - 9. Dictionary - 10. Bibliography (selective listing, p.839-861) - 11. Atlas - 12. Who's who - 13. Directory - 14. Indexes (polyglot glossary of religious terminology; names of countries in 6 languages; names of God in 900 languages; index of people and languages; Christian abbreviations, acronyms and initials; photographic index; standard and definitive locations index). *Class No:* 230(031)

[513]

Encyclopedia of early Christianity. Ferguson, E., *and others, eds.* New York, Garland, 1990. 983p. illus. $95. (*Garland reference library of the humanities, 846.*) ISBN: 0824057457.

997 entries by 135 scholars, covering persons, places, doctrines, practices, art, liturgy, heresies, and scisms of the first 600 years of Christianity. Entries vary in length from a few lines to *c.*4000 words. Cross-references. Bibliographies appended to most entries. *Class No:* 230(031)

Handbooks & Manuals

[514]

The Lion handbook of Christian belief. Organising editor: Robin Keeley. Tring, Herts., Lion Publishing; Sutherland, N.S.W., Albatross Books, 1982. 480p. 212 illus (15 col.), charts, diagr. £11.95; A$19.95. ISBN: 0856483214, UK; 0867604190, Australia.

Covers the whole sweep of Christian beliefs and their development down the centuries. Orthodox standpoint. 100 authors have contributed articles on the key beliefs. 6 parts: 1. How can we know? - 2. Jesus Christ - 3. God - 4. Creation: humanity and the world - 5. A new creation - 6. Christian belief in the making. Glossary (p.463-475). Detailed index (p.476-480). User-oriented and colourful presentation. *Class No:* 230(035)

[515]

NOLAN, M.L. *and* NOLAN, S. **Christian pilgrimage in modern Western Europe.** Chapel Hill, N.C., The University of North Carolina Press, 1989. xix,422p. illus., tables. $34.95. ISBN: 0807818143.

7 sections: Shrines of Western Europe - Pilgrimage in the European tradition - Periods of pilgrimage shrine formation - Holy persons: the subjects of devotion - Sacred objects: focal points for veneration - Wondrous events, miracles, and legends: original stories examined - Location and

....*(contd.)*

environment: shrines as holy places. Notes, p.339-380. Bibliography, p.381-402. Index, p.403-422.
Class No: 230(035)

Dictionaries

English

[516]
METFORD, J.C.J. Dictionary of Christian lore and legend. London, Thames & Hudson, 1983. 283p. illus. £12.50. ISBN: 0500110204.

Over 1700 articles spanning the whole field of Christian lore ('the learning and background knowledge which underpins Christian culture') and legend ('the historical, traditional or symbolic content of Christianity without prejudging its veracity'). Entries vary in length from 2-3 lines to a column (*e.g.* 'Immaculate conception': 13 lines; 'Eden, Garden of': 16 lines; 'David, King': 37 lines). *Class No:* 230(038)=20

Reviews & Abstracts

[517]
ASSOCIATION OF BRITISH THEOLOGICAL AND PHILSOPHICAL LIBRARIES. Bulletin ... London, Heythrop College Library, for the Association, 1956-66; New series, 1974- 3pa. £12pa; $20pa. ISSN: 0305781x.

A forum for professional exchange and development in the fields of theological and philosophical librarianship. Most issues include a review section (*i.e.* v.2(5), January 1989 has 5 reviews, p.28-36). *Class No:* 230(048)

[518]
The Heythrop journal: a review of philosophy and theology. 1960-. v.1, no.2- 4pa. Oxford, Blackwell, (previously Heythrop College, University of London; Chipping Norton, Oxfordshire, The Fathers of the Jesuit Faculties of Philosophy and Theology), 1960-. £35. $48 pa. ISSN: 00181196.

Includes features on contemporary philosophical and theological issues, including the Bible, eccliastical history, and the sociology of religion. Also book reviews and notices of books received. *Class No:* 230(048)

[519]
—Theologische Literaturzeitung. Monatsschrift für das gesamte Gebiet der Theologie und Religionswissenschaft. Berlin, Evangelische Verlagsanstalt GmbH, 1876-. Monthly. DM.198pa. ISSN: 00405671.

The leading Protestant Evangelical reviewing journal, with *Bibliographisches Beiblatt,* 1921 to 1942 (1922-43). 'Nearly indispensible'. (*Library trends,* v.15(3), January 1967, p.474). *Class No:* 230(048)

Quotations

[520]
CASTLE, T., *comp.* **The Hodder book of Christian quotations.** London, Hodder & Stoughton, 1982. [4], 293p.. £8.95. ISBN: 0340323396.

4115 quotations culled from a wide variety of sources, ancient and modern, English and American, Protestant and Catholic, by over 1000 authors. Grouped by 450 theme

....*(contd.)*

headings, A-Z (Abandonment ... Zeal), with several quotes under each heading. Each entry indicates author. Cross-references. Author index, p.267-293. *Class No:* 230(082.2)

[521]
CASTLE, T.C., *comp.* **The New book of Christian quotations.** New York, Crossroad, 1983. 272p. $10.95. ISBN: 08245005514.

4110 quotations by 1200 authors, arranged under 450 topics. 'See also' references. Lacks a keyword index. *Class No:* 230(082.2)

Histories

[522]
LATOURETTE, K.S. Christianity in a revolutionary age: a history of Christianity in the nineteenth and twentieth centuries. London, Eyre & Spottiswood, 1959-63. (Reprinted Greenwood Press, 1973). 5v. £144.50 the set. ISBN: 0837157005.

1: *The nineteenth century in Europe: background and the Roman Catholic phase* (xiv, 498p.); 2. *The nineteenth century in Europe: the Protestant and Eastern churches* [1], [1], 532p.); 3: *The nineteenth century outside Europe: the Americas, the Pacific, Asia and Africa* (viii, [1], 527p.); 4: *The twentieth century in Europe: the Roman Catholic, Protestant and Eastern churches* (viii, 568p.); 5: *The twentieth century outside Europe: the Americas, the Pacific, Asia and Africa; the emerging world Christian community* (viii, 568p.).

Discusses all aspects of Christianity throughout the world since 1815 - theology, organization, devotional life and influence on the social, political and education scene. Well documented (*e.g.* the chapter on Latin America in v.3 has 187 footnotes); each volume carries an annotated bibliography of *c.*17 pages of works cited more than once. Analytical index. *Class No:* 230(091)

[523]
LATOURETTE, K.S. A History of Christianity. New York, Harper & Row, 1975. 2v. (1552p.). $20 each volume. ISBN: 0060649526, v.1; 0060649534, v.2.

First published 1954 (xxviii, 1516p.).

62 chapters, each with a selected bibliography. Each volume has supplemented bibliography of books since 1950 (v.1, p.684-6; v.2, p.1507-14). 19 maps. Index to each volume. A tracing of the development of Christianity in the setting of human history. *Class No:* 230(091)

[524]
MANSCHRECK, C.L. History of Christianity in the world. 2nd ed. Englewood Cliffs, N.J., Prentice-Hall, 1985. viii,357p.illus. $38; £26.70. ISBN: 0133893545.

First published 1974.

21 chapters, arranged chronologically: 1. Presuppositions in the beginning of Christianity - 2. Conflict with Rome ... - 8. Eastern orthodoxy... 13. Reformation ... 18. The age of reason and piety ... 21. Retrenchment, outreach, reappraisal and uncertainty. General bibliography, p.336-344. Index, p.345-357. *Class No:* 230(091)

[525]

The Oxford illustrated history of Christianity.
McManners, J., *ed.* Oxford, Oxford University Press, 1990. xi,726p. illus., maps. £25. ISBN: 0198229283.

19 chapters arranged in 3 parts: From the origins to 1800; Christianity since 1800; Christianity today and tomorrow. Contributions, by a team of 18 leading scholars, based on latest research. Further readings, p.667-685 (by chapter). Chronology, p.680-705. 150 illustrations, 32 colour plates, and 12 maps. Sources are given. Detailed analytical index, p.707-724. Editor is Regius Professor of Ecclesiastical History, Oxford University. *Class No:* 230(091)

Europe—Western

[526]

Religion and society in early modern Europe, 1500-1800.
Greyerz, K. von, *and others.* London, George Allen & Unwin, for the German Historical Institute, 1985. x,281p. £35. ISBN: 0049400789.

17 chapters in 5 parts: 1. Religion as a cultural phenomenon - 2. The reform of popular culture and religion - 3. Religion and social control - 4. Religion and the community - 5. Historiography, sacred or profane?. Appendix: German, French and Italian works cited above available in English translation. 17 contributors. Many notes, including references, after each chapter. Index, p.275-281. *Class No:* 230(400)

England

[527]

DAVIES, H. Worship and theology in England. Princeton, N.J., Princeton University Press, 1961-75. 5v. illus., facsims.

Vol.1: *From Cranmer to Hooker, 1534-1603 - 2. From Andrewes to Baxter, 1603-1690 - 3. From Watts and Wesley to Maurice, 1690-1850 - 4. From Newman to Martineau, 1850-1900 - 5. The ecumenical century, 1900-1965.* V.1 (xix, 482p.) has 12 foot-noted chapters (1. Catholics and Protestants in controversy (1534-1568) ... 12. Spirituality: Catholic, Anglican, Puritan. Bibliography, p.443-62. Indexes of persons and of places (including churches). V.5 adds an index of topics. *Class No:* 230(420)

[528]

HASTINGS, A. A History of English Christianity, 1920-1985. London, Collins, 1986. 720p. £25. ISBN: 0002152118.

42 chapters in 7 parts: I. 1920 and before - II. The 1920s - III. The 1930s - IV. 1939-1945 - V. 1945-1960 - VI. The 1960s - VII. 1970-1985. Includes many portraits of personalities. Notes (p.673-703) are mainly references and arranged in chapter order. Index (p.704-720) includes 'see' references. '... this finely printed, vigorously written, industrially researched, sensibly opinionated yet cosmically fair survey of a very complex and hard-to-judge phenomenon... ' (*Church times,* 3 October 1986, p.6). *Class No:* 230(420)

India

[529]

NEILL, S. A History of Christianity in India. Cambridge, Cambridge University Press, 1984-85. 2v. (xxi,583; xvii,578p.). £45 each vol. ISBN: 0521243513, v.1; 0521303761, v.2.

V.1 is subtitled *the beginnings to A.D. 1707,* v.2 *1707-1858.* Aims to be comprehensive, with 15 chapters in v.1 and 18 in v.2, all subdivided. Over 160 pages of notes, arranged by chapter, include a wealth of bibliographical detail of writings in many languages. Each volume has appendices, select bibliographies, and indexes. *Class No:* 230(540)

Africa

[530]

OFORI, P.E. Christianity in tropical Africa: a selective, annotated bibliography. Nendeln, Netherlands, KTO Press, 1977; Westport, CT., Greenwood Press, 1982. [5],461p. ISBN: 3262006027.

The 2nd vol. of a 3-volume work. V.1 was titled *Black African traditional religions and philosophy* and the 3rd vol. will be on Islamic religion in Africa.

2859 numbered, unannotated entries arranged by countries, A-Z, preceded by sections on reference and bibliographical works, general works, and Africa (general). Includes a list of journals and periodicals on Christianity in Africa. Name index, p.426-461. *Class No:* 230(6)

Theology

Bibliographies

[531]

Bibliography of British theological literature, 1850-1940.
Hadidian, D.Y., *comp.* Pittsburgh, Pa., Barbour Library of Pittsburgh Theological Seminary, 1985. xxix, 453p. $34. (*Bibliographia Tripotamopolitana.*) ISBN: 0931222117.

18-page introduction to the British theological scene, followed by an A-Z list of *c.*3000 authors, subdivided by their main works, also arranged A-Z, with place and date of publication. Few annotations. Spacious layout to enable the addition of more titles. '... undoubtedly a major contribution to the librarianship of British theology but ... with more care ... could have produced an even more useful publication ...' (*Bulletin of ABTAPL,* no. 37, November 1986, p.8). *Class No:* 230.1(01)

[532]

BOLLIER, J.A. The Literature of theology: a guide for students and pastors. Philadelphia, Pa., Westminster Press, 1979. 208p. $5.95. ISBN: 0664242257.

Annotated entries for 543 reference tools, primarily English-language and recent (bibliographies, encyclopedias, dictionaries, indexing and abstracting services, guides and manuals, catalogues, commentaries and a few monographs with extensive bibliographies). General section (with biographies, almanacs, directories, yearbooks, quotation and poetry indexes, style manuals) is followed by coverage of Biblical studies, systematic theology, historical studies and practical theology. Primary coverage: the Judeo-Christian tradition, including both Protestant and Catholic approaches. 'The kind of book all Bible students and pastors should have in their personal libraries' (*Choice,* v.16(9), November 1979, p.1148). *Class No:* 230.1(01)

[533]
KEPPLE, R.J. **Reference works for theological research:** an annotated selective bibliographical guide. 2nd ed. Washington, University Press of America, 1981. xiv, 283p. $32.25. ISBN: 0819116793.

First published 1978.

About 800 entries, with concise, evaluative annotations. 39 chapters in 2 parts: 1. The general & general/religious/theological lists - 2. The subject area lists. Index to authors/editors and joint authors/editors, titles and alternative titles. A distinct drawback is the lack of a subject index. Some US slant, with special chapters on US bibliography and American church history. 'Because of the existance of James McCabe's useful work, *A critical guide to Catholic reference books* (2nd ed., 1980), this guide has been highly restrictive in including works about the Roman Catholic Church or produced under its auspices' (*General introduction*). 50% more entries than Bollier and generally more evaluative in its annotations. *Class No:* 230.1(01)

[534]
LONGSTAFF, T.R.W. *and* THOMAS, P. A. comps. and eds. **The Synoptic problems:** a bibliography, 1716-1988. Macon, GA., Mercer University, 1989. 235p. $35. (*New gospel studies, 4.*) ISBN: 0865543216.

A comprehensive bibliography covering the entire history of the so-called 'synoptic problems'. The author and title index includes a full bibliographical information as well as a printing and translation history of each item. Also a keyword index. *Class No:* 230.1(01)

Encyclopaedias

[535]
The Blackwell encyclopedia of modern Christian thought. McGrath, A, *ed.* Oxford, Blackwell, 1993. 700p. £60. ISBN: 0631168966.

Covers the period 1700 to the present day, containing articles on significant Christian history during and since the Enlightenment. Full bibliographical support for further reading. *Class No:* 230.1(031)

[536]
Theologische Realenzyklopädie. Krause, G. von *and* Müller, G., *eds.* Berlin & New York, de Gruyter, 1976-.v.1-. To be in 25v. and index (in fascicules).

V.1-17 (1976-1988): A-TRE.

Lengthy, signed and well-documented articles (*e.g.* 'Auferstehung' [Resurrection]: 130p.; 'Atheismus': 90p.; 'Augustine': nearly 90p.). Protestant standpoint. *Class No:* 230.1(031)

Dictionaries

[537]
ANGELES, P.A. **Dictionary of Christian theology.** New York, Harper & Row, 1985. 211p. $17.95. £16.25. ISBN: 0060602376.

Follows the format of the author's *Dictionary of philosophy* (*qv*) with etymologies and frequent cross-references. Brief definitions for a wide range of Christian concepts, some rather remotely connected with theology. Terms mainly primarily of interest to Roman Catholics. Typical length of definitions is 30 to 50 words, but some are much longer (*e.g.* 'Christology' and 'Eucharist' have 3 pages each). Useful for ready reference. *Library journal* (15

....(contd.)
April 1985, p.66) considers Rahner & Vorgrimler's *Dictionary of theology* (*qv*) more narrowly focused, scholarly, and thorough. *Class No:* 230.1(038)

[538]
Evangelical dictionary of theology. Elwell, W.A., *ed.* Grand Rapids, Mich., Baker Book House, 1984; Basingstoke, Hants., Marshall Pickering, 1985. xxii,1204p. $29.95; £24.95. ISBN: 0801034132, US; 0551012722, UK.

Designed to succeed *Baker's Dictionary of Theology* (1960).

1200 entries, written in popular language, encompassing the whole spectrum of theological discussion - dogmatic; historical philosophical; biblical moral-including current movements with broader implications, and historically significant personages. Scholarly entries are usual comprehensive and balanced handbook' (*Library journal*, January 1985, p.74). *Class No:* 230.1(038)

[539]
KOMONCHAK, J.A., *and others, eds.* **The New dictionary of theology.** Dublin, Gill & Macmillan; Wilmington, DE., Michael Glazier, 1987. viii,1112p. I£50; $59.95. ISBN: 0717115526, Ireland; 0894536095, US.

Articles ranging in length from a single paragraph to 15 double-columned pages, by distinguished scholars. Written from the point of view of the Roman Catholic Church. Articles includes 'see' references and bibliographies. 'Its purpose is to present Roman Catholic theology in the light of the teaching of the Second Vatican Council ... It particularly notes the decisions made by the American bishops in the light of the Vatican Council' (*Church times*, no.6531, 15 April 1988). *Class No:* 230.1(038)

[540]
RAHNER, K. *and* VORGRIMLER, H., *eds.* **Concise theological dictionary.** 2nd ed. Tunbridge Wells, Kent, Burns & Oates, 1983. [8], 541p. £15. ISBN: 0860121097.

First English edition 1965. Translated from *Kleines Theologisches Wörterbuch* (10th ed. Verlag Herder, Freiburg, 1976).

A revised and amplified edition, containing brief explanations (6 or 7 lines to 2p.) of the most important concepts of modern Catholic dogmatic theology. Entries arranged A-Z (Absolute ... Yahweh), with 'see' references. *Class No:* 230.1(038)

[541]
RICHARDSON, A. *and* BOWDEN, J., *eds.* **A New dictionary of Christian theology.** New ed. London, S.C.M. Press; Philadelphia, Pa., Westminster Press, 1989. 632p. £15. $24.95. ISBN: 0334022088, UK.

First published 1969. Title of both editions in US is *Westminster dictionary of Christian theology.*

About 800 signed entries by 175 contributors from many denominations. Short bibliographies for lengthier articles. Cross-references. A thorough revision and reworking of the first edition, with a nice balance between information and analyses. Drops biographical entries, 'focusing instead on theological thinking against a historical background rather than on historical events or figures (*Preface*). *Class No:* 230.1(038)

Reviews & Abstracts

[542]

Theological book review. October 1988-. Guildford, Surrey, Feed the Mind, 1988-. 3pa. £15; $30. ISSN: 09542191.

Claims to cover about 250 books from the UK, US and Third World in each issue. Subject arrangement. Author index and list of publishers in each issue. Michael Walsh found the entries in v.1(1) 'rather too uniformly fulsome' (*Bulletin of the ABTPL*, v.2(5), June 1989, p.35).
Class No: 230.1(048)

Histories

[543]

LANE, T. The Lion concise book of Christian thought. Tring, Herts, Lion Publishing; Sutherland, N.S.W., Albatross Books, 1984. 240p. illus. (line drawings). £5.95. Aus. $11.95. ISBN: 0856485055, UK; 0867604972, AUS.

'... primary purpose of this book is to introduce leading thinkers from the past (and present) and to whet the appetite by giving abstracts from their writings' (*Introduction*). Contains brief introductions to 90 of the most formative thinkers, together with extensive quotations, and 25 important creeds and confessions, etc. summarized. 5 sections: The Church of the Fathers to AD 500 - The Eastern tradition from AD 500 - The medieval West, 500-1500 - Reformation and reaction, 1500-1800 - Christian thought in the modern world, 1800 onwards. Bibliography (p.233-235) arranged A-Z by author. Index (p.237-238).
Class No: 230.1(091)

[544]

PELIKAN, J. The Christian tradition: a history of the development of doctrine. Chicago, University of Chicago Press, 1971-1989. 5v. v.1: $12.95; v.2: $10.95; v.3 & 4: $27.50 each; v.5: $29.95. v.1 & 2: £19.95 each; v.3 & 4: £21.95 each. ISBN: 0226653706, v.1; 0226653722, v.2; 0226653749, v.3; 0226653765, v.4; 0226653781, v.5.

V.1: *The emergence of the Catholic tradition (100-600);* v.2: *The spirit of eastern Christendom (600-1700);* v.3: *The growth of medieval theology (600-1300);* v.4: *Reformation of church and dogma (1300-1700);* v.5: *Christian doctrine and modern culture (since 1700).* Each volume starts with a list of primary sources and ends with a Biblical and general index (analytical). Early references are given in the left-hand margin of the text. *Class No:* 230.1(091)

19th Century

[545]

SMART, N., and others, eds. Nineteenth-century religious thought in the West. Cambridge, Cambridge University Press, 1985. 3v. (1038p.). £35 each volume. ISBN: 052122831x, v.1; 0521228328, v.2; 0212011149, v.3.

V.1: *Theology - 19th century* (Immanual Kant - Ludwig Feuerbach and Karl Marx); v.2: *Theology, doctrinal - history - 19th century* (Samuel Taylor Coleridge - William James and Josiah Royce); v.3: *Religion - history - 19th century* (Religion and science - Ernst Troeltsch). Each essay ends with a long list of notes, including references, and a bibliographical essay. Index to each volume.
Class No: 230.1(091)"18"

20th Century

[546]

FORD, D.F., ed. The Modern theologians: an introduction to Christian theology in the twentieth century. Oxford, Basil Blackwell Ltd., 1989. 2v. (xvi,342; xii,330p.). £35. each vol. ISBN: 0631153713, v.1; 0631168079, v.2.

'Aims to introduce the thought of most leading 20th-century Christian theologians and movements in theology' (*Preface*). Each volume has 14 chapters in 5 parts. V.1. Part 1. Corresponding to Revelation - 2. Existentialism and correlation - 3. Transcendential theology - 4. Tradition and beauty - 5. History and eschatology. V.2. Part 1. British theologies - 2. Theology in the United States - 3. Evangelical and orthodox theology - 4. New challengers in theology - 5. Theology and religious diversity. Each volume has a list of dates, a glossary, and an analytical index.
Class No: 230.1(091) "19"

Biographies

[547]

BOWDEN, J. Who's who in theology. London, SCM Press, 1990. 152p. £5.95. ISBN: 0334024641.

An A-Z guide for students and the general reader to the names that appear in theological works. Not a substitute for weightier works, of which there is a list at the beginning of the book. Entries vary in length, averaging about 6 to a page, and a typical entry includes person's dates, biographical details, and account of his or her works. No value judgements. Appendix on the Popes of Rome, in chronological order. 1-page alphabetical index. '... compact, concise, well-balanced and clear (both in form and content) ...'(*Reference reviews*,v.5(2),1991, p.9).
Class No: 230.1(092)

South Africa

[548]

BORCHARDT, C.F.A. and VORSTER, W.S., eds. South African theological bibliography... Pretoria, University of South Africa, 1980. xxvii, 398p. ISBN: 0869811851.

'The aim ... is to index all Festschrifts and periodical literature published in South Africa covering the field (*Preface*). 6088 unannotated entries, arranged in 8 sections: Bibliological subjects - Systematic theology - Historical subjects - Practical theology - Science of religion - Science of missions - Apologetics - Sects - and an addendum. Author index, p.370-398. *Class No:* 230.1(680)

Miracles

[549]

BREWER, E.C. A Dictionary of miracles, imitative, realistic and dogmatic. London, Chatto & Windus, 1884 (Reprinted Detroit, Mich., Gale Research Co., 1966). 632p. ISBN: 0810343533.

The only reference book of its kind, intended to reproduce in a handy form impartial information about a mode of religious thought. Three parts: miracles of saints, relating to Scripture miracles or secular stories; realistic miracles, founded on literal interpretation of Scripture; and dogmatic miracles, to prove ecclesiastical dogmas. Full index.
Class No: 231.73

Mariology (Virgin Mary)

Dictionaries

[550]
ATTWATER, D., *comp*. **A Dictionary of Mary.** London, Longmans, Green, 1957. vii,312p.

Originally published 1956 (New York, Kennedy).

The aim is 'to provide the reader, whether a member of the Catholic Church or not, with a quick reference to matters connected with the many aspects of the life, significance and veneration of the Blessed Virgin Mary in ordinary non-technical language' (*Preface*). *Class No:* 232.931(038)

[551]
DE FIORES, S. *and* MEO, S. **Nuovo dizionaria di Mariologia.** 2nd ed. Milano, Edizioni Paoline, 1986. xxvii,1561p. ISBN: 8821509885.

First published 1985.

Lengthy signed essays commence with a summary and end with notes and bibliography. 65 contributors. Italian only. *Class No:* 232.931(038)

Angels

[552]
DAVIDSON, G. **A Dictionary of angels,** including the fallen angels. New ed. New York, Free Press, 1972. xxxii,387p. illus., facsims., charts. $22.95. ISBN: 0029069408.

First published 1967.

About 7,000 very brief entries (A'albiel ... Zuriel), with many references to angels in literature, art and mythology. Well documented, Many cross-references from alternatives names. Lengthy introduction (p.xi-xxix) has 46 footnote references. Many appendices, p.335-62 (*e.g.* 'The orders of the celestial hierarchy'). Bibliography, p.363-87. *Class No:* 235

Demonology

Dictionaries

[553]
GETTINGS, F. **Dictionary of demons:** a guide to demons and demonologists in occult lore. North Pomfret, VT., Trafalgar Square Publishing, 1988. 255p. illus., tables. $24.95. ISBN: 094395505x.

A compendium of historical, biographical and factual information. An introduction explains the historical evolution of demonological traditions. Arranged A-Z, the dictionary includes pagan, occult, pre-Christian, and Christian evil spirits and devils, explaining the origin of each and its representation in different traditions. Entries vary in length from a line to several pages. 'See' references connect name variants. Bibliography listing titles referred to in the text. Considered 'More scholarly than *Man, myth and magic* (1984)' (*Reference books bulletin*, 15th December 1988, p.689). *Class No:* 235.1(038)

Saints

[554]
METFORD, J.C.J. **The Christian year.** London, Thames & Hudson, 1991. 144p. £12.95. ISBN: 0500110212.

A companion to the holy days, festivals and seasons of the ecclesiastical year. Select bibliography, with some comment, p.129-30. Glossary, p.131-40. Detailed index. Scholarly

.... (contd.)
discussion of origins, reasons and theological background. A calendar of saints' days would have been a helpful addition! *Class No:* 235.3

[555]
ROEDER, H. **Saints and their attributes:** with a guide to localities and patronage. London, Longmans, Green, 1955. xxviii, 391p.

Saints' emblems and symbols as depicted in pictorial representations and statuary, arranged by subjects A-Z. Sub-arranged under saints' names (giving date of death; religious order). Indexes of saints, patronage and localities; short bibliography, p.xiv. *Class No:* 235.3

[556]
—POST, W.E. **Saint's signs and symbols.** 2nd ed. London, S.P.C.K., 1975. 96p. illus. £3.99. ISBN: 028102894x.

First published 1964.

Four or more illustrations per page, with descriptive captions. 'Crosses' (p.56-60): 60 types. Index, p.85-96. *Class No:* 235.3

Bibliographies

[557]
Analecta Bollandiana: revue critique d'hagiographie. Brussels, Société des Bollandistes, 1882-. 2pa (previously quarterly). F.2800pa; $60pa. ISSN: 00032468.

Contains criticisms of recent works on questions relating to the lives of the saints. The work of a group of Belgian Jesuits. Also has commentaries, texts, etc., supplementary to the monumental *Acta sanctorum quotquot toto orbe coluntur* (1643-; Paris ed., 1863-1940, 85v. in 67, and supplements), a collection of biographies and legends of the saints, in calendar order. Inventories of the collection appear in: *Bibliotheca hagiographica graeca* (Brussels, 1895; 3rd ed. 1957. 3v.), *Bibliotheca hagiographica latina* (Brussels, 1898-1901. 2v.), and *Bibliotheca hagiographica orientalis* (Brussels, 1910). More recent is Analecta Bollandiana's *Inventaire hagiographique des tomes 1 à 100 (1882-1982)* (Brussels, Société des Bollandistes, 1983. 443p.). *Class No:* 235.3(01)

[558]
METZGER, B.M., *comp*. **Index to periodical literature on the Apostle Paul.** 2nd ed. Leiden, E.J. Brill, 1970. xvi,184p. Gld.41. ISBN: 9004015477.

First published 1960.

*c.*3000 entries in 6 sections: 1. Bibliographical articles on Paul - 2. Historical studies on the life of Paul - 3. Critical studies of the Pauline literature - 4. Pauline Apocrypha - 5. Theological studies - 6. The history of the interpretation of Paul and his work. Includes articles from *c.*135 journals in many languages. Author index. *Class No:* 235.3(01)

Dictionaries

[559]
The Book of saints: a dictionary of servants of God canonized by the Catholic Church. Benedictine monks of St. Augustine's Abbey, Ramsgate, *comps*. 6th ed. rev. & updated. London, A. & C. Black, 1989. 624p. 135 black-and-white illus. £19.95. ISBN: 071363006x.

5th ed. published *c.*1966.

Brief biographical details, achievements, feast days, and emblems of *c.*10,000 saints of the Catholic Church, revised

....(contd.)

according to the recommendations of the Church. Includes many modern saints. Arranged A-Z. Also lists patron saints and a list of emblems, relating them to the saints.
Class No: 235.3(038)

Quotations

[560]

ADELS, J.H. The Wisdom of the saints: an anthology. New York, Oxford University Press, 1987. 233p. $21.95. ISBN: 0195041526.

A collection of the saints' own words, thematically arranged. 60 items (Saints - God ... Mystic Union) with brief entries. Biographical notes, p.205-233.
Class No: 235.3(082.2)

Biographies

[561]

BUTLER, A. The Lives of the saints. New ed., rev. and copiously supplemented by H. Thurston *and others.* London, Burns, Oates, 1926-38. 12v. & supplement.

A greatly expanded edition of a work published 1756-9, intended for the general reader. Lives of *c.*2500 saints. 1 volume per month, biographies being arranged according to the saint's day. Short bibliographies are appended. A general index to the rev. ed. (giving date for each saint) is published as *A dictionary of saints ...* compiled by D. Attwater. (New ed. London, Burns & Oates, 1958, vii, 280p.).
Class No: 235.3(092)

[562]

—BUTLER, A. Butler's lives of the saints: edited, revised and supplemented by H. Thurston and D. Attwater. 3rd ed. London, Burns & Oates, 1981. 4v. (700p.). ISBN: 0860121127.

In this edition certain abbreviations have been made to the 1926-38 text (*e.g.* Butler's daily exhortations have been discarded). Each volume has an index, v.4 including a cumulated index. *Class No:* 235.3(092)

[563]

—WALSH, M., *ed.* Butler's lives of the saints: concise edition. London, Burns & Oates, 1985. 484p. £12.95. ISBN: 0860121402.

One-volume abridgement of the above. For each day of the year one saint is given, suitable for devotional reading as well as for historical background to Church history. Also reproduces full index from complete edition, with saints included in this volume highlighted in bold type. Contains the most recent canonizations as well as revised dating.
Class No: 235.3(092)

[564]

—WALSH, N., *ed.* Butler's lives of patron saints. Rev. ed. London, Burns & Oates, 1987. xvi, 476p. illus. £14.95. ISBN: 0860121577.

Over 250 saints from legendary to modern times, showing how their patronages have become both popularly accepted and officially recognized. Arranged A-Z, giving a short biography of the patron saint, preceded by the history of each patronage. 3 indexes: by country, place, profession, occupation, and social or medical condition; a list of saints and their feast days; and an index of the saints and their patronages listed by the dates of their feast days.
Class No: 235.3(092)

[565]

COULSON, J., *ed.* The Saints: a concise biographical dictionary. London, Burns & Oates, 1958. 496p. illus. (inc. 16 col. plates).

About 2500 entries arranged A-Z by anglicized form of Christian name. Entries vary in length from 3-4 lines to 3 columns (*e.g.* St. Thomas Aquinas: 2½ columns; St. Teresa of Avila: 2¼ columns, plus an illustration). Many cross-references. 'Calendar of feast days', p.473-85: 'For further reading', p.489-91. Articles unsigned; the impressive list of some 65 contributors does not indicate the specific contributions. *Class No:* 235.3(092)

[566]

—ATTWATER, D. The Penguin dictionary of saints. 2nd ed. by C.R. John. Harmondsworth, Mddx., Penguin Books, 1983. 352p. £6.99. ISBN: 0140511237.

First published 1965.

Identifies more than 750 saints, especially those of Great Britain and Ireland. Many other individuals are mentioned in the biographical sketches, with cross-references. 'Short general bibliography', p.18. Glossary, p.19-26.
Class No: 235.3(092)

[567]

The Oxford dictionary of saints. Farmer, D.H. 3rd ed. Oxford, Oxford University Press, 1992. xxvii,530p. £7.99. $14.95. ISBN: 0198691491.

First published 1978.

Concise accounts of the lives, cults, and artistic associations of *c.*1250 saints who lived or died or have been venerated in Great Britain and Ireland. Increased coverage of Greek and Russian saints in the 2nd ed. Arranged A-Z ('Joan of Arc': 3 columns; 10 references). 3 appendices (I. Some unsuccessful English candidates for canonization; II. Principal patronages; III. Principal iconographical problems). Index of places in Great Britain and Ireland associated with particular saints. Calendar of feasts. Valuable introduction refers to the 1969 reform of the Roman Calendar. 'Excellent value and as a single volume work based on critical principles is unlikely to be rivalled' (*Heythrop journal,* v.20, 1979, p.466, on the first edition).
Class No: 235.3(092)

Europe

[568]

SHARP, M. A Traveller's guide to saints in Europe. London, Evelyn, 1964. xv, 251p.

Identifies more than 400 European saints, arranged A-Z, with chronological list of saints (by century and then date of death). Entries give names, dates, attributes in art, and patron. Bibliography (p.vii); glossary of terms (p.viii); index of churches containing relics (by countries, p.241-51). The *Times literary supplement,* no. 3241, 9 April, 1964, p.297, notes some omissions and misspellings. *Class No:* 235.3(4)

Wales

[569]

HENKEN, E.R. Traditions of the Welsh saints. Woodbridge, Suffolk, Boydell & Brewer, 1987. vii,368p. £29.50; $53. ISBN: 0859912213.

'... a survey of narrative traditions concerning the lives of the Welsh saints ... examines Welsh hagiographical traditions rooted in local lore as represented by a variety of

....*(contd.)*

sources, both written and oral' (*Introduction*). Deals with 47 Welsh saints, mainly real men and women of the 5th and 6th centuries. Extensive footnotes. Bibliography, p.311-320, A-Z by author. Index of saints' traditions, p.321-368. *Class No:* 235.3(429)

Creeds

Histories

[570]

CURTIS, W.A. A History of creeds and confessions of faith in Christendom and beyond. Edinburgh, Clark, 1911. xx, 502p.

An admirable survey of religious creeds throughout the ages, with extensive and representative quotations from the authoritative documents, bibliographies, and appendices of historical tables. Index.

The 3rd ed. of J.N.D. Kelly's *Early Christian creeds* was issued in a new edition in 1982 (Longman, 460p. 058249219x). *Class No:* 238(091)

Ethics

[571]

CAMPBELL, A.V., *ed*. A Dictionary of pastoral care. London, SPCK Ltd., 1987. xi,300p. £20. ISBN: 0281042608.

'... a concise but comprehensive guide to the concepts and problems most likely to be encountered in pastoral care and counselling' (Book jacket). 300 entries by *c.*185 contributors, experts in their fields, arranged A-Z by subject (Abortion and abortion counselling ... Worship and pastoral care). Bibliographies are appended to each entry. Cross-references. *Class No:* 241

[572]

MACQUARRIE, J. *and* CHILDERS, J.F., *eds*. A New dictionary of Christian ethics. London, S.C.M. Press; Philadelphia, Pa., Westminster Press, 1990. 698p. £17.50. $34.95. ISBN: 0334022045, UK; 0664209408, US.

First published 1967 as *A dictionary of Christian ethics* in the UK and as *Westminster dictionary of Christian ethics* in US.

167 contributors, representing Protestant, Anglican, Roman Catholic, Orthodox and Jewish faiths. Signed articles and brief follow-up bibliographies for longer items (*e.g.* 'Jesus, Ethical teachings of': 7½ cols; 4 references). Wide range of subjects (*e.g.* Pride; Prison reform; Hippocratic oath; Industrial relations; Neoplatonism), including entries under moralists (*e.g.* Schleiermacher). Many additional entries in the new edition; articles updated; bibliographies revised; more cross-references. '... major contribution that reflects contemporary ideas on Christian ethics and moral theology ... distinguished reference work'. (*Reference books bulletin,* 1986/87, p.52-53). 'Major omission is biographical entries, though movements associated with individuals remain' (*Library journal,* 15 March 1986, p.62). *Class No:* 241

Christian Art & Symbols

Handbooks & Manuals

[573]

CHILD, H. *and* COLLES, D. Christian symbols, ancient and modern: a handbook for students. London, Bell, 1971. xxi, 269p. illus. (incl. pl.). £17.50. ISBN: 0713519606.

18 sections: Symbolism - The Cross - The Trinity - Images of Christ - The Virgin Mary: her place in art - The nativity of Jesus Christ - Living water - The Holy Spirit - The Eucharist - Angels - Good and evil - Forerunners and followers - The four living creatures - The Evangelists - Benedicite omnia opera - The Church in work and time - Categories (*e.g.* The seven virtues and the seven vices) - The liturgy and the crafts. 'List of books', p.256-9. Non-analytical index. Excellent illus. (33 pl., 114 line-drawings, with descriptive captions). *Class No:* 246(035)

[574]

RÉAU, L. Iconographie de l'art chrétien. Paris, Presses Universitaire de France, 1955-59 (Reprinted Nendeln, Kraus-Thomson, 1974). 3v.

V.1: *Introduction générale*; v.2: *Iconographie de la Bible* (2 parts: Ancien Testament. Nouveau Testament); v.3: *Iconographie des saints* (3 pts. A-F, G-O, P-Z). A detailed survey, with section bibliographies. V.3 includes 80 plates and a general bibliography of hagiographies, etc. (p.1382-4), as well as sections: 'Les noms des saints'; 'Les patronages'; 'Les attributs', and a general index. Indispensible for research on Christian iconography. *Class No:* 246(035)

[575]

SILL, G.G. A Handbook of symbols in Christian art. New York, Macmillan, 1975. xii,241p. illus.

50 categories, A-Z (Angel ... Zodiac), follow a short introductory essay. Clear illustrations of 162 works of art, with captions. Select bibliography, with a long list of sources and credits. Copious cross-references. 'An indispensable reference work, especially for public collections' (*ARLIS/NA Newsletter,* v.4(1), December 1975, p.14, a review on which this annotation is based. *Class No:* 246(035)

Dictionaries

[576]

BOTTOMLEY, F. The Church explorer's guide to symbols and their meaning. London, Kaye & Ward, 1978. xvi, 176p., 320 illus. £1.95. ISBN: 0718211871.

A-Z entries on the symbolism of decorations, furniture and fabrics of churches, in terms of the Church's history and teaching. Further reading, p.161. Marginal illus., 2 or more per page. Index. 'The result of many years exploring churches in all parts of the country' (Note). *Class No:* 246(038)

[577]

Lexikon der christlichen Ikonographie. Kirschbaum, E., *and others*. Freiburg, Herder, 1968-1975,. 9v. illus.

V.1-4: Allgemeine Ikonographie (on Biblical concepts and persons, A-Z); v.5-9: Ikonographie der Heiligen (saints, A-Z, plus indexes of attributes, localities and artists in v.9). *Class No:* 246(038)

Spirituality

Bibliographies

[578]
CARSON, A. Feminist spirituality and the feminine divine:
an annotated bibliography. Crossing Press, 1986. 125p.
$39.95. ISBN: 0895942003.

Aimed at both lay and scholarly audiences. Over 700
entries, mainly books, for works produced by the women's
spirituality movement and inspired by it. Wide subject field
(history, folklore, mythology, religion, psychology,
witchcraft, occult sciences, lesbian feminism, etc.).
Arrangement is A-Z by author (periodicals by title). Average
length of annotations is 40 words. Excellent subject index,
but no title index. *Class No:* 248(01)

Dictionaries

[579]
VILLER, M., and others, eds. Dictionnaire de spiritualité,
ascétique et mystique, doctrine et histoire. Paris,
Beauchesne, 1937-. v.1-.

V.1-13 (1937-88) A-Ryelandt, published so far. A
scholarly work, with long signed articles; rich in
biographies. Bibliographies appended to articles include
references to sources. The article on St. Bernard of
Clairvaux, for instance, occupies p.1454-99 of v.1 and is in
5 sections (life; spiritual works; source of teaching; doctrine
(20 pages); influence on spirituality) and has 1½ columns of
bibliography. That on Jakob Boehme runs to 6 columns (life
and work; doctrine) and has ½ column of bibliography
(works; literature on). *Class No:* 248(038)

[580]
WAKEFIELD,, G.S., ed. A Dictionary of Christian
spirituality. New ed. London, SCM Press, 1983 (reprinted
in paperback, 1988). xvi.400p. £15; $22.95. ISBN:
0334019672.

First published 1971. Published by Westminster Press in
the US as *Westminster dictionary of Christian spirituality.*

The standard reference work on the subject. Includes 358
articles, written by a team of 153. Entries are signed, include
bibliographical references, and are often lengthy (*e.g.*
'Asceticism': 6 cols., 5 references; 'Penitence': 2 cols., 6
references; 'Ecstasy': 1¼ cols., 4 references). Includes
biographies. Cross-references. Clearly and concisely
written, defining spiritual concepts, practices, schools and
important persons. 'A fascinating exposition ... ' (Theology,
v.87(717), May 1984. p.207-9). *Class No:* 248(038)

Histories

[581]
BOUYER, L., and others. A History of Christian
spirituality. Burns & Oates, 1968. Tunbridge Wells, Kent
(Reprinted 1982). 3v. (1404p.). £39.50 the set. V.1 & 2:
£16 each; v.3: £10. ISBN: 0860121135, v.1; 0860121143,
v.2; 0860121151, v.3; 0860121259, set.

Translated from the French 1960-65 ed.

V.I: *The Spirituality of the New Testament and the Fathers*
has 19 chapters, an index of subjects, and a biblical index
(p.534-541) divided into ancient authors and modern
authors. V.II: *The spirituality of the Middle Ages* has 18
chapters, an appendix on Byzantine spirituality, and an index

....(contd.)
of names (persons and places). V.III: *Orthodox spirituality*
and Protestant and Anglican spirituality has 6 chapters,
Conclusion, and list of names. *Class No:* 248(091)

Meditation

[582]
JARRELL, H.R. International meditation bibliography,
1950-1982. Metuchen, N.J. Scarecrow Press, and The
American Theological Library Association, 1985. x,432p.
$32.50. (*ATLA bibliography series, no.12.*) ISBN:
0810817594.

Entries for about 1000 books, 900 journal and magazine
articles, and over 200 dissertations and masters' theses,
arranged A-Z, for items published between 1950 and 1982
with some 1983 references. Brief annotations are included
for the articles. Articles are in English, some books in other
Western languages; dissertations and theses in English and
German. Also includes 32 motion pictures, 93 recordings,
and 32 societies and associations. Subjects include Christian
meditation, Zen-Buddhist meditation, relaxation techniques,
Yoga meditation, and transcendential meditation. Author,
title and subject indexes. *Class No:* 248MED

Pilgrimage

[583]
BARBER, R. Pilgrimages. Woodbridge, Suffolk &
Rochester, NY, Boydell & Brewer Ltd., 1991. 160p. 12
plates. £16.95; $29.95. ISBN: 0851155197.

A survey of the major pilgrimage traditions of all the great
religions of the world, outlining the history and nature of the
different ideas and rites of pilgrimage. *Class No:* 248.1

[584]
DAVIDSON, L.K. and DUNN-WOOD, M. Pilgrimages in
the Middle Ages: a research guide. New York, Garland,
1993. 480p. $74. (*(Garland medieval bibliographies,16).*)
ISBN: 0824072219.

Topically organized bibliographical essays; a research
guide; and an annotated, descriptive bibliography of over
1000 entries. No indexes. *Class No:* 248.1

Christian Church

Handbooks & Manuals

[585]
WORLD COUNCIL OF CHURCHES. Handbook: member
churches. 2nd rev. ed. Geneva, the Council, 1985. x, 289p.
£9.95. ISBN: 28225407259.

First published 1982.

A handy compendium of important information on
churches, national and religious councils of churches and
Christian world communions. Lists over 300 churches by
continent, region and country, giving name and address,
telephone number, number of members, number of
congregations, number of pastors, publications, general
secretary, and description. Indexed by countries, names of
member churches, and English names of member churches.
Class No: 26/28(035)

Dictionaries

[586]

CROSS, F.L. *and* LIVINGSTONE, E.A. **The Oxford dictionary of the Christian Church.** 2nd ed. London, Oxford University Press, 1974. xxxi, 1518p. £35. ISBN: 0192115456.

First published 1957.

About 6000 entries particularly strong on biographies (*e.g.* Zwingli: 2 cols., including ½ col. of bibliography). Appended 'Chronological list of popes and antipopes'. Some 250 contributors. A corrective to the High Anglican stance, 'establishmentarianism and antiquarian attachment to the ways of the Western Church; (*T.L.S.*, 20 April 1973, p.448) of the 1st ed. Thus, the 2nd ed., while allotting 'Church of England' 6 cols. (including nearly 1 col. of bibliography), more justice is done to, for example, the Eastern Orthodox Church (3 cols. including 2/3 of bibliography). The 2nd ed. was designed to take full account of recent years (*e.g.* Pope Paul VI: 1¾ cols.; Vatican Council, The Second: '1½ cols. (14 lines of bibliography); World Council of Churches: 1+Q cols.; 10 lines of bibliography). Addressed 'to the educated public as a whole' (*Preface* to the 1st ed). 'The most useful quick-reference tool for the teachers of theology, and their hard-pressed students' (*Heythrop journal*, v.15, 1974, p.362).

The Concise Oxford dictionary of the Christian Church, edited by E.A. Livingstone (O.U.P., 1977. vi, 570p. £6.95. ISBN 0192830147), based on the above, has over 5000 brief entries, shortened and modified to suit the lay reader. *Class No:* 26/28(038)

[587]

DOUGLAS, J.D., *General editor*. **The New international dictionary of the Christian Church.** Exeter, Devon, Paternoster Press, 1978. xiv, 1074p. £21.95. ISBN: 0310238307.

First published 1974.

Nearly 200 contributors. 5000 articles, nearly all signed. 'Aachen, Synod of' ... 'Zwingli'. Many biographies, with references appended (*e.g.* Ignatius of Loyola: 1 col., 6 references; John Wesley: nearly 2 cols., 21 lines of references). 'Music, Christian': 7 cols., ½ col. of bibliography; 'Epistles, Pauline': 4 cols., ½ col. of bibliography; 'Mormonism': 1½ cols., 11 lines of references. Ample cross-references. Aims at impartiality, and a 'middle path between academic textbook and popular introduction' (*Preface*). *Class No:* 26/28(038)

Yearbooks & Directories

[588]

WORLD COUNCIL OF CHURCHES. **Directory of Christian Councils.** 4th ed. Geneva, the Council, 1985. xii, 244p. ISBN: 2825408468.

Arranged by continent or region, subdivided by country A-Z, and then arranged A-Z by name. Information given : name and address; telephone number, cable, telex; general secretary, other full-time executive staff, part-time and honorary staff; president; membership (list of affiliated and associate members); date of foundation; basis of membership; aims and functions, main concerns and activities; organization of the council; sources of budget; ecumenical relationships. List of regional and inter-regional conferences. No index. *Class No:* 26/28(058)

England

[589]

EDWARDS, D.L. **Christian England.** London, Collins, 1981-1984. 3v. (1249p.). (Reprinted by Fount Publications, 1989). £10.95. ISBN: 0006274048.

A survey of Christian England to the end of the first world war. V.1. Its story to the Reformation (pt.1. The first England; pt.2. The Middle Ages): v.2 From the Reformation to the eighteenth century (pt.1. Christians under the Tudors; pt.2. A war between believers; pt.3. Religions in the age of reason. Outline of events); v.3. From the eighteenth century to the first world war (pt.1. Revival; pt.2. The Victorian Christians. Outline of events). Copious footnotes throughout; Lists for further reading after each part; and an 8-page index to each volume. '... an enthralling story told with lucidity, vividness and the most judicious discernment'. (*Church times*, August 17, 1984, p.6). *Class No:* 26/28(420)

Ecumenical Movement

[590]

Dictionary of the Ecumenical movement. Lossky, N., *and others, eds.* Grand Rapids, Mich., Eerdmans, 1991. 1196p. illus. $79.95. ISBN: 0802824265.

Prepared under the auspices of the World Council of Churches, the volume aims 'to draw together a record of the ... movement in the twentieth-century'(*Introduction*). Over 650 signed articles, A-Z, covering important ecumenical themes and events, organizations and personalities, in each region of the world and in the various denominations. Articles have brief bibliographies and some photographs. Cross-references. 50-page index. 'A Christian/Protestant point of view is apparent throughout' (*RQ*, v.31(3), Spring 1992, p.415-6). *Class No:* 261.8

Bibliographies

[591]

WORLD COUNCIL OF CHURCHES. Geneva. Library. **Classified catalog of the ecumenical movement.** Boston, Mass., G.K. Hall, 1972. 1st supplement, 1981. 2v. and supplement. $185 for 2v.; $105 for supplement. ISBN: 0816109257; 0816103607, Supplement.

20,200 photolithographed catalogue cards covering *c.*11,000 titles on the ecumenical movement in the Library. Arranged according to a modified Dewey Decimal scheme. *Class No:* 261.8(01)

Histories

[592]

ROUSE, R. *and* NEILL, S.C., *eds*. **A History of the ecumenical movement.** London, S.P.C.K., on behalf of the Committee on Ecumenical History, Geneva, 1954-70. 2v.

1: *1517-1948* (1954. 3rd rev. ed. 1986. 864p.). 2: *The ecumenical advance ... 1948-1968,* edited by H.E. Fey. (1970. 544p.). V.1 stresses the influence of evangelical revivals; bibliography, p.745-801. V.2 has chapter bibliographies (p.449-508), with index of authors cited; analytical general index. *Class No:* 261.8(091)

Liturgy & Worship

Bibliographies

[593]

A Bibliography of Christian worship. Thompson, B., *ed.* Metuchen, N.J. and London, American Theological Association and Scarecrow Press, 1989. xiii,786p. $79.50. (*ATLA bibliography series, 25.*) ISBN: 0810821540.

51 sections arranged in 6 parts: 1. Reference works and general works - 2. Worship and the liturgy in the Christian tradition (covering more than half the book) - 3. Word and sacraments: theology, liturgy and spirituality - 4. The daily office and the church year - 5. Worship and the arts - 6. Church music and hymnology. Includes periodical articles as well as books. Author/editor, p.741-782. Church bodies/ conference/organizations index, p.783-786. 'International in scope, its comprehensiveness and depth make this a truly outstanding work' (*Choice*, v.27(10), January 1990, p.1645). *Class No: 264(01)*

[594]

GRIMES, R.L. Research in ritual studies: a programmatic essay and bibliography. Metuchen, N.J., Scarecrow Press; The American Theological Library Association, 1985. 165p. $15. (*ATLA bibliography series, 14.*) ISBN: 0810817624.

Over 1600 entries for books and journal articles on ritual (in the disciplines covered by religion, anthropology, sociology, psychology and literary criticism) grouped in 4 sections: Ritual components - Ritual types - Ritual descriptions - General works. Includes festivals, pilgrimages, ritual objects, rituals of exchange, and civil ceremonies. An overview of the current state of the study precedes. '... unique because it does not classify rituals by particular group ...' (*Choice*, v.23(1), September 1985, p.81). *Class No: 264(01)*

Dictionaries

[595]

DAVIES, J.G. A New dictionary of liturgy and worship. Rev. & expanded ed. London, S.C.M. Press; Philadelphia, Pa., Westminster Press, 1986. xv, [1], 544p. £19.50. $29.95. ISBN: 033402207x, UK; 0664212700, US.

First published 1972. Title in US is *The new Westminster dictionary of liturgy and worship.*

Over 100 contributors, Emphasis is on Christian worship (baptism, eucharist, etc.), with brief treatment of other religions. 'The separate articles are not confined to simple definitions but give the historical background to the subject treated and seek to relate this to the contemporary scene' (*Preface* to 1st ed.). Signed articles; references in text and/or appended. It strikes a more ecumenical note than the *Oxford dictionary of the Christian church.* 'Students will come to find it extremely useful (especially in revision), both for its factual material and for the stimulation of faith' (*Heythrop journal*, v.15, 1976, p.240). '... will prove invaluable ...' (*British book news*, April 1986, p.211). *Class No: 264(038)*

Vestments

[596]

MAYO, J. A History of ecclesiastical dress. London, Batsford, 1984. 192p. 112 illus. (6 in colour). £20. ISBN: 0713437642.

Traces the origins and development of ecclesiastical dress (liturgical vestments, choir dress, and outdoor or general

....(contd.)

dress where it differs from contemporary fashionable dress). A chronological account is followed by a detailed and illustrated glossary in which individual items and their origins are described. *Class No: 264-03*

[597]

NORRIS, H. Church vestments: their origin & development. London, Dent, 1949. xv, 190p. illus.

A work which grew out of the author's *Costume and fashion* (1927-38), dealing with classical garments that were the ancestors of church vestments. Attention given to accurate dating; coloured, and black-and-white illustrations; brief historical data; index. *Class No: 264-03*

Hymns

Bibliographies

[598]

PARKS, E.D. Early English hymns. Metuchen, N.J., Scarecrow Press, 1972. 168p.

Lists and locates over 900 hymns written in English before Isaac Watts. Many of the titles do not appear in Julian's *Dictionary*. Data: metre, number of stanzas, author, date published, number and/or page where hymn located; and on tune and composer. Author, composer and tune indexes. *Class No: 264-068(01)*

[599]

—**DIEHL, K.S.** Hymns and tunes - an index. Metuchen, N.J., Scarecrow Press, 1966. lv, 1185p. $70. £52.50. ISBN: 0810800624.

An index to songs found in 78 hymnals, chiefly in English and representing British and North American Jewish-Christian institutions. Part 1: The hymns; part 2: The tunes. *Class No: 264-068(01)*

[600]

—**McDORMAND, T.B.** *and* CROSSMAN, F.S. Judson concordance to hymns. Valley Forge, Pa., Judson Press, 1965. 375p.

Indexes nearly 2400 hymns from 26 hymnals of major US and Canadian denominations. The user is referred from the keyword in any line to the 'Line index' and thence to the first line of the hymn. *Class No: 264-068(01)*

[601]

PERRY, D.W. Hymns and tunes indexed, the first lines, tune names and metres. Compiled from current English hymnbooks. Croydon, The Hymn Society of Great Britain and Ireland, and the Royal School of Church Music, 1980. ix,306p.

Indexes 37 hymnals (listed p.vii-viii). Index of first lines, p.121; index of tunes, p.123-229; index of metres, p.230-306. 'Intended as a comprehensive reference book for all who deal in hymns, whether as 'amateurs' or 'professionals' and will be especially valuable for those working with members of other denominations' (*The Church times*, 28 November, 1980, p.viii). *Class No: 264-068(01)*

[602]

TURNER-EVANS, H. **A Bibliography of Welsh hymnology.**
Caernarfon, Arfon/Dwyfor Library HQ., 1977. [ii], 206p.
£4.

Based on the author's Library Association thesis,
Bibliography of Welsh hymnology to 1960 (1964). About 200
entries for individual hymn-writers (Adams, David ...
Wynne, Ellis; p.15-206). Data include: biographical sketch;
works; hymn(s) in Welsh. No index of hymns. Prefixed list
of Bardic names and pseudonyms; bibliography of books,
periodical articles and manuscripts in hymnology.
Mimeographed. *Class No:* 264-068(01)

Dictionaries

[603]

JULIAN, J. **A Dictionary of hymnology,** setting forth the
origin and history of Christian hymns of all ages and nations
... Rev. 2nd ed., with new supplement. London, Murray,
1907 (Reprinted, 1958, 2v.; Gordon Press, 4v. 1977). $600
the set. ISBN: 884901719x.

First published 1892.

Includes biographical and critical notices of authors and
translators, historical articles on national and denominational
hymnody, breviaries, etc., the English language being the
keynote. Lists of contributors, MSS., abbreviations; indexes
of first lines and names. Still the standard work.

Class No: 264-068(038)

Biographies

[604]

HAYDEN, A.J. *and* NEWTON, R.F., *eds*. **British hymn
writers and composers:** a check-list, giving their dates and
places of birth and death. Guildford, Hymn Society of Great
Britain & Ireland, 1977. [94]p. £3. ISBN: 0950558907.

Lists *c.*2,500 names, A-Z, includes 'the names of those
who were born or died in a known year in the British Isles
and who wrote or shared in the making of a hymn in English
or a tune (*not* a harmonisation or a descant-setting only)
included in a major British hymn-book published between
January 1901 and December 1975' (*Compilers' Preface*). 35
hymn-books were consulted. *Class No:* 264-068(092)

Prayer Books

[605]

The Oxford book of prayer. Appleton, G., *ed*. Oxford,
Oxford University Press, 1985. 399p. £10. ISBN:
0192132229.

Aims to be a reasonably representative collection of
prayers. 7 sections: I. Prayers of adoration - II. Prayers from
the scriptures - III. Prayers of Christians: personal and
occasional - IV. Prayers of the Church - V. Prayer as
listening - VI. Prayer from other traditions of faith (Jewish,
Indian, etc., 10 in all) - VII. Prayer towards the unity of
mankind. Appendix: Notes on the development of
Eucharistic prayer. Index of authors and sources, p.391-396;
index of subjects, p.397-399. *Class No:* 264-1

Missionary Work (Christian Church)

Bibliographies

[606]

International review of mission. Geneva, Commission on
World Mission and Evangelism of the World Council of
Churches (previously London, International Missionary
Council). 1911-. v.1, no.1-. Quarterly. S.Fr.41.50. $28.90
pa. ISSN: 00208582.

V.78, no. 31, April 1989 includes a section of Book
reviews (p.226-236) and the regular 'Bibliography on
mission studies' on p.237-256 (*c.*360 entries). 11 sections: 1.
Bibliographies and studies; 2. Surveys of the Christian
situation; 3. History of theology of mission; 4. Religion,
religions and dialogue; 5. The context of mission -
environment and society; 6. The structure of mission -
churches and mission; 7. The practice of mission - forms of
ministry and witness; 8. Africa; 9. The Americas; 10. Asia;
11. Europe. *Class No:* 266(01)

Dictionaries

[607]

NEILL, S., *and others*, *eds*. **Concise dictionary of the
Christian world missions.** London, United Society for
Christian literature, Lutterworth Press, 1970. xv,682p.

Covers Protestant and Catholic missionary activities
throughout the world. About 250 contributors. Many of the
signed articles have brief bibliographies, Includes
biographies (*e.g.* Livingstone: 2½ cols.; 2 references),
countries (*e.g.* Pacific Islands; p.459-65; 20 lines of
bibliography), forms (*e.g.* missionary atlases, dictionaries
and journals), events, etc. Includes entries for 'Islam' and
'Buddhism'. Many cross-references. 'There is no
comparable tool available in the field' (*Library journal,*
v.96(13), July 1971, p.2296). *Class No:* 266(038)

Histories

[608]

LATOURETTE, K.J. **A History of the expansion of
Christianity.** London, Eyre & Spottiswoode, 1938-47.
7v.maps.

1. *The first five centuries, to 500 A.D.* 2. *Thousand years
of uncertainty, 500-1500 A.D.* 3. *Three centuries of
advance, 1500-1800 A.D.* 4. *The Great Century: Europe and
the U.S.* 5. *The Americas, Australasia and Africa.* 6. *North
Africa and Asia.* 7. *Advance through storm, 1914 and after.*

A work of encyclopaedic range, by a well-known authority
on Christian missions, likely to remain the standard history
for many years to come, on the missionary enterprise of
Christianity from its earliest times up to the present day.
Each volume has its own index, full bibliography, and maps.
'Latourette handles temperately, charitably and with
immense erudition every part of Christian expansion -
Roman Catholic, Protestant, and Orthodox' (Neill, S. *A
History of Christian missions* (1965), p.579).
Class No: 266(091)

Religious Associations & Societies

Bibliographies

[609]
CRUMB, L.N. **The Oxford movement and its leaders:** a bibliography of secondary and lesser primary sources. New York, American Theological Library Association and Scarecrow Press, 1988. 706p. $62.50. (*ATLA bibliography series, 24.*) ISBN: 0810821419.

Lists over 500 titles in chronological order to the end of 1987. Author and subject indexes. *Class No:* 267(01)

[610]
RIC: **Répertoire bibliographique des institutions de religions - croyances. Bibliographical repertory of Christian institutions.** Strasbourg, CERDIC Publications, 1966-. semi-annual. F.600. ISSN: 00799300.

*c.*3000 entries in each issue. Part 1: bibliographical references arranged by region or country, A-Z, subdivided by authors, A-Z; pt.2: General subject index in English,followed by French, German, Spanish and Italian terms. *Class No:* 267(01)

Yearbooks & Directories

[611]
NATIONAL CENTRE FOR CHRISTIAN COMMUNITIES AND NETWORKS. **Directory of Christian groups, communities and networks.** 2nd ed. London, the Centre, 1984. vi, 94p. £2.50.

First published in 1980, as *A directory of Christian communities and groups.*

A selective list of 384 groups, arranged A-Z by name in two sections - More recently established groups - Religious orders and congregations. Information includes name and address, telephone number, ecumenical date, numbers of staff and residents, brief description of denominational allegiance, aims, etc. Geographical index (by country, A-Z). Subject index (p.38-94). *Class No:* 267(058)

Benedictines

[612]
A **Benedictine bibliography:** an author-subject union list. Kapsner, O.L., *ed.* 2nd ed. Collegeville, MN., St. John's Abbey Press, at the American Benedictine Academy, 1962. 2v. ([11],664p.;[10],479p.).

First published in 1952. Compiled for the Library Science Section of the American Benedictine Academy.

V.1 has 13,428 unannotated items arranged A-Z; v.2 is a subject and author index. A 1st *Supplement* was published in 1982 (Collegeville, MN., Liturgical Press. 832p. $20. £29.95. ISBN 081461258x. *Class No:* 267BEN

Salvation Army

[613]
MOYLES, R.G. **A Bibliography of Salvation Army literature in English (1865-1987).** Lewiston, N.Y., E. Mellen, 1988. 209p. $49.95. (*Texts and studies in religion, 38.*) ISBN: 0889468273.

Aims to be comprehensive, including both primary and secondary sources (books, periodical articles, novels, plays, poetry) about the Salvation Army. Omits personal ephemera. 9 subject sections, 3 of which are subdivided by specific

....(contd.)
topic, and all subdivided chronologically. No annotations, but each section has a brief overview of the topic. Author index. *Class No:* 267.12

[614]
The **Salvation Army year book, 1994.** London, International Headquarters of the Salvation Army, 1993. [4], 300p. illus. Annual. ISBN: 0854126090. ISSN: 0080567x.

First published 1906.

Part 1 has 4 articles of special interest; pt.2. Facts and figures; pt.3 Reports, staff lists and addresses; 4. Rolls of Honour; Who's who in The Salvation Army. Index. *Class No:* 267.12

[615]
—The **History of the Salvation Army.** Sandall, R. *and* Wiggins, A.R. *and* Coutts, F. London, Nelson/Hodder & Stoughton, 1947-88. 7v. v.7: £12.95. ISBN: 0340390875, v.7.

A detailed official account of the organization. V.1-2, 4 carry the narrative from 1865 to 1904; v.3 is subtitled '1883-1953: Social work and reform'; v.5 covers 1904-1914; v.6: 1914-1946; and v.7: 1944-1977. Each v. has a bibliography and an analytical index. *Class No:* 267.12

Church History

[616]
CHADWICK, O. **The Pelican history of the Church.** Later volumes are titled *The Penguin history of the Church.* Harmondsworth, Middlesex, Penguin Books, 1964-93. 7v.

1. *The early Church,* by Henry Chadwick. 1968.

2. *Western Society and the Church in the Middle Ages,* by R.W. Southern. 1970.

3. *The Reformation,* by O. Chadwick. 1964.

4. *The Church and the Age of Reason, 1648-1789,* by G.R. Cragg. 1972.

5. *The Church in an age of Revolution, 1789 to the present day,* by A.R. Vidler, 1971.

6. *History of Christian missions,* by S. Neill. 1964.

7. *The Christian Church in the Cold War,* by O.Chadwick, 1993.

V.3 (463p.) has 3 parts: 1. The protest - 2. The Counter Reformation - 3. The Reformation and the life of the Church. 'Suggestions for further readings', p.466-9. V.7 is the final volume, dealing with organized Christianity since the early 1970s, from survival of the Church in Communist Poland to the decline of the mainstream churches in Western Europe. 'It will certainly be one of the largest and most comprehensive Church histories of our time' (*The Church times,* 20 March 1981, p.6). *Class No:* 27

[617]
Encyclopedia of the early Church. di Berardino, A., *ed.* New York, Oxford University Press, 1991. 2v.(1130p). 320 illus (some col). 44 maps. $175. ISBN: 0195208927.

First published in Italian in 1982.

Encyclopedic guide to the first seven or eight centuries of Christianity, from the time of Jesus to that of Bede (673-735) and John of Damascus (*c.*675-*c.*759). 167 contributors. Many entries carry substantial (and updated since 1982) bibliographies. Appended 3-column chronological table. 'This covers more topics, and, for topics common to both, generally treats them in greater depth than Ferguson's *Encyclopedia of early Christianity'*(*qv*). *Class No:* 27

[618]

Oxford history of the Christian Church. Chadwick, H. *and* Chadwick, O., *eds*. Oxford, Clarendon Press, 1976-.

To be in some 20 volumes, published over several years. 'It will certainly be one of the largest and most comprehensive church histories of our time' (*The Church times*, 20 March 1981, p.6.).

Intended to provide a full survey of the Christian Churches and their part in the religious heritage of humanity, particular attention being paid to the place of the churches in surrounding society, the institutions of church life and the manifestations of popular religion, the link with forms of national culture, and the intellectual tradition within and beyond Europe. So far published are: *A history of the churches in the United States and Canada,* by R. Handy (1976. 486p. maps. £40. ISBN 0198269102); *The Frankish church,* by J.M. Wallace-Hadrill (1983. 472p. map. £45. ISBN 0108269064); *Religion in England, 1688-1791,* by Gordon Rupp (1986. 596p. £45. ISBN 0198269188); *The Orthodox Church in the Byzantine Empire,* by J.M. Hussey (1986. 428p. £45. ISBN 0198269013); *The Popes and European revolution,* by Owen Chadwick (1981. 656p. £40. ISBN 0198269196); and *The Papal monarchy: the Western Church from 1050 to 1250,* by Colin Morris (1989. 688p. £55. ISBN 0198269072). *Class No:* 27

Bibliographies

[619]

BAKER, D., *ed.* **The Materials, sources and methods of ecclesiastical history.** Oxford, Blackwell, for the Ecclesiastical History Society, 1975. xii,370p. (*Studies in Church history, 11.*)

Papers read at the 12th Summer meeting and the 13th Winter meeting of the Society. Topics: particular documents or types of document; methodology and historiography: the contribution to church history of archaeological socio-linguistic and socio-cultural techniques. 3 major papers, including the presidential address, 'attempt to assess the place and role of the contemporary church historian, his problems and opportunities' (*Heythrop journal* v.19, 1978, p.205-6). *Class No:* 27(01)

[620]

Revue d'histoire ecclésiastique. Louvain, Université Catholique de Louvain, 1900-. v.1, no.1-. Quarterly. Fr.B.3500pa. $76pa. ISSN: 00352381.

V.84, no.1 Jan-March 1989, contains 4 articles; Comptes rendus ...; Chronique (country surveys); and Bibliographie (p.1-185 with 3014 items). *Class No:* 27(01)

Dictionaries

[621]

BRAUER, J.C. The Westminster dictionary of church history. Philadelphia, PA., Westminster Press, 1971. xii,887p. $27.50. ISBN: 0664212859.

'... purpose is to give an immediate, accurate introductory definition and explanation concerning the major men, events, facts, and movements in the history of Christianity' (*Preface*). Covers the early church (to A.D.600), the medieval church (600-1300), the Reformation church (1300-1700), and the modern church (1700 to present), giving greatest emphasis on the modern period. Over 140 contributors. Includes biographies. Entries vary in length from brief identifications to short articles with bibliographies

....(contd.)
(*e.g.* 'Canon law': 1½ cols.; 5 references; 'Cluny': 3 cols.; 5 references; 'Holy Roman Empire': 4¼ cols.; 7 references). Cross references. *Class No:* 27(038)

Maps & Atlases

[622]

Atlas of the Christian church. Chadwick, H., *ed.* 2nd rev. ed. Oxford, Phaidon, 1990. 240p. £19.50.

First published 1987.

In 6 parts: 1. The early church ... 6. The Christian church today. 302 illus (236 col.): 42 highly coloured maps: chronological table: gazetteer (tiny print). Bibliography, p.229-31. Index, p.237-40. *Class No:* 27(084.3)

Biographies

[623]

BARKER, W.P. Who's who in Church history. Grand Rapids, Mich., Baker Book House, 1977. 319p.

Biographies of over 1500 men and women who left an imprint on the history of the Christian Church. Excludes living persons. 'Provides a concise, inexpensive reference tool recommended for libraries for the churchman and layman'. (*American reference books annual*, 1979, item 1076). *Class No:* 27(092)

Scotland

[624]

Dictionary of Scottish church history and theology. Cameron, R., *ed.* London, Marshall Pickering, 1992. 800p. £35. ISBN: 0551022930.

Aims to provide a single source of reference for the history and theology of the Scottish church, with major coverage of biographies, missions, the development of Scottish theology, ecclesiastical history, art and architecture. *Class No:* 27(411)

[625]

DONALDSON, G. Scottish church history. Edinburgh, Scottish Academic Press, 1985. xii,250p. 25 illus. (incl. 14 pl.). £18.75. ISBN: 0707303613.

17 chapters dealing with various topics from the Dark Ages to the 20th century drawing on material ranging from archaeological and linguistic evidence, through record sources, to some lessons drawn from Inter-Church Discussions in which the author took part: 1. Scotland's earliest church buildings - 2. Bishops' Sees before the reign of David I ... 5. The Church Courts ... 8. The Parish Clergy and the Reformation ... 12. The foundations of Anglo-Scottish union ... 16. The emergence of schism in seventeenth-century Scotland - 17. Church and community. Index, p.239-245. *Class No:* 27(411)

USA

[626]

Religion and society in North America: an annotated bibliography. Brunkow, R. de V., *ed.* Santa Barbara, CA., ABC-Clio Press, 1983. xi,515p. $65; £58.25. (*Clio bibliographical series, no.12.*) ISBN: 0874360420.

4304 annotated entries selected from v.11-18 of *America: history and life,* arranged in 21 sections: 1. United States and

....*(contd.)*

Canada - 2. Americanizations of institutions - 3. Business (including Protestant ethic) - 4. Communal movements and utopian thought - 5. Ecumenism and intergroup relations - 6. Education - 7. Family - 8. Government and politics - 9. Health - 10. Labour - 11. Missionary impulse ... 21. Religious groups (37 + anti-religious movements). Annotations between 50 to 100 words in length. Subject index, p.323-501; author index, p.502-510; list of periodicals, p.511-513. *Class No:* 27(73)

Ancient Times

Manuscripts & Incunabula

[627]
BARDENHEWER, O. Geschichte der altkirchlichen Literatur. Darmstadt, Wissenschaftliche Buchgesellschaft, 1962. 5v.

V.1 covers the period from the end of the Apostolic era to the close of the 2nd century (xii, 633p.). V.5 (ix,423p.) includes a section on the oldest Armenian document. Arrangement is by authors, with biographical data and quotations. Thus 'Boethius' (p.250-64) is dealt with under five headings, each with a bibliography; 'De consolations philosphiae' has ¾p, listing editions, translations, commentaries and studies on it. Semi-analytical name index to each volume. *Class No:* 27"-"(093)

Tudor & Stuart Times

Bibliographies

[628]
BAINTON, R.H. *and* **GRITSCH, E.W. Bibliography of the Continental Reformation:** materials available in English. 2nd ed., rev. & enl. Hamden, CT., Archon Books: Shoe String Press, 1972. xix,220p. $24.50; £19.60. ISBN: 0208012192.

First published 1935.

About 3,000 references (Bibliographies - Encyclopedia articles - Collected essays on the Reformation - Sources in translation - General histories of the Reformation - Special phrases of Reformation history - Roman Catholic reform - Martin Luther ... Doctrinal settlements, including the Augsburg Confession ... Zwingli ... Anabaptists ... Calvin (p.163-84) ... The Reformation in France - The Italian Reformers ... Erasmus ... The Reformation in Norway and Sweden ... The Reformation in Hungary and Poland). Many periodical articles. No indexes. *Class No:* 27"1485-1760"(01)

[629]
COMMISSION INTERNATIONALE D'HISTOIRE ECCLÉSIASTIQUE COMPARÉE. Bibliographie de la Réforme, 1450-1648: ouvrages parus de 1940 a 1955. Leiden, E.J. Brill, 1958-. fasc.1-.

fasc.1: Allemagne, Pays-Bas. (1958. 2nd ed. 1961. Gld.32. $16. ISBN 9004002057).

fasc.2: Belgique, Suède, Norvege, Danemark, Ireland, États-Unis. (1960. Gld.37. $18.50. ISBN 9004002065).

fasc.3: Italie, Espagne, Portugal. (1961. Gld.41. $20.50. ISBN 9004026541).

fasc.4: France, Angleterre, Suisse. (1963. Reprint under consideration).

fasc.5: Pologne, Hongrie, Tchécoslovaquie, Finlande

....*(contd.)*

(1965. Gld.41. $20.50. ISBN 9004002081).

fasc.6: Autriche. (1967. Gld.18. $9. ISBN 9004002103).

fasc.7: Écosse. (1970. Gld.69. $34.50. ISBN 9004067639).

Sponsored by the International Commission of Ecclesiastical History, part of the International Committee of Historical Sciences. The section on Germany, by G. Franz, in fasc.1, comprises 1745 unannotated entries plus 4 indexes (1. Begriffe und Institutionen - 2. Deutsche Länder und Städte - 3. Ausland - 4. Biographien); 38 journals are cited. *Class No:* 27"1485-1760"(01)

[630]
—**COMMISSION INTERNATIONALE D'HISTOIRE ECCLÉSIASTIQUE COMPARÉE.** The Bibliography of the Reform, 1450-1648, relating to the United Kingdom and Ireland for the years 1955-70. Baker, D., *ed.* Oxford, Blackwell, 1975. [x], 242p.

Compiled for the British Sub-Commission of the Commision.

2579 entries for England and Wales, 498 entries for Scotland, and 260 for Ireland (plus interpolations) in A-Z author order in each case. Supplements the entries in fascs, 4 & 7 (above). *Class No:* 27"1485-1760"(01)

Religious Orders & Communities

[631]
CONSTABLE, G. Medieval monasticism: a select bibliography. Toronto, University of Toronto Press, 1976. [xxi], 171p. (*Toronto medieval bibliographies, 6.*)

1036 references. Parts: 1. Reference - 2. Monastic history - 3. Monastic life and institutions. Closely subdivided. Includes a section on women in religious life. 'A standard reference tool for the study of many aspects of medieval culture' (*Library journal,* v.101(12), 15 June, p.1406). *Class No:* 271

[632]
GREENE, J.P. Medieval monasteries. Leicester, Leicester University Press (distributed in USA & Canada by St. Martins Press, New York), 1992. xiii,255p. illus. £47.50 (Archaeology of medieval Britain)

Covers the application of new archaeological techniques, describing the methods and resulting information about monastic life in 9 chapters. Postscript: 'The future of monastic archaeology'. Glossary, p.233-5. Bibliography, p.236-44. Index, p.245-55. *Class No:* 271

Encyclopaedias & Dictionaries

[633]
KAPSNER, O.L. Catholic religious orders, listing conventional and full names in English, foreign languages and Latin; also, abbreviations, date and country of origin, and founders. 2nd ed., enl. Collegeville, Minn., St. John's Abbey Press, 1957. xxxviii, 594p.

First published 1948.

Sponsored by the Catholic Library Association and 'Primarily ... intended for the use of library cataloguers' (*Preface*). 1777 main entries; abbreviations are cross-referred to full names. Glossary, p.xiii-xxvi; list of authorities consulted, p.xxvii-xxxvii. *Class No:* 271(03)

Histories

Bibliographies

[634]

POLGÁR, L. **Bibliography of the history of the Society of Jesus** ... Rome, Jesuit Historical Institute; St. Louis, Mo., St. Louis University., 1967. 207p. (*Sources and studies for the history of the Jesuits, v.1.*)

963 entries, some with bibliographical notes. 3 parts: 1. History of the entire Order - 2. History of the Order in various regions - 3. Published sources (*e.g. Monumenta historica S.L.*). Author index. *Class No:* 271(091)(01)

Scotland

[635]

COWAN, I.B. *and* EASSON, D.E. **Medieval religious houses: Scotland,** with an appendix on the houses in the Isle of Man. 2nd ed. London & New York, Longman, 1976. xxviii, 246, [6]p. £15. ISBN: 0582120691.

First published 1957.

2nd ed. is the result of 'further research, particularly in the Vatican Archives, into the history of the Medieval Church in Scotland' (*Preface*). 10 Sections: Early Christian foundations - Houses of monks - Houses of regular canons - Houses of the mendicant orders - Houses of nuns - Houses of the military orders - Hospitals - Cathedral (secular; monastic) - Secular colleges - Academic secular colleges. Sources. p.32-45 (*c.* 400 items). Appendices: 1. The religious houses of the Isle of Man; 3. The incomes of the Scottish religious houses: sources. A closely documented study.

Class No: 271(411)

Eire

[636]

GWYNN, A. *and* HADCOCK, R.N. **Medieval religious houses: Ireland;** with an appendix to early sites. New ed. Blackrock, Co. Dublin., Irish Academic Press, 1988. 492p. map. £27.50. ISBN: 0716524163.

Identifies and locates over a thousand religious foundations from the 5th to the 17th century. 22 sections, plus 'Unclassified'. A detailed bibliography of books on Irish monasteries precedes. O.S. map of monastic Ireland. *Class No:* 271(417)

England & Wales

[637]

KNOWLES, D. *and* HADCOCK, R.N. **Medieval religious houses:** England and Wales. 2nd ed. London, Longmans, 1971. xv, 565p. tables, maps.

First published 1953 (a much-expanded revision of D. Knowles' *Religious houses of medieval England* (1940).

Arranged by orders (Benedictines, etc.), then A-Z by name of house. Details for each house: county; rank (*e.g.* abbey; priory); income in 1535; date of foundation and dissolution; parent house. Appendices: 1. Religious houses existing at periods before 1066 - 2. Tables showing increase and decrease in various orders. 'A very stimulating inventory to handle' (*Journal of ecclesiastical history,* v.23, no.3, July 1972, p.276-7). A basic list of religious and secular communities. *Class No:* 271(42)

[638]

—KNOWLES, D., *and others.* The Heads of religious houses: England and Wales, 940-1216. Cambridge, Cambridge University Press, 1972. xlvii, 278p.

Gives the names under the various orders (The Benedictine houses ... The Gilbertine canons and nuns), with dates of accession and death, the details of careers. List of MSS referred to, and list of printed books and authors cited precede. Appendix 3: List of pre-Conquest charters used. Index of heads; index of religious houses.

Modern religious houses are listed and described in P.F. Anson's *The religious orders and congregations of Great Britain and Ireland* (Worcester, Stanbrook Abbey Press, 1949, 423p.). *Class No:* 271(42)

England

[639]

KNOWLES, D. **The Monastic order in England:** a history of its development from the times of St. Dunstan to the Fourth Lateran Council, 940-1216. 2nd ed. Cambridge, Cambridge University Press, 1963. xxii, 780p. £55. ISBN: 0521054796.

First published 1940.

An account, historical rather than antiquarian, of English monastic life during an important period of religious history; based on contemporary sources, quoted in full where space allows. Detailed bibliography and notes. Continued in: *Class No:* 271(420)

[640]

—Monasticon Anglicanum. Dugdale W., Sir. London, Bested, 1817-30 (Reprinted Gregg International, 1970). 8v. £950. ISBN: 0576785377.

First published in 1693.

Assessed by J.L. Hobbs (*Local history and the library,* p.200) as an essential source book; it 'details the charters of foundation and other deeds of monasteries and religious houses, with a historical summary of each'. *Class No:* 271(420)

[641]

KNOWLES, D. **The Religious orders in England.** Cambridge, Cambridge University Press, 1948-59. 3v.

The old orders, 1216-1314. 2. The end of the Middle Ages. 3. The Tudor age. Includes the history of the Friars of England. V.3 has a bibliography and detailed index, plus valuable appendices (*e.g.* 2. Religious houses suppressed by Wolsey; 10. Regulars as bishops (a list). *Bare ruined choirs: the dissolution of the English monasteries,* by D. Knowles (C.U.P. 1976. illus. ISBN 0521707126) is an abridged and illustrated edition of v.3.

The standard work, making use of many published records of episcopal visitations. *Class No:* 271(420)

Persecutions

[642]

VEKENÉ, E. van der. **Bibliographie der Inquisition:** ein Versuch. Hildesheim, Olms, 1963. viii,323p.

1963 entries in all, arranged chronologically, 1483-1961, including periodical articles and sections/chapters of books (*e.g. Cambridge medieval history*). 26 European library locations. Index of journals. Sources, p.297-301. Index of authors and titles. *Class No:* 272

Patrology (Church Fathers)

Bibliographies

[643]
ALTANER, B. Patrology. Freiberg, Herder; Edinburgh & London, Nelson, 1960. xxiv,660p.

A translation by Hilda C. Graef, based on the 5th German edition of *Patrologie* (1958), revised and augumented.

Not a 'mere bibliography of patrology', but rather a literary history, with brief biographies and extensive bibliographical references. The section of St. Jerome, for example, covers p.462-77. Index. 'This indispensable manual for patristic studies is notable for the completeness of coverage and for its separate bibliographies for individual writers and subjects' (*Heythrop journal,* v.1(3), October 1960, p.359). *Class No:* 276(01)

[644]
Bibliographia patristica: Internationale patristische Bibliographie, 1956-. Berlin, de Gruyter, 1959-. v.1-. Annual. ISSN: 05232252.

V.28 lists 3172 articles, etc. (including reviews) on the early Church Fathers for 1983 (published 1987). Entries subdivided: 1. Generalia - 2. Novum Testamentum atque Apoocrypha - 3. Auctores - 4. Liturgica - 5. Iuridica, symbola - 6. Doctrina auctorum et historia dogmatum - 7. Gnostica - 8. Patrum exegesis Veteris et Novi Testamenti - 9. Recensiones. Author index. *Class No:* 276(01)

[645]
QUASTEN, J. Patrology. Westminster, MD, Newman Press; Utrecht, Spectrum, 1950-60 (reprinted 1983 by Christian Classics, Westminster, MD). 3v. in 4. $93.95. ISBN: 0870611410.

1: *The beginnings of Patristic literature.* (1950). 2: *The ante-Nicene literature after Irenaeus.* (1953). 3: *The golden age of Greek Patristic literature, from the Council of Nicaea to the Council of Chalcedon.* (1960). An important bibliography, designed to inform both specialist and student on the literature of the subject; the latter comprises (1) critical editions (2) translations, especially into English, and (3) articles and monographs. The fullest collection of Patristic texts is that produced by J.-P. Migne - *Patrologiae cursus completus* (Latin series. Paris, 1844-64, 221v. : Greek series (Greek text with Latin translation). Paris, 1857-66. 166v. Index. 1912. Index locupletissimus. 1928-45. 2v.; Latin texts of Greek authors. Paris, 1856-67. 81v. 'Its vast scope leaves it still unique and valuable, where other editions of special works do not exist' (*Encyclopaedia Britannica* (11th ed.), v.18p.426). *Class No:* 276(01)

[646]
—Corpus Christianorum. Series Latina. Turnhout, Brépols, 1954-.

To be published in 175v. and to cover all Patristic texts in Latin. *Class No:* 276(01)

Dictionaries

Greek

[647]
LAMPE, G.W.H., *ed.* **A Patristic Greek lexicon.** Oxford, Clarendon Press, 1961-67. (Reprinted in one volume by Oxford University Press, 1969). 5 fasc. in 1v. £125. ISBN: 019864213x.

A summary history of the use of all theologically

....(contd.)
important words by the Greek Christian writers of the period from the Apostolic Fathers to A.D.800. Each fascicule has *c.*300 pages. 'Basic and unique lexicon for patristic study' (*Religion & theology,* (1981), p.86). *Class No:* 276(038)=77

Christian Churches

---

[648]
The Good church guide, 1989. London, Marshall Pickering, 1988. x,527p. ISBN: 0551017694.

Brings together details of more than 2000 churches throughout the United Kingdon, collected by questionnaire. Arrangement is geographical: England (subdivided by county, A-Z; London; Northern Ireland; Scotland; Wales; Isle of Man; Channel Islands; English-speaking churches abroad (by country, A-Z). Information given includes church name, denomination, address, historical interest, membership, worship, and symbols showing services conducted. *Class No:* 28

Dictionaries

[649]
BURGESS, S.M., *and others, eds.* **Dictionary of Pentecostal and charismatic movements.** Grand Rapids, MI., Zondervan, 1989. 914p. illus. $29.95. ISBN: 0310441005.

Some 800 entries by 66 contributors focusing on movements in North America and, to some extent, in Europe. Includes biographies of people and descriptions of specific denominations with over 2000 members. Lengthy articles are prefaced by outlines of the text. All entries have bibliographies. Cross-references, but no index. *c.*200 black-and-white photographs, mainly portraits. '... successful both as a reference source ... and as a broadly based introduction to a relgious movement ...' (*Reference books bulletin,* September 1989, v.86(1), p.102-3). *Class No:* 28(038)

Great Britain

[650]
UK Christian handbook, 1994/95. Bromley, Kent, Christian Research Association, l993. 900p. tables, maps. £29.99. ISSN: 09476971.

First published 1964. Annual.

Sections on: Accommodation - Bookshops - Churches - Education - Leadership - Media - Overseas - Services - other useful addresses. Personnel index (p.643-695). Location index (p.697-736). Organization index (p.737-807). *Class No:* 28(410)

Scotland

[651]
BURLEIGH, J.H.S. A Church history of Scotland. London, Oxford University Press, 1960. x,456p. maps.

A survey from the coming of Christianity down to 1957. Addressed to the general reader and not to the specialist (*Preface*). The selective bibliography (p.423-4) is a guide to the more important literature available for consultation.

....*(contd.)*

Includes a very useful diagram showing the Church's divisions and reunions, 1690-1929. Detailed index, p.427-456. *Class No:* 28(411)

Ireland

[652]

KENNEY, J.F. The Sources for the early history of Ireland: an introduction and guide. v.1.$aEcclesiastical. New York, Columbia University Press, 1929. (Reprinted New York, Octagon, 1966). xvi, 807p. maps. $57.50. ISBN: 0374945608.

659 numbered, annotated items in 8 chapters, arranged chronologically up to the 12th century. Many footnotes. References to manuscripts and to printed editions and commentaries, plus notes. General bibliography, p.91-109. Analytical index. No more published. *Class No:* 28(415)

England

Histories

[653]

OWEN, D.M. 'What to read in English religious history'. In *The local historian,* v.16(3), August 1984, p.151-155.

Lists 50 items, and follows an earlier bibliography by the author in *The local historian* (v.8(7), 1969). Author is Keeper of the Archives at the Library of the University of Cambridge. *Class No:* 28(420)(091)

America—North & Central

Encyclopaedias

[654]

LIPPY, C.H. *and* **WILLIAMS, P.W.,** *eds.* **Encyclopedia of the American religious experience:** studies of traditions and movements. New York, Macmillan/Charles Scribner's Sons, 1988. 3v. (xvli, 1872p.). $225 the set. ISBN: 0684180626.

105 commissioned essays on topics dealing with all aspects of the religious experience in the US (and to a limited extent in Canada), both historical and current, and including all denominations, faiths and sects. Arranged in 9 sections organized by broad topic and theme. Essays are lengthy, averaging 12-pages long and include excellent bibliographies. Good cross-references. Exhaustive index. '... valuable as a reference source for information about religious leaders, churches and sects.' (*Reference books bulletin,* 15 May 1988, p.1579-80). 'An outstanding achievement ... will become the standard reference tool in American religion'. (*Choice,* v.25(9), May 1988, p.1380). *Class No:* 28(71/73)(031)

Histories

[655]

HANDY, R. A History of the churches in the United States and Canada. Oxford, Clarendon Press, 1976. ix, [1], [1], 471p. maps. £45. (*Oxford history of the Christian Church.*) ISBN: 0198269102.

12 chapters (2. Conflict and diversity in Colonial Christianity (1650-1720) - 3. The era of the Great Awakening in Colonial America ... 10. Roman Catholic, Lutheran, Eastern Orthodox and other churches in America

....*(contd.)*

(1860-1920) - 11. Alternative visions of a Christian Canada (1867-1925) - 12. North American churches and the decline of Christendom (with 49 footnotes). Bibliography, p.429-49 (running commentary). Detailed index, p.455-71. *Class No:* 28(71/73)(091)

USA

[656]

MELTON, J.G. *and* **GEISENDORFER, J.V. Religious bodies in the United States.** 2nd ed. New York, Garland, 1992. 312p. $55. (*Religious information systems series, v.1).*.) ISBN: 081530806x.

First published in 1977 as *A Directory of religious bodies...*

Compiled from the files of the Institute for the Study of American Religion. Lists groups active in the Summer of 1991, giving addresses and major publications. A-Z index includes alternative names. *Class No:* 28(73)

Biographies

[657]

BOWDEN, H.W. Dictionary of American religious biography. 2nd ed, rev & enl. Westport, CT., Greenwood Press, 1993. 720p. $75. ISBN: 0313278253.

First published in 1977.

550 biographies of deceased persons 'drawn from three centuries of American religious life, each profile containing capsule summary of figure's life, discussion of historical content of contribution, bibliography of works by and about. Appended bibliographies of material on and by the biographee. 'An excellent acquisition for reference collections' (*Library journal,* v.102(10), 15 May 1977, p.1167.) of the first edition. *Class No:* 28(73)(092)

[658]

—Who's who in religion. 3rd ed. Chicago, Ill., Marquis Who's Who Inc., 1985. 439p. $99.50.

Instead of increasing the size for a 3rd ed. a more rigorous selection criteria has been used (2nd ed. covered 18,000 persons). New ed. includes 7000, only those who have 'attained conspicuous achievement' or who hold significant positions in major church or religious organizations. Brief entries indicate name, title, denomination, birthdate, parentage, marriage, children, education and ceritification, professional career, related activities, writings, political affiliations, etc. Also home and office address.

A 4th ed. for 1992-93 was issued in 1992 (768p. $129. ISBN 0837916046). *Class No:* 28(73)(092)

[659]

MELTON, J.G. Biographical dictionary of American cults and sect leaders. New York, Garland, 1986. xii,354p. $39.95. (*Garland reference library of social science, 212.*) ISBN: 0824090373.

Sketches of over 200 individuals, mainly 19th and 20th century (deceased before 1983) who were founders or outstanding leaders of religious group that can be defined as a cult or sect. Well-written entries of about 1½ pages, summarising the person's life and career and including a bibliography of works by and about him/her. General index, and list of leaders by religions, family traditions, birthplace and religious background. *Class No:* 28(73)(092)

Eastern Churches

[660]

The Coptic encyclopedia. Atiya, A.S., *ed. in chief.* New York, Macmillan, 1991. 8v.(2372+371p). $800. ISBN: 002897025x.

2500 signed entries by over 299 contributors. V.1 has a general bibliography. V.8 includes 12 maps and lengthy appendix on the Coptic language. '... its unique focus and depth will fill a real lacuna to reference publishing.'(*College & research libraries*, v.33(5),September 1992, p.418). *Class No:* 281

[661]

KING, A.A. The Rites of Eastern Christendom. London, Burns & Oates, 1950. 2v. illus., map.

Intended as a manual for those (other than the expert liturgical scholar) who want information on the rites of the Eastern Orthodox Church, including the separated Churches. Historical, ritual and ceremonial detail is given, with liturgical tests, bibliography and index to each volume. *Class No:* 281

[662]

—WARE, T. The Orthodox Church. Harmondsworth, Mddx, Penguin Books, 1963 (latest of many reprints with revisions, 1983). 352p. illus. map. £3.50; $4.95. ISBN: 0140205926.

16 chapters on history, faith and worship. 'Further reading', p.335-340. Index, p.341-352. 'Clear and factual account by a convert' (*Religion and theology 4.* (S.C.M. Press, 1979, p.33). *Class No:* 281(035)

Histories

[663]

ELLIS, J. The Russian Orthodox Church: a contemporary history. London, Croom Helm, 1986. [4],531p. £27.50. (*Keston book, 22.*) ISBN: 0709915675.

13 chapters in 2 parts: part 1 (1. Churches and dioceses - 2. Parish life - 3. The clergy - 4. Theological education - 5. Monasticism - 6. Publications - 7. The laity - 8. The episcopate - 9. Church and state relations). Part 2 (Prologue - 10. The rise of orthodox dissent: up to 1974 - 11. The growth of orthodox dissent, 1974-6 - 12. The flowering of orthodox dissent, 1976-9 - 13. The repression of orthodox dissent, 1976-80. Concluding summary: up to 1985). Notes, p.455-507, by chapter. Bibliography, p.508-539, of books, periodicals, samizdat (selected), legislation, and archives. Analytical index, p.520-531. A new ed. was published by Routledge in 1990. (544p. ISBN 0415034671). *Class No:* 281(091)

Roman Catholic

[664]

Catholic almanac, 1971-. Huntington, Indiana, Our Sunday Visitor, 1969-. Annual. ISBN: 0879732679. ISSN: 00691208.

Previously as *National Catholic almanac* (1904-1970).

Although primarily for the US, it covers the Catholic church worldwide. Includes a chronology and glossary, list of periodicals and encyclicals, statistics, and patron saints, popes, etc. Extensive index precedes. *Class No:* 282

[665]

DEEDY, J. The Catholic fact book. T. More, 1986. 412p. $23.95. ISBN: 0883471868.

Brings together facts from several annual editions of the *Catholic almanac*(formerly *National Catholic almanac* 1904-. Huntingdon, IN, Our Sunday Visitor Inc). 'A potpourri of information about the Roman Catholic Church arranged under various headings, according to history, tenets, saints, famous Catholics and several miscellanies' (*Choice* v.24(5) January 1987, p.739). *Class No:* 282

Bibliographies

[666]

Catholic periodical and literature index. Haverford, Pa., Catholic Library Association, 1930-. 6pa; cumulated 2-yearly. ISSN: 00088285.

Takes over from *Catholic periodical index* (covering 1930-67) and the *Guide to Catholic literature* (covering 1888-1940).

Author and subject indexes to *c.*160 Catholic periodicals, mostly American. Indexes also book and film reviews, conciliar and papal documents. *Class No:* 282(01)

[667]

McCABE, J.P. Critical guide to Catholic reference books. 3rd ed. Englewood, Co., Libraries Unlimited, 1989. xiv,323p. $47.00. (*Research studies in library science, no.20.*) ISBN: 0872876217.

First published 1971; 2nd ed. 1980.

Over 1500 main entries for publications on the teaching, history and mission of the Roman Catholic Church. 5 chapters, each closely subdivided: General; Theology; Humanities; Social science; History. Most entries are annotated, all are in European languages and available in North America. '...continues to be a mainstay for libraries supporting scholarly research on Catholicism' (*Reference books bulletin*, 1989-1990, p.37). *Class No:* 282(01)

[668]

MUSTO, R.G. The Peace tradition of the Catholic Church: an annotated bibliography. New York, Garland, 1987. 590p. $67. (*Garland reference library of social science, v.339.*) ISBN: 0824088841.

The 2nd vol. of the author's 'three-part study that hopes to document the history of the peace tradition in the Roman Catholic Church from the Gospels to the twentieth century' (*Preface*). The 1st part was *The Catholic peace tradition* (Orbis, 1986), a narrative history. The 3rd part is to be an anthology of texts.

1485 entries, mostly annotated, the annotations varying in length from a few sentences to several paragraphs. Covers the tradition from biblical concepts of peace and peacemaking from the Gospels and early church, the Middle Ages, the Renaissance, the age of colonization, and the modern period into the era of Vatican II in Europe, the US and the Third World. Includes items published through November 1986 in English, French, German, Italian, Spanish, Portuguese and Latin. Classified arrangement. Author, personal name, and title indexes. 'Not another source has the scope and depth of Musto's work' (*R.Q.*, v.27(4), Summer 1988, p.576). *Class No:* 282(01)

Encyclopaedias

[669]
MEAGHER, P.K., *ed.* **Encyclopedic dictionary of religion.**
Palatine, Ill., Corpus Publications, 1978. 3v. $69.95 the set.
ISBN: 0960257233.

Over 500 contributors. About 25,000 signed articles, primarily concerning Roman Catholicism, but also covering Protestant denominations, Judaism, philosophy, psychology, sociology, archaeology. 'Will be one of the most comprehensive and up-to-date references in the field of religious knowledge. It should be particularly useful for those libraries that cannot afford the *New Catholic encyclopedia* (1967)' (*RSR,* v.6(2), April/June 1978, p.18).
Class No: 282(031)

[670]
New Catholic encyclopedia: an international work of reference on the teachings, history, organization and activities of the Catholic Church, and on all institutions, religions, philosophies, and scientific and cultural developments affecting the Catholic Church from its beginning to the present. Catholic University of America, editorial staff. New York, McGraw-Hill, 1967; supplements, 1974-79 (Reprinted Palatine, Ill., Publishers Guild, 1981). 15v. (15,350p.), illus., maps. Plus 3 supplementary vols. $875 for 18v. ISBN: 007010235x.

About 17,000 articles by *c.*4,800 contributors; 7,400 illus. (32 col.pl.) and 300 maps. V.15 is an index of 300,000 entries (including entries for maps and illus.). All articles carry select bibliographies, some briefly annotated. 'St. Anselm of Canterbury': 51/3 cols,; 2 illus.; 15 lines of bibliography. Wide coverage (*e.g.* 'Psychiatry': 13 cols.; 'Zionism': 3 cols.; 'Hungarian art': 6p.; 20 lines of bibliography). Some unusual articles (*e.g.* 'Translation literature, Greek and Arabic'). No biographies of living persons. Especially valuable on scholastic philosophy and theological writers. Excellently produced and illustrated. V.16-18 update and supplement. *Class No:* 282(031)

[671]
—The Catholic encyclopedia. New York, Encyclopedia Press, 1907-22; Gilmore Society, 1950-59. 18v.

Superseded by the above, but this title is still of value to the student of the Middle Ages as well as Catholic doctrine and history. *Class No:* 282(031)

[672]
—CLIFTON, C.S. Encyclopedia of heresies and heretics. Santa Barbara, CA, ABC-Clio, 1992. 156p. $50. ISBN: 0874366003.

Focuses on Christian heretics from the beginnings of the Church to the Reformation, distinguishing between heretics and reformers. Includes many individuals not in *New Catholic encyclopedia* (*qv*), which it supplements. Literate articles. Biographies. Ample illustrations. Cross-references. *Class No:* 272

[673]
Sacramentum mundi: an encyclopaedia of theology. Rahner, K., *ed. and others.* New York, Herder & Herder; London, Burns & Oates, 1968-70. 6v.

About 1000 signed articles, A-Z, on the central themes of modern religious thought, by over 600 specialists. Bibliographies are appended (*e.g.* 'Zionism': v.6, p.393-6; ½ col. of bibliography; 'Islam;: v.3, p.165-70, 5 sections; ½ col. of bibliography). Short general index in v.6. An international theological dictionary, published in English,

....(contd.)
Dutch, French, German, Italian and Spanish. A significant contribution to the field of Roman Catholic lexicography.
Class No: 282(031)

[674]
—Encyclopedia of theology: the concise '*Sacramentum mundi*'. Rahner, K., *ed.* London, Burns & Oates, 1975. xiv, 1850p. £35. ISBN: 0860120066.

Contains revised versions of the major articles on theology, Biblical science and related topics from *Sacramentum mundi,* together with a large number of articles from the major German works, *Lexikon für Theologie und Kirche* and *Theologisches Taschenlexikon,* 'and entirely new articles on topics of major importance written for the occasion ...' (*Prefatory note*). Nearly 500 signed articles, 'Afterlife' ... 'Worship'. Biblical and other references in text. Non-Biblical sources listed, p.xiii-xiv. 'Recommended to all who wish to have a handy compendium of theology on their desks' (*Heythrop journal,* v.17, 1976, p.240).
Class No: 282(031)

Dictionaries

[675]
HARDON, J.A., *S.J.* **Modern Catholic dictionary.** London, Robert Hale, 1981. xiii, 619p. £12.50. ISBN: 0709193815.

An abbreviated ed., *Pocket Catholic dictionary* was issued in 1985 by Doubleday Image. (ISBN 038523281).

In two parts; part 1 is a dictionary of 5000 terms, directly or indirectly dealing with Catholic faith, worship, morals, history, canon law, and spirituality. The terms, even those from psychology and the social sciences, are described from the Roman Catholic point of view. Includes biographies, some 50 organizations and societies. Cross-references. Entries vary in length from 2-3 lines to a column or more. Part 2 is an appendix, containing the Credo of the People of God; a listing of popes from Peter to John Paul II; updated ecclesiastical calendars of both the Roman and Byzantine rites with saints for each day of the year; and a listing of religious communities and secular institutes in the United States and Canada. *Class No:* 282(038)

Quotations

[676]
CHAPIN, J., *ed.* **The Book of Catholic quotations,** compiled from approved sources, ancient, medieval and modern. London, J. Calder, 1957. xi, 1073, [1]p. £6.95. ISBN: 0714501360.

More than 10,400 quotations, arranged alphabetically by subject. Quotations, p.1-932; detailed analytical index of subjects, p.933-1056; index of sources, p.1057-73; corrigenda appended. *Class No:* 282(082.2)

Histories

[677]
HOLMES, J.D. *and* **BICKERS, B.W. A Short history of the Catholic Church.** Tunbridge Wells, Kent, Burns & Oates, 1983. 315p. £6.95. ISBN: 0860121267.

Replaces a book with the same title by Philip Hughes first published in 1964.

A one-volume history of the church from the origins of the church in the New Testament to the accession of Pope John Paul II in 1978. Divided into 7 broad chapters (1. The

....(contd.)

origins and early history of the Christian church to 461-2; 2. The development of the Western church and its final separation from the East, 461-1198; 3. Papalism and Conciliarism, 1198-1455; 4. The Protestant Reformation and the progress of Catholic reform, 1455-1648; 5. The age of rationalism and absolutism, 1648-1789; 6. The church, revolution and reaction, 1789-1914; 7. The church and the modern world, 1914-1978). There follows a table of major events in church history; a table of Popes and their reigns; notes for further reading (p.300-306); and a name index (p.307-315). *Class No:* 282(091)

Biographies

[678]

DELANEY, J.J. *and* **TOBIN, J.E. Dictionary of Catholic biography.** Garden City, N.Y., Doubleday, 1961; London, Hale, 1962. xi, 1245p.

Biographies of *c.*13,000 leading Roman Catholics (churchmen and laymen), from the founding of the Church to the present day. Bibliographies appended; numerous cross-references. Appendices: the saints as patrons of vocations; the saints as patrons of places; symbols of the saints in art; 12-page chart correlating papal and secular reigns. *Class No:* 282(092)

Great Britain

[679]

GILLOW, J. A Literary and biographical history, or bibliographical dictionary, of the English Catholics, from the breach with Rome, in 1534, to the present time. London, Burns & Oates, 1885-1902. Reprinted New York, Franklin, 1961. 5v.

'The object ... is to present ... a concise record of the literary efforts, educational struggles and the sufferings for religion's sake of the Catholics in England down to the present time'. (*Preface,* v.1). A good example of biobibliography. Following the biographical sketch are given brief references to biographical dictionaries, histories, etc. for further material and then a full numbered list of works (*c.*15,000 items). *Index to Gillow's bibliographical dictionary of the English Catholics,* edited and published by J. Bevan, Ross-on-Wye, was issued in 1985 (£20. ISBN 0951090801). *Class No:* 282(410)

[680]

—BOSSY, J. The English Catholic community, 1570-1850. London, Darton, Longman & Todd, 1975 (Reprinted 1979). 464p. tables, maps. £6.95. ISBN: 0232514402.

In 4 parts, with footnoted chapters (*e.g.* 10: Missionary questions, p.205-49; 103 footnotes). Sources, p.432-4. Detailed, non-analytical index. *Class No:* 282(410)

Scotland

[681]

The Catholic directory for Scotland, 1991. Glasgow, John S. Burns & Sons, 1991. 535p. £16.50. ISSN: 03065677.

First published 1829. Annual.

Contents: Liturgical calendar - The hierarchy - The Church of Scotland - The dioceses in Scotland - The clergy of Scotland - Catholic societies and institutions - Diocesan statistics. Index of places. *Class No:* 282(411)

Ireland

[682]

Irish Catholic directory, 1992. Dublin, Veritas Publications for the Hierarchy, 1992. Annual. 376p., excluding diary. £24.50. ISSN: 00750735.

First published 1838.

Contents: Hierarchy of Ireland - Episcopal commissions and advisory bodies - Dioceses of Ireland - Religious orders and congregations - Organizations and societies - Other Christian churches in Ireland - Religious periodicals - Clergy of Ireland, alphabetical list - Main towns index - Parish index - General index. *Class No:* 282(415)

England & Wales

[683]

The Catholic directory of England and Wales for ... 1993. 154th year of issue. Manchester, Gabriel Communications, 1993. 832p. illus., tables. £19. ISBN: 0949005819. ISSN: 00691224.

First published 1838.

Chief sections: Dioceses and provinces (p.113-537) ... Priests of England and Wales (p.652-788) ... Statistical section. General index and index of places. *Class No:* 282(42)

USA

[684]

DELANEY, J.J. Dictionary of American Catholic biography. Garden City, New York, Doubleday, 1984. 624p. $24.95. ISBN: 0385178786.

A compendium of factual information about 1500 Roman Catholic lay people and clergy who have made a 'significant' contribution to the Church and nation. All entrants are deceased and mainly clergy. Arranged A-Z by name, with some cross-references. Succinct entries. '... unique biographical source'. (*Library journal,* 15th November 1984, p.2142). *Class No:* 282(73)

[685]

ELLIS, J.T. *and* **TRISCO, R. A Guide to American Catholic history.** 2nd rev. ed. Santa Barbara, CA., ABC-Clio Press, 1982. xiii,265p. $31. ISBN: 0874363187.

First published 1959.

1258 annotated entries arranged in 9 sections: 1. Guides - 2. General works - 3. Studies in diocesan, sectional, and parish history - 4. Biographies, correspondence, and memoirs - 5. Religious communities - 6. Education - 7. Special studies - 8. Periodicals - 9. Historical societies. Index, p.205-265. Omits section on manuscript repositories, which was in 1st ed. Heavily clerical. '... an excellent compilation which will prove invaluable to scholars' (*Bulletin of ABTAPL,* no.28, November 1983, p.11). *Class No:* 282(73)

The Popes

Biographies

[686]

KELLY, J.N.D. The Oxford dictionary of Popes. Oxford, Oxford University Press, 1986. xiii,347p. £12.95. ISBN: 0192139649.

'A Papal who's who' (*Preface*) precedes short biographies of 266 officially recognised Popes and 39 antipopes,

....(contd.)
arranged in chronological order (St. Peter ... John Paul II). Entries include birth and death dates, details of family background, pre-Papal career and activities in office, plus bibliographical sources. There is an appendix on Pope Joan. Extensive index, p.331-347, has cross-reference. 'The entries themselves are little gems of concise and pungent scholarship' (*British book news,* May 1986, p.283-4). *Class No:* 282POP(092)

[687]
—JOHN, E., *ed.* The Popes: a concise biographical history. London, Burns & Oates, 1964. 496p. illus. (incl. col.pl.).
Gives precise information on each papal reign, from St. Peter to Paul VI. 9 contributors. 130 good black-and-white illus., plus 16 col.plates. Annotated list of books for further reading, p.481-482. Index, p.483-496. *Class No:* 282POP(092)

[688]
—MANN, H.K. The Lives of the Popes in the early Middle Ages. London, Kegan Paul, 1903-32. 18v. in 19.
Deals with the period 590-1305, but the work is 'disfigured by complete lack of impartiality' (Sonnenschein, W.S. *The best books.* 3rd ed., 1910. v.1, p.252). *Class No:* 282POP(092)

[689]
—PASTOR, Freiherr von L. The History of the Popes, from the close of the Middle Ages. London, Hodges; Kegan Paul; Routledge & Kegan Paul, 1891-1953. 40v.
Translated from the German and edited by F.I. Autrobus and others.
A monumental history, drawn from the secret archives of the Vatican and other original sources. Commences with Clement V (1305-14); v.40 deals with Pius VI (1775-99). 2v. are devoted to some popes (*e.g.* Leo X, Paul III, Clement VIII, Pius VI). Each volume carries a list of most cited works; each is heavily footnoted and has an index of names, 'Unlikely ever to be superseded' (John E. *The Popes,* p.482). *Class No:* 282POP(092)

Protestant

[690]
The Church of England year book, 1993. The official year book of the General Synod of the Church of England. 109th ed. London, Church House Publishing, 1993. Annual. xxxix, 445p. £18. ISBN: 0715180827. ISSN: 00693987.
8 parts. 1. Central structure - 2. Dioceses- 3. General - 4. Organizations - 5. Anglican communion - 6. Ecumenical - 7. Who's who - 8. Index. *Class No:* 283/289

Bibliographies

[691]
Christian periodical index: an index to subjects and authors and to book reviews and media reviews, 1959-. West Seneca, NY., Cedarville, Ohio, Association of Christian Librarians Inc., 1959-. 3 pa.including annual. $95 pa. ISSN: 00693871.
Indexes 85 conservative evangelical periodicals. Includes a periodical index and an index to reviews. *Class No:* 283/289(01)

Anglican

Histories

[692]
WELSBY, P.A. A History of the Church of England, 1945-1980. Oxford, Oxford University Press, 1984. xii, 300p. £27.50. ISBN: 0192132318.
A comparatively brief account of the many changes in the Church's structure and attitude to doctrine. Contents: Part 1: 1945-1959 (Reconstruction - Putting the house in order - Theology, worship, and morals - Church relations); part 2: The sixties (The bewilderment of the sixties - Theological and moral radicalism - Parishes, priests, and people - Liturgies, music, and cathedrals - The continuing search for unity); part 3: The seventies (Church and nation - Government by Synod - Church and State - Doctrine, worship, and the life of the spirit - Ministry and mission - One Church, one mission, one world); Epilogue. Bibliography (p.293-296) arranged in 3 parts. Index (p.297-300). *Class No:* 283(091)

Great Britain

[693]
Crockford's clerical directory, 1993/94: a directory of the clergy of the Church of England, the Church in Wales, the Scottish Episcopal Church, the Church of Ireland. 93rd issue. London, Church House Publishing, 1993 (early editions published by Oxford University Press), for the Church Commissioners for England and the Central Board of Finance of the Church of England. 1084p. (adverts not separately numbered). maps. £39. ISBN: 0715180800.
First published 1858. Preceded by *Clerical guide,* 1817-36, and *Clergy list* (1840?-).
Biographical notes under clergy (*c.*22,000), A-Z, p.1-778. Index of English benefices and churches; Index of Welsh benefices; of Scottish incumbencies; Irish benefices. Index of cathedrals and collegiate churches. Service, prison and hospital chaplains. Bishops of Anglican dioceses overseas. Addresses of provincial offices, Episcopal succession lists. An essential source on all matters relating to Anglican clergy; primarily concerned with those ordained in the British Isles. *Class No:* 283(410)

[694]
—Guide to bishops' registers of England and Wales: a survey from the Middle Ages to the abolition of episcopy in 1646. Smith, D.M., *ed.* London, Royal Historical Society, 1981. 448p. £15. *Class No:* 283(410)(058)

[695]
Directory of orthodox parishes and clergy in the British Isles. Welshpool, Powys, Stylite Publishing Ltd. and the Orthodox Fellowship of St. John the Baptist, 1984. 68p. maps. £2.50. ISBN: 0947805087.
Arranged A-Z by town/city and jurisdiction, listing names and addresses of parish/church/community; names and addresses of clergy; names and addresses of persons to contact for details of services (times of services/languages/additional information). Index to clergy; index to towns/cities. *Class No:* 283(410)

England & Wales

[696]

ANSTRUTHER, G. The Seminary priests: a dictionary of the secular clergy of England and Wales, 1558-1850. Greenwood, SC., Attic Press, 1968-77. 4v. $18.50 each vol. ISBN: 0879210591, v.1; 0855970820, v.2; 0855971169, v.3; 0855971185, v.4.

Contents: v.1 Elizabethan, 1558-1608 (1968. 422p.); 2. 1603-59 (1975. 424p.); 3. 1660-1705 (1976. 318p.); 4. 1716-1800 (1977. 368p.). *Class No:* 283(42)

Histories

[697]

STEPHENS, W.R.W. *and* **HUNT, W.,** *eds.* **A History of the English Church.** London, Macmillan Press, 1899-1910 (and reprints). 8v. in 9. maps.

The standard history, based on a careful study of original authorities, and the best ancient and modern writers, in moderate-sized volumes. Goes beyond purely ecclesiastical history (*e.g.* v.2, chapter 16: 'Popular religion, learning and art'). Each volume is by a specialist in the period covered, with its own analytical index, chronological tables and maps. A list of sources is appended to each chapter. *Class No:* 283(42)(091)

England

Biographies

[698]

LE NEVE, J. Fasti Ecclesiae Anglicanae, 1066-1300. London, University of London, Institute of Historical Research, Athlone Press, 1968-77. 3v.

V.1: St. Paul's, London, 1066-1300. (1968. xx,115p.). v.2: Monastic cathedrals. (1971. 136p.). v.3: Lincoln. (1977). *Class No:* 283(420)(092)

[699]

—LE NEVE, J. Fasti Ecclesiae Anglicanae, 1300-1541. New and expanded ed. London, University of London, Institute of Historical Research, Athlone Press, 1962-67. 12v.

First published 1716; rev.ed. by T.D. Hardy (covering the period from the earliest times to *c.*1850, 1854 (3v.).

A diocese-by-diocese list of every known bishop, canon and dignitary for the periods covered. 1. *Lincoln diocese* 2. *Hereford diocese* - 3. *Salisbury diocese* - 4. *Monastic cathedrals (Southern Province)* - 5. *St. Paul's London,* - 6. *Monastic Cathedrals (Northern Province: York, Carlisle, Durham* - 7. *Chichester diocese* - 8. *Bath and Wells diocese* - 9. *Exeter diocese* - 10. *Coventry and Lichfield diocese* - 11. *The Welsh dioceses* - 12. *Introduction, errata and index.* V.3, *Salisbury diocese* (x,117p.) has a list of references (words in print; manuscript) preceding the calendar (bishops, deans, subdeans, archdeacons, percentors, chancellors, treasurers, prebendaries, with dates of collation, election and death, and sometimes fuller notes; detailed indexes of persons and places. *Class No:* 283(420)(092)

[700]

—LE NEVE, J. Fasti Ecclesiae Anglicanae, 1541-1857. London, University of London, Institute of Historical Research, Athlone Press, 1969-.

1. St. Paul's, London, 1541-1857 (1968) - 2. Chichester diocese (1971) - 3. Canterbury, Rochester and Winchester

....(contd.)

diocese (1974) - 4. York diocese. Rev. ed. (1975) - 5. Bath and Wells diocese (1979) - 6. Salisbury diocese (1986). *Class No:* 283(420)(092)

[701]

—STUBBS, W. Registrum sacrum Anglicanum: an attempt to exhibit the course of episcopal succession in England from the records and chronicles of the Church. 2nd ed., with an appendix of Indian, Colonial and missionary consecrations; collected and arranged by E.E. Holmes. Oxford, Clarendon Press, 1897. xvi,248p. *Class No:* 283(420)(092)

Official Records

[702]

Councils and synods, with other documents relating to the English Church. Oxford, Oxford University Press, 1964-1981. 2v. in 3. (1151p.1200p.). ISBN: 0198223943, v.2.

Planned under the general editorship of F.W. Powicke, in continuation of A.W. Haddan and W. Stubbs' *Councils and ecclesiastical documents of Great Britain and Ireland* (Oxford, Clarendon Press, 1969-78. 3v.).

V.1: *AD871-1204,* ed. by D. Whitelock and others (1981) is in 2v.; pt.1. 871-1066; pt.2. 1066-1204. V.2: *AD1205-1313,* ed. by Sir. F.M. Powicke and C.R. Cheney (1964) is in 2 parts. Pt.1 covers AD1205-1265; pt.2 the later years and including an index of manuscripts and a general analytical index. *Class No:* 283(420)(093.2)

[703]

—PURVIS, Canon J.S. An Introduction to ecclesiastical records. London, St. Anthony's Press, [1953]. 96p.

Deals fully with the records to be found in diocesan record offices - archbishops' and bishops' registers; visitations; records of ecclesiastical courts, etc. *Class No:* 283(420)(093.2)

[704]

OWEN, D.M. The Records of the Established Church in England, excluding parochial records. London, British Records Association, 1970. 64p. £2. (*Archives and their use, no.1.*) ISBN: 0900222018.

The Records: Description ((a) The Diocese, the archdeaconry and the peculiar jurisdictions; (b) The province; (c) The National church; (d) Capitular bodies) - Location of records. Index of terms used. *Class No:* 283(420)(093.2)

16th & 17th Centuries

Bibliographies

[705]

Cathedral libraries catalogue: books printed before 1701 in the libraries of the Anglican cathedrals of England and Wales. v.1. Books printed in the British Isles and British America and English books printed elsewhere. London, British Library, in association with the Bibliographical Society, 1985. (Limited edition). xxi, 442p. £30. ISBN: 0712300384.

In 6 sections: Locations of English books to 1640 as enumerated in Pollard & Redgrave's *Short-list catalogue;* ... 1641-1700 as enumerated in Wing's *STC;* English books to 1640 not in Pollard & Redgrave; ... from 1641-1700 not in Wing; Locations of periodicals published 1641-1700; Locations of Statutes published 1641-1700. Brief references

....*(contd.)*

are given for titles in Pollard & Redgrave and Wing; full bibliographical references for those not in those volumes. *Class No:* 283"15/16"(01)

Lutheran

Encyclopaedias

[706]

BODENSIECK, J.H., *ed*. **The Encyclopedia of the Lutheran Church.** Minneapolis, MN., Augsburg Publishing House, 1965. 3v.

Published under the auspices of the Lutheran World Federation.

*c.*3000 entries (A-E,F-M,N-Z), contributed by 723 Lutheran scholars and specialists from 34 countries. Includes 1000 biographical sketches and articles on places, etc., pertinent to Lutherism. Bibliographies.

Class No: 284.1(031)

[707]

—BENZING, J. Lutherbibliographie. Verzeichnis der gedruckten Schriften Martin Luthers bis zu dessen Tod... Baden-Baden, Heiz, 1965-66. xi,512p.

A chronological list of Luther's writings, with locations. A supplement was published in 1982 (Gotha, 1982. 226p.).

Class No: 284.1(01)

[708]

—Lutheran cyclopedia. Lueker, E.L., *ed*. Rev. ed. St. Louis, Miss., Concordia, 1975 (reprinted 1987). 845p. $22.95. ISBN: 0317604880.

First published 1954.

Has over 12,000 short articles, not confined to Lutherism. 246 contributors. *Class No:* 284.1(031)

Non-Conformist

[709]

The Church of Scotland year-book, 1992. Edinburgh, Saint Andrew Press for the Church of Scotland, 1992. Annual. 412p. illus. £9.95. ISSN: 00693995.

First published 1884.

Directory information on synods, presbyteries and parishes; alphabetical list of ministers, probationers and lay missionaries. Index of personnel; index of places; index of subjects.

The United Free Church of Scotland issues *The handbook* biennially (Glasgow, United Free Church of Scotland, 1930-.

Class No: 285/288

Bibliographies

[710]

DEXTER, H.M. The Congregationalism of the last 300 years, as seen in its literature. New York, Harper, 1880. (Reprinted 1988 by Gregg International Publications). 1072p. £120. $240.00. ISBN: 0685140989.

Consists of 12 lectures, with a bibliographical appendix (326p.): 'Collections toward a bibliography of Congregationalism'. *Class No:* 285/288(01)

[711]

DR. WILLIAMS'S LIBRARY, London. **Early Nonconformity, 1566-1800:** a catalogue of the books in Dr. Williams's Library. Boston, Mass., G.K. Hall, 1968. 12v. $495 the set. ISBN: 0816107971.

31,000 author cards, 33,000 subject cards and 14,000 chronological cards. Concerned with early Nonconformity in England and Elizabethan Puritanism to the end of the 18th century, and books and pamphlets printed 1566-1800.

Class No: 285/288(01)

[712]

—Nonconformist congregations in Great Britain: a list of histories and other material in Dr. Williams's Library. London, Dr. Williams's Trust, 1973. vii,[1],151p.

*c.*2000 entries, including periodical articles as well as books. Geographical arrangement. *Class No:* 285/288(01)

Histories

[713]

BROWN, K.D. A Social history of the Nonconformist Ministry in England and Wales, 1800-1930. Oxford, Clarendon Press, 1988. xi, 244p. tables. £25. ISBN: 0198227639.

An investigation into the private and professional lives of protestant nonconformist ministers, based on the statistical analysis of a sample of several thousand ministers of 5 denominations (Baptist, Congregational, Wesleyan, Primitive and United Methodist). 7 chapters: 1. Origins - 2. Training, 1800-*c.*1860 - 3. Training, *c.*1860-1914 - 4. An unsettled ministry? - 5. Private lives - 6. Public lives - 7. Postscript. Footnotes throughout. Select bibliography, p.235-241, by chapter. Index, p.241-244. '...an important contribution to British social and religous history ... most fascinating and scholarly study of a group of individuals who at one time wielded immense influence in society' (*Economic history review,* v.42(3), August 1989, p.411-2).

Class No: 285/288(091)

United Reformed Church

[714]

The United Reformed Church year book, 1994. London, United Reformed Church in the United Kingdom, 1993. Annual. 291p. map. ISBN: 085346135x. ISSN: 00698849.

First published 1973.

Includes sections: Assembly officers, committees and departments - Provincial moderators, past moderators, recognised colleges and affiliations - List of churches in provinces and districts (p.16-129) - Summary of statistics - Roll of Ministers - Deaconesses - U.R.C. personnel serving overseas - Deceased Ministers and obituaries - Index of churches. *Class No:* 285.42

Baptist

[715]

BRACKNEY, W.H. The Baptists. Westport, CT., Greenwood Press, 1988. 352p. $49.95. (*Denominations in America series,* 2.) ISBN: 0313238227.

Focuses primarily on American Baptists. 2 sections: 1. Overview of the Baptist tradition - 2. Biographical sketches of over 100 prominent Baptist leaders, A-Z, describing events in their lives and careers, and including short bibliographies of works on and by the person. Other

....(contd.)

inclusions are a chronology; statistical data on Baptist Church membership; a bibliographical essay; and an index to persons and organizations. *Class No:* 286

Bibliographies

[716]

STARR, E.C. A Baptist bibliography; being a register of printed material by and about Baptists; including works written against Baptists. Philadelphia, Pa., Judson Press; subsequently Rochester, N.Y., American Baptist Historical Society, 1947-76. 25v. $400 the set.

About 125,000 entries in all, under authors A-Z. Each volume has an index of joint authors, translators, Baptist publishers, distinctive titles, and subjects. Location of copies. *Class No:* 286(01)

[717]

WHITLY, W.T. Baptist bibliography; being a register of the chief materials for Baptist history, whether in manuscript or in print, preserved in Great Britain, Ireland and the Colonies ... ; compiled for the Baptist Union of Great Britain and Ireland. London, Kingsgate Press, 1916-22 (Reprinted in 1984 by George Olms Verlag, Hildesheim, Zürich & New York). 2v. in 1. £66.25. ISBN: 3487074567.

V.1: 1526-1776; v.2: 1777-1837, and addenda for 1613-53. Chronological arrangement, with indexes of anonymous pamphlets, authors, places and subjects. Locations are given for 30 libraries in England and Wales, and one library in US. *Class No:* 286(01)

Yearbooks & Directories

[718]

Baptist Missionary Society: directory of missionaries and other information relating to current work of the Society. London, the Society, 1986. 56p.

The directory (p.8-13) is an A-Z listing, with UK addresses, postings, etc. Very brief. *Class No:* 286(058)

[719]

The Baptist Union directory for 1992-93. 131st year. Council of the Baptist Union of Great Britain, *ed.* London, Baptist Church House, 1992. Annual. 349p. £5.50. ISSN: 03023184.

Directory information on the Baptist Union of Great Britain, with list of associations and churches; Baptist Missionary Society; Lay pastors and preachers. Index of churches (England, Scotland, Wales) etc. *Class No:* 286(058)

Church of God, Seventh Day

Bibliographies

[720]

BJORLING, J. The Church of God, Seventh Day: a bibliography. New York, Garland, 1987. xix, 296p. $48. (*Sects and cults in America, bibliographic guide 8.*) ISBN: 082408537x.

1627 unannotated entries arranged in 8 subject chapters, all subdivided. Each chapter has historical and biographical background information followed by listings of primary and secondary material. Footnotes. A highly specialized bibliography. Author index, p.291-296. *Class No:* 286CHU(01)

Methodist

[721]

GARLICK, K.B., *ed.* **Garlick's Methodist registry, 1983.** London, B. Edsall & Co. Ltd., 1983. 373, [2], xiii, [1], xvi, [1], vip. £17.50. ISBN: 090262332x.

Contents: Exortium - A brief survey of Methodist history - Methodist ministers (biographical notes presented by the ministers themselves) (p.43-371) - Abbreviations. 3 appendices: 1. Presidents, Secretaries, etc., of the Wesleyan Methodist Conference, 1744-1932; 2. Presidents, Vice-presidents, Secretaries, divisions, lectures, etc., of the Methodist Conference, 1932-1982; 3. The Independent Methodist Church, The Wesleyan Reform Union ... Glossary. *Class No:* 287

Bibliographies

[722]

Methodist Union catalog: pre-1976 imprints. Rowe, K.E., *ed.* Metuchen, N.J., Scarecrow Press, 1975-. v.1-. £21.75. $29 each volume, for v.1-6. ISBN: 0810808803, v.1; 0810809206, v.2; 0810810670, v.3; 0810812258, v.4; 0810814544, v.5; 081081725x, v.6.

V.1-6 (1975-1985); A-I. To be in 20 vols.

A repertory of the catalogued holdings (under author/anonymous title) of more than 200 libraries in the US, Canada, Great Britain and serveral other European countries. Includes works on Methodist history, biography, doctrine, polity, missions, education and sermons. Confined to books, pamphlets and theses, excluding manuscripts, periodicals and serials (for which see Batsel, J. and L. *Union list of United Methodist serials, 1773-1973.* 1974). A preliminary edition, *Methodist Union catalog of history, biography, disciplines .and hymnals,* edited by B.B. Little, was issued in 1967 (Lake Junaluska, N.C., Association of Methodist Historical Society. xxl. 478p.). *Class No:* 287(01)

Histories

[723]

DAVIES, R. *and* **RUPP, G.,** *eds.* **A History of the Methodist Church in Great Britain.** London, Epworth Press, 1965-1988. 4v. (c.2000p.). ISBN: 0716203960, v.1; 0716209014, v.2; 0716203871, v.3; 0716204444, v.4.

V.1 has 10 contributors and covers the 18th century in 9 chapters; bibliography of primary and secondary sources, p.317-9. Indexes of subjects, names and places. V.2 has 7 contributors and covers the first half of the 19th century; ample footnote references, but no bibliography. Analytical index. V.3 covers in depth the years from the middle of the 19th century to 1932 and the coming into operation of the Methodist Church Act in 1976. V.4 assembles primary documents of Methodist history from its beginnings, sections arranged chronologically; and includes a bibliography (p.650-800) arranged in 7 subject sections, all subdivided. Two appendices: 1. Chapter conversion table; 2. Index of authors and editors (p.803-830). Index of documents and source material (p.831-838). *Class No:* 287(091)

[724]

—The Encyclopedia of world Methodism. Harmon, N.B., *ed*. Rev. ed. Nashville, United Methodist Publishing House, 1974. 2v. (2814p.). illus. $89.50. ISBN: 0687117844.

Sponsored by the World Methodist Council and the Commission on Archives and History of the United Methodist Church.

Includes a bibliography, p.2721-66. *Class No:* 287(091)

The Brethren

Encyclopaedias

[725]

The Brethren encyclopedia. Dumbaugh, D.F. Ambler, PA., Brethren Encyclopedia, 1984. 3v. (2126p.). illus., tables, maps. $130 the set; $75 each vol. ISBN: 0318004878.

Comprehensive coverage of all aspects of Brethren life, practice, belief and history. *c.*6000 articles in v.1 & 2, as well as illustrations (including historic photographs), and each article is supported by a bibliography. V.3 has lists, maps, statistics, etc., including a 256-page bibliography of books, articles, theses and unpublished material about the Brethren; 'impossible to find' information (lists of congregations, Annual meetings, institutions, ministries); and statistics from 1770 to the 1980 US census. Thorough and carefully researched. *Class No:* 287BRE(031)

Unitarian

[726]

GENERAL ASSEMBLY OF UNITARIAN AND FREE CHRISTIAN CHURCHES. Directory, 1985/86. London, Unitarian HQ., 1985. [2], 78p.

6 sections, including: Directory of congregations [in England (inc. Isle of Man), Wales, Scotland, non-subscribing Presbyterian Church of Ireland, overseas] (p.9-48); Directory of ministers - Ministry students - Lay preachers - Affiliated societies - Obituaries. *Class No:* 288

Other Churches & Sects

Shakers

[727]

McKINSTRY, E.R., *comp*. **The Edward Deming Andrews Memorial Shaker collection.** New York, Garland, 1987. 357p. $67. ISBN: 0824094301.

The major collection of Shaker material. Arranged in 5 divisions: Printed material, including bibliographic description of 468 items written or published by the Shakers and 246 secondary works, A-Z by author - Manuscript material, including 497 individual manuscripts, collections of letters, etc. - Photographic material - Artifacts - Andrews archives. 'This excellent guide to an important research collection ... is also a useful reference tool' (*College & research libraries,* v.49(1), January 1988, p.59-60, on which this entry is based). *Class No:* 289SHA

Unification Church

[728]

MICKLER, M.L. The Unification Church in America: a bibliography and research guide... New York, Garland, 1987. 227p. $36. (*Sects and cults in America, bibliographic guides, 9. Garland reference library of social science, 201.*) ISBN: 0824090403.

Includes bibliographies and background essays. The bibliographies include materials of all kinds (pamphlets, speeches, theses, popular magazine articles, and critical materials). Items, original documents, scholarly books and articles) published between 1960 and 1985 in the US. No annotations. Author index to the bibliographies. *Class No:* 289UNI

Church of Jesus Christ of the Latter-Day Saints (Mormons)

Bibliographies

[729]

FALES, S.L. *and* **FLAKE, C.J.,** *comps*. **Mormons and mormonism in the US government documents:** a bibliography. Utah, 1989. 357p. $30. ISBN: 0874803128.

1467 annotated entries for items published between 1830 and 1930, the years of persecution by the Federal Government. Arrangement is chronological. Subject, title and series indexes. 'This excellent bibliography demonstrates the contribution such a work can make to scholarship' (*Choice,* v.27(3), November 1989, o.460). *Class No:* 289.3(01)

[730]

FLAKE, C.J., *ed*. **A Mormon bibliography, 1830-1930:** books, pamphlets, periodicals and broadsheets relating to the first century of Mormonism. Salt Lake City, University of Utah Press, 1978. xxxi,[i],825p. illus. $80. ISBN: 0874800161.

The standard source, 10,145 numbered items (plus 56 in addenda) arranged A-Z by author, with brief descriptions for some entries and also locations. Index by date (year) refers to item numbers. A ten-year supplement by Flake and L.W. Draper (426p. $30. ISBN 0874803381) was issued in 1990. *Class No:* 289.3(01)

[731]

—SHIELDS, S.L. The Latter Day Saint churches: an annotated bibliography. New York, Garland, 1987. 281p. $45. (*Bibliography on sects and cults in America, 11. Garland reference library of social science, 337.*) ISBN: 0824085825.

1538 citations to literature relating to the Mormon Church and splinter groups. Selective coverage of works by and about the Church of Jesus Christ of Latter Day Saints (Mormon Church) and the Reorganized Church of Jesus Christ of Latter Day Saints (RLDS Church); comprehensive coverage of the writings relating to over 60 smaller existing churches or movements within a similar religious origin. Author index, but no subject index. Intended to supplement the above. *Class No:* 289.3(01)

Encyclopaedias

[732]

Encyclopedia of Mormonism: the history, scripture, doctrine and procedure of the Church of Christ of Latter-day Saints. Ludlow, D.H., *ed.* New York, Macmillan, 1992. 5v..(2333p). illus, tables. $340. ISBN: 002904040x.

Presents research efforts of committed believers on a host of topics relating to the founding and growth of the Church. V.1-4 contain *c*.1500 articles by over 730 contributors. A synoptic outline organizes entries under 5 major headings. Cross-references. Detailed subject index in v.4. 13 appendices and a glossary. V.5 reproduces the standard works of the Church. The apologia approach 'in no way negates the overall values of the encyclopedia'(*Library journal*, 15 February 1992, p.158). *Class No:* 289.3(031)

Histories

[733]

SHIPPS, J. Mormonism: the story of a new religious tradition. Urbana & Chicago, University of Chicago Press, 1987. xviii,212p. illus. $22.95. ISBN: 0252011597.

Reconstructs the signal events of early Mormonism as perceived from inside the faith. 8 chapters: 1: Prologue - 2-7 are historical - 8: A chronology of 19th century Mormonism. Extensive notes, p.169-192. Bibliography, p.193-202. Index, p.203-212. *Class No:* 289.3(091)

Quakers (Society of Friends)

Bibliographies

[734]

SMITH, J. A Descriptive catalogue of Friends' books, or books written by members of the Society of Friends... London, J. Smith, 1867. Supplement published by Hicks, 1893. 2v.

An author catalogue, covering broadsheets as well as books. The heading 'Periodical publications' is followed by a list of contents of issues of various periodicals. Editions and reprints are recorded. Analytical notes are provided as necessary, as well as very brief biographical data. *Class No:* 289.6(01)

[735]

—TURNER, A. A Bibliography of Quaker literature, 1893-1967. 2v. (792p.,247p.).

A thesis accepted for L.A. Fellowship in 1974. 5700 entries, many with brief bibliographical or explanatory notes, in 14 classes. Excludes all Society of Friends publications. Index of authors and subjects. *Class No:* 289.6(01)

Yearbooks & Directories

[736]

RELIGIOUS SOCIETY OF FRIENDS. Handbook of the Religious Society of Friends, 1982. 8th ed. London, Friends World Committee for Consultation, 1982. 128p. £3. ISBN: 0901856061.

First published 1955. Issued 5-yearly since 1962.

Subtitled 'Finding friends around the world'. Lists Societies of Friends around the world, arranged geographically. Data on meetings, lists of Quaker schools, study centres, publications, libraries. *Class No:* 289.6(058)

Jehovah Witnesses

[737]

BERGMAN, J. Jehovah's Witnesses and kindred groups: a historical compendium and bibliography. New York, Garland, 1984. xli,[i],370p. $58. (*Sects and cults in America. Bibliographical guides, 4. Garland reference library of social science, 180.*) ISBN: 0824091094.

Arranged in 5 sections: 1. Official Watchtower Bible and Tract Society literature (A. Books; B. Song, hymn and poem books ... M. Indexes; N. Convention reports; O-R. articles) - 2. Material associated with the Russell Movement (subdivided A-H) - 3. Material about Jehovah's Witnesses (subdivided A-J) - 4. Offshoots of the Watchtower Bible and Tract Society (subdivided A-K) - 5. Non-American Bible student groups (Britain; Europe; Canada; Australia). An appendix gives addresses for Jehovah's Witnesss and their offshoots. Author index, p.353-369. '... important and unique bibliography of the religious sect ...' (*Choice*, v.22(5), January 1985, p.658). *Class No:* 289.954

29 Non-Christian Religions

Non-Christian Religions

[738]
PARRINDER, G., *ed*. **An Illustrated history of the world's religions.** London, Newnes, 1983. 528p. illus. ISBN: 0600337982.

21 chapters (1. Prehistoric religions ... 21. Islam. Conclusion). 20 specialist contributors. Bibliography, by chapters, p.516-9. Marginal text references to illustrations. Index (tiny print). Comparative religion for the new comer as well as the scholar. *Class No:* 29.0

Dictionaries

[739]
PARRINDER, G. **Dictionary of non-Christian religions.** 2nd ed. Amersham, Bucks, Hulton Educational Publications Ltd., 1981. 320p. illus. £7.95. ISBN: 0717509729.

First published 1971.

'This dictionary covers the whole field of the religions of the world, with the exception of Christianity and the Bible' (*Introduction*). About 3000 brief entries, including biographies. Special attention is paid to Hinduism, Buddhism and Islam, and other Far Eastern religions; also Near Eastern, Celtic, Teutonic and Scandinavian religions, the beliefs and customs of ancient American culture, Mayas, Aztecs and Incas, plus those of Australasia and Africa. Judaism is referred to in detail in the post-Biblical period. Ample cross-references. Over 300 drawings and photographs. No references to authorities consulted. Further reading list, p.318-9. Well produced. For undergraduates and the general reader. *Class No:* 29.0(038)

Great Britain

[740]
HUTTON, R. **The Pagan religions** of the ancient British Isles: their nature and legacy. Oxford & Cambridge, Mass., Blackwell, 1991. 288p. 150 illus. £20. $29.95. ISBN: 0631172882.

Claims to be the first survey of religious beliefs in the British Isles from the Old Stone Age to the coming of Christianity. *Class No:* 29.0(410)

America — North

Encyclopaedias

[741]
HIRSCHFOLDER, A. and MORIN, P. **The Encyclopedia of native American religions.** New York, Facts on File, 1992. 367p. illus. Maps. $40. ISBN: 0816020175.

Claims to be the first encyclopedia of native *North American* religions. Wide range. Entries A-Z, each 1-2 paragraphs, and including biographies of religious leaders

....(contd.)
and Christian missionaries. Extensive bibliography of popular and scholarly books, government publications and periodical articles. A unique compendium. *Class No:* 29.0(71+73)(031)

Handbooks & Manuals

[742]
MELTON, J.G. **Encyclopedic handbook of cults in America.** 2nd rev. ed. New York, Garland Publishing Inc., 1992. 424p. $65.00. (*Garland reference library of social science, 213.*) ISBN: 0815305028.

Aims to be a concise summary of the most accurate information available on the more important of the alternative or non-conventional religious movements. 6 sections, each having an appended short bibliography (1. What is a cult? [surveys the broad range of issues surrounding the topic] - 2. The established cults - 3. The new age movement - 4. The newer cults - 5. Counter-cult groups - 6. Violence and the cults) Index, p.265-272. *Class No:* 29.0(71+73)(035)

Comparative Studies

Encyclopaedias

[743]
KLAUSER, T., *ed*. **Reallexikon für Antike und Christentum.** Sachwörterbuch zur Auseinandersetzung des Christentums mit der antiken Welt. Leipzig (subsequently Stuttgart), Anton Hiersemann, 1950- v.1- illus.

V.1-14 (1950-1988): A-HEXE. An encyclopedia of the classical world and its relationship to early Christianity. Scholarly, signed articles, sometimes lengthy, with bibliographies (*e.g.* Constantine the Great is subject of a monograph (v.3, p.306-79), sectionalised A-G, with subdivisions, nearly two columns of bibliography, apart from references in the text). Occasional line-drawings. Each vol. has *c.*1280p. *Class No:* 291(031)

Handbooks & Manuals

[744]
FRAZER, J.G. **The Golden bough:** a study in magic and religion. 3rd ed. rev. & enl. London, Macmillan Press, 1911-15 (Reprinted in 13v., 1980). 13v. (5380p.). $250 the set. ISBN: 0333012828.

1st ed. 1890; 2nd ed. 1900.

1: *The magic art and the evolution of kings* (1911. 2v.); 2: *Taboo and the perils of the soul* (1911); 3: *The dying God* (1911); 4. *Adonis, Attis, Osiris* (1914. 2v.); 5: *Spirits of the corn and of the wild* (1912. 2v.); 6: *The scapegoat* (1913); 7. *Balder the beautiful. The fire-festivals of Europe and the doctrine of the external soul* (1913. 2v.); 8: *Bibliography and general index* (1915); *Aftermath: a supplement to the 'Golden bough'* (1936). A monumental contribution on

....*(contd.)*

primitive beliefs and customs, and their place in the comparative history of religion. The general index provides an adequate key to the many examples and analogies. Much of what is called 'primitive religion' is classified as magic by Frazer, and his views have accordingly been attacked as unscientific.

=2The Making of 'The Golden bough'=* was issued in 1990 (Macmillan. 256p. 5 illus. £45. ISBN 0333496310) *Class No:* 291(035)

[745]
—FRAZER, J.G. The New golden bough: a new abridgment of the classic work. Gaister, T.H., *ed.* New York, Criterion, [1959]. 758p. $39.95. ISBN: 0875990363.

Updates the original in the light of recent discoveries, plus further notes. Comprehensive index. *Class No:* 291(035)

Mythology

[746]
COTTERELL, A. The Illustrated encyclopedia of myths and legends. London, Cassell, 1992. 260p. illus. £14.95. ISBN: 0304341819.

An anthology, covering the popular myths and legends of 20 world cultures. Micropedia (p.180-248). Further reading (p.249-50). Index (p.251-259). *Class No:* 292/293

Bibliographies

[747]
'The Classical world' bibliography of philosophy, religion and rhetoric. New York, Garland Publishing Inc. 1978. 396p. $51. (*Garland reference library of the humanities, v.95.*) ISBN: 0824098781.

19 bibliographic essays (some with critical comments) on Greek and Roman philosophy, Roman religion and ancient rhetoric (*e.g.* 'Early Roman religion ...' reprinted from the monthly *Classical world* (Classical Association of the Atlantic States, Pittsburgh, Pa.). 'This book will be of great use to the researcher as well as the teacher and students' (American reference books annual, v.10, 1979. item 1080). *Class No:* 292/293(01)

[748]
SMITH, R. Mythologies of the world: a guide to sources. Urbana, Ill., National Council of Teachers of English, 1981. 347p. $13.95. ISBN: 0814132227.

The bibliographical essays are arranged in 6 broad geographical categories, subdivided by ethnic groups and further subdivided by types of material. Emphasis is on the myth as a tale, and only material in English is included. No indexes. Light-hearted. *Class No:* 292/293(01)

[749]
SOUTH, M., *ed.* Mythical and fabulous creatures: a source book and research guide. New York, Greenwood Press, 1987. xxxv, 393p. illus. $49.95. ISBN: 0313243387.

The editor's introduction, which includes a bibliographic essay, is followed by 20 chapters on individual creatures arranged in 4 sections: Birds and beasts - Human-animal composites - Creatures of the night - Giants and fairies. The chapters are written as bibliographic essays. The second part of the book includes 'A Miscellany' and 'A Taxonomy'

....*(contd.)*

which have information on another 43 creatures. Glossary. General bibliography. Index with 'see' references. '... a breadth of coverage that is both impressive and delightful' (*Choice*, v.24(11/12), July/August 1987, p.1678). *Class No:* 292/293(01)

Encyclopaedias

[750]
GORDON, S. The Encyclopedia of myths and legends. London, Headline, 1993. 512p. 32 illus. £19.99. ISBN: 0747206236.

A compilation of world folklore from 'Aboriginal myths' to 'Zodiac'. *Class No:* 292/293(031)

[751]
JORDAN, M. Encyclopedia of gods: over 2500 deities from both ancient and modern cultures. New York, Facts on File, 1993. 337p. $40. ISBN: 0816029091.

Brief sketches of gods and goddesses from both ancient and modern cultures.Arranged A-Z by name of deity. Subject index lists deities by function and type. Civilization index lists deities by specific culture. *Class No:* 292/293(031)

[752]
MERCATANTI, A.S., *ed*. The Facts on File encyclopedia of world mythology and legend. New York, Facts on File, 1988. xviii,807p. illus. $95; £55. ISBN: 0816010498.

Aim is to provide a quick reference to world myth, fairy tale, and legend, thus giving a better understanding of 'the thematic contents of the world's masterpieces of art, music and literature'. Over 3000 entries with concise definitions and background information, arranged A-Z by the most common English spelling. Annotated bibliography, p.699-716; Key to variant spellings, p.717-722; Cultural and ethnic index, p.723-740; General index, p.741-807. Includes 450 illustrations. *Class No:* 292/293(031)

Handbooks & Manuals

[753]
GRAY, I.H., *ed*. Mythology of all races. Boston, Mass., Archaeological Institute of America, Marshall Jones Co., 1916-32. (Reprinted New York, Cooper Square Publishers, 1964. 13v. illus.

Contents: V.1: *Greek and Roman,* by W.S. Fox (1916); 2: *Eddic,* by J.A. McCulloch (1930); 3: *Celtic,* by J.A. McCulloch; *Slavic,* by J. Machal (1918); 4: *Finno-Ugric. Siberian,* by U. Holmberg (1927); 5: *Semitic,* by S.H. Langdon (1931); 6: *Indian,* by A.B. Keith; *Iranian,* by A.J. Carnoy (1917); 7: *Armenian,* by M.H. Ananikian; *African,* by A. Werner (1925); 8: *Chinese,* by J.C. Ferguson; *Japanese,* by M. Anesaki (1928); 9: *Oceanic,* by R.B. Dixon (1916); 10: *North American,* by H.B. Alexander (1916); 11: *Latin American,* by H.B. Alexander (1920); 12. *Egyptian,* by W.M. Müller; *Indo-Chinese,* by J.G. Scott (1918); 13. Complete index to v.1-12 (1932). Each volume carries some 20-50 plates, in addition to figures in the text; also some 20 pages of bibliography. The detailed index runs to 477 pages,. Valuable for its truly extensive geographical coverage, backed by a full index. *Class No:* 292/293(035)

[754]

Guide to the gods Jones, M.O. *and* Cattermole-Tally, F., *eds.* Santa Barbara, CA, ABC-Clio;London & Detroit, Gale Research International,1992. xi,995p. $150. £95. ISBN: 0874365910, US; 1873477856, UK.

20,000 deities listed, arranged by 8 main subject divisions, each subdivided. Each brief entry conprises name, function, attributes, and bibliographical reference, referring to a comprehensive 15-page bibliography. A-Z index of names. 'a finding list, not an encyclopedia'(p.x of volume). *Class No:* 292/293(035)

[755]

Larousse world mythology. Grimal, P., *ed.* Rev. ed. London, Hamlyn, 1982. 569p. illus., (incl.col.pl.). £7.95.

Translated from the French by G.P. Beardmore. Originally published as *Mythologies* (Paris, Larousse, 1963).

23 specialist contributions (Prehistory - Egypt - Sumer - Babylon - The Hittites - Greece - Rome - Persia - India - The Celts - Germans - Slavs - Ugric Finns - China - Japan - North America - Siberia). Profusely illustrated with 40p. of colour plates and 600 black-and-white illus. Bibliography of selected readings, p.546-7. Index. Lacks maps. *Class No:* 292/293(035)

[756]

—New Larousse encyclopedia of mythology. New ed. London, Hamlyn, 1969. 508p. £8.95. ISBN: 0600023508.

First published as *Larousse mythologie générale* (1935). Translated from the French by R. Aldington and D. Ames. Less scholarly than the above. *Class No:* 292/293(035)

[757]

LEACH, M. Guide to the gods. Andover, Hants, Gale Research International, 1993. 1008p. £95. ISBN: 1873477856.

Originally published in US in 1992 by ABC-Clio.

A guide to more than 20,000 gods, from pre-history to the present, arranged by function or other attribute under 8 major headings (Cosmogonical deities - Celestial deities - Atmospheric deities - Terrestrial deities - Life/death cycle deities - Economic activities - Socio-cultural concepts - Religion) each subdivided. Each short entry has information under some or all of the headings: Primary or secondary functions of the deity; aspects and attributes; alternative names and spellings; relationships with other mythical figures; culture and country of origin; bibliographical references. Bibliography of 1600 works, and separate list of 45 learned journals. *Class No:* 292/293(035)

[758]

MONAGHAN, P. The Book of goddesses and heroines. Rev. ed. New York, Dutton, 1990. 456p. $17.95. ISBN: 0875425739.

A helpful list of goddesses by family and geographic location precedes the main part of the work, which is arranged A-Z by name (A ... Zuleika). A thorough bibliography follows. 'An excellent source for collections of comparative religions and women's studies' (*Library journal,* July 1981, p.1405) on the first edition. *Class No:* 292/293(035)

Dictionaries

[759]

COTTERELL, A., *ed.* A Dictionary of world mythology. Originally published by Windward, imprint of W.H. Smith, Reprinted 1986 by OUP in Oxford paperback series. [2], 320p. illus. maps. £4.95. ISBN: 0192177478.

Arranged in 7 main sections: West Asia; South and Central Asia; East Asia; Europe; America; Africa; and Oceania. Introduction to each section highlights history, lifestyle, and ideology of an ancient people, and the landscape in which they lived. In each section myths and mythologies are A-Z, entries ranging from 100 to 500 words. 'Further reading' is included for the introduction and each section. Cross-references. Double column index, p.303-14. *Class No:* 292/293(038)

[760]

JOBES, G. Dictionary of mythology, folklore and symbols. New York, Scarecrow Press, 1961-62. 3v. (1759p. + 482p.). ISBN: 0810820366.

Vols. 1 and 2 are the dictionary: 1. A-Jephthah; 2. Jephuneh - ZZZ, and also a bibliography (p.1736-1759), A-Z by author. V.3 is the index, in 2 parts: A. Table of deities, heroes and personalities; B. Table of mythological affiliates. *Class No:* 292/293(038)

[761]

LURKER, M. Dictionary of gods and goddesses, devils and demons. New York, Routledge & Kegan Paul, 1987. 451p. $45; £16.95. ISBN: 0710208774.

First published in Stuttgart in 1984 as *Lexikon der Götter und Däomen: Namen, Funktionen, Symbole/Attribute.*

c.1800 articles, their length proportionate to their importance, on the gods, and other supernatural persons from all the world's religions. Followed by indexes of varient names, secondary names, and by-names; of functions, aspects and areas of influence; and of symbols, attributes and motives; and a select bibliography. *Class No:* 292/293(038)

[762]

SYKES, E., *comp*. Everyman's dictionary of non-classical mythology. 3rd ed. London, J.M. Dent, 1961 (Reprinted Biblio. Dist., 1977). 298p. illus. $13.50. (*Everyman's reference library*.) ISBN: 0460030108.

Previous edition 1952.

Comprises c.2000 short articles, with cross-references and a brief general bibliography. Covers Chinese, Japanese and American mythology, as well as Scandinavian, Teutonic and Near Eastern, but omits *One thousand and one nights* as a source. *Class No:* 292/293(038)

Biographies

[763]

HART, G. Dictionary of Egyptian gods and goddesses. London, Routledge & Kegan Paul, 1986. A paperback ed. was issued in 1990. ISBN 0415059097. 229p. illus. £12.95. ISBN: 0710209657.

An outline time-chart and 2 maps precede the dictionary, arranged by name A-Z (Aken ... Yamm). The author has 'tried to include all the important deities that figure in magical medicine and daily life' (*Preface*). Entries are detailed and clearly written; some lengthy. (e.g., 'Aten': 10 pages; 'Osiris': 15 pages) but others only 2 or 3 lines. Short

....(contd.)
'Select further reading' (p.227) and 'Alternative renderings of divine names' (p.229) complete the book.
Class No: 292/293(092)

[764]
SENIOR, M. The Illustrated who's who in mythology. London, Macdonald Illustrated, 1985 (reprinted 1990). 224p. illus. £12.95. ISBN: 0356197298.

Short entries arranged A-Z featuring more than 1200 figures from the world's myths, with more than 240 black and white and coloured illustrations. Main sources are given. Index of themes, p.219-223. *Class No:* 292/293(092)

Great Britain

[765]
ASHE, G. Mythology of the British Isles. London, Methuen, 1990. 304p. 153 illus (50 col.). £17.99. ISBN: 0413629902.

Each section deals with topic first as presented in legend or story-telling or speculation; then a commentary discusses sources, facts, underlying ideas, etc. Sections: The peoples and their origins - Mysteries of early Britain - Dynasties - Magic and secret lore - The Roman era - Transition - Arthurian Britain - The birth of Scotland — The English inheritance. Epilogue. Bibliography, p.294-297. Index, p.298-304. *Class No:* 292/293(410)

Ireland

[766]
ELLIS, P. B. A Dictionary of Irish mythology. Santa Barbara, CA., ABC Clio, Oxford, University Press, 1989. 240p. $34.95. ISBN: 0874365538, US; 0192828711, UK.

Aimed at the enthusiast and the lay reader, but academics could find it useful. A lengthy introductory essay on the history of the Celts, the sources of their sagas and romances, precedes the dictionary, which covers gods, human heroes, titles, sites, objects, etc. A select bibliography is appended. *Choice* (v.27(2), October 1989, p.285) suggests an indication of pronunciations should be considered for a later edition. *Class No:* 292/293(415)

[767]
SMYTH, D. Guide to Irish mythology. Blackrock, Co. Dublin, Irish Academic Press, 1988. 176p. 98 illus. £6.95. ISBN: 0716524341.

A guide arranged A-Z (Aed ... Uisneach) to mythological places and things. Includes a list of 67 items of source material; special notes; p.158-163; and index, p.167-176. *Class No:* 292/293(415)

Scandinavia

[768]
LINDON, J. Scandinavian mythology: an annotated bibliography. New York, Garland, 1988. 593p. $25. (*(Garland folklore bibliographies, no.13).*.) ISBN: 0824081736.

Lists over 3000 books and periodical articles published between the 1830s and 1982. Most items are in German or one of the Scandinavian languages. *Class No:* 292/293(48)

Asia

[769]
HACKIN, J., *and others*. **Asiatic mythology:** a detailed description and explanation of the mythologies of all the great nations of Asia. London, Harrap, 1832. (Reprinted 1963). 459, [1]p. illus (incl.pl.).

Deals in turn with the mythologies of Persia, the Kafirs, Buddhism in India, Brahmanic mythology (p.100-146), the mythology of Lamaism, of Indo-China and Java, Buddhist mythology in Central Asia, mythology of modern China (p.252-384), the mythology of Japan (p.385-448). Some footnote bibliographical references. Detailed analytical index. 16 col.pl. and 354 other illus. *Class No:* 292/293(5)

China

[770]
WALTERS, D. Chinese mythology: an encyclopedia of myth and legend. Aquarian Press, 1992. 240p. illus. £7.99. ISBN: 1855380803.

Covers the most prominent human, animal and supernatural figures of Chinese legend, folklore and religious beliefs. *Class No:* 292/293(510)

[771]
WERNER, E.T.C. Dictionary of Chinese mythology. Shanghai, Kelly, 1932 (Reprinted Longwood Press, 1976). xvii,[i],627p. $60. ISBN: 0893410349.

'A who's who of the Chinese other world, compiled from the Chinese and foreign works named in the bibliography (p.625-27) from personal observations in Chinese temples, houses and streets, and conversations with Chinese scholars, priests and peasants' (*Preface*) Gives Chinese characters, following English head-word. Numerous cross-references. Index to myths. Bibliography, p.625-7.
Class No: 292/293(510)

India

[772]
Indian mythology: an encyclopedia of myths and legends. Knappert, J. London, Aquarium Press, 1991. 287p. illus. £8.99. (*World mythology*.) ISBN: 1855380404.

Draws on a 5,000 year history of Indian culture, looking at mythology in both the Hindu and Buddhist traditions. Includes the deities, epic heroes, prophets and saints; the creation of the world; and religious concepts of the afterlife. The encyclopedia, arranged A-Z, is preceded by 7 introductory sections (p.9-27): The myths - The language - Prehistory - The peoples - Literature - The sources - History - Further reading - A guide to pronunciation.
Class No: 292/293(540)

Australasia & Oceania

[773]
CRAIG, R.D. Dictionary of Polynesian mythology. New York, Greenwood Press, 1989. 456p. map. $55. ISBN: 0313258902.

Covers an area from Hawaii in the north to New Zealand in the south and Easter Island in the east. A nearly comprehensive listing of the goddesses, gods and ancient heroes chronicled in the legends of the Polynesians. Bibliography of almost 300 sources. Highly recommended as a 'significant new work ... for Pacific studies and

....(contd.)

comparative mythology collections' (*RQ*, v.30|(1), Fall 1990, p.112. from which this entry is taken).
Class No: 292/293(9)

[774]
KNAPPERT, J. **Pacific mythology:** an encyclopedia of myth and legend. London, Aquarian/Thorsons, 1992. 336p. illus. Map. £8.99. $17. ISBN: 1855381338.

An A-Z guide (Abang Salamat ... Yusup), with entries from a few lines to a page. 'See' references. Bibliography, p.333-336. Capitalising on the growing interest in the Pacific. *Class No:* 292/293(9)

Classical Mythology

[775]
BULFINCH, T. **Myths of Greece and Rome.** Holme, B., *ed.* London, Allen Lane/Penguin Books Ltd., 1980. 308p. illus. (some col.). ISBN: 0713912901.

In 1855 Thomas Bulfinch wrote *The Age of fable* to instruct readers in classical mythology, and this is a new edition. 33 chapters: (1. Stories of the gods and heroes - 2. Prometheus and Pandora ... 11. Cupid and Psyche ... 21. Bacchus and Ariadne ... 32. The infernal regions. The Sibyl - 33. Aeneas in Italy ...) followed by a chart, The Descent of the gods, and a name index, p.305-308. *Class No:* 292

[776]
FERGUSON, J. **The Religions of the Roman Empire.** London, Thames & Hudson, 1970 (Reprinted 1982 in paperback). 296p. illus., chron, table. £5.95. (*Aspects of Greek and Roman life,* 5.) ISBN: 050027276x.

12 chapters (1. The Great Mother - 2. The Sky-father - 3. The Sun-god (56 references; 8 illus) - 4. The divine functionaries ... 7. Personal religion - 8. Beyond death ... 11. Philosophers and gods - 12. Syncretism and confrontation. Various quotations. 'Bibliography and references', p.244-74. 87 illus. in all. Chronological table. 800 B.C. - 461 A.D. *Class No:* 292

Encyclopaedias

[777]
ROSCHER, W.H. **Ausführliches Lexikon der griechischen und römischen Mythologie.** Leipzig & Berlin,. Teubner, 1884-1937 (reprinted Hildeshein, Verlagshandlung Olms, 1965. 6v. & 4 supplements, illus.

A scholarly work, the most detailed of its kind (7647p.); for the large library. Signed articles, with extensive references to sources as well as to secondary material. Many illustrations. *Class No:* 292(031)

[778]
STONEMAN, R. **Greek mythology:** an encyclopedia of myth and legend. London, HarperCollins, 1991. 192p. illus. Maps. £7.99. $13.95. ISBN: 0850309344.

Claims to include all major figures of Greek mythology. Black and white line drawings. Short entries making a handy but comprehensive guide for newcomers to the subject. Bibliography, p.187-92. *Class No:* 292(031)

Handbooks & Manuals

[779]
BURKERT, W. **Greek religion in the archaic and classical periods.** Oxford, Basil Blackwell, 1985. 512p. £29.50. ISBN: 0631112413.

A survey intended for classical scholars and students, drawing upon literature and myth, vase paintings and archaeology, and building up a picture of the current state of knowledge about the religions of the ancient Greeks. 7 chapters, followed by notes, a bibliography, and indexes. *Class No:* 292(035)

[780]
LYTTELTON, M. *and* FORMAN, W. **The Romans, their gods and their beliefs.** London, Orbis Publishing Ltd., 1984. 128p. 120 col. illus. £15. ISBN: 0856134732.

Concerned with Roman life and religion from *c.*100 B.C. to A.D. 100. 6 chapters: The changing image of the city - The traditional gods of Rome - Rites of sacrifice and divination - Augustus's religious revival - Private life and personal religion - The mystery religions. Suggestions for further reading (10 books). Index, p.126-128. *Class No:* 292(035)

[781]
MORFORD, M.P.O. *and* LENARDON, R.J. **Classical mythology.** 4th ed. New York, Longman Group Ltd., 1991. xxi, 703p. illus. maps. $28.95; £15.99. ISBN: 0801304652.

First published 1971.

3 parts (26 chapters): 1. The myths of creation; The Gods - 2. The Greek sagas; Greek local legends - 3. The survival of classical mythology (*e.g.* 26. Classical mythology in music and film). Select bibliography, p.671-674; also bibliographies at the end of the introduction (p.35-38) and appended to chapters. Indexes: A. Mythological and historical persons, subjects and placenames; B. Authors, artists, composers, subjects and titles. *Class No:* 292(035)

[782]
ROSE, H.J. **A Handbook of Greek mythology,** including its extension to Rome. 6th ed. London, Methuen, 1958. ix, 363p. £9.95 (paperback edition issued in 1964). ISBN: 0416682006.

First published 1928.

A standard, scholarly manual by the then Professor of Greek in the United College of St. Salvator and St. Leonard, St. Andrews. Chapter footnotes and bibliographical references (*e.g.* chapter 9, 'The legends of Greek lands', has 82 references); bibliography, p.335-9. Index of mythological names; index of real names. *Class No:* 292(035)

Dictionaries

[783]
BELL, R.E. **Dictionary of classical mythology.** Santa Barbara, CA., ABC-Clio Press, 1982. xi,390p. illus. $31.75. ISBN: 0874363055.

A dictionary of symbols, attributes and associations. Under each term, arranged A-Z, are listed associated persons (*e.g.* under 'Abandonment' are listed 'Ariadne','Dido', and 'Oenone', each with a short description). Cross-references. Lists of surnames, epithets and patronymics (p.287-330), Heroic expeditions (p.331-350), Guide to persona (p.351-390). *Class No:* 292(038)

[784]

BELL, R.E. Place-names in classical mythology: Greece.
Santa Barbara, CA., ABC-Clio, 1988. 350p. $48.50. ISBN: 0874365074.

About 1000 entries for ancient names, listed in their Latin spellings with modern name in parenthesis. Cites specific references to standard sources. Includes a list of modern place-names associated with ancient locations; a guide to personae; and a brief bibliography. No. map. Some of the entries are lengthy (*e.g.* 'Athens' has 18 pages).
Class No: 292(038)

[785]

GRIMAL, P., ed. The Dictionary of classical mythology.
Oxford, Basil Blackwell Ltd., 1986. 603p. illus. £22.50. $34.95. ISBN: 0631132090.

First published as *Dictionnaire de la mythologie grecque et romaine* (Paris, Presses Universitaires de France. 6th ed., 1979).

Identifies the gods, goddesses, heroes and mortals of Greek and Roman mythology. Entries are arranged by the form of name commonly used in English, with the Greek (in Greek characters) and Latin names in parenthesis. Entries range in length from a paragraph to 14 pages, and each entry explains its subject's genealogy and summarizes the legends about it. Footnote references to sources. Cross-references. 40 genealogical tables included in an appendix. Scholarly.
Class No: 292(038)

[786]

—**GRIMAL, P., ed.** A Concise dictionary of classical mythology. Oxford, Blackwell, 1990. 456p. £19.95; $34.95. ISBN: 0631166963.

A concise version of the above, translated by A.R. Maxwell-Hyslop, with entries concentrated on the principal versions of the myths and including only major variations.
Class No: 292(038)

[787]

TRIPP, E. Dictionary of classical mythology. Rev. ed. London, Collins, Publishers, 1988. [14], 631p. maps & geneological charts. £4.95. ISBN: 0004343808.

First published 1970.

Over 2000 entries, A-Z, varying in length from 2 or 3 lines to 5 pages. Includes names of people and places as well as terms. Includes stories telling of the myths of Greece and Rome in readable and convenient form (*e.g.* 'Oedipus': 2½p.; 'Pan': 1¼p.; 'Media': 4¼p.; 'Zeus': 5p.). 'See' references. Pronouncing index. 5 maps of the classical world. 5 genealogical charts of great royal lines.
Class No: 292(038)

Biographies

[788]

BELL, R.E. Women in classical mythology: a biographical dictionary. Santa Barbara, CA, ABC-Clio, 1991. 462p. $49. ISBN: 0874365813.

2600 entries, arranged A-Z by most standard name and spelling, of mortal, immortal and divine beings, monsters, hermaphrodites and transectuals. Entries vary in length from a sentence or paragraph to 4 pages (*e.g.* Athena, Helen). Cross-references. Special index: 'The men in their lives'. 'Because there is little written on women in classical

.... *(contd.)*
literature, this will be a useful addition to the reference collection ... (*Booklist*, v.88(6), 15 November 1991, p.652).
Class No: 292(092)

[789]

GRANT, M, and HAZEL, J. Who's who in classical mythology. London, Weidenfeld & Nicolson, 1973. 447p. illus., maps.

Fairly lengthy entries (*e.g.* Odysseus; Theseus; - each 10p.). Many cross-references. 400 illus. (16 in colour). Greek and Latin writers referred to. 'Handsome as well as scholarly' (*Financial times*. 25 October, 1973, p.33). No bibliographies, but indebtedness to Tripp and Rose is acknowledged. *Class No:* 292(092)

Eastern Religions

---

[790]

The Rider encyclopedia of Eastern philosophy and religion: Buddhism, Hinduism, Taoism, Zen. Schumacher, S. *and* Woerner, G., *eds*. London, Rider Books, 1989. xv,[i],468p. illus., tables. ISBN: 0712611924.

Originally published in German by Otto-Wilhelm-Barth Verlag in 1986.

The A-Z encyclopedia (p.1-444) has over 4000 entries and over 100 illustrations (*e.g.* 'Nirvana': 3¼ columns. illus.). Appendix: Ch'an/Zen lineage chart; bibliography, p.457-468 (grouped: Buddhism-Zen; subdivided into primary and secondary sources). 4 contributors: I. Fischer-Schreiber (Buddhism & Taoism); F.K. Ehrhard (Tibetan Buddhism); K. Friedrichs (Hinduism); M.S. Diener (Zen). A scholarly survey of the teachers, traditions and literature of Asian writers. *Class No:* 294/299

[791]

The Sacred books of the East. Translated by various Oriental scholars and edited by F. Max Müller. Oxford, Clarendon Press, 1879-1910. (Reprinted by Chronica Botanica India (State Mutual), 1988). 50v. $2000 the set.

A major collection of translated Eastern religious literature, including the Upanishads, Sacred Laws of the Aryas, Texts of Confucianism, Zend-Avesta, Pahlavi Texts, Qur'an and Institutes of Vichnu. V.50 is the general index to the series by M. Winternitz.

Another important collection is the *Harvard Oriental series*, edited by C.R. Lanman and others (Cambridge, Mass., Harvard University Press, 1891-1950. 44v.).
Class No: 294/299

[792]

WINTERNITZ, M., *comp*. A Concise dictionary of Eastern religion: being the index volume to The sacred books of the East. Oxford, Clarendon Press, 1910, (reprinted 1925). xvi, 683p.

Forms V.50 of *The Sacred books of the East* (*q.v.*). A remarkably detailed analytical index (*e.g.* 'Prayers': 15 columns, set solid). Many cross-references. Designed on the basis of a 'scientific classification of religious phenomena'.
Class No: 294/299

Hinduism

[793]

The Sacred books of the Hindus. Allahabad, The Panini Office, 1909-37 (Reprinted by Baman Das Basu). Originally in 32v.; reprinted in 47v. $1575.50. ISBN: 0404195482.

In this valuable collection, as in Müller's *Sacred books of the east*, the most notable Hindu scriptures appear as complete documents. Some 30 extensive works have been translated and published in the two collections. (*A reader's guide to great religions*, ed. C.J. Adams (1965), p.47). *Class No: 294*

Bibliographies

[794]

DANDEKAR, R.N. Vedic bibliography: an up-to-date, comprehensive and analytically arranged register of all important work done since 1930. in the field of Veda and allied antiquities, including Indus Valley civilisation. Bombay, Karnatak Publishing House (Rater Poona, University of Poona), 1946-73, v.1-3.

Sequel to *Bibliographie védique*, by L. Renou (Paris, Adrien-Maisonneuve, 1931. v.339p.), with its 6750 items. V.1 lists *c*.3500 books and periodical articles in Western and Indian languages. Some entries are annotated. Subject arrangement. Index to titles and subjects. V.2 (Poona, 1961) has 6500 entries, mostly annotated, for books and periodical articles published 1946-60. V.3 has over 700 entries. *Class No: 294(01)*

[795]

DELL, D.J., *and others*. **Guide to Hindu religion.** Boston, Mass., G.K. Hall, 1981. 434p. $47. ISBN: 0816179034.

Subject bibliography. Categories: Hindu history; religious thought and practice; sacred scriptures and rituals; popular practices; arts; mythology; Hinduism in social and political life; research aids. *Class No: 294(01)*

Encyclopaedias

[796]

Encyclopaedia of the Upanishads. Subrahmanian, N.S. London, Oriental Group, 1986. xii,564p. £35. ISBN: 074650005x.

Prints, describes and explains each of the 108 Upanishads now extant. Part 1 has the 10 major ones, pt.2 the lesser ones. Appendices: 1. On creation; 2. Yoga; 3. The Mudrās; 4-13. List of 108 upanishads. Index, p.547-564. *Class No: 294(031)*

Dictionaries

[797]

STUTLEY, M. *and* **STUTLEY, J. A Dictionary of Hinduism:** its mythology, folklore and development, 1500 B.C. - A.D. 1500. London, Routledge & Kegan Paul, 1977 (Paperback ed. published 1985). xvii,372p. map. £25. ISBN: 0710205872.

Published by Harper & Row in the US as *Harper's dictionary of Hinduism*.

c.2500 subject entries ('Jaina': 2 cols., 10 references). Bibliography, p.353-68. Diacriticals are shown. 'This

....(contd.)

outstanding work will be a standard reference tool in libraries for many years to come' (*American reference books annual*, 1978, entry no. 983). *Class No: 294(038)*

[798]

—WALKER, B. **The Hindu world: an encyclopedic survey of Hinduism.** London, Allen & Unwin, 1968. 2v. (xiii,609p.;xi,696p.).

A-L, M-Z. About 600 articles, documented (*e.g.* 'Suttee'; over 9p.; 6 references; 'Jainism': v.1. p.492-6; 9 references; 'Buddhism': v.1. p.183-7; 16 references). Includes bibliographies (*e.g.* 'Ganésa': 2p.; 2 references). V.2 has a detailed index of articles and subjects. Cross-references. Articles are unsigned. 'The substance of this book is derived largely from the standard works of recognised authorities, supplemented by material drawn from traditional Indian sources'. *Class No: 294(038)*

[799]

—WILKINS, W.J. **Hindu mythology: Vedic and Puranic.** 2nd ed. London, Curzon Press, 1973. xviii,500p. illus.

Facsimile reprint of 2nd ed. (Calcutta, London, Thacker, Spink, 1901).

Part 1 discusses the Vedic deities; pt.2 the Puranic deities; pt.3, the inferior deities. Many illustrations. Detailed index. Supplements Stutley pictorially. *Class No: 294(038)*

Indian Religions

[800]

CHOPRA, P.M., *ed*. **Religions and communities of India.** London, East-West Publications (UK), 1982. 316p. illus (photographs). £12.50. ISBN: 0856920819.

9 chapters, all divided and subdivided: 1. Hinduism - 2. Jainism - 3. Buddhism in India - 4. Sikhism - 5. Islam - 6. Christianity in India - 7. Zoroastrianism - 8. The Armenian community - 9. Judaism and the Jewish community. Glossary, p.270-291. Bibliography, p.292-297, by religion. Index, p.303-316. *Class No: 294.0/295*

Buddhism

[801]

BROWN, K. *and* **O'BRIEN, J.,** *eds*. **The Essential teachings of Buddhism:** daily readings from the Sacred texts. London, Rider, 1988. 304p. £8.95. ISBN: 0712616748.

An anthology of daily readings from Buddhist texts and commentaries which explain fundamental ideas behind Buddhism for the non-Buddhist. Clear explanation of history, theology and spirtualism of Buddhism. *Class No: 294.3*

[802]

HARVEY, B.P. An Introduction to Buddhism: teachings, history and practices. Cambridge, Cambridge University Press, 1990. 350p. illus, diagrs. £55. $64.95. ISBN: 0521308151.

Aims to be a comprehensive introduction to Buddhist

....(contd.)

tradition as it has developed in three major cultural areas in Asia, and as it is now developing in the West. Primarily intended for students. *Class No:* 294.3

[803]

Sacred books of the Buddhists, translated by various Oriental scholars ... London, H. Frowde. Oxford University Press, 1895-1974. 30v.

Previous edition, 1942. *Class No:* 294.3

[804]

—GODDARD, D., *ed.* A Buddhist Bible. 2nd ed., rev. & enl. Thetford, Vermont, D. Goddard, 1938 (Reprinted Beacon Press, 1991). viii,677p. $14.95. ISBN: 080705951x.

First published 1932.

A collection of translations of texts from Pali, Sanscrit, Chinese and Tibetan sources and from Japanese modern collections. Appendix of bibliographical and other notes. The 2nd ed. adds the work of Bhikshu Wai-tao and other Buddhist scholars. *Class No:* 294.3

Bibliographies

[805]

REYNOLDS, F.E., *and others*. **Guide to Buddhist religion.** Boston, Mass., G.K. Hall, 1981. 440p. $57.50. ISBN: 081617900x.

Subject bibliography. Categories: Historical development; religious thought; authoritative texts; popular beliefs and literature; the arts; social, economic and political aspects; religious practices and rituals; ideal beings; hagiography and biography; mythology (including sacred history), cosmology and basic symbols; sacred places; soteriological experience and processes; path and goal; research aids.

Class No: 294.3(01)

[806]

VESSIE, P.A. Zen Buddhism: a bibliography of books and articles in English, 1892-1975. Ann Arbor, Mich., University Microfilms International, under the aegis of the East Asia Library, University of Washington, 1976. xiv, 81 leaves. $12.75. ISBN: 0835701735.

762 numbered entries, with occasional brief annotations. 2 parts. 1: General works ... Zen sects: Rinzai and Solo - 2. Zen and archery; Zen and the arts; Zen and Christianity ... Zen training; Zen and the West; Miscellaneous; Zen periodicals. *Class No:* 294.3(01)

[807]

YOO, Y. Buddhism: a subject index to periodical articles in English, 1728-1971. Metuchen, N.J., Scarecrow Press, 1973. 184p.

1261 numbered items from over 200 periodicals; author and title indexes. Appended list of Buddhist societies and associations. *Class No:* 294.3(01)

[808]

—YOO, Y. Books on Buddhism: an annotated subject guide. Metuchen, N.J., Scarecrow Press, 1977. 251p.

A companion volume to the above, with 1300 entries under 38 headings. All items are in English.

Class No: 294.3(01)

Dictionaries

[809]

HUMPHREYS, C.A. A Popular dictionary of Buddhism. Rev. ed. London, Curzon Press, 1976. (Reprint 1984). 224p. £3.50. ISBN: 0700701842.

First published 1962.

Gives definitions and brief explanations of *c.*1000 terms (*e.g.* 'Four Paths': ½p.). Includes brief biographies; references to the literature. Modified diacriticals. Author is Founder-President of the Buddhist Society.

Class No: 294.3(038)

[810]

—LING, T.O. A Dictionary of Buddhism: India and South-East Asia. New ed. Calcutta, K.P. Bagchi (South Asia Books), 1986. [4],202p. $15. (*Bagchi Indological series, 2.*) ISBN: 0836414365.

First published 1972.

Complementary to Humphreys, defining fewer terms more extensively; bibliographical references. Terms were the author's contribution to S.G.F. Brandon's *A dictionary of comparative religion* (1970). *Class No:* 294.3(038)

[811]

PREBISH, C.S. Historical dictionary of Buddhism. Metuchen, NJ,Scarecrow Press, 1993. 387p. $42.50. ((*Historical dictionaries of religions, philosophies, and movements, 1.*)) ISBN: 0810826984.

Preliminaries include preface, pronunciation guide, overview of Buddhist scriptures, chronology and map of Asia showing Buddhist sites. The dictionary (p.36-288) has A-Z arrangement of persons, places, events, texts, doctrines, practices, institutions and movements. A bibliography of nearly 100 pages is especially valuable.

Class No: 294.3(038)

Yearbooks & Directories

[812]

BUDDHIST SOCIETY. The Buddhist directory: a directory of Buddhist groups and centres in the United Kingdom and Ireland and other related organisations. 4th ed. London, the Society, 1987. 75p. ISBN: 090103228x.

First published 1979.

5 sections: Societies and organizations (subdivided England, Ireland, Scotland, Wales, and again by counties, A-Z, giving names, descriptions, addresses and telephone numbers); Other related organizations; the Buddhist Union of Europe (representatives names and addresses); Libraries; Buddhist literature - some retailers. Index of organizations, p;72-75. *Class No:* 294.3(058)

[813]

International Buddhist directory. London, Wisdom Publications, 1985. 120p. £5.95; $8.95. (*A Wisdom reference book.*) ISBN: 0861710258.

In 2 parts: part 1: Confirmed addresses; pt.2: Unconfirmed addresses. Lists some 1800 Buddhist centres in 63 countries. 500 confirmed addresses include name and address, telephone number, which tradition of Buddhism, the spiritual director, whether centre is in city or country, or has resident teacher, accommodation, regular teachings, meditation and retreat facilities, library, bookshop, newsletter. Unconfirmed list includes some 1300 names and addresses. Arranged A-Z in both sections; tabular data in section 1. *Class No:* 294.3(058)

China

[814]
SOOTHILL, W.E. *and* HODOUS, L. **A Dictionary of Chinese Buddhist terms**, with Sanscrit and English equivalents. New ed. Delhi, Motilal Banarsidass, 1987. 510p. £20. ISBN: 8120803193.

First published 1937, London, Kegan Paul.

'Indexed by the number of strokes in the Chinese symbol, with definitions in clear and concise English' (Diehl, K.S. *Religions, mythologies, folklores* (2nd ed., 1962), item no. 931). *Class No:* 294.3(510)

Japan

[815]
NAKAMURA, H., *and others, comps. & eds.* **Japanese-English Buddhist dictionary.** Tokyo, 1965. xv,383p.

Over 5000 terms, arranged in order of Japanese syllabary. *Class No:* 294.3(52)

Sikhism

[816]
COLE, W.O. *and* SAMBHI, P.S. **A Popular dictionary of Sikhism.** London, Curzon Press, 1990. 174p. £4.50.$14.95. ISBN: 0700702026.

30-page introduction includes a historical sketch of Sikhism, with time charts and maps, and a bibliography for further reading. Entries go beyond mere definitions. '... concise, inexpensive but authoritative and well-*written...* '(*Choice*, v.28(5),January 1991). *Class No:* 294.51

[817]
COLE, W.O. *and* SAMBHI, P.S. **The Sikhs: their religious beliefs and practices.** London, etc., Routledge & Kegan Paul, 1978. xxvii, 210p. illus., maps. £9.50. ISBN: 0710088434.

9 chapters (*e.g.* 2. The place of the Ten Gurus in the Sikh religion; 6. Daily life, ceremonies and festivals: 8. The attitude ot Sikhism towards other religions. 'Primary sources for the study of Sikhism, p.xv-xvii. Glossary. Secondary sources (running commentary) and additional bibliography, p.196-204. Detailed non-analytical index. A new ed. was published in 1991 (ISBN 0415040280). *Class No:* 294.51

[818]
RAI, P.M., *comp.* **Sikhism and the Sikhs:** an annotated bibliography. Westport, CT., Greenwood Press, 1989. xv,257p. $69.95. (*Bibliographies and indexes in religious studies, 13.*) ISBN: 031326130x.

1150 numbered and annotated entries arranged in 7 chapters: 1. General works - 2. Sikh history - 3. Sikh gurus - 4. Sikh sculptures and philosophy - 5. Sikh politics and social-economic conditions - 6. Sikhs abroad - 7. Source materials. Author, title and subject indexes. *Class No:* 294.51

Yoga

[819]
ELIADE, M. **Yoga:** immortality and freedom.

Trask, W.R., *translator.* 2nd ed. Princeton, N.J., Princeton University Press, 1970 (Reprinted 1991); London, Arkana (Penguin Group), 1989. xxii,536p. (*Bollinger series, v.56.*) ISBN: 0691017646, (US); 0140191585, (UK).

First published in US in 1958; 2nd ed. in 1969.

'A scholarly treatment of yoga philosophy, which gives an exhaustive survey of the history and main schools of thought' (Thompson, I. *Alternative medicine* (1981)). List of works cited, p.433-480. Index p.481-536. *Class No:* 294.527

[820]
FEUERSTEIN, G. **Encyclopedic dictionary of Yoga.** New York, Paragon House, 1990. 430p. illus. (90 black & white photographs). $24.95. (*Living traditions series.*) ISBN: 155778244x.

Defines more than 2000 words, expressions and concepts found in the study of Yoga, arranged in English A-Z order. Entries range in length from a few lines to several pages. English keywords refer to Sanscrit equivalents. Includes brief biographies. Bibliography (p.427-430) is in two parts: 1. Reference; 2. Recommended reading. *Class No:* 294.527

[821]
JARRELL, H.R. **International yoga bibliography, 1950-1980.** Metuchen, N.J., Scarecrow Press, 1981. ix,221p. $22.50; £13.85. ISBN: 0810814722.

Numbered entries of books, journal articles, magazine articles, and yoga periodicals, arranged A-Z in each of the four sections. Includes works published in English, French, German, Spanish, Portuguese, Italian and Dutch over the last 31 years, and also reprints, new editions, etc., of books originally printed before that time. No annotations. Author index, p.155-174; title index, p.175-211; subject index, p.212-221. *Class No:* 294.527

[822]
WOOD, E.E. **Yoga dictionary.** New ed. Harmondsworth, Mddx., Penguin Books, 1977. 328p. (*Pelican books.*)

Originally published in New York, by Philosophical Library, in 1956.

Includes both definitions and longer notes. All technical terminology taken from Sanscrit words. *Class No:* 294.527

Zoroastrianism

[823]
BOYCE, M. **A History of Zoroastrianism.** Leiden, E.J. Brill, 1975-. To be in 4v. v.1. Gld.165; $94.50. v.2. Gld.144; $82.50. v.3. Gld.380; $217.25. ISBN: 9004088474, v.1; 9004065067, v.2; 9004092714, v.3 505.00/00$aV.1: *The early period* (1975. xvi,349p. Rev. ed. 1988); v.2: *Under the Achaemenians* (1982. xvi,306p.); v.3: *Zoroastrianism under Macedonian and Roman rule* ; v.4: *Zoroastrianism under the Parthians and early Sasamans* (in preparation). *Class No:* 295

[824]

BOYCE, M. **Zoroastrians:** their religious beliefs and practices. London, Routledge & Kegan Paul, 1979. 252p. £10.50. (*Library of religious beliefs and practices.*) ISBN: 0710001215.

14 chapters (2. Zoroaster and his teaching - 3. The establishment of Mazda worship ... 5. Under the Achaemenians - 6. Under the Seleucids and Sassanids ... 10. Under the Caliphs ... 13. Under the Qajars and British - 14. In the twentieth century. Chapter bibliographies, p.229-36 (with some notes). Glossary, p.xv-xvii. *Class No:* 295

Jewish Religion (Judaism)

Bibliographies of Bibliographies

[825]

SHUNAMI, S. **Bibliography of Jewish bibliographies.** 2nd ed. enl. Jerusalem, The Magnes Press, The Hebrew University, 1965. xxiv,992,xxiip.

First published 1936.

4,727 numbered items, with very brief annotations, in 27 sections (including 1. Encyclopaedias - 2. Bibliography of bibliography - 3. General bibliographies - 4-5. Catalogues of public and private collections - 6. Booksellers' and publishers' catalogues (a selection) - 7. Bibliographical periodicals - 8. Lists of periodicals - 9-25. Subject sections - 26. Manuscripts - 27. Personal bibliographies). Index of names and subjects; index of Hebrew titles. The 2nd ed. has entries on the Dead Sea Scrolls and the holocaust of the Nazi régime. A supplement (1975. xvii,464,xvip.) lists entries 4751-6859, also in 27 sections. *Class No:* 296(009)

Bibliographies

[826]

CUTTER, C. *and* OPPENHEIM, M.F. **Jewish reference sources:** a selective, annotated bibliographic guide. New York, Garland, 1982. 180p. $24. ISBN: 082409347x.

Supersedes H. Zafran's *Jewish reference books: a select list* (1970).

371 numbered items arranged in 2 sections: General reference- Subject reference. Arrangement is A-Z with some subdivisions. Short descriptive annotations. Hebrew titles transliterated. Cross-references. '... fills a unique need' (*Bulletin of ABTPL,* v.2(4), March 1989, p.21-22). *Class No:* 296(01)

[827]

FRANK, R.S. *and* WOLLHEIM, W. **The Book of Jewish books:** a reader's guide to Judaism. New York, Harper & Row, 1986. xiv,320p. illus. $15.95. ISBN: 0060630086.

*c.*500 annotated entries listing books on the Bible, Jewish thought, Jewish history, the Holocaust, the arts, Israel, prayer books, etc. Essays precede each section. List of Jewish periodicals; list of Jewish bookstores. Glossary. 'Despite the few questionable inclusions and omissions inevitable in undertakings of this nature, this collection is a fairly solid work' (*Library journal,* v.lll(18) November 1, 1986, p.87). *Class No:* 296(01)

[828]

LUBETSKI, E. *and* LUBETSKI, M. **Building a Judaica library collection:** a resource guide. Littleton, Col., Libraries Unlimited, 1983,. 185p. $30. ISBN: 0872873757.

Arranged in 2 parts: Selection - Acquisitions. The 1st part is non-evaluative bibliographic guide to selection aids for Judaica materials; the 2nd part is an annotated international directory of publishers, etc. in the field. Index. *Class No:* 296(01)

[829]

—RUDAVSKY, A. 'Sources for a Judaica reference collection'. In *RSR,* v.12(3), Fall, 1984, p.13-30.

Compilation of a core collection of Jewish reference sources, arranged by form: Bibliographies - Encyclopedias - Indexes and specialized bibliographies - Almanacs, yearbooks, directories - Biographical dictionaries - Histories - 'Popular' sources - Proverbs and folklore - Atlases. *Class No:* 296(01)

[830]

NEW YORK PUBLIC LIBRARY. **Dictionary catalog of the Jewish collection** of the New York Public Library, Reference Department. Boston, Mass., G.K. Hall, 1960. First supplement, 1975. 14v; supplement, 8v.

371,000 photolithographed catalogue cards in all, 'for publications in all European languages as well as in Hebrew and Yiddish, on the history and traditions of the Jewish people throughout the ages and in all lands. It covers archaeological and Biblical studies as well as *belles-lettres,* rabbinic and philosophic texts' (G.K. Hall & Co. *Catalog of publications,* 1979-80, p.32-33). *Class No:* 296(01)

[831]

ROTH, C. **Magna bibliotheca anglo-judaica:** a bibliographical guide to Anglo-Jewish history. New ed., rev. & enl. London, Jewish Historical Society of England, 1937. xiii,464p.

First published as *Bibliotheca anglo-judaica,* by J. Jacobs and L. Wulf (1888).

About 3000 items, 2 main parts: 1. Histories (sections A1-14, including biography and periodicals) - 2. Historical material (B1-22). Items in the Mocatta Library and allied collections in University College, London, are asterisked. Author index. The sequel is: *Class No:* 296(01)

[832]

—LEHMANN, R.P. **Anglo-Jewish bibliography, 1937-1970.** London, Jewish Historical Society of England, 1973. xi,364p.

27 sections(1. Bibliographies and works of reference - 2. Periodicals ... 25. Biography). Includes works in Hebrew and periodical articles. Analytical entries. Detailed analytical index, p.337-64. A volume covering 1971-90 was published in 1992 (£35. ISBN 0902528262. *Class No:* 296(01)

[833]

SPECTOR, S.A. **Jewish mysticism:** an annotated bibliography of the Kabbalah in English. New York, Garland, 1984. 399p. $45. (*Garland reference library of social science, 210.*) ISBN: 082409042x.

Lists English-language works, including festschrifts, reference books, serials, and monographs for the period 1659-1983, arranged by subject. Entries include quotations from the prefaces of cited works. 3-part index to primary materials, secondary materials and subjects. No title index. Only other published bibliography is G.G. Scholem's *Bibliographia Kabbalistica* (1927). *Class No:* 296(01)

Encyclopaedias

[834]

Encyclopaedia Judaica. Roth, C. *and* Wigoder, G., *eds*. Jerusalem, Keter Publishing House,1971; New York, Macmillan, 1972. 16v.(12,128p).illus. facsims. charts. maps.

The 16v. encyclopaedia has 25,000 entries. Major articles are signed. Over 1800 contributors. V.16: UR-Z, plus supplementary entries on ' Chronology', 'Migration', etc. The entry 'Hebrew language' (columns 1559-1662) has over 6 cols. of bibliography. V.1 carries the general index (249,580 references) with supplementary lists of newspapers and periodicals. Over 8000 illus., some in colour. Glossaries are appended to each volume. A well-printed, handsome set. 'The latest, most comprehensive and in many ways, most authoritative summary of research in all areas of Jewish scholarship.'(*Library journal*, August 1972, p.2582). It supplements but does not supersede the *Jewish encyclopaedia* (12v. 1901-6), *Encyclopaedia Judaica* V,1-10, *c*.1928-34) or the 10v. *Universal Jewish encyclopaedia* (1939-43).

Encyclopaedia Judaica yearbook decennial book, 1973-1982 (1982). *Class No:* 296(031)

[835]

The Encyclopedia of Judaism. Wigoder, G., *ed*. New York, Macmillan, 1989. 768p. illus. $75. ISBN: 0026284103.

Articles (unsigned) vary in length according to significance (*eg*'Torah':2p.;'Hilel'(the saga), 2p.). Hebrew translation/transliteration is often given. A feature: *c*.300 illus.(including colour) and a 15-page index. 'It provides a concise introduction to many topics; at the same time, it is more comprehensive than older one-volume works on Judaism' (*Reference books bulletin*, 1989-90, p.60.). *Class No:* 296(031)

[836]

The Jewish encyclopedia: a descriptive record of the history, religion, literature and customs of the Jewish people from the earliest times to the present day ... Singer, I., *ed*. New York, Funk & Wagnalls, 1901-1906. (Reprinted Gordon Press, 1976). 12v. illus. $998.95 the set. ISBN: 0849021014.

Contents include Assyriology, Egyptology, archaeological investigation in Palestine in the 19th century, the relation of the Hellenistic literature to the Jewish and Greek thought of the period, and the literature of the New Testament. Signed articles; extensive bibliographies; 2000 plates. Less scholarly than the *Encyclopedia Judaica* (Berlin, Verlag Eschkol [*c*.1928-34]. Illus. v.1-10: A-LYRA) for the topics covered by the latter, it is also somewhat dated. Biographical and historical data are still invaluable, nevertheless. *Class No:* 296(031)

[837]

UNTERMAN, A. Jews; their religious beliefs and practices. London, Routledge & Kegan Paul, 1981. xiii,272p. £16.95. ISBN: 0710007434.

'... about the religion, ritual and attitudes of the Jews' (*Preface*). Part 1 has six chapters on religious beliefs; Part 2 has 8 chapters on Jewish ritual and practice, the home, the synagogue and the ritual year. There follows a glossary, notes to the chapters, a select bibliography (p.257-262), and an index (p.263-272). 'Scholarly' (*Church times*, September 1981, p.7). *Class No:* 296(031)

[838]

WIGODER, G., *ed*. **Everyman's Judaica:** an encyclopedic dictionary. London, W.H. Allen, 1975. xi,673p. illus. (incl. col. pl.). facsims, ports, tables, maps.

15,000 short entries. 'A guide to the Bible, to Israel old and new, to Jewish communities throughout the world, to famous Jews, to Jewish concepts and customs, to Jewish history and literature' (*Introduction*). 65 lists and tables (*e.g.* List of Kibbutz, p.339-40; Common Jewish abbreviations, p.3-5; Blessings and benedictions, p.73). Appendices include 'Hebrew-English basic vocabulary'; 'Daily calendar'. Many brief biographies. 200 illus. (many in colour). Planned as complimentary to the 16v. *Encyclopedia Judaica* and its *Yearbooks. Class No:* 296(031)

[839]

—ROTH, C. *and* WIDOGER, G., *eds*. Concise Jewish encyclopedia. New York, New American Library, 1981. 576p. $8.95. ISBN: 0452005264. *Class No:* 296(031)

[840]

WIGODER, G., *editor-in-chief*. **The New standard Jewish encyclopedia.** 7th ed. New York, Facts on File, 1992. [vi],1001p. illus, ports, facs, tables. $59.95. ISBN: 0816026904.

Covers *all* aspects of Jewish history, religion amd culture, not merely Judaism. Many brief entries and cross-references. 'Holocaust', only 9 lines. Well illustrated; well produced. Unsigned articles, no maps. *Class No:* 296(031)

Dictionaries

[841]

COHN-SHERBOK, D. The Dictionary of Judaica. Oxford, Blackwell, 1992. 650p. illus. £50. $74.95. ISBN: 0631166157.

Over 7000 concise entries on Jewish history, civilization and religion. Intended as a single-volume dictionary for students and the general reader. Entries for Yiddish, Hebrew and Aramaic terms are spelled out as Sephardic terms. 59% of entries are of people. 2-page chronological table. '... concise definitions that reflect strong scholarly research ...' (*Choice*, v.30(9), May 1993, p.1436). *Class No:* 296(038)

[842]

COHN-SHERBOK, D. A Dictionary of Judaism and Christianity. London, SPCK, 1991. [v],180p. ISBN: 0281045380.

Aims to provide vital information about Judaism and Christianity in direct and simple language, making important connections between the two faiths. Entries vary in length from a few lines to 3 columns or more. Cross-references. For the general reader. 'The first dictionary to explain and compare key concepts, beliefs and practices of both Judaism and Christianity' (*British book news*, September 1991, p.607). *Class No:* 296(038)

Yearbooks & Directories

[843]

The Jewish year book, 1994/5754-5755. London, Valentine, 1994. Annual. 315p. £18.50. ISBN: 0853032742. ISSN: 00753769.

First published 1896.

Directories of synagogues; religious organizations; memorials; cemeteries; educational organizations; welfare organizations; clubs and cultural societies; miscellaneous

....(contd.)

organizations in London, the regions, other countries, Israel; Jewish statistics. 'A Jewish book list'; Who's who, p.224-301. Obituary. Index, p.304-313. *Class No:* 296(058)

Quotations

[844]

BARON, J.L., *ed.* **A Treasury of Jewish quotations.** New York, A.S. Barnes, 1966 (Reprinted 1985). 623p. $25. ISBN: 0876688946.

First published 1956.

A dictionary of quotations about Judaism and Jewish history, from the Bible to the present. Arranged under topics A-Z. Precise references to sources. Many of the quotations have never been published in English. *Class No:* 296(082.2)

Histories

[845]

BARON, S.W. A Social and religious history of the Jews. 2nd ed., rev. & enl. New York, Columbia University Press, 1952-80. 17v. $41.60 each vol.

First published 1937 in a 3-vol. ed.

Content: V.1: *To the beginning of the Christian era* (1952. vi,436p.); 2: *Christian era: the first five centuries* (1952. vi,436p.); 3: *Heirs of Rome and Persia* (1957. x,340p.); 4: *Meeting of east and west* (1957. 352p.); 5: *Religious controls and dissensions* (1957. 416p.); 6: *Laws, homilies and the Bible* (1958. 486p.); 7: *Hebrew languages and letters* (1958. 329p.); 8: *Philosophy and science* (1958. 405p.); 9: *Under Church and Empire* (1965. x,350p.); 10: *On the Empire's periphery* (1965. 432p.); 11. *Citizen or alien conjurer* (1967. 359p.); 12: *Economic catalyst* (1967. 359p.); 13: *Inquisition, Renaissance, and Reformation* (1969. vi,463p.); 14: *Catholic restoration and wars of religion* (1969. 412p.); 15: *Resettlement and exploration* (1973. 550p.); 16: *Poland - Lithuania, 1500-1650* (1976. 460p.); 17: *Byzantines, Mamelukes, and Maghribians* (1980. 450p.). Each volume has notes and references to sources. Index to v.1-8 (1960. xi,163p.). *Class No:* 296(091)

[846]

The Blackwell companion to Jewish culture: from the eighteenth century to the present. Abramson, G., *ed.* Oxford, Blackwell, 1989. xxiii,853p. illus (ports). ISBN: 0631151117.

Over 1100 entries by a group of *c.*230 scholars. '... covers wide geographical, intellectual, and artistic areas, and offers material for every kind of reader, from the scholar to the casual browser (*Preface*, p.vii). Subjects include films, folklore, cinema industry, etc., but mainly people. 'Further reading' after entries, and bibliographies after some entries. Cross-references. Index, p.833-53. *Class No:* 296(091)

[847]

The Cambridge history of Judaism. Davies, W.D. *and* Finkelstein, L. Cambridge, Cambridge University Press, 1984-. To be in 4v. V.1. xvi,461,[3]p. figs., map; v.2. 800p. 6 illus. v.1. £70; v.2. £85.. ISBN: 0521218802, v.1; 0521219299, v.2.

To be in 13 chapters in 4v. Contents: Chapters 1-3. *Introduction. The Persian period* are in v.1. Other chapters planned are: 4. The Persian Empire and the political and social history of Palestine in the Persian period; 5. The archaeology of Persian Palestine; 6. Hebrew and Aramaic in

....(contd.)

the Persian period; 7. The Jewish community in Palestine in the Persian period; 8. Prophesy and psalms; 9. Wisdom literature; 10. Jewish religious life; 11. Persian religion in the Achemenid age; 12. Iranian influence on Judaism; 13. The Diaspora (A. Babylonia in the Persian age; B. The Babylonian captivity; C. Egypt, Persian satrapy; D. The Jews in Egypt).

V.1 covers the geography of Palestine and the Levant in relation to its history; Numismatics; Calendars and chronology. Extensive footnotes. Bibliographies, p.401-446, arranged by chapter, subdivided by subject and form, subdivided again by author. Analytical index, p.447-461. *Class No:* 296(091)

[848]

POLIAKOV, L. The History of anti-Semitism. London, Elek Books, 1966-85. 4v. v.2 £19.50; v.3 £25; v.4 £20. (*The Littman library of Jewish civilization.*) ISBN: 0197100260, v.2; 0197100279, v.3; 0197100384, v.4.

Translated from the French by Richard Howard.

Traces in detail the development of anti-Semitism in 4 chapters: 1. From the time of Christ to the court Jews; 2. From Mohammed to the Marranos; 3. From Voltaire to Wagner; 4. Suicidal Europe, 1870-1933. *Class No:* 296(091)

Bibliographies

[849]

The Jewish world in modern times: a selected annotated bibliography. Edelheit, A.J. *and* Edelheit, H., *eds.* London, Mansell Publishing; Boulder, Col., Westview Press, 1988. xix, 569 p. £55. $ 85. ISBN: 072011988x, UK; 0813305721, US.

Aims to place Jewish history in both its universal and its local contexts, broadly covering modern Jewish life from the mid-17th century to the present. An introduction summarizing the most important events, people and places, precedes the annotated bibliography, which is in two parts. Part 1: *The Jewish World*, has surveys of Jewish history, social history, religious trends, culture trends, antisemitism, etc., arranged in 9 subject chapters. Part 2: *The Jewish Community* is arranged by geographical region. The final chapter 19 lists bibliographies and guides. 2170 entries in all. Glossary, p. 460 - 463, author, title and subject indexes, p. 464 - 569, complete the volume. ' ... an important work ... '. (*College and research libraries*, v.50 (1), January 1989, p.85). 'These biographies not only cover their subject thoroughly but provide succinct and critical annotations in a well-organized, amply cross-referenced and indexed volume' (*Choice*, v.26 (5), January 1989, p.780). *Class No:* 296(091)(01)

America—North & Central

[850]

Encyclopedia of Jewish institutions: United States and Canada. Rosen, O., *ed.* Tel Aviv, Mosadot, 1983. 501p. $55.

Lists *c.*6000 Jewish institutions, ranging from national organizations to local synagogues and community centres, arranged geographically. Entries include full name; address; telephone number; a description of the institution, its aims

....(contd.)

and activities; membership; number of employees; history; facilities; officers; publications. Index of institutions. *Class No:* 296(71/73)

USA

Histories

[851]

KORROS, A.S. *and* **SARNA, J.D. American synagogue history:** a bibliography and state-of-the-field survey. New York, Markus Wiener, 1989. 247p. $29.95. ISBN: 0910129908.

Lists *c.*1100 monographs, journal articles and pamphlets on synagogue and community histories, arranged by US State. Includes a separate bibliography of 69 items on synagogue architecture. Select bibliography of secondary sources. Author index. 'The value of the volume is enriched by a thoughtful introduction by noted historian Jonathan D. Sarna ... and a 40-page survey by Daniel J. Elazar, "The development of the American synagogue"' (*Choice,*) v.27(1), September 1989, p.82). *Class No:* 296(73)(091)

Biographies

[852]

NADELL, P.S. Conservative Judaism in America: a biographical dictionary and sourcebook. Westport, CT., Greenwood Press, 1988. 409p. $56. ISBN: 0313242054.

The first of a projected series on the Jewish denominations in America.

The introduction, a 24-page historical essay, is followed by about 130 one or two page sketches of key rabbis, educators, scholars, and lay readers, each entry giving basic biographical information, indicating the person's contribution to conservative Judaism, and listing works by or about the person. There are 3 further historical essays on the Jewish Theological Seminary, the Rabbinical Assembly, and the United Synagogue. Glossary. Bibliographies. Index. '... main drawback is of an ideological nature ... author's personal bias very evident ... Nevertheless, this is an important contribution' (*Choice,* v.26(6), February 1989,p.924). *Class No:* 296(73)(092)

Libraries

[853]

HOOGEWOUD, F.J., *and others.* **A Guide to libraries of Judaica and Hebraica in Europe.** Copenhagen, Det Kongelige Bibliotek, for the Association of Libraries of Judaica and Hebraica in Europe, 1986. 124 leaves, 15 of which are markers & only bear the name of the country. DKr.150. *c.*£13. ISBN: 8770235554.

Arranged A-Z by country, subdivided by city or town, A-Z. Information given: 1. Name, address, telephone number, librarian - 2. Size and contents - 3. Access to holdings - 4. Collection services - 5. Additional information. 3 appendices: 1. Hebrew manuscript collections in Europe on microfilm - 2. Hebrew incunabula in European libraries: a provisional list of bibliographical tools - 3. Names and addresses of national associations concerning Jewish studies. No pagination and no index; printed on one side of each leaf only. Correction sheets and additional information leaves to be supplied free of charge. *Class No:* 296:061:026/027

Talmud, Midrash etc.

[854]

The Babylonian Talmud; translated, with notes, glossary and indices. Epstein, I., *ed.* London, Soncino Press, 1935-52. 35v. (including index vol.).

The complete English translation of the Talmud. Comprehensive index; covering all cited Scriptural passages. Lists foreign-language glossaries and abbreviations and gives a complete list of Rabbis mentioned in the Talmud, with their sayings. *Class No:* 296.80

[855]

—A Concordance of the Septuagint, giving various readings from Codices Vaticanus, Alexandrinus, Sinaiticus, and Ephraemi; with an appendix of words, from Origen's 'Hexalpa', etc.; not found in the above manuscripts. Morrish, G., *comp.* Grand Rapids, Mich., Zondervan Publishing House, 1976. (Reprint). viii,[1],284p. $25.95. ISBN: 0310203007. *Class No:* 296.80

[856]

—Soncino books of the Bible. Cohen, A., *ed.* London, Soncino Press, 1945-52. (Reprinted by Bloch). 14v. $165 the set. ISBN: 0900689234.

Published in association with the Jewish Publication Society of America.

Hebrew text and English translation plus expositions based on the classical Jewish commentaries. Soncino Press has also published *The Midrash* (the classical Jewish commentaries), translated into English, with notes, glossary and indexes; and edited by H. Freedman and M. Simon (1951. 10v.). *Class No:* 296.80

[857]

The Talmud: the Steinsaltz edition. V.3: a reference guide. New York, Random House, 1989. 3v. $40 each volume.

The complete 8v. translation has extensive introductions and commentaries. V.3, 'A reference guide', provides the essential guidelines for Talmud studies. Rabbi Steinsaltz's description of the setting and structure of the Talmud, is followed by appendices and a general index. *Class No:* 296.80

Dictionaries

Hebrew

[858]

JASTROW, M. Dictionary of the Targumin, the Talmud Babli and Yerushalmi, and the Midrashic literature. with an index of Scriptural quotations. London, Luzac, 1903 (Reprinted New York, Pardes Publishing House, 1950). 2v. (xx,1736p.).

First published 1886.

Includes many quotations, with exact references to sources and translation. A scholarly work; the standard Talmudic Hebrew-English dictionary. Well produced. *Class No:* 296.80(038)=924

Islam

[859]
AL-TABARĪ, Abu Ja'far Muhammad bin Jarir. **The commentary on the Qur'ān.** Cambridge, Cambridge University Press, 1987-. To be in 5v. V.1: £45; v.2: £35. ISBN: 0521326621, v.1; 0521350018, v.2.

An abridged translation of the whole of Tabari's commentary on the Qur'ān. V.1: The reign of Abu Ja'far al-Mansur, AD 754-775 (published 1987. 283p.); v.2: The son and grandsons of al-Mansur - the reigns of al-Mahdi, al-Hadi and Harun-al-Rashid, AD 775-808 (published in 1989. 360p). *Class No:* 297

[860]
Islam and Islamic groups: a worldwide reference guide. Shaikh, F., *ed.* Harlow, Longman, 1992. ix,316p. Map. £85;$155. ISBN: 0582091462.

105 signed entries by 11 contributors, arranged under country or region, and covering all politically significant national and international organizations. Bibliography. Short glossary. *Class No:* 297

[861]
KASSIS, H.E. **A Concordance of the Qur'an.** Berkeley, CA., University of California Press, 1984. 1440p. $115. ISBN: 0520043278.

The first concordance of the Koran in English. 2 sections: 1. All the verses in which the divine name appears (based on Arberry's *The Koran interpreted*) - 2. the remaining vocabulary. The vocabulary is arranged by root, subarranged grammatically. *Class No:* 297

Bibliographies

[862]
BINARK, L. *and* EREN, H. **World bibliography of translations of the meanings of the Holy Qur'an:** printed translations, 1515-1980. London, Routledge, 1988. 600p. £65. ISBN: 0710302290.

Contains details of every translation of the Qur'an from Arabic into every known language between 1515 and 1980. Full bibliographical entries of references and sources. *Class No:* 297(01)

[863]
GEDDES, C.L. **Guide to reference books for Islamic studies.** Denver, Col., American Institute of Islamic Studies, 1985. 429p. $45. (*American Institute of Islamic studies, no. 9.*) ISBN: 0933017006.

1069 annotated entries for reference books on the history, culture, society, and faith of Muslim peoples from the time of Muhammed to 1924. Includes some works in Western European and Asian languages as well as English. 79-page author, title and subject index. *Choice* (v.23(10), June 1986, p.1520) considers coverage of some subjects inadequate, many omissions, and no criteria for inclusion indicated. *Class No:* 297(01)

[864]
Guide to Islam. Ede, D., *ed.* Boston, Mass., G.K. Hall, 1983. 288p. $65.50. ISBN: 0816179050.

Annotated bibliography of primary and secondary materials on the Islamic faith and civilization from A.D. 600 to 1976. Includes translations, literary anthologies, travel accounts, biographies, ancient and modern histories, and theological and mystical writings. Arranged in 7 sections: Historical development, religious thought, religious practice, sacred places, institutions, art and architecture, and research aids. 'A particularly welcome feature is the inclusion of English-language translations of Muslim works' (*Library journal,* 15 November 1983, p.2151). *Class No:* 297(01)

Encyclopaedias

[865]
The Encyclopaedia of Islam. New ed., prepared by a number of leading Orientalists, under the patronage of the International Union of Academies. Leiden, E.J. Brill, 1954-. v.1, fasc.1-. illus., plans, maps. To be in about 10v. Gld.396-620; $198-310 each vol. ISBN: 9004061576, v.1; 9004070265, v.2; 9004061584, v.3; 9004057215, v.4; 9004078193, v.5; 9001418127, v.6.

First published 1913-1936; reprinted 1987 in 9v. (5164p. illus., tables, 110 pl.) in view of the many years still needed to complete the new ed. (Gld.1500; $750. ISBN 9004082654).

Published primarily in double fascicules and then in volumes. V.I - V (Fasc.1-98a): A - Mahi (1954-86); V.VI (Fasc.99-108) (1986-88) in 5 parts. Signed articles, with bibliographies. Many biographies and entries under localities (*e.g.* 'Afghanistan': has 5 sections: geography; ethnography; languages; religion; history - each with bibliography; folded black-and-white map). The article 'Crusades' has bibliography of 1¼ columns, with running commentary. A minor difficulty is the entry of articles under the appropriate Arabic word instead of the English (*e.g.* mosques - under 'Masdjid'). Diacritical markings. A definitive scholarly work. An index to the first five volumes and supplement has been published (1989. vii,295p. Gld.120. $60. ISBN 9004088490). *Class No:* 297(031)

[866]
GLASSÉ, C. **Concise encyclopedia of Islam.** London, Stacey International; New York, Harper Row, 1989. 472p. 40 illus (col.). ll maps. £30. $59.95. ISBN: 0060631236, US; 0905743520, UK.

Nearly 1200 entries (Aaron ... Zekiel). Appended chronology, and bibliography (p.468-72). *Class No:* 297(031)

[867]
The Shorter encyclopedia of Islam. Gibb, H.A.R. *and* Kramer, J.H., *eds.* Leyden, Brill, 1953 (Reprinted 1993). vii,671p. 7 pl., 2 plans. Gld.99; $63.00. ISBN: 9004006818.

Comprises all the articles in the 1st ed., and supplement of the *Encyclopaedia of Islam* (1913-33) relating particularly to the religion and law of Islam. Most of these articles have been reproduced without material alteration; some have been shortened or revised; a few new entries have been added. Bibliographies have been brought up-to-date. Included is a 'Register of subjects', which gives the English translation of Arabic words used as headings. A-Z index of articles, stating authors. Invaluable. *Class No:* 297(031)

Handbooks & Manuals

[868]

WEEKES, R.V. **The World of Islam:** a world ethnographic survey. 2nd rev. ed. Westport, CT., Greenwood Press, 1985. xii,546p. tables, maps. £85.50. ISBN: 0313233926.

lst ed., 1978, as *Muslim people*.

71 contributors. Articles A-Z, on the life and culture of all major ethnic groups (with Muslim population in excess of 100,000), 30 Muslim culture groups. 'Somali' (tribe), p.364-9 (bibliography, p.365-9). Appended bibliographies include periodical articles and theses. Maps show locations of ethnic groups. 3 appendices: 1. Muslim nationalities of the world; 2. Muslim ethnic groups within nations; 3. Major Muslim ethnic groups. 'A timely reference work for both public and academic libraries' (*Library journal*, 15 April 1979, p.587). *Class No:* 297(035)

Dictionaries

[869]

NETTON, I.R. **A Popular dictionary of Islam.** London, Curzon Press; Atlantic Highlands, NJ, Humanities Press International, 1992. 279p. £9.99. ISBN: 0700702334, UK; 0391037560, US.

'Abasa'(Ar) … al-Zumar (Ar). Includes people, places, parts of the Quran, etc. Length of entries varies (*eg* 'Muhammad' has over a page; 'Mecca' 12 lines). Guide to further reading, p.269-79. *Class No:* 297(038)

[870]

PENRICE, J. **A Dictionary and glossary of the Koran,** with copious grammatical references and explanations of the text. London, Curzon Press, 1971. vi,168p. £7.50. ISBN: 0700700013.

'Using Penrice in conjunction with the reprinted Flügel text and Arberry's translation, many students with a basic foundation in Arabic grammar will discover for themselves the beauties and the profundities of the Koran' (*T.L.S.*, 14 July 1972, p.823). Sources, p.vi. *Class No:* 297(038)

Arabic

[871]

MIR, M. **Dictionary of Qur'ānic terms and concepts.** New York, Garland, 1987. 244p. $40. (*Garland reference library of the humanities, 693.*) ISBN: 0824085469.

Lists over 500 terms found in the Qur'ān. English translations of the terms are arranged A-Z with cross-references from the transliterated Arabic. Definitions vary in length from several lines to 2 or more pages. Entries refer to specific passages in the Qur'ān where the term is used and explain its significance. A 20-page list of terms included follows the text. *Class No:* 297(038)=927

Histories

[872]

LAPIDUS, I.M. **A History of Islamic societies.** Cambridge, Cambridge University Press, 1988. xxxi,1002p. 30 illus., 37 maps. £35. ISBN: 0521225523.

A study of the civilization and patterns of life of Muslims throughout the world. Part 1 examines the formative era of Islamic civilization from the revelation of the Qu'ran to the 13th century; pt.2 traces the diffusion of the Middle Eastern Islamic paradigm from the 10th to the 19th centuries; and pt.3 treats the disruption of Islamic societies by economic

…. (contd.)

decline, internal religious conflict, and the establishment of European domination in the 19th and 20th centuries. Glossary, p.918-928. Extensive bibliography, p.929-970. Index, p.971-1002. *Class No:* 297(091)

[873]

RAHMAN, H.U. **A Chronology of Islamic history, 570-1000 C.E.** London, Mansell Publishing Ltd.; Boston, Mass., G.K. Hall, 1989. 256p. 3 maps. £25; $45. ISBN: 0720119820, UK; 0816190674, US.

Lists and describes the events that marked Islam's rise. Chronological entries are self-contained and there are frequent cross-references. Dates refer to the Gregorian calendar and formulas for transposing Gregorian into Muslim dates included. Footnotes. Index, p.169-181. *Class No:* 297(091)

Europe—Western

[874]

GERHOLM, T. *and* LITHMAN, Y.G., *eds*. **The New Islamic presence in Western Europe.** 2nd ed. London, Mansell Publishing Ltd., 1991. 304p. 8 illus. £19.99. ISBN: 0720120918.

Stems from a conference in Stockholm in 1986, organized by the Centre for Research in International Migration and Ethnicity at the University of Stockholm and the Royal Swedish Academy of Letters, History and Antiquities.

16 chapters arranged in 3 parts: 1. The institutionalization of Islam in various countries - 2. Migration and changes in the religious experience - 3. Additional themes for future research. Notes and references follow each chapter. Glossary, p.278-280. Subject index, p.281-288; name index, p.289-291; index of Muslim organizations, p.292-293. *Class No:* 297(400)

USSR

[875]

BENNINGSEN, A. *and* WIMBUSH, S.E. **Muslims of the Soviet empire:** a guide. Muskogee, OK., Indiana University Press, 1986. 294p. tables, 3 maps. $29.95. ISBN: 0253339588.

In 3 parts, part 1 discusses the historical roots of Islam; part 2 examines the history, culture, politics and demography of Soviet Muslims, grouped by religions; and part 3 is a selected bibliography of sources, English and Russian titles mostly. 'No comparable volume presents such a wealth of information in such a systematic, compact, and lucid form' (*Choice*, April, 1987, p.1194). *Class No:* 297(47)

Africa—North

Bibliographies

[876]

SHINAR, P. **Essai de bibliographie sélective et annotée sur l'Islam:** Maghrébin contemporain: Maroc, Algérie, Tunisie, Libye (1830-1978). Paris, Éditions du CNRS, 1983. 506p. F.280. ISBN: 2222027039.

2025 items, including 295 bibliographies and reference sources on 'Islam' in its broad cultural sense. Part I is basically an annotated list of source material used to compile the bibliography proper (Part II). Part II is arranged in 5

....*(contd.)*

sections (General, and for each country), the sections being further divided by subject. Works in all formats (books, articles in journals, and congress proceedings) and in various languages (English, French, Arabic, Spanish, Italian and German) are included selectively. Each entry includes complete bibliographical information, annotation, and list of reviews. Library locations are also given for books. Author, detailed subject, cited personal name, geographical name, and Arabic or Berber term indexes.
Class No: 297(61/65)(01)

Babism

Handbooks & Manuals

[877]

SMITH, P. The Babi and Baha'i religions: from messianic Shi'ism to a world religion. Cambridge, Cambridge University Press, 1987. xiv,[3],243p. illus., diagrs., tables, maps. £25. ISBN: 0521301289.

10 chapters in 3 parts: 1. Babism - 2. The Baha's faith in the East, *c.* 1866-1921 - 3. The Baha's faith as a world religion. Chapter notes, p.296-299. Appendices: Glossary. Chronology. A note on the sources and a guide to further reading. Index, p.239-243. *Class No:* 297BAB(035)

Celtic Cults

[878]

GREEN, M. The Gods of the Celts. Totowa, N.J., Barnes & Noble Books; Gloucester, A. Sutton Publishers, 1986. [8], 257p. 103 illus. $27.50. £14.95. ISBN: 0389206725, US; 0862992923, UK.

A guide to Celtic beliefs in Britain and Europe 'drawing on the latest research and covering all aspects of the gods' ritual customs, cult objects, and sacred places. 7 chapters: The Celts and religion - Cults of sun and sky - Fertility and the Mother-Goddesses - War, death and the underworld - Water-gods and healers - Animals and animism - Symbolism and imagery in Celtic cult expression. Notes/references (p.226-235), bibliography (p.236-249), Index (p.250-257). *Class No:* 299.16

[879]

HUBERT, H. The Greatness and decline of the Celts. Rev.ed. London, Constable, 1987. xxii, 314p. 3 maps. £12.95. ISBN: 0094678006.

First published in French in 1932, as *Les Celtes depuis l'èpoque de la Tène.*

13 chapters arranged in 3 parts: 1. Celtic expansion in the La Tène period; 2. The end of the Celtic world; 3. The civilization of the Celts. Conclusion: The heritage of the Celts. Footnotes. Bibliography (p.281-299) in 13 sections (Sources - Inscriptions - Periodicals - Miscellaneous - Language - Literature - General works - and then by countries) each subdivided A-Z by author. Index (p.301-304). With the author's *The Rise of the Celts* (q.v.) a 2v. history of the Celts. *Class No:* 299.16

[880]

—**HUBERT, H. The Rise of the Celts.** New ed. London, Constable, 1987. xxxiii,335p. 43 illus., 12 maps. £12.95. ISBN: 0094677905.

First published 1934.

10 chapters divided between 2 parts: pt.1: What the Celts were; pt.2: Movement of the Celtic peoples. Bibliography, p.303-322. Index, p.323-335. *Class No:* 299.16

[881]

NICHOLS, R. The Book of Druidry: history, sites and wisdom. Wellingborough, Northants, Aquarian Press, 1990. 320p. illus. £16.99. ISBN: 085030900x.

In 8 chapters, each subdivided: Stones, wood and culture - The Celts - Cymric takeover - How far underground: a study of aims and festivals in France and Britain - Nine groups of Druidic concepts - Greater sites of the Britannic Islands - Druidic wisdom - The eight-fold year-plan. Epitome. Bibliography, p.311-3. Index, p.315-9. *Class No:* 299.16

Dictionaries

[882]

ELLIS, P. B. A Dictionary of Celtic mythology. Santa Barbara, CA, ABC-Clio, 1992. 325p. 24 illus. $52. £44.95. ISBN: 0874366097.

Compares the Irish, Welsh, Manx, Scottish, Cornish and Breton cultures. Good introduction, followed by thorough and well-written entries. Selective bibliography.

Author also wrote *A Dictionary of Irish mythology* (ABC-Clio, 1991). *Class No:* 299.16(038)

[883]

GREEN, M.L. Dictionary of Celtic myth and legend. London, Thames & Hudson, 1992. 240p. 243 black & white illus. £16.95; $35. ISBN: 0500015163.

Over 400 entries, A-Z, on Celtic religious life, the Druids, animal and human sacrifice, and other aspects of the Celtic people, 500BC-400AD. Preceded by a 'Reader's guide': a lengthy introduction. Major sources are cited and full bibliographical references included. Subject index. 'An excellent source ...'(*Choice*, v.29(11/12), July/August 1992, p.1656). *Class No:* 299.16(038)

Chinese Religions

Bibliographies

[884]

THOMPSON, L.G. Chinese religion in Western languages: a comprehensive and classified bibliography: publications in English, French and German through 1980. Tucson, Ariz., University of Arizona for the Association for Asian Studies, 1985. xlix,302p. $19.95. (*Monograph of the Association for Asian studies, 41.*) ISBN: 0816509263.

A retitled version of the author's *Studies of Chinese religion* (1976), which covered publications to 1970.

Aimed primarily at researchers and includes coverage of Chinese Buddhism as well as the native Han religion. In 3 parts: 1. Bibliographies and general studies - 2. Chinese religion exclusive of Buddhism (45 chapters: 1. Terminology - 2. Antiquity - 3. Mythology ... 45. Miscellenous) - 3. Chinese Buddhism (22 chapters: 1. Reference works - 2. General studies - 3. Texts in translation ... 22.

....(contd.)

Miscellaneous). No annotations. Cross-references. Index of authors, editors, compilers, translators, photographers and illustrators, p.269-302. *Class No:* 299.5(01)

[885]
YU, D.C. *and* **THOMPSON, L.G. Guide to Chinese religion.** Boston, Mass., G.K. Hall, 1985. 200p. $50. (*Asia philosophies and religious resource guide.*) ISBN: 0816179026.

Deals with religions that originated on Chinese soil, and includes material from 1500B.C. to 1977. *c.*3000 short annotated entries, covering all aspects and periods of religion from folk beliefs to rituals to Maoism and to conflicts between religious institutions. Index.
Class No: 299.5(01)

Japanese Religions

[886]
READER, I. Religion in contemporary Japan. London, Macmillan, 1991. xv,277p. £40. ISBN: 0333523210.

Aims to give the reader an overview of the contemporary nature of religion in Japan, in particular looking at religious behaviour and the ways in which religious themes are found in the lives of Japanese people. Notes (p.244-259); references cited (p.260-267); index (p.268-277).
Class No: 299.52

Bibliographies

[887]
EARHART, H.B. The New religions of Japan: a bibliography of Western-language materials. 2nd ed. Ann Arbor, Mich., University of Michigan, Center for Japanese Studies, 1983; New York, Harper & Row, 1985. 158p. $7; £4.95. (*Michigan papers in Japanese studies, 9.*) ISBN: 0939512130.

First published 1970 (96p.).

1450 annotated entries arranged in 2 parts: General bibliography, A-Z by author; Bibliography of individual new religions, by name of religion. Many cross-references. Index of authors, translators and editors; topical index, Appendix on suggestions for locating Western-language materials. Highly recomended by *Choice,* November 1983, p.400.
Class No: 299.52(01)

[888]
HOLZMAN, D., *and others.* **Japanese religion and philosophy:** a guide to Japanese reference and research material. Ann Arbor, Mich., Michigan University Press, 1959 (Reprinted 1975). vii, 142p. $22.50. (*Michigan University Center for Japanese Studies. Bibliographic series, no.7.*) ISBN: 0837179106.

992 numbered items, giving author and title in Japanese, with English translation. Limited to Japanese books on the doctrines and histories of the religions and philosophies of Japan published since the Meijiera. Most entries are annotated briefly. Sections: 1. General - 2. Shinto - 3. Buddhism - 4. Confucianism - 5. Bushidó, Kokugaku and Yogaku - 6. Christianity - 7. Meiji and after. Appendices: List of publishers; List of authors and editors; subject index.
Class No: 299.52(01)

[889]
—Meiji taishô shôwa Shintô shoseki mokuroku. [A Bibliography of Shintoism of the Meiji, Taishô and Showâ eras.] Katô, G., ed. Tokyo, Meiji Jingû Shamusho, 1953. 707p.

Lists *c.*16,000 items. *Class No:* 299.52(01)

[890]
—Shintô shoseki mokuroku. [A Bibliography of Shintoism.] Katô, G., ed. 2nd ed. Tokyo, Meiji Seitoku Kinen Gakkai, 1943. 646p.

Lists *c.* 150,000 items up to 1940. *Class No:* 299.52(01)

Handbooks & Manuals

[891]
JAPAN. Agency of Cultural Affairs. **Japanese religion:** a survey. Tokyo & Palo Alto, Kodansha International Ltd., 1972 (reprinted 1981). 276p. illus. $12.95. ISBN: 0870111833.

9 contributors (all Japanese). Part 1: Description and interpretation (2. Shinto; 3. Buddhism; 4. Christianity; 5. New religious movements; 6. Confucianism; 7. Folk religion...) - Part 2: Specific religious organizations - Part 3: Statistical tables. Index, p.265-72, includes Japanese characters. A survey of major religious organizations, with particular reference to their present circumstances.
Class No: 299.52(035)

African Religions

[892]
PARRINDER, G. Africa's three religions. 2nd ed. London, Sheldon Press, 1976. 256p. map. £3.95. ISBN: 0859690962.

First published 1969 as *Religion in Africa.*

4 parts (20 chapters): 1. Traditional religions - 2. Christianity - 3. Islam - 4. Conclusion (18. Other religions; 19. Relationship of Africa religions; 20. Characteristics of religion in Africa). Bibliography, p.239-42 (3 sections). Non-analytical index. *Class No:* 299.6

Bibliographies

[893]
MITCHELL, R.C. *and* **TURNER, H.W. A Comprehensive bibliography of modern African religious movements.** Evanston, Ill., Northwestern University Press, 1966. lxv,132p.

1313 items, many with annotations; arranged by countries (south of the Sahara), plus sections on 'Theory' and 'Africa, General'. Covers religious interpretations of such movements as Mau Mau, as well as Christian deviations. Omits Islamic movements. Author and ethnic indexes. Continued in periodic supplements in the *Journal of religion in Africa* (Leiden, E.J. Brill, ISSN 00224200).
Class No: 299.6(01)

[894]

WILLIAMS, E.L. *and* **BROWN, C.F. The Howard University bibliography of African and Afro-American religious studies,** with locations in American libraries. Wilmington, Del., Scholarly Resources, [1977]. 525p. $55. ISBN: 0842020802.

Entries for over 13,000 books, periodical articles and parts of books. 5 main divisions: Africa heritage - Christianity and slavery in the New World - Black religious life in the Americas - The civil rights movement - The contemporary religious scene. At least one American library location per item; list of manuscripts and their locations. Appendix of biographies and autobiographies. Author index. Sources range from scholarly to popular accounts in national weeklies. *Class No:* 299.6(01)

Inca Religion

[895]

COBO, B. Inca religion and customs. Hamilton, R., *trans. & ed.* Austin, Texas, University of Texas Press, 1990. 303p. $27.50. ISBN: 0292738544.

Completed in 1653, Father Bernabe Cobo's *Historia del nuevo mundo* is an important source of information on pre-conquest and colonial Spanish America. This translation of part of Cobo's work covers such topics as language, food and shelter, marriage and childbearing, agriculture, warfare, medicine, practical crafts, games and burial routines. *Class No:* 299.85

Oceanic Religions

[896]

POIGNANT, R. Oceanic mythology: the myths of Polynesia, Micronesia, Melanesia, Australia. 2nd rev. ed. London, Newnes, 1985. 144p. illus. (incl.col.pl.). £7.95. ISBN: 0600342832.

4 regional sections, as in title, with subdivisions. Many sub-sections. 148 illustrations, 48 in colour. 'Further reading list'. Index. *Class No:* 299.9

[897]

SWAIN, T. Aboriginal religions in Australia: a bibliographical survey. Westport, CT., Greenwood Press, 1991. 336p. $55. ((*Bibliographies and indexes in religious studies, 18)*.) ISBN: 0313260443.

Over 1000 references in Western languages. An encyclopedic, interpretive survey of the literature is followed by a bibliography, arranged in the 10 standard regions of Aboriginal habitats and subdivided topically (*eg*. institutions, women, myth). Annotations are evaluative and there are extensive 'see also' references. Author, title and general subject indexes. '... easily the most comprehensive bibliography on its topic.'(*Choice*, v.29(11/12), July/August 1992, p.1662). *Class No:* 299.9

3 Social Sciences

Social Sciences

[898]

International current awareness services/ICAS. British Library of Political and Economic Science, at the London School of Economics, *comp.* London, Routledge, November 1991-. 4 series, each monthly. ISSN: 09601511, Anthropology; 0960152x, Economics; 09601538, Political science; 09601546, Sociology.

Aims to provide rapid international coverage of the world's most significant social science literature. Entries are drawn from a total of 13000 current serials, plus an extensive monograph collection. Coverage is worldwide, in 30 languages from over 60 countries. *Class No:* 30

Databases

[899]

RABEN, J. *and* **MARKS, G.,** *eds.* **Data bases in the humanities and social sciences:** I.F.I.P. Working Conference proceedings. Oxford, North-Holland, 1980. xii, 330p. 36 illus., 8 tables. £37.54. ISBN: 0444854991.

58 short papers, mostly on specific databases. (Review in *Aslib information*, September 1981, p.211).
Class No: 30(003.4)

Bibliographies of Bibliographies

[900]

Chicorel index to abstracting and indexing services: periodicals in the humanities and social sciences. 2nd ed. New York, American Library Publishing Co., 1978. 2v. (922p.).

c.33,000 entries from 135 services. Arranged A-Z by title of periodical, giving titles of indexing and abstracting services that cover them. List of addresses of services. List of inverted terms. International in scope. *Class No:* 30(009)

[901]

GRAY, R. A. Serial bibliographies in the humanities and sciences. Ann Arbor, Mich., Pierian Press, 1969. xxiv. 345p. $29.50. ISBN: 0876500041.

Annotated list of nearly 1500 current and discontinued serial bibliographies, classified by Dewey. Coverage includes philosophy, religion, political science, economics, education, law and other related subjects. Indexes: titles; authors; sponsors and publishers; subjects and keywords in context; characteristics (ie, form). *Class No:* 30(009)

Bibliographies

[902]

APAIS: Australian public affairs information service: a subject index to current literature. Canberra, National Library of Australia, 1945- Monthly (except December), cumulated annually (since 1955). AUS$180. ISSN:

....(contd.)
07278926.

'APAIS' is a current guide to material on Australian political, economic, social and cultural affairs. The March 1989 issue had over 500 items, arranged under subjects, A-Z, with sub-divisions. c.200 periodicals published both in Australia and overseas, indexed comprehensively. Some annual reports of government agencies and other important organizations are also indexed.
Australian social science abstracts (Melbourne, Australian National Research Council, nos. 1-18, March 1946- November 1954, 2pa) was systematically arranged, with c.300-350 abstracts pa and annual index. *Class No:* 30(01)

[903]

COUNCIL OF PLANNING LIBRARIANS. CPL bibliographies. Chicago, Ill., the Council, 1958-. no.1-. $285.

A series of subject bibliographies, mainly in the social sciences, compiled by individuals or groups of individuals in academic organizations. Recent bibliographies include: 180. *Community development resources: a selected and annotated bibliography* (1986. [2], 67p. $16. ISBN 0866021809). 181. *Congregate housing for the elderly: a selective and annotated bibliography* (1986. [4],27p. $12. ISBN 0866021817). 182. *Adaptive reuse of school buildings: a selective and annotated bibliography* (1986.[3],13p. $10. ISBN 0866021825). A comprehensive index to nos. 1-1565, 1958-July 1978, was published in 1979 in 3 vols. (subject, author and numerical listings). *Class No:* 30(01)

[904]

Current contents: social and behavioral sciences. Philadelphia, Pa., Institute for Scientific Information, 1969-, v.1, no.1-. Weekly. $390 pa. ISSN: 00926361.

Originally as *Current contents: behavioral, social and management sciences* and *Current contents: education.*

Reproduces tables of contents of several hundred domestic and foreign journals, c.150 journal issues covered in each weekly part. Coverage: Anthropology - Area studies - Business - Communications - Economics - Education - Geography - History - Information science - International relations - Law - Library science - Linguistics - Management - Planning and development - Political science - Psychology - Psychiatry - Public health - Rehabilitation - Social issues - Social medicine - Social work - Sociology - Special education. Weekly title word index; author index; address directory. Original Article Tear Sheet (OATS) service. Available online (BRS, DIALOG). *Class No:* 30(01)

[905]

—Current contents. Address directory. Social sciences/Arts and humanities. 1987 ed. Philadelphia, Pa., Institute for Scientific Information, 1988. 1324p. $195. ISSN: 08822379.

Generated from I.S.I.'s citation indexes and current contents publications. *Class No:* 30(01)

[906]
ESRC DATA ARCHIVE. The ESRC Data Archive catalogue. Cambridge, Chadwick-Healey Ltd., 1986. 2v. £80.00 the set. ISBN: 0859641805.

An abbreviated guide to the then Social Science Research Council Survey Archive's holdings was issued in 1979 by Essex University.

A fully indexed listing of the entire holding of the Economic and Social Science Research Council archives, the largest collection of machine-readable social science data in the UK, with over 2,500 data sets ranging from major national surveys to single research projects. Indexes by subject category, name, title, geography, and population. *Survey archive bulletin* (3 pa.) has news of recently acquired survey material. *Class No:* 30(01)

[907]
FONDATION NATIONALE DES SCIENCES POLITIQUES. Bibliographie courante d'articles de périodiques postérieurs à 1944 sur les problemes politiques, économiques et sociaux. Boston, Mass., G.K. Hall, 1968-72. 17v. plus supplements. $1420. for 17v. Supplements, $225 for each set of 2v., Complete set: $1850.

Main bibliography reproduces 302,000 catalogue cards, arranged initially by countries or areas and then by a decimal classification. *Class No:* 30(01)

[908]
GABROVSKA, S., *and others, comp. & eds*. European guide to social science information and documentation services. Oxford, Pergamon Press, 1982. v, 234p. £31. ISBN: 0080289274.

Compiled and edited for European Cooperation in Social Science Information and Documentation.

An alphabetical list of countries precedes the list of 215 institutions providing social science information in 22 European countries. Arrangement is A-Z by country, subdivided A-Z by title of organization. Entries include address, date started, official status, telephone number, functions, subject coverage, library and publications. Indexes of institutions and subjects. *Class No:* 30(01)

[909]
GRANDIN, A. Bibliographie générale des sciences juridiques, politiques, économiques et sociales de 1800 à 1925/6. Paris, Recueil Sirey, 1926; Supplements 1-19, 1926-50. 1928-51. 3v. plus 19 supplements.

Systematic arrangement, with 16 subject groups. The bibliography is of books and only those in the French language, published in France or elsewhere. Includes theses and government publications. No annotations but frequent cross-references. Subject and author indexes. Aspects of law preponderate.

Continued, for economics, in Mossé, R. and Potier, M. (at 33(01)). *Class No:* 30(01)

[910]
HOSELITZ, B.F., *ed*. A Reader's guide to the social sciences. Rev. ed. London, Collier-Macmillan, 1970. (New York, Free Press issued a paperback version in 1973). xiv, 425p. $3.95. ISBN: 0029149908.

First published 1967.

Chapters: 1. Sociology (p.1-40) - 2. Anthropology (p.41-90) - 3. Psychology (p.91-127) - 4. Political science (p.129-237) - 5. Economics (p.239-91) - 6. Geography (293-318). General bibliography (p.319-425) by major sections, each with 'Miscellaneous sources' appended. 7 contributors. In

.... *(contd.)*
each chapter the ramifications and development of the subject are explained, plus a running commentary on the literature. *Class No:* 30(01)

[911]
LI, T-ch. Social science reference sources: a practical guide. 2nd ed., rev. & enl. Westport, CT, Greenwood Press, 1990. 590p. $75. (*Contributions in librarianship and information science, 68.*) ISBN: 0313255393.

685 annotated reference sources arranged in 14 chapters. Entries are extensive bibliographic essays and constitute the bulk of the book, each being devoted to one particular discipline. Comparisons are made between two or more titles covering much the same information. Well-designed and well-written. Less comprehensive but more up-to-date than W.H. Webb's 'sources of information in the social sciences'(3rd ed. 1986) (*qv*). '... will be the mainstay for the nineties ...'(*Wilson library bulletin*, April 1991, p.1132). *Class No:* 30(01)

[912]
A London bibliography of the social sciences ... British Library of Political and Economic Science, *comp. and ed*. London, Mansell (previously London School of Economics, London University), 1931/32-90. ISSN: 0076051x.

V.1-5 record works in 9 libraries; v.6: 4 libraries. Holdings in v.7 onwards are confined to B.L.P.E.S. and the Edward Fry Library of International Law at L.S.E. Suppt.6 onwards published by Mansell; computer-produced annual suppts. since Suppt.9 (v.32: 1974.1975). The largest subject (A-Z) bibliography of its kind; subject headings conform with Library of Congress subject headings; arrangement is chronological under subjects of their country/topic sub-divisions. Bibliographical details in entries are brief, but presence of a bibliography in a work is indicated. Particularly strong on US and UN material The library has *c*.600,000 books and pamphlets, being one of the largest libraries in the world devoted to its subjects. The total number of separate items is estimated at over 2½ million. Publication ceased with the 1989 edition. *Class No:* 30(01)

[913]
PAIS international in print: a selective list of the latest books, periodical articles, government documents, pamphlets, microfiche, and reports of public and private agencies relating to business, economic and social conditions, public policy and administration, and international relations, published in English, French, German, Italian, Portuguese and Spanish throughout the world. New York, Public Affairs Information Service, 1915-. v.1, no.1-. Monthly, with 3 quarterly and annual cumulations. $495 pa; $1600 on CD-ROM. ISSN: 10514015.

Previously titled *Public affairs information service bulletin* and then *PAIS bulletin* and *PAIS foreign language index* until 1991.

Indexes *c*.3000 periodicals. The annual volume carries an author index. The annual entry 'Directories' provides a handy check-list directory of publishers and organizations in cumulations. Because of its frequent cumulation and wide coverage of material, it is the major indexing service in the social sciences. PAIS on CD-ROM is available from 1972. Also online (BRS, Data-Star, DIALOG, etc.). *Class No:* 30(01)

[914]

—PAIS subject headings. Woods, L.J., *and others, ed*. New York, Public Affairs Information Service, 1984. 319p. $45.

A listing of the controlled vocabulary terms used to index the other PAIS publications. *Class No:* 30(01)

[915]

ROBERTS, N., *ed*. **Use of social science literature**. London, Butterworths, 1977. [x], 326p.

15 contributors (librarians and academics). 14 chapters: 1. Communication and bibliographical system of the social sciences - 2. The information needs and sources of economics - 3. The literature of sociology and the pattern of research and retrieval - 4. Politics, and data archives (largely on methodology) - 5. The literature and sources of social anthropology - 6. Management research - 7. The literature and sources of education - 8. Environmental planning information - 9. The literature and sources of public administration - 10. Criminology and its literature - 11. Exploiting social science journals - 12/14. Exploiting the official publications of the UK, foreign countries, and international organizations. Some chapters have selected references appended (that on 'Management research' has, exceptionally, 7½p. of references). Takes a narrow approach to the social sciences (omits law, business information). Brief index covers only subject fields, institutions and types of literature (*e.g.* abstracts, statistical sources).

Noted: Burrington, F.A. *How to find out about the social sciences*. (Pergamon, 1975. vii, 144p. £11.75. ISBN 0080182895). *Class No:* 30(01)

[916]

The Social sciences: a cross-discipinary guide to selected sources. Herron, N.L., *ed*.   Englewood Cliffs, CO, Libraries Unlimited, 1989. 287p. $36. (*(Library text series)*.) ISBN: 0872877256.

790 annotated entries in 12 disciplines (political science - economics and business - history - law - anthropology - sociology - education - psychology - communications - geography - statistics - demography). Lively, evaluative annotations. Author, title and subject indexes. '... a trustworthy textbook for library students ...' (*RQ*,v.30(1), Fall 1990, p.154). *Class No:* 30(01)

[917]

Social sciences citation index. 1970-. Philadelphia, PA., Institute for Scientific Information, 1973-. 3pa. (3rd issue as bound annual cumulation). $4300pa. (5-year cumulations also available). ISSN: 00913707.

The annual cumulation, in 5v., comprises 3 indexes: *Citation index* (the main index, listing, A-Z, authors and titles of items cited in the *Source index*); *Source index* (listing, A-Z, authors and titles of citing articles); and *Permuterm subject index* (based on permuted words of titles of articles)., Titles are drawn from *c.*2,000 journals in the social sciences. Also available online (DIALOG, SOCIAL SCISEARCH) and on CD-ROM. *Class No:* 30(01)

[918]

Social sciences index, New York, H.W. Wilson, 1974-. v.1-. Quarterly, with bound cumulation. Sold on a service basis. ISSN: 00944920.

One of two indexes superseding *Social sciences & humanities index* (1916-1974).

Author and subject entries to English-language periodicals in anthropology; area studies; community health and medical

....(contd.)

care; geography; gerontology; law & criminology; minority studies; planning and public administration; police science and corrections; policy sciences; psychiatry; psychology; social work and public welfare; sociology; urban studies, and related subjects. Author listing of citations to book reviews. 342 key periodicals currently indexed. Clear typography: good paper. Available online and CD-ROM. *Class No:* 30(01)

[919]

Social scisearch. Philadelphia, PA., Institute for Scientific Information, 1972-.

An online database, up-dated monthly, is a 'citation index of worldwide periodical literature covering all social science descriptions. *Class No:* 30(01)

[920]

UNITED NATIONS. Dag Hammarskjöld Library. **Current bibliographical information**. New York, 1971-. v.1, no.1-. 22 issues pa. $75 pa. ISSN: 00417343.

Succeeds *New Publications in the Dag Hammarskjöld Library* (1950-70) - previously *New publications in the United Nations Headquarters Library*.

Planned as a practical finding list rather than as a bibliography or a list of suggested readings. Excludes U.N. and Specialized Agency publications. A selective listing of articles from over 700 periodical titles. About 500 items per issue arranged in subject groups: Political and legal affairs - economic affairs - natural resources - agriculture, forestry and fisheries - industry - transport - trade - population - family planning - human settlements - health - employment - humanitarian aids - social affairs - human rights - women - cultural affairs - information systems - science and technology - general reference works. Author and subject indexes. List of recently acquired serials. List of non-Roman alphabet materials. *Class No:* 30(01)

[921]

UNITED   NATIONS.   Library.   Geneva.   **Monthly bibliography**. Part 1: Books, official documents, serials. Geneva, 1928-. Bi-monthly. $60 pa. ISSN: 02516616.

Formerly as *Monthly list of books catalogued in the Library of the United Nations,* 1946-77; originally *... League of Nations,* 1928-45.

A subject compilation of newly acquired books, official documents and periodicals, which serves as the Library's monthly acquisition list as well as a current awareness list. Personal and corporate author index; a subject index which includes geographical terms; and a title index. *Class No:* 30(01)

[922]

UNITED   NATIONS.   Library.   Geneva.   **Monthly bibliography**. Part 2: Selected articles. Geneva, 1929-. Bi-monthly. $60 ISSN: 02516624.

Up to 1977 as *Monthly list of selected articles*.

About 600 current-information items on periodical literature and contributions to collective works of interest to the United Nations and the international community. About 1000 titles regularly scanned. Excludes short news items and statistical notes. Subject arrangement: Political and legal affairs - economic affairs - natural resources - agriculture, forestry and fisheries - industry - transport - communications - trade - population - human settlements - health -

....(contd.)

employment - humanitarian aid - social affairs - cultural affairs - science and technology. A current awareness service. Author, subject and title indexes. *Class No:* 30(01)

[923]

—League of Nations and United Nations Monthly list of selected articles: cumulation, 1920-1970. Field, N.S., *ed.* Dobbs Ferry, N.Y., Oceana, 1971-5. 14v. $910 the set. ISBN: 0379411507.

Lists selected articles on international, constitutional and administrative law, politics and economics from *c.*3000 journals worldwide. Volumes have 3 broad subject groups: *Political questions* (v.1: 1920-1928; v.2: 1929-1945; v.3: 1946-1960; v.4: 1961-1970; v.5: Special problems, 1920-1970) - *Legal questions* (v.1: Public international law; private international law; v.2: National law - countries) - *Economic questions* (v.1: Economic conditions, 1920-1955; v.2: Economic conditions, 1956-1970; Economic conditions - food and agriculture, 1956-1970; Economic conditions - textiles, mining, coal, metals. 1920-1970; v.4: Economic conditions - petroleum, 1920-1970; Economic conditions - miscellaneous industries, 1920-1970; v.5: Commercial policy, 1920-1970; v.6: Economic policy, 1920-1970).
Class No: 30(01)

[924]

WEBB, W., *and associates.* **Sources of information in the social sciences:** a guide to the literature. 3rd ed. Chicago, Ill., American Library Association, 1986. x, 777p. $70. £35. ISBN: 083890405x.

Supersedes C.M. White's *Sources of information in the social sciences* (Chicago, A.L.A., Preliminary ed. 1959; 1st ed. 1964; 2nd ed. 1973. xviii, 702p.).

A thorough updating of White's standard sources, describing the literature; some sections reworked, others merely updated. 8110 numbered entries (2nd ed. 4527), mostly annotated, in 9 main classes: 1. Social science literature - 2. History - 3. Geography - 4. Economics and business administration - 5. Sociology - 6. Anthropology - 7. Psychology - 8. Education - 9. Political science. 20 contributors. Each chapter commences with a survey of the field, followed by a survey of the reference works, subject grouped. Cross-references. Extensive index (p.585-776) has subject, author-title and title entries. 'Focuses on form rather than function' (*Choice*, v.24(5), January 1987, p.749).
Class No: 30(01)

Encyclopaedias

[925]

Encyclopaedia of the social sciences. Seligman, E.R.A., *ed.* New York & London, Macmillan, 1930-35. (Reprinted 1951. 15v. in 8; Reprinted by Encyclopaedia Britannica Inc. in 5 vols. 5v. $129. ISBN: 0878273557.

A comprehensive work, projected under the auspices of 10 learned societies; signed articles by specialists. Some subject articles are lengthy and are provided with lists of contents (*e.g.* 'Agriculture'; 9 sections; 8 contributors); treatment is usually systematic (*e.g.* a subject will be introduced by giving historical background surveyed in various countries, and then discussed in terms of its problems). Although about one half of the articles are biographies, these are usually comparatively brief, being chiefly concerned with the person's achievements in the social sciences. Bibliographies,

....(contd.)

generally excellent, even if dated, are appended to articles. Includes an index and a classification of the articles in subject and biography groups. *Class No:* 30(031)

[926]

International encyclopedia of the social sciences. Sills, D.L., *ed.* New York, Macmillan Co. & The Free Press, 1968. (Reprinted by Collier-Macmillan, New York, 1977, in 8v. set, including Biographical supplement). Originally in 17v. plus v.18 (Biographical supplement). Reprint in 8v. including supplement. £495 the set. ISBN: 0028955404.

1900 articles by *c.*1500 contributors. 'First and foremost the work of social scientists' (*Preface*) and designed to complement, not to surplant its predecessor, *Encyclopaedia of the social sciences* (Macmillan, 1930-35). Emphasises theory and methodology, psychology and sociology. Historical topics are not plentiful; as against 4000 biographies in the earlier *Encyclopaedia,* here there are only a few hundred. No living person is included who was born after 1890.

Articles average 1500 words. 'Karl Marx': 7 columns of text plus 4 of bibliography; 'Urban revolution': 20p., each of the 3 sections having a bibliography of ½ column or more. Numerous cross-references. V.17, the index, has *c.*40,000 analytical entries, and a classified list of articles. A standard encyclopedia, with articles of lasting significance.
Class No: 30(031)

[927]

KUPER, A. and **KUPER, J.,** *eds.* **The Social science encyclopedia.** London, Routledge & Kegan Paul, 1985. xxviii, 916p. £29.95. $75. ISBN: 0710200080.

Over 700 essays dealing with theories, issues and methods in the social sciences, and many others devoted to the life and work of individual scholars. Covers all the social sciences and related disciplines. Contributions by 500 international scholars in the field. Most entries followed by a list of references and suggestions for further reading. Some cross-references. No index. 'The range is vast, the overall level of erudition is impressive ... level of entries varies ... (*British journal of educational studies.* October 1986, p.280-281). 'This somewhat eccentric work ... includes biology, medicine, philosophy and psychiatry ... semantics ... Editorial control seems lacking. (*Library journal*, 15 April 1986, p.72). *Class No:* 30(031)

Dictionaries

Polyglot

[928]

LOGIE, G., *ed.* **International planning glossaries.** Amsterdam, Elsevier Science Publishers (previously Hemel Hempstead, International Planning Glossaries) 1978-. £78.18 each vol.

A continuing series, v.1: Population (1978. xviii, 266p. 0444417303); v.2: Transport (1980. xxviii, 196p. 0444418881); v.3: Employment and industry (1982. xxx, 290p. 0444420649); v.4: Glossary of land resources (1984. xxviii, 304p. 0444422811); v.5: Glossary of planning and development (1986. xxvii, 254p. 0444426086).

English, French, Italian, Dutch, German and Swedish. Arranged alphabetically by English term with indexes of terms in other languages. *Class No:* 30(038)=00

English

[929]

GOULD, J. *and* KOLB, W.K., *eds*. **A Dictionary of the social sciences.** London, Tavistock Publications, 1964. xvi, 761p.

Compiled under Unesco auspices.

About 270 British and US social scientists treat 1022 terms and concepts, especially in political science and sociology. Aims at extended discussion of each concept, its role in the social sciences and its historical development. Signed articles, sectionalized for different meanings; literature references in text; cross-references (*e.g.* 'Gold standard': nearly 4 columns; sections A-D; 3 references in text; cross-references). Well produced. 'Undoubedtly the best one-volume dictionary of the language of the social scientist available today' (*Library journal*, v.90(2), 15 January 1965, p.231). *Class No:* 30(038)=20

[930]

READING, H.F. **A Dictionary of social sciences.** London, Routledge & Kegan Paul, 1977. 231p.

Concisely defines 7500 terms, covering 'all the social sciences with the exception of economics and linguistics' (*Preface*). Intended for students of the social sciences, public and social administration, and social work. Dedicated to 'all those who remain unconvinced by the argument for restricting scientific method in its application to the social sciences'. *Class No:* 30(038)=20

German

[931]

DIETL, E.-E., *and others*. **Wörterbuch für Recht, Wirtschaft und Politik. Dictionary of legal, commercial and political terms.** 2nd rev. ed. Munich, C.H. Beck; Albany, NY, Matthew Bender, 1988-90. 2v.

Rev. & enl. ed. of the dictionary by G. Erdsiek and C.-E. Dietl.

V.1: English-German (5th rev. ed., 1990. lxiv,937p. £133.75). v.2: German-English (3rd rev. ed., 1988. xxii,821p. £126.60). Terms illustrated by examples, explanations and commentaries. Incorporates American usage. *Class No:* 30(038)=30

[932]

—DIETL, E.-E., *and others*. Wirtschaftswörterbuch: Wörterbuch für den Wirtschafts-, Handels- und Rechtsverkehr .../Commercial dictionary: dictionary of commercial, business and legal terms - including the terminology of the European Communities. Wiesbaden, Gabler, 1985-87. 2v. (409 & 404p.). £39.60 each vol. ISBN: 3409199004, v.1; 3409198997, v.2.

Part 1: German-English; part 2: English-German. *Class No:* 30(038)=30

[933]

KOSCHNICK, W.J. **Standard dictionary of the social sciences.** München, K.G. Saur, 1984-92. 3v. (x,664p.; ix,785.; x,780). DM.120-; £75 each vol.

V.1: English-German; v.2: German-English: Part 1: A-L; part 2: M-Z. *c*.20,000 terms from all areas of the social sciences, particularly sociology, psychology, statistics, communications research, psychiatry. anthropology, political science and research methodology. Definitions range in length from a few words to a paragraph or more. Identifies authors who originated or were closely associated with particular terms. Cross-references. '... likely to be the

.... (contd.)

standard English-German social science dictionary for some time' (*Choice*, v.23(5), January 1986, p.728). *Class No:* 30(038)=30

[934]

Market economy and planned economy: an encyclopaedic dictionary. Földi, T., *and others, eds*. London, K.G.Saur, 1991 (available from Bowker-Saur). xxxix,1045p. £105. ISBN: 3598110707.

Trilingual dictionary of 661 entries and over 1000 sub-entries for those interested in comparisons between very different economic systems, especially between capitalist and communist economies. Some terms are basic, but most refer to concepts revelant to the book's main purpose. Entries are arranged A-Z in German, with definitions and interpretation in German, English and Russian. Cross-references. Favourable review in *Reference reviews*, v.6(3), 1992. *Class No:* 30(038)=30

French

[935]

BRANCHIARD, M. **Dictionnaire économique et social: dictionnaire Thomas Suavet.** 11. éd., entièrement revue et corrigée. Paris, Économie et Humanisme, 1978. 582, 19p. ISBN: 270820209x.

First published 1961; 1st-10th eds. by T.H. Suavet.

Analyses *c*. 1600 key-words, definitions plus comment and usually a bibliography; (*e.g.* 'Malthusianisme': 2 cols., bibliography has anti-Malthusian items; 'Coopérative': 6 cols., including a ½-column bibliography). Appended chronology, 1830-1977. Numerous cross-references. No biographies, but a table of names of persons mentioned plus associated idea, theory, movement or group. *Class No:* 30(038)=40

[936]

EUROPEAN COMMUNITIES. Council. **Glossaire des Communautés Européennes.** European Communities glossary. Anglais-Français. English-French. 8th ed. Luxembourg, Office for Official Publications of the European Communities, 1986. vii, 707p. £14. $20.50. ECU.19.70. ISBN: 9282404102.

7th ed. published 1979.

Arranged A-Z by subject, connected terms indented.

A French-English companion volume is also available (8th ed. 1984. 1589p. £15.70. $22. ECU.26.38). *Class No:* 30(038)=40

Arabic

[937]

KHAN, M.A. **A Glossary of Islamic economics.** London, Mansell, 1990. 154p. £25; $45. (*Mansell Islamic studies.*) ISBN: 072012042x.

500 terms, including legal and technical terms, mostly in Arabic but also in Urdu, Persian and Turkish, defined in English. *Class No:* 30(038)=927

[938]

SABIQ, J. **Majama'al-lughat:** qamus al-iqtiṣad, al-huquq, al tarbiya wal-ta'lim ... Beirut, the Author, 1971. 1189p.

Trilingual dictionary (Arabic-French-English; French-English-Arabic; English-French-Arabic) covering economics, law, sociology, statistics, political and diplomatic sciences. *Class No:* 30(038)=927

Chinese

[939]

English-Chinese glossaries, v.1-5. Prepared by the Chinese Language Division of the Home Affairs Department. Hong Kong, 1981-1986. 5v.

V.1: Education (1981. 79p. *c*.2000 entries which are special terms used in government departments on subjects relating to education; v.2: Housing and land (rev. ed., 1986. 131p. Some 2700 entries ...); v.3: Finance (1983. 233p. *c*.4000 terms in finance and economy); v.4: Civil service (1985. 101p. 2000 terms); v.5: Internal transport, part 1 - Land transport. *Class No:* 30(038)=951

Theses

[940]

BILBOUL, R.R. *and* **KENT, F.L.,** *eds*. **Retrospective index to theses of Great Britain and Ireland, 1917-1950.** v.1: Social sciences and humanities. Santa Barbara, CA.; Oxford, ABC-Clio, 1977. [xviii], 393p. facsim. £78.

About 12000 entries. Subject index (subject; title; author; degree; date; university). Author index (author; title; degree; date; university). *Class No:* 30(043)

[941]

Dissertation abstracts international: Section A. The humanities and social sciences. Ann Arbor, Mich., University Microfilms International, 1938-. Monthly. $275pa US & Canada; $450pa elsewhere, including cumulative author index. ISSN: 04194209.

Formerly Dissertation abstracts.

Sections on communications and the arts; education; language, literature, linguistics; philosophy, religion and theology; social sciences. Author-prepared abstracts are of doctoral dissertations and contain up to 350 words; they are submitted by nearly 500 participating institutions in North America and the world. Information for each entry includes title; author's name; degree; date awarded; institution granting degree; no. of pages; UMI order no. Author and keyword title indexes. Available online (BRS; DIALOG) and on CD-ROM. *Class No:* 30(043)

Reviews & Abstracts

[942]

ASSIA: Applied social sciences index and abstracts. East Grinstead, Bowker-Saur Ltd., 1987 -. v.1, no.1 -. Bimonthly, plus annual cumulation. £493. $930 pa. ISSN: 09502238.

Monitors over 500 English-language journals, mainly published in the United Kingdom (*c*.40%) and the United States (*c*.46%). Covers the whole range of the applied social sciences. Informative abstracts of up to *c*.150 words in length are arranged under subject headings, often subdivided. Extensive cross-referencing. Available online (Vendors: Data-Star (file ASSI)). *Class No:* 30(048)

[943]

Book review index to social science periodicals. Ann Arbor, Pierian Press, 1978. 4v. $75 each vol.; $275 the set. ISBN: 0876500262, v.1; 0876501102, v.2; 0876500491, v.3; 0876501145, v.4; 0686770668, set.

Companion guide to *Book reviews in the humanities.*

Contains references to book reviews in more than 400

.... (contd.)
journals in the social sciences. V.1 - 1964-70; v.2. - 1971; v.3. - 1972; v.4 - 1973-74. Continued in *Social science index* (see at 3(01). *Class No:* 30(048)

[944]

FONDATION NATIONALE DES SCIENCES POLITIQUES. Bulletin analytique de documentation politique, économique et sociales contemporaines. Paris, Fondation Nationale des Sciences Politiques (previously Presses Universitaires de France), 1946-. Monthly. FFr.700pa. ISSN: 00074171.

Preceded by *Bulletin bibliographique de documentation internationale contemporaine.*

Over 5000 indicative abstracts pa of periodicals and also official documents. An abstract sometimes has appended to it the titles of other articles on the same topic. Systematic arrangement: 1. Etudes nationales (subdivided by country/ area) - 2. Etudes régionales - 3. Etudes générales mondiales ou internationales. Cross references. Annual subject index and list of periodicals scanned. *Class No:* 30(048)

Periodicals

[945]

Political and social science journals: a handbook for writers and reviewers. Santa Barbara, CA., ABC-Clio, 1983. xxx, 236p. $24.95. £17.50. (*Clio guides to publishing opportunities series, no.2*.) ISBN: 0874360269.

Entries describe editorial focus and list frequency, editor, address, circulation, readership characteristics, indexing, manuscript requirements, referee system, and book reviewing policies for both reviewers and publishers. Indexed by discipline and broad topics. *Class No:* 30(051)

Bibliographies

[946]

HARZFELD, L.A. Periodical indexes in the social sciences and humanities: a subject guide. Metuchen, N.J., Scarecrow Press, 1978. xiv, 174p. $16.50. £13.15. ISBN: 0810811332.

Succeeds J.A. Kujoth's *Subject guide to periodical indexes and review indexes* (Scarecrow Press, 1969).

Annotated entries for more than 200 abstracting and indexing services, contents - listing journals, plus periodic bibliographies in journals and elsewhere. Data: number of periodicals indexed; arrangement; availability of cumulations, or databases. 48 subject sections. Mostly English-language titles. Accurate and reasonably priced. 'Recommended for academic libraries' (*Library journal,* v.103(20), 15 April 1978, p. 2324). *Class No:* 30(051)(01)

Yearbooks & Directories

[947]

Directory of alternative communities in the British Isles; compiled by Michèle and Kevin of The Teachers, Bangor, North Wales. 4th ed. Bangor, North Wales, Teacher Printing and Publishing, 1983. 199p.

First published 1977.

A list of over 100 communities operating in the British Isles, arranged A-Z by name of community (Ampleforth Abbey - Whitbourne Hall Community). Contains both a

....*(contd.)*

discussion of community life and details of size, social and economic organization, as well as a general description of aims and activities of each community. *Class No:* 30(058)

[948]

WHITAKER, J. An Almanack for the year of Our Lord ...
1868- (Annual). 126th, 1994. London, Whitaker, 1993. 1280p. illus., maps. £25. ISBN: 0850212383.

Previous editions included a sub-title: 'containing an account of the astronomical and other phenomena and a vast amount of information respecting the government, finances, population, commerce, and general statistics of the various nations of the world, with an index containing nearly 10,000 references'. Includes British government and public offices (ministers and senior civil servants, with their salaries), lists of peers, baronets, knights, M.P.'s, judges, sheriffs (county and borough), holders of the V.C. and George Cross, societies. Data on churches, armed forces, education (public schools, universities, professional education), insurance companies and their rates, postal regulations, tide tables, income tax, national insurance, legal notes, conservation and heritage, etc. Index using computer technology, at end of volume (p.1248-1277). Still no cross-references. Invaluable in any library or home; particularly useful for the variety of miscellaneous information available through the detailed index. *Class No:* 30(058)

[949]

The World almanac & book of facts, 1993. New York, World Almanac, 1993 960p. illus. maps. Annual. ISBN: 1401000795. ISSN: 00841382.

First published 1868.

Similar content to *Whitaker's almanack* and equally dependent on a detailed index (p.3-31). Includes a full annual chronology, memorable dates, US associations and institutions, US population statistics for places of 2500 or more, and has sections on noted personalities (not all US), foreign countries, A-Z, and sporting events. Quotes sources of statistics. 16p. of coloured flags and maps. The nearest approach to a general US yearbook. *Class No:* 30(058)

Quotations

[950]

The Macmillan book of social science quotations: who said what, when and where. Sills, D.L. *and* Merton, R., *eds*. New York, Macmillan, 1992. 458p. $25; £19.95. ISBN: 0028973976.

Over 2500 quotations from *c.*1000 authors, mainly famous social scientists but also some literary figures. Arranged A-Z by names. Each entry includes nationality, discipline, date of birth and (where relevant) death, the quotation (often in longer paragraphs of text to show proper context) and its sources. Keyword subject index and 67-page bibliography. Adjunct to the 18v. *International encyclopedia of the social sciences* (1968-80. Macmillan and Free Press).
Class No: 30(082.2)

Histories

[951]

INTERNATIONAAL INSTITUUT VOOR SOCIALE GESCHIEDENIS, AMSTERDAM. Alfabetische catalogus van de boeken en brochures. Alphabetical catalog of the books and pamphlets of the International Institute of

....*(contd.)*

Social History. Boston, Mass., G.K. Hall, 1970. 1st supplement. 1975. 12v., plus 2v. supplement. $1220 & $250. ISBN: 0816108072, the set of 12v; 0816110336, supplement.

310,000 cards, photolithographically reproduced. One of the largest special collections of social history, the library has *c.*350,000v., of which 40,000 are Slavonic holdings. *Class No:* 30(091)

[952]

International review of social history. Internationaal Instituut voon Social Geschiedenis, *ed.* Assen, Netherlands, Van Gorcum Ltd., 1956-. v.1-. 3 pa. Fl.85 pa. ISSN: 01650629.

Previously (1937-40, 1950-55) as *Bulletin of the International Institute of Social History.*

Each issue contains about 50 pages of bibliography, over 100 items, systematically arranged. (General issues (social theory and social science, history, contemporary issues); Continents and countries (sub-divided by region, then country, A-Z. Annotations or abstracts average *c.*100 words. Annual author and geographical indexes. *Class No:* 30(091)

Biographies

[953]

International encyclopedia of the social sciences. v.18: Biographical supplement. Sills, D.L., *ed.* New York, Free Press, 1979. xxxviii, [1], 820p. $90. ISBN: 0028955102.

The biographical supplement to the 17v. encyclopedia. The biographical supplement to the 8v. edition was published in 1989 (Free Press, $85. ISBN 0028956907). *See* 3(031)=20 for information on the encyclopedia.

Over 200 signed biographical sketches, 'placing' each biographee. 'Jean Piaget': 10½ columns (works by: 1 col.; supplementary biographies: 7 items). *Class No:* 30(092)

Official Records

[954]

GREAT BRITAIN. Public Record Office. **Records of interest to social scientists, 1919 to 1939:** introduction. London, HMSO., 1971. viii, 282p. (*Public Record Office handbooks, no. 14.*)

Sections (each subdivided by Ministry, Office, etc.): Central direction - Finance - Foreign affairs - Industry and trade - Land - Social services - Law and order - Defence - Common services. Bibliography, p.281; glossary, p.282. *Class No:* 30(093.2)

Scotland

[955]

People and society in Scotland. Edinburgh, John Donald Publishers Ltd. in association with The Economic and Social History Society of Scotland, 1988-1990. 3v. (900p.) illus. £12.50. ISBN: 0859762106, v.1; 0859762114, v.2; 0859762122, v.3.

Vol.I: 1760-1830, ed. by T.M. Devine & R. Mitchison; v.2: 1830=1914, ed. by W.H. Fraser & R.J. Morris; v.3: 1914 to the present day, ed. by A.R. Dickson & J.H. Treble. *Class No:* 30(411)

Wales

Research Projects

[956]

Contemporary Wales: an annual review of economic and social research, 1987-. Rees, G. *and* Day, G., *eds*. University of Wales Press, on behalf of the board of Celtic Studies of the University of Wales. V.5: 160p. £7.50; $14.00. ISSN: 09514937.

Analysis of economic and social development in Wales. *Class No:* 30(429):061:061.62.005

USSR

[957]

A Researcher's guide to sources on Soviet social history in the 1930s. Fitzpatrick, S. *and* Armonk, L.V., *eds*. New York, M.E.Sharpe, 1990. 296p. illus. tables. $43.95. ISBN: 0873324978.

Western and Soviet specialists assess the potential of sources available for the Stalinist period in the USSR, with bibliographic essays on topics such as archives, laws, statistics, collectivization and industrialization. Subject index. *Class No:* 30(47)

[958]

Soviet studies guide. Konn, T., *ed*. London, Bowker-Saur, 1992. xviii,237p. Map. £39. ISBN: 0862917905.

A critical reference guide to the political, economic and social sciences literature in English on the Soviet Union. 10 chapters, each ending with a bibliography: Land, environment and people - Soviet history - Society and culture - Government and politics - International relations - Armed forces - The economy - Business - Science and technology - General reference. Index, p.229-37. *Class No:* 30(47)

Education Institutions

[959]

RUBLE, B.A. *and* **TEETER, M.J. A Scholars' guide to humanities and social sciences in the Soviet Union and the Baltic States;** the Academies of Sciences of Russia, Ukraine, Belorussia, Moldova, and Transcausasian and Central Asian republics, and Estonia, Latvia and Lithuania. 2nd ed. Harlow, Essex, Longman Group Ltd., 1992. 256p. £134. ISBN: 0582987008.

Jointly compiled by the American Council of Learned Societies and the Soviet Academy of Sciences' Commission on the Humanities and Social Sciences.

A guide to institutions belonging to the USSR Academy of Sciences which study the humanities and social sciences. Entries include name, address, telephone numbers, history, bibliographies, areas of research, staffing, contacts, and co-operation with other countries. *Class No:* 30(47):061:37

China

Tables & Data Books

[960]

China's social statistics, 1986. New York, Praeger, 1989. 275p. $75. (*China statistics series*.) ISBN: 0275932737.

c. 300 statistical tables arranged by subject: General survey - Population and family - Labour - Income and consumption - Housing and services - Labour insurance and social welfare - Education - Scientific research - Health care

....(contd.)
- Environmental protection - Culture - Physical culture - Social order and security - Participation in political and social activities - Daily time allocation.
Class No: 30(510)(083)

India

Maps & Atlases

[961]

A Social and economic atlas of India. Oxford, Oxford University Press, 1988. 254p. £37.50; $65. ISBN: 0195620410.

Maps and information on land, physical features, urbanization, population, society, language, literacy, religion, employment, natural resources, climate, infrastructure (welfare, education, transport, communications, banking, irrigation and power), produce, tourism, and economy (including India's dependency on other nations and regions). Maps, on a relatively small scale, for each section. 'This is a no-nonsense, technically proficient volume, permitting at a glance a view of where India is now, and where its future lies' (*Choice*, v.26(5), January 1989, p.788). *Class No:* 30(540)(084.3)

Africa

Periodicals

[962]

Index of African social science periodical articles. V.1-, 1989-. Dakar, CODESRIA (Council for the Development of Economic and Social Research in Africa), 1989-. ISSN: 08509379.

An abstracting service. V.2/3, 1990-1991, published in 1993, has 549 entries for articles from 49 journals. Author, title, description in English and French sequences. No meaningful order so indexes are important. Indexes of authors, English descriptions, French descriptions, periodicals, and titles of articles. *Class No:* 30(6)(051)

Latin America

Biographies

[963]

Who's who in Latin America: government, politics, banking and industry. Corke, B., *ed*. 3rd ed. N.Ross, 1993. 391p. $99. ISBN: 0883542242.

*c.*2000 biographies of contemporary leaders in 35 Latin American and Caribbean countries, arranged A-Z by country and then biographee. Name index indicates relevant country. No cross-references. Spanish and Portuguese names can cause difficulties in locating entries.
Class No: 30(729.99)(092)

USA

Bibliographies

[964]

McALLISTER, J. 'Colonial America, 1607-1776'. In *The economic history review,* Second series, v.42(2), May 1989, p.245-259).

An essay in bibliography and criticism, including 156 references to books and journal articles.
Class No: 30(73)(01)

Writing & Lecturing

[965]

MULLINS, C.J. A Guide to writing and publishing in the social and behavioral sciences. New York, Wiley, 1977 (Reprinted by Krieger, 1983). 448p. $29.50. ISBN: 0898746434.

'Written primarily for students and professionals in the social and behavioral sciences, but also for their typists, editors and publisher'. 4 parts: 1. Outlines, first drafts, revisions and resources - 2. Authors, articles and scholarly journals - 3. General instructions for preparing a book manuscript: monographs, textbooks and edited collections - 4. Publishers, prospectuses and contracts: the forthcoming book. Table 7.1: 'Characteristics of journals (540 in all) in the social and behavioral sciences', p.134-55. Bibliography, p.411-7. *Class No:* 30:001.81

Research Methods

[966]

KANE, E. Doing your own research: basic descriptive research in the social sciences and humanities. London, Marion Boyars, 1984 (Reprinted 1987). 220p. £15.95. ISBN: 0714528439.

Aimed at people with little or no experience in social research. Part 1: What do you want to know? - 2: How do you find it - 3: Preparing the results - 4: Counting the cost. References cited, p.215-217. Index (double column), p.218-220. *Class No:* 30:001.891

Dictionaries

[967]

MILLER, P.M. *and* **WILSON, M.J. A Dictionary of social science methods.** Chichester, Wiley, 1983. 124p. illus. £18.55. $39.95. ISBN: 0471900354.

Aims to be a comprehensive dictionary of terms and methodologies used in all major social science disciplines. Explains and sets each term in its practical context in addition to providing simple definitions. Fully cross-referenced. 'Excludes concepts drawn from learning theory and behavior therapy or those used in the philosophy of science'. (*Choice,* v.21(3), November 1983, p.404). British orientation. *Class No:* 30:001.891(038)

Thesauri

[968]

AITCHISON, J., *comp.* **Unesco thesaurus:** a structured list of descriptors for indexing and retrieval literature in the field of education, science, social science, culture and communication. Paris, UNESCO, 1977. 2v. (485;530p.). F.250 the set. ISBN: 9231014692.

....(contd.)
V.1: Introduction. Classified thesaurus. Permuted index. Hierarchical display. V.2: Alphabetical thesaurus.
Class No: 30:025.43

[969]

The Contemporary thesaurus of social science terms and synonyms: a guide to natural language computer searching. Knapp, S.D., *comp.* Oryx, 1993. xxi,401p. $95. ISBN: 0897745957.

Lists synonyms and related terms for more than 6000 concepts and terms in the social sciences, listing them logically, clearly and thoroughly with a large number of 'see' and 'see also' references. Appendix B: British spellings. Selected sources used to compile the thesaurus, p.399-400. Favourable review in *Choice,* v.30(10), June 1993, p.1606. *Class No:* 30:025.43

Libraries

[970]

Subject directory of special libraries and information centers. v.1 Business, government and law libraries. Darnay, B.T. *and* DeMaggio, J., *eds.* 17th ed. Detroit, Mich., Gale Research Co., 1993. $275. ISBN: 0810380137.

One of 3 subject volumes related to the *Directory of special libraries and information centers, 1990.*

Over 3000 entries for business and law libraries, including military libraries. Information includes name of library, sponsoring institution, address, name and title of person in charge and other professional personnel, collection statistics, description of subjects covered, policies regarding use of collection, services provided, special collections, automated operations, publications and special catalogues, and special indexes. Alphabetical title and alternative name index, and subject index. *Class No:* 30:061:026/027

Great Britain

[971]

Aslib directory. Codlin, E.M., *ed.* 5th ed. London, Aslib, 1982-84. 2v. ([5], 789p. & [5], 1000p.). v.1: £46; v.2: £60. ISBN: 0851421660, v.1; 0851421849, v.2.

First published 1928: 4th ed. 1977-80.

V.1: *Science, technology and commerce;* V.2: *Social sciences, medicine and the humanities,* 2954 numbered entries in v.1, and 3583 in v.2, covering the United Kingdom and Eire. Arranged under names of organizations, A-Z, with generous references from changed or alternative names. Very brief data for each: name and address; enquiries to ... ; subject coverage; publication(s). Abbreviation and subject indexes (p.757-789) in v.1, and p.955-1000 in v.2. *Class No:* 30:061:026/027(410)

[972]

LEVINE, H.M. *and* **OWEN, D.B. An American guide to British social science resources.** Metuchen, N.J., Scarecrow Press, 1976. xii, 281p. $18.50; £14.60. ISBN: 0810809508.

Basic information about important British social science library resources, designed to serve as a reference source for American social scientists conducting research in Britain. A general section on travel and living in Britain precedes a list of over 200 libraries with social science collections, with

....(contd.)
details of holdings, access requirements, hours of opening, facilities available. Also listed are 35 other organizations and universities. *Class No:* 30:061:026/027(410)

Institutions & Associations

[973]
World directory of social science institutions, 1990: research, advanced training, documentation, professional bodies. 5th ed. Paris, Unesco, 1990. xv,1211p. £15.00. (*World social science information directories: 2.*) ISBN: 9230025526.

First consolidated ed., 1977, from basic loose-leaf index of 1970, plus updatings in the quarterly *International social science journal.* Now produced from Unesco's DARE BANK.

In 4 parts: - Section I is an alphabetical index of official names and acronyms of institutions, with the relevant entry number; Section II has full details of each institution, listed A-Z, preceded by international and regional organizations, with address, date of establishment, name of head, senior researchers, staff, subject coverage, type of organization, activities, finance, research facilities, method of data processing, and publications; Section III is an index, A-Z by name of head of institution; Section IV is an index by subject and geographic coverage, with indication of the host country of the institution. *Class No:* 30:061:061.2

Conferences

[974]
Directory of published proceedings. Series SSH: Social sciences/humanities. Harrison, N.Y. InterDoc Corporation, 1968-. v.1, no.1-. Quarterly. $335pa. ISSN: 00123307.

Chronological list of proceedings of conferences and meetings on social sciences and humanities. 4-year cumulations contain editor, location and subject/sponsor indexes. *Class No:* 30:061:061.3

[975]
Index to social sciences and humanities proceedings. Philadelphia, PA., Institute for Scientific Information, 1978-. No.1-. 3 quarterly issues and annual cumulation. $625. pa. ISSN: 01910574.

Indexes over 21,000 individual papers a year from published proceedings of conferences throughout the world. A category index precedes the detailed contents of proceedings. 5 more indexes follow - author/editor; sponsor; meeting location; permutation subject; and corporate. *Class No:* 30:061:061.3

[976]
World meetings: social and behavioral sciences, human services, and management. New York, Macmillan Publishing Co., 1971-. Quarterly. $150 pa. ISSN: 01946161.

A companion to *World meetings: United States and Canada* and *World meetings outside US and Canada.*

Each issue lists *c.*500 meetings to take place during the 2-year period following the date of the issue, with notes on languages used and availability of preprints or transactions. *Class No:* 30:061:061.3

Research Establishments

[977]
Directory of social research organisations in the United Kingdom. Sykes, W., *and others.* Poole, Dorset, Mansell Publishing, 1993. 448p. £35. ISBN: 0720121655.

11 short essays on aspects of social research precedes the directory proper, which lists, A-Z by name, over 1000 organizations currently carrying out social research in the United Kingdom. Includes those in central and local government, quangos, universities and other higher education establishments, independent research units, charities, market research companies, and management consultants. Data given for each is name, address, description of organization, director/head, number of researchers, fields and methods of research, details of a few recent projects, research services, training opportunities, and contact information. Also separate lists of freelance researchers, philanthropic funding bodies, professional associations, etc. There are various indexes, which could be unnecessarily time-consuming. *Class No:* 30:061:061.62

Research Projects

[978]
BRITISH LIBRARY. Current research in Britain: social sciences. 8th ed. London, Longman, for the British Library, 1993. xxvi,694p. ISBN: 0582236711. ISSN: 02671964.

Supersedes *Research in British universities, polytechnics and colleges, government departments and other institutions, v.3: Social sciences,* which superseded the British Library's (and earlier the Department of Education and Science's) *Scientific research in British universities and colleges.* V.3 *Social sciences,* which in turn superseded in part Warren Spring Laboratory's *Register of research in the human sciences,* first published in 1967.

A register of current research in universities, colleges and other institutions. An introduction is followed by a Department index and an index of institutions. The main sequence, Research in progress, is arranged in subject groups, and is followed by name, study area, and keyword indexes. *Class No:* 30:061:061.62.005

[979]
Comparative social research: an annual publication. Greenwich, CT., Jai Press, 1978-. Annual. Individually priced. V.10, 1987: $56.50.

Contributors mainly North American academics. V.1-5 (1978-82) did not have separate titles: v.6: *The welfare state,* 1883-1983: v.7: *Demography, development, dependency theory and policy;* v.8: *Deviance;* v.9: *Historical studies;* v.10: *Religion and belief systems* (1987. ISBN 0892327375) has 9 articles with copious references and notes, plus author and subject indexes for vols. 6-10. *Class No:* 30:061:061.62.005

[980]
HEILIGER, W.S. Bibliography of the Soviet social sciences, 1965-1975. Troy, N.Y., Whitston, 1978. 2v. (v, 996p.). $65 the set. ISBN: 0878751114.

Comprises citations, in English translation, for publications of the 15 major research institutes in the social sciences affiliated to the Academy of Sciences, USSR. For each institution, a listing of the contents of its journal, arranged by year, precedes a listing of the other publications sponsored by that institute. Subject and author indexes. A critical review in *Soviet studies* (v.30(4), October 1978,

....(contd.)

p.596-8) complains of carelessness, translation errors, etc., but *Choice* (v.15, no.5/6, July/August 1978, p.668) welcomes 'the availability of Soviet social science literature to English readers for the extremely important period following the resolution of the 23rd party congress in 1966 that approved and initiated new directions in social science research'. *Class No:* 30:061:061.62.005

[981]
Register of current social science research in Ireland, 1988.
O'Sullivan, F., *comp.* Dublin, The Economic and Social Research Institute, 1989. xvi, 73p. IR£3. ISBN: 0707001013.

Lists the names and addresses of organizations active in research in 1988. Arranged in 16 subject sections, including Business, industrial and management studies; Economics; Education; Regional studies; Statistics. The entries for each organization include information on department, researchers, and a brief indication of subject. Based on a questionnaire. Index to researchers. *Class No:* 30:061:061.62.005

Education Institutions

Yearbooks & Directories

[982]
Directory of social science information courses. Unesco. Social and Human Sciences Documentation Centre *and* International Federation of Documentation's Social Science Information and Documentation Committee (FID/SD). Oxford, Berg Publishers Ltd., for Unesco, 1988. xxxii,167p. F.100; £25; $50. ISBN: 0854062409, UK; 9230025259, Unesco.

Intended to provide details of the major academic and practical courses in social science information. 4 sections: 1 is an index of names and acronyms of institutes; 2 lists courses by country (international and regional institutions, then national institutions); 3 lists contact people (p.155-7); and 4 is an index of disciplines and subjects with indications of the host country of the institutions (p.159-167). An annex contains the questionnaire used in the survey. *Class No:* 30:061:37(058)

Sociology

Bibliographies

[983]
ABY, S.H., *comp.* **Sociology:** guide to reference and information sources. Littleton, Col., Libraries Unlimited, 1987. xv, 231p., (Reference sources in the social sciences series). $43.50; £36. ISBN: 0872874982.

659 entries in 3 parts - General social science reference sources (71 entries for guides, bibliographies, indexes and abstracts, handbooks and yearbooks, dictionaries and encyclopedias, statistics, directories, biographies); social science disciplines (69 entries in the fields of education, economics, psychology, social work, anthropology and history; and sociology (519 general reference sources and sources in sociological fields, *e.g.* clinical sociology, population and demography, race and ethnic relations, women's studies). Entries are annotated. Up-dates Charles

....(contd.)

Mark's *Sociology of America* (Gale, 1976). Author/title index, p.203-16; subject index, p.217-31. '... an excellent up-to-date guide to the major reference sources of sociology ...' (*Choice,* v.24(11/12), July/August, 1987. p.1671). *Class No:* 301(01)

[984]
Alternatives in print: an international catalog of books, pamphlets, periodicals and audiovisual materials, compiled by the Task Force on Alternatives in Print, Social Responsibilities Round Table, American Library Association. 6th ed. New York, Neal-Schuman Publications, Inc; London, Mansell. xii, 668p. £35. ISBN: 0918212200, USA; 0720115191, UK.

First published in 1970.

Catalogue of publishers, A-Z by name of publisher, followed by address and titles of publications (p.1-330). Title index (books & pamphlets/periodicals/audiovisual recordings/films/slideshows/videotapes), author index, subject index and geographical index to publishers, key to publishers' abbreviations. *Class No:* 301(01)

[985]
BOTTOMORE, T.B. Sociology: a guide to problems and literature. 3rd ed., completely revised and rewritten. London, Allen & Unwin, 1987. xii, 372p. £25. ISBN: 0043001084.

First published 1962, second ed. 1971.

"An introduction to sociology in a world context and a sophisticated guide to the major themes, problems and controversies in present day sociology". (*Jacket*). In 6 parts (each with 'Notes on reading' appended; 1. The Scope and methods of sociology - 2. Population and social groupings - 3. Social institutions - 4. The regulation of behaviour - 5. Social change - 6. Sociology and social practice. Numerous footnote references. Bibliography (p.323-361) A-Z by author. Non-analytical index of subjects and names. *Class No:* 301(01)

[986]
—McMILLAN, P. *and* KENNEDY, J.R. Library research guide to sociology: illustrated research strategy sources. Ann Arbor, Mich., Pierian Press, 1981. x, 67p. facsims. $25. (*Library research guide series, no.5.*) ISBN: 0876501218.

Appendix 2 is 'Basic reference sources in sociology', p.51-65, in 18 sections. Items asterisked are those described in the text. *Class No:* 301(01)

[987]
Combined retrospective index to journals in sociology, 1894-1974. Washington & Inverness, Carrollton Press; Reading, Berks., Newspaper Archive Developments Ltd., 1978. 6v. $615.

Includes over 105,000 articles and 87 catalogues. V.1 has journal codes; v.1-5 are arranged by subject; v.6 by author. Within each subject group the arrangement is Keyword - reference title - author - year/vol. - journal - page. Author index has Author - reference title - year - vol. - journal - page. *Class No:* 301(01)

[988]
Current sociology ... the journal of the International Sociological Association. London, Newbury Park, CA., Sage Publications (previously UNESCO (1952-57) and then Blackwell), 1952-. 3pa. $87.; £53 pa. ISSN: 00113921.

An international bibliography of sociology. Each volume comprises a trend report plus supporting bibliography. V.36, no.1 Spring 1988: 'Cults, converts and charisma: the sociology of new religious movements; by Thomas Robbins (trend report, p.1-207; bibliography (A-Z by author) of c.700 items, p.208-248); v.37, no.2, Summer 1989: 'The present state of sociology in Italy, 1', by Franco Ferrarotti (trend report, p.1-111; bibliography (A-Z by author) of c. 350 items, p.123-137). *Class No:* 301(01)

[989]
Finding the source in sociology and anthropology: a thesaurus-index to the reference collection. Brown, S.R., *comp.* Westport, CT, Greenwood Press, 1987. xv,269p. $49.95. (*(Finding the source, no.1).*.) ISBN: 0313252637.

In two sections: 'Bibliographic citations to selected reference books' has 586 citations (General sources - social science - anthropology - sociology - population and life style - racial, ethnic and social groups - sexuality - social issues - social forces - social welfare) all subdivided); 'Thesaurus-index to the contents of the books cited' has a title-subtitle index (p.55-67), an author index (p.69-75), and a thesaurus index (p.77-269). '...distinguished by its thesaurus-index' (*Choice*, v.24(11/12), July/August 1987, p.1672).
Class No: 301(01)

[990]
FRANCIS 521. Sociologie. Paris, Centre National de la Recherche Scientifique. Sciences humaines, 1947-. Quarterly. F.455 pa. ISSN: 07651465.

Formerly part of *Bulletin analytique. Philosophie (v.1-9, 1047-55), Bulletin signalétique. 19. Philosophie, Sciences humaines,* (1956-1960), then *Bulletin signalétique. 521.*

Over 5000 indicative abstracts and references a year, arranged in 16 subject sections: 1. History, theory and methodology - 2. Social psychology - 3. Social organization, social system, social structure ... 16. Social problems and social welfare, social work. Each issue has a list of journals abstracted; an index of 'concepts'; and a list of authors. Available online (Telesystems, Questel) and on CD-ROM.
Class No: 301(01)

[991]
GUTTSMAN, W.L. The Literature of social anthropology. In Roberts, N., *ed.* Use of social sciences literature (1977), p.56-79.

Discusses the relationship between the character of the sociological discipline, its expansion and its growing sophistication over a period of a century. Describes the formal structure of the literature and evaluates the retrieval tools, indexes, and literature-surveys recently published. 29 references.

Another chapter in *Use of social sciences literature,* - 'The literature of social anthropology', by J. Urry (p.101-17) has sections on: Anthropology and literature; Journals; Monographs; Books; Bibliographies, indexes and abstracts; Libraries and collections; Archival sources; Field notes; Current research and theses. *Class No:* 301(01)

[992]
International bibliography of social and cultural anthropology. London, Tavistock Publications, 1955, v.1-. Annual. (*International bibliography of the social sciences.*) ISSN: 00852074.

V38: 1992 (1993. lxxix,215p.) has *c.* 1700 numbered entries, arranged in 10 subject sections (*e.g.* D. Ethnographic studies of people and communities - E. Social organization and relationships - G. Problems of knowledge, arts and sciences, folk traditions - H. Studies of culture and personality - I. Problems of acculturation and social change). Author and analytical subject indexes. *Class No:* 301(01)

[993]
International bibliography of sociology ... British Library of Political and Economic Science, *comp.* London and New York, Routledge, 1952-. v.1-. Annual. ISSN: 00852066.

References to books, periodical articles, and documents, arranged in 11 sections, each subdivided: A. Social sciences. Research. Documentation - B. Methodology. Theory - C. Individuals, groups, organizations - D. Culture. Socialization. Social life - E. Social structure - F. Population. Family. Ethnic group - G. Environment. Community: Rural, Urban - H. Economic life - I. Labour - J. Politics. State. International relations - K. Social problems. Social service. Social work. Author and subject indexes. V.42: 1992 published in 1993 (lxxxvii, 358p. ISBN 0415092140). Supported by *Thematic list of descriptors: sociology, 1989* (Routledge, 1989. xix,475p. ISBN 0415017793) and updated by *International current awareness service: sociology and related disciplines* (November 1990-. monthly). Also available online (QL Systems). *Class No:* 301(01)

[994]
WEPSIEC, J. Sociology: an international bibliography of serial literature, 1880-1980. London, Mansell, 1983. 198p. £29; $55. ISBN: 072011652x.

Lists over 2300 serial publications from sociology and related fields, A-Z by title. Each entry has complete bibliographical description, and indications of where indexed or abstracted. International in scope, with romanization of foreign-language titles as necessary. Cross-references from varient titles. Subject index. *Class No:* 301(01)

Encyclopaedias

[995]
Encyclopedia of sociology. Borgatta, E.F. *and* Borgatta, M.L., *eds.* New York, Macmillan, 1992. 4v.(2359p.) charts, tables. $340 the set. ISBN: 0028970519.

370 well-documented signed articles of 2 to 18 pages, by 337 academics (mostly American sociologists). Arranged A-Z, the articles reflect sociology in all its diverse manifestations and include titles for further study. Many cross-references. Excellent detailed subject/name index of 74 pages in v.4. Intellectual level 'somewhat challenging for undergraduates' (*Library journal*, July 1992, p.76). 'The field of sociology now has a current and authoritative standard encyclopedic work' (*Choice*, v,29(11/12). July/ August 1992, p.1654). *Class No:* 301(031)

[996]

The International encyclopedia of sociology. Mann, M., *ed.* New York, Crossroads/Continuum, 1984. 434p. $34.50. ISBN: 0826402380.

*c.*2000 entries arranged A-Z in single listing. Includes both subject terms and individuals related to sociology. Extensive cross-references. *Choice* review (v.22(1), September 1984, p.64) has reservations, considering many entries present superficially. *Class No:* 301(031)

[997]

Macmillan student encyclopedia of sociology; ed. by Michael Mann. London, Macmillan Press, 1983 (Reprinted 1987). xii, 434p. (Macmillan dictionary series). £25. (paperback ed. issued 1991. £9.95). ISBN: 0333281934.

Aimed at all students of social science, with over 2000 entries, A-Z, of all important sociological terms, theories, concepts, and proper names. Entries vary from 100 to 300 or more words. Cross-references. '...wide-ranging... in fact, encyclopedic'. (*The Times educational supplement,* 18 March, 1984, p.36). *Class No:* 301(031)

Handbooks & Manuals

[998]

Handbook of sociology. Smelser, N. J., *ed.* Newbury Park, CA., Sage Publications Ltd., 1988. 824p. $89.95. ISBN: 0803926650.

Aims to supersede *Handbook of modern sociology* by R. E. L. Faris (1964).

22 Chapters arranged in 4 parts: 1. Theoretical and methodological issues - 2. Bases of inequality in society - 3. Major institutional and organizational settings - 4. Social process and change. Each chapter contains a lengthy, up-to-date bibliography. Subject index, p.775-791. Name index, p.792-824. US view of sociology. ' ... an excellent collection ... no better handbook of contemporary sociology' (*Choice* V.26 (7) March 1989, p.1122). ' ... uniformly high quality of contributions ... exceptionally rich in its coverage of fields of sociological specialisation, data sources, bibliographical material and theoretical expositions' (*The Sociological review,* v.37 (3), August 1989, p.551-3). *Class No:* 301(035)

[999]

PHILLIPS, B. Sociology, from concepts to practice. New York, London, etc., McGraw-Hill, 1979. xvii, 524p. illus., diagrs., tables. $40.95. ISBN: 0070497877.

8 parts: 1. Sociology: the science of society — 2. Introduction to personality structure — 3. Theory and methods — 4. Stratification — 5. Institutions — 6. Groups and organizations — 7. Biological and physical structures — 8. Social change. 20 sections, each with summary, glossary and suggested readings (annotated). References (A-Z authors), p.489-500; Glossary, p.501-10. Name and subject indexes. *Class No:* 301(035)

Dictionaries

[1000]

The Blackwell dictionary of twentieth-century social thought. Outhwaite, W. *and* Bottomore, T., *eds.* Oxford, Blackwell, 1992. 864p. $49.95. ISBN: 0631152628.

*c.*1000 entries, averaging 500-1000 words, on the main themes of social thought, broadly conceived, but including Western European thinkers only. Each entry includes a short

.... (contd.)

reading list. A bibliography lists all books and articles referred to in the text. Biographical appendix. General index. *Class No:* 301(038)

Polyglot

[1001]

ENDRUWEIT, G. Dreisprachiges Wörterbuch der Soziologie (Deutsch/Englisch/Französisch): ... Trilingual dictionary of sociology (German/English/French). 2e, erw.Aufl. Königstein/Fs, Athenäum Verlag GmbH, 1982. 133p. £3.95. (*Athenäum Taschenbücher: 4065: Sozialwiss.*) ISBN: 3445011648.

First published 1975.

In three parts - German-English-French; English-French-German, and French-German-English. *Class No:* 301(038)=00

English

[1002]

ABERCROMBIE, N., *and others.* **The Penguin dictionary of sociology.** 2nd ed. London, Allen Lane Penguin Books Ltd., 1988, xii,324p. £6.99. ISBN: 0140511849.

First published 1984. 505.00/00$aDesigned to appeal to students of the subject from O-level to undergraduates. *c.* 500 entries discuss the issues involved in, and alternative approaches to, the central concepts and theories of sociology. Includes entries for the principal writers in sociology. Bibliography. *Class No:* 301(038)=20

[1003]

MITCHELL, G.D., *ed.* **A New dictionary of sociology.** London, Routledge, for Department of Sociology, University of Exeter, 1989. viii, 244p. £10.99 ISBN: 0415043018.

First published in 1968 as *A dictionary of sociology.*

46 contributors. Signed articles, with references (*e.g.* 'Ethology': 1/3p; 4 references, 2 cross-references; 'Social psychology'; 11/3p., 5 references, 1 cross-reference; 'Malthusian theory'; 1p., 3 cross-references). Includes biographies (*e.g.* 'Malinowski; 1½p.). Very readable text. *Class No:* 301(038)=20

[1004]

SEYMOUR-SMITH, C. Macmillan dictionary of anthropology. London, Macmillan Press; Boston, Mass., G.K. Hall, 1986. vi,305p. £25; $39.95. ISBN: 0333365909, UK; 0816188173, US.

Title in the US is *Dictionary of anthropology.*

About 2000 entries, usually lengthy. Includes short biographies. Ample cross-references. 'intended to convey the critical spirit of anthropological enquiry to students of social and cultural anthropology and to the interested lay reader. Emphasis placed on theoretical and conceptual issues, as well as the clarification of technical terms ...' (*Foreword*). 'Selective bibliography for further reading' (authors, A-Z), p.293-305. *Class No:* 301(038)=20

[1005]

THEODORSON, G.A. *and* **THEODORSON, A.G.** **A Modern dictionary of sociology.** New York, Crowell, 1969 (Reprinted Harper & Row, 1970). x, 469p. $7.95. (*Everday handbooks.*) ISBN: 0064634833.

About 2500 entry-words, with *c.*50-100 words of concise definition. Ranges over related fields of psychology, anthropology, and statistics. 'Free will': 2/3p.;

....(contd.)

'Nonparametic statistics': ½p. Liberal use of cross-references. *Library journal* (v.94(13), July 1969, p.2593) complains that definitions are not supported by concrete examples. *Class No:* 301(038)=20

German

[1006]

FUCHS, W., *and others, eds.* **Lexikon zur Soziologie.** 2. ed. Opladen, Westdeutscher Verlag, 1978. 890p.

First published 1973.

7,500 terms in the sociology and related fields, including politics, psychology, philosophy, psychoanalysis, anthropology, behavioural science, economics and statistics. *Class No:* 301(038)=30

French

[1007]

BOUDON, R. *and* BOURRICAUD, F. **Dictionnaire critique de sociologie.** Paris, Presses Universitaires de France, 1982. xv,651p.

93 terms and lengthy articles in French which include bibliographical references and cross-references to other terms. Includes names (*e.g.* 'De Tocqueville': 2½p.; 'Socialisme': 7¼p.). Bibliography. General thematic index, p.627-651. *Class No:* 301(038)=40

[1008]

—BOUDON, R. *and* BOURRICAUD, F. **A Critical dictionary of sociology,** selected and translated by Peter Hamilton Chicago, Ill., University of Chicago; London, Routledge. 1989. xii,438p. £40; $49.50 ISBN: 0226067289.

Translation of an abridged version of the above from a predominently French point of view. A collection of 73 articles on a number of major concepts in the social sciences. *Class No:* 301(038)=40

Theses

[1009]

Sociology theses register. 3rd ed., 1980. London, Social Science Research Council; British Sociological Association, 1981. viii, 166p. £4. ISBN: 0862260558, SSRC; 0904569071, BSA.

First published 1976.

About 1560 entries under 20 subject headings. Index of institutions. Subject classification. Subject index (2p.). *Class No:* 301(043)

Reports Literature

[1010]

L'Année sociologique. Paris, Alcan, 1896-1925: Paris, Presses Universitaires de France, 1948-. Annual. Fr.335 pa. ISSN: 00662399.

More than half of each annual is a selective survey of the significant literature of sociology. V.38 has such a bibliography in 5 sections (p.343-485): Political science - Sociology of science and technology - Sociology of crime - Sociology of education - Sociology of work. Also included are 11 lengthy reviews. A-Z list of authors, periodicals and collective volumes; contents table. *Class No:* 301(047)

[1011]

—**Annual review of sociology.** Palo Alto, CA., Annual Reviews Inc., 1975-. v.1-. Annual. $31 pa. ISSN: 03600572.

Contains well-documented articles on topical subjects in each issue. V.14, 1988 (ix, 545p.) has 10 such articles. Subject indexes. Cumulative index of authors and chapter titles. *Class No:* 301(047)

Reviews & Abstracts

[1012]

Geographical abstracts: human geography. Norwich, Elsevier/Geo abstracts, 1966-. Monthly. £308pa. ISSN: 09539611.

*c.*800 abstracts in each issue of articles from over 1000 leading journals, books, conference proceedings, reports, and theses. Informative abstracts (author abstracts used where possible) arranged in subject groups (Methodology and theory - Techniques - Environment - Environmental resources - Historical - Population - People and regions - Rural studies - Urban studies - Regional and community planning - Exchange and development - Agriculture - Industry - Transport and communications - Recreational geography - Regional index). Also on line in GEOBASE. *Class No:* 301(048)

[1013]

Sociological abstracts. Brooklyn, N.Y., subsequently San Diego, CA., Sociological Abstracts, Inc., 1952-. v.1, no.1-. 5 issues pa. $475pa including cumulated index. ISSN: 00380202.

Sponsored by the International Sociological Association.

About 4000 indicative and informative abstracts pa. Main sections: 0100. Methodology and research technology - 0200. Sociology: history and theory - 0300. Social psychiatry ... 0800. Mass phenomena ... 1000. Social differentiation ... 1900. The family and socialization ... 2100. Social problems and social welfare ... 2400. Policy, planning, forecasting ... 2900. Feminist/gender studies - 3000. Marxist sociology - 9000. Papers presented at sociology meetings. Supplement section (International review of publications in sociology) contains book abstracts and a listing of book reviews that appear in the serials abstracted in the issue). Subject, author and periodical indexes. Also online from 1961, updated quarterly. (BRS(SOCA), DIMDI, DIALOG and CD-ROM. *Class No:* 301(048)

Yearbooks & Directories

[1014]

Collins dictionary of sociology. Jary, D. *and* Jary, J. London & New York, Harper Collins Publishers, 1991. 768p. illus. £7.99; $13. ISBN: 0064610365.

Includes terms most likely to be met from associated disciplines (*e.g.* psychology, economics, anthropology and political science), and methodological terms and research techniques. Also biographical entries. Cross-references. *Class No:* 301(058)

Quotations

[1015]

BARDIS, P.D. Dictionary of quotations in sociology. Westport, Conn., Greenwood, 1985. xiv, 356p. $45. £42.95. ISBN: 0313237786.

Arranged A-Z by general concepts, followed by quotation(s) in chronological order with provenance in brackets. Includes historical, cross-cultural and international sources, 25% of quotes being in areas related to sociology. Selected bibliography, A-Z by author (p.315-25). Well indexed by name (p.327-43) and subject (p.345-56). *Choice,* v.23(9), May 1986, p.1368 points out that there are 24 instances of self-quoting, and that the dictionary is '... useful mainly as the only work of its type ... Recommended with reservations...' *Class No:* 301(082.2)

Histories

[1016]

MITCHELL, G.D. A Hundred years of sociology. London, Duckworth, 1968. xiii, 310p. (Hundred years series).

A very readable survey of 18 chapters (1. Introduction - 2. Early social science in America, Britain and France - 3. Evolutionary sociology ... 10. The social survey tradition ... 16. Macrosociology ... 18. Current trends). Footnote references; sources ('Acknowledgements'), p. xiii. Index of names; index of chapters and sub-titles. *Recent British sociology,* by J. Eldridge (London, Macmillan, 1981. 276p. £22.50. ISBN 0333266390) is a critical essay (and bibliography) analysing trends over the past 20 years). *Class No:* 301(091)

[1017]

SWINGEWOOD, A. A Short history of sociological thought. 2nd ed. London, Macmillan Press, 1991. 359p. £35. ISBN: 033355860x.

'... neither a history of sociology nor sociological theory but a selective history of sociological thought from its origins in eighteenth-century philosophy, history and political economy ... an awareness of society as a distinctive object of study ...' (*Introduction*). 12 chapters are arranged in 3 parts: Part 1. Foundations; pt.2. Classical sociology; pt.3. Modern sociology. Further reading relates to chapters. Bibliography is A-Z by author. Index. *Class No:* 301(091)

Great Britain

[1018]

ABERCROMBIE, N., *and others.* **Contemporary British society:** a new introduction to sociology. 2nd rev. ed. Cambridge, Polity Press, 1994. 538p. illus., diagrs., graphs, tables, maps. £45; £12.95. ISBN: 0745610608.

12 chapters: 1. Introduction - 2. Work - 3. Class - 4. Gender - 5. Ethnicity and racism - 6. Families and households - 7. Towns, cities and the countryside - 8. Education - 9. Health - 10. Culture and media - 11. Deviance, crime and control - 12. Politics. Bibliography, p.520-531. Detailed order. Boxed information and summaries are a feature of this textbook. *Class No:* 301(410)

USSR

[1019]

Contemporary Soviet society: a statistical handbook. Ryan, M., *comp. & translator.* Cheltenham, Edward Elgar Publishing, 1990. ix,283p. £45. ISBN: 1852783494.

Statistical tables for selected years to 1989 arranged in 13 subject sections. Sources are given. Data is by country, republic, town, etc.Index. *Class No:* 301(47)

Writing & Lecturing

[1020]

DOBKIN, U.S. Handbook for the teaching of social studies. 2nd ed. Newton, Mass., Allyn & Bacon Inc., 1985. x, 323p. £26.75. ISBN: 0205081495.

First published 1977.

14 chapters (Goals and objectives - Planning - The art of questioning - Independent study - Dealing with values - Reading skills - Writing skills - Media - Simulation activities - Testing and evaluation - Electives and curriculum consideration - Mainstreaming - Professional growth - Professional evaluation. Examples are given in many chapters; end notes (including references) are added to all chapters. Index, p.317-323. *Class No:* 301:001.81

Social Change

Bibliographies

[1021]

FREY, F.W., *with others, eds.* **Survey research on comparative social change:** a bibliography. Cambridge, Mass., M.I.T. Press, [1969]. 77p. ISBN: 0262060272.

2,174 annotated items in 9 groups (1. General descriptions, and comparisons of groups - 2. Group and interpersonal relations - 3. Cognition, personality and behavior - 4. Family, childbearing, gerontology, demography, women as a group - 5. Social change, communications, education - 6. Political institutions, attitudes, and behavior - 7. Economic behavior and institutions - 8. Special topics - 9. Methodology). Computer-printed. Author, title, subject index. *Class No:* 301.15(01)

[1022]

SADLER, J.D. Families in transition: an annotated bibliography. Archon/Shoestring Press, 1988. 251p. $30. ISBN: 0208021809.

Topics include families of those in prison, surrogate parentage, and latchkey children, etc. Arrangement is by topical chapters, subdivided by books and articles, then A-Z by author. An appendix lists associations and organizations. Author, subject and title indexes. *Class No:* 301.15(01)

[1023]

The Social and economic impact of new technology, 1978-84: a select bibliography, compiled by L. Grayson. Letchworth, Herts, Technical Communications, 1984. [9]. 80p. ISBN: 0946655014.

*c.*700 references "... bringing together American, British and European literature on the social and economic effects on government, industry, business and the home" (Introduction). Subject arrangement: The overall picture - National and international initiatives, policies and political manifestos - Social impacts - Economic structure and policy - Impact of new technology on business, industry and communications - Administrative impact and industrial

....*(contd.)*

relations: impact of new technology. No index. This has been followed by a review publication with the same titles. First issue, June 1985, updated quarterly. *Class No:* 301.15(01)

Social Psychology

[1024]

Advances in experimental social psychology. San Diego, CA., Academic Press, 1964-.v.1-. Irregular. ISSN: 00652601.

Each issue has several articles by prominent scholars in the field, providing overviews and theoretical integrations of specialized areas of research. Extensive lists of references usually follow the articles. Subject index and contents lists of earlier volumes. *Class No:* 301.151

[1025]

European review of social psychology, no.3. Stroeke, W. *and* Hewstone, M., *eds.* No.1 issued 1990. Annual. New York, Wiley, 1992. 336p. $120. ISBN: 0471932019. ISSN: 10463283.

Aim is to reflect the dynamism of social psychology in Europe and the attention now being paid to European ideas and research. V.3 explores such issues on the discontinuity effects, long-lasting cognitive and social consequences of emotion, features of asymetry and stereotypes. *Class No:* 301.151

Public Opinion

[1026]

Index to international public opinion, 1978/79-. Westport, CT., Greenwood Press, 1980-. Annual. ISSN: 0193905x.

Prepared by Survey Research Consultants International Inc.

The 8th edition, 1985-1986 (published 1987, xxi, 655p. $175. ISBN 0313255954) is in two parts: Single nation surveys (agriculture - business and industry ... crime and justice - economic affairs ... government ... marriage and family ... military affairs ... transportation); Multinational surveys. Bibliography, p.621-626. Indexes by topical categories, by countries and regions. Brings together many of the important surveys conducted by researchers throughout the world. *Class No:* 301.153

Bibliographies

[1027]

KRUGER, A.N. Argumentation and debate: a classified bibliography. 2nd ed. Metuchen, N.J., Scarecrow Press, 1975. 520p. $27.50. ISBN: 0810807491.

First published 1964.

Lists c.6,000 books, periodical articles and theses under 22 subject heads. Author and subject indexes. "The standard comprehensive bibliography in the field" (*Wilson library bulletin,* September 1975, p.76). *Class No:* 301.153(01)

[1028]

MILLER, A.J. Confrontation, conflict and dissent: a bibliography of a decade of controversy, 1960-1970. Metuchen, N.J., Scarecrow Press, 1972. 567p. $30; £24.35. ISBN: 0810804905.

Over 5,000 items are listed, some with annotations. Topics include Vietnam, abortion, Women's Lib and racism. US slanted. *Class No:* 301.153(01)

[1029]

SMITH, B.L. *and* **SMITH, C.M. International communication and political opinion:** a guide to the literature. Prepared for the Rand Corporation by the Bureau of Social Science Research, Washington, D.C. Princeton, N.J., Princeton University Press, 1956 (Reprinted by Greenwood, 1972). xi, 325p. $22.50. ISBN: 0837160073.

2,563 numbered, annotated entries (annotations average *c.*100 words). 7 sections: 1. Theoretical and general writings relevant to international communication and censorship - 2. Political persuasion and propaganda activities (by country of origin) - 3. Specialists in political persuasion - 4. Channels ('Media') of international communication (to, from and in particular areas) - 5. Audience characteristics - 6. Methods of research and intelligence - 7. Bibliographies. Appendix A is a note on current sources, and B, a list of journals. Author and subject index. *Class No:* 301.153(01)

[1030]

WALDEN, G.R. 'Public opinion polls': a guide to assessing the literature. In *Reference Services Review,* v.16(4) 1988, p.65-74.

Introduction - Published polls (Gallup Organization, etc.) - Polling indexes and abstracts (journals) - Further readings (15 annotated titles) - Notes (27 items referring to the text). *Class No:* 301.153(01)

Handbooks & Manuals

[1031]

LAKE, C.C. *and* **HARPER, P.C. Public opinion polling:** a handbook for public interest and citizen advocacy groups. Washington, Island Press, [1987]. 166p. $29.95. ISBN: 0933280327.

How to plan, administer and analyse a poll. 10 chapters take the reader step-by-step through the polling process, each chapter including tips for success, warnings of potential problems, and checklists summarizing important points. Also, annotated bibliography, sample questionnaires, grids and tabulations, short glossary, and index. *Class No:* 301.153(035)

[1032]

Pros and cons: a debater's handbook. Jacobson,, M.D., *ed.* 17th ed. London, Routledge & Kegan Paul, 1987. x, 278p. £4.95. ISBN: 0710210442.

First published 1896.

Objective is to give debaters a useful guide to for-and-against arguments on a wide range of controversial issues. Topics A-Z ('Advertising, public control and taxation' ... 'Written constitution'). Pro and con points on each topic in adjacent columns per page. The index groups topics under 21 heads (Agriculture ... Women). *Class No:* 301.153(035)

Great Britain

[1033]
HEALD, G. *and* WYBROW, R.J. The Gallup survey of Britain. Beckenham, Kent, Croom Helm, 1986. [4], 303p. £19.95. ISBN: 0709938462.

8 chapters, mainly relating to 1985: 1. The year begins - 2. Domestic politics - 3. The economy - 4. The environment - 5. Law and order - 6. International affairs - 7. Social and other non-political issues - 8. Britain 20 years on. There follow 4 appendices (A. How scientific polls are conducted - B. Diary of events - C. Gallup's election record, 1945-1983 - D. Party fortunes, 1984-1985) and a 3-page index. Aims to be issued annually. *Class No:* 301.153(410)

[1034]
WYBROW, R.J. Britain speaks out, 1937-87: a social history as seen through the Gallup data. London, Macmillan Press, 1989. 224p. tables. £40. ISBN: 0333396634.

Based on a fraction of the available data, the author attempts to create a picture of British society over the 50-year period. 8 chapters are arranged chronologically and there is an appendix of tables. Author is Director of Gallup. 'This is a wonderful book - a real treasure trove of opinion poll results across a huge range of subjects ... ' (ESRC Data Archive. *Bulletin* No.45, Spring 1990, p.31).
Class No: 301.153(410)

Adolescents

[1035]
Encyclopedia of adolescence. Lerner, R.M., *and others, eds.* New York, Garland, 1991. 2v. (*c.*1223p.). ISBN: 0824043782.

Over 200 articles (2 to 10 pages each) surveying the emotional upheaval and transformations that mark the passage from childhood to young adulthood. Bibliographies included at end of each article. Cross-references. Subject index. 'Highly recommended' (*Library Journal*,, 15 May 1991. p.77). *Class No:* 301.18-053.7

Aged People

[1036]
Old age: a register of social research, 1982-84. Todd, H., *ed.* London, Centre for Policy on Aging, 1985. 280p. £12. ISBN: 0904139433.

First published 1955, and issued annually and later bienially. Compilation of a new ed. started 1989.

Information on current and recently completed British studies on the social and behavioural aspects of old age. Major projects are fully detailed. Research notes; indexes to subjects, organizations and individuals; and a review of research trends. *Class No:* 301.18-053.9

Bibliographies

[1037]
ADAY, R.H., *comp*. Crime and the elderly: an annotated bibliography. Westport. CT., Greenwood Press, 1988. 118p. $35.95. (*Bibliographies and indexes in gerontology, 8.*) ISBN: 0313254702.

361 references arranged in 10 topical chapters (Criminal justice issues - The elderly as victims - Fear of crime - Elder abuse and neglect - Crime prevention problems - Old age and crime - Elderly crime patterns - Causes of criminal behavior - Aging prisoners - Rehabilitative programs.

.... (contd.)
Includes books, journal articles, conference proceedings, research reports, Congressional hearings, unpublished MS, and dissertations. Annotations are short. Author and subject indexes. Highly recommended by *Choice* (v.26(10),June 1989). *Class No:* 301.18-053.9(01)

[1038]
BALKEMA, J.B., *ed*. Aging: a guide to resources. Syracuse, N.Y., Gaylord Professional Publications, 1983. 232p. $34.95. ISBN: 0915794489.

An annotated bibliography in a clear and logical arrangement. Annotations are brief and descriptive. Includes books, pamphlets and journal articles. Title, name and subject indexes. *Class No:* 301.18-053.9(01)

[1039]
COLEMAN, P.G. 'Social gerontology' In *British book news,* November 1984, p.650-655.

A book survey and listing of 128 items in subject sections: Social policy - Social care services - Social work - Support to families - Voluntary work - Residential care - Sheltered housing - Health care, including geriatric medicine - Mental illness and infirmity - Nursing - Dying - Social sciences - History of aging - Psychology - Other fields - Introductory books - General literature. *Class No:* 301.18-053.9(01)

[1040]
—Select bibliographies on aging. London, Centre for Policy on Aging, 1984-. ISSN: 02670348.

An occasional series designed to bring together a wide range of annotated references on a variety of topics. No.1: *Social planning for the elderly,* compiled by Barbara Meredith (1984. 44p. £3.50) has over 250 references on the services older people use at local government level, the final section listing government policy documents. No.2: *Education and older people,* compiled by Dianne Norton (1987. 50p. £4.50) explores the existing literature of ideas on aging and education, and catalogues the work that is being undertaken to make more opportunities available. *Class No:* 301.18-053.9(01)

[1041]
New literature on old age: a guide to new publications, courses and conferences on aging, 1977- no. 1-. London, Centre for Policy on Aging. 6pa. £10 pa. ISSN: 01402447.

About 100 entries (often briefly annotated) per issue. Covers new books and periodical articles, central and local government reports and circulars, statistical reports, semi-published research documents, and informal publications issued by voluntary groups, Mainly British literature. Cross-references. Headings: General - Attitudes to aging - Women - Health - Physical disability - Falls - Nutrition - Psychology - Mental illness and services to the mentally ill - Alcohol and aging - Social characteristics - Retirement - Education in later life - Leisure - Services - Social work - Income maintenance - Housing - Residential care - Health services - Primary health care - Medications - Community care - Family care - Ethnic minorities - Crime/security/abuse - Reference works - Annual reports. *Class No:* 301.18-053.9(01)

[1042]

ORIOL, W.E., *comp*. **Federal public policy on aging since 1960:** an annotated bibliography. Westport, CT., Greenwood Press, 1987. xiv, 127p. $52.95. (*Bibliographies and indexes in gerontology, no.5*.) ISBN: 0313252866.

750 briefly annotated references dating from 1960 to 1986. Part 1: Federal agency policy: general critiques, key themes; part 2: Specific programmes and issues (income and retirement policy - health and long-term care - housing ... minorities - research ... women). Appendix: Sources of information: Congressional committees and national organizations. Author index (p.115-122) and subject index (p.123-127). '... a well-executed bibliographical guide'. (*RQ*, v.27(4), Summer 1988, p.5734). *Class No:* 301.18-053.9(01)

[1043]

—GUTTMAN, D., *comp*. **European American elderly:** an annotated bibliography. Westport, CT., Greenwood Press, 1987. 122p. $42.95. (*Bibliographies and indexes in gerontology, 6*.) ISBN: 0313255830.

A bibliography of 310 English-language titles published in the United States in the past 15 years. Includes journal articles, chapters in monographs, and dissertations. Arranged in topical sections with subdivisions. Includes *c.*35 nationalities and ethnic groups. *Class No:* 301.18-053.9(01)

Retirement

[1044]

MILETICH, J.J., *comp*. **Retirement:** an annotated bibliography. New York, Greenwood Press, 1986. xvii, 147p. $29.95. (*Bibliographies and indexes in gerontology, no.2*.) ISBN: 031324815x.

Selected references, annotated and numbered, dating from 1975 through 1985, that examine many aspects of retirement. Arranged in 9 topical sections: 1. Planning and counselling for retirement - 2. Retirement adjustment, health and leisure - 3. Financial aspects of retirement - 4. Housing and transportation for the retired - 5. Crime and the retired - 6. Executives, the professions and retirement - 7. Women and retirement - 8. Work after retirement - 9. Old age and death. Entries arranged A-Z by author within the subject sections. References are mainly to journal articles. Author index (p.125-131); subject index (p.132-147). 'Annotations are succinct and identify accompanying special features such as tables, figures, and references' (*Choice*, v.24(5), January 1987, p.746). *Class No:* 301.18-053.9(01)RET

Encyclopaedias

[1045]

MADDOX, G.L., *and others*. **The Encyclopedia of aging.** New York, Springer Publishing Co., 1987. 890p. illus., tables. $96. ISBN: 0826148409.

Concise, descriptive articles on *c.*500 subjects in the field, including biological, psychological and sociological aging, life experience of the elderly. Written for the non-specialist, it lists references to classical and recent works. Over 200 contributors from academic, medicine and health-related agencies. Entries, arranged A-Z, vary in length from 1-7 pages. Cross-references. Bibliography of over 2000 references to sources cited in the text. Comprehensive index. '... an authoritative reference source ...' (*Library journal*, 15 April 1987, p.75). *Class No:* 301.18-053.9(031)

Handbooks & Manuals

[1046]

BINSTOCK, R.G., *and others*. **Handbook of aging and the social sciences.** 3rd ed. San Diego, Academic Press, 1990. 489p. tables. $79.95. (*The Handbooks of aging*.) ISBN: 012099190x.

First published 1977.

'Designed to provide comprehensive information and major reference sources and to suggest contemporary research issues'. 23 chapters arranged in 4 parts: 1. Aging and social structure - 2. Aging and the life source - 3. Aging and social institutions - 4. Aging and social intervention. Many references appended to each chapter. Author index, p.455-474; analytical subject index, p.475-489. 'A necessary acquisition for all colleges and universities as a basic reference tool in the field' (*Choice*, September 1977, p.832, of the first ed.). Other volumes in the 'Handbooks of aging' series are: Schneider, E.L. and Rowe, J.W. *Handbook of the biology of aging*; and Birren, J.E. and Schaie, K.W. *Handbook of the psychology of aging (qv)*. *Class No:* 301.18-053.9(035)

[1047]

BIRREN, J.E. *and* SCHAIE, K.W., *eds*. **Handbook of the psychology of aging.** 3rd ed. San Diego, Academic Press, 1990. xviii,552p. tables. $79.95. ISBN: 0121012808.

Focuses on the psychology of adult development and aging, with 28 chapters written by 45 expert contributors covering a wide range of topics. Chapters arranged in 4 parts: 1. Theory and measurement in the psychology of aging. 2. Influences of behavior and aging - 3. Behavioral processes in aging - 4. Application to the individual and society. Summaries precede and extensive references follow each chapter. Author index, p.503-530; analytical subject index, p.531-552. *Class No:* 301.18-053.9(035)

[1048]

PATMORE, E., *ed*. **International handbook of aging:** contemporary developments and research. Westport, CT., Greenwood Press, 1980. xviii, 529p. illus., tables. $50.95. ISBN: 0313208905.

The International Association of Gerontology requested scholars in 28 countries to submit evaluative essays on the gerontological work in their respective countries. Each essay discusses the roles and status of the aged in the given country, the history of gerontological research, programmes for the aged, and sources of further information. Bibliographies of major works end each essay. Two appendices - names and addresses of major organizations concerned with gerontological research and problems. Index. 'Articles informative and readable, enhanced by tables summarizing the statistical data'. (*College & research libraries*, July, 1981, p.354). *Class No:* 301.18-053.9(035)

Dictionaries

Polyglot

[1049]

GIBSON, J.S. *and* NUSBERG, C., *eds*. **International glossary of social gerontology.** New York, Van Nostrand Reinhold Co., 1985. $31.95. ISBN: 0442242824.

Published under the auspices of the International Federation of Aging.

Aim is to assist the international exchange of information and cross-national research on aging by assembling basic

....*(contd.)*

terms that are required to apply gerontological principles across national boundaries. *c.*40 contributors. Definitions in English, French, German and Spanish. *Class No:* 301.18-053.9(038)=00

Reviews & Abstracts

[1050]

Abstracts in social gerontology: current literature on aging. Newbury Park, Sage Publications (for the National Council on Aging). $126. ISSN: 10474862.

Prior to 1991 title was 'Current literature on aging'.

Indexes and abstracts selected books and journals on gerontology, including demography, economics, family relations, government policies and health. Books are a part of NCOA/s library; *c.*80 core journals are indexed cover-to-cover. Arrangement is A-Z by subject. Cumulated author and subject indexes included in last issue each year.

Class No: 301.18-053.9(048)

Periodicals & Progress Reports

[1051]

HESSLEIN, S.B., *comp.* **Serials on aging:** an analytical guide. Westport, CT., Greenwood Press, 1986. 176p. $32.95. (*Annotated bibliographies of serials: a subject approach, 9.*) ISBN: 0313247099.

An exhaustive bibliography that identifies a broad range of serials, including newsletters and government publications, that have a substantial amount of information on aging. International, US State and regional English-language sources are cited. arranged by general disciplinary sources first and then by speciality areas. Descriptive annotations. 4 indexes - geographical, publisher and sponsoring organization, title, and subject. 'Hesslein has compiled the best source for serials on aging' (*Choice,* March 1987, p.1032). *Class No:* 301.18-053.9(05)

Yearbooks & Directories

[1052]

CENTRE FOR POLICY ON AGING. CPA world directory of old age. Harlow, Longman, 1989. [8],208p. £35. ISBN: 0582044243.

In 2 parts: 1. International; 2. Country by country (Afghanistan ... Zimbabwe). For each country information is given on population, life-expectancy, socio-economic data, followed by organizations, A-Z by name of organization (and translation into English if necessary), address, telephone number, fax number, director, contact, formation, activities, international affiliates, publications). Index, p.201-8. *Class No:* 301.18-053.9(058)

[1053]

DARNBOROUGH, A. *and* **KINRADE, D. Directory for older people:** a handbook of information and opportunities for the over-55s. Cambridge, Woodhead-Faulkner, 1990. 215p. £19.95. $45.

Lists organizations concerned with money, house/home, aids to daily living, welfare, bereavement, voluntary work, learning, etc. A-Z index. *Class No:* 301.18-053.9(058)

[1054]

Directory of resources for aging, gerontology, and retirement. 2nd ed. Mankate, MN., Minnesota Scholarly Press, 1987. 400p. $75. ISBN: 0933474415.

First published 1979.

Contains 6 directories: Reprint of *A directory of State and area agencies in aging* (4th ed. Washington, GPO, 1985), listing 57 State and 672 area agencies; and lists of 100 national associations, research centres, foundations, political action groups, and social service agencies; 100 local associations; 100 legal services; 150 colleges and universities offering degrees in gerontology and aging: and 55 international organizations. Glossary. Index. *Class No:* 301.18-053.9(058)

[1055]

Directory of services for elderly people in the UK. Lodge, K., *ed.* Harlow, Essex, Longman and Public Service Management in collaboration with the Centre for Policy on Aging, 1990. xxxi,321p. £49.50. (*Community information guides.*) ISBN: 0582087856.

Aims to bring together information on organizations which provide care, support and facilities for the elderly. Arranged in 7 sections, with full contact details. Index. *Class No:* 301.18-053.9(058)

Retirement

[1056]

BROWN, R. Good retirement guide, 1994. London, Kogan Page, 1994. 544p. £14.95. ISBN: 0749410981.

First published 1987.

Topics include money management, budget planning, your home, leisure activities, starting your own business, looking for paid work, voluntary work, health, holidays, caring for elderly parents, wills, etc. Also a list of organizations that can help. Index. *Class No:* 301.18-053.9(058)RET

Research Methods

[1057]

ZITO, D.R. *and* **ZITO, G.V. A Guide to research in gerontology: strategies and resources.** Westport, CT., Greenwood Press, 1988. 144p. $35.95. ISBN: 0313259046.

Intended for information specialists and professionals concerned with gerontology in all its aspects - psychological, social and medical. Explains how to design a research strategy; how to evaluate different information sources; and the role of various kinds of reference sources in research. Examples are given. Also explains how to get information from other organizations, listing them. 4 appendices listing and annotating reference books, indexes and abstracts, databases, and journals. Subject index. 'A title index would have been a useful addition; (*Reference books bulletin*, July 1989, v.81(21), p.1883). *Class No:* 301.18-053.9:001.891

Race Relations

Bibliographies

[1058]

GILBERT, V.F. *and* **TATLA, D.S. Immigrants, minorities and race relations:** a bibliography of theses and dissertations presented at British and Irish universities, 1900-1981. London, Mansell, 1984. xxxiii, 153p. £20. ISBN: 0720116910.

....(contd.)

Some 1700 entries, unannotated, arranged in two main sections: General theoretical and historical studies; and Theses relating to a particular region or country. Each section is divided into some 200 subject subdivisions. Time span ranges from ancient history, through medieval immigrant communities, slavery and the slave trade, to contemporary topics. An introductory essay by Colin Holmes surveys the history of immigrants in Great Britain, concentrating on immigration since World War II. Author index (p.138-153); subject index (p.105-137). *Class No:* 301.18-054(01)

[1059]
HALLMAN, C.N. *and* LISTER, L.F. **White supremacy and its associated groups:** an annotated bibliography. In *RSR*, v.17(4),1989, p.7-18,28.

55 annotated entries plus 32 listed books and reports. Includes sections on white supremacy, Aryan nations, Ku Klux Klan, skinheads, justice system/civil rights, media, and law enforcement. *Class No:* 301.18-054(01)

[1060]
HEBREW UNIVERSITY OF JERUSALEM. Vidal Sassoon International Center for the Study of Anti-Semitism. **Antisemitism:** an annotated bibliography, v.1. Cohen, S.S., *ed.* New York, Garland, 1987-. v.1.- Biennial. xxix, 392p. $47. (*Garland reference library of social science, v.366-.*) ISBN: 0824085329.

V.1 covers 1255 books, dissertations, masters theses, and periodical articles published 1984-1985, anti-Semitism being defined as 'antagonism toward Jews and Judaism as expressed in writings ... in the visual arts ... and in actions.' (*Introduction*). Clear and concise annotations of materials published in English, European languages, Hebrew and Yiddish (English translations of works in less wellknown languages). Arranged A-Z under broad chronological headings, subdivided for the modern period by regions or countries. Includes a section on bibliographies and reference works. 2 appendices: a list of anti-Semitic periodicals with publishers names and addresses; a check list of bibliographies published on anti-Semitism and the Holocaust before 1984. Subject and author indexes and list of periodicals and collections cited. *Class No:* 301.18-054(01)

[1061]
PRUCHA, F.P. **A Bibliographical guide to the Indian-White relations in the United States.** Chicago, Ill., University of Chicago Press, 1977. $30. ISBN: 0226684768.

In two parts: part 1 is a guide to sources - national archives, government documents, manuscripts, newspapers, oral history, travel accounts and library catalogues. Part 2 cites published works, including periodical literature, under 12 major subject and numerous sub-sections. *Class No:* 301.18-054(01)

[1062]
—PRUCHA, F.P. **Indian-White relations in the United States:** a bibliography of works published, 1975-1980. Nebraska, 1982. 179p. $14.95. ISBN: 0803236654.

3400 unannotated citations, updating the above. Citations are arranged under 15 topical headings, including Guides to sources. Extensive index of subjects and names. 'These two volumes constitute the most comprehensive bibliographic treatment of the field.' (*Choice*, v.19(11/12), July/August 1982, p.1542). *Class No:* 301.18-054(01)

[1063]
World racism and related inhumanities: a country-by-country bibliography. Weinberg, M., *comp.* New York & Westport, CT, Greenwood Press, 1992. xiii,1048p. $99.50. (*Bibliographies and indexes in world history,26.*) ISBN: 0313281092.

Covers 135 countries, A-Z, plus a chapter for each continent, a short section on the ancient world, and a section of other related bibliographies. No annotations. Emphasis is on recent literature in English, French, German and Spanish. Author index, p.915-1020. Thematic subject index, p.1021-48. '... researchers concerned with racism will find no comparable compilation.'(*Choice*, v.30(3), November 1993, p.451). *Class No:* 301.18-054(01)

Handbooks & Manuals

[1064]
SIGLER, J., *ed.* **International handbook of race and race relations.** Westport, CT., Greenwood Press, 1987. 512p. $95; £56.95. ISBN: 0313247706.

Studies of the conditions which are extant in many of the world's societies and accounts of the movements in race and race relations throughout the world. *Class No:* 301.18-054(035)

Dictionaries

[1065]
CASHMORE, E.E., *and others.* **Dictionary of race and ethnic relations.** 3rd rev. ed. London, Routledge, 1993. 336p. £45. ISBN: 041510291x.

First published 1984.

A view of race and ethnic relations, including events and individuals significant to race relations as well as topics, theories and practices. Clearly written; long, signed articles, with reading lists appended. Cross-references. *Class No:* 301.18-054(038)

Reviews & Abstracts

[1066]
Sage race relations abstracts. London, Sage Publications, on behalf of the Institute of Race Relations, 1975-. v.1-,no.1-. Quarterly. £125pa. ISSN: 03079201.

Formerly *Race relations abstracts* (1968-74).

Over 1,000 indicative and informative abstracts pa, drawing on books and *c.*200 journals. 33 sections (Bibliographies - Adjustment and integration - Area studies ... Culture and identity ... Education (general, pre-school; further; higher; policy and planning; syllabuses) - Employment ... Housing ... Race relations (general; law and legislation; history and ideologies) ... Young people ... Ephemera. List of journals abstracted. Author and subject indexes. *Class No:* 301.18-054(048)

Great Britain

[1067]
GORDON, P. *and* KLUG, F. **Racism and discrimination in Britain:** a select bibliography, 1970-83. London, The Runnymede Trust, 1984. viii, 143p. £3.50. ISBN: 0902397508.

A basic unannotated guide to the material, books, pamphlets, official reports, journal articles published in

....*(contd.)*

Britain since 1970 and some important earlier material and material published abroad. 13 sections (1. Racism and discrimination; 2. Politics and race; 3. Immigration and nationality; 4. Women, race and racism; 5. Employment and unemployment; 6. Education, race and racism; 7. Housing and the inner city; 8. The Health Service; 9. Social and welfare services; 10. Policing and racial violence; 11. The criminal justice system; 12. The media; 13. Films and filmstrips. Finally an appendix listing organizations. *Class No:* 301.18-054(410)

[1068]
—AMIN, K., *and others*. Racism and discrimination in Britain: a select bibliography, 1984-1987. London, Runnymede Trust, 1988. [3], 98p. £3.95. ISBN: 0902397753.

Lists books, pamphlets, offical reports and journal articles in 12 subject sections, each subdivided and subdivided again by form. Contents: 1. Racism and discrimination - 2. Politics and race - 3. Immigration and nationality - 4. Women, race and racism - 5. Employment and unemployment - 6. Education - 7. Housing and inner city - 8. The Health Service - 9. Social and welfare services - 10. Policing, racial violence and urban disorder - 11. Criminal justice and the legal system - 12. The media. Appendix lists addresses of publishing organizations. Supplements *Racism and discrimination in Britain: a select bibliography*, by P. Gordon and F. Klug, which covered 1970-83. No annotations and no index. *Class No:* 301.18-054(410)

South Africa

[1069]
OMOND, R. The Apartheid handbook. 2nd ed. Harmondsworth, Mddx., Penguin Books, 1986. 283p. £3.95.

First published 1985.

Cover subtitle: 'A guide to South Africa's everyday racial policies'. 41 subject chapters, including Racial terminology - Race classification - Social segregation - Education - The Homelands - Banned gatherings - Radio and television - Books - State of Emergency. Bibliography and sources, p.257-258. References (really a subject index), p.259-271. Index of legislation. General index, p.277-282 (12 column). *Class No:* 301.18-054(680)

[1070]
SOUTH AFRICAN INSTITUTE OF RACE RELATIONS. Race relations survey. Broomfontein, the Institute, 1951/52- Annual.. ISSN: 02587246.

Early title was *Survey of race relations in South Africa*

'A valuable summary review of developments and trends in legislation, government action and opposition' (Musiker, R. *South Africa* (1979),. entry no.329). *Class No:* 301.18-054(680)

Bibliographies

[1071]
KALLEY, J.A. South Africa under Apartheid: a selected and annotated bibliography. Westport, CT., Meckler, 1989. 544p. $85. ISBN: 088736506x.

1123 references to books and articles produced over the last 30 years, with emphasis on the last decade. Good author index and useful subject index arranged in broad categories. Fuller than S.E. Pyatt's *Apartheid: a selective annotated*

....*(contd.)*

bibliography, 1979-1987 (Garland, 1990. 160p.), although the latter has an appendix on major South African laws and regulations. *Class No:* 301.18-054(680)(01)

[1072]
LIMB, P. The ANC and black workers in South Africa, 1912-1992: an annotated bibliography. London, Hans Zell, 1993. 380p. £48. ISBN: 1873836953.

Entries for *c.*3000 books, pamphlets and periodical articles arranged A-Z by author (or title if no author), followed by *c.*1000 entries for periodicals, newspapers, government publications, theses, conference papers, bibliographies and reference works. Subject index. *Class No:* 301.18-054(680)(01)

[1073]
POTGIETER, P.J.J.S. Index to literature on race relations in South Africa, 1910-1975. Boston, Mass, G.K. Hall, 1979. 555p. $56. (*Bibliographies and guides in African studies.*)

Compiled for the Potchefstroom University for Christian Higher Education.

More than 5,000 entries, mainly post-1948 when the policy of 'Separate development' was officially decreed. Entries limited to select books, periodicals and official publications, one third in Africaans, Dutch and German. Author and subject indexes. No cross-references or annotations. *Class No:* 301.18-054(680)(01)

[1074]
SCHAPERA, I., *comp*. Select bibliography of South African native life and problems. London, Oxford University Press, 1941. vii. 249p. Supplements 1956-74.

Compiled for the Inter-university Committee for African Studies.

*c.*2,500 briefly but critically annotated items in 6 sections, including: Physical anthropology; Ethnography (p.36-109:714 items); Modern status and conditions (p.110-204). The 4 Supplements cover 1939-1970. Author index only. *Class No:* 301.18-054(680)(01)

Histories

[1075]
ELLIS, S. The ANC in exile. In *African affairs*, v.90, no.360. July 1991, p.439-47.

Brief history of the ANC from its establishment in 1912, which concentrates on the period 1960-1990. *Class No:* 301.18-054(680)(091)

[1076]
HOLLAND, H. The Struggle: a history of the ANC. London, Grafton, 1989. 252p. illus., ports. (inc. 8p. of pl.). £4.50. ISBN: 0586206132.

A sympathetic and up-to-date history of the African National Congress, the political group fighting 'apartheid' inside and outside South Africa. *Class No:* 301.18-054(680)(091)

Latin America

[1077]
LEVINE, R.M. Race and ethnic relations in Latin America and the Caribbean: an historical dictionary and bibliography. Metuchen, N.J., Scarecrow Press, 1980. 260p. $17.50. ISBN: 0810813246.

....(contd.)

Over 1200 terms with short definitions, and 1300 geographically arranged bibliographical citations, unannotated. Intended to facilitate the study of racial and ethnic issues in Latin American and Caribbean history. No index. *Class No:* 301.18-054(729.99)

USA

Bibliographies

[1078]
Black American families, 1965-1984: a classified, selectively annotated bibliography. Editor-in-chief: W.R. Allen. Westport, Conn., Greenwood, 1986. xxxi, 480p. (Bibliographies and indexes in Afro-American and African studies, no. 16). $45. ISBN: 0313256136.

More than 1100 entries, arranged A-Z, a quarter being annotated, published between 1965 and 1984, with a few issued in 1985. The majority of items are from scholarly journals, with some books, dissertations, government publications, etc. 'The strength of this work is its indexes which make up to 1/3rd of the book' (*Reference books bulletin*, 1986/87, p.59). A keyword index (150p.) based on titles cited, a classified subject index, and an author index. More comprehensive than '*The black family ...*'. *Class No:* 301.18-054(73)(01)

[1079]
DAVIS, L.G., *comp.* **The Black family in the United States:** a selected bibliography of annotated books, articles and dissertations on black families in America. Rev. ed. Westport, Conn., Greenwood, 1986. x, 234p. Bibliographies and indexes in Afro-American and African studies, no. 14). $ 39.95. ISBN: 0313252378.

First published 1978.

Lists 722 books, articles and dissertations, arranged by these forms subdivided by specific topics, most items dating from 1960 to 1985. Annotations are informative, with quotes from authors in many cases. All dissertations and the majority of the books and articles are American. Author and subject index. '... list of bibliographic sources searched would have been helpful'. (*Reference books bulletin,* 1986/87, p.58). *Class No:* 301.18-054(73)(01)

[1080]
DAVIS, N., *comp & ed.* **Afro-American reference:** an annotated bibliography of selected resources. Westport, CT, Greenwood Press, 1985. xiii, 288p. $49.95. (*Bibliographies & indexes in Afro-American and African studies, 9.*) ISBN: 031324930x.

An annotated guide to reference books useful in black studies. 105 general reference sources; 537 books in the topical chapters. 'A guide to the best of the field's vast monographic list'. (*Wilson library bulletin.* April 1986, p.62). *Class No:* 301.18-054(73)(01)

[1081]
MILLER, W.C. *and* **VOWELL, F.N.,** *and others.* **A Comprehensive bibliography for the study of American minorities.** New York, New York University Press, 1976. 2v. (xix, 690p.; xix, 691-1380). $150. ISBN: 0814753736.

29,300 entries. V.1: From Africa and the Middle East. From Europe (*e.g.* 'The Irish-American experience', p.381-422). From Eastern Europe and the Balkans. V.2: From Asia. From the Islands (*e.g.* Cuba). Typical subsections: Bibliographies; periodicals; history; sociology; economics;

....(contd.)

politics; education; religion, biography and autobiography; literary criticism; fiction; poetry and drama; music; English-language material; concise annotations; introductions to sections. Select list of general sources (p.969-70). V.2 includes author and title indexes. *Class No:* 301.18-054(73)(01)

[1082]
—Ethnic information sources in the United States: a guide to organizations, agencies, foundations, institutions, media, commercial and trade bodies, government programmes, research institutions, libraries and museums, etc. Wasserman, P. *and* Kennington, A.E., *eds.* 2nd ed. Detroit, Mich., Gale Research Co., 1983. 2v. (xix,1380p.). $165. ISBN: 0810303671.

First published 1976.

Arranged by ethnic group, A-Z, excluding Blacks, American Indians and Eskimos. Organizations and publications indexes. 'A primary source book ... on foreign nationalities [in the US]. (*RQ*, v.16(2), Winter 1976, p.181, of the 1st ed.).

A 3rd ed. is to be published in 1995. *Class No:* 301.18-054(73)(01)

Maps & Atlases

[1083]
ALLEN, J.P. *and* **TURNER, E.J. We the people:** an atlas of America's ethnic diversity. New York, Macmillan, 1988. 315p. $85. ISBN: 0029014204.

A comprehensive guide to the immigrant, ethnic, and racial groups in the US. 13 chapters on European, Asian, South American and African immigrants and native North Americans. Each chapter contains historical information, statistics, and maps depicting settlement patterns. An appendix lists the ancestries of state populations and ethnic populations for states and countries. Indexes of places and ethnic populations. More up-to-date and contains more detailed statistical data than the *Harvard encyclopedia of American ethnic groups* edited by S. Thermstron and others (Cambridge, Mass., Harvard University Press, 1980. 1076p. tables, maps, $90. 0674375122). *Class No:* 301.18-054(73)(084.3)

Jews

[1084]
LERMAN, A., *ed.* **The Jewish communities of the world:** a contemporary guide. 4th ed. London, Macmillan Press, in association with the Institute of Jewish Affairs, 1989. 224p. £35. ISBN: 0333480708.

3rd rev. ed. was published in 1971.

Based on material from the archives of the Institute and on detailed information from the communities obtained through the network of contacts of the World Jewish Congress. Provides up-to-date and comprehensive information on Jewish life and institutions in 98 national communities. Entries include a brief historical outline, the composition of the community, its legal status, communal organizations, religious life, education, cultural activities, libraries, museums, press, welfare and historical sites. Arranged by countries, A-Z. Table of world Jewish population. Glossary. *Class No:* 301.18-054(=924)

Black Races

[1085]
DIGGS, E.L. **Black chronology,** from 400 BC. to the abolition of the slave trade. Boston, Mass., G.K. Hall, 1983. 312p. $45. ISBN: 0816185433. *Class No:* 301.18-054(=96)

[1086]
Index to black periodicals. Boston, Mass. G. K. Hall, 1972-. Annual. $95.00. ISSN: 08896253.

Previously, from 1960 - *Index to periodical articles by and about blacks. Index to periodical articles by and about negroes,* and *Index to selected periodicals.*

An index to Afro-American periodicals of general and scholarly interest. Arrangement is A-Z by subject/author in the same sequence. Reviews are indicated.
Class No: 301.18-054(=96)

[1087]
The Negro almanac: a reference work on the Afro-American. Ploski, H.A., *and others, eds.* 5th ed. Boston, Mass., Gale Research, 1989. 1622p. illus., tables, graphs. $79.95. ISBN: 0810377063.

First published 1967. First 4 eds. published by Wiley Interscience.

A massive compilation of information on all aspects of black life in America and around the world. Treats nearly 500 years of history with an emphasis on the current situation of blacks in American society in 33 chapters. Includes a 100-page chronology of black history to 1989.
Class No: 301.18-054(=96)

[1088]
NEW YORK PUBLIC LIBRARY, *Schomburg Collection.* **Dictionary catalog of the Schomburg Collection of Negro Literature and History.** Boston, Mass., G.K. Hall, 1962 (Reprinted 1973). 9v. (8474p.). $830 the set. ISBN: 0816106320.

Over 250,000 photolithographically reproduced catalogue cards for monographs, periodicals, pamphlets, manuscripts, photographs, pictures, newspaper clippings, etc. One of the world's most important collections for the study of peoples of African descent.

Supplements; 1st (1970. 2v. $120. ISBN 0816107351); 2nd (1972. 4v. $400. ISBN 081610820x); 1974 (published 1976. $110. ISBN 0816100624). *Class No:* 301.18-054(=96)

[1089]
—Bibliographic guide to black studies, 1975-. Boston, Mass., G.K. Hall, 1976-. Annual. $110. ISSN: 03602710.

Supplements the above. *Class No:* 301.18-054(=96)

Amerindians, North

[1090]
HUNTINGTON FREE LIBRARY AND READING ROOM, NEW YORK. **Dictionary catalog of the American Indian collections.** Boston, Mass., G.K. Hall, 1977. 4v. (2455p.). $435.00. ISBN: 0816100659.

51,500 photolithographed catalogue cards, covering 35,000 v. and pertinent periodical articles. Coverage includes anthropology, ethnology, art, archaeology, history and current affairs of the Indian in both North and South America. *Class No:* 301.18-054(=97)

Amerindian

[1091]
KLEIN, B.T. **Reference encyclopedia of the American Indian.** 6th ed. New York, Todd Publications, 1993. 679p. $125. ISBN: 0915344300.

First published 1967.

A series of directories relating to native Americans (USA and Canada) including government agencies; reservations; museums, monuments & parks; Indian health services, etc.; a list of shops dealing with Indian arts and crafts; a bibliography and a biographical dictionary.

The *Native American information directory*, edited by J. Furtaw (Detroit, Gale, 1993. 371p. $75. ISBN 0810388545) covers similar ground. *Class No:* 301.18-054=97

Urban Communities

[1092]
MELVIN, P.M., *ed.* **American community organizations:** a historical dictionary. Westport, CT., Greenwood Press, 1986. xvi, 236p. $45. ISBN: 0313240531.

Relates to the subject over the past 100 years, from the settlement house movement in the 1880s to the present. Arranged A-Z is information on 59 significant community organizations, 8 federal laws that have affected organizing activities in urban areas, and 43 biographical sketches of key figures in the community organization movement. Ample cross-references. Subject and name indexes. 3 appendixes - chronological list of organizations, list of significant legislation, and list of prominent individuals. There is also a bibliographical essay on accessible published materials in the history of community organization. 'Should prove to be a valuable resource' for those interested in neighborhood activism and its history' (*Reference books bulletin*, 1986/87, p.63). *Class No:* 301.185.2

Bibliographies

[1093]
DINER, H.R., *ed.* **Women and urban society:** a guide to information sources. Detroit, Mich., Gale Research Co., 1979. xii, 138p. $65. ISBN: 0810314258.

An annotated bibliography of articles and books on the effect of urbanization on women and the family situation, arranged in 6 sections: 1. Women and urbanization - 2. Women in urban families - 3. Urban fertility - 4. Employment and urban women - 5. Women's roles in urban societies: social and psychological implications - 6. Views of urban women. Appendices: A. Selected bibliography of books - B. Abstracts and indexes - C. Periodicals. Author, title and subject indexes. *Class No:* 301.185.2(01)

[1094]
FILIPOVITCH, A.J. *and* REEVES, E.J., *eds.* **Urban community:** a guide to information sources. Detroit, Mich., Gale. 1978. x, 286p. $65. ISBN: 0810314290.

Annotated bibliography of books and periodical articles, dealing primarily with recent American and British experience of urban community and research done since 1970. 5 major sections (each with a prefatory bibliographic essay) dealing in turn with theories of community, the community as a physical entity and as a social group, specific problems (*e.g.* safety, quality of life, physical design, and community power) and problems of community planning (*e.g.* citizen participation; new towns). Author, title and subject indexes. *Class No:* 301.185.2(01)

Dictionaries

[1095]
ROSENBERG, P.M. *and* DURR, W.T. The Urban information thesaurus: a vocabulary for social documentation. Westport, Conn., Greenwood, 1977. 374p. $45. ISBN: 0837194830.

A computer-based thesaurus developed by the Baltimore Region Institutional Studies Center as the subject authority list for the Center's archival collection. Based on HUD's 'Urban vocabulary' and the metropolitan Council of Government's 'Urban affairs and planning thesaurus'. Focuses on terms related to planning, urban development, human services, and social history. Main index includes scope notes and references, and there is also a KWOC index, a section of terms arranged in hierarchical order, a list of geographical codes, and a list of qualifiers. '... the most comprehensive and sophisticated source available and is highly recommended for appropriate reference collections. (*RQ*, v.18 no.2, Winter, 1978. p.214-5).
Class No: 301.185.2(038)

Great Britain

Bibliographies

[1096]
BIRMINGHAM UNIVERSITY. School of Public Policy. **Publications list.** Birmingham, the University, 1989. [30p.]. free.

Annotated lists of the publications of the Centre for Urban and Regional Studies, the Institute of Local Government Studies, and the Development Administration Group.
Class No: 301.185.2(410)(01)

USSR

[1097]
WHITE, P.M. **Soviet urban and regional planning:** a bibliography with abstracts. London, Mansell, 1979. ix, 276p. £20; $39.95. ISBN: 0720109000, UK; 0312749120, USA.

A classified bibliography of books and articles in English, French and German (mainly English), including both Soviet materials published in English and Western translations of Russian materials, as well as Western studies. Introduction (30p.) on the theory and practice of Soviet planning.
Class No: 301.185.2(47)

China

[1098]
China urban statistics. State Statistical Bureau. People's Republic of China, *comp.* rev. ed. London, Longman Group and China Statistical Information and Consultancy Service Group, 1988. 504p. tables. £75. ISBN: 0582997569.

First published 1985.

Part 1. has profiles of 34 major Chinese cities. Part 2: General surveys: statistics of 295 cities (demography, agriculture, industry, transport and telecommunications, urban development, trade and commerce, education and culture, public health, labour, public finance). Part 3. Appendix: Weights and measures. Glossary of city names in English and Chinese. *Class No:* 301.185.2(510)

India

[1099]
BOSE, A. **Bibliography on urbanization in India, 1947-1976.** New Delhi, Tata McGraw-Hill for the Institute of Economic Growth, New Delhi, 1977. xxxi, 179 p.

A by-product of continuous research in the field, the work lists 2,711 titles relating to important writings in the post-independence period, including books, monographs, reports, research papers, journal articles, a few selected newspaper articles, and important unpublished material. Sections on urban demography; urban economics; urban geography; urban history, politics and administration; urban housing, development and planning; a survey of literature, trend reports, etc; and an addenda. Author and subject indexes.
Class No: 301.185.2(540)

Africa

[1100]
AJAEGBU, H.I. **African urbanization:** a bibliography. Edinburgh University, Centre for African Studies; London, International African Institute, 1972. (Reprint 1984). vi, 78p. £6.10.

Replaces Edinburgh University. Department of Social Anthropology's *African urbanization: a reading list ...* (1965).

Nearly 3000 items, intended as a guide to research into the process of urbanization and urban problems in African countries south of the Sahara; scope is mainly sociological, economic and demographic. An alphabetical index of towns cited and a list of abbreviations are followed by 25 other bibliographies, and then by the main bibliography, arranged A-Z by author under region, country and town sections. Author index. *Class No:* 301.185.2(6)

Rural Communities

Bibliographies of Bibliographies

[1101]
BERNDT, J. **Rural sociology:** a bibliography of bibliographies. Metuchen, N.J., Scarecrow Press, 1986. viii, 177p. $17.50; £17.50. ISBN: 0810818604.

Attempts to list and annotate, in about 100 words, all English-language bibliographies concerned exclusively with social aspects of rural life published since 1970. 454 numbered entries arranged in 15 subject divisions, then A-Z by author. Personal and corporate name index (p.153-9), title index (p.160-74), and geographical index (p.175-7).
Class No: 301.185.20(009)

Bibliographies

[1102]
Village studies: data analysis and bibliography. Compiled by Mick Moore [and others]. Edited by Clare M. Lambert. London, Mansell, 1977-78. 2v.

Published originally by Bowker for the Institute of Development Studies, Univ. of Sussex. 1: *India, 1950-1975.* 1976. 351p. 2: *Africa, Middle East and North Africa, Asia (excluding India), Pacific Islands, Latin America, West Indies and the Caribbean, 1950-1075.* 1978. 346p. Aims to present information on studies of single villages, and

....(contd.)

especially to inform the researcher of the availability of primary data. Separate indexes of authors, institutions and topics. *Class No:* 301.185.20(01)

Plantations

[1103]

KIRK, C. People in plantations: a review of the literature and annotated bibliography. Brighton, Sussex, Institute of Development Studies, 1987. xxviii, 286p. £10.50. (*Research report 18.*) ISBN: 0903354780.

Part I has introductory pages, including a conclusion. Part II is a mainly annotated bibliography of 925 items, arranged A-Z by author. Annotations are descriptive and each entry has codes to indicate subject matter (14 subject codes). Index of subjects, countries, and commodities. *Class No:* 301.185.20(01)PAL

Hunger

[1104]

DRÈZE, J. *and* **SEN, A. The Political economy of hunger.** Oxford, Clarendon Press, 1991. 3v.(1277p). v.1 & 2: £40 each; v.3: £45. ISBN: 019828635x, v.1; 0198286368, v.2; 0198286376, v.3.

Essays addressing a wide range of policy isues relating to the role of public action in combating hunger and deprivation in the modern world. *Class No:* 304.9

[1105]

Hunger in history: food shortage, poverty and deprivation. Newman, L., *general ed.* Oxford, Blackwell, 1989. xiii, 429p. 10 figures. 5 maps. £45. $29.95. ISBN: 1557860440.

Members of the World Hunger Program at Brown University have brought together 15 original and specially commissioned articles on the study of hunger. 15 chapters are arranged in 6 parts: 1. Introduction; 2. Hunger in prehistoric societies; 3. Hunger in complex societies; 4. Hunger in the emerging world system; 5. Hunger in the recent past; 6. Conclusions. Analytical index, p. 411-429. *Class No:* 304.9

Bibliographies

[1106]

BALL, N., *ed.* **World hunger:** a guide to the economic and political dimensions. Oxford, Clio Press; Santa Barbara, CA., ABC-Clio, 1981. xxii, 386p. 6 charts. £39.30; $46.50. (*War/peace bibliography series, no. 15.*) ISBN: 087436308x.

Explains and chronicles the literature of food production and distribution from economic and political perspectives. Items mostly in English. Introductions to the chapters on the major elements of the topic, highlighting particular problems, 'Highly recommended...' (*RQ*, v.21(2), Winter 1981. p.207). *Class No:* 304.9(01)

[1107]

KUTZNER, P.L. World hunger: a reference handbook. Santa Barbara, CA, ABC-Clio, 1991. xii, 359p. $39.50. ISBN: 0874365589.

An extensive analytical review of reference material for concerned people. 7 sections: 1. Overview; 2. Chronology (p.57-119); 3. Biographies (p.121-53); 4. Facts and data; 5. Organizations; 6. References in print; 7. Nonprint sources. Glossary, p.323-37. Index, p.339-59. '... researcher looking for a general guide would be well served.'*Choice*, v.29(3), November 1991, p.418). *Class No:* 304.9(01)

Social Climate

[1108]

KINLOCH, G. C. Social stratification: an annotated bibliography. New York, Garland, 1987. 357p. $55. (*Garland library of sociology, 11. Garland reference library of social science, 393.*) ISBN: 0824098056.

Over 1700 annotated and numbered entries arranged in broad categories. Most entries relate to journal articles published between the 1960s and the 1980s. Categories are general bibliographies and research trends; theoretical and conceptual issues; methodological issues; historical studies of stratification; stratification in the US; and stratification in other societies. Author and subject indexes. *Class No:* 308

Bibliographies

[1109]

SILIDAY, G.L., *ed.* **History of the family and kinship;** a select international bibliography. Millwood, N.Y., Kraus International Publications, 1980. 410p. $45. ISBN: 0527844519.

The published result of a special project of the *Journal of family history,* contains 6200 entries grouped by regional/national units published through 1976. World-wide and systematic coverage. Name index. *Class No:* 308(01)

[1110]

STREATFIELD, D. Social work: an information sourcebook: a guide to publications and other information sources. Edinburgh, Capital Planning Information Ltd., 1982. 165p. (CPI sourcebooks, no. 2). £17. ISBN: 0906011167.

Intended mainly for local authority social services staffs, voluntary agencies staff, and community workers. Part 1: Fieldworkers and their information world; part 2: Problems and information sources; part 3: Information workers; Appendix A: Organising a local information system; Appendix B: Some useful organisations. Author, title and subject index, p.148-162. *Class No:* 308(01)

Men's studies

[1111]

AUGUST, E.R. Men's studies: a selected and annotated interdisplinary bibliography. Littleton, Col., Libraries Unlimited, 1985. 232p. $36. £30. ISBN: 0872874818.

Describes nearly 600 English-language books in 10 topical chapters, including autobiographies, bibliographies and anthologies. Topics include men's awareness, divorce and custody, health and related matters, crime and sexual violence, women and men, masculine gender roles,

....*(contd.)*

sexuality, homosexuality, men in families, men in literature, art and religion. Works range from scholarly to popular. Cross-references at end of chapters. *Class No:* 308(01)MEN

Encyclopaedias

[1112]

Encyclopedia of social inventions. Albery, N. *and* Yale, V., *eds*. London, The Institute of Social Inventions, 1991. 298p. £19.99.

New and imaginative solutions to social problems (*e.g.* pneumatic bicycle seats; using wild dolphins to help treat mental illness), 500 in all. The most worthwhile or controversial inventions are commented upon by experts in the field, and each entry has a contact name, address and telephone number. The Institute runs an annual £1000 prize competition for the best social inventions. (Entry taken from *The good book guide*, v.53, July/August 1991, p.17). *Class No:* 308(031)

Handbooks & Manuals

[1113]

THOMSON, A. and **PLATT, R. Help yourself:** an everyday survival handbook. 2nd ed. London, Impact Books, 1993. 192p £4.95 ISBN: 1874687110.

First published 1985.

Facts, tips and advice for young people about getting a job, working for a wage, beating unemployment, claiming benefit, managing money, education and training, rights and laws, having a say, mind and body, shelter, time out. Index. *Class No:* 308(035)

Reviews & Abstracts

[1114]

Geographical abstracts. D: Social and historical geography. Norwich, Geo Abstracts Ltd., 1974-?. 6pa. ISSN: 02687909.

Preceded by *Geographical abstracts*. D: *Social geography* (1966-7), thereafter *Geo abstracts*. D. *Social geography and cartography* (1968-73).

About 2500 indicative and informative abstracts pa. Sections: Social - Population distribution - Population change - Population migration - Population fertility - Man and environment - Natural hazards - Perception - Medical - Regional - Cultural - Historical: field evidence - Historical: documentary evidence - Historical: regional - Political - Urban - Rural - Methodology - Biography - Education. Author and regional indexes for each part appear in the last issue each year. *Class No:* 308(048)

[1115]

Sage family studies abstracts, 1979-. Newbury Park, CA. & London, Sage Publications Inc., 1979-. $232. £117 pa. ISSN: 01640283.

Sections: Trends in marriage, family and society - Gender roles - Issues concerning reproduction - Singlehood, mate selection & marriage - Early socialization: infancy & childhood - Childcare, problems & treatment = Late socialization: adolescence - Life cycles: adulthood, aging & the family - Family relations & problems - Family services, counselling & therapy - Divorce - Economics & the family -

....*(contd.)*

Minority & cross-cultural relations - Theory & method. Author and subject indexes. (V.15(3), August 1993, has 41 abstracts). *Class No:* 308(048)

Yearbooks & Directories

[1116]

WEEKS, G., ed. Family directory: information resources on the family. London, British Library, 1986. xii,183p. £12.50. (*BLIG 1.*) ISBN: 0712220755.

Part I: Organizations, databases and publications; part II: The family in perspective. The first part lists British organizations, non-British and international organizations, online databases, and publications relevant to family studies. The second part includes 4 essays, each with notes or references appended. *Class No:* 308(058)

Worldwide

Tables & Data Books

[1117]

UNITED NATIONS. Statistical Office, *and others.* **Compendium of social statistics and indicators, 1988.** New York, United Nations, 1991. x,686p. tables. (*Statistical papers, series K, no.9.*)

Earlier editions were issued for 1963, 1967 and 1977.

Data on population size, composition and change; human settlements; households and families, marital status; education and literacy, education services, culture and communications; health and nutrition, disabled services, health services; economic participation and population not economically active; national and household income and expenditure, social and consumption expenditure; participation in public affairs; crime and criminal justice. Annex - subject fields, p.675-684. Statistical sources, p.685-6. *Class No:* 308(100)(083)

Developing Countries

Yearbooks & Directories

[1118]

Third World resource directory. Fenton, T.P. *and* Heffron, M.J., *eds.* Maryknoll, N.Y., Orbis Books, 1984. 283p. illus. $82 70. ISBN: 0883445093.

A guide to organizations and publications. In 3 parts: pt.1. Areas (ch.1. Third world - 2. Africa - 3. Asia and the Pacific - 4. Latin America and Caribbean - 5. Middle East); pt.2. Issues (*e.g.* 6. Food, hunger, agribusiness - 7. Human rights - 8. Militarism, peace, disarmament - 9. Transnational corporations - 10. Women); pt.3. Indexes (Organizations - Books - Periodicals, pamphlets and articles - Audiovisuals - Audiovisual bibliographies, catalogues and guides - Bibliographies, directories and curriculum resources - Simulated games). 'The book is a guide to resources about the Third World and the United States involvement in the affairs of the Third World nations and peoples' (*Preface*). *Class No:* 308(4/9-77)(058)

Europe

Histories

[1119]

CASEY, J. **The History of the family.** Oxford, Basil Blackwell, 1989. 192p. £25. ISBN: 0631146687.

Concerns the changing interactions between family and social, political and religious structures over the last 1,000 years of European history. 7 Chapters: 1. The meaning of family - 2. The role of the ancestors - 3. The politics of family - 4. The arranged marriage - 5. The nature of passion - 6. The economics of the household - 7. The rise of domesticity. 'Suggestions for further reading'; 'Reference list of works cited in the text'; and glossary of kinship terms. *Class No:* 308(4)(091)

[1120]

A **History of private life.** Ariès, P. *and* Duby, G., *general eds.* Cambridge, Mass., & London, Harvard University Press, 1991. 5v.(3000p.). $39.95; £29.95 each vol. ISBN: 0317561685, v.1; 0674399765, v.2; 0674399773, v.3; 0674399781, v.4; 067439979x, v.5.

Contents: V.1: From pagan Rome to Byzantium; v.2: Revelations of the medieval world; v.3: Passions of the renaissance; v.4: From the fires of revolution to the Great War; v.5: Riddles of identity in modern times. *Class No:* 308(4)(091)

Great Britain

[1121]

Atlas of British social and economic history since *c.*1700. Pope, R., *ed.* London, Routledge, 1990. xiii,250p. diagrs., maps. £13.99. ISBN: 0415056330.

Maps and text illustrating historical development. 12 sections: 1. Agriculture - 2. The textile and chemical industries - 3. Metal, vehicle and engineering industries - 4. Coal, gas and electricity - 5. Transport and trade - 6. Demographic changes, 1901-1981 - 7. Employment and unemployment - 8. Urbanization and living conditions - 9. Labour movements - 10. Education - 11. Religion - 12. Leisure. Further reading, p.236-45 (by chapter). Detailed, analytical index ('Education': 1 column), p.246-50. 255 diagrs. and maps. A neat production. *Class No:* 308(410)

[1122]

The **Cambridge social history of Britain, 1750-1950.** Thompson, F.M.L., *and others, eds.* Cambridge, Cambridge University Press, 1991. 3v (1493p) £15.95 each vol.; £39.95 the set. ISBN: 0521257883, v.1; 0521257891, v.2; 0521257905, v.3; 0521438136, the set.

V.1 Regions and communities - v.2. People and their environment - v.3. Social agencies and institutions. Each volume has 6-8 contributions. V.3 includes chapters on education, health and medicine; crime, authority and the policemans work; religion; philanthropy; clubs, societies and associations. Each volume has bibliographies and an index. *Choice* (v.28(6), February 1991, p.982) considers it serves best as a reference work to be dipped into selectively. A comprehensive index to all three volumes is called for. *Class No:* 308(410)

[1123]

The **General household survey ... an inter-departmental survey ... 1987.** Office of Population Censuses and Surveys. London, HMSO., 1989. vi,291p. tables. £13.90. ISBN: 0116912871.

First published 1971. Annual. Sponsored by the Central Statistical Office.

A continuous survey based each year on a sample of the general population resident in private households in Great Britain. Section 1: 'Introduction and main findings' precedes the report, which is in two main parts: Part 1, section 2. People, households and families - 3. Housing - 4. Health - 5. Sterilisation and infertility - 6. Entertainments, libraries, forests - 7. Occupational pension scheme coverage - 8. Share ownership. Part 2: Tables. 4 appendices (A. Definitions and terms - B. Household and individual interview schedules - C. Summary of main topics including a questionnaire - D. List of tables). *Class No:* 308(410)

[1124]

MITCHELL, A. **The New Penguin guide to personal finance:** make your money work for you. 3rd ed. London, Viking, 1992. 370p. illus. £17.99. ISBN: 0670847712.

Covers the whole spectrum of personal finance - savings and investment, tax, financing a family. 30 chapters in 3 parts: pt.1 has advice on building a capital sum by regular savings and investment; pt.2 is concerned with taxes; pt.3 has 18 chapters on family finance. Each chapter has a summary of contents, and cross-references to other chapters. *Class No:* 308(410)

Bibliographies

[1125]

WESTERGAARD, D.J., *and others.* **Modern British society:** a bibliography. 2nd ed. London, Frances Pinter (Publishers) Ltd., 1977. 199p. £12.50.

First published 1974.

'Intended as a fairly detailed guide to the literature and research on contemporary British social structure and its immediate historical background' (*Introduction*). About 2,000 unannotated entries. Sections, further divided: A. General - B. Historical introduction - C. Class structure - D. Economic and industrial organization - E. Education - F. Government and politics - G. Social policy - H. Population, family and stages of life - I. Sex roles and the position of women - J. Migration and minority groups - K. Urbanism and rural communities - L. Crime and punishment - M. Culture, leisure and communication - N. Religion. 'References to journal articles have been kept to a minimum' (but a list of essential journals would be helpful). No index. 'A comprehensive, though necessarily selective, guide to the literature of sociology' (*Library review,* v.27, Spring 1978, p.70). *Class No:* 308(410)(01)

Yearbooks & Directories

[1126]

Social policy review, No.5, 1993. London, Social Policy Association, 1993. 330p. £9.95. ISBN: 0951889516.

First published 1971 as *The Year book of social policy in Britain;* title changed in 1990.

The publication examines current issues and developments in social policy and social administration. This issue has an article, *Evolving state of welfare* by R. Page & J. Baldock. No index. *Class No:* 308(410)(058)

Tables & Data Books

[1127]

Family spending: a report for the 1992, family expenditure survey. Department of Employment. London, HMSO., 1993. iv,125p. tables. £24. ISBN: 0116206004. ISSN: 09651403.

First published for 1957. Annual.

Based on a representative sample of about 11,500 private households in the UK. 41 tables with data on household characteristics, household expenditure, household income, regional income and expenditure. 3 appendices: B. Definitions; C. Index to tables, 1988-1992.

Class No: 308(410)(083)

[1128]

Social trends, [no] 24, 1994. Central Statistical Office. London, HMSO., 1994. 199p. diagrs., graphs, tables, maps. £27. ISBN: 0116206047. ISSN: 03067742.

First published 1970. Annual.

Sections: Population - Households and families - Education - Employment - Income and wealth - Expenditure - Health and personal social services - Housing - Environment - Leisure - Participation - Crime and justice - Transport. Appendix: definitions and terms. Subject index.

Class No: 308(410)(083)

[1129]

—Key date. Great Britain. Central Statistical Office. 1993/94 ed. London, HMSO, 1993. 116p. illus., charts, tables, maps. ISBN: 0116205997.

Published annually as a student version of *Social trends.* Cover title adds 'UK business and social statistics ...'.

Over 130 tables, maps and coloured charts, accompanied by reference sources. Data is for several years to 1992. Index. *Class No:* 308(410)

Histories

[1130]

HALSEY, A.H., ed. British social trends since 1900: a guide to the changing structure of Britain. 2nd ed. London, Macmillan Press, 1988. xxviii,650p. tables. £45. ISBN: 0333345215.

Updates Halsey's *Trends in British society since 1900...* (1972).

18 contributors, aiming to produce a volume which would complement *Social trends* by presenting longer time series and covering additional topics, drawing on both official and non-official statistics. 417 tables and graphs, providing an overview of trends since World War II.

Class No: 308(410)(091)

Institutions & Associations

[1131]

MOSS, L. The Government Social Survey: a history. London, HMSO, 1991. viii,297p. £16. ISBN: 0116913029.

A detailed study of how the Survey's work has evolved and developed over 40 years. Part 1 describes changes in the situations in government which provided the framework within which the Survey grew; pt.2 describes the main subject areas in which work was done and how changes and innovations in methods were developed.

Class No: 308(410):061:061.2

Eire

[1132]

McGILVRAY, J. Social statistics in Ireland: guide to their sources and uses. Dublin, Institute of Public Administration, 1977. x, 204p. £3.50.

A guide to the main sources of social statistics published in Ireland, and the use of their statistics in social investigation and analysis. Contains chapters on basic demographic statistics; vital statistics; health; housing; education; social security; incomes, expenditures and the standard of living; other social statistics. The final two chapters explain some statistical concepts of statistical methods and sample survey techniques. *Class No:* 308(417)

England & Wales

[1133]

CARR-SAUNDERS, A.M., and others. A Survey of social conditions in England and Wales, as illustrated by statistics. 3rd rev. and extended ed. Oxford, Clarendon Press, 1958. xxi, 302p. tables.

First published in 1927 as *A survey of the social structure of England and Wales.*

Presents a picture of some of the more important aspects of social life so far as they can be illustrated by statistics, including population, households and housing, regional distribution, education, employment, health, etc.

Class No: 308(42)

London

[1134]

O'DAY, R. and ENGLANDER, D. Mr. Charles Booth's inquiry: life and labour of the people in London reconsidered. London, Hambledon Press, 1993. viii,246p. £35. ISBN: 1852850795.

20 chapters in 3 parts: 1. The poverty series; 2. The industry series; 3. The religious influence series. 6 appendices. A select bibliography. Index of names and places. Index of subjects. *Class No:* 308(421)

[1135]

SAWYER, P. and FRASER, J. Bridges: directory of African, Caribbean, Asian, Latin American and Mediterranean community groups in Greater London, 1988. London, London Voluntary Service Council, 1988. ISBN: 0901171638.

Over 800 groups and organizations were contacted for this first edition. Arrangement is first by area and then by name of organization, A-Z. Also lists Community Relations Councils and Councils for Voluntary Service.

Class No: 308(421)

[1136]

SHEPHERD, J., and others. A Social atlas of London. Oxford, Clarendon Press, 1974. 128p. maps, illus. £4.95 (paperback ed. Hardback o.p.). ISBN: 0198740301.

Maps and text cover the history of London, land use, housing, age and sex, structure of population, immigrant groups, socio-economic groups, industry, shopping centres, transport, education, health and welfare, and local elections. Bibliography. 48p. of maps. Statistics are based on the 1971 census. 'Represents remarkably good value as an intellectual challenge ...' (*The economist,* 12 July 1975, p.110).

Class No: 308(421)

Wales

[1137]
Welsh social trends/Tueddiadau Cymdeithasol, 1991. Welsh Office. No.8. Cardiff, Welsh Office, 1991. £9.50. ISBN: 0750400501. ISSN: 01409018.

First published 1977. Biennial.

Statistics of population, vital statistics, social characteristics (*e.g.* household data and migration); economic characteristics; health and social security; social services; education; leisure; housing; justice and crime; finance. Appendices on sources and definitions.
Class No: 308(429)

Germany

[1138]
MERRITT, A.J. *and* **RICHARD, L. Politics, economics and society in the two Germanies, 1945-75:** a bibliography of English-language works. Urbana, Ill., University of Illinois Press, 1978. xix, 268p. $24.95. ISBN: 0252006844.

A selective bibliography of 8548 items arranged according to primary focus in a number of discrete categories. Author index. *Class No:* 308(430)

France

[1139]
Histoire de la population française. Dupâquier, J., *Directeur*. Paris, P.U.F.(Presses Universitaires de France), 1988. 4v. tables, graphs. ISBN: 2130401090, v.1; 2130413838, v.2; 2130419283, v.3; 2130420702, v.4.

4 chapters, each subdivided, with notes and bibliographies after each chapter: 1. Des origines à la Renaissance; 2. De la Renaissance à 1789; 3. De 1789 à 1914; 4. De 1914 à nos jours. A general index for each volume. *Class No:* 308(44)

[1140]
MAGRAW, R. A History of the French working-class. Oxford, Blackwell, 1992. 2v.(768p.). £80. ISBN: 063118046x.

V.1: 1815-70; v.2: 1871-1939. Surveys the changing structures and examines working-class politics and culture.
Class No: 308(44)

USSR

[1141]
MICKIEWICZ, E. Handbook of Soviet social science data. New York, Free Press, 1973. xxvi, 225p. $30. ISBN: 0029211905.

202 statistical tables in 9 sections (1. Demography - 2. Agriculture - 3. Production - 4. Health - 5. Housing - 6. Education - 7. Elite recruitment and mobilization - 8. Communications - 9. International interactions (*e.g.* trade, COMECON). Notes: sources. No index. Tables to 1968.
Class No: 308(47)

[1142]
RYAN, M. *and* **PRENTICE, R. Social trends in the Soviet Union from 1950.** London, Macmillan, 1987. 120p. tables, diagrs., maps. £29.50. ISBN: 0333408412.

Intended to provide easy access to a range of information about the Soviet Union since 1950, presented in tabulated form with accompanying text. Data is broken down by Union Republics where possible. Sections: Population change - The growth of towns - Migration - Patterns of

....(contd.)
child-bearing - The family and marriage - Ethnic composition - Education - Health care. List of abbreviated titles used in the tables. Notes and references.
Class No: 308(47)

Asia—Middle & Near East

Bibliographies

[1143]
BANUAZIZI, A. *and* **PROUCHESTIA, G. Social stratification in the Middle East and North Africa:** a bibliographic survey. London, Mansell Publishing Ltd.,1984. xviii,248p. £25. ISBN: 0720117119.

A bibliography of sources published in English and French, 1946-82. An introduction is followed by a list of journals and periodicals consulted; the bibliography is arranged geographically (Middle East & North Africa: general and comparative studies - Afghanistan ... The Yemens). Subdivisions within each country are chronological. No annotations. Subject and author indexes.
Class No: 308(53+56)(01)

Caribbean

[1144]
OBERG, L.R. Human services in postrevolutionary Cuba: an annotated international bibliography. Westport, Conn., Greenwood Press, 1984. 433p. $45. ISBN: 0313231257.

'Human services' includes education, public health, housing and sports, education being the main theme. Includes books, book chapters, pamphlets, journal articles, government and international agency publications, dissertations, and encyclopedia entries, also bibliographies. Annotations vary from brief descriptions to lengthy comments on intellectual content, bias, strengths and weaknesses. Author, title and detailed subject indexes. '... this significant bibliography...' (*College and research libraries*, July 1985, p.351-2). *Class No:* 308(729)

Latin America

[1145]
Welfare, poverty and development in Latin America. Abel, C. *and* Lewis, C.M., *eds.* London, Macmillan, 1993. 380p. £45. ISBN: 0333517377.

Describes the social consequences of recent development strategies in Latin America; social welfare and poverty during the 20th century. Issues are addressed from several different disciplines. *Class No:* 308(729.99)

31 Statistics

Statistics

[1146]
HUTCHINSON, T.P. *and* KE, Y. **An Index to corrections, addenda, and comments that were published in statistical journals, 1970-1991.** Sydney, NSW, Rumsby Scientific Publishing, 1992. AUS$55. £25.

78 major English-language journals were searched and 3200 items found. *Class No:* 310

Databases

[1147]
CD-ROM and online statistical databases. Brittin, M., *comp.* London, Aslib, 1993. 136p. £26. ISBN: 0851423000.

Lists 210 databases worldwide, including online, diskette, magnetic tape, and CD-ROM. A-Z arrangement, with information on format, content, language, countries covered, time span, frequency of update, hosts, producer or distributor, and costs. Subject index. *Class No:* 310(003.4)

Encyclopaedias

[1148]
International encyclopedia of statistics. Kruskal, W.H. *and* Tanur, J.M., *eds.* New York, Macmillan and Free Press, 1978. 2v. $80. each vol; $155. the set. ISBN: 002917970x, v.1; 0029179807, v.2; 0029179602, the set.

Includes articles from the *International encyclopedia of the social sciences* (*qv.*), such articles being revised, corrected and updated. 75 of the articles are on statistics proper, and of these 5 are new. Of the 57 biographies, 12 are new. Detailed, analytical index. 'This unique set will be used in undergraduate and graduate libraries' (*Library journal*, 1 May 1979, p.1044). 'This carefully edited compendium, useful to the student or researcher at any level'. (*College and research libraries*, v.40(4), July 1979, p.350-1). *Class No:* 310(031)

Dictionaries

[1149]
MARRIOTT, F.H.C. **A Dictionary of statistical terms.** 5th rev. ed. London, Longman Group, for the International Statistical Institute, 1990. xiii,222p. tables. £12.95. ISBN: 0582019052.

First published 1957. The first four eds. were compiled by M.G. Kendall and W.R. Buckland.

Defines over 3000 statistical terms. Entries range from 25 to 150 words. Author and date citations are given for more recent terms. Formulae and cross-references figure. As in the 3rd ed. (1971), the glossary of French, German, Italian and English terms in the 2nd ed. (1960) is omitted. 'Authoritative compilation of generally accepted definitions'

....(contd.)
(Webb, W.H. and others. *Sources of information in the social sciences* (3rd ed. 1986), entry A405) of the 4th ed. *Class No:* 310(038)

[1150]
MULHALL, M.G. **The Dictionary of statistics.** 4th ed., rev. to November 1898. London, Routledge, 1899 (Reprinted Gregg International). [vi], 853p. tables. $62.10. ISBN: 0576531847.

Arrangement is by subjects, A-Z; numerous tables. Period covered is from A.D. 300 to 1898. List of books of reference, p.822-25. Index of places and topics. Sources are sometimes quoted for the statistics cited, but their general omission is a serious drawback. Supplemented by Webb (q.v.). *Class No:* 310(038)

[1151]
WEBB, A.D. **The New dictionary of statistics:** a complement to the fourth edition of Mulhall's *Dictionary of statistics.* London, Routledge, 1911. (Reprinted Gale, 1971). xii, 682p. tables. $75. ISBN: 0810339889.

Covers the period 1899-1919. Similar in pattern to Mulhall, but does not give sources for all figures cited. On the other hand, Webb only cites data for which he can quote chapter and verse, thereby excluding a certain amount of useful information. The 325 sources cited are listed on p.648-54. *Class No:* 310(038)

Polyglot

[1152]
Dreisprachiges Verzeichnis statistischer Fachausdrücke Wiesbaden, Statistisches Bundesamt 1969 (Reprinted 1980) 201p. £.4.90.

Three-language index of statistical technical terms: German-English-French. *Class No:* 310(038)=00

French

[1153]
NIXON, J.W. **Glossary of terms in official statistics,** English-French, French-English. Edinburgh, Oliver & Boyd, for the International Statistical Institute, 1964. xiv,106p.

Pt.1. English-French (p.3-43); Pt.2. French-English (p.47-104); *c.* 3500 and 4500 specialised entry-words respectively, with equivalents. Appendix 1: 'List of principal sources consulted'; 2: 'Existing glossaries or dictionaries giving terms in English and French used in official statistics'. Clear layout; good use of bold type. *Class No:* 310(038)=40

Russian

[1154]
KOTZ, S. **Russian-English/English-Russian glossary of statistical terms.** Edinburgh & London, Oliver & Boyd for the International Statistical Institute, 1971. vii, 87p.

Selection of *c.*2,500 terms included in the 3rd edition of

....(contd.)

Kendall and Buckland's *Dictionary of statistical terms* (Oliver & Boyd, 1971). Some terms are given brief explanations. 'Not a book for the beginner, either in statistics or Russian' (*Nature*, v.239, 8 Sept. 1972, p.114-5).
Class No: 310(038)=82

Worldwide

[1155]

The Economist book of vital world statistics... Smith-Morris, M., *ed.* London, Hutchinson Business Books Ltd., 1990. 256p. tables, map. £19.99. ISBN: 0091746523.

A view of how countries of the world compare on everything. Sections: Demography - Economic strength - Agriculture and food - Energy - Commodities - Transport and communications - Government finance - Inflation and finance - Trade and balance of payments - Debt and aid - Employment - Education - Health - Family life - Environment. Glossary, p.255. Sources, p.256.
Class No: 310(100)

[1156]

Pocket world in figures. The Economist, *comp.* 2nd ed. London, Random Century Ltd., 1993. 208p. illus. £6.99.

First published 1991.

Part 1 gives world rankings (natural facts; population; economic strength, economic growth, etc. Part 2 has country profiles. *Class No:* 310(100)

[1157]

KURIAN, G.T. New book of world rankings. 3rd ed. updated by J. Marti. New York, Facts on File, 1991. xxi,324p. $40. ISBN: 0816019312.

First published 1979 as *The book of world rankings.*

Is 'designed as an international scorecard that compares & ranks over 190 nations of the world according to their performance in some 300 key areas' (*Introduction*). 23 subject chapters: Geography and climate - Vital statistics - Population dynamics and the family - Race and religion - Politics and international and international relations - Foreign aid - Military power - Economy - Finance and banking - Trade - Agriculture - Industry and mining - Energy - Labour - Transport and communications - Consumption - Housing - Health and food - Education - Crime rate - Media - World cities - Culture. Country profiles. Bibliography, p.319. Index, p.321-324. *Class No:* 310(100)

[1158]

World tables, 1991. World Bank. 6th updated ed. Baltimore, MD., Johns Hopkins University Press, for the World Bank, 1991. xvi,655p. ISBN: 0801842520. ISSN: 10435573.

First published 1971.

Collections of economic and social time series data for most countries of the world. Topical pages have 20 tables by subject, subdivided by country with data for 1970-1989 or 1990. Country pages include data on national accounts, foreign trade, balance of payments, external debt, manufacturing, money and fiscal, social indicators.
Class No: 310(100)

Bibliographies

[1159]

International directory of non-official statistical sources, 1990. London, Euromonitor Publications Ltd., 1990. x,155p. £135. ISBN: 0863383548.

*c.*1000 regularly produced titles arranged A-Z by organization or journal title name for countries outside Western Europe. Data includes title of the statistics, frequency, contents/coverage summary, information on availability, language, machine-readable version of source, price in currency of originating country, contact and address of department when available, telephone/telex/fax numbers where applicable. Subject index, p.135-146; geographical index of publishers, p.147-155. *Class No:* 310(100)(01)

[1160]

KURIAN, G.T. Sourcebook of global statistics. New York, Facts on File; Harlow, Essex, Longman Group, 1985. xi,413p. $85; £60. ISBN: 0582902665.

Information on 209 statistical publications, most of which are serials issued by international organizations (*e.g.* UN, OECD, EC). Arrangement is A-Z by title and includes year of publication, language, number of pages, edition, indexes, base period, updating, scope, sources of data, organization, contents, new features, graphs-tables-charts, evaluation, publisher, most recent price, availability on tape, database, etc. *International affairs* (v.63(1), Winter 1986/87, p.178) comments that the index is unsatisfactory and the format could be improved. *Class No:* 310(100)(01)

Yearbooks & Directories

[1161]

UNESCO. Unesco statistical yearbook, 1993. Paris, Unesco, 1993. [*c.*700p.], chiefly tables. ISBN: 9230028878.

First published, 1964. Annual. Continues the biennial *Basic facts and figures* (Unesco, 1952-62).

The 1993 edition covers *c.*200 countries; computer-produced tables. Sections: Reference tables - Education - Education by level and by country - Educational expenditure - Science and technology - Culture and communications - Printed matter (Libraries - Book production - Newspapers and other periodicals - Cultural paper (*e.g.* newsprint) - Cultural heritage - Film and cinema - Broadcasting - International trade in printed matter.
Class No: 310(100)(058)

[1162]

—**Unesco statistical digest: a statistical summary of data on education, science and technology, culture and communication, by country, 1988.** Paris, Unesco, 1988. xxiv,335p. tables. F.40. ISBN: 9230025623.

First published 1982. Annual.

Basic statistics on a country-by-country basis.
Class No: 310(100)(058)

[1163]

UNITED NATIONS. Department of International Economic and Social Affairs. Statistical Office. **Statistical yearbook/ Annuaire statistique, 1990/91.** 38th ed. New York, UN., 1993. xiv,1109p. ISBN: 9210611527. ISSN: 00828459.

First published 1949. Continues *Statistical year-book of the League of Nations*, 1926-42/44 (Geneva, 1927-45).

Covers over 200 countries and areas. 131 tables; time series: 1975, covers 1981-1990 or 1982-91 usually. Sections: World and region summary - 2. Population and social statistics (population & human settlements; education

....(contd.)

and literacy; health & child-bearing, nutrition; culture) - 3. Economic activity (national accounts; government finance; labour force; wages and prices; agriculture, forestry, fishing; mining and quarrying; manufacturing; transport & communications; energy, environment and land use; science & technology; intellectual property) - 4. International economic relations (international trade; international tourism; balance of payments; international finance; development assistance). Sources, notes appended to tables. Annex 1: Country & area nomenclature; 2. Conversion coefficients and factors. In English and French. Statistical sources & references (p.1096-1100). Index (English only) p.1101-09).Supplemented by *Monthly bulletin of statistics* (1947-. $180pa.) Each issue has *c.*250p. of tables. Special tables feature regularly. A *Supplement* of definitions and notes is issued every few years. *Class No:* 310(100)(058)

[1164]

—UNITED NATIONS. Department of International Economic and Social Affairs. Statistical Office. World statistics in brief, 1992. 14th ed. New York, United Nations, 1992. xiii,114p. $7.50; £5. (*Statistical papers, series V.*.) ISBN: 9211613442.

First published 1976. Annual.

A pocketbook with data on *c.*150 countries, plus world and regional data for 1989 with 1980 and 1985.

Class No: 310(100)(058)

[1165]

World facts and figures. Showers, V. 3rd ed. New York, John Wiley & Sons, 1989. xii, 721p. illus. tables. $74.95. ISBN: 0471857750.

First published in 1973 as *The World in figures.*

Mainly tabular data, allowing for comparisons to be made on 218 countries, 2664 of the largest and best-known cities, and nearly 3000 geographical and cultural features. 11 main chapters (chapter 1 has 11 tables on demography, economy, transport, communications and educational activities in all 218 countries; 2. City tables; 3. Country comparisons; 4. City comparisons - 5. Comparisons of cultural features; 6. Seas; 7. Islands; 8. Rivers; 9. Mountains; 10. Lakes; 11. Waterfalls). Selected bibliography of 258 items. Index, p.651-721. *Class No:* 310(100)(058)

Bibliographies

[1166]

WESTFALL, G. Bibliography of official statistical yearbooks and bulletins. Alexandria, VA., Chadwyck-Healey Inc., 1986. [18],247p. $75.£48. (*Government documents bibliographies.*) ISBN: 0859641244.

Supersedes P. C. Carter's *Statistical yearbooks; an annotated bibliography ...* and *Statistical bulletins: an annotated bibliography ...* (Washington, Library of Congress, 1953 and 1954).

374 titles, from more than 180 countries, arranged by continent, subdivided by country. Data includes title, translation of title where necessary, date first published, compiler language, history of changes, factual description of particular edition/issue, any other information, publisher, and price. Limited to statistical yearbooks and bulletins. *Class No:* 310(100)(058)(01)

Histories

[1167]

MITCHELL, B.R. International historical statistics: the Americas, 1750-1988 . 2nd ed. London, Macmillan Press, 1993. 960p. £135; $250. ISBN: 0333585151, UK; 1561590622, US.

The third volume in the series *International historical statistics.* First published 1983 and including Australasia.

Covers the principal areas of economic and social activity in the Americas, each section having a short introductory commentary and extensive notes and footnotes. Contents: Introduction - Climate - Population - Labour force - Agriculture - Industry - External trade - Transport and communications - Finance - Prices - Education - National accounts. *Choice* (v.31(2), October 1992, p.270) considers broader and more consistent coverage is needed in future editions but says 'This volume and series remain the most important general historical statistical sources for the Americas and the world'. *Class No:* 310(100)(091)

[1168]

—MITCHELL, B.R. International historical statistics: Africa and Asia. London, Macmillan; New York, New York University Press, 1982. 800p. £75. $74.50. ISBN: 0333316304.

The second volume of *International historical statistics.*

Includes data for about two centuries (1800-1975) for all the principal areas of economic and social activity in 38 African and 34 Asian countries. 11 sections: Climate - Population and vital statistics - Labour force - Agriculture - Industry - External trade - Transport and commerce - Finance - Prices - Education - Environment, Extensive footnotes. *Class No:* 310(100)(091)

[1169]

MITCHELL, B.R. International historical statistics: Europe, 1750-1988. 3rd ed. London, Macmillan Press, 1992. 860p. £125. ISBN: 0333568729.

2nd ed. published 1980. Title of first two editions was *European historical statistics.*

Data for over two centuries for all principal areas of economic and social activity in all ountries of Western and Eastern Europe. 10 sections cover population and vital statistics, labour force, agriculture, industry, external trade, transport and communications, finance, prices, education and national accounts. Each section has an introduction, notes and footnotes. *Class No:* 310(100)(091)

Government Organizations

[1170]

GREAT BRITAIN. Department of Trade and Industry. Export Market Information Centre. **National statistical offices of the world, 1991.** London, the Centre, 1991. 41p. £20.

New eds. are issued at intervals.

Lists the statistical offices of 176 countries, A-Z by country, with cross-references. Distinguishes, where appropriate, between offices for foreign trade statistics and those for other statistics. Appended are offices of international organizations which publish statistics. *Class No:* 310(100):061:061.1

Developing Countries

[1171]

EUROPEAN COMMUNITIES. Statistical Office. **ACP-basic statistics, 1988.** Luxembourg, Office for Publications of the European Communities, 1989. 253p. ECU9.50. ISBN: 928258867x.

First published 1981. Annual.

Presents a selection of the most important statistics of the ACP countries (African, Caribbean and Pacific countries, signatories of the Lomé convention and associates of the EEC countries). Includes data on population, national accounts, production, foreign trade, prices, finance, aid, and standard of living. *Class No:* 310(4/9-77)

[1172]

INSTITUTE OF DEVELOPING ECONOMIES. **Catalogue of statistical materials of developing countries.** 10th ed. Tokyo, Asia Economic Press, 1990. 607p.

First published in 1968 as *Bibliography of statistical materials ...*

Entries grouped by country, subdivided by general and 9 subject groups. Appendix 1 lists publications from international organizations and statistical institutes in developing countries; Appendix 2 is a directory of statistical organizations of developed countries. *Class No:* 310(4/9-77)

Europe

Bibliographies

[1173]

HARVEY, J.M. **Statistics Europe:** sources for social, economic and market research. 5th ed. Beckenham, Kent, CBD Research Ltd., 1987. xii, 320p. £47.50. $130. ISBN: 0900246480.

First published 1969.

2427 entries for Europe as a whole and for individual countries of Europe, both East and West, (*e.g.* Sweden: p.261-268: Central Statistical Office; Libraries; Libraries and information services abroad; Bibliographies; Statistical publications (nos. 2159-2218). UK: nos. 1167-1553). Data include bibliographical information; time factor; price; pagination. Arranged in 9 subject groups for each country (general, production, external trade, internal distribution and service trades, population, social and political, finance, transport and communications, environment) many subdivided. Indexes of organizations, titles, and subjects. New ed. in progress. *Class No:* 310(4)(01)

Yearbooks & Directories

[1174]

The Economist pocket Europe. Butler, P., *ed.* London, Economist Books, 1992. 224p. £9.99 ISBN: 071269806x.

In 4 parts: 1. Country profiles (Albania ... Yugoslavia); 2. Country comparisons (area & population, economy, personal expenditure, life & leisure); 3. Country facts (statistics on the economy, structure of manufacturing, inflation & exchange rates, balance of payments & debt, government, people, society); 4. The organizations (The European Community, the institutions, aims and characteristics of other organizations). Notes on data and sources, p.214-7. Index, p.218-24. *Class No:* 310(4)(058)

Europe—Western

[1175]

European directory of non-official statistical sources, 1988. Mort, D. London, Euromonitor Publications, 1988. x,281p. £135; $160. ISBN: 0863382584.

Lists over 2000 non-official sources of time series statistics for Western European countries, particularly the UK, France and the German Federal Republic. Citations include statistical publications on particular markets, industries, products and sectors; opinion surveys, market research, salary surveys, etc. Arranged A-Z by name of publishing organization of journal, entries include publication title, frequency, content or coverage summary, availability, price, language details, and availability of machine-readable version. Index to publishers, by country. Subject index. *Class No:* 310(400)

[1176]

MORT, D. **Western European statistics.** London, Pitman, 1992. 608p. £90. ISBN: 0273037366.

Evaluates and collates official and non-official sources of statistics and market information for EC countries and selected industries across the manufacturing and service sector. Each entry is evaluated in terms of ease of location, ease of use, strengths and weaknesses, time and cost factors. *Class No:* 310(400)

[1177]

RAMSEY, A., *comp*. **Eurostat index:** a detailed keyword subject index to the statistical series published by the Statistical Office of the European Communities with notes on the series. 5th rev.ed. Stamford, Capital Planning Information, 1992. 250p. £45.. ISBN: 0906011833.

First published 1981.

Lists the statistical series by subject (1. General statistics ... 9. Miscellaneous), followed by the keyword subject index. Bibliography, p.269-280. 7 appendices (4. Alphabetical list of Eurostat titles contained in the text). *Class No:* 310(400)

Periodicals

[1178]

Sigma: the bulletin of European statistics, no.1, Sept/Oct 1991-. Superseded *Eurostat news*, 1976-1991. Luxembourg, Eurostat, 1991-. 6pa. ISSN: 10185739.

Provides up-to-date information from a statistical viewpoint on the progress of measures taken in the run-up towards European integration. Supplemented by *Just published*, listing titles published during the month. *Class No:* 310(400)(051)

Yearbooks & Directories

[1179]

EUROPEAN COMMUNITIES. Commission. Statistical Office. **Eurostat review, 1977-1986.** Luxembourg, Office for Official Publications of the Community, 1988. 221p. ECU.21. ISBN: 9282581497.

First published for 1970/1979. Annual.

Time series for the principal statistical domains covered by Eurostat. In 7 sections: 1. European Community institutions - 2. Economy and finances - 3. Population and social conditions - 4. Energy - 5. Agriculture, forestry and fisheries - 6. Foreign trade - 7. Services and transport. *Class No:* 310(400)(058)

[1180]

EUROPEAN COMMUNITIES. Eurostat. **Basic statistics of the Community, 1993.** 30th ed. Luxembourg, Office for Official Publications of the European Communities, 1993. 335p. ECU 11. ISBN: 9282662195.

First published 1960. Annual.

A selection of the most important recent statistics, including those of US, USSR, and other countries. Also available online. *Class No:* 310(400)(058)

[1181]

EUROPEAN COMMUNITIES. Eurostat. **Regioner: statistisk årbog ... Regions: statistical yearbook ... 1993.** Luxembourg, Office of Publications of the European Communities, 1993. xxxi,184p. map. ECU23.20. £18.75. ISBN: 9282623521.

First published 1971. Annual. Early title was *Yearbook of regional statistics.*

Comparable statistics for main regional indicators, demography, population activity and unemployment, economic aggregates, agriculture, energy, transport, living standards. Glossary. In 5 languages.

Class No: 310(400)(058)

Histories

[1182]

FLORA, P., *ed.* **State, economy and society in Western Europe, 1815-1975.** London, Macmillan Press; New York, St. James Press; Frankfurt A.M., Campus Verlag, 1983-1987. 2v.(633, 758p.). £90 the set; $140 the set. ISBN: 0333359445, UK; 0912289066, US; 3593329107, Germany.

V.1: *The growth of mass democracies and welfare states;* v.2: *The growth of industrial societies and capitalist economies.* Includes statistical tables on population, suffrage, housing, labour disputes, bureaucracy, military personnel, education, public income and expenditure, gross national product, income distribution, etc. Has some advantages over Mitchell's *European historical statistics,* but 'Flora's presentation of data in reverse chronological order unnecessarily confusing' (*Choice,*v.25(4), December 1987, p.605). *Class No:* 310(400)(091)

Europe—Eastern

[1183]

COMECON data, 1990. Vienna Institute for Comparative Economic Studies,, *ed.* London, Macmillan Press, 1991. 440p. £50. ISSN: 02633701.

First published in Austria in 1979 by the institute, updating *RGW in Zahlen/CMEA data* (1978).

Presents information on the economies of the European CMEA countries. A summary and a register of sources are followed by the main tables arranged in broad subject groupings subdivided more specifically by subjects and then by individual countries: Main indicators - I. Production (employment & wages, investment, industry) - II. Consumption and standard of living - III. Foreign trade - IV. Finance - V. Energy. Data is for various years from 1960 to 1986. Available online (Wilw database, Vienna)

Class No: 310(401)

[1184]

SHOUP, P.S. **The East European and Soviet data handbook:** political, social and developmental indicators, 1945-1975. New York, Columbia University Press, 1981. c.350p. tables. $115. (*Hoover Institute publications series.*) ISBN: 0231042523.

Aims to give an overview of social change and elite development in the Soviet bloc since World War II. Lengthy introduction detailing problems involved in obtaining data used and determining its reliability, followed by information arranged in 8 major categories: Population - Party membership - National and religious affiliations - Educational attainment - Class structure - Party leadership - Occupations - Development indicators. 12-page bibliography supplemented by a narrative summary of the sources used for each table. '... impressive handbook'. (*Library journal,* 1 May 1981, p.963-4). *Class No:* 310(401)

Great Britain

Bibliographies

[1185]

GREAT BRITAIN. Central Statistical Office. **Guide to official statistics.** 5th ed. London, HMSO, 1986. (Revised in 1990). v,191p. ISBN: 0116203943.

First published 1976.

Meant to cover all official and significant non-official sources published in the last 5 years. Annotated entries; also running commentary. 16 sections: 1. General - 2. Area, climate, environment - 3. Population, vital statistics - 4. Social statistics - 5. Labour - 6. Agriculture - 7. Production industries - 8. Transport - 9. Distribution and other services - 10. Public services - 11. Prices - 12. The economy - 13. General and public finance - 14. Business and financial institutions - 15. Overseas transactions - 16. Isle of Man & Channel Islands. Bibliography (titles, A-Z), p.143-156. Government department contact points (name & address; telephone no.). Alphabetical keyword index (analytical; 'Agriculture': nearly 1 column). *Class No:* 310(410)(01)

[1186]

—GREAT BRITAIN. Government Statistical Service. **Government statistics: a brief guide to sources.** 1993 ed. London, HMSO, 1993. Annual. 50p. *Gratis.*

Short descriptions of the latest editions, arranged by subject: General background and reference - General digests - The economy - Defence - External trade - Transport, distribution and other services - Society - Environment - Overseas aid - Departmental responsibilities and contact points. *Class No:* 310(410)(01)

[1187]

GREAT BRITAIN. Interdepartmental Committee on Social and Economic Research. **Guides to official sources.** London., HMSO, 1948-61,nos.1-6.

1. *Labour statistics* (3rd ed., 1958) - 2. *Census reports of Great Britain, 1801-1931* (1051) - 3. *Local government statistics*(1953) - 4. *Agricultural and food statistics* (1961. Superseded by *Select list of reference books in agriculture, fisheries and food*) - 5. *Social security statistics* (1961) - 6. *Census of production reports*(1961) 'Intended to assist research workers, students and others who have occasion to use the extensive range of information on economic and social matters made available by government departments in official reports and papers'. *Class No:* 310(410)(01)

[1188]

MORT, D. Sources of unofficial UK statistics. University of Warwick. Business Information Service, *ed.* 2nd ed. Aldershot, Hants., Gower Publishing Co. Ltd., 1990. xi, 413p. £45. ISBN: 056602795x.

First published 1986, compiled by D. Mort and L. Siddell.

A detailed guide to the main unofficial statistical sources in the UK of interest to business and industry. Part 1: The Statistics (Abacus Data Services ... Zinc Development Association). Data on 1077 sources/services (organization; title; coverage; availability; cost; comments; address; telephone number). Part 2: Title index. Part 3: Subject index. Patchy on issues, but excellent annotations, according to a review in *Library Association record,* (v.92(8), August 1991). *Class No:* 310(410)(01)

[1189]

—MORT, D. 'Non-official statistics - an important source of business information'. In *Business information review,* v.1(4), April 1985, p.6-10.

During an 18-month period (1983-84), Warwick Statistics Service carried out a survey of regular titles published in the UK (1112 titles) and this article outlines the main results of the survey, covering the number and range of non-official statistics, the subject range of the titles, sources and reliability of statistics, and availability.

Class No: 310(410)(01)

[1190]

Reviews of United Kingdom statistical sources. Maunder, W.F. (to 1987) *and* Fleming, M.C. (from 1985), *eds.* London, Chapman & Hall (v.1-5 published by Heinemann Educational Books; v.6-21 by Pergamon Press), 1974- v.1-.

Succeeds M.G. Kendall's *Sources and nature of the statistics of the United Kingdom* (1952-1957. 2v.). Sponsored by The Royal Statistical Society and The Economic and Social Research Council.

1:1. Personal social services. 2. Voluntary organizations in the personal social service field. 1974.

2:3. Central government routine health statistics. 4. Social security statistics. 1974.

3:5. Housing in Great Britain. 6. Housing in Northern Ireland. 1974.

4:7. Leisure. 8. Tourism. 1975.

5:9. General sources of statistics, by G.F. Lock. 1976.

6:10 Wealth. 11. Personal incomes. 1978 (£35. ISBN 6080224504).

7:12. Road passenger transport. 13. Road goods transport. 1978.

8:14. Land use. 15. Town and country planning. 1978.

9. Health surveys and related studies. 1979. (£75. ISBN 0080224598).

10. Ports and inland waterways; and civil aviation. 1978.

11. Coal; gas; and electricity. 1979.

12. Construction and the related professions. 1980.

13. Wages and earnings. 1980. (£40. ISBN 0080240607).

14. Rail and sea transport. 1981. (£44. ISBN 0080261051).

15. Crime. 1981. (£52. ISBN 0080261043).

16. Iron and steel. 1984. (£23. ISBN 0080301916).

17. Weather and water. 1985. (£52. ISBN 0080318444).

18. Ports and telecommunications. 1986. (£29. ISBN 0080339670).

19. Intellectual property. 1986.(ISBN 0080339026).

20. Religion. Recurrent Christian sources; Non-recurrent Christian data; Judaism; Other religions. 1987 (£97. ISBN

....(contd.)
0080347789).

21. Financial data of banks and other institutions; Life assurance and pension funds. (ISBN 0080347800).

22. Printing and publishing. l987. ISBN 0080347819)

23. Agriculture. 1988. (£35. ISBN 0412316706).

24. Local government. 1988. (£42.50. ISBN 0412316803).

25. Family planning. 1988. (£35. ISBN 0412316900).

26. International aspects of UK economic activities. l991. (£49. ISBN 0412356503).

27. Research and development. 1993. (ISBN 0412356406)

28. The food industries. 1993. (ISBN 0412356600)

Class No: 310(410)(01)

[1191]

United Kingdom statistical sources: a selection guide for libraries. McShane, P., *ed.* 4th ed. London, Library Association's Information Services Group, for the Committee of Librarians and Statisticians, 1985. 24p. £5. ISBN: 0946347069.

'Basic minimum list' (10 annotated items), p.6-8. Extended list, (163 items), p.9-24. Subject sections: General statistical compilations - Agriculture, fishery and food ... Education, science and technology - Energy - Banking, insurance and finance - Foreign trade and balance of payments - Health , personal social services, social security - Housing, construction and property - Industrial production, distribution and other services - Justice and crime - Labour - Population, households and vital statistics - Public finance and taxation - Tourism, entertainment and leisure - Transport and communications. No index. *Class No:* 310(410)(01)

Periodicals

[1192]

Statistical news: developments in British official statistics. London, HMSO., 1968-. no.1-. Quarterly. £33pa; £8 single issue. ISSN: 00173630.

Each issue contains 2 or more articles dealing with a subject in depth. Shorter notes give news of latest developments in many fields, including international statistics. Cumulative analytical index. Lists recently available statistical series and publications.

Class No: 310(410)(051)

Yearbooks & Directories

[1193]

Annual abstract of statistics, 1994. Central Statistical Office. No.130. London, HMSO, 1994. Annual. x,348p. tables. £23. ISBN: 0116206055. ISSN: 00725730.

First published 1946. Continues *Statistical abstract,* 1st, 1840/53- 83rd, 1924/38, compiled by the Board of Trade.

The 1994 ed. gives annual figures, so far as available, for 1981-92. 18 chapters: 1. Area - 2. Population and vital statistics - 3. Social conditions - 4. Law enforcement - 5. Education - 6. Employment - 7. Defence - 8. Production - 9. Agriculture, fisheries and food - 10. Transport and communications - 11. Distributive trades. Research and development - 12. External trade - 13. Balance of payments - 14. National income and expenditure - 15. Personal income, expenditure and wealth - 16. Home finance - 17. Banking, insurance, etc. - 18. Prices. Sources appended to tables. Index of sources (by chapters), p.333-339. Index. Indispensable for British libraries. *Class No:* 310(410)(058)

[1194]

—Monthly digest of statistics. Central Statistical Office. London, HMSO, 1946-. £7.50 each; £85pa incl. supplement. ISSN: 03086666.

Supplements many of the tables in the *Annual abstract,* and its January issue carries a supplement: *Definitions and explanatory notes. But the Annual abstract* generally gives greater detail for comparable series and includes many other series that, by their nature, can only be included in an annual publication. *Class No:* 310(410)(058)

[1195]

Regional trends, 1993. Central Statistical Office. London, HMSO, 1993. Annual. 220p. maps, tables. £26. ISBN: 0116205962. ISSN: 02611783.

First published 1965. Nos. 1-17 were titled *Regional statistics.*

Brings together detailed information highlighting regional variations in the United Kingdom data covering a wide range of social, demographic and economic topics. The 1993 issue has 15 sections: 1. Regional profiles - 2. European Community regional statistics - 3. Population - 4. Housing - 5. Education - 6. Health - 7. Employment - 8. Income and spending - 9. Criminal justice - 10. Transport - 11. Environment - 12. Regional accounts - 13. Industry and agriculture - 14. Sub-regional statistics - 15. Districts. Appendix. Subject index (217-220).

Class No: 310(410)(058)

Histories

[1196]

MITCHELL, B.R. British historical statistics. Cambridge, Cambridge University Press, 1988. 886p. 322 tables. £80. ISBN: 0521330084.

Supplants the author's two previous volumes, *Abstract of British historical statistics* and *Second abstract of British historical statistics.*

Contains the major economic and social statistical series for the British Isles from the earliest available, in the 12th century to 1980/81. Tables are grouped under 16 subject headings: Population and vital statistics - Labour force (including wages) - Agriculture - Industry (5 sections) - External trade - Transport and communications - Public finance - Financial institutions - Consumption - Prices - Miscellaneous (inc. crime and education) - National accounts. Subject index. A standard reference work.

Class No: 310(410)(091)

Scotland

[1197]

GREAT BRITAIN. Scottish Office. **Scottish abstract of statistics, 1992.** No.21. Edinburgh, HMSO., 1993. £22.

First published 1971. Annual. Together with the *Scottish economic bulletin,* it replaces *Digest of Scottish statistics* (1953-71).

Data arranged in 16 subject sections (1. Population and vital statistics - 2. Social security - 3. Health services … 9. Labour … 12. Industrial activity … 15. Finance - 16. Environment). Footnotes. *Class No:* 310(411)

[1198]

HORN, M. Scottish Office statistical publications. In *Statistical news,* no.l, Winter 1990, p.91.5-91.9.

Describes the statistical publications of the Scottish Office and advises how to obtain them. *Class No:* 310(411)

Northern Ireland

Bibliographies

[1199]

COLLETT, R.J. Northern Ireland statistics: a guide to principal sources. Belfast, Queen's University, Department of Library and Information Studies, 1979. [ix],79p.

Arrangement is in subject groups, supported by a bibliography and a subject index. *Class No:* 310(416)(01)

[1200]

—A Guide to Northern Ireland statistics. Policy Planning and Research Unit, Department of Finance and Personnel. Belfast, the Unit, 1988. [4],131p. (*PPRU occasional paper.*) ISSN: 02674025. *Class No:* 310(416)(01)

Yearbooks & Directories

[1201]

NORTHERN IRELAND. Department of Finance. **Digest of statistics, Northern Ireland.** Belfast, HMSO., March 1954-.no.1-. 2pa.

The latest to be published is for 1980.

Followed the pattern of the *Annual abstract of statistics* for the UK. *Class No:* 310(416)(058)

[1202]

NORTHERN IRELAND. Department of Finance. Policy, Planning and Research Unit. **Northern Ireland annual abstract of statistics, 1990.** Stormont, the Department, 1982-. no.1-. ISSN: 02676044.

The 1990 ed. (1993. 169p.£16.50) has 17 subject sections with nearly 200 tables. Data is for several yesars to 1991. Final page has a list of publications giving statistical and other information on the social and economic life of Northern Ireland. *Class No:* 310(416)(058)

Eire

[1203]

EIRE. Central Statistics Office. **Statistical abstract of Ireland, 1992.** 54th ed. Dublin, Stationery Office, 1992. 418p. £30. ISSN: 07909381.

First published 1931. Annual.

Data arranged in 14 subject sections, with an introduction to each section, relating to 1991. List of sources. Appendix: Northern Ireland (34 tables). Subject index.

Supplemented by the quarterly *Statistical bulletin* (title change from *Irish statistical bulletin*) (1926-. ISSN 07908344). *Class No:* 310(417)

Wales

[1204]

GREAT BRITAIN. Welsh Office. **Digest of Welsh statistics, 1992.** No.38. Cardiff, the Office, 1992 (previously HMSO). 184p. tables, map. £7. ISSN: 02628295.

First published 1954. Annual.

A statistical review of Welsh affairs (population and vital

....(contd.)

statistics, social conditions, education, labour, production and distribution, transport and communications, finance, income and expenditure, environment). *Class No:* 310(429)

[1205]
—WILLIAMS, J. Digest of Welsh historical statistics.
Department of Economic and Social History, University College of Wales, Aberystwyth. Cardiff, The Welsh Office, 1985. 2v. (x,359; x,356p.). maps. ISBN: 0863481205, v.1; 086348140x, v.2.

In English and Welsh. Data is arranged in 13 sections, all subdivided, covering various years. *Class No:* 310(429)

Federal Republic of Germany

[1206]
GERMANY (FEDERAL REPUBLIC). Statistisches Bundesamt. **Statistisches Jahrbuch für die Bundesrepublik Deutschland, 1993.** Stuttgart, Metzler-Poeschel Verlag (previously Mainz, Kohlhammer), 1993. 790p. DM.125. ISBN: 3824603608.

First published 1952-. Annual.

27 subject sections. Data is for several years to 1991 or 1992. List of German official statistical publications. Subject index. In German only.

Supplemented by the monthly *Wirtschaft und Statistik* (1949-. DM.189pa. ISSN 00436143) the second half of which consists of *Statistisches monatszahlen.*

Class No: 310(430.1)

German Democratic Republic

[1207]
GERMANY (DEMOCRATIC REPUBLIC). Staatlichen Zentralverwaltung für Statistik. **Statistisches Jahrbuch der Deutschen Demokratischen Republik, 1989.** Berlin, Staatxverlag der DDR, 1989. xv,434,96,13p.

First published 1955. Annual.

On somewhat the same lines as the *Statistisches Jahrbuch für die Bundesrepublic Deutschland.* Arranged in 8 subject sections (24 sub-sections), with data for various years to 1988. In German only.

The *Statistical pocketbook of the German Democratic Republic* consists of extracts from the yearbook in English (1960-. 1987. 160p. has data for several years to 1986).

Class No: 310(430.2)

Luxembourg

[1208]
LUXEMBOURG. Service Central de la Statistique et des études Économiques. **Annuaire statistique ... 1992.** Luxembourg, STATEC, 1992. various pagings. FLux ll00 ISSN: 00761575.

First published 1955. Annual.

Arranged in 22 subject sections and an international section, with tables for 1987 or 1987/88 and earlier years. Subject index. *Class No:* 310(435.9)

Austria

[1209]
AUSTRIA. Statistisches Zentralamt. **Statistisches Jahrbuch für die Republik Österreich, 1993.** 44th ed., new series. Vienna, the Office, 1993. xxxi,595p.

First published 1950. Annual.

Arranged in 36 subject chapters, plus an international chapter on yellow-tinted paper, with data for 8 years or more to 1992.

Supplemented by the monthly *Statistisches Nachrichten* (1946-. S.1250pa). *Class No:* 310(436)

Czechoslovakia

[1210]
CZECHOSLOVAKIA. Federální Statistický Úřad. **Statistická ročenka Československé Socialistické Republiky, 1992.** Praha, the Office, 1992. 736p. Kčs.78. ISBN: 8070490411.

First published 1934-38, 1957-. Annual.

The Federal Statistical Office's statistical yearbook of the Czechoslovak Socialist Republic. Arranged in 27 subject chapters. Tables are for various years to 1990 or 1991. In Czech, but an English translation of the text is available separately.

Supplemented by the monthly *Statistické přehledy* (Kčs.6 each issue. ISSN 03227537). *Class No:* 310(437)

Poland

[1211]
POLAND. Glówny Ürzad Statystyczny. **Rocznik statystyczny, 1990.** Warsaw, the Central Statistical Office, 1991. lxvii,612p. Zl.15000. ISSN: 00792780.

First published 1941. Annual.

Includes *c.*150 tables arranged in subject sections, with data for several years to 1989. Subject index. In Polish, but a translation of the text is available separately in English. Supplemented by the monthly *Biuletyn statystyczny.*

Class No: 310(438)

Hungary

[1212]
HUNGARY. Központi Statisztikai Hivatal. **Magyar statisztikai evkönyv. Statistical yearbook ... 1992.** Budapest, 'Kultura', 1993. xx,402p. Ft.1540. ISSN: 00734039.

First published in 1965. Annual.

Contains 27 subject sections, with statistical tables for 1991, 1992 and earlier years in some sections.

Supplemented by the monthly *Statisztikai havi közlemények* (ISSN 0018781x). There is also *Statistical pocket book for Hungary*, published annually. *Class No:* 310(439)

[1213]
Statisztikai adatforrások: bibliografia 1945-1985/Sources of statistical data: bibliography, 1945-1985 ... Budapest. Központi Statisztikai Hivatal, Könyvtár és Dokumentációs Szolgálat [Central Statistical Office, Library and Documentation Service],1987. 431 p. ISBN: 9633408261.

Information on the Hungarian statistical services in Hungarian, English and Russian. 6 Sections: 1. Publications of a general character - 2. Economic statistical publications - 3. Social statistical publications - 4. Regional statistical publications - 5. International statistical publications - 6. Statistical activity, statistical organization. Translations, but

....(contd.)

no annotations. 2 appendices. I. Publications of the CSO institutions; II. Hungarian title index. (p363-431).
Class No: 310(439)

France

[1214]
FRANCE. Institut National de la Statistique et des Études économiques. **Annuaire statistique de la France, 1993.** Paris, the Institute, 1994. xxiv,856,30p. F.590. ISBN: 211066116x.

First published 1978. Annual.

Data arranged in 16 subject sections, all subdivided, with statistics for several years to 1991 or 1992. A list of tables, an index, and sources (organizations) are printed on tinted paper.

Supplemented by the *Bulletin mensuel de statistique* (1950-. ISSN 00074713). *Class No:* 310(44)

Italy

[1215]
ITALY. Istituto Centrale di Statistica. **Annuario statistico italiano, 1993.** Roma, the Institute, 1993. 565p. L.55,000. ISSN: 00664545.

First published 1878. Annual.

Supplemented by the monthly *Bollettino mensile di statistica* (1926-. L.18,000 each issue. ISSN 00213136). *Compendio statistico italiano* (L.27,000 for 1993 ed. ISSN 00697958) is a shortened version of the yearbook.

Data arranged in 21 subject sections, with a 22nd section of international statistics. Statistics are mainly for 1992 or 1991, with earlier years in some sections. Notes on methods. *Class No:* 310(450)

Malta

[1216]
MALTA. Central Office of Statistics. **Annual abstract of statistics, 1990.** Valletta, the Office, 1992. 244p. £M.2.

First published 1947. Annual.

Data arranged in 13 subject sections, with statistics to 1990. Detailed contents list, but no index.

Supplemented by the Office's *Quarterly digest of statistics* (1960-. 75c. each issue). *Class No:* 310(458.2)

Spain

[1217]
SPAIN. Instituto Nacional de Estadística. **Anuario estadístico de España, 1990.** V.65. Madrid, the Institute, 1991. 915p. maps. Ptas.5200. ISSN: 08930003.

First published 1913. Annual.

In two parts: part 1 has national statistics in 16 subject sections, plus an international section; part 2 has regional data. Subject index. Statistics for several years to 1987 or 1988.

Supplemented by the monthly *Boletin de estadística* (1918-. ISSN 00386391). *Class No:* 310(460)

Portugal

[1218]
PORTUGAL. Instituto Nacional de Estatística. **Anuário estatístico, 1991.** Lisbon, the Institute, 1992. *c*.300p. Esc.6615. ISSN: 00794112.

First published 1875. Annual. Prior to independence of the Portuguese colonies in 1974, the yearbook was in 2v., the second volume dealing with Portuguese territories overseas.

Data arranged in 22 including one for international statistics, with data for Portugal, the Azores, and Madeira. Statistics for 1991 or the latest available, and some earlier years. Subject index. In Portuguese and French.

Supplemented by the *Boletin mensal de estatística* (1929. Esc.29400pa. ISSN 00325082), which includes a list of publications of the institute. *Class No:* 310(469)

USSR

[1219]
LEWYTZKYJ, B., *ed*. The Soviet Union: facts, figures, data. New York, K.G. Saur, 1979. xxxvi,614p. ISBN: 3598070403.

German title: *Die Sowjetunion.* Parallel texts in English, German and Russian.

A statistical handbook providing a wide range of information on the administration and state structure of the USSR, including population, the Communist Party, the economy, labour, social structure, science, education, printing and publishing, living standards, public organizations and religion. Mainly in tabular form, coverage is from the beginning of the 20th century to the present. '... value limited by a failure to specify criteria for selection or exclusion and by the unforgivable failure of the compiler to indicate sources' (*Choice*, v.17(5/6), July/August 1980, p.654). *Class No:* 310(47)

[1220]
POCKNEY, B.P. Soviet statistics since 1950. Aldershot, Hants, Dartmouth Publishing Company, 1991. 352p. illus. £19.05. ISBN: 1855211068.

Sets out to provide a consistent series of data over a time period from 1850 to the end of the 1980s, for a number of areas including population, industry, agriculture, education, energy, and foreign trade. *Class No:* 310(47)

Bibliographies

[1221]
KASER, M.C. 'Soviet statistical abstracts... In *Soviet affairs*, number 4 (St. Antony's papers, no.19), p.134-55.

A cumulation of the 8 lists (comprising 431 abstracts that appeared annually in the January issue of *Soviet studies* (v.10(3), January 1959, p.312-9, and thereafter). 8 library holdings are cited (Library of Congress, United Nations Library (Geneva) and 6 in Britain). The series continued with M.C. Kaser's 'Ninth list of Soviet statistical tables', in *Soviet studies*, v.18(3), January 1967, p.394-6. This lists 41 abstracts, incorporating entries in *Knizhnaya letopis*, up to no.33, 1966; all are re-issues, with later material. 'Fifteenth list...' by P. Fletcher (*Soviet studies*, v.24(3), 1973, p.462-6) ... 'Twentyfirst list...' by B.S.H. Rees (*Soviet studies*, v.31(3), 1979, p.463-6) has 50 titles of publications grouped in All-Union sector, regional general, regional sector, and international ... 'Thirtieth list...' by B.S.H. Rees, with 82 titles, was published in *Soviet studies*, v.40(4) October 1988,

....*(contd.)*
p.687-690... 'Thirtysecond list...' by J. Johnson, was published in *Soviet studies*, v.43(1), 1991, p.207-209. *Class No:* 310(47)(01)

Yearbooks & Directories

[1222]
Russia & Eurasia facts & figures annual (formerly *USSR facts and figures annual*). Karasik, T.W., *ed.* v.18. Gulf Breeze, FL, Academic International Press, 1988. xxxi,523p. tables, maps. $72. ISBN: 0875691722. ISSN: 01487760.
First published 1972.
An annual review of developments in the countries of Russia and Eurasia, providing recent basic data on government, political parties, military and security, health and welfare, energy and environment, foreign trade and aid, or as much as is available. Chapter 1 is on the Commonwealth of Independant States; ch.2 on Russia; ch.3-16 on individual states, A-Z (Armenia...Uzbekistan). Data is to 1990 or 1991. *Class No:* 310(47)(058)

[1223]
Statistical handbook: states of the former USSR. Washington, World Bank (Country department III, Europe and Central Asia Region), 1992. ix,504p. ISBN: 0821322648.
Comparative tables (p.1-17) are followed by international transaction tables (1. Balance of payments in convertible currencies; 2. External debt in convertible currencies of the former USSR), and country tables (Armenia...Uzbekistan) with general data, population, employment and labour force, national accounts, foreign trade, public finance, monetary statistics, industry, agriculture, prices and wages. Data is for 1985-91. Bibliography, p.455. *Class No:* 310(47)(058)

[1224]
USSR. Tsentral'noe Statisticheskoe Upravlenie. **Narodnoe khozyaistvo SSSR ... statisticheskii ezhegodnik, 1990.** Moscow, Statistika, 1991. 752p. 9r.
Published annually from 1956 to 1990.
A comprehensive annual survey of the Soviet economy. This issue is for a jubilee year (70 years). Tables are grouped in 27 main headings, with figures for 1985 or 1986 and earlier years. Explanatory notes; index.
Vestnik statistiki (1949-. Monthly. 1r.50k. each issue. ISSN 03208068) is not a statistical bulletin in the accepted sense but a review on statistical methodology, with some articles on special statistical data. *Class No:* 310(47)(058)

[1225]
—**The USSR in figures ... brief statistical handbook, 1990.** The State Committee of the USSR on Statistics. Information and Publications Centre, *comp.* Moscow, Finansy i Statistika Publishers, 1991. 320p. 2r.
An English version of *SSSR v tsifrakh ... kratkii: statisticheskii sbornik*.
A pocket-sized version of the statistical yearbook published annually from l956 to l990.
Class No: 310(47)(058)

[1226]
—**USSR.** Tsentral'noe Statisticheskoe Upravlenie. Narodnoe khozyaistvo SSSR, 1922-1982. Moscow, Statistika, 1982. 623p. 2r.30k.
Includes extensive statistical data on Soviet economy and culture, plus retrospective tables on changes in each of the

....*(contd.)*
14 constituent republics since the union (1922), plus data on the autonomous republics and national districts forming part of a number of the Union republics. *Class No:* 310(47)(058)

Scandinavia

[1227]
NORDIC STATISTICAL SECRETARIAT, *ed.* **Yearbook of Nordic statistics, 1992.** v.31. Copenhagen, Nordic Council of Ministers and the Nordic Statistical Secretariat, 1992. 427p. ISSN: 00781088.
First published 1962. Annual.
Statistical tables in 25 sections, covering all the important economic and social statistics for Denmark, Finland, Iceland, Norway and Sweden. Tables are retrospective for 5-10 years. Explanatory footnotes; sources; bibliography; list of statistical reports; English/Swedish vocabulary; measures and weights. Introduction and headings in English and Swedish. *Class No:* 310(48)

Finland

[1228]
FINLAND. Tilastokeskus. **Suomen tilastollinen vuosikirja, 1993.** v.88. Helsinki, Tilastokeskus, 1993. 620p. Fmk.260. ISBN: 9514776062. ISSN: 00815063.
First published 1879.
The Finnish Central Statistical Office's statistical yearbook of Finland, has 31 subject chapters plus an international section on yellow-tinted paper, with statistical tables for several years to 1991 or 1992. Lists of official statistical publications. Subject index. In Finnish, Swedish and English. Supplemented by the monthly bulletin of statistics, *Tilastokatsauksia* (1924-. ISSN 00152390).
Class No: 310(480)

Norway

[1229]
NORWAY. Statistisk Sentralbyra. **Statistisk årbok/Statistical yearbook of Norway, 1992.** 111th ed. Oslo, the Bureau, 1992. 494p. NKr.90. ISSN: 03778908.
First published 1880. Annual.
Arranged in 7 main sections, each subdivided: Survey of geography - Natural resources and environment - Socio-demographic subject matters - Industrial subject matters - General economic matters - Social organizations — International tables. In Norwegian and English.
Supplemented by the monthly *Statistisk månedshefte* (1882-. ISSN 00293636), also in Norwegian and English. *Class No:* 310(481)

Sweden

[1230]
SWEDEN. Statistiska Centralbyrån. **Statistisk arsbok för Sverige.** Stockholm, the Bureau, 1914-. Annual. ISSN: 00815381.
The 1993 ed. (1992. 565p. map. SKr/430) has 22 subject sections, with *c*.450 tables, plus an international section, relating to the year 1991 and several earlier years. Detailed list of Swedish official statistical publications. Subject index. In Swedish and English.
Supplemented by the monthly *Allmän mañadsstatistisk*

....(contd.)
(1963-.). For historical statistics there is the Bureau's *Historisk statistisk för Sverige* (1. Befolkning, 1720-1967; 2. Vdaderlek ... climate, land surveying, agriculture, forestry, fisheries, to 1955; 3. Utrikeshandel, 1732-1970).
Class No: 310(485)

Denmark
[1231]
DENMARK. Danmarks Statistik. **Statistisk arbog:** Statistical yearbook. København, Danmarks Statistik, 1887-. Annual. Kr.245 (1993 issue). ISBN: 8750108700. ISSN: 00703567.
The 1993 edition (1993. 566p.) has sections on Denmark as a whole and 13 subject sections. Also sections for the Faroe Islands, Greenland, and international data. List of official statistical publications. Index of subjects (in English and Danish). Supplemented by the monthly *Statistisk månedsoverigt*. (Kr.825pa. ISSN 01085603).
Class No: 310(489)

Netherlands
[1232]
NETHERLANDS. Centraal Bureau voor de Statistiek. **Statistical yearbook of the Netherlands, 1881-.** Voorburg, the Bureau, 1882-. Annual. ISSN: 03036448.
The 1993 yearbook (1993. 567p.) has 27 subject chapters with data for 1991 and selected earlier years. Published only in English. Subject index. List of official statistical publications. *Class No:* 310(492)

Belgium
[1233]
BELGIUM. Institut National de Statistique. **Annuaire statistique de la Belgique, 1990.** v.110. Brussels, the Institute, 1990. 1560p. BF.1250. ISSN: 07700415.
First published 1870. Annual.
29 subject chapters plus an international section, with data for 1989 and earlier figures in some tables. Subject index.
Supplemented by the monthly *Bulletin de statistique* (1909-. BF.1410pa.) which includes some regional statistics. *Class No:* 310(493)

Switzerland
[1234]
SWITZERLAND. Eidgenössisches Statistisches Amt. **Statistisches Jahrbuch der Schweiz/Annuaire statistiques de la Suisse, 1993.** 101st year. Berne, The Bureau, 1993. 445p. maps. SwF 95. ISSN: 00815330.
First published 1891. Annual.
The *Monatsbericht* (SwF.40pa) of the Schweizerische Nationalbank is a mainly statistical publication, and can be used to update the above.
20 main subject sections, with statistical tables for several years to 1991. Subject index. *Class No:* 310(494)

Liechtenstein
[1235]
LIECHTENSTEIN. Amt für Volkswirtschaft. **Statistisches Jahrbuch, 1992.** Vaduz, the Office, 1992. 352p. *Gratis.*
First published 1960. Annual.
Arranged in 22 subject sections, with data for several years to 1986. *Class No:* 310(494.9)

Greece
[1236]
GREECE. Ethnike Statistike Yperesia. **Statistical yearbook of Greece, 1989.** Athens, National Printing Office, 1992. 543p. maps. diagrs. Drs.2000 $22.
First published 1930. Annual.
Title varies. In Greek and English. The 1989 ed. has 23 subject chapters plus an international chapter, with data for various years to 1988 or 1989.
Supplemented by the Bank of Greece's *Monthly statistical bulletin* (ISSN 11050519) in English and Greek, with tables and graphs. *Class No:* 310(495)

Yugoslavia
[1237]
YUGOSLAVIA. Savezni Zavod za Statistiku. **Statisticki godisnjak FNRJ, 1992.** 39th year. Belgrade, the Office, 1992. 476p. maps. ISSN: 05851920.
First published 1954. Annual.
32 subject sections plus an international review. Data is for 1990 and some earlier years, and covers Montenegro and Serbia. In Serbian. An edition in Russian and English is also available (ISBN 8674790186).
Supplemented by the monthly *Indeks* (ISSN 00193585). *Class No:* 310(497.1)

Bulgaria

Yearbooks & Directories
[1238]
BULGARIA. Tsentralno Statistischesko Upravlyenie. **Statisticheski godishnik na Narodna Republika Buylgariya, 1992.** Sofia, the office, 1993. xv,455p. Leva 289.48. ISSN: 02044838.
First published 1956. Annual.
A general overview has 22 subject sections, followed by a sectoral overview of 14 sections and 7 sections of international statistics, with data to 1991. Detailed table of contents, but no subject index. In Bulgarian. Supplemented by the office's Statisticheski isvestia [statistical news] (quarterly ISSN 0204563x). *Class No:* 310(497.2)(058)

Rumania
[1239]
ROMANIA. Direcţia Centrala de Statistica. **Anuarul statistic al Republicii Socialiste România. Romania statistical yearbook, 1992.** Bucharest, the Office, 1992. xxxii,678p.
The 1992 yearbook has 18 subject chapters, with statistics up to 1990/91 or 1991/92. Detailed chapter headings, but no index. Supplemented by the quarterly *Buletin statistic trimestrial* (1958-). *Class No:* 310(498)

Asia

Bibliographies

[1240]

HARVEY, J.M. Statistics: Asia & Australia: sources for social, economic and market research. 2nd ed. Beckenham, Kent, CBD Research Ltd., 1983. xiv, 440p. ISBN: 0900246413.

First published 1974.

2777 entries. Asia & Australasia (in general), nos. 1-420; then by countries, A-Z (Australia, nos. 449-674; Central Statistical Office; Libraries; Libraries and information services abroad; Bibliographies; Statistical publications, A-H (A. General; B. Production; C. External trade; D. Internal distribution and service trades; E. Population; F. Standard of living; G. Finance; H. Transport and communcation). Indexes of organizations, title and subjects.

Class No: 310(5)(01)

Yearbooks & Directories

[1241]

UNITED NATIONS. Economic Commission for Asia and the Pacific. **Statistical yearbook for Asia and the Pacific, 1992.** Bangkok, the Commission, 1993. 468p. £68. ISBN: 9211196108. ISSN: 02523655.

First published 1970. Annual. Prior to 1974 the name of the Commission was Economic Commission for Asia and the Far East and of the publication *Statistical yearbook for Asia and the Far East.*

Covers 42 countries, arranged A-Z, with figures up to 1987. Each country entry is divided into sections (Population - Labour - National accounts - Agriculture, forestry, fishing - Industry - Energy - Transport and communications - External trade - Wages, prices and consumption - Finance - Social statistics). Updated by the *Quarterly bulletin of statistics for Asia and the Pacific* (1971-. ISSN 01250019).

Class No: 310(5)(058)

China

[1242]

China: facts and figures annual, 1993 Friske, J.D., *ed.* v.17. Gulf Breeze, FL., Academic International Press, 1993. xx,462p. $90. ISBN: 087569165x.

First published 1979. Annual.

Content varies each year. V.17 has 28 sections: 1. Survey - 2. Summary of social and economic indicators... 4. Government - 5. Party - 6. International relations - 7. Military - 8. Population ... 10. Economy - 11. Resources - 12. Energy - 13. Industry ... 27 Sports - 28. Society.

Class No: 310(510)

[1243]

CHINA. State Statistical Bureau. **Statistical yearbook of China, 1993.** Beijing, State Statistical Bureau of the PRC; Hong Kong, Longman, 1993. 763p. ISBN: 9627349186.

First published 1981. Annual.

Arranged in 19 subject chapters, with national and provincial data for economic and social development for 1992, and time series for 1949-1992. The English edition of the Chinese language *Zhongguo tongji nianjian.*

Supplemented by the State Statistical Bureau's *Monthly bulletin of statistics - China* (1986-). *Class No:* 310(510)

[1244]

China statistical abstract, 1990. New York, Praeger, 1991. 128p. £52.50. ISBN: 0275938697.

Data taken from statistical publications of the Statistical Bureau of the People's Republic of China.

Key statistics for principal sections of the national economy from 1978 to 1989. 9 sections: General survey - Population and labour force - Agriculture - Industry - Transportation, postal and telecommunications services - Investment in fixed assets - Finance, trade and prices - People's livelihood - Education, science and culture, public health and sports. *Class No:* 310(510)

Hong Kong

[1245]

HONG KONG. Census and Statistics Department. **Hong Kong monthly digest of statistics, 1978-.** Hong Kong, the Department. HK$48 each issue.

First published 1978, complementing *Hong Kong Statistics, 1947-1967* (1969).

Part 1: Regular tables in 11 subject sections, each subdivided; pt.2: Periodic tables; pt.3: special review articles, one in each of about five issues a year.

Class No: 310(512.317)

Japan

[1246]

JAPAN. Statistics Bureau. Management and Coordination Agency. **Japan statistical yearbook, 1991.** 41st ed. Tokyo, the Bureau, 1991. xxxii,842p. Yen.13,500. ISBN: 4620850012.

First published 1949. Annual.

650 tables and 30 charts in 23 chapters, plus an international chapter, with data for 1988 and 1989. In English and Japanese. 2 appendices (1. Key statistics - 2. Guide to sources (in Japanese only)). Index is in Japanese only.

Supplemented by *Monthly statistics of Japan* (1947-.).

Class No: 310(52)

[1247]

TSUNETA YANO MEMORIAL SOCIETY. Nippon: a charted survey of Japan, 1989/90. 34th ed. Tokyo, Kokusei-sha, 1989. 355p. ISBN: 4875493096.

First published for 1936. Annual.

An English-language version of *Nihon Kokusai-Zue* (1927-). Data are mostly statistical. 45 chapters in 5 parts: 1. General aspects - 2. Economy in general - 3. Industries - 4. Social life and trends. Statistical sources, p.348-349. Index, p.351-355. *Class No:* 310(52)

India

[1248]

INDIA. Central Statistical Organisation. **Statistical abstract of the Indian Union, 1990.** New Delhi, Manager of Publications, 1992. xiii,590p. 500.00/00 First published for 1949. Annual. Superseded the Department of Commercial Intelligence and Statistics' *Statistical abstract relating to British India.* (1840-1943).

Contains 248 tables and 16 charts in 39 subject sections. Sources are stated; includes footnotes and explanatory notes. Supplemented by the *Monthly abstract of statistics* (1947-). *Class No:* 310(540)

Sri Lanka

[1249]

SRI LANKA. Department of Census and Statistics. **Statistical abstract of the Democratic Socialist Republic of Sri Lanka, 1991.** 29th ed. Colombo, the Department, 1991. xvi,504p.

First published for 1949. Annual.

Over 300 statistical tables in 25 subject chapters, for 1986/87. In Sinhalese, Tamil and English. Includes sources and footnotes. Subject index. An annual *Statistical pocketbook* (1967-. 23rd ed. 1990. ISBN 9555770425) is also available. *Class No:* 310(548.7)

Pakistan

[1250]

PAKISTAN. Federal Bureau of Statistics. **Statistical pocket book of Pakistan, 1990.** Karachi, the Bureau, 1990. xi,400p. Rs.30.

First published 1962. Annual.

A general section is followed by 18 subject sections with data for 1987/88 to 1989/90. Also a list of 'Important addresses' and 'A list of selected publications of the Federal Bureau of Statistics. Supplemented by *Monthly statistical bulletin* (Rs.40 each issue). *Class No:* 310(549)

Bangladesh

[1251]

BANGLADESH. Bureau of Statistics. **Statistical yearbook of Bangladesh, 1991.** 12th ed. Dhaka, the Bureau, 1991. xvii,729p. Taka 200. $40.

First published 1975. Annual. Continues *Statistical digest,* published from 1966-1974.

750 tables arranged in 15 subject chapters. Data is for 1988/89. Updated by the *Statistical bulletin of Bangladesh* (monthly. Taka 55. US$14). An annual *Statistical pocket book of Bangladesh* (1978-. 1989 ed. Taka 50. $12) is also available. *Class No:* 310(549.3)

Turkey

[1252]

TURKEY. Devlet Istatistik Enstitüsü. **Türkiye istatistik yıllığı. Statistical yearbook of Turkey, 1989.** Ankara, the Institute, 1990. 459p. maps. US$46.95. ISBN: 9751902274. ISSN: 0082691x.

First published 1928. Annual.

24 subject chapters, followed by a 25th of international statistics. Data is for several years to 1986. Sources of data, p.477. Detailed list of contents but no subject index. In Turkish and English, Supplemented by the monthy bulletin, *Aylık istatistik bülteni.* (1952-. ISSN 00414263). *Class No:* 310(560)

Cyprus

[1253]

CYPRUS. Department of Statistics and Research. **Statistical abstract, 1989 & 1990.** nos.35 & 36. Nicosia, Printing Office of the Republic, 1991. xxiii,601p. maps. C£6. ISSN: 0253875x.

First published 1955. Annual.

Arranged in 22 subject sections, the 22nd being devoted to

.... (contd.)

international statistics, with data for several years to 1989. Supplemented by *Monthly economic indicators* (C£4 each issue. ISSN 02538555). *Class No:* 310(564.3)

Israel

[1254]

ISRAEL. Central Bureau of Statistics. **Statistical abstract of Israel, 1993.** No.44. Jerusalem, the Bureau, 1993. [920]p. ISSN: 00814679.

First published 1950. Annual.

In two parts, English and Hebrew. 27 subject chapters with data to 1992. Chapter 27 is on Judea, Samaria and Gaza Area. Supplemented by the *Monthly bulletin of statistics* (ISSN 00211982). *Class No:* 310(569.4)

Thailand

[1255]

BANK OF THAILAND. **Quarterly bulletin.** Bangkok, the Bank, 1961-. B.650; $25. ISSN: 0125605x.

Includes a statistical section of 63 tables in each issue, on money and banking, public finance, foreign trade and payments, business capital, production and prices, rates of exchange, and the price of gold. Data is given for several years and quarters. *Class No:* 310(593)

[1256]

—WILSON, C.M. Thailand: a handbook of historical statistics. Boston, Mass., G.K. Hall, 1983. 360p. $80. ISBN: 0816181152.

Data collected between 1850 and 1979 is arranged under various chapter headings, including climate and land base, population, education, health, labour, transportation, communications, politics and government, money and banking, industry, and culture. *Class No:* 310(593)

Malaysia

[1257]

MALAYSIA. Department of Statistics. **Yearbook of statistics.** Kuala Lumpur, the Department, 1988. xxxi,334p. maps. Ringgit.12. ISSN: 01272624.

First published 1964. Early title was *Annual statistical bulletin, Malaysia.* Annual.

Brings together statistics for Sabah, Sarawak, and Peninsular Malaysia as well as data for Malaysia as a whole. Arranged in 19 subject sections with data for 4 or 5 years to 1985 or 1986. *Class No:* 310(595)

Africa

Bibliographies

[1258]

HARVEY, J.M. **Statistics Africa:** sources for social, economic and market research. 2nd ed. Beckenham, Kent, CBD Research Ltd., 1978. xii, 374p. £25. $80. ISBN: 090024626x.

First published 1970.

1461 entries covering the whole continent and adjacent islands. Sections: Africa, then countries A-Z. Data on central statistical offices, libraries with collections of statistical publications, principal bibliographies, and major

....(contd.)

statistical publications arranged in 8 subject groups (general, production, external trade, internal distribution and service trades, population, social, finance, transport and communication). *Class No:* 310(6)(01)

Yearbooks & Directories

[1259]

UNITED NATIONS. Economic Commission For Africa. **Statistical yearbook, 1990/91.** New York, United Nations, 1993. 4v. $50 each vol. ISBN: 9210250354.

First published 1973 (1974). Annual.

V.1. Pt.1: North Africa; Pt.2: West Africa; v.2. Pt.3: Eastern and Southern Africa; Pt.4. Central Africa. Data for each country on population and employment, national accounts, production, transport and communications, foreign trade, prices, finance, and social statistics. Data for several years to 1986 or the latest available. Footnotes.
Class No: 310(6)(058)

Egypt

[1260]

ARAB REPUBLIC OF EGYPT. Central Agency for Public Mobility and Statistics. **Statistical yearbook, 1952-91.** Cairo, the Agency, 1992. xvi,296p.

First published for 1952-64. Annual.

Sections: Population and consumption - Agriculture - Industry and petrol... Tourism - Economy - Useful information - International population information.
Class No: 310(620)

Mali

[1261]

Mali: a handbook of historical statistics. Imperato, P.J. *and* Imperato, E.M. Boston, Mass., G.K. Hall, 1982. 364p. $86. ISBN: 0816181470.

Chapter headings include climate and landbase, population, education, labour, transportation, communications, politics and government, money and banking, industry and culture. *Class No:* 310(662.1)

Zimbabwe

[1262]

ZIMBABWE. Central Statistical Office. **Statistical yearbook of Zimbabwe, 1989.** Harare, the Office, 1989. 266p.

First published 1986.

Statistical data arranged in 15 subject chapters, each beginning with a list of the tables in that chapter. Data is for several years to 1988. Supplemented by *Quarterly digest of statistics. Class No:* 310(689.1)

America

Bibliographies

[1263]

HARVEY, J.M. Statistics America: sources for social, economic and market research (North, Central and South America). 2nd ed., rev. & enl. Beckenham, Kent, CBD Research Ltd., 1980. xiv, 385p. £43.50. $185. ISBN: 0900246332.

....(contd.)

First published 1973.

1592 entries. 'America', nos. 1-335: Some international organizations publishing statistics; Libraries and information services; Bibliographies; Statistical publications (A. General; B. Production; C. External trade; D. Internal distribution and service trades; E. Population; F. Social; G. Finance; H. Transport and communication). 56 countries, A-Z. Entries are annotated; prices given; language(s) of publication stated. Many cross-references. Indexes of organizations, titles and subjects. A basic source in this field.
Class No: 310(7)(01)

America — North

Bibliographies

[1264]

Statistics sources, 1990. O'Brien, J.W. *and* Wasserman, S.R. 13th ed. Detroit, Mich., Gale Research Inc., 1989. 2v. (lxvi,3733p.). $305. ISBN: 0810346990. ISSN: 0585198x.

First published 1962.

Over 72,000 citations arranged under 20,000 specific subject headings, including geographic headings for states and individual countries, in a single alphabetical sequence. Citations mainly to United States and Canadian publications, with a few publications of international organizations (*e.g.* the United Nations Statistical Office's *Statistical yearbook*). Directory of federal statistical telephone contacts, guiding users to experts within the federal government.

The 17th ed. was published in 1993 (2v. $345. ISBN 0810381621). *Class No:* 310(71+73)(01)

Canada

Bibliographies

[1265]

CANADA. Statistics Canada. **Statistics Canada: catalogue:** updated to January 1, 1993. Ottawa, Statistics Canada, 1993. 442p. ISSN: 08384223.

Issued annually.

In 8 parts: 1. General - 2. Primary industries - 3. Manufacturing - 5. Transport, communications & utilities - 6. Commerce, construction, finance and prices - 7. Employment, unemployment and labour income - 8. Education, culture, health and welfare - 9. Census publications. Subject/title index. Brief annotations to the entries. *Class No:* 310(71)(01)

[1266]

Directory of statistics in Canada, 1985-. McClelland, R., *ed.* Toronto, Micromedia Ltd., 1986 - Annual. Can $190.

Formerly *Canadian statistics index.*

Initially included only English-language or bilingual material from Statistics Canada and other federal or provincial government bodies, but the scope is to be expanded. *Class No:* 310(71)(01)

Yearbooks & Directories

[1267]

CANADA. Statistics Canada. **Canada year book ... a review of economic, social and political developments in Canada, 1994.** Ottawa, Statistics Canada, 1994. various pagings, maps. ISBN: 0660151863.

....(contd.)

First published 1905. Annual.

22 subject chapters, including many tables with the text. 6 appendices. Detailed analytical index.
Class No: 310(71)(058)

Cuba

[1268]

CUBA. Dirección Central de Estadística. **Anuario estadístico de Cuba, 1987.** Habana, Comité Estatal de Estadística, 1988. 696p.

First published for 1966/67. Annual.

The 1987 edition has 18 chapters (the 18th has international statistics) with 531 tables. In Spanish. Supplemented by the quarterly *Boletín estadístico de Cuba.*
Class No: 310(729.1)

[1269]

—Cuba: a handbook of historical statistics. Schroeder, S. Boston, Mass., G.K. Hall, 1982. 589p. $98.50. ISBN: 0816132132.

Chapter headings include climate and land base; Population; Education; Health; Labour; Transport; Communications; Politics and government; Money and banking; Industry; and Culture. *Class No:* 310(729.1)

Jamaica

[1270]

JAMAICA. Statistical Institute of Jamaica. **Statistical yearbook of Jamaica, 1991.** 15th ed. Kingston, the Institute, 1992. [9],415p. maps.

First published 1973. Annual.

Arranged in 20 subject chapters, with an introduction to each chapter. Statistical data for various years to 1990.
Class No: 310(729.2)

Latin America

[1271]

UNITED NATIONS. Economic Commission for Latin America and the Caribbean. **Anuario estadístico para América Latina y el Caribe ... Statistical year-book for Latin America and the Caribbean, 1992.** New York, United Nations, 1992. lxxxii,[7],778p. $65; £43. ISBN: 9210210328. ISSN: 02519445.

First published for 1973. Annual.

An introduction, technical notes, and a list of sources precede the main part of the volume. Pt.1. Indicators of economic and social development ... (6 subject sections, with 105 tables). Statistical series ... (11 sections with over 374 tables). Statistics are given for the area as a whole and for individual countries for several years to 1989.
Class No: 310(729.99)

USA

Databases

[1272]

EVINGER, W.R., *comp.* **Federal statistical data bases:** a comprehensive catalog of current machine-readable and on-line files. Phoenix, AZ., Oryx, 1988. 671p. $132.50. ISBN: 0897742559.

....(contd.)

Updates US department of Commerce's *Directory of Federal statistical data files* (1981).

Files arranged by agency or department producing them. Entry for each file contains description of information in the file, and technical description of file characteristics (*e.g.* structure, size and tape format). Also A-Z listing of files by title. *Class No:* 310(73)(003.4)

Bibliographies

[1273]

American statistics index: a comprehensive guide and index to the statistical publications of the United States government. Washington, Congressional Information Service, 1973-, v.1-. Annual, with monthly and quarterly cumulations; bound annual supplements. price varies. ISSN: 00911658.

Each issue is in two parts: Index and Abstracts. The index volume has indexes by subjects and names, categories, titles, and agency report numbers; the abstracts volume has numbered abstracts arranged by government department, subdivided by division, service, etc., then by form (annuals & biennials, special & irregular publications, publications in series, reports, etc.); *c.*500 abstracts per issue. Database covers 1973- (DIALOG), also on CD-ROM (Statistical Masterfile). *Class No:* 310(73)(01)

[1274]

—Statistical reference index: to current American statistical publications from sources other than the US Government. Bethesda, MD., Congressional Information Service Inc., 1980-. v.1,no.1-. Monthly; quarterly and annual cumulations. (Also 5-year cumulated indexes). ISSN: 0278694x.

A companion serial to *American statistics index* (*qv*). Indexes and abstracts serial and monograph statistical publications of trade and professional associations, business organizations, commercial publishers, university and independent research centres, and state government agencies. Published in 2 parts: *Index,* providing access to the abstracts through 4 basic indexes (subjects and names, categories, issuing sources, and titles); and *Abstracts,* containing full bibliographical data and detailed descriptions of the items. Also available on CD-ROM (Statistical Masterfile). *Class No:* 310(73)(01)

[1275]

Guide to US government statistics. Andriot, D., *and others, eds.* 5th ed. McLean, VA., Documents Index, 1986. ix,686p. $215. ISSN: 04349067.

4th ed. published in 1973.

Identifies and annotates 11,945 recent monographic and serial publications reporting statistical data. Arranged by issuing agency in SuDocs order. Each agency has brief description of its creation and authority and address for further information. Each statistical publication, listed under its agency, has title, issuing agency, collation, item number, stock number, Library of Congress number, Dewey number, SuDocs number, price, ISSN, L.C. card number, OCLC number, and notes. Preferred to Wasserman's *Statistics sources* (10th ed. Gale, 1986) by *Reference books bulletin* (1986/87) who consider competitor is *American statistics index* (monthly). *Class No:* 310(73)(01)

[1276]
STRATFORD, J. *and* STRATFORD, J.S. **Guide to statistical materials produced by government and associations in the United States.** Alexandria, VA., Chadwyck-Healey Inc., 1987. 279p. £100. (*Government documents bibliographies.*) ISBN: 0859641279.

Intended as a bibliographical guide and acquisitions tool, the volume lists more than 700 statistical publications issued by US federal and state governments and membership associations. Includes only those publications that recur biennially or more frequently, and omits censuses. For each publication - citation, ISSN and LC card numbers, frequency, price, availability, annotation; for GPO publications also class number and depository item number. 5 appendixes, 3 on addresses of issuing sources, a glossary, and list of abbreviations used. Title and subject indexes (p.233-279). 'A useful supplement to existing statistical source books ...' (*Choice*, v.25(3), November 1987, p.460). *Class No:* 310(73)(01)

Yearbooks & Directories

[1277]
Statistical services directory: a guide to the organizations, corporations, professional and trade associations, research centers, universities, publishers, foundations and government agencies that provide statistical services. 2nd ed. Detroit, Mich., Gale Research Co., 1984. 461p. $150. ISBN: 0810306689. ISSN: 07326971.

First published 1982.

Over 2000 gatherers of statistical information are arranged A-Z by organization name, with address; telephone number; contact person; brief description of the organization, including subjects covered; methods of disseminating statistics; available formats; time period covered; dates of release and frequency; and cost of service. Over 500 subject areas covered. 4 indexes: subject index; geographic index; contact name index; and title index. *Class No:* 310(73)(058)

[1278]
UNITED STATES. Bureau of the Census. **Statistical abstract of the United States, 1993.** 113th ed. Washington, US Government Printing Office, 1993. xxv,1009p.

First published for 1878. Annual.

*c.*1500 tables and charts arranged in 31 sections: 1. Population ... 3. Health and nutrition ... 9. State and local government finances and employment ... 16. Banking, finance and insurance ... 19. Energy ... 25. Mining and mineral products ... 27. Manufactures - 28. Domestic trade and services - 29. Foreign commerce and aid ... 30. Outlying areas - 31. Comparative international statistics. 7 appendices: (1. Guide to sources of statistics ... 3. Statistical methodology and reliability). Detailed index, p.958-1009. A basic statistical tool. *Class No:* 310(73)(058)

[1279]
—UNITED STATES. Bureau of the Census. Historical statistics of the United States: colonial times to 1970. Washington, US Government Printing Office, 1976 (Reprinted 1989 by Kraus International Publications, White Plains, N.Y.). 2v. $58.50. ISBN: 0527917567.

Contains over 12,500 statistical time-series, largely annual, on American social, economic, political and geographic development, 1610 to 1970. Includes definitions of terms, descriptive text, specific source notes. Detailed subject index. *Class No:* 310(73)(058)

Brazil

[1280]
BRAZIL. Instituto Brasileiro de Geografia e Estatística. **Anuário estatístico do Brasil, 1992.** v.53. Rio de Janeiro, the Institute, 1993. 1117p. ISSN: 01001299.

First published 1936. Annual.

Arranged in 7 broad groups: Geographical area - Population - Agriculture and fisheries - Industry - Services, trade, transport and communications - Prices, wages, indices - Macroeconomics (money and finance). Data is for 1990 or earlier. Text in Portuguese.

Brazil: a handbook of historical statistics, by A. K. Ludwig (Boston,Mass., G K Hall, 1985. 536 p. $83. ISBN 0816181888) indicates Brazil's social, economic and political development through the perspective of its historical statistics. *Class No:* 310(81)

Chile

[1281]
Historical statistics of Chile. Mamalakis, M.J., *comp.* Westport, CT, Greenwood Press, 1978-89. 6v. tables. $175. £125 each volume. ISBN: 0313206198, v.1; 0313208549, v.2; 0313208565, v.3; 0313208565, v.4; 0313251363, v.5; 0313265631, v.6.

V.1: National accounts; v.2: Demography and labour force; v.3: Forestry and related activities; v.4: Money, prices and credit services; v.5: Money, banking and financial services; v.6: Government services and public sector, and a theory of services. Mainly statistical tables, but also a number of brief essays. *Class No:* 310(83)

Indonesia

[1282]
INDONESIA. Biro Pusat Statistik. **Statistik Indonesia/ Statistical yearbook of Indonesia, 1991.** Djakarta, the Central Bureau of Statistics, 1992. xlix,587p. ISSN: 01262912.

First published for 1975. Annual.

*c.*400 tables arranged in 12 subject chapters, with data for 1986-1989. In Indonesian and English. *Class No:* 310(910)

New Zealand

[1283]
NEW ZEALAND. Department of Statistics. **Official yearbook, 1993.** 96th ed. Wellington, the Department, 1993. xii,560p. illus., tables, maps. $59.95.

First published 1892.

26 subject chapters have data for various years to 1991/92. Appendices include a glossary of statistical terms; weights and measures; Department of Statistics publications; Index (p.551-560). Supplemented by *Key statistics: a monty abstract of statistics* (1914-. NZ$295pa. ISSN 01142119). *Class No:* 310(931)

[1284]
—BLOOMFIELD, G.T. New Zealand a handbook of historical statistics. Boston, Mass., G.K. Hall, 1984. 252p. $65. ISBN: 0816181683.

Contains data from 1840 to the early 1980s, chronicling the nation's growth and development. *Class No:* 310(931)

Australia

Bibliographies

[1285]
HAGGER, A.J. A Guide to Australian economic and social statistics. Sydney, Pergamon Press, 1983. ix,116p. (*Guides to Australian information sources.*) ISBN: 0080298338.

7 sections: 1. Australian economic and social statistics: the broad picture - 2. Population - 3. Social statistics - 4. Economic accounts - 5. Labour and prices - 6. Public finance, industry and overseas trade - 7. Economic and social statistics produced outside the ABS. Index.
Class No: 310(94)(01)

Yearbooks & Directories

[1286]
AUSTRALIA. Bureau of Statistics. **Year book of Australia,1994.** No.76. Canberra, the Bureau, 1994. xii,869p.tables,maps. ISSN: 08108633.

First published 1908. Annual.

The 1994 year book has 28 subject chapters of text, with many maps and tables, and an appended statistical summary with data mainly for 1992-1993. Analytical index, p.827-869. List of special articles published in previous issues. Updated by *Monthly summary of statistics, Australia* (1912-. Early issues were quarterly. ISSN 07271689).
Class No: 310(94)(058)

Statistical Theory

[1287]
CHAPMAN, M. *and* MAHON, B. Plain figures. Cabinet Office (Management and Personnel Office) *and* Civil Service College. London, HMSO., 1986. 110p. £5.50. ISBN: 0114300011.

'The aim of this book is to demonstrate and discuss ways of presenting numbers effectively so that their value can be realised in full. A subsidiary aim is to help the reader interpret all data more competently and confidently' (*Introduction*). Contents: 1. General principles for presenting data - 2. Summary of recommendations - 3. Structure and style of tables - 4. Demonstration tables - 5. Reference tables - 6. Charts - 7. Effective charts for general use - 8. Words. Appendices: A. Tables and charts as visual aids - B. Further reading (p.107) - C. Research evidence - D. Bibliography (p.109-110). *Class No:* 311

Bibliographies

[1288]
Short book reviews. Voorburg, Netherlands, International Statistical Institute, 1981-. 3pa. $12 pa. ISSN: 02547694.

Prior to 1981 reviews were carried in the Institute's *Revue internationale de statistique* (1933-1971) and then *International statistical review*, 1972-.

Provides a rapid book review service for statisticians covering books on statistics and related subjects published throughout the world. *Class No:* 311(01)

Dictionaries

Polyglot

[1289]
PAENSON, I. Systematic glossary of the terminology of statistical methods. Oxford, Permanon Press, 1970. xxxviii,517p. £96.

The glossary is in English-French-Spanish-Russian.
Class No: 311(038)=00

Histories

[1290]
STIGLER, S.M. The History of statistics: the measurement of uncertainty before 1900. Cambridge, Mass., Belknap Press of Harvard University Press, 1986. xvi,410p. illus., figs., tables. $27. ISBN: 0674403401.

10 chapters in 3 parts: 1. The development of mathematical statistics in astronomy and geodesy before 1827 - 2. The struggle to extend a calculus of probabilities to social sciences - 3. A breakthrough in studies of heredity. Appendices A & B are syllabuses. Suggested readings, p.370-373, by chapter. Bibliography p.374-398, A-Z. Index, p.399-410. '... an incredibly rich source of ideas ... (*Contemporary psychology,* v.33(4), April 1988, p.293-295).
Class No: 311(091)

Population

Bibliographies

[1291]
Population index. Princeton, N.J., Office of Population Research (previously School of Public Affairs), for Population Association of America, 1935-. v.1-. Quarterly. charts, tables. $85pa. ISSN: 00324701.

Fall 1991 issue has 842 indicative, analytical abstracts. Contents include 'Current items' (documented), 'Bibliography': A. General population studies and theories - B. Regional population studies - C. Spatial distribution - D. Trends in population growth and size - E. Mortality - F. Fertility - G. Nuptiality and the family - H. Migration - I. Historical demography and demographic history - J. Characteristics - K. Demographic and economic interrelations and natural resources - L. Demographic and non-economic interrelations - M. Policies - N. Methods of research and analysis including models - O. The production of population statistics - P. Professional meetings and conferences - Q. Bibliographies, directories, and other information services - R. New periodicals - S. Official statistical publications - T. Machine-readable data files. Geographical and author indexes (cumulated annually). A first-class example of an annotated bibliography in a special field, covering periodical articles, monographs, statistical yearbooks and new journals. Available online (National Library of Medicine) and CD-ROM. *Class No:* 312(01)

[1292]
—'Population index' bibliography: cumulated 1969-1981, by authors and geographical areas ... Boston, Mass, G.K. Hall, 1984. 4v. $310.

Continues *'Population index' bibliography cumulated, 1935-1968, by authors and geographical areas* (Boston, Mass., G.K. Hall, 1971. 9v.).

V.1: author index; v.2: 1975-77; v.3/4: 1978-81.
Class No: 312(01)

[1293]

TEXAS UNIVERSITY. Population Research Center. **International population census bibliography.** Austin, Texas, Bureau of Business Research, University of Texas, 1965-67. 6v. Supplement, 1968.

V.1 Latin America and the Caribbean; v.2. Africa; v.3. Oceania; v.4. North America; v.5. Asia; v.6. Europe. Foreword to each volume mentions more general sources. V.5 deals with 47 countries, A-Z, with items in chronological order. Prefatory note on each country; parts of multi-volume works are detailed. Coverage of national, provincial, state and city censuses (India:102p.).

Updated in Goyer, D.S. *The international population census bibliography: revision and update, 1945-1977: Texas bibliography II* (New York, Academic Press, 1980. 20, 576p. (Studies in population, University of Wisconsin). *Class No:* 312(01)

[1294]

—DOMSCHKE, E. *and* GOYER, D.S. The Handbook of national population censuses. V.2: Africa and Asia. Westport, CT., Greenwood Press, 1986. xiii,[1],1032p. $195. £120. ISBN: 0313253617.

For each sovereign state or geographically separated area is provided a historical overview of the censuses conducted and a brief description of the content and geographic coverage of each specific national survey. No demographic data is included. Topographical index. *Class No:* 312(01)

[1295]

—DOMSCHKE, E. *and* GOYER, D.S. The Handbook of national population censuses. [V.1] Latin America and the Caribbean, North America and Oceania. Westport, CT., Greenwood Press, 1983. xii,711p. $125.00. £69.96. ISBN: 0313213526.

A companion volume to the above. *Class No:* 312(01)

[1296]

—GOYER, D.S. *and* DRAAIJER, G.E. The Handbook of national population censuses [v.3]: Europe. Westport, CT, Greenwood Press, 1992. 544p. $95. ISBN: 0313284261.

Includes all Europe, west of and including USSR, completing the series. 'A specialized but excellent guide ...'(*Choice*,v.30(6), February 1993, p.940). *Class No:* 312(01)

Encyclopaedias

[1297]

ROSS, J.A., *ed*. **International encyclopedia of population.** 2nd ed. New York, The Free Press; London, Collier Macmillan, 1982. 2v. (850p.). illus., tables, figs., maps. £116; $145. ISBN: 0029274400, v.1; 0029274609, v.2; 0029274303, set.

Concerned with the basic areas of population study (marriage, mortality, morbidity, migration, etc.) as well as interdisciplinary subjects (*e.g.* abortion). Includes corporate entries, which cover several related topics in the same article, and core entries, which define individual terms or concepts. Bibliographies follow all essays. Cross-references. '... should prove a basic reference source ...' (*Library journal*, 1 November 1982, p.2086). *Class No:* 312(031)

Handbooks & Manuals

[1298]

RHIND, D., *ed*. **A Census user's handbook.** London & New York, Methuen, 1983. xx,393p. £14.95. ISBN: 0416305105.

'Designed to be a guide to what is in and what can be obtained from the census; to what is good practice in analysing such data and what is definitely unwise' (*Introduction*). A list of tables, a list of figures, and a glossary of abbreviations precede 11 chapters (1. Censuses past and present - 2. The 1989 census and its results - 3. User needs: an overview - 4. Univariate analysis: presenting and summarizing single variables - 5. Creating new variables and new areas from the census - 6. Mapping census data ... 10. Linking census and other data - 11. Microdata from the British census). 8 appendices. Bibliography, p.375-388, A-Z by author. Name and subject indexes. *Class No:* 312(035)

Dictionaries

[1299]

PETERSEN, W. *and* PETERSEN, R. **Dictionary of demography:** terms, concepts and institutions. Westport, CT., Greenwood Press, 1984. 2v,. (*c*.1248p.). £125 for 2v. ISBN: 0313241341.

Relates to the past and present determinants and consequences of population trends throughout the world. The dictionary runs A-Z through the two volumes (A-M; N-Z), entries varying in length from a few lines to 2 or more pages. References, p.1015-6. Appendix: Classified list of institutes, organizations and associations. Index, p.1059-1154. *Class No:* 312(038)

[1300]

PRESSAT, R., *ed*. **Dictionary of demography.** Wilson, C., *ed*. Oxford, Basil Blackwell Ltd., 1985. 368p. diagrs. £35. $60. ISBN: 0631127461.

First published in French (*Dictionnaire de démographie.* Paris, Presses Universitaires de France, 1979).

A dictionary of theories, concepts, techniques and technical terms relating to every aspect of contemporary and historical demography. The English edition has been adapted and includes many new entries from a team of some 30 international contributors. Entries range in length from 100 to 1000 words, illustrated where necessary with graphs and diagrams, and all but the shortest are followed by suggestions for further reading. Cross-references. British orientation; lacks some standard US concepts. Subject index. '... impressive, covers the subject well, and offers useful models, formulas, and graphs to illustrate specific points.' (*Choice*, February 1986, p.853). *Class No:* 312(038)

Polyglot

[1301]

LOGIE, G. **Glossary of population and housing.** Amsterdam, Elsevier, 1978. xxvii,266p. £89.90. (*International planning glossaries, v.1*.) ISBN: 0444417303.

Originally (1975) as 2v. in English, Dutch and German only.

825 English-base terms, with French, Italian, Dutch, German and Swedish equivalents. 17 subject sections (Demography - Migration - Statistics - Individuals - Populations - Age groups - Households - Family - Society - Housing policy - Slum area - Ownership - Housebuilding - Dwellings - Rooms - Density - Living climate). Signs denote

....*(contd.)*

terms that are only an approximate equivalent, and those officially recommended or disapproved. Bibliography (grouped). 6 language indexes. Favourably reviewed in *The Incorporated linguist*, v.18(4), Autumn 1979, p.118-9. *Class No:* 312(038)=00

[1302]
—COMMITTEE FOR INTERNATIONAL COORDINATION OF NATIONAL RESEARCH IN DEMOGRAPHY (CICRED). Population multilingual thesaurus ... Paris, CICRED/FNUAP, 1979. [3v.].

One volume is in English/French/Spanish; the other two have French and Spanish as the first language.
Class No: 312(038)=00

[1303]
PETERSEN, W. *and* PETERSEN, R. **Dictionary of demography:** a multi-lingual glossary. New York, Greenwood Press, 1985. [2],260p. $100. ISBN: 0313251398.

Over 400 basic demography terms are listed A-Z in English, with translations into French, Spanish, Russian, Italian, German, Chinese and Japanese. The Russian is transliterated and the Japanese and Chinese terms are in European characters. Indexes refer from the other languages to English. *Class No:* 312(038)=00

Periodicals

[1304]
Population bulletin of the United Nations. United Nations. Department of International Economic and Social Affairs. New York, the Department, 1951-.no.1-. Bi-annual. ISSN: 04979133.

Publication was suspended from 1964 to 1975, recommencing in 1976 in a different format.

Presents brief articles on population which are aimed at research institutions and individuals who are engaged in social and economic research. (No.33. 1992, 125p. $9.00. ISBN 9211512425). *Class No:* 312(051)

Yearbooks & Directories

[1305]
TRZYNA, T.C., *ed*. **Population:** an international directory of organizations and information sources. Claremart, CA., Public Affairs Clearing House, 1976. xviii, 132p. $18.75. ISBN: 0912102225.

A 'user's guide to who's doing what' to over 600 governmental and non-governmental national and international organizations on population, family planning, abortion, and programmes, etc. Bibliography of other directories and published sources. Indexes of organizations, subjects, acronyms and initialisms. 'A valuable reference tool' (*Library journal*, v.102(5), 1 March 1977, p.594-5). *RQ* (v.17(3), Spring 1978, p.278) finds indexing inadequate and the price high. *Class No:* 312(058)

[1306]
UNITED NATIONS. Statistical Office. **Demographic yearbook, 1991.** 43rd ed. New York, United Nations, 1992. x,567p. ISBN: 9210510801.

First published for 1949. Annual.

Returns from =2c.=*216 countries or areas. Tables published annually (tables 1-25); World summary - Population - Natality ... Infant and maternal mortality ...

....*(contd.)*

Subject matter index, p.512-565. *Demographic yearbook: historical tables* was published in 1981 (1178p.).
Class No: 312(058)

Histories

[1307]
WRIGLEY, E.A. *and* SCHOFIELD, R.S. **The Population history of England, 1541-1871:** a reconstruction. New ed. Cambridge, Cambridge University Press, 1989. xxxvii,779,[2]p. tables. maps. £24.95. ISBN: 0521356881.

First published in 1981.

11 chapters in 2 parts: 1. From parish register to national vital series; 2. English population history. The first part of the book describes how statistics were assembled for three centuries (mid-16th to mid-19th); the second part is devoted to an analysis of the series to discover the course of population change in early modern England. 16 appendices. Bibliography, p.741-57 (Section 1: A-Z by author; Section 2 has statistical publications and county maps). Related publications are listed on p.xxxi-xxxiv. Analytical index, p.759-79. *Class No:* 312(091)

Worldwide

Histories

[1308]
ORGANISATION FOR ECONOMIC CO-OPERATION AND DEVELOPMENT. **Demographic trends, 1950-1990.** Paris, OECD, 1980. 145p. graphs, tables. £3.80. $8.50. ISBN: 9264120211.

Earlier volumes covered 1951-1971, 1956-1976, 1965-1980, & 1970-1985.

A study containing projections for total population and active population in OECD countries.
Class No: 312(100)(091)

Europe—Western

Yearbooks & Directories

[1309]
EUROPEAN COMMUNITIES. Statistical Office. **Demographic statistics, 1993.** Luxembourg, Office for Official Publications of the European Communities, 1993. xlix,312p. tables. ECU18.50. £21. ISBN: 9282658864.

First published 1978 for 1960/76. Annual.

Comparable information for individual member countries as well as the Community as a whole. Includes all the principal series of demographic statistics (population change, population structure, EC and its regions, EC in the world, fertility, marriage and divorce, mortality, foreign residents, population projections (to 2020)). *Class No:* 312(400)(058)

Great Britain

Bibliographies

[1310]
BENJAMIN, B. **Population statistics:** a review of UK sources. Aldershot, Hants, Gower Publishing Co. Ltd., 1989. xi,355p. tables, maps. £45. ISBN: 056605731x.

A guide to sources of information over the whole field of

....(contd.)

demography relating to the population of the UK and including birth, death, marriage and divorce, migration, sickness, censuses and surveys (the position that obtained at the end of 1986). In 12 chapters, 10 of which describe the sources and include information on mode of collection, method of construction of standard indices, possible sources of error or bias, and guidance in the choice of information for particular purposes. Chapter 11 contains maps; chapter 12 is on desirable improvements; and there is a postscript. Index, p.351-355. Author is Emeritus Professor of Actuarial Science at the City University. *Class No:* 312(410)(01)

[1311]
GREAT BRITAIN. Office of Population Census and Surveys *and* **GENERAL REGISTER OFFICE FOR SCOTLAND. Guide to census reports: Great Britain, 1801-1966.** London, HMSO, 1977. 7,279p.

Based on *Guides to official sources no.2., Census reports of Great Britain 1861 - 1931 (qv).* In 7 sections: 1. Introduction and list of reports. - 2. Significant developments in scope and organisation - 3. Questions and schedules for each census - 4. Selected subjects of census enquiry (showing the gradual elaboration and refinement of the various social measurements concerned in the 14 subject areas dealt with) - 5. Enumeration of special groups. - 6. Areas for which populations have been given - 7. Using census reports.. *Class No:* 312(410)(01)

[1312]
—HAKIM, C. Census data and analysis: a selected bibliography. London. Office of Population Censuses and Surveys, 1978. [ii],30p. (*OPCS occasional paper 6.*)

A selective annotated listing of 105 books and journal articles, arranged A-Z by author/institution. '... aimed at those who wish to make use of census data, whether to obtain a few tables or figures, or to analyse census statistics in some detail ... ' (*Preface*). No index.
Class No: 312(410)(01)

[1313]
GREAT BRITAIN. Office of Population Censuses and Surveys. **Government publications. Sectional list 56: Office of Population Censuses and Surveys.** Revised 1 September 1987. London, HMSO, 1987. 17p. Gratis.

Major sections are on: Census, 1981; Population trends; Reference series; OPCS monitors; Studies on medical and population subjects; Handbooks and survey reports.
Class No: 312(410)(01)

[1314]
INTERDEPARTMENTAL COMMITTEE ON SOCIAL AND ECONOMIC RESEARCH. Guide to official sources. No.2: Census reports of Great Britain, 1801-1931. London, HMSO., 1951. iv, 119p. tables.

'The aim ... is to give a brief account for research workers and others of the development of the Census and of the wide range of information and analyses published in the long series of official reports'. Chapter 5: Selected subjects of census enquiry. Numerous tables and reproductions.
Class No: 312(410)(01)

Periodicals

[1315]
Population trends. Office of Population Censuses and Surveys. London, HMSO, Autumn 1975-. v.1-. Quarterly. £50pa. ISSN: 03074463.

The journal of OPCS, with articles on a variety of population and medical subjects, and also regular series of tables on population, components of population change, vital statistics, live births, marriages, divorces, migration, deaths, and abortions.

Beginning with 1974 data, OPCS data are published in subject volumes: series FM: Family statistics (1-2) - DH: Deaths (1-5) - MB: Morbidity (1-5) - PP: Population estimate and projections (1-3) - AB: Abortion statistics - MN: International migration - VS: Vital statistics: local and health areas - EL Electoral statistics - DR: Demographic review - DS: Decennial supplement - LS: Longitudinal study - LFS; Labour force survey - GHS: General household survey.
Class No: 312(410)(051)

Tables & Data Books

[1316]
GREAT BRITAIN. General Register Office for Scotland. **Census, 1991.** Edinburgh, HMSO, 1991-93.

Census publications include:.
Report for Scotland. 2v. (Part 1: £65. ISBN 0114951195); part 2: £33. ISBN 0114951209).
Report for new towns 2v. (£53. ISBN 0114952248).
Class No: 312(410)(083)

[1317]
GREAT BRITAIN. Office of Population Censuses and Surveys. **Census 1991** London, HMSO, 1992-94

A census has been taken every ten years since 1801
Census 1991 publications include:
Definitions (£13.80. ISBN 0116913614).
Users'guide (xvii,398p. £19,80. ISBN 0116915277).
Report for Great Britain (2 parts. £85 & £40) ISBN 0116915366 & 0116915269).
Historical tables (34p. £7.60. ISBN 0116915099).
Household composition (£27.40.ISBN 0116915609).
Ethnic group and country of birth (£45.40. ISBN 0116915188).
County reports (one for each county in England and Wales in 2 parts). *Class No:* 312(410)(083)

[1318]
GREAT BRITAIN. Office of Population Censuses and Surveys. **Population projections ... [1985 -2001. England].** London HMSO, 1988. iv.72p. tables. £7.40. (*Series PP3.*) ISBN: 0116912375.

First published for 1970-2010.
Data by area, sex and age, from mid-1985.
Class No: 312(410)(083)

[1319]
NORTHERN IRELAND. General Register Office. **Census of population, Northern Ireland, 1971.** Belfast, HMSO, 1971-76.

First census was taken in 1801.
The 1971 census publications include.
Summary tables.
County reports (7 reports).
Housing and household composition tables.
Religion tables, Northern Ireland.
Education tables. *Class No:* 312(410)(083)

Maps & Atlases

[1320]

DURHAM UNIVERSITY., *Department of Geography. Census Research Unit.* **People of Britain:** a census atlas. London, HMSO, 1981. 132p. tables, maps. £15. ISBN: 0116906189.

Prepared in collaboration with the Office of Population Censuses and Surveys and the General Register Office, Scotland.

Presents a unique and easy-to-grasp picture of the population of Great Britain, showing population distribution and information on major characteristics, bringing out national, regional and local patterns from the wealth of detail provided in the 1971 census of population. Pt.1 has 34 national maps on population, birthplace, demographic characteristics, socio-economic characteristics, travel to work, households and housing. Pt.2 is in 7 regional sections, each subdivided by population density, born outside UK, multi-car households, and bath-deficient households. Appendices give explanations; introduction explains computer mapping, etc. *Class No:* 312(410)(084.3)

Manuscripts & Incunabula

[1321]

HIGGS, E. **Making sense of the census:** the manuscript returns for England and Wales, 1801-1901. Public Record Office. London, HMSO, 1989. 156p. £9.95. ISBN: 0114402191.

Provides researchers with a guide to the records. A general introduction and a means of reference when working on the records, which it describes in detail. Also comments on the nature and reliability of the information. *Class No:* 312(410)(093)

Ireland

Maps & Atlases

[1322]

HORNER, A.A., *and others.* **Population in Ireland:** a census atlas. Dublin, University College Dublin, Department of Geography, 1987. ix, 165p. tables, maps. IR£15. ISBN: 1870089103.

200 maps, together with text and tables, cover the Republic of Ireland and Northern Ireland. Using computer plotting techniques the volume displays the many spatial variations of population structure and distribution in Ireland in 1981. 'Most complete analysis of Irish census material yet to appear' (*The geographical journal,* March 1989, p.126-7). *Class No:* 312(415)(084.3)

Northern Ireland

Maps & Atlases

[1323]

COMPTON, P.A., *and others.* **Northern Ireland; a census atlas.** Dublin, Gill and Macmillan,1978. [2], 169p. diagrs, tables, maps.

A series of 115 computer-drawn maps summarizing the main spatial characteristics of the population of Northern Ireland and the urban area of Belfast in 1971, based on census data collected that year. Spans 3 broad themes - the demography of the province, the social and economic

....(contd.)
characteristics of the people, and household data. Short bibliography of 11 items. Detailed index. *Class No:* 312(416)(084.3)

Eire

[1324]

EIRE.Central Statistics Office. **Census of population of Ireland, 1991.** Dublin. Stationery Office, 1991-.

First census was taken in 1821. Excludes Northern Ireland.

Results of the 1991 census are n ow being published, including 'Preliminary results'; Local,population reports - 1st series (nos.1-28); 'Small area population statistics (SAPS).

A census was taken in 1986, and a preliminary report was issued in that year. The final report is in 8v. (V.1. Population classified by area (£10)). *Class No:* 312(417)

England & Wales

Bibliographies

[1325]

GIBSON, J.S.W., *comp.* **Census returns on microfilm. Directory to local holdings, 1841-1881.** Banbury, Oxfordshire, Federation of Family History Societies, 1982. 44p. £1.25. Paperback issued in 1987. ISBN: 090709919x.

First published 1979 as *Census returns, 1841, 1851, 1861, 1871, on microfilm ...*

Covers England and Wales, under counties A-Z. The holdings of the five census years are now released to the public under the '100 years' rule. *Class No:* 312(42)(01)

Histories

[1326]

NISSEL, M. **People count:** a history of the General Register Office. London, HMSO, 1987. [4], 157p. illus. (col.). £5.75. ISBN: 0116911832.

11 chapters (Registration before 1837 - Establishing the General Register Office - The civil registration system - Social commentary - The population controversy and the first population census - The census: the first 100 years of the General Register Office - The census: the last 50 years - Social surveys - Health statistics: the early years of the General Register Office - Health statistics: later developments - Population). 4 appendices: Chronology of main events in the history of the Office; Registrars-General, 1837-1987; Some recent OPCS publications; Historical tables. Index, p.156-7. 'A potted history of social change in the past 150 years'. (*Library association record,* v.89(11), November 1987). *Class No:* 312(42)(091)

Biographies

[1327]

PETERSEN, W. *and* PETERSEN, R. **Dictionary of demography:** biographies. New York, Greenwood Press, 1985. 2v. (xx,1365p.). £142.50. ISBN: 0313214190.

Short biographies of 3363 nationals of 99 countries are arranged A-Z in the 2 volumes (A-L; M-Z). Average length

....(contd.)
of each biography is ½ page, including references. Appendix: classification of nationality. References, p.1187-1198. Index, p.1199-1365. *Class No:* 312(42)(092)

China

[1328]
New China's population. China Financial & Economic Publishing House. New York, Collier Macmillan, 1988. xxiv,232p. tables, charts. $90. £82. ISBN: 0029054710.

A condensation in English of a 32v. survey in Chinese, summarizing the most important findings. 12 chapters: 1. Introduction - 2. The Chinese population: its size and growth - 3. Trend and differences in China's fertility rate - 4. The trend and difference of mortality of China's population - 5. Internal migration - 6. Urbanization - 7. Distribution of Chinese population - 8. Sex and age composition of China's population - 9. Marriage and family - 10. Working population - 11. Population of minority nationalities - 12. China's population policy and family planning. Data is based on the 1953, 1964 and 1982 censuses and the fertility sample survey of 1982. Extensive index. *Class No:* 312(510)

[1329]
The Population atlas of China. Population Census Office of the State Council of China *and* Institute of Geography of the Chinese Academy of Sciences. Hong Kong, Oxford University Press, 1988. 216p. 152 col. maps. £30. ISBN: 0195840925.

Based on the 1982 census of the People's Republic of China, the atlas covers population distribution and change, nationalities, sex and age, marriage and fertility, the level of education, and occupations. Hong Kong and Taiwan are included in so far as comparable data are available. *Class No:* 312(510)

Africa

Bibliographies

[1330]
PINFOLD, J.R., *comp. & ed.* **African population census reports:** a bibliography and check-list. München, K.G. Saur; Oxford, Hans Zell Publishers, on behalf of SCOLMA, 1985. xii, 100p. £15. DM60-. ISBN: 0905450191, UK; 3598105711, Germany.

Arranged A-Z by the names of African countries. Population censuses and other national demographic surveys are listed in chronological order. Regional and urban population censuses are included when there is no national survey. Covers a wide variety of sources, including statistical yearbooks, United Nations publications, periodicals, etc. Locations are given (25 libraries in Britain; 9 major collections in Europe). Cross-references between old and new names of countries. *Class No:* 312(6)(01)

[1331]
Union list of African censuses, development plans, and statistical abstracts. Evalds, V.K., *comp.* Oxford, Hans Zell; Munich, K.G. Saur, 1985. xiv,232p. £22.50; DM.88. ISBN: 0905450205, UK; 3598105762, Germany.

Lists the holdings of 13 major North American libraries, but not the Library of Congress, of government documents concerned with African censuses, development plans, and statistical abstracts from 1945 to 1983. *Class No:* 312(6)(01)

USA

[1332]
BOGUE, D.J. The Population of the United States: historical trends and future projections. New York, Free Press, 1985. 728p. tables. $70. ISBN: 0029047005.

An eminently readable portrait of the people of the United States from 1790 to 1980 in 20 chapters. Includes detailed bibliographies, clear definitions of terms, and a guide to obtaining further information. Hundreds of charts, graphs, pie charts, etc. are included. 'An excellent accompaniment to the *Statistical abstract* and *Historical statistics of the United States (Library journal,* 15 April 1986, p.36). *Class No:* 312(73)

[1333]
WELLS, R.V. The Population of the British colonies in America before 1776: a survey of census data. Princeton, Princeton, University Press, 1976. xii,342p. tables. $44. ISBN: 0691046166.

In 8 sections: 1. Subject, sources, methods - 2. The northern colonies - 3. New England - 4. The middle colonies - 5. The southern colonies - 6. The island colonies - 7. Colonial patterns - 8. Household size and composition. Includes 88 tables. References are give in footnotes. Analytical index. *Class No:* 312(73)

Bibliographies

[1334]
SCHULTZE, S. Population information in nineteenth-century census volumes. Phoenix, AZ., Oryx Press, 1983. 456p. illus., maps. $82. ISBN: 0897741226.

An index to tables containing population information in the first 11 federal censuses (1790-1890). For each census the bibliographical data and a table of contents are preceded by a short essay on its history and scope. *Class No:* 312(73)(01)

[1335]
—**SCHULTZE, S.** Population information in twentieth-century census volumes... Phoenix, AZ., Oryx Press, 1985-88. 2v. (289p.; 328p.), illus., maps. $82 each vol. ISBN: 0897741641; 0897744004.

Similar information to the above for 1900-1940 and 1950-1980. *Class No:* 312(73)(01)

Maps & Atlases

[1336]
Atlas of demographics: from the 1980 census. Boulder Co., Infomap Inc., 1982. 60p. 16 maps, tables. $175. ISBN: 0910471002.

Based on the 1980 census data, graphically presents socio-economic data at county level on population and housing. Data includes population density, age, race, housing. A table lists specific demographic data, A-Z, by State and counties within States. No. index. Recommended by *Choice,* (v.20(8), April 1983, p.1106). *Class No:* 312(73)(084.3)

Histories

[1337]
GERHAN, D. R. *and* **WELLS, R. V.,** *comps.* **A Retrospective biography of American demographic history from colonial times to 1983.** Westport CT., Greenwood Press, 1989. 474p. $65. (*Bibliographies and indexes in American history. 10.*) ISBN: 0313231303.

....*(contd.)*

Intended for user groups with more than a casual interest in the subject. 3840 entries are arranged in subject groupings corresponding to the author's earlier *Revolutions in Americans' lives* (1982). 6 chapters, all subdivided and with short introductions: 1. Introduction and general background - 2. Marriage and fertility - 3. Health and death - 4. Migration, pluralism and local patterns - 5. Family and demographic history - 6. Population, economics, politics and society. Author, place and subject indexes. A second volume is to cover material published since 1983.
Class No: 312(73)(091)

Research Establishments

[1338]
Directory of demographic research centers. 2nd ed. Paris, Committee for International Co-operation of National Research in Demography (CICRED), 1980. [2], 273p.

First published in 1974 in a loose-leaf edition.

Country arrangement, A-Z, with one page for each organization in questionnaire format, giving the name and address of the organization, its functions, objectives, research, personnel, publications, etc.
Class No: 312:061:061.62

Births & Deaths

[1339]
PRESTON, S.H., *and others.* **Causes of death:** life tables for national populations. San Diego, CA., Academic Press, 1972. xi, 787p. $49.50. £37. (*Studies in population.*) ISBN: 0127856641.

Sections (each with references): Method of calculation - Accuracy and comparability - Guide to life tables - Causes of death: life tables. 8 types of table per entry (age and sex). 180 populations. Australia ... Yugoslavia. Time series (*e.g.* Canada: 1921, 1931, 1941, 1951, 1960, 1964). Sources of data, p.54-65. *Class No:* 312.1/.2

[1340]
SINGER, R.B. *and* **LEVINSON, L.,** *eds.* **Medical risks:** patterns of mortality and survival. A reference volume ... Lexington, Mass., Lexington Books, 1976. v.p., tables. $44. ISBN: 0669982288.

Sponsored by the Association of Life Insurance Medical Directors of America and the Society of Actuaries.

Part 1: Text (172p.): 16 chapters, with references (*e.g.* 5. Cancer: 8. Hypertension; 16. Endocrine and metabolic diseases). Part 2 (over 1000 tables, with text left, facing): Tabular abstracts: References - Subjects studied - Follow up - Results - Comment. Subject index to text and tables.
Class No: 312.1/.2

Tables & Data Books

[1341]
ALDERSON, M. International mortality statistics. London, Macmillan; New York Facts on File, 1981. 524p. (380p. of tables). £45. $55. ISBN: 0871965143.

Comparative international data on causes of death during the 20th-century for 33 countries (US, Canada, Australia, New Zealand, Japan, Chile, Turkey, Europe, except Germany) and 178 causes of death. Mainly computer-produced serial mortality tables containing data in the form of age-standardized indexes. Each table devoted to a single

....*(contd.)*

cause of death for one sex. Preceded by explanatory material and state-of-the-art reviews on trends in mortality statistics, and on validity of data. Extensive bibliographical citations.
Class No: 312.1/.2(083)

Marriage & Divorce

[1342]
DICANIO, M. The Encyclopedia of marriage, divorce and the family. New York, Facts on File, 1989. 607p. $45. ISBN: 081601695x.

Some 600 essays, A-Z, on specific topics (*eg*,Alcoholics; Cohabitation), their historical, legal, psychological and sociological aspects. Cross-references. 8 directory-type appendices. Index. US slanted. '... offers convenient access to short, objective explanations of the myriad phenomena pertaining to contemporary life.'(*Wilson library bulletin*, v.64(3), November 1989, p.115). *Class No:* 312.3

Bibliographies

[1343]
ALDOUS, J. *and* **HILL, R. International bibliography of research in marriage and the family, 1900-1964.** Minneapolis, University of Minnesota Press, 1967. 508p.

Nearly 13000 citations in 6 sections. KWIC index; classified index; author and periodical lists. 'Substantially valuable to social scientists' (*Library journal*, v.92(8), 15 April 1967, p.1001), noting that the compilers relied heavily on *International bibliography of sociology, Psychological abstracts* and *Sociological abstracts,* 'obviating the need for searching there'. 'Impressive, but poorish printing and layout' (*RQ*, v.6(4), Summer 1967, p.190-3). Continued in *International bibliography of research in marriage and the family, v.2: 1965-1972.* edited by J. Aldous and N. Dahl, then *Inventory of marriage and family literature* (qv).
Class No: 312.3(01)

[1344]
Inventory of marriage and family literature. V.17, (published 1992). St. Paul, MN., National Council on Family Relations (previously Minnesota University Press; Minnesota University, Family Social Science Department; and Sage Publications), 1967-. v.1-. $129.95 pa. ISBN: 091617431x.

Earlier vols.: v.1. 1900-1964 (1967); v.2. 1965-1972 (1974); v.3. 1973-1974 (1975); v.4. 1975-1976 (1977) ...

A computer produced subject guide and subject index precedes the author index, which has full bibliographical references, a keyword-in-title index, and a periodical list. Over 600 journals are covered. *Class No:* 312.3(01)

[1345]
SELL, K.D. *and* **SELL, B.H.,** *eds.* **Divorce in the United States, Canada and Great Britain:** a guide to information sources. Detroit, Mich., Gale, 1978. xvi, 298p. $66. ISBN: 0810313960.

Contains 13 chapters devoted to subject bibliographies, basic reference books, statistical sources, legal texts, etc. Author, title and subject indexes. 'A brilliantly organized compendium of published and unpublished, print and non-print, retrospective and current sources dealing with divorce and such related issues as child custody, alimony, re-marriage of divorced persons, and the like' (*RQ*, v.18(4), Summer 1979, p.410).

....(contd.)

A similar book is M. McKenney's *Divorce: a selected annotated bibliography* (Metuchen, N.J., Scarecrow Press, 1975. 163p. ISBN 0810907777). *Class No:* 312.3(01)

[1346]

—SELL, K.D., *comp.* Divorce in the 70s: a subject bibliography. Phoenix, AZ., Oryx Press, 1981. viii,191p. $32.50; £25. ISBN: 0912700815.

Complements and to some extent supersedes the above. An unannotated bibliography of 4762 items published in the US in the 1970s, arranged in 7 sections (1. Social and behavioural science literature - 2. Legal literature - 3. Judeo-Christian literature - 4. Popular literature - 5. Non-print materials on divorce - 6. Addendum and appendix - 7. Indexes (author, geographical and analytical subject). *Class No:* 312.3(01)

32 Politics

Politics

[1347]
DERBYSHIRE, J.D. *and* DERBYSHIRE, I. **World political systems:** an introduction to comparative government. London, Chambers, 1992. 380p. £5.99. ISBN: 0550207538.

An introduction to philosophies, systems and structures, economics and society of every country of the world. *Class No:* 320

[1348]
EVANS, G. *and* NEWNHAM, J. **The Dictionary of world politics:** a reference guide to concepts, ideas and institutions. Hemel Hempstead, Herts., Harvester Wheatsheaf; New York, Simon & Schuster, 1991. xiv,449p. £60; $25.50. ISBN: 0745002749, UK; 0132105276, US.

Over 600 entries, ranging from a few lines to 2 pages, providing information on concepts and institutions essential to an understanding of contemporary politics, including important terms likely to be found only in specialized texts or journals. Cross references. Omits South Africa, Iran and Cambodia. Well-designed and up-to-date. Usable in conjunction with Munro and Day's *A world record of major conflict areas* (*qv*). 'An essential purchase for most libraries' (*Library journal,* December 1990, p.116). *Class No:* 320

[1349]
The Oxford companion to politics of the world. Krieger, J., *and others, eds.* Oxford, Oxford University Press, 1993. xxxi,1056p. £35. $49.95. ISBN: 0195059344.

650 mini-essays from nearly 500 contributors from 40 countries (mostly US). Covers international relations and domestic politics worldwide, with emphasis on post-1945 events. Most articles conclude with cross-references and sources. '... will become indispensable for all academic libraries.' (*Library journal,* 15 March 1993, p.72). *Class No:* 320

[1350]
Political geography in the twentieth century: a global analysis. Taylor, P.J., *ed.* London, Belhaven Press; New York, Wiley, 1993. [11],269p. £35. ISBN: 1852931965, UK; 0470219661, US.

5 chapters: 1. Geopolitical world orders; 2. Political geography of war and peace; 3. The rise and decline of the corporate-welfare state; 4. Colonialism, post-colonialism and the political geography of the Third World; 5. The United States and American hegemony. Epilogue: *Fin de siècle* geopolitics. Towards a geographical dialogue. *Class No:* 320

Bibliographies

[1351]
ABC Pol Sci: a bibliography of contents: political science and government. Santa Barbara, CA., ABC-Clio, 1969-. v.1, no.1-. 5 pa plus annual index. Subscription based on service rate principal. ISSN: 00010456.

Current awareness service, reproducing table of contents pages of over 300 core journals (both foreign and domestic) on political science and government, law, sociology, and economics, etc. Arranged by journal titles, A-Z. 'Subject profile' and author indexes in each issue, cumulated annually and five-yearly, plus list of periodicals. *Class No:* 320(01)

[1352]
CRIS the combined retrospective index to journals in political science, 1886-1974. Wile, A.N., *ed.* Washington, Carrollton Press, 1977-78. 8v. $880. ISBN: 0840801866.

Indexes 115,000 articles from over 170 English-language periodicals under more than 130 subject headings in theoretical and applied political science, international relations, public administration and urban studies. Volumes are: 1. International affairs and organizations; 2. General studies and methodology; 3/6. Public administration; 7/8. Authors [index]. *Class No:* 320(01)

[1353]
ENGLEFIELD, D. *and* DREWRY, G., *eds.* **Information sources in politics and political science: worldwide.** London, Butterworths, 1984. xviii, 509p. £38. (*Butterworths guides to information sources.*) ISBN: 0408114703.

Aims to be a critical assessment of a large English library on both the study and the practice of the subject (*Preface*). In 4 parts: 1. Resources - 2. Approaches to the study of politics and government - 3. Politics and government: United Kingdom - 4. Politics and government: overseas. The 24 contributors are academics and librarians, and the chapters are essays covering the various aspects of political studies (*e.g.* political behaviour, political thought, comparative politics), of government, and of politics in the UK and the rest of the world by regions. Subject index, p.503-509. *Class No:* 320(01)

[1354]
FOUNDATION NATIONALE DES SCIENCES POLITIQUES. **Bibliographie courante d'articles de périodiques** postérieurs à 1944 sur les problèmes politiques, économiques et sociaux/Index to post-1944 periodical articles on political, economic and social problems. Boston, Mass., G.K. Hall, 1968. 17v. (14,391p.). *Supplements* (annual). 1-20.

Main volumes and supplements contain over 500,000 photolithographed catalogue-card entries. About 1500 periodicals (one-third in French) are currently received; over 20,000 new entries pa. Classified by countries or areas, with reverse-chronological sub-arrangement. *Class No:* 320(01)

[1355]

HARMON, R.B. Political science: a bibliographic guide to the literature. Metuchen, N.J., Scarecrow Press, 1965-76. 2v. (388p.; x, 233p.). ISBN: 0810805588, v.1; 0810809036, v.2.

Previously as 1965 edition, plus 3 supplements, 1968-74. The 1965 volume as *c*.2000 entries (some annotated) in 10 chapters. Brief introductions to sections. Scope includes law and jurisprudence, public administration and industrial relations. Author-title index; subject index. *Class No:* 320(01)

[1356]

—**HARMON, R.B.** Developing the library collection in political science. Metuchen, Scarecrow Press, 1976. x, 198p. $19.50. ISBN: 0810808986.

Aims primarily 'to provide librarians with a selection device for most types of materials in political science' (*Preface*), particularly for small to medium-sized libraries. 'Selected reference materials', p.122-54; 'The periodical literature', p.155-162. Author and title index. Very brief annotations. *Class No:* 320(01)

[1357]

HEROLD, J. 'Political science reference sources'. In *RSR*, v.10(3),Fall,1982,p 45-53.

A book survey including a bibliography of 46 books. *Class No:* 320(01)

[1358]

HOLLER, F.L. Information sources of political science. 4th ed. Santa Barbara, CA., ABC-Clio, 1986. xvii, 417p. $65. £54.50. ISBN: 0874363756.

First published 1971; 3rd rev. ed. 1981.

2423 annotated citations of printed and computerized reference works in political science and related social sciences and humanities. In 3 parts: Pt. 1 is an extended discussion of the author's political reference theory. Pt. 2 is the main body of the work, with citations covering general references; the social sciences; American government, politics and public law; international relations and organizations; comparative government and area studies; political theory; and public administration. Citations are numbered and listed A-Z within the sections, containing bibliographical information and descriptive annotations of 1-2 paragraphs. Pt.3 has author, title, subject and typology indexes, the latter identifying reference sources by their genre (*e.g.* abstracts, bibliographies, directories, etc.). 'Every possible type of reference source is included, fully annotated, and easily located ... All in all, an indispensible volume for anyone doing political research'. (*College & research libraries*, v.48(1), January 1987, p.69). *Class No:* 320(01)

[1359]

International bibliography of political science. British Library of Political and Economic Science, *comp.* London and New York, Routledge 1954-. v.1-. Annual. ISSN: 00852058.

References to books, periodical articles, and documents, arranged in 6 subject sections, each subdivided: A. Political science. General studies and methods - B. Political thought - C. Political systems - D. Political life - E. Government policy - F. International life. Author and subject indexes. V.40: 1990 was published in 1992 (xxxix,467p. ISBN 0415674584). Supported by *Thematic list of descriptors:*

....(contd.)
political science, 1989 (Routledge 1989. 480p. ISBN 0415017785) and updated in *International current awareness service ...* (*qv*). *Class No:* 320(01)

[1360]

MARDALL, B. How to find out in politics and government. London, LLRS Publications, 1976. [1], [1], 40p. table, chart. £2. ISBN: 090426422x.

'Intended mainly as a guide to those "tools" of bibliographic and data organisation which constitute the means by which you [the student] *can find your own material* on a topic' (*Introduction*). 18 sections, (Encyclopaedias and dictionaries - How to trace books ... Publications of international organisations ... Statistical data ... Politics and government in London libraries ... Research in progress - Reference books - Further reading). Appended cross-reference chart of Dewey Classification. *Class No:* 320(01)

[1361]

WYNAR, L.R. Guide to reference materials in political science. Rochester, N.Y., Libraries Unlimited Inc., 1967-68. 2v. (318p., 342p.). (*Library science text series.*)

First published 1966.

Several thousand annotated entries. V.1 has 4 sections (Social science general reference sources; political science general reference sources; political theory; ideology). V.2, 6 main sections (International relations; public administration; political behavior, public opinion, political parties and electoral processes; comparative political systems; government documents; reference sources in law). Each volume has an index. Comparable in scope to Harmon (qv). *Class No:* 320(01)

[1362]

—**BROCK, C.** The Literature of political science: a guide for students, librarians and teachers. New York, Bowker, 1969. (Available from Books Demand, UMI). xii, 232p. illus., facsims. $46.40. ISBN: 0317103547.

About 500 brief annotated entries for bibliographies and other reference sources. Preliminary chapters on information sources and how to use them. Author-title index. US slanted. 'Does not supersede Harmon and Wynar (qqv), but it does supplement them' (*RQ*, Summer 1970, p.354-5). *Class No:* 320(01)

[1363]

YORK, H.E. Political science: a guide to reference and information sources. Englewood Cliffs, Co, Libraries Unlimited Inc., 1990. 249p. $38. (*Reference services in the social sciences, 4.*) ISBN: 0872877949.

650 evaluative as well as descriptive entries, 80-200 words each, arranged in 6 chapters. Sources include databases, periodicals and organizations. Author, title and subject indexes. 'This is an easily accessible, well-developed tool' (*Choice*, v.28(9), May 1991, p.1471) '... first choice guide for introducing students to political science reference literature and for evaluating political science reference collections' (*Wilson library bulletin*, v.65(8), April 1991, p.121). *Class No:* 320(01)

Encyclopaedias

[1364]

SEGAL, G., *ed*. **Political and economic encyclopedia of the Pacific:** a world guide. Harlow, Essex, Longman, Group; Chicago, St. James Press, 1989. [6],293p. maps on endpapers. £65; $85.00. (*Longman international reference series*.) ISBN: 0582051614, UK; 1558620338, US.

Entries focus on terms and subject areas central to current affairs, covering all the countries of the Pacific and the Pacific Rim, including Japan, China, and the Pacific dimensions of the US and USSR. Arrangement is A-Z by name of person, place or subject (Akihoto, Emperor - Alitas, Ali - Aluminium - American Samoa - Andean Pact - Antarctic Treaty ... Yi Kun Mo). Length of entries ranges from a few lines to several columns (Vietnam, Socialist Republic of: 8½ cols.). General index, p.287-293.
Class No: 320(031)

[1365]

WILCZYNSKI, J. **An Encyclopedic dictionary of Marxism, socialism and Communism:** economic, philosophical, political and sociological theories, concepts, institutions and practices - classical and modern, east-west relations included. London, Macmillan, 1981. [4], 608p. £35. ISBN: 0333306899.

Over 2300 entries on theories, practices and institutions of left-wing ideologies. *Class No:* 320(031)

Handbooks & Manuals

[1366]

NAGEL, S. **Policy-studies handbook.** Lexington, Md., Lexington Books, 1981. 238p. diagrs., tables. $27. ISBN: 066903777x.

Identifies training programmes, research centres, publishing outlets and government agencies for policy-studies scholars. 28 tables. *Class No:* 320(035)

[1367]

Political handbook of the world, 1990. Annual. Banks, A.S., *ed.* 62nd ed. Binghamton, N.Y., C.S.A. Publications, for Center for Education and Social Research, State University of New York, 1990. 956p. $89.95.. ISBN: 0933199066. ISSN: 0193175x.

First published in 1927 as *Political handbook of Europe*. Title varies. Until recently, sponsored by the Council on Foreign Relations.

Covers government and intergovernmental organizations as of March 1988 (with major political developments noted to 1 Jan 1990). Reports for each country include general data, the constitution, foreign relations, current issues, political parties, the legislature, the cabinet, news media, and inter-governmental representation of each country. A second part deals with intergovernmental organizations, including their history, structure, activities, official and/or working languages. Appendices: A chronology of major events, 1945-1989. Chart showing membership of the United Nations and agencies. A convenient source for quick reference.

A 63rd ed. was issued in 1993 (1200p. $104.50. ISBN 0933199090). *Class No:* 320(035)

Dictionaries

[1368]

A New dictionary of political analysis. Roberts, G. *and* Edwards, A., *eds.* London, Edward Arnold, 1991. [5],153p. £10.95. ISBN: 0340528605.

A guide to the current terminology of the subject, including concise definitions of basic terms and longer entries for more complex terms. 'Indicates subtle, but often significant differences in words which are sometimes misused.'(*British book news*, October 1991, p.682).
Class No: 320(038)

[1369]

ROBERTSON, D. **A Dictionary of modern politics.** 2nd. ed. completely rev. & updated. London, Europa Publications, 1993. 500p. £35. ISBN: 0946653755.

First published in 1985.

A guide to the complex ideology and terminology which surrounds the world of politics. Over 500 extensive entries on political theories, dogmas, issues and institutions. 'Concise, straightforward definitions' (*British book news*, April 1993, p.251). *Class No:* 320(038)

[1370]

SAFIRE, W. **Safire's political dictionary:** an enlarged, up-to-date edition of *The new language of politics*. 3rd. ed. (A 4th ed., *Safire's new political dictionary* was published in 1993. $30.50. 0679420681). New York, Random House, 1978. 845p. $17.95. ISBN: 0394502612.

First published 1968.

About 1200 entries, briefly defining over 1600 political terms or phrases, plus explanations placing source and period. Omits terms covered by ordinary dictionaries in favour of American catchwords, slogans and the like. 'A useful and amusing lexicon of political (not governmental) words and phrases' (*Wilson library bulletin*, v.47(3), November 1972, p.292, of earlier edition).
Class No: 320(038)

[1371]

SPERBER, H. *and* TRITTSCHUH, T. **American political terms:** an historical dictionary. Detroit, Mich., Wayne State University, 1962. x, 516p. $29.95. ISBN: 0814311873.

On *OED* lines: definitions, different meanings; changes in usage, with quotations (*e.g.* 'loco foco'; 'egghead'). About 1000 entries. A few politically unimportant words are included solely because they did not appear in *OED* etc.
Class No: 320(038)

Polyglot

[1372]

BACK, H., *and others*. **Polec: dictionary of politics and economics** ... 2. verbesserte und erw. Aufl. Berlin, de Gruyter, 1967. xvi,1037p. DM 61 £35.90.

16,000 English, French and German terms in one A-Z sequence, with definitions and frequently descriptive data, plus adequate cross-references. The definition and data are in the language of the entry-word, the equivalent of which is then given in the other two languages. Includes many abbreviations, also entries under the names of States and political parties. English entry-words are sometimes suspect (e.g. 'sudden trip'; 'exceptional law') and English definitions can be awkwardly phrased (e.g. 'VVB' is translated as 'Society of people's owned industry').
Class No: 320(038)=00

French

[1373]

CHAUDESAIGUES-DEYSINE, A.E. *and*
DREUILHE, A.E. Dictionnaire anglais-français et lexique français-anglais des termes politiques, juridiques et économiques. Paris, Flammarion, 1978,. 354p.

About 4-5,000 English entry-words, with French definitions, in the first and major part. Many idioms; numbered applications. US and British-English terms given. French-English index, p.291-354. *Class No:* 320(038)=40

[1374]

—SANDAHL, P. *and* DEBEA, L. Dictionnaire politique et diplomatique. Paris, Libraires Techniques, 1976. x,193p.

Explains *c.*360 political and diplomatic terms in French. Appended list of principal international organizations, with data on origins, purpose, HQ, and number of member countries. *Class No:* 320(038)=40

Chinese

[1375]

LAU, Y.-F., *and others.* **Glossary of Chinese political phrases.** Hong Kong, Union Research Institute, 1977. 590p.

'Contains over 2000 phrases in Chinese, with an English equivalent and explanation of political significance. Terms date from the beginning of the Communist period in China. Stroke-count index' (*RSR*, v.6(4), October/December 1978, p.66). *Class No:* 320(038)=951

Reviews & Abstracts

[1376]

International political science abstracts. Documentation politique internationale. Paris, International Political Science Association, under the auspices of the International Social Science Council, in co-operation with the International Committee for Social Science Information & UNESCO. (previously Oxford, Blackwell), 1951-. 6pa (previously quarterly. F.1350 (institutions); F.400 (individuals) pa. ISSN: 00208345.

About 6000 indicative and informative, but not evaluative, abstracts of *c.*150 words, arranged in 6 main sections: 1. Political science: methods and theory - 2. Political thinkers and ideas - 3. Government and administrative institutions - 4. Political process: public opinion, attitudes, parties, forces, groups and elections - 5. International relations - 6. National and area studies. English abstracts of articles in English, otherwise French abstracts. Covers *c.*400 journals (listed in each issue). Subject index in each issue; annual author and cumulated subject index. Complementary to the *International bibliography of political science* (qv), in that it concentrates on periodical articles, is annotated, and is more frequent. *Class No:* 320(048)

[1377]

Neue politische Literatur: Berichte über das internationale Schriftum. Stuttgart, Franz Steiner Verlag, 1956-?. 3pa. ISSN: 00283320.

Contains long articles that are surveys of the international literature on a particular topic, and shorter reviews of new books. Reviews are in German, books reviewed mainly in German, but a few in English or French. V.34(1), 1989 has 5 articles and 56 book reviews. Annual index of authors of articles and books reviewed appears in the first issue the following year. *Class No:* 320(048)

Yearbooks & Directories

[1378]

People in power. Harlow, Essex, Longman Group, 1987. 1v. loose-leaf. £90. $160. pa. (includes 2-monthly up-dates). ISBN: 0582017831.

A directory of the current political leadership in the sovereign countries of the world. Arranged by country, A-Z, outlines the current political system, including details of the head of state, full composition of the cabinet or council of ministers, and, where relevant, the leadership of the ruling party, ruling council, or military junta. Name and address of each country's ambassador or high commission in the UK also included. *Class No:* 320(058)

Almanacs

[1379]

The Facts on File world political almanac. Cook, C., *comp.* 2nd ed New York and Oxford, Facts on File, 1992. v, 490p. tables. $40 £25. ISBN: 0816026033.

First published 1989.

Key facts and figures on the major political developments since 1945. 11 chapters: International political organizations and movements - Heads of State and governments - Legislatures and constitutions - Treaties, alliances and diplomatic agreements - Political parties (by country, A-Z) - Elections - The violent world (inc. conflicts, wars, civil strife, terrorism) The nuclear age - Populations and urbanization - Dictionary of political terms (p.384-432) - Biographical dictionary. Analytical index. 'Unique in its specialized chronologies of international and civil conflicts, acts of terrorism, nuclear events and heads of state' (*Library journal*, 15 April; 1989, p.66), of the first ed. A 3rd ed is promised for 1994. *Class No:* 320(059)

Quotations

[1380]

BAKER, D.B., *ed.* **Political quotations.** Detroit, Mich., Gale Research International Ltd, 1990. 508p. ISBN: 0810349205.

More than 5000 notable quotations on politics, from antiquity to the present, with emphasis on the 20th century. Author and keyword indexes. '... indisputably useful in its field ...' (*Wilson library bulletin*, v.65(4), December 1990. p.155). *Class No:* 320(082.2)

[1381]

MONTGOMERY, H. *and* **CAMBRAY, P.G. A Dictionary of political phrases and allusions.** London, Sonnenschein, 1906. (Reprinted Detroit, Mich., Gale, 1968). 406p. ISBN: 081033092x.

Mainly British political phrases and allusions, but includes some foreign and US. Short bibliography. *Class No:* 320(082.2)

[1382]

RATHBONE, C. *and* **STEPHENSON, M. Guide to political quotations.** 2nd ed. Harlow, Essex, Longman Group Ltd., 1985. [4], 247p. £3.95. (*Longman pocket companion series.*) ISBN: 0582892090.

First published 1983.

Arranged in 19 sections (1. Some principles - 2. On the attack - 3. Historic phrases ... 8. On America ... 12. Women - 13. Wise words ... 18. In praise - 19. In memorium. Each

....(contd.)
entry begins with the quote, followed by the name of the person quoting and an explanation. Index, p.243-247.
Class No: 320(082.2)

[1383]
STEWART, R., *comp.* **A Dictionary of political quotations.** London, Europa Publications, 1984. viii, 226p. £18.50. ISBN: 0905118812.
*c.*2500 quotations arranged A-Z by the name of the person quoted, with explanation of who he is/was, followed by the quote and the source, if known. Most entries are of British, European or American origin and, although some classical authors are included, mainly from 1700 onwards. Key-word index (p.179-224) and supplementary index (p.225-226).
Class No: 320(082.2)

Tables & Data Books
[1384]
LANE, J.-E., *and others.* **Political data handbook:** OECD countries. New York, Oxford University Press, 1991. viii,257p. tables. £35. (*Comparative European politics.*) ISBN: 0198277180.
Statistics on 24 OECD countries' government and politics, plus social and economic background information. Data for a selection of years to 1985. Bibliographical references, p.255-7. *Class No:* 320(083)

Histories
[1385]
BRACHER, K.D. Age of ideologies: history of political thought in the twentieth century. London, Weidenfeld & Nicolson, 1984. xii, 305p. £20. ISBN: 029778434x.
Translated from the German by Ewald Osers. Published in German by Deutsche Verlags-Anstalt GmbH, Stuttgart in 1982.
21 chapters in 3 parts: I. The turn of the century - II the inter-war years - III. The present. Index of names, p.279-291. Analytical general index, p.293-305.
Class No: 320(091)

[1386]
HAMPSHER-MONK, I. A History of modern political thought: major political thinkers from Hobbes to Marx. Oxford, Blackwell, 1992. xiii,609p. £45. ISBN: 1557861463.
A guide to the ideas and writings of major thinkers, plus background comment. 10 chapters: Thomas Hobbes - John Locke - David Hume - Jean-Jacques Rousseau - 'Publius': the Federalist - Edmund Burke - Jeremy Bentham - John Stuart Mill - G.W.F.Hegel - Karl Marx. Bibliography (p.563-92) by chapters, each in two parts: A. Original works; B. Subsidiary works. Analytical index, p.593-609.
Class No: 320(091)

Biographies
[1387]
BLONDEL, J. *and* **WALKER, C.,** *comps. & eds.* **Directory of European political scientists.** 4th rev. ed. Oxford, H. Zell, for the European Consortium for Political Research, University of Sussex, 1985. vi,640p. £48. ISBN: 0905450124.
3rd ed. published 1979.

....(contd.)
*c.*3000 numbered entries, A-Z, covering academics working on a permanent or semi-permanent basis in Europe, including scholars who are not European citizens. Data includes information on careers, degrees, publications, and fields. Field index (African studies - American/Canadian studies ... Third world studies - Women's studies).
Class No: 320(092)

[1388]
Who's who of women in world politics. London, Bowker-Saur, 1991. xxii,311p. tables. £55. $95. ISBN: 0862916275.
Over 1500 entries for women in world legislatures and other national and regional leadership roles in 115 countries. Arrangement is A-Z by name, and includes personal and professional achievements, biographical details in normal who's who format, and address. Biographies are followed by a statistical section showing the number of women elected to positions within the government, legislature, political parties and trade unions of each country. A biography index is arranged A-Z by country, subdivided by surnames, A-Z.
Class No: 320(092)

Developing Countries
[1389]
WILLIAMS, G. Third-World political organizations: a review of developments. 2nd rev. ed. London, Macmillan Press, 1987. xiii,150p. tables. £29.50. ISBN: 0333362969.
First published 1981.
A review of organizations that help the Third-world. Includes UNCTAD conferences, the Non-aligned movement, special sessions of the United Nations, OPEC, and the Conference on International Economic Co-operation. An appendix is a data chart of the main events affecting the Third-world, 1944-1985. Notes, p.137-142, grouped by chapters. Select bibliography, p.143-44. Index, p.145-150.
Class No: 320(4/9-77)

Europe
[1390]
COOK, C. *and* **PUGH, G.** **Sources in European political history.** London, Macmillan Press, 1987-90. 3v. (749p.). v.1. £38; v.2. £45; v.3. £35. ISBN: 0333239962, v.1; 0333277759, v.2; 0333423690, v.3.
V.1. *The European left;* v.2. *Diplomacy and international affairs;* v.3. *War and resistance* V.1. is a wide-ranging guide to the surviving personal papers of over 1000 individuals active on the European Left during the last century, including anarchists, syndicalists, pacifists, trade unionists, socialists and communists. Arrangement is A-Z (Abate ... Zyromsky), with brief information on the person and notes on the papers. V.2. provides a wide-ranging guide to the surviving private papers of over 1000 statesmen, politicians and diplomats who played a part in the shaping of modern Europe. Each volume includes a select bibliography.
Class No: 320(4)

Encyclopaedias & Dictionaries
[1391]
Political and economic encyclopedia of Western Europe. Nicholson, F., *ed.* Harlow, Essex, Longman; Chicago, St. James Press, 1991. vii,411p. maps. £75. $85. ISBN: 0582068487, UK; 1558620729, US.

....(contd.)

Data on the events, organizations and personalities shaping the future of Western Europe. 'The low price, generally high quality of the articles, and handbook format make this ... publication a useful purchase ...' (*Choice*, v.28(10), June 1991, p.1622). *Class No:* 320(4)(03)

Encyclopaedias

[1392]

ROSSI, E.E. *and* McCREA, B.P., *eds.* **The European political dictionary.** Santa Barbara, CA., ABC-Clio, 1986. xxii, 408p. 2 maps. $42.50. £37.40. (*Clio dictionaries in political science, 7.*) ISBN: 0874360463.

Preceded by a 'Guide to countries' the entries are grouped in 5 sections: 1. The United Kingdom - 2. France - 3. The Federal Republic of Germany - 4. Western European regionalism - 5. The Soviet Union. Sections on the major nations are divided into 'Historical perspectives', 'Social and economic background', 'Government institutions and processes', 'Political parties and elections', and 'Domestic and foreign politics'. Each of the 325 entries consists of 'Definition' and 'Significance' paragraphs. Cross-references follow the entries. Index, p.377-408. 'Useful for background information ... not complete enough for a real reference work' (*Parliamentary affairs*, v.41(2), April 1988, p.303). *Class No:* 320(4)(031)

Handbooks & Manuals

[1393]

COOK, C. *and* PAXTON, J. **European political facts,** 1918-90. London, Macmillan, 1992. vii,322p. tables. £47.50. (*Macmillan historical and political facts.*) ISBN: 0333547764.

The fourth in a chronological series. Earlier titles covered 1648-1789 (by Babuscio & Dunn. 1984. 350p. £33. $24.95. ISBN 0333321111 (UK) & 0871969920 (US); ... 1789-1848 (1982. 300p. £29.50. ISBN 0333216970); and ... 1848-1918 (1978. 300p. £10. ISBN 0333151003).

Contains statistical tables, annotated bibliographical lists, and brief summaries regarding governmental structure and political activity in each European country that has existed since World War I. 10 chapters: International organizations - Heads of State - Parliaments - Ministers - Elections - Political parties - Justice - Defence and treaties - Dependencies - Population. Within each chapter organization is A-Z by country. Index, p.316-322. '... useful compendium of facts and background information ...' (*Reference books bulletin,* 1986/87, p.66) of Cook & Paxton's 1986 ed. *Class No:* 320(4)(035)

Biographies

[1394]

Who's who in European politics. 2nd ed. London, Bowker-Saur, 1993. xxiii,1016p. £159. ISBN: 1857390210.

lst issued for 1990/91.

Entries for nearly 8200 politicians from 43 countries. A-Z biography section (p.1-839) has entries of a few lines to half a column or more. Followed by A-Z country directory and index (p.843-1016). Better coverage of Western Europe than Eastern Europe. *Class No:* 320(4)(092)

Great Britain

[1395]

COOK, C. **Sources in British political history, 1900-1951.** London, Macmillan Press, 1976-85. 6v. ISBN: 0333387899, set; 0333150368, v.1; 0333150376, v.2; 0333150384, v.3; 0333191609, v.4; 0333221249, v.5; 0333265688, v.6.

V.1. *A guide to the archives of selected organizations and societies; v.2. A guide to the papers of selected public servants; v.3. A guide to the private papers of Members of Parliament, A-K; v.4. ...L-Z; v.5. A guide to the private papers of selected writers, intellectuals, and publicists; v.6. First consolidated supplement. Class No:* 320(410)

Handbooks & Manuals

[1396]

BUTLER, D. *and* BUTLER, G. **British political facts, 1900-85.** 6th ed. London, Macmillan Press Ltd., 1986. xix, 536p. tables. £35. (*Macmillan historical and political facts.*) ISBN: 033339948x.

First published 1963.

23 sections: Ministers - Parties - Parliament - Elections - Political allusions - Civil Service - Royal Commissions, Committees of inquiry and tribunals - Administration of justice - Social conditions - Employment and trade unions - The economy - Nationalisation - Royalty - British Isles - Local government - The Commonwealth - International relations - Britain and Europe - Armed forces - The press - Broadcasting authorities - Religion - Bibliographical note (sources, p.519-522). Analytical index (p.523-536). A valuable compendium of data. 'Itself a national institution' (*TLS*, no.4021, 18 April, p.1148, on 5th ed.). *Class No:* 320(410)(035)

Almanacs

[1397]

WALLER, R. **The Almanac of British politics.** 4th ed. London, Routledge, 1991. 638p. tables. £60. ISBN: 0415064341.

2nd ed. published 1983.

'... attempts to describe the political geography or electoral anatomy of the United Kingdom (*Introduction*). A comprehensive seat-by-seat analysis of all the parliamentary constituencies, describing their social, economic and political character. Each profile also gives the seat's recent electoral history and looks forward to their prospects. *Class No:* 320(410)(059)

[1398]

—WALLER, R. Atlas of British politics. London, Croom Helm, 1985. ix.205p. 148 maps. £16.95. ISBN: 0709936087.

Complementary to the author's *Almanac of British Politics* and also a contribution in its own right.

Based on evidence provided by the 1983 General Election and the 1981 census of population. 13 geographical sections, all subdivided: 1. National maps - 2. South West - 3. South - 4. London ... 11. Wales - 12. Scotland - 13. Northern Ireland. Data include winners, Conservative support, Labour, Alliance, middle-class workers, professional and management workers, owner-occupied housing, local authority housing, non-white voters, unemployment, car ownership, educational qualifications, agricultural workers, coal mining. *Class No:* 320(410)(059)

Chronologies

[1399]

FOOTE, G. A Chronology of post war British politics. London, Croom Helm, 1988. [3], 280p. £7.95. ISBN: 0709949227.

Covers from January 1945 to June 1987, and includes elections, government changes, significant legislation, internal party developments, social and economic developments, and international policies, documenting the major changes in British politics. No index. No introduction. A useful background reminder. *Class No:* 320(410)(090)

Ireland

[1400]

MITCHELL, A. and Ó SNODAIGH, P., eds. Irish political documents, 1916-1949. Blackrock, Co. Dublin, Irish Academic Press, 1985. 254p. ISBN: 0716505886.

Lists 147 documents on political affairs, arranged chronologically. *Class No:* 320(415)

[1401]

—MITCHELL, A. and Ó SNODAIGH, P., eds. Irish political documents, 1869-1916. Blackrock, Co. Dublin, Irish Academic Press, 1989. 195p. ISBN: 0716524228.

A companion volume to the above. 100 documents, chronologically arranged. '... traces the emergence of the Irish nation and responses to that development ... an effort to present a broad spectrum of political and constitutional issues' (*Introduction*). *Class No:* 320(415)

Quotations

[1402]

O'CLERY, C. Phrases make history here: political quotations in Ireland, 1886-1987. Rev.ed. O'Brien Press; Boston, Mass., G.K. Hall, 1987. 236p. £6.95; $25. ISBN: 0816189390, US.

First published in 1986, covering 1886-1986. Published in US as *The Dictionary of political quotations on Ireland, 1886-1987: phrases make history here.*

Over 1700 quotations, ranging from the significant to the trivial. Chronological arrangement. Attribution to each quotation. *Class No:* 320(415)(082.2)

Northern Ireland

[1403]

FLACKES, W.D. and ELLIOTT, S. Northern Ireland: a political directory, 1968-88. 3rd ed. rev & updated. Belfast, Blackstaff Press, 1989. 400p. £16.95. ISBN: 0856404179.

First published 1980.

A chronicle of events precedes an alphabetical dictionary of people, parties, organizations and key places, election results, systems of government in Northern Ireland, and the security system. *Class No:* 320(416)

Wales

[1404]

The Wales yearbook, 1993. Balsom, D., ed. 3rd ed. Aberystwyth, HTV Cymru Wales, 1992. 380p. ports. £9.95. ISBN: 0950042943.

Critical review of the year in Wales and month-by-month chronology of principal news stories in Wales; analysis of

.... (contd.)

1992 General Election in Wales with economic, cultural and linguistic profiles of all Parliamentary constituencies; guide to Welsh Office and local government directory of over 800 organizations, pressure groups, public bodies, and Welsh media, etc. *Class No:* 320(429)

France

[1405]

BELL, D., and others. A Biographical dictionary of French political leaders since 1870. Hemel Hempstead, Herts, Harvester Wheatsheaf, 1989; New York, Simon & Schuster, 1990. 600p. £85. $85. ISBN: 0719810148; 0130846902.

Prepared under the auspices of the Association for the Study of Modern and Contemporary France.

c. short, readable biographies of leading men and women in French politics since Napoleon III. Basic biographical data is combined with an explanation of why the figure is important to our understanding of French politics, and the shaping of modern France. Helpful appendices list presidents, prime ministers and important party leaders. Intended for students, the general reader and researchers. *Class No:* 320(44)

Spain

[1406]

DONAGHY, P.J. and NEWTON, M.T. Spain: a guide to political and economic institutions. Cambridge, Cambridge University Press, 1987. xiii,242p. £27.50. ISBN: 0521300320.

A guide to the major political and economic institutions established in Spain since the death of Franco. 14 chapters: 1. Introduction: political and economic background - 2. The Constitution of 1978 - 3. The monarchy - 4. Parliament - 5-8. Government and order - 9. Public sector enterprise - 10. Political parties - 11. Trade unions - 12. Business and professional organizations - 13. Financial organizations - 14. Geneal conclusions. All chapters are subdivided. 2 appendices (Chronological resumé of Spanish history since 1939; Elections since 1977). Select bibliography, p.229-232. Index of institutions, p.233-242. *Class No:* 320(460)

USSR

[1407]

McAULEY, M. Soviet politics, 1917-1991. New York, Oxford University Press, 1992. 160p. $21.95. ISBN: 0198780664.

An analysis of the developments which sustained, and then finally undermined, the Communist regime: revolution - state-building - party rule - terror - elections. *Class No:* 320(47)

[1408]

V.I. Lenin: an annotated bibliography of English-language sources to 1980. Egan, D.R., and others, eds. Metuchen, N.J., Scarecrow Press, 1982. 516p. $39.50; £29.65. ISBN: 0810815265.

Aims to include all English-language publications irrespective of place of publication or author's creed. Most entries have short annotations and the most important publications are marked with an asterisk. Book reviews are listed along with the works they review. Valuable for the study of 20th century Russian political science and history as

....(contd.)

well as for the study of Lenin. 'A quite extraordinarily detailed guide to the English end product' (*Library review*, Winter 1983, p.305). '... not only a welcome but even an indispensable contribution to Russian studies...' (*Choice*, v.20(7), March 1983, p.955). *Class No:* 320(47)

Asia

[1409]

KIM, E. *and* **ZIRING, L.,** *eds.* **The Asian political dictionary.** Santa Barbara, CA., ABC-Clio, 1986. xx, 438p. tables, maps. $40. £32.95. (*Clio dictionaries in political science 10.*) ISBN: 0874363683.

Focuses on south, southeastern and eastern Asia, including the Indian Ocean, 27 countries and territories in all. Over 3000 terms arranged in 8 chapters (political geography - political culture and ideology - political parties and movements - political institutions and processes - militarism and the armed forces - modernization and development - diplomacy - international relations and conflict). Maps, tables, index. *Class No:* 320(5)

[1410]

Who's who in Asian and Australasian politics. London, Bowker-Saur, 1991. xvii,475p. £99. $175.

In 2 parts: part 1 has over 3000 biographies of politicians in the top and midle ranking levels, from over 25 countries; pt.2 is a political directory and index. *Class No:* 320(5)

Japan

[1411]

WARD, R.E. *and* **WATANABE, H. Japanese political science:** a guide to Japanese reference and research materials. Rev. ed. Ann Arbor, Mich., University of Michigan Press, 1961. (Reprinted Greenwood Press, 1978). xi, 210p. tables, maps. $59.75. ISBN: 0313204365.

1759 annotated items in 27 sections, each with an introduction (1. Bibliographies - 2. General reference works - 3. Periodicals - 4-27. Subject aspects (*e.g.* Constitutional law; National diet; Allied occupation of Japan). Author's name in entry is first given in romanized form, then in Japanese characters, and similarly with title. Cross-references. Index of authors and editors. *Class No:* 320(52)

Asia—Middle & Near East

[1412]

SHIMONI, Y., *ed.* **A Political dictionary of the Arab world.** Rev. ed. New York, Macmillan, 1988. 520p. illus., tables, charts, maps. $50; £40. ISBN: 0029164222.

Revised and updated version of *Political dictionary of the Middle East in the 20th century* (1972 & 1974).

600 entries prepared by a team of specialists from Tel Aviv University Centre for Middle Eastern and African Studies. Covers 21 Arab countries. Entries are arranged A-Z on a wide range of subjects from biographies to national political histories, movements and conflicts. 'Generally well researched and documented, the book is a useful tool for a wide ranging audience...' (*Library journal*, 15 February 1988p. p.161). *Class No:* 320(53+56)

[1413]

ZIRING, L. The Middle East political dictionary. Rev.ed. Santa Barbara, CA., ABC-Clio, 1992. 401p. tables, maps. $56.50. (*Clio dictionaries in political science, 5.*) ISBN: 0874366127.

Over 300 entries arranged in topical chapters (political geography - Islam - ethnicity - political parties and movements - the Arab-Israeli conflict - diplomacy and conflict). Cross-references. *Class No:* 320(53+56)

Israel

[1414]

ROLEF, S.H., *ed.* **A Political dictionary of the State of Israel.** 2nd ed. New York, Macmillan, 1993. 417p. illus (75 half-tones; 15 line-drawings), tables, charts, maps. $65. ISBN: 0028971930.

Part-successor to Shimoni and Levine's *Political dictionary of the Middle East in the 20th century* (Rev. ed., 1974).

*c.*500 signed articles covering all aspects of Israel's political life, including political institutions, events, personalities and terminology. Length of entries varies from single-paragraph definitions to 10,000-word analyses. Contributors are prominent Israeli academics, journalists and politicians. '... succinct discussions of Israeli political issues ... and explanations of the specialized terminology and slogans of Israeli political discourse'. (*Choice,* v.25(8), April 1988, p.1224). A reprint of the first edition except for the addition of a 68-page supplement covering the period 1987 through December 1992. *Class No:* 320(569.4)

Africa

Bibliographies

[1415]

A Bibliography for the study of African politics. Waltham, Mass., Crossroads Press (new African Studies Association), 1977-. v.1-.

Published so far are:-

1, by R. Shaw and R.L. Sklar (1st published 1973 by University of California Press), 1977.

2, by A.C. Solomon, 1978.

3, by Eric Siegal, 1983. $18. ISBN 0918456479.

V.1 has 3951 entries for monographs and periodical articles, almost all in English and covering the period up to 1970. Complex arrangement: 2 main divisions - General works; Regions and states - with 90 sections. Extensive 30-page index. 'An excellent reference tool for anyone interested in African affairs' (*RQ,* v.13(2), Winter 1973, p.179).

V.2, also with over 300 entries and similarly arranged, is a supplement to v.1, covering the period 1971-75. V.3 is a second supplement. *Class No:* 320(6)(01)

Encyclopaedias & Dictionaries

[1416]

PHILLIPS, C.S. The African political dictionary. Santa Barbara, CA., ABC-Clio, 1984. xxvii,245p. $34; £25.25. (*Clio dictionaries in political science, 6.*) ISBN: 0874360366.

Over 225 terms grouped in chapters by subject, subdivided A-Z. Each term has a 'definition' and a

....(contd.)
'significance' paragraph, highlighting the historical, geographical, economic, sociological, philosophical and religious characteristics. Cross-references. Index.
Class No: 320(6)(03)

[1417]
Political and economic encyclopedia of Africa. Arnold, G., *ed.* Harlow, Longman, 1993. x,342p. £80. ISBN: 0582209951.

Four types of entry in A-Z order - country (54 countries and islands) - organizations - individuals (personalities and political parties) - general (problems or topics on more than one country). Cross-references. Cut-off point is early 1993. Index, p.323-342. *Class No:* 320(6)(03)

Handbooks & Manuals
[1418]
COOK, C. *and* **KILLINGRAY, D. African political facts since 1945.** 2nd ed. London, Macmillan; New York, Facts on File, 1990. 288p. £33. $35.00. £45. (*Macmillan historical and political facts.*) ISBN: 0333439856, UK; 0816024189, US.

First published 1983.

A chronology of key events is followed by sections on governors and heads of state - chief ministers - constitutions and parliaments - political parties - trade unions - armed forces and coups - foreign affairs and treaties - population and ethnic groups - basic economic statistics - biographies. Bibliography, p.257. Index, p.258-263.
Class No: 320(6)(035)

Biographies
[1419]
WISEMAN, J.A. Political leaders in Black Africa: a biographical dictionary of the major politicians since Independence. Aldershot, Hants, Edward Elgar, 1991. xxiii,248p. £50. ISBN: 1852780479.

Alphabetical list of entries and list of abbreviations and acronyms precedes. Short biographical essays on 485 politicians who have shaped the development of Africa since Independence. Entries vary in length from ½p. to a page. Chronology of major events since 1960. Geographical index,p.247-8. *Class No:* 320(6)(092)

South Africa
[1420]
GASTROW, S, *ed.* **Who's who in South African politics** 4th ed. Munich & London, Hans Zell, 1993. xxxviii,333p. illus. £55. ISBN: 1873836066.

1st published 1985.

119 profiles (1000-word essays) of people involved in South African politics on both the left and the right in and out of Parliament. Each profile ends with a list of sources. Includes list of politicians who appeared in previous editions but who no longer commanded a place. *Class No:* 320(680)

America — Central
[1421]
GUNSON, P., *and others.* **The Dictionary of contemporary politics of Central America and the Caribbean.** London, Routledge, 1991. 416p. illus. maps. £35. $45. ISBN: 0415024455.

A guide to the most important organizations, personalities, events and themes in the contemporary politics of the area. Countries covered are Mexico, Guatemala, Belize, British Honduras, El Salvador, Nicaragua, Costa Rica, Panama, Cuba, Dominican Republic, Haiti, Jamaica, Trinidad & Tobago, Barbados, Grenada, St. Vincent, St. Lucia, Dominica, St. Kitt's, Nevis, Antigua and Puerto Rico. 'This excellent reference work by three British journalists who specialize in Latin America' (*Library journal*, 15 April 1992, p.43-44). *Class No:* 320(728)

Latin America

Dictionaries
[1422]
ROSSI, E.E. *and* **PLANO, J.C. Latin America: a political dictionary.** Santa Barbara, CA., ABC-Clio, 1980. 242p. $56.50. ISBN: 0874366089.

Replaces *The Latin American political dictionary.*

10 chapters, each with entries A-Z (1. Geography, population and social structure - 2. Historical perspective - 3. Political culture and ideology - 4. Revolutionary and counter-revolutionary forces - 5. Political parties, pressure groups and elections - 6. The military - 7. Governmental institutions and processes - 8. Economic modernization and political development - 9. International law and organization - 10. United States-Latin American relations). Each entry is in two parts: definition, aim, etc. (plus cross-references); significance. Detailed analytical index. 'Entries are concise yet clearly written and convey essential introductory information' (*Choice* v.30 (10) June 1993 p.1608). *Class No:* 320(729.99)(038)

USA

Reviews & Abstracts
[1423]
United States political science documents. Pittsburgh, Pa., Industrial Applications Center, University of Pittsburgh, 1976-. v.1-. Annual. $395. ISSN: 01486063.

V.13 (published 1988) has over 3400 abstracts of political and social science articles from *c.*150 journals. Each issue is in two parts: Part 1 has a list of journals. Author/contributor index, rotated subject descriptor index, and subject index. Part 2 has the document description listing (abstracts). Also online from 1975-. *Class No:* 320(73)(048)

Almanacs
[1424]
JEE, S., *ed.* **The World almanac of US politics, 1993-1995.** New York, World Almanac (distributed by St. Martin's Press), 1993. 416p. $29.95. ISBN: 0886877091. ISSN: 10431535.

Designed to contain everything every citizen should know about who and what governs the country. Mainly a state-by-state directory of senators and representatives, with several

....(contd.)

lines of personal and political biography, committee memberships, voting data, as well as address and telephone number. '... a handy, inexpensive ready-reference guide to US government' (*Reference books bulletin,* 15 September 1989, v.86(2), p.211), of the 1989 ed.
Class No: 320(73)(059)

Biographies

[1425]

American political scientists: a dictionary. Utter, G.H. *and* Lockhart, C., *eds.* Westport, CT, Greenwood Press, 1993. 362p. $85. ISBN: 0313278490.

Lists 171 political scientists who represent the origins and early years of the academic discipline, as well as the contemporary period. Entries arranged in A-Z order by name and are 2 to 3 pages each in length. Focus is on main themes, theories and major works of each scholar, and the most important publications by and about them are listed. Select bibliography. Appendices list the political scientists by university and by major field. *Class No:* 320(73)(092)

America—South

Encyclopaedias & Dictionaries

[1426]

GUNSON, P., *and others.* **The Dictionary of contemporary politics of South America.** London, Routledge, 1989. xi,314p. 14 maps. £19.95. (*Dictionaries of contemporary politics.*) ISBN: 0415028086.

A guide to the most important organizations, figures, events and themes in the contemporary politics of South America. Cross-references. Countries covered: Chile, Argentina, Paraguay, Colombia, Venezuela, Ecuador, Bolivia, Peru, Uruguay, Brazil, Surinam and Guyana. Includes list of entries by country, p.309-314.
Class No: 320(8)(03)

[1427]

Political and economic encyclopedia of South America and the Caribbean. Calvert, P., *ed.* New York, St. James Press, 1991. v,363p. Maps (on end papers). $85. (*Longman current affairs.*) ISBN: 1858621601, US; 0582085284, UK.

A chronology precedes the main A-Z listing. Includes countries and people. Length of entries varies (*eg* Brazilia (nearly 7 columns); Castro (3 columns); CARECOM (Caribbean Community and Common Market) (55 col.). General index, p.355-63. *Class No:* 320(8)(03)

Australasia & Oceania

[1428]

Who's who in Asian and Australasian politics. London, Bowker-Saur, 1991. xvii,475p. £99. $175.

In 2 parts: Part 1 has over 3000 biographies of politicians in the top and middle ranking levels, from over 25 countries; pt.2 is a political directory and index. *Class No:* 320(9)

Thesauri

[1429]

BECK, C., *and others, comps.* **Political science thesaurus.** Washington, Political Science Association, 1975. (Available from Books Demand UMI). 463p. $117.80. ISBN: 0317102354.

Main section records *c.*6000 terms, each followed by broader, narrower or related terms. 38 major concepts. Permuted and hierarchical indexes. 'An essential reference tool for academic and government libraries' (*Library journal,* v.100(21), 1 December 1975, p.2232).
Class No: 320:025.43

Institutions & Associations

[1430]

BOGDANOR, V., *ed.* **The Blackwell encyclopedia of political institutions.** Oxford, Basil Blackwell Ltd., 1987. xvi, 667p. £45; $65. ISBN: 0631338412.

Contains 247 contributions from 13 Western industrialized countries. As well as political institutions, includes entries on many concepts and on deceased key political thinkers. Entries range from short paragraphs to 4-page articles (e.g., 'Civil rights': 3 cols.; 'European Community': 3 cols.; 'Monnet, Jean': 2 cols). Cross-references. Bibliographical references follow most entries. Contributors focus on their own world plus USSR and Eastern Europe. Index, p.647-667. '... the work is valuable because its main stream approach is more extensive and comprehensive than the various political science dictionaries available.' (*Choice,* v.26(1), September 1988, p.74). *Class No:* 320:061:061.2

Political Theory

[1431]

The Blackwell encyclopaedia of political thought. Miller, D., *ed.* Oxford, Blackwell, 1987. xiii,570p. ISBN: 0631140115.

350 entries, both substantial articles and brief definitions, analysing concepts in political thought that influence the contemporary world, and outlining the thought of leading political theorists, past and present. Mainly Western traditions. Cross-references. 134 contributors. '... a solid reference work' (*Reference books bulletin,* 1987/88, p.591). *Class No:* 320.001

[1432]

—**ASHFORD, N.** *and* **DAVIES, S.** A Dictionary of conservative and libertarian thought. London & New York, Routledge, 1991. 320p. £35; $49.95. ISBN: 0415003024.

Examines the ideas and arguments produced by the intellectual traditions of both conservatism and classical liberalism. 11 signed sections, each with brief bibliographies. An important supplement to the above. *Class No:* 320.001

[1433]

A Companion to contemporary political philosophy. Goodin, R.E. *and* Pettit, P., *eds.* Oxford, Blackwell, 1993. 679p. £60. (*Blackwell companions to philosophy.*) ISBN: 0631179933.

A guide to current thinking, focusing on normative issues. Explores the contribution that different disciplines have made to current debates, analyses political ideologies, and discusses major concepts. *Class No:* 320.001

[1434]
PAREKH, B. **Contemporary political thinkers.** Oxford, Martin Robertson, 1982. x,219p. £17. ISBN: 0855203374.

'Explores the current state of political philosophy as reflected in the writings of some of its ablest practitioners' (*Preface*). Chapters on 7 philosophers (Hannah Arendt - Isiah Berlin - C.B. Macpherson - Herbert Marcuse - Michael Oakeshott - Karl Popper - John Rawls) and a final chapter, 'Some reflections'. Notes (p.202-214) are arranged by chapter and include citations. Bibliography (p.215). Index (p.216-219). *Class No:* 320.001

[1435]
PLANT, R. **Modern political thought.** Oxford, Blackwell, 1991. 352p. £40. ISBN: 0631142231.

Reviews and analyses the major developments in political thought over the past 15 years (legitimacy of the state; rights, justice, power, welfare, equality, etc.). *Class No:* 320.001

Dictionaries

[1436]
PLANO, J., *and others*. **Dictionary of poltical analysis.** 2nd ed. Santa Barbara, CA., ABC-Clio, 1982. xvi, 197p. $17; £20.45. (*Clio dictionaries in political science, 3.*) ISBN: 0874363314.

First published 1973.

A-Z listing of terms, with cross-references. Each major entry is in two parts, a paragraph of definition, followed by a significance paragraph providing illustrations, examples, and applications for each defined concept. Selected bibliography, p.169-184. Index, p.185-197. *Class No:* 320.001(038)

[1437]
RIFF, M., *ed*. **Dictionary of modern political ideologies.** Manchester, Manchester University Press; New York, St. Martin's Press, 1987. xiv, 226p. £27.50; $37.60. ISBN: 071901882x, UK; 0312009283, US.

'... not a dictionary or encyclopedia of political concepts or doctrines ... an attempt to make clear how ideals and principles in fact lie at the heart of our political experience and aspirations.' (*Introduction*). 42 essays arranged A-Z by subject (African nationalism - Anarchism - European integration - Fascism ... Keynesianism - Kuomintang ... Zionism). Short bibliographies of books (author & title only) conclude each essay. R. Scruton's *Dictionary of political thought* (1982) is considered to be better for simple explanations of political concepts and ideologies. *Class No:* 320.001(038)

[1438]
The **Routledge dictionary of twentieth-century political thinkers.** Benewick, R. *and* Green, P., *eds*. London, Routledge, 1992. 244p. £40. $59.95. ISBN: 0415043719.

165 signed articles by over 85 contributors on political theorists (and some practitioners, such as Lenin, Mao, Hitler). Articles vary in length from a sentence to several pages, and each is followed by cross-references and a selected bibliography of primary and secondary works. 'A useful, somewhat revisionist, supplement to other sources ...'(*Choice*, v.31(1), September 1993, p.88). *Class No:* 320.001(038)

[1439]
SCRUTON, R., *ed*. **A Dictionary of political thought.** London, Macmillan Press Ltd., 1982. [7], 499p. £25. ISBN: 0333334396.

'... intention has been to extract, both from active debate, and from the theories and intuitions which surround it, the principle ideas through which modern political beliefs find expression. The emphasis of the dictionary is conceptual rather than factual ...' (*Preface*). Includes over 1000 entries, ranging in length from 100 to 450 words. Includes biographies, but only when they cast light on intellectual conceptions. Cross-references. *Class No:* 320.001(038)

Histories

[1440]
Political thought since 1945: Philosophy, science, ideology. Tivey, L. *and* Wright, A., eds. Cheltenham, Edward Elgar, 1992. 240p. £38.50. ISBN: 1852783117.

Accounts of the views of seven major thinkers - Arendt, Dahl, Habermas, Hayek, Macpherson, Oakeshott and Rawls. An introductory chapter sets out the ideas of other thinkers. *Class No:* 320.001(091)

[1441]
SABINE, G.H. **A History of political theory.** 4th ed., rev. Hinsdale, Ill., Dryden Press, 1973. [xvii], 871p. $34.95. ISBN: 0030803055.

First published 1937.

3 parts: 1. The theory of the city state - 2. The theory of the universal community - 3. The theory of the national state (p.311-849). 36 chapters (35. Communism; 36. Fascism and National Socialism). Each chapter has footnotes and 'Selected bibliography'. Analytical index. Standard textbook, giving acceptable short analyses of major works concerned. *Class No:* 320.001(091)

Islamic Peoples

[1442]
ENAYAT, H. **Modern Islamic political thought:** the response of the Shi'i and Sunni Muslims in the twentieth century. London, Macmillan, 1982. 240p. £14. ISBN: 0333279689.

Aimed at those who wish to understand the often bewildering political situation in the Islamic world. Following a short introduction outlining how the traditional Islamic heritage has affected the development of modern intellectual currents, the author deals with an analysis of the differences and points of agreement between the two groups and also discusses the concept of the Islamic State. '... a lucid and detailed account of the most important religio-political movements in the Islamic world in the 20c. ... sheds valuable light on many of the problems which face the crucial area today.' (*British book news*, November 1982, p.670). *Class No:* 320.001(=95.297)

Middle Ages

[1443]
The **Cambridge history of medieval political thought, c.350-1450.** Burns, J.H., *ed*. Cambridge, Cambridge University Press, 1988. viii,808p. £60. ISBN: 0521243246.

Aims to be the contemporary successor to Gierke and Carlyle. 19 chapters in 5 parts: 1. Foundations; 2. Byzantium; 3. Beginnings: *c*.350-*c*.750; 4. Formation;

....(contd.)

c.750-c.1150; 5. Development: c.1150-1450; Conclusion. Within the parts treatment is largely thematic. Biographies (notes on medieval authors (p.690-777); index of names and persons (p.779-790); analytical subject index (p.791-808). '...quality of scholarship presentation uniformly high'. (*Political studies*, v.37(1). 1989. *Class No:* 320.001"01/14"

Tudor & Stuart Times

[1444]

The Cambridge history of political thought, 1450-1700. Burns, J.H., *ed.* Cambridge, Cambridge University Press, 1991. 800p. £75. ISBN: 0521247160.

A sequel and complement to the above. 21 chapters in 5 parts: 1. Renaissance and counter-renaissance; 2. Religion, civil government, and the debate on constitutions; 3. Absolutism and revolution in the sevemteenth century; 4. The end of Aristotelianism; 5. Natural law and utility. Conclusion. Biographies. Bibliography (for each part). Indexes of names of persons and of subjects. *Class No:* 320.001"1485-1760"

Government

[1445]

Federal systems of the world: a handbook of federal, confederal and autonomy arrangements. Elazar, D.J., *ed.* Harlow, Essex, Longman, 1991. xxx,402p. £69. ISBN: 0582086949.

Based on data collected by the Jerusalem Center for Public Affairs.

Main part is arranged A-Z by countries with federal, federacy/associated state and home rule arrangements (Basic introductory material, standard sections on government structure and the constitution, political dynamics/recent constitutional developments). Bibliography for each country. A second section examines confederal arrangements of ASEAN, Benelux, Caricom, the EC and the Nordic Council and Council of Ministers. '...useful addition to reference collections.'(*International affairs*, v.68(4), October 1992, p.721). *Class No:* 321

Encyclopaedias

[1446]

Encyclopedia of government and politics. Hawkesworth, M. *and* Kogan, M., *eds.* London, Routledge, 1992. 2v.(1404p.). £125. $230 the set. ISBN: 0415030927.

84 detailed essays on theoretical and factual change of the last three decades, arranged under nine main headings (political theory - central concepts - contemporary ideologies - contemporary political systems - political institutions - political forces and political processes - centripetal and centrifugal forces in the nation-state - policy-making and policies - international relations - major issues in contemporary politics). Each topic includes extensive bibliographies and suggestions for further reading. Index of topics and people. 'This up-to-date and well-executed work provides a sound introduction to all aspects of political study' (*Choice*, v.30(7), March 1993, p.1110). *Class No:* 321(031)

Biographies

[1447]

Regents of nations: a systematic chronology of states and their political representatives past and present; a biographical reference book. Truhart, P. München, K.G. Saur, 1984-88. 3v. in 4 (4258p.). Dm960; $525. ISBN: 359810491x.

Part 1. Africa/America; pt.2. Asia/Australia - Oceania; pt.3/1. Middle-, Eastern-, Northern-, Southern-, Southeastern Europe; pt.3/2. Western Europe. Bibliography, index, addenda to parts 103. Includes biographical information on c.30,000 heads of state and premiers from 1000 nations, along with information on territorial and provincial governors of nations back to the Middle Ages. Also includes information on the historical development of present nation states and a review of political structures of the past 5000 years. *Class No:* 321(092)

Japan

Biographies

[1448]

Who's who in Japanese Government, 1988/89. 2nd ed. Tokyo, International Cultural Association, 1988. viii, 414p. ISBN: 4900477028.

Includes a profile of the Japanese political system, Lower House members, Upper House members, Committees of the Lower House, Committees of the Upper House, Political parties organizational charts. Political parties officials, and important addresses and telephone numbers. Index of personal names. *Class No:* 321(52)(092)

Dictatorships

[1449]

SNYDER, L.L. Encyclopedia of nationalism. New York, Paragon House, 1990. 445p. $35. ISBN: 1557781672.

250 scholarly and well-documented entries on movements, theories, proponents, scholars and goals, A-Z. Length of entries varies from a paragraph to 8 pages. Cross-references, but no index. Bibliographies are attached to the main entries and there is a short general bibliography. 'This inexpensive volume fills a gap in the reference literature on a topic of continuing broad interest ...'(*Choice*, v.28(2), October 1990, p.288). *Class No:* 321.6

Fascism

[1450]

LAQUEUR, W., *ed.* Fascism: a reader's guide: analysis, interpretations, bibliography. London, Wildwood House, 1978 (Reprinted by Wildwood House, 1988). x, 478p. £8.95. ISBN: 0704501902.

12 contributors. 6 parts: 1. Some notes towards a comparative study of Fascism in sociological historical perspective - 2. Italy and Germany - 3. Local Fascisms (E. Europe; Latin America; Western Europe) - 4. Fascist ideology - 5. Fascism and the economy - 6. Interpretations. Well documented (*e.g.* Italian Fascism; p.125-50; 77 references). Analytical index. 'The essays are thorough and analytical. They provide an excellent evaluation of the literature' (*Journal of politics*, v.40(2), May 1978, p.567). *Class No:* 321.64

[1451]

—REES, P. Fascism in Britain. Atlantic Highlands, N.Y., Humanities Press, 1980. 243p.

A bibliography of Fascism in Britain, 1023-77. 'An invaluable starting point for research digging, most likely to be used at university level' (*Choice,* v.18(8), April 1981, p.1077). *Class No:* 321.64

[1452]

REES, P. **Fascism and pre-Fascism:** a bibliography of the extreme right in Europe, 1890-1945. Brighton, Sussex., Harvester Press; Totowa, N.J. Barnes & Noble, 1984. xxii, 330p. £65. ISBN: 0710803729 (UK); 0389204722 (US).

A select bibliography on the ideology and practice of the extreme right, including books, journal articles and dissertations published since 1945. An introductory chapter precedes a chapter on Fascism generally and chapters on East and West European countries (*e.g.* Germany, p.233-315). Individual chapters focus on parties, movements and prominent figures, presented roughly in chronological order. Index of names, p.316-330. " ... the first useful general bibliography on European Fascism" (*Choice* v.22(6) February 1985 p.798). *Class No:* 321.64

Internal Relations

Jews

Bibliographies

[1453]

SINGERMAN, R. **Anti-semitic propaganda:** an annotated bibliography and research guide. New York, Garland, 1982. 448p. $60. (*Garland reference library of social science, 112.*) ISBN: 0824092708.

A major reference tool. Comprehensive, with informative but not evaluative annotations. Arranged in two unequal sections. The first section lists *c.*2000 English-language works (books, pamphlets, and dissertations) in chronological order from 1870 to the present. Includes one holding institution for each entry and reviews of major works. The second smaller section is a research guide of works on anti-semitism classified by subjects. 'An important acquisition for every college library'. (*Choice,* v.20(3), November 1982, p.412). *Class No:* 323(=924)(01)

Minorities

[1454]

ASHWORTH, G., *ed.* **World minorities.** Sunbury-on-Thames, Mddx., Quartermaine House Ltd., 1977-78. 2v. (167p. 192p.).

V.1 has 44 groups, A-Z: 1. The Adivasis: the 'scheduled tribes' of India - 2. The Afars and the Assas ... 8. The Bedouin ... 10. The Bretons ... 13. The Catalans ... 17. The Corsicans ... 28. The Kashmiri ... 31. The Maoris of New Zealand ... 34. Pakistan's Hindus ... 43. The Ukrainians - 44. Yugoslav's minorities. Contributed by various hands; each contribution has selected bibliography. Index, p.163-167. *Class No:* 323.1

[1455]

—ASHWORTH, G., *ed.* World minorities in the eighties: a third volume in the series. Sunbury-on-Thames, Quartermain House Ltd., 1980. xvii, 174p. £4.25. ISBN: 0905878117.

37 groups, A-Z: (1. Aboriginal peoples of Siberia ... 10. Fiji ... 22. Migrant workers in the Gulf States ... 37. The Welsh in Argentina). Index, p.171-174. *Class No:* 323.1

[1456]

World directory of minorities. Minorities Rights Group, *ed.* Harlow, Essex, Longman; Chicago, Ill., St. James Press, 1990. xvi,427p. 29 maps. £78; $85. (*Longman international reference.*) ISBN: 1558620168, US; 0582036194, UK.

Updates the MRG's *World minorities* (Quartermaine House Ltd., Minorities Rights Group, 1977-80. 3v.) and their 80 plus MRG reports.

11 regional groupings, each region introduced by Patrick Thornberry. Within the groups, more than 150 ethnic or radical minorities are listed, A-Z, with a few salient facts (alternative names - location - population - percentage of population - religion - language) in 200-5000 words. Appendices are abstracts from original documents. Index, p.419-427. Essential for locating individual minority groups. *Class No:* 323.1

Europe—Eastern

Handbooks & Manuals

[1457]

HORAK, S.M., *and others.* **Eastern European national minorities, 1919-1980:** a handbook. Littleton, Col., Libraries Unlimited Inc., 1985. xv, 353p. tables. $47.50. ISBN: 0872874168.

Covers the treatment of national minorities; statistical data; the political, social, economic and educational aspects and changes that have occurred during the 3 periods: Interwar - World War II - Post-World War II. 10 chapters, the first 9 of which are each divided into 'Historical summary' and 'Bibliography', the bibliographies being annotated, selective, international, and representing different views and interpretations. Chapters: 1. Eastern Europe national minorities, 1919-1980 - 2. National minorities in Poland, 1919-1980 - 3/6 & 8/9 cover Czechoslovakia, Hungary, Romania, Yugoslavia, Bulgaria and Albania - 7. The Slovene and Croat minorities in Italy and Austria, 1945-1980 - 10. National research centers in Eastern European countries. Author/short title index, p.331-353. *Class No:* 323.1(401)(035)

USA

Bibliographies

[1458]

COUTTS, B.E., *comp.* **Ethnics in American society.** In *Booklist,* v.80(21), July 1990, p.2109-2112.

A briefly annotated bibliography highlighting some of the best recent reference sources on ethnic minorities in American society, with special emphasis on African Americans, Asian Americans and Hispanic Americans. *Class No:* 323.1(73)(01)

[1459]

Minorities in America: the annual bibliography, 1976-. Miller, W.C., *ed.* Pennsylvania State University Press, 1985-?. Irregular. 1976 ed. published 1985, $100. ISSN: 07482302.

Follows Miller's *A comprehensive bibliography for the study of American minorities* (1977).

The 1976 ed. has *c.*7500 entries drawn from over 900 journals, and also including books, government publications and dissertations. Arrangement is in 41 subject groups, and includes people of European background as well as coloured people, indigenous and immigrant. Annotations of *c.*100 words. Author index. *Class No:* 323.1(73)(01)

[1460]

MOMENI, J.A. Demography of racial and ethnic minorities in the United States: an annotated bibliography with a review essay. Westport, CT. Greenwood Press, 1984. 293p. $35. (*Bibliographies and indexes in sociology, 2.*) ISBN: 0313239754.

688 entries for books, periodical articles, dissertations and master's theses. Except for Jewish Americans, white American ethnic groups are excluded. Includes a 40-page review essay giving an overview of historical, political and social events affecting minorities. Author and minority/subject index. *Class No:* 323.1(73)(01)

[1461]

—MOMENI, J.A. Housing and racial/ethnic minority status in the United States: an annotated bibliography with a review essay. Westport, CT., Greenwood Press, 1987. 310p. $45. (*Bibliographies and indexes in sociology, 8.*) ISBN: 0313248206.

1007 citations to monographs and journal articles on housing for minorities, with summaries or abstracts for each title. *Class No:* 323.1(73)(01)

Yearbooks & Directories

[1462]

Minority organizations: a national directory. 4th ed. Garrett Park, MD., Garrett Park Press, 1992. 690p. $50. ISBN: 0912048301.

First published 1978.

The directory's real strength is in the large number of regional and local groups it lists, as well as the national ones. Includes 7700 active organizations and 2800 'lost' ones. *Class No:* 323.1(73)(058)

Resistance & Revolution

[1463]

DEGENHARDT, H.W., *ed.* **Revolutionary and dissident movements:** an international guide. 3rd ed. London, Longman Group, 1991 (Distributed in US and Canada by Gale Research Co.). 408p. £85. $145 (*A Keesing's reference publication.*) ISBN: 0582009863, UK; 0810320568, US.

First published 1983 as *Political dissent.*

Details of the activities, leadership, policy and affiliation of more than 1000 underground movements, national liberation or secessionist movements and human rights groups, arranged A-Z, by country (Afghanistan ... Zimbabwe - International revolutionary groupings). Coverage is through mid-1987. A brief introductory section to each country describes the political realities there, then details the various dissident groups. Select bibliography,

.... (contd.)
p.427-430, arranged general, then by region, and A-Z by author. Detailed index of countries, individuals and revolutionary organizations, p.433-466. Aim is to up-date 5-yearly. 'Better country balance than *The Radical right ...*' (*Reference books bulletin,* 1 September 1988). *Class No:* 323.2

[1464]

JESSUP, J.E. A Chronology of conflict and revolution, 1945-1985. Westport, CT., Greenwood Press, 1989. x,943p. $85. £73.10. ISBN: 0313243085.

The chronology covers the period September 1945 to December 30, 1985. Brief information is given under the entries for each date. No cross-references. A glossary of abbreviations, and an index (p.847-942) complete the work. *Class No:* 323.2

[1465]

MUNRO, D. *and* **DAY, A.J. A World record of major conflict areas.** London, Edward Arnold Publishers Ltd.,; Chicago, Ill., St. James Press, 1990. [vi],374p. maps. £45. $85. ISBN: 0340522976, UK; 1558620664, US.

'The purpose is to describe and elucidate, in an easy reference format, some 28 current conflicts in different parts of the world' (*Preface*). Arranged in 5 regions (1. Africa - 2. Middle East - 3. Asia/Far East - 4. Americas - 5. Europe), each subdivided by country. Chapters on specific conflicts follow a standard structure, beginning with a map and profile of the relevant country or territory, historical background, current status of conflict with chronology of events, followed by directory sections. General bibliography. p.374. *Class No:* 323.2

[1466]

SZAJKOWSKI, B. Encyclopedia of conflicts, disputes and flashpoints in Eastern Europe, Russia and the successor states. Harlow, Essex, Longman. 1993. 416p. illus. £85. (*Longman current affairs.*) ISBN: 058221002x. *Class No:* 323.2

Bibliographies

[1467]

BLACKEY, R. Modern revolutions and revolutionists: a comprehensive guide to the literature. Rev. ed. Santa Barbara, CA., ABC-Clio, 1982. 488p. $55.75. (*War/peace bibliography series, 17.*) ISBN: 0874363306.

First published 1976.

Aims to gather together the most important English-language writings on some 140 revolutions, most occurring in the 19th and 20th centuries. Following an introductory essay the chapters cite scholarly articles, books, collections of documents, and published primary sources. After the first chapter, 'Concepts and aspects', the arrangement of chapters is chronological order, the modern period being sub-divided geographically. Author/editor and subject indexes. Chronology of revolutions. '... a laudable accomplishment ...' (*Choice,* v.21(1), September 1983, p.58). *Class No:* 323.2(01)

[1468]

BOWMAN, J.S., *and others*. **Professional dissent:** an annotated bibliography. New York, Garland, 1984. 322p. $39. (*Public affairs and administration series, 2. Garland reference library of social science, 128.*) ISBN: 0824092171.

The subject is 'whistle-blowing' in government and business. The author's definition is 'an employee who reveals information about illegal, inefficient, or wasteful action that endangers the health, safety, or freedom of the public'. Nearly 1400 entries, covering books, periodical and newspaper articles, and government reports, are organized in chapters on business, government, science and engineering, selected professions, etc. Literature included is mainly US, and published during the past 15 years to 1982. More than half the entries are annotated. A resource section lists basic journals, directories, etc., and there are listings of works that offer personal guidance to employees, and relevant organizations. *Class No:* 323.2(01)

[1469]

From radical left to extreme right: a bibliography of current periodicals of protest, controversy, advocacy, or dissent, with dispassionate content-summaries to guide librarians and other educators. Skidmore, G. *and* Spahn, T.J. 3rd ed., completely rev. Metuchen, N.J., Scarecrow Press, 1987. 503p. $59.50. ISBN: 0810819678.

First published 1967; 2nd ed. 1970-76.

280 annotated entries for periodicals with political content, grouped under 21 general chapter headings. Each chapter is introduced by a brief essay about the subject area and its publications. Content-summaries are preceded by such information as address, editor, price, frequency of publication and indexing. Geographical, subject, and title/editor/publisher indexes. *Choice*, October 1987, p.290, reports that it has only 280 detailed entries as against 1200 in the 2nd ed. but many others are listed, and that it is 'A commendable attempt, but far from successful'.
Class No: 323.2(01)

Terrorism & Persecution

[1470]

SCHMID, A.P. **Political terrorism:** a research guide to concepts, theories, data bases and literature. 2nd ed. New Brunswick, N.J., Transaction Books, 1988. 625p. $59.95. ISBN: 0444856595.

First published 1984.

Arranged in 4 main sections, the first examining the major concepts, definitions and elements of political violence and terrorism; the second on major theoretical conceptions, with detailed bibliographies; the third discusses global databases available and includes an appendix listing every major terrorist group by country, with description, leadership, ideological position, etc. The final part is an annotated bibliography. *Choice* (v.22(2), October 1984, p.254), on which this entry is based, comments on the book's uneven quality but considers it an important reference work. *Class No:* 323.28

[1471]

SOBEL, L.A., *ed*. **Political terrorism.** Oxford, Clio Press, 1975-78. 2v. [vii], 309p.; [vii], 279p.). £10.50 each; £18.90 the set. ISBN: 0871962322, v.1; 0871962330, v.2.

'The word terrorism is employed to specify acts of violence for political coercion' (Introduction, v.1). Each volume has 8 contributors. A detailed, factual record, under countries and episodes. V.1 covers the first half of the 1960s up to the 1970s (The Middle East ... Yugoslavia. International action). V.2: Terrorists and others - The Middle East - Latin America - The United States - Other areas. Each vol. has a detailed analytical index. Helpfully assembles scattered sources, being based largely on *Facts on File* weekly reports. *Class No:* 323.28

[1472]

—LAQUEUR, W. Terrorism. London, Weidenfeld & Nicolson, 1977. [vii], 277p. £12.50. $15. ISBN: 0316514705.

Has 5 chapters: 1. The origins - 2. The philosophy of the bomb - 3. The sociology of terrorism - 4. Interpretations of terrorism - 5. Terrorism today. Notes. Bibliography, p.257-64 (grouped). Analytical index, p.265-77. *Class No:* 323.28

[1473]

WILKINSON, P. *and* STEWART, A.M., *eds*. **Contemporary research on terrorism.** Aberdeen, Aberdeen University Press, 1987. xx,634p. £45. ISBN: 0080350682.

The published proceedings of a conference held at Aberdeen University in April, 1986.

6 chapters, each subdivided: 1. Definitional and conceptional aspects - 2. Moral and religious aspects - 3. Trends and pattern in the history of terror - 4. Behavioural aspects - 5. Terrorism and the media - 6. National and international responses. A quarter of the book is devoted to chapter 3. 36 expert contributors. Selected English-language bibliography, p.599-623. Name index, p.625-631; index of terrorist movements and groups, p.633-634. ' .. wide coverage of facts and of sophisticated arguments; (*International affairs*, v.64(2), Spring 1988, p.274-275). *Class No:* 323.28

Bibliographies

[1474]

EL-SHERBINI, M. **Terrorism: current readings.** In *RSR*, v.18(4), 1990, p.49-63,48.

91 entries in sections: general works, psychological aspects, religious aspects, combating terrorism, periodicals, online batabases, and bibliographies. *Class No:* 323.28(01)

[1475]

LAKOS, A. **International terrorism:** a bibliography. London, Mansell; Boulder, Col., Westview, 1986. xii, 481p. £30. $37.50. ISBN: 072011862x, UK; 0813371570, US.

Claims to be the 'definitive bibliography of the literature of terrorism'. Includes over 5600 entries of English-language materials covering terrorist activities over the past two decades. No annotations. Arrangement of entries primarily by subject: 1. Reference works (sub-divided by form) - 2. General works - 3. Theories of terrorism - 4. Psychological and social aspects of terrorism - 5. Strategies and tactics of terrorism - aspects - 6. Counter measures to terrorism - 7. Domestic and international law aspects - 8. Media and terrorism - 9. Nuclear terrorism threat - 10. Geographical, subdivided by regions and then countries. Author index,

....(contd.)
p.417-445; subject index, p.447-481. '... easy-to-read, handsome mixture of type faces and point sizes, and a modest purchase price.' (*Choice,* April 1987, p.1201). *Class No:* 323.28(01)

[1476]
—LAKOS, A. Terrorism, 1980-1990: a bibliography. Boulder, CO, Westview Press, 1991. x,443p. $55. ISBN: 0813380359.
5850 entries in the same format as the above. Chapters 2-9 deal with broad subject categories; chapter 10: Geographical subdivision. *Class No:* 323.28(01)

[1477]
MICKOLUS, E., *comp*. The Literature of terrorism: a selectively annotated bibliography. Westport, CT., Greenwood Press, 1980. xi,553p. $67.95. ISBN: 0313222657.
3395 entries, mostly annotated. Sectionalised topics (*e.g.* the responses to terrorism; relationship between terrorism and the media and literature); also country sections. Some significant French, German and Italian titles included. Well indexed. 'Highly recommended for academic and large public libraries' (*Library journal*, 15 January 1981, p.136-7, on which the above annotation is partly based). Adversely reviewed in *Choice* (v.18(10), May 1981, p.1238), which finds the annotations sparse and of very little help, and the publication expensive. *Class No:* 323.28(01)

[1478]
MICKOLUS, E., *comp*. Terrorism, 1980-1987: a selectively annotated bibliography. Westport, CT., Greenwood Press, 1988. ix,314p. $55; £42.25. (*Bibliographies and indexes in law and political science, no.8.*) ISBN: 0313262489.
Concentrates on material written in the 1980s. 'In addition to surveying journalistic, social scientific and traditional historical studies in some dozen languages, the book also includes fictional literature of terrorism' (Advert.). *Class No:* 323.28(01)

[1479]
—MICKOLUS, E. Terrorism, 1988-1991: a chronology of events and a selectively annotated bibliography. Westport, CT., Greenwood Press, 1993. 916p. $125. (*(Bibliographies and indexes in military studies,6).*.) ISBN: 0313289700.
Together with the above, aims to provide the most comprehensive bibliography on terrorist violence available in print. This vol. is in 3 parts: Update on incidents between 1960 and 1987 - Review of the incidents, 1988-91 - Bibliography of books and journal articles (including fiction) in many languages. Highly commended in *Choice*(v.31(2), October 1993, p.270). *Class No:* 323.28(01)

[1480]
MILLER, R. 'The Literature of terrorism'. In *Terrorism,* v.11(1), 1988, p.63-87.
12 notes and 33 references, A-Z by author, follow the text of the literature review, dealing with traditional literature, historical studies, normative-judicial/legal studies, behaviourist literature, psychological studies, socio-economic studies, and public policy studies.
Class No: 323.28(01)

[1481]
ONTIVEROS, S.R., *ed*. Global terrorism: a historical bibliography. Santa Barbara, CA., ABC-Clio, 1986. xiii, 168p. $49.50. (*ABC-Clio research guides, no. 16.*) ISBN: 0874364531.
598 abstracts of periodical articles published between 1965 and 1985, drawn from the publisher's history database. Includes some articles in foreign languages. Emphasis is on post-World War II terrorism generally. Arranged in 7 geographic chapters and including topics such as the use of terrorism as a means of political or economic coercion, terrorist groups, terrorist conspiracies by nations, and types and uses of terrorism. Lengthy, clearly written abstracts. Subject index, p.115-139; author index, p.141-144; chronology of terrorist events, p.145-168. 'Useful starting place for research on a timely topic'. (*Library journal,* v.111(15), 1 September 1986, p.190). *Class No:* 323.28(01)

[1482]
SCHECHTERMAN, B. *and* SLANN, M. 'Political terrorism, 1981-1987'. In *Choice,* v.26(3), November 1988, p.444-452.
Emphasises recent study in the last decade or so, although it does not purport to be all-inclusive. 82 works arranged A-Z by author follow the bibliographical essay.
Class No: 323.28(01)

Encyclopaedias

[1483]
LENTZ, H. M. Assassinations and executions: an encyclopedia of political violence, 1865-1986. Jefferson, N.C., McFarland & Company, 1988. 275p. $29.95 £22.45. ISBN: 0899503128, US; 1558621008, UK.
Aims to present concise worldwide reference to political assassinations, political executions, and also unsuccessful attempts against major figures. Chronological arrangement. Entries detail the manner, the motive, the assailant (when known) brief biographical information on the victims, the immediate effects on the political climate of the day, and in some cases, the final fate of the assassin. Index to personal and country names. *Class No:* 323.28(031)

[1484]
THACKRAH, J.R. Encyclopedia of terrorism and political violence. London, Routledge & Kegan Paul, 1987. xi, 308p. £16.95. $35. ISBN: 0710206593.
Designed to provide information about theories and terms used in the rapidly growing academic study of terrorism and political violence. 200 entries of which about half focus on specific events, individuals, groups and nations. Virtually all entries relate to the post-World War II era, and vary in length from about 500 to 1000 words. Arranged A-Z (Abu Nidal ... Zimbabwe African People's Union (ZAPU). References and select bibliography of books and articles from the 1970s to 1986, p.290-294, with 'see also' references also after entries. Index, p.295-308. '... will be of use to researchers studying terrorism and to anyone trying to make some sense of terrorist activities reported in the daily press'. (*Reference books bulletin,* 1 March 1988, p.1119). *Class No:* 323.28(031)

Yearbooks & Directories

[1485]
JANKE, P. *and* SIM, R. **Guerrilla and terrorist organisations:** a world directory and bibliography. Brighton, Sussex, Harvester Press, 1983. 560p. £85. ISBN: 0710800134.

Brief descriptions of almost 600 violent intergovernmental organizations worldwide, grouped by region and country of origin. Introductions to the geographical sections also list the major analytical and historical works on the subjects, providing a useful bibliography. List of organizations cited, but no other index. 'This comprehensive work is to be praised for its thoroughness and detail and for the clarity of its organization'. (*Choice,* v.21(8), April 1984, p.1112, 1114). *Class No:* 323.28(058)

[1486]
ROSIE, G. **The Directory of international terrorism.** Edinburgh, Mainstream Publishing Co. (Edinburgh) Ltd., 1986. 310p. £14.95. ISBN: 1851580212.

Surveys more than a century of revolution, terror and counter-terror. A long introduction on terrorism (p.13-36) with 20 references, is followed by an A-Z listing of people (terrorists, people terrorized), operations, etc. Entries vary in length from a few lines to a page. Up-to-date basic information that is not easily available elsewhere. Select bibliography, p.307-310. 'A ready reference guide to the major events and players, but its lack of an index and sparse and inconsistant use of alphabetical cross-references diminish usefulness for this purpose'. (*Choice,* April 1987, p.1203). *Class No:* 323.28(058)

Chronologies

[1487]
MICKOLUS, E.F., *and others*. **International terrorism in the 1980s:** a chronology of events. Iowa State University, 1989-. 2v.(v.1:541p.). V.1. $49.95. ISBN: 0813800242 V.1; 0813801729 v.2.

Continues the author's *Transnational terrorism: ... 1968-79* (1981).

V.1. covers 1980-1983; V.2. will cover 1984 - 1987. Comprehensive descriptions of terrorist incidents throughout the world, the length of the descriptions varying from a few lines to several pages. Sources are not indicated. 2 appendices to V.1. (I. lists terrorist groups; II. is a reprint of ITERATE 3 data codebook). *Class No:* 323.28(090)

Elections

Bibliographies

[1488]
CATT, H. **'Diverse routes to electoral comprehension'.** In *Parliamentary affairs.* v.42(1), January 1989, p.123-127.

A review article listing 8 items on electoral studies. *Class No:* 324(01)

Handbooks & Manuals

[1489]
ARMS, T.S. *and* RIDLEY, E., *eds*. **World elections on file.** New York, Facts on File, 1987. 2v.(loose-leaf), with quarterly up-date. $195 pa. ISBN: 0816017662.

.... (contd.)
A loose-leaf service of information on the latest election results and related political information for 165 nations. *Class No:* 324(035)

[1490]
Elections since 1945: a worldwide reference compendium. Gorvin, I., *ed*. Harlow, Essex, Longman; Chicago, St. James Press, 1989. ix,420p. £85. $150. ISBN: 0582036208, UK; 1558620176, US.

Arranged A-Z by country (Afghanistan ... Zimbabwe) and including all national presidential and legislative elections, in sovereign states, since 1945 or, in the case of former colonies, since accession to independence. Additional section covers elections to the European Parliament. Appendix describes principal systems of proportional representation. *Class No:* 324(035)

[1491]
INTER-PARLIAMENTARY UNION. **Chronicle of parliamentary elections and development; 1 July 1986/30 June 1987.** Geneva, International Centre for Parliamentary Documentation, 1987. 163p. SwF.30.

First published for July 1 1966/June 30, 1967.

Brief notes on developments in various countries, followed by information on 38 parliamentary elections (electoral systems and results), distribution of MPs by sex, profession, age, etc. *Class No:* 324(035)

Maps & Atlases

[1492]
LEONARD, D. *and* NATKIEL, R. **World atlas of elections:** voting patterns in 39 democracies. London, The Economist Publications Ltd., 1986 (distributed in North America by Gale Research Co.). [4] 160p. 197 maps 66 diagr & charts, all in col. £46; $85. ISBN: 0850580897.

Democracies covered were selected on the basis of size (minimum population: 500,000; independence: minimum five years; and freedom: minimum five years). For each country: short essay on government and elections, list of main political parties, election dates, map showing parliamentary seats. Entries vary in length from one to nine pages, mostly two to three pages. Includes brief bibliography of related materials and list of sources of country information (p.5-8). Intended to complement Mackie and Rose's *International almanac of electoral history* (*qv*). Mixed reviews; ' ... an excellent, easy-to-use handbook ...' (*Reference books bulletin, 1986/87, p.149);* ' ... *doubtful whether there is a need for this book' (Parliamentary affairs,* v.41(2), April 1988, p.302); ' ... difficult to assess the readership the work is aimed at. Specialists will feel the need to verify data' (*International affairs,* v.63(4), Autumn 1987, p.725). *Class No:* 324(084.3)

Histories

[1493]
MACKIE, T.T. *and* ROSE, R. **The International almanac of electoral history.** 3rd complete rev. ed. London, Macmillan, 1990. [9], 448p, tables. £50. ISBN: 0333452798.

First published 1974.

Sections on 24 countries (1. Australia since 1901 ... 23. United Kingdom since 1828; 24. United States of America since 1828). 19 of the countries are in Western and Northern

....(contd.)

Europe; the others are Australia, Canada, Israel, Japan, New Zealand and US. The section on Italy (p.216-227) contains a brief history, political parties in Italy, 1895-1979, data on elections, 1895-1979, statistics of total votes, party votes, number and percentage of seats won; 9 tables in all. Sources are cited at the end of each section. *Class No:* 324(091)

Europe

[1494]
MACKIE, T.T. *and* CRAIG, F.W.S., *eds.* **Europe votes 3: European Parliamentary election results, 1989.** Aldershot, Hants. Dartmouth Publishing Co. Ltd., 1990. £37.50.

Full information about the 1989 elections, including brief outlines of the electoral system, notes on the less well-known parties, and results by constituencies. *Class No:* 324(4)

Maps & Atlases

[1495]
SALLNOW, J. *and* JOHN, A. **An Electoral atlas of Europe, 1968-1981:** a political geographic compendium including 76 maps. London, Butterworth Scientific, 1982. [8], 149p. maps, fig., tables. £22.50. ISBN: 0408108002.

Developed from a series of articles published by the authors in the *Geographical magazine* in 1977 and 1978, the book attempts to show the degree of electoral support in major administrative divisions of European countries. Chapter 1: Western and Southern Europe: a political overview; 2: Central Europe; 3: Maritime Europe; 4: Mediterranean Europe; 5: Nordic Europe; Appendix 1: Results of referendums in Denmark, Norway, Ireland and the United Kingdom on accession to the European Community; Appendix 2: The electoral systems of Europe. Index and index of political parties. *Class No:* 324(4)(084.3)

Europe—Western

Histories

[1496]
CARSTAIRS, A. McL. **A Short history of electoral systems in Western Europe.** London, Allen & Unwin, 1980. [5],236p. tables. £18. ISBN: 0043240062.

18 chapters in 6 parts: 1. Electoral systems - 2. Belgium and the Netherlands - 3. The Nordic countries - 4. Austria and Switzerland - 5. The great powers on the Continent [Italy, Federal German Republic, France] - 6. The United Kingdom and Ireland. An introduction (p.1-6), with references sets the scene from 1864. References also follow each chapter. Select bibliography, p.225-231, A-Z by author. Index, p.232-236. *Class No:* 324(400)(091)

Great Britain

[1497]
British elections and parties year-book. Denver, D., *and others, eds.* Hemel Hempstead, Harvester Wheatsheaf, 1991-. Annual.

The 1993 volume (xiii,242p. tables. ISBN 0745914968) opens with an account of the 1992 General Election campaign and results. Studies elections, parties and public opinion in Britain. *Class No:* 324(410)

[1498]
British electoral facts, 1832-1987. Craig, F.W.S. Aldershot, Hants., Dartmouth Publishing Co., Ltd., 1989. 232p., £30. ISBN: 0900178302.

First published 1968 as *British Parliamentary election statistics, 1918-70*; 2nd ed. 1976 as *British Parliamentary election facts, 1885-1975*, published by Parliamentary Research Services.

Facts and statistics on all of the 40 General elections and more than 3600 by-elections that have taken place in the UK since the passing of the Reform Act in 1832. *Class No:* 324(410)

[1499]
British general election manifestos, 1900-1987. Craig, F.W.S. 3rd ed. Aldershot, Hants., Dartmouth Publishing Co., Ltd., 1989. 600p. £45. ISBN: 0900178345.

First published 1970 by Political Reference Services, covering 1918-66; 2nd ed., 1975, covering 1900-1974. Contains a complete collection of the full official texts issued by the Conservative, Labour and Liberal Parties at all general elections since 1900. *Class No:* 324(410)

[1500]
British Parliamentary election results, 1974 - 1983. Craig, F.W.S., *comp. & ed.* 2nd ed. Aldershot, Hants, Dartmouth Publishing Co. Ltd., 1984. 382p. £60. ISBN: 090017823x.

Earlier editions are for 1832-1885 (2nd ed., 1989. 1st pub. 1977. 768p. £60. ISBN 0900178264); 1885-1918 (2nd ed., 1989. 1st pub. 1974. 704p. £60. ISBN 0900178272); 1918-1949 (3rd ed. 1983. 804p. ISBN 090017896x); and 1950-1973 (2nd ed. 1983, 780p. £60. ISBN 0900178078).

Data is given for the 3 countries, counties, boroughs and universities. Indexes to candidates and constituencies. *Class No:* 324(410)

[1501]
—Chronology of British Parliamentary by-elections, 1983-1987. Craig, F.W.S. Aldershot Hants, Dartmouth Publishing Co. Ltd., 1987. 400p. £50. ISBN: 0900178310. *Class No:* 324(410)

[1502]
BUTLER, D. *and* KAVANAGH, D. **The British general election of 1991/2.** 14th in the series; 5th by present authors. London, Macmillan, 1992. 300p. £40. ISBN: 0333568125.

First was for 1945.

Covers salient events of the Parliament, planning of the parties' campaign strategies, the election campaign itself, and the treatment of the campaign by the mass media and opinion polling agencies. Also provides extensive and analytical statistical appendix. *Class No:* 324(410)

[1503]
BUTLER, D. **British general elections since 1945.** Oxford, Blackwell, for the Institute of Contemporary British History, 1990. viii,133p. illus. tables. maps. £10.99. (*(Making contemporary Britain)*.) ISBN: 0631160523.

13 chapters examining 13 post-war elections, the mechanics of voting, timing of elections. cost, the media, local electioneering, etc. 2 appendices: 1. Election results, 1945-1987; 2. Election peaks and troughs. Bibliography, p.125-8. Index, p.129-33. *Class No:* 324(410)

[1504]

CRAIG, F.W.S., *comp & ed*. **Britain votes. 5: British Parliamentary election results, 1988-1992.** Aldershot, Hants., Dartmouth Publishing Co., Ltd., 1993. x,214p. £45. ISBN: 0900178361.

First published 1977.

Intended to provide an interim supplement to the series *British Parliamentary election results* (qv). Gives the name and party of each candidate, the number of votes polled, the percentage of the total poll and the majority. Boundary changes and lost deposits indicated. Tables and appendices give details of total votes cast, turnout, etc. Index to candidates. *Class No:* 324(410)

[1505]

KINNEAR, M. **The British voter:** an atlas and survey since 1885. 2nd ed. New York, St. Martin's Press, 1981. 173p. maps. $40. ISBN: 0312105630.

First published 1968.

Comprehensive coverage of British general elections from 1885 to the 1970s, with special analyses of the effects of redistributions, of migrations of voters among parties, and of voting patterns by occupational and religious groups. Also the Common Market referenda and elections to the European Parliament. Special sections on Wales and Scotland and Northern Ireland. Excellent annotated bibliography. Maps somewhat overcrowded. '... a unique and valuable work ...' (*Choice,* March 1982, p.892). *Class No:* 324(410)

Scotland

[1506]

PARRY, R. **Scottish political facts.** Edinburgh, T. & T. Clark, 1988. 154p. £9.95. ISBN: 0567291235.

Contains parliamentary constituency results since 1945 and local election results since 1974; lists current Scottish Members of Parliament; and includes 100 key socio-economic indicators comparing Scotland and England. *Class No:* 324(411)

Ireland

[1507]

WALKER, B.M., *ed*. **Parliamentary elections results in Ireland, 1801-1922.** Dublin, Royal Irish Academy, 1978. xvi,438p. IR£8.10.

Fourth volume in the series of publications ancillary to *A New history of Ireland,* edited by T.W. Moody, and others (Oxford, Clarendon Press, 1976-), and conceived at the same time as the second volume, *Irish historical statistics, population, 1821-1971. Class No:* 324(415)

[1508]

—Parliamentary elections results in Ireland, 1918-1992: Irish elections to Parliaments and Parliamentary assemblies at Westminster and Belfast, Dublin, Strasbourg. Dublin, Royal Irish Academy; Belfast, The Institute of Irish Studies, Queen's University of Belfast, 1992. 358p. Maps. ISBN: 0901714968. *Class No:* 324(415)

Commonwealth

Bibliographies

[1509]

BLOOMFIELD, V. **Commonwealth elections, 1945-1970:** a bibliography. Westport, CT., Greenwood Press, 1977. xvi, 306p. $46.95. ISBN: 0837190673.

5654 numbered, unannotated entries, covering more than 760 elections and referenda held at national, state and provincial level in the Commonwealth countries and dependencies. 15 geographical areas (Commonwealth and general - Americas ... Pacific area). List of journals cited, p.267-74. Author and name index. 'A model of how such a work should be produced' (*African research & documentation,* no.14, 1977, p.36). *Class No:* 324(41-44)(01)

France

[1510]

COLE, A. *and* CAMPBELL, P. **French electoral systems and elections since 1789.** 3rd ed. Aldershot, Hants., Gower, 1989. xii,202p. tables. £25. ISBN: 0566056968.

9 chapters in 3 parts: I. Introduction; II. French electoral system and elections, 1789-1958; III. French electoral systems and elections in the Fifth Republic. Conclusion. 6 appendices: A. General surveys; B. Overseas deputies; C. Elections to Upper Chamber; D. Election of President; E. Local and regional elections; F. Tables of reference. Bibliography, p.193-97. Index, p.198-202. *Class No:* 324(44)

USA

[1511]

Presidential elections since 1789. 5th ed. Washington, D.C., Congressional Quarterly Inc., 1991. 235p. tables, maps. $19.95. ISBN: 0871876094.

First published 1975.

Consists largely of tables, maps, brief biographies of candidates. Deals with every presidential election since 1789 and every primary since 1912. *Class No:* 324(73)

[1512]

RENSTROM, P.G. *and* ROGERS, C.B. **The Electoral politics dictionary.** Santa Barbara, CA., ABC-Clio, 1989. 365p. $44.50. ISBN: 0874365171.

*c.*400 selected entries pertaining to electoral politics in the US, including words, concepts, organizations, court decisions, etc. grouped in chapters relating to political culture and public opinion, political participation, campaigns, elections, political parties, interest groups, and the media. Entries are lengthy and include 'significance' paragraphs. Cross-references. Considered to be a useful supplement to J.M. Shafritz's *The Dorsey dictionary of government and politics* (qv). *Class No:* 324(73)

[1513]

YOUNG, M.L. **The American dictionary of campaigns and elections.** Lanham, MD, Hamilton Press (distributed by University Press of America 1987). 246p. $24.95. ISBN: 0819154466.

Defines 725 terms used by US political campaigners. Clear, brief entries. Cross-references. Bibliography. Subject index. *Class No:* 324(73)

Migration

Tables & Data Books

[1514]

WILLCOX, W.F., *ed*. **International migrations.** New York, Gordon & Breach, 1929 (Reprinted 1969-70). 2v. (1112p., 715p.). tables, diagrs. v.l: $l60. v.2: $l88. ISBN: 0677022107.

V.1: Statistics: v.2: Interpretations. V.1 contains international migration statistics for 16 countries, from the beginning of the record of each country until 1924. Annotated tables, preceded by descriptive and historical commentary. *Class No:* 325(083)

Europe

[1515]

COUNCIL OF EUROPE. **People on the move:** new migration flows in Europe. Brussels, Council of Europe, 1992. 250p. ISBN: 9287120208.

Describes migration patterns, especially from east to west during the last five years; also national and United Nations policies. Includes bibliographical references. *Class No:* 325(4)

[1516]

The New geography of European migrations. King, R., *ed*. London & New York, Belhaven Press, 1993. 240p. 20 illus. £35. ISBN: 1852932910.

A study of population migrations following the collapse of the Soviet Bloc. Contributors are British, European and United States demographers. *Class No:* 325(4)

Biographies

[1517]

Biographisches Handbuch der deutschsprachigen Emigration nach 1933/International biographical dictionary of Central European emigrés, 1933-45. Institut f. Zeitgeschichte München/Research Foundation of Jewish Emigration Inc., New York., *comp*. Munich, K.G. Saur, 1980-83. 3v. (933p.; 1398p.; 301p.). DM.960.- the set. V.1 & 2: $175 each; v.3: $125. ISBN: 3598100876, set; 3598100884, v.1; 3598100892, v.2; 3598100906, v.3.

V.1 covers politics, economics, government and living; v.2 covers science, arts and literature; v.3 is the index. V.1 & 2 are in German; v.3 is in German and English. *Class No:* 325(4)(092)

USA

Bibliographies

[1518]

BUENKER, J.D. *and* BURCKEL, N.C., *eds*. **Immigration and ethnicity:** a guide to information sources. Detroit, Mich., Gale Research Co., 1977. xii, 305p. $68. (*American government and history information guide series*.) ISBN: 0810312026.

Nearly 1500 entries, mostly annotated, for primarily English-language items. 7 main sections: General accounts and miscellaneous - Old immigration - New immigration - Orientals - Recent ethnics - Post 1920s - Acculturation, assimilation, ethnicity and restrictions - Centers,

....(contd.)
repositories, societies, documents and journals (listing ethnic organizations and their publications). US-based. *Class No:* 325(73)(01)

Histories

[1519]

Dictionary of American immigration history Cordasco, F., *ed*. Metuchen, NJ, Scarecrow Press, 1990. xxv,784p. $97.50. ISBN: 0810822415.

More than 2500 entries by *c*.100 contributors, mainly American social scientists. Arranged A-Z, entries range in length from a few lines to 7p. (*eg*White slave trade and immigrants). Includes information on most of the ethnic groups, important individuals, immigration societies, mutual aid societies, legislation and restrictions relating to immigrants. Cross-references. Appendix: Selected bibliography,p.776-84. *Class No:* 325(73)(091)

[1520]

ROSE, P.I. **The New immigration.** In *Choice*, v.27(7), March 1990, p.1284-1291.

Bibliographic essay considering the works of some of those who have been examining immigration history. Includes sociological studies, ethnographies, and personal accounts of the new immigration that is changing the character of America. 122 titles. *Class No:* 325(73)(091)

Black Races

Bibliographies

[1521]

Black immigration and ethnicity in the United States: an annotated bibliography. University of Michigan. Center for Afro-American & African Studies Staff, *comps*. Westport, CT., Greenwood Press, 1985. xi, 170p. $36.95. (*Bibliographies and indexes in Afro-American and African studies, 2*.) ISBN: 0313243662.

Entries for 1049 books, articles, government documents, dissertations, master's theses and chapter essays published through 1982, arranged in 6 topical main sections: Bibliographies and literature surveys - General works on immigration and ethnicity - United States immigration legislation and policies - Aspects of black immigration - Studies of individual groups - Selected list of works on black immigrants to Canada and Great Britain. About half the entries have descriptive annotations. Author and subject indexes. '... a useful bibliography'. (*College & research libraries*. January 1986, p.73). Highly recommended by *Choice*, (v.22(11/12), July/August 1985, p.1609). *Class No:* 325(73)(=96)(01)

Colonial Administration

[1522]

Colonialism in Africa, 1870-1960. Stanford, CA., Hoover Institution on War, Revolution and Peace, 1969-75. 5v. tables, maps. ISBN: 0521073731, v.1; 052107732x, v.2; 052107844x, v.3; 0521086418, v.4; 0521078598, v.5.

1: *The history and politics of colonialism. 1870-1914;* edited by L.H. Gann and P. Duignan. 1969. 532p. ($87.50). 2: *The history and politics of colonialism, 1914-1960;* edited by L.H. Gann and P. Duignan. 1970. 563p. ($84.50). 3: *Profiles of change: African society and colonial rule;* edited

....*(contd.)*

by V. Turner, 1971. 455p. ($74.50). 4: *The economics of colonialism;* edited by P. Duignan and L.H. Gann. 1975. 719p. ($99.50). 5: *A bibliographic guide to colonialism in sub-Saharan affairs,* by P. Duignan and L.H. Gann. 1973. 552p. ($84.50). V.5 (2,516 entries) ranges over anthropology, law, literature, medicine, natural science, politics and religion, as well as including *c.2,000* items, arranged by colonial power, region and colony. General introductory section (*c.*300 entries) on general reference material, bibliographies, etc. Index of authors, titles, organisations, agencies, colonies and main geographical areas. Includes an amount of non-English language material. 'In all this is a scholarly work which will be invaluable to anyone studying Africa over the last hundred years' (*International affairs,* v.50, no.3, July 1974, p.517). *Class No:* 325.3

[1523]
HENIGE, D.D. Colonial governors, from the fifteenth century to the present: a comprehensive list. Madison, University of Wisconsin Press, 1970. xx, 461p. $50. ISBN: 0299054403.

Under colonizing countries, A-Z (Belgium - Denmark - France (bibliography, p.63-65) -Germany - Great Britain (bibliography, p.191-195) - Italy - Japan - Netherlands - Portugal - Russia - Spain - Sweden - US (bibliography, p.359). General index; index of governors' names, p.375-461. *Class No:* 325.3

Bibliographies

[1524]
HALSTEAD, J. P. *and* **PORCARI, S. Modern European imperialism:** a bibliography of books and articles, 1815-1972. Boston, Mass. G. K. Hall, 1974. 2v. (xiv, 508p.; xiv, 501p.).

V.1. *General and British Empire;* V.2. *French and other empires. Regions.* V.1, divided geographically, has *c.*15,000 unannotated entries, including many periodical articles (*c.*100 journals cited: 20 English, 7 French, and 3 US journals searched comprehensively). 'British South Africa' (p.242-93) is closely subdivided (General; Atlases; Bibliographies; Documents and papers; Economic and financial; Federation and Union; Fiction and literary comment; Great Boer War; Historiography; Race relations and native policy; High Commission Territories ...). No index. *Class No:* 325.3(01)

Commonwealth

[1525]
MANSERGH, N. The Commonwealth experience. 2nd ed. London, Macmillan Press, 1982. 2v. (288p.; 308p.). £35 each vol. ISBN: 0333331583, v.1; 0333331605, v.2; 0333331680, set.

First published in one vol., 1969.

V.1 *The Durham report to the Anglo-Irish treaty;* v.2. *From British to multiracial Commonwealth.* V.1 has 7 chapters in 2 parts: 1. The foundation members and the nature of their association - 2. The British Commonwealth of Nations, 1914-21. V.2 has 7 chapters in 3 parts: 1. The British Commonwealth of Nations, 1921-47 - 2. The Commonwealth since 1947 - 3. Retrospect 1838-1981: the historical experience. Each volume has extensive notes by chapter and an analytical index. *Class No:* 325.3(41-44)

British Colonies

Bibliographies

[1526]
GREAT BRITAIN. Colonial Office. Library. **Catalogue of the Colonial Office Library, London.** Boston, Mass., G.K. Hall, 1964-79. 15v. + 7v. of supplements. $1490 the set of 15v. 1st. supplement: $140; 2nd ... $220; 3rd ... $545. ISBN: 0816106886, the set of 15v; 0816107297, 1st supplement; 0816108439, 2nd supplement; 0816100101, 3rd supplement.

187,000 photolithographed catalogue entries in v.1-15 (1-2: Author catalogue: pre-1950 accessions - 3-6: Author and title catalogue: post-1950 accessions - 7-8: Subject catalogue: pre-1950 accessions - 9-13: Subject catalogue: post-1950 accessions - 14-15: Classified catalogue: post-1950 accessions). *c.*100,000 entries in the 3 supplements (1st supplement: 1963-1967; 2nd supplement (1972. 2v.); 3rd supplement (1979. 4v.). No key to the classified catalogue (v.14-15), which follows the Library of Congress classification. 'All aspects of organization and development of those countries which form or have formed part of the Commonwealth, are covered by this catalogue, which reflects the changing interests and activities of the Colonial Office over the past 300 years' (*Introduction*). An invaluable catalogue of books, pamphlets, reports, official publications and periodical titles. *Class No:* 325.3(41-5)(01)

Handbooks & Manuals

[1527]
GREAT BRITAIN. Colonial Office. **The Corona Library.** London, HMSO, 1952-71. 13v. illus., maps.

A series of well-produced, illustrated volumes dealing with the United Kingdom's former dependent territories, the way their people live and how they were governed: Basutoland, Bechuanaland, British Guiana, British Honduras, Fiji, Hong Kong, Jamaica, North Borneo, Nyasaland, Sierra Leone, Swaziland, Uganda, Western Pacific Islands. Designed 'to fill the place between official Blue Books on the one hand and the writings of occasional visitors on the other, to be authoritative and readable' (Series note). *Class No:* 325.3(41-5)(035)

Histories

[1528]
MORGAN, D.J. The Official history of colonial development. London, Macmillan, 1980. 5v. tables, maps. each £33. ISBN: V. 1-5, 0333262247, 0333262301, 0333262328, 0333262336, 0333262344.

1. *The origins of British aid policy, 1924-1945.*
2. *Developing British colonial resources, 1945-1951.*
3. *A reassessment of British aid policy, 1951-1965.*
4. *Changes in British aid policy, 1951-1970.*
5. *Guidance towards self-government in British colonies, 1941-1971.*

V.5 (xvii, 382p.) has 11 chapters (8. 'Decolonialization, 1963-1966', p.207-50. 'Sources', 1-90). 5 appendices (1. Administrations and ministers concerned with colonial affairs, 1924-1974). Analytical index. Author is lecturer in Economics, Univ. of London. 'A valuable preview of unused evidence of a subject of great contemporary interest and importance' (*British book news,* December 1980, p.728). *Class No:* 325.3(41-5)(091)

Biographies

[1529]

KIRK-GREENE, A.H.M. A Bibliographical dictionary of the British Colonial Service, 1939-1966. Oxford, Hans Zell, 1990. ISBN: 0905450965.

Consisting of almost 10,000 entries, this is an A-Z register of all members of the Colonial Office whose names appeared in the *Colonial Office lists* in the period stated. It covers the Professional Services (education, forestry, medical, police, public works) as well as the Administrative Service, serving in all colonial territories. A substantial introduction assesses the annual *Colonial Office lists* as a primary biographical source for the social, administrative and career history of the Colonial Service. *Class No:* 325.3(41-5)(092)

Africa

[1530]

KIRK-GREENE, A.H.M. Decolonization in British Africa. In *History today*, v.42, January 1992, p.44-50.

A historiographical survey, which refers to important books on the subject in the text. *Class No:* 325.3(6)

[1531]

WESTFALL, G. French colonial Africa: a guide to official sources. London, Hans Zell, 1992. x,226p. ISBN: 1873836600.

Descriptive guide to guides and bibliographies; French colonial archives; publications of the Central Administration; semi-official publications; and colonial government publications. Bibliography of official publications of individual colonies,p.113-198. *Class No:* 325.3(6)

Slavery

[1532]

MILLER, J.C. Slavery: a worldwide bibliography, 1900-1982. White Plains, NY, Kraus International Publications, 1985. xxvii, [1], 451p. $40.00. ISBN: 0527636592.

5177 consecutively numbered entries grouped in 11 sections (General and comparative; North America; Spanish mainland; Brazil; Caribbean; Africa; Muslim; Ancient; Medieval and early modern Europe; other areas; the slave trade). Includes books, chapters in books, journal articles, and doctoral dissertations, mainly in Western European languages. No annotations. Author index, p.391-423. Subject/keyword index, p.425-451. Annual supplements planned for publication in the journal *Slavery and abolition.* *Class No:* 326

Histories

[1533]

WALVIN, J. Black ivory: a history of British slavery. London, HarperCollins, 1992. 384p. illus. maps. £20. ISBN: 0246138912.

Using contemporary accounts, the author shows how British maritime trade and power were transformed by the Atlantic slave trade. Also describes the brutal conditions of the trade and its legacy of racism. *Class No:* 326(091)

Africa

[1534]

HOGG, P.C. The African slave trade and its suppression: a classified and annotated bibliography of books, pamphlets and periodical articles. London, Cass, 1973. xvii, 409p. £45. ISBN: 0714627755.

Originally as thesis for the L.A. fellowship, accepted 1970, with title 'A classified bibliography ... on the African slave trade'.

4,675 numbered entries. Part 1: 'Slave trade' (A. Collection of evidence - B. General accounts - C. West Africa - D. Sudan - E. East Africa - F. Slaving voyages - G. Medical conditions - H. Laws and official documents - I. Economic controversy - J. Economic history - K. Biographies of slaves - L. Ethnic origin of slaves). Part 2: 'Abolition and suppression' (M. Abolition controversies ... R. Laws and official documents - S. Naval blockade ... W. History of abolition ... Y. Biographies of abolitionists - Z. Imaginative literature. Appendix 1: Unpublished theses - 2. Addenda. Author, personal name, geographical name and anonymous title indexes.

The same author's *Slavery - the Afro-American experience* (British Library, 1979. 52p. illus. (incl. col.), map. £1.95) is an introduction - using British Library resources - 'to the history of slavery in the British colonies in America and the West Indies from the 17th century to the early 19th centuries' (*British library news,* no.48, December 1979, p.2). *Class No:* 326(6)

[1535]

MANNING, P. Slavery and African life: occidental, oriental, and African slave trades. Cambridge, Cambridge University Press, 1990. xi,236p. illus. tables, charts. Maps. (*(African studies series, 67).*) ISBN: 0521343968.

Prologue ('Tragedy and sacrifice in the history of slavery') is followed by 8 chapters: 1. The political economy of slavery in Africa; 2. Why Africans? The rise of the slave trade to 1700; 3. Slavery and the African population; 4. The quantitative aspect of the slave trade, 1700-1900; 5. The economics and morality of the slave supply; 6. Patterns of slave life; 7. Transformation of slavery and society, 1650-1900; 8. The end of slavery in the world and Africa. Appendices: 1. Slave prices; 2. The demographic simulation. Notes, p.182-211. Bibliography, p.212-26. Index, p.227-34. *Class No:* 326(6)

America

[1536]

SMITH, J.D., *comp.* **Black slavery in the Americas:** an interdisciplinary bibliography, 1865-1980. Westport, CT., Greenwood Press, 1982. 2v. (1847p.). $95 the set. ISBN: 0313231184.

15667 unannotated citations arranged in 25 chapters (*e.g.* African background, slave trade, geography, economics, Indian slave owners, conditions of slave life, family, religion, culture, resistance). Author and subject indexes (subject index weak: needs sub-divisions). 4394 cross-references. A massive bibliography, but computer-printout is difficult to read, however '... will surely be the most comprehensive compilation on slavery for a long time to come'. (*Choice,* v.20(10), June 1983, p.1438). *Class No:* 326(7)

USA

[1537]
MILLER, R.M. *and* SMITH, J.D., *eds*. **Dictionary of Afro-American slavery.** Westport, CT., Greenwood Press, 1988. 866p. tables, maps. $95; £68.50. ISBN: 0313238146.

*c.*300 individual articles, A-Z, on people, places and themes during the first English settlement in America to the Reconstruction of the Civil War, over 200 written by recognized authorities on the subject of slavery. Emphasis is placed on the social, institutional, intellectual and political aspects of slavery. Each article includes a select bibliography for further reading. Helpful tables. Index. '... a magnificent reference compilation ...' (*Choice,* v.26(8), April 1989, p.1302). *Class No:* 326(73)

Foreign Relations

[1538]
HOLLIS, M. *and* SMITH, S. **Explaining and understanding international relations.** Oxford, Clarendon Press, 1990.$bv,226p.$c£25. ISBN: 0198275889.

An introduction to theoretical debates on international relations and as a contributiom to those debates. 9 chapters in 3 parts: Growth of the discipline since 1918 - The international system, state, bureaucracies, decision-making individuals - Proposal for theoretical agenda. Short bibliographic essay as a guide to further reading. '... well-structured and clearly written ...'(*International affairs,*v.67(3), July 1991, p.565). *Class No:* 327

Bibliographies

[1539]
CONOVER, H.F., *comp*. **A Guide to bibliographic tools for research in foreign affairs.** 2nd ed., with supplement. Washington, D.C., Library of Congress, 1958 (reprinted Greenwood Press, 1970). iii, 145,15p. $250. ISBN: 0840191765.

351 main entries, with much other material referred to in annotations. Sorely needs updating. *Class No:* 327(01)

[1540]
COUNCIL ON FOREIGN RELATIONS, INC., New York City. **Catalog of the Foreign Relations Library.** Boston, Mass, G.K. Hall, 1969 (First supplement, 1979). 9v. + supplementary vol. $870. Supplement: $340. ISBN: 0816108404, (9v.); 0816103062, supplement.

148,000 lithographed catalogue cards in dictionary form, for books and pamphlets. Subject and bibliography analytics are a feature. *Class No:* 327(01)

[1541]
'Foreign affairs' bibliography: a selected and annotated list of books on international relations, 1919/1932. New York, Bowker (previously Harper), for the Council on Foreign Relations, 1933-.

Decennial volumes: 1919/1932; 1932/1942-.

'Based largely on the annotated lists appearing quarterly in *Foreign affairs'*(*Foreword*). Covers international relations in the broadest sense, including recent history, economic, military, social and cultural affairs, and political developments in all countries. The 1962-72 volume has *c.* 10,000 entries in 3 parts: 1. General international relations (1. General works ... 8. War and peace) - 2. The world since 1914. (1. General ... 4. Second World War) - 3. The world by regions. Cross-references. Index to authors; index

....(contd.)
to title entries. Restricted to books and documents; valuable for its brief (*c.*15 word) critical annotations. *Class No:* 327(01)

[1542]
—'Foreign affairs' 50-year index: volumes 1-50, 1922-1972. New York, Bowker, for the Council on Foreign Relations, 1973. 1282p.

Described (*Library Journal* 15 March 1974, p.744) as a work of 'extraordinary thoroughness'. *Class No:* 327(01)

[1543]
—The 'Foreign affairs' 50-year bibliography: new evaluations of significant books on international relations., 1920-1970. Dexter, B, Ed. New York, Bowker for the Council on Foreign Relations, 1972. xxvii, 936p.

A selection, by more than 400 specialists, of 2130 items, based on hindsight. Arrangement is as in the decennial volumes. 'A valuable reference tool useful for collection evaluation as well' (*Library journal* v.98(8), 15 April 1973, p.1246). *Class No:* 327(01)

[1544]
GREAT BRITAIN. Foreign Office. Library. **Catalogue of the Foreign Office Library, 1926-1968.** Boston, Mass., G.K. Hall, 1972. 8v. $790. ISBN: 0816109982.

About 135,000 photolithographed catalogue-cards, representing the complete collections of the Foreign Office and Commonwealth Office libraries for 1926-1968 (the two offices merged in 1968). 4 separate sequences: Author, Subject, Title, Class. Includes many British and foreign government publications. *Class No:* 327(01)

[1545]
GREAT BRITAIN. HM Stationery Office. **Government publications: Sectional list 69, revised April 1987. Overseas affairs.** London, HMSO, 1985. 29p. Gratis.

4 parts: 1. Classified list of subjects - 2. Country list (A-Z) - 3. Series (British Atlantic Survey ... Background briefs) - 4. Periodicals. Kraus reprints. *Class No:* 327(01)

[1546]
LAKOS, A. **International negotiations: a bibliography.** Boulder, CO, & London, Westview Press, 1989. xii,417p. $54.50. £43.95. ISBN: 0813375584.

Aims to identify and classify materials (books, journal articles, documents and reports) pertaining to the processes of diplomatic negotiation. 5419 entries arranged in 12 sections: Negotiations, processes and theories - Psychological and sociological aspects - Game theory - Mediation - Multilateral negotiations - Arms control negotiations - Summit meetings - International trade negotiations - Diplomacy - Soviet diplomacy & negotiating behavior - American diplomacy - Case studies. No annotations. Author and subject indexes. *Class No:* 327(01)

[1547]
PFALTZGRAFF, R. **The Study of international relations:** a guide to information sources. Detroit, Mich., Gale Research Co., 1977. 155p. $68. (*International relations information guide series, v.5. Gale information guide library.*) ISBN: 0810313316.

360 titles, mostly post-1945, and annotated. Topics: the nature and scope of international relations as a discipline; the international system; foreign policy and diplomacy; power and theory of conflict; military strategy; integration and alliance themes. *Class No:* 327(01)

[1548]
ROYAL INSTITUTE OF INTERNATIONAL AFFAIRS.
Library. **The Classified catalogue of the Royal Institute of International Affairs for international relations, defence, diplomacy, international law, politics and economics...**
Oxford, Oxford Microform Publications Ltd.

A catalogue of 170,000 catalogue cards on microfiche. In 2 parts: 1. International and general classification (8 major subjects with subdivisions); 2. Regional classification (11 major areas grouped into their regions, subdivided into countries and their parts). 26 microfiches in the first part and 163 in the second. There is a printed introduction and guide. *Class No:* 327(01)

[1549]
ROYAL INSTITUTE OF INTERNATIONAL AFFAIRS.
Library. **Index to periodical articles, 1950-1964 ...** Boston, Mass., G.K. Hall, 1964. 2v. $225. ISBN: 0816107114.

The Library, now the leading specialist collection in Britain dealing with international affairs from 1918 onwards, currently receives *c.*600 periodicals. The *Index* is to *c.*31,500 articles taken from these, for the period January 1950 to October 1964. Arranged by the Chatham House scheme of classification (class A-H (general and subject), J-T (regions)). Preceding the index proper: list of principal periodicals indexed; guide to the classification scheme; geographic index; subject index. *Class No:* 327(01)

[1550]
—ROYAL INSTITUTE OF INTERNATIONAL AFFAIRS.
Library. Index to periodical articles, 1965-1972 ... Boston, Mass., G.K. Hall, 1974. xxix, 879p. $120. ISBN: 081611062x.

Index to *c.*15000 articles from some 200 periodicals, on *c.*16400 photolithographed cards, 21 per page. Classified arrangement, as in the main volumes. List of 60 principal periodicals indexed. Subject index. *Class No:* 327(01)

[1551]
—ROYAL INSTITUTE OF INTERNATIONAL AFFAIRS.
Library. Index to periodical articles, 1979-1989. Published at intervals - 1950/64; 1965/72; 1973/78... Boston, Mass., G.K. Hall, 1990. $250. ISBN: 0816117845.

The 1973/78 issue has index to *c.*15000 articles, similarly arranged. List of principal periodicals indexed (66). *Class No:* 327(01)

[1552]
WRIGHT, M., *and others*. **Essay collections in international relations:** a classified bibliography. New York, Garland, 1977. 172p. $29. (*Reference library of social science, v.45.*) ISBN: 0824098684.

Indexes essays in 'non-current multi-author works published between 1945 and 1975', listed under authors, subjects and into 22 groups. There is 'no comparable volume' (*Choice*, v.14(10), December 1977, p.1342). *Class No:* 327(01)

Handbooks & Manuals

[1553]
Defense and foreign affairs handbook, 1988-89.
Copley, G.R., *ed.* New York, International Media, 1988. 1400p. illus. $197.

3rd ed. published 1978.

Political, economic and defence data on *c.*200 countries (Afghanistan ... Zimbabwe). *Class No:* 327(035)

Dictionaries

English

[1554]
PLANO, J.C. *and* OLTON, R. **The International relations dictionary.** 4th ed. Santa Barbara, CA., ABC-Clio, 1988. xxiii,446p. $42.95. ISBN: 0874364779, US; 058203096x, UK.

First published 1969 by Holt, Rinehart & Winston Inc., New York.

A 'Guide to major concepts' (p.xiii-xxiii) precedes the 12 subject chapters of the dictionary: 1. Nature and role of foreign policy - 2. Nationalism, imperialism and colonization - 3. Ideology and communication - 4. Geography and population - 5. International economics - 6. War and military policy - 7. Arms control and disarmament - 8. Diplomacy - 9. International law - 10. International organizations - 11. American foreign policy - 12. Patterns of political organization. For each there is a paragraph of definitions and one headed 'significance'. 570 entries in all, ranging in length from a half page to a page. No bibliographies. Index, p.423-446. *Class No:* 327(038)=20

[1555]
UNITED STATES. Department of State. Library Division.
International relations dictionary. 2nd rev.ed. Washington, D.C., Government Printing Office, 1980. 80p. $4.75. (*Department and foreign service series, 221. Department of State publication, 9.72.*)

First published 1978.

Substantial definitions of more than 200 current phrases, acronyms, catchwords, and abbreviations dealing with foreign affairs, accompanied by notes documenting the sources of the terms (*e.g.* Carter Doctrine, Eurodollars, MX (Missile experimental)). Many 'see' and 'see also' references. Does not aim to be comprehensive, merely supplements other reference works. *Class No:* 327(038)=20

[1556]
WEIGALL, D. **Britain and the world, 1815-1986:** a dictionary of international relations. London, Batsford Ltd., 1987. 240p. + 12p. of maps. £17.95.505. ISBN: 0713447532.

A-Z entries on topics related to British foreign policy and international relations (Aberdeen - Abyssinian War ... Zinoviev letter - Zulu War). Cross-references. Entries range in length between 100 and 3000 words (*e.g.* Germany and Britain: 6½ cols. 10 references; 'Gladstone': 3 cols.; 'League of Nations': 2 cols.; 'Pearl Harbour' 1/3col.). Chronology of international relations, p.227-240. 12 maps. *Class No:* 327(038)=20

Arabic

[1557]
EL'ADAH, S.F. **A Dictionary of diplomacy and international affairs:** English-French-Arabic. New ed. Beirut, Librairie du Liban, 1979. 566p. £30. ISBN: 0948690569.

First published 1974.

About 5,000 English base-terms, with French and Arabic equivalents and indexes. Arabic equivalents/definitions are sometimes stated at length (*e.g.* 'Spying: Espionage: Arabic explanation of 1½ columns). *Class No:* 327(038)=927

Reviews & Abstracts

[1558]

International affairs. Cambridge. Cambridge University Press (previously Oxford University Press, then Butterworths) for the Royal Institute of International Affairs, 1922-. v.1, no.1-. Quarterly. £45 pa. ISSN: 00205850.

About a quarter in each issue comprises review articles, book reviews, 'Other books received' and an author index of books reviewed. V.69(4), October 1993 has 56 main articles, plus 115 signed book reviews (p.743-825) in sections: International relations and organizations - Security and arms control - Politics, social affairs and law - Political economy, economics and development - Energy and environment - History - Western Europe ... Latin America and the Caribbean - Bibliography and reference. 'Other books received'.

Cumulative index, 1922-76 to International affairs, edited by L. Adolphus and F.L. Kent (Abingdon, Oxford, Learned Information (Europe), 1978. 78p. ISBN 0904933121) is noted. *Class No:* 327(048)

Yearbooks & Directories

[1559]

Die Internationale Politik und Wirtschaft, 1985/1986: Jahrbucher der Deutschen Gesellschaft für Auswärtige Politik. München, R. Oldenbourg Verlag, 1988. 503 p. DM.98. ISBN: 3486546015.

First published 1955. Irregular.

The yearbook seeks to provide informed exposition and analysis of contemporary trends and developments in the global political system. This volume has 9 sections: 3 thematic sections (global problems - world economy in crisis - superpowers and East-West relations) and 6 regional sections (the Western community - developments in Eastern and Southern Europe - conflicts in the Middle East and North Africa - development crises and unrest in Africa - continuity and change in Asia - democratization and conflict in Latin America). D.G.A.P. is one of the most prestigious and authoritative international affairs research institutes in the Federal Republic of Germany. *Class No:* 327(058)

Histories

[1560]

NORTHEDGE, F.S. *and* **GRIEVE, M.J. A Hundred years of international relations.** London, Duckworth, 1971. x, 397p. 7 maps. ISBN: 0715605755.

Assumes that there exists, and has existed for two or three centuries, the international system of sovereign states in continuous mutual interaction, and is a study of the development of that system over the past 100 years. 16 chapters, arranged chronologically, on the period since 1870. 1. The epoch of peace - 2. Growth of the European powers - 3. Early imperialism ... 12. Birth and death of the Cold War - 13. The United Nations and world economics - 15. The transcendence of sovereignty - 16. Conclusions. Chapter and footnote references. 'Further reading', p.371-380. Detailed, partly analytical index, p.381-97. *Class No:* 327(091)

[1561]

RENOUVIN, P., *ed.* **Histoire des relations internationales.** Paris, Hachette, 1953-58. 8v. maps.

1. *Le moyen âge,* by F.-L Ganshof. 1953. 2. *Les Temps modernes* I. *De Christophe Colomb à Cromwell* by G Zeller. 3. *Les temps modernes* II. *De Louis XIV à 1789* by G. Zeller. 4. *La révolution française et l'empire napoléonien.* by A. Fugier. 5. *Le XIX siècle* I. *De 1815 à 1871* by A. Renouvin. 1954. 6. *Le XIXe siècle.* II *De 1871 à 1914* by A. Renouvin, 1955 7. *Les crises du XXe siècle.* I. *De 1914 à 1929* 1957. 8. *Les crises du XXe siècle* I. *De 1929 à 1945.* 1958. A standard work that does not confine itself to political and diplomatic history, but provides the economic, social and cultural setting. It also goes beyond European international relations. Chapter bibliographies. *Class No:* 327(091)

[1562]

ROYAL INSTITUTE OF INTERNATIONAL AFFAIRS. Survey of international affairs, 1920/23-66. London, Oxford University Press, for the Institute, 1925-77. tables, maps.

Pre-war series 1920-1938 by A.J. Toynbee, and others. 1925-53, 17v. *War-time series* 1939-1946 edited by A.J. Toynbee, 1952-58, 11v. *Post-war series* since 1947, by P. Calvocoressi, and others. 1952-77. Annual (1963 v. 1977). *Consolidated index to the 'Survey of international affairs' 1920-1938* compiled by E.M.R. Ditmas, 1967, 272p. (*Indexes, 1920-30* reprinted Johnson Reprint). Volumes in the war-time series deal with particular aspects over a period of years (*e.g. The Middle East, 1945-1950; The Far East, 1942-1946*). The Post-war series consist of annual surveys. That for 1961 was published in 1965. The surveys, by specialists in the various periods or regions, are characterised by their well-documented factual narratives and analytical indexes. *Class No:* 327(091)

Biographies

[1563]

Who's who in international affairs. London, Europa Publications Ltd. (Distributed by Gale in the US), 1990. 590p. £150. ISBN: 0946653631.

*c,*7000 biographies of key figures in international affairs, including diplomats, foreign ministers, heads of state, academics, and officials of international organizations. Entries give nationality; position; address; telephone, telex, & fax numbers; education and career progression; publications. Index by nationality. Index by organizations (over 600). '... rather expensive for a down-market edition of the International who's who, but useful nonetheless.' (*International affairs,* v.67(3), July 1991). *Class No:* 327(092)

Official Records

[1564]

ROYAL INSTITUTE OF INTERNATIONAL AFFAIRS. Documents on international affairs, 1928-1963. Wheeler-Bennett, J.W., *and others.* London, Oxford University Press for the Institute, 1929-73.

Intended to accompany and supplement the *Survey of international affairs* (*qv*), although it can now be used independently, thanks to the notes prefacing each section. A collection of available state papers, exchanges of notes, statements, speeches and other source material of a wide

....(contd.)

range of countries. The 1963v. (1973) was the last to be published by Chatham House.

Consolidated index to the 'Survey of international affairs'. 1920-1938, and 'Documents on international affairs', 1920-1938 (1967). *Class No:* 327(093.2)

Europe

[1565]

MESSICK, F.M., *comp*. **Primary sources in European diplomacy, 1914-45:** a bibliography of published memoirs and diaries. Westport, CT., Greenwood Press, 1987. xxii, 222p. map. $39.95. (*Bibliographies and indexes in world history series, no. 6*.) ISBN: 031324555x.

An introduction and list of frequently consulted sources are followed by a bibliography of 636 briefly annotated entries, arranged A-Z by author, which are sources of personal experience of those in the European arena from World War I to World War II. Predominantly English-language material. Appendix A: Authors by nationality; appendix B.i: Selected diplomatic events, 1914-1945; ii: Chronology. Cross-references. Subject index, p.202-221. *Class No:* 327(4)

Official Records

[1566]

THOMAS, D.H. *and* **CASE, L.M. The New guide to the diplomatic archives of Western Europe.** Philadelphia, Pa., University of Pennsylvania Press, 1975. 441p. $22.95. ISBN: 0812276973.

First published in 1959 as *Guide to the diplomatic archives of Western Europe*.

22 contributors. 'Western Europe' embraces Greece, Finland, the Vatican City, the UN, ILO, etc. A directory of archival repositories; data on each include history, organization and classification, availability, bibliography. 'Essential for all graduate libraries' (*Choice*, v.13(3), May 1976, p.351). *Class No:* 327(4)(093.2)

Europe—Eastern

[1567]

REMINGTON, R.A., *ed*. **The International relations of Eastern Europe:** a guide to information sources. Detroit, Mich., Gale Research Co., 1978. xvi, 273p. $68. (*International relations information guide series, v.8*.) ISBN: 0810313200.

An annotated bibliography. Part 1 covers sources that relate to Communist Eastern Europe as a region (bibliographies, references, basic texts ... The Warsaw Treaty Organization). Pt.2 provides specific country approach for Albania, Bulgaria, Czechoslovakia, East Germany, Hungary, Poland, Rumania, and Yugoslavia. Author, title and subject indexes. 'An indispensable ... tool for the subject librarian, despite many spelling errors and misprints' (*American reference book annual,* 1980, entry 515). *Class No:* 327(401)

Great Britain

Official Records

[1568]

TEMPERLEY, H. *and* **PENSON, L.M.,** *eds*. **A Century of diplomatic blue books, 1814-1914.** London, Cambridge University Press, 1938 (reprinted by F. Cass, 1966). xvi, [2], 600p. £30. ISBN: 0714615196.

Lists titles of all Parliamentary papers published between 1814 and 1914, bearing directly on British foreign policy, with historical introduction. *Class No:* 327(410)(093.2)

[1569]

—**TEMPERLEY, H.** *and* **PENSON, L.M.,** *eds*. A Century of diplomatic blue books, 1914-1936. London, Cambridge University Press, 1938 (reprinted by P.Cass, 1966). xviii,600p. £30. ISBN: 0714615196.

Continues the above. *Class No:* 327(410)(093.2)

[1570]

—**VOGEL, R.,** *ed*. A Breviate of British diplomatic blue books, 1919-1939. Montreal, McGill University Press; Leicester, Leicester University Press, 1963. xxxv, 474p. $16.50. ISBN: 0773500057.

Continues the Temperley and Penson list. 1836 numbered items, chronologically arranged. Titles in full, with additional dates or notes, but no summary of contents. Analytical subject and country index, p.437-74. *Class No:* 327(410)(093.2)

19th Century

Histories

[1571]

The Cambridge history of British foreign policy, 1783-1919. Ward A.W., Sir *and·* Gooch, G.P., *eds*. Cambridge, Cambridge University Press, 1922-23. 3v.

Modelled on the *Cambridge modern history*. A connected narrative based on official documents which gives the history of British foreign policy from the national point of view. Each volume has appendices of supporting documents and chapter bibliographies, and an index. Chapter 8 of v.3 deals with the history of the Foreign Office during the whole period. *Class No:* 327(410)"18"(091)

20th Century

[1572]

GREAT BRITAIN. Cabinet Office. **British foreign policy in the Second World War.** Woodward, Sir L. London, HMSO, 1970-76. 5v.

V.1. covers the period from the German invasion of Poland, on 1 September 1939, to the opening of the German attack on the U.S.S.R. on 22 June 1941. v.2-3 cover Anglo-Russian, Anglo-Japanese, Anglo-French, Anglo-Italian, etc., relations, Anglo-American relations, etc., V.4. covers British relations with Allied and neutral countries. V.5. deals mainly with British and Allied policy and planning for the post-war world, especially the treatment of Germany after her surrender. Also an abridged ed. in 1v. (HMSO, 1962. lv.592p). *Class No:* 327(410)"19"

Official Records

[1573]
Documents on British policy overseas. Bullen, R. *and* Pelly, M.E. London, HMSO, 1984-.

A collection of documents from the archives of the Foreign and Commonwealth Office. Published so far are:- Series I (1945-1950).

V.I The Conference at Potsdam, July-August 1945 (1984. 1388p.+26 microfiches. £85. ISBN 0115916822).

V.II. Conferences and conversations, 1945: London, Washington and Moscow (1985, 1002p.+9 microfiches, £75. ISBN 0115916830).

V.III. Britain and America: negotiation of the United States loan, 3 August-7 December 1945. (1987. 453p.+microfiche. £35. ISBN 0115916849).

V.IV. Britain and America: atomic energy, bases and food, December 1945-July 1946. (1987.454p. £35. ISBN 0115916857).

V.V. Germany and Western Europe. 11 August - 31 December 1945 (1990. £55. ISBN 0115916865).

V.VI. Eastern Europe, 1945-1946.

Series II (1950-1955).

V.I The Schuman Plan, the Council of Europe and Western European integration, 1950-1952 (1986. 1096p. £70. ISBN 011591692x).

V.II The London conferences, 1950 (1987. 500p.+ microfiche. £35. ISBN 0115916938).

V.III. German rearmament, September-December 1950. (In preparation).

V.IV. Korea, 1950-1951. (ISBN 0115916954).

Class No: 327(410)"19"(093.2)

[1574]
GREAT BRITAIN. Foreign Office. **Documents on British foreign policy, 1919-1939.** London, HMSO, 1946-.

1st series: 1919-1939. (1949-. 37v. so far). 1st series A: 1925-1930 (1966-1976. 7v.). 2nd series: 1930-1938 (1946-1978.21v.). 3rd series: March 1938-September 1939 (1949-61.10v.). A more inclusive collection for the period than that provided by the Royal Institute of International Affairs' *Documents on international affairs*. 2nd series, v.9: *The Far Eastern crisis, 1931-1932* (lxv,713p.1965) reproduces 667 documents with a tabular summary-index preceding (p.xiii-xlv): number, name of sender, date, main subject, page. *Class No:* 327(410)"19"(093.2)

[1575]
WATT, D.C. 'United States documentary resources for the study of British foreign policy, 1919-1939'. In *International affairs.* v.38(1), January 1962, p.63-72.

Describes diplomatic papers in Washington and elsewhere. *Class No:* 327(410)"19"(093.2)

Research Methods

[1576]
ASTER, S., *comp.* **British foreign policy, 1918-1945: a guide to research and research materials.** Wilmington, DE., Scholarly Resources, 1984. 324p. $20. ISBN: 0842021760.

5 main chapters: I. Introduction (provides the historical background, including lists of Secretaries of State and Ambassadors to selected countries) - II. The Foreign Office and foreign policy - III. Research libraries and archives (A. Information and publications; B. General guides, directories, and union lists; C. Manuscript research) - IV. Bibliography

....(contd.)
of over 1600 selected references (A. General; B. Parliamentary and government; C. Memoirs, biographies; D. Secondary literature; E. Peacemaking and detente, 1918-1933; F. Diplomacy in crisis; G. The approach of war, 1937-1939; H. The Second World War, 1939-1945) - V. Index of authors, editors and compilers, p.301-324. Many entries are annotated. Mainly British publications, but some German and French. 'An important handbook ...' (*Choice,* v.22(5) January 1985, p.657). A revised ed. was published in 1991 (382p. ISBN 0842023100). *Class No:* 327(410):001.891

Eire

Bibliographies

[1577]
MAGUIRE, M., *comp.* **Bibliography of published work on Irish foreign relations, 1921-78.** Dublin, Royal Irish Academy, 1981. viii,136p. IR£4.02. ISBN: 0901714151.

1314 unannotated entries arranged in 5 sections: 1. General works; 2. Foreign relations; 3. Defence; 4. Related areas; 5. Index of authors. Section 2: Foreign relations is subdivided A-H, geographically, and I-O by international organizations. *Class No:* 327(417)(01)

Germany

20th Century

Bibliographies

[1578]
CARLSON, A.R. German foreign policy, 1890-1914, and colonial policy to 1914: a handbook and annotated bibliography. Metuchen, N.J., Scarecrow Press, 1970. 333p. $19.80. £13.10. ISBN: 0810812961.

Over one-half of the volume consists of an extensive annotated bibliography. *Class No:* 327(430)"19"(01)

[1579]
—KIMMICH, C.M., *comp. & ed.* German foreign policy, 1918-1945: a guide to research and research materials. Rev. ed. Wilmington, DE., Scholarly Resources, 1991. 300p. $40. ISBN: 0842023119.

1st published 1981.

In 5 sections: 1. Introduction; 2. The foreign ministry and foreign policy; 3. Archives and libraries; 4. Bibliography (1025 entries arranged by subjects, p.97-280); 5. Index, p.281-293. 'This admirable research guide continues the bibliographic coverage ... begun by Andrew R. Carlson's *German foreign policy, 1890-1914 (College & research libraries,* January 1983, p.53). Bibliographies in footnotes and chapters have, in particular, been updated in the revised ed. *Class No:* 327(430)"19"(01)

Official Records

[1580]
GREAT BRITAIN. Foreign Office. **Documents on German foreign policy, 1918-1945.** London, HMSO, 1950-.

Documents from the archives of the German Foreign Ministry. Series C: 1933-37, v.1-5 (1958-66): January 30th 1933-October 31st 1936; v.5-6: *The Third Reich: first phase.*

....(contd.)

1966-83. Series D: 1937-45. v.1-13 (1950-64). *The War years begins with v.8.* V.13: The War years, June 23 1941-December 11, 1941 (1964). *Class No:* 327(430)"19"(093.2)

[1581]
KENT, G.O. A Catalog of files and microfilm of the German Foreign Ministry archives, 1920-1945. Stanford, CA., Hoover Institution Press, 1962-72. 4v.

Prepared under the auspices of the US Department of State and the Hoover Institution.

'Analyses *c.*300 tons of records discovered by US and British troops in Germany' (*Library of Congress information bulletin.* 27 April 1973, p.152).
Class No: 327(430)"19"(093.2)

France

Bibliographies

[1582]
YOUNG, R.J. French foreign policy, 1918-1945: a guide to research and research materials. Rev. ed. 260.00/00$aWilmington, DE., Scholarly Resources, 1991. 280p.c40.00. ISBN: 0842023089.

First published 1981.

Intended as a handbook to help scholars plan their work to guide them on their visits to archives and libraries. Includes a bibliography of reference works, dissertations, documents, memoirs, biographical sources, journal articles and monographs. Also provides sketches of French archives and other depositories of primary source materials. Subject and name indexes. List of prominent officials, and organizational charts of the French Foreign Ministry. '... Young has provided a good introduction ...' (*Choice,* June 1982, p.1387). *Class No:* 327(44)(01)

Italy

Bibliographies

[1583]
CASSELS, A. Italian foreign policy, 1918-1945: a guide to research and research materials. Rev.ed. Wilmington. Del.,Scholarly Resources, 1991. 261p. $40.00. (*Guides to European history research and research materials.*) ISBN: 0842023070.

3 main chapters: the first describes the structure and functions of the Foreign Ministry and includes list of prominent diplomats; the second lists archives, libraries and repositories in Italy and other countries, describing the various papers available in them; the third chapter is a bibliography of selected material (reference works, bibliographical aids, documents, memoirs, etc. in all major Western European languages. Index of authors, serials, and major document collections. 'A valuable guide ...' (*Choice,* v.19(11/12), July /August 1982, p.1534).
Class No: 327(450)(01)

Spain

Bibliographies

[1584]
CORTADA, J.W., *comp.* **A Bibliographic guide to Spanish diplomatic history, 1460-1977.** Westport, CT., Greenwood Press, 1977. xii, 390p.

About 5000 unannotated entries; over half of them for the period 1808-1977, and mostly in Spanish, French and English. 21 chapters (1: Archives and bibliographies; 2-21: Periods). Author index. No annotations. Includes theses. 'The highly uneven quality of the sources cited, the absence of annotations' - these limit the bibliography's value for undergraduate students (*Choice,* September 1978, p.838). *Class No:* 327(460)(01)

USSR

Bibliographies

[1585]
HAMMOND, T.T., *ed.* **Soviet foreign relations and world Communism:** a selected annotated bibliography of 7,000 books in 30 languages. Princeton, N.J., Princeton University Press, 1965. xxiv, 1240p. $105. ISBN: 0691087148.

Three main sections: Soviet foreign relations since 1917 (subdivided into periods) - World Communism (regions and countries) - Special topics. Compiled by area and subject specialists. A judicious selection, with careful, frequently evaluative annotations. The leading ten items in each subsection are marked 'A', and the next twenty 'B'. Detailed index of authors and anonymous titles. Well produced. *Class No:* 327(47)(01)

[1586]
—**SWORAKOWSKI, W. S. The Communist International and its front organizations:** a research guide and checklist of holdings in American and European libraries. Stanford, CA., Hoover Institution on War, Revolution and Peace, 1965. 493p. $20. ISBN: 0817922113. *Class No:* 327(47)(01)

Asia—South & South East

[1587]
KOZICKI, R.J., *ed.* **International relations of South Asia, 1947-80:** a guide to information sources. Detroit, Mich., Gale Research Co., 1981. xiv,166p. $68. ISBN: 0810313294.

A section on bibliographies and reference works (p.3-5) is followed by the 4 main sections: 1. South Asia as a region - 2. India - 3. Pakistan - 4. Bangladesh, Sri Lanka, Nepal, Bhutan, Afghanistan. Entries are annotated, and sections are subdivided (monographs - articles and essays). An appendix lists basic books, A-Z (p.145-153). Author and subject indexes. *Class No:* 327(54+59)

India

[1588]
Yearbook on India's foreign policy, 1984-85 and 1985-86. Kumar, S., *ed.* New Delhi & Newbury Park, CA., Sage Publications, 1987:1988. 246p. £30. ISBN: 8170361206, India; 0803995830, US.

First published for 1982/83. Annual.

Could be considered a successor to the defunct *Documents on India's foreign policy,* edited by S. Kumar. 4 sections: 1.

....(contd.)

India and the world (trends and events) - 2. The major issues (analysed by Indian academics) - 3. Country profiles (Nepal) - 4. Statistical and documentary profile. '... series is a handy starting point for information on and analysis of India's foreign relations, especially seen from the Indian point-of-view. More documents would, however, be welcome ... a useful addition to reference material on India' (*International affairs*, v.65(2), Spring 1989, p.395). *Class No: 327(540)*

Asia—Near East

[1589]

SCHULZ, A., *ed*. **International and regional politics in the Middle East and North Africa:** a guide to information sources. Detroit, Mich., Gale Research Co., 1977. xiv, 244p. $68. (*International relations information guide series, v.6.*) ISBN: 081031326x.

Bibliographical essays in the form of 5 topical chapters (Regional issues - The foreign policies of Middle Eastern states - External powers in the Middle East - The Arab-Israeli conflict - Petroleum), followed by 2 chapters on reference materials (bibliographies and indexes, biographical indexes, chronologies, yearbooks and atlases) and on periodicals. Author, title and subject indexes.
Class No: 327(56)

Africa

[1590]

Année africaine, 1963-. Paris, Editions A. Pedone, 1965-. Annual. ISSN: 05701937.

Deals mainly with external affairs of the territories of Africa south of the Sahara. *Class No: 327(6)*

[1591]

DELANCEY, M.W. **African international relations:** an annotated bibliography. Boulder, Col., Westview Press, 1981. xviii, 365p. $38.50. ISBN: 0891586806.

2840 entries for books, journal articles, pamphlets and a few documents arranged in broad subject categories and sub-categories, and giving titles and brief annotations. Period covered is 1960-78 and some items to 1980. 'See' references. Analytical subject index, p.339-365.
Class No: 327(6)

America

[1592]

TRASK, D.F., *and others, eds*. **A Bibliography of United States-Latin American relations since 1810:** a selected list of eleven thousand published references. Lincoln, University of Nebraska Press, 1968. 441p. $32.50. ISBN: 0803201850.

Two main sections: a chronological survey, and a country-by-country survey. Books and periodical articles. Also specialised chapters, with lists of guides and aids, general studies, works on the Inter-American movements, etc.

M. C. Meyer edited a supplement to the above (University of Nebraska Press, 1979). *Class No: 327(7)*

America—North & Central

[1593]

SCHOOLEY, H. **Conflicts in Central America.** Harlow, Essex, Longman Group (UK) Ltd., 1987. xxiii,326p. maps. £25. (*Keesing's international studies.*) ISBN: 0582902746.

Covers Guatemala, Honduras, El Salvador, Nicaragua, Costa Rica, and Panama. In 6 main sections: 1. Political history (1.1: The region; 1.2-1.7 by region) - 2. Economic and social dimensions (subdivided by subjects, then country) - 3. Internal and cross-border conflict (subdivded as for above) - 4. Refugees, human rights and the Indian question (subdivided as before) - 5. Foreign involvement in Central America - 6. Central American peace initiatives. Includes a bibliography, p.316-317; name index, p.321-326; and subject index, p.319-320. *Class No: 327(71/73)*

Government Publications

[1594]

TURNER, C.A., *comp*. **Directory of foreign document collections.** Government Documents Round Table *and* American Library Association. White Plains, N.Y., Kraus Publications; UNIPUB, 1985. vii, 148p. $20. ISBN: 0890590451.

A list of major library collections in the United States and Canada containing publications of foreign governments and international agencies. Arranged A-Z by State (US) and Province (Canada). Includes information on the size and scope of the collection; access, loan and copying privileges; names of staff working with foreign publications; and National Union Catalog codes for each library. Indexed by country of origin. Libraries listed by State or Province, subdivided by name of institution, but no direct index to institutions or personal names. Overlaps with Kile & Taylor's *Directory of government documents collections and librarians* (4th ed., 1984). *Class No: 327(71/73)(061.1)*

Latin America

[1595]

FINAN, J.J. *and* CHILD, J. **Latin America: international relations:** a guide to information sources. Detroit, Mich., Gale Research Co., 1981. xviii, 236p. $38. (*International relations information guide series, v.11.*) ISBN: 0810313251.

Over 1400 items of interest to the general reader and the student arranged in 3 parts; 1. Bibliographies and aids - 2. General - 3. Countries (A-Z). Includes books and periodical articles only, mainly in the English language. Each item has a brief description of one or two lines. Author index, p.213-225; subject index, p.227-236. *Class No: 327(729.99)*

USA

Bibliographies

[1596]

PLISCHKE, E., *ed*. **US foreign relations:** a guide to information sources. Detroit, Mich., Gale Research Co., 1980. xviii, 715p. $68. (*Gale information guide library. American government and history information guide series, v.6.*) ISBN: 0810312042.

Annotated bibliography in 3 parts: 1. Diplomacy and diplomats-general - 2. Conduct of US foreign relations (15 chapters) - 3. Ready reference to Federal official sources,

....*(contd.)*

resources and guides, Presidential addresses and papers, publications of the Department of State, etc., Senate and House documents, journals and enactments, etc. *Class No:* 327(73)(01)

Histories

[1597]

FINDLING, J.E. **Dictionary of American diplomatic history.** 2nd rev. & expanded ed. Westport, CT., Greenwood Press, 1989. xviii,622p. $66. ISBN: 0313260249.

First published 1980.

Attempts to provide 'basic factual information on over 500 persons associated with US foreign policy from the Revolution through 1978, and descriptions or definitions of more than 500 non-biographical items connected with American diplomacy, ranging from crises to catchwords' (*Preface*). Entries average ½p. in length. 5 appendices (A. Chronology of American diplomatic history - B. Key diplomatic personnel listed by presidential administration - C. Initiation, suspension, and termination of diplomatic relations - D. Place of birth - E. Locations of manuscript collections and oral histories). Index, p.591-622.

Class No: 327(73)(091)

Bibliographies

[1598]

BEMIS, S.F. *and* GRIFFIN, G.G. **Guide to the diplomatic history of the United States, 1775-1921.** Washington, D.C., Government Printing Office, 1935. 979p.

Notes books and articles in many languages; source material, printed and manuscript; indexes collections of personal papers and authors. Also valuable for international relations as a whole. *Class No:* 327(73)(091)(01)

[1599]

—BRUNE, L.H. Chronological history of United States foreign relations, 1776-January 20 1981. New York, Garland, 1985. 2v. (1320p.), 24 maps. $150. ISBN: 082409056x. *Class No:* 327(73)(091)

[1600]

—BURNS, R.D., *ed.* Guide to American foreign relations since 1700. Santa Barbara, CA., ABC-Clio, 1983. xxvi,1311p. illus., map. $135. ISBN: 0874363233.

40 chapters, each with a contents list and introduction; 1. Reference aids - 2. Overviews: diplomatic surveys, themes and theories - 3. Colonial and imperial diplomacy to 1774 - chapters 4-38 follow chronologically - 39. Economic issues and foreign policy - 40. The armed forces, strategy and foreign policy. Cross-references. 2 Appendices (I. Makers of American foreign policy; II. Secretaries of State, 1781-1982). Author and subject indexes. Designed to supplement the above guide. ' ... a worthy successor indeed' (*Library journal*, 1 February 1983, p.196).

Class No: 327(73)(091)(01)

[1601]

—DE CONDE, A., *ed.* Encyclopedia of American foreign policy: studies of the principal movements and ideas. New York, Scribner's, 1978. 3v. (1202p.). $l95. ISBN: 0684155036.

Has 1050 entries (about half of these biographical sketches) for the period from the American Revolution to 1978. *Class No:* 327(73)(091)(01)

Australia

[1602]

AUSTRALIA. Department of Foreign Affairs and Trade. **Documents on Australian foreign policy, 1937-1949.** Canberra, Australian Government Publishing Service.

V.III (1944) was published in 1988 (lvi,749p. ISBN 0644056657) with a chronological list of documents, followed by the documents. Appendices include: III. Bibliographical guide (p.727-32). Indexes of persons and subjects. *Class No:* 327(94)

Cold War

[1603]

BLACK, J.L. **Origins, evolution, and nature of the Cold War:** an annotated bibliographic guide,. Santa Barbara, California, and Oxford, ABC-Clio, 1986. xxviii,173p. indexes. $49. (*The War/peace bibliography series.*) ISBN: 0874363918.

13 separately contributed bibliographies totalling 1367 entries on all aspects of the Cold War: 1. History - 2. Origins - 3. Image of the enemy - 4. The actors - memoirs and biography - 5. Canada and the early Cold War - 6. American-Soviet relations - 7. The Soviet perspective - 8. Critical issues - 9. Critical issues - Policy - 10. Regional influences and developments - 11. Eastern Europe - 12. Institutions and alliances - 13. Collections, documents, and bibliographies. Author and subject indexes.

Class No: 327.54

[1604]

YOUNG, J. 'The Origins of the Cold War', *The Historian*, no.13, Winter 1986/87, p.10-13.

Survey of recent publications. *Class No:* 327.54

Espionage

Bibliographies

[1605]

BLACKSTOCK, P.W. *and* SCHAF, F.L. **Intelligence, espionage, counterespionage, and covert operations:** a guide to information sources. Detroit, Mich., Gale Research Co., 1978. xv, 255p. $68. (*International relations information guide series, v.2.*) ISBN: 0810313235.

Annotated bibliography of mainly English-language books, periodical articles and newspaper accounts. 4 parts (21 chapters): General bibliographic resources - Strategic intelligence - Espionage and counter espionage - Covert operations. International coverage. Appended 'Selected bibliography of fifty titles' for a personal library or core collection. Author and title indexes. 'A useful tool for large bibliographical service units faced with tracing fugitive materials' (*Library review*, v.28, Autumn 1979, p.187).

Class No: 327.84(01)

[1606]

CONSTANTINIODES, G.C. Intelligence and espionage: an analytical bibliography. Boulder, Col., Westview Press, 1983. 559p. $60. ISBN: 0865315450.

Annotated bibliography of c. 500 major non-fiction books on intelligence and related subjects published from the 17th to the 20th centuries, mainly English-language. Arrangement is A-Z by author, and entries range in length from ½ to 1½ pages. Cross-references. Glossary and abbreviations, p.511-518. Title index, p.519-536; subject and author index, p.537-559. ' ... an original and enduring work' (*Choice*, v.21 (9), May 1984, p.1273). *Class No:* 327.84(01)

[1607]

Scholar's guide to intelligence literature: bibliography of the Russell J. Bowen Collection in the Joseph Mark Lavinger Memorial Library, Georgetown University. Cline, M.W., *and others.* University Press of America, for the National Intelligence Study Center, 1983. 236p. $40. ISBN: 0890935408.

More than 5000 titles on topics concerning intelligence and related matters. Worldwide scope, coverage being from events B.C. to the 1980s. Includes entries for monographs, journals and journal articles, biographies, case histories, military field and technical manuals, fiction, etc., Author and title indexes. *Class No:* 327.84(01)

[1608]

SMITH, M.J. The Secret wars: a guide to sources in English. Santa Barbara. CA., ABC-Clio, 1980-1981. 3v. (938p.). $32.95 each vol. (*War-Peace bibliography series, nos. 12,13,14.*) ISBN: 0874362717 v.1; 0874363039 v.2; 0874363047 v.3; 0317588052 set.

V.1.*Intelligence, propaganda and psychological warfare, resistance movements and secret operations, 1939-1945.* (I. Reference works - II. Propaganda and psychological warfare - III. Intelligence: general works and secret services - IV. Military intelligence; land, sea and air - V. Selected military campaigns and battles influenced by intelligence operations - VI. Special forces - VII. Secret operations: resistance movements, special forces, intelligence agents and paramilitary units - VIII. Some personalities of the secret wars. V.2. deals with 1945-1980 (I. Reference works - II. Propaganda ... - III. Intelligence, espionage and covert operations - IV. Some personalities). V.3. *International terrorism 1968-1980* (I. Reference works - II. General works: violence and terrorism, 1968-1979 - III. Philosophy and psychology of terrorism - IV. Terrorist tactics - V. Terrorist armaments - VI. Domestic and international support for and countermeasures against terrorism. - VII. International law and terrorism - VIII,. Terrorism around the world, 1968-1980). Each chapter has an introduction and each volume a chronology. No annotations. Author and subject indexes. *Class No:* 327.84(01)

Encyclopaedias & Dictionaries

[1609]

BURANELLI, V. *and* BURANELLI, N. Spy/counterspy: an encyclopedia of espionage. New York, McGraw-Hill Book Company, 1982. 361p. $24.95; £18.95. ISBN: 0070089159.

Profiles of the major figures and organizations of international intelligence from the Renaissance to the present. Over 400 articles on espionage and related information, arranged A-Z, including biographical sketches of spymasters and spies, descriptions of intelligence

.... (contd.)

organizations, indentification of networks and secret societies, explanations of historical events, clandestine techniques, and vocabulary. Information is authoritative, accurate, complete with dates. Many articles cite suggestions for further reading. Extensive index. *Class No:* 327.84(03)

[1610]

MINNICK, W.L. Spies and provocateurs: a worldwide encyclopedia of persons conducting espionage and covert action, 1946-1991. Jefferson, NJ, McFarland, 1992. 310p. $45. ISBN: 0899507468.

Short biographical dictionary aimed at providing quick information on the people involved in the post-World War II Soviet-Western spy wars. Numbered entries of varying lengths arranged A-Z. Emphasis is on personalities outside the Communist countries. Each entry ends with a list of books consulted, and there is an extensive bibliography of English-language reference books, monographs and periodical articles. Chronology of major Cold War espionage events. *Class No:* 327.84(03)

Dictionaries

[1611]

BECKET, H. The Dictionary of espionage: spookspeak into English. New York, Stein & Day, 1986. 203p. $17.95. ISBN: 0812830687.

Explains over 2000 cant terms used by the international spy community, those peculiar to the underground world of spies and also those that have surfaced into everyday language. Entries are enlivened by anecdotes explaining the terms' origins. '... this dictionary will be very useful to any serious student of espionage; it will also come in handy when readers of spy novels need an explanation of a technical term'. (*Wilson library bulletin*, April 1986, p.64). *Class No:* 327.84(038)

Biographies

[1612]

DOBSON, C. *and* PAYNE, R. The Dictionary of espionage. London, Harrap Limited, 1984. xiv, 234p. 30 illus. £10.95. ISBN: 0245542019.

Published in US as *Who's who in espionage* (New York, St. Martin's Press, 1985. $15.95. 0312874324.

A biographical dictionary with biographical sketches of more than 300 spies, spymasters and victims involved in spying or intelligence work since World War II. Supplemented by brief histories of intelligence organizations in 17 countries, a short glossary, and a bibliographical listing. '... a very esoteric style' (*International affairs*, v.61(1), Winter 1984/85, p.190). 'The bibliography provides a listing but no guidance on further reading' (*Library journal*, 1 June 1985, p.116). *Class No:* 327.84(092)

[1613]

MAHONEY, M.H. Women in espionage: a biographical dictionary. Santa Barbara, CA, ABC-Clio, 1993. 283p. illus. $65. ISBN: 0874367433.

150 essays on women, A-Z, varying in length from a few paragraphs to several pages. Cross-references and also 'see' references to alliases. A few sources are given at the end of each entry. International in scope, but mostly American and European, and mainly 20th century. Black and white

....(contd.)

portraits. Personal name and subject index. Written for a lay audience. Author is a former CIA operative. *Class No:* 327.84(092)

USSR

[1614]

ROCCA, R.G. *and* **DZIAK, J.J.,** *and others*. **Bibliography on Soviet intelligence and security services.** Boulder, Col., and London, Westview Press, 1985. xi, 203p. $16.00; £19.00. (*Westview special studies*.) ISBN: 0813370485.

A guide to Russian activities in intelligence, espionage, propaganda and psychological warfare. Includes 518 English-language sources, some translated Russian-language works, published since the Russian revolution. Sources grouped under 5 main headings (Selective bibliographies and other works; Russian/Soviet accounts; Defector/First-hand accounts; Secondary accounts; Congressional and other government documents). Each entry is numbered for reference from the indexes. Detailed annotations. Appendices: Glossary of abbreviations and terms; KGB and GRU leadership; and a chart depicting the growth of Soviet intelligence and security services. Author/source index, p.174-186. Title index, p.187-203. 'Strength lies not in its comprehensiveness ... but in extremely informative analysis provided in the extremely detailed annotations'. (*Choice,* v.23(2) October 1985, p.276). *Class No:* 327.84(47)

USA

[1615]

O'TOOLE, G.I.A. The Encyclopedia of American intelligence and espionage: from the Revolutionary War to the present. New York, Facts on File, 1988. 539p. $50. ISBN: 0816010110.

Nearly 700 articles arranged A-Z and cross-referenced. Some 70% of entries are biographical and include biographee's full name, birth and death dates, education, and intelligence and non-intelligence careers. Biographical and other sources appended. Remaining entries are on intelligence organizations, major events, techniques and devices, and the role of strategic/tactical intelligence and espionage in both peace and war. Longest article is an 18-page one on the CIA. Extensive subject index. 400-item unannotated bibliography of English-language books, articles and government documents. *Class No:* 327.84(73)

Parliaments

Great Britain

Bibliographies

[1616]

MENHENNET, D. *and* **WAINWRIGHT, J. 'POLIS' in Parliament:** computer-based information retrieval in the House of Commons Library'. In *Journal of documentation.* v.38(2), June 1982, p.72-93.

Describes the organization of the House of Common Library and history of POLIS (the Parliamentary on-line information system) operational from 1980. Includes 8 references and the House of Commons thesaurus. (POLIS database is now managed by Meridian Systems Management

....(contd.)

Ltd. who charge 'a very high monthly rental to external users'. (*Refer,* v.5(4), Autumn 1989, p.22). *Class No:* 328(410)(01)

[1617]

PATTERSON, S.C. 'Understanding the British Parliament'. In *Political studies,* v.37(3), September 1989, p.449-462.

A review article with 64 footnotes, including titles. Text is in 5 sections: MP-constituency linkages - MPs political orientation - MPs voting behaviour - Committee-centre studies - Conclusion. *Class No:* 328(410)(01)

[1618]

RUSH, M. Parliament and government: an annotated bibliography of government publications for the 1986-87 Parliamentary session'. In *Parliamentary affairs,* v.41(4), October 1988, p.556-565.

Covers Parliamentary procedure, Parliamentary privilege, services and facilities, broadcasting of Parliamentary proceedings, the Ombudsman, Parliament and the EEC, Parliamentary control of the executive, the Civil Service, elections and electoral reform, official information and rights, the register of members' interests. Similar bibliographies were published for the 1978-1979 and 1982-83 sessions. *Class No:* 328(410)(01)

Handbooks & Manuals

[1619]

GRIFFITH, J.A.G. *and* **RYLE, M. Parliament: functions, practice and procedures.** London, Sweet & Maxwell, 1989. xxvii,538p. £21. ISBN: 042143970x.

Notes on references, table of Statutes, table of Standing Orders, and detailed contents list precede the 13 chapters in 5 parts: 1. Functions, powers and membership - 2. The framework of Parliament - 3. The use of opportunities - 4. The Lords - 5. Evaluations. Footnotes. Bibliography, p.525-7. Analytical index, p.529-38. *Class No:* 328(410)(035)

[1620]

SHELL, D. The House of Lords. 2nd ed. Hemel Hempstead, Herts, Harvester Wheatsheaf, 1992. xi,276p. illus. £40; $68. ISBN: 0745012019.

1st published 1988 by Barnes & Noble.

Describes and discusses the House of Lords and constitutional development, membership, the role of political parties, procedure and organization, legislative work, treatment of government legislation, (1979-1990), deliberative work, select committees and secondary legislation. *Class No:* 328(410)(035)

Periodicals & Progress Reports

[1621]

GREAT BRITAIN. House of Commons. Public Information Office. **Weekly information bulletin.** London, HMSO, £88.80pa; £2.30 each issue. ISSN: 02619229.

Information on the work of the House for the period of the bulletin and on forthcoming business for the following week. A users' guide is available from the Office also (Factsheet no.29). *Class No:* 328(410)(05)

[1622]
—GREAT BRITAIN. House of Commons. Public Information Office. Sessional information digest. 1991-92. London, HMSO, 1992. [3],47p. £6. ISSN: 02668343.

First published for 1983/84.

An index and companion publication to the above, as well as providing additional information. Issued about 10-12 weeks after the end of the Session. *Class No:* 328(410)(05)

Commonwealth

Histories

[1623]
GREY, I. **The Parliamentarians:** the history of the Commonwealth Parliamentary Association, 1911-1985. Aldershot, Hants. Gower Publishing Group Ltd., 1986. 336p. £29.45. ISBN: 0566051990.

Founded by leading Commonwealth statesmen and MPs, the original aim was to forge closer bonds between the parliamentary democracies of the world, and the book records the development and expanding activities of the Association. Chapters are arranged chronologically, and are followed by appendices and an index. *Class No:* 328(41-44)(091)

USA

Bibliographies

[1624]
The Speakers of the US House of Representatives: a bibliography, 1789-1984. Baltimore, MD., Johns Hopkins University 1986. xxx,323p. $37.50. ISBN: 0801827868.

Sponsored by the US Capitol Historical Society.

4280 partly-annotated books, journal articles, dissertations and also manuscript collections. An overview of the Office of Speaker precedes the bibliography, which is arranged in 4 chronological sections, each containing a general bibliography, followed by bibliographies of the 46 individual Speakers. Author index. Detailed subject index, and also detailed table of contents. *Class No:* 328(73)(01)

Encyclopaedias

[1625]
Congress A to Z: CQ's ready reference encyclopedia. 2nd ed. Washington, DC., Congressional Quarterly, 1993. 650p. $110. ISBN: 0871878267.

First published 1988.

Aims to be a comprehensive encyclopedia concerning the structure and operations of Congress. Includes explanations (several pages for each) of 30 basic processes (*e.g.* legislation, impeachment, lobbying, reapportionment). Also 250 definitions of terms; committee profiles; biographies of selected members; and historical facts. A 75-page appendix has historical lists of members of Congress; historical statistics on re-elections; party affiliations; vetoes; etc. Index of names and topics. '... indispensible source book ...' (*Choice,* v.26(7), March 1989, p.1120) of the 1st ed. *Class No:* 328(73)(031)

Tables & Data Books

[1626]
STANLEY, H. *and* NIEMI, R. **Vital statistics on American politics.** 3rd ed. Washington, Congressional Quarterly, 1991. 403p. $29.95. ISBN: 0871874606.

13 topical chapters, each concluding with study questions, presenting statistical data on such subjects as state governors' terms and limits on succession, public opinion on the death penalty and abortion, apportioning among the states of seats in the House of Representatives, etc. Annotated bibliography arranged by topical sections. Index. ' ... although designed as a textbook ... has uses as a reference book' (*Wilson library bulletin,* October, 1988, p.105, on which this entry is based). *Class No:* 328(73)(083)

Biographies

[1627]
Biographical directory of the United States Congress, 1774-1989. 15th ed. Washington, D.C., Government Printing Office, 1989. 2104p. $82.

First published 1859 under the title 'Dictionary of Congress'.

In 2 sections, Preliminary and Biographical. The Preliminary section includes a complete list of members of each Presidential cabinet, membership and leadership of the Congresses, etc. The Biographical section (¾ of the book) is arranged A-Z by individual's surname and includes biographies of senators, representatives, delegates, resident commissioners, and vice-presidents. Data includes office held, State or territory represented, place and date of birth, education, profession, jobs held, party affiliation, election history. Entries average a paragraph in length. No photographs or portraits. *Class No:* 328(73)(092)

Libraries

Great Britain

[1628]
MENHENNET, D. **The House of Commons Library:** a history. London, HMSO, 1991. xi,162p. illus. £25. (*(House of Commons Library document no.21).*) ISBN: 010850641x.

A history of the library from earliest beginnings - appointment of the first librarian (1818) - developing from when it served mainly as a gentleman's club library to the research library it is now. *Class No:* 328:061:026/027(410)

Lobbying

Europe—Western

[1629]
PHILIP, A.B., *ed.* **Directory of pressure groups in the European Community.** Harlow, Essex, Longman, 1992. 380p. £95. ISBN: 0582086973.

Profiles of *c.* 800 pressure groups operating at EC level. Organized by country, each entry includes details of the constitutional structure, election summary, data on political parties and major pressure groups (contact details, structure, funding, activities, achievements, and assessment of group's influence). *Class No:* 328LOB(400)

Great Britain

[1630]

DUBS, A. Lobbying - an insider's guide to the Parliamentary process. London, Pluto Press, 1988. ix, 221p. tables, figures. £30. ISBN: 0745301371.

A handbook to provide ordinary people with the knowledge they need to exert pressure on those in power in order to get results. 14 chapters (*e.g.* 4. Raising an issue in the House - 5. Legislation - 6. How an MP can help in other ways - 8. How to use election campaigns - 9. Influencing political parties - 10. House of Lords - 11. The European Parliament and other international bodies - 12. Councillors - 14. Commercial lobbying). 5 appendices (1. Commons glossary - 2. Lords glossary - 3. European glossary - 4. Political lobbying companies; specialist public affairs companies ; public relations companies offering lobbying services; Monitoring services - 5. Useful addresses and phone numbers). Bibliography. p.224-225. Index. p. 226-228. *Class No:* 328LOB(410)

[1631]

JORDAN, G. 'Insider lobbying': the British version. In *Political studies,* v.37(1), 1989, p.107-113.

Includes 8 references and footnotes.

Class No: 328LOB(410)

[1632]

MILLER, C. Lobbying: understanding and influencing the corridors of power. 2nd ed. Oxford, Blackwell, 1990. xv,250p. £40. ISBN: 0631172122.

lst published in 1987 as *Lobbying government.*

A manual of the techniques of access to and influence over power. In 3 chapters: 1. Government - the components of power; 2. Decision-makers - how do they work? 3. Dealing with government. 5 appendices. Index, p.245-250.

Class No: 328LOB(410)

Lobbyists

USA

[1633]

The American lobbyists directory. Wilson, R., *ed.* Detroit, Mich., Gale Research Company, 1989. 1588p. $194.93. ISBN: 0810348144.

A guide to American registered lobbyists and their concerns. Includes a list of Federal lobbyists, arranged A-Z, *c.*9000 organizations represented by 6000 active lobbyists; a list of State lobbyists, arranged State-by-State, subdivided by the organizations and the *c.*35,000 lobbyists that represent them; and an appendix listing State and Federal government offices regulating lobbying activities. Indexes by name of lobbyist, by organization represented, and by subject areas of interest. *Class No:* 328LOB(73)

[1634]

—Beacham's guide to key lobbyists: an analysis of their issues and impact. Beacham, W., *and others, eds.* Washington, D.C., Beacham Publishing, 1989. 632p. illus. $195. ISBN: 093383313x.

A directory of lobbyists considered to be the most effective and influential on Capital Hill. Each profile has a black-and-white photograph, address, issue specialities, clients, party affiliation, history of lobbying activities, etc. '... more anecdotal than analytical ... more useful than the bare-bones biographies in many directories ... (*Choice*, November 1989, v.27(3), p.455). *Class No:* 328LOB(73)

[1635]

Washington's representatives ... who does what for whom in the nation's capital. Close, A.C., *and others, eds.* 17th ed. Annual. Washington, Columbia Books,1993. 723p. $70. ISBN: 1880873036.

A directory of lobbyists, listing over 12000 individuals and 11000 companies, interest groups and public relations firms. A-Z list of companies and organizations (names and addresses) - Index of companies and organizations grouped by subject or industry group - Country-by-country listing of foreign governments and representatives in Washington. 6-page introduction gives an overview of lobbying in the capital. *Class No:* 328LOB(73)

Parties & Movements

Worldwide

[1636]

DAY, A.J., *and others.* **Political parties of the world.** 3rd ed. rev. & updated. Harlow, Essex, Longman Group; New York, St. Martin's Press, 1988. x, 776p. £70. (*A Keesing's reference publication.*) ISBN: 0582026261, UK; 0912289945, US.

First published 1980.

A guide to over 2000 political parties (Bangladesh has 127) worldwide, arranged A-Z (Afghanistan ... Zimbabwe), with brief introduction on each country. Little data given for some parties but the aim is to give information on historical development; structure; leadership; membership; policy; publications; international affiliations when available. Appendices on international party organizations. Index of people, organizations & countries, p.649-776.

Class No: 329(100)

[1637]

DELURY, G.E., *ed.* **The World encyclopedia of political systems and parties.** 2nd ed. New York, Facts on File; Harlow, Essex, Longman Group, 1987. 2v.(1410p.;697p.). £120; $175. ISBN: 0816015392.

First published 1983.

Covers 170 states and 8 dependent territories in articles of varying lengths. Arrangement is A-Z by country (v.1. Afghanistan ... Mozambique; v.2 Nepal ... Zimbabwe and smaller countries and microstates). Includes data on the history of the party system, organization, membership and/or constituency, leadership, and prospect. *Class No:* 329(100)

Histories

[1638]

BRAUNTHAL, J. History of the International.

Clark, J., *translator.* London, Nelson, 1967. 2v. illus.

V.1 covers 1864-1914; v.2, 1914-1943. 'Will become as essential for students of the European Labour movement as the late G.D.H. Cole's classic *History of socialist thought'* (*TLS* no.3440, 1 February 1968, p.105).

V.3, *History of the International: world socialism, 1943-1968* (London, Gollancz; Westview Press, 1980. 656p. $61. ISBN 0891583696) concludes the work. One section deals with the expansion of Socialism and Communism in Asia since 1945. *Class No:* 329(100)(091)

Communism

[1639]

FURTAK, R.K. The Political systems of the Socialist States: an introduction to Marxist-Leninist regimes. Brighton, Sussex, Harvester/Wheatsheaf, 1986. xi,308p. tables. £40; $70.80. ISBN: 0745000487.

A brief introductory survey of the characteristics and common features of Socialist States precedes in-depth studies of 15 individual countries (Albania, Bulgaria, Republic of China, Cuba, Czechoslovakia, German Democratic Republic, Hungary, Korea, Laos, Mongolia, Poland, Rumania, USSR, Vietnam, Yugoslavia). Notes for further reading are given at the end of each chapter. Name index, p.300-301; subject index, p.302-308.

Class No: 329(100)COM

[1640]

HOBDAY, C. Communist and Marxist parties of the world. Santa Barbara, CA., ABC-Clio; Harlow, Essex, Longman Group, 1986. [5], 529p. $70; £48. (*A Keesings reference publication.*) ISBN: 0874364760, US; 0582902649, UK.

Section 1: Historical and international perspectives, includes a historical essay on the rise and evolution of Communist and Marxist parties; Section 2: Communist and Marxist parties, the bulk of the book, is a descriptive list ofinternational Communist organizations arranged in 8 geographical areas subdivided by country, A-Z, and again subdivided by name of organization, A-Z. Section 3: Appendices, has a lengthy list of documents, with extracts, from Marx to 1986 (p.411-507), and a select bibliography (p.508-513) grouped as in Section 2, subdivided A-Z by author. Index of names (p.513-529). 'Easy to use, clearly written' (*Library journal,* v.111 (18), 1 November 1986, p.87). '... Communist and Marxist parties in the broadest sense ...' (*International affairs,* v.62(4), Autumn 1986, p.719).

A 2nd ed. by R. East was published in 1990 (596p. £85;$85. ISBNs 1558620737 (US), 0582060389 (UK).

Class No: 329(100)COM

[1641]

Marxist governments: a world survey. Szajkowski, B., *ed.* London, Macmillan Press; New York, St. Martin's, 1981. 3v. (1761p.), maps. £20 each vol.; $27.50 each vol. ISBN: 0312518579, v.1; 0312518587, v.2; 0312518587, v.3.

V.1 Albania - The Congo; v.2. Cuba - Mongolia; v.3. Mozambique - Yugoslavia. 25 regimes, self-described. Each includes a history of the country's transition from colonialism or capitalism to Marxist; a description of the country's party and government structure; biographies of leading officials; and military, economic and demographic data. China and USSR are only given 119p. but coverage is adequate for lesser-known regimes. Limited bibliographies. 'Indispensable for anyone interested in comparative Communism or individual Marxist governments' (*British book news,* December 1981, p.727). '... a good reference tool for students' (*Library journal,* 1 November 1981, p.2128). *Class No:* 329(100)COM

[1642]

WHITE, S., *and others.* **Communist and post-Communist political systems:** an introduction. 3rd rev. ed. London, Macmillan Press, 1990. xi,357p. figs., tables. £40. ISBN: 0333535472.

First published 1982.

A comparative study of 16 states. 8 chapters: 1. The comparative study of Communist and post-Communist states

....(contd.)

- 2. Histories, societies and political cultures - 3. Structure of government - 4. The party system - 5. The leaderships - 6. The policy process 7. Democracy and citizen politics - 8. Communist and post-Communist states in comparative perspective. Bibliography, p.337-352. Index, p.353-357.

Class No: 329(100)COM

[1643]

Yearbook on international Communist affairs: parties and political movements, 1991. Staar, F., *ed.* 25th ed. Stanford, CA., Hoover Institution Press, 1991. 675p. $59.95. ISBN: 0817991611.

First published 1968 (covering 1966).

Describes the activities of 107 organizations during the previous year. The party profiles are arranged geographically by region subdivided by country, some including directory type information and there are 12 biographies. Includes the Warsaw Treaty Organization, the C.M.U.A., and 12 International Communist Front organizations. Select bibliography. Index of names of persons. 'The volume should prove very valuable in any reference library specialising in political affairs' (*International affairs,* v.54(3), July 1978, p.549, of an earlier edition). *Class No:* 329(100)COM

Radical Right

[1644]

Ó'MAOLÁIN, C., *comp.* **The Radical right:** a world directory. Harlow, Essex, Longman Group Ltd., 1987 (distributed in US by ABC-Clio). 500p. £73.95. (*Keesing's reference publications.*) ISBN: 0582902703.

The radical right is here viewed as comprising ultra-conservatism, anti-communism, and right-wing extremism. About 3,000 organizations are listed in all. Profiles of about 1,500 parties, movements and groups in over 100 countries known to have far-right organizations, including anti-semitic and racist groups, right-wing guerrilla groups, right-wing conservative fringe groups and extreme nationalist groups, are arranged A-Z by country or territory. Each country section begins with a brief survey of recent political history and the evolution of the far right. Information for each organization includes name in the vernacular and in English, address, history, structure, membership, ideology, activities, finances, publications, and national and international affiliations. There are also brief notes on defunct organizations, lesser-known groups, and unaffiliated individuals. 'There is no comparable work' (*Choice,* v.26(1), September 1988, p.86). '... The most comprehensive listing...' (*Reference books bulletin,* 1 September 1988).

Class No: 329(100)RAD

Europe

[1645]

McHALE, V.E. *and* **SHOWRORSKI, S.,** *eds.* **Political parties of Europe.** Westport, CT., Greenwood Press, 1983. 2v. (1400p.). illus. $125 the set. (*Historical encyclopedia of the world's political parties series, v.2.*) ISBN: 0313244050.

V.1: Albania ... Norway; v.2: Poland ... Yugoslavia. Aims to provide a comprehensive reference guide to all significant parties in Europe through brief biographical sketches of the parties, covering such information as date and circumstances of foundation, evolution of ideology and programme, evolution of organization (including splits,

....(contd.)

mergers, associations and alliances), and impact of government and society. 39 distinct party systems are included. Country sections by contributing scholars have introductory essay and bibliography preceding the A-Z listing of the country's parties, which includes cross-references for varient and successive party names, initials and translations. *Library journal* (15 March 1983, p.577) considers the information given to be 'essentially factually correct and generally adequate for quick reference' but the bibliographies inadequate. *Class No:* 329(4)

Europe—Western

[1646]

DAALDER, H., *ed.* **Party systems in Denmark, Austria, Switzerland, the Netherlands and Belgium.** London, Frances Pinter Publishers, 1987. xiii,372p. tables. £25. (*European party systems series.*) ISBN: 0861873696.

Studies of continuity and change in the party systems of five smaller European democracies from the aftermath of World War II to the present. Notes and references are given after each chapter. There are five chapters, one for each of the countries studied. Index, p.365-372. *Class No:* 329(400)

[1647]

JACOBS, F., *ed. & comp.* **Western European political parties:** a comprehensive guide. Harlow, Essex, Longman Group, 1989. 730p illus., tables, maps. £95. ISBN: 0582001137.

Aim is to provide up-to-date information on all the major and minor political parties currently active in Western Europe. Two main sections cover the countries of the European Community and the other democracies, a third section outlining the continent's various multi-party political groupings. Arrangement is A-Z by country; for each country a map showing its political divisions, a historical and current overview of its political institutions and activities (with statistical tables), and a detailed examination of its political parties. '... a superb achievement ... (*Library Association record,* v.92(4), April 1990, p.345). *Class No:* 329(400)

Europe—Eastern

Encyclopaedias

[1648]

Political and economic encyclopedia of the Soviet Union and Eastern Europe. White, S., *ed.* Harlow, Essex, Longman; Chicago, St. James Press, 1990. xii,328p. illus. Maps. £65. $85. ISBN: 0582060362, UK; 1558620702, US.

A description of the political and economic histories and systems, from 1945 to 1990, of Albania, Bulgaria, Czechoslovakia, East Germany, Hungary, Poland, Romania, and the Soviet Union. Clear and detailed entries for each country and on leading personalities. Cross-references. Chronological table precedes the encyclopedia. Index of entries, p.325-8. '... a very useful reference work ... against a background of recent fundamental change' (*International affairs,* v.67(3), July 1991, p.608). *Class No:* 329(401)(031)

Communism

[1649]

STAAR, R.F. Communist regimes in Eastern Europe. 5th ed. Stanford, CA., Hoover, 1988. 369p. $11.95. ISBN: 0817988122.

First published 1967.

Covers events to mid-1988, with separate chapters on the 8 East European socialist countries, as well as the Warsaw Pact, the Council for Mutual Economic Assistance, and intra-bloc relations. Standard text in the field - but out of date already. *Class No:* 329(401)COM

Great Britain

[1650]

BEER, S.H. Modern British politics: parties and pressure groups in the collectivist age. 3rd ed. London, Faber & Faber, 1982. xiv, 434, xivp. £4.95. ISBN: 0571180647.

First published 1965. First and second editions were sub-titled *'a study of parties and pressure groups'*.

Mainly concerned with the rise of collectivism from the late 19th century to the early 20th century. 13 chapters in 3 parts (1. Five types of politics - 2. The Labour party - 3. The Conservative party) are followed by a Conclusion, an Epilogue, and a detailed index (p.i-xiv). *Class No:* 329(410)

[1651]

The Blackwell biographical dictionary of British political life in the twentieth century. Robbins, K., *ed.* Oxford, Blackwell Reference, 1990. 449p. illus. £30. ISBN: 0631157689.

Main focus is on politicians, but also includes information on the careers of church leaders, writers, the Royal Family, scientists, soldiers and businessmen, including some pre-1900 and Irish figures. Gives guidance on further reading. Has fewer facts than in *Dod's Parliamentary companion* or the *Civil Service yearbook,* but has much more qualitative comment. Full index. *Class No:* 329(410)

[1652]

REES, P. Biographical dictionary of the extreme right since 1890: an international biographical dictionary. Hemel Hempstead, Herts, Harvester Wheatsheaf, 1990. xx,418p. ISBN: 0710810199.

Profiles of 500 major figures on the radical right, extreme right and revolutionary right from 1890 to the present, arranged A-Z by surname. Entries include short bibliographies. *Class No:* 329(410)

Histories

[1653]

BALL, A.R. British political parties: the emergence of a modern party system. 2nd ed. London, Macmillan, 1987. xviii, 268p. £27.50. ISBN: 0333445015.

First published 1981.

A historical account of the development of the modern British party system from its origins to the late nineteenth century, written for students and others with little prior knowledge. 12 chapters in 4 parts: Part 1: The making of the British party system, 1867-1922 - pt.2: The inter-war party system, 1922-40 - pt.3: The party system and consensus politics, 1940-64 - pt.4: The challenge of the two-party system after 1964. Appendices list important dates since

....(contd.)

1867, and leaders of British political parties. Select bibliography (subject grouped), p.251-261. Index, p.262-268. *Class No:* 329(410)(091)

[1654]

HILL, B.W. The Growth of British parliamentary parties, 1689-1742. London, George Allen & Unwin Ltd., 1976. 265p. £30. ISBN: 0049421492.

Traces the development of the early parties in the new situation brought about by the Revolution of 1688. 12 chapters in 3 parts: 1. The shaping of the parties - 2. The heydey of the parties - 3. The parties in the age of Walpole. A conclusion is followed by Notes (p.232-247) arranged by chapter; a select bibliography (p.248-254) divided into MS collections, printed sources, and secondary works; and an index (p.255-265). *Class No:* 329(410)(091)

[1655]

—HILL, B.W. British parliamentary parties, 1742-1832, from the fall of Walpole to the first Reform Act. London, Allen & Unwin, 1985. x,272p. £18. ISBN: 0049421875.

A sequel to his previous book, *The growth of British parliamentary parties, 1689-1742.*

13 chapters in 4 parts: 1. Introductory - 2. The early parties in decline - 3. Party tradition versus Court tradition - 4. The revival of the Tory party. An appendix, 'Later allegiance of 113 Tories elected in the 1761 General Election' is followed by Notes (p.239-254) arranged by chapters; Select bibliography (p.255-260); and analytical index (p.261-272). *Class No:* 329(410)(091)

Conservative Party

[1656]

A History of the Conservative Party. London, Longman Group, 1978-. v.1-. £24.50 each. ISBN: 058250712x, v.1; 0582507138, v.2; 0582507146, v.3.

To be in 4v. V.1 & 3 are published; v.2 is promised for March 1991; no date for v.4.

V.1: *The foundation of the Conservative Party, 1830-1867,* by R. Stewart (xviii, 427p.); v.2: *The rise of democracy, 1867-1902;* v.3: *The age of Balfour and Baldwin, 1902-1940,* by J. Ramsden (xiv, 813p.); v.4: *From affluence to disillusion, 1940-1975.* V.1 deals not only with the leading figures but also minor characters, as well as party organization. Bibliography p.393-406. V.3 'will be regarded as a standard work for a long time' (*History,* v.65, 1980, p.149). *Class No:* 329(410)CON

[1657]

—LINDSAY, T.F. and HARRINGTON, M. The Conservative Party, 1918-1979. 2nd ed. London, Macmillan, 1979. 295p.

First published 1974 (New York, St. Martin's Press).

Provides chronological treatment in 19 chapters. Bibliographies, p.287-9. Non-analytical index.

Class No: 329(410)CON

Labour Party

[1658]

HINTON, J. Labour and Socialism: a history of the British labour movement 1967 - 1974. Brighton, Sussex, Wheatsheaf Books Ltd., 1983. ix, 212p. £19.95. ISBN: 071080184x.

Traces the changing relationship between the Labour movement and the broader working-class constituency. 11

....(contd.)

chapters (working-class organization in mid-Victorian Britain; Society, politics and the Labour movement, 1875-1914; Socialism and the new unionism, 1884-95; The Labour Alliance, 1895-1914; The labour unrest, 1910-1914; The impact of war, 1914-1921; Working-class organization between the wars; Labour governnment and general strike 1924-31; The thirties; Labour and the nation, 1939-51; The Labour movement in crisis, 1951-74. Further reading, p.201-206. Index. p.207-212. *Class No:* 329(410)LAB

[1659]

MORGAN, K. O. Labour people: leaders and lieutenants: Hardie to Kinnock. 2nd ed. Oxford, Oxford University Press, 1992. x,372p. illus. £8.99. ISBN: 0192852701.

First published 1987.

Examines *c.*30 key personalities in the history of the British labour movement between 1900 and 1987. 28 sections, each devoted to one or more personalities are grouped in 4 chapters: 1. The founding fathers, 1900-1931 - 2. Towards Jerusalem, 1931-1945 - 3. The years of power, 1945-1970 - 4. Retreat and renewal - 1970-1987. Select bibliography, p.346-360, Index. p.361-372.

Class No: 329(410)LAB

[1660]

PELLING, H. A Short history of the Labour Party. 10th ed. London, Macmillan, 1993. 225p. illus., plates. £35. ISBN: 0333594754.

A brief introductory account of the Labour Party from its foundation to the present. 11 of the 12 chapters chronlogically arranged (from 1906 to 1992, the 12th chapter being conclusions. 4 appendices: A. Party membership; B. General election results; C. Chairmen and leaders of the Parliamentary party; D. Party secretaries. Index. *Class No:* 329(410)LAB

Liberal Party

[1661]

COOK, C. A Short history of the Liberal Party, 1900-88. 3rd ed. (A 4th ed. covering 1900-1992 was issued in 1993. 250p. illus. £40. ISBN 0333558219). London, Macmillan Press, 1989. 192p. £33. ISBN: 0333448839.

Covers the electoral fortunes of the party, personalities and the policies that have constituted an integral part of the party since 1900. 3 appendices: I. Major holders of party office, 1900-1988; II. The Liberal vote, 1918-1988; III. Liberal by-election victories since 1945. Bibliographical note. Index. *Class No:* 329(410)LIB

[1662]

DOUGLAS, R. The History of the Liberal Party, 1895-1970. London, Sidgwick & Jackson, 1971. xx, 330p. illus.

15 chapters, well footnoted, followed by biographical notes (p.303-13). Short bibliography, p.315-8 (1. Private papers - 2. Periodicals, etc. - 3. Books). Non-analytical index, p.319-30. *Class No:* 329(410)LIB

Scotland

[1663]

KELLAS, J.G. The Scottish political system. 4th ed. Cambridge, Cambridge University Press, 1989. xii, 286p. diagr., 28 tables, map. £12.50. ISBN: 0521363195.

First published 1973. 3rd ed., 1984, was completely revised.

....*(contd.)*

14 sections: 1. Scotland as a political system - 2. The constitutional inheritance ... 5. Parliament - 6. Political parties and electoral behaviour - 7. Nationalism - 8. Devolution ... 12. The policy-making process - 13. The Highland periphery - 14. Conclusion. Notes, p.273-286, are arranged by chapter and include references. Bibliography, p.287-289, is A-Z. Index, p.291-296. *Class No:* 329(411)

Biographies

[1664]

Scottish labour leaders, 1918-1939: a biographical dictionary. Knox, W., *ed.* Edinburgh and Washington, Mainstream Publishing Co., (Edinburgh) Ltd., 1984. 304p. tables. £10. $39.95. ISBN: 0906391407.

Introduction, p.1-57 with 235 notes, is followed by the biographical entries. Entries, mostly 3-4 pages long, all end with lists of writings and sources. Entries marked with an asterisk denote information taken from the *Dictionary of labour biography* (*qv*). *Class No:* 329(411)(092)

France

[1665]

FREAR, J.R. Political parties and elections in the French Fifth Republic. London, C. Hurst; New York, St. Martin's Press, 1977. 292p. tables. $25. ISBN: 0312623313.

17 chapters, each with notes, on the period 1945-77: 1. French politics and the role of parties ... 4/5. Parties of the Majorité ... 12. Presidential elections in the Fifth Republic ... 15. Referenda - 16. Aspects of electoral behaviour - 17. Conclusion. 8 appendices (8. Glossary: elections, assemblies, etc.). Bibliographies, p.279-86. Analytical index. *Class No:* 329(44)

USSR

Encyclopaedias & Dictionaries

[1666]

LAIRD, R.D. *and* **LAIRD, B.A. A Soviet lexicon:** important concepts, terms, and phrases. Lexington, Mass., Lexington Books, 1987. 224p. $27; £10. ISBN: 066916738x.

Includes a list of members of the Politburo, 1917-1987, the Constitution and the Rules of the Communist Party. *Class No:* 329(47)(03)

[1667]

—ZEMTSOV, I. Encyclopedia of Soviet life. New Brunswick, NJ, Transaction, 1991. 376p. $59.95.

*c.*250 fairly lengthy entries which include Russian terms, colloquialisms, euphemisms and idioms. Russian and English subject indexes. An updated version of the author's *Lexicon of Soviet political terms* (1984). Complements the above entry. *Class No:* 329(47)(03)

Official Records

[1668]

GILL, G., *ed*. The Rules of the Communist party of the Soviet Union. London, Macmillan, 1988. xi, 264p. £29.50. ISBN: 0333387910.

Includes the texts of all the rules that have been adopted by the Soviet Communist party between its foundation 1898

....*(contd.)*

and the XXVII Congress of 1986, plus amendments adopted at various stages of the party's history. All rules have been freshly translated for this volume with indications of amendments made. A substantial introduction traces the evolution of party rules. Glossary. 'This is the fullest treatment of the subject now available in English ...' (*Political studies,* v.37(1), March 1989, p.147). *Class No:* 329(47)(093.2)

Asia

[1669]

Political parties of Asia and the Pacific. Fukui, H., *ed.* Westport, Conn., and London, Greenwood Press, 1985. 2v. (xviii, 678p. and viii, 679p.) tables. $145; £165.50 the set. ISBN: 031321350x.

Arranged by country, A-Z (v.1: Afghanistan-Korea; v.2: Laos-Western Samoa), covering 82 countries. 72 academic specialist contributors. For each country; concise overview, selective bibliography, and detailed party histories. Cross-references. Coverage up to late 1983 in most cases. Clear and consistant style. 3 appendices; Chronology of events; Genealogy of parties; Typology of parties. Index of people, organizations, ideologies and events (p.1269-1346). "In depth and scope this ... is the most comprehensive available" (*Choice,* v.23(10), June 1986, p.1824). *Class No:* 329(5)

China

Communism

[1670]

HSÜEH, C.-T. The Chinese Communist movement, 1937-1949. Stanford, Calif., Hoover Institution on War, Revolution and Peace, Stanford University, 1962. x, 311p. $8.95. ISBN: 0817921125.

23 sections in 3 parts, all entries being annotated: 1. General works - 2. The war period, 1937-1945 - 3. The post-war period. In each part a general section precedes sections on specific aspects of the subject. Appendices list personal, geographic and corporate names appearing in the annotations, and a list of publishers.

An earlier volume covers the years 1921-1937 (1960, vii, 131p. $6.95. ISBN 081792082x) and follows the same pattern. *Class No:* 329(510)COM

Africa

[1671]

Political leaders of contemporary Africa south of the Sahara: a biographical dictionary. Glickman, H., *ed.* Westport. CT, Greenwood Press, 1992. xxii,362p. $65. ISBN: 0313267812.

Biographies of 54 'contemporary' political leaders (*e.g.* since the mid-1950s), with bibliographies after each entry. Daniel Arap Moi (6p);Jomo Kenyatta (over 5p.); Desmond Tutu (5p). (Nelson Mandela is not included). Chronology. Bibliographical references, p.[337]-339. Index. *Class No:* 329(6)

America

[1672]

ALEXANDER, R.J. Political parties of the Americas: Canada, Latin America, and the West Indies. Westport, CT., Greenwood Press, 1982. 2v. (864p.. $65 the set,. (*Greenwood historical encyclopedia of the world's political parties.*) ISBN: 0313214743.

Arranged A-Z by country (v.1 Anguilla ... Grenada; v.2. Guadeloupe ... Virgin Islands of the United States). For each country there is an introduction with information on history, race, politics, labour, etc., followed by a select bibliography and a list of political parties by their English-language designations, with information on origin, development and leaders. Comprehensive index. 'Includes precise party histories, especially useful regarding Latin American politics' (*Wilson library bulletin,* May, 1983, p.789). '... highly recommended ...' (*Choice,* v.20(10), June 1983, p.1436). *Class No:* 329(7)

[1673]

—Political parties of the Americas, l980s to l990s, Canada, Latin America and the West Indies. Ameringer, C.D., *ed.* Westport, CT, Greenwood Press, 1992. 697p. $99.50. ISBN: 0313274185.

Intended to complement the above. Contains updated country essays and bibliographies, and an inventory of active political parties, with a description of each. Each chapter written by an expert. Arrangement is by country, each entry including a narrative followed by a bibliography and a list of parties. Extensive cross-references. Appendix has a chronology. 'Highly commended for all reference collections' (*Library journal,* 15 March 1993, p.72,74). *Class No:* 329

Canada

[1674]

HEGGIE, G.F. Canadian political parties, 1867-1968: a historical bibliography. Toronto, Macmillan, 1977. 603p.

8850 annotated entries; chronological/topical arrangement. Detailed subject index. 'Very thorough coverage ... Essential for every university-level library and every Canadian library of any pretensions whatsoever' (*Choice,* v.15(3), May 1978, p.374). *Class No:* 329(71)

Latin America

Bibliographies

[1675]

Latin American politics: a historical bibliography. Santa Barbara, CA., ABC-Clio, 1984. 290p. $75. (*Clio bibliography series, 16.*) ISBN: 0874363772.

Lists *c.*3000 journal articles on Latin American and Caribbean politics and political history published between 1973 and 1982. Some entries have short abstracts. Arranged geographically, subdivided chronologically. Items taken from the ABC-Clio database. Author index, cross-referenced subject index, and list of journal titles covered. *Class No:* 329(729.99)(01)

Handbooks & Manuals

[1676]

Ó MAOLÁIN, C. Latin American political movements. Harlow, Essex, Longman Group, 1986. 296p. £15.95. ISBN: 0582902754.

Data on *c.*700 legal and illegal political parties, left-wing and right-wing guerrilla movements, human rights pressure groups, politically active trade unions, and externally based groups (*e.g.* the Cubans in the US) active in continental and insular Latin America. Detailed information on each party is given, and also an account of the political background of each country. Index of names. *Class No:* 329(729.99)(035)

Biographies

[1677]

ALEXANDER, R.J., *ed.* Biographical dictionary of Latin American and Caribbean leaders. New York, Greenwood Press, 1988. x, 509p. $75. ISBN: 0313243530.

Intended as a partial companion to the 1982 *Political parties of the Americas.*

'Over 450 biographical sketches of the most important political figures in the 19th and 20th centuries in Latin America and the Caribbean' (Preface). Emphasis is on leaders (presidents, dictators, prime ministers) but more minor figures are often mentioned in the signed essays. Entries include bibliographies. No cross-references. Appendix A: Chronology of political events; appendix B: Biographies by countries. Index of people and places, p.481-506. List of contributors, p.507-509. '... useful for thumbnail sketches of specific political figures'. (*College & research libraries,* v.50(1), January 1989, p.85). *Class No:* 329(729.99)(092)

USA

Encyclopaedias

[1678]

Encyclopedia of the American Left. Buble, M.J., *and others, eds.* New York, Garland, 1990. 928p. illus. $95. (*Garland reference library of the social sciences, 502.*) ISBN: 0824047818.

'American Left' defined as 'that segment of society which has sought fundamental changes in the economic, political and cultural systems'. *c.*600 articles by *c.*300 contributors. Includes people, organizations and events associated with movements of radical social change and leftist positions on general topics (*e.g.* Abortion ... Utopianism). Majority of articles about a page in length and include 3 to 5 references. Glossary of terms and acronyms. Name and subject indexes. '... offers a fine introduction to many subjects otherwise difficult to find in reference works...the organization of the work is less praiseworthy than its content, however, and may cause difficulties for readers unfamiliar with radical history and vocabulary ... nonetheless strongly recommended ...'(*Choice,* v.28(2), October 1990, p.281). *Class No:* 329(73)(031)

Maps & Atlases

[1679]

MARTIS, K.C. The Historical atlas of political parties in the United States Congress, 1787-1988. New York, Collier Macmillan, 1989. 368p. illus., charts, maps. $160; £128. ISBN: 0029201705.

Continues Martis's *Historical atlas of the United States Congressional districts, 1789-1983,* published in 1983, which delineates district boundaries for the first 97 Congresses and names representatives from each district.

A complete history of political representation in America, claiming to be the first accurate, documented source of information about political party membership in the history of the US congress to the 100th (1989). Multicolour maps for each Congress show party representation by district; smaller maps on the same pages show party representation in the Senate. Pages facing the maps list the senators and representatives from each State and district with their party designations. The remainder of the work is explanatory text and a 700-item bibliography. 'This rich, beautifully presented compilation is a wellspring for research' (*Choice,* v.27(1), September 1989, p.84-88).
Class No: 329(73)(084.3)

Biographies

[1680]

JOHNPOLL, B. *and* **KLEHR, H.,** *eds.* **Biographical dictionary of the American Left.** Westport, CT., Greenwood Press, 1986. xiv,493p. $65. ISBN: 0313242003.

A collection of esssays on 275 individuals, mostly born between 1870 and 1920 and prominent in the major left wing organizations of the first half of the 20th century, and the history of the parties to which they belong(ed). Entries normally 1-2 pages in length, some 4 pages. 6 appendices (A. Chronology of key events - B. Major radical party affiliation and year of entry - C. Place of birth - D. Birthdate (with date of death) - E. Those who abandoned the radical movement - F. Ethnic origin). Index, p.465-489. List of contributors. 'Objective, scholarly tone...' (*Wilson library bulletin,* January 1987, p.76). *Class No:* 329(73)(092)

[1681]

Who's who in American politics, 1993-94. 14th ed. New York, R.R. Bowker, 1993. 2v. $225. ISBN: 0835237859.

First published 1967. Issued biennially.

About 25000 biographical sketches of US office-holders, persons active in party politics, campaigners, etc. Information gathered primarily from answers to questionnaires includes party affiliations; birth date and place; names of parents; spouse; children; education; political, governmental and business positions held; memberships; voting residence; address; etc.
Class No: 329(73)(092)

[1682]

—MORRIS, D. *and* MORRIS, I. Who was who in American politics: a biographical dictionary of over 4,000 men and women who contributed to the United States political scene, from colonial days up to and including the immediate past. New York, Hawthorn Books, 1974. 637p.

Complementary to the above. *Class No:* 329(73)(092)

Australia

[1683]

JAENSCH, D. *and* **TEICHMANN, M.** **Macmillan dictionary of Australian politics.** 4th ed. Crow's Nest, NSW, Macmillan of Australia, 1992. 256p. £35. ISBN: 0732914450.

Third ed. was published in 1988.

Guide for both student and lay person, providing a deeper understanding of the background to current events.
Class No: 329(94)

Socialism

[1684]

NICHOLLS, D. *and* **MARSH, P.,** *eds.* **Biographical dictionary of modern European radicals and socialists:** Vol.1: 1780-1815. New York, St. Martin's Press, 1988. 291p. $44.95. ISBN: 0312019688.

To be in 7 vols.

187 biographies of political radicals who helped to transform Europe's social and political order. 48 contributors. Each biography commences by giving the subject's nationality, occupation, and membership or role in radical groups, then summarizes the subject's life and radical activities, and analyses his/her political philosophy and its relationship to others' ideas, concluding with suggestions of books by or about the person. The biographies are arranged A-Z by name of biographer. '... a high standard ...' (*Wilson library bulletin,* October 1988, p.106). *Class No:* 329SOC

Working class movements

Great Britain

Biographies

[1685]

BAYLEN, J.O. *and* **GOSSMAN, N.J.,** *eds.* **Biographical dictionary of modern British radicals.** Hassocks, Sussex, Harvester Press (later Hemel Hempstead, Herts., Harvester Wheatsheaf), 1976-88. 3v. in 4. (2112p.). V.1&2: £85 each; v.3: £150. ISBN: 0855274042, v.1; 0855274948, v.2; 0710813198, v.3.

V.1: 1770-1830; v.2: 1830-1870; v.3 (in 2v.): 1870-1914. Biographies of *c.*900 British radicals active between 1770 and 1914, 'Radicals' covering middle as well as working class radicals in numerous radical, social, economic and religious groups and movements. Each entry details the subject's career and writings, and includes a bibliography of both primary and secondary sources.
Class No: 329WOR(410)(092)

[1686]

GREAVES, R.L. *and* **ZALLER, R.,** *eds.* **Biographical dictionary of British radicals in the seventeenth century.** Brighton, Sussex, Harvester Press, 1982-1985. 3v. ISBN: 0855271337, v.1; 071080430x, v.2; 0710804865, v.3.

An informative introduction on radicals of the 17th century precedes the lengthy biographies (*e.g.* Ashley, 1st Earl of Shaftesbury: over 7 columns; Henry Ireton (Cromwell's man): 8 cols.; Oliver Cromwell: over 7 cols.). V.3 has a supplementary bibliography, p.349-351, 3½ page corrigenda relating to v.1 and 2, and an index, A-Z by name of radicals included in the dictionary, p.356-371.
Class No: 329WOR(410)(092)

33 Economics

Economics

Bibliographies of Bibliographies

[1687]
International bibliography of bibliographies in technology, science and economics/ Internationale Bibliographie der Fachbibliographien für Technik, Wissenschaft und Wirtschaft. 9.-2. Ausg. Munich, K.G. Saur, 1969. 2v. (*Handbuch für Dokumentation, 3.*)

A. Einmalig erscheinende Bibliographien. 9. Ausg. (viii,887p.). B. Periodisch erscheinende Bibliographien. 2. Ausg. (viii,817p.). Volume A lists *c.*2200 systematically arranged entries (in 10 classes) for non-periodical bibliographies, catalogues and other lists covering science, technology and economics. Indexes of authors, editors, countries, subjects and publishers. *Class No:* 330(009)

Bibliographies

[1688]
BLACK, R.D.C. A Catalogue of pamphlets on economic subjects published between 1750 and 1900, and now housed in Irish libraries. Belfast, Queen's University, 1969. [xi], 632 p.

10,011 numbered items; 17 library locations. 'The work is in fact a union catalogue of pamphlets of economic interest published anywhere between 1st January 1750 and 31st December 1900' (*Introduction*). Chronological order. Full titles. Author, title and societies and institutions indexes. Well produced. *Class No:* 330(01)

[1689]
BROWNSTONE, D.M. *and* **CARRUTH, G. Where to find business information:** a world-wide guide for everyone who needs the answer to business questions. 2nd ed. New York, Wiley, 1982. 632p. $80. ISBN: 047108736x.

First published 1979.

Lists over 5000 publications in the English language on all subjects of interest to the world of business, describing briefly what kind of information each source contains. Only current sources included, particularly periodic publications and services. In 3 sections: source finder (A-Z list of over 2500 subjects, cross-referenced, and referring to item numbers in 3rd section; publishers index (listing all their publications); sources, A-Z by title, each with an item number. *Class No:* 330(01)

[1690]
Business periodicals index. New York, H.W. Wilson & Co., 1958-.v.1-. Monthly, except August; annual bound cumulation. ISSN: 00076961.

Its parent is *Industrial arts index,* 1914-57, from which both *Business periodicals index* and *Applied science and technology index* have stemmed.

Subject fields include: 'accounting, advertising and public relations, banking, building and buildings, chemicals,

....(contd.)
communications, computer technology and applications, drugs and cosmetics, economics, electronics and electricity, finance and investments, industrial relations, insurance, international business, management and personnel administration, marketing, occupational health and safety, paper and pulp, petroleum and gas, printing and publishing, real estate, transportation, and other specific businesses, industries and trades' (*Prefatory note*). Subject index, with full cross-references. *Class No:* 330(01)

[1691]
Contents of recent economics journals. London, HMSO, for the Department of Trade and Industry Library, 1971-. Weekly. £90 pa. ISSN: 00456368.

A current-awareness service, comprising facsimile reproduction of contents-tables of *c.*250 leading journals written solely or partly in English. Intended to fill a bibliographical gap. Annual list of names and addresses of publishers. *Class No:* 330(01)

[1692]
—**Contents of current journals** ... London, London Business School Library, 1977-. Monthly in each of 8 subject sections. £30pa each title, except *Economics* and *Finance and accounting* which are £70 pa, and *Organisational behaviour*, which is £50pa.

Photocopied contents-pages of journals in the Library in the fields of: Decision sciences - Economics (including economic forecasting) - Finance and accounting - Information management (including information technology) - Marketing (including design management) - Strategic and international management - Organizational behaviour - Operations management. *Class No:* 330(01)

[1693]
DANIELLS, L.M. Business information sources. New ed. Berkeley, CA., University of California Press, 1985. xvi, 673p. $35; £22.95. ISBN: 0520053334.

First published 1976.

21 chapters of annotated entries relating primarily to American sources, with chapter introductions. 1. Methods of locating facts - 2. Basic time-saving sources - 3. U.S. business and economic trends - 4. Basic U.S. statistical sources ... 14. Corporate finance and banking ... 16. International management ... 18. Marketing ... 20. Production and operations management - 21. A basic bookshelf (p.549-554). Full author and title indexes (p.555-673).

A 3rd completely revised ed. was published in 1993. (725p. $35. ISBN 0520081803). *Class No:* 330(01)

[1694]

—STRAUSS, D.W. Handbook of business information: a guide for librarians, students and researchers. Littleton, Col., Libraries Unlimited, 1988. 537p. $37.50. ISBN: 0872876071.

Arranged in 18 chapters in 2 sections, the first section dealing with guides, bibliographies, periodicals, newspapers, loose-leaf services, and electronic forms of business information. The second section deals with special fields of business, including marketing, banking, real estate, etc. Sample pages are included for illustration. Good index. '... a very useful and detailed handbook that complements ... Daniells' *Business information sources'.* (*Choice*, v.26(10) June 1989, p.1668). *Class No:* 330(01)

[1695]

Economics working papers bibliography, 1975-. Dobbs Ferry, N.Y., Trans-Media Oceana Publications Ltd., in association with the University of Warwick, Coventry, 1976-. Semi-annual. $115pa; $780 including bibliographic service. ISSN: 00946451.

Prior to 1977 the bibliography contained only unpublished working papers in broadly defined areas of economics and management received in the University of Warwick Library, but the subject scope has since been widened to include all the social sciences. Working papers are defined to include 'papers variously called discussion papers, research papers, seminar papers and working papers which are privately published, restricted in circulation, and often difficult to obtain'. In 3 parts: author index, series index, and analytical subject index, full descriptions being in both the author and subject indexes. No cumulations. A microfilm service for copies of original papers is available. *Class No:* 330(01)

[1696]

Encyclopedia of business information sources. Woy, J. 9th ed. Detroit, Mich., Gale Research Company, 1992. c.900p. $245.00. ISBN: 0810374897.

First published 1965 as *Executive's guide to information sources.*

Sources listed under 1000 business-related subjects, A-Z, subdivided by type of information. Live, print and electronic sources are covered, and including abstracting services, encyclopedias and dictionaries, periodicals, trade and professional associations, manuals and handbooks, etc. *Class No:* 330(01)

[1697]

FIELD, B.C. and WILLIS, C.E. Environmental economics: a guide to information sources. Detroit, Mich., Gale, 1979. 243p. (Man & the environment information guide series, vol. 8). $68. ISBN: 0810314339.

In 2 parts: 1.'Conceptional foundations' covers introductory readings, theoretical foundations and studies, environmental parameters, and socialist and future perspectives: 2. 'Empirical studies and applications' is concerned with principles in measurement, environmental media studies, and institutional and industrial studies, and the entries in this second part are annotated. '... a valuable and excellent resource ... will prove to be a reliable and dependable tool for environmental information research' (*RQ*, v.19, no.3., Spring 1980, p.294-5). *Class No:* 330(01)

[1698]

FLETCHER, J., *ed.* **Information sources in economics.** 2nd ed. London, Butterworth, 1984. xii, 339p. (Butterworths guides to information sources). £39. ISBN: 0408114711.

First published 1971 as *The use of economics literature.*

24 chapters (2. Libraries and making a literature search - 3. Using the economics library - 4. Reference and bibliographic tools - 5. Periodicals - 6. Unpublished material ... 13. History of economic thought - 14. Economic history - 15. Economic theory ... 19. Labour economics ... 23. International economics - 24. Social economics. Index, p.333-39. British slant. *Class No:* 330(01)

[1699]

HARVARD UNIVERSITY. Graduate School of Business Administration. Baker Library. **Author-title catalog.** Boston, Mass., G.K. Hall, 1971. 22v.

388,000 photolithographed catalogue cards. The Baker Library, one of the largest business libraries in the world, has 150,000v. A 'First supplement' adds 45,300 cards. *Class No:* 330(01)

[1700]

—HARVARD UNIVERSITY. Graduate School of Business Administration. Baker Library. Subject catalog. Boston, Mass., G.K. Hall, 1971. 10v.

228,000 photolithographed catalogue cards. The 'First supplement' adds 30,500 cards. *Class No:* 330(01)

[1701]

—HARVARD UNIVERSITY. Graduate School of Business Administration. Baker Library. Recent additions to Baker Library. Boston, Mass., the Library, v.13, 1973- Monthly. $18pa.

Previous title was *New books in business and economics.* Arranged in broad subject areas. *Class No:* 330(01)

[1702]

HARVARD UNIVERSITY. Graduate School of Business Administration. Baker Library. **The Kress Library of Business and Economics. Catalogue** covering material published through 1776, with data upon cognate items in other Harvard libraries. Boston, Mass., Baker Library, Harvard Graduate School of Business Administration, 1940. x,414p.

Supplement... 1776 (1956.vi,175p.); *Catalogue, 1777-1817* ... (1957.[x],397p.); *Catalogue,1818-1848* (1964.viii,397p.); *Catalogue supplement, 1473-1848* (1967.[iv],453p.).

The 1940 volume has 7279 items, including 23 incunabula; 6 locations. Supplement: 2569 items, plus errata; 6 locations. 1957 vol.:7085 items; 10 locations., 1964v. 7642 items; 8 locations. Arranged chronologically by year, then A-Z by author. The 1957v. has a narrower interpretation of 'economics' than the previous volumes. The 1964v. omits government publications except those of chambers of commerce or boards of trade, but it includes books and pamphlets in the main Baker Library. *Class No:* 330(01)

[1703]

Index to economic articles in journals and collective volumes, 1886/1924-, v.1-. Homewood, Ill., Richard D. Irwin Inc., 1961-.

Prepared under the auspices of *The Journal of economic literature* of the American Economic Association. Prior to the 1966 ed., title was *Index of economic journals* and each ed. covered two or more years.

....*(contd.)*

V.29, 1987 (published 1990) lists, by subject and author, *c.*40,000 articles published in 312 major economic journals and in collective volumes published in 1987, in English or with English summaries. Includes a list of journals and collective volumes indexes, the 4-digit classification scheme used and a topical guide to the classification schedules. Subject and author indexes. *Class No:* 330(01)

[1704]
Index to Indian economic journals. Calcutta, Information Research Academy, 1966-. Monthly. Rs.175 $60 pa.

Includes book reviews as well as articles. Cumulative index. *Class No:* 330(01)

[1705]
—RATH V. Index to Indian economic journals, 1916-1965. Poona Gokhale Institute of Politics and Economics, [1971]. 302p.

Indexes 32 journals, including official journals, in a subject arrangement. Author index. *Class No:* 330(01)

[1706]
International bibliography of economics. British Library of Political and Economic Science, *comp.* London and New York, Routledge, 1955-. v.1-. Annual. ISSN: 0085204x.

References to books, periodical articles, and documents, arranged in 15 sections, each subdivided: A. Preliminaries - B. Methods - C. General and basic works - D. History of economic thought - E. Economic history - F. Economic activity - G. Organization of production - H. Production (goods and services) - I. Prices and markets - J. Money and finance - K. Income and income distribution - L. Demand (use of income) - M. Social economics and policy - N. Public economy - O. International economics. Author and subject indexes. V.41: 1992 was published in 1993 (xxxii,450p. ISBN 0415692124). Supported by *Thematic list of descriptors: economics, 1989* (Routledge, 1989. 494p. ISBN 0415017777) and updated by *International current awareness service: economics and related disciplines* (November 1990-. Monthly. ISSN 0960152x).
Class No: 330(01)

[1707]
LONDON UNIVERSITY. Library. **Catalogue of the Goldsmiths' Library of economic literature.**
Canney, M., *and others, comps.* V.1 & 2, Cambridge, Cambridge University Press, for the University of London Library; v.3 & 4, University of London, Athlone Press. 4v.

V.1: *Printed books, to 1800* (1970, xxiii, 838p.); v.2: *Printed books, 1801-1850* (1975. vii, 772p.); v.3: *Periodicals which began before 1851, manuscripts, and additions* (1982. 223p.); v.4: *Index to entire catalogue* (1984. 459p.). One of the world's leading collections of early literature on the subject. *Class No:* 330(01)

[1708]
Management contents, 1975-. New York, Find-SVP (previously Skokie, Ill., Management Contents Ltd.), 1975-. Semi-monthly. $102 per hour.

Tables of contents of more than 320 business magazines and journals. Available only online (BRS, DIALOG, DataStar). *Class No:* 330(01)

[1709]
The Official index to the *Financial times*. Reading, Berks, Research Publications Ltd., 1981-. £610. ISSN: 02636891.

Prior to 1988 issue, title was *Annual index to the financial times*.

Compiled from the final London edition, plus references from the international (Frankfurt) edition. Cross-references. Date, page and column references are given. Also available on CD-ROM. *Class No:* 330(01)

[1710]
—Monthly index to the *Financial times*. London, Financial Times Business Information Ltd., 1981-. £297pa.

Electronically compiled index in 3 sections: corporate; general (including book reviews); personalities. Cross-referenced. Entries include brief descriptions of subjects covered, issue date, page number, and item identification. Published about 4 months after the month of the issues. Also available online (DIALOG, Information Services Inc.)
Class No: 330(01)

[1711]
SCIMP: European index of management periodicals. Manchester, distributed by Manchester Business School Library for the European Business School Librarians Group, 1978-. 10pa. £75pa. FIM 650. ISSN: 01415077.

SCIMP (Selective Co-operative Index of Management Periodicals) is a co-operative effort of 18 European business school libraries. Indexes over 160 journals, the main ones exhaustively, covering the fields of management, finance and economics, industry and marketing, and associated subjects. Articles are listed in broad subject groups, with detailed permuted subject and author indexes (the subject index is cumulated 3 times a year). Articles in English from Scandinavian journals are included in particular issues 4 times a year. List of periodicals indexed in each issue. Also available for searching online on the database at Helsinki School of Economics, and on CD-ROM. *Class No:* 330(01)

[1712]
—SCIMP/SCANP thesaurus. Vernon, K.D.C. *and* Newman, S.J., *eds.* London, London Graduate School Library, 1980. (Available from Mr. Geoffrey Cleave, University of Warwick, Coventry CV4 7AL). 124p.

Primarily an indexing tool for retrieving information on-line from the database at Helsinki. *Class No:* 330(01)

[1713]
THWEATT, W.O. Classical political economy: a survey of recent literature. Boston, Mass., Kluwer-Academic Publishers, 1988. viii,275p. $50. ISBN: 0898382297.

Updates Schumpeter's *History of economic analysis*.

5 main chapters, each dealing with a leading classical political economist (Adam Smith, Malthus, Ricardo, J.S. Mill and Marx), plus a chapter devoted to six 'minor' figures. Each chapter surveying the literature is followed by a commentary. 'Its comprehensiveness, its lively style, the scholarship of its contributors, make it valuable to both novice and master in the history of economic thought, as well as an excellent reference' (Journal of economic history, v.69(1), March 1989, p.252-4). *Class No:* 330(01)

Encyclopaedias

[1714]

GREENWALD, D., *ed.* **Encyclopedia of economics.** 2nd ed. New York, McGraw-Hill Book Company, 1993. 1120p. illus. $99.50; £80.95. ISBN: 0070244103.

First published 1982.

A detailed contents list precedes over 300 signed articles on wide- ranging topics by eminent contributors, with up-to-date authoritative discussions. References are appended to each article, which provides a definition and explanation of the subject, discusses its importance, its relationship to other concepts and opposing viewpoints. No biographies. 2 appendices: I: Classification of articles by economic fields; II: Time table of economic events. Name index. Subject index is analytical. US slanted. *Class No:* 330(031)

[1715]

PALGRAVE, R.H.I. The New Palgrave: a dictionary of economics. Eatwell, J., *and others,* eds. London, Macmillan Press; New York, Stockton Press, 1988. 4v. (3500p.). £395; $650. ISBN: 0333372352, UK; 0935859101, US.

First published 1894-96 as the *Dictionary of political economy,* reprinted 1984, 1896 & 1899; new ed. published 1923-26 as *Palgrave's Dictionary of political economy.*

The new edition 'like its predecessor, attempts to define the state of the discipline by presenting a comprehensive and critical account of economic thought' (Publisher's note, v.1, p.vii). About 900 scholars participated. *c.*2000 signed entries in the 4 volumes (1300 subject entries and 900 biographical entries). Length of articles varies (*e.g.* 'Econometrics', 11p.; 'Mathematical economics', 4p.) as do the bibliographies at the end of each article (less than 10 to over 200 items). The biographies, of economists born before 1st January 1916, list both selected works of the biographee and works about him/her. Extensive cross-references. Detailed analytical index, and appendix classifying entries by major subject area. '... succeeeds in its attempt to be a modern treatise on economics. It will undoubtedly become the classic for this century that its predecessor was for the preceding one. However, its scholarly and mathematical approach to the material means its usefulness is limited to serious researchers in economics and related social sciences'. (*Reference books bulletin,* 1st April 1988, p.1320). *Class No:* 330(031)

[1716]

—The New Palgrave dictionary of money and finance. Newman, P., *and others,* eds. London, Macmillan; New York, Stockton Press, 1992. 3v.(2621p.). illus. £350; $595. ISBN: 156159041x, US; 0333527224, UK.

Companion to the above. Over 1000 essays by 800 contributors ('absolute priority rule'...'Zero coupon bonds'). Cross-references. Appendices include a list of entries, A-Z; subject classification; and a list of 104 subheadings. 'The especially fine write-up on Japan constitutes a minitreatise' (*Library journal,* January 1993, p.104,100). *Class No:* 330(031)

Dictionaries

[1717]

The Macmillan dictionary of modern economics. Pearce, D.W., *ed.* 4th ed. London, Macmillan Press, 1992. 560p. £35. (*Macmillan dictionary series.*) ISBN: 0333576026.

First published 1981. *Published in USA by MIT as The*

....(contd.)
MIT dictionary of modern economics. (3rd ed. ISBN 0262161044 (USA).

Designed for the needs of students of economics, and useful to students of business and the social sciences. Over 2,800 entries and 14 contributors. Entries (A-Z) include biographies (*e.g.* 'J.M. Galbraith': over 1½ col., including brief summaries of major works. 'International Monetary Fund': 3½ cols.). No bibliographies. Review of the American edition states 'For currency and readability, this work supersedes Douglas Greenwald's 'McGraw-Hill dictionary of modern economics' (3rd ed., 1983) and Douglas A.L. Auld's 'American dictionary of economics' (1983) (*Choice,* v.24 (11/12), July/August 1987, p.1678). *Class No:* 330(038)

[1718]

PAENSON, I., *comp.* **Systematic glossary, English-French-Spanish-Russian, of selected economic and social terms.** Oxford, Pergamon Press, 1963. xxxv, 414p. diagrs., Loose leaf. £47. ISBN: 0080164358.

A co-operative effort involving NIESR, Institut National de Statistique et des Études Économiques, UNECLA and Institute of World Economy and International Relations, Moscow.

About 7,000 terms are defined and explained (sometimes at length) in all 4 languages. 8 chapters, with detailed subdivisions: 1. Demand - 2. Production - 3. Business economics - 4. Labour and social security questions - 5/6. Financial questions - 7. Economic theories - 8. International trade and other forms of international economic relations. A-Z index for each language. *Class No:* 330(038)

[1719]

—MUNNIKSMA, F. International business dictionary in nine languages/... English/Esperanto/Deutsch/Español/Français/ Italiano/Nederlands/Portuguese/ Svensk. London, Harrap, 1974. xvi,535p.

2812 English-base entries, with English and Esperanto explanations, equivalents in the other 7 languages, and indexes in 8 languages. *Class No:* 330(038)=00

[1720]

RUTHERFORD, D. Dictionary of economics. London, Routledge, 1992. 530p. £50. ISBN: 0415065666.

*c.*4300 A-Z entries for the key terms, issues, theories and concepts of mainstream economic theory and related disciplines. Includes biographies of eminent economists, profiles of organizations, acronyms and jargon. Concise and authoritative definitions, illustrated by graphs, models and diagrams as necessary. Cross-references. Classified index. '... a dictionary for economists rather than a dictionary of economics ...' (*Introduction*). *Class No:* 330(038)

Polyglot

[1721]

BERNARD, Y *and* **COLLI, J.-C. Dictionnaire économique et financier:** Français-anglais-allemande-espagnol. 5e éd. Paris, Éditions du Seuil, 1989. 1438p. £57.

First published 1975.

A dictionary of economic, social and financial terms, each term fully defined and explained in French, with equivalents in the other 3 languages. *Class No:* 330(038)=00

[1722]

—BERNARD, Y *and* COLLI, J.-C. Vocabulaire économique et financier. 6th rev. ed. Paris, Editions du Seuil, 1989. 372p. £5.70.

Abbreviated version of the above.
Class No: 330(038)=00

[1723]

—BERNARD, Y *and* COLLI, J.-C. Wörterbuch der Wirtschaft und Finanzen... Paris, Editions du Seuil,1989. 458p. £17.25.

An abbreviated version of the French original. Terms defined in German. Multilingual index.
Class No: 330(038)=00

[1724]

DE JONG, F.J., *and others, eds*. Quadrilingual economics dictionary: English/American, French, German, Dutch. The Hague, Netherlands, Martinus Nijhoff; Deventer/Antwerp, Kluwer, 1980. ix, 686p. Dfl.95.; £48.50; $48. ISBN: 9024722438.

*c.*11,000 terms altogether (2400 Dutch, 2900 French) arranged in 4 sections: 1. English/American terms, A-Z, each term followed by equivalents in the other three languages; 2. French terms ...; 3. German terms ...; 4. Dutch terms ... Words included are current as of the mid-1970s. *Class No:* 330(038)=00

[1725]

EUROPEAN PARLIAMENT. Translation Division. Terminologie économique (français/italien/anglais/allemand/néerlandais/danois). 3e.éd. Luxembourg, the Parliament, 1979. 287; 163p. £6.30.

First published 1968.
A-Z listing of French terms with definitions, corresponding terms and indexes in the other 5 languages.
Class No: 330(038)=00

[1726]

HERBST, R. Dictionary of commercial, financial and legal terms pertaining to trade and industry... Thoune (Switzerland), Translegal, 1979-1985. 3v. £93.50 each vol.

First published 1955-1965.
V.1: English-French-German (1985, 4th ed. 1155p.); v.2: German-English-French (1989 4th ed. 1147p.); v.3: French-German-English (1982, 2nd ed. xii,958p.). About 30,000 head-words in each volume. Separate entries for different meanings of words. Differentiates between British and US English, Swiss and German German. Compounds are entered under both parts. *Class No:* 330(038)=00

[1727]

IMF glossary: English-French-Spanish. IMF Bureau of Language Services, *comp*. 3rd rev. ed. Washington, DC., International Monetary Fund, 1986. vii, 286p. £11.25. ISBN: 093993471x.

First published 1979.
About 2000 words, phrases and institutional titles most commonly encountered in IMF documents in areas such as money and banking, public finance, balance of payments and economic growth, arranged A-Z by English name. French and Spanish indexes lead to numbered English entries. Appendixes include: III: Multilingual index of abbreviations and acronyms; IV: Currency units of various countries and areas. *Class No:* 330(038)=00

[1728]

ISAACS, A. Multilingual commercial dictionary. New York, Facts on File, 1980 (available from Books Demand UMI). 400p. $123.

*c.*3,000 commercial words and phrases in common commercial use with equivalent terms in other languages (English/American, French, German, Italian, Portuguese, Spanish). *Class No:* 330(038)=00

[1729]

KOHLS, S., *ed*. Dictionary of international economics: German, Russian, English, French, Spanish. Leiden, Netherlands, Sijthoff & Noordhoff International Publishers, 1976. 620p. Dfl.65; £26.50; $32.50. ISBN: 9028605053.

Main part has 6500 German entries, A-Z, with equivalents in the other languages (9700 in Russian, 9300 in English, 9500 in French, & 9400 in Spanish). Indexes in the other languages refer to the German entries.
Class No: 330(038)=00

[1730]

NASR, Z. An English/French/Arabic dictionary of economics. London, Macmillan, 1980. xii,212p. £12.95. ISBN: 0333231090.

Arranged A-Z by the English headword, giving French and Arabic translations. No indexes.
Class No: 330(038)=00

English

[1731]

AMMER, C. *and* AMMER, D.S. Dictionary of business and economics. 2nd ed. New York & London, Collier Macmillan, 1984. 507p. $29.95; £26.50. ISBN: 0029007909.

First published 1977.
An encyclopedic dictionary of over 3,000 entries covering general theory of economics, history of economics and business, prices and income, banking and finance, accounting, law, investments, econometrics, labour, consumer economics, tax laws, microcomputers, etc. Includes biographies of important economists with emphasis on their ideas. Substantial descriptions but with a definite US slant (examples are all from US publications; includes terms peculiar to USA). *Class No:* 330(038)=20

[1732]

BANNOCK, G., *and others*. Dictionary of economics. 5th ed. London, Penguin Books, 1992. 480p. £6.99. ISBN: 0140312551.

First published 1972.
Over 1600 entries (definitions and short articles, *e.g.* 'International liquidity': 1¾p.; 'Inflation accounting': 1p.). Biographies included (*e.g.* 'Keynes': 2p.). Aimed at both the general reader and at students up to the second year of a university course in the subject. Extensive cross-references.
Class No: 330(038)=20

[1733]

BROWNSTONE, D.M., *and others*. The VNR dictionary of business and finance. New York, Van Nostrand Reinhold, 1980. 293p. $35.

Defines keywords and phrases from all major business, financial and related subject fields, including industrial relations, marketing, real estate, insurance, statistics, etc.
Class No: 330(038)=20

[1734]
DEANE, P. *and* **KUPER, J.,** *eds*. **A Lexicon of economics.**
London, Routledge, 1988. xxviii,380p. £9.95. (*Social
science lexicons.*) ISBN: 0415002346.

One of a series of social science lexicons based on the
Social science encyclopedia.

A lengthy historical introduction to economics (p.xv-xxvii)
is followed by articles on specific economics arranged by
subject and including biographies. References for 'further
reading' are given after the introduction and each entry. 81
contributors. There is a contents list of subjects.
Class No: 330(038)=20

[1735]
GREENWALD, D., *ed*. **The McGraw-Hill dictionary of
modern economics:** a handbook of terms and organizations.
3rd ed. New York, McGraw-Hill, 1983. xiii, 632p. illus.
$57.50; £49.95. ISBN: 007024376x.

First published 1965.

Simple definitions of *c.*1400 frequently used modern
economic terms, plus references to sources; followed by
descriptions of *c.*200 private, public and non-profit
associations and research organizations. Heavily US slanted.
'A welcome updating of a useful work' (*Wilson library
bulletin,* v.48(1), September 1973, p.84, of the 2nd ed.).
Class No: 330(038)=20

[1736]
—GREENWALD, D. The Concise McGraw-Hill dictionary of
modern economics. New York, McGraw-Hill, 1984. 396p.
$19.95; £16.50. ISBN: 0070243875.

Based on the 3rd ed. of *The McGraw-Hill dictionary of
modern economics,* but has fewer descriptions of actual
organizations and does not contain some 250 terms largely
related to the accounting profession and insurance industry.
Class No: 330(038)=20

[1737]
—NEMMER, E.E. Dictionary of economics and business.
Enl.ed. Totowa, N.J., Littlefield, Adams, 1978. 523p.
$12.50. ISBN: 0822600331.

First published 1959.

Over 5000 brief entries, with numerous cross-references.
Enters organizations under known abbreviated form, cross-
referring from the full form. Primarily for use in US
colleges. *Class No:* 330(038)=20

[1738]
HANSON, J.L. A Dictionary of economics and commerce.
6th ed., rev. & updated. London, Pitman Publishing Ltd.,
1986. [4], 396p. illus. £7.50. (*M & E professional
dictionaries.*) ISBN: 0712104305.

First published 1965.

Over 5,000 explanations and definitions of current
economic and commercial terms and phrases. Covers
economic theory, applied economics, economic history and
commerce. Includes abbreviations and acronyms in current
use, and also organizations (e.g., banks). Many cross-
references. 'Balance of payments': 2 columns, 1 table.
British slant. Useful to students. *Class No:* 330(038)=20

[1739]
MOFFAT, D. Economics dictionary. 2nd ed. Amsterdam,
New York, Oxford, Elsevier, 1983. xiii,[1],331p. tables.
£37.54; $38; Dfl.125. ISBN: 0444007989.

First published 1976.

Over 5000 concise entries, with extensive cross-
references. Separate section for abbreviations. Mathematical
appendix gives details relevant to analytical methods, plus
weighted price indexes and weighted aggregative indexes.
Entries vary in length (*e.g.* 'Balance of payments': 5 cols. &
2p. of tables; 'Collusion': 2 lines; 'Gross national product':
nearly 1 col.; 'Sanctions': 12 lines).
Class No: 330(038)=20

[1740]
PASS, C., *and others*. **Dictionary of economics.** London,
Collins, 1993. 576p. 190 illus. tables. £7.99. ISBN:
0004703723.

Over 2500 entries defined and explained, both for the
general reader and for the student of economics, and many
including explanatory diagrams. Longer entries summarize
some of the major theoretical principles of economics. New
terms are included (*ie* 'Big Bang', 'insider trading'). Cross-
references. Appendix of mathematical symbols.
Class No: 330(038)=20

[1741]
**Reuter's glossary: international economic and financial
terms.** Harlow, Essex, Longmann, 1989. vii, 213p. £12.95.
ISBN: 0582042860.

First published l982 by Heinemann.

Compiled by Reuter's own staff. Over 2000 entries of
specialized definitions of terms used in banking, shipping,
brokerage, trading and business management. 7 sections
(general market terms - economy, currency - lending -
equities - commodities - energy - shipping). A-Z in each
section. Cross-references. Abbreviations and acronyms
(p.181-183). Double-column index (p.185-213). A
comprehensive revision. *Class No:* 330(038)=20

[1742]
SELDON, A. *and* **PENNANCE, F.G.** **Everyman's
dictionary of economics.** 2nd ed. London, Dent, 1976
(Paperback edition published 1980). 416p. £6.95. ISBN:
0460030280.

First published 1965.

Sub-title 'an alphabetical exposition of economic concepts
and their application'. About 500 entries, including
biographies (*e.g.* 'Hayek'). 'Mercantilism': 2 columns:
'Journals, economic': 11/3 col.: 'Social ownership': 3 cols.:
'Stagflation': 1/3 col. 'Related subject index' (grouping
entries under 14 heads), p.xi-xxiii, Reading lists, p.xxiii-
xxiv. A handy reference tool for all types of library.
Class No: 330(038)=20

[1743]
The World Bank glossary... 3rd rev. ed. Washington, D.C.,
The World Bank, 1986. 2v. (457 + + 445. p.). v.1 £44.50;
$.95. v.2. £33.95. $37.95. Reprinted 1991. ISBN:
0821317334, v.1; 0821317342, v.2.

Intended to assist the Bank's translators and interpreters,
and other Bank staff. Includes terms used in economics and
finance plus terminology common in such sections of Bank
work as agriculture, education, energy, urban development,
public health, transport, etc. Also lists acronyms frequently
found in Bank texts and has a list of international, regional
and national organizations. *Class No:* 330(038)=20

German

[1744]

EICHBORN, R., *von*. Cambridge-Eichborn German dictionary: economics, law, administration, business, general. Cambridge, Cambridge University Press, 1983. 2v. (xii,1163p.viii,1399p.). £100 each vol. v.1: $130; v.2: $140. ISBN: 0521258456, v.1; 0521258464, v.2.

First published as *Wirtschaftswörterbuch* 1947; later editions titled *Der Grosse Eichborn* (Düsseldorf, Econ-Verlag GmbH.).

V.1: English-German; v.2: German-English. about 50,000 main entry words in each volume, the most comprehensive English-German/German-English dictionary of legal, economic, business and administrative terms and phrases available to date. A particular strength lies in the distinctions given between the British and American equivalents of German words and their different usages. Also includes a large number of common or specialized phrases and colloquialisms. *Class No:* 330(038)=30

[1745]

—EICHBORN, R., *von*. Shorter Cambridge-Eichborn German dictionary: business and business law. economics, administration. Cambridge, Cambridge University Press, 1984. 2v. (xi,868; ix,977p.). £20 each vol. ISBN: 0521258138, v.1; 0521258146, v.2.

The condensed version of the above, with 140,000 entries per vol., based on a study of specialist works, newspapers, journals and official documents' (*Foreword*). *Class No:* 330(038)=30

[1746]

RENNER, R. *and* SACHS, R. Wirtschaftssprache/ Economic terminology (German/English; English/German). 4. Aufl., 4th ed. München, Max Hueber Verlag, 1982. 543p. £20.60. ISBN: 3190062013.

First published in 1965.

About 7,000 items in 25 sections (with subsections), ranging from general economics, money and currencies, banking and bookkeeping, through bankruptcy, international trade, advertising and publishing, to transport, insurance and statistics, with an appendix on office equipment. Each section has English and German translation exercises, a key to the exercises being available separately. *Class No:* 330(038)=30

Swedish

[1747]

GULLBERG, I.F. Svensk-engelsk fackordbok för näringsliv, förvaltning, undervisning och forskning/A Swedish-English dictionary of technical terms used in business, industry, administration, education and research. 2. revid uppl., med suppl. Stockholm, Norstedt, 1977. xix,[i],1722p.

First published 1964.

The 2nd ed. has an extensive supplement of *c.*40,000 new terms, giving a total of *c.*175,000 categorised terms. Rich in idioms. Includes many proper names ('Internationella': nearly 36 colums). British and US usages not differentiated. Includes abbreviations; list of important dictionaries in 50 languages. Well-produced and a fine example of its kind. *Class No:* 330(038)=397

French

[1748]

BREMOND, J. *and* GELEDAN, A. Dictionnaire économique et social: 100 articles thématiques, 1200 définitions. Paris, Hatier, 1981. 392p. F.37.50. (*Collection J. Bremond.*) ISBN: 2218051559.

Articles are lengthy, including comments, explanations, etc. (*e.g.* 'Inflation': 9p.; 'Emploi': 6p.). Cross-references. Index, p.384-392. Favourable review in *Bulletin bibliographique de France* (v.27(3), March 1982, p.480). *Class No:* 330(038)=40

[1749]

KETTRIDGE, J.O. French-English and English-French dictionary of commercial and financial terms, phrases and practice. 3rd ed. London, Routledge & Kegan Paul, 1973 (Reprinted 1978). xii, 655p. £25.

First published 1931.

About 12,000 main entries in each half, appendices of conventional signs, French syllabification, abbreviations and conversion tables. Many phrases (*e.g.* 'actions': 3½ columns); also cautionary notes on usage in French and explanatory text in both languages. *Class No:* 330(038)=40

[1750]

REDFERN, J. Basic terms of business and finance: English/ French, French/English. Lanham, MD, University Press of America, 1985. 578p. $45.25; £48.50. ISBN: 081914360x.

Clear, concise equivalents of French and English business terms, definitions being brief but sufficient. Under each item are listed related usages in finance and business, A-Z, allowing for quick retrieval. Similar to *Harrap's French and English business dictionary* (*qv*). Includes separate lists of French and English acronyms and abbreviations. 'Recommended for easy use and clear typography' (*Choice*, v.22(8), April 1985, p.1147). *Class No:* 330(038)=40

Italian

[1751]

EDLER, F. Glossary of mediaeval terms of business. Italian series, 1200-1600. Cambridge, Mass., Mediaeval Academy of Sciences, 1936 (Kraus Reprint). xx, 430p. $36. ISBN: 052701690x.

Glossary of c.2,000 terms, each with some six samples of usages, on OED lines. Classified list appended. List of primary and secondary sources precedes, p.1-17. *Class No:* 330(038)=50

[1752]

MOTTA, G. Dizionario commerciale, inglese-italiano, italiano-inglese: economica-legge-finanza. Milano, Signorelli, 1961 (Reprinted 1975). x,[i], 1051p. £18.95.

English-Italian, p.1-515; Italian-English, p.519-1051. About 15,000 main entries in each half. Many compounds and idioms (*e.g.* 'Account':2½ columns; 'Parts':1). English nouns are categorised; stress in Italian not shown. Intended for Italian rather than British users. English terms are sometimes suspect. *Class No:* 330(038)=50

[1753]

PICCHI, F. Economics and business: dizionario enciclopedico economico e commerciale; inglese-italiano, italiano-inglese. 2nd revised ed. Bologna, Nicola Zanichelli, S.p.A., 1990. 1594p. £53.

Entries, A-Z, in the English language with definitions in

....*(contd.)*

Italian, followed by Italian terms, A-Z, referring to English equivalents (straight translations, with no definitions).
Class No: 330(038)=50

Spanish

[1754]

LOZANO IRUESTE, J.M. **Diccionario bilingüe de economía empresa.** Madrid, J.M.L.I., 1989. 799p. £38.80.
Nearly 30,000 words and expressions in Spanish and English. Includes Spanish-American terms in use.
Class No: 330(038)=60

Portuguese

[1755]

LEWIS, T., *and others, eds.* **Harrap's English-Brazilian Portuguese business dictionary.** London, Harrap's, 1982. [6], 283, [33]p. £35. ISBN: 0245538208.
A basic translating tool for everyday business language, including terms and expressions used in a wide range of commercial contexts such as banking, stock exchange, accountancy, insurance, commerce and law, drawing upon commercial correspondence, company reports, contracts, newspapers and magazines, etc. Translates only from English into Brazilian Portuguese. Cross-references.
Class No: 330(038)=690

Russian

[1756]

ANIKIN, A.V., *ed.* **Anglo-russkii ekonomicheskii slovar .../ English-Russian economics dictionary.** Moscow, Russian Language Publishers, 1977. 728p.
About 60,000 English terms and phrases, A-Z, with Russian equivalents and alternatives. Includes some proper names (*e.g.* Pigou) with explanations of who they were in the economics field. A list of abbreviations, with expansions in both English and Russian (p.698-727).
Class No: 330(038)=82

Arabic

[1757]

HALEEM, M.A.A. *and* KAY, E. **English-Arabic business dictionary.** London, Graham & Trotman, 1984. xxxii, 263p. £22. ISBN: 0860104486.
About 5000 terms arranged by the English form, A-Z, with transliteration of the Arabic, and then in Arabic script. Some basic grammatical points, a few basic phrases for everyday use, and a listing of Arabic numerals precede the main dictionary. A section at the end lists countries and currencies of the major countries of the world with Arabic equivalents and transliterations. *Class No:* 330(038)=927

Chinese

[1758]

BROADBENT, K.A. **A Chinese-English dictionary of China's rural economy.** Farnham Royal, Hants, Commonwealth Agricultural Bureaux, 1978. xiii,406p.
Terms are listed in both Chinese characters and Roman letters. Includes a glossary of current terms and an English-Chinese index. *Class No:* 330(038)=951

Japanese

[1759]

Oriental economist's new Japanese-English dictionary of economic terms. Tokyo, Oriental Economist, 1977. 561,79p.
Earlier eds. published 1970 and 1974.
Both Roman and Japanese characters, with English translations of the terms. Reported to be of high quality.
Class No: 330(038)=956

[1760]

—FUJITA, J. **Kenkyusha's English-Japanese dictionary of trade and industry.** New ed. Tokyo, Kenkyusha, 1970. xv,1181p.
This dictionary is also well thought of.
Class No: 330(038)=956

Theses

Bibliographies

[1761]

The Comprehensive dissertation index (1861-1972). Vols. 25-26: Business and economics. High Wycombe, Bucks., University Microfilms, 1973. 2v. (734p.).
An index of 22,500 dissertations, copies of the majority of which are available from University Microfilms. Supplements are published annually by University Microfilms, Ann Arbor, Mich. (v.4, part 2 includes business and economics) and there are also five-& ten-year indexes (1973-82; 1983-87). *Class No:* 330(043)(01)

Reviews & Abstracts

[1762]

The Economic journal: the quarterly journal of the Royal Economic Society. Oxford, Basil Blackwell Ltd. (previously Cambridge, the Society), 1891-. v.1, no.1-. £60.50pa; $112.50pa. ISSN: 00130133.
A valuable bibliographical tool, a substantial amount of each issue being devoted to reviews and lists of books and articles. The June 1989 issue (v.99, no.396) reviews 18 items (p.491-514), and has sections 'Book notes' (p.515-550) and 'Books received' (p.551-559). An annual index includes book reviews, A-Z by authors of books, and also an index of reviewers. *Class No:* 330(048)

[1763]

Economic titles/abstracts: semi-monthly review (with annual index) providing concise information of interest to business, trade, industry, economic libraries and research institutes. Dordrecht, Netherlands, Martinus Nijhoff, for the Netherlands Foreign Trade Agency EVD of the Ministry of Economic Affairs, V.1-18, 1974-1991. ISSN: 01665057.
A continuation of *Economic abstracts* 1953-1973) and *Economic titles* (1973).
Compiled by the staff of the Library of the Economic Information Service, the Netherlands Ministry of Economic Affairs. About 500 abstracts per issue, arranged by UDC, of items in more than 1800 of the world's leading economic journals, trade journals, bank letters, and professional journals of all sectors and branches of industry, as well as books, special studies, and reports in the same fields. Bibliographical data for entries is 1-4 keywords in English and an abstract in the original language of the publication. Analytical subject index in each issue and cumulative annual

....(contd.)

subject index. The printed version of the online Foreign Trade & Economic Abstracts database, *Economic abstracts international*. Vendors: Belindis, Data-Star, DIALOG. *Class No:* 330(048)

[1764]
—Economic abstracts international. The Hague, Netherlands, Ministry of Economic Affairs, 1974-.

The online database, updated semi-monthly. *Class No:* 330(048)

[1765]
—Key to economic science: semi-monthly review of abstracts in economics, finance, trade, industry, foreign aid, management, marketing, labour. Dordrecht, Netherlands, Martinus Nijhoff, 1953-87. ISSN: 01654748.

Offers a selection of the abstracts published in *Economic titles/abstracts*. Annual index. *Class No:* 330(048)

[1766]
Journal of economic literature. Nashville, Tenn., American Economic Association, 1963-. v.1, no.1-. Quarterly. $130pa., including *American economic review*. ISSN: 00220515.

Incorporating *The journal of economic abstracts.*

A guide for economists to ongoing research and publications. Focuses on research topics. Available online (DIALOG) and on CD-ROM. *Class No:* 330(048)

[1767]
—Economic literature index (ELI), 1969-. Nashville, Tenn., American Economic Association.

Online database for *Journal of economic literature*. Coverage is from 1969 to date, updated quarterly. A 'core' specialist database currently available on interactive public systems. *Class No:* 330(01)

[1768]
World agricultural economics and rural sociology abstracts (WAERSA). Wallingford, Oxon, CAB International, 1958-. Monthly. £320pa. $602pa. ISSN: 00438219.

About 7000 abstracts pa. 10 main sections: Agricultural economics - Agricultural policy - Supply, demand and prices - Marketing and distribution - International trade - Finance and credit policy - Farm economics - Cooperatives and collectives - Education, extension and resource - Rural sociology. Author and subject indexes per issue and annually. Annual geographical index. Online through CAB ABSTRACTS database, and also available on floppy disk.. *Class No:* 330(048)

Periodicals

[1769]
Economic journals and serials: an analytical guide. Sichel, B. *and* Sichel, W., *comps.* Westport, Conn., Greenwood Press, 1986. 285p. $45.00; £45.00. (*Annotated bibliographies of serials, 5.*) ISBN: 0313238103.

An alphabetical listing of 450 economic journals and serials published more than once a year. Each entry is in 3 parts (concise bibliographical information; narrative covering scope of content, editorial objectives, authority of contributors, technical level, and where applicable, comparison to related publications; format, number of articles, special features). Titles mainly from commercial publishing houses and university presses, but important US government and international organization's publications and

....(contd.)

some newsletters are also included. '... excellent notations that are both descriptive and evaluative' (*Library journal*, v.111(12), July 1986, p.73). *Class No:* 330(051)

Yearbooks & Directories

[1770]
CAPIE, F. Directory of economic institutions. London, Macmillan; New York, Stockton Press, 1990. xii,472p. £95. $190. ISBN: 0333464680, UK; 0935859411, US.

Institutions involved in economic research, policy debate and dissemination of ideas are arranged by country (Argentina ... Yugoslavia). Data includes name, address, telephone number, when founded, chairman/president, nature, objectives, research interests, publications, and activities. *Class No:* 330(058)

Quotations

[1771]
JACKMAN, M., *ed*. The Macmillan book of business and economic quotations. New York, Macmillan, 1984. 302p. $19.95. ISBN: 0025582208.

*c.*5000 quotations arranged under 62 A-Z subject categories, and taken from about 1000 sources. Chronological arrangement within each category. Citations include the quotation, the speaker/writer, and the year, but not the source. Period covered is from 400 B.C. to A.D. 1984. Keyword and name indexes. *Class No:* 330(082.2)

[1772]
JAMES, S., *ed*. A Dictionary of economic quotations. 2nd ed. London, Croom Helm; Totowa, N.J., Barnes & Noble, 1984. xi,240p. £25. ISBN: 0709914296, UK; 0389202304, US.

First published 1981.

A collection of *c.*2000 quotations arranged by topic in 133 subject sections, A-Z (Advertising ... Work). As well as economics, covers related areas of economic history, law, mathematics, politics and statistics. Keyword index, p.201-232. Author and source index, p.233-240. *Class No:* 330(082.2)

Histories

[1773]
CAMERON, R. A Concise economic history of the world: from Paleolithic times to the present. 2nd ed. Oxford, Oxford University Press, 1993. xxi,464p. illus., maps. £35. ISBN: 0195074459.

First published 1989.

Intended for the student and the general reader, the work is in two parts. The first part surveys world history, with emphasis on Europe, from ancient times to the end of the 18th century. The second half investigates, in greater detail, the related processes of industrialization and urbanization in the 19th and 20th centuries. *Class No:* 330(091)

[1774]
CARUS-WILSON, E.M. **Essays in economic history:** reprints edited for the Economic History Society. London, Arnold. 1954-62. (Reprinted 1969, New York, St. Martin's Press). 3v. V.1&3: $10.95 each; v.2: $14.95. ISBN: 0312260059, v.1; 0312260407, v.2; 0687011884, v.3.

V.1 contains reprints selected from the first twenty years of *Economic history,* 1926-41, and *Economic history review,* 1927-, articles substantially incorporated in later published work have not been included. 'The aim of the present collection therefore is to make easily accessible in one volume a selection of those articles which have proved most in demand from students'. Articles in v.2-3 'range widely over a century of writing about economic history in a dozen different periodicals and one symposium'.
Class No: 330(091)

[1775]
—SCHLEIFFER, H. *and* CRANDALL, R. Index to economic history essays in Festschriften, 1900-1950. Cambridge, Mass., Harvard University Press, 1953. 68p.

Arranged by broad subject headings; index of authors and proper names. *Class No:* 330(091)

[1776]
HOWEY, R.S., *ed.* **A Bibliography of general histories of economics, 1692-1975.** Regents Press of Kansas, 1982. xii,244p. $29.95. ISBN: 0700602194.

Citations for 998 book-length histories are detailed and include information on later editions, translations, comments, and location of copies. 3 appendices, including citations for 215 essay-length histories taken from general treatises on economics. *Class No:* 330(091)

Reviews & Abstracts

[1777]
The Journal of economic history. Cambridge, Cambridge University Press, for the Economic History Association, 1941-. Quarterly. £42;$75pa. ISSN: 00220507.

V.53(4), December 1993 contains 7 articles; Notes and discussion (3 items); 1 review article and 40 signed reviews of books, arranged by geographical region.
Class No: 330(091)(048)

Jews

[1778]
POLLINS, H. **Economic history of the Jews in England.** Rutherford, Fairleigh Dickinson University Press; London & Toronto, Associated University Presses, 1982. 339p. tables. £20. (*The Littman library of Jewish civilization.*) ISBN: 0838630332.

An introductory chapter deals with the brief period when a medieval Jewish community existed in England, followed by 15 chapters investigating the economic pursuits of the Jews in Britain from the 17th century to the present day. Notes, by chapter, p.254-296. Glossary, p.322. Bibliography, p.297-321, arranged by bibliographies; unpublished parliamentary papers; books and articles, A-Z by author. Index, p.323-339. *Class No:* 330(091)(=924)

Biographies

[1779]
BLAUG, M. **Great economists since Keynes:** an introduction to the lives and works of one hundred modern economists. Hemel Hempstead, Herts, Wheatsheaf Books Ltd.,; New York, Barnes & Noble, 1985. [6],267p. illus. £50.$88.50. ISBN: 0710807554, UK; 0389205176, US.

Alphabetical list of entries precedes the sketches of careers and professional contributions of living or recently deceased (post-1970) economists, including representatives of the major contrasting 'schools', as well as practitioners of distinctive methodological approaches. Lightly written but seriously conceived vignettes and, as the author intended, a reference work useful to students in early stages of their studies in economics. Secondary literature is listed after each biography. Index of names; index of subjects (p.263-7).
Class No: 330(092)

[1780]
—BLAUG, M. Great economists before Keynes: an introduction to the lives and works of 100 great economists of the past. Hemel Hempstead, Herts., Harvester Wheatsheaf Books Ltd., 1986. xi,286p. £50; $39.95. ISBN: 0745001602, UK; 0391033816, US.

A companion volume to *Great economists since Keynes (qv)* in the same format. *Class No:* 330(092)

[1781]
BLAUG, M., *ed.* **Who's who in economics:** a biographical dictionary of major economists, 1700-1987. 2nd ed. Cambridge, Mass., M.I.T. Press; Hemel Hempstead, Herts., Wheatsheaf Books Ltd., 1986. xxiii, 936p. $115; £95. ISBN: 0262022567, US; 0745002307, UK.

First published 1983, covering 1700-1981.

More than 1400 economists ('one who publishes more or less regularly in one of the hundreds of learned journals of economics'), including 1000 living economists who supplied the data in this volume themselves. Information for each biography includes name, year and place of birth, current and previous positions, education, prizes, principal fields of interest, list of publications, brief statements about their principal contributions to the science. Economists included from 25 countries, but half of them from US. Appendices: Index of principal fields of interest; Index of country of residence if not US; Index of country of birth if not US; Names without entry. Editor is the Professor of Economics of Education at London University. *Class No:* 330(092)

[1782]
MAI, L.H. **Men and ideas in economics:** a dictionary of world economists past and present. Totowa, N.J., Littlefield Co., 1975 (Reprinted by Littlefield/Quality Paperbacks). xiii, 270p. $9.95. ISBN: 0822602849.

Preceded by an introduction on the growth of economic thought, the biographical profiles of men and women in economics and selected influential personalities in related fields are arranged A-Z by name. Appendices are a brief state of the art essay on the present generation of economists, a historical outline of the schools of economic thought, and a short bibliography (less than 2 pages). '... a handy reference tool for the undergraduate student ... and for the lay reader ...' (*Library journal,* 15 January 1976, p.327-8). *Class No:* 330(092)

Developing Countries

[1783]

Dictionary of development: Third World economy, environment, society. Welsh, B.W.W. *and* Butorin, P., *eds*. New York, Garland, 1990. 2v. (lxv,1194p.). $130. ISBN: 0824014472.

V.1: A-I; v.2: I-Index. Introduction and 'Developing countries indicators' (by countries, A-Z, providing economic and statistical data concerning Third World societies and economies) precede the dictionary, which contains short definitions of terms, with origins, plus articles. Profuse cross-references. List of periodicals devoted to development topics, with publishers' addresses, completes the volume. *Class No:* 330(4/9-77)

Handbooks & Manuals

[1784]

Third World economic handbook. Sinclair, S. 2nd ed. London, Euromonitor Publications, 1989. 250p. tables. £45; $80. ISBN: 0863381634.

First published 1986.

Covers major economic developments and opportunities in third world countries and highlights short and long term economic opportunities. Regional analysis over 4 groups (Latin America, West Asia, South Asia, East Asia) is followed by detailed overviews for each country. Includes *c.*150 statistical tables. *Class No:* 330(4/9-77)(035)

Europe

Histories

[1785]

ALDCROFT, D.H. *and* **RODGER, R.,** *comps.* **Bibliography of European economic and social history.** 2nd ed. Manchester, Manchester University Press, 1993. 192p. £45. ISBN: 0719034922.

First published 1984.

10,000 entries for English-language books, articles and conference proceedings published in 30 European countries arranged geographically (Europe - Western Europe - East, Central and South - Eastern Europe - Southern Europe - Scandinavia - The Baltic States). Each geographical section subdivided by subject (General economic and social history - agriculture and rural society - industry and external trade ... money, banking and finance ... population and migration ...urban history ... economic aspects of war ... historiography and bibliography - statistical series). Period covered is 1700-1939. No annotations. *Class No:* 330(4)(091)

[1786]

—**TAYLOR, B.,** *comp.* Society and economy in early modern Europe, 1450-1789: a bibliography of post-war research. Manchester, Manchester University Press, 1989. 303p. ISBN: 0719019486.

About 4000 annotated entries representing the most important and useful books and journal articles written since 1945 on the subject. Arranged under 14 topical headings, subdivided by topic and countries. Includes works in French, Italian, Spanish and German as well as English. Annotations are brief but significant and the longer ones include references to review articles. Indexes of authors and place names. Complements the above. *Class No:* 330(400)(091)

[1787]

HACKEN, R.D., *comp.* **Central European economic history from Waterloo to OPEC, 1815-1975:** a bibliography. Westport, Conn., Greenwood Press, 1987. xviii, 270p. (Bibliographies & indexes in economics and economic history, 6). $45. ISBN: 0313254605.

5,373 unannotated, numbered entries arranged in five broad subject areas: Economic conditions - Agriculture - Industry - Business and commerce - Finance. Each area subdivided geographically and chronologically. Author index, p.237-270. Purports to cover all Central Europe but focuses on the German-speaking countries and Germany in particular. Mainly German language material. *Class No:* 330(4)(091)

Europe—Eastern

Histories

[1788]

KASER, M.C. *and* **RADICE, E.A.,** *eds.* **The Economic history of Eastern Europe, 1919-1975.** Oxford, Clarendon Press, 1986-. To be in 5v. tables, maps. V.1 & 2: £45 each; v.3: £32.50. ISBN: 0198284446, v.1; 0198284454, v.2; 0198284462, v.3.

V.1. *Economic structure and performance between the two wars* (1986. 636p.); v.2. *Interwar policy: the war and reconstruction* (1987. 680p.); v.3. *Institutional change within a planned economy* (1987. 328p.). Promises to be a monumental history of Eastern Europe (Albania, Bulgaria, Czechoslovakia, German Democratic Republic, Hungary, Poland, Romania and Yugoslavia) in the 20th century. Aims to be a definitive analysis. Less than favourable review essay in *Economic history review* (v.41(4), November 1988, p.592-602) which does, however, state that 'The erudition ... is not in question ... may overwhelm the inexperienced reader ... Very much for scholars in the best continental tradition'. *Class No:* 330(401)(091)

Great Britain

[1789]

Who's who in British economics: a directory of economists in higher education, business and government. Sturges, P. *and* Sturges, C., *eds.* Aldershot, Hants, Edward Elgar Publishing Ltd., 1990. ix,627p. £75. ISBN: 185278105x.

For each name included gives address, post, qualifications, offices, expertise, publications, the information provided by the people themselves. Nearly 1700 entries. Subject index, p.563-627. *Class No:* 330(410)

Periodicals

[1790]

Bank of England quarterly bulletin. London, Economics Department of the Bank, 1960-. £27. ISSN: 00055166.

First published 1960.

Invaluable on the British economy. Includes articles and an annex of statistics, some of which are not available elsewhere. *Class No:* 330(410)(051)

Histories

[1791]

British business history: a bibliography. Zarach, S., *ed.* London, Macmillan Press, 1993. 304p. £50. ISBN: 0333592875.

Lists over 2500 business histories.
Class No: 330(410)(091)

Italy

[1792]

BARUCCI, P. *and* CARPENTER, K., *comps.* **Italian economic literature in the Kress Library, 1475-1850.** Cambridge, Mass., Kress Library, Harvard University, 1985. 2v. (xxii, 490p.). $25.

1203 titles arranged chronologically by date of publication, then A-Z by author's name. Some entries are different editions of the same work. Cross-references. Several indexes. Includes a 13-page bibliography of Italian economic history. *Class No:* 330(450)

Scandinavia

Libraries

[1793]

RUOKONEN, K *and* RINNE, B. **Economic and business libraries in Scandinavia.** 3rd ed. Helsinki, Helsinki School of Economics Library, 1987. [3],123,[9], 8p. $25. (*Helsinki School of Economics, Reports and catalogues, F;49.*) ISBN: 9517003242.

First published 1976.

Data for 68 libraries arranged by country (Denmark, Finland, Iceland, Norway, Sweden) subdivided by name of library, A-Z. Entries include address, telephone number, date established, person in charge, hours, conditions of use, major library units, number of staff, size of collection, subjects, special collections, classification systems, services offered, library publications, automated operations in use, and co-operative projects. Excludes university libraries. Indexes of library names, English names of libraries, personal names and subjects.
Class No: 330(48):061:026/027

Japan

[1794]

MIECZKOWSKI, B. '**Approaches to the Japanese economic "miracle"'.** (*Choice,* v.21(10), June 1984, p.1417-21, 1424-28 and v.21 (11/12), July/August 1984, p.1567-73).

In two parts: Part 1: The domestic economy (116 references to books); pt. 2: International economic relations (64 references to books, 8 to periodicals).
Class No: 330(52)

USA

Handbooks & Manuals

[1795]

HOEL, A.A., *and others.* **Economic sourcebook of government statistics.** Lexington, Mass., Lexington Books, 1983. xv,272p. tables. £25. ISBN: 066906579x.

Explains how the many statistical series are compiled,

....(contd.)

their strengths and weaknesses, what they describe and do not describe (warnings of pitfalls). 6 sections 1. Measures of inflation - 2. Profits: indicators of general business conditions - 3. Interest rates and other financial indicators - 4. Measures of employment, unemployment and earnings - 5. Indicators of international finance and trade - 6. Indicators of government influence. 4 appendices (A. Selected sources of business and financial information; B. Financial statements; C. The Standard Industrial Classification; D. Value added and gross national product). Glossary. Index, p.264-71. Intended for the use of journalists.
Class No: 330(73)(035)

Writing & Lecturing

[1796]

The Economist style guide. London, Business Books, 1991. 128p. £12.99.

Based on *The Economist's* own house-style manual. Includes a new 'fast-checking section' with a glossary, covering everything from the stock markets to the laws of nature, science and economics. *Class No:* 330:001.81

Information Management

[1797]

INTERNATIONAL ECONOMIC ASSOCIATION. **The Organisation and retrieval of economic knowledge:** proceedings of a conference held ... at Kiel, West Germany. Perlman, M., *ed.* London, Macmillan, 1977. xiii, 520p. £50. ISBN: 0333217071.

26 papers presented to the conference in 1975 by economist and librarians, arranged in four parts: 1. The technology of the library industry and its use for economic research - 2. The economics of the economics library industry and its implications - 3. The information needs of researchers and their implications for the organization of economic knowledge. Index. *Class No:* 330:025.4

Classification Systems

[1798]

BAKEWELL, K.G.B. *and* COTTON, D.A., *eds.* **The London classification of business studies.** 2nd ed. rev. London, Aslib, 1979. 253p. £21. ISBN: 0851421245.

First published 1970, ed. by K.G.B. Bakewell & V. Lang.

A thesaurus of indexing terms in the areas of business and management, as well as a classification scheme, with *c.*4000 terms. *Class No:* 330:025.44

Institutions & Associations

[1799]

MEERHAEGHE, M.S.G., van. **International economic institutions.** 5th rev. ed. Dordrecht, Netherlands, Martinus Nijhoff, 1987 (distributed by Kluwer Academic Publishers). xxviii,368p. tables. £70. ISBN: 9024735130.

First published in German in 1964; in English 1966.

Introduction on the United Nations and its special agencies, the Bank for International Settlements, regional integration, etc. Part 1 with world organizations (KNF, World Bank, International Development Association, IFC. GATT, commodity agreements). Part 2 with European organizations (Benelux, OECD, CMEA, European

....(contd.)

Communities and EFTA). Origins, objectives, functions, operations, are given for each organization; bibliographies for most of them. Author and subject indexes. *Class No:* 330:061:061.2

Poverty

[1800]

World poverty: an economic survey of the 20th century. Pollard, G.S., *ed.* London, Harrap, 1990. 256p. illus., charts, tables. £18.95 ISBN: 024560023x.

Arranged in 6 periods: 1900-14. 1014-29, 1929-45, 1945-60, 1960-73 (The consumer boom), 1973-89 (The worldwide network). Biographies, p.230-47. Glossary. Further reading, p.250. Editor is Emeritus Professor of Economics at Bielefeld, West Germany. *Class No:* 330.16

Reviews & Abstracts

[1801]

Human resources abstracts. Newbury Park, CA., Sage Publications Inc., 1975-. Quarterly. 37.00/00 (institutions); $85pa (individuals). ISSN: 00992453.

Continues *Poverty and human resources abstracts.* v.1-9, 1966-74. Published with the co-operation of the Institute of Labor and Industrial Relations, University of Michigan and Wayne State University.

About 200 journals, mainly US, are scanned and each issue contains *c.*250 abstracts of journal articles, books and reports on employment and related topics such as economic structure and planning, labour markets and participation, labour and industrial relations, earnings and benefits, human resources and society, immigration and migration. Broadly classified arrangement in *c.*15 categories. Author and subject indexes in each issue and cumulated annually. 'A reference tool of high quality' (*Reference services review*, v.7(4), 1979, p.70). *Class No:* 330.16(048)

Economic Theories

[1802]

Companion to contemporary economic thought. Greenaway, D., *and others, eds.* London & New York, Routledge, 1991. 858p. £85. ISBN: 0415026121.

Articles are structured to survey today's economic concerns. Thematically arranged, the 41 essays cover a wide range of issues within the field and associated disciplines. Detailed notes, extensive bibliographies, and suggestions for further reading. *Class No:* 330.8

[1803]

A Modern guide to economic thought: an introduction to comparative schools of thought in economics. Mair, D. *and* Miller, A., *eds.* Aldershot, Hants, Edward Elgar, 1991. xi,281p. figures. £45. $39.95. ISBN: 1852783230.

Describes the main schools of contemporary economic thinking, stated in their own terms, their aims on issues, and the reasoning behind those aims. 9 chapters: 1. Introduction; 2. The philosophy and methodology of economics; 3. The Austrian school; 4. The Neoclassical school; 5. The macroeconomics of the Chicago school; 6. The orthodox Keynesian school; 7. The post-Keynesian school; 8. The Institutionalist (evolutionary) school; 9. Marxism and radical economics. 11 contributors. Bibliography, p.263-74. Index, p.275-81. *Class No:* 330.8

[1804]

ROSTOW, W.W. Theorists of economic growth from David Hume to the present: with a perspective on the next century. Oxford, Oxford University Press, 1990. xx,712p. tables. £35. ISBN: 0195058372.

21 chapters in 4 parts: 1. Six classical economists: David Hume to Karl Marx; 2. Growth theory moves to the periphery, 1870-1939; 3. Growth analysis post-1945: a three-ring circus; 4. Problems and prospects. Appendix: Models of economic growth. Notes, p.571-682. Author index, p.682-688, subject index, p.689-712. *Class No:* 330.8

Bibliographies

[1805]

BATSON, H.E., *comp.* **A Select bibliography of modern economic theory, 1870-1929.** London, Routledge, 1930 (Reprinted 1968 by Kelley). 224p. $27.50. ISBN: 0678065098.

About 2000 entries. Pt.1: Subject bibliography (annotated); pt.2: Author bibliography (English authors; German authors; French authors), including periodical articles and reviews, items not in the British Library of Political and Economic Science are asterisked. Index of authors. A standard guide to the literature of the period. *Class No:* 330.8(01)

Histories

[1806]

GIDE, C. *and* **RIST, C. A History of economic doctrines,** from the time of the Physiocrats to the present day. Authorised translation by R. Richards. 2nd English ed., with additional matter from the latest French edition, translated by E.F. Row. London, Harrap, 1948. 800p. O.P.

First published 1915. The original, *Histoire des doctrines économiques,* was first published in 1909.

The 2nd English edition includes matter from the 7th French edition. Footnote references; analytical index. The standard history. *Class No:* 330.8(091)

[1807]

ROLL, E. A History of economic thought. 5th ed. London, Faber, 1992. xiv,592p. £20. $29.95. ISBN: 0571165532.

First published 1938.

13 chapters: 1. The beginnings - 2. Commercial capitalism and its theory ... 8. Modern economics - 9. The beginning of American economics ... 11. Macroeconomics and economic management - 12. The age of doubt and the new counter-revolution - 13. A new certainty? Conclusion. Index, p.580-92. For this edition, Lord Roll has revised the early chapters and added new material; later sections have been expended and updated. Essential reading. *Class No:* 330.8(091)

Bibliographies

[1808]

FUNDABURK, E.L., *ed.* **The History of economic thought and analysis:** a selective international bibliography. v.1: *The development of economic thought and analysis.* Metuchen, N.J., Scarecrow Press, 1974. 931p. $30. ISBN: 0810805804.

6 volumes were projected but only one published.

Over 10,000 references (including major periodical articles). Sections: General works - Specific works - Periods

....(contd.)

and schools. Author-subject index; short title index. 'The work is designated as selective but no criteria for the inclusion of different items are given' (*RQ,* v.13(4), Summer 1974, p.355). *Class No:* 330.8(091)(01)

[1809]
HUTCHINSON, W.K. History of economic analysis: a guide to information sources. Detroit, Mich., Gale, 1976. xii, 243p. Economics information guide series, vol. 3). $68. ISBN: 0810312956.

Covers the period from 1600 to 1940, citing more than 1,000 sources in the English language. 6 chapters are devoted to the forerunners of classical economics, Keynesian economics, and 20th century British economic thought. Appendices list major organizations concerned with the subject, and journals that print articles pertaining to the field. Author, title and subject indexes. *Choice*(v.14,no.1, March 1977,p.44) recommends it as 'a handy sourcebook for undergraduate and graduate students and professors', but the review in *The Economic Journal* (v.87, no.2, 1977, p.407) mentions numerous gaps in coverage, judgements that do not inspire confidence in the compiler's ability to act as a guide, and the mixture of 'extracts, textbooks and ephemeral articles [that] jostle side by side with classic contributions ...'. *Class No:* 330.8(091)(01)

Official Records
[1810]
STURGES, R.P. Economists' papers, 1750-1950: a guide to archive and other manuscript sources for the history of British and Irish economic thought. London, Macmillan, 1975. xxiv, 140p. ISBN: 082230337x.

Compiled for the Committee of the Guide to Archive Sources in the History of Economic Thought, Royal Economic Society.

A finding list of personal papers and correspondence of the most distinguished British economists (*e.g.* Sir James Stewart (1712-80), R.H. Tawney (1882-1962)), indicating the nature and location of the archival material and the principal published collections. 'A well-designed search-guide' *(The Economic journal,* v.85, 1975, p.974). *Class No:* 330.8(093.2)

Labour & Employment

Bibliographies
[1811]
AZEVEDO, R.E. Labor economics: a guide to information services. Detroit, Mich., Gale Research Co., 1978. xii, 261p. (Economics information guide series, v.8). $62. ISBN: 0810312972.

51 specialized subject sections *(e.g.*Automation; Collective Bargaining;) are preceded by a section on textbooks and general works, and one on general journals, government publications, and information services. In each section an introduction precedes an annotated list of books and journals. US slant. Author, title and subject indexes. *Class No:* 331(01)

[1812]
INTERNATIONAL LABOUR OFFICE. Annotated bibliography on clandestine employment. Geneva, I.L.O., 1987. iii,132p. SFr.17.50; £7.70; $12.25. (*International labour bibliography, no.2.*) ISBN: 9221057267.

Provides a wide range of references to publications on the subject of clandestine employment and related issues, including monographs, journal articles, reports and conference proceedings. *Class No:* 331(01)

[1813]
INTERNATIONAL LABOUR OFFICE. Bibliography of published research of the World Employment Programme. 9th edition. Geneva, ILO., 1991. ix, 130p. SFr.17.50; £7.70; 505.00/00 Presents information on research published up to March 1991 in the form of studies, monographs, articles and World Employment Programme research working papers. ISBN: 9221077462. ISSN: 10108206. *Class No:* 331(01)

[1814]
INTERNATIONAL LABOUR OFFICE. Catalogue of publications in print, 1994-95. Geneva, ILO Publications, 1994. 246p. *Gratis.* ISBN: 922106090x. ISSN: 10110569.

Lists ILO publications and documents available in English and offered for sale. Includes monographs, international comparative studies, manuals, codes of practice and reports of conferences and meetings, etc. Updated by the quarterly *ILO publications.* *Class No:* 331(01)

[1815]
International labour review. Geneva, International Labour Office, 1921-. Bi-monthly. SFr.17.50pa;$60pa. ISSN: 00207780.

Includes articles and notices of new books. V.132(5-6), 1993, 5 has news briefs and news features, 7 articles, and a bibliography (new ILO publications, with descriptions). *Class No:* 331(01)

[1816]
UNITED STATES. Department of Labor. Catalog ... Boston, Mass., G.K. Hall, 1975. 38v. (27, 638p.).

829,000 photographically reproduced catalogue cards, covering books, periodicals, reports, microfilm, microfiche and cassettes. The Library 'is the largest, most complete, and probably the oldest special library in its field' (G.K. Hall & Co. *Catalog of publications, 1979-1980,* p.58). *Class No:* 331(01)

Handbooks & Manuals
[1817]
WALSH, K. *and* **PEARSON, R. UK labour market guide.** 2nd ed. Aldershot, Hants., Gower Publishing Co., 1984. xi, 268p. £18.50. ISBN: 0566007185.

First published 1980.

Aim was to structure the guide so that the user can quickly and easily identify the range of labour market information available to meet the specific need, and then to select the most appropriate published sources or points of further contact. Part 1: Introduction; pt.2: Sources of labour market information (25 sections: How to use this section; Population and related statistics; Economic activity; Employment ... Training ... Labour mobility ... Earnings ... Industrial disputes); pt.3: Reference section (Labour market institutions; Other organizations providing information;

....(contd.)

index to key publications). List of abbreviations. Glossary (p.255-258). Index to numbered items (p.259-268). *Class No:* 331(035)

[1818]

WARREN, C. Personnel administration manual. London, Kogan Page, 1991. 400p. £35. ISBN: 0749401354.

Sections: Recruitment - Training, development and career progression - Maintaining standards of performance and conduct - Severance of the employment relationship - Money matters and the employee - Safety and security - Standard letters - Miscellaneous policies and procedures. *Class No:* 331(035)

Dictionaries

Polyglot

[1819]

KUNHARDT, U. von and LLISTOSELLA-MATZKY, I., comps. Elsevier's dictionary of the labour market: in English, German, Swedish, Spanish and French. Amsterdam, Elsevier Science Publishers, 1988. xii, 366p. Dfl.400; $210.50. ISBN: 0444428844.

Aimed at those working in the field of labour relations, and based on terminology that has largely been collected in the course of the authors' practical work. Includes multiword expressions, conference terminology, and names of institutions, government agencies and international organizations. A bibliography of dictionaries (p.xi-xii) precedes the 'Basic table' listing entries A-Z in English, each numbered, followed by equivalents in the other four languages. 4 indexes in those languages refer to the numbered English section. *Class No:* 331(038)=00

Reviews & Abstracts

[1820]

International labour documentation (New series). Geneva, International Labour Office, Central Library and Documentation Branch, 1949-. Monthly. SFr.90; £39.60; $72pa. ISSN: 00207756.

Frequency has varied.

An abstracting bulletin based on current acquisitions in the I.L.O. Central Library, covering the fields of industrial relations, labour law, employment, working conditions, management, vocational training, labour-related aspects of economics, social development, rural development, technological change, etc. Quarterly indexes. *Labordoc* (1965-, monthly update) is the machine-readable version, available for interactive and retrospective online searching. *Class No:* 331(048)

Periodicals

[1821]

HARRISON, R., *and others, comps*. The Warwick guide to British labour periodicals, 1790-1970: a check list ... Hassocks, Sussex, Harvester Press; Atlantic Highlands, N.J., Humanities Press, 1977. xxiii, 685p.

Lists 4,125 labour periodicals arranged A-Z by title, with dates and place of publication, editors and publishers, some indication of content if title not explicit, price, and library holdings information for 138 British repositories. 'Labour periodicals' are defined by the editors as those produced 'by

....(contd.)

an organised body ... of wage-earners or collectively dependent employees', papers produced 'in the avowed interest of the working class ...', and those 'produced for wage-earners by members of other social classes who sought to improve them, instruct them, or entertain them'. Chronological and thematic indexes. A review in *Social history* v.3. 1978. p.413-4) generally welcomes the guide but points out a number of omissions and criticizes the alphabetical arrangement. *Class No:* 331(051)

[1822]

INTERNATIONAL LABOUR OFFICE. Register of periodicals in the ILO library. Geneva, ILO., 1987. 420 frames. SFr.35. ISBN: 922106171x.

On COM microfiche.

Over 10,000 titles, listed by title and country. Journals scanned for input to *International labour documentation* are flagged. *Class No:* 331(051)

[1823]

INTERNATIONAL LABOUR ORGANISATION. Bibliography of periodicals on the quality of life. Geneva, ILO, 1983. x,88p. SFr.15; £5; $8.55. ISBN: 9221034755.

Selective bibliography, with international coverage. Subjects include labour law, personnel management, ergonomics, industrial psychology and sociology, in addition to government documents and employer and worker organization publications. *Class No:* 331(051)

Yearbooks & Directories

[1824]

Conditions of work and quality of working life: a directory of institutions, edited by Linda Stoddart, assisted by Kristine Falciola. 2nd ed. Geneva, ILO, 1986. xxi, 306p. £14.55; SFr.40. ISBN: 9221053288.

First published 1981.

Lists 288 institutions in 56 countries, including government agencies, employers' organizations, trade unions, research institutions, university departments, etc. Each entry has details on staff, funding, information services, training programmes, research projects, meetings and publications. Arranged by area or country, A-Z, subdivided by organizations, A-Z. *Class No:* 331(058)

Histories

[1825]

SOCIETY FOR THE STUDY OF LABOUR HISTORY. Labour history review. Sheffield, the Society, 1960- 3pa. £20pa. ISSN: 09615652.

Originally the Bulletin of the Society.

V.54(1), 1989 issue includes an essay in bibliography, 'Working women in the United States' (p.37-53); 14 lengthy essays in review, many with references and notes; and short notices of books (p.103-133) of about a page each. *Class No:* 331(091)

Theses

[1826]

GILBERT, V.F., *comp*. Labour and social history theses: American, British and Irish university theses and dissertations in the field of British and Irish labour history presented between 1900 and 1978. London, Mansell

....(contd.)

Publishing Ltd., 1982. x, 194p. £13.50. ISBN: 0720116473.

2626 items arranged A-Z by subject, subdivided A-Z by author. A contents list provides the subject approach. Brief information is given (name, title, award, year of award). Indexes of persons, places, subjects and authors. Since 1978 refer to annual lists of these and dissertations on British labour history in Autumn issues of the *Bulletin of the Society for the Study of Labour History. Class No:* 331(091)(043)

USA

[1827]

NEUFELD, M.E. *and* LEAB, D.J. **American working class history:** a representative bibliography. New York, Bowker, 1983. 356p. $39.95. ISBN: 0835217523.

First published in 1964 as *A representative bibliography of American labor history.*

A revised and greatly expanded edition. Lists nearly 7,300 items published through January 1983, including books, periodicals, certain government publications and films. Arranged in classified order, with a detailed table of contents and an author index. *Class No:* 331(091)(73)

Archives

[1828]

INTERNATIONAL LABOUR OFFICE. **International labour conventions and recommendations, 1919-1991, with supplements 1992-1993.** Geneva, ILO, 1992. 2v. (xlv, 762; xxi, 718) SFr.95; £41.80; $76. ISBN: 922107756x.

First published in 1966, covering the first 50 sessions, since when 30 conventions and 38 recommendations have been adopted. *Class No:* 331(093.20)

Worldwide

Tables & Data Books

[1829]

BEAN, R., *ed.* **International labour statistics:** a handbook,. guide, and recent trends. London, Routledge, 1989. xi,306p. £75. ISBN: 0415021790.

Part 1 is a guide to the use of labour statistics in 9 chapters by subject, pt.2 has 2 chapters on labour statistics from individual countries. Sources and examples are given. An appendix lists membership of the international trade secretariats. Index, p.294-306. *Class No:* 331(100)(083)

[1830]

INTERNATIONAL LABOUR OFFICE. **Bulletin of labour statistics.** Geneva, ILO., 1965-. Quarterly, with 4 supplements a year. SwF.100pa. ISSN: 00074950; 03785505, supplements.

Contains articles and notes relevant to the production and analysis of labour statistics, as well as the most recent time series on employment, unemployment, hours of work, consumer prices. Methodological descriptions are included. Data is for several quarters and years to the latest available. The supplements provide interim release of the most recent information available on the basic statistical series. *Class No:* 331(100)(083)

[1831]

INTERNATIONAL LABOUR OFFICE. **Yearbook of labour statistics, 1993.** 52nd issue. Geneva, ILO., 1993. xix,1225p. SwF.195. ISBN: 9220073420. ISSN: 00843857.

First published 1936 (for 1935/36).

31 tables, with explanatory notes, in 9 chapters (1. Total and economically active population - 2. Employment - 3. Unemployment - 4. Hours of work - 5. Wages - 6. Labour cost - 7. Consumer prices - 8. Occupational injuries - 9. Strikes and lockouts). Statistics cover 1983-1992. Covers *c.*180 countries. Appendix includes International standard industrial classification of all economic activities (ISIC) and International classification of occupations (ISCO. References and sources, p.1187-1208. Index of countries, territories and areas.

Complemented by data presented each quarter in the *Bulletin of labour statistics.* (ISSN 00074950).

Class No: 331(100)(083)

[1832]

WALSH, K. *and* KING, A. **Handbook of international manpower market comparisons.** New York, New York University (distributed by Columbia), 1987. 318p. $90. ISBN: 0814792170.

Annual statistics for the last decade on population, labour force, unemployment, educational supply, industrial relations, labour costs, and consumer prices, grouped by country for the European Community, Norway, Sweden, Japan, and United States. An appendix gives selected indicators for each category. Another appendix lists sources, which are not included at the foot of each table.

Class No: 331(100)(083)

Great Britain

Bibliographies

[1833]

BURNETT, J., *and others, eds.* **The Autobiography of the working class:** an annotated critical bibliography. New York, New York University Press (distributed by Columbia); Brighton, Sussex, Harvester Press, 1984-89. 3v. (1203p.). $125 each vol. £80 each vol. ISBN: 0710806809, UK; 0811471079, US; 0710806970, UK; 0814710948, US; 0710811675, UK.

V.1 covers 1750-1900; v.2 1900-1945; v.3 is a supplement, covering 1750-1945. Over 2000 autobiographies of members of the British working class are included in v.1 and 2, including unpublished diaries, typescripts, newspaper and magazine serializations, as well as published accounts. All critically analysed and annotated. Entries are numbered and information includes full bibliographical data, family life, occupations, activities and comments. 7 appendices (A. Miscellaneous - B. Oral - C. Politics - D. Military - E. Work - F. Collections - G. Diaries). 6 indexes (general - places - occupations - education - dates - appendix authors). 'An extremely valuable tool...' (*Choice,* v.25(3), November 1987, p.452). *Class No:* 331(410)(01)

[1834]

GREAT BRITAIN. HM Stationery Office. **Government publications: Sectional list 21: Employment, health and safety..** Revised May l990. London, HMSO, 1990. 40p. Gratis.

Main sections: Employment - Health and safety.
Class No: 331(410)(01)

Yearbooks & Directories

[1835]

Personnel managers yearbook, 1994. London, A.P.Information Services, 1993. Annual. £49.75.

Lists over 15,000 named senior managers and 7500 companies and organizations in the United Kingdom. Also lists 4500 firms supplyimg such services , such as management consultancy, training, personnel computer systems, counselling, recruitment consultancy, etc.
Class No: 331(410)(058)

Tables & Data Books

[1836]

Employment gazette. Department of Employment. London, Harrington Kilbride plc.(previously HMSO) 1971-. tables. Monthly. £52.50pa; $4.95 single issue. ISSN: 02647052.

Succeeds *Ministry of Labour gazette* (1893-1968), thereafter as *Employment and productivity gazette* (1968-1970) and *Department of Employment gazette* (1971-1979).

V.102(1), January 1994, includes News; Special features (3 items); Questions in Parliament; Labour market statistics (on tinted paper) with information on employment, unemployment, vacancies, industrial disputes, earnings, retail prices, labour force survey; tourism; training and enterprise programmes; Reviews (5 short items); LFS (Labour force survey) help-line (on tinted paper). Index.
Class No: 331(410)(083)

[1837]

LEE, C.H. **British regional employment statistics, 1841-1971.** Cambridge, Cambridge University Press, 1980. 428p. ISBN: 052122666x.

Reclassifies data from the censuses of population into two series of employment tables, one from 1841 to 1911 and the other from 1901 to 1971, devised to give the longest possible time span without losing internal consistance. Data is broken down by the counties and regions of GB and into 27 industrial areas based on the current government industrial classifications. 'This is a thorough and scholarly work' (*Journal of the Royal Statistical Society,* Series A, v.143(3), 1980, p.370). 'Dr. Lee has made the census of occupations and employment much more accessible for testing hypotheses about the development of the economy' (*Economic history review,* v.33(3), 1980, p.430).
Class No: 331(410)(083)

Histories

[1838]

HUNT, E.H. **British labour history, 1815-1914.** London, Weidenfeld & Nicolson, 1981. xiv,428p. £18.50. ISBN: 0297777858.

The first part of the book discussed the character and condition of labour in 5 chapters (1. Work and the workers - 2. Population: births and deaths - 3. Wages and living standards - 4. Poverty - 5. Migrants, emigrants and

....(contd.)

immigrants). The second part is concerned with the organized responses of labour to the changing conditions in 4 chronologically arranged chapters. Notes, p.343-398, are by chapter. 'Further reading', p.399-406, also by chapter. Index, p.407-428. 'It is a strength of this book that it seeks to see labour as it was ...' (*Economic history review,* November 1981, p.657). *Class No:* 331(410)(091)

[1839]

LUNN, K. **A Social history of British labour, 1870-1970.** London, E. Arnold, 1992. 224p. £7.99. ISBN: 0713164786.

Considers union and party policy vis-à-vis leisure, the family, health, welfare and economic change in the context of the aspirations and life-styles of its members. Work on the history of the subject is reflected in the analysis.
Class No: 331(410)(091)

Biographies

[1840]

BELLAMY, J.M. *and* SAVILLE, J. **Dictionary of labour biography.** London, Macmillan Press, 1972-93. 9v. V.1-7; £30 each; v.8: £35; v.9: £55: 9-volume set: £445. ISBN: 0333131800, v.1; 0333140389, v.2; 0333144155, v.3; 0333197046, v.4; 0333220153, v.5; 0333240952, v.6; 0333331818, v.7; 0333387821, v.8; 033338783x, v.9.

Covers not only the national personalities of the British Labour movement, but also the activists at regional and local level. Based on data collected by G.D.H. Cole. Time span: *c.*1790 to the present day. Each volume is self-contained, although volumes after v.1 have a 'Consolidated list of names'. The first seven volumes covered a wide range of entries from most periods of labour history, with v.6 specializing on the radical movements of the early 19th century, and vol.7 mainly concerned with personalities of the 20th Century. V.8 spans two centuries of radicals, trade unionists and socialists. v.9 is especially concerned with 20th century activists and intellectuals. Each volume has its own index. *Class No:* 331(410)(092)

Official Records

[1841]

GREAT BRITAIN. Public Record Office. **Records of interest to social scientists, 1919-1939: Employment and unemployment.** Swann, B. *and* Turnbull, M. London, HMSO, 1978. v. 590p. (*Public Record Office handbooks, no.18.*)

7 chapters: 1. Introduction - 2. General policy - 3. Spheres of government activity (p.86-173) - 4. Cabinet and Departmental records: Code R (p.174-382) - 5. Cabinet annd Departmental records: Code C (p.383-532) - 6. Legislation: Code L (annotated) - 7. Parliamentary Papers: Code P. Appendices: 1. Abbreviations; 2. Unemployment figures; 3. Unemployment Act, 1934. *Class No:* 331(410)(093.2)

Laws

[1842]

WALTON, F., *comp.* & *ed.* **The Encyclopedia of employment law and practice.** 2nd ed. London, Professional Publishing, 1985. loose-leaf. ISBN: 094655921x.

A guide to aspects of employment legislation in the UK, kept up-to-date by a quarterly amendment service. Main

....(contd.)

index (31p.) and table of cases (21p.) are followed by the encyclopedia, A-Z (Advisory, Conciliation and Arbitration Service (ACAS) ... Youth training scheme). As an example, the entry for 'Lock-out' is in 6 sections: 1. Definition - 2. Lock-outs as breaches of contracts of employment - 3. Dismissal of lock-out employees - 4. Meaning of 'directly interested' in a dispute - 5. Status of the contract of employment during lock-outs - 6. Action by an employer contemplating a lock-out. *Class No:* 331(410)(094.1)

Dictionaries

[1843]

CHANDLER, P. An A-Z of employment and safety law. London, Kogan Page, 1981. ix, 516p. facsims., tables. £16.95. ISBN: 085038446x.

3 parts: 1. A-Z of employment and safety law (Abrasive wheels ... Young persons, employment of), including abstracts of regulations and summaries of Acts. - 2. Key codes of practice (e.g., Code of industrial relations practice; Picketing) - 3. Addresses and sources of further information. Appendix: Computing a period of continuous employment. Analytical index, p.502-16. Compact; well produced. *Class No:* 331(410)(094.1)(038)

[1844]

SELWYN, N. Dictionary of employment law. London, Butterworths, 1985. [4], 165p. £15. ISBN: 0406207909.

Aims to provide a quick reference to key words and phrases used in modern employment law, with special emphasis on how the courts and tribunals interpret the various statutory provisions. Entries range in length from two or three lines to a page or more. Cross-references. Entries often refer to cases. *Class No:* 331(410)(094.1)(038)

Scotland

[1845]

MacDOUGALL, I. A Catalogue of some labour records in Scotland and some Scots records outside Scotland. Edinburgh, Scottish Labour History Society, 1978. xvi, 598p. £11.50. ISBN: 0950693308.

A comprehensive catalogue of primary and secondary sources relating to labour history of Scotland. In 7 sections: Records and publications of 1800 friendly societies - History of Co-operative Society records - 500 labour political organisations' records - Trade union organizations - Miscellaneous organizations and activities - Newspapers annd periodicals published in England, Ireland and Scotland: holdings in Scottish libraries - [People] in working class movements. Favourably reviewed in the Society for the Study of Labour History's *Bulletin.* no. 38. p.49. *Class No:* 331(411)

Ireland

[1846]

ELLIS, P.B. History of the Irish working class. New ed. London, Pluto Press, 1985. 372p. £5.50. ISBN: 074530009x.

First published 1972 by Gollancz.

16 chapters: 1. Celtic Communism - 2. Feudalism - 3. The plantations - 4. A century of unrest - 5. The united Irishmen - 6. Pioneers of socialism - 7. O'Connell - the enemy within ... 10. The rise of organised labour - 11. The Dublin lock-

....(contd.)

out ... 14. The Irish Free State - 15. The dictionary republic - 16. The northern revolution. Written from the Irish viewpoint. Notes, p.344. Select bibliography, p.354 + addendum to 1985 ed. Index, p.360. *Class No:* 331(415)

Latin America

[1847]

GREENFIELD, G.M. *and* **MARAM, S.L.,** *eds*. **Latin American labor organizations.** Westport, Conn., Greenwood, 1987. 929p. $125. ISBN: 0313228345.

Short histories of all Latin American republics and Puerto Rico, Cuba, French Guiana, Guyana, Haiti, Jamaica, Suriname and Belize, focusing on labour relations and including information on the various unions, co-operatives, sindicatos and mutual aid societies. Detail given varies from country to country. There are appendices on international labor organizations, a country-by-country chronology of major events, and a country-by-country glossary of terms, people and events, plus a 98-page index. '... indispensable work for any collection on Latin America ... cannot be too highly recommended ...' (*Choice*, v.25(11/12), July/August 1988, p.1675). *Class No:* 331(729.99)

USA

Bibliographies

[1848]

Labor in America: a historical bibliography. Santa Barbara, CA., ABC-Clio, 1985. viii, 307p. $69; £66.70. (*Clio bibliography series, no 18.*) ISBN: 0874363977.

Information taken from the ABC-Clio database.

2865 abstracts of articles published between 1973 and 1983. In 5 chronological chapters (1. Labor in America: multiperiod - 2. Early American labor, to 1865 - 3. Labor in post-bellum America, to 1900 - 4. Labor in the new century, 1900 to 1945 - 5. Modern labor, 1945 to 1982). Each chapter is subdivided topically (*e.g.* General: the worker - The labor movement, government programs, policies and politics - Racial, ethnic and sex discrimination - Economic statistics of labor). Analytical subject index, p.201-294; author index, p.295-301; List of periodicals, p.303-305. *Class No:* 331(73)(01)

Yearbooks & Directories

[1849]

Training and development organizations directory. McLean, J., *ed.* 5th ed. Detroit, Mich., Gale Research Co., 1991. 684p. $310. ISBN: 0810343495.

Lists over 2300 training firms offering seminars and workshops, videos, and other training programmes that can enhance skills and personal development. Data for each firm includes name, address, telephone number, names of principals, staff size, areas of course emphasis, typical clients/target audience, course titles and fees. Arrangement is A-Z by company or organization name. Geographical, subject, and principal officers' names indexes. Available online. *Class No:* 331(73)(058)

Thesauri

[1850]
INTERNATIONAL LABOUR OFFICE. ILO Thesaurus: labour, employment and training terminology. 4th ed. Geneva,ILO,1992. xxxix, 557p. SFr.90. £39.60. $72. ISBN: 9220064294.

First published in 1976.

A thesaurus of English/French/Spanish descriptors used in the ILO library for information processing. An alphabetical index of terms (separate sequences for the three languages) refers to a systematic display using ILO's faceted classification scheme. *Class No:* 331:025.43

Institutions & Associations

[1851]
Employers' organizations of the world. Upham, M., *ed.* Harlow, Longman; New York, St. James Press, 1993. xiv,237p. £75. (*International reference*.) ISBN: 0582060370, UK; 1558620680, US.

Arranged by country, A-Z (Afghanistan ... Zimbabwe), with background information, followed by organizations with addresses, telephone numbers, leadership, total membership, affiliations, government bodies in which represented, aims and objectives, services provided to members, publications, date of foundation. International organizations. Select list of acronyms. Index of major employers' associations, p.234-7.

A new edition was issued in 1993 (loose-leaf, *c.*608p. £245. ISBN 0582100380). *Class No:* 331:061:061.2

Manpower

Worldwide

[1852]
ORGANISATION FOR ECONOMIC CO-OPERATION AND DEVELOPMENT. Labour force statistics, 1970-1990. Paris, OECD, 1992. 510p. tables, graphs. £24; $43; F.395. ISBN: 9264036857.

First published 1968. Annual. Superseded *Manpower statistics,* published from 1961 to 1965.

Definitions, symbols employed, sources precede the 3 main sections: I. General tables and graphs - II. Country tables - III. Participation rates and unemployment rates. Data is given for each of the member countries and includes population, labour force, unemployment and employment.

Updated by *Quarterly labour force statistics* (1975-. £24.pa. $43pa. F.195pa ISSN 02553627).

Class No: 331.024(100)

Great Britain

[1853]
YOUNG, J. D. Socialism and the English working class: a history of English labour, 1883-1939. Hemel Hempstead,Herts., Harvester Wheatsheaf, 1989. x,273 p. £28.50 $50.45. ISBN: 0710812051.

Explores the connection between the social history of the English working class and the history of the Labour Movement. 8 chapters (Labour historiography and the English working class; English working class attitudes to State intervention and the labour unrest, 1906-1914 ... Militancy, English Socialism and The Ragged Trousered

.... (contd.)
Philanthropists ... English workers, mass unemployment and the Left, 1924-1939. 600 notes, all referring to publications, p.234-264. Index, p.265-273. *Class No:* 331.024(410)

Industrial Relations

[1854]
GREAT BRITAIN. Department of Employment. Directory of employers; associations, trade unions, joint organisations, etc. London, HMSO. Semi-annual. £11.25 (September 1992 issue). ISSN: 09659633.

'Provides comprehensive lists of United Kingdom organizations whose objects include the negotiation of, or making of recommendations on wages and working conditions, or which provide representatives of organizations which are so concerned (*Introduction*). Organizations are grouped according to industries in which they function (SIC 1980 revision). Main sections: Employers' Associations - Trade union federations, trade union and other employees associations - Joint organizations, wages, councils, and arbitration boards, etc. Index. *Class No:* 331.1

Bibliographies

[1855]
BAIN, G.S. *and* **WOOLVEN, G.B. A Bibliography of British industrial relations.** Cambridge, Cambridge University Press, 1979. xxiii, 665p.

Aims 'to bring together all the secondary source material, except that of an ephemeral or strictly propagandist nature, published in English between 1880 and 1970 on British industrial relations. It includes books, pamphlets, articles in learned and professional journals, theses and government reports' *(Preface)*. 15,056 numbered items; 7 parts, closely subdivided (1. General (bibliographies, guides and archival sources) - 2. Employees: industrial attitudes and behaviour - 3. Employee organisation - 4. Employers and their organisation - 5. Labour-management relations - 6. The labour force, labour markets and conditions of employment (p.205-413) - 7. The State and its agencies. Index of authors, subjects, periodical titles (*c.*500). etc. 'A large and most impressive book' *(British book news,* October 1979, p.812).

A welcome supplement has now been issued (A bibliography of British industrial relations, 1971-1979, by G.S. Bain and J.D. Bennett. Cambridge University Press, 1985. xix, 258p. £42. ISBN 0521266998). Since 1980 this is updated by annual articles in the *British journal of industrial relations. Class No:* 331.1(01)

[1856]
BENNETT, J. *and* **FAWCETT, J.,** *comps*. **Industrial relations:** an international and comparative bibliography. London, Mansell Publishing Ltd., 1985. xi,172p. £18.50. ISBN: 0720117879.

Compiled for the British Universities Industrial Relations Association.

Entries for major works are arranged A-Z by country, subdivided by chronological arrangement and then A-Z by author. Includes material on collective bargaining, industrial conflict, the institutions of industrial relations, labour economy, labour history, labour law, and the management of labour. Books, journal articles, essays in books of readings, and a few theses are included, mainly in English-language, but some French, German and Spanish. Author index, p.143-163. Subject index, p.164-172. *Class No:* 331.1(01)

[1857]

PETTMAN, B.O. **Industrial democracy:** a selected bibliography. Bradford, Yorks, MCB Publications, 1979. vii, 95p. £29.95. ISBN: 0905440617.

A selective listing of over 3000 items (articles, books, theses and reports) published between 1950 and 1978, divided into general, comparative, and country studies. Author index. *Class No:* 331.1(01)

[1858]

WALSH, R.M. *and* BIRKIN, S.J. **Job satisfaction and motivation:** an annotated bibliography. Westport, Conn., & London, Greenwood Press, 1979. viii, 643p. $50.95; £40.50. ISBN: 031320635x.

946 items relating to research and field studies published between 1970 and 1979. Some books, dissertations, documents, etc. are included but emphasis is on journal articles in disciplines such as psychology, management and public administration. Arranged in 3 parts: author index, subject (keyword in context) index, and abstracts for each of the items. *Class No:* 331.1(01)

Handbooks & Manuals

[1859]

A **Handbook of industrial relations practice:** practice and law in the employer relationship. Towers, B., *ed.* 2nd ed. London, Kogan Page, in association with the Institute of Personnel Management, 1987. xvii,386p. £18.95. ISBN: 185091334x.

First published 1979, edited by K. Hawkins.

17 chapters in 3 parts, pt.1 relates to the background of the subject; pt.2 The practice of industrial relations; pt.3 The law in industrial relations. List of cases cited. Useful addresses. Analytical index, p.369-386.

Class No: 331.1(035)

[1860]

International **handbook of industrial relations:** contemporary developments and research. Blum, A.A., *ed.* Westport, CT., Greenwood Press; London, Aldwych Press, 1981. xiv, 690p. illus., tables. $67.95; £34.50. ISBN: 0313213038, US; 0861720105, UK.

27 essays, arranged A-Z by country, attempt 'to describe how workers and managers around the world deal with their problems at the workplace' (*Preface*). Includes both Western European countries and developing countries. 29 contributors. Select bibliography on comparative industrial relations. Index, p.679-696. *Class No:* 331.1(035)

[1861]

TORRINGTON, D.P., *ed.* **Handbook of industrial relations.** Epping, Essex, Gower Press, 1972. xix,328p. illus.

'An attempt to help managers in their handling of industrial relations within the organization they run' (*Preface*). In 4 parts, with 14 contributors, on the national and company framework, the union viewpoint, and the social framework. Bibliography, p.313-8. Non-analytical index. D.P. Torrington's *Who's who in personnel administration and industrial relations* (1973. 518p.) has over 2500 biographies of leading individuals in the field.

Class No: 331.1(035)

Dictionaries

English

[1862]

KELLY, M.A. **Labor and industrial relations:** terms, laws, court decisions, and arbitration standards. Baltimore, Johns Hopkins University Press, 1987. 200p. $26.50. ISBN: 0801833108.

A basic glossary of labour-related terms and a compendia of labour relations law, protective labour legislation, and major court decisions and arbitration standards. US oriented. Good index. More selective than Shafritz's *Facts on file dictionary of personnel management and labor relations* (*qv*). 'Definitions of terms are precise ...' (*Choice*, October 1987, p.286). *Class No:* 331.1(038)=20

[1863]

MARSH, A. **Concise encyclopedia of industrial relations,** with bibliography. Aldershot, Hants, Gower Press, 1979. [vi], 423p. £26. ISBN: 0566020955.

Originally issued as *Dictionary of industrial relations* in 1973.

About 3,000 entries. 'Donovan Commission': over 2 columns, with 2/3 col. of references. 'Transport and General Workers' Union: 3 cols. (amalgamations, in chronological order). Profuse references to Acts, Command Papers, Reports etc. Cross-references. Bibliography, p.355-423, listing all books and periodical articles cited in the text. British slant, but includes Ireland. 'An essential work of reference for librarians and teachers concerned with British industrial relations' (*British book news*, August 1979, p.650). *Class No:* 331.1(038)=20

[1864]

ROBERTS, H.S. **Robert's dictionary of industrial relations.** Industrial Relations Center. University of Hawaii at Manoa, *ed.* 3rd ed. Washington, DC, BNA Books, 1986. xxi, 811p. $65. ISBN: 0871794888.

First published 1966; rev. ed. 1971.

More than 4400 entries, including significant court cases and legislation, international unions, and government agencies, as well as terms and phrases used in labour-management relations. No biographical entries. '... a helpful, up-to-date source of information on terms, cases and organizations involved in industrial relations'. (*Reference books bulletin*, 1986/87, p.72). *Class No:* 331.1(038)=20

French

[1865]

DION, G. **Dictionnaire canadien des relations du travail.** 2e. rev. Quebec, Les Presses de l'Université Laval, 1987. 993p. £63.

First published 1976.

Has French definitions and an English-French index. Appendices include abbreviations in English and French of numerous North American and international employer, employee and government organizations; chronologies of Canadian and Quebec legislation and of important industrial relations events, etc. Bibliography of relevant dictionaries. *Class No:* 331.1(038)=40

Reviews & Abstracts

[1866]

Employee relations bibliography and abstracts.
Marsh, A., *ed. and comp.* Oxford, Employee Relations
Bibliography and Abstracts, 1985, plus 3 supplements, 1986-
1987. xxxi,667p. Supplements 679, 260&280p. With
supplement 1. £93.75; supplements 2 & 3. £37.50 each.
ISBN: 094787500x, inc. suppl.1; 0947875026, suppl.2;
0947875034, suppl.3.

Classification and keyword index precede the
bibliography, which is in 8 sections (General - Union-
management relations - Relations at the place of work -
Remuneration - Labour force - Trade unions - Industry -
Psychology and sociology - Countries). 17103 entries.
Author index. *Class No:* 331.1(048)

[1867]

—Employee relations bibliography and abstracts. 1989-. v.1-.
Quarterly. Marsh, A., *ed. & comp.* Oxford, Employee
Relations Bibliography and Abstracts, 1989-. ISSN:
09549064.

Continues the above.

*c.*2000 items each issue. Arrangement is as above except
that there is a 9th section for United Kingdom regions.
Class No: 331.1(048)

[1868]

Work related abstracts Detroit, Mich., Information
Coordinators Inc., 1950-. Monthly. $455pa including subject
heading list). ISSN: 02733234.

Formerly *Employment related abstracts*

A guide to current materials in labour relations and
personnel management. About 6000 informative and
indicative abstracts pa from over 275 labour, government
and business journals, arranged by broad topic. Subject
index to each issue, cumulating annually. *Work related
abstracts subject heading list* (1972-. $15.) is issued
biennially. *Class No:* 331.1(048)

Periodicals

[1869]

British journal of industrial relations. London School of
Economics. London, London School of Economics
(previously Oxford, Basil Blackwell, 1963-. quarterly
(previously 3pa.). £72; $130pa. ISSN: 00071080.

V.31(4), December 1993 has 7 articles, 10 book reviews
and a listing of books received (p.641-42). Indexed annually.
Class No: 331.1(051)

Great Britain

Bibliographies

[1870]

**GOTTSCHALK, A.W., *and others.* British industrial
relations:** an annotated bibliography. Nottingham,
University of Nottingham, Department of Adult education,
[1969?]. 72p. £0.75. ISBN: 0902031031.

About 750 entries, briefly annotated, in 5 sections: 1.
Industrial relations at the place of work - 2. Industry wide
bargaining - 3. The parties to collective bargaining - 4.
Industrial relations: wider aspects - 5. Case studies and
sources of information.

Employment relations in the United Kingdom, compiled by
M. MacCafferty (London, Aslib, 1976. vi, 48p. £5.00.

....(contd.)
0851420834) has 455 references to books, periodical and
press articles covering January 1974-December 1975.
Author index. *Class No:* 331.1(410)(01)

Histories

[1871]

**WRIGLEY, C., *ed.* A History of British industrial
relations.** Brighton, Sussex, Harvester Wheatsheaf, 1982-
87. 2v. (xv,269p.; vii,328p.) tables, graphs. £42.50 each
vol; $75.20 each vol. ISBN: 0710803168, v.1; 0710809336,
v.2.

V.1: 1875-1914; v.2: 1914-1939. V.1 has 12 essays (1.
Some aspects of the labour market in Britain ... 2. The rise
of the mass labour movement ... - 3. Rank-and-file dissent -
4. Strikes, 1870-1914 - 5. Employers and managers ... - 6.
Trade unions and the law - 7. The government and industrial
relations - 8. Government administration - 9-12 are industrial
relations case studies on 4 industries. Index, p.266-269. V.2
has 6 essays on the impact of State intervention on industrial
relations during World War I; the interwar trade union
development; rank-and-file movements and unions; the
growth of white-collar trade unionism; employers'
organizations and management strategy; the role of
governments and the importance of social welfare. Also 3
industrial relations case studies. V.2 is considered
disappointing, not maintaining the standard of v.1, but
'Taken together, the chapters represent a useful addition to
the literature of interwar industrial relations ...' (*Economic
history review,* November 1987, p.666).
Class No: 331.1(410)(091)

Germany

Bibliographies

[1872]

**CHAMBERLIN, W. Industrial relations in Germany, 1914-
1939:** annotated bibliography of materials in the Hoover
Library on War, Revolution and Peace and the Stanford
University Library. Stanford, Calif., Stanford University
Press, 1942 (Reprinted New York, AMS Press, 1974). xv,
403p. $35.00. ISBN: 0404564003.

A note on German labour law precedes the bibliography,
which is divided into 7 chapters of documents, society
publications, newspapers and periodical publications; and
then monographs, studies and articles generally for 1914-
1918, and 1933-1940. Index. *Class No:* 331.1(430)(01)

Recruitment

[1873]

**HACKETT, P., *and others.* The Daily Telegraph
recruitment handbook:** the complete step-by-step guide to
successful recruiting. 3rd ed. London, Kogan Page, 1990.
224p. £18.95. ISBN: 0749402032.

First published 1979, written by M. Armstrong and P.
Hackett.

12 Chapters: 1. Analysing recruitment needs - 2. Defining
requirements - 3. Sources of candidates - 4. Advertising - 5.
Using consultants and agencies - 6. Recruitment from
education and training establishments - 7. Setting up

....*(contd.)*

procedures and sifting candidates - 8. Interviewing - 9. Testing - 10. Obtaining references and medical check - 11. The final decision 12. Induction. Index. *Class No:* 331.11

Tribunals

[1874]

GOODMAN, M.J. Industrial tribunals: practice and procedure. 4th ed. London, Sweet and Maxwell, 1987. xxv, 120p. £15. ISBN: 0421391200.

First published 1976 as *Industrial tribunal's procedure.*

Aimed at helping the non-legal practitioner through the intricacies of industrial tribunal rules, regulations and procedure, providing an overall view of the tribunal's principal jurisdictions and detailed analyses of practice and procedure. Updated to include changes in the law since 1985, particularly the Wages Act 1986. Author is part-time chairman of the industrial tribunals and Social Security Commissioner. *Class No:* 331.15

Salaries & Wages

Great Britain

[1875]

Incomes data report. London, Incomes Data Services Ltd., 1966-. Semi-monthly. £125. pa. ISSN: 00193461.

An intelligence service on wages and incomes in Britain, including reviews of current activities in industries and of firms, settlements, intelligence reports on various subjects, and statistical tables of economic forecasts, labour turnover, and a data check (time series). *Class No:* 331.2(410)

[1876]

New earnings survey. Department of Employment. London, HMSO, 1968-. Annual. 6 parts each year. £12.50 each part; £69 the set. ISSN: 02620553.

Contents: A: Streamlined and summary analyses. Description of the survey; B: Analysis by agreement; C: Analyses of industry; D: Analyses by occupation; E: Analyses by region. Analyses by age group; F: Distribution of hours. Joint distributions of earnings and hours. Analysis of earnings and hours for part-time women employees. *Class No:* 331.2(410)

Occupations & Careers

[1877]

DIBDEN, K. *and* **TOMLINSON, J., eds. Information sources in education and work.** Sevenoaks, Kent, Butterworth, 1981. xiii, 166p. £22.50. (*Butterworths Guides to information sources.*) ISBN: 0408709235.

Directed at those responsible for advising young people and young people themselves on career choices. 11 chapters in 6 sections: 1 Setting the scene - 2 & 3. The right answer at the right time (before and in 6th form, beyond school, at university) - 4. Vocational and professional training - 5. Choosing and finding a job - 6. Information sources for the careers adviser. Bibliography relates to each chapter (pp. 150-166). No index. *Class No:* 331.5

[1878]

INTERNATIONAL LABOUR OFFICE. International standard classification of occupations. Rev, ed, Geneva, I.L.O., 1990. vii,457p. illus. SFr.65. $52. £28.60. ISBN: 9221064387.

Structured on the basis of type of work performed. *Class No:* 331.5

[1879]

Occupations, 93. Davies, K. Sheffield, Careers and Occupational Information Centre (COIC), 1992. 640p. £21.50. ISBN: 0861106342.

Entries for *c.*600 jobs and careers, with information on the work involved, the work environment, pay and conditions, vacancies, prospects for promotion, entry requirements, training courses, and address for further information. Subject index. *Class No:* 331.5

Handbooks & Manuals

[1880]

DONALD, V. How to choose a career. 3rd rev. ed. London, Kogan Page, 1993. 128p. £6.99. (*(Kogan Page careers series).*) ISBN: 074940910x.

1st published 1986.

Advice not only on traditional career paths, but also on new growth areas likely to provide a career. 10 sections in 4 parts: 1. Good prospects - 2. What do you want from a career? - 3. Training - 4. Where to go for further career advice. 'Further reading' (11 items published by Kogan Page). Index, p.123-7. *Class No:* 331.5(035)

[1881]

GOLZEN, G. Working abroad: the *Daily telegraph* guide to working and living overseas. 16th ed. London, Kogan Page, 1993. 336p. £9.99. ISBN: 0749410612.

Contains practical advice and detailed information on the overseas job market, including salary level comparisons, pensions, national insurance contributions, financial and tax planning, moving house, educating children, etc. *Class No:* 331.5(035)

[1882]

Working holidays: the complete international guide to seasonal job opportunities, 1993. London, Central Bureau, 1992. Annual. 320p. £7.95; $18.95. ISBN: 0900087891.

Published each December and valid only for the following year.

Practical information (*e.g.* Visas/work permits, travel insurance, advertising for a job); Jobs index, arranged geographically (Africa, Asia, Australia ... Yugoslavia, Worldwide) each subdivided and giving useful addresses, information, regulations, etc., for each. *Class No:* 331.5(035)

Yearbooks & Directories

[1883]

The Directory of jobs and careers abroad. Lipinski,, A. 7th ed. London, Vacation work, 1989. x,342p. £10.95. ISBN: 1854580132. ISSN: 01433482.

First published 1971.

In 3 parts: The general approach (Discovering your employment potential - Getting the job - Rules and regulations - Learning the language - Preparation and follow-up - Home letting) - Specific careers (17 sections, all subdivided) - Worldwide employment (by regions,

....*(contd.)*

subdivided by country; contacts; etc.). 5 appendices, including a Bibliography (p.327-328); Application procedure; Worldwide taxation; Worldwide living standards; Key to company classifications. Index to organizations, p.336-341.

An 8th ed. by A.De Vries was issued in 1993 (388p. £15.95. ISBN 1854580256). *Class No:* 331.5(058)

[1884]
Summer jobs abroad, 1989. Woodworth, D., *ed.* 20th annual ed. Oxford, Vacation Work, 1989. 214p. £7.95. ISBN: 1854580051.

Earlier title was *Directory of summer jobs abroad*.

Aims to help students and other young people find jobs outside Britain during their long summer vacations. Valid for the 1989 summer season only. Lists 30,000 varied vacancies in over 40 different countries, excluding US, stating salaries, hours and periods of work, under countries A-Z: 'au pair, paying guests, and exchange visits'; 'visa, residence and working regulations, useful publications, travel and holidays'.

Also published by this publisher are *Summer employment directory of the US; Emploi d'été en France; Kibbutz volunteer; International directory of voluntary work* (see 362(100)(058)). *Class No:* 331.5(058)

Great Britain

[1885]
ROUTH, G. **Occupations of the people of Great Britain, 1801-1981:** with a compendium of a paper 'Occupations of the people of the United Kingdom, 1801-81' by Charles Booth. London, Macmillan, 1987. xiv, 98p. figs., tables. £29.50. ISBN: 0333434978.

Extends Charles Booth's analysis to 1981, and presents a retrospect of the transformation that has occurred in 180 years. 6 chapters: 1. Charles Booth's paper - 2. 1881-1911 - 3. 1911-1951 - 4. 1951-1981 - 5. Retrospect - 6. Britain in its world setting. Appendix: Allocation of 1981 occupational units to occupational classes. Bibliography, A-Z by author, p.95-96. Index, p.97-98. Author is a former Reader in Economics at University of Sussex. *Class No:* 331.5(410)

Handbooks & Manuals

[1886]
BURSTON, D., *ed.* **An A-Z of careers and jobs.** 6th ed. London, Kogan Page, 1994. 432p. £9.99. ISBN: 0749422291.

First published 1984.

'... aimed primarily at young people still at school ...' (*Introduction*). Covers a range of careers and jobs, 350 different occupations from accountant to zoologist. Information given is description of job, qualifications and training, personal qualities, starting salary, further information (organizations and addresses), and publications. Cross-references. 2 appendices: 1. Youth Training Scheme - 2. Useful addresses. Index. *Class No:* 331.5(410)(035)

[1887]
—The Jobfinders book: the *Daily Telegraph* guide. Sandys, R. *and* Stace, A. 5th ed. London, Kogan Page, 1987. 165p. £4.95. ISBN: 0850911258.

A step-by-step guide to the mechanics of finding a job. *Class No:* 331.5(410)(035)

[1888]
Handbook of free careers information in the UK. 4th ed. Richmond, Surrey, & London, Careers Consultants Ltd., 1987. vii, 311p. ISBN: 0856601195.

First published 1978.

Intended for careers advisers and teachers, the handbook includes nearly 300 organizations. Subject arrangement. Entries include name and address, telephone number, person or department to contact, leaflets and booklets available, services offered by the organization. Organizations included are mainly professional bodies. A-Z index of organizations. *Class No:* 331.5(410)(035)

[1889]
Which subject? Which career? a guide to subjects and courses at ages 14, 16 and 18 and the careers to which they can lead. Jamieson, A., *ed.* 4th ed. London, Which? Books: Consumers' Association; Hodder & Stoughton, 1992. 576p. £10.95. ISBN: 0340564830.

1st published 1987.

21 sections in 2 parts: 1. School courses; 2. Further and higher education. A Part 3, the bulk of the book, is an A-Z of careers (Accountancy ... Zookeeping). *Class No:* 331.5(410)(035)

Yearbooks & Directories

[1890]
Careers encyclopedia. Segal, A., *ed.* 13th ed. London, Cassell, 1991. xxiv, 1280p. £35. $70. ISBN: 030431675x.

First published 1952.

Designed to be read to provide a broad general survey of the state of careers and employment, and the related areas of education and training. 11 sections (each subdivided, with appended 'Further reading',and 'Further information'): Academic and vocational qualifications - Academic and vocational studies and where they can lead - The world of work. The information society - Commerce, administration and finance - Creative, cultural and entertainment work - Land- and environment-related work - Central and local government and the armed forces - Manufacturing and production - Professional, scientific and social services - The service industries - Working overseas. 2 appendices: I: Organizations providing further information; II: Higher and further education institutions. Index to advertisers. Index, p.1231-1244. *Class No:* 331.5(410)(058)

[1891]
Graduate careers services directory, 1991-92. 6th ed. Manchester, University and Polytechnic Careers Advisory Services (Central Services Unit), 1991. 224p. £8.45.

An index of institutions precedes the main directory, which is arranged A-Z under the names of the colleges, universities and polytechnics to which the careers services are attached. Information given includes name of service, address, personnel, term dates, directions, graduating force for 1990. There follows a section relating to disabled graduates. Index of personnel; index of term dates. *Class No:* 331.5(410)(058)

[1892]

Jobfile 89: the comprehensive careers handbook. Miller, I.M., *and others, comps.* London,. Hodder & Stoughton, 1989. 571p. £22.99. ISBN: 0340587652.

First published 1988.

Annually revised career guide designed to give careers staff, teachers, students and others the chance to identify a realistic range of job opportunities. A-Z index of types of work (p.541-571), Careers areas index (p.509-524), Jobfile sections index (p.525-540) precede profiles of 642 jobs, with description of job, qualifications, skills, notes, references, adult notes for each. *Class No:* 331.5(410)(058)

USA

Bibliographies

[1893]

Professional careers sourcebook. Dorgan, C.A., *and others, eds.* 3rd rev. ed. Detroit, Mich., Gale Research International Ltd. 1993. 1049p. $80.44 £47.50 ISBN: 0810375737.

First published 1990.

Presents over 100 professional career profiles, including information on general career guides, career information and services provided by professional associations, standards and certification agencies, directories of educational programmes and institutions, basic reference guides and handbooks related to the profession, professional and trade periodicals, etc. A master index lists all publications, organizations and information sources. *Class No:* 331.5(73)(01)

Yearbooks & Directories

[1894]

Career discovering encyclopedia. Primm, E.R., *ed.* Supersedes Hopke, W.E., ed. The Encyclopedia of careers and vocational guidance. 7th ed. 1988. Chicago, Ill., Ferguson, 1990. 6v. illus. $99.95. ISBN: 0894341065.

Describes 504 careers, A-Z. Each career has a 2-page spread and includes information on type of work, education and training required, salary, future prospects, sources of further information, other related occupations. Index and glossary for all volumes at end of each volume. V.6 also indexes careers by cluster. '... clearly written, attractive, and well organized.' (*Booklist*, 15 May 1990, p.1836). *Class No:* 331.5(73)(058)

[1895]

VGM's careers encyclopedia. Norback, C.T. 3rd ed. Lincolnwood, Ill., National Textbook Co./VGM Careers Books, 1991. 464p. $39.95. ISBN: 0844261327.

Details of nearly 200 Careers, A-Z, including general descriptions, places of employment, qualifications, working conditions, education and training, advancement, income, etc. Index. *Class No:* 331.5(73)(058)

Unemployment

Bibliographies

[1896]

FARMER, P., *comp. & ed.* **The Social and economic impact of unemployment, 1979-85:** a select bibliography. Letchworth, Herts, Technical Communications, 1985. xix, 176p. ISBN: 0946655057.

....(contd.)

Over 1,100 entries. Entries on UK press comment are followed by sections on Social impact - Physical and psychological effects - Economic and technological impact - Alternatives to unemployment - Employer and trade union attitudes to unemployment - Future projections on unemployment. For each entry there is title, author, publisher and price, and pagination, or journal or report details, and annotation. Corporate organizations index and author index. *Class No:* 331.56(01)

Great Britain

Official Records

[1897]

GREAT BRITAIN. Public Record Office. **Records of interest to social scientists: unemployment insurance 1911-1939.** London, HMSO., 1975. 268p. £4.50. (*Public Record Office handbooks, no.16.*) ISBN: 0114400636.

8 chapters, documenting the policy changes of successive governments (Liberal government, 1908/1914 ... National government, 1931/1939). Royal Commission on Unemployment Insurance, 1930-32. Committees dealing with unemployment insurance. 9 appendices (*e.g.* 6. Statistics; 9. Précis of Acts of Parliament dealing with unemployment insurance). *Class No:* 331.56(410)(093.2)

Technical Training

Dictionaries

Polyglot

[1898]

INTERNATIONAL LABOUR OFFICE. Vocational **training:** glossary of selected terms. Rev. ed. Geneva, I.L.O. 1986. vii,132p. SFr.15. ISBN: 9221054578.

First published 1975.

Defines, in English, *c.*300 terms selected on the basis of need for precise definitions of modern vocational training terms. Translations in French and Spanish. *Class No:* 331.86(038)=00

English

[1899]

MANPOWER SERVICES COMMISSION. Training Services. **Glossary of training terms.** 3rd ed. London, HMSO, for the Commission, 1981. [9],93p. £4.50. ISBN: 0118885111.

First published 1967,. 1st and 2nd eds. produced by the Department of Employment.

Defines over 300 terms, including names of organizations. 3 appendices: A. Abbreviations and acronyms - B. Industrial Training Boards and other training organizations - C. Names and addresses of organizations. *Class No:* 331.86(038)=20

Reviews & Abstracts

[1900]

Technical education abstracts from British sources. Leicester University. Library, *comp.* Abingdon, Oxon. Carfax (previously London, National Federation for Educational Research in England and Wales, and later

....(contd.)

Liverpool, Information for Education Ltd.), 1961-. v.1, no.1-. Quarterly. £112pa. ISSN: 00400920.

c.50 indicative and informative abstracts pa, drawn from *c*.50 major journals, monographs, reports and conference proceedings. Arranged in 24 subject divisions: Administration - Adult education - Business studies ... Teacher education ... Special education - Tourism. Author and subject indexes, cumulating annually. Intended for those working in science, technical and further education, including education and training for industry and commerce. *Class No:* 331.86(048)

Great Britain
[1901]

The **Training directory** 2nd ed. London, Kogan Page, in association with BACIE, 1993. 296. £25. ISBN: 0749409568.

First published 1989.

Details government initiatives and proposals for vocational training in the United Kingdom; operations of TECs and LECs, government funding for employee training and industrial training groups; lists of suppliers of training materials and equipment. *Class No:* 331.86(410)

Trade Unions
[1902]

Trade unions of the world, 1992-93. Upham, M., *ed.* 3rd ed., rev. & updated. Harlow, Essex, Longman Group, 1991; (distributed by Gale Research Co., in US and Canada). viii, 579p. £75.00; $130.00. (*Longman current affairs.*) ISBN: 0582081947, UK.

First published 1987.

An international guide to trade unions and their activities. Arrangement is by country and territory, and for each there is background information, a discussion of trade unionism there, and full details of the central trade unions and other unions active there. For each trade union the information given includes the original and English translation of title; address; leadership; telephone, fax., telex, cable numbers; history and character; structure; publications; and international affiliations. A separate section gives information on international organizations. There is also a select index of acronyms, and an index of trade union organizations. 'A handy compendium of basic information on the worldwide status of the labor movement' (*Choice*, v.25(7), March 1988, p.1072, review of the first edition). *Class No:* 331.881

Dictionaries

Polyglot
[1903]

EUROPEAN COMMUNITIES. Commission. Glossary of labour and the trade union movement. Luxembourg, Office for Official Publications of the European Communities, 1983. 216p. £11.50. ECU 17.41.

400 terms in 10 languages on labour terminology and the vocabulary used in the trade union movement. Short definitions. Names and abbreviations of the most important trade union organizations are also listed. *Class No:* 331.881(038)=00

Periodicals
[1904]

TRADE UNION CONGRESS. Library. List of current trade union periodicals. London, the Library, 1991. 15p. Gratis.

Mimeographed.

A-Z list of unions publishing periodicals, with the titles of the periodicals they publish, with frequencies. Title index. *Class No:* 331.881(051)

Europe—Western

Biographies
[1905]

ANDREUCCI, F. *and* **DETTI, T. Il movimento operaio italiano: dizionario biografico, 1853-1943.** Roma, Editori Riuniti, 1975-1978. 5v.

A biographical dictionary of the Italian labour movement, arranged A-Z by biographee throughout the 5v. *Class No:* 331.881(400)(092)

Great Britain
[1906]

JONES, J. *and* **MORRIS, M. A-Z of trade unionism and industrial relations.** New ed. London, Sphere Books Ltd., 1986. 368p. £5.95. ISBN: 0434909009.

First published 1983 by Heinemann.

'Aims to fill the absence of a *single* source of basic information on what may be broadly described as the world of labour (*Preface*). Detailed contents list precedes the main A-Z listing (Ability to pay ... Zero rating). 2 appendices: a list of trade unions in England and Scotland, A-Z under each country; and a list of names and addresses of institutions. 'Compact source book of basic definitions and background information covering *c*.500 terms used in discussions of trade unionism and industrial relations'. (*British book news*, March 1983, p.160, of the 1st edition). *Class No:* 331.881(410)

[1907]

Trade Union Congress directory. London, T.U.C., 1989. 56p. £3.

Lists: County associations of trade councils - TUC affiliated societies - TUC publications - TUC journals - Regional education offices - International societies and institutions. *Class No:* 331.881(410)

Bibliographies
[1908]

SMITH, H., *ed.* **The British labour movement to 1970:** a bibliography. London, Mansell, 1981. 268p. £30. ISBN: 0720109248.

3,838 numbered entries for books, pamphlets and periodical articles in English, published 1945-70. 140 periodicals are indexed. Arranged in sections: General (including biographical sources (making extensive use of Boase and *DNB*) and sources for research, study and teaching) - Socialism: history and theory - Early radicalism (*e.g.* Chartism) - Labour Party and Labour governments - Labour movement - Other organizations (*e.g.* Fabian Society; Communist Party) - Trade Unionism - Co-operation (*e.g.* Co-operative Society histories). Bibliographies, p.xv-xviii. Detailed index, p.221-50.

....(contd.)

The same compiler's article. 'From Chartism to Callaghan; historiography and bibliography' (*Library review*, v.29, Winter 1980. p.271-4) surveys writings on the history of the British labour movement, with special mention of the *Dictionary of labour biography, Warwick guide to British labour periodicals. 1790-1970*, and the Scottish Labour Historical Society's *A catalogue of some Labour records in Scotland and some Scots records outside Scotland*, compiled and edited by Ian McDougall. *Class No:* 331.881(410)(01)

Yearbooks & Directories

[1909]

MARSH, A. *and* **RYAN, V. Historical directory of trade unions.** Aldershot, Hants., Gower Publishing Co Ltd., 1980-88. 4v. £45.00 each vol. ISBN: 0566021609, v.1; 0566021617, v.2; 0566021625, v.3; 0566021635, v.4.

Lists over 5,000 British trade unions, past and present. Entries in each volume A-Z by name of union, with information on foundation date, name changes, amalgamations, cessations, characteristics of policy, membership characteristics and numbers, sources of information (books, articles, minutes, etc.) and location of documentation. Cross-references. Index at end of vol.4. Contents: v.1: Non-manual unions; v.2: Trade unions in engineering. Coal-mining and iron and steel, agriculture, chemicals; v.3: Trade unions in building and allied trades, leather workers, enginemen and tobacco workers; v.4: Trade unions in textiles, printing, retail distribution, government and general unions, miscellaneous industries. *Class No:* 331.881(410)(058)

[1910]

MARSH, A. Trade union handbook: a guide and directory to the structure, membership, policy and personnel of the British Trade unions. 5th ed. Aldershot, Hants, Gower Press, 1991. 350p. tables. £38. ISBN: 0566029758.

First published 1979.

4 parts: 1. The trade union movement in the United Kingdom - 2. Trade union organizations - 3. Directory of 402 trade unions - 4. Addresses of other industrial relations institutions. This edition updated to the beginning of 1987. A bibliography, included in earlier editions, has been omitted because such information is available from the author's *Employment relations bibliography and abstracts* (published 6-monthly). Author is Fellow in Industrial Relations at St. Edmund Hall, Oxford. *Class No:* 331.881(410)(058)

Histories

[1911]

CLEGG, H.A., *and others*. **A History of British trade unions since 1889.** Oxford, Clarendon Press, 1964-. v.1-. v.1: ix, [1], 514p. tables. v.2: xiii, 619p. v.1: £45; v.2: £40. ISBN: 019828229x, v.1; 0198283075, v.2.

To be in 3v. but v.2 appeared 20 years after v.1 and was written by H.A. Clegg alone.

V.1: *1889-1910;* v.2: *1911-1933*. The only previous history of note is Sidney and Beatrice Webb's *History of trade unionism* (1894), the later editions of which (*e.g.* 1920) add little of value. This scholarly continuation, to be in 3v., is a detailed survey with profuse footnote references and notes, and bibliography. Partly analytical indexes. *Class No:* 331.881(410)(091)

[1912]

PELLING, H. A History of British trade unionism. 5th ed. London, Macmillan Press Ltd., 1992. 360p. illus. £40. ISBN: 0333577663.

First published 1963.

A standard work, revised and updated to take account of recent research and to explain the course of events up to the early 1990's. In 3 main parts: 1. The emergence of trade unions; 2. The consolidation of labour; 3. Problems of national integration. A statistical table covering the years 1893-1985 has numbers of trade unions, members, affiliations to the TUC, stoppages, and working days lost. Further reading is in 3 sections: 1. General; 2. Histories of individual unions; 3. Additional sources for particular topics (by chapters). There is a detailed index.

Class No: 331.881(410)(091)

[1913]

PROCHASKA, A. History of the General Federation of Trade Unions, 1899-1980. London, George Allen & Unwin, 1982. xiv,274p. £15. ISBN: 0043310877.

7 chapters: 1. The beginnings to the General Federation of Trade Unions, 1890-1900 - 2. Growth: internal affairs, 1900-10 - 3. The General Federation in a wider world, 1900-10 - 4. The turbulant decade. The challenges of syndicalism and war, 1910-20 - 5. International affairs and the exclusion of the General Federation from British representation, 1913-22 - 6. Between the wars - 7. From the 1940s to the 1970s. Appendix: membership of the General Federation of Trade Unions, 1899-1980. Sources and select bibliography, p.254-261. Index, p.262-274. *Class No:* 331.881(410)(091)

Official Records

[1914]

BENNETT, J. *and* **STOREY, R. Trade union and related records.** Coventry, University of Warwick Library, 1979. 30p. illus.

Details the principal groups of trade unions' and related records outside the custody of the union headquarters. Arranged A-Z by trade unions, indicating locations. *Class No:* 331.881(410)(093.2)

England

[1915]

BROWN, D. The English labour movement, 1700-1951. Dublin, Gill & Macmillan, 1982. [3], 322p. £20. ISBN: 717108708.

Outlines the development of working class organization in England since the industrial revolution.

In 8 chapters: 1. Trade unionism to *c.*1840-2 - 2. The making of the working class? - 3. Chartism - 4. The years of adjustment, 1850-75 - 5. Trade unionism and socialism, *c.*1875-1900 - 6. The emergence of labour, 1900-21 - 7. Triumph and defeat, 1921-27 - 8. Depression and apathy, 1927-39 - Postscript: Cradle to grave? Labour, 1939-51. 658 notes (mainly bibliographical sources on which book is based). Index, p.317-22 double column.

Class No: 331.881(420)

Bibliographies

[1916]

POTTS, A. *and* JONES, E.R., *comps*. **Northern labour history:** a bibliography. London, Library Association, Reference, Special and Information Section 1981. [3],ii.122p. £22.50.

Covering Cleveland, Cumbria, Durham, Northumberland and Tyne and Wear, the bibliography is arranged in 12 subject sections: Friendly and benefit societies, Co-Operatives, Political movements, Trade unionism, Strikes and disputes, Unemployment, Education and recreation, 20th century working class publications, and Individuals. (biographies, autobiographies, private papers, etc.). Includes printing and secondary sources. *Class No:* 331.881(420)(01)

Germany

[1917]

BARTEL, H., *ed*. **Sachwörterbuch der Geschischte Deutschlands und der deutscher Arbeiterbewegung.** Berlin, Dietz, 1969 - 1970. 2v. (1055 p. 877 p.) illus., maps.

An encyclopedia of the history of Germany and of the German working-class movement. V.1: A-K; v.2: L-Z. *Class No:* 331.881(430)

France

[1918]

MAITRON, J., *ed*. **Dictionnaire biographique du mouvement ouvrier français de 1789-1939.** Paris, Éditions Ouvrières, 1964-93. v.1-4. 4 parts (43 volumes.). Prices vary (*e.g.* Tome 27 (1986), FrF.230; £25).

1: (v.1-3): 1789-1864. De la Révolution français à la fondation de la Première Internationale; 2: (v.4-9): 1864-1871. De la fondation de la Première Internationale à la Commune; 3: (v.10-15): 1871-1914. De la Commune à la Grande Guerre; 4: (16-43): 1914-1939. De la Première à la Seconde Guerre Mondiale. Pt.1 contains 12,000 biographies A-Z. 'Important source material for the writing of the biographies was provided by the 10,000 dossiers relating to the June 1848 Rising and the Paris Commune of 1871 kept in the archives of the War Ministry and never previously used for the purposes of historical research' (*Times literary supplement*, no.3367, 8 September 1966, p.819). Biographies are unsigned, but lists of works, bibliography and iconography, as appropriate, are appended. V.10 (1973) has *c.*2500 short biographies, A-BOU, preceded by lists of delegates to congresses. Part 4 is now published. *Class No:* 331.881(44)

USA

Handbooks & Manuals

[1919]

FINK, G.M., *ed*. **Labor unions.** Westport,Conn., Greenwood, 1977. 544p. $50.95. (*Greenwood encyclopedia of American institutions.*) ISBN: 0837189381.

A handbook of historical sketches of more than 200 national labour unions, selected for importance as part of the American labour movement. Entries, arranged A-Z by name of union, are several pages in length, some signed, and all including suggestions for further reading. 5 appendices on national affiliations, chronology, union genealogies, executive leadership (of selected unions), and membership

....(contd.)

(of selected unions). Glossary and detailed index. Companion volume to the editor's *Biographical dictionary of American labor leaders (qv). ' ...* an excellent first choice for a good overview or survey ... (RQ, v.17, no.4, Summer 1978, p.360-61)...Original, useful, and altogether commendable reference work.' *(Library journal,* v.102, no.1, January 1, 1977, p.90). *Class No:* 331.881(73)(035)

Histories

[1920]

AMERICAN FEDERATION OF LABOR. **American Federation of Labor:** history, encyclopedia, reference book. New ed. New York, Greenwood Press, 1977 (now issued by the Federation). 3v. in 5. illus. $197.75 the set. ISBN: 0837195683, the set.

Originally published by authority of the 1916 and 1917 conventions. A reprint of the edition published by the Federation in Washington in 1919 and reprinted in 1960. *Class No:* 331.881(73)(091)

[1921]

—McBREARTY, J.C., *eds*. American labor history and comparative labor movements. A selected bibliography. Tucson, AZ., University of Arizona Press, 1973. (Available from Books Demand UMI). x, 262p. $68. ISBN: 0317105531. *Class No:* 331.881(73)(091)

Biographies

[1922]

FINK, G.M., *ed*. **Biographical dictionary of American labor.** Rev. ed. updated and expanded. Westport, CT., Greenwood Press, 1984. xvii,767p. ilus. $56.95 £45. ISBN: 0313228655.

First published 1974 as *Biographical dictionary of American labor leaders.*

Career biographies of *c.*734 men and women who have had a significant impact on the American labour movement. A main section, A-Z, by name, is supplemented by several appendices. Index. 'Essential for most academic and research libraries' (*Library journal*, 1 October 1984, p.1840), but *Choice* (v.22(9),May 1985, p.1302) complains that it is not representative. *Class No:* 331.881(73)(092)

Strikes

Bibliographies

[1923]

PETTMAN, B.O. **Strikes:** a selected bibliography. Bradford, Yorks., distributed by MCB Books for the Institute of Scientific Business Ltd., 1976. vii, 64p. £29.95. ISBN: 0903763184.

1,230 references from 32 countries, relating to literature published between 1970 and 1975. Covers not only the industrial relations aspects but also the economic, sociological, psychological and legal aspects of strikes. Entries arranged by country, subdivided as books and monographs, articles, theses, or government reports. Author index. *Class No:* 331.89(01)

Land & Property

Bibliographies

[1924]

DENMAN, D. R., *and others*. Bibliography of rural land economy and land ownership, 1900-1957: a full list of works relating to the British Isles and selected works from the United States and Western Europe. Cambridge, Cambridge University Press, 1958. xii, 412p.

A list of *c*.6500 works, first in classified order (p.1.-259). 8 classes: A. History - B. General works - C. Rural economy - D. Land economy - E. Estate economy - F. Research and education - G. Reference works - H. Foreign works; then under authors. Subject index.
Class No: 332(01)

[1925]

GREAT BRITAIN. HM Stationery Office. **Government publications. Sectional list 43, revised February 1992.** London, HMSO, 1992. vii,12p. tables. Gratis.

Land Registry forms are listed and described. Also includes list of revelant official publications.
Class No: 332(01)

[1926]

HARRIS, L. A. The Real estate industry: an information sourcebook. Phoenix, AZ., Oryx Press, 1987. 170 p. $39.50. (*Oryx sourcebook series in business and management, 5.*) ISBN: 0897742621.

About 900 entries for reference works, textbooks, periodicals, government publications and professional books on the subject, mainly published in English in the 1980s. Entries are annotated. Author, table and subject indexes.
Class No: 332(01)

[1927]

NURCOMBE, V.J. International real estate valuation, investment and development: a select bibliography. London, E. & F. Spon, 1987. viii, 232p. £15. ISBN: 0419136908.

3768 unannotated entries. An introduction (with 9 references) is followed by subject sections (General - Techniques - Technical topics (subdivided by subjects) - Industrial land and building (subdivided by countries) - Commercial property (subdivided by countries) - Retail property (subdivided by countries) - Residential property - Rural leisure and other property (subdivided by subject) - Property market (subdivided by countries) - Real estate practice - Finance and investment). Appendices of dictionaries and encyclopedias and of journals. Author index, p.181-207; analytical subject index, p.208-232.
Class No: 332(01)

Dictionaries

[1928]

ABBOTT, D. Encyclopedia of real estate terms. Aldershot, Hants, Gower Technical Press, 1987. xiii, 1102p. £120. ISBN: 0291397026.

Definitions and explanations of over 5,000 terms and phrases used in real estate. Primarily UK usage but also includes terms used in US and France. Many entries are supported by reference to legal decisions. Cross-references.

....(contd.)

Appendices include a bibliography (p.1061-1099) arranged in subject groupings, and tables of measurement.
Class No: 332(038)

English

[1929]

FRIEDMAN, J.P., *and others*. Dictionary of real estate terms. Woodbury, NY., Barron's, 1984. 320p. $5.95. ISBN: 0812025210.

Similar to *Barron's real estate handbook,* except that the handbook has an additional 251p. of tables.

Over 1400 concise definitions of real estate and related legal, financial and architectural terms, with examples and, in some cases, diagrams, sketches, and calculations used to explain terms. 10-page appendix includes mortgage tables, measurement tables, and mathematical formulae. *Choice* (v.22(9), May 1985, p.1304) recommends that libraries purchase the Handbook. *Class No:* 332(038)=20

[1930]

THOMSETT, M.C., *comp*. Real estate dictionary. Jefferson, NC., McFarland & Company Inc., 1988. 220p. illus., charts, diagrs. $29.95; £22.45. ISBN: 0899503217.

Over 1100 entries, including words and phrases, legal concepts and rules, agencies, associations and regulatory bodies involved in real estate. Concentrates on residential and commercial property, real estate investment, mortgage loans, and legal terms. Succinct definitions and helpful charts, tables and diagrams. Cross-references. Also includes a buyers' checklist, amortization tables, and remaining balance tables. A handy source for consumers.
Class No: 332(038)=20

[1931]

Webster's new world illustrated encyclopedic dictionary of real estate. Gross, J.S., *ed.* 3rd ed. Englewood Cliffs, N.J., Prentice-Hall, 1987. 418p. illus. $12.95. ISBN: 0139473181.

Previous ed. was *Illustrated encyclopedic dictionary of real estate.*

Includes a 251-page dictionary and 165-page portfolio of real estate forms. Entries in the dictionary are for real estate jargon, construction terms, and legal terminology for the layman; they vary in length from a sentence to a third of a page, and many have simple line-drawings for illustration. US-slanted. *Class No:* 332(038)=20

Spanish

[1932]

GOLDSTONE, H.P. Real estate/Bienes raíces: a bilingual dictionary, Spanish-English and English-Spanish... Jefferson, N.C., McFarland & Co., 1986. 136p. $15.95; £11.95. ISBN: 0899501966.

Includes about 4000 entries in each section.
Class No: 332(038)=60

England & Wales

Handbooks & Manuals

[1933]

Walmsley's rural estate management: compendium at the service of agricultural landowners, practising land agents, and students for the profession in England and Wales. Miles, C.W.N., *and others*. 6th ed. London, Estates Gazette, 1979. xxvi, 589p. £20. ISBN: 0728200414.

First published 1948.

A list of references for further reading is appended to each chapter. Analytical index. *Class No:* 332(42)(035)

Common Land

[1934]

HOSKINS, W.G. *and* **STAMP, L.D. The Common lands of England and Wales.** London, Collins, 1963. xvii, 366p. illus. maps. (*The new naturalist.*)

The authors were members of the Royal Commission on Common Land, 1955-58. 25 chapters (1-7, by W.G. Hoskins; 8-25 on detailed regions by L.D. Stamp). Appendix: The commons of England. County lists, p.243-350 (name; acreage, nature; rights ownership). Favourably reviewed in *Geographical review*, v.55, no.4, October 1965, p.583-4. *Class No:* 332.24.33

Property Market

Dictionaries

[1935]

AMERICAN INSTITUTE OF REAL ESTATE APPRAISERS. The Dictionary of real estate appraisal. 2nd ed. Chicago, Ill., the Institute, 1989. 366p. $28.50. ISBN: 0911780939.

First published 1984.

*c.*3000 words and phrases related to the valuation of all types of real property, including accounting, arbitration, banking, construction, finance, insurance, law, and urban planning, etc. Short, concise definitions. Cross-references. List of information sources. *Class No:* 332.72(038)

[1936]

WEST, B. W. *and* **DICKINSON, R. L. Street talk in real estate.** Alameda, CA., Unique Publishing Co., 1987. vi. 216 p. $9.95. ISBN: 0934189013.

*c.*1500 standard, technical and colloquial words and phrases, expressions, and acronyms commonly used in real estate transactions. U.S. usage. *Class No:* 332.72(038)

Yearbooks & Directories

[1937]

Barron's real estate handbook. Harris, J.C. *and* Friedman, J.P., *eds.* 2nd ed. (A 3rd ed. was issued in 1993. 700p. $2995.). New York, Barron's, 1988. 700 p. illus., tables. $ 19.95. ISBN: 0812057589.

Combines a glossary of real estate terms with guides for buyers, sellers, professionals, and potential professionals. Several text chapters precede the glossary of *c.*1500 terms, covering finance, law, architecture, construction, associations and organizations. Brief descriptions, often followed by examples. Over 200-pages of mortgage tables,

....(contd.)

measurement tables, sample forms and worksheets. Bibliography. 3-page index. A comprehensive reference source. *Class No:* 332.72(058)

[1938]

Kemp's property industry year book, 1987. Solihull, West Midlands, Kemp's Group Ltd., 1987. [1891]p. ISBN: 086259104x.

First published 1974. From 1974 to 1979 as *Kemp's estate agents yearbook and directory*. Annual.

Directory of estate agents and specialist services in the UK; Development and investment companies; Pension funds; and Property services. Each section arranged in classified order. *Class No:* 332.72(058)

Great Britain

Bibliographies

[1939]

Property information source book, 1989. Moody, M., *comp.* London, Estates Gazette Ltd., 1988. 128p. £32.50. ISBN: 0728201275.

'... identifies and describes reports, surveys and services which contribute to our knowledge about the way the communal property market works, and how it performs'. (p.5). 14 sections: Office markets; Detail markets; Industrial markets; Leisure; Agriculture; Topical issues; Property finance and investment; Independent research companies; Online databases and information services; Marketing services and the players in the market; Property law; Auctions; Property press surveys; the Development Corporations. No index. *Class No:* 332.72(410)(01)

[1940]

RAMSAY, A., *comp.* **Property development and management into the nineties:** a guide to sources of information. London, British Library, 1988. [4], 59p. £19.50. ISBN: 071230763x.

10 chapters, each with an introduction and bibliography (arranged by author, A-Z, and unannotated): 1. Agents involved in property - 2. Development planning - 3. Project appraisal - 4. Property promotion - 5. Property management - 6. Management of property in general - 7. Management of residential property - 8. Management of commercial and industrial property - 9. Management of property in communal use - 10. Land management. Appendix: Directory of relevant organizations. *Class No:* 332.72(410)(01)

[1941]

SCARRETT, D., ed. **Sources of property market information:** a bibliography of practice-based market research reports and indices. Aldershot, Hants, Gower Publishing Ltd., 1988. viii,64p. £25. ISBN: 0566056631.

First published by Leicester Polytechnic Press in 3 eds., 1984, 1986, 1987.

Itemises the sources of information and also points to useful reports issued by stockbrokers and others. Part I: Agents reports; pt. II: Stockbrokers' reports; pt. III: Technical specifications of property indices. Index, p.58-64. *Class No:* 332.72(410)(01)

Cooperative Movements

Great Britain

[1942]
SMETHURST, J.M., *ed*. **A Bibliography of co-operative societies' histories.** Manchester, Co-operative Union, 1973. vi, 122p. £3. ISBN: 0851950949.

Section 1: General books on co-operation with particular reference to those which relate to societies and the history of the movement; 2: Histories of consumer co-operation societies; 3: Agricultural, manufacturing, production and co-partnership co-operative societies. Section 1 includes a few annotated items. Author index to each section.
Class No: 334(410)

Business Relationships & Organization

[1943]
Kelly's business directory, 1994 107th ed East Grinstead, W. Sussex, Reed Information Services Ltd, 1993. xxxv,2186p. ISBN: 061000641x. ISSN: 02699265.

About 82000 industrial product and service companies in the UK are listed. Arranged in 4 sections: Reader reply section (reply paid cards for product literature); Industrial products and services section (with details of manufacturers, merchants, wholesalers and firms offering an industrial service, arranged under classified trade and professional headings); Oil and gas industry section (arranged similarly); Company information section (companies listed A-Z, with trade description, address and telecommunications details).
Class No: 334.7

[1944]
Kompass United Kingdom: register of British industry and commerce, 1993/94. East Grinstead, Reed Information Services, in association with the Confederation of British Industry (CBI), 1993. 6v. £924.

First published 1962. Annual.

Lists manufacturers, suppliers, distributors, products and services. V.I has *c*.41,000 different products and services offered by British industrial companies; v.II. Corporate information on 43,500 leading companies in British industry; [v.III]. Financial data; [v.IV]. Parents and subsidiaries; [v.V]. Industrial trade names; [v.6]. Quality assessed companies. Also available on CD-ROM. *Class No:* 334.7

Abbreviations & Symbols

[1945]
TOWELL, J.E., *ed*. **Business acronyms:** a selection of approximately 25,000 acronyms, initialisms, abbreviations, contractions, alphabetic symbols, and similar condensed appellations. 1st ed. Detroit, Mich., Gale Research Co., 1988. 414p. $74.75. (*Acronyms, initialisms & abbreviations dictionary subject guide series, 2.*) ISBN: 0810325497.

Definitions are taken from *Acronyms, initialisms & abbreviations dictionary* (Gale, 2nd ed., 1987-88. 3v.) and include all aspects of business, including banking, finance, commerce, trade, economics and statistics, plus stock exchange symbols, etc. 2 listings - by acronym and by term or phrase. *Class No:* 334.7(003)

Databases

[1946]
NOBARI, N.S., *ed*. **Books and periodicals on line:** a guide to publication contents of business and legal data bases, V.1., Part 1-, 1987-. New York, Library Alliance Inc. 1987-. Annual. $249. ISSN: 0951838x.

Aims to help researchers to use online time efficiently by providing them with a directory of over 6800 periodicals and serials which are available on such databases. In 4 sections: Alphabetical listing of periodicals and serials (name of publication; country of origin if not US, and journal code; name of publisher; name of database; name of producer; scope of editorial coverage, including starting date (and ending date if applicable); name of vendors) - Publishers' names and addresses - Producers' and vendors' names and addresses - Books and periodicals by database (A-Z by database, subdivided by A-Z list of titles). Available online and on CD-ROM. *Class No:* 334.7(003.4)

[1947]
Online/CD-ROM business sourcebook. Foster, P. *and* Foster, A. Headland, Clevedon, Headland Press, 1989-. 2pa. £129. $259. ISSN: 09535055.

'... an evaluative guide to electronic business databases ... designed to indicate ... those databases which are likely to be of most use in searching for a particular category of information; (*Preface*). 20 sections: 1. Introduction - 2. Recent highlights - 3. Online hosts indepth - 4. Major CD-ROM publishers - 5. Company directories...10. Business news...14. Prices - 15. Market research...17. Economics and finance - 18. International trade - 19. Business management literature - 20. Trade marks and trade names. Information given can include the service, producer, host, type, time span, sources of information, updates, coverage, search options, conditions of access, costs, alternative delivery methods, and comment, but many entries have much less information. 'Further reading', p.314. Index, p.330-336. *Class No:* 334.7(003.4)

Bibliographies

[1948]
BAKEWELL, K.G.B. **Business information and the public library.** Aldershot, Hants, Gower Publishing Company Ltd., 1987. viii,309p. illus. £22.50. ISBN: 0566035375.

Part 1: Business information (the nature of business information, how to meet user's needs, methods of presentation); part 2: The public library's role (organization and promotion of business information services in public libraries); part 3: Some major sources (directory). There follows a section of 60 bibliographical references (p.137-265), abstracting and indexing services first and then subject arrangement, A-Z, with many cross-references. Index (p.273-309) is arranged A-Z under subject and cited persons relating to the main text (parts 1 & 2) and bibliographical references are under author, indicated by 'b'.
Class No: 334.7(01)

[1949]
BALL, S. **The Directory of international sources of business information.** 2nd ed. London, Pitman, 1991. 864p. £125. ISBN: 0273032844.

First published 1989.

Arranged in 3 main sections: country data sources; industry data sources; online data bases; preceded by an introduction and a section on European business information

....(contd.)

brokers and Euro-Info centres. The section on country data sources covers 32 countries, mostly European, arranged A-Z, with each entry including stock exchange members, chambers of commerce, embassies, major government offices devoted to commerce, and sources of statistics. The industry data sources section is arranged in 11 broad industrial groups, listing major international associations dealing with each group, directories, market research services, and journals. 4 appendices (1. Publishers of market research reports - 2. Data base hosts and producers - 3. Data base country coverage - 4. International telephone codes, etc.). 'The descriptions are well-written and provide sufficient information for users to make basic evaluative decisions' (*Choice*, v.27(2), October 1989, p.278) of the 1st ed. *Class No:* 334.7(01)

[1950]

Business index. Menlo Park, CA., Information Access Corporation, Sept. 1980-. Monthly. $1860pa. ($3500 on CD-ROM). ISSN: 02733684.

Indexes, cover-to-cover, the contents of over 325 business periodical titles, in addition to the *Wall street journal*, *Barron's National business and financial weekly*, and the financial section of *The New York times*, plus selected articles containing business information from over 1100 general and legal periodical and business books and reports from the Library of Congress MARC database. End of film has abstracts from *Management contents* database. Computer output microfilm. Available online (DIALOG, BRS, Mead Data Centre). *Class No:* 334.7(01)

[1951]

Business information alert. January 1989-. v.1,no.1-. Chicago, Ill. Alert Publications Inc., 1989- 10pa. $115pa. ISSN: 10420746.

Designed to keep libraries and related information professionals informed of new literature and information services in the field of business. Newsletter format. In 4 sections: Lead article - New publications (descriptive and critical book reviews, which take up about half the issue) - Database news - FYI section (brief descriptions of other news and resources 'for your information'). *Class No:* 334.7(01)

[1952]

OWEN, T. Mind your own local business: where to find and how to use local economic and business information. 2nd ed. Newbury, Berks, Eurofi, 1988. xiii,450p. charts. £37.50. ISBN: 0907304435.

First published 1986.

8 chapters: 1. The tools for the job (sources of information and document supply - 2. Getting to know your area (regional and local statistics) - 3. Who are the local businesses? (information on individual enterprises) - 4. Who is going to buy? (marketing and product information sources) - 5. Answering the impossible questions (online information services) - 6. Who will back it? (guide to sources of finance) - 7. Dealing with the EEC (sources of information on the EEC) - 8. Is it clean? (contract compliance and ethical investment). There follows a complete guide to all the information sources discussed. Subject index, p.421-450. Comprehensive and readable. *Class No:* 334.7(01)

[1953]

RYANS, C.C. International business reference sources: developing a corporate library. Lexington, Mass., Lexington Books, 1983. xvii,195p. ISBN: 0669066125.

'Presents a representative list of the more essential sources of information useful to companies involved in doing business overseas' (*Introduction*). 4 chapters: 1. Government publications - 2. Subscriptions and continuations (journals, annuals, loose-leaf services) - 3. International business data sources (directories, almanacs, handbooks) - 4. International business books (marketing, finance, economics). All arranged A-Z by title. Data includes publication date or starting date and frequency, price, publisher's name & address, and brief description. Appendix: Additional names and addresses of organizations where country and product data may be obtained (subdivided by type of organization). Index, p.185-195. *Class No:* 334.7(01)

Handbooks & Manuals

[1954]

Secretarial administration. Birds, J., *and others, eds.* Bristol, Jordans, 1993. 1800p.(looseleaf). £95. Updating releases are published twice a year (*c*.£45 each). ISBN: 0853080747.

An authority on company procedure. For company secretaries on company law and procedure. 10 chapters, each subdivided: 1.The position of secretary - 2. Constitution and organisation of a limited company - 3. Procedures - 4. Officers of a company - 5. Company meetings - 6. Public companies and investment regulation - 7. Insolvency - 8. Employment law - 9. Corporate insurance - 10. EEC. 5 appendices. Index. *Class No:* 334.7(035)

Dictionaries

[1955]

PASS, C., *and others*. Collins dictionary of business. London, Collins, 1991. [5],656p. illus. £16.95. ISBN: 0004343743.

For students taking a business-studies course at school or in further education, or as a professional seeking further qualifications. *Class No:* 334.7(038)

Laws

[1956]

MARSH, S.B. *and* BAILEY, J.B. Terminology of business and company law. London, Kogan Page, in association with the Chartered Institute of Management Accountants, 1987. [3], 119p. £8.95. (*Kogan Page professional paperback*.) ISBN: 1850914133.

Aimed at students of business law and company law. Definitions vary in length from 1 line to 12 lines. Some common abbreviations included. *Class No:* 334.7(038)(094.1)

Polyglot

[1957]

APPLEBY, B.L., *comp*. Elsevier's dictionary of commercial terms and phrases in five languages: English, German, Spanish, French and Swedish. Amsterdam, Elsevier Science Publishers, 1984. [4],1083p. Dfl.515; £154.65; $271. ISBN: 0444422706.

....*(contd.)*

An 'attempt to bring together in one volume terms and expressions from the multitude of different fields, accounting, banking, computing, economics, etc., which are intimately involved with the world of modern business (*Preface*). 10,163 terms are included, the basic table being English, followed by translations in the other four languages. Indexes in all five languages refer to the numbered English entries in the basic listing. *Class No:* 334.7(038)=00

[1958]

Harrap's five-language business dictionary. Angerer, M., *and others*. London, Harrap, 1991. 448p. ISBN: 0245603476.

Arranged in one A-Z sequence, the dictionary has 20,000 key business words from English, French, German, Italian and Spanish. *Class No:* 334.7(038)=00

[1959]

Law and commercial dictionary in five languages: definitions of the legal and commercial terms and phrases of American, English and civil law jurisdictions. English, German, Spanish, French & Italian. Epstein, R., *ed*. St. Paul, MN, West Publishing Company, München, Beck, 1985. 2v. (xvi,885p.; xvi;899p.).

One volume has a pronunciation guide followed by the dictionary, A-J; the other continues the dictionary, K-Z and includes a list of legal abbreviations. Entries are for the English terms and phrases, with definitions, with the German, Spanish, French and Italian equivalents listed below. Includes terms related to systems in the other four countries. '... most unusual, but most practical ...' (*International journal of legal information*, v.15(5 & 6), p.77). *Class No:* 334.7(038)=00

[1960]

A Multilingual commercial dictionary. London, Pan Books, 1978. 636p.

Lists some 300 words and phrases in common use in 6 languages (English/American - German - Spanish - French - Italian - Portuguese). Arranged in one A-Z sequence, each term followed by equivalents in the other 5 languages. *Class No:* 334.7(038)=00

[1961]

Six language business dictionary. British Chamber of Commerce. Cambridge, Colt Books Ltd., with the Association of British Chambers of Commerce, 1978 (reprinted 1991). 637p. £25. ISBN: 0905899032.

First published by Pan Books in 1978 as *Multilingual commercial dictionary*.

English, French, German, Italian, Portuguese and Spanish terms in one A-Z listing, each term folowed by its equivalents in the five other languages. *Class No:* 334.7(038)=00

English

[1962]

A Concise dictionary of business. Market House Books, *comp*. Oxford, Oxford University Press, 1990. 504p. £17.50. ISBN: 0192852310.

Over 4000 entries covering all the traditional areas of business, as well as the new terminology that has grown up around the globalization of stock, commodity, and financial markets. *Class No:* 334.7(038)=20

[1963]

Harrap's dictionary of business and finance. London, Harrap Ltd., 1988. [5],369p. £8.95 ISBN: 024554660x, .

'... concentrates on words and phrases in everyday business usage, and endeavours to make clear not only their meaning, but also, where appropriate, the way in which they are used'. (*Preface*). *Class No:* 334.7(038)=20

[1964]

STEER, M. Dictionary of business studies. 2nd ed. London, Pitman Publsihing, 1989. xvii, 286p. £5.95. ISBN: 0273030779.

First published 1985.

Intended for students but useful to the general reader. Aims to provide a comprehensive reference companion for students of business studies at intermediate and advanced levels. Clear, detailed explanations. Extensive cross-references. *Class No:* 334.7(038)=20

French

[1965]

COLLIN, P.H., *and others*. **Dictionary of business, English/French, French/English.** Teddington, Surrey, P. Collin, 1990. [ix],351+335+[19]p.

About 3500 main entries in each half ('Mail': 1 column). 'Supplement' (19p): La France. les régions ... United Kingdom - Weights and measures - Numbers - Business letters - Curriculum vitae. Examples and quotations showing usage. *Class No:* 334.7(038)=40

[1966]

LAURENDEAU-COLLIN, F., *and others, eds*. **Harrap's business French-English dictionary:** dictionnaire Anglais-Français. 3rd rev ed. London & Paris, Harrap, 1991. xvi,604p. £19.95. ISBN: 0245542531.

Aims to provide a basic translating tool for everyday business language. Emphasis is on providing practical examples to show terms and phrases used in context. Gives only the strictly commercial meanings of the words. Also includes some useful supplementary material concerning international organizations, international currencies, typical American business expressions, comparisons between English and French balance sheets. *Class No:* 334.7(038)=40

Arabic

[1967]

SABA & CO. The English-Arabic dictionary of professional business terms. London, Middle East Economic Digest (MEED), 1987. [3],210p. ISBN: 0946510334.

Includes *c*.11,000 terms, phrases, names of major organizations, government bodies, and formal titles of qualifications and positions A-Z in English, followed by the Arabic equivalents. '... should be considered a supplement to a standard English-Arabic dictionary ... structured for maximum convenience ...' (*Introduction*). *Class No:* 334.7(038)=927

Japanese

[1968]

MITSUBISHI CORPORATION, *comp*. **Japanese business language:** an essential dictionary. London, K.P.I. Ltd., 1987 (Distributed by Routledge & Kegan Paul). xiii,221p. £9.95. ISBN: 0710301995.

Analyses over 500 key words and phrases that are essential for doing or understanding business in Japan. Clarifies many points of verbal and social misunderstanding, and provides insights into differences in Japanese and Western business practices. *Class No:* 334.7(038)=956

[1969]

Tatemae and honne: distinguishing between good form and real intention in Japanese business culture. Mitsubishi Corporation. New York, Free Press, 1988. 182p. $19.95. ISBN: 0029215919.

A revision of *Japanese business glossary*(1983), which was based on the 'Business glossary' column in the *Tokyo newsletter*.

A glossary of *c.*500 words and idiomatic phrases used in the Japanese company world, which could be misunderstood or misinterpreted by non-Japanese. Includes a 'simplified pronunciation guide'. Cross-references. Index of English words with Japanese equivalents and page numbers. *Class No:* 334.7(038)=956

Reports Literature

Bibliographies

[1970]

Index to business reports. Hunter, N.R., *comp*. Harrogate, North Yorks., Quarry Press (previously Headland Press), 1978-. 2 pa. £16.95 pa. $32.95 pa. ISSN: 02660180.

Indexes reports in a wide range of newspapers and journals. About 400 reports indexed in each issue and each January-June issue is superseded by the following January-December issue. Arrangement is by subject term, A-Z, followed by the journal abbreviation, day, month, year, and page number of the issue. *Class No:* 334.7(047)(01)

Yearbooks & Directories

[1971]

Political risk yearbook. Coplin, W.D. *and* O'Leary, M.K., *eds*. Syracuse, NY, Political Risk Services, 1992 (distributed outside US by Bowker-Saur). 7v. £750. ISBN: 1852711949.

A country-by-country analysis of risk instability, turmoil, economic and trade restrictions, all based on standardized data. Also data on heads of government, government officials, legislature, elections, economy, trade and social indicators, etc. For each country there are 18-month and 5-yearly forecasts of changes of regime, turmoil, and risks to international business with supporting data of all kinds. The 7v are arranged by continents, then A-Z by country. Each entry is of standard length and amount of data. '... a magnificent example of value-added in information analysis making it a quite invaluable reference item.'(*Reference reviews*, v.6(5), 1992, review 321, p.11). *Class No:* 334.7(058)

Quotations

[1972]

A **Dictionary of business quotations.** James, S. *and* Parker, R., *comps*. London, Routledge; New York, Simon & Schuster, 1990. vii,172p. £17.99; $40. ISBN: 0415020301, UK; 0132101548, US.

Over 2500 quotations from across the globe, for browsing and reference. Arranged by 215 topics, A-Z (Accounts ... Workers). Includes 'see-also' references under topic headings. Very wide coverage. Index of authors and sources. Index of keywords. *Class No:* 334.7(082.2)

[1973]

HAY, P. **Harrap's book of business anecdotes.** London, Harrap; New York, Facts on File, 1988. viii,296p. $22.95. ISBN: 0045847436, UK; 0816015228, US.

The title of the US edition is *The Book of business anecdotes*.

Anecdotes are arranged in 12 subject groups, all subdivided (1. About money - 2. Banks and bankers ... 11. Business and the Muses - 12. Rewards). Extensive bibliography, p.279-290. Index, p.291-296. *Class No:* 334.7(082.2)

[1974]

MANSER, M., *comp*. **Chambers book of business quotations.** London, Chambers, 1987. 220p. 20 illus. £12.95. ISBN: 0550204881.

'Sayings from the famous, unknown and unacknowledged'. *c.2000* quotations on business and related subjects, arranged under 900 topics in 9 main sections. Illus. are line-drawings. Index. *Class No:* 334.7(082.2)

Tables & Data Books

[1975]

Key note guides: official business statistics. 1st ed. Hampton, Middx., Key Note Publications Ltd., 1988. iii,125p. tables. ISBN: 1850566046.

10 chapters, most having key data available, key sources, contacts, the sources, the statistics (1. An overview - 2. Product and market statistics - 3. Industry statistics - 4. Import and export statistics - 5. Economic and financial statistics - 6. Labour market statistics - 7. Socio-economic statistics - 8. The reliability of official statistics - 9. Government contact points - 10. Trade association statistics). Appendices (Selective bibliography - Business monitors: the complete list - HMSO information and services). *Class No:* 334.7(083)

Biographies

[1976]

International businessmen's who's who. Kay, E., *ed*. 3rd ed. Cambridge, International Biographical Centre, 1986. [6],383p. £75. ISBN: 0900332387.

First published 1967. 1st & 2nd eds. published by Burke's Peerage Ltd.

Gives biographical data (business activities and appointments held, past positions, recreational and community activities) on *c.*3000 business executives in some 60 of the world's largest countries. About 10-30 lines each, longer entries than in previous editions. By no means definitive; slanted towards Britain, North America, Europe, Japan, Australia and New Zealand. *Class No:* 334.7(092)

Great Britain

[1977]

BIENKOWSKI, M., *and others*. **Government support for British business.** 5th ed. Glasgow, Centre for the Study of Public Policy, University of Strathclyde, 1986. xiv,719p. £25.00. ISBN: 0907243223.

Aim is to provide up-to-date information about the financial aids and other government support available to business in the United Kingdom. Part 1 has summary descriptions by objective (employment and training; general investment/development; advisory/consultancy services; research and development; export services; tourism, recreation, miscellaneous). Pt.2 has detailed descriptions. List of Government departments. Other awarding bodies. United Kingdom assisted areas. Index, p.709-719.

Class No: 334.7(410)

[1978]

GREAT BRITAIN. Department of Trade and Industry. **DTI QA register: the United Kingdom register of quality assessed companies.** London, HMSO, [1993]. 3v.(2494p.). tables. £145 (incl. supplements for the year). ISBN: 0115153179.

Compendium of lists of manufacturers world wide whose quality management systems, and sometimes their products, have been assessed by a number of UK independent third party assessment bodies and significant purchasers. V.1. lists products; V.2 - 3 list companies, A-Z. *Class No:* 334.7(410)

[1979]

HARRISON, A., *ed*. **New sources of grants and aid for businessmen in the UK:** a practical guide to the financial support and advisory services available to UK companies from central government, local authorities and regional agencies. London, Weka Publishing, 1987. loose-leaf unpaged. maps, forms. £68. ISBN: 185303004x.

In 10 parts: 1. Guide to the reader - 2. Current information - 3. Capital investment - 4. Research and technology - 5. Marketing and business advisory services - 6. Employment - 7. Exporting - 8. Energy - 9. Local schemes - 10. Other schemes. General index and contents list to each part. Kept up-to-date by supplements.

Class No: 334.7(410)

Databases

[1980]

BATER, P. *and* PARKINSON, H., *eds*. **Business and company databases, 1988.** 1st ed. London, Aslib, 1988. [6],86p. £18. ISBN: 0851422314.

Selective list of some of the best known databases available in the UK. International coverage. A-Z listing by name of database, with information on content, updating, producer, hosts, cost, user aids, and further information. Database, subject and host indexes.

Class No: 334.7(410)(003.4)

Reports Literature

[1981]

GREAT BRITAIN. Department of Trade and Industry. **Companies in 1992-93;** report for the year ended 31 March 1993. London, HMSO, 1993. [4],62p. tables. £14.50. ISBN: 0115153403.

First published 1890- as *Companies: general annual report* of the Board of Trade. Annual.

....(contd.)

Information on the administration of the Companies Act, plus statistics on registration of companies during the previous 10 years, by classes and amount of nominal capital. *Class No:* 334.7(410)(047)

Periodicals

[1982]

London gazette. London, HMSO., 1665-. 4 per week, excluding supplements annd indexes. £365pa., excluding supplements. ISSN: 03743721.

Apart from State intelligence and public notices, contains official notices relating to companies, bankruptcies, partnerships, dissolutions. Supplements are normally concerned with naval, military and civil awards (*e.g.* lists of New Year's honours, of Queen's Birthday honours, of Premium Bond winners). *Class No:* 334.7(410)(051)

Yearbooks & Directories

[1983]

Key British enterprises, 1993: Britain's top 50,000 companies. London, Dun & Bradstreet, 1993. Annual. 6v.

V.1, 2 & 3 have alphabetical listing of companies actively trading, with address, telephone/telex/fax numbers, named managing director and senior executives, line of business, sales turnover, export markets, capitalisation/ownership, number of employees, etc. V.4 has industrial and geographical cross-references; v.5 has trade names, export markets, director's names; and v.6 has business rankings. Updates are issued twice a year. *Class No:* 334.7(410)(058)

[1984]

TUDOR, J. **Macmillan directory of UK business information sources.** 3rd ed. London, Macmillan Publishers, 1992. xi,435p. £35. ISBN: 0333572718.

First published 1987.

A compendium of sources and resources: How to use this book; Finding business information; Directory of business information sources and centres; Foreign trade organizations of the UK (A-Z.); British trade press and their editorial offices (subject arrangement); Alphabetical index to NACE classification (SIC codes) and organization sources (both of these serve as indexes); and main directory, arranged by subject (SIC), subdivided by UK and European sources and information centres, with names, addresses, telephone numbers, contacts, and brief indication of activities in some entries. A-Z index to information centres. Classified list of NACE categories. *Class No:* 334.7(410)(058)

Histories

[1985]

ORBELL, J. **A Guide to tracing the history of a business.** Aldershot, Hants., Gower Publishing Co. Ltd., for the Business Archives Council, 1987. x,116p. £15. ISBN: 0566055910.

Arranged in 3 parts: 1. Locating the business and research strategy (Sources for locating the business - Research strategy - Approaching the business); 2. Locating records of the business (Records deposited in record offices - Registers of business records - Published guides to business records); 3. Information sources outside the records of the business (records of suppliers of goods and services, records of government departments, records of associations, printed

....(contd.)

sources, personal records, visual sources. Bibliography, p.90-100, is A-Z by author. Addresses of record offices, museums, libraries, societies, etc., quoted in the text, p.101-110. Double-column index, p.111-116.
Class No: 334.7(410)(091)

Biographies

[1986]

JEREMY, D.J., *ed.* **Dictionary of business biography:** a biographical dictionary of business leaders active in Britain in the period 1860-1980. London, Butterworth, 1984-86. 5v. and Supplement. £150 each vol. ISBN: 0406273413, v.1; 0406273421, v.2; 040627343x, v.3; 0406273448, v.4; 0406273456, v.5; 0406273405, set.

Based on the work of the Business History Unit at London School of Economics, funded by the Economic and Social Research Council.

Aimed to cover the whole spectrum of business (mining, manufacturing, public utilities, construction, services, distribution) excluding academics, civil servants, trade unionists, etc. if involvement in the business world was incidental. Includes those who had a good impact for good or bad, from larger or small businesses (*e.g.* Thomas Beecham, Horatio Bottomley, Billy Butlin). Arranged A-Z by biographee: V.1: A-C; v.2: D-G; v.3: H-L; v.4: M-R; v.5: S-Z, and indexes, list of contributors, errata. A supplement to v.1-5 was published in 1986 (120p. ISBN 0406273405). *Class No:* 334.7(410)(092)

Scotland

Bibliographies

[1987]

REID, C.D. 'Business information needs in Scotland'. In *Aslib proceedings,* v.38(2), February 1986, p.51-64.

Paper presented to joint conference organized by the Library Association, R.S. & I. Section (Scottish Group) and Aslib (Scottish Branch) on *Business information problems and prospects, 1985,* which includes a checklist of sources of business information (p.61-64). *Class No:* 334.7(411)(01)

Italy

Bibliographies

[1988]

CUCCHI, L. 'How to find Italian business information'. In *Business information review,* v.4(2), April 1988, p.16-27.

Evaluates the major sources, including directories, statistics, market research organizations, and online databases. *Class No:* 334.7(450)(01)

USSR

Bibliographies

[1989]

KONN, T. 'The Soviet Union': commercial and technical information sources. In *Business information review,* v.4(3), January 1988, p.1526.

Outlines the changes in the foreign trade structure, followed by an introduction to the main Russian and English

....(contd.)

language sources of commercial and technical information relating to the Soviet Union. Includes guides, national economic plans, newspapers, journals, updating services, trade statistics, reports, online databases and organizations. *Class No:* 334.7(47)(01)

Asia

Periodicals & Progress Reports

[1990]

JUNGE, A.R. 'Business information sources in Asia'. In *Special libraries,* v.70(2), December 1979, p.82-90.

A review article on periodicals published by banks, trade organizations, companies, etc., which supplement the standard business information sources.
Class No: 334.7(5)(05)

Japan

Bibliographies

[1991]

EDWARDS, S. *and* **THOMPSON, K. Japanese business publications in English, 1987:** a select annotated list of recent publications held by the British Library. 2nd ed. London, British Library, 1987. [2],i,55p. £10. ISBN: 0712307435.

First published 1986.

232 entries arranged by form (Directories - Statistics, market information and industry surveys - Trade and business journals - Bibliographies and abstracting journals - Company reports), the first three sections subdivided by subject. These are followed by lists of suppliers of literature published in Japan, and alternative sources of information. Index of titles and organizations. *Class No:* 334.7(52)(01)

Africa

Bibliographies

[1992]

African trade: a bibliography of information sources. 1st ed. Berkhamstead, Trade Research Publications, for The Association of African Trade Promotion Organisations, 1988. 219p. £35; $75. ISBN: 0904783251.

Aims to be a guide to reference books of use to the business community. More than 600 references arranged in 4 sections: A. AATPO publications - B. International publications - C. Publications relating to Africa as a whole and regions of Africa - D. Publications by country. Entries have full bibliographical description; description of publication; language; price; brief note of publication; last date published, frequency; SITC number. 15-page subject index. *Class No:* 334.7(6)(01)

America — North

[1993]

Standard and Poor's register of corporations, directors and executives, 1994. 67th ed. New York, Standard and Poor, 1993. 3v. plus cumulative supplements and user's companion. ISSN: 03613623.

First published in 1928.

.... *(contd.)*

Lists *c.*55,000 corporations and 500,000 officers, directors, etc. Contents: V.1: Corporations; v.2: Key to abbreviations. Register of directors and executives; v.3: Executives. Also includes Standard and Poor's 500; US and Canadian securities exchanges and administration; Standard industrial classification index and codes; Geographic index; Corporate family indexes (cross-reference index; ultimate parent index); Obituary section; New individuals in this edition; New companies in this edition.
Class No: 334.7(71+73)

USA

Bibliographies

[1994]

SMITH, G. 'How to find US business information'. In *Business information review,* v.4(1), July 1987, p.3-11.

Reviews major sources - directories, company information, statistics, market research sources, magazines and newspapers, indexes and abstracts, databases, online vendors, libraries and information services, and research guides. *Class No:* 334.7(73)(01)

Periodicals & Progress Reports

[1995]

GEAHIGAN, P.C. *and* ROSE, R.F. Business serials of the US government. 2nd ed. Chicago, Ill., American Library Association, 1988 (Distributed by Eurospan. 86p. $11.95; £8.50. ISBN: 0838933491.

First published 1979.

183 business serial publications of the US government are listed, with descriptive and evaluative annotations. Arrangement is in 14 broad subject categories, and information includes Superintendent of Documents class number, title changes, issuing authority, frequency, supplements (if any), but not prices. Detailed subject and title index includes alternative and previous titles.
Class No: 334.7(73)(05)

Histories

[1996]

LARSON, H.M. Guide to business history: materials for the study of American business history and suggestions for their use. Cambridge, Mass., Harvard University Press, 1948 (Reprinted Boston, Mass., Canner, 1964). xxvi,1181p. $22.50. ISBN: 0910324042.

4904 numbered and annotated terms in 7 parts (87 sections): 1. General introduction - 2. Historical background and setting of American business - 3. Business administrators, biographical and autobiographical books, pamphlets and articles - 4. The history of individual business units - 5. History of industries - 6. General topics in business history - 7. Research and reference materials. Detailed, analytical index, p.1057-1181. An excellent compilation, with introductory notes in each section.
Class No: 334.7(73)(091)

[1997]

—LOVETT, R.W., *ed.* American economic and business history information sources ... Detroit, Gale Research Co., 1971. 323p. $68. ISBN: 0810308231.

6 sections: economic, business, agricultural and labour history, history of science and technology, and general reference works. *Class No:* 334.7(73)(091)

[1998]

PUSATERI, C.J. A History of American business. 2nd ed. Arlington Heights, Ill., Harlan Davidson Inc.; London, Eurospan, 1988. xiii,444p. 14 illus. ISBN: 0882958445.

First published 1984.

14 chapters arranged in 4 sections: I. Panorama - II. The age of the merchant - III. The age of transition - IV. The age of managerial capitalism. 'Some suggestions for further reading' (p.371-374) are followed by 3 appendices (A. A chronology of American business; B. The 25 largest industrial corporations; C. Roster of 50 major business leaders), notes, a glossary of American business terms (p.417-424), and an index (p.425-444).
Class No: 334.7(73)(091)

Libraries

[1999]

HYDE, M. Library and information services to business and industry: study on levels of service, related costs and charging systems. London, British Library Research & Development Department, 1988. viii, 103p. £5. (*British Library research paper, 48.*) ISBN: 0712331743.

In 3 parts: 1. Background: aims and objectives of the project; the 'levels of service' approach; user response to 'levels of service', costs and charging; 2. Guidlines to 'levels of service'; 3. Financial management, conclusions and recommendations. *Class No:* 334.7:061:026/027

[2000]

LIBRARY ASSOCIATION. Industrial Group. Industrial and commercial libraries: an introductory guide. the Group, 1986. viii,44p. £10. (*Library Association pamphlet 39.*) ISBN: 0853655774.

8 sections: The library in the industrial and commercial environment - Relationship with the parent organization - Staff - User education - Resources and services - Funding - Equipment and furniture - Accommodation and space requirements. 2 appendices: 1. Points of contact; 2. Further reading. Index. *Class No:* 334.7:061:026/027

Private Firms

Great Britain

[2001]

Macmillan's unquoted companies, 1994. ICC Business Publications Ltd., *comp.* London, Macmillan Press, 1994. Annual. 2v. (1800p.). £199 the set. ISBN: 0333599071. ISSN: 02674378.

V.1: A-J; v.2: K-Z. Alphabetical listing of the top 20,000 companies. Include only companies with individual turnovers in excess of £3m. pa., and data reflects a 3-year trading period with individual sector performance tables to enable comparisons between companies. Geographical and SIC index. *Class No:* 334.722(410)

USA

[2002]
Macmillan directory of leading private companies. 4th ed. Wilmette, Ill., National Register Publishing Co., 1989. 679p. $427. ISBN: 0872170705.

Over 9500 US companies, with nearly 4200 subsidiaries, with sales of $10 million or more. Detailed information given for parent companies is address, telephone/fax, type of business, major officers, principal owners, assets, liabilities, net worth, sales, date of fiscal year end, number of employees, state of incorporation, number of US and foreign offices or manufacturing facilities, computer system hardware, wholly-owned subsidiaries, and names of outside services used. Main directory is arranged A-Z by name of parent company. A-Z cross-referencing index; geographic and SIC indexes. *Class No: 334.722(73)*

Multinationals

Bibliographies

[2003]
UNITED NATIONS. Centre for Transnational Corporations. **UNCTC bibliography, 1974-1987.** New York, United Nations, 1988. v,83p. illus. $12; £8. *(CT/CTC/88.)* ISBN: 9211042186.

Arranged by subject in 18 main sections (I. Trends in the activities of transnational corporations ... VII. Manufacturing and extractive sectors - VIII. Service sector and transborder data flows ... XV. Data and information systems and sources ... XVIII. The *CTC reporter* and other journals. *Class No: 334.726(01)*

Dictionaries

[2004]
HOOGVELT, A. *and* PUXTY, A. **Multinational enterprise:** an encyclopedic dictionary of concepts and terms. Consultant editor: John Stopford. London, Macmillan, 1987. 261p. £29.95; $52.50. *(Macmillan reference library.)* ISBN: 033373603x, UK; 0893972495, USA.

Attempts to provide definitions for the specialized and multidisciplinary vocabulary used in the world of international business and multinational enterprises. Brings together relevant concepts and terms from economics, international law, management theory, sociology, and politics. Also included are entries for international organizations, regulations, codes and treaties and major national legislation. Includes a full bibliography, index and resource file of libraries, databases and research organizations. 'The definitions are often gems of concise insight ... '(*Choice*, June 1987, p. 1538). *Class No: 334.726(038)*

Yearbooks & Directories

[2005]
Directory of multinationals. Stopford, J., *ed.* 4th ed. London, Macmillan, 1992. 2v.(1600p). £295. ISBN: 0333577566.

First published 1980.

Information on 428 industrial enterprises with global turnover in excess of £1 billion. Company profiles include

....(contd.)
name, address, directors, structure, products, background and current situation, 5-year financial data. *Class No: 334.726(058)*

Small Businesses

[2006]
The 1990 guide to government grants for business. Swindon, Wilts., Associated Management Services, 1989. 91p.

Purpose is to give a clear picture of what is obtainable, the objectives and benefits of each scheme, how much is available, etc. In 7 sections: The Enterprise Initiatives - Business Growth Training - British Overseas Trade Board - Job Centres; Disablement Advisory Service - Energy Efficiency Office - Regional grants - Loan Guarantee Scheme. *Class No: 334.746.4*

[2007]
MANCUSO, J. **Mancuso's small business resource guide.** New York, Prentice-Hall, 1988. 557p. $39.95. ISBN: 0138130809.

An updated and expanded version of Mancuso's *Small business survival guide* (1981).

Arranged A-Z by topical chapters (*e.g.* Advertising ... Venture capital) the guide describes associations, books, journals, government agencies and private sources which will assist those running small businesses. 'An excellent source ... (*Choice*) v.26(5), January 1989, p.785). *Class No: 334.746.4*

Bibliographies

[2008]
KRYSZAK, W.D. **The Small business index.** Metuchen, N.J., Scarecrow Press, 1978-85. 2v. (228p.;320p.). ISBN: 0810811502; 0810818175.

Indexes American and Canadian books, pamphlets and periodicals which contain information on starting a small business. Subject index includes more than 250 kinds of business. *Class No: 334.746.4(01)*

[2009]
The London Business School small business bibliography. Edwards, H. *and* Hughes, D., eds. 1989 ed. London, London Business School Library, 1990. xii,153p. £25. ISBN: 0902583204.

First published 1980.

A listing of *c.*1500 items, adding to the 12,000 collected in the five previous volumes. Arranged in 3 main parts: Part 1. Literature review on employment and unemployment relations in the small enterprise. Part 2. Subject bibliography in 15 sections, mostly subdivided (1. Entrepreneurship - 2. Starting new businesses - 3. Managing the on-going small business - 4. Business policy and organizational development - 5. Education, training, information, advice and consultancy. 6. Financing the small business ... 11. Particular types of small business - 12. Employment and small business ... 14. The small firm and its environment in the UK - 15. The small firm and its environment in other countries). Part 3. Author bibliography. Appendices: List of journals from which articles have been included; List of institutions. *Class No: 334.746.4(01)*

[2010]

MIESENBOCK, K.J. 'Small businesses and exporting: a literature review'. In *International small business journal*, v.6(2), January-March 1988, p.42-61.

Includes 140 references, A-Z, mainly to journal articles, but some books. *Class No:* 334.746.4(01)

[2011]

RYAN, C.C. Small business: an information sourcebook. Phoenix, Arix., Oryz, 1987. 286p. $37. ISBN: 0897742729.

Lists more than 1500 sources in 38 subject categories, relating to starting and operating a small business. Mainly current books and US government publications, with some pamphlets and journal articles. US bias.

Class No: 334.746.4(01)

[2012]

Small business sourcebook. Dorgan, C.A., *ed.* 3rd ed. Detroit, Mich., Gale Research Co., 1988. 2v. (1913p.). $180. ISBN: 0810326485.

First published 1983.

Covers 163 specific small businesses. Information sources: general; counselling; financial. Specific businesses (Accounting ... Word processing). Organizations (government; state; trade and professional organizations; educational institutions; etc.). Comprehensive index.

A 6th ed. by C.A.Schwarz was published in 1992 ($220. ISBN 0810380765). *Class No:* 334.746.4(01)

[2013]

—The Small business guide: sources of information for new and small businesses. Rev. ed. London, Oryx Press, 1984. 399p. ISBN: 0563211105.

First published 1982.

12 sections (*e.g.* 2. Sources of direct help and advice - 3. Business opportunities ... 6. Raising the money - 7. Business and the law - 8. Training for business ... 10. Starting up overseas - 11. Glossary of key business terms (p.347-52). Index of enterprise agency sponsors. General index.

Class No: 334.746.4(01)

Handbooks & Manuals

[2014]

How to set up & run your own business. 2nd ed. London, Telegraph Publications, 1986. [xii],227p. facsims., diagrs., forms, tables. (*'The Daily telegraph' business enterprise book*.) ISBN: 086367030x.

First published 1983.

18 contributors. 10 sections 1. What types of capital are there? - 2. Presenting your case - 3. Finding the right premises - 4. Marketing and sales - 5. Control and finance management - 6. Bookkeeping and administration systems - 7. NIS, corporation tax and VAT - 8. Planning the tax and using the incentives? - 9. Recruitment and employment law - 10. Starting off in export. 4 appendices (1. The costs of different methods of raising finance ... 3. Select bibliography (p.208, 210-1) - 4. Useful addresses). Index. Index of advertisers. *Class No:* 334.746.4(035)

[2015]

MORGANO, M. How to start and run your own business. 7th ed. London, Graham & Trotman, 1989. vii,158p. £8.75 (*Better business series*.) ISBN: 1853332887.

A practical handbook of essential advice and information. 11 chapters: 1. Making a start - 2. Investigating the market - 3. Finding start-up money and using it effectively - 4.

.... *(contd.)*

Getting the business going - 5. Taking professional advice - 6. Sales and marketing - 7. Exporting - 8. Planning and financial control - 9. Obtaining further finance - 10. The importance of people - 11. Growing larger. Useful addresses. Appendix: Budget update. Index, p.155-158.

Class No: 334.746.4(035)

Europe—Western

[2016]

HASKINS, G., *and others*. A Guide to small firms assistance in Europe. Aldershot, Hants., Gower, 1986. vii,363p. £35. ISBN: 056605082x.

Edited and co-ordinated for the European Foundation for Management Development and the European Association for National Productivity Centres.

In 3 parts: I. Reviewing the services: comparative analysis and the scope for transfer of ideas - II. Country overviews - III. Assistance in key areas. Includes a directory of all major national and regional organizations providing small firm services in 17 European countries; special tables showing the support provided for exports, start-ups, technological innovation, and research and development, etc.

Class No: 334.746.4(400)

USA

[2017]

Directory of federal and state business assistance: a guide for new and growing companies. National Technical Information Services, *ed.* National Technical Information Service (NTIS), 1986. xii,159p. $19. ISBN: 0934213038.

First published in 1984 as *Guide to innovative resources and planning for small business*.

2 main sections: Federal assistance section - State assistance section. The Federal assistance section has 182 entries from 47 federal departments, arranged A-Z by department, and entries include a one-sentence description of services offered to business, together with name and address, telephone number, sometimes a contact name, and 6 possible terms to designate type of assistance. The State assistance section has 406 entries and is similarly organized. 7 appendices list federal offices, etc. Subject index.

Class No: 334.746.4(73)

Monopolies

Dictionaries

[2018]

ORGANISATION FOR ECONOMIC CO-OPERATION AND DEVELOPMENT. Glossaire de termes relatifs aux pratiques communicales restrictives/Glossary of terms relating to restrictive business practices. Paris, OECD, 1965. 100p. £2.20; $5.

60 terms are defined, with commentary (*e.g.* 'Unfair competition': 25-word definition plus 1½p. of commentary including quotation from a Convention of 1883). Four chapters. A. Terms relating to economic concentration - B. Terms relating to arrangements between enterprises - C. Actions by enterprises - D. Other terms. Index.

Class No: 334.75(038)

Mergers

[2019]
COOKE, T.E. **International mergers and acquisitions.** London, Blackwell, in association with Arthur Young International, 1988. [5],516p. tables. £70. ISBN: 0631147489.

Provides detailed information on mergers and acquisitions in 12 key geographical areas, including UK, USA, Europe and Japan. Details forms of business organizations, merger registrations and controls, taxation and accounting implications, foreign investment and exchange controls, etc. *Class No:* 334.751

[2020]
EATON, J. **Source guide to mergers and acquisitions information.** London, London Business School Information Service, 1991. 764p. £20. ISBN: 0951440144.

Details of 91 publications arranged by type (*e.g.* databases (online - CD-ROM - diskette), annual directories, official publications, and online hosts. Followed by a miscellaneous section and sections on books, reports and surveys, periodicals and reference works. Does not claim to be comprehensive. *Class No:* 334.751

[2021]
GEORGE, K.D., *ed.* **Macmillan's mergers and acquisitions yearbook.** London, Macmillan Press, 1988. xxxv,799p. tables. £150. ISBN: 0333458656.

Takes a chronological look at events in the field in 6 key articles, followed by a section on 'How to use the book and read the financial data' and a 'Company information section' in 4 parts: 1. Mergers - 2. Acquisitions - 3. Divestments - 4. Management buyouts. Each section is arranged A-Z by name of company and includes information on bidder, target, diary of announcement, terms, financial statistics, and financial advisers. SIC code index. General index by name of company, p.795-799. *Class No:* 334.751

Finance

[2022]
CROPLEY, J. **Directory of financial information sources.** London, Woodhead-Faulkner, 1991. xii,308p. £65. ISBN: 0859415643.

Each entry provides data on institutions, databases and publications. Arrangement is in 10 sections, mostly subdivided: 1. The financial scene - 2. Markets - 3. Financial institutions and credit operations - 4. Corporate institutions and operations - 5. Investment media - 6. Trade - 7. Law and regulations - 8. Economics - 9. People, systems and services - 10. Addresses. Author and title index, p.264-302. Subject index, p.303-308. *Class No:* 336

[2023]
International banking and financial centers. Park, Y.S. *and* Essayyad, M., *eds.* Dordrecht, Kluwer Academic Publishers, 1989. xiv,271p. tables. Dfl.135; £35.25. ISBN: 0792390164.

A study to reflect recent trends and to present an in-depth look into the various aspects of IFCs: definitions; organization; competition; innovations; and evaluation of their contributions to international financing and investment and to the economies of host countries. 16 chapters in 4 parts: 1. Recent developments in international financial

....(contd.)
centers - 2. Cost/benefit analysis of international financial centers - 3. New appraisal of international banking facilities - 4. Global perspective of international financial centers. References are included at the end of each chapter. Index, p.269-271. *Class No:* 336

Databases

[2024]
Business-line finance: the international directory of online financial information. EDI Ltd. (Publishing),, *comp. & ed.* London, EDI:Euromonitor Publications Ltd., 1987. ISBN: 0863382339.

Database directory arranged by subject, A-Z (Accounting - Banking services and information - Commodities/futures - Economics - Financial and insurance services - General business news and information - Insurance - Investment - Money markets - Over the counter listings - Stock market and securities). Indexes of hosts, producers and addresses. *Class No:* 336(003.4)

[2025]
Online databases in the securities and financial markets. New York, Cuadra/Elsevier, 1987. xxii,322p. $39.95. ISBN: 0444012761.

Descriptions of the databases are arranged A-Z by name, with information on type, subject, producer, online service, conditions, content, language, coverage, time span, updating (*i.e.,* monthly). There follows addresses of online databases, and indexes (subject, subdivided by database titles; online service/gateway index; master index). *Class No:* 336(003.4)

Bibliographies

[2026]
BREALEY, R.A *and* EDWARDS, H. **A Bibliography of finance.** Cambridge, Mass., M.I.T., 1991. 822p. $60. ISBN: 0262023199.

Over 12,000 entries (over half for articles published 1980-89) taken from *c.*120 periodicals in finance and related fields. Entries grouped in 40 chapters, further subdivided into 373 individual subjects. Contents list; author and keyword indexes. Both authors at the London Business School. '... a large and impressive work ...'(*Choice*, v.28(11/12), July/August 1991, p.1754). *Class No:* 336(01)

[2027]
COHEN, J. **Special bibliography in monetary economics and finance.** London, Gordon & Breach, 1976. xiii,200p. £61.90. ISBN: 067700690x.

Covers the years 1953-73. In 7 sections (1. Monetary and financial theory - 2. Banks - 3. Financial intermediaries - 4. Financial markets - 5. Monetary statistics - 6. General texts - 7. Bibliographies; reference works). *Class No:* 336(01)

[2028]
LESTER, R.G. *and* CROPLEY, I., *eds.* **Information sources in finance and banking.** Sevenoaks, Kent, Bowker-Saur, 1994. To be in 2v. £55. ISBN: 1857390377, v.1.

V.1: Data sources; v.2: Evaluating financial information. V.1 is arranged by subject, entries including brief notes on sources, frequency of publication, price and serial information. *Class No:* 336(01)

[2029]
ROCK, J.M. **Money, banking and macroeconomics: a guide to information sources.** Detroit, Mich., Gale, 1977. 304p. $68. (*Economics information guide series, v.11.*) ISBN: 0810313006.

A selective, annotated bibliography of books and journal articles on inflation, the relation between income and prices, fiscal policy, and the history of macro-monetary theory. A general chapter (overview; introduction; general; special and secondary sources) precedes the four main chapters relating to financial intermediaries, macro-monetary theory, central banking, and stabilisation policy. Author, title and subject indexes. *Class No:* 336(01)

Encyclopaedias

[2030]
Enzyklapädisches Lexikon für das Geld- Bank- und Borsenwesen. Achterberg, E. *and* Lanz, K., *eds.* 3.Aufl.redigiert und ergänzt. Frankfurt am Main, Knapp, 1967-68. 2v. (xi,1894p.).tables.

First published 1957.

V.1: A-H; v.2: I-Z. Includes country entries (*e.g.* U.S.: 5 pts., 34 sections, p.1686-1723). Includes some biographies (*e.g.* 'Smith, Adam': ½col.; 'Keynes': 2 cols., plus bibliography of 17 lines). International panel of 200 contributors. *Class No:* 336(031)

[2031]
MUNN, G. G. **Encyclopedia of banking and finance.** Woefel, C.J., *ed.* 9th ed. New York & London, McGraw-Hill Book Company 1991. xxvi,1097p. tables, charts. £89; $95. ISBN: 0077073940.

First published 1924; 8th ed. 1983.

c. 4200 lengthy entries, in addition to thousands of basic banking, business and financial terms. 'The in-depth entries provide a wealth of valuable information, such as historical background, analysis of recent trends, illustrative examples, statistical data, and citations to applicable laws and regulations (*Publisher's foreword*). Cross-references, but no index to this edition. *Class No:* 336(031)

[2032]
—DAVIDS, L.E. Dictionary of banking and finance. Totowa, N.J., Rowman & Littlefield, 1979. 229p. $8.95. ISBN: 0822603365.

Concentrates on developments since the mid-1960s in banking, defining *c.* 5400 terms and phrases. Suggested (*Choice* April 1979, p.200,202) as a quick-reference tool and supplement to Munn. *Class No:* 336(031)

[2033]
—RACHLIN, H. The Money encyclopedia. New York, Harper & Row, 1984. 669p., tables. $26.50. ISBN: 0061817112.

Less comprehensive than Munn, but a clear, readable source of information on economic terms commonly encountered by the general public. Entries written by experts from the banking, securities and insurance fields. *Class No:* 336(031)

Handbooks & Manuals

[2034]
GARNER, P., *and others, eds.* **Financial management handbook.** 3rd ed. Brentford, Middx., Kluwer Publishing Ltd., 1988. Loose-leaf, with updates. ISBN: 0903393336.

First published in 1977, edited by G.M. Dickinson and J.E. Lewis.

Part 1: Corporate strategy and financial planning - 2: Evaluation of capital outlays - 3: Financing and dividend policy - 4: Sources of external funds - 5: The management of working capital - 6: Financial control systems and the measurement of performance - 7: Mergers and takeovers - 8: International financial management - 9: Financial management and its economic environment - 10: Using business computers. Each part contains several signed contributions, many by well-known contributors, which include bibliographies. The loose-leaf format is for regular updating. 30-page index. *Class No:* 336(035)

[2035]
MASON, S. **The McGraw-Hill handbook of British finance and trade.** Maidenhead, Berks, McGraw-Hill Book Company (UK) Ltd., 1983. [8] 467p. £29.95p. ISBN: 0070845905.

Preface claims that it includes practically all basic information for businesses. 16 chapters:- 1. Money and interest rates - 2. The national economy - 3. Financial incentives, governnment and institutional aid - 4. International trade - 5. Taxation - 6. Investment - 7. Company structure/company demise - 8. Management analysis and techniques - 9. The mechanics of finance - 10. Sources and methods of finance - 11. The City of London: its institutions and markets - 12. Banks and banking institutions - 13. Commercial and financial institutions - 14. Developments in finance - 15. Miscellaneous financial organizations and activities - 16. Contact points. *Class No:* 336(035)

[2036]
ROWLEY, E.E. **The Financial system today:** understanding financial information. Manchester, Manchester University Press, 1987. ix,228p. tables. £22.50. ISBN: 0719014875.

A practical guide in 9 sections: 1. British government securities - 2. Measuring share price changes - 3. The retail price index - 4. The European currency unit - 5. Evaluation of a company - 6. London traded share options market - 7. Investment trusts and unit trusts - 8. The markets for foreign currencies - 9. The Eurocurrencies market. Index, p.223-228. Notes follow each chapter and include references. *Class No:* 336(035)

Dictionaries

[2037]
A World Bank glossary: a glossary of finance and debt. Washington, World Bank, 1991. vii,213p. $18.95; £17.95. ISBN: 0821316443.

Supersedes *Borrowing and lending terminology*(1984).

Main section (in English) defines terms used in major world financial markets, and also provides equivalent words or phrases in French and Spanish. Also includes a list of relevant acronyms in English, French and Spanish, and glossaries (with no definitions) translating French and Spanish terms into English. *Class No:* 336(038)

Polyglot

[2038]
DE MUNTER, M. *and* BAUDUIN, C. **Elsevier's fiscal and customs dictionary in five languages:** English/American, French, Dutch, and German. Amsterdam, Elsevier Science Publishers, 1988. xxxii,718p. Dfl.500; $285.50 ISBN: 0444428917.

Aimed at theoreticians and practitioners of fiscal law (including customs law), officials of tax administration, etc. 4845 numbered terms (words and phrases) in the English language, followed by French, Dutch and German equivalents. A bibliography (p.xv-xxxi) precedes, with dictionary item numbers in brackets for connection with legal, etc., documents. Includes certain legal and economic as well as purely fiscal terms. Indexes in all 4 languages. *Class No:* 336(038)=00

[2039]
EUROPEAN PARLIAMENT. **Glossary of fiscal terminology:** French/Italian/English/German/Dutch. Luxembourg, European Parliament, 1975. 253p. £6.50.

Arranged under French terms, with keyword indexes in the other languages referring to the main sequence. A supplement, 'List of taxes and duties levied in the member states' includes the Danish language. *Class No:* 336(038)=00

[2040]
GOLDSMITH, DEVOLVÉ ET ASSOCIÉS, *and others*. **Multilingual glossary of tax, financial and commercial terms.** London, Oyez, Longman Group, 1983. 164p. £8.50. ISBN: 0851207618.

Arrangement is A-Z under the English-language terms, followed by French, German and Spanish equivalents in neighbouring columns. No indexes. *Class No:* 336(038)=00

[2041]
The IFR financial glossary. 3rd ed. London, IFR Publishing Ltd., 1992. 354p. £33. ISBN: 1873446012.

Covers terms used in short-term money, equity and bond markets; loans; financial instruments; Japanese, American, German and French terminology now internationally used; institutions and associations and their acronyms, differentiating between those words that have different meanings in different markets. Length of entries varies from 2 or 3 lines to over 20 lines. Extensive cross-references. *Class No:* 336(038)=00

[2042]
THOMSON, F.J. **Elsevier's dictionary of financial terms in English, German, Spanish, French, Italian and Dutch.** Amsterdam, Elsevier Scientific Publishing Ltd., 1979. [6], 496p. Dfl.290. $152.75. ISBN: 0444417753.

2379 numbered entries in English, followed by translations into the other five languages. Indexes in the other five languages followed by the entry numbers. No descriptions, but alternative terms are given. *Class No:* 336(038)=00

English

[2043]
AVEYNON, E.A., *ed*. **Dictionary of finance.** New York, Collier-Macmillan, 1988. 486p. illus., tables, charts. $50. ISBN: 0029164206.

Definitions for over 6000 terms in the area of finance and

....(contd.)
topics relating to finance (*e.g.* banking, law, marketing, economics). Entries include multiple meanings for many terms. Cross-references. *Class No:* 336(038)=20

[2044]
BANNOCK, G. *and* MANSER, W. **International dictionary of finance.** London, Hutchinson, in association with Economist Books, 1989. 220p. £19.95. ISBN: 0091743443.

Concerned not only with international finance but with domestic financial matters in major countries, particularly UK and US. Main subjects covered are money markets, commodity markets, securities markets, banking and insurance, and terms and phrases are limited to the specialized terminology of finance. Entries vary in length from 2 lines to ½-page. Cross-references. List of abbreviations precedes the dictionary. 'Comprehensive and concise reference guide for those wanting to be well-informed about the international world of finance' (*British book news,* January 1990, p.38). *Class No:* 336(038)=20

[2045]
BROSTER, E.J. **Glossary of applied management and financial statistics.** London, Gower Press, 1974. [v], 243p. illus., tables. £22.50. ISBN: 0716101742.

Defines a few hundred terms, some at length (*e.g.* Index numbers, 5 pages). Cross-references, examples and formulae. Annotated bibliography of 16 general works and 30 special works in 11 subject sections. *Class No:* 336(038)=20

[2046]
PERRY, F.E., *ed*. **A Selected vocabulary of financial terms.** London, Waterlow Publishers Ltd., 1981. [3],125p. £4.50. ISBN: 0900791705.

An A-Z listing (Acceptancee credit ... Zero budgeting) of terms, with cross-references. Descriptions vary in length from a line to 1½ pages. Includes organizations. UK orientated. *Class No:* 336(038)=20

[2047]
ROSENBERG, J.M., *ed*. **Dictionary of banking and financial services.** 3rd ed. New York, Wiley, 1993. 369p. illus. $39.95. ISBN: 047157435x.

First published in 1982 with the title *Dictionary of banking and finance.*

Includes *c.*7500 words, phrases and abbreviations in an A-Z sequence. Entries vary in length from 3 or 4 words to about 150 words, and include definitions and alternative words. Excellent clear and concise definitions. 'Terms added, but - unfortunately - others dropped.'(*Wilson library bulletin,* v.67(8), April 1993, p.118). *Class No:* 336(038)=20

[2048]
WALMESLEY, J. **Dictionary of international finance.** 2nd ed. London, Macmillan, 1985. [5], 222p. £27.50. (*Macmillan dictionary series.*) ISBN: 0333370708.

First published 1979.

Several hundred entries for terms in trade finance, foreign exchange and economics. Al ... Zero coupon. 'Special drawing rights': ¾p., with 4 references; 'Eurodollar': 2/3p., with 6 references. Includes abbreviations and organizations (*e.g.* Carribean Community and Common Market; Association of South-East Asian Nations). The author is a vice-president of Barclays Bank. "The jargon of international

....*(contd.)*

trade, insurance, economics and securities trading is clearly, completely, yet succinctly defined" (*RQ,*v.19, no. 4, Summer 1980, p.390 on first ed.). *Class No:* 336(038)=20

German

[2049]

GUNSTON, C.A. *and* **CORNER, C.M. German-English glossary of financial and economic terms.** 8th ed. Frankfurt am Main, Knapp, 1983. xviii,918p. £54.

First published 1953.

About 20,000 main entries, including abbreviations and names of German associations and organizations. Swiss, US, etc. terminology is differentiated. Some explanation of scope of terms. Well spoken of by translators. New ed. in preparation. *Class No:* 336(038)=30

French

[2050]

LAMBERT, D.-C. Dictionnaire français-anglais de l'économie monétaire. 2e.éd. Paris, Éditions Économie et Humanisme, 1975. 261p. £9.90.

First published 1970.

About 500 entries, including biographies and abbreviations. The text of the entry comprises an explanation of the word, and a brief outline of the practice in various countries. Definitions are in French. French and English indexes. *Class No:* 336(038)=40

Spanish

[2051]

DONAGHY, P.J. *and* **LAIDLER, J.,** *comps.* **Dictionary of the language of financial reports:** Spanish-English, English-Spanish. Bilbao, Ediciones Deusto, 1983 (distributed by Christopher Percival, Durham City). 222p. £11.50. ISBN: 8423405435.

Also available under the Spanish title *Diccionario de terminos usados en informes financieros...*

Translations of *c.*8000 specialized terms found in annual reports of companies, annual financial statements, etc. *Class No:* 336(038)=60

Arabic

[2052]

ABDEEN, A. English-Arabic dictionary of accounting and finance, with an Arabic-English glossary. Beirut, Librairie du Liban; Chichester, Sussex, John Wiley & Sons, 1981. xi,226,[41]p. ISBN: 0471276731.

Gives explanations of terms in English and Arabic, supported by examples and illustrations. Terms arranged A-Z in English. Appendices: 1. Financial ratios; 2. Currencies in the Arab world; 3. Metric conversion tables; 4. Illustrations. Finally, an Arabic-English glossary. *Class No:* 336(038)=927

Japanese

[2053]

WILLIAMS, D. A Dictionary of Japanese financial terms. Japan Library: Paul Norbury, 1992. 200p. £35. ISBN: 1873410115.

Each entry in phonetic English, kanji and English, plus brief supporting text. *Class No:* 336(038)=956

Periodicals & Progress Reports

[2054]

FISHER, W.H. Financial journals and serials: an analytical guide to accounting, banking, finance, insurance & investment periodicals. Westport, CT. Greenwood Press, 1986. 201p. $65.00. (*Annotated bibliography series, no.6.*) ISBN: 0313241953.

Over 500 English-language journals, briefly annotated. Arranged in 6 chapters, A-Z by title within each: Accounting, auditing and taxation - Banking - Finance - Insurance - Investments - Indexes and abstracts. Geographical, title, publisher and subject indexes. 'The depth of analysis, frequently several paragraphs in addition to the usual bibliographical data, is the basis for acquiring this work' (*Choice,* December 1986, p.606) but the review also mentions that there are some glaring omissions. *Class No:* 336(05)

Tables & Data Books

[2055]

International financial statistics. New York, International Monetary Fund, 1948-. v.1,no.1-. graphs, tables. Monthly. $218pa for 12 issues and yearbook; $50 for yearbook. ISBN: 1557752974, 1993 yearbook. ISSN: 02507463.

Preliminary pages have data on the IMF, exchange rates; fund accounts; international liquidity; international banking; money and banking; interest rates; prices, wages, production and employment; international transactions, government finance; national accounts and population; world tables. 'Country pages' covers *c.*100 countries (excluding Sino-Soviet bloc), Afghanistan ... Zimbabwe, followed by notes on tables. The February 1994 issue (v.47(2) gives time series 1988-92 yearly; 1992 & 1993 quarterly; latest 5 or 6 months, monthly. *Class No:* 336(083)

[2056]

ORGANISATION FOR ECONOMIC CO-OPERATION AND DEVELOPMENT. Published official sources of financial statistics. Paris, OECD, 1980. 132p. £4.90; $11. ISBN: 9264020950.

Information on the offical institutions in 17 countries publishing financial statistics, including their publications. Also information on the financial statistical publications of four international organizations, including OECD. *Class No:* 336(083)

Bibliographies

[2057]

BALACHANDRAN, M. A Guide to statistical sources in money, banking and finance. Phoenix, Ariz., Oryx, 1988. 119p. $45. ISBN: 0897742656.

A selected and annotated bibliography of 480 serial publications dealing with banking and monetary statistics. Arranged in 6 chapters: State services - Regional sources - National sources - Foreign country sources - International

....(contd.)

sources - Databases (63 entries). Annotations vary from one sentence to half a page. Omits USSR in foreign country section. Title and subject index. Directory of publishers. '... excellent source' (*RQ*, v.27(3), Spring 1988, p.429). 'A useful bibliography for business collections' (*Choice*, v.25(10), June 1988, p.1529). *Class No:* 336(083)(01)

Laws

Great Britain

[2058]

MILLER, J. Dictionary of financial regulations, 1988/89. London, London & International Publishers, under licence to The International Stock Exchange of the United Kingdom and the Republic of Ireland Ltd., 1988. xxvi,238p. £29.95. ISBN: 0948209291.

A guide to the vocabulary adopted in the regulation of financial services under the Financial Services Act, 1986. An overview, describing the way in which the headwords of the main text relate to the regulating system and to one another, is followed by the dictionary of over 900 entries, with extensive cross-references. Index of headwords, p.231,233-238. *Class No:* 336(094.1)(410)

Europe

Histories

[2059]

KINDLEBERGER, C.P. A Financial history of Western Europe. 2nd ed. New York, Oxford University Press, 1993. xviii,524p. illus. (cartoons), tables, maps. £35. $29.95. ISBN: 0195077377.

First published 1984.

Introduction, p.1-14, includes chronologies (1. Wars - 2. Monetary events - 3. Banking landmarks - 4. Financial events), is followed by 24 chapters in 5 parts: 1. Money - 2. Banking - 3. Finance - 4. The interwar period - 5. After World War II. Each part has an introduction and each chapter ends with 'Suggested supplementary reading'. Glossary, p.465-473. Bibliography, p.477-511, A-Z by author. Index, p.513-525. *Class No:* 336(4)(091)

Great Britain

Tables & Data Books

[2060]

Financial statistics. Central Statistical Office. London, HMSO, 1962- no.1-. tables. Monthly. £120pa including explanatory handbook. £10 each issue. ISSN: 0015203x.

Prepared in collaboration with the Statistics Divisions of government departments and the Bank of England.

Brings together key financial and monetary statistics of the United Kingdom. 14 sections: 1. Financial accounts ... 3. Central government ... 6. Banks and building societies - 7. Other financial institutions - 8. Companies - 9. Personal sector - 10. Overseas sector ... 13. Exchange rates, interest rates and security prices - 14. Sectoral balance sheet. Supplementary tables. data and information (for figures in CSO databank). Index. *Financial statistics: explanatory handbook* is published annually. *Class No:* 336(410)(083)

Histories

[2061]

COLLINS, M. Money and banking in the U.K.: a history. London, Croom Helm, 1988. [12], 640p. tables, figs. £49.50. ISBN: 0709907605.

16 chapters in three parts covering the period 1826-1985: 1. 1826-1913;2. 1914-1939; 3. 1939-1986. Deals for each period with the general economic and legislative context determining the growth of monetary and financial assets; the developing form of banking business; the domestic monetary policy, and international monetary factors affecting the UK. Notes and further reading follow each chapter. Bibliography (p.593-626) of books, official publications and reports, articles, essays and papers. General index (p.627-638) and index of names (p.639-640). *Class No:* 336(410)(091)

London

Yearbooks & Directories

[2062]

The City directory, 1992. Cambridge, Woodhead-Faulkner, 1992. 328p. £98. ISBN: 0859417735.

First published 1976 by the *Investor's chronicle* and Woodhead-Faulkner, and later editions by Woodhead-Faulkner.

A comprehensive guide to the banks, financial organizations and other companies and services which make up the City of London. *Class No:* 336(421)(058)

France

Histories

[2063]

SAINT MARC, M. Histoire monetaire de la France, 1800-1980. Paris, Presses Universitaire de France, 1983. 441p. tables.

A thorough study of monetary history in France in 3 parts: Part 1 has the data (series of annual monetary statistics mainly from primary sources); pt.2 is historical; pt.3 is theoretical and empirical. Each chapter has a bibliography and the work is illustrated with graphs and tables. No index. '... presents a useful account of the historical evolution of money'. ... a valuable addition to the literature' (*Economic history review*, v.37 (1984), p.455). *Class No:* 336(44)(091)

Japan

[2064]

SUZUKI, Y, ed. The Japanese financial system. Oxford, Clarendon Press, 1987. £35. xi,358p. tables. ISBN: 0198285965.

Prepared by the staff of the Monetary and Economic Studies, Bank of Japan.

Part I outlines the features and changes in the Japanese financial system and economy after World War II; pt. II gives detailed descriptions of various assets, rates, financial institutions and monetary policy. Bibliography (62 items). Subject index, p.349-358. *Class No:* 336(52)

Asia—Near East

Bibliographies

[2065]

NICHOLAS, D. **The Middle East: its oil, economics and investment policies:** a guide to sources of financial information. London, Mansell, 1981. xxiv,199p. £45. ISBN: 0720109078. *Class No:* 336(56)(01)

Yearbooks & Directories

[2066]

The MEED/TAIC Middle East financial directory, 1986. London, Middle East Economic Digest, in association with The Arab Investment Company SAA, 1985. xi,453p. £60. ISBN: 0946510164. ISSN: 02662094.

First published 1975 as *Middle East financial directory;* from 9th ed., 1985 under the current title. Annual.

For 24 Middle East countries, arranged A-Z, general information, and information on central banks, commercial banks, specialized banks, and other financial institutions. Data includes addresses and telephone numbers, activities, management, head office, directors, finance, branches, and subsidiaries. Also a section on banks and other financial institutions in other countries (p.221-322). Indexes of institutions and persons. Glossary of acronyms and abbreviations. *Class No:* 336(56)(058)

Islamic World

Yearbooks & Directories

[2067]

PRESLEY, J.R., *ed.* **A Directory of Islamic financial institutions.** Croom Helm, 1988. 304p. $120; £50. ISBN: 0709913478.

In 4 sections: Part 1 has 7 articles on the theoretical bases and practical operations of Islamic banking; pt.2 is a directory of Islamic financial institutions, arranged by country, and listing for each institution address; telephone/telex/cable numbers for head and branch offices; names of directors and senior management; financial statistics; number of employees; and areas of operation, objectives, types of investment accounts and banking operations, and future developments. Pt.3 has case studies in Islamic banking and banking laws for certain Islamic countries translated into English; and pt.4 is on ownership, control and management of Islamic banks. Recommended by *Choice* (v.26(7), March 1989, p.1120) for comprehensive collections. *Class No:* 336(5.297)(058)

USA

Yearbooks & Directories

[2068]

The Financial 1000: a directory of who runs the leading 1000 US financial organizations. Marsh, J.E., *ed.* New York, Monitor Publishing Co., 1988. 553p. $100. ISSN: 08947627.

An A-Z list of companies, with names of officers, management, boards of directors, major subsidiaries and divisions, and telephone numbers. Covers banks, thrift

....(contd.)

institutions, insurance companies, and Wall Street firms. 3 indexes: geographical; individual names; by financial services rendered. *Class No:* 336(73)(058)

Public Finance

Bibliographies

[2069]

Financial sourcebooks' sources: the directory of financial research, marketing surveys, and services. Napierville, Jl., Financial Sourcebooks, 1987. 454p. $165.00. ISBN: 0942061004. ISSN: 08927812.

Directory of more than 500 reports, published by over 100 organizations, that range from free government and association publications to surveys from private research firms (priced at $30,000 upwards). Reports grouped in 8 chapters: The consumer - Consumer segments - Consumer financial products - Business and institutional services - Institutions - US geographical area information - International sources - Marketing, advertising and media. Each chapter is subdivided, subject-wise. Entries contain description of report, publishers address, frequency or date of publication, and in most cases length of report and price. Covers 1984- plus census data from the 1980 census. Appendices include a list of reports by publisher, a publisher's directory, and a directory of contacts at the US Census Bureau for demographic and economic information. US oriented. *Class No:* 336.1(01)

Tables & Data Books

[2070]

Government finance statistics yearbook, 1992. v.16. Washington, DC., International Monetary Fund, 1992. 710p. tables. $48. ISBN: 1557753008. ISSN: 02507374.

First published 1977. Annual.

Data for *c.*120 countries for 1977 to 1990, with 1991 estimates. 'United Kingdom': Table A: Revenues and grants; B. Expenditure by function; C. Expenditure and lending; D. Financing, by type of debt holder; E. Financing, by type of debt instrument; F. Outstanding debt by type of debt holder; G. Outstanding debt by type of debt instrument. Data is based on *A Manual on government financial statistics* (Rev. ed., 1986. $10). Also available on CD-ROM. *Class No:* 336.1(083)

[2071]

INTERNATIONAL MONETARY FUND. **A Manual on government finance statistics.** Washington, DC., the IMF, 1986. vii,[1],373p. illus., tables. %c $93.80. ISBN: 0939934442.

Compiled to assist those who are called upon to organize statistics of government finance for various purposes. In 6 chapters: I. Coverage (has sections A-K) - II. Selection and preparation of data - III. Analytical framework - IV.Classification - V. Relationships with other data systems - VI. Nonfinancial public enterprises and the nonfinancial public sector. List of tables; bridge tables; list of working tables; list of charts. *Class No:* 336.1(083)

Europe—Western

[2072]

EUROPEAN COMMUNITIES. Commission. **The European monetary system:** origins, operation, and outlook. Ypersele, J. van *and* Koeune, J.-C. Luxembourg, Office for Official Publications of the European Communities; Cambridge, Woodhead-Faulkner, 1985. 139,[4]p. tables. ECU.25. ISBN: 9282534685, EC; 0859413136, UK.

5 chapters: I. International motives for the EEC initiative - II. The ebb and flow of European monetary integration - III. The EMS and the conditions for its proper operation - IV. Five years with the EMS - V. The future of the EMS. 4 annexes (Timetable of events - Act of foundation of the European Monetary System - Versailles summit - European Parliament resolution of 16 February 1984).
Class No: 336.1(400)

USA

Bibliographies

[2073]

MARSHALL, M.B. **Public finance;** an information sourcebook. Phoenix, AZ., Oryx Press, 1987. xviii,287p. $39.50. (*Oryx sourcebook series in business and management,* 6.) ISBN: 0897742761.

A briefly annotated bibliography of 1205 entries, focusing on policy issues and theory of public finance. Subject arrangement. Detailed table of contents and excellent indexes (Author index, p.253-260; title index, p.261-278; analytical subject index, p.279-287). 'A helpful feature is a core collection of important sources... ' (*Choice,* v.25(9), May 1988, p.1384). *Class No:* 336.1(73)(01)

Budgets

[2074]

BRITTAIN, H. **The British budgetary system.** London, Allen & Unwin, 1959. 320p.

A standard work. The composition of the budget is closely discussed item by item and is followed by a chapter on the national debt. Finally, the control of government expenditure by Parliament and the Treasury is explained in detail. Detailed index: no bibliography. *Class No:* 336.12

[2075]

PREST, A.R. *and* BARR, N.A. **Public finance in theory and practice.** 7th rev. ed. by N.A. Barr. London, Weidenfeld & Nicolson, 1985. 576p. £20. ISBN: 0297787527.

First published 1960.

More general in scope than Brittain (q.v.) as a text book, and includes chapters on US and Canada. *Class No:* 336.12

Accounts

Worldwide

Tables & Data Books

[2076]

ORGANISATION FOR ECONOMIC CO-OPERATION AND DEVELOPMENT. **National accounts of OECD countries, 1955/64-.** Paris, OECD, 1966-. tables. Annual. ISSN: 02567571.

Two volumes each year: v.1. *Main aggregates, 1960-1991.* (1993. 160p. F.150. £25. $38.00.); v.2 *Detailed*

.... (contd.)
tables, 1979-1991 (1993. 588p. F.530. £87. $125.). V.1 shows for each member country the main aggregates calculated according to either the present or the former system of national accounts. V.2 shows each country's detailed statistics. Annex 1 is a glossary of the technical terms used in the system of national accounts; annex 2 gives a full set of English and French translations of the item descriptions in the detailed country tables. Updated by *Quarterly national accounts* (1976-. F.320. £40. $68pa.).
Class No: 336.126(100)(083)

[2077]

UNITED NATIONS. Department of International Economic and Social Affairs. Statistical Office. **Yearbook of national accounts statistics, 1990:** main aggregates and detailed tables. New York, United Nations, 1992. 2v. ISBN: 9211613515.

First published 1957. Annual.

International coverage of statistical data on national accounts estimates for 170 countries and areas, giving specific data on gross domestic product, national income and capital transactions, government and consumer expenditures, social security and household funds. One volume devoted to main aggregates; the other to detailed tables. Issued separately is *National accounts statistics: analysis of main aggregates,* presenting in the form of statistical tables, a summary of main national aggregates.
Class No: 336.126(100)(083)

Great Britain

Tables & Data Books

[2078]

GREAT BRITAIN. Central Statistical Office. **United Kingdom national accounts, 1993.** London, HMSO, 1993. vii,168p. tables. £15.50. ISBN: 0116205889. ISSN: 02678691.

First published for 1938/40. Prior to 1984 title was *National income and expenditure.* Known as *The Blue book.* Annual.

17 chapters in 5 sections: 1. The national accounts - 2. The main analyses - 3. The sector accounts - 4. Capital formation and capital stocks - 5. Other analyses and derived statistics. A 6th section has supplementary information (Glossary of terms; methodological notes; revisions; and index). Data is for several years to 1992.
Class No: 336.126(410)(083)

[2079]

—COPEMAN, H. The National accounts: a short guide. London, HMSO., 1981. various pagings. £5.50. (*Studies in official statistics, no.36.*) ISBN: 0116200006.

Provides a broad description of the accounts and a detailed commentary on their structure.
Class No: 336.126(410)(083)

Taxation

[2080]

PLATT, C.J. **Tax systems of Africa, Asia and Middle East:** a guide for business and the professions. Aldershot, Hants, Gower Publishing Company, 1982. xxii, 240p. £27. ISBN: 0566023350.

Summarizes tax arrangements in 35 countries of Africa,

....*(contd.)*

Asia, and the Near and Middle East. A companion volume to the one on Western Europe. Similar arrangement to companion volume by Platt at 336.2(4). *Class No:* 336.2

[2081]

PLATT, C.J. Tax systems of Western Europe: a guide for business and the professions. 3rd ed. Aldershot, Hants, Gower, 1985. xxii, 171p. £15; $30.50. ISBN: 0566025345.

First published 1980.

Summarizes tax arrangements in 23 European countries, arranged A-Z. Each entry begins with a brief 'tax profile' followed by a summary of taxes in force (income tax, corporation tax, capital tax), notes on legislation, detail of income tax (basis of assessment, computation of taxable income, current allowances, etc.), details of corporation tax, notes on double taxation agreements and rates of tax. *Class No:* 336.2

Laws

[2082]

DIAMOND, W.H. *and* DIAMOND, D.B., *eds*. International tax treaties of all nations. Dobbs Ferry, N.Y., Oceana,1975-83. 34v. (Series A, 14v.; series B, 25v.). Series A plus loose-leaf index $710; Series B $1290. ISBN: 0379007258.

950 bilateral treaties, originally published by the United Nations, in sequence of their dates of issue by the League of Nations and the United Nations, together with individual editorial commentary, current effective status, etc. Supplement and cumulative index was published in 1983 (loose-leaf. $50. ISBN 0379007452).

Class No: 336.2(094.1)

Europe

[2083]

Supplementary service to European taxation. Amsterdam, International Bureau of Fiscal Documentation, 1963-. Loose-leaf in 14 binders. Dfl.2400 for basic volume, binders & monthly updates for the year; Renewal: Dfl.860. ISSN: 00395927.

Includes tax tables (corporation and individual) for each European country; English-language texts of tax treaties; texts (in English) of official reports, including E.C. directives on taxation; and worldwide bibliography of new tax documents and publications. The Bureau also issues a series of loose-leaf guides to European taxation: v.1, *Taxation of patent royalties, dividends, interest in Europe;* v.2, *The taxation of companies in Europe;* v.3, *The taxation of private investment income;* v.4, *Value added tax in Europe;* and v.5, *Taxation in European Socialist countries.* *Class No:* 336.2(4)

Great Britain

Bibliographies

[2084]

GREAT BRITAIN. HM Stationery Office. **Government publications. Sectional list 29, revised January 1992. Inland Revenue.** London, HMSO., 1992. vi,14p. *Gratis.*

Includes references to the Tax Acts, tax cases and leaflets, tax reports, etc. *Class No:* 336.2(410)(01)

Encyclopaedias

[2085]

British tax encyclopaedia. Lawton, P., *ed.* London, Sweet & Maxwell, 1970-. 6v. (looseleaf). Annual service. £625. (including service).

First published 1921.

V.1 is a narrative treatise on the definition of income for tax purposes. V.2-5 contain the relevant statutory material, fully annotated. V.6 has a comprehensive index to the whole work, full tables, current up-dating releases, etc. Plentiful and detailed cross-references. *Class No:* 336.2(410)(031)

Handbooks & Manuals

[2086]

BROOKE-TAYLOR, D. Guide to stamp duties. Bicester, Oxfordshire, CCH Editions Ltd., 1988. xiii,378p. £19.50. ISBN: 0863251153.

Claims to be a straighforward and all-round guide to stamp duties. In 4 parts: 1: General principles; 2. Individual duties - conveyancing; 3: Individual duties - companies; 4: Individual duties - miscellaneous. Appendices: I: Table of duties; II: Companies Act forms; III: Relevant legislation. Case table. Legislation finding list. Double-column subject index, p.359-378, relating to paragraph numbers. *Class No:* 336.2(410)(035)

[2087]

Butterworth's yellow tax handbook, 1993-94: Taxes Acts relating to income tax, corporation tax and capital gains tax... Sadikali, M., *ed.* 33rd ed. London, Butterworths, 1993. £20. (*A Butterworth taxbook annual.*) ISBN: 0406015937.

First published 1962. Annual.

'Provides plain text of the Taxes Acts relating to income tax, corporation tax and capital gains tax. *Moore & Rowlands yellow tax guide* (1989-90 ed. 1988. 1301p. £27.95. ISBN 0406366039. ISSN 09518231) explains the practical effects of all the legislation contained in the above. *Class No:* 336.2(410)(035)

[2088]

—Butterworth's orange tax handbook, 1993-94... inheritance tax, National Insurance contributions, stamp duties, value added tax. London, Butterworth, 1993. £20 ISBN: 0406015945.

First published 1976.

Companion volume to *Butterworths yellow tax handbook, Moores & Rowland orange tax guide* (1989-90. 1988. 1293p. £27.95. ISBN 0406365032. ISSN 09518223) explains the practical effects of all the legislation contained in the above. *Class No:* 336.2(410)(035)

[2089]

Tolley's tax guide, 1993-94: practical tax advice for the non-expert. Homer, A. *and* Burrows, R. 11th ed. Croydon, Surrey, Tolley Publishing Company Ltd., 1993. 870p. £23.95. ISBN: 0854597263.

First published for 1983/84. Annual.

Aims to provide clear and concise guidance on all aspects of taxation. *Class No:* 336.2(410)(035)

[2090]

The Touche Ross tax guide for the self-employed.
Packer, B. *and* Sandy, C.   4th ed. London, Macmillan
Press, 1988. xiv,213p. £4.95. ISBN: 0333468368.

First published 1985.

Written by two tax specialists at Touche Ross, the guide
aims to include every inmportant tax aspect of self-
employment and running a small business, including setting
up the business, salaries versus profits, national insurance,
VAT registration and payment, tax records, capital
expenditure, employees, raising finance, and pension plans,
plus a series of tax-planning guidelines and hints.
Class No: 336.2(410)(035)

[2091]

WEBB, H.B.   *and*   COLLIER, R.   **Butterworth's   stamp
duties guide.** London, Butterworths, 1988.   xiv,163p.
£21.95. ISBN: 0406260303.

An introduction to stamp duty, capital duty, and stamp
duty reserve tax, written for the non-specialist. 8 chapters (1.
The three duties in outline - 2. Stamp duty ... 7. Procedure,
appeals and enforcement - 8. The new approach and future
developments). Table of Statutes. 5 appendices (I. Outline of
main heads of change for stamp duty; II. Specimen forms;
V. Stamp offices - addresses and phone numbers). Index,
p.147-163. *Class No:* 336.2(410)(035)

Dictionaries

[2092]

HART, G. **Dictionary of taxation.** London, Butterworth,
1981.   v,   236p.   £16.50.   (*Butterworth's professional
dictionaries series.*) ISBN: 040652159x.

Defines about 900 words and phrases, including
definitions from the Finance Act, 1981. Entries vary from 2
lines to 2 pages in length, and sources (*e.g.* Acts, etc.) are
given. Cross-referenced. *Class No:* 336.2(410)(038)

Yearbooks & Directories

[2093]

Butterworth's UK tax guide, 1993-94. Tiley, J., *ed.* 10th ed.
London, Butterworths, 1993. 1680p. £17.95. ISBN:
0406015929.

Now issued annually, soon after each year's Finance Act.

'Developed from Tiley's *Revenue law,* it is designed to be
both a comprehensive tax textbook and a pointer, by means
of extensive cross-referencing, to the more detailed narrative
in Butterworths loose-leaf tax encyclopedia' (Preface). In 11
parts I: Introduction; II: Income tax; III: Capital gains tax;
IV: Corporate tax; V: Savings; VI: Anti-avoidance; VII: The
international dimension; VIII: Inheritance tax; IX: National
insurance contributions; X: Stamp duty and stamp duty
reserve tax; XI: Value added tax. Tables of Statutes and
tables of cases are followed by a 139p. index.
Class No: 336.2(410)(058)

Laws

[2094]

HARRISON, E.R. **A Digest and index of tax cases ...** being
a judicial dictionary of the law. Garland, C.E., *ed.* 6th ed.
London, HMSO, 1949-. 2v. (loose-leaf) with cumulative
supplements.

Cases indexed are those reported in the official *Reports of
tax cases,* 1875-, although other reports are included. V.2 is

....(contd.)

a supplementary volume, updating v.1 and cumulated by
periodical addition and replacement by new sheets. Each
volume has 3 sections: tables of tax cases, names of parties
and subject matter. This last is arranged A-Z by subject and
gives a brief account of each relevant case, plus judicial
finding. *Class No:* 336.2(410)(094.1)

China

[2095]

MOSER, M.J. *and* ZEE, W.K. **China tax guide.** 2nd ed.
Hong Kong, Oxford University Press, 1993. xii,316p. £35.
ISBN: 0195857240.

lst published 1988.

An introduction to a complex tax system. Chapter 2 is on
forms of doing business in China; Ch.3 on individual income
tax; the following chapters are on various business taxes.
Includes specimens of tax forms; and a listing of 'selected
legislation'. *Class No:* 336.2(510)

Customs & Excise

[2096]

GREAT BRITAIN. HM Customs and Excise. **Integrated
tariff of the United Kingdom.** 1993 ed. London, HMSO.,
1993. 3v.(1200 leaves). £120pa including amendments.
ISBN: 0117292052. ISSN: 02620421.

Earlier title was *Tariff and overseas trade classification in
the United Kingdom.* Annual.

V.1 General information; v.2. Schedules of duty and trade
statistical descriptions, codes and rates; v.3. Customs freight
procedures. *Class No:* 336.4

Commercial Finance

Bibliographies

[2097]

LISTER, J. *and* LISTER, R.E. **Annotated bibliography of
corporate finance.** London, Macmillan Press, 1979. v,
240p.

1270 annotated entries for English language works of
lasting interest and directly relevant to the theory and
practice of corporate financing decisions. The bibliography
is preceded by a list of the 117 periodicals consulted and the
classification scheme employed for arrangement. Author and
subject indexes. *Class No:* 336.6(01)

[2098]

**London Business School bibliography of financial markets,
1987/88.** Edwards, H., *ed.*   London, London Business
School Library, 1989. 365p. £35. ISBN: 0902583115.

First published for 1985/86. Annual.

*c.*5000 references to books, journal articles, working
papers, reports and reference works published in English. In
3 main parts: Part 1. Subject bibliography (1. Financial
markets - 2. Financial intermediation - 3. Market efficiency -
4. Common stocks - 5. Portfolio investment ... 10.
Corporate finance ... 13. Information technology in financial
markets - 14. Reference works). All sections are subdivded.
Part 2. Country bibliography (by contents, subdivided by
countries, A-Z). Part 3. Author bibliography. No
annotations. Appendices list journals covered and there is
also a list of institutions. *Class No:* 336.6(01)

Handbooks & Manuals

[2099]

DIBBEN, M. The Guardian money guide. 3rd ed. London, William Collins & Sons Ltd., 1988. 256p. £5.95. ISBN: 0004104498.

First published 1984.

18 chapters: 1. Budgeting - 2. Banking - 3. Savings - 4. Borrowing - 5. Buying your home - 6. How to sell a house ... 13. Wills ... 17. Holidays - 18. The law. Useful addresses, p.248-250. Index, p.251-256. '... offers straightforward advice on all the usual financial activities ...' (*Banking world,* October 1988, p.44). *Class No:* 336.6(035)

[2100]

DOWNES, J. *and* **GOODMAN, J.E. Barron's finance and investment handbook.** Woodbury, NY., Barron's, 1986. xiv, 994p. charts, tables. $18.95. ISBN: 0812057295.

In 5 major parts: Part 1 explains 30 types of personal investment; part 2 is on how to read an annual report; part 3 is on how to read more important daily financial pages and ticker tape; part 4 has definitions of more than 2500 financial and investment terms, and includes examples and illustrations taken from financial sources; and part 5 is a directory listing some 4700 companies, A-Z. '... the best introductory handbook for public and academic libraries'. (*Reference books bulletin,* 1986/87, p.75).

Class No: 336.6(035)

[2101]

GEISST, C.R. A Guide to financial institutions. London, Macmillan, 1987. 144p. tables. £27.50. ISBN: 033338623x.

Provides a description of the major types of financial institution in both the United States and the United Kingdom, showing the inter-relationship between the major types of institution beginning with international financial institutions, and continuing with commercial banking, investment banking, building associations, life insurance companies and pension funds, and American federal agencies. There is also an 11-page index. *Class No:* 336.6(035)

Yearbooks & Directories

[2102]

Macmillan directory of global financial markets. Graham, J, *and others.* London, Macmillan Press, 1989. 464p. £95. ISBN: 0333483234.

In 3 parts: 1. Introduction to global financial markets - 2. Directory guide to market participation (introduction - UK organizations - US organizations - Japanese organizations) - 3. Dictionary of terminology and techniques (UK, US and Japanese). Aim is to provide a fully integrated guide to the structural and operational dynamics of the emerging global financial markets, the participant financial organizations, the techniques of financial engineering in complex global markets, and information systems technology. Includes a bibliography and index. *Class No:* 336.6(058)

Laws

[2103]

LOMNICKA, E. *and* **POWELL, J.L. Encyclopedia of financial services law.** London, Sweet & Maxwell, 1987-. 2v. (loose-leaf). £220 (inc. service to end of 1988). ISBN: 0421368802.

V.1 contains an introductory section; full text of the Financial Services Act 1986, with annotations; Statutes

.... (contd.)

related to the Act; Orders and Regulations made under the Act; full text of the SIB's rule book, including explanatory notes and a list of definitions; relevant EEC directives and selected abstracts from the SIB's annual reports. V.2 has the rules of the recognised self regulating organizations, the recognised investment exchanges, and the recognised professional bodies. Both volumes are to be updated with specialist commentary. *Class No:* 336.6(094.1)

Worldwide

[2104]

SMOLKA-DAY, M.I. Bibliographic guide to the legal aspects of international finance. In *International journal of legal information,* v.18(3), Winter 1990, p.205-214.

A selection of some important or representative general materials in English, the emphasis being on recent publications. General material - International monetary system - International investments - Financing international trade - Eurobonds and Eurocurrency markets. *Class No:* 336.6(100)

Europe—Western

Yearbooks & Directories

[2105]

European directory of financial information sources. London, Euromonitor, 1990 (distributed in US by Omnigraphics Inc.). xiv,386p. £160. $335. ISBN: 0863383696.

In 6 sections: 1. Financial services in Europe: a new era - 2. Company information sources (Pan-Europe, then by country, A-Z) - 3. Major banking and financial information - 4. Major banking and financial trade journals - 5. Major banking and finance associations - 6. Major financial operations, by country subdivided by type of business. *Class No:* 336.6(400)(058)

[2106]

Major financial institutions of Europe, 1994. Whiteside, R.M., *ed.* 3rd ed. London, Graham & Trotman, 1993. 336p. £195. ISBN: 1853339660.

Covers 17 Western European countries. Arranged A-Z by country, subdivided A-Z by name of institution. Entries give name and address of institution; telephone, cable, telex numbers; management; principal activities; financial information; principal shareholders; trade names; and number of employees. Index. *Class No:* 336.6(400)(058)

Great Britain

Yearbooks & Directories

[2107]

Sunday telegraph **business finance directory, 1987:** the guide to sources of corporate finance in Britain. 3rd ed. London, Graham & Trotman, 1987. [5],319p. £90; $158. ISSN: 02682249.

First published 1985. Annual.

Lists sources of finance, including banks, venture capital companies, stockbrokers, licensed dealers, finance houses, leasing companies, investment trusts, etc. Indexes of institutions, A-Z, institutions by category, and a classified index. *Class No:* 336.6(410)(058)

Biographies

[2108]
Who's who in the City, 1993. Williams, L., *ed*. London, Macmillan, under licence from the International Stock Exchange of the United Kingdom and the Republic of Ireland, 1993. 800p. £95. ISBN: 0333564057.

First edition 1988.

Brief biographical profiles of over 10,000 people, mainly directors or partners, in the financial community, A-Z by name. Two indexes list companies, A-Z, with address, telephone number, telex and fax numbers, and names of senior personnel; and list companies grouped by sector. *Class No:* 336.6(410)(092)

Scotland

[2109]
DRAPER, P., *and others*. **The Scottish financial sector.** Edinburgh, Edinburgh University Press, 1988. xiv, 347p. tables. £45. (*Scottish industrial policy, series 4.*) ISBN: 0852245505.

Outlines the past, present and future development of capital markets and financial intermediation in Scotland in 12 chapters: 1. Historical and economic perspective; 2. Financial flows and employment in the financial sectors in Scotland; 3. Scottish financial markets; 4. The Scottish clearing banks; 5. Retail deposit institutions; 6. Other banking and deposit institutions; 7. Insurance funds and insurance broking; 8. Investment management; 9. Public venture capital; 10. Innovation in financial markets and institutions; 11. Summary; 12. Conclusions. Bibliography (p.337-41, 105 items, A-Z by author); Double column index (p.342-7). *Class No:* 336.6(411)

London

[2110]
McCULLOGH, V. Pocket guide to the new City. Oxford, Basil Blackwell and The Economist Publications, 1988. [4],121p. illus. £15. ISBN: 0631162836.

An A-Z guide to the types of people, activities, institutions and instruments which populate the 'Square Mile' [the City of London], post the Big Bang. Cross-references. Entries vary from 2 lines to half a page, and are entertaining as well as informative. *Class No:* 336.6(421)

USA

Biographies

[2111]
Who's who in finance and industry, 1992-1993. 27th ed. Chicago, Ill., Marquis Who's Who, 1991. 942p. $220. ISBN: 0837903270.

First published 1936 as *Who's who in commerce and industry*, later as *World who's who in finance and industry*.

An extension of *Who's who in America*. Biographical sketches of American leading men and women in finance and industry. Profiles the top executives of America's largest corporations as well as leaders of small and medium-size firms. *Class No:* 336.6(73)(092)

Capital & Investment

Bibliographies

[2112]
WALLACE, C.D., *ed*. **Foreign direct investment and the multinational enterprise:** a bibliography. Dordrecht, Martinus Nijhoff, 1988. xi,355p. Dfl.195 $100. £59. ISBN: 9024736579.

*c.*3500 unannotated entries arranged in 23 subject and geographical categories, A-Z by author. Includes monographs, journal articles, some government and international agency documents, and a few newspaper articles, mainly in English. ' ... excellent bibliographic survey ... ' (*International journal of legal information*,v.17 (1), Spring 1989, p.70-71). *Class No:* 336.60(01)

Handbooks & Manuals

[2113]
CROSSAN, R. and **JOHNSON, M. The Guide to international capital markets, 1991.** London, Euromoney Publications plc, 1991. [6],270p. 75. ISBN: 1855640708.

An earlier ed. was issued in 1988, edited by B. de Caires.

26 chapters: 1. Introduction - 2-22, each on a country's currency (Australian dollar...US dollar), with data on growth and development of the market, market size; breakdown of investors by type; regulations affecting investment; listing, payment and delivery; secondary market activity - 23. Swaps - 24. Commercial paper - 25. Medium term notes - 26. Corporate bond defaults and default rate. *Class No:* 336.60(035)

Dictionaries

[2114]
ROSENBERG, J.M. Dictionary of investing. New York, John Wiley & Sons, 1993. 368p. $39.95. ISBN: 0471574333.

First published l986 as *The Investor's dictionary*

*c.*8000 terms used by the securities exchange system, the commodity and futures exchange system, and the more recent development in US financial markets, are defined. Also includes commonly-used symbols, acronyms and abbreviations. Cross-references. Many words given multiple definitions based on their utilization in various fields of activity. Short definitions (*c.*2 to *c.*15 lines). '... both current and comprehensive'. (*RQ,* v.26(4), p.517) of the earlier edition. *Class No:* 336.60(038)

Great Britain

[2115]
1992 guide to grants for business. Martin, M., *comp*. Swindon, Associated Management Services, 1992. 119p. £39.50

UK government grants; grants from the EC; assistance from local government in the UK. Each type of grant treated according to a standard format - title, objective, benefits, eligibility, amount available, your costs, whom to contact. Compiler is a consultant for the DTI Enterprise Initiative (Marketing). Favourably reviewed in *Reference review,* v.6(3), 1992. *Class No:* 336.60(410)

[2116]

Government funding for United Kingdom business: a complete guide to sources, grants and application procedures. Walker, R., *and others, eds.* 8th ed. London, Kogan Page, 1993. 668p. £50. ISBN: 0749409614.

Aims to provide detailed information on the many financial assistance schemes available for business development from government departments and other public sector agencies. 8 main sections: General investment/business development - Employment and training - R & D - Exporting - Tourism and recreation - Community and social projects - Transport and freight - Agriculture, forestry and fisheries support. Information for each scheme is in 14 sections. Cross-references. Text is taken directly from the AIMS online grants information service of the European Policies Research Centre. *Class No:* 336.60(410)

Handbooks & Manuals

[2117]

Handbook of market leaders. London, Extel Financial Ltd., 1976- 2pa. *c.*750p each issue. £185pa.

A comprehensive reference book detailing 650 British companies listed in the *Financial times actuaries all share index.* Arranged A-Z by firm, with a page allocated to each. Information includes chairman, registered office, profit and loss record, ordinary share record, net asset value, cash flow, dividend, etc. *Class No:* 336.60(410)(035)

Monetary System

Worldwide

[2118]

FRASER, R., *comp.* **The World financial system, 1944-86;** a comprehensive reference guide. Harlow, Essex, Longman Group, Phoenix, Ariz., Oryx, 1987. xiv, 582p. £50; $95. (*A Keesing's reference publication.*) ISBN: 0582902789, UK; 089774473x, US.

A guide to the evolution of the international monetary system, including extracts from key documents and decisions of the period. Part 1 is a comprehensive historical analysis of international monetary relations from the Second World War to 1986 in 23 chapters; part 2 has information on over 50 major international or regional organizations in the monetary or financial sphere grouped into general economic organizations, monetary and development organizations, and trade associations; part 3 outlines the International Development Strategy for the Third UN Development Decade (1981-90) and the New International Economic Order together with the programme of action. Appendices include data on membership growth of the UN and IMF, and patterns of currency fluctuation, 1970-86. Select bibliography, p.565. Detailed general index, p.567-82. '... well-produced ... a concise and very comprehensive guide to the increasingly complex world monetary system' (*Reference reviews,* v.2(1), March 1988, p.9).

A 2nd ed., which claims to be fully updated, was issued in 1992 by Longman Group and by Gale International Research Co.in 1992 (600p. £95;$165. ISBNs 0582209064 (UK) & 0882096529 (US)). *Class No:* 336.7(100)

Biographies

[2119]

Who's who in international banking. 6th ed. London, Bowker-Saur, 1993. xvii,625p. £125. $225. ISBN: 1857390407.

Concise biographical information on *c.*4000 leading bankers worldwide, plus a banking directory spanning 130 territories. The biographies cover the main aspects of the entrant's personal and professional life, with special emphasis on professional career and interests. The directory includes full contact details and an index of senior executives of the banks. *Class No:* 336.7(100)(092)

Europe—Western

[2120]

Banking in the EC: structure and sources of finance. London, Financial Times Business Information, 1991. xvi,363p. tables. ISBN: 1853341428.

Arranged by country, A-Z. For each country an introduction is followed by sections on banking control and supervision; banking institutions; banking associations; organizations which mobilise and guarantee credit; financial intermediaries; the markets; financing of firms by banks; export finance; business organization; banks [in the country]. *Class No:* 336.7(400)

Great Britain

Handbooks & Manuals

[2121]

TEMPERTON, P. A Guide to UK monetary policy. London, Macmillan Press, 1986. xxiv,165p. tables, diagrs., figs. £35. ISBN: 0333392084.

Aims to be the definitive guide to the current analysis and operation of monetary policy in the UK. A glossary of terms precedes the 9 chapters (Background to the introduction of monetary targets in the UK - Monetary targets in the UK - Analysing broad money - Analysing narrow money - Setting short term interest rates: the policy process - Setting short term interest rates in the money market - Funding the PSBR and monetary growth - The gilt edged market - Conclusion). Two appendices: 1. Official interest rates, 1932 to 1985; 2. Monetary policy measures, 1970 to 1985. Index, p.159-165. *Class No:* 336.7(410)(035)

Histories

[2122]

CAPIE, F. *and* **WEBBER, A. A Monetary history of the United Kingdom, 1870-1982.** Vol.1: Data, sources, methods. London, Allen & Unwin, 1985. xxiv,596p. tables. £40. ISBN: 004332097x.

Research project undertaken by the Centre for Banking and International Finance, City University, for The Economic and Social Research Council. Vol.2 will provide analyses.

In 3 parts: 1. Monetary aggregates and proximate determinants - 2. Components of the monetary aggregates and monetary measures - 3. Money and banking data series. 4 appendices. Bibliography, p.580-588. Index, p.589-596. '... provides all the sources of the primary data and outlines

.... *(contd.)*

in painstaking detail the methodology and the transformations employed' (*Economic history review,* August 1986, p.475-6. *Class No:* 336.7(410)(091)

Banking

Bibliographies

[2123]

BURGESS, N. **How to find out about banking and investment.** Oxford, Pergamon Press, 1969. xii, 300p. facsims. £7.00. ISBN: 0080130453.

27 chapters; 1. Careers - 2. Dictionaries and encyclopedias - 3. Libraries and guides to libraries - 4. Bibliographies and literature guides - 5. Periodical literature - 6/27 (subject chapters, using the Dewey classification). Appendices: 1. Proceedings of the International Banking Summer School - 2. Societies and institutions. The detailed index (p.287-300) includes author/title entries. British slanted. *Class No:* 336.71(01)

[2124]

WELCH, J.M. **Free bank letters as sources of economic and financial information.** In *Journal of business and finance librarianship,* v.1(2), 1990. p,5-17.

Includes an appendix 'List of bank letters by country'. U.S., then by country, A-Z, with name of bank and title of newsletter only. *Class No:* 336.71(01)

[2125]

WILSON, C.R. **The World Bank Group:** a guide to information sources. New York, Garland, 1991. xviii,322p. $45. ISBN: 0824044290.

A bibliography citing books, articles, pamphlets, reports and dissertations by and about the International Bank for Reconstruction and Development, the International Development Association, and the International Finance Corporation of the World Bank Group. Over 1000 entries for items published or translated into English (mainly US sources) from 1944 through 1988 or later. Annotated. Cross-references. Indexes of names, divisions/affiliates, subjects and titles. *Class No:* 336.71(01)

Dictionaries

[2126]

Banking terminology. 3rd ed. Washington, American Bankers Association, 1989. 409p. $34. ISBN: 0899823602.

Concise definitions (1-5 sentences in length) of terms and concepts used in banking. Cross-references. 5 appemdices includes a list of acronyms and abbreviations, bank performance ratios, and a glossary of economic indicators. '... does a good job defining some of the more popular terms and concepts used in banking ...' (*Booklist,* v.86(15), 1 April 1990, p.1573). *Class No:* 336.71(038)

[2127]

COLLIN, P.H. **Dictionary of banking and finance.** London, Peter Collin Publishing, 1991. [v],260,[17]p. £6.95 ISBN: 0948549122.

Vocabulary of *c.*4000 words and expressions covering a range of topics relating to personal and corporate finance. Quotes for examples are given in boxes. British and American usage. *Class No:* 336.71(038)

Polyglot

[2128]

RICCI, J. **Elsevier's banking dictionary:** English/American, French, Italian, Spanish, Portuguese, Dutch and German. 3rd rev & enl. ed. Amsterdam, Elsevier, 1990. x, 360p. £85. ISBN: 0444886674.

2765 numbered entries in English/American, with equivalents and indexes in the other 6 languages. Includes phrases such as 'Mutilated cheque' and 'Token payment'. *Class No:* 336.71(038)=00

[2129]

SCHARF, T. *and* SHETTY, M.C. **Dictionary of development banking:** a compilation of terms in English, French and German, with definitions in English. Amsterdam, Elsevier, 1972. vii, 214p. £66.18. ISBN: 0444410287.

First published in 1969.

Over 1,200 terms arranged in 3 broad sections: the environmental framework - development banking - development banks. Each section subdivided. Indexes in each of the 3 languages. *Class No:* 336.71(038)=00

English

[2130]

HANSON, D.G. **Dictionary of banking and finance:** a commentary on banking, financial services and corporate and personal finance. London, Pitman Publishing, 1985. x,691p. £39.95. ISBN: 0273018590.

Successor to *Thomson's dictionary of banking* (12th ed. 1974), first published in 1912.

Provides comprehensive coverage of the whole range of financial activities, both corporate and personal. Many cross-references. *Class No:* 336.71(038)=20

[2131]

PERRY, F.E. **Dictionary of banking.** 4th ed. revised by G. Klein. London, Pitman Publishing, in association with The Chartered Institute of Bankers, 1992. 368p. £14.95. ISBN: 0273037889.

First published 1977, by Macdonald & Evans.

A comprehensive dictionary of *c.*7000 words and expressions, including jargon, a wide selection of French and German terms, and many cross-references. Fully updated, and directed towards bankers in any position, with particular emphasis on British bankers serving abroad in one or other countries of the European Community. *Class No:* 336.71(038)=20

German

[2132]
FELDBAUSCH, F.K. Bankwörterbuch/Banking dictionary.
Deutsch-Englisch, Englisch-Deutsch. 3rd ed. München,
Verlag Modern Industrie, 1984. 400p. £27.90. $85. ISBN:
3478512409.
First published 1972.
About 10,000 terms in each part, German-English and
English-German. Terms are those used in the US, Britain,
Germany, Austria and German-speaking Switzerland.
Country origin of terms is shown.
Class No: 336.71(038)=30

[2133]
ZAHN, H.L. Wörterbuch für das Bank- und Börsenwesen.
Deutsch-Englisch, Englisch-Deutsch. Dictionary of
banking and stock trading. 3rd ed. Frankfurt am Main, F.
Knapp; London. Pitman, 1984. viii,440p. New ed. in
preparation, 1994. ISBN: 3781920224, German;
071215471x, UK.
First published 1982.
Contains *c.*11,000 terms in current use and practice.
Primary sources were documentation used by banks,
financial dailies and reports of international lending
activities. A specialist dictionary, economic terms outside the
field of banking and stock trading being omitted. Short
explanations of terms given as necessary. Designed to meet
the needs of bankers and translators.
Class No: 336.71(038)=30

[2134]
—**KLAUS, H.**, *ed.* Banking dictionary: English-German. 7th
rev. ed. Bern, P. Haupt: London, Macdonald & Evans,
1990. 220p. £16.95. *Class No:* 336.71(038)=30

French

[2135]
KLAUS, H., *ed.* **Banking dictionary:** English-French/French-
English. Association Suisse du Employés de Banque. Bern,
P. Haupt, 1987. 264p. £20.50. ISBN: 3258033404.
Class No: 336.71(038)=40

Reviews & Abstracts

[2136]
World banking abstracts, 1984-. Oxford, Blackwell, for the
Institute of European Finance, 1984-. 6 pa. £250 pa. ISSN:
02659484.
over 400 current banking finance magazines and journals,
plus research reports and studies, are reviewed for each
issue. Sections, each subdivided, are: Institutions -
Instruments and markets - Operations and services -
Management, accounting and technology - Policy, law and
regulations- International and national economics - Principles
and methods. There is a list of periodicals and an index.
Class No: 336.71(048)

Yearbooks & Directories

[2137]
The Bankers' almanac and year book ... 1993. 148th year.
East Grinstead, London, Reed Information Services, 1993.
Annual. 3v. ISBN: 0611008149.
V.1 & 2 is a directory of some 4000 major international
banks and their 165,000 branches worldwide arranged A-Z

....(contd.)
(name, address, telephone/telex/fax numbers, history,
ownership, president, managing director, head of
international division, correspondents, consolidated balance
sheet, meetings (dates), wholly-owned subsidiaries), etc. V.3
has a geographical listing of those banks and their branches.
Also an index of banks in the Almanac for the first time and
those which have merged or changed name since the last
edition. *Class No:* 336.71(058)

[2138]
Directory of European banking and financial associations.
Molyneux, P., *comp.* Cambridge, Woodhead-Faulkner;
Chicago, St. James Press, 1990. xxi,217p. $65. ISBN:
0859416534, UK; 155862077x, US.
Details of the financial infrastructure of 20 European
countries. Introduction: Trends and developments in
European banking. Part 1: Europe - general; pt.2: Europe by
country (Austria ... West Germany). Each section
subdivided - banking; capital markets; insurance; other
associations and organizations. Appendix of late entries.
Index of offices, p.203-6. Index of organizations, p.207-14.
Index of publications, p.215-7. *Class No:* 336.71(058)

[2139]
Who owns what in world banking. Power, E., *ed.* 3rd ed.
London, Financial times business information, 1993. x,180p.
ISBN: 1853342017.
First published in 1983.
A directory of the world's major banks, their subsidiaries
and affiliates and, in the case of consortia, their shareholder
banks. Information on each includes name, address,
description, financial summary, subsidiaries and associate
companies, etc., and foreign offices. No introduction. Index
of banks, p.143-180. *Class No:* 336.71(058)

Almanacs

[2140]
Banker's almanac 3000 world ranking, 1994. 11th ed. East
Grinstead, Sussex, Reed Information Services, 1993. £121.
ISBN: 0611008076.
First published 1985. Annual.
A list of main exchange rates used precedes the 3 main
sections, each section on a different coloured paper. On
yellow paper is an A-Z index of 3400 banks. On white
paper, the country rankings of 160 individual countries, A-Z
by country, with information on current and previous rank,
name of bank, location of registered office, total assets in US
dollars, indication where figures consolidated, growth in
assets from previous year, capital in US dollars, date of
balance sheet. On green paper, world rankings, rankings by
assets of *c.*3100 international banks with similar information
to the above. *Class No:* 336.71(059)

Histories

Bibliographies

[2141]
VAN DILLEN, J.G. History of the principal public banks.
London. Frank Cass, 1934 (reprinted 1964). xii, 480 p. £28.
ISBN: 0714612553.
Includes extensive bibliographies of the history of banking
and credit in 11 European countries (p.355-480). Also
'Modern bibliography of banking and currency (British

....(contd.)

Empire) from the XVth century to 1815', compiled under the direction of J. H. Clapham (p.449-56).
Class No: 336.71(091)(01)

Laws

[2142]

Paget's law of banking. Megrah, M. *and* Ryder, F.R., *eds.* 9th rev. ed. London, Butterworths, 1982. lxxv,678p. £60. ISBN: 0406333521.

26 sections arranged in 4 parts: I: Banker & customer; II: Cheques and other orders for payment; III: Security for advances; IV: Commercial credits: international banking. Appendices : Uniform customs and practice for documentary credits; The Cheque Act, 1957. Detailed subject index, p.607-678. *Class No:* 336.71(094.1)

Great Britain

Histories

[2143]

GRADY, J. *and* **WEALE, M. British banking, 1960-85.** London, Macmillan, 1986. vii, 232p. tables. £29.50. ISBN: 0333375084.

Describes the evolution of the banking system since 1960 in 9 chapters: 1. An overview of the economy - 2. Risk and financial institutions - 3. Bank of England control and supervision - 4. The traditional banking system - 5. The accepting houses - 6. The new money markets - 7. The other British non-clearing banks - 8. International problems - 9. Conclusions. Notes and references to the chapters, p.207-211. Glossary, p.213-5. Bibliography of 162 items and 21 statistical sources. Index. *Class No:* 336.71(410)(091)

Archives

[2144]

PRESSNELL, L.S. *and* **ORBELL, J.,** *and others.* **A Guide to the historical records of British banking.** Aldershot, Hants., Gower Publishing Ltd., 1985. xxv,1300p. £25. ISBN: 0566035421.

Describes the surviving records of over 600 operating or defunct banks in England, Scotland and Wales. A section on the use of the guide (Archive resources of the British banking community - Functions and structure of British banking - Use of historical records of banks) precedes the A-Z list of records, which gives the name of the bank, location, history, records and records location. Information relates to 639 banks. Select bibliography, p.118-122, arranged A-Z by author. Index to lists of records, p.123-130. *Class No:* 336.71(410)(091)(093.20)

Germany

[2145]

MARSH, D. The Bundesbank: the bank that rules Europe. London, Heinemann, 1992. 359p. £18.99. ISBN: 0434451169.

A detailed account of the nature and role of the organization, together with an examination of the political and economic changes, including German unification. *Class No:* 336.71(430)

Bank of England

Histories

[2146]

CLAPHAM, J. The Bank of England: a history. Cambridge, Cambridge University Press, 1944 (reprinted 1958). 2v. (x, 305p.; [4], 460p.).

V.1, 1694-1797; v.2, 1797-1914, with an *Epilogue: The Bank as it is,* which takes the history to immediately before the Second World War. Written at the invitation of the authorities, treatment is chronological, tracing in detail the growth of bank practices (the use of bills and discounts, the insurance of currency, establishment of the reserve rates, use of cheques) and also records the role of the Bank in relation to contemporary political and economic happenings. Numerous footnotes. V.1 has 8 chapters and 6 appendices (F: The books of the Bank, to end of eighteenth century). V.2 also has 8 chapters and 6 appendices, mainly financial tables. Also an analytical index to both volumes, p.443-460. *Class No:* 336.711(091)

[2147]

—ACRES, W.M. The Bank of England from within, 1694-1900. London, printed for the Governor and Company of the Bank of England by Oxford University Press, 1931. 2v.

Deals more with internal and staff matters than does Clapham. V.2 includes a list of directors of the Bank, and of principal officials, 1694-1900, plus a 'List of the principal banks, pamphlets, etc. referred to in the text' (p.633-40). General, analytical index also in v.2. Numerous footnote references are listed in v.1, p.xv-xvi. *Class No:* 336.711(091)

[2148]

SAYERS, R.S. The Bank of England, 1891-1944. Cambridge, Cambridge University Press, 1976. 3v. (409, 313, 411p.). New ed. in 1v. (1986. 680p. £30. ISBN 0521310229). ISBN: 0521214750.

A history of the Bank. V.1 and 2 have 22 chapters arranged chronologically, followed by a list of publications cited in the text (p.655-659) and an analytical index. V.3 contains 42 appendices relating to the text of v.1 and 2, the final ones being a list of governors and other officers of the bank, a chronological list of events with chapter references, a list of committees, and references to unpublished sources. '... this most stimulating and enjoyable contribution to monetary (and economic) history by the doyen of monetary historians' (*The Economic journal,* v.,87, March 1977, p.145). *Class No:* 336.711(091)

Savings Banks

[2149]

HORNE, H.O. A History of savings banks. London, Oxford University Press, 1947. xv, 407p. ports., maps. *Class No:* 336.72

Building Societies

[2150]

Building societies year book: official handbook of the Building Societies Association, with Council of Mortgage Lenders yearbook. 1993-94 ed. London, Franey & Co Ltd., 1927-. Annual. 848p. £58. ISBN: 0900382694. ISSN: 00683566.

Data on each building society include names of directors

....*(contd.)*

and abridged balance sheet. Geographical list of building society offices. List of members of the Building Societies Association and Building Societies Institute. Geographical directory of surveyors, valuers, auctioneers, estate agents. *Class No:* 336.732

[2151]
NORKETT, P. The Building societies facts file. Harlow, Essex, Longman Group Ltd., in conjunction with Tekron Publications Ltd., 1987. [4], 232p. £100. ISBN: 0582022363.

Designed to give a complete overview of the financial performance of all building societies in the United Kingdom. Arranged in three categories: large (total assets over £250m), medium (£25m-£250m), and small (under £25m). The societies are ranked according to total assets, and there is a financial data sheet for each, giving annual results for 5 years to 1986 in a standard format for easy comparison, and percentage analyses of income, expenditure and balance sheet items. An appendix lists all societies, A-Z. *Class No:* 336.732

Money (Currency)

[2152]
DUNKLING, L. *and* ROOM, A. The Guinness book of money. New York, Facts on File, 1990. 191p. 24 illus. $19.95. ISBN: 0816025207.

Aimed at those only averagely versed in business and finance, a compilation of facts and literary quotations about money. Mini-glossaries define monetary slang throughout the ages. 2 indexes: quotations and references - subjects. 'A good addition to a reference collection' (*RQ*, v.31(1), Fall 1991). *Class No:* 336.74

[2153]
WESTON, R. Gold: a world survey. Beckenham, Kent, Croom Helm, 1983. ix,406p. charts, tables. £40. ISBN: 0709902026, UK; 0312331584, Australia.

6 parts: 1. The role of gold in the international monetary system, 1960-1980 - 2. The demand for gold, its forms and uses - 3/4. The supply of gold - 5. Spot and future market for gold - 6. How the price of gold is determined. Index. 'This book will be of great benefit to the specialist student of international economics. At the same time it is highly recommended for professional and financial analysts and advisers' (*British book news,* March 1984, p.169). *Class No:* 336.74

Bibliographies

[2154]
The International Monetary Fund. Salda, A.C.M., *comp.* Oxford, Clio Press, 1992. xxxviii,295p. £41. (*(International organizations,4)*.) ISBN: 1851091491.

A bibliography of books and articles, mostly in English. Indexes of authors, titles and subjects. *Class No:* 336.74(01)

[2155]
—JOHNSON, M.E. The International Monetary Fund, 1944-1992: a research guide. New York, Garland, 1993. 486p. $73. (*(Research and information guides in business, industry and economic institutions, 9)*..) ISBN: 0815302304.

An annotated bibliography of English-language monographs and articles. *Class No:* 336.74(01)

Handbooks & Manuals

[2156]
EDWARDS, A.D.P. The Exporter's and importer's handbook on foreign currencies. London, Macmillan, 1990. 192p. £40. ISBN: 0333534190.

22 chapters, including: A background to foreign exchange - The Eurocurrency market ... Selling and buying currencies ... What is a forward rate? ... Currency options - Financial futures ... The Treasury function ... Buying from UK importing agents - Conclusion. Glossary. *Class No:* 336.74(035)

[2157]
SUTTON, W. The Currency options handbook. Cambridge, Woodhead-Faulkner, 1988. [5], 208p. £45. ISBN: 0859413233.

Describes how options are traded and discusses their uses. Part 1. Inside currency options; part 2. Hedging foreign exchange risk using currency options; part 3. Currency option trading strategies; part 4. Conclusion. Glossary of terms. Bibliography (21 items). Index (p.207-8). Author is in charge of foreign currency options trading in London for Merrill Lynch.

A 2nd ed. was issued in 1990 (224p. £65. ISBN 0859416658). *Class No:* 336.74(035)

Dictionaries

[2158]
EATWELL, J., *and others, eds*. Money. London, Macmillan Press, 1989. 352p. £17.50. ISBN: 0333495268.

A series of reprints from *The New Palgrave: a dictionary of economics* (*qv*), gathering together 42 essay-length contributions on the subject of money. *Class No:* 336.74(038)

Yearbooks & Directories

[2159]
COWITT, P.P., *ed*. World currency yearbook. 24th ed. Brooklyn, NY., International Currency Analysis Inc., 1985. 974p. illus., tables. $225. ISBN: 0917645015.

Continues *Pick's currency yearbook*, published from 1955 to the 22nd ed. 1977-1978 (1979).

Descriptions of 145 major currencies, under countries, A-Z, preceded by a monetary glossary (p.10-13), 9 essays on currencies and a supplementary currency list. Also includes an essay on the Eurocurrency Market, and a central bank directory. Index (p.967-74) is of countries and currencies.

A 26th ed. for 1988/1989 was issued in 1991 (900p. $250. ISBN 0917645030). *Class No:* 336.74(058)

[2160]
—PICK, F. *and* SÉDILLOT, R. All the monies of the world: a chronicle of currency values. New York, Pick Publishing Corporation, 1971. xviii,, 613p.

Original ed. as *Toutes les monnaies du monde. Dictionnaire des changes,* by R. Sédillot (Paris, Sirey, 1955. 555p.). Translated by Carol J. Golden.

About 1500 concise entries, arranged A-Z under countries and currencies, with definitions and historical accounts of monetary systems. Cross-references. Bibliography, p.612-3. *Class No:* 336.74(058)

Histories
[2161]
A New history of the Royal Mint. Challis, C.E., *ed.* Cambridge, Cambridge University Press, 1992. 816p. illus. 92 tables. 79 maps. £95. ISBN: 0521240263.

The development of English minting from its origins in the 7th century down to the highly mechanised factory production of today. 5 chapters on the location of minting, the chronology and size of output, mint personnel and organization, and the main technology employed. 2 appendices: Output from 1200 to 1985; Mint contracts for 1279-1817. Select bibliography. *Class No:* 336.74(091)

[2162]
VILAR, P. A History of gold and money, 1450-1920. London, Verso Editions, 1984. 360p. 5 maps. £6.95. ISBN: 0860917983.

First English ed. 1976. Translated from the Spanish by J. White.

36 chapters, chronologically arranged, giving a comprehensive account of the role of bullion and currency since the beginning of the early modern epoch. A survey of the role of gold in its various forms of currency used in the ancient world and middle ages precedes an analysis of the gold and silver drive behind the voyages of discovery to Africa, America and Asia. Then traces banking and financial institutions. *Class No:* 336.74(091)

Bank Notes (Paper Money)

Great Britain
[2163]
MACKENZIE, A.D. The Bank of England note: a history of its printing. London, Cambridge University Press, 1953. x,163p. illus.

Covers the history of English banknote production up to the Second World War. More recently, *The search for the inimitable note,* by Clive Goodacre (*Penrose,* v.74, 1982, p.8-82) is an article on the subject profusely illustrated in colour. Whilst the classic work on the history of English coinage and paper money is A.E. Feaveayear's *The pound sterling: a history of English money* (2nd ed. rev. by E.V. Morgan. London, Oxford University Press, 1963, 458p.). *Class No:* 336.747(410)

Exchange Rates
[2164]
FLIGHT, H. *and* LEE-SWAN, B. All you need to know about exchange rates. London, Sidgewick & Jackson, 1988. 208p. £14.95. ISBN: 0283996269.

Aims to set out, for the layman, the intricacies of how the

....(contd.)
international monetary system functions. 17 chapters (Dispelling exchange rate myths - Setting the scene - Appraising currency movement - The balance of payments - The role of the Euromarkets ... Currency hedging instruments - Exchange rates and equity investment ... Man-made currencies ... Exchange-rate systems - The future outlook). Glossary, p.195-203. Analytical index, p.205-208. *Class No:* 336.748

Stock Markets & Exchanges

[2165]
The Money book: sources of finance and business information for businesses - from start-up to conglomerates. London, Mercury, 1993. 192p. £25. ISBN: 1852521120.

Aimed at professionals and lay people involved in raising money for new, emergent and established businesses. *Class No:* 336.76

Abbreviations & Symbols
[2166]
ROSENBERG, J.M. McGraw-Hill dictionary of Wall Street acronyms, initials, and abbreviations. New York, McGraw-Hill, 1992. 235p. $24.95. ISBN: 0070539340.

Over 10,000 entries for terms relevant to the stock and commodity markets. Overlaps with the *McGraw-Hill dictionary of business acronyms, initials, and abbreviations* (*q.v.*). *Class No:* 336.76(003)

Handbooks & Manuals
[2167]
GEISST, C.R. A Guide to the financial markets. 2nd ed. London, Macmillan Press, 1989. vi,164p. tables. £29.50. ISBN: 033348990x.

First published 1982.

Written from the investor's point of view, the guide discusses the 6 major financial markets - stock markets - money markets - bond markets - commodity future markets - options markets - new financial markets. Each chapter commences with basic definitions and ends with current problems. Notes follow each chapter. Index. *Class No:* 336.76(035)

[2168]
The Handbook of world stock and commodity exchanges. Oxford, Blackwell, 1993. Annual. [18],585p. 250. ISBN: 0631188886.

In 2 parts: Part 1 has 27 short essays. Pt.2 has market indices - International security market - then by country A-Z (Argentina ... Yugoslavia), with data on exchanges, including address, principal officers, brief history, structure, official trading hours, number of securities listed, securities traded, trading system, selling and clearing, commission rates and other client costs, taxation and regulations affecting foreign investors. Abbreviations and acronyms. Glossary. Indexes of personnel, contracts, exchanges, trading systems, and information vendors. *Class No:* 336.76(035)

Dictionaries

Polyglot

[2169]

THOLE, B.L.L.M., *comp*. **Elsevier's lexicon of stock-market terms.** English/American-French-German-Dutch. Amsterdam, Elsevier, 1965. [viii], 131p.

c. 1000 numbered English/American specialised terms relating to investment, bonds, shares and other securities, payments, coupons, dividends and conversions, etc., with equivalents and indexes in French, German and Dutch. Includes phrases *e.g.* 'Raise a dividend', 'General meeting of shareholders'), and states genders. Critically reviewed in *Lebende Sprachen* (v.14(2), March/April 1969,p.59) for omissions and mistranslations. *Class No:* 336.76(038)=00

[2170]

VALENTINE, S. **International dictionary of the securities industry.** 2nd ed. London, Macmillan Press, 1989. 300p. £45; $49.95. ISBN: 0333449738.

First published 1985.

Defines *c*.2000 terms and phrases used on the stock exchanges in North America, Great Britain, Netherlands, Japan, Italy, France, Germany and the Spanish-speaking world. Cross-references. Some single-item bibliographies. Revised and expanded principally because of the restructuring of the London stock market following the deregulation of The Stock Exchange, but the coverage of terms used in the other countries has also been revised and expanded. The author is Economic Adviser to The Stock Exchange. *Class No:* 336.76(038)=00

Yearbooks & Directories

[2171]

BATTLEY, N. **McGraw-Hill world futures and options directory, 1991-92.** Maidenhead, Berks, McGraw-Hill, 1991. 663p. £65. $95. ISBN: 0077073436.

8 sections: A. Exchanges - B. Agricultural contracts - C. Financial contracts - D. Metal contracts - E. Petroleum/gas-engineering contracts - F. Stock index and equity contracts - G. Miscellaneous contracts - H. Membership listings. Each section starts with a listing of contracts. '... well-produced ... providing clearly laid out information in a standardized format.'(*Reference reviews*, v.5(2), 1991, p.14). *Class No:* 336.76(058)

[2172]

Directory of world stock exchanges. Bootle, R., *ed.* Baltimore, MD., Johns Hopkins University Press; Cambridge, Woodhead-Faulkner Ltd., for The Economist, 1988. [6],469p. $89.50. ISBN: 0801837170, US; 085058275x, UK.

Data collected by questionnaire from 45 countries, is geared to professionals engaged in international trading. Entries include addresses of the stock exchanges; telephone/telex/cable/fax numbers; information on trading hours; the organization; type of securities traded; regulatory and tax regimes; lists of publications; historical background; and statistics of trading volume. *Class No:* 336.76(058)

[2173]

FITZGERALD, M.D. **Directory of financial futures exchanges.** London, Macmillan, 1987; New York, Stockton Press, 1988. xxv, 251p. £90; $180. ISBN: 0333390806 UK;; 0935859039 USA.

Intended to be a comprehensive directory of financial futures and options exchanges worldwide. Three introductory chapters explain the basic features of the financial futures market, followed by a directory section divided into exchanges, listing the types of contracts traded, and giving details of the members. There is a short bibliography of important books and articles, and a glossary of terms. *Class No:* 336.76(058)

[2174]

Handbook of world commodity and stock exchanges. Oxford, Blackwell, 1991. 482p. £225; $245. ISBN: 0631179313.

Part 1 has 31 brief essays dealing with the history and present concerns of various exchanges. Pt.2 is the directory of stock, equity, commodities, futures and option exchanges in 50 countries. Each is arranged by country, then name. Entries include address, telephone number, principal officers, brief history, structure, official hours, etc. A glossary defines unfamiliar terms. Commodity index. *Class No:* 336.76(058)

[2175]

The International Stock Exchange official yearbook, 1934-. 1993-1994 ed. London, Macmillan; New York, Stockton Press, 1993. lxiii, 958p. ISBN: 0333586980, UK; 156159105x, US. ISSN: 09536329.

Published by Skinner, 1934-1980; Macmillan, under licence from the International Stock Exchange of the United Kingdom and the Republic of Ireland 1981-. Annual. Title was *The Stock Exchange official yearbook* until 1987.

Contains details of all officially listed securities, fully indexed. Main sections are: The securities market in the UK; Overseas stock exchanges; Companies and public corporations in alphabetical order; List of companies in administration; List of companies in receivership; List of companies in liquidation; Register of defunct and other companies. Index (p.943-958). *Class No:* 336.76(058)

[2176]

—Register of defunct companies. London, Macmillan Press, in association with the London International Stock Exchange, 1990. 320p. £65. ISBN: 0333515293.

Lists companies removed from the London International Stock Exchange yearbook and its predecessors. *Class No:* 336.76(058)

[2177]

The Spicer and Oppenheim guide to securities markets around the world. Oliver, P.J. *and* Press, J., *eds.* New York, Wiley, 1988. vii,248p. $19.95. £17.50. ISBN: 0471612898.

First published 1986.

Focuses on 26 of the most important securities markets in the world, arranged A-Z (Australia ... United States of America), each with sections on stock exchanges - overview of bond and equity markets - futures and options trading - regulations affecting new entrants to the markets - outline of tax considerations - prospective developments. Also an actuaries world index; pound sterling index; securities markets around the world - a quick comparison; and

....(contd.)

international securities industry contact partners (names; addresses; telephone, telex and fax data).
Class No: 336.76(058)

Europe

Handbooks & Manuals

[2178]

STONHAM, P. Major stock markets of Europe. Aldershot, Hants, Gower Publishing Company, 1982. xv, 244p. diagr., tables. £40.50. ISBN: 0566003791.

Aims to assess the scale, importance and efficiency of six major European stock markets - Belgium, France, Germany, Italy, Netherlands and the United Kingdom. Presents information for each country on company financing; central government and local authority financing; structure and practice of stock exchange; performance and efficiency of stock market; new legislation and stock market reform; other prescriptions for stock market reform; and fiscal, company and savings/investment incentives. A summary is followed by notes and references. *Class No:* 336.76(4)(035)

Great Britain

[2179]

Studies in capital formation in the United Kingdom, 1750-1920. Feinstein, C. *and* Pollard, S., *ed.* Cambridge, Clarendon Press: C.U.P., 1988. £48. ISBN: 019828408x.

A comprehensive and highly specialized collection of essays. This study 'supplies the first comprehensive set of national estimates of capital formation and capital stocks from the Industrial Revolution to the First World War.'(*British book news*, March 1991, p.154).
Class No: 336.76(410)

Tables & Data Books

[2180]

The Stock Exchange daily official list. London, Extel Financial Ltd., on behalf of the Council of the London Stock Exchange, 1843-. Daily.

Cites the quotations for securities, plus data on business actually transacted. Government, then commercial and industrial companies arranged in broad groups under various subject headings. The *List* is a complete and official record of price movements from day to day. Important not only in investment activities but also as the accepted basis for estate duty, probate valuations and investment holding-values in balance sheets. *Class No:* 336.76(410)(083)

[2181]

—Weekly official intelligence. London, Extel Financial Ltd. on behalf of the Council of the London Stock Exchange, 1882-. £186 per half-year.

Until recently titled 'Stock Exchange weekly official intelligence'.

Contains the official notices of the Council and various data, including dividends, meetings, new issues, etc.
Class No: 336.76(410)(083)

Eire

[2182]

THOMAS, W.A. The Stock exchanges of Ireland. Liverpool, Francis Cairns, 1986. [8],273p. 9 illus. plus 8 black & white plates. £30. (*Studies in financial and economic history, v.1.*) ISBN: 0905205340.

The history of the Irish stock exchanges in 12 chapters, beginning in the late 18th century and reaching, in chapter 11, the unificiation of British and Irish exchanges in 1973 and the 'Big Bang' in 1986. Chapter 12 is on the Belfast Stock Exchange. Appendices have information about public loans raised in Ireland, limited company registrations, turnover on the exchanges, etc. Sources used include offical reports, business archives, the *Journal of the House of Commons*, etc. *Class No:* 336.76(417)

Investment

[2183]

CHAPMAN, K. Investment statistics locator. Phoenix, Ariz., Oryx Press, 1988. 182p. $45.00. ISBN: 0897743679.

An annotated list of 22 basic sources of statistics about stocks, bonds, and other investment vehicles, describing their characteristics and offering hints for efficient use. Detailed A-Z index lists topics and identifies sources that publish statistics on those topics. There is also a list of title abbreviations used in the index. US slanted. A welcome update of James Woy's *Investment information: a detailed guide to selected sources* (Gale, 1970). '... important for effective retrieval of financial statistics'. (*Wilson library bulletin*, May, 1988, p.111). *Class No:* 336.767

[2184]

MASEY, A. Financial Times guide: investment trusts. London, Financial Times Business Information, 1988. [6],195p. £8.95. ISBN: 1853340189.

21 chapters (1. Introduction to investment trusts - 2. What is an investment trust? ... 4. How investment trusts work - 5. Investment trusts versus unit trusts ... 13. How to choose investment trusts ... 16. Reading the charts and ratios - 17. How to read the reports and accounts ... 21. The future. 5 appendices, mainly statistical plus a directory of management companies. Glossary, p.178-185. Index, p.187-195.
Class No: 336.767

[2185]

STOPP, C. Financial Times guides: unit trusts. London, Financial Times Business Information, 1988. [7],176p. £8.95. ISBN: 1853340170.

10 chapters (Why should you buy unit trusts? - What are you buying - Looking at performance - How to choose a unit trust - Unit trusts for income - How to deal in units - Getting advice - Getting technical: pricing, distribution, and tax - Unit trusts or insurance bonds - The future for unit trusts). Appendices: 1. Guide to the groups; 2. Guide to the stock markets. Glossary, p.159-167. Index, p.169-176.
Class No: 336.767

[2186]

WILLIAMSON, G.K. The Longman investment companion: a comparative guide to market performance. Harlow, Essex, Longman, 1990. vi,162p. 71 illus. £20.50. ISBN: 0884628329.

7 topical chapters on bonds, currencies, interest rates, market indicators, mutual funds, stocks, and tangibles. Each

....*(contd.)*

entry describes the investment vehicle (over 70 in all), plus 20-year and year-by-year performance tables. *Class No:* 336.767

Dictionaries

[2187]
HILDRETH, S.S. The A to Z of Wall Street: 2500 terms for the street smart investor. Harlow, Essex, Longman Group Ltd., 1988. 299p. tables, charts. $13.95; £9.95. ISBN: 088462711x.

2500 investment terms defined in non-technical language. Overlaps considerably with *Words of Wall Street* and *More words of Wall Street.* 'Main problem involves the precision and fullness of its definitions' (*Reference books bulletin,* 1 March 1988, p.1101). *Class No:* 336.767(038)

[2188]
SCOTT, D.L. Wall Street words. Houghton Mifflin, 1988. xi,404p. $18.95. ISBN: 0395437474.

Defines 3600 investment terms encountered in US financial journals and newsletters. Definitions are in non-technical language. Includes a brief annotated bibliography of outstanding books on the investment field. *Library journal* (15 February 1988, p.160) prefers *Barron's finance & investment handbook (q.v.). Class No:* 336.767(038)

[2189]
—PESSIN, A.H. *and* ROSS, J.A. More words of Wall Street: 2000 investment terms defined. New York, Dow-Jones-Irwin, 1986. v,269p. $35. ISBN: 087094701x.

Companion volume to *Words of Wall Street,* defining terms in lay language. Includes abbreviations, acronyms, slang, basic investment words and phrases. Entries often amplified with examples. Cross-references. *Class No:* 336.767(038)

[2190]
—PESSIN, A.H. *and* ROSS, J.A. Still more words of Wall Street. New York, Business One Irwin , 1990. 292p. $18. ISBN: 1556233299.

A sequel to the above. *Class No:* 336.767(038)

[2191]
THOMSETT, M.C., *comp.* **Investment and securities dictionary.** Jefferson, NJ, McFarland, 1986. vii, 328p. charts, tables. $29.95. ISBN: 0899502253.

Definitions of more than 2000 technical words and phrases used by US investment professionals and financial planners. Definitions are clear and concise, often with tables, charts and graphs. Cross-references. The dictionary proper is followed by an alphabetical list of more than 170 abbreviations used in the securities industry; a section describing for lay persons what is contained in prospectuses or offering documents; and a bond classification list showing various classes of debt securities and distinctions between them. *Class No:* 336.767(038)

Yearbooks & Directories

[2192]
Allied Dunbar investment and savings guide, 1993. Robinson, C.P., *ed.* London, Longman Group Ltd., 1993. 468p. £19.99. ISBN: 0752000209.

First published for 1980/81. Annual.

Contains a wide range of investment know-how. 8 main

....*(contd.)*

sections, all subdivided: 1. The investor and his investment policy - 2. Real property - 3. Securities - 4. Business ventures (without pariticpation in management) - 5. Collective investment media - 6. Life assurance - 7. Commodities - 8. Alternative investments. Most sections end with lists of sources of further information. Useful addresses, p.300. Index, p.301-317. *Class No:* 336.767(058)

[2193]
Macmillan directory of international asset managers. Scott-Roberts, F. London, Macmillan Press, 1989. 300p. £95. ISBN: 0333494156.

Directory of the leading investment fund managers, A-Z by name. Data includes address; telephone/telex/fax numbers; company history; profiles of investment managers; size of funds under management; list of major clients; management fees; expenses; management policy and objectives; global asset allocation; statistical performance and performance ranking. *Class No:* 336.767(058)

Great Britain

Yearbooks & Directories

[2194]
Unit trust year book, 1993. London, Financial Times Business Information, 1993. Annual. 587p. £95. ISBN: 1853340707.

The year book is published in April each year and there is an *Autumn update* published in September.

The official year book of the Unit Trust Association, it covers 160 management groups and 1215 authorised unit trusts funds. In 3 sections: 1: Unit trusts:commentary and reference; 2: Statistics; 3: Management groups and unit trust details. Section 3 includes a directory of management groups (giving details of address, telephone number, telex, fax; funds managed; history) and details of the unit trusts (group, trustee, date formed, type of fund, investment, number of securities, unit accounts, portfolio distribution, trust record, etc.). *Class No:* 336.767(410)(058)

USSR

[2195]
SLAVENS, T.P. Sources of information for investors in the Commonwealth of Independent States (formerly: The Soviet Union). In *The Reference Librarian,* no.40, 1993, p.107-119.

Sections: Periodicals - Statistics - Economic theory - Economic conditions - Commerce - Dictionaries - Bibliographies. Short descriptions. *Class No:* 336.767(47)

USA

Venture capital

[2196]
SILVER, D.A. Who's who in venture capital. 3rd ed. New York, John Wiley & Sons, 1986. 468p. $29.95. £28.95. ISBN: 047101172x.

First published 1984.

In two sections: the first has four chapters on opinion, fact, concepts, ideas, etc.; the second, of 350 pages, has details of more than 600 funds and more than 1100 venture

....(contd.)

capitalists throughout the United States. 'As a reference book for both entrepreneurs, fund managers, and private investors looking for funds in the United States, it is extremely useful'. (*International small business journal,* v.6(2), January-March 1988, p.85-86). *Class No:* 336.767(73)VEN

Economic Surveys

[2197]
WORLD BANK. World development report, 1993. 16th. New York, Oxford University Press, for the World Bank, 1993. xii,329p. tables. ISBN: 0195208900. ISSN: 01635085.

First published 1978 (1979).

Designed to provide a comprehensive, continuing assessment of global development issues. The 1993 report examines the role of financial systems in development, preceded by a chapter reviewing recent trends. Bibliographical note. Statistical appendix. *Class No:* 338

Handbooks & Manuals

[2198]
Chisholm's handbook of commercial geography. Entirely rewritten by Sir Dudley Stamp. Blake, G.N. *and* Clark, A.N., *eds.* 20th ed. London & New York, 1980. xxxii,984p. tables, maps.

First published 1889.

4 main sections: 1. General factors affecting the production and distribution of commodities - 2. Circumstances connected with the exchange of commodities (transport, etc.) - 3. Commodities - 4. Regional geography (Europe ... Australia, New Zealand and the Pacific Islands, p.319-905). 6 appendices (1. Distribution maps (13); 3. International trade (statistics); 6. Conversion tables. Analytical index, p.933-84. 106 tables in main text. Standard text-book. *Class No:* 338(035)

Reports Literature

[2199]
CITY UNIVERSITY. Business School. Working paper series, 1977-. London, City University, 1977-. 4pa.

A series of working papers on the subject of research in business and management studies, some of which are bibliographies (*e.g. The recruitment and retention of hospital auxiliary staff: a review of the literature and bibliography,* by A.P.O. Williams and others (1977), *The marketing of financial services: a bibliography.* by F.A. Johne and J. Montgomery-Smith (1978), and *Product policy and development in manufacturing firms: an annotated bibliography,* by F.A. Johne and Patricia A. Snelson (1987). *Class No:* 338(047)

Maps & Atlases

[2200]
Oxford economic atlas of the world. Jones, D.B., *ed.* 4th ed. London, Oxford University Press, 1972. viii, 239p. tables, maps. £20. ISBN: 0198941064.

Prepared by the Cartographic Department of the

....(contd.)

Clarendon Press, and first published 1954.

91p. of maps in colour. 13 sections: Environment - Crops - Livestock - Forestry and fishing - Fibres and textiles - Energy - Minerals and metals - Transport industries - Manufacturing industries - Demography - Disease - Society and politics - Surface and air communications. Index-gazetteer of *c.*4000 names of places and specific sites (*e.g.* mines, dams). Statistical supplement, p.117-239): countries, A-Z; statistics largely for 1963-65, with 1953-9 comparisons. Page size, 37.5 x 28.5 cm. Oxford regional economic atlases: *Western Europe* (1971. 162p.);*U.S.S.R. and Eastern Europe* (New ed., 1971. 140p.); *India and Ceylon* (1953. 141p.); *Pakistan* (1955. 142p.); *Middle East and North Africa* (1960. 143p.); *Africa* (1971. 230p.); *United States and Canada* (2nd ed. 1975. 176p. *Class No:* 338(084.3)

Histories

[2201]
The Cambridge economic history of Europe. Cambridge, Cambridge University Press, 1941-89. 8v. in 9v. illus., tables, maps. £45-£75. ISBN: 0521045053, v.1; 0521087090, v.2; 0521045061, v.3; 052104507x, v.4; 0521087104, v.5; 0521045088, v.6; 0521215900 & 0521215919, v.7-2 vols; 0521225043, v.8.

1: The agrarian life of the Middle Ages (2nd ed. 1966) 2: Trade and industry in the Middle Ages (2nd ed. 1987) 3: Economic organization and policies in the Middle Ages 1963) 4: The economy of expanding Europe in the sixteenth and seventeenth centuries (1967) 5: The economic organization of early modern Europe (1977) 6: The industrial revolutions and after: incomes, population and technical change (1965) 7: The industrial economies: capital, labour and enterprise. 1. Britain, France, Germany and Scandinavia (1978) 2. The United States, Japan, and Russia (1978) 8: The industrial economies: the development of economic and social policies (1989). Originally planned by Sir John Clapham and Eileen Power, aiming to provide an authoritative survey of an aspect omitted from the Cambridge medieval and modern histories. Terminal date is mid-20th century. *Class No:* 338(091)

[2202]
HEICHELHEIM, F. M. An Ancient economic history, from the Palaeolithic Age to the migrations of the Germanic, Slavic and Arab nations. Rev. and complete English ed. Leiden, 1958-70. 3v.

Original as *Wirtschaftgeschichte des Altertums* (1938, 2v; bibliography, p.863-1277). Translated by Mrs Joyce Stevens. *Class No:* 338(091)

Periodicals & Progress Reports

[2203]
The Economic history review, v.1, no.1-. 1927-. Oxford, Basil Blackwell Ltd., for the Economic History Society (previously by several other publishers). £54;$95 pa. ISSN: 00130117.

2nd series, v.47(1), February 1994 contains 5 articles (*e.g.* 'The industrial revolution and British imperialism, 1750-1850';'The Australian role in Britain's return to the gold standard'); one article in a series 'Surveys and speculations'. A book review section contains 24 book reviews; and there is a review of periodical literature, 1992.

....(contd.)

The 4th issue each year includes 'List of publications on the economic and social history of Great Britain and Ireland published in the previous year'. Keys to earlier volumes: *Economic history review: an index to the first series, v.1-18, 1927-48* (Utrecht, Oosthoek, 1965. 59p. £4.50); *Economic history review: index to second series, v.1-23, 1948-70* (Welwyn Garden City, Broadwater Press Ltd., 1972. £7.95). *Class No:* 338(091)(05)

Worldwide

Bibliographies

[2204]

ORGANISATION FOR ECONOMIC CO-OPERATION AND DEVELOPMENT. Catalogue of publication. Paris, OECD. Annual (previously biennial), with quarterly supplements. *c.*100p. Gratis.

A sales list of OECD publications. 12 sections in the 1989 edition (published early 1989 and including publications on sale as at 1st January 1989): General economic analysis and forecasting - Energy - Development and aid - Labour market and social problems - Industry: science and technology - Financial and fiscal affairs - Accounting standards, competitions and consumer policy - Education - Environment - Regional development, public management - Food, agriculture, fisheries - Transport, tourism. A-Z of series, titles and authors. *Class No:* 338(100)(01)

[2205]

Predicasts F & S index Europe. Cleveland, Ohio, Predicasts Inc., 1978-. Monthly. Quarterly and annual cumulations. ISSN: 02704536.

A companion volume to *Predicasts F & S index international.*

Indexes articles and news items relative to the European Communities countries, other Western European countries, and Eastern Europe. Database 1970-.

Class No: 338(100)(01)

[2206]

—**Predicasts F & S index United States.** Cleveland, Ohio, Predicasts Inc., 1960-. Quarterly. Annual cumulations. $850pa. ISSN: 02704544.

Title was *F & S index of corporations and industries* from 1960 to 1978.

Indexes articles and news items on US corporations and industries. Database, 1970-. *Class No:* 338(100)(01)

[2207]

Predicasts F & S index international. Cleveland, Ohio, Predicasts Inc., 1967-. Quarterly. Annual cumulation. $800pa. ISSN: 02704528.

Formerly F & S international.

Indexes articles and news items, being complementary to *Predicasts F & S index United States.* In 3 sections: 1. Industry and product (arranged by industry group, preceded by list of groups and subdivisions); 2. Countries, by region; 3. Companies, A-Z. Now limited to Canada, Latin America, Africa, Middle East, and Oceania. Also available online. *F & S index plus text* (1991-) is the CD-ROM version.

Class No: 338(100)(01)

[2208]

World development. Oxford, Pergamon Press, 1972-. Monthly. £462pa. ISSN: 0305750x.

A multidisciplinary journal on the social, economic and political consequences of development, focusing on reforms and co-operative efforts to eliminate disease, poverty and illiteracy. Includes a section of 'Book notes'.

Class No: 338(100)(01)

Handbooks & Manuals

[2209]

GREAT BRITAIN. Department of Trade and Industry. Hints to exporters visiting... London, the Department. £6 each.

Continues *Hints to businessmen.*

About 100 country reports, revised bienially. Topics include preparation for the trip, travel and currency information, economic factors, import and exchange control regulations, methods of doing business and general information. Maps. *Class No:* 338(100)(035)

Reviews & Abstracts

[2210]

ECONOMIST INTELLIGENCE UNIT. Country reports. London, the Unit, 1952-. diagrs., charts, tables. £160. $315 pa for 4 quarterly issues per country.

Early title was *Quarterly economic review series.*

There are reviews for 180 countries, each containing an executive summary; an outlook section on political and economic prospects for the next 12-18 months; a 10-20p. review section analysing political developments, government policies, trends in production and demand, monetary and fiscal conditions, etc.; statistical appendices. Valuable, if expensive, economic digests. *Class No:* 338(100)(048)

Yearbooks & Directories

[2211]

ORGANISATION FOR ECONOMIC CO-OPERATION AND DEVELOPMENT. OECD economic surveys. Paris, OECD, 1953-. illus., tables. Annual. £110; $195 pa. ISSN: 03766438.

Previously as *Economic conditions in member and associated countries* and originally part of the O.E.C.D. annual report, 1949-52.

Country surveys, mostly north and western European, but including Japan, US, Canada, Yugoslavia, Turkey, Australia and New Zealand in a full year, although some countries are surveyed every other year (*e.g.* 17 countries were surveyed in 1989/90). Such published reports are agreed documents, and analyse recent developments and immediate prospects (demand; output; wages and prices; money and capital markets; balance of payments; government policies and the problems facing them. *Class No:* 338(100)(058)

[2212]

—**ORGANISATION FOR ECONOMIC CO-OPERATION AND DEVELOPMENT. OECD economic outlook.** Paris, OECD, 1960-. 2pa. £29.00; $25; Ff.150. ISSN: 04745574.

Published in June & December each year.

Surveys the latest economic developments in the OECD area and assesses future prospects. Includes up-to-date statistical information on the growth of real GNP and GDP, development of domestic demand, employment, output, foreign trade, productivity, etc. *Class No:* 338(100)(058)

[2213]

—ORGANISATION FOR ECONOMIC CO-OPERATION AND DEVELOPMENT. OECD economic outlook - historical statistics, 1960-1989. 3rd ed. Paris, OECD, 1991. 170p. £14; $26; Ff110 ISBN: 9264033483.

First published 1987, covering 1960-1985.

Shows how OECD countries' economies have evolved since 1960, expressed in terms of rates of change or percentage shares. The statistics provide the historical background to the *O.E.C.D. economic outlook's* current analysis and forecasts. *Class No:* 338(100)(058)

[2214]

UNITED NATIONS. Department of International Economic and Social Affairs. **World economic survey, 1993: current trends and policies in the world economy.** New York, United Nations, 1993. 273p. tables, graphs. $55. £42. ISBN: 9211091268. ISSN: 00841714.

First published 1949-. Annual. Initially *World economic report,* a continuation of the League of Nations *World economic survey* (1927-44. 11v.).

7 chapters: 1. The state of the world economy - 2. Trends in global output and policies - 3. International trade - 4. Saving, investment and the international transfer of resources - 5. Energy - 6. Conversion and the peace dividend - 7. Entrepreneurship. Annex: 39 tables. Explanatory notes precede, and sources are given in footnotes.

Class No: 338(100)(058)

Tables & Data Books

[2215]

LIESNER, T. **One hundred years of economic statistics.** New ed. of *Economic statistics, 1900-1983,* revised and expanded to 1987. London, Economist Publications,1990. viii,344p. charts, tables. ISBN: 0850582792.

Presents time series, mainly from the 1950s, for UK, USA, Australia, Canada, France, Germany, Italy, Japan and Sweden. Includes trends and cycles in the total economy; growth of output by sector and commodity; capital formation; income and expenditure; prices; earnings and productivity ; employment and unemployment; population; education; trade and balance of payments; finance; transport; and energy. Data taken predominantly from official sources. Detailed notes explain how the series were constructed from diverse sources and normalized. Final section shows cross-national comparisons for 16 variables.

Class No: 338(100)(083)

[2216]

MOORE, G.H. *and* MOORE, M.H. **International economic indicators:** a sourcebook. Westport, CT. Greenwood Press, 1985. ix,373p. $45; £42.50. ISBN: 0313219893.

An in-depth study of the economic indicators of the world's major industrialized nations, undertaken as part of the long-term project of The Center for International Business Cycle Research (CIBCR). '... a most useful body of data to apply to a variety of historical analyses' (*Journal of economic history,* June 1986, v.46(2), p.580).

Class No: 338(100)(083)

[2217]

ORGANISATION FOR ECONOMIC CO-OPERATION AND DEVELOPMENT. **Main economic indicators, 1965-. Monthly.** Paris, OECD. £144pa; $195pa; F.950pa. ISSN: 04745523.

Contains *c.*1500 economic indicators appearing in major statistical bulletins published by OECD member countries. 1. Indicators by subject - 2. Indicators by country - 3. Appendix: Gross domestic product; purchasing power parities; comparative price levels; exchange rates; population. A historical volume is published from time to time: *Main economic indicators: historical statistics,* 1962-1991 (1993, 368p. $58. F.240. ISBN 9264038736).

Class No: 338(100)(083)

[2218]

—Indicators of industrial activity. Paris, Organisation for Economic Co-operation and Development, 1979-. Quarterly. £26.30; F.225; $50pa. ISSN: 02504278.

Continues *Industrial production: quarterly supplement to 'Main economic indicators'*.

Provides an overall view of short-term economic developments in different industries for all OECD member countries, including indices of output, orders, prices and employment. *Class No:* 338(100)(083)

Bibliographies

[2219]

VERWEY, G. *and* RENOOIJ, D.C. **The Economist's handbook:** a manual of statistical sources. Amsterdam, Economist's handbook, 1934. Supplement, 1937. (Reprinted in 1.v. Detroit, Mich., Gale Research Co., 1971). viii,1460p.; iii, 79p. $65. ISBN: 0810337282.

The main section consists (p.39-200) of subjects, arranged A-Z with country sub-division. Column form is used to facilitate reference, sources of information being given in the right-hand column. An equally extensive section follows (p.203-415) listing the sources quoted (general; then by countries A-Z; then by frequency of publication - annual, quarterly, monthly, etc.) with notes on their scope. Finally, an A-Z index of sources. Countries drawn upon are: Belgium, France, Germany, Netherlands, Switzerland, the UK and USA. The Supplement lists additional source material and gives corrigenda. Now largely of historical value only. *Class No:* 338(100)(083)(01)

Developing Countries

Yearbooks & Directories

[2220]

Third World directory. Stubbs, L., *ed.* 2nd ed. London, Directory of Social Change, 1993. *c.*130p. £9.95. ISBN: 187386003x.

lst published in 1990.

A guide to over 200 development organizations, covering their history, geography, major projects, and future plans. Also volunteering opportunities and research into trusts. Index. *Class No:* 338(4/9-77)(058)

Europe

Bibliographies

[2221]
Sources of European economic and business information.
University of Warwick. Business Information Service. 5th
ed. Aldershot, Gower Publishing Group, 1989. 288p. £75.
ISBN: 0566026589.

First published 1974.

*c.*6000 entries, covering 32 countries of Western and
Eastern Europe. Part 1 lists source publications
(International, then A-Z by country, subdivided by title. For
each numbered entry - publisher, country coverage,
frequency, language, and brief description). Pt.2 lists the
publishing bodies. Indexes list the sources alphabetically, by
subject, and by country. *Class No:* 338(4)(01)

Yearbooks & Directories

[2222]
UNITED NATIONS. Economic Commission for Europe.
Economic survey of Europe, 1992-1993. New York,
United Nations, 1993. ix,291p. tables, map. £42. ISBN:
9211165555. ISSN: 00708712.

First published for 1946/47. Annual.

5 chapters: 1. The transition economies in 1992-1993: an
overview - 2. Macro-economic developments and outlook -
3. International economic relations - 4. The hard road to
market economy: problems and policies - 5. Explaining
unemployment in the market economies: theories and
evidence. 6. Statistical appendices (A. Western Europe and
North America; B. Eastern Europe with the Soviet Union;
C. International trade and payments). Tables and charts
throughout. Data for 1992-93. Kept up-to-date by the
Economic Bulletin for Europe (1948-. Quarterly).
Class No: 338(4)(058)

Histories

[2223]
The Fontana economic history of Europe. Cipolla, C.M., *ed.*
London, Collins/Fontana Books, 1973-76. 6v. graphs,
tables, maps.

V.1 *The Middle Ages* - 2. *The sixteenth and seventeenth
centuries* - 3. *The Industrial Revolution* - 4. *The emergence
of industrial societies* - 5. *The twentieth century* (in 2 parts) -
6. *Contemporary economies* (in 2 parts). Designed to fill a
gap, by covering Europe both as a whole and in terms of
individual countries, 'concise enough for convenient use and
yet full enough to include the results of individual and
detailed scholarship' (Series note). *Class No:* 338(4)(091)

Bibliographies

[2224]
WILSON, C. *and* **PARKER, G.,** *eds.* **An Introduction to
the sources of European economic history, 1500-1800.
V.1: Western Europe.** London, Weidenfeld & Nicolson,
1977; Cornell University Press, 1978. xxx, 256p. diagrs.,
tables. $32.50. (*World economic history series.*) ISBN:
0801411092.

Was to be in two volumes, the second volume dealing with
Northern, Central and Eastern Europe.

7 chapters on Italy, Spain the Low Countries, the British
Isles, France and Germany, each divided by subjects,

....(contd.)
including population, industry, currency and finance, wealth
and social structure, etc. 90 tables and 104 diagrams; notes
and references (p.224-245). 13 contributors.
Class No: 338(4)(091)(01)

Europe—Western

[2225]
Western Europe 1993: a political and economic survey.
London, Europa, 1993. 500p. £165 ISBN: 0946653747.

A series of essays on important issues and topics relating
to the region as a whole, is followed by detailed country
surveys (geography - recent history and politics - economy -
social affairs - media - transport - tourism) containing text,
statistics, directory material and maps for each Western
European country. Additionally, there is a list of addresses,
and a select bibliography for each country (most references
are to English-language publications). *Class No:* 338(400)

Handbooks & Manuals

[2226]
West European economic handbook. London, Euromonitor
Publications Ltd., 1987. xii, 184p. tables, charts. £45.
ISBN: 0863381421.

Examines the political, economic and social structure of
the European Communities and the other principal countries
of Western Europe. 9 chapters: 1. West Europe: an
international perspective - 2. The European Communities: its
economic role in Europe today - 3. Political and defence
issues - 4. Pan-European economic trends - 5. Finance and
banking in Europe - 6. Industrial development in Europe - 7.
External trade flows and patterns - 8. The European market -
9. Future outlook. *Class No:* 338(400)(035)

Europe—Eastern

Bibliographies

[2227]
ABSEES (Abstracts: Soviet and East European series): a
journal of Soviet and East European economic affairs.
London, British Association for Slavonic and East European
Studies (previously Oxford, Pergamon Press and Glasgow
University Institute of Soviet and East European studies),
1970-. v.1, no.1-. 3 pa (previously quarterly). $695 pa.
ISSN: 00445622.

Primarily a microfiche journal; each issue has printed
summaries.

Subject coverage: Agriculture - COMECON - Economic
planning - Economic policy and theory - Finance - Foreign
trade and payments - Industry and construction - Labour and
wages - Management - Science and technology - Social
questions - Tourism - Trade and services - Transport and
communications. Subject index only.
Class No: 338(401)(01)

[2228]
O'RELLEY, Z.E. Soviet-type economic systems: a guide to
information sources. Detroit, Mich., Gale Research Co.,
1978. 228p, $68. ISBN: 0810313065.

Lists and annotates books and journal articles in English
relating to the economies of Bulgaria, Czechoslovakia,
German Democratic Republic, Hungary, Poland, Rumania

....(contd.)

and the Soviet Union. Arrangement is under broad subject headings (*e.g.* prices and inflation, labour force, foreign trade, efficiency and productivity). *Class No:* 338(401)(01)

Handbooks & Manuals

[2229]

East European economic handbook. Smith, A.H. London, Euromonitor Publications Ltd., 1985. vi,325p. tables, 8 maps. £45; $70. ISBN: 0863380298.

A regional overview precedes separate chapters on the economies of 7 nations: Bulgaria, Czechoslovakia, German Democratic Republic, Hungary, Poland, Romania and Yugoslavia. Consideration is given to political factors affecting economic performance, the country and its people,. government and political organization, economic growth, economic planning, etc. A 'Fact file' has 20 statistical tables comparing the countries along various economic variables. *Class No:* 338(401)(035)

Great Britain

[2230]

ALDCROFT, H. The British economy. v.1.$aThe years of turmoil, 1920-1951. Hemel Hempstead, Herts., Wheatsheaf Books Ltd., 1986. vii,264p. £28.50. ISBN: 0710801149.

The first volume of what is intended to be an extended study of the British economy from 1920 to the present day.

8 chapters (Chequered decade: the 1920s - Depression and recovery, 1929-1939: an overview - Economic policy and recovery: external policy - Macroeconomic policy in the 1930s - Regional and industrial policies - Natural forces of recovery - The war economy and its consequences - Facing the future with Labour, 1945-1951), with 102 notes. Select reading, p.253. Political glossary - chief economic Ministers, p.254-258, chronological arrangement. Index, p.259-164. *Class No:* 338(410)

Bibliographies

[2231]

GREAT BRITAIN. HM Stationery Office. **Government publications. Sectional list 3, revised June 1988: Energy, trade and industry.** London, HMSO, 1988. iv, 36p. *Gratis.*

Lists, with prices, publications of the Departments of Energy and of Trade and Industry. Sections: Serial publications and annual reports - Energy - Trade and industry (including Business Monitor). Index. *Class No:* 338(410)(01)

[2232]

—GREAT BRITAIN. Department of Trade and Industry. Libraries. Publications London, Department of Trade and Industry Headquarters Library and Information Centre. Annual. *Gratis.*

An annual list of publications issued by the Department of Trade and Industry, Department of Energy (now merged with the Department of Trade and Industry), Monopolies and Mergers Commission, Office of Electricity Regulation, Office of Fair Trading, Office of Gas Supply, and Office of Telecommunications, issued by the Departments and through HMSO. *Class No:* 338(410)(01)

Handbooks & Manuals

[2233]

MORT, D., *comp*. **The Counties and regions of the United Kingdom:** a statistical and economic review. Warwick Statistics Service. Rev. ed. Aldershot, Hants., Gower Publishing Company Ltd., 1988. 224p. £27.50. ISBN: 0566027550.

First published 1983.

A study of the main demographic, economic and employment trends in the 54 counties of England and Wales, the 12 regional and island areas of Scotland and Northern Ireland and its districts. Provides key statistics on population trends and characteristics, district sizes, unemployment, earnings, housing, industrial structure, and local authority expenditure. Bibliography. List of selected libraries/information services. *Class No:* 338(410)(035)

Tables & Data Books

[2234]

CAPIE, F. *and* **COLLINS, M. The Inter-war British economy:** a statistical abstract. Manchester, Manchester University Press, 1983. [5],118p. tables. £32.50. ISBN: 0719009014.

Mainly tables (142) and arranged in 8 sections: 1. Production - 2. Prices and retail sales - 3. Level of business activity - 4. Labour - 5. Overseas trade and shipping - 6. Money and banking - 7. Interest rates - 8. Capital. Index, p.117-118. *Class No:* 338(410)(083)

[2235]

Economic trends. Central Statistical Office. London, HMSO,.,1953-. no.1-. diagrs., charts, tables. Monthly. £155pa; £12.75 each issue. ISSN: 00130400.

Brings together all the main economic indicators, time series and graphs over the last five years or so. Preceded by several pages of current information, and followed by an analysis of indications in relation to the business cycle over the last 20 years. Other articles comment on and analyse economic statistics. *Class No:* 338(410)(083)

[2236]

First releases. London, Central Statistical Office: Press Office; Newport, Gwent, Business Statistics Office Library. *c.*100pa. Prices vary.

Continues *Business bulletins* from 1st January 1994.

Provides the statistical data previously published in *British business,* covering both sectoral and cross-sectoral data, as well as information of more general interest to business and commerce. *Class No:* 338(410)(083)

[2237]

—Business briefing. London, Association of British Chambers of Commerce. Weekly. .

Aims to provide business-related news items drawn from government and private sector sources, together with some statistical information. An attempt to replace in part the defunct *British business. Class No:* 338(410)(05)

Maps & Atlases

[2238]

Atlas of industrializing Britain, 1780-1914. Langton, J. *and* Morris, R.J., *eds.* London, Methuen, 1986. 272p. illus., tables, maps. £25. ISBN: 0416302904.

Aimed at teachers, the atlas is arranged in 31 chapters (Physical environment - Population - Regional structure and

....*(contd.)*

change - Agriculture - Rural settlement - Wages - Wind and water power - Coal and steam power - Transport - Sea trade - Textiles - Chemicals - Brewing and distillary - Leather footwear - Iron and steel - Shipbuilding - Engineering - Services - Banking and finance - Wealth and the wealthy - Poor law and pauperism - Urbanization - Retail patterns - Labour protest, 1780-1859 - Unionization - Popular institutions - Sport - Languages and dialects - Education - Religion - The electoral system). Sources of maps listed on p.228-235. Bibliography, p.236-246, A-Z by author.
Class No: 338(410)(084.3)

Histories

[2239]
FLOUD, R. *and* **McGLOSKEY, D.**, *eds*. **The Economic history of Britain since 1700.** 2nd ed. Cambridge, Cambridge University Press, 1984. 3v. (432; 536; 400p.). tables. ISBN: 0521459613.

First published 1981 in 2v.

V.1. 1700-1860; v.,2 1860 to the 1970s; v.3 1939-1992. V.1 has 13 chapters in 5 overlapping chronological divisions, each division, except the last, beginning with a general survey followed by a number of chapters which consider the main problems which have arisen in the historical interpretation of that period. Each division, except first and last, conclude with chapters dealing with the social history of the period in relation to economic change. V.2 and v.3 follow the same pattern. Each volume has bibliographies, indexes and glossaries.
Class No: 338(410)(091)

Bibliographies

[2240]
CHALONER, W.H. *and* **RICHARDSON, R.C.,** *comps*. **Bibliography of British economic and social history.** New ed. Manchester, Manchester University Press, 1984. xiv, 208p. £36. ISBN: 0719008883.

First published in 1976 as *British economic and social history: a bibliography*.

5780 numbered entries for books and periodical articles. Sections: General works - England, 1066-1300 - England, 1300-1500 - England, 1500-1700 (General works; Population; Agriculture and rural society; Industry; Towns; Alien migrants; Commerce and colonization; The concept of mercantilism; Communications and internal trade; Prices, public finance, banking and financial dealings; Government policy and administration, law and order; Classes and social groups; Poor relief; Charity and the Poor Law; Labour; Standards of living; Civil War; Interregnum, Restoration and Revolution, 1640-89; Religion; Education and learning) - England, 1700-1970 (p.83-155) - Wales before 1700 - Wales after 1700 - Scotland before 1700 - Scotland after 1700 - Ireland before 1700 - Ireland after 1700. Index of authors and editors, p.186-208. A bibliography easy to consult.
Class No: 338(410)(091)(01)

Middle Ages

[2241]
BOLTON, J.L. The Medieval English economy, 1150-1500. London, Dent, 1980 (Reprinted 1985, Everyman Univ. Pubs.). 416p. £7.95. ISBN: 0460152742.

A general survey of 10 chapters: 1. Introduction: settlement and society - 2. Patterns of demand - 3. Overcrowded island - 4. The growth of the market - 5. Supplying the market - 6. Towards a crisis - 7. Crisis and change in agrarian reform - 8. Freedom versus restriction: town and countryside in the later Middle Ages - 9. English trade in the late Middle Ages: the triumph of the English - 10. Economics and ideas. Followed by conclusion, notes, a bibliography (p.357-378); and an index. 'An exemplary guide; (*TLS*, 26 September 1980, p.1069).
Class No: 338(410)"01/14"

19th Century

[2242]
PORTER, G.R. The Progress of the nation in its various social and economic relations from the beginning of the nineteenth century. 3rd ed. 1851 (Reprinted New York, Kelley, 1970). xvi, 735p. $5032. ISBN: 0678005389.

First published 1836; 2nd ed. 1846.

A statistical and descriptive study of the social, economic, commercial and fiscal changes which took place in the United Kingdom during the first half of the 19th century.
Class No: 338(410)"18"

Scotland

Periodicals & Progress Reports

[2243]
Scottish economic bulletin. Scottish Office. Edinburgh, HMSO, 1971-. no.1-. 2pa. £11.50 each issue.

No.48, Winter 1993/94 (ISBN 0114952353) includes an Economic review; Consumer prices in the Highlands and Islands; Scottish results of the 1991 census of employment: a statistical note; Charts and statistics: Main quarterly economic series; Main annual economic series; Articles published in recent issues of *Scottish economic bulletin*.
Class No: 338(411)(05)

Histories

[2244]
MARWICK, W.H. 'A Bibliography of Scottish economic history during the last decade: 1963-1970'. In *Economic history review*, 2nd series, v.24(3), 1971, p.469-479.

An evaluative running commentary. Sections: General - Medieval - The seventeenth century - The eighteenth century - The nineteenth and twentieth centuries. Preceded by the author's contributions to *Economic history review*, 2nd series, v.16(1), 1963, p.147-54; v.4(3), 1952, p.377-82; and v.3(1), 1931, p.117-37. *Class No:* 338(411)(091)

Ireland

Tables & Data Books

[2245]

KIRWAN, F. *and* **McGILVRAY, J. Irish economic statistics.** Dublin, Institute of Public Administration, 1983. 225p. illus., tables, map. £7.95. ISBN: 0906980143.

First ed., by J. McGilvray, published in 1968.

Designed as a guide to the sources, of collection, presentation and analysis of the major branches of economic statistics in Ireland. Bibliography, p.213-221. Index. *Class No:* 338(415)(083)

Northern Ireland

Histories

[2246]

KENNEDY, L. *and* **OLLERENSHAW, P.,** *eds.* **An Economic history of Ulster, 1820-1940.** Manchester, Manchester University Press, 1985. [6],248p. tables, maps. £25. ISBN: 0719017505.

Arranged in 7 chapters (1. The rural economy, 1820-1914 - 2. Industry, 1820-1914 - 3. Transport, 1820-1914 - 4. Population change and urbanisation, 1821-1911 - 5. Industrial labour and the labour movement, 1920-1914 - 6. The Northern Ireland economy, 1914-1939 - 7. The economic history of Ulster: a perspective. Many notes, including references, at the end of each chapter. Select bibliography, p.241-242, by chapter. Index of places, p.243-245; index of subjects, p.246-248. *Class No:* 338(416)(091)

Eire

Bibliographies

[2247]

PAGE, R. Sources of economic information: Ireland. Dublin, Institute of Public Administration, 1985. [5],112p. $19.95. ISBN: 0906980410.

Arranged in 21 subject sections A-Z: 1. Agriculture and fisheries 2. Balance of payments ... 19. Transport - 20. Data banks - 21. Journals, newspapers. Each section divided into official publications; other publications: Irish; other publications: British; publications of international organizations. Subject, title and author indexes. *Class No:* 338(417)(01)

Yearbooks & Directories

[2248]

EIRE. Department of Finance. **Economic review and outlook.** Dublin, Stationery Office, 1988. 56p. £2.60.

Published annually each summer.

Contains a detailed report on economic trends and includes an appendix of economic statistics. *Economic background to the budget,* published each January, is a companion volume summarizing economic development over the past year and assessing pre-budgetary prospects for the following year. *Class No:* 338(417)(058)

England

Histories

[2249]

CLAPP, B.W., *ed.* **Documents in English economic history: England from 1000 to 1760.** London, Bell, 1977 (Paperback ed. Bell & Hyman, 1984). 576p. £7.95. ISBN: 0713524693. *Class No:* 338(420)(091)

[2250]

—CLAPP, B.W., *ed.* Documents in English economic history: England since 1760. London, Bell, 1976. 544p.

For each volume the documents, and some comment, are arranged in 10 chapters: 1. General view - 2. Agriculture - 3. Evolution of industry - 4. Transport and internal trade - 5. Finance - 6. Foreign trade - 7. The workers - 8. Poor law and public health - 9. The consumer - 10. Economic policy and taxation. 'A valuable reference work' (*New history,* no.7, p.7). *Class No:* 338(420)(091)

Bibliographies

[2251]

WILLIAMS, J.B. A Guide to the printed materials for English social and economic history. 1750-1850. New York, Columbia University Press, 1926, (Reprinted Dublin, Irish University Press, 1968). 2.v.

About 7,500 selected entries - Pt.1., 'Works of general reference' (including bibliographies and catalogues; encyclopedias; local histories; biographies; in 11 sections) - pt.2, Special subjects (economic theory; economic conditions and questions; industry; social and economic conditions and movements; social political theory and movements; sections 12-16). All items are briefly annotated. V.2. includes author (plus brief title) and non-analytical subject indexes. *Class No:* 338(420)(091)(01)

Middle Ages

[2252]

HALL, H., *ed.* **A Select bibliography for the study, sources and literature of English mediaeval economic history.** London, King, 1914 (reprinted New York, B. Franklin, 1960). xiii, 350p. $23.50. (*Studies in economics and political science. Series of bibliographies, 41.*) ISBN: 0833715488.

Compiled by a seminar of the London School of Economics under the supervision of Hubert Hall.

A classified bibliography of 3200 items, with author and title index. Appended list of learned social journals and of periodicals. Still of considerable value on manuscript sources. *Class No:* 338(420)"01/14"

Wales

Yearbooks & Directories

[2253]

Welsh economic trends/Tueddiadau'r economi, 1992. Welsh Office. No.13. Cardiff, the Office, 1993. £10. ISBN: 0750402016.

First published for 1974. Annual.

Over 100 tables in 9 sections: Population - Regional income and expenditure - Earnings and hours - Personal incomes - Household income and expenditure - Industrial

....(contd.)

activity - Aids to industry - Capital expenditure - Public expenditure. Sources of further information are included in an appendix. *Class No:* 338(429)(058)

Germany

Periodicals

[2254]

Wirtschaft und Statistik. Stuttgart, Verlag Metzler-Poeschel, for Statistisches Bundesamt, 1921-. Monthly. DM.184pa. ISSN: 00436143.

About 50 pages of survey articles (economic survey; graphs on economic developments; economic indicators; price index) and 80-odd pages of statistical tables, with figures for previous months and years and cumulative statistical contents for the year. *Class No:* 338(430)(051)

German Democratic Republic

[2255]

The East German economy. Jeffries, E., *and others.* Beckenham, Kent, Croom Helm, 1987. [8],328p. figs., tables. £35. ISBN: 0709914695.

Surveys the current state of the East German Economy in 14 chapters: 1. The GDR in historical and international perspective - 2. Command planning and the production unit ... 4. The economic strategy of the 1980s and the limits to possible reforms ... 8. Product and process renewal in GDR economic strategy ... 10. The GDR financial system ... 13. The role of the GDR in Comecon: some economic aspects - 14. Economic reform of the GDR: causes and effects. 12 contributors. Glossary, p.306-313. References, p.314-322. Index, p.323-328. *Class No:* 338(430).2

[2256]

GERMAN INSTITUTE FOR ECONOMIC RESEARCH. Handbook of the economy of the German Democratic Republic. Pohl, R., *ed.* Farnborough, Hants., Saxon House, 1979. xxiv, 366p. tables. £27.50. ISBN: 0566002566.

First published in German in 1977.

Aims to give a comprehensive view of East German achievements and problems. In 7 chapters: 1. Economic development and basic factors - 2. Economic organizations and planning system - 3. National accounts - 4. Production in the individual economic sectors - 5. Use and distribution of product and incomes - 6. Foreign economic relations - 7. The GDR and the CMEA. Appendix of tables. Index. *Class No:* 338(430).2

Hungary

Bibliographies

[2257]

HORCHLER, G.F. Hungarian economic reforms: a selective, partially annotated bibliography. New Brunswick, The Hungarian Research Center, 1977. 190p. $8.95. (*Hungarian reference shelf, no.3.*) ISBN: 0686234057.

1620 entries, arranged by topics, are preceded by an initial section of references. bibliographical and serial publications. Covers books and articles, including those in a number of Western and Eastern European languages. Author index. *Class No:* 338(439)(01)

[2258]

—HANÁK, P. 'Short survey of recent literature on Hungarian economic history'. (in *Economic history review,* 2nd series, v.24(4), 1971, p.677-81).

An evaluative essay and select bibliography of 122 items in various languages. 3 sections: 1. Historical demography and historical statistics - 2. Economic history - 3. Social history. *Class No:* 338(439)(01)

France

Histories

[2259]

CARON, F. An Economic history of modern France. Translated from the French by Barbara Bray. London, Methuen, 1979 (Reprinted 1983). [xi],384p. illus., tables. £8.95. ISBN: 0416364705.

Part 1: The nineteenth century (1815-1914) (8 chapters, *e.g.* 5. The development of trade; 6. Agriculture) - Part 2. The twentieth century (Chapters 9-14; 14. State policy and business management, 1950-1973). Conclusions. Analytical index, p.371-84. Chapter bibliographies (mostly books and articles cited or directly used). Many tables. *Class No:* 338(44)(091)

Spain

[2260]

LIEBERMAN, S. The Contemporary Spanish economy: a historical perspective. London, Allen & Unwin, 1982. xiii,378p. tables, figs. £20. ISBN: 0043390269.

An introduction, 'Institutions and economic development: the Spanish case', is followed by 7 chapters: 1. Contemporary Spanish agriculture in historical perspective - 2. Agricultural policy since 1939 - 3. The long road to Spain's industrial revolution - 4. The Spanish industrial revolution of the 1960s - 5. The economic crisis of the 1970s - 6. The restoration of free trade unions - 7. Quo Vadis, Hispania? Notes and references follow each chapter. Bibliography, p.360-365, A-Z by author. Index, p.366-378. *Class No:* 338(460)

Bibliographies

[2261]

MACKAY, J. 'Recent literature on Spanish economic history'. In *Economic history review,* 2nd series, v.31(1), 1978, p.129-45.

Evaluative commentary, followed by a select bibliography of 204 titles in Spanish, arranged A-Z by author and indicating relevant pages as necessary. *Class No:* 338(460)(01)

[2262]

—HARRISON, J. 'Spanish economic history from the restoration to the Franco regime (essays in bibliography and criticism)'. In *Economic history review,* 2nd series, v.33(2), May 1980, p.259-75.

Follows up the earlier contribution by Mackay (*qv*) and includes 194 entries in the select bibliography. *Class No:* 338(460)(01)

Histories

[2263]

HARRISON, J. An Economic history of modern Spain. Manchester, Manchester University; New York, Holmes & Meier, 1978. xi,187p. £26.50; $32.50. ISBN: 0719007046, UK; 0841904111, US.

7 chapters take the history chronologically from the middle of the 18th century to early 1978, while an 8th chapter is devoted to the rise of organized labour from the beginning of the 1930s. Good bibliography of English-language works, mainly American. *Class No:* 338(460)(091)

[2264]

—**VIVES, J.V.,** *ed.* An Economic history of Spain. 3rd ed. Princeton, N.J., Princeton University Press, 1969. xii,825p.

Translated from the Spanish by F.M. López-Morillas, and first published in 1955. Includes an extensive bibliography. *Class No:* 338(460)(091)

USSR

Yearbooks & Directories

[2265]

USSR economic handbook. Scrivener, R.S., *ed.* London, Euromonitor Publications Ltd., 1986. viii,246p. tables. £45; $80. ISBN: 0863381561.

Examines the economy of the USSR from 1917 to the present day. 10 chapters: Soviet economic history and growth - The Soviet Union in a world context - Resources and planning - Industrial growth and production - Transport and communications - Agriculture, forestry and fisheries - Foreign trade and tourism - Finance and banking - The USSR a market for consumer goods - Outlook. Index and list of tables. *Class No:* 338(47)(058)

Tables & Data Books

[2266]

CLARKE, R.A. *and* **MATKO, D.J.I. Soviet economic facts, 1917-80.** 2nd ed. London, Macmillan Press, 1983. 244p. £33. ISBN: 0333333624.

First ed. by Clarke, covered 1917-1970, published in 1972.

A statistical compilation containing the most important economic statistics of the Soviet Union since the Revolution, and providing a set of recalculated figures by Western scholars for comparison. Compiled exclusively from Soviet original sources. *Class No:* 338(47)(083)

[2267]

—**TREML, V.G.** *and* HARDT, J.P., *eds.* Soviet economic statistics. Durham, N.C., Duke University Press, 1972. xii,457p. $37.50. ISBN: 0822502519.

A collection of 18 papers in 6 topic sections concerned with the evaluation of availability, credibility and reliability of Soviet statistical data, and with the intepretation of methodological and classification problems. *Class No:* 338(47)(083)

Maps & Atlases

[2268]

KISH, G. Economic atlas of the Soviet Union. 2nd ed. rev. Ann Arbor, University of Michigan Press; London, Cresset Press, 1971. 90p.

First published, 1960.

4 general maps of the Soviet Union. (vegetation, administrative divisions; air lines; population distribution), plus maps of 15 regions, 4 per region: A. Agriculture and land use - B. Mining and minerals - C. Industry - D. Transportation and cities. 3-colour clear maps; regional map scales vary from 1:6,000,000 to 1:12,000,000. Brief text on each region. Appended bibliography (mainly Russian sources) and index-gazetteer to regional maps. Page size, 26 x 26 cm. *Class No:* 338(47)(084.3)

Histories

Bibliographies

[2269]

KAZMER, D.R. *and* **KAZMER, Y. Russian economic history:** a guide to information sources. Detroit, Mich., Gale Research Company, 1977. x,520p. $68. (*Economic information guide series, v.4.*) ISBN: 0810313049.

Annotated, selective bibliography; 36 subject chapters on Russian economic history during the pre-revolutionary and Soviet periods. English-language sources published 1900-1974 (but omitting JPRS *Translations on USSR economic affairs*). *Class No:* 338(47)(091)(01)

20th Century

[2270]

HILL, R.J. The Soviet Union: politics, economics and society, from Lenin to Gorbachov. London, Frances Pinter, 1985. xix,232p. illus., tables, map. (*Marxist regime series.*) ISBN: 0861874463.

Basic data (p.xv-xvii) and glossary and list of abbreviations (p.xix) precede the 5 chapters: 1. History and political tradition - 2. Social structures - 3. The political system - 4. The economic system - 5. The regime's policies. Bibliography, p.211-223,. Index, p.224-232. *Class No:* 338(47)"19"

Finland

Yearbooks & Directories

[2271]

FINLAND. Ministry of Finance. Economics Department. **Economic survey.** Helsinki, Valtion Painatuskeskus, 1949-. Annual. Fmk 100.

Supplement to the annual budget proposal. The 1992 issue surveys the economy for recent years and forecasts it for 1993. 40 tables. Full Finnish and Swedish editions, abridged in English. *Class No:* 338(480)(058)

Sweden

[2272]

The Swedish economy. Stockholm, Konjunkturinstitut, 1960- 2pa. not priced. ISSN: 00397296.

Articles and statistical tables on the general economy. Many tables and graphs, sources and notes. English and Swedish editions. *Class No:* 338(485)

Asia

Bibliographies

[2273]

BLAUVELT, E. *and* DURLACHER, J. **Sources of Asian/ Pacific economic information.** Farnborough, Hants, Gower Publishing Co., Ltd., 1980. 2v.(408 p.; 384 p.). £35. ISBN: 0566022958.

A bibliography of sources (over 5000 descriptive entries). Areas covered include Japan, China, Australia, New Zealand, South Korea, Taiwan, Hong Kong, Thailand, the Philippines, Malaysia, Singapore, Indonesia, India, Pakistan, Sri Lanka, Bangladesh, Papua New Guinea annd the Pacific Islands. Title and subject (subdivided by country) indexes. *Class No:* 338(5)(01)

[2274]

CHEN, V. **The Economic conditions of East and Southeast Asia:** a bibliography of English-language materials, 1965- 1977. Westport, CT., Greenwood Press, 1978. lii,788 p. $125. ISBN: 0313205655.

Entries, mainly for journal articles, are arranged in a section for general works, and then in sections for the countries to which they refer, A-Z (Burma, Hong Kong, India, Japan, Malaysia, Philippines, Singapore, South Korea, Taiwan and Thailand), the entries in each section being preceded by an introduction mentioning important titles and including bibliographies. In each section entries are arranged by detailed subject headings, A-Z. Lists of journals and a list of subject headings are included. *Class No:* 338(5)(01)

[2275]

LEE, M.K.S.C., *ed.* **East Asian economics:** a guide to information sources. Detroit, Mich., Gale Research Company, 1979. x,326p. $68. ISBN: 0810314274.

An annotated bibliography of 1,700 selected English- language materials relating to the economies of China, Japan, South Korea and Taiwan, from 1900 to the present. In 7 chapters: 1-5 for Asia and the individual countries, each subdivided into general and 6 subject sections (Agriculture - Commerce and industry - Economic growth - International economics and trade - Labour - Finance); chapters 6 and 7, for journals and serials, and bibliographies, each subdivided geographically. Author, title and analytical subject indexes. *Class No:* 338(5)(01)

Handbooks & Manuals

[2276]

Asian economic handbook. Wong, J. London, Euromonitor Publications Ltd., 1987. [6],272p. tables, charts. £45; $80. ISBN: 0863381413.

A regional overview precedes economic profiles for 18 nations of the continent's four major regions: East Asia (Taiwan, Hong Kong, North Korea, South Korea, Macao), ASEAN countries (Malaysia, Indonesia, Singapore, the Philippines, Thailand), Indochina (Vietnam, Laos, Burma,

....(contd.)
Kampuchea), and the Indian sub-continent (India, Pakistan, Bangladesh, Sri Lanka). A statistical 'Factfile', with comparative statistics, supplements other statistical data included in the handbook. Index. *Class No:* 338(5)(035)

[2277]

The Pacific Basin: economic handbook. Sinclair, S. London, Euromonitor Publications Ltd., 1987. x,204p. tables, map. £45. ISBN: 0863381391.

10 chapters: 1. The Pacific Basin: the region and its importance to the world - 2. Political and economic issues - 3. Commodities and commodity trade - 4. Energy - 5. Banking and capital markets - 6. Social issues - 7. Manufacturing - 8. Trade - 9. The future of the Pacific Basin: problems and opportunities - 10. Statistical datafile (4 charts, 74 tables). List of tables. Index, p.195-204. *Class No:* 338(5)(035)

China

Bibliographies

[2278]

SCHMIDT, M. **Economic reforms in the People's Republic of China since 1979:** a bibliography of articles and publications in English-language magazines and newspapers. West Cornwall, CT., Locust Hill Press, 1987. xvi, 177p. $25. ISBN: 0933951108.

1898 unannotated items from more than 280 journals and newspapers in a classified arrangement (General economics - Economic growth, development, planning, fluctuation - Quantitative economic methods and data - Domestic monetary and fiscal theory and institutions - International economics - Administration, business finance, marketing, accounting - Industrial organization, technical change, industry studies - Agriculture: natural resources - Manpower, labour, population - Welfare programs, consumer economics, urban and regional economics). No sub-divisions. Author index. 'Heavy emphasis on well- known sources, but others included' (*Choice,* October 1987, p.290). *Class No:* 338(510)(01)

Handbooks & Manuals

[2279]

China economic handbook. Grummit, K.P. London, Euromonitor Ltd., 1986. 246p. tables, charts. £45. ISBN: 0863381553.

Includes 9 chapters covering the various aspects of China's economy: The historical background: Socialist economic development - The four modernizations - Human resources - Agriculture and rural developments - Industry and energy - Transport and communications - Foreign trade and tourism - Finance and banking - The new consumer markets. Also includes a bibliography (p.135-138); a directory of useful names and addresses; and statistical data from 1949 to about 1984. Index. *Class No:* 338(510)(035)

Japan

Yearbooks & Directories

[2280]

Japan: economic almanac, 1989. Tokyo, Japan Economic Journal: Nihan Keizai Shimbun Inc., 1989. 304p. illus. ISBN: 453205589x.

Formerly *Industrial review of Japan* (1956-84). First published 1985. Annual.

Includes sections on the economy, key trends, major industries, and a data file (chronology - directory - statistics (p.285-304). *Class No:* 338(52)(058)

[2281]

JAPAN. Economic Planning Agency. **Economic survey of Japan.** Tokyo, Japan Times Ltd., 1969-. Annual. 3900 yen; $23. ISSN: 00214833.

Superseded *Japanese economic statistics*.

The English-language edition of the Economic Planning Agency's annual economic white paper.

Class No: 338(52)(058)

[2282]

—BANK OF JAPAN. Economic statistics annual. Tokyo, the Bank, 1966-. ISSN: 09106006.

Contains annual statistics on money and banking, securities and public finance, balance of payments, and foreign exchange. Supported by the Bank's *Economic statistics monthly* (1946-). *Class No:* 338(52)(058)

Asia—Middle & Near East

Bibliographies

[2283]

BLAUVELT, E. *and* **DURLACHER, J., *eds.* Sources of African and Middle Eastern economic information.** Aldershot, Hants., Gower Publishing Co. Ltd., 1982.

Arranged in 2 parts: pt.1: Source publications; pt.2: The publishing bodies. Part 1 lists the sources by Middle Eastern country: part 2 has 2 indexes: 1. Sources listed alphabeticaly - 2. Sources by subject and country.

Class No: 338(53+56)(01)

Handbooks & Manuals

[2284]

Middle East economic handbook. Sinclair, S. London, Euromonitor Publications Ltd., 1986. [6],487p. tables, charts, maps. £45; $70. ISBN: 086338126x.

A regional overview precedes 19 chapters on individual Middle Eastern countries (Algeria ... United Arab Emirates), with discussions on the country's economy, political system, etc. A 'Factfile' of statistical data compares various economic aspects of the countries.

Class No: 338(53+56)(035)

Reports Literature

[2285]

The Middle East review: economic and business report, 1989. 15th ed. Saffron Walden, Essex, World of Information, 1989. 191 p. tables, maps. £25. ISSN: 03053210.

First published 1974. Annual.

A general chapter precedes chapters on individual

....(contd.)

countries, arranged A-Z (Afghanistan ... Yemen,PDR). For each chapter an introductory article is followed by key facts, key indicators, country profile, and business guide.

Class No: 338(53+56)(047)

Gulf States

Tables & Data Books

[2286]

KUBURSI, A. The Economics of the Arabian Gulf: a statistical sourcebook. Beckenham, Kent. Croom Helm, 1984. xi,206p. £45. ISBN: 0709915438.

A list of the 154 tables and an introduction precede the 10 subject sections of tables: 1. General statistics - 2. National statistics - 3. Oil and gas - 4. Trade and international transactions - 5. Population and employment - 6. Public finance - 7. Agriculture - 8. Industry - 9. Money and credit - 10. Education. Each section has a brief introduction and sources are indicated. *Class No:* 338(536)(083)

India

Yearbooks & Directories

[2287]

INDIA. Ministry of Finance (Economic Division). **Economic survey ... 1993-94** New Delhi, Government of India Press, 1993. 162p.+ 115p. of statistics. Rs.10; £2; $4.

Annual.

9 chapters on the economic situation are followed by an appendix of statistical tables, arranged in 9 subject sections, all subdivided. Data is for 1992/93.

Class No: 338(540)(058)

Histories

[2288]

The Cambridge economic history of India. Cambridge, Cambridge University Press, 1982-83. 2v. diagrs, tables, maps. v.1 £60; v.2. £80. ISBN: 0521226929, v.1; 0521228026, v.2.

V.1: *c.*1200-1750; edited by T. Raychaudhuri and L. Habib; v.2: *c.* 1757-*c.*1970; edited by D. Kumar and M. Desai.

Brings together the work of economists, historians, sociologists, social anthropologists and demographers, to summarize existing knowledge and undertake new research.

Class No: 338(540)(091)

[2289]

ROTHERMUND, D. An Economic history of India. London, Routledge & Kegan Paul, 1988. iv, 224p. £40. ISBN: 0709942281.

A summary of the structure and dynamics of the Indian economy from pre-colonial times to 1986. 12 chapters: 1. The structure of the traditional economy - 2. The development of maritime trade and the beginnings of colonial rule - 3. The agrarian State and the Company ... 10. India's dilemma; dynamic industrialization and static agriculture - 11. The 'Green Revolution' and the industrial recession -12. Population growth and economic development. Index. 'Focuses on 20th rather than 19th century and on issues of

....(contd.)

India's aborted growth and restricted development' (*The Economic history review*, second series, v.42(2), May, 1989. *Class No:* 338(540)(091)

Bibliographies

[2290]

Annotated bibliography on the economic history of India (1500 AD to 1947 AD). Gokhale Institute of Politics and Economics *and* Indian Council of Social Science Research. Colombia, Mo, South Asia Books, 1978. 4v.

V.1:(1) Selections from the records; (2) Survey and settlement reports; (3) Gazetteers; (4) Acts and regulations. V.2: (5) British parliamentary papers; (6) Reports of committees and commissions. V.3: (7) Census reports; (8) Serials. V.4: (9) Books; (10) Articles; (11) Theses. V. 1-3 are in the form of source materials, v.4 mostly research work. Statistical content annotated exhaustively. Subject, region and author indexes at the end of each part.
Class No: 338(540)(091)(01)

Thailand

Yearbooks & Directories

[2291]

BANK OF THAILAND. Annual economic report, 1991. Bangkok, the Bank, 1992. [4], 135p. *Gratis.*

First published 1943. Annual.

Contains a summary report on developments in 1991 and outlook for 1992. Also a report on the activities of the Bank in 1991. A statistical section has data to 1991. Information is updated by the Bank's *Quarterly Bulletin* (previously *Monthly bulletin*). 1961 -. ISSN 0125605x).
Class No: 338(593)(058)

Malaysia

Periodicals

[2292]

BANK NEGARA MALAYSIA. Quarterly bulletin, 1968-. Kuala Lumpur, the Bank. not priced. ISSN: 01278428.

Early title was *Quarterly economic bulletin.*

A review of economic conditions in Malaysia precedes a statistical section of 63 tables relating to money and banking, foreign trade and payments, production and prices, etc., with data for more than 10 years to the present.
Class No: 338(595)(051)

Islamic World

Bibliographies

[2293]

SIDDIQI, M. N. Contemporary literature on Islamic economics: a selected classified bibliography of works in English, Arabic and Urdu up to 1975. Jeddah. International Centre for Research on Islamic Economics; Leicester, Islamic Foundation 1978. [2], 69p. (*Research report.1.*)

700 entries arranged in 7 sections: Economic philosophy of Islam - Economic system of Islam - Islamic critique of contemporary economics - Economic analyses in Islamic framework - History of economic thought in Islam -

....(contd.)

Miscellaneous - Bibliographies. English translations of Arabic and Urdu titles are given in brackets. Author index.
Class No: 338(5.297)(01)

Africa

Bibliographies

[2294]

BLAUVELT, E. *and* **DURLACHER, J.,** *eds.* **Sources of African and Middle Eastern economic information.** Aldershot, Hants., Gower Publishing Co. Ltd., 1982. 320p.

Arranged in 2 parts: pt.1: Source publications; pt.2: The publishing bodies. Part 1 lists the sources by African country; part 2 has 2 indexes: 1. Sources listed alphabetically - 2 Sources by subject and country.
Class No: 338(6)(01)

Handbooks & Manuals

[2295]

African economic handbook. Hodd, M. London, Euromonitor Publications Ltd., 1986. [6],335p. tables, charts. £45; $70. ISBN: 0863380883.

A regional overview is followed by sections on East, West, Central and Southern Africa, covering Kenya, Sudan, Tanzania, Ghana, Ivory Coast, Nigeria, Cameroon, Congo, Zaire, South Africa, Zambia and Zimbabwe. For each country economic profiles with in-depth statistical data. No index. *Class No:* 338(6)(035)

Histories

[2296]

KONCZACKI, Z.A. *and* **KONCZACKI, J.,** *eds.* **An Economic history of tropical Africa.** London, Cass, 1977. 2v. (xx,310 & xv,260p.) illus., maps. £22.50 each vol. ISBN: 0714629197, v.1; 0714629154, v.2.

V.1: The pre-colonial period; v.2: The colonial period. Each volume reprints selected articles; v.1 having 28 articles in 7 subject groups, and v.2 having 22 articles in 5 subject groups. Index to each v. *Class No:* 338(6)(091)

Egypt

Periodicals

[2297]

Economic review. Cairo, Central Bank of Egypt, 1961-. Quarterly. ISSN: 00089249.

Each issue contains 1 or 2 articles, and sections on national developments, international developments, and statistics. The statistical section is mainly concerned with financial statistics, but also includes economic data.
Class No: 338(620)(051)

Africa—East & Equatorial

Bibliographies

[2298]
KILLICK, A. The Economies of East Africa: a bibliography, 1963-1975. Boston, Mass., G.K. Hall, 1976. xxiv, 150p.

Nearly 1000 entries for English-language printed publications, plus mimeographed items and government documents, on the economies of Kenya. Tanzania and Uganda. Arranged by subject areas. Two indexes - to subjects and places, and to authors, editors and chairmen. *Class No:* 338(67)(01)

[2299]
—KILLICK, A., *and others*. The Economies of East Africa: a bibliography, 1974-1980. Boston, Mass., G.K. Hall, 1984. $55. ISBN: 0816185832.

Nearly 2000 entries published between 1974-1980, focusing broadly on the economies of Kenya, Tanzania and Uganda. Brief introductory essays compare 1872 entries in this work with 968 entries in the previous one. 8 broad subject categories, each subdivded. Useful indexes and appendices include a list of abbreviations, about 30 frequently cited serials, author index and subject index. *Class No:* 338(67)(01)

South Africa

[2300]
JONES, S. *and* **MUELLER, A. The South African economy, 1910-1990.** London, Macmillan, 1992. 380p. 47.50. Maps. ISBN: 0333515307.

27 chapters in 3 parts: A: Laying the foundations of a modern economy; B: The open economy; C: The modern economy takes shape since 1961. Index. *Class No:* 338(680)

Handbooks & Manuals

[2301]
HOUGHTON, D.H. The South African economy. 4th ed. Cape Town, Oxford, Oxford University Press, 1976. xiii, 310p. illus., graphs tables, map. £12.50. ISBN: 0195700805.

First published 1964.

12 chapters relate the economic story of South Africa from the beginnings to 1975, the final chapter being on conditions for sustained progress. A statistical appendix of 25 tables, a select reading list (p.294-304) arranged according to chapters, and an analytical index. Intended primarily for South African readers. *Class No:* 338(680)(035)

America—North & Central

Handbooks & Manuals

[2302]
Central American economic handbook. London, Euromonitor Publications Ltd., 1987. x,172p. tables, charts. £45. ISBN: 0863382185.

Examines the socio-economic trends and developments in several central American countries. 11 chapters: 1. Central America in a world context - 2. Regional interdependence - 3. Mexico - 4. Costa Rica - 5. El Salvador - 6. Guatemala -

.... (contd.)
7. Honduras - 8. Nicaragua - 9. Panama - 10. Future outlook - 11. Factfile (statistics). Index, p.165-172 (double-column, with tables indicated in bold). *Class No:* 338(71/73)(035)

Canada

Bibliographies

[2303]
BROWN, B.E., *ed.* **Canadian business and economics:** a guide to sources of information. Rev. ed. Ottawa, Canadian Library Association, 1984. 469p. Can$90. ISBN: 0888021615.

First published 1976.

Over 6500 entries for government publications, monographs, reference works, serials and theses, plus business databases and services. Omits periodical articles, newspapers, and most government statistical series, and highly specialized reports. 22 subject areas. Many cross-references. Dictionary index in English and French, listing subjects, titles, authors and publishers. '... a valuable, comprehensive, and unique reference tool' (*RQ*, Fall, 1984, p.102). *Class No:* 338(71)(01)

Histories

Bibliographies

[2304]
DICK, T.J.O. Economic history of Canada: a guide to information sources. Detroit, Mich., Gale Research Co., 1978. vii,174p. $68. ISBN: 0810312921.

Nearly 1000 items listed in 5 chapters: 1. Interpretive and bibliographic sources - 2. From colonial times to the present - 3. The colonial period to 1867 - 4. Confederation (1867) to 1920 - 5. From 1920 to the present. Each chapter and section has a short introduction and is subdivided into general works, statistical records, theses of economic growth, sectors and industries, economic organization, technology and productivity change, and welfare resources. Author, title and subject indexes. *Class No:* 338(71)(091)(01)

Caribbean

Handbooks & Manuals

[2305]
Caribbean economic handbook. Fraser, P.D. London, Euromonitor Publications Ltd., 1985. vi,241p. tables. £45; $70. ISBN: 0863380891.

Aims to covert all aspects of the economies of the major islands of the region, including the Bahamas, Bermuda, Barbados, Cuba, the Dominican Republic, Haiti, Jamaica, Puerta Rico, and Trinidad and Tobago. 3 chapters: The Caribbean in a world context - Regional overview - Outlook. A 'Factfile' has comparative statistical data in 28 tables on population, distribution, retail sales, imports, health care, etc. *Class No:* 338(729)(035)

Latin America

Handbooks & Manuals

[2306]
UNITED NATIONS. Economic Commission for Latin America and the Caribbean. **Economic survey of Latin America and the Caribbean, 1985.** New York United Nations, 1987. 660p. $65. ISBN: 9211211352.

First published 1948. Annual.

Reviews trends in the Latin American and Caribbean economic situation, including inflation, trade, output, external finance, and foreign trade. Data for the whole region and individual countries. *Class No:* 338(729.99)(035)

Histories

[2307]
CORTÉS CONDE, R. *and* STEIN, S.J., *eds.* **Latin America: a guide to economic history, 1830-1930.** Berkely, CA., University of California Press, 1977. xviii, 685p. $75. ISBN: 0520029569.

Commissioned by the Joint Committee on Latin American Studies of the ACLS, the SSRC and the Consejo Latinamericano de Ciencia Sociales.

4450 mostly annotated items, in 8 sections; each written by a Latin American or US scholar: a historiographical introduction (in Spanish and English) - General bibliography (English) - Argentina (Spanish) - Brazil (Portuguese) - Chile (Spanish) - Colombia (English) - Mexico (Spanish) - Peru (Spanish). Each section begins with an introductory essay, followed by a section on reference works and major archival sources, and 8 topical sections. Author and journal indexes. '... an indispensible research tool for the student ...' (*Journal of social history,* Summer 1980, p.664-6). *Class No:* 338(729.99)(091)

[2308]
—GRIFFIN, C.C., *ed.* Latin American: a guide to historical literature. Austin, Texas, University of Texas Press, 1972 (Reprinted 1979 by University of Wisconsin Press). xxx,700p. $35. ISBN: 0299082202.

Published for the Conference on Latin American History and issued as Publication no.4 of the Conference ...

Contains 7087 annotated entries in 7 chronological sections. Includes references to items on education, government and parties, foreign relations, law, society and labour. *Class No:* 338(729.99)(091)

USA

[2309]
PORTER, G., *ed.* **Encyclopedia of American economic history.** New York, Scribner's, 1980. 3v. (xii,1286p.). $225. ISBN: 0684162717.

In 5 sections: 1. The historiography of American economic history - 2. The chronology of American economic history - 3. The framework of American economic growth - 4. The institutional framework - 5. The social framework. Includes 72 interpretative and signed articles (e.g., on slavery, prices and wages, the automobile, immigration, women). Glossary. Comprehensive index. 'A superb addition to the reference literature on American economic history' (*RQ,* v.20(1), Fall 1980, p.93). *Class No:* 338(73)

Handbooks & Manuals

[2310]
O'HARA, F.M. *and* SICIGNANO, R. **Handbook of United States economic and financial indicators.** Westport, CT., Greenwood Press, 1985. vi,224p. $42.95; £35. ISBN: 0313239541.

Brings together reference data on more than 200 major standard measures of economic activity in the US, arranged in dictionary format (Accession rate, manufacturing ... Workweek, average manufacturing). Entries include description, derivation, publisher, announced in, cumulations (tables), projections, more information. 3 appendices: Nonquantitative indicators - Abbreviation list & guide to sources - List of compilers of indicators. Index, p.215-224. *Class No:* 338(73)(035)

Tables & Data Books

[2311]
Economic indicators. US Congress, for the Joint Economic Committee. Prepared by the Council of Economic Advisers. Washington, DC., Government Printing Office, 1948-. tables, graphs, Monthly. $28pa.

Data on prices, wages, production, business activity, purchasing power, credit money and Federal finance. Available online (DIALOG). *Class No:* 338(73)(083)

[2312]
Survey of current business. US Department of Commerce. Bureau of Economic Analysis. Washington, DC., the Department, 1921-. Monthly. $29pa. ISSN: 00396222.

Consists of a general survey and articles, with invaluable centre pages on blue-tinted paper - 'Current business statistics'. Each issue carries a detailed subject index to sections and individual series of statistics. Available online (DIALOG) *Class No:* 338(73)(083)

Histories

[2313]
OLSON, J.S. **Dictionary of United States economic history.** Westport, CT, Greenwood Press, 1992. 667p. $85. ISBN: 0313265321.

Over 1300 concise entries, averaging 250-500 words each and including brief bibliographies. Wide subject coverage, including biographies of prominent people. Selected bibliography. Brief chronology. Name and subject index. '... useful tool ...' (*Choice,* v.20(7), March 1993,, p.1118). *Class No:* 338(73)(091)

[2314]
POULSON, B.W. **Economic history of the United States.** New York, Macmillan Publishing Co. Ltd., 1981. x,672p. tables. ISBN: 0023962208.

A textbook of 23 chapters arranged chronologically in 3 sections: 1. Economic growth in the colonial and early national period: to 1790- 2. The transition to modern economic growth: 1790-1890 - 3. A mature economy: 1890 to the present. Footnotes, and suggested readings after each chapter. Index, p.661-672. *Class No:* 338(73)(091)

Bibliographies

[2315]

HUTCHINSON, W.K., *ed*. **American economic history:** a guide to information sources. Detroit, Mich., Gale Research Co., 1980. xii, 296p. $68. ISBN: 0810312875.

Covers American economic history from the colonial period to about 1960. Arranged in 10 chapters (e.g., Population and labor force - Land and agricultural development - Industrial growth and structure - Monetary and financial developments) within which annotated entries are complemented by unannotated listings of works for further study. Appendices list the major organizations concerned with American economic history and the major journals in the field. *Class No:* 338(73)(091)(01)

[2316]

ORSAGH, T., *and others, eds*. **The Economic history of the United States prior to 1860:** an annotated bibliography. Santa Barbara, CA., Clio Press, 1975. xiii, 100p.

799 entries for monographs and journal articles, arranged in 16 subject groupings, preceded by a general section. Most of the entries are annotated, if only briefly. Author and subject indexes. *Class No:* 338(73)(091)(01)

America—South

Handbooks & Manuals

[2317]

South American economic handbook. Blakemore, H. London, Euromonitor Publications Ltd., 1986. [5],274p. tables, charts. £45; $80. ISBN: 0863381251.

A regional overview precedes economic profiles for the 13 nations of South America (Argentina, Bolivia, Brazil, Chile, Colombia, Ecuador, the Guianas, Paraguay, Peru, Uruguay, Venezuela). *Class No:* 338(8)(035)

Uruguay

[2318]

FINCH, M.H.J. **A Political economy of Uruguay since 1870.** London, Macmillan Press; New York, St. Martin's Press, 1981. xiii,339p. tables, figs., map. £35; $29.95. ISBN: 0333278526, UK; 0312622449, US.

Published in association with the Center for Latin American Studies.

9 chapters: 1. The ideology of Batllismo, 1870-1970 - 2. Population and society - 3. Agrarian structure and performance - 4. Taxation and agricultural stagnation - 5. Exports and the meat industry - 6. Imports and industrialisation - 7. Public utilities and public corporations - 8. The economic crisis - 9. The military regime since 1973. Appendix: Foreign trade data. Notes (p.279-309) by chapter. Select bibliography (p.310-328), A-Z by author. Index (p.329-339). *Class No:* 338(899)

Australia

Periodicals

[2319]

The Australian economic review. Parkville, Institute of Applied Economic and Social Research, University of Melbourne, 1963-. Quarterly. A$145pa. ISSN: 00049018.

Each issue contains a summary of the economic situation and several chapters on specific economic and social issues.

....(contd.)

Lists special articles, monographs by members of the Institute's staff, and technical papers. Modelled on the *National Institute economic review*. *Class No:* 338(94)(051)

Institutions & Associations

[2320]

FRASER, R. **Western European economic organizations.** Harlow, Essex, Longman, 1992. 448p. $145; £85. ISBN: 0582068452.

Data on international organizations precedes information on economic policy making in 19 Western European countries. Includes central banks, government agencies, regulatory bodies, stock exchanges and other organizations with input into economic policy making. Data includes postal address, telephone & fax numbers, principal officers, structure, funding, aims and objectives, history, affiliations, publications. Index of country and organization names. *Class No:* 338:061:061.2

Economic Policies & Controls

China

[2321]

HOWE, C. *and* WALKER, K.R. **The Foundations of the Chinese planned economy:** a documentary survey, 1953-65. London, Macmillan Press, 1989. 384p. £45. ISBN: 033346186X.

Traces the important changes in China in that period, through the medium of Chinese economic documents, most of which have not previously been translated. In 4 parts: 1. Strategy and planning - 2. Industrial development and organization - 3. Agricultural development - 4. Population and labour and urbanization. Index. *Class No:* 338.1/.5(510)

Economic Development

[2322]

Development index. East Kilbride, Glasgow (previously London), Overseas Development Administration, Library Services. 1967-. Monthly.

A list of periodical articles indexed by the Library of the Overseas Development Administration for current awareness. About 150 briefly annotated entries per issue, arranged under topics (*e.g.* Agricultural credit ... Women workers), on Third World countries. The country index is no longer provided. *Class No:* 338.1

[2323]

—Development contents. Glasgow, Overseas Development Administration Library. Monthly.

Contents pages of 'core' journals in the field of economic development. Reference numbers are given for articles listed in the above. *Class No:* 338.1(01)

Bibliographies

[2324]

GORMAN, G.E. *and* **MAHONEY, M.**, *comps. & eds*. **Index to development studies literature.** Wokingham, Van Nostrand Reinhold (UK) Co Ltd., 1985. xxix,266p. £33. ISBN: 0442306342.

4452 items, arranged in subject groups, each sub-divided (International co-operation/international relations - economic policy/social policy/planning - economic conditions/ economic research/economic system - institutional framework - culture/society - education/training - agriculture - industry - trade - transport - public finance/banking/ international monetary relations - management/productivity - labour - demography/population - biology/food/health - environment/natural resources - earth science/space sciences - science/research/methodology - information/ documentation). Author index, p.205-238. Keyword index, p.239-266. *Class No:* 338.1(01)

[2325]

GREAT BRITAIN. Department of Trade and Industry. Index to development plans. London, the Department, [1989]. [10]p. *Gratis.*

New eds. published at intervals.

A comprehensive list of current development plans available in the Export Market Information Centre of the Department. *Class No:* 338.1(01)

[2326]

International development abstracts. Norwich, Geo Abstracts, 1982-. 6pa. £250pa (including annual index). ISSN: 02620855.

Compiled by members of the staff at the Centre for Development Studies, University College of Swansea.

Arranged in 22 subject sections, including urbanization, regional and spacial planning; education and training; international relations, conflict, cooperation and aid; and trade. Worldwide coverage. The annual *International development index* has author, subject and regional indexes. Available online (DIALOG) *Class No:* 338.1(01)

Handbooks & Manuals

[2327]

METRA CONSULTING. Handbook of national development plans. Gorle, P., *ed.* 2nd ed. London, Graham & Trotman, 1987. 2v.(400p.). loose-leaf., + supplements. £70. ISBN: 0860108376; 0860108384 Supp.1; 0860108392 Supp.2.

First published 1963, with updating supplements.

Summaries of national development plans for over 70 countries, arranged A-Z by country. For each country a fact sheet with background data, comments on previous plans, summary of present plan (main assumptions - plan's strategy - priorities), allocation of funds by sectors, expected effect of plan on GDP, recent performance of plan. Half-yearly supplements. *Class No:* 338.1(035)

Dictionaries

[2328]

FRY, G.W. *and* **MARTIN, G.R. The International development dictionary** Santa Barbara, CA, ABC-Clio, 1991. 445p. $49. ISBN: 0874365457.

458 terms, arranged A-Z under four major subject categories (Development thinkers/theorists, leaders and

....(contd.)

practitioners - Basic development concepts - Analytical concepts - Development movements, projects and organizations). Entries vary in length from one half to 3 pages. Numerous cross-references,a detailed index, and an A-Z list of entries facilitate access. Substantial bibliography of c350 books and articles. *Class No:* 338.1(038)

Polyglot

[2329]

SCHARF, T. *and* **BALIN, M.**, *comps*. **Dictionary of development economics:** economic terminology in three languages: English, French, German. Amsterdam, Elsevier, 1969. xiii,268p.

3122 entries, in 12 chapters (1. Developing - 2. Planning - 3. Agriculture ... 12. Development statistics). English, French and German indexes. 'Slightly padded with matter extraneous to the subject, and in some cases carelessly edited, this is a useful little book which fills a definite need' (*Finance and development,* 1970, no.1, p.53-54). *Class No:* 338.1(038)=00

[2330]

—**Dictionary of development banking.** Amsterdam, Elsevier, 1972. vii,214p. Dfl.150; $79. ISBN: 0444410287.

1257 terms with English definitions, and French and German indexes. *Class No:* 338.1(038)=00

French

[2331]

UNITED NATIONS. Industrial Development Organization (UNIDO), Vienna. Thesaurus of individual development terms (English-French). Viet, J., *comp.* Vienna, the Organization, 1976. xi. 152p.

Also a French-English version. *Class No:* 338.1(038)=40

Developing Countries

Bibliographies

[2332]

Industrial development abstracts. United Nations. Industrial Development Organization (UNIDO), Vienna. New York, United Nations, 1971-. 2-4pa. price varies. (*UNIDO industrial information system INDIS.*) ISSN: 03782654.

About 200 indicative abstracts per issue of 'printed publications, such as major studies and reports, publications in series, and selected articles; from the reports and proceedings of expert working groups, workshops and seminars; internal studies; public information series; and reports related to technical assistance'. (*Introduction*). Arranged by computer access number. Subject and personal author indexes precede. *Class No:* 338.1(4/9-77)(01)

Great Britain

Bibliographies

[2333]

STONEY, P.J.M. *and* **PATERSON, A.T.** A Bibliography of studies in regional industrial development. Liverpool, University of Liverpool, Department of Business Studies, 1978. Supplement 1979. x,145p. £5. Supplement £1.50.

....*(contd.)*

ISBN: 0950631701; 095063171x, supplement.

Emanated from an empirical study of the Merseyside regions, but includes shorter sections of entries for other British regions and for the rest of the world. For Merseyside and the North West, the bibliography is a listing of titles arranged A-Z by author under subjects subdivided by form: Trade and industry - Regional science - Structure planning and development strategy - Urban studies. Author index. *Class No:* 338.1(410)(01)

Forecasting

Bibliographies

[2334]
FILDES, R., *ed*. **World index of economic forecasts.** 3rd ed. Aldershot, Hants, Gower Press, 1988. 400p. £75. ISBN: 056602702x.

First published in 1978, the first and second eds. edited by G.R. Cyriax.

A guide to econometric-based forecasting work of interest to businessmen and professional economists. Includes details of 470 forecasting groups in over 170 countries, together with their coverage, method and published output. *Class No:* 338.246(01)

Production

Worldwide

Tables & Data Books

[2335]
UNITED NATIONS. Department of International Economic and Social Affairs. **Industrial statistics yearbook, 1988.** 22nd ed. New York, United Nations, 1990. 2v. $50 each vol. ISBN: 9211613205 v.1; 9210611373 v.2; 9211613213 set.

First published for 1938/62. Early title was *Growth of world industry* then *Yearbook of industrial statistics.*

V.1. *General industrial statistics*; v.2. *Commodity production statistics, 1979-1988.* V.1. contains general industrial statistics providing the basic country data as well as a selection of indicators showing global and regional trends in industrial activity. V.2. deals specifically with annual statistics of production of individual commodities. *Class No:* 338.3/.4(100)(083)

Great Britain

Tables & Data Books

[2336]
GREAT BRITAIN. Department of Industry. Business Statistics Office. **Historical record of the census of production, 1907-1970.** London, HMSO, 1979. 402, lxvp. tables.

Contains 11 tables (*e.g.* 6. Analysis of employment, wages and salaries within industry, 1907 to 1970). 3 appendices (1: S.I.C., revised 1968). Bibliographies: A. Bibliography of census of production reports: B. Bibliography of associated publications. *Class No:* 338.3/.4(410)(083)

[2337]
—GREAT BRITAIN. Department of Industry. Business Statistics Office. Annual census of production reports ... 1970 -. London HMSO, 1971 -.

Continues *Report on the census of production* ... (1907-1968), which was normally five-yearly, covering mining and quarrying, manufacturing, construction, gas, electricity and water.

Annual census, 1971-; results for each industry published separately in the 'Business monitor: production series'(PA).

Others in the 'Business monitor: production series' give more up-to-date quarterly or annual production statistics for particular industries. *Class No:* 338.3/.4(410)(083)

[2338]
—Guides to official sources. No.6: Census of production reports. Interdepartmental Committee on Social and Economic Research. London, HMSO, 1961. x,86p.

Covers 'statistics prepared by the Board of Trade and published in the reports of the Census of Production and the Import Duties Act Inquiries for years from 1907 to 1958 (*Introduction*). *Class No:* 338.3/.4(410)(083)

Tourism

[2339]
ORGANISATION FOR ECONOMIC CO-OPERATION AND DEVELOPMENT. **Tourism policy and international tourism in OECD member countries, 1990-1991.** Paris, OECD, 1993. 202p. tables. F.180; £30; $42. ISBN: 9264138293.

Published annually since the 1970 ed.

Information on government policies in the field of tourism, accompanied by a statistical annex on recent trends (tourist flow, accommodation, payments, motives, transport, employment and prices). *Class No:* 338.48

[2340]
Travel trade gazette directory. 37th ed. London, Morgan-Grampion plc., in association with *Travel trade gazette,* 1993. £55. ISBN: 0862132193. ISSN: 09664297.

Sections, each starting with A-Z index: Travel agents - Car travel - Coach travel - Sea travel - Air travel - Travel trade information (National tourist and information offices; visa and passport offices; U.K. resort and regional information offices; associations, organizations and societies; national travel association) - Travel trade services - Tour operators - Special interest holidays - Hotels. Index to advertisers. *Class No:* 338.48

Bibliographies

[2341]
OVERTON, D. **Tourism:** a guide to sources of information. 2nd ed. London, Capital Planning Information, 1988. vi,82p. £16.50. (*CPI Information Reviews; no.4.*) ISBN: 0906011493.

1. Introduction (scope and purpose; general books; tourism textbooks) - 2. Sources of data - 3. Administration of tourism - 4. Tourist management, development and planning - 5. Environment - 6. Tourism for the disadvantaged - 7. Recreational and educational tourism - 8. Conference and business tourism - 9. Training - 10. Jobs - 11. Accommodation. Very sound literature guide. *Class No:* 338.48(01)

Handbooks & Manuals

[2342]

BAR-ON, R. **Travel and tourism data:** a comprehensive research handbook on the world travel directory. London Euromonitor, 1989. ix,366p. ISBN: 0863381316.

8 sections: 1. Travel and tourism: an overview - 2. International and domestic tourism: their scope and definition - 3. The principal sources of tourism data - 4. Methods of collecting tourism data - 5. The presentation, analysis and forecasting of time series - 6. Classification of travel and tourism data - 7. World tourism statistics, 1982-1986 - 8. Public sources of tourism data. Bibliography, p.339-351. Index to countries and subjects, p.359-366.

Class No: 338.48(035)

Tables & Data Books

[2343]

ORGANISATION FOR ECONOMIC CO-OPERATION AND DEVELOPMENT. **National and international tourism statistics, 1974-1985.** 1st ed. Paris, OECD, 1989. 727p. £45; $80; F.380. ISBN: 9264032215.

Tables and graphs showing the trend of national and international demand over nearly two decades. In 2 parts: National tourism, by country of OECD plus US, Canada and Japan, A-Z; International tourism, similarly arranged. Data includes arrivals, nights spent, receipts, expenditures, etc.

Class No: 338.48(083)

[2344]

WORLD TOURISM ORGANIZATION. **Yearbook of tourism statistics, 1992.** 44th ed. Madrid, Organizacion Mundial del Turismo, 1992. 929p. tables. $80.

First published for 1947. Early title was *World travel and tourism statistics: yearbook.*

V.1. World aggregates subdivided by region and country (World summary - Tourism from abroad - Domestic tourism - Tourism payments - Transport - Tourist motivations - Tourist accommodation - Explanatory notes). V.2 Breakdown by country of total arrivals, overnight stays, mode of transport, purpose of visit, tourism receipts and expenditures. Covers 150 countries and territories, and includes data for several years to 1991.

Class No: 338.48(083)

[2345]

—WORLD TOURISM ORGANIZATION. **Compendium of tourism statistics, 1987-1991.** 13th ed. Madrid, Organizacion Mundial del Turismo, 1993. x,216p. tables. $50;£38. ISBN: 9284400049. ISSN: 10141744.

First published for 1976.

Provides in a condensed form the basic statistical series on national and international tourism supply and demand in the various countries and regions of the world. Following the main statistical section are: World and regional totals (on tinted paper); Technical notes; and Main sources of information, p.214. Both the above are updated by the quarterly *Travel and tourism indicators.*

Class No: 338.48(083)

Prices & Costs

Worldwide

[2346]

UNION BANK OF SWITZERLAND. **Prices and earnings around the globe:** a comparison of purchasing power in 52 cities. Zurich, the Bank, 1988. 44p. tables, illus. *Gratis.* (*UBS publications on business, banking and monetary topics, no.108.*) ISBN: x21091010x.

International price comparison (of 14 items); wages and salaries around the world (5 sections); appendix of 27 tables (p.29-44). *Class No:* 338.5(100)

Trade & Commerce

Bibliographies

[2347]

NICHOLAS, D. **Commodities futures trading:** a guide to information sources and computerized services. London, Mansell, 1985. x,144p. £18. ISBN: 0720117038.

Arranged in 6 sections (Market trading and price distribution services - newspapers - newsletters - journals and magazines - yearbooks, directories and reference works - books). There are introductions to each section and subsection, and arrangement within sections is A-Z by service or title. An appendix gives addresses of online database hosts. Index, p.139-144. Mainly relates to computerized services, mainly in UK and US, some Netherlands. *Class No:* 339(01)

Protectionism

[2348]

LUTZ, J.M. **Protectionism:** an annotated bibliography with analytical introductions. Ann Arbor, Mich., Peiron Press, 1989. 207p. $40. (*Resources on contemporary issues.*) ISBN: 0876502494.

Each chapter has in introduction and ends with an annotated bibliography of *c.*20-200 items. Topics covered include the rise of protectionism, tariffs, non-tariff barriers to trade, hegemony, the General Agreement on Tariffs and Trade (GATT), customs unions, free trade areas, trading blocs, etc. As well as the US, other industrialized countries and developing countries are covered. Chronology since World War II. Glossary. Author and title indexes. '... a thorough treatment of protectionism as an economic tool since World War II in an easy-to-read format' (*Choice,* v.26(10), July 1989, p.1664). *Class No:* 339(01)PRO

Dictionaries

[2349]

BRANCH, A.E., *ed.* **Dictionary of commercial terms** and abbreviations. London, Witherby & Co., 1984. xiii,458p. £9.50. ISBN: 0900886900.

Aimed at students and includes terms found in accountancy, advertising, commerce, computers, economics, insurance, international trade, law, marketing, personnel management, real estate, selling, statistics, tourism and transport. Definitions are brief. 5 appendices (A. Further recommended textbook reading - B. Addresses and roles of professional institutions/associations - C. World currencies -

....(contd.)

D. Conversion weights and measures and conversion factors - E. List of chambers of commerce in the UK.).
Class No: 339(038)

Polyglot

[2350]

Multilingual dictionary of commercial international trade and shipping terms: English-French-Spanish-German. Branch, A.E., *and others.* London, Witherby, 1990. 255p. £19.95 ISBN: 0948691905.

Lists some 2200 English terms used in the daily conduct of international trade and commerce with, under each term, the French, Spanish and German equivalents.
Class No: 339(038)=00

Spanish

[2351]

RODRIGUES, L.J. *and* BERNET SOLER, J. **Harrap's glossary of English and Spanish commercial and industrial terms.** London, Harrap, 1990. 288p. £14.99. ISBN: 0245600183. *Class No:* 339(038)=60

Arabic

[2352]

BRANCH, A.E. *and* HAKMEH, J.A. **Dictionary of English-Arabic commercial, international trade and shipping terms.** London, Witherby & Co., Ltd. 1988. 257p. £21. ISBN: 0948691611.

Wide coverage of the business sector, including commerce, customs, documentation, economics, exports, tourism, etc. *Class No:* 339(038)=927

Reviews & Abstracts

[2353]

Wilson business abstracts. New York, Wilson, 1982-.

Claims to provide cover-to-cover indexing and abstracts for the 350 most-demanded business periodicals. Indexing coverage from July 1982; abstracting coverage from June 1990. Available only online, on CD-ROM and on magnetic tape. *Class No:* 339(048)

Periodicals

Bibliographies

[2354]

European directory of trade and business journals. London, Euromonitor Publications Ltd., 1990. [6],339p. £135. ISBN: 0813383394.

Arranged geographically (a Pan-European and International section, followed by 17 West European countries), then subdivided by journal title, A-Z. Data include name of publisher, address, circulation, scope of readership, periodicity and editorial content. Included are the 'main journals which can be accessed for companies, organizations and individuals interested in finding information on Western European markets and industries, particularly in member countries of the forthcoming Single European Market' (*Foreword*). General index, p.289-308; subject index, p.309-339. *Class No:* 339(051)(01)

Europe

Handbooks & Manuals

[2355]

The European marketplace Hogan, J., *ed.* London, Macmillan, 1990. 650p. 50. ISBN: 0333518586.

Step-by-step business information path through the European market as a whole and 12 individual member states. 7 parts: 1. The European marketplace - 2. The economics of Europe - 3. Financing European business - 4. European Community law - 5. Training and education - 6. Official information sources - 7. Published information sources. Bibliography. Index. *Class No:* 339(4)(035)

Great Britain

Yearbooks & Directories

[2356]

MILLARD, P., *ed.* **Trade associations and professional bodies** of the United Kingdom. 12th rev. ed. Andover, Hants., Gale Research International, 1993. 800p. £75. ISBN: 187347721x.

First published 1962. First 9 editions by Pergamon Press.

An alphabetical and subject classified guide, arranged in 3 parts: Alphabetical list of trade associations and professional bodies; Chambers of commerce, trade, industry and shipping; Overseas chambers of commerce with offices in the UK. Subject index (p.557-606); Geographic index by town (p.607-648). The Part 1 listing is arranged by name, with address and telephone/telex/fax numbers.
Class No: 339(410)(058)

Tables & Data Books

[2357]

GREAT BRITAIN. Central Statistical Office. **Overseas trade statistics of the United Kingdom.** London, HMSO, 1970-. Monthly. £385pa.

First published 1848. Previously (1965-69) as Board of Trade's *Overseas trade accounts of the United Kingdom.* Now issued in the Business Statistics Office's *Business monitor* series, MM20.

Detailed statistics of exports and imports compiled from declarations made to HM Customs and Excise by importers and exporters and their agents. Tables: General summary - Summary of imports and exports by area and country - Imports summary by commodities and countries - Imports by commodities and countries - Imports by detailed commodities - Exports summary by commodities and countries - Exports by commodities and countries - Exports by detailed commodities. Index of commodities. Monthly issues give cumulative totals, the December issue having annual figures. *Class No:* 339(410)(083)

[2358]

—Guide to the classification for overseas trade statistics. Central Statistical Office. London, HMSO, 1992. 375p. £34. (*Business monitor, MA21.*) ISBN: 0115351787.

Arranged by Standard International Trade Classification number (SITC), followed by Commodity code number, and trade description. Subject index. *Class No:* 339(410)(083)

USSR

Handbooks & Manuals

[2359]
KNIGHT, M.G. **How to do business with Russians:** a handbook and guide for Western world business people. New York, Quorum Books, 1987. xxiv,311p. £40.50; $45. ISBN: 0899302114.

24 chapters arranged in 2 parts: 1. Trading with the Soviet Union: the way it operates - 2. The structure of Soviet foreign trade operations and orders of a business transaction. *Class No:* 339(47)(035)

Libraries

[2360]
European directory of business information libraries. Euromonitor, 1990. xi,193p. £160. ISBN: 086338367x.

A Pan-European and international section is followed by country sections. A-Z, (Austria ... United Kingdom - West Germany), subdivided by name of organizations.Data includes address; telephone, fax & telex numbers; contact; availability; stock; and services. General and subject indexes. *Class No:* 339:061:026/027

Institutions & Associations

[2361]
EUROPEAN COMMUNITIES. Commission. **Directory of European Communities trade and professional associations.** 5th ed. Luxembourg. Office for Official Publications of the European Community, 1992. 516p. ISBN: 9282641627. ISSN: 07717865.

In French, English and German. 11 sections, some subdivided: Chambers of commerce and industry; Industry; Crafts; Small & medium-sized enterprises; Trade; Transport; Professional; Other activities; Unions; Consumer and other organizations; Miscellaneous. Entries give addresses, telephone and fax numbers, date started, chairman, secretary general. Index of acronyms and abbreviations. Analytical index, p.494-508. Name index, p.509-16. *Class No:* 339:061:061.2

Balance of Payments

[2362]
INTERNATIONAL MONETARY FUND. **Balance of payments yearbook, 1938, 1946, 1947-.** Washington, D.C., I.M.F., 1949-. tables. $56pa for the 1993 2-part yearbook). ISSN: 02523035.

Continues the series of figures issued by the League of Nations, covering 1926 (1910 in a few cases) to 1938, and the United Nations, covering 1939 to 1945.

Covers *c.*140 countries, A-Z. Part 1 has aggregated and detailed tables,standard presentation for each country giving data under headings in 8 subdivided sections (A. Current account - B. Direct investment and other long-term capital - C. Other short-term capital - D. Net errors and omissions - E. Counterpart items - F. Exceptional financing - G. Liabilities constituting foreign authorities' reserves - H. Total change in reserves.). Notes on tables. Part 2 has 55 tables of area and world totals of balance of payments components and aggregates.Information on countries is based partly on requirements laid down in the *Balance of payments manual* (4th ed., 1977). *Class No:* 339.053

Great Britain

[2363]
GREAT BRITAIN. Central Statistical Office. **United Kingdom balance of payments, 1993.** London, HMSO., 1993. Annual. 89p. £13.25. ISBN: 0116205970. ISSN: 09507558.

10 sections: 1. General description of accounts - 2. Visible trade - 3. Invisibles: services ... 6. Invisibles: earnings on UK external assets and liabilities. 7 Transactions in UK external assets and liabilities ... 10. Exchange rates. Glossary. Index. Known as the 'Pink book'. *Class No:* 339.053(410)

Businesses

[2364]
Who owns whom, 1993: United Kingdom and Republic of Ireland. High Wycombe, Bucks, Dun & Bradstreet International, 1993. 2v. ISBN: 0901491314. ISSN: 01404040.

First published 1958. Annual, with quarterly supplements.

Designed to help anyone needing to know about company connections. V.3 lists subsidiaries and associates of parent companies registered in the UK and in the Republic of Ireland; foreign parent companies and their subsidiaries and associates in the UK and Ireland. V.4 is an A-Z index of subsidiary and associated companies, showing their parents. Parent companies are also listed and marked 'Parent entry'. Who owns whom online is also available via the publisher.

Similar volumes are published for Continental Europe (now issued as V.1 & 2 of the volumes for Continental Europe, V.3 & 4 being those listed above), North America, and Australia and the Far East. *Class No:* 339.1

Databases

[2365]
BASCH, R. **Finding foreign firms:** a survey of international company directories. In *Database,* v.12(2), April 1989, p.13-25.

On the capabilities - and quirks - of company directory databases. Compares 25 databases (numbers of companies included, information given, price, reliability, etc.). Appendix A lists additional international business directory-type databases. *Class No:* 339.1(003.4)

[2366]
The Instant guide to company information online: Europe. Spencer, N., *ed.* 2nd ed. London, The British Library, *Science Reference and Information Library,* 1993. [iii],64p. tables. £35. ISBN: 0712308032.

First published 1991.

Tabulates *c.*100 databases containing company data for each of 16 Western European countries (EC members, Austria, Switzerland, Norway and Sweden), indicating industry, product, codes, number of employees, profit and loss, etc. Separate A-Z listing of databases gives contact details, coverage, language and special features. *Class No:* 339.1(003.4)

[2367]

RYAN, F.J. **Company information online:** buyer's guide to British directory databases. In *Business information review,* v.1(2), October 1984, p.26-43.

Discusses 4 databases in detail (ICC British company directory; ICC British company financial datasheets; JLS - Jordan line services; File KBE - Key British enterprises) and adds information on a fifth (EKOL - European Kompass online). *Class No:* 339.1(003.4)

Bibliographies

[2368]

Legal industrial espionage: a sourcebook and guide to finding company information. Newbury, Berks, Eurofi plc., 1988. [3],195p. £42.50. ISBN: 0907304427.

8 chapters: 1. Covert intelligence - 2. Statutory information - 3. Published sources (directories and yearbooks, periodicals, card index services, trade literature) - 4. Online access to information - 5. Patents, trade marks and industrial design - 6. Specialized information services - 7. Market research reports and services - 8. Libraries. Aims to show how anyone can set about obtaining detailed and in-depth company information by legal means. Index, p.189-195. *Class No:* 339.1(01)

[2369]

Research index: the fortnightly library service which indexes the news, views and comments on industries and companies. Dorset, Broadmayne, Business Surveys Ltd., 1965- Fortnightly, with half-yearly cumulation. £250pa. ISSN: 00345296.

Indexes *c.*100,000 articles and news items pa in *c.*130 British business, economic and trade periodicals, and the national press. Section 1 (pink pages) covers industrial and commercial news and reports not dealing specifically with a particular company. A-Z headings, *c.*180, Accountancy ... Yugoslavia. Section 2: Company, A-Z. A current awareness service. *Class No:* 339.1(01)

Dictionaries

Polyglot

[2370]

EUROPEAN PARLIAMENT. **Terminologie le la société anonyme européenne/Terminology of the European company.** 3rd ed. Luxembourg. the Parliament, 1981. . 319p. £8.50.

First published, 1968.

A six - language list of words and expressions. (English/French/German/Italian/Dutch/Danish). First listing in English with equivalents in the other languages. Indexes in the other languages referring to the English list. *Class No:* 339.1(038)=00

Histories

[2371]

DERDAK, T., *ed.* **International directory of company histories.** Chicago, Ill., St. James Press, 1987-. To be in 5v., plus supplementary vols. £85. $130 each vol. ISBN: 0912289104, v.1; 1558620125, v.2; 1558620591, v.3; 1558620605, v.4; 1558621768, v.5; 1558620346, set.

Compiled with the assistance of the Faculty of History, University of Chicago.

....(contd.)

Basic information and short company histories for *c.*1250 leading companies in the United States, Canada, Great Britain, Europe and Japan, arranged A-Z by business category (Advertising ... Utilities). Each entry is about 1500-3000 words in length and includes basic information (Headquarters, capitalization, subsidiaries, etc.) and a company history written by a trained historian. A v.6 (ISBN 1558621768) is the first of the supplementary volumes, to be published twice a year, containing additional company entries and revised entries. *Class No:* 339.1(091)

[2372]

GRANT, D. **Business histories and biographies** an introduction. In *Business information review,* v.4(2), October 1987, p.29-32.

Evaluates the use of business histories and biographies as source materials, and provides a bibliography of 20 up-to-date sources. *Class No:* 339.1(091)

[2373]

ROOM, A. **Corporate eponymy:** a biographical dictionary of persons behind the names of major American, British, European and Asian businesses. Jefferson, NC, & London, McFarland, 1992. xx,280p. $35. £29.75. ISBN: 0899506798.

Arranged A-Z by name of business (*e.g.* Cadbury; Jack Daniels; Steinway; Ritz; Barclay). Short entries with basic information on who, where, when and how businesses were named, with concise description of products. Mainly the English-speaking world. Short selected bibliography. Complements Room's *Dictionary of trade name origins* (1982) which is broader in scope. '... worthwhile addition to any business collection and will intrigue many who happen to pick it up.'(*Booklist,* v.89(7), 1 December 1992, p.687). *Class No:* 339.1(091)

Official Records

[2374]

ARMSTRONG, J. *and* JONES, S. **Business documents** their origins, sources and uses in historical research. London, Mansell Publishing Ltd., 1987. xvi,251p. illus. £30. ISBN: 0720118468.

An introduction for the archivist and researcher to business documents and their value for historical research. 15 sections, preceded by an introduction on document creation: 1. Prospectuses - 2. Articles of association - 3. Board minute books - 4. Letter books - 5. Chairman's statement - 6. Registers of directors - 7. Registers of members - 8. Diaries - 9. Book-keeping records: journals and ledgers - 10. Balance sheets and profit and loss accounts - 11. Staff records - 12. Patents - 13. Licences - 14. Premises records - 15. Dealers and agency agreements. Bibliography, p.231-235. List of useful addresses. Analytical index, p.239-251. Authors are with the Business Archives Council. '... clear, readable guide to the subject of company records ...' (*Business history,* v.30(2), April 1988). *Class No:* 339.1(093.2)

Archives

[2375]

FLEMING, E. **Companies Registration Office:** the long road to public access. In *Business information review,* v.1(2), October 1984, p.13-20.

Documents the long and ultimately successful campaign to force the Companies Registration Office to fulfill its obligations by supplying company records by post at reasonable cost. Includes information on terms of the Postal Sales Service. *Class No:* 339.1(093.20)

Worldwide

Yearbooks & Directories

[2376]

Business rankings annual, 1993: lists of companies, products, services and activities compiled from a variety of published sources. Brooklyn Public Library. Business Library Staff, *comp.* Detroit, Mich., Gale Research International, 1993. Annual. xviii,759p. ISBN: 0810353474. ISSN: 10437908.

First published as *Business rankings and salaries index* in 1988.

An outline of contents, guiding the user to the special subjects covered, precedes the listing of about 3000 rankings and lists that have been published in business publications and specialised periodicals. Index, p.575-742. Bibliography, p.743-59. *Class No:* 339.1(100)(058)

[2377]

DUNNING, J.H. *and* PEARCE, R.D. **The World's largest industrial enterprises, 1962-83.** 2nd. rev. ed. Aldershot, Hants., Gower Publishing Co, 1985. v.186p.tables. £57.50. ISBN: 0566006405.

First published 1981.

Details of the world's largest industrial enterprises in 1983, and for the years 1962, 1967, 1972, and 1982, classified into 20 industrial sectors. Sections: Introduction; The data for 1983; Changes in the sample composition, 1962-1982; Employment of the world's largest enterprises; Concentration, size and diversification; Profitability and growth, 1962-82; International operations; Research and development expenditures of the world's largest enterprises. Appendices: tables. *Class No:* 339.1(100)(058)

[2378]

The International corporate 1000. 3rd ed. London, Graham & Trotman Limited, 1990. 627p. £145; $280. ISBN: 1853333093.

First published 1988. Annual.

Lists the 1000 leading companies outside the US. Arranged by region (Europe, Far East and Australasia, Middle East and Africa, Latin America, and Canada). Data include names and titles of executives of the corporations; names of board members; address, telephone - telex - fax numbers; description of business and subsidiaries. *Class No:* 339.1(100)(058)

[2379]

The Times 1000 ... 1994: the indispensable annual review of the world's leading industrial and financial companies. London, Times Books, 1994. Annual. 128p. £29.50. ISBN: 0723005133. ISSN: 00824429.

First published for 1979-1980.

Listings of 1. World's top 50 industrial companies...7. The UK's top 1000 - 8. Europe's top 1000 - 9. USA's top

....(contd.)

1000 - 10. Japan's top 1000...18. UK's top 25 banks - 19. Europe's top 25 banks - 20. UK's top 30 insurance companies - 21. UK's top 25 property companies - 22. UK's top 25 building societies - 23. UK's top 50 investment trusts. Index. *Class No:* 339.1(100)(058)

[2380]

World business directory. O'Meara, M. *and* Patterson, K., *eds.* 1st ed. Detroit, Mich, & Andover, Hants, Gale, 1992. 4v.(5314p). £250. ISBN: 0810377152.

Over 105,000 businesses involved in international trade (company name and variations; address; telephone, fax and telex numbers; WTC affiliation; key officers; revenue data; number of employees; type of business; year established; products; parent company). Industry, company name and product indexes. 3v. arranged by country; v.4 has indexes. *Class No:* 339.1(100)(058)

Europe

[2381]

European business rankings: lists of companies, products, services and activities compiled from a variety of published sources. Newman, O. *and* Foster, A., *comps.* Detroit & Andover, Hants, Gale Research International Ltd., 1992. 437p. $140. £95. ISBN: 1873477007.

Includes 2260 lists from more than 800 periodicals, newspapers, financial services, directories, statistical annuals, etc., held by Manchester Business School Library. Contents list (subject headings) serves as a finding list. Sources of lists cited and bibliography of sources included. *Class No:* 339.1(4)

Yearbooks & Directories

[2382]

Directory of European business. Cambridge Market Intelligence, *comp.* New York, Bowker-Saur, 1992. xxv,366p. tables. $195. ISBN: 0862916178.

User's guide, currency table, and list of abbreviations precedes. *c.*4000 leading business firms - service companies, organizations, government agencies and top manufacturing companies in 35 countries of East and West Europe, arranged A-Z by country (Albania ... Commonwealth of Independent States ... United Kingdom ... Yugoslavia}. Introduction to each country section on business environment (political system, economic policy, accounting rules, standards, tax system), followed by list of business services (subdivided by subject: Accounts ... Public relations companies); business organizations (Chambers of Commerce, professional bodies, trade associations); leading companies; government (foreign representation, ministeries, regulatory agencies); business information (statistical sources, national newspapers, business periodicals). *Class No:* 339.1(4)(058)

[2383]

European business services directory. Huellmantel, M.B., *ed.* Detroit, Gale, 1993. 1374p. $275. ISBN: 0810379163.

Lists business service providers that service other companies in 30 European countries, including former Soviet republics. In 3 sections: Service listing, profiles more than 20,000 comlanies arranged by topic according to their major service (*eg*, advertising, construction, finance);

....(contd.)

Geographic listing, with entry numbers referring to profiles; and A-Z list of companies, also with entry numbers referring to profiles. Preceding are an introduction and user's guide in English, French and German; a list of symbols and abbreviations; a table of currency abbreviations; and a list of SIC codes. Also available on magnetic tape and floppy disk. *Class No:* 339.1(4)(058)

Biographies

[2384]

Who's who in European business . East Grinstead, West Sussex, Bowker-Saur, 1993. 432p. £99. ISBN: 0862917956.

Biographies of the 5000 business leaders in 37 countries of Eastern and Western Europe. Entries arranged A-Z and tailored for the business user, with emphasis on professional career details. *Class No:* 339.1(4)(092)

Europe—Western

Handbooks & Manuals

[2385]

Guide to European company information: EEC countries. London Business School Information Service. 3rd ed. London, London Business School, 1989. [3],124p. map. £45. ISBN: 0951440101.

First and second editions were produced as handouts for seminars.

In 3 sections. 1st section has 12 country chapters (one for each of the 12 EEC countries) giving brief outlines of the main legal forms of companies, the disclosure requirements, and how to access these public filings. Followed in each chapter, apart from UK. by detailed descriptions of the directories, and online databases which are the main source of company information for each country. A pan-European chapter describes sources for more than one country. The 2nd section is on UK library resources, giving details of over 50 publicly available collections of these directories, together with summaries of the services they offer. The 3rd section has data on agencies that will obtain company accounts information, and describes the services offered by the major business and credit reporting agencies in terms of what they can provide, how long it takes, and cost. *Class No:* 339.1(400)(035)

[2386]

The Tavistock handbook and directory: business centres and managed workspace, 1993. Goodwin, G., *ed.* London, Kogan Page, 1993. 236p. maps. £14.95. ISBN: 0749409304.

Key to the areas covered precedes the introduction (Advantages of short-term accommodation over conventional office space; How to find the right accommodation for your business). Entries are arranged by region, subdivided by towns, and includes name of organization, address, telephone & fax numbers, type of accommodation offered. Index, p.221-36. *Class No:* 339.1(400)(035)

Yearbooks & Directories

[2387]

Dun's Europa, 1990: 35,000 leading companies in Europe. Parsippany, NJ, Dun & Bradstreet International, 1990. 3v. (1439; 1059; 659p). $495. ISBN: 0872404033. ISSN: 09575812.

Profiles the leading companies in 12 EC countriues, Austria and Switzerland. V.1 & 2 have company data by country, subdivided by name of company, A-Z, with address, telephone & telex numbers, principal executives, SIC code signifying main types of business, nominal and issued capital, number of employees, annual sales, net loss or gain, etc. V.3 provides, for the top 10,000 companies, rankings by sales and business activity; statistical profiles; company and business activity indexes; and SIC code tables. *Class No:* 339.1(400)(058)

[2388]

Major companies of Europe, 1993/94. 13th ed. London, Graham & Trotman, 1993. 3v. (1552p.). £599 the set; v.1 £320; v.2 & 3 £160 each. (*Major companies of the world series* ..) ISBN: 1853338893, set; 1853335969, v.1; 1853335977, v.2; 1853335985, v.3. ISSN: 0266934x, v.1; 02684667, v.2; 02684675, v.3.

First published 1980.

A directory of 9000 of Europe's largest companies. V.1: Continental European Community; v.2: United Kingdom; v.3: Western Europe outside the European Community. Data includes addresses; telephone/cable/telex/fax numbers; board of directors; senior executives; principal activities; trade names; subsidiary companies; principal bankers; financial information; and number of employees. *Class No:* 339.1(400)(058)

[2389]

—Medium companies of Europe, 1993-94. London, Graham & Trotman, 1993. 3v. £599. ISBN: 1853338932. ISSN: 09601449.

lst published 1990. Annual.

c.7000 entries for medium-sized companies, following a similar format to the above. *Class No:* 339.1(400)(058)

Europe—Eastern

Yearbooks & Directories

[2390]

East European business directory. Didik, F.X., *ed.* Andover, Hants & Detroit, Gale Research International Ltd., 1991. lx,962p. £185. ISBN: 0810384019.

A guide to *c.5000* of the largest business, commercial enterprises and special interest associations in Bulgaria, Czechoslovakia, Hungary, Poland, Romania, the western USSR, and the former East Germany. Classification is by products and services, and entries include full address of the organization; telephone, telex & fax numbers; contact name; details of product or service in which the business specializes. Production service section, A-Z by products. Geographical section, A-Z by country, subdivided by city or region. Alphabetical listing by company name. *Class No:* 339.1(401)(058)

Great Britain

Yearbooks & Directories

[2391]

Britain's privately owned companies. Bristol, Avon, Jordan, 1989. 3v. £125 each volume.

Formerly titled *Britain's top 2000 private companies*.

V.1 and 2 cover the larger companies, including 2000 companies in each vol. V.3 also has 2000 smaller companies. For each company financial data is given, including fixed assets, current assets, current liabilities, stock/work in progress, cash, numbers employed, total wage bill, average remuneration per employee.
Class No: 339.1(410)(058)

[2392]

Extel Financial UK listed companies. London, Extel Financial Ltd., 1927-. Daily. £3970pa.

Details of *c.*2500 British quoted companies listed on the Stock Exchange. For each company there is an annual card showing the company's activities, balance sheets, board members, capital (with history), chairman's statement, dividend record, profit and loss account, yield earnings, etc. Cumulative new cards are issued for each company as and when dividends are announced or other news justifies. Extel also offers other services, including 'Extel European company service' and 8 overseas company services.
Class No: 339.1(410)(058)

[2393]

GREAT BRITAIN. Central Statistical Office. **United Kingdom directory of manufacturing businesses, 1993.** London, HMSO, 1993. 759,xlviiip. £160. (*(Business monitor PO 1007A).*) ISBN: 0115363084.

First published 1989. Annual.

*c.*19800 entries, compiled from the CSO's register of businesses. Arranged by subject (SIC), subdivided by name of firm, A-Z. Name and address only. Includes key to the SIC (1980 Standard Industrial Classification).
Class No: 339.1(410)(058)

Histories

[2394]

Debrett's bibliography of business history. Zarach, S., *ed.* London, Macmillan Press in association with Debrett's Business History Research Ltd., 1987. xv,278p. £35. ISBN: 0333424042.

Over 2000 titles are listed, arranged A-Z by subject (Accountancy … Wines and spirits). Under each subject, general titles are followed by company histories arranged A-Z by name of company. Information given is author, title, publisher, date of publication, no. of pages. No annotations. Confined to histories published or printed in this century and '… no attempt to pass judgement on their value' (*Preface*). A list of 'Books of general use to the business historian' (p.251-253) is A-Z by author. Index of companies, p.254-278. *Class No:* 339.1(410)(091)

[2395]

FANNING, D. 'Business history and biography'. In *British book news*, February 1986, p.78-82.

A book survey followed by a bibliography of 89 books, arranged A-Z by author. The survey is in 5 sections: Outstanding contributions; Collected biography; Individual biographies; Individual corporate history; and Business and industrial history. *Class No:* 339.1(410)(091)

[2396]

GOODALL, F. A Bibliography of British business histories. Aldershot, Hants., Gower, 1987. v,638p. £45. (*Business history series, v.3.*) ISBN: 0566053071.

A preface and user's guide precedes the 'Author index', which is the bibliography of works published during the last 150 years. Entries include title, publisher, name(s) of firm(s), description of content, SIC, and source library. Extensive cross-references. Company index, p.455-533. Industry classification index. p. 535-638.
Class No: 339.1(410)(091)

[2397]

HEALD, T. By appointment: 150 years of the Royal Warrant and its holders. London, Macdonald: Queen Anne Press. 1990. £40. ISBN: 0356170993.

The Royal Warrant holders number over 850 companies who are allowed to display the Royal Arms with the words 'By Appointment'. Includes descriptions of these 'Best of Britain' companies. *Class No:* 339.1(410)(091)

Biographies

[2398]

The Directory of directors … a list of the directors of the principal public and private companies in the United Kingdom, with the names of the concerns with which they are associated, 1993. 114th ed. East Grinstead, West Sussex,Reed Information Services Ltd., 1992. 2v. ISBN: 0611008157.

First published 1880.

V.1 lists *c.*58,000 directors, A-Z, the name being followed by companies of which the person is a director. V.2 lists *c.*16,000 companies and *c.*85,000 board members. Company information includes name, subject, address, telephone number, telex number, parent company, directors, date of accounts, financial data showing up to 3 years of accounts.
Class No: 339.1(410)(092)

Archives

[2399]

RICHMOND, L. *and* STOCKFORD, B. Company archives: the survey of the records of 1000 of the first registered companies in England and Wales. Aldershot, Hants., Gower Publishing Co. Ltd., 1986. xxi,593p. £48. ISBN: 0566035472.

The survey was undertaken by the Business Archives Council with support from the Economic and Social Research Council.

The survey traced 1000 of the oldest surviving limited companies in England and Wales, embracing all kinds of business activity. An introduction and a user's guide precede the list of records, and are followed by name, place and subject indexes. '… a wonderful book for business historians'. (*Business history*, October 1986, p.126).
Class No: 339.1(410)(093.20)

Eire

Yearbooks & Directories

[2400]

EIRE. Department of Industry and Commerce. **Directory of Irish company names, 1988.** Dublin, Stationery Office, 1988. 2v.([8],1808p.). IR£100.

V.1: A-J; v.2:K-Z. Listing gives the company's registered number, its name (A-Z) and address. Indications are given if a company is in liquidation, receivership or dissolved. *Class No:* 339.1(417)(058)

England

Histories

[2401]

BELLAMY, J.M., ed. Yorkshire business histories: a bibliography. Bradford, Bradford University Press, in association with Crosby Lockwood, London, 1970. xxii,480p.

Edited for the Yorkshire Group, Reference, Special and Information Section of the Library Association.

Nearly 4000 firms, A-Z (p.1-386); 42 library locations. Industrial analysis, p.395-446 (24 classes). Data: name of firm; type of business; town; reference. Appendices: 1. General business histories, theses, etc. - 2. Periodical locations - 3. List of periodicals indexed. *Class No:* 339.1(420)(091)

[2402]

GUILDHALL LIBRARY. London. **London business house histories:** a handlist. London, Corporation of City of London, [1965]. [56]p.

Four sections: 1. Index of firms - 2. 715 items, under trades, A-Z - 3. Collective histories (items 716-33) - 4. Archives (items 734-801). Addenda (7 items). Many of the items were issued privately and not to be found in standard bibliographies. (The Guildhall Library has an interleaved and updated reference copy). *Class No:* 339.1(420)(091)

[2403]

HORROCKS, S., comp. Lancashire business histories. Manchester, Joint Committee on the Lancashire Bibliography, 1971. xii,116p. (*A contribution towards Lancashire bibliography, 3.*)

General histories, p.1-16 (260 items); business histories, p.16-99 (979 entries). Includes many periodical articles; numerous cross-references. Indexes: name (personalia; organizations and firms); industrial; topographical (general; industrial localities). Locations in 58 libraries. *Class No:* 339.1(420)(091)

[2404]

ROWE, D.J., ed. Northern business histories: a bibliography. London, Library Association, Reference, Special and Information Section, 1979. [1],[1],7,191p. £27.50. ISBN: 0853659001.

3092 numbered entries (with locations in 38 libraries), under authors, companies, etc., A-Z. Appendix 1: Record Office holdings of business archives - 2. Law reports - 3. General histories (6 sections, including 6: Journals). 'Industrial analysis (*i.e.,* detailed subject index), also grouped under 23 heads (*e.g.* 20: Distributive trades: 7 columns, further subdivided). *Class No:* 339.1(420)(091)

Germany

[2405]

COVILL, L. Germany's top 300: a guide to Germany's largest corporations. London, Kogan Page, 1992. [424]p. £60. ISBN: 0749406577.

First published in 1991 by *Frankfurter Algemeine Zeitung*.

A *c.*50-page introduction to modern German commerce is followed by descriptions of 300 companies in detail, with date of establishment, address, contact numbers, business activities, SIC codes, locations, management personnel, employees, subsidiaries and participations, capital, major shareholders, turnover and pre-tax profits. Company, industry and location indexes. *Class No:* 339.1(430)

USSR

[2406]

SIBD, 92-93: the business directory for the Soviet region. North River, FYI Information Sources/Cooperative Reserve, 1992. 2v.(894p). $240. ISBN: 0963226304.

Update of the *Soviet independent business directory*: SIBD 1991 ed.

Purpose is to allow business people to 'identify, contact, evaluate, and communicate with potential business associates [in the Soviet Union]'(*Preface*). Lists over 2000 companies, A-Z, with indexes by products, geographical location, leaders (company officers), and business activities. An appendix lists the 500 largest enterprises. *Class No:* 339.1(47)

Asia—Far East

[2407]

Major companies of the Far East and Australasia, 1993-94. 10th ed. London, Graham & Trotman, 1993. 3v. 370 or $1030 the set. (*Major companies of the world series.*) ISBN: 1853338982.

First published 1984.

V.1 South East Asia (Brunei, Indonesia, Malaysia, The Philippines, Singapore, Thailand); v.2. East Asia (People's Republic of China, Hong Kong, Japan, Republic of Korea, Taiwan); v.3. Australasia. *c.*5000 companies selected on a basis of business activity or business importance within the country. Each entry lists company name; address; telephone number; and principal activities. When available, also offices, establishment date, telex, cable and fax numbers; branches; principal agencies; shareholders; bankers; number of employees; and associate, parent or subsidiary company. Financial data is included in many entries. Indexes to each volume of company names, company names listed by country, and business activities. *Class No:* 339.1(51/52+57)

Japan

Yearbooks & Directories

[2408]

Japan company handbook. Tokyo, Toyo Keizai Inc., 1974-. 2v. issued quarterly (previously 2pa). Yen18400; $204pa.

First section covers Blue Chip companies; nthe second section covers younger growth companies. One page for each company, grouped by industries, services, banks, etc.

.... *(contd.)*

For each company there is general information, financial information, business results, etc. Company index, A-Z by name. *Class No:* 339.1(52)(058)

Islamic World
[2409]
Major companies of the Arab world, 1993/94. 17th year. London, Graham & Trotman, 1993. 1152p. £360; $560. (*Major companies of the world series.*) ISBN: 185333894x.

First published for 1976/77.

Lists *c.*6700 top Arab companies. Arrangement is by countries, A-Z, subdivided alphabetically by name of company. Data given include address, principal activities, financial information, branches, date of foundation, number of employees, etc. Indexes by name of company, by country, and by business activity. *Class No:* 339.1(5.297)

Canada
[2410]
The Globe and Mail report on business: Canada company handbook, 1992. 4th ed. Austin, Texas, Reference Press, 1992. 590p. charts, tables. $39.95. ISBN: 0921925212.

Basic business information on more than 1300 of Canada's largest companies. Full-page profiles are included for more than 400 of them, with summary stock market information, statistical information, business description, current news synopsis, and general information for investors. Arrangement is by industry, subdivided A-Z by company. Tinted pages have company address, type, industry, description of business, and total revenue from latest annual report. *Class No:* 339.1(71)

Latin America
[2411]
Dun & Bradstreet's key business directory of Latin America, 1993/94. Bethlehem, PA, Dun & Bradstreet, 1993. 2v.(xxiv,6021p).

Previously *Dun's Latin America's top 25,000 companies.*

V.1: Businesses geographically (A-Z); businesses alphabetically; v.2: Businesses by industry classification (on tinted paper); Top 1000 businesses ranked by employee size. Data includes name and address; telephone and telex numbers; employee total; sales; SIC number; director/president, etc. *Class No:* 339.1(729.99)

USA

Bibliographies
[2412]
Corporate America: a historical bibliography. Santa Barbara, CA., ABC-Clio Information Services, 1984. xii,341p. $34; £26.35. (*ABC-Clio research guides, no.5.*) ISBN: 0874363624.

An annotated bibliography of 1358 short abstracts of articles on American business, published between 1973 and 1982, taken from *c.*2000 periodicals issued in 90 countries. 10 sections (1. Multinationals, conglomerates, and big business - 2. Banking, investments and service industries - 3. Transportation - 4. Communications - 5. Energy - 6. Food and fiber - 7. Mining - 8. Manufacturing and merchandising

.... *(contd.)*

- 9. Social effects and environmental impacts - 10. Government regulation and intervention). Items drawn from the ABC-Clio Information Services database. Detailed subject index, p.255-334; author index, p.335-341. *Class No:* 339.1(73)(01)

[2413]
KLEIN, B., *ed.* **Guide to American directories:** a guide to the major directories of the United States, covering all industrial, professional, and mercantile categories. 13th ed. West Nyack, N.Y., Todd Publications, 1993. 600p. $95. ISBN: 091534422x.

10th ed. was published in 1979.

Describes over 6000 industrial, mercantile, and professional directories. Each concise entry includes publisher's name and address, date of publication, number and type of name listed, and price. Subject and title indexes. *Class No:* 339.1(73)(01)

Yearbooks & Directories
[2414]
Business organizations, agencies, and publications directory. Ehr, C.M. *and* Estell, K., *eds.* 7th ed. Detroit, Mich., Gale Research International Ltd., 1993. 1423p. £225. $330. ISBN: 0810383551.

First published, 1980.

26,000 entries covering 39 types of business information source in the US, arranged in 5 broad categories: US and international organizations - Government agencies and programmes - Facilities and services - Research and education facilities - Publications and information services. Master name and keyword indexes. *Class No:* 339.1(73)(058)

[2415]
Major companies of the USA, 1989/90. 3rd ed. London, Graham & Trotman, 1989. 1100p. £350; $665. (*Major companies of the world series.*)

First published 1987.

Covers 5200 major companies, arranged A-Z by company names. Data includes address; telephone/cable/telex/fax numbers; board of directors; senior executives; principal activities; trade names; subsidiaries; principal bankers; financial information and number of employees. *Class No:* 339.1(73)(058)

[2416]
Ward's business directory of US private and public companies, 1994. Detroit, Mich., Gale Research Company, 1994. Annual. 5v. V.1-4 $1045; v,5 $710. ISSN: 10488707.

Data on over 85,000 US businesses. V.1-3 have alphabetical and geographical listings in a single A-Z sequence, regardless of company size. V.4 has special features and geographical listing. V/5 has companies ranked by sales. Also available on magnetic tape and floppy disk. *Class No:* 339.1(73)(058)

Biographies
[2417]
Business master biography index. McNeil, B. *and* Unterberger, A., *eds.* Detroit, Mich., Gale Research Company, 1987. 630p. $180. (*Gale biographical index series, no.10.*) ISBN: 0810314991.

....(contd.)

A spin-off from Gale's *Biography and genealogy master index* and its supplements. Refers to 26,000 biographical sketches. *Class No:* 339.1(73)(092)

[2418]
INGHAM, J.W., *ed*. **Biographical dictionary of American business leaders.** 2nd ed. Westport, CT. Greenwood Press, 1983. 4v. (xvii,2026p.). $225; £187.95 the set. ISBN: 0313213623.

835 biographical entries provide information on 1159 historically significant individuals, ranging from colonial to contemporary times. Includes colonial merchants, early national fur-traders, late 19th century iron and steel barons, early 20th century financiers, aircraft manufacturers, etc. 8 appendices list the entrepreneurs in a variety of ways. Lengthy index. Favourable review in *Business history* (July 1986, p.153-4) from which this annotation is taken. *Class No:* 339.1(73)(092)

Australia

Biographies

[2419]
The Business who's who of Australia, 1983. 17th ed. Crown's Nest, NSW., Riddell Publishing Pty Ltd., 1983. 848p. A$305. $245. ISSN: 00684503.

First published 1964.

Data on *c*.9000 companies, including addresses, activities, directors, capital, etc., listed A-Z by names of companies. In a separate section a 'directory of directors' lists, in a single alphabet, the names of all directors and the name(s) of the firm(s) with which they are associated. There is also a listing by the names of subsidiary companies, indicating the parent companies. Additional material includes information about Australian government offices and departments, diplomatic representatives,etc. *Class No:* 339.1(94)(092)

Market Structure

Licences and Permits

[2420]
BAILLIE, I.C. **Licensing:** a practical guide for the businessman. Harlow, Essex, Longman Group Ltd., 1987. xi,120p. £75. ISBN: 0851211321.

In 15 sections, written from the businessman's point of view: 1. Licensing and its alternatives - 2. What to license - 3. Government regulations - 4. Exclusion agreements - 5. Establishing and negotiating licenses - 6. Confidentiality - 7. The nature of a licensing agreement - 8. Style of agreement - 9. Structure of an agreement - 10. Considerations (payout) - 11. Managing a license - 12. Disputes - 13. Termination of the agreement - 14. Revision of the agreement - 15. Special types of licensing. Author is a member of the New York Bar and a Chartered Patent Agent. *Class No:* 339.13.025

Foreign Trade

Handbooks & Manuals

[2421]
BROOKE, M.Z. *and* BUCKLEY, P.J., *eds*. **Handbook of international trade.** London, Macmillan Press, 1988. xiv,460p. £125. ISBN: 0333453336. ISSN: 09536248.

First published 1982.

A survey of sources of information arranged in 9 sections: 1. Strategic issues - 2. Export and import - 3. Licensing, franchising, and other contractual arrangements - 4. Foreign investment - 5. Key markets - 6. Special industrial sectors - 7. Influence of treaty organizations - 8. Sources of information - 9. Indexes (subjects; abbreviations; countries and regions; treaties; companies and other relevant organizations; publications). *Class No:* 339.5(035)

[2422]
World trade resources guide: a guide to resources on importing from and exporting to the major trading nations of the world. Estell, K., *ed*. Detroit, Gale International Research Company, 1992. 891p. $169. ISBN: 0810384043.

A directory of more than 1000 foreign trade contacts and information sources in 80 of the largest and most significant trading nations of the world. The first section is arranged A-Z by country. Each country section begins with a map and brief profile, including population, GDP, foreign trade balance, etc., followed by entries for government agencies, chambers of commerce, banks, research services, trade associations, free trade zones, port authorities, airports, shipping lines, freight forwarders, publications, statistical sources, databases, libraries, comsultants, etc.Keyword and name index. *Class No:* 339.5(035)

Dictionaries

Polyglot

[2423]
INTERNATIONAL CHAMBERS OF COMMERCE. **Key words in international trade.** 3rd ed. Paris, ICC Publishing SA., 1989. 416p. £25.

First published 1981.

A glossary of *c*.1500 technical English words and phrases dealing with international commerce, arranged A-Z, with equivalents in German, Spanish, French and Italian. Indexes in German, Spanish, French and Italian. The 2nd ed. is also available with Arabic instead of Italian (£21). *Class No:* 339.5(038)=00

Tables & Data Books

[2424]
UNITED NATIONS. Statistical Office. **International trade statistics yearbook, 1990.** New York, United Nations, 1993. 2v. $125. ISBN: 9210611446.

First published for 1950. Annual.

V.1, Trade by country; v.2. Trade by commodity matrix tables. International coverage of foreign trade statistics through summary tables showing overall trade by regions and countries; world exports by origin and area of destination as well as by product. *Class No:* 339.5(083)

Europe—Eastern

Yearbooks & Directories

[2425]
Directory of foreign trade organizations in Eastern Europe: Bulgaria, Czechoslovakia, East Germany, Hungary, Poland, Romania and the USSR. San Francisco, CA., International Trade Press, 1989. 293p. $85. ISBN: 0926476009.

Lists chambers of commerce, banks, trade ministries, state committees and agencies that trade and deal in manufactured goods; joint ventures, agencies providing consumer goods. Information is limited to addresses and telephone numbers.
Class No: 339.5(401)(058)

Tables & Data Books

[2426]
COMECON foreign trade data, 1986. Vienna Institute for Comparative Economic Studies,, *ed.* London, Macmillan Press, 1988. 552p. tables, graphs. £30. ISBN: 0333369289. ISSN: 02633701.

First published 1980. Final issue was for 1986. Annual.

A register of sources (p.30-31) is followed by the tables in 3 sections: I. CMEA countries' and Yugoslavia's foreign trade according to their national statistics (Comprehensive indicators. Foreign trade by country) - II East-West trade according to OECD and other Western statistics - III. CMEA foreign trade by commodity groups, based on United Nations statistics. Data for 1960, 1970, 1975, 1982-85.
Class No: 339.5(401)(083)

China

Yearbooks & Directories

[2427]
Trade contacts in China: a directory of import and export corporations. London, Kogan Page, in association with Prospect Publishing House, China, 1987. 374p. £60; $110. ISBN: 1850913404.

An enlarged version of United States International Trade Administration's *Doing business with China* (1983).

Introductory chapter on traders in trading corporations, special Economic Zones, import duties and regulations, business laws and regulations, etc,; followed by a guide to over 600 trading corporations in Mainland China interested in developing international trade. Information includes name; address; telephone, telex and cable numbers; key personnel; business activities; subsidiary and branch offices. Indexes by industry, name and province. *Class No:* 339.5(510)(058)

Trade Fairs

[2428]
International tradeshow directory, 1993/94. Frankfurt am Main, M & A Publishers for Fairs, Exhibitions and Conventions Ltd., 1993. 2 pa. £130 each issue; £180 pa.

First published 1919- in German.

Advertisers index and introduction (on how to use the directory) precede the main contents, which are divided into 'registers': 1. Trade fairs by country, subdivided A-Z by city or town, then chronologically. Contact addresses are given but other information varies - 2. Chronological listing of trade fairs and exhibitions to November 1995 - 3. A-Z index of 150 topics - 4. A-Z list of official names and abbreviations

....(contd.)
of events. Parts 2-4 refer back to part 1, which has entry numbers. Also available on electronic book and floppy disk.
Class No: 339.52

[2429]
Trade shows worldwide, 1993. Webster, V.J., *ed.* Detroit, Mich., & Andover, Hants, Gale Research International, 1992. Annual. 1430p. £130. ISBN: 081037630x.

Profiles of 5796 trade shows fully described and with contact data. Also includes a directory of more than 4600 organizers and sponsors of trade shows, and lists of exhibion builders, hotel and motel chains, visitor and convention bureaux. professional asociations, consultants and published sources of industry information, etc. Key information is indexed by date, location and theme of event. Master index of all events, facilities and service providers.
Class No: 339.52

Imports

Great Britain

Yearbooks & Directories

[2430]
The Directory of British importers. Mcleod, S., *ed.* 8th ed. Berkhamsted, Herts., Trade Research Publications, 1993. 2v.(800p.). £120. ISBN: 0904783324.

Sponsored by The British Importers Confederation.

V.1: Editorial and indexes; v.2: Register of importing firms. Indexes are by products imported/importing firms; countries imported from/importing firms; associates abroad/importing firms; brand and trade names/importing firms. The register of importing firms is arranged by name of firm, A-Z, address, telephone-telex-fax number, type of goods imported, import turnover (an indication), and countries imported from. *Class No:* 339.562(410)(058)

Exports

[2431]
MATTHEWS, R. Finding export markets: a guide to methods and information sources in the UK and worldwide. Berkhamspstead, Herts, Trade Research Publications, 1986. various pagings. ISBN: 0904783197.

Includes list of countries covered, information sources for each country, and list of publishers. *Class No:* 339.564

Dictionaries

[2432]
DORSCHEID, P. Elsevier's dictionary of export financing and credit insurance, in English, German and French. London, Elsevier, 1989. viii,314p. £85.90; Dfl.263; $150.50. ISBN: 0444874968.

*c.*2100 terms of export credit insurance.
Class No: 339.564(038)

Great Britain

Yearbooks & Directories

[2433]

British exports, 1994. 26th ed. East Grinstead, West Sussex, Kompass-Reed Information Services, 1993. xxxii,3221p. ISBN: 0862682827. ISSN: 13506986.

Prior to the 24th edition, title was *Kelly's United Kingdom exports.*

Lists more than 10,000 major UK exporters under 16,500 product and service classifications. V.1. Products and services (Indices to products. Product and service section). V.2. Company information (Product information pages. Trade names section. Company information section, with their overseas agents, branches and subsidiaries).
Class No: 339.564(410)(058)

[2434]

The Directory of export buyers in the UK. 6th ed. Berkhamsted, Herts., Trade Research Publications, 1988. 360p. £65. ISBN: 0904783316.

First published 1978.

The register is arranged A-Z by name of firm, with address, telephone,-telex-fax number, products bought, and countries bought for. 3 indexes: Countries/export buyers; Foreign firms bought for/export buyers; and services provided by export buyers. Also international freight services for exporters. *Class No:* 339.564(410)(058)

[2435]

The Export handbook, 1992. London, Kogan Page: London Chamber of Commerce, 1992. 450p. £30. ISBN: 0749406356.

Directory of export services for over 150 subject areas, offering information on embassies and government agencies, and including practical articles on all aspects of exporting.
Class No: 339.564(410)(058)

Laws

[2436]

SCHMITTHOFF, C.M. The Export trade: the law and practice of international trade. 9th ed. London, Stevens & Sons, 1986. £53. ISBN: 042048180x.

First published 1948.

A well-known text, aimed at both lawyers and laymen. 5 chapters: 1. International sale of goods - 2. Representations abroad - 3. Matters incidental to exporting - 4. Long-term contracts - 5. Customs law. Appendices on insurance of exports, carriage of exports by sea and air, exchange control, and freight forwarders. Analytical index.
Class No: 339.564(410)(094.1)

65 Business & Management

Business Schools

[2437]

AMBA guide to business schools. Paliwoda, S.J. *and* Harrison, A.C., *comps*. 7th ed. London, Pitman Publishing, 1988. viii,256p. £8.95. ISBN: 0273029436.

First published 1970. Early title was *The B.G.A. guide to business schools, for prospective students and employers.*

Includes information on how to make an application, sources of funding, and employment prospects. Main part of the guide is an analysis of MBA and post-graduate diploma courses on offer at over 130 business schools around the world, including information on type of courses, methods of teaching, fees, age range and business experience of existing students, local cultural and social activities, etc. Covers 19 countries, including the UK. Bibliography, p.245-247. 'Useful contacts', p.248-256. *Class No:* 650:061:378.9

Business Methods & Organization

[2438]

ALLEN, M. *and* **HODGKINSON, R. Buying a business:** a guide to the decisions. 2nd ed. London, Graham & Trotman, 1989. xvi,209p. 39.50. $75. ISBN: 1853332771.

lst published 1986.

29 chapters each subdivided: 1. Synopsis - 2. Strategic ground rules ... 8. Valuation - 9. Financing ... 13. Legal protection ... 19. Acquiring abroad - 20. The aftermath. 3 appendices: I: Issues management guide; II: Areas to investigate before buying; III: Outline warranties and indemnities. Index. *Class No:* 650.011

[2439]

LOOSE, P., *and others*. **The Company director:** powers and duties. 7th ed. Bristol, Jordans, 1992. 583p. £34.95. ISBN: 085308162x.

Includes the Companies Act of 1989 and other recent developments. *Class No:* 650.011

Abbreviations & Symbols

[2440]

Business acronyms. Towell, J.E., *ed*. Detroit, Mich., Gale, 1988. xxiv, 414p. $60. ISBN: 0810325497.

25,000 acronyms and abbreviations, drawn from the 450,000-entry *Acronyms, initialisms and abbreviations dictionary*, plus additions. Two sequences, one arranged by acronyms, the other by definitions. *Class No:* 650.011(003)

[2441]

ROSENBERG, J.M. McGraw-Hill dictionary of business acronyms, initials, and abbreviations. New York, McGraw-Hill, 1992. 352p. $29.95. ISBN: 0070537348.

More than 15,000 entries from the area of general business, including science, technology and the latest government acronyms and abbreviations. *Class No:* 650.011(003)

Databases

[2442]

FOSTER, A. *and* **SMITH, G. Online business sourcebook.** Hartlepool, Headland, 1985. Looseleaf. ISBN: 090688912x.

Delineates 8 types of business database: A. Company information; B. Business news; C. Prices; D. Product and market data; E. Economics and finance; F. Trade; G. Media and consumer data; H. Business management. Data include cost of online connect time. *Class No:* 650.011(003.4)

[2443]

NEWHAM, G., *and others*. **'Choosing a business database: the expert approach.'** In *Business information review* v.5(1), July 1988, p.27-41.

Outlines the results of a pilot research project carried out at Loughborough University. First choice, basic bases: PTS Promt. 13 references; 8 tables, 1 chart. *Class No:* 650.011(003.4)

Bibliographies

[2444]

BAKEWELL, K.G.B. How to organize information: a manager's guide to techniques and sources, with a checklist for secretaries and assistants. Aldershot, Hants., Gower, 1984. 225p. £17.50. ISBN: 0566023970.

4 parts. 1. The information overload - 2. Using outside sources (libraries; abstracts, indexes and contents lists; fee-based information services; on-line services; videotext systems; other sources of information) p.11-73 - 3. The information file - 4. Directory of sources (Abstracting and indexing services ... Word processing). Loose insert; 'checklist for secretaries and assistants'. A concise, practical guide. *Class No:* 650.011(01)

[2445]

Bibliographic guide to business and economics, 1975-. Boston, Mass., G.K. Hall, 1976-. Annual. $550. ISSN: 03602702.

Each annual bibliography comprises an A-Z sequence of authors, titles, series and subjects of relevant publications catalogued by the New York Public Library, plus additions from Library of Congress MARC tapes. Coverage includes transportation and communication, commerce, business administration and finance, as well as serial titles. No language bar. *Class No:* 650.011(01)

[2446]

BRITISH LIBRARY. Science Reference and Information Service. **Business information:** a brief guide to the reference resources of the British Library. London, British Library, Business Information Service, 1987. 32p. illus., plan, chart. *Gratis.* ISBN: 0712307443.

Business stock location marks (directories, business books and market research reports, journals, abstracts) - Company information - Product information - Market information - Journals, house journals and newspapers - Statistics - Stockbrokers' reports - Abstracting and indexing services - Online database search service - Selected publicly available sources of business information in the UK - Guides to the business literature held at SRIS. Detailed index. An excellent example of a guide to a library's business resources. *Class No:* 650.011(01)

[2447]

—BROOKS, M. Sources of free business information. 2nd ed. London, Kogan Page, 1988. 91p. £5.95. ISBN: 1850914923.

First published 1986.

Has 11 sections, *e.g.* 5. General economic and business information; 6. Information and advice for smaller businesses; 8. Computers; 11. Names and addresses of providers of information. Details of more than 500 booklets 'Further reading from Kogan Page'. Subject index. Index of information providers. *Class No:* 650.011(01)

[2448]

BROWNSTONE, D.M. *and* CARRUTH, G. **Where to find business information:** a worldwide guide for everyone who needs the answers to business questions. 2nd ed. New York, etc., Wiley, 1982. 632p. $80. ISBN: 047108736x.

First published 1979.

3 sections, the third being an annotated title list of over 5,000 numbered entries for periodicals, directories, government publications, loose-leaf services, databases, etc. The first section functions as a subject index (often with geographical subdivision); the third, - a publisher index. US slanted. *Class No:* 650.011(01)

[2449]

Business and economics books, 1876-1983. New York, Bowker, 1983. 4v. (5256p.). $199. ISBN: 0835216144.

1-3. *Subject index.* 4. *Title index.*

Lists virtually every title on business and economics published or distributed in the US, 1876-1983, - more than 150,000 entries. V.1-3 adopt 50,000 Library of Congress subject headings. *Class No:* 650.011(01)

[2450]

—Business and economics books and serials in print, 1981. New York, Bowker, [1981]. 1836p. ISBN: 0835218060.

First published 1973.

Provides author, title and subject access to *c.*50,000 in-print and forthcoming books. A separate section lists over 7,500 periodicals under 250 subject headings. Online through DIALOG. *Class No:* 650.011(01)

[2451]

DANIELLS, L.M. Business information sources. 2nd rev. ed. Berkeley, Calif., Univ. of California Press, 1985. xv, 673p. $40. ISBN: 0520053354.

First published 1976.

21 chapters (1. Methods of locating facts ... 3. US business and economic trends ... 5. Foreign statistics and economic trends ... 10. Management ... 16. International

....(contd.)

management ... 20. Production and operations management - 21. A basic bookshelf, p.549-54 (briefly annotated)). Detailed analytical index. Confined to English-language sources. A standard work, US-slanted.

A 3rd ed. was published in 1993 (xix,725p. $35. ISBN 0520081803). *Class No:* 650.011(01)

[2452]

—The Good book guide for business, from the publishers of *The Good book guide* and *The Economist.* Braithwaite, P. and Taylor, B., *eds.* Harmondsworth, Middx., Penguin Books, 1984. 320p. £9.95. ISBN: 0140511415.

Annotated entries for *c.*600 books. 5 sections: 1. The world business environment - 2. The management of organisations - 3. The individual in business - 4. Business as it happened [history] - 5. Reference, p.273-301, (International business information; Key facts on major countries, regions, industries; Dictionaries, atlases, encyclopedias). 'Guide to buying business books', p.319-20. Aimed at the British practising manager. Limitation to books is a definite drawback, because of their lack of currency. The *Guide* claims to give 'more weight to immediate business relevance than to academic merit' (*Introduction*). *Class No:* 650.011(01)

[2453]

Encyclopedia of business information sources. Woy, J., *ed.* 9th ed. Detroit, Mich., Gale, 1992. $245. ISBN: 0810374897.

Arranged under topics, Abbreviations ... Zinc industry. Sources in each case include 'Abstract services and indexes', 'Online data bases', 'Research centers and institutes', 'Statistics sources', 'Trade associations and professional societies'. Numerous cross-references. Index of headings precedes. *Class No:* 650.011(01)

[2454]

HARVARD UNIVERSITY. Graduate School of Business Administration. Baker Library. **Core collection: an author and subject guide, 1970/71-.** Boston, Mass., Baker Library, 1971-. Annual.

Bibliography of 4,000 titles, based on reading lists used on business courses at Harvard. Annual revision, with monthly updating in *Recent additions to Baker Library.* *Class No:* 650.011(01)

[2455]

HOGAN, J. **Macmillan directory of EC business information sources.** London, Macmillan, 1992. xxi,294p. £75. ISBN: 0333372726.

Guidance to both published and organized sources, stressing practicality throughout. Sections: 1. Directory of EC industry contacts (arranged by NACE product classification system)- 2. EC on-line databases - 3. EC-funded research and development programmes - 4. Business co-operation network (BC-NET) - 5. European business network (BICs) - 6. Economic and social committee members - 7. Glossary of abbreviations, acronyms, commercial, scientific and technical terms (over 700 terms in European languages). Index. *Class No:* 650.011(01)

[2456]
Information sources in management and business.
Vernon, K.D.C., *ed.* 2nd ed. London, etc., Butterworths, 1984. xviii, 346p. tables. £37.50. (*Butterworths Guides to information sources.*) ISBN: 0408013451.

First published as *The use of management and business literature* (1975).

14 contributors. 3 parts (19 chapters, mostly with appended references): 1. The literature, the library and bibliographical tools for finding information - 2. Business information in various forms (company information; statistical publications, online services; market research reports; research in progress) - 3. Subject surveys of the literature (accounting and finance; organization studies; market; strategic management and planning; operations management; quantitative business analysis; business law). A basic guide on the subject. *Class No:* 650.011(01)

[2457]
Japanese business publications in English 1987: a select, annotated, list of recent publications held by the British Library. Edwards, S. *and* Thompson, K. 2nd ed. London, Science Reference and Information Service, 1987. [v], 55p. £10. ISBN: 0712307435.

232 numbered entries. Sections: Directories - Statistics, market information and industry surveys - Trade and business journals - Bibliographies and abstracting journals - Company reports - Suppliers of literature published in Japan - Alternative sources of information. A-Z list of titles and organizations. *Class No:* 650.011(01)

[2458]
LAVIN, M.R. Business information: how to find it, how to use it. 2nd ed. Phoenix, AZ, Oryx, 1992. 499p. tables. $49.95. ISBN: 0897745566.

First published 1987.

Designed to provide in-depth descriptions of major business publications, including electronic products and especially CD-ROM. Title and subject indexes.
Class No: 650.011(01)

[2459]
SCHLESSINGER, B.S., *and others, eds.* **The Basic business library:** core resources. 3rd ed. New York, Oryx, 1994. 256p. $39.50 ISBN: 0897747399.

3 sections: 1. Core list of printed business reference sources; 2. The literature of business reference and business libraries. Part 3 contains 10 state-of-the-art essays concerning business reference sources and services. Useful for its annotated bibliography on business reference and business librarianship and the essays on business reference sources and services. *Class No:* 650.011(01)

[2460]
TUDOR, J. Macmillan directory of business information sources. 3rd ed. London, Macmillan Publishers Ltd., 1992. 500p. £75. ISBN: 0333579718.

Sections: Finding business information (primary sources; secondary sources; computer-based information services; libraries; business related databases: selected list covering UK industries) - Directory of business information sources and centres (based on Standard Industrial Classification) - Foreign trade organisations in the UK - British trade publications and their editorial offices. Alphabetical index to Standard Industrial Classifications - Alphabetical index to organisation sources. Aims 'to provide guidance on both the

....(contd.)
published and organisational sources relevant to the needs of the non-professional business researcher' (*Preface*).
Class No: 650.011(01)

Dictionaries

[2461]
ADAM, J.H. Longman dictionary of business English. 2nd rev. ed. Harlow, Essex, Longman, 1989. xvi, 564p. £15.99. ISBN: 0582050294.

Defines *c.*2,000 words and phrases used in current business and commerce. Includes abbreviations, organizations and brief biographical notices. Full cross-references. Appended 'Useful information' (15 tables of measures, weights, etc.). Clear and simple definitions, showing terms in context. Specially suitable for students of English. *Class No:* 650.011(038)

[2462]
—**COLLIN, P.H.** English business dictionary. Teddington, Middx., the Author, 1986. 358p. £5.95.

Defines 4,500 words and phrases claimed to provide 'the basic business vocabulary of British and American English'. Gives examples of usage, quoting from business newspapers and magazines. Intended primarily for non-native speakers of English. Good value. *Class No:* 650.011(038)

[2463]
GREENER, M. The Penguin business dictionary. New ed. Harmondsworth, Middx., Penguin Books; Viking, 1987. [xv], 316p. £5.99. ISBN: 0670814245.

About 3,000 entries. Includes international bodies, organizations, economic and commercial phrases (*e.g.* 'Kennedy Round'). Ample cross-references. Lengthy list of abbreviations precedes. *Class No:* 650.011(038)

[2464]
Macmillan dictionary of business and management. Lamming, R. *and* Bessant, E. London, Macmillan, 1987. 320p. diagrs., graphs, maps. £30. ISBN: 0333390547.

About 4,000 concise entries and cross-references, omitting some of the more basic terms. Includes entries for abbreviations, organizations, Acts and some biographies. 'European Community': 6½ columns; 'Line management': ½ column. 'It is intended as a handy general reference tool for all occasions' (*Preface*). *Class No:* 650.011(038)

[2465]
ROSENBERG, J.M. Dictionary of business and management. New revision. New York, etc., Wiley, 1993. 374p. tables. $39.45. ISBN: 0471578126.

First published 1978.

About 7500 concise definitions of terms, phrases, acronyms and symbols. Appendices include tables, quotations and a chronology of major US business and economic events. *Class No:* 650.011(038)

German

[2466]
Collins business German: a dictionary of 12,000 essential words and phrases. London, HarperCollins, 1992. xvi,271p. £7.90. ISBN: 0004336240.

Word lists in over 20 fields, under topic (*eg*, accounting,

....(contd.)

advertising, computing, EEC finance, import/export, insurance, manufacturing, marketing, sales). German-English glossary, p.221-271. *Class No:* 650.011(038)=30

[2467]
NEUHAUS, K. *and* **HALTERN, M.** **Euro-business: German.** Bochum, ILT-Verlag, 1991. £7.95;DM17.80. (Euro-business - Sprachführer) ISBN: 3927899011.

Guide to the language of commerce, industry and services for the businessman (exhibitions, sales, marketing, advertising, promotion, meetings, data processing, joint ventures, personnel, import and export). Also useful general phrases for conversation, background information on Germany and its customs, over 150 essential addresses for travellers, etc. *Class No:* 650.011(038)=30

French

[2468]
Harrap's business French-English dictionary. Laurendeau-Collin, J.P., *and others, eds.* 3rd ed. London, Harrap, 1991. xvi, 604p. map. £19.95. ISBN: 024560149x.

Early ed. as *Harrap's French and English business dictionary* (1981).

English-French, French-English dictionary, with *c.*3,000 entries in each part. Includes terms used in banking, stock exchange dealings, accountancy, insurance, commerce, law, etc. Appended abbreviations, conversion tables. *Class No:* 650.011(038)=40

Italian

[2469]
RAGAZZINI, G. *and* **GAGLIARDELLI, G.** **Harrap's business Italian dictionary. Italian-English.** London, Harrap, 1990. xiv,672p. £15.95.
Class No: 650.011(038)=50

Reviews & Abstracts

[2470]
Business periodicals index. New York, H.W. Wilson, 1958-. 11pa.; cumulated 4pa. and annually. ISSN: 00076961.

Its parent is *Industrial arts index*, 1913-57, from which both *Business periodicals index* and *Applied science and technology index* have stemmed.

Subject index to articles in over 250 English-language periodicals of which *c.*12 are British. Full cross-references. Appended 'Book reviews'. Available online through WILSONLINE and also available on CD-ROM.
Class No: 650.011(048)

[2471]
Business publications index and abstracts. Detroit, Mich., Gale, 1983-. Monthly, with quarterly & annual cumulations.

Continues *Management contents* (1975-82).

1985: *c.*24,000 abstracts, covering periodical articles and book chapters. The 1985 cumulation occupies 4v.: *Abstracts* (2v.); *Subject/author citations* (2v.). Covers over 700 periodicals, - more extensive than either its predecessor (*c.*375 titles) or H.W. Wilson's *Business periodicals index* (*c.*275 titles). Forms the printed version of the *Management contents* database. *Class No:* 650.011(048)

Periodicals

[2472]
Business information review. Headland, Cleveland, Headland Press, 1984-. 4pa. $99pa.

Includes articles written by field exports about business information sources - print and electronic. Analyses information sources in specific industry sectors and countries, and the use of business information.
Class No: 650.011(051)

Histories

[2473]
Business history of the world: a chronology. Robinson, R., *comp.* Westport, CT, Greenwood Press, 1993. 562p. $75. ISBN: 031326094x.

Aim was to include representative trend-setting occurrences, and most of those included are European. Formal chronology runs from 10,000 BC to AD 1988 in general. Early entries are, perforce, brief, but later ones can be several pages long. From 1600 material is divided into 'General events' and 'Business events'. Index of names, places and subjects. *Class No:* 650.011(091)

Biographies

[2474]
Dictionary of business biography: a biographical dictionary of business leaders active in Britain in the period 1860-1980. Jeremy, D.J., *ed.* London, Butterworth, 1984-86. 5v. & Supplement. facsims, ports. £72ea. ISBN: 0406273189, v.1; 0406273421, v.2; 040627343x, v.3; 0406273448, v.4; 0406273456, v.5; 0406273405, 5v, with supplement.

5v.: A-C, D-G, H-L, Mc-R, S-Z. Supplement: Indexes, contributors, errata. About 1,000 signed biographies in all, with emphasis on business careers. V.1, p.547-54 is devoted to George Cadbury, with appendix on writings and sources (unpublished and published). Living businessmen are included only if they have now retired from full-time office. Serves to supplement entries in *The Times* obituary columns and the *Dictionary of national biography*, which tend to pass over businessmen. The editor: Research Fellow, Business History Unit, London School of Economics and Political Science. *Class No:* 650.011(092)

[2475]
Dictionary of Scottish business biography, 1860-1960. Slaven, A *and* Checkland, S., *eds.* Aberdeen, Aberdeen University Press, 1986 - 1989. 2v. illus. v.1. £44; v.2. £48. ISBN: 0080303986 v.1; 0080303994 v.2.

V.1.:*The staple industries* is arranged in 9 sections, by industry (Extractive industries - Metals ... Shipbuilding ... Clothing ... Leather and footwear), each section having an essay, followed by a bibliography, A-Z by biographee. Personal name and subject indexes. V.2. *Processing, distributing, services* is arranged in 10 chapters (Food, drink and tobacco ... Construction ... Distributive trades - Banking, insurance and finance). *Class No:* 650.011(092)

Information Management

[2476]
Manual of business library practice. Campbell, M.J., *ed.* 2nd rev. ed. London, Bingley, 1985. x, 238p. £30. ISBN: 0851573606.

First published 1973.

....(contd.)

9 contributors. 13 chapters (2. Organization and administration: objectives, planning and staffing; 5. Directories and company information sources; 9. Management literature; 12. The use of external sources of information - 13. The impact of information technology). References and further reading, p.201-11. Appendix: Databases, p.212-14. Detailed, analytical index, p.215-38. *Class No:* 650.011:025.4

[2477]

—VERNON, K.D.C. *and* LANG, V. The London classification of business studies: a classification and thesaurus for business libraries. 2nd ed., revised by K.G.B. Bakewell and D.R. Cotton. London, Aslib, 1979. 253p. ISBN: 0851421245.

First published by the London Graduate School of Business Studies. *Class No:* 650.011:025.4

Institutions & Associations

[2478]

Business organizations, agencies and publications directory. Ehr, C.M. *and* Estell, K., *eds.* 7th ed. Detroit, Mich., Gale, 1993. 1423p. £225. $330. ISBN: 0810383551. ISSN: 08881413.

First published 1980.

26,000 entries covering 39 types of business in the United States, arranged in 5 broad categories: US and international organizations (subdivided by type) - Government agencies and programmes - Facilities and services - Research and education facilities - Publications and information services. Master name and keyword index. *Class No:* 650.011:061:061.2

[2479]

The International directory of business information sources and services. London, Europa Pubns., Ltd., 1986. ix, 578p. £45.00. ISBN: 0946653186.

A directory of business organizations in 23 countries (Australia - USA), plus international organizations. Subdivisions: Chambers of commerce; International trade; Government organizations; Independent organizations; Research organizations; Sources of statistical information; Business libraries. Data on each organization include date of founding; chief staff; activities, statistics; publications. Detailed index, p.353-78. *Class No:* 650.011:061:061.2

[2480]

TUDOR, J. Macmillan directory of business information sources. 3rd ed. Basingstoke, Macmillan Publishers, 1992. 500p. £75. ISBN: 0333579718.

First published 1987.

Directory of business information sources (journals, etc.) and centres, is followed by foreign trade organizations in the UK and British trade publications and their editorial offices. A-Z index to Standard Industrial Classification (SIC Code), A-Z index to organization sources. *Class No:* 650.011:061:061.2

Mechanization

[2481]

Key abstracts, business automation, 1989-. Stevenage, Herts, INSPEC, IEE, 1989-. Monthly. £90. $165 pa. ISSN: 09549153.

48 subject sections in the fields of communications,

....(contd.)

computers and office systems in business and commerce, including banking, financial markets and retailing. *c.50* abstracts in each issue. Subject index. Also available online (BRS,CEDOCAR, CISTI, Data-Star, Dialog, etc.). *Class No:* 650.011.54

Operational Research

[2482]

A Guide to operational research. Duckworth, W.E., *and others.* 3rd ed. London, Chapman & Hall, 1977. ix, 205p. ISBN: 0412135000.

First published 1962.

12 chapters: 1. What operational research is and does - 2. Measuring uncertainty - 3. Queuing problem - 4. Business forecasting (12 references; bibliography of 9 items) - 5. Simulation and Monte Carlo methods - 6. Stock and production control models - 7. Resource allocation - 8. Planning projects - 9. Analysing decisions - 10. Operational gaming - 11. Other research techniques - 12. Conclusions. Name index; general index. Favourably reviewed in *Aslib book list*, April 1978, entry 216. *Class No:* 650.012.122

Psychology

[2483]

McCORMICK, E.J. *and* **ILGEN, D.R. Industrial and organizational psychology.** 8th ed. London, Allen & Unwin, 1987. xii, 468p. diagrs., tables, graphs. £63.15. ISBN: 0044450028.

First published 1952.

6 sections: 1. Introduction - 2. Job-related behavior and its measurement - 3. Personnel selection - 4. Personnel training and development - 5. The organizational and social context of human work - 6. The job and work environment. 4 appendices: A. Elementary descriptive statistics ... D. Representative personnel tests. Bibliographies appended to each chapter. *Class No:* 650.013

Work Study

[2484]

BRITISH STANDARDS INSTITUTION. Glossary of terms used in work study and organizational methods (O & M). London, the Institution, 1979. 36p. diagr. £25.60. (*BS 3138:1979.*)

Defines terms for operator and machine-controlled work, with sections on organization study, method study, work management and work performance control. Examples of construction of standard time. BS 3375: parts 1-4: 1984-86 is also relevant. It deals with organization and method study, work measurement, and work performance control. *Class No:* 650.015

Office Practice

[2485]

BAILEY, P. Mastering office practice. 2nd ed. London, Macmillan, 1985. xiii, 350p. (*Macmillan master series.*) ISBN: 0333388488.

First published 1982.

....(contd.)

24 sections (each with questions appended): 2. Layout of business letters ... 5. Telecommunications - 6. Shorthand and audio systems - 7. Typewriters - 8. Computers - 9. The purchase and sale of goods ... 14. Filing ... 18. Copying and duplicating - 19. The training and qualifications required for office work ... 22. Wages, salaries and other forms of remuneration ... 23. Sources of information (including 'Reference books', p.317-22) - 24. Visual aids. 2 appendices. Detailed, analytical index. Aims to be a complete self-contained course for individual study or classroom work. *Class No:* 651

[2486]

GARTSIDE, L. **Modern business correspondence:** a comprehensive business guide to business writing and related office services. 4th ed. London, Pitman, 1986. x, 529p. illus. ISBN: 0273025759.

3rd ed., 1976.

2 parts (23 chapters): 1. The English background (principles of good business writing: style; presentation; spelling) - 2. Business correspondence (including filing and indexing systems; office machine systems; typing; letter styles). 4 appendices (C. Glossary of business terms, p.429-97; D. Abbreviations used in business). Detailed, analytical index. 48 illus. *Class No:* 651

[2487]

MILLS, G., *and others*. **Modern office management.** 7th ed. London, Pitman, 1986. xii,496p.

First published 1953; title for first 6 eds. was *Office organization and method..*

8 parts (30 chapters): 1. Administration and organization - 2. Communications - 3. Other office services - 4. Data processing - 5. Financial and accounting services - 6. Environment - 7. Personnel - 8. Planning and control. Glossary of terms, p.478-87. Bibliography, p.385-7. Analytical index, p.488-96. Aims to provide a compact work for reference for company secretaries, accountants, cost accountants and administrative managers generally, and a textbook for students. *Class No:* 651

[2488]

TITMAN, L. **The Effective office:** a handbook of modern office management. London, Cassell, 1991. 544p. £45. $90. ISBN: 0304316768.

A guide to modern office techniques, including traditional techniques, electronic and technological aspects of office management. Chapters: The basics - Technology enlacement - Managerial tools - Method - Design - Work quantification - Support techniques - Final notes - Index. *Class No:* 651

Dictionaries

Polyglot

[2489]

CENTRE DE TERMINOLOGIE DE BRUXELLES. **Elsevier's dictionary of office automation in four languages.** Amsterdam, Elsevier, 1991. xxi,462p. ISBN: 0444880658.

In English, German, French and Dutch. Numbered descriptions are given in English followed by translations of the terms in the three other languages. Term lists in those languages refer to the numbered entries in English. Cross-references. Bibliography precedes (p.xi-xxi).

Class No: 651(038)=00

Equipment

[2490]

BARCOMB, D. **Office automation:** a survey of tools and technology. 2nd ed. Bedford, Mass., Digital Press, 1989. viii, 339p. illus., diagrs.

2 parts: 1. Overview of office automation - 2. The tools of office automation (5. Text management and graphics ... 7. Electronic mail systems ... 9. Micrographics) - 3. Putting it all together (10. Integrated office automation systems ... 12. Coming soon to an office near you). Short bibliographies for each chapter. Glossary, p.311-26. *Class No:* 651.2

[2491]

BATE, J. St. J. **Management guide to office automation.** London, Collins, 1987. 228p. diagrs., tables. £85. ISBN: 0003833534.

16 chapters: 2. Management's role in office management projects; 8. Technologies in the office; 14. Office automation as a support function: 16. Office automation - a threat or an opportunity? Glossary, p.218-26. Brief index. Aimed at senior and middle management in commercial, administrative and financial organizations. *Class No:* 651.2

[2492]

Business equipment digest. Wallington, Surrey, BED Business Books, 1961-87. Monthly.

Covers all aspects of office business equipment, supplies and services. Addressed to senior executives who are responsible for puchasing office equipment, supplies and services. *Class No:* 651.2

[2493]

SAFFADY, W. **The Automated office:** an introduction to the technology. Silver Spring, Md., National Micrographics Association, 1981. viii, [1], 241p. illus. ISBN: 0892580720.

7 chapters (1. Office automation: an introduction - 2. Word processing - 3. Computers and office automation - 4. Micrographics - 5. Retrographics - 6. Electronic mail and message systems - 7. Integrating and implementing automated office systems). Glossary, p.207. Notes (chapter references), p.215-34. Detailed, non-analytical index. *Class No:* 651.2

Secretarial Work

[2494]

HUTCHINSON, L. **Standard handbook for secretaries.** 8th ed. New York, etc., McGraw-Hill, 1969. x, 638p. $16.95.

A mine of information on a variety of topics: letter and letter writing; dictation; typewritten work; copy for the press; filing; legal papers; patents and trademarks; copyright; government information; business and banking papers; securities; foreign exchange; financial statements; petty cash; insurance. Abbreviations; various tables; reference books. Detailed, analytical index. A basic title on the more conventional aspects of secretarial work. *Class No:* 651.44

[2495]

Webster's secretarial handbook. Springfield, Mass., Merriam-Webster, 1984. 550p. diagrs. $10.95. ISBN: 0877791368.

15 chapters cover communications, career-path development, meetings and conference arrangements, dictation, automated equipment, business correspondence,

....*(contd.)*

business English, management of business records, secretarial accounting, telecommunications. Cross-references. Bibliography. Index. *Class No:* 651.44

Correspondence

[2496]

FORMAN, J. *and* KELLY, K.A. **The Random House guide to business writing.** New York, McGraw-Hill, 1990. xxiii,856p. £20.95. (*(McGraw-Hill English language series).*) ISBN: 0075572214.

15 chapters: 1. Introduction ... 4. The basics of business letters: writing to readers outside the organization ... 6. Letters that persuade - 7. Goodwill letters - 8. Memos - 9. The basics of report writing ... 12. Speaking - 13. Visual aids ... 15. The business writer and the computer. 2 appemdices: 1. Writing responses to cases; 2. A brief guide to grammar and punctuation. Notes, p.833-7. Index, p.839-56. *Class No:* 651.7

[2497]

HARVARD, J. **Bilingual guides to business and professional correspondence.** Oxford, etc., Pergamon Press, 1965-72 (and reprints).

English-German, by J. Harvard. 1965. x, 140p. *German-English*, by J. Harvard. 1965. [ix], 140p. *English-French*, by J. Harvard, and F. Rose. 1969. 236p. *French-English*, by J. Harvard, and F. Rose. 1965. ix, 140p. *English-Italian*, by J. Harvard, and M.M. Miletto. 1972. 232p. *Italian-English* by J. Harvard, and M.M. Miletto. *English-Spanish*, by J. Harvard, and I.F. Ariza. 1970. 236p. *Spanish-English*, by J. Harvard, and I.F. Ariza. 1970. 236p.

The *French-English* guide has 9 sections: 1. The layout of a French business letter - 2. The contents of a French business letter - 3. Business organisations - 4. Business transactions ... 8. Inquiry and information - 9. Applications and references. English page on left, French facing. English and French abbreviations. Differences between British and American vocabulary and spelling included. *Class No:* 651.7

[2498]

HORTEN, H.E. **Export-import correspondence in four languages.** London, Gower Press, 1970. xi, 2-316p. £25. ISBN: 0716100274.

The first part consists of a four-way parallel text, (English, French, German and Spanish) on topics such as orders, dispatch notice, acknowledgement of payment (p.2-87) which aims to help the business man to compose his own letters. English, French, German and Spanish indexes. Part 2 consists of 4 parallel dictionaries, each with *c.*1,000 entry-words. *Class No:* 651.7

[2499]

WHITEHEAD, G. *and* WHITEHEAD, D.H. **Pitman business correspondence.** London, Pitman Business Ltd., 1982. xii, 372p. £5.95. ISBN: 0273017977.

23 sections (2. The layout of a business letter; 5. Orders; 8. Complaints and their adjustment; 14/15. Export trade; 21. Organising a business correspondence department. Glossary of terms, p.363-8. Detailed, analytical index, p.369-72. Furnishes numerous examples (1 per page) of business letters and in-house memos serving the whole range of business activity.

A later ed. was issued in 1988. *Class No:* 651.7

Bibliographies

[2500]

Better said and clearly written: an annotated guide to business communication sources, skills and samples. Belanger, S.E., *comp.* Westport, CT, Greenwood Press, 1989. xiv,196p. $37.95. (*Bibliographies and indexes in mass media and communications,3.*) ISBN: 0313266417.

Over 1000 sources listed, including books, periodicals, databases and programmed-instructive workbooks. In 2 parts: 1. Research guides, resources, information; 2. Communication skills. Aimed primarily at business and engineering students, faculty, librarians and other working professionals. *Class No:* 651.7(01)

Dictionaries

Polyglot

[2501]

DUTTWEILER, C. *and* DUTTWEILER, G. **The 20000 sentences and expressions of business and personal correspondence.** OTT Verlag, Switzerland, 1989. 3v.(493+459+422p). £33.90 each vol.; £99 the set.

Volumes are for German-French-English; French-German-English; English-German-French. Each volume has examples of usage in the first language of the volume. *Class No:* 651.7(038)=00

[2502]

The Multilingual business handbook: a guide to international correspondence. Ferney, D., *and others.* 2nd rev. ed. London, Macmillan, 1990. 352p. illus. £27.50; £9.99. ISBN: 0333512480, HB; 0333512499, pbk.

First published in 1983 by Pan Books, edited by P. Hartley and others.

A glossary of commercial expressions used in business correspondence in English, French, German, Spanish and Italian. Covers sales and distribution, agencies, customers, property, sales, rentals, hotel and travel reservations, and vocabulary relating to banking, post office, telephone, etc. *Class No:* 651.7(038)=00

Spanish

[2503]

GIRAUD, A.F.-S. **Diccionario comercial español-inglés, inglés-español. El secretario.** 3rd ed. Barcelona, Editoria Juventud, 1977. 158;137p.

First published 1940.

Intended for commercial correspondence. Includes about 4000 headwords in each half. Particular attention is given to terms and phrases used in commercial correspondence. *Class No:* 651.7(038)=60

Italian

[2504]

DAVIES, S. *and* ARDUINI, A.M. **Manuale bilingue di corrispondinza e comunicazione commerciale. Italiane-Inglese.** Hemel Hempstead, Herts, Prentice-Hall, 1989. viii,210p. £6.50.

First part is Italian-English, the second part English-Italian. Each in 3 sections: A. Commercial correspondence - B. Business communication - C. Business and cultural briefing on Italy. Cross-references. List of abbreviations. *Class No:* 651.7=50

Typing

[2505]

BENNETT, P. The Typewriting dictionary. Maidenhead, Berks, McGraw-Hill Book Company (UK) Ltd., 1987. 99p. £3.50. ISBN: 0070849927.

Complete dictionary of typewriting terms, rules and standard practice. Abbreviations - Accents - Accuracy speed tests ... Guide keys - Half-space correcting ... Paper sizes ... Words or figures. *Class No:* 651.923

[2506]

MACKAY, E. The Typewriting dictionary. London, Pitman, 1977. [iv], 269p. facsims. ISBN: 0273317210.

Originally as *Dictionary of typewriting* by M. Crooks (1919).

Entries, sometimes lengthy, A-Z ('Parts of a typewriter' and their uses, p.190-7, with references from the actual parts, *e.g.* 'Alignment', 'Legal typing', p.121-7; 'Literary work', p.147-52; 'Errors, their causes and remedy,' p.82-7; 'Drills', p.63-9; 'Letters', p.129-46, with specimens). 53 illus. (facsims.). *Class No:* 651.923

Shorthand

[2507]

The Pitman 2000 dictionary of English and shorthand. London, Pitman, 1982. 848p. £19.99. ISBN: 0273016180.

Based on the original work by Sir Isaac Pitman, *Stenographic soundhand* (1837).

Total number of shorthand outlines is now over 75,000. '*Pitman 2000* shorthand is a modified form of Pitman's shorthand as it has been known and practised in its New Era form over the past fifty-nine years' (*Preface*). *Class No:* 651.93

[2508]

—Gregg shorthand dictionary. Gregg, J.R. 2nd ed. New York, etc., McGraw-Hill, 1974. 408p. (*Diamond Jubilee series*.)

Has outlines for 35,000 words, and *c.*4,000 names and geographical expressions. Now includes syllabication. *Class No:* 651.93

Accountancy

Bibliographies

[2509]

Current accounting literature, 1971-74: a catalogue of books and pamphlets in the Members' Reference Library of the Institute of Chartered Accountants in England and Wales... London, Mansell, 1972-82. 4v. £10 each.

8,188 author entries for material, mostly post-1960. Subject index. Annual supplements are union catalogues of recent accessions of the libraries of the Association of Certified Accountants, Institute of Chartered Accountants in Ireland, Institute of Chartered Accountants of Scotland, Institute of Cost and Management Accountants, and Liverpool Society of Chartered Accountants.

Earlier items are covered in the ICA's *Historical accounting literature* (Mansell, 1975. 360p.), listing *c.*3,000 entries for 2,500 works on accounting published since the late 15th century. Author index. *Class No:* 652.7(01)

[2510]

MOWAT, M. 'Information sources on accountancy and finance'. In *Business library review*, v.3(2), October 1986, p.3-9.

A helpful survey of relevant journals, directories, annuals and abstracting services (ANBAR; *ICMA abstracts*; *Research index*). Also mentions government publications, publications from professional bodies and accounting firms, specialist publishers and information services, business libraries and online information services. 1 reference. *Class No:* 652.7(01)

[2511]

PRYCE-JONES, J.E. Accounting in Scotland: a historical bibliography. Edinburgh, The Institute of Chartered Accountants of Scotland/Scottish Committee on Accounting History, 1974. 96p. illus.

323 entries, most of them annotated. 3 parts: 1. Books printed in Scotland, 1683-1320 - 2. Printed transcripts of accounts (books printed) - 3. History of Scottish accounting. Indexes of authors and titles. *Class No:* 652.7(01)

Handbooks & Manuals

[2512]

Handbook of modern accounting. Davidson, S. *and* Weil, R.L., *eds.* 3rd ed. New York, etc., McGraw-Hill, 1983. 1408p. illus. ISBN: 0070154929.

First published 1970.

42 briefly documented chapters by specialists (Accounting concepts and principles, and auditing standards and opinions ... Accounting for nonprofit organizations). Index. A comprehensive handbook.

From the British angle,-. *Class No:* 652.7(035)

[2513]

—BROWN, J.L. *and* HOWARD, I.R. Principles and practice of management accountancy. 3rd ed. London, Macdonald and Evans, 1975. xii, 756p. diagrs., tables.

A comprehensive manual that makes extensive use of examples. *Class No:* 652.7(035)

Dictionaries

[2514]

BROCKINGTON, R. A Concise dictionary of accounting and finance. London, Pitman, 1986. vii, 127, [8]p. (*M & E Professional dictionaries*.) ISBN: 0712106847.

About 1,200 terms defined. American terminology is differentiated. 7 appendices (5. The contents of a company's annual report and accounts). Intended as a work of reference for those studying the literature of accounting and finance, and for the reader of the financial press. *Class No:* 652.7(038)

[2515]

Dictionary of accounting. Estes, R., *ed.* 2nd ed. Cambridge, Mass., MIT Press, 1985. 162p. ISBN: 0262050323.

First published 1981.

Concentrates on *c.*1,000 terms and phrases, often documented and with adequate cross-references. 'More suitable as an appendix to a textbook on accounting' (*Choice*, June 1981, p.1393, on the 1981 ed.). *Class No:* 652.7(038)

[2516]
FRENCH, D. Dictionary of accounting terms. New ed.
Kingston upon Thames, Surrey, Croner Publications, 1991.
xii,296p. £14.95. ISBN: 1855240459.
First published by Financial Training Publications in 1985.
Defines more than 3,500 words and expressions used with
a special meaning in accountancy. Includes abbreviations,
synonyms. 'Profit and loss account': nearly ½p.; 'Holding
company': 2/3p. *Class No:* 652.7(038)

[2517]
Kohler's dictionary for accountants. 6th ed., edited by W.W.
Cooper and Y. Ijiri. Englewood Cliffs, N.J., Prentice-Hall,
1983. xi, 574p. ISBN: 0135166586.
First published 1952; 5th ed. 1975.
20 contributors. 4,538 terms defined (5th ed.: *c.*3,000
entries). The entries - well over half, new material - range in
length from 75 to 100 words. Examples of usage. The
standard dictionary of accountancy. *Class No:* 652.7(038)

[2518]
—PARKER, R.H. Macmillan dictionary of accounting. 2nd ed.
London, Macmillan Press, 1992. 200p. £40. ISBN:
0333455487.
First published in 1984.
Has *c.*1,000 entries ('Depreciation': 2 columns; 'Merger
accountancy': 1½ columns. Abbreviations and acronyms,
p.vii-xi. For students, teachers and practitioners of
accountancy. *Class No:* 652.7(038)

Polyglot

[2519]
**UNION EUROPÉENNE DES EXPERTS COMPTABLES
ÉCONOMIQUE ET FINANCIERS. Lexique UEC.** 2.éd.
Düsseldorf, Institut der Wirtschaftsprüfer-Verlag, 1974.
879p. ISBN: 3802100735.
First published 1961.
A dictionary of *c.*1,300 accountancy terms in French,
German, English/American, Dutch, Danish, Italian, Spanish
and Portuguese. Main A-Z sequence of terms, with
definitions and indexes in each language.
Class No: 652.7(038)=00

Arabic

[2520]
**ABU-GHAZALEH, T. The Abu-Ghazaleh English-Arabic
dictionary of accountancy.** London, Macmillan, 1978.
210p. ISBN: 0333214684.
Arabic translation of the English entry-word appears in
both Latin and Arabic characters.
Class No: 652.7(038)=927

Reviews & Abstracts

[2521]
Accounting and finance abstracts. Bradford, Yorks.,
ANBAR Management Publications, in association with the
Institute of Chartered Accountants in England and Wales,
1971-. monthly, previously 8pa. $1549.95 including
cumulative index and *Compleat Anbar.* ISSN: 00014796.
Supersedes *Accounting + data processing abstracts,*
previously *Anbar management services abstracts.*
Abstracts of articles from more than 300 international

....(contd.)
management journals. Covers financial accounts, software,
internal and external auditing, computer management, capital
investment, and data transmission. *Class No:* 652.7(048)

[2522]
Accounting and tax index: a bibliography of accounting
literature. New York, American Institute of Certified Public
Accountants, 1921-. Quarterly, with annual cumulation.
About 10,000 references pa. to periodical articles, books,
government publications, etc. Author and subject sequence.
Comprehensive coverage of accountancy, auditing, data
processing, finance, investments, law, management and
taxation. Restricted to English-language material. Also
available online (Orbit Search, Service (ACCT) and CD-
ROM. *Class No:* 652.7(048)

Periodicals

[2523]
SPICELAND, J.D. *and* **AGRAWAL, S.P. International
guide to accounting journals.** New York, Markus Wiener
Publishing, 1988. 291p. ISBN: 0910129630.
A 2nd ed. was issued in 1993 (320p. $49.95. ISBN
1558760679).
Covers journals in 33 countries and is concerned mainly
with journals for research. 2 sections: information listed
alphabetically by journal and journals by country. The first
section includes information on primary readership,
language, circulation, publisher, style, length, sponsor and
percentage of articles on accounting topics.
Class No: 652.7(051)

Yearbooks & Directories

[2524]
European accountancy yearbook, 1992. lst ed. London,
Graham & Trotman, 1991. 400p. £125. $240.
Lists *c.*2000 offices of major accountancy firms in Europe,
with addresses; telephone, fax & telex numbers; names of
partners and functions; nature of firm's European coverage;
fee income by sector and total; main services; major public
company clients; history; etc. *Class No:* 652.7(058)

Biographies

[2525]
Who's who in accountancy. [London], Chapter 3
Publications, in association with Longman, 1987. xiv, [1],
394p. £27.00. ISBN: 0851210627.
3 parts: 1. Index of individual entries in alphabetical order
- 2. Indices of a more specialised nature (*e.g.* 4. Accountants
who are members of Parliament; 7. Editors of accountancy
journals) - 3. Index of accountants according to the Industrial
Classification (Accountancy services ... Transport).
Class No: 652.7(092)

Great Britain

Yearbooks & Directories

[2526]
INSTITUTE OF CHARTERED ACCOUNTANTS OF ENGLAND AND WALES. Directory of firms. Macmillan Press, 1994. 950p. £63. ISBN: 0333585178.
Detailed information on the specialization of chartered accountancy firms, arranged A-Z by towns, plus an overseas section. *Class No:* 652.7(410)(058)

Book-keeping

[2527]
Spicer and Pegler's book-keeping and accounts. Spicer, E.E. *and* Pegler, E.C. 22nd ed. London, Butterworth, 1993. 608p. £17.95. ISBN: 0406022364.
26 chapters (1. Incomplete records ... 26. Special reports including Stock Exchange situations). Detailed contents. Detailed, analytical index, p.557-66. 'Prepared with the examination needs of the student primarily in mind' (*Preface*). *Class No:* 652.71

Costing

Dictionaries

[2528]
INSTITUTE OF COST AND MANAGEMENT ACCOUNTANTS. Terminology of management and financial accountancy. London, Institute of Cost and Management Accountants, 1974. x, 95p.
Third major revision of *Costing terminology*, first published in the Institute's *Journal.* Defines *c.*400 terms; includes basic and full contextual classifications. Detailed analytical index, p.77-95. *Class No:* 652.747(038)

Reviews & Abstracts

[2529]
Management and accounting research. London, Academic Press, for the Chartered Institute of Management Accountants, 1983-. Quarterly. ISSN: 10445005.
Title previously *ICMA abstracts bulletin.*
Aims to encourage scholarship and empirical research in management accounting by providing a vehicle for publishing original research in the field.*c.*100 abstracts per issue on cost and financial accountancy; finance and financial management; industry, services and computer applications. Author and subject indexes per issue and annually. *Class No:* 652.747(048)

Auditing

[2530]
ATTWOOD, F.A. *and* **STEIN, N.D. De Paula's auditing.** 17th ed. London, Pitman, 1986. xiv, 682p. ISBN: 0273025015.
First published 1970.
24 chapters (1. How to study auditing ... 24. Investigations). Appendix: Auditing standards and guidelines, and other professional announcements. Detailed, analytical index, p.675-82. Student orientated. *Class No:* 652.76

[2531]
Cashin's handbook for auditors. Cashin, J.A., *and others.* 2nd ed. by P.D. Neuwirth and J.F. Levy. New York, etc., McGraw-Hill, 1985. 1376p. illus. £85. ISBN: 0070102643.
First published 1971 (1344p.).
7 parts (with documented chapters by specialists): 1. Principles, standards and responsibilities - 2. Principal types of auditing - 3. Planning, evaluation and administration - 4. Audit program objectives and procedures - 5. Analytical methods - 6. Conclusion, review and reporting - 7. Professional developments. Index. *Class No:* 652.76

[2532]
CHARTERED INSTITUTE OF PUBLIC FINANCE & ACCOUNTANCY. Glossary of audit terms. London, Chartered Institute of Public Finance & Accountancy, 1988. [v], 40p. £14.25. ISBN: 0852993684.
Defines *c.*300 terms (Access control ... Working files). *Class No:* 652.76

[2533]
SPICER, C.C. *and* **PEGLER, E.C. Spicer and Pegler's practical auditing.** 17th ed. London, Butterworths, 1985. xi, 365p. diagrs., charts, tables. £13.50. ISBN: 0406678014.
2 parts (28 chapters): 1. The firm's audit account - 2. Approach to specific areas (*e.g.* 14. Expenditure; 19. Tangible and intangible fixed assets; 23. Taxation; 24. Group accounts). Glossary of terms, p.351-7. Detailed, analytical index, p.359-65. Includes quotations and abstracts from the Institute of Chartered Accountants in England and Wales' auditing standards and guidelines, etc. Standard textbook; well laid out. *Class No:* 652.76

Management

Databases

[2534]
HOWITT, DORAN AND WEINBERGER, MARVIN, Inc. **Databasics:** your guide to online business information. New York, etc., Garland, 1984. xx, 614p.
5 parts, of which part 2 (chapters 13-23) is 'A guide to selected business databases', p.93-286. The major hosts are DIALOG, DATA-STAR, DATASOLVE, PERGAMON INFOLINE and FINSBURY DATA SERVICES. *Class No:* 652.8(003.4)

Bibliographies

[2535]
ASHRIDGE MANAGEMENT COLLEGE. Management for the future: a bibliography, undertaken on behalf of, and sponsored by, the Federation for Management Education. Ashridge, Bucks., Ashridge Management College, 1986. v.p.
About 800 entries, each with descriptors and abstracts. 6 sections: A. The future - general issues & trends - B. Management: general - C. Strategic management, corporate planning & operational/functional implications - D. Other organizational issues - E. People management & human resources issues - F. Individual companies, (divided by type of industry, *e.g.* Food and drink; Construction). Author and company indexes. *Class No:* 652.8(01)

[2536]
Information sources in management and business.
Vernon, K.D.C., *ed.* 2nd ed. London, etc., Butterworths, 1984. xviii, 346p. tables. £37.50. (*Butterworths Guides to information sources.*) ISBN: 0408013451.

First published as *The use of management and business literature* (1975).

14 contributors. 3 parts (19 chapters, mostly with appended references): 1. The literature, the library and bibliographical tools for finding information - 2. Business information in various forms (company information; statistical publications, online services; market research reports; research in progress) - 3. Subject surveys of the literature (accounting and finance; organization studies; marketing; strategic management and planning; operations management; quantitative business analysis; business law). A basic guide on the subject. *Class No:* 652.8(01)

Encyclopaedias

[2537]
The Encyclopedia of management. Heyel, C., *ed.* 3rd ed. New York, Van Nostrand Reinhold, 1982. xxx, [1], 1371p. diagrs., graphs, tables, maps. ISBN: 0442251653.

Over 200 contributors. More than 350 documented articles, A-Z, ranging in length from half a page to 30p. 'Quality control and quality assurance': p.998-1009, carrying 7 exhibits, 35 references and 5 cross-references. 3 appendices: A. Universities and colleges (all US); B. Sources of information (organizations, A-Z); C. Sources of information (journals cited). Detailed analytical index, p.1361-71. 'A much-needed compendium of management information' (*Reference books bulletin*, 1983-1984, p.84).
Class No: 652.8(031)

[2538]
Encyclopedia of professional management. Bittel, L.R., *ed.* New York, McGraw-Hill, 1978. xl, 1304p. illus. ISBN: 0070054789.

Nearly 250 contributors, and as many entries. Articles provide definition, history of development, applications, problems, and list of sources. Grouped list of articles. Well organized. US-slanted. *Class No:* 652.8(031)

[2539]
Penguin management handbook. 4th ed., edited by T. Kempner. Harmondsworth, Middx., Penguin Books, 1987. xxxi, 624p. diagrs., graphs, tables. £9.99. ISBN: 0140091254.

First published as *Handbook of management* (Weidenfeld & Nicholson, 1971).

16 contributors. Synoptic index of entries precedes the A-Z sequence; 11 headings: 1. Business policy and corporate planning ... 11. Production management. About 1,000 signed entries, usually with 1-3 appended references. Cross-references. For both managers and students. A bargain. *Class No:* 652.8(031)

Handbooks & Manuals

[2540]
APPLEBY, R.C. Modern business administration. 4th ed. London, Pitman, 1987. xvi, 478p. diagrs., tables. ISBN: 0273025058.

First published 1969.

Part 1 (chapters 1-6): Management principles; Part 2 (7-

....(contd.)
10): Management in action. Each chapter has appended 'Review questions' and bibliography. 'Further review problems', p.451-452. Detailed, analytical index. Written particularly for students preparing for examination.

A 5th ed. was issued in 1991. *Class No:* 652.8(035)

[2541]
ARMSTRONG, M. A Handbook of management techniques. London, Kogan Page, 1986. 578p. diagrs., graphs, tables. £18.95. ISBN: 1850910774.

10 parts (124 sections): 1. Introduction - 2. Corporate management - 3. Marketing management - 4. Operations management - 5. Financial management - 6. Personal management - 7. New technology (section 103: The electronic office) - 8. Management science - 9. Planning and resource application - 10. Efficiency and effectiveness. Each section starts with a definition of the technique and continues with application, appraisal, and - at times - further reading (*e.g.* 101. Systems analysis: p.440-50; 4 diagrs.). Detailed, analytical index, p.561-78. Highly organized study of management skills, procedures and activities.
Class No: 652.8(035)

[2542]
Company administration handbook. Beattie, D., *ed.* 7th ed. Aldershot, Hants., Gower, 1990. xxiii,1005p. illus., plans, tables. £65. ISBN: 0566028557.

First published 1970.

28 contributors. 6 parts (34 documented chapters): 1. The constitution and conduct of companies - 2. Accounting and finance - 3. Commercial functions - 4. Office administration - 5. The company and its employees - 6. The management of physical assets. Detailed analytical index. A comprehensive textbook for company secretaries, managers and personnel executives. *Class No:* 652.8(035)

[2543]
The Complete guide to managing your business. Cheltenham, Stottard & Co., 1988-. v.p. Loose-leaf; updating service.

22 contributors. 20 chapters (*e.g.* 2. Financial planning and management; 4. Buying and selling a business; 17. Selling your product or service; 18. Marketing and advertising; 19. Exporting overseas). Includes forms, useful addresses and some publications. 39-p. index.
Class No: 652.8(035)

[2544]
Croner's executive companion. New Malden, Surrey, Croner, 1988. Loose-leaf. ISBN: 0900319615.

12 sections. 1. Sources of law in the UK. Consumer protection; 2. Legal aspects, finance, taxes; 3. Taxation; 4. Communications; 5. Exporting & importing; 6. Property; 7. Government departments & industry; 9. Social security; 10. Manpower; 11. Economic review; 12. General information. 16-p. index. For managers, company secretaries, supervisors and administrators. *Class No:* 652.8(035)

[2545]
Handbook of human factors. Salvendy, G., *ed.* New York, Wiley, 1987. 1874p. illus. $150. ISBN: 0471880159.

Gives 'information about the effective design and use of systems requiring the interaction among human, machine (computer) and environment' (*Preface*). 68 documented chapters by specialists. Index. *Class No:* 652.8(035)

[2546]
Handbook of management. Lock, D., *ed.* 3rd ed. Aldershot, Hants, Gower, 1992. xli,1002p. 271 illus. £60. ISBN: 056602974x.

First published 1983.

73 chapters in 10 parts: 1. Principles, policy & organization; 2. Financial management; 3. Marketing; 4. Research, engineering & design; 5. Purchasing & inventory management; 6. Manufacturing management; 7. Logistics management; 8. Administration; 9. Human resource management; 10. The skills of management. 68 contributors. 'Further reading' after each chapter. Analytical index (double-column), p.989-1002. *Class No:* 652.8(035)

[2547]
Handbook of management skills. Stewart, D.M., *ed.* 2nd ed. Aldershot, Hants, Gower, 1992. xxvi,537p. 161 illus (figures & charts) £42.50. ISBN: 0566029693.

First published 1987.

33 chapters in 4 parts: 1. Managing yourself - 2. Managing other people - 3. Managing a specialist department - 4. Managing the business. 33 contributors. Analytical index, p.529-37 (double-column). '... this book is the one to keep in your desk drawer ... [until] you need the information' (the editor). *Class No:* 652.8(035)

[2548]
The New manager's handbook: a reference guide. Armstrong, M., *ed.* London, Kogan Page, 1990. 438p. tables, charts. £19.95. ISBN: 0749402563.

Designed for quick reference, with chapters on the European Community, human resources management, sales and marketing, production and operations management, financial planning, and strategic management. Includes case studies. Appendices contain useful addresses, details of foreign currencies, time zones, travel information, etc. *Class No:* 652.8(035)

[2549]
SIEGAL, J.G., *and others.* **The McGraw-Hill pocket guide to business finance:** 201 decision-making tools for managers. New York, McGraw-Hill, 1992. 354p. $29.95. ISBN: 0070575770.

'a handy reference' for financial professionals. 'Tools' are some of the most commonly used financial computations ranging from basic ratios to complex multiple regression tests. For each tool there is a brief definition, statement of computational method, examples of practical use, and identification of professions most likely to use it. Clear, well-organized entries. Well indexed. 'A good supplement to more in-depth financial handbooks'(*Choice*, v.30(3), November 1992, p.450). *Class No:* 652.8(035)

Dictionaries

[2550]
BLAKE, J. *and* **LAWRENCE, P. The ABC of management:** a handbook of management terms and concepts. London, Cassell, 1989. [3],133p. £6.95. $12.95. ISBN: 0304322288.

International in scope, with more detailed explanations than a simple dictionary. As well as defining terms, it provides details on key figures in business and management. Cross-references. Aimed at managers at all levels. *Class No:* 652.8(038)

[2551]
FRENCH, D. *and* **SAWARD, H. Dictionary of management.** 2nd ed. London, Pan Books, 1984. x, 470p. ISBN: 0330285122.

First published 1975.

Defines *c.*4,000 terms 'that are likely to be encountered or read about, or discussing, management topics'. Reference in text to 70 sources. Entries include abbreviations and organizations. *Class No:* 652.8(038)

[2552]
—BLOOR, S.G. Reference guide to management techniques and activities. Oxford, etc., Pergamon Press, 1987. xi, 80p. £17.25. ISBN: 008034268x.

Mainly an A-Z list of terms, p.1-61. 50-250-word definitions; cross-references. Further reading, p.63-74. Index, with grouped headings. *Class No:* 652.8(038)

[2553]
ROSENBERG, J.M. Dictionary of business and management. New revision. New York, etc., Wiley, 1993. 374p. tables. $39.45. ISBN: 0471578126.

First published 1978; 2nd ed. 1983.

Defines over 7,500 terms for such areas of business as accounting, banking and finance, data processing, labour relations, management, marketing, real estate and transportation. Appendices A-M of tables of measures, interest, etc. Provides more terms than other such dictionaries, although some definitions are gratuitous. *Class No:* 652.8(038)

[2554]
—JOHANNSEN, H. *and* PAGE, G.T. International dictionary of management. 4th ed. London, Kogan Page, 1990. 388p. illus. £20. ISBN: 0749400153.

First published 1975.

Has over 6000 brief entries for terms, organizations, abbreviations and acronyms. 'It has both omissions and errors' (*Choice*, v.19(6), February 1982, p.744), of the 3rd ed. Use to supplement other business dictionaries. *Class No:* 652.8(038)

German

[2555]
COVENEY, J., *and others.* **Harrap's glossary of business management terms. German-English, English-German.** London, Harrap, 1991. 256p. £4.50. ISBN: 0245603573.

Includes terms not usually found in existing general dictionaries. Covers the main areas of management interest. *Class No:* 652.8(038)=30

[2556]
SOMMER, W. *and* **SCHÖNFELD, H.-M. Management dictionary:** dictionary of accountancy, economic and tax law, and data processing. 4th-5th rev. ed. New York, de Gruyter, 1978-79. ISBN: 3110077086, v.1.

1. *English-German.* 5th rev. and enld. ed. 1979. 620p. 2. *Deutsch-Englisch.* 4th rev. and enld. ed. 1978. 542p. *Class No:* 652.8(038)=30

French

[2557]

**QUEBEC OFFICE DE LA LANGUE FRANÇAISE.
Terminologie de la gestion:** vocabulaire des imprimés administratifs lexique, français et anglais. Quebec, Office de la langue française, 1974. 311p.

French-English, English-French dictionary of management terms. *Class No:* 652.8(038)=40

Theses

[2558]

Selected list of UK theses and dissertations in management studies. Sheffield City Polytechnic Library, for the British Business Schools' Libraries Group, 1975-. Annual. ISSN: 01407414.

12th annual listing, 1987, ([7], 472p.) lists *c.*1,500 theses and dissertations, with locations. 3 parts: 1. Subject grouping; 2. Author index; 3. Subject index. 19 Library locations. *Class No:* 652.8(043)

Reviews & Abstracts

[2559]

Compleat ANBAR. Bradford, Yorks, ANBAR Management Publications, 1972-. Annual.

Reproduces all the abstracts appearing throughout the year in 5 ANBAR abstracting services, - *Accounting and finance abstracts, Marketing and distribution abstracts, Personnel and training abstracts, Top management abstracts, Operations + production abstracts.* Cumulated abstracts are grouped: 1. Users; 2. Techniques; 3. Applications; 4. Equipment, premises, suppliers. Indexes: subjects; authors (books). Bibliography (list of monographs, etc.). *Class No:* 652.8(048)

[2560]

Management and marketing abstracts. Leatherhead, Surrey, PIRA [Paper Industry Research Association], in association with British Institute of Management, 1976-. Monthly. $846. ISSN: 03082172.

Formerly *Marketing abstracts.*

Over 3600 abstracts a year in 26 sections, including management techniques, personnel, education and training, marketing, etc. Author and subjects pa. Stresses practical aspects. Online: PERGAMON INFOLINE, DIALOG, ORBIT (1973-). *Class No:* 652.8(048)

[2561]

Management bibliographies and reviews. Bradford, Yorks., ANBAR Management Publications, 1987-. 8 pa (previously quarterly). £999.95. $2629.95 pa. ISSN: 09535713.

Continues *Anbar management publications* and *The ANBAR management bibliography.*

Provides up-to-date information on new developments and thinking in management practice and serves as a resource for research workers and practicing managers. *Class No:* 652.8(048)

[2562]

Management contents: the semi-monthly compilation of tables of contents from more than 320 business magazines and journals. Niles, Ill., Find/SVP, 1976-87. 24pa. ISSN: 03602400.

V.12(23), 4 September 1987 issue provides contents pages of 31 journal titles grouped: General - Business - Economics & finance - Management science & operations research -

....(contd.)

Marketing - Personnel. Appended list of *c.*300 journal titles (*c.*100 British) contents-listed over the year. Subject index. Available online, BRS(MGMT), DATA-STAR (MGMT), DIALOG, MEAD DATA CENTRAL, ORBIT. *Class No:* 652.8(048)

[2563]

SCIMP [Selective cooperative index of management periodicals]: European index of management periodicals. European Business School Librarians Group. Helsinki, Helsinki School of Economics Library, previously Manchester, Manchester Business School Library, 1978-. 10pa. £75;FIM650pa. ISSN: 07822979.

Over 5,000 references pa.; *c.*150 journals scanned. Subject classes (100 General management; 200 Finance and economics; 300 Industry and marketing; 400 Associated subjects (*e.g.* Psychology; Communications). Author, company, and permitted subject indexes per issue, cumulated 3 times a year. A truly international effort: indexing is shared amongst 7 different countries; the database functions at Helsinki, editing at Delft, printing at Manchester, and the *SCIMP/SCAMP thesaurus* at the London Business School Library. Also available on CD-ROM. *Class No:* 652.8(048)

[2564]

Top management abstracts. Bradford, Yorks.,ANBAR Management Publications, in association with the British Institute of Management, 1971-. monthly (previously 8 pa). £689.95 pa. ISSN: 00494100.

Supersedes in part *ANBAR management services abstracts.*

About 120 short abstracts per issue, with critical comments italicized (*e.g.* "A bit of plugging for the author's organization here"). Brief subject index ('At a glance'). Cross-references. Asterisked items are mentioned in an introductory 'Highlights'. Some 250 journals are monitored. Annual index. Intended for directors, senior managers and senior staff officers. *Class No:* 652.8(048)

[2565]

Women in management review and abstracts. Equal Opportunities Commission. Bradford, Yorks., ANBAR Publications, Ltd., 1985-. 7 pa (previously quarterly). ISSN: 09558357.

Includes articles, news items, and book reviews, as well as *c.*50 abstracts per issue of articles in other management journals. Leavitt, J.A. *Women in management: an annotated bibliography and sourcelist* (Phoenix, Ariz., Oryx Press, 1982. 197p.) covers items published/written 1970-81, in 20 sections, with author index. *Class No:* 652.8(048)

Progress Reports

[2566]

Current research in management. Hammond, V., *ed.* London & Dover, N.H., Frances Pinter (Publishers), for the Association of Teachers of Management, 1985. xv, 265p. £30. ISBN: 086187546x.

24 contributors. 5 parts (16 well-documented chapters): 1. Understanding organisations and culture - 2. Understanding managers and their needs - 3. Developments in personnel and industrial relations - 4. New directives in business - 5. Research into practice. Complete list of papers presented at Current Research in Management Conference, p.261-5. *Class No:* 652.8(055)

Audio-Visual Materials

[2567]

Films and videograms for managers: British National Film & Video catalogue. Brown, M., *ed.* London, British Film Institute, 1984. vi, 181p. (*British national film and video catalogue subject listing no.2.*) ISBN: 0851701698.

'A subject listing of recent films and videograms on management and selected topics drawn from the published records of the British National Film and Video catalogue for the year 1980 to 1983 inclusive'. *Class No:* 652.8(086)

[2568]

Management media directory: an annotated guide of commercially available audiovisual programs for business and management schools, in-house training and development programs, management consultants and human resource managers. Proven, J. *and* Glogowski, M.P., *eds.* Detroit, Gale Research Co., 1982. vi, 506p. $200. ISBN: 0810301709.

Data on over 3,500 programmes used by American business and management schools. Media include films, sound filmstrips, audiocassettes and videos. More than 230 distributors. Title and subject indexes. *Class No:* 652.8(086)

Information Services

[2569]

LONG, L. Management information systems. Englewood Cliffs, N.J., Prentice-Hall, 1989. $42.67. ISBN: 0135515988.

In 5 parts: Information - Computing institutions - MIS (Management Information Systems) concepts - Planning and implementation - Managing information and computing resources. Geared to undergraduate and graduate students. *Class No:* 652.8:061:025.5

Personnel Management

[2570]

ARMSTRONG, M. A Handbook of personnel management. 3rd ed. London, Kogan Page, 1988. xix, 712p. tables. ISBN: 1850913366.

7 sections: 1. Personnel management - an overview - 2. Organizational behaviour - 3. Organizational planning and development - 4. Employee resourcing - 5. Employment and personnel administration - 6. Reward management - 7. Employee relations. Appendicies A-L (A. Personnel policies … H. Disciplinary procedure … L. Assessment centres). Bibliographies throughout. *Class No:* 652.83

[2571]

—**An International dictionary of personnel terms.** 2nd ed. London, European Association of Personnel Management, 1980. 157p.

Provides equivalents of terms in 10 languages, - French, Norwegian, English, Spanish, Finnish, German, Portuguese, Dutch, Swedish and Danish - in a grouped sequence. The index covers all 10 languages. A separate Italian section completes coverage of Western and Northern Europe. *Class No:* 652.83

[2572]

The Human resources management yearbook, 1993. London, A.P.Information Services, 1993. Annual. £22.50 ISBN: 0814581607. ISSN: 03066673.

First published 1969 by Kogan Page.

In 6 parts: Part 1 has articles by leading experts; pt 2 is a survey of major areas of employment, trade union and health and safety legislation; pts 3,4,5 are directories of course providers, consultancy and service providers, officials and public bodies of HRD; and pt 6 is a bibliography of recent books and journals on human resource management, grouped under 18 headings. *Class No:* 652.83

[2573]

Personnel + training abstracts. Bradford, Yorks, Anbar Publications Ltd., in association with The Institute of Personnel Managament, 1971-. monthly (previously 8 pa). $1549.95 including cumulative index and *Compleat Anbar* ISSN: 0305067x.

Supersedes in part *Anbar management services abstracts.*

Abstracts of articles selected from over 300 international management journals. Covers such topics as health and safety, management development, industrial relations. *Class No:* 652.83

[2574]

TORRINGTON, D. *and* **EARNSHAW, J. Pocket employer.** Oxford, Basil Blackwell and the Economist Publications, 1988. [ii], 252p. ISBN: 0631153896.

Contains *c.*300 terms related to the management of employment. Definitions and explanations of terms from employment law, academic research, and personnel management methods. Cross references and suggestions for further reading contained in text. *Class No:* 652.83

Dictionaries

[2575]

BENNETT, R. Dictionary of personnel and human resources management. London, Pitman Publishing, 1992. [ii],231p. £12.99. ISBN: 027303877x.

Over 3500 definitions covering the practical and utilitarian aspects of the personnel function (laws and regulations, methods, systems, procedures and techniques, plus broader topics concerned with organizational behaviour, human resources, planning, strategy and control. Intended for both student and practitioner. Fully cross-referenced. Includes acronyms. *Class No:* 652.83(038)

[2576]

TRACEY, W.R. The Human resources glossary: a complete desk reference for HR professionals. New York, AMACOM, 1991. 416p. $49.95. ISBN: 0814450113.

Over 3000 terms relating to human resources specializations, plus key terms from selected business and management disciplines, with explanation of context, use and managerial implications. Index of key terms. 'There are few glossaries one would wish to read cover to cover. This is one of them. It reads well, is thoughtfully organized …' (*Choice*, v.29(2). October 1991, p.267). *Class No:* 652.83(038)

Ergonomics

[2577]

Ergonomics abstracts. Basingstoke, Hants, Taylor & Francis, for the Ergonomics Information Analysis Centre, School of Manufacturing and Mechanical Engineering, University of Birmingham, 1969-. 6pa. £393:$677pa. ISSN: 00462446.

*c.*750 abstracts per issue on working efficiency of human beings. Irregular author and subject indexes. Available on microform from MIM. *Class No:* 652.83.04

Production Management

[2578]

BRITISH STANDARDS INSTITUTION. Glossary of production planning and control terms. London, The Institution, 1975. 40p. (*BS 5191: 1975.*)

Lists and defines general terms used in quality assurance, with an appendix defining related common words. *Class No:* 652.85

[2579]

—BURBRIDGE, J.L. IFIP glossary of terms used in production control. Amsterdam, North-Holland, 1987. ix, 113p. diagrs. ISBN: 0444702873.

3 parts: 1. Introduction - 2. Classified glossary (A. - J.: A. Management ... D. Purchasing ... J. Secretarial) - 3. Alphabetical glossary. Index. *Class No:* 652.85

[2580]

Industrial engineering handbook. Maynard, H.B., *ed.* 3rd ed. New York, etc., McGraw-Hill, 1971. [xvii, 1891]p. illus., diagrs., tables. $132. ISBN: 0070410844.

First published 1956.

About 75 contributors. 13 sections: 1. The industrial engineering function - 2. Methods - 3. Work measurement techniques ... 6. Wage and salary administration ... 8. Planning and control procedures ... 12. Industrial engineering tools - 13. Industrial engineering applications. Based on US practice. *Class No:* 652.85

[2581]

Operations + production abstracts. Bradford, Yorks, Anbar Publications, Ltd., in conjunction with the Institute of Management Services, 1973-. monthly (loose-leaf). $1549.95 including the *Compleat Anbar* ISSN: 09524614.

Formerly *Work study + O and M abstracts.* Supersedes in part *Anbar management services abstracts*, and later *Management services + + production abstracts.*

Abstracts selected from over 300 international management journals, covering productivity, industrial engineering, work measurement, operational research, safety, and production methods. *Class No:* 652.85

[2582]

—Work Research Unit Information Service news and abstracts. London, the Service, 1978-. 6pa. *Gratis.*

Provides 30 items per issue on aspects of working conditions, including automation and robotics. *Class No:* 652.85

Quality Control

[2583]

EUROPEAN ORGANISATION FOR QUALITY CONTROL. Glossary Committee. Glossary of terms used in the management of quality control, with their equivalents in Arabic, Chinese, Czech, Danish, Dutch,

....(contd.)

Finnish, French, German, Greek, Hungarian, Italian, Japanese, Norwegian, Polish, Portuguese, Russian, Spanish, Swedish. 6th ed. Bern, the Organisation, 1989. 777p. £49.95.

First published in 1965.

457 English-based terms, with definitions (p.9-82), and equivalents and indexes in the other 18 languages. *Class No:* 652.856

[2584]

Juran's quality control handbook. Juran, J.M., *ed.-in-chief.* 4th ed. New York, etc., McGraw-Hill, 1988. [1774]p. illus. £93.50. ISBN: 0070331766.

3rd ed. 1974. [1600]p.

Revised and updated 4th ed. includes chapters on companywide planning for quality; quality improvement; quality costs; computers and quality; managing human performance; training for quality; quality programmes in service industries; marketing; upper management and quality. Index. *Class No:* 652.856

[2585]

LOCK, D., *ed.* **Gower handbook of quality management.** Aldershot, Hants, Gower, 1990. xxi,649p. £50 ISBN: 0366027704.

Contributions by professionals on a broad range of issues. 'It provides a full and instructive discussion of quality programmes and their implementation. Comprehensive'. (*British book news,* September 1990, p.575). *Class No:* 652.856

[2586]

Quality control and applied statistics: international literature digest service. Davenport, Iowa, Executive Sciences Institute, 1956-. Monthly. $148pa. ISSN: 00335207.

Formerly *Quality control and applied statistics, including Operations research, yearbook,* 1960-62.

50 abstracts per issue. 5 sections: Statistical process control - Mathematical statistics and possibility theory - Experimentation and correlation - Managerial applications - Reliability of complex assemblies. Appended list of publications abstracted. Author, subject and classification code indexes. *Class No:* 652.856

[2587]

UNITED NATIONS. Industrial Development Organization (UNIDO), Vienna. **Information sources on industrial quality control.** New York, United Nations, 1973. xii, 57p. $4.00. (*UNIDO guides to information sources, no.6.*)

10 sections. 1. Addresses of professional, trade and research organizations, learned societies and special information services - 2. Basic handbooks, textbooks and manuals - 3. Monograph series - 4. Current periodicals - 5. Current abstracting and indexing services - 6. Proceedings, papers and reports - 7. Specialized dictionaries and encyclopedias - 8. Bibliographies - 9. Films, filmstrips and slides - 10. Other potential sources of information. Bibliographical sources used. Sections 2-4, 6, 9-10 have annotated entries. Subject index. *Class No:* 652.856

Purchasing

[2588]

Purchasing and materials management. Dobler, D.W., *and others*. 4th ed. New York, etc., McGraw-Hill, 1984. 736p. $33.95. ISBN: 0070370427.

6 parts: 1. The functions of purchasing and materials management - 2. Fundamentals - 3. Related materials functions - 4. Management - 5. Institutional and government purchasing - 6. Cases for study and analysis. Appendices. Indexes. *Instructor's manual* is also available.
Class No: 652.87

Marketing & Sales

[2589]

Macmillan dictionary of marketing and advertising. Baker, M.J., *ed.* 2nd ed. London, Macmillan Press, 1990. [vi],271p. £20. ISBN: 0333516044.

First published in 1984.

About 2000 initialled entries, by 26 contributors, of terms commonly used in marketing and advertising, including thumb-nail sketches of key concepts and ideas. Fully cross-referenced. Intended readership: practitioners, managers, students and lay persons. *Class No:* 652.88

Bibliographies

[2590]

The European directory of marketing information sources, 1991. 2nd ed. London, Euromonitor, 1991. xix, 674p. charts, tables. ISBN: 0863384005.

First published 1987.

Over 2,000 entries, arranged in 10 main sections, all subdivided by country: 1. Official sources and publications; 2. Libraries and information services; 3. Leading market research companies; 4. Leading consumer research publishers; 5. Information databases and databanks; 6. Abstracts and indexes; 7. Major business and marketing journals; 8. Major business and marketing associations; 9. European business contacts; 10. Socio-economic profiles. Coverage: 17 Western European countries. Subject and A-Z indexes. *Class No:* 652.88(01)

[2591]

HEROLD, J. Marketing and sales management an information sourcebook. Phoenix, Ariz., Oryx, 1988. $39.50. (*Oryx sourcebook series in business and management.*) ISBN: 0897744063.

Contains 1,000 entries on reference works, indexes, abstracting journals, periodicals, serials, statistical sources, databases and vendors, CD-ROMS, and associations. Covers English-language material only from 1980 to the present. Numbered entries with annotations. Final chapter, 'Core Library Collection'. *Class No:* 652.88(01)

[2592]

International directory of marketing information sources 1988. London, Euromonitor, 1988. xxi, 362p. ISBN: 0863381618.

8 broad sections: 1. Official sources and publications - 2. Major reference libraries - 3. Leading market research companies - 4. Information databases - 5. Abstracts and indices - 6. Major business and marketing journals - 7. Leading general business and marketing associations - 8. International business contacts. General index, p.335-62.
Class No: 652.88(01)

Handbooks & Manuals

[2593]

BUELL, V.P. Handbook of modern marketing. 2nd ed. New York, McGraw-Hill, 1986. [1312]p. illus. $84.95. ISBN: 0070088543.

First published 1970.

107 essays on a wide range of marketing topics, by practitioners and academics. 19 subject areas. 'Of limited value to faculty and graduate level researchers, but useful treatment for students and practitioners' (*Choice*, v.24(3), November 1986, p.521). *Class No:* 652.88(035)

Dictionaries

[2594]

HART, N.A. *and* **STAPLETON, J.** **The Marketing dictionary.** 4th ed. London, Butterworth-Heinemann, in association with the Chartered Institute of Marketing,1992. 240p. £12.95. ISBN: 0750602082.

First published 1977. The first 3 eds. were titled *Glossary of marketing terms.*

Contains *c*.3,000 terms used in present-day marketing and associated terminology, including research management, export, packaging, advertising, raw materials, selling, public relations, law, etc. Aimed at students taking diploma and degree examinations in the marketing field.
Class No: 652.88(038)

[2595]

IVANOVIC, A. Dictionary of marketing. Teddington, Peter Collin Publishing, 1989. 207p. ISBN: 0948549084.

Contains *c*.3,500 terms and phrases used in marketing services and goods, *e.g.* market research, presentation and packaging, publicity and television advertising. Extensive use of bold type throughout text when giving examples. Supplement includes: British socio-economic groups ... Technical information for a periodical.
Class No: 652.88(038)

[2596]

IVANOVIC, A., *and others*. **English-German dictionary of marketing.** Teddington, Mddx, Peter Collin, 1991. 350p. £25. ISBN: 094854922x.

Transation of the *Pons Fachwörterbuch Marketing*. Terms are defined in English. *Class No:* 652.88(038)

[2597]

OSTROW, R. *and* **SMITH, S.R. The Dictionary of marketing.** New York, Fairchild Publications, 1988. 258p. illus. $25.00. ISBN: 0870055739.

Has *c*.1,900 definitions of words and phrases. Some graphs and charts plus numerous cross-references. Also contains profiles of principal marketing trade associations.
Class No: 652.88(038)

Glossaries

[2598]

CLEMENTS, M.N. The Marketing glossary: key items, concepts and applications in marketing management, advertising, sales promotion, public relations, direct marketing, market research, sales. New York, AMACOM, 1992. 392p. illus. charts, diagrs. $34.95. ISBN: 081445030x.

Over 1400 definitions for terms in marketing, arranged A-Z by key term. Cross-references. Appendices includes

....*(contd.)*

addresses and telephone numbers of marketing and advertising trade publications. Bibliography. *Class No:* 652.88(038.1)

Reviews & Abstracts

[2599]

Marketing + distribution abstracts. Bradford, Yorks., ANBAR Publications Ltd, 1971-. monthly (previously 8pa). £689.95 pa. ISSN: 03050661.

About 100 abstracts per issue. Some items are asterisked, for mention in the 'Highlights' introduction. Others may be given critical comment, italicized (*e.g.* "Rather involved"; "A well presented article in an area of increasing importance"). Subject index precedes, cumulated annually. Items are drawn from a core list of *c.*250 journals, listed in April and October issues. *Class No:* 652.88(048)

Worldwide

[2600]

International marketing data and statistics. London, Euromonitor Publications, Ltd., 1975-. Annual. tables. £145. ISSN: 03082938.

17th annual ed., 1993 (viii, 652p.) covers all major and selected minor countries, except European countries (in another volume). 25 data sections in the fields of population, employment, production, trade, economy, standard of living, consumption, housing, health, education, communications, transport, tourism, etc. Footnoted sources. Statistics are the latest available at time of publication. 'An essential source for international studies and marketing collections'(*Choice*,v.30(10), June 1993, p.1604). *Class No:* 652.88(100)

[2601]

International marketing handbook. 3rd ed., edited by F.E. Bair. Detroit, Mich., Gale, 1988. 3v. (4036p.). charts, tables, maps. $235.

Detailed marketing profiles for 141 countries. Trade and economic data on each country include foreign trade outlook; industry trends; transportation and utilities; distribution and sales channels; advertising and research; credit; trade regulations; investment; guidance for business visitors; sources of economic and commercial information.

A 4th ed. is planned for late 1995 (3v. $235. ISBN 0810373122). *Class No:* 652.88(100)

Europe

[2602]

European marketing data and statistics, 1992. 27th ed. London, Euromonitor Publications, Ltd., 1992. Annual. xiii,462p. tables, maps. $295. £150. ISBN: 086338403x. ISSN: 00712930.

First published 1964.

Covers the 33 countries of Eastern and Western Europe. Profiles of the countries are followed by some 24 subject areas containing statistics on marketing geography, demographic trends and forecasts, economic indicators, finance and banking, external trade, labour force indicators, industrial resources and output, energy resources and output, defence, environmental data, consumer expenditure patterns,

....*(contd.)*

retailing, advertising, consumer markets, housing, health, education, agriculture, telecommunications, transport, tourism and culture. Subject index. *Class No:* 652.88(4)

Europe—Western

[2603]

Guide to European market information: EC countries. London, London Business School Information Service, 1991. £50. $100. ISBN: 0951440136.

11 chapters aranged by country (excluding UK) provide details of published market research studies, marketing and advertising journals, statistical series on trade and industry, online sources of market data, subscription services, trade and official bodies. The most important industries are listed for each country, with leading media and marketing organizations. Also, a Pan-European chapter covering international sources. Subject, title and type of source indexes. *Class No:* 652.88(400)

Bibliographies

[2604]

FOSTER, P. How to find information 1992: the European Single Market. In *Business information review,* v.5(4), April 1989, p.3-19.

Reviews the major sources of information on the European Single Market, covering books, pamphlets, directories, journals, newsletters, looseleaf services, current awareness services, EC official publications, market reports, information packs, seminars, information services, consultancy and seminars, care services, videos and online databases (*Author abstract*). *Class No:* 652.88(400)(01)

Great Britain

[2605]

Compendium of marketing information sources. London, Euromonitor Publications, 1989. xi,258p. ISBN: 0863382495. ISSN: 09572376.

'... a comprehensive one-stop guide to assessing the UK marketplace with classified entries identifying primary sources of market information available from official and unofficial sources on UK markets' (*Foreword.* In 7 sections, all subdivided and with brief annotations or descriptions: 1. Libraries and information services - 2. Abstracts and indexes - 3. Online databases and databanks - 4. Official sources - 5. Non official sources - 6. Market research agencies - 7. Company information. Products and services index; General index. *Class No:* 652.88(410)

Japan

[2606]

Japan marketing handbook. London, Euromonitor, 1988. 160p. $160. ISBN: 0863382134.

6 sections: Market overview - Economic and government policies - Japanese industry, technology and markets - Business and management - The Japanese consumer market - Conclusions. Appendices: Fact file - A to Z of Japanese markets - Some useful addresses. *Class No:* 652.88(52)

Market Research

[2607]
ASSOCIATION OF BRITISH MARKET RESEARCH COMPANIES. ABMRC handbook and guide to commissioning market research surveys 1991. London, Carrick James Market Research. 207p.

Main section: Industrial companies. Other sections include index by type of research, index by services offered, cfd index, personnel index, companies working overseas, index of publications, index of software packages. Chief aim of the Association is to assist clients in the selection of a research agency to meet their needs. *Class No:* 652.880

[2608]
BRITISH LIBRARY. Science Reference and Information Service. **Market research: a guide to British Library holdings.** Leydon, M., *ed.* 7th ed. London, SRIS, 1991. ix, 194p. (*Key to British Library holdings series*.) ISBN: 0712307745.

Sub-title varies.

List over 2000 current reports, arranged by subject. Subject index precedes (p.v-ix) the list of research reports, industry surveys and county profiles (p.1-168). Publishers' directory, p.169-194. British Library reference and loan copies (from the British Library Documents Supply Centre) are indicated. *Class No:* 652.880

[2609]
DICKINSON, J.R. The Bibliography of marketing research methods. Lexington, Mass., D.C.Heath, for Marketing Science Institute, 1986. xxxi,[1],758,[1]p.

Over 9200 entries, classified under *c.*800 headings and subheadings. Arranged in 3 broad categories: Market research function; data collection methods; data analysis techniques. Despite 'methods' in title, 'applications' subheadings are used, by way of illustration. *Class No:* 652.880

[2610]
A Guide to marketing research in the UK. London, Key Note Publications, Ltd., 1987. [iii], 141p. diagrs. ISBN: 1850564264.

Two main sections: 1. Marketing and marketing research (1.3: Types of marketing research) - 2. Sources of marketing information (2.2: Company directories; 2.5: Market research companies; 2.7: Trade associations; 2.10: Libraries and information systems; 2.11: On-line information (21 sources)). *Class No:* 652.880

[2611]
International directory of market research organizations. Fuller, J.R., *ed.* 11th ed. London, Market Research Society, 1993. xx,[776]p. ISBN: 0906117143. ISSN: 09606718.

10th ed. was published in 1990.

Nearly 2000 companies in over 80 countries are listed. Arranged A-Z by country (Argentine ... Zimbabwe) subdivided by names of organizations. Data includes company address, telephone & fax numbers, contact, parent or subsidiary, membership [of organizations], research facilities, data services, product group expertise, international experience, staff, turnover, company description. 8 appendices including A. Principal market research associations; C1. Index of research facilities by country; C2. Index of data collection and processing services by country; D1.Publications by company; D2. Publications by title. *Class No:* 652.880

[2612]
Market research abstracts. London, Market Research Society, 1963-. 2pa. 60pa. ISSN: 00253596.

About 400 abstracts pa., covering market surveys, statistics, advertising and media research, psychology, etc. Subject and author indexes per issue. Online DEMOTAB. Available on microfilm from UMI. *Class No:* 652.880

[2613]
Market research: international directory of published market research. 16th ed. London, Arlington Management Publications Ltd., 1992. Annual. 751p. tables. £69.75.

First published 1976.

Lists *c.*700 major consulting and market research firms worldwide, A-Z; *c.*19,000 professional market reports covering over 100 countries; Organizations, firms and other producers of reports, A-Z. Products and services index. Price includes supplementary publication each September and a telephone enquiry service for new reports. *Class No:* 652.880

[2614]
—Marketsearch: international directory of published market research. 17th. ed. London, Arlington Management Publications Ltd., 1993. Annual. 640p. £69.75. ISBN: 090661614x.

*c.*17,000 research studies of which many are completely new works. Worldwide coverage of over 150 countries. Semi-annual supplement published in the second half of the year updates. *Class No:* 652.880

Wholesale Selling

[2615]
American wholesalers and distributors directory: a comprehensive guide offering industry details on more than 18,000 wholesalers and distributors in the United States. Burek, D.M., *ed.* Gale, 1992. 1745p. $150. £95. ISBN: 0810382482.

Main arrangement is A-Z by name of firm, with access to entries by SIC code or geographically. Each entry includes all contact details, SIC code, major product lines, number of employees, estimated sales, and principal executives. A statistical section ranks the top 50 companies in each SIC section by sales. '... no other single comparable directory of this type.'(*Choice*,November 1992). *Class No:* 652.886

[2616]
European wholesalers and distributors directory. Irwin, L., *and others, eds.* Detroit, Gale, 1992. 677p. $175. ISBN: 0810383543.

Profiles more than 5000 major wholesalers and distributors in *c.*40 European countries. Arranged in four sections: by SIC subdivided by country; by specific product line; by countries in which company distributes products, subdivided by SIC; and A-Z by company name. Each main entry includes address; telephone, fax and telex numbers; executives; primary and additional SICs; number of employees; products and territories of distribution. *Class No:* 652.886

Retail Selling

[2617]

Macmillan dictionary of retailing. Baron, S. *and* Jones, P., *eds.* London, Macmillan, 1991. 312p. £35. ISBN: 0333537580.

Defines terms emanating from the Department of Retail Marketing at Manchester Polytechnic and top companies in retailing. *Class No:* 652.887

[2618]

Retail directory 1994. 48th ed. London, Newman Books, Ltd., 1993. 1300p. 900 maps. £139. ISBN: 0707969646. ISSN: 03054012.

Earlier title: *Stores, shops, supermarkets: retail directory*.

2 major parts: *Company details*, by type of retail operation: stores, shops and hypermarkets. High Street and out of town. Specialized outlets and groups - *Shopping street areas*, in over 500 towns: England (9 areas), Wales, Scotland, Northern Ireland, Republic of Ireland. Index to advertisers. Outline maps and town plans. *Class No:* 652.887

[2619]

Retail trade international. London, Euromonitor Publications Ltd., 1992. 3v. tables. £650. $1300 the set. ISBN: 0863384072, v.1 & 2; 0863384471, v.3. ISSN: 09510737, v.1 & 2; 09510745, v.3.

Data on trends in retailing; consumer spending; retail sales by commodity, outlets, organizations (including mail order). V.1 & 2 cover Western European countries, A-Z, followed by Eastern European countries; v.3 has international data. *Class No:* 652.887

[2620]

Retailing in the European single market, 1993. Luxembourg, Office for Official Publications of the European Community, 1993. xii,213p. tables, diagrams. £34. $52. ECU 40. ISBN: 9282654583.

In 3 parts: I. Retail trade in Europe: structure, strategies, prospects (5 sections, all subdivided) - II. Retail trade in the single market: country reports (for each country key statistics, employment, activity, etc.) - III. Glossary. Data sources, p.211-2. Symbols and abbreviations. *Class No:* 652.887

Handbooks & Manuals

[2621]

BAILLIEU, D. Streetwise franchising: everything you need to know about taking up and running a successful franchise. London, Hutchinson Business, 1988. xvi,187p. £16.95. ISBN: 0091736803.

Aims to provide a guide to the issues and problems. 12 chapters: 1. Franchising as a legal concept ... 3. Raising finance - 4. Organizations to consult ... 11. Other sources of information - 12. The future of franchising; growth and new developments. 8 appendices include: Summary of franchise listing; sources of finance; Franchising trade associations. Index. *Class No:* 652.887(035)

[2622]

BARROW, C. *and* GOLZEN, G. Taking up a franchise: the *Daily telegraph* guide. 6th ed. London, Kogan Page, 1989. 283p. £6.99. ISBN: 1850919925.

Explanation of the meaning of franchising. 12 sections: 1. What franchising means - 2. Advantages and disadvantages of taking up a franchise ... 6. Financing a franchise ... 8.

.... (contd.)

Current franchising opportunities: a guide ... 11. The British Franchise Association - 12. Useful organizations and publications. Index, p.267-275. '... somewhat journalistic format' (*International small business journal,* v.7(3), April/June, 1989, p.88). *Class No:* 652.887(035)

[2623]

MENDELSOHN, M. The Guide to franchising. 5th ed. London, Cassell, 1992. 368p. £45;$80. ISBN: 0805019766.

16 sections: The concept of franchising - History and development - Why franchise your business? ... How to become a franchiser ... Legal aspects ... Franchising internationally ... The British Franchise Association - Franchise consultants and their profession. Appendix. *Class No:* 652.887(035)

Yearbooks & Directories

[2624]

Markets year book: a list of markets in England, Wales and Scotland, with market days, owners and superintendents, etc. 28th ed. Oldham, the "World's Fair", Ltd., 1988. 239p. £6.50. ISSN: 00764647.

Directory (one alphabetical sequence), Aberdare ... Ystradgyrlais p.15-121. Wholesalers (Northern; Midland; South East; Bristol, p.125-98). Market operations. List of market venues in England, Scotland and Wales, indexing counties and days, p.203-18. Map; holiday dates; etc. Index to advertisers. *Class No:* 652.887(058)

[2625]

Markets yearbook. 33rd ed. Oldham, The 'World's Fair' Ltd., 1993. 264p. £8.

A list of markets in England, Wales and Scotland, with market days, owners and superintendents, etc. Directory (one alphabetical sequence), Aberdare ... Ystradgyrlais, p.17-191. Wholesalers directory, p.192-246. Market operators, p.247-252. List of market venues, p.253-257. Index to advertisers. *Class No:* 652.887(058)

[2626]

Worldwide franchise directory: a guide offering details for comparing franchises and franchise investment opportunities around the world. Martin, S.B., *ed.* Detroit, Gale, 1991. 620p. $129.50. ISBN: 0810378051. ISSN: 1056456x.

Lists of 1600 franchising companies in 15 countries (*c.*1000 in US); lists of *c.*80 franchise consulting firms and *c.*40 franchising associations, are followed by the main entries for franchising firms, arranged A-Z by types of business (Accounting/tax services ... Weight control). Information for each includes name, address, telephone number, year franchise began, number of outlets, initial franchise fee, general description, background of franchising company, and franchise agreement information. Master name and keyword index, p.535-68. Geographical index. Personal name index, p.607-20. *Class No:* 652.887(058)

USA

[2627]

FOSTER, D.L. The Encyclopedia of franchises and franchising. New York, Facts on File, 1989. 465p. $65. ISBN: 0816020817.

A-Z arrangement includes franchise histories, biographical sketches of business leaders, industry capsules (*eg* fast food), summaries of franchise regulations, and legal

....(contd.)

explanations and forms. Appendices include investment data, a ranking of 583 franchises by number of outlets, a list of franchises by type of business, and an index. A sequel to the author's *Rating guide to franchises* (1988).
Class No: 652.887(73)

Mail Order Selling

[2628]
The Royal Mail direct mail handbook. Andrews, L., *ed.* 2nd ed. Watford, Herts., Exley, 1988. 284p. illus. (incl. col.), ports., forms. £19.95. ISBN: 1850150729.

8 chapters. 1. The why and wherefore of mailing lists - 2. Direct mail production ... 7. Direct mail, the law, and advertising standards - 8. A guide to Royal Mail services. Bibliography, p.251-5. Glossary. Index.
Class No: 652.887.2

Publicity

Advertising

[2629]
Advertiser's annual, 1994. East Grinstead, Reed Information Services Ltd. 1993. 3v. £162 the set; £99 each volume. ISBN: 0611008262. ISSN: 00653578.

First published 1915. (Business Pubns., Ltd.).

Data on over 2,500 advertising agencies, sales promotion consultants, sponsorship consultants, recruitment advertising agents, and public relations companies. V.1: Agencies and advertisers - v.2: Media (newspapers and periodicals; TV and radio; outdoor advertising) - v.3: Overseas media. Index to classified headings. Services and supplies. New sections in this ed.: advertising agencies; new agency contact companies. Nearly 3,500 major national advertisers are now listed. *Class No:* 652.91

Encyclopaedias & Dictionaries

[2630]
GRAHAM, I. Encyclopedia of advertising: an encyclopedia containing more than 1,100 entries relating to advertising, marketing, publishing, law, research, public relations, publicity and the graphic arts ... for everyday use by advertisers, agencies, advertising practitioners, businessmen and students. New York, Fairchild, 1969. xiii, 494p. illus. $132.60. ISBN: 0317581651.

First published 1952.

3 sections: 1. Advertising terminology, A-Z - 2. Terms grouped according to subject matter - 3. Directory of associations. No index. 'A useful source of information about graphic arts, commercial TV, copywriting and other aspects of advertising' (*Library journal,* 1 March 1970, p.864). *Class No:* 652.91(03)

[2631]
GRUBER, C.M. Wörterbuch der Werbung und des Marketing, Englisch-Deutsch, Deutsch-Englisch. [Dictionary of advertising and marketing.] Munich, Hueber, 1977. 312p., tables.

About 4,500 entry-words in each half. Arrangement is A-Z by keywords, with other terms arranged hierarchically under the keywords. Includes tables of paper sizes, etc., and lists of type sizes, etc. *Class No:* 652.91(03)

[2632]
JEFKINS, F. Dictionary of advertising, direct response marketing and sales promotion. London, Pitman, 1990. 236p. ISBN: 0273031368.

Contains *c.*1,500 definitions. Includes abbreviations, *e.g.* CAVIAR, EPOS. Cross references in upper case throughout text. Also includes entries for the more important advertising publications and legislation. *Class No:* 652.91(03)

[2633]
PAETZEL, H.W. Complete multilingual dictionary of advertising, marketing and communications: English, French, German. Lincolnwood, Ill., Passport Books, 1984. 606p. $39.95. ISBN: 0844291110.

First published 1972 (Essen, Stamm-Verlag, GmbH).

About 8,.000 terms; in three sequences, English, French and German, each with equivalents in the other two languages. *Class No:* 652.91(03)

[2634]
URDANG, L. Dictionary of advertising terms. Chicago, Ill., Tatham-Laird & Kudner, 1977. 209p. illus.

About 4,000 entries, with brief definitions, for terms and abbreviations in advertising and marketing. 'Especially valuable is the inclusion of special meanings of ordinary words, words unique in a single speciality and extensive cross-references for abbreviations, acronyms and synonyms' (*Library journal,* v.102(15), September 1977, p.1748). *Class No:* 652.91(03)

Yearbooks & Directories

[2635]
European advertising, marketing and media yearbook...a directory and source book. 2nd ed. London, Euromonitor, 1992 (distributed in US by Gale). Annual. xxxvi,771p. £195. $390. ISBN: 0863384129.

First published 1989.

Advertising profiles of 16 West European countries and limited data on 8 East European markets, including the former USSR and East Germany. Part 1 has historical and some forecasted data on demographic information, trends in gross domestic product and retail sales, consumer spending, advertising expenditures, and media by specific country. Part 2 is a directory, by country, of advertising agencies, top advertisers, publishers, broadcasters, and market research firms. Part 3 has brief overviews of advertising regulations in West European countries. No index, but detailed table of contents. *Class No:* 652.91(058)

[2636]
—European advertising, media and marketing data, 1990: a directory and sourcebook. lst ed. London, Euromonitor, 1989. xxx,629p. £135. ISBN: 0863382274.

Examines advertising expenditure patterns, media availability, basic consumer marketing parameters in 16 European countries. Sections: 1. European comparisons; 2.

....*(contd.)*

Austria ... 16. United Kingdom; 17. West Germany. Figures are followed by directory sections, giving details of the leading agency and media operators, as well as the leading advertisers themselves, and useful points of contact for further information. Appendix: 'Stats pack'.
Class No: 652.91(038)

[2637]
Graphis design: international annual of design and illustration. Zurich, Graphis Press Corp. illus., (incl. col.). SFr.123. $69.

Early title was *Graphis annual. Class No:* 652.91(058)

[2638]
Standard directory of international advertisers & agencies, 1993. Stokie, Ill., National Register Pubg. Co., 1964-. Annual.. 1560p. $325. ISBN: 0872171442. ISSN: 00814229.

International in scope, with data on *c.*17,000 companies (*e.g.* kind of media used; products; trademarks).
Class No: 652.91(058)

[2639]
World advertising review. Kleinman, P., *ed.* London, Cassell; Holt, Rinehart & Winston, 1924-91. Annual. v.p. illus. (mostly col.). ISBN: 0304318205.

Previously as *Modern publicity,* first published as *Posters and their designers* (1924).

21 sections - (Alcoholic drinks - Automotive - Clothing and footwear ... Toiletries and cosmetics - Travel and tourism). List of credits. Index of agencies and studios. Index of advertisers. 425 well-captioned illus. International in scope. *Class No:* 652.91(058)

Great Britain

[2640]
NEVETT, T.R. Advertising in Britain: a history. London, Heinemann, on behalf of The History of Advertising Trust, 1982. xii, 213p. illus. (incl. ports.). facsims., ports., and tables. ISBN: 0434496421.

11 chapters (4. Advertising takes shape, 1800-1855; 6. Criticism and control in the nineteenth century; 8. The inter-war period. 3 appendices (A. Organisations whose representatives constitute the Code of Advertising Committee; C. Table of legal cases). References (by chapters, p.215-7). Grouped bibliography, p.213-5. Non-analytical index. *Class No:* 652.91(410)

Media Advertising

[2641]
BRAD/British rate and data: media facts at your fingertips. London, Maclean Hunter, for British Rate and Data, 1954-. Monthly. £230. ISSN: 02633515.

The November 1991 issue has 4 main sections: Newspapers - Consumer and special interest publications - Business and professional publications, subjects, A-Z) - Other media (*e.g.* cinema advertising; radio stations; television data; video tape publications). Data include advertising rates per page, part of page, etc. Primarily for advertising, but also valuable for near-current facts on several thousand British newspapers and periodicals. Standard Rate and Data Service (Skorkie, Ill.) provides a more extensive US rate-and-advertising data, now in 13

....*(contd.)*

sections, varying in frequency. The original *Standard rate and data service* ran between 1919 and 1950.
Class No: 652.913/.916

[2642]
British television advertising: the first thirty years. Henry, B., *ed.* London, Century Benham, 1986. 527p. illus. (mostly col.), port., diagrs., graphs, tables, maps. ISBN: 0091658004.

14 contributors. The history (1955-), p.2-237; The television commercial; an essay, p.251-85; The agency viewpoint (3 contributors), p.419-53. Glossary of abbreviations, p.454-70. 12 appendices, A-M (Acts; Committees; Finance; M: 'Top twenty television advertising spenders by brand'). Detailed index, p.522-7. Well organized. *Class No:* 652.913/.916

Dictionaries

[2643]
DUVILLIER, F. *and* **GRÜBER, U. Dictionnaire bilingue de la publicité et de la communication.** London, Grant & Cutler, 1990. 464p. £49.25.

French and English, with terms defined in French.
Class No: 652.913/.916(038)

Visual

Inn Signs

[2644]
LARWOOD, J., pseud. (*i.e* H.D.J. van Schevichaven) *and* **HOTTEN, J.C. English inn signs.** being a revised and modernized version of 'History of signboards', with a chapter on the modern inn sign, by G. Millar. Exeter, Blaketon Hall, 1985. xv, 336p. illus. ISBN: 0907854982.

Reprint of 1965 ed.

This edition is confined to inn signs, although earlier editions (1866-1907) included tradesmen's signs, - now covered partly by Heal, Sir A. *Signboards of old London shops* (1947). Larwood includes a brief bibliography, p.316.
Class No: 652.9133

[2645]
LILLYWHITE, B. London signs: a reference book of London signs from earliest times to about the mid-nineteenth century. London, Allen & Unwin, 1972. xviii, 696p. illus. ISBN: 0049421018.

A-Z index to over 17,000 signs in the 19 manuscript volumes bequeathed by the compiler for use at the Guildhall Library. Data include location, approximate dates when in use and, often, notes on meaning or rarity of a sign. 'These must be of inestimable value to students of London topography, history and social life' (*TLS,* no.3678, 25 August 1972). *Class No:* 652.9133

Management Consultancy Services

[2646]
BRITISH CONSULTANTS BUREAU. Directory, 1993-94.
London, the Bureau, 1993. 516p. £49.50. ISBN:
0950562130.

List of 275 BCB members in 8 sections, by type of
activity: Engineers - Architects, planners - Management and
economic consultants - Surveyors - Mining, minerals,
geotechnical and geological consultants - Agricultural and
fisheries consultants - Specialist categories - Nationalised
industries' overseas group. Appendix: list (blue pages) of all
members irrespective of their fields of activity.
Class No: 652.92

[2647]
Consultants and consulting organizations directory a
reference guide to more than 20,000 concerns and
individuals engaged in consultation for business, industry
and government. 14th ed. Detroit, Mich., Gale, 1993. 2v.
(3026p.). $460. ISBN: 0810380455.

First published 1966.

Entries for 20,311 North American organizations and
individuals, in more than 120 special fields. Geographical,
subject and personnel indexes. *New consultants* provides
interim supplements (2pa.) between editions.
Class No: 652.92

[2648]
Directory of management consultants in the UK, 1993.
Lambert, H., *comp. & ed.* 9th ed. London, TFPL
Publishing, 1992. Annual. 497p. £75. ISBN: 1870889126.

First published 1983 (1983/84 ed.).

1500 management consulting firms, A-Z, with details of
company activities. Index of specializations; Industry area
index; Geographical index; Index of directors, partners,
principals. *Class No:* 652.92

[2649]
European consultants directory, 1991. Koek, K.E., *ed.*
Andover, Hants & Detroit, Mich., Gale Research
International, 1992. 1038p. £150. $225. ISBN: 0810383136.

Companion volume to *Consultants and consulting
organizations directory* covering the US and Canada.

Lists *c.*7500 consultancies operating in 34 European
countries. Arranged in country order, subdivided by 15
headings (Agriculture, forestry and landscaping to the
Environment and Politics). Details for each consultancy
includes full contact information, date of formation of
company, number of employees, names of senior consulting
staff, annual turnover, indication of areas of specialization
and geographical areas covered, branches, and variant
names. Four indexes: Named consultants; Thesaurus of
terms; Consulting activities; A-Z index of all consulting
firms. *Class No:* 652.92

[2650]
European **technical** **consultancies.**
Tomlinson, D.M., *consultant ed.* Harlow, Essex, Longman
Group, 1988. 352p. £75. ISBN: 0582031877.

Directory of more than 700 technical consultancies, in
country order. Data (with effective use of symbols) on each
consultancy include names of senior staff, roles and
industrial categories. 4 indexes: company names, senior
executives, consultancy services, industries served.
Class No: 652.92

Public Relations

[2651]
BLACK, S. *and* SHARPE, M.L. **Practical public relations:**
common-sense guidelines for business and professional
people. 5th ed. London; Englewood Cliffs, Prentice-Hall,
1983. ix,214p. ISBN: 0136935311.

First published 1962.

4 parts (21 chapters): 1. Defining the subject: theory and
practice - 2. Methods of public relations - 3. Public relations
in action (including case histories) - 4. Educational,
organisational, historical. Appendices: 1. Examinations in
public relations; 2. Codes of professional conduct and ethics;
3. Public relations organizations. Bibliography, (p.223-4; 9
sections). Analytical index. *Class No:* 652.94

[2652]
Hollis UK press & public relations annual, 1993-94. 25th ed.
Sunbury-on-Thames, Mddx., Hollis Directories Ltd., 1993.
xciii,1010p. £65. ISBN: 0900967005. ISSN: 00733059.

First published 1967 as 'Contact'.

Arranged in 12 sections, each on a different tinted paper:
1. Media sources - 2. Media and corporate sources - 3.
Reference and research - 4. Official and public information
sources - 5. Consultancy specializations - 6. Public relations
consultancies (UK and Ireland) - 7. Public relations: UK
regional guide - 8. Public relations: overseas - 9.
Sponsorship consultants - 10. Government relations and
Parliamentary consultants - 11. Services - 12. Master index.
Advertisers' index. *Class No:* 652.94

[2653]
Public relations consultancy...Public relations year book,
1992. Financial Times Business Information, for Public
Relations Consultants Association, 1992. 311p. £40. ISBN:
1853340324.

Members of PRCA, A-Z with data on number of
employees and range of services offered. Index of clients;
index of directors and partners; index of holders of public
office. Biographies of 650 PR partners and directors.
Class No: 652.94

[2654]
Public relations handbook. 3rd ed. Englewood Cliffs, N.J.,
Prentice-Hall, 1983. 718p. illus.

First published 1950.

7 sections of chapters: 1. What public relations is and does
- 2. What public relations includes - 3. How an organization
utilizes public relations - 4. Analysis and preparation - 5.
The techniques of communication - 6. The practice of public
relations - 7. Emergency principles and trends.
Bibliography. Glossary. Codes of ethics. List of
associations. Index. *Class No:* 652.94

[2655]
Who's who in public relations. 2nd ed. Ayr, Carrick
Publishing, 1985. 173p. £15. ISBN: 0946724105.

First published for 1984-85. *Class No:* 652.94

[2656]

WRAGG, D.W. The Public relations handbook. Oxford, Blackwell, 1992. xiii,354p. £55. ISBN: 0631184589.

51 chapters in 11 sections: 1: An introduction to public relations; 2. Media relations; 3. Financial and corporate relations; 4. Employee communications; 5. Political and community relations; 6. Sponsorship; 7. Events; 8. The application of public relations; 9. Developing public relations skills and activities; 10. Ancillary services; 11. Public relations today and tomorrow. Appendix: The IPR's code of professional conduct: PRCA professional charter. Index, p.352-4. *Class No:* 652.94

Dictionaries

[2657]

Glossary of public relations terms in seven languages (English-French-German-Spanish-Dutch-Finnish-Italian). Nally, M., *ed.* 2nd ed. Paris, CERP: European Public Relations Confederation, 1990. 83p. £23.50.
Class No: 652.94(038)

34 Law

Law

Abbreviations & Symbols

[2658]
FONG, C. *and* EDWARDS, A.J. **Australian and New Zealand legal abbreviations.** Sydney, Australian Law Librarians Group, New South Wales Branch, 1988. A$16. ISBN: 0959135952.

Aims to include abbreviations for Australian and New Zealand published law reports and journals and also for journals, from other countries regularly publishing articles of Australian and New Zealand interest. Clearly and simply laid out in 3 columns (Abbreviations - Interpretation - Period of coverage). Cross-references. *Class No:* 340(003)

[2659]
SPRUDZS, A., *comp.* **Italian abbreviations and symbols:** law and related subjects. Dobbs Ferry, N.Y., Oceana, 1969. [iii],124p. $20. ISBN: 0379004518.

Aims to provide a simple key to the multitude of Italian abbreviations and symbols as they are found in contemporary Italian writings on law and related subjects. About 2600 abbreviations; no English translation of full Italian terms. 4 categories: (1) Legal, commercial and related terms; (2) Law reviews; (3) Names of Italian trade unions, political parties, etc.; (4) Italian names of European and international organizations concerned with law and related matters. Other volumes by A. Sprudzs: *Benelux abbreviations and symbols: law and related subjects* (1971. iii.129p. $20. ISBN 0379001209); *Foreign law abbreviations: French* (1967. ii.103p.). *Class No:* 340(003)

Databases

[2660]
NOBARI, N.S., *ed.* **Books and periodicals on line:** a guide to publication contents of business and legal data bases, V.1., Part 1-, 1987-. New York, Library Alliance Inc. 1987 -. Annual. $249. ISSN: 0951838x.

Aims to help researchers to use online time efficiently by providing them with a directory of over 6800 periodicals and serials which are available on such databases. In 4 sections: Alphabetical listing of periodicals and serials (name of publication; country of origin if not US, and journal code; name of publisher; name of database; name of producer; scope of editorial coverage, including starting date (and ending date if applicable); name of vendors) - Publishers' names and addresses - Producers' and vendors' names and addresses - Books and periodicals by database (A-Z by database, subdivided by A-Z list of titles). Available online and on CD-ROM. *Class No:* 340(003.4)

[2661]
RAPER, D., *ed.* **Law databases, 1988.** London, Aslib, 1988. [3],70p. £15. (*An Aslib online guide.*) ISBN: 0851422284.
First published 1983.

Details of 35 databases 'from the material supplied, in the main, by database producers' (*Introduction*). Information includes name, content, period of coverage, updating, producer, host, cost. There is a list of countries covered by the databases, and a list of host/producer addresses. A bibliography of 23 items completes the book. *Class No:* 340(003.4)

Bibliographies of Bibliographies

[2662]
FRIEND, W.L. **Anglo-American legal bibliographies:** an annotated guide. Washington, DC., Government Printing Office, 1944. (Reprinted by Rothman) ($15. 0837721288) and AMS Press ($15. 0404025994).

Lists nearly 300 legal bibliographies and bibliographical writings in books and journals. *Class No:* 340(009)

[2663]
LANSKY, R. **Bibliographische Handbuch der Rechts- und Verwaltungswissenschaften:** erläuteinde Bibliographie nationaler und internationaler Bibliographien/Bibliographical handbook on law and public administration: annotated bibliography of national and international bibliographies and other reference guides and information sources. Frankfurt am Main, Vittorio Klostermann, 1987-. To be in 3v. V.1: DM.156-.

V.1 was published in 1987; v.2 will be published 'in a few years'; v.3 will contain supplement and general index.

V.1: *General part and Europe* has 1269 annotated entries for bibliographies of bibliographies issued as books, bibliographical articles, library catalogues, and on-going listings in journals. Also includes basic reference aids such as encyclopedias and dictionaries, handbooks, biographical indexes, institutional directories, etc. Arranged by geographical region, subdivided A-Z by country, then by form or subject category. Entries are numbered, have full bibliographical description, concise annotation, and one location indication. Annotations are informative rather than critical. 'Not only a bibliography of bibliographies but a veritable vade mecum through the maze of legal reference materials in the areas of foreign, comparative and international law' (*International journal of legal information,* v.16(1), Spring 1988, p.24-27). *Class No:* 340(009)

Bibliographies

[2664]
ANDREWS, J.A. *and* HINES, W.D. **'Recent periodicals and source materials in law'.** In *British book news,* September 1988, p.644-647, 649.

Reviews the more significant serial publications that have

....(*contd.*)

appeared in the last 10 years. 45 titles listed in the bibliography. Written with the interest of overseas readers in mind. *Class No:* 340(01)

[2665]
Bibliographic guide to law. 1975- Annual. Library of Congress Staff. Boston, Mass., G.K. Hall (*Biblioguides*), 1991. 2v.(1053p) $340 ISBN: 0816170746.
Formerly *Law book guide.* First published 1975. Annual.
Lists all material catalogued during the year by the Library of Congress, covering all aspects of law, including that of the United States, international law, international organizations, criminology and forensic medicine. One A-Z sequence. *Class No:* 340(01)

[2666]
CAMBRIDGE UNIVERSITY. Squire Law Library. **The Squire Law Library: law catalogue.** Lekner, M.A., *comp.* Dobbs Ferry, N.Y. Oceana Publications, 1974. 15v.
V.1. Classification scheme - List of periodicals - Collections of legislation - Collections of law reports - Collections of treaties - United Kingdom: Parliamentary papers. V.2-7: Authors (*c.* 30,000 entries). V. 8-14: Subjects. V.15: Classification scheme: a list of subject headings for the Squire Law Library. *Class No:* 340(01)

[2667]
COLEMAN, K. Legal reference work in non-law libraries: a review of the literature. In *Special libraries,* v.71(1), January 1981, p.51-58.
Reviews library literature pertaining to the development and use of legal materials in non-law libraries in the US and Canada. Includes descriptions of model programmes and staff training workshops; recommendations for effective library service with law books; and bibliographical essays describing legal material appropriate for laymen. 22 citations. *Class No:* 340(01)

[2668]
Current law index: multiple access to legal periodicals in print. Belmont, CA., Information Access Company, with the American Association of Law Libraries, 1980-.v.1-. Monthly. $395pa. ISSN: 01961780.
Covers *c.*700 law journals published in the US, Canada, UK, Ireland, Australia and New Zealand, and includes allied disciplines such as criminology and accounting. March, June and September issues are quarterly cumulations and the December issue is the annual 2-volume cumulation. Part A: Subject index, has bibliographical details, brief descriptions, and cross-references. Part B: Author/title index, table of contents, table of statutes. Also available online (BRS, DIALOG, etc.). *Class No:* 340(01)

[2669]
DANE, J. and THOMAS, P.A. How to use a law library, with specialist contributions on Community law [and] public international law. 2nd ed. London, Sweet & Maxwell, 1987. xvii,274p. facsims, charts. £16.50. ISBN: 0421360305.
First published 1979.
12 chapters, with running commentary: 1. Using a library - 2. Law reports - 3. Legislation - 4. Periodicals - 5. Government publications - 6. How to find information on a subject (p.88-139) - 7. Using computers to find the law - 8. Scots law - 9. Northern Ireland law - 10. Republic of Ireland - 11. European Community law - 12. Public international law. Chapter 6, with its facsimiles, flow charts and exercises on specific problems, is particularly helpful. 3 appendices

....(*contd.*)

(1. Abbreviations of reports, series and periodicals; 2. Words and abbreviations in English and Latin; 3. A summary of sources for English law). Author index, p.263-269. Detailed, analytical subject index, p.271-274. Authors are respectively the Law Librarian and a Senior Lecturer in Law at University College, Cardiff. 'An essential reference book for new law students and new law library staff ... But it must be regarded as an elementary manual' (*The Law librarian,* v.10(3),. December 1979, p.56, of the 1st ed).
Class No: 340(01)

[2670]
Index to legal books, 1989. New York, Bowker, 1989. Annual. 6v. $600 the set. ISBN: 0835226522.
Arranged in major legal subject categories, cites entries for leading law books, national in scope and importance. Cross-references. *Class No:* 340(01)

[2671]
Index to legal periodicals, 1908-. New York, H.W. Wilson Company, in co-operation with the American Association of Law Libraries, 1909-. Monthly (except September), cumulating quarterly, annually and 3-yearly. $180pa. ISSN: 00194077.
Subject and author index to more than 400 legal periodicals from common-law countries (US and Commonwealth). Separate indexing of legal cases commented on (under plaintiff's name A-Z) and of book reviews. Pronounced US slant. Also available online, WESTLAW, Wilsonline and CD-ROM. *Class No:* 340(01)

[2672]
—Index to foreign legal periodicals. London, Institute of Advanced Legal Studies, in co-operation with the American Association of Law Libraries, 1960-,v.1,no.1-. Quarterly, cumulating annually & 3-yearly. $450pa. ISSN: 0019400x.
Complementary to *Index to legal periodicals,* in that it covers public and private international law, comparative law and municipal law of countries other than the US and Commonwealth. Covers *c.*300 leading legal periodicals. Comprises subject, geographical, book-review and author indexes. *Class No:* 340(01)

[2673]
Index to legal periodicals: thesaurus. New York, H.W. Wilson Company, 1988. 80p. $65. ISBN: 0824207629.
A ready-reference guide to the subject terms used in *Index to legal periodicals.* Includes broad, narrow and related terms in one list. *Class No:* 340(01)

[2674]
Index to periodical articles related to law: selected from journals not included in the 'Index to legal periodicals'. Dobbs Ferry, N.Y., Glanville Publications Inc., 1958-. Quarterly. $45pa. ISSN: 00194093.
A subject index to substantial articles published throughout the world that in the opinion of the editors are of research value, and are not in *Current law index, Index of foreign legal periodicals, Index to legal periodicals, Legal resource index,* or *Legaltrac.* The final issue each year is cumulative, and a 30-year index (1958-1988. v.1-30) has been published (4v. $450. ISBN 0878020632) which replaces the 10 and 5-year indexes. *Class No:* 340(01)

[2675]
Law books, 1876-1981: including books and serials on law and its related subjects. New York, Bowker, 1982. 4v . (5039p.). $425; £413. ISBN: 0835213978.

Comprehensive guide to *c.*130,000 titles in 39,000 law and law-related areas. Includes case books, texts, statutes, biographies, handbooks, commission reports, political treatises, etc. Subject, author, title and publisher indexes. *Class No:* 340(01)

[2676]
—International legal books in print, 1993-94: an annotated bibliography. 2nd ed. Biennial. New York, Bowker-Saur, 1993. 2v.(487;488p). $375. ISBN: 1857390016.

*c.*29,000 descriptively annotated entries for English-language books on the law of individual countries and states of the United Kingdom, the Commonwealth and Western Europe. V.1 has the author and title list; v.2 has a subject index and list of publishers. *Class No:* 340(01)

[2677]
—Law books and serials in print: a multimedia sourcebook. New York, Bowker, 1992. 3v.(2345p.). $575.

Attempts to list all legal titles available within the US and, to a lesser extent, those published internationally. Over 53,000 publications listed, emphasis being on English-language publications. Indexed in 3 ways (v.1. by subject (Library of Congress subject headings); v.2. Author and title indexes; v.3. Separate subject and title indexes for serials, non-print media, microforms. List of publishers, distributors and producers. *Class No:* 340(01)

[2678]
Law books in print: law books in English published throughout the world and in print through 1993. Triffin, N., *comp. & ed.* 7th ed. Dobbs Ferry, N.Y., Glanville, 1994. 6v. $750. ISBN: 087802039x.

V.1-2: Author/title list; V.3: Series; v.4-5: Subject list; v.6: Publishers' list. 'A unique information tool, well-suited to law librarians, legal scholars and practicing attorneys' (*International journal of legal information,* v.15(5-6), October-December 1987). Supplemented by *Law books published* (1969- 3pa.). *Class No:* 340(01)

[2679]
Law books in review: a quarterly journal of reviews of current publications in law and related fields. Dobbs Ferry, NY., Glanville, 1974-. Quarterly. $55pa. ISSN: 08860408.

*c.*150 reviews pa. Arranged by subject, A-Z, and including sections on Legal law; Legal reference; International law; Reviews in brief. Author/title index and addresses of publishers. *Class No:* 340(01)

[2680]
Legal contents: the bi-weekly compilation of tables of contents from law: reviews, journals and symposia. New York, Find/SVP, 1972-. Monthly. ISSN: 02795787.

Previously as *Contents of current legal periodicals,* incorporating *Survey of law reviews.* and *CCLP: Contents of current legal periodicals.* Also available online.

Covers more than 320 business magazines and journals. *Class No:* 340(01)

[2681]
Legaltrac, 1980-. Foster City, CA., Information Access Company, with American Association of Law Libraries, 1980-. Monthly. $3500pa.

Issued on microfilm, and also available online.

Early title was *Legal resource index.*

Comprehensive guide to law journals, legal newspapers and articles selected from the general press. US-slanted. *Class No:* 340(01)

[2682]
LOGAN, R.G., *ed.* **Information sources in law.** London, Butterworth, 1986. xiv, 370p. £38. (*Butterworths guides to information sources.*) ISBN: 0408114746.

'A bibliographical survey of the whole range of general and specialist literature which is available to those engaged in legal study and research' (*Preface*). In 4 parts divided into 23 chapters. Chapters 1 & 2 are introductory and describe material and methodology. Chapters 3-14 treat sources of English law and the literature of its various subdivisions (*e.g.* 3. Statute law - 4. Case law ... 7. Revenue law - 8. Criminal law and procedure ... 11. Family law ... 14. Commercial law). Chapters 15-20 describe the bibliography of other legal systems of direct interest to English lawyers. Chapter 21: Legal bibliographies and reference books; 22: Computer assisted research; 23: Law books for non-lawyers. Subject and title index, p.359-370. '... undoubtedly a useful work for anyone who regularly uses legal sources, whether in practice or for study, since it both indicates the range of available material and is critical in its discussion.' (*British book news,* June, 1986, p.342). *Class No:* 340(01)

[2683]
LONDON UNIVERSITY. Institute of Advanced Legal Studies. **Catalogue of the Library** of the Institute of Advanced Legal Studies. Boston, Mass., G.K. Hall, 1978. 6v. (5085p.). $595. (*Hall library.*) ISBN: 0816100993.

106,700 photolithographed catalogue cards. The Library has extensive collections of public international law, English and Commonwealth law (including South African) and law of the European Communities, Western European countries and North America. 130,000v. of serials and monographs. *Class No:* 340(01)

[2684]
PRICE, M.O., *and others.* **Effective legal research.** 4th ed. Boston, Mass., Little, Brown & Co., 1979. xxx,643p. $33. ISBN: 0316718327.

First published 1953.

'The book is an essential working tool for all law librarians' (*International journal of law libraries,* v.8(2), April 1980, p.73). *Class No:* 340(01)

[2685]
RAISTRICK, D. Lawyers' law books: a practical index to legal literature. 2nd ed. Abingdon, Oxon., Professional Books, 1985. xxxv, 604p. £28. (*Professional Books law reference library, vol.1.*) ISBN: 0862050723.

First published 1977.

Contains a list of subject headings and cross-references (p.xi - xxxv); and 'A practical index to legal literature'(p. 3-491, Abbreviations ... Zambia). About 8,000 unannotated entries (author, title, edition and date, but not publisher). Lengthier topics have sub-headings (*e.g.*, 'International law', p.248-257). Regnal years of English sovereigns(p.495); Law reports of the United Kingdom and Ireland (p.499-515); and an author and short-title index (p.519-604). Clearly intended

....(contd.)

for those in the legal profession rather than librarians, since bibliographical data omit place of publication and number of pages/volumes. 'It is an extremely useful reference work that should fill a widely felt need' (Review of 1st ed. in *International journal of law libraries*, v.6(1), 1978, p.113). *Class No:* 340(01)

[2686]

RAISTRICK, D., *ed.* **'Recommended holdings for law libraries'.** London, Sweet & Maxwell, 1983, and in *The Law librarian* (Special issue), January 1983, p.i-xii, as Appendix VI-XI of 'Standards for law libraries'. £2.95. ISBN: 0421317205.

Appendix VI: Primary sources: basic collection; VII: Primary sources: additional legislation, reports and journals; VIII: Treatises; IX: Bibliographies; X: Librarianship collection; XI: Reference collection. *Class No:* 340(01)

[2687]

REYNOLDS, R.F. **'Indexing of legal journal literature and the history and development of the *Index to foreign legal periodicals*'.** In *The law librarian*, v.15(3), December 1984, p.38-46.

Sections on the need for an index to foreign legal periodicals, planning the index, other indexing services, followed by a bibliography of 63 references. *Class No:* 340(01)

[2688]

SMITH, N. Legal research techniques. Hebden Bridge, Yorks., Legal Information Resources Ltd., 1987. ii,40p. £4.50. ISBN: 1870369017.

Includes sections on Preliminary search; Finding textbooks and articles on a subject; Finding cases; Finding Statutes; Finding Statutory Instruments; Words and phrases; EEC law. Appendix: Law report series. A must for public libraries and the lay person. *Class No:* 340(01)

[2689]

SZLADITS, C., *comp.* **A Bibliography of foreign and comparative law:** books and articles in English, 1953-1980. Dobbs Ferry, N.Y., Oceana, for the Parker School of Foreign and Comparative Law, Columbia University, 1955-82. 5v.+7 supplements. Supplements; $32.50-$35 each.

Chiefly concerned with foreign (*i.e.,* other than that of the common-law jurisdictions) and private international law. Each volume has *c.*13,000 entries. *Class No:* 340(01)

Encyclopaedias

[2690]

WALKER, D.M. The Oxford companion to law. Oxford, Clarendon Press, 1980. ix,[1],1366p. £25. ISBN: 019866110x.

Concise information 'about some of the principal legal institutions, courts, judges and jurists, systems of law, branches of law, legal ideas and concepts, important doctrines and principles of law, and other legal matters ...' (*Preface*). Coverage extends to English-speaking and Western European countries. 'South African law' (sectionalised): p.1159-62; 9 references. Brief biographies (*e.g.* Montesquieu: ½ column; 1 reference). Appendix 1: 'List of the holders of various offices since 1660' (UK, p.1316-62); 2: 'Bibliographical notes' (p.1363-66—: 1. Bibliographies - 2. Indexes to periodical literature - 3. Legal biography and profession - 4. Legal history - 5.

....(contd.)

Jurisprudence - 6. Comparative legal studies - 7. International law and institutions - 8. European Communities law - 9. Commonwealth law - 10. Particular countries (Australia ... USA). Not a concise legal encyclopaedia of the law of any country; 'still less ... a layman's Home Lawyer' (*Preface*). Note occasional double entries, *e.g.* both 'Tender, legal' and 'Legal tender' - by different contributors. *Class No:* 340(031)

Handbooks & Manuals

[2691]

MOYS, E.M., *ed.* **Manual of law librarianship:** the use and organization of legal literature. 2nd ed. Aldershot, Gower, in association with the British and Irish Association of Law Librarians, 1987. xxxv,915p. £47.50. ISBN: 056603512x.

First published 1976.

20 contributors and 3 consultants. 4 parts (18 chapters): 1. Introduction (2 chapters: Law libraries and their users; Legal systems and legal literature) - 2. Legal literature of the British Isles and other common law systems (Primary sources: legislation; Primary sources: law reports; Secondary sources; Government publications; Historical sources; Commonwealth and the US; Reference sources: common law systems) - 3. Legal literature of other legal systems - 4. Law library practice. Bibliographies for further reading are appended to each chapter. Glossary. Extensive index of works cited, p.801-891 (*c.*5000 entries); substantial subject index, p.892-915. Main coverage is still the British Isles, but now includes chapters on the European Community and the Commonwealth. A standard guide to the intricacies of legal literature. '... the only comprehensive general treatise in this area of librarianship ...' (*Library Association record*, January 1988, p.49). '... most highly recommended to anyone who wishes to know about law librarianship' (*The law librarian,* v.18(3), December 1987, p.105). *Class No:* 340(035)

Dictionaries

[2692]

MARTIN, E.A., *ed.* **A Concise dictionary of law.** 2nd ed. Oxford, Oxford University Press, 1990. 448p. £6.99. (*Oxford paperback reference.*) ISBN: 0192852076.

Intended not for lawyers, but for those who need some legal knowledge in their work. *c.*1700 terms, concepts, processes and organizations of the law are defined and explained, a typical entry containing a succinct definition followed by further explanation. Includes foreign terms (italicised). 'Based on the expertise of a team of academic and practising British lawyers, this work amasses an array of substantive articles ...' (*Choice,* v.22(2), October 1984, p.246), of the first edition. *Class No:* 340(038)

[2693]

STROUD, F. Stroud's judicial dictionary of words and phrases. James, J.S., *ed.* 5th ed. London, Sweet & Maxwell, 1986. 6v. £380 (1993 supplement: £28.50). ISBN: 0421366303; 0421371307, supplement.

First published 1890; 4th ed. 1971-75, with supplements.

A dictionary of words and phrases that have been interpreted by the judges, giving their interpretations. Statutory definitions not judicially interpreted are referred to. Cross-references. V.1: A-C; v.2: D-H; v.3: I-O; v.4: P-R; v.5: S-Z; v.6: Tables of cases and statutes. The first

....(contd.)

supplement is now issued annually. Rearrangement of the articles has improved access to the contents. 'This dictionary enjoys a well-merited reputation and the frequently heard question 'have you checked Stroud?' is a tiny indication of this. It has the authority of reliability and comprehensiveness achieved over nearly one hundred years and through five editions ...' (*Law librarian*, v.18(2), August 1987, p.68-69). *Class No:* 340(038)

Polyglot

[2694]

BUTLER, W.E. *and* **NATHANSON, A.T.,** *eds.* **Mongolian-English-Russian dictionary of legal terms and concepts.** The Hague, Nijhoff, 1982. 745p. £103.50. ISBN: 9024157778.

Terminology also touches upon most branches of the social sciences, military affairs, medicine and some areas of the natural sciences. *Class No:* 340(038)=00

[2695]

DOUCET, M. Dictionnaire juridique et économique. Wörterbuch der Rechts ... Fleck, K.W., *ed.* 4 éd. rev. et remaniée. München, C.H. Beck'she Verlagsbuchhandlung, 1988. 2v. (xix,634p.; xvi, 656p.). ISBN: 3406314104, v.1; 3406098614, v.2.

2nd ed. published 1967-80.

French-German and German-French dictionaries of law and economics. *Class No:* 340(038)=00

[2696]

EGBERT, L.D. *and* **MORALES-MACEDO, L. Multilingual law dictionary,** English-français-español-Deutsch. Alphen aan den Rÿn, Sÿthoff; Dobbs Ferry, N.Y. Oceana, 1978. xxii,551p. £34.95.

6300 English-base terms, with French, Spanish and German equivalents and indexes. Where equivalents are lacking in the other languages (*e.g.* for 'Writ of scire facias'), explanations may be given. 4 appendices (1. Select list of definitions; 2. Law dictionaries, p.511-4; 3. Select references to law literature, p.515-6. Aimed at practising lawyers, legal scholars and language specialists. 'Certainly achieves a great deal' (*International journal of law libraries,* v.6(3), November 1978, p.312). *Class No:* 340(038)=00

[2697]

EUROPEAN PARLIAMENT. Legal terminology of the European Communities. Luxembourg, Office for Official Publications of the European Community, 1976. 2v. (873 p.). £6.

Terms in French-Italian-English-German-Dutch-Danish, arranged under 632 classified French keywords, followed by equivalents in the other languages. V.2. is the index. *Class No:* 340(038)=00

[2698]

GARCÍA, I.R. Diccionario de términos juridicos. 2nd ed. rev. London, Butterworths, 1985. xi,704p. £39.50. (*Butterworths legal publications.*) ISBN: 0880635002.

English-Spanish; Latin-Spanish; French-Spanish. Terms are explained in Spanish, and there is a 237-page section of words and phrases defined by the Supreme Tribunal of Puerto Rico. *Class No:* 340(038)=00

[2699]

LE DOCTE, E. Dictionnaire de termes juridiques en quatre langues ... Legal dictionary in four languages. 4th ed. Antwerp, Maklu; London, Sweet & Maxwell Ltd., 1987. [16], 822p. £74. ISBN: 0421378204, UK; 9062151639, Belgium.

First published 1978.

*c.*12,000 words & phrases: French-base, with Spanish, English and German equivalents across a double-page. Very brief definitions, but includes alternative terms. Indexes in Spanish, English and German refer to page numbers. A section on judicial systems of Spain, Belgium, Luxembourg, Netherlands, Germany, Austria, England, Ireland, US and Canada, p.731-749. *Class No:* 340(038)=00

English

[2700]

COLLIN, P.H. English law dictionary. Teddington, Mddx., Peter Collin Publishers, 1986. [4], 319p. £5.95. ISBN: 0948549017.

Some 6000 words and phrases, the basic vocabulary in British and American law, are explained, using a limited vocabulary of 500 words. Examples are given as necessary. Cross-references. *Class No:* 340(038)=20

[2701]

GARNER, B.A. A Dictionary of modern legal usage. Oxford, Oxford University Press, 1987. xviii,[3],587p. £25; $35. ISBN: 0195043774.

A dictionary of American and British usage. Classification guide, pronunciation guide, and list of abbreviations precede the dictionary. Entries range in length from one line to over a column ('Metaphors': 4 columns), point out distinctions among variant forms and include brief essays on special topics. Cross-references. Select bibliography, p.585-587. 'Its strengths are depth in explanations, careful distinctions, and engaging style' (*Library journal*, 15 September 1987, p.74). *Class No:* 340(038)=20

[2702]

SAUNDERS, J.B., *ed.* **Words and phrases legally defined.** 3rd ed. Butterworth and Co., (Publishers) Ltd., 1988-89. 4v. £220 the set. ISBN: 0406080402, Set; 0406080410, v.1; 0406080429, v.2; 0406080437, v.3; 0406080445, v.4.

First published about 1950.

An A-Z listing over the four volumes (e.g., v.1: A-C) aiming at accurate definitions of legal terms. Scope of the 3rd ed. broadened by the addition of selections of statutory definitions and extracts from textbooks (*e.g. Halsbury's laws of England*). Cross-references. Indications given when a term relates to a particular country such as Canada or Australia. A useful companion to *Halsbury's laws ....* *Class No:* 340(038)=20

[2703]

—**BURTON, W.C.,** *ed.* Legal thesaurus. 2nd ed. New York, Macmillan, 1992. 1011p. $40; £21. ISBN: 0028970772.

First published 1982.

Designed to augment the 1st edition and is very similar. 'If properly updated, this thesaurus would have enjoyed most use, but it will not be needed by libraries that have the first edition'. (*Choice*, v.30(6), February l993, p.936). *Class No:* 340(038)=20

[2704]

—CURZON, L.B. A Dictionary of law. 4th ed. London, Pitman Publishing, 1993. 480p. £13.99. ISBN: 0273601016.

First published 1979; 1st and 2nd eds. published by Macdonald & Evans.

A classic concise dictionary, compiled primarily for students, both in the UK and overseas, as a guide to the specialised vocabulary of the principles, practices and procedures of English law. Full references are given to cases and Statutes. *Class No:* 340(038)=20

[2705]

—Mozley & Whiteley's law dictionary. Ivamy, E.R.H., *ed.* 11th ed. London, Butterworth & Co., (Publishers) Ltd., 1993. vii,511p. £8.95. ISBN: 0406014205.

First published 1876.

A concise legal dictionary with over 3000 entries and cross-references. Its purpose is to give an exposition of legal terms and phrases of past and present use. 10th ed. adds definitions of terms used in the commercial and business world. *Class No:* 340(038)

[2706]

—OSBORN, P.G. Concise law dictionary. Bird, R., *ed.* 7th ed. London, Sweet & Maxwell, 1983. vi,390p. £9.25. ISBN: 0421296704.

Considered one of the best concise law dictionaries. Includes definitions of legal words and phrases, Roman law terms and maxims, and a list of law reports together with their abbreviations. *Class No:* 340(038)=20

German

[2707]

BESELER, D. von *and* JACOBS-WÜSTEFELD, B. Englisch-deutsches und deutsch-englisches Wörterbuch der Rechts und Geschäftssprache. Law dictionary: technical dictionery of the Anglo-American legal terminology, including commercial and statistical terms. 4th rev. ed.0 Berlin, de Gruyter, 1986-91. 2v. (xxii,1932p.). Eng.-Ger. 4th rev. ed. 1986. £176.95. Ger.-Eng. 4th ed., 1991. £264.95.

A technical dictionary of the Anglo-American legal terminology, including commercial and statistical terms. *Class No:* 340(038)=30

Scandinavian

[2708]

ANDERSON, R.J.B. Anglo-Scandinavian law dictionary of legal terms used in professional and commercial practice. Oslo, Universitetsforlaget, 1977. 137p. £12.95. ISBN: 8200023656.

Prepared under the auspices of the Royal Norwegian Ministry of Justice.

English base-term definitions, with equivalents in Swedish, Norwegian and Danish, followed by Norwegian - English - Swedish - Danish; Swedish - Norwegian - Danish - English; and Danish - English - Norwegian - Swedish sequences. *Class No:* 340(038)=395

French

[2709]

BAKER, J.H. Manual of law French. Aldershot, Hants., Avebury Publishing Co., 1979. 208p. £18.50. ISBN: 0859677443.

Claims to be the first law French glossary to be produced since 1779, and is intended for students and practitioners concerned with English legal history. An introduction to law French (history, study, grammar, common abbreviations and contractions) is followed by a 'Bibliography of aids to interpretation' (1. Law French and Anglo-Norman glossaries - 2. Dictionaries of old French and French etymologies - 3. English dictionaries - 4. Latin dictionaries - 5. Translations and parallel texts - 6. Guides to grammar and morphology). Glossary, p.43-205, A-Z French and English translations. Index of persons, p.207-208. *Class No:* 340(038)=40

[2710]

QUEMNER, Th. A. Dictionnaire juridique, nouveau dictionnaire ... français/anglais, English/French: administration, assurances, bourse, commerce, douanes, droit ... Baleyte, J., *ed.* 6.ré éd. Paris, Editions de Navarre, 1977. 311, 415p. £30.20.

First published 1953-55.

Wide-ranging, covering legal, financial, commercial, fiscal and allied terms. Appendix of Latin and English/French legal terms. Pays particular attention to differences between Anglo-American concepts and those prevailing in France. *Class No:* 340(038)=40

Italian

[2711]

FRANCHIS, F. de. Dizionario giuridico. Law dictionary. Milano, Giuffrè Editore, 1984. xi, 1545p. L.100,000; £67.50. ISBN: 8814003165.

Over 10,000 entries of English/American law terms, with descriptions in Italian, covering constitutional law, administrative law, civil and criminal procedures, commercial law and the newest contractual techniques, international law, etc. Descriptions are often small essays (*e.g.* 'Bankruptcy': 10 cols; 'Company': 15 cols.). Bibliographies are attached to many entries. Italian-English dictionary is in preparation. *Class No:* 340(038)=50

Spanish

[2712]

ROBB, L.A., *and others.* Diccionario de términos legales. Spanish-English and English-Spanish dictionary of legal terms. New York, Wiley, 1955. xii,228p. £34.85.

Includes terms used in Latin American countries (indicating name of country), and economic terminology. Well set out. Very favourably reviewed in *The Incorporated linguist.* v.18(1), Winter 1979, p.27. *Class No:* 340(038)=60

Latin

[2713]

Latin for Lawyers. 3rd ed. London. Sweet & Maxwell, 1960. viii,287p.

First published 1915.

Includes vocabulary of over 1000 Latin maxims, etc., with English translation. *Class No:* 340(038)=71

Russian

[2714]
PRISCHEPENKO, N.P. Russian-English law dictionary.
New York University School of Law, *ed.* New York,
Praeger, 1969. vii,146p.

9700 entries for Russian technical legal terms. Russian-
English only. *Class No:* 340(038)=82

Polish

[2715]
POLISH ACADEMY OF SCIENCES. Institute of State and
Law. Polish/English dictionary of legal terms. Warsaw,
Ossolineum, 1986. [6],211p. £11.95. ISBN: 8304018977.

The first of four versions planned of the *Foreign-language
dictionary of legal terms.* The others will be Polish/Russian,
Polish/German, and Polish/French.

A-Z listing of *c.*11,000 headwords in Polish with English
translations or equivalents. English-Polish index.
Class No: 340(038)=84

[2716]
RYDLEWSKA-SZEWCZYKOWA, D.   *and*
ZACZKIEWICZOWA, J. Slownik prawniczy polsko-
angielski/Polish-English dictionary of legal terms.
Wroclaw, Zaklad Narodowy im Ossolinskich, 1986. 211p.

Published under the auspices of the Polish Academy of
Sciences Institute of State and Law. The first of a series of
foreign language dictionaries of legal terms planned to be
published in Poland.

*c.*11,000 main entries arranged A-Z by the Polish term,
with English equivalents. Supplemented by an index of the
main English/Polish noun headwords.
Class No: 340(038)=84

Welsh

[2717]
LEWIS, R. Termau cyfraith/Welsh terms ... gyda rhagair
gan Alglwydd Morris o Borth-Y-Gest. Llandysul, Gwasg
Gower, 1972. xxxiii,226p. ISBN: 0850881404.

Parallel Welsh and English text. Bibliography, p.219-216.
Class No: 340(038)=916.6

Arabic

[2718]
FARUQI, H.S. Faruqi's law dictionary, English-Arabic,
meanings and definitions of terms of English and American
jurisprudence (ancient and modern). 2nd rev. ed. Beirut,
Librairie du Liban, 1970. xvi,758p.

Wide-ranging coverage, including terms in forensic
medicine, commerce, banking, insurance, civil aviation,
diplomacy and petroluem. *Class No:* 340(038)=927

[2719]
—FARUQI, H.S. Faruqi's law dictionary, Arabic-English,
containing terms of jurisprudence (ancient and modern),
forensic medicine, commerce, banking, insurance, civil
aviation, diplomacy and petroleum. Beirut, Librairie du
Liban, 1972. [9],388,[288]p.

Listed by the Arabic terms, with English equivalents.
Class No: 340(038)=927

Reviews & Abstracts

[2720]
Legal reference services quarterly. New York, Hawarth
Press Inc., 1981-. v.1(1)- $105pa. ISSN: 0270319x.

As well as articles, it contains book reviews and an
annotated bibliography on a specific subject in each issue.
Class No: 340(048)

Periodicals & Progress Reports

[2721]
International journal of legal information: the official
journal of the International Association of Law Librarians.
1973-. 3pa. Washington, DC., The Institute for International
Legal Information. $80pa. ISSN: 07311265.

Early title was *International journal of law libraries,*
published by the International Association of Law Libraries.

Includes articles on legal perspectives and law
librarianship, bibliographies, notes and comments, periodical
reviews, international documentation, book reviews, books
received and noted. *Class No:* 340(05)

[2722]
The Law librarian: journal of the British and Irish Association
of Law Librarians. London, Sweet & Maxwell, for the
Association, 1970-. 4pa. £35pa. ISSN: 00239275.

Early sub-title was *bulletin....*

V.24(1), March 1993 (52p.) is devoted to the use of
information technology in law libraries; 15 case studies by
law librariansry'); a 'Current awareness' section
(Bibliographical guides ... Dictionaries ... Legal research
and method...Periodicals (new)...Statistics. Lengthy signed
book reviews, p.44-52. *Class No:* 340(05)

Periodicals

[2723]
WYPYSKI, E.M. Legal periodicals in English. Dobbs Ferry,
N.Y., Glanville Press, 1976. 5 binders. $525 the set. ISBN:
0878020543.

Succeeds L.W. Marse's *Checklist of Anglo-American legal
periodicals* (1962).

A page is allocated to each title, with data on frequency,
previous title(s) (if any), subject, and where indexed,
reprinted, microfilmed or cited. Cumulative indexes.
Class No: 340(051)

[2724]
—MERSKY, R.M., *and others, eds.* Author's guide to
journals in law, criminal justice and criminology. New York,
Haworth Press, 1979. 243p. $32.95. ISBN: 0917724062.

Includes 'only those journals that accept manuscripts from
outside sources' (*American book review annual,* 1980, item
519). 4 sections, covering general and specialized law-school
reviews, association publications and commercial journals.
Class No: 340(051)(01)

Bibliographies

[2725]
Legal journals index. Hebden Bridge, Legal Information
Resources, 1986-. Monthly, with quarterly and annual
cumulations. Annual issue is bound vol. £560pa. ISSN:
09504206.

Indexes over 155 British legal journals, including all
items, case reports, comments and legislation, nearly 4000

....(contd.)

items in each issue. A list of journals indexed precedes the subject index, with items arranged A-Z by subject, full citations and cross-references. This is followed by an author index, case index, legislation index, and book review index. *Class No:* 340(051)(01)

[2726]
LONDON UNIVERSITY. Institute of Advanced Legal Studies. **Union list of periodicals.** 4th ed. London, the Institute, 1978. xx,316p.

First published in 1949 as *A survey of legal periodicals held in British libraries.*

Lists nearly 3000 titles of legal periodicals held in 114 libraries in the UK, with details of holdings, Excludes law reports, treaty collections, legislation and ephemera such as news letters. *Class No:* 340(051)(01)

Quotations

[2727]
JAMES, S. *and* **STEBBINGS, C.,** *comps.* *&* *eds.* **A Dictionary of legal quotations.** London, Croom Helm, 1987. xiv,209p. £12.95. ISBN: 0709913032.

Arranged A-Z by 160 subject terms (Accomplice ... Witnesses). Quotations under each subject are numbered and give source of quotation. 'Comprehensibility' has 16 quotations; 'Law' has 210, and 'see' references to Civil law, Common law, International law, Jurisprudence and Legislation. Index of authors and sources, p.178-184. Index of key words, p.185-209. *Class No:* 340(082.2)

[2728]
Oxford dictionary of American legal quotations. Shapero, F.R., *ed.* New York, Oxford University Press, 1993. xv,582p. $49.95. £35. ISBN: 0195058593.

3500 quotations, arranged by broad topic. Appendix: The Constitution. Author and rotated keyword indexes. 'Essential for law libraries that want a traditional and timely resource (*Choice*, v.31(2), October 93, p.273). *Class No:* 340(082.2)

Festschriften

Bibliographies

[2729]
DAU, H., *comp.* **Bibliographie juristischer Festschriften und Festschriftenbeträge:** Deutschland, Schweiz, Österreich/Bibliography of legal Festschriften: titles and contents, Germany, Switzerland, Austria. Berlin, Berlin Verlag Arno Spitz, 1962-87. 6v. V.5: DM.150-.

Now covers 120 years: Band O: *1864-1944* (1984); 1: *1945-1961* (1962); 2: *1962-1966* (1967); 3. *1967-1974* (1977); 4. *1975-1979* (1981); 5. *1980-1984* (c.1987). V.5 is in 4 main sections: A. Bibliography of Festschriften, arranged under 44 subject headings in A-Z order; B. Analytical bibliography of Festschriften; C. Indexes (author, name, geographical, subject); D. Supplement of Festschriften published in 1985/86. The very detailed subject index (p.526-617) is in German, but there is a useful listing of major subject areas in English, with German equivalents. *Class No:* 340(082.20)(01)

Histories

Bibliographies

[2730]
GILISSEN, J., *ed.* **Introduction bibliographique à l'histoire du droit et à l'ethnologie juridique/Bibliographical introduction to legal history and ethnology.** Bruxelles, Éditions de l'Institut de Sociologie, 1965-1988. 9v. (Loose-leaf binders). (*Études d'histoire et d'ethnologie juridiques.*)

Some chapters not published. The majority of the sections are in English or French. *Class No:* 340(091)(01)

Developing Countries

Bibliographies

[2731]
LANSKY, R. **Handbuch der Bibliographien zum Recht der Entwicklungsländer/Handbook of bibliographies on the laws of developing countries.** Hamburg, Übersee - Dokumentation im Verband der Stiftung Deutsches Übersee - Institut, 1981. xxxiii, 633p. ISBN: 3465014464.

Preliminary edition published 1977.

Annotated entries for 1494 bibliographies and reference tools in various languages. Arranged in geographical order (A. Multiple regions - B. Middle East (Islamic legal systems) in general - C. Africa - D. Asia - E. Oceana - F. Latin America). Items starred with one asterisk - important, items with two - very important. Titles in original languages, descriptions in German. Summary, p.515-532; Index, p.533-615, in English & German in one sequence; Supplement, p.616-633. *Class No:* 340(4/9-77)(01)

Europe

Yearbooks & Directories

[2732]
Yearbook of European law, 1981-. Oxford, Clarendon Press, 1982-.

V.11, 1991/92, (1992. xvii,682p. £90. ISBN 0198257791) contains 14 essays (*e.g.* 'The future of the Court of Justice of the European Communities'; 'The Europe of universities') and 6 annual surveys (Legal developments in the European Parliament - Competition law - European political co-operation, 1989-91 - The Brussels Convention - Council of Europe legal co-operation in 1991 - The European Convention on Human Rights). 18 book reviews - Books received - Table of cases - Commission decisions on competitions. Index. *Class No:* 340(4)(058)

Middle Ages

[2733]
ULLMANN, W. **Law and politics in the Middle Ages:** an introduction to the sources of medieval political ideas. Cambridge, Cambridge University Press (first published by The Sources of History Ltd). 1975. 320p. £17. (*Sources of history series.*) ISBN: 0521214599.

8 chapters: 2. The Roman law - 3. The scholarship of Roman law - 4. Canon law - 5. The scholarship of Canon law - 6. Non-Roman secular law - 7. Governmental doctrines in literary sources - 8. The new science of politics. Footnotes. Select bibliography. p.307-10 (by chapters). Non-

....(contd.)

analytical index. 'One of the first attempts to present the principal sources of medieval political ideas in an integrated and coherent manner' (*Preface*). *Class No:* 340(4)"01/14"

Europe—Western

Bibliographies

[2734]

GRAULICH, D. *and* GRAULICH, C. **Guide to foreign legal materials: Belgium, Luxembourg, Netherlands.** Dobbs Ferry, N.Y., Oceana, 1968, for the Parker School of Foreign and Comparative Law, Columbia University. 258p. $17.50. (*Parker School studies in foreign and comparative law, v.3.*) ISBN: 0379117533. *Class No:* 340(400)(01)

[2735]

LONDON UNIVERSITY. Institute of Advanced Legal Studies. **Union list of West European legal literature:** publications held by libraries in Oxford, Cambridge and London. London, the Institute, 1966. viii,426p. (*Union catalogue no.5.*)

Covers the holdings of 8 libraries. Sections: General reference material. General periodicals (p.2-5) - Part A. Country sections - Part B. Western Europe: integration & cooperation. General author, serial and subject indexes. *Class No:* 340(400)(01)

[2736]

SZLADITS, C. **Guide to foreign legal materials, French, German, Swiss.** New York, Oceana Publications, for Parker School of Foreign and Comparative Law, Columbia University, 1959. xv,599p. $30.00.

A 2nd ed. is being compiled in several parts. See 340(44)(01) for the guide to French materials, and 340(43)(01) for German materials.

French law, p.3-116; German law, p.118-330; Swiss law, p.333-507. In the case of Swiss law, subdivision is: pt.1, Sources of law; pt.2, Repositories of the law (bibliographies; legislative materials and commentaries; case law; encyclopedias and dictionaries; doctrinal writings; list of legal abbreviations). Many footnote references. Index of authors and titles; index to subjects. A guide for the common-law lawyer to the use of foreign legal materials - laws, reports, books. *Class No:* 340(400)(01)

Great Britain

[2737]

Current law London, Sweet & Maxwell and Stevens, 1946-. Monthly. £190pa (with yearbook and citators: £265pa; with Statutes, yearbook and citators: £335pa). ISSN: 0011362x.

Cumulated annually. The yearbook is an annual consolidation of the monthly citation indexes to all developments since 1947, covering case law, Statute law, and Statutory instruments.

A survey by subject, believed to be complete, of all legal developments, legislation, decisions and literature. Full references to law reports, periodicals, etc., are given, and full indexes are provided, including case and Statute citators (*i.e.,* tables of earlier cases and Statutes affected by current development, legislative, judicial or literary). The making of orders, etc., under powers conferred by a Statute is shown in

....(contd.)

the citator. *Current law statutes annotated* (1948-. Annual) contains the Statutes and Church Assembly Measures passed during the calendar year. *Class No:* 340(410)

[2738]

Every man's own lawyer, by 'A barrister'. 71st ed. London, Macmillan Press, 1981. vp. £3.95. ISBN: 0333318358.

First published 1863.

A short elucidation of those parts of English law that are of most interest to the private citizen and written for the non-specialist. In general, 'the law ... in force during the first half of the year 1979' (*Preface*). 25 chapters (*e.g.* 2. Personal rights and remedies; 7. The law of property; 10. Criminal law; 15. Wills and trusts; 25. A short dictionary of legal terms). Table of cases; table of Statutes. Analytical index. Well-sectionalised and footnoted. *Class No:* 340(410)

[2739]

GREAT BRITAIN. **Statutory Instruments. 1890-.** London, HMSO, 1890-.

Initially (and until 1947) as *Statutory Rules and Orders* ('S.R. & O.'). Cumulation, to December 31, 1948 (HMSO, 1949-52. 25v.), as *S.R. & O. and S.I. revised.*

Statutory Instruments ('S.I.'),. each issued separately and cumulated annually (less local S.I.s and revocations), consist of subordinate legislation, - Orders in Council and Orders, rules, regulations, etc. made by Ministers and others. A biennial subject index is provided in *Index to Governmental Orders in force* ... The annual *Table of Government Orders* is in numerical order. *Class No:* 340(410)

[2740]

GREAT BRITAIN. Statutory Publications Office. **The Public General Acts and General Synod Measures.** London, HMSO, [1831]-. Annual (formerly sessional).

Early title was *The Public General Acts and Church Assembly Measures.* *Class No:* 340(410)

[2741]

Halsbury's Statutes of England and Wales. 4th ed. London, Butterworths, 1985-92. 50v. ISBN: 0406214093.

First published 1930. Companion to *Halsbury's Laws of England* (*qv*).

Aim is to provide the user with an up-to-date version of the amended text of every Public General Act or Ecclesiastical Measure in force in England and Wales, with detailed annotations to each section and schedule. Arrangement is A-Z by subject and there is an index to each volume. V.50 includes Treaties of the European Communities. *Cumulative supplement,* 1989 (1989. ISBN 0406043442). *Tables of Statutes and general index, 1989-90* (1989. ISBN 0406214727) refers to v.1-39 & 41-50. 'Particularly useful for tracing Acts on a particular subject' (Dane, J., and Thomas, P.A. *How to use a law library* (1979),p.51) of the 3rd ed. *Class No:* 340(410)

Bibliographies

[2742]

CHLOROS, A.G., *ed.* **Bibliographical guide to the law of the United Kingdom, the Channel Islands and the Isle of Man.** 2nd ed. London, University of London, Institute of Advanced Legal Studies, 1973. xvii,301p. £7.50. ISBN: 0901190144.

First published 1956. Published in co-operation with the United Kingdom National Committee of Comparative Law,

.... *(contd.)*

and under the auspices of Unesco and the International Association of Legal Science.

Contributions by more than 30 lawyers. 21 chapters, sectionalised, with introductions and select bibliographies (1. Bibliographies and general accounts - 2. The sources of English law ... 7. Civil law (entries for books written primarily for students are single-asterisked; those for students coming to the subject for the first time are double-asterisked) ... 12. International law - 13. Northern Ireland - 14. Scots law ... 17. The Commonwealth ... 21. Common Market). Index of authors and editors; subject index. 'Prepared mainly in order to introduce English law to foreign lawyers and especially to "Civilians" (*Foreword*). *Class No:* 340(410)(01)

Reports Literature

[2743]

All England law reports. London, Butterworths, 1936-. Weekly.

A series of reports of decisions of all the courts; in suitable cases editorial notes are given, explaining the legal significance. Cases are speedily reported. Annual cumulative index and 'noter-up'. This also contains a table of cases, a table of statutes judicially considered, and a table of cases judicially noticed in later editions.

All England law reports reprint, 1558-1935 (London, Butterworths, 1966-68. 36v. and index. ISBN 040600000x) is a selection in the same styles as the *All England law reports.*

LEXIS, a computer-based legal research service, launched by Butterworths in 1980, contains the full text of all English cases reported in the main series of law reports since 1945. *Class No:* 340(410)(047)

[2744]

DICKMAN, P. and **MISKIN, C.,** *eds.* **Daily law reports index.** Hebden Bridge, West Yorks., Legal Information Resources Ltd., July, 1988-. Weekly. £285 including bound annual volume.

A quick access index to law reports appearing in UK daily newspapers (*e.g., The Times, Financial times, Independent, Guardian* and *Daily telegraph*). Each issue appears in the week following the last week of the fortnight covered. Indexed by case, keywords and legislation judicially considered. Individual issues are filed behind numbered tags in a loose-leaf binder; bound cumulations also contain a checklist of cases, and a Case report index, detailing cases subsequently reported fully in the major series (*e.g., Law reports, Criminal appeal reports, Local government reports, Tax cases,* etc.). 'The editors ... have filled a very important gap in aids available to legal research' (*The Law librarian,* v.20(2). August 1989, p.70). *Class No:* 340(410)(047)

Yearbooks & Directories

[2745]

British directory of legal services, 1990/91. 3rd ed. Issued every two years. Oxford, Varsity Publications, 1990. 216p. £15. ISSN: 09519181.

1st published for 1987/88.

Lists companies able to offer specific services to solicitors and barristers in the fields of arbitration, accident,

.... *(contd.)*

investigation and analysis, company information and searches, consulting and expert witnesses, etc. A-Z index. Subject index. Index of countries. *Class No:* 340(410)(058)

[2746]

Butterworth's legal services directory, 1993. 3rd ed. East Grinstead, West Sussex, Thomas Skinner Directories, 1993. 300p. £28. ISBN: 1857390962.

First published 1988.

Covers investigators, expert witnesses, company registration agents, process servers, bailiffs, etc. *Class No:* 340(410)(058)

[2747]

Legal 500: a client's guide to UK law firms. Pritchard, J., *ed.* 6th ed. London, Legalease, 1993. 912p. £39. ISBN: 1870854098.

First published 1988. Annual.

Aims to be an introductory guide to leading law firms, the factual information being supplied by the firms. A regional survey, by area, precedes the listing of 500 firms, A-Z, by name, followed by address, recruitment, agency work, types of work undertaken. Then a list of foreign law firms in London, a list of recruitment agencies, etc. *Class No:* 340(410)(058)

Histories

[2748]

BLAND, D.S., *comp.* **A Bibliography of the Inns of Court and Chancery.** London, Seldon Society, 1965. xi,75p. £10. ISBN: 0854231161.

Comprises 862 numbered items, with many cross-references. 15 sections, including A. Manuscript sources- B. Histories, descriptions and general works - J. Drama - K. Literature, general - L. Libraries - M. Education - N. 19th century reform - O. The legal profession. Indexes of authors, subjects and persons. *Class No:* 340(410)(091)

[2749]

YALE, D.E.C. and **BAKER, J.H.,** *eds.* **A Centenary guide to the publications of the Seldon Society.** London, Seldon Society, 1987. xxiv,242p. £30.

Supersedes the *General guide to the Society's publications,* by Kiralfy & Jones (1960).

A detailed index and summary of the contents of the Introductions to volumes 1-102 of the main series of the Society's publications, and also the supplementary series and the occasional publications. V.1 was published in 1887. Thorough indexes of names and subjects. The Seldon Society aims to study the history of law, prints, and ancient records, and the editors are literary directors of the Society. An informative review of the Society and the guide by Peter Luther is published in *The Law library,* v.20(1), April 1989, p.90-91. *Class No:* 340(410)(091)

Bibliographies

[2750]

HINES, W., *comp.* **'Bibliography on British and Irish legal history (works published after 1985)'.** In *Cambrian law review,* v.18, 1988, p.80-90.

An unannotated bibliography of 195 items, mainly journal articles but some books. In 7 sections (General and miscellaneous works - Medieval (before 1500) - Early modern (1500-1800) - Modern (from c.1800) - Ireland -

....*(contd.)*

Scotland - Wales). Arrangement within sections is A-Z by author. No introduction. Works published before 1985 were listed in earlier issues of *Cambrian law review.*

Class No: 340(410)(091)(01)

Laws

[2751]

GREAT BRITAIN. Chronological table of the Statutes, covering the legislation from 1235 to the end of 1990. London, HMSO, 1990. 2v. (ix,874; 875-1946p.). £170. ISBN: 0118403222.

Issued annually.

Part 1: 1235-1950; pt.2: 1951 to end of 1990. Does not include local or personal Acts. *Class No:* 340(410)(094.1)

[2752]

GREAT BRITAIN. Statutory Publications Office. Statutes in force. London, HMSO, 1972-. Loose-leaf, with 64 binders.

Replaces *The Statutes revised.*

A series of booklets, in subject groups, A-Z.

Class No: 340(410)(094.1)

[2753]

Is it in force? 1993: a guide to the commencement of the Statutes of England and Wales and of Scotland passed since 1 January 1965. Butterworth's Editorial staff. London, Butterworths, 1993. Annual. viii,615p. £21. ISBN: 0406015880.

Arranged chronologically, 1965-, subdivided by the Acts, arranged A-Z by short title, with chapter number, date of Royal Assent, list of provisions, etc.

Class No: 340(410)(094.1)

Scotland

Handbooks & Manuals

[2754]

WALKER, D.M. The Scottish legal system: an introduction to the study of Scots law. 6th ed. Edinburgh, W. Green, 1992. 552p.8 illus. £35. ISBN: 0414010124.

First published 1959.

Written primarily as a textbook for the introductory course in the legal curriculum of Glasgow University. 15 chapters, each with 'further readings' (3. The branches of legal science - 4. The development of Scots law ... 7. The modern judicial system ... 10. The sources of Scots law - 11. The repositories of Scots law ... 14. The administration of criminal justice - 15. The making of new law. Many footnotes referring to books, articles, case law, and Statutes.

Class No: 340(411)(035)

Dictionaries

[2755]

GIBB, A.D. Students glossary of Scottish legal terms. Duncan, A.G.M., *ed.* 2nd ed. Edinburgh, W. Green & Son Ltd., 1982. 100p. £6. ISBN: 0414006968.

First published 1946.

A list of books of reference precedes the glossary, which has short, clear definitions of about 15 words for *c.*1000 terms. (Concerned almost exclusively with legal expressions

....*(contd.)*

which are truly and exclusively lawyers' expressions' (*Introduction* to 1st ed.). Adequate cross-references.

Class No: 340(411)(038)

Yearbooks & Directories

[2756]

Scottish current law year book ... 1948-. Edinburgh, W. Green & Sons, 1949-. Annual. £320. ISSN: 02656159.

Annual cumulation of the monthly *Current law* (Scottish ed.). Sold only with *Scottish current law citator.*

The 1984 *year book* has tables of cases, statutory instruments and abbreviations, followed by subjects (Administrative law ... Workmen's compensation). Appended: 'Books and articles' (78p. under subjects, A-Z). Analytical index. *Class No:* 340(411)(058)

[2757]

—Encyclopaedia of the laws of Scotland. Viscount Dunedin, *and others, eds.* Edinburgh, W. Green & Sons, 1926-35. v.1-16; supplementary volume, pts.1-2, and Appendix, 1949-52. 3v.

No further volumes published. Should be supplemented by *Scottish current law year book. Class No:* 340(411)(058)

Histories

[2758]

WALKER, D.M. A Legal history of Scotland. v.1. The beginnings to AD 1286. Edinburgh, W. Green, 1988. xxi,435p. £64. ISBN: 0414008162.

An account of the historical development of legal institutions and the system of concepts, doctrines and principles in Scottish law, both public and private. A chronological approach, with 2 chapters on the early period and 15 chapters on the feudal period. Bibliography (p.409-420) is divided into reference books, general histories, record publications, sources, and literary sources, each subdivided A-Z by author. Analytical subject index (p.421-435). *Class No:* 340(411)(091)

Manuscripts & Incunabula

[2759]

STAIR SOCIETY. An Introductory survey of the sources and literature of Scots Law. Edinburgh, Stair Society, 1936. 486p.

The inaugural volume of the Stair Society, presenting the first comprehensive survey of the sources of Scots law which has ever been essayed. A complete guide, well documented and equipped with bibliographies. 38 contributions by specialists in 4 sections: Native sources - Non-native sources - Indirect sources - Special subjects. *Index,* compiled by J.C. Brown (Edinburgh, Stair Society, 1939, 66p.), in two parts: index of cases cited; index of subjects.

Class No: 340(411)(093)

Laws

[2760]

SCOTLAND. PARLIAMENT. The Acts of the Parliaments of Scotland, 1424-1707. 2nd rev. ed. Edinburgh, HMSO, 1966. lix,191p. tables.

First published 1908.

....(contd.)

The 1908 ed. contains a chronological table of all the Acts, the text of Acts of a public nature and still in force, and a digested index of those still in force. Omits local and personal Acts (Minto, J. *Reference books* (1929), p.72). Insert: *Index of short titles of the current Acts of the Parliament of Scotland, 1424-1707* (1967.4p.).
Class No: 340(411)(094.1)

Northern Ireland

Manuscripts & Incunabula
[2761]
NORTHERN IRELAND. The Statutes revised, Northern Ireland, AD1226-1950 inclusive (as amended up to the end of 1954). Belfast, HMSO, 1956. 16v.

V.1: Legislation pre-1800 - 2-8. UK enactments, 1801-1920; 9-12: UK enactments, 1921-1950; 13-16: Northern Ireland enactments, 1921-1950. These volumes contain all the enactments affecting Northern Ireland. *Chronological table of the Statutes* (covering 1226 onwards) and *Index to the Statutes in force* are issued at 3-yearly intervals.

Subordinate legislation is published singly and bound annually as *Statutory rules and orders of Northern Ireland. Index to the Statutory rules and orders of Northern Ireland in force on 31 December 1992* (1993. £150. ISBN 0337902925). *Class No:* 340(416)(093)

Eire

Bibliographies
[2762]
PAWLOSKI,, B.M. 'Gaelic law in early and medieval Ireland; a bibliography' In *Law library journal.* v.79(2), Spring 1987, p. 305-31.

A bibliography of 365 books and articles on all aspects of early Irish law (pre-history to the Elizabethan era), arranged in 15 sections: 1. The Brehon law system; II. The King; III. Courts; IV. Irish parliament; V. Local law and administration; VI. Law of the family; VII. Honour and status; VIII. Land law; IX.. Charters and deeds; X. Agriculture; XI. Sick-maintenance; XII. Distraint; XIII. The Church; XIV. Influence of English Law; XV. Other influences. Double column author index, p. 332-3.
Class No: 340(417)(01)

Handbooks & Manuals
[2763]
DOOLAN, B. Principles of Irish Law. 2nd ed. Dublin, Gill & Macmillan, 1986. xix,395p. £12.50. ISBN: 0707114384.

First published 1981.

Claims to be the standard introduction to Irish law, each major area of law being comprehensively treated with a jargon-free explanation. Details given for over 120 statutes and more than 600 cases decided in Irish courts which together form the body of Irish law. Arranged in 9 parts (1. The Irish legal system - 2. The law of contract - 3. Criminal law - 4. The law of torts - 5. Equity and trusts - 6. Land law - 7. Family law and succession - 8. Commercial law - 9. Employment law), preceded by tables of statues and tables of cases. Index. *Class No:* 340(417)(035)

Dictionaries
[2764]
MURDOCH, H. A Dictionary of Irish law. Dun Loaghaire, Co. Dublin, Topaz Publications, 1988. xiii,569p. IR£38. ISBN: 0951403206.

Provides in one volume definitions of the principal words and phrases which are encountered in Irish law giving, in most instances, the legal sources of the definitions, whether statutory or judicial, and a brief introduction to the relevant law. '... designed primarily for busy practising lawyers, whether barrister or solicitor, who want an *aide memoire* or an introduction to an area of law with which they are not immediately familiar ...' Endeavours to cover all areas of law. Extensive cross-references. 3 appendices: 1. Books on Irish law referred to in the dictionary (A-Z by author); books on UK law, of relevance to Irish law, referred to in the dictionary; 2. Law reports; 3. Law Reform Commission's reports/working papers. *Class No:* 340(417)(038)

Laws
[2765]
EIRE. Actanna an Oireachtais/The Acts of the Oireachtais passed in the year ... consisting of the Public General Acts and the Private Acts, with tables and index. Dublin, Stationery Office, 1922-. Annual.

Irish and English on opposite pages.

Index to the legislation passed by the Oireachtais ... 1922 to 1975 (Dublin, Stationery office, 1977) is updated at intervals. Subordinate legislation is issued singly and bound annually as *Statutory Rules, Orders and Regulations for Eire,* with cumulative indexes. *Class No:* 340(417)(094.1)

Commonwealth
[2766]
Law reform in the Commonwealth: law reform proposals and their implementation, 1987. London, Commonwealth Secretariat, 1988. v,191p. £7.50.

First published 1981. Annual.

A register of Commonwealth law reform agency proposals in law reform, and monitors the progress made in the implementation of such proposals. Also lists government departments concerned with legal research.
Class No: 340(41-44)

Bibliographies
[2767]
NEWTON, V. Commonwealth Caribbean legal literature: a bibliography of primary sources to date and secondary sources for 1971-85. 2nd ed. Cave Hill, Barbados, Faculty of Law Library, University of the West Indies, 1987. xxiv, 492p. $50; Barbados$70.

First published as *Legal literature and conditions affecting legal publishing in the Commonwealth Caribbean: a bibliography* (1979).

3439 numbered entries, arranged by different types of sources (*e.g.* Constitutions; Law reports; Bibliographies; Theses). Most materials cited held in the University's libraries, but also includes materials held in other Caribbean law libraries. '... well suited to supporting research comparing the law of different Caribbean countries in

....(contd.)
particular fields and for checking collections by topic' (*International journal of legal information*, v.16(1), Spring 1988, p.38-39). *Class No:* 340(41-44)(01)

Reviews & Abstracts

[2768]
English and Empire digest, with complete and exhaustive annotations. Stickland, P., *ed.* Rev. ed. London, Butterworth, 1971. 66v. £2350. ISBN: 0406025002, the set.

Cumulative annual supplements, continuation and replacement volumes.

Digests every English case reported in a law report or series of reports, from early times onwards and (in smaller type) of many cases decoded in Commonwealth countries. A note of the decision is always given, with references to all published reports of the case, plus reference to later cases in which it has been judicially noticed. Cases are arranged systematically under broad subject headings (*e.g.* 'Contract'; 'Evidence'; 'Companies'; 'Negligence'; 'Criminal law and procedure'). *Class No:* 340(41-44)(048)

Yearbooks & Directories

[2769]
Annual survey of Commonwealth law, 1965-1977, v.1-13. Oxford, Clarendon Press, 1966-1978. 13v.

Various contributors to each issue. Covers all types of law, providing commentary on judicial decisions from most of the jurisidications of the Commonwealth and collections of legislative material. Heavily footnoted. Analytical subject and territorial indexes to each vol. *Class No:* 340(41-44)(058)

[2770]
Commonwealth law bulletin. London, Commonwealth Secretariat, 1975-. v.1,no.1-. Quarterly. £20pa. ISSN: 03050718.

Contains details of legislation, judicial decisions, international agreements, law reform. A 'Miscellaneous' section includes review of books, a list of recent periodical articles. The editorial note that precedes highlights developments. *Class No:* 340(41-44)(058)

England & Wales

Reports Literature

[2771]
Weekly law reports. London, Incorporated Council of Law Reporting for England and Wales, 1953-. Weekly. £175pa. ISSN: 00193518.

The series contains decisions of all courts, the most important of them being reported more fully in the *Law reports,* later. Here cases are reported speedily.

The annual cumulative index covering this series and *Law reports* also contains tables of cases and statutes judicially considered. Also available online.

The history of *Law reports* and other law series is described in section 5. 'The reports, abridgements, digests, collections of cases and statutes, and dictionaries', in v.15 (1965) of Sir W. Holdsworth's *A history of English law.* Also available online. *Class No:* 340(42)(047)

Laws

[2772]
Halsbury's Statutory Instruments; being a companion work to *Halsbury's Statutes of England.* Butterworth's Legal Editorial staff. 4th re-issue. London, Butterworth, 1979-. 23v. £400. ISBN: 0406045003.

Annotated edition of all Statutory Rules and Orders and Statutory Instruments in force, arranged under topics. Not all Instruments in force are reprinted in full. Updated by looseleaf supplementary service. *Class No:* 340(42)(094.1)

England

Bibliographies

[2773]
WILLIAMS, G. Learning the law. 11th ed. London, Stevenson & Sons, 1982. viii,241p. £4.25. ISBN: 0420462902.

First published 1945; 10th ed. 1978.

Handbook for the law student, to prepare him/her for reading legal textbooks. 14 chapters (1. The divisions of the law ... 5. Technical terms ... 7. The interpretation of the statutes ... 12. Legal research ... 14. General reading (p.226-237, in 10 subject sections)). Index, p.239-241. *Class No:* 340(420)(01)

Encyclopaedias

[2774]
Halsbury's Laws of England. Lord Hailsham, *ed.* 4th ed. London, Butterworths, 1973-. 56v. *Annual abridgemer* (v.1, 1974-); *Cumulative supplement* (2 parts, 1980; Current service *Monthly review. Monthly re... £35pa.* ISSN: 03084388, Annual abridgement; 0209821, Monthly review.

First published 1907-17; 3rd ed. 1952-64 (43v.).

An encyclopaedia of English law, consisting of separate treatises on individual subjects, A-Z. The article 'Juries' (v.26, p.313-39, paras 601-654/700) is subdivided: 1. Constitution and duties of juries - 2. Qualification, exemption and excusability of juries - 3. Summoning of jurors - 4. Proceedings before juries - 5. Payment of jurors - 6. Common law offences. V.23 (1978) is devoted entirely to 'Income taxation' (1298p.), with a detailed index (p.1225-89) and a 'Words and phrases' index. Definitions; footnoted Acts and case law. V.53 (2v.) is a consolidated table of Statutes; v.54 (2v.) a consolidated table of cases; v.55-56 a consolidated index. *Class No:* 340(420)(031)

[2775]
—Halsbury's Laws of England: a user's guide. London, Butterworths, 1983. 30p.

Contents: Introduction - Component parts of Halsbury's Laws - keeping Halsbury's Laws up to date - Halsbury's annual abridgement - How to use Halsbury's Laws - Tables of titles (to the 4th ed.). Index key. *Class No:* 340(410)

[2776]
JOWITT W.A., 1st earl Jowitt *and* **WALSH, C. The Dictionary of English law.** Burke, J., *ed.* 2nd ed. London, Sweet & Maxwell, 1977. 2v. (1952p.). £144 for 2v. & 1985 supplement. Supplement only, £23. ISBN: 0421230908, the set; 0421293705, supplement only.

First published 1959.

Substantial definitions and explanations of English legal terms, A-K, L-Z, plus references to the relevant statutes,

....(contd.)

cases and standard text books. Many cross-references. 'Witness': 2 columns. Some biographies are included, with emphasis on legal careers or writings (*e.g.* Bracton). Bibliography (A-Z, authors), p.1923-35. 'It is thoroughly recommended to law librarians and to professional and business offices throughout the common law world ...' (*British book news*, June 1977, p.452).
Class No: 340(420)(031)

Handbooks & Manuals

[2777]

PRITCHARD, J. **The New Penguin guide to the law:** your rights and the law explained. 3rd ed. London, Viking, 1992. 960p. £20. ISBN: 0670845906.
First published 1981.
Reflects changes in English law that have occurred over the past decade. *Class No:* 340(420)(035)

Dictionaries

[2778]

McFARLANE, G. **The Layman's dictionary of English law.** London, Waterlow Publishers Ltd., 1984. vi,[2],319p. £12.95. ISBN: 0080391613.
Designed to give speedy explanations of legal words and phrases used in newspapers and broadcasting, etc., and in legal offices and documents. Very brief definitions. Includes Latin and French terms. *Class No:* 340(420)(038)

Quotations

[2779]

NORTON-KYSHE, J.W. **The Dictionary of legal quotations:** or, Selected dicta of English Chancellors and judges, from the earliest periods to the present time. With explanatory notes and references. Reprint of 1904 edition published by W.S. Hein, Buffalo, N.Y., 1984. xxi,344p. $40. ISBN: 0899413757. *Class No:* 340(420)(082.2)

Histories

[2780]

HOLDSWORTH, W.S. **A History of English law.** Rev. ed. London, Methuen; etc., 1956-72. 17v. £39. each vol. ISBN: 0421051604, v.1; 0421050209, v.2; 0421050306, v.3; 0421050403, v.4; 0421050500, v.5; 0421050608, v.6; 0421050705, v.7; 0421050802, v.8; 042105090x, v.9; 0421051000, v.10; 0421051108, v.11; 0421051205, v.12; 0421041900, v.14; 0421042001, v.15; 042105140x, v.16; 0421175605, v.17.
V.1: *The judicial system.* 7th ed.; revised by S.B. Chrimes and others. 1956. Index to v.1-9, by E. Potten; v.13 was published posthumously in 1953; v.16 (1966) is the final volume. V.17: *General index* (Sweet & Maxwell, 1972. 551p.). The great history of English law; indispensable for detailed information. *Class No:* 340(420)(091)

[2781]

MANCHESTER, A.H. **Sources of English legal history:** law, history and society in England and Wales, 1750-1950. New ed. London, Butterworths, 1984. xiv,443p. tables. £36. ISBN: 0406516596.
First published in 1980 as *A modern legal history of England and Wales, 1750-1950.*
Systematically covers the sources of the law, the legal profession, courts, criminal law, civil liability, the law of property and family law. The 15 chapters are preceded by a table of Statutes and list of cases. Each chapter commences with references to Statutes, cases, etc. Analytical index, p.435-443. *Class No:* 340(420)(091)

[2782]

SAINTY, J., *comp.* **A List of English law officers, King's Counsel and holders of patents of procedure.** London, Seldon Society, 1987. xviii,330p. £32. (*Seldon Society supplementary series, v.7.*)
Compiled for the Seldon Society.
'Lists are arranged in chronological order of appointment: Lists of holders of the offices of King's Serjeants at law (1278-1866); King's Prime or Ancient Serjeant (1623-1866); Attorney General (1315-1984); Solicitor General (1461-1984); Advocate General (1604-1872); King's Counsel (1604-1984); and holders of patents of precedence (1687-1897). Includes a few samples of letters patent, and a full list of names from each section. Each list preceded by a brief introduction giving details of the method of appointment, tenure and renumeration, and including reference to sources where history of each office can be found' (*The Law Librarian*, v.19(3), December 1988, p.114).
Class No: 340(420)(091)

Official Records

[2783]

WINFIELD, P.H. **The Chief sources of English legal history.** Cambridge, Mass., Harvard University Press, 1925 (Reprinted in 1972 by B. Franklin and in 1983 by W.S. Hein). xviii, 374p. $40. (*Historical reprints in jurisprudence and legal literature series.*) ISBN: 0899412556.
Based on a course of lectures delivered in the Harvard Law School in 1923, this essential guide discusses problems involved in the study of English legal history and the equipment needed to face them; to each chapter is appended a critical list of printed sources and secondary works. Subjects: Existing bibliographical guides, Anglo-Saxon law, influence of Roman law on English law, statutes, public records, case law, abridgements, textbooks and books of practice. *Class No:* 340(420)(093.2)

[2784]

—COWLEY, J.D. A Bibliography of abridgements, digests, dictionaries and indexes of English law to the year 1800. London, Quarich, 1932 (now available from the Seldon Society). xcv,[1],196p. illus. £22. ISBN: 0854231080.
Class No: 340(420)(093.2)

[2785]

—LOGAN, R.G. 'Bibliographical guide to early British law books'. In *Law librarian*, v.4(1), April/July 1973, p.9-12.
Class No: 340(420)(093.2)

Laws

[2786]
GREAT BRITAIN. **Index to local and personal Acts;**
consisting of classified lists of the local and personal and
private Acts and special Orders and special procedure
Orders 1801-1947. London, HMSO, 1949. viii,1140p.

Repeals and amendments are shown, but the information
about repeals, etc. prior to 1901 is not complete. An earlier
ed., covering 1801-1890, contains Irish entries omitted from
the 1801-1947 ed. The local and personal Acts themselves
are published individually, with annual tables and index.
*Supplementary index to the local and personal Acts, 1948-
1966: classified list of the local and personal Acts (together
with alphabetical and chronological lists) for the years 1948-
1966 inclusive* (Prepared in the Statutory Publications Office
under the authority of the Statutory Law Committee.
London, HMSO, 1967.228p.). The Statutory Publications
Office's *Chronological list of the local and personal Acts,
1887-1947* also appeared in 1967 (200p.). According to J.L.
Hobbs (*Local history and the library* (1962), p.39), the best
guides to earlier private Acts are Vardon's *Index to local
and personal and private Acts (1798-1840)* and Bramwell's
Analytical table of private Statutes (1813. 2v.).
Class No: 340(420)(094.1)

Germany

Bibliographies

[2787]
KEARLEY, T. *and* FISCHER, W. **Charles Szladits' guide**
to foreign legal materials: German. 2nd rev. ed. Dobb's
Ferry, NY, Oceana Publications Inc., 1990. xxiii,318p. $75.

Follows the format of the original (see 340(400)(01)) but
also adds a description of legal education and the legal
profession in West Germany, covering private and
commercial law, procedural and penal law, public and
administrative law, legal history, legal philosophy, statutes,
customary law, judicial decisions, legal writings, and general
principles of law in 12 chapters. List of abbreviations. List
of English-language titles cited. Author-title and subject
indexes. *Class No:* 340(430)(01)

Handbooks & Manuals

[2788]
COHN, E.J., *and others*. **Manual of German law.** Rev. ed.
Dobbs Ferry, N.Y., Oceana, 1968-71. 2v. (350p.;311p.).
V.1: $34; v.2: $23; set: $58. ISBN: 0379002965, v.1;
0379002973, v.2; 0686968204, set.

V.1 describes the structure and history of the German
legal system and deals with civil law. V.2 covers commercial
law, conflicts, civil procedure, bankruptcy, German law of
nationality and East German law, plus indexes, glossary of
German terms, and table of cases. *Class No:* 340(430)(035)

[2789]
—The German civil code, as amended to January 1, 1975.
Amsterdam, North-Holland Publishing Co., 1975.
xxxvii,434p.

Translated from the German. *Class No:* 340(430)(035)

Austria

Bibliographies

[2790]
FOX, J.R. **'A Guide to Austrian legal research'.** In *Law
library journal,* v.80(1), Winter 1988, p.99-113.

An overview of the Austrian legal system, including a
bibliography of primary and secondary source materials in
Austrian law (constitutional law, federal and provincial
statutes and administrative law, courts and procedure, the
civil code, health and safety law, business and tax law, and
criminal law). Also lists Austrian law reviews and
publishers. *Class No:* 340(436)(01)

Hungary

[2791]
Bibliography of Hungarian legal literature, 1945-1980.
Nagy, L., *ed.* Budapest, Akadémiai Kiadó, under the
auspices of the International Association of Legal Science
and the International Committee for Social Science
Information and Documentation, for the Institute for Legal
and Administrative Sciences of the Hungarian Academy of
Sciencess, 1988. 429p.

Previous edition, covering 1945-65, was issued in 1966.

A learned and informative introduction precedes 19
subject chapters with a wide selection of books, articles and
papers in Hungarian and other languages on the various
fields of law. Each subject chapter has a concise introduction
written by a well-known Hungarian specialist. 3316 entries
have full bibliographical information and English translations
of titles. List of abbreviations. Author index and broad
subject index according to the language of the works listed.
'... this very impressive bibliography ...'(*International
journal of legal information,* v.17(2), Summer 1989, p.164-
5). *Class No:* 340(439)

France

Bibliographies

[2792]
DUNES, A. **Documentation juridique.** Paris, Dalloz, 1977.
viii,158p. (*Méthodes du droit.*)

Part 1 considers the functions of documentation, with
particular reference to law. Part 2 deals with types of
material (compendia; codes; reviews; monographs).
Appended contents list and subject index. Recommended as
a 'refresher' for French law-librarians and documentalists
(*Bulletin des bibliothèques de France,* v.23(8), August 1978,
item 1657). *Class No:* 340(44)(01)

[2793]
—COMBE, D.A. 'French legal bibliographies'. In
International journal of law libraries, v6(2), July 1978,
p.183-204. *Class No:* 340(44)(01)

[2794]
SZLADITS, C. *and* GERMAIN, C.M. **Guide to foreign
legal materials: French.** 2nd rev. ed. Dobbs Ferry, N.Y.,
Oceana, 1985. xi, 205p. $35. ISBN: 0379117541.

First published 1959.

A guide for common law lawyers to the use of French
legal materials. 10 chapters in 2 parts. Part 1 describes
sources, their character and position in the French legal
system (I. Legislation - II. Custom - III. Case law - IV.

....(contd.)

Legal science - V. General principles and equity). Part 2. (2/3rds of the work) is bibliographical (VI. Bibliographies (current bibliographies, retrospective bibliographies, guides to legal research, guides to libraries) - VII. Legislative materials - VIII. Case law (jurisprudence) - IX. Encyclopedias and legal dictionaries - X. Doctrinal writings). All chapters are subdivided. Conclusions, are followed by a list of legal abbreviations (p.171-182), a subject index (p.183-191), and an author/title index (p.193-205). *Class No:* 340(44)(01)

Handbooks & Manuals

[2795]

KAHN-FREUND, O., *and others.* **A Source-book on French law:** system, methods, outlines of contract. 2nd ed. Oxford, Clarendon Press, 1979. xxviii,550p. £18.95. ISBN: 0198760884.

First published 1973.

Part 1: Sources and methods, includes chapters on major sources of law, categories of law, the courts and the legal profession. Part 2: Contract, has chapters on essentials, methods, and breach. Bibliography, p.583-546. Index, p.547-550.

A 3rd ed. by B. Rudden was issued in 1991 (xxix,523p. £40. ISBN 0198762488). *Class No:* 340(44)(035)

Italy

[2796]

CERTOMA, G.L. The Italian legal system. London, Butterworth, 1985. xxiii,520p. £29.50. (*Butterworth's legal systems of the world.*) ISBN: 040639993x.

Aims 'to present the first comprehensive study of the Italian legal system. A table of the principal legislation Acts is followed by 12 chapters in 5 parts: 1. The historical development of the ... system - 2. Public law - 3. Private law - 4. Hybrid categories of law - 5. The research of Italian law. Legal research and bibliographical notes, p.491-500. Analytical index, p.501-520. *Class No:* 340(450)

Bibliographies

[2797]

GRISOLI, A. Guide to foreign legal materials: Italian. Dobbs Ferry, N.Y., Oceana, 1965, for the Parker School of Foreign and Comparative Law, Columbia University. xv,272p. $17.50. (*Parker School studies in foreign and comparative law, v.2.*) ISBN: 0379117525.

Primarily for the common-law lawyer. Part 1, Sources of Italian law (chapters 1-6); part 2, Repositories of the law (1. Bibliographies - 2. Legislative materials - 3. Case law - 4. Encyclopedias, form books and legal dictionaries - 5. Doctrinal). Appendices: Current legal abbreviations, abbreviations of periodicals. Index to subjects. Index to authors and titles. *Class No:* 340(450)(01)

Handbooks & Manuals

[2798]

GIANNANTONIO, E. Italian legal information network: a handbook ... Milano, Dott. A. Giuffrè Editore, 1984. xii,181p. ISBN: 881400143x.

A handbook on how to use databases in the system. In 4

....(contd.)

parts: 1. Introduction to Italian law - 2. The information retrieval system - 3. Databases - 4. Retrieval aids. Appendix: Terminals connected via Euronet or via the public telephone network: initial procedure. Index, p.179-181.

Class No: 340(450)(035)

USSR

[2799]

BUTLER, W.E. Soviet law. 2nd rev. ed. Butterworth, 1988. 432p. £27.95. (*Butterworth's legal systems of the world.*) ISBN: 0406562601.

First published 1953.

20 chapters: 1. Soviet law in comparative legal studies - 2. The pre-revolutionary heritage - 3. The ideological foundations of Soviet law - 4. Sources of Soviet law (p.39-60) - 5. Soviet legal education - 6. Soviet legal profession ... 19. Foreign relations law - 20. Notes on additional reading (p.350-360). Footnotes. Analytical index, p.361-374.

Class No: 340(47)

Bibliographies

[2800]

KAVASS, I.I. Soviet law in English: research guide and bibliography, 1970-1987. Buffalo, N.Y., W. Hein, 1988. vii,653p. $48.50. ISBN: 0899416314.

Aims to provide a guide to research on Soviet law and a bibliography on English-language publications. In 3 sections: an introductory essay, 'Researching Soviet law'; a subject bibliography of publications; and an annotated bibliography by author. The subject bibliography is arranged under about 80 headings, each subdivided, but there is no subject index. The author bibliography includes books, journal articles, essays from collections, translations of laws, foreign legal and non-legal journals which include articles in English, journals of translations, and multivolume compendia. Full bibliographical data are given and the annotations are reasonably detailed. '... at treasure trove of primary source materials ... Kavass has promised to supplement his contribution 'on a periodic basis to include more current literature'. (*International journal of legal information,* v.16(1), p.72). *Class No:* 340(47)(01)

Encyclopaedias & Dictionaries

[2801]

Encyclopaedia of Soviet law. Feldbrugge, F.J.M., *ed.* 2nd ed. Leiden, Nijhoff, 1985. 964p. £124.75.

First published 1973.

Entries arranged A-Z by subject heading, most have subdivisions, all are signed, and end with 'see also' references to other headings. A select list of statutory materials is also included. *Class No:* 340(47)(03)

Greece

Bibliographies

[2802]

SPIROU, C.D.C. English, French, German, and Italian language materials relating to Greek law: a selected annotated bibliography. In *International journal of legal information,* v.17(1), Spring, 1989, p.10-31.

....(contd.)

305 entries relating to books and articles, most material dating from 1980. Arranged A-Z by main entry. Subject-keyword index to numbered entries. *Class No:* 340(495)(01)

China

Bibliographies

[2803]

LANGEVOORT, J.J. **Chinese law in English:** a selected bibliography. In *International journal of legal information,* v.14(3-4), June-August 1986, p.111-154.

An unannotated list of 498 citations, arranged A-Z in each section, of books and articles on the law of Mainland china published in English from 1980. Part I. Primary source material; II. Other books and articles. Subject and keyword index, p.150-154. *Class No:* 340(510)(01)

Chinese

[2804]

BILANCIA, P.R. **Dictionary of Chinese law and government: Chinese-English.** Stanford, CA., Stanford University Press, 1981. xv,822p. $75. ISBN: 0804708649.

Claims to have entries for 25,000 terms, with 15,000 examples of usage and 30,000 cross-references (*The Bookseller,* 8 August 1981. p.648).

Class No: 340(510)=951

India

Bibliographies

[2805]

JAIN, H.C. **Indian legal materials:** a bibliographical guide. Bombay, N.M. Tripathe; Dobbs Ferry, N.Y., Oceana, 1970. xxiii,123p. $8.50. ISBN: 0379004666.

Class No: 340(540)(01)

Israel

[2806]

SNYDER, E. M. 'Guide to Israel legal bibliography: primary sources' In *Law library journal* v.70(1), February 1977, p.14-29.

Covers statutes, regulations and decisions published officially and by private publishers - 'pre-State materials since 1917, and publications after the establishment of the State in 1948, including brief discussions of the Knesset, the national legislature and the court structure. A separate section briefly touches upon Jewish law' (*Abstract*) Index.

Class No: 340(569.4)

Islamic World

Bibliographies

[2807]

MAKDISI, J. 'Islamic law bibliography'. In *Law library journal,* v.78(1), Winter 1986, p.103-189.

A survey of the publications of primary sources of islamic law (in Arabic) and secondary sources (in English and French). Introduction discusses the basic sources of the law

....(contd.)

and schools of legal doctrine, and provides a brief treatment of the development of Islamic law. 865 references. Author index. *Class No:* 340(5.297)(01)

Handbooks & Manuals

[2808]

FYZEE, A.A.A. **Outlines of Muhammadan law.** 4th ed. New Delhi, Oxford University Press, 1974. xix,520p. diagrs., table.

Previous ed. published 1964.

Includes a bibliography, p.487-493, and index.

Class No: 340(5.297)(035)

Africa

Bibliographies

[2809]

MWALIMU, C. 'A Bibliographic essay of selected secondary sources on the common law and customary law of English speaking Sub-Saharan Africa'. In *Law library journal,* v.80(2), Spring 1988, p.241-289.

In 5 parts: I. Introduction - II. The reception, influence, and impact of common law on African traditional legal systems, 1954-85 - III. African customary law in its interaction with common law, the results of interaction, and judicial approaches to the resolution of conflicts, 1954-85 - IV. Integration, unification, harmonization, and codification of laws of English-speaking Sub-Saharan Africa, 1897-1972 - V. Key provisions of legislation on the application of common law and customary law in English-speaking Sub-Saharan Africa (subdivided by country). 189 footnotes, many indicating sources. 2 appendices of sources (A. The legal profession and legal education in English-speaking Sub-Saharan Africa, 1967-81; B. General African law materials relevant to common law and customary law in the legal systems of English-speaking Sub-Saharan Africa, 1962-85.

Class No: 340(6)(01)

Canada

Bibliographies

[2810]

MacELLVEN, D.T. **Legal research handbook.** 2nd ed. Toronto, Butterworths, 1986. xxiv,411p. Can$49.95. ISBN: 0409847798.

19 chapters, all subdivided: 1. Legal research concepts - 2. Law reports - 3. Digests and indexes for law reports - 4. Statutes - 5. Subordinate legislation - 6. Statutes and case citations - 7. Legal encyclopedias - 8. Legal periodicals and legal periodical indexes - 9. Other secondary literature research sources - 10. Computerized legal research ... 18. Social science and government publications research - 19. Improving legal writing. 3 appendices (B. Selected sources for further study; C. Glossary of legal research terms and concepts). Index. *Class No:* 340(71)(01)

[2811]
Canadian legal directory, 1987. Hintauer, S., *ed.* 77th ed. Richard de Boo Publishers (distributed in US by Gale Research Co.), 1987. xii,1138p. $70. ISBN: 0888202407.
First published 1911. Annual.
The standard reference book for information about Canada's attorneys and law firms, relevant government offices, departments and judicial systems. Also includes details of law firms based outside Canada that are licenced to practice law in Canada. *Class No:* 340(71)(058)

Latin America

Laws

Bibliographies

[2812]
UNITED STATES. Library of Congress. Law Library. **Index to Latin American legislation,** 1950 through to 1960. Boston, Mass., G.K. Hall, 1961. 2v. Supplements 1-3 (1970-78). $195.00; $120 each supplement. ISBN: 0816105944.
30,900 catalogue cards photolithographically reproduced. Covers the principal laws, decrees, regulations and administrative rulings of twenty Latin American republics. Arranged by country, then by subject and chronologically thereafter. The 3 supplements add *c.*70,000 cards.
Earlier material is covered by *Bibliografia juridica de América latina (1810-1965);* compiled by Alberto Villalón (Santiago, Editorial Juridica de Chile, [1970]. 5v.).
Class No: 340(729.99)(094.1)(01)

USA

Bibliographies

[2813]
Encyclopedia of legal information sources. Baker, B.L. *and* Petit, P.J., *eds.* 2nd ed. Detroit, Mich., Gale Research Co., 1993. xxv,1083p. $165. ISBN: 0810374390.
First published 1988.
*c.*29,000 citations on 480 law-related subjects, arranged A-Z by subject (Actions and defenses ... Zoning and planning). Intended to meet the needs of both professionals and laypersons. Includes laws, loose-leaf services, reference works, indexes, newsletters, statistics and audiovisual material, mainly published since 1980. Emphasis is on federal law and national organizations, but sections listing sources for each State are included. Detailed outline of contents, but no title or organization indexes. Cross-references. Supplements are planned to update the work.
Class No: 340(73)(01)

[2814]
KARP, R.S. Law books for lazy people. In *Booklist,* September 15, 1991, p.185-189.
44 cited sources, all US, in 9 sections (Guides to the field - Legal research - Encyclopedias and dictionaries - Handbooks - Writing aids - Directories - Legal summaries - General resources - Do-it-yourself resources). *Class No:* 340(73)(01)

[2815]
NIXON, J.M. 'Legal reference service in the public library': a guide to primary-source legal material. In *RQ,* v.24(2), Winter 1984, p.195-203.
Discusses the material (laws, regulations, and court decisions) useful for public libraries. Outlines the structure of legal literature, identifies the most important tools needed for legal research, and show how they relate to one another. *Class No:* 340(73)(01)

[2816]
REAMS, B.D., *and others.* **American legal literature:** a guide to selected legal resources. Littleton, Col., Libraries Unlimited, 1985. 239p. $27.50. ISBN: 0872875148.
Intended for the layman. 3 sections (List of primary materials such as statutes, case reports and finding aids useful for finding such - List of legal reference materials such as law dictionaries, directories of lawyers, bibliographies, and research guides - List of monographs on the law accessible to a reader with no legal training). Short appendices include one on major American law book publishers. Unannotated. *Class No:* 340(73)(01)

Encyclopaedias

[2817]
The Guide to American law: everyone's legal encyclopedia. St. Paul, MN., West Publishing Co., 1983-85. 12v. (6446p.). illus. $660 the set. ISBN: 0314732241.
Intended for students and the general reader rather than the professional. Articles range in length from long signed essays to short unsigned contributions. Definitions are in small open boxes. Includes historical and biographical entries and famous trials. Numerous case citations. Each volume has an index and a cumulated index is included in V.12. V.11 relates to classical legal documents.
Class No: 340(73)(031)

[2818]
—The Guide to American law yearbook, 1987: everyone's legal encyclopedia. St. Paul, MN, West Publishing Co., 1987. xvi, 580p. illus. $95. ISSN: 08950989.
Supplements the above by both updating some entries and adding new ones, its aim being 'to examine the major legal documents of recent years'. Mainly covers 1984 to early 1987. *Class No:* 340(73)(031)

Handbooks & Manuals

[2819]
Encyclopedia of the American judicial system: studies of the principal institutions and processes of law. Janosik, R.J., *ed.* New York, Charles Scribner and Sons, 1987. 3v. (1420p.). $225. (*American civilization.*) ISBN: 0684178079.
Intended to meet the need for easier access to the subject matter of the American legal system. 88 lengthy essays analysing a wide array of aspects of American law are arranged in 6 subject sections (legal history - substantive law - institutions and personnel - process and behaviour - constitutional law and issues - methodology). Each article lists relevant court cases, a select bibliography, and cross-references to related articles, and averages 15 pages in length. Index at end of 3rd vol. *Class No:* 340(73)(035)

Yearbooks & Directories

[2820]
National directory of legal services. Davidson, R.L., *ed.*
Englewood Cliffs, N.J., Prentice Hall Press, 1989. 589p.
$79.95. ISBN: 0136093973.

Lists over 700 businesses serving the legal profession,
providing attorneys and law officers with listings of
individuals and organizations that can serve important needs
of a law practice (*e.g.* expert witnesses; investigators;
detectives; model makers; photographers), In 4 sections:
Glossary of abbreviations and acronyms used - 'Discovery
key indexing' (641 subject headings, each divided into
general services and computer services) - General services
listing - Computer services listing. Under the last 2 sections,
organizations are arranged A-Z by name.
Class No: 340(73)(058)

[2821]
WASSERMAN, S. *and* **O'BRIEN, J.W.,** *eds.* **Law and legal
information directory.** 5th ed. Detroit, Mich., Gale
Research Co., 1988. 1120p. $280. ISBN: 0810326477.
ISSN: 0740090x.

First published 1981.

13,500 entries grouped in 21 chapters (9 of the 21 consist
mainly of entries from other Gale publications): National and
international organizations - Bar associations ... Federal
Court system ... Law schools ... Special libraries -
Information systems and services - Research centers - Legal
periodicals - Book and media publishers ... Small Claims
Court - Corporation departments of State. Chapters
individually indexed.

A 7th ed. was published in 1992 in 2v.
Class No: 340(73)(058)

Laws

Bibliographies

[2822]
LONDON UNIVERSITY. Institute of Advanced Legal
Studies. **Union list of United States legal literature:**
holdings of legislation, law reports and digests in libraries in
Oxford, Cambridge and London. 2nd ed. London, the
Institute, 1967. xii,82p.

Covers federal and state Statutes, the code of federal
regulations, law reports and digests of cases. Treatises and
periodicals are excluded, but reports of decisions of
administrative tribunals and agencies are shown. Details of
the years held are given. *Class No:* 340(73)(094.1)(01)

New Zealand

Bibliographies

[2823]
PALMER, K.A., *ed.* **Index to New Zealand legal writing
and cases.** 2nd ed. Auckland, N.Z. Legal Research
Foundation Inc., 1982-87. 2v. V.1. NZ$24.20; v.2. NZ$66.
First published 1977.

V.1: 1954-1981; V.2. 1982-1985. Detailed coverage of
writings on New Zealand law, including material published
outside New Zealand. Entries arranged by subject, mostly
subdivided. Cross-references. Each volume is in 2 parts; the
first part indexes books, theses, dissertations, journal

....(contd.)
articles, law reform publications, and selected government
publications; the second part indexes case notes, with
reference to published reports, etc. *Class No:* 340(931)(01)

18th Century

Bibliographies

[2824]
ADAMS, J. *and* **AVERLEY, G.** **A Bibliography of
eighteenth century legal literature:** a subject and author
catalogue of law treatises and all law related literature held
in the main legal collections in England. Newcastle-upon-
Tyne, Avero Publications Ltd., 1982. 924p. with six
microfiche. £220. ISBN: 0907977014.

Arranged by a special detailed classification scheme
created for the work. 14 libraries were searched (locations
given) as well as publishers' catalogues, etc. Entries are in 3
parts: Authors name - title, class no. - imprint information
for every edition held in the source libraries (in
chronological order). Separate author catalogue in fiche form
in pocket. Somewhat difficult to use. *Class No:* 340"17"(01)

Research Methods

[2825]
JACOBSTEIN, J.M. *and* **MERSKY, R.M.** **Fundamentals of
legal research.** 3rd ed. New York, Foundation Press, 1985.
705p. $22.95. (*University textbook series.*) ISBN:
0882772457.

First published 1977 as a successor to E.H. Pollack's
Fundamentals of legal research (4th ed. 1973).

Designed as an aid to students learning to do legal
research, especially in Anglo-American law. Includes
information on computers and microforms, etc. Also helpful
for research work. *Class No:* 340:001.891

Information Services

[2826]
MISKIN, C. **Library and information services for the legal
profession.** London, British Library Research and
Development Department, 1981. iv,68p. £8. (*B.L.R & D
Report, no.5633.*) ISBN: 0905984730.

In 9 sections: Introduction and methodology - The legal
database - Law publishers - The legal profession - Library
services and information units - Law librarians - Online
systems (subdivided by country) - User studies - Conclusions
and recommendations - References, p.52-55 (79 items).
Class No: 340:061:025.5

[2827]
—**LOGAN, R.G.** 'Law libraries in Oxford'. In *The Law
librarian,* v.20(2), August 1989, p.49-54.
Class No: 340:061:025.5

Libraries

[2828]
MISKIN, C., *ed.* **Directory of law libraries in the British
Isles.** 3rd ed. Hebden Bridge, West Yorks, Legal
Information Resources Ltd., 1988, for the British and Irish
Association of Law Libraries. ix,120p. £15. ISBN:
1870369025.

....(contd.)

First published 1976 by the Association and edited by B. Mangles.

Entries for 317 libraries, based on replies to a postal questionnaire, with supplementary information. Arranged by place (England; Ireland; Scotland; Wales; Channel Islands and other islands). Data: name and address; telephone-telex-fax numbers; opening hours; terms of admission; loans; facilities and services; stock; subject coverage; affiliation, etc. 4 indexes - by name of organization, type of organization, contact name, special collection name. 'Presentation and layout is excellent; (*The Law librarian,* v.20(2), May 1989, p.71). *Class No:* 340:061:026/027

Research Projects

[2829]

Legal research in the United Kingdom, 1905-1984: classified list of legal theses and dissertations successfully completed for postgraduate degrees awarded by universities and polytechnics in the United Kingdom from 1905 to 1984. University of London. Institute of Advanced Legal Studies. London, the Institute, 1986. various pagings. £12.50. ISBN: 0901190292.

Supersedes all earlier eds.

Nearly 2700 numbered entries listed in A-Z order of subject, subdivided chronologically. Each entry includes name of scholar, degree granting institution, degree, year awarded, and full title of thesis. Includes both an A-Z and a classified list of subject headings. Author and geographical indexes. *Class No:* 340:061:061.62.005

Bibliographies

[2830]

CORBIN, J. Find the law in the library: a guide to legal research. Chicago, Ill., American Library Association, 1989. 327p. $58. ISBN: 0838905021.

'... responds to students' needs to locate primary legal sources (*e.g.* statutes and court decisions) and to use secondary legal sources (*e.g.* encyclopedias and treatises) in dealing with legal research problems and writing library research reports ... excellent guide ...' (*Choice,* v.27(5), January 1990, p.766). *Class No:* 340:061:061.62.005(01)

Law Schools

[2831]

TSENG, H.P. The Law schools of the world. Buffalo,N.Y., W.S. Hein, 1977. ix, 419p. $47.50. ISBN: 0930342097.

'A current and fairly accurate international directory of law schools' (*International journal of law libraries,* v.6(3), November 1978, p.329). *Class No:* 340:061:378.4

Legal Aid

[2832]

Legal aid handbook. Legal Aid Board. 1993 ed. London, Sweet & Maxwell, 1993. 504p. £11.50. ISBN: 0421497602.

First published 1950 by HMSO. From 1990 ed. by Sweet & Maxwell.

Sets out the 1988 Legal Aid Act and the references, together with eligibility tables, list of legal aid forms, and an updated version of the Law Society's *Notes for guidance.* Index. *Class No:* 340.028

Jurisprudence

[2833]

DIAS, R.W.M. A Bibliography of jurisprudence. 3rd ed. London, Butterworth, 1979. ix,453p. £22.95. ISBN: 0406574286.

A companion to his *Jurisprudence* (4th ed. 1976).

About 3500 briefly annotated entries in 22 sections: 1. General - 2. Advantages and disadvantages - 3. Justice perspectives of power and liberty ... 6. Precedent - 7. Statutory interpretation - 8. Custom - 9. Values - 10. Duty - 11. Conduct - 12. Persons - 13. Possessions - 14. Ownership - 15. Legal change - 16. Positivism. British theories - 17. The pure theory - 18. Historical and anthropological approaches - 19. Economic approach - 20. Sociological approaches - 21. Modern realism - 22. National law. Bibliographical index (authors, A-Z); case index; general index. *Class No:* 340.143

Bibliographies

[2834]

DREWRY, G. 'Judiciary and government'. In Englefield, D and Drewry, G's *Information sources in politics and political science: a survey worldwide* (Butterworth, 1986, p.209-225).

In 6 parts: Partial revival of a lost tradition? - The judicial process - Judicial institutions and the machinery of justice - Administrative law - Present trends in law and politics - Law reports and lawyers' journals. *Class No:* 340.143(01)

Scotland

Biographies

[2835]

WALKER, D.M. The Scottish jurists. Edinburgh, W. Green & Sons Ltd., 1985. xv,492p. illus. £39. ISBN: 0414007573.

29 chapters on the major jurists of the 15th to 20th centuries, arranged chronologically (1. The concept of a Scottish jurist - 2. The early jurists - 3-27. on individual jurists, one per chapter - 28. The minor jurists of the 20th century - 29. The contribution of the Scottish jurists to the science of law in Scotland. Textual and bibliographical footnotes. An appendix reports on decisions of the Court of Session, etc. A bibliography (p.451-466) is extensive and includes works of reference, historical papers, Parliamentary papers, and writings of Scottish jurists. Excellent index (p.467-492). No bibliography of the works of the jurists but these are accessible through the index. '... a welcome addition to the literature of Scottish legal history ...' (*International journal of legal information,* v.15(1-2), February-March, 1987, p.72-3).
Class No: 340.143(411)(092)

Comparative Law

Encyclopaedias

[2836]

INTERNATIONAL ASSOCIATION OF LEGAL SCIENCE. International encyclopedia of comparative law. New York, Kluwer Academic (early issues by Sijthoff & Noordhoff); Tübingen, J.C.B. Mohr; The Hague, Martinus Nijhoff Publishers, 1972-1989. 17v. $100-$138.50 each vol.

Contents: 1. National reports on the legal system of the

....(contd.)

world's states - 2. The legal systems of the world/their comparison and unification - 3. Private international law - 4. Persons and family - 5. Succession ... 11. Torts ... 13. Business and private organizations ... 15. Labour law - 16. Civil procedure - 17. State and economy. Heavily footnoted; bibliographies. *Class No:* 340.5(031)

Handbooks & Manuals

[2837]
DAVID, R. *and* **BRIERLEY, J.E.C. Major legal systems of the world today:** an introduction to the comparative study of law. 3rd ed. London, Stevens & Sons, 1985. xvi,624p. £28. ISBN: 0420473408.

First published 1978. Translation of *Les Grands systèmes de droit contemporains.*

4 parts: 1. The Romano-Germanic family - 2. Socialist laws - 3. The common law (English law; law of the US) - 4. Other conceptions of law and the social order (Muslim law; Law of India; Laws of the Far East; Laws of Africa and Malagasy). Appendix 1: 'Bibliographical information' (brief notes; 9 sections: Bibliographical tools ... Unification and harmonisation of law), p.577-609. Appendix 2: 'Useful information and references' (Centres of comparative law; Comparative law studies; Comparative law libraries). Bibliography, p.577-613. Index, p.615-624.
Class No: 340.5(035)

Medical Jurisprudence

[2838]
WILSON, C. Written in blood: a history of forensic medicine. London, Grafton Books, 1991. 533p. 16 illus. £14.95. ISBN: 1853360554.

Analytical table of contents, followed by 10 chapters: 1. The science of detection; 2. The power of poison; 3. The discovery of fingerprints; 4. Whose body? 5. If blood could speak; 6. Every bullet has a fingerprint; 7. The microscope as detective; 8. The sexual criminal; 9. The craft of the manhunter; 10. The soul of the criminal. Select bibliography, p.505-10. Index, p.511-23. *Class No:* 340.6

Bibliographies

[2839]
MERSKY, R.M., *and others, comp. & ed*. **A Manual on medical literature for law librarians.** Dobbs Ferry, N.Y., Oceana, 1973. 180p. $35. ISBN: 0878101902.

A handbook and bibliography in 7 sections: Medical bibliography - Terminology - Suggested citation style - Cataloguing and indexing tools - Selected and current literature on medicine and the law - Regional medical library network - Directory of related health science libraries. US slanted. *Class No:* 340.6(01)

[2840]
—SYNDER, L. Homicide investigation: practical information for coroners, police officers, and other investigators. 3rd ed. Springfield, Ill., C.C. Thomas, 1977. 397p. $54. ISBN: 0398036322.

Mentioned as 'a true classic in forensic pathology' by R.Q. Kelly in his article *A basic guide to medicolegal reference sources,* published in *RSR,* v.7(3), July/September 1979, p.61-66. *Class No:* 340.6(01)

Encyclopaedias

[2841]
LANE, E. The Encyclopedia of forensic science. London, Headline Book Publishing, 1992. [9],415p. illus. £17.99. ISBN: 0747205892.

123 entries A-Z (Acid ... Voiceprints), each subdivided and many including case studies. Introduction includes a chronology to 'some of the landmarks in the history of forensic science' (p.9). Index, p.407-15.
Class No: 340.6(031)

Dictionaries

[2842]
BANDER, E.J. *and* **WALLACH, J. Medical legal dictionary.** Dobbs Ferry, N.Y., Oceana, 1970. vii,114p. $17.50. ISBN: 0379141019.

'This dictionary defines medical terms for the lawyer and legal terms for the physician. It contains many references to legal resources to enable the practitioner to obtain further information' (*Bibliography, documentation, terminology,* v.20(2), March 1970, p.83). *Class No:* 340.6(038)

International Law

Bibliographies

[2843]
BERNAL, M.-L.H. 'Reference sources in international law'
In *Law library journal.* 76(3), Summer 1983, p. 427-35.

Brief survey of the historical origin and developmennt of international law, followed by a bibliographic essay on reference tools in international law. 31 books are discussed and listed, selection limited to English-language sources.
Class No: 341(01)

[2844]
BEVERLY, E. Public international law: a guide to information sources. London, Mansell, 1991. 334p. £60; $90. ISBN: 0720120829.

Part 1: Sources of information: a documentary typology of public international law; pt.2: Sources of information & selected subject bibliography: topical approach. 'Scholarly treatment' (*Library association record,* v.91(11), November 1991, p.760). *Class No:* 341(01)

[2845]
CAMBRIDGE UNIVERSITY. Squire Law Library.
Catalogue of international law. Lekner, M.A., *comp.*
Dobbs Ferry, N.Y., Oceana, 1972. 4v. $200 the set. ISBN: 0379200309.

About 12,000 entries; v.1-2: Author catalogue; v.3-4: Subject catalogue. V.4 includes a list of periodicals, collections of legislation, law reports, treaties, UK Parliamentary papers and UN documents. Primarily late 19th-century and early 20th-century materials in the Western world, with sparing cross-references in the author catalogue, according to *Choice,* v.9(9), November 1972, p.1115-6. Type (computer print-out) could be more legible.
Class No: 341(01)

[2846]

MERRILL, J.G. **A Current bibliography of international law.** London, Butterworth, 1978. xx,277p. £30. ISBN: 0406623767.

Confined to English-language monographs (including translations) and especially periodical articles published since 1960, thus excluding some important foreign literature. Author index; no subject index, but a detailed list of contents. *Class No:* 341(01)

[2847]

—DELUPIS, I. Bibliography of international law. New York, Bowker, 1976. 670p.

Lists over 5000 books and periodical articles in major European languages, published 1920-1974. 14 sections, each with introduction highlighting important works, states *Library journal,* v.101(13), July 1976, p.1512). *Class No:* 341(01)

[2848]

Public international law: a current bibliography of articles. New York and Berlin., Springer-Verlag, for Max-Planck Institute for Comparative Public Law and International Law, 1975 -. 2pa. DM120. $88.50 pa. ISSN: 03407349.

Lists foreign and English books and articles on public international law. *Class No:* 341(01)

Canada

[2849]

WIKTOR, C.L. **Canadian bibliography of international law.** Toronto, University of Toronto Press, 1984. 767p. $95. ISBN: 0802056156.

A major bibliography reflecting Canada's international legal practice from its beginnings through the early 1980s. Over 9000 entries arranged under topical headings, following the outline of many international law textbooks. Many subjects reflect particular Canadian emphasis. Citations include books, articles, documents and official papers, chapters and proceedings. Includes both English- and French-language literature. No annotations. Introduction provides a statistical analysis of citations by subject and period. 'A valuable guide ...' (*Choice,* v.22(5), January 1985, p.668). *Class No:* 341(01)(71)

Encyclopaedias

[2850]

Encyclopedia of public international law. Bernhardt, R. Amsterdam, North-Holland Publishing Company, 1981-. To be in 12 instalments, and ultimately in 4v.

Published under the auspices of the Max-Planck-Institute for Comparative Public Law and International Law.

First issued in subject instalments: 1. Settlement of disputes - 2. Decisions of international courts ... - 3. & 4. Use of force ... - 5. International organizations in general ... - 6. Regional co-operation ... - 7. History of international law ... - 8. Human rights and the individual in international law. International economic relations - 9. International relations ... - 10. States. Responsibility of States ... - 11. Law of the sea - 12. Geographical issues. Instalment 8 (1985. xv,551p.) has 129 entries by 87 authors. 'Lists of articles' in each instalment is a subject list relating to the complete work. Articles are signed and include bibliographies. Cross-references. *Class No:* 341(031)

Dictionaries

Polyglot

[2851]

LINDBERG, G. **International law dictionary** English/French/German. Blackstone Press, 1992. vii,439p. £18. ISBN: 1854311190.

Gives brief translations of all the major legal terms. Includes basic legal terminology, plus the most frequently used law-related terms from banking, finance, insurance, industry, and taxation. Also includes supplements of Latin and EC abbreviations. *Class No:* 341(038)=00

[2852]

PAENSON, I. **Manual of the terminology of public international law (peace) and international organization: En/Fr/Sp/Russ.** Bruxelles, Bruylant, for Institut Universitaire de Hautes Études Internationales, Geneve; Derventer, Kluwer Academic, 1983. xlviii, 846 p. £163 $295. ISBN: 2802702831 Belgium; 9065440526 Netherlands.

Terms are listed in English-French-Spanish-Russian across the pages, and are arranged in 8 subject chapters, all subdivided. Terms are fully defined in all 4 languages. For each language there is a general index, an index of bi- or multilateral international transactions, an index of declarations and of resolutions of international organizations, an index of international conferences, and an index of cases submitted to international tribunals. Footnotes. *Class No:* 341(038)=00

English

[2853]

BLEDSOE, R. *and* BOCZEK, B.A. **The International law dictionary.** Santa Barbara, CA., ABC-Clio, 1987. 422p. $45. (*Clio dictionaries in political science series, no.11.*) ISBN: 087436406x.

368 key terms in international law, including concepts, major treaties, international conventions, and theories. Organized thematically in 12 chapters. The 2-part entries first define the term and then explain its significance and implications through historical and current examples. Most entries are brief essays. 'See also' references. Good index. 'A must for law collections ...' (*Wilson library bulletin,* November 1987, p.94). *Class No:* 341(038)=20

[2854]

PARRY, C., *and others, eds.* **Encyclopedic dictionary of international law.** Dobbs Ferry, N.Y., Oceana, 1986. xix,564p. $60. ISBN: 0379208288.

Designed for the contemporary student. Short, concise articles giving thorough information on the subjects covered. Includes not only the concepts of international law, but also important cases, treaties, and select biographies of major literary figures, but omits all topics of international law on war and the law of international organizations. Extensive cross-references. A documents section has the Charter of the United Nations and other contemporary international instruments. *Class No:* 341(038)=20

German

[2855]

GILBERTSON, G. **Harrap's German and English glossary of terms in international law.** London, George G. Harrap & Co. Ltd., 1980. xi,355p. £25. ISBN: 0245535241.

Over 9000 headwords, phrases and contextual examples used in theoretical international law and international law as codified in treaties and agreements. 3 main parts: I. German-English section - headword entries arranged in strict alphabetical order; subheadings indented; II. 21 annexes (*e.g.* a selection of extended extracts from a variety of international instruments); III. English register, referring to Part I. 12,500 precise references for all English terms in parts I & II. Cross-references. *Class No:* 341(038)=30

Yearbooks & Directories

[2856]

The British year book of international law, 1990. Brownlie, I. *and* Bowett, D.W., *eds.* 60th ed. Oxford, Clarendon Press, 1991. 672p. £85. ISBN: 0198257260.

First published 1920. Annual.

Contains articles, book reviews, summaries of decisions in English and European Courts. Analytical index. *Class No:* 341(058)

Law of International Organizations

Bibliographies

[2857]

BAER, G.W., *comp. & ed.* **International organisations, 1918-1945:** a guide to research and research materials. Wilmington, DE., Scholarly Press Inc., 1981. 261p. $30. ISBN: 0842021795.

Over 1600 entries, many with annotations. Chapter 1 commences with an overview, followed by a list of 117 selected works on international affairs, organizations, law, and diplomacy; ch.2 has details of the archives of international organizations; ch.3 & 4 describe archival and other related resources in the US, UK, France and other European countries, including resources of libraries and international affairs institutions. 13 other chapters deal with aspects of the League of Nations, etc., and the final chapter is on World War II conference diplomacy and the founding of the United Nations. *Class No:* 341.1/.8(01)

[2858]

HAMERTON, D.N. **'Exploiting the publications of international organisations'.** In *Use of social science literature,* edited by N. Roberts (1977) p.303-322.

A valuable concise running commentary. Contents: Introduction - International organisations - League of Nations - International Labour Organization - World Court - United Nations - International Court of Justice - Documentation - Intergovernmental regional organisations - European Community - O.E.C.D. - Council of Europe - Organization of American States - Organization of African Unity - Defence organisations - Conferences - Periodicals - Conclusions. *Class No:* 341.1/.8(01)

[2859]

International bibliography: publications of intergovernmental organizations. White Plains, N.Y., Kraus International Publications; Oxford, Marsten Book Services Ltd. 1973-. Quarterly. $100pa. ISSN: 02561042.

Until 1983 title was *International bibliogaphy, information, documentation: publications of international organizations,* published by Bowker.

'Bibliographic record': *c.*500 annotated entries in each issue under broad subject headings (Agriculture and related subjects ... Youth). 'Periodicals record': contents-listing of over 100 periodicals. Subject index. Organizations index. Title index. Indexes cumulate annually. *Class No:* 341.1/.8(01)

[2860]

World bibliography of international documentation. Dimitrov, T. D., *comp. and ed.* Pleasantville, N.Y., UNIFO, 1981. 2v (826p.). $95. ISBN: 0891110100.

V.1: *International organizations* is in 2 parts: pt.1. 'International organizations. Activities, structure, policies, document control' has 4 chapters (1. Nature, structure and activities of international governmental organizations - 2. Basic documents ... - 3. Secretaries-General - 4. Policies and research on international documentation); pt.2. 'Bibliographic control of international documents'. V.2. *Politics and world affairs* is in 3 parts: I. Multinational diplomacy and international relations - II. International periodicals - III. Annexes (1. Major intergovernmental conferences.). Author index, p.323-340. Index of organizations, p.341-348. Subject index, p.349-352. " ... a work of considerable value ... ' (*International affairs* v.58(4), Autumn 1982, p.737). *Class No:* 341.1/.8(01)

Official Records

[2861]

PEASLEE, A.J., *ed.* **International governmental organizations: constitutional documents.** Xydis, D.P., *ed.* 3rd ed. The Hague, Martinus Nijhoff, 1974-1979. 5v.

First published 1956; 2nd ed. 1961.

Contents: 1. *General and regional, political economic, social, legal defense* (1974. 2v. (xiii,xv,1479p.) - 2. *Agriculture, commodities, fisheries, food, plants* (1975. xii,633p.) - 3. *Education, culture, copyright* (1979) - 4. *Science, health* (1979) - 5. *Communications, transport, travel* (1976. xi,686p.). Texts of the basic constitutional documents of leading international organizations, plus background data and select bibliographies. 'An invaluable source' (D.N. Hamerton, in *Use of social sciences literature,* edited by N. Roberts (1977), p.304). *Class No:* 341.1/.8(093.2)

Archives

[2862]

Guide to the archives of international organizations. v.1: the United Nations system. Unesco. Paris, Unesco, 1984. 279p. £14.25 F.95. (*Documents, libraries and archives: bibliographies and reference works, 8.*) ISBN: 9231020900.

A preliminary version was published in 1979.

Data on the archives of 34 United Nations agencies and their subordinate institutions, and other bodies. Information includes address, opening hours, working languages, administrative history, structure, select bibliography, and description of the archives. *Class No:* 341.1/.8(093.20)

League of Nations

Bibliographies

[2863]
BIRCHFIELD, M.E. Consolidated catalog of League of Nations publications offered for sale. Dobbs Ferry, N.Y., Oceana, 1976. ix,477p. $55. ISBN: 0379003287.

A guide to both series and monographs, arranged by the 17 League of Nations publications categories (Assembly; Council; Library; Information and general questions; Periodicals; and subject divisions of the Secretariat). 3 indexes: official number, sales number and subject. 'A comprehensive checklist and index' (*RQ*, v.16(3), Spring 1977, p.253). *Class No:* 341.121(01)

[2864]
—GHÉBALI, V.Y. *and* GHÉBALI, C., *comps. & eds.* A Repertoire of League of Nations serial documents, 1919-1947. Dobbs Ferry, N.Y., Oceana, 1973. 2v. (773p.). $85. ISBN: 0379003716.

Complements the above. Limited to serial documents but does include publications not for sale, unnumbered series and commission, conference and Secretariat documents. *Class No:* 341.121(01)

Histories

[2865]
WALTERS, F.P. A History of the League of Nations. London, Oxford University Press, under the auspices of the Royal Institute of International Affairs, 1952 (Reprinted in one vol. in 1986 by Greenwood Press). xvi,833p. ISBN: 0313250561.

First published 1952 in 2v.

The standard work on the League of Nations. An objective account by a member of the Secretariat, 1919-40. 67 chapters, taking the narrative up to 1946. No bibliography, but a rather general appendix note on sources. Supported by a very good analytical index. *Class No:* 341.121(091)

United Nations

Handbooks & Manuals

[2866]
The Encyclopaedia of the United Nations and international agreements. Osmánczyk, E.J.   2nd ed. London & Philadelphia, Taylor & Francis, 1985. xv, 1059p. £170. $295. ISBN: 0850668336.

First published 1974 in Polish (Warsaw); 2nd ed. in Spanish, 1976.

A compendium of political, economic and social information, including data on the structure of the United Nations; its specialised agencies, and the many intergovernmental and non-governmental organizations that co-operate with the UN. Over 7000 entries, more than half of them having short explanations of words or names; other entries comprise descriptions of all the States in the world, and vary in length from a third to a full page. Sources are given for most entries. Also includes 'World population statistics, 1985-2025'; a list of acronyms and abbreviations; a selective index (p.975-1046); and an index to agreements, conventions and treaties (p.1047-1059). '...continues to be a convenient one-stop source...' (=2Booklist=*, v.87(12), 15/2/91, p.1248). *Class No:* 341.123(035)

[2867]
UNITED NATIONS. Department of Public Information. Basic facts about the United Nations. 8th ed. New York, United Nations, 1992. 291p. $5. ISBN: 9211004993.

8 chapters: 1. Origins of the United Nations; 2. Organization of the United Nations; 3. International peace and security; 4. Economic and social development; 5. Human rights and humanitarian assistance; 6. Decolonization; 7. International law; 8. Intergovernmental agencies related to the United Nations. Appendices include 'For further reading' (p.276-77). Index, p.279-291. *Class No:* 341.123(035)

Histories

[2868]
A Chronology and fact book of the United Nations, 1941-1991. Hovet, T. *and* Trover, E.L.   8th ed. by Kumiko Matsuura and others. Dobbs Ferry, N.Y.. Oceana, 1992. 598p. $75.00. (*Annual review of United Nations affairs series.*) ISBN: 0379212005.

4th ed. published 1976, covering 1941-1976.

A chronology with subject index list of members of UN organs and agencies, and texts of the Charter and of the General Assembly's rules of procedure. 'An indispensable starting point for research on UN activities and organization' (*International affairs*, April 1977, p.335, of the 4th ed). *Class No:* 341.123(091)

[2869]
Everyone's United Nations a handbook on the work of the United Nations. 10th ed. New York, United Nations Department of Public Information, 1986. [6],484p. $14.95. ISBN: 9211002737.

First published in 1948 as *Everyman's United Nations*.

Exposition of the work of the U.N. and its associated 18 intergovernmental agencies in 9 chapters: 1. The organization - 2. Peacemaking - 3. Peace-keeping - 4. Disarmament - 5. Economic and social development - 6. Human rights - 7. Decolonization - 8. International law - 9. Intergovernmental organizations. U.N. Charter p.429-50. Statutes of the International Court of Justice p.451-461. Universal Declaration of Human Rights p.462-6. Index, p.467-484. *Class No:* 341.123(091)

[2870]
LUARD, E. A History of the United Nations. London, Macmillan Press, 1982-. v.1:£35; v.2: £45. ISBN: 0333243897, v.1; 0333244249, v.2.

V.1. *The years of Western domination, 1945-1955* (1982. 416p.); v.2. *The age of decolonization, 1955-1965* (1989. 592p.). V.1 is a critical account of the planning and setting up of the UN and of its responses to the various problems with which it found itself confronted during the first 10 years. V.2 deals with the period when the UN was involved with major crises throughout the world, and includes four of its peace-keeping operations. *Class No:* 341.123(091)

Biographies

[2871]
Who's who in the United Nations and related agencies. New York, Ayer & Co. Publishers, 1975. xxxiii785p. $65. ISBN: 040506490x.

About 4500 entries. Appendices include: organizational roster; installations of the United Nations system; member

....*(contd.)*

States of the UN, 1946-1974; United Nations depository libraries; UN budget, 1944-75. Index to the biographical section, p.749-85.

A 2nd ed. by S.R. Greenfield was published in 1992 by Omnigraphics Inc. (800p. $185. ISBN 1558887628).
Class No: 341.123(092)

Official Records

Bibliographies

[2872]
UNDOC: current index. United Nations documents index. New York, and Geneva, United Nations Publications, 1979-. v.1, no.1/2-. Quarterly, with annual cumulations on microfiche. $150 for complete service. ISSN: 02505584.

Comprehensive coverage of UN documentation, including full bibliographical descriptions. Subject, author and title indexes. Also a check-list of new UN documents received at headquarters. *Class No:* 341.123(093.2)(01)

Unesco

Bibliographies

[2873]
UNESCO. Bibliography of publications issued by Unesco or under its auspices (1946-1971). Paris, Unesco, 1973. xviii,385p. F.30. ISBN: 9230010375.

Over 5000 entries for books and journals, grouped by subjects. Coverage: 1946 to the end of 1971.
Class No: 341.16(01)

[2874]
—UNESCO. Unesco publishing catalogue, 1993. Paris, Unesco, 1993. 162p. illus. *Gratis.*

Published annually.

Sections: Books - Periodicals - Electronic publishing - Publications of Unesco's regional offices. Alphabetical index and price list of titles in English, French and Spanish (p.129-143). *Class No:* 341.16(01)

[2875]
—Unesco lists of documents and publications, 1972/76-. Paris, Unesco, 1979-.

Published every three years. 1987/89 volume was published in 1993 (ISBN 9230028401).

Each is issued in 2 volumes: 1. Annotated list of documents and publications; 2. subject index; personal name index; conference index. *Class No:* 341.16(01)

European Community

[2876]
CENTRE FOR EUROPEAN POLICY STUDIES. Annual review of European Community affairs, 1992. First issued for 1990. Annual. London, Brassey's (UK) Ltd., 1992. 475p. £40. ISSN: 09623868.

Aims to provide EC specialists, students and general readers with a comprehensive and authoritative account of EC developments. *Class No:* 341.174

[2877]
The European Communities encyclopedia and directory, 1992. London, Europa, 1991. (distributed in US and Canada by Gale Research Ltd.). xix,390p. tables. £155; $325. ISBN: 0946653658.

In 4 parts: 1 has information on the European Communities, arranged A-Z, covering personalities, politics, programmes, reports and committees, acronyms, catch terms and phrases, etc. Pt.2 is a collection of essays by British academics on the political, legal, and social activities of the EC. Pt.3 is a detailed statistical survey. Pt.4 is a directory of EC institutions, including MEPs. Appendices summarize 3 original treaties, list measures involved in the implementation of the internal market, and give information on EC databases. *Class No:* 341.174

[2878]
The European Community 1991/92: the professional reference book for business, media and government. Morris, B., *ed.* 3rd ed. London, Macmillan, 1991. 500p. tables. £50. ISBN: 0333398386.

First published 1981.

The essential guide to what's what and who's who in the E.C. The introduction is followed by sections on: Europe 1990 - Member States of the European Community - The European Community framework - A-Z of European Community issues - European directory. Index. The first ed. was named best new business reference book of the year by Aslib. *Class No:* 341.174

[2879]
The European Community 1992: annual review of activities. Nugent, N., *ed.* Annual. In *Journal of Common Market studies*, v.31, 1993, p.1-163.

Includes a bibliography. *Class No:* 341.174

Abbreviations & Symbols

[2880]
RAMSAY, A. Eurojargon a dictionary of EC acronyms, abbreviations and soubriquets. 3rd ed. Stamford, Capital Planning Information, 1991. 90p. ISBN: 0906011787.

Arrangement is A-Z by acronyms, etc., with 'see' references. Bibliography (3 items). *Class No:* 341.174(003)

Databases

[2881]
HANSON, T. Directory of European Cummunity and related databases. European Information Association, 1991 (available from Barbara Vickery, University of Nottingham Library, NG72RD). 78p. ISBN: 0948272244.

Introduction is followed by database records (p.3-69); index by database category; and index by host of distributor. Bibliography, p.77-8 *Class No:* 341.174(003.4)

Bibliographies

[2882]
HOPKINS, M., *ed.* European Communities information: its use and users. London, Mansell, 1985. xiii,304p. £22.50. ISBN: 0720117011.

A lengthy introduction of background information, followed by 14 chapters in two parts: Part 1. The nature of European Communities information; 2. Sources of European Communities information and their use. 16 contributors.

....(contd.)

References and notes at the end of each chapter. Appendix lists European Documentation Centres and Depository Libraries in the United Kingdom. Analytical subject index, p.293-299; title index, p.300-304. Recommended for the Besterman Medal for 1985. *Class No:* 341.174(01)

[2883]

—HOPKINS, M., *ed.* Policy formation in the European Communities: a bibliographical guide to Community documentation, 1958-1978. London, Mansell, 1981. 360p. £30. ISBN: 0720115973.

Gives details of over 600 'important reports, communications and memoranda prepared by the Commission' (*Aslib information,* v.9(11/12), November/December 1981, p.275). *Class No:* 341.174(01)

[2884]

JEFFRIES,, J. A Guide to the official publications of the European Communities. 2nd ed. London, Mansell, 1981. xiv,i, 318p. £21; $36. ISBN: 0720115960.

First published 1978.

10 sections: 1, Introduction - 2. Publications of the European Communities - 3. Commission: general publications (*e.g.* Official journal; Treaties) - 4. Commission; non-statistical publications - 5. Eurostat - 6. Council of Ministers - 7. European Parliament - 8. Court of Justice of the European Communities - 9. Other bodies - 10. Bibliographic aids (*e.g., Euro abstracts; European bibliography*). 3 appendices (2. European documentation centre and depository libraries; 3 Further reading on the European Communities p284-7. Detailed, analytical index. Includes titles up to the end of 1979. Attractively produced. A historical volume is *Reports of the European Communities, 1952-1977:* an index to authors and chairmen; compiled by June Neilson (London, Mansell, 1981. 576p. £35. ISBN 0720115922). (qv). *Class No:* 341.174(01)

[2885]

THOMSON, I. The Documentation of the European Communities: a guide. London, Mansell Publishing, 1989. 396p. £35; $60. ISBN: 0720120225.

Describes the many publicly available printed documents, many in series, that emanate from the Community. Also information on the structure of all its institutions. Appendices cover such topics as EEC online databases, EC information centres, and depository libraries. *Class No:* 341.174(01)

Encyclopaedias

[2886]

Encyclopedia of European Community law. Simmonds, K.R., *ed.* London, Sweet & Maxwell, 1973-. 3v.(loose-leaf). V.A: £335; V.B: £480; V.C: £990. ISBN: 0421193506, v.A; 0421193603, v.B; 0421207604, v.C.

Vol. A: United Kingdom sources (2 loose-leaf binders); v.B: European Community treaties (3 loose-leaf binders); v.C: Community Secondary legislation (7 loose-leaf binders). Text, with commentary in smaller type; definitions. Brief bibliographies. Kept up-to-date with amendments.

Secondary legislation (regulations, directories, decisions, recommendations and opinions made by the Council of the European Communities) is published in *Official journal of the European Communities). Class No:* 341.174(031)

[2887]

Oxford encyclopaedia of European Community law. Oxford, Clarendon Press, 1990-. To be in 3v. V.1:xcviii,550p. £75. ISBN: 0198255896.

V.1, *Institutional law,* has over 300 concise and lucid entries, A-Z, each explaining a particular concept or point of law, fully documented with case and treaty references. Also suggestions for further reading. *Class No:* 341.174(031)

Handbooks & Manuals

[2888]

ARBUTHNOT, H. *and* EDWARDS, G., *eds*. A Common man's guide to the Common Market. 2nd ed. London, Macmillan Press, 1989. 248p. tables. £37.50. ISBN: 0333409132.

First published 1979.

Aim is to explain, as clearly as possible, how the policies of the Community are meant to achieve its primary objectives. 17 chapters: The institutions of the European Community - The policy-making process in the European Community - Community law - The Common Market ... Social policy ... The common commercial policy ... Political cooperation ... Abbreviations commonly used in the Community-Major sources of information on the Community and its policies. Index. *Class No:* 341.174(035)

[2889]

COE, A. *and* FURLONG, P. A Modern companion to the European Community: a guide to key facts, institutions and terms. Aldershot, Hants, Edward Elgar, 1992. 327p. £35. ISBN: 1852785160.

Includes a brief historical overview of the development of the EC and a description of the major Directorates and policy making functions. Also included are basic statistics on population, GNP, trade performance, and the economic potential of each member country; and explanations of over 1000 commonly used acronyms and abbreviations. *Class No:* 341.174(035)

[2890]

LEONARD, D. Pocket guide to the European Community. Oxford, Basil Blackwell Ltd; London, Economist Publications, 1988. xiii,210p. tables, graphs. £15; $29.95. ISBN: 0631162844.

An introduction to the history, institutions and functions of the European Community. 4 sections: The background - The institutions - The competances - Special problems. Cross-references. 8 appendices (1. Basic statistics of member states; 2. Presidents of the High Authority and the Community; 5. Elections to the European Parliament; 7. The single European Act; 9. Eurojargon). Suggestions for further reading, p.201-202. Index, p.203-210. *Class No:* 341.174(035)

[2891]

MATHIJSEN, P.S.R.F. A Guide to European Economic Community Law. 4th ed. London, Sweet & Maxwell, 1985. xl,284p. £17. ISBN: 0421339209.

First published 1972.

Aims to give an overall view of the state of development of Community law. Tables of cases, Commission decisions, European treaties, Community secondary legislation, and United Kingdom legislation, precede the 7 chapters (1. The European Communities - 2. History - 3. The institutions and other organs of the Community - 4. Community Acts - 5.

....*(contd.)*

The sectoral treaties: ECSC and Euratom - 6. The European Economic Community - 7. Community law). Footnotes. Analytical index, p.273-284. *Class No:* 341.174(035)

[2892]
OVERTON, D. **Common Market digest: an information guide to the European Communities.** London, Library Association, 1983; New York, Facts on File, 1984. xlvii,387 p. £32 $45. ISBN: 0853655537.

Describes the agencies, giving brief historical background and providing bibliographical citations to English-language sources about the European unity movement. Arranged in 8 chapters: 1. The European Communities - 2. The organizations of the Communities - 3. Common economic and agricultural developments - 4. Common industry and energy policies - 5. Common social and environmental development - 6. Common technology and research - 8. Additional information (includes a chronology). *Class No:* 341.174(035)

Dictionaries

[2893]
DINAN, D. **Historical dictionary of the European Community.** Metuchen, NJ, Scarecrow Press, 1993. 319p. charts, maps. $37.50. (*(International organizations).*) ISBN: 0810826666.

160 brief descriptive and analytical entries on politicians, statesmen, events and organizations in the history of the European Community. Includes short pieces on each member state, but 25% of the entries are biographical, with emphasis on how individuals influenced the EC's development. Each entry has 250-300 or more words. Cross-references. Lengthy introduction precedes. Classified bibliography lists monographs and official documents. Detailed chronology; 20p. of tables and graphs; and 5 political maps complete the dictionary. *Class No:* 341.174(038)

[2894]
PARKER, G. *and* PARKER, B. **A Dictionary of the European Communities.** London, Butterworth, 1981. [4], 84p. ISBN: 0408107332.

Concise definitions of terms relating to the European Communities, covering institutions, policies and people, as well as including many miscellaneous terms in common use. Cross-references. Reading list of 13 items. *Class No:* 341.174(038)

[2895]
PAXTON, J., *ed.* **A Dictionary of the European Communities.** 2nd ed. London, Macmillan Press, 1982. 240p. £25. ISBN: 0333334388.

First published in 1977 as *A dictionary of the European Economic Community.*

Entries A.A.S.M. ... Zollverein. Lengthier articles (*e.g.* 'Rome, Treaty of' p.219-221) are sectionalised. That on 'Referendum, United Kingdom, p.222-226, has detailed breakdown by counties of voting. Includes brief biographies, and abbreviations. Cross-references, *e.g.* from French terms to English. Select bibliography (grouped), p.279-282. A handy quick-reference tool. *Class No:* 341.174(038)

Polyglot

[2896]
EUROPEAN COMMUNITIES. Council. **Multilingual glossary of abbreviations.** 2nd ed. Luxembourg, Office for Official Publications of the European Communities, 1982. xxxii,589p. £10.30. ECU 18.62.

First published 1980.

A glossary in 6 languages (French/German/English/Italian/Dutch/Danish) containing *c.*8000 multilingual entries, plus their abbreviations, on the internal and external activities of the European Community. Includes technical terms, concepts, international bodies and Community institutions. *Class No:* 341.174(038)=00

Reports Literature

[2897]
NEILSON, J., *comp.* **Reports of the European Communities, 1952-1977: an index to authors and chairmen.** London, Mansell Publishing, 1981,. xiv, 561p. £27.50. ISBN: 0720115922.

Author index with over 2200 entries, A-Z, with full bibliographical details. English and/or French translations of titles. Coverage is to the end of 1977. Detailed subject index, p.503-561, refers to numbered entries in the author (and chairmen) index. *Class No:* 341.174(047)

Periodicals & Progress Reports

[2898]
European access, February 1989-. Cambridge, Chadwick-Healey; in association with the United Kingdom Offices of the European Commission, 1989-. Bi-monthly. £110pa. ISSN: 02647362.

A current awareness guide to the development, activities and policies of the European Communities. 1989(2), April issue has 119p. and contains: Chronology of events in the European Community - The European Parliament in election year - Commentary - Education and R & D funding news - European Community information developments - Documentation of the European Communities - Bibliographic review - Recent references (brief entries) - Alphabetical list of subject headings - List of useful addresses. *Class No:* 341.174(05)

Yearbooks & Directories

[2899]
The Europe 1992 directory: a research and information guide. London, HMSO, for the Information Technology Consultancy Unit, Coventry Polytechnic, 1992. 97p. £10.95.

First published 1989.

Sections: Glossary - Organizations - Principal Community documents - Books, monographs, pamphlets - Journals (including list of major articles on 1992), periodicals, magazines - Speeches (on 1992) - Research and training programmes - Databases for 1992 - Audio-visual material - Management consultancies - Legal consultancies - European documentation centres in the UK - Who's who in the European Commission. Index. *Class No:* 341.174(058)

[2900]
EUROPEAN COMMUNITIES. Commission. **Directory of the Commission of the European Communities (September 1988).** Luxembourg, Office for Official Publications of the European Community, 1988. 132p. ECU 3.50 £2.50.

A directory of the services and key personnel of the Commission. *Class No:* 341.174(058)

[2901]
MARTENS, H. **EC direct:** a comprehensive directory of EC contacts. Oxford, Blackwell, 1992. xiv,230p. $34.95. ISBN: 0631187960.

A handbook for companies interested in the European Community and in the EC Commission. 12 chapters, all subdivided: 1. Introduction: the single market - 2. The EC Commission: institutions and persons - 3. Other EC institutions to contact ... 5. Private organizations ... 8. Financial support and grants - 9. Databases - 10. Economic data for EC countries ... 12. Glossary of terms and abbreviations. Further reading, p.204. Index, p.205-19. Name index, p.220-30. *Class No:* 341.174(058)

Tables & Data Books

Bibliographies

[2902]
EUROPEAN COMMUNITIES. Statistical Office. **Eurostat catalogue: publications and electronic services.** Luxembourg, the Office. Annual. *Gratis.*

Lists each title with bibliographical details and a brief description of contents. *Class No:* 341.174(083)(01)

Maps & Atlases

[2903]
HUDSON, R., *and others*. **An Atlas of EEC affairs.** London, Methuen, 1984. xiv,158p. illus., maps, tables.

Account in 6 chapters of the Community's history, organizational structure, population, labour market, economic performance and resources, social conditions, and prospects for the year 2000 A.D. 'A most welcome contribution to a field in which little has been published' (*International affairs,* v.61,no.1, Winter 1984-85, p.189-190). *Class No:* 341.174(084.3)

Laws

[2904]
EUROPEAN COMMUNITIES. Commission. **Directory of Community legislation in force** and other Acts of the Community institutions (recompiled and updated every six months) - all institutions. 19th ed. Luxembourg, Office for Offical Publications of the European Communities, 1992. 2v. (1064p.). ECU 90. £64 for 2v.

V.1 Analytical register; v.2. Chronological index. Alphabetical index. Enables the user to find the current instruments of Community legislation. *Class No:* 341.174(094.1)

Asian Regional Organizations

Official Records

[2905]
HAAS, M., *ed*. **Basic documents of Asian regional organizations.** Dobbs Ferry, N.Y. Oceana, 1974-85. 9v. v.1-8: $47.50 each; v.9: $50. Set: $430. ISBN: 0379001772.

V.1-7 are concerned with documentary history of international organizations with headquarters in Asia. V.8 has analytical treatment of the history, structure and functioning of the various Asian intergovernmental organizations. V.9 puts the data available from the preceding 8v. into a format to facilitate comparisons. *Class No:* 341.175(093.2)

African Regional Organizations

Official Records

[2906]
SOHN, L.B., *ed*. **Basic documents of African regional organizations.** Dobbs Ferry, N.Y., Oceana, for the Inter-American Institute of International Legal Studies, 1971-73. 4v. $190 the set. ISBN: 0379003619.

Texts of constitutions and other relevant documents, backed by bibliographies of books, periodical articles and documents. Main subdivisions: Organization of African Unity - African Development Bank - Regional groups in French-speaking Africa - Regional co-operation in West Africa - Maghreb Permanent Consultative Committee - East African organizations - Association of African States with the European Community. *Class No:* 341.176(093.2)

Frontiers

[2907]
DAY, A.J. **Border and territorial disputes.** 3rd ed. Harlow, Essex, Longman Group, 1992. (distributed in US and Canada by Gale Research Co.). x, 562p. 67 maps. £135 $245. (*Keesing's reference publication.*) ISBN: 0582209315, UK.

First published 1982.

Details of some 84 contemporary border and territorial disputes throughout the world. Coverage is limited to land-based disputes which are of territorial and/or political significance and involve contentious territorial claims by one nation against another. In five sections: Europe; Africa; Middle East; Asia and Far East; The Americas and Antarctica. Comprehensive index and a select bibliography. Noteworthy for "its lengthy in-depth explanations of each dispute's history, significant efforts and resolution, legal bases, etc. (*Wilson library bulletin,* V.67(8), April 1993, p.118). *Class No:* 341.222

[2908]
DOWNING, D. **An Atlas of territorial and border disputes.** London, New English Library, 1980. 121p. £7.95. ISBN: 0450048047.

30 maps arranged by region (Asia, the Middle East, Africa, the Americas, Europe). Examines, in textual and cartographic form the border disputes most likely to disturb the local or the international peace in the 1980s. Bibliography, p.116. Index, p.119-120. *Class No:* 341.222

[2909]
Maritime boundaries and ocean resources. Blake, G., *ed.* Beckenham, Kent, Croom Helm Ltd., 1987. [14],284p. tables, figs., maps. £27.50. ISBN: 0709939744.

Produced for the International Geographical Union Study Group on the World Political Map.

15 chapters by 15 contributors: 1. Worldwide maritime boundaries delimitation: the state of play - 2. Delimitation of maritime boundaries: emergent legal principles and problems - 3. Straight and archipelagic baselines ... 8. European national and regional concepts of fishing limits in the European Community ... 14. Defining the undefinable: Antarctic maritime boundaries - 15. Beyond the bounds? A consideration of local government limits in the coastal zone of England and Wales. Select bibliography, p.257-271, A-Z by author. Index, p.272-284. *Class No:* 341.222

[2910]
PRESCOTT, J.R.V. The Maritime political boundaries of the world. London, Methuen, 1985. xv,[1],377p. tables, diagrs. £35. ISBN: 0416417507.

14 chapters, each with conclusions and references: 1. Political geography of the oceans - 2. The physical nature of oceans and coasts - 3. National maritime claims - 4. International maritime boundaries - 5. International maritime zones - 6-14. on individual oceans and seas. Suggested reading list p.355-360, by chapter subject. Glossary, p.361-366. Name index, p.367-368; analytical subject index, p.369-377. *Class No:* 341.222

Africa

[2911]
BROWNLIE, L. *and* **BURNS, I.R. African boundaries:** a legal and diplomatic encyclopaedia. London, C. Hurst; Berkeley & Los Angeles, University of California Press, for the Royal Institute of International Affairs, 1979. xxvi, 1355p. 8 maps. £70. ISBN: 0903983877.

5 parts: 1. States of the Mediterranean littoral (15 boundaries) - 2. States of West Africa and the Western Sahara (28) - 3. The succession States of French Equatorial Africa, with Cameroun, Equatorial Guinea and Zaire (24) - 4. Sudan, Ethiopia, Somalia and East Africa (18) - 5. Southern Africa, including Angola, Zambia, Malawi and Mozambique (20). Rhodesia (Zimabawe) - Zambia: p.1304-12 (General provenance; Alignment; Evidence, including Schedule; Current issues; Bibliography of 19 items). At least one sketch map accompanies each separate alignment; plus 8 other maps. Introduction concludes with a 'Select general bibliography', p.22-24. *Class No:* 341.222(6)

Law of the Sea

[2912]
Maritime affairs: a world handbook. Gold, E., *ed.* 2nd ed. Harlow, Essex, Longman, 1991. xxv,479p. £95. ISBN: 0582086930.

First published 1985, edited by H.W.Degenhardt.

A reference guide for modern ocean policy and management. 14 chapters: 1. Maritime affairs: the setting; 2. The modern law of the sea; 3. Maritime organizations and institutions...10. The coastal zone; 11. The Polar areas...13. The resolution of maritime disputes; 14. Maritime education and training. Appendices: A. United Nations Convention on

....(contd.)
the Law of the Sea; C. Selected maritime periodicals listing; D. Selected maritime reference bibliography. Index, p.471-9. *Class No:* 341.225

[2913]
WANG, J.C. Handbook on ocean politics and law. Westport, CT. & London, Greenwood Press, 1992. 592p. tables, charts, maps. $95. £85. ISBN: 0313264341.

A comprehensive work, with chapters surveying physical aspects of the oceans, international conferences on the law of the sea, living and non-living resources (with their economic and political management, environmental protection and pollution, military uses, navigation and transport, and marine scientific research. The author expresses his own opinion and summarizes those of others. Each chapter has bibliographical references and there is also a select bibliography. 7 appendices. Index. *Class No:* 341.225

Bibliographies

[2914]
The Law of the Sea: a selected bibliography, 1991. Annual. United Nations. Office for Ocean Affairs and the Law of the Sea. New York, United Nations, 1993. 61p. £15. ISBN: 9211334519.

Divided into 22 subject categories based mainly on the major topics in the United Nations Convention on the Law of the Sea. Author index. *Class No:* 341.225(01)

[2915]
—**UNITED NATIONS.** Office for Ocean Affairs and the Law of the Sea. The Law of the Sea: a bibliography on the law of the sea, 1968-1988: two decades of lawmaking, state practice and doctrine. New York, United Nations, 1991. 472p. $25. ISBN: 9210330684. *Class No:* 341.225(01)

[2916]
PAPPADAKIS, N. *and* **GLASSNER, M.,** *eds.* **International law of the sea and marine affairs:** a bibliography. The Hague, Martinus Nijhoff, 1984. xxvi,579p. £88.95. ISBN: 9024728150.

Arranged in 9 sections: I. Introduction - the marine environment and the Law of the Sea - II. Maritime zones and maritime jurisdiction - III. The legal regime of the sea bed ... - IV. Main resources - V. Protection and preservation of the marine environment - VI. Marine scientific research - VII. Military uses and arms control - VIII. Ocean policy making - IX. Settlement of disputes. 2 appendices (1. Bibliographies, reference works, indexes, directories, dictionaries and guides to documents on the Law of the Sea and marine affairs, p.491-499 (343 items); 2. List of journals and periodical publications consulted). Author index. Index to documents, etc. *Class No:* 341.225(01)

Dictionaries

Russian

[2917]
ZHELTOV, L.M. *and* **KNIAZEV, V.S. Anglo-russkii i russko-angliiskii slovar po morskomu pravu/English-Russian and Russian-English law of the sea dictionary.** Moskva, Voen, 1988. 207p. Rub.1.80.
Class No: 341.225(038)=82

Independence of Nations

Official Records

[2918]

BLAUSTEIN, A.P., *and others, comps*. **Independence documents of the world.** Dobbs Ferry, N.Y., Oceana, 1977. 2v. $85. ISBN: 0379007940, v.1; 0379007959, v.2.

Texts, mostly in full and all translated into English, of documents covering 150 of some 160 nations of the world; introductory brief political histories. 'An excellent compilation' (*Choice*, v.14(12), February 1978, p.1624). *Class No:* 341.231(093.2)

Alliances & Treaties

[2919]

BOWMAN, M.J. *and* HARRIS, D.J., *eds*. **Multilateral treaties:** index and current status. London, Butterworth, 1984. 516p. £60.

An index to more than 800 of the most important multilateral treaties, relating to both public and private international law, that were concluded between 1856 and June 1983. Listing is in chronological order. Information in each entry includes entry into force, duration, signatories, parties, territorial scope, reservations, amendments, authentic texts, and sources of publication. Cross-references. Subject and word indexes. *Class No:* 341.232/.24

[2920]

MILLER, T.B., *ed*. **Current international treaties.** London, Croom Helm, 1984. [9],558p. £35. ISBN: 0709917589.

'... attempt to bring together in a single volume the texts of the main bilateral and multilateral treaties which form the legal skeleton of so much of current international relations ...' (*Preface*). Entries broadly grouped by subject (The convention of international diplomacy - Global political institutions - Economic treaties - Regional agreements - The control of nuclear weapons - Security treaties - Human rights), each group subdivided. Preambles and less essential clauses usually omitted and commentary kept to a minimum. 2 appendices: A. Signatories to multilateral instruments in this volume; B. Bilateral treaties in this volume. Index, p.553-558. 'Chief deficiency is omission of date and place of signatures' (*International affairs*, v.61(1), Winter 1984/85). *Class No:* 341.232/.24

[2921]

Treaties and alliances of the world. Rengger, N., *ed*. 5th ed. Harlow, Essex, Longman Current Affairs, 1990. x,579p. diagrs., tables, maps. £85. ISBN: 0582057337.

First published 1968. H.W. Degenhardt edited the first four eds.

Compiled with the cooperation of the editorial team of Longman and *Keesing's Contemporary archives* (now *Keesing's Record of world events*). 5 parts: 1. The analysis of treaties and alliances in world politics - 2. International organizations - 3. Treaties and alliances of the Cold War - 4. Regional agreements - 5. Trans-regional and informal groupings. 13 maps. Grouped bibliography, p.567-70. Index. *Class No:* 341.232/.24

[2922]

UNITED NATIONS. **Treaty series: treaties and international agreements registered or filed and recorded with the Secretariat of the United Nations ... 1946/47-.** New York, United Nations, 1947-.v.1-. ISSN: 03798267.

Texts are in the original languages, with English and French translations. Cumulative indexes are produced from time to time (v.1-100, 101-200...) comprising chronological and subject indexes. *Class No:* 341.232/.24

[2923]

—**Multinational treaties deposited with the Secretary-General as at 31 December 1985.** New York, United Nations, 1986. xxiv. 871p. $60 £60. (*ST/LEG/SER.E/4.*) ISBN: 9211332931.

Lists 833 treaties in chronological order, concluded from 1856. *Class No:* 341.232/.24

Handbooks & Manuals

[2924]

REUTER, P. **Introduction to the law of treaties.** London, Pinter Publishers, 1989. xii,236p. £39.50. ISBN: 0861879546.

Originally a publication of the Graduate Institute of International Studies, Geneva. 1st French ed. published by Armond Colin, 1972; 2nd ed., 1985. Translated by José Mico and Peter Haggenmacher.

In-depth treatment of the subject in 4 chapters, all subdivided: 1. Treaties (1. Historical aspects - 2. Fundamental legal aspects - 3. Definition and classification of international treaties - 4. Work on international treaties); 2. Conclusion, entry into foreign participation; 3. The effects of treaties; 4. Non-application of treaties. Notes, p.156-163, and after some chapters. Index, p.231-236. *Class No:* 341.232/.24(035)

Dictionaries

Polyglot

[2925]

EUROPEAN COMMUNITIES. Commission. **European treaty vocabulary.** 2nd ed. Brussels, the Commission, 1983. 414p. £13.50.

French - German - English - Italian - Dutch - Danish. Indexes in each language. *Class No:* 341.232/.24(038)=00

Histories

[2926]

HARVARD UNIVERSITY. Law School. Library. **Index to multilateral treaties:** a chronological list of multi-party international agreements, from the sixteenth century through 1963, with citations to the text. Mostecky, V. Dobbs Ferry, N.Y., Oceana, 1965. x,301p. $40.00. ISBN: 0379003848.

3859 numbered items, 1596-1963. Entries state number, date, subject and sources. 'Subject and regional guide' (p.253-301), listing each treaty under one or more of the following: topic, area (if regional), country or city, place of signature and date (if popularly known), name of person(s) instrumental in drafting, and name of international organization (in English), if the treaty is a charter, etc., of that organization. 'While the list is comprehensive for the period preceding 1960, it is necessarily incomplete for the

....(contd.)

most recent years because the texts of some treaties were not available in printed form at press time' (*Preface*).
Class No: 341.232/.24(091)

[2927]
TOSCANO, M. The History of treaties and international politics. Baltimore, MD., Johns Hopkins Press, 1966. (Available from Books Demand UMI). xv,[1],685p. $160. ISBN: 0317423592.

English translations of *Storia dei trattati e politica internazione. 1, Parte generale* (Turin, Giappichelli, 1963), expanded edition of *Lezioni di storia dei trattati e politica internazionale. 1, Parte generale* (Turin, Giappichelli, 1958).

An indispensable, evaluative guide to the source material of 20th-century international history. Particularly valuable, states *International affairs* (v.43(3), July 1967, p.537) on documents on the literature of World Wars I and II and memoir sources for the two wars. 'The Italian side understandably receives great emphasis'.
Class No: 341.232/.24(091)

Official Records

[2928]
The Consolidated treaty series, 1648-1918: annotated. Parry, C., *ed.* Dobbs Ferry, N.Y., Oceana Publications, 1970-77. 243v. in 12v. indexed set. $11,000 the set. ISBN: 0379130009.

Extends from the Peace of Westphalia (1648) to the beginning of the League of Nations. Texts of treaties in original languages, plus English or French translations/ summaries. Some annotations. Arranged chronologically.
Class No: 341.232/.24(093.2)

Great Britain

[2929]
GREAT BRITAIN. Foreign and Commonwealth Office. **British and foreign state papers,** with which is incorporated [in v.116-157] Hertslet's Commercial treaties. London, Ridgway (then HMSO), 1841-1976. 170v.

v.1.(1841) covered 1812-14; v.169 (1976) covered 1967-68 v.170: index to v.166-169. This completes the series.

Items are arranged chronologically and consist of texts of agreements, treaties to which Great Britain was a partner. Orders in Council, appropriate Acts of Parliament (*e.g.* European Payments Union (Financial provisions), letters patent, etc.). Chronological index precedes. Subject and country indexes per volume and interim-cumulative (*e.g.* v.65 is index to v.139-164). An important source.
Class No: 341.232/.24(410)

[2930]
GREAT BRITAIN. Foreign Office. **Treaty series, 1892-.** London, HMSO, 1892-. Annual.

Treaties to which the United Kingdom is a party and which have come into force are published as Command Papers in a special series. They have their Command number and their Treaty series number (beginning with no.1. each year). They are published individually as presented to Parliament. Many treaties are published as Command Papers outside the Treaty series when concluded but before they have come into force; when they have come into force, they are again published in the Treaty series with a different Command number. *Class No:* 341.232/.24(410)

[2931]
PARRY, C. *and* **HOPKINS, C.,** *comps.* **An Index of British treaties, 1101-1968.** London, HMSO, 1970. 3.v. (xvi, 1407p.).

Compiled and annotated under the auspices of the International Law Fund and the British Institute of International and Comparative Law.

V.1. contains the index of multilateral treaties by subjects; index of bilateral treaties by country, etc,; and index of bilateral treaties by subjects. V.2. Chronological list of treaties, 1101 - 1925. V.3. Chronological list of treaties, 1926 - 1968. Dates of entry into force and Command Paper number are given in V. 2-3. *Class No:* 341.232/.24(410)

[2932]
—GREAT BRITAIN. Foreign and Commonwealth Office. Index to treaty series. London, HMSO.

Continues the series of treaty indexes listed in HMSO's *Sectional list No.7: Treaty series, 1910-1962* The Index for 1992 (1993) was issued as Cm.2352 (£4.50. ISBN 0101235224). *Class No:* 341.232/.24(410)

USA

[2933]
KAVASS, I.I. *and* **SPRUDZS, A. A Guide to the United States treaties in force.** Buffalo, N.Y., W.S. Hein, 1992. 2v. $142.50. ISBN: 0685573419, v.1; 089941768x, v.2.

V.1. Numerical list of bilateral and multilateral treaties and agreements of the United States in force; v.2 Multilateral treaties and other agreements. 'May stand alone as handy reference but will be most useful as a complement to *Treaties in force* (1983), the standard Department of State list of agreements still in effect' (*Choice,* v.22(3), November 1984, p.402-3) of an earlier edition. *Class No:* 341.232/ .24(73)

19th Century

[2934]
HURST, M., *ed.* **Key treaties for the Great Powers, 1814-1914.** Newton Abbot, Devon, David & Charles, 1972. 2v. (948p.).

Provides the text of 194 documents. Analytical index, p.918-948. *Class No:* 341.232/.24"18"

20th Century

[2935]
GRENVILLE, J.A.S. The Major international treaties, 1914-1945 a history and guide with texts. London, Methuen, 1987. xviii,268p. 4 maps. £40. ISBN: 0416080928.

Supersedes, in part, Grenville's *The major international treaties, 1914-1973 ...* (1974).

An introduction is followed by 10 chapters: 1. Secret agreements and treaties of the first world war - 2. The peace settlements and the League of Nations - 3. France, Britain, Italy and Germany, 1921-33 - 4. France and the eastern allies, 1921-39 - 5. The Soviet Union and her neighbours, 1919-37 - 6. The collapse of the territorial settlements of Versailles, 1931-8 - 7. From peace to world war in Europe and Asia, 1937-41 - 8. The Grand Alliance: Britain and the United States and the Soviet Union, 1941-45 - 9. The Allied conferences and the political settlement of Europe, 1943-5 - 10. The alliance and alignments of the United States from the

....(contd.)

League of Nations to the United Nations. Source references for the principal treaties, p.256-261. Analytical index, p.263-268. *Class No:* 341.232/.24"19"

[2936]
—GRENVILLE, J.A.S. *and* WASSERSTEIN, B. The Major international treaties since 1945: a history and guide with texts. London, Methuen, 1987. xiv,528p. £50; $85. ISBN: 0416380808.

Supersedes, in part, J.A.S. Grenville's *The major international treaties, 1914-1973 ...* (1974).

An introduction on international treaties is followed by 10 chapters: 1. The foundations of post-war diplomacy - 2. The United States treaty system - 3. The Soviet treaty system - 4. The German question - 5. West European integration - 6. South and East Asia and the Pacific - 7. Africa - 8. The Middle East and East Mediterranean - 9. Latin America and the South Atlantic - 10. Détente and arms control. Appendix: Multilateral treaties on human rights and the environment. Sources for treaty texts, p.500-506. Analytical index, p.507-528. *Class No:* 341.232/.24"19"

[2937]
LEAGUE OF NATIONS. Treaty series: publications of treaties and international engagements registered with the Secretariat of the League. Geneva, League of Nations; London, Harrison, 1920-46. (Reprinted Dobbs Ferry, NY., Oceana, 1970). 9v. *Class No:* 341.232/.24"19"

[2938]
ROHN, P.H. World treaty index. 2nd ed. Santa Barbara, CA., ABC-Clio, 1984. 5v.(4271p.). $999 the set. ISBN: 0874361419.

First published 1975 in 6v.

V.1 Reference volume - 2. Main entry section, 1900-1959 - 3. Main entry section, 1960-1980 - 4. Keyword index - 5. Party index. Information includes: Type of agreement; date signed; registered; articles; language; head note; topic; concepts; parties (countries). *Class No:* 341.232/.24"19"

Aid & Development

Abbreviations & Symbols

[2939]
CARROLL, M., *comp.* Acronyms relating to international development/Liste de sigles en développement international/Sigles relacionadas con desarrollo internacional. Ottawa, International Development Research Centre, 1980. (Available from Unipub). 162p. $9.50. ISBN: 0839362084.

About 1500 entries (AAACU ... ZPG) giving abbreviations, full name, place and country. *Class No:* 341.232(003)

Dictionaries

[2940]
GREAT BRITAIN. Overseas Development Administration. ABC of aid and development: some terms and institutions. 4th rev. ed. London, ODA, 1986. 100p. Gratis.

First published 1971.

About 320 terms are defined, with background information, (*e.g.* 'Inter American Development Bank (IDB)': 2/3p.). 'Aims to explain as simply as possible phrases, terms and organizations commonly referred to by

....(contd.)

those who are involved in overseas aid and development' (*Preface*). Cross-references. Abbreviations, p.5-13). *Class No:* 341.232(038)

Yearbooks & Directories

[2941]
Development aid: a guide to national and international agencies. Sevenoaks, Kent, Butterworths; Newbury, Berks, Eurofi, 1988. [22],583p. 55. ISBN: 0408009918.

Listings of agencies providing aid for development. In two sections: 1. International agencies - 2. National agencies, arranged by continent, subdivided by countries, A-Z. For each entry: executive summary, followed by precise details of the nature and scope of the funding available. Includes addresses, telephone and telex numbers. *Class No:* 341.232(058)

Great Britain

Yearbooks & Directories

[2942]
Development guide: a directory of non-commercial organisations in Britain entirely concerned in overseas development and training. 3rd ed. London, Overseas Development Institute; Hemel Hempstead, Herts, Allen & Unwin, 1978. ix,216p. £10. ISBN: 0043600476.

First published 1962.

200 organizations (Action in Distress (AID) ... Young Women's Christian Association (YWCA) of Great Britain), p.3-202 - 1 per page. Data: name and address; aims; number of members; research; education; training; information and advice; publications; when founded; how financed; name of president. 'Overseas sources of information; (countries, A-Z), p.205-8. Index (partly analytical). *Class No:* 341.232(410)(058)

Atlantic Alliance

[2943]
The North Atlantic Treaty Organisation: facts and figures. llth ed., fully rev. & re-set with new graphics & an extended alphabetical index. Brussels, NATO Information Service, 1989. xii,575p. ISBN: 9284500419.

First published 1955 under title *NATO: the first five years*; 10th ed., 1981.

Includes an index and bibliographical references. *Class No:* 341.232.1

Bibliographies

[2944]
GORDON, C. The Atlantic Alliance: a bibliography. London, Frances Pinter, 1978. 216p. £20. ISBN: 0903804328.

About 3000 references, drawn from British, Canadian, US, Scandinavian and Soviet sources. General bibliographical introduction (background material, p.11-15). 4 sections: 1. The genesis of the Alliance, 1945-1955; 2. The years of strain and stress, 1955-1962; 3. The search for a *modus vivendi,* 1962-1970; 4. The onset of *Détente,* 1970-1977 (books; economic and social aspects; legal aspects; industrial aspects; national and regional aspects; politico-

....(contd.)

military aspects; military-strategic aspects; reports, papers and pamphlets are similarly divided). Each of the 4 sections has an introduction. *Class No:* 341.232.1(01)

[2945]

NORTON, A.R., *and others*. **NATO: a bibliography and resource guide.** New York, Garland, 1985. xiii,252p. $50. ISBN: 0824093313.

A general section, with entries arranged chronologically in 5-year periods to 1979, then 1980-81, is followed by entries for member states (A-Z), 'Issues in NATO'. 'Doctrines, strategies and military issues', 'Alliance politics', and 'Warsaw Pact'. No annotations. Index, p.227-252. *Class No:* 341.232.1(01)

Handbooks & Manuals

[2946]

Jane's NATO handbook, 1991/92. George, B., *ed.* Coulsdon, Surrey, Jane's Information Group, 1991. 450p. £125. ISBN: 0710609760.

Includes a chronology, directory of personalities, and documentation section. '...constitutes an all-embracing NATO scrapbook' (*The RUSI journal,* Spring 1990, p.84). *Class No:* 341.232.1(035)

International Court of Justice

Bibliographies

[2947]

INTERNATIONAL COURT OF JUSTICE. Library. **Bibliographie de la Cour ... Bibliography of the International Court of Justice.** The Hague, International Court of Justice, 1947-. No.1-.

A continuation of the lists published in chapter 9 of the *Yearbook* and *Annuaire* of the Court from 1946/47 to 1963/64, using the same grouping (sections A-L) and continuing numbering. Each annual issue has *c.*250 entries and profuse cross-references. Name and analytical subject indexes. (No.40, 1986, p.149-180, xxviip. £2.75. ISBN 0119097435). *Class No:* 341.646(01)

Yearbooks & Directories

[2948]

INTERNATIONAL COURT OF JUSTICE. **Year book, 1987-88.** No. 42. The Hague, the Court, 1989. xii,193p.

First published 1947. Annual.

Contains general information in 8 chapters on the organization, jurisdiction, activities and administration of the Court. *Class No:* 341.646(058)

Disarmament

[2949]

MENOS, D., *comp.* **Arms control fact book.** Jefferson, N.C., McFarland, 1985. 140p. $15.95. ISBN: 0899501583.

According to the *Preface,* the aim is to help the general reader to understand the basic issues underlying arms control, its accomplishments to date, and the challenges for the future. The first half is a dictionary of frequently used terms in the arms control literature, each entry about half-page in length. There follows a directory, arranged A-Z, of

....(contd.)

selected national and international organizations active in arms control and disarmament. There is also a chronology of key arms control events. *RQ* (v.25(3), p.387) reports inconsistencies and incomplete indexing, but says there is no comparable work so it fills a definite need. *Class No:* 341.67

[2950]

—GAY, W. *and* PEARSON, M. **The Nuclear arms race.** Chicago, Ill., American Library Association, 1988. 270p. $29.95. (*Last quarter century, no.1.*) ISBN: 083890467x.

An overview of major issues (nuclear policies, nuclear war, arms control, deterrence, strategic theory, etc.). An annotated bibliography of books, articles, reports, etc., and a list of sources are included in each chapter. 'A comprehensive, well-conceived and well-organized sourcebook' (*Library journal,* v.113(7), April 1988, p.32-33). *Class No:* 341.67

[2951]

The Nuclear almanac: confronting the atom in war and peace, edited by J. Dennis, Massachusetts Institute of Technology. Reading, Mass., Addison - Wesley, 1984. 546p. photos. tables. $35. ISBN: 0201053314.

A factual account of the discovery, development and use of nuclear energy, and a critical evaluation of possible issues raised by nuclear armaments and nuclear power. Signed essays are grouped under major headings: The history of nuclear weapons - The effects of nuclear weapons - Atomic warfare, its technologies and its consequences - International issues, including arms control negotiations - The non-military uses and abuses of nuclear energy - Public response - Scientific background. Each essay includes photographs, chronologies, tables, documentary excerpts, etc., as well as short 'Suggested readings' lists. Detailed index. *Class No:* 341.67

Bibliographies of Bibliographies

[2952]

CARROLL, B.A., *and others*. **Peace and war:** a guide to bibliographies. Santa Barbara, CA., ABC-Clio, 1983. xxi,580p. $42.50; £32.75. (*War and peace bibliography series, 16.*) ISBN: 0874363225.

Produced in co-operation with California State University Center for the Study of Armament and Disarmament.

Includes 1398 bibliographies published separately or as parts of books and articles, etc. from 1785 to 1980. Arranged under 34 subject groups (*e.g.* Women, peace and war; Peace education; Economic aspects of war). Gives detailed bibliographical information, number of items included, main language, proportion of items annotated, kinds of material included, and descriptive rather than evaluative annotations of *c.*30 words. Author index. *Class No:* 341.67(009)

Bibliographies

[2953]

ATKINS, S.E. **Arms control and disarmament, defense and military, international security and peace:** an annotated guide to sources, 1980-1987. Santa Barbara, CA., ABC-Clio 1988. 411p. $65. ISBN: 0874364884.

Nearly 1600 important works are annotated, mostly in English, and published between 1980 and 1987. Includes

....(contd.)

microform sets and textbooks, as well as printed sources. '
... very welcome and surprisingly unique in its capture of all
four major subtopics' (*Choice* v.26 (11/12), July-August,
1989. p. 1805-6). *Class No:* 341.67(01)

[2954]

BURNS, R. D., *comp.* **Arms control and disarmament:** a
bibliography. Santa Barbara, CA, ABC-Clio, 1977. xv.
430p. (*The War/peace bibliography series, no.6.*)

8847 numbered references (many to periodical articles)
arranged in 13 chapters in 2 parts. Each chapter is prefaced
by an essay. Part 1. Views, overviews and theory (1.
Research resources, and arms control and disarmament
organizations ... 3. Historical surveys and contemporary
views - 4. League of Nations and United Nations - 5. Special
issues: inspection, verification, and supervision ...); Part 2.
Accords, proposals and treaties (... 12. Controlling
proliferation of nuclear weapons - 13. Rules of war and
stabilizing the international environment). Subject and author
indexes. *Class No:* 341.67(01)

[2955]

**Card catalog of the Peace Palace Library, The Hague.
Microfiche edition.** Bethesda, MD., C I S Academic
Editions, 1988. 1090 fiche and 724 fiche. $3545 and $2030.
$4350 for both.

Comprises a universal bibliographical catalogue (a file
containing *c.*350,000 entries for books, pamphlets and other
materials, including correspondence) and a periodicals
reference guide (an index to the contents of more than 2300
journals currently received, plus those no longer published).
Class No: 341.67(01)

[2956]

FERMANN, G. **Bibliography** **on** **international
peacekeeping.** Dordrecht, The Netherlands, & London,
M.Nijhoff, 1992. xiii,291p. £59. ISBN: 0792320115.

1148 numbered items covering academic literature from
banks, reports and journals, etc. Arranged in 14 chapters of
which 1 to 10 are general, theoretical and conceptual,
including case studies and brief reviews of operations.
Chapter 11. Biographies and memoirs; 12. Book reviews;
13. Documentary collections; 14. Bibliographies. Data is
from 1946/47 onwards. Subject index, p.256-71. General
index, p.272-87. Journals & yearbooks, p.288.
Class No: 341.67(01)

[2957]

McHUGH, D. Peace information sources: a guide to 31
British collections with comprehensive subject index.
London, Infoshare Project, 1987. [4],83p. £2.50.

Listings of 23 national peace organizations, A-Z by name,
and 9 peace centres (A-Z by town). For each entry: name
and address, telephone number, access, aims, activities,
publications, overview (main types of material, archives,
human expertise), detailed analysis (subjects/important
materials, organization/accessibility) of the various
resources. Detailed subject index, p.67-83.
Class No: 341.67(01)

[2958]

PASKINS, B. 'Peace studies and disarmament.' In *British
book news*, July 1985, p. 387-91.

A literature survey with sections on The new peace
movement, The effects of nuclear war, Ideas of deterrence,
History and power politics, Philosophers and theologians,
Psychologists and economists, Civil nuclear power, and
finally, General guides and bibliographies. A bibliography
lists the 98 book titles and two periodical titles referred to in
the text. *Class No:* 341.67(01)

[2959]

RIDINGER, R.B.M. The Peace Corps: an annotated
bibliography. Boston, Mass., G.K. Hall & Co., 1989. 384p.
$35. ISBN: 0816189129.

A guide to the history of the United States Peace Corps
from its inception in 1961 to 1986. Lists over 1400 selected
sources, including books, newspaper and periodical articles,
videotapes, memoirs, dissertations, research monographs
and government documents, all annotated. 3 sections: 1.
History of the Peace Corps; 2. Country programs; 3.
Returned volunteers. 2 appendices: List of the Directors of
the Peace Corps, 1961-1986; Periodicals of the Peace Corps.
Name and subject index. *Class No:* 341.67(01)

[2960]

WOITO, R.S., *ed.* **To end war** a new approach to
international conflict. 6th ed. New York, Pilgrim Press,
1982. 755p. $25. ISBN: 0829804641.

First published 1967.

21 chapters, each with an introductionary essay of *c.*10p.,
preceding a bibliography on a particular subject (military,
political, economic, ethical, religious, etc., connected with
peace studies. Also includes a 200p. section of practical
guidance, listings of organizations and resources. 'Not only
the best bibliography by far on peace studies but also a
superb guide to many issues ...' (*Choice,* v.20(8), April
1983, p.1114). *Class No:* 341.67(01)

Encyclopaedias

[2961]

Encyclopedia of arms control and disarmament. Burns, R.
D., *ed.* New York, Scribner, 1993. 3v. $280. ISBN:
0684192810.

Includes 76 original articles and 150 excerpts of treaties.
V.1 has signed articles in 2 parts: 1. has detailed histories of
military activity and peace movements; 2. on a variety of
themes and institutions, V.2 surveys historical dementions to
1945 and covers covert arms control activities since 1945.
V.3 has a chronology of treaties and excerpts from treaties;
a list of the 83 contributors; a list of acronyms; and a
detailed index. Annotated bibliographies are included at the
end of each article. *Class No:* 341.67(031)

[2962]

World encyclopedia of peace. Laszlo, E. *and* Yoo, J.Y., *eds.*
Oxford, Pergamon Press, 1986. 4v. (1930p.). illus. £295;
$530. ISBN: 0080326854.

Over 3000 literary references by over 200 experts from
more than 30 countries, predominantly Western European
and American. V.1-2 has a 36p. essay of introduction and
history of peace encyclopedias, followed by a series of *c.*500
articles arranged A-Z by subject. V.3 has reprints of texts of
peace treaties and conventions since 1919, a chronology of
the peace movement, and Nobel Peace Prize laureates. V.4
lists peace organizations and institutions, A-Z by country; a

....*(contd.)*

bibliography arranged thematically (p.69-135); a list of journals arranged thematically (p.136-155) and devoted to peace research, peace activism, and international relations; and a list of contributors. Also a name index (p.173-230) and an analytical subject index (p.231-294) to the whole work. 'As the introductory essay ... suggests, this is a unique endeavor in many ways: it is also a fair achievement and deserves a place in all but the smallest reference collections' (*College & research libraries*, v.48(4), July 1987, p.358). '... includes some noteworthy flaws' (*Choice*, October 1987, p.292). *Class No: 341.67(031)*

Handbooks & Manuals
[2963]
Peace resource book: a comprehensive guide to issues, groups and literature, 1986, edited by E. Bernstein and others for The Institute for Defense and Disarmament Studies. Cambridge, Mass., Ballinger Publishing Company 1986. 414p. $14.95. ISBN: 0887300383.

Supersedes *American peace directory*, 1984.

Issued as a working tool for those who are active in efforts for arms control, disarmament, and world peace. Arranged in 3 parts: 1. Peace issues and strategies (a useful 27-page introduction to the world military system, to government arms control negotiations, and to peace movement alternatives); 2. Directory of US peace organizations, listing about 400 national peace groups and 100 peace-oriented educational programmes. Also 5,700 national and local groups, arranged by A-Z and by Zipcode; 3. A briefly annotated bibliography of some 800 books, pamphlets and documents published between 1980 and 1985, arranged by topic. An author index and a list of publishers and distributors. Favourable review in *Choice*, v.23(7), March 1986, p.1042. *Class No: 341.67(035)*

Dictionaries

Polyglot
[2964]
Disarmament terminology. Foreign Office of the Federal Republic of Germany. Berlin, de Gruyter, 1982. xii,645p. £34.60. (*Terminological series, v.1.*)

2459 numbered terms and phrases related to disarmament, as well as designations of relevant organizations, authorities, conferences, bilateral and multilateral agreements. Listed A-Z in English, each entry followed by equivalents in German, French, Spanish and Russian. Indexes in all 5 languages. (A Chinese index is also available, £21.95). *Class No: 341.67(038)=00*

English
[2965]
ELLIOT, J.M. *and* **ELLIOT, R.R. The Arms control, disarmament and military security dictionary.** Santa Barbara, CA, ABC-Clio, 1989. 349p. $44.50. ISBN: 0874364302.

268 numbered entries, designed to complement by definition and organization those terms noted in standard texts on the topics. Arrangement is A-Z within subject-matter chapters. Extensive cross-references. US slant. Includes 24p. of notes. *Class No: 341.67(038)=20*

Russian
[2966]
DMITRICHEV, T.F. English-Russian dictionary on disarmament: about 12,000 terms ... Anglo-Russkii terminologicheskii slovar po voprasam razoruzhaniia. Moskva, Russky Yazuk Publishers, 1987. 377p.

Terms and sub-terms arranged A-Z by the English language terms, followed by the Russian equivalents. 5 annexes: I. Multilateral and bilateral agreements and other documents concerning arms limitation and disarmament. II. Peace initiatives of the Soviet Union and other Socialist countries in the field of arms limitation - III. Conferences, meetings and other international forums for peace and disarmament - IV. International and national bodies - V. International and national non-governmental organizations, research institutes, etc. A Russian-English volume was published in 1990 (560p. £7.965). *Class No: 341.67(038)=82*

Reviews & Abstracts
[2967]
Peace research abstracts journal. Newbury Park, CA., Sage Publications (Dundas,. Ontario, Peace Research Institute until l994 issues), 1964-. v.1, no.1-. Bi-monthly. $193pa. ISSN: 00313599.

About 5000 abstracts pa of papers, articles and books dealing with questions of war and peace. Arranged in 10 subject sections, subdivided geographically as necessary. Author and subject indexes. *Class No: 341.67(048)*

Yearbooks & Directories
[2968]
MEYER, R.S. Peace organizations, past and present: a survey and directory. Jefferson, N.C., McFarland, 1988. 266p. $24.95. ISBN: 0899503403.

Profiles of 92 selected peace organizations, mainly US-based or international with US branches. Information included varies in length and content, but usually covers history, and political, philosophical or religious thrust, with examples of efforts and accomplishments. Final chapter has author's observations on the organizations and his thoughts on search for peace. 'Main value is in profiles of lesser-known groups' (*Choice*, v.26(7), March 1989,. p.1128). *Class No: 341.67(058)*

[2969]
—**TRZYNA, T.C.,** *ed.* International peace directory. Californian Institute of Public Affairs, in co-operation with the University of Peace, Ciudad Colon, Costa Rica., 1984. 63p. $19.95. (*Who's doing what series, no. 10. University of Peace information guides, 1.*) ISBN: 0912102721.

A directory of leading organizations working for peace. *c.*100 entries, A-Z by name. Entries vary in length from a column to a page. Highly selective. *Class No: 341.67(058)*

[2970]
Peace movements of the world: an international directory. Day, A.J., *ed.* Harlow, Essex, Longman Group; Phoenix, Ariz., Oryx, 1987. viii,398p. £48; $74.50. ISBN: 0582902681, UK; 0897744381, US.

Provides factual and objective data on over 1000 peace and anti-nuclear movements throughout the world. Arranged A-Z by country within broad geographical areas. Includes details of the origin, precise aims and activities of each

....(contd.)

movement, placed within the context of a description of prevailing issues in the particular country or continent. Index of movements, p.373-392; index of publications, p.392-398. '... useful directory of groups working for peace and disarmament' (*Choice,* v.25(8), April 1988, p.1224). '... by far this is the best source of information on peace organizations' (*Wilson library bulletin,* v.62(6), February 1988, p.102). *Class No:* 341.67(058)

[2971]

SIPRI: yearbook: world armaments and disarmament, 1993. Stockholm International Peace Research Institute. 24th ed. Oxford, Oxford University Press, for SIPRI, 1993. 600p. tables. £40; $75.00. ISBN: 0198291663. ISSN: 09530282.

1st issue (1970) covered 1968/69.

Up-to-date information on war, strategic and peace studies, and international relations. In 4 parts: 1. Weapons and technology - 2. Military expenditure, the arms trade and armed conflicts - 3. Developments in arms control - 4. Special features. Annexes: A. Major multilateral arms control agreements; B. Chronology. Abstracts. Index. *Class No:* 341.67(058)

[2972]

—SIPRI yearbooks: world armaments and disarmament, 1968-1979: cumulative index. London, Taylor & Francis Ltd., 1980. vii,90p. £25. ISBN: 0850661897. *Class No:* 341.67(058)

[2973]

The United Nations disarmament yearbook, 1992. V.17. New York, United Nations, 1992. 393p. $50. ISBN: 9211421934. ISSN: 02525607.

First published 1976. Annual.

Covers the deliberations, negotiations and actions related to documents occurring during the year concerned in the UN or under the auspices of the UNO and in committees on disarmament. *Class No:* 341.67(058)

[2974]

WOODHOUSE, T., *ed*. **The International peace directory.** Plymouth, Northgate House Publishers Ltd., 1988. 189p. £19.95; $52.50. ISBN: 0746303793.

Covers *c*.600 peace organizations. Arranged in 4 parts: Part 1.: Introduction; pt.2: The organizations (A-Z by country, subdivided A-Z by name of organization, giving name and address, telephone number; membership and affiliations; meetings, publications, library; objectives; functions; placements; grants; issues); pt.3: Peace literature (comprising directories and guides; bibliographies; guide to current periodicals); pt.4: Statistical and reference analyses of returns (organizations identified by issues covered, by membership type; organizations making awards, prizes, scholarships and fellowships; organizations accepting voluntary work, placements, internships). Index to organizations. *Class No:* 341.67(058)

[2975]

—KINCADE, W.H. *and* HAYNER, P.B., *eds*. The Access resource guide: an international directory of information on war, peace and security. Cambridge, Mass., Ballinger Publishing Company, 1988. xxxvii,238p. $14.95; £23.50. ISBN: 0887302602.

c.600 organizations are listed, giving address, telephone number, membership, publications, meetings, internships, objectives and issues of concern. *Class No:* 341.67(058)

Biographies

[2976]

JOSEPHSON, H., *ed*. **Biographical dictionary of modern peace leaders.** Westport, Conn., Greenwood Press, 1985. 1133p. $145. ISBN: 0313225656.

Surveys the field of peace activism from 1800 to 1980. 750 biographical essays by over 250 authors from 15 nations, focusing on individuals who viewed the issues of war and peace from various approaches. Each essay contains an introductory paragraph including information about birth, death, education and career, followed by a study of the subject's work, thought and activity as a peace leader, and concludes with a bibliography. Wide definition of peace leadership (includes Czar Nicholas II, Kwame Nkrumah, and Haile Sellassie), but ' ... provides a useful source for quick, general reference ...' (*RUSI journal,* v.133(1), Spring 1988, p.91). *Class No:* 341.67(092)

USA

Yearbooks & Directories

[2977]

FINE, M. *and* **STEVEN, P.M.,** *eds*. **American peace directory.** Institute for Defense & Disarmament Studies. 1st ed. Cambridge, Mass., Ballinger Publishing Company, 1984. ix,225p. ISBN: 0884109968.

In 2 parts, preceded by a 'Users'; guide'. Part 1 has alphabetical lists of peace groups in 5 sections; pt.2, 'Reference sections', has a list of groups by State and Zip-code, and US house of Representatives for 1984. Indexes (Peace forces - Structure - Constituency - Alphabetical). *Class No:* 341.67(73)(058)

Research Establishments

[2978]

UNESCO. Social and Human Sciences Documentation Centre *and* International Federation of Documentation's Social Science Information and Documentation Committee (FID/SD). **World directory of peace research and training institutions, 1991.** 7th ed. Paris, Unesco, 1991. xiii,[2],351p. ISBN: 9230027529.

First published 1973 as *International repertory of institutions for peace and conflict research.* Title changes slightly with each ed.

Includes institutions wholly or partly engaged in peace and conflict research and also institutions that support or promote such research in 66 countries. 7 sections: 1. Index of names and acronyms of institutions - 2. List of entries. International/regional institutions. National institutions - 3. Index of research subjects with indication of host country of the institution - 4. Geographical index - 5. Index by senior staff involved in peace activities - 6. Index of courses and subjects taught with indication of host country - 7. Index of institutions providing scholarships. *Class No:* 341.67:061:061.62

Constitutional Law

[2979]
DERBYSHIRE, J.D. *and* DERBYSHIRE, I. **Political systems of the world.** London, Chambers, 1989. xii,932p. tables, maps. £40 ISBN: 0550210083.

A guide to the political philosophies, systems and structures of every country of the world. In 3 parts: 1. The comparative approach; 2. Political systems of the world's nation-states (p.136-762); 3. Towards one world. Appended: Data sources. Detailed analytical index (p.895-904). 165 notes on geographical regions plus 55 semi-sovereign states, colonies and dependencies. A 'political system' implies operation of a statistical office, a legislative body, and a national bank. *Class No:* 342

Dictionaries

[2980]
CHANDLER, R., *and others*. **Constitutional law dictionary.** Santa Barbara, ABC-Clio, 1985-87. 2v. (1244p.). v.1: $47.50; £35.25. v.2: $50; £41.50. (*Clio dictionaries in political science, 8 & 13*.) ISBN: 0874360315, v.1; 087436440x, v.2.

V.1 *Individual rights;* v.2. *Governmental powers.* V.1 focuses on concepts of constitutionalism, words and phrases common to American constitutional law, and leading case decisions by the United States Supreme Court. V.2 summarizes important cases in US legal history. Cross-references. Index. *Class No:* 342(038)

Worldwide

Government State Papers

[2981]
BLAUSTEIN, A.P. *and* FLANZ, G.H. **Constitutions of the countries of the world.** Dobbs Ferry, N.Y., Oceana, 1971-. 20 binders. Loose-leaf. $1500 for 20v. + supplement binder. ISBN: 0379004674.

Each binder has full text (translated, as necessary) of *c.*10 constitutions. Each text is accompanied by a concise chronology of events leading up to its adoption and a brief annotated bibliography for further reference. *Class No:* 342(100)(093.200)

[2982]
—BLAUSTEIN, A.P. *and* BLAUSTEIN, E.B. Constitutions of dependencies and special sovereignties. Dobbs Ferry, N.Y., Oceana, 1975-76. 7 binders, and yearly supplements. $625. ISBN: 0379002787.

Covers British, French and American dependencies. *Class No:* 342(100)(093.200)

Europe—Western

[2983]
WEATHERILL, S. *and* BEAUMONT, P. **EC law:** the essential guide to the legal working of the European Community. London, Penguin Books, 1993. 846p. £20. ISBN: 0140145070.

An in-depth analysis of the constitutional law of the law and legislation of EC countries. *Class No:* 342(400)

USA

Bibliographies

[2984]
KURLAND, P. B. *and* LERNER, R., *eds*. **The Founders' constitution.** Chicago, University of Chicago Press, 1988. 5v.(3250p.). $300. ISBN: 0226463877.

Contains documents, letters, broadsides, etc., bearing on the creation of the United States Constitution, and its first 12 amendments from the 17th-century to the first third of the 19th-century. V.1. deals with philosophical and theoretical principles; v.2 - 4 proceed from the Preamble through the Articles; v.5. deals with Amendments I-XII. *Class No:* 342(73)(01)

[2985]
McCARRICK, E.M., *ed*. **US constitution:** a guide to information sources. Detroit, Mich., Gale Research Co., 1980. x,390p. $65; £14.50. (*American government and history information guide series, 4*.) ISBN: 0810302134, US; 0874362040, UK.

Annotated bibliography in chapter form. Chapters 1-5 cover general sources; background; framing, etc,; general interpretative works; basic principles. Chapters 6-12 deal with specific articles of and amendments to the US constitution. *Class No:* 342(73)(01)

[2986]
—MEYERS, A. 'Reference sources on the US Constitution.' In *Reference books bulletin*, 1986/1987, p.18-19.

Includes 20 annotated entries for encyclopedias and dictionaries, bibliographies, sources, Supreme Court decisions, etc. *Class No:* 342(73)(01)

Encyclopaedias

[2987]
LEVY, L.W., *and others*. **Encyclopedia of the American Constitution.** New York, Macmillan Publishing Company; London, Collier-Macmillan, 1987. 4v.(1500p.). $400. the set. Supplement 1 (1992. 616p. $90). ISBN: 0029186102.

Over 2200 articles by nearly 300 scholarly contributors (historians, lawyers and political scientists) on all aspects of the American Constitution. Entries vary in length from a paragraph to several pages (*e.g.* 'Constitutional interpretation': 14¼ cols., 15 references; 'Watergate and the Constitution': 2 cols., 3 references; 'Humphrey, Hubert H. (1911-1978)': 1 col., 1 reference; 'Johnson, Lyndon B. (1908-1973)': over 60 cols., 4 references). Fully cross-referenced. Bibliographies appended to many articles. V.1 has a preface, a list of articles and a list of contributors preceding the encyclopedia entries. The final volume has a glossary and 3 indexes (general, names, and cases). 'This is certainly one of the most innovative, ambitious, and useful of the scholarly publications celebrating the bicentennial of the US Constitution' (*Library journal*, v.111(20), December 1986, p.96). *Class No:* 342(73)(031)

[2988]
PLANO, J.C. *and* GREENBERG, M. **The American political dictionary.** 8th ed. Fort Worth, Holt, Rinehart Winston Inc., 1989. x,608p. ISBN: 0030028442.

First published 1962.

Entries A-Z within 14 chapters: 1. Political ideas - 2. United States constitution and the federal union - 3. Parties, politics, pressure groups, and elections - 4. The legislative process: Congress and the state legislatures - 5. The

....(contd.)

Executive Office and powers - 6. Public administration: organization and personnel - 7. The judicial process: courts and law enforcement - 8. Civil liberties, civil rights, immigration and citizenship - 9. Finance and taxation - 10. Business and labor - 11. Agriculture, energy and environment - 12. Health, education and welfare - 13. Foreign policy and national defense - 14. State and local government. About 1000 entries in all (definition; significance to overall operations, theories and problems of American government; cross-references). The Constitution of the United States. Index, p.577-608. A standard encyclopedic dictionary. *Class No:* 342(73)(031)

[2989]

—SMITH, E.C. *and* ZURCHER, A.J. Dictionary of American politics. 2nd ed. New York, Baines & Noble, 1968. vii, [1]. 434p. illus., maps. $26.50. ISBN: 0064808033.

First published 1888.

*c.*4500 entries, giving definitions, categories, usage, plus etymology (where relevant). Appendices include text of American constitution, statistical data on the 50 states (with their nicknames), and a list of presidents.

Class No: 342(73)(031)

Handbooks & Manuals

[2990]

LEES, J.D. **The Political system of the United States.** 3rd. London, Faber & Faber, 1983. 406p. £6.95. ISBN: 057118068x.

First published 1969.

12 chapters (*e.g.* 3. The nature of American federalism; 8. The Congress: legislative representation and action; 12. The political system and social change). Appendices: A. The Consititution; B. Presidents of the United States; C. Election results, 1944-80; D. Notes on further reading (by chapters, with general introduction, p.386-392). Analytical index, p.393-406. 'An attempt to provide an introduction to American politics which is as useful to students of the United States as to students of politics' (*Acknowledgements* in the 2nd ed.). *Class No:* 342(73)(035)

Parliaments

Handbooks & Manuals

[2991]

Parliaments of the world: a comparative reference compendium, prepared by the Inter-Parliamentary Union. 2nd ed. Aldershot, Hants, Gower Publishing Company Ltd; New York, Facts on File, 1986. 2v. (1440p). tables. £135. ISBN: 0566053810, (UK); 0810611869, (US).

First published in 1976 by Macmillan Press.

A comparative study of the structure and operation of parliaments throughout the world. An introduction is followed by chapters on The parliaments of the world - Parliament and its membership - Parliamentary procedure - Proceedings and debates - Parliamentary groupings - Parliamentary committees - Parliament and its means of information - Parliament and the media - Legislation - The budget - Parliament and the Government - Parliament and emergency - Constitutionality of laws - Dissolution of Parliament - Judicial and other functions of Parliament. Index. ' ... a potpourri of useful and otherwise difficult-to-

....(contd.)

locate information about this branch of government in 83 countries ...' (*Reference books bulletin*, 1986/7, p.68). *Class No:* 342.53(035)

[2992]

PAXTON, J., *ed*. **World legislatures.** London, Macmillan, 1974. xiii,169p. £10. ISBN: 0333148495.

Concise data on the formal procedures and constitutions of the world. A-Z (legislative authority; frequency of election; initiation of bills; referenda; etc.). Covers states (*e.g.* USA, Australia), provinces (*e.g.* Canada), Länder (*e.g.* West Germany) and republics (*e.g.* USSR). Selected bibliography, p.159-64; glossary, p.165-9. *Class No:* 342.53(035)

Europe—Western

[2993]

COCKS, B. **The European Parliament:** structure, procedure & practice. London, HMSO, 1973. [xi],336p.

Parts : 1. Structure of the European Parliament - 2. The external relations of the Communities - 3. Procedure of the European Parliament (chapters 9-19). Appendices A-D (A. Treaty establishing the E.E.C. (80p.)) ... C. Principal debates, reports and resolutions of the Parliament, 1958-1972 - D. Presidents of the Parliament). Index, p.321-36. 'Designed to help Members of the United Parliament' (*Preface*). The author is Clerk of the House of Commons. 'An indispensable guide' (*International affairs*, v.49,no.3, July 1973, p.528). *Class No:* 342.53(400)

[2994]

European handbook of organisations. London, Whurr Publications, 1992. £29.95. ISBN: 1870332296.

Each entry starts with mention of a treaty or convention that established the organization, followed by clear sections on purpose, members countries, structure and activities. Brief chronology, up to the Maastricht Treaty. Country-by-country tabulation of who belongs to what. List of acronyms. Similar to Vachers (*qv*) but Whurr has better descriptions of what bodies do, according to *Refer*, v.9(2), Spring 1993, p.27. *Class No:* 342.53(400)

[2995]

The Times guide to the European Parliament, June 1989. Wood,, A., *ed*. 3rd ed. London, Times Books, 1989. 287p. £25. ISBN: 0723002584.

First published 1979.

Detailed results of the 1989 direct elections to the European Parliament held in the 12 member states of the European Community. Contains: Leaders of the political groups - Members elected to the European Parliament - Women in the European Parliamennt - Member state political parties - European Parliament committee membership - Election campaigns - Review of the European Parliament, 1984-89 ... Results of the voting ... The European Parliament (Illustrated biographies of MEPs - Manifesto summary - The European Commission - Presidents of the European Parliament. *Class No:* 342.53(400)

[2996]

Vacher's European companion: a diplomatic, political and commercial reference book. Berkhampstead, Herts., Vacher's Publications, 1972-. no.1-. Quarterly. £35.50pa. ISSN: 09580336.

A directory. Contents: The European Communities (The Commission, the European Parliament, the Court of Justice,

....(contd.)

Directorates General); other international organizations; National sections; European Documentation Centres and Deposit Libraries. Glossary of abbreviations. No index. *Class No:* 342.53(400)

Great Britain

[2997]
GREAT BRITAIN. House of Commons. The Parliamentary debates. Fifth series. House of Commons: official report 1909-. London, HMSO, 1909-.

Originally published as a private venture. (Cobbett's *Parliamentary History of England from ... 1066 to 12th August 1803.* London, Hansard, 1806-20. 36v., and its continuations). It became an official report in 1909: substantially verbatim.

Issued daily during the session; cumulated in bound volumes, with general detailed index (speakers and topics) to each session. A.J.P.Taylor (*English History, 1914-1945,* p.606) notes two limitations to Hansard. 'The reporters do not include casual cries, unless these contributed to the progress of the debate; hence, for instance, they omitted Amery's famous call to Greenwood on 2 September 1939. Nor was any record kept of the secret sessions, held in both World Wars - unlike the French Chamber, which kept a secret record, published later.' Also available on CD-ROM. *Class No:* 342.53(410)

[2998]
GREAT BRITAIN. House of Lords. The Parliamentary debates. Fifth series. House of Lords: official report, 1909-. London HMSO. 1909-.

Issued daily during the session; cumulated and indexed similarly to the House of Commons *Debates.* Also available on CD-ROM. *Class No:* 342.53(410)

[2999]
—GREAT BRITAIN. House of Lords. Journals, 1509-. London, HMSO.

The *Journals* of the House of Lords, issued sessionally, are a record of what was done in the House of Lords, not what was said. *Class No:* 342.53(410)

[3000]
Manual of procedure in the public business: laid on the table by Mr. Speaker for the use of Members. House of Commons. 13th ed. London, HMSO, 1984. xix, 287 p. £14.95. ISBN: 0108360156.

Contents of chapters: 1. Meetings of Parliament - 2. Election and admission of Members - 3. The Speaker and Chairmen of Committees - 4. Officers and Departments of the House - 5. Sittings of the House and arrangement of business - 6. Matters taken ... - 7. General rules of procedure - 8. Public bills - 9. Committees - 10. Financial business - 11. Relations between the two Houses - 12. Communications between the Crown and the House - 13. Witnesses ... - 14. Accounts and papers - 15. Records of the House - 16. Miscellaneous - 17. Private bills - 18. Special procedure orders - 19. Procedure under the Parliament Acts of 1911 and 1949 - 20. European legislation and international assemblies. *Class No:* 342.53(410)

[3001]
RADICE, L., *and others.* **Member of Parliament:** the job of the backbencher. London, Macmillan, 1990. 208p. £40. ISBN: 0333491211.

Chapters: The role of the Honourable Member - Getting in - The job in Parliament - A Parliamentary day - Pay and conditions - The job outside the House - Backbench views of the job - A month in the life of four backbenchers - Changes. Bibliography. Index. *Class No:* 342.53(410)

[3002]
The Times guide to the House of Commons, June 1992. Wood, A., *ed.* London, Times Books, 1992. 368p. illus. £25. ISBN: 0723004978.

First published in 1880.

Results of the 1987 general election, arranged under constituencies, A-Z. Who's who and portraits of winning candidates; brief notes on others. Data: constituency; number of electorate, 1983, 1987; candidates and election results, 1983, 1987. Election manifestos, p.288-350. Survey of the voting. Index of candidates. *Class No:* 342.53(410)

Bibliographies

[3003]
FORD, P. *and* **FORD, G. A Guide to Parliamentary Papers;** What they are, how to find them, how to use them. 3rd ed. Shannon, Irish University Press, 1972. 87p. £12.50. (*Southampton University Studies in Parliamentary Papers.*) ISBN: 0716514184.

First published 1955.

'Our main aim is to familiarise the researcher with the different kinds of papers, to explain the apparatus for finding them and to indicate the most profitable way of extracting information from them' (*Preface to the third edition*). Bibliographical aids, p.71-80; index, p.81-85. A valuable introduction to a complex subject. *Class No:* 342.53(410)(01)

[3004]
GOEHLERT, R.U. *and* **FENTON, S.M. The Parliament of Great Britain:** a bibliography. Lexington, Mass., Lexington Books, 1983. 240p. $30. (*Lexington Books special series on libraries and librarianship.*) ISBN: 0669057002.

Includes works dealing with the history, development and legislative processes of the Parliament, coverage being limited to works in English published in the last 100 years, monographs, essays in collections, journal articles, and dissertations and theses. Not evaluative, but introduction suggests basic introductory works. Author and subject indexes. *Choice* (v.20(9), May 1983, p.1264) suggests it could be used in conjunction with Wilding & Laundy's *An encyclopaedia of Parliament* (*q.v.*). *Class No:* 342.53(410)(01)

[3005]
GREAT BRITAIN. House of Commons. A Bibliography of Parliamentary debates of Great Britain. London, HMSO, 1956. 62p. (*House of Commons Library document no.2.*)

A bibliography of debates of both Houses of Parliament, including not only the standard sets of debates, both official and unofficial, but also information from diaries, etc. 94 numbered items. Helpful evaluative notes; a chronological chart of debates, diaries and proceedings, 1066-1953, assists quick reference. Debates in the Irish House of Commons are covered in an appendix. *Class No:* 342.53(410)(01)

[3006]

JONES, D.L. Debates and proceedings of the British Parliaments: a guide to printed sources. London, HMSO., 1986. vi,152p. £9.10. (*House of Commons library document, no.16.*) ISBN: 0108506150.

Lists, with suitable annotations, the printed sources of the proceedings (the record of what is done) and for the debates (the record of what is said) of the Parliaments held in the United Kingdom. The work is divided into sections based on the different Parliaments: the Parliaments at Westminster, the Irish Parliament, Parliamentary institutions in Northern Ireland, and the Scottish Parliament. Entries are arranged chronologically within each section by the earliest date of the work. Index referring to the principal elements of the text, p.145-152. *Class No: 342.53(410)(01)*

[3007]

Subject catalogue of the House of Commons Parliamentary papers, 1801-1900. Cockton, P., *comp.* Cambridge; Alexandria, VA., Chadwyck-Healey, 1988. 5v.(4500p.). $1500; £900. ISBN: 0859641333.

The papers are divided into 19 subject areas (*e.g.* Central government and administration; National finance and financial institutions; Population and demography;; Statistics; Agriculture and rural society; Industry and industrial society), each subject area being subdivided (Central government and administration has 4 sections). Then arranged according to traditional classification of Bills, Reports of select committees, Reports of commissions, Accounts and papers, arranged A-Z by descriptors, an index of descriptors is at the end of v.5. '... careful and scholarly approaches ... essential tool for study of 19c. Britain' (*Parliamentary affairs,* v.42(1), January 1989, p.134). *Class No: 342.53(410)(01)*

Handbooks & Manuals

[3008]

Erskine May's Treatise on the law, privileges, proceedings and usage of Parliament. Boulton, C., *ed.* 21st ed. London, Butterworths, 1989. xliv,1079p. ISBN: 0406114714.

First published 1844; 18th ed. 1971.

Parts: 1. Constitution, powers and privileges of Parliament (chapters 1-11) - 2. Proceedings in Parliament: public business (12-34) - 3. Proceedings in Parliament: private business. Table of abbreviations (references to sources), p.xxxix-xliv. Detailed table of contents. Appendix: House of Commons Standing Orders relative to public business. Detailed, analytical index, p.1025-1079. 'Erskine May' is not official; next to the *Journals* of both Houses, it is accepted as the great secondary authority. For the parliamentary and constitutional specialist; whereas *Abraham and Hawtrey's Parliamentary dictionary* (3rd ed., by S.C. Hawtry and H.M. Barclay. London, Butterworth, 1970. viii,248p.) is for the general political audience (*T.L.S.* no.3625, 20 August 1971, p.985).

For the historical development of parliamentary procedure: Campion, G.F.M., 1st baron Campion. *An introduction to the procedure of the House of Commons* (2nd ed. London, Macmillan, 1950. 348p.); and, complementary, from the historical viewpoint, to Erskine May, - Redlich, J. *The procedure of the House of Commons: a study of its history and present form* (London, Constable, 1908. 3v.). *Class No: 342.53(410)(035)*

[3009]

MENHENNET, D. The Journal of the House of Commons: a bibliographical and historical guide. London, HMSO, 1971. viii,96p. facsims. (*House of Commons Library document no.7.*)

1. Introduction - 2. The official Record of Proceedings - 3. Origins: the Commons manuscript *Journal,* 1547 to 1800 - 4. The printing of the *Journal* - 5. The indexing of the *Journal* - 6. Contents and historical value of the Commons *Journal.* 3 appendices (1. Availability of the present Commons *Journal* volumes and of the general indexes, p.52-7; 25 locations). Analytical index. Bibliography, p.92-94. The House of Commons *Journals,* published each session, are a record of what was done in the House of Commons, not what was said. They also record all papers laid before the House. The *Journals* constitute the authentic record of the proceedings of the House and primary authority on parliamentary procedure. House of Commons' *Standing Committee debates* is issued daily when Committees meet; - a verbatim report of proceedings in Standing Committee published by HMSO since 1919. *Class No: 342.53(410)(035)*

Dictionaries

[3010]

HAWTREY, S.C. *and* **BARCLAY, H.M. Abraham and Hawtrey's parliamentary dictionary.** 3rd ed. London, Butterworth, 1970. viii, 248p.

First published 1956 as *A Parliamentary dictionary*, by L. A. Abraham and S. C. Hawtrey.

An A-Z guide to expressions in common usage in the Houses of Parliament with explanation and comment. Understood to refer to House of Commons unless the context obviously requires otherwise. Some footnotes. Cross-references. Detailed, analytical index, p.241-8. *Class No: 342.53(410)(038)*

Periodicals

[3011]

The House magazine. London, Parliamentary Communications, Ltd., 1976-. v.1,no.1-. Weekly. £115pa.

The weekly journal of the House of Commons, with sections on the Commons diary; The week; The week in Washington; 'Committee corridors', features (*e.g.* the issue for 11 June 1990 includes several items on prisons). 'Parliamentary and European business' is printed on blue-tinted paper. *Class No: 342.53(410)(051)*

Yearbooks & Directories

[3012]

The Almanac of British politics. 4th ed. London, Routledge, 1991. 736p. £60. ISBN: 0415064341.

Attempts to describe the political geography or electoral anatomy of the United Kingdom, individual constituency profiles assessing what influences the various parts of the country to vote as they do. Preliminary matter precedes the geographical arrangement - Greater London; Metropolitan counties, A-Z; non-metropolitan counties, A-Z; Scotland, Wales, Northern Ireland. *Class No: 342.53(410)(058)*

Published Series

20th Century

[3013]
RODGER, F. Serial publications in the British Parliamentary Papers, 1900-1968. London, Library Association, 1971. xix, 146p. £7.50. ISBN: 0838900860.

1273 entries in all, aiming 'to list by issuing agency all serials which have appeared in the House of Commons Sessional Papers at any time during the present century and to indicate briefly their publishing history: earliest and latest dates of issue, relationship to other publications and details of non-parliamentary publications when this occurs' (*Introduction*). Great Britain, excluding Ireland: p.1-119 (1207 items); Ireland: p.113-8. Detailed analytical index of subjects , bodies, areas/countries. 'A guide of inestimable value to the annual reports, accounts, statistics and other serial publications of government departments which are embodied in this century's sessional papers of the House of Commons' (*Library Association record*, v.74(3), March 1972, p.62). *Class No:* 342.53(410)(082.1)"19"

Tables & Data Books

[3014]
CREWE, I. *and* **FOX, A. British Parliamentary constituencies:** a statistical compendium. London, Faber and Faber, 1984. 397p. tables, maps. £25. ISBN: 0571132367.

Up-to-date electoral, political and socio-economic information on each of the 650 constituencies, in the 1983 election results. *Class No:* 342.53(410)(083)

Histories

[3015]
BUTT, R. A History of Parliament. V.1: The Middle ages. London, Constable, 1989. xxiii,662p. 22 illus (1 col). £30. ISBN: 0094706301.

'... describes growth of medieval Parliament by placing it in a continuous narrative of political history ...' (*Preface*, p.xv). Footnotes. Select bibliography, p.635-8. Analytical index, p.639-62. *Class No:* 342.53(410)(091)

[3016]
HISTORY OF PARLIAMENT TRUST. The History of Parliament. London, HMSO, 1964-. Secker & Warburg, 1983-. (Alan Sutton Publishing from l991).

It is planned to cover the Westminster Parliament from 1264 to the present day. The introductory surveys (each with its index) and especially the biographies are particularly valuable. The latter are signed, have quotations, and give sources. Published so far:- The House of Commons, 1715-1754, by Romney Sedgwick (2v. 1970. £50); The House of Commons, 1754-1970, by Sir Lewis Namier and John Brook (3v. 1964. £80); The House of Commons, 1660-90, by B.D. Henning (1983, 3v. £120. ISBN 0436192748); The House of Commons, 1509-1558, by S.T. Bindoff (1983. 3v. ISBN 0436042827); The House of Commons, 1558-1603, by P.W. Hasler (1982. 3v. £95. ISBN 0118875019); The House of Commons, 1790-1820, by R.G. Thorne (1986. 5v. £225): The House of Commons, 1386-1421, by J.S. Roskill and others(1993. 4v. 276p. ISBN 086299943x).
Class No: 342.53(410)(091)

[3017]
WEDGEWOOD, J.C. History of Parliament, 1439-1509. London, HMSO, 1936-38. 2v.

V.1: Biographies of members of the Commons House, 1439-1509; v.2: Register of the ministers and of the members of both Houses, 1439-1509.
Class No: 342.53(410)(091)

Biographies

[3018]
STENTON, M., *ed*. Who's who of British Members of Parliament: a biographical dictionary of the House of Commons, based on annual volumes of *Dod's parliamentary companion*, and other sources. Brighton, Sussex, Harvester Press, 1976-1981. 4v each vol. ISBN: 0855273151, v.2; 0855273259, v.3; 0855273356, v.4.

Contents: V.1: 1832-1885; v.2: 1886-1918; v.3: 1919-1945; v.4: 1945-1979. *Dod's parliamentary companion* (*q.v.*) began publication in 1832. This biographical dictionary adds more career data, including date of death. Since earlier volumes of *Dod's* are not readily available, this work has its place. 'However, Stenton's efforts at revision and updating are disappointingly sparse' (*Library journal*, 1 May 1977, p.1005). *Class No:* 342.53(410)(092)

[3019]
—Dod's Parliamentary companion. 161st year. Hurst Green, East Sussex, Dod's Parliamentary Companion, 1993. xlvii,1102p. illus. ISBN: 0905702204. ISSN: 00707007.

First published 1832.

Sections: The Royal Family - Biographies of Peers (A-Z, p.l-365) - composition of the House of Lords - Biographies of Peers of Ireland who are not Peers of Parliament - Precedence - Addressing letters - Biographies of Members of the House of Commons (A-Z, p.427-653) - Constituencies and polling, etc. - The Ministerial responsibilities - Government and public offices. Index.
Class No: 342.53(410)(035)

[3020]
—Vacher's parliamentary companion: a reference book for Parliament, national organisations and public offices. Berkhamstead, Herts., Vacher's Publications, 1831-. Quarterly. £23. ISSN: 09580328.

Provides more concise information more frequently than the above. A-Z list of members of both Houses, with members' town addresses, constituencies, etc. Also available on microform from UMI. *Class No:* 342.53(410)(092)

[3021]
—ZETTER, L. Vachers biographical guide, 1990. London, A.S.Kerswill, 1990. 370p. £25.

Includes sections on members of both Houses of Parliament and British members of the European Parliament. Each entry lists name, political allegiance, date of birth, marital status, education, previous occupation(s), political career, and political and personal interests.
Class No: 342.53(410)(092)

Official Records

[3022]
BOND, M.F. Guide to the records of Parliament. London, HMSO, 1971. x,352p. illus.

'This guide describes the complete range of records preserved within the Palace of Westminster: the records of

....(contd.)

both Houses of Parliament; all documents which have been presented to the two Houses or purchased by them; - and the papers which have accumulated in the various Parliamentary and non-Parliamentary offices of the Palace' (*Preface*). 6 parts; 1. Records of the House of Lords (p.13-194) - 2. Records of the House of Commons of Westminster. Appendices: 1. List of Clerks of the Parliaments; 2. List of Clerks of the House of Commons. Table of Acts cited. Detailed, analytical index, p.313-52. A comprehensive guide; well produced. *Class No:* 342.53(410)(093.2)

[3023]
POLDEN, P. Guide to the records of the Lord Chancellor's Department. Brunel: the University of West London. London, HMSO, 1988. xxx,376p. £35. ISBN: 0113800150.

21 chapters arranged in 4 main sections: 1. The Lord Chancellor and his office - 2. The administration of justice - 3. Reforms in the law - 4. Church and State. Introductions to each section; short prefaces to chapters and notes after them. 4 appendices: 1. The Lord Chancellors and their staff, 1872-1951 - 2. Reports of committees - 3. Statutes and bills - 4. Decided cases. Bibliographies of books, p.371-374, and articles and lectures, p.374-376. No index. A comprehensive and accessible guide to the records.
Class No: 342.53(410)(093.2)

17th Century

[3024]
HAYTON, D. *and* **JONES, C.,** *eds.* **A Register of Parliamentary lists, 1660-1761.** Leicester, University of Leicester, History Dept., 1979. xxvi,168p. illus., plan. Mimeographed.

6 contributors. Sections: The House of Lords - The House of Commons - The Parliament of Ireland - The Parliament of Scotland, Valuable commentary. 'Principal abbreviations used' (*i.e.*, sources), p.xv-xviii. 5 ground-plans.
Class No: 342.53(410)"16"

[3025]
KEELER, M.F. The Long Parliament, 1640-1641: a bibliographical study of its members. Philadelphia, Pa., American Philosophical Society, 1956. ix,410p.

In three parts: 1. Portrait of a Parliament - 2. Elections and returns - 3. Biographical directory of the Parliament Men (p.81-404; *c.*650 entries, A-Z). Profuse footnotes (*c.*20 per page). Index to part 1. *Class No:* 342.53(410)"16"

18th Century

[3026]
Hansard's catalogue and breviate of Parliamentary Papers, 1696-1834. Ford, P. *and* Ford, G. Oxford, Blackwell, 1953. 220p.

Reprinted in facsimile.

A classified list, together with a breviate of the Papers arranged under subject headings. This reprint includes a select list of House of Lords Papers not in Hansard's *Breviate*. There is a very full index to the papers, and a helpful introduction. *Class No:* 342.53(410)"17"

[3027]
JUDD, G.P. Members of Parliament, 1734-1832. New Haven, CT, Yale University Press; London, Oxford University Press, 1955. Reprinted 1972 by Shoestring. vii,389p. $43.50 ISBN: 0208012303.

Attempts to show the relationship between the British ruling class 'a cohesive group ... toughly knit' and the House of Commons, 1734-1832 by a detailed statistical analysis of 5034 Members. 10 chapters (*e.g.* 4. The age of members - 5. Length of service - 6. Social status and family background, etc.), followed by 'Check list of members (p.95-385). This list consists of 5034 numbered entries (full name; dates of birth and death; position(s) held; parliamentary career (seat(s) and date(s)); sources (*e.g.* D.N.B., G.E.C. [Cokayne], *Alumni Oxon.*), with many cross-references. analytical index to chapters 1-10.
Class No: 342.53(410)"17"

[3028]
LAMBERT, S., *ed.* **Sessional Papers of the eighteenth century: George I and II.** Wilmington, Del., Scholarly Resources Inc., 1975. 20v. diagrs., graphs, charts, maps.

Claims to provide a complete collection of the Parliamentary Papers of the period, covering trade, taxation, colonies, crime, religion and politics under the early Hanoverians. 'Indispensable' (*Choice*, v.13(12), February 1977, p.1570). *Class No:* 342.53(410)"17"

[3029]
—**LAMBERT, S.,** *ed.* Sessional Papers of the eighteenth century: George III. Wilmington, Del. Scholarly Resources Inc. 1975. 127v. *Class No:* 342.53(410)"17"

19th Century

[3030]
FORD, P. *and* **FORD, G. Select list of British Parliamentary Papers, 1833-1899.** Rev. ed. Shannon, Irish University Press, 1970. xxii,166p. £17.50. ISBN: 0716505746.

First published 1953.

A classified list of reports and other material 'issued by commissions or similar bodies of investigation into economic, social and constitutional questions, and matters of law and administration'. Valuable subject index, over 4500 papers listed; references are to the House of Commons' volume arrangement. *Class No:* 342.53(410)"18"

20th Century

[3031]
FORD, P. *and* **FORD, G. A Breviate of Parliamentary Papers, 1900-1916:** the foundation of the Welfare State. Oxford, Blackwell, 1957 (Reprinted Shannon, Irish University Press, 1969). xlix,470p. £27.50. ISBN: 0716505754. *Class No:* 342.53(410)"19"

[3032]
—**FORD, P.** *and* **FORD, G. A Breviate of Parliamentary Papers, 1917-1939.** Oxford, Blackwell, 1951 (Reprinted Shannon, Irish University Press, 1969). [1],xlviii,571p. £27.50. ISBN: 0716505762. *Class No:* 342.53(410)"19"

[3033]

—FORD, P. *and* FORD, G. A Breviate of Parliamentary Papers, 1940-1954: War and reconstruction. Oxford, Blackwell, 1961. [1],515p.

Each volume consists of summaries of selected Parliamentary Papers, - 'the reports of committees, royal commissions and similar bodies in matters which have been, or might have been, the subject of legislation or have dealt with public policy' (*Introduction*, 1917-1939 vol.). The 1940-1954 vol. is arranged in 16 sections (17 in the 1900-1916 vol., which includes 'Irish Papers'): 1. Machinery of government - 2. National finance - 3. Monetary and economic policy, financial institutions- 4. Agriculture and food supply - 5. Trade and industry - 6. Coal, fuel, power, water - 7. Transport - 8A. Post Office, telegraphy - 8B. Broadcasting, the press - 9. Inventions, patents, copyright - 10. Labour - 11. Social security - 12. Health - 13A. Housing - 13B. Town and country planning - 14. Education - 15A. Population - 15B. Social problems - 16. Legal administration, police, law. *Class No:* 342.53(410)"19"

[3034]

Ford list of British Parliamentary papers, 1974-1983, together with specialist commentaries. Marshallsay, D. Cambridge, Chadwick-Healey, 1989. xlviii,694p. £70. (*(Southampton University studies in Parliamentary papers).*)

Includes reports and published evidence of all types of committee, commission, working party and other enquiry bodies, plus White and Green Papers. Selected reports of the Foreign Affairs Committee are listed for the first time. Commentaries, editor's note, abbreviations, and subject classification of papers precedes. Appendices: 1. Select list of annual reports; 2. Select list of research series. Alphabetical subject/title index, p.655-83. Chairmen and author index, p.684-94. *Class No:* 342.53(410)"19"

Scotland

[3035]

YOUNG, M.D., *ed.* **The Parliaments of Scotland.** Edinburgh, Scottish Academic Press, 1992-93. 2v. illus. £35 each vol. ISBN: 0707307058.

Biographies of the burgh and shire commissioners of Scotland, 1357-1707 (the Treaty of Union). V.1:A-K; v.2:L-Z. *Class No:* 342.53(411)

Ireland

[3036]

ENGLEFIELD, D. **Printed records of the Parliament of Ireland, 1613-1800:** a survey and bibliographical guide. London, Lemon Tree Press, 1978. 52p.
Class No: 342.53(415)

Northern Ireland

[3037]

MALTBY, A. **The Government of Northern Ireland, 1922-72:** a catalogue and breviate of Parliamentary Papers. Dublin, Irish University Press, 1974. xxii,235p. £19.50; $35. ISBN: 0716521512.

16 classes: 1. Machinery of government - 2. National finance ... 16. Legal administration, police, the law. Appendix 1: Westminster reports concerning Northern

.... (contd.)

Ireland. 2: Select list of annual and other recurring reports. Index of chairmen and authors; title index.
Class No: 342.53(416)

Eire

[3038]

EIRE. Dail Eireann. **Diosbóireachtai pairliminte/ Parliamentary debates:** tuairsig oifigiúil/official report, 9th September 1922-. Dublin, Stationery Office, 1922-. v.1-.

Daily parts, followed by bound volumes. Each volume is indexed. *Class No:* 342.53(417)

19th Century

[3039]

MALTBY, A. *and* MALTBY, J. **Ireland in the nineteenth-century:** a breviate of offical publications. Oxford, Pergamon Press, 1979. 269p. £37. ISBN: 008023688x.

Lists and digests over 600 nineteenth-century reports relating to Ireland, under broad subject headings. 'Combines scholarship and liveliness' (*Library review*, v.29, Winter 1980, p.51). *Class No:* 342.53(417)"18"

20th Century

[3040]

FORD, P. *and* FORD, G. **A Select list of reports of enquiries of the Irish Dáil and Senate, 1922-1972.** Dublin, Irish University Press, 1974. 64p. v £12.50. (*Southampton University studies in Parliamentary Papers.*) ISBN: 0716522365.

In 17 classes (1. Machinery of government - 2. National finance ... 17. Legal administration, police, law). Analytical subject index. Aims 'to help students to follow the development of thought in Eire's main lines of domestic policy since the foundation of the State' (*Scope and arrangement*). *Class No:* 342.53(417)"19"

Commonwealth

Encyclopaedias

[3041]

WILDING, N. *and* LAUNDY, P. **An Encyclopaedia of Parliament.** Completely rev. 4th ed. London, Cassell, 1971. ix,931p.

First published 1958.

'Abjuration Act' ... 'Zinoviev letter'. Covers British and Commonwealth Parliaments, giving definitions of terms (*e.g.* 'Closure'), background history (*e.g.* 'Elizabeth I (1533-1603) and Parliament'), and notes on procedure, privileges and customs of Parliament. Lengthier articles have brief bibliographies, for further reading. 34 appendices (2. Salaries of Ministers, Speakers and Members ... 34. Bibliography, p.892-931 with subdivisions). Well produced. Both authors were members of the Federal and Southern Rhodesian Parliaments. The standard work.
Class No: 342.53(41-44)(031)

France

[3042]

PICKLES, D. The Government and politics of France.
London, Methuen, 1972-73. 2v.(xii,453p.;xii,500p.).
V.1: *Institutions and parties;* 2: *Politics.* V.1 has 11
chapters on institutions, and parties and interest groups.
Appendix 2: The French Constitution of 4 October 1958.
Notes, p.321-410. Bibliography of French and English
items. Analytical index, p.417-53. V.2 has 3 parts: 1.
Internal politics; 2. Foreign policy; 3. Reflections by way of
conclusion. Notes, p.356-476. Bibliography (grouped),
p.477-83. Analytical index. Covers events up to 1973. A
standard work. *Class No:* 342.53(44)

[3043]

WRIGHT, V. The Government and politics of France. 3rd
ed. London, Unwin-Hyman; New York, Holmes & Meier,
1989. xii,402p. £9.95; $44.50. ISBN: 0091731437, UK;
0841912394, US.
First published 1978.
A leading text on the government and politics of France,
taking account of events up to and including the presidential
elections of 1988. *Class No:* 342.53(44)

USA

Bibliographies

[3044]

**HALL, K.L. A Comprehensive bibliography of American
constitutional and legal history, 1896-1979.** Millwood,
NY, Kraus International Publications, 1984. 5v.(3443p.).
$650 for 5v. Supplement 1980-1987 (1991. $155. 021.00/00
0527374083
68063 numbered entries for books, journal articles, and
doctoral dissertations published in English in the United
States, journal articles accounting for a high percentage of
citations. Items grouped in topical subdivisions within 7
chapters: 1. General surveys and texts - 2. Institutions - 3.
Constitutional doctrine - 4. Legal doctrine - 5. Biographical -
6. Chronological - 7. Geographical. Some duplication of
entries. Supplements promised. *Class No:* 342.53(73)(01)

[3045]

**REAMS, B.D. *and* YOAK, S.D. The Constitution of the
United States** a guide and bibliography to current scholarly
research. Dobbs Ferry, N.Y., Oceana Publications Inc.,
1987. xvii,[4],545p. $65. ISBN: 0379208881.
Produced to mark the celebrations of the Bicentenary of
the signing of the US Constitution in 1787.
An unannotated bibliography arranged according to
sections and amendments of the Constitution, listed in
reverse chronological order. Covers essays, articles and
books in one sequence, and government documents in
another, published between 1970 and 1986. Also includes
selected general texts, other bibliographies, and a selection
of government documents. Author, title and subject indexes.
Class No: 342.53(73)(01)

[3046]

—REAMS, B.D. *and* YOAK, S.D. The Constitutions of the
States: a state by state guide and bibliography to current
scholarly research. Dobbs Ferry, N.Y., Oceana Publications
Inc., 1988. 554p. $60. ISBN: 0379209705.
A companion volume to the above.
Each chapter devoted to the Constitution of a State.

.... (contd.)
Coverage almost entirely a survey of periodical literature.
Indexes by title, author and case name.
Class No: 342.53(73)(01)

[3047]

ZWIRN, J. Congressional publications: a research guide to
legislation, budgets and treaties. Littleton, Col., Libraries
Unlimited, 1983. 195p. $22.50. ISBN: 0872873587.
An explanation of how political, social and economic
forces shape national public policy, followed by chapters on
the relationship of congressional strategy to its information
gathering and producing role. The main part of the book
deals with the legislative process (policy research, hearings,
reports, debates, voting, bills and resolutions). Basic sources
are included at the end of most chapters. Document and
subject indexes. '... marred by poor proofreading and the
author's convoluted sentence structure' (*Choice,* v.20(10),
June 1983, p.1440). *Class No:* 342.53(73)(01)

Handbooks & Manuals

[3048]

**Congressional quarterly's guide to the Congress of the
United States.** 3rd ed. Washington, Congressional Quarterly
Inc., 1982,. xx, [1],1185p. illus. $90. ISBN: 0871872390.
First published 1971.
Carefully defines and explains, with full footnotes, the
complex procedures and issues of the US House of
Representatives and Senate. 7 chapters: 1. The origins and
development of Congress - 2. Powers of Congress - 3.
Congressional procedures - 4. Housing and support of
Congress - 5. Congress and the electorate - 6. Pressures on
Congress - 7. Qualifications and conduct. Several appendices
(Biographical index of members, 1789-1982; Constitution;
Documents of the pre-Constitutional period; Congressional
statistics; Congressional rules; Glossary of Congressional
terms; Lobbying; etc.). Detailed index. 'An essential
reference work' (*Choice,* May 1977, p.344, of the 2nd ed.).
Class No: 342.53(73)(035)

Reviews & Abstracts

[3049]

CIS/Index. Congressional Information Service/Index to
publications of the United States Congress. Washington,
D.C., Congressional Information Service, 1970 - . Monthly;
quarterly and annual cumulations. Service basis. ISSN:
00078514.
Abstracts and indexes US Congressional hearings, reports,
committee prints, and other Congressional papers issued
during the previous month. Very detailed indexing. 'In every
respect the master index to the total prolific output of the US
Congress' (*RQ,* v.11(1), Fall, 1972, p.32). Available on CD-
ROM (Congressional Masterfile).
Class No: 342.53(73)(048)

Yearbooks & Directories

[3050]

The Almanac of American politics, 1990: the Senators, the
Representatives, the Governors - their records, States and
districts. New York, National Journal (previously Dutton),
1989. 1500p. $56.95. ISBN: 0892340436.
First published 1972. Biennial.

....(contd.)

Data under States (Alabama ... Wyoming) and Congressional districts. Senate and House of Representatives committees. Name index. *Class No:* 342.53(73)(058)

Maps & Atlases

[3051]

MARTIN, K.C. The Historical atlas of the United States Congressional Districts, 1789-1983. New York, Macmillan/ Free Press, 1982. 302p. $150.

Includes an index to members of the House of Representatives, identifying the Congress(es) each served in. *Class No:* 342.53(73)(084.3)

Libraries

[3052]

World directory of national parliamentary libraries. Dietz, W., *ed.* IFLA, Section of Parliamentary Libraries, 1985. x,379p.

Entries arranged by countries, A-Z, by the English names (Albania ...Zimbabwe), with 'see references' from earlier names. Information given includes library address, telephone number, person in charge; parliamentary papers (*e.g.* Hansard, Votes and proceedings, Standing orders, Bills, Committee papers, journals, etc.); publications concerning the library; and publications by the library. Descriptions are brief. *Class No:* 342.53:061:026/027

Human Rights

Bibliographies

[3053]

ANDREWS, J.A. *and* **HINES, W.D. Keyguide to information sources on the international protection of human rights.** London, Mansell; New York, Facts on File, 1987. 169p. £28; $40. ISBN: 0720118735, UK; 0816018227, US.

An introduction to the international and regional protection of human rights, and to its literature. Part 1. General background, has overviews of the history of human rights, international treaties and conventions, and individual rights; pt.2 is an annotated bibliography arranged by general topics (*e.g.* treaties, constitutional protection) and by format (*e.g.* by law reports, bibliographies); and p.3 has brief descriptions of a wide range of organizations. Index to authors, titles, subjects and organizations. 'An essential and timely research tool' (*International affairs,* v.63(4), Autumn 1987, p.725). 'Highly recommended' (*Choice,* v.25(6), February 1988, p.881). *Class No:* 342.7(01)

[3054]

ANDREWS, J.A. *and* **HINES, W.D. 'The Literature of human rights'.** In *British book news,* July 1984, p.390-3.

Sections on sources of material, periodicals, theoretical and general works, textbooks on international protection, human rights in Europe, and human rights in UK law. Lists 44 books and 10 reports and journals. *Class No:* 342.7(01)

[3055]

COLUMBIA UNIVERSITY. Center for the Study of Human Rights. **Human rights:** a topical bibliography. Boulder, Col., Westview, 1983. xii,299p. $29.95. ISBN: 086531571x.

2500 entries arranged in over 150 categories. Main sections, each subdivided, are: 1. General and introductory works - 2. Philosophical and theoretical works - 3. National and international perspectives - 4. Specific rights (47 subdivisions) - 5. Related topics - 6. Teaching human rights - 7. Reference sources (collected documents, bibliographies, directories, selected journals, organizations providing regular human rights reports). Index of authors, p.271-296; brief subject index, p.297-299. *Class No:* 342.7(01)

[3056]

FRIEDMAN, J.R. *and* **SHERMAN, M.I.,** *eds. & comps.* **Human rights:** an international and comparative law bibliography. Westport, CT., Greenwood Press, 1985. xxvi,868p. $76.95; £64.50. (*Bibliographies and indexes in law and political science, no.4.*) ISBN: 0313247676.

Authorised by the Division of Human Rights and Peace of Unesco.

In 3 parts: 1. Rights - 2. Institutions - 3. Source guide. Part 1 is arranged A-Z by subjects (Aliens - Associations - Asylum ... Children - Civil and political rights - Conscience - Cultural rights - Detention ... Privacy - Peace ... Women) subdivided A-Z by authors. 4306 citations, in over 20 languages with English translation in brackets for all other languages except French. Part 2 covers organizations, procedures, doctrines, and practices, etc. Author index, p.809-854; secondary subject index, p.855-868 is not sufficiently detailed. *Class No:* 342.7(01)

[3057]

Human rights bibliography. Geneva,United Nations Centre for Human Rights, 1992. 5v.(2086p.). $95 (CD-ROM, 1980-93. $190). ISBN: 9211003776.

Bibliography of UN documents and publications on human rights, racial discrimination, apartheid, etc., published from 1980-1990. Over 9000 entries grouped according to the human rights classification, subdivided A-Z by title. Each entry includes title, publication place and date, pagination, notes on document content, and other relevant information.. Author and subject indexes. *Class No:* 342.7(01)

[3058]

Human rights sourcebook. Blaustein, A.P., *and others.* New York, Paragon House, 1987. 970p. $55. ISBN: 0887022022.

Lists the principal documents published on human rights throughout the world. *Class No:* 342.7(01)

[3059]

VERSTAPPEN, B., *. comp. and ed.* **Human rights reports:** an annotated bibliography of fact-finding missions. New York, K.G. Saur Inc., 1987. xiii,393p. $75. DM198. ISBN: 0905450353, US; 3598107456, Germany.

Prepared under the auspices of the Netherlands Institute of Human Rights.

An annotated bibliography reporting on fact-finding missions sponsored by both governmental and non-governmental organizations. Covers a wide range of subjects, including arrest and detention, prison conditions, religious freedom and the position of the churches, refugees and displaced persons, trade unions and freedom of

....(contd.)

association. *c.*550 reports conducted between 1970 and 1986, classified by country or region. Subject and organization indexes. *Class No:* 342.7(01)

[3060]
WHALEN L. **Human rights:** a reference handbook. Santa Barbara, CA, ABC-Clio, 1989. 218p. $37. ISBN: 0874360935.

Primary purpose is to bring together those materials on human rights that would be useful to researchers, teachers, students, activists and others interested in the subject. An annotated bibliography of print and non-print materials on the subject produced betwen 1982 and 1988, including indexes and abstracts, directories, anthologies, monographs, periodicals, films, videos, filmstrips, audiotapes, and databases. The bibliography is preceded by a chronology from 1941 to 1988, a 14-page biographical section on 15 people, and an annotated directory of human rights organizations. Also included are texts of important human rights documents. Index of authors, subjects and organizations. *Class No:* 342.7(01)

Encyclopaedias

[3061]
Encyclopedia of human rights. Lawson, E.H., *ed.* Washington, Taylor & Francis, 1991. 1907p. $275. ISBN: 0800280032.

A major compendium, arranged A-Z. Includes over 300 original texts of international and regional treaties; reports on general and specialized subjects (*eg* health care, the environment, women's and children's rights, rights of minorities and indigenous peoples); specialized conventions and declarations on apartheid, terrorism, etc.; guarantees of fundamental rights around the world and an overview of the human rights situation in more than 150 countries; plus information on over 130 non-governmental and intergovernmental organizations (*e.g.* UN, OAS). Fully cross-referenced. 100-page bibliography. 10 appendices. 'No other work approaches the massive scope of this encyclopedia'(*Booklist*, v.99(6), 15 November 1991, p.642). *Class No:* 342.7(031)

Handbooks & Manuals

[3062]
BROWNLIE, I. **Basic documents on human rights.** 3rd ed. Oxford, Clarendon Press, 1992. x,631p. £20. ISBN: 0198256833.

First published in 1971; 2nd ed. 1981.

Designed to provide a collection of sources on human rights issues in the form of a handbook. Covers recent UN declarations and conventions, European institutions, the contribution of the ILO, and developments in the Third World. *Class No:* 342.7(035)

[3063]
World human rights guide. Humana, C., *comp.* 2nd ed. New York, Facts on File; London, Hodder & Stoughton, 1986. xviii,344p. tables, charts, maps. $35; £19.95. ISBN: 0816014043, US; 0850580757, UK.

First published 1983.

Assesses information about human rights in 120 major countries, from data compiled from a 40-item questionnaire based on 3 UN documents (Universal Declaration of Human

....(contd.)

Rights. International Covenant on Economic, Social and Cultural Rights. International Convenant on Civil and Political Rights). Arranged A-Z by country and including human rights rating; life expectancy; infant mortality; form of government; UN covenants ratified; income per head; percentage of gross national product on military; state of health; education; factors affecting human rights; summary. The amount of information depending on what could be collected by questionnaire and extensive literature search. *Class No:* 342.7(035)

Dictionaries

[3064]
EUROPEAN PARLIAMENT. **Terminology of human rights:** English/French/German/Italian/Dutch/Danish/Greek. 3rd ed. Luxembourg, European Parliament, 1982. 342p. £11.

Rev. ed. published 1977.

English-based terms with equivalents and reverse indexes in the other languages. 'This valuable glossary' (*The Incorporated Linguist*, Autumn 1976, p.106, of the revised 1977 ed.). *Class No:* 342.7(038)

[3065]
Human rights organizations and periodicals directory, 1993. Ginger, A.F., *and others, eds.* 7th ed. Irregular in the past, now biennial. Berkeley, CA, Meiklejohn Civil Liberties Institute, 1993. 232p. $44.95.

Over 1000 entries arranged A-Z, describing US-based organizations, periodicals, publishers and library collections that focus on human rights, civil rights, and civil liberties, etc. Directory information and brief descriptions are based on replies to a questionnaire and on the Federal agencies guide. Indexes by subject and type of activity, by periodical title, and by geographical area. *Class No:* 342.7(038)

[3066]
MARIE J.-B. **Glossaire des droits de l'homme:** termes fondamentaux dans les instruments universels et régionaux: Français-Anglais. Glossary of human rights: basic terms in universal and regional instruments: English-French. Paris, Editions de la Maison des Sciences de l'Homme, under the auspices of Institut International des Droits de l'Homme, 1981. 339p. £13.35. *Class No:* 342.7(038)

Yearbooks & Directories

[3067]
Human rights directory: Latin America, Africa, Asia. Wiseberg, L.S. *and* Scoble, H.M., *eds and* Human Rights Internet staff, *comp.*. 2nd ed. Garrett Park, Washington, Human Rights Internet, 1987. 243p. $30. ISBN: 0939338009.

First published 1981.

*c.*400 organizations, including 32 PEN affiliates and 20 Amnesty International affiliates, from *c.*70 countries. Emphasis is on Latin America, The Caribbean, Africa, the Middle East, Asia and the Pacific, but there is also a listing of 70 organizations based in Europe and North America. Amount of information varies from simple name and address to entries including origin, purposes, programmes, publications, presidents, etc. Initial arrangement is by countries. Indexes of English-name, non-English name, acronyms and subjects. *Class No:* 342.7(058)

[3068]
—WISEBERG, L.S., *and others, eds*. Human rights directory: Latin America and the Caribbean. Cambridge, MA, Human Rights Internet (USA), Harvard Law School, 1990. 528p. $50. ((*Human rights internal reporter, l3, no.2-3*).)

First published 1981. Early editions also covered Africa, Asia, etc. (see above).

34 chapters (area, individual countries, international organizations). More than 800 organizations, primarily non-governmental, operating inside or outside Latin America, whose primary concern is human rights in that region. Civil, political and economic prerogatives of the individual, *and* also rights specific to women, children, indigenous peoples, refugees, etc. Omits 'universal' organizations (included in the 1987 volume). Bilingual text. Cross-references. Index. *Class No:* 342.7(058)

[3069]
Yearbook on human rights, 1987. First published 1946. Annual. New York, United Nations, 1992. 158p. $45. ISBN: 9211540879.

Extracted texts and summaries of significant national constitutional, legislative and judicial developments on personal, civil, political,economic, social and cultural rights. Covers national developments in 30 countries, the activities of the supervisory bodies on racial discrimination, and international developments in the United Nations and Specialized Agencies. *Class No:* 342.7(058)

USA

Yearbooks & Directories

[3070]
O'CONNOR, K. *and* EPSTEIN, L. **Public interest law groups:** institutional profiles. Westport, CT., Greenwood Press, 1989. 261p. $45. ISBN: 0313247870.

Detailed profiles for *c*.170 US public interest groups concerned with the protection of civil rights, legal aid, conservation, consumer interest, abortion, and capital punishment. Information includes a brief history of the organization, sometimes with discussion of legal cases with which it has been concerned. Entries average 1-page, and usually include references. Appendix A has brief descriptions of *c*.50 more groups. Index of cases cited. *Class No:* 342.7(73)(058)

Thesauri

[3071]
STORMORKEN, B. *and* ZWAAK, L. **Human rights terminology in international law:** a thesaurus. Dordrecht, Martinus Nijhoff, 1988. 234p. Dfl.100; £30.95.

Based on actual texts of 8 most important human rights conventions. 4 sections: Master listing (the thesaurus) - A-Z listing of all terms - KWOC listing - Articles listing by convention in abbreviated form. Stormorken is Head of the Human Rights Documentation Centre of the Council of Europe in Strasbourg. *Class No:* 342.7:025.43

Education Institutions

[3072]
World directory of human rights teaching and research institutions. Social and Human Sciences Documentation Centre and the Division of Human Rights and Peace. Paris, Unesco/Berg, 1988. xxiv,216p. F.125; $49.95. ISBN: 923102504x, Unesco; 0854962298, Berg.

An inventory of all · human rights higher education programmes which contain the academic, technical and financial information required by potential candidates. Field codes and an index of countries precedes the directory, which is in 5 sections: I. Index of names and acronyms of institutions - II. List of entries (divided into 2 groups: International and regional institutions - National institutions; and including name, address, date created, staff, type of organization, human rights education programme) - III. Index by research subject, with indication of host country of the institute - IV. Index of courses and subjects taught, with indication of the host country of the institution - V. Index of institutions providing scholarships.

A 2nd ed. was published in 1992. *Class No:* 342.7:061:37

Citizens Rights

Great Britain

[3073]
NATIONAL COUNCIL FOR CIVIL LIBERTIES. **Civil liberty:** the NCCL guide to your rights. Grant, L., *and others*. 3rd ed. Harmondsworth, Mddx, Penguin Books, 1978. 618p. illus. £1.95.

First published 1972.

29 sections: 1. The powers of the police - 2. Your rights in the criminal courts ... 5. Motorists - 6. Drugs - 7. Sex - 8. The worker and the law - 9. Consumer rights - 10. Race discrimination - 11. Your rights in the civil courts ... 13. Censorship and secrecy - 14. Industrial privacy ... 22. Housing - 23. Medical rights - 24. Death ... 26. Complaints against government, public authorities and the professions ... 29. European Commission on Human Rights. 3 appendices (*e.g.* Organizations which give help and advice; Index of Acts of Parliament). Analytical index, p.605-18. *Class No:* 342.71(410)

[3074]
Reader's Digest you and your rights: an A to Z guide to the law. Williams, D.W., *ed*. 9th ed. London, Reader's Digest Association Ltd., 1986. 752p. illus. £16.95.

A to Z entries (Abandoned vehicle ... Zebra crossing). Written in simple language and well sectionalised, it makes good use of two-colour illustrations, facsimiles, and cross-references. Quotes cases and decisions. 'How to make a complaint', p.736-752. Index. A 10th ed. was published in 1991 (ISBN 0276420055). *Class No:* 342.71(410)

Bibliographies

[3075]
MORBY, G. **Know how to find out about your rights.** 2nd ed. London, Pluto Press & Library Association Publishing Ltd., 1982. 188p. £3.95. ISBN: 0861043596.

First published as *Know how guide to information training and campaigning materials for information and advice workers*.

A critical guide to the literature. Sections: General reference and information services - Immigration, nationality

....*(contd.)*

and race - Sex and sexual discrimination - Battered women and refuges - Family law - Housing - Money, tax and debt - Consumer rights - Health, mental health and drugs - Retirement, death, and coping with bereavement - The police and the criminal law - The legal system and general principles of law - Children, young people's rights and education - Employment and unemployment - Group work, campaigning and fund raising - Training materials - Publishers and their addresses. Index, p.174-188.

Class No: 342.71(410)(01)

Criminal Justice

[3076]

Vandalism: a state of the art review and guide to sources of information. Farmer, P. 2nd ed. Stamford, Lincs., Capital Planning Information, 1987. 61p. £7.75. (*CPI Topicguide, no.5.*) ISBN: 0906011434.

First published 1982. *Class No:* 343.1

Bibliographies

[3077]

BEST, R.A. *and* **PICQUET, D.C. Computer crime, abuse, liability and security: a comprehensive bibliography, 1970-1984.** Jefferson, N.C., McFarland & Co, 1985. iv,155p. $33. £24.75. ISBN: 0899501486.

1704 unannotated entries for journal articles and 293 books, for the subjects in the title plus privacy, patents, copyright, antitrust and trade regulation. Books arranged A-Z by author, articles by title. No subdivisions. English-language material only. Co-author and detailed subject indexes. *Class No:* 343.1(01)

[3078]

Criminal justice periodical index. Ann Arbor, Mich., University Microfilms International, Serials Index, 1975-. 3pa. (Base vol. & semi-annual update.). $260pa. ISSN: 01465818.

Lists *c.*30,000 references a year under subjects, A-Z, from *c.*100 titles (mostly US) covering criminal law, criminology, drug abuse, family law, juvenile justice, police studies, prison administration, rehabilitation, security systems, etc. Includes book reviews. Extensive cross-references. Author index each issue. 3rd issue each year is cumulation for the year. Also available online. *Class No:* 343.1(01)

[3079]

DEIGHTON, S., ed. The New criminals: a bibliography of computer related crime. 2nd ed. London, Institution of Electrical Engineers, 1979. [44p.]. £10. ISBN: 0852964560.

112 annotated entries arranged in two main sections, each subdivided: 1. Computer abuse (1. Books - 2. General - 3. The crime - 4. The criminals); 2. Protection and security (1. Books - 2. General - 3. Security systems - 4. Auditing - 5. Legal aspects - 6. Insurance). References were taken from INSPEC and the *Quarterly bibliography of computers and data processing,* and include all relevant material in the joint library of the IEE and the British Computer Society. *Class No:* 343.1(01)

Encyclopaedias

[3080]

Encyclopaedia of world crime, criminal justice, criminology and law enforcement. Nash, J. R. Wilmette, Il., Crime Books Inc. (distributed by Marhsall Cavendish), 1990. 6v (5500p.) illus. $600 the set. ISBN: 0923582002.

V.1-4 have over 50,000 articles, with 4000 illustrations, including stories of criminals, prosecutors, executioners, legal theorists, assassination victims, notorious prisons, organized crime syndicates, crime fighters, and fictional works based on real crime. Length of articles varies from a few sentences to several pages. V.5 is a dictionary of 20000 terms from law enforcement, the underworld, current slang, etc., and also includes summaries of court decisions and legislation. V.6 has an index of proper names; a subject index, and a bibliography of over 25000 books. 'An important work ...' (*RQ* v.30(3), Spring 1991, p.416). *Class No:* 343.1(031)

[3081]

KADISH, S.H., ed. Encyclopedia of crime and justice. New York, Collier Macmillin, 1983. 4v.(1790p.). $300. ISBN: 0029181100.

286 articles organized topically, which present all sides of the cogent arguments. Reading lists are given after each article. Several multi-articles on the biggest problem areas (*e.g.* sentencing (10 articles); police (9 articles); prisons (6 articles)) All are well-written. Cross references. Glossary of terms, and excellent index. 'An invaluable interdisciplinary study of the field of criminal justice.' (*Library journal,* v.109(1) January 1984, p.74). *Class No:* 343.1(031)

Reviews & Abstracts

[3082]

Criminal justice abstracts. Monsey, N.Y., Willow Tree Press Inc. (previously the National Council on Crime and Delinquency), 1968-. Quarterly. $140pa. ISSN: 01469177.

Continues *Crime and delinquency literature.* previously as *Selected highlights of crime and delinquency literature* and *Information review on crime and delinquency.*

About 400 informative abstracts in each issue. Claims to cover all criminal justice literature from all disciplines. Subject and geographical index. Author index. Indexes cumulate annually. Cumulated author and subject index, 1968-1985, was published in 1988 (ISBN 0960696059). US slanted. *Class No:* 343.1(048)

[3083]

Criminology, penology & police science abstracts. Criminologica Foundation, the University of Leiden, and Joint Bureaus for Dutch Child Welfare (WIJN), Utrecht., *eds.* Amstelveen, Netherlands, Kugler Publications b.v., for the Criminologica Foundation, London, 1961-. v.1-. 6pa. Dfl.630 pa. $450pa.

Formed by a merger of *Police science abstracts* and *Criminology and penology abstracts.* The former was previously *Abstracts on police science*; the latter *Excerpta criminologica* (v.1-8. 1961-68) and *Abstracts on criminology and penology...* (v.9-19. 1969-79).

Covers the etiology of crime and juvenile delinquency, the control and treatment of offenders, criminal procedure, the administration of justice, and forensic and police science, including forensic medicine. indexes. *Class No:* 343.1(048)

Worldwide

Yearbooks & Directories

[3084]

International directory of private investigators, private detectives, process servers, security guards, security equipment suppliers, security services, debt collecting agencies, covering also certificated bailiffs, status enquiry agents and trade protection societies, 1986-87. 20th ed. Folkestone, Kent, Regency International Publications, 1986. 480p. £19.50. ISBN: 0900618728.

First published 1967. Annual. *Class No:* 343.1(100)(058)

[3085]

A World directory of criminological institutes. Santoro, C.M., *ed.*   5th ed. Rome, United Nations Interregional Crime and Justice Research Institute, 1990. xxxiii,661p. $54. ISBN: 9290780096.

First published 1974; 4th ed. 1986.

Lists *c.*400 criminological organizations and institutes, many international in scope, located in 55 countries. International bodies are followed by countries, A-Z (Argentine ... Zaire - CERDAS - Kinshasa), subdivided by names of organisations, A-Z. Entries have full name and address, history, method of governance, type of activities, staff, finances and publications. *Class No:* 343.1(100)(058)

England & Wales

Tables & Data Books

[3086]

GREAT BRITAIN. Home Office. **Criminal statistics, England and Wales, 1992.** London, HMSO, 1993. Annual. 230p. tables. £22.70. (*Cm.2410.*.) ISBN: 010124102x.

8 sections: 1. Introduction and summary - 2. Notifiable offences recorded by the police - 3. Notifiable offences in which firearms were reported to have been used or stolen - 4. Homicide - 5. Offences cautioned or found guilty - 6. Court proceedings - 7. Sentencing - 8. Use of police bail and court remand. 7 appendices (*e.g.* 5. Standard list offences - 6. Glossary of terms - 7. Statistics on the criminal justice system. *Class No:* 343.1(42)(083)

USA

[3087]

WALSH, J. Crime and criminal justice reference sources. In *Booklist*, v.88(10), January 15, 1992, p.363-4,966.

Lists guides to the literature, bibliographies, dictionaries and encyclopedias, directories, statistical sources, and electronic reference sources. *Class No:* 343.1(73)

Handbooks & Manuals

[3088]

BAILEY, W.G., *ed.* **The Encyclopedia of police science.** New York, Garland, 1989. 718p. illus. $77. (*Garland reference library of social science, 413.*) ISBN: 0824066278.

143 entries on American law enforcement topics, covering technology, administration, history, values and future trends. Intended to be an introduction to the subject, the entries are general in scope and 2 to 14 pages in length. Bibliographies are appended to each entry and two other bibliographies are included: 'Bibliography of police history', including books,

....(contd.)

dissertations and articles, and 'Bibliography of bibliographies' listing 71 works in chronological order by publication date. 2 Sections of black-and-white photographs. Complementary to J.J. Fay's *Police dictionary and encyclopedia* (1988). *Class No:* 343.1(73)(035)

Criminal Law

Bibliographies

[3089]

DE SCHUTTER, B. *and* **ELIAERTS, C. Bibliography on international criminal law.** Leiden, Sijthoff, 1972. li,423p.

5201 numbered items (books, periodical articles, typescripts) in 11 sections (1. General studies - 2. Extraterritorial jurisdiction - 3. Extradition - 4. Transmission of prosecutions ... 7. War crimes - 8. Other international crimes - 9. Humanitarian law - 10. International Criminal Court - 11. United Nations concern with international criminal law). Index of persons; subject index. *Class No:* 343.5(01)

[3090]

WERNER, J. 'Recent literature on organized crime'. In *International journal of legal information,* v.14(3-4), June-August 1986, p.155-169.

A 2-page essay precedes the bibliography, which is arranged in 3 parts: Books & TV material; Articles; Bibliographies. *c.*250 entries, unannotated, arranged A-Z within the 3 sections. *Class No:* 343.5(01)

Periodicals & Progress Reports

Bibliographies

[3091]

RANK, R. 'Criminal law and criminology': a bibliography of periodicals. In *Law library journal,* v.60(3), August 1967, p.249-71.

Part 1: 320 titles, A-Z, with details of start and frequency; includes ceased journals. Part 2 is a list of titles, under 41 countries. 'Especially useful for "dead" periodicals' (*Use of social sciences literature,* ed. by N. Roberts (1977), p.225). *Class No:* 343.5(05)(01)

England

Histories

[3092]

RADZINOWICZ, L. A History of English criminal law and its administration from 1750. London, Stevens & Sons, 1948-86, under the auspices of the Pilgrim Trust. 5v. £100 each vol. ISBN: 0420374604, v.1; 0420374470, v.2; 0420374809, v.3; 0420415904, v.4; 0420462805, v.5; 0420475206, set.

Volumes are: 1. The movement for reform - 2. The clash between private initiative and public interest in the enforcement of law - 3. Cross-currents in the movement for the reform of the police - 4. Grappling for control - 5. The emergence of penal policy. *Class No:* 343.5(420)(091)

Industrial Espionage

[3093]

CORNWALL, H. The Industrial espionage handbook. London, Ebury, 1992. 131p. £9.99

First published 1990.

A handbook on the collection and compilation of commercial intelligence - how to spy, how others could be spying on you, and the resources, disciplines, techniques and technologies available in the service of the industrial espionage operative. 6 appendices, including a list of terms, online services, costs, and useful addresses. Bibliography, p.125-6. Index, p.127-31. *Class No:* 343.534

Murder

Bibliographies

[3094]

ABEL, E., *comp.* **Homicide** a bibliography. Westport, CT., Greenwood Press, 1987. xiii,169p. $29.95. (*Bibliographies and indexes in sociology, no.11.*) ISBN: 0131259011.

1919 unannotated entries relating to articles, monographs and documents on homicide from the scientific literature, arranged A-Z by author. Most citations are from the late 1970s or early 1980s, plus a few classics. Subject index, p.157-169, has broad headings. *Class No:* 343.611(01)

[3095]

CHARNY, I,W,, *ed.* **Genocide:** a critical bibliographic review. London, Mansell Publishing Ltd., 1988. xiv,273p. £36.50. ISBN: 072011876x.

A publication of the Institute of the International Conference on the Holocaust and Genocide.

'Each chapter ... is intended to present an authoritative, encyclopedia-like statement of the knowledge base in a given field or area of study of genocide, and an annotated critical bibliography' (*Introduction*). 13 chapters: 1. The study of genocide - 2. Intervention and prevention of genocide - 3. The history and sociology of genocidal killings - 4. The Holocaust ... 5. The Armenian genocide - 6. Genocide in the USSR ... 11-13. are on literature, art and film. Bibliographies follow each chapter. Index, p.257-273. *Class No:* 343.611(01)

[3096]

NEWTON, M. Mass murder: an annotated bibliography. New York, Garland, 1988. 378 p. $45. (*Garland reference library of social science, 427.*) ISBN: 0824066197.

A bibliography and biographical dictionary of men and women who have perpetrated murders and killings. Over 600 annotated entries, avoiding sensational works ' ... a welcome research guide' (*Choice*, v.25(10), June 1988, p. 1538). *Class No:* 343.611(01)

Encyclopaedias

[3097]

WILSON, C. *and* **PITMAN, P. Encyclopaedia of murder.** Rev. ed. London, Pan Books, 1984. 672p. illus. £4.95. ISBN: 0330283006.

First published 1961 by Arthur Barker Ltd.

A detailed contents list is followed by 2 essays ('The study of murder' by Colin Wilson and 'Why an encyclopaedia of murder?' by Patricia Pitman). The main part of the book

....(contd.)

consists of biographies of murderers, arranged A-Z by name followed by a select bibliography and a classified index. *Class No:* 343.611(031)

[3098]

—**WILSON, C.** *and* **SEAMAN, D.** Encyclopaedia of modern murder, 1962-82. London, Arthur Barker Ltd., 1983. xx,267p. illus. £10.95. ISBN: 0213168766.

'The age of murder', an introductory essay by Colin Wilson, is followed by the main section of the work, 'A-Z of murderers, terrorist organizations and victims' which has 102 names, mainly UK and US. A select bibliography, p.255-256; a classified index, p.257-258; and a name index, p.259-267 complete the book, which is a sequel to *Encyclopaedia of murder (qv). Class No:* 343.611(031)

Biographies

[3099]

GAUTE, J.H.H. *and* **ODELL, R. New Murderer's who's who.** New ed. London, Headline, 1989. 512p. illus. £7.99. ISBN: 0747232709.

Biographical sketches of 360 murderers (mostly British; 85 are American). Limited to crimes on which books have appeared. Bibliography of 746 items fails to state publishers and dates of publication. Arrangement and faulty subject index are criticised in *Library review* (v.29. Autumn 1980, p.217). 'Still, an essential reference book' (*Library journal* 1 May 1979, p.1042). *Class No:* 343.611(092)

Suicide

Bibliographies

[3100]

LESTER, D., *and others.* **Suicide:** a guide to information sources. Detroit, Mich., Gale Research Company, 1980. xiv. 294p. $68. (*Social issues and social problems information guide sources,v.3.*) ISBN: 0810314150.

The first and main part covers the various sources on the subject in general (*e.g.* bibliographies; basic reference sources; dissertations and theses; statistics; the news media). The 4 remaining parts concern Theories of suicide; Social and environmental correlates of suicide; Psychological correlates and analyses of suicide; and Suicide prevention. Included: a checklist of doctoral dissertations, of authors who committed suicide, and of suicide in literature and mythology. Author, title and subject indexes. *Class No:* 343.614(01)

[3101]

—**McINTOSH, J.L.,** *comp.* Research on suicide: a bibliography. Westport, CT., Greenwood Press, 1985. xiii,323p. $35. (*Bibliographies and indexes in psychology, no.2.*) ISBN: 0313239924.

Updates and expands Lester's work. Over 2300 entries, mainly 1970-, arranged in 10 chapters, all subdivided: 1. Overview works - 2. Definitions and the variety of self-destructive behaviour - 3. Historical background - 4. Theories of suicide - 5. Demography and epidemiology of suicide: statistics and risk factors - 6. Prevention, intervention, treatment, assessment and prediction of suicidal behaviour - 7. The need for education about suicide - 8. Ethics of suicide: moral, philosophical, religious and legal aspects - 9. After suicide: prevention - 10. Suicide literature

....(contd.)

directed to specific gatekeepers and suicide and art. Noteworthy items and uninformative titles only are annotated. Selected sources have asterisks. Author index, p. 288-314. Subject index, p.315-323. *Class No:* 343.614(01)

[3102]

—PRENTICE, A.E. Suicide: a selective bibliography of over 2,200 items. Metuchen, N.J., Scarecrow Press, 1974. 227p. $19. ISBN: 0810807734.

Covers English-language material, mostly published 1960-73, and is narrower in scope as well as being less current than the above. *Class No:* 343.614(01)

[3103]

Suicide and the elderly: an annotated bibliography and review. Osgood, N.J. *and* McIntosh, J.L. Westport, CT., Greenwood Press, 1986. xiii,193 p. $59.95. (*Bibliographies and indexes in gerontology . 3.*) ISBN 0313247862.

A 36-page literature review is followed by an annotated list of bibliographical sources, with fairly lengthy descriptions, and a list of non-English works, some annotated. An appendix gives sources of demographic data. Author and subject indexes ' ... an excellent source ... ' (*Choice* v.24(7), March 1987 p.1034). *Class No:* 343.614(01)

Encyclopaedias

[3104]

EVANS, G. *and* **FARBEROW, N.L. The Encyclopedia of suicide.** New York. Facts on File, 1988. 434p.tables,charts. $40. ISBN: 0816013977.

Intended as a companion volume to the publisher's encyclopedias on alcohol and drug abuse.

An introduction giving an overview of suicide as a social, cultural and historical phenomenon, precedes the encyclopedia of over 500 entries treating the various aspects of the subject. Entries range in length from a few sentences to long essays, averaging about 700 words. Includes biographies of famous suicides, noted authors and researchers, as well as historical events involving suicide. Extensive bibliography as well as publications mentioned in the text. Subject index. ' ... comprehensive work on a socially prevalent and disturbing problem' (*Reference books bulletin*, 15 November 1988, p 552). *Class No:* 343.614(031)

Prisons

Histories

[3105]

McCONVILLE, S. A History of English prison administration. v.1: 1750-1877. London, Routledge & Kegan Paul, 1981. 535p. £34.50. ISBN: 0710006942.

To be in 2v. V.1, at its best in covering the centralization of the local prison system and the emergence of a national convict-prison system between 1834 and 1877. V.2 will presumably bring the narrative up to the present. 'The two great door-stoppers will take their place on the shelves as standard works of reference' (*TLS*, no. 4099, 23 October 1981, p.1230). *Class No:* 343.81(091)

USSR

[3106]

ROSSI, J. The Gulag handbook: a historical dictionary of Soviet penitentiary institutions and terms related to the forced labour camps. London, Overseas Publications Exchange Ltd., 1987. 546p. ISBN: 0903868970.

Published in USSR in 1987, and in New York in 1988 as *The Gulag handbook: an encyclopedic dictionary of Soviet penal institutions ...,* translated by William Burhans (Paragon House. 608p. $55. ISBN 1557780242).

A linguistic, encyclopedic guide, cross-referencing thousands of terms invented by, for and about the Gulag. *Class No:* 343.81(47)

Libraries

Bibliographies

[3107]

HARTZ, F.R., *and others.* **Prison librarianship:** a selective, annotated, classified bibliography, 1945-1985. Jefferson, N. Carolina, McFarland & Company, 1987. ix,115p. £19.95. ISBN: 089950258x.

185 lengthy entries arranged in 19 sections and including Administration and planning of correctional libraries; Background reading; Bibliographies; Censorship issues; Libraries and educational rehabilitation; Law libraries; and Library services. Author and subject indexes. US slant. *Class No:* 343.81:061:026/027(01)

Criminology

[3108]

RADZINOWICZ, L. The Cambridge Institute of Criminology: its background and scope. London, HMSO, 1988. 96p. £11.50. ISBN: 0113408846.

Outlines the early problems of the Institute, established 1959, examines the scope and content of courses offered, and looks at how the work has evolved over the years. *Class No:* 343.9

Bibliographies of Bibliographies

[3109]

DAVIES, B.L. Criminological bibliographies: uniform citations to bibliographies, indexes and review articles of the literature of crime study in the United States. Westport, CT., Greenwood Press, 1978. xxvi,182p. $36.95. ISBN: 0313205450.

Over 1400 references, in 7 subject sections. Indexed by subject, compiler and issuing body. *Class No:* 343.9(009)

Bibliographies

[3110]

Criminology and forensic sciences: an international bibliography, 1950-1980. Vomende, R., *comp.* Munich, K. G. Saur, 1981-82. 3v. (xv, 2389p.). £110. DM420. $300. ISBN: 3598103743.

An extended survey of 30 years' publication in criminology and related sciences, law and humanities in *c.* 50 countries. Includes *c.* 400,000 published items arranged A-Z by author, with citations in the original language of

....(contd.)

publication. Books, journal articles, collective works, conference papers, etc., are included. No subject or classified listing. *Class No:* 343.9(01)

[3111]
HOWARD LEAGUE FOR PENAL REFORM. John Howard Library of Criminology and Penology. **Catalogue, 1963.** London, the League, 1963,. 82p.

A list of nearly 3000 items in 8 main sections: 1. Social problems and social services - 2. Crime and criminals - 3. Child welfare and juvenile delinquency - 4. Law and penal procedure - 5. Treatment of offenders and penal institutions - 6. Capital punishment - 7. Biography and memoirs - 8. Miscellaneous: philosophy; psychology. Offical journals and statistics received. Author index. The John Howard Library no longer exists. *Class No:* 343.9(01)

[3112]
PERRY, R. 'Criminology and its literature' In *Use of social sciences literature* ., edited by N. Roberts (1977), p.219-39.

Sections: Introduction - Guide to the literature, bibliographies and library catalogues - Abstracting and indexing services - Periodicals - Official publications - Statistics - Legislation - Conference and Congress proceedings - Books of readings, Festshriften and other collections - Encyclopedias, dictionaries and other reference works - Information and current awareness services - Research in progress. 5 references. Helpful running commentary. *Class No:* 343.9(01)

[3113]
RADZINOWICZ, L. *and* **HOOD, R.G. Criminology and the administration of criminal justice:** a bibliography. London, Mansell; Westport, CT., Greenwood Press, 1976. 414p. ISBN: 0837190681.

Main sequence of *c.*4500 entries, primarily covering literature published within the last 20 years. 19 subject headings, with chronological sub-arrangement. A supplement (1500 entries) updates to 1976. Concerns the sociology of crime, criminal justice and penology. Author index. 'Much more concerned with issues of policy and research on criminals than with day-to-day practical matters' (*British book news,* April 1977, p.274-5). 'Highly commended' (*Library journal,* v.102, no.12, 1 September 1977, p.1747). Winner of the 1977 Joseph L. Andrews Bibliographic Award of the American Association of Law Libraries. *Class No:* 343.9(01)

[3114]
WRIGHT, M., *ed.* **Use of criminology literature.** London, Butterworth, 1974. [xii], 242p. (*Information sources for research and development.*)

16 contributors. 13 sections (1. Conducting a search for information on criminology - 2. Sociological aspects of criminology - 3. Psychiatric aspects of crime - 4. Criminological aspects of psychology - 5. Alcoholism and crime: an introductory bibliography - 6. Introduction to the literature of drug dependence - 7. The treatment of offenders - 8. Criminal law and administration of criminal justice - 9. Police literature - 10. Criminal and related statistics - 11. The history of prisons and penal practice - 12. Illustrations in criminological and penal literature - 13. Official publications. Running commentary; well sectionalised chapters. Subject and name index only. 'A useful guide to literature and information in the whole field of criminology, concentrating on British publications, but also referring to

....(contd.)

some foreign material' (*Brtish book news,* November 1978, p.871). Author was Director of the Howard League for Criminal Reform. *Class No:* 343.9(01)

Handbooks & Manuals

[3115]
International handbook of contemporary developments in criminology. Johnson, E.H., *ed.* Westport, CT., Greenwood Press, 1983. 2v. illus. \$125 the set. V.1. \$65; V.2.\$85. ISBN: 0313210594 v.1; 0313238030 v.2.

V.1. *General issues and the Americas*; v.2. *Europe, Africa, the Middle East and Asia.* Essays on criminology as it is carried out in the differing political-legal contexts of the US and 39 other countries. Collectively, the two volumes are an inventory of variations in the conceptions and work of criminologists around the world. Most articles are followed by bibliographies and many bibliographical entries are annnotated. 'This handbook is unique in its intellectual richness and transnational criminological perspective. (*Choice,* March 1984, p.954). *Class No:* 343.9(035)

Dictionaries

[3116]
DE SOLA, R. Crime dictionary. 2nd ed., rev. & expanded. New York, Facts on File, 1988. xiii,222p. \$24.95; £18.50. ISBN: 0816018723.

First published 1981.

Over 10,000 terms, including 1500 new entries, used by criminals and law enforcement professionals, including legal, medical and psychiatric terms; abbreviations; weapons; nicknames of prisons; criminal gangs and terrorist groups; government crime-fighting agencies; criminal and drug-culture slang; criminal and white-collar crime; etc. 3 appendices (Foreign terms - Place-name nicknames - Selected sources. US oriented. *Class No:* 343.9(038)

Polyglot

[3117]
ADLER, J.A., *ed.* **Elsevier's dictionary of criminal science in eight languages:** English/American - French - Italian - Spanish - Portuguese - Dutch - Swedish - German. Amsterdam, London, etc., Elsevier, 1960. xv,1460p.

10,930 numbered English/American terms, with one-word equivalents in the other 7 languages across the double page, and keys to those languages. Coverage: 'the prevention, detection and suppression of crime, including the physical state, physical conditions and special circumstances of law-breakers, witnesses, and victims' (*Preface*). Terms are categorised. The review in *Babel* (v.9(1-2), p.110-1) notes mistranslations and omissions. *Class No:* 343.9(038)=00

English

[3118]
WALSH, D. *and* **POOLE, A.,** *eds.* **A Dictionary of criminology.** London, Routledge & Kegan Paul, 1983. xi,242p. £14.95. ISBN: 071009549x.

Intended for students, this guide to concepts and terminology frequently used in criminology, includes terms selected from the fields of psychology, psychiatry, penology, sociology, social work, and the law of England and Wales.

....(contd.)

Cross-references. British slant. 34 contributors. 'Too many entries are merely legal definitions' (*Times educational supplement,* 18 May 1984, p.31). *Class No:* 343.9(038)=20

French

[3119]

INGLETON, R. Elsevier's dictionary of police and criminal law: English-French and French-English. Amsterdam & New York, Elsevier, 1992. viii,592p. $157. Dfl.275. ISBN: 0444891021.

12500 terms relating to the organization and functions of the police, the criminal law and rules of evidence, traffic control, drugs, terrorism, accidents and disasters. Includes many slang and jargon terms. *Class No:* 343.9(038)=40

USA

Bibliographies

[3120]

Crime and punishment in America: a historical bibliography. Santa Barbara, CA., ABC-Clio, 1984. 346p. $38.50. ISBN: 0874363632.

Information taken from the ABC-Clio database.

1396 abstracts of periodical articles published between 1973 and 1982 on crime, criminals, and criminal justice in America from Colonial times to the present day. Topics arranged in 8 chapters and within each chapter arranged by author, A-Z. Subject index with terms rotated. Author index. '... a good basic starting point for research in particular topics in the field ...; (*Choice*, v.21(10), June '1984, p.1440). *Class No:* 343.9(73)(01)

Mafia

[3121]

CAMBRIDGE UNIVERSITY. Institute of Criminology. **Mafia:** a selected annotated bibliography. Trott, L. *and* Smith, D. C., *comps.* Cambridge, the Institute, 1977. [viii], 141p. Mimeographed.

*c.*1000 annotated entries. Classes A - I (A: Mafia as a criminal organization that operates internationally ... C: Mafia's share in US crime ... F: Mafia seen as a Sicilian sub-culture - G: Mafia as a state of mind rather than an organization - H: Mafia represented in art - I: Unannotated and unclassified references. Author and short title index, p. 114-41. *Class No:* 343.91

Commercial Law

Dictionaries

English

[3122]

FOSTER, S. Business law terms. Edinburgh, W. & R. Chambers Ltd. 1988,. [4],115p. £2.50. ISBN: 0550180656.

A compact guide to the key business law words and phrases used in the commercial world. Short, clear explanations are given. *Class No:* 347.7(038)=20

[3123]

HUDSON, A.H. Dictionary of commercial law. London, Butterworth & Co (Publishers) Ltd., 1983. [4],289p. £9.95. (*Butterworth's professional dictionary series.*) ISBN: 0406681600.

Intended to provide ready access to basic information relating to the terminology of most of the principal topics of both commercial law and intellectual property, describing rather than merely defining words and phrases. Cross-references. 'Copyright' itself: 2 pages, but with Copyright exemptions, in sound recording, literary, dramatic, etc.: 6 pages. 'Form of contract': 2 pages. 'Guarantee': 2 pages. *Class No:* 347.7(038)=20

[3124]

IVAMY, E.R.H. Dictionary of company law. 2nd ed. London, Butterworth, 1985. 264p. £14. (*Butterworths professional dictionary series.*) ISBN: 0406681635.

First published 1983.

Words and phrases used in company law, each entry containing a concise statement of the relevant provisions of the Companies Acts and of significant case law. Entries vary in length (*e.g.* Debenture, 6½ pages; Deed of settlement, 3½ lines; Fraudulent trading, *c.* 600 words). Cross-references. This second edition brings the dictionary up-to-date with the Companies Act, 1985, Companies Securities (Insider Dealing) Act, 1985, and the Business Names Act, 1985. *Class No:* 347.7(038)=20

German

[3125]

BECKER, U. von. Rechtswörterbuch für die gewerbliche Wirtschaft: Deutsch-Englisch-Französisch, mit dreisprachigen index. 2. Aufl. Frankfurt am Main, Fritz Knapp Verlag, 1980. 985p. £64.60.

First published 1966.

A dictionary of commercial law, particularly concerned with terms found in legal documents (*e.g.* conditions of sale, tenders). Systematically arranged in subject chapters. Trilingual index (German, English, French) and a bibliography. *Class No:* 347.7(038)=30

[3126]

ROMAIN, A., *and others.* **Dictionary of legal and commercial terms.** v.1: 4th rev. ed.; v.2: 2nd. rev. ed. London, Butterworths; München, C. H. Beck'sche Verlagsbuchhandlung, 1985-1989. 2v .(viii,854; viii,883). £45 each vol. ISBN: 0406038112 v.1.(UK); 0406038120 v.2.(UK); 0406038103 set.

First published 1975. German title is *Wörterbuch der rechts- und wirtschaftssprache.*

v.1. English-German; v.2. German-English. A very detailed dictionary. *Class No:* 347.7(038)=30

Persian (Farsi)

[3127]

FAHIM, K., *and others.* **English-Persian dictionary of legal and commercial terms.** Leiden, E.J. Brill, 1989. xviii,81p. Gld.150; $75. ISBN: 9004084150.

Compiled primarily for the use of the Iran-United States Claims Tribunal at the Hague.

Lists *c.*5000 key legal and commercial English terms and their equivalents in Persian. A companion Persian-English volume is in preparation. *Class No:* 347.7(038)=915.5

Worldwide

[3128]

Digest of commercial laws of the world. Kohlick, G., *ed.* Dobbs Ferry, N.Y., Oceana, for National Association of Credit Management, 1966-72. 11 loose-leaf binders, including forms of commercial agreements and state variations. $850 + supplementary service. ISBN: 0379010003.

Each volume covers a set of countries; each digest deals with such matters as contracts, agency and representation, forms of business organizations, bills of exchange, and recognition of foreign judgement. *Class No:* 347.7(100)

Europe—Western

Handbooks & Manuals

[3129]

MEINHARDT, P. Company law in Europe. 3rd ed. Farnborough, Hants., Gower Publishing Co. Ltd., 1982. 656 p. (loose-leaf). £50. ISBN: 0566022451.

First published, 1975.

A full survey of the law relating to companies within individual countries of Europe, the information given extending from general data to detailed notes on specific subjects. Each country section concludes with a bibliography listing further sources of information. Countries covered are Austria, Belgium, Denmark, France, Germany, Italy, Jersey, Liechtenstein, Luxembourg, Netherlands, Sweden and Switzerland. 'Aim is to give a 'panoramic view' of company law in Europe' (*Preface*). *Class No:* 347.7(400)(035)

Great Britain

Bibliographies

[3130]

CLINCH, P. Business law: an introduction to information sources. In *Business information review*, v.5(1), July 1989, p.3-17.

The sources of business law, including statutes, staturory instruments, case law and extra-legal sources, are described and evaluated with, in addition, practical advice on their use in enquiry work. (Author's abstract).
Class No: 347.7(410)(01)

Handbooks & Manuals

[3131]

Butterworths company law handbook, 1993. Walmsley, K., *ed.* 9th ed. London, Butterworths, 1993. xvii,2066p. ISBN: 0406020078.

'The aim is to make available in a convenient and up-to-date form the full text of the most important company law statutes, statutory instruments and European legislation'(Introduction). In 6 parts: 1. Company legislation; 2. Other legislation; 3. Statutory instruments; 4. Selected stamp duties provision; 5. Securities and Investment Board rules and regulations; 6. European Community legislation. Index (to paragraph numbers), p.2027-63. Glossary, p.2065-6. *Class No:* 347.7(410)(035)

[3132]

MEINHARDT, P. *and* **DAVIS, N. Company law in Great Britain.** Aldershot, Hants., Gower Publishing Co. Ltd., 1982. 300p. £22.50. ISBN: 056602389x.

Sets out the main features of company law in Britain in 26 sections: 1. Basic law - 2. Formation of a limited company ... 8. Capital ... 10. Allotment and transfer of shares ... 13. Minority rights and investigation - 13A. Insider dealing ... 20. Audit ... 24. Private companies ... 26. Reform. Select bibliography (2p.). Index (18p.). *Class No:* 347.7(410)(035)

[3133]

Palmer's company law. Schmitthoff, C.M., *and others, eds.* 25th ed. London, Sweet & Maxwell, 1992-. 5v. (looseleaf). £295, updating service: £180 pa. ISBN: 0420446605.

V.1 & 2 have narrative texts (16 parts); v.3 & 4 are on the Companies Acts and other measures (pts A-K); v.5 has tables and index. *Class No:* 347.7(410)(035)

Canada

Handbooks & Manuals

[3134]

FRASER, W. Fraser's handbook of Canadian company law. 7th ed. Toronto, Carswell Co. Ltd., 1985. 733p.

6th ed., 1975.

Presented in logical sequence in 23 chapters. Covers the law of several provinces as well as Federal law. Table of fees. List of Statutes applicable in the Dominion. Table of contents. Index. 'Each subject thoroughly explained and discussed and the wealth of information so accumulated is presented in a clear and readable form' (*International journal of legal information,* v.14(1-2), February-April 1986, p.73). *Class No:* 347.7(71)(035)

Consumer Protection

Bibliographies

[3135]

FOREMAN, S. Consumer monitor: an annotated bibliography of British government and other official publications relating to consumer issues. Aldershot, Hants., Gower Publishing, 1987. 460p. £35. ISBN: 0566054019.

Prepared on behalf of the National Consumer Council.

*c.*2000 annotated entries in broad subject arrangement, aiming to be comprehensive for the period 1980 to 1 April 1986, and also including some older material. Detailed subject index. 'A little extra background text and explanation would not have gone amiss.' (*Library Association record,* v.89(7), July 1987, p.338). *Class No:* 347.731(01)

[3136]

—**GOUKER, D.** 'Consumer information sources'. In *Reference books bulletin,* July 1988, p.1791-2, 1794, 1796, 1798, 1800, 1802, 1806-7.

Over 80 titles arranged by general sources (indexes and abstracts, directories, periodicals, and loose-leaf services), followed by individual product groups.
Class No: 347.731(01)

Handbooks & Manuals

[3137]

HARRIES, J.N. **Consumers: know your rights.** 3rd ed. London, Oyez Longman, 1983. xii, 235p. £5.95. ISBN: 0851207804.

Chapters: 1. The consumer bargain - 2. Buying goods - 3. Consumer safety - 4. Credit - 5. Contractors, repairers and other services - 6. Business practices - 7. Manufacturers' liability for defective products - 8. Who can help? - 9. The European Economic Community. Analytical index, p.227-235. Sectionalised chapters; good use of bold type.
Class No: 347.731(035)

Ownership & Property

Handbooks & Manuals

[3138]

WILLIAMS, J.F. **A Manager's guide to patents, trade marks & copyright.** London, Kogan Page, 1986. 168p. £12.95. ISBN: 1850912033.

16 chapters written in clear, non-legal language: 1. What is 'intellectual property'? ... 3. Advisers ... 7. Trade marks - 8. Copyright - 9. Registered designs - 10. Industrial design copyright - 11. Ownership of rights ... 16. The future. 14 appendices (8. Summary of copyright rules; 13. Further reading; 14. Useful names and addresses). Index, p.165-168.
Class No: 347.77(035)

Dictionaries

Polyglot

[3139]

MIATELLO, A. **Glossario trilingue della proprietà industriale ... Trilingual glossary on industrial property.** Torino, Albert Meynier, 1985. 93p. L.60,000; SwF.80.

Includes over 500 terms and phrases relative to industrial property. In 3 sections: French-Italian - English-Italian - Italian-French-English. *Class No:* 347.77(038)=00

Copyright

[3140]

GOLDSTEIN, P.M. **Copyright:** principles, law and practice. Boston, Mass., Little, Brown, & Co., 1989. Supplement: 1991. 3v. and cumulative supplement (xi,486p). ISBN: 0316319651, v.1; 0316319643, v.2; 0316319651, v.3; 0316319694, supplement.

First published in 1949.

16 chapters in v.1 & 2 dealing with rights, infringements, defences, remedies, procedures, other sources of protection, etc. V.3 has Appendices: A: Statutes, legislation, reports & regulations; B: Copyright conventions; C: Forms. Table of cases. Table of statutes. Index, p.949-91.The supplement updates and is superseded from time to time.
Class No: 347.78

[3141]

STONE, P. **Copyright law in the United Kingdom and the European Community.** London, Athlone Press, 1990. x,233p. (*(European Community law series)*).

'... seeks both to expound the new British law of copyright under the 1988 Act ... and to examine ... the relevant existing rules of Community law ...' (*Preface*). 8 chapters: 1. Introduction - 2. Subsistence - 3. Infringement - 4.

....(contd.)

Remedies - 5. Licences - 6. Moral right - 7. Performers' rights - 8. Industrial design. Notes, p.172-223. Bibliography, p.224. Table of cases, p.225-231. Index, p.232-3.
Class No: 347.78

Handbooks & Manuals

[3142]

Copinger and Skone James on copyright, including international copyright. Skone James, E.P., *ed.* 13th ed. London, Sweet & Maxwell, 1991. 1598p. £168. ISBN: 0421392002.

First published 1870.

11 parts (32 chapters: 1. Introductory and historical - 2. Copyright in literary, dramatic, musical and artistic works and published editions - 3. Related forms of protection - 4. Copyright in cinematographic films, sound recordings and broadcasts - 5. Copyright in special circumstances (*e.g.* public lending right) - 6. European Economic Community - 7. Transitional provisions - 8. Arrangements between authors and publishers, etc. 9. International copyright and the protection of works originating outside the United Kingdom - 10. Copyright law of America and other foreign countries - 11. Forms and precedents. Appendices A-F (A. U.K. Statutes; B. U.K. Orders; C. Copyright conventions and agreements; F. Treaty of Rome). Analytical subject index, p.1129-91. The basic manual on the subject.
Class No: 347.78(035)

[3143]

FLINT, M.F. **A User's guide to copyright.** 5th ed. London, Butterworth, 1990. xxv,370p. 100 illus., 1 form. £23.95. ISBN: 0406200750.

First published 1979.

In 2 parts: 1. Copyright law generally (chapters 1-14; *e.g.* Infringement of copyright) - 2. Copyright in use (15-33; *e.g.* 19. Reprography; 20. The music industry; 24. Television and radio stations; 29. Advertising agencies; 31. Computer software; 32. Character merchandising). Appendices: 1. Relevant organizations; 2. Conventions and international agreements to which the UK is a party; 3. Countries which have adhered to the Berne Convention and/or Universal Copyright Convention. Analytical index, p.351-70.
Class No: 347.78(035)

[3144]

THORN, E.A. **Understanding copyright:** a practical guide. Tunbridge Wells, Jay Books, 1989. 128p. illus. £4.95. ISBN: 1870404033.

Arranged in 8 sections: 1. Defines ownership of copyright, including significance of the copyright symbol - 2. Photocopying and duplication - 3. Copyright of books, film and video rights, etc. Public Lending Right - 4. Sound recordings - 5. Television and video - 6. Problems with copyright for computer programs and software piracy - 7. Artistic works (including photographic work) - 8. Live performances. 7 appendices (Examples of copyright notices - useful organizations - recorded music libraries - signatories to the Berne Convention - further reading (10 items)). Index, p.127-128. Written in non-legal language. Biassed towards the view of the publisher or other owner of the copyright.
Class No: 347.78(035)

Dictionaries

Polyglot

[3145]

WORLD INTELLECTUAL PROPERTY ORGANISATION. **WIPO glossary of terms of the law of copyright and neighbouring rights.** Geneva, WIPO, 1980. 281p. £19.50.

In English/ French/Spanish. Also available in English/ French/Arabic and English/French/Russian. *Class No:* 347.78(038)=00

Laws

[3146]

Copyright laws and treaties of the world. Unesco *and* World Intellectual Property Organization (WIPO), *and others.* Paris, Unesco; Washington, Bureau of National Affairs Inc., 1956-. Annual Supplements. 3v. (loose-leaf). $ 655 for 3 loose-leaf vols. updated to 1987, including supplements.

'A compilation of the laws, orders, rules, regulations, conventions and treaties which establish, in and between the different countries of the world, the legal provisions for the protection of copyright' (*Explanatory notes*). Arranged by countries. A-Z. *Class No:* 347.78(094.1)

Air Law

Bibliographies

[3147]

HEERE, W.P. **International bibliography of air law, 1900-1971.** Leiden, Sijthoff; Dobbs Ferry, N.Y., Oceana, 1972. xxvi,569p. $40. ISBN: 0379000105.

Supplements 1972-1976 (1976. xxii, 169p. $22); 1977-1980 (1981. 394p. $69.50. ISBN 90224725550); 1981-1984 (Deventer, Kluwer and Taxation Publishers, 1985. xxxiv, 250p.).

About 10,000 entries in the main work. 16 chapters: 1. General subjects - 2. Organizations in the field of civil international aviation - 3. The administration of national and international aviation - 4. The aviation industry - 5. Aircraft - 6. Aviation personnel - 7. Airports and air navigation facilities - 8. Air transport - 9. Damage to third parties - 10. Accidents, towage and salvage - 11. Insurance - 12. Criminal law - 13. Acts on board aircraft - 14. Military aviation - 15. The laws of war and neutrality - 16. Miscellaneous. Index of names; analytical subject index. The supplements are similarly arranged. *Class No:* 347.8(01)

[3148]

LONDON UNIVERSITY. Institute of Advanced Legal Studies. **Union list of air and space law literature** in the libraries of Oxford, Cambridge and London. 2nd ed. London, the Institute, 1975. xii,301p. (*Union catalogue no.4, 2nd ed.*)

First published 1956.

About 2000 items with locations in 22 libraries. Part 1: Background works and source materials (dictionaries, bibliographies, etc.) - 2: Works on air and space law in general and on specific topics (*e.g.* legal aspects of military aviation and astronautics). Index of authors and editors, corporate author index; subject index. *Class No:* 347.8(01)

Legal Procedures & Personnel

[3149]

Stone's justice's manual, 1993. Richman, J. *and* Draycott, A.T., *eds.* 125th ed. London, Butterworth & Co (Publishers) Ltd.; Shaw & Sons Ltd., 1993. 3v. ISBN: 040601602x.

First published 1842.

Detailed authoritative information. 10 parts in 3v. V.1. Part 1. Magistrate's Courts, procedure - II. Evidence - III. Sentencing - IV. Family law - V. Youth Courts - VI. Licensing. V.2. Part VII. Offences, matters of complaint, etc. V.3. Part VIII. Transport - IX. Precedents and forms - X. Miscellaneous legislation. Table of Statutes and treaties. A-Z table of Statutory Instruments and EEC regulations. Chronological list of S.I.'s. Table of cases. Index, p.401-731. *Class No:* 347.9

Encyclopaedias

[3150]

REDDEN, K.R. **Modern legal systems cyclopedia.** Buffalo, N.Y., William S. Hein & Co., 1984. 10v. (loose-leaf, various pagings). $1375 the set; $175 each vol. ISBN: 0899413005, the set.

Designed as a standard reference source for practicing attorneys and academic institutions. Each volume covers a particular geographic region:- 1. North America - 2. Pacific Basin - 3. Western Europe (EEC countries) - 4. Western Europe (non-EEC countries) - 5. Middle East - 6. Africa - 7. Central America and Caribbean - 8. Eastern Europe - 9. Asia - 10. South America. Annotated bibliography follows each chapter. Value is enhanced by periodic supplementation and regional coverage, according to *International journal of legal information,* v.14(5-6), October-December, 1986, p.236). *Class No:* 347.9(031)

Ireland

Bibliographies

[3151]

O'HIGGINS, P. **Bibliography of Irish trials and other legal proceedings.** Abingdon, Oxon, Professional Books, 1986. 300p. £42.50. ISBN: 0862050804.

Nearly 2000 entries in 12 sections: 1. Digests - 2. Law reports - 3. Reports of single trials by named reporters - 4. Anonymous reports of trials - 5. Election cases - 6. Fishery cases - 7. Judge's charges to Grand Juries - 8. Books containing reports of trials - 9. Speeches by Counsel - 10. Speeches from the dock - 11. Counsel's opinion - 12. Miscellaneous. Indexes of cases, persons, and subjects. *Class No:* 347.9(415)(01)

Costume & Dress

[3152]

HARGREAVES-MAWDSLEY, W.N. **A History of legal dress in Europe** until the end of the eighteenth century. Oxford, Clarendon Press, 1963. xii,151p. illus.

Chapters: 1. Italy, Spain and Portugal - 2. France - 3. Great Britain and Ireland - 4. German-speaking countries, the Low Countries, Switzerland, Scandinavia, Hungary and Poland. Short glossary of terms, with line-drawings. Most of

....(contd.)

the illustrations are half-tones, not particularly clear or numerous, but backed by handy descriptions (*e.g.* of the dress of the Chief of Police in France). The 'Critical bibliography' (p.121-9) covers manuscripts and books but it is not annotated. Analytical index. *Class No:* 347.90:391

Civil Proceedings

[3153]
The Encyclopedia of forms and precedents other than court forms. Walton R., Sir. 5th ed. London, Butterworths, 1985-93. ISBN: 0406023603, the set.

3rd ed. 1945-50. 20v.; 4th ed. 1964-73, 24v.

Aim is 'to provide a form for at least every ordinary transaction which occurs in practice and for all those except such as are purely academic. To present these forms in a simple and straightforward manner so that the nature and effect can be understood at a glance. To collect and arrange them so that they can be found with the utmost facility' (*Publishers'* note). Arranged under topics, A-Z. *A consolidated index, 1988/89, to published volumes* was issued in 1989. Also two loose-leaf 'service' volumes. *Class No:* 347.91/.98

[3154]
—Atkin's encyclopaedia of court forms in civil proceedings. Jacob J.I.H., Sir, *and others, eds.* 2nd ed. London, Butterworth, 1961-. 41v. loose-leaf supplementary service. £966. ISBN: 040601020x.

First published 1937 in 16v.

Arranged under topic, A-Z. *Class No:* 347.91/.98

Arbitration

Bibliographies

[3155]
ZAGORIN, J.S. Bibliography of books and articles on international commercial arbitration. In *International journal of legal information*, v.17(3), Winter 1989, p.233-54.

Based on the library collection of bBaker & McKenzie, New York. 9 sections: General - Arbitrability - Coice of law - Procedure - Awards - Enforcement - Treaties - Local and regional arbitration. Includes a list of serials which regularly publish articles on arbitration, and a list of national arbitration associations and their publications. *Class No:* 347.918(01)

Dictionaries

[3156]
LEE, E.H. Dictionary of arbitration law and practice. London, Mansfield Law Publishers, 1986. [5],185p.

Claims to be the first of its kind to be devoted to the subject. Table of contents, by subject A-Z, precedes the dictionary, which includes terms and phrases familiar and less familiar relating to the subject. Also terms connected with arbitration law and practice. Entries may be definitions or judicial interpretations. Cross-references. Table of cases and table of Statutes and Rules of the Supreme Court. *Class No:* 347.918(038)

[3157]
SEIDE, K., *ed.* **A Dictionary of arbitration and its terms.** Dobbs Ferry, N.Y., Oceana, for the American Arbitration Association, 1970. 334p. $21. ISBN: 0379003864.

Defines *c.*700 arbitration terms, with source and case citations. Cross-references. Appendices on rules of arbitration procedures, arbitration statutes and uniform laws, international conventions, plus extensive bibliographies of commercial arbitration, international public arbitration and labour arbitration. *Class No:* 347.918(038)

Lawyers, Solicitors & Legal Officials

Worldwide

Yearbooks & Directories

[3158]
Kime's international law directory for 1993-94... Matthews, J.M., *ed.* London, Longman Law, Tax and Finance, previously Kime's International Law Directory Ltd., 1993. 1448p. £48. ISBN: 0851218768.

First published 1892.

Practitioners' names are arranged under continents, countries, states and towns. Separate sequences for foreign lawyers resident in London, New York and Paris; international commissioners, etc. *Class No:* 347.96(100)(058)

Great Britain

Yearbooks & Directories

[3159]
Butterworths law directory, 1993: a directory of solicitors and barristers in private practice, commerce, local government and public authorities in England, Scotland and Wales. 9th ed. London, Martindale-Hubbell, in association with the Butterworth Group, 1993. xi,1767p. £45. ISBN: 1857390717.

A-Z indexes, with contact details, of solicitors in private practice, in commerce, and firms in private practice. Agency commissions. A-Z indexes of barristers in private practice, in commerce. Geographical list of chambers. List of organizations employing solicitors and barristers. Scottish section. International section. Members of the Institute of Legal Executives. *Class No:* 347.96(410)(058)

[3160]
Directory of solicitors and barristers, 1992. London, The Law Society, 1992. 1313p. £48. ISBN: 1853280631.

Succeeds *The Law list* (1641-1976), *The Bar list* (1977-1989), and *The Solicitor's and barrister's directory.*

Contents include: Solicitors (solicitors firms in London, in England & Wales,overseas; Employed solicitors; firms index; solicitors index; notaries index); Barristers (chambers; individual barristers); Legal executives (A-Z listing). *Class No:* 347.96(410)(058)

[3161]
Hazell's guide to the judiciary and the courts with the Holborn Law Society's Bar list by chambers with index, 1987. Editorial Staff of R. Hazell & Co., *eds.* 3rd ed. Henley-on-Thames, Oxon, R. Hazell & Co., 1988. xi[1],335p. £17. ISBN: 0901718416. ISSN: 02663597.

First published 1985.

....(contd.)

In 9 sections: The judiciary - The courts in England and Wales (Circuits, Crown courts, Country courts, Magistrates' courts, Crown prosecution service) - Bar list by chambers - Northern Ireland - Scotland - Isle of Man - Jersey - Guernsey and Alderney - Police forces in England and Wales, Scotland, Northern Ireland, Isle of Man and the Channel Islands. A handy source of information. *Class No:* 347.96(410)(058)

Scotland

Yearbooks & Directories

[3162]

The Scottish law directory, 1987. 96th ed. Glasgow, W. Hodge & Co. Ltd., for the Law Society of Scotland, 1987. £25. ISSN: 00808083.

First published 1895.

Covers certificated solicitors practising in Scotland by authority of the Law Society of Scotland. *Class No:* 347.96(411)(058)

Courts

[3163]

The County court practice, 1993. Thompson, P.K.J., *ed.* London, Butterworth, 1991. Annual. clxxxiv,2013,54p. ISBN: 0406016127.

Part 1: General jurisdiction (relevant Acts; County court rules, 1981; Procedural tables) - 2. Special jurisdiction (Admiralty ... Consumer credit ... Water). 3. Costs and fees - 4. Forms. Appendix (County court directory).Analytical index, 54p. The Law is generally stated as at 1 January 1993. *Class No:* 347.97/.99

[3164]

A Reference guide to the United States Supreme Court. Elliott, S.P., *ed.* New York, Facts on File, 1986. 476p. illus. $50. ISBN: 0816010188.

6 major sections: The role of the Supreme Court - The constitutional powers of the branches of federal government - Division of power - Individual rights - Landmark cases - Biographies of the Justices (a concise biography, A-Z, of every Justice who has served on the Supreme Court). Several appendices of chronological listings. The bibliography includes books on the Court itself as well as on individual Justices. Index to cases, individuals and subjects. Supplements Congressional Quarterly's *Guide to the United States Supreme Court*(1979). *Class No:* 347.97/.99

[3165]

SKYRME, T. History of the Justices of the Peace. Chichester, West Sussex, Barry Rose, 1991. 3v. £75 each volume. ISBN: 1872328458, v.1; 1872328504, v.2; 1872328555, v.3.

History of JPs and magistrates from medieval England to date, including chapters on development in the United Kingdom and in Commonwealth countries. V.1. England to 1689 - v.2. England, 1689-1989 - v.3. Territories beyond England. Includes bibliographies and indexes. *Class No:* 347.97/.99

England & Wales

[3166]

The Supreme Court practice. Jacob, I.H., *ed.* 10th ed. Sweet & Maxwell and Stevens, 1992. 3v. (3961p.). ISBN: 0421464003. ISSN: 00395978.

First published 1967. New eds. were issued at 3-yearly, but now two-yearly intervals, kept up-to-date by biannual cumulative supplements.

V.1: pt.1. Rules of the Supreme Court (orders 1-115). ccxxvi, 1742p. V.2: pts. 2-18 (paras 1-6174). xix,1687p. V.1 includes tables of cases and Statutes (but not of Statutory Instruments). V.2, pts.: 2. Forms - 3. Practice directions and tables - 4. Court fees and stamps - 5. Court Funds Office rules and practice - 6. Admiralty jurisdiction and proceedings - 7. Family proceedings - 8. European jurisdiction - 9. Court of Protection - 10. Probate jurisdiction and proceedings - 11. Solicitors - 12. Legal aid - 13. Trustees - 14. Miscellaneous parties and proceedings - 15. Miscellaneous matters of practice - 16. House of Lords appeals - 17. Supreme Court Act 1981 and other Statutes and regulations - 18. Miscellaneous Statutes. V.3: Index (p.1-153). Table of Statutes (p.155-236). Chronological table. Table of Statutory Instruments (p.237-266). Table of cases (p.267-395). *Class No:* 347.97/.99(42)

Handbooks & Manuals

[3167]

OKE, G.C. Oke's Magisterial formulist ... Pearson, J.E., *ed.* 20th ed. London, Butterworth, 1985. 700p. in 2 loose-leaf binders. £125. ISBN: 040632400x.

First published 1850; 19th ed. 1979.

A companion volume to *Stone's Justice's manual.* Part 1. deals with forms for use before Magistrate's Courts; part 2. deals with precedents for offences, matters of complaint, search warrents, etc., divided A-R. Table of penalties. Tables of Statutes, Statutory Instruments. Detailed index, p.101-184, to divisions and paragraph numbers. Kept up to date. *Class No:* 347.97/.99(42)(035)

Yearbooks & Directories

[3168]

GREAT BRITAIN. Lord Chancellor's Department. County Courts Branch. **County Court districts (England and Wales): index of place names.** 14th ed. London, HMSO, 1992. [iv],181p. £15.95. ISBN: 0113800525.

Over 30,000 place-names, A-Z, with county and place of County Court. *Class No:* 347.97/.99(42)(058)

[3169]

—Shaw's directory of courts in the United Kingdom, 1993-94. London, Shaw & Sons, 1993. 456p. £27. ISBN: 0721914004.

First published 1973. Annual. *Class No:* 347.97/.99(42)(058)

USA

[3170]

BLANDFORD, L.A. *and* **EVANS, P.R.,** *eds.* **Supreme Court of the United States, 1789-1982:** an index of opinions. Millwood, N.Y., Kraus International, 1983. 2v. (1182 p.). $85. ISBN: 0527279528.

Arranged chronologically by the term of each justice. Opinions are classified in 7 categories (majority opinions -

....(contd.)

concurring opinions - dissenting opinions - opinions announcing judgement (plurality opinions) - separate opinions (views of individual justices) - statements (reasons for decisions based on precedents - opinions as circuit justices (opinions written during justice's service in such courts). 'Meticulous work' (*College and research libraries*, v.45 (1), January 1984, p.54 - 55).

First supplement, l981-l991 (l993. ISBN 0527279552). *Class No:* 347.97/.99(73)

[3171]

Guide to the US Supreme Court. 2nd ed. Washington, Congressional Quarterly, 1989. 1060p. $179.95 ISBN: 0685335585.

First published l979.

Guide to the origins, development, operation and decisions and impact of the Supreme Court. 'Members of the Court' provides brief biographies of the 101 Supreme Court justices. 'Major decisions of the Court, 1790-1979' summarises Supreme Court rulings. 'Case index' - Appended documents, glossary and detailed subject index. (Based on entry in *College & research libraries* July 1980, p.345-6). *Class No:* 347.97/.99(73)

[3172]

The Oxford companion to the Supreme Court of the United States. Hall, K.L., *ed*. New York, Oxford University Press, 1992. 1028p. illus. $49.95. ISBN: 0195058356.

A political, economic, cultural and legal history of the Court. Over 1000 entries by *c*.300 contributors, including biographies, court decisions, terms, etc. Cross-references. Case-name and topical indexes and extensive appendices. *Class No:* 347.97/.99(73)

Canon Law

[3173]

Canon law abstracts: a half-yearly review of periodical literature in canon law. By members of the Canon Law Society of Great Britain and Ireland. Melrose, the Society, 1959-. no.1-. 2pa. £10pa. ISSN: 00085650.

The 1988, no.2 issue (no.60) covers articles on the canon law of the Roman Catholic Church in journals appearing in July-December, 1987. Sections: General subjects - Oriental law - Historical subjects - Book 1: General works ... Book 7: Processes. *Class No:* 348

[3174]

The Code of canon law in English translation. London, Collins Liturgical Publcations, 1983. xv,319p. £4.95. ISBN: 000599750x.

7 Books (chapters): General norms - The people of God - The teaching office of the Church - The Sanctifying office - The termporal goods of the Church - Sanctions in the Church - Processes. Table of Canons. Glossary. Separate index published 1984 by Collins (112p. £1.95). *Class No:* 348

[3175]

CORIDEN, J., *and others, eds*. **The Code of canon law:** a text and commentary. New ed. London, Cassell, 1990. 1184p. £35. ISBN: 0809128373.

First published by G. Chaopman, 1985.

A commentary on the revised code of canon law, written and edited by members of the Canon Law Society of America. Each section is followed by a bibliography. Complete analytical index. *Class No:* 348

35 Public Administration

Public Administration

Bibliographies

[3176]
BUTCHER, T. 'Public administration and policy studies'. In *Information sources in politics and political science ...* (ed. by Englefield & Drewry. Butterworth, 1986.) p.189-208.

An introduction precedes 10 sections: Approaches to the study of public administration - Traditional approaches - Public administration as the study of organizations - Policy studies - British public administration - Central administration - The Civil Service - Control of the administration - Policy studies in Britain - Other literature and information sources. *Class No:* 350(01)

[3177]
CALIFORNIA UNIVERSITY. Institute of Governmental Studies Library. **Subject catalog...** Boston, Mass., G.K. Hall, 1970. 26v. (21,981p.). First supplement. 1978. 5v. (4051p.). $2830 the set. ISBN: 0816109079.

813,000 photolithographed catalogue cards. 'A collection of pamphlets, government documents, and periodicals covering a wide range of subjects of public interest, both past and present'. (G.K. Hall & Co. *Catalog,* 1979-1980, p.34). *Class No:* 350(01)

[3178]
GREAT BRITAIN. Overseas Development Administration. Library Services. **Public administration:** a select bibliography. 7th ed. London, the Library, 1987. [26p.]. *Gratis.*

First published 1967.

152 numbered items in 26 sections: Administrative law ... Government and public administration - Legislatures ... Management ... Population planning ... Rural development ... Urban and regional planning. Does not now include official publications which are included in *Technical co-operation.* Bibliographies; author and geographical indexes. *Class No:* 350(01)

[3179]
WRIGHT, M. 'The Literature and sources of public administration'. In *Use of social sciences literature* (ed. N. Roberts. London, Butterworth, 1977), p.192-218.

Running commentary. Sections: Public administration as a discipline - Approaches to the study of public administration [central and local government] - Information for research (Official documents; Unpublished material; Research; Government publications; Statistics; Secondary sources (journals). *Class No:* 350(01)

Dictionaries

[3180]
CHANDLER, R. *and* PLANO, J. **The Public administration dictionary.** 2nd ed. Santa Barbara, CA., ABC-Clio, 1988. 430p. $39.50. (*Clio dictionaries in political science.*) ISBN: 0874364991.

First published 1982 by Wiley.

330 two-part entries grouped in thematic chapters. Entries each cover a page or more, the first part explains what an idea, organization or principle is and cites related terms; the second part explains the defined idea's significance as it has been applied in practice. A bibliography is included but is not thematically linked with the dictionary. Index. *Class No:* 350(038)

[3181]
COLLIN, P.H. **Dictionary of government and politics.** Teddington, Mddx., Peter Collin Publishing, 1988. [3],225,[23]p. £5.95. ISBN: 094854905x.

*c.*5000 main words and phrases covering national legislatives, elections, local government, parliamentary and council procedure, international affairs and political parties and theories. Aims to cover both British and American terminology. A supplement gives information about the political and legislative systems in both Britain and the United States, together with the reproduction of relevant documents. Examples given. *Class No:* 350(038)

[3182]
SHAFRITZ, J.M. **The Facts on File dictionary of public administration.** New York, Facts on File, 1986. [9], 610p. $29.95. ISBN: 0816012660.

Short entries covering a great many terms and concepts in the traditional A-Z arrangement. Many entries include references to books and journals for further study. Includes short biographies of prominent persons in the field; court decisions, statutes, regulations, organisations and journals. Many cross-references. Also information on indexes, abstracts, databases, etc. relevant to public administration; a list of significant journals in the field; and a historical list of significant textbooks. Appendices include a copy of the US Constitution. 'A masterly codification by an eminent authority in public administration' (*Choice,* July/August 1986). *Class No:* 350(038)

Reviews & Abstracts

[3183]
FRANCIS. 528. **Bulletin signalétique.** 528. Bibliographie internationale de science administrative. International bibliography of administrative science. Paris, Institut de l'Information Scientifique et Technique, Science Humaines et Sociales. Centre National de la Recherche Scientifique, 1971-.v.1-. Quarterly. F.560pa. ISSN: 01508695.

Previously *Bulletin signalétique. 528. Science administrative,* 1947-1970, then *Bulletin signalétique. 528. Bibliographie interational de science administrative.*

V.42(4) (1988): Items 3335-4232 of indicative abstracts

.... *(contd.)*

and references. Sections: 01. Administrative science - 02. History - 03. Methods of administrative science - 04. Administrative structures - 05. Civil Service - 06. Means of action of administration - 07. Control of public order - 08. Public enterprise. List of journals scanned, index of concepts, index of authors per issue and annually. Contents list in English and French, but abstracts only in French. Available online (Telesystems, Questel) and on CD-ROM. *Class No:* 350(048)

[3184]
International review of administrative sciences. Brussels, International Institute of Administrative Sciences, 1928-. v.1, no.1-. Quarterly. £60pa.; $99pa. ISSN: 00208523.

An English-language edition has been published by Sage Publications since 1957. There is also a Spanish edition.

Includes a selective bibliography of between 60 and 100 books each issue, arranged by subject. *Class No:* 350(048)

[3185]
Sage public administration abstracts. Newbury Park, CA., Sage Publications, 1974-. Quarterly. $235pa. ISSN: 00946958.

Each issue has *c.*250 abstracts of books, pamphlets, government publications, significant speeches, legislative research studies and periodical articles from *c.*200 English-language periodicals in a wide range of subject fields relating to public administration. Many author abstracts. Arranged in 13 subject groups. Author and subject indexes (cumulated in the 4th issue each year) plus 'related citations' (lists of articles and books not abstracted). Journals and subject matter predominently North American. *Class No:* 350(048)

Scotland

Yearbooks & Directories

[3186]
The Scottish government yearbook, 1992. Paterson, L. *and* McCrone, D., *eds.* Edinburgh, University of Edinburgh, Unit for the Study of Government in Scotland, 1992. 282p. £8.95. ISBN: 0951805304.

First published 1979.

20 sections. The editors' introduction is followed by 2. The political year in Westminster, 3-8 are articles on constitutional issues, 9-11 on education, 12-15 on general matters, 16-19 on reference (opinion polls, Scottish legislation, structure of the Scottish Office, Parliamentary by-elections. 20 is on recent publications (452 items on Scottish government and politics).

From 1993 the title changed to *Scottish affairs.* issued quarterly. *Class No:* 350(411)(058)

USA

Bibliographies

[3187]
CAIDEN, E.G., and others. American public administration: a bibliographical guide to the literature. New York, Garland, 1983. xvii,201p. $30. (*Public affairs and administration series, v.3. Garland reference library of social science, v.169.*)

1220 items with descriptive annotations, arranged in 4 sections: 1. The scope of American public administration -

.... *(contd.)*

2. Abstracts, indexes and continuing bibliographies in public affairs and administration - 3. Professional journals in public affairs and administration - 4. A select bibliography of books. Index of abstracts, indexes and continuing bibliographies; index of journals; and author index. Intended for students of American public administration. One of *Choice's* outstanding academic books, 1984-85. *Class No:* 350(73)(01)

Handbooks & Manuals

[3188]
SHAFRITZ, J.M. The Dorsey dictionary of American government and politics. Chicago, Dorsey Press, 1989. xxxii,661p. illus., tables. $34.95. ISBN: 0256056390.

Over 4000 entries on Federal, State and local government and politics. Entries include important US Supreme Court decisions, political slang, and biographies, and most have bibliographical references. 5 appendices (including one treating online databases). Key concept list organizes all entries under wide headings. 'The work's careful scholarship, ease of use, comprehensiveness, and depth recommend it highly...' (*Choice,* October 1988, p.296). *Class No:* 350(73)(035)

[3189]
—SHAFRITZ, J.M. The HarperCollins dictionary of American government and politics. New York, HarperCollins, 1992. 656p. illus. tables, charts. $50. ISBN: 0062700316.

About half of the material has been taken from the Dorsey dictionary (see above), but *c.*1000 new terms are included, including current slang. Over 5000 entries, from a sentence to 250 words in length, noting the term's origins. Cross-references. Boxed features with many entries with lists, statistical summaries, quotes, and primary source material. 'Anything but dry, it is both erudite and readable.' (*Booklist,*v.88(17), 1 May 1992, p.1623). *Class No:* 350(73)(035)

Biographies

[3190]
American leaders, 1789-1991: a biographical summary. Washington, D.C., Congressional Quarterly, 1991. 450p. $27.95. ISBN: 0871875942.

Summary biographies of from two to six lines each, containing facts about American leaders at Federal and State levels (only governors at State level). 'A general potpourri ... useful at general reference desk' (*Choice,* v.25(4),December 1987, p595) of the first edition. *Class No:* 350(73)(092)

Libraries

[3191]
SIMMLER, O., *ed*. World directory of administrative libraries: a guide to libraries serving national, state, provincial and Länder libraries. Munich, K.G. Saur (previously Verlag Dokumentation), 1976. 475p. DM60. ISBN: 3794044274.

A directory, under countries A-Z; entries 1 per page for major libraries. Data stress specialisation, stock, service. Index of libraries; index under countries; index of official and English names. Includes entries for all European Community libraries. *Class No:* 350:061:026/027

Government Bodies

Worldwide

[3192]

State economic agencies of the world: an international directory of governmental organizations concerned with economics development and planning. Day, A.J., *ed.* Harlow, Essex, Longman, 1985. (Dist. in US & Canada by Gale Research Co.). x, 546p. £48; $78. (*Keesing's reference services.*) ISBN: 0582902533, UK; 0810321041, US.

Issued in the US as 'Governmental economic agencies of the world ...'.

*c.*2,000 state and parastatal agencies and organizations throughout the world active in economic spheres (*e.g.* national, regional and sectoral planning, industrial development, agrarian reform, export promotion etc.). Covers 170 countries, arranged A-Z, with, for each one, basic economic data and a brief résumé of the prevailing political and economic conditions preceding the listing of the economic agencies (*e.g.* trade agencies, central banks, nationalized banks, trading organizations, chambers of commerce, central statistical offices).

Class No: 350.07(100)

Great Britain

[3193]

GREAT BRITAIN. Cabinet Office. **Public bodies, 1993.** London, HMSO, 1993. xii,81p. tables. £12. ISBN: 0114300933.

First published 1988.

Lists nationalized industries, public corporations, non-departmental public bodies, and National Health Service authorities, and gives some basic facts about them, including information about annual reports published, addresses of sponsor departments, number of members appointed and their remuneration, other financial information, etc. Index.

Class No: 350.07(410)

Yearbooks & Directories

[3194]

Councils, committees & boards: a handbook of advisory, consultative, executive & similar bodies in British public life. Glanville, M.P., *ed.* 8th ed. Beckenham, Kent, CBD Research Ltd., 1993. xv,389p. £110. $200. ISBN: 0900246588.

First published 1970.

About 1270 entries (Aberdeen and District Milk Marketing Board ... Youth Committee for Northern Ireland). Includes Crown Agents, BBC and National Health Service (p.203-206). Data on each body: name; abbreviation; validity indication; address; telephone & telex number; establishment and membership; terms of reference, objects or duties; activities and supplementary information; publications; notes re imminent or proposed changes which will affect status/functions. Cross-references. Abbreviations index; index of chairmen, presidents and chief executives; subject index. 'An essential reference tool' (*Trade and industry,* 25 November 1977, p.386, on the 3rd ed.).

Class No: 350.07(410)(058)

USSR

Biographies

[3195]

LAZITCH, B.M. and **DRACHKOVITCH, M.M. Biographical dictionary of the Comintern.** New, rev. & expanded ed. Stanford, CA., Hoover Institution Press, 1986. lv,532p. $44.95. ISBN: 0817984011.

First published 1973.

A new introduction is followed by 753 biographical sketches ranging in length from several lines to several pages, of which some 230 have been updated and corrected. There follows a guide to abbreviations, a list of biographees, and a list of 435 pseudonyms. Does not indicate sources or include suggestions for further reading. 'The work should prove invaluable to those looking for information about persons who played little publicized roles in the Communist International' (*College & research libraries,* v.36(1), January 1975, p.63-4, of the 1st ed.).

Class No: 350.07(47)(092)

USA

Handbooks & Manuals

[3196]

United States government manual, 1992-93. Office of the Federal Register, National Archives and Records Service. Washington, Bernan Press, 1993. 1000p. tables, map. $29. ISBN: 0890590168.

First published 1935. Annual.

The official handbook of the Federal government. Describes the purposes and programmes of most government agencies and lists top personnel. *Class No:* 350.07(73)(035)

Meetings

[3197]

Shackleton on the law and practice of meetings. Shearman, I., *ed.* 8th ed. London, Sweet & Maxwell, 1991. xxxix,330p. £50. ISBN: 0421408707.

First published 1934.

5 parts: 1. Public meetings - 2. Meetings for the transaction of business: general rules 3. Meetings relating to companies - 4. Meetings of local authorities - 5. Defamatory statements. Analytical index, p.321-330.

Class No: 350.077.5

[3198]

—YELLAND, J., *ed.* The Conduct of meetings. 22nd ed. Bristol, Rose-Jordan, Ltd., 1982. xvii,206p. £6. ISBN: 0907313019.

First published 1910.

Authoritative, concise information on the conduct and procedure in holding both formal and informal meetings, with emphasis on statutory regulations and requirements. *Class No:* 350.077.5

[3199]

WARD, S. A-Z of meetings: how they work and how to run them. London, Pluto Press, 1985. ix,241p. illus., forms. £3.95. (*Pluto handbook.*) ISBN: 0745301037.

In 10 chapters: 1. Constitutions and rules - 2. Standing orders - 3. Alternative standing orders - 4. Meetings in practice - 5. Alternative practice for meetings - 6. Annual General Meetings - 7. Large conferences - 8. Running your

....*(contd.)*

own conference - 9. Discussion conferences - 10. The Law. Appendices: 1. Meetingspeak; 2. A guide to etiquette; 3. Sample trust deed. Index, p.211-214. *Class No:* 350.077.5

China

[3200]

LIEBERTHAL, K.G. *and* DICKSON, B.J. **Research guide to central party and government meetings in China, 1949-1986.** Rev. & expanded ed. Armonk, N.Y., M.E. Sharpe Inc., 1989. 339p. $50. ISBN: 0873324927.

First published 1976 covering 1949-75.

Covers over 500 meetings that could be documented. Information given includes dates, type of meetings (*e.g.* Party Congress, Politburo, Report meetings, etc.), place, attendance, major items on the agenda, speeches and reports, documents passed, other decisions or actions, and additional comments. Chronological arrangement. Index of people, places, organizations and issues. '... a unique and invaluable resource for China students and scholars' (*Choice*, v.27(4), December 1989, p.613p.).

Class No: 350.077.5(510)

Civil Service

Great Britain

[3201]

DREWRY, G. *and* BUTCHER, T. **The Civil Service today.** Oxford, Basil Blackwell, 1988. x,259p. tables. £29.95. ISBN: 0631154280.

A prologue: some crises of the 1980s, precedes 11 chapters (1. Charting the territory - 2. How things came to be - 3. Some facts and figures - 4. The universal department - 5. Recruitment and training - 6. Conditions of service - 7. The working context - 8. Ministers and civil servants - 9. The public face of private government - 10. Slimmer and fitter: the quest for efficiency and effectiveness - 11. Conclusion: the Civil Service at the crossroads?. 422 notes, by chapter headings, p.222-244. Select bibliography, by subject sections with no annotations, p.245-252. Index, p.253-259. (A 2nd ed. was issued in 1991. x,281p. £12.99. ISBN 0631181725). *Class No:* 350.08(410)

[3202]

GREAT BRITAIN. Committee on the Civil Service, 1966-68. Chairman: Lord Fulton. **[Report on the Civil Service].** London, HMSO, 1968-9. 5v. in 7.

1: Report of the Committee. 1968. (Cmnd.3638); 2: Report of a Management Consultancy Group. (1968); 3: (2 pts): Surveys and investigations; 4: Factual, statistical and explanatory paper (1968); 5: (2 pts): Proposals and opinions (1968). *Class No:* 350.08(410)

Bibliographies

[3203]

GREAT BRITAIN. HM Stationery Office. **Government publications. Sectional list 44, revised January 1991: Treasury and Civil Service.** London, HMSO, 1991. viii,139p. Gratis.

Includes sections on the Civil Service College - Civil Service Department - Committee of enquiry into Civil Service Pay - Equal Opportunities Division - Treasury and Civil Service Committee. *Class No:* 350.08(410)(01)

Yearbooks & Directories

[3204]

The Civil Service year book, 1993. Cabinet Office. London, HMSO., 1993. viii.885,ix-lxxxip. £19.50. ISBN: 0114300755.

Issued annually.

6 chapters: 1. The Royal Household - 2. Parliamentary Offices - 3. Ministers, Departments and Executive Agencies - 4. Libraries, museums and galleries. Research councils. Other organizations - 5. Departments and other organizations (Northern Ireland; Scotland; Wales) - 6. Salary tables. Entries briefly state scope of office and give telephone numbers for contacting. Index to individual officers. Index to departments and sub-departments precedes. Subject index, p.xliii-lxxvi. Essential to any reference library.

Class No: 350.08(410)(058)

Police

Bibliographies

[3205]

LOS ANGELES PUBLIC LIBRARY. **Catalog of the Police Library.** Boston, Mass., G.K. Hall, 1972. 2v. (1546p.). $200. ISBN: 0816109648.

35,000 photolithographic reproductions of a card dictionary catalogue, covering books, pamphlets and periodical articles, The collection is strong in criminology, scientific investigation, crime and criminals, riots, violence and police history. First supplement published l980 ($255. ISBN 0816103281 *Class No:* 351.74(01)

[3206]

Police science abstracts: an international abstracting service covering police science, the forensic sciences and forensic medicine. Amstelveen, Netherlands, Kugler Publications, for Criminologica Foundation, (early issues published by Kluwer D.V.), 1973-?. v.1-?. 6pa. ISSN: 01666282.

Continues *Abstracts on police science* (1973-1979). Prepared by Criminologica Foundation in co-operation with the University of Leiden and the Netherlands Institute for Advanced Training of Senior Police Officers, Warnsveld. Now superseded by *Criminology, penology and police science abstracts*.

About 1500 indicative and informative abstracts and references pa. 14 sections: 1. General - 2. Police organization - 3. Police personnel - 4. Police equipment - 5. Finances, budget - 6. Police power - 7. Police operations - 8. Traffic and traffic control - 9. Crime prevention - 10. Crime control, criminal investigation - 11. Police work in relation to special kinds of persons - 12. Police work in relation to special types of offences - 13. Forensic science - 14. Forensic medicine. Cross-references. Cumulative author and subject indexes. List of journals received for abstracting. *Class No:* 351.74(01)

[3207]

—WHITEHOUSE, J.E. A **Police bibliography.** New York, AMS Press, 1980. 2v.(525p.). $95. (*Studies in criminal justice, no.3.*) ISBN: 0404160409.

17,400 entries. Useful for retrospective coverage, with emphasis on the 1960-1970 period. *Class No:* 351.74(01)

Encyclopaedias

[3208]

KURIAN, G.T. World encyclopedia of police forces and penal systems. New York, Facts on File, 1989. 582p. tables, charts. $95. ISBN: 0816010196.

Data on law enforcement systems and correction systems in 183 countries. Countries are listed A-Z within 3 categories - major, smaller, micro. Entries for each country include a basic fact sheet with information on area, population, type of government, population per police officer, and police expenditure per 1000 inhabitants. Length of entries varies (UK:15p.; US:52p.) and for smaller countries, merely the basic fact sheet, plus short descriptions. For larger countries there are 4 headings (History and background - Structure and organization - Recruitment, education and training - The penal system). 4 appendices: Interpol (12p.); Directory of addresses of police HQs in 141 countries; Bibliography (34 titles, unannotated); Table of comparative statistics on police protection covering 125 countries. 'Although the information it contains is largely undocumented ... [the] encyclopedia ... brings together in one source much useful material' *Reference books bulletin*, v.86(2), 15 September 1989, p.211).
Class No: 351.74(031)

[3209]

—**FAY, J. Police dictionary and encyclopedia.** Springfield, Ill., C.C. Thomas, 1988. 378p. $29.75. ISBN: 0398054940.

4500 brief entries, including more than 6300 terms. International in coverage. ' ... a dictionary in format and contents ... '(*Library journal*, 15 April 1989, p.68).
Class No: 351.74(031)

Dictionaries

[3210]

INGLETON, R. Elsevier's dictionary of police and criminal law: English-French, French-English. Amsterdam & New York, Elsevier, 1992. viii,592p. Dfl. 275; $157. ISBN: 0444891021.

12,500 terms relating to the organization and functions of the police, the criminal law, and rules of evidence, traffic control, drugs, terrorism, accidents and disasters. Includes many slang and jargon terms. *Class No:* 351.74(038)

Yearbooks & Directories

[3211]

ANDRADE, J. World police and paramilitary forces. London, Macmillan Press,; New York, Stockton Press, 1985. xiii,245p. illus. £55.; $90. ISBN: 0333386299, UK; 0943818141, US.

Directory of police forces in almost every country of the world. 177 entries covering the history, organization and strength of each force and its role in maintaining internal security, criminal statistics, and operations and equipment. Part 1: Introduction; 2: Country-by-country survey, A-Z, plus Interpol; 3: Directory of internal security equipment. Select bibliography, p.xiii. 'Expensive, but worth the money' (*Reference books bulletin*, 1986/87).
Class No: 351.74(058)

Great Britain

[3212]

Police and constabulary almanac; official register of police forces and organizations in the United Kingdom for 1993. Henley-on-Thames, Oxon., R. Hazell & Co., 1993. 352p. £20.50 ISBN: 0901718602. ISSN: 04772008.

First published 1861.

A directory of Home Office officials, police organiozations; police forces; chief police officers; defence services, transport and local police; prisons, etc.; motor licence authorities and index; police and professional societies, associations, etc.; gazetteer; civil defence, emergency planning; fire brigade; ambulance services; charitable societies, associations, etc.; advertisements. Index, p.354 in 2 columns. Courts (p.i-xxiv) on yellow paper. *Class No:* 351.74(410)

Bibliographies

[3213]

BRETT, D.T., *comp.* **The Police of England and Wales:** a bibliography. 3rd ed. Bramshill, Hartley Wintney, Hants., Police Staff College, 1979. [i],[1],129p. £0.30. ISBN: 0903727927.

First published *c.*1964.

About 1000 unannotated entries under 7 heads (*e.g.* General information sources; Office of constable; General history and description; Committee reports; Police forces and areas). Little or no reference to special branches or departments such as the CID or women police.
Class No: 351.74(410)(01)

Security

Dictionaries

[3214]

FAY, J.J., *ed.* **Butterworth's security dictionary:** terms and concepts. Stoneham, MA., Butterworths publishers, 1987. [5], 277p. illus. (16 line drawings). $24.95. £35. ISBN: 0409900338.

Intended for security personnel who need to know the language used in all areas. Arranged in 3 sections: Procedural concepts - Legal concepts - Organizational concepts. Includes disciplines of law, investigations, risk management, personnel administration, safety, and electronics technology. Explains and describes terms and phrases rather than merely defining them, and includes examples where needed. Bibliography of *c.*120 items. Appendices include a list of terrorist groups; electronic security symbols, conversion tables, properties of flammable liquids and gases, etc. *Class No:* 351.75(038)

[3215]

KIDD, S. Dictionary of industrial security. London, Routledge, 1987. 141p. £16.95; $39.95. ISBN: 0710207948.

*c.*1000 entries for terms, phrases, acronyms, abbreviations, and names of associations and institutions related to the industrial security industry. Clearly written. Intended for managers of security firms, crime prevention agencies and the like. Includes a select bibliography and an appendix on UK and US security standards. Author is a British security manager. *Class No:* 351.75(038)

Yearbooks & Directories

[3216]

International security directory, 1987-88. 20th ed. Henley-on-Thames, Oxon., R. Hazell & Co. (Court & Judicial Publishing) 1987. [4],108p. £19.50. ISBN: 0901718424. ISSN: 00747890.

Annual since 1963.

Sections on international organizations (UN, NATO, Commonwealth Secretariat, ICPO Interpol) and national days (for all countries) precede the main section, Countries of the world (United Kingdom - Afghanistan ... Zimbabwe), with information for each country on population, alliance, defence, police and fire HQs, associations, and companies. Index of products, services and suppliers.
Class No: 351.75(058)

USA

[3217]

HAINES, G.K. *and* **LANGBART, D.A. Unlocking the files of the FBI:** a guide to its records and classification system. Wilmington, Del, Scholarly resources, 1993. xviii,348p. $60. ISBN: 0842023380.

Designed for researchers who require access to the extensive records and papers of the Federal Bureau of Investigation. Provides number, title, description, extent of records, date span, location, disposition, and procedures required to gain access. There are 278 classifications in the system. Includes bibliographical references and index. 'A welcome finding aid ...'(*Choice*, v.30(11), July/August 1993, p.1749). *Class No:* 351.75(73)

Housing

Dictionaries

[3218]

SAYEGH, K.S. Housing a multidisciplinary dictionary. Ottawa, ABCD-Academy Book, 1987. 626p. $31. ISBN: 0921139012.

c. 28,000 terms giving clear, concise and useful definitions from a wide variety of disciplines.
Class No: 351.778.5(038)

Europe

Tables & Data Books

[3219]

UNITED NATIONS. Economic Commission for Europe. **Annual bulletin of housing and building statistics for Europe ... 1991.** V.35 New York, United Nations, 1992. 129p. $25. ISBN: 9210162684.

First published 1957. Annual.

Statistical data on dwelling construction, materials used, employment in the construction industry, and wholesale price indices of building materials in Europe, Canada and the United States. *Class No:* 351.778.5(4)(083)

Great Britain

Bibliographies

[3220]

A Housing bibliography. Newson, T., *ed.* 5th ed. Birmingham, University of Birmingham, School of Public Policy, 1988. 214p. £12.

First and second eds. (1976 & 1978) published by Lancaster University; 3rd & 4th eds. by Birmingham University, Centre for Urban and Regional Studies. Early editions compiled by J.M. Stewart.

A comprehensive listing of literature published on British housing policy over the last five years. Subject and author indexes. *Class No:* 351.778.5(410)(01)

Yearbooks & Directories

[3221]

Housing year book, 1993. Harlow, Essex, Longman Group (UK) Ltd., 1993. Annual. xxxi,445p. £60. ISBN: 0582095042. ISSN: 02645181.

First published 1983.

A guide to local and central government departments, institutions, and people concerned with housing issues and problems in the UK. Preliminaries, including a gazetteer, are followed by 21 sections relating to local authorities, housing, rent and rates, etc., and including 20: Sources of information. Index,p434-444; Advertisers' index.
Class No: 351.778.5(410)(058)

Tables & Data Books

[3222]

GREAT BRITAIN. Department of the Environment. Scottish Development Department and Welsh Office. **Housing and construction statistics, 1982-1992, Great Britain.** 14th ed. London, HMSO., 1993. vii[2],226p. illus. tables. £24. ISBN: 0117528862.

First published for 1969-1979.

Designed to provide a broad perspective on developments over the past decade. Includes data on orders, output, labour, structure, materials and investment on construction; housebuilding, renovations, slum clearance, stock of dwellings, finance, rents, etc. relating to housing.

A 2-part quarterly, also titled *Housing and construction statistics* (1972-. £30pa. ISBN 03089819) has monthly and quarterly statistical data for the main series published in the annual. *Class No:* 351.778.5(410)(083)

England

Histories

[3223]

BURNETT, J. A Social history of housing, 1815-1985. Rev. ed. London, Methuen, 1986. 387p. £35. $39.95. ISBN: 0416367704.

First published by David & Charles in 1978, covering the years 1815-1970.

11 chapters, in 3 main periods: 1. 1815-1850 (1. People and houses; 2. The cottage homes of England; 3. The housing of the urban working classes; 4. Middle class housing) - 2. 1850-1914 - 3. 1918-1985. Chapter 11:

....(contd.)

Retrospect and prospect. Chapter notes and references, p.346-373. Index (small type), p.374-387.
Class No: 351.778.5(420)(091)

Economic Legislation

Dictionaries

[3224]
DRAZIL, J.V. Quantities and units of measurement: a dictionary and handbook. London, Mansell Publishing, 1983. [V],313p. £15. ISBN: 0720116651.

Supersedes the author's *Dictionary of quantities and units* (1971).

In 3 parts: 1. A dictionary of units of measurements, their symbols and abbreviations - 2. A dictionary of quantities and selected constants - 3. Symbols denoting qualities and constants. 4 appendices (2. UK and US units; 4. Bibliography (p 287-294). French and German indexes with references to corresponding English terms in pt.2.
Class No: 351.82(038)

Weights & Measures

[3225]
The Economist desk companion. London, Century Business/ Economist Books, 1992. 272p. £20. ISBN: 0712698167.

Adapted from *The World measurement guide.* Mostly conversion tables. In 4 parts: pt.1 is an introduction describing the three major world measurement systems; pt.2 has definitions, special measurements, formulae and calculations for 24 subject areas; pt.3 has 175 pages of conversion tables; and pt.4 has appendices. 'This is 'top desk publishing', but probably not a book for the layman' (*Library association record*, v.94(10), October 1992, p.668).
Class No: 351.821

[3226]
NAFT, S *and* **SOLA, R.de. International conversion tables.** Rev. and enl. ed. by P.H.Bigg. London, Cassell, 1965. liii,351 p.

First published 1961. Originally S. Naft's *Conversion equivalents in international trade* (1931).

6 sections: 1. Conversion factors - 2. Conversion tables - 3. Compound conversion factors - 4. Special measures used in various industries, commerce and engineering (Automobiles ... Water. Typographical point system. Clothing and shoe sizes: English, US and continental/metric) - 5. Geography of weights and measures (84 countries) - 6. Other useful data (alphabets; chemical elements; electrical units; international standards; signs and symbols). Detailed contents list; no index. Key passages are in French, German, Italian and Spanish, as well as English. *Class No:* 351.821

[3227]
The World measurement guide. 4th ed. London, The Economist Newspaper, 1980. 240p. illus. £30.; $55. ISBN: 085058040455.

First published as *The Economist' guide to weights and measures* in 1954. 3rd ed. (1975) was titled *'The Economist measurement guide and reckoner'.*

A guide to conversions between measuring systems; explains, defines, comments on and illustrates national and

....(contd.)

international measures and statistics. Quick reference - Systems of measurement (metric, UK, US, other countries) - Conversion tables - Special measurements (space and time; agriculture, fishing and forestry; industry) - Useful definitions and formulae - General tables (annual percentage rates, interest rates, growth rates, etc.) - Glossary (p.224-229) - Index (p.234-240). *Class No:* 351.821

Dictionaries

Polyglot

[3228]
CLASON, W.E., *comp.* **Elsevier's lexicon of international and national units;** English/American - German - Spanish - French - Italian - Japanese - Dutch - Portuguese - Polish - Swedish - Russian. Amsterdam, Elsevier, 1964. 75 p. (*Elsevier lexica.*)

299 English/American terms, with definitions, plus equivalents (but not indicating genders or plural forms) in 10 other languages. A second section lists units (300-368) used in different parts of the world, A-Z by 69 countries.' Index of international and national units' (p.61-72), covering 10 of the 11 languages in one A-Z sequence; 'Russian index ... ', p.73-74. Appended is a bibliography of dictionaries, glossaries and vocabularies, and of textbooks.
Class No: 351.821(038)=00

French

[3229]
DOURSTHER, H. Dictionnaire universel des poids et mesures anciens et modernes, contenant des tables des monnaies de tous les pays. Bruxelles, Hayez, 1840. (reprinted Amsterdam, Meridian Publishing Co., 1965). iv,604p.

Extremely full A-Z list of units, with French, English and decimal equivalents; for monetary units gives French and English weights, content and value. About 10-20,000 different units in all. Invaluable on Asiastic, historical and obscure currencies of weights and measures (*e.g.* Paolo; Ghersch; Platt; Batman; Line; Mud; Muck; Mun).
Class No: 351.821(038)=40

Great Britain

Yearbooks & Directories

[3230]
BRITISH STANDARDS INSTITUTION. British standards catalogue, 1993. London, BSI., 1993. xxi,798p. £36; loose-leaf ed. £52. Supplement (usually monthly): £108 pa. ISBN: 0580219704. ISSN: 09530339.

First published 1937. Title varies. Originally *Handbook of information.*

A numerical, briefly annotated list of current British Standards: General series (p.1-452), followed by BS CECC publications - BS QC publications - Codes of practice (p.453-472) - Automobile series - Marine series - Aerospace series - Handbooks - Published documents - Drafts for development - Education publications - British Standards Society publications - European standards - ETSI publications - Information service publications - BSI QA publications - Miscellaneous items - Corresponding

....(contd.)

international/British standards index. 'Complete sets of British Standards maintained for reference in the United Kingdom' (p.xiii). Subject index, p.621-798.
Class No: 351.821(410)(058)

Histories

[3231]
CONNOR, R.D. The Weights and measures of England. London, HMSO, 1987. xxvi,422p; illus. £30. ISBN: 0112904351.

14 chapters (1. From early beginnings to Roman times - 2. The natural and drusian foot - 3. The Saxon gyrd, the rod, and the acre ... 7. The early currency - 8. The origins of the units of commercial weight ... 13. The onset of metrication: The nineteenth century - 14. Britain goes metric: the twentieth century). 4 appendices (*e.g.* D. Tables of pre-metric British measures). Glossary of unit terms. Bibliography, p.373-387, A-Z by author. Analytical index, p.388-422. *Class No:* 351.821(410)(091)

[3232]
ZUPKO, R.E. British weights and measures: a history from antiquity to the seventeenth century. Madison, University of Wisconsin Press, 1977. xvi,248p. tables. ISBN: 0299073408.

Arranged in four chapters, all subdivided: 1. Roman, Anglo-Saxon, and Norman legacies - 2. Medieval times: refinement and proliferation - 3. The Tudor era - 4. Epilogue. 4 appendices include: B. British pre-Imperial units; C. British Imperial Units; D. Pre-metric weights and measures in Western and Eastern Europe. Bibliography (p.193-234) is arranged in four sections (MS., Monographs, Articles, Documents, Reference works, other works). Analytical index, p.235-248. *Class No:* 351.821(410)(091)

[3233]
ZUPKO, R.E. A Dictionary of English weights and measures, from Anglo-Saxon times to the nineteenth century. Madison, University of Wisconsin Press, 1968 (Available from Books Demand UMI). xvi,224p. $60. ISBN: 031708979x.

Dictionary, p.3-184 ('Acre' ... 'Yoke of land'). 'Pennyweight': 1½p. (etymology; definition; quotations). Ample cross-references; references. *Library journal* (v.93(16), 15 September 1968) notes that much material is drawn from *Oxford English dictionary* but there is new material as well. Valuable annotated bibliography, p.195-224. Appendix 2: Fundamental English laws on weights and measures. *Class No:* 351.821(410)(091)

Metric System

Dictionaries

[3234]
BRITISH STANDARDS INSTITUTION. Vocabulary of legal metrology: fundamental terms. London, BSI, 1971. 184p.

French ed. 1969, by Organisation Internationale de Metrologie Légale (93p.).

Defines *c.*280 terms on metrology, organizations and services, activities, documentation and markings for the

....(contd.)

service of legal metrology, quantities and units of measurement ... A-Z index in English and French. *Class No:* 351.821.1(038)

[3235]
—BRITISH STANDARDS INSTITUTION. Glossary of terms used in metrology. Rev. ed. London, BSI, 1986. 28p. (*BS 5233:1986.*)

First published 1975.

Defines fundamental terms, basic to all aspects of measurement. *Class No:* 351.821.1(038)

Local Government

[3236]
YOUNGS, F.A. Guide to the local administrative units of England. London, Royal Historical Society, 1980-1991. 2v. (xx,830p.;xx,919p.). ISBN: 0901050679, v.1; 0861932781, v.2.

Vol I. Southern England; vol II. Northern England. Each volume in 4 parts: 1. The parishes of England (V.I p.1-554; v.II. p.1-635) - 2. Local government units - 3. Parliamentary constituencies - 4. The dioceses of England. Parts 2-4 summarise the information in pts. 1 of each volume. Dividing line between volumes is roughly from the Severn to the Wash. Detailed lists of sources. *Class No:* 352

Bibliographies

[3237]
HILL, D.M. 'Local government'. In *Information sources in politics and political science ...* (Englefield & Drewry, eds., 1986), p.226-241.

An introduction is followed by sections on: Theories and definitions - Historical works and texts - Area studies, including London - Comparative studies - Representation and participation - Functions - Finance - Management - Central-local relations - Reform - Official material and bibliography. *Class No:* 352(01)

[3238]
INTERNATIONAL UNION OF LOCAL AUTHORITIES. Bibliographia: new publications in the library. The Hague, the Union, 1963-. no.1-. 6pa.

About 100 items (usually annotated) per issue. Annotations are in the language of the original. Sections, A-Z, by subject. No index. *Class No:* 352(01)

Handbooks & Manuals

[3239]
ROWAT, D.C. International handbook on local government reorganization: contemporary issues. Westport, CT., Greenwood Press, 1980. xv, 626p. illus. tables. $76.95. ISBN: 0313212694.

A comparative study, worldwide. 5 parts: 1. The government of metropolitan areas - 2. Regional or county government - 3. The basic units in developed countries - 4. The basic units in developing countries - 5. Conclusion, trends and problems. Appended list of comparative materials. *Class No:* 352(035)

Europe—Western

[3240]

European municipal directory, 1991-92. London, European Directories Ltd., [1991?]. lxiv,1191p. ISBN: 0951752006. ISSN: 09627820.

Key to entries; General note on listings; Local authorities and the European Community's institutions, precede the directory, which is arranged by country, A-Z. Each country listing is introduced by an explanation of how local government works in that country; what spending and other powers are available, and how budgets are raised. In English and 8 other European languages. *Class No:* 352(400)

Great Britain

Bibliographies

[3241]

GREAT BRITAIN. HM Stationery Office. **Government publications. Sectional list 5, revised August 1991: Environment.** London, HMSO, 1991. viii,68. *Gratis.*

Covers publications issued principally by the Department of the Environment (including those of its predecessor, the Ministry of Housing and Local Government, which are still available.

Covers in-print publications on the environment (local government, housing, conservation, polution control, etc.) available from HMSO, and also includes relevant publications from other organizations.

Class No: 352(410)(01)

[3242]

LOGA: local government annotations service. Romford, Essex, Havering Public Libraries, 1966-. Bi-monthly (previously monthly). £10pa. ISSN: 00236349.

Issued on behalf of the Association of London Chief Librarians in co-operation with other London public libraries.

Entries arranged A-Z by subject sections (General - Accidents ... Youth, youth employment and youth services). V.21, 1988/89 has 1142 indicative abstracts, covering journal articles, monographs and reports. 78 periodical titles are scanned (listed on back cover). Index to subjects.

Class No: 352(410)(01)

[3243]

—WATSON, J., *comp.* Bibliography of ephemeral community information materials. Leeds, Leeds Polytechnic School of Librarianship, Public Libraries Management Research Institute, 1979. 2v. (*British Library Research and Development report, 5521.*)

Part 1: A sources guide; part 2: An assessment of BNB coverage of housing and education titles from January 1977 to April 1979. *Class No:* 352(410)(01)

Handbooks & Manuals

[3244]

HARRISON, T. Access to information in local government. London, Sweet & Maxwell, 1988. xv,107p. £12.50. ISBN: 0421384107.

'Designed as a concise and practical guide to the law governing access to information held by local authorities and access to meetings generally'. Contents: 1. Access by the public (I. The Local Government (Access to Information) Act, 1985; II. Access to outside the 1985 Act) - 2. Access by

....(contd.)
local authority members - 3. Personal information - access and confidentiality - 4. The Data Protection Act, 1984 - 5. The Access to Personal Files Act, 1987. App.1: Text of the 1985 Act; App.2: List of enactments conferring rights to attend meetings or inspect documents.

Class No: 352(410)(035)

Yearbooks & Directories

[3245]

Longman directory of local authorities, 1993. London, Longman Law, Tax and Finance, 1993. 224p. £19.50. ISBN: 0851219675.

First published 1961.

Part 1. *Local authorities in England and Wales,* and part 2: *Local authorities in Scotland* both list county councils and district authorities, followed by a section giving names and alphabetical list of parishes, villages and other smaller places. Part 3. *General information and addresses* aims to help the user in the course of conveyancing work.

Class No: 352(410)(058)

Tables & Data Books

Bibliographies

[3246]

MORT, D. 'How to find UK local statistics'. In *Business information review,* v.5(1), July 1988, p.3-14.

Outlines the range of sources produced by local authorities, CIPFA, Chambers of Commerce, TV companies, market research companies and specialist consultants, etc. *Class No:* 352(410)(083)(01)

Histories

[3247]

KEITH-LUCAS, B *and* **RICHARDS, P. G. A History of local government in the twentieth century.** London, Allen & Unwin, 1978. 268p. (*New local government series, 17.*)

11 chapters, on constitution, functions, popularisms, councillors and permanent staff, party politics, central control, local government associations, 20th-century reorganizations, Local Government Act, 1972 and the changed system it created. ' ... The standard work on the subject' (*British book news,* November 1978, p.904).

Class No: 352(410)(091)

Scotland

[3248]

Scotland's regions, incorporating *County & municipal year book for Scotland,* 1994. 62nd ed. Coupar Angus, Perthshire, Wm Culross & Son Ltd., 1993. xi,390p. ISBN: 1873891148.

The ... *County & municipal year book for Scotland* was first published in 1934.

4 parts: 1. Offices and staff of government departments - 2. Scotland's regions: Regional, District Council and Development Corporation officials - 3. Scottish Health Service (p.125-217). National and local authority associations (p.218-382) - 4. Advertisers (by names and trades). *Class No:* 352(411)

England & Wales

Handbooks & Manuals

[3249]

GREAT BRITAIN. Department of the Environment *and* Welsh Office. **Local government in England and Wales:** a guide to the new system. London, HMSO, 1974. iv,275p. tables, maps. £4. ISBN: 0117508470.

The re-organization came into full operation on 1 April 1974. 10 sections: 1. General outlines of the new system - 2. Local authority functions in England and Wales - 3. Areas of the new local authorities - 4. Parishes, communities, etc. - 5. Electoral arrangements - 6. Chief executives and addresses of principal authorities - 7. National Health Service reorganization - 8. Water reorganization - 9. Names and addresses of bodies at national level - 10. Selection of publications (p.272-5). 3 folding maps: administrative, health and water areas. *Class No:* 352(42)(035)

[3250]

LABOUR PARTY. Local government handbook, England and Wales. 6th ed. London, Labour Party, 1977. xiv,381p. tables. (loose-leaf). £2.50.

First published 1920.

18 sections: 1. Structure of local government in England and Wales - 2. How local authorities work - 3. Councillors' rights and responsibilities ... 5. Local government finance - 6. Education - 7. Housing - 8. Social services - 9. Planning - 10. Transport ... 13. Environmental health - 14. Consumer protection - 15. Information services ... 17. Regional administration - 18. The Labour Group. Periodicals. *Class No:* 352(42)(035)

England

Histories

[3251]

REDLICH, J. *and* **HIRST, F.W. The History of local government in England.** 2nd ed. London, Macmillan, 1970. (Facsimile ed., by Kelley, 1980). xv,261p. £18. ISBN: 0678070059.

A re-issue of Book 1 of 'Local government in England' (1903), edited with an introduction and epilogue by B. Keith-Lucas.

The best account of the development of local government in the 19th century. Excellent evaluative footnote references to the literature; bibliography, p.253-6.

The massive *English local government, from the Revolution to the Municipal Corporation Act,* by Beatrice and Sidney Webb (London, Longmans, 1909-29, 11v.) was reprinted in 1963 (London, Cass), V.1, *The parish and the county* (xxxiv,664p.) has footnote references, an index of subjects of authors and other persons, and index of places. *Class No:* 352(420)(091)

USA

Bibliographies

[3252]

SHEARER, B.S. *and* **SHEARER, B.F. Periodical literature on United States cities:** a bibliography and subject guide. Westport, CT., Greenwood Press, 1983. xi,574p. $56.95. ISBN: 0313235112.

4919 periodical articles on the 170 US cities having a

....(contd.)

population of 100,000 or more, arranged by name of city, A-Z. Includes articles published between 1970 and 1981, selected by value of information and availability. 8 categories (not all used for each city): General - Architecture and the arts - Education and the media - Environment - Government and politics - Housing and urban development - Social and economic conditions - Transportation. List of cities by States, with entry numbers. Author and subject indexes. 'A most useful selection' (*College & research libraries,* v.45(1), January 1984, p.52-53). *Class No:* 352(73)(01)

Information Services

Great Britain

[3253]

GRAYSON, L. Library and information services for local government in Great Britain. London, Library Association, 1978. 242p. £11.50; $15. ISBN: 0853658102.

9 chapters, each with 'References and notes': 1. Developments promoting information flow in local government ... 4. The development of documentary information services ... 7. Co-operation between information services ... 9. The future. Appendix: 'Local government and other organisations involved in the provision of documentary information services', p.170-4. Bibliography of 283 annotated items, p.175-228. Analytical index, p.229-42. Useful to local councillors as well as librarians. *Class No:* 352:061:025.5(410)

Urban Areas (Towns & Cities)

[3254]

MARLIN, J.T., *and others*. **Book of world city rankings.** New York, Free Press, 1986. 604p. 82 tables. $29.95. ISBN: 0029202302.

Supersedes *The book of city rankings* (1984).

Information on the quality of life and work in over 100 metropolitan areas around the world, using vital statistics, demographics, economy, health, crime, and many other important social criteria to ascertain rankings. In 2 parts: 1. Cities subdivided by geographical regions - 2. Comparative data on land and environment, demography, economy, transport, health, housing, education and crime. Useful table of contents but no general index. Bibliographical references follow each section. *Class No:* 352.075.1

Reviews & Abstracts

[3255]

Sage urban studies abstracts. Newbury Park, CA., Sage Publications, 1973-. v.1-. Quarterly. $232pa. ISSN: 00905747.

*c.*250 indicative and informative abstracts in each issue. Sections: Trends in urbanization and urban society - Urban history - Architecture and urban design - Housing - Urban development and redevelopment - Urban planning and land use - Environment and resource conservation - Transportation and communication - Crime, criminal justice, and law enforcement - Urban economics - Social and public services - Government, administration and politics - Urban fiscal and budgeting policy - Social issues and trends - Urban

....*(contd.)*

theory and research. Author and subject indexes. List of periodicals abstracted and cumulative index published in the 4th issue each year. *Class No:* 352.075.1(048)

Yearbooks & Directories

[3256]

Urban history yearbook, 1991. Reeder, D.A., *ed*. Leicester, Leicester University Press, 1991. 300p. £39.50. ISBN: 0718560914.

First published 1974. Annual.

A research tool and forum of discussion for urban historians. *Class No:* 352.075.1(058)

Histories

[3257]

CHANDLER, T. Four thousand years of urban growth: an historical census. Rev. ed. Lewiston, N.Y., St. David's University Press, 1987. 656p. tables. $129.95. ISBN: 0889462070.

First published 1974 as *3000 years of urban growth,* by Chandler and Fox.

Covers the period from 2250 BC. to AD. 1975. Time series population data is given for the years available for individual cities. Sources are cited and indications given to which figures are estimated. Other tables rank cities by population. An introductory chapter on methodology precedes the main part of the work, which is arranged in broad geographic areas, subdivided by country or region. Historical names are used. Index of city, country and regional names, but no cross-references to current names. *Class No:* 352.075.1(091)

Europe

Histories

[3258]

BARLEY, M.W., *ed.* **European towns:** their archaeology and early history. London, New York, Academic Press, for the Council for British Archaeology, 1977. xxvii,521p. illus. (incl. pl.). £74. ISBN: 0120788500.

30 contributors. 3 parts: 1. Country surveys (1-18; *e.g.* 2. Urban archaeology in Scotland, p.19-35. 30 references. Résumés in French and German) - 2. Origins of towns (16-23; *e.g.* 22. Novgorod, p.391-403; bibliographical note of ½p.) - 3. The town as a political centre (*e.g.* 27. Northern Italy, p.475-85. 12 notes). Index (non-analytical), p.511-21. *Class No:* 352.075.1(4)(091)

Europe—Western

Histories

[3259]

GUTKIND, E.A., *and others*. **International history of city development.** London, Collier-Macmillan, 1964-72. 8v. illus., facsims., plans, maps. £40. each vol. ISBN: 0029132509, v.1; 0029132606, v.2; 0029132703, v.3; 0029132800, v.4; 0029133009, v.5; 0029133106, v.6; (no information on v.7); 0029133300, v.8.

Contents: v.1. Urban development in Central Europe (1964); v.2 Urban development in the Alpine and

....*(contd.)*

Scandinavian countries (1965); v.3. Urban development in Southern Europe: Spain and Portugal (1967); v.4. Urban development in Southern Europe: Italy and Greece (1969); v.5. Urban development in Western Europe: France and Belgium (1970); v.6. Urban development in Western Europe: the Netherlands and Great Britain (1971); v.7 Urban development in East-Central Europe: Poland, Czechoslovakia and Hungary (1972); v.8 Urban development in East Europe: Bulgaria, Romania and the U.S.S.R. (1972). V.6 (xv,512p.) devotes p.127-473 to Great Britain (chapters: 5. Origin and spread of settlement; 6. The Roman interlude; 7. Invasion and settlements; 8. The Middle Ages; 9 Utopia. Reality. Subtopia; 10. City survey (24 cities); bibliography, p.492-504). V.6 has 294 captioned illus. in all. *Class No:* 352.075.1(400)(091)

Great Britain

Reviews & Abstracts

[3260]

Urban abstracts. London Research Centre. Research Library, *comp.* London, Research Centre (previously London, Greater London Council Research Library, and later Letchworth, Herts., Technical Communications), 1974-. v.1-. Monthly. £98pa. ISSN: 0305103x.

Previously compiled by the Greater London Council's Research Library.

About 3000 indicative abstracts pa., arranged under 16 subject headings: Government and politics - Local government - Education - Emergency services and planning - Health - Housing - Industry and employment - Leisure and recreation - Personnel and training - Social issues and policy - Social services - Urban and regional planning - Transportation - Building, construction and architecture - Engineering and electronics - Environment and pollution. Also available on ACOMPLINE and URBALINE databases, and on CD-ROM.. *Class No:* 352.075.1(410)(048)

Yearbooks & Directories

[3261]

The Municipal year book and public service directory. 1994 ed. London, Municipal Journal Ltd., 1994. 2v. maps. Annual. £140 for 2v. ISBN: 0900552612. ISSN: 03055906.

First published 1898.

46 sections of general information on public services. V.1. Functions and officers (35 sections: 1. Administrative and legal services ... 31. Water - 32. National associations of local authorities - 33. Organizations - 34. Maps - 35. Late information). V.2 Authorities and members (sections 36 to 46: 36. County councils of England ... 46. Central government of England).General index; index to local authorities; index to advertisers. *Class No:* 352.075.1(410)(058)

Histories

[3262]

GROSS, C. A Bibliography of British municipal history. 2nd ed. Leicester, Leicester University Press, 1966 (Reprinted New York, B. Franklin). vi,xvi,vii,xxxiv,461p. $32.50. ISBN: 8833714651.

First published 1897 by Harvard University Press.

.... (contd.)

3092 numbered items (with interpolations) - books, pamphlets, articles - on the constitutional history of British boroughs. Introductory 'Survey of principal public and local records for municipal history and town chronicles'. Part 1: General works (including bibliographies, sources, secondary works) on municipal history (including countries), arranged by period and by subject. Part 2: Works on individual towns, A-Z (p.150-430). Particularly important items (*e.g.* Anderson) are asterisked. Index, p.433-461. A basic critical bibliography. The 2nd ed. is a reprint, with an essay on Gross and his contributions to urban studies, by G.H. Martin. *Class No:* 352.075.1(410)(091)

[3263]
—MARTIN, G. H. *and* McINTYRE, S. A Bibliography of British and Irish municipal history. v.1: General works. Leicester, Leicester University Press, 1972. lviii,806p. £30. ISBN: 0718510933.

Excludes titles cited in Gross, which it supplements. 6006 entries cover the period from earliest times to 1966. Main sections (closely subdivided): Bibliographies and guides - General printed records: texts and calendars - General history - The urban community - Municipal administration (p.295-544) - Wales, Scotland, Ireland (p.545-703). Valuable general introduction; numerous sectional prefaces. Author and subject index, p. 717-806.
Class No: 352.075.1(410)(091)

England

[3264]
BERESFORD, M.W. *and* FINBERG, H.P.R. English medieval boroughs: a hand-list. Newton Abbot, Devon, David & Charles, 1973. 200p. tables.

Introduction (p.21-57; 10 sections, *e.g.* 10: Nature of sources for first evidence) - Handlist of English medieval boroughs, arranged by counties, p.65-193. 'A gazetteer of places which in their day were reckoned to be boroughs' (*Introduction*). Entries consist of date, brief description, source. Call numbers are given for classes of documents cited from the Public Record Office.
Class No: 352.075.1(420)

[3265]
—REYNOLDS, S. An Introduction to the history of English medieval towns. Oxford, Clarendon Press, 1977. xiv,234p. illus. (pl.), maps. £17.50. ISBN: 0198224559.

Concerns towns, not boroughs. Refers to European parallels. Bibliography, p.202-23. Index. 'For the undergraduate and the interested layman' (*British book news,* January 1978, p.74). *Class No:* 352.075.1(420)

[3266]
PATTEN, J. English towns, 1500-1700. Folkestone, Dawson, 1978. 360p. 15 tables, 25 figs., maps. £14; $30. ISBN: 0712907939, UK; 0208617216, US.

Concentrates on themes of population, occupation and town-and-country relationships during the period, following examination of medieval town patterns and antecedents. The concluding chapter focuses on a comparative study of towns in Norfolk and Suffolk. *Class No:* 352.075.1(420)

Africa

Bibliographies

[3267]
O'CONNOR, A.M. Urbanization in tropical Africa an annotated bibliography. Boston, Mass., G.K. Hall, 1981. xxx,380p. maps (on end papers). $46. (*Bibliographies and guides in African studies.*) ISBN: 0816182620.

Annotated entries for scholarly literature written in English or French and published between 1960 and 1979 in the disciplines of sociology, demography, geography and urban planning. Geographical arrangement subdivided by countries, then cities. Cross-references. Includes a list of periodicals, and indexes by place names and authors. *Class No:* 352.075.1(6)(01)

USA

Bibliographies

[3268]
BUENKER, J.D., *and others.* Urban history: a guide to information sources. Detroit, Mich., Gale Research Co., 1981. 448p. $68. (*American government and history information guide series, 9.*) ISBN: 0810314797.

*c.*1900 entries, divided into topical chapters: General studies - The urbanization process - The city in American thought - Regional studies - Studies of colonial cities and towns - Urban institutions - Planning, architecture and urban renewal - Class, ethnicity and race - Urban politics and government - Bosses, machines and urban reform. Author, title and subject indexes. *Class No:* 352.075.1(73)(01)

[3269]
Index to current urban documents. Westport, CT., Greenwood Press, 1973-. Quarterly, with annual cumulations. $350pa. ISSN: 00468908.

Documents are listed geographically by US state and city or county, subdivided by government agency. Short annotations appended as necessary to convey content. Subject index. Also available online.
Class No: 352.075.1(73)(01)

[3270]
—HECKART, R.J. 'A Fresh look at the *Index to current urban documents* and the *Urban documents microfiche collection*'. In *RSR,* v.17(3), Fall, 1989, p.79-82.

'Despite the fact that these two resources constitute the only ongoing, fully indexed national resource for local government documents, many libraries fail to use them' (the author). The article explains how they can be used, and includes 6 references. *Class No:* 352.075.1(73)(01)

[3271]
UNITED STATES. Department of Housing and Urban Development. Library and Information Division. Dictionary catalog of the United States Department of Housing and Urban Development Library and Information Division. Boston, Mass., G.K. Hall, 1972-75. 19v. (14,936p.); 2 supplements (2v. each). $1880 for 19v.; $220 for supplements. ISBN: 0816110077, the set of 19v; 0816111359, the set of supplements.

About 350,000 photolithographically reproduced catalogue cards. Includes over 12,000 Comprehensive Planning Reports and Model Cities Reports. The HUD Library is the national information resource for urban regional planning

....(contd.)

literature, covering housing, urban renewal, race relations, community development environment, law and legislation. *Class No:* 352.075.1(73)(01)

Reviews & Abstracts

[3272]

Urban affairs abstracts. Washington, National League of Cities, 1971-. Weekly, with semi-annual and annual cumulations. $275pa. ISSN: 03006859.

Draws upon 400 journals on urban affairs. Mainly US. Subject arrangement. *Class No:* 352.075.1(73)(048)

Yearbooks & Directories

[3273]

The Municipal year book, 1993. V.60. Washington, DC., ICMA, 1993. 416p. charts, tables. $79.95. ISBN: 0873269683. ISSN: 00772186.

First published 1934.

The basic reference annual on United States local government. In 6 sections: 1. Five substantial articles on selected current issues - 2. Four surveys of intergovernmental developments - 3. Salary surveys - 4. Profiles of individual cities and counties in tabular form - 5. Ten directory listings of local government associations, top municipal officials, etc., and descriptions of 73 organizations providing professional services. Also includes a bibliography with references under 17 headings (reference - statistical sources - 15 functional areas); an annotated list of books and reports, followed by periodicals and descriptions of online services; a list of publishers' addresses.

Class No: 352.075.1(73)(058)

Counties

England & Wales

Histories

[3274]

STEPHENS, E., *comp.* **The Clerks of the Counties, 1360-1960.** London, Society of Clerks of the Peace of Counties and of Clerks of County Councils, 1961. xiv,[1],274p. illus.

Lists *c.*2800 names, arranged A-Z according to counties, of those known to have held office of Clerk of the Peace in the counties of England and Wales, 1360-1960, and the office of the Clerk of the County Council from 1889 to 1960 (p.51-193). 7 columns, stating period of office, name, dates of birth and death, and biographical notes. 5 appendices. Index of names of Clerks of the Counties.

Class No: 353(42)(091)

USA

Dictionaries

[3275]

ELLIOTT, J.M. *and* **ALI, S.R. The State and local government political dictionary.** Santa Barbara, CA., ABC-Clio, 1988. 325p. $37.50. (*Clio dictionary in politics.*) ISBN: 0874364175.

The author describes the work as a 'dictionary, reference guide, study guide, supplement to a textbook, source of

....(contd.)

review material and/or a social science aid. '... a useful and well-organized tool that defines and describes the significance of major concepts and terms used to study American state and local government' (*Choice,* v.26(5), January, 1989, p.780). *Class No:* 353(73)(038)

Yearbooks & Directories

[3276]

The Book of the States, 1992-93. Lexington, KY, Council of State Governments, 1992. 720p. illus. $79.00. ISBN: 0872929639. ISSN: 00680125.

First published 1935. Biennial.

A general survey of the constitution, organization, financing and functioning of State governments is followed by data on individual States (*e.g.* nickname, motto, flower, bird, tree, song). *Class No:* 353(73)(058)

Biographies

[3277]

SOBEL, R. *and* **RAIMO, J., eds. Biographical directory of the governors of the United States, 1789-1978.** Westport, CT., Meckler Books, 1978. 4v.

117 contributors. Entries are in chronological order under States, A-Z. Biographical data include names and occupations of parents; family; religion; political affiliation; election results; political and private careers; accomplishments in office; bibliography (including location of governor's papers). 'This excellent set' (*Choice,* December 1978, p.1344). *Class No:* 353(73)(092)

[3278]

—RAIMO, J.W., *ed.* Biographical directory of the governors of the United States, 1978-1983. Westport, CT., Meckler Books, 1985. 352p. $45.

Continues the above. *Class No:* 353(73)(092)

Central Government

[3279]

The Economist dictionary of political biography. London, Economist Books Ltd., 1990. 335p. ISBN: 009174847x.

Over 2000 entries, including brief biographies (*e.g.* 'Mitterand': 1¾ columns. A glossary and list of abbreviations follow. The index arranges entries under countries, Afghanistan ... Zimbabwe. Very readable text. *Class No:* 354

Worldwide

[3280]

BLONDEL, J. The Organization of governments: a comparative analysis of governmental structures. Beverley Hills, CA., Sage Publications, 1980. [6],242p. illus. $28. (*Political executives in comparative perspective: a cross-national empirical study, v.2.*) ISBN: 0803997760.

Arranged in 8 chapters, followed by a select bibliography (p.235-6). Index, p.237-242. *Class No:* 354(100)

[3281]

TAPSELL, R.F. **Monarchs, rulers, dynasties and kingdoms of the world.** New York, Facts on File, 1983. 512p. illus. $35. ISBN: 0871961210.

Part 1 has a 1200-item dictionary of states and dynasties (Abbadids of Seville ... Zurayids of Yemen); part 2 lists are arranged geographically and chronologically. A chart indicating family relationships precedes the lists. Includes minor states and, except for the US presidents, includes only rulers who were members of established lines or dynasties. Bibliography of sources. Supplements *Kings, rulers and statesmen*, by E.W. Egan and others (1977).
Class No: 354(100)

Handbooks & Manuals

[3282]

World guide to foreign services, 1986-87. Jackisch, M., *ed*. First ed. Weissensberg, Germany, World Guides Internationale, 1986. xiv, 838p. $155. ISBN: 3926393009.

A directory of ministries of foreign affairs, embassies, consulates, high commissions, missions, legations, delegations and representations. Lists 18,400 diplomatic and consular services of 170 nations. For each office it gives the office's name, address, telephone & telex numbers, office hours, jurisdiction, and names and titles of diplomatic staff members. Arrangement is A-Z by country. '... an accurate source of information on the world's diplomatic posts as of August 1986' (*Wilson library bulletin,* May 1987, p.68). 'There is no directory quite like this one' (*Choice,* June 1987, p.1540). *Class No:* 354(100)(035)

Yearbooks & Directories

[3283]

BIDWELL, R., *comp. & ed*. **Bidwell's guide to government ministers.** London, Frank Cass & Co. Ltd., 1973-74. 3v. (606p.). tables. £25 ech vol. ISBN: 0714629774, v.1; 0714630012, v.2; 0714630179, v.3.

V.1 *The major powers and Western Europe, 1900-1971*; V.2 *The Arab world, 1900-1972; V.3 The British Empire and successor states, 1900-1972.* Positions given for each country: head of state; heads of government; ministers of foreign affairs, war/defence, the interior, finance, justice; the navy; trade, commerce, industry and economic affairs; colonies/overseas territories; permanent representatives at UNO. Notes are appended to each volume.
Class No: 354(100)(058)

[3284]

BLONDEL, J. **Government ministers in the contemporary world.** London, Beverley Hills., CA., Sage, 1985. viii,291p. 1 illus., tables, charts. £25. (*Political executives in comparative perspective: a cross-national empirical study, v.3.*) ISBN: 0803997507.

Devoted to an anatomy of ministerial careers throughout the governments of the world since 1945. In 3 parts: I. Background (the social background of ministers; the routes to ministerial office) - II. The duration of ministers in office - III. Ministers in government (including amateurs and specialists, long-lasting ministers, one-post ministers). Appendix I. The sources of this study; II. Country characteristics of ministers, 1945-1982. Bibliography, p.282-283. Index, p.284-290. *Class No:* 354(100)(058)

[3285]

BLONDEL, J. **World leaders:** heads of government in the post-war period. Beverley Hills, CA., Sage Publications, 1980. [4],282p. $28. (*Political executives in comparative perspective: a cross-national empirical study, v.1.*) ISBN: 0803998309.

An introduction is followed by 9 chapters arranged in 3 parts: 1. The institution of chief executive - 2. The leaders - 3. The 'Long' leaders. Notes are appended to the end of chapters. Appendix: Notes on sources (p.271-272). Bibliography (p.273-274). Index (p.275-282).
Class No: 354(100)(058)

[3286]

Countries of the world and their leaders, 1994. Detroit, Mich., Gale Research Company, 1993. Annual. 2v.(1990p.). illus., 70 maps and other illus. ISBN: 081038227x. ISSN: 01962809.

Basic social, political and economic data for 170 countries of the world, provided by the US State Department and other government sources. Also other information of use to American businessmen and other travellers, including the CIA's list of 'Chiefs of State and Cabinet members of foreign governments' and reports on OAU, NATO, OECD, UN, ASEAN and the EC. *Class No:* 354(100)(058)

[3287]

DA GRAÇA, J. **Heads of state and government:** a comprehensive international historical directory. New York, New York University Press; London, Macmillan, 1985. [7], 265p. $65; £33. ISBN: 0814717780, US; 0333392817, UK.

Updates *Rulers and governors of the world,* ed. by B. Spuler (New York, Bowker, 1977-78), which was a translation of *Regenten und Regierungen der Welt* (Würzburg, Ploetz, first published 1953).

Arranged in two main sections: A. Major international organizations (Arab League - ASEAN- Caribbean Community - Commonwealth of Nations - CMEA - Council of Europe - European Community - NATO - UAU - OAS - Organization of the Islamic Conference - South Pacific Commission - UN); B. Countries and regions, A-Z, (Afghanistan ... Zimbabwe). Under each organization, country or region is a chronological list of names and dates of office of all the leaders, each entry being preceded by a concise historical note and some general facts about the country, etc. Covers over 500 countries, regions and territories, and contains the names of nearly 10,000 leaders. Index, cross-referenced. *Class No:* 354(100)(058)

[3288]

The International directory of government. London, Europa, 1990 (distributed by Taylor & Francis in the US). 697p. £140. $275. ISBN: 0946653569.

Over 10,000 entries for government ministries, departments, agencies and corporations, plus key personnel. Arranged A-Z by country (Afghanistan ... Zimbabwe). Standard format, each chapter being headed by a 'power map' relating to the head of state and legislation. Telephone and telex numbers and full addresses are given. 'A very substantial addition to the Europa reference series'(*International affairs,* v.67(3), July 1991, p.571). *Class No:* 354(100)(058)

[3289]

The Times survey of foreign ministries of the world. Steiner, Z, *ed.* London, Times Books; Westport, CT., Meckler Publishing Inc., 1982. 624p, illus. £40; $87.50. ISBN: 0723002452, UK; 0930466373, US.

A 32-page introduction precedes 24 essays by experts, covering 10 members of the European Community, the rest of Europe, Australia, Canada, China, Japan, Turkey, the Soviet Union and USA, 24 countries in all. Essays include a history of the origins and growth of the foreign ministry in question, an account of how the foreign service works today, a bibliography, and a diagram of the foreign ministry establishment. 'A standard source in diplomatic history, although omitted countries deserve a companion volume (*Wilson library bulletin*, October 1982, p.176).

Class No: 354(100)(058)

Europe

[3290]

Who's who in European politics. 2nd ed. London, Bowker-Saur, 1993. xxiii,1016p. £149. $215. ISBN: 1857390210.

Section 1 has 8170 short biographies of active politicians (heads of state, members of government, national legislatures, political parties, trade unions, and prominent regional leaders) arranged A-Z in one sequence. Section 2 is a country by country political directory and index, listing heads of State, all members of national governments, leading political party members, etc. *Class No:* 354(4)

Great Britain

[3291]

The New Whitehall series. London, Allen & Unwin, for the Royal Institute of Public Administration, 1954-79. No. 16 is available from the Institute, £10.

1. *The Home Office,* by Sir F.A. Newsam, 1954; 2nd ed. 1955. 2. *The Foreign Office,* by First Baron Strong, and others. 1955. 3. *The Colonial Office,* by Sir C. Jeffries. 1956. 4. *The Ministry of Works,* by Sir H. Emmerson. 1956. 5. *The Scottish Office, and other Scottish government departments,* by Sir D. Milne. 1957. 6. *The Ministry of Pensions and National Insurance. 1958. 7. The Ministry of Transport and Civil Aviation,* by Sir G. Jenkins. 1959. 8. *The Ministry of Labour and National Service,* by Sir G. Ince. 1960. 9. *The Department of Scientific and Industrial Research,* by Sir H. Melville. 1962. 10. *Her Majesty's Custom & Excise,* by Sir J. Crombie. 1962. 11. *The Ministry of Agriculture, Fisheries and Food,* by Sir J. Winnifrith. 1962. 12. *The Treasury,* by Lord Bridges, 1966; 2nd ed. 1967. 13. *The Inland Revenue,* by Sir A. Johnston, 1965. 14. *The Ministry of Housing and Local Government,* by Lady E. Sharp. 1969. 15. *The Central Office of Information,* by Sir F. Clark. 1970. 16. *The Department of Education and Science,* by Sir W.D. Pile. 1979. Authoritative description of the work of major central government depts., past and present; each with list of ministers, etc., footnote references and an analytical index. Nos. 12 and 14 are praised (in *Use of social sciences literature* (1977. p.205), as rising above the level of being 'dull, pedestrian and uninformative'. All titles except the last in the series are op. *Class No:* 354(410)

[3292]

SAINTY, J.C. Office-holders in modern Britain. London, Athlone Press, for the University of London, Institute of Historical Research, 1972-79. 8v. £4-£7 each vol. ISBN: 0485171414, v.1; 0485171422, v.2; 0485171430, v.3; 0485171449, v.4; 0485171457, v.5; 0901179353, v.6; 0901179531, v.7; 0901179558, v.8.

1: *Treasury officials, 1660-1780* (1972. xiv,161p.). 2: *Officials of the Secretaries of State, 1660-1780* (1973. xii,119p.). 3: *Officials of the Board of Trade, 1660-1870.* (1974. xiv,124p.). 4: *Admiralty officials, 1660-1870,* (1975. xiv,159p.). 5: *Home Office officials, 1782-1870.* (1975. xv,62p.). 6: *Colonial Office officials: Officials of the Secretary of State for War and Colonies, 1801-1854, and of the Secretary of State for Colonies, 1854-1879.* (1976. x,52p.). 7: *Navy Board officials, 1660-1832,* by J.M. Collinge. (1979. 165p.). 8: *Foreign Office officials, 1782-1870,* by J.M. Collinge. (1979. 93p.). Each volume contains chronological and A-Z lists of officials, with notes and a scholarly introduction. *Class No:* 354(410)

[3293]

—COLLINGE, J.M. Officials of Royal Commissions of Inquiry, 1815-70. University of London, Institute of Historical Research, 1984. vii,108p. £8. ISBN: 0901179809. *Class No:* 354(410)

[3294]

—PICKERILL, D.A. Ministers of the Crown. London, Routledge & Kegan Paul, 1981,. 280p.

Lists public office-holders under the Crown from earliest available records to the present day. *Class No:* 354(410)

Bibliographies

[3295]

GREAT BRITAIN. HM Stationery Office. Government publications. Sectional list 26, (revised September 1987): Home Office. London, HMSO, 1987. 16p. *Gratis.*

Sections: Animals - Betting, gaming and lotteries - Broadcasting - Charities - Children - Civil defence - Community relations - Criminal matters - Drugs - Elections - Fire - Firearms - Immigration and nationality - Northern Ireland - Police - Prisons, probation and after-care, parole - Research and Planning Unit publications - Safety - Shops - Miscellaneous. The Home Office Information and Library Services issues a list, annually, of publications of the Office not handled by H.M. Stationery Office.

Class No: 354(410)(01)

Yearbooks & Directories

[3296]

The London diplomatic list (incorporating *Directory of international organizations*). Foreign and Commonwealth Office. London, HMSO., 1964-. 2pa (previously quarterly). £3.95 each issue. ISSN: 09506918.

Alphabetical list of all the representatives of foreign States and Commonwealth countries in London, with names and descriptions of the persons returned as composing their diplomatic staff. Includes addresses and telephone numbers of each department, and list of representatives in order of their precedence. *Class No:* 354(410)(058)

Histories

[3297]

GREAT BRITAIN. Public Record Office. **The Cabinet Office, to 1945.** Wilson, S.S. London, HMSO, 1975. vii,252p. £6. (*Public Record Office handbook, no. 17.*) ISBN: 0114400342.

10 sections: 1. Introduction - 2. The general procedures of the Cabinet Office, 1917-1945 - 3. The Cabinet and Committee of Imperial Defence before 1917 - 4. The War Cabinet, 1916-1919, and the Lloyd George administration to October 1922 ... 8. Imperial and International Conferences, 1915-1939 - 9. The War Cabinet, 1939-1945 - 10. The Historical Section. Annexes 1-12 (11: List of committees). Index, p.244-52. *Class No:* 354(410)(091)

[3298]

JENNINGS, J. **Cabinet government.** 3rd ed. Cambridge, Cambridge University Press, 1959. x,587p.

First published 1936.

A description of the central administration and its historical development during the last hundred years, in 15 chapters. Appendix 1: Governments since 1835. Appendix 4: Biographical and bibliographical notes (p.546-70). Covers material available up to the middle of 1957.

Class No: 354(410)(091)

Eire

[3299]

O'DONNELL, J.D. **How Ireland is governed.** 6th ed. Dublin, Institute of Public Administration, 1979. vii,152p.

First published 1965.

16 chapters (*e.g.* 4. The House of the Oireachtas; 9. Local government; 11. The judiciary; 14. The Government of Northern Ireland). Appendices A-E (A: The Departments and major offices). Partly analytical index.

Class No: 354(417)

England

[3300]

BELL, G.M. **A Handlist of British diplomatic representation, 1509-1688.** London, Royal Historical Society, 1990. viii,306p. £25;$52. ISBN: 0861931238.

Continues *Lists of British diplomatic representatives (1689-1789)*, edited by D.M.Horn (London, 1932) and *Lists of British diplomatic representatives (1789-1852)*, edited by S.T.Bindoff (London, 1934).

Names of England's 602 diplomats and their 1320 missions. Each entry gives brief career details, with dates, plus sources (instructions, correspondence). List of abbreviations and symbols for sources. Index of persons, p.295-306. *Class No:* 354(420)

Wales

[3301]

BALSOM, D. *and* BURCH, M. **A Political and electoral handbook for Wales.** Farnborough, Hants, Saxon House, 1980. viii,195p. £25. ISBN: 0566002361.

5 parts: 1. Basic features of Welsh politics - 2. Central government - 3. Local government - 4. Electoral statistics - 5. Constituency profiles (A-Z, p.112-87). Bibliography, po.188-95 (1. Reference works; 2. Books and articles; 3. Government documents). *Class No:* 354(429)

USSR

[3302]

Current Soviet leaders ... a cumulative guide to officials and notables in the USSR. Oakville, Ontario, Mosaic Press, 1974-1982. 2pa. ISSN: 03182037.

Based on official Soviet sources and compiled by the Borys Lewytzkyj Research Bureau.

Sections: 1. Communist Party of the Soviet Union (USSR; Union Republics) - 2. Soviet government (USSR; Union Republics) - 3. Public organizations (*e.g.* Komsomol; Trade Unions) - 4. Foreign trade agencies and organizations - 5. Soviet delegations abroad - 6. Activities of L.I. Brezhnev and A.N.Kosygin - 7. Honours - 8. Deaths - 9. Index. Changes in position and of occupants are noted.

Class No: 354(47)

[3303]

SCHWARTZ, C.A. **'Post-Stalin Soviet leadership studies'.** In *Choice*, v.27(2), October 1989, p.266-273.

Sections on individual leaders (Krushchev ... Gorbachev) - Grand analyses - Collective essays - Specialized and Soviet studies - Reference works - Conclusions. 89 works cited, A-Z by author. *Class No:* 354(47)

Denmark

[3304]

Kongelig dansk Hof- og Statskalender, 1993. Statshåndbog for kongeriget Danmark... København, Schultz, 1734-. Annual. ISSN: 00852589.

Detailed directory of Danish government departments and officials, plus organizations, universities, etc. Name index and subject index. *Class No:* 354(489)

Belgium

[3305]

Annuaire administratif et judiciaire de Belgique et de la capitale du royaume. Brussels, Bruylant. Annual. BFr.57100. ISSN: 00662461.

Detailed directory of Belgian central and local government departments and officials. Includes a list of Brussels streets, communes, and faubourgs. Index of departments and subjects. *Class No:* 354(493)

China

[3306]

LAMB, M. **Directory of officials and organisations in China, 1963-1983.** 3rd ed. Armonk, N.Y., & London, M.E. Sharpe Inc., 1984. xxxii,717p. £65.05; $100. ISBN: 0873322770.

Also published in Australia in 1983 by the Australian National University.

Intended for analysts of political and organizational developments in China since the Cultural Revolution. In 5 sections: A. The Communist Party of China (subdivided by committees, commissions, departments, institutes, etc.); B. The State structure; C. Ministers and commissions of the State Council; D. Abolished ministers and commissions; E. Bureau and specialized agencies subordinate to the State Council. *Class No:* 354(510)

[3307]

SAICH, T. **China: politics and government.** London, Macmillan Press, 1981. xiii,265p. tables, map. £8.50. ISBN: 0333287436.

11 chapters: 1. From revolution to liberation: the emergence and triumph of the Chinese Communist Party - 2. The first seventeen years ... 3. The Cultural Revolution and its aftermath - 4. Marxism-Leninism-Mao Zedong thought - 5. The Chinese Communist Party - 6. The State structure - 7. The People's Liberation Army - 8. Social and political control - 9. Urban China - 10. Rural China - 11. Epilogue. References to chapters and footnotes, p.229-253. Selected further reading (by chapter), p.254-261. Analytical index, p.262-265. '... authoritative ...' (*British book news,* April, 1982, p.221). *Class No:* 354(510)

India

[3308]

RANA, M.S., *ed.* **Indian government and politics:** a bibliographical study. v.1: 1885-1980. New Delhi, Wiley Eastern Ltd., 1981. xxviii,648p. £30. ISBN: 0852267630.

To be in 2 v.

*c.*11,000 items arranged in 8 subject sections: I. Ancient political thought and institutions - II. Medieval political thought and institutions - III. Modern political developments - IV. Political thinkers and leaders - V. Collected biographies - VI. Nationalism - VII. Democracy. Political ideologies. Political movements. Politico-social issues. Muslim politics - issues and ideas - VIII. A classified list of PhD theses. Author index, p.595-648. *Class No:* 354(540)

Asia—Near East

[3309]

Political leaders of the contemporary Middle East and North Africa: a biographical dictionary. Reich, B., *ed.* Westport, CT., Greenwood Press, 1990. 557p. £69.95. $85. ISBN: 0313262136.

Profiles 70 men and women who have had a significant impact on the political development of the Arabic-speaking countries of the area since World War II. Each entry (7-10p.) is signed and concludes with a list of additional sources as well as noting the political leader's own writings. A chronology of the region, up to 1989, precedes a bibliography of general sources and a detailed index. 'Strongly recommended'. (*Choice,* v.27(11/12), July-August 1990, p.1810). *Class No:* 354(56)

Africa

[3310]

BIDWELL, R.L. **Guide to African ministers.** London, Rex Collings, 1978. [iv], 79p. tables. £10. ISBN: 0860360644.

6 tabular sections: Heads of State (including, where appropriate, Colonial governors) - Prime Ministers - Ministers of Foreign Affairs - Ministers of War or Defence - Ministers of the Interior or of Local Government - Ministers of Finance. Each section is subdivided into 8 groups, 'representing countries grouped together for geographical or historical reasons' (*e.g.* groups D & E: Francophone Equatorial and West Africa). Period: 1950-1976. Exact dates are given. 60 notes. No index. *Class No:* 354(6)

USA

Bibliographies

[3311]

VOSE, C.E. **A Guide to library resources in political science: American government.** Washington, DC., American Political Science Association, 1975. viii,135p. illus. $6.50. (*Instructional resource monographs, no.1.*) ISBN: 0915654032.

Essays on how political scientists might garner knowledge from libraries. In 3 parts: 1. American national government (Government publications - the Constitution - Congress - The Executive Branch - Federal Courts); 2: General reference books (Almanacs - biographies - political dictionaries - encyclopedias); 3. Library basics (files, archives and manuscripts). Bibliographies attached to each essay. 'A selection tool rather than a reference work' (*R.Q.,* v.15(2), Winter 1975, p.180). *Class No:* 354(73)(01)

Yearbooks & Directories

[3312]

CONGRESSIONAL QUARTERLY INC. **Washington information directory, 1993-94.** Washington, D.C., Congressional Quarterly, 1993. Annual. 1100p. $89.95. ISBN: 0871877720.

First published 1976.

Names, telephone numbers, addresses and responsibilities of more than 5000 key personnel and agencies located in Washington, arranged in subject chapters, each followed by a bibliography. Subject index; agency and organization index. 'An invaluable guide to the working of official and unofficial Washington' (*American reference book annual,* 1980, entry 490). *Class No:* 354(73)(058)

[3313]

—Encyclopedia of governmental advisory organizations. Batten, D. *and* Dresser, P., *eds.* 9th ed. Detroit, Mich., Gale Research Company, 1989. $505. ISBN: 0810374609.

First edition 1973-75.

Reports on the advisory organizations at work in the US today. Nearly 6000 entries describing the activities and personnel of the committees advising the President and various departments and bureaus of the Federal government (organization name and address; telephone number; executive secretary's name, history and authority; programme; membership; staff; etc.). Also includes information on White House conferences and other conferences sponsored by the Federal government, groups under contract doing studies for the Federal government, and Congressional committees doing studies of current topical interest. 5 indexes; alphabetical and keyword, personnel, publications and reports, organizations by Federal department or agency, organizations by Presidential administration. *Class No:* 354(73)(058)

[3314]

LARSON, D.R. **Guide to US government directories.** Phoenix, AZ., Oryx Press, 1981-1985. 2v. (436p.). $60.50; £45 each vol. ISBN: 0912700637, v.1; 0897741625, v.2.

V.1: 1970-1980; v.2: 1980-1984. Includes all types of publications (serials, appendices, articles, as well as individual volumes (with some 'location identification or contact codes' for the names of people, groups or places. Extensive analytical subject index to each volume. *Class No:* 354(73)(058)

Biographies

[3315]

SOBEL, R., *ed*. Biographical directory of the United States executive branch, 1774-1989. 2nd rev. ed. Westport, CT., Greenwood Press, 1990. 600p. $95. ISBN: 0313265933.

First published 1971.

Contains biographical data on *c.*500 persons.

Class No: 354(73)(092)

Diplomatic Service

Worldwide

Handbooks & Manuals

[3316]

FELTHAM, R.G. Diplomatic handbook. 6th ed. London, Longman Group (UK) Ltd., 1993. ix,180p. £10.99. ISBN: 0582099528.

First published 1970.

10 sections: 1. Diplomatic relations (*e.g.* the establishment of diplomatic missions and of permanent diplomatic missions) - 2. The Ministry of Foreign Affairs - 3. The diplomatic mission - 4. Protocol and procedure - 5. Diplomatic privileges and immunities - 6. Consular offices and consular posts - 7. The United Nations - 8. International organizations and agreements outside the UN - 9. International law and practice - 10. Conferences. Appendices A-E (E: Glossary of diplomatic, consular, legal and economic terms). Analytical index. Author is former Director of the Foreign Service Programme at the University of Oxford. 'An exceptionally handy little book' (*International affairs,* v.56(4), Autumn 1980, p.682) of the 3rd ed. *Class No:* 354DIP(100)(035)

[3317]

—Satow's guide to diplomatic practice. Gore-Booth, Lord . 5th ed. London, Longman, 1979. xix,544p. £29.95. ISBN: 0582501091.

First published 1917.

5 books (44 chapters): 1. Diplomacy in general - 2. Diplomatic agents in general - 3. Consular matters - 4. International transactions - 5. International organizations. 6 appendices (*e.g.* 1. Definitions and terms; 4. Specialized agencies). Chapter notes, p.489-521; bibliography, p.522-31; index, p.532-44. A more detailed, legalistic approach than Feltham's *Diplomatic handbook.*

Class No: 354(100)(035)

Great Britain

Yearbooks & Directories

[3318]

The Diplomatic Service list, 1993. Foreign and Commonwealth Office. 28th ed. London, HMSO., 1993. 334p. £18.50. ISBN: 0115917446. ISSN: 04191714.

Succeeds *The Foreign Office list* (1806-1965). Issued twice a year.

In 4 parts: 1. Home departments - 2. British representatives overseas - 3. Chronological lists, from 1972, of Secretaries of State, Ministers of State, Permanent Under-Secretaries, Ambassadors, High Commissioners and permanent representatives to international organizations - 4. Biographical notes, and lists of staff (of Senior Grade to

....(contd.)

Grade 10 of the Diplomatic Service, officers of Grades S1-S3 of the Secretarial Branch and officers of the Security Officer Branch). *Class No:* 354DIP(410)(058)

Armed Forces

[3319]

WISE, T. A Guide to military museums. 5th rev. ed. Doncaster, S. Yorks., Athena Books, 1988. [80]p.

First published 1969.

211 main entries, arranged under regiments (descriptive notes; hours, curator, approaches; marginal badges of regiments). Index of special museums (*e.g.* German occupation: Channel Islands). 72 entries on 'other places of interest'. *Class No:* 355

[3320]

World defence forces, 1989: a compendium of current military information of all countries of the world. Pope, B.H., *ed.* Santa Barbara, CA, ABC-Clio Press, 1989. 137p. $28.95;£17.15. ISBN: 0874362733. *Class No:* 355

Abbreviations & Symbols

[3321]

Defence terminology: an A-Z of military abbreviations, acronyms and special-purpose words. Lee, R.G., *ed.* London, Brasseys (UK) Ltd., 1991. vi,225p. £15.95. ISBN: 008041320x.

A compilation of current terms (including combat terms, mnemonics and special-purpose words), abbreviations and acronyms. Over 4200 definitions from '"A" weighting' to 'Zoom systems'. Includes army, navy and air force terms from both sides of the Atlantic. *Class No:* 355(003)

[3322]

PRETZ, B., *ed*. Dictionary of military technological abbreviations and acronyms. London, Routledge & Kegan Paul, 1983. [2],496p. £37.50. ISBN: 0710092741.

*c.*50,000 abbreviations and acronyms used by the British, American, German and Soviet military. Covers all the services and their technology. A-Z throughout.

Class No: 355(003)

[3323]

SCOTT, B.K.C. Dictionary of military abbreviations. Hastings, Tamarisk Books, 1982. [4], 117p. £7. ISBN: 0907221017.

Over 5000 abbreviations and acronyms used by and about the military forces of the UK, Europe and Commonwealth, past and present, that may be found in official documents, on items of equipment, in military histories or contemporary accounts. *Class No:* 355(003)

Bibliographies

[3324]

Air University Library index to military periodicals. Alabama, Maxwell Air Force Base, Air University Library, 1949-, v.1, no.1-. Quarterly. ISSN: 00022586.

As *Air University periodical index,* 1949-62.

'A subject index to significant articles, news items and editorials appearing in 76 English-language military and

....*(contd.)*

aeronautical periodicals' (*Preface*). Arranged A-Z authors and subjects in one sequence, with further subdivision as necessary, and finally A-Z by title. *Class No:* 355(01)

[3325]
COCKLE, M.J.D. A Bibliography of English military books up to 1642. New ed. London, Holland Press, 1982. xl,269p. illus. £25. ISBN: 0900470704.

First published 1900.

Entries nos.1-166 consist of books in English, arranged chronologically; nos. 500-950 cover foreign books, arranged according to subjects A-Z, with final chronological order. Nos. 167-499 are not used. Index (p.251-68) includes names of English printers. *Class No:* 355(01)

[3326]
Current military and political literature. Oxford, The Military Press Ltd., 1983-. 6pa. £60pa. ISSN: 09543589.

Early title was *Current military literature*.

Comment, abstracts and citations of important articles from journals and monographs about international strategic and defence studies, military science, political science and international affairs. Arranged in subject sections. Author, source journals and geographical indexes.
Class No: 355(01)

[3327]
SCRIVENER, D. *and* **SHEEHAN, M. Bibliography of arms control verification.** Aldershot, Hants, Dartmouth Publishing Company, 1990. [6],176p. £30. ISBN: 1855210444.

Bibliography of recent research on arms control verification, both Western sources and Soviet writings. Also includes two essays on the problems of verification and the difference between Western and Soviet attitudes . Bibliographical data includes books and articles, unannotated. *Class No:* 355(01)

Encyclopaedias

[3328]
International military and defense encyclopedia. Dupuy, T.N., *and others, eds.* Washington, Brassey's (US), 1993. 6v.(3132p). $1250. ISBN: 0028810112.

785 articles (including 129 for regions or countries complete with historical data) each of 100-10,000 words in length, by over 400 authors. Articles are arranged in 17 major subject areas (*e.g.* Aerospace forces; Logistics; Combat). Emphasis is on current events, theories, etc., but there are numerous historical and biographical articles also. Each article carries a bibliography. V.1 lists all authors and articles. Lists of acronyms and abbreviations are in each volume. Meticulous, easy-to-use index of more than 25,000 index terms. 'This work is essential for military, government, and academic collections and is highly recommended for large public libraries.(*Library journal*, 15 March 1993, p.70). *Class No:* 355(031)

[3329]
MACKSEY, K. *and* **WOODHOUSE, W. The Penguin encyclopedia of modern warfare,** 1850 to the present. Harmondsworth, Mddx., Viking, 1991. x,373p. diagrs, maps. £18.99. ISBN: 0670826987.

More than 30 maps and a useful chronology covering the last 150 years. Bibliography, p.361-2. Index, p.363-73. 'A

....*(contd.)*

useful desk-reference book, supporting Dupuy's *The Encyclopedia of military history*'(1986). (*Library journal*, 1 November 1991, p.90.). *Class No:* 355(031)

Histories

[3330]
WARRY, J. Warfare in the classical world: an illustrated encyclopedia of weapons, warriors and warfare in the ancient civilisations of Greece and Rome. New York, St. Martin's Press; 1981. 224p. illus, diagrs., maps. $24.95. ISBN: 0312856148.

First published in London in 1980 by Salamander Books Ltd.

15 chapters on the soldiers of Greece and Rome from the rise of Mycenae to the decline of the Roman Empire, 1600 BC - AD 800: The pronunciation of ancient languages - Homeric and Mycenaean warfare - The Persian wars ... Alexander the Great ... Pompey and his epoch - Julius Caesar ... The coming of the Barbarians. Glossary, p.218-219. Detailed analytical index, p.220-224. Includes over 125 photographs, the majority in colour, 50 battle plans, and tactical diagrams. 'A magnificent colour encyclopedia ...' (*Library journal,* August 1981, p.1528).
Class No: 355(031)(091)

Russian

[3331]
Sovetskaya voennaya entisiklopediya. Moscow, Voennoe Izdat. Ministerstva Oborony SSSR, 1976-80. 4v.illus. (some.col.), tables, maps.

'Soviet military encyclopedia'. Entries A-Z (*e.g.* 'Samokhodnaya artilleriiskaya' [artillery self-propelled gun]: 3p., 9 illus., 1 table). Campaign maps (*e.g.* World War II) are a feature. Cross-references. Coloured illustrations of flags, etc. Each volume has *c.*650p.
Class No: 355(031)=82

[3332]
—ROMER, J.-C. Le Dictionnaire encyclopédique militaire soviétique: d'une édition à l'autre. In Strategique, no.35, 1987, p.5-23.

Discusses changes in the new 1986 edition of the Soviet military encyclopedia. *Class No:* 355(031)=82

Handbooks & Manuals

[3333]
Defense and foreign affairs handbook, 1988-89. Copley, G.R., *ed.* New York, International Media, 1988. 1400p. illus. tables. maps. $197. ISBN: 0096093268.

3rd ed. published 1978 by Copley & Associates, S.A.

Political, economic and defence data on *c.*200 countries.
Class No: 355(035)

[3334]
ROBERTSON, D. Guide to modern defense and strategy: a complete description of the terms, tactics, organizations and accords of today's defense. Detroit, Mich., Gale Research International Ltd., 1988. xii. 324p. $65. ISBN: 0810350432.

A handbook of defence terms and concepts, emphasising 'modern' and 'strategy'. Long definitions and discussions of broad military and naval terms and concepts, half a page to a

....(contd.)

page or more in length. Cross-references. List of *c.*150 acronyms. No index and no bibliography. British slant, but US topics and concepts included. *Class No:* 355(035)

Dictionaries

Polyglot

[3335]

Brassey's multilingual military dictionary. Oxford, Pergamon & Brassey's Defence Publications, 1987. Reprinted 1989. xvii,815p. £48. ISBN: 0080270328.

*c.*7000 key military words and phrases in the English language, with definitions in English, numbered, and followed by equivalents in French, Spanish, German, Russian and Arabic. 6 indexes, one in each of the languages, including English, refer to the numbered items. Index of definitions and equivalents in British English and US usage, p.447-457. Appendices (*e.g.* A. Ranks; B. Units/ formations). *Class No:* 355(038)=00

English

[3336]

AMMER, C. Fighting words: from war, rebellion, and other combative capers. New York, Paragon House, 1989. 256p. illus. $19.95. ISBN: 1557780560.

Definitions of originally military terms in short informative essays. *Class No:* 355(038)=20

[3337]

Department of Defense dictionary of military and associated terms: incorporating the NATO (English and French). United States. Joint Chiefs of Staff. Washington, G.P.O., 1990-.

First published 1972, 1979 & 1988 by the Hemisphere Publishing Corporation. Now to be updated by supplements.

c. 6000 entries for military and 'Pentagonese' terms arranged in subject groups. Many cross-references. An appendix is a directory of departments, agencies and facilities of the Department of Defense and the Coast Guard. 'may be useful in the interpretation of military documents' (*Choice*, v.25 (10), June 1988, p.1532).

Class No: 355(038)=20

[3338]

Dictionary of military terms. US Joint Chiefs of Staff. 2nd ed. Elstree, Herts., Greenhill Books, 1990. 420p. £25. ISBN: 1853670858.

At head of title-page - US Department of Defense. First published by the Joint Chiefs of Staff as JCS Pub.1.

More than 6000 concise entries for current military and associated terms. Symbols indicate the origin of the terms. *Class No:* 355(038)=20

[3339]

DUPUY, T.N., *and others, comps.* **Dictionary of military terms:** a guide to the language of warfare and military institutions. New York, H.W. Wilson, 1986. vii,237p. $30; £17.50. ISBN: 0824207173.

*c.*2500 briefly defined terms relating to modern military affairs and military history from ancient times to the present. Covers all aspects of military and naval affairs, including strategy, tactics, weapons, fortifications, ranks and administration. Some slang terms, nicknames, acronyms and

....(contd.)

initialisms are also included. International coverage of English-language terms. Cross-references. *Class No:* 355(038)=20

[3340]

ELLIOT, J.M. *and* **ELLIOT, R.R. The Arms control, disarmament, and military security dictionary.** Santa Barbara, CA., ABC-Clio, 1989. $44.50. (*Clio dictionaries in political science*.) ISBN: 0874364302.

268 definitions for treaties, laws, organizations, and terms, each entry in 2 parts, definition and significance paragraphs. *Class No:* 355(038)=20

[3341]

Jane's dictionary of military terms. Hayward, P.H.C., *comp.* London, Macdonald & Jane, 1975. [iv],201p.

*c.*2500 concise entries, some terms having a number of meanings (*e.g.* 'Cluster' has 5). Cross-references. Appendix 1: Abbreviations, p.179-98; 3: The order of precedence of corps and regiments of the Regular Army. British slant. *Class No:* 355(038)=20

[3342]

SHAFRITZ, J.M., *and others.* **The Facts on File dictionary of military science.** New York, Facts on File, 1989. 498p. $40. ISBN: 0816018235.

Over 5000 entries, primarily those associated with strategy, logistics, military law, weapons, technology, administration and weapons procurement from the age of Napoleon to the 1980s. Systematic sequence: (1) Headword (2) Definition number when more than one meaning (3) Definition. Many 'see also' references and full bibliographical references. '... a useful reference work ...'(*Reference books bulletin*, 1 November 1989, p.606). *Class No:* 355(038)=20

German

[3343]

EITZEN, K.H. German-English, English-German military dictionary, with detailed lists of abbreviations, American and British tables of measurements, coins and weights, ranks, calibres, conversion tables, NATO-ABC, etc. 4th ed. London, Atlantic Press, 1957. 549p. Reprinted 1988 as *The military Eitzen.* £22.90.

Each half has *c.*10,000 entries, including many compounds. Particularly strong on colloquialisms (especially US). Some 2,000 abbreviations are explained on p.467-530, with references to the main text. *Class No:* 355(038)=30

Norwegian

[3344]

MARM, L. Engelsk-Amerikansk-Norsk, Norsk-Engelsk-Amerikansk... militeir ordbok. Oslo, Fabritius, 1977. x,276p.

English/American - Norwegian, Norwegian - English/ American military dictionary. More recent is: *Class No:* 355(038)=396

[3345]

—**ARK, O.I.** English-Norwegian military dictionary. New York; French and European Publications, 1985. 459p. $95; £29.50. ISBN: 0828819076.

English into Norwegian. *Class No:* 355(038)=396

French

[3346]

NATO glossary of terms and definitions (English and French), listing terms of military significance and their definitions for use in NATO, together with an index of NATO agreed documents containing specialist terms and definitions. [Brussels], NATO, 1988. (*Allied administrative publications/North Atlantic Treaty Organization, 6.*)
Class No: 355(038)=40

Russian

[3347]

Russian-English military dictionary. Joint Technical Language Service of the War Office. London, HMSO, 1983. 688p. £25. ISBN: 0112300189.

Produced for military translators and interpreters, this revised ed. is the first to be made available to the public.
Class No: 355(038)=82

Arabic

[3348]

Arabic military dictionary: English-Arabic, Arabic-English. Multi-lingual International Publishers Ltd.,, *comp and* Kay, E., *ed.* London, Routledge & Kegan Paul, 1986. [7],171,[133]p. £30. ISBN: 0710204582.

Compiled for use by military personnel and by anyone who is directly or indirectly involved in military technology. Includes the terms and phrases in everyday use in the field or in headquarters. No definitions. Includes abbreviations. The first section has the terms, A-Z in English, with transliterated Arabic and Arabic script; the second section has terms in Arabic script, with English translations.
Class No: 355(038)=927

[3349]

KAYYALI, M.S. Modern military dictionary: English-Arabic, Arabic-English. London, Third World Centre for Research and Publishing; Beirut, Arab Institute for Research and Publishing, 1986. 118,[135]p. £22. ISBN: 0861990218.
Class No: 355(038)=927

Chinese

[3350]

LOWE, J. D-H. A Dictionary of military terms and military intelligence phrases: Chinese-English, English-Chinese. Boulder, Col., Westview Press, 1992. 725p. maps. $95
Class No: 355(038)=951

Reviews & Abstracts

[3351]

Abstracts of military biography. Ramirez Mitchell, R.A., *ed.* Buenos Aires, Ruben A. Ramirez Mitchell, 1967-., v.1, no.1-. Quarterly. $70pa.

Former titles were *Resumenes analyticos sobre defensa y seguridad nacional* and *Resúmes analiticos de bibliografia militar,* published by Instituto de Publicaciones Navales.

World coverage of literature (books, periodicals, government reports) on warfare, national defence and international relations. A-Z subject order. Abstracts are in Spanish and English. *Class No:* 355(048)

Periodicals

Bibliographies

[3352]

IMPERIAL WAR MUSEUM. Department of Printed Books. List of current journals,1991. London, the Museum, 1991. 83p. £14.

Includes *c.*500 titles, A-Z, followed by a 26-page subject index. *Class No:* 355(051)(01)

Yearbooks & Directories

[3353]

R.U.S.I. and Brassey's defence yearbook, 1991. Royal United Services Institute for Defence Studies, *ed.* 101st ed. London, Brassey's U.K. Ltd., 1991. viii,336p. illus. ISBN: 0080407102.

First published jointly 1974 (1974/56 ed.). 1886-1949 as *Brassey's naval and shipping manual.*

Up-to-date surveys and analyses of the defence world. This ed. has 18 articles by well-known experts, arranged in 5 subject sections: European security - Security policies and military concepts - Defence industries and the market place - The place of the military in regional stability - Signposts (3 items including a directory of educational establishments teaching strategic studies, and statistics of NATO defence expenditure, 1985-1989. Notes including bibliographical references, follow each article. One of the most authoritative sources on the defence field. *Class No:* 355(058)

Quotations

[3354]

A Dictionary of military quotations. Royle, T., *comp.* London, Routledge; New York, Simon and Schuster, 1990. [xii],210p. $40. ISBN: 0415041384, UK; 0132101130, US.

Nearly 3500 quotations arranged in 5 major categories: 1. Captains and kings - 2. Battles and wars - 3. Armies and soldiers - 4. War and peace - 5. Last post. Author index, p.191-198. Subject index, p.199-210. *Class No:* 355(082.2)

[3355]

HEINL, R.D. Dictionary of military and naval quotations. Annapolis, MD., U.S. Naval Institute Press, 1966. xl,[i],367p. ports. $21.95. ISBN: 0870211498.

About 6000 quotations from more than 1400 individuals under 800 subjects, A-Z; range extends chronologically from Homer to Liddell Hart. Gives sources and date of quotation, where known and applicable. Index of authors of quotations. *Class No:* 355(082.2)

[3356]

SHAFRITZ, J.M. War on words: including quotations from ancient times to the present. Englewood Cliffs, NJ, Prentice-Hall, 1990. 559p. $29.35. ISBN: 013209875x.

Far more helpful to students than M. Hastings (1985) or J. Wintle (1987), and more of a follow-up to the classic *Dictionary of military and naval quotations,* by R.D.Heinl, (*q.v.*) according to *Choice,* December 1990, p.616.
Class No: 355(082.2)

[3357]
TSOURIS, P.G. **Warriors' words: a quotation book:** from Sesostris III to Schwarzkopf, 1871 BC to AD 1991. London, Arms & Armour Press, 1992. 534p. £15.99. $29.95. ISBN: 1854090887.

Quotations from more than 250 military personalities who have 'exercised the profession of arms', arranged in c.350 subject areas ('War' has 12 subheadings). Entries list author, title, date of source, translator, complete bibliographical details being given at the end of the book. Biographical index of sources provides brief summaries of military career. *Class No:* 355(082.2)

Histories

[3358]
DUPUY, R.E. *and* DUPUY, T.N. **The Encyclopedia of military history,** from 3500 B.C. to the present. 4th rev. ed. New York & London, Harper-Collins, 1993. 1654p. illus. maps. $65;£30. ISBN: 0062700561, US; 0004701437, UK.

First published 1970. Title in USA is The Harper encyclopedia of military history...

21 chapters (1. The dawn of military history ... 21. Superpowers in the nuclear age, 1945-1991). Each begins with an essay assessing military trends, leaders, weapons, etc., followed by data chronologically arranged. Thus, ch. 14, 'The beginning of modern warfare, 1600-1700', deals with military trends, then major wars (*e.g.* Thirty Years' War, 1618-48, with events chronologically tabulated), and finally with areas and countries (Western Europe ... Spanish America, Portuguese America). Bibliography by chapters. 150 illus., 75 campaign and other maps. General index (c.15,000 entries); index of battles and sieges; index of wars. A valuable contribution. *Class No:* 355(091)

[3359]
JESSUP, J.E. *and* COAKLEY, R.W. **A Guide to the study and use of military history.** Center of Military History, United States Army. Washington, D.C., Government Printing Office, reprinted 1982. xv,507p. $250.00.

23 chapters in 4 parts: 1. Military history, its nature and use - 2. Bibliographical guide - 3. Army programs, activities, and uses - 4. History outside the US Army. 2 appendices: A: Reference works: a select list; B: Historical journals and societies. Index, p.457-507. Footnotes, and lengthy bibliographies after each chapter. '... designed to foster appreciation of the value of military history and explain its uses and the resources available for study' (*Preface*). *Class No:* 355(091)

Maps & Atlases

[3360]
HARTMAN, T *and* MITCHELL, J. **A World atlas of military history, 1945-1984.** London, Leo Cooper/Secker & Warburg, 1984. xi, 108p. tables. 93 maps. £16. $24.95. ISBN: 0436191474.

Covers the major and minor wars fought since 1945 in Europe, the Middle East, the Gulf, Africa, India, China and Korea, South East Asia, Central and South America. Includes text, statistical tables and maps. Name index, p. 93-96. Gazetteer, p.97-108. *Class No:* 355(091)(084.3)

Biographies

[3361]
KEEGAN, J. *and* WHEATCROFT, A. **Who's who in military history,** from 1453 to the present day. New ed. London, Hutchinson, 1987. 376p. illus. £25. ISBN: 0091705207.

First published, 1976. by Weidenfeld and Nicolson.

'We have dealt with the Great Captains at length, as they deserve; but beyond them we have written as the interest or curiosity of the topic demanded' (*Introduction*). For popular consumption. *Class No:* 355(092)

Worldwide

Encyclopaedias

[3362]
The International military encyclopaedia. Tobias, N., *ed.* Gulf Breeze, Ill., Academic International Press, 1992-. To be in c.50v. v.1: $37. ISBN: 0875691595, v.1.

Primarily a work of military history and affairs, with emphasis on the post- World War II period. V.1 has 197 entries (A...). *Wilson library bulletin* (February 1993, p.105) considers the *Encyclopedia of military history* will suffice for most libraries. *Class No:* 355(100)(031)

Handbooks & Manuals

[3363]
The Military balance, 1993-94. Oxford, Brassey's for the International Institute for Strategic Studies, 1993. Annual. 268p. illus., tables. £36. ISBN: 1857530381. ISSN: 04597222.

First published 1959 as *The Soviet Union and the NATO powers: the military balance.*

In 2 parts: 1. Countries and principal facts - 2. Tables and analysis. Provides an authoritative assessment of the military strength and defence spending of every country possessing armed forces. Country entries detail military organization and list equipment holdings, manpower and relevant economic data. *Class No:* 355(100)(035)

[3364]
Strategic survey, 1992-93. International Institute for Strategic Studies. First published 1967. Annual. London, Brassey's (UK), 1992. 248p. £21; $29. ISBN: 1857530039.

The Institute's annual analytical review of international security-related events, and likely future international developments. *Class No:* 355(100)(035)

Yearbooks & Directories

[3365]
International defence directory. Thompson, S., *ed.* 11th ed. Coulsdon, Surrey, Jane's, 1993. xci.1223p. £250. $395. ISSN: 02567822.

Lists c.15000 defence companies and c.350000 key personnel in 172 countries. Entries include company name, key personnel, product and service description. Quick reference section (on tinted paper) precedes. Product/service index. Product supplier link. Also available on CD-ROM. *Class No:* 355(100)(058)

[3366]

KEEGAN, J., *ed*. **World armies**. 2nd ed. London, Macmillan; Detroit, Mich., Gale Research Co., 1983. xlvi, 688p. £45; $80. ISBN: 0333340795, UK; 0810315157, US.

First published 1979.

18 contributions. Data on the armies of 150 countries, Afghanistan ... Zimbabwe (*e.g.* Finland, p.183-6. History and introduction - Strength and budget - Command and constitutional status - Role commitment, deployment and recent operations - Organization - Recruitment, training and reserves - Equipment and arms industry - Rank, dress and distinctions - Current developments). Appendices: 1. The armies of Africa; 2. The armies of India, Pakistan, Burma, Sri Lanka and Bangladesh. Adds flesh to the bare bones provided by *The Military balance* (International Institute for Strategic Studies) (*qv*), but the latter has the decided advantage of being annual. *Class No:* 355(100)(058)

Tables & Data Books

[3367]

World military and social expenditure, 1991. Sivard, R.L. 14th ed. Washington, World Priorities Inc., 1991. (available also from the Armament and Disarmament Information Unit, University of Sussex). 64p. $7.00. ISSN: 03634795.

First published 1974. Annual.

A report on the use of world resources for two kinds of priorities: military power and human needs. Includes factual background data for *c.*150 countries, with comparative figures not readily available elsewhere.

Class No: 355(100)(083)

Great Britain

[3368]

GORDON, L.L. **British battles and medals:** a description of every campaign medal and bar awarded since the Armada, with the historical reasons for their awards, and the names of all the ships, regiments and squadrons of the Royal Air Force whose personnel are entitled to them. Joslin, E.C., *ed*. 6th ed. London, Spink & Son, 1988. viii,299p. illus. (some col.). £38. ISBN: 0907605257.

First published 1947.

10 sections: Campaign medals from 1588 to 1982 listed in chronological order - Polar medals - United Nations medals - Indian Army ranks and British equivalents - List of regiments and corps as at 1987 - Precedence of corps and infantry regiments - Cavalry and infantry regiments - Bibliography - Index of medals - Index of bars. Profusely illustrated in black-and-white, and 4 pages of bars in colour. A standard reference work for medal collectors.

Class No: 355(410)

Handbooks & Manuals

[3369]

CHANT, C. **Handbook of British regiments**. London, Routledge, 1988. xi,313p. illus. £20. ISBN: 0415002419.

Information on *c.*85 regiments and corps which form the current British Army 'from the Household Cavalry to the Royal Dental Corps, from the SAS to Queen Alexandra's Nursing Corps and the Royal Army Chaplain's Department' (book jacket). Each has a separate entry giving factual details in a standardized layout for easy comparison, including current title, colonel-in-chief, battle honours,

.... (contd.)

uniform, history, nicknames, mottoes and marches, and illustration of cap badge. Index to corps and regiments, p.310-313. *Class No:* 355(410)(035)

[3370]

FREDERICK, J.B.M., *comp*. **Lineage book of British land forces, 1660-1978:** biographical outlines of cavalry, yeomanry, armour, artillery, infantry, marines and air force land troops of the regular and reserve forces. 2nd ed. Pontefract, W. Yorks., Lofthouse Publications, 1987. 2v. (532p.,534p.). £25 each vol. ISBN: 1851170073, v.1; 1851170081, v.2; 185117009x, set.

First published 1969 by Hopefarm Press, Cornwallville, N.Y.

Skeleton histories of well-known and also little-known regiments of the British Army, including those formed for short periods of war service. Under each regiment - regular units, militia, special reserve, territorials and volunteers, as well as new armies and war-formed units. Also a section on disbanded regiments and corps. *Class No:* 355(410)(035)

Yearbooks & Directories

[3371]

Brassey's armed services careers yearbook, 1987/88. London; Brassey's Defence Publishers, 1988. xxii,345p. 12 illus. £35; $52.50. ISBN: 0080335985.

Arranged in 3 parts: 1. The Royal Navy and Royal Marine - 2. The Army - 3. The Royal Air Force. In each part there is information on organization and role, opportunities, selection and training, career development for commissioned and non-commissioned officers. Appendices have more specific details. *Class No:* 355(410)(058)

[3372]

British defence directory. Lycett—Gregson D.C., *ed*. London, Brasseys (UK) Ltd., 1982-. Quarterly. £228 pa. ISSN: 02724782.

Quarterly computerized directory of senior service and civilian personnel in the Ministry of Defence, Royal Navy, Army, *eg*Royal Air Force, NATO and Diplomatic service. Includes hierarchical charts. Comprehensive address code index. Name index. *Class No:* 355(410)(058)

Official Records

[3373]

HIGHAM, R., *ed*. **A Guide to the sources of British military history**. London, Routledge; Berkeley, CA., University of California Press, 1971. xxi,630p. (*Conference in British studies, no.1.*) ISBN: 0710072511, UK; 0520016742, US.

25 chapters, by various hands (1. Introduction - 2. Military developments from prehistoric times to 1485 - 3. Military developments of the Renaissance - 4. The Navy, to 1714... 11. Colonial warfare, 1815-1970... 16. The development of the Royal Air Force, 1909-1945... 24. The evolution of naval medicine - 25. The history of military and martial law. Includes information on access to special collections and private archives. Appended bibliography of 362 items. No index. 'Nearly all 25 chapters are very good and some are outstanding' (*Journal of modern history*, v.45(1), March 1973, p.92-93. *British military history: a*

....*(contd.)*

supplement to Robin Higham's guide... (New York, Garland, $67. xii,586. ISBN 0824084500) was published in 1988. *Class No:* 355(410)(093.2)

Germany

[3374]
SEATON, A. The German army; 1933-45. London, Weidenfeld & Nicolson, 1982. xxiv. 310p. 7 maps. £16.50. ISBN: 0297780328.

A full length analytical study in 12 chapters, arranged chronologically (1. The Legacy - 2. In the grip of fear ... 7. New commitments, 1941 - 8. Barbarossa ... 12. The collapse). 3 appendices (1. Army groups in the West and South; 2. Army groups in the East; Notes on the main German arms). Notes and sources, p.270-282, by chapter; Bibliography, p.283-292; Name and general indexes, p.293-310. *Class No:* 355(430)

Histories

[3375]
MEIER-WELCKER, H. Handbuch zur deutschen Militärgeschichte, 1648-1939. Militärgeschichtlichen Forschungsant durch Friedrich Forstmeier ... [et all]. München, Bernard & Graefe, 1979-1981. 6v.

A handbook of German military history.
Class No: 355(430)(091)

[3376]
SHOWALTER, D.E. German military history, 1648-1982: a critical bibliography. New York, Garland Publishing Inc., 1984. xxxiii,331p. $45. (*Military history bibliographies, 3. Garland reference library of social science, 113.*) ISBN: 0824092686.

A historical preface is followed by 4055 numbered entries, arranged in 10 chapters, each chapter having an introduction: 1. General works - 2. The age of absolutism: 1648-1789 - 3. Revolution and reform: 1789-1815 - 4. Confederation and unification: 1815-1871 - 5. The Second Empire: 1871-1914 - 6. The Great War: 1914-1918 - 7. The Weimar Republic: 1918-1933 - 8. The Nazi years: 1933-1945 - 9. The Wehrmacht, institutions and operations: 1933-1945 - 10. The two Germanies, 1945-1980. Author index, p.309-331. *Class No:* 355(430)(091)

France

Histories

[3377]
HEGGOY, A.A. and HAAR, J.M. The Military in imperial history: the French connection. New York, Garland, 1984. x,302p. $50. (*Military history bibliographies, 4. Garland reference library of social science, 192.*) ISBN: 0824090608.

Claims to be the first English-language guide devoted exclusively to literature on French overseas military affairs from the Crusades to the present. Arranged in 20 chapters by topic and geographic location: I. French military organization and theory - II. French colonization and imperialism - III. French foreign legion... - IV-XVIII deal with overseas territories - XIX Comparative and general works on imperialism - XX. Bibliographies, serials. Each section has an introduction. 'Some conclusions' are followed

....*(contd.)*

by a chronology of selected events in French imperialist history; a short bibliography (p.269-272); and an index (p.273-302). *Class No:* 355(44)(091)

[3378]
ROSS, S.T. French military history, 1661-1799: a guide to the literature. New York, Garland Publishing, 1984. 305p. $54. (*Military history bibliographies, 6. Garland reference library of social science, 190.*) ISBN: 0824090624.

In 3 parts, general works, the old regime, and the French revolution. Each part is divided into 4 sections, each treating a different theme. Informative essays begin every part and section and conclude with bibliographical listings. Author, but no subject, index. 'This approach is very helpful in outlining and providing expert commentary on historiographic developments in a maze of sources, many of which are in French' (*Choice* v.22(6) February 1985, p.798, on which this entry is based). *Class No:* 355(44)(091)

USSR

[3379]
SCOTT, H.F. and SCOTT, W.F. Armed forces of the USSR. 2nd ed. rev. & updated. London, Arms and Armour Press, with the Royal United Services Institute for Defence Studies, 1981. xxiv.447p. illus. tables. £14.95. ISBN: 0853682879.

First published, 1979.

12 chapters, arranged in 3 parts: 1. Fundamentals of Soviet military doctrine and strategy - 2. Military force for the nuclear age -3. A nation in arms. Many footnotes, including bibliographical references. Selected bibliography, p.401-412. Name index, p.423 -430. Subject index. p.431-447. *Class No:* 355(47)

[3380]
The Soviet military encyclopedia. Green, W.C. and Reeves, W.R., eds. Westview Press, 1993. 4v.(404,403,407,222p). $375. ISBN: 0813314321.

Abridged English-language edition of an 8v. Russian-language encyclopedia published by the Soviet Ministry of Defence between 1976 and 1980. V.1-3 have signed entries arranged A-Z by English terms (with Russian in parenthesis), many entries including lengthy lists of references. V.4 is the index in two sections - English terms and Russian terms used in the original edition. No cross-references. '... a treasure trove of insights into Soviet military organization, doctrine and tactics ...'(*Choice*, v.31(5), January 1994, p.762). *Class No:* 355(47)

Yearbooks & Directories

[3381]
Soviet armed forces review annual. Jones, D.R., ed. Gulf Breeze FL., Academic International Press, 1988. 375p. $71. ISBN: 0875691005.

First published 1977. Annual. The responsibility of Russia Research Center at Dalhousie University in Nova Scotia.

A survey of Soviet military developments for the past decade, with data to 1987. Detailed charts on people, weapons and policies. (... the SAFRA series remains unique and handy ... ' (*International affairs*, v.65(3) Summer 1989 p.607). *Class No:* 355(47)(058)

[3382]

—The Military-naval encyclopedia of Russia and the Soviet Union. Jones, D. R., ed. Gulf Breeze, FL., Academic International Press, 1978-. V.1-. ISBN: 0875690289 set.

Projected in c.50v., each with c.250p. and c.200 documented articles (lengthier articles being signed. Aim was to complete at the rate of 2-3v. pa., but editor 'badly need(s) co-operation of scholars and specialists ... '.

So far published: v.1. "A" (Gliders) - Administration, Military (1978); v.2. Administration, Military, Science of - Admiral Makarov (ship); v.3. Admiral Murgescu (ship) - Adp. Adp-tail 1981; v.4. Adrian I Nataliia (ship) - Adzhariia (1984) [deals largely with Russian tactical formations]. 'This is an excellent, though specialized, reference work of great utility to university libraries' (*Choice* v.16 (11), January 1980, p. 1422). *Class No:* 355(47)(058)

Balkan States

[3383]

JESSUP, J.E. **Balkan military history:** a bibliography. New York, Garland, 1986. xii,478p. $66. (*Military history bibliography, 8. Garland reference library of social sciences, 234.*) ISBN: 0824089634.

Lists unannotated citations of literature on Balkan military history from the 14th century to 1983. Includes what is now Albania, Bulgaria, Greece, Hungary, Romania, Yugoslavia, European Turkey, Serbia, Macedonia and Montenegro. A section on sources for the region as a whole is followed by 8 chronological chapters. Each chapter has an informative essay on sources and then a bibliographic listing of books, monographs, journal articles, essays, documents, dissertations, etc. in Balkan and Western European languages. Author and subject indexes. *Class No:* 355(497)

Japan

[3384]

KONDO, S. **Japanese military history:** a guide to the literature. New York, Garland, 1984. xii,88p. $35. (*Military history bibliography series, 5.*) ISBN: 0824090578.

6 sections: 1. Survey histories of the modern period - 2. From the ancient era to the restoration of 1868 - 3. From the creation of a modern army to the China Incident - 4. The Pacific War (1): survey histories - 5. The Pacific War (2): campaign and combat histories - 6. The history of the conclusion of the war, memoirs and biographies. Bibliography of 443 items, A-Z (p.51-81). Index (p.83-88). *Class No:* 355(52)

Israel

[3385]

WALLACH, J.L. **Israeli military history:** a guide to the sources. New York, Garland, 1984. xii,291p. $39. (*Military history bibliographies 1. Garland reference library of social science, 191.*) ISBN: 0824090616.

1715 entries arranged in 11 chronological chapters from c.1300 B.C. to 1974 and after. Each chapter begins with an informative essay on the sources and concludes with a bibliographical listing of books, monographs, journal articles, dissertations and documents published in Western languages. Appendix: Archives, libraries, museums, periodicals. Author index, p.273-291, but no subject index. *Class No:* 355(569.4)

Latin America

[3386]

ENGLISH, A.J. **Armed forces in Latin America:** their histories, development, present strength and military potential. London, Jane's, 1984. 490p. illus. £30. ISBN: 0710603215.

Covers the countries of Central and South America, and also Haiti, Jamaica, Cuba, and Trinidad and Tobago. Data for each country includes vital statistics, historical outline, politico-strategic position, general structure of armed forces (army, navy, air force), paramilitary forces, sources of supply, defence production, summary and prospects. Glossary in English, Spanish and Portuguese. Select bibliography, p.481-486, arranged by chapter. Index, p.487-490. *Class No:* 355(729.99)

USA

Yearbooks & Directories

[3387]

American military defense annual, 1987. Kruzel, J., ed. Lexington, Lexington Books, 1987. 228p. illus.,charts,tables. $35.£27. ISBN: 0669150916.

First published for 1985-1986. Annual.

Claims to be a definitive, up-to-the-minute guide by recognised experts with a wide range of views on the latest topics in defence. 11 chapters: 1. Perspectives - 2. US Defense strategy: a debate - 3. The defense budget - 4. Strategic forces - 5. Theater forces: US defense policy in NATO - 6. Seapower and projections forces - 7. Manpower - 8. Organization and management - 9. Arms control - 10. Special supplement: the Strategic Defense Initiative - 11. Special supplement: low intensity conflict. Defense bibliography, 1984, p.241-250. Notes. Index. *Class No:* 355(73)(058)

Histories

[3388]

Reference guide to United States military history. Shrader, C.R., ed. New York, Facts on File, 1993-. To be in 5v. illus. maps. $50 each volume. ISBN: 0816018375, v.2; 0816018383, v.3.

V.1 deals with the period 1607-1815; v.2 with 1815-1865; v.3 with 1865-1919; v.4 with 1919-1945; and v.5 with 1945-1993. First half of each volume is an overview of major trends and developments in the US military for that period, followed by six chronological narrative chapters, and then by brief biographical and 'battles and events' sections. Each volume has a short bibliography and an index. '... concise introductions ... but do not supersede existing standard and specialised reference sources.'(*Choice*,v.31(3), November 1993, p.438). *Class No:* 355(73)(091)

Bibliographies

[3389]

LANE, J.C., *ed.* **America's military past:** a guide to information sources. Detroit, Mich., Gale Research Co., 1980. xi,280p. $68. (*American government and history information guide series, 7.*) ISBN: 0810312050.

1743 items, with short annotations, arranged A-Z in each of 8 chapters: 1. Foundations of the American military experience - 2. Origins of the American military experience -

....(contd.)

3. The military in the new republic (1783-1815) - 4. The military in the era of nationalism and westward expansion (1815-1877) - 5. The military and America's rise to world power - 6. The military in the age of total war (1914-45) - 7. The military in the nuclear age (since 1945) - 8. The military and the limited wars. Author index, p.253-267; subject index, p.269-280. *Class No:* 355(73)(091)(01)

Reviews & Abstracts

[3390]

KINNELL, S.K., *ed.* **Military history of the United States:** an annotated bibliography. Santa Barbara, CA., ABC-Clio, 1986. x,333p. $88.95. (*Clio bibliography series, 23.*) ISBN: 0874364744.

A collection of 3825 abstracts of scholarly journal articles originally published in *America: history and life* between 1974 and 1985. Subject arrangement, with subject and author indexes. Complements *A Guide to the sources of United States military history,* ed. by R. Higham (*qv*).
Class No: 355(73)(091)(048)

Biographies

[3391]

SPILLER, R.J. *and* DAWSON, J.G., *eds.* **Dictionary of American military biography.** Westport. CT., Greenwood Press, 1984. 3v. (xv,1368p.). $175 £136.50. ISBN: 0313214336.

*c.*400 biographical essays, written by *c.*200 scholarly contributors, of pertinent individuals from the French and Indian Wars to the Vietnam war. Includes both native Americans and non-Americans, and all branches of the military are represented. Arrangement is A-Z by name of biographee. Essays average *c.*1500 words, include factual information (birth, death dates, etc.,) and brief bibliographies. Cross-references. Appendices. Subject index. 'A well-constructed scholarly publication that will appeal to the casual reader of American military history' (*Choice* v.22(9) May 1985., p 1303.). 'A good starting place for research on a person or period ... ' (*Library journal* December 1984, p.2264). *Class No:* 355(73)(092)

[3392]

Webster's American military biographies. McHenry, R., *ed.* Springfield, Mass., Meriam 1978 (reprinted 1984 by Dover). xi 548p. $11.95. ISBN: 0486247589.

1033 capsule biographies. MacArthur: 22/3 columns; Ulysses S. Grant: 3½ cols. Addenda (p.498-548): 1. Secretaries of War ... Commanders of NATO forces, 1960-; 2/4. Army, Navy, Marine Corps (Chief Officers. Chronology and Commanders), Air Force (Chief Officers, Commanders); Career categories (A/Z, p.544-8).
Class No: 355(73)(092)

20th Century

[3393]

CARVER, Field Marshall Lord. **Twentieth century warriors:** the development of the armed forces of the major military nations in the twentieth century. London, Weidenfeld & Nicolson, 1987. [4], 468p. 6 maps. £16.95. ISBN: 0297791605.

Aims to trace the development of the armed forces of the major military nations of the century, with a chapter for each

....(contd.)

country (Britain - France - Germany - Russia - the Soviet Union - USA - Japan - China) and a ninth chapter of conclusions. Select bibliography, p.447-450, by chapter; notes, p.451-452; analytical index, p.453-468.
Class No: 355"19"

Decorations

Great Britain

[3394]

ABBOTT, P.E. *and* TAMPLIN, J.M.A. **British gallantry awards:** the standard reference work on awards for gallantry or distinguished service, 1855-1979. Hayward, J.B., *ed.* 2nd ed. London, Nimrod Dix Co., 1981. xx,316p. illus. £25. ISBN: 0902633740.

First published 1971 by Guiness Superlatives Ltd.

44 selected awards, A-Z (Air Force Cross ... Victoria Cross). Information given for each includes origin and development; description; verifications and citations; numbers awarded; illustrative award (showing reason for award in a particular instance); illustrations (some in colour). Includes information on 'copies' and 'fakes'. Bibliography, p.xvii-xviii. *Class No:* 355.134(410)

[3395]

CREAGH, O'M. *and* HUMPHRIS, E.M., *eds.* **Victoria Cross, 1856-1920:** a complete record of the recipients of the Victoria Cross, 1856-1920, with citations, services and other biographical and related details. New ed. of 1924 ed. Colchester, J.B. Hayward & Son, 1985. 350p. 722 illus. £35. ISBN: 0903754223.

Compiled from official publications and despatches, letters from commanding officers and other contemporary accounts, and from information from private sources.
Class No: 355.134(410)

[3396]

—CREAGH, O'M. *and* HUMPHRIS, E.M., *eds.* Distinguished Service Order, 1886-1923: a complete record of the recipients of the Distinguished Service Order, 1886-1923, with citations, services and other biographical and related details. New ed. of 1924 ed. Colchester, J.B. Hayward & Son, 1978. 777p. 1020 illus. £50. ISBN: 0903754126.

Companion volume to the above. *Class No:* 355.134(410)

[3397]

LESLIE, N.B. **The Battle honours of the British and Indian armies, 1695-1914.** London, Leo Cooper, 1970. xiii,145p.

Regiments of the British army - Regiments of the Indian army - Battle honours: (a) Europe; (b) Asia; (c) Africa; (d) America; (e) West Indies; (f) Antipodes. Careful detail (name and date of battle; abbreviated title of regiment; title; date of award - Army Ordnance and date). 'An extremely valuable ... reference book' (*TLS*, 2 April 1971).

Two older works are still of value: J.H. Mayo's *Medals and decorations of the British army and navy* (London, Constable, 1897, 2v. illus. (incl. col. pl.)), detailing all British and Indian medals and decorations issued up to date of publication, and reprinting official warrants and orders in full; and C.B. Norman's *Battle honours of the British army,* from Tangier, 1662 to the commencement of the reign of King Edward VII (London, Murray, 1911. xxviii,500p. illus.

....(contd.)
maps), with notes on the battles for which honours were awarded to British regiments, recording numbers taking part, casualties, etc. *Class No:* 355.134(410)

Uniforms & Insignia

Worldwide
[3398]
CAMPBELL, B.L. *and* REYNOLDS, R. **Marine badges and insignia of the world,** including marines, commandos and naval infantrymen. Poole, Dorset, Blandford, 1983. 191p. illus. £8.95; $16.95. ISBN: 0713711388.

Arranged in 19 sections, by country (US; UK; European countries; other). Text concentrates on describing the badges and insignia and includes a certain amount of background history. There are 48 colour plates of over 1000 badges and insignia on centre pages, as well as black and white illustrations in the text. Index, p.189-191, has references to illustrations in italics. *Class No:* 355.14(100)

[3399]
ROSIGNOLI, G. **Air Force badges and insignia of World War 2.** Poole, Dorset, Blandford Press, 1976. 200p. illus (col.).

Covers 19 countries (Great Britain, p.11-16, plates 1-6; USSR, p.118-20, pl.15-20; US, p.135-47, pl.29-39). Brief historical background is provided. Index (under countries). *Class No:* 355.14(100)

[3400]
ROSIGNOLI, G. **Army badges and insignia of World War 2:** Great Britain, Poland, Belgium, Italy, USSR, US, Germany. 2nd ed. London, Blandford Press, 1974. 288p. illus. £8.95. ISBN: 071370697x.

First published 1972.

88 plates, many in colour. Index of countries, subdivided by type of badge, etc. *Class No:* 355.14(100)

[3401]
—ROSIGNOLI, G. Army badges and insignia of World War 2, Book 2:$bBritish Commonwealth, Canada, South Africa, British African territories, India, British overseas territories, Finland, France, Japan, Netherlands, Yugoslavia, China, Denmark, Czechoslovakia. London, Blandford Press, 1975. 198p. illus. ISBN: 071370747x.

80 colour plates, illustrating over 2000 badges. Index, by country. *Class No:* 355.14(100)

[3402]
THOMPSON, L. **Badges and insignia of the elite forces.** London, Arms and Armour Press, 1991. 144p. illus. £19.95. ISBN: 1854091298.

Arranged by region (Africa - The Americas - Asia - Middle East - Europe), each subdivided by country. Brief descriptions and history of badges and insignia, with colour plates. *Class No:* 355.14(100)

Handbooks & Manuals
[3403]
KNÖTEL, R. **Uniforms of the world:** a compendium of army, navy and air force uniforms, 1700-1937. Knötel, H. *and* Sieg, H., *eds.* Rev. & enl. ed. New York, Scribner; London, Arms and Armour Press, 1980 (reissued by Arms and Armour Press in 1988). 483p. illus. $30; £5.99. ISBN:

....(contd.)
0684103047, US; 1850791090, UK.
Originally published 1896. Translated from the 1956 ed. by R.G. Bell.

Broad chronological and geographical coverage. 1600 illus. 'Leans rather heavily on the uniforms of the preunified states of Germany ... Recommended for all libraries' (*Choice,* v.18(4), December 1980, p.507-8). *Class No:* 355.14(100)(035)

[3404]
—KANNIK, P. Military uniforms in colour. English ed., edited by W.Y. Carman. London, Blandford Press, 1968. 278p. illus.

Translated from the Danish, *Alverdens uniformer i farver* (1967).

International in scope, with pride of place to the Napoleonic Wars. Comparatively meagre on British colonial and Indian units. Military terminology, p.257-70. Analytical index, under countries. 512 small coloured illus. (4 per page), chronologically from the Papal Swiss Guard of 1506 to 1960 units (including UN troops, 1950). Editor was Assistant Director, Imperial War Museum. *Class No:* 355.14(100)(035)

[3405]
—MOLLO, A. *and* SMITH, D. World army uniforms since 1939. London, Blandford Press, 1981. 359p. 122p. of col. illus., with 260 illus in all. *Class No:* 355.14(100)(035)

Europe—Eastern
[3406]
WIENER, F, *comp.* **Army, navy and air force uniforms of the Warsaw Pact.** London, Arms and Armour Press, 1978. 64p. illus. (inc. col. pl.).

Translated from the German original *Die Armeen der Warscheven-Pakt-Staaten* (M. Lehmanns, 1975).

Brief text supported by 654 illus. (including 16p. of col. plates). Covers current uniforms, badges and insignia. Warsaw Pact countries: USSR, Bulgaria, East Germany, Poland, Czechoslovakia, Hungary, Romania and Yugoslavia. *Class No:* 355.14(401)

[3407]
—Soviet army uniforms and insignia (1945-75). London, Arms and Armour Press, 1981. 149p. illus.

Originally produced under the direction of Chief of Imperial General Staff, War Office, London. Has 9 p. of plates and nearly 300 drawings. *Class No:* 355.14(47)

Great Britain
[3408]
CHICHESTER, H.M. *and* BURGES-SHORT, G. **The Records and badges of every regiment and corps in the British Army.** 2nd ed. London, Greenhill Books, 1986. 984p. 24 col. illus. £30. ISBN: 0947898220.

First published in 1900 by Gale & Polden, Aldershot.

An authoritative account of British regiments and corps, and their predecessors, up to 1900, with data on badges, lists of unit histories, and information on uniforms, colours and standards. *Class No:* 355.14(410)

[3409]
DAVIS, B.L. British army cloth insignia: 1940 to the present: an illustrated reference guide for collectors. London, Arms & Armour Press, 1985. 72p. 600 illus. £7.95. ISBN: 0853687099.

A price guide, mainly illustrations. Bibliography, p.17-18. *Class No:* 355.14(410)

[3410]
EDWARDS, T.T. Regimental badges. 6th ed. London, Charles Knight, 1974. xiv,361p. illus.

First published 1951.

An illustrated record of cap badges of regiments and corps of the British Army, with notes on origin. Sections: 1. Regular Army - 2. Territorial and Army Volunteer Reserve - 3. Departments and Corps - 4. Miscellaneous - 5. Officers Training Corps - 6. Some discontinued badges. 5 appendices (The Garter ... The bugle). Brief index. *Class No:* 355.14(410)

[3411]
—**KIPLING, A.L.** *and* **KING, H.L.** Head-dress badges of the British Army. London, F. Muller, 1973-79. 2v. illus. V.1: £50; v.2: £35. ISBN: 0584109474, v.1; 0584109490, v.2.

The two volumes have 3100 black and white illustrations. V.1 has 36 sections (1. Early badges ... 36. The marching regiments of foot, 1914). V.2 has 22 sections, from the end of the Great War to the present day. Each volume has an index. *Class No:* 355.14(410)(035)

[3412]
JARRETT, D. British naval dress. London, Dent, 1960. 148p. illus.

Four sections: 1. Before 1748; 2. 1748 to 1829; 3. 1830 to 1900; 4. After 1900 . Profusely illustrated (86 plates and 19 line-drawings), many of the originals being in the National Maritime Museum. Illustrations also include badges. Detailed index. 'A most interesting book for the general reader as well as a handbook for film and theatrical producers and for historical illustrations; (*The Naval review,* v.49(1), January 1961, p.88). *Class No:* 355.14(410)

[3413]
—**MOLL, J.** Uniforms of the Royal Navy during the Napoleonic Wars. London, Evelyn, 1965. [7],43p. illus.

Contains 20 coloured plates in the form of modern silhouettes and includes a bibliography. *Class No:* 355.14(410)

[3414]
WILKINSON, F. Badges of the British Army, 1820 to the present, an illustrated reference guide for collectors. 8th rev. ed. London, Arms and Armour Press, 1992. 95p. illus. £12.99. ISBN: 1854096352.

First published 1969.

A guide for the collector, with 450 black-and-white photographs and a price guide. Also information on badge collections, how to purchase, sell. store, renovate and record them. *Class No:* 355.14(410)

Handbooks & Manuals

[3415]
DAVIS, B.L. British army uniforms and insignia of World War II. Rev. ed. London, Arms and Armour Press, 1992. 276p. £16.95. ISBN: 085409159x.

First published 1983.

Arranged in 6 parts: 1. Ranks and appointments - 2.

....(contd.)
Badges and insignia - 3. Uniforms and clothing - 4. Specialist and protective clothing - 5. Equipment - 6. Local Defence Volunteers and the Home Guard. 3 appendices (1. Glossary; 2. The Army Council; 3. Army numbers). Profusely illustrated. No index. *Class No:* 355.14(410)(035)

Illustrations

[3416]
ARMY MUSEUMS OGILBY TRUST. Index to British military costume prints, 1500-1914. London, the Trust, 1972. 493p. illus.

2584 numbered items; an index to published prints, recording more than 15,000. Two parts: 1. Sets; 2. Single prints. Index to artists, authors, engravers, lithographers, printers and publishers; index to regiments, corps and subjects; index to persons and plates. Good reproductions (51 plates). 'An exceptionally full and thorough checklist' (*British book news,* September 1972, p.784). *Class No:* 355.14(410)(084.1)

[3417]
—**CARMAN, W.Y.** British military uniforms from contemporary pictures: Henry VII to the present day. London, Spring Books: Hamlyn, 1968 (a reprint of the 1957 volume published by Leonard Hill). xiv,168p. illus.

Has 109 monochrome and colour plates; sources stated. Detailed lists (*e.g.* 'Dress of infantry', p.160-2: regiment/ uniform/piping). Index. *Class No:* 355.14(410)(084.1)

Histories

[3418]
LAWSON, C.C.P. A History of the uniforms of the British army, from its beginnings to 1760. London, Norman Military Publications, 1940-67. 5v. illus. (incl. col. pl.), tables.

An authoritative record, based on official records and warrants. V.3 (1961) has a chapter on the Amerian colonies and a bibliography. V.4 (1966), covering *c.*1797-1815, introduces the foreign regiments in British Service. Profusely illustrated (*e.g.* v.4 has 4 colour-plates and 150 black-and-white drawings). Effective use of tables (*e.g.* p.115-7: 'Scottish fencibles'; tabulated data: regiment; date; facings; dress; lace; details; reference). *Class No:* 355.14(410)(091)

Scotland

[3419]
COCHRANE, P. Scottish military dress. London, Blandford Press, 1987. 128p. 92 illus. (90 in col.). £12.95. ISBN: 0713717386.

Arranged chronologically in 6 chapters (Late Middle Ages - 17th century - 18th century - The French wars, 1793-1815 - 19th century - 20th century. An appendix lists regimental titles and numbers. Bibliography of sources consulted (p.116-117). Index (p.122-128). *Class No:* 355.14(411)

Germany

[3420]

ELLIS, C. A Collector's guide to the history and uniform of Das Heer: the German Army, 1933-45. Addlestone, Surrey, Ian Allan, 1993. 160p. 170 illus. £10.99. ISBN: 0711021937.

A historical account of the German Army through the years of Nazi domination. *Class No:* 355.14(430)

[3421]

STEIN, H.-P *and* **OTTMER, H.-M. Symbole und Zeremoniell in deutschen Striekräften vom 18. bis zum. 20. Jahrhundert.** Herford, Mittler, 1984. 320p. illus (inc. 18 col. pl.). (*Entwicklung deutscher militärischer Tradition, Band 3.*) ISBN: 3813201619.

Arranged in 3 main sections, each subdivided. A general section of military symbols and ceremonial (4 parts) is followed by a section on symbols (10 parts) and a section on ceremonial (4 parts). Bibliography, p.310-314. Index. p.315-318. *Class No:* 355.14(430)

USA

[3422]

DAVIS, B.L. United States Army cloth insignia: 1941 to the present day. London, Arms & Armour Press, 1987. 68p. 370 illus. £6.95. ISBN: 0853688508.

A price guide, mainly illustrations. *Class No:* 355.14(73)

[3423]

EMERSON, W.K. Chevrons: illustrated history and catalogue of U.S. Army insignia. Washington, DC., Smithsonian Institute Press, 1983. 298p. illus. tables. $49.50. ISBN: 0874744121.

Designed for use by military personnel, historians, museum curators, and uniform buffs. 8 chapters: 1. The story of chevrons, uniforms and service stripes - 2. Evolution of early chevrons, pre- 1872 - 3. History, 1872-1902 - 4. Catalog of 1872-1902 - 5. History, 1902-1920 - 6. Catalog, 1902-1920 - 7. History, post 1920 - 8. History and catalog of special chevrons, awards and insignia. Includes illustrations of 637 chevrons, inc. 50 in colour. 3 appendices (Summary of manufacturing code letters; Alphabetical listing of rank titles with corresponding catalog numbers). Notes after each chapter. *Class No:* 355.14(73)

Standards & Colours

Commonwealth

[3424]

EDWARDS, T.J. Standards, guidons and colours of the Commonwealth forces. Aldershot, Gale & Polden, 1953. xvi,239p. illus (15 col. pl.).

Provides a historical commentary on the official warrants, regulations and orders relating to regimental colours. Well documented, with excellent illus. *Class No:* 355.15(41-44)

Battles & Battlefields

Dictionaries

[3425]

BRUCE, G. The Paladin dictionary of battles. London, Paladin, 1986. viii,356p. £4.95. ISBN: 0586085297.

First published 1904 as *Dictionary of battles,* by T. Harbottle; in 1971 and 1979 as *Harbottle's dictionary of battles,* by G. Bruce.

Entries A-Z (Aachen. World War II ... Zuyder Zee. Netherlands War of Independence) includes sieges, raids and relatively minor actions, mainly because these minor actions represent the tactical moves which so often led up to the main battles. Data: 'the War/campaign of which part; the date it began; who commanded; how many men on each side, the tactics and sometimes the weapons employed; to whom went victory; the casualties, and, when it can be said, what was the ultimate outcome' (*Preface*). Appended cross-references name associated battles, where possible. 'Vietnam War': 6 columns. Guerilla wars up to 1985 are included in this latest edition. Partly analytical index for both personal names and wars, p.329-357. *Class No:* 355.422(038)

[3426]

EGGENBERGER, D. Encyclopedia of British battles, 1479 to the present. New ed. London, Dover Publications, 1986. 546p. 50 illus., maps. £13.45. ISBN: 0486249131.

First published 1967 as *A dictionary of battles.*

Recreates the scenes and actions of nearly 1600 military engagements in the period covered. 'Suggestions for further reading'. Detailed index of all persons and places mentioned. *Class No:* 355.422(038)

[3427]

LAFFIN, J. Brassey's battles: 3,500 years of conflict, campaigns and wars from A to Z. London, Oxford, Brassey's Defence Publications: Pergamon Press, 1986. 500p. 80 illus., maps. £22.50; $29.95. ISBN: 0080311857.

A dictionary of over 7000 entries for battles, campaigns and wars. Contents: Chronicle from Greek-Persian wars to W.W.II (p.1-21); Major wars and 'incidents' since 1945 (p.24). List of battles, campaigns and wars (p.27-482) A-Z by name of battle. 'Textual entries are clear, concise and informative and quality of design and production is first class' (*British book news,* May 1986, p.293). *Class No:* 355.422(038)

[3428]

SWEETMAN, J. A Dictionary of European land battles: from the earliest times to 1945. London, Hale, 1984; New York, Macmillan, 1985. 309p. £10.50; $19.95. ISBN: 0029317002, UK.

Ready reference to *c.*2400 European land battles. In 4 parts, the main 266-page section listing the battles with concise descriptions and details of strategy, weapons, casualties, the political background and the ramifications of the outcome. There follows a list of wars and battles fought within them; a select bibliography (1½p.); and index of persons involved in the battles described, including biographical data. *Class No:* 355.422(038)

Histories

[3429]

CHANDLER, D.G. Battles and battlescenes of World War Two. New York, Macmillan, 1989. 160p. illus., maps. $19.95. ISBN: 0028971752.

Information on 52 selected engagements, arranged A-Z by title of battle or battlefield. Entries include essential facts such as date, location, object, opposing sides, forces engaged, casualties, and result. Also a list of suggested readings and a 2-3 page narrative about the engagement. Small black-and-white maps and photographs accompany each entry. Chronological table. Index.
Class No: 355.422(091)

[3430]

CONNOLLY, P. Greece and Rome at war. London, Macdonald, 1981. 320p. illus (col). £15.95. ISBN: 035606798x.

The author has recast his 3 earlier books to make this general sketch of the historical background from early Greek times to the fall of the Roman Empire. The text has been expanded in places to recount the course of some individual battles and campaigns in detail. In 4 parts: Greece and Macedonia - Italy and the Western Mediterranean - The Roman Empire - The later Empire, AD200-450. 3 appendices: War at sea - Fortifications and siege warfare - Roman military costume. Profusely illustrated. Bibliography, p.314. Index, p.316-20. *Class No:* 355.422(091)

[3431]

CORDESMAN, A.H. *and* WAGNER, A.R. The Lessons of modern war. Boulder, Col., Westview Press; London, Mansell Publishing Ltd., 1989-90. 3v. $88. £35 each volume. ISBN: 0813309549, v.1 (US); 0720120454, v.1 (UK); 0813309557, v.2 (US); 0720120446, v.2 (UK); 0813309565, v.3 (US); 0720120438, v.3 (UK).

Focuses on military events and lessons, the politics, strategy and tactics of five recent major conflicts. V.1: The Arab-Israeli conflicts, 1973-1989; v.2: The Iran-Iraq war; v.3: The Afghan and Falklands conflicts.
Class No: 355.422(091)

[3432]

SEYMOUR, W. Great sieges of history. London, Brassey's (UK), 1991. xviii,338p. illus, maps. ISBN: 0080376967.

List of maps and illustrations, and glossary precedes. An introduction is followed by 17 chapters, except for ch.1 each on a siege: 1. The mechanics of a siege - 2. Acre 1189-91 ... 7. Londonderry 1689 ... 11. Ladysmith 1899-1900 ... 14. The Alcásar of Toledo, July-September 1936 ... 16. Leningrad September 1941-January 1944 - 17. Dien Bien Phu ... Appendix: Notes for visitors to the sites of the sieges. Bibliography (by chapter), p.324-9. Index, 330-338.
Class No: 355.422(091)

[3433]

WEIGLEY, R.F. The Age of battles: the quest for decisive warfare from Breitenfeld to Waterloo. Bloomington & Indianapolis, Indiana University Press, 1991. £25. ISBN: 0253363802.

A narrative history that considers all aspects of the topic, the historical circumstances and political conditions of the adversaries, strategic thinking, personalities of the commanders,tactical maneuvers on the field, the role of armaments and technology, etc. 20 chapters in 3 parts: 1. The profession of officership and the birth of modern war; 2.

.... (contd.)
The eighteenth century: classical epoch of modern war; 3. Thunderstrokes of battle: the French revolutionary and Napoleonic wars. *Class No:* 355.422(091)

Great Britain

[3434]

SEYMOUR, W. Battles in Britain, and their political background. London, Sidgwick & Jackson, 1975. 2v. (232p.; 231p.). illus, plans, charts.

V.1: 1066-1547; V.2. 1642-1746. V.1. has chapter bibliographies, plus a list of books studied in connection with armour, weapons, and uniforms. V.2. has 11 chapters. 'Marston Moor', p.83-107, with 2 illus. 1 plan. 4p. shows types of weapons used in the Civil War. Bibliography, p.225-7. Each volume has a non-analytical index.
Class No: 355.422(410)

[3435]

—**GREEN, H. Guide to the battlefields of Great Britain and Ireland.** Rev. ed. London, Constable, 1983. 288p. 32 illus., 49 maps. £6.50. ISBN: 0094645205.

First published 1973.

A brief account and sketch map of 52 battles, often with photographs showing how the ground looks today.
Class No: 355.422(410)

[3436]

SMURTHWAITE, D., *ed*. Ordnance Survey complete guide to the battlefields of Britain. Exeter, Devon, Webb & Bower, 1984. 224p. 140 illus. (50 col.), 133 maps (col.). £8.95. ISBN: 0863501575.

Chronological arrangement (The Romans in Britain, 55 BC-AD 409 - Early England, 410-1060 - The Middle Ages, 1066-1450 - The age of the Wars of the Roses, 1450-1550 - The English Civil War, 1642-51 - Warfare in the age of reason, 1660-1746 - The Battle of Britain: the Royal Air Force, 1918-40). Tables of regiments. Gazetteer. Glossary. Further reading (p.221). Analytical index, p.222-224.
Class No: 355.422(410)

France

Dictionaries

[3437]

CHANDLER, D.G. Dictionary of the Napoleonic wars. London, Arms & Armour Press, 1979. xxxvi,570p. ports., maps.

Entries for 1200 battles and campaigns, A-Z ('Austerlitz': p.31-36: 4 maps. Also biographies (Wellesley: p.487-9). Appendix: Napoleon's military movements, 1796-1815 (date; from; to; via; events), p.496-557. Bibliography, p.558-70 (authors, A-Z). Chronological tables, p.xxiii-xxxvi. 85 maps. No index. 'An authoritative and valuable book which historians of the future will neglect at their peril' (*RUSI journal*. June 1980, p.75.
Class No: 355.422(44)(038)

USA

[3438]

MACDONALD, J. Great battles of the American Civil War. London, Michael Joseph, 1988. 200p. illus. ISBN: 0718131029.

Introduction on the nation divided, followed by 18 chapters on individual battles (including Fredericksburg, Gettysburg, Chattanooga, etc.), and final chapter on the nation reunited. Gazetteer, p.192-4. Bibliography, p.195. Index, p.196-99. *Class No:* 355.422(73)

Strategy

[3439]

HOUSE, J.M. Military intelligence, 1870-1991: a research guide. Westport, CT, Greenwood Press, 1993. 165p. $55. (*(Research guides in military studies, 6).*)

English-language books and articles arranged in 5 chapters (General and strategic intelligence - Institutional studies - Tactical intelligence - Human intelligence - Counter intelligence) subdivided by author, A-Z. Most entries have short, but frequently critical annotations. Introduction discusses the nature and history of military intelligence. Author and subject indexes. '... a very useful source.'(*Choice*,v.31(3), November 1993, p.434).

Class No: 355.43

[3440]

Jane's C31 systems. Rackham, P., *ed.* Coulsdon, Surrey, Jane's, 1993. 380p. £145. ISBN: 0710610734.

A guide to command, control, communication and major sub-systems. Also on CD-ROM. *Class No:* 355.43

Bibliographies

[3441]

Current world affairs: a quarterly bibliography. Alexandria, VA., John C. Damon (previously Boston, VA, American Security Council Education Foundation of the Center for International Security Studies), 1977-. no.1-. $140pa. ISSN: 10504850.

Prior to 1989 title was *Quarterly strategic bibliography*, which superseded *Current bibliographic survey of national defense*.

*c.*800 references per issue, arranged under Periodicals (titles, A-Z): Congressional documents; Books; Other documents, Appended list of periodicals consulted. Glossary. Subject index. *Class No:* 355.43(01)

[3442]

LAWRENCE, R.M. Strategic defense initiative: bibliography and research guide. Boulder, Col., Westview Press, in co-operation with the Center for Space Law and Policy, University of Colorado at Boulder; London, Mansell, 1987. xiii,352p. $29.50; £27.50. ISBN: 0813372291, US; 0720118689, UK.

*c.*1000 citations that reflect the full spectrum of thought on the issue. In 3 sections: Technical background of the debate - Arguments in favour of SDI - Arguments against SDI. Each section includes an essay integrating and amplifying the information presented in the abstracted materials. No annotations. No indexes. *Class No:* 355.43(01)

[3443]

—TUTTLE, A.C. 'The Strategic defense initiative'. In *Choice*, v.27(1), September 1989, p.61-63, 66-73.

A bibliographic essay citing 63 items. Sections on historical context, early proponents, SDI technology, SDI and the USSR, SDI and the American economy, ethics of SDI, SDI and the future; SDI and the strategic policy debate. *Class No:* 355.43(01)

Dictionaries

[3444]

ROBERTSON, D. A Dictionary of modern defense and strategy. London, Europa Publications, 1987. xii,324p. £12.95. ISBN: 0946653674, UK.

Distributed in US & Canada by Gale Research Co., under the title *Guide to modern defense and strategy*.

Over 400 entries describing the terms, tactics, organizations, and accords governing today's defence. Entries arranged A-Z and each defined by an essay of *c.*350 words. Extensive cross-references. Uses non-technical language. British bias. A new ed. was published in 1990 (ISBN 0946653674). *Class No:* 355.43(038)

[3445]

WALDMAN, H. The Dictionary of SDI. Wilmington, Del., Scholarly Resources, 1988. 182 p. $35. ISBN: 0842022813.

c. 800 concise definitions of words and phrases relating to the 'strategic defense initiative' (SDI), including some personal and organizational names. Includes text and agreed statements of the 1972 Antiballistic Missile Treaty and a list of members of the Defensive Technologies Study Team. *Class No:* 355.43(038)

Polyglot

[3446]

SCHWARZ, U. *and* **HADIK, L. Strategic terminology:** a trilingual glossary. New York, Praeger, 1966. 157p. $12.50. ISBN: 0686572173.

Published under the auspices of the Graduate School of International Studies, Geneva.

About 4000 English, French and German terms are defined in those languages, with supporting quotations from 29 authorities (*e.g.* Clausewitz; *Dictionary of United States military terms* ... (1964). The English term and definition plus quotation(s) are followed by the French and German entries (normally supported by citations from authorities in those languages). French and German indexes (including equivalents); bibliography of authorities cited, p.155-7. *Class No:* 355.43(038)=00

Maps & Atlases

[3447]

CHALIAND, G. *and* **RAGEAU, J-P. A Strategic atlas:** comparative geopolitics of the world powers. Translated by Tony Berrett; maps by Catherine Petit. 3rd rev. and updated ed. New York, Harper & Row, 1993. 224p. maps. $40:00. ISBN: 0062715542.

First published in France in 1983 as *Atlas stratique*.

Shows the economic, political, cultural and military relationships of the world in a special and geographical context, emphasizing the geopolitical position in which individual nations and groups of nations see themselves in

....(contd.)

today's world. Extensive maps and charts, circular polar projection maps introduced to avoid distortion. A readable text accompanies the maps. *Class No:* 355.43(084.3)

[3448]
FREEDMAN, L. **Atlas of global strategy.** London, Macmillan Press; New York, Facts on File, 1985. 192p. 90 illus., tables, 120 maps. £18.95; $22.95. ISBN: 0333384164, UK; 0816010587, US.

Examines the role of war in the modern world. An extensive introduction (p.9-24) is followed by 6 sections (The changing international order - The changing pattern of warfare - The nuclear arms race - Conventional war - Warfare since 1945 - What's to be done?). Chronology, 1945-1985. Bibliography, p.185-187. Index, p.189-192. 'An atlas for quick reference on strategic concerns', the author 'overcomes the picture-book format ... by combining an unbiased narrative of the superpower relationship with innovative cartography' (*Library journal,* v.111(3), 15 February 1986, p.173). *Class No:* 355.43(084.3)

USA

[3449]
DANIELS, G., *ed*. **A Guide to the reports of the United States strategic bombing survey ...** London, Boydell & Brewer, for the Royal Historical Society, 1981. xxvi, 115p. £12; $22. (*Guides and handbooks. Supplementary series 2.*) ISBN: 0901050717.

1. European survey (p.3-66) - 2. Pacific survey (p.69-115). A closely classified inventory, providing contents of each report, its documentary exhibits and appendices. Valuable historical introduction. No indexes, but a detailed contents list. *Class No:* 355.43(73)

[3450]
—COULTER, E. 'Evolution of nuclear strategy in the United States'. In *Choice,* v.25(10), June 1988, p.1519-1527.

A bibliographical essay, with sections on the generalists, foreign generalists, the hardliners, the skeptics, the philosophers. 93 cited works listed A-Z by author. *Class No:* 355.43(73)

Army

[3451]
The Army list. 1814-. London, HMSO, 1914-. Frequency varies. 2v. (xii,534p.;780p.). Part 1 £18; part 2 £24. ISBN: 0117726575, Part 1 (1993 ed.); 0117720585, Part 2 (1993 ed.).

Part 1 is in 4 sections: 1. Queen and Royal Family; 2. Defence councils, Army commands, Establishments; 3. Regular Army; 4. Territorial Army. Index of names (p.411-533). Subject index (p.534). Part 2 lists officers in receipt of retired pay. *Class No:* 356

[3452]
The World's armies: an illustrated review of the armies of the world. Westhorp, C., *ed*. London, Salamander Books Ltd., 1991. 143p. illus (col). maps. £18.95. ISBN: 0861015878.

Chapters by area (North America - Central & South America - Asia & the Far East - Oceania - Europe - North Africa & Middle East - Sub-Saharan Africa), subdivided by country. Deals with the composition and capabilities of each

....(contd.)

army. Text is accompanied by equipment tables of principal items in service, colour flags and maps, diagrams and colour photographs. *Class No:* 356

Encyclopaedias

[3453]
HOGG, I.V. **The Illustrated encyclopaedia of artillery.** London, Stanley Paul & Co. Ltd., 1987. 256p. illus. (photos, some in col.)., diagrs. £16.95. ISBN: 0091726549.

In two sections: a short history of artillery from 1325, and (c.200p.) an A-Z encyclopedia covering weapons, technical terminology, gunner shorthand, and notable personalities involved in the development of artillery weapons. Covers all nations, some sketchily (*e.g.* USSR). Clear and concise layout. Presumably aimed at the layman, but equally of interest to the professional or military historian. *Class No:* 356(031)

Handbooks & Manuals

[3454]
WEEKS, J., *comp*. **Jane's pocket-book: armies of the world.** London, Jane's, 1981. 224p. illus. £5.95. (*Jane's pocket book.*) ISBN: 0710601492.

Sections arranged A-Z by country (Afghanistan ... Zimbabwe), with details of strength of the army, military service, background, structure, and equipment. *Class No:* 356(035)

Maps & Atlases

[3455]
BANKS, A. **A World atlas of military history to 1500.** New ed. London, Secker & Warburg, 1984. 12.95. ISBN: 0436032295.

154 clear, easily understood, black-and-white maps, some with double-page spread. Adequate legends. Some battles are shown in phases (*e.g.* Cannae: 3 phases, p.56). Includes general as well as war maps. Index of battles, sieges, wars, campaigns, etc.; index of individuals; index of races, tribes and all named groups of people. Page size, 22 x 17 cm. *Class No:* 356(084.3)

[3456]
—BANKS, A. **A World atlas of military history, 1861-1945.** London, Seeley Service, 1978. [ix],160,[22]p. ISBN: 0854221409.

145 maps, covering the American Civil War, the European, colonial and Far Eastern wars, 1860 - 1914, and World Wars I and II. ' ... an easily accessible and handy guide to the strategic and tactical geography of the wars of the 19th and 20th centuries' (*British book news,* June 1978, p468). Page size, 22 x 17 cm. *Class No:* 356(084.3)

[3457]
—CHANDLER, D.G. **Atlas of military strategy: the art, theory and practice of war, 1618-1878.** London, Arms and Armour Press, 1980. 208p. illus., maps.

200 two-colour maps, including campaign and battle plans. Bibliography. Over 120 illus. *Class No:* 356(084.3)

Histories

[3458]
BARTHORP, M. The Armies of Britain, 1485-1980.
London, National Army Museum; Guernsey, Seagull S.A., [1981]. 296p. illus., maps. £4.50. ISBN: 0901721069.

A popular account in 22 chapters. Appendices: 1. Regiments and corps of the British army in 1979 and their chief forbears; 2. Command of the army, 1485-1980. Chapter references, p.290-8. Index to text and illus.

For detailed period histories of army organization and administration, best sources are: Cruickshank, C.G. *Elizabeth's army* (1946); Fifth, Sir C.H. *Cromwell's army* (3rd ed., 1932); Walton, C. *History of the British standing army, 1660-1700* (1894); Curtis, E.E. *The organization of the British army in the American revolution* (1926); Oman, Sir C. *Wellington's army* (1912); and Dunlop, J.K. *The development of the British army, 1899-1914* (1938).
Class No: 356(091)

Great Britain

Bibliographies

[3459]
BRUCE, A.P.C. A Bibliography of the British Army, 1660-1914. 2nd ed. London, Munich, New York, K.G. Saur, 1985. xii,422p. £35; DM.120; $45. ISBN: 0862912873, UK; 0862912873, US; 3598105746, German.

First published 1975 as *An annotated bibliography of the British Army, 1660-1914* (New York, Garland).

5656 entries, some annotated, arranged in 24 chapters in 4 parts: 1. Bibliographies, indexes and general works - 2. Organization, management and personnel - 3. Military theory, tactics, drill and equipment - 4. Military operations and overseas garrisons (arranged geographically, then by subject). No introductions to either chapters or parts. Author index, p.351-390. Subject index, p.391-422. 'In all, it gives fine coverage of a somewhat narrow topic' (*Library journal,* v.101(13), July 1976, p.1512, of the 1st ed.).
Class No: 356(410)(01)

[3460]
—BRUCE, A. A Bibliography of British military history, from the Roman invasion to the Restoration, 1660. Munich, K. G. Saur, 1981. x, 350p. Dm.56-. $31. £18.50. ISBN: 359810359x.

3280 annotated entries arranged in 17 chapters in 4 parts: 1. Guides, indexes and sources - 2. General military works - 3. Organizations, campaigns and military leaders - 4. Fortifications, castles, weapons and uniforms. Each part and chapter begins with a brief introductory paragraph followed by an A-Z list by author. Strong emphasis on books and periodical articles, including the popular. Very short annotations. Follows the same selection criteria as the above.
Class No: 356(410)(091)

[3461]
STRACHAN, H. 'The British Army, 1815-1856: recent writing reviewed'. In *Journal of the Society for Army Historical Research,* Summer 1985, p.68-79.

Includes references to c.84 books, articles and theses.
Class No: 356(410)(01)

[3462]
—SPIERS, E.M. 'The British Army, 1856-1914: recent writing reviewed'. In *Journal of the Society for Army Historical Research,* Winter 1985, p.194-207.

Includes references to over 150 items.
Class No: 356(410)(01)

Encyclopaedias

[3463]
GRIFFIN, D. Encyclopaedia of modern British army regiments. Wellingborough, Northants. P. Stephens, 1985. 236p. illus. £16.50. ISBN: 0850597080.

Deals, in order of seniority, with each of the regiments left in the modern army. Includes information on insignia, honours, anniversaries, customs, mascots, dress distinctions, marches, etc., plus a 'family tree' for each regiment showing its lineage. Many photographs and other illustrations.
Class No: 356(410)(031)

[3464]
PEEDLE, R. Encyclopaedia of the modern territorial army. Wellingborough, Patrick Stephens, 1990. 232p. illus. diagrs, maps. £22.50. ISBN: 0850599385.

Explains the role of the Territorial Army, its history and structure. Chapters: A brief history - The Territorial Army today - The Yeomanry - The Artillery - The Corps of Royal Engineers - The Infantry - Airborne units - The corps and services. 5 appendices: 1. Chronological table of significant dates; 2. Sandhurst; 3. Council of TAVRAs; 4. Some Victoria Crosses of the Territorial Army; 5. Territorial Army order of precedence; 6. Regimental quick marches. Index, p.229-232. *Class No:* 356(410)(031)

Handbooks & Manuals

[3465]
ASCOLI, D. A Companion to the British Army, 1660-1983.
London, Harrap Ltd., 1983. 319p. illus. £14.50. ISBN: 0245539603.

A *vade-mecum* to the Army's origins and development from the first standing regiments of Charles II to the present day. A lengthy introduction (p.13-57) and an A-Z listing of regiments, titled *The Spinal column,* precedes the 6 main sections: A. Orders of precedence - B. Information on regiments - C. The anatomy of the Army - D. Battle honours - E. Headdress badges - F. Chronology of political and military control. Select bibliography, p.313-314. Analytical index, p.315-319. *Class No:* 356(410)(035)

[3466]
BRERETON, J.M. A Guide to the regiments and corps of the British Army on the regular establishment. London, The Bodley Head, 1985. 288p. illus. £10.95. ISBN: 0370305787.

'... unravels at a glance the complex amalgamations underlying the present day units. All regiments and corps ever raised are listed if they subsist in the units of today's British regular army. The Royal Marines are also included'. (Dust jacket). A select bibliography of 19 items, explanatory notes, and a list of precedence of regiments and corps, precedes the main part of the guide. This includes information in respect of each unit, whether existing or previously merged: date of raising, successive titles, battle

....(contd.)
honours, motto, uniform, regimental marches, journal, headquarters, museum, nicknames, and cap badge. Index to regiments and corps, p.183-288. *Class No:* 356(410)(035)

[3467]
HALLOWS, I.S. Regiments and corps of the British Army. London, Arms & Armour Press, 1991. 320p. illus. £19.95.

A useful general reference work tracing the history and traditions of every regiment and corps in the Army's 1991 Order of Battle. Covers dress, regimental marches, battle honours and anniversaries. Includes addresses of museums and associations, and a bibliography of each regiment and corps. *Class No:* 356(410)(035)

Dictionaries

[3468]
GANDER, T. Encyclopedia of the modern British army. 3rd ed. Wellingborough, Northants, P. Stephens, 1986. 312p. 650 illus., diagrs. £19.95. ISBN: 085059684x.

First published 1980.

In 4 sections: The British army since 1945 (p.6-18) - Organization (p.19-99) giving information and hierarchy diagrams of each of the regiments - Weapons and equipment (p.100-287) - Uniforms and insignia (p.288-306). 4-columned index (p.307-312) is combined with a glossary of abbreviations. Cross-referenced. *Class No:* 356(410)(038)

Histories

[3469]
DIETZ, P. The Last of the regiments: their rise and fall. London, Brassey's (UK), 1990. viii,271p. 10 illus. £31.50. ISBN: 0080347614.

A study of the creation of the British military tradition and of the regimental system in particular. 10 chapters: 1. The origins of the British Army ... 3. The golden age of the regiments ... 5. The regiments in India ... 8. Action, reaction and intervention - 9. The long armistice and the second world war - 10. The end of the family. 4 appendices. Notes and references. Bibliography, p.255-8. Index, p.259-71. *Class No:* 356(410)(091)

[3470]
FORTESCUE, J.W. A History of the British Army. London, Macmillan, 1899-1930. (Reprinted by AMS Press). 13v. with 6v. of maps. ISBN: 0404025501, the set.

Usually accepted as the standard work on British Army history. It suffers, however, from a lack of proportion: the majority of the volumes are devoted to the period between 1763 and 1810. Furthermore, it contains little or no information on the development of army organizations and administration. *Class No:* 356(410)(091)

[3471]
WHITE, A.S., *comp.* **A Bibliography of regimental histories of the British Army.** Rev. ed. London, London Stamp Exchange, 1988. viii,317p. £16.95. ISBN: 094813061x.

First published in 1965 by the Society for Army Historical Research, with The Army Museums Ogilby Trust.

*c.*2500 briefly annotated entries. Sections: 1. General - 2. Regular army - 3. Departments, Corps - 4. Auxiliary forces - 5. Miscellaneous (*e.g.* Women's corps; Disbanded regiments). Appendix shows present day titles of regiments.

....(contd.)
Index, p.309-317.

An addendum was issued in 1992 (viii,331p. £24.95). *Class No:* 356(410)(091)

Scotland

Histories

[3472]
BARNES, R.M., *and others.* **The Uniforms and history of the Scottish regiments:** Britain - Canada - Australia - New Zealand - South Africa, 1625 to the present day. London, Seeley Service, [1956]. 351p. illus. (12 col. pl.), tables.

16 chapters, 12 of which cover the history, 1625-1954, by periods. Chapter 13: Early Scottish weapons; 14: The pipes; 15-16: Uniforms of the Scottish regiments. Appendices consist of abbreviated regimental histories (Scottish regiments of Britain, of Canada, of Australia, etc.) noting H.Q. or depot, brief chronology, uniforms, battle honours, number of battalions in 1914-18, regimental march and motto, and affiliated or allied regiments. No bibliography. Index, giving names of regiments in capitals. 83 uniforms illustrated in colour on 12 plates; 26 line-drawings. *Class No:* 356(411)(091)

British Colonies

Histories

[3473]
Regiments of the Empire: a bibliography of their published histories. Perkins, R., *comp.* Newton Abbott (privately published), 1989. 382p. illus. £24.50. ISBN: 0950642916.

A glossary of acronyms and abbreviations precedes the bibliography of over 800 items arranged in 8 geographical groups: 1.Colonies, protectorates and other territories; 2. Africa; 3. India; 4. Canada; 5. New Zealand and Australian forces in Korea; 6. New Zealand and Australian forces in South Vietnam; 7. New Zealand; 8. Australia. Index is by chapter. *Class No:* 356(41-5)(091)

France

Histories

[3474]
HORWARD, D.D., *ed.* **Napoleonic military history:** a bibliography. London, Greenhill Books, Lionel Leventhal Ltd.,; New York, Garland, 1986. xiii,689p. £30.00. (*Garland reference library of social science, 194. Military history bibliographies, 9.*) ISBN: 0947898441.

7740 entries arranged in 24 chapters, each chapter having an introduction: I. Introduction to Napoleonic research - II. Armies of the Napoleonic period ... V. The Egyptian campaign (1798-1801) ... VII. England at war (1798-1815) ... XVI. St. Helena and the Napoleonic legend... XXIV. The Ottoman Empire. *Class No:* 356(44)(091)

USSR

[3475]

HERSPRING, D.R. The Soviet High Command, 1967-1989: personalities and politics. Lawrenceville, NJ, Princeton University Press, 1990. 296p. $45 ISBN: 0691078440.

A study, based on primary written source materials, of the evolutions of civil-military relations in the Soviet Union from 1967, including the ideas and personalities of the 8 key military leaders. *Class No:* 356(47)

Bibliographies

[3476]

SMITH, M.J. The Soviet army, 1939-1980: a guide to sources in English, with a historical introduction by John Erickson. Santa Barbara, CA., ABC-Clio, 1982. lviii,551p. $26.25. ISBN: 0874363071.

Brief historical introduction precedes the unannotated bibliography of 5743 items arranged in 5 sections: 1. Reference works (subdivided A-Z; Bibliographies - Abstracts ... Biographies) - 2. The era of World War II, 1939-1945 -3. The Soviet economy and defense establishments - 4. The Soviet ground forces, 1946 to the present - 5. The Soviet army and military assistance around the globe, 1945 to the present. Each section has a short introduction. 2 appendices (I. List of journals consulted; II. Selected Soviet military lives: a bibliographical directory (p.475-522). Author index, p.523-551. 'An excellent general reference tool for non-specialized research on the Soviet military ... ' (*Choice* v.20(9), May 1983 p.1270). *Class No:* 356(47)(01)

Canada

Bibliographies

[3477]

COOKE, O.A., *ed*. The Canadian military experience, 1867-1983: a bibliography. Department of National Defence of Canada. 2nd ed. Ottawa, Canadian Government Publishing Centre, 1984. xix,329p. Can.$11.95. (*Department of National Defence, Directorate of History, monograph series, no.2.*) ISBN: 0660526492.

First published 1979. The 2nd ed. has an added section covering the period since the amalgamation of the Canadian services in 1968.

Now in 6 sections: Bibliography - Defence policy and general works - and sections on each of the three services (subdivided chronologically) and one on the combined forces since 1968. No annotations. Subject index, p.270-293; persons index, 294-295. Services, branches, formations, units, p.296-329. 'Overall ... this is a valuable update of a valuable handbook ...' (*RUSI journal*, v.130(1), March 1985, p.82). *Class No:* 356(71)(01)

USA

Bibliographies

[3478]

FLETCHER, M. The Peacetime army, 1900-1941: a research guide. Westport, CT. Greenwood Press, 1988. 177p. $37.95. (*Research guides in military studies, 1.*) ISBN: 0313259879.

Over 900 annotated entries, chronologically subdivided into 1900-1917 and 1919-1941. A substantial introduction

....(contd.)

precedes the bibliography of English-language books, scholarly and popular journal articles, and dissertations. Omits first-hand narratives, naval studies, and accounts of the rise of air power. Includes a chronology. Author/subject index. 'A high-quality work ...' (*Choice*, v.26(10), June 1989, p.1660). *Class No:* 356(73)(01)

Histories

[3479]

HIGHAM, R., *ed*. A Guide to sources of US military history. Hamden, CT., Archon: Shoestring Press, 1981. xiii,559p. ISBN: 0208014993.

19 chapters - bibliographical essays on major sources by specialists: 1. Introduction - 2. European background of American military affairs - 3. Colonial forces, 1607-1776 - 4. The American revolution ... 6. The Navy in the nineteenth century, 1789-1889 ... 10. Science and technology in the twentieth century ... 12. Military and naval medicine ... 17. The Army, 1945-1973 - 18. The Navy, 1941-1973 - 19. Museums as historical resources. Lengthy bibliographies after each essay (*e.g.* 17. The Army: 390 references, A-Z). Introductory essay ends with suggestions for further research, then a bibliography. 6431 bibliographical references in all.

2 supplements have been published - 1. by Shoestring Press (1981. xiv,332p. ISBN 020801750x); 2-3. by Archon Books (1993. 531p. ISBN 0208022147). *Class No:* 356(73)(091)

Air Force

[3480]

FLINTHAM, V. Air wars and aircraft: a detailed record of air combat, 1945 to the present. New York, Facts on File, 1990. 415p. illus. tables. maps. $50. ISBN: 0816023565.

Aims to identify aircraft used in major and minor wars worldwide since 1945. Conflicts are arranged chronologically within 12 geographical regions. Entries describe political and social problems causing armed conflict and detail how military aircraft were used. Includes *c.*100 tables, 221 black & white photographs, and 100 maps. Glossary of abbreviations. Bibliography. *Class No:* 358.4

Worldwide

Encyclopaedias

[3481]

TAYLOR, M.J.H. Encyclopedia of the world's air forces. New York. Facts on file; Wellingborough, Northants. Patrick Stephens Ltd., 1988. 216p. $35 £21.50. ISBN: 0816020043 US; 1852601353 UK.

Largely updates M. Hewish's *Air forces of the world* (1979).

'Details of the world's aircraft from single aircraft operated by the Comores Air Force to the many thousands operated by the super powers' (*Stephen's catalogue*). Arranged A-Z by country, each country entry includes a map showing geographical location and a brief history of its air force, followed by information on current strength, air bases, commitments, budgets, and air policies, etc.,

....*(contd.)*

Comparative specifications for aircraft types are in data tables at the end of the book. The author is a noted British aviation authority. *Class No:* 358.4(100)(031)

Great Britain

[3482]
NESBIT, R.C. An Illustrated history of the R.A.F. London, Hutchinson, 1990. illus. £25. ISBN: 0091746566.

Published to commemorate the 50th anniversary of the Battle of Britain. Includes over 600 black and white and full-colour photographs and illustrations, with detailed captions. *Class No:* 358.4(410)

Handbooks & Manuals

[3483]
GANDER, T. Encyclopaedia of the modern Royal Air Force. 2nd ed. Wellingborough, Northants, Patrick Stephens, 1987. 256p. illus. £19.95. ISBN: 0850598591.

First published 1984.

A guide to the organization, structure, role and equipment of the RAF today, including aircraft, bombs, guns, missiles, and uniforms. Profusely illustrated with black-and-white photographs and diagrams. *Class No:* 358.4(410)(035)

Yearbooks & Directories

[3484]
The Air Force List, 1994. London, HMSO, 1993. viii,493. £18.50. ISBN: 0117726338. ISSN: 02668610.

First published 1949. Annual. Previously *The Monthly Air Force list* February, 1919-1939.

Arranged by Commands/Branches, etc.; R.A.F. Voluntary Reserve. Index of names. Also 'The Royal Air Force retired list' (1994. 383p. £15. ISBN 0117726346). *Class No:* 358.4(410)(058)

Histories

[3485]
ROBERTSON, B. The RAF: a pictorial history. London, Hale, 1978. 256p. illus., map.

Traces the history up to 1976. About 2 illus, with detailed captions, per page. Clubs and associations, p.250-1. Map gives Military Air Traffic Organization (MATO) locations. Index, in tiny print. *Class No:* 358.4(410)(091)

[3486]
—**LEWIS, P.** Squadron histories: R.F.C., R.N.A.S. and R.A.F., 1912-59. London, Putnam, 1959. 208p. illus. (incl. col. pl.).

Provides very brief squadron histories (nos.1-695), p.11-124. 13 appendices, including: 1. Aircraft used as equipment or for service trials by squadrons (keyed to squadrons 1-695) - 2. Aircraft specifications - 3. Titles of squadron ... 7. Squadron and unit code lettering. Illus. of flight-squadron markings. *Class No:* 358.4(410)(091)

France

Bibliographies

[3487]
CHRISTIENNE, C., *and others.* **French military aviation:** a bibliographical guide. New York, Garland, 1989. 255p. $35. (*Military history bibliographies, 11. Garland reference library in the humanities, 381.*) ISBN: 0824085183.

Intended as a guide for researchers in the field of French military aeronautics. In 2 parts; the first part containing an 84-page treatise by General Christienne on the development of French military aviation and the research challenges and opportunities offered. The second part is a bibliography of *c.*2000 books, articles, documents, and dissertations, almost all in French. *Class No:* 358.4(44)(01)

USSR

Bibliographies

[3488]
SMITH, M.J. The Soviet air and strategic rocket forces, 1939-1980: a guide to sources in English. Oxford, Clio Press, 1981. xliv, 321p. £22.85 $45. (*War/peace bibliography series 10.*) ISBN: 0874363063.

3350 unannotated entries arranged in 7 sections, each section having a brief introduction and subdivisions: 1. Reference works - 2. The era of World War II, 1939-45 - 3. The Soviet economy and defense establishments - 4. Soviet aerospace forces, 1946 to the present - 5. Soviet aerospace weapons systems - 6. Arms competition, arms control, and the balance of power. - 7. Soviet aerospace arms and assistance around the globe. Includes books., journal articles, documents, papers and reports. 4 appendices (Late entries; List of journals consulted; Selected Soviet aerospace biographies; Charts). Author index, p.305-321. Well researched and detailed bibliography. *Class No:* 358.4(47)(01)

Navy

[3489]
OBIN, A. Bibliography of nautical books, 1991. 6th ed. Warsash, Southampton, Warsash Nautical Bookshop, 1991. 478p. ISBN: 0948646063.

First ed. published 1985. Computer printout, one line per title. 2 supplements issued for this edition.

11 sections: 1. Books, main listing by title (p.9-120) - 2. Books, main listing by author - 3. Books, main listing by subject - 4. Hydrographic Department (Admiralty) - 5. International Maritime Organization - 6. Statutory instruments - 7. M notices (Department of Transport) - 8. British standards - 9. Journals and periodicals - 10. Video cassettes - 11. Publishers and suppliers (addresses and telephone numbers). Coverage of shipping, naval, maritime, yachting, and marine engineering items in print, forthcoming, and out of print. *Class No:* 359

[3490]
PEMSEL, H. Atlas of naval warfare: an atlas and chronology of conflict at sea, from the earliest times to the present day. London, Arms and Armour Press, 1977. 176p. illus., tables, maps.

First German ed. 1975.

4 sections: The age of galleys - The age of sail - The iron and steel - The nuclear age. Traces events up to 1973 (the

....*(contd.)*

Arab-Israeli 'Yom Kippur' war). 'The war in the Pacific', 1941-42: p.125-8; 8 maps; 8 illus. of ships. 9 appendices (*e.g.* 'The world's naval powers', by number of ships, 1859-1977). Select bibliography, p.165-6. Index. 'An excellent work, well researched and attractively put together' (*American reference books annual,* 1979, v.10, item 1604). *Class No:* 359

[3491]
—LLOYD, C. Atlas of maritime history. London, Hamlyn, 1975. 144p. illus. (some col.), maps.

Divided into chronological periods (from Phoenicians and Greeks to the nuclear submarine); 2p. per period, consisting of map, text and illus. 6-colour maps. Some British slant. 'Recommended enthusiastically for the undergraduate and graduate library; (*Choice,* April 1976, p.204,206 - on which the foregoing is based). *Class No:* 359(084.3)

Abbreviations & Symbols

[3492]
WEDERTZ, B., *comp.* **&** *ed.* **Dictionary of naval abbreviations.** 3rd ed. Annapolis, Md., Naval Institute Press, 1984. [6], 330p. $21.95; £13.95. ISBN: 0870211552.

First published 1969.

Contains over 45,000 abbreviations, including a complete listing of US Marine Corps and Coast Guard abbreviations, terms which may have been of army origin but now navy. *Class No:* 359(003)

Bibliographies

[3493]
GREAT BRITAIN. Ministry of Defence. **Author and subject catalogues of the Royal Navy Library,** Ministry of Defence, London. Boston, Mass., G.K. Hall, 1967. 5v. $495. ISBN: 0816107556.

Claimed to be the world's largest collection of naval and maritime books, mainly devoted to naval and general history, voyages, hydrographic surveys and the like. 78,000 entries, photolithographically reproduced from cards. Entries include charts and maps. *Class No:* 359(01)

Handbooks & Manuals

[3494]
MILLER, D. The World's navies. London, Salamander Books, 1992. 160p. 250 illus. £13.95. (*(Armed forces, v.3).*) ISBN: 0861016424.

Details by region, with brief notes on equipment, size and organization of such services. Highlights major warships, submarines and weapons. *Class No:* 359(035)

Dictionaries

[3495]
GRANVILLE, W. A Dictionary of sailors' slang. London. Andre Deutsch, 1962 (reprinted 1972). 136p.

'... slang and colloquial speech of the Royal and Merchant Navies, the fishing fleets, yachtsmen, lightshipmen and the crews of the barges and 'narrow boats' ... also records of speech habits of dock workers, harbourmen, and those who

....*(contd.)*

labour on the fringes of maritime endeavour' (*Preface*). Omits Cockney rhyming slang. Explanations, as well as definitions, are given when necessary. *Class No:* 359(038)

[3496]
HARD, J. Royal Navy language. Lewis, Sussex, The Book Guild Ltd., 1991. 310p. £12.50. ISBN: 0863325580.

Over 3000 terms and expressions are explained briefly, each entry being from a line to 5 or 6 lines in length. Arranged in 23 chapters: 1. The Royal Navy, Naval Reserve & assorted services - 2. Ships and aircraft ... 5. Ranks, rates and jobs - 6. Dress...12. Parts of a ship and equipment ... 17. Boats ... 21. Traditional tallies (nicknames) - 22. Royal Navy slang - 23. The language of the sea ashore. Cross-references. *Class No:* 359(038)

[3497]
PALMER, J., *comp.* **Jane's dictionary of naval terms.** London, Macdonald & Jane's. 1975. [iv],342p. ISBN: 035608258x.

Over 6000 entries for maritime military terms, terms of general seamanship and some purely mercantile terms ('Davit': ¾col.; 'Shackle': 1 column). Different meanings are numbered. Many cross-references. Sources (p.2) include Royal Navy, US Navy and NATO manuals. *Class No:* 359(038)

[3498]
—NOEL, J.V. Naval terms dictionary. 5th ed. Annapolis, Md., Naval Institute Press, 1988. 336p. 80 illus. £21.95. ISBN: 087021571x.

First published 1952.

*c.*6000 entry-words, - US Navy colloquialisms, slang and technical terminology, including abbreviations. 5 appendices (*e.g.* ship, aircraft and missile designation systems; electronic nomenclature. *Class No:* 359(038)

Yearbooks & Directories

[3499]
JONES, J.M. Historic warships: a directory of 140 museums and memorials worldwide. Jefferson, NJ, McFarland, 1993. 245p. illus. $45. ISBN: 0899507794.

Describes 144 warships built between the 16th and 20th centuries, which are now in parks or museums in 25 countries. Entries, arranged by country where located (about half in the US), include battle record, technical information, black and white photographs, and information on the museums, etc. where situated, with address and telephone number. *Class No:* 359(058)

[3500]
SILVERSTONE, P.H. Directory of the world's capital ships. London, Ian Allan, 1984. 496p. illus. £35. ISBN: 0711012229.

Aim was to produce an illustrated work of reference, covering the capital ships of 21 of the world's most important navies, from the mid-nineteenth century to the late twentieth century. Includes 1000 ships in some 500 classes. Definition of capital ships is broad and includes battleships, battle cruisers, monitors, coastal defence ships, aircraft carriers, etc. A preliminary section, 'How to use this book', includes lists of operations of the US Civil War, W.W.1 and W.W.2, A-Z by name of operation, and a list of shipbuilders, A-Z by name plus town and country. The main part of the directory is arranged A-Z by country (Argentine

....*(contd.)*

... USA) with, for each country, brief background information; class details (displacement, dimensions, armour, complement, etc.); individual ships (A-Z by name, with data on history of its career, type, class, nomenclature (meaning of name), details of construction, war service, ultimate fate). Index, p.491-496. *Class No:* 359(058)

Histories

[3501]

MARCUS, G.J. **A Naval history of England.** London, Allen & Unwin, 1961-71. 2v. (xii,494p.; 523p.). maps.

V.1: *The formative years [to 1973]*; v.2: *The age of Nelson.* V.2. is well formulated and has chapter bibliographies. p.505-20. Non-analytical index, but ships are listed in detail. Very readable narrative. Aims to be a compromise between the short and the full-scale history. '... a must for all secondary schools and libraries' (*British book news*, June 1971, p. 498). *Class No:* 359(091)

[3502]

—NATIONAL MARITIME MUSEUM. The Commissioned sea officers of the Royal Navy, 1660-1815. London, the Museum, 1954. 3v.

Provides a complete list of naval officers for the period. *Class No:* 359(410)(091)

[3503]

SWEETMAN, J., *ed*. **American naval history:** an illustrated chronology of the U.S. Navy and Marine Corps, 1775 - present. 2nd ed. Annapolis, Md., Naval Institute Press, 1991. 376p. illus., maps. $36.95. ISBN: 1557507856.

First published 1984.

Year-by-year summary of major events in the history of the US Navy and Marine Corps from the American Revolution to the late 1980s. Covers battles, warships, personnel, exploration, etc. *c.*200 illustrations and several specially drawn maps. Bibliography. Calendar, vessel and general indexes. *Class No:* 359(091)

[3504]

WARNER, O. **Great sea battles.** Spring Books, 1963. 303p. illus (some col). ISBN: 0600016501.

5th impression 1973.

Describes the strategy and tactics, freaks of wind and weather, which decided 26 famous battles from Lepanto and the Armada to Trafalgar, Jutland and Midway. Profusely illustrated. *Class No:* 359(091)

Bibliographies

[3505]

ALBION, R.G. **Naval and maritime history:** an annotated bibliography. 4th ed. rev. & expanded. Mystic, CT., Munson Institute of American Maritime History, the Marine Historical Association, Inc., 1972. ix,370p. $10. ISBN: 0913372056.

First published 1951.

Lists *c.*5000 books in English, plus PhD. theses. In 7 main sections: 1. Reference works (A-G, including F: Lists of ships; G: Lists of men) - 2. Merchantmen and warships - 3. Captains and crews - 4. Maritime science, exploration and expansion - 5. Commerce and shipping - 6. Navies (naval history, by periods, p.229-302) - 7. Special topics (*e.g.* Auxiliary services; Main American maritime museums). Books asterisked represent 'the select minority of the more

....*(contd.)*

substantial and useful'. Author and subject indexes. 'An indispensable companion to any writer on maritime subjects' (E.G.R. Taylor, on the 3rd ed., in *Journal of the Institute of Navigation,* v.17(2), April 1964, p.211). US-slanted. *Class No:* 359(091)(01)

Europe

[3506]

LEWIS, A.R. *and* RUNYAN, T.J. **European naval and maritime history, 300-1500.** Bloomington, Ind.,Indiana University Press, 1985. 208p. $22.95. ISBN: 0253320828.

Focuses on Western Europe, including the Baltic, North Sea and Atlantic traditions, and on the Mediterranean, particularly Byzantine and Moslem naval history. Scholarly. *Class No:* 359(4)

Great Britain

[3507]

RASOR, E.L. **British naval history since 1815:** a guide to the literature. New York, Garland, 1990. xxi,841p. $90. (*(Military history bibliographies, v.13).*) ISBN: 0824077350.

Part 1: Historiographical narrative (1. Introduction & sources - 2. Naval writers and historians - 3. Strategy, sea power, and international relations - 4. Intelligence - 5. Admiralty, logistics, warships & naval aviation - 6. Human resources, war and society - 7. The Merchant Marine and the fishing fleet - 8. Imperialism and reconnaisance - 9. Chronology - 10. Genre). Part 2: Bibliographical listing (3125 entries by name). *Class No:* 359(410)

[3508]

WEIGHTMAN, A.E. **Heraldry in the Royal Navy:** crests and badges of H.M. ships. Aldershot, Gale & Polden, 1957. xviii,514p. illus.

Arrangement is by name of ships, A-Z. Diagrams of badges are accompanied by heraldic descriptions, origin and notes on historical background and battle honours. *Class No:* 359(410)

Encyclopaedias

[3509]

BEAVER, P., *ed*. **Encyclopaedia of the modern Royal Navy:** including the Fleet Air Arm and Royal Marines. 3rd ed. Wellingborough, Northants, Patrick Stephens, 1987. 329p. illus., maps, tables. £19.95. ISBN: 0850598605.

First published 1982.

'Aims to illustrate the many facets of the modern Royal Navy ... remains the only comprehensive guide to all these elements' (*Introduction*). The introduction is followed by essays on the Royal Navy since 1945, organization and role, Royal Navy warships, the Fleet Air Arm, the Royal Marines, auxiliary services, other services, naval equipment weapons and services, uniforms and insignia. Also a glossary and an index. *Class No:* 359(410)(031)

Handbooks & Manuals

[3510]

THOMAS, D.A. A Companion to the Royal Navy. London, Harrap Ltd., 1988. xvi,443p. illus., maps. £19.95. ISBN: 0245545727.

The story of the Royal Navy in 5 sections: 1. The Admiralty - 2. Ship's names and badges (A-Z by name of ship) - 3. Naval battles (chronological, then A-Z by name) - 4. Battle honours (name of battle & date; list of ships) - 5. Naval chronology, 1660-1987. No index.
Class No: 359(410)(035)

Yearbooks & Directories

[3511]

GREAT BRITAIN. Ministry of Defence. Navy Department. The Navy list: containing lists of ships, establishments and officers of the Fleet, 1993. London, HMSO, 1993. vi,357p. £17.50. ISBN: 011772632x. ISSN: 01416081.

First published April 1814. Annual. Not published for sale between September 1939 and May 1949. July and January supplements cover selective promotions, Queen's Birthday and New Year honours, and changes.

Contents include: 2. Alphabetical list of officers - 3. Seniority lists of officers on active list - 4. Key Royal Navy personnel - 5. Ships and units of the fleet and establishments - 6. Key addresses - 7. Reserves - 8. Obituary ... Also *The Navy list of retired officers* ... (1989. xii,215p., ISBN 0117726141). *Class No:* 359(410)(058)

Histories

[3512]

CLOWES, W.L. The Royal Navy: a history from the earliest times to the present. London, Sampson Low, 1897-1903. (Reprinted by AMS Press). 7v. illus., maps. $290 the set; $41.50 each vol. ISBN: 0404016405, the set.

V.7 has a sub-title '... to the death of Queen Victoria', and goes up to 1900. A most detailed work. And the standard history; full index, and many appendices of flag officers and of ships lost, etc. *Class No:* 359(410)(091)

[3513]

COLLEDGE, J.J. Ships of the Royal Navy: complete record of all fighting ships of the Royal Navy from the 15th century to the present. Rev. ed. London, Greenhill Books, 1987. 388p. £30. ISBN: 0947898751.

Rev. ed. of *Ships of the Royal Navy: an historical index* (David & Charles, 1969-70) V.1: major ships (excluding trawlers, drifters, tugs, etc.).

Preliminaries describing the scope of the book are followed by a listing, A-Z by type or name of ship ('A' class submarines ... Zulu). Includes over 13,000 names.
Class No: 359(410)(091)

[3514]

—COLLEDGE, J.J. Ships of the Royal Navy: an historical index. V.2: Navy-built trawlers, drifters, tugs and requisitioned ships. Newton Abbot, Devon, David & Charles, 1970. 400p.

*c.*11,000 names are listed, stating tonnage, dimensions, armament, dates, shipyard, etc. *Class No:* 359(410)(091)

[3515]

—MANNING, T.D. *and* WALKER, C.F. British warship names. London, Putnam, 1959. 498p.

*c.*20,000 entries, A-Z, giving name, meaning/derivation and a 1-2 line history. Ships of the same name are numbered under each name entry. When gaps occur in the enumerated sequence, the ships 'do not qualify for inclusion'. A history of names rather than of warships as such.
Class No: 359(410)(091)

[3516]

—YOUNG, J. A Dictionary of ships of the Royal Navy of the Second World War. Cambridge, Stephens, 1975. . 192p. illus.

Records over 2000 vessels, 27 photographs.
Class No: 359(410)(091)

[3517]

LYON, D.J. The Sailing Navy list: all the ships of the Royal Navy (built, purchased and captured), 1688-1855. Conway, Maritime, 1993. 352p. 300 illus. £60. ISBN: 0851776175.

Arranged by types and classes, with notes on design and designer. D.J.Lyon is Curator, National Maritime Museum.
Class No: 359(410)(091)

[3518]

The Royal Navy day by day. Sainsbury, A.B., *ed.* Shepperton, Surrey, Ian Allan Publishing, in association with the National Maritime Museum, 1992. vi,424p. illus. £29.95 ISBN: 0711021236.

A history, in diary form, of daily events (not just great battles) in the Navy's 700-year tradition. Bibliography, p.365-77. General index, p.378-424.
Class No: 359(410)(091)

[3519]

SMITH, P.C. *and* **OAKLEY, D. The Royal Marines - a pictorial history, 1664-1988.** Tunbridge Wells, Kent, Spellmount, 1988. 256p. 366 illus. (16 in col.). £25. ISBN: 0946771324.

11 chapters chronologically arranged, 50/50 text and illustrations. Includes a short bibliography (p.247) and index (p.248-256). *Class No:* 359(410)(091)

[3520]

WARNER, O. Battle honours of the Royal Navy. London, Philip, 1956. 199p. illus.

A tabulated list of naval actions from 1588 to 1953, and details of single ship actions, listed alphabetically. Lists, with battle honours, follow of ships of the Royal and Commonwealth Navies now in commission, of Fleet Air Arm squadrons which have been in action, and of regiments with naval battle honours. A final section gives illustrations of ships' badges. *Class No:* 359(410)(091)

Biographies

[3521]

Naval who's who, 1917. Polstead, Suffolk, J.B. Hayward & Son, 1981 (Distributed by London Stamp Exchange Ltd, London). 344p. £19.

A facsimile of the 1st ed., originally titled *The Royal Navy list of Who's Who in the Navy.*

Uninteresting data and advertising material deleted and text of Admiral Jellicoe's Despatch for the Battle of Jutland added, together with a casualty roll of all ranks. Includes a list of abbreviations, etc.; a chronological list of notable naval events, 1213-1914; Services, honours and special

....(contd.)

qualifications of officers, active and retired; and *War supplement,* giving service details and acts of gallantry which, although they may have culminated in an award, did not always appear in the *London gazette.*
Class No: 359(410)(092)

Germany

[3522]
BIRD, K.W. German naval history: a guide to the literature. New York, Garland, 1985. xx,1121p. $154. (*Military history bibliographies, 7. Garland reference library of social science, 215.*) ISBN: 0824090241.

Includes 4871 citations devoted to literature on the German navies from before Bismarck to 1983. 9 chapters discuss the craft and sources of German naval history, each beginning by examining current research themes and proceeding to a bibliographic essay keyed to the bibliography proper, and ending with suggestions for further research. The bibliography is arranged by author, A-Z, and there is no subject index. '... one of the finest naval bibliographies available on any foreign fleet' (*Choice,* v.22(8), April 1985, p.1136, on which this annotation is based). *Class No:* 359(430)

France

[3523]
POLAK, J. Bibliographie maritime française depuis les temps les plus reculés jusquà 1914. Grenoble, Éditions de Quatre Seigneurs, 1976. 367,[1]p. facsims.

9627 numbered entries arranged under authors, A-Z. Bibliographical and source notes. Ships index; subject index (non-analytical). List of sources precedes.
Class No: 359(44)

[3524]
—JENKINS, E.H. History of the French Navy, from its beginnnings to the present. London, Macdonald and Jane's, 1973. 364p. illus. (inc. 17p. of pl.)., ports., maps, plans.
Bibliography, p.349-51. *Class No:* 359(44)

USSR

[3525]
POLMAR, N. Guide to the Soviet Navy. 4th ed. London, Arms and Armour Press, 1986. xiv,536p. 425 illus., charts, tables. £35. ISBN: 0853688214.

First published 1977.

Arranged in 33 sections: 1. State of the fleet - 2. Glossary of terms - 3. Soviet ship classes ... 8. Naval aviation ... 10. Personnel training - 11. Fleet development ... 29. Bases and ports - 30. Shipbuilding and shipyards - 31. Merchant marine - 32. Fishing fleet - 33. Warsaw Pact navies. Appendices: Senior naval officers; Commanders-in-Chief; Soviet order of Battle, 1945-1985; Soviet ship transfers; Reading list; General index; Ship name and class index. Emphasis is on naval weapons and electronics as well as missions and tactics, operations and exercises, personnel, aviation, shipyards and bases. Up-dated at 3-yearly intervals.
Class No: 359(47)

Bibliographies

[3526]
SMITH, M.J. The Soviet navy, 1941-1978: a guide to sources in English. Santa Barbara, CA., ABC-Clio Press, 1980. xiv,211p; illus (incl.pl.). $26.25. (*War/peace bibliography series, 9.*) ISBN: 0874362652.

About 1750 entries for monographs, periodical articles and theses, indexed by authors. 'A valuable and extensive bibliography for both general and specific research needs at all academic levels' (*Choice,* December 1980, p.512).
Class No: 359(47)(01)

Handbooks & Manuals

[3527]
JORDAN, J. An Illustrated guide to the modern Soviet navy. London, Salamander Books Ltd., 1982. 159p. illus. £4.95. ISBN: 0861011465.

A popular work, with more than 150 photographs (70 in colour) and 30 dawings. Sections on the organization of the Soviet surface navy, and on ocean-going ships, are followed by chapters by class of ship, and then weapons and sensors, ship-borne aircraft, and weapons by type.
Class No: 359(47)(035)

Latin America

Histories

[3528]
SCHEINA, R.L. Latin America: a naval history, 1810-1985. Annapolis, MD., Naval Institute Press, 1987. xv,442p. $34.95; £25.25. ISBN: 0870212958.
Class No: 359(729.99)(091)

USA

[3529]
JORDAN, J. An Illustrated guide to the modern US Navy: the world's most advanced naval power. London, Salamander Books Ltd., 1982. 159p. illus. £4.95. ISBN: 0861011511.

Chapters arranged by classes of vessels - aircraft carriers, cruisers, destroyers, frigates, patrol combatants, amphibious warfare vessels, support ships, replenishment ships, weapons and sensors. Popular rather than scholarly.
Class No: 359(73)

Bibliographies

[3530]
SMITH, M.J., *comp.* **The United States Navy and Coast Guard, 1946-1983:** a bibliography of English-language works and 16mm films. Jefferson, N.C., McFarland & Company, 1984. xx,539p. $65; £48.75. ISBN: 0899501222.

10,057 entries arranged topically. No annotations. A historical note and list of periodicals consulted are followed by the bibliography in 8 sections: 1. Reference works - 2. The American Defense Establishment - 3. The US Navy and US Coast Guard - 4. The balance of power and arms control - 5. The US Navy and Coast Guard operations - 6. Warships, warplanes and hardware. 16mm film guide, Author index, p.473-519; subject index p.520-539.
Class No: 359(73)(01)

Histories

[3531]

BAUER, K.J. *and* **ROBERTS, S.S. Register of ships of the U.S. Navy, 1775-1990: major combatants.** New York & London, Greenwood Press, 1991. xxiii,350p. illus. $85. £79.95. ISBN: 0313262020.

1: The sail navy, 1775-1853; 2: The old steam navy, 1814-1876; 3: The new navy, 1883-1990. Bibliography, p.299-302. Hull number index. Index, p.309-350. The first of 3v. designed to update Bauer's *Ships of the Navy, 1775-1969* (Rensselaer Polytechnic Institute, 1969).
Class No: 359(73)(091)

[3532]

NORRIS, J.M. History of the US Navy. Feltham, Middx., Hamlyn, 1984. (Distributors for Bison Books Ltd.). 224p. illus., plans, ports. (some col.). £9.95. ISBN: 0600385914.

Introduction (p.6-13) is a brief history, and is followed by 10 chapters in 3 parts (I. A reluctant naval power - II. A naval power born to glory - III. New naval missions). Profusely illustrated. Index, p.222-224.
Class No: 359(73)(091)

Bibliographies

[3533]

A Bibliography of American naval history. Coletta, P.E., *ed.* Annapolis, Naval Institute Press, 1981. 453p. $15.95; £9. ISBN: 0870211056.

Includes diplomatic, political, economic and social history, as well as the history of US Navy, Marine Corps and Coast Guard (when part of the Navy Department). 4822 entries for English-language works (journal articles, essays, books, theses, government publications, oral history reviews). Arrangement is chronological, subdivided by type of publication, preceded by an international section of bibliographical aids and reference works. Subject index. Complements Myron Smith's books.
Class No: 359(73)(091)(01)

[3534]

—**A Selected and annotated bibliography of American naval history.** Coletta, P.E., *ed.* Lanham, MD; London, University Press of America, 1988. xi,523p. $34.50. ISBN: 0819171115.

Updates the above by providing new titles in military literature that have appeared since the end of 1979. Entries arranged in 23 special topics (*eg* Amphibious operations ... Women in the Navy) as well as titles in chapters that proceed in chronological order. *Class No:* 359(73)(091)(01)

[3535]

UNITED STATES. Department of the Navy. US Naval History Divison. **US naval history sources in the United States.** Allard, D.C., *and others, eds.* Washington, DC., United States Government Printing Office, 1979. viii,235p. illus.

'... seeks to aid students of naval history by identifying manuscripts, archival and other special collections deposited in more than 200 American archives and libraries'. Arrangement is by US state, A-Z (Alabama ... Wyoming), subdivided by the name of the library of other organization. Lists of papers are given by name, date and volume. Index, p.207-235, of names and places.
Class No: 359(73)(091)(01)

36 Social Services & Welfare

Yearbooks & Directories

Charities & Foundations

Bibliographies

[3536]

HARRIS, M. *and* **BILLIS, D. Organizing voluntary agencies:** a guide through the literature. London, Bedford Square Press, 1986. [4],125p. £7.95. ISBN: 0719911478.

An introduction precedes the bibliographic section, arranged A-Z by author. Entries are annotated, varying in length from 2 lines to a page, covering the relevant literature published during the ten years to 1984 generally. Cross-references. Also includes a user's guide to topics and issues; a list of journals cited; and a list of useful addresses. *Class No:* 36.075(01)

[3537]

LAYTON, D.N. Philanthropy and voluntarism: an annotated bibliography. New York, Foundation Center, 1987. 308p. $18.50. ISBN: 0879541989.

Entries for 1614 items, 244 annotated, on the philanthropic tradition.

The author is mainly concerned with the history, philosophy and theory of philanthropy in the US, the UK and other countries. Includes 1614 items, of which about a sixth are annotated, on the philanthropic tradition, drawn from writings in history, economics, sociology, journalism and statistics. *Class No:* 36.075(01)

Handbooks & Manuals

[3538]

The Complete fundraising handbook. Clarke, S., *ed.* London, Directory of Social Change, in association with the Institute oof Charity Fundraising Managers, 1993. 256p. £9.95. ISBN: 090716465x.

First published in 1992.

6 sections, all subdivided: 1. Introduction - 2. Getting started - 3. Sources - 4. Techniques - 5. Skills - 6. Sources of information (Useful addresses - Bibliography - Community trusts - Codes of practice of the Institute). Index, p.253-6. *Class No:* 36.075(035)

[3539]

EAGLESHAM, N. Researching local charities: a practical guide to making better use of charitable resources. London, Directory of Social Change, 1988. v,73p. £3.95. ISBN: 0907164382.

4 sections: Local charities [a description of what they are, etc.]; Sources of information [index of charities and other sources]; Building a charity profile; Producing a finished profile, 6 appendices include the Charities Acts 1960 & 1985. *Class No:* 36.075(035)

Yearbooks & Directories

[3540]

Directory of grant-making trusts, 1991. 12th ed. A 13th ed. was issued in 1993 (£50. ISBN 0904757749). Tonbridge, Kent, Charities Aid Foundation, 1991. xxvi, 1038p. £45. ISBN: 0904757528.

First published 1968 by National Council of Social Service, Charities Aid Fund.

4 parts: 1. Classification of charitable purposes - 2. Trusts listed under classifications (p.7-19). Alphabetical list of trusts empowered to give to general charitable trusts - 3. Register of grant-making charitable trusts (p.351-983). Trusts deleted from Part III - 4. Geographical index of trusts (p.986-1024). Alphabetical index of subjects (p.1025-1038). Some entries include titles of publications (*e.g.* Oxfam, p.776). *Class No:* 36.075(058)

[3541]

Donors directory of registered charities, 1986. 1st ed. Morden, Surrey, Trade & Technical Press Ltd., 1986. xvi, 246p. ISBN: 854611169.

Data on some 1000 registered charities actively engaged in raising funds for their worthy causes. Part I: Index of charities, A-Z with name, address, phone number, contact, registered charity number, bank account, and solicitors. Part II: Classified list (Education and science; Health and medical; Humanities; Religion; Environment; Welfare) each divided by more specific subjects, A-Z. Part III: Geographical index. *Class No:* 36.075(058)

[3542]

International encyclopedia of foundations Kiger, J.C., *ed.* New York, Greenwood Press, 1990. 470p. $75. £59.85. ISBN: 0313259836.

Essays on 145 major foundations in 31 countries outside the USA, with history and operations. Includes founding, purpose, activities, financing, governance and location. All entries contain bibliographical references or additional sources of information. Chronology. Genealogy. Index. Complements N.M.Keele and J.C.Kiger's *Foundations. The international foundation directory* (5th ed.1990) covers more countries but provides less background. *Class No:* 36.075(058)

[3543]

The International foundation directory. Hodson, H.V., *ed.* 5th ed. London, Europa Publications Ltd.; Detroit, Mich., Gale Research Co., 1991. xxvii,526p. £39; $95. ISBN: 0946653666, UK.

First published 1974.

A directory of about 900 institutions in 50 countries, A-Z, covering foundations, trusts and similar non-profit institutions in many fields. Data on each: name and address; founding data; brief history; activities; finance; names of officers; publications (if any). Bibliography: index. Coverage is wide-ranging, including science, medicine, education, social welfare, the arts and humanities, aid to less-developed countries, and international relations. *Class No:* 36.075(058)

Great Britain

Handbooks & Manuals

[3544]

Charities and broadcasting: a guide to radio and television appeals and grants. Parker, N., *ed.* London, Directory of Social Change, 1988. vi, 250p. £5.95. ISBN: 090716434x.

Provides practical information about every television company, radio station and cable operator in the United Kingdom, with details of their policy towards charities and voluntary groups. Part 1: The background; part 2: Regional and local classification (for each company, showing information on total raised for charity, donations, appeals, social action broadcasts, etc.). 3 appendices (1. Rules and guidelines; 2. Further information (Broadcasters - further names and addresses; Useful contacts; Suggested further reading). Index of television companies, radio stations, and cable operators precedes. *Class No:* 36.075(410)(035)

[3545]

NORTON, M. **A Guide to the benefits of charitable status.** 2nd ed. London, Directory of Social Change, 1988. [5], 230p. £5.95. ISBN: 0907164269.

First published 1983.

Provides information on all the important tax reliefs and other benefits available to charities. 9 sections: 1. Value added tax; 2. Rates; 3. Investment of charity funds; 4. Individual giving; 5. Gifts of capital; 6. Grants and donations; 7. Lotteries, gaming and competitions; 8. Charity trading; 9. Salaries. 8 appendices (Appendix 8; Resources: useful publications and organizations (p.225-230). No index, but detailed table of contents. *Class No:* 36.075(410)(035)

Yearbooks & Directories

[3546]

Charities digest: an alphabetical digest of charities, 1991. 99th ed. London, Family Welfare Association, 1993. Annual. 368p. £14.95. ISBN: 0900954507.

First published 1882 as *The annual charities register and digest.* Title varies.

A detailed directory of *c.*2000 charitable trusts and associations for special and general classes. Sections: Charities in the UK - Registry of Friendly Societies - Giving to charity - Alphabetical list of charities registered under the Act - Some organizations not registered - Adoption societies - Almshouses - C.A.B. - Councils for voluntary service - Legal advice centres - Local associations for the deaf - Local associations for disabled people - Local associations for the blind - Subject index - Advertisers' index.
Class No: 36.075(410)(058)

[3547]

Handbook of charities, no.5, 1988-1989: a guide to charities for use by the education profession and community service officers. London, Charity Data Services, 1988. 127p. ISBN: 1870914015.

First published 1984.

Entries for the charities have 1-2 pages each, with name, address, description, what it offers, what it needs. Arrangement is not alphabetical. Fields index and regional index precede a list of charities offering speakers. Alphabetical index. *Class No:* 36.075(410)(058)

Laws

[3548]

CRACKNELL, D.G. **Charities: law and practice.** 3rd ed. London, Longman Group (UK) Ltd., 1987. xxxix,299p. £29.50. ISBN: 0851213006.

First published in 1983 as *Law relating to charities.*

12 chapters: 1. Meaning of "charity" - 2. Creation of charities - 3. Special charities - 4. Registration of charities - 5. Central authorities - 6. Charity trustees - 7. Powers and duties of charity trustees - 8. Breaches of trust - 9. Amendment of charitable trusts - 10. Charity proceedings - 11. Fund-raising - 12. Financial privileges. Main chapters are preceded by tables of cases, statutes, and statutory instruments, each arranged A-Z by title. 10 appendices (4. Addresses ... (p.275-276); 5. Charity Commission leaflets). Analytical index, p.293-299. *Class No:* 36.075(410)(094.1)

England & Wales

Histories

[3549]

CROWTHER, M.A. **The Workhouse system, 1834-1929:** a history of an English social institution. London, Methuen & Co. Ltd., 1983. 316p. £8.95. ISBN: 0416369804.

First published 1981 by Batsford Academic and Educational Ltd.

10 chapters in 2 parts: I: Administrators (ch.1-7); II: Inmates (ch.8-10); followed by Conclusions. Notes (p.273-291) include references. Select bibliography (p.292-295). Index (p.296-316). *Class No:* 36.075(42)(091)

USA

Yearbooks & Directories

[3550]

Corporate 500: the directory of corporate philanthropy. 12th ed. San Francisco, CA., Public Management Institute, 1994. 1400p. $365. ISBN: 0916664570. ISSN: 0197937x.

First published 1982.

Factual information on the funding programmes of the 580 American corporations with the most active programmes. Includes profiles of 70 corporations responsible for gifts of $95m. to non-profit organizations.
Class No: 36.075(73)(058)

[3551]

Foundations. Keele, H.M. *and* Kiger, J.C., *eds.* Westport, CT., Greenwood Press, 1984. 516p. illus. $56.95. (*Greenwood encyclopedia of American institutions, 8.*) ISBN: 0313225567.

Lists 230 foundations, selected from the core group of *c.*3400 large foundations described in the 9th ed. of the Foundation Center's *Foundation directory.* Descriptions, up to 3p. long, are on the history and current giving interests. 227 of the foundations selected have assets of over $30 million; 199 are private, independent foundations; 31 are company-sponsored or community foundations. Entries vary widely in quality. Arrangement is A-Z by the first word of the foundation's name. *Class No:* 36.075(73)(058)

Social Services

[3552]
BUNCH, A. **Community information**. In *Printed reference material* (3rd ed., 1990, edited by P.W. Lea and A. Day), p.324-359.
General sources - Government publications - Subject areas (careers ... women). 6 references. An important and timely contribution. *Class No: 362*

[3553]
BUNCH, A.J. **Community information services**: their origin, scope and development. London, Clive Bingley Ltd., 1982. viii, 168p. £20. ISBN: 0851573185.
7 chapters: 1. Community information - meaning and origins; 2. The United States - the information and referral model; 3. Community information services in Britain - non-public library; 4. Public library community information services in Britain; 5. Community information services to rural areas; 6. Developments in community information services in other countries; 7. Community information and new technology. References are appended to each chapter. Index, p.164-168. *Class No: 362*

[3554]
Social services year book, 1993. London, Longman Group (UK) Ltd., 1993. Annual. lxii,882p. ISBN: 0582091977. ISSN: 0307093x.
First published 1972 (for 1972/73).
30 sections (*e.g.* 7. Local government, England and Wales (including social services and allied departments) ... 8. London ... 12. Health authorities ... 18. Advice and counselling - 19. Voluntary service - 20. Elderly people's welfare organizations ... 29. Social services and allied organizations - 30. Buyer's guide. Index, p.859-882'. Bibliography precedes, p.xlviii-lv, arranged by subjects. A mine of information. *Class No: 362*

Abbreviations & Symbols

[3555]
CENTRAL COUNCIL FOR EDUCATION AND TRAINING IN SOCIAL WORK. **Glossary of abbreviations.** 2nd ed. the Council, 1986. [1],21p. (spiral binding). £1. ISBN: 0904488063.
First published 1985.
Arranged A-Z (AA Alcoholics Anonymous ... YWCA), giving only full title (no address). Titles in brackets no longer exist or have been changed or incorporated into those of other organizations. Also includes CCETSW's awards and programmes, and former awards. *Class No: 362(003)*

Databases

[3556]
MENDELSOHN, H.N. **'Social work online'.** In *Database*, v.7(3), August 1984, p.36-49.
Examines online coverage of the literature of social welfare. The subject profile technique was used to search 13 social science databases in order to compare the extent of subject coverage, and journal coverage comparison data was obtained by searching 20 social welfare titles with databases to see which journals are indexed in the respective databases. *Class No: 362(003.4)*

[3557]
Online information sources on social and community issues. Harman, J., *comp.* New ed. Berkhamsted, Volnet UK, 1993. 43p. illus. Spiral binding. £7.50. ISBN: 1897708459.
First issued in 1992 as an online pack.
Sources of online information (hosts and databases) in the field are listed and and described. Alphabetical and subject index to databases. *Class No: 362(003.4)*

Bibliographies

[3558]
CONRAD, J.H. **Reference sources in social work:** an annotated bibliography. Metuchen, NJ., Scarecrow Press, 1982. vi,201p. $17.50; £13.85. ISBN: 0810815036.
656 entries, with very short annotations, arranged in 6 groups: 1. General - 2. History of social work - 3. Allied fields (A. Psychiatry and psychology; B. Sociology and anthropology; C. Economics; D. Political science; E. Urban affairs) - 4. Fields of service (Adoption ... Women) - 5. Service methods - 6. Social work profession. Appendices list social work journals, social service organizations, and social work libraries. Author, title and subject indexes. US slant. *Class No: 362(01)*

[3559]
CROWN, A.D., *comp*. **A Bibliography of the Samaritans.** 2nd ed. Metuchen, N.J., Scarecrow Press, and The American Theological Library Assocation, 1992 338p. $39.50. (*ATLA bibliography series, no.10.*) ISBN: 0810826461.
An expansion of Leo A. Meyer's *Bibliography of the Samaritans*, edited by D. Broadribb (1964).
Nearly 6000 annotated items, with class numbers after the entries giving a clue to the subject. Subject index with class numbers and subject terms. *Class No: 362(01)*

[3560]
MENDELSOHN, H.N. **A Guide to information sources for social work and the human services.** Phoenix, Ariz., Oryx, 1987. viii,136p. $28.50. ISBN: 0897743385.
Aims to systematically present pertinent sources that social work practitioners, educators and students can use to locate information in libraries. 11 bibliographic essays, some on types of material, some on techniques, some on topics. Each chapter ends with a bibliography. Title, organization and subject index. '... an excellent introductory source for social work students' (*Wilson library bulletin*, December 1987, p.92). 'This well-conceived bibliographic guide fills a gap ...' (*Reference books bulletin*, 1 March 1988, p.1120). *Class No: 362(01)*

Dictionaries

[3561]
BARKER, R.L. **The Social work dictionary.** 2nd ed. Washington, NASW Press, 1991. xv,287p. $26.95. ISBN: 0871011905.
lst published 1987.
Defines nearly 5000 terms used in social work administration, research, policy development and planning, health, etc. *Class No: 362(038)*

[3562]

CLEGG, J. **Dictionary of social services:** policy and practice. 3rd ed. London, Bedford Square Press for the National Council for Voluntary Organisations, 1980. x, 148p. £5.95. ISBN: 0719910390.

First published 1971.

Defines c.500 words, phrases and names of government departments commonly used in social services, 'Ability ... Zoning'. Outlines reorganization of local government and the National Health Service in 1974. *Class No:* 362(038)

Reviews & Abstracts

[3563]

Social service abstracts: monthly summaries of selected documents. Department of Health and Social Security. Library Services. London, HMSO (previously the Library), 1972-. Monthly. £98. ISSN: 03094693.

Includes over 2000 abstracts a year. Sections: Social policy - Social services - Social work - Services for the elderly and the handicapped - Services for children and young people - Services for other special needs - DHSS circulars - Bibliographies. Author and analytical subject index per issue; cumulated annually. Covers the whole range of the personal social services, with particular emphasis on literature originating in Britain. *Class No:* 362(048)

[3564]

Social work research and abstracts. Washington, NASW Press (previously New York, National Association of Social Workers, 1965-. Quarterly. $100pa. ISSN: 01480847.

Early title was *Abstracts for social workers.*

Nearly 2000 abstracts pa from about 200 journals. Arranged in 4 main subject sections, each subdivided; Social work profession - Theory and practice - Area of service - Social issues/social problems. 2 essays and a list of journals scanned precedes. Author and subject indexes. Available online (BRS) and also on microform from UMI. *Class No:* 362(048)

Yearbooks & Directories

[3565]

International directory of voluntary work. 5th ed. Oxford, Vacation Work, 1993. 264p. £14.95. ISBN: 1854580868. ISSN: 01433474.

First published 1979.

Residential work, long and short term, subdivided geographically (United Kingdom, by type of activity; Europe, subdivided by country; North America, Israel and the Middle East; Africa; Asia and Australia.

Non-residential work, by type of activity. Further reading. Index of organizations. *Class No:* 362(058)

[3566]

Voluntary agencies directory, 1993/94. 13th rev. ed. London, NVCO Publications (previously Bedford Square Press), 1993. xii,270p. £12.95. ISBN: 071991339x.

Previously as *Voluntary social services: a directory of national organisations* (first published 1928) and *Voluntary organizations: an NCVO directory.*

A directory of over 2000 organizations, including voluntary organizations, charity and pressure groups, arranged A-Z. Data: address; chairman's name; contact name; date of foundation; objectives; activities; publications;

....(contd.)

etc. Useful addresses, p.167-170; abbreviations and acronyms, p.171-177; classified index, p.179-224. *Class No:* 362(058)

Great Britain

Bibliographies

[3567]

BUNCH, A.J. **Sources of community information.** St. Albans, Branch and Mobile Libraries Group of the Library Association, [1986]. [3],64p. £3. (*Basic library guides, 8.*) ISBN: 0946461066.

Arranged in 4 sections: Introduction - General sources - Official sources - Non-official sources. Each section includes information on organizations and agencies, annotated entries for reference books and periodicals, and information on databases. No index. *Class No:* 362(410)(01)

[3568]

STEWART, G., *comp.* **Personal social services bibliography.** 2nd ed. London, Library Association, 1980. xiii, 129p. £12.50. ISBN: 0853655138.

First published 1978.

3,435 references, covering the literature from 1977 to May 1980. Subject area: 'Domicillary fieldwork and residential local services ...' (*Introduction*). 43 sections, with extensive subdivision , and cross-references (*e.g.* 1. General - 2. Advice centres - 3. Alcoholism ... 6. Children ... 16. Elderly ... 27. Offenders ... 30. Racial minorities ... 41. Youth). Many periodical articles. About 75% of the references are British; 25%, North America. Appended: Abbreviations. Compiler is Lecturer in Social Policy, Univ. of Lancaster. *Class No:* 362(410)(01)

Handbooks & Manuals

[3569]

The FIAC directory of independent advice centres. Thackeray, A. *and* Jones, M. London, Federation of Independent Advice Centres, 1988. £8.95. ISBN: 1871181003.

Lists the 450 independent advice agencies and organisations who are members of FIAC, a coordinating, resource and service agency. Geographical arrangement, subivided as necessary. Each entry has name and address, telephone number, services offered, subjects on which advice can be given, representation, languages, translators, and users. Several indexes. *Class No:* 362(410)(035)

[3570]

Guide to the social services, 1988. 76th ed. London, Family Welfare Association, 1988. x, 354p. £8.95. ISBN: 0900954388.

First published 1882, as part of *Charities digest.*

14 sections: 1. Organization and administration of the social services - 2. Personal social services - 3. The physically and mentally disabled and the elderly - 4. The National Health Service ... 8. Housing services - 9. Education - 10. Employment and industry - 11. The law and legal services ... 13. Information, advice and other consumer services 14. Self-help services. 4 appendices (4: Select bibliography, p.335-7). Subject index, p.338-354. Detailed coverage of statutory and voluntary social services on an annual basis, and cheaply. *Class No:* 362(410)(035)

Theses

[3571]

TAYLOR, M. *and* PRESLEY, F. **Community work in the UK, 1982-1986:** a review and digest of abstracts. London, Library Association Publishing Ltd., in association with C.P.F. (Community Projects Foundation) and Calouste Gulbenkian Foundation, 1987. [4], 148p. £20. ISBN: 0853659974.

An introductory review (p.1-24) is followed by the digest (p.25-122), with 16 subject sections of abstracts (A,. Directories ... C. Community work theory - D. Community work practice ... H. Race and sex equality ... P. Funding and legal). Author and selected subject indexes. Lists of organizations and abbreviations. Selected journals list. *Class No:* 362(410)(043)

Yearbooks & Directories

[3572]

The Self-help guide: a directory of self-help organizations in the United Kingdom. Knight, S. *and* Gann, R. London, Chapman & Hall, 1988. [6],125p. £6.95. ISBN: 0412293706.

Lists over 500 organizations arranged in 5 sections: 1. Introduction (with 16 references) - 2. Organizing and using self-help information - 3. Self-help literature (A-Z, numbered items. Name, address, telephone number and contact, publications, aims) - 4. Where to go for more information - 5. Directory of self-help groups. 2-page subject index. Directory index (refers to numbered items). *Class No:* 362(410)(058)

[3573]

The Social work and social welfare yearbook, 1991. Carter, P., *and others, eds.* Milton Keynes, Open University Press, 1991. viii,216p. £19.99. ISBN: 0335097960.

First published 1989. Annual.

Provides a range of critical commissioned articles on current concerns in social work and social welfare. 16 essays *e.g.* 2: Social work, justice and common good - 5. Family centres - 9. Drug problems in social work - 12. How social fund officers make decisions. *Class No:* 362(410)(058)

Laws

[3574]

CANS (Citizens Advice Notes): a service of information ... compiled from authoritative sources. Cumulative ed. to 1993. London, NCVO (National Council for Voluntary Organisations), CANS Department, 1991. 3v. plus supplements. 1st year's subscription: £95; annual renewal: £62. Loose-leaf.

First published as *Notes on new emergency regulations, 1939.*

Continuously updated digest of social legislation. 16 sections: 1. Administration of justice ... 3. British nationality and migration - 4. Business and industry - 5. Consumer protection ... 7. Education - 8. Employment ... 11. Housing, general - 12. Housing: Rent Acts - 13. Local government and public health - 14. Married persons and children ... 17. Personal health and welfare services ... 21. Town and country planning - 22. Transport (Roads). Index precedes, p.1-109. *Class No:* 362(410)(094.1)

Scotland

[3575]

Directory of national voluntary organisations in Scotland. Saunders, M. *and* Scott, M. Edinburgh, Scottish Council for Voluntary Organisations, 1987. 135p. illus. £5.50. ISBN: 0903589974.

Lists over 400 organizations, A-Z. Each entry includes name of organization, address, telephone number, contact name, and brief description of the organization's work, aims, and activities. Title index and classified index. *Class No:* 362(411)

[3576]

ENGLISH, J., *ed.* **Social services in Scotland.** 3rd ed. Edinburgh, Scottish Academic Press, 1988. vi,238p. diagrs., tables. £8.95. ISBN: 0707305179.

First published 1979.

Provides an introduction to all the main social services in Scotland. Contains chapters on central and local government, social security, health services, mental health services, housing, personal social services, children's hearings, education, employment services, services for the elderly and for the physically handicapped, urban social policy. References and 'further reading' follow each chapter. Index, p.234-238. *Class No:* 362(411)

USA

Bibliographies

[3577]

TRATTNER, W.L. *and* ACHENBAUM, W.A., *eds.* **Social welfare in America:** an annotated bibliography. Westport, CT., Greenwood Press, 1983. xxxiii,324p. $36.95. ISBN: 0313230021.

Over 1400 annotated entries relating to major works written since 1956 on the subject of public welfare in America. Arranged in topical subject groups, subdivided chronologically. Subject and author indexes. '... remarkably thorough collection of sources ...' (*Choice*, v.21(8), April 1984, p.1117-8). *Class No:* 362(73)(01)

Encyclopaedias

[3578]

Encyclopedia of social work. Minahaw, A., *ed.* 18th ed. Silver Springs, Md., National Association of Social Workers, 1987. 2v. (xii,2048p.). $75 (including supplement). ISBN: 0871011417; 0871011425, supplement. ISSN: 00710237.

16th ed., 1971-. Continues *Social work year book* (Russell Sage Foundation, 1929-.).

225 topical articles (about 1/3 from the 17th ed.) on social work and social welfare activities in the US, written by specialists in the field. Arranged in 8 sections covering fields of practice, populations, social issues and problems, social work practice, social institutions, human development, research, professions, etc. Cross-references. Includes biographies in a separate section of v.2. Detailed index. A statistical supplement, *Face of the nation, 1987* (1987. 124p. charts, tables) is a separate volume for frequent updating. 'There are no similar sources to which this invaluable collection of information can be compared' (*Choice*, v.14(11), January 1978, p.1478, of the 17th ed.). *Class No:* 362(73)(031)

Yearbooks & Directories

[3579]

Volunteerism: the directory of organizations, training, programs and publications. Kipps, H.C., *ed*. 3rd ed. New York. Bowker,1991. 1164p. $104.95. ISBN: 0835227391.

Previously published in 1980 as *411: community resource tie line* and *Community green sheets*, and in 1984 as *Community resources directory* (Gale Research Co.).

In 3 sections: 1. Resource groups and publications (listed generally by types of assistance such as Health, Employment and Consumer Services) - 2. Training programs (arranged by States) - 3. Program profiles (emphasizing those organizations that administer volunteer groups). Indexes of organizations and program emphasis. Identifies more than 5000 organizations. Index access by type of organization, organization name, and geographical location. *Class No:* 362(73)(058)

Histories

[3580]

BLAIR, K.J. The History of American women's voluntary organizations, 1810-1960: a guide to sources. Boston, Mass., G.K. Hall, 1988. 363p. $45. ISBN: 0816186480.

678 annotated entries for books and journal articles, arranged A-Z by author and coded to show whether a work concentrates on a charitable organization or one dedicated to peace, patriotism, religion, suffrage, temperence, etc. List of sources consulted. Subject and name index. No geographical index. Publisher claims this to be the first annotated bibliography on the subject ... 'from 1810, when women first began to gain influence in the public sphere through the formation of clubs, to 1960, when the contemporary women's movement emerged'. *Class No:* 362(73)(091)

Biographies

[3581]

TRATTNER, W.I., *ed*. **Biographical dictionary of social welfare in America.** Westport, CT., Greenwood Press, 1986. 897p. $76.95; £75. ISBN: 0313230013.

Biographical sketches of some 300 prominent Americans who were active in social work or other related endeavours. Women and minorities well-represented. Excludes theorists, philanthropists and persons still living. Most entries concisely and clearly written, containing relevant remarks about a person's importance in the history of social reform and social welfare. Includes a list of current sources for further information. (Information based on a review in *Choice* (v.24(2), October 1986). *Class No:* 362(73)(092)

Health & Welfare

[3582]

National health systems of the world. Oxford, Oxford University Press, 1991-93. 2v. (663,356p.). V.1.£65; v.2.£45. ISBN: 0195053206, v.1; 0195078454, v.2.

V.1: The countries; v.2: The issues. Examines health systems in 68 countries. Introduction explains benefits from a comparison of the systems, followed by sections on individual countries grouped in three major categories (industrialized - transitional - very poor). Length of entries

....(contd.)
varies from short ones for Eastern European countries to 23p. for the US. '... indispensable ...'(*Choice*,v.29(2), October 1991,p.263) on V.1. *Class No:* 362.1

Bibliographies

[3583]

BLADES, C.A., *and others*. **The International bibliography of health economics:** a comprehensive annotated guide to English language sources since 1914. New York, Macmillan; Brighton, Sussex, Wheatsheaf, 1986. 2v. (xviii,1092p.). $180; £90. ISBN: 0028959906, US; 074500086x, v.1 UK; 0745001599, v.2 UK.

First published in 1977 as *An annotated bibliography of health economics*.

5180 numbered entries for books, chapters of books, government publications, and articles from *c*.440 journals, on health economics published between 1914 and 1982. Part 1: General works - Demand/need for health care - Supply of health services - Estimating the contribution of health services. Part 2: Finance and organization of health services - Planning whole systems - Bibliographies - Supplementary entries. Entries are annotated with 50-100 word descriptions. Author and very detailed subject indexes. *Class No:* 362.1(01)

[3584]

ELLING, R.H., *ed*. **Cross-national study of health systems - countries, world regions, and special problems:** a guide to information sources. Detroit, Mich., Gale Research Co., 1980. xviii,687p. $68. (*Health affairs information guide series, v.3.*) ISBN: 0810314533.

Complementary to *Cross-national study of health systems - concepts, methods and data sources*. (Transaction Books, 1980).

Identifies 17 types of special problems in health systems. Specific countries (including Canada, Cuba, People's Republic of China, Sweden, UK and USSR - but not USA, dealt with elsewhere in the Health affairs series), and other world regions are then covered. The annotated bibliography records research monographs, periodical articles, official reports and unpublished dissertations. *Class No:* 362.1(01)

[3585]

Encyclopedia of health information sources. Wasserman, P., *ed*. 2nd ed. Detroit, Mich., Gale Research Company, 1993. *c*.500p. $165.00. ISBN: 0810369095.

First published 1987.

13,000 citations for *c*.450 health-related topics, listed A-Z. Under each topic heading are listed the citations for up to 14 types of sources, including abstract services, annuals, associations, bibliographies, biographical sources, dictionaries, directories, encyclopedias, institutes, online data bases, periodicals, professional societies, statistical sources, textbooks. Cross-references. List of subjects. A 3rd ed. is planned for 1996. *Class No:* 362.1(01)

[3586]

HASSELBAUER, K.J. A Research guide to the health sciences: medical, nutritional, and environmental. New York, Greenwood Press, 1987. 657p. $49.95. (*Reference sources for the social sciences and humanities, 4.*) ISBN: 0313235309.

Over 2000 citations in 4 parts: General works - Basic sciences - Social aspects of the health sciences - Medical specialties. The first part includes research guides,

....(contd.)
bibliographies, indexes, bibliographical sources, directories, encyclopedias. The other three parts also include textbooks. *Class No:* 362.1(01)

[3587]
REES, A.N. *and* JANES, J. **The Consumer health information source book.** 2nd ed. New York, R.R. Bowker, 1984. xiii,530p. £44; $44.95. ISBN: 0835218775.
First published 1981.
Includes annotated entries for 935 books and 1500 booklets and pamphlets, arranged in 2 main parts: 1. Reference and research aids; 2. The literature (in 14 subject sections). Cross-references. Appendix 1: Directory of 220 pamphlet suppliers; 2. Directory of publishers. Title and subject indexes. *Class No:* 362.1(01)

[3588]
ROPER, F.W. *and* BOURKMAN, J.A. **Introduction to reference sources in the health sciences.** 2nd ed. Chicago, Ill., Medical Library Association Inc., 1984. [7], 302p. $27. ISBN: 0912176164.
First published 1980.
16 chapters in 3 parts, each chapter discussing the general characteristics of the type of source being considered, followed by examples of the most important tools in the area. Part I. The reference collection; pt.II. Bibliographic sources; pt.III. Information sources. Index, p.287-302. '... does an excellent job of discussing various types of reference and information sources and their use in reference work in the health sciences' (*Journal of academic librarianship,* v.11(4), September 1985, p.255). *Class No:* 362.1(01)

Dictionaries

[3589]
DEARLING, A. **The Social welfare word book.** Harlow, Longman, 1993. xxiii,203p. £12.95. ISBN: 0582219760.
A 13-page list of acronyms and abbreviations precedes. The main dictionary entries are about a paragraph in length, with description, background and context. Many have examples, and all end with references to related headings. *Class No:* 362.1(038)

[3590]
HOGARTH, J. **Glossary of health care terminology.** Copenhagen, World Health Organization, Regional Office for Europe, 1975. 476p.
About 350 main entries with references to many other terms; designed to promote the standardization of public health terminology. Coverage: health services; resources; finance; manpower; buildings; drugs; management; planning; statistics. Detailed index. *Class No:* 362.1(038)

[3591]
TIMMS, N. *and* TIMMS, R., *eds.* **Dictionary of social welfare.** London, Routledge & Kegan Paul, 1982. vi, 217p. £37.50. ISBN: 0710090846.
*c.*300 entries, arranged A-Z. Each entry indicates the meaning or range of meanings of the word, and then outlines its application in welfare, and use by practitioners. Most entries conclude with references to works which deal with the subject. Cross-referenced. *Class No:* 362.1(038)

Reviews & Abstracts

[3592]
Health service abstracts. London, Department of Health and Social Security Library, 1974-. no.1-. Monthly. £29pa. ISSN: 02680459.
Succeeds *Current literature on personal social services* and, later, *Current literature on health services.* As from May 1985 incorporates *Hospital abstracts* and *Current literature on general medical practice* also.
About 150 brief summaries of journal articles, reports, books, and references per issue. Headings: Services for special groups (Maternity - Children - Elderly - Terminally ill - Physically handicapped - Psychiatric services - Mentally handicapped - Ethnic minorities - Prison medical services); Services for special diseases; NHS reports; DHSS publications; Circulars and other guidance material. Cross-references. Author and subject indexes. Database is DATASTAR. *Class No:* 362.1(048)

[3593]
Quality assurance abstracts. DHSS Library and King's Fund Centre, Quality Insurance Project. London, Department of Health and Social Security Library *and* King Edward's Hospital Fund for London, 1986-92. 6pa. ISSN: 0269297x.
Over 800 abstracts pa. Arranged in 28 broad subject divisions: General items and comment ... Quality assurance in the United Kingdom ... Hospitals (various subdivisions) ... Primary health care ... Nursing ... Bibliography and reference materials. Subject and author indexes. Produced for DHSS-DATA, the DHSS Library database. *Class No:* 362.1(048)

Yearbooks & Directories

[3594]
The Health and safety directory, 1993/94. Hastings, M.R., *and others.* London, Croner Publications (previously Brentford, Middx., Kluwer Publishing Ltd.), 1993. 900p. £28.15. ISBN: 1855242400.
Aims to be a comprehensive collection of names and addresses of organizations and people interested in, or involved with, health and safety. 26 sections in 6 parts: A. Regulatory authorities and national bodies - B. Regional and local public services - C. Organizations world-wide - D. Health and safety in industry - E. Professional bodies, safety organizations and training - F. Miscellaneous. Keyword index of individuals, p.921-982; keyword index of committees, p.983-985; General keyword index, p.986-1025. Classified section. *Class No:* 362.1(058)

Tables & Data Books

[3595]
World health statistics annual ... 1992. Geneva, World Health Organization, 1993. xxiii,463p. tables. £55. SFr.100. ISBN: 9240679200. ISSN: 02503794.
Initially as *Annual epidemiological and vital statistics.* Until recently issued in 3v. First published for 1939/46, then annually.
In 4 main sections: A. Global overview - B. Special topic (in this issue 'Implementation of the global strategy for health for all by the year 2000: regional perspectives of achievement') - C. Vital statistics and life tables - D. Causes of death (subdivided by region and country). 2 Annexes (II. List of member states of WHO, by region). Data is for 1991

....(contd.)

and also earlier years in some tables.

Supplemented by *World health statistics quarterly* (1978-. SFr.100pa.). *Class No:* 362.1(083)

Laws

[3596]

The Journal of social welfare law and family law. London, Sweet & Maxwell, Stevens Journal, 1978-. 6pa. £72 pa. ISSN: 01418033.

Each issue usually includes 3-4 articles; Recent legislation and reports; Recent Social Security Commissioners' decisions; and one or two lengthy book reviews. *Class No:* 362.1(094.1)

Developing Countries

[3597]

GABRIEL, T. Who's for health? Community health in developing countries. In *British Book News*, April 1990, p.236-9.

A survey reviewing a selection of books on various aspects of health and how it may be improved in developing countries. Includes 63 items. *Class No:* 362.1(4/9-77)

Great Britain

[3598]

The Health directory, 1990-91. 2nd ed. London, Bedford Square Press, 1990. 121p. £6.95

lst published 1979.

Lists *c.*700 established national bodies, voluntary groups and other societies and institutions connected with health. Arranged A-Z, data includes address; telephone, fax & telex numbers; and objects. Subject index. *Class No:* 362.1(410)

[3599]

The Hospitals and health services yearbook ... an annual record of the hospitals and health services of Great Britain and Northern Ireland, incorporating *Burdett's Hospitals and charities,* founded 1889. 1993 ed. London. Institute of Health Services Management, 1993. Various pagings. ISBN: 0901003867.

23 sections, including directories of health authorities in England, in Wales and in Scotland; Statutory instruments and circulars; Summaries of reports; Health Service literature; a short bibliography; and Directory of hospital suppliers. Indexes (on green paper); Health authorities, hospitals; general index; advertisers. *Class No:* 362.1(410)

[3600]

LAING, W. Laing's review of private health care ... and directory of independent hospitals, residential and nursing homes and related services 1992. 4th ed. London, Laing & Buisson Publications, 1992. 1220p., tables, map. £95. ISBN: 185440024x. ISSN: 09539050.

Lists *c*12,000+ private and voluntary homes for the elderly, plus independent hospitals, screening clinics, and homes and hospitals for the mentally ill. *Class No:* 362.1(410)

[3601]

The NHS handbook. National Association of Health Authorities and Trusts. 7th ed. London, Macmillan Press, 1991. xxiii,267p. ISBN: 033353736x.

First ed. published 1980.

Aims 'to make N.H.S. easily understood by those without prior knowledge of its structure and to provide an up-to-date reference document for those already working in the N.H.S. and related fields ...' (*Publisher's catalogue*). Sections: The N.H.S. today - Management - Funding - Trends in health care - Health care provision - Support services - Personnel - Care in the community - Partnerships with the N.H.S. Also a quick reference section and an index. *Class No:* 362.1(410)

Bibliographies

[3602]

GREAT BRITAIN. HM Stationery Office. **Government publications. sectional list 11, revised December 1988: Department of Health and Social Security.** London, HMSO., 1989. 35p. *Gratis.*

Two lists of items currently in print: 'Health and social services' (sections include: Children and child abuse; Drugs and pharmaceuticals; Health equipment notes; Hospitals, administration and organization; Medical practitioners; National Health Service; Social services; Statistical and research reports) - 'Social security' (*e.g.* National insurance (industrial injuries); Pensions; Occupational pensions). *Class No:* 362.1(410)(01)

[3603]

Health education index and guide to voluntary and other support organisations and self-help groups concerned with health care. Edsall, B., *comp. & ed.* 9th ed. London, B. Edsall & Co., 1988. 414p. £40. ISBN: 0902623508. ISSN: 01403273.

First published 1970.

Lists over 13,000 references to health education material (p.18-359) arranged in 170 subject areas, A-Z. Includes booklets and pamphlets, books, films, film strips and slides, flannelgraphs, lecture notes, loops, transparencies, tapes and tape cassettes, posters, video cassettes, wallcharts, etc. Sources of supply index, p.7-15. Also lists professional organizations (p.361-362) and 'People who help, index of voluntary and other support organizations ...' (p.363-413). *Class No:* 362.1(410)(01)

[3604]

HUSTWIT, J. *and* **WEBLEY, M. Information in social welfare:** a survey of resources. London, National Institute for Social Work, 1977. 95p. £2.50. (*NISW no. 6.*) ISBN: 0902789090.

Based on a report on information resources in social welfare prepared for the British Library Research and Development Dept.

Pt. 1: Development in social welfare information resources in the 1970's - Pt. 2: Social welfare information resource - a guide (142 references). Appendix A: Current awareness sources - B. A short bibliography of social welfare and related information research (1968-), by date. *Class No:* 362.1(410)(01)

Handbooks & Manuals

[3605]

NATIONAL CONSUMER COUNCIL. You and your dentists: a guide to patients' rights. London, HMSO, 1987. 116p. illus (cartoons). £2.50. ISBN: 0117013439.

Aims to answer questions consumers most often ask, and explains in some detail how dentists work in the NHS, their responsibilities, and what patients can reasonably expect of them. Main sections: The family dentist (choosing a dentist, length of treatment, referral to specialists, home visits) - Charges - Special services - Information and consent - Complaints and redress - Preventive dentistry - Consumer representation - Contacts: useful addresses. References. *Class No:* 362.1(410)(035)

[3606]

Registered Nursing Home Association: reference book, 1990/91: registered nursing homes, clinics and hospitals in the UK. 15th ed. Birmingham, the Association, 1990. 210p. maps.

Contents: Summary of National Health Service beds - List of N.H.S. in region/district order - Regional health authorities/boards - Alphabetical list of members of the R.N.H. Association - Town/district locations of members of the R.N.H. Association. *Class No:* 362.1(410)(035)

Yearbooks & Directories

[3607]

Croner's care homes guide. New Maldon, Croner Publications, 1987. 2v. £28.50 each vol. ISBN: 0900319518, South; 0900319526, North & Midlands. ISSN: 09525157.

One volume covers the South of England, the other the North and Midlands. Each volume is arranged by counties and then alphabetically by town in postal address. Together they list over 10,000 homes. Each entry includes full name of home, date established, full postal address, telephone number, name of proprietor, ownership status, special services offered, visiting arrangements, fees, number of residents, conditions of acceptance, licensing authority, details of accommodation available, arrangements for meals, lifts, TV, telephone, heating, etc. A-Z index by names of homes. *Class No:* 362.1(410)(058)

[3608]

Directory of health centres, 1986. Harlow, Essex, Longman Group, 1985. [5], 486p. £65. ISBN: 0582903602.

Arranged A-Z by place and name of centre, giving address, telephone number, administrator/manager/secretary name, practitioners names, dentists names, community nursing officers names, services and facilities. Health centres listed by regional and district health authorities, p.463-486. *Class No:* 362.1(410)(058)

[3609]

Directory of independent hospitals and health services, 1994. London, Longman Group, with the Independent Healthcare Association, 1993. iv,791p. £96. ISBN: 0582231566. ISSN: 09510561.

First published 1980. The first 5 eds. published by Medical Marketing Information Ltd. Former title was *Directory of private hospital and health services.*

Includes chapters on independent hospitals, screening clinics, private bed accommodation in NHS hospitals, private nursing homes, voluntary homes, dual registered homes. Arrangement is A-Z by organization, with address,

....(contd.)
telephone, matron's name, etc. Followed by guides to English health regions, health authorities, and English counties; a buyers' guide, general index, and index of advertisers. *Class No:* 362.1(410)(058)

[3610]

The Helping handbook. St. Michael's, Lancs., Silver Link Publishing Ltd., 1988. 95p. £3.95. ISBN: 0947971238.

A directory of information and addresses for the sick, disabled, and their families and friends. Includes chapters on rehabilitation units for severe disabilities and less severe physical disabilities; residential accommodation for the physically disabled; residential and educational centres for epileptics; residential care for the mentally disabled; facilities for the disabled; techniques of communication; employment of the disabled; training and education of the disabled; mobility; information services; self-help groups; pressure groups; unions and trade associations; holiday centres; organizations for the blind and for the deaf. A-Z index; regional index; index of specialised groups; and subject index. *Class No:* 362.1(410)(058)

Scotland

Bibliographies

[3611]

GREAT BRITAIN. HM Stationery Office. **Government publications. Sectional list 71: revised 1 June 1989. Scotland.** London, HMSO, 1989. 45p. *Gratis.*

Includes a section on the Scottish Home and Health Department (p.24-29). Sections: Home affairs (Criminal matters - Fire - Licensing ... Police - Prisons); Health (Alcohol - Child health ... Food, hygiene, nutrition - Health buildings and equipment ... Mental health and welfare ...). *Class No:* 362.1(411)(01)

England & Wales

Tables & Data Books

[3612]

Health and personal social service statistics for England, 1992. Department of Health and Social Security. London, HMSO., 1992. 144p. maps. £11.50. ISBN: 0113215398.

First published 1969. Annual.

13 sections: 1. Population and vital statistics - 2. Finance - 3. Manpower - 4. N.H.S. hospital administrative service - 5. Family Practitioner Committee services - 6. Community health service - 7. Personal health services - 8. Maternity and child health and social services - 9. Psychiatric services - 10. Preventive medicine - 11. Morbidity - 12. Abortions notified under the Abortion Act, 1967 - 13. Miscellaneous health statistics. Appendices: 1. General notes; 2. List of publications; 3. Regional health authority areas. *Class No:* 362.1(42)(083)

[3613]

—Health and personal social services statistics for Wales, 1991. Welsh Office. no.18. Cardiff, E & S. S Division, Welsh Office, 1991. £5. ISBN: 0750401982.

First published 1969. Annual.

Similar content to the above, with 12 sections and 2 appendices. *Class No:* 362.1(42)(083)

USA

Yearbooks & Directories

[3614]

Directory of nursing homes: state-by-state listing of facilities and services. Mongeau, S., *ed.* 5th ed. Phoenix, AZ., Oryx Press, 1993. 1620p. $225 Diskette: $2500). ISBN: 1880678098.

First published 1982.505.00/00$aLists over'18,000 state-licenced long-term-care facilities. All entries have name, address, telephone number, number of beds, level of care, and names of administrators. Some entries also have information on facilities and activities, types of ownership, languages spoken, number of staff, and admission requirements. Arranged A-Z by State, subdivided by cities, A-Z. Indexes of nursing home names and regions/fraternal-maternal affiliations. *Class No:* 362.1(73)(058)

[3615]

Medical and health information directory. Backus, K., *ed.* 7th ed. Detroit, Mich., Gale Research Co., 1994. 3v. $485 the set; $195 each vol. ISBN: 081037868x. ISSN: 07499973.

First published 1977.

V.1: Organizations, agencies and institutions - v.2: Libraries, publications, audiovisuals, and databases - v.3: Health services. Intended for US medical and health professionals, government officials, librarians, consumers, and others. Each volume is self contained.
Class No: 362.1(73)(058)

Libraries

[3616]

Directory of medical and health care libraries in the United Kingdom and Republic of Ireland, 1990. Wright, D.J., *for the Medical, Health and Welfare Libraries Group of the Library Association.* 7th ed. London, Library Association Publishing Ltd., 1990. xiv,295p. ISBN: 0853657793.

First published 1957, the 1st-4th editions being titled *Directory of medical libraries in the British Isles*.

Lists over 600 specialist libraries, with details of address, telephone and fax numbers, electronic mailing addresses, librarian, readers, stock policy, opening hours, publications, branches, holdings, etc. 2 appendices, including 1. List of members of NHS Regional Libraries Group. List of libraries arranged A-Z by town. Indexes of personal names, establishments, counties, and named collections. Subject index to special collections. Selected subject index to libraries. *Class No:* 362.1:061:026/027

National Health Service

[3617]

NATIONAL CONSUMER COUNCIL. Patients' rights: a guide for NHS patients and doctors. London, HMSO, 1983. 60p. illus. £1.50. ISBN: 0117010448.

Contents: 1. Becoming a patient - 2. Choice and consent - 3. Information - 4. Children - 5. Representation - 6. Complaint and redress - 7. Contacts.
Class No: 362.1:061:061.1

[3618]

A Patient's guide to the National Health Services. Hessayon, A., *comp.* London, Consumers' Association and Hodder & Stoughton, 1983. 223p. £3.95. ISBN: 0340335467.

Topics covered include: How to choose your GP, dentist, optician; Maternity and child health services; All aspects of going into hospital; Mental health services; The care of the elderly; The roles of different health workers; Questions of medical records and confidentiality, and consent and medical research. Further chapter considers the pros and cons of private treatment. Finally, there is a chapter on the structure of the NHS; a list of useful addresses (p.215-8); and an index (p.219-223). *Class No:* 362.1:061:061.1

Hospitals

Reviews & Abstracts

[3619]

Hospital literature index. Chicago, Ill., American Hospital Association, 1945-. Quarterly (from 1945 to 1961, 2pa.) 4th quarter is annual hard-bound issue. 5-year cumulations. $290pa. ISSN: 00185736.

From 1978 compiled with the co-operation of the National Library of Medicine.

About 10,000 references pa from *c.*500 English-language journals. An A-Z author-subject index of literature about hospital administration, planning and financing, and administrative aspects of medical, paramedical, etc., fields. Includes references to significant books as well as periodical articles. Also available online; Vendors: DIMDI; National Library of Medicine. *Class No:* 362.11(048)

Great Britain

[3620]

Directory of hospitals. 5th ed. Edinburgh, Churchill Livingstone Medical Journals, 1992. 490p. £34. ISBN: 058209626x.

Lists all hospitals in the United Kingdom and Eire (NHS and independent) plus names of consultants for each hospital by specialities. Features RHS/DHA/FHSA addresses, NHS Trusts. Index of consultants by medical specialty.
Class No: 362.11(410)

Libraries

[3621]

Directory of domiciliary and hospital patients' library services in the United Kingdom. Collison, J., *and others, eds.* Manchester, Library Association, Medical, Health and Welfare Libraries Group *and* Department of Library and Information Studies, Manchester Polytechnic, 1984. viii,854p. £12. ISBN: 0950989703.

Geographical arrangement: Domiciliary library services (Public library services in the UK - Other public libraries in the British Isles); Hospital public library services (England: Regional health authorities, by authority - Northern Ireland: Health and personal social services, by authority - Northern Ireland: Health and personal social services, by authority - Scotland: Health boards, by authority - Wales: Regional health authority - Isle of Man and Channel Islands - London

....(contd.)
post-graduate teaching hospitals - Special hospitals). Index of hospitals, district health authorities and place names. *Class No:* 362.11(410):061:026/027

England

Middle Ages

[3622]
CLAY, R.M. **The Mediaeval hospitals of England.** London, Methuen, 1909 (Reprinted by Cass, 1966). xxii,357p. illus. £25. ISBN: 0714612928.

The most valuable part of this history lies in appendix B, which is a list of nearly 800 houses for wayfarers, sick, aged, infirm, insane, and lepers founded before 1547, arranged by counties. Appended list of sources. Well produced. 'It should be available in every historical and good general library' (*British medical journal,* no.5503, 25 June 1966, p.1590. *Class No:* 362.11(420)"01/14"

Family Planning

[3623]
LOUDON, N. *and* NEWTON, J., *eds.* **Handbook of family planning.** Edinburgh, Churchill Livingstone, 1985. xiv,334p. illus. £18.95. ISBN: 0443024804.

17 chapters: 1. Family planning - the United Kingdom: services and training - 2. Choice of method ... 4. Combined oral contraceptive pills ... 7. Intrauterine contraceptive devices ... 10. Sterilization ... 14. Medicolegal aspects of family planning ... 17. Family planning in general practice. Addresses. Analytical index, p.327-334. A 2nd rev. ed. was published in 1991 (484p. illus. ISBN 044303964x). *Class No:* 362.178

Reviews & Abstracts

[3624]
Latest literature in family planning. London, Family Planning Information Service, 1974-90. 6pa. ISSN: 03088774.

Formerly *Current literature in family planning.*

About 100 abstracts pa, drawn from English-language books, pamphlets, periodicals, monographs and reports. Subject fields: Family planning - medical and non-medical. *Class No:* 362.178(048)

Developing Countries

[3625]
ROSS, J.A., *and others*. **Family planning and child survival:** 100 developing countries. New York, Center for Population and Family Health, Columbia University, 1988. 247p. Gratis (later eds. $5 each). ISBN: 0962095206.

Intended to be issued biennially. Successor to *Population and family planning programs*, Population Council fact book series issued 1969-1985.

Statistical data compiled from returned questionnaires and standard secondary sources. (*e.g.* UN's Demographic yearbook). No index. Useful table of contents. *Class No:* 362.178(4/9-77)

Disabled & Handicapped

Bibliographies

[3626]
LANE, E. *and* LANE, J. **'Reference materials for the disabled'.** In *RSR* v.10(3), Fall, 1982, p.73-76.

Includes 23 annotated citations and also organizations, etc., that help, arranged in 6 sections (Guides - Aids for independent living - Service agencies - Library resources - Specialized formats - Utilizing technology. US oriented. *Class No:* 362.4(01)

[3627]
LANE, P. **'Books on disability'.** In *British book news,* April 1984, p.199-204.

A literature review, with sections on Children; Toys; Education; Employment; The sociology of disability; The Snowball effect of Snowdon; Social work and community care; Careers with disabled people; Attitudes; Self-help; Leisure; Access and design; Aids costs, Women; Preventable disability; Third world; Libraries. Also a bibliography of the 129 books referred to in the text. *Class No:* 362.4(01)

[3628]
NATIONAL LIBRARY FOR THE HANDICAPPED CHILD. **Catalogue of library holdings.** London, the Library, 1986. 800p. £7.50. ISBN: 0948664002.

A list of books, computer software, sound tapes, slides, film strips, 16mm film, videos, jigsaws, pictures and multi-media packs. Includes details of books on the care and education of handicapped children. Listed by author, by title, and by handicap. *Class No:* 362.4(01)

Dictionaries

[3629]
INTERNATIONAL LABOUR OFFICE. **Vocational rehabilitation and the employment of the disabled:** a glossary. Geneva, ILO., 1981. 182p. Sw.F.15. £6.60. ISBN: 922002571x. *Class No:* 362.4(038)

[3630]
LINDSEY, M.P. **Dictionary of mental handicap.** London, Routledge, 1989. vi,345p. £35. ISBN: 0415028108.

Bringing together terms and concepts from a wide variety of fields, this is '... an attempt to demystify the terms so that they can be more readily understood by lay people, unqualified staff, and staff from the same and other disciplines.' (*Preface*). Short descriptions vary in length from a few lines to a page. Cross-references. References for further reading are added to many entries. *Class No:* 362.4(038)

Yearbooks & Directories

[3631]
Directory for the disabled: a handbook of information and opportunities for disabled and handicapped people. Darnborough, A. *and* Kinrade, D., *comps.* 4th ed. Cambridge, Woodhead-Faulkner, in association with the Royal Association for Disability and Rehabilitation, 1985. x, 358p. £11.50. ISBN: 0839412555.

First published 1977.

16 sections ... 2. Financial benefits and allowances - 3. Aids: their provision and availability ... 7. Employment - 8. Mobility and motoring ... 11. Sport and leisure ... 16.

....*(contd.)*

Helpful organizations. 2 appendices: A. Selected further information, including bibliographies; B. Addresses of publishers and stockists mentioned. Index, p.349-53). *Class No:* 362.4(058)

[3632]
HALE, G., *ed*. **The New source book for the disabled:** an illustrated guide to easier and more independent living for physically disabled people, their families and friends. 2nd ed. London, Heinemann, 1983. 288p, illus. £9.95. ISBN: 0434311596.

First published in 1979 by Paddington Press.

A quarto which includes sections on resources (*e.g.* organizations; general reference books; periodicals; leisure activities). Index. *Class No:* 362.4(058)

[3633]
SANDHU, J., *and others. eds*. **Directory of non-medical research relating to handicapped people, 1987.** 4th ed. Newcastle-upon-Tyne, Handicapped Persons Research Unit, Newcastle Polytechnic, 1987. [6], 479p. £15. ISBN: 0906721296.

First published 1932.

Sections on education, communication, family, post school, recreation, social and personal, services, community care, institutional care, health care, rehabilitation, functional/clinical assessment, elderly, mobility, miscellaneous. Information given for each project is project title, aims and methods, institution/organization (name, address, telephone no.), investigator's name, funded by, starting date, publications/progress report. Indexes of workers, institutions, and subjects.

A new ed. was issued in 1993 as *Directory of non-medical research on disability, 1989-93*, edited by E.Humphries & O.Paget (University of Northumbria at Newcastle, 210p. £9. ISBN 0906721555). *Class No:* 362.4(058)

The Blind

Bibliographies

[3634]
AMERICAN FOUNDATION FOR THE BLIND. New York City. M.C. Migel Memorial Library. **Dictionary catalog of the M.C. Migel Memorial Library ...** Boston, Mass., G.K. Hall, 1970. 2v. $156 the set. ISBN: 081610705x.

A catalogue of 23,000 photolithographically reproduced cards, on every phase of blindness. Typical subject headings include Preschool child, Reading, Public school classes, Space perception, Personality development, Counseling, Vocational guidance and placement, the Deaf-blind, and the War-blinded. *Class No:* 362.41(01)

[3635]
—ROYAL NATIONAL INSTITUTE FOR THE BLIND. Reference Library. Works on blindness and associated subjects. London, the Institute, 1962, with supplements in 1964, 1969, 1971.

Since 1974 the Library has produced select accessions lists. *Class No:* 362.41(01)

The Deaf

Dictionaries

[3636]
Gallaudet encyclopedia of deaf people and deafness. Van Cleve, J.V., *ed*. New York, McGraw-Hill, 1987. 3v. (xiii,1322p.). illus. $300 the set. ISBN: 0070792291.

Sponsored by Gallaudet University.

273 entries discussing the sociology, audiology, law, education, psychology, history and rehabilitation of deaf people. Articles are signed, vary in length between half a page to 30 pages, with subsections and bibliographies. 10 associate editors and 400 distinguished contributors in all. Includes biographical entries. International in scope. 'Excellently done' (*Library journal*, v.111(17), 15 October 1986, p.86). '... an encyclopedia on and for the deaf that is likely to become the standard work in its field' (*Choice*, April 1987, p.1198). '... a unique set with no competition ... written in a clear and generally accessible manner ...' (*Reference books bulletin*, 1986/87, p.84). *Class No:* 362.42(038)

Poor & Destitute

Bibliographies

[3637]
HENSLIN, J.M. **Homelessness:** an annotated bibliography. New York, Garland, 1993. 2v.(1092p). $125. ISBN: 0824041151.

V.1 has 3300 annotated entries arranged by author, A-Z, each entry being from a sentence to a paragraph in length. V.2 lists the same citations in 41 subject sections (Advocacy ... Homeless women), with full citations but no annotations. Author index. '... brings together a wide array of sources on a critical global social issue'(*Booklist*, v.90(1), 1 September 1993, p.88). *Class No:* 362.5(01)

Child Welfare

[3638]
UNICEF. **State of the world's children, 1992.** Adamson, P. *and* Adamson, L. Oxford, Oxford University Press for UNICEF, 1992. [xi], 96p. tables, charts. ISBN: 0192622285. ISSN: 0265718x.

Annual, first published 1980.

In 2 parts: A report sumbitting 10 specific propositions for ending the poverty of one quarter of mankind, and a section of statistical tables (p.69-89); footnotes to tables (p.90-96). *Class No:* 362.7

Bibliographies

[3639]
HAAG, E.E. **Research guide for studies in infancy and childhood.** Westport, CT., Greenwood Press, 1988. 430p. $55. (*Reference sources for the social sciences and humanities, 8.*) ISBN: 0313247633.

Section 1 has chapters on search strategy, databases, and general reference works, by type. Section 2 has specialised subject bibliographies on families; child care; communication; cognition; behaviour, social/cultural, physical and atypical development; and creativity. Each

.... *(contd.)*

section is subdivided. Annotations are descriptive. Subject, title and author indexes. Complements Woodbury's *Childhood information sources* (1985). *Class No:* 362.7(01)

[3640]
PARDECK, J.T., *and others, comps*. **Child welfare training and practice:** an annotated bibliography. Westport, CT., Greenwood Press, 1982. 143p. $36.95. ISBN: 0313233837.

In 7 sections: Abuse and neglect - Law and court - Substitute care - In-home services and parent education - Institutions and special-needs children - Minority clients - Training and interviewing methods. Annotated entries. Non-print media included. Cross-references. Author, institutional, audiovisual and subject indexes. *Class No:* 362.7(01)

[3641]
SCHEIMAN, D.L. *and* SLONIM, M. **Resources for middle childhood;** a source book. New York, Garland, 1988. 138p. $27. (*Garland reference library of social sciences, 433.*) ISBN: 0824077776.

Concerned with children who are 6 to 12 years old. Arranged in 8 broad groupings (Physical development - psychosocial development - cognitive development - family interaction - play - peer relationships- schooling - societal impact). Each section has an essay, followed by an annotated bibliography. Author and title indexes, but no subject index. *Class No:* 362.7(01)

[3642]
WOODBURY, M. **Childhood information resources.** New York, Information Resources, 1985. 593p. $45. ISBN: 087815051x.

789 annotated entries for information published by all kinds of child study agencies, in all disciplines regarding children. Each chapter has a 3-5 page introduction describing coverage, subject category, research methodology, etc. Covers 150 periodicals, 173 organizations, and 40 databases. Lengthy author/title/subject index. ' ... a useful sourcebook ... ' (*Choice* v.23(2) October 1985 p.278). *Class No:* 362.7(01)

USA

Yearbooks & Directories
[3643]
POSNER, J.L. **CWLA's guide to adoption agencies:** a national directory of adoption agencies and adoption resources. New York, Child Welfare League of America, 1989. 668p. tables. $15.95. ISBN: 0878683453.

Lists both public and private adoption agencies in the US. Arranged by State, subdivided by name of agency. Data includes address of agency, director's name, adoption procedures, programme summary, accreditation, children placed (age, ethnicity, etc.), requirements for adoptive parents (age, religion, marital status, etc.), and average cost and waiting time. *Class No:* 362.7(73)(058)

Youth Welfare
[3644]
Directory of youth services and child care in the UK. 2nd ed. Harlow, Essex, Longman, 1992. xvii,346p. £40. (*Longman community information guide.*) ISBN: 0582087864.

First published 1990.

.... *(contd.)*

A comprehensive, detailed listing of local authority, independent and voluntary organizations. In 2 parts: 1. Public and statutory services, central and local government, England, Wales, Scotland and Northern Ireland - 2. Voluntary, private and non-statutory services. Index, p.340-345. *Class No:* 362.8

[3645]
Youth movements of the world. Angel, W.D. Harlow, Essex, Longman, 1991. 700p. illus. £99. (*Longman current affairs.*) ISBN: 0582062713.

Lists over 1000 youth organizations and government and non-government agencies under countries A-Z. Introduction on each country gives statistics (demography, education, employment and health) and information on government youth ministries and youth policies. On each organization: contact; office holders; membership; history; aims; activities; affiliations. *Class No:* 362.8

Bibliographies
[3646]
DERRICK, D., *comp*. **Selected and annotated bibliography of youth, youth work and provision for youth.** Leicester, National Youth Bureau, 1976. ix,411p. £3.50. ISBN: 0902095269.

Over 2000 entries, with concise, expository annotations. Classes A-S (with further subdivision): A. Social studies - B. Psychology and human behaviour - C. Social services - D. Community development - E. Education - F. Adolescence - G. Transition from school to work - H. Leisure - I. Handicapped - J. Delinquency - K. Young volunteers - L. Drugs - M. Counselling - N. Sex - O. Detailed youth work - P. The youth service - Q. Training for youth and community work - R. Training - S. Management. Key to publishers. Indexes of authors and subjects. *Class No:* 362.8(01)

[3647]
Young people now. Leicester, National Youth Agency, 1973- First 6pa, then monthly. £22.80pa. ISSN: 09562842.

As *Youth service information centre digest,* 1969-73. Incorporated *Youth social work bulletin,* then *Youth in society* umtil l988. Current title from l990. Focuses on issues that affect young people and those who work for them. *Class No:* 362.8(01)

Counselling
[3648]
FELTHAM, C. *and* DRYDEN, W. **Dictionary of counselling.** London, Whurr Publishers Ltd., 1993. xii,216p. £19.50. ISBN: 1870332083.

A list of 8 consultants, conventions used, and a list of abbreviations precede the dictionary. Entries are from 2 or 3 lines to over a column in length ('Counselling skills': nearly a column). References [a bibliography], p.212-6. *Class No:* 364.44

Insurance

Bibliographies

[3649]
CHARTERED INSURANCE INSTITUTE. Library.
Insurance reading list: a selection of useful books and periodicals on insurance and related subjects. 7th ed. London, the Library, 1986. 23p. £2.

First published 1972 as *Select list of useful books....*

About 300 unannotated entries (but stating prices, or if op). 17 sections (with subdivisions): General ... Marine ... Fire ... Life ... Pensions ... Accident ... Liability ... Aviation ... Periodicals.

The *Journal* of the Institute (6pa each £2.) regularly carries a feature 'In print', - a checklist for books and periodical articles. Prices are given for photocopying articles. The Institute also issues *gratis* select subject bibliographies (*e.g. Householders' insurance; Life insurance*). *Class No:* 368(01)

[3650]
CUNNEW, R. The Insurance sourcebook. Harlow, Essex, Longman, 1991. x,246p. £40 ISBN: 058208556x.

Comprehensive guide to sources of information on and for insurance, in the UK and internationally. *Class No:* 368(01)

Dictionaries

Polyglot

[3651]
DE LUCCA, J.L. Elsevier's dictionary of insurance and risk prevention in English, French, Spanish, German and Portuguese. Amsterdam, Elsevier, 1992. xii,430p. £118.18. $185.50. Dfl.325.

Deals with 3962 terms. *Class No:* 368(038)=00

[3652]
DRUDE, G. *and* SACHS, W, *eds.* Lebensversicherungs-technisches Wörterbuch, Deutsch-Englisch-Französisch-Italienisch-Spanisch. Dictionary of actuarial and life insurance terms. 3.Aufl. Karlsruhe, Verlag Versicherungswirtschaft, 1983. 611p. £45.50.

2nd ed. published 1964 with supplement, 1972.

A dictionary of actuarial and life insurance terms, with equivalents. Five sequences: German-English-French-Italian-Spanish; English-French-Italian-Spanish-German; French-Italian-Spanish-German-English; Italian-Spanish-German-English-French; and Spanish-German-English-French-Italian. *Class No:* 368(038)=00

[3653]
MÜLLER-LUTZ, H.L., *ed.* Four-language insurance dictionaries. Rev. eds. Karlsruhe, Verlag Versicherungswirtschaft e.V., 1971-90. £16.50 each.

A series of polyglot insurance dictionaries; English, French and German equivalents figure in each dictionary, the other languages being, respectively: Bulgarian, Chinese, Czech, Danish, Dutch, Greek, Hungarian, Japanese, Norwegian, Polish, Portuguese, Romanian, Russian, Swedish, Turkish. Each dictionary has *c.* 270 p. *Class No:* 368(038)=00

[3654]
—MÜLLER-LUTZ, H.L. *and* CHIDIAC, J.S. Insurance dictionary: English-French-Arabic, French-English-Arabic, Arabic-English-French. Karlsruhe, Verlag Versicherungswirtschaft e.V., 1971. 134, 64p. *Class No:* 368(038)=00

English

[3655]
BENNETT, C. Dictionary of insurance. London, Pitman, 1992. viii,385p. £13.99. ISBN: 0273033271.

Over 3500 fully cross-referenced insurance and insurance-related terms. 6 appendices include abbreviations, special terms, and useful addresses, plus specimen policies, p.373-85. No index. *Class No:* 368(038)=20

[3656]
BROWN, R.H. Dictionary of marine insurance terms and clauses. 5th ed. London, Witherby & Co. Ltd., 1989. 656p. £25. ISBN: 0948691433.

First published 1962.

About 4000 entries for terms, abbreviations and clauses. Concise definitions, and references to Acts. Cross-references. This edition includes summaries of the new sets of clauses which have been published by the Institute of London Underwriters, and comments on most of the individual clauses. *Class No:* 368(038)=20

[3657]
COCKERELL, H. Dictionary of insurance. 2nd ed. London, Witherby & Co. Ltd., 1987. viii,235p. £14.50. ISBN: 0900886501.

First published 1980 as *Witherby's dictionary of insurance*.

About 2000 terms, with brief (*c.*20-word) definitions. List of abbreviations precedes. Appendix. 'Institutions of insurance', p.207-35. 'Intended to help people who practice insurance or who need to read about it, to understand the terms and abbreviations they may encounter. It is not encyclopedic' (*Preface*). *Class No:* 368(038)=20

[3658]
DAVID, L.E. Dictionary of insurance. 5th rev. ed. Totowa, Littlefield, Adams & Co., 1983. xv,[i],338p. $24.95. ISBN: 0847673405.

First published 1959.

Over 3000 entries for terms and abbreviations, varying in length from 2 to 20 lines. Covers all fields of insurance, including life, health, property, liability, marine, pensions, surety, social, real estate, and municipal and federal regulating agencies. US slant. Includes a directory of State Commissioners of Insurance. An excellent source. *Class No:* 368(038)=20

[3659]
THOMSETT, M.C., *comp.* Insurance dictionary illustrated. Jefferson, N.C., McFarland, 1989. 243p. $29.95. ISBN: 0899503918.

Includes over 1000 words and phrases used in the insurance industry. Definitions are clear even though complex. Covers all types of insurance but the emphasis is on those most likely to be needed by consumers. Includes examples and cross-references. Includes a directory of addresses. Fewer terms than L.E. David's *Dictionary of insurance* (6th ed., 1984) and H. Rubin's *Dictionary of insurance terms* (1987). *Class No:* 368(038)=20

German

[3660]

STOCKS, K.-H. **Wörterbuch für alle Sparten der Versicherung.** Düsseldorf, Buchverlag Annaliese Rettinghausen, 1988. 2v. (634p.). ISBN: 3980155404, v.1; 3980155412, v.2.

Bande I: Deutsch-Englisch; Bande II: Englisch-Deutsch. Includes *c.*7500 terms, including *c.*200 technical words. Keywords (headwords) are followed by indented connections. *Class No:* 368(038)=30

French

[3661]

DINSDALE, W. A. *and* PEARCE, E A. **French for insurance officials,** with French-English and English-French glossaries. Jory, G. A., ed. 3rd ed. London, Chartered Insurance Institue, 1968. xii, 13-313p. £4.

Chapters 1-7: Introduction - Accident insurance - Fire insurance - Life insurance - Marine insurance - Aviation insurance - Reinsurance. Letters, policy forms, etc., in French. French-English technical terms (*c.* 1000) p.232-72, plus common abbreviations; English-French technical terms, p 277-313. Appendices: 1. Miscellaneous forms, p. 177-224. 2. Bibliography p.225-7. *Class No:* 368(038)=40

[3662]

LESOBRE, J. *and* SOMMER, H. **Lexique: risque, assurance, réassurance: français - anglais/américain, anglais/américain - français. Lexicon: risk, insurance, reinsurance.** 2nd é. Paris, Berger-Levrault, 1981. 396p. ISBN: 2701304059.

Includes 5300 terms and expressions, 1600 abbreviations, and 98 pages of technical tables. Part 1. English/American - French; French - English/American; part 2. Abbreviations and initials: (1. English and American; 2. French); part 3. Tables; part 4. Bibliography, p.387-394.

Class No: 368(038)=40

Spanish

[3663]

BROWN, A.C.S. *and* DINSDALE, W.A. **Spanish for insurance officials.** with Spanish-English and English-Spanish glossaries. London, Chartered Insurance Institute, 1957. vii,9-189 p. £4.

Chapters 1-5: Introduction - Accident insurance - Fire insurance - Life insurance - Marine insurance (p.9-135). Letter forms, policy forms etc., in Spanish. Appendix; bibliography, p.136-8. Glossaries: Spanish-English technical terms (*c.* 1500 words), p.142-65; English-Spanish, p.166-88. Very brief index of subjects. *Class No:* 368(038)=60

Arabic

[3664]

TREKY, T.H., *ed*. **Dictionary of insurance terms. In English and Arabic.** London, Witherby & Co. Ltd., 1985. 395p. £30. ISBN: 090088696x.

Gives the Arabic equivalent of various insurance terms, explaining them in simple clear language. Various usages are given. *Class No:* 368(038)=927

Biographies

[3665]

Who's who in world insurance Harlow, Essex, Longman; Chicago, St. James Press, 1991. xiii,280p. £135. (*Longman business information.*) ISBN: 0582085209, UK; 1558621687, US.

Details principal corporate insurance personnel, to provide insurance professionals with key contacts within the industry. Preceded by lists of abbreviations and company designations, is an A-Z listing of 3421 personnel, with name, current appointment, current employer, business address, telephone, telex, cable and fax numbers. Company index, p.229-60. Geographical index (countries A-Z. subdivided by personnel, A-Z), p.263-80. *Class No:* 368(092)

Worldwide

Yearbooks & Directories

[3666]

Financial Times world insurance year book, 1993. Harlow, Essex, Longman Group (UK) Ltd.; Detroit, Gale, 1993. xxi,580p. £125. ISBN: 0582217369.

Entries for 1143 companies and 50 associations in 84 countries, arranged geographically (Argentina ... Zimbabwe). Each country section is prefaced by selected statistics and details of leading national insurance associations and institutes. Information for each insurance firm is foundation, head office, directors, management, classes written, activities, capital, ownership, financial results (data for the last three years available). Preliminary sections are: Currency conversion rates and abbreviations - Company designations - Financial terms defined - Lloyds of London. Indexes of classes written (p.479-508), companies (p.509-576), international professional services, and advertisers (p.580). *Class No:* 368(100)(058)

[3667]

Lloyd's Nautical year book, 1993. Colchester, Essex, Lloyd's of London Press, 1992. 430p. illus., maps. £35. ISBN: 1850444293. ISSN: 09525394.

Published from 1892 - annually. Early title was *Lloyd's nautical year book and calendar.*

Contains current information relating to offshore and onshore ship management. Sections: The shipping industry (includes an annual review of developments and trends in all aspects of ship management) - Lloyd's and insurance (including marine insurance) - Legal/international regulations - General information (including shipping, insurance and legal terms) - A-Z index. *Class No:* 368(100)(058)

Great Britain

Yearbooks & Directories

[3668]

The Insurance directory and year book (*Post magazine green book***).** London, Bouverie Data Services, on behalf of Buckley Press Ltd., 1992. Annual. 3v. (xxx,1958p.). £235 for 3v.; v.1 & 2 £65 each; v.3 £145. ISBN: 090023637x, v.1; 0900236388, v.2; 0900236450, v.3; 0900236469, set. ISSN: 00740691.

First published 1842.

V.1: Insurance companies, Lloyd's syndicates, unit trusts; v.2: Brokers and intermediaries; v.3: Statistics. *Class No:* 368(410)(058)

[3669]

REW, J. *and* STURGE, C. **Macmillan directory of Lloyds of London.** London, Macmillan Press, 1989. 310p. tables. £60. ISBN: 0333491815.

Claims to be a directory explaining the working of Lloyds without technical jargon. Editorial review of the year, with tables and statistics, is followed by a directory of agencies, Lloyd's brokers, Lloyd's departments, Lloyd's associations, back-up services, and professional bodies. Index.
Class No: 368(410)(058)

Tables & Data Books

[3670]

ASSOCIATION OF BRITISH INSURERS. **Insurance statistics, 1988-1992.** London, the Association, 1993. 28p. tables. ISSN: 09503668.

First published for 1981-1985. Annual.

Long-term business (premiums and benefit - individual life insurance - individual pensions - individual annuities - health insurance - occupational pensions and life insurance schemes); General business (worldwide premium income - UK motor insurance - UK non-motor insurance - overseas insurance - marine, aviation and transport insurance - worldwide reinsurance - overall trading results - invisible earnings investments - family spending). Sources of further statistics. *Class No:* 368(410)(083)

Archives

[3671]

COCKERELL, H.A.L. *and* GREEN, E. **The British insurance business, 1547-1970:** an introduction and guide to historical records in the United Kingdom. London, Heinemann Educational Books, 1976. xiii,142p. illus. (pl.), tables.

The historical scope of business (chapters 1-5) - pt.2 A guide to insurance archives in the United Kingdom, p.76-132. 4 sections: 1. The archives of British assurance companies (brief inventory; business; linkages; records; locations); 2. Marine insurance underwriters: a guide to risk books; 3. Local insurance agents: a guide to research in the UK; 4. Insurance institutions: a guide. Further reading, p.133-4. Analytical index. *Class No:* 368(410)(093.20)

Laws

[3672]

IVAMY, E.R.H. **Dictionary of insurance law.** London, Butterworth, 1981. [3],166p. £9.95. (*Butterworth's professional dictionary series.*) ISBN: 0406603006.

Includes terms in general use in marine and non-marine insurance which have been legally defined, either in Statute or case law. Excludes general legal terms. When possible includes detailed extracts from relevant legal decisions to support the meaning given. Copiously cross-referenced.
Class No: 368(410)(094.1)

Social Security

Bibliographies

[3673]

Bibliographie universelle de securité sociale/World bibliography of social security. Genève, Association Internationale de la Sécurité Sociale/International Social Security Association, 1963-. no.1-. 2pa (previously quarterly). SFr.50pa. ISSN: 00061476.

*c.*3000 references pa. Arranged A-Z by country, subdivided by subjects, followed by international and regional sections, also subdivided by subjects. French, English, Spanish and German indexes refer to the numbered items. *Class No:* 368.4(01)

Dictionaries

Polyglot

[3674]

EUROPEAN PARLIAMENT. **Terminologie de la sécurité sociale ...** Luxembourg, the Parliament, 1974. [234]p. £2.50.

Replaces the 1967 ed., adding English and Danish terminology.

237 French-base terms, A-Z, with equivalents and indexes in Italian, English, German, Dutch and Danish.
Class No: 368.4(038)=00

Great Britain

Tables & Data Books

[3675]

Social security statistics, 1993. Department of Social Security. London, HMSO, 1993. viii,335p. illus. charts. tables. £25. ISBN: 0117821013.

First published for 1972. Annual. Replaces tables previously included in the annual report of what was then the Department of Health and Social Security.

In 8 sections: A. Income related benefits - B. Elderly - C. Unemployment - D. Incapable of work because of sickness - E. Disabled and carers - F. War pensions and industrial injuries - G. Mothers, widows and families - H. Other statistics. Data is for several years to 1992 or 1993. 4 appendices (*e.g.* 3. Useful publications - 4. Description of standard regions. *Class No:* 368.4(410)(083)

Laws

[3676]

O'HIGGINS, P. *and* PARTINGTON, M. **Social security law in Britain and Ireland:** a bibliography. London, Mansell Publishing Ltd., 1986. xxiv, 417p. £65. ISBN: 0720117941.

Includes more than 5500 items, arranged in broad subject categories, drawing together books, pamphlets and periodical articles published up to and including 1983. 4 main sections, all subdivided: 1. History of social security to 1946; 2. Social security since 1946; 3. Social security: International and European influences; 4. Miscellaneous works. Author index. 'The main fault ... lies in its format, and the resulting difficulty in being able to access information quickly'. (*Library review,* Spring, 1987, p.70).
Class No: 368.4(410)(094.1)

Unemployment Insurance

Great Britain

Official Records

[3677]

GREAT BRITAIN. Public Record Office. **Records of interest to social scientists: unemployment insurance 1911-1939.** London, HMSO, 1975. 268p. £4.50. (*Public Record Office handbooks, no. 16.*) ISBN: 0114400636.

8 chapters, documenting the policy changes of successive governments (Liberal government, 1908/1914 ... National government, 1931/1939). Royal Commission on Unemployment Insurance, 1930-32. Committees dealing with unemployment insurance. 9 appendices (*e.g.* 6. Statistics; 9. Précis of Acts of Parliament dealing with unemployment insurance). *Class No:* 368.44(410)(093.2)

37 Education

Education

[3678]

The International encyclopedia of education: research and studies. Huson, T. *and* Postlethwaite, T.N., *eds.* London, Pergamon Press, 1985. 10v. (6068p.). 500 illus. £1425. ISBN: 0080281192.

15,000 entries cover 17 major areas of education (adult education, counselling, curriculum, economics, administration, policy, educational technology, evaluation, higher education, national systems, pre-school education, education research, special education, teaching, vocational education, and industrial education). Strong US emphasis. Lengthy entries (*e.g.* 'Adolescence': 10½ cols., 8 sections, 8 references; 'Audiovisual equipment': over 8 cols., 7 sections, 3 references). Vol. 10 contains a classified list of entries, a list of contributors, author and subject indexes, and a list of major educational journals. *Supplementary volume 1* (1989. xxvi,864p. £108. ISBN 0080349749) is the first of a series intended to extend and update the work. *Class No:* 370

[3679]

—Encyclopedia of comparative education and national systems of education. Postlethwaite, T.N., *ed.* Oxford, Pergamon Press, 1988. 806p. 200 illus. £85. (*Advances in education.*) ISBN: 0080308538.

1200 entries, thematically organized. Detailed descriptions of the educational systems in 159 countries, and articles outlining major aspects of comparative education. Also based on the above. *Class No:* 370(031)

[3680]

—The International encyclopedia of educational technology. Eraut, M., *ed.* Oxford, Pergamon Press, 1989. xxii,654p. £60. ISBN: 0080334091.

Also based on the above. Provides state-of-the-art reports covering the whole field of educational technology from a largely international perspective. 114 entries. Contributors, name and subject indexes. *Class No:* 370(031)

Bibliographies of Bibliographies

[3681]

HOUNSELL, D., *and others.* **Bibliographic services in education:** a survey and analysis of secondary services in the United Kingdom. Lancaster, University of Lancaster, Centre for Educational Research and Development, 1978. vi,66p. diagrs., charts, tables. (*BL R & D report no. 5447.*)

Report to the British Library Research and Develpment Department on Project SI/CT/011.

Pt.1: Survey of recurrent secondary services in education; pt.2: Analysis of selected secondary services in education (detailed examination of *British education index, Research into higher education abstracts, Sociology of education abstracts,* and *Technical education abstracts.* Appendix 1:

....(contd.)

'An annotated list of British secondary services covering the literature of education', p.57-62 (33 indexing and abstracting services). *Class No:* 370(009)

[3682]

—BESTERMAN, T. Education - a bibliography of bibliographies. Totowa, N.J., Rowman & Littlefield, 1971. 306p.

Extracted from the author's *A world bibliography of bibliographies* (1965-66. 4v. and index).
Class No: 370(009)

[3683]

—HOUNSELL, D., *and others.* Bibliographic and information services in education: final report to the British Library R & D Department on Project SI/CT/011. Lancaster, University of Lancaster, Centre for Educational Research and Development, 1980. [6],110.[51]p. (*BL R&D report no. 5610.*)

7 sections: Personnel in education and training - ERIC feasibility study - An inventory of information services - Bibliographic services in education - the *Current index to journals in education* - The experimental information service - Concluding comments. References (2p.). 16 appendices. *Class No:* 370(009)

[3684]

SHANKS, D. Guide to bibliographies on education. Winnipeg, University of Manitoba, Department of Educational Administration and Foundations, Faculty of Education, 1982. 144p. Can$6. (*Monographs in education, 7.*)

947 entries arranged by the L Schedule of the Library of Congress classification scheme. An explicit introduction precedes the entries, which are for publications issued between 1964 and 1980 (continuing T. Besterman's *Education: a bibliography of bibliographies* (1971) which covered to 1964. Author, title and subject indexes. 'Though modest in size, this bibliography is a welcome addition to the field, both for its coverage and for its ease of use' (*Choice,* v.20(7), March 1983, p.960). *Class No:* 370(009)

Bibliographies

[3685]

ALTBACH, P.G., *and others.* **International bibliography of comparative education.** New York, Praeger, 1981. xvii,300p. $52.95; £26. (*Praeger special studies series in comparative education.*)

Includes an extensive essay on comparative education, followed by two bibliographies, a general one on the definition and development of the discipline and topics of major interest within the field, and one on education in various countries of the world, excluding the US. Over 3000 unannotated bibliographical citations of books and journal articles, arranged under broad categories or geographical areas. Cross-referenced subject index. *Class No:* 370(01)

[3686]
ALTBACH, P.G., *and others*. **Research on foreign students and international study:** an overview and bibliography. New York, Praeger, 1985. 403p. $35.95. (*The Praeger special studies series in comparative education.*) ISBN: 0030719224.

Published in co-operation with the Comparative Education Center at Suny, Buffalo.

Over 2800 entries arranged in 37 topical categories (*e.g.* economic aspects, academic performance, cross-cultural issues), subdivided by form (books, articles, dissertations, theses, government documents, reports). Most entries are annotated and the majority in English, published over the last 20 years. No. index. *Class No:* 370(01)

[3687]
AMBERT, A.N. *and* MELENDEZ, S.E. **Bilingual education:** a sourcebook. New York, Garland, 1985. 355p. $45. (*Garland reference library of social science, v.197.*) ISBN: 0824009551.

11 chapters: Bilingual education program models - Legal issues - English as a second language - Assessment - Reading - Bilingual special education - Bilingual vocational education - Program evaluation - Parental involvement and participation - Teachers and teacher training - Antibilingualism. Clearly written and readable. US slant. *Class No:* 370(01)

[3688]
BAATZ, C.A. **The Philosophy of education:** a guide to information sources. Detroit, Mich., Gale Research Co., 1980. 344p. $68. (*Education information guide series, v.6.*) ISBN: 0810314525.

Partly annotated bibliography of recent works from the mid-1960s to the mid-1970s, following a concise and well-written introduction. *Choice*, (v.18(5), January 1981, p.631) reports that annotations are not complete, nor are they uniform, but 'It is a real help to faculty and students alike...' *Class No:* 370(01)

[3689]
BERRY, D.M. **A Bibliographic guide to educational research.** 2nd ed. Metuchen, N.J., Scarecrow Press, 1980. 215p. £18.75. ISBN: 081081742x.

First published 1976.

772 annotated entries for books, periodicals, research studies, government publications, textbooks, tests, audiovisual materials, etc., arranged by type of publication (*e.g.* Instructional materials), subdivided by subject categories. Designed for students on education courses. Excellent subject index, and also author and title indexes.

A 3rd ed. was issued in 1990 (508p. $49.50. ISBN 0810823438). *Class No:* 370(01)

[3690]
Bibliographical aids and reference tools for the literature of education: a guide to works relating to education held by Southampton University Library. Balakrishnan, M. *and* Chadwick, C., *eds.* 6th ed. Southamptonn, University of Southampton Library, 1986. [4],54,[3]p. £5. ISBN: 0854322736.

The 4th ed. was published in 1978.

340 briefly annotated entries. 12 sections: Guides to the literature of education - Guides to British governmental and official publications - Directories and yearbooks, with a section on entry requirements and courses in adult and higher education - Dictionaries, encyclopaedias and surveys

.... *(contd.)*
- Indexing and abstracting periodicals - Guides to the research literature (research registers; surveys of research) - Research methods - Statistical methods - Statistics of education: guides and sources - Preparing research papers and publications, with a note on copyright - The law of education - Bibliographies - Tests: bibliographies. Name index. A basic user's guide. *Class No:* 370(01)

[3691]
BLAUG, M. **Economics of education:** a selected annotated bibliography. 3rd ed. Oxford, Pergamon Press, 1978. vi, 421p. £33. ISBN: 0080206273.

First published 1966.

2002 briefly annotated entries in 4 main sections: A. Developed countries (1. General surveys ... 4. Educational planning ... 8. The economics of health) - B. Developing countries - C. Bibliographies (items 1880-1937) - D. Items (65) received too late for classification. Includes French and German items. Brief evaluative section introductions. *Class No:* 370(01)

[3692]
British education index. 1954-.v.1-. Leeds, University of Leeds (previously London, Library Association, then British Library Bibliographic Division), 1954-58; 1968-. 3 quarterly issues and annual cumulation. £92pa. ISSN: 00070637.

An index of articles of permanent educational interest, published in a wide range of English-language periodicals. Arranged by author, with full bibliographical citations, then by subject. List of indexed journals. Also available online. Vendors: DIALOG. *Class No:* 370(01)

[3693]
Bulletin of the International Bureau of Education. Geneva, Unesco for the International Bureau of Education, 1926-. no.1-. Quarterly. SFr.65pa. ISSN: 10141715.

Formerly *International Bureau of Education bulletin*, later *Education documentation and information: bulletin of the International Bureau of Education*. Now incorporates the bulletin, and *Awareness list* and *Cooperative education abstracting service*.

Each issue is devoted to a particular theme. Thus, no.250, 63rd year, 1st quarter 1989: 'Computers in education: the shape of things to come; (p.7-88) including an annotated bibliography of 302 items in 5 sections (General reference - National policies - Training teachers and the development of human resources - Informatics as a subject for education and culture - Computerized ways and means for education). Index of authors and editors. *Class No:* 370(01)

[3694]
CLARKE, P.B. **Find out in education:** a guide to basic reference sources. 3rd ed. Glasgow, Jordanhill College of Education Library, 1979. v,92p.

First published 1976.

A selected annotated guide. 4 main sections: General reference sources - Bibliographies - Periodicals - Education research. 3 appendices (2. Select list of topics in education with their Dewey Classification; 3. How to compile a bibliography, with 22 references). An evaluative survey that covers many more general sources (*e.g.* general encyclopedias). No index, but detailed contents list. *Class No:* 370(01)

[3695]

—FOSKETT, D.J. 'The Literature and sources of education'. In *Use of social sciences literature,* ed. by N. Roberts (1977), p.149-75.

Succinctly covers many aspects of educational literature and organizations. *Class No:* 370(01)

[3696]

CLARKE, P.B. **Finding out in education:** a guide to sources of information. 2nd rev. ed. Harlow, Essex, Longman, 1993. ix,217p. £95. ISBN: 0582217970.

Annotated entries, arranged in form rather than subject sections. 29 sections in all: 1. Introduction ... 3. Guides to libraries ... 7-17 General reference sources - 18-20. Bibliographies - 21-24. Periodicals - 25-26. Educational research - 27. Conclusion - 28. Title index (p.194-211) - 29. Subject index (p.212-217). No author index. Author was formerly librarian at Jordanhill College of Education, Glasgow. *Class No:* 370(01)

[3697]

Contents pages in education. Abingdon, Oxon, Carfax, 1986-. Monthly. £276. $569 pa. ISSN: 02659220.

Covers over 700 international journals; *c.* 2000 contents pages in each annual volume. *Class No:* 370(01)

[3698]

Core list of books & journals in education. O'Brien, P. *and* Fabiano, E., *eds.* Phoenix, Ariz., Oryx, 1990. 125p. $39.95. ISBN: 0597745590.

Mainly limited to English-language imprint material. Entries have detailed annotations. 3 indexes: author/title; title; subject. *Class No:* 370(01)

[3699]

Education index. New York, H.W. Wilson, 1932-. v.1-. Monthly (except July and August), cumulates quarterly and annually (July-June). Service basis. ISSN: 00131385.

An index to *c.*350 selected educational journals, proceedings and yearbooks. A-Z order of subjects and authors, list of book reviews appended. Journals covered are predominantly US. Also available online. (Vendors: Wilsonline (EDI)) and on CD-ROM. *Class No:* 370(01)

[3700]

—Education literature, 1907-1932. Facsimile ed. New York, Garland, 1979. 12v. $40. ISBN: 0824037111.

Usefully precedes *Education index.* Over 44,000 references; separate volume of cumulated proper name and subject index. *Class No:* 370(01)

[3701]

HUMBY, M. **A Guide to the literature of education.** London, University of London, Institute of Education Library, 1975. vi, 142p. £1. (*Education libraries bulletin, Supplement 1. 3rd ed.*) ISBN: 0900008202.

Based on *A guide to the literature of education,* by S K. Kimmance (2nd ed., 1961),first published 1958. Aims 'not to provide a comprehensive bibliography, but to give selected examples of the various types of printed material to be found in an education library'(*Introduction*). 572 concisely and well-annotated entries, arranged in 15 sections: 2. Guides to the literature of education - 3. Bibliographies of education - 4. Educational research - 5. Encyclopedias of education - 6. Dictionaries of education - 7. Educational directories and yearbooks - 8. Educational organizations - 9. Educational periodicals (including indexing and abstracting services) - 10. Biographies in

.... (contd.)

education - 11. Official publications concerning education - 12. Education statistics - 13. School textbooks and other teaching aids - 14. Classification schemes for education - 15. Education libraries and information services. Index of authors and titles. *Class No:* 370(01)

[3702]

KENNEDY, J.R. **Library research guide to education:** illustrated research strategy and sources. Ann Arbor, Mich., Perian Press, 1979. x, 77p. illus., facsim. $25. (*Library research guides, 3.*) ISBN: 0876501153.

12 brief chapters, well illustrated, on research strategy (*e.g.* 6. Collecting current information; 11. Using other libraries). 'Basic reference sources for undergraduates and masters courses in education', p.57-74. Index of titles. US-slanted. *Class No:* 370(01)

[3703]

MONROE, W.S. **Bibliography of education.** New York, Appleton, 1897. (Reprinted Detroit, Mich., Gale, 1968). 228p. $35. ISBN: 0810333376.

A bibliography of 3200 books and pamphlets; restricted to books in English. According to the 1968 introduction by Dr. Cordasco, it 'continues to serve as a major initial source in education bibliography. *Class No:* 370(01)

[3704]

RAMSAY, P.G., *and others.* **Multicultural education:** a source book. New York, Garland, 1989. 177p. .$25. ISBN: 0824085582.

Theoretical, research and practical information related to the implementation of a multicultural education programme in pre-school and elementary school classrooms. Omits bilingual education. Each chapter reviews major issues, historical changes, and related research in its subject area and includes an annotated list of 30-50 titles. Includes literature published since 1976. US slant. ' ... a fine sourcebook ... '(*Choice* v.26(11/12), July-August 1989, p.1818). *Class No:* 370(01)

[3705]

UNITED STATES. Department of Health, Education and Welfare. Department Library, Washington. **Subject catalog.** Boston, Mass., G.K. Hall, 1965. 20v. (17,301p.). First supplement, 1973. 4v. (2,941p.).

424,700 photolithographed catalogue cards. Special strengths in education include historical materials on all levels, textbooks in all subject fields and grade levels through secondary school, and foreign titles'. *Class No:* 370(01)

[3706]

WOODBURY, M. **A Guide to sources of educational information.** 2nd ed., completely rev. Arlington, VA., Information Resources Press, 1982. xii,430p. facsims. £36.80. ISBN: 0878150412.

First published 1976.

636 annotated entries. 5 main parts (19 chapters): 1. Effective research - 2. Printed research tools (dictionaries, encyclopedias, thesauri; directories; yearbooks, monograph series, periodicals, news letters; bibliographies and review sources; statistical sources; abstracting, indexing and current awareness services) - 3. Special subjects (*e.g.* special education; tests and assessment instruments) - 4. Non-print sources (*e.g.* directory and institutional information sources; computerized retrieval sources) - 5. Follow-through (guides

....(contd.)

to routers). Well annotated. Analytical index. US-slant. 'The best guide to education's reference literature' (*Wilson library bulletin,* February, 1986, p.60). *Class No:* 370(01)

[3707]

—BUTTLAR, L.J. Education: a guide to reference and information souces. Littleton, Col., Libraries Unlimited, 1989. 258p. $35. (*Reference sources in the social sciences, series 2.*) ISBN: 0872876195.

Describes *c.*750 major sources of educational information from the elementary level to higher education. Arranged in 20 broad subject-orientated chapters, subdivided by type of material. Includes online databases, educational research centres and other organizations, and periodical titles, as well as printed sources. Annotations are evaluative and descriptive. Emphasis is on US works published since 1980. *Class No:* 370(01)

Encyclopaedias

[3708]

BLISHEN, E., *ed.* **Blond's encyclopedia of education.** London, Blond Educational, 1969. xi,882p.

'A-level' ... 'Zoning'; *c.*2150 entries, with numerous cross-references; *c.*150 contributors. Some articles carry short bibliographies (*e.g.* 'South Africa, Education in': 7 items). 6½ columns on 'School leaving age'. Includes biographies. Deals primarily with British educational practice, plus brief notes on other countries. 15 appendices (14. Educational journals - 15. Selected museums and art galleries). *Class No:* 370(031)

[3709]

DEJNOZKA, E.L. *and* **KAPEL, D.E. American educators' encyclopedia.** Revised ed. Westport, CT., Greenwood Press, 1991. xvii,597p. illus. $95. ISBN: 0313252696.

First published 1982.

Over 2000 articles arranged A-Z by subject. Covers all aspects of education and includes names as well as topics and terms most frequently used in elementary, secondary and higher education. Suggestions for further study follow most entries. Cross-references. Topical index. 27 appendices provide variety of tabular information. *Class No:* 370(031)

[3710]

The Encyclopedia of education. Deighton, L.C., *ed.* New York, Macmillan and the Free Press, 1971. 10v. (*c.*6000p.). $199 the set. ISBN: 0028953002.

About 1000 contributors. In more than 1000 articles it offers a view of institutions and people, of the processes and products, found in educational practice. 'The articles deal with the history, theory, research, and philosophy, as well as the structure and fabric of education' (*Preface*). Well documented ('Test reliability': v.9, p.143-53, with nearly a column of bibliography). The article on education bibliographies gives an 'excellent brief overview of bibliographies, indexes, abstracts, encyclopedias, directories, government publications' (*Wilson library bulletin,* v.46(4), December 1971, p.365-6). V.10 includes 'Guide to articles', p.117-228, and an index with *c.*50,000 entries. Strongly US-slanted. *Class No:* 370(031)

[3711]

MONROE, P., *ed.* **A Cyclopedia of education;** edited with the assistance of departmental editors and more than 1,000 individual contributors. New York, Macmillan Press, 1911-13. (Reprinted by Gale in 1969; available now from Omnigraphics Ltd.). 5v. (3928p.). illus. $425 the set. ISBN: 0810335379.

A scholarly, comprehensive encyclopedia with over 7000 signed articles of varying, but sometimes considerable, length, each with a bibliography. V.5 includes a subject index grouping articles under broad subject headings. Its date limits its usefulness, but many articles are still valuable in their own right and the work as a whole gives an excellent picture of early 20th-century educational thought in America. *Class No:* 370(031)

German

[3712]

Lexikon der Pädagogik. Willmann-Institut, München-Wein. Leitung der Herausgabe: Heinrich Rombach. Neue Ausg. Freiburg in Briesgau, Herder, [1970] -1971. 4v. (*c.* 2000 p.).

First published 1930-32; 2nd ed. 1960-64.

More international in scope than previous editions, although the viewpoint is Roman Catholic. Most articles carry bibliographies (*e.g.* 'Kuba': 21/3 columns; 11½ lines of bibliography). 'It is not an exhaustive dictionary of pedagogics, but contains selected entries in which foreign educational thinking figures as prominently as German. It has a triple reference system: cross-references to key terms selected as headings; cross-references between words in the entry texts and their headings; and cross-references at the end of the entries to headings dealing with a related subject' (*Bibliography, documentation, terminology,* v.13, No.1. January 1973, p. 39). General index of persons and subjects appended to v.4. A standard work. *Class No:* 370(031)=30

Handbooks & Manuals

[3713]

A Parents' guide to education. London, Fontana/Collins, 1986. 352p. £3.95. ISBN: 0006368069.

First published by Hodder & Stoughton in 1983.

In 6 chapters: 1. The educational system - 2. The pre-school child - 3. The primary child - 4. The secondary pupil - 5. Beyond sixteen - 6. Children with problems. Address and book list, p.335-340. Index, p.341-352. *Class No:* 370(035)

Dictionaries

English

[3714]

BARNARD, H.C. *and* **LAUWERYS, J.A.,** *comps.* **A Handbook of British educational terms** including an outline of the British educational system. London, Harrap, 1963. 210p.

'Primarily intended for readers in foreign or overseas countries who are interested in the British educational system and its institutions and history' (*Preface*). About 10-100 word definitions of *c.*1400 terms, including colloquialisms. Cross-references. Abbreviations, p.206-10. *Class No:* 370(038)=20

[3715]

BARROW, R. *and* **MILBURN, G. A Critical dictionary of educational concepts:** an appraisal of selected ideas and issues in educational theory and practice. 2nd ed. New York, St. Martin's Press; Hemel Hempstead, Herts, Harvester Wheatsheaf Publications, 1990. 350p. $43.95. £50. ISBN: 0807730580, US; 0745009190, UK.

Essay length entries analysing such major subjects as assessment, culture, emotional development, teacher effectiveness, development theory, knowledge, learning, curriculum, etc. References are attached to the longer entries. Cross references. Bibliography, A-Z by author. *Class No:* 370(038)=20

[3716]

COLLINS, K.T., *and others*. **Key words in education.** London, Longmans, 1973. [iii],240p.

Arranged A-Z (Abacus-Aberdare Report (1881) ... Youth service (references to 2 reports). Includes brief biographies. Cross-references. Appendix 1: The educational system in Great Britain - 2: Important Education Acts in England and Wales - 3: Important Education Reports since 1926 - 4: Education journals. *Class No:* 370(038)=20

[3717]

DEJNOZKA, E.L. Educational administration glossary. Westport, CT., Greenwood Press, 1983. xii,247p. $50.95. ISBN: 0313233012.

*c.*1400 terms in educational administration are defined. The glossary is supplemented by 15 appendices, including the American Association of School Administrators' code of ethics; a list of major school administration journals; the names of institutional members of the University Council for Educational Administration; and a listing of all nationally accredited school administration programs. *Class No:* 370(038)=20

[3718]

GORDON, P. *and* **LAWTON, D. A Guide to English educational terms.** London, Batsford Academic and Educational Ltd., 1984. xvii, 220p. £14.95. ISBN: 0713443758.

Aim is to provide concise definitions of those terms most likely to be encountered in current discussion on educational matters. Many entries have short well-chosen bibliographies for further reading. 'An outline of the educational system in England and Wales: 2½p,;' 'Landmarks in the development of English education since 1800': 6p.; 'Education acronyms': 5½p.; 'Ministers of education': 1¾p. '... this really is a good job, sensible and helpfully done' (*The Times educational supplement,* 18 May 1984, p.32). *Class No:* 370(038)=20

[3719]

HILLS, P.J., *ed*. **A Dictionary of education.** London, Routledge & Kegan Paul,1982. 5,284p. £15. (*Routledge education books*.) ISBN: 0710008716.

A 'conceptual dictionary' for students, teachers, administrators and the general reader. 2 parts: Part 1: Areas of education (brief articles on topics such as 'educational research', 'curriculum development', with references for further reading. Part 2 is the dictionary proper, with terms fully explained. *Class No:* 370(038)=20

[3720]

LAWTON, D. *and* **GORDON, P. Dictionary of education.** London, Hodder & Stoughton, 1993. viii,200p. £12.99. ISBN: 0340531797.

A guide to the language of education. In 3 sections: 1. Discussion of some key concepts - 2. The dictionary: an alphabetical list of definitions - 3. Acronyms and abbreviations. The dictionary incorporates recent changes, has short definitions from one or two lines to half a page (nearly a page for 'Local government acts'), and has cross-references. *Class No:* 370(038)=20

[3721]

PAGE, G.T. *and* **THOMAS, J.B. International dictionary of education.** London, Kogan Page, 1977. 381p. diagrs. £14.95. ISBN: 0850383013.

Over 10,000 entries, ranging from the fine points of curriculum development and educational research to the colloquialisms of the classroom and lecture theatre (*Introduction*). Brief definitions (maximum: *c.*150 words); numbered meanings. Very concise bibliographies; entries for international organizations and major national institutions and associations. Appendix of abbreviations, and of American honor societies, professional fraternities and sororities. British and US emphasis. *Class No:* 370(038)=20

[3722]

ROWNTREE, D. A Dictionary of education. London, Harper & Row; Totowa, N.J., Barnes & Noble, 1981. viii, 354p. £15.95 $22.50. ISBN: 0063181576 UK; 0389202630 US.

Over 3000 entries providing a guide to the intricacies of educational jargon in the US and UK. Includes brief entries on educationalists and descriptions of educational reports. Definitions are short, *c.*1-10 lines, and indicate US or UK usage. Cross-references. *Class No:* 370(038)=20

Theses

Bibliographies

[3723]

British education theses index (BETI), 1950-1980. Johnston, J.B.V. *and* Marder, J.V., *eds.* Leicester, Librarians of Institutes and Schools of Education, 1980. Microfiche 48X, with a full-size hard-copy introduction. £33. A thesaurus was published in l986 (l50p. £13.50. ISBN 090l92217x). *Class No:* 370(043)(01)

[3724]

—British education theses index. Thesaurus. Johnston, J.B.V. *and* Marder, J.V., *eds.* Leicester, Librarians of Institutes and Schools of Education, 1986. 150p. £13.50. ISBN: 090192217x.

Developed from the ERIC thesaurus for use with *British education theses index. Class No:* 370(043)(01)

Reviews & Abstracts

[3725]

Current index to journals in education. Phoenix, AZ., Oryx Press (previously New York, CCM Information Sciences Inc.), 1969-. v.1,no,.1-. Monthly. $235pa.; semi-annual indexes, $198. ISSN: 00113565.

Published in co-operation with the Educational Resources Information Center (ERIC) of the US Office of Education.

....(contd.)

Covers *c.*740 major education and education-related journals. About 2000 articles are indexed monthly. 4 sections: main entry section (using ERIC descriptors), with 3 indexes - subject, author and journal content. Has references to textbooks in each issue. More comprehensive, by far, than *British education index* and *Education index. Current index to journals in education: cumulated author index, 1969-1984* was published by Oryx Press in 1985 (2218p. $100. ISBN 0897742354). The on-line database ERIC (Washington, Educational Resources Information Center, 1966-), covering both periodical articles and reports, is updated monthly. *Class No:* 370(048)

[3726]
Educational administration abstracts. Beverley Hills, CA., Sage Publications, in cooperation with the University Council for Educational Administration, 1966-. Quarterly. $175; £134pa. ISSN: 00131601.

Previously *Educational abstracts.*

*c.*250 abstracts each issue of articles from more than 140 professional journals. Broad topical arrangement (*e.g.* personnel, curriculum, school-community relations, supervision, minority group relations, professional education, etc.). Cross-references. Author index.

Class No: 370(048)

[3727]
FRANCIS. 520. Bulletin signalétique. 520. Sciences de l'éducation. Paris, Centre National de la Recherche Scientifique: Centre de Documentation Sciences Humaines, 1947-. v.1-.no.1-. Quarterly. F.520pa. ISSN: 0223341x.

Previously *Bulletin analytique. Philosophie* (v.1-9, 1947-55, *Bulletin signalétique. 19: Philosophie, Sciences humaines* (1956-60), and *Bulletin signalétique. 20: Psychologie. Pédagogie* (in 19-24: *Sciences humaines. Philosophie* (1961-)), later as *Bulletin signalétique. 520. Sciences de l'éducation.*

*c.*4000 indicative abstracts and references a year. Classes: 01. History and philosophy of education - 02. Educational policy - 03. Planning and economics of education - 04. Educational organization - 05. Life-long education and employment - 06. Educational research - 07. Teaching methods - 08. Teaching aids - 09. Educational personnel - 10. School life - 11. School work, docimology, guidance - 12. Maladjustment - 13. Education and psychology - 14. Sociology of education. Cumulative list of journals searched. Indexes of concepts and authors. Available online (Telesystem, Questel) and CD-ROM. e *Class No:* 370(048)

[3728]
Multicultural education abstracts. Abingdon, Oxon, Carfax Publishing, 1982-. v.1,no.1-. Quarterly. ISSN: 02609770.

A current awareness service drawing on a wide range of international sources. Non-evaluative abstracts. *c.*400 abstracts pa, mainly of journal articles but includes some books. *c.*750 journal titles are scanned. Author and subject indexes to each issue, cumulated annually.

Class No: 370(048)

[3729]
Sociology of education abstracts. Abingdon, Oxon, Carfax Publishing Co., (previously Liverpool, Information for Education Ltd.), 1965-. v.1,no.1-. Quarterly. ISSN: 00380415.

*c.*600 indicative and informative abstracts pa, arranged

....(contd.)

under authors, A-Z. Includes abstracts of books and journal articles, *c.*400 journal titles being scanned. Author and subject indexes, cumulating annually. *Class No:* 370(048)

Periodicals & Progress Reports

Bibliographies

[3730]
COLLINS, M.E., comp. Education journals and serials: an analytical guide. Westport, CT., Greenwood Press, 1988. 355p. $49.95. (*Annotated bibliography serials: a subject approach series, no.12.*) ISBN: 0313245142.

An aid to selection of serials for library collections. Includes serials published abroad in English, and interdisciplinary journals with substantial coverage of education. Entries are numbered and grouped under broad headings. Annotations are in 2 parts: general topical areas covered and description of contents; they include starting date, frequency, price, publishers' address, circulation, and former titles. Features noted included index, book reviews, adverts, major indexes and databases that index the journal, and target audience. 'Well-organized, thoroughly indexed, and easy to read...' (*Choice*, v.26(1), September 1988, p.76). *Class No:* 370(05)(01)

Yearbooks & Directories

[3731]
World year book of education, 1994. London, Kogan Page, 1994. 260p. £32. ISBN: 0749410795.

First published 1932. From 1965 to 1974 issued by Evans Bros. Ltd.

Each issue is devoted to a special theme (1987 'Vocational education'; 1988 'Education for the new technologies'; 1989 'Health education'; 1994 'The gender gap in higher education') and reviews the nature and practice of health education in over 15 countries. *Class No:* 370(058)

Histories

Bibliographies

[3732]
HIGSON, C.W.J., ed. Sources for the history of education: a list of material (including school books) contained in libraries of the Institutes and Schools of Education, together with works from the libraries of the Universities of Nottingham and Reading. London, Library Association, 1967. x,196p. Supplement. (for 1965-74). 1976. x,221p.

Sections A-D cover books, textbooks and children's books published up to 1870, by periods; E: Government publications up to and including 1918. About 5500, British-slanted items in all. Detailed, analytical subject index; author index to government publications. The *Supplement* lists *c.*4000 items, with 22 locations, for sections F-J (covering the same periods as in the parent work). Subject index; author index to government publications.

Class No: 370(091)(01)

[3733]
McCARTHY, J.M. An International list of articles on the history of education published in non-educational serials, 1965-1974. New York, Garland, 1977. xxv,228p. $33. ISBN: 0824099095.

2817 references in 8 sections: 1. Ancient world and general - 2. Europe (p.5-93: General; countries, A-Z) - 3. Mid-East (General. Israel, Lebanon. Syria. Turkey) - 4. Africa (General; countries, A-Z) - 5. Asia - 6. Oceania - 7. South America - 8. North America (US: p. 149-201). Cross references. Author index. Complementary to Higson, in covering only periodical articles. *Class No:* 370(091)(01)

Worldwide

Encyclopaedias

[3734]
World education encyclopedia. Kurian, G.T., *ed.* New York, Facts on File, 1988. 3v. (1720p). illus., tables, charts, maps. $175. ISBN: 0871967480.

181 countries are divided into major, middle or minor according to the amount of information available, and arranged A-Z in each category. V.1. Major countries. Algeria - Hungary; V.2. Major countries; Iceland - Sri Lanka; V.3. Major countries; Sudan - Zambia. Middle countries. Minor countries. So far as information is available, the essays for each country include recent history, background, legal foundations, an overview, pre-primary and primary schooling, secondary education, higher education, non-formal education, the teaching profession, a glossary, and a brief bibliography. The aim is to compare and analyse the various education systems, but not to evaluate, criticize or judge them. 67 contributors. Appendices (I. Global education rankings; II. Global and regional bibliography). Index, p. 1685-1720. 'The strength of the encyclopedia lies in the consistency with which it presents its data'(*Reference books bulletin*, 1 November 1989, p. 722-3). *Class No:* 370(100)(031)

Handbooks & Manuals

[3735]
International handbook of educational systems. Chichester, Wiley, 1983-84. 3v. (738+906+854p.). illus. v.1: £35.95. v.2: £38. v.3. £38.90. ISBN: 0471900788, v.1; 0471900796, v.2; 0471902144, v.3.

V.1: *Europe and Canada,* ed. by B. Homes; v.2: *Africa and the Middle East,* by J. Cameron and P. Hirst; v.3: *Asia; Australia and Latin America,* by Robert Cowen and Martin McClean. Contain a wealth of valuable information concerning the education systems of 60 countries, including historical developments, social structure, economics. Systematically arranged so that comparisons between countries can be made. Statistical data and information on relevant legislation is included when available. *Class No:* 370(100)(035)

Developing Countries

Bibliographies

[3736]
CLAYTON, D. *and* JAMESON, E., *comps*. Bibliography of policy related education documents in selected countries in Africa, Asia, the Caribbean and the Pacific. 2nd ed. London, Overseas Development Administration, 1988. 2v.

V.1 Africa and the Caribbean; v.2. Asia and the Pacific. Arranged by countries, A-Z, under each region. Publications, mainly of the countries themselves, are arranged in 5 sections for each country: 1 Development plans - 2. Statistics, annual reports, yearbooks and directories - 3. Legislation and policy statements - 4. Reports of committees and commissions - 5. General education documents. Where applicable, a further section covering curriculum and syllabuses is added. A-Z by author in each section. List of locations at end of each volume. No index. *Class No:* 370(4/9-77)(01)

Europe

Histories

[3737]
BOWEN, J. A History of Western education. London, Methuen, 1972-81. 3v. (416p.;xxii,504p.;630p.). illus., maps. v.1. £35; v.2. £27.50; v.3. £32.50. ISBN: 0416161103, v.1; 0416161200, v.2; 0416161308, v.3.

V.1: *The ancient world: Orient and Mediterranean, 2000B.C.- A.D.1054* (1972); v.2: *Civilization of Europe, sixth to sixteenth century* (1975); v.3: *The modern West: Europe and the New World* (1981). A comprehensive account of theories, educational institutions and practices. Include bibliographies and analytical indexes in each volume. Scholarly, with many quotations from primary sources. *Class No:* 370(4)(091)

Great Britain

Bibliographies

[3738]
GREAT BRITAIN. HM Stationery Office. Government publications. Sectional list 2. Revised May 1988: Education and science. London, HMSO, 1988. 28p. *Gratis.*

Part 1: General, adult and further education ... curriculum and examinations - health and physical education - higher education - middle schools - primary education - safety - school meals ... secondary education - special education - statistics - teachers - youth - series lists - Assessment of Performance Unit. Pt.2: University Grants Committee. Pt.3: Legislation. Title index (excluding legislation). *Class No:* 370(410)(01)

Yearbooks & Directories

[3739]
The Education authorities directory and annual, 1991. 90th year of publication. Merstham, Redhill, School Government Publishing Ltd., 1993. lxxx,1290p. £58. ISBN: 0900640316. ISSN: 00709131.

First published 1909.

Various sections: Government departments, public offices, examination organizations - Local education authorities -

....(contd.)

Secondary and middle schools (p.156-559) - Teachers' centres - Further education - Polytechnics and Scottish central institutions - Institutes/colleges of higher education (teacher training) - Universities - Special schools and homes for the handicapped - Special community homes - Directors of social services - Educational psychological service - Careers centres - Public library authorities - Organizations concerned with education (p.1198-1249) - Education publishers and equipment suppliers - Commonwealth education departments and universities (p.1264-1280). Preliminary pages include: Index to local education authorities and secondary schools; General index (p.xi-xxvi); Index to place names; Index to advertisers; Buyer's guide; 'Coming events in education, 1991'.
Class No: 370(410)(058)

[3740]
The Education factbook: an A-Z guide to education and training in Britain. Pates, A., *and others*. London, Macmillan Press, 1983 (Reprinted 1986). ix, 268p. £14.95. (*Macmillan reference books*.) ISBN: 0333274695.

Main body of the work is a list of terms, arranged A-Z, and including names, initials, phrases, etc., each briefly described and explained. Length of entries varies from 2-3 lines to 2 columns. Address list, p.240-264. Book list, A-Z by author, p.266-268. *Class No:* 370(410)(058)

[3741]
Education year book, 1994. Harlow, Essex, Longman Group UK Ltd., 1993. li,742p. maps. ISBN: 0582091985.

First published 1939. Previously *Education committees year book.*

A detailed compendium in 29 sections, including: 3. County Council Education departments - 4. London district education departments - 8. Independent secondary schools - 11. Higher, further and vocational education - 17. Employment and careers - 18. Teachers' and other educational organizations - 24. Overseas education - 26. Broadcasting, audio-visual education and computers in education - 29. Buyers' guide. Index, p.720-741. Index to advertisers. *Class No:* 370(410)(058)

Government Publications

[3742]
ARGLES, M. and VAUGHAN, J.E. British government publications concerning education during the 20th century. 4th ed. Lancaster, History of Education Society, 1982. iii,60p. £4.50. (*Guides to sources in the history of education, no.7.*) ISBN: 0905090144.

First published 1963.

Running commentary and literature in closely divided sections. A. Short bibliography and book list of helpful works - B. Introduction - C. The central authorities: a historical note - D. United Kingdom Departments of State, etc., which issue or have issued documents relating to education - E. Official literature of education - F. Two special periods, 1900-1946; 1969-1980 - G. Reports: a list of popular (chairmen's) names and official titles - H. Short selective index of bodies and topics mentioned in the text and not listed under 'contents'. *Class No:* 370(410)(061.1)

[3743]
—ARGLES, M. British government publications in education during the 19th century. Lancaster, History of Education Society, 1971. 20p. £0.25. ISBN: 0950106437.
Class No: 370(410)(061.1)

Tables & Data Books

[3744]
Education statistics for the United Kingdom, 1993. Department of Education and Science, Welsh Office, Scottish Education Department, Department of Education for Northern Ireland, University Grants Committee. London, HMSO, 1993. 98p. tables. £13.50. ISBN: 0112708102.

First published 1967. Annual.

Contents: Population - Number of institutions - Finance - Teaching staff - Schools - Curriculum - Post-compulsory participation rates - Further and higher education - Qualifications and destinations. *Class No:* 370(410)(083)

Scotland

Bibliographies

[3745]
CRAIGIE, J., ed. A Bibliography of Scottish education before 1872. New ed. Scottish Council for Research in Education, 1984. 251p. £7.50. (*Publications of the Scottish Council for Research in Education, 60.*) ISBN: 0901116599.

First publisheed 1970, by University of London Press.

Draws on 24 library collections. 4 parts: 1. Works of general reference. General histories of Scottish education - 2. Acts of the Parliament of Scotland ... 3. Administration. Biographies. Curriculum ... Historical studies. Local history ... 4. The Scottish universities. Indexes of writers, subject, places. *Class No:* 370(411)(01)

[3746]
—CRAIGIE, J., ed. A Bibliography of Scottish education, 1872-1972. New ed. Scottish Council for Research in Education, 1984. 279p. £7.50. ISBN: 0901116629.

First published in 1974 by University of London Press.

Continues the above. *Class No:* 370(411)(01)

England & Wales

Histories

[3747]
ARMYTAGE, W.H.G. Four hundred years of English education. Cambridge, Cambridge University Press,1964. viii,353p.

Covers the period 1563-1963 in 12 chapters. Chapter notes, p.270-324; references to general sources used, p.vii-viii. Analytical index. Author was Professor of Education, University of Sheffield. *Class No:* 370(42)(091)

[3748]
LOWNDES, G.A.N. The Silent social revolution: an account of the expansion of public education in England and Wales, 1895-1935. London, Oxford University Press, 1937. xii,274p.

A standard work, dealing mainly with the development of elementary and secondary education during the period

....(contd.)

covered, but with a chapter on technical and further education. Extensive chapter bibliographies. *Class No:* 370(42)(091)

[3749]

—BIRCHENOUGH, C. History of elementary education in England and Wales, from 1800 to the present day. 3rd ed. London, University Tutorial Press, 1938. xxi,572p.

The most comprehensive history of elementary education for that period. *Class No:* 370(42)(091)

[3750]

—CUNNINGHAM, P. Local history of education in England and Wales: a bibliography. Leeds, University of Leeds, Museum of the History of Education, 1971 (Reprinted in paperback, 1976). 190p. £2.50. ISBN: 0904427056.

*c.*3000 entries, with very occasional explanatory notes), arranged by counties and towns. Appended sections on the Isle of Man and the Channel Islands. *Class No:* 370(42)(091)

[3751]

MACLURE, J.S. **Educational documents in England and Wales, 1816 to the present day.** 5th ed. London, Methuen, 1986. x,445p. £9.95. ISBN: 0416394701.

First published 1965.

Aim is to bring together selected extracts from the leading official documents which plot the development of a public system of education in England and Wales since 1816. A lengthy introduction precedes 65 excerpts arranged chronologically, with bibliographical details. Index of members of committees, assessors, etc. Short general index, p.437-439. '... an essential companion for those who wish to learn from primary sources of the most crucial developments in public education ... since the early years of the nineteenth century'. (*British journal of educational studies,* February 1987, p.89). *Class No:* 370(42)(091)

Biographies

[3752]

CHRISTOPHERS, A. **An Index to nineteenth-century British educational biography.** London, University of London, Institute of Education, 1965. xii,88p. £1.05. (*Education libraries bulletin. Supplement 10.*) ISBN: 0900008067.

Sections: 1. Collected biography (19 items) - 2. Individual biography (450 numbered items, under biographees, A-Z). Subject index. Dates and very brief notes on careers of biographees are given in section 2. Includes many analyticals (*e.g.* references to entries in DNB). No annotations. *Class No:* 370(42)(092)

Germany

[3753]

RUST, V.D. **Education in East and West Germany:** a bibliography. New York, Garland, 1984. 227p. $35. (*Reference library of social science, 202.*) ISBN: 0824090500.

Long introductory essay on the history of German education precedes a bibliography of over 1100 English-language books and periodical articles on all phases of German education, mainly regarding the period since 1945. Arrangement is in 11 general subject categories, and most

....(contd.)

items have annotations. Journal, name and subject indexes. '... a valuable annotated bibliography ...' (*Choice,* v.22(8), April 1985, p.1147). *Class No:* 370(430)

China

[3754]

FRASER, S.E. *and* HSU, K.-L. **Chinese education and society:** a bibliographic guide: the cultural revolution and its aftermath. White Plains, N.Y., International Arts and Sciences, 1972. (available Books Demand Unlimited). 204p. $53.50. ISBN: 0317102338.

14 sections, sections 4-14 concerned specifically with education. Entries usually annotated. Many of the items listed were originally written in Chinese; full references to translations. Favourably reviewed. *Class No:* 370(510)

Japan

[3755]

BEAUCHAMP, E.R. *and* RUBINGER, R. **Education in Japan:** a source book. New York, Garland, 1989. 300p. $42. (*Reference books in international education, 5. Garland reference liibrary of social science, 329.*) ISBN: 082408635x.

A successor to Herbert Passin's *Japanese education: a bibliography of materials in the English language.* (1971).

About 2000 entries arranged in 14 chapters, each preceded by an essay on the major themes and developments. Many entries are annotated. Historical emphasis is from the Tokugaswa period (1603-1867) forward, and a third are pre-1970. The main Western and Japanese scholars are cited. Subject index. 'Essential for graduate collection in international education' (*Choice,* v.27(1), September 1989, p.76). *Class No:* 370(52)

[3756]

TEICHLER, U. *and* VOSS, F. **Bibliography of Japanese education/Bibliographie zum japanischen Erziehungswesen: postwar publications in Western languages.** Munich, K.G. Saur, 1974. 294p.

Over 2000 entries, under 25 subject heads. Items are mostly in English, followed by German and French. *Class No:* 370(52)

India

[3757]

GREAVES, M.A. **Education in British India, 1698-1947:** a bibliography and guide to the sources of information in London. London, University of London, Institute of Education, 1967. xx,182p. maps. £1.50. (*Education libraries bulletin. Supplement 13.*)

1379 unannotated items. Books, pamphlets, reports and theses are listed under authors, A-Z; index to those items with specific subjects; select list of journals; manuscripts and records. A select list of reference works used in compiling the bibliography precedes. Continued in part by S.R. Mittal's *Bibliography of Indian education, 1947-1966,* a thesis accepted for the LA diploma. *Class No:* 370(540)

Islamic World

Bibliographies

[3758]
PANTELIDIS, V.S. Arab education, 1956-78: a bibliography. London, Mansell Publishing Co., 1982. xviii,552p. £45; $96. ISBN: 0720115884.

Lists over 5600 sources of information on education in the 21 countries of the Arab world. Arrangement is by country, then subject (Accountability - Administration and supervision - Adult education ... Bibliographies ... Women's education - Writing), not in A-Z order. Items are numbered and cover books, journal articles, dissertations, conference and working papers, government and non-government reports, information and other pamphlets, photographs and maps in books and articles. English-language materials only. Generous cross references. Items are *very* briefly annotated. Author, title and subject index (p.481-552) related to item numbers. 'It will become a standard in its field' (*Choice*, v.20(3), November 1982, p.409). *Class No:* 370(5.297)(01)

Africa

Bibliographies

[3759]
COUCH, M., *comp.* **Education in Africa:** a select bibliography. London, University of London, Institute of Education, 1962-65. 2v. (121p. xii, 116p.). v.1. £0.65; v.2. £1.05. (*Education libraries bulletin, supplement 5,9.*) ISBN: 0900008008 v.1; 0800008016 v.2.

1. *British and former British territories in Africa.*1962. x, 121p. 2. *French-speaking territories (former French and Belgian colonies); Portuguese and Spanish territories; Ethiopia and Eritrea; Liberia; and general African references, 1962-64.* 1965, xii, 116p. Pt 1 (*c.* 1,300 entries) excludes the Republic of South Africa. It is selected from the catalogue of the Library of the Department of Education in Tropical Areas of the Univ. of London, Institute of Education, and contains material listed to the end of 1961. General; then countries A-Z, with subdivisions (*eg.* Nyasaland: General - Primary - Secondary - Higher - Adult - Women and girls) and final chronological order. Pt.2. is similarly arranged; items starred were not available for checking by the compiler. Each pt. has a list of more than 200 periodicals cited. *Class No:* 370(6)(01)

Latin America

Bibliographies

[3760]
LAUERHASS, L. *and* **HAUGSE, V.L. Education in Latin America:** a bibliography. Boston, Mass., G.K. Hall; Los Angeles, CA., UCLA Latin American Centre Publications, University of California, 1981. xviii,431p. $63.50. (*UCLA Latin American Center Publications, Reference series, v.9.*) ISBN: 0816185166.

Designed as an introductory reference volume for research on education in Latin America in all its formal and nonformal aspects from its beginning in pre-Columbian times to the mid-1970s. 4 main sections: Latin America: general - Middle America and the Caribbean (subdivided by countries) - Spanish South America (subdivided by countries) - Brazil. 9866 numbered, unannotated entries with, for each division,

....(contd.)
sections on serials and reference sources; education in general; in-school education; out-of-school education and special programmes; educational planning and administration. Index, p.369-431. *Class No:* 370(729.99)(01)

USA

Bibliographies

[3761]
American education: a guide to information sources. Durnin, R.G., *ed.* Detroit, Mich., Gale Research Co., 1982. xvi,247p. $68. (*American studies information guide series, v.14.*) ISBN: 0810312654.

107 topical chapters (Art ... Utilization of teachers) each listing up to 40 books, mostly annotated, and in some cases relevant bibliographies. Includes a bibliographic essay with a list of the most influential books on education published in the last 200 years. 'On balance, the editor has done a good job of choosing the important books on most topics, although significant omissions are almost inevitable in a work of this scope' (*Library journal,* 14 January 1983, p.121). *Class No:* 370(73)(01)

Reviews & Abstracts

[3762]
Resources in education (RIE), 1975-. v.10, no.1-. ERIC, *comp.* Washington, Superintendent of Documents, Government Publishing Office. Monthly. $94pa. ISSN: 00980897.

Previously as *Research in education* (Washington, Education Resources Information Center (ERIC), US Office of Education, 1966-74.

About 15,000 digests pa of documents (largely US) in education, giving ERIC clearinghouse numbers/ED number cross-references, plus descriptors and identifiers. Subject arrangement in broad groups. Semi-annual indexes (subject, author, institution, type of publication).

The online database ERIC (Washington, Education Resources Information, 1966-), covers both reports and periodical articles, and is up-dated monthly. *Class No:* 370(73)(048)

Yearbooks & Directories

[3763]
KLEIN, B.T., *ed.* **Guide to American educational directories.** 7th ed. New York, Todd Publications, 1993. 350p. $75.

First published 1963. A 'spin-off' of the publisher's *Guide to American directories.*

Lists *c.*3000 US and Canadian directories, under *c.*100 subjects A-Z. Broad subject arrangement. Each entry of 30-50 words has title, brief description of contents, pagination, publisher's address and telephone number, and price. Title index. *Class No:* 370(73)(058)

Biographies

[3764]

OHLES, J.F. Biographical dictionary of American educators. Westport, CT. Greenwood Press, 1978. 3v. (1666p.). $65 each vol.; $150 for 3v. ISBN: 0837198941, v.1; 083719899x, v.2; 0837198968, v.3; 0837198933, set.

470 contributors. Biographical sketches of 1665 leaders in American education from the 1700s to the present day. Entries contain references to other sources (*e.g.* general biographical dictionaries; obituaries). Appendices group names by birth-places and dates, States and specializations. Usefully assembles data scattered elsewhere.
Class No: 370(73)(092)

Research Methods

Handbooks & Manuals

[3765]

Educational research, methodology, and measurement: an international handbook. Keeves, J.P., *ed.* Oxford, Pergamon Press, 1988. xxi,832p. £75; $125. ISBN: 0080365108.

Arranged in 4 sections (1. The methods of educational enquiry - 2. The creation, diffusion, and utilization of knowledge - 3. Measurement of educational research - 4. Research techniques and statistical analysis. Each section has an introductory essay. According to *Choice* (v.26(10), June 1989) 115 of the 139 articles are taken from the *International encyclopedia of education* with little updating.
Class No: 370:001.891(035)

Thesauri

[3766]

British education thesaurus. Marder, J.V., *ed.* Leeds, Leeds University Press, 1988. xii, [2],426p. £40. ISBN: 0853161445.

Alphabetical descriptor display, p.1-254, is followed by Rotated descriptor display, p.255-426. Preliminary items include 'Indexing and retrieval in the British education databases', 'Thesaurus construction and format' and 'How to search effectively using the British Education Thesaurus'.
Class No: 370:025.43

[3767]

EUDISED; multilingual thesaurus for information processing in the field of education. English version. Viet, J. *and* Slype, G.van. New ed. Berlin, Mouton Publishers, 1984. xix[307]p. ISBN: 3110098474.

Previous ed. published 1982. Also available in French, German, Spanish and Dutch.

Designed by the European Documentation and Information System for Education (EUDISED), using documentary language specially conceived for the processing of information in member states. An introduction precedes the structured alphabetical thesaurus, terminographs, list of terminographs, and rotated alphabetical thesaurus.
Class No: 370:025.43

[3768]

EUROPEAN CENTRE FOR THE DEVELOPMENT OF VOCATIONAL TRAINING (CEDEFO). Thesaurus of vocational training. Viet, J., *and others.* 2nd ed. Luxembourg, Office for Official Publications of the European Communities, 1988. xiii,234p. ECU12. ISBN: 9282580482.

First published 1986. Also available in 7 other languages.

An introduction precedes the structured alphabetical thesaurus, a list of 'top terms', a permuted index, and a list of 'candidate descriptors'. *Class No:* 370:025.43

[3769]

Unesco:IBE education thesaurus: a list of terms for indexing and retrieving documents and data in the field of education, with French and Spanish equivalents. International Bureau of Education. 4th rev. ed. Paris, Unesco, 1984. xvi,345 p. £9. (*Ibedata series.*) ISBN: 9231020617.

First published 1973.

Covers the field of 'education and training' for use in the computerized indexing and retrieval of educational information at an international level. *Class No:* 370:025.43

[3770]

—EDUCATIONAL RESOURCES INFORMATION CENTRE (ERIC). Thesaurus of ERIC descriptors. Houston, J.E., *ed.* 11th ed. Phoenix, AZ., Oryx Press, 1986. 640p. $65. ISBN: 0897741595.

A-Z list of descriptors - rotated descriptor display - hierarchical term display - descriptor group display.
Class No: 370:025.43

[3771]

—FOSKETT, D.J. *and* FOSKETT, J. The London education classification: a thesaurus/classification of British educational terms. 2nd ed. London, University of London, Institute of Education Library, 1974. [i], 165 p. (*Education Library bulletin. Supplement 6.*) *Class No:* 370:025.43

Information Services

[3772]

Directory of educational documentation and information services. Unesco. International Bureau of Education. 5th ed. Paris, Unesco, 1988. x,114p. ISBN: 9230025186.

In 4 sections: 1. National services - 2. Regional services - 3. International services - 4. Other member institutions. Data for each service include name (official and translated); address; country; year of creation; parent organization; present head; size of staff, type of activities; people served; services given; fields covered, size of collection; methods of data processing; classification systems; audio-visual material; reprographic services; periodical publications. Within the 4 sections, the organizations are arranged A-Z by country. Entries in English, French or Spanish; title page and preliminaries in all 3 languages. *Class No:* 370:061:025.5

Research Projects

[3773]

Review of educational research. Washington, American Educational Research Association, 1931-. Quarterly (previously 5pa). $46pa (institutions); $37pa (individuals). ISSN: 00346543.

Each issue consists of lengthy, well-documented

....(contd.)

contributions on topical themes (until June 1970 articles on 15 major themes were updated triennially).
Class No: 370:061:061.62.005

[3774]
SACHS, M. EUDISED R & D bulletin, no.1,1976-.
Quarterly. Munich, K.G. Saur, for EUDISED, Council of Europe. £55pa. ISSN: 03787192.

Each issue contains *c*.250 reports on current or recently completed projects in the field of educational research and development. Also available online.
Class No: 370:061:061.62.005

Encyclopaedias

[3775]
MITZEL, H.E., *and others, eds.* **Encyclopedia of educational research.** 5th ed. London, Collier Macmillan; New York, Free Press, 1982. 4 v. (2126 p.) illus. £315. ISBN: 0029004500.

First published in 1941. Sponsored by the American Educational Research Association.

Presents a critical synthesis and interpretation of reported research in the field. 256 lengthy articles by 300 specialists, with extensive bibliographies (*e.g.* 'Bilingual education': 18 cols., with 'see also' references and 39 bibliographical references; 'Computer-based education': 29 cols. in 15 sections, with 'see also' references and including 7½ columns of bibliographical references. Cross references. ' ... an essential purchase for libraries serving students and professionals in education' (*Library journal*, 1 January, 1983, p.42).

A 6th ed. was issued in 1992, edited by M.C. Alkin, with 257 new and revised articles, and suggestions for further reading (4v (1606p). $330. ISBN 0029004314).
Class No: 370:061:061.62.005(031)

[3776]
—Handbook of research on social studies teaching and learning. Shaver, J., *ed.* New York, Macmillan, 1991. 603p. $63. ISBN: 0028957903.

A project of the National Council for the Social Studies modelled on the aging *Encyclopedia of educational research* (*qv*). 53 topical chapters. Appended bibliographies.
Class No: 370:061:061.62.005(031)

Women

Developing Countries

Bibliographies

[3777]
KELLY, D. H. Women's education in the Third World - an annotated bibliography. New York, Garland, 1989. 478p. $52. (*Reference books in international education, 5. Garland reference library of social science, 544.*) ISBN: 0824086341.

1200 annotated entries, mainly from 1970 onwards, including journal articles, monographs, chapters of books, arranged in 15 topic groups, subdivided geographically. Cross-references. Excellent introduction and introductory essays to each topic. Items mainly in English, but do include

....(contd.)

some Spanish, French, Portuguese and German publications. Author and geographic indexes. *Class No:* 370-0055.2(4/9-77)(01)

Education Theory

[3778]
DUFOUR, B., *ed.* **New movements in the social sciences and humanities.** London, M.T. Smith, 1982. xii,287p. £13.50. ISBN: 0851171931.

Surveys new developments in the study and teaching of the whole range of the subjects and also interdisciplinary areas. 19 chapters in 2 parts: Part 1. The social sciences in higher education: academic developments in the subjects; pt.2. The social sciences and humanities in secondary education: the subjects in the schools. References, p.237-260. arranged by chapter. Further reading and useful addresses, p.261-284. Notes on the contributors, p.285-287. *Class No:* 370.01

[3779]
HILGARD, E.R. *and* **BOWER, G.H. Theories of learning.** 5th ed. Englewood Cliffs, N.J. Prentice-Hall, 1981. 640p. illus. $41; £43.85. ISBN: 0139144323.

First published 1948.

A scholarly introduction to the major current theories of learning. Extensive bibliography. *Class No:* 370.01

[3780]
—CURTIS, S.J. *and* BOULTWOOD, M.E.A. A Short history of educational ideas. 5th ed. London, University Tutorial Press, 1978. x,685p.

4th ed. published 1965.

21 chapters, each with 'suggestions for further reading'. Chapter 17: 'John Dewey (1859-1952). Footnote references. Index of names and titles mentioned in the text.
Class No: 370.01

Religious Education

Bibliographies

[3781]
HUNT, T.C. *and* **CARPER, J.C. Religious colleges and universities in America:** a selected bibliography. New York, Garland, 1988. 374p. $54. (*Garland reference library of social science, 422.*) ISBN: 0824066480.

Arranged in 24 chapters, the first one having *c*.400 annotated entries on religion and higher education, as well as government aid to, and regulation of church-affiliated institutions. The following 23 chapters are organized by denomination, with *c*.1900 partially annotated entries. 35 contributors. Index to topics and individual institutions. 'No other book approaches this in coverage of the subject'. (*Choice*, v.26(6), February 1989, p.920). A companion work is *Religious schools in America: a select bibliography*, by T.C. Hunt and others (1986. 416p. $47. 0824085833).
Class No: 370.014.52(01)

Dictionaries

[3782]
SUTCLIFFE, J.M., *ed.* **A Dictionary of religious education.** London, SCM Press, in association with The Christian Education Movement, 1984. xvi,[1],376. £14.95. ISBN: 0334019680.

....*(contd.)*

A guide to religious education around the world, concentrating 'on methods of teaching rather than the content of what is taught' (*Preface*). Lengthy signed entries of ¼ to 3 pages, each having a short bibliography. Select bibliography, p.373-374. Name index, p.375-376. *Class No:* 370.014.52(038)

Educational Psychology

Bibliographies

[3783]
BAATZ, O.K. *and* BAATZ, C.A., *eds*. **The Psychological foundations of education:** a guide to information sources. Detroit, Mich., Gale Research Co., 1981. 481p. $68. (*Educational information guide series, v.10.*) ISBN: 0810314673.

Topical arrangement in 9 chapters; within each chapter the authors include objective; curriculum design; the role of learners, parents, teachers and schools; process, structure and methods of teaching and learning; theory, research sources, and teacher education and preparation. Many entries have descriptive and evaluative annotations. Author, title and subject indexes. *Class No:* 370.015.3(01)

Dictionaries

[3784]
HARRÉ, R. *and* LAMB, R., *eds*. **The Dictionary of developmental and educational psychology.** Oxford, Basil Blackwell Ltd., 1986. xi,271p. £25. ISBN: 0631146032.

Based on material from *The encyclopedic dictionary of psychology* (1983), material being selected and up-dated, bibliographies revised and new entries added, and including more biographies. 97 contributors. Short bibliographies follow most entries. Cross-references. 'Absence from school and truency': 6 cols., 16 references in bibliography; 'Freud, Sigmond': 6½ cols., 15 references; 'Ontogenetic sequence': ¼ col. *Class No:* 370.015.3(038)

Teachers & Teaching

Bibliographies

[3785]
HAYWOOD, P.G., *comp*. **A Bibliography of adult teaching, psychology and research:** a sourcebook. Nottingham, University of Nottingham, Department of Adult Education, 1981. [2],48p. £1.50. ISBN: 0902031678.

Unannotated bibliography on student motivation and learning application in 4 sections: 1. a. General works; b. Mature students - 2. Teaching methods and evaluation (subdivided, A-E) - 3. University and adult education - 4. Education in retirement. *Class No:* 371(01)

Encyclopaedias

[3786]
The International encyclopedia of teaching and teacher education. Dunkin, M.J., *ed*. Oxford, Pergamon Press, 1987. 900p. £65. (*Advances in education.*) ISBN: 008030852x.

Based on *The International encyclopedia of education: research and studies*, ed. by T. Huson and T.N. Postlethwaite (1985) (*qv*).

2000 literary references, thematically organized in 124 articles on all aspects of the subject. *Class No:* 371(031)

Great Britain

[3787]
Treasure chest for teachers: services available to teachers and schools. 12th ed. Kettering, Northants., The Teachers Publishing Co. Ltd., [1988]. [4],204p. £3.50. ISBN: 0900642351.

First published 1960.

5 parts: 1. Societies and associations providing services and materials for teachers and schools (p.2-56; data; name & address; secretary; subscription; activities; aims) - 2. Materials and services relating to individual countries from embassies, legations and bodies for the promotion of travel and good relations - 3. Commercial, industrial and nationalized concerns providing services and materials for teachers and schools - 4. Places to visit (A-Z under country headings) - 5. Educational equipment manufacturers and suppliers. Classified index to parts 1-3 (p.186-194). General index, mainly of organizations, p.196-204. *Class No:* 371(410)

Education & Training

[3788]
University courses in education open to students from overseas, 1990-91. London, University Council for the Education of Teachers, 1989. 156p. £3.75. ISBN: 0903509121.

Lists advanced courses available in United Kingdom universities, and short courses for teachers, identifying those unikversities that offer tailor-made courses. *Class No:* 371:377.8

Teaching Materials

[3789]
Audiovisual and microcomputer handbook: the SCET guide to educational and training equipment. Henderson, J. *and* Humphreys, F., *eds*. 4th ed. London, Kogan Page, 1983. 160p. £12.95. ISBN: 0850387817.

First published 1980.

A products directory for equipment, software, services, etc., giving names, addresses and telephone numbers. Also listings of training and information organizations, professional organizations, film libraries, professional and trade journals, a selective bibliography (p.118-129), and a microcomputer supplement. *Class No:* 371.64/.69

Bibliographies

[3790]

El-Hi textbooks and serials in print: including related teaching materials, 1993. New York, Bowker, 1993. 1555p. $133. ISBN: 0835233448. ISSN: 00000825.

First published 1969. Annual.

Bibliographic information on *c.*30,000 texts, text series, reference and professional books, arranged by subject. Indexed by author, title and series. *Class No:* 371.64/.69(01)

Yearbooks & Directories

[3791]

Educational media and technology yearbook, 1993. v.19. Englewood Cliffs, Col., Libraries Unlimited, 1993. 380p. $60. ISBN: 1563081539. ISSN: 87552094.

First published 1973. Annual.

Provides an up-to-date overview of the subjects, including information on professional associations, graduate programmes, foundations and funding sources. *Class No:* 371.64/.69(058)

Audio-Visual Aids

[3792]

COPPEN, H.E., *comp*. **Survey of British research in audio-visual aids, 1945-71.** 3rd ed. London, National Committee for Audio-Visual Aids in Education, Educational Foundation for Visual Aids, 1972. iii,271p. £1.50. Supplements 1-5: £0.70-£1.50.

First published 1965.

Bibliography is in 10 sections: 1. Films - 2. Still projected media ... 8. Television - 9. Programmed learning and teaching machines - 10. Unclassified. Abstracts are similarly grouped. *Class No:* 371.67

Bibliographies

[3793]

WICKS, P. 'Audio-visual aids in education'. In *British book news,* May 1988, p.340-343.

A book survey on the subject, including a list of 18 book titles, some free booklets, and 5 periodical serial titles. *Class No:* 371.67(01)

Education Technology

[3794]

International yearbook of educational and training technology, 1991. Osbourne, C., *ed*. 9th ed. London, Kogan Page, in association with the Association for Educational and Training Technology, 1991. Annual. 508p. ISBN: 0749403780. ISSN: 03709732.

First published in 1976. Previously as *APLET yearbook of educational and instructional technology, 1972/73* (1972).

Arranged in 4 parts: 1. International and regional centres of activity - 2. Centres of activity in the United Kingdom - 3. Centres of activity in the United States (by State, A-Z) - 4. Centres of activity worldwide (by country, A-Z). Each section lists organizations actively involved in the development of educational and training technology and includes addresses, telephone and telex numbers, contact names, area of interest, details of current and future research and development projects, main services offered, keywords

....(contd.)
summarizing the organization's activities, and recent publications by staff or personnel. Index of institutions. *Class No:* 371.68/69

Dictionaries

English

[3795]

ELLINGTON, H. *and* **HARRIS, D. Dictionary of instructional technology.** London, Kogan Page; New York, Nichols Publishing Company, 1986. 189p. illus. £15.95; $34.50. (*AETT occasional publication, no.6.*) ISBN: 1850910723, UK; 0893972436, US.

Aims to be a comprehensive glossary of the most important terms that educational and training technologists are liable to come across in their daily work. Includes both British and US terms, as well as terms used in other English-speaking countries. Over 2800 terms from instructional technology, educational psychology, statistics, film & TV production, photography, reprography, computing and information technology. Many cross-references. *Class No:* 371.68/69(038)=20

French

[3796]

Glossary of educational technology terms. Methods, Materials and Techniques of Education Section, Unesco, for the International Bureau of Education. 2nd. ed. rev. & enl. Paris, Unesco, 1988. 263 p. F60 £9. ISBN: 9230025178.

First published 1984.

Groups in one volume the terms related to educational technology. English-French edition, with each term defined in both languages. (English-Spanish and English-Russian editions are also available). *Class No:* 371.68/69(038)=40

Reviews & Abstracts

[3797]

Educational technology abstracts. Abingdon, Oxon, Carfax Publishing Company, 1985-. 6pa. £45; $120pa. ISSN: 02663368.

Provides *c.*900 indicative abstracts pa from a wide range of international journals and books. About 3400 journals scanned. Arrangement is by broad subject groups: Design and planning - Teaching methods - Instructional media - Instructional resources - Learning - Assessment and evaluation. List of journals covered. Author and subject indexes. *Class No:* 371.68/69(048)

Games & Simulators

[3798]

BELCH, J., *ed*. **Contemporary games:** a directory and bibliography covering games and play situations or simulations used for construction and training by schools, colleges and universities, government, business and management. Detroit, Mich, Gale Research Co., 1973-74. 2v. (560p.; 408p.). v.1: $110; v.2: $98. ISBN: 0810309688, v.1; 0810309696, v.2.

v.1: Directory; v.2: Bibliography. V.1 lists and describes *c.*900 games, under titles A-Z, with references. V.2 has 2375 entries in 3 main subject groups. *Class No:* 371.69

[3799]

GIBBS, G.I. Dictionary of gaming, modelling & simulation.
Beverly Hills, CA., Sage Publications, 1979 (Available from
Books Demand UMI). 159p. illus. $43.50. ISBN:
0317110195.

Provides illustrations to bring out the meanings of some
terms, plus mathematical formulae for the many statistical
tests included. 'A small, attractive work' (*Choice,* v.17(1),
March 1980, p.48). *Class No:* 371.69

Schools

Bibliographies

[3800]

BURGESS, R.G. 'Studying schooling'. In *British book news,*
April 1988, p.254-7,259.

A book survey in 4 sections: Basic texts - Social and
political context - Studies of schools and classrooms - Studies
of curriculum and assessment. Includes a bibliography of 75
books. *Class No:* 373(01)

[3801]

The School administrator's resource guide. Clay, K., *ed.*
Phoenix, AZ., Oryx Press, 1988. viii,104p. $22. ISBN:
0897744462.

An annotated bibliography of 548 entries, arranged in 9
overlapping chapters. Document format (journal articles,
microfiche documents, books, dissertations) relating mainly
to 1982-1987. Author, subject and title indexes. '... the best
and most current thinking in the field of school
administration' (*Reference books bulletin,* 1 May, 1988).
Class No: 373(01)

Dictionaries

[3802]

GORTON, R.A., *and others, eds.* **Encyclopedia of school
administration & supervision.** Phoenix, AZ., Oryx Press,
1988. 352p. $74.50. ISBN: 089774232x.

Intended for administrators in elementary and secondary
schools. 300 practical or theoretical topics arranged A-Z by
subject. Entries are signed, average length is one page,
include cross-references and bibliographies of up to 3 books
or journal articles. 200 contributors. 'A guide to related
topics' groups titles of individual articles under broader
headings. *Class No:* 373(038)

Reviews & Abstracts

[3803]

School organization and management abstracts. Abingdon,
Oxon, Carfax, 1982-. V.1(1)-. Quarterly. £112. ISSN:
02612755.

In 3 sections: Abstracts of journal articles: Abstracts of
books; Abstracts of theses and dissertations. Aims to focus
particularly on the organization and management of the
school as a complex institution. Journals covered (*c.* 200)
are listed in each issue. Author and subject indexes, which
are cumulated and bound in the final issue of each volume.
Class No: 373(048)

Great Britain

Yearbooks & Directories

[3804]

**The Gabbitas, Truman & Thring guide to boarding schools
and colleges, 1988/89.** Henderson, M., *ed.* Plymouth,
Northcote House, 1988. 374p. £8.95. ISBN: 1869863070.
ISSN: 0951872x.

First published 1987/88.

Includes over 900 independent and state boarding schools,
arranged in 5 sections: Pre-prep and preparatory schools -
Senior independent schools - State maintained boarding
schools - Boarding at 16 and over - International schools in
the UK and overseas. A guide for parents, which also
contains a number of articles contributed by experts.

A 7th ed. was published by John Catt in 1993 for 1994,
edited by D. Bingham. (370p. 130 illus. 17 maps. £9.95.
ISBN 1869863453). *Class No:* 373(410)(058)

[3805]

Independent schools yearbook, 1993-94. boys' schools -
girl's schools - co-educational schools and and preparatory
schools. 87th year. London, A. & C. Black, 1993. Annual.
400p. £19.99. ISBN: 0713637501.

Prior to 1992-93 edition, separate volumes for girls'
schools and for boys' schools, co-educational schools and
preparatory schools.

Full details of all the schools in the Headmasters
Conference, Girls' Schools Association schools.
Class No: 373(410)(058)

Biographies

[3806]

The Schools' who's who, 1987. 1st ed. Ayr, Carrick
Publishing, 1986. [3],187p. £20. ISBN: 0946724164.

Aims to provide a comprehensive guide to key figures in
secondary education throughout the UK. Includes
biographies of almost 2000 headmasters, representing the
most prominent schools. Arrangement is A-Z by surname
and includes details of professional career and personal
background and interests. Information is based on
information supplied by the respondents themselves.
Class No: 373(410)(092)

USA

Yearbooks & Directories

[3807]

Private schools of the United States. Council for American
Private Education (CAPE) Schools. Shelton, CT., Market
Data Retrieval, 1988. 2v. $75. ISBN: 0897705025, v.1;
0897705033, v.2.

Information on 15,000 elementary and secondary private
schools, members of 13 diverse national private school
associations. The first vol. lists the schools A-Z by State,
subdivided A-Z by school name. All entries have school
name, address, telephone no., grades, principal's name and
enrollment; some entries include more specific information.
The second vol. has indexes to schools by association
membership and by grade level, and a complete A-Z listing
of schools. *Class No:* 373(73)(058)

Libraries

[3808]

HERRING, J.E. **School librarianship.** 2nd ed. London, Clive Bingley Ltd., 1988. xii,81p. £11.95. ISBN: 0851574238.

A general survey of the place of school librarianship within education, management, organization and the provision of information. Bibliography, p.78-80, A-Z by author. Index, p.81. *Class No:* 373:061:026/027

Catholic Schools

Handbooks & Manuals

[3809]

Catholic education: a handbook. 12th ed. London, Catholic Education Council for England and Wales, 1984. £4. ISBN: 0950156248.

Basically a 'General list of schools by diocese and local education authorities' (p.25-149), preceded by an index. Appended, lists of Catholic boarding schools, special schools for handicapped pupils, and community homes (providing educational and training facilities). *Class No:* 373:283(035)

Primary Schools

England & Wales

[3810]

The Routledge compendium of primary education. Campbell, R.J., *ed.* London, Routledge & Kegan Paul, 1988. x,250p. £6.95. ISBN: 0415002206.

Designed as a guide and reference source to the theory, practice and policy in primary education. Part 1 consists of 14 extended analyses and discussions of the main ideas in the field, such as classroom processes, home-school relationships, and children's development and learning. Part 2 is a glossary, including definitions of complex or controversial ideas; a list of 'Further reading', and outlines of important reports, surveys, Education Acts, and leading figures in primary education. *Class No:* 373.3(42)

Secondary & Sixth Form Schools

Great Britain

[3811]

The Parents' guide to independent schools, 1989/90. Tyrrell, C., *ed.* 9th ed. Maidenhead, Berks., SFIA Educational Trust, 1989. 2v. in 1. (990p.+44p. of maps). ISBN: 0906695139.

First published 1981.

V.1 consists mainly (p.77-893) of nearly 1300 school profiles; arranged by countries and counties. Data on each school: type (*e.g.* girls - board; day); name of head; entry; curriculum; reports and consultation; leavers; sports; activities; religious service; comment. 44 coloured maps. Preliminary 14 sections deal with the independent school system, choice of school, schools for children with special needs, abilities, and disabilities; glossary. V.2, largely tables, reviews and details schemes designed for the financing of school fees. Tables 895-955) of comparative school details, supporting the school profile in v.1. Index of school types; index of schools, by categories; index of

....(contd.)

schools, by religious denominations.

1993-94 edition (1993. 902p. £31.95. ISBN 090669518x).
Class No: 373.5(410)

Eire

[3812]

EIRE. Department of Education. **Liosta a iarbhunscoileanna (List of post-primary schools). 1987-88.** Dublin. Stationery Office, 1988. . £2.25. *Class No:* 373.5(417)

Adult Education

Bibliographies

[3813]

FRENCH, J. **Adult literacy:** a source book and guide. New York. Garland, 1987. 435p. $58. (*Garland reference library of social science, 346. Sourcebooks on education, 14.*) ISBN: 0824085744.

A literature review precedes 591 numbered and annotated entries for books, journal articles, documents, federal and state monographs published in the last five years. Arrangement is by topic, subdivided A-Z by author. Author and subject indexes. US bias. 'Informative, easy to use, and more comprehensive than other literary bibliographies ... ' (*Choice* v.25(6),February 1988, p.886). *Class No:* 374.7(01)

[3814]

HAYWOOD, P., *comp.* **Bibliography of comparative adult education:** a source book. 2nd ed. Nottingham, University of Nottingham, Department of Adult Education, 1983. xi,203p.(spiral binding). £12.50 ISBN: 0902031686.

First published 1981.

A subject index (p I-XI) precedes the main text, which is arranged geographically (General and international - Africa - Americas - Asia - Australasia - Europe). 2467 unannotated entries in all, mainly related to 1960-. Includes 5 supplements. *Class No:* 374.7(01)

Handbooks & Manuals

[3815]

DRODGE, S. **Adult education.** Newcastle-under-Lyme, AAL Publishing, 1988. [2],53p. £6. ISBN: 0900092696.

Sections: Information about adult classes - Providing resources for adult classes - Adult basic education - Provision for independent learners - Supporting open learning packages - Education guidance services - Twenty-five practical ways to work with adult learners - References and further reading (p.52-3). *Class No:* 374.7(035)

[3816]

STEPHENS, M.D., *ed.* **International organizations in education.** New York, Routledge, 1989. 165p. $42.50. ISBN: 0415021839.

A collection of 10 authoritative essays dealing with various aspects of organizations involved in adult education on an international scale, including 2 overviews, 3 articles on

....(contd.)

broadly international organizations, and 5 essays on regional organizations. Essays are analytical and evaluative.
Class No: 374.7(035)

Histories

Great Britain

[3817]

KELLY, T. A History of adult education in Great Britain. 3rd ed. Liverpool, Liverpool University Press, 1991. liv,425p. £20. ISBN: 0853234078.

First published 1962.

A revised 38-page prologue is followed by 26 chapters, with footnotes, and a bibliography to 1990 (p.397-9). Detailed, analytical index (p.40l-425).
Class No: 374.7(091)(410)

Biographies

[3818]

International biography of adult education. Thomas, J.E. *and* Elsey, B., *eds.* Nottingham, University of Nottingham, Department of Adult Education, 1985. xxii,709p. £27. (*Nottingham studies in the theory and practice of the education of adults.*) ISBN: 1850410011.

A world wide collection of biographies of people who have played a significant part in the development of adult education. Arranged A-Z by name (Abdullah, Hagia Dadasore (b.1917) ... Zilsel, Edgar (1891 - 1944), the entries are signed and vary in length from one to 8 pages, usually ending with one or two references. Thematic index, p. 686 - 705; subject index, p. 706 - 709.
Class No: 374.7(092)

Europe

Bibliographies

[3819]

KULICH, J. Adult education in continental Europe: an annotated bibliography of English-language materials, 1983-1985. Vancouver, University of British Columbia, Centre for Continuing Education, 1987. [5].ii,145 p. Can$ 18. (*Monographs on comparative and area studies in adult education, 12.*) ISBN: 088843135x.

First ed. was for 1945-1969 (1971); followed by eds. for 1971-1974 (1975), 1975-1979 (1982), 1980-1982 (1984).

661 unannotated entries, arranged by country, subdivided by subject. Index. ' ... most useful volume' (*Adult education,* v.60 (4)). *Class No:* 374.7(4)(01)

Great Britain

Bibliographies

[3820]

DALE, S. *and* CARTY, J. Finding out about continuing education: Sources of information and their uses. Milton Keynes, Open University Press, 1985. vi[1] 101p. £7.95. ISBN: 0335150241.

In 7 sections (1. Introduction - 2. Libraries - 3. Literature search procedure - 4. Bibliographical tools - 5. Audio-visual

....(contd.)

materials - 6. Organizations and associations - 7. Conclusions. Finally,'A corollary: libraries in continuing education. No index. *Class No:* 374.7(410)(01)

[3821]

A Select bibliography of adult continuing education in Great Britain, including works published to the end of the year 1981. Thomas, J.E. *and* Davies, J.H., *eds.* Leicester, National Institute of Adult Continuing Education, 1984. xvi,158p. ISBN: 0900559470.

First published 1952; 3rd ed. 1974, edited by T. Kelly.

1156 numbered entries, some annotated and referring to other items. 4 main parts: 1. General - 2. The social and educational background - 3. History and organization of adult education (p.12-91) - 4. Theory and method. Includes periodical articles. Cross-references. Author and subject indexes. *Class No:* 374.7(410)(01)

England & Wales

Yearbooks & Directories

[3822]

Returning to work: a directory of education and training for women. Johnson, M., *ed.* 5th ed. London, Kogan Page, in association with The Women Returners Network, 1991. 416p. £12.95. ISBN: 0749404698. ISSN: 09574808.

A glossary of acronyms precedes the directory of courses and county contacts, arranged by county. Followed by 'sources of information: national schemes and organizations' and 'Useful publications'. Subject, college and advertisers' indexes. *Class No:* 374.7(42)(058)

Information Services

[3823]

UNESCO. Directory of adult education documentation and information services. 3rd ed. Paris, Unesco, 1984. x,76p. F.20. ISBN: 9230021881.

2nd ed. published 1980.

Data on *c.*160 documentation services world wide, including national, regional and international services. An annex lists adult-education abstracting services.
Class No: 374.7:061:025.5

Open Learning

Yearbooks & Directories

[3824]

Open learning directory, 1994. Brooke Association (Manchester) Ltd. Oxford, Pergamon Open Learning and the Employment Department Group, 1993. xxiv,676p. £32.50. ISBN: 6080421555.

Details of over 2500 open learning training courses, arranged in 4 sections: 1. Introduction - 2. Delivery centres, consultancies - 3. Materials (agriculture, horticulture and animal care...Transport services and vehicle engineering - 4. Indexes (p.591-676), 4 for support services; 6 for materials.
Class No: 374.7OPE(058)

Great Britain

Yearbooks & Directories

[3825]

ADAMS, M., ed. **Libraries and open learning:** a directory of college libraries involvement with open learning. Library Association, Colleges of Further and Higher Education Group, 1988. [3], 51p. £5. ISBN: 186997705x.

114 entries, giving name of college, address, telephone number, name of contact, position, provision, library involvement, and comment. Further surveys are promised. *Class No:* 374.7OPE(410)(058)

Special Education

Bibliographies

[3826]

DAVIS, W.E. **Resource guide to special education:** terms, laws, assessment procedures, organizations. 2nd ed. Newton, Mass., Allyn & Bacon, 1986. 329p. $37.95. ISBN: 0205085466.

First ed. was titled *Educators' resource guide to special education.*

5 sections: 1. Terms employed in special education and related areas - 2. A list of commonly used acronyms and abbreviations - 3. A listing and description of educational and psychological tests and inventories - 4. Concise summaries of key pieces of legislation and litigation affecting the handicapped - 5. A list of organizations and agencies concerned with exceptional persons. US emphasis. *Class No:* 377(01)

[3827]

GREENLAW, M.J. and McINTOSH, M.E. **Educating the gifted:** a sourcebook. Chicago, Ill., American Library Association, 1988. viii,469p. $45; £35.25. ISBN: 0838904831.

'... purpose is to serve as a concise, clear reference tool for persons interested in the gifted individual. (*Preface*). 8 chapters: 1. A historical look at gifted education - 2. Who are the gifted? - 3. Indentification of the gifted - 4. Counseling the gifted and those around them - 5. Programming for the gifted - 6. Academic curriculum for the gifted - 7. Education for teachers of the gifted - 8. Parenting gifted children. Selected bibliographies follow each chapter. US-slant. Index, p.459-469. *Class No:* 377(01)

[3828]

Special education: a source book. Sternlicht,, M., comp. New York, Garland, 1987. 431p. $50. (*Garland reference library of social science, 375.*) ISBN: 0824085248.

Annotated bibliography on special education for teachers of exceptional students and others interested in the field. Arranged in 10 chapters (Mental retardation - Giftedness - Visual impairments - Hearing impairments - Learning disabilities - Brain damage - Speech and language inpairments - Orthopedic and other physical impairments - Emotional and behavioural impairments - and mainstreaming. Each chapter prefaced by an information survey article. Most citations are to periodical articles. Author and subject indexes. '... fills a gap in special education scholarship ...' (*Choice*,v.25(3), November 1987, p.458). *Class No:* 377(01)

Encyclopaedias

[3829]

REYNOLDS, C.R. and MANN, L., eds. **Encyclopedia of special education:** a reference for the education of the handicapped and other exceptional children and adults. New York, Wiley, 1987. 3v. (1793 p.). $250 £180. ISBN: 0471828580.

Designed to present a comprehensive view of what special education is about in a readable, understandable, usable and summative form. Worldwide coverage but with US bias. Topics covered include clinical disorders and syndromes, testing, intervention techniques, education methods and legal considerations. Biographies of prominent practitioners and theorists. Articles are followed by bibliographical references. Name index, p.1719-1776. Subject index, p.1777-1793. 'An invaluable resource' (*Library journal* v.113(7), 15 April 1988, p.32). ' Despite some flaws, a well-designed and up-to-date source' (*Choice*, v.25(8), April 1988, p. 1220). *Class No:* 377(031)

[3830]

—REYNOLDS, C.R. and FLETCHER-JANZEN, E. Concise encyclopedia of special education. New York, Wiley, 1990. 1215p. $89.95. ISBN: 0471515272.

An abridged version, based on the above. Articles are unsigned and most, according to the editors, have been 'condensed and streamlined to give basic facts and reference ideas'. *Class No:* 377(031)

Handbooks & Manuals

[3831]

Handbook of special education. Kauffman, J.W. and Hallahan, D.P., eds. Englewood Cliffs, N.J., Prentice-Hall, 1981. xv,807p. illus. ISBN: 0133817563.

Aimed at students, professionals and practitioners involved in the education of exceptional children. Chapters are arranged in 5 sections: Introduction (covers history, trends and European practice) - Conceptual foundations (disabilities and special characteristics) - Delivery systems - Curriculum and methods - Environmental management. Includes bibliographies. Index. *Class No:* 377(035)

[3832]

Handbook of special education: research and practice. Wang, M.C., and others, eds. Oxford, Pergamon Press, 1987. 3v. (xi,387p.;xi,392 p.;ix,376 p.). £50 each vol.; £140 the set. ISBN: 0080333834 Vol.1; 0080333842 Vol.2; 0080333850 Vol.3.

V.1. Learner characteristics and adaptive education; v.2. Mildly handicapped conditions; v.3. Low incidence conditions. The 3 vols. contain 45 chapters in 9 sections, each summarizing the well-confirmed knowledge in a particular area, giving attention to the research literature, tested experience and practice of leading professionals. Each vol. has a bibliography, author and subject index. Synthesis of findings published 1990 (236p. ISBN 0080402380; 0080402372). *Class No:* 377(035)

Dictionaries

[3833]

WILLIAMS, P., ed. **A Glossary of special education (children with special needs).** Milton Keynes, Open University Press, 1987. 192p. £20. ISBN: 0335159966.

....*(contd.)*

Brief explanations of the terminology of education, psychology, medicine and social work used in special education. *Class No:* 377(038)

Polyglot

[3834]

BRUNET, L., *and others.* **Terminology of special education.** Rev. ed. Paris, Unesco: International Bureau of Education, 1983. 368p. F.30; £11.50. (*Ibedata series.*) ISBN: 923002127x.

First published 1977.

English, Spanish, French and Russian terms in 4 separate glossaries, following a preliminary section, 'Group clusters'. English glossary has over 500 terms: English definitions with Spanish, French and Russian equivalents. Spanish, French and Russian glossaries are on the same pattern. *Class No:* 377(038)=00

English

[3835]

MOORE, B.C., *and others.* **A Dictionary of special education terms.** Springfield, Ill., C.C.Thomas, 1980. 128p. (spiral binding). $17.00. ISBN: 0398040095.

Includes mental retardation, emotional handicap, hearing, vision and learning disability, speech handicap, physical handicaps, and giftedness. *Class No:* 377(038)=20

Reviews & Abstracts

[3836]

Exceptional child education resources. Reston, VA., Council for Exceptional Children, 1968-. Quarterly. $90pa. ISSN: 01604309.

As *Exceptional child education abstracts* until May 1977.

Abstracts periodical articles from over 250 journals, as well as books, reports, surveys, doctoral dissertations, and nonprint professional media. Covers education of both handicapped and gifted children. Numerical order, with author, subject and title index, per issue and annually. The Council acts as a clearinghouse for ERIC programmes in this field. On-line database available, 1966- (updated quarterly). *Class No:* 377(048)

Yearbooks & Directories

[3837]

Directory of special education. International Bureau of Education. Paris, Unesco, 1986. 104p. $5; F.25; £3.75. ISBN: 9230024139.

First published in 1969 as *Special education.*

'Special education' is designed as 'covering all general or vocational education given to children who are physically handicapped, mentally handicapped, socially maladjusted or are in other special categories' (1969 ed.). Lists governmental and non-governmental agencies responsible for the provision of special education in 136 countries and territories. Arranged A-Z by English names. *Class No:* 377(058)

Executive Education

[3838]

McNULTY, N.G., *ed.* **International directory of executive education.** Oxford, Pergamon Press, 1985. 528p. £84; $125. ISBN: 0080309887.

In-depth descriptions of 4 aspects of executive education and training services in 92 countries (Programmes in general management; Programmes in functional management; In-company training; Master's degree programmes for executives). Management consultancy services. Description of schools. Index of acronyms of schools; Index to acronyms and terms used in text; Matrix index of programmes by country. *Class No:* 377.3

Further & Higher Education

Bibliographies

[3839]

ALTBACH, P.G. Comparative higher education abroad: bibliography and analysis. New York, Praeger, with the International Council for Educational Development, 1976. xii,274p. $5.50. ISBN: 0891922229.

More than 1700 unannotated references to books, periodical articles and dissertations on countries in Africa, Asia, Canada, Europe, Latin America, the Middle East, and Oceania. Includes two bibliographical essays and an annotated list of relevant books published in 1974. *Class No:* 378(01)

[3840]

—**ALTBACH, P.G. Comparative higher education: research trends and bibliography.** London, Mansell, 1979. xi,[1],206p. ISBN: 072010825x.

The essay on recent trends (p.3-113) indicates directions for future research and is well footnoted. Bibliography of 1116 numbered entries with interpolations. Topic cross-reference index; country and region index; author index. *Class No:* 378(01)

[3841]

ALTBACH, P.G. and **KELLY, D.H. Higher education in international perspective:** a survey and bibliography. London, Mansell Publishing Ltd., 1985. xviii,583p. £40. ISBN: 0720117070.

The two reports of the survey, *Perspectives on comparative higher education, a survey of research and literature* and *Research on higher education in European socialist countries* includes 82 and 210 references respectively. The bibliography of 6901 items, has 22 subject sections, each subdivided by geographical regions, then by books and articles, and finally A-Z by author, followed by bibliographies, again by region. *Class No:* 378(01)

[3842]

MENGE, R.S. and **MATHIS, B.C. Key resources on teaching, learning, curriculum and faculty development:** a guide to the higher education literature. San Francisco, CA., Jossey-Bass Publishers, 1988. xix,406p. $35; £32. (*Higher education series.*) ISBN: 1555421180.

686 annotated items, books and periodical articles, on teaching, learning, curriculum and faculty development in colleges and universities. Arranged in subject chapters, each with an introduction, references, and bibliography,

....(contd.)

subdivided by general and then subject and A-Z by author. Cross-references. Includes information on periodicals and databases. Author index, p.373-384; analytical subject index, p.385-406. *Class No:* 378(01)

[3843]
—REID, B.J. 'Higher education', 1980-85. In *British book news,* August 1985, p.450-58.

A review of recent books covering a wide subject area (General - Learning and teaching - Entry to higher education - Students study courses in particular disciplines - Higher education staff, research, finance and management - Distance education - Industry and employment - Books and libraries - Overseas students and higher education overseas - Adult education). Includes 206 books, 2 serials, 3 abstracting and indexing journals, and 4 directories. *Class No:* 378(01)

Encyclopaedias

[3844]
The International encyclopedia of higher education. Knowles, A.S., *ed.* Washington, Jossey-Bass Publishers, 1977. 10v. (5208p.). $700 the set. ISBN: 0875893236.

V.1. *Contents. Contributors, Acronyms. Glossary.* v.2-9. A-Z entries. v.10. *Index.* About 500 named contributors. Appended to each substantial article are lists of (a) major international and national organizations; (b) principal information sources. 'Adult education': v.2. p.120-73: 7 sections, plus two appendices (p.168-73). Country entries are a feature. V.9 concludes with 'International directory' (p.4477-4588). V.10: *Index* comprises a name index and a subject index (p.4633-5208). Somewhat elaborate layout. For the very large reference library. 'A unique source for state-of-the-art surveys, and particularly for comparative studies ... (*Library journal,* 15th April 1979, p.886). *Class No:* 378(031)

[3845]
—ALTBACH, P.G. International higher education: an encyclopedia. New York, Garland, 1991. 2v.(1165p.) $150. £110. ISBN: 0824048474, US; 1558621520, UK.

52 country and regional profiles (mainly underdeveloped areas) arranged by countries, blend description and analysis into short overviews of 10 to 20 pages, covering historical developments, current trends, structure and governance, higher education's relationship with political systems and labour markets, etc. Also included are 15 cross-cultural topics, including foreign education, graduate education, private higher education, and academic freedom. Updates, in part, the above, aging encyclopedia. *Class No:* 378(031)

Reviews & Abstracts

[3846]
Research into higher education abstracts. Abingdon, Oxon, Carfax Publishing Co., for the Society for Research into Higher Education, 1967-. v.1,no.1-. 3pa (previously quarterly). £112. ISSN: 00345326.

About 200 abstracts per issue. Sections: A. General - B. Systems and institutions - C. Teaching and learning - D. Students - E. Staff - F. Student assessment and course evaluation - G. Continuing education - H. Information

....(contd.)

technology and networks. Over 500 journals scanned. Author and subject indexes each issue, cumulating in the 3rd issue each year. *Class No:* 378(048)

Yearbooks & Directories

[3847]
Directory of technical and further education, 1993. 27th ed. Harlow, Longman, 1993. xi,509p. illus. £65. ISBN: 0582096049.

Includes both public and private education in the United Kingdom, with courses and careers from 16 to restart, and from adult education to polytechnics. 11 chapters: 1. Central government; 2. Regional framework for further education; 3. Local government education departments; 4. Further education colleges; 5. Tertiary colleges; 6. Sixth form colleges; 7. Correspondence colleges; 8. Examining bodies; 9. Employment and careers; 10. CBI; TUC; 11. Allied organizations. Subject, geographical and general indexes. *Class No:* 378(058)

[3848]
Vacation study abroad, 1991. Howard, E., *ed.* 41st ed. Institute of International Education, 1991. 278p. $26.95. (*The learning traveller, 2.*) ISBN: 0872061795.

First published 1951. Annual.

Designed to assist students planning summer study abroad, with relevant information on more than 850 study abroad programmes. *Class No:* 378(058)

Developing Countries

Bibliographies

[3849]
ALTBACH, P.G. Higher education in developing nations: a select bibliography, 1969-1974. New York, Praeger, with the International Council for Educational Development, 1975. iv,229,[1]. $6. ISBN: 0891922210.

Continues the author's *Higher education in developing countries* (Cambridge, Mass., Harvard University, Center for International Affairs, 1970).

Bibliography of 2438 references (general perspectives; developing countries; regions and countries; Africa (Botswana ... Zambia); Asia; Latin America; Middle East and North Africa) - largely for periodical articles. Appended list of bibliographies and journals. Cross-reference index. Appendix: International and regional agencies concerned with research and education in higher education. *Class No:* 378(4/9-77)(01)

Europe

Handbooks & Manuals

[3850]
RASHDALL, H. The Universities of Europe in the Middle Ages. Powicke, F. M. *and* Emden, A. B., *eds.* new ed. London, Oxford University Press, 1936,(reprinted 1987). 3.v.(1587p.)illus. v.1. £55; v.2.£35; v.3. £50. ISBN: 019822981x v.1; 0198229828 v.2; 0198229836 v.3.

First published 1895.

A scholarly account, heavily footnoted. Bibliographies precede accounts of individual universities (*e.g.* Vienna, in

....(contd.)
v.2:one page of bibliography). Appendices of documents and notes. General index in v.3. p.497-558. Folding map.
Class No: 378(4)(035)

Europe—Western

Handbooks & Manuals

[3851]
MOHR, B., *ed.* Higher education in the European Community: student handbook. 6th ed. Luxembourg, Office for Official Publications of the European Communities; London, Kogan Page; Phoenix, AZ, Oryx Press, 1990. 516p. BFr.750. £14.95. $32.50. ISBN: 9282607399, EC; 0749401281, UK; 0897746570, US.

First published 1977.

A directory of courses and institutions in the 12 countries. Arranged by country, information for each is organizations of higher education (type, student statistics, organization and validity of courses); admission and registration; knowledge of the language of instruction, language courses, and other courses; financial assistance and scholarships; entry and residence regulations; social aspects (social security and health insurance, advisory services, student employment, cost of living, accommodation, etc.). Appendix to each entry lists organizations and institutions from which further information and application forms may be obtained, a bibliography of national information material and, in most cases, a table of subjects taught at each institution. Also includes information on the European University Institute, Florence; College of Europe; Bruges; and information on the Erasmus programme, ECTS, Comett, Lingua and Naric.
Class No: 378(400)(035)

Great Britain

Handbooks & Manuals

[3852]
College administration a handbook. Locke, M., *and others.* 2nd ed. Longman Group UK Ltd., in association with NATFHE, 1988. xii, [1], 498p. £19.95. ISBN: 0582901170.

First published 1980.

Describes in detail the administration of public sector post-school education in England and Wales. 4 basic sections: 1. The administrative framework - 2. The institutions and the staff - 3. Curriculum and students - 4. Buildings. Cross-references. References, A-Z by author, p.477-485, with further reading lists attached to many subsections. Triple-column detailed index, p.490-498. *Class No:* 378(410)(035)

[3853]
The NATFHE handbook: the handbook of initial teacher training, 1994. Central Register and Clearing Houses Ltd., *comp.* London, National Association of Teachers in Further and Higher Education, 1992. Annual. 250p. maps. £12. ISBN: 0901390410.

First published 1954.

Detailed guide to courses of training for teaching, and a wide range of other courses. For each institution; general information; courses offered; method of application. Lists courses within the CRCH scheme, A-Z by name, followed by entries for colleges of dance, music, drama, etc. Index of subjects and courses (p.229-248). Index of institutions, p.249-50. *Class No:* 378(410)(035)

Reports Literature

[3854]
GREAT BRITAIN. Committee on Higher Education. Report of the Committee appointed ... under the chairmanship of Lord Robbins. 1961-1963. London, HMSO, 1963. 7v. *(Cmnd 2154.)*

The Report is accompanied by 5 Appendices: 1. The demand for places in higher education - 2. Students and their education (2 pts.) - 3. Teachers in higher education - 4. Administrative, financial and economic aspects - 5. Higher education in other countries (10 countries; 'Principal written sources', p.300-6). *Class No:* 378(410)(047)

Yearbooks & Directories

[3855]
The Gabbitas-Thring guide to independent further education. 1989/1990. 3rd ed. London, John Catt Ltd., 1989. £7.95. ISSN: 0269588x.

First published 1986.

Lists a wide variety of schools and colleges, including tutorial colleges and professional/vocational training establishments. *Class No:* 378(410)(058)

USA

Bibliographies

[3856]
BEACH, M., *comp.* A Subject bibliography of the history of American higher education. Westport, CT., Greenwood Press, 1984. vii,165p. $36.95. ISBN: 0313232768.

A bibliography of major books, journal articles and dissertations on the subject, arranged A-Z by subject (Academic costume ... Zoology). Unannotated. Author and subject indexes. A companion volume to the author's *Bibliographic guide to American colleges and universities* (1976). *Class No:* 378(73)(01)

[3857]
PARKER, F. and PARKER, B.J. US higher education: a guide to information sources. Detroit, Mich., Gale Research Co., 1980. xii,675p. $68. (*Gale information library: Education information guide series, v.9.*) ISBN: 0810314762.

Annotated bibliography of books and reports on the history, philosophy, administration, finance, governance, curriculum, student life, library and audiovisual services, and custodian concerns of the field. Author arrangement, with detailed subject index. *Class No:* 378(73)(01)

Research Establishments

[3858]
International directory of research institutions on higher education. European Centre for Higher Education (CEPES). 2nd rev. ed. Paris, Unesco, 1988. xv,134p. F.30; £6. (*IBEDATA series.*) ISBN: 923002576x.

First published 1981 as *International directory of higher education research institutions.*

Particular emphasis on the research and publication functions of institutions, listing extensively the books, periodicals, documents and papers which they have published since 1983. *Class No:* 378:061:061.62

Education Institutions

Worldwide

[3859]
Academic year abroad, 1991/92. Howard, E.M., *ed.* 20th ed. New York, Institute of International Education, 1991. 418p. $31.95. ISBN: 0872061809.

First published 1964. Annual.

Arranged in 2 parts, part 1 providing information on *c.*2100 programs sponsored by colleges and universities with US accreditation; part 2 listing programs sponsored by institutions without US accreditation. Geographical arrangement of each part by region, subdivided by country, city, and sponsoring institution. Information includes dates, subjects offered, credit eligibility, language of instruction, highlights, costs, housing, contact person, etc. Indexes by sponsoring body and by field of study. '... the most comprehensive source ...' (*Reference books bulletin,* 1 November 1989, p.598),. *Class No:* 378:061:37(100)

Academic Dress

[3860]
FRANKLYN, C.A.H. Academical dress, from the Middle Ages to the present day, including Lambeth degrees. Hassocks, Sussex, the Author, 1970. vii,254p. illus.

15 chapters, devoted to the academical dress of graduates (1. The origin of academical dress ... 8. The University of Oxford - 9. The University of Cambridge - 10. The University of London - 11. Other universities ... 15. Bibliography (58 items). Small black-and-white illustrations. *Class No:* 378:391

[3861]
HAYCRAFT, F.W., *comp.* **Degrees and hoods of the world's universities.** 5th ed., rev. and enl. by F.R.S.Rogers and others. Hassocks, Sussex, C.A.H.Franklyn, 1972. xvii,162p.illus.

First published 1923.

Short historical introduction. Main section gives, under each country, its universities and under each university its degrees and details of the shape and colours of its degree hoods. Separate sections for theological colleges and learned societies. Illus. include hoods in full colour and a section showing hood shapes. A comprehensive index is provided. *Class No:* 378:391

[3862]
SMITH, H. *and* **SHEARD, W. Academic dress and insignia of the world:** gowns, hats, chains of office, hoods, rings, medals and other degree insignia of universities and other institutions of learning. Cape Town, Balkema, 1970. 3v. (1843p.). illus.

V.1: *General introduction. British Commonwealth, Irish Republic (Eire) & Republic of South Africa;* v.2: *Europe, Africa, Asia, United States of America, Central and South America;* v.3: *Glossary and definitions.* Hood identification tables (p.1646-1771; by colours). US Inter Collegiate Code. Abbreviations, Index (p.1825-41). Detailed full-page black-and-white illus. 442 plates, with notes usually facing. *Class No:* 378:391

Europe

[3863]
HARGREAVES-MAWDSLEY, W.N. A History of academical dress in Europe until the end of the eighteenth century. Oxford, Clarendon Press, 1963. (Reprinted Greenwood Press, 1978). xiii,235p. illus (21 pl.). £22.50. ISBN: 0313202508.

Chapters: 1. Italy, Spain, Portugal and Malta - 2. France - 3-4. Great Britain and Ireland - 5. German-speaking countries, the Low Countries, Switzerland, Scandinavia, Hungary and Poland. A scholarly survey, with profuse footnotes. Glossary of terms (p.190-5); critical bibliography (p.196-210: A. Manuscripts - B. Printed books). Analytical index. Not very fully illustrated (colour frontispiece and 21 black-and-white half-tones, 17 drawings), but descriptions are detailed. *Class No:* 378:391(4)

Great Britain

[3864]
SHAW, G.W. Academical dress of British universities. Cambridge, Heffer, 1966. vii,120p. illus.

Descriptions and diagrams of gowns, hoods, robes and caps worn by graduates and undergraduates. Index of universities and degrees; useful list of abbreviations of degrees (p.13-16) which indicates, *e.g.* which university grants a degree as Master of Dental Surgery. Illustrations are black-and-white, but may be supplemented by the coloured illustrations in *Academic dress of the University of Oxford,* by D. R. Venables and R. E. Clifford (2nd ed. Oxford, Shepherd & Woodward, 1967, [2] 33p. col.ill.). *Class No:* 378:391(410)

Degrees & Qualifications

Worldwide

Handbooks & Manuals

[3865]
International guide to qualifications in education. National Academic Recognition Information Centre, British Council. 3rd ed. London, Mansell Publishing, in association with the British Council, 1992. 880p. £90. ISBN: 0720120853.

First published 1984.

Chapters on each of *c.*150 countries, arranged A-Z, from which students come to Britain for further study, training or employment. For each country, a brief introduction to education there, evaluation of recognition normally accorded to key qualifications, description of marking systems used at secondary and tertiary levels, and a survey of the structure of education in the country. Appendices on examination bodies and international organizations. *Class No:* 378.2(100)(035)

Great Britain

[3866]
British qualifications: a complete guide to educational, technical, professional and academic qualifications in Britain. 24th ed. London, Kogan Page, 1993. Annual. liii,784p. ISBN: 0749411058. ISSN: 01415972.

First published 1966.

A comprehensive guide to educational, technical, professional and academic qualifications in Britain. 7 parts:

....(contd.)

1. Teaching establishments - 2. Secondary school examinations - 3. Further education examinations - 4. Awards made by universities and designated institutions - 5. Qualifications, listed by trades & professions (*c*.200 career fields and professions (Accountancy ... Youth and community service) - 6. Bodies crediting independent institutions - 7. Study associations and the 'learned societies'. Detailed index, p.716-784, preceded by index of advertisers. *Class No:* 378.2(410)

[3867]

Degree course guides, 1993/94: guides to first-degree courses at UK universities, polytechnics and other institutions. Cambridge, Hobsons Publishing plc., for CRAC (Careers Research and Advisory Centre), 1988. Annual. *c*.1400p. tables. ISBN: 1853241016.

21 subject guides (Agriculture ... Veterinary science - Engineering technology) by various hands).
Class No: 378.2(410)

[3868]

Which degree? a complete guide to all full-time and sandwich lst degree courses, 1993. 25th ed. East Grinstead, The Newpoint Publishing Company Ltd., 1992. Annual. 5v. £64.95 the set. ISBN: 0862631599, full set; 0862631548, v.1; 0862631556, v.2; 0862631564, v.3; 0862631572, v.4; 0862631580, v.5.

Successor to *Which university?*.

A subject listing of over 12,000 degree courses in the UK, stating content and entrance requirements followed by sections on universities, polytechnics and colleges, stating amenities, etc. Volumes are arranged by subject: 1: Arts, humanities, languages - 2. Engineering, technology, the environment - 3. Mathematics, medicine, sciences - 4. Business, education, social sciences - 5. Lists all higher education institutions, A-Z, with information on town where situated and the institution itself. Essential reading. Indexes to all 5 vols. *Class No:* 378.2(410)

USA

[3869]

Peterson's guide to certificate programs at American colleges and universities. Lopos, G.J., *and others, eds.* Princeton, N.J., Peterson's Guides, 1988. 343p. $35.95. ISBN: 0878667415.

Developed in co-operation with the National University Continuing Education Association.

Information on over 1400 programmes, representing nearly 300 US four-year colleges & universities, arranged A-Z by state, subdivided by programme classification. Each entry has programme content, format, evaluation criteria, enrollment requirements, cost, student services, contact person. Geared towards adult part-time learners and heavily career-oriented. Indexes to institutions and programmes. *Class No:* 378.2(73)

Scholarships & Postgraduate Awards

[3870]

The Awards almanac: an international guide to careers, research and education funds. Schmidt, G.W. *and* Singson, K.P., *eds.* Detroit & London, St. James Press, 1993. xi,749p. £61. $90. ISBN: 155862144x.

Aimed at individuals (not organizations) requiring funds to

....(contd.)

continue education or to carry out activities related to their career. Arranged A-Z under the name of the grant-awarding body, each entry has contact names and addresses, brief description of purpose of award, areas of study it encompasses, details of requirement of award, method of application, deadlines, amounts awarded, ratio of applicants and awards offered. Indexes of awards by name and by subject covered, granting organizations, and keywords. *Class No:* 378.3

[3871]

BRITISH COUNCIL. Scholarships abroad: scholarships offered to British students by overseas governments and universities, 1991/92. London, for British Council, 1990. Annual. 58p. £4.95. ISBN: 0117015008.

Lists over 300 foreign government awards available to British postgraduate students, with details of how to apply. Arranged by country, A-Z. Followed by information on the Commonwealth Scholarship and Fellowship Plan, Council of Europe, and NATO. *Class No:* 378.3

[3872]

The Grants register, 1993-95. Williams, L., *ed.* 13th ed. London, Macmillan, 1992. 864p. £85. ISBN: 0333532546. ISSN: 00725471.

First published 1969 (for 1969-70). Editor of early issues was C.A.Lerner.

Details of awards and grants worldwide. Subject index, p.xi-xxv; index of awards and awarding bodies, p.769-794. Complementary to Unesco's annual *Study abroad (qv)*. *Class No:* 378.3

[3873]

Study abroad: international scholarships and courses. 28th ed. Paris, Unesco, 1993. £13.25.

First published 1948.

A directory of more than 3000 opportunities for further study and training in all academic and professional fields, offered by international organizations, governments, private and public foundations, universities and other institutions in more than 124 countries. *Class No:* 378.3

Great Britain

Handbooks & Manuals

[3874]

Directory of post-graduate and post-experience courses, 1988-89. London, Council for National Academic Awards (CNAA), 1988. Annual. vii,86p. *Gratis.* ISSN: 02668459.

Arranged by subject, A-Z. Under each subject heading are listed the colleges dealing in that subject, type of award, title of course, and description of course in many cases. College and subject indexes. *Class No:* 378.3(410)(035)

Yearbooks & Directories

[3875]

The Educational grants directory: voluntary and charitable help for children and students in need. Fitzherbert, L. *and* Eastwood, M. London, The Directory of Social Change, 1988. [3],217p. £12.50. ISBN: 0907164293.

Details 220 national and general sources of help, A-Z by name; 900 local and parochial educational charities; and nearly 100 companies sponsoring degree courses. Details are given of eligibility, policy/practice, grants, correspondent,

....(contd.)

and address. Other sections: musical education (choir schools, music scholarships); assisted places scheme; education authorities; and sources of further information and advice. Index. Other grant guides from the same publisher include: *Guide to grants for individuals in need,* ed. by L. Fitzherbert & H. Bellofatto (1987. 208p. map. £9.95 ISBN 0907164285); *Guide to company giving,* ed. by M. Norton (3rd ed. 1989. £25. ISBN 0907164447); and *Guide to the major trusts.* ed. by L. Fitzherbert & M. Eastwood (2nd ed. of *Guide to the major grant-making trusts.* 1989. £25. ISBN 0907164455).

A later ed. by M.Eastwood & D.Casson was issued in 1992 (£14.95. ISBN 0907164773).

Class No: 378.3(410)(058)

USA

Yearbooks & Directories

[3876]

Directory of research grants, 1994. Phoenix, AZ., Oryx Press, 1994. 1328p. $125. ISBN: 0897747690.

First published for 1983. Annual.

Arrangement is by subject areas. A tool for scholars, grants administrators, faculty members and any person or organization looking for a way to get support for research projects. *Class No:* 378.3(73)(058)

Universities, Polytechnics & Colleges

[3877]

The Encyclopedia of higher education. Clarke, B.R. *and* Neave, G.R., *eds.* Oxford, Pergamon Press, 1992. 4v.(2530p). £750. $1500. ISBN: 0080372511.

V.1 analyses more than 135 national systems of higher education; v.2 & 3 have papers on an extensive range of issues and problems in the fields; and v.4 offers a unique and comprehensive review of the development of core academic disciplines. In all, over 300 essays. Indexes of contributors, names and subjects. '... a monumental achievement ...' (*Choice,* v.30(6), February 1993, p.938). *Class No:* 378.4/.6

[3878]

History of universities. Brockliss, L., *ed.* Oxford, Oxford University Press, 1981-. Annual. *c.*£50 each volume. ISSN: 01445138.

V.11, published in 1992 (viii,336p. illus. £50. ISBN 0198220014) has 8 essays, including studies of medieval Paris and the 20th-century Hebrew University of Jerusalem, an item of research in progress, 9 conference reports, an essay review, 21 book reviews, and a bibliography of publications on university history since 1977. Index. *Class No:* 378.4/.6

[3879]

International handbook of universities. International Association of Universities. 12th ed. London, Macmillan Press, for the Association, 1990. 1302p. £90. ISBN: 0333436431.

First published 1959.

Includes over 6500 universities in 115 countries, arranged A-Z by country, with brief descriptions of faculties and departments, names of deans and principals, admission

....(contd.)

requirements, degrees and diplomas awarded, publications, number of academic staff, student enrollment, library (stock and publications). Index. *Class No:* 378.4/.6

Yearbooks & Directories

[3880]

European education yearbook: the annual guide to study abroad, 1993. Swanley, Kent, Nexus Business Connections Ltd., 364p. and supplement, 'Course and program selector'. ISSN: 0968168x.

Details of over 700 universities, colleges and institutions worldwide. Index of institutions and courses guide precede. Main section is 'Studying in Europe' (A-Z by country, with an introduction to the country followed by a list of universities, etc.); 'Higher education overseas'(profiles of institutions); and 'Learning English overseas'. Many advertisements of educational institutions. *Class No:* 378.4/ .6(058)

[3881]

The World list of universities/Liste mondiale des universités, 1989-1991. International Association of Universities, *comp.* 18th ed. London, Macmillan Press, for the association, 1989. 638p. £50. ISBN: 0333474880.

11th ed. 1973.

Directory of over 6000 universities and other institutions of higher education in over 150 countries and a guide to the principal national and international organizations concerned with higher education. Part 1: Institutions and national organizations - Part 2: International and regional organizations. University vacations. Appendix: The International Association of Universities (officers; members; publications). Index. In English and French.

The 19th ed., 1991/93, was issued in 1991 (760p. £65. ISBN 0333540107). *Class No:* 378.4/.6(058)

[3882]

The World of learning, 1994. 44th ed. London, Europa Publications, 1994. Annual. xv,2094p. £190. ISBN: 0946653925. ISSN: 00842117.

A directory of universities, colleges, libraries, learned societies, museums, art galleries and research institutes in more than 150 countries, arranged A-Z (International - Afghanistan ... Zimbabwe). Includes over 26,000 institutional names, addresses, etc., and lists more than 150,000 individuals. The international section has details of more than 400 international educational, scientific and cultural organizations. Includes 'open' and 'free' universities. Index of institutions, p.1991-2094. *Class No:* 378.4/.6(058)

Histories

[3883]

The Illustrated history of Oxford University. Prest, J., *ed.* Oxford, Oxford University Press, 1993. 500p. 224 illus. 5 maps. £25. ISBN: 0198201583.

Contains separate chapters on Oxford's contribution to religion, classical studies, the arts, and the life and physical sciences. Chronology. Guide to further reading. Index. *Class No:* 378.4/.6(091)

Europe

[3884]

BOSWICK, S. **Guide to the universities of Europe.** New York, Facts on File, 1991. 296p. $35. ISBN: 081602359x.

A directory of 275 universities in 26 European countries, arranged A-Z by country. Information for prospective applicants includes admission requirement, application procedures and deadlines, degree requirements, visas, costs, scholarships available, etc. Aimed at North American applicants. Both public and private universities are included. Universities of Eastern Europe are treated separately.

Class No: 378.4/.6(4)

Europe—Western

[3885]

Directory of higher education institutions in the European Community. London, Kogan Page; Luxembourg, Office for official Publications of the European Community, 1992. 544p. illus. maps. £25. ISBN: 0749404892, UK; 9282627500, EC.

Over 4000 entries, giving address, number of students, and subject areas covered. In English and French.

Class No: 378.4/.6(400)

Great Britain

Handbooks & Manuals

[3886]

ASSOCIATION OF COMMONWEALTH UNIVERSITIES. **Higher education in the United Kingdom, 1992-93.** Harlow, Essex, Longman Group UK Ltd., 1992. Biennial. 312p. illus. £14.95. ISBN: 0582081955. ISSN: 03061744.

First published 1936.

A guide for overseas students wishing to study in Britain and their advisers. Lists 150 subjects, A-Z, with, under each subject heading, a list of courses available and where offered. A list of useful addresses. A list for further reading.

Class No: 378.4/.6(410)(035)

[3887]

British universities guide to graduate study, 1993-94. London, Pitman, for the Committee of Vice-Chancellors of the Universities of the United Kingdom,1993. 480p. £19.95. ISBN: 0948890282.

First published 1973. Formerly *Postgraduate courses in United Kingdom universities* and *Schedule of post graduate courses in the United Kingdom.*

A directory of *c*.3,000 graduate courses lasting at least six months, arranged in 54 subject groups. Short descriptions of course content, method of assessment, length, fees, grants and awards. *Class No:* 378.4/.6(410)(035)

[3888]

Graduate studies, 1993/94: the complete guide to over 6000 post-graduate courses in the UK. CRAC (Careers Research and Advisory Centre). Cambridge, Hobson Publishing Plc., 1993. 1264p. £99.75. ISBN: 1853247251.

First published 1972. Annual.

Summaries of research facilities and courses and basic information about the institutions in which postgraduate study is available. In 4 parts: 111 subject sections, A-Z (Accounting and finance...Zoology), each entry naming the institutions concerned, with title of course of study area. qualifications, period of study, any specific entrance

....(contd.)

requirements, and a brief synopsis - Institutions address list - Research establishments - Research institutes... Index of course titles (p.1133-1224). Index of subject headings (p.1225-1264).adnd applied sciences. Each entry gives the name of the institution, title of course or study area, qualification, period of study, any specific entrance requirements, and a brief synopsis. Cross-references. Institutions address list, p.875-901; Index of course titles, p.905-965; Index of subject headings, p.967-1004; and index of advertisers. *Class No:* 378.4/.6(410)(035)

[3889]

Polytechnic courses handbook, 1993-94: full-time and sandwich and advanced courses. 22nd ed. London, The Committee of Directors of Polytechnics, 1992. 660p. £14. ISBN: 187200704x.

Brief account of each polytechnic's background, its purposes and pattern of courses offered. *Class No:* 378.4/ .6(410)(035)

[3890]

The Student book, 1994: the... applicant's guide to UK colleges and universities. Boehm, K. *and* Wellings, N. 16th ed. London, Macmillan Press, 1993. Annual. 828p. illus., maps. £12.99. ISBN: 0333585143.

First published 1979.

A book for those applying for a degree course in UK colleges, polytechnics and universities. Content: How to go about it - Where to study - Maps - Subject/place index - What to study. Index (p.819-828). *Class No:* 378.4/ .6(410)(035)

[3891]

The Student's guide to graduate studies in the UK, 1994. Radcliffe, B *and* Massey, L., . *eds.* Cambridge, Hobson's for CRAC, 1993. 752p. £18.95 ISBN: 1853247944.

Courses are listed (p.71-651) in 111 subject sections. A-Z, each in three subdivisions: Higher degrees by research and thesis - Higher degrees by instruction and examination - Certificates and diplomas. In each subsection are names of institutes, with course title or research area, and qualifications awarded. Other listings include institutes' address list; research establishments, and research institutes and departments. Subject index, p.703-38. *Class No:* 378.4/ .6(410)(035)

[3892]

University entrance, 1993: the official guide. 6th ed. London, Association of Commonwealth Universities, for the Committee of Vice-Chancellors and Principals of the Universities of the United Kingdom, 1992. 504p. illus., tables. £13.95. ISBN: 0851431356.

First published in 1987. Successor to *Compendium of university entrance requirements.*

Lists over 11500 courses and their entrance requirements. Also profiles and pictures of 80 admitting universities and university colleges in the UK and of the 19 higher education colleges offering university-validated courses. Subject index. *Class No:* 378.4/.6(410)(035)

[3893]
Where to study in the UK: a guide to British professional qualifications. 2nd ed. London, Kogan Page, 1988. 217p. £8.95. ISBN: 1850913870.

First published 1986.

Contains information relating to the qualifications of professional associations and examining bodies, with details of the colleges and schools in the independent and public sectors which prepare students for the professional associations' examinations. In 5 parts: 1. The professional associations; 2. Business, commercial, secretarial and technical examining bodies; 3. Colleges offering professional courses; 4. Post-experience and postgraduate courses; 5. English language colleges. A list of useful addresses is followed by indexes of professional assocations and advertisers. *Class No:* 378.4/.6(410)(035)

Yearbooks & Directories

[3894]
'The Times' good universities guide: the definitive guide to Britain's universities. O'Leary, J. *and* Cannon, T. London, Bartholomew & Times, 1993. 216p. £8.99.

A complete list of all 96 UK universities, each with facts, figures, and a short profile. Also rankings (league tables of performance according to clear criteria), and listing 'top' universities by subject. (Entry taken from *The good book guide*, v.63, July/August 1993, p.15). *Class No:* 378.4/.6(410)(058)

Histories

[3895]
GABRIEL, A.L. Summary bibliography of the history of the universities of Great Britain and Ireland up to 1800, covering publications between 1900 and 1968. Notre Dame, Indiana, Medieval Institute, University of Notre Dame, 1974. 154p. (*Texts and studies in the history of medieval education, no.14.*)

1514 entries, in 6 sections, on the history of education in Europe and England up to 1800, and on English. Scottish, Welsh and Irish universities. Author and subject indexes. *Class No:* 378.4/.6(410)(091)

[3896]
—The History of British Universities, 1800-1969: a bibliography, excluding Oxford and Cambridge. London, Society for Research into Higher Education, 1970. xv,264p.

7 general sections, followed by entries on the universities, A-Z (p.59-250). 'University of York' (p.248-50: 40 entries). Data on each, as appropriate: (a) books and pamphlets; (b) theses and dissertations; (c) reports; (d) periodical articles; (e) bibliographies. Author index. *Class No:* 378.4/.6(410)(091)

[3897]
The History of the University of Oxford. Oxford, Oxford University Press, 1984-. To be in 8v.

A completely new and full-scale history, from its obscure origins in the 12th century to the late 20th century. 8 chronologically arranged volumes are planned: two on the Middle Ages; three spanning the early modern period to 1800; two on the 19th century; one on the 20th century. Published so far: v.1: *The early Oxford Schools,* ed. by J.I. Catto (1984. 670p. £55); v.II: *Late medieval Oxford* ed. by J.I. Catto & T.A.R. Evans (1992. 823p. illus. £90); v.III:

....(*contd.*)
The collegiate university, ed. by James McConica (1986. 800p. £65); v.V: *The eighteenth century,* ed. by L.S. Sutherland and L.G. Mitchell (1986. 968p. illus.£75). *Class No:* 378.4/.6(410)(091)

[3898]
LEADER, D.R. A History of the University of Cambridge. V.1: The University to 1546. Cambridge, Cambridge University Press, 1988. xxi,399p. illus. (18 half-tones), 2 maps. £35. ISBN: 0521328829.

To be in 4v. V.1: *The University to 1546,* by D.R. Leader; v.2: *1546-1750,* by V. Morgan; v.3: *1750-1870,* by P. Searby; v.4: *1870-1990,* by C. Brooke.

V.1. has 13 sections: 1. Origins - 2. Hostels, convents and colleges - 3. Teaching - 4. The trivium - 5. The Quadrivium - 6. The philosophers - 7. Theology - 8. Law - 9. Medicine - 10. Interlude and expansion - 11. Internal reform - 12. John Fisher and Lady Margaret - 13. The Henrician reformation. Bibliography, p.352-379. Index, mainly of people, p.381-399. *Class No:* 378.4/.6(410)(091)

Biographies

[3899]
Universities' who's who, 1988. Ayr, Carrick Publications, 1988. [3],252p. £20. ISBN: 0946724202.

Brief biographies of *c.*3000 senior academic staff in United Kingdom universities. In 3 sections: England and Wales; Scotland; Northern Ireland, each subdivided A-Z by surname of biographee, with professional and personal information (*e.g.*degrees, job, society and committee membership, birthdate, marriage, education). *Class No:* 378.4/.6(410)(092)

Scotland

Biographies

[3900]
WATT, D.E.R. A Biographical dictionary of Scottish graduates, to AD 1410. Oxford, Clarendon Press, 1977. 607p.

Biographical data on *c.*1100 graduates who attended universities in England and the continent before the foundation in 1411 of St. Andrews, the oldest of the Scottish universities. 'Will take its place naturally on the reference shelves of all libraries with any pretence to holdings in medieval history' (*Library review*, v.27, Winter 1978, p.264). *Class No:* 378.4/.6(411)(092)

Commonwealth

Yearbooks & Directories

[3901]
Commonwealth universities yearbook, 1993: a directory to the universities of the Commonwealth and the handbook of the Association. 69th ed. London, Association of Commonwealth Universities, 1993. 4v.(3500p.). £136. ISBN: 0851431399. ISSN: 00697745.

First published 1914.

Information on over 500 universities in 31 countries. V.1: Australia ... Hong Kong. V.2: India ... Nigeria. v.3: Pakistan ... United Kingdom ... Zimbabwe. v.4:

....(contd.)

Appendices. Abbreviations. Indexes (General: Institutions and organizations: Subjects of study: Personal names)(p.3111-3597). *Class No:* 378.4/.6(41-44)(058)

Japan

[3902]
Japanese colleges and universities, 1989: a guide to institutions of higher education in Japan. Association of International Education, Japan., *comp. & ed.* Tokyo, Marazon Co. Ltd., 1989. xviii,781p. diagrs. maps. ISBN: 4621033573.

3 sections: 1. National colleges and universities (A-Z by name); 2. Local public colleges and universities; 3. Private colleges and universities. Other sections include: School fees; Scholarships; Programs. Japanese-English names list of the colleges and universities. Index. *Class No:* 378.4/.6(52)

Africa

Yearbooks & Directories

[3903]
Directory of African universities. Association of African Universities. 5th ed. Accra North, A.A.U. Documentation Centre, 1988. [4],viii,495p.

3rd ed. published 1983.

Arrangement is A-Z by country, subdivided A-Z by name of university. Information includes address, telephone number, academic year, foundation date, language of instruction, senior staff, council, statistics of personnel (administrative and teaching), number of students, faculties, conditions of admission, libraries, publications. Entries are in the European language of the country. *Class No:* 378.4/.6(6)(058)

America—North & Central

Yearbooks & Directories

[3904]
The Faculty directory of higher education. 1st ed. Detroit, Mich., Gale Research Co., 1988. 12v.(6635p.). $785 the set. (individual subject vols. available separately). ISBN: 0810327503. ISSN: 08949476.

Classified directory of names, addresses and titles of courses taught by some 623,000 faculty members in more than 31000 US and 220 Canadian colleges and universities. 11 discipline-oriented volumes cover business, economics and law; communications; computer science and data processing; education; engineering; fine and applied arts; humanities; language and literature; medicine and nursing; science and mathematics; and social sciences. Each volume has a short guide to subject coverage and a key to abbreviations. V.12 is the master A-Z index of faculty members, and also has a list of institutions. Competes with *The National faculty directory*. 'Primary value will be as a marketing aid' (*Choice*, v.25)7), March 1988, p.1062). *Class No:* 378.4/.6(71/73)(058)

Caribbean

Bibliographies

[3905]
Universities in the Caribbean region - struggles to democratize: an annotated bibliography. Waggoner, B.A. *and* Waggoner, G.R., *comps.* Boston, Mass., G.K. Hall, 1986. 368p. $55. ISBN: 0816181594.

Over 1600 annotated entries on the rapid growth of higher education in the Caribbean after World War II. *Class No:* 378.4/.6(729)(01)

USA

Yearbooks & Directories

[3906]
American universities and colleges. 14th ed. New York, deGruyter, 1992. 2200p. $149.95. ISBN: 0899258611. ISSN: 00660922.

First published 1928.

Describes over 1900 institutions in detail. Profiles are arranged by state and include information on history, admission requirements, programmes offered, degrees conferred, enrollment, fees and financial aid, faculty size, administration, buildings and grounds, etc. Institution and general indexes. *Class No:* 378.4/.6(73)(058)

[3907]
Faculty white pages, 1991. CMG Information Services, *comp.* Detroit, Mich., Gale Research Co., 1991. 1837p. Annual. $135. ISBN: 0810371782.

Lists names, addresses and telephone numbers of more than 510,000 teaching faculty at over 3,000 US colleges, universities and other institutions of higher learning. Arranged in 41 subject sections, and A-Z by name within each section. A guide to subject coverage lists over 300 specific disciplines that are covered in the general subject sections. 'Roster of colleges and universities' provides name, city, State, and zipcode for each of the institutions covered. *Class No:* 378.4/.6(73)(058)

[3908]
The National faculty directory, 1995, an alphabetical list, with addresses, of approximately 660,000 members of teaching faculties at junior colleges, colleges, and universities in the United States and at selected Canadian institutions. Detroit, Mich., Gale Research Co., 1994. 3v. $630. ISBN: 081038518x. ISSN: 00774472.

First published 1970.

Covers about 3200 junior colleges, colleges and universities in the US and 120 selected Canadian institutions. Single A-Z sequence of entries, which give individual's name, department, institution, address, city, state, and zip code. Geographic listing of the institutions covered. Six-monthly supplement updates the main edition. *Class No:* 378.4/.6(73)(058)

[3909]
Yearbook of American universities and colleges, 1986-1987. Kurian, G.T., *ed.* New York, Garland, 1988. c1637p. charts, tables. $95. ISBN: 0824079426. ISSN: 08961034.

First published for 1986-1987. To be annual.

A review of major developments in US higher education in 15 sections: 2. Principal sectors of higher education - 3.

....(contd.)
    Issues - 4. Statistics - 5. People ... 10. Selected state reports
    on higher education... 15. Bibliography (p.615-632). Index,
    p.633-653. *Class No:* 378.4/.6(73)(058)

39 Customs & Traditions

Costume

Bibliographies

[3910]
ANTHONY, P. *and* **ARNOLD, J. Costume: a general bibliography.** London, Costume Society, c/o Department of Textiles, 1974. vi,42p. £1. ISBN: 090340706x.
First published 1966.
A selection of *c.*500 periodical articles, books and journals, mainly published after 1900, dealing primarily with the history of Western European costume. (*Introduction*). 35 sections of briefly annotated entries (sections by form and by subject). No index. *Class No:* 391(01)

[3911]
Costume index: a subject index to plates and illustrated text. Monro, I.S. *and* Cook, D.E. New York, H.W. Wilson Co., 1937. Supplement, 1957. x,338p. Supplement. x,210p.
Indexes illustrations of costume in 615 books; entries are under countries, types of people wearing costume, and specific articles. Locations in 33 libraries. The supplement adds 347 titles. *Class No:* 391(01)

[3912]
HILER, H. *and* **HILER, M.,** *comps.* **Bibliography of costume:** a dictionary catalog of about eight thousand books and periodicals. Cushing, H.G., *ed.* New York, Wilson, 1939 (Reprinted New York, Arno Press, 1976). xl,911p.
Author, title, subject, editor, illustrator, engraver and other entries in one alphabet; *c.*8400 items. The fullest information, including non-evaluative annotation, is given in the author entry. 'The items listed include books, periodicals and portfolios of plates dealing with dress, jewelry, and decoration of the body, in general and for special occasions, of all countries, times, and peoples ... In addition to books on costume many books of travel, history and antiquities are listed since they include text or illustrations of costume value' (*Preface*). *Class No:* 391(01)

Encyclopaedias

[3913]
IRELAND, P.J. Encyclopedia of fashion details. London, Batsford, 1989. 264p. 512 illus. £17.99. ISBN: 071346433x.
Fashion details (*e.g.* pleats, tucks, piping, pockets, collars). Arrangement is A-Z and illustrates some of the ways in which style and decorative effects may feature in the design of a garment. *Class No:* 391(031)

[3914]
PLANCHÉ, J.R. A Cyclopaedia of costume; or, Dictionary of dress, including notices of contemporaneous fashions on the continent; and a general chronological history of the costumes of the principal countries of Europe, from the commencement of the Christian era to the accession of George the Third. London, Chatto & Windus, 1876-79 (Reprinted Gale Research Co., Detroit, 1969). 2v. illus (some col.).
V.1 contains the dictionary and covers a wide variety of costumes, material, armour, etc., from lace, hood, sleeves, pin and wimple to crozier, helmet, gauntlet and sword; many quotations; some footnote references. V.2 is a history from 53B.C. to A.D.1760. Despite its age, it is still valuable for details of costume of the medieval and renaissance periods. *Class No:* 391(031)

[3915]
RACINET, A. The Historical encyclopedia of costumes. New York, Facts on File, 1988. 320p. illus. (some col.). $40. ISBN: 0816019762.
Originally published in 20 instalments, *c.*1876-86, in *Le costume historique.* In 1888 a 2000-page work in 6 vols. was fashioned from the earlier periodical instalments.
The 1888 work was the basis for the English ed., condensed to one vol., edited in chronological order, and redesigned into a more accessible form. In 4 parts: *The ancient world - Nineteenth century antique civilizations - Europe from Byzantium to the 1800s - Traditional costumes of the 1800s.* Each part is subdivided geographically. Index by country. 'The scope of the work is impressive' (*RQ*, v.28(4), Summer 1989, p.565). *Class No:* 391(031)

[3916]
—**BOUCHER, F. 20000 years of fashion:** the history of costume & personal adornment. New ed. Abrams, 1987. 356p. illus. $45. ISBN: 0810916932.
Devoted only to Western fashion, but covers more chronological ground than the above, having been updated to include the 1970s and 1980s. *Class No:* 391(031)

Handbooks & Manuals

[3917]
ARNOLD, J. A Handbook of costume. London, Macmillan Press, 1973 (Reprinted 1978). 336p. illus., facsims., ports. ISBN: 0333244893.
1. Primary sources (1. Paintings - 2. Sculpture... 6. Monumental brasses... 9. Dolls - 10. Tapestries, embroidery, printed and woven textiles - 11. Archival material, literary sources, periodicals and newspapers) - 2. Dating costumes from construction techniques - 3. Costume conservation, storage and display - 4. Costume for children and students (use of library and museums; collection of reproductions showing primary source material) - 5. Custume for the stage - 6. Costume bibliography (p.217-32; 18 sections; *c.*500 items) - 7. Collections of costume and costume accessories in England, Scotland and Wales (over

....*(contd.)*
80 collections under places, A-Z, p.233-336). Each part of section 1 has list and notes of books with 'useful' illustrations or a list of primary source books. Over 240 illus. (photography; line drawings) in all. No index. A valuable guide to sources. *Class No:* 391(035)

[3918]
ARNOLD, J. **Patterns of fashion.** London, Macmillan Press, 1972-85. 3v. (72p., 88p., 128p.). £12.95 each vol. ISBN: 0333136063, v.1; 0333136071, v.2; 0333382846, v.3.
V.1 is sub-titled 'Englishwomen's dresses and their construction, *c.*1660-1860'; v.2 '... *c.*1860-1940' v.3 'the cut and construction of clothes for men and women, *c.*1560-1620. *Class No:* 391(035)

[3919]
DE LA HAYE, A. **Fashion source book.** London, Macdonald & Co (Publishers) Ltd., 1988. 191p. illus. (col.). £17.50. (*A Macdonald Orbis book.*) ISBN: 0356159280.
Designed and produced by Quarto Publishing plc., London.
Brief text discusses the consumption, production and retailing of fashion and fashion design from 1900-1908 to the 1980s, chronologically arranged. The bulk of the book is pictorial and illustrates women and children's clothing, plus a few men's clothing in the 1980s. Index, p.188-191. *Class No:* 391(035)

[3920]
HOUCK, C. **The Fashion encyclopedia:** an essential guide to everything you need to know about clothes. New York, St., Martin's Press, 1982. 236p. illus. $22.50. ISBN: 0312284004.
A highly readable survey of the field of fashion, covering style, personalities, production, care, and purchasing of material, clothing and accessories. Arranged A-Z by topic. Many black-and-white illustrations. *Class No:* 391(035)

[3921]
YARWOOD, D. **Costume in the Western world:** pictorial guide and glossary. New York, St. Martin's Press; London, Lutterworth Press; 1981. 192p. illus. $17.50; £7.95. ISBN: 0312170130, US; 0718824784, UK.
Supplements 'The encyclopedia of world costume' (1979). Focuses on fashion and costume in the Western world and North America from the early Middle Ages to the present, emphasising in particular the sixteenth to nineteenth centuries. *Class No:* 391(035)

[3922]
—YARWOOD, D. **The Encyclopedia of world costume.** London, Batsford, 1978. (Reprinted 1986). 472p. illus. £14.95. ISBN: 0713413409.
This work, in A-Z order, has 2164 careful line-drawings and 8p. of coloured illustrations. 'Sleeves' (p.377-84): 39 illus.; 'Lace' (p.264-72) includes specific laces and lace terms. Bibliography (grouped), p.454-9. Detailed index. 'This book should be in every school and public library' (*New history*, no.11., 1979, p.8). *Class No:* 391

Dictionaries

[3923]
PICKEN, M.B. **The Fashion dictionary:** fabric, sewing and apparel in the language of fashion. Rev. & enl. ed. New York, Funk & Wagnall, 1973. xii,[1],434p. illus.
First published 1939 as *The Language of fashion*. Rev. ed.

....*(contd.)*
1957.
More than 10,000 words briefly defined, with pronunciation. 109 group terms (*e.g.* Linens, Heels). Includes obsolete terms. 'Sleeves': 5½ columns in the 1959 ed., describing *c.*50 types of sleeve, with 11 small line-drawings. 202 half-tones, plus *c.*2 line-drawings per page. Analytical index of illustrations. Adequate cross-references. A standard work in its field. *Class No:* 391(038)

[3924]
WILCOX, R.T. **The Dictionary of costume.** London, Batsford, 1992. 416p. illus. £19.99.
Over 3200 entries and over 2000 line drawings. Covers all periods worldwide. All aspects of costume from 'aal' (source of red dye) to 'zukin' (Japanese scarf); accessories, underwear, hairstyles, cosmetics, clothing materials, embroideries, lace, etc. *Haute couture*, folk costume, military and ecclesiastical dress, tailoring and dressmaking tools. *Class No:* 391(038)

Reviews & Abstracts

[3925]
Costume: the journal of the Costume Society. London, the Society, 1967-. Annual. £15. ISSN: 05908876.
The history of clothing. Includes numerous short articles, *c.*30 book reviews, lists of new books (including museum publications) and periodical articles. *Class No:* 391(048)

Yearbooks & Directories

[3926]
LAMBERT, E. **World of fashion:** people, places, resources. New York, R.R. Bowker, 1976. 361p. $18.95. ISBN: 0835206270.
Arrangement is geographical, entries for each country including a brief history and economic survey of the industry. This is followed by a biographical directory of leading designers and firms, a section of 'Fashion influentials' (editors and writers, fashion historians, photographers, illustrators, merchandisers), trade associations, awards, schools and colleges, costume museums, and fashion periodicals. Bibliography. Index. *Class No:* 391(058)

Histories

[3927]
BOEHN, M.von. **Modes and manners from the Middle Ages to the end of the eighteenth century.** London, Harrap, 1932-5 (reprinted by Blom Publications, 4v. in 2). 4v. illus. $50. ISBN: 0405082800.
Translation of the original German, *Die Mōde, Menschen und Modern* (München, Bruckmann, 1923-28. 8v. in 5).
1: *From the decline of the ancient world to the Renaissance;* 2: *The sixteenth century;* 3. *The seventeenth century;* 4. *The eighteenth century. Class No:* 391(091)

[3928]

—BOEHN, M. von *and* FISCHEL, O. Modes and manners of the nineteenth century. Rev. ed. London, Dent, 1927 (Reprinted by Blom Publications, 4v. in 2). 4v. illus. $50. ISBN: 0405082835.

Covers 1790-1914, by periods; illustrated from contemporary sources. 'Especially valuable for its illustrations from works of art often unfamiliar to English students' (*Art libraries journal*, v.1(3), Summer 1976, p.6). *Class No:* 391(091)

[3929]

BOUCHER, F. A History of costume in the West. Rev. ed. London, Thames & Hudson, 1987. 464p. 1300 illus. (365 in col.). £32. ISBN: 0500014167.

Translation of *Histoire du costume en occident, de l'antiquité à nos jours* (Paris, Flammarion, 1965), by John Ross.

A particularly well-illustrated history, arranged chronologically by periods from prehistory to 1964, 12 chapters, each with short bibliography appended. General bibliography in 4 form sections. Index. *Class No:* 391(091)

[3930]

BRUHN, W. *and* TILKE, M.A. A Pictorial history of costume: a survey of costume of all periods and peoples from antiquity to modern times, including national costume in Europe and non-European countries. Tübingen, Wasmuth; London, Zwemmer, 1955. 277p. 200 illus. (120 col.). £32.50. ISBN: 0302002693.

Based on the German edition, *Das Kostümwerk* (1941). The colour plates illustrate about 4000 costumes up to the end of the 19th century. *Class No:* 391(091)

[3931]

—TILKE, M. Costume patterns and designs a survey of costume patterns and designs of all periods and nations, from antiquity to modern times. London, Magna Books, 1990. 128p. 112 illus. £19.99. ISBN: 1854221965.

Planned as a supplement to Bruhn and Tilke. Many of the plates are in colour, explanatory text preceding. The drawings are mostly to scale 1:10. *Class No:* 391(091)

[3932]

CUNNINGTON, C.W. *and* CUNNINGTON, P. The History of underclothes. Mansfield, A.D. *and* Mansfield, V., *eds.* New rev. ed. London, Faber & Faber, 1981. 185p. illus. £13.50. ISBN: 0571117473.

First published 1951.

Chronical treatment in 14 chapters (1. Medieval period; 2-13. periods 1585-1939; 14. 1940-1950). 157 black-and-white illus. Appendix on clothes rationing. Glossary of materials. Bibliography of primarily and secondary sources (2p.). Sources of illus. Detailed index, p.183-185. *Class No:* 391(091)

[3933]

EWING, E. History of twentieth-century fashion. Mackrell, A., *ed.* 3rd ed. London, Batsford, 1992. xii,300p. 307 illus (some col.). £25. ISBN: 0713468181.

Written by E.Ewing, this edition revised and updated by A. Mackrell. Looks behind the scenes for an understanding of the social, economic and technical changes which have made fashion available to all.Bibliography precedes, p.iv-v. Index, p.299-300. *Class No:* 391(091)

[3934]

GORSLINE, D. A History of fashion. London, Fitzhouse Books (an imprint of B.T. Batsford), 1991. xiii,266p. illus. ISBN: 0713465921.

First published in 1953; first published in Great Britian by Batsford in 1955.

A historical and visual study of dress from the ancient world to the middle of the 20th century. In 3 parts, all subdivided: I. Costume of the ancient world; II. European costume; III. American costume. Detailed contents list precedes. *c.*1800 illustrations. Bibliography, p.249-256. Sources, p.257-266. Essentially pictorial with a minimum amount of explanatory material. 'A reference for professionals and students alike' (*British book news*, January 1991, p.64). *Class No:* 391(091)

[3935]

HANSEN, H.H. Costume cavalcade: 689 examples of historic costume in colour. 2nd rev. ed. London, Methuen, 1972. 160p. illus. (mostly col.). £6.50. ISBN: 0413288005.

First published 1956, a translation of *Klaededratsen kavalcade* (Copenhagen, Politikens Forlag).

Text in chronological periods (Egypt. *c.*3000-500 B.C. ... Twentieth century, 1900-1970. 689 six-colour photolithographed illus. (re-drawn from original dress), plus small line-drawings. 'Some books on costume', p.[6]. 'Sources used for the illustrations', p.[7]. Bibliography, p.156. Index. *Class No:* 391(091)

[3936]

PEACOCK, J. Costume, 1066-1966. London, Thames & Hudson, 1986. 128p. illus. £4.95. ISBN: 0500274045.

A sketchbook of dress arranged under the reigns of English kings and queens. Each page has 8 sketches; no text, apart from an introduction, the aim being to make each costume self-explanatory, but there are brief notes around each sketch. Sources of sketches are not indicated. List of books for further reading. *Class No:* 391(091)

[3937]

SMITH, G. Inspiration and information: sources for the fashion designer and historian. In *Art librarian's journal*, 1989, 14/4, p.11-16.

Text of a paper presented to the IFLA Sectionn of Art Libraries, at Paris, August 1989. 50 references to sources other than books on costume history. *Class No:* 391(091)

[3938]

A Visual history of costume. London, Batsford, 1984-86. 6v. illus. £12.95 each vol. Volumes for the 19th & 20th centuries were reprinted (revised and reprinted) in 1992 (£15.99 each vol.). ISBN: 0713440937; 0713440953; 0713448571; 0713448598; 0713440996; 0713440910.

Devised for those who need reliable, easy-to-use reference material on the history of dress. The central part of each volume is a series of illustrations taken from the time of the dress itself. Clothes described and significance explained. Arranged chronologically. Glossaries designed to also act as indexes. Volume titles: *14th & 15th centuries*, M. Scott. (1986. 152p. 150 illus); *16th century*, by J. Ashelford. (1983. 144p. 156 illus (8 col.)); *17th century* (1983. 144p. 158 illus (8 col.)); *18th century,*by A. Ribeiro (1983. 144p. 156 illus (8 col.)); *19th century* (1984. 144p. 158 illus (8 col.)); *20th century*, by P. Byrde (1986. 152p. 162 illus.). *Class No:* 391(091)

Biographies

[3939]

STEGEMEYER, A., *comp.* **Who's who in fashion.** 2nd ed. New York, Fairchild, 1988. 243p. illus. (inc. 16 col.pl.). $15.50. ISBN: 0870055747.

First published 1980.

The 208 people chosen for inclusion are '... designers with an international track record ...'. Entries, which vary in length from a paragraph or two to 2 or 3 pages, include date and place of birth (and death), fashion awards, background, education, philosophy, career, etc. A-Z arrangement by name. 3-page bibliography. Index. *Class No:* 391(092)

[3940]

Who's who in fashion: a biographical encyclopedia of the International Red Series containing some 6000 biographies. Strute, K. *and* Dolken, T., *eds.* 2nd ed. New York, Bowker; Zurich, Who's who in the International Red Series, 1983. 3v. (1000p.).

First published 1982.

A directory of important personalities and institutions related to fashion in Western European countries. V.1 covers fashion, v.2-3 cover beauty and jewelry.
Class No: 391(092)

Europe

Bibliographies

[3941]

SNOWDON, J. **European folk dress:** a guide to 555 books and other sources of illustrations and information. London, The Costume Society, 1973. 60p. £2.50. (*Bibliography, no.2.*) ISBN: 0903407043.

Entries for bibliographies, periodicals, and general works are followed by entries grouped in European areas, subdivided by countries. For each entry, author, title, place of publication and publisher, year of publication. Many entries also have brief descriptions or comments. No indexes. *Class No:* 391(4)(01)

Handbooks & Manuals

[3942]

SNOWDON, J. **The Folk dress of Europe.** London, Mills & Boon Ltd., 1979. 160p. illus. £8.95. ISBN: 0263063976.

Arranged by country, A-Z (The Austrian-Hungarian Empire - Czechoslovakia ... Spain - Portugal). Includes 145 black-and-white illustrations in the text and 24 colour plates. Bibliography, p.153-160. *Class No:* 391(4)(035)

Histories

[3943]

PEACOCK, J. **The Chronicle of Western fashion.** New York, Abrams, 1991. 224p. illus. $29.95. ISBN: 0810939533.

*c.*1000 full-colour, detailed drawings in chronological order (ancient civilisation grouped by nationalities, later nationalities mingle). 8-10 figures a page, with descriptions of each figure accompanied by small outline replicas). Bibliography. Illustrated glossary. *Class No:* 391(4)(091)

England

Dictionaries

[3944]

CUNNINGTON, C.W., *and others.* **A Dictionary of English costume. 900-1900.** London, Black, 1960. (Reprinted 1982). 292p. illus. £7.50.

Concise descriptions of all items of English costume from contemporary sources, plus approximate date of their coming into fashion and in many cases a quotation to illustrate their nature and function. Extensive glossary of materials and over 300 illustrations.
Class No: 391(420)(038)

Histories

[3945]

BROOKE, I. **English costume...** London, Black, 1929-50. 7v. £4.50 each volume.

English costume of the early Middle Ages: the 10th to the 13th centuries ... the later Middle Ages: the 14th and 15th centuries ... in the age of Elizabeth; the 16th century ... the seventeenth century ... the eighteenth century ... the nineteenth century ... English children's costume since 1775. A popular series that aims to be a useful guide and not a serious text-book. Uniform pattern. Thus, *English costume of the seventeenth century* has 89 pages, plus 40 pages of illus. (8 in colour), with descriptive text facing; treatment is chronological, by 10-year periods. No Index.
Class No: 391(420)(091)

Middle Ages

[3946]

OWEN-CROCKER, G.R. **Dress in Anglo-Saxon England.** Manchester, Manchester University Press, 1986. xi,241p. illus. £35. ISBN: 0719018188.

Arranged chronologically and profusely illustrated: 1. Introduction - 2. Germanic tradition - 3-8. are devoted to women's and men's costumes in the 5th & 6th, 7th to 9th, 10th & 11th centuries - 9. Textile production - 10. Conclusions. Appendix, p.203-208, old English garment names. Notes, p.211-225, by chapter. Bibliography, p.227-234, A-Z. Index, p.235-241. *Class No:* 391(420)"01/14"

Africa

[3947]

EICHER, J.B. **African dress:** a select and annotated bibliography of subSaharan countries. East Lansing, Michigan State University, African Studies Center, 1969. xii,134p.

Lists over 100 sources in English. *Class No:* 391(6)

USA

[3948]

WARWICK, E., *and others.* **Early American dress;** the Colonial and Revolutionary periods. New York, Blom, 1965 (Reprinted by Alexander Wyckoff and other. 428p. illus., maps. $45. (*History of American dress, v.2.*) ISBN: 0943276101.

Based on *Early American costume* (1929), By E. Warwick and H.C. Pitz.

A chronological survey in 9 chapters, from the founding

....(contd.)
of the colonies to the US of 1790. Costume of men and
women are given separate treatment in chapters 2-7; 8:
'Children in North America, 1785-1790'; 9: 'Frontier life'.
Well produced, careful drawings from original sources.
Major items in the bibliography, p.389-98. Evaluative
annotations. Analytical index, p.399-425,.
Class No: 391(73)

19th Century

[3949]

BYRDE, P. Nineteenth century fashion. London, Batsford,
1992. 192p. 138 illus (8 col). £30. ISBN: 0713455462.

Traces the evolution of men's, women's and children's
clothes throughout the age. Illustrations, in black & white
and in colour, include contemporary portraits, cartoons,
fashion plates, advertisements, etc. *Class No:* 391"18"

20th Century

[3950]

The Guinness guide to 20th-century fashion. Bond, D. 2nd
ed. Enfield, Middx., Guinness Publishing Ltd., 1985
(Reprinted 1988). 240p. illus (some col.). £32.95. ISBN:
0851123562.

First published 1981.

Chapters for each of the decades from the 1900s to the
1980s, the text describing the decade and fashions,
supported by the many illustrations. Index, p.237-240.
Class No: 391"19"

[3951]

PEACOCK, J. 20th century fashion: the complete
sourcebook. London. Thames & Hudson, 1993. 240p. illus.
£18.95. ISBN: 0500015643.

Detailed history and sourcebook, with 1100 coloured
illustrations, charts the development of women's fashion in
all its aspects (couture wear, day wear, underwear, leisure
wear, evening wear, bridal wear, and accessories).
Designers and designs. *Class No:* 391"19"

Stage Costume

[3952]

KESLER, J. Theatre costume: a guide to information
sources. Detroit, Mich., Gale Research Co., 1979. 308p.
(*Performing arts information guide series, v.6.*)

Over 1700 titles, concisely and accurately annotated.
Class No: 391:792

[3953]

PRISK, B. Stage costume handbook. New York, Harper &
Row, 1966 (Reprinted Greenwood Press, 1979). x,198p.
illus. $52.50; £38.50. ISBN: 031320912x.

Arranged by countries. Particular features - the scale of
patterns for cutting and helpful specific notes. Favourably
reviewed in *Library journal*, v.93(10), 15 May 1968,
p.1990. *Class No:* 391:792

[3954]

—BROOKE, I. Western European costume ... and its relation
to the theatre. London, Harrap, 1939-40. 2v. illus (incl. pl.).

V.1 covers 13th-16th century; v.2, 17th-19th century. 32
colour plates, 176 black-and-white illustrations in all. Aims
'to give some of the more usual styles and fashions worn
since the theatre commenced to be a leading interest in
Western Europe' (*Introduction*). No bibliographies; index in
v.2. *Class No:* 391:792

[3955]

—TRUMAN, N. Historic costuming. London, Pitman, 1936.
2v. illus.

A chronological survey, 550 B.C. - A.D. 1910. Numerous
keyed black-and-white illustrations and 1 colour plate. Of
value to theatrical producers and designers, covering civil,
ecclesiastical and military dress. *Class No:* 391:792

Yearbooks & Directories

[3956]

Directory of theatre resources. A guide to research
collections and information services. Howard, D., *comp.*
2nd ed. London, Library Association Information Services
Group and The Society for Theatre Research, 1986. 144p.
£10.50. ISBN: 0946347085.

A survey was carried out in 1985/86 to provide
information for the Working Party on Library Provision for
Theatre Research.

In 2 parts: part 1 is a directory of public and private
collections open to the public, 256 entries arranged A-Z by
place; part 2 has entries for those societies and associations
serving the theatre which provide information services. 46
entries arranged by name of organization. Information was
collected by questionnaire and is uneven, but entries name a
contact, give opening hours and note conditions of
admission; some give details of catalogues, indexes and
publications. Index to collections, p.134-137; subject index,
p.139-142. *Class No:* 391:792(058)

Men's Fashions

[3957]

Esquire's encyclopedia of 20th century men's fashions.
Schoeffler, O.E. *and* Gale, W. New York, McGraw-Hill,
1973. xi,709p. illus. (incl. col.). xi,709p. illus. (incl. col.).

51 sections on all items of men's clothing (Suits ...
Designers), illustrated from *Esquire*, etc. Captions give
dates. 'Footwear': p.292-320, subdivided into decades, to
show fashion changes; 38 illus. plus 1 col.plate. Later
sections cover materials and manufacture of fabrics.
Glossary, well illustrated, p.644-89. Analytical index, p.690-
709. *Class No:* 391.1

[3958]

WAUGH, N. The Cut of men's clothes, 1600-1900. London,
Faber & Faber, 1964. 160p. illus., diagrs. £15. ISBN:
0571057144.

A chronological survey, in three main periods: 1600-1680,
1680-1800, 1800-1900. Includes quotations from
contemporary sources. Bibliography (c.35 books; 4
journals); list of museums with costume collections (p.157).
List of artists, engravers and illustrators. Index (accessories
and detail, *e.g.* buttons; cravet; ruffles). 29 plates and
frontice-piece; 42 cutting diagrmas; 27 tailors' patterns.
Class No: 391.1

Women's Fashions

[3959]
BRADFIELD, N. **Costume in detail: women's dress, 1730-1930.** New ed. London, Harrap, 1981. ix,391p. illus. £15.95. ISBN: 0245536086.

First published 1968.

Chronological treatment, in 5 chapters. 'The Charles Wade Collection at Snowhill Manor, now a property of the National Trust, proved a valuable starting point for local research, and from there the circle widened' (*Introduction*). 370 full-page drawings (colour plates were included in the 1st ed.) and highly detailed studies, together with scholarly and informative text. Detailed, non-analytical index, p.386-91. 'Books consulted', p.384-5. 'Most valuable for anyone studying fashion and design, and for those concerned with the dating, conversation and repair of historic costume' (*British book news*, January 1969, p.23) of the 1st ed. *Class No: 391.2*

[3960]
COLEMAN, E.A. **The Opulent era: fashions of Worth, Doucet and Pingat.** London, Thames & Hudson, [1989]. 208p. 192 illus (52 in col.). £24. ISBN: 0500014760.

A survey of *fin de siècle* couture, including many reproductions of the most sumptious gowns. Designs, fabrics and clients are discussed and compared, setting their work in a larger social and cultural context. Author is an American museum curator. *Class No: 391.2*

[3961]
WAUGH, N. **The Cut of women's clothes, 1600-1930.** London Faber & Faber, 1968. 336p. illus., diagrs. £20. ISBN: 0571085946.

A chronological survey in 4 parts (17th-20th centuries). 75 cutting diagrams; 54 tailors' patterns; 71 plates. 'The diagrams have been chosen as far as possible from existing patterns in order to show a sequence of cut' (*Introduction*) Hair-styles and accessories are included. Bibliography, p.320-1, with a separate list of technical books and a selection of journals. Partly analytical index, p.323-36. *Class No: 391.2*

Encyclopaedias

[3962]
O'HARA, G. **The Encyclopedia of fashion from 1840 to the 1980s.** New York, Abrams, 1986. 272p. illus. $27.50. ISBN: 0810908824.

Covers the multifarious subject from 1840, when sewing machines came into use, and concentrates on the five major fashion capitals of the 19th and 20th centuries, Paris, London, New York, Rome, and latterly, Milan. More than 1000 entries, A-Z, including individuals in the fashion industry or influencing it, styles, trends, fabrics, furs, retailers etc. Numerous cross-references. 365 illustrations, 27 in colour. Length of entries varies from 2 lines to half a page. Bibliography, p.269-272 (General, dictionaries & encyclopedias, books about fashion and costume design, books by fashion and costume designers, magazines, etc.). *Class No: 391.2(031)*

Dictionaries

[3963]
Fairchild's dictionary of fashion. Calasibetta, C.M. 2nd ed. New York, Fairchild, 1988. 749p. illus. $50. ISBN: 0870056352.

First published 1976.

A significantly revised and updated edition of 10,000 entries, A-Z, for organizations, persons, slang terms, trademarks, clothing, hair styles, jewelry and fabrics. Numerous cross-references. Black-and-white drawings illustrate the terms, and there are 16 full-colour pages with 50 illustrations of costume from Ancient Egypt to 1988 America. An appendix of 171 brief biographical entries for fashion designers is followed by black-and-white portraits of some 64 of them. 'Authoritative, well-designed ...' (*Reference books bulletin*, 15 December 1988, p.690). *Class No: 391.2(038)*

Children's Fashions

England

[3964]
CUNNINGTON, P. *and* BUCK, A. **Children's costume in England, 1300-1900.** London, Black, 1965. 236p. 15 illus. £9.50. ISBN: 0713603712.

One chapter per century; many contemporary quotations. Deals with children from infancy to the age of *c.*16. Particularly rich in illus. Bibliography, p.226-9 (manuscript sources; printed manuscripts and books; dress and domestic economy; journals; secondary sources). Non-analytical index. *Class No: 391.31(420)*

Hairstyles

Histories

[3965]
CORSON, R. **Fashions in hair:** the first five thousand years. London, Owen, 1965. 701p. illus. (incl. pl.). £38.50. ISBN: 0720632838.

A well-illustrated historical survey, with 167 plates and 3500 black-and-white illus. Plates are on rectos, with descriptive notes facing. Chapters: 1. The wheel of fashion - 2. Ancient civilizations ... 6. The fifteenth century ... 14. The twentieth century: women. Sources, p.678-86 (Museums and libraries; Books and periodicals). Index covers plates. *Class No: 391.5(091)*

Regalia

England

[3966]
HOLMES, M. *and* SITWELL, H.D.W. **The English regalia:** their history, custody & display. London, HMSO., 1972. ix,83p. illus. (pl.).

The history of the regalia - The history of the Crown jewels and their custody. References, p.82-83. Lists: 'Keepers of the Crown jewels before the Civil War'; 'Musters and Treasurers of the jewels and plate of the Jewel House, 1660-1782'; 'Keepers of the Jewel House at the Tower of London': etc. 42 well-coloured plates. Attractive production. *Class No: 391.7(420)*

Customs

[3967]

KIGHTLY, C. The Customs and ceremonies of Britain: an encyclopaedia of living traditions. London, Thames & Hudson, 1986. 248p. illus., map. £12.50; $24.95. ISBN: 0500250960.

Over 200 entries describing English, Scottish and Welsh customs and ceremonies (*e.g.* 'Pig-face Sunday', 'Cheese rolling', 'Whuppity Stourie') arranged A-Z by name of custom or ceremony (or under a group title whenever a custom does not warrant a separate entry). Entries include dates, times and locations of the ceremonies when appropriate. Over 200 illus. (12 in col.). Cross-references. Includes a calendar of customs; a select (brief) bibliography (1p.); a regional map; and a regional gazeteer (England divided into 12 regions; Scotland and Wales separate) listing customs and places where they occur. '... fascinating ...' (*Choice*, v.24(2), October 1986, p.280). *Class No:* 392

Festivals

[3968]

COOPER, J.C. The Aquarian dictionary of festivals. Wellingborough, Northants, 1990. 224p. illus. £7.99. $12.75. ISBN: 0850308488.

A detailed history of all festivals celebrated by humankind from tribal communities to urban societies. Reflects the origins of ancient beliefs and customs. Cross-references. Bibliography, p.221-4. *Class No:* 394.2

[3969]

MacDONALD, M.R. The Folklore of world holidays. Detroit, Gale, 1992. xxix,[1],739p. $80. ISBN: 081037577x.

Entries for each day of the year; country/countries plus references. Over 340 holidays and festivals for over 150 countries, being particularly strong on non-European countries. Detailed index, p.699-739. A useful companion to *Holidays and anniversaries of the world*' (2nd ed., Gale, 1990). *Class No:* 394.2

[3970]

SPICER, D.G. The Book of festivals. Detroit, Mich., Gale Research Co., 1969 (Reprinted by Omnigraphics Inc., 1990). xiv,429p. $52. ISBN: 1558888411.

Part 1: The festivals of different peoples (p.3-347; A-Z; 'Festivals of Albania' ... 'Festivals of Yugoslavia'). Pt.2: The story of the calendars (Armenian, Chinese, Gregorian, Hindu, Jewish, Julian, Mohammedan). Appendix: 'Glossary of familiar religious and festival terms'. Selected bibliography on festivals, p.389-420 (by countries). Index of festivals. *Class No:* 394.2

[3971]

—MERIN, J. *and* BURDICK, E.B. International directory of theatre, dance and folk festivals. Westport, CT., Greenwood Press, 1978. 480p. $35. ISBN: 0313209936.

Sponsored by the International Theatre Institute of the United States.

Records over 850 festivals in 56 countries, with brief description of programmes and attractions offered. *Class No:* 394.2

Handbooks & Manuals

[3972]

Festivals in world religions, edited by Alan Brown on behalf of the Shap Working Party on World Religions in Education, compiled by A. Brown. New ed. London & New York, Longmans, 1993. x, 290p. illus. £9.99. ISBN: 0582361974.

First published 1986.

Explains in detail how many religions and many countries celebrate their major festivals. Chapter 1: Introduction (Feasts and festivals, Natural cycles and festivals. Sacred history. Sacred times. Sacred places. The Gregorian calendar) is followed by chapters on Baha'i, Buddhist, Chinese, Christian, Hindu, Jaina, Japanese, Jewish, Muslim, Sikh, Zoroastrian (Parsi), National and secular festivals, and Observing festivals in schools. 16 specialist contributors. Bibliography of 11 items plus 6 on Shap Working Party. Double column index, p.283-89. *Class No:* 394.2(035)

Scotland

[3973]

McNEILL, F.M. The Silver bough: a four-volume study of the national and local festivals of Scotland. Glasgow. Maclellen, 1957-90. 4v. V.1. & v.4: £7.50 each. ISBN: 0853351619, v.1; 0948474041, v.3; 0853350027, v.4.

V.1: *Scottish folk-lore and folk-belief* (1957); 2: *A calendar of Scottish national festivals, Candlemas to Harvest Home* (1959); 3: *A calendar of Scottish national festivals. Halloe'en to Yule* (1990); 4. *The local festivals of Scotland* (1970). V.2-4 deal with festivals in calendar order. V.1 carries a brief bibliography; that in v.2 is a little fuller (but authors and titles only). V.2 is well illustrated and carries many quotations. 'A valuable compendium of information' (*Scottish studies,* v.4, 1960, p.219-22). *Class No:* 394.2(411)

England

[3974]

WHISTLER, L. The English festivals. London, Heinemann, 1947. 241p. illus.

The calendar festivals described in some detail, with helpful bibliographical footnotes. An appendix indexes carols in several collected volumes. *Class No:* 394.2(420)

Yearbooks & Directories

[3975]

SPICER, D.G. Yearbook of English festivals. New York, Wilson, 1954 (Reprinted Westport, CT. Greenwood Press, 1973). xxv,298p. map. $16.50.; £16.95. ISBN: 0837161320.

Part 1: Chronological survey; part 2: The Easter cycle. In calendar order; gives very readable, rather popularised accounts of current festivals, thus supplementing Chambers; *Book of days.* Glossary; bibliography; indexes of customs, counties and regions. *Class No:* 394.2(420)(058)

USA

[3976]

COHEN, H. *and* COFFIN, T.P., *eds.* The Folklore of American holidays: a compilation of more than 400 beliefs, legends, superstitions ... 2nd ed. Detroit, Mich., Gale Research Co., 1991. *c.*450p. $85. ISBN: 0810376024.

....(contd.)

Concentrates on the lore and legend associated with c.125 American calendar holidays and festivals. Describes the way they are celebrated, historical origin, general characteristics, etc., followed by 'Sources and comments' (Bibliographical information for published sources, informant information for oral sources), and comments from editors. Entries vary from one to 5 pages in length. 5 indexes (Subject - Ethnic and geographic - Collectors, informants and translators - Song titles and first lines - Motifs and tale types). '... impressive reference work ...' (*Reference books bulletin*, 1986/87, p.92). '... seems a rag-bag ...' (*Library journal*, 1 April 1987, p.138). *Class No:* 394.2(73)

[3977]

Festivals sourcebook: reference guide to fairs, festivals and celebrations in agriculture; antiques; the arts, theatre and drama, arts and crafts; community; dance; ethnic events; film; folk; food and drink; history; Indians; marine; music; seasons and wildlife. Wasserman, P., *ed.* 2nd ed. Detroit, Mich., Gale Research Co., 1984. 736p. $135. ISBN: 081030323x.

Lists more than 4000 festivals. *Class No:* 394.2(73)

[3978]

—HILL, K.T. **Festivals USA.** New York, Wiley, 1988. 242p. $12.95. ISBN: 0471626368.

Lists the nation's best 1000 festivals, as identified by the author. Arranged geographically by region, subdivided by State and then by month. Includes date and location of festival, description of the event, foods served, and (because designed as a travel guide) information on accommodation, restaurants, etc. Glossary of local terminology and jargon. Subject index. *Class No:* 394.2(73)

[3979]

SHEMANSKI, F. A Guide to fairs and festivals in the United States. Westport, CT., Greenwood Press, 1984. viii,339p. $42.95. ISBN: 0313214379.

Identifies several hundred of the main United States events, arranged by State, then city or town. Appendix by type of event and a calender of events by State and month. *Class No:* 394.2(73)

Special Days

[3980]

GROSS, E. This day in religion. New York, Neal-Schuman, 1990. 294p. $39.95. ISBN: 1555700454.

A chronological 'book of days' for religion. Covers every day of the year, the time period being c.300 CE to 1989. Describes in 1-2 sentences religious events that happened on each day. Non-Christian religions included. Index of names and subjects. Brief glossary. Bibliography. '... offering more current and diverse information on religion than any similar work available'(p.6). *Class No:* 394.268

[3981]

Holidays and anniversaries of the world. Mossman, J., *ed.* 2nd ed. Detroit, Mich., Gale Research Co., 1990. 1080p. ISBN: 0810348705.

First published 1985.

Lists 23000 regional, national and international holidays and anniversaries for each of the 366 days of the Gregorian year. Includes birthdates of famous people of all ages; days

....(contd.)

of the Saints, Holy Days and other days of religious significance; historical events; etc. Glossary of time words. Index. *Class No:* 394.268

Dictionaries

[3982]

DUNKLING, L. A Dictionary of days. London, Routledge & Kegan Paul; New York, Facts on File, 1988. xiii,156p. £14.95; $21.95. ISBN: 0415002397, UK; 0816019169, US.

A compendium of over 850 named days celebrated in literature and in real life in the English-speaking world. 27 categories. Entries generally brief, usually less than 300 words. Includes occasional quotations, and references are cited. List of specifically dated days in calendar order. 'Eminently readable source' (*Library review*, v.37(2), 1988, p.62). *Class No:* 394.268(038)

USA

[3983]

GREGORY, R.W. Anniversaries and holidays. 4th ed. Chicago, Ill., American Library Association, 1983. xiii,262p. $25; £18.50. ISBN: 0838903894.

First published 1928.

'The purpose... is to provide a quick identification of notable anniversaries, holy days, holidays and special event days, and to link outstanding days to books for further information or background' (*Preface*). Arranged in 3 parts: 1. Calendar of fixed days - 2. Calendar of movable days - 3. Books related to anniversaries and holidays (p.184-244. 875 briefly annotated entries, A-Z). Index, p.245-262. *Class No:* 394.268(73)

[3984]

HATCH, J.M. The American book of days. 3rd ed. New York, Wilson, 1978. 1214p. $75. ISBN: 0824205936.

2nd ed. 1948, by G.W. Douglas.

Over 700 articles, each of 300-8000 words. Covers holidays, anniversaries, religious and secular festivals, celebrations, birthdays of prominent Americans, etc. 'Recommended as an essential purchase for all academic libraries' (*Choice*, v.16(5/6), July/August, 1979, p.648). *Class No:* 394.268(73)

Official Ceremonies

[3985]

GARNER, J.F. Civic ceremonial: a handbook of practice and procedure. Waldram, G.N., *ed.* 3rd ed. London, Shaw & Sons, 1979 (reprinted 1984). xiv,204p. £10. ISBN: 072190162x.

First published 1953.

9 chapters: 1. Historical background - 2. The office of mayor or chairman - 3. The ceremonial position of mayor or chairman - 4. The expenses of office - 5. Royal and State visits - 6. Civic ceremonies and functions - 7. Town twinning - 8. Civic insignia - 9. Ceremonial officers. 2 appendices: A. Specimen orders of procedure; B. Attendance of mayor/chairman at non-civic functions - specimen forms. Index of towns. Alphabetical index. No illustrations. *Class No:* 394.4

England

Histories

[3986]

MILTON, R. **The English ceremonial book:** a history of robes, insignia and ceremonies still in use in England. Newton Abbot, Devon, David & Charles, 1972. 216p. illus.

6 chapters: The heralds and the college of Arms - 2. The coronation: the royal robes and regalia - 3. Robes and coronets of the peers - 4. Robes of judges, serjeants and barristers - 5. Knighthood: insignia and robes of orders of chivalry - 6. Civic robes and insignia. Chapter notes and short bibliography, p.208. Authorities personally consulted, p.209. Detailed index. 61 illustrations (8 in colour).
Class No: 394.4(420)(091)

Chivalry

[3987]

BARBER, R. *and* BARKER, J. **Tournaments, jousts, chivalry and pageants in the Middle Ages.** Woodbury, Suffolk, Boydell Press, 1989. 240p. illus. £19.95. ISBN: 0851154700.

Aims to present a coherent picture of the tournament from its beginnings in the 12th century until the close of the medieval period. Includes 40 coloured and 80 black-and-white illus. *Class No:* 394.7

Dictionaries

[3988]

BROUGHTON, B.B., *comp.* **Dictionary of medieval knighthood and chivalry:** concepts and terms. New York, Greenwood Press, 1986. 614p. illus. $67.95; £65. ISBN: 0313245525.

Intended as a resource for medievalists at all levels and areas of interest. Topical arrangement of entries, which have quick definitions and in-depth discussions of chivalry and knighthood as practiced in England and France. Extensive cross-referencing. Most entries include one or more bibliographical references and there is also a lengthy bibliography. Calendar of feast days and saint's days. Index. *Class No:* 394.7(038)

[3989]

BROUGHTON, B.B., *comp.* **Dictionary of medieval knighthood and chivalry:** people, places and events. New York, Greenwood Press, 1988. 774p. charts. $55. ISBN: 0313253471.

Companion volume to *Dictionary of medieval knighthood and chivalry: concepts and terms* (1986) above.

Over 700 entries with wide coverage of Britain and France. Extensive cross-reference to items in both this and the previous volume. Entries are fairly short and include bibliographical references. Separate bibliography of 249 items of mainly secondary sources. Appendices include genealogical charts of reigning families. 70-page double-column index. *Class No:* 394.7(038)

[3990]

UDEN, G. **A Dictionary of chivalry.** London, Longmans, 1968. viii,352p. illus., ports.

Over 1000 entries, 'Abatement of honour' ... 'Zutphen, Honour of'. Lavishly and well illustrated in margins; 96 illus. in colour. Articles concern arms and armour, battles and warfare, tournaments and pennons, sports and pastimes,

....(contd.)

biographies of knights (*e.g.* Sir Philip Sidney: 1 column). Few references to sources; no bibliography. For the young. *Class No:* 394.7(038)

Etiquette

[3991]

COLLETT, P. **Foreign bodies:** a guide to European mannerisms. London, Simon & Schuster, 1992. 368p. £14.99. ISBN: 067171063x.

Explores the way Europeans behave towards each other - revealing much about the British national character. *Class No:* 395

[3992]

DE COURCY, A. **A Guide to modern manners.** London, Thames & Hudson, 1985. 160p. 25 illus. £5.95. ISBN: 050001373x.

'In this book I have tried to define some major social groupings, together with pitfalls unknown to earlier manuals of correct behaviour - in short, to write a guide to truly modern manners; (*Introduction*). 23 chapters, amusing and lightly written. *Class No:* 395

Handbooks & Manuals

[3993]

Debrett's etiquette and modern manners: current behaviour for every sphere of social and business life. Donald, E.B., *ed.* New ed. Headland, Cleveland, Headline Publications, in association with Debrett's Peerage Ltd., 1992. 400p. illus. £20. ISBN: 0747206570.

First published 1981.

16 sections, giving precise guidance: 1. Births and the ceremonies of childhood ... 3. Weddings ... 6. Table manners - 7. Parties - 8. Invitations, letters and talk - 9. Visitors and houseguests ... 11. Public occasions and events ... 13. Courtship - 14. Household staff - 15. Sports and games - 16. Dress. Appendix: Initials and abbreviations of rank, honours and degrees: Precedence in England and Wales; Scotland. Analytical index (p.391-399). 'The first comprehensive book of etiquette to be issued since the social revolution of the sixties' (*The Times,* 25 June 1981, p.1). *Class No:* 395(035)

[3994]

POST, E.P. **Emily Post's etiquette.** 14th ed. New York, Harper, 1984. 1018p. $24.45. ISBN: 0061816833.

First published 1922.

The standard US handbook, legislating for every conceivable social occasion. This edition updates the 1975 ed. (published by Funk & Wagnell), paying more attention to behaving on the job and to business situations than earlier editions, and less attention to dress. Includes a new section on unmarried couples living together and expands the section on divorce. *Class No:* 395(035)

[3995]

—The Amy Vanderbilt complete book of etiquette: a guide to contemporary living. Baldridge, L., *ed.* New York, Doubleday, 1978. 879p. illus. $18.95. ISBN: 0385133758.

Complementary to Post. 'The emphasis, where appropriate, is on handling the sometimes difficult and awkward situations that arise as a result of changing attitudes

....(contd.)

towards marriage, divorce, living together, sex and feminism' (*American reference book annual*, 1980, item 1100). *Class No:* 395(035)

[3996]
—EDWARDS, A. *and* BEYFUS, D. Lady behave: a guide to modern manners. London, Cassell, 1969. 380p.

4th ed. published 1957.

A British equivalent to Emily Post. Modern, practical and reasonably comprehensive, amusing as well as informative. Examples of invitation cards, etc. Appendix: 'How to address titled people' (p.307-19). Analytical index. *Class No:* 395(035)

Dictionaries
[3997]
BÄUML, B.J. *and* BÄUML, F.H. A Dictionary of gestures. Metuchen, N.J., Scarecrow Press, 1975. 284p. illus. $22.50; £15.75. ISBN: 0810808653.

'Culturally transmitted (semiotic) gestures' (*Introduction*), as cited in works of literature and art. 53p. of finger gestures. Bibliography of 512 sources. Indexed by significance of gesture and body part (*e.g.* Neck). Negligible illus. 'An impressive compendium of erudite research' (*Choice*, v.14(1), March 1977, p.40, on which this annotation is based). *Class No:* 395(038)

Forms of Address
[3998]
Debrett's correct form: standard modes of address for everyone from peers to presidents. Montague-Smith, P., *comp. & ed.* New rev. ed. Headland, Cleveland, Headline, l992. 432p. £20. ISBN: 0747206589.

First published 1970.

7 parts: 1. The Royal Family - 2. The Peerage - 3. Other titles and styles - 4. Styles by office (*e.g.* Legal) - 5. Official and social occasions - 6. American usage - 7. Usages in other foreign countries. Appendices: Rules for hoisting flags ... Pronunciation of titles and surnames. Detailed, analytical index, p.413-423. *Class No:* 395.6

Great Britain
[3999]
Titles and forms of address: a guide to their correct use. 19th rev. ed. London, A & C Black, 1990. xxxviii,185p. £5.50. ISBN: 0713631325.

First published 1918.

Sections: Royalty - The peerage - Dukes and duchesses - Marquesses and marchionesses - Earls and countesses - Viscounts and viscountesses ... Chiefs of Scottish clans ... Ecclesiastical - The Royal Navy - The Army - The Royal Air Force ... Law, diplomatic and government - Honours, qualifications and appointments - The universities. Some pronunciations of proper names. Analytical index, p.179-185. Confined to English titles, including those of the church and civic dignitaries. *Class No:* 395.6(410)

Women & Society
[4000]
CARTER, S. *and* RITCHIE, M. Women's studies: a guide to information sources. London, Mansell; Jefferson, NC., McFarland, 1990. 278p. £50. $39.95. ISBN: 0720120586, UK; 0899505341, US.

Over 1000 English-language works published mainly between 1978 and 1988. Arranged in 3 main sections: General material (*e.g.* reference sources, biographies, women's studies) - Women in the world (subdivided geographically) - Special subjects (13 topics). Annotations vary in length from two lines to two paragraphs. Indexed by author, title and subject. Updates S.E. Searing's *Introduction to library research in women's studies* (1985) and K. Loeb's *Women's studies: a recommended core bibliography* (1987). *Class No:* 396

[4001]
HUMM, M. The Dictionary of feminist theory. Hemel Hempstead, Herts., Harvester Wheatsheaf Publications; Columbus, Ohio, Ohio State University Press, 1989. xvi,278p. £30; $39.95. ISBN: 0710811489 UK; 0814205062, US.

'A broad, cross-cultural and international account of contemporary feminist thought' (*Preface*). Claims to be the first fully cross-referenced guide to bring together, clarify and explain the concepts and ideas about women and their views of the world. Bibliography, p.251-278. *Class No:* 396

Databases
[4002]
Women online: research in women's studies using online databases. Atkinson, S.D. *and* Hudson, J., *eds.* Redding, CA, Hawthorn Press Inc., 1990. 420p. $19.95. ISBN: 1560240377.

Chapters on online searching, by specialists, are followed by a directory of the online services mentioned. Database Matrix (not exhaustive). (Neither *Women's studies abstracts* nor *Women's abstracts* is online). *Class No:* 396(003.4)

Bibliographies of Bibliographies
[4003]
BALLOU, P.K. Women: a bibliography of bibliographies. 2nd ed. Boston, Mass., G.K. Hall, 1986. 288p. $30. ISBN: 0816187290.

First published 1980.

A mainly annotated list of 906 books, parts of books, pamphlets, journal articles, microforms and documents published between 1970 and June 1985. Items selected for scope, availability, organization and commentary. A wide range of topics, with 200 subject headings. Cross-references. Subject, title and author indexes. 'An excellent starting point, the volume will be useful to both beginning and advanced women's studies researchers' (*Choice*, March 1987, p.1025). *Class No:* 396(009)

[4004]

RICHIE, M., *comp*. **Women's studies:** a checklist of bibliographies. London, Mansell, 1980. xv, 107p. £15. ISBN: 0720109183.

489 unannotated entries. Sections: General (including special issues of periodicals; library-holdings) - Anthropology - Area studies - Arts - Criminology - Economics -, Education - Geography - Health and medicine - History - Language - Law and women's rights - Literature - Politics - Psychology and psychiatry - Religion - Science - Sex roles - Sociology. Appendix. Author and keyword indexes. *Class No:* 396(009)

Bibliographies

[4005]

BARROW, M. **Women, 1870-1928:** a select guide to printed sources in the United Kingdom. London, Mansell; New York, Garland, 1981. 249p. £25; $73. ISBN: 072010923x, UK; 0824094506, US.

Originally as a thesis accepted for Fellowship of the Library Association, 1977, with its 4 major sections: 1. Archives (Collections; Education; Emigration ...) - 2. Printed works (Collections; Bibliographies; Biographies; Diaries ...) - 3. Non-book material (*e.g.* artefacts; films; oral history) - 4. Index. *Class No:* 396(01)

[4006]

—OAKES, E.H. *and* SHELDON, K.E. A Guide to social science resources in women's studies. Santa Barbara, CA, Clio Books, 1978. xi,162p.

Items arranged by academic discipline, with subdivisions as warranted. Includes books, bibliographies, and other resources. Author and subject indexes. *Class No:* 396(01)

[4007]

Bibliofem: a joint library catalogue and continuing bibliography on women. London, City & London Polytechnic, Fawcett Library, 1978-1986. Monthly. (Microfiche). ISSN: 01416456.

Co-sponsored by the Equal Opportunities Commission. *Class No:* 396(01)

[4008]

A **Bibliographic guide to studies on the status of women:** development and population trends. Paris, Unesco; New York, UNIPUB; Epping, Essex, R.R. Bowker, 1983. xii,292p. F.175; $41; £14.95. ISBN: 9231021222, France; 0859350673, UK; 0890590281, US.

597 annotated items arranged in regional sections (including Western and Eastern Europe, North America, Latin America, Africa, Asia and the Arab States), subdivided into thematic sub-sections. The sub-sections each provide an overview and list the main existing bibliographies, followed by items on women's work and labour force participations, family and household concerns, education and demography. Includes theses and unpublished documents as well as books and other sources of information. Country, subject and author indexes. *Class No:* 396(01)

[4009]

Building women's studies collections. Ariel, J., *ed*. Middletown, CT., *Choice,* in co-operation with the Women's Studies Section, Association of College and Research Libraries, A.L.A. 1987. $12 pre-paid. ISBN: 0914492071.

A 48-page guide listing up-to-date information on sources for acquiring women's studies materials: review media,

....(contd.)

feminist publishers, publishers' series, non-print sources, electronic databases, book dealers and distributors, and service organizations. *Class No:* 396(01)

[4010]

EVANS, M. *and* MORGAN, D. **Work on women** a guide to the literature. London, Tavistock Publications, 1979. [viii],83p. £7.95. ISBN: 0422771309.

About 750 unannotated entries. 11 sections (with section and subsection introductions): Feminism and the women's movement - Domestic life and labour - Women and paid work - Health, education and welfare - Law and politics - Crime and deviance - Literature, art and popular culture - Cross-cultural studies - Social psychological perspectives - Additional bibliographies, general reviews of literature, feminist journals. *Class No:* 396(01)

[4011]

GILBERT, V.F. *and* TATLA, D.S. **Women's studies: a bibliography of dissertations, 1870-1982.** Oxford, Blackwell Reference, 1985. xiv,496p. £57.50. ISBN: 0631137149.

Over 12,000 unpublished dissertations relevant to women's studies, retrieved from the archives of American British and Irish universities. Subject guide, a very detailed contents list, is followed by the bibliography, arranged in 23 subject sections (Arts - Criminology - Demography - Education ... Feminism - Health ... Philosophy - Physiology - Politics ... Religion - Reproduction - Sexuality - Sociology ... Women in the Third World. Each section subdivided and subdivided again by authors, A-Z. No annotations. 'See also' references at beginning of each subsection. Checklist of bibliographical and reference sources, p.461-466. Index, p.467-496. *Class No:* 396(01)

[4012]

HUGHES, M.M. **The Sexual barrier:** legal, medical and social aspects of sex discrimination. Washington, Hughes Press, 1977. $70. ISBN: 0912560045.

Rev. ed. of his *The sexual barrier: legal and economic aspects of employment* (1970).

Over 8000 entries for English-language books, pamphlets, periodical and newspaper articles and documents. 17 alphabetical subject sections (aging; bibliographies; child care; condition of women; economic status; education; employment; family relations; fertility; health; international; legal status; lesbianism/homosexuality; minority women; occupations; religion; sex role). 'Overall, this is a worthwhile addition to a reference collection' (*College & research libraries,* January 1979, p.51-52. *Class No:* 396(01)

[4013]

HUMM, M. An **Annotated critical bibliography of feminist criticism.** Boston, Mass., G.K. Hall, 1987. 240p. $35. ISBN: 0816189374.

An annotated list of 907 English-language books and articles published in the United States and Great Britain between 1950 and 1985. Entries chronologically arranged within 8 subject areas (Theory and sexual politics; literary criticism; sociology; psychology; history; anthropology and myth; education; and women's studies). Indexes to subjects (topics and authors) and contributors. Includes works not in Stineman and Loeb, but has fewer entries. 'Recommended as a supplement to Stineman and Loeb', (*Choice,* v.25 (7), March 1988, p.1066). *Class No:* 396(01)

[4014]

KRICHMAR, A., *and others*. **The Women's movement in the seventies:** an international English-language bibliography. Metuchen, N.J., Scarecrow Press, 1977. 891p. $47.50; £35.60. ISBN: 0810810638.

Continues Krichmar's *The women's rights movement in the United States, 1848-1970: a bibliography and source book* (1972. 436p.), plus international coverage.

Over 8600 entries (often briefly annotated) for books, pamphlets, articles, dissertations, research reports and government documents published 1970-76. Arranged geographically, then by subject and political divisions. Subject index - lacking in M.M. Hughes' *The sexual barrier (qv)*, which it complements. 'Both are necessary' (*Choice*, v.15(5/6), July/August 1978, p.670). *Class No: 396(01)*

[4015]

LOEB, K., *and others*. **Women's studies:** a recommended core bibliography, 1980-1985. Littleton, Col., Libraries Unlimited, 1987. xvi, 538p. $85; £55. ISBN: 0872874729.

An abridged edition was also published in 1987 (c.250p. £23.50; $28. 0872875989).

Annotated entries for 1154 English-language books and 57 periodicals relating to women. Arranged in 18 broad categories, the entries are both descriptive and evaluative. Author, title and subject indexes, the latter rich in multiple levels of access. '... offers an excellent review of current scholarship ...' (*Choice*, June 1987, p.1536).

A predecessor, E. Stineman's 'Women's studies: a recommended core bibliography' was published in 1979 and included 1,763 annotated entries. *Class No: 396(01)*

[4016]

ROSENBERG, M.B. and BERGSTROM, L.V., *comps. & eds*. **Women and society:** a critical review of the literature, with a selected annotated bibliography. Beverley Hills, CA., Sage Publications, 1975 (Available from Books Demand UMI). [vi], 354p. $90. ISBN: 0317106198.

3612 briefly annotated entries in 12 sections: 1. Sociology - 2. Political science (entries 878-1542) - 3. History - 4. Women in philosophy and religion - 5. Women in medicine and health - 6. Women in biography, autobiography and memoirs - 7. Women in literature and the arts - 8. Women in psychology - 9. Women in anthropology - 10. Women in economics - 11. General reference works on women (A. Bibliographies; E. Women's collections and libraries) - 12. Addendum. Indexes: author organization; journal issues entirely devoted to women; persons not cited as authors; indexes of places, subjects and topics. *Class No: 396(01)*

[4017]

STAFFORD, B. **'Best reference works for the study of minority and third world women'.** In *Special collections*, v.3(3/4), Spring/Summer, 1986, p.173-189.

Aims to provide an overview or guide to the best women's studies reference sources published within roughly the past five years. Sections: Afro-American women in North America - Native American women - Latins in the United States - Asian-American women - Jewish women - Muslim women - Women in international development - Subsaharan Africa - The Arab world - South Asia - China - Korea and Japan - South-east Asia - Latin America - General. *Class No: 396(01)*

[4018]

WARREN, M.A. **The Nature of women:** an encyclopedia & guide to the literature. Point Reyes, CA., Edgepress, 1980. 708p. $20. ISBN: 0918528070.

Describes and analyses the scholarly works that shaped the western tradition with regard to thought about women. 'Authors and topics' (A/Z, monographs). 'Anthologies and sourcebooks'; (broad categories); followed by a directory of periodicals, a bibliography, glossary and comprehensive index. 'While her impressive work lacks bibliographic precision, it is, for extensive analysis of individual works, an achievement unequaled in the women's studies area (*Library journal*, v.107(6), 15 March 1980, p.712-3). *Class No: 396(01)*

Encyclopaedias

[4019]

TUTTLE, L., *ed*. **Encyclopedia of feminism.** Harlow, Essex, Longman Group UK Ltd.; New York, Facts on File, 1986. 399p. £9.95; $24.95. ISBN: 0582893461, UK; 0816014248, US.

Aims to provide, in one volume, ready access to major events, people, ideas, organizations and publications in the contemporary and past women's movements. Emphasis on America and Western Europe. Arrangement is A-Z, length of entries varying from c.30 words to 2½ columns (*e.g.*, 'Holloway brooch':1 col; 'Housework': 2½ cols.' 'Liberal feminism': 2½ cols.). Many entries are about people. Good cross-reference structure. Extensive bibliography, p.375-399, by authors, A-Z. 'An excellent reference guide to a vast body of information;' (*Choice*, v.24(8), April 1987, p.1204). *Class No: 396(031)*

[4020]

Women studies encyclopedia. Tierney, H., *ed*. Westport, CT., Greenwood Press, 1989-91. 3v. v.1. 433p. v.2. 384p. v.3. 531p. $112.00 for v.1&2; $65 for v.3. ISBN: 0313267251, v.1; 031327357x, v.2; 0313273588, v.3.

V.1 Views from the sciences; v.2. Literature, art and learning; v.3. History, philosophy and religion. Focuses on recent feminist research in the natural, behavioural and social sciences, health and medicine, economics, linguistics, political sciences, and the law. Articles provide a definitive historical overview and current research findings. Most articles include selected references. *Class No: 396(031)*

Reviews & Abstracts

[4021]

Studies on women abstracts. Abingdon, Oxon, Carfax Publishing Co., 1983-. v.1, no.1-. 6pa. £136. ISSN: 02625644.

c.800 indicative and informative abstracts pa. Covers books and journal articles in all main areas of women's studies (education, employment, women in the family and community, medicine and health, female sex and gender role socialization, social policy, social psychology of women, female culture, media treatment of women, biography, literary criticism, and historical studies. List of books received for inclusion. List of journals covered (396). Author and subject indexes, cumulated annually. *Class No: 396(048)*

[4022]
Women studies abstracts. Rush, N.Y., Rush Publishing Co., 1972-.no.1-. Quarterly. $56pa. ISSN: 00497835.

About 200 indicative and informative abstracts per issue, arranged in 22 subject sections: Education, localization - Sex roles, characteristics, differences and similarities - Employment - Sexuality - Family ... History - Literature and art ... Women's Liberation Movement. Appended is an extensive listing of book reviews. Author and subject indexes, cumulating in the 4th issue each year. 'Recommended for the basic women's studies collection in college libraries (*Choice*, v.12(12), February 1976, p.1544). Also available on microform from UMI. *Class No:* 396(048)

[4023]
—Women's studies index. 1989-. Boston, Mass., G.K. Hall, 1991-. Annual. $165. ISSN: 10586369.

Covers over 100 journal titles, ranging from popular to scholarly. Whereas *Women's studies abstracts* offers depth, this index offers breadth. Author and subject access. *Class No:* 396(048)

Periodicals & Progress Reports

[4024]
DOUGHAN, D. *and* **SANCHEZ, D.,** *comps.* **Feminist periodicals, 1855-1984:** an annotated, critical bibliography of British, Irish, Commonwealth and international titles, compiled by David Doughan and Denise Sanchez. Brighton, Harvester Press, 1986; New York, New York University Press (Dist. by Columbia), 1987. 316p. £60; $75. ISBN: 0710809921, UK; 0814717985, US.

920 titles, 229 antedating 1960, arranged chronologically, of journals, broadsheets and other periodicals relating to women. Include brief annotations and locations in major London libraries. Includes an essay on women's periodicals, a short bibliography and indexes of persons, titles, subjects and dates. A good source guide for working on 19th and 20th century social and feminist histories. David Doughan is librarian of the Fawcett Library. *Class No:* 396(05)

Yearbooks & Directories

[4025]
COWLEY, R. What about women? Information sources for women's studies. Manchester, Fanfare Press, 1984. [4],103p. £2.85. ISBN: 0947813004.

Includes nearly 140 addresses of British and foreign organizations of importance to women, plus details of their resource centre holdings and their services. Arranged in 3 sections: I. Directory of organizations (England, Scotland, Wales, international, some overseas governmental organizations) - II. Developing a resource collection, 1: Basic resource list for women's studies - III. Developing a resource collection, 2: Organization of materials. The directory in section I includes for each organization, name, address, telephone number, aims, publications, stock and policy, services offered. *Class No:* 396(058)

Quotations

[4026]
PARTNOW, E. The New quotable woman. New York, Facts on File, 1992. 714p. $40. ISBN: 0816021341.

Combines, revises and updates two previous volumes, *The Quotable woman from Eve to 1979*(1986) and *The Quotable*

....(contd.)
woman...1800-1981(1983).

Organized chronologically by birthdates, subdivided by speakers. Sources given. Biographical index indicates subject, career and occupation, ethnicity and nationality. *Class No:* 396(082.2)

Tables & Data Books

[4027]
Statistical record of women worldwide Schmittroth, L., *comp. & ed.* Detroit, Gale, 1991. 763p. $89.50. ISBN: 0810383497.

Coverage claims to be international, but about 50% of the 814 tables deal only with the US. Draws on a variety of sources, whereas C. Taeuber's *Statistical handbook on women in America*(Onyx, 1991) and the UN's *The world's women trends and statistics, 1970-1990*(1991) rely on official documents. Source notes are given for each table. Subject and geographic index. *Class No:* 396(083)

Maps & Atlases

[4028]
SEAGER, J. *and* **OLSON, A. Women in the world** an international atlas. Touchstone, Simon & Schuster; London, Pan Books, 1986. 128p. illus., tables, maps. $19.95; £7.95. ISBN: 0671602977, US; 0330291939, UK.

Global information on the lives of women arranged in 40 chapters within 10 central topics (The second sex - marriage - motherhood - work - resources - welfare - authority - body politics - change - statistical politics). Maps and short tables, supported by text, showing the differences and similarities among women throughout the world. Country table. Notes on maps. Bibliography, p.121-126. Index, p.127-128. 'A major tool' (*Library journal, v.111(19)*, 15 November 1986, p.87). *Class No:* 396(084.3)

Histories

[4029]
KANNER, B., *ed.* **The Women of England,** from Anglo-Saxon times to the present: interpretative bibliographical essays. Hamden, CT., Archon; Shoestring, 1979; London, Mansell, 1980. 429p. $37.50; £30. ISBN: 0208016392, US; 0720115647, UK.

13 contributors. 12 bibliographical essays (*e.g.* 'Women in Norman and Plantagenet times', p.83-123; 55 notes; bibliography, p.113-23. 'A survey of primary sources and archives for the history of early twentieth-century English women', p.388-409; 21 notes; bibliography (*i.e.*, library and society sources), p.410-8). Index. 'This belongs in any library used by students of literature, history, or the social sciences. (*Library journal*, v.104(14), August 1979, p.1552). *Class No:* 396(091)

[4030]
O'DAY, R. 'The History of women and the family'. In *British book news,* July 1986, p.383-386.

A literature survey of 55 books, arranged in 4 sections: Demographic history; The 'sentiments' school; The 'household economics' approach; Other works on women. *Class No:* 396(091)

Bibliographies

[4031]

FREY, L., *and others, comps.* **Women in Western European history:** a select chronological, geographical and topical bibliography from antiquity to the French Revolution. Westport, CT., Greenwood Press, 1982. lv,760p. $49.95.

A historical outline and topical guide to citations, p.xv-l, (serves as a detailed contents list) is followed by a Guide to quotations (names A-Z & pages on which quoted). The bibliography is arranged in 6 sections: 1. Historical surveys - 2. Antiquity - 3. Middle Ages - 4. Renaissance/ Reformation - 5. Seventeenth century - 6. Eighteenth century. Entries are numbered and arranged by subject in each section, subdivided by authors, A-Z. No annotations. Subject index, p.633-639; name index, p.641-660; author index, p.661-760. *Class No:* 396(091)(01)

[4032]

—**FREY, L.,** *and others, eds. & comps.* Women in Western European history: a select chronological, geographical and topical bibliography, the nineteenth and twentieth centuries. Westport, CT., Greenwood Press, 1984. liv,1025p. $85. 021.00/00 0313228590

Similar arrangement to the above, with 4 sections: 1. Nineteenth and twentieth centuries - 2. Nineteenth century (c.1789-1914) - 3. Early twentieth century, 1914-1945 - 4. Twentieth century since 1945. A first supplement (1986. 699p. 0313251098) supplements the two earlier volumes, with more recently discovered or published material. *Class No:* 396(091)(01)

Laws

[4033]

CHARLES, N. *and* **JAMES, J.** The Rights of women: the essential question and answer guide to women's legal problems. London, Arrow Books, 1990. 224p. ISBN: 0099662302.

Gives answers to queries about women's legal problems, from sexual harassment at work to compensation claims. *Class No:* 396(094.1)

Developing Countries

Bibliographies

[4034]

BYRNE, P.R. *and* **ONTIVEROS, S.R.,** *eds.* **Women in the Third World:** a historical bibliography. Santa Barbara, CA., ABC-Clio, 1986. 152p. $28. ISBN: 0874364590.

600 annotated entries for journal articles, selected from *c.*2000 journal titles and published between 1970 and 1985. Arranged by geographical area (Africa - Asia - Middle East - Pacific region - Latin America - West Indies). Subject and author indexes. *Class No:* 396(4/9-77)(01)

[4035]

FENTON, T.P. *and* **HEFFRON, M.J.,** *comps. & eds.* **Women in the Third World:** a directory of resources. Maryknell, N.Y., Orbis Books, 1987. 160p. $9.95. ISBN: 0883445301.

In 5 sections, annotated entries for books, periodicals, pamphlets and articles, audiovisual materials, and organizations, with unannotated supplementary lists in each section. Material mainly published between 1971 and 1986.

....(contd.)

'An excellent complement to Byrne & Ontivero's *Women in the Third World: a historical bibliography* (1986)' *(Choice,* v.25(1), September 1987, p.86). *Class No:* 396(4/9-77)(01)

[4036]

TOWNSEND, J. **Women in developing countries;** a select annotated bibliography for development organisations. Brighton, Sussex, Institute of Development Studies, 1988. v,190p. £7.50 + £1.50 p & p. *(Development bibliography series, 1.)* ISBN: 0903354802.

Assembled with the help of IDS, War on Want, and Oxfam.

Items arranged by country, with a general section for each continent, and also a final general section. All items annotated and relative importance is indicated. *Class No:* 396(4/9-77)(01)

Europe

Almanacs

[4037]

SNYDER, P. The European women's almanac. New York, Columbia, 1992. 399p. $35. ISBN: 0231080646.

A 'snapshot' of women's status and conditions in 26 countries. Chapters are arranged A-Z by country, each beginning with a map and description of political and cultural status, followed by statistics for 1987-91 of vital issues (equal rights, health care, parental leave, lesbian rights, employment, education). Comparative tables give information on women's life expectancy, no. of TV sets in homes, women's suffrage, etc. *Class No:* 396(4)(059)

Great Britain

[4038]

SMITH, H.L. **British feminism in the twentieth century.** Aldershot, Hants, Edward Elgar, 1990. x,214p. £28.50. ISBN: 1852780967.

11 specially commissioned essays arranged in 3 parts, with extensive notes after each chapter: 1. Feminism in the early 20th century; 2: Feminism in the interwar years; 3: Feminism from the second world war to the present. Select bibliography (books and articles), p.205-7. Index, p.209-14. *Class No:* 396(410)

[4039]

SMITH, H.L. **British women in the 20th century.** In *Choice,* v.31(6), February 1994, p.900-08.

116 citations arranged A-Z by author in the following sections: The suffrage movement - WWI and the interwar years - WW2 and the postwar years - Contemporary feminism - Social and policy issues - Work, family and the law - Women in Scotland, Wales and Ireland. *Class No:* 396(410)

Biographies

[4040]

BANKS, O. **The Biographical dictionary of British feminists:** v.1. 1800-1930. Brighton, Harvester Wheatsheaf, 1985. 256p. £70. $133. ISBN: 0710801327.

Entries arranged under 32 broad headings/categories. *Class No:* 396(410)(092)

[4041]

—BANKS, O. The Biographical dictionary of British feminists. V.2: A supplement, 1900-1945. Hemel Hempstead, Herts, Harvester Wheatsheaf, 1990. 243p. £65. $114. ISBN: 0745001122.

Adds new material on Fabian women and feminist writers. Subject index covers more than 300 specific topics.

Class No: 396(410)(092)

Scotland

Bibliographies

[4042]

MARSHALL, R.K. **Virgins and virago:** a bibliography of women in Scotland from 1080 to 1980. London, Collins, 1983. 365p. 8 illus. (ports). ISBN: 0002160390.

An attempt to examine the activities of women in Scotland. 14 chapters in 4 parts: 1. To 1560: the passive woman? - 2. 1560-1709: wives and mothers - 3. 1707-1830: women in society - 4. 1830-1980: the active woman. Notes, p.317-340, by chapters, include refeences. Index, p.341-365.

Class No: 396(411)(01)

Ireland

Bibliographies

[4043]

BRADY, A., *comp.* **Women in Ireland:** an annotated bibliography. Westport, CT., Greenwood Press, 1988. xxxiii,478p. $45. (*Bibliographies and indexes in women's studies, 6.*) ISBN: 0313244863.

2312 briefly annotated entries for books, book chapters, periodical articles, theses and dissertations and treat all aspects of Irish women's lives. Arranged A-Z by author under subject categories (Biography and Autobiography - Literature, folklore and mythology (entries 824-1003) - Education - Religion and witchcraft - Community studies - Marriage and the family - Human sexuality, reproduction and health - Psychology - Law - Employment and economic life - History - Politics - Revolutionary movements - Perspectives on women's literature - General - Doctoral dissertations - Masters' theses). Each category begins with a scope note on contents. Annotations are descriptive and most items included are in English. Author index, p.421-438; subject index, p.439-478, is analytical.

Class No: 396(415)(01)

England

Bibliographies

[4044]

KANNER, B. **Women in English social history, 1800-1914:** a guide to research. New York, Garland, 1990. 3v. ISBN: 0824092015, v.1; 0824092058, v.2.

*c.*20,000 primary and secondary sources from the onset of the 19th century to World War I. Entries are mainly annotated and evaluative,and include journal articles. V.3 has autobiographical writings. Index to each volume.

Class No: 396(420)(01)

China

Bibliographies

[4045]

WEI, K.T. **Women in China:** a selected and annotated bibliography. Westport, CT., Greenwood Press, 1984. 250p. $65. (*Bibliographies and indexes in women's studies, 1.*) ISBN: 0313242348.

Expanded version of the author's bibliographical essay published in *Choice,* November 1982.

Over 1100 annotated entries of books, periodical articles, theses, dissertations and reports. Arranged in broad subject chapters (*e.g.*education, legal status). Cross-references listed at end of each chapter. Most items in English, some in European languages; Chinese publications are transliterated into English. Emphasis is on 19th and 20th century publications. Lacks a specific subject index. 'One of the more important reference tools on the subject ...' (*Choice,* v.22(6), February 1985, p.801). *Class No:* 396(510)(01)

Japan

[4046]

HUBER, K.R. **Women in Japanese society:** an annotated bibliography of selected English language materials. Westport, CT, Greenwood Press, 1992. xviii,485p. $65. ((*Bibliographies and indexes in women's studies*).) ISBN: 0313252963.

19 sections of journal articles, book chapters and books published through 1990 arranged in 5 groups: Women's place - Women in the private sphere - Women in the public sphere - Women as artists, performers and writers - Other. Concise informative annotations. Chronology of historical periods. Indexes by author, title, translater, interviewee; by title phrase, series, proceedings; and by subject.

Class No: 396(52)

Asia—South & South East

[4047]

SAKALA, C. **Women in South Asia: A guide to resources.** New York, Kraus International, 1980. 517p. $40. ISBN: 0527785741.

Sponsored by The Association for Asian Studies.

'This book organizes an unprecedented and perhaps unanticipated wealth of materials related to South Asian women. The materials cover both historical and contemporary South Asia, which includes India, Pakistan, Bangladesh, Sri Lanka and Nepal' (*the author*). In 2 sections: *Published resources* is a bibliography of *c.*4600 Western language entries for books, films, recordings, etc., most of which were examined and are annotated; and *Libraries, archives and other local sources.*

Class No: 396(54+59)

USA

[4048]

BASS, D.C. *and* BOYD, S.H. **Women in American religious history:** an annotated bibliography and guide to sources. Boston, Mass., G.K. Hall, 1986. xiv,155p. $30. (*Reference publications in women's studies.*) ISBN: 0816181519.

Claims to be the first to list and extensively annotate writings about women in religion from colonial times through 1985, exploring the connection between the history

....(contd.)

of American women and religion in America. 568 items, including books, parts of books, reference works, and periodicals. Cross-references. Index to proper names, authors, editors and historical figures. 'A scholarly addition ...' (*Reference books bulletin,* 1986/87, p.55).
Class No: 396(73)

[4049]
HILDENBRAND, S., *ed.* **Women's collections:** libraries, archives and consciousness. New York, Howarth Press, 1986. 194p. $32.95. ISBN: 0866562737.

Describes the major library holdings of women's collections in the United States, as well as excellent private collections. Also examines the history of women's collections through the years. *Class No:* 396(73)

Bibliographies

[4050]
COYLE, J.M., *comp.* **Women and aging:** a selected, annotated bibliography. Westport, CT., Greenwood Press, 1989. 135p. $35.95. (*Bibliographies and indexes in gerontology,9.*) ISBN: 0313260214.

622 annotated items arranged in 13 sections (Roles and relationships - Economics - Employment - Retirement - Health - Sexuality - Religion - Housing - Racial and ethnic groups - Policy issues - International concerns - Middle age - General), subdivided A-Z by author in format categories in each section (books - articles - films - government documents - dissertations). Primary focus is on the older American woman, but includes the middle-aged. Author and subject indexes. ' ... although the subject index does not always include items under all relevant listings' (*Choice,* v.27(1), September 1989, p78). *Class No:* 396(73)(01)

[4051]
Women's history sources: a guide to archives and manuscript collections in the United States. Hinding, A., *ed. in association with the University of Minnesota.* New York, R.R. Bowker, 1979. 2v. $189.95. ISBN: 0835211037.

Devotes V.1 (Collections) to descriptions of over 18,000 collections held by 2000 depositories, arranged under States, then towns, A-Z. V.2 forms the index.
Class No: 396(73)(01)

Reviews & Abstracts

[4052]
HARRISON, C.L. **Women in American history:** a bibliography. Byrne, P.R. Santa Barbara, CA., ABC-Clio, 1975-85. 2v.(374p.383p.). v.1 $15; v.2 $75. (*Clio bibliography series, nos. 5 & 20.*) ISBN: 0874362601, v.1; 0874364507, v.2.

V.1 covers the period 1964-77; v.2 1978-84. Abstracts and annotations pertaining to American and Canadian women, chosen from *c.*600 international serials and anthologies, are arranged topically in 11 headings (*e.g.* Women and ethnicity; Women and religion), each subdivided. Subject indexes are cross-referenced. Author index. List of periodicals. *Choice,* (v.23(8), April 1986, p.1196) says it will not replace *Women's studies abstracts* but it is easy to use. *Class No:* 396(73)(048)

Yearbooks & Directories

[4053]
DOSS, M., *ed.* **Women's organizations:** a national directory. 2nd ed. Garrett Park, MD., Garrett Park Press, 1986. 302p. $25. ISBN: 0912048425.

An expanded version of *The directory of special opportunities for women* (1981).

Some 2,000 organizations and their branches, including professional and trade associations, networking groups, government commissions, community and college-based women's centres, and resource and research centres specialising in women's issues and concerns. Arranged A-Z, with address, telephone number, code letter for category, and brief (4-5 sentence) explanation of purpose if one is known. Index by state and by broad subject category. Comprehensive in scope. '... some indexing eccentricities' (*Wilson library bulletin,* February 1987, p.68).
Class No: 396(73)(058)

Histories

[4054]
TINLING, M. **Women remembered:** a guide to landmarks of women's history in the United States. Westport, CT., Greenwood Press, 1986. 810p. $76.95. ISBN: 0313239843.

Entries are from 1 to 4 paragraphs long and concentrate on the accomplishments of the women. Arrangement is geographical, eventually subdivided by personal name, A-Z. At the end of each State listing are bibliographical notes. Finally, a general bibliographical essay on women's studies. 'A major ready reference source... ' (*Library journal,* 1 October 1986, p.88). *Class No:* 396(73)(091)

Negro-African

Bibliographies

[4055]
SIMS, J.L., *comp.* **The Progress of Afro-American women:** a selected bibliography and resource guide. Westport, CT., Greenwood Press, 1980. 387p. $36.95. ISBN: 0313220832.

The first major bibliography in the field since L.G. Davis's *The black woman in American society* (1976).

*c.*4000 unannotated items, including books, magazine and newspaper articles, dissertations, theses and government documents, arranged in 34 subject sections, each subdivided. Coverage is from slavery to participation in the women and rights movement. *Class No:* 396(73)=96(01)

Jews

Bibliographies

[4056]
RUUD, I.M. **Women and Judaism:** a select annotated bibliography. New York, Garland, 1988. 232p. $45. (*Garland reference library of social science, 316.*) ISBN: 0824086899.

Over 800 informatively, but uncritically annotated entries for monographs, journal articles, essays and dissertations, mainly published in the twentieth century. English, French and Scandinavian language material, but no Hebrew. Arrangement is A-Z by author, and items are numbered.

....(contd.)

Topographical, author and subject indexes. 'A significant contribution to a growing field ...' (*Choice*, v.25(11/12), July/August 1988, p.1677). *Class No:* 396(=924)(01)

Islamic Peoples

Bibliographies

[4057]

MEGHDESSIAN, S.R., *comp*. **The Status of the Arab woman:** a select bibliography. London, Mansell; Westport, CT. Greenwood Press, 1980. 176p. £19.50; $32.50. ISBN: 0720115175.

Compiled under the auspices of the Institute for Women's Studies in the Arab World, Beirut University College, Lebanon.

1616 entries mainly in English or French, for journal articles, books, dissertations, reports, etc., published since 1950. General items are grouped (Cultural and social background of the Middle East - Conferences and seminars on the Arab woman - Women in Islam and the law - Women in the Arab Middle East - Women in North Africa), followed by items on specific Arab countries (by country, A-Z)). Author index, p.159-171, and a poor subject index, p.173-176, with long lists of item numbers under each term. *Class No:* 396(=95.297)(01)

Thesauri

[4058]

CAPEK, M.E.S., *ed*. **A Women's thesaurus:** an index of language used to describe and locate information by and about women. The National Council for Research on Women. New York, Harper and Row, 1987. xxxv,1052p. $37.50. ISBN: 0060157755.

A section on thesaurus construction and use precedes the displays (alphabetical, rotated, hierarchical, subject groups, use/do not display, delimiters display). *Class No:* 396:025.43

Libraries

[4059]

SEARING, S.E. **Introduction to library research in women's studies.** Boulder, Col., Westview Press, 1985. xiii,257p. $48.00. (*Westview guides to library research.*) ISBN: 0865312672.

In 2 parts: Part 1: *Using the library* is in 5 sections, with notes. Part 2: *The tools of research* is a selective, annotated bibliography describing the major tools (guides, bibliographies and indexes, catalogues, biographical sources, directories, microforms, online sources, periodicals, handbooks). 3 appendices, including C. Review essays in Signs. Author, title and subject indexes. Photolithographic typescript. *Class No:* 396:061:026/027

Institutions & Associations

[4060]

Encyclopedia of women's associations worldwide: a guide to over 3400 national and multinational nonprofit women's and women-related organizations Barrett, J.K. *and* Malonis, J.A., *eds*. Detroit, Gale, 1993. 471p. $80. ISBN: 1873477252.

....(contd.)

Lists 3435 (mostly US) established and emerging women's associations intended to be used to promote communication and networking. Geographical arrangement, with some countries having only one entry. Activities index. *Class No:* 396:061:061.2

Research Projects

[4061]

FRANSELLA, F. *and* FROST, K. **On being a woman:** a review of research on how women see themselves. London, Tavistock Publications, 1977. 237p. £9.95. (*Tavistock women's studies.*) ISBN: 0422760706.

Chapters cover such topics as the development of self-esteem, research on pregnancy and childbirth, and female mental health. In each chapter research findings are summarised, plus a useful commentary. 'All in all, it is a very valuable volume, packed with information and references, and offering succinct summaries of countless different topics' (*British book news,* November 1977, p.847). *Class No:* 396:061:061.62.005

Gypsies

[4062]

FRASER, A. **The Gypsies.** Oxford, Blackwell,1993. x,359p. 48 illus. 5 maps. £19.99. (*The Peoples of Europe.*) ISBN: 0631159673.

Sections: 1: Bibliographical works; 2: Periodicals; 3: General studies; 4. Asian backround; 5: Particular European countries; 6: Pre-1800 European history; 7: 19th & 20th centuries; 8: North America; 9: Physical anthropology; 10: Language; 11: Music; 12: Folktales; 13: Pollution code; 14: Religion; 15: Other travellers; 16: Gypsies in art and literature. Bibliography, p.319-339. Index, p.340-359. *Class No:* 397

Bibliographies

[4063]

BINNS, D. **A Gypsy bibliography:** a bibliography of recent books, pamphlets, articles, broadsheets, theses and dissertations pertaining to gypsies and other travellers that the author is aware of at the time of printing. Manchester, Dennis Binns Publications, 1982. [108]p. ISBN: 0950829005.

1306 items (1289 arranged A-Z by author; the rest are of records currently available). Includes materials from 1500 to the present day, but pre-1914 titles are omitted if unattainable or obscure or in a foreign language. *Class No:* 397(01)

[4064]

BLACK, G.F. **A Gypsy bibliography.** London, Quaritch, for the Gypsy Lore Society, 1914. vii,226p. (*Gypsy Lore Society monographs, no.1.*)

Preliminary ed., 1909 (139p.).

4577 items in author order, with subject index. *Class No:* 397(01)

[4065]

—LIVERPOOL UNIVERSITY. Library. A Catalogue of the gypsy books collected by the late Robert Andrew Scott Macfie. Liverpool, the University, 1936. 178p.

Brief author catalogue only; appendix of songs and music. *Class No:* 397(01)

[4066]

KENNINGTON, D. **Gypsies and travelling people:** a select guide to documentary and organisational sources of information. 5th ed., revised by D. Barton & edited by M Ashcroft. Stamford, Lincs., Capital Planning Information, 1992. iii,73p. £15. (*CPI topic guide, no. 1.*) ISBN: 0906011833. ISSN: 01421859.

3rd ed., l986.

In 10 sections: Historical background - The travelling population - Official publications and legislation (subdivided by area, etc.) - Social characteristics, history and traditions - Planning, legal and environmental issues - Education of travellers - Bibliographies - Organizations - Local authority liaison officers/advisers - Libraries and information sources. Entries include brief annotations. Name index.
Class No: 397(01)

[4067]

LEEDS UNIVERSITY. Brotherton Library. **Catalogue of the Romany Collection** formed by D.U. McGrigor Phillips and presented to the University of Leeds. Edinburgh, Nelson, for the Brotherton Collection, 1962. xii,[1],227p.

20 sections, including drawings and paintings, photographs, gramophone records, letters, playbills and press cuttings. International coverage. Section 1. Bibliographies and other general works; 2. Official documents. 1234 numbered items, each with brief bibliographical descriptions. Index. *Class No:* 397(01)

Handbooks & Manuals

[4068]

OKELY, J. **The Traveller-gypsies.** Cambridge, Cambridge University Press, 1983. xii,254p. 16 illus., 9 diagrs., 15 tables. £22.50. (*Changing cultures.*) ISBN: 0521246415.

12 chapters examine the historical origins of the gypsies, their economy, travelling patterns, self ascription, kinship and political groupings, and their marriage choices, upbringing and gender divisions. References, p.241-247, by author, A-Z. Glossary (including Romany terms), p.249-250. Analytical index, p.251-254. *Class No:* 397(035)

Dictionaries

[4069]

WEDECK, H.E. **Dictionary of gypsy life and lore.** London, Peter Owen, 1973. vi, 518p. illus. £4.50. ISBN: 0720601630.

Includes material from the collection of *The Journal* of the Gypsy Lore Society.

Spans the history of gypsies in each continent where they exist, chronicling their origins, beliefs, customs, folklore and related subjects. A-Z arrangement. Entries mainly short from 2 to 3 lines to a page. *Class No:* 397(038)

Folklore & Folktales

Bibliographies

[4070]

ASHLIMAN, D.L. **A Guide to folktales in the English language:** based on the Aarne-Thompson classification system. New York, Greenwood, [1987]. 368p. $79.50 (*Bibliographies and indexes in world literature, no. 11.*) ISBN: 0313259615.

Aims to help readers find reliable texts of any given folktale, not only in its best-known version, but also in less familiar variants (*Introduction*). Short plot summaries for the stories are followed by lists of several collections in which versions of the stories are included. There is a separate list of titles of Grimm's tales; a list of folk-tale collections; and an index of titles of better-known stories and keywords from typical plots. 'More selective than N.O. Ireland's 'Index of fairy tales ...' but plot summaries and arrangement make identifying stories easier' (*College and research libraries*, v.49(4), July 1988, p.345). *Class No:* 398(01)

[4071]

AZZOLINO, D.S. **Tale type- and motif-indexes:** an annotated bibliography. New York, Garland, 1987. 105p. $33. (*Garland folklore bibliographies, v.11. Garland reference library of the humanities, v.565.*) ISBN: 0824087887.

186 entries, arranged A-Z by author, of type and motif indexes with which folklorists can arrange tales and elements in tales in numeric sequences, which make comparisons easier (Best known is the Aarne-Thompson classification system). Subject and geographical indexes.
Class No: 398(01)

[4072]

BONSER, W. **A Bibliography of folklore, as contained in the first eighty years of the publications of the Folklore Society.** London, W. Glaisher, for the Folklore Society, 1961. Supplement, 1969. xv, 126p. Supplement, 54p. £4.50. Supplement, £6. ISBN: 0903515024; 0903515032, Supplement.

Preceded by N.W. Thomas's *Bibliography of anthropology and folklore* (London, Nutt, for the Folklore Society, 1906-7. 2v.).

2626 entries in the main volume; a classified index to *Folk-lore record, Folk-lore journal, Folk-lore* and the Society's extra publications, 1878-1957. Classes A-P: A. General topics - B. Folklore of the British Isles - C. Folklore of other countries and races - D. Mankind - E. Human activities - F. Natural history - G. Natural phenomena - K. Calendar customs - L. Religious folklore & the supernatural - M. Miscellaneous aspects of folklore - N. Narrative folklore - P. Folklore in literature and art. Brief notes explain or expand titles of articles. Indexes: authors, topography of the British Isles; foreign countries, races and tribes; subjects. The supplement covers 1958-1967; the original volume, 1878-1957. *Class No:* 398(01)

[4073]
CARNES, P. **Fable scholarship:** an annotated bibliography. New York, Garland, 1985. 382p. $65. (*Garland folklore bibliographies, v.8. Garland reference library of the humanities, v.367.*) ISBN: 0824092295.

Fables defined as literary tales 'generally assumed to comfortably fit under the rubric "Aesopic"' (*Introduction*). 1452 items of scholarly works appearing in books, dissertations and journal articles published between 1880 and 1982. Extensively annotated. Many cross-references. Arranged A-Z by author, with separate indexes for names and subjects, listing of fables by Perry number, and motif index. 'Complexity of indexes and most criticism cited not in English indicates limited to scholars' (*College & research libraries*, January 1987, p.68). 'This work's greatest strength ... lies in the number and variety of the entries - embracing monographs, articles, and both domestic and foreign dissertations' (*Choice*, v.23(5), January 1986, p.724). *Class No:* 398(01)

[4074]
CLEVELAND PUBLIC LIBRARY. John G. White Department. **Catalog of folklore, folklife and folk songs.** 2nd ed. Boston, Mass., G.K. Hall, 1978. 3v. (2456p.). $255. ISBN: 081610249x.

First published 1965.

51,500 photolithographed catalogue cards for over 36,000v. of monographs and serials. Most entries are for subjects (over 1100 subject headings), including analytical entries. International in scope, embracing 'Märchen, jests, legends, exempla, fables, and heroic fairy and etiological tales, ballads, folk songs, children's songs, folk dances, proverbs, riddles, wit and humour, and the folklore of physical objects ...' (G.K. Hall & Co., *Catalog of publications, 1979-80*, p.27). *Class No:* 398(01)

[4075]
—ZIEGLER, E.B. **Folklore:** an annotated bibliography and index to single editions. Boston, Mass., Fazon, 1973. 203p. $12. ISBN: 087305100x.

Confined to singly published editions of folklore, as opposed to stories in collections. Arranged by titles. Separate indexes for subject, motif, country, type of folklore and illustrator. *Class No:* 398(01)

[4076]
Internationale volkskundliche Bibliographie/International folklore and folklife bibliography/... 1939/41-. Bonn, (previously Basle), Rudolf Habelt Verlag GmbH, for Société Internationale d'Ethnologie et de Folklore, 1949-.Biennial. ISSN: 00749737.

Under the auspices of the Conseil International de la Philosophie et des Sciences Humaines, with Unesco support. Continues *Volkskundliche Bibliographie* (Berlin, de Gruyter, for Verband Deutsche Vereine für Volkskunde, 1919-41. v.1-13: 1917-36, which itself continues *Catalogus* van Volklorein de Koninklijke Bibliotheek (The Hague, Drukkerij 'Humanitas', 1919-22. 3v. in 2).

The 1985-1986 volume, published 1991, has *c.*11,600 items in 21 classes (1. Folklore and folklife in general - 2. Settlement - 3. Buildings - 4. Objects - 5. Signs - 6. Technology, arts and crafts, industries - 7. Characteristics and types of people - 8. Costume, - 9. Food - 10. Manners and customs, festivals, pastimes - 11. Social groups, common law - 12. Popular beliefs - 13. Folk medicine - 14. Popular science - 15. Folk literature - 16. Popular poetry -

....(contd.)

17. Music and dance - 18. Folk-tales, myths, legends ... 21. Popular speech. List of periodicals precedes. Author and subject indexes. *Class No:* 398(01)

[4077]
SHANNON, G.W.B., *comp.* **'Folk literature and children':** an annotated bibliography of secondary materials. Westport, CT., Greenwood Press, 1981. 124p. $36.95. ISBN: 0313228086.

465 annotated entries for essays, monographs, articles, portions of books, dissertations, theses, etc., that deal with folk literature and its effect on children. Introduction summarises arguments both for and against folk tales, followed by the bibliography in 3 main sections (Literature - Education - Psychology) covering the period 1693-1979. Author, title and subject indexes. 'A valuable reference tool ...' (*Choice*, v.19(9), May 1982, p.1220). *Class No:* 398(01)

[4078]
STEINFIRST, S. **Folklore and folklife:** a guide to English-language reference sources. New York, Garland, 1992. 2v.(1208p). $120. (*Folklore bibliographies, v.16.*.) ISBN: 0815300689.

A general bibliographical survey aimed at the beginner in research. Entries include descriptive annotations. Sections have bibliographical essays. One chapter discusses folklore associations and periodicals. Author, title and subject indexes. *Class No:* 398(01)

[4079]
The Storyteller's sourcebook: a subject, title and motif index to folklore collections for children. MacDonald, M.R. 1st ed. Detroit, Mich., Gale Research Co., 1982. xviii,818p. $95. ISBN: 0810304716.

An index to children's folktales in 556 collections and 389 picture books published during the last 20 years. 4 main parts: Motif index, following the folktale indexing system designed by Stith Thompson - Tale title index - Subject index - Ethnic and geographic index, arranged by geographical area, subdivided and followed by an ethnic group index. 2nd ed. is promised for 1995. *Class No:* 398(01)

[4080]
THOMPSON, S., *ed.* **Motif-index of folk-literature:** a classification of narrative elements in folk tales, ballads, myths, fables, medieval romances, exempla, fabliaux, jest books, and local legends. Rev. ed. Copenhagen, Rosenkilde & Bagger; Bloomington, Indiana State University Press, 1955-58. 6v. $250 the set. ISBN: 0253338875.

First published Bloomington, 1932-36. 6v.

A systematic thematic index, covering a vast collection of folk-literature; references and some source material are cited. A-Z index and list of sources. The scope of the revised ed. is extended to include Icelandic sagas, early Irish literature, and oral tales of India. V.6, as before, provides a detailed A-Z index of motifs. An indispensable study of the subject. *Class No:* 398(01)

Encyclopaedias

[4081]
Enzyklopädie des Märchens. Handwörterbuch zur historischen und vergleichenden Erzählforschung. Hrsg.von Kurt Ranke [u.a.]. Berlin, de Gruyter, 1977-.v.1-. prices vary.

....(contd.)

To be in 12v. (v.5 issues were published in 1985/86).

Articles on specific figures (*e.g.* Faust), tales, customs, supernatural, etc. Biographies of folklorists are a special feature. Most contributors are from German-speaking countries. 'The set is indispensable for any folklore collection;' (*American notes & queries*, v.23(16), January - February 1985, p.89. *Class No:* 398(031)

Reviews & Abstracts

[4082]

Abstracts of folklore studies. Austin, Texas, University of Texas Press, for the American Folklore Society, 1963-1975, v.1-13. Quarterly.

About 1000 indicative and informative abstracts were arranged pa under periodical titles, A-Z (*Alabama review ... Zeitschrift für Volkskunde*). 49 journals featured in the Winter 1975 issue. Final section listed book reviews. Annual author and subject indexes. *Class No:* 398(048)

[4083]

Folklore. London, Folklore Society, 1959-. 2pa. £24pa. ISSN: 0015587x.

The journal of the society, with scholarly articles on all aspects of traditional culture in Britain, Europe and related cultures, plus a review section. *Class No:* 398(048)

Yearbooks & Directories

[4084]

Folk directory, 1965-. 1994-95 ed. London, English Folk Dance and Song Society. 176p £5.95 ISBN: 0946247005.

Includes a calendar of traditional customs; and lists of conferences and lectures; Folk festivals; district secretaries of the society; performers; films; archives, libraries and museums; and folk organizations (national, regional, international). *Class No:* 398(058)

Great Britain

[4085]

ALEXANDER, M. British folklore, myths and legends. London, Weidenfeld & Nicolson, 1982. 224p. 90 illus. (24 in colour). ISBN: 0297781510.

Examines the survival of different legends and customs and charts the evolution of folk belief. 9 sections: The magical island - Stones, graves and chalk images - 'There were giants in the earth' - The fabulous bestiary - The secret commonwealth - The Devil's congregation - The ghostlore of Britain - Rebels and champions - The Pagan inheritance. Picture sources. Index. *Class No:* 398(410)

[4086]

Folklore, myths and legends of Britain. 2nd ed. London, Reader's Digest Association, 1977. 552p. illus. (some in colour). ISBN: 0340163979.

First published 1973.

In 3 parts: 1. Lore of Britain - 2. Romance of Britain - 3. People of myth. 28 contributors. Detailed index, p.542-550. Lavishly illustrated. *Class No:* 398(410)

[4087]

The Folklore of the British Isles. Newell, V.J., *ed.* London, Batsford, 1973-1977. 18v. illus., examples, maps.

Cornwall, by T. Deane and T. Shaw. 1975. *The Cotswolds*, by K. Briggs. 1974. *Devon*, by R.Whitlock. 1977. *East Anglia*, by E. Porter. 1974. *Hampshire and the Isle of Wight*, by W. Boase. 1976. *Hertfordshire*, by D. Jones-Baker. 1977. *Ireland*, by S. O'Sullivan. 1974. £6.95. (David & Charles). *The Isle of Man*, by M. Killip. 1975. *The Lake District*, by M. Rowling. 1976. *Orkney and Shetlands*, by E.W. Marwick. 1975. £6.95. *The Scottish Highlands*, by A. Ross. 1976. *Somerset*, by K. Palmer. 1976. *Staffordshire*, by J. Raven. 1978. *Sussex*, by J. Simpson. 1973. *Warwickshire*, by R. Palmer. 1976. *The Welsh Border*, by J. Simpson. 1976. *Wiltshire*, by R. Whitlock. 1976. *Legends from Ireland*, by S. O'Sullivan. 1974. The volume *The folklore of Staffordshire*, by J. Raven (1978. 223p.) has 9 chapters (1. Ghosts and graves ... 6. The turning year ... 9. Sports and pastimes), with chapter notes, p.183-209. Quotes rhymes, charters, church records, etc. Bibliography, p.210-11. Index of tale types. Motif index (following Stith Thompson's *Index* (1966) and E. Baughman's *Type and motif index of the folktales of England and North America* (1966). General index, p.217-23. *Class No:* 398(410)

[4088]

FOLKLORE SOCIETY. British calendar customs. London, Glaisher, 1936-46. 7v.

Content: *England*, ed.by A.R.Wright & T.E.Jones. 3v. 1936-40. (v.1. Movable festivals; 2-3. Fixed festivals). Index in v.3. *Orkneys and Shetlands*, ed.by M.M.Banks, 1946. *Scotland*, ed by M.M.Banks. 3v. 1937-41. (v.1. Movable festivals; v.2-3. Fixed festivals). Index in v.3. Arranged in calendar order; lists of authorities. *Class No:* 398(410)

[4089]

GOMME, A.B. The Traditional games of England, Scotland and Ireland, collected and annotated by Alice Bertha Gomme. New York, Dover, 1964 (Reprinted London, Thames & Hudson, 1984, in one vol.). 1016p. illus. $18.95.

Unabridged reprint of *Dictionary of British folk-lore* (London, Nutt, 1984-8. 2v.).

More than 800 games are listed (A-Z), described and analysed. Rhymes are given in full, with local versions. 'Memoir on the study of children's games', p.458-531. The standard authority. *Class No:* 398(410)

[4090]

McINTYRE, F. What was that dance? Aylesbury, Bucks, the Author, 1993. £9.65.

Based on an earlier book with the same title produced by Bob Howe in 1968.

An index to 3000 folk dances, indicating for each the dance type, the music, a published source, and availability on record or cassette.(Information taken from *Refer*, v.9(1), Winter 1993). *Class No:* 398(410)

Bibliographies

[4091]

BAER, F.E. Folklore and literature of the British Isles: an annotated bibliography. New York, Garland, 1986. 355p. $43. (*Folklore bibliographies, no.11.*) ISBN: 082408660.

Entries for 1039 books, journals articles and dissertations published between 1890 and 1980 on the relation of folklore to English literature. Includes scholarly and popular items,

....(contd.)

arranged A-Z and numbered. 84-page general index. Annotations are descriptive and range in length from a phrase to *c.*200 words. 'An excellent and welcome addition ... (*Choice,* v.24(8), April 1987, p.1193).
Class No: 398(410)(01)

Encyclopaedias

[4092]

BRAND, J. Brand's popular antiquities of Great Britain. Faiths and folk-lore: a dictionary of national beliefs, superstitions and popular customs, past and current, with their classical and foreign analogues, described and illustrated. London, Reeves & Turner, 1905 (Reprinted New York, Blom; London, Blond, 1967. 2v. illus.

Forming a new edition of *The popular antiquities of Great Britain,* by Brand and Ellis, largely extended, corrected and brought down to the present time and now first alphabetically arranged by W.C. Hazlitt. Brand's original work: *Observations on popular antiquities* (1777), had a new edition by Sir Henry Ellis in 1813.

In the Hazlitt edition, the editor makes his own comments and retains many illustrative passages from the obscurer Elizabethan and Jacobean writers. Entries A-Z (Abbot of Bon Accord ... Yule log), and far easier to use than Brand's *Observations. Class No:* 398(410)(031)

Dictionaries

[4093]

BRIGGS, K.M. A Dictionary of British folk-tales in the English language, incorporating the F.J. Norton Collection. New ed. London, Routledge & Kegan Paul, 1991. 2v.(1472p.) £35 each vol. £65 the set. A paperback edition in 2 vols. was published in l991 (Pt.A: Folk narratives (1168p. £35. ISBN 0415066948); Pt.B: Folk legends (1472p. £35. ISBN 0415066956). ISBN: 0710002076.

A: Folk narratives (1168p.) B: Folk legends (1472p.). . Folk-tales are narrated in full and embrace verse tales (*e.g.* Child's *English and Scottish ballads*), giving source, type and motifs and comment, if considered necessary. 'Recommended for public and academic libraries' (*Library journal,* 1 December 1976, p.2470).
Class No: 398(410)(038)

[4094]

HOLE, C. A Dictionary of British folk customs. London, Paladin, 1976. 349p. tables, maps. £3.95. ISBN: 058608293x.

Originally as *British folk customs* (1976).

Customs (p.25-336): All Fool's Day ... Yule Candle (over 4p.). Select calandar. Select bibliography (A-Z authors), p.337-42. Index. Succinct; very readable.
Class No: 398(410)(038)

Ireland

[4095]

O SÚILLEABHÁIN, S. A Handbook of Irish folklore. Dublin, Educational Co. of Ireland, Ltd., for the Folklore of Ireland Society, 1942 (Reprinted Detroit, Mich., Singing Tree: Gale Research Co., 1971). xxxi,699p. $58. ISBN: 6810335611.

14 chapters (1. Settlement and dwelling ... 13. Popular oral literature - 14. Sports and pastimes). No index, but a

....(contd.)

detailed contents list (p.xix-xxxi); no sources. 'The main purpose ... is to serve as a guidance for collectors of Irish oral tradition' (*Introduction to collectors*). A mine of information and also, because of the many questions listed, a guide for further research. *Class No:* 398(415)

[4096]

—Ó DANACHAIR, C., *comp.* A Bibliography of Irish ethnology and folk tradition. Dublin & Cork, The Mercier Press, 1978. 95p. £13. ISBN: 085342490x.

In 2 parts: pt.1. Subjects (Settlement and dwelling - Livlihood and household support - Communications and trade - The community - Human life - Nature - Medicine - Time - Principles and rules of popular belief and practice - Mythological tradition - Historical tradition - Religious tradition - Folk narrative and the verbal wit - Folk poetry - Sports and pastimes - Miscellanies - Study and reesearch. Pt.2 is an alphabetical list of authors. Entries are arranged according to the O Súilleabháin handbook.
Class No: 398(415)(01)

[4097]

O'HOGAIN, D. Myth, legend and romance: an encyclopaedia of the Irish folk tradition. London, Harrap: Ryan Publishing, 1990. 500p. illus. £19.95. ISBN: 1870805119.

Covers all of the stories in the narrative history of the Irish tradition. 284 entries, A-Z, incorporate the mythological cycle, the Ulster cycle, the Fianna cycle, the King's cycle, as well as the hagiography, folktales and customs of Ireland. List of sources in abbreviated form follow each entry, referring to the complete bibliography forming a separate part of the volume. There are several indexes, a short introduction to Gaelic, and a pronunciation guide.
Class No: 398(415)

England

[4098]

CHANDLER, K. Morris dancing in the English South Midlands, 1660-1900: a chronological gazetteer. Enfield Lock, Mddx, Hisarlik Press, 1993. 208p. £10.95. (Publications of the Folklore Society: Tradition 2) ISBN: 1874312079.

A county-by-county listing of the 147 confirmed performance locations of morris dancing in the region during the period. Each entry includes, where available, chronology of performance, with details of context and activity, participants, musicians, etc. *Class No:* 398(420)

[4099]

CHANDLER, K. "Ribbons, bells and squeaking fiddles": the social history of morris dancing in the English South Midlands. 1660-1900. Enfield Lock, Mddx, Hisarlik Press, 1993. 208p. £12.95. (Publications of the Folklore Society: Tradition 1) ISBN: 1874312060.

Examines the historical development and performance aspects of the dance. *Class No:* 398(420)

Wales

[4100]

RHYS, J. Celtic folklore: Welsh and Manx. New ed. London, Wildwood House, 1980. 2v.(400p.;318p.). v.1 £5.50; v.2. £4.95. ISBN: 0704504057, v.1; 0704504103, v.2.

....(contd.)

First published 1901, by Clarendon Press, Oxford.

A pioneer treatment of Welsh folklore, with a useful list of bibliographical references appended. *Class No:* 398(429)

Handbooks & Manuals

[4101]
OWEN, T.M. **Welsh folk customs.** 5th ed. Llandysul, Dyfed, Gomer Press, 1987. 197p. 16p. of plates (black & white). £4.95. ISBN: 0863833470.

First published 1959, 1st to 4th eds. published by the National Museum of Wales, Cardiff.

Chapters: 1. The Christmas season - 2. Candlemas and the movable festivals - 3. May and midsummer - 4. Harvest and winter's eve - 5. Birth, marriage and death. Select bibliography (p.187-189) A-Z by author. Index (p.190-197). 'The text provides an integrated study of the subject based on the literature, on replies to questionnaires and on information collected in the field' (*Foreword* to an earlier edition). Well documented. *Class No:* 398(429)(035)

China

Bibliographies

[4102]
TING, N.-T. *and* TING, L.-H. **Chinese folk narratives:** a bibliographical guide. San Francisco, CA., Chinese Materials Center, Inc., 1975. 68p. (*Bibliographical aids series, no.4.*)

A selective annotated bibliography of primary sources, confined to publications in major American and West European libraries, and in the authors' private collection. 3 parts: bibliographies; classical literary versions (title entry); modern oral versions (author entry; under title if authorship is corporate). Titles appear in romanised form, plus Chinese script form and often with English translations. *Class No:* 398(510)(01)

[4103]
YIN-LIEN C. CHIN, *and others.* **Traditional Chinese folktales.** Armonk, New York, M.E. Sharpe Inc.,1989. 184p. illus. $17.95. ISBN: 0873325079. *Class No:* 398(510)(01)

Japan

Bibliographies

[4104]
ALGARIN, J.P. **Japanese folk literature:** a core collection and reference guide. New York, R.R. Bowker, 1982. 226p. $29.95. ISBN: 0835215164.

Annotated bibliography of mainly English-language sources of Japanese folk literature. An introduction tracing its developments precedes the bibliography, which is in 3 parts: Works on Japanese folklore (63 titles) - Japanese folktale anthologies (48 titles) - Classic folktales of Japan (27 titles), which summarises the best-known tales. Indexes include a folktale index. 'The work fills a gap in the bibliographies of Japanese studies' (*Choice,* v.20(6), February 1983, p.805). *Class No:* 398(52)(01)

America

Bibliographies

[4105]
FLANAGAN, C.C. *and* FLANAGAN, J.T. **American folklore:** a bibliography, 1950-1974. Metuchen, N.J., Scarecrow Press, 1977. vi,406p. $27.50; £20.60. ISBN: 0810810735.

3639 numbered entries, with very brief annotations for some 16 sections: 1. List of magazines and abbreviations - 2. Festschriften, symposia, collections - 3. Bibliography, dictionaries, archives - 4. Folklore: study and teaching - 5. General folklore - 6. Ballads and songs - 7. Tales and narrative material - 8. Legends (theory; history; collections) - 9. Myth and mythology - 10. Beliefs, customs, superstitions, cures - 11. Folk heroes - 12. Folklore in literature - 13. Proverbs, riddles, Wellerisms, limericks - 14. Speech, names, cries, etc. - 15. Minor genres (*e.g.* rhymes; graffiti) - 16. Obituaries (of prominent folklorists). Includes some Canadian, Mexican and Caribbean material. *Class No:* 398(7)(01)

Canada

Bibliographies

[4106]
BLANCHETTE, J.-F., *and others.* 'Une Bibliographie de la culture materielle traditionelle au Canada, 1965-1982/A Bibliography of folk material culture in Canada, 1965-1982'. In *Canadian folklore Canadien,* v.4(1-2), 1984, p.107-146.

Lists works on the material culture of 'People who came to Canada after the fifteenth century'. *Class No:* 398(71)(01)

Latin America

Bibliographies

[4107]
BOGGS, R.S. **Bibliography of Latin American folklore.** New York, Wilson, 1940 (Reprinted Detroit, Mich., Ethridge, 1975). x,109p.

643 numbered, briefly annotated entries in 15 sections: Bibliography - Periodicals, serial publications and organizations - General and miscellaneous works (Argentina ... Venezuela) - Mythology, legends and traditions - Folktales - Poetry, music, dancing and games - Festivals and games - Drama - Arts and crafts, including dress and ornament - Food and drink - Belief, witchcraft, medicine and magic - Folk speech - Proverbs - Riddles. Subdivision by countries throughout. Detailed index. Supplemented by entries in 'Folklore bibliography' (*Southern folklore quarterly,* 1941-. ISSN 00384127). *Class No:* 398(729.99)(01)

USA

Bibliographies

[4108]
KIBBEE, J. **American folklore** a guide to reference sources. In *R.S.R.,* v.17(3), Fall, 1989, p.37-44.

39 references which it is suggested could serve as a core collection of reference materials on American folklore for

....*(contd.)*

both scholars and the general public, reflecting the scope of folk studies as it has evolved during the past 100 years. *Class No:* 398(73)(01)

Handbooks & Manuals

[4109]

DORSON, R.M., *ed.* **Handbook of American folklore.** Bloomington, Indiana University Press, 1983. xix,584p. illus. $35; £21. ISBN: 0253327067.

About 70 essays present the state of the art, with evaluations of the scholarly literature and other pertinent work. Bibliographical notes are appended to each chapter, and there is a 23-page general bibliography. General index. 'A basic work' (*American notes and queries,* v.23(16), January/February 1985, p.90). *Class No:* 398(73)(035)

[4110]

PUCKETT, N.N., *comp.* **Popular beliefs and superstitions:** a compendium of American folklore. Hand, W.D., *and others.* Boston, Mass., G.K. Hall, 1981. 3v. (1903p.). $125. ISBN: 0816185859.

36,209 entries, interpreting nearly every imaginable human experience. Aimed at serious students of American culture, anthropology and folklore. *Class No:* 398(73)(035)

Theses

[4111]

DUNDES, A. Folklore theses and dissertations in the United States. Austin, Texas, University of Texas Press, for the American Folklore Society, 1976. 610p. $27.50. ISBN: 0292724136.

Chronological listing of over 7000 dissertations and masters' essays accepted by US universities before 1969. Indexes of authors and institutions. 'All in all this is a very useful, well-executed bibliography' (*College & research libraries,* v.38, July 1977, p.328). *Class No:* 398(73)(043)

Films

[4112]

American folklore films and video tapes: a catalog. Center for Southern Folklore Staff. New York, R.R. Bowker, 1982. 424p. $39.95; £34.75. ISBN: 0835215369.

An earlier catalogue was published by the Center with the title *American folklore films and video tapes: an index* (1976. $15. ISBN 0892670002).

Lists over 2000 films, etc., available for rental or sale, with details of title, length, format, date, producer, distributor, and brief synopsis. Detailed subject index. *Class No:* 398(73)(084.122)

Australia

[4113]

The Oxford companion to Australian folklore. Davey, G.B. *and* Seal, G., *eds.* Oxford, Oxford University Press (Australia), 1993. xvii,381p. illus. A$49.95; £30. ISBN: 0195530578.

Attempts 'to draw together the various threads of what is known' (*Preface*). Covers the major genres and ethnic groups, longer articles being signed and many including

....*(contd.)*

bibliographies. Also includes biographical entries, descriptions of institutions, and publications. *Class No:* 398(94)

Jews

[4114]

YASSIF, E. Jewish folklore: an annotated bibliography. New York, Garland, 1986. 341p. $65. (*Garland folklore bibliographies, 10. Garland reference library of the humanities, 450.*) ISBN: 082409039x.

Choice (v.24(2), October 1986, p.289) considers that '*A bibliography of Jewish folkloristics* would be a more appropriate title for this critical annotated study, which focuses on the scholarly contributions about folklore of all Jewish groups rather than actual texts'. More than 1300 informative and evaluative annotations for books and articles published over the last 100 years are arranged A-Z by author, with an appendix of late additions. Bibliographic information omits publishers. Few cross-references. Subject (keywords from titles) and name index. 'A major contribution to the study of Jewish folklore' (*Choice,* v.24(2), October 1986, p.290). *Class No:* 398(=924)

Children

[4115]

OPIE, L. *and* **OPIE, P. The Lore and language of school-children.** Oxford, Clarendon Press, 1959 (Paperback issued 1987). 438p. £4.95. ISBN: 0192820591.

'The present study is based on the contributions of some 5000 children attending seventy schools, primary, secondary modern and grammar, in different parts of England, Scotland, and Wales, and one school in Dublin' (*Preface*). Riddles, topical rhymes, nicknames, pranks, street names, superstitions, first-line and general indexes. 11 distribution maps. Fully illustrated by examples. *Class No:* 398-0053

Metrical Romances

Bibliographies

[4116]

Arthurian legend and literature: an international bibliography. Reiss, E., *and others.* New York, Garland, 1984-. 2v. V.1: $48; V.2: $34. (*Garland reference library in the humanities, v.415.*)

V.1: *The Middle ages,* has *c.*400 entries arranged by broad subject headings. Author and title index. V.2 covers post-medieval treatment of Arthurian legend. Updates and complements Loumis's *Arthurian literature in Middle Ages* (1959). *Class No:* 398.22(01)

[4117]

Bulletin bibliographique des études arthuriennes. Paris, Société International Arthurienne; Seattle, W.A., University of Washington, International Arthurian Society, 1949- Annual. $20. ISSN: 00267929.

Includes lists of books, articles and theses published in *c.*15 countries. Indexes of authors and subjects; list of members. *Class No:* 398.22(01)

[4118]

Clwyd Library Service catalogue of the collection of Arthurian literature. Davies, G., *ed.* [ii]. 2,83, 591p.

Cover title: 'Casgliat Arthuraidd'.

Two sequences: 1. Authors and titles, A-Z (*c.*2500 entries) - 2. Classified. *Class No:* 398.22(01)

[4119]

FLETCHER, R.H. The Arthurian material in the Chronicles, especially those of Great Britain and France. 2nd ed. New York, B. Franklin, 1966 (Reprinted 1973). ix,335p. $28.50. ISBN: 0833711539.

First published 1906. The 2nd ed. was expanded by a bibliography and critical essay for the period 1905-1965, by L.S. Loomis.

Aims to show what Arthurian material is contained in the European Chronicles, especially those of Great Britain and France. Treats more than 200 Chronicles, ranging from mid-6th to end of 16th century. 12 chapters (*e.g.* 3. Geoffrey of Monmouth, p.43-115). Numerous footnote references to the literature. Supplementary bibliography, 1905-65, p.333-5. *Class No:* 398.22(01)

[4120]

PICKFORD, C.B. *and* LAST, R. The Arthurian bibliography. Woodbridge, Suffolk, Boydell & Brewer Ltd., 1981-. To be in 3v. V.1: 820p., v.2: 352p. V.1: £35; v.2: £25. ISBN: 0859910695, v.1; 0859910997, v.2.

V.1 was published in 1981, v.2 in 1983. Publication of v.3 has been delayed.

Claims to be a complete listing of all critical writing on King Arthur and the Arthurian romance down to 1975. Computer-compiled. V.1: Author listing; v.2: subject index; v.3: Author listing: subject order. *Class No:* 398.22(01)

Encyclopaedias

[4121]

LACY, N.C., *and others, eds.* The New Arthurian encyclopedia. 2nd ed., completely rev. and expanded. New York, Garland, 1991. xxxviii,577p.100 black & white illus. $90. (*Garland reference library of the humanities, v.585.*) ISBN: 0824043774.

First ed. published in 1986.

Over 1200 essay entries and a large number of brief and informative entries, by 130 contributing scholars. Treats major authors and texts as well as broad subjects, covering the Arthur legend from the earliest tales to the present day in literature, history, art, music, films, etc. Each essay has a short bibliography of 1-4 items appended. Cross-references. Subject list of entries by category, p.xiii-xxv. Index, including all authors, artists, and important themes and motifs, p.535-577. Recommended as 'an important beginning in Arthurian studies' (*Library journal,* 1 Sept., 1991, p.182). *Class No:* 398.22(031)

Handbooks & Manuals

[4122]

LACY, N.J. and ASHE, G. The Arthurian handbook. New York, Garland Publishing, 1988. 300p. $47. ISBN: 0824079418.

Aims to provide both an introduction for the general reader and a useful summation for the specialist. A chronology precedes 5 chapters: 1. Origins - 2. Early

....(contd.)

Arthurian literature - 3. Modern Arthurian literature - 4. Arthur in the arts - 5. An Arthurian glossary. Index. *Class No:* 398.22(035)

Dictionaries

[4123]

MOORMAN, C. *and* MOORMAN, R. An Arthurian dictionary. University Press of Mississippi, 1978. 117p. $10.95. ISBN: 0878050833.

Entries for 'mythological and literary characters, historic personages, authors, works and place names in terms of their connection with the historic and literary Arthur'. (*Choice,* v.16(2), April 1979, p.206). Short bibliography. *Class No:* 398.22(038)

Histories

[4124]

LOOMIS, R.S., *ed.* Arthurian literature in the Middle Ages: a collaborative history. Oxford, Clarendon Press, 1959. xvi,574p. illus.

41 chapters (1. The Arthur of history ... 5. The Welsh Triads ... 12. The origin and growth of the Tristan legend ... 15. Chrétien de Troyes ... 21. The origin of the Grail legend ... 29. The troubadours ... 34. The Dutch romance ... 37. The English rimed and prose romances ... 40. St. Thomas Malory - 41. Arthurian influence on sport and spectacle. Epilogue. Detailed, non-analytical index. Gives quotations. Pays tribute to James Douglas Bruce's *Evolution of Arthurian Romance from the beginnings down to the year 1300* (1923). *Class No:* 398.22(091)

Superstitions

Encyclopaedias

[4125]

Zolar's encyclopaedia of omens, signs and superstitions. Englewood Cliffs, N.J. Prentice Hall Press, 1989. 400p. $11.95; £6.95. ISBN: 0671653172.

Explains the origin, hidden meaning, and significance of more than 650 omens, signs and superstitions. *Class No:* 398.3(031)

Dictionaries

[4126]

OPIE, I. *and* TATEM, M., *eds.* A Dictionary of superstitions. Oxford, Oxford University Press, 1989. xiii,[1],494p. £17.50. ISBN: 0192115979.

1600 entries, arranged A-Z by subject, that treat superstitions of the British Isles that have survived to the nineteenth and twentieth centuries. Each superstition is illustrated by one or more quotations in chronological order to show the history and development of the superstition, the quotations being from a wide range of published and unpublished sources. Geographical locations and other clarifying information is given in brackets. Extensive cross-references. Entries vary in length from 2 or 3 lines to over a

....(contd.)
column. Select bibliography of 16th to 20th-century books and periodicals, p.455-462. Analytical index, p.463-494. *Class No:* 398.3(038)

Fallacies

[4127]
ACKERMANN, A.S.E. Popular fallacies: a book of common errors explained and corrected, with copious references to authorities. 4th ed. London, Old Westminster Press, 1950 (reprinted Detroit, Mich., Gale,1970). xv,843p. $74. ISBN: 0810332957.

A hotchpotch of curious information, not always authoritative but frequently useful. *Class No:* 398.3FAL

[4128]
WARD, P. A Dictionary of common fallacies. 2nd ed. Cambridge, Oleander Press, 1980 (reprinted New York, Prometheus, 1989 in 1v.). 2v.(viii,303;xii,313). Reprint:636p. £10 each vol. $49.95 for reprint. ISBN: 0900891653, set; 0900891637, v.1; 0900891645, v,2; 0879755113, Reprint.

First published 1978 in 1v.

Each volume has entries, A-Z, covering commonly-held beliefs and sayings (*e.g.* that Aethelred was 'unready', 'The earth is flat' and 'History repeats itself'), as well as phenomena (*e.g.* Ectoplasm). Keywords are used for entry, which may be the name of a person. Each volume has a bibliography of authorities and an index. *Class No:* 398.3FAL

Fairies & Goblins

Bibliographies

[4129]
EASTMAN, M.H. Index to fairy tales, myths and legends. 2nd ed. Boston, Faxon, 1926. Supplement, 1937; 2nd supplement, 1952. ix,610p. (1st supplement, ix,566p.; 2nd supplement, 370p.). $14. ISBN: 0873050282.

About 30,000 references in an alphabetical analytical index, with list of books analysed; geographical list; bibliography of books on the art of story telling. Includes some modern stories. Continued by: *Class No:* 398.43(01)

[4130]
—IRELAND, N.O. Index to fairy tales, 1949-1972 including folklore, legends and myths in collections. Westwood, Mass., Faxon, 1973. (Available Metuchen, N.J. Scarecrow). 741p. Supplements, 1973-77 (1979. 259p.) and 1978-1986 (1989, 575p.), both published by Scarecrow. $39.50. Supplement: $26. ISBN: 0810820110; 0810818558; 081082194x.

Main work indexes 406 books. Innovations are the comprehensive subject index of stories and the single A-Z sequence. *Class No:* 398.43(01)

Dictionaries

[4131]
BARBER, R. *and* RICHES, A. A Dictionary of fabulous beasts. New ed. Ipswich, Boydell Press, 1975. 168p.

First published 1971 by Macmillan Press.

Fabulous beasts, A-Z, from the Asbaia to the Zû. Bibliography of over 200 items, with references from the text, is arranged chronologically. The black-and-white illus. are few and far between, and *RQ* (v.12(1), Fall, 1972, p.86) recommends, for illus., *A fantastic bestiary*. by Ernest Lehner, with over 300 illus. *Class No:* 398.43(038)

[4132]
BRIGGS, K.M. A Dictionary of fairies, hobgoblins, brownies, bogies and other supernatural creatures. New ed. London, Penguin, 1993. 512p.illus. £8.99. ISBN: 0140176586.

First published by Allen Lane in l976.

Entries A-Z include such unlikely headwords as 'Faults condemned by fairies'. Also entries for W.B. Yeates and Milton, but not Shakespeare, for his Ariel. 'Wizards': over 2p., with appended motif numbers. 'Tom Tit Tot' has an entry, with the tale reproduced in full. Book-list (A-Z authors), p.455-62. 'A note on the pronunciation of Celtic names'. Index of types and motifs, using the Antti-Aarne + Stith Thompson standard method of cataloguing folk-tales. *Class No:* 398.43(038)

Singing Games

[4133]
OPIE, I. *and* OPIE, P. Children's games in street and playground; chasing, catching, seeking, hunting, racing, duelling, exerting, daring, guessing, acting, pretending. London, Oxford University Press, 1969 (paperback ed., 1984). xvi,371p. illus, maps. £3.95. ISBN: 0192814893.

Concerned solely with games that children (aged about 6-12) play of their own accord when out of doors, and usually out of sight. About 2500 names of games and game-rhymes appear in the index (p.345-71); over 10,000 children were interviewed. Notes on histories of individual games. *Class No:* 398.8

[4134]
OPIE, I. *and* OPIE, P. The Singing game. Oxford, Oxford University Press, 1985. xxii,521p. 28 illus. £15. ISBN: 0192115626.

'Presents the singing games and clapping games that used to be, or still are, played by children in Great Britain, with as much of their histories as could be discovered. Information chiefly drawn from the nationwide surveys undertaken in the 1950s and 1960s' (*Preface*). Chapter 1. The singing game - 2. Chains and captives - 3. Match-making - 4. Mating - 5. Wedding rings - 6. Cushion dances ... 12. Mimicry ... 16. Static circles - 17. Eccentric circles ... 20. Clapping. Music and verses are included in the text. List of illustrations; list of abbreviations; select bibliography (p.481-483); general index (p.485-488); A-Z index of songs, games and dances (p.489-521). *Class No:* 398.8

[4135]

The Oxford dictionary of nursery rhymes. Opie, L. *and* Opie, P., *eds.* Oxford, Clarendon Press, 1951 (Reprinted, with corrections, 1952). xxvii,467p. illuys (incl. pl.). £15. ISBN: 0198691114.

Entries on more than 500 rhymes and songs traditionally handed on by young children. Entry is usually under the most prominent word or subject; data on history of each rhyme, parallels and first appearance, source and variations. The illustrations are taken from drawings or old ballad sheets. Index of notable figures; index of first lines. *Class No:* 398.8

[4136]

—NORTHAL, G.F. English folk-rhymes: a collection of traditional verses relating to places and persons, customs, superstitions, etc. London, Kegan Paul, Trench, Trübner, 1892. xii,565p.

17 subject sections (*e.g.* 11. Games - 12. The almanac - 13. Weather), plus 18. Additions and corrections. Many quotations; references to sources. Sources, p.ix-xii. *Class No:* 398.8

Proverbs

[4137]

The Concise Oxford dictionary of proverbs. Simpson, J.A., *ed.* New ed. Oxford, Oxford University Press, 1992. 316p. £12.95. $22.95. ISBN: 0198661770.

First published 1982.

Nominally an abridgement of the standard work, *The Oxford dictionary of English proverbs* (3rd ed. 1970). Includes over 1000 proverbs in common use in the 20th century in Britain and America, giving full documentary information from the point when each proverb entered the English language. Many illustrative quotations. 2½-page bibliography of major proverb collections and works cited from modern editions, A-Z by author. Thematic index. '...abundant cross-references, and the attractive layout make the book more enjoyable to browse than many older, standard sources.'(*Choice*, v.30(7) March l993, p.1122). *Class No:* 398.9

[4138]

FERGUSON, R. The Penguin dictionary of proverbs. London, Allen Lane: Penguin Books Ltd., New York, Facts on File, 1983. xii, 331p. £8.95; £3.95; $24.95. ISBN: 0713915404, UK; 0871962985, US.

Published in the US as *The facts on file dictionary of proverbs.*

A collection of over 6000 proverbs, numbered, from all over the world, arranged in 188 categories, A-Z (Absence ... Corruption ... Love ... Royalty ... Writing), each category subdivided into various aspects of the main theme. Identification of the origins of the proverbs and explanations of the meanings are given as necessary. Index, p.271-331, indexes each proverb under its first keyword, followed by the complete phrase or opening phrase, with category and item number. 'The proverbs, displaying their folkloric foundings, range from the mundane to the witty' (*Wilson library bulletin*, November 1983, p.225). *Class No:* 398.9

[4139]

FLEXNER, S. *and* FLEXNER, D. Wise words and wives tales: the origins, meanings and time-honored wisdom of proverbs and folk sayings, olde and new. New York, Avon, 1993. 218p. $9. ISBN: 0380762382.

Entries note the earliest recorded appearance of each saying, followed by variations in form and meaning as they evolved. Limited to the English-speaking world. Cross-references. *Booklist* (v.90(1), 9/1/93, p.92) comments that a thematic index would have been a useful addition. *Class No:* 398.9

[4140]

GLUSKI, J., *comp.* & *ed.* Proverbs/Proverbes/Sprichwörter/Proverbi/Proverbios/Poslovity: a comparative book of English, French, German, Italian, Spanish and Russian proverbs, with a Latin appendix. Amsterdam, Elsevier, 1971 (paperback ed. 1989). xxxviii,448p. £48.75; Dfl.95. ISBN: 0444409041; 0444873503.

More than 1100 proverbs and proverbial phrases, more or less current, in each of the 6 languages, under 48 topic-sections (1. Words and deeds - 2. Truth:lie ... 47. Ethics: practical philosophy - 48. Miscellaneous). 6 language indexes (indexed by catchwords). Entries asterisked in the main sequence have equivalents in the Latin appendix (p.433-46). *Class No:* 398.9

[4141]

STEVENSON, B.E. Stevenson's book of proverbs, maxims and familiar phrases. New York, Macmillan, 1948; London, Routledge, 1949 (Reprinted 1965). viii,2957p.

Contains more than 73,000 proverbs, maxims and phrases. Subject arrangement, with dates; full index of keywords. Overlaps considerably with Stevenson's *Book of quotations.* Gives precise citations; international in scope. Proverbs in foreign languages are first translated, then given in the original. The 1965 reprint has the title *Macmillan book of proverbs, maxims and familiar phrases. Class No:* 398.9

England

[4142]

The Oxford dictionary of English proverbs. Wilson, F.P., *ed.* 3rd ed. rev. Oxford, Clarendon Press, 1970. xv,[1], 930p. £19.50; $45. ISBN: 0198691181.

First published 1935.

About 14,000 entries, A-Z, under first significant word. Cites variants (*e.g.* 'House is his castle. A man's (Englishman's)'). Cross-references from other key words, but not necessarily from first word of proverb. Cites sources and users, chronologically, with dates. Sources, p.xi-xv. Smallish print; entries not sufficiently conspicuous. Many new entries, thanks to permitted unrestricted use of M.P. Tilley's *A dictionary of the proverbs in England in the sixteenth and seventeenth centuries* (1950). No index.

Two older storehouses of proverbs, English and foreign, are: *Lean's Collectanea*, by V.S. Lean (1902-04), classified in various ways by country, calendar, subject-matter, etc.; and H.G. Bohn's *Handbook of proverbs* (1889), based on the collections of John Ray (1670) and David Ferguson (1641). *Class No:* 398.9(420)

[4143]

TILLEY, M.P. A Dictionary of the proverbs in England in the sixteenth and seventeenth centuries: a collection of the proverbs found in English literature and the dictionaries of the period. Ann Arbor, Mich., University of Michigan Press; London, Oxford University Press, 1950. (Reprinted AMS Press). xiii,854p. $115. ISBN: 0404188990.

Subject entry, items A-Z thereunder, citing sources; bibliography of works quoted, p.769-802. Indexes of significant words in proverbs (p.809-54; and a Shakespeare index (p.803-08), giving exact references. About 11,780 proverbs are listed. *The Oxford dictionary of English proverbs* (3rd ed., 1970, p.x) refers to Tilley's work as 'exemplary for clarity, for references, particularly to Shakespeare, and for paucity of errors'.
Class No: 398.9(420)

[4144]

WHITING, B.J. *and* **WHITING, H.W. Proverbs, sentences and proverbial phrases, from English writings mainly before 1500.** Cambridge, Mass., Belknap Press of Harvard University Press; London, Oxford University Press, 1968. li,733p. $51. ISBN: 0674719506.

About 10,000 entries, A-Z by keyword, and then chronologically, with exact citation to source. Where appropriate, references to other standard collections are cited. Indexes: important words; proper nouns. 'It will not be superseded' (*Library journal,* v.93(21), 1 December 1968, p.4543). *Class No:* 398.9(420)

[4145]

—WHITING, B.J. Modern proverbs and proverbial sayings. Cambridge, Mass., Harvard University Press, 1989. 709p. $39.95. ISBN: 0674580532.

5567 entries of material published between *c.*1930 to the early 1980s, arranged by keyword, with bibliographical sources indicated. A very wide variety of sources were scanned throughout the years for this compilation. Unfortunately, only one keyword, usually the first noun, is used for each proverb; no definitions are given, even for abstract or metaphorical proverbs; and no oral proverbs are included. However, 'No other compilation of proverbs covers the twentieth century with such comprehensiveness ... Whiting's crowning work will become a standard reference source for proverbs and should delight both the scholar and the casual browser' (*Reference books bulletin,* November 15, 1989, p.696). *Class No:* 398.9(420)

Wales

[4146]

VAUGHAN, H.H., *ed.* **Welsh proverbs with English translations.** London, Kegan Paul, Trench, 1889 (Reprinted Detroit, Mich., Gale Research Co., 1969). vi,378p. $43. ISBN: 0810332051.

A collection of 2259 Welsh proverbs in metrical English, with Welsh originals. *Class No:* 398.9(429)

[4147]

—EVANS, J.J. Welsh proverbs, in English and Welsh. Llandyssul, Cardiganshire, Gomerian Press (J.D. Lewis & Sons Ltd.), 1965. 147,59p.

About 1400 selected entries, under first words, A-Z of the proverbs in Welsh. Parallel Welsh and English text.
Class No: 398.8(429)

China

[4148]

SCARBOROUGH, W. A Collection of Chinese proverbs. 2nd ed. Shanghai, Presbyterian Misson Press, 1926 (Reprinted New York, Paragon Book Reprint Corp., 1964). vi,381,xivp.

Grouped under broad headings, with a topical index. Proverbs in Chinese script, with transliteration and translation. *Class No:* 398.9(510)

USA

[4149]

TAYLOR, A. *and* **WHITING, B.J. A Dictionary of American proverbs and proverbial phrases, 1820-1880.** Cambridge, Mass., Belknap Press of Harvard University Press, 1958. xxii,[1],418p.

Arranged A-Z by keyword, with full references to book and page. Includes proverbs used by American authors of the period, even if the proverbs are not American in origin. 10-page bibliography of texts and reference works (p.xiii-xxii). *Class No:* 398.9(73)

[4150]

—WHITING, B.J. Early American proverbs and proverbial phrases. Cambridge, Mass., Harvard University Press, 1977. 576p. $42.50. ISBN: 0674219813.

Covers 1620-1820. Arranged under keywords, A-Z, p.1-506, with cross-references to similar sayings and to entries in standard collections of English proverbs. Bibliography of sources, p.xxiii-lxiv. Index of keywords. The period was one in which 'proverbs were used seriously to instruct, warn, cajole or just grumble about life in general' (*TLS,* no.3969, 28 April, p.483). *Class No:* 398.9(73)

90 Archaeology

Archaeology

[4151]
Ancient peoples and places. London, Thames & Hudson, 1957-. illus., tables, maps, bibliogs.

A series of concise and well-illustrated surveys by distinguished archaeologists and historians, examining what has been discovered and what has been deduced about ancient civilizations. 'They're not gee-whiz books, but are directed at the literate general reader, as well as providing up-to-date material for scholars in other fields' (*Sunday Telegraph,* 22 December 1968). V.100 in the series was Glyn Daniel's *A short history of archaeology* (1981).
Class No: 902

[4152]
RENFREW, C. *and* **BAHN, P. Archaeology** theories, methods, and practice. London, Thames and Hudson, 1991. 544p. illus., diagrs., maps, bibliog., index. pbk. £18.95. ISBN: 0500276056.

Comprehensive introduction to what archaeology is and to what archaeologists do. 3 main parts: 1. Framework of archaeology - 2. Discovering the variety of human experience - 3. The World of archaeology. 87 special features on key topics *e.g.* underwater archaeology, radiocarbon dating, origins of farming, collapse of civilizations, and summaries of 25 significant excavations. 'Serves as an important showcase for modern archaeological science' (*Antiquity,* v.66, no.250, March 1992, p.272-3).
Class No: 902

[4153]
WYMER, J. The Palaeolithic age. London, Croom Helm, 1982. 310p. illus., tables, bibliog. ISBN: 070992710x.

7 chapters: 1. Time, change and method; 2. The first humans; 3. Unspecialised hunter-gatherers; 4. Specialised hunter-gatherers; 5. The transition from savagery to barbarism; 6-7. Advanced hunting communities of the Upper Palaeolithic. Bibliography p.273-293. Index of sites p.294-300. General index p.301-310. 'In many ways a *tour de force*' (*Antiquity* v.58, no.222, March 1984, p.76-77).
Class No: 902

Bibliographies

[4154]
Annuario bibliografico di archaeologia (opere e periodici entrati in Biblioteca con la data di pubblicazione del 1952. Modena, Società Tipografica Modenese, 1954-. v.1-. Annual.

V.6: 1957 (published 1960) has 2,514 numbered, annotated and systematically arranged entries. 14 classes, with country, subject, etc., subdivisions: 1. Archaeologia cristiana e bizantinologia - 2. Architettura e topografia - 3. Arti minori e industria - 4. Ceramica - 5. Epigrafia - 6. Filologia - 7. Numismatica - 8. Pittura e mosáico - 9. Preistoria e protoistoria - 10. Religione. Etnologia - 11.

....*(contd.)*
Scavi e notizie archeologiche (1. Generalia; 2. Africa e Oriente; 3. Grecia e Italia; 4. Europa (tránne Grecia e Italia): items 1864-2091) - 12. Scultura - 13. Storia. Vita pubblica e privata - 14. Varia. Author and subject indexes. A list of the 600 periodicals from which articles are indexed (or abstracted) appears on p.5-14. *Class No:* 902(01)

[4155]
Archäologische Bibliographie. Berlin, Walter de Gruyter, 1913-. Annual. ISSN: 03418308.

Succeeded bibliographies printed in *Jahrbuch Deutschen Archäologischen Instituts* (1886-88) and *Archäologischer Anzeiger* (1889-1912).

1992v. (1993. lii,484p.) 13146 references in 24 subject sections (*e.g.* Praxis und Institutionen; Topographie; Urgeschichte). Systematic subject index. A comprehensive and authoritative bibliography of mammouth proportions.
Class No: 902(01)

[4156]
Bulletin signalétique. 525: Préhistoire et protohistoire. Paris, Centre National de la Recherche Scientifique, 1947-. Quarterly.

Lists articles (most with abstracts) covering prehistory from the origins of man to the invention of writing. About 450 archaeological and 200 general periodicals are covered. Sections: 01. Généralités - 02. Méthodologie et études générales - 03. Europe - 04. Asie - 05. Afrique - 06. Amérique et régions arctiques - 07. Océanie. France and neighbouring countries are covered in detail. Annual cumulative index. *Class No:* 902(01)

[4157]
Bulletin signalétique. 526. Art et archéologie Proche Orient - Asie - Amérique. Paris, Centre National de la Recherche Scientifique, 1947-. Quarterly.

List of articles (most with abstracts) from 400 archaeological and *c.*200 multidisciplinary journals. Sections: 01. Généralités - 02. Civilisations anciennes du Proche-Orient - 03. Islam - 04. Asie - 05. Civilisation américaines. Author and subject indexes. *Class No:* 902(01)

[4158]
DEUTSCHES ARCHÄOLGISCHES INSTITUT. Katalog der Bibliothek des Deutschen Archäologisches Instituts. Boston, Massachusetts, G.K. Hall, 3v., 1969.

Autoren- und Periodica Kataloge. 7v. (5,465p.). 92,000 cards. *Systematischer Katalog.* 3v. (2,568p.). 84,000 cards, $355. *Zeitschriften-Autorenkatalog.* 3v. (2,067p.). 37,000 cards. The collection embraces the entire Mediterranean region, Near Eastern and Egyptian archaeology, a large part of European prehistory, period of the great migrations, and early Christian and Byzantine archaeology. The *Systematischer Katalog* classifies under *c.*1,200 heads (some further subdivided) monographs, articles, festschriften, etc., beginning with publication date 1956. The *Zeitschriften-Autorenkatalog* lists authors of articles, festschriften contributions and review articles, 1956-. *Class No:* 902(01)

[4159]

HEIZER, R.F. **Archaeology: a bibliographical guide** to the basic literature. New York, Garland Publishing, 1980. 434p. index. $48.00. ISBN: 0824098269.

4,818 unannotated items. 5 sections: Nature and purpose of archaeology - History of archaeology - The work of the archaeologist - Archaeology as a profession - Sources of primary data. Author index, but no title index. 'The most thorough review of the archaeological literature available' (*Library Journal*, 15 January 1981. p.136.

Class No: 902(01)

[4160]

WOODHEAD, P. **Keyguide to information sources in archaeology.** London, Mansell, 1985. xiv,219p. diagr. £25. ISBN: 0720117453.

Part 1. Overview of archaeology and its literature in 7 chapters: 1. History and scope - 2. Archaeological information - 3. Who, what, where? - 4. Keeping up to date with current publications, developments and events - 5. Finding out about the literature - 6. The literature of archaeology - 7. Other sources of information. Pt. 2 Bibliographical listing (an annotated bibliography of reference sources). Pt. 3 List of selected organizations. 'A work of great interest and quite widespread usefulness' (*Library Review*, v.35, no.2, Summer 1986, p.136-7).

Class No: 902(01)

Encyclopaedias

[4161]

The Cambridge encyclopedia of archaeology. Sherratt, A., *ed.* Cambridge, Cambridge Univ. Press, 1980. 495p. illus., charts, maps, plans.

55 contributors. 3 parts (10 sections; 62 chapters): 1/1. The development of modern archaeology ... 2/2. Man the hunter; 2/3. The postglacial revolution; 2/4.The early empires of the western Old World; 2/5. Empires in the eastern Old World; 2/6. Old empires and new forces; 2/7. On the edge of the Old World; 2/8. The New World (*e.g.* chapter 59: Andean South America); 2/9. Pattern and process ... 3/10. Framework; dating and distribution. Chronological atlas, p.437-52 (36 col. maps). Bibliography (by chapters), p.453-65. Further reading (by parts and sections), p.416-31. Analytical index, p.468-95. 500 illus. (150 col.), with descriptive captions. Omits industrial archaeology.'The selection of topics is excellent and as comprehensive as positive' (*Choice*, v.18, no.2, October 1980, p.220). 'A volume with wide appeal' (*Nature*, v.288, 6 November 1980, p.42). 'More likely to be used for browsing than for quick reference' (*College & Research Libraries*, January 1981, p.49). *Class No:* 902(031)

[4162]

Larousse encyclopedia of archaeology. Charles - Picard, G., *ed.* London, Hamlyn, 1987. 432p. illus., (some col.), maps, tables, bibliog., index. £7.95. ISBN: 0600554252.

First published as *L'archéologie découverte des civilisations disparues* (Paris, Librairie Larousse, 1969). 1st English ed. 1972. 2nd ed. 1983.

18 essays by 13 French specialists; for the non-specialist reader. The first part defines the discipline and traces its development; the second part has chapters on various periods from different parts of the world. *Library journal* (v.98, no.9, 1 May 1973, p.1471) finds the work particularly

.... (contd.)

inadequate in essays on prehistoric archaeology. Essentially a picture book. About 1,000 illus., including 36 fine coloured illus., with a very loose relationship to the text. Emphasis on great places rather than everyday things. Bibliography p.421-3. *Class No:* 902(031)

[4163]

TATTERSALL, I., *and others, eds.* **Encyclopedia of human evolution and prehistory.** New York Garland Publishing, 1988. xxxvi, 603p. illus., diagrs., maps. $87.50. ISBN: 0824093755.

40 academic contributors. 1200 A-Z topic heading entries about half being cross-references to associated articles. Entries are initialled and all but the shortest carry bibliographical references. Main subject areas covered include Fossil and archaeological localities; Archaeology (general terms and concepts); and Archaeological sites. Subject list by topics (summary of major subject areas) p.xiii-xxiv. 'A comprehensive and authoritative source, filling a unique niche, that will be essential to academic libraries' (*Booklist,* v.85, no.11, 1 February 1989, p.922+924). *Class No:* 902(031)

Handbooks & Manuals

[4164]

DAY, A.E. **Archaeology** a reference handbook. London, Clive Bingley; Hamden Connecticut, Linnet Books, 1978. 319p. index. £22.50. ISBN: 0851572421, UK; 0208016724, US.

639 entries, A-Z, for titles of books, articles and periodicals, names of organizations, antiquarians, archaeologists, publishers and series. Title and author index. Useful but has decided limitations *e.g.* no subject approach and dispersive nature of alphabetical order.

Class No: 902(035)

[4165]

Handbuch der Vorgeschichte. Müller-Karpe, H. München, C.H. Beck, 1966-. V.1-.

1. *Altsteinzeit* 1966; 2nd ed. 1977. xi, 359p.+274p. plates and drawings. 2. *Jungsteinzeit Text.* 1968. xiii, 612p. *Tafeln* 1968. vi, 327p. 3. *Kupferzeit Text* 1974. xiii, 770p. 3406054218. *Regesten* 1974. 771-1124p. 3406054226. *Tafeln* 1974. 746p. 3406054234. 4. *Bronzezeit Text.* 1980. vii, 496p. 340679415. *Text und Register.* 1980. 497-866p. 3406079423. *Tafeln.* 1980. 602p. 340607943 3v. DM548. To be completed with an Iron Age volume. This monumental series provides an account of world prehistory, continent by continent, country by country, with a distinct European bias. Each chapter begins with a historical survey of archaeological work. 'Almost unreadable as a book, because of the vast array of cross-references and footnotes, nonetheless there is buried here an immense learning' (*Antiquity*, v. LVI, no.218, November 1982, p.233-234). *Class No:* 902(035)

[4166]

LEROI-GOURHAN, A. **La Préhistoire.** 3rd ed. Paris, Presses Universitaires de France, 1977. 368p. ISBN: 2130352537.

3 parts: 1. La documentation (sources, *i.e.,* sites, with commentary); bibliographies (455 items: reviews, series, congresses; manuals, treatises and general works - Europe, Asia, Africa, America, Oceania and Australia, Methodology,

....(contd.)

Art; no annotations) - 2. Nos connaissances - 3. Problèmes et directions de recherche. Footnote references; index. 54 small but clear illustrations. *Class No:* 902(035)

Dictionaries

[4167]

BAHN, P., *ed.* **Collins dictionary of archaeology.** Glasgow, Harper Collins, 1992. iv,654p. maps, bibliog. £15.99. ISBN: 0004341570.

3,000 entries including definitions of archaeological terms, worldwide sites and artefacts, explanations of archaeological theory and methods, biographical sketches of important archaeologists. Map section p.556-641. Bibliography p.642-50. *Class No:* 902(038)

[4168]

BRAY, W. *and* TRUMP, D. **Penguin dictionary of archaeology.** 2nd rev. ed. London, Allen Lane: Penguin Press, 1982. 283p. illus., maps, index. pbk. £5.95. ISBN: 0140511164.

First published as *A dictionary of archaeology* (London, Allen Lane, 1970).

Over 1600 A-Z entries for archaeological terms, sites, techniques and for prehistoric peoples. Excludes classical and medieval archaeology. English slanted but 'otherwise probably the best nonspecialized guide to archaeological terms and concepts in English' (*Library Journal,* v.97,no.18, 15 April 1972, p.1385). *Class No:* 902(038)

[4169]

CHAMPION, S.A. **A Dictionary of terms and techniques in archaeology.** Oxford, Phaidon, 1980. 144p. illus., diagrs., graphs, maps.

Deliberately excludes names of cultures and artifacts. 'In general, terms have been included if they describe a technique applied to archaeological material either in the past or as part of modern analysis' (*Introduction*). Terms: 'Absolute dating' ... 'X-ray milliprobe'. References appended to some entries (*e.g* 'Radio-carbon dating': 2p., 1 illus., 1 graph, 1 reference). Appended: Sources for line drawings - Further reading. A neat production. Less comprehensive but more up to date than Bray and Trump (*Library Journal,* 15 October 1980, p.2190). 'Suitable for purchase by large academic or public libraries' (*Choice,* March 1981, p.1068). *Class No:* 902(038)

[4170]

Dictionnaire de préhistoire. Leroi-Gourhan, A., *ed.* Paris, Presses Universitaires de France, 1988. x,1221p. illus., maps, tables, bibliog. 495F. ISBN: 2130414591.

Almost 5,000 entries from 114 different hands on prehistoric sites, methods and techniques, and general articles (e.g. Archaïque maritime) covering the Palaeolithic period to the Metal Ages worldwide. Many entries end with specific bibliographies. General bibliography p.1149-59. Major French-language work. *Class No:* 902(038)

[4171]

WHITEHOUSE, R.D., *ed.* **The Macmillan dictionary of archaeology.** London, Macmillan Press, 1983. xi,597p. bibliog., index. £25.00. ISBN: 0333271904.

Over 3500 entries covering the themes, concepts, and discoveries in archaeology. Bibliography p.592-97. Subject index. *Class No:* 902(038)

Reviews & Abstracts

[4172]

Art and archaeology technical abstracts. London, The Getty Conservation Trust in association with the International Institute for Conservation of Historic and Artistic Works, 1966, no.1-. Quarterly and subsequently 2pa. v.9-. ISSN: 06042994.

V.28, no.2, 1991. 889p. has 2886 indicative and informative abstracts in 8 sub-divided sections. Section C Archaeology has 10 sub-sections. Second part in the year includes author, subject and source index. The first 5 volumes were published under the title of *Abstracts of the technical literature on archaeology and fine arts* usually known as *IIC abstracts*. *Class No:* 902(048)

[4173]

Répertoire d'art et d'archéologie. Paris, Morancé (now Centre National de la Recherche Scientifique) 1910-. Annual. ISSN: 00800953.

Publié sous la direction du Comité Française d'Histoire de l'Art, avec une subvention de l'UNESCO sur la recommandation du Conseil International de la Philosophie et des Sciences Humaines.

The 1987v. (N.S. t.22; Ancienne série t.91) has 10377 indicative abstracts and references (mainly on art). 5 main sections: 01: Principes et organization (A. Ouvrages; B. Théories et science de l'art; C. Iconographie; D. Techniques et restauration; E. Institutions savantes et enseignement; F. Collections) - 02. Histoire générale de l'art - 03. Moyen Age - 04. Renaissance XVII et XVIII siècles - 05. XIX et XX siècles. List of over 1000 journals scanned. Quarterly indexes of artists, subjects and authors. *Class No:* 902(048)

Periodicals

[4174]

MUSTY, J. **The Origins of the archaeological periodical** *Current Archaeology.* v.9, no.5. June 1986, p.142-143.

Notes on UK journals 1665-1979. *Class No:* 902(051)

Maps & Atlases

[4175]

BRANIGAN, K., *ed.* **The Atlas of archaeology.** London, Macdonald, 1982. 240p. illus., (many col.), maps. ISBN: 0356062538.

46 significant excavations from various periods and world regions. Although a large map for each of 8 geographical sections is provided, and there are additional site maps and town plans, this is not really an atlas in the conventional sense of the word. Gazetteer p.228-234. Glossary p.234-235. Index p.236-240. 'Good buy for school libraries' (*Antiquity* v.57, no.219, March 1983, p.70-71). *Class No:* 902(084.3)

[4176]

HAWKES, J. **Atlas of ancient archaeology.** London, Heinemann; New York, McGraw Hill, 1974. 272p. maps, index.

22 contributors; 7-8 regions, town plans and sites being a feature, with maps supporting: Africa - British Isles (England, p.26-34: Creswell Crags, Cheddar Gorge, Grime's Graves, Hetty Pegler's Tump, the Avebury District, the Stonehenge District; Maiden Castle) - France - Germany & Netherlands - Scandinavia - Eastern Europe - Iberia - Central Mediterranean - Greece and the Aegean - Anatolia

....(contd.)

and Soviet Armenia - Egypt - Mesopotamia, Iran and the Persian Gulf - Syria, Lebanon and Palestine - India - South East Asia - North America - Mesoamerica - South America. 176 sites; *c*.180 coloured maps. Chronological chart. Glossary, p.268-9. 'Commended - apart from surpirisng omission of most of Asia outside the Fertile Crescent and North India' (*Geographical Journal*, November 1975, p.506-7). *Class No:* 902(084.3)

[4177]

HAWKES, J. and TRUMP, D. The Atlas of early man. London, Macmillan; New York, St. Martin's Press, 1976. 255p. illus., tables, maps, index.

A synoptic view of the events and personalities during 'the 40,000 or so years from the full emergence of *Homosapiens* down to AD500' (*Introduction*). A review of world happenings is followed by a map and illus. of objects, etc. for technology, architecture, art, and a chart to show the state of the economy, main centres, events and developments, people, religion, technology and inventions, architecture and art for 8 regions of the world. Atlas of archaeological site maps, p.230-45, plus gazetteer. No bibliography. Fully illustrated in colour. A beautifully produced book of real reference value.

Class No: 902(084.3)

[4178]

Past worlds The Times atlas of archaeology. Scarre, C., ed. London, Times Books, 1989. Distributed in the US by Hammond Inc. 320p. col. illus., col. maps, tables, bibliog, index. £29.50, $85.00. ISBN: 0723003068.

90 academic contributors (31 from Cambridge University). 122 double page pictorial and cartographic features arranged in 7 main sections: 1. Understanding the past - 2. Human origins 16 million-10,000BC. - 3. The agricultural revolution 10,000-4,000BC. - 4. The first cities and states 4000-1000BC. - 5. Empires of the Old World 1000BC-AD650 - 6. The New World 10,000BC-AD1600 - 7. Towards the modern world AD650-1800. Chronology in 5 colour code for geographical regions p.11-21. Glossary p.281-4. Bibliography p.285-8. 750 col. illus.

A series of articles by George Hill appeared in *The Times* immediately prior to publication *viz* 1. Uncovering the secrets, 27 Sep, 1988, p.10-11; The Age of the great explorers, 28 Sep, p.11; Separate worlds, same ideas, 29 Sep, p.12; and Man and the fathers of invention, 30 Sep, p.12. 'Without question, this is now the standard archaeological atlas' (*Wilson Library Bulletin*), v.63, no.5, January 1989, p.127). *Class No:* 902(084.3)

[4179]

WHITEHOUSE, D. and WHITEHOUSE, R. Archaeological atlas of the world. Maps drawn by J.B. Woodcock. London, Thames & Hudson, 1975. 272p. maps.

Sections: 1. Palaeolithic sites in the Old World (17 sub-sections, each with 'Further reading' and map) - 2. Africa - 3. Western Asia - 4. The Mediterranean basin - 5. Europe, with Russia (*e.g.* 'Rock-cut tombs in Europe': 2½ cols. of text; 5 items of 'Further reading'; 2-p. map spread, for locations) - 6. South and East Asia, Australasia and the Pacific - 7. The Americas. Index of sites, with grid references, p.237-72, pinpointing over 5,000 sites. 103 two-colour maps. *British Book News* review (September 1975, p.668) finds choice of Latin American sites 'frankly

....(contd.)

capricious'. 'More comprehensive though less detailed than Jacquetta. Hawkes' *Atlas of ancient archaeology'* (*qv*) (*New History*, July 1975, p.3). *Class No:* 902(084.3)

[4180]

The World atlas of archaeology. Flon, C., ed. London, Mitchell Beazeley International Ltd., Boston, G.K. Hall, 1985. 423p. col.illus., col. maps, bibliog., index. £29.95; $83.00. ISBN: 0855335538, UK; 0816187479, US.

English language edition of *Le grand atlas de l'archéologie* (Encyclopaedia Universalis, 1985).

Over 90 contributors present a superb visual survey closely integrated with authoritative text arranged in chronological, thematic and regional chapters: Prehistoric Europe - The Classical World - The early Middle Ages - Middle Ages - Byzantine World - Islam - Near East - Egypt and Sudan - Scythia and the Steppes - Central Asia - The Indian World - Southeast Asia - China - Vietnam - Korea and Japan - Africa - The Americas - Oceania - Modern period (Archaeological background ... Archaeology and East-West exchange ... Industrial archaeology). Glossary p.405-418. Bibliography p.394-403. More than 100 maps. Over 1000 photographs. Emphasis is on social aspects i.e., food and drink, clothing, everyday life, commercial interchange etc. 'A most useful and necessary work for the professional scholar' (*Antiquity*, v.60, no.229, July 1986, p.154).

Class No: 902(084.3)

Chronologies

[4181]

GRASLUND, B. The Birth of prehistoric chronology dating methods and dating systems in nineteenth century Scandinavia. Cambridge, Cambridge University Press, 1987. iv, 132p., illus., bibliog., index. £25.00. $39.50. (*New studies in antiquity*.) ISBN: 0521322499.

15 Well documented chapters analysing the basic elements of archaeological dating systems and tracing the origins and development of those sytems. *Class No:* 902(090)

Histories

[4182]

DANIEL, G. A Hundred and fifty years of archaeology. 2nd ed. London, Duckworth, 1975. 410p. bibliog., index.

First published as *A hundred years of archaeology* (1950).

11 sections: 1. The antiquarian background - 2. The antiquarian and geological revolutions - 3. The birth of archaeology: 1840-70 - 4. Archaeology comes of age: 1870-1900 - 5. The development of technique and method before 1900 - 6. The discovery of the Near-Eastern civilizations - 7. European prehistory, 1900-50 - 8. The development of world prehistory - 9. The development of techniques and methods: 1900-50 - 10. Retrospect and prospect - 11. Archaeology, 1945-70 (1. World prehistory; 2. Prehistoric Europe; 3. America; 4. Science and technology; 5. Historic archaeology; 6. archaeology; new and false). Glossary: 'Archaeological table of main events' (up to 1973), p.385-400. Bibliography, p.401-6. *Class No:* 902(091)

[4183]
DANIEL, G. **A Short history of archaeology.** London, Thames & Hudson, 1981. 232p. illus., (some col.), bibliog. (*Ancient Peoples and Places.*) ISBN: 0500021015.

100th volume in Ancient Peoples and Places series.

1. The birth of archaeology - 2. Antiquaries and archaeologists (1797-1867) - 3. Excavators and explorers (1867-1914) - 4. Archaeology comes of age (1914-1929) - 5. New and not-so-new archaeology (1939-1950) - 6. The great themes. Bibliog. p.217-219. Index p.225.232.

Daniel G. and Renfrew, C. *The Idea of Prehistory* (Edinburgh Univ. Press, 2nd ed., 1988. £19.50. ISBN 0852245327) traces the conceptual development of archaeology from its antiquarian origins to the 1980s. Important bibliography p.205-13. *Class No:* 902(091)

[4184]
TRIGGER, B.G. **A History of archaeological thought.** Cambridge, Cambridge Univ. Press, 1989. xv,500p. illus., bibliog., index. ISBN: 0521328780.

'A history of archaeology from medieval times to the present in world-wide perspective'. 1. Relevance of archaeological history - 2. Classical archaeology and antiquarianism - 3. Beginnings of scientific archaeology - 4. The imperial synthesis - 5. Culture-historical archaeology - 6. Soviet archaeology - 7. Functionalism in Western archaeology - 8. Neo-evolutionism and the New Archaeology - 9. The explanations of diversity - 10. Archaeology and its social context. Bibliographical essay p.412-28. References p.429-76. Analytical index. 'The best intellectual history of the discipline to date' (review article, *Journal of Field Archaeology,* v.18, no.1, Spring 1991, p.106-11). *Class No:* 902(091)

Pacific Ocean

[4185]
BELLWOOD, P. **Man's conquest of the Pacific** the prehistory of Southeast Asia and Oceania. Auckland, Collins, 1978. 462p. illus., maps, bibliog., index. £20.00. ISBN: 0002169118.

13 chapters: 1. Introduction; 2. Human populations - past and present; 3. Cultural foundations; 4. The cultures of Southeast Asia and Oceania; 5. The linguistic history of the Pacific area; 6. Subsistence pattern and the prehistoric implications; 7. Neolithic and Early Metal Age cultures on the Southeast Asian mainland; 8. Neolithic and Early Metal Age Inland Southeast Asia; 9. The prehistory of Melanesia; 10. Prehistory of Micronesia; 11-12. Prehistory of Polynesia; 13. Prehistory of New Zealand. Glossary p.424. Important bibliography p.425-451. *Class No:* 902(265)

[4186]
IRWIN, G. **The Prehistoric exploration and colonisation of the Pacific.** Cambridge, Cambridge Univ. Press, 1992. viii,240p. maps, tables, bibliog., index. £30. ISBN: 0521403715.

'Concerned with two distinct episodes of voyaging and colonisation. The first began some 50,000 years ago in the tropical region of Island Southeast Asia, the continent of Australia and its Pleistocene outliers ... The second episode began after 3,500 years ago and was a burst of sophisticated maritime and neolithic settlement in the remote Pacific' (*Introduction*). Bibliography p.223-31. Analytical index. *Class No:* 902(265)

Ancient Egypt

Bibliographies

[4187]
Annual Egyptological bibliography/Bibliographie Egyptologique annuelle/Jährbuch Ägyptologische bibliographie. Zonhoven, L.M.J., *ed.* Leiden, International Association of Egyptologists in cooperation with the Nederlands Instituut voor het Nabije Oosten, 1948-. Annual.

The 1984v. (1987. xi, 251p. 9072147030) has 1331 numbered abstracts sytematically classified in 10 sections: 1. General (History of Egyptology, Obituaries, Present day Egyptology, Reports, Methodology, Research tools) - 2. Scripts and language - 3. Texts and philology - 4. History - 5. Art and archaeology - 6. Religion - 7. Society and culture - 8. Science and technology - 9. The country and neighbouring areas - 10. Nubian studies. Author and title indexes. Published on the recommendation of the International Council for Philosophy and Humanistic Studies, with the financial assistance of UNESCO and the Nederlandse organistie voor zuiver-wetenschappenijk onderzoek ZWO.

Janssen, J.M.A. *Annual Egyptological Bibliography indexes 1947-1956.* Leiden, E.J. Brill, 1960. xviii, 475p. *Class No:* 902(32)(01)

Encyclopaedias

[4188]
Lexikon der Ägyptologie. Helck, W. *and* Westendorf, W., *eds.* Wiesbaden, Otto Harrassowitz, 6v., 1975-1986.

V.6: *Stele-Zyppresse* (1986.1455p. ISBN 3447026634). International cooperative encyclopedia of immense scholarly distinction. Initialled articles end with lists of reference. Nachtragsartikel continue in fascicules. *Class No:* 902(32)(031)

Handbooks & Manuals

[4189]
VANDIER, J.V. **Manuel d'archéologie égyptienne.** Paris, Picard, 1952-. v.1-. (*Grands Manuels Picard.*)

Published under the auspices of the Centre Nationale de la Recherche Scientifique. Continues G. Jéquier's *Manuel d'archéologie égyptienne* (Paris, Picard, 1924).

1. *Les époques de formation.* Pt.1. *La préhistoire*; pt.2. *Les trois premières dynasties* 2v., 1988 (1952). 1044p. ISBN 2708401602. 2. *Les grands époques.* Pt.1. *L'architecture funéraire*; pt.2. *L'architecture religieuse et civile.* 2v., 1954. 2708401610. 3. *La statuaire.* 2v., 1959. 4/5. *Bas-reliefs et peintures: scènes de la vie quotidienne.* 4v., 1964-69. 6. *Bas-reliefs et peintures: scènes de la vie agricole.* 1978. 2708400150.

An illustrated guide to the study of the monuments and artifacts of ancient Egypt, dealing only incidentally with its religion, literature and history. V.5, pt.2 (vi, 1038p.) has 48 plates and 235 figures. *Class No:* 902(32)(035)

Biographies

[4190]

Who was who in Egyptology: a biographical index of Egyptologists; of travellers, explorers and excavators in Egypt; of collectors and dealers in Egyptian antiquities; of consuls, officials, authors, benefactors, and others whose names occur in the literature of Egyptology, from the year 1500 to the present day, but excluding persons now living. 2nd ed. London, Egypt Exploration Society, 1972. xiv,315p. port.

First published 1952.

About 1,000 entries. 'Champollion': p.58-60; 9½ lines of bibliography. 'Flinders Petrie': p.228-30; 13½ lines of bibliography. 'Maspero': p.197-8; 14 lines of bibliography. Bibliographies cite periodical articles, papers, unpublished diaries, etc. Sources, p.x-xiv. *Class No:* 902(32)(092)

[4191]

WORTHAM, J.D. British Egyptology 1549-1906. Newton Abbot, Devon, David & Charles, 1972. xi,171p. illus., maps.

11 chapters (1, Egyptology during the Renaissance - 2. English travellers in Egypt during the Renaissance ... 10. The Egyptian Exploration Fund - 11. Sir Flinders Petrie and the development of scientific exploration). Bibliography, p.149-65. Non-analytical index. *Class No:* 902(32)(092)

Mesopotamia

[4192]

LLOYD, S. The Archaeology of Mesopotamia from the Old Stone Age to the Persian conquest. London, Thames & Hudson, 1978. 252p. illus., ports., maps, plans, index. (*The World of Archaeology.*)

10 chapters (1. The land and its rivers - 2. The twilight of Neolithic man ... 9. The late Assyrian period - 10. Babylon: the last Mesopotamian monarchy). Notes on the text, p.232-7. Bibliography p.238-43 (under authors). 'Analyses systematically the wealth of material produced by major and minor excavations since 1900 ... an invaluable reference work' (A.J. Abdulrahman. *Iraq*, 1984 Entry 144). *Class No:* 902(35)

Persia, Ancient

Bibliographies

[4193]

PEARSON, J.D., ed. A Bibliography of pre-Islamic Persia. London, Mansell, 1975. 288p.

Compiled under the auspices of the Royal Institute of Translation and Publication of Iran.

Over 7,000 entries, in 4 main parts (1: Languages and literatures - 2. History, including numismatics, chronology, historical geography, law - 3. Religions, including folklore and Iranian epic - 4. Art & archaeology (general; archaeological travels; exhibition catalogues; history of art; artifacts). Attempts to list 'all the printed literature in Western European languages' (*Introduction*) - books and periodical articles - on the pre-Islamic period locatable in relevant libraries, museums and periodicals. *Class No:* 902(355)(01)

Ancient Greece & Rome

[4194]

GRANT, M. The Visible past Greek and Roman history from archaeology 1960-1990. London, Weidenfeld and Nicolson, 1990. xvii,258p. illus., maps, bibliog., index. £17. ISBN: 0297820397.

9 chapters arranged chronologically in 2 parts (1. The Greeks - 2. Italy and the Roman Empire) describe and assess 50 archaeological sites or projects, including underwater archaeology and the findings of air photography, that have transformed our knowledge of classical history. Chapter references p.186-92. Notes p.193-216. Bibliography p.220-40. 9 maps. *Class No:* 902(37/38)

[4195]

STILLWELL, R., and others eds. The Princeton encyclopaedia of classical sites. Princeton, New Jersey, Princeton Univ. Press, 1976. xxi, 1019p. $215. ISBN: 0691035423.

Data on over 2,800 archaeological sites. Aardenburg ... Zoster. About 400 contributors. Period: 750BC-AD565. All entries, however, short, have references, ('Corinth'; 6 columns; 2/3 col. of bibiliography; 'Carthage': 1¼ cols., 5 references; 'Katana' (Catania, Sicily); 21/3 cols. of bibliography). Map references to 24p. of 3-colour maps; map indexes, p.1011-19. Glossary of technical terms. Scholarly, readable text. A handsome volume. 'This first-class reference book' (*Library Journal*, v.101, 1 October 1976, p.2050). *Class No:* 902(37/38)

Bibliographies

[4196]

COULSON, W.D.E. Greek and Roman art, architecture, and archaeology: an annotated bibliography. 2nd ed. New York, Garland, 1987. viii, 204p. (*Garland Reference Library of The Humanities No.580.*) ISBN: 0824087569.

This edition is a completely new work.

349 critically annotated entries primarily relating to in print material suitable for undergraduate courses and organized in 8 chapters: 1. General - 2. Archaeology (methods and techniques) - 3. Prehistoric - 4. Greek - 5. Etruscan - 6. Roman - 7. Sites of multiple periods - 8. Additional resources. *Class No:* 902(37/38)(01)

Reviews & Abstracts

[4197]

Fasti archaeologici annual bulletin of Classical archaeology. Firenze, Licosa-Libreria Commissionaria for the International Association for Classical Archaeology. 1948. V.1-.

Vs. 34-35: 1987 (1979-80, xvii, 1570p. illus., plans, indexes.) contains 19,031 indicative and imformative abstracts in 6 main sections (with regional *etc.*, subdivisions): 1. General - 2. Prehistoric and Classical Greece - 3. Italy before the Roman Empire - 4. The Hellenistic world and the Eastern provinces of the Roman Empire - 5. The Roman West - 6. Christianity and late antiquity. Profuse cross-references. 5 indexes including 4. Lexicalia and 5. Literary and epigraphical sources. 40 plates. *Class No:* 902(37/38)(048)

Maps & Atlases

[4198]

FINLEY, M.I. Atlas of classical archaeology. London, Chatto & Windus, 1977. 256p. illus., plans, maps.

Period covered is mainly 1000B.C.-500A.D. Sections: Introduction - Roman Britain - The Roman Rhine - Danube frontier - Provence - The Iberian Peninsula - North Africa - Sicily - Italy - Illyricum, Moesia and Dacia - Greece (p.141-83) - Cyprus - Black Sea - Asia Minor - Syria - Palestine - East of Palmyra. Each section has reference appended. Appended: Chronological table; Roman emperors; Glossary; Greek vase types; The Greek architectural orders. Excellent photographs and ground plans; small diagrams and maps. *Class No:* 902(37/38)(084.3)

[4199]

HEYDEN, A.A.M. *and* **SCULLARD, H.,** *eds.* **Atlas of the Classical World.** London, Nelson, 1959. 221p. illus., maps, index.

'Not intended primarily for professional scholars' (*Foreword*). 70 coloured maps, plus insets; 475 photogravure plates, including many aerial photographs. It illustrates the centuries from prehistoric Greece to the decline of the Roman Empire before the barbaric immigrations of the 4th century. Information is presented in three ways: maps, giving religious, economic, military, literary, artistic and political statistics; illustrations (line-drawings and photographs); descriptive articles, covering geography, history and culture. Maps include town plans, and a number have lengthy legends; scales are not often indicated. *Shorter atlas of the Classical world,* compiled by H.H. Scullard and A.A.M. van der Heyden (London, Nelson, 1962 [*i.e.* 1963] 239p. illus., maps.) is not a mere abridgement. Prof. Scullard has provided a new 40,000 word account of the Greek and Roman civilizations. But the chief features are the 200 or so excellent illustrations of landscape and culture. The 10 coloured maps occupy a rather inconspicuous place. *Class No:* 902(37/38)(084.3)

[4200]

THOMSON, J.O. Everyman's classical atlas with an essay on the development of ancient geographical knowledge and theory. new ed. London, J.M. Dent, 1961. lxxp. 56pl. of maps, 59-125p. illus.

First published as *Everyman's Atlas of ancient and Classical geography,* 1907; rev. ed. 1952.

The text consists of the essay, together with notes on some of the battlefields of antiquity. The 56 maps (by Bartholomew) and 5 sketch maps of various sizes and scales. The index-gazetteer carries some 3,500 entries and is followed by 29 pages of illus. The small page-size (20x12.5cm) is not enhanced by the 1" margin for maps and much white space for illus. *Class No:* 902(37/38)(084.3)

Europe

[4201]

CHAMPION, T., *and others.* **Prehistoric Europe.** London, Academic Press, 1984. x, 359p. illus., maps, bibliog., index. £37.00.

Comprehensive synthesis of new interpretations (based on recent archaeological data) in 9 chronological chapters each equipped with numerous maps and drawings. References p.327-35. 'It will at once take its place as a new standard

....(contd.)

work, for it is quite simply the best introduction to European prehistory which is currently available' (*Nature,* v.314, no.6006, 7 March 1985, p.28-29). *Class No:* 902(4)

[4202]

COLLIS, J. The European Iron Age. London, B.T. Batsford, 1984. 192p. illus., map, bibliog. £19,95. ISBN: 0713434511.

General introduction demonstrating the links between the classical Mediterranean world and the more shadowy regions of Central Europe. Notes and bibliography p.181-188. Index p.189-192. 'A magnificent survey of a whole continent' (*Current Archaeology,* v. ix, no.2, July 1985, p.46). *Class No:* 902(4)

[4203]

GAMBLE, C. The Palaeolithic settlement of Europe. Cambridge, Cambridge Univ Press, 1986. xix, 471p. illus., tables, bibliog. £45.00. ISBN: 0521245141.

Surveys the hunter-gatherer societies of Europe in 9 chapters (1. European paleolithic studies: history and approaches; 9. The palaeolithic settlement in Europe). Extensive bibliography p.411-459. Site index p.460-462. General index p.463-471. *Class No:* 902(4)

[4204]

SCHUTZ, H. The Prehistory of Germanic Europe. New Haven, Yale Univ Press, 1983. viii, 421p. illus., (some col.), maps, tables, index. $60.00. £45.00. ISBN: 0300028636.

Systematic survey of Central European cultural history in 7 chapters: 1. The Palaeolithic; 2. The Ceramic Age; 3. The Bronze Age; 4. Hallstatt; 5. The La Tene culture; 6. Northern genesis; 7. Conclusion. Chapter notes p.355-399. Bibliography p.400-407. Aim is to make accessible a summary of modern research to students and scholars. *Class No:* 902(4)

[4205]

SKLENAR, K. Archaeology in Central Europe the first 500 years. Leicester, Leicester Univ. Press; New York, St. Martin's Press, 1983. viii, 182p. illus., maps. ISBN: 0718512049, UK; 0312047215, US.

The development of prehistoric and protohistoric archaeology in Central Europe and in each of the countries concerned. Bibliography p.170-174. Index p.176-182. *Class No:* 902(4)

[4206]

WHITE, A.W.R. Neolithic Europe a survey. Cambridge, Cambridge Univ. Press, 1985. xiv,363p. illus., maps, bibliog. £27.50. (*Cambridge World Archaeology.*) ISBN: 0521247993.

Wide ranging survey of the archaeological evidence 8000-2000BC Each chapter reviews nature of the evidence, the environment, chronology and cultural sequences, settlements, and social context of production. Bibliography p.342-355. Index p.356-363. 'A balanced and well-referenced summary of the subject' (*Choice,* v.23, no.7, March 1986, p.1126). *Class No:* 902(4)

Encyclopaedias

[4207]

FILIP, J. Enzyklopädisches Handbuch zur Ur- und Frühgeschichte Europas. Stuttgart, Kohlhammer, 2v., 1966-69. xv, 1756p. illus. (incl. pl.), tables, maps, bibliogs.

1: A-K; v.2: L-Z und Nachträge.

About 250 contributors. Many short articles on the prehistory, and early history of Europe, some of them signed; references appended. Helpful entries under 'Inventaria archeologia', 'Izvestija'. 'Bretagne': 5 cols; 'Kroatien': 6 cols. listing publications produced locally; 'England': nearly 4 cols., with ½col. of bibliography. Includes biographies (*e.g.* Müller-Karpe, H.: ½col.). Numerous small, good line-drawings; 92 plates appended. *Class No:* 902(4)(031)

Great Britain

[4208]

Archaeology in Britain. London, Council for British Archaeology, 1977-. Annual. ISSN: 03088456.

Before 1977 published with C.B.A.'s *Annual Report.*

1991 volume edited by Morris, R. and Heyworth, M. (1992, vi,143p. illus., index. ISBN 1872414362) includes directory information and annual reports of official bodies (*e.g.* Cadw. Welsh Historic Monuments; Department of the Environment for Northern Ireland; English Heritage; Historic Scotland, *etc.*); Nautical bodies (*e.g.* C.B.A. Nautical Archaeology Society); Research Projects; and city, county, district and regional organizations. *Class No:* 902(410)

[4209]

The Archaeology resource book 1992. Halkon, P., *and others*, eds. London, English Heritage and Council for British Archaeology, 1992. iii,146p. softcover. £6. ISBN: 1872414230.

Expands and replaces M.J. Corbishley's *Archaeological resources handbook for teachers* (London, CBA., 2nd ed., 1983).

1. Archaeology in education (including National Curriculum, Examinations, Careers) - 2. Archaeology in Action (National agencies, Professional units and trusts, National, regional and local archaeological societies, Museums) - 3. Research (reading archaeology, Audio-visual materials, computer software). *Class No:* 902(410)

[4210]

CUNLIFFE, B. Iron Age communities in Britain an account of England, Scotland and Wales from the seventh century BC until the Roman Conquest. 3rd ed. London, Routledge, 1991. xii,685p. illus., maps, drawings, bibliog., index. ISBN: 0415054168.

1st ed. 1974; 2nd ed. 1979.

Comprehensive account of the British Iron Age. 21 chapters in 4 parts: 1. Introduction (development of Iron Age studies) - 2. Space & time (from a chronological and regional standpoint) - 3. Themes (pattern of settlement, development of hill-forts etc.) - 4. Systems (Iron Age society and social change). Appendix A. Pottery - B. Selected radiocarbon dates - C. List of principal sites (p.609-23). Chapter notes p.624-6. Bibliography p.631-73. This edition is substantially revised. *Class No:* 902(410)

[4211]

GREAT BRITAIN. Ordnance Survey. Field archaeology in Great Britain. 5th ed. Southampton, Ordnance Survey, 1973. 184p. illus. £5.00. ISBN: 0319000222.

First published 1921 (HMSO).

8 sections: 1. Archaeological field work - 2. Time scales - 3. Prehistoric antiquities - 4. The Roman period - 5. The Dark Ages and the early medieval period - 6. The medieval and post-medieval period - 7. Industrial archaeology - 8. Miscellaneous (1-4; *e.g.* 2: Trackways). Analytical index. 30 text figures. *Class No:* 902(410)

[4212]

Medieval Archaeology Journal of the Society for Medieval Archaeology. London, Society for Medieval Archaeology, 1957-. Annual. ISSN: 00766097.

Regular feature 'Medieval Britain and Ireland' includes Specialist Group reports and Excavation Reports (A-Z by site) for England, Northern Ireland, Republic of Ireland, Scotland, and Wales. V.36. 1992. has B.S. Nenk and others, 'Medieval Britain and Ireland in 1991' (p.194-308). *Class No:* 902(410)

[4213]

MEGAW, J.V.S. and SIMPSON, D.D.A. Introduction to British prehistory from the arrival of *Homo Sapiens* to the Claudian invasion. Leicester, Leicester Univ. Press, 1979. xv, 560p. illus., plans, tables, maps, pbk. £12.95. ISBN: 0718511727.

7 contributors. 7 chapters: 1. The environmental background to British prehistory - 2. Exploitation and adaptation in pre-agricultural communities - 3. The first agricultural communities (*c.*3,500-2,500BC) - 4. The Later Neolithic (*c.*2,500-1,700BC) - 5. The Early Bronze Age (*c.*2,000-1,300BC) - 6. The Later Bronze Age (1400-500BC) - The Iron Age (*c.*BC-AD200) (p.344-501). Some chapter notes. Abbreviations (sources. Bibliography (A/Z authors), p.503-44. Analytical subject index; index of places. Well produced; finely drawn illus. *Class No:* 902(410)

[4214]

Post-medieval archaeology. London, The Journal of The Society For Post-Medieval Archaeology, 1968-. Annual. ISSN: 00794326.

Regularly includes 2 features: 'Post-medieval Britain and Ireland' consisting of excavation reports (ecclesiastical buildings; military and naval earthworks and structures; towns and corporate buildings; villages; manors, country houses *etc.* farms and small domestic buildings; industry; communications; sport and amusements) and 'Post-medieval Britain in periodic literarure' A-Z periodical title. *Class No:* 902(410)

[4215]

SELKIRK, A. The Riches of British archaeology. Cambridge, Cambridge Univ. Press, 1988. 208p. illus., maps, index. ISBN: 0521321328.

50 significant sites excavated in Britain over the last 20 years, on double-paged spreads, arranged in 5 chronological sections: Earlier prehistory - Later prehistory - Roman Britain - The Dark Ages - Saxon and Medieval Britain. With a glossary and list of sites and museums to visit. *Class No:* 902(410)

Bibliographies

[4216]
Archaeological bibliography for Great Britain and Ireland.
London, Council for British Archaeology, 1950-1980.
Biennially 1950-51 and 1952-53; then annually.

Replaced CBA's *Archaeological bulletin for the British Isles* (1940-49). Discontinued in 1980 because of financial stringencies.

In 2 sections: a topographical section under county, period, and subject headings followed by a bibliography A-Z by author. Drew upon *c.* 150-200 British and Irish periodicals and covered the British Isles from the earliest times to 1600. A sad loss. *Class No:* 902(410)(01)

[4217]
BONSER, W. A Prehistoric bibliography. Extended and edited by Jane Troy. Oxford, Blackwell, 1976. xvi, 425p. ISBN: 0631170901.

Companion to Bonser's *Romano-British bibliography* (1964) and *Anglo-Saxon and Celtic bibliography* (1957).

9,020 entries for books and periodical articles, many drawn from British local history, archaeological and antiquarian society publications. Topical arrangement under 5 main heads: A. Men and methods in archaeology - B. Field archaeology - C. Specific sites - D. Material funds - E. Culture. (B.C. and D. are further divided into 6 geographical zones of the British Isles). Index of authors and subjects. Long list of *corrigenda* issued.
Class No: 902(410)(01)

[4218]
British archaeological bibliography. London, British Archaeological Bibliography, 1992-. Two issues per year. ISSN: 09647104.

BAB was set up by a consortium of the Council for British Archaeology, English Heritage, the Royal Commission on the Ancient and Historical Monuments of England, and the Society of Antiquaries.

1992 (2 issues) contain 1,728 items arranged in 9 heavily sub-divided sections: 1. General, multi-period, undated - 2. Palaeolithic and Mesolithic - 3. Neolithic - 4. Bronze Age - 5. Iron Age - 6. Roman Britain - 7. Migration and Early Medieval - 8. Medieval - 9. Post-medieval, industry, recent. Each issue also includes an author index, and directories of periodicals and monographs, of book publishers, and of other abstract publications and serial bibliographies relevant to archaeology and its related disciplines. The second issue also carries a subject index. The perceived role, aims and objectives of *BAB* is spelled out in v.1, no.1, April 1992, p.14-15. *Class No:* 902(410)(01)

[4219]
DYER, J., ed. British archaeology an introductory booklist. 2nd ed. London, Council for British Archaeology, 1987. 36p. pb. £2.50. ISBN: 0906780705.

Previous edition 1976.

In 3 sections: 1. General (works of general importance, principles and methods, prehistoric, Romano-Britain, migration and early medieval, post-medieval); 2. Regional; 3. Young people. For students, teachers and amateurs.
Class No: 902(410)(01)

[4220]
GOMME, G.L., *and others*. Index of archaeological papers 1665-1890. London, Constable, 1907. xi, 910p.

Prepared for the Congress of Archaeological Societies and the Society of Antiquaries of London. Continued annually for the years 1891-1910 under the same auspices (Constable, 1892-1914). The main work is an index under authors to articles in 94 journals of archaeological and historical content. The supplements include further indexes of subjects and places mentioned, referring back to the author sequence.

Continued by *Index to archaeological papers published in 1891-1910* (Constable, 1892-1914).

The series is incomplete in the historical side, many local societies having been omitted, and it is superseded for 1901 onwards by Mullins' *Guide to the historical publications of the societies of England and Wales. Class No:* 902(410)(01)

Handbooks & Manuals

[4221]
ADKINS, L and ADKINS, R.A. The Handbook of British archaeology. London, Macmillan, 1983. 319p. illus. bibliog., pbk. £7.95. ISBN: 0333348435.

First published by David & Charles and in the US by Barnes & Noble in 1982 under the title of *A thesaurus of British archaeology.*

8 chronological chapters from the palaeolithic to the medieval period are followed by 2 others, 'Archaeological Techniques' and a miscellaneous chapter. Text entries end with sources for further reading and there is an extensive bibliography (p.285-296). Index p.292-319. More than 500 line drawings. 'Excellent detailed work explaining the technical terms and jargon found in British archaeology' (Woodhead: *Keyguide to information sources in archaeology*, 1985). *Class No:* 902(410)(035)

Reviews & Abstracts

[4222]
British archaeological abstracts. London, Council for British Archaeology, 1967-. no.1-. 2 *pa.* £35.00. individuals. £75.00 institutions. ISSN: 00070270.

1989: 1892 abstracts on the archaeology of Great Britain and Ireland. Arranged by periods: 1. General, multi-period undated - 2. Palaeolithic and Mesolithic - 3. Neolithic - 4. Bronze Age - 5. Iron Age - 6. Roman Britain - 7. Migration/ Early medieval - 8. Medieval - 9. Post-medieval/Industrial. Recent, then by subjects. Annual author and subject indexes. When CBA's *Archaeological bibliography for Great Britain and Ireland* folded with the 1980 issue coverage of abstracts ceased to be selective and comprehensivity is now attempted from *c.*165 British and 130 foreign journals. There is a microfiche edition. *Archaeological site index to radiocarbon dates for Great Britain and Ireland*, 1971-1982 is a supplement to *British archaeological abstracts.* Lavell, C. *British archaeological thesaurus for use with British archaeological abstracts and other publications in British archaeology* (CBA, 1989). 69p. refs., pbk. £4.95. ISBN 0906780772 is 'a standard list of words in current use in British archaeology' (*British archaeological abstracts* Entry 89/893). *Class No:* 902(410)(048)

Gazetteers

[4223]

MEANEY, A. A Gazetteer of early burial sites. London, Allen and Unwin, 1964. 304p. map.

Entries A ... York, (plus Scotland, West Lothian), giving grid references, sources, museum, date and detailed description. 'Sutton Hoo': nearly 3 columns. Aims to place the burials in their historical context 'and to give some account of the burial customs used by the heathen English'. *Class No:* 902(410)(083.86)

Maps & Atlases

[4224]

HELLYER, R. 'The Archaeological and historical maps of the Ordnance Survey', *The Cartographical Journal,* v.26, no.2, December 1989. p.111-133. figs, plans, tables.

Important research article. 'Discusses the making of these maps and cites the known cartographical, bibliographical and manuscript sources relevant both to the published maps and to those which failed to reach publication' (*Abstract*). Bibliography p.131-3. Table 1: Period maps prepared by the O.S. *Class No:* 902(410)(084.3)

[4225]

MANLEY, J. Atlas of prehistoric Britain. Oxford, Phaidon, 1989. 160p. illus., (some col.), maps, bibliog., index. £22.50. ISBN: 0714825697.

A chronological approach, 'no more than a rough guide' (Preface) to 'the principal concentrations of major prehistoric monuments in Britain and Ireland'. Date charts p.152-53. Sites to visit p.154-57. Bibliography p.157. 139 illus. (41 in colour). *Class No:* 902(410)(084.3)

Roman Times

Handbooks & Manuals

[4226]

COLLINGWOOD, R.G. *and* **RICHMOND, I. The Archaeology of Roman Britain.** Rev. ed. London, Methuen, 1969. xxv, 350p. illus. (inc. pl). (*Methuen's Handbooks of Archaeology.*)

First published 1930.

16 chapters (1. Roads - 2. Camps - 3. Fortresses and forts - 4. Signal stations, lighthouses and fortlets - 5. Frontier works - 6. Towns - 7. Villas - 8. Temples - 9. Tombs - 10. Native settlements - 11. Inscriptions - 12. Coins - 14. Samian ware of terra sigillata - 14. Coarse pottery - 15. Brooches - 16. Weapons, tools and utensils). 'An indispensable and exceptionally fine contribution to Romano-British studies' (*British Book News*, August 1969, p.639-40). *Class No:* 902(410)"0055-0449"(035)

Maps & Atlases

[4227]

GREAT BRITAIN. Ordnance Survey. Roman Britain. 4th ed. Southampton, Ordnance Survey, 1978. 31p.

Scale, 1:625,000. Depicts Roman Britain, AD 43-410 locating land and water communications, settlements, temples, villas and other buildings; symbols for military, civil and industrial sites. Explanatory text has 2 supplementary maps, chronological table, Roman place-names and topographical indexes, with National Grid

....(contd.)

references. 'Well up to their usual standard' (*Bulletin of the Institute of Archaeology*, no.17, 1980, p.146). *Class No:* 902(410)"0055-0449"(084.3)

Middle Ages

[4228]

MUIR, R. The Lost villages of Britain. London, Michael Joseph, 1982. 285p.+16p. col. plates. illus., diagrs., bibliogs., index. £11.95. ISBN: 0718120361.

12 thematic chapters *e.g.* 2. Meeting the medieval village ... 7. The Highlands made desert ... 9. The price of a park. Appendix 1. Reading on p.271-2 - 2. Main sites, A-Z by county p.273-8. For the non-specialist reader. 'Fills a notable gap on the archaeologist's bookshelf' (*Current Archaeology*, v.8, no.4, June 1983, p.123-4). *Class No:* 902(410)"01/14"

Modern Times

[4229]

CROSSLEY, D. Post-medieval archaeology in Britain. Leicester, Leicester Univ. Press, 1990. ix,328p. illus., plans bibliog., index. £52.50; $49. ISBN: 0718512855.

Overview in 12 chapters: 1. Post-medieval rural landscape - 2. Post-medieval town - 3. Church archaeology - 4. Fortifications - 5. Shipwrecks - 6. Sources of power before the invention of the steam engine - 7/8. Metals - 9. Mining and quarrying - 10. Other industries - 11. Glass - 12. Ceramics. Bibliography p.291-308. 'To have written a book which encapsulates current research in post-medieval archaeology so clearly is a considerable achievement, but to direct the reader so firmly to the tasks for the next generation of scholars is of even greater benefit. It ensures that its value as a work of reference is greatly enhanced' (*Post-Medieval Archaeology*, no.25, 1991, p.189-91). *Class No:* 902(410)"15/19"

20th Century

[4230]

LONGWORTH, I.H. *and* **CHERRY, J. Archaeology in Britain since 1945** new directions. London, British Museum Publications, 1986. 248p. illus., map, bibliog., index. pbk. £12.50. ISBN: 0714120359.

Progress review by 7 contributors surveying the most important achievements in British archaeology over the past 30 years. 1. Prehistoric Britain - 2. A Roman province - 3. Anglo-Saxon England - 4. Technology, towns, castles and churches 1100-1600 - 5. The medieval countryside. Glossary p.237-8. Bibliography p.239-44. *Class No:* 902(410)"19"

Scotland

[4231]

Discovery & Exploration in scotland an annual survey of Scottish archaeological discoveries, excavation and fieldwork. Edinburgh, Scottish Regional Group Council for British Archaeology, later The Council For Scottish Archaeology, 1955-. ISSN: 0419411x.

1990 volume edited by Proudfoot, E.V.W. and Proudfoot, B.E. (1992. 64p.) illus., map, charts, indexes, sd. ISBN 090135211x) includes brief reports of excavations A-Z by locality within regions/districts; report of Royal Commission

....(contd.)

On the Ancient and Historical Monuments of Scotland (Archeology and Buildings programmes and accessions to the National Monument Record of Scotland). *Class No:* 902(411)

[4232]
HANSON, W.S. *and* SLATER, E.A., *eds.* **Scottish archaeology** new perceptions. Aberdeen Univ. Press, 1991. xi,228p. illus., maps, tables, bibliogs., index. limp cover. £14.95. ISBN: 0080412122.

13 papers by different hands, each ending with a bibliography, provide authoritative overviews on the current state of knowledge of all periods of Scottish archaeology *e.g.* 2. Skara Brae: revisiting a Neolithic village in Orkney ... 4. Future of Roman Scotland ... 7. Surveying for the future: RCAHMS archaeological survey ... 13. Managing output rather than input? The implications of computerising the National Museum of Scotland's archaeological information. *Class No:* 902(411)

[4233]
RITCHIE, G. *and* RITCHIE, A. **Scotland: archaeology and early history.** London, Thames & Hudson, 1981. 192p. illus., map, bibliog. (*Ancient peoples and places.*) ISBN: 0500021007.

8 chapters: 1. Hunters and fishers; 2. Early farming communities; 3. Henge monuments and stone circles; 4. The first metalworkers; 5. Warrior Celts; 6. Roman Scotland; 7. Britons, Angles and Scots; 8. The Pictish kingdom. Extensive bibliography p.183-186. Index p.159-192. 'Scholars will consult it many times' (*Choice*, v.19,no.2, October 1981, p.292). *Class No:* 902(411)

Ireland

[4234]
EDWARDS, N. **The Archaeology of early medieval Ireland.** London, B.T. Batsford, 1990. 256p. illus. bibliog., index. £35.00. ISBN: 0713453672.

1. The Roman impact on Ireland - 2. Settlement: ring forts - 3. Other settlement types - 4. Food and farming - 5. Craft - 6. The Church - 7. Art - 8. The Vikings. New critical introduction to the archaeological evidence. *Class No:* 902(415)

[4235]
MACALISTER, R.A.S. **The Archaeology of Ireland.** 2nd ed. London, Methuen, 1949. xx, 386p. illus., bibliog.

1st ed. 1927.

In addition to a general index, has an index of Irish topography (arranged by counties, followed by towns A-Z) and an index of authorities cited. The latter gathers together the footnote references and serves as an informal bibliography (p.383-6). *Class No:* 902(415)

[4236]
O'KELLY, M.J. **Early Ireland:** an introduction to Irish prehistory. Cambridge, Cambridge Univ. Press, 1989. xiii, 375p. illus., maps, plans, bibliog., index. £35.00. ISBN: 0521334896.

12 chronological and thematic chapters: 1. The Ice Age ... 10. The Iron Age - 11. Later prehistoric settlement - 12. Iron Age burial. 4 Appendices: Radio-carbon dating; Dendochronology; Pollen analysis; and Calibration of radio-carbon dating. Bibliography p.353-70. *Class No:* 902(415)

Bibliographies

[4237]
BRADLEY, J. **A Bibliography of Irish archaeology 1980-1982.** Belfast, Ulster Archaeological Society, 1983. 15p. index. sd. ISSN: 0265329x.

371 unannotated entries arranged A-Z within 18 sections: 1. Bibliographical - 2. Festschriften - 3. Guidebooks and local surveys - 4. Museums - 5. General Irish archaeology ... 8. Mesolithic ... 14. Post-medieval and industrial. Excavates much material from journals. *Class No:* 902(415)(01)

Northern Ireland

[4238]
GREAT BRITAIN. Department of Environment for Northern Ireland. **Pieces of the past** archaeological excavations by the Department of the Environment for Northern Ireland 1970-1986. Hamlin, A. *and* Lynn, C. Belfast, HMSO, 1988. xxi, 109p. col. illus., col. maps, diagrs., bibliog., index. £6.90. ISBN: 0337082162.

Describes 35 excavations. Appendix 1. Archaeological excavations organized by the Department 1970-1986. Glossary p.99-102. Bibliography p.102. For the general reader. *Class No:* 902(416)

[4239]
GREAT BRITAIN Department Of The Environment (Northern Ireland). **Finding and minding** a series of reports on archaeological work in Northern Ireland. Belfast, HMSO, 1990. 16p. col. illus., pbk. £2.90. ISBN: 0337082456.

How Northern Ireland's heritage is identified, excavated, recorded, and protected. *Class No:* 902(416)

[4240]
MALLORY, J.P. *and* McNEILL, T.E. **The Archaeology of Ulster** from colonization to plantation. Belfast, The Institute of Irish Studies, The Queen's Univ. of Belfast, 1991. 367p. illus., maps, diagrs., bibliog. index. £15. ISBN: 0853893527.

Chronological narrative and interpretation of archaeology in Ulster c.7000 BC - 1800 AD. Important bibliography p.338-56. Mainly confined to the 9 counties of modern Ulster although some details of archaeological sites in Donegal, Cavan, and Monaghan. 'A very valuable up-to-date discussion on the archaeology of Ireland in general, and not just Ulster alone' (*Antiquity*, v.66, no.251, June 1992, p.559). *Class No:* 902(416)

England

[4241]
WILSON, D.M., *ed.* **The Archaeology of Anglo-Saxon England.** London, Methuen, 1976. xvl,532p. illus., facsims., tables, plans, index.

11 contributors. 10 sections: 1. Agricultural and rural settlement - 2. Buildings and rural settlement - 3. Towns - 4. Ecclesiastical architecture - 5. Monastic sites - 6. Crafts and industry - 7. The pottery - 8. The coins - 9. The animal resources - 10. The Scandinavians. Appendices (A-C (A: Gazetteer of Anglo-Saxon settlement sites (tabulated under 9 heads; p.405-52). List of sources, p.463-511. *Class No:* 902(420)

Middle Ages

[4242]

CLARKE, H. The Archaeology of medieval England. London, British Museum Publications, 1984. 224p. illus., maps, bibliog. £12.95. ISBN: 0714180386.

Reviews knowledge of medieval England derived from archaeological sources. Chapter notes p.195-201 and valuable bibliography p.204-218. Index p.221-224.

Class No: 902(420)"01/14"

Channel Islands

[4243]

The Channel Islands an archaeological guide. Chichester, Sussex, Phillimore, 1981. xv.144p.illus.(inc.16p.plates), maps, diagrs. bibliog. index. £14.95. ISBN: 0850333954.

Part 1 is a summary account of the state of archaeological knowledge in 9 sections *e.g.* Palaeolithic man ... The Roman period ... Antiquities and scholars. Part 2 Sites and Monuments, is a complete gazetteer of sites. Bibliography p,.137-140. 40 plates. 71 figures. 'Essential for all visitors with any interest in the Islands' past' (*British Book News,* December 1981,p.766). *Class No:* 902(423.4)

Wales

[4244]

STANFORD, S.C. The Archaeology of the Welsh Marches. 2nd ed. Ludlow, Salop, S.C. Stanford, 1991. ii,190p. illus., maps, bibliog., index. £7.95. ISBN: 0950327158.

First published London, Collins, 1980.

'An essay on the problems of community survival within the geographical and political limitations of the Welsh Marches' (*Preface*). 2. Palaeolithic hunters and their descendants - 3. Neolithic settlers and traders ... 9. Castles in the Marches ... 11. Archaeology of rural industries. Places to visit p.171. Bibliography p.172-8.

Class No: 902(429)

Germany

Encyclopaedias

[4245]

HOOPS, J. Reallexikon der germanischen Altertumskunde. Berlin & New York, W. de Gruyter, 1968-. Lieferung 1-. illus., (incl. pl.), plans, tables, maps.

First published 1911-19 (4v.).

v.1-6. (1973-1986). Aachen-Einbaum. An encylopaedia of German archaeology to be completed in 8v. Longer articles are sub-divided into sections, each with a bibliography. A scholarly work. *Class No:* 902(430)(031)

Czechoslovakia

[4246]

SKLENAR, K. The History of archaeology in Czechoslavakia, chap. 14, *Towards a history of archaeology* edited by Glyn Daniel (Thames & Hudson, 1981). *Class No:* 902(437)

Poland

[4247]

'A Panorama of Polish archaeology', *Antiquity*, v.65, no. 248, September 1991, p.583-721. illus., diagrs., maps, bibliogs.

11 papers by separate hands surveying recent discoveries and excavations methods introduced by the title paper which includes sections on historical and ethnic geography, the origins of growth of archaeology in Poland.

Class No: 902(438)

France

[4248]

Archéologie de la France 30 ans de découvertes. Paris, Éditions de la Réunion des musées nationaux, 1989. 495p. illus. (many col.), drawings, maps, bibliog., indexes. A4 soft cover. 390F. ISBN: 2711822516.

39 chapters organized in 8 main sections: 1. Paléolithique inférieur et moyen - 2. Paléolithique supérieur - 3. Le Néolithique - 4. L'Âge du Bronze - 5. L'Âge du Fer - 6. La Gaulle Romaine - 7. Antiquité tardive et début de Moyen Âge: L'évêque et le Compte - 8. Moyen Âge et temps modernes: La construction de la France. 8 Annexes: 1. Organisation et réglementales de la recherche archéologique en France (p.462-3) - 2. Les Musées d'archéologie en France (p.264) - 3. Archéologie et archéometrie - 4. Glossaire (p.466) - 5. Tableau chronologie (p.467-74) ... 8. Bibliographie (p.479). Produced as a catalogue of an exhibition organized by La Réunion des Musées Nationaux, La Direction due Patrimoine, and La Direction des Musées de France in 1989. *Class No:* 902(44)

[4249]

BENDER, B. The Archaeology of Brittany, Normandy and the Channel Islands an introduction and guide. London, Faber, 1986. 246p. illus., maps, bibliog. £14.95. ISBN: 0571099572.

A detailed up-to-date account of the archaeological background precedes a systematic guide: Brittany (p.65-162); Normandy (p.163-217); Channel Is. (p.218-243). Glossary p.245. Bibliography p.246-247. Index p.249-254. *Class No:* 902(44)

[4250]

SCARRE, C., ed. Ancient France 6,000-2,000 BC Neolithic societies and their landscape. Edinburgh, Edinburgh Univ. Press, 1984. viii, 390p. illus., maps, bibliog. £25.00. ISBN: 085224441x.

8 regional chapters relate the story of France's early farming societies. Each chapter includes a brief geographical account and a short history of previous research. Important bibliography p.344-380. Index p.383-390. 'An excellently factual and stimulating reference work' (*Antiquity*, LXVIII, no.223, July 1984, p.146). *Class No:* 902(44)

Bibliographies

[4251]

Gallia informations: préhistoire et histoire. Paris, Éditions du Centre National de la Recherche Scientifique, 1990-. 2pa. ISSN: 09948899.

Derives from features in *Gallia* v.1-15 (1943-1957) and *Gallia Préhistoire* v.1-32 (1958-1990).

Descriptive excavation reports and bibliographies region by region in progressive volumes. 1990. 1++2 (1990.

....(contd.)
319p. illus., maps, drawings. F270. ISBN 2222046165) covers Bretagne and Provence-Alpes - Côte d'Azur.
Class No: 902(44)(01)

Maps & Atlases

[4252]
Carte archéologique de la Gaulle. Paris, Édition Academie Des Inscriptions Et Belles-Lettres. maps, bibliog.
v.41 *Le Loire-et-Cher.* 1988 ISBN 2877540030. 'Une collection de l'Institut de France ... créée en 1930-, qui, relancée en 1987, se propose d'effectuer l'inventaire le plus complet et le plus scientifique possible de toute la documentation et de toutes les connaissances acquises sur les sites archéologiques gaulois, du début de l'Age du Fer au Haut Moyen Age'. *Class No:* 902(44)(084.3)

[4253]
Carte archéologique de la Gaulle Romaine.
Editées par les Presses Universitaires de France 1. Partie orientale (carte et texte complet) du département des Alpes-Maritimes by P. Couissin; *... des Basses-Alpes* by H. de Gérin-Ricard. 1931. 2. *...du département du Var* by P. Couissin and others. 1932. 3. *...du département de la Corse* by A. Ambrosi. 1933. 4. *...Carte de la partie occidentale du département du Var et de la partie orientale du département des Bouches-du-Rhône* by P. Couissin, 1936. 5. *Carte (parte occidentale) et texte complet du département des Bouches-du-Rhône* by F. Benoit. 1936. 6. *Carte et texte du département des Basses-Alpes* by H. de Gérin-Picard and A. Blanchet. 1937. 7. *...du Vaucluse* by J. Sautel. 1939. 8. *Texte complet du département du Gard* by M. Louis and A. Blanchet. 1941. 9. *Carte et texte du département de l'Aveyron* by E. Bonnet and A. Blanchet. 1944. 10. *Texte complet du département de l'Hérault* by E. Bonnet and A. Blanchet. 1946.
Editées par le CNRS 11. Carte et texte complet du département de la Drôme by J. Sautel. 1957. 12. *...de l'Aude* by A. Grenier. 1959. 13. *...d'Indre et Loire* by J. Boussard. 1960. 14. *...de la Haute Vienne* by J. Ferrier. 1964. 15. *...de l'Ardèche* by A. Blanc. 1975. 16. *...de la Corrèzze* by G. Lintz. 1981. 147p. illus. (pl.), index. ISBN 2222028434. *Class No:* 902(44)(084.3)

Italy

[4254]
SPIVEY, N. *and* **STODDART, S. Etruscan Italy** an archaeological account. London, Batsford, 1990. 168p. illus., bibliog., index. £29.95. ISBN: 0713465212.
1. Physical environment and prehistoric background - 2. Settlement and territory - 3. Subsistence technology and production - 4. Trade and exchange - 5. Myth, language and literacy - 6. Ritual - 7. Warfare - 8. Social organization. Traveller's gazetteer p.153-7. Glossary p.158-9. Bibliography p.160-3. *Class No:* 902(450)

Scandinavia

[4255]
KLINDT-JENSEN, O. A History of Scandinavian archaeology. London, Thames & Hudson, 1975. 144p. illus., facsims, ports, plans, maps, index. (*The World Of Archaeology.*)

....(contd.)
A survey of the past 400 years with biographical sketches of key figures. Bibliography p.139-41. 129 illus.
Class No: 902(48)

Denmark

[4256]
JENSEN, J. The Prehistory of Denmark. London, Methuen, 1983. xviii, 330p. illus., maps, bibliog. ISBN: 041634190x.
19 interdisciplinary chapters examine the whole of Denmark's cultural prehistory from Stone Age hunters *c.*11,000 BC to the end of the Iron Age 800 AD. An extensive bibliography (p.287-321) enhances an 'outstanding and important book' (*Antiquity* v.57, no.221, November 1983, p.230). Index p.322-330. *Class No:* 902(489)

[4257]
ROESDAHL, E. Viking age Denmark. London, British Museum Publications, 1982. 172p. illus., map, bibliog., index. ISBN: 0714150270.
Covers the period *c.*800-1050 in 12 thematic chapters *e.g.* 4. Settlement and survival ... 8. Arms and fortifications ... 9. Pagans and Christians. Appendix: Finds list. Viking Age settlements in present day Denmark traced archaeologically p.249-50. Extremely useful bibliography p.255-268. 51 plates. Analytical index. *Class No:* 902(489)

Albania

[4258]
ANDREA, Zh. 'Archaeology in Albania', *Archaeological Reports For 1991-1992*, p.71-88. illus., maps.
'Archaeology in Albania 1973-83' was published in *Archaeological Reports 1983-84.* p.102-19.
Descriptive reports of excavations by district and by site. *Class No:* 902(496.5)

Rumania

[4259]
MacKENZIE, A. Archaeology in Romania the mystery of the Roman occupation. London, Robert Hale Ltd., 1986. 183p. illus., bibliog. £14.95. ISBN: 0709027249.
Preoccupied for political reasons with establishing the pattern of events in Dacia after the withdrawal of Roman troops and administration by the Emperor Aurelian AD271-275. Chronology p.8-9. Bibliography p.170-173. *Class No:* 902(498)

China

[4260]
CHANG, Kwang-Chih. The Archaeology of ancient China. 4th ed. New Haven, Yale Univ. Press 1987. xxv, 450p. illus., maps, tables, bibliog. $52.00. £50.00. ISBN: 0300037821.
First published 1963. 'This edition ... bears very little resemblance to its previous incarnations ... I no longer intend to cover the whole field and cite every available reference ... now ends with the rise of civilization and no longer includes the very rich and complex period of ancient history after about 1000 BC.'
Introduction (geographical review, traditional historiography and antiquarianism, modern and

....(contd.)

contemporary archaeology) - 1. Palaeolithic foundations - 2. The early farms - 3-4. Neolithic developments - 5. The Chinese interaction sphere and the foundations of civilization - 6-7. The first Chous. Glossary of Chinese characters p.423-438. Bibliography p.443-450. *Class No:* 902(510)

[4261]

JIA LANPO *and* **HUANG WEIWEN. The Story of Peking Man** from archaeology to mystery. Beijing, Foreign Language Press; Hong Kong, Oxford Univ. Press, 1990. vii,270p. illus., map, index. £19.50; $29.95. ISBN: 0195851889.

An illustrated account of the excavation of the fossilized remains of Peking Man at Zhoukoudian in 1929. Jia Lianpo was one of the excavation team. *Class No:* 902(510)

[4262]

KEIGHTLEY, D.N. The Origins of Chinese civilization. Berkeley, Univ. of California Press, 1983. xxix, 617p. illus. maps, tables. index. $50. ISBN: 0520042298.

17 academic contributors giving a multidisciplinary approach to the early cultural development of China. Arranged in 4 parts: environment and agriculture; culture and peoples; language and writers; tribe and state. Extensive English and Chinese language references to each chapter. Finding list of Carbon - 14 dates cited p.583-585. Index and glossary p.587-617. *Class No:* 902(510)

Japan

[4263]

AIKENS, C.M. *and* **TAKAYASU HIGUCHI. Prehistory of Japan.** New York, Academic Press, 1982. xv, 354p. illus., maps, bibliog., index. $39.50. £26.50. ISBN: 0120452804.

6 chapters describe the archaeological evidence of human activity in the Japanese islands from Palaeolithic times to the emergence of the historic Yamato states *c.* AD 700. Bibliography A-Z by author, p.339-347. 'Welcomed as a general textbook and for reference use' (*Antiquity*, v.56, no. 218, December 1982, p.238). *Class No:* 902(52)

[4264]

PEARSON, R.J., *and others, eds*. **Windows on the Japanese past:** studies in archaeology and prehistory. Ann Arbor, Michigan, Center for Japanese Studies, Univ. of Michigan, 1986. 629p. maps, bibliog. $48.95. ISBN: 0939512238.

32 Japanese and American academic contributors. 'The volume's 110-page glossary of place-names, personal names, site names, type names, and technical terms constitutes an important reference aid for the field of Japanese archaeology' (Shulman, F.J. *Japan*. 1989. Entry 109). *Class No:* 902(52)

[4265]

Recent archaeological discoveries in Japan. Tsuboi Kiyotari, *ed.* Paris, UNESCO; Tokyo, Centre for East Asian Cultural Studies, 1987. Available in UK from HMSO. xiii,108p.+ 20p. col. pl. illus., maps, bibliog. pbk. ISBN: 9231024515, UNESCO; 4896564030, CEACS.

A summary of the results of surveys in different regions of Japan by government agencies and various institutes in 6 chapters by different hands: 1. Palaeolithic age - 2. Jomon culture - 3. Protection of archaeological sites in Japan. Chronology p.101-2. Bibliography p.103-6. *Class No:* 902(52)

Asia—Middle & Near East

Encyclopaedias

[4266]

Reallexikon der Assyriologie und vorderasiatischen Archäologie. Edzard, D.O., *ed.* Berlin & New York, Walter de Gruyter, 1928-. Lieferung 1-. illus., charts.

Published first in fascicules and consolidated in bound volumes at 4-yearly intervals. V.1-7: A-Medizin (1931-1990). A scholarly archaeological encyclopaedia of Assyriology and archaeology of the Near East. Articles are signed and end with lists of references. Bd.7 Libanukšabaš-Medizin. 1990. xxvii,631p. ISBN 3110104377. *Class No:* 902(53+56)(031)

India

[4267]

AGRAWAL, D.P. The Archaeology of India. London and Malmo, Curzon Press, 1982. Distributed in North America by Humanities Press and in India by India Book House of Bombay. xvi, 294p. illus. maps, bibliog., index. £9.50. $50.00. (*Scandinavian Institute of Asian Studies monograph series*.) ISBN: 0700701400. ISSN: 00691712.

Complete survey of Indian prehistory in 10 chapters. Introduction includes a brief survey of Indian archaeology. Bibliography p.281-90. *Class No:* 902(540)

[4268]

ALLCHIN, B. *and* **ALLCHIN, R. The rise of civilization in India and Pakistan.** Cambridge, Cambridge Univ. Press, 1982. xiv,379p. illus., maps, tables, bibliog., index. £25.00. (*Cambridge World Archaeology*.) ISBN: 0521242444.

Lineal descendant of *The Birth of Indian civilization* (1968).

Introductory chapter 'Archaeology in South Asia', then 13 chapters (grouped in 3 sections: 1. Constituent elements - 2. Indus urbanism - 3. The legacy of the Indus civilization) tracing 'the origins and development of culture in India and Pakistan from its earliest roots in Palaeolithic times, through the rise and disintegration of the great Indus civilization, to the emergence of regional cultures and the arrival and spread of Indo-Aryan speaking peoples'. Bibliography (by chapter) p.362-371. *Class No:* 902(540)

[4269]

THAPER, B.K. Recent archaeological discoveries in India. Paris, Unesco, and Tokyo, The Centre for East Asian Cultural Studies, 1985. Available in UK from HMSO. xiii,159p. +12p. col. pl. illus (some col.), bibliog., pbk. £16.50. ISBN: 9231023853, Unesco; 4896564022, CEACS.

A state of the art review of Indian excavation and publication highlighting recent advances in knowledge of the cultural history of each period: Palaeolithic, Mesolithic, Neolithic, the Indus civilization, Megalithic, and the historical period. Bibliography p.149-59. *Class No:* 902(540)

[4270]

WHEELER, Sir M. The Indus civilization supplementary volume to the *Cambridge History of India*. 3rd ed. Cambridge, Cambridge Univ. Press, 1968. xi,144p. illus. (incl.pl.), plans, bibliog.

First published 1953.

The 3rd ed., extensively rewritten and enlarged,

....(contd.)

incorporates notes on new sites and recent research down to 1967. Bibliography p.141. 34 excellent plates. *Class No:* 902(540)

Bibliographies

[4271]

Annual bibliography of Indian archaeology. Leiden, Kern Institute, 1926- Irregular.

V.22: *1970-1972* (Dordrecht, D. Reidel, 1984. xxiv, 241p.). 2788 entries organized in 5 main parts: 1. General - 2. India and the regions within its cultural influence - 3. The Indian sub-continent (A. General; B. Archaeology; C. Historical studies; D. Arts) - 4. Regions within the sphere of Indian cultural influence (A. General; B. Sri Lanka; C. South-East Asia; D. Indonesian archipelago; E. Afghanistan and Central Asia; F. Nepal; G. Tibet) - 5. Commemorative and obituary notices. Index p.219-241.

Class No: 902(540)(01)

Encyclopaedias

[4272]

An Encyclopedia of Indian archaeology. Ghosh, A., *ed.* New Delhi, Munshiram Manoharlal, 1989; Leiden and New York, E.J. Brill, 2v., 1990. xvi,413p. +470p. illus., bibliogs., index. $228.57. ISBN: 8121500877, India; 9004092641, Holland & US.

V.1: Subjects; v.2: A Gazetteer of explored and excavated sites. Over 100 Indian anthropologists, archaeologists and historians examine the findings of 150 years of excavation in 20 subject based sub-divided chapters (e.g. dating, rock art, cultures, technology, coins and seals, settlements, pottery, writing). Sections within chapters end with bibliographies. V.2 is a gazetteer of sites in v.1 with expansive treatment of the larger and more important sites. 'This work should take its place as the classic statement of Indian archaeology for many years' (*Library Journal*, v.116, no.7, 15 April 1991, p.82). *Class No:* 902(540)(031)

Bangladesh

[4273]

CHAKRABARTI, D.K. Ancient Bangladesh a study of the archaeological sources. Delhi, Oxford Univ. Press India, 1992. xii,200p.+ 8p. plates. £17.50. ISBN: 0195628799.

1. Introduction (Geographical background, Ancient Historical Geographical units) - 2. Prehistory (inc. inventory of sites and artifacts) - 3. Early history - 4. Excavated data - 5. Miscellaneous data on ancient settlements - 6. Summary. Bibliography p.186-7. Systematic review of the pre-Islamic archaeological data. *Class No:* 902(549.3)

Cyprus

Biographies

[4274]

ÅSTRÖM, P. Who's who in Cypriote archaeology biographical and bibliographical notes. Göteborg, Åström, 1971. 88p. illus. (*Studies in Mediterranean Archaeology.*)

'Very valuable indeed within its limited field' (*TLS*, no.3657, 31 March 1972, p.370).

Class No: 902(564.3)(092)

Iraq

Maps & Atlases

[4275]

BEEK, M.A. Atlas of Mesopotamia a survey of the history and civilization of Mesopotamia from the Stone Age to the fall of Babylon. London, Nelson, 1962. 164p. illus., maps.

Text on the civilizations of Sumeria, Assyria and Babylonia in 16 sections 'The accompanying maps provide comprehensive information concerning ancient empires, the chief excavation sites and the major discoveries' (A.J. Abdulrahman. *Iraq*, 1984, Entry 92). 296 photogravure illus. and 22 maps. *Class No:* 902(567)(084.3)

Israel

[4276]

AHARONI, Y. The Archaeology of the land of Israel from the prehistoric beginnings to the end of the First Temple period. New York, Westminster, 1982. xx, 344p. $27.50. ISBN: 0664213847.

First Hebrew edition published in Jerusalem by Shikmona Publishing in 1978.

Well-documented survey of the important findings of archaeological research especially valuable for material previously available only in Hebrew. *Class No:* 902(569.4)

[4277]

AMIHAI MAZAR. Archaeology of the land of the Bible 10,000-586 B.C.E. New York, Doubleday, 1990. Published for Center for Judaic-Christian Studies, Dayton, OH. xxx,572p. illus., maps, bibliog., indexes. $30. (*The Anchor Bible Reference Library.*) ISBN: 038523970x.

Comprehensive chronological overview of the archaeological research of Old Testament Palestine from the earliest settlements to the Babylonian destruction of the first temple. Bibliographical note and abbreviations p.xix-xxiii. Glossary of geographic terms (Hebrew, Arabic, English) p.xxx. 11 maps. 'Of special value ... is Mazar's superb 34-page introduction to the technical realia of Palestinian archaeology; nothing better is currently in print; (*Choice*, v.28, no.4, December 1990, p.688). *Class No:* 902(569.4)

[4278]

AMNON BEN-TOR, *ed.* The Archaeology of ancient Israel. New Haven, Yale Univ. Press, 1992. xxi,398p. +41p. col. pl. maps, tables, bibliog., index. £30. ISBN: 0300047681.

Translation by R. Greenberg of the original Hebrew edition published by The Open University of Israel.

7 Academic contributors. Survey of a century of research into the history of ancient Israel from the Neolithic era to the fall of Jerusalem and the destruction of the Temple in 586 BC. Introduction reviews the past 40 years of archaeological activity in Israel. Bibliography p.377-84. Supersedes W.F. Albright's *The archaeology of Palestine* (3rd ed. 1956), K. Kenyon's *Archaeology in the Holy Land* (1965), and Y. Aharoni's *The archaeology of the land of Israel* (1982). *Class No:* 902(569.4)

[4279]

The New encyclopedia of archaeological excavations in the Holy Land. Stern, E., *ed.* New York, Simon & Schuster, 4v., 1993. 1600p. col.illus., maps, plans. $355; £199. ISBN: 0132762889.

Updated and enlarged edition of *Encyclopedia of archaeological excavations in the Holy Land* edited by M. Avi-Yonash (Prentice Hall, 1976-8).

....(contd.)

Describes and analyses excavations at 420 sites. 'Scholars and researchers will find this reference set indispensable' (*Library Journal*, v.118, no.14, 1 September 1993, p.173-4). *Class No:* 902(569.4)

Encyclopaedias

[4280]

NEGEV, A., *ed.* **Archaeological encyclopedia of the Holy Land.** New York, Putnam; London, Weidenfeld & Nicolson, 1980. 355p. illus., tables, maps. ISBN: 0899610048.

Reprint of 1972 ed.

20 contributors. 600 unsigned articles, mostly on archaeological sites, supported by good illus. and maps. Adequate cross-references, but no bibliographical references. Some sites on the excavation maps do not appear in the text (*Library Journal*, v.98, no.11, 1 January 1973, p.61-62). *Class No:* 902(569.4)(031)

Asia—South East

[4281]

HIGHAM, C. The Archaeology of mainland Southeast Asia from 10,000 BC to the fall of Angkor. Cambridge, Cambridge Univ. Press, 1989. xvi,387p. illus., maps, plans, bibliog., index. £35. (*Cambridge World Archaeology.*) ISBN: 0521255236.

Scholarly prehistory of the area covered by the valleys of the Red, Mekong and Chao Phraya rivers and the intervening terrain, *i.e.* Thailand, Vietnam, Kampuchea, Laos and adjacent areas. Chronological table p.xv-xvi. References p.363-77. *Class No:* 902(59)

Africa

[4282]

The Archaeology of Africa food, metals and towns. Shaw, T., *and others, eds.* London, Routledge, 1993. xxxvii,857p. illus., maps, diagrs., tables, bibliog., index. £75. (*One World Archaeology.*) ISBN: 041508444x.

61 contributors. Academic archaeological and palaeoenvironmental survey of change in Africa, principally over the last 10 millenia, in 40 chapters. Important bibliography p.750-833. Analytical index. *Class No:* 902(6)

[4283]

PHILLIPSON, D.W. African archaeology. 2nd rev. ed. Cambridge, Cambridge Univ. Press, 1993. 300p. illus., maps, bibliog., index. £40. ISBN: 052144103x.

Up to date survey in 8 chapters (2. The emergence of man in Africa ... 5. Beginnings of permanent settlement ... 8. The second millenium AD in sub-Saharan Africa). Bibliography p.212-27. *Class No:* 902(6)

[4284]

ROBERTSHAW, P., *ed.* **A History of African archaeology.** London, James Currey, 1990. viii,378p. illus., maps, bibliog., index. £35. ISBN: 0852550200.

Primarily a regional survey but also includes the personal memoirs of Desmond Clark, Peter Shinnie and Thurstan Shaw and essays on early prehistory, rock art, and African archaeology in a world perspective. Bibliography p.310-71.

....(contd.)

Criticised for its exiguous coverage of some regions in *Antiquity*, v.65, no.246, March 1991, p.174-5. *Class No:* 902(6)

Maps & Atlases

[4285]

CLARK, J.D., *comp.* **Atlas of African prehistory.** Chicago, Univ. of Chicago Press, 1967. 62p. maps.

12 base-maps (1. Topography; 2. Geology; 3. Soils; 4. Mean annual rainfall; 5. Main vegetation types; 6/7. Hypothetical rainfall; 8/11. Hypothetical vegetation zones; 12. Simplified vegetation), 11 of them 1:20 million. 38 transparent overlays (*e.g.* 9/11. Fossil man in Africa; 24 Neolithic industries of sub-Saharan Africa; 25/26. Prehistoric art; 27. Distribution of white rhinoceros). Page size, 42.5 x 50cm. A 62p. booklet includes a gazetteer, listing sites by countries, subdivided by industries or culture, with geographical co-ordinates. *Class No:* 902(6)(084.3)

America

[4286]

FAGAN, B.M. The Great journey the peopling of ancient America. London, Thames and Hudson, 1987. 228p. illus., bibliog., index. £14.95. $19.95. ISBN: 0500050457.

'A quest for early artifacts and human fossils, for indisputable proof of the antiquity of humankind in the Americas.' Further reading p.263-276. 'A conservative and very carefully reasoned overview' (*Choice*, v.25, no.8, April 1988, p.1282). *Class No:* 902(7)

[4287]

FIEDEL,, S.J. Prehistory of the Americas. 2nd ed. Cambridge, Cambridge Univ. Press, 1992. xix,400p, illus., maps, table, bibliog., index. £40. ISBN: 0521415322.

1st ed. 1987.

1. The development of American archaeology - 2. From Africa to Siberia: early human migration in the old world - 3. The Paleo-Indians - 4. The Archaic:post Pleictocene foragers - 5. The origins of agriculture and village life - 6. Chiefdoms and states - 7. Parallel worlds. References p.358-378. Author and subject indexes. Chronology p.xv-xix. Bibliography p.367-91. *Class No:* 902(7)

Maps & Atlases

[4288]

COE, M., *and others.* **Atlas of ancient America.** New York and Oxford, Facts on File, 1986. 284p. illus., maps, bibliog., index. $40.00. £18.95. ISBN: 0816011990.

20 thematic and 25 site features arranged in 6 sections: The new world - The first Americans - North America - Mesoamerica - South America - The living heritage. Bibliography p.226-7. Gazetteer p.228-236. 200 colour illus. 60 maps. 'Instructive to refer to and a delight to dip into' (*Bulletin Society of University Cartographers*, v.22, no.1, 1988, p.40-41). *Class No:* 902(7)(084.3)

Chronologies

[4289]

TAYLOR, R.E. *and* MEIGHAN, C.W., *eds*. **Chronologies in New World archaeology.** New York and London, Academic Press. xiii,587p. maps, tables, bibliogs., index. chronological charts on endpapers. $49.50. (*Studies in Archaeology*.) ISBN: 0126857504.

Chapter 1. 'Dating methods in New World archaeology followed by 15 chronological chapters, each by a different hand, and each furnished with its own bibliography. General bibliography p.558-563. 'General chronology for the whole of the New World with a view toward providing a general reference work that can allow more reading, understanding and comparison of chronological information for New World archaeology'. *Class No:* 902(7)(090)

America — North

[4290]

FAGAN, B.M. **Ancient North America:** the archaeology of a continent. London, Thames and Hudson, 1991. 480p. illus., maps, diagrs., bibliog., index. £19.50. ISBN: 0500050597.

22 chapters narrative account of the diverse prehistoric societies of North America, from first settlement c.12,000 BC to the period of European contact, arranged in 7 parts: 1. Background (inc. Discovery and Culture history and North American archaeology) - 2. Palao-Indians - 3. Great Plains - 4. Far North - 5. The West - 6. Eastern woodlands - 7. After Columbus. Each chapter ends with list of further reading. Bibliography p.459-70. 345 illustrations. *Class No:* 902(71+73)

Handbooks & Manuals

[4291]

ROBBINS, M. **The Amateur archaeologist's handbook.** 3rd ed. New York, Harper & Row; Toronto, Fitzhenry & Whiteside Ltd., 1981. xi, 306p. illus., maps, diagrs., tables, bibliog., index. $15.45. ISBN: 0690019769.

Standard guide to methods and techniques. Primarily limited to North America. Appendix 1. Archaeological sites open to the public (p.240-249); 2. Archaeological societies and related organizations (p.250-255); 3. Museums and special collections (p.256-264); 4. Study courses (p.265-269); 5. Antiquities Laws (p.270-276); 6. Radiocarbon correction table (p.277-280). Glossary p.281-285. Bibliography p.286-300. 'It is gratifying that such a book is available' (*Choice*, v.18, no.11-12, July-August 1981, p.1594). *Class No:* 902(71+73)(035)

Dictionaries

[4292]

JELKS, E.B., *ed*. **Historical dictionary of North American archaeology.** Westport, Connecticut, Greenwood Press,1988. xvii, 760p. Bibliog., index. $95.00. £77.95. ISBN: 0313243077.

151 contributors. Over 1800 signed entries of varying length relating to significant sites, artifacts, and major prehistoric cultures, each concluding with a list of selected sources. Dictionary p.1-546. Appendix: Sites listed geographically p.547-553. Sources A-Z by author p.569-705. Analytical index. 'Indispensable in reference work and collection development' (*Booklist*, v.85, no.2, 15 September 1988, p.136+138). *Class No:* 902(71+73)(038)

20th Century

[4293]

American archaeology past and future a celebration of the Society for American Archaeology 1935-1985. Meltzer, D.J., *and others, eds.* Washington DC, Smithsonian Institution Press, 1986. 479p. refs. $35.00. £31.25. ISBN: 0874746922.

Papers read at 50th anniversary symposium: 1. Themes in the history of archaeology - 2. New looks at past problems - 3. Current trends and future prospects. Five decades of American archaeology p.23-49. 'Cumulatively, the book adds up to a lively and conspicuously well written critique of the strengths and weaknesses of archaeology in North America' (*Nature*, v.322, no.6083, 28 August 1986, p.784). *Class No:* 902(71+73)"19"

Mexico

[4294]

BERNAL, J. **A History of Mexican archaeology** the vanished civilizations of Middle America. London & New York, Thames and Hudson, 1980. 208p. illus., maps, bibliog., index. £12.50. (*The World of Archaeology*.) ISBN: 0500780080.

8 chapters *e.g.* 1. American-Indian origins ... 3. Research in the archives ... 5. Historians and travellers (1825-1880) - 6. Museums and the protection of antiquities. Bibliography p.190-203. *Class No:* 902(72)

America — Central

Bibliographies

[4295]

BERNAL, I. **Bibliografía arqueología y etnografía: Mesoamérica** y norte de México. Mexico, Instituto Nacional de Antropología e Historia, 1962. 634p. maps.

13,134 items on the pre-Spanish conquest civilizations of Mexico and Central America. Main subject sections: common cultural areas; pre-ceramic periods; codices, chronology and general inscriptions of regional groups; relations with other world areas; history of science, literature; bibliography and biography. Includes references to reviews. Author index. 'The most complete bibliography ... ever assembled on the pre-Hispanic culture of Mesoamerica and northern Mexico' (*Handbook of Latin American studies*, v.25, 1963, p.6-7). Rather uneven; weak on Southern Mesoamerican ethnography. *Class No:* 902(728)(01)

Bahamas

Bibliographies

[4296]

GRANBERRY, J.A. **Bibliography of Bahaman prehistory.** 2nd ed. Nassau, Bahamas Archaeological Team, 1988. 1st ed. 1982.

103 unannotated items. New editions are planned on a quinquennial basis. *Class No:* 902(729.6)(01)

Peru

[4297]

KEATINGE, R.W., *ed*. **Peruvian prehistory** an overview of pre-Inca and Inca society. Cambridge, Cambridge Univ. Press, 1988. xvii, 364p. illus., figs., tables, maps, bibliog., index. £35.00. $49.50. ISBN: 0521255600.

Supersedes *A reappraisal of Peruvian archaeology* edited by W. Bennett (Society for American archaeology, 1948) as the standard work.

11 papers from different hands either review a specific period of Peruvian history or examine recent research results *e.g.* 8. Progress and prospect in the archaeology of the Inca -9. From event to process: the recovery of late Andean organizational structure by means of Spanish colonial written records ... 11. A summary view of Peruvian prehistory. Bibliography p.319-355. *Class No:* 902(85)

Australasia & Oceania

[4298]

WHITE, J.P. *and* O'CONNELL, J.F. **A Prehistory of Australia, New Guinea and Sahul.** Sydney, Academic Press, 1982. xii,286p. atlas, maps, tables, bibliog., index. ISBN: 0127467505.

1. Perspectus - 2. Land, people and research - 3. Sahul early prehistory ... 5. Australia the last 10,000 years - 6. New Guinea - 7. Sahul - 8. Update. Bibliography p.237. References p.239-66. *Class No:* 902(9)

Indonesia

[4299]

BELLWOOD, P. **Prehistory of the Indo-Malaysian archipelago.** Sydney, Academic Press, 1985. x, 370p. illus., maps, bibliog., index. A$34.50. £45.00. ISBN: 0120853701.

10 chronological chapters relating the human prehistory of the islands of Indonesia from the initial hominid settlement to the eve of the historical Hindu and Buddhist civilizations. 'A balanced, thorough and reasonable presentation on the state of Indo-Malaysian prehistoric research' (*Antiquity*, v.61, no.232, July 1987, p.325-326). *Class No:* 902(910)

New Zealand

[4300]

ANDERSON, A. 'The Chronology of colonization in New Zealand', *Antiquity*, v.65, no.249, December 1991, p.767-95, map, tables, refs.

Assesses the likely period of the prehistoric colonization of New Zealand according to radio carbon dates. References p.793-5. *Class No:* 902(931)

[4301]

DAVIDSON, J. **The Prehistory of New Zealand.** 2nd ed. Auckland, Longman Paul, 1987. iv, 270p. illus., maps. ISBN: 9582718120.

1st ed. 1984.

10 extensively documented chapters *e.g.* 2. Maori origins ... 5. Material culture ... 6. Subsistence economics ... 10. From East Polynesia to Maori: conclusion and prospect. Bibliography p.227-41. Glossary of Maori and other Polynesian words p.243. List of sites and places of archaeological interest p.247-59. Authoritative state of the art review. *Class No:* 902(931)

[4302]

PRICKETT, N., *ed*. **The First thousand years** regional perspectives in New Zealand archeology. Palmerston North, The Dunmore Press, 1982. 204p. maps, illus., bibliog. $27.95. ISBN: 090856483x.

10 regional chapters by 8 contributors record progress in New Zealand archaeology since 1957. Bibliography p. 179-199. Index of sites p.201-202. 'A useful summary of the present state of New Zealand archaeology' (*Antiquity* v.58, no.224, November 1984, p.234-235). *Class No:* 902(931)

Australia

[4303]

CONNAH, G. **Of the hut I builded:** the archaeology of Australia's history. Cambridge, Cambridge Univ. Press, 1988. xvi, 176p. illus., diagrs., bibliog., index. Aust$35.00; £19.50. ISBN: 0521345677.

10 chapters *e.g.* 1. The material heritage of Australian history - 2. The historical archaeology of precolonial contact ... 9. Information from industrial relics - 10. Potential of Australian historical archaeology. Bibliography p.164-168. Author is Professor of Archaeology and Palaeoanthropology, Univ. of New England in Armisdale. *Class No:* 902(94)

[4304]

FLOOD, J. **Archaeology of the dreamtime.** Sydney, Collins, 1983. 288p., illus., (some col.), bibliog. ISBN: 0002164442.

18 chapters in five sections (Introduction; Human origins; Ice Age beginnings; The rising of the seas; The last two thousand years) examine what is known of Australian prehistory. Incorporates the results of much recent archaeological work. Chapter notes p.254-256. Glossary p.267-274. Further reading p.275-277. Index p.278-288. 'A generally clear, well-informed and well-balanced account of Australian prehistory' (*Antiquity*, v.58, no.224, November 1984, p.232-233). *Class No:* 902(94)

Arctic

Bibliographies

[4305]

DEKIN, A.A. **Arctic archaeology** a bibliography and history. New York, Garland, 1978. 279p.

An A-Z author list of over 1,200 references covering the 1800s up to 1977. 'The most complete compilation of material on arctic and subarctic archaeology available' (*Choice*, December 1978, p.1346). *Class No:* 902(98)(01)

Nautical Archaeology

[4306]

MUCKLEROY, K. **Maritime archaeology.** Cambridge, Cambridge Univ. Press, 1978. x, 270p. illus., tables, maps, bibliog. ISBN: 0521220793.

In 2 parts: 1. The scope of maritime archaeology. 2. Towards a theory of maritime archaeology. A 'statement ... of which problems constitute the proper concern of maritime archaeology, the extent to which recent work has tackled such writers, and the directions in which future studies might profitably proceed' (*Preface*). Bibliography p.255-67. 61 illus. *Class No:* 902.034

[4307]
PEARSON, C., *ed*. **Conservation of maritime archaeological objects.** London, Butterworth, 1987. iv,297p. illus. £55.

Compendium of 12 essays from 8 contributors on the marine environment; the deterioration of materials and the corrosion of metals; on-site and off-site conservation treatments; and environmental and storage factors.
Class No: 902.034

Bibliographies

[4308]
KERBER, J.E. **Coastal and maritime archaeology.** Metuchen, N.J., Scarecrow Press, 1991. viii,400p. index. $42.50. ISBN: 0810824655.

2,800 unannotated entries, A-Z by author, in 4 sections: 1. Prehistory worldwide - 2. North American Atlantic - 3. Shellfish and shell middens - 4. History and ethnography. Excludes shipwrecks. *Class No:* 902.034(01)

Handbooks & Manuals

[4309]
DEAN, M., *and others, eds*. **Archaeology underwater** the NAS guide to principles and practice. Denbigh, Clwyd, Nautical Archaeological Society and Archetype Publications, 1992. ix,336p. illus., diagrs., bibliog., index. ISBN: 1873132255.

19 contributors. Comprehensive guide and textbook. Topics include project planning, recording, position fixing, search methods, surveying, investigative techniques, post-fieldwork recording, analysis, and publication. Chapter reading lists. Bibliography p.282-98.
Class No: 902.034(035)

[4310]
GREEN, J. **Maritime archaeology:** a technical handbook. London & San Diego, Academic Press, 1990. xx,282p. illus., diagrs., bibliog., index. $27. ISBN: 012298630x.

With the emphasis on technical matters this handbook covers 5 broad areas: searching for sites; recording sites; excavation; management of collections; and study, research and publication. Bibliography p.267-78. Analytical index. 'There is a heavy bias towards shipwrecks, and relatively modern ones at that' (*Preface*). *Class No:* 902.034(035)

Maps & Atlases

[4311]
MUCKLEROY, K., *ed*. **Archaeology under water** an atlas of the world's submerged sites. New York and London, McGraw-Hill, 1980. 192p. illus. (some col.), maps, bibliog. index. ISBN: 0070439561.

1. Techniques and approaches - 2. Mediterranean wreck sites and classical seafaring - 3. European shipwrecks over 3000 years - 4. Shipwrecks in the wake of Columbus - 5. Structures under water - 6. Preservation. Bibliography p.188-189. Analytical index. 'A broad picture of how and where underwater archaeology has advanced' (Prologue). A good state of the art report. *Class No:* 902.034(084.3)

Indian Ocean

[4312]
RAO, S.R., *ed*. **Marine archaeology of Indian Ocean countries:** proceedings of the First International Conference on Marine Archaeology of Indian Ocean countries, October 1987. Goa, National Institute of Oceanography, 1988. xlvi,164p. illus. (some col.). Rs500. ISBN: 819007408.

60 papers by geologists, geophysicists, oceanographers and archaeologists in 2 sections: 1. Organization of the Conference, general problems, and the future of marine archaeology - 2. Research areas (problems of marine archaeology; ancient shipping and shipwrecks; exploitation of submerged ports; underwater survey techniques; sea-level fluctuations; marine art; ancient ports in India; conservation; the underwater cultural heritage of Indian Ocean countries; and marine technology in archaeology).
Class No: 902.034(267)

America

[4313]
BASS, G.F. **Ships and shipwrecks of the Americas** a history based on underwater archaeology. London, Thames and Hudson, 1988. 272p. illus. (many col.), maps, bibliog., index. £24.95. $40.00. ISBN: 050005049x.

12 essays by different hands record the triumphs of marine archaeology in the New World in chronological order: Viking longboats to the Titanic. Glossary p.260-61. Brief guide to museums and research institutes p.261-62. Bibliography p.263-67. 376 illus. (80 col.).
Class No: 902.034(7)

Australia

[4314]
HENDERSON, G. **Maritime archaeology in Australia.** Nedlands, Univ. of Western Australian Press, 1986. ix, 201p. illus., tables, bibliog., index. £12.00. ISBN: 0855642416.

Complete account of the archaeological resource and an overview of the progress of the discipline in Australia, with some pointers to future directions in 10 chapters e.g., 3. Ships in Australian waters before European settlement - 4. After European settlement - 5. Finders and the law - 6-9. Maritime archaeology in the various States - 10. Reflective overview and prospects. Appendix: Shipwrecks declared under legislation p.173-8. Bibliography p.179-85.
Class No: 902.034(94)

Fieldwork Techniques

Bibliographies

[4315]
Radiocarbon dating literature: the first 21 years, 1947-1968 an annotated bibliography. Polach, D., *comp*. London, Academic Press, 1988. x,370p. indexes. ISBN: 0125592906.

2715 items arranged in 14 form, thematic, and regional chapters: 1. Bibliographical works - 2. Theoretical works - 3. Techniques and instrumentation - 4. Geology - 5. Glacial geology - 7. Pleistocene - 8. Archaeology. Africa - 9.

....(contd.)

America - 10. Asia - 11. Europe - 12. Oceania - 13. Conferences - 14. Date lists. Author, subject and location indexes. *Class No:* 902.2(01)

Great Britain

[4316]

BINKS, G., *and others eds.* **Visitors welcome** a manual on the presentation and interpretation of archaeological excavations. London, HMSO, 1988. 162p. illus. (some col.), bibliog., index. pbk. £25.00. ISBN: 0117012106.

Part 1. Section 1. Why invite visitors to your dig? The benefits of presentation and interpretation - 2. What is it realistic to provide for the visitor? Planning the interpretative programme - 3. Who is really likely to visit ... and what will they be interested in? - 4. How are you going to get your interpretation across to visitors? - 5. Encouraging school visits - 6. Opportunities for generating income - 7. Who can help? Grant aid and sponsorship - 8. Public relations. Part 2. Technical Appendix (*e.g.* funding ... useful addresses ... setting up a trading company ... guided tours ... publication design ... audio systems). Bibliography p.156-9.
Class No: 902.2(410)

[4317]

JONES, B. Past imperfect the story of Rescue Archaeology. London, Heinemann, 1984. xii, 164p. illus., tables, bibliog.

10 chapters surveying the development of Rescue Archaeology *i.e.* excavation of sites and monuments preceding destruction. Bibliography p.159-62.
Class No: 902.2(410)

[4318]

WOOD, E.S. Collins field guide to archaeology in Britain. 5th ed. London, Collins, 1979. 389p. illus. (inc.pl.), maps, indexes. ISBN: 0002192357.

1st ed. 1963.

4 parts: 1. General background - 2. Types of field antiquities; fixtures (p.88-246; Caves and rock shelters ... Deceptive natural features) - 3. Types of field antiquities: surface findings (*e.g.* flint; pottery) - 4. Books to read (sectionalised; running commentary; p.350-66). A key to over 200 varieties of earthworks. Neat production.
Class No: 902.2(410)

America — North

[4319]

McMILLON, B. The Archaeology handbook a field manual and resource guide. New York, John Wiley, 1991. iv,259p. illus., bibliog., index. $24.95; £10.95. ISBN: 0471530514.

Excavation guide for North American amateur archaeologists and archaeological volunteers. Resource section (travel agencies; museums; sites; excavations; field schools; state archaeologists and state historical reservation officers; archaeological organizations) p.142-248. Bibliography p.249-53. 'A good practical guide to archaeological techniques' (*Reference Reviews,* v.6, no.2, 1992, p.44). *Class No:* 902.2(71 + 73)

Antiquities

[4320]

CLEERE, H.F., *ed.* **Archaeological heritage management in the modern world.** London, Unwin, Hyman, 1989. xxiv, 318p. maps, tables, diagrs., bibliogs., index. £35.00. (*One World Archaeology series, no.9.*) ISBN: 0044450281.

33 contributors from 18 countries. Compendium of papers arranged in 4 sections: 1. Approaches to heritage management - 2. Regional and country studies - 3. Case studies - 4. Training and qualification of archaeologists for heritage management. Most papers have lists of references appended. *Class No:* 904

[4321]

JOUSSAUME, R. Dolmens for the dead : megalith building throughout the world. Translated by A. and C. Chippindale. London, B.T. Batsford Ltd., 1988. 320p. illus., maps, bibliog., index. £19.95. ISBN: 0713453699.

First published in Paris by Hachette as *Les dolmens pour les morts* 1985.

13 geographical chapters with marked European emphasis but with worldwide coverage nevertheless: 8. Africa, the Arabian peninsula, and Madagascar - 9. Syria, Lebanon and Israel - 10. The Caucasus - 11. India - 12. China, Korea and Japan - 13. South America. Introduction (p16-24) attempts a definition of dolmen whilst Translator's preface (p.11-15) distinguishes between British and continental usage. Bibliography p.299-315. 26 plates and 65 drawings.
Class No: 904

[4322]

MOHEN, J-P. The World of megaliths. London, Cassell, 1989; New York, Facts On File, 1990. 318p. illus. (some col.), maps, bibliog., index. $35. ISBN: 0304318795, UK; 0816022518, US.

Originally published as *Le Monde des mégalithes* (Tournai, Casterman, 1989).

Worldwide survey of menhirs, dolmens and cromlechs together with a discussion of current views of megalithic societies. 9 chapters in 4 sections: Sites and legends - Three thousand years of building - Secret of the builders - Sacred world of megaliths. Chronological table p.284. Table of contemporaneous megalithic cultures p.285. Glossary p.290-8. Bibliography (with French and German language titles p.286-9). Geographic index p.299-318. *Class No:* 904

Worldwide

[4323]

The Collections of the British Museum. Wilson, D.M., *ed.* London, British Museum Publications, 1989. 304p. illus. (many col.), bibliog., index. ISBN: 0714116823.

Descriptive handbook to British Museum antiquities arranged by Departments: 1. Classical collections - 2. Coins and medals - 3. Egyptian antiquities - 4. Ethnographic collection - 5. Medieval and modern collection - 6. Oriental collections - 7. Prehistoric and Roman Britain - 8. Prints and drawings - 9. Western Asiatic antiquities - 10. Conservation and scientific research. Bibliography p.289-90. Galleries of the BM. p.291-4. *Class No:* 904(100)

Ancient Greece & Rome

Dictionaries

[4324]
DAREMBERG, C. *and* SAGLIO, E. **Dictionnaire des antiquités grecques et romaines,** d'après les textes, et les monuments, contenant l'explication des termes qui se rapportent aux moeurs, aux institutions, à la religion ... et en général à la vie publique et privée des anciens. Paris, Hachette, 5v. and index, 1873-1919.

Reprinted Graz, Akademische -u. Verlagsanstalt, 1962. 8464p. ISBN 3201002828.

Scholarly and well documented, covering all phases of ancient Greek and Roman life, customs and institutions. Excludes biography and literature. Signed articles. Useful indexes of authors, Greek words, Latin words, and subjects.

Excels possibly even Pauly-Wissowa's *Real-Encyclopädie* presentation of material; 'is still an unequalled source of reference on many topics such as arms, dress, furniture, ceramics, cultural practices, sport, architecture, deities, etc.' (Ad Orientem. *Books on Africa and the Orient Catalogue five*, 1966, entry no. 1963). *Class No:* 904(37/38)(038)

[4325]
SEYFFERT, O. **A Dictionary of Classical antiquites:** mythology - religion - literature - art. Nettleship, H. *and* Sandys, J.E., *Rev. and ed.* London, Allen & Unwin, 1957; Magnolia, Montana, Peter Smith. vi, 716p. illus. index. $19.

Founded on Seyffert's *Lexikon der classicher Altertumskunde* (1882). The 1957 edition is a reprint of the 3rd ed. (1894) of the English translation.

A standard work, compact yet readable. Adequate cross-references; some references to sources.
Class No: 904(37/38)(038)

Europe

[4326]
BALFOUR, M. **Megalithic mysteries** an illustrated guide to Europe's ancient sites. Limpsfield, Sy. Dragon's World, 1992. 192p. col. illus., maps, diagrs., bibliog., index. £19.95. ISBN: 1850281637.

Selective A-Z gazetteer by area and country which includes road directions and map references. 'Europe' includes parts of North Africa; British sites are well represented. 'All the well-known monuments in Europe are here and plenty which are scarcely known at all' (*Reference Reviews*, v.7, no.3, 1993, p.42). *Class No:* 904(4)

[4327]
SERVICE, A. *and* BRADBERY, J. **The Standing stones of Europe** a guide to the great megalithic monuments. Rev. ed. London, Dent, 1993. 287p. illus., maps, bibliog., index. ISBN: 0460861158.

First published by Weidenfeld & Nicolson 1979.

Descriptive gazetteer and guidebook to Northern and Southern Europe. Megalithic sites to visit in British Isles p.254-64. Glossary p.270-2. References and bibliography p.273-9. Map sources for locating megalithic sites (by country) p.280-1. *Class No:* 904(4)

Great Britain

[4328]
AUBREY, J. **Monumenta Britannica.** Fowles, J., *ed.* Sherborne, Dorset, Dorset Publishing Co., 2 vols., 1982. 1143p. facsims. maps, indexes. £95.; $250. each vol. ISBN: 0902129406, v.1; 0902129503, v.2.

Monumenta Britannica: a miscellanie of British antiquities remained in manuscript form from 1693 to its first printing in this limited edition of 595 copies.

A survey of British field antiquities from the prehistoric to the medieval period commissioned by Charles II. Aubrey's manuscript is here reproduced in facsimile with a facing modern English printed text. *Class No:* 904(410)

[4329]
BURL, A. **The Stone circles of the British Isles.** New Haven, Yale Univ. Press, 1976. xxii,410p. illus., maps, diagrs., tables, bibliog., index. £40.00. ISBN: 0300019726.

9 chapters *e.g.* 1. The earlier work on stone circles - 2. Origins - and regional chapters 4-9. Appendix 1. A county gazetteer of the stone circles of the British Isles p.335-71. Bibliography p.376-95. *Class No:* 904(410)

[4330]
CANBY, C. **A Guide to the archaeological sites of the British Isles.** New York and Oxford, Facts on File, 1988. 358p. illus. index. $24.95. £13.95. (*Guide to the archeological sites of Europe & the Mediterranean no.1.*) ISBN: 0816015708.

750 cross-referenced entries relating to monuments, churches, castles, towns and cities, Palaeolithic period to 12th century, A-Z in 3 sections: England and Wales, Scotland and Ireland. Sites are located by distance from the nearest major town. No bibliography. Intended as a travel book and as an archaeological reference work but 'while it has some reference value, public libraries serving travellers will not find it a worthwhile addition as a guidebook' (*Booklist*, v.85, no.14, 15 March 1989, p.1265-6). *Class No:* 904(410)

[4331]
CASTLEDEN, R. **Neolithic Britain** New Stone Age sites of England, Scotland and Wales. London, Routledge, 1992. xiv,432p. illus., plans, bibliog., index. £40. ISBN: 0415058457.

1,100 domestic, ceremonial, and burial sites, some of them recently discovered, belonging to the period 4700-2000 BC, are described A-Z within the 'new counties'. Appendix: radiocarbon dates p.403-4. Bibliography p.405-9. *Class No:* 904(410)

[4332]
CLAYTON, P. **Guide to the archaeological sites of Britain.** 2nd ed. London, B.T. Batsford, 1985. 239p. illus., bibliog., index. £14.95. ISBN: 0713448431.

First published as *Archaeological sites of Britain* Weidenfeld & Nicolson, 1976.

250 of the more notable sites described in 7 regional sections (1. The South East ... 7. The North). Some museums to visit p.232-5. Glossary p.230-1. Bibliography p.229. 180 illustrations. *Class No:* 904(410)

[4333]

ELLIS, P.B. A Guide to early Celtic remains in Britain. London, Constable, 1991. 272p. illus., bibliog., index. £11.95. ISBN: 0094692009.

Divided into 9 regions this guide contains descriptions of the visible remains of the Early Celtic period from the 8th century BC to the arrival of the Romans in the 1st centry AD. All the most scenic and the most significant sites - hillforts, cliff castles, hillside carvings, burial mounds *etc.* - are included. Glossary p.255-9. Bibliography p.260-4. *Class No:* 904(410)

[4334]

HAWKES, J. The Shell guide to British archaeology. London, Michael Joseph, 1986. 320p. illus. (some col.), maps, bibliog. £14.95. ISBN: 0718124480.

"A History of archaeology in Britain" and "Prehistoric and Roman Britain" precede a gazetteer of sites divided regionally. A general survey of the prehistory and archaeology of each region opens each section. Site entries explicate its archaeological age, importance, plan, and use, noting significant artifacts found and their present whereabouts. Regional maps, a glossary, and a list of the most important museums complete a compact and comprehensive guide. *Class No:* 904(410)

[4335]

HAYES, A. Archaeology of the British Isles with a gazetteer of sites in England, Wales, Scotland and Ireland. London, Batsford, 1993. 206p. illus., maps, bibliog., index. £25. ISBN: 0713472278.

Popular account of Britain's archaeological heritage from 250,000 BC to AD 1500. Gazetteer of 450 sites p.159-200. Bibliography p.201-2. *Class No:* 904(410)

[4336]

HOGG, A.H.A. Hill-forts of Britain London, Hart-Davis, Macgibbon, 1975. xvi. 17p + 304 p. illus. (inc. pl.), ground plans, maps, index.

12 chapters. 1. Names - 2. Modern research ... 5. Distribution and regional types ... 7. Building the hill-fort ... 10. The interior - 11. The Romans and after - 12. Four important hill-forts. Bibliography. 103-11. Gazetteer. A-Z, p.112-299 (with ground plans, grid references, bibliographical references). Illus. include aerial views, location maps. *Class No:* 904(410)

Bibliographies

[4337]

GREAT BRITAIN. HM Stationery Office. **Government Publications: Sectional List 27, revised 1 April 1982: Ancient monuments and historic buildings in the care of the state.** London, HMSO. *gratis.*

Lists items with prices: official guidebooks; Royal Commission publications; miscellaneous publications; departmental publications - England, Scotland, Wales and Northern Ireland. *Class No:* 904(410)(01)

Roman Times

[4338]

COLLINGWOOD, R.G. *and* **WRIGHT, R.P. The Roman inscriptions of Britain:** 1. Inscriptions on stone. Oxford, Clarendon Press, 1965. 824p. illus. (incl.pl.).

A finely produced work, with details of 2,400 inscriptions; entries arranged under regions and counties, then towns. In

....(contd.)

each case, a reproduction of the original plus transcription and translation. 'Milestones' are covered in items 2219-2400. Short glossary and translation of military terms; index of sites. Bibliography (p.xix-xxxiii): A. Abbreviations of periodicals and serial works - B. Manuscript sources - C. Separate works - D. Museum catalogues.

Goodburn, R. and Waugh, H. *Inscriptions on stone. Epigraphic indexes.* Gloucester, Alan Sutton. 1990. 128p. £18. 0862990262. Key to analysis of inscriptions' contents: 64 separate indexes in 16 major reference groups. *Class No:* 904(410)"0055-0449"

[4339]

—**COLLINGWOOD, R.G.** *and* **WRIGHT, R.P.** The Roman inscriptions of Britain: 2. Minor inscriptions. Gloucester, Alan Sutton, 1990-1991.

Volume 2. Instrumentum domesticum. Gloucester, Alan Sutton *Fascicule 1. The military diplomata; metal ingots, tesserae, dies; labels; and lead sealings.* Edited by S.S. Frere, M. Roxan, and R.S.O. Tomlin. 1990. xiv,126p. + + 8p. pl. £35. ISBN 0862997755. Bibliography p.xiii-xiv.

Fascicule 2. Weights, gold vessels, silver vessels, bronze vessels, lead vessels, pewter vessels, shale vessels, glass vessels, spoons. Edited by S.S. Frere and R.S.O. Tomlin. 1991. xiii,146p. + + 8p. plates (twice). £35. 0862998204. Bibliography p.xiii.

Fascicule 3. *Brooches, rings, gems, bracelets, helmets, shields, weapons, iron tools, baldric fittings, votives in gold, silver and bronze, lead pipes, roundels, sheets and other lead objects, stone roundels, pottery and bone roundels, other objects of bone.* Edited by S.S. Frere and R.S.O. Tomlin, 1991. xiii,176p. + + 16p. pl. £35. 0862999359. Bibliography p.xiii.

Fascicule 4. *Wooden barrels, stilus tablets, leather stamps, oculists stamps, wall plaster, mosaics, handmills, stone tablets, balls, pebbles, etc.* Edited by S.S. Frere and R.S.O. Tomlin. 1992. 244p. £35. 0750900865. The definitive publication of Roman written sources for Britain. *Class No:* 904(410)"0055-0449"

[4340]

DE LA BÉDOYÈRE, G. The Finds of Roman Britain. London, B.T. Batsford, 1989. 242p. illus. (inc. some col. pl.), tables, bibliog., index. £19.95. ISBN: 0713460822.

Emphasis on artefacts sharing a common function: 1. The Roman army in Britain - 2. Crafts, trade and industries - 3. Household life - 4. The individual - 5. Public and social life - 6. Religion and superstition - 7. Death and burial - 8. Christianity - 9. Coinage. Appendix: Museums p.209-22 (list of most important holding Romano-British collections). Table of events p.212-13. Bibliography p.227-37. Over 500 illustrations. *Class No:* 904(410)"0055-0449"

[4341]

WILSON, R.J.A. A Guide to the Roman remains in Britain. 3rd ed. London, Constable, 1988. xvi, 453p. illus., maps, bibliog., indexes. £8.95. ISBN: 0094686507.

1st ed. 1978.

Survey of all visible antiquities in 10 regional chapters. Sites are grouped according to their nature and not to their proximity. Introduction (p.1-30) includes sections on Roman army in Britain; Military remains (by type); Historical outline; and Glossary (p.26-30). Appendix 1. Gazetteer of visible remains not mentioned in text p.408-19 - 2. Some museums displaying Romano-British material (p.420-1) - 3. Bibliography p.422-444. Index of sites and types of

....*(contd.)*

monument. Designed primarily for the ordinary individual who has an interest in the Roman past but no prior specialized knowledge. *Class No:* 904(410)"0055-0449"

Bibliographies

[4342]
DOBSON, B. *and* BREEZE, D. 'Books Hadrians Wall 1979-89' *Current Archaeology.* v.10, no.9, August 1989, p.295-7.

Literature review encompassing books, journals and magazines. *Class No:* 904(410)"0055-0449"(01)

Scotland

[4343]
Exploring Scotland's heritage. Edinburgh, HMSO for Royal Commission on the Ancient and Historical Monuments of Scotland, 1985-1987. illus., maps, bibliog., index, pbk. £6.95. each.

Popular but authoritative handbooks introducing Scotland's most interesting and best preserved monuments which are grouped according to character and date. The use of O.S. 1:50,000 Landranger maps is recommended. Ritchie, G. and Harman, M. *Argyll and the Western Isles.* 1985. ISBN 914924295. Stevenson, J.B. *The Clyde Estuary and Central Region.* 1985. ISBN 0114924546. Baldwin, J. *Lothian and the Borders.* 1985. ISBN 0114924341. Ritchie, A. *Orkney and Shetland.* 1985. ISBN 0114924589. Snell, G. *Dumfries and Galloway.* 1986. ISBN 0114924597. Shepherd, I.A.G. *Grampian.* 1986. ISBN 0114924538. Close-Brooks, J. *The Highlands.* 1986. ISBN 0114924600. Walker, B. and Ritchie, G. *Fife and Tayside.* 1987. ISBN 011492435x. 'Essential to complete the libraries of tourist guides, antiquarians and historians, and intelligent visitors to Scotland' (*Local Historian,* v.17, no.3, August 1986, p.184). *Class No:* 904(411)

[4344]
FOJUT, N. *and* PRINGLE, D. The Ancient monuments of Shetland. London, HMSO, 1993. 64p. col. illus. pbk. £3.95. ISBN: 0114942005.

Illustrated gazetteer to the antiquities of Shetland from Neolithic settlements to 18th century coastal defences. *Class No:* 904(411)

[4345]
GREAT BRITAIN. Historic Buildings And Monuments Scotland. A List of ancient monuments in Scotland 1990. Edinburgh, Scottish Development Department, 1990. 51p. ISBN: 0748003274.

A-Z regional guide arranged according to local authority areas. Data: 1:50,000 O.S. sheet and National Grid number within broad categories: prehistoric ritual and funerary; domestic and defensive; Roman; Crosses and canal stones; Ecclesiastical; secular; industrial. List of addresses of national organizations and regional archaeologists inside end cover. *Class No:* 904(411)

[4346]
JENNER, M. Scotland through the ages. London, Mermaid, 1989. 256p. illus. (many col.), maps, bibliog., index. £10.95. ISBN: 0718132807.

First published by Penguin 1987.

Historical background with maps and gazetteers to over 400 major archaeological and historic sites. *Class No:* 904(411)

[4347]
MacSWEEN, A. *and* SHARP, M. Prehistoric Scotland. London, Batsford, 1989. 208p. illus., maps, bibliog., index. £15.95. ISBN: 071346173x.

A lavishly illustrated guide to over 100 outstanding prehistoric sites to stand as exemplars of the various types: settlement, defence, tombs and burial; ritual, and stones & henges. An introductory chapter summarizes the periods of Scottish prehistory. Glossary p.195-8. Gazetteer p.199-203. Bibliography p.204. *Class No:* 904(411)

[4348]
Reports and inventories. Great Britain. Royal Commission on the Ancient and Historical Monuments of Scotland. Edinburgh, HMSO,1909-.

1.*Berwick,* 1909. 2. *Sutherland.* 1911. 3. *Caithness.* 1911. 4/5. *Galloway.* 1912-14. 2v. 6. *Berwick.* Rev. issue. 1915. 7. *Dumfriesshire.* 1920. 8. *East Lothian.* 1924. 9. *Outer Hebrides, Skye and the Small Isles.* 1928. 10. *Midlothian and West Lothian.* 1929. 11. *Fife, Kinross and Clackmannan.* 1933. 12. *Orkney and Shetland.* 1946. 3v. 13. *City of Edinburgh.* 1951. 14. *Roxburghshire.* 1956. 2v. 15. *Selkirkshire.* 1957. 16. *Stirlingshire.* 1963. v.1-2. £15. 17. *Peebleshire.* 2v. £10; £17.50; $20.00. 18. *Argyle.* v.1: *Kintyre.* 1972; v.2: *Lorn.* 1975; v.3: *Mull, Tiree, Coll & N. Argyle*; v.4: *Iona.* 1982; v.5: *Islay, Jura, Colonsay & Oronsay.* 1984. £45. 0114917280; v.6: *Mid-Argyll & Cowal.* 1988. v.7: *Mid Argyll & Cowal: medieval and later monuments.* 1992. £120. 0114940940; 19/20. *Lanarkshire.* 1978. (v.20. £20). *North-east Perth: an archaeological landscape.* 1990. £35. 0114934460 is the first in a series of RCAHMS archaeological surveys. Occasional publications designed to give fuller treatment to subjects which cannot be embraced within the normal course of the Commission's publication programme include: *Late medieval monumental sculpture in the West Highlands.* 1977. 230p.+45p., plates. £14.50. *Monuments of industry: an illustrated historical record.* 1986. xiii, 248p. £28.00. 0114924570.

In the numbered series descriptions are arranged by parish. Until 1938 monuments erected up to 1707 were included; in 1938 The Commissioners were empowered to cover up to 1815; after 1948 the terminal date has been left to their discretion. S.P. Halliday and J.B. Stevenson's 'Surveying for the future: RCAHMS Archaeological Survey 1908-1990', *Scottish Archaeology: new perceptions.* 1991. p.129-39. bibliog. relates its development and progress. See also: 'The Royal Commission on the Ancient and Historical Monuments of Scotland: the first eighty years', *Transactions Ancient Monuments Society,* v.36, 1992, p.13-77. *Class No:* 904(411)

[4349]

—GREAT BRITAIN Royal Commission on the Ancient and Historical Monuments of Scotland. National Monuments Record of Scotland Jubilee a guide to the collections, 1941-1991. Edinburgh, HMSO, 1991. xvii,77p. illus., index. £14.95. ISBN: 0114941254.

A-Z cumulative descriptive list of NMRS's historical collections. Does not include NMRS Library or material emanating from RCAHMS' field investigations. *Class No:* 904(411)

[4350]

RITCHIE, A. *and* BREEZE, D.J. **Invaders of Scotland** an introduction to the archaeology of the Romans, Scots, Angles and Vikings, highlighting the monuments in the care of the Secretary of State for Scotland. Edinburgh, HMSO for Historic Buildings and Monuments, 1991. vi,58p. col. illus., map on endpaper, bibliog., indexes, flexicover. £4.95. ISBN: 011494136x.

Colourfully illustrated descriptive guide to Scotland's most interesting and important archeological sites. Bibliography p.56. *Class No:* 904(411)

[4351]

RITCHIE, A. **Picts** an introduction to the life of the Picts and to the carved stones in the care of the Secretary of State for Scotland. Edinburgh, HMSO, for Historic Buildings and Monuments, 1989. 64p. col. illus. pbk. £3.95. ISBN: 0114934916.

Illustrated introduction to Pictish Scotland 400-800 AD. and a guide to the surviving antiquities. *Class No:* 904(411)

[4352]

RITCHIE, A. **Viking Scotland.** London, Batsford for Historic Scotland, 1993. 143p. col.illus. to maps, bibliog., index. (*Historic Scotland, no.1.*) ISBN: 0713472251.

Illustrated guide to major Scottish archaeological monuments. 'A substantial amount of text, written by a highly respected Scottish archaeologist ... a selective but commendably up-to-date bibliography, a thoroughly professional index, a useful select glossary of technical terms, and a helpful catalogue of monuments and museums to visit' (*Reference Reviews,* v.8, no.2, 1994. p.47). *Class No:* 904(411)

[4353]

ROBERTSON, A.S. **The Antonine Wall:** a handbook to the surviving remains. Revised by L. Keppie. 4th ed. Glasgow Archaeological Society, 1990. v,113p. illus., maps, bibliog., index. ISBN: 0904254127.

1st ed. 1960.

Authoritative and detailed guide. Bibliography p.102-9. Museums holding Antonine Wall material p.109-110. *Class No:* 904(411)

Gazetteers

[4354]

PIGGOTT, S. *and* RITCHIE, G. **Scotland before history with a gazetteer of ancient monuments.** 2nd ed. Edinburgh, Edinburgh Univ. Press, 1982. 196p. illus., map, pbk. £13.50. ISBN: 0852244703.

Non-technical account of human settlement and development from the earliest times to the Roman occupation accompanied by a gazetteer of 255 sites of the best preserved, most dramatic, and most typical field monuments,

....(contd.)

arranged A-Z by region and district. Index of sites. Favourable reception in *Antiquity*, v.57, no.221, November 1983, p.230-231. *Class No:* 904(411)(083.86)

Roman Times

[4355]

KEPPIE, L. **Scotland's Roman remains:** an introduction and handbook. Edinburgh, John Donald, 1986. ix, 188p., illus., maps, plans, diagrs., bibliog., index, pbk. £7.50. ISBN: 0859761576.

Part 1: Romans in Scotland has 9 chapters *e.g.* 1. Scotland on the eve of the Roman invasion - 2. Romans in Scotland: an historical outline ... 9. Impact of Romans. Part 2. Visiting Scotland's Roman remains (p.72-170) is in 3 geographical regional chapters. Bibliography p.173-84. *Class No:* 904(411)"0055-0449"

[4356]

RITCHIE, A. **Scotland BC** historical buildings and monuments. Edinburgh, H.M. Stationery Office, 1988. Published for Scottish Development Department (Historic Buildings and Monuments). 80p. illus. (some col.), pbk. £3.95. ISBN: 0114934274.

Description of stone circles, tombs, rock carvings, Celtic forts *etc.,* (many in state care and open to the public) on mainland Scotland and on the Northern and Western Isles. *Class No:* 904(411)"0055-0449"

Ireland

[4357]

EVANS, E. **Prehistoric and early Christian Ireland** a guide. London, Batsford, 1966. xii, 241p. illus., maps, index.

The archaeological background (p.5-40) - Gazetteer (of the more remarkable sites, p.41-214; arranged under counties A-Z); glossary (p.215-21); bibliography (p.223-30). Index of monuments and illustrations; non-analytical subject index. *Class No:* 904(415)

[4358]

McNALLY, K. **Standing stones.** Belfast, Appletree Press, 1991. 128p. illus. IR£6.99. ISBN: 0862812011.

Guide to Irish field monuments illustrated by over 70 photographs. *Class No:* 904(415)

[4359]

WEIR, A. **Early Ireland** a field guide. Belfast, Blackstaff Press, 1980. vii, 245p. illus., index. £7.95. ISBN: 0856402125.

In 2 distinct sections: a chronological survey incorporating the dating of prehistoric monuments and the archaeological background; and a gazetteer (p.93-233) arranged A-Z by counties. Only those monuments offering the visitor/general reader some visual reward find a place. Glossary p.235-239. Place-name index p.241-245. *Class No:* 904(415)

Northern Ireland

[4360]

HAMLIN, A. **Historic monuments of Northern Ireland.** 6th ed. Belfast, HMSO for Department of the Environment (Northern Ireland), 1988. xii,168p. illus. (some col.), map, bibliog., index. pbk. £6.90. ISBN: 0337082162.

1st ed. 1926.

.... *(contd.)*

Traces the province's prehistoric and historic background and covers 154 sites in state care A-Z by county and lists over 250 other monuments. Bibliography p.157-60.

Class No: 904(416)

Eire

[4361]

HARBISON, P. Guide to the national monuments in the Republic of Ireland: including a selection of other monuments not in state care. 2nd ed. Dublin, Gill and Macmillan, 1982. 284p.+8p. maps, bibliog., index. £8.95. ISBN: 717107582.

First published 1970. May be regarded as a very much altered and expanded edition of *The national monuments of Ireland* published by *Bord Failte* (Irish Tourist Board) and now out of print.

Arranged A-Z by counties (p.1-260). Entries provide a map reference, access details, a description, and references to relevant publications. Glossary p.261-264. Bibliography p.269. List of selected museums and folk parks p.270.

A revised and updated edition, *National monuments of Ireland* (1992), is completely redesigned and for the first time includes details of the principal monuments in Northern Ireland. *Class No:* 904(417)

England & Wales

[4362]

HAWKES, J. A Guide to the prehistoric and Roman monuments in England and Wales. 2nd ed. London, Chatto & Windus, 1973.

First published 1951.

'Attempts to reveal the monuments always in their proper setting of the countryside' (*Preface*). Arranged by areas (*e.g.* South-east; Wessex; South-west; Oxfordshire to the Forest of Dean; Wales and Monmouthshire; Eastern England; North of England). 'Gazetteer of sites described in this Guide', p.291-315 (name of site and page references; national grid reference), - over 600 sites. General index. 16 colour pl., 24 illus.; 5 maps as loose inserts. *Class No:* 904(42)

[4363]

The Penguin guide to prehistoric England and Wales. Dyer, J. Harmondsworth, Allen Lane, 1981. 384p. illus., maps.

Published in Penguin Books 1982.

Descriptive guide to prehistoric monuments, 3-4 entries to the page grouped under 'new' county sections. Each entry is provided with a national grid reference number and the use of Ordnance Survey 1:50,000 maps is recommended. Map section p.18-27. References p.363-366. Glossary p.369-372. Index of sites p.374-384. 'Extensive, detailed, informative and in general acurate and reliable' (*Antiquity*, v.56, no.216, March 1982, p.74-75). *Class No:* 904(42)

England

[4364]

COLVIN, H.M., ed. The History of the King's Works. London, H.M. Stationery Office, 6v., 1973-1982.

1-2. *The Middle Ages.* 1976. £52.00 (these volumes are not sold separately). 0116704497. 2. *1485-1660* Pt.1. 1975. 011670568x. 4. *1485-1660* Pt.2. 1982. £55.00. 0116708328. 5. *1670-1782.* 1976. £32.00. 011670571x. 6. *1782-1851.*

.... *(contd.)*

1973. £40.00. 0116702869. Portfolio plans V-VII complementing v.4-5 sold separately from volumes of text. £11.00. 0116711167. Surveys royal building in England from the era of Offa's Dyke to the establishment of the Victorian Office of Works in 1851. *Class No:* 904(420)

[4365]

DARVILL, T. Ancient monuments in the countryside: an archaeological management review. London, Historic Buildings & Monuments Commission for England, 1987. viii,188p. illus., maps, plans, tables, bibliog., index. Softcover. £12.50. (*Archeological Report, no.5.*) ISBN: 1850741670.

A detailed framework for the enjoyment, preservation, and conservation of ancient monuments in rural areas ranging from prehistoric sites to 19th century industrial remains. 1. Archaeology and management (archaeological evidence; development of the countryside; resource management; legislative background) - 2/3. Semi-natural and man-made landscapes - 4. Looking forward. Appendix A: Names and addresses of archaeological organizations in England - B. Ancient Monuments and related legislation - C. Code of practice for mineral operators. Notes p.174-8. Glossary P.179-80. Bibliography p.181-8. *Class No:* 904(420)

[4366]

English Heritage series. Johnson, S., *ed.* London, B.T. Batsford/English Heritage, 1989-. illus. (some col.), maps, diagrs., bibliog., index.

Nearly 30 titles have now been published including de la Bëdoyère, G. *Roman towns in Britain* (1992. 143p. 0713469839); Richards, J.D. *Viking Age England* (1991); and Welch, M. *Anglo-Saxon England* (1992). *Class No:* 904(420)

[4367]

GREAT BRITAIN. Royal Commission on the Ancient and Historical Monuments of England. **Inventories.** London, HMSO, 1910-. illus., maps, plans.

Buckinghamshire, 2v., 1912-13. *City of Cambridge*, 2v., 1959. reprinted 1988. 500p. pbk. £35. ISBN 0113000235. *County of Cambridge*, 2v., 1968-72. *Dorset*, 5v., 1952-75. *Essex*, 4v., 1916-23. *Hertfordshire*, 1911. *Huntingdonshire*, 1926. *London*, 5v., 1924-30 including v.3 *Roman London*, 1928. *Middlesex*, 1937. *Lincolnshire: Town of Stamford*, 1977. 0117007129. *County of Northamptonshire*, 6v., 1975-84. *City of Oxford*, 1939. *City of Salisbury*, v.1. 1980. 0117008494. *Gloucestershire. 1. Iron Age and Romano-British monuments in the Gloucestershire Cotswolds.* 1977. 282p. 0117007137. *Shielings and Bastles*, 1970. *Westmorland*, 1936. *City of York*, 5v., 1962-81. *County of Cambridgeshire*, v.1: *West Cambridge* (1968. lxix,256p.) covers 37 civil parishes, each with village plan, description, parish church, etc. Sectional preface (natural background, building materials, ecclesiastical buildings, earthworks, etc.). Armorial index; glossary; analytical index. 120 maps, plates, ground plans.

The Royal Commissions on Historical Monuments of England, Scotland and Wales were set up to make an inventory of the ancient and historical monuments and constructions connected with or illustrative of the contemporary culture, civilization and living conditions of ordinary people. *Class No:* 904(420)

[4368]

THOMAS, N.A. A Guide to prehistoric England. 2nd ed. London, B.T. Batsford, 1976. illus., bibliog., index.

Covers the major pre-Roman earthworks of England. Glossary of archaeological terms, p.38-42. Gazetteer (Avon: Palaeolithic; Neolithic; Bronze Age; Iron Age ... Yorkshire, West). Bibliography (including periodical articles, p.258-64). Index to sites, p.265-70. 70 half-tone illus. *Class No:* 904(420)

Isle of Man

[4369]

MANX MUSEUM AND NATIONAL TRUST. The Ancient and historic monuments of the Isle of Man: a general guide including a select list with notes. 4th ed. Douglas (I.of M.), Manx Museum and National Trust. 49p. illus., map, index. pbk. £0.50p. ISBN: 0901106135.

1st ed. 1958; 3rd ed. 1967.

Contents: The early history of the Isle of Man - Suggestions for further reading (p.17) - The ancient monuments - Administration in the Isle of Man - Illustrations (p.19-30) - Map of sites - The Ancient and historical monuments of the Isle of Man: a selected list with notes (p.31-47). Alphabetical index to sites. *Class No:* 904(428.9)

Wales

[4370]

BARBER, C. and WILLIAMS, J.G. The Ancient stones of Wales. Abergavenny, Gwent, Blorenge Books, 1989. 192p. illus., bibliog., index. ISBN: 095104446x.

Guide to all known Welsh prehistoric stone monuments classified into 3 main groups (standing stones, stone circles, dolmens) but with separate sections on Legends, Arthurian monuments, The Church and the stones, Preservation *etc.* Gazetteer A-Z by 'new' counties p.101-85. Data: name of parish, monument, short description, O.S. map reference number. Glossary p.188. Bibliography p.189. Index of sites p.190-2. *Class No:* 904(429)

[4371]

GREAT BRITAIN Cadw: Welsh Historic Monuments. **A Guide to ancient and historic Wales.** London, HMSO for Cadw, 1991-. illus., maps, bibliogs., index.

1. Rees, S. *Dyfed.* 1992. x,241p. illus., pbk. £11.95. ISBN 0117012203. 2. Whittle, E. *Glamorgan and Gwent.* 1992. 244p. illus. pbk. £11.95. ISBN 0117012211. In preparation *Gwynedd* and *Clwyd and Powys.* Descriptive A-Z county gazetteers of sites and buildings in the care of CADW. Dyfed has 8 chapters: 1. Earliest prehistoric periods ... 5. Roman period ... 8. Medieval churches. Summary of dates p.218-20. Glossary p.221-4. Bibliography p.225-9. 3 maps. *Class No:* 904(429)

[4372]

GREAT BRITAIN. Royal Commission on Ancient And Historical Monuments In Wales. Inventories. Cardiff, H.M. Stationery Office, 1911-.

1. *Montgomery* 1911. 2. *Flint* 1912. 3. *Radnor* 1913. 4. *Denbigh* 1914. 5. *Carmarthen* 1917 6. *Merioneth* 1921. 7. *Pembroke* 1925. 8. *Anglesey* 1937. 9. *Caenarvon* 3v., 1956-64. *Glamorgan* v.1: *Pre-Norman. Pt.1. The Stone and Bronze Ages.* 1976 xxx,144p. ISBN 0117005886. *Pt.2 The Iron Age and the Roman occupation.* 1976. xxx,135p.16p.pl. 0117005894. *Pt.3 The early Christian period.* 1976.

....(contd.)

xxx,80p.15p.pl. 0117005908. V.3: *Medieval secular monuments. Pt.1A: The early castles from the Norman Conquest to 1217.* 1991. xv,391p. 0113000359. *Pt.2. Non-defensive.* 1982. xxxviii,397p.44p.pl. 011701141x. V.4: *Domestic architecture from the Reformation to the Industrial Revolution. Pt.1. The Greater houses.* 1981. xl,379p. 0117007544. *Pt.2. Farmhouses and cottages.* 1988. xviii,661p. 0113000200.

Glamorgan: v.1: *Pre-Norman. Pt.1. The Stone and Bronze Ages.* 1976. xxx,144p. ISBN 0117005886. *Pt.2 The Iron Age and the Roman occupation.* 1976. xxx,135p.16p.pl. 0117005908. *Pt.3. The early Christian period.* 1976. xxx,80p. 15p.pl. 0117005908. V.3: *Medieval secular monuments. Pt.2. Non-defensive.* 1982. xxxviii,397p. 44p.pl. 011701141x. V.4: *Domestic architecture from the Reformation to the Industrial Revolution. Pt.1. The Greater houses.* 1981. xl,379p. 0117007544. *Pt.2. Farmhouses and cottages.* 1988. xviii,661p. 0113000200.

11. *Brecknock. V.1: The prehistoric and Roman monuments. Part 2. Hill forts and Roman remains.* 1987. xxxii,196p. 18p.pl. £45.00. 0113000030. All volumes arranged by parishes with glossaries, numerous illustrations and maps. *Class No:* 904(429)

[4373]

GREGORY, D. Wales before 1066: a guide. Llanrwst, Gwynedd, Gwasg Carreg Gwalch, 1989. 144p. illus., maps, bibliog., index. pbk. £30. ISBN: 0863811175.

4 chronological parts, each comprising a general historical survey followed by a descriptive guide to surviving ruins and monuments: 1. Prehistoric times - 2. Roman interlude - 3. Celtic church - 4. External threats. Short bibliography p.139. 4 maps. *Class No:* 904(429)

[4374]

HOULDER, C. Wales: an archaeological guide the prehistoric, Roman and early medieval field monuments. London, Faber, 1974. 207p. illus., plans, maps, bibliog., index. (*Archaeological guides.*)

8 regional sections (1. North-west Wales ... 5. South central Wales ... 8. South-west Wales), covering 48 areas. National grid references are given for sites. Concise data. References to literature are cited only for major sites. Bibliography, p.194-7, 29 plates; 40 other illus. (of artifacts, site plans). *Class No:* 904(429)

[4375]

ROBINSON, D. Heritage in Wales : a guide to the ancient and historic sites in the care of Cadw: Welsh Historic Monuments. London, Macdonald Queen Anne Press, 1989. 208p. illus. (many col.), index. £14.95. ISBN: 0356172783.

Introduction: The work of Cadw (p.8-9) is followed by A-Z county descriptive gazetteer. Biographical notes: key historical figures p.181-7. Glossary p. 188-93. Gazetteer: the location of properties and details of access p.194-200. Bibliography (200-201) includes list of Cadw's official guidebooks. *Class No:* 904(429)

Maps & Atlases

[4376]

GREAT BRITAIN Cadw: Welsh Historic Monuments. **Map of Wales** a map and gazetteer to the ancient & historic sites in the care of Cadw: Welsh Historic Monuments. Cardiff, Cadw: Welsh Historic Monuments, 1990. single sheet folded, col. illus. £1.25. ISBN: 0948329513.

....(contd.)

A comprehensive guide to over 120 properties of major importance in the direct care of the Secretary of State for Wales. The gazetteer gives brief historic notes, details of rail and road access, and an indication of those sites with exhibitions or other displays. *Class No:* 904(429)(084.3)

Germany

Roman Times
[4377]
VON ELBE, J. *and* VON ELBE, D. **Roman Germany** a guide to sites and museums. Mainz, Verlag Philipp von Zabern, 1975. 523p. folding map in pocket, bibliog.

141 locations. 'More than a mere guidebook ... also a companion to the study of Roman Germany, with well-written authoritative descriptions and explanations of archaeological sites, museum holdings, and their historical significance' (D.S. and J.E. Detweiler. *West Germany,* 1987. Entry 37). *Class No:* 904(430)"0055-0449"

Italy
[4378]
COARELLI, F. **Guida archeologica di Roma.** 5th ed. Milano, Arnoldo Mondadore Editore, 1989. 357p. illus (some col.), maps, plans, geneal., tables, bibliog., index. L38,000. ISBN: 8804118962.

1st ed. 1974.

Comprehensive and well-produced descriptive guide of 17 sections arranged in 3 parts: 1. Le grandi opere pubbliche - 2. Il centro monumentale - 3. Le regioni auguste. Appendix: La tecnica edilizia e i materiali costruzione. Imperatori romani p.343. Bibliography p.345-51. 129 illustrations. *Class No:* 904(450)

Bibliographies
[4379]
McILWAINE, I.C. **Herculaneum: a guide to printed sources.** Napoli, Bibliopolis, 2v., 1988. 1029p. maps, plans, index. L200,000. ISBN: 8870882099.

Monumental work with 3 chaps: 1. Excavation of Herculaneum - 2. Papyri - 3. Impact of the discovery - and 14 sections: 1. Source materials - 2. Campania, Naples and Vesuvius - 3. Herculaneum: history and excavation - 4. The town and its buildings - 5. People - 6. Neapolitan Academies - 7. National Museum - 8. Art in general - 9. Paintings and mosaics - 10. Sculpture - 11. Other fine and applied arts and technologies - 12. Epigraphy and wax tablets - 13. Papyri - 14. Biographical sources. 12 Appendices. Chronology p.27-29. Name and subject indexes p.917-1028. A scholarly work of high distinction. *Class No:* 904(450)(01)

Asia—Near East
[4380]
CANBY, C. **A Guide to the archaeological sites of Israel, Egypt and North Africa.** New York and Oxford, Facts On File, 1990. vi,272p. illus., maps, plans, index. £13.95. $29.95. ISBN: 0816010544.

Description of 300+ sites in Israel, Egypt, Libya, Tunisia, Algeria and Morocco. Data: location; history and excavations; important finds; museums. Introductory essays

....(contd.)

provide a chronological framework. 'Suffers from a lack of chronological and geographic coherence and sufficient detail for the serious traveller' (*Booklist,* v.86,n o.19, 1 June 1990, p.1923-4). *Class No:* 904(56)

Maps & Atlases
[4381]
ROAF, M. **Cultural atlas of Mesopotamia and the Ancient Near East.** New York and Oxford, Facts On File, 1990. 238p. col. illus., col. maps, bibliog., index. £19.50. ISBN: 0816022186.

Pictorial atlas covers the geography, history, archaeology of the Near East from prehistory to 330 BC, combining text, maps and photographs in 3 parts: 1. Villages - 2. Cities - 3. Empires. Also 24 special features (*e.g.* Archaeology in the Near East ... Origins of writing ... Discovery of Mesopotamia); 20 site features (*e.g.* Jericho ... Nineveh ... Persepolis); 16 King Lists; and 46 maps. Chronological table p.8-9. Bibliography p.224. Glossary p.225. Gazetteer p.230-2. The author was Director of the British School of Archaeology in Iraq 1981-85. *Class No:* 904(56)(084.3)

Syria
[4382]
BURNS, R. **Monuments of Syria** a historical guide. London, I.B. Tauris, 1993. 350p. illus., maps, plans. £49.50. ISBN: 1850434964.

Gazetteer and encyclopedic architectural and historical survey of all main and secondary sites and monuments. *Class No:* 904(569.1)

Israel
[4383]
PEARLMAN, M. *and* YANNAI, Y. **Historical sites in Israel.** London, W.H. Allen, 1964. 247p. illus. (many col.), map, bibliog., index.

Historical background to the most important archaeological and historical sites in Israel presented in rough geographical order. Chronological table p.231-6. Bibliography p.237-42. *Class No:* 904(569.4)

Egypt
[4384]
REEVES, N. **The Complete Tutankhamun:** the king, the tomb, the royal treasure. 260 London, Thames & Hudson, 1990. 224p. illus. (many col.), maps, bibliog., index. £15.95. ISBN: 0500050589.

1. Tutankhamun and his time - 2. Search and discovery - 3. Archaeology of the tomb - 4. Pharaoh's burial - 5. Treasures of the tomb. Chronology and family relationships p.8-9. The story of the tomb (dates of burial, discovery, and location of objects discovered) p.210-1. Bibliography p.214-7. Lavishly illustrated handbook. *Class No:* 904(620)

Australia

[4385]

FLOOD, J. The Riches of ancient Australia: a journey into prehistory. St. Lucia, Univ. of Queensland Press, 1990. xxii,373p. illus., maps, table, index. pbk. Aust$34.95. ISBN: 0702222593.

Guide to the prehistoric sites of Australia in 20 chapters region by region. 'Each chapter summarizes the prehistory of an area and then tells where the sites are and how to reach them, well informed and well illustrated (*Antiquity,* v.65, no.248, September 1992, p.726). *Class No:* 904(94)

Industrial Antiquities

[4386]

ALFREY, J. *and* **PUTNAM, T. The Industrial heritage** managing resources and uses. London, Routledge, 1992. xii,327p. illus., bibliog., index. £40. ISBN: 041504068x.

The assessment, conservation, interpretation, financing and management of the heritage of industrial cultures. Bibliography p.310-20. *Class No:* 904:6

[4387]

HUDSON, K. World industrial archaeology. Cambridge, Cambridge Univ. Press. 1979. 247 p. illus. maps, bibliog. index. (*New Studies In Archaeology..*) ISBN: 0521219914.

Introduction. The aims and state of industrial archaeology. Section 1. The techniques appropriate to the study. 2. The range of current work (by industry). Select bibliography p.237 - 241 especially useful for list of periodicals containing articles on various aspects of the study. Limited to Europe, North and South America, and South Africa. 'As an international survey this book will be of great value' (*Industrial Archaeology Review,* v.5. no.1. Winter 1980-81, p.60-61). *Class No:* 904:6

Encyclopaedias

[4388]

The Blackwell encyclopedia of industrial archaeology. Trinder, B., *ed.* Oxford, Blackwell, 1992. xxii,964p. illus., maps, bibliogs., index. £100. ISBN: 0631142169.

59 contributors. Signed articles of varying length and ending with a list of locations and a bibliography provide a guide to the monuments, settlements, landscapes, and museums holding industrial artefacts. National articles for 31 countries: Albania, Australia, Austria, Belgium, Bulgaria, Canada, Czechoslovakia, Denmark, England, Finland, Germany, Greece, Hungary, Iceland, Ireland, Italy, Netherlands, New Zealand, Norway, Poland, Portugal, Romania, Scotland, Spain, Sweden, Switzerland, Turkey, USSR, USA, Wales, and Yugoslavia. Also biographical entries for significant industrial pioneers 1650-1950 and articles on technology in 18 subject groups (*e.g.* transport, chemicals, public utilities). Appendix: guide to contents by subject p.861-72. Bibliography p.873-930. Analytical index. Editor is Lecturer and Historical Adviser, Institute of Industrial Archaeology, Ironbridge. *Class No:* 904:6(031)

[4389]

LINES, C. Companion to the Industrial Revolution. New York and Oxford, Facts On File, 1990. x,262p. illus., maps, tables, bibliog. ISBN: 0816021570.

Over 1000 A-Z entries (200-1000 words in length) relating to people, places, events and technological achievements of

....(contd.)

historical significance. Many entries identify places to visit or end with suggestions for further reading. Chronology (1702-1867) p.246-56. *Class No:* 904:6(031)

Europe

Bibliographies

[4390]

GREENWOOD, J. Industrial archaeology in Western Europe: a bibliography, *Industrial Archaeology Review,* v.6, no.2, Spring 1982, p.125-139.

Books and articles (excluding those relating to British Isles) A-Z by country after a brief general section. *Class No:* 904:6(4)(01)

Great Britain

[4391]

BUCHANAN, R. A. Industrial archaeology in Britain. 2nd ed. London, Allen Lane, 1980. 475 p. illus(inc 86 plates). maps. bibliog. index. ISBN: 0713909560.

First published in Pelican Books, 1972.

Part handbook, part gazetteer organized in 4 sections (16 chapters)and a regional survey: 1. Introduction (1. Definitions and techniques; 2. The Historical framework) - 2. The industrial categories - 3. Power, transport, and public services - 4. The progress of industrial archaeology (15. The organization of the subject; 16. The study of industrial archaeology) - 5. Regional survey: Scotland, North England,Wales, English Midlands, South-East England, and South-West England each with map and bibliography. Notes and bibliographical references. p.437-452. *Class No:* 904:6(410)

[4392]

COSSON, B.P. The BP book of industrial archaeology. 2nd ed. Newton Abbot, Devon, David & Charles, 1987. 384p. illus. bibliog. £16. ISBN: 0715389319.

First published 1975.

17 chapters: 1. Nature of industrial archaeology; 2. The industrialization of Britain; 3. Wind and water power; 4. Steam and internal combustion engines; 5. Coal; 6. Iron and steel; 7. Engineering 8. Non-ferrous metals; 9. Stone, clay and glass; 10. Textiles; 11. The chemical industries; 12. Public utilities; 13. Roads and bridges; 14. Rivers and canals; 15. Railways; 16. Ports and shipping; 17. Conclusion.

4 Appendices: 1. Gazetteer of sites p.323-350; 2. Museums of industry p.351-360; 3. Useful addresses p.361-364; 4. Bibliography p.365-376. Index p.377-384. 246 illus. 'A vast amount of information both verbal and visual, both for the casual reader and for the dedicated student' (*Industrial Archaeology Review,* v.10, no.1, Autumn 1987, p.100-101. *Class No:* 904:6(410)

[4393]

MINCHINTON, W. Guide to industrial archaeology sites in Britain. London, Granada, 1984. 192p. illus., maps, bibliog., index. £10.95. ISBN: 0246117818.

Almost 100 sites of major importance arranged in 7 regional sections (sub-divided by county). Lists of other sites worth visiting for each county. Bibliography p.181-3. 'Easy

....(contd.)

to follow, eminently readable and within the limited choice of sites, quite informative' (*Industrial Archaeology Review*, v.8, no.2, Spring 1986, p.217). *Class No:* 904:6(410)

Gazetteers

[4394]

The National Trust guide to our industrial past. Burton, A. London, George Philip in association with The National Trust and The National Trust for Scotland, 1983. 240p. illus. (some col.), maps, bibliog. £12.50. ISBN: 0540010723.

9 chapters. Gazetteers of sites and monuments open to the public in United Kingdom arranged by modern counties p.187-226. Bibliography p.227-228; maps, p.230-234; index p.235-240. 'Everything is superficial, and nothing is treated in depth' (*Industrial Archaeology Review*, v.6, no.3, Autumn 1982, p.249-250). *Class No:* 904:6(410)(083.86)

Scotland

[4395]

GREAT BRITAIN Royal Commission on the Ancient and Historical Monuments of Scotland. **Catalogue of records, Scottish Industrial Archaeology Survey 1977-85.** Edinburgh, Royal Commission on the Ancient and Historical Monuments of Scotland, 1989. 106p. £2. ISBN: 0748003053.

1500 industrial sites arranged in 3 sections: Topographical; Industrial classification; Thematic surveys. Data: site name, industrial classification, type of site, National Grid reference, and parish or burgh. 'Whilst the book is not a comprehensive gazetteer it presents a useful record of demolished or threatened sites on mainland Scotland ... and as such will be a valuable source of reference' (*Industrial Archaeology Review*, v.12, no.2, Spring 1990, p.223-4). *Class No:* 904:6(411)

Northern Ireland

[4396]

McCUTCHEON, W.A. The Industrial archaeology of Northern Ireland. Belfast, HMSO; 1980. Fairleigh Dickinson, 1984. xlv, 395p. illus., tables, bibliog., indexes. £55. $75. ISBN: 0337081549, UK; 0838631258, US.

A major conspectus of the industrial history and landscape of Northern Ireland in 7 chapters each furnished with extensive notes and bibliographical references: 1. Roads and bridges - 2. Canals and internal navigations - 3. Railways - 4. Animal, wind and water power - 5. Flax and linen - 6. Tyrone coalfield - 7. Conservation and preservation. Appendix of 35 plates covers topics and themes which for lack of space could not be the subject of separate chapters. 177 figures. 156 plates. 35 tables. Author is Director of the Ulster Museum. 'This book is a major contribution ... it sets a standard of coverage and research that is very much higher than we have seen. It could prove to be a pivotal book - the trend of publishing and even of industrial archaeology itself may well come to move along new lines' (*Industrial Archaeology*, v.16, no.1, Spring 1981, p.84-89). *Class No:* 904:6(416)

England

Bibliographies

[4397]

GREENWOOD, J. Industrial archaeology and industrial history series. Cranfield, Kewdale Press, 1985-.

1. *Industrial archeology and industrial history of Northern England: a bibliography.* 1985. 300p. index. ISBN 0951038907. 3050 entries in 7 regional chapters. 2. *-of the English Midlands: a bibliography.* 1987. 410p. index. 0951038915. 3. *-of London: a bibliography.* 1988. 259p. index. 0951038923. 4. *-of South-eastern England: a bibliography.* 1990. 450p. indexes. 0951038931. 5151 numbered entries (books and articles from 420 periodicals). *Class No:* 904:6(420)(01)

Gazetteers

[4398]

ALDERTON, D. *and* **BOOKER, J. The Batsford guide to the industrial archaeology of East Anglia:** Cambridgeshire. Essex. Norfolk. Suffolk. London, B.H. Batsford, 1980. 192p. illus., maps, bibliog., index. (*The Batsford Guide to the Industrial Archaeology of the British Isles.*) ISBN: 0713422335.

Introductory chapter p.13-34 relates the region's basic changes in industries, communications and economic structure. Descriptive gazetteer A-Z by county. Bibliography p.181-183. Glossary p.183. Index of sites by industry p.184-192. 65 photographs, 5 maps. *Class No:* 904:6(420)(083.86)

[4399]

ALDERTON, D. The industrial archaeology of regions in the British Isles. No.1. East Anglia. *Industrial Archaeology Review*, v.7, no.1, Autumn 1984, p.7-23. illus. maps, refs.

The industrial aspects of agricultural change - transport system and the sea - the utilities - textiles and the successor trades - the East Anglian contribution. *Class No:* 904:6(420)(083.86)

[4400]

ASHMORE, O. The Industrial archaeology of North-west England. Manchester, Manchester Univ. Press, 1982. 241p. illus., maps., bibliog., index. £9.95. ISBN: 0719008204.

Descriptive gazetteer of industrial archaeological sites in 4 A-Z sequences: Cheshire, Greater Manchester, Merseyside, and Lancashire selected to illustrate their range and type, geographical distribution, and historical development. Bibliography (by industrial type) p.230-235. Subject index. 'The publisher can fairly claim that this is an essential reference gazetteer for enthusiasts, students, teachers, planners and environmentalists' (*British Book News*, January 1883, p.35). *Class No:* 904:6(420)(083.86)

[4401]

A Brief guide to the industrial heritage of West Yorkshire. Thompson, W.J., *ed.* Telford, Salop, Association for Industrial Archaeology, 1989. 52p. illus., maps, bibliog. sd. ISBN: 0950844837.

5 contributors. Essays and descriptive gazetteer of sites for Calderdale, Kirklees, Bradford, Leeds, and Wakefield. Bibliography inside back cover. Published on the occasion of the Association's annual conference in Huddersfield in 1989. *Class No:* 904:6(420)(083.86)

[4402]

BROOK, F. **The Industrial archaeology of the British Isles 1. The West Midlands:** Hereford-Worcester. Shropshire. Staffordshire. Warwickshire. West Midlands. London, B.T. Batsford, 1977. 223p. illus., maps, diagrs., bibliog., index. (*The Industrial Archaeology of the British Isles.*) ISBN: 071340924x.

Introduction (p.15-39) surveys the region's major industries. A-Z gazetteer of 1200 sites in 5 county sequences. Bibliography p.211-213.
Class No: 904:6(420)(083.86)

[4403]

DAY, J. **A Guide to the industrial heritage of Avon and its borders.** Telford, Shropshire, Association for Industrial Archaeology, 1987. 51p. (inc. covers). illus., maps, bibliog., index. sd.

Descriptive gazetteer of 268 sites grouped in 10 area sections *viz* Bath; Bristol; Bristol Port; Kingsdown; Northavon; Wansdyke; Woodspring; Gloucester; Wiltshire and Somerset borders. Bibliography p.50. Subject index. Published on the occasion of the Association for Industrial Archaeology's annual conference, University of Bath, September 1987. *Class No:* 904:6(420)(083.86)

[4404]

HASELFOOT, A.J. **The Batsford guide to the industrial archaeology of South-East England:** Kent Surrey East Sussex West Sussex. London B.T. Batsford, 1978. 152p. illus., maps, bibliog., index. (*The Batsford Guide to the Industrial Arcaeology of the British Isles.*) ISBN: 0713415614.

Introduction surveys extractive industries, power supplies and services, transport, and miscellaneous industries. Gazetteer A-Z by county. Bibliography p.147-148. Glossary p.149. 65 photographs. 3 maps. Unfavourable review in *Industrial Archaeology Review,* v.3,no.3, Summer 1979, p.276 which concludes 'nevertheless it is worth buying .. because it does draw attention to a number of interesting sites'. *Class No:* 904:6(420)(083.86)

[4405]

MOORE, P. **The industrial archaeology of regions in the British Isles. No.2. Hampshire,** *Industrial Archaeology Review,* v.8, no.1, Autumn 1985, p.28-41. illus. refs.

Maritime activities - defence supply - agriculture - staple industries - transport and public utilities.
Class No: 904:6(420)(083.86)

[4406]

WRIGHT, N.R. **A Guide to the industrial archaeology of Lincolnshire** including South Humberside. Telford, Shropshire, Association for Industrial Archaeology and The Society for Lincolnshire History and Archaeology, 1983. 40p. (inc. covers). illus., maps, bibliog. sd. 95p. ISBN: 0903582007.

A-Z gazetteer of sites and museums at 97 locations. Bibliography p.3-4. Published on the occasion of the Association for Industrial Archaeology's annual conference, Lincoln, September 1983. *Class No:* 904:6(420)(083.86)

Wales

Gazetteers

[4407]

HUGHES, S. *and* REYNOLDS, P. **Industrial archaeology of the Swansea region.** Telford, Shropshire, Association for Industrial Archaeology, in association with the Royal Commission of Ancient and Historical Monuments in Wales and the South West Wales Industrial Archaeology Society, 1988. 55p. (inc. covers) illus. map. bibliog. sd. £1.95. ISBN: 0950844829.

Gazetteer of 173 sites arranged in industrial groups. Site plan p.24-29. Bibliography, museums and conservation societys, p.55. Published for the Association for Industrial Archaeology's Annual Conference, Swansea, 1988.
Class No: 904:6(429)(083.86)

Netherlands

[4408]

NIJHOF, P. **Industrial archaeology in the Netherlands** *Industrial Archaeology Review,* v.13, no.2, Spring 1991 p.103-13.

Early days - Involvement of local institutions - Surveys and documentation ... Museums - Company archives. Appendix: Classification of industrial and technological monuments. *Class No:* 904:6(492)

Belgium

[4409]

BAETENS, R. **Industrielle archeologie in Vlaanderen** :theorie en praktijk. Antwerpen, Standard Uitgeverij, 1988. 271p. illus. Fr.1980. ISBN: 9002152787.

Contents: definitions, methodology and progress of industrial archaeology since 1965 - documentary and other sources - list of monuments classified by industry - provincial case studies. Favourably reviewed in *Industrial Archaeology Review,* v.12, no.1, Autumn 1988, p.101-102.
Class No: 904:6(493)

South Africa

[4410]

HARRIS, D.E. **'Some notes on the industrial archaeology of South Africa',** *Industrial Archaeology,* 1980, p.359-365.
Class No: 904:6(680)

New Zealand

[4411]

THORNTON, G. **Industrial archaeology in New Zealand** *Industrial Archaeology Review,* v.10, no.1, Autumn 1987, p.23-39. 26 plates, map, refs.

Review of the industrial archaeology of 18 industries plus a final section on the present position of industrial archaeological studies. *Class No:* 904:6(931)

Australia

[4412]

DONNACHIE, I. **Industrial archaeology in Australia.** *Industrial Archaeology Review,* v.5, no.2, Spring 1981, p.96-113. illus. refs.

'Examines something of the development and progress of

.... (contd.)

industrial archaeology in Australia, the recording of its industrial heritage, the range of survivals, the achievements in excavation and conservation, the work of museums and universities, and the growing volume of literature.' 38 refs.
Class No: 904:6(94)

[4413]
DONNACHIE, J. The industrial heritage of Australia and New Zealand: an essay in bibliography and criticism, *Industrial Archaeology Review*, v.7, no.2, Spring 1985, p.200-209. illus. refs.

Review article of recent works of note.
Class No: 904:6(94)

Institutions & Associations
[4414]
Industrial Archaeology institutions and societies *Industrial Archaeology* Index to v.1-15. (1964-1980).1984.

Directory and activity information of 17 of the most influential institutions, associations and societies.
Class No: 904:6:061:061.2

908 Area Studies

Worldwide

[4415]

The Guinness world data book. Enfield, Mdx, Guinness Publishing, 1991. 192p. col. illus., col. maps, tables, index. £9.99. ISBN: 0851129609.

Succinct information on 1. Physical world (comparative geographical facts) - 2. Political world (United Nations; regional organizations; environment issues; languages *etc.*) - 3. Economic world (populations, national economies *etc.*) - 4. Countries of the World A-Z (Basic facts plus details of government, geography, and recent history). Admirable quick reference for all library information points.

Class No: 908(100)

[4416]

SEGAL, G. The World affairs companion the essential one-volume guide to global issues. 3rd ed. London, Simon & Schuster, 1991. xxiv,310p. maps, tables, bibliogs., index. pbk. £8.99; $24.95.

Overview of world affairs since 1945 concentrating on current issues in a series of c.1000 word essays arranged in 9 subdivided thematic and regional sections: 1. Power of politics - 2. Shaping the new agenda - 3. Modern warfare - 4. The new Europe ... 8. The Middle East - 9. Africa. Section bibliographies. *Class No:* 908(100)

Bibliographies

[4417]

The World bibliographical series. Santa Barbara, California and Oxford, Clio Press, 1978-.

'A series of selective national bibliographies which will eventually include every country in the world. Each critically annotated bibliography covers the literature on a single country and reflects the culture, unique qualities and background to that country'.

'The series has a uniform format that enables readers to compare countries and to locate literature on similar subjects throughout a range of countries. This format is nevertheless flexible enough to reflect national idiosyncracies and to impart the genuine 'flavour' of each country'.

'Each bibliography contains: a Table of Contents; an Introduction; 600-1000 Entries; an extensive index; and a Map. Where necessary, cross-references are provided at the end of chapters and a Glossary is sometimes included. Subjects covered include: The Country and its People; Geography; Flora and Fauna; History; Population and Social Structure; Customs and Folklore; Social Change; Religion; Education; Politics and Government; Law and Constitution; Foreign Relations; Military Affairs and Defence; Economy; Agriculture; Industry; Housing; Newspapers and Periodicals; Transport and Communications; Language and Literature; Art; Music; The Media; Reference Works and Bibliographies'. (*Clio Press catalogues*).

Class No: 908(100)(01)

Encyclopaedias

[4418]

Worldmark encyclopedia of the nations: a practical guide to the geographic, historical, political, social & economic status of all nations, their international relationships, and the United Nations system. Sachs, M.Y., *ed.* 7th ed. New York and Chichester, Sussex, Wiley-Interscience, 5v., 1988. 1800p. illus., maps (some col.), bibliogs., index. $285.00; £245.00. ISBN: 0471624063.

First published in 1v., 1960; 6th ed. 1984.

V.1: United Nations; v.2 Africa; v.3 Americas; v.4 Asia & Oceania; v.5 Europe. Comprehensive geographic, historical, political, and economic data on 176 nations and 80 dependencies arranged under 50 numbered headings e.g., 1. Location - 2. Topography ... 12. History ... 47. Tourism - 48. Famous persons ... 50. Bibliography. 192 maps.

Class No: 908(100)(031)

Handbooks & Manuals

[4419]

Cities of the world: a compilation of current information on cultural, geographical, and political conditions in the countries and cities of six continents, based on the Department of State's Post Reports. Young, M.W. *and* Stetler, S.L., *eds.* 3rd ed. Detroit, Gale Research Co., 4v., 1988. 3268p. illus., maps. index. $281.75. ISBN: 0810325284, set. ISSN: 08592741.

1st published in 1982. Based on official briefings issued as *Post reports* by the US Department of State.

1. *Africa*. 843p. $80.50. ISBN 081032539x. 2. *Western Hemisphere (excluding US)* 776p. $80.50. ISBN 0810325403. 3. *Europe and the Mediterranean Middle East.* 844p.. $80.50 ISBN 0810325411. 4. *Asia, the Pacific, and the Asiatic Middle East.* 805p. $80.50. ISBN 081032542x. 140 background country articles cover social, political and economic conditions, population, history, commerce and industry, *etc.* With reports on over 1500 cities. Countries where the United States maintains no direct diplomatic representation are excluded *i.e.* Angola; the Comoros; Libya; Namibia; Sao Tome and Principe; Spanish Sahara in v.1. Guadeloupe and French Guiana (pt. of Martinique) in v.2. Albania in v.3 and Kampuchea, Vietnam, Iran and Taiwan in v.4. Cumulative index in v.4.

A *Supplement*, 750p. $92.00. ISBN 0810325292. provides newly issued information. *Class No:* 908(100)(035)

[4420]

Handbook of the nations. A brief guide to the economy, government, land, demographics, communications, and national defense establishment of each of the 249 nations and other political entities. 12th ed. Detroit, Gale Research Co. 1992. 420p., 13p. maps, tables. ISBN: 0810374862. ISSN: 01943790.

A reprint of *The World factbook* (previously *National basic intelligence factbook*) produced annually by the US Central Intelligence Agency.

Country entries (1-2p. in length) provide factual

....(contd.)

information on geography, the people, government, economy, communications and defense forces Afghanistan-Zimbabwe. Appendix A: The United Nations system - B. International organizations - C. Country membership of international organizations - E. Cross-reference list of geographic names. 13 regional maps.

'The material not classified, but not provided directly to the public by the CIA, is made available in this publicly circulated edition so that students and private researchers may access it without undue difficulty' (*Foreword*).

Class No: 908(100)(035)

[4421]
Political handbook of the world. Banks, A.S., ed. 61st ed. Binghampton, New York, CSA Publications, 1989. 890p. maps on endpapers, index. $89.95. ISBN: 0933199058. ISSN: 0193175x.

First published as *A political handbook of Europe* in 1927 then with various titles.

Part 1. Governments Afghanistan - Zimbabwe (and Palestine Liberation Organization). Basic information (political status, area, population, urban centers, official language, monetary unit); Legislature; Cabinet; News media - 2. International Organizations. Appendix A. Chronology of major events 1945-1988 - B. Membership of United Nations and its specialized and related agencies.

Class No: 908(100)(035)

[4422]
UNITED STATES. Department of The Army. Country studies. Washington, Headquarters Department of The Army, 1957-. (*Area Handbook Series/American Univ. Foreign Area Studies.*)

Over 100 volumes on individual countries, some now in revised editions. The series aims 'to provide a compact and objective composition and analysis of the dominant social, political and economic characteristics ... Topics covered include: government, population, topography, language, religion, health, climate, justice, economics, trade, communications, transportation, international affairs, and armed forces' (US Government Reports Announcement, AD-739-131). Volumes include *Afghanistan; Albania; Algeria; Angola; Argentina; Australia; Austria; Bangladesh; Belgium; Bolivia; Brazil; Bulgaria; Burma; Burundi; Cambodia; Cameroon; Chad; Chile; China; Republic of China; Colombia; Congo; Costa Rica; Cuba; Cyprus; Czechoslovakia; Dominican Republic; Ecuador; Egypt; El Salvador; Ethiopa; Finland; East Germany; Federal Republic of Germany; Ghana; Greece; Guatemala; Guinea; Guyana; Haiti; Honduras; Hungary; India; Indian Ocean; Indonesia; Iran; Iraq; Israel; Italy; Ivory Coast; Jamaica; Japan; Jordan; Kenya; North Korea; South Korea; Laos; Lebanon; Libya; Malawi; Malaysia; Mauritania; Mexico; Mongolia; Mozambique; Morocco; Nepal; Bhutan; Sikkim; Nicaragua; Nigeria; Oceania; Pakistan; Panama; Paraguay; Persian Gulf States; Peru; Philippines; Poland; Portugal; Romania; Rwanda; Saudi Arabia; Senegal; Sierra Leone; Singapore; Somalia; South Africa; Soviet Union; Spain; Sri Lanka; Sudan; Syria; Tanzania; Thailand; Trinidad & Tobago; Tunisia; Turkey; Uganda; Uruquay; Venezuela; North Vietnam; South Vietnam; The Yemens; Yugoslavia; Zaire; Zambia. Class No:* 908(100)(035)

Yearbooks & Directories

[4423]
The Europa world year book, 1994. 35th ed. London, Europa Publications, 2v., 1993. Available in North America from Gale Research Co. xix,3299p. maps, tables, index. £310. ISBN: 0946653879. ISSN: 09562273.

First published 1926. Under various titles, latterly *Europa yearbook: a world survey.* From 1960 as an annual publication in 2v.

1. Pt.1 International organizations. Pt.2. Country surveys Afghanistan-Jordan. 2. Kampuchea-Zimbabwe. Pt.1. ecompasses more than 1650 organizations *e.g.* The United Nations ... The Commonwealth ... The European Communities. Data includes history, publications and activities. Pt.2. consists of surveys of over 200 countries which follow a set pattern: 1. Introductory survey covering recent history, economic affairs, social welfare and brief geographical details - 2. Statistical survey retrospective and, up to 12988 or 1989) - 3. Directory information on the consitution, government legislature, political organizations, diplomatic representation, judicial sysem, religion, press, radio and television, finance, trade and industry, transport, tourism, atomic energy. 'A consistently reliable and comprehensive reference work, essential to both general and special libraries. (*International Affairs,* v.61, no.4, Autumn 1985, p.737). *Class No:* 908(100)(058)

[4424]
The International year book and statesman's who's who 1993/94. 41st ed. East Grinstead, W. Sussex, Reed Information Services, 1953-. cxxviii,752p.++ 675p. tables. ISBN: 0611008327.

1. International and national organizations - 2. States of the world and Dependent states and territories, p.1-752, in a single A-Z sequence (*e.g.* Republic of Kirghizstan: constitution and government; area and population; finance; banks; production; industry and commerce; education; communications; religion; newspapers) - 3. Biographical section (632p.). No index. *Class No:* 908(100)(058)

[4425]
The Statesman's year-book statistical and historical annual of the states of the world for the year 1993-1994.. Hunter, B. 130th ed. London, Macmillan Reference Books, x;v,1710p. *c.*1730p. tables, diagrs., graphs, maps. £37.50. ISBN: 0333558367.

Pt.1. International organizations. Pt.2. Countries of the world A-Z. Commonwealth of Independent States has separate sections for Former USSR/CIS; Russia; Ukraine; Belorussia; Armenia, Azerbaijan; Moldavia; Central Asia; Kazekhstan; Kirghizia; Tajikstan; Turkmenistan; and Uzbekistan. *Class No:* 908(100)(058)

Nomenclatures

[4426]
WILCOCKS, J. Countries and islands of the world a guide to nomenclature. 2nd ed. London, Clive Bingley, 1985. vii, 124p. bibliog. £11.50. ISBN: 0851573835.

First published 1981.

'A reference guide to the many changes in name and government in states all over the world in modern historical times'. *Class No:* 908(100)(083.72)

Maps & Atlases

[4427]

BOYD, A. An Atlas of world affairs. 9th ed. London, Routledge, 1991. 240p. maps, index. £35. ISBN: 0415066247.

1st ed. 1957 published by Methuen; 8th ed. by Routledge in 1987.

Arranged in 10 thematic sections (*e.g.* oil, nuclear geography) and 63 geo-political sections (*e.g.* Russia's territorial gains, Northern Seas, Suez and Indian Ocean). Long-serving general guide to international affairs since 1945. Still no mention of international terrorism or maritime piracy. Appendix: Countries and currencies p.219-23. 97 maps. *Class No:* 908(100)(084.3)

[4428]

CHALIAND, G. and RAGEAU, J-P. Strategic atlas: world geopolitics. Harmondsworth, Middlesex, Penguin Books, 1986. 224p. col.maps, col.diagrs., tables. pbk. £6.95. ISBN: 014501175x.

First published as *Atlas stratégique* by Librarie Artheme Fayard (1985). 1st English ed. by Harper & Row (New York, 1985).

Views of the world - The geopoliticians - Cultural factors - Historical context of the contemporary world - A world of oceans - Security perceptions of the United States, the U.S.S.R., and regional and middle powers - National constraints - Economic data - Population factors - North-South - The military balance. World statistical survey p.219-23. Bibliographic references p.224. *Class No:* 908(100)(084.3)

Atlantic Ocean

Bibliographies

[4429]

KING, H.G.R. Atlantic Ocean. Santa Barbara, California and Oxford, Clio Press, 1985. xix, 250p.+2p. map, index. £36.50. $41.50. (*World Bibliographical Series; no. 61.*) ISBN: 1851090045.

913 annotated entries. 16 sections: The Atlantic region in general - History - The Atlantic as a strategic military area and contemporary foreign relations ... Tourism ... Research institutions, libraries, art galleries, museums and archives ... Atlantic islands in general - North Atlantic Islands - South Atlantic islands. Author, title and subject index. *Class No:* 908(261)(01)

Pacific Ocean

Bibliographies

[4430]

MAURICIO, R., *comps*. Pacific Basin and Oceania. Fry, G.W. Santa Barbara, California and Oxford, Clio Press, 1987. xxxvi, 468p. + 2p. maps, index. £64.95; $55.00. (*World Bibliographical Series, no.70.*) ISBN: 1851090150.

1178 annotated entries. 38 sections: The Pacific region in general - History - Law of the sea ... Tourism and travel accounts - Small boat voyages - Periodicals - Research institutions, libraries and archives - The Pacific Islands in general - Prehistory and archaeology - Geography - History ... Libraries, archives, and museums - Periodicals - Bibliographies - Contemporary foreign relations - Melanesia

.... (contd.)
- The islands of Melanesia - Micronesia - The islands of Micronesia - Polynesia - The islands of Polynesia - Other Pacific Islands. Single author, title, subject index. *Class No:* 908(265)(01)

Indian Ocean

Bibliographies

[4431]

CRAWCOUR, P. *and* HOLT, S., *eds*. The Indian Ocean a select bibliography of resources for study in the National Library of Australia. Canberra, National Library of Australia, 1979. ix, 190p. index, softcover. ISBN: 0642991502.

Over 6200 entries arranged in 7 sections with form, thematic and geographical sub-divisions: 1. History and social sciences - 2. Island studies - 3. Science - 4. Manuscripts - 5. Confidential prints - 6. Pictorial material - 7. Maps and charts. 'The only comprehensive bibliography of the Indian Ocean region available at present' (J.J. Gotthold. *Indian Ocean.* 1988. Entry 656). *Class No:* 908(267)(01)

[4432]

GOTTHOLD, J.J., *comp*. Indian Ocean. Santa Barbara, California and Oxford, Clio Press, 1988. xxix, 329p.+2p., map, index. £47.95. $55.00. (*World Bibliographical Series; no.85.*) ISBN: 1851090347.

804 annotated entries. 12 sections: The Indian Ocean in general - History (8 subdivisions) ... Atlases, maps and charts ... Encyclopaedias, yearbooks, indexes and gazetteers ... Bibliographies - Indian Ocean island groups. *Class No:* 908(267)(01)

Developing Countries

Encyclopaedias

[4433]

KURIAN, G.T. Encyclopedia of the Third World. 4th ed. New York, Facts on File, 3v., 1992. lv,2363p. illus., diagrs., tables, maps, bibliog., index. £125. ISBN: 0816022615.

First published in 2v. 1979; revised edition 3v. 1981.

Europa year-book type data and discursive text describing the dominant political, economic and social systems of 126 countries A-Z. Bibliography p.2241-56. *Class No:* 908(4/9-77)(031)

Handbooks & Manuals

[4434]

ARNOLD, G. Third World Handbook. London, Cassell, New York, St. James Press 1989. 221p. illus., maps. index. £14.95; $45. ISBN: 0304321915, UK; 1558621490, US.

9 chapters: 1. End of empires - 2. The United Nations - 3. The Third World and non-alignment - 4. The (six) regional groupings (p.56-136) - 5. Aid and its agencies - 6. OPEC and oil power - 7. A new international economic order - 8. The population factor - 9. Resources and exploitation. Country gazetteers (statistical informtion) p.189-205. *Class No:* 908(4/9-77)(035)

[4435]
Third World guide 93/94. Montevideo, Instituto del Tercer Mundo, 1992. Available in UK, Oxford, Oxfam Publications. 631p. maps, diagrs., tables, bibliog., index. £19.95. ISBN: 0855982160, UK. ISSN: 07974779.

First published published in Mexico as *Guia de tercer mundo* (1979). First English language edition 1985.

Issues and perspectives (p.31-112) includes demography, children and education, food, labour, migration, human rights, indigenous peoples, sport, health, power and poverty, debt, non-alignment, cartography *etc.* Countries of the world A-Z p.191-583. Profiles (external debt, history, geography, demography) and Indicators (population, education, commerce, armed forces, economy public expenditure). '*Third World Guide* can be characterized as a *Europa Yearbook* written from a Third World perspective. Clearly, it does not provide an objective treatment, but libraries seeking an alternative perspective may find this volume useful.' (*Booklist,* v.86, no.12, 15 February 1990, p.119).
Class No: 908(4/9-77)(035)

Dictionaries

[4436]
HADJOR, K.B. Dictionary of Third World terms. London, I.B. Tauris, 1992. 303p. £24.95. ISBN: 1850433461.

Additional entries in *Penguin dictionary of Third World Terms.* 1993. £6.99. 0140512934.

Entries include short factual items, biographical data on key Third World figures, information on economic and social realities, and discursive and critical summaries of controversial words and concepts. *Class No:* 908(4/9-77)(038)

[4437]
KURIAN, G.T. Glossary of the Third World: words for understanding Third World peoples and cultures. New York and Oxford, Facts On File,1989. 300p. $45.00. ISBN: 0816018421.

This A-Z list of mostly non-English terms is intended 'to survey, explore, and illustrate the rich variety of Third World cultures' and to complement the author's *Encyclopedia of the Third World.* Its organization, conceptual basis, and contents are described as limited in *Choice* (v.27, no.3, November 1988, p.466).
Class No: 908(4/9-77)(038)

Maps & Atlases

[4438]
KURIAN, G.T. Atlas of the Third World. 2nd ed. New York and Oxford, Facts on File, 1989. 400p. maps, tables, bibliog., index. $175.00. ISBN: 0816019304.

1st ed. 1983. Companion to *Encyclopaedia of the Third World.*

Comprehensive selection of maps and statistical information in graphic form. 1. Introduction provides a review and interpretation of the data presented - 2. Thematic profiles: 14 topics identified as critical issues in Third World development - 3. 80 Country profiles A-Z concentrating on natural resources, population, and social and economic performance. Over 600 maps and 2000 charts and graphs. 'Because of the mamy revisions and the new countries that were not in existence in 1982, the *Encyclopedia* is a worthwhile purchase even for libraries that own the earlier edition. The dynamic conditions in much of the Third World

....(contd.)
merit the publication and purchase of a new edition every five years'. (*Reference Books Bulletin 1987-1988,* p.140).
Class No: 908(4/9-77)(084.3)

Europe

Bibliographies

[4439]
KREWSON, M.B. The German-speaking countries of Europe a selective bibliography. 2nd ed. Washington, Library of Congress, 1989. 318p.

1st ed. 1985.

Entries on Austria, East Germany, West Germany, Liechtenstein and Switzerland arranged in 7 sections: 1. Bibliographies and reference works - 2. Description and travel - 3. Economy - 4. Intellectual and cultural life - 5. Politics and government - 6. Religion - 7. Society.
Class No: 908(4)(01)

Europe—Western

[4440]
Western Europe 1993 a political and economic survey. 2nd ed. London, Europa Publications, 1992. xiv,640p. £165. (*Regional Surveys of the World.*) ISBN: 0946683747. ISSN: 09536906.

1st ed. 1989.

Section 1. 7 introductory essays presenting an overview of important and topical issues relating to the region as a whole. Section 2. Analytical surveys A-Z by country or territory under 8 subject headings: Geography; Recent history and politics; Economy; Social (health and welfare, immigration, education, religion); Media; Transport; Tourism; and a select bibliography. Covers all member countries of the European Communities and of the European Free Trade Association plus Cyprus, Malta and Turkey. Revised editions are expected every 2 years. 'These surveys are a prime source for informed, to the point and up-to-date information on all the countries covered in the volume'. (*Reference Reviews,* v.7, no.7, 1993, p.40).
Class No: 908(400)

Yearbooks & Directories

[4441]
MAYNE, R., *ed.* **Western Europe.** London, Muller; New York, Facts on File, 1986,. xvii,699p. $45.00. ISBN: 0584700075.

29 contributors. Pt.1: The Countries of Western Europe (basic information for each country A-Z). Pt.2: General (*i.e.,* political, social and economic affairs essays). Pt.3: Western European integration (complete guide to the structure and functioning of all principal Western European organizations).
Class No: 908(400)(058)

Europe—Eastern

Bibliographies

[4442]
The American bibliography of Slavic and East European studies. Prepared at the Library of Congress for American Association for the Advancement of Slavic Studies, 1972 - Annual. ISSN: 00943770.

Succeeds *American bibliography of Russian and East European studies,* 1955-66 (Bloomington, Indiana Univ., 1957-67, 11v.).

1985 (1987). Index. 5474 entries from US and Canadian publications divided into 17 sections *e.g.* 1. General ... 6. Geography, demography, travel ... 8. History - 9. International relations ... 17. Obituaries.
Class No: 908(401)(01)

[4443]
Bibliographic guide to Soviet and East European studies. Boston, Mass., G.K. Hall, 1978-. Annual.

1992 (3v.), 1993. viii,587p.,541p.,653p. ISBN 0816116822 lists all publications on or from the Soviet Union and Eastern Europe catalogued during the past year by the Research Libra;ries of New York Public Library with additional entries from LC MARC tapes. It is, in effect, an annual supplement to the New York Public Library's *Dictionary catalog of the Slavonic Collection* (2nd ed. G.K. Hall, 1974, 44v). *Class No:* 908(401)(01)

[4444]
JOHANN-GOTTFRIED-HERDER-INSTITUT Marburg. **Alphabetischer Katalog der Bibliothek.** Boston, Mass., G.K. Hall, 5v., 1964. 3022p. $495.00 (Export $598.00). ISBN: 0816106983.

First Supplement. 1971. 4 reels. $215.00 (Export $260.00). ISBN 0816113998 is no longer available in printed book form. *Second Supplement.* 3v., 1981. 1608p. $365.00 ($440.00). ISBN 0816102775. Total of 135,700 photolithographed catalogue cards. The Bibliothek des Johann-Gottfried-Herder-Instituts, founded in 1950, is the reference library of the largest research institute for East Central Europe in the Federal Republic of Germany. Its holdings encompass older as well as current books on East Central European political, legal, economic, and cultural history; geography; and ethnography. In scope and size, the Herder Library is considered unique in the Western world.
Class No: 908(401)(01)

[4445]
MAGOCSI, P.R. Carpatho-Rusyn studies: an annotated bibliography. New York, Garland, 1988-. viii, 143p. maps, index. (*Garland Reference Library of The Humanities; no. 824.*) ISBN: 0824058364.

V.1 *1975-1984* (1988). V.2 planned for publication 1995. 649 extensively annotated entries arranged on an annalistic basis. 4 Appendices: Transliteration tables; Language, subject and places of publication. The Carpatho-Rusyn area is defined as far western Ukraine, the Lemko region of Poland, the Prešov region of north-east Czechoslovakia, and the Vojvodinian villages of Yugoslavia. The present intention is for future volumes to appear at 10 year intervals.
Class No: 908(401)(01)

[4446]
NEW YORK PUBLIC LIBRARY. RESEARCH LIBRARIES. Dictionary catalog of the Slavonic Collection. 2nd ed. Boston, Mass., G.K. Hall, 44v., 1974. 1st ed. 1959.

Now available only on microfilm (88 reels). $3960.00 (Export $4790.00). ISBN 0816112649. 727,000 photlithographed catalogue cards covering works written in Slavonic or Baltic languages. Supplemented annually by the *Bibliographic guide to Soviet and Eastern European studies.*
Class No: 908(401)(01)

[4447]
Slavic studies a guide to bibliographies, encyclopedias, and handbooks. Croucher, M., *comps.* Wilmington, Delaware, Scholarly Resources, 2v., 1993. xiv,986p. ISBN: 0842023747.

5210 items relating to Slavic studies in English, German, French and Slavic languages. Vol.1: Area studies, Eastern Europe and the Balkans, Bulgaria, Czechoslovakia, Poland. Vol.2: Soviet Union, Former Yugoslavia, General references. Author and title indexes. 'It contains only reference works that, arranged by subject, allow researchers to find materials in their areas of interest without having to know the author or title of any specific work' (*Introduction*).
Class No: 908(401)(01)

Encyclopaedias

[4448]
KURIAN, G. and KARCH, J. Encyclopedia of the Second World. New York and Oxford, Facts On File, 1991. 614p. maps,. charts, tables, bibliog., index. $95. £85. ISBN: 0816012326.

National profiles (at Janaury 1990) of Albania, Bulgaria, China, Czechoslovakia, East Germany, Hungary, Mongolia, Poland, Rumania, Soviet Union, and Yugoslavia, provide information on over 30 subject fields (*e.g.* geographical features, historical background, human rights, defence, foreign policy). By virtue of unfortunate timing now largely outdated by events although it remains 'a valuable source of historical information on the rise and reign of communism in these eleven countries' (*Wilson Library Bulletin,* v.65,no.10, June 1991, p.134). *Class No:* 908(401)(031)

Handbooks & Manuals

[4449]
HORAK, S.M., *and others.* **Eastern European national minorities 1919-1980: a handbook.** Littleton, Colorado, Libraries Unlimited, 1985. xi, 353p. index. £60.25; $47.50. ISBN: 0872874168.

Chapter 1 brings national minorities into focus. Chapters 2-9 discuss their treatment in the countries of Eastern Europe and the Balkans. Chapter 10, Nationality Research Centres. 'An excellent research tool' (*Choice,* v.22, no.11/12, July/ August 1985, p.1614). *Class No:* 908(401)(035)

Yearbooks & Directories

[4450]
Eastern Europe and the Commonwealth of Independent States 1992. London, Europa, 1991. Distributed in North America by Gale Research Co. 512p. maps, tables, bibliogs. £185. (*Regional Surveys of the World.*) ISBN: 0946653771.

Over 30 specialist contributors. Part 1. Background to the

....(contd.)

region *i.e.* introductory essays *e.g.* Nationalism in the USSR - 2. Eastern Europe. Individual country chapters A-Z on Albania, Bulgaria, Czechoslovakia, Hungary, Poland, Romania and Yugoslavia, with sections on the constituent republics within federal countries, including a geographical profile, chronology, essays on recent history and the economy, statistical survey and directory material on the constitution, government, defence and military, foreign embassies, judicial system, news media, finance, trade, tourism, industry, *etc.* and a bibliography - 3. USSR containing 11 essays covering political and economic affairs and similar sections to those in Part 2. - 4.Key personalities of the region, brief biographical details of major political figures. *Class No:* 908(401)(058)

Great Britain

[4451]

BRITISH COUNCIL. Studying and living in Britain 1991. Plymouth, Northcote House in association with the British Council, 1991. Annual. 90p. pbk. £3.25. ISBN: 0746306237.

Completely revised in 1984 and updated annually.

Information and advice for overseas students and other first-time visitors to Britain on how to make the decision to come, arriving, how to find accommodation, costs, customs and services, and on the British way of life. *Class No:* 908(410)

[4452]

The Guinness UK data book. Caprenter, C., *ed.* Enfield, Mdx., Guinness Publishing, 1992. 192p. col. illus., col. maps, col. diagrs., col. tables, index. £9.99. ISBN: 0851125220.

Compendium of statistics, analyses and overviews of all aspects of contemporary Britain: 1. United Kingdom - 2. Physical geography - 3. Environment - 4. Royal Family - 5. Government - 6. Local government - 7. Cities - 8. Social trends - 9. Economy - 10. Law - 11. Defence - 12. International affairs - 13. Transport - 14. Education - 15. Religion - 16. Arts - 17. Media - 18. Sport. *Class No:* 908(410)

Bibliographies

[4453]

JACKSON, P. British sources of information: a subject guide and bibliography. London and New York, Routledge & Kegan Paul, 1987. xvii, 526p. £35.00. ISBN: 0710206968.

4 Parts: 1. The select bibliography (40 chaps.) e.g., Commonwealth and Europe ... Geography ... History ... Northern Ireland ... Scotland ... Travel and tourism in Britain ... Wales - 2. Periodicals, journals, magazines (24 chaps.) - 3. Sources of Information (33 chaps.) - 4. Teaching resources. 'This subject guide to books and sources aims to provide assistance above all to the general reader but also to the student and teacher in locating texts, information and teaching resources on major aspects of British life, society and culture' (*Preface*). *Class No:* 908(410)(01)

Encyclopaedias

[4454]

GASCOIGNE, B. Encyclopaedia of Britain. London, Macmillan, 1993. 720p. £29.95. ISBN: 0333547640.

6000 A-Z cross-referenced entries covering every aspect of British life and history with specific fact-box items. 'A highly successful attempt to distil virtually a reference library into a single book' (*Reference Reviews,* v.8, no.1, 1994, p.43. *Class No:* 908(410)(031)

Dictionaries

[4455]

JACOBS, A. *and* **MONK, J.,** *eds.* **The Cambridge illustrated dictionary of British heritage.** Cambridge, Cambridge Univ. Press, 1987. viii,484p. illus., maps, bibliog., index. £14.95; $24.95. ISBN: 0521302145.

'Encapsulates the essence of Britain and British life in 1500 entries, 200-300 words in length. Fields covered include arts; buildings; ceremonies; cuisine; customs; education; finance; geography; government; history; languages; law; monarchy; monuments; organizations; religion; societies; and sports. Bibliography (by topic) p.480-3. *Class No:* 908(410)(038)

Yearbooks & Directories

[4456]

GREAT BRITAIN Central Office of Information. **Britain 1994** an official handbook. 45th ed. London, HMSO, 1993. vii,518p. col. illus., maps, diagrs., tables, index. £21. ISBN: 0117017590.

All the latest facts, figures, and developments about British life in 31 sections arranged in 6 groups: 1. Britain and its people - 2. Government and administration - 3. Economic affairs - 4. External Affairs - 5. Environment - 6. Social and cultural affairs. Appendix: Government Departments and Agencies; Recent legislation; Britains economy: statistical annex; Citizen's Charter initiative; Obituaries. *Class No:* 908(410)(058)

Scotland

Bibliographies

[4457]

GRANT, E.G., *comp.* **Scotland.** Santa Barbara, California and Oxford, Clio Press. 1982. xxi, 408p.+1p., map, index. £49.95. $55.00. (*World Bibliographical Series; no.34.*) ISBN: 090345064x.

1408 annotated entries. 34 sections: The country and its people - Geography and geology - Tourism - Travel, topography and local history ... Prehistory and archaeology - History - Genealogy, clans and military history ... Libraries, museums and art galleries ... Bibliographies. Addresses of Scottish publishers p. xvii-xxi. Author, title and subject index. *Class No:* 908(411)(01)

[4458]

GREAT BRITAIN. HM Stationery Office. **Government Publications Sectional List 71, revised June 1989: Scotland.** London and Edinburgh, HMSO, 1989. 46p. index, sd. *gratis.*

HMSO publications relating to Scotland in print December

....*(contd.)*

1988 listed by relevant Department: Ancient Monuments Board for Scotland - Scottish Tourist Board. *Class No:* 908(411)(01)

Ireland

[4459]

Facts about Ireland. 6th ed. Dublin, Department of Foreign Affairs, Government of Ireland, 1985. 225p. col.illus., col.maps, tables, index. £5.75. ISBN: 0906404215.

1st ed. 1963.

General overview of Irish life in 7 main sections: 1. Land and people - 2. The Irish State - 3. Culture and the sciences - 4. The economy - 5. Services (e.g., education, health service, social services) - 6. Northern Ireland - 7. Ireland and the world. Bibliography p.251-2. *Class No:* 908(415)

Bibliographies of Bibliographies

[4460]

EAGER, A.R. A Guide to Irish bibliographical material a bibliography of Irish bibliographies and sources of information. 2nd ed. London, Library Association, Westport, Connecticut, Greenwood Press, 1980. xv, 502p. £55. ISBN: 0853659311, UK; 0313223432, US.

1st ed. 1964.

9,517 unannotated entries (5,700 more than 1st ed).

Sections: General works (bibliography; librarianship; periodicals; newspapers; directories and almanacs; museums; manuscripts; incunabula; binding; censorship) - Philosophy - Religion - Sociology - Philology - Science - Useful arts - Fine arts - Literature - Geography, travel - Biography - History (by period; Ulster, Connaught; Leinster; Munster; The Irish abroad).

Object: 'to provide a bibliographic index covering Irish enumerative bibliography and aims to serve as a quick reference guide to all who are interested in Irish studies and research studies' (*Introduction*). Includes unpublished material and work in progress. 'This excellent guide ... can be recommended enthusiastically' (*Choice*, v.18 no.9 May 1981, p.1234). *Class No:* 908(415)(009)

Bibliographies

[4461]

SHANNON, M.O. Modern Ireland: a bibliography on politics, planning, research, and development. Westport, Connecticut, Greenwood Press; London. The Library Association. 1981. xxvi, 733p. indexes. £55.00; $67.95. ISBN: 0853659141, UK; 0313229031, US.

5425 entries (some briefly annotated), with particular emphasis on items relating to the 20th century, grouped in 29 sections e.g., 1. General (reference works and bibliographies) - 2. History ... 7. Islands ... 23. Major regions of the Republic - 24. Dublin ... 26. Belfast - 27. Selected counties and towns of Northern Ireland. Name, subject and geographical indexes. *Class No:* 908(415)(01)

Encyclopaedias

[4462]

DE BREFFNY, B. Ireland: a cultural encyclopaedia. London, Thames & Hudson, 1983. 256p. illus., map. ISBN: 0500013047.

45 contributors Over 600 initialled cross-referenced entries reflecting the 'aesthetic endeavour of a people and the manifestation of their intellectual, artistic and even social development' (*Introduction*). Bibliographical references to most entries. *Class No:* 908(415)(031)

Northern Ireland

Bibliographies

[4463]

DEUTSCH, R.R. Northern Ireland a select bibliography. New York, Garland, 1975. viii, 142p. ISBN: 0824010604.

About 1,000 concisely annotated entries. A. Non-fiction (1. Bibliographies and reference works; 2. Official publications (UK; Republic of Ireland); 3. Newspapers; 4. General works; 5. Selected works; 6. Relevant chapters; 7. Articles; 8 Pamphlets) - B. Fiction (Novels, Plays, Poetry, Songs) - C. Index of authors. Chronology, p.v-viii. 'Most important for students of Irish or British history' (*Library journal*, v.100, no.18, 15 October 1975, p.1907).
Class No: 908(416)(01)

[4464]

GREAT BRITAIN. HM Stationery Office. **Government Publications Sectional list 72, revised 1 November 1987: Northern Ireland.** London and Belfast, HMSO, 1988. 16p. sd. *gratis.*

HMSO publications for all Northern Ireland government departments A-Z. Does not include Northern Ireland Assembly titles. *Class No:* 908(416)(01)

[4465]

SHANNON, M.O., *comp.* **Northern Ireland.** Santa Barbara, Calif., and Oxford, 1991. xxxviii,603p. +1p. map. indexes. £79. (*World Bibliographical Series, no. 129.*) ISBN: 1851090320.

1962 annotated entries in 52 sections: Province and its people - Geography - Tourism and travel guides - City and regional guides ... Prehistory - Archaeology - History - Biography ... Military, police and security forces ... Encyclopaedias and directories - Bibliographies. Glossary p. xxxi-xxxviii. *Class No:* 908(416)(01)

Eire

Bibliographies

[4466]

SHANNON, M.O., *comp.* **Irish Republic.** Santa Barbara, California and Oxford, Clio Press, 1986. xxiv, 404p. +1p. map, index. £59.95. $55.00. (*World Bibliographical Series; no.69.*) ISBN: 1851090142.

1459 annotated entries. 48 sections: The country and its people - Geography - Travellers' accounts - Tourism and travel guides - City and regional studies ... Prehistory - Archaeology - History ... Genealogy ... Libraries ... Encyclopaedias and directories - Bibliographies. Glossary p.xxiii-xxiv. Author, title and subject index.
Class No: 908(417)(01)

Yearbooks & Directories

[4467]

Ireland: a directory 1990. O'Donnell, J., *ed.* 24th ed. Dublin, Institute of Public Administration. An Foras Riaracháin, 1989. 448p. ports., index. ISBN: 1872002250. ISSN: 00739596.

'A complete directory of Irish life, covering the private as well as the public sector': Legislature, executive and judiciary - Diplomatic representation - Civil service - Defence forces - Garda Siochána - Local administration - Public voluntary hospitals - State-sponsored bodies - Financial institutions - Major companies and corporations - Communications - Higher education - Religious denominations - Trade & professional organizations - Social, cultural and political organizations - Northern Ireland - European Community - International organizations - Institute of Public Administration - Statistics - General information. *Class No:* 908(417)(058)

Commonwealth

[4468]

The Commonwealth Ministers reference book 1989/90. MacLeish, M., *ed.* London, Kensington Publications in conjunction with the Commonwealth Secretariat, 1989. 583p. illus.

Apart from the list of Commonwealth Ministers, A-Z by member state (p.13-19) there is very little of true reference value in this publication. Most of its 18 sections are essentially promotional literature contributed by various major commercial or industrial firms. *Class No:* 908(41-44)

[4469]

LARBY, P.M. *and* **HANNAM, H. The Commonwealth.** Oxford, Clio Press, 1993. xxxvii,254p.+ 3p. maps, index. (*International Organizations Series, no.5.*) ISBN: 1851091866.

970 annotated entries under 36 headings: Countries of the Commonwealth ... History ... Constitutional development ... Archives and manuscripts - Bibliographies ... Reference works - Research. Author, title and subject index. Both authors are senior librarians well versed in Commonwealth studies. *Class No:* 908(41-44)

Bibliographies

[4470]

The Catalogues of the Library of the Institute of Commonwealth Studies, University of London. Cambridge, Chadwyck-Healey, 1979. 1. £180.00. 2. £250.00. 3. £10.00. 4. £100.00. Complete set £475.00.

Author catalogue: 55,000 catalogue cards on 136 microfiche - Subject catalogue: 81,000 cards on 195 fiche - Periodicals catalogue: 1,500 cards on 5 fiche - Bibliography of bibliographies: 9,000 pages on 30 fiche. Individual catalogues are available separately. Subject coverage includes the history of the Commonwealth and its member states since 1850; relations between them; and political, economic and social problems. Since the 1960s the Library has specialised in acquisitions from the Commonwealth Caribbean. *Class No:* 908(41-44)(01)

[4471]

HANNAM, H. *and* **LARBY, P.M.** 'Commonwealth Studies' *British Book News,* November 1985, p.578-83.

Literature review on modern Commonwealth under 8 subject headings including 1. Empire into Commonwealth - 2. Commonwealth Secretariat. Bibliography p.581-3. *Class No:* 908(41-44)(01)

[4472]

ROYAL COMMONWEALTH SOCIETY. Subject catalogue of the Library of the Royal Empire Society, formerly the Royal Colonial Institute. Lewin, E., *comp.* London, The Society, 4v., 1930-37. Reprinted Dawsons Pall Mall Press 1967.

1: *British Empire generally, and Africa.*

2: *Australia, New Zealand, South Africa. General voyages and travels, Arctic and Antarctic.*

3: *Canada, Newfoundland, West Indies, Colonial America.*

4: *Mediterranean dependencies, Middle East, India, Burmah, Ceylon, Malaya, East Indies, Far East.*

The Royal Commonwealth Society Library contains an estimated 400,000 items. Geographical areas are divided by subjects; final chronological order. Although the Society's library was damaged in World War II, and the catalogue no longer strictly applies to it, the listing remains an indispensable bibliography. 'Perhaps the finest private library on imperial history in the world' (Flint, J.E. *Books on the British Empire and Commonwealth* (1968), Foreword).

Supplemented by: *Biography catalogue of the Library of the Royal Commonwealth Society,* edited by Donald H. Simpson (1961, xxiii, 511p. and *Manuscript catalogue of the Library of the Royal Commonwealth Society,* also edited by Donald H. Simpson (London, Mansell, 1975).

The *Subject catalogue* and *Biography catalogue* are updated in *Subject catalogue of the Royal Commonwealth Society* (Boston, Mass., G.K. Hall, 1971, 7v.; *First supplement.* 1977. 2v.) reproducing a total of 157,000 catalogue cards. *Class No:* 908(41-44)(01)

Handbooks & Manuals

[4473]

The Commonwealth factbook: facts and figures about Commonwealth countries. 5th ed. London, Commonwealth Secretariat, 1992. 76p. map, tables, diagrs. £5.00.

Factual geographical, political, social, economic and statistical information in 3 pts: 1. Member countries - 2. Associated states and dependencies - 3. Tables and charts. *Class No:* 908(41-44)(035)

Theses

[4474]

INSTITUTE OF COMMONWEALTH STUDIES. University of London. **Theses in progress** a cumulative list November 1989. London, the Institute, 1989. v.57p. ISSN: 02674513.

Not published since October 1986, but it is now hoped regular annual publication will be resumed.

'Contains all titles believed to be still in progress noted to October 1989' (*Introduction*). Sections: Commonwealth - Africa - Americas - Asia - Mediterranean and Middle East - Pacific area - Other material. Restricted to British theses although Appendix 1. lists overseas students admitted to the Institute 1986-1989. *Class No:* 908(41-44)(043)

Yearbooks & Directories

[4475]

The Commonwealth yearbook 1992. 6th ed. London, HMSO. vii,541p. col. illus., pbk. index. £22.50. ISBN: 0115917101.

Formerly *A yearbook of the Commonwealth* (1969-1986) itself a successor to the *Commonwealth Office yearbook.*

Pt.1: The Commonwealth in 1991 (Evolution of the modern Commonwealth; Organization of British Government relations with other Commonwealth countries and administration of dependent territories) - 2. Government offices in London - 3. Commonwealth Secretariat and other institutions - 4. Member countries of the Commonwealth A-Z - 5. Dependent territories. - 6. Statistics (geographical, economic, trade *etc.*), national days, and British parliamentary and non-parliamentary Papers of Commonwealth interest - 7. The Overseas Development Agency. A compendious outline of member countries; history, geography, constitution, government, trade, and international policy. *Class No:* 908(41-44)(058)

Manuscripts & Incunabula

[4476]

ROYAL COMMONWEALTH SOCIETY. The Manuscript catalogue of the library ... Simpson, D.H., *ed.* London, Mansell, 1975.

'The word *"manuscript"* has been somewhat liberally interpreted' (*Introduction*) and embraces minute books, letter books, correspondence, autographs and portraits. Sections: Collections (library talks; Walter Frewen Lord Prize essays) - General material (*e.g.* Voyages and travel) - Europe - Asia - Africa (p.77-129) - The Americas - Australasia. Cross-references. Notes on character and provenance of each item. Index of names; index of subjects and organizations. The fourth supplement, 'Manuscripts newly catalogued 1983-1989', is printed in Royal Commonwealth Society *Library Notes*, no. 293 (new series), October 1989, p.1-5. Previous supplements appeared in issues nos. 217, 225 and 253. 'Certainly no research library in a Commonwealth or ex-Commonwealth country can afford to be without it' (British Book News, September 1975, p.622). *Class No:* 908(41-44)(093)

England

Bibliographies

[4477]

DAY, A.E., *comp.* **England.** Santa Barbara, Calif., and Oxford, Clio Press, 1998. xvii,591p. +1p. map, index. £87.50. (*World Bibliographical Series, no.160.*) ISBN: 1851090401.

2,364 annotated entries arranged in 44 sections: Country and its people - Travellers' accounts - Geography and geology ... Tourism and travel guides - Prehistory and archaeology - History ... Monarchy ... Armed forces and defence ... Directories - Bibliography. Author, title and subject index. *Class No:* 908(420)(01)

London

Bibliographies

[4478]

ADAMS, B. 'London in print', *British Book News,* August 1981, p.455-460.

Review article: General works, guides and pictorial souvenirs; Past, present and future; The Setting: architecture and architects; Communications and open spaces; Living in London; and Bibliography p.458-460. *Class No:* 908(421)(01)

Wales

Bibliographies

[4479]

HUWS, G. *and* **ROBERTS, D.H.E.,** *comp.* **Wales.** Santa Barbara, Calif., and Oxford, Clio Press, 1991. xv,247p. +1p. map, indexes. (*World Bibliographical Series, no.122.*) ISBN: 1851091181.

876 annotated entries arranged in 33 sections: Country and its people - Geography and geology - Tourism and travel ... Prehistory and archaeology - History and genealogy ... Welsh overseas - Libraries, art galleries, museums and archives - Books ... Directories - Bibliographies. Author, subject and title indexes. *Class No:* 908(429)(01)

[4480]

JONES, S.R., *comp.* **Books of Welsh interest.** Aberystwyth, Cyngor Llyfrau Cymraeg/Welsh Books Council, 1977. 236p. 75p. ISBN: 0950230553.

908 concisely annotated entries. 2 main sections. 1. General (Bibliographies - Geography, geology and natural history ...History and archaeology ... Architecture and fine arts ... Biography and autobiography - Children's books) - 2. Literature (Cultural studies and histories - Anthologies - Works by individual authors and critical studies on them). Index of authors, translators and adaptors; title index; series index. Supplementary list of titles published between September 1976 and March 1977. *Class No:* 908(429)(01)

Germany

[4481]

Berlin handbuch das Lexicon der Bundeshauptstadt. Berlin, Fab Verlag, 1992. 1584p. illus. (some col.), col. plans, col. maps, tables. ISBN: 3927551279.

12 Feature articles and 1440 dictionary entries cover all aspects of Berlin, the revived capital of a united Germany. *Class No:* 908(430)

[4482]

Facts about Germany. Hoffman, A., *ed.* Frankfurt/Main, Societäts-Verlag, 1992. 416p. illus. (many col.), maps, tables, index. ISBN: 3797305222.

Translated from *Tatsachen über Deutschland* (ISBN 3797305125).

Pocketsize handbook: Country and people - History - Political system, constitution, law - Germany in the world - Economy - Society - Education, science, culture. *Class No:* 908(430)

[4483]

German studies: British resources papers presented at a colloquium at the British Library 25-27 September 1985. Organized in conjunction with the Institute of Germanic Studies of the University of London. Paisley, D., *ed.* London, The British Library, 1986. xiv, 321p. £19.50. (*British Library Occasional Papers, no.8.*) ISBN: 0712300961.

Over 600 papers concerned with British Library resources; other UK library resources; training; supply of German publications; and the users perspective. *Class No:* 908(430)

[4484]

PASLEY, M., *ed.* **Germany:** a companion to German studies. 2nd ed. London, Methuen, 1982. viii,690p. maps, geneal. tables, index. pbk. £16.95. ISBN: 0415037042.

First published in 1972 when it was edited by J. Bithell.

A well-documented survey of the main fields of German studies in 10 chapters by different hands *e.g.* 1. The German language ... 3. German history 911 to 1618 - 4. Making of modern Germany 1618-1870 - 5. From Bismarck to the present. Chapter bibliographies. Analytical index. 'The volume should find its place readily on the library shelves' (*Modern Languages,* v.55,no.2, June 1974, p.104). *Class No:* 908(430)

Bibliographies

[4485]

HERSCH, G., *comp.* **A Bibliography of German studies 1945-1971.** Germany under Allied occupation, Federal Republic of Germany. German Democratic Republic. Bloomington, Univ. of Indiana Press, 1972. xvi, 603p. $155.30. ISBN: 0317107860.

About 5,000 entries in 7 sections: 1. Germany under Allied Occupation - 2. The German question - 3. The Federal Republic of Germany (p.54-373) - 4. The German Democratic Republic (p.374-498) - 5. Biographical materials on contemporary Germans - 6. Government publications - 7. German newspapers and periodicals. Author, title and subject indexes. *Class No:* 908(430)(01)

[4486]

WALLACE, W., *comp.* **Berlin.** Santa Barbara, Calif., Oxford, Clio Press, 1993. c.180p. map, index. £28. (*World Bibliographical Series, no.155.*) ISBN: 1851091424.

c.429 annotated entries on many aspects of the city including tourism, flora and fauna, transport, planning, literature, and architecture. *Class No:* 908(430)(01)

Federal Republic of Germany

Bibliographies

[4487]

DETWEILER, D.S. *and* **DETWEILER, J.E.,** *comps.* **West Germany** The Federal Republic of Germany. Santa Barbara, California and Oxford, Clio Press, 1987. xv, 353p.+1p. map, index. £49.95. $55.00. (*World Bibliographical Series; no.72.*) ISBN: 1851090177.

534 annotated entries. 35 sections: The country and its people: Reference and general works - Geography ... Prehistory and archaeology - History ... West Berlin and it special status ... Archives, libraries and museums - Directories and encyclopaedias - Bibliographies. Author,

....(contd.)

title and subject index. 'An essential bibliographical guide' (*Choice,* v.26, no.11-12, July-August 1989, p.1809). *Class No:* 908(430.1)(01)

German Democratic Republic

[4488]

Information GDR the comprehensive and authoritative reference source of the German Democratic Republic. The GDR Academy of Sciences, Panorama DDR and Intertext Berlin, GDR, *comps.* Oxford, New York, Frankfurt, Pergamon Press, 2v., 1989. xxi,819p. illus. (many col.), col. maps, tables, bibliog., index. £200. (*Countries Of The World Information Series.*) ISBN: 0080370659.

34 contributors. Part 1. Land and people - 2. History (p.85-205) - 3. Foreign policy - 4. System of government - 5. National economy - 6. Science - 7. Environment - 8. Living conditions - 9. Health and social services - 10. Education - 11. Arts and media - 12. Religious affairs - 13. Sport - 14. Tourism. Bibliography p.781-90. 36 colour plates. 8 maps. Subject index p.781-819. 'Presents the GDR's view of itself' (*Preface*). Now an historical curiosity. *Class No:* 908(430.2)

Bibliographies

[4489]

WALLACE, J. East Germany. Santa Barbara, California and Oxford, Clio Press, 1987. xviii, 293p.+1p., map, index. £40.95. $51.50. (*World Bibliographical Series, no.77.*) ISBN: 1851090231.

739 annotated entries. 36 sections: The country and its people - Geography - Tourism and travel guides - Travellers' accounts and descriptions of East Germany by GDR citizens, émigrés from GDR and Westerners ... History ... Berlin (East), the Wall and escapes ... Reference works - Bibliographies - Documentary collections. Author, title and subject index. *Class No:* 908(430.2)(01)

Handbooks & Manuals

[4490]

DDR Handbuch. Bundesministerium für innerdeutsche Beziehungen, *ed.* Köln, Verlag Wissenschaft und Politik, 2v., 1985. xlviii, 1660p. tables, softcovers. ISBN: 3804686427.

First published 1975.

Well-documented encyclopaedic dictionary (Checkpoint Charlie, 12 lines; Energiewirtschaft, 8p.). Chronology 1945-1984 p.1560-1615. Bibliography (1300 titles organized under 27 subject headings). p.1616-60. *Class No:* 908(430.2)(035)

Luxembourg

Bibliographies

[4491]

HURY, C. *and* **CHRISTOPHORY, J.,** *comps.* **Luxembourg.** Santa Barbara, California and Oxford, Clio Press, 1981. xx, 184p.+1p. map, index. £24.50. $31.25. (*World Bibliographical Series; no.23.*) ISBN: 0903450372.

487 annotated entries. 39 sections: The country and its

....(contd.)
people - Geography ... Prehistory - Archaeology - History ... Libraries, archives and museums ... Bibliographies. Author, title and subject index. *Class No:* 908(435.9)(01)

Austria

[4492]
Austria, facts and figures. Wien, Federal Press Service, 1984. 239p.

Outline of landscape, climate, vegetation, population. Separate section on each of the 9 provinces. History - Government and politics - Austrian economy - Social services - Sport and recreation - Education - Science - Arts - The media. 'This is a most valuable and authoritative documentary source on Austrian life today and is normally updated at roughly five-yearly intervals ... can be warmly recommended as a definitive background reference work' (D. Salt and A.F. Radley *Austria*, 1986. Entry 375). *Class No:* 908(436)

Bibliographies

[4493]
SALT, D. *and* **RADLEY, A.F.,** *comps.* **Austria.** Santa Barbara, California and Oxford, Clio Press, 1986. xxxviii, 318p. + 1p. map, index. £46.95; $52.25. (*World Bibliographical Series, no. 66.*) ISBN: 1851090096.

847 unannotated entries. 34 sections: The country and its people - Geography- Traveller's accounts ... Prehistory and archaeology - History ... Encyclopaedias, directories and reference works - Museums, libraries, art galleries and archives ... Bibliographies. Glossary p.xxxi-xxxiv. Austrian rulers p.xxxv-xxxviii. Author, title and subject index. *Class No:* 908(436)(01)

Yearbooks & Directories

[4494]
Österreichisches Jahrbuch 1990. Wien, Verlag der Österreichischen Staatsdruckerei. Annual. xvi,783p. tables.

First published 1928.

Government and politics - Domestic and Foreign Policy - Law - Education - Social security - Banking - Economic development - Industry - Trade. Also sections on provincial affairs. Statistics. *Class No:* 908(436)(058)

Czechoslovakia

Bibliographies

[4495]
SHORT, D., *comp.* **Czechoslovakia.** Santa Barbara, California and Oxford, Clio Press, 1986. xxv, 409p.+1p. map, index. £57.50. $55.00. (*World Bibliographical Series, no.68.*) ISBN: 1851090118.

1,000 annotated entries. 41 sections: The country and its people - Geography - Travellers' accounts - Tourism and travel guides ... Prehistory and archaeology - History - Nationalities and minorities ... Encyclopaedias and directories - Archives and libraries - Bibliographies - Document collections. A note on the language of Czechoslovakia p.xxiii-xxv. Author, title and subject index. *Class No:* 908(437)(01)

Poland

Bibliographies

[4496]
KANKA, A.G. Poland: an annotated bibliography of English language sources in English. New York, Garland, 1988. 395p. indexes. $47.00. (*Garland Reference Library of The Humanities, no. 743.*) ISBN: 0824084926.

1585 items relating to books on Poland and the Poles published 1770-1986. Divided into 2 sections: 1. General works and 2. Special works (subdivided under 90 A-Z subject headings). Author and title indexes. *Class No:* 908(438)(01)

[4497]
SANFORD, G. *and* **GOZDECKA-SANFORD, A.,** *comps.* **Poland.** 2nd ed. Santa Barbara, California and Oxford, Clio Press, 1993. xxiii,250p.++1p. map, index. £40.50. (*World Bibliographical Series; no. 32.*) ISBN: 1851091807.

1st ed. 1984.

914 annotated entries: 35 sections: The country and its people - Geography - Tourism and travel ... Prehistory and archaeology - History - Poles abroad ... Encyclopaedias and directories - Bibliographies ... Libraries, archives and museums. *Class No:* 908(438)(01)

Hungary

Bibliographies

[4498]
KABDEBO, T., *comp.* **Hungary.** Santa Barbara, California and Oxford, Clio Press, 1980. lvi, 280p.+1p. map, index. £38.95. $34.75. (*World Bibliographical Series; no.15.*) ISBN: 0903450283.

1094 annotated entries. 37 sections: The country and its people - Geography - Prehistory, archaeology - History ... Libraries, art galleries, museums and archives ... Encyclopaedias, directories - Bibliographies. Glossary p.liv-lvi. Author, title and subject index. *Class No:* 908(439)(01)

Handbooks & Manuals

[4499]
HALÁSZ, Z., *ed.* **Hungary:** a guide with a difference. 3rd ed. Budapest, Corvina Press, 1983. 474p. illus., ports., tables, maps.

1st ed. 1978.

21 contributors. Sections: A brief historical survey - Geography - State organizations of the Hungarian People's Republic - Foreign policy - Recent changes in society - Economy - Foreign trade - Health - Scientific life - Public education and culture - Literature, past and present - Fine arts - Music - Theatre - Film - The mass-media - Sports - Travel guide. Statistics. *Class No:* 908(439)(035)

France

Bibliographies

[4500]
CHAMBERS, F., *comp.* **France.** 2nd ed. Santa Barbara, California and Oxford, Clio Press, 1990. xv,290p.++1p. map, indexes. £52.00; $31.50. (*World Bibliographical Series; no.13.*) ISBN: 1851090827.

1st ed. 1980.

....(contd.)

942 entries in 49 sections: Country and its people - Paris - Maps, atlases and gazetteers - Travel guides ... Prehistory and archaeology - Historiography - History ... Nationalities and minorities ... Fashion - Food and Drink ... Reference works - Bibliographies. Author, title and subject indexes. *Class No:* 908(44)(01)

[4501]
DEUTSCHES - FRANZÖSISCHES INSTITUT Ludwigsburg. **La France contemporaine** guide bibliographique et thématique. Laserre, R., *ed.* Tübingen, Max Niemeyer Verlag, 1978. xii, 743p. bibliog., indexes. ISBN: 3484500913.

526 works examined in detail and 1500 others listed in 8 categories: Histoire - Vie politique - Economie - Travail et vie sociale - Information - Education - Vie culturelle - Littérature et société. Annexe: Liste des ouvrages cités édités en langue allemande p. 695-706. *Class No:* 908(44)(01)

Handbooks & Manuals
[4502]
CHARLTON, D.G., *ed.* **France:** a companion to French studies. 2nd rev. ed. London, Methuen, 1983. 690p. illus., map, pbk. £14.95. ISBN: 0416723101.

1st ed. 1972.

11 contributors. 'Seeks to provide a detailed introduction and guide to the history and culture of France from the time of the Renaissance to the present day' (*Preface to the first edition*). Chapters: 1. Introduction - 2. The Renaissance in France: history, thought and literature - 3. French history and society from the Wars of Religion to the Revolution ... 6. French thought in the nineteenth and twentieth centuries ... 9. French literature since 1870 - 10. French painting, sculpture and architecture since 1500 - 11. French music since 1500 - 12. Contemporary France; politics, society and institutions. French language is not covered. The short chapter-bibliographies in the 1st ed. are replaced by more extended bibliographical essays (*e.g.* 4. 'French history and society from the Revolution to the Fifth Republic', p.119-221, has 4½ pages of bibliography, with commentary. 34 black-and-white plates. Detailed analytical index. Editor is Professor of French in the University of Warwick. A scholarly compendium, well-produced. *Class No:* 908(44)(035)

Monaco
Bibliographies
[4503]
HUDSON, G.L., *comp.* **Monaco.** Santa Barbara, Calif. and Oxford, Clio Press, 1991. xxxiii,193p. +1p. map. index. £30; $70. (*World Bibliographical Series, no.120.*) ISBN: 1851091173.

511 annotated entries arranged in 30 sections: The Principality and its people - Geography and tourism - Travellers' accounts ... Archaeology and prehistory - Genealogy and heraldry ... Casino ... Archives, libraries and museums ... Bibliographies. Reigns of the Lords and Princes of Monaco, House of Grimaldi p.xxix-xxxi. Author, subject and title index. *Class No:* 908(449.49)(01)

Italy
Bibliographies
[4504]
GARVIN, B., *comp.* **Italy.** Santa Barbara, Calif.; Oxford, Clio Press, 1994. (*World Bibliographical Series, no.30.*) ISBN: 0903450445.

Publication announced. *Class No:* 908(450)(01)

[4505]
LOVETT, C.M. Contemporary Italy a selective bibliography. Washington, D.C., Library of Congress, 1985. viii, 106p. indexes, pbk. ISBN: 0317599909.

1280 unannotated entries (books and monographs) organized under 16 subject headings. 90% of entries relate to Italian-language material. For academic researchers in humanities and social sciences. *Class No:* 908(450)(01)

[4506]
SANNA, S.A. Sardinien - Bibliographie. Sardegna una bibliografia. München, Verlag Dokumentation, 1974. 136p. map, index, pbk. ISBN: 3794031806.

1125 unannotated entries arranged under 28 subject headings *e.g.* Altertumswissenschaft ... Geographie ... Geschichte. Author index. *Class No:* 908(450)(01)

Vatican City
Bibliographies
[4507]
WALSH, M.J. Vatican City State. Santa Barbara, California and Oxford, Clio Press, 1983. xxxv, 105p.+2p. plan, index. £18.95. $22.00. (*World Bibliographical Series; no.41.*) ISBN: 0903450720.

368 annotated entries. 18 sections: The city and its citizens - Guides for visitors - Archaeology - History ... Papal Office and Court ... Diplomacy ... Services to culture and scholarship ... Reference works. Introduction (p.xv-xxxv) includes The states of the church; The Popes and their capital; The Roman question; Constitution; Legal status; Administrative organization; College of Cardinals *etc*. Author, title and subject index. *Class No:* 908(456.31)(01)

Yearbooks & Directories
[4508]
L'Attivit à della Santa Sede. Vatican City, Libreria Editrice Vaticana (later Tipografia Poliglotta Vaticana). Annual.

Chronology of the activities of the Pope and of the various Departments of the Vatican during the previous year. 'A useful book for the students of Vatican affairs' (M.J. Walsh. *Vatican City State*, 1983. Entry 365). *Class No:* 908(456.31)(058)

Malta
Bibliographies of Bibliographies
[4509]
XUEREB, P. A Bibliography of Maltese bibliographies. Msida, Univ. of Malta Library, 1978. 18p. index.

121 items based on the Bibliography section of the author's *Melitensia* (Malta Univ. Press, 1974). 24 sections (General then by subjects: Archaeology ... History ... Towns and villages). *Class No:* 908(458.2)(009)

Bibliographies

[4510]

THACKRAH, J.R., *comp*. **Malta.** Santa Barabara, California and Oxford, Clio Press, 1985. xviii, 162p. + 1p. map, index. £25.95. $31.00. (*World Bibliographical Series; no. 64.*) ISBN: 185109007x.

588 annotated entries. 35 sections: The country and its people - Geography and geology - Travellers' accounts - Travel guides and tourism ... Prehistory, archaeology and ethnography - History - Knights of St. John - Genealogy and heraldry... Bibliographies. Theses and dissertations on Malta p. xvii-xviii. Author, title and subject index.

Class No: 908(458.2)(01)

Handbooks & Manuals

[4511]

Malta handbook. Valletta, Information Division, Maltese Government, Annual.

Historical and current data submitted by ministries and government departments. Economic and social conditions, cultural affairs, tourist information.

Class No: 908(458.2)(035)

Yearbooks & Directories

[4512]

Malta year book 1989. Clews, B.H.A., *ed.* Sliema, St. Bonild's School, De la Salle Brothers Publications, 1989. 442p. bibliog., index. softcover.

First published 1953.

Informative annual compendium with historical data, roundup of events, and information on all major aspects of Maltese life and society *e.g.* Malta in prehistory and history p.61-3; Notable dates in Maltese history p.64-6; Libraries p.277-82. Malta bibliography p.280-290. Gozo bibliography p.305-7. Analytical index of articles appearing in the Malta year book 1953-88, p.295-304. Not an official publication.

Class No: 908(458.2)(058)

Spain

[4513]

RUSSELL, P.E., *ed.* **Spain** a companion to Spanish studies. Rev. ed. London, Methuen, 1973. xv, 592p. geneal. tables, maps.

Entirely new version of E. Allison Peers' work (1929). 12 contributors. 12 chapters, each with bibliography. 1. Spain and the Spanish language - 2. Muslim Spain (711-1492) - 3. The medieval kingdoms of the Iberian peninsula - 4. Monarchy and Empire (1474-1700) - 5. Spanish history from 1700 - 6. Spanish literature and learning to 1474-7. Medieval Catalan literature - 8/9. Spanish literature - 10. Spanish American literature - 11. The visual arts in Spain (p.473-542; nearly 7p. of bibliography). Analytical index.

'An invaluable work' (*British Book News*, January 1980, p.74-77). *Class No:* 908(460)

[4514]

Spain 1992. Madrid, Ministerio del Portavoz del Gobierno, 1992. 344p. col. illus. col. map, tables. ISBN: 8487243312.

Published in Spanish, English and French editions.

Official handbook: Geography - Population - History - Culture - Politics - Foreign Affairs - Economy -

....(contd.)

Infrastructure and environment - Health - Social Services - Education - Science and technology - The Media - Spain and the World. *Class No:* 908(460)

Bibliographies

[4515]

SHIELDS, G.J. **Spain.** Santa Barbara, California and Oxford, Clio Press, 1985. xxvi, 340p. + 1p. map, index. £48.95. $55.00. (*World Bibliographical Series; no.60.*) ISBN: 1851090037.

982 annotated entries. 42 sections: The country and its people - Travellers' accounts - Geography - Tourism and travel guides ... Archaeology and prehistory - History - Empire ... Nationalities and minorities ... Armed forces ... Libraries, museums and archives. Encyclopaedias and directories - Bibliographies. Chronology p.xxi-xxiii. Rulers of Spain p.xxv-xxvi. Author, title and subject index.

Class No: 908(460)(01)

Andorra

Bibliographies

[4516]

TAYLOR, B., *comp.* **Andorra.** Santa Barbara, Calif., Oxford, Clio Press, 1993. (*World Bibliographical Series.*) Publication announced. *Class No:* 908(467.2)(01)

Gibraltar

Bibliographies

[4517]

GREEN, M.M. **A Gibraltar bibliography** based on the holdings of the British Library Reference Division and of the libraries of: Royal Institute of International Affairs; Commonwealth Institute; Ministry of Defence; Foreign and Commonwealth Office, Gibraltar Garrison Library; Imperial War Museum; Rhodes House, Oxford; and Royal Commonwealth Society. London, Institute of Commonwealth Studies, Univ. of London, 1980. vi,108p. Mimeographed.

984 unannotated entries. Sections: General - Religion and the church - Sociology - Foreign relations - History (including Warfare) - Science (including Fortifications) - Fine arts - Literature - Travel and description - Biography. Gives up to 3 locations in the libraries concerned. Includes periodical articles. Index of authors and titles of anonymous works. *Supplement* 1981. 30p. *Class No:* 908(468.2)(01)

[4518]

SHIELDS, G.J., *comp.* **Gibraltar.** Santa Barbara, California and Oxford, Clio Press, 1987. xxxiii, 100p. + 2p. map, index. £18.50. (*World Bibliographical Series, no.87.*) ISBN: 1851090452.

260 annotated entries. 28 sections: The Rock and its people - Geography and geology - Travellers' accounts - Guidebooks and maps ... Archaeology and prehistory - History ... Anglo Spanish dispute ... Libraries and museums ... Yearbooks and directories - Bibliographies - Theses and Dissertations. Chronology p.xxxi-xxxiii. Author, title and subject index. *Class No:* 908(468.2)(01)

Yearbooks & Directories

[4519]

The Gibraltar Year Book and Finance Centre handbook.
Garcia, J., *ed*. Gibraltar, Mediterranean Sun Publishing
Co., 1988. 112p. illus. (inc.col.), index.

Events of the year - Calendar - Gibraltar administration -
Treaties and agreements - Reference (*i.e.,* general
information) - Gibraltar Finance Centre.
Class No: 908(468.2)(058)

Portugal

Bibliographies

[4520]

UNWIN, P.T.H. **Portugal**. Santa Barbara, California and
Oxford, Clio Press, 1987. xxxlx, 269p. + 1p. map, index.
£40.95. $50.50. (*World Bibliographical Series; no.71.*)
ISBN: 1851090169.

787 annotated entries. 29 sections: The country and its
people - Geography and geology ... Travellers' accounts -
Tourism - Prehistory and archaeology - History - Overseas
territories ... Bibliographies and catalogues. Author, title and
subject index. *Class No:* 908(469)(01)

USSR

[4521]

AUTY, R. *and* OBOLENSKY, D., *eds*. **Companion to
Russian studies** v.1. Introduction to Russian history.
Cambridge, Cambridge Univ. Press, 1976. xvi, 403p.
general tables, maps. £32.50. ISBN: 0521208939.

10 academic contributors. 10 chapters, each with running
commentary and 'Guide to further reading'. 1. The
geographical setting - 2. Kievan Russia - 3. Appanage and
Muscovite Russia - 4. Imperial Russia: Peter I to Nicholas I -
5. Imperial Russia: Alexander II to the Revolution - 6. Soviet
Russia (p.272-314; 'Guide to further reading'. p.308-14: 14
sections) - 7. The Church - 8. The structure of the Soviet
State: Government and politics - 9. The structure of the
Soviet State: the economy - 10. The Soviet Union and its
neighbours. Partly analytical index, p.393-403. 'Aims at
providing a first orientation for those embarking on the study
of Russian civilization, past and present, in its most
important aspects' (*Preface*), although it does omit military
history. 'A particularly substantial introduction to the study
of Russia, whether for readers within the academic world or
outside' (*Soviet Studies*, v.29, no.2, 1977, p.341).
Class No: 908(47)

[4522]

SCHOPFLIN, G., *ed*. **The Soviet Union and Eastern
Europe**. New York and Oxford, Facts On File, 1986. xviii,
637p. illus. tables, bibliog., index. £30.00; $45.00.
(*Handbooks To The Modern World*.) ISBN: 0816012601.

First published by Anthony Blond in 1970.

33 contributors. 34 essays (*e.g.* The Soviet Union and the
Warsaw Pact: military and security affairs ... Tourism in the
Soviet Union and Eastern Europe ... The Baltic Republics)
arranged in 4 parts: Historical, Political, Economic, Social to
form a concise encyclopaedia providing basic information
and informed comment about the Eastern bloc countries.
Analytical index. 'A truly indispensable reference work for
all serious libraries, academic or public' (*Choice,* v.23,
no.11-12, July-August 1986, p.1661). *Class No:* 908(47)

Bibliographies

[4523]

JONES, D.L., *comp*. **Books in English on the Soviet Union,
1917-73** a bibliography. New York, Garland, 1975. 331p.

Lists over 4,500 books under topics. Not confined to US
and British publications. Detailed name index. 'Should be
quite helpful to the beginning student or general reader who
needs a point of departure for study' (*Library journal*, 15
January 1976, p.327). *Class No:* 908(47)(01)

[4524]

KERN-SIMIRENKO, C. *and* WAWRO, W. '**Reference
materials in Russian and Soviet area studies, 1987-88**',
The Russian Review, v.49.no.2, April 1990, p.175-81.

Discursive bibliographical essay in 5 sections: 1. Guides
to collections and general bibliographies - 2. History and
social sciences - 3. Literature - 4. Linguistics and
dictionaries - 5. Theatre and art. *Class No:* 908(47)(01)

[4525]

Soviet studies guide. Konn, T., *ed*. London, Bowker Saur,
1992. xvi,237p. maps, bibliogs., index. £39. (*Area Study
Guide Series, no.1.*) ISBN: 0862917905.

10 thematic bibliographical essays by different hands: 1.
Land, environment, people - 2. History - 3. Society and
culture - 4. Government and politics - 5. International
relations - 6. Armed Forces - 7. Economy - 8. Business - 9.
Science and technology - 10. General reference. Each essay
ends with consolidated annotated bibliography. Although
collapse of USSR overtook publication this guide retains
considerable reference value. *Class No:* 908(47)(01)

[4526]

THOMPSON, A., *comp*. **Russia/USSR** a selective annotated
bibliography of books in English. Santa Barbara, California
and Oxford, Clio Press, 1979. xiii, 286p. + 2p. map, index.
£39.95. (*World Bibliographical Series; no.6.*) ISBN:
0903450186.

A revised edition, compiled by L. Pitman, is announced
for 1994. £35. ISBN 1851091858.

1,247 annotated entries. 22 sections: General works -
Geography - History ... Biography ... Law, justice and
human rights ... General bibliography. Author, title and
subject index. *Class No:* 908(47)(01)

Encyclopaedias

[4527]

**The Cambridge encyclopedia of Russia and the Soviet
Union.** Brown, A., *and others, eds*. Cambridge University
Press, 1982. 492p. illus. (some col.), maps (some col.),
tables, bibliog., index. ISBN: 0521231698.

112 academic contributors. Well presented encyclopedia
of essential information arrayed in 12 main sections: 1.
Territory and peoples - 2. History - 3. Religion - 4. Art and
architecture - 5. Language and literature - 6. Music, theatre,
dance and film - 7. Sciences - 8. Soviet political system - 9.
Economy - 10. Society - 11. Military power and policy - 12.
World role. Glossary p.11. Bibliography (by section) p.485-
91. More scholarly than *Cultural atlas of Russia and the
Soviet Union*. *Class No:* 908(47)(031)

[4528]

McGraw-Hill encyclopedia of Russia and the Soviet Union.
Florinsky, M.T.   New York and London, McGraw-Hill, 1961. xiv, 624p. illus., diagrs., tables, maps, bibliogs., index.

'The object of the Encyclopedia is to present, within the relatively brief space of a single volume, a mass of useful information on Russia before and after the revolution of 1917' (*Editor's Preface*). 91 contributors, the lengthier articles being signed. The article on Komsomol runs to 3 columns, with a bibliography of 3 items; that on Stalin runs to 2 columns, with a bibliography of 5 items. Bibliographies are confined to English-language material. Very well illustrated, with more than 400 illustrations, diagrams, maps, etc. Its main weakness, according to *Library Journal*, v.87, no.2, 15 January 1962, p.210-1, is neglect of the pre-Soviet period. Strong in biography, economics and technology; weak in factual detail, cross-references and geographical coverage (Neiswender, R. *Guide to Russian reference and language aids* (1962), p.37-38. *Class No:* 908(47)(031)

Handbooks & Manuals

[4529]

KATZ, K., *and others*, *eds*. Handbook of major Soviet nationalities. New York, The Free Press; London, Collier Macmillan, 1975. xiv, 451p. tables, maps. $25.00. ISBN: 0029170907.

Well-documented essays by 14 contributors on each of the 17 nationalities in the USSR. Introduction: The nationality problem. Parts: 1. The Slavs (*e.g.* The Ukraine and the Ukrainians - 2. The Balts - 3. The Transcaucasians - 4. Central Asia - 5. Other nationalities (*e.g.* The Jews in the Soviet Union; Moldavia and the Moldavians), 'Lithuania and the Lithuanians' (p.118-40); General information; History; Demography; Culture; External relations; Media (language data; local media; educational institutions; cultural and scientific institutions); National attitudes. References, p.138-40; 5 tables. 'Clearly presented, well researched ... A very valuable reference tool' (*Library journal* v.100, no.16, 15 September 1975, p.1617). *Class No:* 908(47)(035)

RSFSR

[4530]

Eastern Europe and the Commonwealth of Independent States 1994. London, Europa, 1994. 718p. maps, bibliogs., tables. £185. (*Regional Surveys of the World*.) ISBN: 0946653860.

Part 1. Background to the region (introductory social, political and economic overviews). Pt.2. Eastern Europe. Individual countries A-Z with geographical profile, recent history, statistical surveys, government and diplomatic directory, judicial system, tourism, and select bibliography. Pt.3 USSR and its successor states including geography, chronology, recent history, and political profiles and career outlines of leading political figures. *Class No:* 908(470)

Baltic States

Bibliographies

[4531]

SMITH, I.A. *and* GRUNTS, M.V., *comps*. Baltic States. Santa Barbara, Calif., Oxford, Clio Press, 1993. c.200p. map, index. £30. (*World Bibliographical Series, no.161.*) ISBN: 1851091963.

Publication announced. c.600 annotated entries relating to Estonia, Latvia and Lithuania. A detailed 20th century chronology is also included. *Class No:* 908(474)(01)

Lithuania

Bibliographies

[4532]

KANTAUTAS, A. *and* KANTAUTAS, F. A Lithuanian bibliography: a checklist of books and articles held by the major libraries in Canada and the United States. Edmonton, Univ. of Alberta Press, 1975. xxxix, 725p. £16.55. ISBN: 0888640684.

10168 entries, classified in 13 categories e.g., 4. Bibliographic aids, general reference works, serials, locating copies. Author and subject indexes.

Supplement to a Lithuanian bibliography: a further checklist... 1979. xxviii, 316p. 0888640684. £5.50. *Class No:* 908(474.5)(01)

Encyclopaedias

[4533]

Encyclopedia Lituanica. Sužiedélis, S. *and* Vesaitis, A., *eds*. Boston, Encyclopedia Lituanica, 6v., 1970-1978.

Based on the same publishers *Lithuanian encyclopaedia* (1953-1969) - the first complete general encyclopedia ever published in Lithuania.

V.6 *V-Z* and *Supplement A-Z*. 1978. 540p. illus., map, index. 38 contributors. Includes list of contributors to entire work. Essential reference source to Lithuania from the earliest times. *Class No:* 908(474.5)(031)

[4534]

Lithuania: an encyclopaedic survey. Demskis, E., *ed*. Vilnius, Encyclopedia Publishers, 1986. 431p. illus. (many col.), col. maps, tables, index.

Over 50 contributors. Illustrated sections on General information - Natural Features - Population and settlements - Constitution and government - History - Communist Party of Lithuania - Economy - Public Health - Sports and tourism - Education - Science - Publishing - TV and radio - Literature and art - Religion - Honorary titles and prizes. *Class No:* 908(474.5)(031)

Ukraine

Bibliographies

[4535]

MAGOCSI, P.R., *comp*. Ucrainica at the University of Toronto Library a catalogue of holdings. Toronto, University of Toronto Press, 2v., 1985. xviii, 1845p. ISBN: 0802034306.

Library catalogue entries arranged in 31 chapters *e.g.* 1. Reference aids and general works - 2. Serials ... 6.

....(contd.)

Guidebooks ... 8. Maps and atlases ... 15. Numismatics, genealogy and sphragistics - 16 Archaeology - 17. History ... 31 Ucrainica abroad. *Class No:* 908(477)(01)

[4536]
WYNAR, B.S. Ukraine a bibliographic guide to English-language publications. Englewood, Colo., Ukranian Academic Press, 1990. xiii, ,406p. index. $85. ISBN: 0872877612.

1084 critically annotated entries, plus thousands of subsumed entries, covering the period early 1950s to mid-1989, arranged in 13 categories (e.g. 1. General reference sources ... 5. Ethnic studies ... 7. Geography and travel - 8. History and political science). Entries include unpublished doctoral dissertations, books, symposia, pamphlets, selected articles in scholarly journals, and, in some instances, review citations. An important reference source.
Class No: 908(477)(01)

Encyclopaedias

[4537]
Encyclopedia of Ukraine. Kubijovyč, V., *ed.* Toronto, Univ. of Toronto Press, for the Canadian Institute of Ukrainian Studies, the Shevchenko Scientific Society, and the Canadian Foundation for Ukrainian Studies. 1984-. illus. maps. ports. bibliogs. $115 (v.1). $125 (v.2).

Revision of *Entsklopediia Ukrainoznavstva*. Preface discusses earlier Soviet and non-Soviet Ukrainian encyclopedias.

v.1 *A-F.* 1984. xv,952p. 0802033628. v.2 *G-K* 1988. 737p. 0802034446 100 scholars are engaged worldwide on a comprehensive guide to the life and culture of the Ukraine. Most of the longer entries include a bibliography. To be completed in 5v. A map/gazetteer with statistical data is published as a supplement to v.1. 'Sets a standard which other such projects will find it difficult to equal' (*Canadian American Slavic Studies*, v.25, nos.1-4, 1991. p.381).
Class No: 908(477)(031)

[4538]
—KUBIJOVYČ, V. *and* SHUKOVSKY, A. Encyclopedia of Ukraine. Map and gazetteer (scale 1:2,000,000). Toronto, Univ. of Toronto Press for the Canadian Institute of Ukrainian Studies, 1984. 30p. folded col. maps tipped in inside back cover. ISBN: 0802033628.

Gazetteer p.10-30. *Class No:* 908(477)(031)

[4539]
—KUBIJOVYČ, V., *ed.* Ukraine a concise encyclopedia. Toronto, Univ. of Toronto Press, 2v. 1963-71.

Based on *Entsyklopediya Ukrainoznavsta* (München & New York, 3v. 1949-52).

Arranged by topics. V.1: physical geography, natural history, population, ethnography, history, culture and literature: v.2 (xiiii, 1394p.): law and government ... social sciences, culture ... concluding with the Ukranian diaspora. V.2 has 87 contributors. *Class No:* 908(477)(031)

Finland

[4540]
Finnish Features. Helsinki, Ministry for Foreign Affairs, 1981-.

Factsheets of 4-6 pages grouped in 15 categories 'produced as part of the Finnish information service abroad'

....(contd.)

and 'intended to be used for reference purposes': 1. The land and the people (The Finnish nature and landscape; Population; Swedish Finland; Roots of the Finnish language) - 2. History (Finland through the ages; Coats of Arms) - 3. Politics - 4. Foreign Policy - 5. Legal system - 6. Government and defence - 7. Business and economics - 8. Social and environmental planning - 9. Social welfare - 10. The Church and religion - 11. Education and the media - 12. Science - 13. Culture, art and design - 14. Leisure and sports - 15. Finnish way of life. Updated at intervals and inserted in a spring binder. *Class No:* 908(480)

[4541]
Suomen valtiokalenteri 1993 /Finlands Statskalender 1992. 182nd ed. 1025p. tables, indexes. ISBN: 9510172189. ISSN: 03552462.

Official governmental and ministerial directory and handbook. *Class No:* 908(480)

Bibliographies

[4542]
SCREEN, J.E.O., *comp.* Finland. Santa Barbara, California and Oxford, Clio Press, 1981. xv, 212p.+1p. map, index. £27.95. $30.50. (*World Bibliographical Series; no.31.*) ISBN: 0903450550.

768 annotated entries. 27 sections: Introductory works - Geography - Prehistory, archaeology and ethnography - History ... Libraries, archives, museums and art galleries ... Encyclopaedias, yearbooks and biographical dictionaries - Bibliographies. Author, title and subject index.
Class No: 908(480)(01)

Encyclopaedias

[4543]
Uppslagsverket Finland. Ekberg, A., *ed.* Helsingfors, Holger Schildts förlag, 3v., 1982-1985.

1. *A-J* 1982. ISBN 915002672 - 2. *K-R* 1983. ISBN 9515002966 - 3. *S-Ö Supplement* 1985. ISBN 9515003318. Swedish language encyclopaedia. 3141 entries. Colour map front endpapers. Finnish flags 1862-1918; Currency; and Flowers and provincial coats of arms on back endpapers.
Class No: 908(480)(031)

Norway

[4544]
Norges statskalender fortegnelse over konstitusjonelle organer og statsforvaltning m.v. 1991. 119th ed. Oslo, Universitetsforlaget, 1990. xii,940p. col. illus., col. port., col. maps on endpapers, tables, indexes. ISBN: 8200212319. ISSN: 08012229.

Official, government, and departmental directory.
Class No: 908(481)

Bibliographies

[4545]
SATHER, L.B., *comp.* Norway. Santa Barbara, California and Oxford, Clio Press, 1986. xxiv, 293p.+1p. map, index. £42.50. $46.95. (*World Bibliographical Series; no.67.*) ISBN: 185109010x.

942 annotated entries. 41 sections: The country and its

....(contd.)

people - Travellers' accounts - Geography - Tourism and travel guides ... Prehistory and archaeology - History - Modern explorers ... Reference books, directories and biographical dicitionaries. Author, title and subject index. *Class No:* 908(481)(01)

Yearbooks & Directories

[4546]

Hvem, Hva, hvor. [Who, what, when.] Oslo, Chr. Schibsteds, 1934-. Annual.

Almanac including summaries of the past years' national events. 'A frequently used reference guide' (L.B. Sother. *Norway,* 1986. Entry 904). *Class No:* 908(481)(058)

Sweden

[4547]

Sveriges statskalender 1993. Stockholm, Allmänna Förlaget, 1993. 834p. indexes. ISBN: 9138128098.

Official directory. 2566 entries in 14 sections. *Class No:* 908(485)

Bibliographies

[4548]

LARSON - FLEMING, S., *and others, eds.* **Books on Sweden in English.** New York, Swedish Information Service, 1983. 61p.

505 titles arranged according to Dewey Decimal Classification. *Class No:* 908(485)(01)

[4549]

SATHER, L.B. *and* **SWANSON, A.,** *comps.* **Sweden.** Santa Barbara, California and Oxford, Clio Press, 1987. xxiv, 370p.+1p. map, index. £49.95. $55.00. (*World Bibliographical Series; no.80.*) ISBN: 1851090355.

1015 annotated entries. 44 sections: The country and its people - Travellers' accounts - Geography - Tourism and travel guides ... Prehistory and archaeology - History ... The social welfare state ... Nobel prizes ... Libraries, archives and museums ... Reference works and directories ... Bibliographies. *Class No:* 908(485)(01)

Denmark

[4550]

Facts about Denmark. 3rd ed. København, Press and Cultural Relations Department, Ministry of Cultural Affairs, 1988. 112p. ISBN: 8770002053.

Brief introduction to all aspects of Danish life and culture. *Class No:* 908(489)

[4551]

Kongelig Dansk Hof-og Statskalender 1993 statshåndbog for Kongeriget Danmark. København, Schultz Information, 1993. 1306p. indexes. ISBN: 8756928939. ISSN: 00852589.

Official directory and calendar. *Class No:* 908(489)

Bibliographies

[4552]

MILLER, K.E., *comp.* **Denmark.** Santa Barbara, California and Oxford, Clio Press, 1987. xix, 216p.+1p, map, index. £31.95. $50.50. (*World Bibliographical Series; no.83.*) ISBN: 1851090428.

730 annotated entries. 33 sections: The country and its people - Geography - Tourism and travel ... Prehistory and archaeology - History ... Libraries and museums ... Encyclopaedias and directories - Bibliographies -The Faroe Islands - Greenland. Author, title and subject index. *Class No:* 908(489)(01)

Iceland

[4553]

Iceland 1986. Nordel, J. *and* Kristinsson, V., *eds.* 3rd ed. Reykjavik, Central Bank of Iceland, 1987. xvi,412p. illus., maps, diagrs., tables, bibliog., index.

New ed. approximately every 10 years.

Handbook to the country and its inhabitants: 1. Country and population - 2. History and cultural heritage - 3. Government and administration - 4. Foreign relations - 5. Industries and energy - 6. Economic policy and finance - 7. Foreign trade and payments - 8. Social conditions - 9. Religion and education - 10. Science and the arts - 11. Recreational activities. Statistical appendix p.337-54. Bibliography p.355-65. Subject index. *Class No:* 908(491.1)

Bibliographies

[4554]

HORTON, J.J., *comp.* **Iceland.** Santa Barbara, California and Oxford, Clio Press, 1983. xxiii, 346p.+2p., map, index. £47.95. $53.00. (*World Bibliographical Series; no.37.*) ISBN: 090345078x.

971 annotated entries. 43 sections: The country and its people - Exploration and travel - Travel guides - Maps - Regional geography ... Archaeology - Geneaology and heraldry - History - Directories - Museums and library services - Catalogues and bibliographies. Author, title and subject index. *Class No:* 908(491.1)(01)

Netherlands

[4555]

Staatsalmanack voor het Koninkrijk der Nederlanden 1993. 's-Gravenhage, Sdu Uitgeverij Plantijnstraat, 1993. variously paginated. ISBN: 9039903948.

Official almanac in 34 lettered sections: A Koninklijke Familie ... F/G. Nederlandse Antillen. Aruba - V. Provinces etc. *Class No:* 908(492)

Bibliographies

[4556]

KING, P. *and* **WINTLE, M.,** *comps.* **The Netherlands.** Santa Barbara, California and Oxford, Clio Press. 1988. xix, 308p.+1p., map, index. £43.95. $52.50. (*World Bibliographical Series; no.88.*) ISBN: 185109041x.

1025 annotated entries. 35 sections: The country and its people - Geography ... Prehistory and archaeology - History - Voyages of discovery and colonies ... Archives, libraries,

....(contd.)
galleries and museums ... Directories - Bibliographies. Glossary p.xix. Author, title and subject index. *Class No:* 908(492)(01)

Almanacs

[4557]

Pyttersen's Nederlandse almanack 1992-'93 Jaarlijks vershijnend handboek van personen en instellingen in Nederland en de Nederlandse Antillen. 91st ed. Bohn Staflen Van Loghum, 1991. 1102p. (variously numbered), index. ISBN: 9031314293.

Directory information in 6 sections: 1. Organizations, institutions, associations - 2. Public authorities - 3. Legal practice - 4. Education - 5. Health services and care of the elderly - 6. Arts and culture. *Class No:* 908(492)(059)

Belgium

Bibliographies

[4558]

RILEY, R.C., *comp.* **Belgium.** Santa Barbara, California and Oxford, Clio Press, 1989. xxxviii, 269p. + 1p. map, indexes. £38.00. (*World Bibliographical Series; No.104.*) ISBN: 1851090991.

819 annotated entries. 37 Sections: The country and its people - Geography and geology ... Archaeology and prehistory - History ... The EEC ... Libraries, art galleries and museums ... Encyclopaedias, directories and reference works - Bibliographies. Theses and dissertations on Belgium p.xxix-xxxviii. Author, subject and title indexes. *Class No:* 908(493)(01)

Switzerland

Bibliographies

[4559]

MEIER, H.K. *and* MEIER, R.A., *comps.* **Switzerland.** Santa Barbara, California and Oxford, Clio Press, 1990. xviii,409 + 1p. map. indexes. £55.95; $65. (*World Bibliographical Series, no. 114.*) ISBN: 1851091076.

974 annotated entries in 42 chapters: The Country and its people - Travel - Geography ... Archaeology and prehistory - History - Genealogy ... Emigration: The Swiss abroad - Languages and dialects ... Tourism ... Museums, libraries and archives - Books and bookmaking ... Reference books - Bibliographies. Author, title and subject index. 'There is nothing comparable available' (*Choice,* v.28, no.9, May 1991, p.1462). *Class No:* 908(494)(01)

Liechtenstein

Bibliographies

[4560]

MEIER, R., *comp.* **Liechtenstein.** Santa Barbara, Calif., Oxford, Clio Press, 1993. 130p. map, index. £24. (*World Bibliographical Series, no.158.*) ISBN: 1851092013.

270 annotated entries including many German language items. *Class No:* 908(494.9)(01)

Greece

Bibliographies

[4561]

AMERICAN SCHOOL OF CLASSICAL STUDIES AT ATHENS. **Catalogue of the Gennadius Library.** Boston, Mass., G.K. Hall, 7v., 1965. First Supplement 1973. Second Supplement 1981. $695.00; Export $840.00; 1st Supplt. $125.00; Export $150.00. 2nd Supplt. $170.00; Export $205.00. ISBN: 0816114986; 0816114994, 1st Supplt; 0816115001, 2nd Supplt.

About 100,000 cards, photolithographically reproduced. A library of nearly 50,000 v. on Greece. According to the publishers, areas of particular strength include: Renaissance editions of Classical and Byzantine authors and of Greek grammars; early modern Greek literature; the beginnings of Classical archaeology (1750-1825); travellers to the Greek East (to 1900); Greek Bibles and the Orthodox Church; early printed materials on Turkish history; Greece under Turkish domination; Greek War of Independence (including Byroniana); the early Kingdom of Greece; and the 'Eastern Question'. Prices are for microfilm edition (9 reels altogether). No longer available in printed book form. *Class No:* 908(495)(01)

[4562]

CLOGG, M.J. *and* CLOGG, R. **Greece.** Santa Barbara, California and Oxford, Clio Press, 1980. xvii, 224p. + 1p. map, index. £26.95. $34.50. (*World Bibliographical Series; no.17.*) ISBN: 0903450305.

830 annotated entries. 33 sections: The country and its people - Geography - Prehistory and archaeology - History ... Greeks overseas ... Encyclopaedias - Bibliographies. Author, title and subject index. *Class No:* 908(495)(01)

Albania

Bibliographies

[4563]

BLAND, W.B., *comp.* **Albania.** Santa Barbara, California and Oxford, Clio Press. 1988. xxxvi, 290p. + 1p. map, indexes. £43.95. $48.00. (*World Bibliographical Series: no.94.*) ISBN: 1851090371.

893 annotated entries. 35 sections: The country and its people - Travellers' accounts - Geography ... Tourism and travel guides ... Archaeology and prehistory - History ... Albanian communities abroad ... Encyclopaedias - Bibliographies. Author, subject and title indexes. *Class No:* 908(496.5)(01)

[4564]

HETZER, A. *and* ROMAN, V.S. **Albania** a bibliographic research survey with location codes. München, K.G. Saur, 1983. 653p. index. $53.00. (*Bibliographies on Regional Geography and Area Studies.*) ISBN: 3598211333.

Section A. General Works (Sources; Cartography and Topography; Area Studies; and Philology). B. History and Politics. C. Law; D. Business and Economics. Index p.615-653. Compiled in Bremen University Library, the working language is German, with introductions to each section in English. 'This outstanding bibliography on Albania makes one wish for authors who can do a similar job for other countries ... probably the most valuable are the introductory

....(contd.)

essays, which give brief and succinct introductions to the literature on the various subjects' (*Choice*, v.21, no.4, December 1983, p.554). *Class No:* 908(496.5)(01)

Encyclopaedias & Dictionaries

[4565]

Fjalori enciklopedik shqipter. [The Albanian encyclopaedic dictionary.] Buda, A., ed. Tirana, Academy of Sciences, 1985. 1243p.

'An invaluable source of information of all kinds on Albania, its history and culture. Of particular value are the biographical details ... not readily available elsewhere' (W.B. Bland. *Albania*, 1988. Entry 860).

Class No: 908(496.5)(03)

Balkan States

Bibliographies

[4566]

Balkan Bibliography. Verrou-Karakosta, T.H. *and* Katzopoulos, K.K., eds. Thessaloniki, Institute for Balkan Studies, 1972-. Annual.

V.9 1980 (1988), xliii, 493p. index. has 3569 entries briefly annotated in Greek. Title page only in English.

Class No: 908(497)(01)

Yugoslavia

Bibliographies

[4567]

HORTON, J. J. Yugoslavia. Rev. and expanded ed. Santa Barbara, California and Oxford, Clio Press, 1990. xxi, 279p. + 1p. map, index. (*World Bibliographical Series, No. 1.*) ISBN: 185109105x.

First published 1977.

921 annotated entries in 41 sections: The country and its people - Travel and description - Geography . . . Archaeology - History ... Nationalities . . . Tourism . . . Directories - Museums and libraries - - Bibliographies. A note on the languages of Yugoslavia p.xxi. Author, subject and title index. *Class No:* 908(497.1)(01)

[4568]

LESKOŠEK, V. Yugoslavia a bibliography. New York, Studia Slovenika, 4v., 1974-82. $36. (set). ISBN: 068628383x, v.1; 0686283864, v.2; 0686267125, v.3; 0938616153, v.4.

'A substantial bibliography of Yugoslavia in the 20th century ... the classified subject arrangement is easy to use but the lack of author and subject indexes makes the volumes more suitable for general browsing than for individual checking' (Horton, J.J. *Yugoslavia*, 2nd ed., 1990).

Class No: 908(497.1)(01)

Bulgaria

Bibliographies

[4569]

CRAMPTON, R.J. Bulgaria. Santa Barbara, California and Oxford, Clio Press, 1989. xxxiii,232p., map, indexes. £39. (*World Bibliographical Series; no.107.*) ISBN: 1851091041.

794 annotated entries. 38 sections: The country and its people - Geography - Tourist guides - Travel accounts - Bulgaria before the Bulgarians - History ... Libraries, museums and archives ... Directories - Bibliographies. Author, title and subject indexes. *Class No:* 908(497.2)(01)

Encyclopaedias

[4570]

Information Bulgaria a short encyclopaedia of the People's Republic of Bulgaria. The Bulgarian Academy of Sciences. Oxford, Pergamon Press, 1985. xxii, 976p. illus. (some col.), col. maps, tables, bibliog., index. £120.00; $155.00. (*Countries of the World Information Series.*) ISBN: 0080318533.

12 Parts: 1. General information - 2. History - 3. Socio-political structure - 4. Armed forces - 5. Economy - 6. Social policies - 7. Education - 8. Science - 9. Culture - 10. Cultural and educational establishments - 11. Mass media - 12. Foreign policy. 'This is obviously the Bulgarian view of Bulgaria ... a useful source' (*International Affairs*, v.61, no.4, Autumn 1985, p.738). *Class No:* 908(497.2)(031)

Rumania

Bibliographies

[4571]

DELETANT, A *and* **DELETANT, D., comps. Romania.** Santa Barbara, California and Oxford, Clio Press, 1985. xviii, 236p. + 1p. map, index. £33.50. $38.00. (*World Bibliographical Series; no.59.*) ISBN: 1851090029.

797 annotated entries. 31 sections: The country and its people - Geography - Prehistory, archaeology and ethnography - History ... Nationalities and minorities ... Encyclopaedias and directories - Libraries and collections - Bibliographies. Author, title and subject index. 'An excellent guide to relevant material ... one of the best so far in the series' (*Choice*, v.24, no.3, November 1986, p.452).

Class No: 908(498)(01)

Asia

[4572]

Asia and Pacific review 1991/92. 12th ed. Saffron Walden, Essex, World of Information; Edison, N.J., Hunter Publishing, 1991. 230p. maps, pbk. ISBN: 0904439852.

54 A-Z country reviews and profiles i.e. current events, key facts, business guide and directory, maps, statistics. *Class No:* 908(5)

Bibliographies

[4573]

Asian bibliography. Bangkok, United Nations Economic Commission for Asia and the Far East, 1952-1974; U.N. Economic and Social Commission for Asia and the Pacific Library, 1975-1982. New York, ESCAP Library, 1983-. 2

.... *(contd.)*

issues pa. ISSN: 04979400.

V.37, no.2. July-December 1988. A select list of ESCAP Library's accessions dealing with Asia and the Pacific in 4 parts: 1. List of 1128 citations grouped under broad subject categories reflecting ESCAP's programmes and activities. 2-4. Author, title and ESCAP area indexes. Publications are listed when acquired by ESCAP Library irrespective of date of issue. *Class No:* 908(5)(01)

[4574]
ASSOCIATION FOR ASIAN STUDIES. **Cumulative bibliography of Asian studies 1966-1970.** Boston, Mass., G.K. Hall, 8v., 1972-1973.

1. *Author Bibliography.* 1973. 3 reels. $415.00 (Export $500.00). ISBN 0816114889. 2. *Subject Bibliography.* 1972. 6 reels. $415.00 ($500.00). ISBN 0816113262. Five-year cumulation of *c.*154,000 entries originally appearing in *Journal of Asian studies* between January 1966 and December 1971.

Preceded by *Cumulative bibliography of Asian studies, 1941-1965: author bibliography and subject bibliography* (1969-70. 8v. listing 107,000 + 100,000 entries.

Aims to provide 'as complete a listing as possible of significant books and articles in European languages concerning the countries of the Far East, Southeast Asia and South Asia' in the humanities and social sciences (G.K. Hall & Co. *Catalog. 1973-1974,* p.30). Now out of print. Available only in microfilm. *Class No:* 908(5)(01)

[4575]
Bibliography of Asian studies 1985. Surdam, W., *ed.* Ann Arbor, Association for Asian Studies, Univ. of Michigan, 1956-. Annual. ISSN: 00677159.

Previously published as *Bulletin of Far Eastern bibliography* 1936-40; and as 'Far Eastern bibliography' in *Far Eastern Quarterly,* 1941-46.

1985 volume (1990. xxxi, 428p.) has 18,002 entries for monographs, periodical articles, articles included in festschriften and commemorative volumes arranged in 34 geographical divisions, subdivided under 16 subject classifications (including Geography, History, Library and Information Sciences) further subdivided under *c.*150 subject headings. Abbreviations of journal titles p.vii-xiv. List of books analyzed p.xv-xxi. Periodicals list p.xxii-xxxi. Author index p.354-428. *Class No:* 908(5)(01)

[4576]
LONDON UNIVERSITY. School of Oriental and African Studies. **Library Catalogue.** Boston, Mass., G.K. Hall, 28v., 1963 (also in 14 separate sections). First supplement 16v., 1968. Second supplement 16v., 1973. Third supplement 19v. 1979. $2665.00 (Export $3225.00) 1st Supplt. $1750.00 ($2120.00). 2nd Supplt. $1750.00 ($1925.00). 3rd Supplt. $2070.00 ($2505.00). ISBN: 081611225; 0816107343, 1st Supplt; 0816112967, 2nd Supplt; 0816102619, 3rd Supplt.

1,053,357 catalogue cards, photolithographically reproduced. A comprehensive catalogue (author, subject and title entries) of material (including periodical articles and analyticals from other collective works) on all aspects of Asia, Oceania and Africa, but excluding the purely scientific, medical and technical. Available as a set or in 14 sections: Author catalogue - Title index - Subject catalogues (General. Africa. Middle East. South Asia. Southeast Asia and Pacific Islands. Far East) - Catalogue of manuscripts and microfilms - Chinese catalogues (Titles. Authors. Subjects) -

.... *(contd.)*

Japanese catalogue - Catalogue of periodicals and series (included in the Author catalogue). No longer available in printed form apart from 1st Supplt. Other prices are for 96 reel microfilm edition. A *Fourth Supplement 1978-1984* (1985) is published in microfiche format by IDC of Zug, Switzerland. The record continues in SOAS's *Monthly list of titles added to the catalogue.* *Class No:* 908(5)(01)

[4577]
NEW YORK PUBLIC LIBRARY. The Research Libraries. **Dictionary catalog of the Oriental Collection of the New York Public Library, Reference Libraries.** Boston, Mass., G.K. Hall, 16v., 1960. First Supplement, 8v., 1976.

1960. 30 reels $1200.00 (Export $1450.00). ISBN 0816112827 *First Supplement,* 8v., 1976. $1000.00 ($1210.00). ISBN 0816107750.

Contains some 318,000 entries for about 65,000 volumes. The Arabic, Indic and Ancient Near East holdings of the Oriental Collection are the largest in the US. 'Other outstanding features are the comprehensive holdings of Japanese technical and scientific periodicals, a unique collection of linguistic works and a fine collection in the field of Oriental religions, especially of Islam and Buddhism'. The main catalogue now available only on microfilm.

Class No: 908(5)(01)

[4578]
NUNN, G.R. **Asia: reference works** a select annotated guide. London, Mansell, 1980. xvi, 365p.

First published 1971 as *Asia: a selected and annotated guide to reference works* (Cambridge, Massachusetts, M.I.T. Press).

Annotated entries for 1,558 reference items. Sections A-T (A. Asia - B. Bangladesh - C. India (including South and Southern Asia) - D. Nepal - E. Pakistan - F. Sri Lanka - G. Southeast Asia - H. Burma - I. Democratic Kampuchea - J. Indonesia - K. Laos - L. Malaysia (including Singapore) - M. Philippines - N. Thailand - O. Vietnam - P. East Asia - Q. China - R. Japan - S. Korea - T. Mongolia). 'A. Asia' is subdivided: Encyclopedias and handbooks; Yearbooks; Directories; Atlases; Bibliography; Theses and dissertations; Subject bibliography (religion and thought; social sciences; natural sciences; art and music; history and geography). Chinese, Japanese and Korean characters are included for titles in the text. Author and title indexes. Omits Middle East, Soviet Asia and Afghanistan; title should therefore read: 'South and East Asia'. 'A scholarly undertaking and will be an invaluable addition to Asian reference collections' (*RQ,* Spring 1981, p.304). *Class No:* 908(5)(01)

Encyclopaedias

[4579]
FRÉDÉRIC, L. **Encyclopaedia of Asian civilizations.** Villecresnes, France, 11v., 1977-1987. illus.

V.1-10 (1977-1987) A-Z plus Corrigenda.

V.1: A-B (429p.) has *c.*20 short entries per page (and rarely more than ½p. each) for people, places, etc. 'Afghanistan': 1¼ columns; 'Brunei': nearly 1 col.; 'Asoka, Emperor': 1 col.; 'Gandhi, M.K.' (v.3): 2/3col. Profuse cross-references. List of Chinese, Japanese, Korean and Vietnamese idiogrammatic characters corresponding to the entries appended to each v. Index in English and French.

....(contd.)

V.11 *Supplement to v.10 and general bibliography* has Bibliography (19 sub-divided geographical sections) p.131-295. *Class No:* 908(5)(031)

Yearbooks & Directories

[4580]

Asia yearbook. Hong Kong, Far Eastern Economic Review, 1960-. Annual. 356p. tables, softcover. ISBN: 9627010332.

Formerly *Far Eastern Economic Review Yearbook.*

An overview of the previous year is followed by a general section (the power game, food and population, refugees, development banks *etc.*) and analyses of events and developments in 31 countries including Soviet Asia, the Maldives, Australia, New Zealand, Papua New Guinea and Fiji. Obituaries p.254-6. *Class No:* 908(5)(058)

[4581]

FENTON, T.P. *and* **HEFFRON, M.J.,** *comps.* **Asia and Pacific: a directory of resources.** Maryknoll, New York, Orbis Books; London, Zed Books, 1986. xx, 137p., bibliogs., indexes, pbk. £18.95; $9.95. ISBN: 088344528x, US; 0862326354, UK.

Updates and expands the Asia and Pacific chapter of *The Third World resource directory* (Orbis Books, 1984).

6 Chapters: 1. Organizations - 2. Books - 3. Periodicals - 4. Pamphlets and articles - 5. Audiovisuals - 6. Other resources. Clearly intended for US use: 'We have probably overlooked significant organizations and resources in Europe, Asia, the Pacific, and elsewhere' (*Introduction,* p.xix). *Class No:* 908(5)(058)

Asia—Far East

Bibliographies

[4582]

Bibliographic guide to East Asian studies. Boston, G.K. Hall. Annual

1993 (1994). 550p. $185.00. 0783820801. Covers Japan, China, North and South Korea, Hong Kong, and Taiwan, with approximately 3500 listings from LC MARC tapes and the Oriental Division of the New York Public Library. It includes publications about East Asia; materials published in any of the relevant countries; publications in the Chinese, Japanese and Korean languages.

Class No: 908(51/52+57)(01)

[4583]

CHICAGO UNIVERSITY. Catalogs of the Far Eastern Library. Boston, Mass., G.K. Hall, 1974-.

1. *Author/title catalog of the Chinese Collection.* 8v., 1974. 16 reels. $980.00 (Export $1135.00). ISBN 0816113327.

2. *Author/title catalog of the Japanese Collection.* 4v., 1974. 8 reels. $535.00 ($645.00). ISBN 0816113211.

3. *Classified catalog and subject index of the Chinese and Japanese Collections.* 6v., 1974. 12 reels. $825.00 ($995.00). ISBN 0816113653. Main catalogue now available only on microfilm.

First Supplement 1981.

1. *Author/title Chinese catalog.* 4v. 2564p. $690.00 ($835.00). ISBN 0816103089.

2. *Author/title Japanese catalog.* 4v., 2032p. $565.00 ($685.00). ISBN 0816103097.

....(contd.)

3. *Classified catalog and subject index.* 4v. 2210p. $615.00 ($745.00). ISBN 0816103100.

The initial collection of the Far Eastern Library was systematically compiled in China with emphasis on basic reference tools, learned journals, and research materials for the study of Chinese literature, history, and institutions, especially of the ancient period. The collection has been expanded by incorporation of the Laufer Collection in East Asiatic languages, the addition on microfilm of 3000 rare books from the National Library of Peking, and the recent large-scale acquisition of materials in Japanese and on modern Chinese social sciences and literature.

Class No: 908(51/52+57)(01)

[4584]

UNIVERSITY OF MICHIGAN. Catalogs of the Asia Library. Boston, Mass., G.K. Hall, 25v., 1978. 19,968p. $2445.00 (Export $2995.00). ISBN: 0816100969.

The Asia Library contains 300,000 volumes and 18,000 reels of microfilm of Chinese, Japanese, and Korean publications. The Chinese Collection, which comprises more than 170,000 volumes/reels, is especially noteworthy for its materials on modern China - some of which are not available in any other collection outside of Asia. The Japanese Collection of more than 140,000 volumes/reels is strong in literature and the social sciences, with outstanding holdings on local history, legislation, education, and statistical compilations. *Class No:* 908(51/52+57)(01)

Yearbooks & Directories

[4585]

The Far East and Australasia 1994. 25th ed. London, Europa, 1993. xxiii,1078p. maps, tables, bibliogs. Annual. £175. (*Regional Surveys of the World.*) ISBN: 0946653909. ISSN: 00713791.

First published 1969.

Over 50 contributors provide a compendium guide and systematic political and economic guide to all the countries and territories of East Asia, Southeast Asia, the Asiatic countries of the former USSR, Australia, New Zealand, and the Pacific Islands. Pt.1 General survey comprises a series of introductory essays (*e.g.* Development problems of Asia; the Pacific century: progress towards the integration of the Pacific Basin) - 2. Country surveys including Physical and social geography, History, Economy, Statistical survey, Directory (*i.e.* constitution, government, political organizations, diplomatic representation, judiciary, religion, the media, finance, tourism, *etc.* with a bibliography) - 3. Regional organizations (*i.e.* comprehensive information on the major organizations active within the region). 'Quite simply it must be regarded as an obligatory annual purchase for all reference and research libraries determined to keep up with world affairs' (*Reference Reviews,* v.5,no.2, 1991, p.40). *Class No:* 908(51/52+57)(058)

China

[4586]

China facts and figures. Scherer, J.L., *ed.* Gulf Breeze, Florida, Academic International Press, 1978 - Annual. (v.9. 1986). x, 390p. maps, bibliog., tables. ISBN: 0875690939.

Reviews developments in the Peoples' Republic. V.9 has 19 sections: 1. Survey - 2. Industrial and agricultural production - 3. Government - 4. Party - 5. Armed forces - 6.

....(contd.)

Demography - 7. Economy - 8. Energy - 9. Industry - 10. Agriculture - 11. Foreign trade - 12. Foreign aid - 13. Transportation - 14. Institutions - 15. Science - 16. Culture and communications - 17. Health, education and welfare - 18. Provinces and cities - 19. Special topics (1985 calendar of events; Space news; Tourism; Obituaries; Key works on the Peoples Republic p.386-390). *Class No:* 908(510)

[4587]

Chinese studies papers presented at a colloquium at the School of Oriental and African Studies, University of London 24-26 August 1987. Sponsored jointly by the British Library, the School of Oriental and African Studies, University of London and the China Library Group. Wood, F., *ed.* London, The British Library, 1988. 232p. illus. £23.50. (*British Library Occasional Papers, No.10.*) ISBN: 0712301569.

25 papers presenting an overview of resources for Chinese studies in UK libraries; paper and book in China; and automation and cooperation. *Class No:* 908(510)

Bibliographies of Bibliographies

[4588]

TSIEN, Tsuen-Hsuin *and* CHENG, J.K.M. **China: an annotated bibliography of bibliographies.** Boston, Mass., G.K. Hall, 1978. xxx, 604p.

Title also in Chinese: *Chung-kuo shu mu chieh t'i hui pien.* Annotated list of *c.*2,500 bibliographies on Chinese studies published to the end of 1976. Emphasis on English, Chinese and Japanese language sources. Includes bibliographies in periodicals and monographs. Name, title and subject indexes, plus a list of periodicals cited.

Class No: 908(510)(009)

Bibliographies

[4589]

CHENG, P., *comp.* **China.** Santa Barbara, California and Oxford, Clio Press, 1983. xx, 390p.+1p. map, index. £49.95. $55.00. (*World Bibliographical Series; no. 35.*) ISBN: 090345081x.

1460 annotated entries. 31 sections: The country and its people - Geography - Tourism and travellers' accounts ... Prehistory and archaeology - History - Biographical works ... Overseas Chinese - Libraries, museums and archives ... Bibliographies and directories. Author and subject index.

Class No: 908(510)(01)

[4590]

CHENG, P., *comp.* **Current books on China 1983-1988:** an annotated bibliography. New York, Garland, 1990. 268p. indexes. $29. ISBN: 0824034368.

626 annotated English-language books, published in UK or US, arranged in 25 broad subject divisions, with the emphasis on Chinese history, politics, government, and foreign relations. Supplements the author's *China,* published in the World Bibliographical Series (*q.v.*).

Class No: 908(510)(01)

[4591]

CORDIER, H. **Bibliotheca Sinica:** dictionnaire bibliographique des ouvrages relatifs à l'Empire Chinois. 2nd ed. Paris, Guilmoto, 4v., 1904-08. Suppl°ment, Paris, Geuther, 1922-24.

Reprinted New York, Burt Franklin, 1965. (with 1961 index).

50,000 entries in main work; 20,000 in supplement. 'The only reasonably complete bibliography for China in any European language' (Ad Orientem. *Catalogue* 6 (1966), p.99). Classified; no annotations. Pt.1 (in v.1-3): La Chine proprement dite - pt.2, Les étrangers en Chine (in v.3) - pts.3-5 (v.4). Relations des étrangers avec les chinois. Les chinois chez les peuples étrangers. Les pays tributaires de la Chine. An author index, lacking in all previous editions and printings, was published separately in New York, 1953 (reprinted 1961). *Class No:* 908(510)(01)

[4592]

LUST, J. *and* EICHORN, W. **Index Sinicus** a catalogue of articles relating to China in periodicals and other collective publications 1920-1955. Cambridge, Heffer, 1964. xxx, 663p.

19,734 numbered, unannotated items. 'Collective publications' comprises memorial volumes, symposia and the like, and proceedings of congresses and conferences. Intended as a contribution towards filling the gap between Cordier's *Bibliotheca Sinica,* the supplementary volume of which covered works published up to 1924, and the monthly list of periodical articles on *The Far East and South-East Asia* [1954-65], and as a supplement to T.L. Yuan's *China in Western literature (qqv).* Includes important reviews and obituary notices as well as substantial articles. Similar pattern to *Index Islamicus.* 27 classes 2-20 being subjects and 21-27, areas (21. Manchuria - 22. Mongols and Mongolia - 23. Tibet - 24. Sinkiang and Central Asian countries - 25. Hsi-Hsia - 26. Hong Kong - 27. Macao). Tibet is subdivided: General - Tibetan studies. Bibliography - Description, Travel - Tibetan and related languages - History. Foreign relations - Social conditions - Folklore - Communications - Religion - Art. Music. Dancing - Sciences and Medicine. *Class No:* 908(510)(01)

[4593]

SKINNER, W.G, *and others,* eds. **Modern Chinese society** an analytical bibliography. Stanford, California, Stanford Univ. Press, 3v., 1973.

1. *Publications in Western languages.* 1644-1972. 802p.
2. *Publications in Chinese* 1644-1969. 801p.
3. *Publications in Japanese* 1644-1971. 531p.

About 31,500 entries in all. 3 analytical indexes (subject index by historical period; subject index by geographical area; local-systems index), as well as conventional author and subject indexes. 'A very extensive critical work' (Univ. of London, School of Oriental and Africa Studies. *Library Guide.* 1980, p.34). *Class No:* 908(510)(01)

Encyclopaedias

[4594]

The Cambridge encyclopedia of China. Hook, B. *and* Twitchett, D., *eds.* 2nd ed. Cambridge Univ. Press, 1991. 512p. illus. (some col.), maps, bibliog., index. £35. $49.50. ISBN: 052135594x.

1st ed. 1982.

79 contributors. Covers all aspects of China: history,

....(contd.)

geography, economics, politics, the arts, wildlife, customs, food and drink, social organization, law, education, literature etc. Arranged thematically, this edition charts the political unrest of 1989. 60 maps. *Class No:* 908(510)(031)

[4595]

THE CHINESE ACADEMY OF SOCIAL SCIENCES.
Information China. James, C.V., *ed for Pergamon Press*. Oxford, New York and Beijing, Pergamon, 3v., 1989. xix, 1621p. illus., col.maps, tables, bibliog., indexes. £450.00 $795.00. (*Countries of the World Information Series*.) ISBN: 0080347649.

V.1: 1. China land and people - 2. History of China - 3. Sociopolitical structure and legal system. V.2: 4. The national economy - 5. Foreign trade and economic relations - 6. Living standards and social welfare - 7. The armed forces - 8. Sport - 9. Medicine and health. V.3: 10. Education - 11. Science and technology - 12. Philosophy - 13. Literature and the arts - 14. Cultural facilities - 15. Mass media - 16. Nationalities - 17. Religious beliefs - 18. Foreign policy - 19. Overseas Chinese affairs - 20. One country, two systems and the unification of the Motherland. Chronology of Chinese Historical periods p.xxix. Chinese names p.xxxiii-xxxv. China in figures p.1427-1563. Bibliography p.1565-9. Name, place-name and subject indexes. Biennial supplementary volumes are planned; the first in 1990. 'An extraordinary reference treasure, except for the lack of further sources for consultation and research' (*Choice,* v.26, no.10, June 1989, p.1664). *Class No:* 908(510)(031)

[4596]

COULING, S. The Encyclopaedia Sinica. Hong Kong, Oxford Univ. Press, 1983. xiv, 633p. bibliog. £18.00. ISBN: 0195815955.

Facsimile edition of a work originally published by Kelly and Walsh, Shanghai, 1917.

A scholarly work still of considerable value. Articles A-Z. with short addenda and corrigenda. A mine of information (*e.g.* on 'Names'); 'Han Dynasty' includes list of rulers with names in Chinese characters as well as in romanised form. Biographies; many cross-references. Author was one-time Honorary Secretary and Editor, North-China Branch, Royal Asiatic Society. *Class No:* 908(510)(031)

[4597]

Encyclopedia of China today. Kaplan, F.M., *and others, eds*. 3rd ed. London, Macmillan Press, 1982. 446p. illus., col.maps on end papers, tables, index. £14.95. ISBN: 0333324471.

Over 40 contributors. 10 Sections: 1. Land and population - 2. Government, law, politics - 3. Prominent figures - 4. Economic system - 5. Business - 6. Education - 7. Medical and social services - 8. Art and culture - 9. Access: travel and tourism - 10. Access to information (published material from China; inventory of Chinese-language periodicals; China related periodicals published outside Peoples Republic of China; Bibliography p.387-403). Three appendices: 1. Constitution (1988) - 2. Constitution of Chinese Communist Party - 3. Glossary. 8 maps. 3 chronologies. 55 tables. 'The most comprehensive and reliable guide to contemporary China available now to Western readers' (*TLS,* no.4131, 4 June 1982, p.618). *Class No:* 908(510)(031)

[4598]

Encyclopedia of New China. Luo Liang, *ed*. Beijing, Foreign Languages Press, 1987. 990p. illus. (mostly col.), col. maps, tables, index. £49.00. ISBN: 0835119696, UK; 711900086-1/217.

38 contributors. 5 main sections: 1. The land and the people - 2. History - 3. Politics - 4. Economy - 5. Culture. Appendix 1. The constitution and other important laws - 2. Brief guide to China's leading officials (p.831-908) - 3. A chronology of the People's Republic of China 1949-1985 (p.911-970) - 4. Miscellaneous tables including Brief chronological table of Chinese history p.973. *Class No:* 908(510)(031)

Handbooks & Manuals

[4599]

MACKERRAS, C. *and* **YORKE, A. The Cambridge handbook of contemporary China.** Cambridge, Cambridge Univ. Press, 1991. x,266p. maps, tables, bibliog., index. £35; $37.50. ISBN: 0521383420.

1. Chronology 1900-April 1990 (p.1-58) - 2. Politics - 3. Eminent contemporary figures (p.73-119) - 4. Classified and annotated bibliography (p.120-45) - 5. Foreign relations - 6. China's economy - 7. Population - 8. Gazetteer (p.183-204) - 9. China's minority nationalities - 10. Education - 11. Culture and Society. Chapter notes p.240-2. *Class No:* 908(510)(035)

Yearbooks & Directories

[4600]

China directory 1988. 16th ed. Tokyo, Radiopress Inc., 1987. 566 + 44 + 48p. index. Annual.

Lists leaders and members of party and government, constitutional, and other official bodies such as 13th Central Committee, National Peoples Congress and the State Council and Commissions. Name index in Pinyin. *Class No:* 908(510)(058)

Maps & Atlases

[4601]

BLUNDEN, C. *and* **ELVIN, M. Cultural atlas of China.** Oxford, Phaidon; New York, Facts on File, 1983. 237p. illus. (mostly col.), col. maps, tables, bibliog., index. £18.50; $40.00. ISBN: 0714823090, UK; 0871961326, US.

1. Space (geographic and demographic context) - 2. Time (survey of Chinese culture from Beijing Man to the present) - 3. Symbols and society (thematic coverage). Bibliography p.225-27. Gazetteer p.229-34. 58 maps. 204 col.illus. *Class No:* 908(510)(084.3)

[4602]

The Contemporary atlas of China. Sivin, N., *ed*. London, Weidenfeld and Nicolson; Boston, Houghton Mifflin, 1988. 200p. col.illus., col.maps, tables, diagrs., indexes. £19.95; $39.95. ISBN: 0297794043, UK; 0395473292, US.

23 contributors. Complete authorized 1:4,000,000 maps of modern China with place names in Pinyin and Chinese transliteration. Chronology of China (p.8-11) - Maps (p.12-35) - China fact file (p.36-7) - 50 pictorial essays: Regions; History; Society; Culture; China today. Maps compiled jointly by the Cartographical Publishing House in China and the Esselte Map Service in Sweden. 'This moderately priced

....(contd.)
and handsome volume deserves a place in both college and research library collections' (*Choice*, v.26, no.7, March 1989, p.1120). *Class No:* 908(510)(084.3)

Hong Kong

[4603]
Research materials for Hong Kong studies. Birch, A., *and others, eds.* Hong Kong, Centre of Asian Studies, Univ. of Hong Kong, 1984. $80.00. ISSN: 04411900, HK.

16 chapters (1. Reference material for Hong Kong studies - 2. Summary of archaeology material excavated in Hong Kong - 3. Cartographic materials ... 11. Facilities for research in the Public Records Office in Hong Kong).
Class No: 908(512.317)

Bibliographies

[4604]
SCOTT, I., *comp*. **Hong Kong**. Santa Barbara, California, and Oxford, Clio Press, 1990. xxiii,248p.++ 1p. map, indexes. £35.95; $64.00. (*World Bibliographical Series, no.115*.) ISBN: 1851090894.

838 annotated entries in 30 sections: Territory and its people - Geography ... Archaeology and prehistory - History ... Urban society and problems ... Bibliographies. Author, title and subject indexes. *Class No:* 908(512.317)(01)

Yearbooks & Directories

[4605]
WITT, H. **Hong Kong 1993**. Hong Kong, Government Information Services, 1993. 478p. col. illus., map on front end paper, index. HK$52.00; £16.50. ISBN: 9620201256.

Official handbook. 26 chapters *e.g.* Travel and tourism ... History. 45 appendices. Calendar of events in 1989 p.1-5. 44 col. plates. Official Yearbook of the Hong Kong Government. *Class No:* 908(512.317)(058)

Macao

Bibliographies

[4606]
Bibliografia macaense. Gomes, L.G., *comp*. 2nd ed. Macau, Instituto Cultural, 1987. 202p. index.

1800 items, mostly Portuguese.
Class No: 908(512.318)(01)

[4607]
EDMONDS, R.L., *comp*. **Macau**. Santa Barbara, California and Oxford, Clio Press, 1989. 1v, 110p.+1p. map, index. £21.00. (*World Bibliographical Series, no.105*.) ISBN: 1851090908.

381 annotated entries. 22 sections: The territory and its people - Geography and geology ... Travellers' accounts - History ... Libraries, art galleries, museums and archives ... Directories ... Bibliographies. Glossary of place names p.lv. Author, title and subject index. *Class No:* 908(512.318)(01)

Tibet

[4608]
CHIME RINPOCHE, *The Venerable Lama*. **Tibetan resources in Great Britain and South Asia**, p.230-238, *South Asian studies* (British Library, 1986).
Class No: 908(515)

Bibliographies

[4609]
PINFOLD, J., *comp*. **Tibet**. Santa Barbara, Calif., and Oxford, Clio Press, 1991. xxvi,157p. +1p. map. indexes. £26.95. (*World Bibliographical Series, no. 128*.) ISBN: 1851091580.

559 annotated entries in 25 sections The country and its people - Geography - Travel and exploration ... History ... Language - Religion ... Human rights ... Bibliographies. Author, title and subject indexes. 'An ideal source for further study ... it will prove a valuable resource for academic, geographical and many general reference collections' (*Reference Reviews*, v,5, 1991, p.36).
Class No: 908(515)(01)

Mongolia

[4610]
Mongolia today. Shirin, Akiner, *ed*. London, Kegan Paul International in association with the Central Asia Research Forum, School of Oriental and African Studies, London, 1989. xxiv,237p. maps, bibliog. £45. ISBN: 0710303459.

Preliminary versions of most of the chapters were originally presented as papers to a conference on 'Mongolia today', held at S.O.A.S., Univ of London, in December 1987.

12 chapters by different hands: 1. Problems of writing Mongolian history - 2. Mongolia and the Mongolians - 3. Between the Kremlin and the forbidden city ... 8. Mongolian Peoples Army ... 10. Shamanism of the Mongols. Specialist bibliographies at end of each chapter and Bibliography p.229-33. *Class No:* 908(517)

Bibliographies

[4611]
NORDBY, J., *comp*. **Mongolia**. Santa Barbara, California and Oxford, Clio Press, 1993. xxix,192p.++ 1p. map, index. £44.00; $75.00. (*World Bibliographical Series, no.156*.) ISBN: 1851091297.

489 annotated entries in 36 sections: Country and its people - Travellers' accounts - Tourism and travel guides - Geography ... Archaeology - History ... Mongolian nationalism ... Bibliographies. Author, title, and subject index. *Class No:* 908(517)(01)

Encyclopaedias

[4612]
Information Mongolia the comprehensive reference source of the People's Republic of Mongolia (MPR). The Academy of Sciences MPR, *comp*. Oxford, New York, and Beijing, Pergamon Press, 1990. xxxviii,505p. illus. (some col.), col. maps, tables, bibliogs., index. £120; $200. (*Countries Of The World Information Series*.) ISBN: 0080361935.

79 contributors. Part 1. Land and people - 2. History of Mongolia - 3. Political system of the Mongolian People's

....(contd.)

Republic - 4. The Armed Forces - 5. National economy. Each part is sustained by a substantial bibliography. 19 maps. 67 tables. Analytical subject index p.483-505. Encyclopedic coverage of all aspects of Mongolian life 'within a detailed historical framework'. 'With information largely through 1989, the book is already dated by the political and social changes in Mongolia, but ... this is still a very useful work' (*Choice,* v.28, no.4, December 1990, p.608). *Class No:* 908(517)(031)

Korea

[4613]

KING, HAN-KYO. Studies on Korea a scholar's guide. Honolulu, Univ. Press of Hawaii, 1980. xxi, 438p. bibliog. index. £24.75; $27.50. ISBN: 0824806735.

16 contributors provide introductory essay and bibliography for Archaeology - History - Philosophy and religion - Language and linguistics - Literature and folklore - Art, music and drama - Education - Geography and natural environment - Maps of Korea (p.247-248) - Government and politics - International relations - North Korea - Russian language materials. Appendix: Major Korean dynasties and rulers p.421-424. 'A well-balanced scholarly overview of Korea' (*Reference Quarterly,* v.20, no.4, Summer 1981, p.430). *Class No:* 908(519)

[4614]

STEINBERG, D.I. The Republic of Korea: economic transformation and social change. Boulder, Colo., Westview Press, 1989. xvi,218p. illus., bibliog., maps, index. (*Westview profiles: Nations Of Contemporary Asia.*) ISBN: 0865317208.

1. Introduction: geography as destiny - 2. Land and people - 3. Origins and early history of the Korean people - 4. Flowering and decline of traditional Korea - 5. Japanese colonial period - 6. Republics of Korea - 7. Society and culture - 8. Politics and administration - 9. Role of the military in Korean society - 10. Economic development 1953 to 1986 - 11. External relations - 12. Future of Korea. Chapter notes p.197-8. Glossary p.119-201. Dramatis personae p.202-4. Bibliography p.205-11. *Class No:* 908(519)

Bibliographies

[4615]

COURANT, M. Bibliographie Coréene. Tableau littéraire de la Corée, contenant la nomenclature des ouvrages publiés dans ce pays jusqu'en 1890 ainsi que la description et l'analyse detaillées des principaux d'entre ces ouvrages. Paris, Leroux, 2v., 1894-96. 2v. Supplément (jusqu'en 1899), 1901. illus. (pl.), index.

Supplément reprinted New York, Lenox Hill, 1966.

3,821 entries, often annotated. V.1: Enseignement, Études des langues. Confucianisme, Littérature - v.2: Moeurs et coutumes, Histoire et géographie - v.3: Sciences et arts, Religions, Relations extérieures. *Class No:* 908(519)(01)

Handbooks & Manuals

[4616]

A Handbook of Korea. 8th ed. Seoul, Korean Overseas Information Service, 1990. 571p. col.illus., col.maps, bibliog., index.

First published 1978.

Sections: Land - People and language - History - Belief, philosophy and religions - Culture and arts - Customs and tradition - Constitution and government - Foreign relations - Unification policy - National defense - Finance - Economy - Industry - Agriculture, forestry and fisheries - Transporation and telecommunications - Science and technology - Education - Mass communications - Social development - Quality of life - Sports - Tourism. Bibliography p.549-61. *Class No:* 908(519)(035)

Yearbooks & Directories

[4617]

Korea Annual 1992. Chun Moon, K., *ed.* 29th ed. Seoul, Yonhap News Agency, 1988. 785p. illus. col.maps, index.

Chronology 1991 p.5-16. Chronology of South Korea in 20th century p.17-38. Review of all aspects of Korean life e.g., government; economic and social affairs; and general information. Who's who p.514-748. *Class No:* 908(519)(058)

Japan

[4618]

Japan Foundation Directory Series. Tokyo, Japan Foundation.

7. *Japanese studies in Europe* 1985.427p. 8. *Directory of Japan specialists in Australia.* rev. ed. 1986. 11. *Japanese studies in Southeast Asia* 1987. 204p. 15. *Japanese studies in the United Kingdom.* 1985. 285p. 16. *Japanese studies in Canada* 1987. 285p. 17 - 18 *Japanese studies in the United States. Part 1. History and present condition* compiled and edited by M. B. Jansen. *Pt 2. Directory of Japan specialists and Japanese studies institutions in the United States and Canada* edited by P. G. Steinhoff. (Ann Arbor, Association for Asian Studies, 3v.1988-89). 'All contain (1) descriptive reports about the historical background, development and current state of Japanese studies within a particular country or region, and (2) directories of institutions and individual specialists - including their addresses, academic affiliation, area of specialisation and current research interests, and major publications about Japan' (Shulman, F. J. *Japan* 1989. Entry 1559). *Class No:* 908(52)

[4619]

Japanese studies: papers presented at a colloquium at the School of Oriental and African Studies, University of London 14-16 September 1988. Brown, Y-Y., *ed.* London, The British Library, 1990. xvi,398p. illus., facsims. (*British Library Occasional Papers, no.11.*) ISBN: 071230178x.

Sessions at the colloquium were devoted to 3 areas: 1. Overview of resources for Japanese studies (*e.g.* Japanese studies in Britain 1945-88. Map and map collections in Japan) - 2. Printing, publishing and the art of the Japanese book - 3. Automation and cooperation. *Class No:* 908(52)

[4620]

Nippon: a charted survey of Japan 1989/90. The Tsuneta Yano Memorial Society (Yano-Tsuneta Kinenkai), *ed.* Tokyo, Kokusei-Sha Corporation, 1989. 355p. tables, index. ISBN: 4875493096.

First published in 1936 as English language version of *Nihon Kokusei-Zue,* an annual publication for Japanese students.

45 chapters covering all aspects of contemporary Japan in 4 sections: 1. General (geography, history, people, law, politics, prefectures and cities, climate and population) - 2. Economy - 3. Industries - 4. Social life and trends. Heavily armed with batteries of statistics. *Class No:* 908(52)

Bibliographies

[4621]

Catalogue of books in English on Japan 1945-1981. Tokyo, The Japan Foundation, 1986. viii, 726p.

8942 unannotated entries in 10 sections: 1. General works - 2. Philosophy - 3. History - 4. Social Sciences - 5. Natural Science - 6. Technology. Engineering - 7. Industry and Commerce - 8. The Arts. Fine Arts - 9. Language - 10. Literature. Author and title indexes. Selected from materials in the National Diet Library, the Japan Foundation Library, and from materials listed in the *Cumulative Bibliography of Asian Studies. Class No:* 908(52)(01)

[4622]

CORDIER, H. Bibliotheca Japonica: dictionnaire bibliographique des ouvrages relatifs à l'Empire Japonais rangé par ordre chronologique jusqu'à 1870, suivi d'un appendice renfermant la liste alphabétique des principaux ouvrages parus de 1870 à 1912. Paris, Leroux, 1912. Reprinted 1968. xiip. 762 cols.

Pioneer and still standard list of materials for Japanese studies. About 3,500 items. *Class No:* 908(52)(01)

[4623]

KOKUSAI BUNKA SHINKOKAI, *comp.* **KBS bibliography of standard reference books for Japaneses studies** with descriptive notes. Tokyo, KBS (and latterly Univ. of Tokyo Press) 1959-.

1: *Generalia,* 1959 Rev. ed. 1971.

2: *Geography and travel,* 1966 (*Geography,* Rev. ed. 1973).

3: *History and biography,* 1965, 3pts.

4: *Religion.*

5A: *History of thought,* 1965, 2pts.

5B: *Education,* 1966.

6A: *Language,* 1961. Rev. ed. 1966.

6B: *Literature* 1966, 5pts.

7A: *Traditional art and architecture,* 1959-60. Rev. ed. 1971.

8: *Manners and customs, and folklore,* 1966.

9: *Politics,* 1970.

9B: *Law,* 1968-70, 2pts.

10: *Economics,* 1969. 2pts.

Each volume has *c.* 200-300 evaluatively annotated entries, systematically arranged. Titles, authors and imprint in Japanese characters as well as romanised. Indexes of authors and editors (romanised, then in Japanese characters). Otherwise text is in English. *Class No:* 908(52)(01)

[4624]

—An Introductory bibliography for Japanese studies. Tokyo, Univ. of Tokyo Press (latterly Bonjin Co. Ltd.) 1975-. v.1.

Continues *KBS Bibliography of standard reference books for Japanese studies (qv).*

V.1: Pt.1. *Social sciences 1969-1972* (1974) Pt. 2. *Humanities 1970-1973* (1975). Similarly v.2 (1976 and 1977); v.3 (1978 and 1980); v.4 (1982); v.5 (1986 and 1987). V.6 Pt.1. *Social sciences 1981-85* (1988). iii, 380p. ISBN 4893580086 contains 9 bibliographical essays: 1. Law - 2. Political sciences - 3. International relations - 4. Economics - 5. Business administration - 6. Sociology - 7. Geography - 8. Cultural anthropology - 9. Education. Author and subject indexes. It is planned to revert to biennial issues after v. 6 is completed. *Class No:* 908(52)(01)

[4625]

PERREN, R. Japanese studies from prehistory to 1990: a bibliographical guide. Manchester Univ. Press, 1992. x,172p. index. £45. (*History and Related Disciplines Select Bibliographies.*) ISBN: 0719024587.

4069 Western language items (many annotated) in 6 uniformly sub-divided sections under 20 thematic headings (*e.g.* population and demography ... foreign trade and culture ... imperialism ... art and culture). *Class No:* 908(52)(01)

[4626]

SHULMAN, F.J. Japan. Santa Barbara, California, and Oxford, Clio Press, 1989. xix, 873p. and 2p. maps, index. (*World Bibliographical Series, no.103.*) ISBN: 1851090746.

1615 annotated entries in 46 sections: The country and its people - Geography and geology ... Travellers' accounts - Tourism and travel guides - Prehistory and Archaeology - History - Biographical and autobiographical accounts ... Minorities: the Ainu, Burakumin, and Koreans - Overseas Japanese ... Libraries and Museums ... Encyclopaedias, directories and subject dictionaries - Bibliographies and research guides. Chronology p.xxi. Author, subject and title index. *Class No:* 908(52)(01)

[4627]

WENCKSTERN, F. von, *comp.* **A Bibliography of the Japanese Empire** being a classified list of all books, essays and maps in European languages relating to Dai Nihon (Great Japan) published in Europe, America and in the East from 1859-93. A.D. (VIth of Ansei - XXVIIth of Meiji). To which is added a facsimile reprint of Léon Pagès' Bibliographie Japonaise depuis le xve siècle jusqu'à 1859. Stuttgart, Anton Hiersemann; Nendeln Liechtenstein, Klaus Reprint, 2v., 1970.

First published in Leiden by E.J. Brill and by Kegan Paul in London 1895-1907. L. Pagès' *Bibliographie Japonaise ou catalogue des ouvrage, relatifs au Japon* was published in Paris by Benjamin Duprat, Librairie-de l'Institut Impérial de France in 1859. V. Palugren's List of Swedish literature on Japan was first published in Tokyo in 1907.

V1: ix, 338p. ISBN 377270334. V.2: xvi, 486p. + 28p. ISBN 377270342 comprises the literature from 1894 to the middle of 1906 with additions and corrections to v.1 and a supplement to Pagès' *Bibliographie Japonaise.* Added is V. Palmgren's *List of Swedish literature on Japan.* In total about 16,000 entries. *Class No:* 908(52)(01)

[4628]

—NACHOD, O. Bibliographie von Japan. Stuttgart, Anton Hiersemann; Nendeln, Liechtenstein, Klaus Reprint, 6v., 1970.

First published in Leipzig by Verlag Karl W. Hiersemann 1928-1940.

33621 entries covering material published 1927-1937. *Class No:* 908(52)(01)

[4629]

—NACHOD, O. Bibliography of the Japanese Empire 1906-1926 being a classified list of the literature issued in European languages since the publication of Fr. von Wenckstern's Bibliography of the Japanese Empire up to the year 1926. London, Edward Goldston; Leipzig. Karl W. Hiersemann, 2v., 1928. xvi, 832p.

4575 entries covering books and articles in English, German, French, Dutch, Italian, Spanish and Portuguese languages and assembled in sections *e.g.* 2. History (A. General works, B. By period prehistory to World War I) p.150-306 - 3. Travel ... 13. Bibliography - 14. Works of reference - 15. Territories (Old Japan; Yezo and Kurile Is.; Sachalin; Ryuku; Formosa and the Pescadores; Korea; Southern Manchuria). *Class No:* 908(52)(01)

Encyclopaedias

[4630]

The Cambridge encyclopedia of Japan. Bowring, R. **and** Kornicki, P., *eds.* Cambridge, Cambridge Univ. Press, 1993. 408p. col. illus., col. maps, tables, diagrs., bibliogs., index. £29.95. (*Cambridge World Encyclopedias.*) ISBN: 0521403529.

54 contributors. *Contents:* Geography - History - Language and literature - Thought and religion - Arts and crafts - Society - Politics - Economy in thematically arranged text with boxed features highlighting important topics. *Class No:* 908(52)(031)

[4631]

Kodansha encyclopedia of Japan. Tokyo, Kodansha International Ltd., 9v. 1983. Distributed in UK by International Book Distributors and in US by Harper & Row. V.1-8. 352p. each; v.9. 288p. $620.00 (set including *Supplement*). ISBN: 0870116207, UK; 4061445316, Japan.

680 Japanese and 524 international contributors. Covers all aspects of Japanese life: technology, economics law and business with the greatest emphasis on history, geography, fine arts, and literature. V.9 is a analytical index: list of contributors p.ix-xxii. 'The long pieces on the major aspects of Japan are of the highest quality, all of them written by top-notch scholars' (Encyclopaedia of Japan, *Choice,* v.21, no. 11-12, July-August 1984, p.1576).

Supplement/1987. 64p. illus. index. $20.00. 'Overviews and in-depth analyses of the newest developments in Japanese society'.

Japan: an illustrated encyclopedia (2v., 1993. 1930p. col. illus., maps, bibliog. £175). is announced as the successor to the *Kodansha encyclopedia of Japan*. It contains 12168 cross-referenced entries from 1100 contributors emphasising contemporary aspects of Japanese society and culture with detailed entries on technology, art, business, and economics. 15p. of maps. 24p. history chart, 10p. bibliography of major English-language works, and 3500 colour plates. *Class No:* 908(52)(031)

Dictionaries

[4632]

DE MENTE, B. Everything Japanese. London, Harrap, 1989. xiv, 319p. illus., map. £14.95.

Almost 1,000 A-Z entries relating to Japanese history, geography, politics, economics, arts, education, business and social customs. Other English language sources p.313-18. *Class No:* 908(52)(038)

[4633]

PERKINS, D. Encyclopedia of Japan: Japanese history and culture, from Abacus to Zori. New York and Oxford, Facts on File, 1991. 410p. illus., maps, charts. £21.95. ISBN: 0816019347.

1,000 + A-Z cross-referenced entries relating to Japanese history, culture, business, government, arts and crafts, language and literature, food, and religion. List of Emperors p.79. Prime Ministers since 1945 p.269. Bibliography p.394-401. 'Well balanced and accurate survey for the general reader' (*Reference Reviews,* v.6, no.5, 1992, p.47). *Class No:* 908(52)(038)

Taiwan

[4634]

COPPER, J.F. Taiwan nation-state or province? Boulder, Colo., Westview Press, 1990. xi,148p. illus., map, bibliog., index. $32.50; £21. (*Westview Profiles Nations of Contemporary Asia.*) ISBN: 081330444x.

1. Land and the people - 2. History - 3. Society and culture - 4. Political system - 5. Economy - 6. Foreign and military policies - 7. Future. Chapter notes p.129-36. Bibliography p.137-41. *Class No:* 908(529)

[4635]

Republic of China reference book. Chang, H., *and others, eds.* Taipei, United Pacific International Inc., 1983. Distributed in United States by Collings Inc. of New York. xvi, 473p. col.illus. index. $30.00.

A continuation of *China yearbook* (1st ed. 1943) in a new format.

55 chapters in 9 sections: 1. General - 2. Government - 3. Territory - 4. Economy and finance - 5. Education, sport and cultural activities - 6. Social activities - 7. Religion - 8. Chronology (p.315-362) - 9. Who's who in China. Section 10 consists of appendices *e.g.* Constitution; Government directory, China and the world *etc.. Class No:* 908(529)

[4636]

WEI-CHIN LEE, *comp.* **Taiwan.** Santa Barbara, California and Oxford, Clio Press, 1990. xxxiv,247p. + + 1p. map, indexes. £38.00; $68.00. (*World Bibliographical Series, no.113.*) ISBN: 1851090916.

825 entries in 37 sections: Country and its people - Tourism and traveller's accounts - Geography ... Prehistory and archaeology - History - Religion ... Indigenous minority peoples ... Military affairs ... Bibliographies and directories. Romanization of Chinese names and terms p.xxix. Author, title and subject indexes. Concentrates on post-1980 English language publications. *Class No:* 908(529)

Bibliographies

[4637]
JACOB, J.B. **Taiwan** a comprehensive bibliography of English-language publications. New York, East Asian Institute, Columbia Univ., 1984. 214p. pbk. $12.50. ISBN: 0913418099.

Unannotated bibliography of about 200 publications 1945-1980 arranged in 18 categories. The Introduction, 'The study of Taiwan', gives excellent background information. *Class No:* 908(529)(01)

[4638]
LEE, K. Siu-chu *and* TAI, A, Choung-mei. **An Annotated bibliography of selected works about Republic of China.** Taipei, Taiwan, Kwang Hwa Publishing Co., 1981. 105p. index. pbk.

249 annotated entries introducing various aspects of Republic of China in 26 sections e.g., 7. Biography ... 15. History ... 26. Tourism. Mostly English-langue material but other Western and Oriental languages also represented. *Class No:* 908(529)(01)

Asia—Middle & Near East

Bibliographies

[4639]
AUCHTERLONIE, P. **Introductory guide to Middle Eastern and Islamic bibliography.** Oxford, Middle East Libraries Committee, 1990. v,84p. index, A4 soft cover. £7.50. (*MELC Research Guides, no.5.*) ISBN: 0948889407.

Basic bibliography (in form sections) providing a concise and straightforward guidance to the range of reference materials available for Middle Eastern studies. *Class No:* 908(53+56)(01)

[4640]
Bibliographic guide to Middle Eastern Studies. Boston, G.K. Hall. Annual.

1993 (1994). 650p. $195. 0783820976. Lists all materials cataloged during the past year by the Library of Congress, the Middle East section of the NYPL's renowned Oriental Division, and the modern Hebrew language books in the BYPL's Jewish Division. *Class No:* 908(53+56)(01)

[4641]
CHICAGO UNIVERSITY. **Catalog of the Oriental Institute Library.** Boston, Mass., G.K. Hall, 16v., 1970.

1970. 32 reels. $1585.00 (Export $1915.00). ISBN 0816112835. *First Supplement (Catalogue of the Middle Eastern Collection, Formerly the Oriental Institute Library).* 962p. $110.00 ($135.00). ISBN 0816100675. 284,000 photolithographed catalogue cards. Author catalogue, interfiled with authority, series, book review and journal analytical-card entries. Holdings are particularly rich in Assyriology, Egyptology and Islam. Main catalogue now available on microfilm. *Class No:* 908(53+56)(01)

[4642]
FENTON, T.P. *and* HEFFRON, M.J., *comps.* **Middle East: a directory of resources.** Maryknoll, New York, Orbis Books, 1988. 144p. indexes, pbk. $9.95. ISBN: 0883445336.

Updates and expands the Middle East chapter in *Third World resource directory* (Orbis, 1984).

1. Organizations - 2. Books - 3. Periodicals - 4. Pamphlets and articles - 5. Audiovisuals. *Class No:* 908(53+56)(01)

[4643]
HOPWOOD, D. *and* GRIMWOOD-JONES, D., *eds.* **Middle East and Islam** a bibliographical introduction. Rev and enlarged ed. Zug, Switzerland, Inter-Documentation Co., 1979. xi,492p. index. (*Bibliotheca Asiatica; no.15.*)

1st ed. 1972 (Bibliotheca Asiatica, no.9)

At head: 'Middle East Libraries Committee'. 25 contributors. Sections (each with introduction): 1. Reference - 2. Islamic studies - 3. Subject bibliographies (Anthropology; Geography; Political science; Recent economic history; Official publications) - 4. Regional bibliographies (Arabia ... Syria and Lebanon) - 5. Arabic language and literature (including Arabic periodicals and newspapers). Auchterlonie, P. *Middle-East and Islam: a bibliographical introduction. Supplement 1977-1983.* 1986. vi,244p. (Bibliotheca Asiatica, no.20). *Class No:* 908(53+56)(01)

[4644]
THE MIDDLE EAST INSTITUTE, Washington DC. **Catalog of the Middle East Institute Library.** Boston, Mass., G.K. Hall, 4v., 1984. 2290p. $650.00 (Export $770.00). ISBN: 0816104301.

48,000 photolithographed catalogue cards covering a wide range of topics including 19th and 20th century history, economics and oil, and 19th century travel accounts. *Class No:* 908(53+56)(01)

Encyclopaedias

[4645]
The Cambridge encyclopedia of the Middle East and North Africa. Mostyn, T. *and* Hourani, A., *eds.* Cambridge, Cambridge Univ. Press, 1988. 504p. illus., (some col.), col. maps., bibliogs., index. £30.00; $49.50. ISBN: 0521321905.

Over 80 contributors. Authoritative essays grouped in 6 parts sub-divided into headed sections: 1. Lands and peoples - 2. History (Ancient history of the Near East to The Middle East and North Africa 1800-1939 in 8 sections) - 3. Societies and economies - 4. Culture - 5. The countries (28) and peoples without countries (Armenians, Kurds, Palestinians) - 6. Inter-state relations. Section bibliogs. 36 maps. 50 colour and 100 black and white illus. 'An authoritative source of information on the history, culture and political situation of the Middle East' (*Reference Reviews*, v.3, no.2, June 1989, p.93). *Class No:* 908(53+56)(031)

Handbooks & Manuals

[4646]
ADAMS, M., *ed.* **The Middle East:** a handbook. 2nd ed. New York and Oxford, Facts On File, 1988. xviii, 865p. maps. bibliog., tables, index. £30.00; $45.00. (*Handbooks to the Modern World.*) ISBN: 0816012687.

First published by Anthony Blond in 1971.

41 mostly academic contributors from 12 countries. Basic information and comparative statistics A-Z by country precede well-documented chapter length essays grouped in 5 sections: 1. General background (*i.e.* historical outline) - 2. Countries of the Middle East - 3/5. Political, Economic and Social affairs. Chapter bibliographies. Analytical index. 'Can be used as a quick reference tool, but really comes into its own as a substantial introduction to Middle Eastern affairs

....*(contd.)*

and a guide to further reading' (*Reference Reviews*, v.2, no.3, September 1988, p.159-60).
Class No: 908(53+56)(035)

[4647]
BACHARACH, J.L. A Middle East studies handbook 570-1974. Seattle and London, Univ. of Washington Press, 1984. x, 160p. maps, index. $20.00. ISBN: 0295961384.

A revised version of the author's *A Near East studies handbook* (1974).

Handbook of terms, maps, names and data of value to teachers and students, writers and researchers arranged in 11 sections: *e.g.* 4. Dynasties ... 6. Chronology ... 8. Historical atlas (51 maps) - 9. Gazetteer (p.131-134) - 10. Glossary (p.135-147). Index for Historical atlas p.148-151. Concentrates on Iran, Turkey, Egypt, Iraq, Syria, Lebanon, Jordan, Israel, and the Arabian peninsula. 'In one neat package all the odds and ends needed for ready reference in Middle East studies' (*Choice*, v.22, no.8, April 1985, p. 1135). *Class No:* 908(53+56)(035)

Yearbooks & Directories

[4648]
The Middle East and North Africa 1994. 40th ed. London, Europa, 1993. Annual. Distributed in North America by Gale Research Co. xxi,988p. maps, tables, bibliogs. £145. (*Regional Surveys of the world*.) ISBN: 0946653895.

Part 1. General survey, authoritative essays on issues of contemporary interest - 2. Regional organizations: comprehensive information on the United Nations and the other major organizations active in the region - 3. Country surveys A-Z: Geography; History; Economy; Statistical survey; Directory (the constitution, government, legislature, political organizations, diplomatic representation, judicial system, religion, press, publishers, radio and TV, finance, trade and industry, transport, tourism, atomic energy, defence, education). 'A reference work of high standard in a remarkably consistent series' (*International Affairs*, v.61,no.2, Spring 1985, p.348). *Class No:*
Class No: 908(53+56)(058)

[4649]
The Middle East annual issues and events. Partington, D.H., *ed.* Boston, G.K. Hall, 1981-. Annual (v.3. 1983). xiii, 269p. maps on endpapers. index.

1983 edition has 6 articles: Islamic fundamentalism - PLO since Beirut - Soviet Union, Syria, and the crisis in Lebanon - Chad - Middle East in the US Media - The year's publications in Middle Eastern studies. Essays included in v.1-2 listed p.269. 'Offers convenient access to authoritative analyses of important issues' (*Wilson Library Bulletin*, v.57, no.8, April 1983, p.708). *Class No:* 908(53+56)(058)

[4650]
Middle East contemporary survey 1987. 11th ed. Boulder, Colo., Westview Press for the Moshe Dayan Center for Middle Eastern and African Studies, The Shiloah Institute, Tel Aviv Univ. xxxviii,710p. maps, tables, index. ISBN: 0813309255.

'An annual record and analysis of political, economic, military and international developments in the Middle East and its peripheral regions'. V.10. (xxxv, 694p. 7 maps, 1988), with 24 contributors, has 2 parts: 1. Current issues (Middle East in perspective; Middle East and World affairs; Arab-Israeli relations; Intra-regional and Muslim affairs;

....*(contd.)*

Palestinian issues; Middle East economic issues) - 2. Country-by-country survey. List of sources p.xix-xxiv.
Class No: 908(53+56)(058)

[4651]
Middle East review. Saffron Walden, Essex, World of Information, 1987-. Annual. 200p. maps. softcover. ISBN: 090443964x.

Formerly *Middle East annual review*. First published 1974.

15 contributors. 6 introductory chapters and 27 A-Z country reviews each comprising essay and profile, key facts, business guide, statistics, and map. 'A useful reference tool' (*International Affairs*, v.57, no.1, Winter 1980/81, p.216). *Class No:* 908(53+56)(058)

Libraries

[4652]
AUCHTERLONIE, P. Collections in British libraries on Middle Eastern and Islamic studies. Durham, University of Durham Centre for Middle Eastern and Islamic Studies, 1981. 98p. bibliog. pbk. ISSN: 03070654.

Resources of the British Library, SOAS, and various University libraries. Also a survey of recent developments in Islamic bibliography in UK.
Class No: 908(53+56):061:026/027

[4653]
DORR, S. Scholar's guide to Washington DC for Middle Eastern studies : Egypt, Sudan, Jordan, Lebanon, Syria, Iraq, the Arabian peninsula, Israel, Turkey, Iran. Washington, Smithsonian Institution Press, 1981. xiii, 540p., bibliog., index. $29.95. (*Scholar's Guide to Washington*.) ISBN: 0874743729.

Directory and evaluation of the resources of more than 500 institutions. Appendix 1. Judaic history collections. 2. Bookstores. 3. Library collections. Bibliography p.513-516. Oral history and personal papers, Library subject-strength, name and subject indexes p.517-540. 'A unique and indispensable reference work on an area of the world of crucial importance to the US'. (*Choice*, v.19, no.10, June 1982, p.1376). *Class No:* 908(53+56):061:026/027

Saudi Arabia

[4654]
FOUAD AL-FARSY. Modernity and tradition the Saudi equation. London, Kegan Paul International, 1990. xxiii,337p. illus., maps, tables, bibliog., index. ISBN: 0710303955.

Supersedes the author's *Saudi Arabia: a case study in development*.

1. The geography of the Kingdom - 2. Historical and cultural background - 3. Islam ... 5. Political system - 6. Kingdom's ministries - 7. Government agencies - 8. Petroleum - 9. Economy - 10. Planning - 11. Industrial development - 12. Agricultural development ... 18. Foreign relations ... 20. How others see us. Bibliography p.322. 4 maps. 'Primary objective of this work is to deal as comprehensively as possible with the development of Saudi Arabia as a political, economic and social system' (*Introduction*). *Class No:* 908(532)

Bibliographies

[4655]

CLEMENTS, F.A., *comp*. **Saudi Arabia.** 2nd ed. Santa Barbara, California and Oxford, Clio Press, 1988. xxix, 354p. + 1p. map, index. £44.95. $55.00. (*World Bibliographical Series; no.5.*) ISBN: 1851090673.

1361 annotated entries (789 in 1st ed.). 34 sections: The country and its people - Exploration and travel - Geography ... History ... Libraries - Bibliographies. Theses and dissertations on Saudi Arabia p.xviii-xxix. Author, title and subject index. *Class No:* 908(532)(01)

[4656]

PHILIPP, H.J. **Saudi Arabia:** bibliography on society politics economics. München, K.G.Saur, 1984. xii, 405p. £33. (*Bibliographies on regional geography and area studies.*) ISBN: 3598211341.

3680 mainly English-language items covering the period commencing with the ascent of Saudi power in 1745 over the territory now known as the Kingdom of Saudi Arabia. 'A no-frills, researcher's bibliography this ... as comprehensive as any on Saudi Arabia' (*Library Review*, v.35, no.2, Summer 1986, p.140-141). *Class No:* 908(532)(01)

Yemen

[4657]

WENNER, M.W. **The Yemen Arab Republic** development and change in an ancient land. Boulder, Colo., Westview Press, 1991. x,194p. illus., map, tables, bibliog., index. $34.95. (*Westview Profiles. Nations Of The Contemporary Middle East.*) ISBN: 0891587748.

1. The land - 2. People and culture - 3. Economic problems and prospects - 4. Before the Republic - 5. The Republic. Bibliography p.175-80. Chronology p.181-3. *Class No:* 908(533)

Bibliographies

[4658]

SMITH, G.R., *comp*. **The Yemens** The Yemen Arab Republic and the People's Democratic Republic of Yemen. Santa Barbara, California and Oxford, Clio Press, 1984. xxiii, 161p. + 1p. map, index. £24.95. $33.00. (*World Bibliographical Series; no.50.*) ISBN: 0903450879.

401 annotated entries. 35 sections: The country and its people - Geography - Tourism - Travellers' accounts ... Prehistory and archaeology - History ... Museums and archives ... Directories - Bibliographies. Theses and dissertations on The Yemens p.xix-xxiii. Author, title and subject index. *Class No:* 908(533)(01)

Oman

Bibliographies

[4659]

CLEMENTS, F.A., *comp*. **Oman.** Santa Barbara, California and Oxford, Clio Press, 1981. xv, 216p. + 1p., map, index. £29.50. $32.50. (*World Bibliographical Series, no.29.*) ISBN: 0903450437.

A revised edition is announced for publication in 1994. ISBN 1851091963.

890 annotated entries. 31 sections: The country and its people - Oman in general works on the Middle East -

.... (contd.)
Exploration and travel - Geography ... Prehistory and archaeology - History ... Oil ... Bibliographies. Author, title and subject index. *Class No:* 908(535)(01)

[4660]

SHANNON, M.O. **Oman and Southeastern Arabia** a bibliogrphical survey. Boston, Mass., G.K. Hall, 1978. 181p.

988 numbered items, - books, articles and reports, entries for the most significant items being annotated. Coverage: all Western literature on Oman and S.E. Arabia from prehistory to the present. Topics include politics and society, geology, geography, maritime affairs, international law and government. Entries for books are ususally annotated. Subject, author, title index. *Class No:* 908(535)(01)

Gulf States

[4661]

COTTRELL, A.J., *ed*. **The Persian Gulf states** : a general survey. Baltimore, John Hopkins Univ. Press, 1980. xiii, 695p. tables. $59.00. ISBN: 0801822041.

22 contributors. 4 parts (18 chapters): 1. The history of the Persian Gulf - 2. Economics and urban development of the Persian Gulf - 3. Culture, religion, language and literature - 4. Arts and society in the Persian Gulf. Each chapter has select bibliography. Footnotes. Appendices A-L (C. Natural regions; H. Demography; I. Education; K. Industrial development; L. Agriculture). Components: Iran, Iraq, Saudi Arabia; Kuwait, Bahrain, Qatar, United Arab Republic Emirates, Oman. A handsome volume. *Class No:* 908(536)

[4662]

Qatar. Whelan, J., *ed*. London, Middle East Economic Digest, 1983. Distributed by Croom Helm. vii, 176p. illus. (some col.), maps, tables, bibliog., index. softcover. £9.95. ISBN: 0950521191.

1. The background (government, biographies of ruling family, history, archaeology etc.) - 2. Practical guide - 3. The expatriate experience - 4. Economy - 5. Doing business - 6. Data and the regions. Bibliography p.171-3. *Class No:* 908(536)

Bibliographies

[4663]

CLEMENTS, F.A., *comp*. **United Arab Emirates.** Santa Barbara, California and Oxford, Clio Press, 1983. xii, 162p. + 1p. map, index. £23.50. $26.00. (*World Bibliographical Series, no.43.*) ISBN: 0903450747.

565 annotated entries. 30 sections: The country and its people - UAE in general works on the Middle East - Exploration and travel - Geography ... Prehistory and archaeology - History ... Bibliographies. Author, title and subject index. *Class No:* 908(536)(01)

[4664]

UNWIN, P.T.H., *comp*. **Qatar.** Santa Barbara, California and Oxford, Clio Press, 1982. xxv, 162p + 1p. map, index. £24.95. $30.00. (*World Bibliographical Series, no.36.*) ISBN: 0903450666.

574 annotated entries. 29 sections: The country and its people - Geography and geology - Travel and exploration ... Prehistory and archaeology - History ... Bibliographies. Author, title and subject index. *Class No:* 908(536)(01)

Bahrain

[4665]

LAWSON, F.H. **Bahrain** the modernization of autocracy. Boulder, Colo., Westview Press, 1989. xiv,146p. illus., map, bibliog., index. (*Profiles Nations Of The Middle East.*) ISBN: 0813301238.

1. Geographical and social structure - 2. Establishment of British Imperial order - 3. Nationalist movements of 1950s - 4. Contemporary politics - 5. Contemporary economic affairs - 6. Foreign relations. Bibliography p.137-42.

Class No: 908(536.5)

Bibliographies

[4666]

UNWIN, P.T.H., *comp.* **Bahrain.** Santa Barbara, California and Oxford, Clio Press, 1984. xxxii, 265p.+1p. map, index. £39.50. $43.50. (*World Bibliographical Series no.49.*) ISBN: 0903450860.

911 annotated entries. 31 sections: The country and its people - Geography and geology - Travel and exploration ... Prehistory and archaeology - History ... Oil industry ... Bibliographies. Author, subject and title index.

Class No: 908(536.5)(01)

Kuwait

[4667]

CRYSTAL, J. **Kuwait** the transformation of an oil state. Boulder, Colo., Westview Press, 1992. xii,194p. illus., map, tables, bibliog., index. (*Nations Of The Contemporary Middle East.*) ISBN: 0813308887.

1. Introduction - 2. History - 3. Oil economy - 4. Kuwaiti society - 5. Political institutions and processes - 6. Foreign policy - 7. Aftermath of the invasion. Chronology (1756-1991) p.179-80. Bibliographic essay, p.181-5.

Class No: 908(536.8)

Bibliographies

[4668]

CLEMENTS, F.A., *comp.* **Kuwait.** Santa Barbara, California and Oxford, Clio Press, 1985. xv, 195p.+1p. map, index. £28.50. $30.00. (*World Bibliographical Series, no.56.*) ISBN: 0903450992.

799 annotated entries. 33 sections: The country and its people - Kuwait in general works on the Middle East - Exploration and travel - Geography ... History ... Oil ... Libraries - Bibliographies. Author, title and subject index.

Class No: 908(536.8)(01)

Asia—South & South East

[4669]

RAHIM, E. **Scholar's guide to Washington D.C. for South Asian studies:** Afghanistan, Bangladesh, Bhutan, India, Maldives, Nepal, Pakistan, Sri Lanka. Washington, Smithsonian Institution Press, 1981. 438p. bibliog., indexes. $27.50; £12.50. (*Scholars Guide to Washington D.C., no.8.*) ISBN: 0874747783.

Basic reference guide for scholars to South Asian resources in the Washington D.C. metropolitan area. Bibliography p.410-3. *Class No:* 908(54+59)

Bibliographies

[4670]

PATTERSON, M.L.P. **South Asian civilizations** a bibliographic synthesis. Chicago, Univ. of Chicago Press, 1981. xxxix, 853p. maps, index. £55.95; $70.00. ISBN: 0226649105.

28017 citations arranged in 5 parts totalling 18 long subdivided chapters relating to India, Pakistan, Bangladesh, Nepal, Bhutan, Sri Lanka, and the Maldive Islands. Pt.5 is Reference resources *viz* general reference; physical and human ecology: a scholar's and traveller's introduction; teaching and study; South Asian research materials: location and access; tools for the study of the literary languages. Author index p.707-808. Subject index p.809-853.

A detailed study of Structure and organization (p.xix-xxiii) and The Outline of Headings (p.1-83) is recommended before use. *Class No:* 908(54+59)(01)

[4671]

PATTERSON M.L.P. *and* INDEN, R.B., *eds.* **Introduction to the civilization of India, South Asia** an introductory bibliography. Chicago, Univ. of Chicago Press, 1962. 448p. (*Bibliotheca Asiatica; no.12.*)

Lists 4,369 publications on India, Pakistan, Ceylon and Nepal, mostly in English. Six major sections: General - History - Social structure and organization - Political and economic structure and political, economic and social change - Religion and philosophy - Literature, science and the arts. *Class No:* 908(54+59)(01)

[4672]

PEARSON, J.D., *ed.* **South Asian bibliography** a handbook and guide. Hassocks, Sussex, Harvester Press; Atlantic Highlands, New Jersey, Humanities Press, 1979. xiii, 381p. ISBN: 0855278919, UK; 0391008196, US.

26 contributors. Sections: Manuscripts. Archives. Theses - Printed books (1. Special forms: Periodicals and newspapers; Official publications, to 1947: Government publications, since 1947; Maps. 2. Subjects: Religions; Anthropology and sociology: Art and archaeology; Music and the dance; Language and literature; Historical writing, Law; Economics; Traditional science and technology; Modern science and technology - 3. Regions and countries (India, Pakistan, Bangladesh, Afghanistan, Ceylon (Sri Lanka), Maldives, Burma, the Himalayas and Tibet). Running commentary in subsections (India: bibliographies; reference books: India in general; the states). Index of authors, p.361-81 - *c.*1,600 entries. An important and scholarly bibliography: awarded the LA's Besterman Medal for 1979. *Class No:* 908(54+59)(01)

[4673]

UNIVERSITY OF MINNESTOA. Ames Library of South Asia. **Catalog of the Ames Library of South Asia.** Boston, Mass., G.K. Hall, 16v., 1980. 10,895p. $185.00 (Export $224.00). ISBN: 0816102759.

228,000 photolithographed catalogue cards of one of the most comprehensive South Asian collections in the US. The collection contains over 90,000 books, periodicals, manuscripts, pamphlets, maps, newspapers, and microforms on South Asia. The Catalog of the Library is in dictionary form, with author, title, and subject cards arranged in one alphabetical sequence. Analytics are generally provided for all serial publications. *Class No:* 908(54+59)(01)

Encyclopaedias

[4674]
The Cambridge encyclopedia of India, Pakistan, Bangladesh, Sri Lanka, Nepal, Bhutan and the Maldives. Robinson, F., *ed*. Cambridge, Cambridge Univ. Press, 1989. 520p. illus., (many col.), maps, tables, index. £30.0; $49.50. ISBN: 0521334519.

69 contributors. 85 authoritative essays grouped in 9 sections: 1. Land - 2. Peoples - 3. History to independence - 4. Politics - 5. Foreign policy - 6. Economics - 7. Religions - 8. Societies - 9. Culture. Section bibliographies. Glossary p.505-7. 75 maps. 69 tables. Analytical index. 'The best available single-volume treatment of South Asia' (*Library Journal*, v.114, no.9, 15 May 1989, p.65).
Class No: 908(54+59)(031)

Almanacs

[4675]
GUNASINGHAM, S., *comp*. **Directory of South Asian library resources in the UK and the Republic of Ireland.** London (?), South Asia Library Group, 1988. 182p. Mimeographed with spiral binding. ISBN: 0951359304.

154 libraries and collections arranged topographically by city and A-Z by library. Data: address; telephone; librarian; access and facilities; brief history of collections; special features; publications. *Class No:* 908(54+59)(059)

Maps & Atlases

[4676]
Fully annotated atlas of South Asia. Dutt, A.K. *and* Geib, M.M. Boulder, Colorado, Westview Press, 1987. xxiii,231p. illus., maps, bibliog. $29.50. ISBN: 0813300444.

Introduction to South Asia followed by 6 national sections on India, Bangladesh, Pakistan, Sri Lanka, Nepal and Bhutan. Bibliography p.225-231. 'More appropriate to have published this text as an introductory textbook on South Asia, rather than an atlas' (*Cartographica* v.25,no.4, 1988, p.92-93). *Class No:* 908(54+59)(084.3)

Libraries

[4677]
GAUR, A., *ed*. **South Asian studies** papers presented at a colloquium on 24-26 April 1986. London, The British Library, 1986. xvii, 327p. £19.50. (*British Library Occasional Papers, No. 7.*) ISBN: 0712300953.

Devoted to 3 main topics: 1. Resources in the United Kingdom (with special reference to the British Library's collections - 2. Bibliographical research, and facilities - 3. Resources in the libraries of South Asia and other countries, and the prospects for international cooperation. 'This is bound to emerge as a standard work in its field' (*Library Association Record*, v.89, no.6, June 1987, p.293).
Class No: 908(54+59):061:026/027

India

Bibliographies

[4678]
BRAY, J. *and* **NAWANG TSERING SHAKSPO. A Bibliography of Ladakh.** Warminster, Wiltshire, Aris & Phillips, 1988. 153p. index. £17.50. ISBN: 085668435x.

Close to 1000 annotated entries listing books, articles, sound discs, tapes and academic theses which appeared before mid-1987 in India, Europe, North America and Japan. The emphasis is on academic studies on Ladakhi history and culture. *Class No:* 908(540)(01)

[4679]
CHAWLA, S. *and* **PANDIT, T.N. Bibliography on Andaman and Nicobar Islands** (covering anthropology, biology, geography, geology, history, statistics etc.). Calcutta, Anthropological Survey of India, 1981. xii, 138p. index.

1301 unannotated entries A-Z by author. Subject index. *Class No:* 908(540)(01)

[4680]
GREAT BRITAIN. India Office Library and Records. **Catalogue of European printed books, India Office Library.** Boston, Mass., G.K. Hall, 10v., 1964. 7225p. $835.00 (Export $1010.00). ISBN: 0816106711.

110,000 photolithographed catalogue cards. Scope is every aspect of the history and culture of the peoples of the Indian subcontinent and contiguous territories of related culture. Particularly strong in art and archaeology, history, philosophy and religion, linguistics, anthropology, and economics and politics, the collection includes many official British and Indian publications. *Class No:* 908(540)(01)

[4681]
GUPTA, B.K. *and* **KHARBAS, D.S.,** *comps*. **India.** Santa Barbara, California and Oxford, Clio Press, 1984. xviii, 364p.+2p., map, index. £37.95. $42.00. (*World Bibliographical Series; no.26.*) ISBN: 0903450380.

A revised edition compiled by I.Derbyshire is announced for publication in 1994. ISBN 1851092005.

835 annotated entries. 31 sections: The country and its people - Geography ... History ... Religion ... Libraries, museums and archives - Bibliographies, abstracts and indexes. Chronology p.xvii-xviii. Author, title and subject index. *Class No:* 908(540)(01)

[4682]
RAMESH CHANDER DOGRA. Jammu and Kashmir: a select and annotated bibliography of manuscripts books and articles together with a survey of its history, languages and literature. Delhi, Ajanta Publications, 1986. viii, 417p. indexes. Rs300. $60.00.

11 introductory essays precede a classified bibliography. 'A most useful cumulation of knowledge' (*Bulletin of School of Oriental and African Studies*, v.51, no.1, 1988, p.193-194). *Class No:* 908(540)(01)

Encyclopaedias

[4683]
Encyclopaedia Indica. Sharma, J.S. 2nd ed. New Delhi, S. Chand, 2v., 1981. viii, 1407p.

First published in 1v. 1975.

About 10,000 entries: 'Indira Gandhi': 2 columns; 'S.R.

....(contd.)

Ranganathan': 1 column; 'Socialist thinking in India': 11 columns. No illus., maps or bibliographies.

Class No: 908(540)(031)

Dictionaries

[4684]

ROY, A.K. *and* GIDWANI, N.N. **A Dictionary of Indology.** New Delhi, Oxford & IBH Publishing; Atlantic Highlands, N.J., Humanities Press, 4v., 1983-1986. iii,327p, 349p, 287p, 337p.

Encyclopedic dictionary of terms and topics relating to, amongst other subjects, ancient geography, archaeology, epigraphy, history, and palaeography.

Class No: 908(540)(038)

Yearbooks & Directories

[4685]

Hindustan yearbook and who's who 1988. Sarkar, S. 56th ed. Calcutta. M.C. Sarkar, 1988. 256p. tables, index. Rs40.00. ISSN: 09701168.

Pt.1. 45 sections *e.g.* Indian chronology; History of India; Geographical information; World gazetteer. Pt.2. States and Territories; Who's who; Directory information; Indian events 1987; Bangladesh 1987; Obituaries; Details of 7th Five Year Plan. *Class No:* 908(540)(058)

Gazetteers

[4686]

The Gazetteer of India. Chopra, P.N., *ed.* New Delhi, Gazetteer Unit, Ministry of Education and Social Welfare, 4v., 1965-78. maps.

V.1 (xii, 657p.) has 10 chapters, with section specialists: 1. Physiography - 2. Weather and climate - 3. Geology - 4. Flora - 5. Fauna - 6. The people - 7. Languages - 8. Religions - 9. Social structure - 10. Social life (20p. only). Index. 'For all its faults, the *Country and people* volume probably contains a wider range of useful information than any work of comparable length' (*Journal of Asian Studies,* v.26. no.2. February 1967, p.318).

Class No: 908(540)(083.86)

Bhutan

Bibliographies

[4687]

DOGRA, R.C., *comp.* **Bhutan.** Santa Barbara, California and Oxford, Clio Press. 1990. xxxiii,124p. + + 1p. map, index. £21. (*World Bibliographical Series, no.116.*) ISBN: 1851091289.

403 annotated entries in 21 sections: Country and its people - Geography and geology ... History ... Foreign relations ... Yearbooks, encyclopedias and directories - Bibliographies. Chronology p.xxi-xxiv. Rulers and dignitaries of Bhutan (1616 to date) p.xxv-xxvi. Glossary p.xxvii=xxxiii. Author, title and subject index.

Class No: 908(541.31)(01)

Nepal

Bibliographies

[4688]

Bibliographie du Népal. Paris, Éditions du Centre National de la Recherche Scientifique. 1969-. Cahiers Népalais.

1. *Sciences humaines. Réferences en langues européenes.* by L. Boulnois and H. Millot. 1969. 289p. Introduction (p.9-10), Sources consulted (p.19), Classification (p.20-21) in English translation. Over 4500 briefly annotated entries in 18 sections: Cartes nos. 1581-1612; Histoire 1766-2631; Biographies 4496-4511. *Supplement 1967-1973.* 1975. 435p. 3991 entries - 2. *Sciences humaines* (en langues orientales) - 3. *Sciences naturelles* pt.1 *Cartes du Népal dans les bibliothèques de Paris et de Londres.* 1973. 117p. maps. pt.2 *Botanique* by J.F. Dobrenez and others. 1972. 126p. *Class No:* 908(541.35)(01)

[4689]

WHELPTON, J. **Nepal.** Santa Barbara, California and Oxford, 1990. xxv,295p. + 1p. map, index. £44.95; $75.00. (*World Bibliographical Series, no.38.*) ISBN: 0903450682.

917 annotated entries in 33 sections: Country and its people - Travellers' accounts - Geography and geology - Tourist guides ... Archaeology and prehistory - History ... Brigade of Gurkhas ... Reference works - Bibliographies. Author, title and subject index. *Class No:* 908(541.35)(01)

Sri Lanka

[4690]

DE SILVA, K.M., *ed.* **Sri Lanka** a survey. Hamburg, Institute of Asia Affairs; London, C. Hurst, 1977. xvi, 496p. tables, maps, index.

11 contributors. 4 parts: (18 chapters, each with references appended). Part 1: The physical environment - 2. Historical survey (p.31-85) - 3. The evolution of a plural society - 4. Review of demographic trends. Part 2: 5. The economy in 1948 - 6. Planning and economic development - 7. Foreign trade - 8. Industrial policy and development since independence - 9. Plantation agriculture - 10. Peasant agriculture - 11. Statistical appendix. Part 3: 12. Politics and political development since 1948 - 13. The constitution - 14. Foreign policy - 15. The administration and judicial system. Part 4: 16. Religion - 17. Education - 18. Literature and the Arts. Glossary. 46 tables. Analytical index.

Class No: 908(548.7)

Bibliographies

[4691]

GOONETILEKE, H.A.I. **A Bibliography of Ceylon** a systematic guide to the literature on the land, people, history and culture published in Western languages from the sixteenth century to the present. Zug, Switzerland, Inter Documentation Co., 5v., 1970-83.

26,000 annotated entries in 30 main sections closely sub-divided covering the literature in 16 Western languages. 'An indispensable tool for the researcher on Sri Lanka' but 'the compiler's goal of comprehensiveness has led to the inclusion of material of questionable value' (V. Samaraweera. *Sri Lanka,* 1987. Entry 264).

Class No: 908(548.7)(01)

[4692]

SAMARAWEERA, V., *comp*. **Sri Lanka**. Santa Barbara, California and Oxford, Clio Press, 1987. xliii, 194p.+1p. map, index. £32.50. $40.50. (*World Bibliographical Series; no.20.*) ISBN: 090345033x.

631 annotated entries. 34 sections: The country and its people - Geography - Travel guides - Travellers' accounts ... Prehistory - Archaeology and epigraphy - History ... Politics ... Libraries, museums and archives ... Bibliographies and indexes. Chronology p.xxxix-xliii. Author, title and subject index. *Class No:* 908(548.7)(01)

Pakistan

[4693]

BURKI, S.J. **Pakistan** the continuing search for nationhood. 2nd ed. Boulder, Colo., Westview Press; Lahore, Pak Book Corporation, 1991. xii,243p. illus., map, tables, bibliog., index. £26.50. (*Profiles. Nations Of Contemporary Asia.*) ISBN: 0813381002.

1st ed. 1986.

1. Birth - 2. Political development - 3. Economic development - 4. Social development - 5. Foreign relations - 6. Future. Bibliography p.221-6. *Class No:* 908(549)

Bibliographies

[4694]

TAYLOR, D., *comp*. **Pakistan**. Santa Barbara, California and Oxford, Clio Press, 1990. xxxi, 259p.+1p. map, indexes. (*World Bibliographical Series, no.10.*) ISBN: 1851090819.

797 annotated entries in 37 sections: The country and its people - Geography ... Travellers' accounts - Tourism - Archaeology and prehistory - History - Biographies and autobiographies ... Armed forces ... Reference works - Bibliographies. Chronology p.xxix-xxx. Heads of State and Prime Ministers p.xxxi. Author, subject and title indexes. *Class No:* 908(549)(01)

Yearbooks & Directories

[4695]

Pakistan: an official handbook. Islamabad, Government of Pakistan Directorate of Films and Publications. Ministry of Information and Broadcasting. Annual.

Originally as *West Pakistan yearbook*.

1991 volume (ix,315p. col.illus. col. port., fold-in-map, index). 1. Pakistan (history) - 2. Foreign relations - 3. Justice - 4. Parliamentary affairs - 5. Federal government - 6. Economy - 7. Industry ... 22. Punjab - 23. Sindh - 24. Northwest Frontier Province - 25. Baluchistan - 26. States and frontier regions - 27. Azad Kashmir - 28. Northern areas. 'A review of government progress and achievements mainly economic ... the tone is inevitably bland but a considerable amount of information can be derived from it'. *Class No:* 908(549)(058)

[4696]

RAFIQUE AKHTAR. **Pakistan year book 1990-91.** 18th ed. Karachi and Lahore, East and West Publishing Co., 1990. 647p. illus., ports., tables, index.

1st ed. 1973.

38 sections deployed under 4 headings 1. The land and people - 2. The cultural heritage (History ... Archaeology ... Tourism) - 3. The Government and its services - 4. The Economy. Analytical index. *Class No:* 908(549)(058)

Bangladesh

[4697]

BAXTER, C. **Bangladesh** a new nation in an old setting. Boulder, Colorado, Westview Press, 1984. xii, 130p. illus. map, bibliog. index. $30.00. (*Nations of Contemporary Asia.*) ISBN: 0865316309.

9 chapters: 1. A delta and its people - 2. Hindu, Buddhists, and Muslims - 3. Bengal under the British - 4. A province of Pakistan - 5. A new nation-state - 6. Administration: civil and military - 7. Economic and social development - 8. Bangladesh in the world system - 9. Prospects: hope or despair? Annotated bibliography p.117-120. *Class No:* 908(549.3)

Bibliographies

[4698]

SATYAPRAKASH. **Bangla Desh:** a select bibliography. New Delhi, Indian Documentation Service, nd. 218p.

About 2500 citations of 135 books and articles, research papers etc. published in 91 Indian journals, and items from *The Times of India,* 1962-1976, arranged in a dictionary pattern. *Class No:* 908(549.3)(01)

Iran

Bibliographies

[4699]

EHLERS, E. **Iran** a bibliographic research survey with comments and annotation. München, K.G. Saur, 1980. xiii, 441p. index. £24.00 $30.00. ISBN: 3598211325.

8 broad subdivided subject chapters (*e.g.* Archaeology and History) are preceded by others listing Bibliographies, Journals and Travel Literature. Text in German and English. *Class No:* 908(55)(01)

[4700]

ELWELL-SUTTON, L.P. **Bibliographical guide to Iran.** Brighton, The Harvester Press; Totowa, New Jersey, Barnes & Nobb, 1983. xxv, 462p. index. £85.00; $35.00. ISBN: 0710804121, UK; 0389203394, US.

More than 30 contributors. 14 sections: 1. The study of Iran - 2. Reference works and bibliographies ... 8. Geography and Topography - 9. History. Short bibliographic essays introduce main sections. 'Fills a large gap in its field' (*Choice,* v.21, no.10, June 1984, p.1437). *Class No:* 908(55)(01)

[4701]

FARHAD DIBA. **A Bibliography of Iran.** Tauris, 2v., 1989. 1200p. index. £100.00. ISBN: 1850431213.

More than 14,000 items in several languages cover Iranian culture, history, politics and economics *etc.*. *Class No:* 908(55)(01)

[4702]

NAVABPOUR, R., *comp*. **Iran**. Santa Barabara, California and Oxford, Clio Press, 1988. xviii, 308p.+1p., map, index. £43.50. $52.00. (*World Bibliographical Series; no.81.*) ISBN: 1851090363.

787 annotated entries. 39 sections: The country and its people - Geography and Geology - Travellers' accounts - Tourism and travel guides ... Prehistory and archaeology - History ... Ayatollah Khomeini and the Iranian Revolution

....(contd.)

... Iranian collections in foreign libraries, museums and galleries ... Bibliographies. Author, title and subject index.
Class No: 908(55)(01)

Encyclopaedias

[4703]
Encyclopaedia Iranica. Yarshater, E., *ed.* New York, Columbia University Press; London, Routledge and Kegan Paul, 8v. 1985-. illus., maps, bibliog., index.
V.1 AB-ANAHID. 1011p. (2 cols.). ISBN 0710090994. $300.00; £200.00. In process of publication in fascicules (6pa.) each of 112 pages with 8 fascicules comprising one volume with the exception of v.1 which has 9. When complete the *Encyclopaedia* will consist of 18v., an index volume, and a single-volume supplement. Research tool covering archaeological, geographical, ethnographic, historical, artistic, literary, religious, linguistic, philosophical, scientific, and folklore studies. Coverage extends to surrounding areas and their cultural relations with Iran. 'As it is an unprecendented enterprise, many of the articles are the first comprehensive and systematic treatment of the topics they cover ... the most important and ambitious scholarly publication ever attempted in the field of Iranian studies' (*Middle Eastern Studies,* v.24, no.3, July 1988, p.391-392. *Class No:* 908(55)(031)

Yearbooks & Directories

[4704]
Yearbook Iran 89/90. Bonn, MB Medien & Bücher Verlagsgesellschaft, 1990. Available in UK from Menas Publishing Co. of Wisbech, Cambridgeshire. various pagination, tables, indexes. ISBN: 3927073032, Ger.
1st ed. 1989.
Comprehensive factbook of all areas of Iranian life in 22 sections *e.g.* 2. Land and people - 3. Government - 4. Foreign relations ... 7. Religion and clergy ... 13. Oil industry. *Class No:* 908(55)(058)

Turkey

Bibliographies

[4705]
GÜÇLÜ, M. Turkey. Santa Barbara, California and Oxford, Clio Press, 1981. xli, 331p.+2p. map, index. £44.50. $49.00. (*World Bibliographical Series; no.27.*) ISBN: 0903450399.
993 annotated entries. 34 sections: The country and its people - Description and travel - Geography ... Prehistory and archaeology - History ... Nationalities and minorities ... Libraries, museums and archives ... Encyclopaedias and directories - Bibliographies. Glossary. p.xxxv-xli. Author, title and subject index. *Class No:* 908(560)(01)

Cyprus

[4706]
The Almanac of Cyprus 1992. Christodoulou, A., *and others, eds.* Nicosia, Press and Information Office, Republic of Cyprus, 1992., 358p. illus. (some col.), tables. ISBN: 9963380581.
Cyprus profile: A. Background - B. History - C. Cyprus

....(contd.)

Republic (constitution *etc.*) - D. Economy - E. Culture and Education. Useful information. Statistics.
Class No: 908(564.3)

Bibliographies

[4707]
KITROMILIDES, P.M. *and* **EVRIVIADES, M.L.,** *comps.* **Cyprus.** Santa Barbara, California and Oxford, 1982. xx, 193p.+2p. map, index. £27.95. $31.00. (*World Bibliographical Series; no.28.*) ISBN: 0903450402.
689 annotated entries. 25 sections: The country and its people - Geography - Travel and tourism ... Prehistory and archaeology - History ... Ethnic groups and ethnic relations ... Directories - Bibliographies. Author, title and subject index. *Class No:* 908(564.3)(01)

Handbooks & Manuals

[4708]
North Cyprus almanack. London, K. Rustem & Brother, 1987. 261p. col. illus., tables, bibliog., pbk. £8.50. ISBN: 9963565085.
35 sections: Turkish Republic of North Cyprus - History-Political and administrative evolution... Cultural heritage ... Tourism - Historical sites ... Information services ... Useful literature. Bibliography p.229-30. Handbook for scholars, students, business and tourist visitors.
Class No: 908(564.3)(035)

Iraq

Bibliographies

[4709]
ABDULRAHMAN, A.J., *comp.* **Iraq.** Santa Barbara, California and Oxford, Clio Press, 1984. xviii, 162p. + 1p. map, index. £26.95 $35.00. (*World Bibliographical Series; no.42.*) ISBN: 0903450739.
A second edition compiled by C.H. Bleaney is announced for publication in 1994.
515 annotated entries. 26 sections: The country and its people - Exploration and travel - Geography ... History ... Encyclopaedias and directories ... Bibliographies. Theses and dissertations on Iraq p. xv - xviii. Author, title and subject index. *Class No:* 908(567)(01)

[4710]
McLACHLAN, K.S. *and* **SCHOFIELD, R.N.** **A Bibliography of the Iran-Irak borderland.** Wisbech, Cambridgeshire, Middle East & Northern African Studies Press, 1987. xii, 383p. index. £30. ISBN: 0906559219.
Almost 3,400 entries arranged in 5 chapters: 1. Geography; 2. Geology and geomorphology; 3. Maps; 4. Modern history and international relations; 5. Treaties, reports and bibliographies. Notes on library resources in London p.viii-xi. 'Attempts to review the literature germane to disputes over the boundary including matters affecting the entire frontier zone.' For recent newspaper and current affairs journal articles readers are referred to A. Mahrad's *Der Iran-Irak Konflikt. Class No:* 908(567)(01)

Encyclopaedias

[4711]

The Encyclopaedia of modern Iraq. Al-Ani, K.A.M., *ed.* Baghdad, The Arab Encyclopaedia House, 3v., 1977.

V.1 covers geography, history, politics and general information. V.2 surveys petroleum, industry and minerals, agriculture and agrarian policies. V.3 has sections on the armed forces, education, health, finance, *etc.* 'A well-produced bilingual publication and an oustanding reference work' (A.J. Abdulrahman. *Iraq.* 1984. Entry 395).

Class No: 908(567)(031)

Syria

Bibliographies

[4712]

BLEANEY, C.H., *comp.* **Modern Syria** an introduction to the literature. Durham, Centre for Middle Eastern and Islamic Studies, Univ. of Durham, 1979. ix, 91p. (*Occasional Papers no.6.*)

Over 980 references in 8 major sub-divided sections: 1. General - 2. Geography - 3. History 1918-1939 - 4. History, World War II to independence - 5. History, post-independence - 6. Politics - 7. Social and economic conditions - 8. Minorities. 'Particularly useful are the sections dealing with the religious and ethnic minorities, and with the French mandate period'. (J.J. Seccombe, *Syria*, 1987. Entry 886). *Class No:* 908(569.1)(01)

[4713]

SECCOMBE, I.J., *comp.* **Syria.** Santa Barbara, California and Oxford, Clio Press, 1987. xxxii, 341p.+2p. map, index. £49.50. $55.00. (*World Bibliographical Series; no. 73.*) ISBN: 1851090185.

903 annotated entries. 32 sections - The country and its people - Travel guides and travelogues - Explorers' and travellers' accounts - Geography ... Prehistory and archaeology - History ... Minorities ... Libraries and archives ... Bibliographies. Author, title and subject index.

Class No: 908(569.1)(01)

Lebanon

Bibliographies

[4714]

BLEANEY, C.H., *comp.* **Lebanon.** 2nd ed. Santa Barbara, California and Oxford, Clio Press, 1991. xxxi,230p.++1p. map, index. £39.; $84. (*World Bibliographical Series; no.2.*) ISBN: 1851091505.

1st ed. 1979 compiled by Shereen Khairallah

724 annotated entries in 34 sections: Country and its people - Geography - Travellers' accounts ... Prehistory and archaeology ... History ... Foreign relations ... Bibliographies. Author, title and subject index. Majority of the new entries in this edition relate to the civil war which broke out in 1975. *Class No:* 908(569.3)(01)

[4715]

SALIBA, M., *comp.* **Index Libanicus** analytical index of publications in European languages on Lebanon. Lebanon, the compiler, 1979. xlv, 510p. indexes.

5,359 entries A-Z by author. About 120 library locations. *Class No:* 908(569.3)(01)

Israel

[4716]

Facts about Israel. Jerusalem, Ministry of Foreign Affairs Information Division, 1985. 137p. col.illus., col.maps, bibliog.

A well-illustrated pocket guide. Sections: The Land - Lifestyles - Roots - Search for peace - The State - Economy - Communities - The year in Israel - Education and Sports - Health and social affairs - Culture. Bibliography p.132-5. *Class No:* 908(569.4)

Bibliographies

[4717]

ALEXANDER, Y, *and others.* **A Bibliography of Israel & Zionism.** New York, Herzl Press, 1981. 263p. indexes.

Thematic arrangement with main emphasis on contemporary social and political life.

Class No: 908(569.4)(01)

[4718]

NEUBERG, A. The State of Israel an annotated bibliography. 2nd ed. Jerusalem, Centre for Public Libraries in Israel, 2v., 1977.

First published in a single-volume ed. 1970.

'A comprehensive listing of books and other materials dealing with Israel, published the world over and found principally in the Jewish National and University Library in Jerusalem' (E.M. Snyder, *Israel*, 1985. Entry 1140).

Class No: 908(569.4)(01)

[4719]

SNYDER, E.M. and **KREINER, E.,** *comps.* **Israel.** Santa Barbara, California and Oxford, Clio Press, 1985. xviii, 272p.+1p. map, index. £35.50. $52.50. (*World Bibliographical Series; no.58.*) ISBN: 0851090010.

A second edition compiled by C.H. Bleaney is announced for publication in 1993. c.340p. £48. ISBN 1851091769. c.1100 entries.

1141 annotated entries. 41 sections: The country and its people - Geography ... Archaeology - History - Zionism - The Arab-Israeli conflict ... Libraries - Museums ... Directories and encyclopaedias - Bibliographies. Author, title and subject index. *Class No:* 908(569.4)(01)

Encyclopaedias

[4720]

PATAI, R. Encyclopedia of Zionism and Israel. New York, Herzl Press, McGraw Hill, 2v. 1971. xxiii, 647p.; v, 649p. illus., ports., facsims., tables.

285 contributors. Three main types of articles: places in Israel; biographies (primarily Zionist leaders and Israeli statesmen and public officials); topical subjects 'Kibbutz movement': v.2, p.666-73; 3 illus.; 'Herzl, Theodor': v.1, p.490-5. Bibliography, v.2, p.1287-92 (Zionism; Israel). No general index. *Class No:* 908(569.4)(031)

Yearbooks & Directories

[4721]

The Israel year book and almanack 1993. 47th ed. Jerusalem, IBRT Translation/Documentation, 1993. iv,308p. illus., tables, index. ISSN: 00751413.

Incorporating *The Palestine yearbook and Israel annual,* formerly published in US for the Zionist Organization of

....(contd.)

America, and the *Anglo-Palestine year book* formerly published in UK.

1. General information (physical data and human resources) - 2. Agriculture - 3. Archaeology (inc. major finds 1992) - 4. Arts - 5. Defense - 6. Economy - 7. Education - 8. Environment - 9. Foreign Affairs - 10. Government - 11. Health - 12. Housing - 13. Immigration - 14. Judea, Samaria and Gaza - 15. Media - 16. National Institutions - 17. Peace progress - 18. Religion - 19. Sports - 20. Tourism - 21. Transportation - 22. Women. *Class No:* 908(569.4)(058)

Jordan

[4722]
GUBSER, P. Jordan crossroads of Middle Eastern events. Boulder, Colo., Westview Press; London, Croom Helm, 1983. xii,139p. illus., tables, maps, bibliog., index. (*Profiles. Nations Of The Contemporary Middle East.*) ISBN: 0891589864, US; 0709911459, UK.

1. Introduction - 2. Environment - 3. People - 4. Economy - 5. History - 6. Contemporary politics and international relations. Bibliography p.131-4. *Class No:* 908(569.5)

Bibliographies

[4723]
SECCOMBE, I.J., *comp.* **Jordan.** Santa Barbara, California and Oxford, Clio Press, 1984. xliii, 278p.+1p. map, index. £42.95. $45.00. (*World Bibliographical Series; no.55.*) ISBN: 0903450925.

834 annotated entries. 34 sections: The country and its people - Travel guides, travelogues and tourism - Explorers and travellers' accounts - Geography ... Prehistory and archaeology - History ... The West Bank since 1967 ... Libraries ... Bibliographies. Author, title and subject index. *Class No:* 908(569.5)(01)

Russia (in Asia)

[4724]
BATALDEN, S.K. *and* **BATALDEN, S.L. The Newly independent states of Eurasia** handbook of former Soviet Republics. Phoenix, Oryx, 1993. 224p. maps, tables. $34.95. ISBN: 0897747631.

Chapters for each state with information on its economic, political, cultural, social and religious background together with an up-to-date map, statistical data, and an analysis of contemporary issues. *Class No:* 908(57)

Bibliographies of Bibliographies

[4725]
ALLWORTH, E. Soviet Asia: bibliographies a compilation of social science and humanities sources on the Iranian, Mongolian and Turkic nationalities. With an essay on the Soviet-Asian controversy. New York, Praeger, 1975. lxiii, 686p. ISBN: 0275287405.

Some 5,200 Russian and Soviet bibliographies, including books and articles containing bibliographies published between 1850 and 1970. Arranged in 4 major geographical regions, subdivided into Union republics, autonomous republics or ethnic groups, and again subdivided by subjects, including anthropology and ethnography, economics,

....(contd.)

education, political science (government) and law, social organizations, etc. 'To the researcher ... this bibliography will appear the timely worthy effort that it is.' (*Soviet studies,* v.29, 1977. p.41). *Class No:* 908(57)(009)

Siberia

[4726]
COLLINS, D.O., *comp.* **Siberia and the Soviet Far East.** Santa Barbara, Calif. and Oxford, Clio Press, 1991. xx,217p.+ 4p. maps, indexes. £35. (*World Bibliographical Series, no. 127.*) ISBN: 1851091572.

735 annotated entries in 27 sections: General works - Travellers' accounts - Travel guides - Geography ... Prehistory and archaeology - History - Ethnography ... Bibliographies - Encyclopaedias and reference works - Periodicals. Ethnonyms p.xv-xvii. Author, title and subject indexes. *Class No:* 908(571)

Afghanistan

Bibliographies

[4727]
JAMIL HANIFI, M. Annotated bibliography of Afghanistan. 4th ed. New Haven, Connecticut, Hraf Press, 1982. xv, 545p. index. $140.30. ISBN: 0875362303.

First published 1956 edited by D.N. Wilber. Rev. eds. 1962 and 1968.

3500 items, more than double in previous editions. 8 sections: 1. General sources - 2. Geography - 3. History - 4. Social organizations - 5. Social evolution - 6. Political and economic structure - 7. Language and literature - 8. Art and archaeology. Author index. Complemented by K. McLachlan and W. Whittaker's *A Bibliography of Afghanistan* (1983) (*q.v.*). *Class No:* 908(581)(01)

[4728]
JONES, S., *comp.* **Afghanistan.** Santa Barbara, Calif., and Oxford, Clio Press, 1992. xxv,279p. +1p. map. indexes. £43.95. (*World Bibliographical Series, no.135.*) ISBN: 1851091405.

1014 annotated entries in 37 sections: Country and its people - Geography and geology - Tourism and guide books - Travel and exploration ... Archaeology - History - Soviet invasion and occupation ... Libraries, galleries, museums and archives ... Reference works - Bibliographies. Author, title and subject indexes. *Class No:* 908(581)(01)

[4729]
McLACHLAN, K. *and* **WHITAKER, W. A Bibliography of Afghanistan** a working bibliography of materials on Afghanistan with special reference to economic and social change in the twentieth century. Wisbech, Cambs., Middle East and North African Studies Press Ltd., 1983. Distributed in North America by Westview. xiii, 671p. maps, indexes. £55.25; $45.00. ISBN: 090655912x.

Based on previously published bibliographies notably *Bibliographie der Afghanistan literatur 1945-1967* (Hamburg. 2v., 1968-1969).

7561 entries of Western language material arranged in 15 sections: 1. Bibliography; 2. General; 6. Geographical studies; 7. Travel, exploration and description; 8. Historical

.... (contd.)

studies; 9. History and politics; 15. Maps. 'Best suited for the advanced researcher in social science fields' (*Choice*, v.22, no.1, September 1984, p.66). *Class No:* 908(581)(01)

Asia—South East

[4730]

CAREY, P. Maritime Southeast Asian studies in the United Kingdom a survey of their post-war development and current resources. Oxford, JASO, 1986. vii, 115p. bibliog., pbk. (*JASO Occasional Papers, no. 6.*)

Pt.1: Survey of post-war developments 1945-1985. Pt.2: Current resources *i.e.* 3 Appendices: 1. Scholars in the UK with major research interests in maritime Southeast Asia, Oceania, and the Indian Ocean region - 2. University departments specializing in teaching and research - 3. Libraries, archives and ethnographic collections ... Principal references cited p.115. *Class No:* 908(59)

[4731]

MAYERCHAK, P.M. Scholar's guide to Washington DC for Southeast Asian studies: Brunei. Burma. Cambodia. Indonesia. Laos. Malaysia. Philippines. Singapore. Thailand. Vietnam. Washington D.C., Smithsonian Institution Press, 1983. xiv, 409p. bibliog., index. $29.95. ISBN: 0874746264.

Overview of over 400 collections, organizations, and agencies. 'While providing the basic directory information ... the Guide is primarily a descriptive and evaluative survey of Washington's research resources'. *Class No:* 908(59)

[4732]

Southeast Asian affairs 1993. 20th ed. Singapore, Institute of Southeast Asian Studies, 1974-. Annual. xvii,372p. maps on endpapers. ISSN: 03775437.

Comprehensive coverage on Southeast Asian politics, economics, and social trends and developments in the form of analyses and writings primarily from contributors in the region. Part 1: Regional and ASEAN overviews; 2: Internal developments in each of 10 ASEAN countries. Bibliographical notes appended to each essay. *Class No:* 908(59)

Bibliographies

[4733]

CHAND, A. Southeast Asia and the Pacific: a select bibliography 1947-1977. New Delhi, Sterling Publishers, 1979. xvi, 378p. index.

The most significant books and periodical articles listed in 15 chapters. *Class No:* 908(59)(01)

[4734]

CORDIER, H. Bibliotheca Indosinica: dictionnaire bibliographique des ouvrages relatifs à la Péninsule Indochinois. Paris, Imprimerie Nationale, 5v., 1912-32. 309p.

Reprinted Hildesheim, G. Olms, 1972.

V.1: *Birmanie, Assam, siam, Laos.* 2. *La Péninsule Indochinoise.* 3-4. *Indochine Française.* 5. *Index.*

A bibliography of *c.*20,000 items covering all fields of works in European languages. The pioneer and still standard bibliography for Indo-China, Burma and Malaya. *Class No:* 908(59)(01)

[4735]

LIM, P., *ed.* **ASEAN A Bibliography.** Singapore, Institute of Southeast Asian Studies, 1984. xxxix, 487p. index. $39.00. ISBN: 9791902745.

11 chapters: 1. Southeast Asia regeneration - 2. A study of regional cooperation - 3. Structure and policies - 4. Perceptions of policies towards ASEAN - 5-6. Intra and extra ASEAN relations - 7. Political cooperation - 8. Economic growth and development - 9. Socio-cultural cooperation - 10. Future trends - 11. Reference materials p.452-6. Entries in Western European and Oriental languages. 'The editor, who laments ASEANS's lack of bibliographical control, promises that this very welcome work will be updated at intervals' (*International Affairs,* v.61, no. 3, Summer 1985, p.567). *Class No:* 908(59)(01)

[4736]

LIM PUI HUEN, P. The Malay world of Southeast Asia a select cultural bibliography. Singapore, Institute of Southeast Asian Studies, 1986. xiii, 456p. index. ISBN: 9971988364.

5327 entries, encompassing Brunei, Indonesia, Malaysia, The Philippines, Singapore, and Thailand, listed in 21 subject chapters arranged in 4 parts: 1. Reference and general works - 2. The setting - 3. The people - 4. Culture and society. *Class No:* 908(59)(01)

[4737]

UNITED STATES. Library of Congress. Oriental Division. Southern Asia Section. Southeast Asia subject catalog. Boston, Mass., G.K. Hall, 6v., 1972. 3932p. ISBN: 0816112347.

82,500 catalogue cards, photolithographically reproduced, representing Western-language materials of Southeast Asia interest. In addition to the section 'Southeast Asia, General', individual country sections have detailed subject divisions, A-Z. *Class No:* 908(59)(01)

Maps & Atlases

[4738]

ULACK, R. *and* **PAUER, G. Atlas of Southeast Asia.** New York Macmillan Publishing Co.; London, Collier Macmillan Publishers, 1989. xvii, 171p. col. illus., col. maps, tables, bibliog., index. $95.00. £45.00. ISBN: 0029332001.

Part 1. Regional overview: 1. Physical environment and resources - 2. Historical and political background - 3. Cultural characteristics - 4. Regional population and urban characteristics. Part 2: 10 chapters on the nation - states of the region. Integrated text, maps and illustrations. Bibliography p.153-157. 70 maps. 'Fills a gap that has existed in the literature for many years' (*Booklist*, v. 85, no.16, 15 April 1989, p.1442-3). *Class No:* 908(59)(084.3)

Libraries

[4739]

Directory of South-East Asian library collections in the United Kingdom and Western Europe. Karni, R.S., *ed.* 3rd ed. Oxford, Hans Zell on behalf of the South East Asia Library Group, 1989. 240p. £35.00. ISBN: 0905450604.

150 libraries and documentation centres with sizeable holdings of printed materials on Southeast Asia. Data: full name and address plus collections, services and facilities information. *Class No:* 908(59):061:026/027

Myanmar

Bibliographies

[4740]
BERNOT, D. **Bibliographie Birmane**. Paris, Centre National Recherche Scientifique.
Années 1950-1960. 1968. 228p. Fr.72. ISBN 222201042x. *Années 1960-1970. Partie méthodique 1962*. 294p. Fr.52. 2222011338. *1963* 326p. Fr.62. 2222012423. *Partie alphabétique A-F*. 384p. Fr.60. 2222035473. *G-L*. 336p. Fr.60. 2222035481. *Class No:* 908(591)(01)

[4741]
HERBERT, P.M., *comp*. **Burma**. Santa Barbara, Calif., and Oxford, Clio Press, 1991. xxiv,327p. +1p. map. indexes. £49. (*World Bibliographical Series, no.132*.) ISBN: 1851090886.
850 annotated entries in 30 sections: Country and its people - Travellers' accounts and guide books - Geography and geology ... Prehistory and archaeology - History ... Religion ... Yearbooks, directories and statistics - Bibliographies and research guides. Author, title and subject indexes. *Class No:* 908(591)(01)

Thailand

[4742]
HOHNHOLZ, J. *and* BECHTOLD, K.H., *eds*. **Thailand** : Geographie. Geschichte. Kultur. Religion. Staat. Gesellschaft. Politik. Wirtschaft. Tübingen, Ehrmann, 1980. 518p. illus. (col.), tables, maps.
34 contributors. Parts: 1. Environment - 2. History, culture, religion - 3. The State and politics - 4. People and society - 5. Economy. Section bibliographies. No index, but detailed contents-list. *Class No:* 908(593)

[4743]
KEYES, C.F. **Thailand**: Buddhist kingdom and modern nation-state. Boulder, Colo., Westview Press, 1987; Bangkok, Editions Duang Kamos, 1989. xviii,252p. illus., maps, tables, bibliog., index.
6 chronological and thematic chapters. 'An accessible introduction to modern Thailand which, remarkably, also offers the specialist insight and information on virtually every page' (*Journal of Southeast Asian Studies*, v.22, no.2, September 1991, p.455-6). *Class No:* 908(593)

Bibliographies

[4744]
WATTS, M. **Thailand**. Santa Barbara, California and Oxford, Clio Press, 1986. xli, 275p. map, index. £41.95. $47.85. (*World Bibliographical Series; no.65*.) ISBN: 1851090088.
818 annotated entries. 32 sections: The country and its people - Geography and geology - Travel, tourism and guidebooks ... Prehistory and archaeology - History ... Narcotics ... Libraries, museums and archives ... Bibliographies. Glossary p.xxix-xxxv. Chronology p.xxxvii-xxxviii. Kings of Thailand p.xxxix. Author, title and subject index. *Class No:* 908(593)(01)

Malaysia

[4745]
Malaysian studies archaeology, historiography, geography, and bibliography. Lent, J.A. *and* Mulliner, K., *eds*. Dekalb, Illinois, Northern Illinois University Center for Southeast Asian Studies, 1986. Distribution by Cellar Book Shop. xi, 240p. bibliog. $14.00. (*Occasional Papers SEA Studies, no. 11*.) ISBN: 0318200708.
7 contributors. 5 essays each with a bibliography: 1. Archaeology in Malaysia, Brunei and Singapore - 2. Historiography of Peninsular Malaysia - 3. Survey and evaluation of the literature on modern Sarawak and Sabah history - 4. Geographical studies of Malaysia - 5. Recent bibliographical activities in Malaysia and Sarawak. 'Recommended for graduate and upper-division collections ... particularly as a guide to essential Malay sources' (*Choice*, v.24, no.9, May 1987, p.1382). *Class No:* 908(595)

Bibliographies of Bibliographies

[4746]
DING CHOO MING. **A Bibliography of bibliographies on Malaysia**. Selangor, Hexagon Elite Publications, 1981. xi, 184p. index.
507 extensively annotated entries assembled in 22 categories e.g., 6. Geography, geology, mining and maps ... 8. History. Author and title indexes. *Class No:* 908(595)(009)

Bibliographies

[4747]
BROWN, I. *and* AMPALAVANAR, R., *comps*. **Malaysia**. Santa Barbara, California and Oxford, Clio Press, 1986. xxxv, 308p.+2p. maps, index. £43.95. $53.50. (*World Bibliographical Series; no.12*.) ISBN: 0903450232.
754 annotated entries, 34 sections: The country and its people - Geography ... Prehistory and archaeology - History ... Indigenous minority peoples ... Libraries ... Directories - General bibliographies. Glossary p. xxxiii-xxxv. Author, title and subject index. *Class No:* 908(595)(01)

[4748]
KARNI, R.S. **Bibliography of Malaysia and Singapore**. Kuala Lumpur, Penerbit Universiti Malaya, 1980. [xxi], 649p. bibliog.
A development of H.A.R. Cheeseman's *Bibliography of Malaya* (Longmans, 1959).
7 sections: 1. General (bibliographies, lists of manuscripts, archives, libraries, museums) - 2. Religion - 3. Social sciences, economics, government, education - 4. Natural sciences - 5. Applied sciences - 6. Architecture - 7. Geography, biography, history. *Class No:* 908(595)(01)

Yearbooks & Directories

[4749]
Malaysia 1986 official year book. 24th ed. Kuala Lumpur, Department of Information, Ministry of Information, Malaysia, 1986. 405p. col.illus., diagrs., tables, softcover. ISSN: 01266098.
Factual account of the administration and national economy in 29 sections: 1. Review - 2. General and historical - 3. Peoples, customs and culture ... 5. Federal

....(contd.)

territory ... 9. Internal affairs ... 12. Economic survey ... 16. Land and regional development ... 26. Public enterprise ... 29. Honours and awards. *Class No:* 908(595)(058)

Singapore

Bibliographies

[4750]

QUAH, S.R. *and* QUAH, J.S.T., *comps.* **Singapore.** Santa Barbara, California and Oxford, Clio Press, 1988. xv, 258p.+2p. maps, indexes. £39.50. $55.00. (*World Bibliographical Series; no.95.*) ISBN: 1851090711.

764 annotated entries. 33 sections: The country and its people - Geography and Tourism ... History ... Finance and banking ... Libraries and museums - Directories ... Bibliographies. Author, title, and subject indexes. *Class No:* 908(595.13)(01)

[4751]

UNIVERSITY OF SINGAPORE LIBRARY. Catalogue of the Singapore/Malaysia Collection. Boston, Mass., G.K. Hall, 1968. 757p. $130.00 (Export $155.00). ISBN: 0816108188.

The Singapore Malaysia Collection is particularly strong in source material tracing the various aspects of development of the Malayan States, Singapore, and the Bornean regions (excluding Brunei and Indonesian Borneo) from their founding through the period of colonial government up to independence and after. *Class No:* 908(595.13)(01)

Yearbooks & Directories

[4752]

Singapore 1992. Singapore, Publicity Division, Ministry of Information and the Arts, 1992. 318p. col. illus., tables, maps on endpapers. S$18.30. ISSN: 0129766x.

22 sections (e.g. Land; People; History; Tourism). *Class No:* 908(595.13)(058)

Vietnam

[4753]

SARDESAI, D.R. **Vietnam** the struggle for national unity. 2nd ed. Boulder, Colo., Westview Press, 1992. xi,192p. maps, bibliog., index. ISBN: 0813381967.

1st ed. 1988 published by Promilla.

1. Ethnicity, geography, and early history - 2. Millenium of freedom - 3. French conquest - 4. Nationalist movement - 5. Roots of second Indochina war - 6. Indochina imbroglio - 7. New Vietnam - 8. International relations - 9. Cambodia question and US-Vietnamese relations. Chronology p.153-7. Chapter notes p.159-64. Bibliography p.165-77. 3 maps. *Class No:* 908(597)

Bibliographies

[4754]

COTTER, M. **Vietnam** a guide to reference sources. Boston, G.K. Hall, 1977. xvii, 272p.

Annotated list of *c.*1,400 books, periodical articles, serials, government publications. Classes; A. General reference sources - B. Humanities - C. Social sciences, political science and government - D. History and related

....(contd.)

subjects - E. Pure and applied science. Based mainly on material at Cornell, Library of Congress, Harvard, and Southern-Illinois Carbondale. 'A must acquisition for any serious library and institution of higher learning' (*Choice,* July/August 1978, p.666). *Class No:* 908(597)(01)

[4755]

JUMPER, R. **Vietnam** an annotated bibliography. Salisbury, North Carolina, Documentary Publications 1980. v, 179p. index. ISBN: 0897120825.

Formerly distributed on a restricted basis to United States military and government agencies as *Bibliography on the political and administrative history of Vietnam 1802-1962.*

964 briefly annotated entries covering the period 1802-1962 arranged in 8 sections: 1. Political history and biography (8 sub-divisions) - 2. Politics and administration - 3. Law - 4. Foreign affairs - 5. Economics - 6. Social conditions - 7. References - 8. Bibliographies. *Class No:* 908(597)(01)

[4756]

MARR, D.G., *comp.* **Vietnam.** Santa Barbara, Calif., and Oxford, Clio Press, 1992. lxxviii,393p. +1p. map. indexes. £65. (*World Bibliographical Series, no.147.*) ISBN: 1851090924.

1038 annotated entries in 32 sections: Country and its people - Traveller's accounts - Geography ... Archaeology and prehistory - History - Biography and autobiography ... Minorities and nationalities ... Foreign relations ... Bibliographies. Chronology p.xlvii-lxxvi. Glossary p. lxxvii-lxxviii. Author, title, and subject indexes. *Class No:* 908(597)(01)

Laos

Bibliographies

[4757]

CORDELL, H., *comp.* **Laos.** Santa Barbara, Calif. and Oxford, Clio Press, 1991. xxxvi, 215p. +1p. map. indexes. £36. (*World Bibliographical Series, no.133.*) ISBN: 1851090754.

548 annotated entries in 34 sections: Country and its people - Travellers' accounts and travel guides - Geography and geology ... Prehistory and archaeology - History ... Ethnic groups ... Annuals and directories - Manuscripts and archives - Bibliographies. Author, title and subject indexes. *Class No:* 908(598)(01)

[4758]

LAFONT, P.B. **Bibliographie du Laos.** 2nd ed. Paris, École Française d'Extrême-Orient, 2v., 1964-1978. 270p.+414p. Fr.200.

1. To 1962. 2. 1962-75. Includes items in Lao, Thai, Vietnamese, Russian, and Western languages. 'The most comprehensive bibliography published on Laos, it endeavours to cover all fields of knowledge ... the starting point for any serious study of Laos' (H. Cordell: *Laos,* 1991. Entry no.547). *Class No:* 908(598)(01)

Islamic World

[4759]

The Cultural atlas of Islam. Al Faruqi, I.R. *and* Al Faruqi, L.L. New York, Macmillan Publishing Co.; London, Collier Macmillan, 1986. xv, 512p. illus., maps, general tables, indexes. $100.00; £92.00. ISBN: 0029101905.

The entire Islamic world, from the Mediterranean to the Pacific presented in 23 chapters grouped in 4 sections - 1. The Origin, the roots of Islam (inc. Chap. 1. Arabia the crucible; 2. Language and Literature; 3. Religion and culture) - 2. The Essence, *i.e.* its fundamental principles - 3. The Form (social life and institutions inc. *The Koran*) - 4. The Manifestation (Islamic beliefs in law, science, philosophy *etc.*). Lacks a consolidated bibliography and glossary. 300 photographs. 'The reference value of the *Cultural Atlas of Islam* lies in its 75 maps and numerous charts and tables on aspects of Islamic culture' (*Reference Books Bulletin 1986-1987*, p.145). *Class No:* 908(5.297)

Bibliographies

[4760]

ANDERSON, M. Arabic materials in English translation. Boston, G.K. Hall, 1981. xiii, 249p. index.

A bibliography of some 1600 works mostly English translations of Arabic originals ranging from the pre-Islamic period to 1977 and covering a comprehensive range of topics. *Class No:* 908(5.297)(01)

[4761]

Index Islamicus 1906-1955 a catalogue of articles on Islamic subjects in periodicals and other collective publications. Pearson, J.D. *and* Ashton, J.F., *comps.* Cambridge, Heffer, 1958 (reprinted Mansell, 1961, with minor corrections). xxxvi,895p. £65.00. ISBN: 0702103800. ISSN: 03069524.

Supplement 1956-1960 (1962) xxviii,316p. £48.00. 0720103819. *Second supplement 1961-1965* (1967) xxx,342p. £48.00. 0720103827. *Third supplement 1966-1970* London, Mansell, 1972. xxxvi,384p. £48.00. ISBN 0720102820. *Fourth Supplement 1971-1975* (1977) xlii,429p. £48.00. 0720106397. ISSN 03069524. *Fifth supplement 1976-1980* (2v., 1983). *part 1. Articles,* xliii,539p. Part 2. *Monographs,* xii,348p. £110.00. 0720116503 set. *Index Islamicus 1981-1985:current books, articles and papers on Islamic subjects* compiled by G.J. Roper, 2v., 1990. 1216p. £100.00. $200.00. 0720120098 set. Some 30,000 items some of which do not appear in the *Quarterly. Index Islamicus: a bibliography of books and articles on the Muslim World* compiled by G.J. Roper. Bowker-Saur, 2v. 1991. 1347p. 6th quinquennial supplement 1981-1985. 34,382 entries. The main volume has more than 26,000 entries drawn from 510 periodicals, plus Festschriften, other collective works and congress proceedings. Aims to cover the whole field of Islamic studies, pure science and technology alone being excluded. Not confined to Islamic countries but includes items of Islamic interest from elsewhere. Restricted to material in Western languages, including Russian. Classified arrangement with main divisions: General works and bibliography - Religion and theology - Law - Philosophy and science - Art - Geography - Ethnology and history - Language - Literature - Education. Author index. Unquestionably the basic bibliographical tool in its field. *The*

....(contd.)

Quarterly Index Islamicus (1976-.) £95.pa (institutions) £24. (individuals) ISSN 03087395 draws on over 1,100 sources in all European languages. *Class No:* 908(5.297)(01)

[4762]

—Index Islamicus, 1665-1905: a bibliography on Islamic subjects in peridoicals and other collective publications. Behn, W.A., *comp.* Millersville, Pennsylvania, Adiyok Publications, 1989. 869p. map on front end papers, indexes. $125.00.

Extends coverage to Pearson's *Index Islamicus* back to the mid-17th century with 21,000 items in Western languages. The compiler was also joint compiler with Pearson on the *Fifth supplement* to the main work (1983). 'A required purchase for all libraries with research-level collections in Middle East studies' (*Choice,* v.27,no.2, October 1989, p.278). *Class No:* 908(5.297)(01)

[4763]

—ROPER, G. The Bibliography of the Arab Middle East with particular reference to Index Islamicus, p.11-37, *Arabic resources acquisition and management in British Libraries* (Mansell, 1986). *Class No:* 908(5.297)(01)

Handbooks & Manuals

[4764]

The Legacy of Islam. Schacht, J. *and* Bosworth, C.E. 2nd rev. ed. Oxford, Clarendon Press, 1974. xiv, 530p. 39p. illus. (pl). £19.95. ISBN: 019821913x.

First published 1931.

17 contributors. 10 sections, with footnotes and bibliographies. 1. The Western image and Western studies of Islam - 2. Islam in the Mediterranean world - 3. Islamic frontiers in Africa and Asia (Africa south of the Sahara; Central Asia; India; Indonesia) - 4. Politics and war - 5. Economic developments - 6. Art and architecture - 7. Literature - 8. Philosophy, theology and mysticism - 9. Law and state (including Islamic political thought) - 10. Science (including music). Partly analytical index, p.506-30. No maps. 63 illus. *Class No:* 908(5.297)(035)

[4765]

WEEKES, R.V., *ed.* **The World of Islam:** a world ethnographic survey. 2nd rev. ed. Westport, Connecticut, Greenwood Press, 1985. xli, 546p. tables, maps, bibliog., index. £85.50. ISBN: 0313233926.

1st ed. 1978.

71 contributors. Articles A-Z, on the life and culture of all major ethnic groups (with a Muslim population in excess of 100,000), - 30 Muslim culture groups, 'Somali' (tribe): p.364-9; (bibliography, p.368-9); 'Berbers': p.99-110 (bibiliography, p.108-10). Appended bibliographies include periodical articles and theses. Maps show locations of ethnic groups. 3 appendices: 1. Muslim nationalities of the world; 2. Muslim ethnic groups within nations; 3. Major Muslim ethnic groups. 'A timely reference work for both public and academic libraries' (*Library Journal*, 15 April 1979, p.587). *Class No:* 908(5.297)(035)

Dictionaries

[4766]

MORSY, M. **Lexique du monde arabe moderne.** Paris, Dalloz, 1986. xix, 183p. maps, tables. pbk. FFR76.00. ISBN: 224700735x.

Definitions and background notes on persons, places, states, and international relations.
Class No: 908(5.297)(038)

Maps & Atlases

[4767]

Atlas of the Islamic world since 1500. Robinson, F. Oxford, Phaidon; New York, Facts On File, 1982. 238p. illus. (mostly col.), maps (mostly col.), bibliog., index. £18.50; $40.00. ISBN: 0714822000, UK; 0871966298, US.

Pt 1. Revelation and Muslim history - 2. To be a Muslim (religious life, Arts of Islam) and 10 specified features *e.g.* 'The Mughal World' and 'Ottoman World'. Chronological table p.8-9. Islamic rulers p.10-11. Glossary p.224-5. Bibliography p.229-31. Gazetteer p.232-4. 50 Maps. 'A mine of information on Islam and the Islamic world since A.D. 1500' (*Choice*, v.20, no.8, April 1983, p.114).
Class No: 908(5.297)(084.3)

[4768]

DEMPSEY, M.W. **The Daily Telegraph atlas of the Arab World.** London, Daily Telegraph, 1983. 124p. col.illus., col.maps. £8.95. ISBN: 0901684929.

Published in North America by Facts On File as *Atlas of the Arab World.* 0871967790.

A concise introduction to the economic, social, political and military affairs with comprehensive A-Z by country gazetteer. 38 double-page coloured maps. 'Will not suffice for any but the most general look at the entire region' (*Choice*, v.21,no.2, October 1983, p.249).
Class No: 908(5.297)(084.3)

Africa

[4769]

Africa today. London, Africa Books Ltd., 1981. xxii, 23-1506p. + 24p. col. maps. tables. (*Know Africa.*) ISBN: 0903274132. ISSN: 02611562.

Companion volume to *Africa today* and *Makers of modern Africa (q.q.v.).*

Compendious reference work on 54 African countries presenting a detailed record of modern African history and the political, economic and social development, from an African viewpoint, arranged in 6 pts: 1. General (geography, languages, religion) - 2. Organizations (political and economic) - 3. A-Z Country surveys - 4. sports - 5. Quick reference - 6. Atlas. *Class No:* 908(6)

[4770]

African studies papers presented at a colloquium at the British Library 7-9 January 1985. Sternberg, I. *and* Larby, P.M., *eds.* London, The British Library in association with SCOLMA, 1986. xix, 332p. bibliogs. softcover. £17.95. (*British Library Occasional Papers.*) ISBN: 0712300503.

'The papers describe the current state of African studies in the United Kingdom, the resources available to researchers, the currency of guides and indexes to those resources, the

....(contd.)

problems of publishing and distributing books in Africa, and possible areas of cooperation between international libraries for the provision of Africana'. *Class No:* 908(6)

[4771]

BAKER, P., *comp.* **International guide to African studies research/Études africaines, guide international de recherches.** 2nd ed. Oxford, Hans Zell for the International African Institute, 1987. 264p. index. £40.00. $76.00. ISBN: 0905450256.

First published 1975.

1137 entries (as compared to less than 500 in the first edition) listed A-Z by country and name of organization. 4 indexes (thematic by area or country; ethnyms and language names; serial publications; personnel).
Class No: 908(6)

[4772]

MORONEY, S., *ed.* **Africa.** New York and Oxford, Facts on File, 2v., 1989. xxii,1208p. maps, tables, index. (*Handbooks To The Modern World.*) ISBN: 0816022003, v.1; 0816022011, v.2; 0816016232, set.

39 contributors. V.1: Basic information (geography, population, constitutional system, recent history, economy, social welfare, education, mass media, biographical sketches, map) on 52 African countries A-Z. V.2: 32 essays on political, economic and social affairs. *Class No:* 908(6)

[4773]

NORTHWESTERN UNIVERSITY. **Catalog of the Melville Herskovits Library of African Studies ... and Africana in selected libraries.** Boston, Mass., G.K. Hall, 8v., 1972. First Supplement 6v., 1978. 5671p.+4380p.

1972. 8 reels. $750.00 (Export 905.00). ISBN 0816114617. Now available only on microfilm. *First Supplement.* 4380p. $500.00 ($605.00). ISBN 0816100829. This collection consists of about 60,000 volumes, including 600 periodicals and newspapers, rare books, microfilms and microfiches, manuscripts, maps, photograph records, photographs, and literary and political ephemera. Materials on all aspects of Africa, irrespective of language, are collected comprehensively, including contemporary literary works in both African and European languages. The Herskovits Library holdings are supplemented by the interfiling of cards from libraries which contribute to the *Joint Acquisitions List of Africana (JALA). Joint acquisitions list of Africana: 1978.* 1980. 764p. $95.00 ($115.00). ISBN 0816103291. *Joint acquisitions list of Africana: 1979.* 1981. 662p. $100.00 ($120.00). ISBN 0816103720. *Joint acquisitions list of Africana: 1980.* 1982. 856p. $130.00 ($155.00). ISBN 0816104115. Since 1962, the *Joint Acquisitions List of Africana (JALA),* administered by Northwestern University, has provided a record of materials cataloged by the leading African Studies Libraries - including the Library of Congress. The New York Public Library, the library of the United Nations, and the libraries of Princeton, Stanford, and Yale Universities.
Class No: 908(6)

[4774]

ZELL, H.M. The African studies companion a resource guide and directory. Oxford, Hans Zell, 1989. 16p. £30. $47.50. ISBN: 0905450809.

Annotated guide to major information sources: bibliographies, journals, major libraries and documentation centres, dealers and distributors of African studies material, research foundations *etc. Class No:* 908(6)

Bibliographies of Bibliographies

[4775]

BESTERMAN, T.A. A World bibliography of African bibliographies. Revised and updated by J.D. Pearson. Totowa, New Jersey, Rowman and Littlefield, 1975. 241 cols. $27.50. ISBN: 0874717493.

The 4th ed. of Besterman's *A world bibliography of bibliographies* (1965-66, 5v.) listed *c.* 1,136 works on African countries and subjects under various heading and subheadings. This edition adds 1,634 further items, published up to the end of 1972. Main arrangement is geographical. Index. The reviewer in RQ (v.15, no.3. Spring 1976, p.264-5) has criticised listing of subdivisions. *Class No:* 908(6)(009)

[4776]

SCHEVEN, Y. Bibliographies for African studies 1970-1986. Oxford, Hans Zell Publishers, 1988. xii, 615p. index. £58.00. ISBN: 0905450337.

Preceded by *Bibliographies for African studies 1970-1975* (Waltham, Mass., Crossroads Press, 1977); *1976-1979* (1980); and *1980-1983* (Oxford, Hans Zell, 1984), all of which are now superseded.

Brief annotations (inc. number of entries) on 3277 separately published bibliographies on Sub-Sahara Africa arranged in 2 sections: 1. Topical (under 36 subject headings) - 2. Geographical (by 9 regions and 48 countries) 'Thorough, meticulously compiled, and totally essential' (*African Research and Documentation*, no.48, 1988, p.40-42). *Class No:* 908(6)(009)

Bibliographies

[4777]

Africa bibliography. Blackhurst, H. in association with International African Institute., *comp.* Manchester, Manchester Univ. Press, 1984 -. 1 - Annual. Distributed in North American by St. Martin's Press.

Records publications principally in the humanities, social sciences, and arts under 33 subject headings. Data sources are the book and periodical acquisitions of the John Rylands University Library of Manchester and material received by the International African Institute in London. 1987 volume includes 4031 entries from works published in 1986 and 1987 and indexes almost 400 journals. Review in *Journal of African History*, v.28, no.1, 1987, p. 175-6 compares its coverage with *International African Bibliography*. *Class No:* 908(6)(01)

[4778]

Africa since 1914. Santa Barbara, California and Oxford, ABC-Clio Information Services, 1985. ix, 402p. indexes. £60.50. $75.00. (*Clio Bibliography Series*.) ISBN: 0874363950.

4329 abstracts of journal articles printed 1973-1982 extracted from the ABC - Clio databank and arranged in 11

....(contd.)

chapters: 1. General - 2. Pan African integration and cooperation - 3. African politics - 4. International relations and trade - 5. Africa in the world wars - 6. Society and culture - plus five regional chapters. 'A worthwhile acquisition for specialist libraries'. (*Journal of African History*, v.28, no.3, 1987, p.469). *Class No:* 908(6)(01)

[4779]

BRIDGMAN, J. *and* **CLARKE, D. German Africa** : a select annotated bibliography. Stanford, California, Hoover Institution, Stanford Univ., 1965. 120p. (*Hoover Institution Bibliographical Series; no.19.*)

907 items published 1870 onwards under 7 subject headings. *Class No:* 908(6)(01)

[4780]

FENTON, T. *and* **HEFFRON, M.J.,** *comps.* **Africa** a directory of resources. New York, Orbis Books, 1987. 144p. pbk. $9.94. ISBN: 0883445328.

Organizations, reference books, pamphlets, articles, and audiovisual materials. 'A useful work that deserves frequent updating' (*Choice*, v.25,no.11-12, July-August 1988, p.1674). *Class No:* 908(6)(01)

[4781]

Index Africanus. Asamani, J.O., *ed.* Stanford, California, Hoover Institution Press, Stanford Univ., 1975. xiii, 659p. ISBN: 0817925317.

24,694 entries for articles in Western languages on Africa and published from 1885 to 1965 in periodicals, festschriften or memorial volumes, symposia and proceedings of congresses and conferences. Geographical arrangement, subdivided by subject. Compiled at the School of Oriental and African Studies, Univ. of London. *Class No:* 908(6)(01)

[4782]

International African bibliography current books, articles and papers in African studies. Hall, D., *ed.* London, Mansell, 1971-. Quarterly. ISSN: 00205877.

Appeared as a supplement to the International African Institute's journal, *Africana*, until 1970. A fuller history of the project up to 1972 appears in R. Jones' introduction to the Institute's *Cumulative bibliography of African studies* (2v., 1973) (*q.v.*).

This quarterly bibliography lists serious and authoritative work in African studies, covering the whole of the African continent (and adjacent islands), except for Egypt. The main focus is on the arts and humanities, but there is some coverage of scientific publications, especially relating to geography, natural resources and environmental issues. Arrangement is primarily geographical, but to aid a subject approach, one or more subject tracings are included at the end of each entry so that the user may rapidly scan the page to pick out a particular subject. The first section, covering Africa in general, is subdivided into broad subject groupings.

International African bibliography 1973-1978: books, articles and papers in African studies edited by J.D. Pearson (Mansell, 1982. xxx,343p. ISBN 0720115655) covers v.3-8 plus 3000 items not recorded in the quarterly issues. *Class No:* 908(6)(01)

[4783]
INTERNATIONAL AFRICAN INSTITUTE London. **Cumulative bibliography of African Studies.** Boston, Mass., G.K. Hall, 2v., 1973.
1. *Author catalog.* 4 reels. $200.00 (Export $240.00). ISBN 0816112525. 2. *Classified catalog.* 6 reels. $300.00 ($360.00). ISBN 0816112533. Contains all titles published in the journal Africa (1929-1970) and in International African Bibliography (1971-72). Main focus is on tropical Africa. Now available only on microfilm. *Class No:* 908(6)(01)

[4784]
McILVAINE, J. **Africa: a guide to reference material.** Oxford, Hans Zell, 1992. xxv,507p. indexes. £75. (*Regional Reference Guides, no. 1.*) ISBN: 0905450434.
Annotated guide to 1766, factual reference works relating to Africa south of the Sahara including encyclopaedias, dictionaries, directories, handbooks, gazetteers, almanacs, yearbooks, topographic reference sources, biographical sources, statistical sources and other categories. Appendix includes Annual Reports on British possessions in Africa from 1846 until date of independence. 'Will be an essential companion to African studies for many years' (*Library Association Record,* v.95, no.10, October 1993, p.574). *Class No:* 908(6)(01)

[4785]
PORGÈS, L. **Sources d'information sur l'Afrique noire francophone et Madagascar:** institutions, répertoires, bibliographies. Paris, Documentation Française, 1988. 380p. index. F150. (*Analyse des sources d'information.*) ISBN: 2110017872. *Class No:* 908(6)(01)

Encyclopaedias

[4786]
OLIVER, R. *and* CROWDER, M. **The Cambridge encyclopedia of Africa.** Cambridge, Cambridge Univ. Press, 1981. 492p. illus. (some col.), maps (some col.), tables, diagrs. £27.50 $35.00. ISBN: 0521230969.
99 contributors. 4 sections: 1. The African continent - 2. The African past before European colonisation - 3. Contemporary Africa - 4. Africa and the World. Bibliography (by chapter) p.485-491. 'There is really no other work on the market at present that is so comprehensive and useful as this handsome publication' (*Choice,* v.19, no.10, June 1982, p.1374). *Class No:* 908(6)(031)

Yearbooks & Directories

[4787]
Africa contemporary record. Annual survey and documents 1987-1988. Legum, C. and Doro, M.E., eds. New York & London, Africana Publishing Co., 1989. xl,A150,B859,C102, xli-lxxp. ISBN: 0841905584. ISSN: 00653845.
First published for 1968-69 (1969). Annual.
Pt.1: Current essays (13: *e.g.* The South African crisis 1987-88 the making of a kind of peace - 2. Country-by-country review (6 regional sections) - 3. Documents (political, social, international, Inter-African, economic affairs). Abbreviations p.xi-xxii. Glossary p.xxiii-xxiv. List of sources p.xxx-xxxiii. 'Its value increases with each new volume published' (*International Affairs,* October 1973, p.695). *Class No:* 908(6)(058)

[4788]
Africa south of the Sahara 1994. 23rd ed. London, Europa, 1993. Annual. Distributed in North America by Gale Research Co. 1012p. maps, tables, bibliogs. £150. (*Regional Surveys of the World.*) ISBN: 0946653887. ISSN: 00653896.
First published 1971.
Part 1. Background to the continent: 8 essays by separate hands (*e.g.* Africa in retrospect and prospect - 2. Regional Organizations, all major organizations working in the region: their aims activities, publications etc. Pt.3. Country surveys A-Z: Physical and social geography; The Economy; Statistical survey; Directory (i.e. constitution; government; political organizations; diplomatic representation; religion; news media; finance; trade/industry; transport; tourism; atomic energy; power; defence; and bibliography. 'An excellent reference tool for detailed information about the countries included' (*Reference Reviews,* v.4, no.1, 1990, p.34). *Class No:* 908(6)(058)

[4789]
African studies information resources directory. Gosebrink, J.E.M., *ed.* Oxford, Hans Zell, 1986. xiii, 572p. bibliog., index. £55.00. $88.00. ISBN: 0905450302.
437 entries comprising an inventory of informational sources for the study of Africa, particularly south of the Sahara, in the United States: 1. Information resources for African studies (*i.e.* an A-Z base guide to collections and information services) - 2. Resources in church and missionary organizations - 3. Bookstores, book dealers etc. - 4. Publishers. Bibliography p.505-519. Published for African Studies Association. 'A most impressive and admirable work, with enormous quantities of information carefully presented' (*African Research and Documentation*, no.43, 1987, p.31-32). *Class No:* 908(6)(058)

[4790]
New African yearbook 1993-1994. Van Buren, L., *ed.* 9th ed. London, I.C. Publications, 1993. 436p. maps, tables. ISBN: 090526858. ISSN: 01401378.
African organizations (directory) p.9-18. 52 A-Z by country summary articles on each country's political history, economy, current events, statistics, and general information. *Class No:* 908(6)(058)

Libraries

[4791]
STANDING CONFERENCE ON LIBRARY MATERIALS ON AFRICA. **SCOLMA directory of libraries and special collections on Africa in the UK and in Europe.** French, T. 5th ed. Oxford, Hans Zell, 1992. 355p. index. £52. ISBN: 0905450892.
First published in 1963. 4th ed. 1993.
Over 300 collections identified and described. Arranged geographically by country. Data includes name of librarian; hours of opening; subject coverage; special services; publications; CD-ROM and online databases *etc.* Detailed index of subjects, territories, authors and organizations. *Class No:* 908(6)(058):061:026/027

Maps & Atlases

[4792]
GRIFFITHS, J.L. **An Atlas of African affairs.** Rev. ed. London, Methuen, 1985. viii, 200p., maps, tables, bibliog., index. pbk. £4.95. ISBN: 0416309402.

57 enviromental, historical, political, economic and southern Africa sections each containing a map or group of maps with 2-4 pages of text *e.g.* 1. Africa: barrier peninsula … 12. Pre-European history … 21. Libya and neighbours … 42. Regional economic groupings … 55. Namimbia: Africa's last colony - 56. Chronology of African independence - 57. States, capitals, changes of government and political leaders of post-colonial Africa. Bibliography p. 193-194. 'Strongly recommended as easily the best of its kind. It is authoritative, unbiased and lucid' (*Geographical Journal*, v. 152, no.1, March 1986, p.93). *Class No:* 908(6)(084.3)

[4793]
MURRAY, J., *ed.* **Cultural atlas of Africa.** Oxford, Phaidon; New York, Facts on File, 1981. 240p. illus. (mostly col.). col. maps. bibliog., index. £17.95. $29.95. ISBN: 0714820458.

1. Physical background (natural geographical phenomena) - 2. Cultural - 3. Nations of Africa, a country by country survey grouped regionally. Also 16 special features (*e.g.* Great Zimbabwe; Source of the Nile debate; Mapping of Africa; Flags-symbols of nationhood). Bibliography p.227-229. Gazetteer p.230-235. 84 maps. 'A great deal of information in an extraordinarily attractive book' (*Choice*, v.19, no.1, September 1981, p.52). *Class No:* 908(6)(084.3)

Black Races

Handbooks & Manuals

[4794]
MORRISON, D.G., *and others.* **Black Africa** a comparative handbook. 2nd ed. New York, Paragon House; London, Collier Macmillan, 1989. 720p. maps, charts, tables. $169.50. £99. ISBN: 0887020429, US; 0333498631, UK.

1st ed. 1972.

Systematic data on 41 nations (32 in 1st ed.). Pt1. Comparative profiles with notes on the uses and limitations of cross-national data; measures, models and meaning in aggregate data; ethnic unit classification and analysis, *etc.* Pt2. Country profiles A-Z. Sources are given; select bibliography for each territory. 'An essential reference work for students, scholars and organizations requiring quantitive comparative information relevant to problems of development in Africa' (*Choice*, v.10, no.3, May 1973, p.429-30). *Class No:* 908(6)(=96)(035)

Africa—North

Yearbooks & Directories

[4795]
Annuaire de l'Afrique du Nord. Aix en Provence, Centre de Recherches et d'Études sur les Sociétés Mediterranéenes, 1964-. Later Paris. CNRS. Annual. maps. ISSN: 02427540.

V.38 (1992) ISBN 2222046033.

1. Étude thématique - 3. L'année au Maghreb - 4. Repères bibliographiques - 5. Références bibliogoraphiques. Bibliographie systématique (9 form and thematic sections) p.1013-1157. Index. *Class No:* 908(61/65)(058)

Tunisia

Bibliographies

[4796]
LAWLESS, R.I., *and others, comp.* **Tunisia.** Santa Barbara, California and Oxford, Clio Press, 1982. xxviii, 251p. map, index. £35.95. $36.00. (*World Bibliographical Series; no.33.*) ISBN: 0903450631.

895 annotated entries. 35 sections: The country and its people - Travel and travel guides - Tourism - Geography and geology … Prehistory and archaeology … Libraries and archives … Bibliographies. Author, title and subject index. *Class No:* 908(611)(01)

Libya

Bibliographies

[4797]
BESCHORNER, N., *comp.* **Bibliography of Libya 1970-1990.** London, Centre of Near and Middle Eastern Studies, SOAS, Univ. of London, and Society for Libyan Studies. vi,110p. softcover. ISBN: 0728601729.

528 unannotated entries for books and pamphlets mainly in Western languages but a few in Arabic script arranged under 9 headings: bibliography, economics, Islam, law, natural resources/environment, politics, sociology, transport, and urbanization. Locations (with shelfmarks) are given for 8 London and 1 Libyan libraries. *Class No:* 908(612)(01)

[4798]
LAWLESS, R.J., *comp.* **Libya.** Santa Barbara, California and Oxford, Clio Press, 1987. xxi, 243p. + 1p. map, index. £35.95. $47.75. (*World Bibliographical Series; no.79.*) ISBN: 1851090339.

626 annotated entries. 31 sections: The country and its people - Travellers' accounts and travel guides - Geography and geology - Prehistory and archaeology - History … Foreign relations … Libraries and archives … Bibliographies. Author, title and subject index. *Class No:* 908(612)(01)

Egypt

Bibliographies

[4799]
MAKER, R.N., *comp.* **Egypt.** Santa Barbara, California and Oxford, Clio Press, 1988. xxxi, 306p. + 1p. map, indexes. £46.95. $55.00. (*World Bibliographical Series; no.86.*) ISBN: 1851090398.

1022 annotated entries. 31 sections: The country and its people - Geography, maps and geology - Tourism and travel guides - Travellers' accounts - History … Libraries and museums - Bibliographies. Chronology p. xxi-xxv. Glossary p. xxvii-xxxi. Author, title and subject indexes. *Class No:* 908(620)(01)

Sudan

Bibliographies

[4800]
DALY, M.W., *comp*. **Sudan**. Rev. and expanded ed. Santa
Barbara, California and Oxford, Clio Press, 1992. 194p. + +
1p., indexes. £24.95. (*World Bibliographical Series; no.40.*)
ISBN: 1851091874.
First published 1983.
708 annotated entries. 29 sections: Land and people -
Geography and Geology - Exploration and travel ... History
- Biography and autobiography ... Libraries and archives -
Bibliographies. Author, title and subject indexes.
Class No: 908(624)(01)

[4801]
HILL, R.L. **A Bibliography of the Anglo-Egyptian Sudan**
from the earliest times to 1937. London, Oxford Univ.
Press, 1939. 213p., indexes.
About 5,000 items, on all aspects of knowledge. History,
p.113-52, includes biography and genealogy, and is
arranged under periods. Indexes of persons and subjects.
Class No: 908(624)(01)

[4802]
—EL NASRI, A.R., *comp*. A Bibliography of the Sudan 1938-
1958. London, Oxford Univ. Press for Univ. of Khartoum,
1962. x, 171p.
Continues R.H. Hill's *A bibliography of the Anglo-
Egyptian Sudan* (1939) (*qv*). 2,763 items, the largest section
being on government and politics. Agriculture,
anthropology, economics, history, language and literature,
medicine also figure. The compiler was librarian of the
Univ. of Khartoum.
Supplemented by 'Sudan bibliography, 1959-1963' and 'A
bibliography of the Sudan, 1964-1966,' by Ibrahim and A.R.
El Nasri, in *Sudan notes and records*, v.46, 1965, p. 130-
66, and v.49, 1968. 162-91: 1,893 unannotated items in all,
under sections. *Class No:* 908(624)(01)

Ethiopia

[4803]
MULATIC WUBNEH *and* YOHANNIS ABATE. **Ethiopia**
transition and development in the Horn of Africa. Boulder,
Colo., Westview Press; London, Avebury, 1988. xvi,224p.
illus., map, tables, bibliog., index. (*Profiles: Nations of
Contemporary Africa.*) ISBN: 0865314268, US;
0566056437, UK.
Recount's Ethiopia's passage from an imperial-feudal
system to one of state socialism: 1. Geographical and
historical setting - 2. Opposition to imperial rule - 3. Military
rule - 4. Economic system - 5. Population, culture and
society - 6. International relations - 7. Prospects for change
and stability. Appendix: Programme of the National
Democratic Revolution (PNDR) of Ethiopia p.205-210.
Bibliography p.213-5. *Class No:* 908(63)

Bibliographies

[4804]
MILKIAS, P. **Ethiopia:** a comprehensive bibliography.
Boston, Massachusetts, G.K. Hall, 1989. 650p. index.
$75.00. Export $85.00. ISBN: 0816190666.
Over 16,000 items listed covering all aspects of Ethiopian

....(contd.)
history, culture and society arranged thematically. Includes
much material previously unrecorded outside Ethiopia.
Class No: 908(63)(01)

[4805]
MUNRO-HAY, S. *and* PANKHURST, R. **Ethiopia**. Santa
Barbara, Calif., and Oxford, Clio Press, 1994. (*World
Bibliographical Series.*) ISBN: 1851091114.
Announced for publication. *Class No:* 908(63)(01)

Morocco

Bibliographies

[4806]
FINDLAY, A.M., *and others, comps*. **Morocco**. Santa
Barbara, California and Oxford, Clio Press, 1984. xxix,
317p. + 1p. map, index. £45.95. $45.00. (*World
Bibliographical Series; no.47.*) ISBN: 0903450844.
927 annotated entries. 34 sections: The country and its
people - Travel guides, modern travelogues and tourism -
Travellers' accounts - Geography and geology ... Prehistory
and archaeology - History ... Foreign relations ... Libraries
and archives ... Bibliographies. Author, title and subject
index. *Class No:* 908(64)(01)

Western Sahara

Bibliographies

[4807]
SIPE, L.F. **Western Sahara** a comprehensive bibliography.
New York, Garland Publishing Inc., 1984. xxxiv, 418p.,
map, index. $54.00. ISBN: 0824091256.
3345 items limited to works in Western languages in 28
subject sections grouped in 4 broad divisions: 1. Human and
physical characteristics - 2. The Spanish Sahara - 3.
International legal aspects of the Western Sahara crisis - 4.
The evolving struggle for Western Sahara.
Class No: 908(648)(01)

Algeria

Bibliographies

[4808]
LAWLESS, R.I., *comp*. **Algeria**. Santa Barbara, California
and Oxford, Clio Press, 1980. xxxiii, 215p. + 1p. map,
index. £28.50. (*World Bibliographical Series; no.19.*) ISBN:
0903450321.
A revised edition is announced for publication in 1994.
ISBN 1851091300.
742 annotated entries. 36 sections: The country and its
people - Tourism and travel - Geography and Geology ...
Prehistory and archaeology - History ... Maghreb unity ...
Libraries and archives ... Bibliographies. Author, title and
subject index. *Class No:* 908(65)(01)

[4809]

LAWLESS, R.I. **Algerian bibliography** English language publications 1830-1973. New York and London, R.B. Bowker in association with the Centre for Middle Eastern and Islamic Studies of the Univ. of Durham, 1976. 136p.

About 1,500 references to books and articles. 12 sections (1. 'Bibliography', includes French titles),. Works considered particularly significant are indicated as such. Author index. 'It will be an essential reference tool for all those wishing to undertake research on Algeria and modern North Africa and for those interested in development studies in general' (*British Book News*, October 1976, p.731).
Class No: 908(65)(01)

[4810]

PLAYFAIR, R.L. **A Bibliography of Algeria and its supplement.** Farnborough, Hampshire, Gregg International, 1971. 271p.

First published London, John Murray, 1898 comprising 'A bibliography of Algeria from the expedition of Charles V in 1541 to 1887' *Royal Geographical Society Supplementary Papers* 1888, p.127-140 and *Supplement to the bibliography of Algeria from the earliest times to 1895.*
Class No: 908(65)(01)

Africa—West

Bibliographies

[4811]

IBADAN UNIVERSITY LIBRARY. **Africana catalogue of the Ibadan University Library.** Boston, Mass., G.K. Hall, 2v., 1972. 1605p.

Author catalogue of some 34,000 items. Emphasis is on West Africa and Nigeria in particular.
Class No: 908(66)(01)

Mauritania

Bibliographies

[4812]

CALDERINI, S., *and others, comps.* **Mauretania.** Santa Barbara, Calif., and Oxford, Clio Press, 1992. xvii,165p +1p. map. indexes. £27.95. (*World Bibliographical Series, no.141.*) ISBN: 1851091521.

405 annotated entries in 29 sections: Country and its people - Travel memoirs and travel guides - Explorers and early travellers' accounts - Geography ... Prehistory and archaeology - History ... Slavery ... Foreign aid ... Bibliographies. Author, title, and subject indexes.
Class No: 908(661.2)(01)

Mali

[4813]

IMPERATO, P.J. **Mali** a search for direction. Boulder, Colo., Westview Press; London, Dartmouth, 1989. xiv,170p. illus., maps, bibliog., index. $29. (*Profiles. Nations Of Contemporary Africa.*) ISBN: 0813303419.

1. Introduction - 2. Early history - 3. Conquest, colonial rule, and independence. 4. Malian politics since independence - 5. Culture and society - 6. Economy - 7. International relations. Chapter notes p.149-58. Bibliography p.159-62. *Class No:* 908(662.1)

Bibliographies

[4814]

BRASSEUR, P. **Bibliographie générale du Mali** (anciens Soudan français et Haut-Sénégal-Niger). Dakar, Institut Français D'Afrique Noire, 1964. 461p. map.

4,902 numbered items, often annotated. Includes many references to periodical articles. 6 main sections: 1. Sources (cartes; périodiques; bibliographies; sources manuscrites; sources imprimées) - 2. Le Soudan - 3. Milieu physique - 4. Milieu humain - 5. Mise en valeur - 6. Biographies (nos.4651-4873). Author, locality and subject (non-analytical) index. *Class No:* 908(662.1)(01)

[4815]

MYERS, R.H., *comp.* **Mali.** Santa Barbara, Calif., Oxford, Clio Press, 1993. (*World Bibliographical Series.*) ISBN: 1851091793.

Publication announced. c.600 annotated items covering all major subject areas. *Class No:* 908(662.1)(01)

Upper Volta

Bibliographies

[4816]

IZARD, F. **Bibliographie générale de la Haute-Volta:** 1956-1965. Paris, Centre National de la Recherche Scientifique, 1967. 300p.

Syustematically arranged chapters, covering books, reports, periodical articles and other sources difficult of access. Author index; systematic index; ethnic and linguistic index; list of consulted periodicals. (*Tropical Abstracts*, v.24, no.5, May 1969, p.342). *Class No:* 908(662.5)(01)

Niger

[4817]

CHARLICK, R.B. **Niger** personal rule and survival in the Sahel. Boulder, Colo., Westview Press; London, Dartmouth, 1991. xv,189p. illus., tables, maps, bibliog., index. £20. (*Profiles Nations of Contemporary Africa.*) ISBN: 0891589686, US; 1855212226, UK.

1. The Sahel and its people - 2. Historical background to contemporary Niger - 3. Nigerien political system - 4. Economy - 5. Niger in the world. Bibliography p.171-5.
Class No: 908(662.6)

Bibliographies

[4818]

ZAMPONI, L.F., *comp.* **Niger.** Santa Barbara, Calif., and Oxford, Clio Press, 1993. c.180p. map, index. £28. (*World Bibliographical Series.*) ISBN: 1851092048.

Publication announced. c.435 annotated entries.
Class No: 908(662.6)(01)

Senegal

Bibliographies

[4819]

EADES, J. *and* DILLEY, R.M., *comps.* **Senegal.** Santa Barbara, Calif., and Oxford, Clio Press, 1993. c.200p. map, index. £32. (*World Bibliographical Series.*) ISBN: 1851091564.

....(contd.)
Publication announced. Covers every aspect of Senegal's history, geography, culture, society, economy and politics. *Class No:* 908(663)(01)

Sierra Leone

Bibliographies

[4820]
BINNS, M. *and* BINNS, T., *comps*. **Sierra Leone.** Santa Barbara, Calif., and Oxford, Clio Press, 1992. xliv,235p. +2p. maps, indexes. £24.50. (*World Bibliographical Series no.148.*) ISBN: 1851091017.
627 annotated entries in 37 sections: Country and its people - Geography ... Environment and conservation - Archaeology - Travellers' accounts - History ... Customs and rituals ... Bibliographies. Author, title, and subject indexes. *Class No:* 908(664)(01)

[4821]
SIERRA LEONE UNIVERSITY Fouray Bay College. **Catalog of the Sierra Leone Collection.** Boston, Mass., G.K. Hall, 1979. *c.*500p.
Dictionary catalogue of *c.*6000 cards for monographs, pamphlets, serials, microfilms and manuscripts.
Class No: 908(664)(01)

Gambia

Bibliographies

[4822]
GAMBLE, D.P., *comp*. **The Gambia.** Santa Barbara, California and Oxford, Clio Press, 1988. xxxiv, 135p.+2p. maps, index. £22.95. $32.50. (*World Bibliographical Series, no.91.*) ISBN: 1851090681.
334 annotated entries. 32 sections: Place names and orthography - The country and its people - Travel guides, travelogues and tourism - Explorers and travellers' accounts - Geography ... Prehistory and archaeology - History ... Libraries ... Bibliographies. Author, title and subject index. 'This is an excellent bibliography' (*Choice*, v.26, no.11-12, July-August 1989, p. 1812). *Class No:* 908(665.1)(01)

[4823]
GAMBLE, D.P. *and* SPERLING, L. **A General bibliography of The Gambia** (up to 31 December 1977). Boston, Mass, G.K. Hall, 1979. xxiii, 266p. indexes. ISBN: 0816181772.
4552 entries under subject headings following the Dewey Decimal Classification. Name, organization, place-name, conferences, and periodical indexes.
Supplement 1. San Francisco, the author, 1987. 185p. Adds 935 entries. *Supplement 1978-1987.* San Francisco, the author, 1987. 404p. Adds a further 2450 items.
Class No: 908(665.1)(01)

Guinea

[4824]
SUNDIATA, I.K. **Equatorial Guinea** colonialism, state terror, and the search for stability. Boulder, Colo., Westview Press, 1990. x,179p. illus., maps, tables, bibliog., index. $29. (*Westview Profiles. Nations Of Contemporary*

....(contd.)
Africa.) ISBN: 0813304296.
1. Land and people - 2. History - 3. Politics - 4. Society and culture. Bibliography p.155-61. *Class No:* 908(665.2)

Bibliographies

[4825]
FEGLEY, R., *comp*. **Equatorial Guinea.** Santa Barbara, Calif., and Oxford, Clio Press, 1991. lvii,118p.+ 1p. map, index. £26. (*World Bibliographical Series, no.136.*) ISBN: 185109167x.
339 annotated entries arranged in 35 sections: Names and orthography - The country and its people - Travel guides - Explorers' and travellers' accounts - Geography ... Migrations, exiles and refugees ... Biographies - Reference works - Bibliographies. Author, subject and title index.
Class No: 908(665.2)(01)

[4826]
JAMES, D., *comp*. **Guinea.** Santa Barbara, Calif., and Oxford, Clio Press, 1993. (*World Bibliographical Series.*) ISBN: 1851091483.
Announced for publication. *Class No:* 908(665.2)(01)

Guinea-Bissau

[4827]
FOREST, J.B. **Guinea-Bissau:** power, conflict and renewal in a West African nation. Boulder, Colo., Westview Press, 1992. x,165p. illus., maps, tables, bibliog., index. ISBN: 0865316813, t/p; 0813316813, rear cover.
1. Historical context - 2. Politics - 3. Economy - 4. Society - 5. Future. Bibliography p.153-4. *Class No:* 908(665.7)

Bibliographies

[4828]
GALLI, R.E., *comp*. **Guinea-Bissau.** Santa Barbara, Calif., Oxford, Clio Press, 1990. xxiv,180p.+ 1p. map. indexes. $57; £27. (*World Bibliographical Series, no.121.*) ISBN: 1851091084.
584 annotated entries in 21 sections: The country and its people - Geography and geology ... History ... Bibliographies - Reference books. Theses and dissertations on Guinea-Bissau p.xiii-xxiv. Author, title and subject indexes. Very useful for its record of Portuguese language material. *Class No:* 908(665.7)(01)

Cape Verde Islands

Bibliographies

[4829]
SHAW, C.S., *comp*. **Cape Verde.** Santa Barbara, Calif., and Oxford, Clio Press, 1991. 190p.+ 1p. map, index. £29. (*World Bibliographical Series, no.123.*) ISBN: 185109119x.
484 annotated entries arranged in 28 sections: The country and its people - Geography ... Tourism and travel guides - Travellers' accounts - History ... Libraries, archives and research ... General reference sources - Bibliographies. Author, title and subject index. *Class No:* 908(665.8)(01)

Liberia

Bibliographies

[4830]

DUNN, D.E., *comp*. **Liberia**. Santa Barbara, Calif., and Oxford, Clio Press, 1993. 220p. map, index. £30. (*World Bibliographical Series, no.157.*) ISBN: 1851091785.

Announced for publication. *Class No:* 908(666.2)(01)

Ivory Coast

Bibliographies

[4831]

DAVID, P., *comp*. **Ivory Coast**. Santa Barbara, Calif., and Oxford, Clio Press, 1994. c.225p. map. index. £36. (*World Bibliographical Series, no.131.*) ISBN: 1851091203.

Announced for publication. 584 annotated entries.

Class No: 908(666.8)(01)

Ghana

Bibliographies

[4832]

BROKENSHA, D. *and* KOTEI, S.I.A., *comps*. 'A Bibliography of Ghana 1958-1964'. *African Studies Bulletin,* v.10, no.2, September 1967, p.35-79.

Follows A.W. Cardinall's *A Bibliography of the Gold Coast: issued as a companion volume to the Census Report* (Accra, Government Printer, 1932. xix,348p.) and A.F. Johnson's *A Bibliography of Ghana* (Accra, Longmans, 1964, 210p.).

Unannotated and unnumbered items arranged under 41 subject headings. *Class No:* 908(667)(01)

[4833]

MYERS, R.A., *comp*. **Ghana**. Santa Barbara, Calif., and Oxford, Clio Press, 1991. xxvii,436p. +1p. map. index. £65.95. (*World Bibliographical Series, no. 124.*) ISBN: 1851091351.

781 annotated entries in 35 categories: The country and its people - Geography and geology ... Prehistory and archaeology - Explorers', travellers' and missionaries' accounts - History ... Ethnic groups ... Archives, libraries and museums ... Encyclopaedias and directories - Bibliographies. Author, title, and subject index.

Class No: 908(667)(01)

Togo

Bibliographies

[4834]

PARKER, F.J., *comp*. **Togo**. Santa Barbara, Calif., Oxford, Clio Press, 1994. c.200p. map, index. £30. (*World Bibliographical Series.*) ISBN: 1851091602.

Publication announced. c.400 annotated entries.

Class No: 908(668)(01)

Benin

Bibliographies

[4835]

EADES, J.S., *comp*. **Benin**. Santa Barbara, Calif., and Oxford, Clio Press, 1994. (*World Bibliographical Series.*) ISBN: 1851091459.

Announced for publication. *Class No:* 908(668.2)(01)

[4836]

ROESE, P.M. *and* REES, A.R. A Bibliography of Benin a commentary on published and unpublished sources written in German. *African Research and Documentation,* no.45, 1987(1988 on cover), p.15-26; no.46, 1988, p.31-39; no.48, 1988, p.23-36.

Printed, manuscript and bibliographical sources.

Class No: 908(668.2)(01)

Nigeria

[4837]

Nigeria 1991 official handbook. 10th ed. Lagos, Federal Ministry of Information, 1991. col. illus., tables, bibliog. ISBN: 9782170143.

1st ed. 1970; 9th ed. 1982.

1. Geography - 2. History - 3. Government ... 5. State (of Nigeria) ... 7. Nigeria and the world ... 11. Culture ... 13. Print and electronic media - 14. Facts and figures *etc.* Bibliography p.393-433. *Class No:* 908(669)

Bibliographies

[4838]

EITNER, K, *comp*. **Nigeria: Auswahlbibliographie.** Hamburg, GFR: Dokumentations - Leitstelle Afrika, Insitut für Afrika Kunde, 2v., 1983. maps, indexes. (*Dokumentationsdienst Afrika. Reihe A, 20/1-2.*)

1. *Landeskunde. Politik. Recht* 131p. 908 briefly annotated references in 13 sections: 1. Country studies - 2. History - 3. Contemporary history and politics - 4. Domestic policy - 5. Foreign policy - 6. Public Health - 7. Education - 8. Research - 9. Information - 10. Culture - 11. Religion - 12. Language - 13. Law. 2. *Wirtschaft. Gesellschaft* 135p. 975 references under 80 subject headings.

Most items are in English. *Class No:* 908(669)(01)

[4839]

MYERS, R.A., *comp*. **Nigeria**. Santa Barbara, California and Oxford, Clio Press, 1989. xxxii, 462p.+1p. map, index. £57.50. $55.00. (*World Bibliographical Series; no.100.*) ISBN: 1851090835.

1150 annotated entries. 39 sections: The country and its people - Geography and geology - Explorers', travellers' and missionaries' accounts ... Prehistory and archaeology - History ... Ethnic groups ... Museums ... Libraries and archives ... Encyclopaedias and directories - Bibliographies. Author, title and subject index. *Class No:* 908(669)(01)

Maps & Atlases

[4840]

BARBOUR, K.M., *and others*. **Nigeria in maps**. London, Hodder and Stoughton, New York, Holmes and Meier, 1982. vii,148p. maps, diagrs., tables, bibliog. ISBN: 0340184256, UK; 0841907633, US.

60 maps with accompanying text divided into general,

....(contd.)
physical geography, prehistory and historical and political evolution, social conditions, agriculture and fishers, rural and urban life, manufacturing and power, commerce, and communications, transport and planning. Glossary p.142. Bibliography p.143-148. 21 contributors mostly drawn from Univ. of Ibadan. 'An extremely well thought-out range of topics included ... one would need an encyclopaedic knowledge of Nigeria to detect errors of substance' (*Geographical Journal,* v.149, no.3, November 1983, p.390-301). *Class No:* 908(669)(084.3)

Cameroon

[4841]
DE LANCEY, M.W. Cameroon dependence and independence. Boulder, Colo., Westview Press; London, Dartmouth, 1989. ix,193p. illus., tables, maps, index. (*Profiles. Nations Of Contemporary Africa.*) ISBN: 1855210533.
1. Introduction - 2. Precolonial and colonial heritage - 3. Political system - 4. Society and culture - 5. Economy - 6. Foreign policy - 7. Cameroon looks to the future. Bibliography p.177-83. 'The chapters on politics and economics are excellent ... A most sensible, well-done book' (*Choice,* v.27, no.9, May 1990, p.1556).
Class No: 908(671.1)

Bibliographies

[4842]
DE LANCEY, M. and DE LANCEY, V.H. A Bibliography of Cameroon. New York and London. Africana Publishing Co., 1975. xxii, 673p. $45.00. (*African Bibliography Series, no.4.*) ISBN: 0841901678.
6,041 entries, some briefly annotated, in 20 sections (Agriculture ... Zoology). Covers in depth the period from the start of German colonisation in 1884, to 1972, plus some 1972-73 material. 3 lengthy indexes: ethnic, linguistic and geographic: authors and personal names; subjects. 'Indispensable to anyone working on Cameroon' (*African research and development, no.13,* 1977, p.25).
Class No: 908(671.1)(01)

[4843]
DE LANCEY, M.W. and SCHRAEDER, P.J., comps. Cameroon. Santa Barbara, California and Oxford, Clio Press, 1986. xxvi, 201p.+1p. map, index. £30.95. $34.40. (*World Bibliographical Series; no.63.*) ISBN: 1851090061.
502 annotated entries. 26 sections: The country and its people - Geography - Travellers' accounts - Tourist guides ... History ... Languages ... Museums, archives and libraries - Bibliographies. Author, title and subject index.
Class No: 908(671.1)(01)

[4844]
DIPPOLD, M.F. Une bibliographie du Cameroun les écrits en langue Allemande. Yaoundé, Éditions CLE, 1971. 343p. bibliog., index.
Over 6000 entries. Subject index.
Class No: 908(671.1)(01)

Gabon

[4845]
AICARDI DE SAINT-PAUL, M. Gabon: the development of a nation. London, Routledge, 1989. x,145p. maps, tables, index. ISBN: 0415039053.
First published by Albatros (Paris, 1987) as *Le Gabon: du roi Denis à Omar Bongo.*
1. The country and its people - 2. From discovery to independence - 3. Institutional, administrative and political framework - 4. Analysis of Gabonese economy - 5. Infrastructures - 6. Social policies - 7. Gabon and the world. Chapter notes p.98-107. Bibliography p.129-38.
Class No: 908(672.1)

Bibliographies

[4846]
GARDINIER, D.E., comp. Gabon. Santa Barbara, Calif., and Oxford, Clio Press, 1992. xxxvii,178p. +1p. map. indexes. £32. (*World Bibliographical Series, no.149.*) ISBN: 1851091742.
549 annotated entries in 32 sections: The country and its people - Geography ... Archaelogy and prehistory - History ... Religions and missions ... Bibliographies. Author, title and subject indexes. *Class No:* 908(672.1)(01)

Congo

[4847]
FEGLEY, R., comp. The Congo. Santa Barbara, Calif., and Oxford, Clio Press, 1993. l,168p.+ 1p. map, index. (*World Bibliographical Series, no. 162.*) ISBN: 1851091998.
536 annotated entries in 34 sections: Country and its people - Travel guides - Explorers' and travellers; accounts - Geography ... Prehistory and archaeology - History ... Ethnic groups ... Reference works and scholarly journals - Bibliographies. Author, title and subject index.
Class No: 908(672.4)

Angola

Bibliographies

[4848]
BLACK, R., comp. Angola. Santa Barbara, Calif, and Oxford, Clio Press, 1992. xxvii,176p. +1p. map indexes. £29.50. (*World Bibliographical Series no.151.*) ISBN: 1851091432.
565 annotated entries arranged in 31 sections: The country and its people - Geography and geology ... Prehistory and archaeology - History ... Foreign relations and foreign intervention ... Directories and Current reference sources. Glossary p.xxv. Theses and dissertations on Angola p.xxvii. Author, subject, and title indexes. *Class No:* 908(673)(01)

[4849]
GOWAN, S.J. Portugese-speaking Africa 1900-1979: a select bibliography. Volume 1. Angola. Braamfontein, South African Institute of International Affairs, 1982. 346p. map, index. (*Bibliographical Series; no.9.*)
2329 references arranged in identical sections for Angola before and after independence: 1. General (including bibliographies) - 2. Politics and government - 3. Foreign relations - 4. Economic development.
Class No: 908(673)(01)

Central African Republic

[4850]

O'TOOLE, T. **The Central African Republic:** the continent's hidden heart. Boulder, Colorado, Westview Press; London, Gower, 1986. xiv,174p. illus., maps, bibliog., index. $34.00; £19.50. (*Profiles/Nations of Contemporary Africa.*) ISBN: 086531647, US; 0566007738, UK.

1. The physical setting - 2. Historical context - 3. The Central African policy - 4. Society and change - 5. Economic and political dependence - 6. The Central African Republic and the world. Bibliography (by chapter) p.152-6. *Class No:* 908(674.1)

Bibliographies

[4851]

KALCK, P., *comp.* **Central African Republic.** Santa Barbara, Calif., and Oxford, Clio Press, 1993. liv,153p.+ 1pl. map, indexes. £36. (*World Bibliographical Series, no.152.*) ISBN: 1851091726.

538 annotated entries (mostly French language) in 22 sections: Country and its people - Geography and geology - Maps - Tourist guides - Expeditions and exploration ... Peoples - Prehistory and History ... Bibliographies - Biographies. Chronology p.xliv-liv. Author, title and subject indexes. *Class No:* 908(674.1)(01)

Chad

Bibliographies

[4852]

ALAWAR, Mohamed A., *and others.* **A Concise bibliography of Northern Chad and Fezzan in Southern Libya.** Cambridge, Arab Crescent Press; Boulder, Colorado, Westview Press, 1983. xxiv, 229p. maps and index. $30.00.

Almost 3000 entries, primarily in English or French, intended to assist students grappling with 'a complex and otherwise uncoordinated literature'. 'A must for anyone engaged in serious scholarship in this important border region' (*African Journal*, v.xiv, no.4, 1983, p.323). *Class No:* 908(674.3)(01)

[4853]

JOFFE, E.G.H., *comp.* **Chad.** Santa Barbara, Calif., and Oxford, Clio Press, 1994. (*World Bibliographical Series.*) Announced for publication. *Class No:* 908(674.3)(01)

Zaire

Bibliographies

[4854]

BUSTIN, É. **Congo-Kinshasa: guide bibliographique.** Bruxelles, Centre d'Études et de Documentation Africaines, 2v., 1971.

Preceded by his 'A study guide for Congo-Kinshasa' (Boston, African Studies Center, Boston Univ., 1970. 167p.), a subject list described as 'an excellent new bibliographic survey' (Duignan, P., ed. *Guide to research and reference works on Sub-Saharan Africa* [1971], entry no.2214). *Class No:* 908(675)(01)

[4855]

HEYSE, T. **Bibliographie du Congo-Belge et du Ruanda-Urundi** (1939-1951). Bruxelles, Camperhout, 2v., 1953.

The basic bibliography on the Congo. 854 pages in all, dealing with specific aspects *e.g.* geology and mines, agriculture, communications, economy, history, culture, etc. *Class No:* 908(675)(01)

[4856]

PARFITT, T.W., *comp.* **Zaire.** Santa Barbara, Calif., Oxford, Clio Press, 1994. (*World Bibliographical Series.*) Publication announced. *Class No:* 908(675)(01)

Encyclopaedias

[4857]

Encyclopédie du Congo Belge. Bruxelles, Éditions Bieleveld, 3v., 1950-53. illus., diagrs., maps.

Systematically arranged. V.1 covers history, prehistory, peoples, geology, climate, soils, botany and agriculture; v.2, forestry, fauna, fishing, stockbreeding, minerals; v.3, public health, agricultural diseases, applied entomology, economics and industry, transport, electricity, water supply, tourism, political administration and judiciary, finances, land tenure, mining, etc. Statistics are given up to 1948. A general index is also included in v.3 (p.847-60). *Class No:* 908(675)(031)

Burundi

[4858]

DANIELS, M., *comp.* **Burundi.** Santa Barbara, Calif., and Oxford, Clio Press, 1992. xxv,135pp.+ 1p. map. indexes. £24.50. (*World Bibliographical Series, no.145.*) ISBN: 1851091947.

463 annotated entries in 25 sections: The country and its people - Geography ... Prehistory and archaeology - History ... Ethnic groups ... Bibliographies. Chronology p.xix,xxv. Author, title and subject indexes. *Class No:* 908(675.97)

Rwanda

[4859]

FEGLEY, R., *comp.* **Rwanda.** Santa Barbara, Calif., and Oxford, Clio Press, 1993. xxxvi,161p.+ 1p. map, index. (*World Bibliographical Series, no.154.*) ISBN: 1851092021.

521 annotated entries in 34 sections: Country and its people - Travel guides - Explorers' and Travellers' accounts - Geography ... Prehistory and archaeology - History ... Reference works and scholarly journals - Bibliographies. Author, title and subject index. *Class No:* 908(675.978)

Uganda

Bibliographies

[4860]

COLLISON, R.L., *comp.* **Uganda.** Santa Barbara, California and Oxford, Clio Press, 1981. xxviii, 159p.+1p. map, index. £22.95. $25.20. (*World Bibliographical Series; no.11.*) ISBN: 0903450178.

521 annotated entries. 29 sections: The country and its people - Geography ... Prehistory and archaeology - History ... Periodicals and yearbooks - Libraries and Museums -

....*(contd.)*

Library catalogues - Bibliographies. Chronology p.xiii-xxv. Glossary p.xxvii-xxviii. Author, title and subject index. *Class No:* 908(676.1)(01)

Kenya

Bibliographies

[4861]

COLLISON, R.L., *comp*. **Kenya.** Santa Barbara, California and Oxford, Clio Press, 1982. xxix, 157p. map, index. £21.55. $25.25. (*World Bibliographical Series; no.25.*) ISBN: 0903450348.

596 annotated entries. 29 sections: The country and its peoples - Geography ... Prehistory and archaeology - History ... Libraries and museums - Library catalogues - Bibliographies. Chronology p.xiii-xxvii. Glossary p.xxix. Author, title and subject index. *Class No:* 908(676.2)(01)

[4862]

WEBSTER, J.B., *and others, comps*. **A Bibliography on Kenya.** Syracuse, New York. Program of Eastern African Studies, Syracuse Univ., 1967. xvii, 461p. indexes. $80.00. (*Syracuse Univ. Eastern African Bibliographical Series; no.2.*) ISBN: 0686709950.

7,210 numbered items in 28 chapters (1. Agriculture - 2. Anthropology and sociology - Archaeology and ancient history ... 12. Geography - 13. Geology ... 17. Language and literature (p.227-90) - Land ... 25. Urban and housing - 26. Women and children - 27. General, miscellaneous and additions - 28. Entry numbers of bibliographies or works which contain bibliographies. *Class No:* 908(676.2)(01)

Somalia

[4863]

LAITIN, D.D. *and* SAMATAR, S.S. **Somalia** nation in search of a state. Boulder, Colo., Westview Press; London, Gower, 1987. xvii,198p. illus., map, bibliog., index. (*Profiles: Nations Of Contemporary Africa.*) ISBN: 0865315558, US; 0566054590, UK.

1. Peopling of the Somali peninsula - 2. Society and culture - 3. Colonialism and the struggle for national independence - 4. Government and politics - 5. Economy - 6. Foreign relations - 7. Into the 1990s. Chapter notes p.171-81. Bibliography p.182-3. *Class No:* 908(677)

Bibliographies

[4864]

Bibliografia Somalia. Carbani, F., *ed.* Roma, Ministero Degli Affari Esteri, 1983. 309p. (*Studi Somali; no.4.*)

7500 unannotated entries (mainly Italian but with English, French and German material) in detailed subdivisions. 'Although citations are often incomplete and make this bibliography somewhat frustrating to use, it should be considered an important research tool' (M.W. De Lancey. *Somalia*, 1988. Entry 568). *Class No:* 908(677)(01)

[4865]

DE LANCEY, M.W. **and others,** *comps*. **Somalia.** Santa Barbara, California and Oxford, Clio Press, 1988. xxviii, 191p.+1p. map, indexes. £32.95. $43.50. (*World Bibliographical Series; no.92.*) ISBN: 185109038x.

584 annotated entries. 26 sections: The country and its people - Geography - Travellers' accounts ... History ... Libraries, museums and archives ... Bibliographies. Author, title and subject indexes. 'Recommended for all research collections' (*Choice*, v.27, no.2, October 1989, p.293-4). *Class No:* 908(677)(01)

[4866]

SALAD, M.K. **Somalia** a bibligraphical survey. Westport, Connnecticut, Greenwood Press, 1977. xvi, 468p. $46.95. (*African Bibliographic Center. Special Bibliography Series; no.4.*) ISBN: 0837184806.

About 4,000 titles, covering agriculture, anthropology, biology, economics, education, history and antiquity, *etc*. *Choice*, (v.14, no.12, February 1978, p.1627) notes 'lack of reference to some of the important scholarship of the last decade'. *Class No:* 908(677)(01)

Djibouti

Bibliographies

[4867]

SCHRAEDER, P.J., *comp*. **Djibouti.** Santa Barbara, Calif., and Oxford, Clio Press, 1991. xxxix,239p.+ 1p. map, index. £38. (*World Bibliographical Series, no.118.*) ISBN: 1851090843.

409 annotated entries arranged under 22 subject headings: The country and its people - Tourist guides - Geography and earth sciences - Travellers' accounts ... History ... Migration and refugees - Ethnicity and population ... Bibliographies. Author, title and subject index. *Class No:* 908(677.1)(01)

Tanzania

[4868]

BENNETT, N.R. **A History of the Arab state of Zanzibar.** London, Methuen, 1978. viii,304p. tables, bibliog., index. £10. (*Studies in African history.*) ISBN: 0416550800.

7 well-documented chapters covering the period from the late eighteenth century onwards with an introduction on early history. Notes p.269-286. Bibliographical essay p.287-297. 'Serves well as background to any study of the island' (*Geographical Journal,* v.145, no.1, March 1979, p.132). *Class No:* 908(678)

Bibliographies

[4869]

BENNETT, N.R. **The Arab state of Zanzibar** a bibliography. Boston, G.K. Hall & Co., 1984. xvii,231p. index. $53.00; £47.50. (*A Reference Publication in African Studies.*) ISBN: 0816184550.

2492 items mainly in Western European languages grouped in 8 categories: General reference; Environment; Description and travel; History and biography; Peoples; Economy; Administration; and Greater Zanzibar (*i.e.,* major sources in continental Tanzania for understanding Zanzibar's role in East Africa in the 19th century). Persons, places,

....(contd.)

subject and author indexes. 'Solid mass of information' (*African Research and Documentation,* no.40, 1986, p.26). *Class No:* 908(678)(01)

[4870]

DARCH, C., *comp.* **Tanzania.** Santa Barbara, California and Oxford, Clio Press, 1985. xxv, 315p.+1p. map, index. £45.50. $48.50. (*World Bibliographical Series; no.54.*) ISBN: 0903450917.

676 annotated entries. 30 sections: The country and its people - Geography ... Archaeology and pre-colonial history - History ... Foreign relations ... Libraries, archives and the book trade ... Bibliographies. Author, title and subject index. *Class No:* 908(678)(01)

Maps & Atlases

[4871]

BERRY, L., *ed.* **Tanzania in maps.** London, Univ. of London Press, 1971. 172p. maps, illus., tables.

61 black-and-white maps, with text facing (1. Tanzania in Africa - 2. Tanzania and her neighbours - 3. Administrative areas ... 22. Cotton ... 33. Railways ... 47. Tribes ... 53/54. Traditional rural settlement ... 61. External trade). General bibliography, p.146; Select bibliography and sources by chapters, p.147-52. 61 tables, *Library Journal* (1 October 1972, p.3138-9) finds most of the maps too small and cluttered but praises the well-written, 'informative and thoroughly researched text'. *Class No:* 908(678)(084.3)

Mozambique

Bibliographies

[4872]

DARCH, C., *comp.* **Mozambique.** Santa Barbara, California and Oxford, Clio Press, 1987. xxvi, 360p.+1p. map, index. £49.95. $55.00. (*World Bibliographical Series; no.78.*) ISBN: 1851090258.

735 annotated entries. 32 sections: The country and its people - Travellers' accounts and exploration - Geography ... Prehistory and archaeology - History ... Foreign and economic relations ... Museums and archives ... Directories and current reference sources - Bibliographies. Author, title and subject index. *Class No:* 908(679)(01)

Africa—Southern

Bibliographies

[4873]

UNITED STATES. Library of Congress. General Reference and Bibliography Division. African Section. **Africa south of the Sahara:** index to periodical literature. Boston, Mass., G.K. Hall, 4v., 1971. First Supplement, 1973. Second Supplement 3v., 1981.

1971. 8 reels. $365.00 (Export $440.00). ISBN 0816112568. *First Supplement.* 1 reel. $110.00 ($135.00). ISBN 0816113513. Covers period January 1971-July 1972. Base catalogue and *First Supplement* now available only on microfilm. *Second Supplement.* 3v., 1243p. $220.00 ($265.00). ISBN 0816102937. Total entries 142,300. Divided by regions A-Z with A-Z subject sub-division. *Class No:* 908(68)(01)

Yearbooks & Directories

[4874]

Southern African annual review. Pycroft, C *and* Munslow, B. Oxford, Hans Zell, 1989-.

1. 1987/88. v.1: Country reviews. 404p. £48. $85. ISBN 0905450035. v.2: Regional reviews. 470p. £48. $85. 0905450043. Set 2v. 1989. £96. $170. 0905450027.

2. 1989. v.1: Country reviews. 320p. £35. $65. 0905450747. v.2 Regional reviews. 320p. £35. $65. 0905450795. Set 2v. 1990. £70. $130. 0905450698.

Volume 1 provides extensive coverage of press sources on the region, whilst Volume 2 deals with the important issues of the period, revealing the motivating forces for regional integration, confrontation, and negotiation. Based on the Southern Africa Computerized Data/Text (SACDT) System developed by the Centre of African Studies in the University of Liverpool. 'Uneven, disjointed, patchy in quality, highly selective and difficult to use' (*Reference Reviews,* v.4,no.3, 1990, p.31-2). *Class No:* 908(68)(058)

South Africa

Bibliographies

[4875]

MUSIKER, R., *comp.* **South Africa.** Santa Barbara, California and Oxford, Clio Press, 1979. xiii, 194p. map, index. £27.50. $25.25. (*World Bibliographical Series; no.7.*) ISBN: 090345016x.

A revised edition is published in 1993.

577 annotated entries. 29 sections: Geography ... Prehistory and archaeology - History ... Politics - Law ... Libraries, archives and museums ... Encyclopaedias - Bibliographies. Author, title and subject index. Excludes material on Namibia, the Transkei. *Class No:* 908(680)(01)

Yearbooks & Directories

[4876]

South Africa 1989-90 official yearbook of the Republic of South Africa. 15th ed. Pretoria, Bureau for Information on behalf of the Department of Foreign Affairs. 842p., col.illus., col.maps, tables, diagrs., bibliog., index. ISBN: 0797017291.

First published 1974.

40 chapters each ending with suggested readings: 1. Physical features - 2. History - 3. People and languages - 4. Demographic trends - 5. Citizenship and immigration - 6. Constitution - 7. Government departments - 8. Political parties - 9. Black political development - 10. Foreign relations - 11. Justice - 12. National security - 13. Railways and harbours - 14. Aviation - 15. Road transport - 16. Posts and telecommunications - 17. Energy - 18. Mining and minerals - 19. Agriculture - 20. Water - 21. Forestry - 22. Marine fisheries - 23. Manpower and industrial relations - 24. Public works and land affairs - 25. National economy - 26. Finance - 27. Guide for foreign investors - 28. Education - 29. Health and welfare - 30. Community development - 31. Research - 32. Cultural life - 33. Literature - 34. Religion - 35. Press and advertising - 36. Radio & TV - 37. Sport and recreation - 38. Wildlife and conservation - 39. Tourism - 40. Calendar 1987 and 1988. Bibliography p.793-806. 37 maps. *Class No:* 908(680)(058)

Botswana

Bibliographies

[4877]
WISEMAN, J.A., *comp*. **Botswana**. Santa Barbara, Calif., and Oxford, Clio Press, 1992. xxvii,187p. +1p. map. indexes. £32. (*World Bibliographical Series, no. 150.*) ISBN: 1851091718.

723 annotated entries in 30 sections: Country and its people - Geography and geology - Travellers' and Explorers' accounts ... Prehistory and archaeology - History ... Peoples of Botswana - Bibliographies and libraries. Author, title and subject indexes. *Class No:* 908(681)(01)

Swaziland

[4878]
DAVIES, R.H. **The Kingdom of Swaziland** a profile. London, Zed Books, 1985. Distributed in US by Biblio Distribution Center, Totowa (New Jersey). x, 82p. tables. £13.95. (*Third World Books.*) ISBN: 0862324491.

Swaziland under colonialism - 2. Process of decolonization - 3 Structure of the Swaziland economy - 4. Outline of the class structure - 5. Political struggles since independence - 6. Swaziland in the regional struggle. Notes p.76-81. *Class No:* 908(683.4)

Bibliographies

[4879]
NYEKO, B., *comp*. **Swaziland**. Santa Barbara, Calif., and Oxford, Clio Press, 1982. xvi,135p. +1p. map. index. £19.50. (*World Bibliographical Series, no. 24.*) ISBN: 0903450356.

478 annotated entries in 19 sections: Country and its people - Travellers' accounts and tourism - Geography and geology ... Archaeology and ancient history - History - Anthropology and sociology ... Archives and libraries. Author, title and subject index. *Class No:* 908(683.4)(01)

Lesotho

[4880]
BARDILL *and* COBBE, J.H. **Lesotho** dilemmas of dependence in South Africa. Boulder, Westview Press, London, Gower, 1985. xii,224p. map,bibliog., index. $34.00. (*Profiles/Nations of Contemporary Africa.*) ISBN: 0865314403, US; 0566051591, UK.

1. The historical setting - 2. Economy - 3. Social dynamics of the labor reserve - 4. Government and politics - 5. Lesotho and the world - 6. Prospects for the future. Bibliography p.203-8. *Class No:* 908(686.1)

Bibliographies

[4881]
WILLET, S.M. *and* AMBROSE, D.P., *comps*. **Lesotho** a comprehensive bibliography. Santa Barbara, California and Oxford, Clio Press. 1980. xliii, 496p.+2p. map, index. £42.50. (*World Bibliographical Series; no.3.*) ISBN: 0903450119.

2562 annotated entries. 24 sections: Geography and travel ... Archaeology - History ... Bibliography. Glossary of Lesotho words p.xxxix-xl. Author, title and subject index. *Class No:* 908(686.1)(01)

Namibia

[4882]
PUTZ, J., *and others*. **Namibia handbook and political who's who**. Windhoek, The Magus Company, 1989. 448p. maps, index. R58; $23. (*Namibia Series, no.2.*)

Includes current data, economic statistics, names of leading officials and administrators by their office, churches, diplomatic missions, trade unions and employers' associations. Also details of every existing political parties, their leaders and programmes. 'All libraries with African collections must get this book for their reference departments' (*African Book Publishing Record,* v.16, no.4, 1990, p.242). *Class No:* 908(688)

Bibliographies of Bibliographies

[4883]
VOGT, M. 'Bibliographical aids for studies on South West Africa' *Basel Africa Bibliographies. Communications.* v.13, 1975, p.21-32.

68 items. *Class No:* 908(688)(009)

[4884]
—HILLEBRANDT, W. 'Bibliographical aids for studies on Namibia' a supplement to Martin Vogt's list, *Basel Africa Bibliographies. Newsletter,* v.6, no.3, May 1982, p.39-54.

A further 150 items. *Class No:* 908(688)(009)

Bibliographies

[4885]
SCHOEMAN, S. *and* SCHOEMAN, E., *comps*. **Namibia**. Santa Barbara, California and Oxford, Clio Press, 1984. xxiv,186p. +1p. map. index. £27.95. (*World Bibliographical Series, no. 53.*) ISBN: 0903450909.

710 annotated entries. 33 sections: The country and its people - Geography ... Archaeology and rock art - History - Biographies ... Politics and the international status issue ... Libraries and archives ... Bibliographies. Author, title and subject index. *Class No:* 908(688)(01)

[4886]
STROHMEYER, E. *and* MORITZ, W., *comps*. **Umfassende Bibliographie der Völker Namibians (Südwestafrikas und Südwestangolas)**. [Comprehensive bibliography of the peoples of Namibia (South West Africa and Southwestern Angola).] Starnberg, Max Planck-Institut, 2v., 1975-80.

V.1 (xix, 349p.) has c.3,000 entries, some annotated, covering ethnology, prehistory, physical anthropology, linguistics, vernacular literature and translations, Christian literature, educational material, vernacular journals and missionary history. Arrangement by tribe, then subject. Includes monographs, articles and manuscript material, with locations for rare items. (Based on review in *African research & documentation,* no.3, 1973, p.29). 'The most comprehensive and up-to-date bibliography on South West Africa' (Musiker, R. *South African bibliography* (2nd ed., 1980), p.27. *Class No:* 908(688)(01)

[4887]
TRUSCHEL, L.W. **German South West Africa**: a centennial bibliographic essay, *African Journal,* v.14, no.4, 1983, p.277-291.

Literature review with consolidated bibliography p.289-91. *Class No:* 908(688)(01)

Zimbabwe

[4888]

SYLVESTER, C. **Zimbabwe** the terrain of contradictory development. Boulder, Colo., Westview Press; London, Dartmouth, 1991. xii,212p. illus., maps, bibliog., index. (*Profiles: Nations Of Contemporary Africa.*) ISBN: 0813306906, US; 1855212560, UK.

1. Historical kaleidoscope - 2. Contradictions of Rhodesia (1923-1979) - 3. State and politics in contemporary Zimbabwe - 4. Political economy of 'growth and equity' - 5. Civil society and state-society relations - 6. Z.'s international profile - 7. Less contradictory future? Bibliography p.191-7. *Class No:* 908(689.1)

Bibliographies

[4889]

POLLAK, O.B. *and* POLLAK, K., *comps.* **Rhodesia/ Zimbabwe.** Santa Barbara, California and Oxford, Clio Press, 1979. xix, 195p.+1p. map, index. £42.50. $25.25. (*World Bibliographical Series; no.4.*) ISBN: 0903450143.

Material drawn from authors' *Rhodesia/Zimbabwe* (Boston, G.K. Hall, 1977). To be superseded by Potts, D. *Zimbabwe* 1993. c.240p. £36. ISBN 1851091955 c.800 entries.

508 annotated entries. 33 sections: General reference books - The people - Geography - History ... Race relations ... African nationalism ... Museums, archives and libraries ... Bibliographies. Author, title and subject index. *Class No:* 908(689.1)(01)

[4890]

POLLAK, O.B. *and* POLLAK, K. **Rhodesia/Zimbabwe** an international bibliography. Boston, Mass., G.K. Hall, 1977. xxxv, 621p.

11,380 computer-compiled, unannotated entries for monographs, articles, essays within books, and theses, - mostly in English. 9 subject sections: Anthropology, ethnology, religion and sociology - Communications - Economics - Education - Fine arts - Geography - History - Natural science - Political science and international relations. Bibliographic sources, p.1-14; *c.*1,200 journals cited. Author index. *Choice* (v.15, no.1, March 1978, p.46) notes curious omissions. *Class No:* 908(689.1)(01)

Encyclopaedias

[4891]

A Concise encyclopedia of Zimbabwe. Berens, D., *ed.* Gweru, Mambo Press, 1988. 444p. illus. (some col.), col.maps, tables, softcover. £6.95. ISBN: 0869224417.

Compact general knowledge book encompassing flora and fauna, history and geography, religion and culture, politics, economics, and social life. *Class No:* 908(689.1)(031)

[4892]

Tabex encyclopedia Zimbabwe. 2nd ed. Stanton, Arlington Business Corporation, 1989. xv,448p., illus., col. maps, index. $42.70. ISBN: 0951450506, UK; 0908306040, Zim.

First published in 1987 by Quest Publishing of Harare.

All aspects of present-day Zimbabwe presented in a single A-Z sequence with the emphasis on sport and the natural sciences. Some entries end with lists of further reading. Zimbabwean chronology p.xiii-xv. 'An excellent single-

....(contd.)
volume reference work appropriate for a wide range of audiences' (*Choice*, v.27, no.11-12, July/August 1990, p.1810). *Class No:* 908(689.1)(031)

Zambia

Bibliographies of Bibliographies

[4893]

WILLIAMS, G.J. 'Zambia a bibliography of bibliographies,' *Zambia Library Association Journal*, v.12, no.1, June 1980, p.25-32. *Class No:* 908(689.4)(009)

Bibliographies

[4894]

BLISS, A.M. *and* RIGG, J.A., *comps.* **Zambia.** Santa Barbara, California and Oxford, Clio Press, 1984. xviii, 233p.+1p. map, index. £33.95. $38.00. (*World Bibliographical Series, no.51.*) ISBN: 0903450887.

829 annotated entries. 34 setions: The country and its people - Geography and geology ... Prehistory and archaeology - History ... Peoples of Zambia ... Libraries, museums and archives ... Bibliographies. Place names in Zambia (old and new) p. xviii. Author, title and subject index. *Class No:* 908(689.4)(01)

[4895]

RAU, W.E. **A Bibliography of pre-independence Zambia.** Boston, Mass., G.K. Hall, 1978. xxix, 357p. (*Bibliographies and Guides in African Studies.*)

Unannotated list of books, articles, essays and unpublished theses written before 1964, and much of it recorded for the first time. 16 major topics in the social sciences, including archaeology, anthropology, linguistics, geography, description and travel, history, economics, government and politics, and wildlife. Cross-references. Indexes of authors, ethno-linguistic groups, and proper names. 'A reference book that all academic libraries will want to have' (*Choice*, v.15, no. 10. December 1978, p.1352). *Class No:* 908(689.4)(01)

Malawi

Bibliographies

[4896]

BOEDER, R.B. **Malawi.** Santa Barbara, California and Oxford, Clio Press, 1979. xviii, 165p. map, index. £23.95. $28.50. (*World Bibliographical Series; no.8.*) ISBN: 0903450224.

557 annotated entries. 25 sections: The country and its people - Geography ... History ... Bibliographies. Author, title and subject index. *Class No:* 908(689.7)(01)

[4897]

BROWN, E.E. **and others,** *comps.* **A Bibliography of Malawi.** Syracuse, New York, Program of Eastern African Studies, Syracuse Univ., 1965. 161p. Index. (*Syracuse Univ. Eastern African Bibliographies; no.1.*)

3000 items organized under 24 subject headings *e.g.* 1. General ... 4. Bibliography ... 6. Description and travel ... 11. Geography ... 14. History. Author and indexes.

....(contd.)

Webster, J.B. and Mohome, P. *A Supplement to a bibliography of Malawi* (Program of Eastern African Studies, 1969). *Class No:* 908(689.7)(01)

Madagascar

Bibliographies

[4898]

BRADT, H., *comp*. **Madagascar**. Santa Barbara, Calif., and Oxford, Clio Press, 1993. c.200p. map, index. £30. (*World Bibliographical Series*.) ISBN: 1851091793.

Announced for publication. c.400 annotated entries including French language items. *Class No:* 908(691)(01)

Seychelles

Bibliographies

[4899]

BENNETT, G. *and* BENNETT, P.R., *comps*. **Seychelles**. Santa Barbara, Calif; Oxford, Clio Press, 1993. c.151p. map, index. £24.50. (*World Bibliographical Series, no.153*.) ISBN: 1851091823.

339 annotated entries cover all aspects of Seychelles history, geography, culture, society, economy and politics. *Class No:* 908(696)(01)

Mauritius

[4900]

BOWMAN, L.W. **Mauritius** democracy and development in the Indian Ocean. Boulder, Colo., Westview Press; London, Dartmouth, 1991. xv,208p. illus., maps, tables, bibliog., index. (*Profiles. Nations of Contemporary Africa*.) ISBN: 081330508x, US; 185521248x, UK.

1. Geographic and physical setting - 2. Historical background - 3. Society and culture - 4. Politics of independent Mauritius - 5. Economy - 6. International relations - 7. Mauritius and the future. Chapter notes p.169-88. Bibliography p.189-95. 2 maps. 'This most informative, well-written book provides a wealth of up-to-date facts ... a valuable addition to the literature on off-shore Africa' (*Journal of Modern African Studies*, v.29, no.4, December 1991, p.715-6). *Class No:* 908(698.2)

Bibliographies

[4901]

BENNETT, P.R. *and* BENNETT, G.J., *comps*. **Mauritius**. Santa Barbara, Calif., and Oxford, Clio Press, 1992. xxv,151p. +2p. maps, index. £26.95. (*World Bibliographical Series, no. 140*.) ISBN: 185109153x.

537 annotated entries in 27 sections: Country and its people - Geography - Travellers' accounts ... History ... Cuisine ... Directories - Bibliographies. Glossary p. xxiii-xiv. Author, subject and title index. *Class No:* 908(698.2)(01)

America — North

Yearbooks & Directories

[4902]

The USA and Canada 1994. 2nd ed. London, Europa Publications, 1993. 600p. maps, tables, bibliogs. £195. (*Regional Surveys of the World*.) ISBN: 0946653933. ISSN: 09560904.

Revised every 2 years.

Separate sections for each country provide introductory historical, geographical and demographic data. There follow essays (plus bibliographies) on the political and administrative system, the economy, social issues, and international relations. Extensive statistical and directory type information is listed under Public affairs; The economy; Society; Transport and utilities; and Tourism. A group of essays examine topics currently affecting US and Canada equally. 'It is difficult to see how any other single volume of comparable size could possibly improve its coverage' (*Reference Reviews*, v.4, no.4, 1990, p.36). *Class No:* 908(71 + 73)(058)

Canada

[4903]

Canada: a portrait. The official handbook of present conditions and recent progress. 53rd ed. Ottawa, Statistics Canada, 1991. biennial. 259p.+ 2p. map, col. illus., tables, bibliog. ISSN: 08406022.

First published 1931. Recently known as *Canada handbook*.

Succinct and popular account published 'to survey the Canadian situation as a whole within a reasonable space, in a popular and attractive format, and at a cost which makes possible a wide distribution' (*Preface*): 1. The Environment - 2. People and their heritage - 3. Society - 4. Economy. Bibliography p.245-54. *Class No:* 908(71)

Bibliographies

[4904]

COOKE, A. *and* CARON, F., *comps*. **Bibliographie de la Péninsule du Québec-Labrador**. Boston, Mass., G.K. Hall, 2v., 1967. 815p. index. $198.00; Export $240.00. ISBN: 0816107580.

This Bibliography of some 9000 monographs, articles, and manuscripts represents a comprehensive survey of the literature of the peninsula formed by northern Québec and Labrador. Collations are given in English or French, according to the language of the entry. *Class No:* 908(71)(01)

[4905]

INGLES, E., *comp*. **Canada**. Santa Barbara, Calif., Oxford, Clio Press, 1990. xxx,393 +1p. map. indexes. £55.95. (*World Bibliographical Series, no.62*.) ISBN: 1851090053.

1316 annotated entries arranged in 37 sections: The country and its people - Geography ... Prehistory - History ... Nationalities and minorities - Aboriginal peoples ... Languages ... National identity ... Libraries, museums and archives - Book industries and trade ... General reference works. Author, title and subject indexes. *Class No:* 908(71)(01)

[4906]

RYDER, D.E., *ed.* **Canadian reference sources** a selective guide. 2nd ed. Ottawa, Canadian Library Association. 1981. viii,311p. index. ISBN: 0888021569.

1st ed. 1973. Supplement 1975.

About 1900 concisely annotated entries that cite further titles. Covers English and French works up to December 1980. Ample cross-references. 5 main classes with mnemonic letters - GR. Reference works; HA. History and allied subjects; HV. Humanities; SC. Science; and SS. Social Science. Appendix A. Canadiana: Canada's national bibliography - B. Government of Canada publications - C. Canadian Periodical Index - D. Canadian Almanac and Directory. Index of authors, titles, and selected subjects. *Class No:* 908(71)(01)

Encyclopaedias

[4907]

The Canadian encyclopaedia. Marsh, J.H., *ed.* 2nd ed. Edmonton, Alberta, Hurtig Publishers, 4v., 1988. Available in US from Gale Research Co. 2784p. illus (many col.), col. maps, bibliog., index. Can $225.00. ISBN: 0888303262, set.

First published in 3v. 1985.

*c.*9500 signed entries, with short reading lists 'to provide coverage of all aspects of life in Canada, of all regions, over a vast time scale from the geological formation of the ancient rocks ... to the most recent political events' (*Preface to 1st ed*). Analytical index. 'There will be no new edition ... until 1992 at the earliest. We are now investigating the possibility of publishing an updated supplementary volume yearly or biennially' (*Foreword to 2nd ed*). A CD-ROM edition is available. CD-ROM Find It TM software and instruction manual. 1990. 0888303424. *Class No:* 908(71)(031)

[4908]

COLOMBO, J.R. Colombo's Canadian references. Toronto, Oxford Univ. Press, 1976. viii, 576p. ISBN: 0195402537.

Over 6,000 brief entries, A-Z Encyclopaedic in scope containing biographies (*e.g.* Jacques Cartier: ½ col., 3 cross-references), historical and geographical data, literary terms, abbreviations, *etc.*, as well as notes on current topics. Handy lists (*e.g.* Canada's prime ministers; winners of the Stanley Cup; Canada's 100 largest companies). Good use of cross-references. 'This excellent mini-encyclopaedia' (*RQ*, Fall 1977, p.72), No illus., maps or bibliographies. *Class No:* 908(71)(031)

[4909]

LANDRY, L. Encyclopédie du Québec un panorama de la vie québécoise. Montréal et Bruxelles, Les Éditions de l'Homme, 2v., 1973. xliii, 1010p. illus., tables, maps. ISBN: 0775903671, v.1; 0775903795, v.2.

A compendium with many statistical data and listings. Unusually arranged in Dewey Classification order (010 Bibliographie. Générale ... 929. Armoiries). Sections include directory material, 1-2 line biographies, bibliographies and statistics. Subject index to each volume (v.1: 0-6; v.2: 7-9). Aimed at student and laymen. *Class No:* 908(71)(031)

Yearbooks & Directories

[4910]

Canada year book 1992. A review of economic, social and political developments in Canada. Ottawa, Statistics Canada, 1993. vi,577p. illus. col. maps, tables, bibliog., index. ISBN: 066014056x.

First published in 1867 as *Year-book and almanac of British North America.*

23 chapters: 1. Physical setting - 2. Demography - 3. Health - 4. Education - 5. Employment - 6. Social security - 7. Housing and construction - 8. Forest, fish and furs - 9. Agriculture - 10. Mines and minerals - 11. Energy - 12. Science and technology - 13. Transportation - 14. Communications - 15. Cultural activities and leisure - 16. Manufacturing - 17. Merchandising - 18. Banking, finance and insurance - 19. Government - 20. Judicial system - 21. External relations, trade and defence - 22. Government finance - 23. Review of the economy. 5. Appendices: A. Government organizations - B. Federal legislation - C. Political update - D. Commissions of Enquiry - E. Constitution. A French edition is also published.

22 chapters arranged in 5 sections: 1. Land - 2. People - 3. Nation - 4. Economy - 5. Art and literature. Bibliography p.593. *Class No:* 908(71)(058)

[4911]

Canadian almanac and directory 1991. 146th year of publication. Toronto, Canadian Almanack and Directory Publishing Co. 1442p. index. £75. ISBN: 189502109x.

First published 1847 as *Scobie & Balfour's Canadian almanac and repository of useful knowledge containing full and authoritative commercial, astronomical, departmental, ecclesiastical, educational, financial, military, naval and general information.*

Facts and figures about Canada and Canadian organizations, institutions, legal services, government departments *etc.* 1. Financial institutions, media directory, transport - 2. Organizations, foundations and trade unions - 3. Education - 4. Political information - 5. Municipalities - 6. General information - 7. Legal. *Class No:* 908(71)(058)

Almanacs

[4912]

The Canadian world almanac & book of facts 1988. Filion, J., *ed.* Toronto, Global Press, 1987. 693p. col. illus., col. maps, tables. ISBN: 0771539924. ISSN: 0833532x.

49 sections *e.g.*. Chronology of the year (p.1-9); Geography; Historical figures; History of Canada; Immigration; Nations of the World; Prime Ministers of Canada; Tourism; World facts. 12p. col. maps and 4p. col. flags insert. *Class No:* 908(71)(059)

[4913]

The 1988 Corpus almanac & Canadian sourcebook. Sova, G., *ed.* 23rd. ed. Don Mills, Ontario, Corpus Information Services, 2v., 1988. illus., ports, maps, coats of arms, tables, bibliogs. ISBN: 0919217478. ISSN: 08231133.

First published 1966. Continues *Corpus directory and almanac.*

V1: 1. Current events - 2. General information - 3. Geography - 4. Natural resources - 5. The people - 6. Religion - 7. Education - 8. Sources of information (libraries and archives; book publishers; magazines; newspapers; associations and societies) - 9. Communications - 10.

....(contd.)

Transportation - 11. Labour - 12. Law - 13. Banking, finance & insurance - 14. Business, industry and trade - 15. Canadian constitution. All but 2 sections have lists of further readings.

V2: The Federal Government - Provincial and Territorial Governments - Intergovernmental agencies - Municipal government. A directory and current encyclopaedia.
Class No: 908(71)(059)

Libraries

[4914]
BLOOMFIELD, V. **Research for Canadian studies in Britain** with some reference to relevant collections in Europe. 2nd ed. London, British Association for Canadian studies, 1983. xxi, 252p. maps. bibliog. £5.00. ISBN: 0950906301.

First published Ottawa, Department of External Affairs, 1979.

264 collections listed (182 in UK; 82 in Europe). A-Z by place and institution. Data: Directory information, details of collections, facilities, and publications. Separate indexes to British and European sections. The author's 'A guide to Resources for Canadian Studies in Britain', p. 97-100, *Canadian studies* (The British Library, 1984) is a comprehensive introduction.
Class No: 908(71):061:026/027

Education Institutions

[4915]
Canadian studies papers presented at a colloquium at the British Library 17-19 August 1986. MacLaren-Turner, P., *ed.* London, The British Library, 1984. vii, 210p. illus. £9.50. (*British Library Occasional Papers No.1.*) ISBN: 0712300392.

Papers outlining the current state of Canadian studies in Canada and the United Kingdom; current bibliographic and research projects, and a coherent philosophy for future development. *Class No:* 908(71):061:37

Newfoundland

Bibliographies

[4916]
O'DEA, A.C., *comp.* **Bibliography of Newfoundland.** Toronto, Univ. of Toronto Press in association with Memorial Univ. of Newfoundland, 2v., 1986. xx,1450p. index. $175.00; £122.50. ISBN: 0802024025.

v.1 5911 entries. Collections and sources p.xvi-xx. v.2 378 annuals. Author, title and subject indexes p.885-1450. Major work 'to record, chronologically, the printed works relating to Newfoundland from the early voyages of discovery to 1975 ... intended to inform or interest the scholar, the intelligent reader, and the collector' (*Preface*). 'Meets an undoubted need, and meets it in a way that can be described as definitive' (*Canadian Historical Review* v.69, no.3, September 1988, p.418-420). *Class No:* 908(718)(01)

Encyclopaedias

[4917]
Encyclopedia of Newfoundland and Labrador. Smallwood, J.R. *and* Pitt, R.D.W. St. Johns, Newfoundland Book Publishers, 1981-.

1. A-E. 914p. illus., maps. 1981. $39.00. ISBN 0920508146. Covers all aspects of life past and present with long articles (with list of references) for major topics. 18p. of maps. 'Much useful information that would be difficult to find elsewhere' (*Choice,* v.19,no.10, June 1982, p.1376).
Class No: 908(718)(031)

Mexico

Bibliographies

[4918]
ROBBINS, N.C., *comp.* **Mexico.** Santa Barbara, California and Oxford, Clio Press, 1984. xii, 165p. + 1p. maps index. £24.50; $35.00. (*World Bibliographical Series, no.48.*) ISBN: 0903450852.

A revised edition (c.800 entries) is announced for publication 1993. ISBN 185109198x.

640 annotated entries. 34 sections: The country and its people - Geography ... Archaeology and prehistory - History ... Indians of Mexico ... Museums and Libraries ... Reference works. Author, title, and subject index.
Class No: 908(72)(01)

Guatemala

Bibliographies

[4919]
WOODWARD, R.L., *comp.* **Guatemala.** Revised and enlarged ed. Santa Barbara, California and Oxford, Clio Press, 1992. xxix,269p. + + 1p. map, indexes. £42.50. (*World Bibliographical Series; no.9.*) ISBN: 1851091882.

First published with W.B. Franklin as compiler in 1984.

843 annotated entries in 34 sections: Country and its people - Geography - Travellers' accounts ... Prehistory and archaeology - History ... Human rights.Bibliographies. Author, title and subject index. *Class No:* 908(728.1)(01)

Belize

Bibliographies

[4920]
WOODWARD, R.L., *comp.* **Belize.** Santa Barbara, California and Oxford, Clio Press, 1980. xxii, 229p. + 1p. map, index. £26.95. (*World Bibliographical Series, no.21.*) ISBN: 0903450410.

A second edition is announced for publication in 1994. ISBN 1851091327.

681 annotated entries. 39 sections: The country and its people - Geography - Traveller's accounts ... Prehistory and archaeology - History ... Libraries and archives ... Encyclopaedias and directories - Bibliographies. Introduction includes a brief history of Belize and a bibliographical essay on the major sources of information. Author, title, and subject index. *Class No:* 908(728.2)(01)

Honduras

Bibliographies

[4921]

HOWARD-REGUINDID, P.F., *comp*. **Honduras**. Santa Barbara, Calif., and Oxford, Clio Press, 1992. xx,258p. +1p. map. indexes. £39.95. (*World Bibliographical Series, no.139*.) ISBN: 1851091378.

788 annotated entries in 38 sections: Country and its people - Geography - Tourism - Travellers' accounts ... Prehistory and archaeology - History ... Ethnic groups and refugees ... Libraries and archives ... Encyclopedias and directories - Bibliographies. *Class No:* 908(728.3)(01)

El Salvador

Bibliographies

[4922]

WOODWARD, R.L., *ed*. **El Salvador**. Santa Barbara, California and Oxford, Clio Press, 1988. xxix, 213p.+1p. map, index. £32.95; $39.00. (*World Bibliographical Series, no.98*.) ISBN: 0851090738.

659 annotated entries. 40 sections: The country and its people - Geography - Travellers' accounts ... Prehistory and archaeology - History ... Human rights ... Libraries, museums and archives ... Encyclopaedias and directories - Bibliographies. Author, title, and subject index. *Class No:* 908(728.4)(01)

Nicaragua

[4923]

WALKER, T.W. **Nicaragua** the land of Sandino. 3rd ed. Boulder, Colo., Westview Press, 1991. xvi,202p. illus., map, bibliog., index. £26.95. (*Westview Profiles: Nations Of Contemporary Latin America*.) ISBN: 0813310903.

1st ed. 1981; 2nd ed. 1986.

1. Introduction - 2. Early history: pre-Columbian period to the mid-1930s - 3. Recent history - 4. Economic dimension - 5. Culture and society - 6. Government and politics - 7. International dimension. Bibliography p.173-84. *Class No:* 908(728.5)

Bibliographies

[4924]

WOODWARD, R.L., *comp*. **Nicaragua**. Santa Barbara, California, and Oxford, Clio Press, 1983. xxiii, 254p.+1p. map, index. £36.95; $40.00. (*World Bibliographical Series, no.44*.) ISBN: 0903450798.

703 annotated entries. 40 sections: The country and its people - Geography - Travellers' accounts ... Prehistory and archaeology - History ... Human rights - Politics - Foreign Relations ... Libraries and archives ... Encyclopedias and directories - Bibliographies. Author, title, and subject index. 'Should be at the top of the must-buy list for nearly every library because it provides such comprehensive coverage' (*Choice*, v.21, no.9, May 1984, p.1284). *Class No:* 908(728.5)(01)

Costa Rica

Bibliographies

[4925]

STANSIFER, C.L., *comp*. **Costa Rica**. Santa Barbara, Calif., and Oxford, Clio Press, 1991. xxiii,292p. +1p. map. indexes. £44.95. (*World Bibliographical Series, no. 126*.) ISBN: 1851090274.

706 annotated entries in 39 sections: The Country and its people - Geography and geology - Travellers' accounts ... Prehistory and archaeology - History ... Human rights ... Libraries, archives and museums ... Biographies - Directories - Bibliographies. Dissertations on Costa Rica p.xix-xxiii. Author, title and subject indexes. *Class No:* 908(728.6)(01)

Panama

Bibliographies

[4926]

LANGSTAFF, E.D., *comp*. **Panama**. Santa Barbara, California and Oxford, Clio Press, 1982. vii, 184p. + 1p. map, index. £25.95; $28.00. (*World Bibliographical Series, no.14*.) ISBN: 0903450267.

641 annotated entries. 34 sections: The country and its people - Geography ... Travel - Prehistory and archaeology - History - Peoples ... Periodicals - Reference Books - Libraries, museums and archives - Bibliography and bibliographies. Author, title, and subject index. *Class No:* 908(728.7)(01)

Caribbean

[4927]

DYDE, B. **Caribbean companion** the A-Z reference. London, Macmillan, 1992. 192p. pbk. £4.75 ISBN: 0333545591.

Includes entries relating to people and places, politics, sport, the arts, and historical events, in a single dictionary sequence. *Class No:* 908(729)

Bibliographies of Bibliographies

[4928]

JORDAN, A. *and* COMISSIONG, B., *comps*. **The English-speaking Caribbean** a bibliography of Bibliographies. Boston, G.K. Hall, 1984. xxiv, 411p. indexes. $61.00. ISBN: 0816186073.

1406 annotated entries divided into 5 bibliographical and 59 (country sub-divided) subject listings *e.g.* Archaeology (entries 517-520); History (766-808); and Geography (732-742). Name and subject indexes. Based on collections of St. Augustine campus library of University of West Indies where the compilers are University Librarian and Deputy Librarian. *Class No:* 908(729)(009)

Bibliographies

[4929]

Bibliography of the English speaking Caribbean books, articles and reviews in English from the arts, humanities and social sciences. Neymeyer, R.J., *ed*. Parkersburgh, Iowa, the editor, 1979-. v.1, no.1-. 2 *pa*.

Each issue (*c*. 600 references) has 20 sections: Reference -

....(contd.)

General - Tourism - Travel and description - Archaeology - History ... Geography - Environment. Geographical index. *Class No:* 908(729)(01)

[4930]

COMITAS, L. **The Complete Caribbeana 1900-1975** a bibliographic guide to the scholarly literature. Nendeln, Liechtenstein/Millwood, New York, KTO Press, 4v., 1978. $265.00. ISBN: 0527188204, set.

Under the auspices of the Research Institute for the Study of Man.

Supersedes his *Caribbeana, 1900-1965: a topical bibliography* (Univ. of Washington, 1968. $18.50); expanded to include the Bahamas and Bermuda. Lists over 17,000 books, monographs, articles, conference proceedings, masters' and doctoral theses, reports and pamphlets published in the 20th century. The 4v.: 1. Introduction the Caribbean. The past. The people - 2. Institutions. Elements of culture. Health, education and welfare. Political issues - 3. Socioeconomic activities and institutions. The environment and human geography. Soils crops and livestock - 4. Author index. Geographical index. Includes the Guianas, Belize, but omits Haiti and the Spanish-speaking territories. 'All in all an invaluable tool' (*West Indies chronicle*, April 1969, p.180-1, on the 19068 ed.). *Class No:* 908(729)(01)

[4931]

HUGHES, R., *comp*. **The Caribbean** a basic annotated bibliography for students, librarians and general readers. London, Commonwealth Institute Library Services, 1987. iv, 73p. index. sd. £2.50. (*Commonwealth bibliographies, no.6.*) ISBN: 0946140324. ISSN: 03061124.

Unnumbered entries in 5 subdivided sections: 1. Caribbean experience - 2. Lifestyle - 3. Communication - 4. Education - 5. Arts. Booksellers p.65-67. Other library collections p.69-71. *Class No:* 908(729)(01)

[4932]

HUGHES, R., *comp*. **Caribbean book list.** London, Commission for Racial Equality, 1984. 47p. maps. ISBN: 090792042x.

Briefly annotated list in 17 sections: Geography - History ... Specialist booksellers. Concentrates on English-speaking islands. For school use. *Class No:* 908(729)(01)

[4933]

UNIVERSITY OF MIAMI. **Catalog of the Cuban and Caribbean Library.** Boston, Mass., G.K. Hall, 6v., 1977. 5047p. $500.00 (Export $605.00). ISBN: 0816100535.

100,000 photolithographed catalogue cards. Contains material not only on the entire Caribbean area, but also on Mexico and Colombia. Subject strength is greatest in history and literature, with particularly rich holdings in nineteenth-century Caribbean history and in twentieth-century Cuban history and literature. *Class No:* 908(729)(01)

[4934]

UNIVERSITY OF PUERTO RICO. Institute of Caribbean Studies. **Caribbean studies.** Rio Pedras, Puerto Rico, 1961-. v.1, no.1-. Quarterly (now 6 *pa*).

Includes 'Current bibliography' of books, pamphlets and articles. Coverage extends to the Antilles, Yucatan, Central America, Panama, Colombia, Venezuela, Belize, Guyana, Surinam. Excludes the natural sciences. *Class No:* 908(729)(01)

[4935]

WEST INDIA REFERENCE LIBRARY. **The Catalogue of the West India Reference Library** Insitute of Jamaica. Milkwood, New York, Kraus International Publications, 6v., 1980.

Over 120,000 photographically reproduced catalogue cards. Arranged under authors, titles and subjects. *Class No:* 908(729)(01)

Encyclopaedias

[4936]

The Cambridge encyclopaedia of Latin America and the Caribbean. Collier, S., *and others, eds.* 2nd rev. ed. Cambridge, Cambridge Univ. Press, 1992. 480p. illus. (some col.), maps, tables. £35. ISBN: 0521413222.

1st ed. 1985.

68 contributors. 6 sections: 1. Physical environment - 2. Economy - 3. Peoples - 4. History - 5. Politics and society - 6. Culture. Glossary p.8-9. Detailed analytical index. Articles append further reading lists. 70 maps. 'Destined to become the standard single-volume work on Latin America' (*Choice*, v.23, no.7, March 1986, p.1036-37). *Class No:* 908(729)(031)

Handbooks & Manuals

[4937]

The Caribbean handbook 1992/93. St. Johns, Antigua, FT Caribbean 1992. 236p. illus. (some col.), maps, tables, bibliog. Softcovers. ISBN: 9768033088.

Section A. Caribbean profile: regional survey, business review - B. Caribbean countries A-Z: Key facts, business/tourist information, location and physical features, travel, official public holidays, the economy, utilities *etc.* Bibliography p.229-4. *Class No:* 908(729)(035)

Yearbooks & Directories

[4938]

MACDONALD, R. *and* TRAVIS, C. **Libraries and special collections on Latin America and the Caribbean:** a directory of European resources. London, Athlone Press for the Institute of Latin American Studies, Univ. of London, 1988. 339p. index. £32. ISBN: 0485177145.

2nd ed. of B. Taylor's *Directory of Libraries and special collections on Latin America and the West Indies* (1975). Completely revised and extended to cover holdings in Europe.

195 UK and 272 European collections recorded (3 times the number in the earlier work) for material relating to regions south of the Rio Grande and reasonably adjacent islands. Main emphasis is on printed material. Full directory information. 'A useful guide to the existence and availability of special research materials' (Reference Reviews, v.2, no.3, September 1988, p.110). *Class No:* 908(729)(058)

Cuba

[4939]

Cuba official guide. Gravette, A.G. London, Macmillan Caribbean in conjunction with Cuba National Institute of Tourism, 1988. x,278p. col.illus., col.maps. ISBN: 0333427033.

10 chapters: 1. An exotic background (geography and

....(contd.)
history) - 2. A cultural melting pot - 3. An effective economy
- 4. The National Order - 5. Travelling tips - 6. Where and
how (accommodation and activities) - 7. The Cuban
experience (beaches and country resorts) - 8. From tip to tail
(provinces, towns and cities) - 9. 7 Cuban towns - 10.
Information. *Class No:* 908(729.1)

Bibliographies

[4940]
PEREZ, L.A. **Cuba** an annotated bibliography. New York,
Garland Press, 1988. xiii, 301p. index. $45.00 £36.95.
(*Bibliographies and Indexes in World History; no.10.*) ISBN:
0313261628. ISSN: 07426852.

1120 items identifying the major written works on Cuba
arranged in 45 categories (*e.g.* 2. Geography ... 5.
Prehistory and archaeology - 6. History (7 subdivisions) - 7.
Genealogy ... 45. Bibliographies. Preference given to works
in English. 'Only titles that are generally available to readers
are included' (*Introduction*). Compiler is Graduate Research
Professor in the Department of History, Univ. of South
Florida. *Class No:* 908(729.1)(01)

Jamaica

Bibliographies

[4941]
INGRAM, K.E. **Jamaica.** Santa Barbara, California and
Oxford, Clio Press, 1984. xxiv, 369p. + 1p. map, index.
£49.95; $55.00. (*World Bibliographical Series, no.45.*)
ISBN: 0903450828.

1182 annotated entries. 36 sections: The country and its
people - Geography ... Prehistory and archaeology - History
and collective biography ... Labour movement and Trade
Unions ... Libraries, archives and information systems ...
General directories and handbooks - Bibliographies. Author,
title, and subject index. *Class No:* 908(729.2)(01)

Cayman Islands

Yearbooks & Directories

[4942]
Cayman Islands annual report 1988. George Town, Grand
Cayman, Government of the Cayman Islands, 1989. 168p.
illus. (some col.), col. maps, tables, softcover.

21 chapters *e.g.* 1. The year in review ... 10. Tourism and
immigration ... 17. History ... 19. The sister islands - 20.
Government officials. Based on reports submitted by
government departments and agencies.
Class No: 908(729.29)(058)

[4943]
Cayman Islands yearbook and business directory 1990.
Winker, C. *and* Martins, D., *eds.* Grand Cayman, Cayman
Free News, 1985-. Annual. 480p. illus. (some col.), tables
index.

1. Cayman Islands and its people (History, geography,
culture, the year in review *etc.*) - 2. Government - 3.
Finance and investment - 4. Business and commerce - 5.
Living and working - 6. Reference (Tourist information A-
Z). *Class No:* 908(729.29)(058)

Dominican Republic

Bibliographies

[4944]
SCHOENHALS, K., *comp.* **Dominican Republic.** Santa
Barbara, California, and Oxford, Clio Press, 1990. xxx,
210p. map. index. (*World Bibliographical Series, no.111.*)
ISBN: 1851091106.

913 annotated entries in 40 sections: The country and its
people - Geography ... Travellers' accounts ... Prehistory
and Archaeology: pre-Columbian inhabitants - History ...
Voodoo ... Encyclopaedias and directories - Bibliographies.
Author, subject and title index. *Class No:* 908(729.3)(01)

Haiti

[4945]
BELLEGARDE-SMITH, P. **Haiti** the breached citadel.
Boulder, Colo., Westview Press, 1990. xxi,217p. illus.,
maps, bibliog., index. $34. (*Westview Profiles. Nations of
Contemporary Latin America.*) ISBN: 0813371724.

1. The nature of Haiti: Land and society - 2. Context of
Haitian development and underdevelopment - 3.
Modernization and dependence - 4. Haitian economy and the
National Security state - 5. Politics and government.
Appendix 1. Significant dates in Haitian history p.181-7.
Chapter notes p.191-7. Bibliographical essay p.199-207. 'A
useful summary of Haiti's history' (*Choice*, v.27, no.10,
June 1990, p.1736). *Class No:* 908(729.4)

Bibliographies

[4946]
CHAMBERS, F., *comp.* **Haiti.** Santa Barbara, California and
Oxford, Clio Press, 1983. xiii, 177p.+1p. map, index.
£24.95. $27.00. (*World Bibliographical Series; no.39.*)
ISBN: 0903450690.

A revised edition is announced for publication in 1994.

558 annotated entries. 37 sections: - The country and its
people - Geography and geology - Travellers' accounts ...
Prehistory and archaeology - History ... Human rights ...
Voodoo ... Libraries and archives ... Encyclopaedias and
directories - Bibliographies. Author, title and subject index.
Class No: 908(729.4)(01)

[4947]
LAGUERRE, M.S. **The Complete Haitiana** a bibliographic
guide to the scholarly literature 1900-1980. Millwood, New
York, Kraus International Publications, 2v., 1982. lxxiii,
xix, 1562p. maps on endpapers, index. ISBN: 0527540404,
set.

A companion work to L. Comitas' *The complete
Caribbeana* (*qv*).

65 chapters divided into 11 general thematic sections: 1.
Introduction to Haiti - 2. Ecological setting - 3. History of
Haiti - 4. Population - 5. Culture - 6. Structure of Haitian
society - 7. Health and medicine - 8. Educational system - 9.
Political and legal processes - 10. Socio-economic system -
11. Rural and urban developments. Includes books, articles,
government documents and essays that form part of a book,
in several languages including Haitian creole. Most
references include a library code indicating location.
Class No: 908(729.4)(01)

[4948]
PRATT, F., *ed*. **Haiti** guide to the periodical literature in English, 1800-1990. Westport, Conn., Greenwood Press, 1991. xiv,310p. indexes. £33.95. ISBN: 0313278555.

Over 5,000 citations arranged chronologically within 9 sections: 1. Physical setting - 2. Human element - 3. Cultural environment ... 5. Geopolitical influence - 6. Historical background ... 8. Bibliographies. Computerized index. *Class No:* 908(729.4)(01)

Dictionaries

[4949]
Dictionnaire géographique et administratif universel d'Haïti illusté ou guide général en Haïti. Paris, Imprimerie Charles Blot, v.1-2, 1892-94. Port au Prince, Imprimerie August A. Heraux, v.3-4, 1927-28.

'Enclopaedic treasury of information on Haitian geography, history, literature and politics' (F. Chambers. *Haiti*, 1983, Entry 548). *Class No:* 908(729.4)(038)

Puerto Rico

Bibliographies

[4950]
CEVALLOS, E.E., *comp*. **Puerto Rico.** Santa Barbara, California and Oxford, Clio Press, 1985. xiii, 193p. + 1p. map, index. £28.50. (*World Bibliographical Series, no. 52.*) ISBN: 0903450895.

605 annotated entries. 34 sections: The country and its people - Geography ... Archaeology and prehistory - History - Folklore ... Migration ... Encyclopaedias - Museums, archives and libraries - Bibliographies. Author, title and subject index. *Class No:* 908(729.5)(01)

[4951]
PEDREIRA, A.S. **Bibliografía Puertorriqueña (1493-1930).** New York, Burt Franklin Reprints, 1974. xxxii, 707p. indexes. (*Bibliography and Reference Series; no.496.*) ISBN: 0833746693.

Reprint of 1932 ed. published by Inprenta de la Libreria y Casa Editorial Hernando, Madrid.

1. Fuentes bibliográficas - 2. Informacion general - 3. Historia natural - 4. La Salud - 5. Economía social - 6. Historia, política y administrativa - 7 Organización cultural - 8. Historia de Puerto Rico (9 main divisions) p.375-486 - 9. Historia Literaria. 'The most complete bibliography on Puerto Rico ever published' (P. Vivó *The Puerto Ricans* 1973. Entry 1:45). *Class No:* 908(729.5)(01)

Encyclopaedias

[4952]
La Gran encicyclopedia de Puerto Rico. Baez, V., *ed*. Madrid, Ediciones R., 14v., 1976. illus., bibliogs., indexes.

Thematic volumes: 1. Historia - 2. Politica ... 14. Diccionario histórico - biográfico. 'Without question, this is a comprehensive encyclopaedia of Puerto Rican cultural, political, and social history' (F.E. Cevallos. *Puerto Rico*. 1985. Entry 574). *Class No:* 908(729.5)(031)

Bahamas

Bibliographies

[4953]
BOULTBEE, P.G., *comp*. **The Bahamas.** Santa Barbara, California and Oxford, Clio Press, 1989. xx, 195p. + 1p. map, index. £37.00. (*World Bibliographical Series; no.108.*) ISBN: 1851091025.

703 annotated entries. 36 sections: The country and its people - Geography ... Travel guides - Travellers' accounts - Tourism ... Prehistory and archaeology - History ... Obeah ... Libraries and archives ... Directories - Bibliographies. Author, title and subject index. *Class No:* 908(729.6)(01)

Handbooks & Manuals

[4954]
Bahamas handbook and businessman's annual 1989. Nassau, Etienne Dupuch, 1988. 478p. illus. (some col.), maps, index. Soft cover. ISBN: 0914755471.

8 glossy sections: 1. Features (including Our prehistoric past) - 2. Leisure and vacations - 3. The family islands - 4. Business and finance - 5. Bahamas information - 8. Government. *Class No:* 908(729.6)(035)

Turks & Caicos Islands

Bibliographies

[4955]
BOULTBEE, P.F., *comp*. **Turks and Caicos Islands.** Santa Barbara, Calif., and Oxford, Clio Press, 1991. xvii,97p. + 1p. map. index. £19. (*World Bibliographical Series, no.137.*) ISBN: 1851091629.

305 annotated entries in 25 sections: The country and its people - Geography ... Travel guides - Traveller's accounts - Tourism ... Prehistory and archaeology - History ... Philately and numismatics ... Libraries Directories - Bibliographies. *Class No:* 908(729.68)(01)

Virgin Islands

Bibliographies

[4956]
MOLL, V.P., *comp*. **Virgin Islands.** Santa Barbara, Calif., and Oxford, Clio Press, 1991. xxv,210p. + 2p. maps, indexes. £34. (*World Bibliographical Series, no.138.*) ISBN: 1851091653.

614 annotated entries in 40 sections: Islands and their peoples - Geography - Travellers' accounts - Tourism ... Prehistory and archaeology - History ... Environment ... Books and publishing ... Bibliographies and abstracts. Author, title, and subject indexes. *Class No:* 908(729.72)(01)

Montserrat

Bibliographies

[4957]
BERLEANT-SCHILLER, R., *comp*. **Montserrat.** Santa Barbara, Calif., and Oxford Clio Press, 1991. xxviii,102p. + 1p. map, indexes. £22. (*World Bibliographical Series, no.134.*) ISBN: 1851091548.

....(contd.)

341 annotated entries arranged under 20 headings: 1. Country and its people - Geography - Tourism and travel ... Natural hazards ... Archaeology - History ... Reference sources. Author, title and subject indexes.
Class No: 908(729.727)(01)

Dominica

[4958]

MYERS, R.A., *comp.* **Dominica.** Santa Barbara, California and Oxford, Clio Press, 1987. xxv, 190p. + 1p. map, index. £31.95' $40.50. (*World Bibliographical Series, v.82.*) ISBN: 1851090312.

493 annotated entries. 28 sections: The country and its people - Geography - Travel guides and tourism ... Amerindians - History ... Libraries and archives ... Encyclopaedias and directories - bibliographies. Author, title and subject index. *Class No:* 908(729.821)

[4959]

MYERS, R.A., *comp.* **A Resource guide to Dominica 1493-1986.** New Haven, Connecticut, Human Relations Area Files, 1987. 649 leaves. maps.

Includes an outline history of Dominica and 25 sections arranged by topic. Also location guide to documents in UK, Europe, US, and West Indian archives. Name and subject index p.580-649. *Class No:* 908(729.821)

St. Vincent & the Grenadines

Bibliographies

[4960]

POTTER, R.B., *comp.* **St. Vincent and the Grenadines.** Santa Barbara, Calif., and Oxford, Clio Press, 1992. xxviii,212p. + 1p. map, indexes. £34.50. (*World Bibliographical Series, no.143.*) ISBN: 1851091831.

631 annotated entries in 33 sections: Country and its people - Geography ... Tourism - Travellers' accounts ... Prehistory - History ... Language and dialect ... Bibliographies. Glossary p.xxvii-xxviii. Author, title, and subject indexes. *Class No:* 908(729.824)(01)

Grenada

[4961]

STEELE, B.A., *comp.* **Bibliography of Grenada.** St. George's, Univ. of the West Indies, Department of Extra Mural Studies, 1983. 119p.

Covers general works, religion, social science, statistics, demography, sociology, women, political and government, economics, tourism, laws, education, linguistics, medicine, agriculture, literature. 'The best existing bibliography on Grenada' (Schoenhals, K. *Grenada,* 1990, Entry 791).
Class No: 908(729.828)

Bibliographies

[4962]

SCHOENHALS, K., *comp.* **Grenada.** Santa Barbara, Calif., Oxford, Clio Press, 1990. xxxviii,179p. + 1p. map, index. £33. (*World Bibliographical Series, no.119.*) ISBN: 1851091262.

793 annotated entries in 37 sections: The country and its

....(contd.)

people - Geography ... Travellers' accounts ... Prehistory and archaeology - History ... Nationalities and minorities ... Encyclopaedias and directories - Bibliographies. Author, title and subject index. Events leading to the US invasion are well summarized in the introduction. *Class No:* 908(729.828)(01)

Barbados

Bibliographies

[4963]

POTTER, R.B. *and* **DANN, G.M.S. Barbados.** Santa Barbara, California and Oxford, Clio Press, 1987. xxxix, 356p. + 1p. map, index. £49.95. $55.00. (*World Bibliographical Series; no.76.*) ISBN: 1851090223.

958 annotated entries. 39 sections: The country and its people - Geography ... Travellers' accounts - Tourism ... Prehistory and archaeology - History ...Constitution and the legal system ... Libraries ... Directories, yearbooks and handbooks - Bibliographies. Glossary p. xxxv-xxxix. Author, subject and title index. *Class No:* 908(729.86)(01)

Trinidad & Tobago

Bibliographies

[4964]

CHAMBERS, F., *comp.* **Trinidad and Tobago.** Santa Barbara, California and Oxford, Clio Press, 1986. xv, 213p. + 1p. map, index. £30.50; $ 35.00. (*World Bibliographical Series, no.74.*) ISBN: 1851090207.

641 unannotated entries. 43 sections: The country and its people - Geography ... Travel guides - Travellers' accounts ... Prehistory and archaeology ... Historiography - History ... Calypso - Festivals - Carnival ... Libraries and archives ... Reference works - Bibliographies. Author, title and subject index. *Class No:* 908(729.87)(01)

Netherlands Antilles

[4965]

KOULEN, I., *and others.* **The Netherlands Antilles and Aruba** : a research guide. Dordrecht, Foris Publications. 1987. viii, 162p. bibliog. (*Koninklijk Insitut Voor Taal-Land-en Volkenkunde Caribbean Series, no.7.*) ISBN: 9067652318.

1. Profile of the Netherlands Antilles and Aruba (geography; history; economy; constitutional development; culture) - 2. Dutch Caribbean studies - 3. Social Science studies 1967-1986 an extensive bibliographical essay (described as the heart of the book) - 4. Conclusions. Chapter notes p.107-113. Bibliography (550 items) p.115-59. *Class No:* 908(729.88)

Bermuda

Bibliographies

[4966]

HALLETT, A.C.H. Bermuda in print a guide to the printed literature on Bermuda. Hamilton, The Author, 1985. 210p.

5 chapters: 1. Literature of Bermuda from discovery to

....(contd.)

1684 - 2. Bermuda books (A-Z by author) p.17-136 - 3. Almanacks - 4. Guide books *etc.* - 5. Newspapers - 6. *Bermuda Historical Quarterly. Class No:* 908(729.9)(01)

Latin America

Bibliographies of Bibliographies

[4967]
GROPP, A.E., *ed*. **A Bibliography of Latin American bibliographies.** Metuchen, New Jersey, Scarecrow Press, 1968. ix, 515p.

An updating of the 2nd ed. (1942) compiled by C.K. Jones.

7,210 numbered, unannotated entries, plus interpolations. C.K. Jones item numbers are referrred to. A 'General works' section is followed by subjects, A-Z. Index of authors, subjects (non-analytical) and places, p.421-515. (*Supplement* 1971. xiii, 277p. adds 1416 items published 1965-1969. *Class No:* 908(729.99)(009)

[4968]
—A Bibliography of Latin American bibliographies. 1980-1984. Loroña,, L.V., *ed*. Metuchen, New Jersey, Scarecrow Press, 1987. xiv, 239p. $25.00. ISBN: 0810819414.

4th Supplement to Gropp's *A bibliography of Latin American bibliographies.* 1633 unannotated entries arranged in a 'General works' section followed by 33 subjects subdivided by countries *e.g.* Biography, Geography/Cartography, History. *Class No:* 908(729.99)(009)

[4969]
—CORDEIRO, D.P., *ed*. A Bibliography of Latin American bibliographies. v.1. Social sciences and humanities. Metuchen, New Jersey, Scarecrow Press, 1979. 272p. $26.50. ISBN: 0810811707.

Supplements A.E. Gropp's Latin American bibliographies. 1750 unannotated entries for both monographs (1969-74) and periodical articles from about 200 periodicals. 36 main subject headings. Subject and author indexes.
Class No: 908(729.99)(009)

[4970]
—GROPP, A.E. A Bibliography of Latin American bibliographies published in periodicals. Metuchen, New Jersey, Scarecrow Press, 2v.,1976. 1031p.

Over 9,700 items published 1929-1965. 76 subject categories, subdivided by country or region.
Class No: 908(729.99)(009)

[4971]
—PIEDRACUEVA, H., *ed*. A Bibliography of Latin American Bibliographies 1975-1979 social sciences and humanities. Metuchen, New Jersey, Scarecrow Press, 1982. 313p. $32.50. ISBN: 0810815249.

Third supplement to Gropp's bibliographies (*vide supra*). Adds 2122 entries published 1975-1979.
Class No: 908(729.99)(009)

Bibliographies

[4972]
Bibliographic guide to Latin American Studies. Boston, G.K. Hall. Annual

1993. 1v., 1994. 1700p. $550. 0783820895. Includes acquisitions catalogued during the past year by the Nettie Lee Benson Latin American Collection at the University of Texas Library, Austin, and the Library of Congress. Coverage of Mexico, Argentina, Brazil, Venezuela, Colombia, Chile, Guatemala, Peru, Bolivia, Cuba, Ecuador, Costa Rica, and Uruguay is particulary strong. A supplement to the *Catalog of the Latin American Collection of the University of Texas Library* (G.K. Hall, 1969) (q.v.).
Class No: 908(729.99)(01)

[4973]
BLAKEMORE, H. *and* BIGGINS, A. **'Latin American studies in Britain'** a selective review of recent publications, *British Book News*, January 1989, p.4-7.
Class No: 908(729.99)(01)

[4974]
British bulletin of publications on Latin America the Caribbean Portugal and Spain. London, The Hispanic and Luso-Brazilian Council, 1950-. v.1-. 2 *pa.* £10.00. *pa.* ISSN: 02682400.

Annotates 200-250 English-language books and lists a large number of periodical articles per issue. Nos.1-45 are available on a 35mm. microfilm (£20.00).
Class No: 908(729.99)(01)

[4975]
FENTON, T.P. *and* HEFFRON, M.J., *comps*. **Latin America and Caribbean:** a directory of resources. New York, Orbis Books; London, Zed Books, 1986. xvi,142p. indexes. $9.95; £18.95. ISBN: 0862326370, UK; 0883445298, US.

An expansion of the Latin American and Caribbean chapter in the compilers' *Third World resource directory* (Orbis, 1984).

1. Organizations - 2. Books - 3. Periodicals - 4. Pamphlets and articles - 5. Audiovisuals - 6. Other resources. Emphasis on 'alternative' sources; some standard works are omitted.
Class No: 908(729.99)(01)

[4976]
HISPANIC COUNCIL *and* LUSO-BRAZILIAN COUNCIL. Canning House Library. **Author and subject catalogues of the Canning House Library.** Boston, Mass., G.K. Hall, 1967. First Supplement 1973.

Hispanic catalogues. 4v. 1967. 2288p. $325.00 (Export $390.00). ISBN 08167107416. *First Supplement.* 1973. 627p. $s115.00 ($140.00). ISBN 0816111251.

Luso-Brazilian catalogues. 1967. 567p. $100.00 ($120.00). ISBN 0816101264. *First Supplement* 1973. 288p. $110.00 ($135.00).

The Canning House Library's 30,000 books are mainly of 20th and 19th-century origin. The *Hispanic catalogues* reproduces 48,000 photolithographed cards, and the *Luso-Brazilian Catalogues,* 12,700 cards.
Class No: 908(729.99)(01)

[4977]

HISPANIC SOCIETY OF AMERICA New York. **Catalogue of the Library of the Hispanic Society of America.** Boston, Mass., G.K. Hall, 10v., 1962. First supplement 4v., 1970. $990.00 (Export $1089.00) Supplement $440.00 ($530.00). ISBN: 0816114749; 0816114757, Suppl.

211,000 photolithographed catalogue cards on 10,048 pages. The Library contains more than 100,000v. on the cultures of Spain, Portugal and colonial Hispanic America. Stresses art, history and literature; includes music, social customs, regional costumes, description and travel, but excludes Indian subjects. The First supplement adds 58,000 cards. No longer available in printed book form; prices quoted are for 24 reel microfilm edition.

Class No: 908(729.99)(01)

[4978]

IBERO-AMERIKANISCHES INSTITUT Berlin. **Schlagwortkatalog des Ibero-Amerikanischen Instituts Preussischer Kulturbesitz in Berlin.** Boston, Mass., G.K. Hall, 30v., 1977. 23,494p. $2810.00 (Export $3400.00). ISBN: 0816100683.

493,000 photolithographed catalogue cards. The Institute's library, one of the world's leading libraries in the field of Latin American studies, comprises *c.*300,000 items (books and periodical articles). The catalogue has general, geographical and biographical sections. Subject and geographical indexes, in English and Spanish.

Class No: 908(729.99)(01)

[4979]

Latin American studies a basic guide to sources. McNeil, R.A., *ed.* 2nd ed. Metuchen, N.J., Scarecrow Press, 1990. xi,458p. indexes. $42.50. £40.40. ISBN: 0810822369.

A rev. ed. of *Latin American bibliography: a guide* edited by L. Hallewell (1978).

36 contributors. A form-based introductory guide to research on Latin America in the humanities and social sciences divided in 6 main parts: 1. Libraries and their use (leading Latin American collections in UK, US and Europe) - 2. Bibliographies - 3. Other printed sources (encyclopedias, handbooks, guides, directories, maps and atlases etc.) - 4. Non print sources - 5. Specialised information - 6. Research and career development. Subject and reference source indexes. Prepared under the auspices of the Standing Committee of National and University Libraries' Advisory Committee on Latin American Materials. 'Essential for any library with a serious interest in Latin America' (*Choice*, v.28,no.1, September 1990, p.78).

Class No: 908(729.99)(01)

[4980]

PAN AMERICAN UNION. Columbus Memorial Library. **Index to Latin American periodical literature, 1929-1960.** Boston, Mass., G.K. Hall, 8v., 1962. First Supplement 2v., 1967. 6000p. $540.00. Export $655.00. Supplement $220.00. Export $265.00. ISBN: 0816105014, 1962 set; 0816107688, supplement.

About 295,000 catalogue cards (authors, subjects and other secondary entries) photolithographically reproduced. Indexes articles from more than 3000 periodicals, these being mostly of Latin American origin.

Class No: 908(729.99)(01)

[4981]

TULANE UNIVERSITY. New Orleans. **Catalog of the Latin American Library of the Tulane University Library.** Boston, Mass., G.K. Hall, 9v., 1970. First Supplement 2v., 1973. Second Supplement, 2v., 1975. Third Supplement, 2v., 1978. 7422p. + 1618p. + 1571[. + 1532p.

1970. 9v. $890.00 (Export $1075.00). ISBN 0816108943. *First Supplement.* 4 reels. $250.00 ($300.00). ISBN 0816112762. *Second Supplement.* 4 reels. $250.00 ($300.00). ISBN 0816113122. These two supplements are no longer available in printed book form. *Third Supplement.* 2v. 15232p. $275.00 ($330.00). ISBN 0816100055.

253,900 photolithographed dictionary-catalogue cards in all on Central America (including Mexico) and the West Indies, as well as Latin America generally. The collection was known until 1962 as the Middle American Research Library. Under the Farmington Plan the Latin American library was primarily responsible for collecting Central American material (except Costa Rica).

Class No: 908(729.99)(01)

[4982]

UNIVERSITY OF FLORIDA Libraries. **Catalog of the Latin American Collection, University of Florida Libraries.** Boston, Mass., G.K. Hall, 13v., 1973. First Supplement. 7v., 1980.

1973. 26 reels. $1345.00 (Export $1625.00). ISBN 0816113165. No longer available in printed book form. *First Supplement* 7v. 4354p. $990.00($1198.00). ISBN 0816110905. The Latin American Collection consists of approximately 120,000 volumes of books, pamphlets, periodicals, and government documents. History is the strongest field, followed by the social and political sciences, literature, and the other humanities. In addition, the University of Florida has the greatest concentration of Caribbean materials held by any university library, with particular strength in Cuban, Haitian, and Dominican Republic materials. This is a dictionary catalog with author, title, subject, and added entries in one sequence.

Class No: 908(729.99)(01)

[4983]

UNIVERSITY OF TEXAS. Austin. **Catalog of the Latin American Collection** of the University of Texas Library. Boston, Mass., G.K. Hall, 31v., 1969. First Supplement 5v., 1971. Second Supplement 3v., 1973. Third Supplement 8v., 1975. Fourth Supplement 3v., 1977. 22854p. + 3561p. + 2004p. + 6254p. + 1968p.

1969. 31 reels. $2960.00 (Export $3580.00). ISBN 0816115117. *First Supplement.* 10 reels. $430.00 ($520.00). ISBN 0816112819. *Second Supplement.* 6 reels. $340.00 ($410.00). ISBN 0816113254. *Third Supplement.* 16 reels. $930.00 ($1125.00). ISBN 0816113602. Catalog and first 3 supplements now available only on microfilm.

Fourth Supplement. 3v. 1968p. $330.00 ($400.00). ISBN 0816111561. Additional supplements appear annually as the *Bibliographic guide to Latin American studies* (*qv*). A dictionary catalogue of authors, titles and subjects for books, pamphlets, periodicals, newspapers and microfilm. The main catalogue consists of 479,000 cards. One of the world's most comprehensive Latin American collections.

Class No: 908(729.99)(01)

[4984]

WILGUS, A.C., *comp*. **Latin America, Spain and Portugal** a selected and annotated bibliographical guide to books published in the United States 1954-1974. Metuchen, New Jersey, Scarecrow Press, 1977. xv, 910p. index. $55.00. ISBN: 0810810182.

9 subdivided pts: 1. Mexico and related parts of the United States - 2. Central America - 3. Caribbean and West Indies - 4. South America - 5. Latin America - 6. Latin America:related - 7. Iberia - 8. Adult fiction - 9. Children's books. *Class No:* 908(729.99)(01)

[4985]

WOODS, R.D. **Reference materials on Latin America in English** the humanities. Metuchen, New Jersey, Scarecrow Press, 1980. xii, 639p. index. $47.50. ISBN: 0810812940.

1,252 entries cover the sub-continent from the colonial period to the present. Primary arrangement by authors A-Z, with separate author, title and subject indexes. 'An exhaustive and extremely useful bibliography' (S.V. Bryant. *Brazil*. 1985. Entry 802). *Class No:* 908(729.99)(01)

Handbooks & Manuals

[4986]

Handbook of Latin American studies. Martin, D.M., *ed*. Austin, Univ. of Texas, 1936-. v.1-. Annual. ISSN: 00729833.

V. 1-3 published by Harvard Univ. Press, then by Univ. of Florida Press. Latterly prepared 'by a number of scholars for the Hispanic Division of the Library of Congress'.

As from v.26 (1964) coverage has been split, 'Humanities' and 'Social sciences' volumes being published in alternative years. Thus v.51 *Social sciences* (1992. xx,901p. 0292751494) has 5109 concisely annotated entries for Bibliography and general works, Anthropology (including Archaeology) - Economics - Education - Geography - Government and politics - International relations - Sociology. 55 contributing editors. V.52 *Humanities* (1993. xxiii,934p. 0292751567) has 5444 entries for Bibliography and general works - Art - Film - History (in 7 main divisions) - Language - Literature - Music - Philosophy. 68 contributing editors. *Class No:* 908(729.99)(035)

Dictionaries

[4987]

NUÑEZ, B., *with the assistance of the African Bibliographical Center*. **Dictionary of Afro-Latin American civilization.** Westport, Connecticut, Greenwood Press, 1980. xxxv, 525p. illus., maps, indexes. $56.95. ISBN: 0313211388.

Historical and descriptive dictionary of more than 4500 entries relating to terms and places, and including biographies of Afro-Latin American political leaders, writers *etc*. involved in Afro-Latin American civilization. From English, French, Portuguese and Spanish sources. 'Provides a unique documentation and illustration of the impact of African civilization and peoples upon - and contributions to - the New World' (*Foreword*). *Class No:* 908(729.99)(038)

Theses

[4988]

LONDON UNIVERSITY. Institute of Latin American Studies. **Research on Latin America on the humanities and social sciences in the universities and polytechnics in the United Kingdom 1984-88.** London, Institute of Latin American Studies. v, 128p. ISSN: 09569014.

Merger of *Theses in Latin American studies at British universities in progress and completed* (1967-) and *Staff research in progress or recently completed in the humanities and the social sciences* (1969-).

1. Staff publications 1984-88 - 2. Staff research in progress 1988-89 - 3. Theses completed 1984-88 - 4. Theses in progress 1988-89. *Class No:* 908(729.99)(043)

Yearbooks & Directories

[4989]

South America, Central America and the Caribbean 1995. 5th ed. London, Europa, 1994. Distributed in North America by Gale Research Co. xv,702p. maps, tables, bibliogs. £155. (*Regional Surveys of the World*.) ISBN: 1857430034.

Previous ed. 1990.

Over 20 specialist contributors. Part 1. Background to the region consists of 8 signed introductory essays (*e.g.* Dictatorship and democracy in South America) - 2. Country surveys: 47 A-Z chapters on all countries and territories containing concise historical, geographical and economic information, using the latest official statistics on finance, industry, agriculture, trade, population, education, transport, tourism, and the news media. Also a government, political and constitutional directory and a bibliography for each of the major countries - 3. Regional organizations *i.e.* all principal organizations working in the region with the emphasis on United Nations activities. 'Has deservedly won generous plaudits for its comprehensive coverage of three quite distinct geopolitical areas' (*Reference Reviews*, v.5,no.2, 1991, p.39-40). *Class No:* 908(729.99)(058)

Libraries

[4990]

GROW, M. **Scholars' guide to Washington DC for Latin American and Caribbean studies.** 2nd ed. Woodrow Wilson Center, John Hopkins Univ. 1992. 427p. $60. (*Scholars' guide to Washington DC, no.2*.) ISBN: 0943875366.

Mainly focussed on social sciences and humanities resources: 1. Collections (libraries, archives, museums, map collections etc.) - 2. Organizations (research centres, information offices, US government agencies, learned societies, media *etc*.). Personal papers, library specialisms, institution indexes. *Class No:* 908(729.99):061:026/027

USA

[4991]

Cities of the United States a compilation of current information on economic, cultural, geographic and social conditions. Straub, D.A., *ed*. Detroit, Gale Research Inc., 4v., 1989. illus., maps, index. $80.44 per volume; $258.75 (set). ISBN: 0810325004, set.

1. *The South* 403p. index. ISBN 0810325010 ISSN 08996075. 2. *The West* 344p. index. ISBN 0810325022. 3.

....(contd.)

The Midwest ISBN 0810325039. 4. *The Northwest* ISBN 0810325047.

Historical and present-day information on over 100 key cities of historical, political, or commercial significance organized in 12 data sections - 1. The city in brief - 2. Geography and climate - 3. History - 4. Population - 5. Municipal government - 6. Economy - 7. Education and research - 8. Health care - 9. Recreation - 10. Convention facilities - 11. Transport - 12. Communications. 'Useful to business researchers, marketing specialists, tourists, history students, and students of urban affairs. Although ... most of the information ... can be derived from other sources, it is always useful to be able to find it in one place' (*Choice*, v.26, no.7, March 1989, p.1118). *Class No:* 908(73)

[4992]
KANE, J.N., *and others, comps.* **Facts about the States.** New York, H.W. Wilson, 1989. 576p. bibliogs., tables. US and Canada $55.00. $65.00 other countries. ISBN: 0824204077.

Chapter for each State (plus Puerto Rico and Washington DC) with information on geography and climate, demography, Government and politics, history, finances, culture and education, *etc.* and a bibliography. Comparative statistics feature population, age, income. *Class No:* 908(73)

[4993]
WELLAND, D., *ed.* **The United States:** a companion to American studies. 2nd ed. London, Methuen, 1987. xii,594p. maps, bibliog., index. £35.00. ISBN: 0416415008. 1st ed 1974.

14 contributors. 15 chapters: 1. Geographical basis of American life - 2. Profile of the American city - 3. Americanism - 4. Immigration and the American economy - 5. Race in American history - 6. American wars - 7. America in world affairs - 8. The United States: constitution and government - 9. American politics, past and present - 10. Emergence of an American literature - 11. Literature of realism - 12. Fiction and poetry since 1918 - 13. Drama and the arts - 14. American media and the denial of history - 15. American thought. A checklist of essential works of reference p.574-6. 9 maps. *Class No:* 908(73)

[4994]
World Almanac of the USA. Carpenter, A. *and* Provorse, C., *eds.* New York, World Almanac, 1993. 400p. col. maps, tables, flags. $18.95. ISBN: 0886877245.

Detailed portrait of each State in the Union: its history, geography, notable sons and daughters, laws, climate, environment, statistics, sport, transport, and religion. *Class No:* 908(73)

Bibliographies

[4995]
American studies a guide to information sources. Marcell, D.W., *ed.* Detroit, Gale Research Co., 1982. xx, 207p. indexes. $68.00. ISBN: 0810312638.

Bibliographic guide in 3 major sections: 1. The History, Theory, Curricula and programs in the discipline - 2. Biography and autobiography; Cultural and social anthropology; Folklore; History; Literature; Women, minorities, ethnic groups; National character; Performing arts; Philosophy, law, religion; Popular and mass culture;

....(contd.)

Regionalism; Science and technology; Visual arts - 3. Others. Author, title and subject indexes. *Class No:* 908(73)(01)

[4996]
BANCROFT LIBRARY University of California, Berkeley. **Catalog of printed books.** Boston, Mass., G.K. Hall, 22v., 1964. First Supplement 6v., 1969. Second Supplement 6v., 1974. Third Supplement, 1979.

1964. 44 reels. $1980.00 (Export $2400.00) ISBN 0816113939. *First Supplement.* 6v. 4133p. $660.00 ($798.00) ISBN 0816108374. *Second Supplement,* 6 reels. $720.00 ($870.00) ISBN 0816113947. *Third Supplement.* 5 reels. $830.00 ($1005.00) ISBN 0816111634. *Catalogue* and *Second and Third Supplements* now available only on microfilm. In total 612,800 photolithographed catalogue cards are reproduced. Holdings of the Bancroft Library concern the area from Alaska to Panama and from the Montana-Texas line westwards to Hawaii and the Pacific Islands. *Class No:* 908(73)(01)

[4997]
HERSTEIN, S.R. *and* **ROBBINS, N.C.,** *comps.* **United States of America.** Santa Barbara, California and Oxford, Clio Press, 1982. xii. 307p.+1p. map, index. £42.50. $45.00. (*World Bibliographical Series; no. 16.*) ISBN: 1851090444.

1126 annotated entries. 36 sections: The country and its people - Geography - Archaeology and prehistory - History - Nationalities and minorities ... Reference works.. *Class No:* 908(73)(01)

[4998]
The Kaiser index to black resources 1948-1986. Kaiser, E.D., *comp.* New York, Carlson Publishing, 5v., 1992. 2600p. $995. ISBN: 0926019600.

Index of 174,000 items relating to articles in newspapers and over 170 periodicals held in the Schomburg Center for Research in Black Culture of The New York Public Library arranged under 15,000 subdivided Library of Congress subject headings. Much of the material is not indexed elsewhere. *Class No:* 908(73)(01)

[4999]
KARKHANIS, S. Jewish heritage in America an annotated bibliography. New York, Garland Press, 1988. xx,434p. indexes. $59. ISBN: 0824075382.

1100 annotated items arranged in 7 sections: 1. Reference and research - 2. Historical perspectives - 3. Antisemitism - 4. Religious traditions - 5. Intellectual and literary traditions - 6. Sociological impact - 7. Political activism. Author, title and subject indexes. *Class No:* 908(73)(01)

[5000]
LOPEZ, M.D. New York: a guide to information and reference sources 1979-1986. Metuchen, N.J., Scarecrow Press, 1987. xi,372p. indexes. £26.25. ISBN: 0810820188.

1065 fully annotated entries arranged in 2 parts (New York State and New York City) and divided under 30 and 36 headings respectively: *e.g.* Biography and Autobiography ... Bibliographies and indexes ... Description and travel ... Geography ... History. Follows the author's *New York: a guide to information and reference sources.* Scarecrow Press, 1980. x,307p. *Class No:* 908(73)(01)

[5001]

MARTEN, J., *comp*. **Texas**. Santa Barbara, Calif., and Oxford, Clio Press, 1992. xxiii,229p. + 1p. map, index. £36. (*World Bibliographical Series, no.144*.) ISBN: 185109184x.

708 annotated entries in 20 sections: State of Texas and its people - Geography and natural history - History - Military affairs ... Ethnic groups ... Reference works and bibliographies. Author, title and subject index.

Class No: 908(73)(01)

[5002]

Native American Bibliography Series. Marken, J.W. Metuchen, N.J., Scarecrow Press, 1980-.

1. Marken, J.W. and Hoover, H.T. *Bibliography of the Sioux*. 1980. 338p. $27.50. ISBN 0810813564.

4. *Anderson, W.L. and Lewis, J.A. A guide to Cherokee documents in foreign archives*. 1983. 768p. $40. 081081630x.

6. Wilson, T.P. *Bibliography of the Osage*. 1985. 172p. $20. 0810818051.

7. Kutsche, P. *A guide to Cherokee documents in the Northeastern United States*. 1986. 541p. $79. 0810818272.

9. Tate, M.L. *The Indians of Texas: an annotated research bibliography*. 1986. 514p. $52. 0810818523.

10 Blumer, T.J. *Bibliography of the Catawba*. 1987. 575p. $59.50. 0810819864.

11. Hoyt, A.K. *Bibliography of the Chickasaw*. 1987. 230p. $25. 0810819953.

12. Edmunds, R.D. *Kinsmen through time: an annotated bibliography of Potawatomi history*. 1987. 237p. $27.50. 081082020x.

13. Dempsey, H.A. and Moir, L. *Bibliography of the Blackfoot*. 1989. 255p. $27.50. 0810822113.

14. Tate, M.L. *The Upstream people: an annotated research bibliography of the Omaha tribe* 1991. 522p. maps. $27.50. 0810823721.

The series of bibliographies on Native American tribes also includes bibliographies of general topics concerning Native Americans. The compilers aim to be comprehensive, annotate the more important items, and produced bibliographies ranging from 2000 to 5000 entries.

Class No: 908(73)(01)

[5003]

SALZMAN, J., *ed*. **American studies** an annotated bibliography. Cambridge, Cambridge University Press. 3v., 1986, xii, 2058p. ISBN: 0521266866, v.1; 0521266874, v.2; 0521266883, v.3; 0521325552, set.

Replaces *An annotated bibliography of works on the civilizations of the United States* (US Information Agency, 1982).

V.1 Anthropology and folklore; Art and Architecture; History (p.237-707). V.2 Literature; Music; Political science; Popular culture; Psychology; Religion; Science, technology and medicine. V.3 Author, title and subject indexes. Prefaces to each section introduce the basic bibliographic resources for research in that discipline. 'A valuable set because of the huge number of books it lists, the meaningful way in which they are arranged, and the prefaces that precede each section' (*Reference Books Bulletin* 1986-1987, p.156). *Class No:* 908(73)(01)

[5004]

SALZMAN, J., *ed*. **American studies** an annotated bibliography, 1984-1988. Cambridge University Press, 1990. xi,1085p. indexes. £75. $95. ISBN: 0521365597.

Interim supplements are printed in *Prospects: an annual of American Cultural Studies*.

Over 200 contributors. This supplement to the original bibliography contains 3,872 annotated items published in US. Similar supplements, a volume for material published outside US, and a volume devoted to journal articles, are planned. Author and title indexes. 'A thoroughly commendable compilation' (*Choice*, v.28,no.4, December 1990, p.614). *Class No:* 908(73)(01)

[5005]

UNIVERSITY OF TEXAS. Austin. **Catalog of the Texas Collection in the Barker Texas History Center.** Boston, Mass., G.K. Hall, 14v., 1979. 10.249p. $1250.00 (Export $1510.00). ISBN: 0816102732.

215,000 photolithographed catalogue cards relating to Texas and Texans. *Class No:* 908(73)(01)

Encyclopaedias

[5006]

The American regional encyclopedia series. New York and Oxford, Facts On File, 1985-. £40.00 each.

1. *New England* 1985. 400p. ISBN 0871967596. 2. *The South*. 1985. 560p. 0871967286. 3. *Midwest*. 1988. 544p. 0816016607. 4. *Central West*. 1990. 488p. 0816016615. 5. *Far West*. 1990. 544p. 0816016623.

A-Z articles on each region in their historical and contemporary contexts. *Class No:* 908(73)(031)

[5007]

The Encyclopedia of New England. O'Brien, R. *and* Brown, R.D., *eds*. New York and Oxford, Facts On File, 1985. ix,613p., illus. (some col.), maps, tables, bibliog., index. $29.95. £26.50. ISBN: 0871967596.

2500 A-Z entries covering history, people, places, industries and landmarks of Connecticut, Maine, Massachusetts, New Hampshire, Rhode Island and Vermont. Map and fact sheet for each state. Appendix 1. A-Z by state list of counties and county seats - 2. State statistics - 3. State governors. Bibliography p.554-57. *Class No:* 908(73)(031)

[5008]

Encyclopedia of Southern culture. Sponsored by the Center for the Study of Southern Culture, Univ. of Mississipi. Wilson, C.R. *and* Ferris, W., *eds*. Chapel Hill, Univ. of North Carolina Press, 1989. 1,634p. illus. (incl. pl.), maps, tables, charts, bibliogs., index.

Over 800 contributors. 1300 signed, well-documented, cross-referenced entries deployed in 24 major thematic sections *e.g.* Agriculture; Art and architecture; Black life; Environment; Ethnic life; Folklore; History and manners; Industry; Language; Law; Media; Music; Politics; Recreation; Religion; Violence; Women's life *etc*. Scope covers the 11 Confederate States of the Civil War and also midwestern and Middle Atlantic states. Includes biographies. 'This compendium has no contemporary rival' (*Booklist*, v.86, no.1, 1 September 1989, p.97-98).

Class No: 908(73)(031)

[5009]
The Encyclopedia of the South. O'Brien, R. *and* Martin, H.H., *eds.* New York and Oxford, Facts On File, 1985. viii, 583p., illus., maps, tables, bibliog., index. £26.50. ISBN: 0871967286.

2500 A-Z entries covering all aspects of Southern life and culture: entire span of history, people, places ('March to the sea', 37 lines; 'Louisiana Purchase', 58 lines; Alamo, 38 lines). Map and fact sheet for each state *i.e.* Alabama, Arkansas, Florida, Georgia, Kentucky, Louisiana, Maryland, Mississipi, Missouri, North and South Carolina, Tennessee, Texas, Virginia and West Virginia. Appendix 1. A-Z by state list of counties and county seats - 2. State statistics - 3. State governors. Bibliography p.519-22. *Class No:* 908(73)(031)

[5010]
The Reference encyclopedia of the American Indian. 5th ed. Santa Barbara, Calif., and Oxford, ABC-Clio, 1990. 999p. bibliog., index. £79. ISBN: 0915344165.

Current information on associations, foundations, government agencies, publications, *etc.* and 2000 profiles of Native Americans prominent in tribal affairs, business, industry, the arts and sciences. *Class No:* 908(73)(031)

[5011]
Worldmark encyclopedia of the States a practical guide to the geographic, demographic, historical, political, economic and social development of the United States. 2nd ed. New York and Chichester, Sussex, John Wiley, 1986. xiv, 690p. maps, tables, bibliogs. $133.70. £95.45. ISBN: 0471832138. 1st ed. 1981.

A detailed portrait of each state, the District of Columbia, Puerto Rico, US Virgin Islands, American Samoa, Guam, and the US Pacific and Caribbean territories and dependencies organized under 50 numbered headings *e.g.* 1. Location ... 11. History ... 47. Tourism ... 49. Famous persons - 50. Bibliography. 'A convenient package of statistical data with general review information. However it is presently revised too infrequently and contains too little unique material to be recommended for purchase by most libraries' (*Reference Books Bulletin 1986-87*, p.155). *Class No:* 908(73)(031)

Periodicals

[5012]
DEERING, C.M., *comp. and ed.* Union list of American Studies periodicals in UK Libraries. Boston Spa, West Yorkshire, The British Library Lending Division in association with the Standing Conference of National and University Libraries, 1983. ISBN: 0712320121.

Companion volume to P. Snow's *The United States: a guide to library holdings in the UK* (1982).

Finding list of *c*.2500 journals related to the study of the United States in British libraries. Data: basic bibliographical information including place of publication, starting date *etc.* *Class No:* 908(73)(051)

Yearbooks & Directories

[5013]
Hispanic American information directory. Detroit, Gale Research Co., 1990. 395p. indexes. $69.50. ISBN: 0810374447.

Selected material in 8 out of 16 chapters was taken from

....(contd.)
other Gale titles and re-edited for this publication.

4700 resources available to Hispanic Americans organized in 16 sections including national associations, library collections, industrial service companies, government programmes, publications *etc*. Name and keyword indexes. *Class No:* 908(73)(058)

Government Publications

Bibliographies

[5014]
PARISH, D.W. Bibliography of State bibliographies 1970-82. Littleton, Colorado, Libraries Unlimited, 1985. xiii, 267p. indexes. ISBN: 0872874664.

1031 annotated entries relating to material published by US State governments arranged A-Z by State and alphabetically within States under broad subject headings *e.g.* Archaeology - Area Studies - Drug use and abuse ... Geography ... History ... Libraries ... Native people ... Politics and government ... Space exploration. Appendix: Acquisition guide and agency addresses p.217-39. Title and subject indexes. *Class No:* 908(73)(061.1)(01)

Libraries

[5015]
SNOW, P., *comp.* The United States a guide to library holdings in the UK. Boston Spa, Wetherby, Yorkshire, British Lending Library Division in association with SCONUL, 1982. xxiii, 717p. index. £14.00. ISBN: 0853501831.

Description of printed, microform and audio-visual materials of over 350 libraries (Aberdeen City Library - University of York) in arts, humanities, and social science subjects and a detailed annex of over 1800 microform and multi-volume works in 30 named major collections. *Class No:* 908(73):061:026/027

Alaska

Bibliographies

[5016]
HALES, D.A. America's last frontier reference books about Alaska. *Reference Services Review* v.13, no.4, Winter 1985, p.23-46.

Review of current information on the resources and people of Alaska. *Class No:* 908(798)(01)

[5017]
TOURVILLE, E.A., *comp.* Alaska a bibliography 1570-1970. Boston, Mass., G.K. Hall, 1874. xviii, 738p. index.

Over 8,500 author entries for Alaskan books including Alaskan inprints and books published on the state. Subject index. *Class No:* 908(798)(01)

Handbooks & Manuals

[5018]
WOERNER, R.K. The Alaska handbook. Jefferson, North Carolina, and London, McFarland & Co., 1986. ix, 220p. illus., ports., maps, tables, index. $19.95. ISBN: 0899502199.

....(contd.)

10 chapters: 1. Alaska: an overview - 2. Land regions - 3. Transport - 4. Land ownership and disposal - 5. National Parklands - 6. Cities - 7. Flying to Alaska - 8. Camping - 9. Floating Alaska's rivers - 10. Wildlife, fishing and hunting. Appendix F. Other information sources.
Class No: 908(798)(035)

Brazil

Bibliographies of Bibliographies

[5019]
BASSECHES, B. **A Bibliography of Brazilian bibliographies/Uma bibliographia das bibliografias brasileiras.** Detroit, Blain Ethridge, 1978. 185p. $16.00. ISBN: 0879170646.

Nearly 2,500 references to books, parts of books and periodical articles. Author/subject index. In Portugese, with introductory matter in English and Portugese. 'A topical/ classified arrangement would have made for great ease of use' (*College & research libaries*, January 1979, p.47).
Class No: 908(81)(009)

Bibliographies

[5020]
BRYANT, S.V., *comp.* **Brazil.** Santa Barbara, California and Oxford, Clio Press, 1985. xii, 244p. + 1p. map. index. £33.95; $37.50. (*World Bibliographical Series, no. 57.*) ISBN: 1851090002.

806 annotated entries. 36 sections: The country and its people - Geography ... Archaeology and prehistory - History ... Nationalities, minorities and immigrants - Museums and libraries ... General bibliographies. Author, title and subject index. *Class No:* 908(81)(01)

[5021]
HARTNESS, A. **Brazil in reference books 1965-1989** an annotated bibliography. Metuchen, N.J., Scarecrow Press, 1991. ix,351p. indexes. $39.50. ISBN: 0810824000.

1669 entries divided into 20 categories *e.g.* Bibliographies ... General sources ... Biography ... Geography - History ... Libraries, archives, museums, and information science ... Statistics. Author and subject indexes.
Class No: 908(81)(01)

Argentina

Bibliographies

[5022]
BIGGINS, A., *comp.* **Argentina.** Santa Barbara, Calif., and Oxford, Clio Press, 1991. xxvi,460p. +1p. map indexes. £65. (*World Bibliographical Series, no.130.*) ISBN: 1851091092.

1350 annotated entries in 42 sections: Country and its people - Geography - Travellers' accounts ... Archaeology and prehistory - History ... The Gaucho ... Falklands Islands dispute ... Encyclopaedias, directories and biographical dictionaries - Bibliographies. Author, title and subject index.
Class No: 908(82)(01)

[5023]
UNIVERSITY OF BUENOS AIRES. **Argentine bibliography:** a union catalogue of Argentinian holdings in the libraries of the University of Buenos Aires. Boston, Mass., G.K. Hall, 7v., 1980. 5000p. $689.00 (Export $830.00). ISBN: 0816103178.

The *Argentine Bibliography* reproduces in book form more than 105,000 cards in the card catalogs of the 53 libraries of the University of Buenos Aires. The Bibliography lists all works written by Argentine authors and works about Argentina published anywhere in the world through 1977. *Class No:* 908(82)(01)

Falkland Islands

[5024]
HEADLAND, R. **The Island of South Georgia.** Cambridge, Cambridge Univ. Press, 1984. xvi, 293p. illus., maps, tables, bibliog. £22.50. ISBN: 0521252741.

9 chapters: 1. Geography, administration and population - 2. Discovery - 3. Early history and the first epoch of sealing - 4. Expeditions, visits and other events - 5. Whaling, second sealing epoch - 6. Travel and communications - 7. Physical sciences, the land, ocean and atmosphere - 8. Natural history - 9. Military action, events on South Georgia in 1982 and the island's future. Bibliography p.270-5. 'A truly splendid book by a knowledgeable scholar, catholic in interest and qualified by extensive personal experience of the island' (*Geographical Journal*, v.151, no.2, July 1985, p.261).
Class No: 908(829.1)

Bibliographies

[5025]
HEADLAND, R. **South Georgia** a bibliography. Cambridge, British Antarctic Survey, 1982. 180p. £3.00. ISBN: 0856650951.

'A definitive work in this field, computer-set and likely to be updated periodically' (H.G.R. King. *The Atlantic Ocean*, 1985. Entry 886). *Class No:* 908(829.1)(01)

[5026]
A **Selective listing of monographs and government documents on the Falkland/Malvinas Islands in the Library of Congress.** Larson, E.E., *comp.* Washington DC, Library of Congress Hispanic Division, 1982. 28p. pbk. *gratis.* (*Hispanic Focus No. 1.*)

Replaces 2 unpublished lists available in the Library of Congress' Main Reading Room: H.F. Conover's 'The Falkland Islands and its dependencies: a list of recent references' (1944) and 'Antarctica and the Falkland Islands: a list of recent references' (1955).

196 entries not restricted to 1982 war in the South Atlantic. *Class No:* 908(829.1)(01)

Chile

Bibliographies

[5027]
BLAKEMORE, H., *comp.* **Chile.** Santa Barbara, California and Oxford, Clio Press, 1988. xiv, 197p. + 2p. maps, indexes. £28.50; $42.50. (*World Bibliographical Series, no. 97.*) ISBN: 1851090266.

642 annotated entries. 29 sections: The country and its people - Geography - Exploration and travel ... Archaeology

....(contd.)
... History ... Government and politics ... Museums and libraries ... Bibliographies. Author, title and subject indexes. *Class No:* 908(83)(01)

Bolivia

Bibliographies

[5028]
YEAGER, G.M., *comp*. **Bolivia.** Santa Barbara, California and Oxford, Clio Press, 1988. xv, 228p.+1p. map. index. £32.95; $41.00. (*World Bibliographical Series, no.89.*) ISBN: 0851090665.
816 annotated entries. 36 sections: The country and people - Geography - Tourism and travel guides - Travellers' accounts ... Prehistory and archaeology - History ... Social conditions ... Bibliographies - Reference Works and encyclopaedias - Dictionaries. Author, title and subject index. *Class No:* 908(84)(01)

Peru

Bibliographies

[5029]
FISHER, R., *comp*. **Peru.** Santa Barbara, California and Oxford, Clio Press, 1989. xvii, 193p.+1p. map, indexes. £34.00. (*World Bibliographical Series; no.109.*) ISBN: 1851091009.
705 annotated entries. 31 sections: The country and its people - Geography - Tourism and travel guides - Exploration and travellers' accounts ... Archaeology and prehistory - History ... Libraries and archives ... Reference works ... Bibliographies. Author, title and subject indexes. *Class No:* 908(85)(01)

[5030]
PERU. NATIONAL LIBRARY. Author catalog of the Peruvian Collection of the National Library of Peru. Boston, Mass., G.K. Hall, 6v., 1979. 4694p. $685.00 (Export $830.00). ISBN: 0816102503.
98,1000 catalogue cards reproduced photolithographically. The Library contains material published 1583 onwards. Appended are lists of *c.*10,000 periodicals by title and of 1,300 maps and charts under places A-Z. *Class No:* 908(85)(01)

Colombia

Bibliographies

[5031]
DAVIS, R.H., *comp*. **Columbia.** Santa Barbara, California and Oxford, Clio Press, 1990. xxi,204 +1p. map. indexes. £29.95. (*World Bibliographical Series, no.112.*) ISBN: 1851090932.
662 annotated entries in 29 sections: Country and its people - Geography and the environment ... Exploration and travellers' accounts - Archaeology and prehistory - History ... La Violencia ... Archives ... Reference works - Bibliographies. Author, title and subject index. *Class No:* 908(86)(01)

Ecuador

Bibliographies

[5032]
Ecuador. Corkill, D., *comp*. Santa Barbara, California and Oxford, Clio Press, 1989. xxi, 155p. + 1p. map. indexes. £32.00; $45.00. (*World Bibliographical Series, no. 101.*) ISBN: 085109069x.
557 annotated entries. 28 sections. The country and its people - Geography - Exploration and travellers' accounts - Tourism and travel guides ... Archaeology and prehistory - History ... Directories and current reference books - Bibliographies - Professional periodicals. Author, title, and subject indexes. *Class No:* 908(866)(01)

Venezuela

Bibliographies

[5033]
WADDELL, D.A.G., *comp*. **Venezuela.** Santa Barbara, California and Oxford, Clio Press, 1990. xviii,206p. map, index. £29.95; $29.95. (*World Bibliographical Series, no.110.*) ISBN: 1851091068.
815 annotated entries in 29 sections. Country and its people - Geography - Description and travel ... Prehistory and archaeology - Native peoples - History ... Bibliographies. Author, subject and title index. *Class No:* 908(87)(01)

Guyana

Bibliographies

[5034]
CHAMBERS, F. **Guyana.** Santa Barbara, California and Oxford, Clio Press, 1989. xv, 206p. + 1p. map. indexes. £31.95; $45.00. (*World Bibliographical Series, no. 96.*) ISBN: 1851090703.
606 annotated entries. 36 sections: The country and people - Geography - Maps, atlases and gazetteers ... Travel guides - Travellers' and explorers' accounts ... Prehistory and archaeology - Historiography - History ... Libraries, archives and museums ... Reference works - Bibliographies. Separate author, title and subject indexes. *Class No:* 908(88)(01)

Suriname

Bibliographies

[5035]
HOEFTE, R., *comp*. **Suriname.** Santa Barbara, Calif., Oxford, Clio Press, 1990. xxx,227p. + 1p. map, index. £34. (*World Bibliographical Series, no.117.*) ISBN: 1851091033.
731 annotated entries in 30 sections: The country and its people - Geography and geology - Travellers' accounts ... Prehistory and archaeology - History ... Languages ... Libraries and archives ... Reference Books - Bibliographies. Author, title and subject index. *Class No:* 908(883)(01)

Paraguay

[5036]

ROETT, R. *and* SACKS, R.S. **Paraguay** the personalist legacy. Boulder, Colo., Westview Press, 1991. xviii,188p. illus., tables, map, bibliog., index. £21.95. (*Profiles. Nations Of Contemporary America.*) ISBN: 0865312729.

1. Introduction - 2. History 1524-1904 - 3. Modern history - 4. Economy - 5. Culture and society - 6. Politics and government - 7. International relations. Bibliography p.171-7. *Class No:* 908(892)

Bibliographies

[5037]

JONES, D.L. **Paraguay: a bibliography.** New York, Garland, 1979. xxiv, 499p.

4,431 unannotated entries. 15 sections: 1. Bibliography and reference works - 2. Religion - 3. History (items 129-2348) - 4. Geography - 5. Anthropology - 6. Economics - 7. Sociology and social administration - 8. Government and politics - 9. Law - 10. Education - 11. The arts and music - 12. Literature - 13. Science - 14. Medicine - 15. Select list of Paraguayan periodicals, p.431-7. Index, p.437-99. 'An invaluable research tool for scholars of Paraguay' (R.A. Nickson. *Paraguay*, 1987. Entry 590). *Class No:* 908(892)(01)

[5038]

NICKSON, R.A., *comp.* **Paraguay.** Santa Barbara, California and Oxford, Clio Press, 1987. xxvi, 212p.+1p. map. index. £31.95; $45.00. ISBN: 1851090282.

600 annotated entries. 33 sections: The country and its people - Geography - Tourism and travel guides - Travellers' accounts ... History ... Human rights ... Libraries and archives ... Biographical dictionaries - Bibliographies. Single author, title, subject index. *Class No:* 908(892)(01)

Uruguay

Bibliographies

[5039]

FINCH, M.H.J. **Uruguay.** Santa Barbara, California and Oxford, Clio Press, 1989. xxix, 232p. + 1p. map, indexes. £34.95. (*World Bibliographical Series, no.102.*) ISBN: 0851090983.

667 annotated entries. 34 sections: The country and its people - Tourism and travel guides - Geography ... Prehistory and archaeology - History ... Politics ... Museums and archives - Directories - Bibliographies. Theses and dissertations on Uruguay p.xxvii-xxix. *Class No:* 908(899)(01)

Australasia & Oceania

[5040]

BARZELATTO, F., *and others.* **Country profiles** Cook Islands, Fiji, Kiribati, Nauru, Niue, Papua New Guinea, Solomon Islands, Tonga, Tuvalu, Vanautu, Western Samoa. Honolulu, Pacific Islands Development Program, 1982. 126p. maps, bibliog.

Basic information on each country: Geography - Government - Economy - Communications - Transport - Foreign Relations - Membership of international and regional organizations. *Class No:* 908(9)

Bibliographies of Bibliographies

[5041]

LEESON, I. **A Bibliography of bibliographies of the South Pacific.** Melbourne and London, Oxford Univ. Press, 1954. 72p.

Published under the auspices of the South Pacific Commission.

Divided first by geographical area and secondly by subject. Includes bibliographies in periodicals; omits bibliographies the contents of which are covered by more important texts on the same subject. 'Though dated, this bibliography is still of value' (G.W. Fry and R. Maurice. *Pacific Basin and Oceania.* 1987, Entry 478). *Class No:* 908(9)(009)

[5042]

THOMPSON, A.G. **The Southwest Pacific:** an annotated guide to bibliographies, indexes and collections in Australian libraries. Canberra, Research School of Pacific Studies, The Australian National University in association with The Academy of Social Sciences in Australia, 1986. x, 127p. indexes, softcover. ISBN: 0867848327.

479 annotated items listed under 6 geographical headings subdivided into broad subject categories. Author and subject indexes. *Class No:* 908(9)(009)

Bibliographies

[5043]

NEW SOUTH WALES. The Mitchell Library. **Dictionary catalog of printed books.** Boston, Mass., G.K. Hall, 38v., 1968. First supplement 1970. $3735.00 (Export $4520). Supplt. $140.00 ($170.00). ISBN: 0816113629; 0816113238, Supplt.

The main catalogue has 603,000 photolithographed cards; the First supplement adds 17,500 entries. The Mitchell Library contains more than 220,000 printed maps, as well as manuscripts, maps, microfilms and pictures. The publishers describe the library as 'the foremost single collection of documentary materials relating to the Australasian and South Pacific region, including the East Indian archipelago and Antarctica'. Prices given are for microfilm editions. Both catalog and supplement are no longer available in printed book form. *Class No:* 908(9)(01)

[5044]

TAYLOR, C.R.H., *comp.* **A Pacific bibliography** printed matter relating to the native peoples of Polynesia, Melanesia, and Micronesia. 2nd ed. London, Oxford Univ. Press, 1965. xx, 692p.

First published 1951 (xxix, 492p.).

More than 16,000 references (to periodical articles as well as books), classified by island groups and by subjects. Covers every island group of Polynesia, Melanesia and Micronesia, and includes New Zealand. According to Ad Orientem *Catalogue nine*, 1967, (p.147). over 13% of the entries concern the Maori, over 5%, Hawaii and 4%, the Fiji Islands. 'One of the major bibliographies on the Pacific' (G.W. Fry and R. Mauricio. *Pacific Basin and Oceania*, 1987. Entry 488). *Class No:* 908(9)(01)

Theses

[5045]

DICKSON, D. *and* **DOSSOR, C.**, *comps*. **World catalogue of theses on the Pacific Islands.** Canberra, Australian National Univ. Press, 1970. xii, 123p.

Over 1,000 entries. Parts: Oceania - Melanesia - Micronesia - Polynesia. Entry states if the item has been published, giving publisher and date. Author index. 'Based mainly on the microfilm library of theses on the Pacific islands maintained by the Department of Pacific history of the Australian National University' (*Library journal*, 15 June 1970, p.2323). First in a planned series of basic reference tools for students of the Pacific area. *Class No: 908(9)(043)*

[5046]

—**COPPELL, W.G.** *and* **STRATIGOS, S.** A Bibliography of Pacific Island theses and dissertations. Canberra, Research School of Pacific Studies, Australian National University in conjunction with The Institute for Polynesian Studies, Brigham Young University Hawaii Campus, 1983. Distributed by Univ. of Hawaii Press. xi, 520p. softcover. ISBN: 0939154331.

Data: author, title, university, degree, year of conferment (to 1980). Author and subject indexes. References p.511-520. An important sequel to Dickson and Dossor's *World catalogue of theses on the Pacific Islands* (*qv*.). *Class No: 908(9)(043)*

Yearbooks & Directories

[5047]

Pacific islands yearbook. Douglas, N. *and* Douglas, N., *eds*. 16th ed. North Ryde, N.S.W., Angus & Robertson, 1989. vi,717p. ISBN: 0207161143. ISSN: 00787523.

Preceded by *Stewart's Handbook of the Pacific Islands: a reliable guide to all the inhabited islands of the Pacific for tourists, traders, settlers* (Sydney, McCarren, Stewart, 1908-1929 annual). Under present title since 1932.

Descriptive gazetteer A-Z by island or island group *e.g.* French Polynesia (Government - Justice - Defence - Education - Labour - Health - The Land - Primary production - Manufacturing and Mining - Tourism - Housing - Overseas trade - Finance - Transport - Communications - Water and electricity - Major office holders - Government ministers and departments) p.145-193. Pacific chronology p.7-10. Obsolete and alternative names for Pacific Islands p.686-95. Current names (with obsolete/alternative names) p.696-705. Index of islands, atolls and inlets p.706-17. *Class No: 908(9)(058)*

Indonesia

Bibliographies

[5048]

AVÉ, J.B., *and others*. **West Kalimantan** a bibliography. Dordrecht, Fons Publications Holland/USA, 1983. x, 260p. maps, index, soft cover. (*Koninklijk Institut Voor Taal-Land-En Volkenkunde Bibliographical Series; no.13*.) ISBN: 9067650412.

1855 items entered in 9 sections: 1. General - 2. Exploration and travels - 3. History - 4. Natural sciences - 5. Technology - 6. Economy - 7. Humanities - 8. Museums - 9. Chinese. Author index. Introduction includes 'West Kalimantan: background information (p.5-8) and 'A guide to the main sources' (p.8-13). *Class No: 908(910)(01)*

[5049]

BUTLER, A. A New Guinea bibliography. Waigani, Univ. of New Guinea Press, 5v, 1984-1990. xxvii, 2604p. index, reproduced from typescript.

'An attempt to list in subject order all the monographs, pamphlets, theses, reports, government documents, seminar papers, journals, *etc.* which are published either in New Guinea or which deal with Papua New Guinea or Irian Jayan topics' (*Preface*). V.5: *Indexes* (1990) includes contents tables for v.1-4; author and name index; and subject index. The *Bibliography* is part of the Papua New Guinea Information Network project. *Class No: 908(910)(01)*

[5050]

FARJON, I. Madura and surrounding islands an annotated bibliography 1860-1942. The Hague, Martinus Nijhoff, 1980. xvi, 109p. index, softcover. (*Koninklijk Institut Voor Taal-Land-En Volkenkunde Bibliographical Series no.9.*) ISBN: 9024724104.

347 entries relating to books and articles on Madura, Bawean and the Kangean and Sapudi archipelogos arranged chronologically. Author and subject indexes. *Class No: 908(910)(01)*

[5051]

FARJON, I., *ed*. **Minahasa and Bolaangmongondow** an annotated bibliography 1800-1942. The Hague, Martinus Nijhoff, 1981. xxvi, 289p. maps. softcover. (*Koninklijk Institut Voor Taal-Land-En Volkenkunde Bibliographical Series no. 10.*) ISBN: 9024761700.

2 separate annotated bibliographies: Minahasa (788 entries); Bolaangmongondow (106 entries) arranged in 18 and 7 categories respectively. 2 Author and subject indexes. *Class No: 908(910)(01)*

[5052]

KRAUSSE, G.H. *and* **KRAUSSE, S.C.E.**, *comps*. **Indonesia.** Santa Barbara, California and Oxford, Clio Press, 1991. xliii,249p. + + 1p. map, index. £42.00; $73.00. (*World Bibliographical Series.*) ISBN: 1851091270.

660 entries in 31 sections: Country and its people ... Geography ... Archaeology and prehistory - History - Sultans ... Tourism and recreation ... Bibliographies and indexes. Chronology p.xxxix-xli. Glossary p.xxxvii-xxxviii. Sultants of Borneo p.xlii-xliii. *Class No: 908(910)(01)*

[5053]

SHERLOCK, K. A Bibliography of Timor including East (formerly Portuguese) Timor and West (formerly Dutch) Timor and the island of Roti. Canberra, Research School of Pacific Studies, Australian National Univ., 1980. xviii, 292p. maps. index. softcover. (*Aids to Research Series no A/4.*) ISBN: 0908160534.

Arranged under 17 broad subject headings. Bibliographies, periodicals published in Timor p.274-280. Author index. *Class No: 908(910)(01)*

[5054]

VAN BOAL, J., *and others*. **West Irian:** a bibliography. Dordrecht, Foris Publications Holland; Cinnaminson, New Jersey, Foris Publications USA, 1984. xiv, 307p. index. (*Koninklijk Institute Voor Taal-Land-En Volkenkunde Bibliographical Series; no.15.*) ISBN: 9067650595.

Approximately 3,000 entries arranged in 9 subdivided chapters: 1. General - 2. Climate, geology - 3. Zoology and botany - 4. Physical anthropology and demography - 5. Linguistics - 6. History (p.41-76) - 7. Cultural anthropology - 8. Ethnology, regional studies - 9. Economics and socio-

....*(contd.)*

cultural development after 1950. Each chapter contains an introduction to and a description of relevant literature followed by a list of titles A-Z by author. Intended as a concise guide, not 'a voluminous work referring to a confusing mass of literature of often uncertain value'. Author index and index of geographical and tribal names.

Appendix: P. Nienhuis' 'Inventaris van het rapportenarchief van het kantooos voor bevolkingszaken (Nederlands-Nieuw Guinea) 1951-1962' *i.e.* an inventory of reports of the Bureau of the Adviser on Native affairs, p.206-307. *Class No:* 908(910)(01)

Handbooks & Manuals

[5055]
Indonesia handbook. Dalton, B. 5th ed. Chico, California, Moon Publishers, 1991. illus., maps, index, 1100p. ISBN: 0918373727.

Survey of geography, flora and fauna, ethnology and culture of all the main Indonesian islands - Java, Sumatra, Bali, Nusa Tennggara, Moluccas, Irian Jaya, Celebes, and Kalimantan. Introduction includes sections on history, government, getting to Indonesia, customs and regulations, and money. Classified booklist p.567-572. Glossary p.573-588. *Class No:* 908(910)(035)

Brunei

[5056]
Brunei Darussalem in profile. London, Shandwick, 1988. Published on behalf of The Government of Brunei Darussalam. 164p. col.illus. col.map. tables, index. ISBN: 095138550x.

Contents: Introduction (Location, size, race, religion; Short history; Key dates; Future) - The Constitution - Structure of government - Heraldry - The Sultans of Brunei - Economic profile - Commercial information - Practical information. 8p. street maps. *Class No:* 908(911.13)

Bibliographies

[5057]
KRAUSSE, S.C. *and* **KRAUSSE, G.H. Brunei.** Santa Barbara, California and Oxford, Clio Press, 1988. xliii, 249p. + 2p. maps, geneal. tables. index. £39.50. (*World Bibliographical Series, no. 93.*) ISBN: 1851090290.

660 annotated entries. 31 sections: The country and its people - Brunei in general works on Southeast Asia - Geography ... Archaeology and prehistory - History - The Sultans - Politics and government ... Tourism and recreation ... Libraries and Museums ... Bibliographies and indexes. Sultans of Brunei: a genealogy p.xlii-xliii. Author, subject and title index. *Class No:* 908(911.13)(01)

Philippines

Bibliographies

[5058]
RICHARDSON, J. Philippines. Santa Barbara, California and Oxford, Clio Press, 1989. xx, 372p.+1p. map. index. £37.00. (*World Bibliographical Series, no.106.*) ISBN: 0851090770.

955 annotated entries. 39 sections: The country and its

....*(contd.)*

people - Tourism and travel guides ... Archaeology and pre-Spanish history - History - Politics since independence - Libraries and Museums ... Encyclopaedias, directories and yearbooks - Bibliographies. Author, title, subject index. *Class No:* 908(914)(01)

Encyclopaedias

[5059]
GALANG, Z.M. Encyclopedia of the Philippines. 3rd ed. Manila, Exequiel Floro, 20v., 1950-1958.

Systematically arranged: v.1-2 Literature; v.3-4. Biography; v.5-6 Commerce and industry; v.7-8. Art; v.9. Education; v.10. Religion; v.11-12. Government and politics; v.13-14. Science; v.15-16. History; v.17-18. Builders; v.19-20. General information. Includes bibliographies. *Class No:* 908(914)(031)

[5060]
ROBERTSON, J.A. Bibliography of the Philippine Islands 1493-1898. Manila, Cacho Hermanos, 1974. 433p.

This is v.53 of E.H. Blair and J.A. Robertson's *The Philippine Islands* originally published Cleveland, Ohio, A.H. Clark, 1908 and reprinted Kraus Reprints 1970.

Deals with printed and manuscript material with a preceding description of the most important archives and collections on the Philippines. *Class No:* 908(914)(031)

Timor

Bibliographies

[5061]
ROWLAND, I., *comp.* **Timor.** Santa Barbara, Calif., and Oxford, Clio Press, 1992. xli,117p. + 2p. maps, index. £32. (*World Bibliographical Series, no.142.*) ISBN: 1851091599.

348 annotated entries in 22 sections: Island and its people - Travel guides - Travellers' accounts - Geography ... Archaeology and prehistory - History - Timorese peoples... Indonesian invasion and foreign relations ... Bibliographies - Periodicals. Chronology. p.xxxix-xli. Author, title and subject index. *Class No:* 908(923.52)(01)

New Zealand

[5062]
Facts about New Zealand. Wellington, Department of Statistics and Daphne Brasell Associates Press, 1992. 222p. maps, tables, index. pbk. ISSN: 11715057.

Concise digest on all aspects of contemporary New Zealand in 9 sections: 1. Land and people - 2. Social organization - 3. Work and leisure - 4. Maori - 5. Women - 6. Primary production - 7. Industry and business - 8. Economics - 9. International comparisons. *Class No:* 908(931)

Bibliographies of Bibliographies

[5063]
NEW ZEALAND LIBRARY ASSOCIATION. A Bibliography of New Zealand bibliographies. Prelim. ed. Wellington, the Association, 1967. iv, 58p.

Lists under subject headings 315 bibliographies concerned

....(contd.)

with aspects of New Zealand - 'its history, government and literature, its economic, industrial and scientific activities, and so on' (*Preface*). *Class No:* 908(931)(009)

Bibliographies

[5064]

GROVER, R.F. **New Zealand.** Santa Barbara, California and Oxford, Clio Press, 1981. xxxvii, 254p. + 2p. maps, index. £27.95; $36.25. (*World Bibliographical Series, No.18.*) ISBN: 0903450313.

878 annotated entries. 40 sections: The country and people - Geography ... History of the Pacific - Prehistory and archaeology - History of New Zealand ... Maori people ... Politics ... Libraries, art galleries, museums and archives ... Encyclopedias and directories - Bibliographies. *Class No:* 908(931)(01)

[5065]

HOCKEN, T.M. **A Bibliography of the literature relating to New Zealand.** Wellington, Newrick Associates, 1973. xii, 619p.

Originally published by J. Mackay, Government Printer, 1909.

Arranged chronologically, 1643-1909 (p. 1-487), with a Maori bibliography appended (p.499-547). About 4,000 annotated entries; index of authors and subjects. *Supplement to Hocken's Bibliography of New Zealand Literature*, compiled by A.H. Johnstone (Auckland, Whitcombe & Tombs, 1927. ii, 73p.) adds items (unannotated) for the period 1694-1909, plus 'Principal additions to New Zealand literature since 1909' (p.50-59). Index of authors and subjects.

Further supplemented, for the period up to 1909, by L.J.B. Chapple's *Bibliographical brochure containing addenda and corrigenda to extant bibliographies of New Zealand literature* (Dunedin, Read, 1938. 47p.). *Class No:* 908(931)(01)

[5066]

MARTIN, M.S. **'New Zealand at 150',** a sesquicentennial booklist, *Choice*, v.27, no.9, May 1990, p.1460-4.

Running commentary with consolidated list of books mentioned on political, historical and social issues (including race and the environment). *Class No:* 908(931)(01)

[5067]

New Zealand a basic annotated bibliography for students, librarians, and general readers. Nesbitt, M., *comp*. London, Commonwealth Institute Staff & Research Library, 1988. vi,62p. sd. (*Commonwealth Institute Bibliographies Series.*) ISBN: 094614043x. ISSN: 03061124.

16 sections *e.g.* General books ... History ... Natural environment. 'A dominant theme in this selection is the description and analysis of the intense social and economic changes of the 1980's. (*Introduction*). *Class No:* 908(931)(01)

Encyclopaedias

[5068]

The Illustrated encyclopedia of New Zealand. McLauchlan, G., *ed.* Auckland, David Bateman, 1990. Distributed in North America by G.K. Hall. 1448p. $75. ISBN: 0869530071, US.

Expanded version of *The Bateman New Zealand*

....(contd.)

encyclopedia (2nd ed. 1988).

*c.*2500 articles cover all aspects of New Zealand life. Chronology of New Zealand history to the end of 1988. Entirely redesigned with pages divided into 3 columns. 2,200 colour and 800 black and white illustrations. Good index serves cross-reference role. 'Articles are well developed, readable, and much more extensive than in *Bateman*' (*Booklist*, v.87, no.6, 15 November 1990. p.682). *Class No:* 908(931)(031)

[5069]

McLINTOCK, A.H., *ed*. **An Encyclopaedia of New Zealand.** Wellington, Owen, Government Printer, 3v., 1966. illus., tables, maps.

Signed articles by *c.*350 countributors, usually with references (*e.g.* 'Otago province': 6½p. 4 maps, 6 references; 'Welfare services'; 4p. 5 references). Some 700 biographies, including 'Expatriates - Biographies' (v.1, p.575-604). The 500 maps are a feature. 96 plates in all, with 3, 4 or 6 illus. per page; also numerous small text illustrations. Analytical index. v.3, p.713-843. Well produced. *Class No:* 908(931)(031)

Yearbooks & Directories

[5070]

New Zealand official yearbook 1993 Te pukapuka Houanga Whaimana o Aotearoa. 96th ed. Auckland, Department of Statistics, 1993. xii,561p. illus., col. maps, tables, diagrs., bibliogs., index. $49.50. ISSN: 00780170.

1st ed. 1893.

Compendium of facts and figures on all aspects of New Zealand's social, economic and cultural life presented in 23 sections: 1. Geography - 2. Government ... 11. Leisure and tourism ... 14. Land and environment, each with its own bibliography. Analytical index. This edition commemorates centenary of women suffragettes. *Class No:* 908(931)(058)

Libraries

[5071]

Australian and New Zealand studies papers presented at a colloquium at the British Library 7-9 February 1984. McLaren-Turner, P., *ed*. London, The British Library, 1985. [x] 213p. £13.95. (*British Library Occasional Papers.*) ISBN: 0712300481.

31 papers mainly devoted to the resources of the British Library and other UK research libraries. *Class No:* 908(931):061:026/027

[5072]

BLOOMFIELD, V. **Resources for Australian and New Zealand studies** a guide to library holdings in the United Kingdom. London, Australian Studies Centre, Institute of Commonwealth Studies, University of London & The British Library, 1986. xvi, 284p. bibliog. index. pbk. £14.95. ISBN: 0712301224.

Detailed description of relevant holdings of printed and audio-visual material of 172 libraries and other institutions. Subject coverage is concentrated on the humanities and social sciences. Main purpose is to facilitate access to research resources for scholars and others. Arrangements is A-Z by place and institution. Bibliography p.264. Analytical index. 'It should ... be added to the basic reference stock or

....*(contd.)*

the directory collection of any library, and its publication is to be warmly welcomed' (*Library Association Record*, v.89, no.6, June 1987, p.292). *Class No:* 908(931):061:026/027

[5073]
—BLOOMFIELD, V. 'Resources for Australian and New Zealand studies in the United Kingdom', p. 67-75, *Australian and New Zealand studies* (The British Library, 1985).

Based on information collected for a *Guide to resources for Australian and New Zealand studies in the United Kingdom*. *Class No:* 908(94):061:026/027

Melanesia

Bibliographies

[5074]
EDRIDGE, S. **Solomon Islands bibliography up to 1980.** Suva Institute of Pacific Studies, University of the South Pacific; Wellington, Alexander Turnbull Library; Honiara, Sol. Is., National Library, 1985. xvi, 476p. maps on endpapers, index. ISBN: 0908702035.

Books, pamphlets and periodical articles published within Solomon Islands, or relating to them, arranged as a classifed catalogue. All works published by Solomon Islanders are included regardless of subject. *Class No:* 908(932)(01)

[5075]
O'REILLY, P. **Bibliographie méthodique, analytique et critique de la Nouvelle - Calédonie.** Paris, Musée de l'Homme: 1955. 361p. index. (*Publications de la Société des Océanistes; no.4.*)

4181 items published 1774-1954 covering all aspects of New Caledonia's life and history - geography, geology, zoology, botany, ethnology, economy, literature *etc.* 'Still a valuable comprehensive annotated bibliography' (G.W. Fry and R. Mauricio *Pacific Basin and Oceania*, 1987. Entry 566). *Class No:* 908(932)(01)

[5076]
—PISIER, G. Bibliographie méthodique, analytique et critique de la Nouvelle - Calédonie 1955-1982. Nouméa, Publications de la Société Études Historiques de la Nouvelle - Calédonie; 1983. 350p. illus., indexes.

Modelled on P. O'Reilly's *Bibliographie ... de la Nouvelle - Calédonie* (1955) which it updates.

3338 references. 20 Sections: 1. Bibliography and general reference works - 2. Geography ... 11. History ... 18. Periodical publications .. *etc.* Author, place and subject indexes. *Class No:* 908(932)(01)

[5077]
O'REILLY, P. **Bibliographie méthodique, analytique et critique des îles Wallis et Futuna.** Paris, Musée de l'Homme, 1964. 68p. (*Publications de la Société des Océanistes, no.13.*)

491 items in subject divisions *e.g.* Geography and climate; Ethnology; History *etc.*, 'This carefully annotated and comprehensive bibliography' (G.W. Fry and R. Mauricio *Pacific Basin and Oceania*. 1987. Entry 1157). *Class No:* 908(932)(01)

[5078]
O'REILLY, P. **Bibliographie méthodique, analytique et critique des Nouvelles-Hébrides.** Paris, Musée de l'Homme, 1958. 305p. (*Publications de la Société des Océanistes; no.8.*)

Mostly annotated entries relating to all aspects of the islands. 'A comprehensive bibliography' (G.W. Fry and R. Mauricio. *Pacific Basin and Oceania*, 1987, Entry 631). *Class No:* 908(932)(01)

Australia

[5079]
ORDONNAUD, G. *and* SÉRIEYX, A. **Australie 88** Bicentenaire ou naissance. Paris. Éditons France-Empire, 1988. Published under the auspices of the Institut du Pacifique and the Comité Français Pour Le Bicentaire De L'Australie. 464p. maps, tables, bibliog. ISBN: 2704805709.

Over 30 contributors (mostly French or Australian). 46 chapters in 4 major sections: 1. Vie et société - 2. Economie -3. Environnement international - 4. La France et L'Australie. Orientation Bibliographique p.452-60. *Class No:* 908(94)

[5080]
Reader's Digest country Australia the land and the people. Sydney, Reader's Digest, 1989. col. illus., diagrs., col. maps. $45.00. ISBN: 0864380526.

Over 800 A-Z entries relating to Australian history, wildlife, lore and legends illustrated with 1300 photographs *etc*. *Class No:* 908(94)

Bibliographies

[5081]
CLINCH, M.A. **Guide to Northern Territory research resources in Northern Territory collections.** Darwin, North Australia Research Unit of the Australian National Univ., 1981. ix, 374p. maps, bibliog.

5 major parts: 1. Directory of collections - 2. Finding list (8200 A-Z by author entries with locations) - 3. Union list of Northern Territory newspapers - 4. Appendices (including B. Brief chronology of the Northern Territory p. 359-62). Maps p.369-74. Bibliography p.374. 'Starting point for anyone ... who wants to find out something about the Territory' (*Foreword*). *Class No:* 908(94)(01)

[5082]
CUMPSTON, J. **Macquarie Islands** a bibliography. Gemorne, New South Wales, The Stone Copying Co., 1958. ii, 32p. map. sd. *Class No:* 908(94)(01)

[5083]
KEPARS, I. **Australia.** Santa Barbara, California and Oxford, Clio Press, 1985. xvii, 289p. + 2p. map, index. £40.95; $43.50. (*World Bibliographical Series, no. 46.*) ISBN: 0903450836.

A revised editgion is announced for publication 1994 ISBN 185109122x.

964 annotated entries. 43 sections: The country and people - Geography ... History ... Defence and military history ... Immigrants and ethnic groups - Australian Aborigines ... Libraries and Museums - Reference works. Author, title and subject index. *Class No:* 908(94)(01)

[5084]

MILLS, C.M. A Bibliography of the Northern Territory. Canberra, College of Advanced Education Library, 1977-. ISBN: 0858990607, set.

1. *Monographs. Pt.1. Sciences, primary industry and recreation.* 1977. xiv, 168p. index. 0858990615. 1236 entries in 12 sections including C. Geography and L. Maps and atlases.

2. *General, Travels, History, Humanities and religion.* 1978. xvi, 465p. index. 0858990828. Over 2000 entries in 15 sections *e.g.* M. General, travels - N. Bibliographies and catalogues - O. History - P. Biographies - Q. Journals, diaries, logs, letters - R. Exploration and survey.

3. *The Social Sciences (excluding material relating to the Aborigines)* 1981, xxii, 174p. 0858990913. 848 entries in 9 sections. Summary of Northern Territory historical events p.xi-xvii.

4. *The Aborigines; plus supplementary entries to Pts. 1-3, to 1981 and consolidated index to the complete bibliography,* 2v., 1983. xii, 751p. 08589902324. 2623 entries in 21 sections including AG. Prehistory and archaeology ... AL. Bibliography - AM. Tribes. Index p.609-751.

Class No: 908(94)(01)

Encyclopaedias

[5085]

The Angus & Robertson concise Australian encyclopedia. rev. ed. North Ryde, New South Wales, Angus and Robertson, 1986. 505p. col. illus., tables, col. maps, index. ISBN: 0207153051.

First published 1983.

Almost 1000 cross referenced entries illuminating the most significant geographical, historical, cultural, social, political and commercial events that have shaped modern Australia. Suitable for home and school use. *Class No:* 908(94)(031)

[5086]

The Australian encyclopaedia. 4th ed. Sydney, Grolier Society of Australia, 12v., 1983. illus. (many col.), maps, diagrs. ISBN: 0959660429.

First published 1925/26. 3rd. ed. 1977.

A comprehensive picture of Australia and its people both past and present. V.12 *Index and Appendix* (p.1-86) includes lists of awards, sporting achievements, and statistical data. 100 new topics in this edition not counting biographical entries. *Class No:* 908(94)(031)

[5087]

The Australian people: an encyclopedia of the nation, its people and their origins. Jupp, J., *gen. ed.* North Ryde, New South Wales, Angus & Robertson, 1988. xvi, 1040p. illus. (some col.), bibliog., tables, index. Aust$80.00; £47.75. ISBN: 0207154279.

250 Contributors. 290 articles deployed in 4 main sections: 1. Aspects of the peopling of Australia (The Aboriginals and the convict period; Imperial settlement; Immigration since the Second World War) - 2. Australian Aborigines (Society; Culture; Economy; Politics *etc.,*) - 3. The Settlers (Afghans to Yugoslavs) - 4. Immigrants and immigration. Appendix 1. 1986 Census data - 2. Chronology (p.973-978). Bibliography p.979-1022. Supported by Australian Bicentennial Authority to lend a multicultural dimension to the Bicentennial publications. For general and academic use. *Class No:* 908(94)(031)

[5088]

The Bateman concise encyclopaedia of Australia. Shaw, J., *ed.* 2nd ed. Bunderim, Queensland, David Bateman. Distributed in North America by G.K. Hall. xxvi, 848p. illus (some col.), col. maps. Aust $39.93; US$54.95. ISBN: 0949135232.

1st ed. 1984 as *Collins Australian encyclopedia.*

Popular, family reference work containing over 1000 cross-referenced articles. Few changes from 1984 edition. *Class No:* 908(94)(031)

[5089]

The Cambridge encyclopedia of Australia. Bambrick, S., *ed.* Cambridge, Cambridge Univ. Press, 1994. 400p. illus., col. maps, tables. £35. (*Cambridge World Encyclopedias Series.*) ISBN: 0521365112.

70 contributors. 8 major sections examine all the key aspects of the continent, past and present: the physical environment, traditional aboriginal society, history since European contact, economy, society, government, culture and the arts, and scientific research. Individual states receive individual attention, but the emphasis throughout is on Australia-wide trends and the way these interact with developments in the world outside, in North America and Europe quite as much as in the Pacific. *Class No:* 908(94)(031)

Yearbooks & Directories

[5090]

Year book Australia 1992. 75th ed. Canberra, Australian Bureau of Statistics, 1991. xii,802p. illus. (some col.), maps, tables, bibliogs. ISSN: 03124746.

First published 1908. Title varies.

28 chapters: 1. Geography and climate - 2. Government - 3. The territories of Australia (Northern Territory, Australian Capital Territory, Norfolk Is., Heard and McDonald Is., Australian Antarctic Territory, Cocos (Keeling) Is., Christmas Is., Coral Sea Is.) Analytical index. 'A continuous record of government policies, international relationships and a concise statistical summary of every facet of Australia's economy and society' *Class No:* 908(94)(058)

Aborigines

Bibliographies

[5091]

THAWLEY, J. *and* **GAUCI, S. Bibliographies on the Australian aborigines** an annotated listing. 2nd ed. Bundoora, Victoria, The Borchardt Library, La Trobe Univ., 1987. v, 44p. index. softcover. ISBN: 0858166623.

1st ed. 1979.

163 entries A-Z by author with subject and geographical index. *Class No:* 908(94)(=995)(01)

Papua—New Guinea

Bibliographies

[5092]

McCONNELL, F. Papua New Guinea. Santa Barbara, California and Oxford, Clio Press, 1988. xxviii, 379p. map, index. £49.95; $55.00. (*World Bibliographical Series, no. 90.*) ISBN: 1851090304.

865 well-annotated entries. 33 sections: The country and its people - Geography ... Prehistory and archaeology -

....*(contd.)*

History - Biographies ... Libraries, museums and archives ... Encyclopaedias, directories and reference works - Bibliographies. Publishers and research institutions p.xxvii-xxviii. *Class No:* 908(954)(01)

[5093]
SACK, P.G., *ed.* **German New Guinea** a bibliography. Canberra, Department of Law, Research School of Social Sciences, Australian National Univ., 1980. 298p. ISBN: 0909596456.

About 3,000 entries A-Z by author relating to German-language literature published 1884-1914. List of periodicals p.288-298. A comprehensive bibliographical essay on the various types of published sources on German New Guinea introduces the main sequence. *Class No:* 908(954)(01)

Encyclopaedias

[5094]
The Encyclopedia of Papua and New Guinea. Ryan, P., *ed.* Melbourne Univ. Press in association with the Univ. of Papua and New Guinea, 2v. and index. 1231p.+83p. illus., maps and index.

About 200 contributors; signed articles. 'Art' (v.1, p.20-50): over 1 column of references; cross-references, 'Port Moresby'; 3½ cols. of bibliographies. V.3 has detailed index, p.33-83; gazetteer of place-names; 10 colour lift out maps. *Choice* (v.9, no.12, February 1973, p.1572) commends the biographical articles as being more evaluative than in most encyclopaedias. Well written and well produced. At various times the prospect of updating the encyclopedia has been discussed but to no avail. *Class No:* 908(954)(031)

Polynesia

Bibliographies

[5095]
DE RIETZ, R. **Bibliotheca Polynesia:** a catalogue of some of the books in the Polynesiana collection formed by the late Bjarne Kroepelian and now in the University Library Oslo. Stockholm, Almquist & Wiksell, 1969. 455p.

'Meticulous analysis of over 1300 items (*TLS*, no.3,564, 18 June 1970, p.669). *Class No:* 908(96)(01)

[5096]
HANSON, F.A. *and* O'REILLY, P., *eds.* **Bibliographie de Rapa, Polynésie Française.** Paris, Musée de l'Homme, 1973. (*Publications de la Société des Océanistes; no.32.*)

259 entries, many annotated. *Class No:* 908(96)(01)

[5097]
HOLMES, L.D., *comp.* **Samoan Islands bibliography.** Wichita, Kansas, Poly Concepts Publishing Co., 1984. vi, 329p. $85.00. ISBN: 0915203006.

A-Z by author entries divided into 44 subject areas *e.g.* Archaeology; Biography; Discovery and Exploration; Geography; History. 'Complex bibliographic entries require considerable disentanglement' (*Choice*, v.22, no.9. May 1985, p.1305). *Class No:* 908(96)(01)

[5098]
O'REILLY, P. *and* REITMAN, R. **Bibliographie de la Tahiti et de la Polynésie française.** Paris, Musée de l'Homme, 1967. 1046p. index. (*Publications de la Société des Océanistes; no.14.*)

10,501 annotated items organized under by subject *e.g.* Bibliographies; Voyages; Geography; Ethnology; History. *Class No:* 908(96)(01)

Encyclopaedias

[5099]
L'Encyclopédie de la Polynésie. Salvat, B, *and others, eds.* Papeete, Christian Gleizal-Multipress, 9v., 1986-1988.

100 contributors. Covers 118 islands but concentrates largely on French possessions. V.1-3 are concernned with the physical environment, climate etc.; v.4-5 consider Polynesian civilization before the arrival of European expeditions; v.6-7 deal with the colonization of Polynesia; whilst v.8-9 focus on the period 1960-1987, especially upon political affairs, new institutions such as L'Université du Pacifique, and the establishment of an economy based on tourism. 4000 col. illus. 'Cette Encyclopédie ... réunit une documentation considérable présentée de façon très agréable, avec notamment une iconographie très abondante, très variée et de grande qualité' (*Cahiers D'Outre-Mer*, no.170, Avril-Juin 1990, p.208). *Class No:* 908(96)(031)

Fiji

Bibliographies

[5100]
SNOW, P.A. **A Bibliography of Fiji, Tonga and Rotuma.** Canberra, Australian National Univ. Press, 1969. xliii,418p. maps.

Over 10,000 entries. Fiji (p.80-295) has 63 sections (1. Bibliography - 2. Biography - 3. Research - 4. Origins and migrations ... 62. Philately). Alphabetical index of names, p.357-418. List of journals and bibliography precede. 'So comprehensive that it should be classified as a national bibliography' (*Library Journal*, v.94,no.21, 1 December 1969, p.4420-1). *Class No:* 908(961.1)(01)

Micronesia

Bibliographies

[5101]
MARSHALL, M. *and* NASON, J.D. **Micronesia 1944-1974** a bibliography of anthropological and related materials concerning Micronesia since World War II. New Haven, Connecticut, HRAF Press, 1976. 337p. maps.

About 2,000 entries, under authors A-Z. Covers Caroline, Mariana and Marshall Islands group, but not the Gilbert Islands. Includes unpublished papers and doctoral theses, but not government and US documents. Indexed by geographical and topical codes. Wide-ranging subject coverage. 'For all research and four-year academic libraries' (*Choice*, v.13, no.7, September 1976, p.798, on which this annotation is based). *Class No:* 908(965)(01)

Hawaii

Bibliographies

[5102]
**BERNICE P. BISHOP MUSEUM. HONOLULU.
Dictionary catalog of the Library of the Bernice P.
Bishop Museum.** Boston, Mass., G.K. Hall, 9v., 1964.
First Supplement 1967. Second Supplement, 1969.
6443p.+676p.+239p. $890.00. Export $1075.00. ISBN:
0816106797.

First Supplement 1 reel. $120.00 (Export $145.00). ISBN
081611448x) and *Second Supplement* reel. $110.00
($121.00). ISBN 0816114498) are now available only on
microfilm. In total 154,100 photolithographed cards. A rich
source of information pertaining to Polynesia, Micronesia
and Melanesia. *Class No:* 908(969)(01)

[5103]
MORRIS, N.J. *and* **DEAN, L.,** *comps.* **Hawai'i.** Santa
Barbara, Calif., and Oxford, Clio Press, 1992. xxxv,324p.
+2p. map. indexes. £49. (*World Bibliographical Series, no.
146.*) ISBN: 1851091750.

812 annotated entries in 36 sections: The islands and the
people - Geography ... Prehistory and archaeology - History
- Voyaging - Maritime history - Specific islands ...
Bibliographies. Chronology p. xxi-xxxv. Author, title and
subject indexes. *Class No:* 908(969)(01)

[5104]
UNIVERSITY OF HAWAII Sinclair Library. **Dictionary
catalog of the Hawaiian Collection.** Boston, Mass., G.K.
Hall, 4v., 1963. 3278p. $355.00 (Export $430.00). ISBN:
0816106509.

68,000 cards, photolithographically reproduced on 3278
pages, representing the world's largest and most complete
collection of Hawaiiana; more than 42,000 items. Includes
Hawaiian government documents since 1915, and over 1,500
Hawaiian serials. *Class No:* 908(969)(01)

Polar Regions

Reviews & Abstracts

[5105]
Polar and glaciological abstracts. Cambridge, Cambridge
University Press, 1990-. Quarterly. £24.00 (Individuals.
£32.00 (Institutions). ISSN: 09575073.

Abstracting service offering comprehensive coverage of
the world's polar regions scanning over 900 serials plus
relevant books, reports and theses. Each issue contains
author, subject and geographic indexes cumulated annually.
Archaeology, history and expeditions and exploration are 3
specialized areas included. *Class No:* 908(98/99)(048)

Arctic

Bibliographies

[5106]
KING, H.G.R. The Arctic. Santa Barbara, California and
Oxford, Clio Press, 1989. xvi, 272p. + 3p. map, indexes.
£39.50; $55.00. (*World Bibliographical Series, no. 99.*)
ISBN: 185109072x.

935 annotated entries. 37 sections: The Arctic Region in
General - Geography ... Prehistory and archaeology -
History - Biographies of Arctic explorers ... Arctic peoples

....(contd.)

... Expedition planning and survival ... Libraries, museums,
archives and academic institutions - Bibliographies -
Svalbard - Jan Mayen - Greenland - Arctic Canada - Alaska
- Soviet Asia/Siberia - Scandinavian Arctic and Lapland -
The Arctic Ocean. Author, subject and title indexes.
Class No: 908(98)(01)

Greenland

[5107]
Greenland past and present. Hertling, K., *and other eds.*
Copenhagen, Edvard Henriksen, n.d. 370p. illus., (some
col.pl.).

31 sections by a variety of hands: Geography of Greenland
- Mapping of Greenland ... History of Greenland since the
time of Hans Egede - Exploration... Life in Greenland.
Internal evidence would indicate a publication date in the
1970s. *Class No:* 908(988)

Bibliographies

[5108]
HØYER, B., *ed.* **Groenlandica. Catalogue of Groenlandica
collection in the National Library of Greenland.** Nuuk,
Nunatta Atnagaateqarfia, 1986. 585p. indexes.

Annotated. Books in Greenlandic - Books on Greenland
and the Arctic. Alphabetical and subject indexes.
Class No: 908(988)(01)

[5109]
MILLER, K.E., *comp.* **Greenland.** Santa Barbara, Calif.,
and Oxford, Clio Press, 1991. xix,111p. +1p. map. index.
£18.95. (*World Bibliographical Series, no. 125.*) ISBN:
1851091394.

375 annotated entries in 18 sections: Greenland and its
people - Explorations - Geography and geology ...
Prehistory and archaeology - History ... Foreign relations ...
Libraries and museums ... Bibliographies. Author, title and
subject index. *Class No:* 908(988)(01)

Antarctic

[5110]
TRIGGS, G.D., *ed.* **The Antarctic Treaty regime:** law,
environment and resources. Cambridge Univ. Press, 1987.
xxii,239p. diagrs., tables, map, bibliog. £30. (*Studies in
Polar Research.*) ISBN: 0521327660.

24 papers from the Proceedings of a conference organized
by the British Institute of International and Comparative
Law, April 1985, examine the legal structure established by
the Treaty and discuss the legal, political and environmental
issues involved. Bibliography (by topic) p.234-5.

A similar work is *The Antarctic legal regime,* edited by
C.C. Joyner and S.K. Chopra, Dordrecht, Martinus Nijhoff,
1985, xi,288p. map, index. This includes 11 papers by
different hands in 2 sections: Law and politics and Resource
regimes and environmental protection. *Class No:* 908(99)

Bibliographies

[5111]

Australian Antarctic bibliography. Hobart, Institute of Antarctic and Southern Ocean Studies, Univ. of Tasmania, 1987. v, 463p. in spiral binding. ISBN: 0859013707.

8 sections: 1. General (expeditions, voyages, travel) - 2. Atmospheric physics - 3. Bases and logistics - 4. Biological sciences - 5. Terrestial sciences - 6. Oceanography - 7. Medical sciences - 8. Socio-economic sciences. No annotation. Relates to Australian Antarctic Territory and the Heard, Macquarie, and McDonald Islands.
Class No: 908(99)(01)

[5112]

HAYTON, R.D. National interests in Antarctica an annotated bibliography. Washington, US Government Printing Office for the US Antarctica Projects Officer, 1959. 137p. map.

Records documents which 'report, assert, interpret, limit or pretend to influence the interests of nations in these regions' (*Introduction*). Arranged A-Z by 28 countries.
Class No: 908(99)(01)

91 Geography, Exploration, Travel

Geography & Travel

Bibliographies

[5113]

A Bibliography of geographic thought. Brown, C.L. *and* Wheeler, J.O., *comps*. Westport, Conn., Greenwood Press, 1989. x,521p. indexes. $55. (*Bibliographies and Indexes in Geography, no.1*.) ISBN: 0313268991. ISSN: 10448349.

A revised and expanded edition of Wheeler's *Bibliography on geographic thought* (1983).

6,196 citations (over 5,500 articles and 453 books listed separately) divided into 9 subsections: 1. Biography - 2. Geography - 3. Geography in other countries - 4. Techniques and models - 5. Philosophy - 6. The profession - 7. Subdisciplines - 8. Applied geography - 9. Educational. Author, subject and biographical indexes. 'Represents an impressive benchmark that documents a lengthy and proud record of geographical scholarship' (*Bulletin, Special Libraries Association Geographical and Map Division*, no.162, December 1990, p.43-4). *Class No: 91.0(01)*

[5114]

GREAT BRITAIN. National Maritime Museum. Catalogue of the library. London. H.M. Stationery Office, 1968-. illus., ports., facsims., maps.

1.*Voyages & travel.* 1968. xi,403p. 2. *Biography.* 2v., 1969. 501p.475p. ISBN 0112900046. 3. *Atlases & cartography.* 2v., 1971. vi,lx, 1166p. 0112900585. 4. *Piracy & privateering.* 1972. ix,175p. 0112901190. 5. *Naval history. pt.1: The Middle Ages to 1815.* 1977. 218p. 0118807609. V.1 has 1,240 numbered entries, usually with annotations or bibliographical notes. Sections (each preceded by a chronological table): Collective voyages - Circumnavigations (items 17-125, chronologically) Africa - America - East Indies - Europe and Mediterranean - Far East - Pacific - Polar: Arctic - Polar: Antarctic - General voyages. Detailed index; index of ships. Well produced. *Class No: 91.0(01)*

[5115]

NELSON, T. and GROSS, A. Good books for the curious traveler. Boulder, Colorado, Johnson Books, 1989. indexes. pbk. $12.95 each.

1. *Europe.* ix, 326p. ISBN 155566038x. 2. *Asia and the South Pacific.* vii, 312p. 1555660401. More than 400 reviews (Europe) and over 350 (Asia) of in print books; mostly published in the 1980s, grouped in 13 and 11 geographical sections subdivided thematically viz. General; Anthropology and archaeology; art and architecture; Cuisine; History; Nature; Performing arts; Young peoples books. For the impending or arm-chair traveller. 'There are some wonderful suggestions and insights in these brightly written reviews (*Booklist*, v.86, no.3, 1 October 1989, p.256). *Class No: 91.0(01)*

Exploration & Travel

[5116]

Guinness book of explorers and exploration. Gavet-Imbert, M., *ed*. Enfield, Mdx., Guinness Publishing, 1991. 285p. col. illus., col. maps, index. £19.95. ISBN: 0851129730.

12 contributors. Recounts travels, discoveries and explorations in 11 historical and continental sections: 1. Antiquity - 2. Medieval adventures - 3. Islamic travellers - 4/8. by continent - 9. The Poles - 10. Mountains and oceans, caves and volcanoes - 11. Space. *Class No: 910*

Bibliographies

[5117]

COX, E.G. A Reference guide to the literature of travel including voyages, geographical descriptions, adventures, shipwrecks and expeditions. Seattle, Univ. of Washington, 3v., 1935-49. Reprinted Westport, Connecticut, Greenwood Press, 1970. $125.00. ISBN: 0837125065, v.1; 0837121620, v.2.

1. *The Old World.* 1935. 2. *The New World.* 1938. 3. *Great Britain.* 1949. Source material is covered up to 1800. Entries, usually annotated are arranged chronologically under sea or subject. V.3 includes chapters on maps and charts, general reference books, and bibliographies. Indexes of personal names in v.2 (covering v.1-2) and v.3. *Class No: 910(01)*

[5118]

MIDDLETON, D. 'Guide to the publications of the Royal Geographical Society 1830-1892', *Geographical Journal*, v.144,no.1, March 1978, p.99-116.

Bibliographical essay on the coverage of the progress of world geographical discovery in the *Journal* and *Proceedings* of The Royal Geographcial Society. *Class No: 910(01)*

Encyclopaedias

[5119]

DELPAR, H., ed. The Discoverers an encyclopedia of explorers and exploration. New York, McGraw-Hill, 1980. viii,471p. illus., ports, facsims, maps. £45.00. ISBN: 0070162646.

28 contributors (5 British). 250 signed articles, with brief bibliographies appended, on world exploration since the 15th century, 'Aerial exploration' ... 'Zagoskin'. 'Maritime exploration': p.225-38; 18 references; 6 cross-references. 'Literature and exploration': p.209-17; quotations; 13 references. 'Women in travel and exploration' has 5 ports. and 18 references. Includes entries under continents and countries. Emphasis on Western European discoverers. 'The volume is beautifully illustrated with photographs,

....(contd.)

engravings, maps and other reproductions' (*Current Geographical Publications*, v.43, no.5, May 1980, p.396). *Class No:* 910(031)

Handbooks & Manuals

[5120]

DAY, A.E. Discovery and exploration: a reference handbook. The Old World. London and New York, K.G. Saur - Clive Bingley, 1980. 295p. £22.50. ISBN: 0851572561, UK; 0896641791, US.

Covers the continents of Europe, Asia and Africa, 455 entries, A-Z, over half of them biographical (Livingstone: nearly 4p.: Marco Polo: 2p.). Also entries for associations, institutions (*e.g.* Hakluyt Society and its publications: 13p.), book and periodical titles. Regional index of discovery and exploration, including names of explorers, books, etc: index of titles. Aimed at sixth form and undergraduate students specialising. 'It will guide young students directly to the more available and useful English printed sources' (*British Book News*, September 1980, p.569). *Class No:* 910(035)

Maps & Atlases

[5121]

Atlas of Columbus and the great discoveries. Nebenzahl, K. Chicago, Rand McNally, 1990. 168p. illus (some col.), maps (some col.), bibliog. $75. col. maps, bibliog. ISBN: 052883407x.

50 late 15th century and early 16th century maps depicting contemporary geographical knowledge and speculation of the world's oceans and new lands. Each map is accompanied by a short documented essay. *Class No:* 910(084.3)

[5122]

DEBENHAM, F. Discovery and exploration: an atlas history of men's journeys into the unknown. London, Hamlyn, 1960. 272p. illus., maps.

Maps, arranged by continents, show well-plotted itineraries of explorers. Brief biographies: gazetteer section. 'Books about explorers and exploration' (p.246-51). General, analytical index. Appropriate and unusual illus. Particularly suitable for upper forms of secondary schools. *Class No:* 910(084.3)

[5123]

NEWBY, E. The Mitchell Beazley world atlas of exploration. London, Mitchell Beazley, 1975. 288p. illus., facsims., ports., plans, maps.

Some full-page, 3-colour maps, but the maps are an adjunct to text and illus. 'South America: a land of scientists', p.180-9 (11 illus., 3 ports., 3 maps). Concludes with 'The last frontier' (outer space), p.266-7; and 'Men of the world' (listing over 600 explorers, subdivided by continents, 6 illus., 9 maps). Bibliography (by continents), p.274-5. Index, p.176-88. Over 600 illus. Page size:29x23cm. 'If it is not strictly speaking an "atlas", it is still a highly desirable book' (*Bulletin of the Society of University Cartographers*, v.13,no.1, 1979, p.63). *Class No:* 910(084.3)

[5124]

ROBERTS, G. Atlas of discovery. London, Aldus Books, 1973. 192p. illus., facsims., maps.

13 chapters (1-3: chronological, from primitive times to first navigation of the world; 4-11: geographical by regions; 12-13: investigation of ocean and of space). 120 well-coloured physical maps, with itineraries plainly marked. Index includes 431 explorers' names. 'A convenient and reasonably priced source of information not readily available in more sophisticated historical atlases' (*RQ*, v.14,no.1, Fall 1974, p.70). *Class No:* 910(084.3)

[5125]

The Times atlas of world exploration. Fernández-Armesto, F., *ed.* London, Times Books, 1991. 286p. col. illus., col. maps, facsims, index. £35. ISBN: 0723003440.

18 contributors. 46 chapters arranged in 12 mainly continent and ocean sections. Chronology in continent time bands p.10-15. Glossary of technical terms p.243-4. Biographical glossary (*c.*400 explorers) p.245-72. Index of place-names (over 12,000 entries) p.273-86. Facsimiles of over 180 period maps and 130 specially commissioned topographical maps showing discovery and exploration routes. Excellent atlas covering over 3,000 years of exploration. Generally superior to *Royal Geographical Society history of world exploration* (*qv*) but with inexplicable omission of any sort of bibliographical apparatus apart from list of antique maps reproduced in the *Atlas* with their sources. *Class No:* 910(084.3)

Histories

[5126]

BAKER, J.N.L. A History of geographical discovery and exploration. 2nd ed. London, Harrap, 1937. 552p. diagrs., maps.

Quotes original sources: liberal maps; valuable bibliographies; full index. The standard work on the subject. *Class No:* 910(091)

[5127]

BEAZLEY, C.R. The Dawn of modern geography: a history of exploration and geographical science ... London, John Murray, 3v., 1897-1906. Reprinted Gloucester, Massachusetts, Peter Smith, 1964.

Part 1: 'from the conversion of the Roman Empire to A.D.900. with an account of the achievement and writings of the early Christian and Chinese travellers and students'. Part 2: from the close of the 9th to the mid-13th century (*c.*A.D.900-1266). Part 3: 1260-1420. with appendix on the leading MS of the principal texts in pts.2 and 3. and an analytical index. Numerous footnote references. A scholarly study. *Class No:* 910(091)

Biographies

[5128]

BAKER, D.B., *ed.* **Explorers and discoverers of the world.** Detroit, Gale Research, 1993. xli,637p. illus., maps, bibliogs., index. ISBN: 0810354217.

Biographies of 320 world explorers in single A-Z sequence. Entries (1-4p. in length) examine historical significance and consequences of discoveries and explorations. Political, economic, and religious contexts assessed. Select bibliography for each entry. Chronology of exploration p.xvii-xxiii (by area). *Class No:* 910(092)

Pacific Ocean

[5129]
BADGER, G. **The Explorers of the Pacific.** Kenthurst, Kangaroo Press, 1988. 248p. illus. (some col.), maps, bibliog., index. ISBN: 0864172117.

Historical narrative in 21 chapters with 8 appendices. Notes p.230-5. Bibliography p.236-42. *Class No:* 910(265)

[5130]
MARTIN, M.S. 'The Other ocean: the discovery and exploration of the Pacific', *Choice*, v.30, no.8, April 1993, p.1277-86.

Bibliographic essay covering non-European and European voyages, navigation, the people, exploration and science, culture contact, and literary responses. Works cited p.1284-6. *Class No:* 910(265)

Biographies

[5131]
DUNMORE, J. **Who's who in Pacific navigation.** Honolulu, Univ. of Hawaii Press, 1991. xvi,312p. bibliog., index. $34. ISBN: 0824813502.

Life and achievements of 256 British, Spanish, French and Dutch voyagers and researchers. Bibliography p.273-300. *Class No:* 910(265)(092)

Tibet

[5132]
WALKER, D. **The Pundits:** British exploration of Tibet and Central Asia. Lexington, Univ. Press of Kentucky, 1990. viii,327p. maps, bibliog., index. $30. ISBN: 081311666x.

Narrative account of the explorations and surveys of Nepal, Sikkim, Bhutan and Tibet, 1866-1885, undertaken by the 'Pundits', the trained native Indian personnel emploped by the Great Trigonometrical Survey of India. 7 maps. 'A major contribution to the history of exploration beyond the Indian frontiers' (*Geographical Journal*, v.157, no.1, March 1991, p.79). Accounts of the more important surveys were first published in the Survey's *General Reports* and subsequently collected in v.8 of the *Records of the Survey of India* (Dehra Dun, 1915). *Class No:* 910(515)

Africa

[5133]
CASADA, J.A. **An Annotated bibliography of exploration in Africa.** Oxford, Hans Zell, 1990. 400p. indexes. £48.00; $85.00. ISBN: 0905450272.

Covers African exploration from the earliest period to modern times and includes major articles as well as books. The emphasis is on English language material but significant works in other languages find a place. A substantial introduction investigates the present state of reference sources on African exploration. *Class No:* 910(6)

Antarctic

[5134]
FOGG, G.E. *and* SMITH, D. **The Explorations of Antarctica** the last unspoilt continent. London, Cassell, 1990. 224p. illus. (mostly col.), bibliog., index. £16.95; $24.95. ISBN: 0304318132.

Combines a history of Antarctic exploration with a

....(contd.)
description of the continent's geography, geology, and its continuing scientific and ecological significance. Bibliography p.218-21. Superbly illustrated. 7 maps. *Class No:* 910(99)

Women

[5135]
TINLING, M. **Women into the unknown** a sourcebook on women explorers and travellers. Westport, Conn., Greenwood Press, 1989. xxvi,356p. maps, bibliogs., index. $55. ISBN: 0313253285.

42 short biographical and travel essays each with a respectable bibliography. Appendix: Books of exploration and travel (written by women) in the English language p.314-42. Bibliography p.343-4. 9 maps. *Class No:* 910-0055.2

Planning & Field Work

[5136]
WINSER, S. *and* McWILLIAM, N. **Expedition planners' handbook and directory 1993-94.** London, Expedition Advisory Centre, Royal Geographical Society, 1992. 319p. illus., bibliogs. £12.95.

1. Expedition planning - 2. Organization - 3. Choosing expedition projects - 4. Scientific fieldwork - 5. Environmental logistics - 6. Expedition techniques - 7. Post-expedition responsibilities - 8. Appendices (Expedition Advisory Centre; Young Explorers Trust) - 9. Expedition Directories (reference sources; grant-giving organizations; equipment and services directory). *Class No:* 910.2

Expeditions, Voyages, Travel

[5137]
GREAT BRITAIN. Department of Health and the Central Office of Information. **Before you go** the traveller's guide to health. London, HMSO, 1989. For a free copy phone (in United Kingdom) 0800 555 777. Bulk copies may be ordered from Health Publications Unit, No.2 Site, Heywood Stores, Manchester Road, Heywood, Lancs., OL10 2PZ. 28p. col.illus., tables, index. sd. *gratis*.

Vital information for people preparing for overseas travel. Pt.1 Overseas in general: Plan well ahead; diseases & precautions; rabies; malaria warning; AIDS; additional vaccination advice; insure your health. Pt.2 Visiting the European Community: Emergency treatment in European Community countries *etc.,*. Information in this pamphlet is updated on Prestel p.50063. *Class No:* 910.4

[5138]
—GREAT BRITAIN. Department of Health and the Central Office of Information. **While you're away** the traveller's guide to health. London, HMSO., 1989. For a free copy phone (in United Kingdom) 0800 555 777. Bulk copies may be ordered from Health Publications Unit, No. 2 Site, Heywood Stores, Manchester Road, Heywood, Lancs., OL10 2PZ. 16p. col.illus. *gratis*.

Vital information on how to avoid getting ill and how to get urgent medical treatment. Pocket size pamphlet with smaller 20p. pamphlet *Health care for visitors to E.C. countries* inserted in back cover foldover. *Class No:* 910.4

[5139]
HARRINGTON, R. **Trouble-free travel:** an insider's guide. 2nd ed. London, WEXAS Ltd., 1987. 96p. illus., pbk. £2.75. ISBN: 0905802039.

1st ed. 1982.

14 chapters *e.g.* 2. Maps: the good and the bad ... 4. Money matters - 5. Travel tip-offs - 6. Visas: a bureaucratic jungle. Practical tips not for total beginners. 'It assumes you are already a 'traveller' - someone who avoids conventional package holidays like the plague and probably has some experience of independent travel in the Third World' (*Introduction*). *Class No:* 910.4

[5140]
KEAY, W. **Expedition guide.** London, The Duke of Edinburgh's Award, 1987. 208p. col.illus., diagrs., bibliog. £7.95. ISBN: 0905425014.

17 chapters (1. Equipment ... 5. Planning ... 7. First aid) providing guidance for trainers, supervisors and assessors, and instructions in expedition skills. Also contains the syllabus, conditions, Course Directors' and Tutors' notes for the Basic Expedition Training Award of the Central Council of Physical Recreation. Bibliography p.205. *Class No:* 910.4

[5141]
SWINGLEHURST, E. *and* ANDERSON, J. **Thomas Cook's A-Z guide to travel.** London, Constable, 1984. 265p. illus. ISBN: 0094646708.

Pt.1: General information: *i.e.* 130 subjects A-Z (p.9-162). Pt.2: Gazetteer (p.163-265). Data: visa requirements; health regulations; currency; language; national holidays; business conditions; office and shop hours; social taboos; internal travel; local time; electricity supply. 'Contains some interesting information but ... it is by no means comprehensive and has no detailed contents or index' (*Geographic Journal*, v.150, no.2, July 1984, p.276). *Class No:* 910.4

[5142]
TULLY, C. **The A-Z guide for lightweight travellers.** Mulbarton, Norfolk, Writer's Block, 1988. 160p. cartoons, pocket-size, pbk. £4.00. ISBN: 0951341006.

Chatty but informative notes. Airports p.118-9. Conversion charts (length, temperature, volume, weight) p.122-4. National Tourist Offices p.125-6. Also visa and vaccination regulations for 180 countries, time zones, short wave radio frequencies *etc*. *Class No:* 910.4

[5143]
'Visas', *Holiday Which*, v.15, no.1, January 1988, p.66-7. tables.

How to get them, forms, photographs, payment. *Class No:* 910.4

Bibliographies

[5144]
GREAT BRITAIN. National Maritime Museum. **Catalogue of the library. V.4: Piracy and privateering.** London, H.M. Stationery Office, 1972. ix,175p. 8p. illus. ports., facsims. ISBN: 0112901190.

585 numbered entries, A-Z authors, concluding with anonyma. Index of names, places and subjects. The basis of this material has been the celebrated Pirate Library founded by the late Philip Gosse and acquired in 1939, with additions subsequently. Very well produced. *Class No:* 910.4(01)

[5145]
SORENSON, J.L. *and* RAISH, M.L. **Pre-Columbian contact with the Americas across the oceans** an annotated bibliography. Provo, Utah, Research Pr., 2v., 1990. 1350p. index. $89. ISBN: 0934893144.

5613 items relating to the theme: 'to what degree were the pre-Columbia American peoples and their cultures dependent on or independent of those in the Old World'. *Class No:* 910.4(01)

[5146]
UNIVERSITY OF WASHINGTON. Fisheries-Oceanography Library. **Selected references to literature on marine expeditions, 1700-1960.** Boston, Massachusetts, G.K. Hall, 1972. iv,517p.

9,000 references, arranged A/Z by ship or name of expedition. No subject or author index; infrequent cross-references. Poor-quality print for some catalogue cards, but accuracy of citation is high (*RQ*, v.13,no.4, Summer 1974, p.354-5). *Class No:* 910.4(01)

Handbooks & Manuals

[5147]
GORMAN, S. *and* BRANDENBURGER, C., *eds*. **The Traveller's handbook.** 5th ed. Bath, Trade & Travel, 1991. xliii, 820p. maps, soft-cover. £11.95. ISBN: 0905802055.

82 contributors. 1. Where and when to travel (places in vogue; countries at war; climate and its relevance to travel. *etc.*) - 2. Finding out more (choosing maps; background reading; a guide to guides) - 3. Great journeys overland - 4-6. Getting there by air, road, and other means - 7. What type of travel - 8. Your special needs - 9. Paperwork - 10. Money - 11. Equipping for a trip - 12. Basic guide to health - 13. A place to stay - 14. Communicating - 15. When things go wrong - 16. Keeping track - 17. Maps - 18. Directory (rules and regulations; medical requirements and advice; travel; climate; equipment; training, help, advice?; Publications and publishers. 'A mass of information, much of which is just about impossible to locate easily elsewhere. An indispensable guide for the independent traveller' (*Reference Reviews*, v.3, no.1, March 1989, p.40-1). *Class No:* 910.4(035)

Quotations

[5148]
YAPP, P., *ed*. **The Travellers' dictionary of quotations:** who said what, about where? London, Routledge and Kegan Paul, 1983. xvi, 1022p.

More than 10,000 quotations, drawn principally from English-language sources, arranged A-Z by existing countries, subdivided by regions and smaller units. 'A wealth of material on a very wide range of places' (*Geographical Journal*, v.150, no.1, March 1984, p.113). *Class No:* 910.4(082.2)

Histories

[5149]
FRANCK, I.M. *and* BROWNSTONE, D.M. **To the ends of the earth** the great travel and trade routes of human history. New York and Oxford, Facts on File, 1984. xiv, 427p. illus. (some col.), maps, bibliogs., index. $35.00. ISBN: 0911818251.

31 chapters trace 45 of the principal routes following their

....(contd.)

history in contemporary accounts *e.g.* The Northeast Passage (p.282-92) has map, 4 illus. and 7 citations. In contrast The Northwest Passage has no entry and only 5 slight references. All chapters are equipped with bibliographies of varying length. *Class No:* 910.4(091)

[5150]

QUINN, D.B., *ed.* **The Hakluyt handbook.** London, the Hakluyt Society, 2v., 1974. xxvi,332p.; xiii,333-707p. facsims, maps. (*Hakluyt Society, 2nd series, nos.144,145.*) ISBN: 0521086949, v.1; 0521202116, v.2; 0521202124, set.

29 essays and bibliographical studies by various hands, arranged in 5 parts, provide 'a reference guide to the publications of Richard Hakluyt (1552-1616) and a critical evaluation of his work in the field of travel literature' (*Geographical Journal*, v.142,no.1, March 1976, p.163-4). Part 1: A Hakluyt perspective (7. Hakluyt's maps - 8. From Hakluyt to Purchase - 9. Tudor travel literature). Part 2: Hakluyt's use of the materials available to him. Part 3: From 1552 to 1616 (A Hakluyt chronology). Part 4: Contents and sources of the three major works. Part 5. Hakluyt's books and sources (27. The primary Hakluyt bibliography - 28. Secondary works on Hakluyt and his circle - 29. Works published by the Hakluyt Society 1846-1973). D.B. Quinn's 'Richard Hakluyt and his followers' in the Society's *Annual Report 1972* is an account of the *Handbook's* conception and birth. Hakluyt Society publications subsequent to the *Handbook* and volumes in preparation are recorded in the Society's annual *List of publications in print*. G.B. Park's *Richard Hakluyt and the English voyages*. New York, American Geographical Society, 1930. (Reprinted in a revised edition New York, Frederick Ungar, 1961) is indispensable for further research. *Class No:* 910.4(091)

[5151]

The Royal Geographical Society history of world exploration. Keay, J., *ed.* London, Hamlyn, 1991. 320p. illus. (some col.), col. maps, bibliog., index. £20.

10 sections by different hands: 1. Early exploration - 2. Asia - 3. Africa - 4. North America - 5. Central and South America - 6. Pacific, Australia and New Zealand - 7. Arctic - 8. Antarctic - 9. Oceanography - 10. Exploration today. Each consists of historical narrative with boxed features on chief explorers, their key routes, and their equipment etc., and a discovery map. A running chronological frieze adorns every page. Bibliography p.314. *Class No:* 910.4(091)

Manuscripts & Incunabula

[5152]

GREAT BRITAIN. National Maritime Museum. **Guide to the manuscripts in the National Maritime Museum.** London, Mansell, 2v., 1977-80. facsims., maps, indexes.

1. *The Personal collections.* edited by R.J.B. Knight. 1977. xxiv,234p. £28.00,. ISBN 0720107148. 2. *Public records, business records and artificial collections.* 1980. 251p. £28.00. 0720115914. V.1 has 300 annotated entries, briefly outlining careers of individuals concerned, plus description of each description. Arranged A-Z under names of persons. Detailed general index; ship index. *Class No:* 910.4(093)

Tropics

[5153]

HATT, J. The Tropical traveller the essential and celebrated guide to travel in hot countries. 2nd ed. London and Syndey, Pan Books, 1985. 267p. illus., bibliog., index. pbk. £3.95. ISBN: 0330288512.

1st ed. 1982.

12 chapters (2. Equipment ... 4. Flying - 5. Health - 6. Animal hazards - 7. On the move - 8. Practical hints - 9. Photography - 10. Human hazards - 11. Culture shock - 12. Taking the plunge). Appendix 1. Further reading (p.245-7). *Class No:* 910.4(213)

[5154]

HÉBERT, J. Travelling in tropical countries a guide for Africa, the South Seas, Latin America, Asia and the West Indies. Edmonton, Hurtig Publishers, 1986. 250p. illus. Can $14.95. ISBN: 0888303033.

Translation of *Voyager en pays tropical* (Montreal, Les Éditions du Boréal Express, 1984).

14 chapters. 1. The tourist - 2. The young traveller - 3. Other kinds of travellers - 4. Passport - 5. Visas, immigration and customs - 6. Baggage - 7. Money, mail - 8. Rules of hygiene - 9. Air travel - 10. Automobile trips - 11. The World's great itineraries - 12. Other kinds of transportation - 13. Respect for other cultures - 14. Appendices. (12 of Canadian interest only). *Class No:* 910.4(213)

Canada

[5155]

Canada travel information (for visitors from the United Kingdom). Ottawa, Tourism Canada, 1988. Published by authority of the Minister of Regional Industrial Expansion. 48p. illus., map, tables, index. *Gratis.*

Deals with entry into Canada; Bringing goods into Canada; Firearms, hunting and fishing; Vehicles and motoring; Provincial and territorial tourist information; Standard time zones; Hints for visitors; Climate; Transportation, maps and charts. *Class No:* 910.4(71)

Treasure Trove

[5156]

HAYDOCK, T. Treasure trove where to find the great lost treasures of the world. London, Fourth Estate, 1986. 160p. illus., maps, tables, index. £9.95. ISBN: 0947795308.

15 sites 'where the exact location of the treasure has been recorded with a promising degree of precision'. *Class No:* 910.4:351.759.5

[5157]

WILSON, J. Undiscovered the fascinating record of undiscovered places, graves, wrecks, and treasure. London, Michael O'Mara Books, 1987. 192p. illus., maps, index. ISBN: 0948397667.

Descriptive accounts of 30 undiscovered locations (e.g. Battlefield of Mt. Badon, the graves of Mallory and Irvine on Everest, the lost White Ship, and King John's jewels). Chronology of the Discoveries p.186-9. *Class No:* 910.4:351.759.5

Maps & Atlases

[5158]
WILSON, D. **The World atlas of treasure.** London, Collins, 1981. 256p. illus. maps. ISBN: 0002168774.

Popular account of the world's buried and sunken treasure. Of limited reference value.
Class No: 910.4:351.759.5(084.3)

Disasters

[5159]
DAVIS, L. **Encyclopedia of natural disasters.** London, Headline, 1993. xii,433p. illus., index. pbk. bibliog. £6.99. ISBN: 0747243433.

1. Avalanches and landslides - 2. Earthquakes - 3. Famines and droughts - 3. Floods ... 5. Plagues and epidemics - 6. Cyclones - 7. Hurricanes - 8. Icestorms and snowstorms - 9. Tornadoes - 10. Typhoons - 11. Storms - 12. Volcanic eruptions and natural explosions. Chapter chronologies. Bibliography p.411-6. Nearly 400 entries.
Class No: 910.4:502.5

[5160]
SMITH, R. **Catastrophes and disasters.** Edinburgh, Chambers, 1992. x,246p. illus., tables, index. pbk. £6.99. ISBN: 0550170154.

Accounts of air disasters; avalanches, rockfalls, mudslides; earthquakes; environmental disasters; famine; fire; floods; industrial disasters; pandemics; road and rail; disasters at sea; space; sporting disasters; Tsunamis; volcanoes; and windstorms. Chronological list of events p.viii-x. *Class No:* 910.4:502.5

Shipwrecks

[5161]
CAHILL, R.A. **Disasters at sea** Titanic to Exxon Valdez. London, Century, 1990. xv,272p. illus., bibliog., index. £16.99. ISBN: 0712638148.

Narrative of maritime diasters by unsafe design, foundering, fire, explosion, collision, and stranding. Chapter notes p.249-59. Bibliography p.259-62.
Class No: 910.4:656.6

[5162]
HOCKING, C. **Dictionary of disasters at sea** during the age of steam including sailing ships and ships of war lost in action 1824-1962. London, London Stamp Exchange, 1989. 779p. £35. ISBN: 0948130725.

First published in 2v. by Lloyd's Register of Shipping in 1969.

Shipping losses on the high seas and in inland waters arranged A-Z by name of ship. Data: owners, launch date, builders, displacement, engine power, maximum speed, and circumstances of loss. *Class No:* 910.4:656.6

Expeditions, Voyages, Travel

Women

[5163]
CHESTER, C. **Going alone:** the women's guide to travel know-how. London, Christopher Helm, 1987. 195p. index, pbk. £4.95. ISBN: 0747004048.

34 countries examined under headings: the male attitude; where to stay; getting around on your own; eating and

.... (contd.)
drinking solo; the safety factor; no-nos; essentials; medical survival; what to do solo; visas and inoculations; useful addresses. *Class No:* 910.4-0055.2

[5164]
MOSS, M. *and* MOSS, G. **Handbook for women travellers.** London, Piatkus, 1987. xii, 260p. illus., bibliog., index. ISBN: 0861886151.

1. Thinking ahead - 2. What to carry - 3. What to wear - 4. Getting ready to go - 5. On the move - 6. Staying healthy - 7. Women only - 8. Travel with children - 9. Disorientation - 10. Making contact - 11. Personal safety - 12. Coming back. Appendix A. The traveller's code - B. Overland tour operators - C. Meeting local women. *Class No:* 910.4-0055.2

Geography

Bibliographies

[5165]
AMERICAN GEOGRAPHICAL SOCIETY. **Research catalogue.** Boston, Mass., G.K. Hall, 15v. and map supplt., 1962. 1043p.

V.1 & 2: General - 3. Regional North America - 4-5. United States - 6-7. Mexico, Central America, Bermuda, West Indies, South America - 8-10. Europe - 11. Africa - 12-13. Asia - 14. Australasia - 15. Polar regions, Oceania, Tropics. Map supplement is merely a map key to the classification used.

First Supplement: Regional catalogue 2v., 1972. 1414p. $260.00 (Export $315.00). ISBN 0816109990. *Topical catalogue,* 2v. 1974. 1483p. is available on microfilm by request. $265.00 ($320.00). *Second Supplement* 2v., 1978. 1300p. $260.00 ($315.00). ISBN 0816100810.

More than 200,000 photolithographed catalogue cards. Particularly strong in periodical-article entries. Includes maps. The Library is the largest of its kind in the Western hemisphere. Updated in *Current geographical publications: additions to the Research catalogue of the American Geographical Society (qv).* *Class No:* 911(01)

[5166]
Bibliographie géographie internationale/International geographical bibliography. Paris, Colin (now Centre National de la Recherche Scientifique Laboratoire d'Information et de Documentation En Géographie avec la collaboration du Centre de Documentation des Sciences Humaines), 1891-. v.1. Annual. Annual subscription. FFr480.

Title varies. Issues for 1891-1914 were published as part of *Annales de Géographie.*

V.91 (1986) has 7259 informative and critical abstracts A-Z by author assembled in 11 sections: 1. General (including General documentation and cartography) - 2. Historical (A. History of geographical sciences and discoveries; B. Historical geography) - 3. Physical geography - 4. Human geography - 5. World multi-regional - 6. Europe - 7. Asia - 8. Africa - 9. America - 10. Oceania - 11. Polar regions. 4 quarterly issues plus an annual index. Cumulative list of periodicals scanned appears in first issue every year. Subject

....(contd.)

index (in French with English references). Index of places (French). Author index. 89 contributors worldwide. *Class No:* 911(01)

[5167]

HARRIS, C.D. Bibliography of Geography. Chicago, Department of Geography, Univ. of Chicago, 1976-. ISBN: 0890650861.

Pt.1: *Introduction to general aids.* 1976. ix, 276p.

585 main entries, some (*e.g.* the 6 major comprehensive current bibliographies of geography, p.25-26) with extensive analysis of contents and all annotated. 16 sections: 1. Bibliographies of bibliographies - 2. Comprehensive current bibliographies - 3. Comprehensive retrospective bibliographies - 4. Specialized bibliographies - 5. Books - 6. Serials - 7. Government documents - 8. Dissertations - 9. Photographs - 10. Maps and atlases - 11. Gazetteers - 12. Place-name dictionaries - 13. Dictionaries - 14. Encyclopedias - 15. Statistics - 16. Methodology. Appendices: 1. Gazetteers of the US Board on Geographic Names; 2. A small geographical reference collection (items 530-85). Detailed index of authors and titles. Prepared primarily for use by geographers.

Pt.2: *Regional v.1 The United States of America.* 1984. viii, 178p. index. $12.00. 0890651124.

Almost 1000 briefly annotated entries in 5 sections: Preliminary (worldwide bibliographies and guides, maps and atlases etc.) - 1. General aids - 2. Physical geography, related earth services, the environment, and resources - 3. Human geography and related social sciences - 4. Regions of the United States. Limited to separately published bibliographies, commercial, university presses, government sources or associations with the emphasis on works printed in the previous 15 years.

Pt.2: *Regional* will eventually comprise 5 sequences, the others to be *USSR; The Americas excluding United States; Europe excluding Soviet Union;* and *Africa, Asia, Australia and the Pacific.*

A worthy successor to J.K. Wright and E.T. Platt's *Aids to geographical research* (1947). *Class No:* 911(01)

[5168]

LOCK, C.B.M. Geography and cartography: a reference handbook. London, Clive Bingley, 1976. 762p.

An integration of *Geography: a reference handbook* (1968; 2nd ed. 1972.529p.) and *Modern maps and atlases* (1969).

1,400 entries, A-Z (titles of works, forms of literature, biographies, topics), with a strong bibliographical and cartobibliographical slant. Extended entries on Cartography (p.159-95); Audio visual aids; Bibliographies, national; Classification; Education in geography and cartography; Globes; Map librarianship (p.427-51); Maps (historical); Abstracts. Extensive index, p.635-762. The work does not fully integrate *Modern maps and atlases*, which should be retained for its coverage of national, regional and thematic maps and atlases (*RQ,* v.16,no.3, Spring 1977, p.258-9). A-Z order of entry has value for quick reference, but it is apt to scatter related material and choice of entry-words can be capricious (*e.g.* 'Man and wildlife'). Sample maps would have been an asset. A bulky but highly rewarding volume; 'for all geographical libraries' (*Library Review,* v.26,1977/8,p.144). *Class No:* 911(01)

[5169]

New geographical literature and maps. London, Royal Geographical Society, 1951-80. nos.1-60. *2pa.*

About 2,500 entries 2pa; annotations for some books. Two regular parts: 1. Accessions to the Library; 2. Accessions to the Map Room. In pt.1 all articles in 20 leading British and foreign geographical journals were indexed, with a selection from others. 'All new books, atlases and current maps received are also catalogued' (*Note*). Annual list of completed theses in geography approved for higher degrees in British university depts. of geography appears as pt.3 in the December issue. Each issue featured new periodical titles added to the Library. A particular virtue of this bibliography is that country and subject descriptors are printed in bold across the page as headings to the entry, - an eye-catching feature that makes for quick reference and compensates partly for lack of an index. An essential tool for libraries in this field, and its lamentable that there was no further publication after no.60, December 1980. *Class No:* 911(01)

Encyclopaedias

[5170]

DUNBAR, G.S., *ed.* **Modern geography: an encyclopedic survey.** New York, Garland; London, St. James Press, 1991. xx,219p. index. $45. £40. ISBN: 0824053435, US; 1558621229, UK.

95 contributors. 'An overview of developments in the field of geography from about 1890 to the present, with emphasis on personalities, institutions, major concepts, subfields, and the evolution of the discipline in various countries' (*Introduction*). Entries are A-Z with some cross-referencing, many have bibliographies (maximum of 6 items). 300 biographies (birth and death dates, highest academic qualification, institutional affiliation, major publications). 'Highest recommendation for all academic libraries' (*Choice,* v.28,no.8, April 1991, p.1292). *Class No:* 911(031)

Dictionaries

[5171]

FISCHER, E. *and* **ELLIOTT, F.E. German & English glossary of geographical terms.** Westport. Connecticut. Greenwood Press, 1977. $35.00; £32.50. ISBN: 0837189942.

First published New York, American Geographical Society, 1950.

Attempts to include the terms that the geographer is most likely to encounter; specialized terms in related sciences have been omitted. Geomorphology is included, since in Germany geomorphology is regarded as an integral part of geography. Short biographies of eminent geographers; entries on peoples and races. Considered (White, C.M., etc. *Sources of information in the social sciences,* entry B369) particularly valuable for its definitions in physical and mathematical geography. Chief source books, p.iv-v. *Class No:* 911(038)

[5172]

MAYHEW, S. *and* **PENNY, A. The Concise Oxford dictionary of geography.** Oxford, Oxford Univ. Press, 1992. 250p. £17.95. ISBN: 0198661576.

Definitions of over 5,000 terms used in all aspects of human and physical geography including cartography, surveying, ecology, population, agriculture, and transport. *Class No:* 911(038)

[5173]
MEYNEN, E., *comp*. **Bibliography of mono-and multilingual dictionaries and glossaries of technical terms used in geography** as well as in related natural and social sciences. Wiesbaden, Franz Steiner, 1974. xx, 246p. index. ISBN: 3515018468.

3212 numbered entries, with bibliographical notes. Author index. *Class No:* 911(038)

[5174]
STAMP L.D., Sir, *ed*. **A Glossary of geographical terms** based on a list prepared by a Committee of the British Association for the Advancement of Science. 3rd ed. London & New York, Longman, 1979. xxix,571p. £29.50. ISBN: 0582352584.

First published 1961; 2nd ed. 1966.

Covers physical, human, economic and political geography. 58 correspondents and collaborators. Various definitions, drawn freely from leading works, with acknowledgements, are given of terms, with 'Comment' added, if called for. Thus, entry for 'Isobase' cites definitions from the *OED*, H.R. Mill (*Catalogue* of the RGS library, 1893) and the *Meteorological glossary*, plus 15 lines of comment, with 2 references. Has some foreign terms (*e.g.* 'Liwa'). No illus., or diagrams. 'List of standard works' referred to, p.xvii-xxv. Appendices of special terms, and Greek and Latin roots. 'A valuable work of reference, with its most useful features preserved' (*The Geographical Magazine*, January 1980. p.316). *Class No:* 911(038)

[5175]
WALKER, A. **A Basic dictionary of geography.** London, Bell and Hyman, 1981. 64p. illus. sd. £1.95. ISBN: 0713512458.

Straightforward definitions of all basic terms that a new student of geography would encounter. *Class No:* 911(038)

[5176]
Westermann Lexikon der Geographie. Braunschweig, Georg Westermann, 5v., 1972-75.

1. *A-E.* 3rd ed. 1975. ISBN 3141640117. 2. *F-K.* 2nd ed. 1973. 3141640125. 3. *L-R.* 2nd ed. 1973. 3141640133. 4. *S-Z.* 2nd ed. 1973. 3141640141. 5. *Register.* 1972. 3141640057.

Entries include biographies of geographers, articles on localities, geographical terms and concepts, and on allied subjects such as cartography, geodesy and ethnography. According to *Geographical Review* (v.60, no.4, October 1970, p.886-7), more concerned with orthodox descriptive geography than with modern analytical geography. *Class No:* 911(038)

Reviews & Abstracts

[5177]
Geo abstracts. Norwich, Elsevier/Geo Abstracts, 1972-.

Preceded by *Geomorphological abstracts* (1960-65) and *Geographical abstracts* (1966-71) comprising 6 sections each 6 *pa*.

1972-1988 in 7 separate sections: A. Landforms and the Quaternary - B. Biogeography and climatology - C. Economic geography - D. Social and historical geography - E. Sedimentology - F. Regional and community planning - G. Remote sensing and cartography. Annual index in 2v. Index to A.B.E. and F. and C.D. and F. These 7 sections are now replaced by:

Physical geography See *Walford's Guide to Reference*

....(contd.)
Material Vol.1 (6th, 1993) items 1584 and 1799.

Human geography (1989-. £165 UK; £180 or $333.00 overseas. ISSN 09539611). 6*pa*. 15 sections: Methodology and theory; Techniques; Environment; Environmental resources; Historical; Population; Rural studies; Urban studies; Regional and community planning; Trade; Agriculture; Industry; Transport and communications; Recreational geography (inc. Tourism). Regional index in each issue. Annual thematic and geographical index and list of journals scanned.

GEOBASE (DIALOG file 292) is the online database of *Geo abstracts*. Over 58% of its records cover physical and human geography 1980-. E.H. Ferrell's 'GEOBASE: the online bibliographical database of Geo Abstracts', *SLA G&M Bulletin*, no.153, Sep. 1988, p.11-13 discusses its search capabilities, finding strategies *etc*. *Class No:* 911(048)

Periodicals

[5178]
HARRIS, C.D. **Annotated world list of selected current geographical serials.** 4th ed. Chicago, Department of Geography, Univ. of Chicago, 1980. [viii], 165p. tables, maps. $12.00. ISBN: 0890651019.

Records 443 current geographical serials from 72 countries (International; Algeria ... Zimbabwe). Contents include 'Geographical serials most cited in geographical bibliographies', p.4-35; and 'Serials not primarily geographical often cited in geographical bibliographies', p.35-52. Concise annotations, stressing coverage. End-paper location maps. *Class No:* 911(051)

[5179]
HARRIS, C.D. *and* FELLMAN, J.D., *comps*. **International list of geographical serials 1980.** 3rd ed. Chicago, Department of Geography, Univ. of Chicago, 1980. vi, 457p. ISBN: 0890651000.

First published 1960; 2nd ed. 1971.

3,455 numbered entries from 107 countries in 55 languages; arranged by areas (international; countries, A-Z; titles in non-Roman scripts). Index and cross-references, p.399-457. 76 collaborators. 'List of principal sources', p.13-25; 'Locations of library holdings through union lists of serials', p.26-39. Serials given semi-enclosed running numbers are those confirmed as current. *Class No:* 911(051)

Bibliographies

[5180]
National Geographic Index 1888-1988. Washington, National Geographic Society, 1989. 1216p. col. illus., col. maps. $24.95. ISBN: 0870447645.

Supersedes 3 previous indexes.

Indexes by subject, title, author, and photographer some 7000 articles published in 1148 issues of *National Geographic Magazine* (subsequently *National Geographic*) . *Class No:* 911(051)(01)

Yearbooks & Directories

[5181]

EHLERS, E., *ed.* *In cooperation with the International Geographical Union.* **Orbis geographicus 1992-1993/ World directory of geography ...** 7th ed. Wiesbaden, Franz Steiner Verlag, 1992. xviii,546p. maps, index. DM108.00. ISBN: 3515043268.

First issued in 1952 on the occasion of the International Geographical Congress, Washington.

Departments of geography - Geographical societies and associations - Geographical institutions and their members A-Z by country. 'Highly useful international directory' (C.D. Harris. *Annotated world list of selected current geographical serials.* 4th ed., 1980, p.55).
Class No: 911(058)

Tables & Data Books

[5182]

Philip's geographical digest 1992-93. Rayner, C., *and others, eds.* London, Heinemann-Philip Atlases, 1992. 128p. maps, tables. £15. ISBN: 0435349562.

World statistical coverage A-Z by country: Summaries (area and population; production; manufactures; trade) - Population - Agriculture - Energy - World trade - Gross National Product - Money exchange rates. Text features: Recent significant political changes - Recent placename changes - Raw materials, engineering, energy projects - Manufacturing - Transport and communications - Conservation and environment - Geographical catastrophes - UK statistics (population, foreign trade, balance of payments). *Class No:* 911(083)

Histories

[5183]

BROWN, E.H., *ed.* **Geography yesterday and tomorrow.** Oxford, Oxford Univ. Press, 1980. x,302p. illus., bibliog. £10.00. ISBN: 0198740964.

The first part is devoted to the achievements of the Royal Geographical Society in the development of academic geography. The remainder surveys the progress of geographical theory in the last 25 years, - 13 short essays, well documented, by leading geographers on difference branches of the discipline. *Class No:* 911(091)

[5184]

CRONE, G.R. Modern geographers: an outline of progress in geography since A.D.1800. 3rd rev. ed. London, Royal Geographical Society, 1970. 56p. with 7pl. and map. £0.50. ISBN: 0902447009.

1st ed. 1959.

The development of geographical theories in the last 150 years, outlined in a series of biographical sketches of leading geographers, from Humboldt to Mackinder and Bowman. *Class No:* 911(091)

[5185]

DICKINSON, R.E. The Makers of modern geography. London, Routledge & Kegan Paul, 1969. 305p. illus. £30.00. ISBN: 0710067755.

'It contains much the best account in English of the lives and thoughts of French and German geographers, and throws many a valuable sidelight on British and American geography' (*Geographical Journal*, v.136,no.2, June 1970,

....(contd.)
p.253-5). A final survey, 'professional growth', covers national societies and publications, plus successive international congresses. *Class No:* 911(091)

[5186]

DICKINSON, R.E. *and* **HOWARTH, O.J.R. The Making of geography.** Oxford, Clarendon Press, 1933. 264p. illus. (pl.)., index.

Chapters 1-15 deal with historical aspects; 16-20: The development of physical geography - The development of human geography - The development of biogeography - The regional concept - Summary and conclusions. Appended selected list (p.254-8) of books and articles that deal specifically with the history of geography (general, and by chapters). Standard works are mentioned in the text paper. 'The best general history of geography' (Church, M., and others. *A basic geographical library* (1966), entry no.188). *Class No:* 911(091)

[5187]

KIMBLE, G.H.T. Geography in the Middle Ages. London, Methuen, 1938. xi,272p. illus., bibliog.

A survey in 10 chapters, with 20 illustrations. Numerous footnote references. The select bibliography (p.245-57) contains valuable lists of texts and of secondary materials, including periodical articles. *Class No:* 911(091)

[5188]

THOMSON, J.O. History of ancient geography. Cambridge, Cambridge Univ. Press, 1948. xi,427p. illus., maps.

12 chapters, ending with the 5th century A.D. A scholarly survey of the beliefs and theories about the cosmos, heavens and earth, by the one-time Professor of Latin in the University of Birmingham. Profuse footnote references, but with citations drastically curtailed. Notes on books, etc., p.392-4, 66 illus. in the text and maps. Detailed index. Very readable: 'the definitive work on the legacy of classicial geographers' (Parry, J.H. *The age of reconnaissance* (1963), p.347). *Class No:* 911(091)

Bibliographies

[5189]

ALTENGARTEN, J.S. *and* **MOLYNEAUX, G.A. The History, philosophy and methodology of geography:** a bibliography selected for education and research. Monticello, Illinois, Council of Planning Libraries, 1976. 56p. index. $5.50.. ISBN: 0686203852.

678 entries in 25 sections: General works ... Environment ... Historic periods *etc.* *Class No:* 911(091)(01)

[5190]

DUNBAR, G.S. The History of modern geography: an annotated bibliography of selected works. New York, Garland, 1985. xvi,386p. index. $53.50. (*Bibliographies of the history of science and technology, no.9.*) ISBN: 0824090667.

1717 entries assembled in 3 Pts. (22 chapters): General and topical; Geography in various countries; Biographical works. Author and subject indexes. 'A guide to the literature in the history of geography from the mid-eighteenth century' (*Introduction*). *Class No:* 911(091)(01)

20th Century

[5191]
JOHNSTON, R.A. *and* CLAVAL, P. **Geography since the Second World War:** an international survey. London, Croom Helm; Totowa, New Jersey, Barnes & Noble, 1984. 290p. £30.00. ISBN: 0709914113, UK; 0389204811, US.

1. Introduction: the international study of the history of geography - followed by individual studies on France, Italy, South-east Europe, Soviet Union, United Kingdom, Poland, the German-speaking countries, North America, the Netherlands, Japan, the Iberian Peninsula and Latin America. Extensive chapter references.
Class No: 911(091)"19"

Biographies

[5192]
LARKIN, R.P. *and* PETERS, G.L. **Biographical dictionary of geography.** Westport, Conn., Greenwood Press, 1993. xii,361p. bibliogs., index. ISBN: 0313276626.

Career profiles and biographical sketches, chronologies, and selected bibliographies of 77 geographers and cartographers of all periods. *Class No:* 911(092)

[5193]
MARTIN, G.J. **Geographers: bibliographical studies.** London and New York, Mansell, 1976-. v.1-. Annual. ISSN: 03086992.

Studies of geographers, cartographers, mariners, surveyors, etc. 'who have made major contributions to the development of geographical thought and of geography as a scientific subject and academic discipline'. Includes names whose significance has hitherto been neglected. Thus v.14. (1992. xii,116p. £40; $80. 0720121167) includes Ibn Battuta, Andrew Hill Clark, Clarence James Glacken, François Emile Matthes, John Muir, Stanislaw Pawlowski, Raphael Pampelly, and Josef Schmithüsen.

Each study describes the education, life and work of its subject, scientific ideas and geographical thought, and the influence and spread of those ideas. In addition, for each individual, there is a bibliography, list of sources, summary chronology of his/her life, and a portrait. An index completes each volume. Over 200 individuals have been profiled since the annual studies started in 1976.
Class No: 911(092)

Europe

[5194]
HOFFMAN, G.W., *ed*. **Europe in the 1990s** a geographic analysis. 6th ed. New York, Wiley, 1989. xxiv,759 +28 index pages. illus., tables, maps, bibliogs. ISBN: 047162280x.

1st ed. 1953; 5th ed. 1983. Formerly titled *A Geography of Europe: Problems and prospects.*

7 contributors. A geographical analysis of Europe's major regions in 12 chapters: 1. Historical geography - 2. Physical environment - 3. Social and economic change - 4. Regional and environmental problems, policies, and institutions - 5. The British Isles - 6/10. Western, Northern, Central, Southern, and Eastern Europe - 11. Soviet Union - 12. Europe in the 1990s. Glossary p.752-4. Chapter bibliographies. 'This edition takes particular note of the dramatic changes that have taken place since the mid-1980s, and it focusses on expected changes in the 1990s. (*Preface*).
Class No: 911(4)

Great Britain

[5195]
CHAMPION, A.G. *and* TOWNSEND, A.R. **Contemporary Britain:** a geographical passport. London, Edward Arnold, 1990. x,310p. bibliog., index. £12.95. ISBN: 0713165804.

12 documented chapters arranged in 4 parts: 1. Faces of change - 2. Geographical impact - 3. Local outcomes and government responses - 4. The next decade. Bibliography p.277-300. *Class No:* 911(410)

Histories

[5196]
FREEMAN, T.W. **A History of modern British geography.** London, Longman, 1980. ix,258p. illus., maps, bibliolg., index. ISBN: 0582300304.

10 chronological chapters trace the development of academic geography, discuss seminal books, individuals and groups, and relate the growth of the discipline to intellectual, social and economic circumstances. Geographical biographies (over 60 leading British geographers) p.205-239. Bibliography p.240-250. Publication coincided with the 150th anniversary of the Royal Geographical Society. *Class No:* 911(410)(091)

[5197]
STEEL, R.W., *ed*. **British geography 1918-1945.** Cambridge, Cambridge Univ. Press. 1987. xi,189p. index. £27.50. ISBN: 052124790x.

12 chapters, each by a different hand, trace the foundations of modern British geography *e.g.* Darby, H.C. 'On the writing of Historical Geography 1918-1945'.
Class No: 911(410)(091)

Ireland

[5198]
GRAHAM, B.J. *and* PROUDFOOT, L.J. **Historical geography of Ireland.** London, Academic Press, 1993. 454p. £24.95. ISBN: 0122948815.

11 Contributors. Period 500-early 1920s covered in 9 thematic chapters (Irish emigration to Britain, US and Australia, urbanization, industrialization). 'Has some revealing insights on the separate development of historical geography in Ireland and in Britain' (*Geographical Journal*, v.159. no.3. November 1993, p.346-7). *Class No:* 911(415)

London

Bibliographies

[5199]
DOPHIN, P., *and others*. **The London Region** an annotated geographical bibliography. London, Mansell, 1981. xvi,379p. maps, indexes. ISBN: 0720115981.

1909 annotated entries in 9 sections: 1. General bibliographies, statistical sources and atlas - 2. General works - 3. Physical environment - 4. Historical patterns of growth and development - 5. Economic structure and patterns - 6. Transport - 7. Social patterns and processes - 8. Planning the metropolis and beyond - 9. Environmental problems: conservation, pollution and control. Appendix: Libraries in London containing collections on the London region (p.322-5). Name and subject indexes. 'This work may

....*(contd.)*

possibly be one of the more important reference tools on London' (*Choice*, v.20 no.2 October 1982, p.242). *Class No:* 911(421)(01)

Federal Republic of Germany

[5200]

Geographie Deutschlands Bundesrepublik Deutschland. Staat-Natur-Wirtschaft. Tietze, W., *and others, eds.* Berlin & Stuttgart, Gebrüder Borntraeger, 1990. xii,687p. illus., maps, tables, bibliog., index.

11 contributors. A. Politisch-geographische Grundlagen - B. Landesnatur - C. Grundlagen und strukturräumliche Entwicklungen der Wirtschaft in der Bundesrepublik Deutschland - D. Kartographische Quellenlage - E. Die Verwendung vond Zahlen der amtlichen Statistik in der geographischen Landeskunde. A monumental work of scholarship. Bibliographies are appended to each section. *Class No:* 911(430.1)

France

[5201]

Atlas et géographie de la France moderne. Papy, L., *ed.* Paris, Flammarion, 16v., 1976-83.

Brétagne by A. Meynier. 1976. *La Region Lyonnaise* by R. Lebeau. 1976. *Alsace et Lorraine* by E. Juillard. 1977. *Normandie* by A. Fremont. 1977. *Paris* by J. Beaujeu-Garnier 2v. 1977. *Haute Bourgogne et Franche-Compté* by P. Claval. 1978. *Midi Touloussain* by F. Taillefer. 1978. *Pays de la Loire* by P. Fenelon. 1978. *Provence, Côte d'Azur et Corse* by R. Livet. 1978. *Alpes Françaises* by Paul G. Veyret. 1979. *Languedoc et Roussillon* by R. Ferras and others. 1979. *Nord et Picardie* by P. Flatres. 1980. *Champagne Pays de Meuse et Basse Bourgogne* by R. Brunet. 1981. *Massif Central* by A. Fel and G. Bouet. 1981. 348p. illus., maps. In 3 sections: Le Massif Central, L'Auvergne, Le Limousin. 32p. maps between p.301 and 306. Statistical tables p.306-317. Place name index p.320-324. Bibliography p.325-338. These attractive volumes are intended for a wide readership; and present 'une image vivante de la France au début du dernier quart du xxième siècle' (*Preface*). *Class No:* 911(44)

[5202]

ESTIENNE, P. La France. Paris, Masson, 4v. 1978-1979. maps, bibliog., index. (*Collection Geographie des États.*)

1. Généralités sur la France. Region du Nord. 1979. 184p. 2. De l'Atlantique aux Vosges. 1978. 215p. 2225482683. 3. Les montagnes françaises et l'axe Rhône-Rhin. 1978. 208p. 2225496765. 4. Les Midis français 1978. 212p. 2225496870. 'An up-to-date, beautifully composed regional geography' (*Geographical Journal*, v.147, no.2, July 1981, p.220). *Class No:* 911(44)

[5203]

PINCHEMEL, P. France a geographical, social and economic survey. Elkins, D. *and* Elkins, T.H., *translators.* Cambridge, Cambridge Univ. Press; Paris, Editions De La Maison Des Sciences De l'Homme, 1986. xxvi,660p. illus., maps, tables, bibliog., index. £40.00. ISBN: 0521249872, UK; 2735101754, Fr.

Originally as *La France* (Paris, Armand Colin, 1980).

39 chapters deployed in 8 main parts: 12. The natural environment - 2. People - 3. Actors and policies in the

....*(contd.)*

spatial structures of France - 4. Resources, economic activity and economic enterprises - 5. The infrastructure of spatial interaction - 6. Landscape and environment in rural France - 7. The urban environment - 8. Conclusion. Bibliography p.605-49. Analytical index. *Class No:* 911(44)

Netherlands

Handbooks & Manuals

[5204]

ZULDER, G.A.M., *ed*. Handboek der geographie van Nederland. Zwolle, Tijl, 6v., 1949-59.

'The standard handbook, now rather dated, but still indispensable for reference' (P. King and M. Wintle. *The Netherlands*, 1988. Entry 33). *Class No:* 911(492)(035)

Institutions & Associations

[5205]

BRYAN, C.D.B. The National Geographic Society 100 years of adventure and discovery. Washington, National Geographic Society; Oxford, Phaidon, 1987. 484p. illus. (mostly col.), bibliog., index. £35. ISBN: 0714824852, UK.

Lavishly illustrated history of the Society: 10 chronological chapters interspersed with 10 thematic chapters *e.g.* polar exploration, archaeology, natural disasters, space exploration. Bibliography p.476. See also G.M. Grosvenor's 'A hundred years of the National Geographic Society', *Geographical Journal*, v.154, no.1, March 1988, p.87-92. *Class No:* 911:061:061.2

Conferences

[5206]

KISH, G., *ed*. Bibliography of international geography congresses 1871-1976. Boston, G.K. Hall, 1979. viii,540p.

6969 papers presented at 23 congresses from Antwerp 1871 to Moscow 1976 listed in chronological order with author and subject indexes. 'Of permanent value to students of the history of geography' (*Geographical Journal*, v.147,no.2, July 1981, p.251). *Class No:* 911:061:061.3

Historical Geography

Europe

[5207]

POUNDS, N.J.G. An Historical geography of Europe. Cambridge University Press, 1990. xiii,484p. maps, diagrs., tables, bibliogs., index. £30. $17.95. ISBN: 0521322170.

12 alternating chapters on the changing pattern of human history during the last 2,500 years of Europe's history. One set of 7 captures Europe at particular celebrated points, the other 5 chapters trace the changes in the intervening periods. Chapter bibliographies. Based on 3v. work of the same title (1973-85). 'A superb summary of Europe's historical geography in one succinct volume' (*Choice*, v.28,no.7, March 1991, p.1205). *Class No:* 911.0(4)

Europe—Eastern

[5208]

TURNOCK, D. **Eastern Europe an historical geography 1815-1945.** London and New York, Routledge, 1989. ix,357p. maps, tables, bibliogs., index. £35.00. ISBN: 0415012694.

8 broad thematic chapters arranged in 2 pts. Pt.1. The century of peace 1815-1914: 1. Political geography - 2. Economic development: Germany and the Hapsburg lands - 4. The Russian and Ottoman Empires - 5. Settlement geography. Pt.2. The Era of World War 1914-1945. 6. Political geography - 7. Economic geography - 8. Transport power and settlement. Extensive chapter bibliographies plus (general) Bibliography p.330-9. *Class No:* 911.0(401)

Great Britain

[5209]

SHAW, G. **British directories as sources in historical geography.** London, Geo Books, 1982. 60p. illus., tables. sd. £5.00. (*Historical Geography Research Series.*) ISBN: 0860941094. ISSN: 0143683x.

An introductory survey in 6 chapters: 1. Introduction - 2. Evolution and development - 3. Contents - 4. Spatial and temporal coverage - 5. Reliability - 6. Use of directory material in urban historical geography. Notes p.54-60. *Class No:* 911.0(410)

Scotland

Bibliographies

[5210]

WHYTE, J.D. *and* WHYTE, K.H. **Sources for Scottish historical geography** an introductory guide. Norwich, Geo Abstracts, 1981. ii,46p. bibliog., sd. £5.00. (*History of Research Series no.6.*) ISBN: 0860940667. ISSN: 0143683x.

1. Introduction (location of source material) - 2. General research aids - 3. Sources (18 categories *e.g.* 12 maps ... 16. Statistical accounts). Bibliography p.38-46. *Class No:* 911.0(411)(01)

England & Wales

[5211]

DODGSHON, R.A. *and* BUTLIN, R.A., *eds.* **An Historical geography of England and Wales.** 2nd ed. New York, Academic Press, 1990. xxi,589p. diagrs., tables, maps, bibliog., index. £39. ISBN: 0122192532.

14 contributors (British academics, etc.). Extends from prehistory to date. Well-documented overview of all aspects of human geography, population changes, agriculture, transport and communications, landscape, towns and industries, and overseas trade. Detailed subject index. 'A most methodical analysis of recent researches into the various themes discussed' (*British Book News*, February 1979, p.171). *Class No:* 911.0(42)

France

[5212]

PLANHOL, X. de. **Géographie historique de la France.** Paris, Fayard, 1988. 635p. maps, figs., bibliog., index.

11 chapters organized in 3 parts: 1. Genèse de la France - 2. L'Organisation traditionnelle de l'Espace Français - 3. Centralisation et diversification de l'Espace Français. Chapter notes p.537-566. Bibliography p.567-591. 'Le sujet a été délib°ment traité per grandes plages chronologiques (*Avant-propos*). *Class No:* 911.0(44)

Scandinavia

[5213]

MEAD, W.R. **An Historical geography of Scandinavia.** London and New York, Academic Press, 1981. xviii,313p. maps, tables, diagrs., bibliogs., index. £41.00; $74.00. ISBN: 0124874207.

12 chapters *e.g.* 2. The concept of Scandinavia ... 4. From Middle Ages to Baroque Empire ... 11. Fin de siècle *c.*1900 - 12. The process and problems of fulfilment. Ch. bibliographies. *Class No:* 911.0(48)

Caribbean

[5214]

WATTS, D. **The West Indies** patterns of development, culture and environmental change since 1492. Cambridge, Cambridge Univ. Press, 1987. xxii,609p. illus., maps, tables, bibliog., index. £50.00. (*Cambridge Studies in Historical Geography no.8.*) ISBN: 0521245559.

3 main themes (total removal of a large aboriginal population; development of plantation agriculture; and resulting environment changes) unravelled in 11 chapters: 1. The environment - 2. Aboriginal settlement and culture - 3. Spanish intrusion and colonization - 4. Early northwest European plantations - 5. Northwest European sugar estates 1645-1665 - 6-9. Extension of the West Indian sugar estate economy 1665-1833 - 10. Post 1833 adjustments - 11. Twentieth-century trends. Notes p.540-52. Bibliography p.553-85. Analytical index. *Class No:* 911.0(729)

USA

Bibliographies

[5215]

GRIM, R.E. **Historical geography of the United States:** a guide to information sources. Detroit, Gale Research Co., 1982. xix,291p. indexes. (*Geography and Travel Information Guide Series.*) ISBN: 0810314711.

686 annotated entries 'limited almost exclusively to the United States from the beginning of the sixteenth century until the early twentieth century' arranged in 21 chapters divided into 3 parts: Cartographic sources; Archival and other historical sources; Selected literature in historical geography. Author, title and subject indexes. Because of its emphasis on 'recent and current literature, *i.e.*, published or reprinted 1965-1980, it complements rather than duplicates D.R. McManis' *Historical geography of the United States* (1965). 'Recommended for all academic libraries (*Choice*, v.20,no.8, April 1983, p.1110). *Class No:* 911.0(73)(01)

Australia

[5216]

POWELL, J.M. An Historical geography of modern Australia. The restive fringe. Cambridge, Cambridge Univ. Press, 1988. xx,400p. illus., maps, tables, bibliog., index. £30.00. (*Cambridge Studies in Historical Geography no.11.*) ISBN: 0521256194.

'A broad interpretative thesis' in 10 chapters *e.g.* 3. Imperialism, protectionism, democratic nationalism ... 5. Science and the frontier ... 9. Agriculture and the modern federation. Notes p.342-76. Bibliography p.377-86. Analytical index. 'A fine achievement, good for historical geography, and good as well for Australia' (*Geographical Journal,* v.158, no.2, July 1992. p.231). *Class No:* 911.0(94)

Research Methods

[5217]

BAKER, A.R.H. *and* **BILLINGE, M. Period and place. Research methods in historical geography.** Cambridge, Cambridge Univ. Press, 1982. x,377p. illus., maps, bibliog., index. £25.00. (*Cambridge Studies in Historical Geography no.1.*) ISBN: 052124272x.

31 papers presented at a workshop organized by the International Geographical Union's Working Group on Historical changes in Spational Organization in Cambridge, July 1979, arranged under 6 headings: 1. Developments in Historical Geography - 2. Reconstructing past geographies - 3. Identification and interpretation of geographical change - 4. Behavioural approaches - 5. Theoretical approaches - 6. Historical sources and techniques. Notes p.313-61. Bibliography p.363-72. *Class No:* 911.0:001.891

Human Geography

Dictionaries

[5218]

GOODALL, B. The Facts on File dictionary of human geography. New York, and Oxford, Facts on File, 1987. 507p. diagrs., graphs. $29.95; £15.00. ISBN: 0816017387.

Over 3000 definitions (1 line to 1 page in length) including some obsolete terms students may still encounter, and in foreign languages if in common international use. 'Inevitably, this volume will be compared - to its detriment - to the *Dictionary of Human Geography* edited by R.L. Johnston' (*Choice,* v.24, no.11/12, July/August 1987, p.1676). *Class No:* 911.3(038)

[5219]

JOHNSTON, R.J., *ed.* **The Dictionary of human geography.** 3rd ed. Oxford, Blackwell Reference, 1993. xxiii,411p. diagrs., graphs, index. pbk. £14. ISBN: 0631181415.

18 contributors. Concerned with English-language words and terms in common usage in contemporary human geography. Many entries end with references, suggested readings, or both. Abbreviations in Human Geography. For this editions the articles are restructured and the bibliographies updated. *Class No:* 911.3(038)

[5220]

WOODCOCK, R. The Hamlyn dictionary of geography. London, Hamlyn, 1989. 287p. illus. pbk. £2.99. ISBN: 060056519x.

More than 1000 cross-referenced geographical terms covering the main aspects of both human and physical geography. For GCE 'O' and 'A' level use. *Class No:* 911.3(038)

912 Maps & Atlases

Bibliographies

Bibliographies

[5221]

Bibliographie cartographique internationale. Paris, Colin (latterly Centre National de la Recherche Scientifique in collaboration with UNESCO and the International Geographical Union), 1938-. Annual.

Previously (1936-1945) titled *Bibliographie Cartographique Française*.

V.28 *1975* (1979. 1197p. 3262006513) has 5420 entries for maps, atlases, charts and plans, organized in 3 separate parts: 1. Monde, Europe - 2. Afrique, Amerique - 3. Asie, Oceanie, Regions polaires. Scales and map sizes are stated. Especially strong on map series. The leading geographical societies of some 20 countries collaborated in its compilation. Now seems to be in abeyance.
Class No: 912(01)

Map Collections

[5222]

ALLISON, B. 'Map acquisitions: the major sources', *Wilson Library Bulletin,* v.60,no.2, October 1985, p.21-24.

Discusses basic cartographic concepts; map collection development policy, and acquisitions. List of US, Foreign, and Antiquarian map sources. *Class No:* 912:026

[5223]

LARSGAARD, M.L. Map librarianship. 2nd ed. Littleton, Colorado, Libraries Unlimited Inc., 1987. xxvii,382p. illus., maps, index. ISBN: 0872875377.

7 chapters: 1. Selection and acquisition - 2. Classification - 3. Cataloguing and computer applications - 4. Storage, care and repair - 5. Reference services - 6. Public relations - 7. Education. 'The focus is on theory, techniques, and practices, and on the practical short-term, and long-term aspects of working with cartographic material; thus the volume may be used as a classroom text, a working manual, and a reference source' (*Introduction*). *Class No:* 912:026

[5224]

NICHOLS, N. Map librarianship. 2nd ed. London, Clive Bingley, 1982. 272p. bibliog., index. £17.50. ISBN: 0851573274.

15 chapters, 3 of which deal with the content of the map collection (current, early and local maps. 5 with classification and cataloguing, and others with storage, the dating and identifying of early maps, care and preservation of maps. Chapter references. Reading list. Detailed, analytical index. 'There is much of value ... for all grades of librarian' (*Geographical Journal*, v.149, no.2, July 1983, p.253). *Class No:* 912:026

Bibliographies

[5225]

NEW YORK PUBLIC LIBRARY. Research Libraries. Map Division. **Dictionary catalog of the Map Division.** Boston, Mass., G.K. Hall, 10v., 1971. 8898p. $990.00 (Export $1198.00). ISBN: 0816107831.

187,000 photolithographed catalogue cards. Represented are the 280,000 sheet maps of the Map Division. Included are nearly 11,000v. other than atlases on the techniques of map making; analytical cards for periodical articles and bibliographies.

Supplemented by *Bibliographic guide to maps and atlases.* 1979-. *Class No:* 912:026(01)

Australia

[5226]

Map collections in Australia: a directory. O'Connor, M., *ed.* 4th ed. Canberra, National Library of Australia, 1991. 146p. indexes. ISBN: 0642104832.

Over 130 entries describing university, national and state, government, and private company library collections including rare and historical maps, hydrographic charts, aerial photographs, and remote sensing images and digital data, arranged by state by collection name. Data: address, opening hours, subject of collection, chronological coverage. Also lists of map publishers and selected cartographic works published since 1980. Subject, geographical, and collection indexes. *Class No:* 912:026(94)

Maps & Atlases

Bibliographies

[5227]

BANCROFT LIBRARY University of California, Berkeley. **Index to printed maps.** Boston, Mass., G.K. Hall, 1964. First Supplement, 1975.

Index. 1964. 521p. $79.00 (Export $95.00). ISBN 0816107041. *First Supplement.* 1975. 581p. $110.00 ($135.00). ISBN 0816111723. Total of 23100 photolithographed catalogue cards. Maps indexed are of the New World with emphasis on the western half of North America, 16th to 20th century. *Class No:* 912.0(01)

[5228]

Bibliographic guide to maps and atlases. Boston, Mass., G.K. Hall, 1979-. Annual.

Supplements *Dictionary catalog of the map division* Research Libraries, New York Public Library (1971).

In 2v. since 1986 edition *1987* ed. (1988) has v, 434p.+437p. Lists materials catalogued during the past year by the New York Public Library Map Division, and the Geography and Map Division of Library of Congress. Includes maps, atlases, charts, plans and globes, as well as

....(contd.)

books about maps and cartography, plus periodicals and periodical articles. 'Not a work of scholarship but merely the commercial exploitation of automated records' (*Geographical Journal*, v.147, no.3, November 1981, p.381). *Class No:* 912.0(01)

[5229]

BOOK MARKETING COUNCIL The Publishers Association. **Catalogue of maps and guides 1990.** London, Book Marketing Council, 1983-. Now annually. viii,56p. illus. map. £5.00. ISBN: 085386165x.

In 2 parts: 1. Britain p.1-20 arranged Britain, England (further subdivided into the 12 Tourist Board areas), Scotland, Wales - 2. Rest of the world A-Z by countries or areas. Each publication is listed under Atlas, Map, or Travel Guide. Data: title, imprint, ISBN, pagination, retail price, map scale. Publishers directory p.54-56. Primarily intended as a book trade tool this is a useful in print bibliography. 'Brings together a lot of material, much of which does not appear in BBIP' (*Refer*, v.2,no.3, Spring 1983, p.11). *Class No:* 912.0(01)

[5230]

BRITISH LIBRARY. Catalogue of printed maps, charts and plans. Photolithographed ed. London, Trustees of the British Museum, 15v., 1967. Corrections and additions. 1967. 7822p. + 55p. £400.00. ISBN: 0714103241.

First published as *Catalogue of the printed maps, plans and charts in the British Museum* compiled by R.K. Douglas (London, 1885. 2v.); supplemented by the annual *Catalogue of printed maps in the British Museum: accessions* (1884-).

The 15v. ed. records British Museum holdings up to 1964 and is in the same format as the *General catalogue of printed books*. Entries have brief bibliographical notes (*e.g.* scale, map size). Arrangement is by localities. A-Z, with subdivision (*e.g.* London, v.9, p.13-202) as relevant.

The British Library catalogue of printed maps charts and plans Ten-year supplement 1965-1974. 1978. 690p. £45.00. ISBN 0714103667.

Catalogue of cartographic materials in the British Library 1975-1988, London, Bowker-Saur, 3v., 1989. 1201p. £36.00. 0862917654. 48,000 entries relating to atlases, single sheet maps, map series, maritime charts, plans, globes, and other relevant material acquired by the British Library Map Library. Also details of 260 digital cartographic and remote sensing databases in the UK located as a result of a British Library sponsored research project. 3 sequences: 1. Geographic names A-Z using BL Map Library headings - 2. Names/titles - 3. Subjects *i.e.* reference works, books and serials relating to all aspects of cartography. Also available on 48 x reduction microfiche.

British Library Catalogue of Cartographic Materials: Accessions 1975-1988. 15 x 1.48 microfiche on Datox sheets filed in a ring-bound folder accompanied by an explanatory introduction. *Class No:* 912.0(01)

[5231]

General reference books for adults authoritative evaluations of encyclopedias, atlases, and dictionaries. Sader, M., *ed.* New York and London, R.B. Bowker & Co., 1988. xvi, 614p. illus., bibliog., index. $69.95. £70.00. (*The Bowker Buying Guide Series.*) ISBN: 0835223930.

Comparative charts 32 atlases p.38-40. Data: title, publisher, edition, pages, maps, index entries, trim size, price. Part 3. Atlases: what to look for in atlases p.149-158; Glossary p.158-161; Evaluations (format, special features,

....(contd.)

currency, scale and projection *etc.*) p. 163-225. Bibliography p.587-589. List of publishers p.591-597. 'British works are reviewed only if they are readily available for purchase in the United States' (*Preface*). 'Reviews are evaluative and do not hesitate to point out both strengths and weaknesses or to compare works for suitability to various purposes' (*Booklist*, v.85, no.10, 15 January 1989, p.849). *Class No:* 912.0(01)

[5232]

GeoKatalog. Stuttgart, Geo Center Internationales Landkartenhause, 2v., 1975-1983. Loose-leaf.

A detailed trade catalogue of national and international maps and atlases, thematic maps and atlases, plans, guides and globes.

GeoKartenbrief (*c.3pa*). no.317, June 1990 notes new maps, atlases and books comprising all topics in the field of regional geography and, at the same time, acts as a Supplement to *GeoKatalog. Class No:* 912.0(01)

[5233]

GREAT BRITAIN. National Maritime Museum. **Catalogue of the Library. Volume 3: Atlases and cartography.** London, HMSO, 2v., 1971. xi, lx, 1166p. illus. facsims.

765 numbered items. V.1: Ptolemy - Italian atlases - Dutch and Flemish atlases - French atlases - British atlases (p.343-524) - German, Russian, Spanish & American atlases - Cartography & historiography. V.2: Index (lx p., p.655-1166), - detailed and analytical. V.1 states contents of *Imago mundi* (annual) and of atlases. (Noting every map and chart). Well produced. *Class No:* 912.0(01)

[5234]

KOEMAN, C., *comp. and ed.* **Atlantes Neerlandici** bibliography of territorial, maritime and celestial atlases and pilot books published in the Netherlands up to 1880. Amsterdam, Theatrum Orbis Terrarum, 5v., 1965-72. 1904p. facsims., diagrs.

1-3 Terrestrial atlases. 4. Celestial and maritime atlases and pilot books. 5. Indexes.

Bibliographical descriptions; locations in *c.*70 collections, worldwide. V.5 indexes; 1a. Index of terrestrial maps - 1b. Index of sea-atlases, rutters and pilot books - 2. Index of terrestrial atlases: sea-atlases, rutters and pilot books in chronological order - 3. Nominal index, names of cartographers, engravers, map-authors and publisher - 4. Index of geographical names (p.89-287). *Class No:* 912.0(01)

[5235]

UNITED STATES. Library of Congress. **A List of geographical atlases in the Library of Congress** with bibliographical notes. Washington, Library of Congress, 8v., 1909-74.

V.1-4 (1909-20), compiled by P.L. Phillips; v.5-6 (1958-63), compiled by C. E. LeGear.

V.6. covering titles 7624-10254, covers nearly 2,500 items received 1956-60, including *800* Oriental publications. Arranged by continent and country. Author lists and topographical indexes in v.2-6, with cumulated index to v.1-4 in v.4 Entries sometimes have biobibligraphical notes, often extensive. V.5 deals with world atlases, special and general. While v.6 records atlases of Europe, Asia, Africa, Oceania, the Polar regions and Oceania, v.7 (1973) lists titles 10255-18435, dealing with the Western hemisphere and individual countries of North and South America. V.8 (1974) is an integrated author list and index. *Class No:* 912.0(01)

Pacific Ocean

[5236]

Atlas of the South Pacific. 2nd ed. Wellington, External Intelligence Bureau of New Zealand, 1986. 48p. col. maps. $NZ59.95.

First published 1978.

Maps (1:40,000 to 1:7.500,000) and descriptive text on facing pages cover Micronesia, Melanesia, Polynesia, and New Zealand. 20 plates. Gazetteer p.40-48.

Class No: 912.0(265)

[5237]

KENNEDY, T.F.A. A Descriptive atlas of the Pacific Islands: New Zealand, Australia, Polynesia, Melanesia, Micronesia, Philippines. 3rd ed. Wellington, A.H. Reed, 1975. 79p. 67p.

1st ed. 1966.

Grey, black-and-white maps only, illustrating each of the principal island groups. Concise supporting text. Written on a very elementary level; designed for use in school and general libraries (*Library Journal*, v.93, no.22, 15 December 1968, p.4641). Page size: 23 x 17.5cm.

Class No: 912.0(265)

Developing Countries

[5238]

CROW, B. *and* **THOMAS, A. Third World atlas.** New ed. Milton Keynes, Buckinghamshire, and Philadelphia, Open Univ. Press, 1984. 72p. col.tables, col.maps, diagrs. £27.50. ISBN: 0335150152.

32 features (maps, text, diagrams) arranged in 3 sections: 1. Definitions of 'Third World' and 'development' - 2. The making of the Third World - 3. The Third World today. Data tables p.68-71. Notes and sources p.72.

Class No: 912.0(4/9-77)

[5239]

The Third World in maps. Stellenbosch, Cape of Good Hope, Department of Development Administration and The Institute for Cartographic Analysis, Univ. of Stellenbosch, 1985. ISBN: 0797200525.

24 single sheet thematic maps. *Class No:* 912.0(4/9-77)

Europe

[5240]

AA Big road atlas. Europe. Basingstoke, Hants, Automobile Association, 1993. 208p. col. maps, index. £10.99. ISBN: 0759519554.

Road maps of 42 European countries. 56 col. town plans.

Class No: 912.0(4)

[5241]

Atlante Enciclopedico Touring. Milano, Touring Club Italiano, 3v-. 1986-.

1. *Italia* 1986. xviii, 160p. 8836502989. Explanatory sections as how maps are made *i.e.,* impact of scale, use of satellite imagery, and Glossary. 4 Major sections: 1. Thematic maps on various scales *e.g.* geomorphology, land use, vegetation, settlement, urban development - 2. Regional analysis: satellite, physical, political, environmental and industrial maps of each of Italy's 6 major regions - 3. National synthesis: general physical, population, migration, industrial employment, energy and regional data for Italy's 20 administrative regions - 4. International comparative maps setting Italy in its E.E.C. and world contexts. Glossary

.... (contd.)

p.131-143. Bibliography p.144-45. 2. *Europa* 180p. 8836502997. 3 major sections: 1. General and thematic maps with essential geographical, economic and political features, mostly at 1:20,000,000 - 2. Principal European regions *e.g.* Scandinavia, Iberia, Italy and the Balkans, Soviet Union at 1:5,000,000 - 3. Physical-political maps at 1:2,500,000 mostly duplicating previous information. Glossary p.135-45. Bibliography p.146-47.

Class No: 912.0(4)

[5242]

Atlas of Central Europe. London, Murray, 1963. 20p. maps, 2, 52p. illus.

Originally a self-contained section of the German edition of the *Grosse Bertelsmann Weltatlas*.

The 20p. of heavily coloured maps, almost all 1:1M., cover Benelux, West Germany, Austria, Switzerland, East Germany, lower half of Danube, and parts of Czechoslovakia, N. Italy and Poland. Conurbations shown. Glossary of German geographical terms; index of English equivalents of names. Gazetteer of *c.*37,000 names with grid references. Page size 32 x 24cm. *Class No:* 912.0(4)

[5243]

Baedeker/AA maps. Basingstoke, Hampshire, The Automobile Association. Double-sided map. Scales ranging from 4 to 8 miles to 1 inch with smaller scales for the multi-country/large area titles. Mostly £3.75.

Alps ISBN 0861454464 - *Austria* 0861454472 - *Belgium/ Luxembourg* 0861454499 - *Denmark* £3.25. 0861454480 - *Europe* 086145443x - *France* £3.95. 0861454375 - *Germany* 0861454421 - *Great Britain* 0861454405 - *Greece* 0861454413 - *Italy* 0861454383 - *Mexico* 0861454529 - *Middle East* £3.95. 0861454545 - *Netherlands* 0861454502 - *Scandinavia* 0861454456 - *Spain & Portugal* 0861454391 - *Switzerland* 0861454510 - *Yugoslavia* 0861454448. Designed to complement guidebook series.

Class No: 912.0(4)

[5244]

Baedeker/AA road atlas of Europe. Basingstoke, Hampshire, The Automobile Association. 268p. maps. £19.95. ISBN: 086145829x.

Covers 25 countries with 12 miles to 1 inch maps. Also route planning maps depicting the major road networks.

Class No: 912.0(4)

[5245]

Collins road atlas Europe 1990. rev. ed. Glasgow, Collins, 1990. 144p. col. maps, index, flexible cover. £7.95. ISBN: 0004477855.

First published 1982.

Route planning maps with distance map and chart p.1-9. Road maps at 1:1,000,000 (include tourist information and motorway services) p.10-76. 28 urban area maps p.77-91. 97 city and town centre plans p.92-118. Index of over 45,000 place names. *Class No:* 912.0(4)

[5246]

Euroguide travel planner 89/90 edition. Bern, Hallweg, 1989. vi,95 double pages, 96-784p. col.illus., col.maps, tables, index. ISBN: 3444004788.

1st ed. 1981.

Road maps (Europe survey maps) p.1-5 - Europe travel maps (1:1,000,000) p.6-85 - Road maps Alps (1:600,000) p.86-95 - Index of places and names p.96-190 - Hotel

....(contd.)

directory (A-Z by country) p.191-781 - Alpine passes and tunnels p.782-3. Contents table in 5 languages.
Class No: 912.0(4)

[5247]

Europe: a thematic atlas. London, Century Business in association with The Economist Books, 1992. 288p. col. illus., col. maps, tables, index. £39.95. ISBN: 071265383x.

Map features assembled in 9 main sections: History, Communications, Business, Finance, Politics, International relations, War and defence, Environment, and People and culture. Country analyses give basic reference information (area, climate, population, government, *etc.*). Chronology p.274-83. Sources p.288. 'This splendid reference work ... gives a thorough overview of Europe as a whole' (*Reference Reviews,* v.7, no.2, 1993, p.43). *Class No:* 912.0(4)

[5248]

Map of the New Europe wallchart. Wetherby, West Yorks, Reader Services Department, The Independent, 1992. col. map. £3.25.

First published in *The Independent on Sunday,* no.107, 9 February 1992, Sunday Review p.31-4.

Following the collapse of the Soviet Union and the break-up of Yugoslavia, a major part of the continent's geographical and geopolitical make-up has altered. The map and guide, with a foreword by Neal Ascherson, aims to set the scene as it is now. Data: flag (col.); constitutional status; population; national and regional capitals.
Class No: 912.0(4)

[5249]

The New Europe an encyclopedic atlas. Blombach-Schäfer, U., *and others eds.* London, Mitchell Beazley, 1992. 288p. col. illus., col. maps, index. £19.99. ISBN: 0855339225.

Published in conjunction with Bertelsmann Lexikon Verlag of Gütersloh/München.

30 contributors. 3 general sections: Europe land and people; European Community origins and the Community today. Relief map and factbox of each nation whilst text summarises its history, environment, culture, tradition, economics, and political system. Profusely illustrated.
Class No: 912.0(4)

[5250]

RAC atlas Europe. 2nd ed. Croydon, RAC Publishing, 1992. 174p. + + 48p. + + 138p. col. maps, index. ISBN: 0862112168.

Road maps for Western Europe on a scale of 1:1,000,000 (16m:1in) and Eastern Europe on 1:2,750,000 (44m:1in) p.1-74. 45 city approach maps. Place-name index. Contents page and other informative material in 5 languages.
Class No: 912.0(4)

Europe—Western

[5251]

The Bartholomew/Warne atlas of Europe: a profile of Western Europe. Edinburgh, Bartholomew; London, Warne, 1974. 128p. diagrs., graphs, tables, maps.

A combination of bar diagrams, graphs and maps, to illustrate the social, economic and political conditions in 18 Western European countries. Physical-political maps (mostly 1:3,250,000) are preceded by excellent thematic maps (density of population; migration; food production; coal and

....(contd.)

iron ore; manufacturing industry; railway network; housing; tourist industry; world trade; strategic position). Appended: Statistical profile - Glossary - Sources and subject index. Index-gazetteer: *c.*3,500 entries. Awarded the Reference Book Prize Award, Nice International Book Fair, 1975. Page size: 30 x 20cm. *Class No:* 912.0(400)

Europe—Eastern

[5252]

Atlas der Donauländer. [Atlas of Danubian lands.] Breu, J., *ed.* Wien, Franz Deutike Verlagsgesellschaft for Österreichisches Ost-und Südosteuropa Institut, 10 lieferung in loose-leaf binder, 1970-1989. $7,200. ISBN: 3700590180.

A massive and monumental thematic atlas, the work of 35 cartographers over two decades, with 48 fold-out plates (95cm x 68cm) each accompanied by a page of text. The area covered extends from the northern boundary of Czechoslovakia to the southern boundary of Albania; from just west of Regensburg in Bavaria to Odessa in the east, thus excluding the Danube headwaters. There are 43 physical, 34 population, and 67 economic and communication maps, whose texts end with bibliographical references. Standard scale is 1:2,000,000. Contents table and introduction printed in German, Russian, French and English. 'A first-rate, innovative, most attractive atlas, unfortunately affordable only [by] the world's leading libraries' (*Cartographica,* v.27, no.1, Spring 1990, p.93-5). *Class No:* 912.0(401)

[5253]

—Atlas der Donauländer. Register. Wien, Österreichisches Ost-und Südosteuropa-Institut, 1989. xxv,139p. ISBN: 370050019x.

Comprehensive multilingual gazetteer of the geographical names in the *Atlas. Class No:* 912.0(401)

[5254]

Atlas Ost-und Südosteuropa /Atlas of Eastern and Southeastern Europe. Jordan, P. *and* Kelnhofer, F., *eds.* Wien, Österreiches Ost-und Südosteuropa- Institut, 1989-. 4 sheets per year. DM28.(DM21. for subscribers to the complete atlas).

Map 5.1 G1. *Administrative subdivision of Eastern and South-eastern Europe.* 1989. DM28.

Map 5.1 H1. *The expansion of tourism from Western countries to Hungary in the eighties.* 1989. DM28.

Atlas in progress: loose-leaf collection of standard size sheets (74 x 59cm), each sheet with one or more maps on a particular theme. Each map sheet is accompanied by a booklet with background text to the map's theme and with methodological notes on its compilation and design. Aims to provide up-to-date information on the nine former socialist countries of Eastern Europe in 5 broad thematic sections: ecology, population, economy, transport, and planning. Titles, legends and text in German and English. 'Likely to become a valuable reference work' (*Cartographica,* v.28, no.1, Spring 1991, p.118-9 from where this information is derived). *Class No:* 912.0(401)

Great Britain

[5255]

AA big atlas of town plans. Basingstoke, Hampshire, Automobile Association, 1990. 96p. col. maps. £5.95. ISBN: 0861458214.

Full colour maps of 232 towns plus central London with detailed route planner and 6 airport plans.
Class No: 912.0(410)

[5256]

AA Great Britain road atlas 1994. Basingstoke, Hampshire, Automobile Association, 1993. xvi, 279p. col.maps, indexes. £17.00. ISBN: 0749506059.

Preliminaries including 5 double-page route planning maps and mileage chart. Road maps (including Ireland). London maps (11p.). 7 airport, 13 seaport and 64 town plans. A primary route map shows service stations. Bestselling road atlas with 'new digitised mapping'. A de luxe edition is available at £25.00 ISBN 0749506083.
Class No: 912.0(410)

[5257]

AA maxiscale atlas of Great Britain 1993. Basingstoke, Hampshire, The Automobile Association, 1993. 192p. maps, indexes. Softcover. £8.95. ISBN: 0749506040.

Scale 2.4 miles to 1 inch with route planner, mileage chart, street map of inner London and a 30,000 place name index. Includes Ireland. 8,000 places of interest noted and 4,000 AA recommended hotels and restaurants listed. Utilizes computerised cartography drawn from satellite imagery and the AA's automaps database. Size 403x285mm.
Class No: 912.0(410)

[5258]

AA road atlas of the British Isles 1993. Basingstoke Automobile Association, 1992. 384p. maps. £20. ISBN: 0749506008.

Includes 48p. Tourist guide to Britain, route planning maps, regional roadworks and bottlenecks, 64 indexed town plans including 11p. for central London. Scale: 3m:1in.
Class No: 912.0(410)

[5259]

The Atlas of Britain and Northern Ireland. Planned and directed by D.P. Bickmore and M.A. Shaw. Oxford, Clarendon Press, 1963. xli,200p. of maps, 22p. of gazetteer.

Standard scale, 1:2M, enlarged by 1:1M and 1:½M for regions, and reduced to 1:8M for small distribution-maps. The 1:2M and 1:1M maps are used for physical geography, agriculture, fisheries, industry, demography, housing, administrative boundaries, communications and trade. Many fascinating and unusual maps, although some aspects are ignored, *e.g.* education, health, culture, history, scenery. Gazetteer has *c.*15,000 entries, with grid references. Separate transparent overlay at 1:2M. Dudley Stamp calls the atlas 'a landmark in the history of British cartography, with originality and freshness of approach as the most striking feature (*Geographical Journal*, v.129, pt.4, December 1963, p.506-7). *Class No:* 912.0(410)

[5260]

Directory of town plans in Britain. Basingstoke, Hampshire, Automobile Association, 1985. 80p.+48p.+96p.+96p. col.maps, indexes. ISBN: 086145278x.

Town plans and street indexes of major towns and cities grouped in 4 regions: Southern England, London, Central England and Wales, Northern England and Scotland. Route planning maps p.iv-xii. *Class No:* 912.0(410)

[5261]

GREAT BRITAIN. Ordnance Survey. **1994 Ordnance Survey motoring atlas of Great Britain.** Southampton, Ordnance Survey and Twickenham, Mdx., Hamlyn, 1993. 152p. col. maps, index, pbk. ISBN: 031900323x.

1. Routeplanning maps - 2. O.S. 3 mile to 1 inch and 5 mile to 1 inch maps - 3. Central London, town centre maps and plans - 4. Index p.131-140. Excellent maps but format a trifle large for convenient use. *Class No:* 912.0(410)

[5262]

GREAT BRITAIN. Ordnance Survey. **Landranger maps.** Southampton, Ordnance Survey. Sheet size: flat 39 x 35 inches; folded 5½ x 9 inches. £3.35.

204 maps cover the country (listed in *Maps, atlases and guides catalogue 1993*). Each map encompasses an area 25 x 25 miles and shows tourist information such as camping and caravan sites, viewpoints *etc.*, as well as footpaths and bridleways. Scale 1¼ inches to 1 mile (1:50,000).
Class No: 912.0(410)

[5263]

GREAT BRITAIN. Ordnance Survey. **Pathfinder maps.** Southampton, Ordnance Survey. Sheet size: folded 5 x 9 inches; flat 39 x 18 inches. £2.99.

Replace renowned 1:25,000 First Series maps. Coverage of the country completed in 1989.

Complete list of 1373 maps in *Maps, atlases and guides catalogue 1993* (*qv.*). Particularly useful for walking and rambling showing rights of way, thus revealing the country's footpath network. Scale: 2½ inches to 1 mile (1:25,000).
Class No: 912.0(410)

[5264]

The National road atlas of Great Britain. London, George Philip, 1988. viii,112p.+61p. maps, index. £9.50. ISBN: 0540055411.

Preliminaries (p.i-viii): Motorways; service areas; M25-London orbital route; distance tables; local radio stations. Maps of Great Britain 5m:1in (p.2-64) - Approaches to London 1m:¾in (p.65-72) - Central London 1m:5in (p.73-80). 54 Town plans p.81-112. Indexes p.1-61.
Class No: 912.0(410)

[5265]

Ordnance Survey road atlas of Great Britain. Southampton, Ordnance Survey/Twickenham, Mdx, Hamlyn, 1993. 194p. col. maps. col. plans, index. ISBN: 0319002993.

First published 1983.

Four sections: 1. Motorways, major routes, route planning maps, and motorists information - 2. Road maps at 1:250,000 and legend - 3. M25 and routes into London, 9 Central London maps at 1:10,000 and street index. 12 major city maps, 16 ferry port approach maps - 4. Index to 4 miles: 1" maps. Recommended for arm-chair and driving-seat use. *Class No:* 912.0(410)

[5266]

Ordnance Survey superscale atlas of Great Britain. Southampton, Ordnance Survey; Twickenham, Mdx, Hamlyn, 1993. 212p. col. maps, index, pbk. ISBN: 0319003116.

Route planning maps and limited interchange motorway junctions. 12 town centre maps and Central London. Distances between principal towns on back endpapers. This is the largest scale single volume atlas currently available.
Class No: 912.0(410)

[5267]

Ordnance Survey touring atlas of Great Britain.
Twickenham, Middlesex, Paul Hamlyn, 1987. xxiv, 240p.
col., illus., col. maps, index. £16.95.

1. Route planning maps, motorways and major routes,
motorway strip maps, road signs p.i-xxii - 2. O.S. 1:19,080
(3 miles to the inch) maps p.1-177 - 3. Central London maps
1:10,000 (1m:6") and street index, 12 Town centre maps, 15
Ferry port and 12 Principal airport approach maps p.178-
206 - 4. Tourist gazetteer and index p.207-240.
Class No: 912.0(410)

[5268]

OWEN, T. *and* **PILBEAM, E. Ordnance Survey** map
makers to Britain since 1791. Southampton, Ordnance
Survey; London, HMSO, 1992. x,196p. illus. (many col.),
col. maps, bibliog., index. ISBN: 0319002497, OS;
0117015075, HMSO.

General history in 14 chapters (1. Origins and early maps
... 14. Market led) published to mark O.S.'s 200th
anniversary. Chronology p.179, 181, 183, 185-6.
Bibliography p.187.

A more detailed history is *A History of the Ordnance
Survey* edited by W.A. Seymour (Folkestone, Dawson,
1980. 394p. 13 maps). which relates O.S.'s origins, the birth
of the topographical surveys, the national grid, and technical
developments in map production. *Class No:* 912.0(410)

[5269]

The Postcode atlas of Great Britain and Northern Ireland
postcode area and district boundaries. Edinburgh,
Bartholomew, 1989. viii,168p. maps, indexes. ISBN:
0702809187.

All postcode boundaries clearly depicted on detailed
background maps. Scale: 4 miles to 1 inch; Greater London
1 mile to 1 inch. *Class No:* 912.0(410)

[5270]

Reader's Digest driver's atlas of the British Isles. Reprint
London, The Reader's Digest Association Ltd., 1991. 368p.
col. illus., col. maps. £21.95. ISBN: 0276412100.

First published 1988.

Successor to Reader's Digest's *Book of the road* and *New
book of the road.*

14 sections: 3. Gazetteer (p.33-79): index of 28,000
locations shown on the road maps - 4. The British Isles by
road (p.80-81): how to use the road maps, index of maps,
and guide to the symbols - 5. Major routes (p.82-89)
including ferry information - 7. Road maps on scale of 3
miles to one inch (p.92-232) - 8. Town places (p.233-301):
street maps of 128 cities and towns - 9. Britain's motorways
(p.302-320): strip plans of the principal motorways showing
interchanges, services, and distances between junctions - 10.
Places to visit (p.321-352): a selective guide (800 locations).
A reversible fold at the end of p.81-242 is designed to bridge
one map to the next; each flap carries local information. In a
comparative review together with *Collin's road atlas Britain
1988; O.S. Motoring atlas of Great Britain 1988;* and *RAC
motoring atlas Britain 1988, Reference Reviews* v.2, no.4,
December 1988, p.224 remarked that this atlas was 'clearest
of all' and that 'having tried all four atlases out in practice,
then (it) is definitely the one I would choose'.
Class No: 912.0(410)

Bibliographies

[5271]

GREAT BRITAIN. Ordnance Survey. **Maps, atlases and
guides. Catalogue 1994.** Southampton, Ordnance Survey,
1993. An annual publication. 32p. col. illus. sd. *gratis.*

Previously published as *Ordnance Survey map catalogue:
maps, atlases, guides and services.*

Contents include descriptive lists of all OS map series
intended for business, educational and leisure use *e.g.*
Routemaster maps, touring and holiday maps, historical
maps and guides, and administrative and geological maps.
Class No: 912.0(410)(01)

Scotland

[5272]

Ordnance Survey touring atlas Scotland. London, Temple
Press, 1988. 144p. col. maps, index. pbk. £7.95. ISBN:
0600556557, Temple Press; 0319001482, O.S.

Introduction (history; landscape; countryside; parks and
gardens) - 12 area tours (p.22-57) - Motorways and major
route maps (p.58-133). Also principal airports, ferry ports
and index of place names (p.139-44). O.S. mapping of the
whole of Scotland including Shetland and Orkney at scale of
3 miles: 1 inch. *Class No:* 912.0(411)

Bibliographies

[5273]

**ROYAL SCOTTISH GEOGRAPHICAL SOCIETY. The
Early maps of Scotland to 1850...** with A History of
Scottish maps by D.G. Moir. 3rd rev. ed. Edinburgh, Royal
Scottish Geographical Society, 2v., 1973-1983. maps,
facsims, bibliogs., indexes.

1. xi,243p. ISBN 0904049000. Pt.1. A History of Scottish
maps (12 chapters, notes and references p.144-153) - 2. The
Early maps of Scotland to 1850 (p.157-234). Over 450 maps
described. 2. vii,310p. 0904049027. Smaller scale maps
(arranged chronologically. Early marine charts - Road maps
- Military road maps - Canal plans - Railway plans -
Agricultural maps - Geology, Historical, County maps -
Town plans. Bibliography p.284-6. Over 2000 items
recorded. Annotated with library locations indicated.
Class No: 912.0(411)(01)

Ireland

[5274]

AA atlas of Ireland. Basingstoke, Hampshire, The
Automobile Association, 1987. xii,52p. col.illus., col.maps,
index. Softcover. £2.99. ISBN: 0861455967.

Scale 5½ miles to the inch. 9 town plans. 3000 place name
index. *Class No:* 912.0(415)

[5275]

Atlas of Ireland. Prepared under the direction of the Irish
National Committee for Geography. Dublin, Royal Irish
Academy, 1979. 104p. illus., table, maps.

Sections: General reference - Geology and geophysics -
Geomorphology and hydrology - Soils - Climate - Flora and
fauna - Settlement (*e.g.* Prehistoric sites) - Population -
Primary production - Manufacturing - Tertiary activities -
Social and culture. Includes 5 town plans. Notes to maps.
Table of English and Irish place-names. Air photographs:
'The Irish landscape'. Index (*c.*800 place-names). Page size:

....(contd.)

33x41.5cm. 'This is an important reference volume on Ireland' (M.O. Shannon. *Irish Republic,* 1986. Entry 57). *Class No:* 912.0(415)

[5276]

GREAT BRITAIN. Department of the Environment for Northern Ireland. Ordnance Survey. **The Ordnance Survey road atlas of Ireland.** Belfast. 47p. maps. £6.40.

36p. maps derived from O.S.N.I.'s 1:250,000 Holiday Series with 29 town plans. A second section divides the whole of Ireland into 16 Touring Areas, each detailing places of interest. *Class No:* 912.0(415)

[5277]

An Illustrated record of the Ordnance Survey in Ireland. Dublin, Ordnance Survey of Ireland; Belfast, Ordnance Survey of Northern Ireland, 1991. 104p. col. illus., col. maps. £5. ISBN: 0904996026.

Gives 'the flavour of the activities, successes and trials of the Ordnance Survey since it was established in Ireland in 1824'. *Class No:* 912.0(415)

[5278]

The Ordnance Survey road atlas of Ireland. Dublin, Gill & Macmillan, 1985. 82p. col.illus., col.maps. £8.95. ISBN: 071711404x.

36 plates of national maps complemented by road and urban area maps, a gazetteer, and basic touring information. *Class No:* 912.0(415)

Bibliographies

[5279]

GREAT BRITAIN. Department of the Environment for Northern Ireland. Ordnance Survey. **Map catalogue** with notes on related publications and services. Belfast, HM Stationery Office, 1988. 36p., maps, sd. *gratis* from O.S., Colby House, Stranmillis Court, Belfast.

First published 1935. Last previous ed. 1986.

Descriptive catalogue of OSNI map series and services. Free Supplements available quarterly. *Class No:* 912.0(415)(01)

Eire

[5280]

EIRE. OIFIG NA SUIRBHEIREACHTA ORDNAIS. Half-inch maps of Ireland. Dublin, Ordnance Survey. £3.35. each.

Sheet no.5 is no longer published. It is replaced by Sheet 5 (Northern Ireland) published by Ordnance Survey of Northern Ireland.

24 maps (1:126,720) primarily intended for motorist and cyclist use. Many unclassified roads not shown on the *Quarter-million* maps are included. *Class No:* 912.0(417)

[5281]

EIRE. OIFIG NA SUIRBHEIREACHTA ORDNAIS. Quarter-million maps of Ireland. New holiday series (1:250,000). Dublin, Ordnance Survey. £3.35. each.

4 sheets each containing overlaps of adjoining sheets. National Primary, Secondary and Regional roads are given with their classification numbers. Inset city and town maps, distance chart and a guide to places of tourist interest are printed on the reverse. *Class No:* 912.0(417)

Commonwealth

[5282]

Atlas of British overseas expansion. Porter, A.N., *ed.* London, Routledge, 1991. x,279p. maps, plans, bibliog., index. £50. ISBN: 0415019184.

92 chronological map/text features chart and chronicle Britain's growth as a maritime commercial power from the late 15th century to the postwar withdrawal from Empire (*e.g.* Bristol and the Atlantic 1480 to 1509 ... Exports from the West Indies ... The Commonwealth 1931 to 1989). Also 20 shorter features on 20 towns and cities of imperial significance. Bibliography p.238-50. 137 black/white maps. More academic in tone and content than C. Bayly's *Atlas of the British Empire. Class No:* 912.0(41-44)

London

[5283]

Greater London street atlas comprehensive edition. 7th rev. ed. London, Nicholson, 1991. 416p. col. maps, indexes. ISBN: 0702812536.

First published by Geographia in 1977.

Street atlas covering 1500 square miles of streets of an extended Greater London area. Information includes hospitals, police stations, sporting venues, museums, galleries, and underground stations. Index includes over 750,000 entries. Scale: Inner London 1:11,520 (5.5 inches: 1 mile); Greater London 1:20,000 inches: 1 mile). *Class No:* 912.0(421)

Bibliographies

[5284]

BRITISH MUSEUM. London: an excerpt from the British Museum *Catalogue of printed maps, charts and plans.* Photolithographic ed. to 1964. London, Trustees of the British Museum, 1967. 202 cols.

About 2,500 entries. Arrangement: General atlases - General plans - Administrative divisions - Commercial, industrial and professions - Communications - Disease and medical (A-Z) - Public services - Religion - Sociology - General views - Particular plans and views - London: City - London; Environs. Appendix: Catalogues, dicitonaries, etc. Topographical index. *Class No:* 912.0(421)(01)

Wales

[5285]

Atlas cenedlaethol Cymru/National atlas of Wales. Carter, H., *ed.* Aberystwyth, University of Wales Press for the Social Science Committee, Board of Celtic Studies, Univ. of Wales, 1981-1984. illus., maps, bibliogs. £250.00. ISBN: 0708307752.

Over 200 thematic map sheets compiled by 20 specialists from universities and other higher education institutions in and beyond Wales. Sheets are grouped and numbered in 9 sections and housed in a stout box folder: 1. Physical environment - 2. Political development - 3. Culture - 4. Economic history - 5. Land use and agriculture - 6. Industry - 7. Services and communications - 8. Population and settlement - 9. Regional policy and planning. Maps are drawn by Geoprojects (UK) Ltd. and the Department of Geography, University College of Wales, Aberystwyth, on a general scale of 8 miles to 1 inch (1:500,000). Transparent reference overlays incorporate National Grid to facilitate

....(contd.)

precise location of the mapped information. The maps are fully bilingual and are accompanied by a commentary text with bibliographies. H.M. Griffiths' 'The National Atlas of Wales', (*Cartographical Journal*, v.26, no.1, June 1989, p.7-14) traces its origins and the factors influencing its development and outlines aspects of its design, compilation and production. *Class No:* 912.0(429)

[5286]
Welsh Office atlas/Atlas y Swyddfa Cymreig. Cardiff, HM Stationery Office, 1972-75. maps.

An atlas of planning maps, 1:425,000, based on Ordnance Survey maps. 23 maps: 1. General reference map - 2. Administrative areas - 3. Parliamentary constituencies - 4. Home population - 7. Forestry - 8.8a. Traffic volumes, 1965, 1972 - 9. Rate support grant, 1971-72 - 10. Local office areas and assisted areas - 11. Water resources - 12. Energy facilities, production and distribution - 13. Derelict land, 1971-72 - 14. Agricultural land - 15. Conservation of the countryside - 16. Population distribution, 1971 - 17. Health facilities - 18. Population density, 1971 - 19. Communications - 20. Annual average rainfall, 1941-1970 - 20a. Climate. Map size, 35.5 x 22cm. *Class No:* 912.0(429)

Germany

[5287]
AA big road atlas Germany. Basingstoke, Hants., Automobile Association, 1993. 224p. col. maps. £12.99. ISBN: 0749506628.

Produced in conjunction with ADAC (German Automobile Club) this large scale atlas has maps on the scale of 2.4 miles to 1 inch. Over 17000 place names are indexed. *Class No:* 912.0(430)

[5288]
Topographischer atlas Berlin Entwicklung und Struktur der Stadt Berlin in 55 Karten und 20 Luftbildern mit erläuternden Texten. Pape, C. *and* Freitag, V., *eds.* Berlin, Dietrich Reimer Verlag, 1987. 189p. illus. (some col.), maps (some col.), bibliog., index. ISBN: 3496008970.

74 explanatory text and maps in double-page features organized in 8 sections: 1. Die geographische Lage Berlins - 2. Das Stadtgebiet im Naturraum - 3. Die Entwicklung des Stadtgebietes - 4. Zentren städtischen Lebens - 5. Typen städtischer Wohngebiete - 6. Raumtypen städtischer Wirtschaft und Verwaltung - 7. Kultur-und Freizeitstätten - 8. Die amtlichen Karten Berlins. Auswahl aus dem neueren Schriftums p.184-89. Published to mark Berlin's 750th anniversary. *Class No:* 912.0(430)

Bibliographies

[5289]
ELKINS, T.H. 'Atlases and maps of Berlin,' *Geographical Journal*, v.154, no.3, November 1988, p.435-437.

Survey of cartographical material published to commemorate the 750th anniversary of the City's foundation. *Class No:* 912.0(430)(01)

Federal Republic of Germany

[5290]
Auto atlas Bundesrepublik Deutschland 1989/90. Berlin, R.V. Reise-und Verkehrsverlag, 1989. xvi, 304p. col.maps. Flexible cover. ISBN: 3575117020.

Karten in Massstab 1:800,000 p.l-xvi. Karten 1:200,000 Die Autokennzeichen sind Abkürzungen, die abgeliefet von Namen der Kreisstädte oder der Kreise p.178-240. Stadtpläne mit Strassenverzeichnis p.241-299. Entfernungstabelle (distance tables) p.300-1. Legends of conventional signs in English and German. *Class No:* 912.0(430.1)

[5291]
Der Grosse ADAC General Atlas. München, ADAC Verlag, 1985. 394p. col.illus., col.maps, index. ISBN: 3870032421.

1. Europa 1:4,500,000 (6 folded maps) - 2. Bundesrepublik Deutschland 1:200,000 (52 folded maps) - 3. Die schönten Reiseziele in der Bundesrepublik Deutschland (p.119-182) - 4. Stadtpläne of 15 cities (p.183-213) - 5. Autobahnkarten 1:600,000 (p.215-233) - 6. Spezialkarten und sonstige Angaben (p.235-246) - 7. Alpenländer 1:750,000 (p.247-57). *Class No:* 912.0(430.1)

[5292]
STATISTISCHES BUNDESAMT, INSTITUT FÜR LANDESKUNDE, AND INSTITUT FÜR RAUMFORSCHUNG. Die Bundesrepublik Deutschland in Karten. Mainz, W. Kohlhammer Verlag, 1965-69. 200 col. maps on 100 loose sheets (mostly 83 x 111 cm.) folded once in custom built wooden map case.

Divided in 5 sections: 1. General overview and administrative districts - 2. Physical geography - 3. Demography and social geography - 4. Economic geography - 5. Regional planning. Scale 1:1,000,000 or 1:2,000,000. 'The most comprehensive cartographical work on Germany' (D.S. Detwiler and I.E. Detweiler. *West Germany*, 1987. Entry 31). *Class No:* 912.0(430.1)

German Democratic Republic

[5293]
Atlas Deutsche Demokratische Republik. Leipzig, Haack Gotha, 1981. Fascicules in metal binder. Index.

5 general (politico-administrative, physical, economic structure, settlement systems, orographical) and 50 thematic maps arranged in 6 sections: physical conditions, population, industry, agriculture and forestry, traffic and trade. Large format national atlas. *Class No:* 912.0(430.2)

Luxembourg

[5294]
Atlas du Luxembourg. Prepared by Department of Geography, Univ. of Nottingham in collaboration with a group of Luxembourg geographers. Luxembourg, Board of National Education, 1971-76. 3pts. loose-leaf.

The completed atlas consists of some 70 sheets. The 42 sheets forming pts. 1-2 are in 6 sections - historical, physical, administrative, demographic, economic and social. The relief and geological sheets are on a scale 1:200,000. Favourably reviewed in *Geography* (v.58, pt.1, no. 258, January 1973, p.100). Sheet size, 37.5x50cm. *Class No:* 912.0(435.9)

Austria

[5295]

Atlas der Republik Österreich. Hrsg. von der Kommission für Raumforschung der (Österreichischen Akademie der Wissenschaften unter der Gesamtleitung ihres Obmannes Hans Bobek. Wien, Kartographische Anstalt Freytag-Berndt und Artaria, 1961-.

85 major maps, 1:1M. 12 sections - general, topographical, climate, hydrology, soil, flora and fauna, economy, population, agriculture and forestry, industry, power, mining, trade, transport and communications, culture. *Class No:* 912.0(436)

Czechoslovakia

[5296]

Atlas Ceskoslovenské Socialistické Republiky. Praha, Ustrední Správa Geodézie a Kartografie, 1966. 16p. 58pl. of maps.

58 maps covering geology, geomorphology, climate, biogeography, population, mining, industries (chemicals; textiles), agriculture, transport, trade, housing, health, social security, education and culture of Czechoslovakia. Headings and explanatory notes on maps in Czech, English and Russian. Index-gazetteer of *c.*5,500 names. Very favourably reviewed in *The Geographical Journal*, (v.136, pt.3, September 1970, p.487). Page size, 49x43.5cm. *Class No:* 912.0(437)

[5297]

Atlas SSR. [Atlas of the Slovak Socialist Republic.] Mazúr, E., *and others, eds.* Bratislava, Slovensá Kartografia, 1980. 1,136p. maps.

161 contributors. General key to the atlas, map titles and texts in the appendix given in English and Russian as well as Slovak. 'This is the first complete Slovak atlas and covers ever aspect of the country's geography' (D. Short. *Czechoslovakia*, 1986. Entry 46). *Class No:* 912.0(437)

Hungary

[5298]

Magyarorszäg nemzeti atlasza/National atlas of Hungary. Budapest, Cartographia, 1968. 112p. maps, charts.

100 pages of maps (179 maps) in 8 chapters: topographic, population, agriculture, industry, transport and communications, trade, social and culture. Prepared in co-operation with the Geographical Committee of the Hungarian Academy of Sciences. Page size, 29x40.5cm. *Class No:* 912.0(439)

France

[5299]

Atlas de France. Comité National de Géographie. 2nd ed. Paris Éditions Géographiques de France, 1951-59. 80pl. of maps.

First published 1933-45.

The 2nd ed. has its 80 sheets divided as follows: Géographie physique (26) - Biogéographie (8) - Géographie économique (29) - Géographie humaine et géographie politique (17). Where information was unchanged, plates were repeated from the 1st ed. Each sheet may contain various maps. Thus, sheet no.80, Santé publique, comprises 14 maps, showing incidence of major diseases, etc. in

.... (contd.)

France. Distributions are mainly shown by départements, in flat tints. More important maps are in 4 sheets at 1:1M. No index gazetteer. Page size, 50x38.5cm. *Class No:* 912.0(44)

[5300]

Atlas de la France et de ses régions un atlas cartographique au 1:250.000. Paris, Sélection du Readers Digest, 1993. 278p. maps. 420F. ISBN: 2709804670. *Class No:* 912.0(44)

[5301]

Atlas des départments français d'Outre-mer. Bordeaux-Talence, Centre d'Études de Géographie Tropicale du CRNS, 1975-.

1. *La Réunion.* 1976. 192p. 250F. ISBN 2222019117. 37 maps (1:150,000). 'The range of subject matter covers virtually every aspect of Réunion's geography and the written material both complements and supplements the cartography' (*Geographical Journal, v.144,no.2, July 1978, p.376-7).* 2. *La Martinique.* 1977. 120p. 430F. 2222021642. 3. *La Guadeloupe.* 1982. 430F. 2222031052. 4. *La Guyane.* 1979. 222202501x. 36 col. map features: 1. Situation - 2. La Région des Guyanes ... 17. Archéologie - 18. Cartes anciennes - 19. Histoire Coloniale. *Class No:* 912.0(44)

[5302]

Atlas Paris par arrondissements. Clermont-Ferrand, Services de Tourisme Michelin, 1988. 70p. col.maps. Softcover. ISBN: 206000151x.

Les rues de Paris p.6-20. Plan de Paris p.21-51 with other maps Boulogne-Billancourt; Clichy, Levallois-Perret, Neuilly-sur-Seine; Saint Ouen p.54-8. Also Métro, Résau Express Régional, Autobus, Lignes Urbaines, and Aéroports p.60-65. Les Bois de Paris p.68-9. *Class No:* 912.0(44)

[5303]

CD-Atlas de France. Paris, Chadwyck-Healey France. CD-ROM, floppy disk and manual in a box. £750.

Developed by GIP Reclus, Argo-Infographie, and the publishers.

Economic, social, demographic and political data by regions, départements, cantons and communes. *Class No:* 912.0(44)

[5304]

Collins road atlas France 1990. rev. ed. Glasgow, Collins, 1990. 128p. col. maps, index, flexible cover. £6.95. ISBN: 000477073.

First published 1987.

Road and tourist maps of France at 1:250,000 p.2-115. Map of Greater Paris at 1:100,000 p.116-7. Plan of Paris and useful information p.118-19. 25 town plans p.120-22. Index of 6,000 places with a post office. Mapping by Institut Géographique National. *Class No:* 912.0(44)

[5305]

Michelin regional maps - France. Harrow, Middlesex, Michelin Tyre PLC., 1990. £2.65.

Brittany - Normandy - Pays de Loire - Poitou. Charentes - Aquitaine - Midi Pyrénées - Nord: Flandre. Artois. Picardie - Paris region - Centre - Auvergne Limousin - Languedoc Rousillion - Champagne Ardennes - Alsace et Lorraine - Bourgogne Franche Comté - Rhône Alpes - Provence Côte D'Azur - Vallée du Rhône. Scale 1:200,000 (1 cm = 2 km). *Class No:* 912.0(44)

[5306]

Michelin road atlas of France. 2nd ed. Twickenham, Middlesex, Paul Hamlyn, 1988. xvi, 337p. col. illus., col. maps, index. £16.95. ISBN: 0600559092.

First published 1987.

Route planning maps; motoring in France; Paris area; snow affected roads p.viii-xvi. Maps of France on a scale of 1:200,000 (3.15 miles to the inch) p.1-269. Index (38,000 names), including 52 plans of cities and principal towns, p.270-337. Definitive road atlas for professional drivers, tourists, and businessmen with symbols locating a wide range of sites and tourist attractions. Designed to be used with other Michelin touring publications.

Class No: 912.0(44)

Italy

[5307]

Atlante stradale d'Italia. Milano, Touring Club Italiano, 3v. L81,000 set. L28,500 single volumes.

3v. road atlas: *Nord*; *Centro*; *Sud*. Scale 1:200,000. A fully annotated review of the more important tourist localities is placed at the beginning of each volume.

Class No: 912.0(450)

[5308]

Atlante tematico d'Italia. Milano, Touring Club Italiano and Consiglio Nazionale delle Ricerche, 4 boxed sets, 1990-. 800p. col. maps, tables, bibliogs. ISBN: 8836504299.

This new social, economic, environmental and cultural profile of Italy has 126 numbered fascicules arranged in 4 thematic boxed sets: 1. Riferimenti generali ed elementi fisico-ambientali - 2. Popolazione e insediamenti - 3. Risorse e attivitá economiche - 4. Patrimonio culturale e ambiente. Each fascicule consists of text, map(s), and sources and bibliography. At the time of compilation 32 fascicules had been issued *e. g.* 3. Italy in the Mediterranean area ... 52. Urban system ... 72. Energy ... 96-7. Folklore (All fascicules have Italian and English titles). Maps: 8 colours. Scale varies 1:1 million - 1:12 million. 'In the Thematic Atlas of Italy will be found in uniquely authoritative and comprehensible form the cartographic expression of the major recent changes in Italy's economic and social geography that are the reality of today's Italy' (*Geographical Journal*, v.158, no.3, November 1992, p.331-2).

Class No: 912.0(450)

[5309]

Collins road atlas Italy 1990. London, Collins, 1990. In association with Instituto Geografio De Agostini. 128p. £7.95. ISBN: 0004477094.

Road maps 1:250,000 (p.4-91) - Town plans (p.92-112). Index to placenames p.113-28. Large size.

Class No: 912.0(450)

Spain

[5310]

Atlas grafico de España Aguilar. 2nd ed. Madrid, Aguilar, 1982. 507p. col.illus., col.maps, index. ISBN: 8403421087.

Sumptuous pictorial atlas with 124 physical and thematic map features. Place name index p.439-507. Most maps on scale 1:250,000. *Class No:* 912.0(460)

[5311]

Atlas nacionale de España. Madrid, Instituto Geográfico y Catastral, 1965-1968.

The atlast consists of 28 topographical 75x52cm and 72 thematic maps in loose sheet form, with transparent overlays. Accompanying these are two bound volumes, - an index of over 40,000 place-names, and 'Reseña geográfica del *Atlas nacional de España,* gives geographical data. *The Geographical Journal* (v.135, pt.2, June 1969, p.310-1) finds the maps 'well above the usual standard of national atlases, being exceptionally clear and well printed'.

Class No: 912.0(460)

[5312]

Gran atlas de Carreteras España Portugal. Barcelona, Plaza & Janes, 1992. ix,320p. col. maps, index. ISBN: 3575188696.

Available from Geo-Center International with cover title of *Euro-road Atlas Spain and Portugal.* £9.99. 357511381

Maps on scale of 1:300,000 and A-Z of places p.10-278. 60 towns plans and index p.279-320. Preliminaries and guide to index in 5 Iberian and 3 Western European languages.

Class No: 912.0(460)

[5313]

Nuevo atlas de España. Madrid, Aquilar, 1961. 455p. illus., tables, graphs, maps.

An excellent reference atlas of maps and illustrations, in 4 sections: general (physical, political and economic maps, at 1:3,250,000); historical, regional; provincial (at 1:600,000), including Spanish colonies (*e.g.* Fernando Po). 'Sintesis geográfia-estadistica', p.21-95. Gazetteer, p.395-455, - c.30,000 entries, with grid references. *Class No:* 912.0(460)

Portugal

[5314]

AMORIM GIRAO, A. de. Atlas de Portugal: continente, ilhas adjacentes e provincias ultramarinas. Coimbra, Instituto de Estudos Geográficos, 1958. 43pl. of maps.

Published in commemoration of the quincentenary of the death of Prince Henry the Navigator. The 43 plates of maps (scale, 1:1M to 1:5M.) cover geology, drainage, climate, population, agriculture, industries, communications, trade, dialects and the overseas provinces. Text and captions in Portuguese and English. Plate size, 42.5x30cm. 'A comprehensive, if now somewhat dated, atlas of Portugal' (P.T.H. Unwin. *Portugal,* 1987. Entry 46).

Class No: 912.0(469)

[5315]

Atlas de Portugal. Lisboa, Cartas do Instituto Geográphico e Cadastral, 1988. (Selecções do Reader's Digest). 159p. illus., col.maps, tables, index.

1. Portugal no mundo - 2. Mapas de Portugal (p.10-40) - 3. Portugal hogie e ortem (geology; parks; vegetation; rivers; temperature and climate; fishing; tourism; agriculture; industry; architecture; Portuguese overseas discoveries p.41-88). 4. Almanaque (geographical tables p.89-104) - 5. Portugal em imagens (pictorial feature p.105-120). *Class No:* 912.0(469)

[5316]
Atlas turístico de Portugal. Lisboa, Lucidus, 1986. 392p. col.illus., col.maps, tables, index.

Less an atlas, more a sumptuously illustrated guidebook which includes Azores, Madeira and Macao. General tourist and geographical data and information p.343-387. Index of places p.389-90. Mostly in Portuguese but occasional short passages in English. *Class No:* 912.0(469)

USSR

[5317]
Atlas SSSR. Mockba, Glavnoe Upravlenie Geodezii i Kartografii pri Sovete Ministrov SSSR, 1983. 25p. col.illus., col.maps.

Previous eds. 1947, 1954, 1955, 1962, 1969.

General atlas of the USSR in 3 main sections: physical maps (p.22-80); maps of natural conditions *viz* geology, tectonics, minerals, geomorphology, climate, soils *etc.* (p.86-121); economic maps *viz* population, electric power, industries (p.128-203). Geographical tables p.204-6. Pagination in Arabic numerals. *Class No:* 912.0(47)

[5318]
DEWDNEY, J.C. USSR in maps. London, Hodder & Stoughton; New York, Holmes and Meier, 1982. vi,117p. maps, diagrs., bibliog., index. £6.95; $29.50. ISBN: 0340244143, UK; 0841907609, US.

49 b/w maps, each accompanied by a comprehensive text, in 4 sections: Physical environment; Human geography; Economic geography; the Regions. An introduction expands on the problems of attempting a cartographic representation of a country of the size of the U.S.S.R. 'Perhaps the best general atlas of the Soviet Union now on the market' (*Choice*, v.20,no.6, February 1983, p.808). *Class No:* 912.0(47)

[5319]
Road atlas of the USSR. Svirskaia, K. *and* Turkina, N., *eds.* Moskva, GUGK, 1989. 176p, maps, plans, index. £9.95.

Russian language atlas which includes distance charts town and city plans, and an index of place names. *Class No:* 912.0(47)

Poland

[5320]
Narodowy atlas Polski. Warszawa, Polska Akademia Nauk, Instytut Geografii, 1973-78. xlp. 127 pl. of maps.

127 folding coloured maps - general, analytical, socioeconomic and sociocultural at scale 1:200,000 and smaller. English language version as *National atlas of Poland* (186p). *Class No:* 912.0(475)

Scandinavia

[5321]
Cappelens bilatlas Norden. [Cappelen's car atlas of the Nordic states.] Oslo, J.W. Cappelens Forlag. 1981. In cooperation with Norges Automobil-Forbund. 287p. maps.

Detailed maps of Norway, Denmark, Sweden and Finland (Scale 1:6,000,000). Text in English, French, German, Dutch as well as Scandinavian languages. *Class No:* 912.0(48)

Finland

[5322]
Fennia suuri Suomi-Kartasto/Kartverk över Finland/ Finland in maps/Finnischer atlas 1:250,000. Helsinki, Maanmittanshallitus (*i.e.*, National Board of Survey) ja Weilin and Göös, 1979. 224p. col.mnaps, index. ISBN: 0513519554.

GT road maps on scale (1:250,000) larger than in any previous atlas of Finland. 102 town plans (1:40,000). Distances tables p.165. Gazetteer of 9000 place names. *Class No:* 912.0(480)

[5323]
Suomen Kartasto/Atlas of Finland/Atlas över Finland. Helsinki, Kustannososakeyhti ö Otava, 1960. viii, 39 pl. of maps.

Originally Atlas de Finlande (Helsinki, Société de Géographie de Finlande, 2v. 1899). Under present title 2v., 1925-29.

39 double plates of special maps of excellent quality; scales, 1:1M., 1:6M., etc. 455 maps, covering altitudes and depths, geodesy and mapping, geology, climate (34 maps), hydrology, fauna, flora, vegetation zones, forests and peatlands, population (37 maps), arable area, agriculture (64 maps), forestry, industry, foreign trade and harbours, traffic, inland trade, co-operative movement, finance, education, health and medical care, history, elections, geographic regions, communications. There are even maps showing distribution of dentists, blue-and-grey-eyed people. Norwegian lemmings, and sausage factories. Largest scale, 1:1M. (population maps); usually each double-plate has several small maps. No subject index, although there is a detailed contents list in Finnish, English and Swedish. Legends are also trilingual. Page size 45 x 36cm.

Separate [*Explanatory notes*] in Finnish (1962. 122p.) describes and supplements the maps. An English edition of this has been promised.

New edition 1976-1985 published by National Board of Survey and Suomen Maantietaellinen Seura. Maps and figures in Finnish, Swedish and English. Accompanying articles in Finnish with Swedish and English in enclosures. *Class No:* 912.0(480)

Sweden

[5324]
Atlas över Sverige. Svenska Sällskapet för Antropologi och Geographi. Stockholm, Generalstabens Litografiska Anstalls Förlag, 1953-71.

Issued in 75 fascicules. 150 full-size coloured maps, with descriptive texts. A regional atlas of Sweden, covering geology, meteorology, mineral deposits, climatology, soil, vegetation, population, agriculture, trade and port traffic. *Class No:* 912.0(485)

Denmark

[5325]
Atlas over Danmark. København, Det Konelige Danske Geografiske Selskab, 1976-. illus., maps, bibliog.

1st series.

1. *Landskabsformerne* (The landscapes). 1949. 32p.; explanatory booklet. 129p.

2. *Befolkningen* (The population). 1961. 2p.; explanatory booklet. 124p.

V.1 has many sectional maps, with text and indexes to

....(contd.)

types of landscape, in Danish and English. V.2 consists of population maps, 1:200,000, each dot respresenting 25 persons. The booklets include illustrations and bibliographies. Page size, 55 x 37.5cm.

2nd series.

1. *Opgivne og tilplantede landburgsarealer:Jylland* (Abandoned and afforested agricultural lands in Central Jutland). 1976. 46p. 10p. pl.

2. *Topografisk atlas Danmark* 1976. 192p. Includes 79 main maps and encompasses Greenland. English summaries of commentary. Bibliography p.178-79. No gazetteer/index. *Class No:* 912.0(489)

[5326]
Danmark 1:100 000 topografisk atlas. 3rd ed. København, Kort-og Matrikelstyrelsen, 1989. 161p. maps, tables, index. ISBN: 8774500686.

60 x double page dated maps supported by 22,000 gazetteer entries. Most detailed map of Denmark. *Class No:* 912.0(489)

Netherlands

[5327]
Atlas van Nederland/Atlas of the Netherlands. Compiled for the Federation for the Scientific Atlas of the Netherlands. 's-Gravenhage, Staatsdrukkerij- en Uitgeverijbedrift, 1963-77. Supplements 1978-1981. diagrs., tables, maps. Looseleaf.

98 map plates (double-page spreads), backed by commentary or other maps. 17 sections (1. Topography and cartography - 2. Geology, geophysics, mineral resources - 3. Geomorphology - 4. Soils (9 plates, 1:200,000) - 5. Climate - 6. Vegetation and biogeography - 7. Water management - 8. Historical geography - 9. Settlements - 10. Dialect and regional - 11. Population - 12. Public utilities - 13. Agriculture - 14. Fisheries - 15. Manufacturing industries - 16. Commerce and transportation - 17. Physical training). No gazetteer. *Class No:* 912.0(492)

[5328]
—Atlas van Nederland. 's-Gravenhage, Staatsdrukkerij/ uitgeverij, 21v. 20 parts each of 24p. col.illus., col.maps, col.graphs, tables, bibliogs, sd. ISBN: 901205006, set.

Under the auspices of the Stichting Wetenschappelijke *Atlas van Nederland* (1977).

1. *Bevolking* - 2. *Bewoningsgeschiedenis* - 3. *Steden* - 4. *Dorpen* - 5. *Wonen* - 6. *Voorzieningen* - 7. *Recreatie* - 8. *Werken* - 9. *Bedrijven* - 10. *Landbouw* - 11. *Poort van Europa* - 12. *Infrastructuur* - 13. *Geologie* - 14. *Bodem* - 15. *Water* - 16. *Landschap* - 17. *Milieu* - 18. *Ruimtelijke ordening* - 19. *Stadsinrichting* - 20. *Landinrichting* - 21. *Registers en indexen*. All volumes are equipped with a glossary and a bibliography. *Class No:* 912.0(492)

[5329]
Pictorial atlas of the Netherlands. The Hague, Information and Documentation Centre for the Geography of the Netherlands, Univ. of Utrecht/Ministry of Foreign Affairs, 1977. 40p. maps.

18 thematic maps and English text. *Class No:* 912.0(492)

[5330]
TAMSMA, R. The Netherlands in 50 maps. Amsterdam, Koninklijk Nederlands Aardrijkskundig Genootschap, 1988. 126p. DFL24.90. ISBN: 9068090623.

Continuation of *The Netherlands in 100 maps* (1977).

Brings together maps first printed in issues of *Tijdschrift voor Economische en Sociale Geografie* with original commentaries. 'An essential compendium of information about the current geography of the Netherlands and is highly recommended because the commentaries ... enhance considerably the value of the original journal maps' (*Bulletin of Society of University of Cartographers*, v.22, no.1, 1988, p.46). *Class No:* 912.0(492)

Belgium

[5331]
Atlas de Belgique/ Atlas van Belgie. De Smet, R.E., *and others.* Bruxelles, Royaume de Belgique Comité National de Géographie, 1950-1972. 266p. bibliogs.

65 maps (50x60cm) grouped under 13 headings: 1. Belgium in Europe - 2. Cartography and geophysics - 3. Soils and sub-soils - 4. Climatology - 5. Hydrology - 6. The North Sea coast - 7. Biogeography - 8. Human geography - 9. Forestry and agriculture - 10. Industry - 11. Transport and commerce - 12. Regional geography - 13. Administrative areas. Each map accompanied by text and bibliography. *Class No:* 912.0(493)

[5332]
Atlas of Belgium. Bruxelles, Belgian Information and Documentation Institute, 1987. 30p. maps.

10 topical maps accompanied by text: 1. Belgium in Europe - 2. Political structure - 3. Population - 4. Agriculture - 5. Metallurgy - 6. Chemicals and textiles - 7. Energy - 8. Roads - 9. Railways - 10. Inland waterways. 'A useful, if general, up-to-date picture of the state of the nation' (R.C. Riley *Belgium,* 1989, Entry 59). *Class No:* 912.0(493)

Switzerland

[5333]
Atlas der Schweiz. Imhof, E. Berne, Verlag der Eidgenössischen Landestopographie, 1965-78. illus., tables, maps. Looseleaf.

General scale (double-spread): 1:½M., with large-scale topographical maps at 1:50,000 of Aletsch Glacier and other selected areas. More than 404 coloured maps. Topographical relief plates from the *Schweizerischer Mittelschulatlas.* Thematic maps on 9 topics, from topography to traffic. Explanatory notes and statistical tables accompany each map. Good choice of colours for contours, rocks, snowfields and glaciers. Page size, 50 x 37.5cm.

'It is no doubt the finest national atlas ever produced' (*The Geographical Magazine*, August 1978, p.772). *Class No:* 912.0(494)

Rumania

[5334]
Atlasul din Republica Socialistă România. Bucharest, Editura Didactică Și Pedagogică, 1978. 140p.

Physical, economic and tourist maps of Bucharest and of Rumania's 38 local administrative areas. *Class No:* 912.0(498)

[5335]

Atlasul Republicii Socialiste România. Bucharest, Editura Academiei Republicii Socialiste România, 1974-79. 5 fascicules.

'This definitive atlas of Romania is divided into thirteen sections containing seventy-six maps which present aspects of the physical, economic and social geography of the country' (A. and D. Deletant. *Romania*, 1985. Entry 29). *Class No:* 912.0(498)

[5336]

România: atlas rutier. Dragomir, V., *and others*. Bucharest, Editura Sport-Tourism, 1982. 204p. maps, index.

73 maps at a scale of 1:350,000. 40p. of town plans. Glossary of road signs. Place-name index 'The most detailed road atlas of Rumania published since the last war' (A. and D. Deletant. *Romania*, 1985. Entry 32). *Class No:* 912.0(498)

China

[5337]

Atlas of China. Chicago, Rand McNally, 1990. 48p. illus., maps, index. pbk. $8.95. ISBN: 0528833855.

Two-page maps of The World, Asia, China, and 4 regional maps of China (1:3,000,000) including Tibet followed by single page maps of areas surrounding major cities (1:1,000,000). Updated from *The international atlas* (1969) showing political capitals and boundaries with cultural, transport, hydrographic and topographic features. Detailed index of 11,000 entries. For home and school use. *Class No:* 912.0(510)

[5338]

Atlas of the People's Republic of China. Yang Dan, *ed.* Beijing, Foreign Languages Press China Cartographic Publishing House, 1989. Distributed by China International Book Trading Corporation, Beijing. variously paginated but 58 mostly double page maps +112p. index. col. maps. $49.95. ISBN: 0835123197; 711900560x.

Based on Chinese pinyin edition 1983.

32 administrative maps of provinces, autonymous regions and Beijing municipality mostly on scale 1:2,000,000 (table of facts or short articles on back of each map covering population, area, climate, major products, and administrative set up December 1987). 17 topographical maps on various scales. Finely produced atlas. *Class No:* 912.0(510)

[5339]

HSIEH CHIAO-MIN. Atlas of China. New York, McGraw-Hill, 1973. xvi,282p.

273 two-colour maps (1. Physical - 2. Cultural [and economic] - 3. Religion [including cities] - 4. Historical. Includes Taiwan). Bibliography (running commentary) and map sources (mostly Chinese), p.263-7. Glossary. Two indexes to maps. 'Has strictly limited value as a reference tool' (*China quarterly*, no.63, September 1975, p.566-7). *Class No:* 912.0(510)

[5340]

The National atlas of China. Chang Chi-yun, *ed.* Taiwan, National War College, 5v., 1960-67. maps.

1. Taiwan - 2. Hsitsang (Tibet), Sinkiang and Mongolia - 3. North China - 4. South China - 5. General maps of China. Thematic maps with place-names and indexes in Chinese and Roman scripts. *Class No:* 912.0(510)

[5341]

Rand McNally illustrated atlas of China. Chicago, Rand McNally, 1972. 282p. illus., diagrs., maps.

Originally as US Central Intelligence Agency, *People's Republic of China atlas* (Washington, Government Printing Office, 1971), prepared for President Nixon's visit to China.

3 main sections: Introduction to China (p.8-31) - Administrative divisions. Population. Ethnic groups. Railroads. Roads and inland waterways. Climate agriculture. Minerals and metals. Fuel and power. Industry (p.32-71) - Human resources and economy. Historical perspective. Peking and environs. Index-gazetteer of *c*.600 place-names. Fine cartography. *Geographical Review* (v.63, no.3, July 1973), p.436-8) praises its 'professionalism and crisp production'. Page size 38 x 22.5cm. *Class No:* 912.0(510)

[5342]

Times atlas of China. Gulan, P.J.M. *and* Twitchett, D.C. London, Times Books, 1974. xl, 144p.+27p. maps.

First published (in part) by Kyobunkaku Ltd., Tokyo, 1973.

Sections: History - Modern China (population: agriculture … China's frontiers) - Physical maps (by Bartholomew) - Provincial maps and notes - 31 city plans (main sheets named). Glossary, p.144. Index-gazetteer of *c*. 25,000 place-names. 'Destined to become the standard in its field' (*Library Journal*, v.101, no.8, 15 April 1976, p.968). 'Hardly a monumental work' (*Geographical Journal*, v.142, pt.2, 1976, p.359). Page size, 36 x 26cm. *Class No:* 912.0(510)

[5343]

Tourist atlas of China. Zhao Xilin, *ed.* Shanghai, Cartographic Publishing House China, 1985. 99p.+12p. col. plates. col. illus., col. maps. softcover. £6.95.

Principal details and coloured maps of 56 main cities and areas open to foreign tourists. Chronology of Chinese historical periods p.3. Information for tourists p.96-99 includes official travel agency travel service details, important anniversaries and holidays in China, climatic data *etc.* Tall pocket size. *Class No:* 912.0(510)

Hong Kong

[5344]

Hong Kong atlas. Hong Kong, Hai Feng Publishing, 1991. 66p.++ 18 unnumbered pages. col. maps, tables, index. £14.25. ISBN: 9622381820.

Includes general, thematic, and street maps. Bilingual introduction, other preliminaries, and street index. *Class No:* 912.0(512.317)

Mongolia

[5345]

Bügd Nairamdakh Mongol Ard Uls ündesnii atlas. [Mongolian Peoples Republic national atlas.] Ulaanbaatar, Academy of Sciences, 1990. 144p.

Physical geography, history, demography, political geography *etc.* thematic maps. Gazetteer. List of contents only in English. *Class No:* 912.0(517)

Japan

[5346]

Atlas of Japan, physical economic and social. Isida, F.M.R., *ed.* Rev. ed. Tokyo, International Society for Educational Information, 1974. viii,64p.64p. of maps.

48 plates of maps. of which 14 deal with the physical geography of Japan; 3 other maps depict the pattern of post-war urbanisation and population change, and the rest mainly on economic geography. Keys in English. *The Geographical Journal* (v.137, pt.3, September 1971, p.422) finds one serious shortcoming, - the system of romanisation used. 64p. of explanatory text in English, French and Spanish. *Class No:* 912.0(52)

[5347]

Edo/Tokyo through maps. Atlas Tokyo. Masai Yasuo. Tokyo, Heibonsha Ltd., Publishers, 1986. 160p. col. maps, index. ISBN: 4582434134.

Tokyo metropolis - Thematic Tokyo - Tokyo close up - Tokyo now. Appendices provide information on areas and population, past and present administrative divisions; chronology of Edo/Tokyo; parks and historic sites. Bilingual Japanese-English text but English is present only as a summary and occasional supplement to the main Japanese text. *Class No:* 912.0(52)

[5348]

Japan: a bilingual atlas. Tokyo, Kodansha. 128p. maps (some col.), index. pbk £11.95. ISBN: 4770015364.

Regional city, tourist, national parks, and transport maps are included. *Class No:* 912.0(52)

[5349]

The National atlas of Japan. Compiled by Geographical Survey Institute, Ministry of Information. Tokyo, Japan Map Center, 1977. x,367, illus., maps.

216 maps (50 at 1:2,500,000; 166 at 1:4,000,000), with explanatory notes and small supporting maps. Nearly half the maps are thematic, covering agriculture, industry, communications and trade. Several maps concern environmental problems. Gazetteer: List of administrative areas; Index to place names (p.359-65; *c.*5,000 entries). 'A superb example of the high standards which characterize Japanese cartography' (*Geographical Journal*, v.144, 1978, p.369). *Class No:* 912.0(52)

[5350]

Teikoku's complete atlas of Japan. 8th ed. Tokyo, Teikoku-Shoin, 1985. 55p. maps, tables, index. Softcover. ISBN: 4807100092.

1st ed. 1964.

1. Large-scale (1:800.000) general maps cover 5 major districts of Japan - 2. Major cities and main cultural and tourist areas - 3. Thematic maps *e.g.* History (p.7-8), agriculture, population *etc.* Map symbols and glossary p.10. *Class No:* 912.0(52)

Asia—Middle & Near East

[5351]

Atlas of the Middle East. Brawer, M., *ed.* New York, Macmillan; London, Collier Macmillan, 1988. 140p. maps, tables, diagrs., bibliog., index. ISBN: 0029052718.

Covers 19 countries from Libya in the West to Iran in the east and Turkey to the north. A regional overview is followed by country surveys *e.g.* Iran p.86-93 has sections

....(contd.)

on topography, climate, population, agriculture, history, government and politics, and 3 maps. *Class No:* 912.0(53 + 56)

[5352]

HALE, G.A. 'Maps and atlases of the Middle East' *Middle East Studies Association Bulletin,* v.3, no.3, 1969, p.17-39. bibliog. *Class No:* 912.0(53 + 56)

Gulf States

[5353]

National atlas of The United Arab Emirates. Al Ain, United Arab Emirates in association with Reading, GEOprojects, 1993. ISBN: 0863511007.

1. Maps of U.A.E. (history of cartographic knowledge; topography; topographical map coverage *etc.*) - 2. U.A.E. from space - 3. International, regional and local - 4. Heritage and history - 5. Geology and geomorphology - 6. Climate - 7. Water resources - 8. Biogeography - 9. Population - 10. Land use - 11. Economic - 12. Transport and communication - 13. Education and Health - 14. Cultural. 154 plates in all. Index of geographic names p.155-64. Large format. *Class No:* 912.0(536)

India

[5354]

An Atlas of India. Muthiah, S., *ed.* Delhi, Oxford Univ. Press, 1990. vi,185p. col. maps, tables, index. £30; $79.95. ISBN: 0195625536.

18 general maps for India then physical geography, administration, population, transport and tourism, agriculture, industry, minerals, economic development, and mass communication maps for each of India's 32 states and union territories, 212 maps in all on various scales. 'The administrative maps that show the district and smaller Taluk boundaries within each state and their principal cities are particularly noteworthy' (*Choice*, v.30, no.2. October 1992, p.267). 'Provides a wealth of data ... the definitive atlas for the world's second most-populous nation' (*Booklist*, v.88, no.22, Aug 1992, p.203 + 4). *Class No:* 912.0(540)

[5355]

The Map's Road atlas of India. Muthiah, S. *and* Arya, R.P. Madras, Tamilnad Printers and Traders PVT Ltd., 1982. 64p. col. maps. pbk.

Includes a map of the major tourist centres; a guide to the States (p.8-20); coloured maps (p.21-57); and maps depicting the national highways, the Indian railway system, and Indian air routes. The publishers also issue a number of State road guides. *Class No:* 912.0(540)

[5356]

National atlas of India. Calcutta, National Atlas and Thematic Mapping Organization, Department of Science and Technology, Government of India, 1984.

Massive work, 25 years in the making, in 8 large loose-leaf volumes: 1. General and political maps - 2. Physical and geomorphological - 3. Climatic and biogeographical - 4. Population and transport - 5. Land use and industrial - 6. Agricultural and economic - 7. Social and regional - 8. Historical and cultural. In all 300 variously dated maps on basic scale 1:6,000,000. Format allows for extracting single or more maps for detailed scrutiny or for class use.

Despite the maps' old-fashioned and cluttered appearance,

.... (contd.)

the atlas remains a colossal achievement, fully justifying the sense of pride evident in S.P. Dasgupta's preface to v.1. *Class No:* 912.0(540)

Bibliographies

[5357]

GOLE, S. **India within the Ganges.** New Delhi, Jayaprints, 1983. 239p. facsims., bibliog., index.

1. Indigenous maps - 2. Early European contacts - 3. Portuguese foothold - 4. Finding the way - 5. European rivalry -6. British conquest - 7. Survey maps. Bibliography p.102. 8. Printed maps in India 1447-1800 p.103-228. Division into 2 parts reflects the book's purpose: as a text on how the maps come to be drawn and, secondly, to serve as a reference guide. *Class No:* 912.0(540)(01)

Nepal

[5358]

SILL, M. *and* KIRKBY, J. **The Atlas of Nepal in the modern world.** London, Earthscan Publications in association with the ETC Foundation. 1991. 159p. illus., maps, tables, bibliog., index. ISBN: 1853830321.

Part 1. Nepal today. Part 2: Natural resources and hazards; water and its uses; tourism and the environment; people and language; towns and industry; land management; land and food; energy; transport; education. Bibliography p.153-6. 'An attempt to provide analytical information that can be used in detailed discussions of environmental and developmental issues' (*Foreword*). *Class No:* 912.0(541.35)

Sri Lanka

[5359]

The **National atlas of Sri Lanka.** Colombo, Survey Department (Ministry of Lands and Land Development) Sri Lanka, 1988. x,142p. col. illus., maps (some col.), diagrs., tables, index. ISBN: 9559059009.

59 mostly double-paged maps, with authoritative accompanying texts, arranged in 9 categories: 1. Location maps - 2. Maps of Sri Lanka (Ancient and modern maps Geodetic control) - 3. Physical - 4. Archaeology and history - 5. People - 6. Agriculture - 7. Industry, power and transport - Commerce - 9. Government, administration and justice. 'Designed to suit users with a good secondary education. It is not meant for specialists in their own fields'. *Class No:* 912.0(548.7)

Turkey

[5360]

Türkiye atlasi/**Atlas of Turkey.** Istanbul, Milli Egitim Basimevi, 1961. 23 double pl.

Publication of the Faculty of Letters, University of Istanbul. The first national atlas of Turkey. No explanatory text. 87 maps and diagrams, mostly based on original research, but some are compilations or are taken from other sources. Thus, the 44 small maps on climate are based on data of the General Directorate of Meteorology. *Class No:* 912.0(560)

Israel

[5361]

Atlas of Jerusalem. The Israel Academy of Sciences and Humanities; the Israel Exploration Society; Department of Geography, Hebrew Univ. of Jerusalem. Berlin, de Gruyter, 1973. ISBN: 3110036231.

113 maps in 10 sections: 1. Region - 2. Quarters and streets - 3. History (15 maps) - 4. Urban structure - 5. Land use - 6. Public institutions - 7. Transportation - 8. Population - 9. Town planning - 10. Changes after 1967. Sheet size 48cm x 65cm.

Amiran, D.K., and others, eds. *Urban geography: a companion to the Atlas of Jerusalem.* 173p. Contents: 1. Building history - 2. Development of Jerusalem (1860-1970) - 3. Evolution of population - 4. Functional structure - 5. Economic development - 6. Human ecology - 7. Transportation - 8. Planning Jerusalem 1917-1968. Appendix: Maps of the atlas: sources, definitions and notes (p.154-72. *Class No:* 912.0(569.4)

[5362]

BAHAT, D. *and* RUBENSTEIN, C.T. **The Illustrated atlas of Jerusalem.** New York, Simon & Schuster, 1990. 152p. illus. col. maps and plans, bibliog., index. $95. ISBN: 0134516427.

First published in Hebrew (Jerusalem, Carta, 1989).

An introductory chapter on topography, and 14 others on the city's history, cover the period from 1,000 BC to the present day. Based on archaeological findings and written sources from each period including *The Bible.* Lavishly illustrated. For this English language edition there is a new section on Jerusalem at the time of Christ and a bibliography (p.148). *Class No:* 912.0(569.4)

[5363]

BENVENISTI, M. *and* KHAYAT, S. **The West Bank and Gaza atlas.** Jersualem (?), West Bank Data Bank Project, 1990. (Distributed in North America by Westview Press). 140p. maps, tables, pbk. ISBN: 9653560026.

60 thematic maps covering topography, Israeli and Arab population growth and distribution, administrative boundaries, roads, transportation, health, land use *etc.* *Class No:* 912.0(569.4)

[5364]

Israel touring and road atlas: with a full index of towns, villages of sites. Brawer, M. *and* Machlis, G., *comps.* Tel Aviv, Yavneh Publishing House Ltd., 1980. iv,38p. tables. sd. maps, tables.

Based on 1:250,000 *Touring map of Israel.* Maps p.1-22. List of settlements, antiquities and sites p.23-34. *Class No:* 912.0(569.4)

[5365]

SURVEY OF ISRAEL. **Atlas of Israel** cartography physical and human geography. 3rd ed. London, Collier Macmillan, New York, Macmillan, 1985. 232p. $175.00. ISBN: 002905050x.

1st Hebrew ed. published in Tel-Aviv by The Survey of Israel 1956-64. 2nd English ed. 1970. contained 550 colour maps including some not to be found in the 3rd ed.

55 contributors (leading Israeli geographers, cartographers *etc.*). This bilingual Hebrew-English edition contains 400 col. maps on 40 sheets (each sheet consisting of a double-page) 2/3 of which are devoted to settlement patterns and economic geography. Following the map sheets is an English language narrative section which includes statistical data and

....(contd.)

bibliographies. 'The currency of the third edition both in terms of data and boundaries, and the new thematic maps ... will require that academic and large public libraries purchase it. The second edition should not be discarded, since the volumes complement each other' (*Reference Books Bulletin 1986-1987* p.149). *Class No:* 912.0(569.4)

Afghanistan

[5366]

National atlas of the Democratic Republic of Afghanistan. Warsaw, Geokart Poland, 1985(?). xiv,36p. col. maps, bibliog., index. ISBN: 8300023275.

Published in cooperation with the Afghan Geodesy and Cartography Head Office in Kabul.

63 maps depict Afghanistan's physical and socio-economic geography. Bibliography p.xiii-xiv. Published in two versions: in English and in Dari. *Class No:* 912.0(581)

Islamic World

[5367]

BOUSTANI, R. *and* FARGUES, F. The Atlas of the Arab World geopolitics and society. New York, Facts on File, 1991. 144p. col. illus., col. maps, col. diagrs., tables, index. ISBN: 0816023468.

First published: Paris, Bordas, *Atlas du monde arabe* (1990).

11 thematic map sections including narrative analysis of issues indicated in sub-title: 1. Borders - 2. Ethnic groups - 3. Population ... 8. Oil and industry - 9. Regional unity - 10. The state - 11. Palestine. References p.142. Maps and their sources p.143-4. *Class No:* 912.0(5.297)

[5368]

CORNU, G. Atlas du monde Arabo-Islamique à l'époque classique ixe-xe siècles. Répertoire des toponymes. Leiden, E.J. Brill, 1985. Publié avec le concours du Centre National de la Recherche Scientifique et l'aide de l'Institut de Monde Arabe, Paris. xv,213p. bibliog. index. ISBN: 9004068740.

Accompanies, and is arranged according to, 20 sheetmaps in binder. Bibliography p.xi-xiv. *Class No:* 912.0(5.297)

Africa

[5369]

CHI-BONNARDEL, R. van. The Atlas of Africa. Paris, éditions jeune afrique, 1973. 335p. maps. ISBN: 0903274035.

Edited jointly by the publishers of *Africa magazine* and *Jeune Afrique*. Maps prepared by L'Institut Géographique National de Paris.

138 six-colour maps (1:1M to 1:10M). Maps on Africa in general are followed by 2 maps on each country and its economy, plus text and statistical data. Gazetteer of less than 6,000 entries; bibliography. 'A timely, vitally essential reference work characterized by a high order of scholarship and cartographic portrayal' (*Best reference books*, ARBA, 1970-1976, entry 223). Page size, 40x30cm. *Class No:* 912.0(6)

Bibliographies

[5370]

Maps and plans in the Public Record Office 3. Africa. Penfold, P.A., *ed.* London, HMSO, 1982. xii, 426p. index. £36.00. ISBN: 0114401098.

3647 items described with PRO order reference number arranged A-Z by country. Illustrate especially the European expansion in the nineteenth and early twentieth centuries, boundary disputes, territorial claims, and settlements. Former colonies with their present names p.vii. Key to record references p.397-399. *Class No:* 912.0(6)(01)

[5371]

NORWICH, O.I. Maps of Africa: an illustrated and annotated carto-bibliography. Bibliographical descriptions by Pam Kolbe. Johannesburg and Cape Town, A.D. Donker, 1983. 444p. illus. (some col.) facsims (some col.) maps on endpapers, index. Rand 95. £65.00. $120.00. ISBN: 0868520284.

345 maps, each with its own cartobibliography, in 8 sections: 1. Continent of Africa - 2. Southern Africa - 3. Cape of Good Hope - 4. Sea charts - 5. North Africa - 6. East Africa - 7. West Africa - 8. Islands, towns, ports, etc. Historical survey of maps of Africa p.13-33. 'Chiefly of interest to collectors and scholars concerned with the authentication of maps' (*Geographical Journal*, v.150, no.2, July 1984, p.289-290). *Class No:* 912.0(6)(01)

Tunisia

[5372]

Atlas de Tunisie. Fakhfakh, M., *ed.* Paris, Jeune Afrique, 1979. 72p. maps, bibliog.

44 thematic maps and accompanying text. 'A very valuable geographical source book' (A.M. Findlay and others. *Tunisia*, 1982. Entry 97). *Class No:* 912.0(611)

Ethiopia

[5373]

National atlas of Ethiopia. Addis Abeba, Ethiopian Mapping Authority, 1988. vii,81p. col. maps., illus., diagrs.

76 map features (facing pages of maps and text): Ethiopia in Africa ... Administrative divisions - Topography ... Tourism - Addis Abeba city ... Ancient Ethiopia c.2800 BC to 1270 AD ... Imperi Abassini Geographica ... Ethiopia and the post-colonial neighbouring states 1910-1987 - Wars and invasions. Gazetteer p.153-7. *Class No:* 912.0(63)

Morocco

[5374]

Atlas du Maroc. Comité de Géographie du Maroc. Rabat, Institut Scientifique Chérifien, 1956-. maps.

A series of loose maps with explanatory handbooks (30-40p.) Some 200 maps covering 54 topics. *Class No:* 912.0(64)

Mauritania

[5375]

Atlas de la République Islamique de Mauritanie. Paris, editions j.a., 1977. 64p. col.maps, tables, bibliog., index. (*les atlas jeune afrique.*) ISBN: 2852580845.

19 thematic maps with text. Documentation et bibliographie p.64. *Class No:* 912.0(661.2)

Mali

[5376]

Atlas du Mali. Paris, éditions jeune Afrique, 1980. 64p. col. maps, bibliog., index.

20 thematic map features including La Bouche du Niger ... Le Delta Intérieur ... Bamako et sa région. Lexique p.62. *Class No:* 912.0(662.1)

Upper Volta

[5377]

Atlas de la Haute-Volta. Paris. éditions ja., 1975. 47p. col.maps. index. ISBN: 2852580144.

15 thematic maps including Histoire ... Tourisme. *Class No:* 912.0(662.5)

Niger

[5378]

Atlas du Niger. Paris, éditions j.a., 1980. 64p. col.maps, tables, bibliog., index. (*les atlas jeune afrique.*) ISBN: 2852581515. ISSN: 03370658.

19 thematic maps with text. Lexique p.62. Documentation et Bibliographie p.64. *Class No:* 912.0(662.6)

Senegal

[5379]

Atlas du Senegal. Pélissier, P., *comp.* 2nd ed. Paris, les éditions jeune afrique, 1983. 72p. col.maps, tables, bibliog., index. (*les atlas jeune afrique.*) ISBN: 2852582880. ISSN: 03370658.

First published 1980.

19 thematic maps with text. Documentation et bibliographie p.72. *Class No:* 912.0(663)

Sierra Leone

[5380]

CLARKE, J.L. **Sierra Leone in maps.** 2nd ed. London, Univ. of London Press, 1969. 120p.

51 black-and-white maps (usually 1:30M), with explanatory text facing each map. 13 contributors. Bibliography, p.115-20, including many periodical articles. *Class No:* 912.0(664)

Liberia

[5381]

GNIELINSKI, S. van, *ed.* **Liberia in maps.** London, Univ. of London Press, 1972. 111p. maps, plans.

Black-and-white maps in 50 sections (1. Liberia in Africa - 2. Liberia and her neighbours - 3. Historical background - 4. Geology ... 12. Wildlife ... 22/23. Urban land use - 32. Economic history - 43. Electric power and water supply ... 49. Ports - 50. External trade). 14. contributors - past and

....(contd.)

present members of the Department of Geography, Univ. of Liberia. Text on left-hand page, facing map. Bibliography, p.109-11. *Class No:* 912.0(666.2)

Ivory Coast

[5382]

Atlas de la Côte d'Ivoire. Vennetier, P., *comp.* 2nd ed. Paris, les éditions jeune afrique, 1983. 72p. col.maps, tables, bibliog., index. (*les atlas jeune afrique.*) ISBN: 2852582872.

First published 1978.

20 thematic maps with text. Bibliographie et documentation p.72. *Class No:* 912.0(666.8)

Cameroon

[5383]

Atlas de la République Unie de Cameroun. Paris, éditions j.a., 1979. 72p. col.maps, bibliog., index. ISBN: 2852581248.

20 thematic map features (inc. Géomorphique ... Histoire ... Ethnies et langues). Lexique p.68-9. Bibliography p.72. *Class No:* 912.0(671.1)

Bibliographies

[5384]

NGO, V.V. **Cartobibliography of the Cameroon** (Survey and mapping of Cameroon 1884-1984). Aberdeen, Department of Geography, Univ. of Aberdeen, 1987. xxiv,436p. map,bibliog., index. pbk. ISBN: 0901832308.

Attempts to bring some order into the complexities of French, German and English colonial mapmakers. *Class No:* 912.0(671.1)(01)

Gabon

[5385]

Géographie et cartographie du Gabon: atlas illustré. Barret, J., *ed.* Paris, EDICEP. 1983. 135p. maps. *Class No:* 912.0(672.1)

Congo

[5386]

Atlas de la République Populaire du Congo. Paris, éditions j.a., 1977. 64p. col.maps, bibliog., index. ISBN: 2852580438.

18 thematic map features (inc. Divisions administratives ... Région du Pool ... Région du Niari ... Congo Septentrional). Bibliography p.64. *Class No:* 912.0(672.4)

Central African Republic

[5387]

Atlas de la République Centrafricaine. Vennetier, P., *comp.* Paris, les éditions jeune afrique, 1984. 64p. col. maps, tables, index. (*les atlas jeune afrique.*) ISBN: 2852583127. ISSN: 03370658.

19 thematic map features (inc. Préhistoire et histoire ... Tourisme). Lexique p.60-61. Bibliographie p.64. *Class No:* 912.0(674.1)

Uganda

[5388]

Atlas of Uganda. Uganda Lands and Surveys' Department. 2nd ed. Kampala, Government Printer Uganda, 1967. 81p. maps, illus.

First published 1962.

40 pages of coloured maps (mostly 1:1,500,000), sometimes 12 to a page, each accompanied by explanatory text. Ranges from external communications, physical geography, climate, flora and fauna, human geography, rural economy, industry and trade, to history. Town plans of Kampala and Jinja. Brief gazetteer. 48 x 51cm. *Class No:* 912.0(676.1)

Kenya

[5389]

KENYA. SURVEY OF KENYA. National Atlas of Kenya. 3rd ed. Nairobi, the Survey, 1970. 103p. illus., maps.

43 plates of maps, mostly at 1:3M, with descriptive text facing, and a comprehensive gazetteer. 'Better, more attractive and more informative than its 1959 precedessor' (*The Geographical Journal*, v.137, pt.4, December 1971, p.590-1). *Class No:* 912.0(676.2)

Africa—Southern

[5390]

Philip's atlas of southern Africa and the world. Cape Town, Jonathan Ball Publishers with George Philip, 1986. 12p.+48p.+96p.+64p. ISBN: 086850131x.

4 sections: The Earth from space; The Universe, earth and man; Maps; Index. Emphasis (32/96 maps) on Southern African and continental regional maps. *Class No:* 912.0(68)

[5391]

Reader's Digest atlas of Southern Africa. Cape Town, Reader's Digest Association of South Africa, 1984. Produced in conjunction with the Directorate of Surveys and Mapping, Department of Community Development. 256p. illus., maps, bibliog. £45.00. ISBN: 09477008020.

213 pictorial map features in 3 sections: 1. Anatomy of South Africa (a compendium of facts and figures) - 2. Africa south of the Sahara (a broader view of the African continent with detailed thematic maps and concise notes on the history, economy, population and government of 42 independent states) - 3. Our land in close up. Gazetteer and index (30,000 names) p.214-54. Extensive bibliography (in very small print) p.255-56. Map scales vary but 1:500,000 most common. *Class No:* 912.0(68)

Bibliographies

[5392]

Braby's maps of Southern Africa/Brabyse kaarte van Suidelike Afrika. Durban, A.C. Brady, nd. 24p. sd.

Descriptive catalogue and price list of maps of Transvaal, Orange Free State, Natal, Cape Province and other areas (inc. South African homelands). *Class No:* 912.0(68)(01)

South Africa

[5393]

TALBOT, A.M. *and* **TALBOT, W.J. Atlas of the Union of South Africa.** Pretoria, Government Printer, 1960. lxiv,177p. maps, tables.

Prepared in collaboration with the Trigonometrical Survey Office and under the aegis of the National Council for Social Research. English and Afrikaans text. All the maps (about 700), except for a few relief, geological and vegetation maps, are black and white, Sections: 1. Relief, geology, mining, soils, vegetation and fisheries - 2. Climate and water resources - 3. Population - 4. Agriculture - 5. Industries and occupations - 6. Transportation - 7. External trade. A scale of 1:8M is used for most maps. Page size. 41 x 56cm. *Class No:* 912.0(680)

Namibia

[5394]

National atlas of South West Africa (Namibia)/ Nasionale atlas van Suidwes-Afrika (Namibie). Van der Merwe, J.H., *ed.* Cape Town. Prepared by the Institute for Cartographic Analysis, University of Stellenbosch for Directorate Development Coordination SWA, 1983. 184 unnumbered pages, tables, diagrs., bibliog. ISBN: 0797200207.

92 full-page maps (each accompanied by a page of text containing a summary of data sources and computational procedures) arranged in 7 sections: 1. Orientation - 2. Natural environment - 3. Settlement structure - 4. Population - 5. Economic structure - 6. Infrastructure - 7. Urban structure. Designed as an official source of spatial information for national and international publication. A short list of reference works is presented 'to gain a perspective of the country as a whole for more background information about specific themes'. *Class No:* 912.0(688)

Zambia

[5395]

DAVIES, D.H., *ed.* **Zambia in maps.** London, Univ. of London Press, 1971. 128p. maps.

55 black-and-white maps, with text facing (1. Political geography ... 10/11. Early man ... 21. Administrative divisions ... 39. Lusaka ... 55. Regional inequalities and the First National Devlopment Plan). 21 contributors. References p.123. *Class No:* 912.0(689.4)

Malawi

[5396]

The National atlas of Malawi. Lilongwe, Malawi Department of Surveys, 1983. 70p. col.maps.

Maps and explanatory text in loose-leaf binder to allow for new or replacement maps. *Class No:* 912.0(689.7)

Madagascar

[5397]

ASSOCIATION DES GÉOGRAPHES DE MADAGASCAR Tananarive. **Atlas de Madagascar.** Sous la direction de F. Le Bourdiec. Tananarive, Bureau pour le Développement de la Production Agricole, Agence de Madagascar, avec la collaboration du Centre de l'Institut Géographique National à Madagascar. 1969-71.

....(contd.)

62 maps, 1:4M; 106p. of commentary. 7 sections; Physical, human and rural geography; resources and industries; vie de relations; équipment divers; synethèse regional. Favourably reviewed in *Africa* (v.42, no.3, July 1972, p.261). Page size 40 x 31 cm. *Class No:* 912.0(691)

Mauritius

[5398]

DEVI VENKATASAMY, *and others.* **Philips atlas of Mauritius.** London, George Philip, 1991. 47p.

'Comprehensive and elaborate in its presentation of the geographical, economic and social features of the islands ... the cartography is of high quality' (Bennett, P.R. and Bennett G.J. *Mauritius,* 1992. Entry no 77).

Class No: 912.0(698.2)

America — North

[5399]

Basic map library. New York, H.W. Wilson. $59.95. (*Map Library*.)

Basic map library contains 30 maps, including 25 road maps that cover all 50 states, regional maps of the Eastern and Western US, a detailed street map of Washington D.C. and wall maps of the US and the world. Interstate highway system, details of roads in major cities and areas of special interest, and toll road & bridges information, are all featured. *Class No:* 912.0(71+73)

[5400]

—Canadian supplement. New York, H.W. Wilson. $29.95. (*Map Library*.)

12 maps and index dividers designed as a supplement either to *Map Library* or *City map library*. Extends coverage to major metropolitan areas and provinces of Canada.

Class No: 912.0(71+73)

[5401]

—City map library. New York, H.W. Wilson. $69.96. (*Map Library*.)

37 maps, case and index dividers. Street maps of major US cities with street indexes. *Class No:* 912.0(71+73)

[5402]

Hammond 1990 road atlas America United States/Canada/Mexico. Maplewood, New Jersey, Hammond, 1990. 96p. maps. $5.95. ISBN: 0843726857.

Maps of all 50 US states and all 10 Canadian provinces with major city area maps; National Park maps and points of interest; and mileage tables. *Class No:* 912.0(71+73)

[5403]

Hammond road atlas and vacation guide of the United States & Southern Canada. Maplewood, New Jersey, Hammond, 1990. 48p. maps, indexes, pbk. $2.50. ISBN: 0843726830.

Includes state and metropolitan area maps; highway mileage distance table; scenic routes and points of interest.

Class No: 912.0(71+73)

[5404]

Rand McNally road atlas United States. Mexico, Canada. Chicago, Rand McNally, 1992. 160p. Pbk. $7.95. ISBN: 0528810626.

350 detailed maps with mileage charts for principal cities plus city, state park, and other special maps.

Class No: 912.0(71+73)

Canada

[5405]

Atlas of Canada. Reader's Digest Association (Canada) in conjunction with the Canadian Automobile Association, 1981. 220p. col.illus., col.maps, tables, graphs, index. £17.95. ISBN: 0888500963.

1. Thematic features (p.6-59) on geography, geology, history, society, population - 2. Facts about Canada: a compendium of basic knowledge (p.60-76) - 3. Maps of Canada (p.77-177) on various scales drawn with cooperation of Surveys and Mapping Branch. Energy, Mines and Resources Canada - 4. Gazetteer index (p.178-219).

Class No: 912.0(71)

[5406]

Canada gazetteer atlas. Toronto, Macmillan of Canada in cooperation with Energy, Mines and Resources Canada and the Canadian Government Publishing Center, Supply and Services Canada, 1980. 164p. index. ISBN: 0770518737.

48 physical maps (Various scales 1:500,000, 1:1,000,000 and 1:2,000,000) giving the name, status, population and position of the populated places recorded in the 1976 Census of Canada. Gazetteer-index p.100-164. Complements *National atlas of Canada,* 4th ed., 1975. A French version. *Canada atlas toponymique,* is published. 'An essential reference tool for all Canadian libraries' (*Choice,* v.18, no.7, March 1981, p.920). *Class No:* 912.0(71)

[5407]

FARLEY, A.L. **Atlas of British Columbia** people, environment and resource use. Vancouver, Univ. of British Columbia Press, 1979. 144p. illus. (some col.), graphs, diagrs, maps.

61 maps sheets (people (11 maps); environment (15); resource use (35). Text, facing map sheets, include references. The reviewer in *Geography* (v.65, pt.3, no.288, July 1980, p.263) considers that the *Atlas* needs more tabulated data and fewer unnecessarily large colour photographs. Page size, 35.5 x 28.5cm.

Class No: 912.0(71)

[5408]

MATTHEWS, G.J. *and* **MORROW, R. Canada and the world** an atlas resource. Scarborough, Ontario, Prentice Hall Canada. 1985. vii, 201p. illus., maps, graphs, tables, bibliog. ISBN: 0131138464.

1. Canada and the world. 2. Canada: 59 mostly double page regional and thematic maps *e.g.* Exploration; the Provinces today; Native peoples; Far North; Great Lakes. 3. World thematic maps. 4. World regional maps. 5. Canadian statistics. 6. World statistics. Glossary p.185-92. Gazetteer p.193-200. Sources p.201. *Class No:* 912.0(71)

[5409]
National Atlas of Canada. 5th ed. Ottawa, Energy Mines and Resources Canada, 1986-. Box $30.00. Each map $5.50.

First published as *Atlas of Canada* by the Department of the Interior in 1906. 4th ed. under the present title issued in 1974 by the Macmillan Company of Canada.

'The 5th edition is planned as a continuing serial publication of separate but related maps, collectively dealing with all aspects of Canada. When comprehensive coverage of about two hundred map subjects is eventually reached, revision of the original maps will also be underway. The production of revised versions of each map will, in general, depend on the national importance of the subject, the state of scientific and scholarly knowledge in the field, and the public demand for such information' (*The fifth edition The National Atlas of Canada. An Information System*, a brochure issued *gratis* by Energy, Mines and Resources Canada, Canada Map Office, 615 Booth Street, Ottawa, Ontario, KIA OE9). A French version, *L'Atlas National du Canada* is available.

'Eventually all National Atlas data will be stored in digital form to allow rapid updating and information transfer as new research material is received into the National Atlas Information System' (*ibid.*). *Class No:* 912.0(71)

[5410]
North of 50°: an atlas of Far Northern Ontario. Toronto, Univ. of Toronto Press for Royal Commission on the Northern Environment on behalf of the Government of Ontario. xviii, 54 plates, 112-119p. col. maps. ISBN: 0802033873.

54 maps in atlas designed to aid decision-making in the development of Northern Ontario. *Class No:* 912.0(71)

[5411]
RICHARDS, J.H. *and* **FUNG, K.I. Atlas of Saskatchewan.** Saskatoon, Univ. of Saskatchewan, 1969. viii, 236p.

51 Canadian academic contributors. Maps grouped in 12 sections each of which deals with 'a specific but not necessarily separate theme' *e.g.* 2. Historical geography ... 4. Physical geography ... 6-10. Economic geography. Chapter references p.199-201. Gazetteer p.202-236. *Class No:* 912.0(71)

Bibliographies

[5412]
NICHOLSON, N.L. *and* **SEBERT, L.M. The Maps of Canada** a guide to official Canadian maps, charts, atlases and gazetteers. Folkestone, William Dawson and Sons Ltd; Hamden (Conn), Archon Books, The Shoe String Press Inc., 1981. x, 251p., illus., maps, tables. £20.00. ISBN: 0712909117, UK; 0208017828, US.

Comprehensive survey in 17 chapters and 8 appendices. Appendix 1. Some significant dates in the evolution of Canadian mapping. 4. Map coverage of the provinces and territories of Canada. 8. Availability of official Canadian maps, charts, atlases and gazetteers. Notes and references (by chapter) p.240-245; glossary of mapping terms p.246-247; index p.248-251. 'Highly recommended' (*Library Journal*, 1 May 1982, p.878). *Class No:* 912.0(71)(01)

Newfoundland

[5413]
McMANUS, G.E. *and* **WOOD, C.H. Atlas of Newfoundland and Labrador.** St. Johns, Breakwater, 1991. vii,77p. illus., diagrs., bibliog. $49.95. ISBN: 1550810006.

23 thematic map features (including text, graphs, diagrams, illus.) covering environment, culture, demography, communications, tourism, fishing, forestry, energy, *etc.* Gazetteer p.55-65. References and credits p.67-77. *Class No:* 912.0(718)

Mexico

[5414]
Atlas of Mexico. Pick, J.B., *and others*. Boulder, Colo., Westview Press, 1989. xxi,367p. maps, tables, bibliog., index. $55. ISBN: 0813376955.

135 black and white maps computer plotted from data derived from 1980 census and subsequent annual statistical reports. All but 13 maps focus on political and administrative units. 93 tables. *Class No:* 912.0(72)

America — Central

[5415]
ARBINGAST, S.A., *and others*. **Atlas of Central America.** Austin, Univ. of Texas, Bureau of Business Research, 1979. 62p. maps, pbk. $18. ISBN: 0877552622.

38 maps covering terrain, administration, population, economic activity, transportation and geology. Colouring is criticised for lack of clarity. Nevertheless, 'a welcome addition to printed sources dealing with Central America' (*Choice* v.17, no.4, June 1980, p.515). *Class No:* 912.0(728)

Costa Rica

[5416]
VALENCIANO, E.C. Atlas cantonal de Costa Rica. San José, Instituto de Fomento y Asesoría Municipal, 1987. 395p. col. maps, bibliog.

Detailed maps of Costa Rica's 7 provinces and of its 81 cantons (counties) each accompanied by a narrative text with information on population statistics, geology, land use, history etc. 'The atlas is a monumental contribution to basic knowledge about Costa Rica and will be of use to researchers and casual students as well as to tourists and investors' (Stansifer, C.L. *Costa Rica*, 1991, entry no.49). *Class No:* 912.0(728.6)

Panama

[5417]
Atlas nacional de la Republica de Panama. 3rd ed. Panama, Instituto Geographico Nacional, 1988. x,222p. maps. $80.

15 sections combining maps, text, graphs and diagrams: 1. General maps - 2. Physical geography - 3. Natural resources - 4. Population - 5. Silviculture and fishing - 6. Agriculture - 7. Industry - 8. Transport and communication - 9. Commerce - 10. Education and culture - 11. Health and social welfare - 12. Elections - 13. Regional and urban maps - 14. Administrative areas - 15. Index. Scale ranges from 1:500,000 - 1:125,000,000 although mostly 1:1 million. 304 maps *in toto*. 'The atlas is better than similar atlases in Latin America and the Third World. The quality of information the

....(contd.)

manner of presentation, the volume and thoroughness of the data are first rate' (*Cartographica, v.*28, no.2, Summer 1991, p.115-6). *Class No:* 912.0(728.7)

Caribbean

[5418]

The Atlas of Central America and the Caribbean. New York, Macmillan; London, Collier Macmillan, 1985. 144p. illus. (some col.); col.maps, col.plans, coats of arms, bibliog., index. $40.00; £50.00. ISBN: 0029080207.

Part 1. Regional profile consisting of 7 brief thematic essays - 2. Central America (12 country essays) - 3. The Caribbean (22 essays). Bibliography p.138-41. 'Plagued by so many problems of both a technical and intellectual nature that it is not possible to recommend the purchase of the atlas for either personal or library use' (*The American Cartographer,* v.14,no.2, April 1987, p.183-4). *Class No:* 912.0(729)

Cuba

[5419]

Atlas de Cuba XX aniversari del triunfo de la Revolución Cubana. La Habana, Instituto Cubano de Geodesia y Cartografía, 1978. 168p. col. maps, index.

71 maps arranged in 6 sections: 1. Introducción (Cuba y los países vecinos; División político - administrativa 1975, 1979) - 2. Mapas de la naturaleza y recursos - 3. De la economía - 4. De la población y cultura - 5. De la historia - 6. Mapa geográfico general. *Class No:* 912.0(729.1)

[5420]

Atlas nacional de Cuba/Natsional'nyi atlas Kuby. Moskva, Glanoe Upravlenie Geodezii i Kartografii MVD SSSR, 1970. 144p. maps.

A co-operative effort of the Cuban and Soviet Institutes of Geography of the Academy of Sciences and the Academia de Ciencias de Cuba.

105 maps. on scales 1:75,000 to 1:1M. General, physical, agricultural, industrial, cultural, historical and population maps, with explanatory text for each group. 23p. of text; 7p. index-gazetteer. (Based on review in *Library of Congress information bulletin,* v.30, no.27, 8 July 1971, p.407). 'An excellent recent atlas' (*Latin American bibliography.* edited by L. Hallewell (1978), p.123. *National atlas of Cuba; complete translation of the Russian-language atlas* (Springfield, Va., 1971, 309p.) (US Joint Publications Research Service. Translations on Latin America, 525) is a translation of the text only. *Class No:* 912.0(729.1)

Jamaica

[5421]

CLARKE, C.G. Jamaica in maps. London, Univ. of London Press, 1974. 104p., diagrs., maps.

42 maps, with text facing (*e.g.* 4. Geology and drainage; 8. Distribution of population; 19. Rural settlement; 22. Selected small towns; 23/25. Kingston (land use; population; housing); 30/32. Export crops; 39. Electricity; 42. External trade. Bibliography p.98-104. Page size 22.5 x 30cm. *Class No:* 912.0(729.2)

[5422]

National atlas of Jamaica. Kingston, Town Planning Department, Ministry of Finance & Planning, 1971. 79p. col. illus., tables, maps.

Maps (on rectos, with descriptive text facing): Location and size - Geology ... Water resources ... Soils and land capability ... Sugar ... Coffee ... Manufacturing - Transportation ... Education ... Monument, historic and archaeological sites - Bathing beaches. 41 tables. Statistical sources. Page size, 30 x 55cm. *Class No:* 912.0(729.2)

Bahamas

[5423]

Atlas of the Commonwealth of the Bahamas. Kingston Publishers. Rev. ed. Nassau, Ministry of Education, 1985. 48p. maps, plans.

38 thematic maps and 45 plans of cities, towns and settlements. *Class No:* 912.0(729.6)

Trinidad & Tobago

[5424]

AKAI, A. *and* **MATADEEN, J. Atlas for Guyana and Trinidad and Tobago.** Rev. ed. London, Macmillan, 1982. 32p. maps.

For school use. *Class No:* 912.0(729.87)

USA

[5425]

The National atlas of the United States. Gerlach, A.C., *ed.* Washington, U.S. Geological Survey, 1970. xiii,417p. maps, diagrs.

765 maps, mostly in colour and many with a two-page spread. General reference maps, followed by thematic maps: physical, climatic and water (74p.); historical (24p.); economic (89p., *i.e.,* 187 maps, including sets); sociocultural (30p.; administrative (24p.); mapping and charting (34p.); political (7p.). One drawback: The tight binding prevents two-page spread maps from being visible at the inner edges. 'Ranks amoung the finest national atlases yet produced' (*Geographical Review,* v.62, no.1, January 1972, p.97). 'The general layout and design is quite superb' (*Cartographic Journal,* v.9, no.1, June 1972, p.65-66). Page size: 47 x 34.5cm. *Class No:* 912.0(73)

[5426]

Rand McNally city map collection. Chicago, Rand McNally. $29.95 complete in laminated case. ISBN: 0528269968, set.

30 city maps covering the largest US metropolitan areas. Individual titles are currently available in the UK from Springfield Books of Huddersfield at £2.50. each. *Class No:* 912.0(73)

[5427]

Rand McNally state map collection. Chicago, Rand McNally. $29.95. complete in laminated case. ISBN: 0528273345.

41 individual road maps covering all 50 US states plus US Interstate Highway map. Available in UK from Springfield Books of Huddersfield at £2.50 each. *Class No:* 912.0(73)

[5428]

USA State maps on file. New York and Oxford, Facts On File, 7v. £250.00 the set or £40.00 each volume. Replacement pages 75p. each.

1200 loose leaf, copyright free outline maps in 7 ring binder volumes: *Mid-Atlantic; Southwest; Mountain and Prairie; West; Midwest; New England;* and *Southeast.* Topics include politics, environment, demographics, physical geography, climate, and history. For school use. *Class No:* 912.0(73)

[5429]

WURMAN, R.S. US Atlas. New York, Access Press, 1990. Distributed by Prentice Hall. 144p. col.maps, index. pbk. $12.95. ISBN: 0130017604.

Divides US into 70 maps each 250 miles by 250 miles at a uniform scale of 1:15,480.000. Also 34 metropolitan maps (50 miles by 50 miles) and 8 downtown cente maps (5 miles by 5 miles). Tourist information includes food and accommodation, museums and amusement parks, architecture, weather extremes, and a calendar of events. Index of *c.*10,000 place names. 'US Atlas is a good road atlas. It would be a useful addition to any reference collection' (*Booklist,* v.86,no.12, 15 February 1990, p.1191-2). *Class No:* 912.0(73)

Micromaterials

[5430]

PC USA Version 2.0. Mildenhall, Suffolk, Global Network. £59.95.

Electronic atlas which provides current and historical information for all 50 states and Puerto Rico. Included is a self-updating time zone map, detailed state and city data, colorful state flags. System requires IBM PC/XT/AT/PS2 or compatibles with min. 640K RAM floppy drive or hard disk DOS 2.0+. *Class No:* 912.0(73)(003.5)

Bibliographies

[5431]

MAKOWER, J., *ed.* **The Map catalog:** every kind of map and chart on earth and even some above it. 2nd ed. New York, Vintage Books, 1990. 364p. illus., maps, facsims. $27.50. ISBN: 0394383264.

1st ed. 1986.

Directory of the map resources of the United States in 10 main sections: 1. Travel - 2. Specific areas - 3. Boundaries - 4. Scientific - 5. History - 6. Utility/Services - 7. Water - 8. Sky - 9. Images - 10. Atlases/Globes (in 41 map themes). This edition is significantly restructured. 'Possibly the very best starting point for anyone who wants to obtain a map or information about maps, especially for uncommon types or remote areas ... every map librarian should have a copy' (*Cartographica,* v.28, no.2, Summer 1991, p.107-8). *Class No:* 912.0(73)(01)

[5432]

MILLER, E.W. 'State atlases': major sources of spatial information;, *Journal of Geography,* v.81,no.1, January/February 1982, p.34-6.

Brief reviews of 7 state atlases and a list of 44 others A-Z by state. *Class No:* 912.0(73)(01)

[5433]

SCHWARTZKOPF, R.B. 'State atlases from the eighties', Special Libraries Association. Geography and Map Division *Bulletin* No.155, March 1989, p.21-25.

Bibliography of current State atlases *i.e.* 1980 onwards arranged A-Z by State. 7 references. *Class No:* 912.0(73)(01)

Amerindians, North

[5434]

PRUCHA, F.P. Atlas of American Indian affairs. Lincoln, Univ. of Nebraska Press, 1990. x,191p. maps, bibliog., tables, index. $47.50. ISBN: 0803236891.

109 black and white maps and statistical information covering 'Native Americans' in United States, but not Canada, arranged by topic *e.g.* population by counties and rural areas, land cessions, reservations, sites of Indian uprisings and military operations, using census data up to 1980. 'Lacks focus, balance or consistency as well as an interpretative framework that would enable to reader to make sense of the author's selection of information' (*Journal of the Early Republic,* v.11, no.3, Fall 1991, p.400-1). *Class No:* 912.0(73)(=97)

Alaska

Bibliographies

[5435]

FALK, M.W. Alaskan maps: a cartobibliography of Alaska to 1900. New York, Garland, 1983. xxiii,245p. $68.00. ISBN: 0824091329.

1. History of Alaskan cartography (1300-1900) p.xi-xv. 2. Alaskan maps listed chronologically p.3-192. Bibliography p.193-201. *Class No:* 912.0(798)(01)

America—South

[5436]

Atlas of South America. Brawer, M., *ed.* New York, Simon & Schuster, London, Macmillan, 1991. 144p. col. illus., diagrs., col. maps, indexes. $65; £35. ISBN: 0130506427, US; 0333559010, UK.

Pt.1: Overview of region. Pt.2: Physical environment, climate, economy, agriculture, industry and minerals, history, government and politics of South American countries and territories. Sources p.131. Annotated bibliography compiled by Linda Vertrees p.132-8. Glossary p.139. Indexes of place-names and persons. *Class No:* 912.0(8)

Brazil

[5437]

Atlas nacional do Brasil. new ed. Rio de Janeiro, Instituto Brasileiro de Geografia e Estatistica, Conselho Nacional de Geografia, 1966.

50 map-plates (chiefly thematic maps), with statistical data and explanatory text. 5 sections; 1. Political and administrative - 2. Physical - 3. Demographic - 4. Economic - 5. Socio-cultural. Map size 57.48cm. *Class No:* 912.0(81)

Argentina

[5438]

Atlas de la República Argentina. 6th ed. Buenos Ayres, Instituto Geográfico Militar, 1989. 81p. col. maps, tables.
1st ed. 1965.
36 col. maps of provinces and major cities supplemented with physical and socioeconomic information.
Class No: 912.0(82)

[5439]

RANDLE, P.H. Atlas del Desarrollo Territorial de La Argentina. Buenos Ayres, Oikos, 3v., 1981. ISBN: 8449948525 (complete set).
Atlas. xvii, 312 plates, 1p. 8449948523. Maps grouped in 4 sections. 1. El territorio se configura (Cartografia antigua; Etnografia; Expediciones exploraciones y viages; Fronteras internas; Jurisdicciones politicas; J. eclesiasticas; J. de la Justicia Federal; Universidades; Limites internacionales) - 2. La produccion y la poblacion - 3. El equipamiento territorial - 4. El proceso de urbanizacion. Massive 53 cm x 35½ cm format. *Memoria.* 146p. 8449948521. Commentary on maps in atlas. *Serie de estidisticas historicas.* ix, 283p. 844994852x. Statistical table to accompany Pt.2. of Atlas: La producion y la poblacion. *Class No:* 912.0(82)

Chile

[5440]

Atlas de la Republica de Chile. 2nd ed. Valparaiso (?) Instuto Geografico Militar, 1983. 352p. maps.
1st ed. 1982.
196 maps deployed in 4 parts: 1. Antecedentes generales - 2. Mapa Físico de Chile - 3. Mapas temáticos nacionales - 4. Mapas temáticos régionales (Tarapacá; Antofagasta; Atacama; Coquimbo; Valparaíso; Santiago; Libertador General Bernardo O'Higgins; Maule; Bío-Bío; La Araucanía; Los Lagos; General Carlos Ibáñez del Campo; Magallanes y de la Antártica Chilena) - 5. Índice de nombres geográficos. *Class No:* 912.0(83)

Bolivia

[5441]

Atlas de Bolivia. Barcelona, Ediciones Geomundo, 1985. xii,227p. col. illus., col. maps. ISBN: 8459957012.
121 maps supported by text and illustrations divided in 5 parts: 1. La Tierra y el Espacio - 2. Bolivia y su desarrollo hisórico - 3. Bolivia y su divisón politica - 4. Mappas temáticos de Boliva - 5. Población y recursos humanos.
Class No: 912.0(84)

Peru

[5442]

DOMINOVICH, A.L. Atlas del Perú. Lima, Librería e imprenta Guiá Lascano, 1964. 68p.
General maps and 24 Department (regional) maps. For school and college use. *Class No:* 912.0(85)

Colombia

[5443]

Atlas de Colombia planeó y dirigió la obra. 3rd ed. Bogotá, Instituto Geográfico Agustin Codazzi, 1977. 283p.
190 maps, most of them in colour. 70p. of maps: *c.*300 illus. on 50 plates. 'Of major interest to geographers is the thematic part of the work' (*The Geographical review*, v.59, no.2, April 1969, p.301-2). For the general public rather than the specialist. Page size, 44 x 31cm.
Class No: 912.0(86)

Venezuela

[5444]

Atlas de Venezuela. 2nd ed. Caracas, Direccion de Cartografia Nacional, Ministerio del Ambiente y de los Recursos Naturales Renovables, 1979. viii,331p. col. illus., col. maps.
First published 1969.
Major atlas of 300 maps and text in 8 sections: 1. Referencias Generales - 2. Venezuela historica - 3. Caracas historica - 4. Cartografia basica - 5. Mapas de las Entidades Federales - 6. Mapas regionales - 7. Cartografia tematica - 8. Miscelaneas. *Class No:* 912.0(87)

Australasia & Oceania

[5445]

ANTHEUME, B. *and* **BONNEMAISON, J. Atlas des îles et états du Pacifique Sud.** Montpellier, GIP Reclus; Paris, Publisud, 1988. 126p. col.maps, tables, bibliog. ISBN: 286600417135; 2869120213.
In 2 main sections: 1. Le Pacifique, les Pacifiques? 14 thematic chapters *e.g.* origins of peoples; discovery; population intensity; migration; trade, commerce, tourism *etc.* 2. Le Pacifique Sud d' île en île: each island described with map, statistical tables, and references. Bibliography p.124-6. 'Cet atlas est un instrument de travail moderne, attrayant, indispensable pour tous ceux qui veulent s'initier aux réalités de Pacifique d'aujourd'hui' (*Les Cahiers D'Outre-Mer*, no.170, Avril-Juin 1990, p.205-60).
Class No: 912.0(9)

Indonesia

[5446]

The Tourist atlas of Indonesia. Enschede, Intermap, 1988. 54p. col. maps, index. ISBN: 9069000083.
12 detailed maps and 12 city plans with accompanying text: General; Java; Bali; Sumatera; Sulawesi; Other islands. Scale 1:800,000 to 1:6,000,000. *Class No:* 912.0(910)

Brunei

[5447]

Primary atlas for Brunei. London, Macmillan Education Ltd., 1983. 32p. index. sd. ISBN: 0333348990.
Thematic and physical maps for school use.
Class No: 912.0(911.13)

Philippines

[5448]

The Philippine atlas. Manila, Fund for Assistance to Private Education, 2v., 1975. illus., diagrs., tables, maps & overlays.

1. *A historical, economic and educational profile of the Philippines.* 304p. 2. *Directory of schools, assistance groupings and index.* 125p. V.1 has good coloured maps, with text facing. V.2 includes distribution maps of universities and institutions (governmental and non-governmental), a glossary and place-name index (*c.*2,500 entries), as well as a general index. Page size, 31 x 38cm. *Class No:* 912.0(914)

New Zealand

[5449]

MacKENZIE, D.W., *ed*. **Heinemann New Zealand atlas.** Auckland, Heinemann in association with the Department of Survey and Land Information, 1987. 31p. of text+117 pages of maps +46 unnumbered pages of gazetteer. $NZ75.00.

117 sectional maps on scale 1:250,000 based on the Department's New Zealand Map Series. Text gives information on plate tectonics, climate, vegetation, forestry, urbanization *etc.* Gazetteer of 20,000 entries. *Class No:* 912.0(931)

[5450]

MARSHALL, B. Atlas of New Zealand boundaries. Auckland, Dept. of Geography, University of Auckland, 2v., 1986. various paginations. Ring binders. (*Occasional Publication n.20.*) ISBN: 0908672071. ISSN: 01121545.

Maps on scale 1:600,000 depicting administrative and statistical boundaries arranged in 13 sections. V.1 includes 1. Territorial and statistical - 2. Environment - 3. Land - 4. Agriculture and fisheries - 5. Forest, power and mineral resources. V.2. 6. Trade and industry - 7. Planning and development - 8. Transport and communications - 9. Judicial - 10. Finance and insurance - 11. Services, welfare and defence - 12. Government and politics - 13. Religion, culture and sport. Ring binder format allows for convenient insertion of updated material. *Class No:* 912.0(931)

[5451]

New Zealand atlas. Wards, I.McL., *ed*. Wellington, A.R. Shearer, Government Printer, 1976,. xx,292p. illus., diagrs., maps.

First published 1959 as *A descriptive atlas of New Zealand,* edited by A.H. McLintock.

80p. of maps (general; sectional; thematic, *e.g.* discovery, patterns of settlements; population; soils, land classification, and use; tourist resources), 12 as double-page spreads. 18p. of black-and-white illus. 78p. of colour illus. Gazetteer, p.258-85 (*c.*7,000 entries); index to subject-matter of text. *Class No:* 912.0(931)

[5452]

New Zealand in maps. Anderson, A.G., *ed*. London, Hodder & Stoughton 1977; New York, Holmes & Meier, 1979. 141p. graphs, tables, maps. £5.50. m42.50. ISBN: 0340185848, UK; 0841903247, US.

Stresses demographic and socio-economic aspects of life in New Zealand. 2 appendices 'give a valuable summary of New Zealand map coverage, metric and non-metric, and a selected bibliography'. (*Bulletin*. Special Libraries Association. Geography and Map Division, no.119, March 1980, p.78). *Class No:* 912.0(931)

Australia

[5453]

Atlas of South Australia. Griffin, T. *and* McCaskill, M., *eds*. Adelaide, South Australian Government Printing Division, 1986. xiv,134p. maps, bibliog., index. A$55.00. ISBN: 0724346880.

55 thematic map features in 5 main sections: 1. Course of settlement - 2. Environment and resources - 3. Production - 4. South Australians - 5. Regional maps. Gazetteer of 2000 place-names (p.121-8). Chronology p.129-30. Map sources p.130-1. Bibliography p.131. 'Should become a milestone of its type in cartography' (*Bulletin. Society of University Cartographers,* v.21, no.2, 1988, p.117). *Class No:* 912.0(94)

[5454]

Atlas of Victoria. Duncan, J.S., *ed*. Melbourne, Victoria Government Printing Office, 1982. xv,239p. col.illus., col.maps, tables, diagrs. A$39.95. ISBN: 0724182551.

40 thematic sections *e.g.* 14. Prehistory ... 15. History ...38. Topography forming an inventory of resources and a portrayal of the State in the late 1970s. Section 39 Gazetteer (names on topographic maps) p.217-225. Section 40 Index. 170 maps and diagrams, 209 illus. 'A handsome work, at once technically impressive and aesthetically pleasing' (*Geographical Journal,*v.149, no.3, November 1983, p.392-4.). *Class No:* 912.0(94)

[5455]

The Australian road atlas. 7th ed. Ringwood, Victoria, Viking O'Neill, 1988. 162p. col.maps. ISBN: 0670901075. 1st ed. 1977.

Detailed maps of all the continental states and territories p.7-127. Index p.128-60. *Class No:* 912.0(94)

[5456]

Philip's illustrated atlas of Australia. Rev. ed. 1981. South Yarra, Victoria, George Philip, 1981. 178p. col. illus., col. maps, col. diagrs. ISBN: 0855507128.

First published 1977 as *The pictorial atlas of Australia.*

The physical, economic and social aspects of each state presented on a scale appropriate to its size. Includes sections on New Zealand, Islands of the West Pacific, and Papua New Guinea. Gazetteer (over 7000 entries) p.150-178. Over 100 maps. For home and school use. *Class No:* 912.0(94)

[5457]

The Reader's Digest Atlas of Australia, produced in conjunction with the Division of National Mapping, Department of National Resources. Sydney, Reader's Digest, 1977. 288p. illus., diagrs., charts, maps. ISBN: 0909486549.

14 contributors. Sections: 'Mapping Australia' - 'The land we live in' (large map of Australia, showing surface features, main cities, towns, roads and railways) - 'Our country in close-up' (150 detailed physical maps, p.12-160, scale 1:1,000,000; including islands) - 'Anatomy of Australia' (small illus., etc. giving social, economic, ethnographic, industrial and political data, p.161-216) - 'Gazetteer to the maps' (nearly 40,000 entries, with coordinates. 'The best Australian atlas ever produced' (*RSR,* v.7, no.2, April/June 1979, p.10). Page size 30 x 40cm. *Class No:* 912.0(94)

Bibliographies

[5458]

Australian maps. Canberra, National Library of Australia, 1968-. Quarterly with annual compilations (1968-1981); annual 1982-. ISSN: 00450677.

1987v. (1988. viii, 171p.+6p. maps.) Aims to provide a comprehensive list of published maps representing areas within Australia and its territories and other maps with Australian associations. Based on acquisitions at the National Library of Australia and arranged according to the classification set out in Boggs. S.W. and Lewis, D.C.*The classification and cataloguing of maps and atlases* (New York, SLA, 1945) with the Australasia area developed by the Mitchell Library of the State Library of New South Wales. Directory of Australian map publishers and retailers p.129-171. *Class No:* 912.0(94)(01)

Papua—New Guinea

[5459]

Papua New Guinea atlas. King, D. *and* Ranck, S., *eds.* Robert Brown (Australia) in conjunction with Univ. of Papua New Guinea, 1980. 109p. col. illus., maps (some col.), bibliogs.

Over 40 contributors. Arranged in 3 parts: 1. The changing face of the nation (archaeology and early man) - 2. The physical environment - 3. Information resources. Well-documented. *Class No:* 912.0(954)

Polynesia

[5460]

Atlas de la Nouvelle - Calédonie et Dépendences. Combroux, J. Paris, Éditions de l'Office de la Recherche Scientifique et Technique Outre-mer, 1981. ISBN: 2709906015.

53 map features in 6 sections: 1. L'Environement géographique et océanique - La Nature dans l'Archipel Nouvelle - Calédonien - 3. Les populations, leur origine et leur implantation - 4. L' Espace rural: son occupation et son utilisation - 5. L'Économie Calédonienne - 6. L'Encadrement, les équipements sociaux, l'urbanisation. *Class No:* 912.0(96)

Micronesia

[5461]

KAROLLE, B. G. Atlas of Micronesia. 2nd ed. New York, Bess Press, 1993. 122p. illus., maps, tables. $21.95. ISBN: 1880188503.

1st ed. 1988.

80 black and white maps in 3 parts: 1. Physical geography, environment, flora, and history - 2. Place-names,. navigation, economic development, climate - 3. Island groups and atolls. 'A required purchase for any library aspiring to provide information about this part of the world' *Booklist,* v.90, no.10, 15 January 1994, p.960). *Class No:* 912.0(965)

Hawaii

[5462]

Atlas of Hawaii. 2nd ed. Honolulu, Univ. of Hawaii Press, 1983. 238p. col.illus. col.maps, tables, bibliog., index. ISBN: 0824808371.

First published 1973.

Nearly 300 reference, environment, cultural, and social maps followed by an extensive Bibliography (46 sections) p.223-230 and Gazetteer p.231-238. 'Characterized by careful scholarship, completeness and vivacity of presentation' (*American Reference Book Annual,* 1974, item 476). *Class No:* 912.0(969)

Polar Regions

[5463]

UNITED STATES. Central Intelligence Agency. **Polar regions atlas.** Washington, Superintendent of Documents, CIA, 1978. 65p. illus., diagrs., maps.

The two Polar regions are dealt with separately but similarly. Each part consists of double-page maps (35 x 45cm.) on 15 'issues' or themes (*e.g.* Arctic, p.6-33: Arctic issues - Discovery - Climate - Physical features - Sea ice - Climatic change - Permafrost - Northern development - Aboriginal people - Fisheries - Mining - Oil and gas - Transportation - Environmental protection - Science programs - Sovereignty problems). Arctic gazetteer/index, p.58-63 (*c.*1,200 entries); Antarctic gazetteer, p.64-65 (*c.*400 entries), - including names of national research stations. Folding map of each region, 1:17,250,000. Well-drawn maps. 'An invaluable summary of the geography of both polar regions' (H.G.R. King *The Arctic,* entry 21). *Class No:* 912.0(98/99)

Antarctic

[5464]

Antarctica great stories from the frozen continent. Sydney, Reader's Digest, 1985. 320p. illus. (many col.), col. maps. £17.95. ISBN: 0949819646.

39 major contributors. 1. Continent and its wildlife (21 species and geographical double-page spreads - 2. The explorers in chronological order - 3. Atlas (p.286-91) and chronology (p.292-91). Good quality pictorial and encyclopedic atlas. *Class No:* 912.0(99)

[5465]

Atlas Antarktike. Moskva, Glavnoe Upravlenie Geodezii i Kartografii, 2v.,1966-67.

V.1 consists of 225 pages of maps; v.2 the text.

V.1 is in 3 parts (introductory, general geographical; regional) and includes geological, climate and ice cover, as well as depicting the history of explorations. Alphabetical index of place names. Claims to be the first complete atlas of the Antarctic. 'It is without doubt the most exciting cartographic document which has ever been produced in the Soviet Union' (*Cartographic Journal,* v.4, no.1, June 1967, p.54), although the pages devoted to map and photographic cover compare unfavourably with the AGS Antarctic map folio series, folio 3 (*qv*). Index-gazetteer of *c.*5,000 place-names. Page size, 60 x 38.5cm.

Soviet geography; review and translation special issue, v.8, no.5-6 (p.261-507) consists of a translation of introduction and legends on maps in v.1. *Class No:* 912.0(99)

World Atlases

[5466]

AA/Rand McNally traveller's world atlas and guide. Basingstoke, The Automobile Association, 1989. 224p. col. maps, index. softcover. £4.95. ISBN: 0861458362.

1. Quick reference (time zone map; international dialling codes; distance chart *etc.*) - 2. Metropolitan area maps p.18-53 - 3. Guide to selected cities p.54-64 - 4. World reference maps p.65-128 - 5. Flags of nations and country profiles p.129-60. Index of 7000 place names. Convenient compact atlas and compendium of geographical data *for home use.* *Class No:* 912.01

[5467]

Atlante internazionale del Touring Club Italiano. 8th ed. Milano, Touring Club Italiano, 2v., 1968.

First published 1927.

173 places of coloured maps, relief being shown by light brown hachuring and hill shading. A number of the 93 maps are folded, giving a lateral spread of 85cm. 74 of the 173 plates concern Europe. Scales vary: 1:1500,000 (Italy) to 1:10,000,000 (Australia). Many large-scale local maps. Lettering clear: transliteration follows BGN/PCGN practice. The separate *Indice dei nomi* locates *c.*250,000 place-names on a close grid system usable only with the *Atlante internazionel;* also a glossary of *c.*3,500 geographical terms. Alone among major atlases, this atlas gives a list of sources. 'One of the most elaborate detailed and cartographically superior of world atlases' (Church, M., and others, comps. and eds. *A basic geographical library* (1966), entry no.43, on the 1956 ed.). Page size: 45x61cm. *Class No:* 912.01

[5468]

The Atlas of the Earth. London, Mitchell Beazley with G. Philip, 1972. 144,303p. illus., maps.

An illustrated natural history of the earth, with an atlas and index-gazetteer supplement. 142p. on 'The good earth' with over 1,200 col.illus., are followed by a world atlas (p.18-187) of physical and thematic maps and by two indexes - to 'The good earth' (p.188-92) and the atlas (p.1-112); *c.*50,000 entries. According to *Geography* (v.58, pt.1, no.258, January 1973, p.99-100) 'is simply a luxury edition of Philip's *University atlas* in a pleasantly toned-down range of colours'. *TLS* (no.3669, 23 June 1972. p.727) questions the value of the atlas and finds the volume expensive. Page size, 37.5 x 27.5cm.

The Mitchell Beazley New concise atlas of the earth (London, Mitchell Beazley, with G. Philip, 1978. 240p. diagrs., maps, first published 1973), has *c.*500 diagrs. and 150 maps. 'Ideal for the school library' (*British Book News,* August 1978, p.664-5). *Class No:* 912.01

[5469]

Bartholomew world atlas. 13th ed. Edinburgh, John Bartholomew, 1985. xvi,100,79p. col.illus., col.maps, index. ISBN: 0702806196.

First published as *The Edinburgh world atlas,* 1st-8th eds. (1954-73) and subsequently under its present title, 9th-12th eds. (1974-82).

1. Introductory features (geographical terms; projections; world climate; communication, exploration *etc.*) - 2. Maps are mainly physical but also with a heavy thematic coverage. 17 different layer colours. Gazetteer of 30,000 place names. An excellent general-purpose world atlas. *Class No:* 912.01

[5470]

Collins atlas of the world. 4th ed. London, Harper Collins, 1993, xl,224p. col.illus., col.maps, index. £14.95. ISBN: 0004470400.

1. Geographical encyclopaedia: 15 double-page spreads *e.g.* Earth structure, Oceans, History of maps, Key to maps, Use of maps. 2. World atlas of 128p. of maps on different large (1:1,000,000 or 1:2,500,000), medium (1:7,500,000), or small scales according to shape, size, and density of detail. 3. Geographical data (world physical and political data, and Nations of the World. Glossary p.136-8. Place-name index (40,000 names) p.141-224. *Collins concise atlas of the world.* 200p. ISBN 000447824x is based on the full atlas and has 96p. of full colour maps. *Class No:* 912.01

[5471]

The Complete world atlas for Australia and New Zealand. 4th ed. London and Melbourne, George Philip, 1984. 47+176+124p. ISBN: 0540054852.

lst ed. 1976.

3 separately paginated sections: geographical features, maps, and index (50,000 entries). General world atlas with emphasis on maps of Australia, New Zealand, and South West Pacific (p.17-64). *Class No:* 912.01

[5472]

Diercke Weltatlas. Mayer, F., *comp. & cartographer.* 1st ed. of 1988 revision. Braunschweig, Westermann, 1988. 275p. col.maps,index.

The atlas includes topographical and thematic maps, graphs, town plans. This edition has '150 Jahre Westermann 1838-1988', an anniversary history. Accompanying the *Weltatlas* is *Diercke Handbuch,* 2nd ed., 1980. 340p. illus. containing map interpretations, learning objectives and instructive comments on the Weltatlas and its abridged version. *Class No:* 912.01

[5473]

The Economist atlas the shape of the world today. London, Business Books, 1991. 384p. col.maps, col.tables, col.diagrs., col.graphs, index. £19.95. ISBN: 0712649336.

First published by Hutchinson 1989.

1. World political and physical maps drawn by Esselte Map Service (Stockholm) p.10-80. 2. World comparisons (thematic maps with text and diagrams) p.82-118. 3. World encyclopedia (220 country and regional profiles) p.120-307. Glossary p.308-10. 'An authoritative text providing a comprehensive overview of the state of the world' (*Reference Reviews,* v.6, no.1, 1992, p.9). *Class No:* 912.01

[5474]

Encyclopaedic atlas of the world. Lye, K., *ed.* London, Apple Press, 1987. 256p. col.illus., col.maps, index. £12.95. ISBN: 1850760160.

Introductory features (p.6-23) on Earth and solar system; The story of Earth; The oceans; Atmosphere, weather and climate; Soil and vegetation; Ecology and conservation; The world in space. Atlas section (p.24-200), arranged by continent, is accompanied by encyclopedic geographical, historical, political, economic and sociological information and a detailed analaysis of each country. Gazetteer p.202-248. Geographical terms p.249. 200 full colour photographs and illustrations. *Class No:* 912.01

[5475]
Goode's world atlas. Espenshade, E.B., *ed.* 18th ed. Chicago, Rand McNally, 1989. Available in UK from Springfield Books (Huddersfield). xvi, 367p. col. illus., col. maps, tables, indexes. $29.95. ISBN: 0528831283.

First published as *Goode's school atlas* (1922) and subsequently as *Goode's world atlas.* 17th ed. 1986.

Emphasis on newly updated physical-political maps and especially on US thematic maps 'addressing current societal concerns: education, wealth, poverty, hazardous waste sites, and health care'. Also world thematic maps (military and economic alliances, nuclear and solar energy, agriculture, minerals) and large-scale maps (1:300,000) of 62 metropolitan areas. 'An excellent supplement to larger atlases ... few atlases of this size are in *Goode's* class' (*General Reference Books for Adults*, 1988, p.208).
Class No: 912.01

[5476]
The Great geographical atlas. London, Mitchell Beazeley in association with Istituto Geografico De Agostini and Rand McNally & Co., 1982. xvi, 256p.+Æ144p. col.illus., col.maps, bibliog., index. £35.00. ISBN: 0855333863.

3 main sections. 1. Encyclopedia in 5 parts: Earth and the universe (astronomy); Making and shaping the earth (geology); The emergence of life (biology and palaeontology); Diversity of life (ecology); and Understanding maps (Mapping old and new, language of maps, how to use maps - 2. International map section (edited and designed by Istituto Geografico De Agostini of Novarra) consisting of 67 double-page maps - 3. United Kingdom and Ireland from Rand McNally's *The International Atlas* (1982) comprising 5 double-page maps. Geographical information and international index (p.A1-A144) (world information table; world geographical tables; major metropolitan areas; population tables etc.). Sources p.A14-A15. Geographical glossary p.A17-A24. International map index p.A75-A144.
Class No: 912.01

[5477]
Der Grosse Bertelsmann Weltatlas. Kartographiches Institut Bertelsmann, *ed.* Güterloh, Bertelsmann, 1965. xxxi, 160 pl. 188p. 52p. maps.

The main sequence of maps (100 pl.) is usually on the scale of 1:5M., and consists chiefly of physical maps, with political maps of continents. The supplementary sequence (20 pl.) deals with 'Mitteleuropa', on a scale of 1:M., this region including the Netherlands and marking conurbations (published in an English ed. as *Atlas of Central Europe* (London, Murray, 1963). Hill shading is rather heavy. The index-gazetteer of 185 pages, with 52 supplementary pages of 'Mitteleuropa', has *c.*150,000 entries. Entries are given for some places not on the maps; these are located in terms of the nearest town on the map, with distance and compass directions. End-paper key-maps. The introduction provides pronunciation keys for various languages and also a glossary (native language, with German equivalents, p.xxv-xxxi). Compares favourably with some post-war one-volume atlases for number and quality of maps and size of gazetteer. Page size 31 x 24cm. *Class No:* 912.01

[5478]
Der Grosse JRO Weltatlas produced by Esselte Map Service. München, JRO Kartografische Verlagsgesellschaft, 1986. 304p. col.illus., col.maps, index.

First published 1949. Frequently revised.

Contents: Enzyklopädie der Erde and Die Welt in Karten. Special emphasis on German speaking Europe. Index-gazetteer of more than 150,000 names. Scales differ.
Class No: 912.01

[5479]
Hammond atlas of the world. Maplewood, N.J., Hammond, 1992. 303p. col. illus., col. maps, tables, index. $65. ISBN: 0843711752.

Maps of the World on various scales (North America 1:3 million, US metropolitan areas 1:1 million, Africa and Latin America 1:6 million) is core section. Incidental material includes Introduction (evolution of cartography and map projections); Global relationships (thematic maps *e.g.* environment, population, economic resources *etc.*); and Geographical reference section (countries A-Z plus area, population, capital and major geographic features). Place-name index has 115,000 entries. 'A superb world atlas ... balanced and very current in its geographic coverage' (*Booklist*, v.89, no.10, 15 Mar 1993, p.940++42).
Class No: 912.01

[5480]
KIDRON, M. *and* **SEGAL, R. The New state of the world atlas.** 4th ed. London and New York, Simon & Schuster, 1991. 159p. col. maps. £16.99. ISBN: 0671710850.

3rd ed. 1987.

50 extensively revised double-page maps covering *au courant* topics *e.g.* AIDS, literacy, greenhouse effect, endangered species, and worldwide political and economic changes. Notes to maps p.118-59. *Class No:* 912.01

[5481]
The Macquarie illustrated world atlas. McMahon's Point, New South Wales, Macquarie Library in association with Division of National Mapping, Canberra, and the Department of Lands and Survey, Wellington, 1984. 512p. col.illus., col.maps, indexes. ISBN: 0949757217.

A world atlas with a strong focus on Australia (covered on a scale of 1:250,000) and its region: Australia p.115-201, New Zealand p.202-219, Papua New Guinea p.220-225, and Pacific Islands p.226-229. Index to Australia and New Zealand p.393-408. Maps and other material from Rand McNally's *The New International Atlas* and *Cosmopolitan World Atlas*. *Class No:* 912.01

[5482]
Meyers neuer Weltatlas. 2nd rev. ed. Mannheim, Meyers Lexikonverlag, 1991. 324p. col. illus., col. maps. ISBN: 3411074922.

1. Satellitenbilder der Erde (*i.e.* col. plates p.10-39) - 2. Geographischer Kartenteil (world and continent maps p.144-76) - 3. Thematischer Kartenteil (p.178-207). Index of 75,000 geographical names p.211-324. *Class No:* 912.01

[5483]
MURPHY, M. 'Atlases of the Eastern Hemisphere' a summary survey. *Geographical Review*, v.64, 1974, p.111-39.

Coverage: Europe; The Soviet Union; Africa; Asia; Australasia and Oceania. Running commentary; 175 footnote references. *Class No:* 912.01

[5484]

—STEPHENSON, R.W. 'Atlases of the Western hemisphere': a summary survey, *Geographical Review*, v.62, no.1, January 1972, p.92-119.

Brief descriptions of 143 regional and thematic atlases published in the Western hemisphere since 1961. Sections: Western hemisphere - North America - Canada - United States (general; thematic; State atlases) - Latin America - Middle America - South America). 136 references.

Class No: 912.01

[5485]

'National Geographic' Atlas of the world. 6th ed. Washington, National Geographic Society, 1991. 404p. col.illus., col.maps, col.graphs, index. $71.50. ISBN: 087044834x.

First published 1963.

Introductory matter includes 1: Pictorial features (universe, heavens, climate *etc.*) - Oceanic floor maps. Continental physical maps and World resources, food, energy, minerals. Nations of the World has text and maps grouped in sections: United States - Canada and Greenland - Mid America - South America - Europe - Asia - Africa - Australia, New Zealand and Antarctica - The Oceans. Geographic data (airline distances, timezones, temperatures and rainfall, population of major cities *etc.*. Glossary of foreign terms. Index of 150,000+ place names. A very attractive large atlas. 'Should not be absent from the shelves of any respectable library' (*Geographical Journal,* v.158, no.1, March 1992, p.95). *Class No:* 912.01

[5486]

The New cosmopolitan world atlas. Chicago, Rand McNally, 1993. 344p. col. illus., col. maps, index. $60. ISBN: 052883553x.

First published 1949. Subsequent editions in 1965, 1966 and 1967 bore the title *Rand McNally's new cosmopolitan world atlas.*

1. Human patterns and imprints - human settlement, industrializaton and economic matters - 2. Environment maps: thematic maps for population, religion, languages, agriculture, forests, fisheries, energy, climate, time zones *etc.* - 3. US travel maps (essentially road maps) - 4. World reference maps with heavy US bias - 5. 12 US metropolitan area maps with separate 3000 entry index listing cities, towns and local area names - 6. US geographical information *i.e.* population statistics for towns, cities and states - 7. World geographical information. Index to world reference maps contains 69,000 entries. Maps at various scales: Europe 1:2,000,000 - 1:4,000,00; US states: 1:700,000 - 1:4,000,000; Rest of world 1:8,000,000 - 1:16,000,000. Heavily biased: 'what purports to be a world atlas is, in effect, a US atlas with maps of other parts of the world' (*General reference books for adults*, 1988, p.202). Includes the recent US census information 1990. *Rand McNally concise world atlas*. 1987. viii, 224p. $24.95. ISBN 0528832859 is even more slanted to North America. 'The maps are useful and accurate but undistinguished' (*Reference Books Bulletin* 1987-1988, p.144). Both atlases are ideal for US school and home use. *Class No:* 912.01

[5487]

The New international atlas. Stokie, Illinois, Rand McNally, 1992. 560p. maps, tables, index. $125. ISBN: 0528835483.

First published 1969.

Rand McNally's flagship atlas. 255 map pages include world, ocean, continental maps; 50 x 16 miles to the inch (1:1,000,000) maps of key regional areas of exceptional economic importance, high density of population, or confronting complex transport needs; and 60 urban maps at scale of 5 miles to the inch (1:300,000) for major world metropolitan areas. Textual matter is in 5 languages: English, French, German, Portuguese and Spanish, with place-names in the local language (country names in English and in local official form). An unusual feature is three-dimensional shadings for mountains and valleys. 168,000 world names (including 35,800 US) are indexed.

Class No: 912.01

[5488]

The New Oxford atlas. Prepared by the Cartographic Department of Oxford Univ. Press. London, Oxford Univ. Press, 1978. 202p. 106p. of maps. ISBN: 0192115723.

First published as *The Oxford atlas* (1951).

Physical and physical-political maps in 6 colours. Relief is shown with layer colour in light tints without contours. Sections: Europe-Asia and USSR - Australasia - Africa - The Americas - World - United Kingdom. Scales for Europe 1:1M, 1:1.6M, 1:2.5M, 1:3.2M, 1:4M, 1:8M. Double-page spreads. Gazetteer of over 60,000 names. Good thematic maps of UK p.104-12. 'Good value for money' (*Geographical Journal*, v.143, no.1, March 1977, p.133). *Class No:* 912.01

[5489]

The Penguin atlas of the world. New York, Viking and Harmondsworth, Middlesex, Viking in association with Rand McNally, 1987. 176p. col.maps, graphs, tables, index. £14.95. ISBN: 0670817155.

1. The World scene (population; religion; languages; climate; surface configuration and Earth structure and tectonics) - 2. Maps (p.18-145) on various scales: continents 1:24,000,000; major regions 1:2,000,000; British Isles 1:1,000,000. World information and Metropolitan areas tables p.116-20. Maps taken from Rand McNally's *New international atlas* For home, office and school use. 'Provides a clear, accurate and comprehensive reference source with a quality of printing and binding that affords excellent value in this price range' (*Geographical Journal,* v.154,no.1, March 1988, p.142-3). *Class No:* 912.01

[5490]

Peters atlas of the world. Harlow, Longman, 1989. 226p. illus., col. maps. bibliog. £29.95. ISBN: 0582035015.

1. The world in 43 double page maps each representing 1/60 of the earth's surface. 2. Nature, man and society *i.e.,* 246 thematic maps (each showing global data by colour, not symbols). 3. Index p.189-226. Principal sources of information on thematic maps p.96. The distinctive feature of this atlas is the use of Arno Peter's own projection, designed to show the Earth in its true proportion, which lends the continental outlines an unfamiliar aspect. 'The very demerits of the Peters world projection could well be commercially helpful for sales of the atlas in developing countries but only the cartographically naive will be deceived and fail to be exasperated by the pretentious and

....(contd.)
misleading claims made for the atlas by the authors and publishers' (*Geographical Journal,* v.155,no.2, July 1989, p.295-7). *Class No:* 912.01

[5491]
—Compact Peters atlas of the world. Harlow, Longman, 1991. 228p. col. maps. £15.99. ISBN: 0582089565.
246 thematic maps. *Class No:* 912.01

[5492]
Philip's great world atlas. London, George Philip, 1990. 48, 176, 144p. illus., (some col.), col. maps, col. charts, index. £35.
Attractively produced atlas in 3 sections: 1. 200 political and physical maps - 2. Thematic maps (*e.g.* agricultural and industrial products, energy sources) - 3. Colour section on solar system, the physical world, climate, food and mineral production, trade and wealth, a double spread for each topic. 'A clear and comprehensive reference work, which for the most part contains up-to-date information' (*Reference Reviews,* v.2, no.4, December 1988, p.223).
Class No: 912.01

[5493]
Rand McNally world atlas of nations. Chicago, Rand McNally, 1988. 208p. col. illus., col. maps. $34.95. ISBN: 0528833154.
Maps of 216 nations, dependencies, protectorates *etc.* presented A-Z and not geographically. 'The arrangement, as text, statistical data, and color photographs are more prominent than the maps' making it 'an effective ready-reference source for basic information and a quick overview' (*Booklist,* v.85, no.10. 15 January 1989, p.853).
Class No: 912.01

[5494]
Reader's Digest atlas of the world. Rev. ed. London and New York, The Reader's Digest Association, 1992. 260p. £24.95.
This edition takes note of political changes in the former Soviet Union, Yugoslavia, Germany, and the Yemen.
A world of wonders *i.e.* 30 pictorial double-page features (*e.g.* The making of earth; Pacific: the vanishing ocean; The wanderings of man) p.4-63. The world in maps (p.64-260) includes United Kingdom and Republic of Ireland, a ten-page atlas within an atlas; World Information Table p.193-6; UK and Ireland gazetteer (over 8,000 names) and World gazetteer (42,000 names). Maps from Rand McNally's *The New International Atlas.* 'Larger in size and number of pages than *The Times Atlas Family Edition,* it contains far more background information on the world's physical and human history, although it is perhaps less easy to use simply for finding places' (*Good Book Guide,* no.44, September-October 1989, p.18). *Class No:* 912.01

[5495]
The Times atlas of the world. Comprehensive ed. 9th ed. London, Times books, 1992. xlvii,122 double+ 1 single plates, 237p. illus., col. maps,. diagrs., index. ISBN: 0723004927.
Comprehensive edition first published 1967. Preceded by *The Times atlas* (1895); *The Times survey atlas of the world* (2v., 1920-22); and *The Times atlas of the world* (Mid-century ed. 5v., 1955-59). Foreign language editions: 1. München, Droemersche Verlagsantalt, *Knaurs Grosser Weltatlas*(German) - 2. Ede, Kluwer Algemene Boeken, *De Grote Times Wereldatlas* (Dutch) - 3. Paris, Sélection du

....(contd.)
Readers Digest, *L'Atlas Universel* (French).
123 plates of maps (nearly all double page spread) include 8 thematic maps *e.g.* 'World climatology and food potential; and 'World mankind', the rest physico - political printed in 8 colours. Various scales: most European countries at scales ranging from 1:500,000 to 1:250,000; most cities and islands inset maps are at 1:250,000. 15 different styles of Times Roman lettering ensures high standards of legibility. Spelling of place names corresponds to the principles and practices of the British Permanent Committee on Geographical names. English conventional names of important places added where space permits. Chinese names in Pinyin style. Preliminaries include 'States and Territories of the World' Geographical comparisons (areas of continents, oceans and seas *etc.*); Star charts; Solar system; Space flight, map projection. Glossary and abbreviations p.1-3. Index-gazetteer *c.*210,000 place names. Includes the new states formed from USSR and Yugoslavia. Map detail updated includes over 2000 name revisions. Maps prepared by John Bartholomew & Son, Edinburgh. 'It will stand for many years to come as one of the leading cartographic sources of reference for the major topographic, social and economic features of our planet in the mid-1980's (*New Scientist,* 2 January 1986, p.46).
Class No: 912.01

[5496]
—The Times atlas of the world. Family edition. 2nd ed. London, Times Books; 1992. 68+156p. maps, tables, index. £17. ISBN: 0723004900, UK.
Introductory section includes states and territories of the world (col. flag, area, population, capital, currency *etc.*), physical maps, solar system, earthquakes and volcanoes, annual rainfall, population and geographic dictionary (p.94-9). Index of 30,000 entries. New nations of Croatia and Slovenia included but not Bosnia. For home, school and office use. 'Excellent value, although obviously less comprehensive than the main edition' (*Good Book Guide,* no.44, September/October 1989, p.18). *Class No:* 912.01

[5497]
—The Times concise atlas of the world. 6th.ed. London, Times Books, 1993. 44p.+148p. maps + 96p. col.illus., col.maps, col.diagrs., index. ISBN: 0723004935, UK; 0812920767, US.
First published 1972. Published in US as *The New York Times atlas of the world.*
148 mainly physical maps. Europe on scale 1:300,000; Asia, Africa, Australasia and South America mostly at 1:600,000. 67 City inset maps at 1:300,000. Preliminary features similar to *The Times atlas of the world* (*qv*). Glossary p.2 (3rd sequence). Index p.3-96 (100,000 names). 'It rivals any atlas on the market today, at any price ... an important title in any atlas collection' (*General reference books for adults,* 1988, p.192). *Class No:* 912.01

[5498]
Today's world a world atlas from the cartographers of Rand McNally. Stokie, Il., Rand McNally, 1992. 200p. col. maps, index. $29.95. ISBN: 0528835009.
New, accurate, large-format political and topographical atlas. National boundaries clearly shown with special markings for disputed, undefined, or indefinite frontiers. Alternative and historical names of cities indicated. Up-to-date information on united Germany, divided Soviet Union, and confused Yugoslavia. Large-scale regional maps of US and Canada. Place-name index of over 45000 entries. 'Does

....(contd.)

an admirable job of portraying the countries of the world with current boundaries' (*Booklist,* v.89, no.11, 1 Feb 1993, p.1005). *Class No:* 912.01

[5499]

"Yavneh" comprehensive atlas with glossary of geographical terms and index. Brawer, M., *ed.* Tel Aviv, "Yavneh" Publishing House, 1985. xxiv,175p.

112p. of coloured physical and political maps ending with the by now obligatory landset images. Multi-lingual glossary of geographical terms p.113-15. Only title page is in English. *Class No:* 912.01

Micromaterials

[5500]

PC Globe version 4.0. Mildenhall, Suffolk, Global Network. £59.95.

An electronic desk-top atlas, which provides instant profiles of 190 countries and dependencies in one source. Annually updated, the profiles include maps, graphics, facts and figures, a picture of the national flag and even a rendition of the national anthem. With world, continent and country maps, the atlas can also display major city locations, landscape elevations, lakes, rivers, mountains. System requires IBM PC/XT/AT/PS2 or compatibles with min. 640K RAM floppy drive or hard disk DOS 2.0+.
Class No: 912.01(003.5)

Bibliographies

[5501]

BRITISH MUSEUM. World: an excerpt from the British Museum 'Catalogue of printed maps, charts and plans.' Photolithographed ed. to 1964. London, Trustees of the British Museum, 1967. cols. 335-806.

About 5,500 entries. Arrangements: General atlases - General maps and charts - Subjects (A-Z, from Agriculture to Zoology). Appendix: Bibliographies, Biographies. Cartography. Catalogues ... *Class No:* 912.01(01)

[5502]

KISTER, K.F. Kister's atlas buying guide General English language world atlases available in North America. Phoenix, Arizona, Oryx Press, 1984. xii,236p. $39.50. ISBN: 0912700629.

105 Atlas profiles, A-Z by title, with a critical evaluation based on published reviews and on the compiler's own assessment. Appendix A: World atlases at a glance: B. Map and atlas bibliography; C. Out of print map and atlas dealers; D. Atlas publishers and distributors. Subject-Title index. 'Useful information for selecting one atlas out of a group of similar works'(*RQ,* v.24,no.1, Fall 1974, p.108). *Class No:* 912.01(01)

[5503]

WALSH, J. 'World atlas survey' Reference Books Bulletin, *Booklist,* v.87, no.7, 1 December 1990, p.769-70, 772-3.

The previous World atlas survey appeared in 'Reference Books Bulletin', 1 September 1983.

24 annotated entries related to comprehensive atlases printed since 1987 and published in the United States. Pocket editions and children's atlases are excluded. *Class No:* 912.01(01)

914/919 Gazetteers & Guide Books

Gazetteers & Guide Books

[5504]

BAEDEKER, K. Handbooks for travellers.
This famous series began when Karl Baedeker took over the The Rheinreisebuch in 1828. Noted for concise, detailed and carefully evaluated descriptions with a wealth of maps, town plans and panoramas. M. Wild's 'The Baedeker guide books', *Book And Magazine Collector,* no.68, November 1989, p.30-38 retells their early history and examines why they earned their splendid reputation. *Baedeker's handbook(s) for travellers: a bibliography of English editions published prior to World War II* (Westport, Connecticut, Greenwood Press, 1985) lists 266 editions of 31 titles. *Class No:* 914/919.9

[5505]

—Baedeker/AA country guides. Basingstoke, Hampshire, The Automobile Association. Average 335p. col. illus., maps, plans, pbk. £9.95.
Australia ISBN 0749504021 - *Caribbean* 0749504013 - *Denmark* 0861456114 - *Egypt* 0861451821 - *France* 0749502754 - *Germany* 0749505753 - *Great Britain* 0861450590 - *Greece* 074950403x - *Ireland* 0861456122 - *Israel* 0749505923 - *Italy* 0861450582 - *Japan* 0861451813 - *Mediterranean Islands* 0861452100 - *Mexico* 0861454162 - *Portugal* 0749504064 - *Scandinavia* 0479506792 - *Spain* 0861450604 - *Switzerland* 0759402770 - *Yugoslavia* 086145708. Latest titles: *Belgium* £11.99. 0749506741 - *Thailand* £11.99. 0749506806 - *Canada* "12.99. 0749505729 - *Netherlands* £12.99. 0749504056 - *Spain* £12.99. 0749504048 - *Tunisia* £12.99. 0749505591. Art, culture, history, climate, places of interest and scenic beauty spots. *Class No:* 914/919.9

[5506]

—HINRICHSEN, A. Baedeker's Reisenhandbücher 1832-1944 bibliographie der deutschen, französischen und englischen Ausgaben. Holzminden, Ursula Hinrichsen, 1981. 72p. bibliog., index. pbk. ISBN: 3922293026.
Detailed guide. Bibliography p.9. *Class No:* 914/919.9

[5507]

Baedeker/AA city guides. Basingstoke, Hampshire, The Automobile Association, 1981-. Average 192p. maps, plans, pbk. £5.95.
Amsterdam 074950278 £6.99 - *Athens* 0749505710 £6 .99 - *Bangkok* 0749504072 £6.99 - *Barcelona* 0749504102 £6.99 - *Berlin* 0749504110 £7.99 - *Budapest* 0759402800 £6.99 - *Copenhagen* 0749505737 £5.99 - *Florence* 0749505745 £6.99 - *Leningrad* 0749502797 £6.99 - *London* 0749502819 £6.99 - *Madrid* 0749504129 £6.99 - *Moscow* 0749502827 £6.99 - *New York* 0749502835 £6.99 - *Paris* 074952843 £6.99 - *Prague* 0749502851 £6.99 - *Rome* 074950286x £6.99 - *San Francisco* 0749504099 £6.99 - *Singapore* 0749505788 £6.99 - *Venice* 0749505796 £6.99 -

....(contd.)
Vienna 0749504080 £6.99. Where to stay, what to do, how to get there, an introduction to cultural background plus a variety of practical information. *Class No:* 914/919.9

[5508]

Blue guides. London, Ernest Benn (later A & C. Black), 1918-. maps, plans.500.00/00 'Blue guides', *Geographical Journal* v.144, no.3, November 1978, p.533 gives the series' background history.
1994 titles: *Albania* 0713637854; *France,* 3rd ed. 0713633867; *Spain,* 6th ed. 0713637315; *Sicily,* 4th ed. 0731637846.
1993 titles: *Amsterdam* ISBN 0713632282; *Belgium & Luxembourg;* 0713637323; *Corsica,* 2nd ed. 0713635894; *Crete,* 6th ed. 0713635886; *Egypt,* 3rd ed. 0713635908; *Holland,* 5th ed. 0713636548; *Morocco,* 2nd ed. 0713635924; *Normandy* 0713637307; *Tuscany* 0713633883; and *Umbria* 0713637056.
1992 Titles: *Athens,* 3rd ed. 0713635061; *Austria,* 3rd ed. 071363382; *Barcelona* 0713632291; *Burgundy* 0713633840; *China* 0713630272; *Czechoslovakia* 0713632305; *Denmark* 071363474x; *Ireland,* 6th ed. 0713634758; *Scotland,* 10th ed. 071363426x; *Paris & Versailles,* 8th ed. 0713635819; *Switzerland,* 5th ed. 0713635592.
Earlier titles: *Channel Is.,* 2nd ed. 0713628359; *Cyprus,* 3rd ed. 0713632747; *England,* 10th ed. 0713630280; *Florence,* 5th ed. 0713633859; *Greece,* 5th ed. 0713627719; *Hungary* 0713633032; *Istanbul,* 3rd ed. 0713632755; *Jerusalem* 0713629444; *London,* 14th ed. 0713632771; *Malta & Gozo,* 3rd ed. 071363233x; *Moscow & Leningrad,* 2nd ed. 0713632763; *New York,* 2nd ed. 0713631694; *Northern Italy,* 9th ed. 0713632763; *Oxford & Cambridge,* 3rd ed. 0713628405; *Portugal,* 3rd ed. 0713629665; *Rome,* 4th ed. 071363149x; *Southern Italy,* 7th ed. 0713631414; *Venice,* 4th ed. 0713631724; *Wales,* 7th ed. 0713631538; *Yugoslavia* 0713630345.
Renowned for detailed coverage of architecture, art history *etc.,* with practical information on accommodation, eating out, and local events and festivals. 'The best guides to have appeared since the nineteenth Baedeckers' (*Reference Reviews,* v.5, no.1, 1991, p.43). *Class No:* 914/919.9

[5509]

Chambers World gazetteer: an A-Z of geographical information. Munro, D., *ed.* 5th ed. Edinburgh and Cambridge, Chambers/Cambridge, 1988. xviii, 733p.+112p. World Atlas. £30.00. $34.50. ISBN: 1852962003.
First published 1895. Last edition (1965) published as *Chamber's World gazetteer and geographical dictionary.* This edition is the most comprehensive revision since the *Gazetteer's* first publication.
Standard international directory of 20,000 world place names: cities, regions, countries, places of touristic interest, notable archaeological and religious sites *etc.* 150 line maps illustrate political divisions and administrative areas. United States countries listed under State headings. Entries include

....*(contd.)*

information on location, pronunciation, topography, history, economic activity and key calendar dates. 120p. colour atlas. 'Generally, more and smaller, place name locations appear in Webster, but the Chambers entries are more informative' (*Choice*, v.26, no.7, March 1989, p.1118).
Class No: 914/919.9

[5510]
FISHER, M. Provinces and provincial capitals of the world.
2nd ed. Metuchen, New Jersey, Scarecrow Press, 1985. ix, 248p. index. £19.50; $21.00. ISBN: 0810817586.

224 countries A-Z. Data: commonly used name of country; official name in its accepted English form; Romanized native form; general location; capital; number and type of major administrative units or provinces; name of these units and their capitals. *Class No:* 914/919.9

[5511]
FITZPATRICK, G.L. *and* **MODLIN, M.J. Direct-line distances.** (1) International and (2) United States editions. Metuchen, New Jersey, Scarecrow, 1986. xliii,275p. maps. £42.50 each or £72.50 for both. ISBN: 0810818728, Int. ed; 081081871x, US ed.

Tables of distances, measured in kilometres, between 1001 cities, towns, islands, and other strategically located places assembled in 50 sections of 20 columns each. Leeds and Manchester (UK) not included although there is an entry for Manchester (New Hampshire). The United States edition includes 312 places in the US not found in the International edition and gives distances in statute miles. 'Will fill a void in reference libraries and collections' (*Geographical Journal*, v.154, no.1, March 1988, p.141).
Class No: 914/919.9

[5512]
GRAESSE, J.G.T. Orbinus Latinus lexikon lateinischer geographischer Namen des Mittelalters und der Neuzeit. Grossausgabe bearbeitet und herausgegeben von H. Plechl. 4th ed. Braunschweig, Klinkhardt & Biermann, 3v., 1972. 685p. + 652p. + 700p.

1st ed, 1909.

Lists medieval Latin place-names and their modern equivalents. *Class No:* 914/919.9

[5513]
The Hutchinson guide to the world. 2nd ed. Oxford, Helicon, 1993. 489p. maps, tables. £15.99. ISBN: 0091775213.

First published as *The Hutchinson paperback guide to the world* (1990).

6000 entries (500 new to this edition) on all the world's major cities, towns, regions, and geographical features, including 18 new sovereign states created since 1991. Cultural and historical detail is added to the usual gazetteer material. 350 location maps. *Class No:* 914/919.9

[5514]
KURIAN, G.T. Geo-data the world almanac gazetteer. Detroit, Gale Research Co., 1982. 624p. $60.00. ISBN: 0810316056.

In 4 major parts: 1. United States (detailed information on 50 states, 3142 counties, and 2492 towns and cities of over 10,000 population) - 2. World countries, cities and administrative divisions - 3. Geographical gazetteer of the world (data on continents, oceans, seas, rivers, islands mountains *etc.*) - 4. Rankings (comparative areas, heights, depths *etc.*). *Choice*, v.20,no.11-12, July-August 1983,

....*(contd.)*

p.1576-7 would have preferred a single A-Z sequence and concludes 'most libraries would be better served by the standard Webster's New Geographical Dictionary'.
Class No: 914/919.9

[5515]
KURIAN, G.T. The World gazetteer of boundaries. Santa Barbara, California, ABC-Clio, 1988. 900p. maps, tables, bibliog. £77.45. ISBN: 087436504x.

Definitive inventory of world land and maritime boundary changes since 1917 arranged by continent or region. Also includes descriptions of current and dormant boundary disputes and summaries of boundary treaties.
Class No: 914/919.9

[5516]
Lonely Planet survival kit series. Hawthorn, Victoria, Lonely Planet Publications.

Over 60 frequently revised single country or small group of countries guides intended for travellers who want to explore beyond the normal tourist routes: Australia and the Pacific - South East Asia - North East Asia - Indian subcontinent - Indian Ocean - West Asia and Middle East - Africa - Northern America and Mexico (4v.) - South America (8v.) and D. Swaney's *Iceland and the islands of the North Atlantic*. 1990. 230p. + + 16p. col. illus. A$15.95; $11.95; £6.95. ISBN 0864420927.

'These guides (*i.e. Turkey* and *Mauritius, Réunion and Seychelles* are particularly fine examples, and are so good that independent travellers who are going to any of these places should not venture abroad without buying one' (*The Independent*, no.1033, 3 February 1990. p.44).

Lonely planet newsletter, 1990-. Quarterly. January 1990-. includes up-to-date travel information and the latest details on new books. 'Lonely Planet's books in particular have set the highest standards of responsible travel advice, and though it doesn't advertise the fact, it has a policy of investing a percentage of its revenue in environmental projects in the countries it covers'. (*Bookseller*, 31 Jan 1992). *Class No:* 914/919.9

[5517]
Philip's world handbook country by country. Widdows, R., *comp.* London, George Philip, 1993. vi,298p. col. maps, tables. ISBN: 0540057290.

1. World maps (different scales) p.1 to 37 - 2. World gazetteer (220++ countries) describing each nation's geography, history, economy, culture, and politics (p.38-232) - 3. World statistics (physical dimensions, demography, cities, energy, gross national product *etc.*).
Class No: 914/919.9

[5518]
Rand McNally world facts & maps. Stokie, Illinois, Rand McNally, 1993. 208p. maps, tables, index. Pbk. $9.95. ISBN: 0528835459.

Quick reference guide 'Hot spots: current events in focus' section (international current affairs) and 'World gazetteer: profiles of nations and places' (population, ethnic groups, religions, history and politics *etc.*). *Class No:* 914/919.9

[5519]
Reader's Digest guide to places of the world. London, The Reader's Digest Association Limited, 1987. 735p. col. illus., col. maps. £26.95. $29.95. ISBN: 0276398262.

Contents: 1. A-Z guide to the nations of the world, places of interest and geographical terms in common use, p.10-730; 2. Flags of the world p.731-733; 3. International organizations and alliances p.734-735.

158 full-colour maps, 250 colour illustrations and 7000 features and articles. 'Heartily recommended as a reference work or as study material for any cartographic office as well as being the ideal home geographical encyclopedia' (*Bulletin of Society of University Cartographers,* v.21, no.2, 1988, p.115-6). *Class No:* 914/919.9

[5520]
ROOM, A., *comp.* **Place-name changes 1900-1991.** 2nd ed. Metuchen, NJ., Scarecrow Press, 1993. 295p. bibliog. $37.50. ISBN: 0810826003.

1st ed. 1979 as *Place-name changes since 1900.*

4500 place-names listed A-Z. Data: type of place (*i.e.* town, river), approximate location, former name(s), and year in which former named ceased to be used.
Class No: 914/919.9

[5521]
The Rough guides London, Harrap Columbus, 1982-. col. illus., maps.

Title in US is 'The Real Guides'.

Intended to be 'a new kind of travel guide that would fill the gap that existed between the *Blue Guide* (which doesn't tell you where the best beaches are) and the *Place x on $20 a day* guide (which don't tell you much more than how to live cheaply)' (*The Independent,* 21 January 1989, p.39).

1992 titles: Greece. (5th edition) - *Hungary.* (2nd edition) - *Provence & the Cote d'Azur.* (2nd edition) - *Thailand.*

Earlier titles: Amsterdam. (3rd edition) - *Barcelona & Catalunya.* - *Berlin.* (2nd edition) - *Brazil.* - *Brittany & Normandy.* (3rd edition) - *California.* (2nd edition) - *Canada.* - *Crete.* (2nd edition) - *Czechoslovakia.* - *Eastern Europe.* - *Egypt.* - *Europe.* - *Florida* - *France.* (3rd edition) - *Germany.* - *Guatemala & Belize.* - *Holland, Belgium and Luxembourg.* - *Hong Kong.* - *Ireland.* (2nd edition) - *Israel.* - *Italy.* - *Kenya.* (3rd edition) - *Mediterranean Wildlife.* - *Mexico.* (2nd edition) - *Morocco.* (3rd edition) - *Nepal.* - *New York.* (3rd edition) - *Nothing Ventured.* - *Paris.* (3rd edition) - *Peru.* (2nd edition) - *Poland.* - *Portugal.* (5th edition) - *Prague.* - *Pyranees.* - *San Francisco. Scandinavia.* (2nd edition) - *Sicily.* - *Spain.* (5th edition) - *Tunisia.* (3rd edition) - *Turkey.* - *Tuscany & Umbria. US.* - *Venice.* - *West Africa.* - *Women Travel.* - *Yugoslavia.* (2nd edition) - *Zimbabwe & Botswana. Class No:* 914/919.9

[5522]
SPAULL, H. New place names of the world. London, Ward Lock, 1970. 64p. maps. ISBN: 0706310578.

Lists names of new towns and other places created since 1945 and also names that have changed since then. 17 maps.
Class No: 914/919.9

[5523]
The Stateman's year book world gazetteer. Paxton, J., *ed.* 4th ed. London, Macmillan Press, 1991. xiii,693p. £39.95. ISBN: 0333525272.

1st ed. 1975; 3rd ed. 1986.

8,000 entries for towns, regions, and geographical landmarks. Data: location, description, history, industries,

....(contd.)
population. Index of 700+ geographical terms p.655-693. 'A valuable reference work, which pleasantly doubles up as a traveller's companion' (*International Affairs,* v.63,no.1, Winter 1986-87, p.177). *Class No:* 914/919.9

[5524]
UNITED STATES. Board on Geographic Names. **Gazetteers.** Washington, Defense Mapping Agency Combat Support Center, 1955-. tables.

A world series of country gazetteers, Afghanistan-Zambia, of standard names approved by the Board on Geographic Names and unapproved variants. The single line entries include coordinates, evaluation of the quality of the names, designations (*i.e.,* cities, mountains, rivers *etc.*), and political administrative unit. Includes undersea features. By far the most comprehensive and detailed of their kind.

Foreign names decisions of the US Board on Geographic Names contains information about recent decisions. They are not cumulative. *Names of political entities of the world* is published approximately every 15 months.
Class No: 914/919.9

[5525]
—Foreign gazetteers of the US Board on Geographic Names, Microfiche Collection. Washington, D.C., Congressional Information Service, 1987. 1505 microfiche (negative polarity) 24:1 reduction ratio. 15p. printed bibliography. $3,000.00.

Only the most current gazetteer for each country is reproduced in this collection.

'Not all these gazetteers were distributed through the Government Printing Office's depository program ... Tragically, several gazetteers from the 1980s have been withled from depository libraries due to bureaucratic definitions of proprietary information ... The printed bibliography is excellent and can stand on its own as a superb reference tool. It alphabetically lists the countries included in the collection, with cross references to previous names of a country (if any) and countries grouped together in one gazetteer' (*Information Bulletin* Western Association of Map Librarians, v.19,no.2, March 1988, p.114-5).
Class No: 914/919.9

[5526]
Webster's new geographical dictionary. Rev. ed. Springfield, Massachusetts, Merriam, 1984. 1568p. tables, maps. $19.95. ISBN: 0877794464.

First published 1949 as *Webster's geographical dictionary.*

A gazetteer, not a dictionary of geographical terms. Over 47,000 place-names entries, plus over 15,000 cross-references. Geographical terms (over 450 in *c.*12 languages),. Entries state pronunciation, word division and basic data (location; features; history) on countries, regions, cities and natural features. 217 black-and-white maps. 'US and Canada have the largest number of entries, and all incorporated places with populations in excess of 2,500 are included' (*RQ,* v.12,no.3, Spring 1973, p.324). Helpful tables (*e.g.* Greater London). 'A must for any reference, school or public library, as well as many commercial and all newspaper offices' (*Times Educational Supplement,* no.3017,23 March 1973, p.23). *Class No:* 914/919.9

Bibliographies

[5527]

HEISE, J.O. *and* RINEHART, J.R. **The Travel book guide to travel guides.** Metuchen, NJ., Scarecrow Press, 1993. 397p. index. £42.50. ISBN: 0810826976.

First published New York, Bowker, 1981.

Evaluation of travel guides published worldwide but very strong North American bias. Less than ethusiastic review in *Reference Reviews*, v.8, no.1, 1994, p.41-42 which points to some serious omissions, patchy coverage, and lack of up-to-date information in some instances.
Class No: 914/919.9(01)

[5528]

MEYNEN, E., *comp.* **Gazetteers and glossaries of geographical names of the member-countries of the United Nations** and the agencies in relationship with the United Nations. Stuttgart, Franz Steiner Verlag, 1984. xvii, 518p. maps. DM98.00. *Class No:* 914/919.9(01)

[5529]

WHITTINGTON, C. 'On the road: an annotated list of travel guides', *Reference Books Bulletin 1987-1988*, p.16-19.

Recommended US travel guide series.
Class No: 914/919.9(01)

Encyclopaedias

[5530]

CANBY, C. **The Encyclopaedia of historic places.** New York, Facts On File; London, Mansell Publishing Ltd., 2 vols, 1984. v,1051p. illus. £85. $160. ISBN: 0720116902, the set; 0720116937, vol.1; 0720116945, vol.2.

Geographic locations of historic significance (towns, cities, countries, provinces and regions, empires, deserts, forts and battle sites, lakes and rivers, mountains, shrines and archaeological sites 'including many places not found in standard reference books' pinpointed in A-Z entries by most common English name. 'Should become librarians' first choice as a source of short histories' (*Wilson Library Bulletin*, v.58, no.10, June 1984, p.753).
Class No: 914/919.9(031)

Europe

[5531]

Baedeker/AA regional guides. Basingstoke, Hampshire, The Automobile Association. Average 244p. col.illus. maps,pbk. £5.95.

Costa Brava ISBN 0861456769 - *Gran Canaria* 0861456777 - *Greek Islands* 0861456149 - *Ibiza/Formentera* 0861456785 - *Loire* 0861452798 - *Mallorca.Menorca* 0861456793 - *Provence/Cote d'Azur* 0861453581 - *Rhine* 0861452801 - *Tenerife* 0861456807 - *Turkish coast* 0861456130 - *Tuscany* 086145281x. Pocket size guides. Detailed gazetteer of towns and places of interest.
Class No: 914

[5532]

EASTMAN, J. **Who lived where in Europe** a biographical guide to homes and museums. New York, Facts on File, 1985. xiv,416p. illus. £20.00; $35.00. ISBN: 0871967499.

8 geographical chapters covering Western Europe concentrating on homes of 300 or so persons 'whose lives had major effects on European society and history'. Detail includes year of construction and destruction, date of

....(contd.)

occupation by the noted inhabitant, and the 1984 status of the home or site. Name index and gazetteer p.381-413; Geographical index p.413-416. *Class No:* 914

[5533]

Michelin green tourist guides. Harrow, Mdx, Michelin Tyre PLC., 1992. pbk. £6.95.

English language: *Austria, Canada, England - The West Country, Germany, Great Britain, Greece, Ireland, Italy, London, Mexico, Netherlands, New England, New York City, Portugal, Quebec, Rome, Scotland, Spain, Switzerland, Washington.*

French language: *Belgique & Luxembourg, Hollande, Londres, Maroc.*

Detailed descriptions of places of interest, local culture, history and touring programmes with plans of towns and buildings. Cross referenced to corresponding Michelin Maps and Red Guides. *Class No:* 914

[5534]

TOURING CLUB ITALIANO. **Guida d'Europa.** Milano, Touring Club Italiano, 16v. illus., maps, plans.

Periodically updated, each volume begins with a comprehensive geographic, artistic and economic overview. This is followed by motoring itineraries and an A-Z gazetteer of places to visit. Also general information on hotels, restaurants, camp sites etc., with plentiful maps, town plans and drawings. *Titles: Spagna e Portogallo*, 502p. L49.000; *Francia*, 444p. L44,000; *Parigi e dintori*, 296p. L39,000; *Gran Bretagna e Irlanda*, 367p. L40,000; *Londra e dintori*, 272p. L39,000; *Germania-Repubblica Federale*, 496p. L49,000; *Belgio, Olanda, Lussemburgo*, 272p. L38,000; *Svizzera*, 280p. L39,000; *Austria*, 290p. L39,000; *Iugoslavia*, 256p. L39,000; *Grecia*, 190p, L40,000; *Bulgaria e Romania*, 240p. L30,000; *Ungheria*, 144p. L28,000; *Cecoslovacchia*, 232p. L30,000; *Mosca e Leningrado*, 192p. L30,000; *Danimarca e Islanda*, L33,000; *Svezia, Norvegia, Finlandia*, L40,000. *Class No:* 914

[5535]

The Traveller's histories. Moreton-In-Marsh, Gloucestershire, Windrush Press, 1989-. illus., maps.

Boatswain, T. and Nicolson, C. *A Traveller's history of Greece.* 320p. £11.95. ISBN 090007521x; Lintner, V. *Italy.* 288p. pbk. £7.95. 0900075600; Cole, R. *France.& 240p.* £10.95. 0900075260; Lalaguna, J. *Spain.* 304p. pbk. £7.95. 0900075503; Fisher, A. *Scotland.* 256p. pbk £7.95. 0900075368; Neville, P. *Russia and the USSR.* 320p. pbk. £7.95. 0900075414. The series offers a history of the country from the earliest times together with a gazetteer cross-referenced to the main text. Major events, chronologies, battles, Prime Ministers, Presidents, Reigning families are all highlighted. *Class No:* 914

Europe—Central

[5536]

BASSETT, R. **A Guide to Central Europe.** New York, Viking, 1987. 256p. illus., maps, bibliog., index. $19.95. ISBN: 0670811130.

'More accurately about those regions that were part of the Hapsburg Empire in 1911 ... this excellent guide expertly leads the reader through the baths of Budapest, Viennese concert halls, and the back streets of medieval Prague; more remote locales are also featured' (*Library Journal*, v.112,no.12, July 1987, p.77). *Class No:* 914.02

Great Britain

[5537]

AA 250 tours of Britain: maps and easy-to-find route instructions for day and weekend drives through England, Wales and Scotland, with descriptions of the natural wonders and man-made attractions to be seen on the way. London, Drive Publications for the Automobile Association, 1986. Distributed by Hodder & Stoughton. 416p. col.illus. col.maps. index. £16.95. ISBN: 090335635x.

8 regional chapters (introduction, text, map and illustrations) p.8-407. Tourist information, national parks, historic plates *etc.,* p.408. Ideal for the experienced non-driving map reader. *Class No:* 914.10

[5538]

AA 365 days out in Britain. Basingstoke, Hampshire, The Automobile Association, 1989. 256p. col.illus., maps, index. £12.95. ISBN: 086145765x.

Over 1000 places to visit arranged in 6 regional sections each with an introduction, a special feature highlighting a particular aspect, a calendar of customs and events, and a location map. Lavishly illustrated. *Class No:* 914.10

[5539]

AA 2000 days out in Britain. Basingstoke, Hampshire, The Automobile Association, 1993. 256p. maps, index. Softcover. £3.95. ISBN: 0749505451.

Previously as *2000 places to visit.*

A-Z gazetteer of places to visit. Data: map reference; brief description; opening hours; admission charges; parking information; refreshments; chairbound access; and location atlas. *Class No:* 914.10

[5540]

AA book of British towns. London, Drive Publications for The Automobile Association, 1982. 432p. illus. (mostly col.), col.maps. £12.95.

First published 1979.

Complete guide to 691 towns and cities (more than 20,000 population) with guided tours of 11 largest. Exploring London p.224-71. Glossary of architectural and historical terms p.430.1. 212 maps in colour. 616 colour and 248 b/w. illustrations. *Class No:* 914.10

[5541]

AA book of British villages a guide to 700 of the most interesting and attractive villages in Britain. Reprinted with amendments. London, Drive Publications for The Automobile Association, 1985. 448p. col.illus., maps, indexes. £16.95. ISBN: 0903356287.

First published 1980.

A-Z gazetteer p.8-416 plus 13 special features e.g., 'Discovering village history' (R. Parker); 'How villages got their names' (M. Gelling); 'Lost villages' (W.S. Hoskins). 13 Regional maps. Gazetteer of village craft centres p.444-47. *Class No:* 914.10

[5542]

AA guide to National Trust properties in Britain. Powell, R., *ed.* Basingstoke, Hampshire, The Automobile Association, 1986. 192p. col.illus., col.maps, index. £9.95. ISBN: 0861451988.

A-Z by location within 7 regional sections. Glossary p.188. Sumptuously illustrated. *Class No:* 914.10

[5543]

AA illustrated guide to Britain's coast. Reprinted with amendments 1987. London, Drive Publications for The Automobile Association, 1984. 383p. col.illus., col.maps, index. £16.95. ISBN: 0903356333.

A richly illustrated mile by mile survey (p.8-349) starting at the Severn estuary near Bristol and continuing anti-clockwise round the entire coastline and the main offshore islands, dividing the coast into 145 sections each covering a strip of coast (typically) of 35 miles. Each section embodies a descriptive text accompanied by a map and boxed local information and places to see inland. 13 special double-pages features, *e.g.* 'Bristol, seafaring city' and 'Coastal lands lost and won'. Also 'Exploring the living world of our seashore' (p.350-369). Key to *Guide* on endpapers. *Class No:* 914.10

[5544]

AA illustrated guide to country towns and villages of Britain. London, Drive Publications for The Automobile Associations, 1985. 448p. col.illus., col.maps, index.

21 major contributors. Descriptive gazetteer of over 500 country towns and villages chosen for their outstanding beauty and interest A-Z in 36 areas. Detailed maps of each area indicate locations of places to visit. Aspects of life (6 special features) p.415-439. Index of towns and villages and general index. *Class No:* 914.10

[5545]

AA/Ordnance Survey leisure guides. Basingstoke, Hampshire, Automobile Association; Southampton, Ordnance Survey, 1985-. 120p. col.illus., col.maps, index. £10.95.

Brecon Beacons and Mid Wales. ISBN 0861458192 - *Channel Islands* 0861455150 - *Cornwall* 0861455126x - *Cotswolds* 0861453492 - *Devon* 0861456653 - *East Anglia* 0861458206 - *Ireland.* 176p. 0861453751 - *Isle of Wight* 0861456661 - *Lake District* 0861452267 - *New Forest* 96p. 0861451740 - *Northumbria* 0861454952 - *North York Moors* 0861454898 - *Peak District* 0861454928 - *Scottish Highlands* 0861452364 - *Snowdonia & North Wales* 0861458036 - *South Downs* 086145667x - *Wessex* 0861456688 - *Wye Valley & Forest of Dean* 0861456696 - *Yorkshire Dales* 0861452348.

Historical and topographical sections precede favourite tourist areas in descriptive A-Z gazetteer form supported by 1 inch to 1 mile O.S. atlas. Other features: a monthly calendar of events, motor tours, walk guides. Softcover versions are also available. *Class No:* 914.10

[5546]

AA/OS Walks and tours in Britain. Basingstoke, Hants., The Automobile Association; Southampton, Hants, Ordnance Survey, 1990. 319p. col. illus., maps, index. Looseleaf in ringbinder. £19.95. ISBN: 074950031x, AA; 0319002098, OS.

A descriptive guide to 244 walks and tours with relevant sections from O.S. Pathfinder, Landranger and Outdoor Leisure maps. Each of 50 tours is followed by a selection of walks within striking distance of the motor routes. National grid reference numbers to walk starting points are provided as are route directions and brief descriptions of major places of interest. 'A useful addition to general touring and topographic collections' (*Reference Reviews,* v.4, no.1, 1980, p.32). *Class No:* 914.10

[5547]

AA places to visit in Britain: a county-by-county guide to more than 2400 castles, stately homes, gardens, theme parks, museums and other places of interest throughout England, Wales and Scotland. London, Drive Publications for The Automobile Association, 1988. 432p. £17.95.

Gazetteer A-Z by counties interspersed with special features on London (16 pages). 10 major towns and cities, and 20 other showpiece sites. Over 650 colour illustrations. 64 county maps. 10 town plans. *Class No:* 914.10

[5548]

AA town and city guides. Basingstoke, Hampshire, Automobile Association, 1987-. 120p. col.illus., col.maps, index. Softcover. £6.95.

Cambridge ISBN 0861456513 - *Dublin* 0861456521 - *Edinburgh* 086145653x - *Glasgow* 086145648 - *York* 086145510x. Detailed maps and large-scale street plans accompany motor tours, walks, practical information and descriptions of places of interest inside and outside the city boundaries. Pocket City guides are also available. *Class No:* 914.10

[5549]

The American guide to Britain. Wright, E., *ed.* Topsfield, Massachusetts, Salem House Publishers in collaboration with The Automobile Association, 1987. 264p.+30p. atlas section, col.illus., maps. $24.95. ISBN: 0881622680.

Marketed in UK as *AA the visitor's guide to Britain* (Exeter, Webb & Bower, 1987. £15.95. ISBN 0863501117).

14 historical essays *e.g.* 'Ancient Britain' and 'Winston Churchill and the Anglo-American marriages' precede detailed A-Z gazetteer of over 1500 towns and places to visit with particular reference to American associations. Over 300 col.illus. 15 double-page maps on scale 10 miles to 1 inch. 'This guide will add little to the number of guides to Britain already available'. (*Reference Reviews*, v.2, no.3, September 1988, p.158-9). *Class No:* 914.10

[5550]

BOGLE, J. Who lies where? a guide to the resting places of the famous. London, Lamp Press, 1989. 108p. index, pbk. £5.99. ISBN: 0551018232.

Brief notes A-Z p.9-99. Of special interest to Americans p.5. Index of place names p.100-108. Covers England, Scotland, Wales and the Channel Islands. *Class No:* 914.10

[5551]

'Britain's national parks', *Holiday Which,* v.11, no.1, January 1984, p.67-83. col.illus, col.maps.

Covers 10 parks - 'what they're like and how to get the best out of them'. Notes on maps and guide books, information services, travel and accomodation. *Class No:* 914.10

[5552]

BROWN, J.W. *and* **BROWN, S.N. Before you go to Great Britain:** a resource directory and planning guide. Camden, Connecticut, Shoe String Press, 1986. xiii,201p. $25.00; £21.895. ISBN: 0208020888.

'After an introductory chapter of facts about Britain as a country, there are chapters that cover resources for planning the trip and getting to Britain, travel guides to the country and areas within it, information sources on getting around within Great Britain, guides to food and drink, resources on sports activities and the arts, tools on special interests such as brass rubbing and antiques, and hints on using one's local library for further study. The chapters are similar in

....(contd.)

arrangement, beginning with a brief discussion of the topic at hand and proceeding through annotated listings of books, pamphlets, maps, audiovisual resources, relevant organizations and associations, and other places to write for information ... a valuable tool for collection development and reader assistance in public and academic libraries' (*Reference Books Bulletin 1986-87,* p.150-1). *Class No:* 914.10

[5553]

David and Charles Touring Companions. Newton Abbot, Devon, David & Charles, 1990. £2.50 each.

104 guides, each for use with a sheet of the Ordnance Survey Landranger map series (1:50,000) of which there are 204 sheets. For 'walkers, motorists, outdoor enthusiasts, naturalists, historians'. 'The idea of linking into the infinitely rich Ordnance Survey mapping is an intriguing one, but I confess to being slightly disappointed by the cheap production and thin texts' (*The Bookseller,* 26 January 1990, p.274). *Class No:* 914.10

[5554]

GAUNT, P. The Cromwellian gazetteer an illustrated guide to Britain in the Civil War and Commonwealth. Gloucester, Alan Sutton and The Cromwell Association, 1987. xiv,241p. illus., maps, geneal tables, index. £14.95. ISBN: 0862992915.

A guide to sites in Britain and Ireland associated with the parliamentary cause 1642-1660 with emphasis on Cromwell himself. Arranged A-Z by country. Appendix: A Cromwell itinerary p.224-228. 9p. of maps. *Class No:* 914.10

[5555]

GOODMAN, A. *and* **CYPRIEN, M. A Traveller's guide to early medieval Britain.** London, Routledge and Kegan Paul; Harrisburg, Pennsylvania, Historical Times Inc., 1986. 128p. illus., map, bibliog. £12.95. ISBN: 0710209428, UK; 0918678161, US.

Gazetteer p.8-122 incl. 11 special essays *e.g.* Magna Carta and the beginnings of parliament, Holidays and Holy-days. List of Kings p. 123-4. Glossary p.125-6. Further reading p.127. *Class No:* 914.10

[5556]

GREAT BRITAIN. Ordnance Survey. The Ordnance Survey gazetteer of Great Britain. 2nd ed. Southampton, Ordnance Survey; London, Macmillan Reference Books, 1989. xiii, 796p. £65.00. ISBN: 0333499999.

1st ed. 1987.

Lists 256,000 named features on O.S. Landranger Map Series (1:50,000 *i.e.* 1½ inches to the mile) covering England, Scotland and Wales on 204 sheets. Data: Name; County; National Grid Reference; Latitude and Longitude; Feature code (antiquity, forest, hill *etc.*); and Sheet number. This edition incorporates 11,000 name changes. 'The sheer scale of the work makes it an invaluable tool' (*Refer,* v.4, no.1, Spring 1986, p.16). *Class No:* 914.10

[5557]

GREAT BRITAIN. Ordnance Survey. Ordnance Survey maritime England a unique and comprehensive guide to the rich and diverse maritime attractions through England ... Southampton, Ordnance Survey, 1982. Single sheet folded map, illus. £1.25.

Published in conjunction with English Tourist Board as part of its 1982-85 Maritime England promotion.

'Locates and briefly describes over 700 maritime

....*(contd.)*

attractions ... ports, harbours, resorts, historic houses, museums, lighthouses'. Scale: 1:625,000 or about one inch to ten miles. *Class No:* 914.10

[5558]
HAMMOND, C. Ricardian Britain a guide to places connected with Richard III. 5th ed. London, Richard III Society, 1988. 48p. map, index. sd. £2.50. ISBN: 0904893138.

1st ed. by V. Giles and C. Hicks (now Hammond) 1968.

88 entries A-Z by historic counties. Data: Description; Hours; Directions. Appendix: Portraits of Richard III. *Class No:* 914.10

[5559]
HUDSON, K. and NICHOLLS, A. The Cambridge guide to the historic places of Britain and Ireland. Cambridge, Cambridge Univ. Press, 1989. viii, [16]p., maps, 326p. illus. (28 col.), indexes. £14.95. ISBN: 0521360773.

Descriptive gazetteer of the amenities and opening hours of 1567 monuments and buildings including all major National Trust and English Heritage sites, industrial monuments, gardens, battlefields, literary shrines, spas, shops, theatres *etc.,* 8 regional double-page location maps. Place and subject indexes. *Class No:* 914.10

[5560]
JACKSON, R. Dark Age Britain: what to see and where. Cambridge, Patrick Stephens, 1984. 208p. illus., maps, index. £10.95. ISBN: 085059622x.

Historical text for the general reader interspersed with descriptions and illustrations of visible Dark Age remains. Arranged in 3 Parts (15 chapters): 1. The British resistance 410-642AD - 2. The Anglo-Saxon kingdoms 642-800AD - 3. 'From the fury of the Northmen, O Lord, deliver us'. List of sites which may be visited p.6-7. 160 photographs. 6 maps. *Class No:* 914.10

[5561]
JOHNSTONE, M. Royal Britain. London, Unicorn Heritage, 1988. 96p. illus. (most col.), col.maps, index. pbk. £3.95. ISBN: 1870968107.

Places with royal associations arranged in 5 regions. List of monarchs p.4. Serviceable pocket handbook. *Class No:* 914.10

[5562]
KERR, N. and KERR, M. A Guide to medieval sites in Britain. London, Grafton Books, 1988. 270p. maps, illus., index. £14.95. ISBN: 0246124709.

160 entries relating to over 200 sites belonging to the period 1200-1485 grouped in 8 geographical regions. Each contains an architectural and historical description and clear map directions. 'As an aid to planning outings rather than as a comprehensive reference work it is an attractive and useful book' (*Reference Reviews,* v.2, no.3, September 1988, p.161). *Class No:* 914.10

[5563]
KERR, N. and KERR, M. A Guide to Norman sites in Britain. London, Granada, 1984. 192p. illus. maps, bibliog. £10.95. ISBN: 0246119764.

156 sites grouped geographically (Southern England p.12-53; East Anglia p.54-79; Central England p.80-107; Wales and the Marches p.108-137; Northern England p.138-159; Scotland and the Borders p.160-185) of the visible physical remains of the period 1066-1200. Each site is located in

....*(contd.)*

detail and is furnished with a six-figure Ordnance Survey grid reference. Glossary p.186-188. Index p.189-192. *Class No:* 914.10

[5564]
LINDOP, C. and FISHER, D. Discover Britain: a practical guide to the language, country and people. 2nd ed. Cambridge, Cambridge Univ. Press, 1988. viii, 168p. illus (some col.), index. pbk. £5.25. ISBN: 0521335949.

First published 1985.

Arriving and leaving - Travel - London - Beyond London - Money - Places to stay - Food - People - Weather and clothes - Shopping - Pubs - Enjoying yourself - Post, places, news - Studying in Britain - Working in Britain - Help! For foreign students, tourists and business people with little English. 'Very uneven; it contains a large amount of useful information, but too much that is sketchy' (*Reference Reviews,* v.2,no.3, September 1988, p.157-8). *Class No:* 914.10

[5565]
MARINE CONSERVATION SOCIETY. The Heinz good beach guide 1993 *the guide to over 500 of Britain's most popular beaches.* London, Vermilion, 1993. 208p. maps, index, pbk. £6.99. ISBN: 0091777151.

First published 1988.

Beaches A-Z by resort graded according to pollution level in 11 regions including Guernsey and Jersey. *Class No:* 914.10

[5566]
MUIR, R. The National Trust guide to Dark Age and Medieval Britain 400-1350. London, George Philip/The National Trust/The National Trust for Scotland, 1985. 256p. maps, illus. (some col), bibliog. £14.95. ISBN: 0540010901.

10 thematic, generously illustrated chapters supported by a gazetteer (p.235-241) introduce surviving monuments and attempt to explain their significance. Maps p.242-250. Bibliography p.251. Index 252-256. *Class No:* 914.10

[5567]
MUIR, R. and WELFARE, H. The National Trust guide to prehistoric and Roman Britain. London, George Philip in association with The National Trust and the National Trust for Scotland. 272p. illus. (a few col.), maps, bibliog., index. £12.50. ISBN: 0540010766.

10 chronological and thematic chapters each ending with an extensive list of places to visit with O.S. grid references and location maps. Bibliography p.261. *Class No:* 914.10

[5568]
MUIR, R. Traveller's history of Britain and Ireland. London, Michael Joseph, 1983. 304p. illus. (mostly col., maps. ISBN: 0718122305.

Descriptions of 54 prominent historic buildings and sites grouped in 8 chronological sections with scores of shorter entries for sites of interest 'Round and About'. Profusely illustrated. *Class No:* 914.10

[5569]
The New Shell guide to Britain. Speaight, G., *ed.* London, Ebury Press in association with The Rainbird Publishing Group, 1985. 416+16p. illus., (many col). maps, index. £14.95. ISBN: 0852234104.

Shell guide to Britain first published by Ebury Press in 1964.

5 introductory essays (The architecture of Britain; Open

....(contd.)

air museums; Walking in Britain; Wildlife; The year in Britain). 3 main sections: England, Wales, Scotland consisting of thematic essays followed by descriptive gazetteers of chief places of interest by county or region. Well produced. *Class No:* 914.10

[5570]

OTTAWAY, P. *and* **CYPRIEN, M. A Traveller's guide to Roman Britain.** London, Routledge & Kegan Paul; Harrisburg, Pennsylvania, Historical Times Inc., 1987. 128p. illus., map, bibliog. ISBN: 0710209438, UK; 0918678196, US.

Gazetteer of sites p.10-124 incl. 11 special articles *e.g.* Emperors in Britain, Towns. List of prominent individuals p.125-6. Glossary of terms p.126-7. Further reading p.128. *Class No:* 914.10

[5571]

PLATT, C. The National Trust guide to late medieval and renaissance Britain: from the Black Death to the Civil War. London, George Philip in association with the National Trust and the National Trust for Scotland, 1986. 239p. illus. (some col.), map, bibliog., index. ISBN: 0540011088.

7 thematic chapters (e.g. High chivalry ... Spoil of the abbeys ... The War of the Three Kingdoms) are supported by a descriptive gazetteer (p.207-25) of some notable buildings of the period with some indications of access. Glossary p.228-31. Bibliography p.230-1. As a guide this beautifully illustrated volume falls down because of its exiguous direction details. *Class No:* 914.10

[5572]

RAC historic Britain and Ireland 1989. Croydon, RAC Motoring Services in association with British Leisure Publications, East Grinstead, 1989. 238p. + 10p. roadmaps. illus. (some col.), index. softcover. £7.95. ISBN: 0862110734.

2500 houses, gardens, castles, museums and art galleries to visit organized A-Z by location in England, Wales, Republic of Ireland, Northern Ireland, and Scotland. Data includes short description, hours and charges. *Class No:* 914.10

[5573]

Reader's Digest touring guide to Britain. London, Reader's Digest, 1992. 320p. col. illus., col. maps. £24.95. ISBN: 0276420314.

Replaces *Illustrated guide to Britain.*

A magnificently produced touring atlas, and descriptive gazetteer guidebook to 4500++ places to visit, things to see, and things to do, closely integrated page by page. A-Z gazetteer of practical information.

Touring guide to Britain p.8-287. 19 town and city guides. 7 x 2 page features *e.g.* Moors of Southwest England. 110 main touring maps. *Class No:* 914.10

[5574]

Reader's Digest town tours in Britain: a walker's guide. London, Reader's Digest Association, 1990. [6p. + 104 folded double p. + 24p.] looseleaf in ring-binder. col. illus., col. maps. £25.95. ISBN: 0276420098.

Pictorial birds-eye view maps outline half-day circular walking tours of 155 towns, all beginning and ending in a central car park (underground station in Central London). Places of interest are clearly marked and are supplemented by detailed notes and colour photographs. Generally each double page is devoted to a single town although,

....(contd.)

occasionally, two smaller towns are accommodated. There are 45 quick tours of other towns. 'A very useful compendium of attractively presented, concise, and up-to-date local information ... of value and interest to a wider audience than the tourist' (*Reference Reviews,* v.4, no.2, 1990, p.37). *Class No:* 914.10

[5575]

ROBINSON, A. *and* **MILLWARD, R. The Shell book of the British coast.** Newton Abbot, Devon, David & Charles, 1983. 560p. illus. (some col.), maps, bibliogs., index. ISBN: 0715381504.

8 introductory essays: 1. Coastal life and habitats - 2. Lost lands - 3. New lands - 4. Coastal curiosities - 5. Pavilions, parades, piers and promenades - 6. Climate: where to holiday and retire - 7. Coastwise sailing - 8. The coast and artist. 13 descriptive regional gazetteers (p.230-550). Scotland: a select bibliography p.551-2. 164 photographs (16 in col). 96 maps. *Class No:* 914.10

[5576]

ROSS, A. *and* **CYPRIEN, M. A Traveller's guide to Celtic Britain.** London, Routledge & Kegan Paul, 1985. 128p. illus., map, bibliog. £9.95. ISBN: 0710206321.

1. Celtic sites in Britain (map) - 2. Celtic Britain, a descriptive gazetteer of 124 significant sites A-Z by location. Glossary of characters p.124-6. Glossary of terms p.127-8. Bibliography p.128. *Class No:* 914.10

[5577]

SMITH, R. Wildest Britain: a visitor's guide to the national parks. Poole, Dorset, Blandford Press, 1983. Distributed in US by Sterling Publishing Co. of New York. 224p. illus. (some col.), maps, bibliog., index. ISBN: 0713712708.

Sections on Dartmoor, Exmoor, Brecon Beacons, Pembrokeshire Coast, Snowdonia, Peak District, Yorkshire Dales, Lake District, North Yorkshire Moors, and Northumberland, each ending with What to do (How to get there, where to stay, places open to the public, Ancient Monuments, Further reading, map *etc.*). 60 col. and 90 b/w plates. 11 maps. *Class No:* 914.10

[5578]

Tourist Information Centres map directory. *Tourist Information Centres in Britain 1993-1994.* London, British Tourist Authority and English Tourist Board, 1993. folded map. 99p. ISBN: 0861431774.

Directory of over 800 centres in the UK and the national and regional tourist boards. *Class No:* 914.10

[5579]

WALTON, J. The National Trust guide to Late Georgian and Victorian Britain: from the Industrial Revolution to World War I. London, George Philip in association with The National Trust, 1989. 269 illus., (some col.), maps, bibliog., index. ISBN: 0540011851.

Pictorial guide to Britain 1750-1914 with chapters on Prestige and property; country houses; factories and industries; transport, travel and trade; towns and cities; urban working class; church, chapel and people; leisure and enjoyment; countryside and people. Emphasis on National Trust properties. Bibliography p.258-61. 3 maps. *Class No:* 914.10

[5580]
WHEATLEY, K. **National Maritime Museum guide to maritime Britain.** Exeter, Webb & Bower, 1990. 206p. illus. (some col.), maps on endpapers, index. £15.95. ISBN: 0863502687.

A region by region account of Britain's maritime history with special emphasis on heritage docks, ship preservation, underwater archaeology, museums, maritime research, the coastline, and leisure. Each regional chapter includes a gazetteer giving local information. *Class No:* 914.10

Standards

[5581]
British Standard specification for codes for the representation of names of counties and similar areas. Milton Keynes, Bucks, 1987. 26p. £19.10.

Replaces Colin Chapman's *Chapman County codes* (Federation of Family History Societies, 1979).

Codes refer to names in use and include all the main names used for UK subdivisions over the years. *Class No:* 914.10(083.74)

Islands

[5582]
The Country Life book of Britain's offshore islands. Shea, M. Richmond upon Thames, Surrey, Country Life Books, 1981. 272p. illus. (some col.), maps. ISBN: 0600367665.

16 descriptive chapters geographically arranged including elements of history, geography, literature, fable and sociology. No bibliography. Index p.266-271. *Class No:* 914.10(210.7)

[5583]
CROOKSTON, P.J. **The Observer island Britain.** London, Macdonald & Co., 1982. 251p. col.illus. col.maps. index. £12.95. ISBN: 0356085406.

Expanded from a series of articles in *The Observer Magazine* in 1980.

20 contributors provide a well illustrated guide to Britain's offshore islands. An appendix Travel Information (p.235-245) includes notes on how to get there, getting around, accommodation, and local information sources. Index, p.247-252. *Class No:* 914.10(210.7)

[5584]
NEWTON, N. **The Shell guide to the islands of Britain.** Newton Abbot, David & Charles, 1992. 224p. illus. (some col.), index, maps. £16.99. ISBN: 0715398830.

Part 1: Early settlements and archeology; islands and Christianity; folklore; commerce and tourism; dispersal and emigration. Part 2: Individual islands, their characteristics, tourist information, and travel directions. *Class No:* 914.10(210.7)

[5585]
The Shell book of the islands of Britain. Booth, D. *and* Perrott, D. London, Guideway/Windward, 1981. 192p. illus., maps, index. ISBN: 0711200874.

Definitive guide to about 150 major islands round the coasts of Britain for tourists and visitors covering history, legend, people, crafts, industry, wildlife, tourist facilities and transport, arranged in geographical order for Scotland,

....(contd.)
England, and Wales, with separate sections for the Isle of Man and the Channel Islands. 325 photographs, 92 maps. *Class No:* 914.10(210.7)

Women

[5586]
LEGGET, J. **Local heroines** a women's historical gazetteer of England, Scotland and Wales. London, Pandora, 1988. xxxiii, 382p. illus., maps, index. £15.95. ISBN: 0863580378.

1. 5 maps p.xxiv-xxxiii. 2. Gazetteer, A-Z by city, town or village, or nearest sizeable community or local landmark. Data: names or events associated with place mentioned, where traced, location, location and brief description of relevant buildings, monuments, gravemarkers, plaques *etc.*, and some information about the women concerned and the nature of the association. 3. Biographical index p.295-367. 4. How to find out more (books, courses, women's historical groups, museums and art galleries, Record Offices and archives, holidays) p.368-375. *Class No:* 914.10-0055.2

Scotland

[5587]
Chambers Scottish guides. Woolnough, K., *ed.* Edinburgh, Chambers, 1992. maps, plans, pbk. £7.99 each.

Smith, R. *Highlands and islands.* xiii,226p. ISBN 0550221026. Woolnough, K. *South-east Scotland* 055002100x; Bathgate, S. *South-west Scotland.* 0550221018.

In 3 sections: 1. National Fact File (activities, food and drink, money, accommodation *etc.*) - 2. Regional Fact File (local features, cinemas, galleries, sport) - 3. Regional Gazetteer (A-Z list of places to visit and things to do with special interest panels and maps). *Class No:* 914.11

[5588]
CROWL, P.A. **The Intelligent traveller's guide to historic Scotland.** London, Sidgwick and Jackson, 1986. xix, 625p. illus., maps, geneal. tables, bibliog., index. £12.95. ISBN: 0283993820.

Pt.1. Narrative history (p.4-371) in 9 sections comprises a chronological account of Scotland's past with an emphasis on its visible and visitable remains. Pt.2. Gazetteer (p.373-571) arranges sites mentioned in Pt.1 in 7 geographical regions sub-divided by historical counties. Bibliography p.579-87. Analytical index. *Class No:* 914.11

[5589]
The Holiday Which? guide to the Scottish Highlands: including the Inner Hebrides. 3rd ed. London, Consumers Association and Hodder & Stoughton, 1988. 219p. maps, index. pbk. £6.95. ISBN: 0340490853.

1st ed. 1984.

14 descriptive road tours *e.g.* Loch Lomond and the Trossachs; Mull and Iona, Skye, Raasay and the Small Isles. Includes accommodation guide and general information. *Class No:* 914.11

[5590]
JOHNSTON, W. *and* JOHNSTON, A.K. **Gazetteer of Scotland** including a glossary of the most common Gaelic names. 3rd ed. revised by R.W. Munro. Edinburgh and London, Johnston & Bacon, 1973. x,353p. maps.

Identifies all named places. Most entries give locational information only. *Class No:* 914.11

[5591]
TRANTER, N. *and* **CYPRIEN, M. A Traveller's guide to the Scotland of Robert the Bruce.** London, Routledge and Kegan Paul, 1985. 128p. illus., bibliog. ISBN: 0710206887.

Illustrated gazetteer to sites including 8 background articles p.8-123. Rivals for the throne and Pride of Bruces (family trees) p.124-7. Bibliography p.128.
Class No: 914.11

[5592]
The Which? guide to Scotland. Leslie, A., *ed.* London, Consumers' Association and Hodder & Stoughton, 1992. 520p. map, index. pbk. £10.95. ISBN: 0340550341.

Introduction (history, religion, birdwatching, golf, travel to Scotland, food and drink) and 123 regional guides each of which includes a gazetteer on places to see and advice on where to stay and where to eat. 'The perfect all-in-one companion to the traveller in Scotland'. *Class No:* 914.11

[5593]
WHYTE, J.D. *and* **WHYTE, K. Exploring Scotland's historic landscapes.** Edinburgh, John Donald Publishers, 1987. v, 314p. illus., maps, bibliog., index, pbk. £10.00. ISBN: 0859761665.

18 trails 'which include a range of landscape features ... important for understanding how the Scottish landscape has developed. A map accompanies each trail. Bibliography p.306-7. *Class No:* 914.11

[5594]
WRIGHT, G., *ed.* **A Guide to the Orkney Islands.** 2nd ed. Edinburgh, Gordon Wright Publishing, 1989. 64p. illus. £2.50. ISBN: 0903065673.

17 sections by various Orcadian hands. 'For anyone planning to visit the Orkneys this will prove an invaluable introduction to what to expect and what to look for - it is equally useful to those non-visitors who simply want to know more about the islands and their culture' (*Library Review*, v.39, no.2., 1990, p.71-72). *Class No:* 914.11

Ireland

[5595]
AA Reader's Digest illustrated guide to Ireland. London, Reader's Digest Association, 1991. 352p. col. illus., col. maps, index. £45. ISBN: 0276420330.

Place by place guide with information on touring centres, local customs, regular events, places of special and historical interest, fishing, golfing, natural history *etc.* 10 route maps. 35 regional maps. 'A good and comprehensive touring companion' (*Traveller*, v.22, no.2, Spring 1992, p.15). *Class No:* 914.15

[5596]
Ireland the complete guide and road atlas. Belfast, Appletree Press, 1993. 144p. col. illus., col. maps, index. Flexible cover. £10.99. ISBN: 0862813778.

1. Introduction (outline history, geography, genealogy, accommodation, further reading) - 2. Motoring in Ireland (10 tours) - 3. 7 regional descriptive gazetteers (p.30-108) - 4. Road atlas. Scale 3 inches to 25 miles (1:443,520). *Class No:* 914.15

[5597]
LEWIS, S. A Topographical dictionary of Ireland comprising the several counties, boroughs, corporate market, and post towns, parishes and villages with historical and statistical descriptions... 2nd ed. Port Washington, New York, Kennikat Press, 2v., and atlas, 1971.

First published London, S. Lewis, 1837. 2nd ed. 1849.

Despite its date, this gazetteer is indispensable for research of any nature involving topographical detail. An atlas volume was also issued but it is now only of historical interest. *Class No:* 914.15

[5598]
Shell guide to Ireland. Killanin, Lord *and* Duignan, M.V., *Updated by Peter Harbison.* Rev. ed. London, Macmillan, 1989. 340p. illus. (some col.), col. maps, bibliog., index. £16.95. ISBN: 0333469577.

1st ed. 1962.

This edition is substantially revised. Bibliography p.340. 'One of the very few reliable and comprehensive guides to the monuments, museums, and culture of the island' (*The Times*, no.63489, p.31). *Class No:* 914.15

Northern Ireland

[5599]
EVANS, R. The Visitor's guide to Northern Ireland. Ashbourne, Derbyshire, MPC Hunter Publishing, 1987. 240p. illus. (some col.), maps. £10.95. ISBN: 0861901835.

Pt.1 Introduction to Northern Ireland (climate, on the road, Ulster at work, historic monuments, towns and architecture, people and places, art and culture, hospitality). Pt.2 Exploring Northern Ireland (seven regional chapters). *Class No:* 914.16

Eire

[5600]
Heritage: a visitors guide Brennan, E., *ed.* Dublin, Office of Public Works, 1992. 208p. col. illus. I£9.95. ISBN: 0707601029.

Annually issued illustrated guide to national monuments, national parks and gardens, nature reserves, and 600 kilometres of inland waterways, in the care of The Office of Public Works. *Class No:* 914.17

[5601]
Ireland guide. Dublin, Gill & Macmillan, 1993. 512p.++ 24p. col. illus., maps, pbk. £8.99. ISBN: 0717119769.

Gazetteer emphasising history, archaeology, and architecture, arranged by province, county and place. Includes Ulster. 3 maps. 'Lies somewhere between the gorgeous *AA/Reader's Digest illustrated guide to Ireland* (over three times the price but six times the value) and the compact *Michelin Green Guide* ... either of which makes this one look a bit old-fashioned and dull' (*Books Ireland*, no.167, April 1993, p.88). *Class No:* 914.17

[5602]
LALOR, B. Ultimate Dublin guide: an A-Z of everything. Dublin, O'Brien Press, 1991. 309p. illus., maps, pbk. IR£6.95. ISBN: 0862782201.

2500 descriptive annotated entries giving basic information on art galleries, churches, cinemas, hostels, hotels, libraries, monuments, museums, music, parks, plaques, pubs,

....(contd.)

restuarants, sport, theatres, and walks. 7 maps. 'A rather appealing mini-encyclopedia of Dublin and environs' (*Books Ireland,* no.150, May 1991, p.99). *Class No:* 914.17

England & Wales

[5603]
GREAT BRITAIN. Office of Population Census and Surveys Census of 1981. England and Wales. **Index of place names.** London, HMSO., 2v., 1985. vii,849p. ISBN: 0116910658.

First produced in the series of Census publications in 1831. This ed. 13th in series.

About 62000 entries in all (A-K, L-Z) including *c.*30,000 villages, hamlets and localities, without legally defined boundaries. Data (tabular): description, county, district, registered district number, national grid reference, and population 1981. Appendix A Topographical arrangement of Registration Districts and Sub-districts. Based on the 1981 Census records updated to include changes to statutory boundaries and/or names up to 1 January 1985.
Class No: 914.2

[5604]
WYATT, J. A Visitor's guide to the National Parks of England and Wales. Exeter, Webb & Bower, 1988. 160p. col. illus., col. maps, bibliog., index. £16.95. ISBN: 0863501559.

Published in association with the Countryside Commission.

11 chapters highlight characteristics of each park. Countryside Access Charter p.153. Bibliography p.154-55.
Class No: 914.2

England

[5605]
AA touring England. Hicks, P., *ed.* Rev. ed. Basingstoke, Automobile Association, 1993. 608p. col. illus., col. maps, index. ISBN: 0749506601.

First published 1987.

Map, text and illustrated motor tours of West Country, South and Southeast England, Central England and East Anglia, and North Country p.34-324. Town plans p.328-443. Atlas p.446-601. Fully up to AA's high standard and lavishly illustrated guidebooks. *Class No:* 914.20

[5606]
GREENWOOD, D. Who's buried where in England. 2nd ed. London, Constable, 1990. xii,352p. illus., map, index. £14.95. ISBN: 0094702802.

1st ed. 1982.

The burial places of over 500 men and women listed in 8 categories: Sovereigns - Royal consorts and nobles - Statesmen, politicians and warriors - Churchmen, philosophers, lawyers and scholars - Scientists, doctors, business men, engineers and industrialists - Authors, playwrights and poets - Actors, artists and musicians - Explorers, sportsmen, reformers, outlaws, heroines, criminals and miscellaneous. Geographical checklist A-Z county p.174-282. *Class No:* 914.20

[5607]
Guide to English Heritage properties. 9th ed. London, Historic Buildings & Monuments Commission for England, 1985. 127p. illus. maps. index. pbk. £2.25. ISBN: 1850744229.

Tour planning guide (*i.e.,* buildings etc. listed A-Z in period categories) p.10-18. County by county guide ('new' counties) of 350 buildings and monuments in the care of English Heritage, with full details of location, opening arrangements and facilities p.20-117. A/B site index.

English Heritage map: a route planner to over 350 places to visit (1989).50p. is a single sheet folded map (1 inch to 20 miles) showing English Heritage sites open to the public.
Class No: 914.20

[5608]
The Holiday Which? guide to the Lake District. Locke, T., *ed.* London, Consumers' Association and Hodder & Stoughton, 1991. 280p. maps, index. pbk. £8.95. ISBN: 0340544112.

Previous ed. 1989.

A practical and informative guide divided into 4 regions. Touring routes are designed to cover major places of interest. Walks p.211-59. Information (Tourist Information Centres; accommodation; entertainment; maps; transport; outdoor activities) p.260-72. Calendar of events p.273-5. Introduced by The Natural Setting p.11-15 and Man's Lakeland History p.16-35. *Class No:* 914.20

[5609]
KERR, N. *and* **KERR, M. A Guide to Anglo-Saxon sites.** London, Granada, 1982. 207p. illus. maps. ISBN: 0246117753.

101 sites selected either as a good example of a particular type of monument, or for its historical associations, or because it enjoys a fine setting, arranged under the major Anglo-Saxon kingdoms: Northumbria p.16-60; Mercia p.62-107; East Anglia p.110-147; Wessex p.150-197. Glossary p.199-203. Museums with important Anglo-Saxon collections p.204. Index 205-207. *Class No:* 914.20

[5610]
KIEK, J. Everybody's historic England a history and guide. London, Quiller Press in association with Sun Life, 1988. 247p. illus., maps, plans, bibliogs., index. pbk. £4.95. ISBN: 0907621880.

Basic information for the history-minded tourist.
Class No: 914.20

[5611]
The King's England. Mee, A., *ed.* Barnsley, Yorkshire, The King's England Press, 41v., 1989-90. £650. Also priced individually.

First published 1936-53 by Hodder & Stoughton. Text for this facsimile edition is usually that of each volume's first printing.

Complete historical and geographical account of England immediately before the Second World War in 41v. Introductory volume *Enchanted land* and one volume per historical county (combined v. for Bedfordshire and Huntingdonshire; Hampshire and Isle of Wight; the Lake Counties; Leicestershire and Rutland; and 3v. for the Yorkshire Ridings). In each volume the places described are arranged A-Z, historical, architectural and biographical notes being included. Richard Dalby's 'Arthur Mee's King's

....(contd.)

England series', _Book and Magazine Collector_, no.36, March 1987, p.20-25 describes the background to this well-loved series. _Class No:_ 914.20

[5612]
PLATT, C. Travellers' guide to medieval England. London, Secker & Warburg, 1985. xix,249p. illus., map, index. £12.95. ISBN: 0436375591.

8 regional weekend/short break tours each with map, background historical text and gazetteer entries. Glossary p.xiii-xix. _Class No:_ 914.20

[5613]
SHIPLEY, D. and PEPLOW, M. England's undiscovered heritage: a guide to 100 unusual sites and monuments. London, Weidenfeld & Nicolson, 1988. 160p. illus. (some col.), maps, geneal tables. £10.95. ISBN: 0297792687.

A-Z descriptive gazetteer of 100 of the least well known monuments in the care of English Heritage. Tour planner county maps p.134-45. Royal houses of England p.146-57. Glossary p.158-60. _Class No:_ 914.20

[5614]
WAINWRIGHT, M. and LOCKE, T. The Which? guide to Yorkshire and the Peak District. London, Consumers' Association and Hodder & Stoughton, 1992. 288p. illus., maps, index. £10.99. ISBN: 034055035x.

8 topographical chapters: 1. West Yorkshire ... 4. North Yorkshire Moors ... 8. Peak District and 9. Walking. Final practical information section includes notes on accommodation, markets, entertainment, and travel _etc._ _Class No:_ 914.20

[5615]
The Which? guide to the West Country. London, Consumer's Association and Hodder & Stoughton, 1991. 337p. maps, index. pbk. £9.95. ISBN: 0340514434.

Points the way to the best West Country attractions. Arranged in 12 topographical sections (11 regional + Walking). Each section ends with 2-tier system highlighting first and second division attractions. Information (p.322-32) includes Tourist Information Centres, public travel details, cinemas, market days _etc._ Covers Somerset, Devon, Cornwall, Isle of Scilly. _Class No:_ 914.20

Bibliographies

[5616]
English places sources of information. London, British Library, 1979. 12p. bibliogs., sd. _gratis._

Introduction to sources of information in the collections of Humanities and Social Sciences division of the British Library: General works and bibliographies; Victoria County History; Directories; Gazetteers and books of travel; Regional surveys; Buildings; Place names; Illustrations; Maps and atlases; Newspapers and general periodicals; Official publications; and Calendars and registers of archives. _Class No:_ 914.20(01)

London

[5617]
The Blue Plaque guide. London, journeyman press in association with English Heritage, 1991. x,132p. illus., indexes. £6.50. ISBN: 1851720057.

Previous ed. published by GLC 1976.

....(contd.)

List of 600 surviving plaques A-Z names of persons commemorated, successively erected by Royal Society of Arts, London County Council, Greater London Council, and English Heritage. London Borough, street, and vocation indexes. English Heritage selection criteria p.14. _Class No:_ 914.21

[5618]
Guide to London docklands. Monahan, P., _ed._ London, William Curtis, 1989. 144p. col.illus. £2.50. ISBN: 1871967066.

Docklands past and present - Residential property - Getting about - Eating out - Good pub guide - Sport - Things to do - Green spaces - Shopping - Consumer services - A place to do business. _Class No:_ 914.21

[5619]
McAULEY, I. Guide to Ethnic London. London, Michael Haag, 1987. 224p. illus., maps, bibliog., pbk. £5.95. ISBN: 0902743465.

A complete handbook to London's 8 major ethnic communities: Italians, Poles, Jews, Irish, South Asians, Afro-Caribbeans, Cypriots, and Chinese. _Class No:_ 914.21

[5620]
NAIRN, I. Nairn's London revisited by Peter Gasson. Rev. ed. London, Penguin Books, 1988. xv,245p. illus., index. pbk. £9.95. ISBN: 0140092641.

450 entries, each of paragraph length, confined to buildings of all descriptions, comprising 'a personal list of the best things in London' (_Preface_) arranged in 11 geographical area chapters. 'Specialists portmanteau (_i.e.,_ subject-index) p.215-27). _Class No:_ 914.21

[5621]
NICHOLSON, L. London: Louise Nicholson's definitive guide. Rev. ed. London, the Bodley Head, 1990. x,382p. maps, bibliog., index, pbk. £9.95. ISBN: 0370314530.

1. Arriving and surviving - 2. Hotels - 3. Instant London: follow my leader - 4. Royalty and pageantry - 5. London day by day: exploring the centre on foot - 6. London on wheels - 7. Rain - 8. London entertains - 9. Food and drink - 10. Spend, spend, spend - 11. Fitness and fresh air. The London year: a month by month directory of events p.352-6. Key dates in London's history p.362-4. Bibliography p.367-9. Winner of the London Tourist Board award: Best London Guide. _Class No:_ 914.21

[5622]
PHILLIPS, T. A London Docklands guide: a gazetteer of historical and architectural interest in St. Katherine's, Wapping, Shadwell, Ratcliff, Limehouse, Poplar, Blackwall, Isle of Dogs, Silvertown, North Woolwich, Beckton, Bermondsey, and Rotherhithe, with maps and photographs. High Wycombe, Buckinghamshire, Peter Marcan Publications, 1986. vi,58p. illus., maps, bibliog. £5.95. ISBN: 0951028952.

A useful guidebook in 8 chapters encompassing the London dockland Boroughs of Southwark, Tower Hamlets, and Newham. Short histories of each region are followed by imaginatively illustrated accounts of their surviving landmarks. Bibliography p.58. 13 individually drawn street maps. _Class No:_ 914.21

[5623]

Quick guide to London. British Tourist Authority. London., British Tourist Authority, 1989. 48p. illus., map, index. sd. *gratis.* ISBN: 0709535880.

Pocket guide featuring Getting around; Sightseer's gazetteer; Maritime London; Sport; Entertainment and nightlife; Shopping; Children's London; Accommodation *etc.. Class No:* 914.21

Women

[5624]

MURPHY, K. **Women's London.** Twickenham, Middlesex, Hamlyn, 1987. 176p. index. pbk. £3.99. ISBN: 0600503704.

Slim pocket-size guide in 16 sections. *Class No:* 914.21-0055.2

Channel Islands

[5625]

STEVENS, J. *and* JEE, N. **The New Shell guide to the Channel Islands.** London, Michael Joseph, 1987. 192p. illus. (many col.), maps, bibliog., index. £12.95. (*New Shell Guides.*) ISBN: 0718127609.

Descriptive gazetteer of 1. The Bailiwick of Jersey (including boxed essays on such topics as the Jersey militia, Museum of La Société Jersiaise) - 2. Guernsey (including Sark, Alderney and the smaller islands). Glossary p.174. Bibliography p.175. 8 maps. *Class No:* 914.234

Wales

[5626]

GREAT BRITAIN Cadw: Welsh Historic Monuments. **A Nation under siege** The Civil War in Wales 1642-48. London, HMSO, 1991. 80p. col. illus. pbk. £6.95. ISBN: 011701222x.

Pictorial guide to over 30 castles and a number of walled towns, great houses, and churches associated with the Civil War. *Class No:* 914.29

[5627]

TOMES, J. **Blue Guide Wales.** 7th ed. London, A & C Black; New York, W.W. Norton, 1990. 326p. illus., maps, index. £12.95. ISBN: 0713631538, UK; 0393306887, US.

Formerly published as *Blue Guide Wales and the Marches.* 1A. Background information (Countries of Wales, Eisteddfod, The Flag (Red Dragon), Industrial archaeology, History p.25-42, Biographical notes p.42-53 etc.) - 1B. Practical information (Organizations like Wales Tourist Board. CADW, Welsh Development Agency) - 2. Detailed descriptions of 46 routes criss-crossing the Principality, illustrated and with maps and plans. An indispensable guide 'excellent on detailed historic and geographical background' (*Observer*, no.10,399, 3 February 1991, p.59). *Class No:* 914.29

Germany

[5628]

ARDAGH, J. **The Shell guide to Germany.** London, Simon & Schuster, 1991. 332p. col. illus., maps, bibliog., index. pbk. £10.99. ISBN: 0671710214.

A guide to Germany in 8 chapters: 1. Introduction

....(contd.)

(Germany today, historical dates, travelling and accommodation etc. including a Glossary of German words p.25-7) - 2. North Rhine/Westphalia - 3. Rhineland/Palatinate - 4. Baden/Württemburg - 5. Bavaria - 6. Hessen - 7. Lower Saxony - 8 Hamburg - 9. Bremen - 10. Schleswig Holstein - 11. Berlin. Bibliography p.328. *Class No:* 914.30

[5629]

Baedeker's Stadtführer. Freiburg, Karl Baedeker.

Paperback guides to German towns and cities: *Augsburg - Baden Baden - Bad Homburg - Bamberg - Basel - Berlin* (separate titles for *Charlottenburg; Kreuzberg; Neukölln; Reinickendorf; Schöneberg; Spandau; Steglitz; Tempelhof; Tiergarten; Wedding Wilmersdorf; Zehlendorf) - Braunschweig - Bremen. Bremerhaven - Celle - Darmstadt - Detmold - Dortmund - Essen - Esslingen - Flensburg - Frankfort am Main - Freiburg - Genf - Graz - Hamburg - Hannover - Heidelberg - Heilbronn - Idar Oberstein - Ingolstadt - Innsbruck - Karlsruhe - Kiel - Koblenz - Köln - Konstanz - Leipzig - Lübeck - Lüneburg - Mainz - Mannheim - München - Münster - Nürnberg - Osnabruck - Passau - Regensberg - Rottweil - Salzburg - Schleswig - Strassburg - Stuttgart - Ulm - Wein - Wiesbaden und der Rheingau - Wuppertal - Würzburg.* Bonn 5th ed. 1987. 139p. maps,plans.index. ISBN 3879540667 is in 4 sections: 1. Praktische Angaben - 2. Gesamtbild und Geschichte - 3. Die Stadtbezirke Bonn und Hardtberg - 4. Die Stadtbezirke Bad Godesberg und Beuel. *Class No:* 914.30

[5630]

Müllers grosses deutsches Ortsbuch Bundesrepublik Deutschland: Vollständiges Gemeinlexicon. 21st ed. Wuppertal, Post-und Ortsbuchverlag, 1982-1983. 1194p.

Revised at intervals of 3-4 years.

A gazetteer of more than 125,000 places in both West and East Germany, and including former German territory that is now Polish. 2-line entries, with map references for each locality in the Federal Republic, based on Mair's Deutsche Generalkarte. 1:200,000. This edition has postal zip codes. *Class No:* 914.30

Federal Republic of Germany

[5631]

Geographisches Namenbuch Bundesrepublik Deutschland. Frankfurt am Main, Institut für Angewandte Geodäsie, 1981. 55+738p. ISBN: 3886480003.

V.1 Introduction: History of the Gazetteer; features and sources used; arrangement; glossary of geographical appellatives and other words required for map reading; references and official sources. V.2 Gazetteer of 14,760 names - populated places, physical features, included on offical Übersichtkarte 1:500,000 maps, arranged in columns under headwords: official spelling, geographical coordinates, population, height above sea level, area (in square kilometres), administrative/geographical area. Prepared and published for the United Nations series of national gazetteers approved at the Conference on the Standardization of Geographical Names, Athens, 1977. *Class No:* 914.301

Hungary

[5632]

NEMETH, G. The Complete guide to Hungary. 3rd ed. Ashbourne, Derbyshire, Moorland, 1989. 320p. illus., maps, index, pbk. £7.95. ISBN: 0861901770.

Opening section comprises lengthy essays on Hungary's history. 'This is a British translation of an indigenous guide, but it is nonetheless lucid, comprehensive, well-illustrated and the maps are excellent' (*Sunday Times*, 19 March 1989, p. 113). *Class No:* 914.39

[5633]

WELLNER, I. Budapest a complete guide. Ashbourne, Derbyshire, Moorland, 1990. 202p. illus., maps, index. £7.99. ISBN: 0861903870.

About Budapest, a short history - Guide to Buda - Guide to Pest - Excursions on the Danube - Mini-dictionary *etc.* *Class No:* 914.39

France

[5634]

AA illustrated guide to France. Basingstoke, Automobile Association, 1992. 256p. col. illus., col. maps, index. £25. ISBN: 0749405001.

Comprehensive guide to all the French regions highlighting where to go and what to see. A special section is devoted to Paris. Michelin mapping. *Class No:* 914.4

[5635]

ARDAGH, H., *ed*. The Collins guide to France. London, Willow Books, 1985. 336p. illus. (some col.), maps, index. ISBN: 0002181649.

Introducing France (France today - History - Architecture - Art - Literature - Gastronomy and wine) p.6-81. Gazetteer divided into 21 tourist regions with extensive background information on the most worthwhile places to visit p.84-236. Tourist information p.327-9. *Class No:* 914.4

[5636]

Dictionnaire de Paris. Paris, Larousse, 1964. 592p. illus., index.

An A-Z encyclopaedic dictionary of events, institutions, monuments and customs by some 20 specialists. 500 illustrations, including reproductions of documents. *Class No:* 914.4

[5637]

Helm French Regional guides. Epernon, A., *series editor*. London, Christopher Helm, 1989-. Distributed by A. & C. Black. col. illus., maps, pbk. £9.95.

Auvergne and the Massif Central. 0747012202; Brittany. *0747006113*; Dordogne & Lot. 2nd ed. 0713635932 Languedoc and Roussillon. 0747030057; The Loire Valley. 0747008027; *Normandy, Picardy and Pas de Calais 0713680237*; *Paris*. 0713680482; Provence and the *Côte d'Azur.* 0747022070; *Rhone Valley and Savoy.* 07136803268; *South-West France.* 0747030219.

Each book includes a lively account of the region's history, a section on food and drink, and a detailed narrative tour of all the region's notable features - cities, villages, chateaux, churches and monuments and areas of outstanding natural beauty. *Class No:* 914.4

[5638]

The Holiday Which? guide to France. Ruck, A., *comp.* 4th ed. London, Consumers' Association and Hodder & Stoughton, 1991. 662p. illus., maps, index, pbk. £10.95. ISBN: 0340550287.

1st ed. 1982.

14 regional profiles (*e.g.* Paris - Isle de France ... Loire Valley - Britanny - Normandy) followed by sections on French history and architecture, eating and drinking in France, and general travel and accommodation information. 'An informative, practical and readable general purpose guide' (*Reference Reviews*, v.5, no.4, 1991, p.32). *Class No:* 914.4

[5639]

Index atlas de la France: liste des localités, nomenclature des communes, cartes départmentales et plans de villes. New ed. Rennes, Oberthur, 1991. 989p. maps, tables, index. ISBN: 2901454022.

In 4 parts: 1. General (Tableau de la France administrative; tableaux des distances kiométriques entre 50 grandes villes; cartes de la France routières) - 2. Index des communes et localités p.32-112. 3. Cartes départementales p.113-304. 4. Nomenclature départementale des communes et localités p.305-432. 5. Plans de villes p.433-992. *Class No:* 914.4

[5640]

Michelin green tourist guides - France. Guides verts touristiques. Harrow, Middlesex, Michelin Tyre PLC, 1990. Annual. £7.25.

French language: *Alpes Du Nord* ISBN 2060030110 - *Alpes du Sud* 2060030218 - *Alsace et Lorraine* 2060037239 - *Auvergne* 2060030412 - *Berry-Limousin* 206003051x - *Bourgogne* 2060030749 - *Bretagne* 2060030935 - *Champagne-Ardennes* 20600312621 - *Châteaux de la Loire* 2060031710 - *Corse* 2060031915 - *Côte D'Azur* 2060032016 - *Flandres-Artois-Picardie* 2060033829 - *France* 2060039010 - *Gorges du Tarn* 2060033713 - *Ile de France* 206003261x - *Jura* 2060033942 - *Normandie-Cotentin* 2060034612 - *Normandie-Seine* 206003471x - *Paris* 206003521x - *Périgord-Quercy* 2060037018 - *Poitou-Vendée-Charentes* 2060037115 - *Provence* 2060036216 - *Purénées-Acquitaine* 2060036712 - *Pyrénées-Rousillon* 206003681x - *Vallée du Rhoine* 206003731x.

English language: *Brittany* 2060131413 - *Burgundy* 2060130816 - *Châteaux of the Loire* 2060132215 - *Dordogne* 2060132312 - *French Riviera* 2060138513 - *Ile de France* 2060134110 - *Normandy-Cotentin* 2060134919 - *Normandy-Seine Valley* 206013501x - *Paris* 2060135435 - *Provence* 2060137519 - *Atlantic Coast* 1993 - *Euro Disney.*

Detailed descriptions of places of interest including town plans. Intended for use with 1:200,000 Michelin regional maps of France (*qv*). 'Are in a class of their own for sightseeing and route planning (*Sunday Times*, 8732, 29 Dec. 1991: p.3:9). *Class No:* 914.4

[5641]

OIZON, R. Dictionnaire géographique de la France: communes, départements, régions, population, économie, tourisme. Paris, Larousse, 1979. 915p. maps.

Records 36,394 communities, noting postal code, population and local features (*e.g.* industry). Unlike comparable gazetteers, has entries for natural regions (*e.g.* Vosges), historical sites (*e.g.* Touraine), tourist attractions (Loire Châteaux), rivers, peaks, national/regional parks, spas and winter sports centres. Overseas départments are

....(contd.)

included. 'It would be difficult to identify a more useful gazetteer for any country' (*American Notes & Queries,* October 1979, p.27). *Class No:* 914.4

[5642]
The Which? guide to Brittany and Normandy. The all-in-one guide to touring, walking, camping and beach holidays in North-West France. London, Consumers' Association and Hodder & Stoughton, 1993. 298p. maps, index. pbk. £11.99. ISBN: 0340564806.

Descriptive gazetteer in 7 regional chapters with final Practical Information section (travel, package holidays, accommodation, weather, *etc.*). *Class No:* 914.4

Italy

[5643]
The Holiday Which? guide to Italy. Morgan, I. rev. ed. London, The Consumers' Association and Hodder & Stoughton, 1992. 560p. illus., maps, index. £10.95. ISBN: 034053897x.

3 introductory essays on History; Art and Architecture; and Food and Wine precede 12 topographical chapters: 1. Lakes and mountains - 2. Venice - 3. Northern cities - 4. Liguria - 5. Florence - 6. Tuscany and Umbria - 7. Rome - 8. Central Italy - 9. Naples and Campania - 10. The South - 11. Sicily - 12. Sardinia. Each chapter contains an introduction 'to give a flavour of what the region or city or island is like'; descriptions of resorts, monuments, places of scenic interest, excursions, *etc.*; and recommended hotel information. A final general information section surveys travel arrangements, recommended books (p.512-5), maps, festivals, and the weather. 'Our aim has been to produce a guide that you won't need to supplement except with road maps and city plans' (*About this guide*). *Class No:* 914.50

[5644]
TOURING CLUB ITALIANO. Guida d'Italia. Milano, Touring Club Italiano. maps, plans, bibliogs.

First published 1914-29.

23 Regional volumes regularly updated. Ideal for detailed exploration of a particular region with very detailed information supported by maps, town plans and a bibliography. Titles: *Piemonte,* 728p. L45.000; *Torino e Valle d'Aosta,* 408p. L47,000; *Lombardia,* 1100p. L65,000; *Milano,* 671p. L54,000; *Veneto,* 740p. L47,000; *Venezia,* 794p. L56,000; *Trento-Alto Adige,* 576p. L47.000; *Friuli-Venezia Giulia,* 573p. L47,000; *Liguria,* 778p. L55,000; *Emilia Romagna,* 787p. L54,000; *Toscana,* 816p. L.55,000; *Firenze e ditorni,* 496p. L47,000; *Marche,* 708p. L52,000; *Umbria,* 552p. L47,000; *Lazio* 830p. L55,000; *Roma e dintorni,* 830p. L54,000; *Abruzzo e Molise,* 534p. L47,000; *Campania,* 716p. L54,000; *Napoli e dintorni,* 640p. L47,000; *Puglia,* 486p. L47,000; *Basilicata e Calabria,* 714p. L54,000; *Sardegna,* 704p. L54,000; *Sicilia,* L65,000. *Rome and Latium,* L15,000 160p. is available in an English language edition. *Class No:* 914.50

[5645]
—TOURING CLUB ITALIANO. Guida illustrata d'Italia. Milano, Touring Club Italiano, 1984. 416p. illus, maps, plans. L42,000.

566 A-Z principal places of interest. 41 maps and plans of tours, archaeological sites, 34p. road maps, and short description of Italy's 20 administrative divisons. 777 col. photographs. Also *Guida ai centri minori-Italia*

....(contd.)

Settentrionale, 368p. L50,000; *Italia Centrale,* 400p. L50,000; *Italia Meridonale,* 400p. L50,000. *Class No:* 914.50

Spain

[5646]
Diccionário geográfico de España. Madrid, Ediciones de Movimiento, 17v., 1956-61.

'The fullest information about Spain yet collected in a single work' (*Times Literary Supplement,* no.3,176, 11 January 1963, p.28). In gazetteer form, entries A-Z, often containing very detailed information. v.17 (xxi,[1], 747p.) includes: 1. 'Plazas de soberania y provincias africanas': 2. 'Poblados nuevos': 3. 'Addenda'. Questionnaires were sent out to all the towns and villages of Spain, to be answered by the local authorities. *Class No:* 914.60

[5647]
The Which? guide to Spain: a panorama of mainland Spain, plus Mallorca, Menorca, Ibiza and the Canary Islands, all in one volume. Belford, R., *and others.* London: Consumers' Association and Hodder & Stoughton, 1991. 631p. maps, bibliog., index. pbk. £12.95. ISBN: 0340521937.

Introduction (history, art and people, environment and wildlife, bullfighting ... eating in Spain, accommodation), 13 regional guides and gazetteers (Andalucia ... Valencia), and Balearic and Canary Islands. Glossary of art, architectural and gastronomic terms p.618-20. Bibliography p.617-8. *Class No:* 914.60

Gibraltar

[5648]
BENADY, T., *ed.* **Gibraltar guidebook.** 2nd ed. Grendon, Gibraltar Books, 1989. 47p. col. illus., maps, bibliog. £1.95. ISBN: 0948466138.

First edition published in 1982 as *Guidebook to Gibralter.* Gibraltar's historical background and places of interest. *Class No:* 914.682

Norway

[5649]
Norway the official guide. Oslo, Nordis, 1988. Available in UK from Springfield Books of Huddersfield. 226p. col. illus., col. maps, pbk. £3.95. ISBN: 3888394015.

Official Norwegian Tourist Board guide. Illustrated features on all regions with suggestions for motor tours. Notes on accommodation and activity holidays. *Class No:* 914.81

Iceland

[5650]
HÁLFDÁNARSON, O., *ed.* **Iceland road guide.** 3rd ed. Reykjavik, Iceland Travel Books, 1981. 440p. maps, pbk.

Based on original Icelandic editions 1973 and 1974.

Single or double-page road sketches cover the whole national network with brief descriptions of all interesting places *en route.* Based on the road numbering system. 2 general and 9 area maps. *Class No:* 914.911

[5651]

SCHEI, L.K. *and* MOBERG, G. **The Faroe Islands.** London, John Murray, 1991. viii,248p. illus. (some col.), map, bibliog., index. £10.95. ISBN: 0719550092.

1. Nature - 2. Early times ... 4. Later history ... 6. People ... 9. Place-names ... 16. The Grind (whales) - 17/28. Island chapters. Glossary p.238-9. Bibliography p.240-1. *Class No:* 914.911

Netherlands

[5652]

AA, A.J. van der. **Aardrijkskundig woordenboek der Nederlanden.** Zaltbommel, Europese Bibliothek, 14v., 1976-80.

First published Gorinchem, Noorduyn, 13v., 1839-51.

Geographical descriptions on all municipalities and other areas of the Netherlands. *Class No:* 914.92

Greece

[5653]

The Holiday Which? guide to Greece and the Greek Islands. Morgan, I., *ed.* London, Consumers Association and Hodder & Stoughton, 1989. 710p. bibliog., maps, index, pbk. £10.95. ISBN: 0340504331.

3 parts: 1. Background information on history and architecture, mythology, wild flowers, eating and drinking - 2. The Mainland (Athens and Attica; The Peloponnese; Central Greece: Macedonia and Thrace) - 3. The Islands (Corfu and the Ionian Islands; The Peloponnese Islands: Evia and the Sporades; The Cyclades; Rhodes and the Dodecanese; The North-East Aegean Islands). Recommended books p.677-78. *Class No:* 914.95

Bulgaria

[5654]

MIHAILOV, D., *and others.* **Bulgaria** a guide. Sofia, Sofia Press, 1986. 264p. col. illus., maps £4.95.

Illustrated guide with suggested routes. Wealth of background information. 'A lively and useful guide to various aspects of life in Bulgaria' (R.J. Crampton. *Bulgaria.* 1989. Entry 38). *Class No:* 914.972

[5655]

MIHAILOV, D. and SMOLENOV, P. **Guide to Sofia.** Sofia, Sofia Press, 1981. 233p. maps. illus. (some col.), pbk. £4.95.

Details of tourist sites and suggested tours. 'An excellent *vade-mecum* for the visitor' (R.J. Crampton. *Bulgaria,* 1989. Entry 44). *Class No:* 914.972

China

[5656]

Collins China guides and Collins illustrated guides. London, Collins, 1985-. col. illus., col. maps, pbk. £8.95.

Collins illustrated guide to all China. 1988. ISBN 0002152398. Other titles: Fuijan; Guilin, Canton and Guangdong; Hangzhou and Zhejiand Province; Jiangsu; The Silk Road: Xian; Yangzi; Yangzi River; Yunnan. *A guide to Beijing.* 1987. 144p. 0002179458 has sections Life in Beijing; Getting to B.; General information for travellers; Climate and clothing; Hotels; Getting around; Recommended

....(contd.)
restaurants; Entertainment; Shopping; History of Beijing. Other titles: *Canton; Fujian; Jiangsu; Shanghai; etc.* *Class No:* 915.10

[5657]

—SCHWARTZ, B. China off the beaten track. London, Collins Harvill, 1985. viii,247+16p. maps, tables, bibliog., index, pbk. £8.95. (*China Guides Series.*) ISBN: 0002721147.

Background historical, political and cultural information and notes on travel arrangements and visas *etc.* precede descriptions of 37 areas and cities grouped in 6 regions: North China, Yellow River, Yangtse Basin, South China, Southwest, and Beyond the Wall (The Silk Road, Inner Mongolia, The Northeast, and Tibet). An appendix includes a phrasebook, main train timetables, a brief glimpse of Hong Kong and Macau, and a Bibliography (p.240-242). List of open cities p.iv. 24 city-centre maps. *Class No:* 915.10

Hong Kong

[5658]

A Guide to Hong Kong. London, Collins, 1987. 144p. £8.95. (*China Guide Series.*) ISBN: 0002179466.

Arriving in Hong Kong; climate and clothing; money; language; getting around; food; shopping; arts and entertainment; night life; museums; festivals; sport; Kowloon; New Territories; Bibliography p.142. *Class No:* 915.123.17

Tibet

[5659]

BATCHELOR, S. **The Tibet guide.** London, Wisdom Publications, 1987. xiv,466p. illus. (mostly col.), maps, diagrs, tables, bibliog., index. £13.95; $26.95. ISBN: 0861710460.

1. Introductory essays on The land and its people; History; and Buddhism p.3-68 - 2. Regional (*i.e.* Lhasa, Central Tibet, Tsang, and Western Tibet) subdivided into a total of 47 sections each dealing with a particular site including travel details, history and description. Travel to Tibet and Getting to Lhasa p.379-395. Iconographical guide p.396-427. Useful words and phrases p.428-434. Glossary p.435-444. Bibliography p.445-450. *Class No:* 915.15

[5660]

BOOZ, E.B. **A Guide to Tibet.** London, Collins, 1986. 208p., col.illus., maps, bibliog., index. £8.95. ISBN: 0002176270.

Visiting Tibet; Lhasa; Shigatse; Gyantse; Tsedang and the Yarlong area; Damxung and Lake Namtso; Western Tibet; Geography and natural history; Festivals; Chronology of events in Tibetan and Chinese history p.186-95. Glossary p.196-9. Bibliography p.200. *Class No:* 915.15

Korea

[5661]

NILSEN, R. **South Korea handbook.** Chico, California, Moon Publications, 1988. 600p. col. illus., maps, charts, bibliog., index, pbk. $14.95. ISBN: 0918373204.

Definitive travel guide. Korean glossary and language notes. Subject and place-name index. *Class No:* 915.19

Japan

[5662]

BISIGNANI, J.D. **Japan handbook.** Chico, California, Moon Publications, 1983. 504p. col.illus., maps, charts, bibliog., index, pbk. $12.95. ISBN: 0960332227.

Cultural and anthropological encyclopaedic guide to every aspect of Japanese life for the tourist and traveller. Appendix on Japanese life and glossary. 112 maps and plans. Subject and place-name index. *Class No:* 915.2

[5663]

McGILL, P. **Tokyo:** the American Express pocket guide. London, Mitchell Beazley, 1988. 216p.+16p. col.maps, illus., index. £5.95. (*The American Express Pocket Travel Guides.*) ISBN: 0855336390.

Basic information (travel notes, customs and etiquette, emergency information, essential Japanese) - Cultural history and background - Planning and walks - A-Z sights,, places of interest, hotels and restaurants - Special information (sports and activities, excursions). *Class No:* 915.2

[5664]

WELCH, T.F. *and* KATO, H. **Japan today!** A Westerner's guide to the people, language and culture of Japan. Lincolnwood, Illinois, Passport Books, 1987. 115p. map, bibliog., pbk. $7.95. ISBN: 0844285013.

Almost 300 A-Z entries on travel, accommodation, common Japanese terms *etc. Class No:* 915.2

Asia—Middle & Near East

[5665]

BLAKE, G., *and others.* **The Cambridge atlas of the Middle East and North Africa.** Cambridge, Cambridge Univ. Press, 1987. vii,124p. col.maps, bibliog. £45.00; $75.00. ISBN: 0521242436.

Maps and accompanying text in 7 sections: 1. Introductory - 2. Physical environment - 3. Cultural - 4. Demographic - 5. Economic - 6. Communications - 7. Special topics. Gazetteer (*i.e.,* country profiles) p.120-1. Bibliography p.122-4. 'A well-executed, scholarly work of enduring value' (*Reference Books Bulletin 1987-1988*, p.146-8). There is a map by map appraisal in *Middle Eastern Studies*, v.27, no.1, January 1991, p.172-9. *Class No:* 915.3+915.6

Asia—South & South East

[5666]

South Asian handbook 1994. Bradnock, R., *ed.* 3rd ed. Bath, Trade & Travel Publications; Chicago, Passport Books, 1993. 1456p. index. £19.95. (*Travellers World Guides.*) ISBN: 0900751479, UK; 0844299804, US.

Traveller's guide to India, Nepal, Bhutan, Pakistan, Sri Lanka, Bangladesh, Maldive Islands with Hints to travellers (travel to and within, documentation and security, etiquette and language, accommodation, general advice) and description of each country's geography, climate, people, handicrafts, art and architecture, music and dance, visitors' information *etc. Class No:* 915.4+915.9

India

Bibliographies

[5667]

SCHOLBERG, H. **The District Gazetteers of British India** a bibliography. Zug, Switzerland, Inter Documentation, 1970. xii, 131p. map, index. (*Bibliotheca Asiatica, no.3.*)

'A complete and orderly list of the district and state gazetteers of British India'. 16 chapters: 1. History - 2. Bengal - 3. Bihar and Orissa - 4. Assam - 5. Madras - 6. Bombay - 7. North-West Provinces and United Provinces - 8. Central Provinces - 9. Central India - 10. Rajputana - 12. North-West Frontier Province - 13. Sind - 14. Baluchistan - 15. Burma - 16. Miscellaneous gazetteers. Series list p.54-94. Author list p.95-109. Place-name index p.110-131.

'A district gazetteer is a comprehensive description of a district or state of British India, published privately, in series, or under the auspices of a governmental body, and including historical, archaeological, political, economic, sociological, commercial and statistical data' (*Introduction*). *Class No:* 915.40(01)

Dictionaries

[5668]

SHARMA, J.S. **The National geographical dictionary of India.** New Delhi, Sterling Publishers, 1972. viii, 223p.

About 2,000 entries, A-Z, with some cross-references and index. Delhi: 2/3p.; Madras ½p. also 2-3 line entries. Unspecified references to classical Indian works; vague locations; no map references. *Class No:* 915.40(038)

Pakistan

[5669]

SHAW, I. **Pakistan handbook.** Chico, California, Moon Publications; London, Murray, 1989. 478p. col. illus., maps, bibliog., index, pbk. £14.95. ISBN: 0719547512.

Detailed and authoritative cultural and travel guide. Bibliography p.452-56. Urdu glossary. 86 maps. Subject and place-names index. *Class No:* 915.49

Turkey

[5670]

FARSON, D. **Turkey.** London, Collins, 1988. 251p. illus., maps, bibliog., index. £5.95. (*Collins Independent Travellers Guide.*) ISBN: 0004109716.

Background information (History, Turkey today, Weather, Travelling, Where to stay, Eating and drinking, Sport, Shopping, General Basics) p.13-69. 7 x A-Z regional gazetteers. Concise, reliable, informative. *Class No:* 915.60

Israel

[5671]

EBER, S. *and* O'SULLIVAN, K. **The Rough guide to Israel and the Occupied Territories.** London, Harrap-Columbus, 1989. x,451p. illus., tables, maps, bibliog., index. Softcover. £5.95. ISBN: 0747101051.

Pt.1 Basics comprises travel information, visas, information and maps (p.10-12) *etc.* Pt.2 Guide encompasses Jerusalem; The West Bank; Tel Aviv and the Southern coast; Haifa and the Central coast; Galilee and the North; Tiberias and the Panhandle; The Golan Heights; The Gaza Strip; and

....(contd.)

Nevev, the South, and Eilat. Pt.3 Context provides an historical framework and an analysis of current issues like Religion in the Holy Land, the Intifada *etc.*, Books p.427-31. Appendix: Hebrew and Arabic glossary p.446-7. 'It is difficult to imagine that there has been or ever will be a better guide to Israel' (*The Independent*, 946, 21 October 1989, p.48). *Class No:* 915.694

Afghanistan

[5672]
Historical and political gazetteer of Afghanistan. Adamec, L.W., *ed.* Graz, Akademische Druck-und Verlagsanstalt, 6v., 1972-1985. 3388p.

Gazetteer of Afghanistan first prepared by General Staff of British India in 1871 as a secret reference source. Subsequent editions in 1882, 1894, 1907 and 1914. This edition consolidates new material up to 1970.

1. *Badakhshan and Northeastern Afghanistan.* 1972. xiii,255p. Glossary p.198-218. 2. *Farah and Southwestern Afghanistan.* 1973. xv,385p. Glossary p.325-45. ISBN 3201008575. 3. *Herat and Northwestern Afghanistan.* 1975. xvi,519p. Glossary. 3201009423. 4. *Mazar-i-Sharif and North-Central Afghanistan.* 1979. xviii,693p. Glossary p.607-27. 320101898. 5. *Kandahar and South-Central Afghanistan.* 1980. xx,667p. Glossary p.579-601. 3201011258. 6. *Kabul and Southeastern Afghanistan.* 1985. xx,847p. Glossary p.825-47. 3201012726. All volumes have substantial unnumbered map sections. The gazetteer combines the most important geographical data with historical, political, and cultural information.
Class No: 915.81

Asia—South East

[5673]
Indonesia, Malaysia & Singapore handbook 1993. Eliot, J., *and others, eds.* Bath, Trade & Travel Publications, 1992. 800p. £13.95. ISBN: 0900751428.

Practical information and advice, with descriptive gazetteers covering Peninsular and East Malaysia, Singapore, Brunei, Sumatra, Java, Bali, Lombok, East Timor, Kalimantan, Maluku, Nusa Tenggara, Sulawesi and Irian Jaya. *Class No:* 915.9

[5674]
Thailand, Indochina & Burma handbook 1993. Eliot, J., *and others, eds.* Bath, Trade & Travel Publications, 1992. 800p. £13.95. ISBN: 090075141x.

Practical travel details and advice, essential in-depth background information with routes through Singapore and Malaysia. *Class No:* 915.9

Africa

[5675]
KIRCHHERR, E.C. Place names of Africa 1935-1986 a political gazetteer. Metuchen, New Jersey, Scarecrow Press, 1987. viii,136p. bibliolg., maps, tables. £13.15. ISBN: 0810820617.

A completely revised, enlarged and updated edition of the author's earlier *Abyssinia to Zimbabwe: a guide to the political units of Africa in the period 1947-1978* (Athens, Ohio, Ohio Univ. Center of International Studies, 3rd ed., 1979).

....(contd.)

Pt.1 General introduction (need for a political gazetteer, notes on the maps *etc.*) - 2. Place names of the principal African states and adjacent islands A-Z (p.7-89) - 3. Supplementary notes and maps - 4. Bibliography p.125-36. 23 maps. 'The layout, the cross-referencing, the maps, the crisp, uncluttered explanations ... bring many disparate facts together' (*Geographical Journal,* v.155, no.2, July 1989, p.253). *Class No:* 916

Bibliographies

[5676]
TAUSSIG, L. Sub-Saharan travel resource guide. Oxford, Hans Zell, 2v., 1992.

V.1: *East & West Africa.* 288p. £40. ISBN 187383503. V.2: *Central & Southern Africa (and Indian Ocean Islands.* 288p. £40. 1873836554. Over 2,000 entries including critically annotated listings of 1500 guidebooks and maps; national parks and historical sites, and language phrasebooks; sections on travel magazines, travel publishers, travel bookshops; and international & African-based conservation and natural history organizations. Concentrates on current material. *Class No:* 916(01)

Africa—North

[5677]
The North Africa handbook (with Moorish Southern Spain) 1994. McLachlan, A. *and* McLachlan, K., *eds.* Bath, Trade and Travel Publications, 1993. 847p. maps, diagrs., tables, index. £14.95. (*Travellers World Series.*) ISBN: 0900751509.

In 3 main sections: 1. Introductory etiquette, languages, cultural, transport and health information - 2. History of North Africa - 3. Detailed regional guides.
Class No: 916.1/916.5

Egypt

[5678]
HANSEN, K. Egypt handbook. Chico, California, Moon Publications, 1992. 500p. col.illus., maps, plans, bibliog., index, pbk.

Cultural and travel compendium emphasising Egyptian history and archaeology. 80 detailed maps and plans to major archaeological sites. Arabic glossary. Subject and place-name index. *Class No:* 916.20

Mauritius

[5679]
BHUCKORY, C.K. Mauritius guide with street maps. Rose Hill, Mauritius, Editions de l'Océan Indien, 1989. 136p. maps.

Brief history - geographical, social and political description - Street maps of every town on the island. 'A very useful practical guide for the Mauritian tourist' (Bennett, P.R. *Mauritius,* 1992. Entry no.83)
Class No: 916.982

America

America—North & Central

[5680]

AAA maps. Falls Church, Virginia, American Automobile Association; Basingstoke, The Automobile Association, 1990. 215x95mm. Softcover. £1.99.

Alabama, Georgia 0749501286 - *Alberta, British Columbia* 0749501405 - *Arizona, New Mexico* 0749501294 - *Boston* 074950143x - *California* 0749501308 - *Central States* 0749501251 - *Chicago* 0749501448 - *Colorado, Wyoming* 0749501316 - *Connecticut, Massachusetts, Rhode Island* 0749501324 - *Delaware, Maryland, Virginia* 0749501448 - *Florida* 0749501340 - *Hawaii* 0749591359 - *Maine, New Hampshire, Vermont* 0749501367 - *Manitoba & Saskatchewan* 0749501413 - *Mexico & Central America* 0749501219 - *Miami, Miami Beach, Fort Lauderdale* 0749501456 - *Nevada, Utah* 0749501383 - *New York State* 0749501375 - *New York City* 0749501472 - *New Orleans* 0749501464 - *Northeastern States & Provinces* 0749501243 - *Northwestern States & Provinces* 0749501227 - *Ontario* 0749501421 - *Southeastern States* 0749501278 - *Southwestern States* 0749501235 - *Texas* 0749501391 - *USA* 0749501200 - *Washington D.C.* 0749501480 - *Western States* 0-74950126x. A comprehensive series of national, regional, state and city maps of the US, Canada, and Central America. *Class No: 917(71/73)*

Canada

[5681]

CANADA. Department of Mines And Technical Surveys. Geographical Branch. **Gazetteers of Canada.** Ottawa, Canadian Government Publishing Centre, 1952-. pbk or mircrofiche.

First published by the Canadian Permanent Committee on Geographical Names (1952-62).

List of place-names with brief description or identification, location and coordinates. *Alberta* C$19.50. ISBN 0660539842 - *British Columbia*, 3rd ed. 1985. C$22.50. 0660527731 - *Manitoba*, 3rd ed. 1981. C$8.00. 0660508486 - *New Brunswick* (Microfiche only) C$3.00 - *Newfoundland*, 2nd ed. 1983. C$12.00. 0660521911 - *Northwest Territories*, 1980. C$7.00. 0660504669 - *Nova Scotia*, 2nd ed. 1977. C$10.00. 0660016745 - *Ontario*, 3rd ed. 1988. C$ 19.95. 0660518644 - *Prince Edward Island*, 2nd ed. 1973. C$1.50 - *Saskatchewan*, 3rd ed. 1985. C$8.00. 0660530481 - *Yukon Territory*, 4th ed. 1981. (Microfiche only) C$2.00. Bilingual. *Class No: 917.1*

[5682]

CHRISTENSEN, D. and **FIEGUTH, M.** **Historic Saskatchewan.** Toronto, Oxford Univ. Press, 1986. 95p. col. illus. ISBN: 0195405625.

Historical sites described in profusely illustrated text in no discernible order. Bibliography p.93-94. List of archival sources p.95. No index. *Class No: 917.1*

Mexico

[5683]

MALLAN, C. Guide to the Yucatan peninsula. 2nd ed. Chico, California, Moon Publications, 1992. 400p. col.illus., maps, charts, bibliog., index, pbk. $11.95. ISBN: 0918373832.

....(contd.)

Detailed travel guide including transport arrangements to Maya archaeological sites. 53 maps. Subject and place-name index. *Class No: 917.2*

[5684]

Mexico and Central American handbook 1994. 5th ed. Bath, Trade & Travel Publications; Chicago, Passport Books, 1993. 800p. £14.95. (*Travellers World Guides.*) ISBN: 0900751460, UK; 0844299774, US. ISSN: 09655492.

Preliminary material includes Introduction and Hints (air travel, documentation and security, accommodation, etiquette and language, general advice *etc.*); Health Information; Pre-Conquest history. Main contents are descriptive gazetteer guides to Mexico, Cuba, Guatemala, Belize, El Salvador, Honduras, Nicaragua, Costa Rica, and Panama. *Class No: 917.2*

Caribbean

Bibliographies

[5685]

POYNTING, J. Caribbean travel resource guide. Oxford, Hans Zell, 1993. 300p. ISBN: 0905450620.

Contents include Travel to the Caribbean: an overview (Resources: bookshops; specialist libraries; museums; publishers & distributors; audio-visual resources; government & business organizations). Books (reference works & bibliographies; travel guides; maps & guides to specific areas; journals & magazines; studies by country; studies by subject). French, Spanish and Dutch-language material is also covered. *Class No: 917.29(01)*

Jamaica

[5686]

PARISER, H.S. Guide to Jamaica including Haiti. Chico, California, Moon Publications, 1985. 174p. col. illus., maps, charts, bibliog., index, pbk. $7.95. ISBN: 0960332286.

Comprehensive guide to the culture, places and peoples of the two islands. 18 maps. Subject and place-name index. *Class No: 917.292*

Puerto Rico

[5687]

PARISER, H.S. Guide to Puerto Rico and the Virgin Islands including the Dominican Republic. Chico, California, Moon Publications, 1986. 225p. col. illus., maps, charts, bibliog., index, pbk. $8.95. ISBN: 0918373085.

Practical travel guide with 25 maps. Subject and place-name index. *Class No: 917.295*

USA

[5688]

American places dictionary a guide to 45,000 populated places and natural features of the United States. Abate, F.R., *ed.* Detroit, Omnigraphics, 5v., 1992. 3500p. tables. $350; $85 each vol. ISBN: 1558887474, set.

1. *Northeast.* 1558881468. 2. *South/Southeast.* 1558881476. 3. *Central.* 1558881484. 4. *West.* 1558881492. 5. *National index.* 1558881247. Information on every state, all 3,141 US countries, nearly 40,000 cities, towns,

....*(contd.)*

townships, boroughs. Indian reservations, and 170 major military installations (*i.e.* every place with a functioning government), includes legal status, ZIP and area code, latitude and longitude, and 1980 and 1990 census population. For larger towns and cities descriptive location, economic, and historical background is given. All main entries are listed in the index volume along with names of individuals, institutions and other text references. *Class No:* 917.3

[5689]

ANDRIOTT, D., *and others, eds.* **Place guide.** McLean, Va., Documents Index, 1990. 561p. pbk. $40.

Complete A-Z list of populated places in US using information derived from US Census Bureau publications. *Class No:* 917.3

[5690]

CANTOR, G. Historic landmarks of Black America. Detroit, Gale Research Co., 1991. 372p. illus., maps, bibliog., index. $29.95; £20. ISBN: 0810378094.

Over 300 significant sites, memorials, historical houses, museums, libraries, colleges, battlefields arranged A-Z by state and city in 6 regions. Idaho, Nevada, Wyoming, and North Dakota are not represented although southern Ontario is covered. Data: historical significance, location, directions, access. Chronology 1539-1919.

Historical black landmarks: a traveler's guide. Visible Ink (Gale), $17.95. ISBN 0810394081 is a paperback edition. *Class No:* 917.3

[5691]

EASTMAN, J. Who lived where in the USA a biographical guide to homes and museums. New York, Facts on File, 1983. xxii,513p. illus., indexes. £20.00. ISBN: 0871965623.

Aims 'to catalog and present data on the American residences of more than 600 persons whose lives had major effects on national society and history; and to enable travelers ... to find and view for themselves the homes or sites associated with these famous persons' (*Introduction*). Data: Year of construction, destruction, dates of occupance, 1982 status of home or site including street address and access information. Sites listed in 6 regions. *Class No:* 917.3

[5692]

A Historical guide to the United States. New York, W.W. Norton, 1986. 601p. illus., index. $25. £19.95. ISBN: 0393023834.

Short essays providing a practical guide (representative rather than exhaustive) to places of historical interest in every State of the Union. Well indexed (p.579-601). 'The strength of this book is that it presents a national overview of the major state and local museums and scenic and historical sites in one volume' (*Choice*, v.24, no.9, May 1987, p.1380). *Class No:* 917.3

[5693]

KANE, J.N. The American counties: origins of county names, dates of creation and organization, area, population including 1980 census figures, historical data, and published sources. 4th ed. Metuchen, New Jersey, Scarecrow Press, 1983. xi,546p. bibliogs. £47.40. ISBN: 0810815583.

1st ed. 1960.

3067 counties listed A-Z: data includes 'capsule bibliographies'. Other sections list counties by State, their date of creation, county seats, and those counties whose

....*(contd.)*

names have changed. Also persons for whom counties have been named, independent cities, and Alaska boroughs. *Class No:* 917.3

[5694]

National Geographic guide to the National Parks of the United States 2nd ed. Washington, National Geographic Society. 432p. col. illus., maps, pbk. £14.95. ISBN: 0870448854.

Guide to 50 scenic parks including itineraries, accommodation, activities, and information on opening times and charges. 72 maps. 429 col. photographs.

America's hidden treasures: exploring our little known National Parks (National Geographic Society. 200p. col. illus. £12.95. ISBN 0870448633) is a guide to the National Parks which are least visited by tourists. *Class No:* 917.3

[5695]

Omni gazetteer of the United States of America. Abate, F.R., *ed.* Detroit, Omnigraphics, 11v., 1991. 9400p. $2,000 (set); $200 (individual volumes). ISBN: 1558883363, set.

1. *New England* - 2. *Northeastern States* - 3. *Southeast* (including Puerto Rico, Virgin Islands, other Caribbean islands) - 4. *South Central States* - 5. *Southwestern States* - 6. *Great Lake States* - 7. *Plains States* - 8. *Mountain States* - 9. *Pacific* - 10. *National Index* - 11. *US Data sourcebook*. Approximately 1.5 million single-line entries for all places of 5,000 population upwards. Data: name, place or feature, state, county, zip code or 1990 Census population, latitude and longitude United States Geological Survey map name. V.10 has detailed A-Z list of every entry in the 9 regional volumes. V.11 is a supplementary collection of 7 specialized lists of vital national data amd other places not noted in the regional volumes. 'The largest compilation of US place names ever published ... essential for large reference collections ... smaller libraries can acquire individual volumes as needed. A landmark reference work' (*Library Journal*, v.166, no.13, August 1991, p.86+88). 'Will be of inestimable value to historians, genealogists, goegraphers, cartographers, and anyone working with demographics' (*ibid*, v.117, no.7,. 15 April 1992, p.45). Included in *Library Journal's* Best Reference Books 1991.

Omni Gazetteer of the United States CD-ROM Version. Edited by Frank R. Abate. Software produced by SilverPlatter. Published by Omnigraphics, Inc., 1992. $2000. ISBN 1558884181. *Class No:* 917.3

[5696]

—Omni gazetteer state series. Abate, F.R., *ed.* Detroit, Omnigraphics, 50v., 1992-. $3750 (Set); $125. (individual volumes).

Extracted from *Omni gazetteer of the United States of America (q.v.).*

First volume published: *Omni gazetteer of New York State: a guide to more than 40,000 place names.* 1992. $125. ISBN 1558887709. Each volume will cover all populated places, structures, facilities, locales, historic places, and named geographic features. *Class No:* 917.3

[5697]
Parks directory of the United States a guide to 3,700 national and state parks, recreation areas, historic sites, battlefields, monuments, forests, preserves, memorials, seashores, and other designated recreation areas in the United States administered by national and state park agencies. Smith, D.L., *ed.* Detroit, Omnigraphics, 1992. 525p. indexes. $65. ISBN: 1558887652.

Data: address; telephone; general directions (for state parks only); Useful compendium of tourist information. *Class No:* 917.3

[5698]
SCOTT, D.L. *and* **SCOTT, K. Guide to the National Park areas Western States.** 2nd ed. Chester, Connecticut, The Globe Pequot Press, 1987. xv, 341p. illus. maps, pbk. $10.95. ISBN: 0871068400.

A revision of *Traveling and camping in the National Park areas: Western States* and *Traveling and camping in the National Park areas: mid-America* (1978).

Over 170 areas operated by the US National Parks Service west of the Mississipi River including historic sites, seashores, battlefields, monuments, memorials, *etc.*, in addition to major national parks, arranged A-Z by state. Entries include description of area, directions, and activities and facilities available. Generously mapped and illustrated. *Class No:* 917.3

[5699]
—SCOTT, D.L. *and* SCOTT, K. **Guide to the National Park areas Eastern States.** 2nd ed. Chester, Connecticut, The Globe Pequot Press, 1987. xv, 251p. illus., maps, pbk. $10.95. ISBN: 0870168389.

Revised edition of *Traveling and camping in the National Park areas: Eastern States* (1979) and *Traveling and camping in the National Park areas: mid-America* (1978).

More than 200 areas east of the Mississipi operated by the National Park Service, arranged A-Z by state, and including historic sites, battlefields, monuments, memorials *etc.* in addition to major national parks. Entries include description, directions, and activities and facilities available. Generously mapped and illustrated. *Class No:* 917.3

[5700]
STANLEY, D. *and* **CASTLEMAN, D. Alaska-Yukon handbook** including the Canadian Rockies. 2nd ed. Chico, California, Moon Publications, 1991. 415p. col. illus., maps, bibliog., index, pbk. $10.95. ISBN: 0918373786.

Superbly illustrated comprehensive travel guide. 94 maps. Subject and place-name index. *Class No:* 917.3

Micromaterials

[5701]
The National register of historic places 1984. Alexandria, Virginia and Cambridge, Chadwyck-Healey, 1984. 300 6497 98-frame silver positive microfiche. £63.50. Individual State registers are available and priced separately.

Supersedes *The National Register of Historic Places 1976.*

150,000 photographs and 130,000 pages of text comprise a record of 27,000 sites and structures of importance in American history, archaeology, architecture and engineering, arranged by State. Information includes name, location, narrative, descriptions, significance, period, geographical data, and major bibliographical references. Includes all properties, registered up to December 1982. The

....(contd.)
National Register is the official list of historic properties recognised by the Federal Government. *Class No:* 917.3(003.5)

Amerindians, North

[5702]
CONFEDERATION OF AMERICAN INDIANS, *comp.* **Indian reservations:** a State and Federal handbook. Jefferson, N.C., McFarland, 1986. 329p. $45. ISBN: 0899502008.

Page-long descriptions of 277 reservations in 31 states. Data: address, tribal land holdings, history, culture, government, population profile, tribal economy, climate, and recreation. 'A unique source' (*Reference Services Review*, v.17,no.4, Winter 1989, p.66-7). *Class No:* 917.3(=97)

America—South

[5703]
South American handbook, 1994. Cox, B., *ed.* 70th ed. Bath, Trade and Travel Publications 1993. 1424p. maps, tables, indexes. £21.95. ISBN 0844299790. ISBN: 0900751444.

Preliminary material includes Introduction and Hints, *i.e.* travel information, money, security *etc.* and Health Information. Main Country Section follows standard pattern: 1. Contents - 2. Description of physical geography (people, history, present form of government) - 3. Survey of cities, towns and places of interest; where to stay; services for visitors - 4. Economic report - 5. Information for visitors - 6. Hotels - 7. Prices. Over 100 detailed text maps and 12p. section of coloured maps. Based on editor's personal travels, contributions from national tourist offices, and on reports from local correspondents. 'The Handbook is, as ever unique. The breadth of its knowledge is little short of disconcerting' (*The Independent* no.629, 15 October 1988, p.43). Winner of the first Thomas Cook Best Travel Guide Award. *Class No:* 918

Falkland Islands

[5704]
GREAT BRITAIN. Foreign and Commonwealth Office. **Gazetteer of the Falkland Islands Dependencies** (South Georgia and the South Sandwich Islands). London HMSO, 1977. 9p. sd.

763 place names A-Z accepted for official use. Supplement 1979. *Class No:* 918.291

Australasia & Oceania

[5705]
MARGOLIS, S. Adventuring in the Pacific The Sierra Club travel guide to the islands of Polynesia, Melanesia, and Micronesia. San Francisco, Sierra Club Publications, 1988. x, 406p. illus., maps, bibliog., index, pbk. $12.95. ISBN: 0871567806.

Complete island by island profile with useful travel data. Bibliography p.400-403. *Class No:* 919

Nomenclatures

[5706]

MOTTELER, L.S. **Pacific island names** a map and name guide to the New Pacific. 3rd ed. Honolulu, Bishop Museum Press, 1986. 91p. maps, index. (*Bishop Museum Miscellaneous Publications, no.34.*) ISBN: 0930897196. ISSN: 08886776.

First published 1960 as *Guide to Pacific Islands* compiled by E.H. Bryan. 2nd ed. 1972 *Guide to islands in the Tropical Pacific*. This edition greatly expanded and in a new format.

Lists 6,000 island names (4500 variants) in 2 sections: 1. Political guide to names - 2. Index. Primary area of coverage: Oceania between Tropics of Cancer and Capricorn with Northwestern Hawaiian islands, Austral Islands (French Polynesia), Pitcairn Island, and the Chilean islands in Southeast Pacific. Sectional maps p.6-12. *Class No:* 919(083.72)

New Zealand

[5707]

AA atlas and touring guide to New Zealand. Auckland, Lansdowne Press, 1985. 196p. col.illus, col.maps. index. £25.00. ISBN: 0868660906.

3 parts: 1. The atlas based on the Lands and Survey 1:500,000 series divided into 24 provincial regions. Each map is complemented by an essay and a town plan - 2. Recreational guide - 3. Touring guide *i.e.,* 46 day tours, each itinerary emphasising historic and scenic landscapes. 300 col.photographs. *Class No:* 919.31

[5708]

AA book of the New Zealand countryside. 6th ed. Auckland, Lansdowne Press, 1984. 191p. col.illus., maps, index. ISBN: 0868660213.

1st ed. 1978. Companion volume to *AA road atlas of New Zealand.*

Where to go and what to see in 35 mainly geographical sections but including 'National and forest parks'; 'Maori art'; 'Gemstones and minerals' *etc. Class No:* 919.31

[5709]

KING, J. **New Zealand handbook.** Chico, California, Moon Publications, 1992. 512p. col.illus., maps, bibliog., index, pbk. $13.95; £13.95. ISBN: 0918373883.

Comprehensive and practical guide to people, places, history and culture. Bibliography p.493-96. 82 maps. Subject and place name index. *Class No:* 919.31

[5710]

The Past today historic places in New Zealand. Wilson, J., *ed.* Auckland, Pacific Publications for the New Zealand Historic Places Trust, 1987. vi, 183p., illus. (many col.), bibliogs., index. ISBN: 0864790015.

17 contributors. 19 chapters regional chapters on places of significance to Maoris and Europeans. Glossary of Maori terms p.173. Chapter bibliographies. For popular use. *Class No:* 919.31

[5711]

SHADBOLT, M. **Reader's Digest guide to New Zealand.** Sydney, Reader's Digest, 1988. 352p. col. illus., col. maps, index. $39.95. ISBN: 0864380372.

20 A-Z regional guides in gazetteer form with useful basic travel data. Special box features highlight wildlife, personalities and historical places. Well produced with 20 maps and over 500 photographs. *Class No:* 919.31

[5712]

Wises New Zealand guide a gazetteer of New Zealand. 8th ed. Auckland, Wises Publications, 1987. xxvi, 481p. col. illus., col. maps. ISBN: 0908794002.

Published as *Wises New Zealand index: every place in New Zealand* 1899-1948. First edition under current title 1952.

Descriptive guide (now incorporating historical detail) to towns, cities, localities, geographical and geological features, Maori folklore, and place-name meanings. General information (p.iv-xxvi) includes Maoris and European discovery, population, climate, main and suburban Post Offices. 23p. of maps. 63 col. plates. *Class No:* 919.31

Australia

[5713]

BARCA, M. **Explore historic Australia** 1200 places. 80 maps. South Yarra, Victoria, Currey O'Neil, 1984. 302p. col.illus. maps. ISBN: 0855505087.

Historic places listed A-Z, with towns of particular historical interest and capital cities especially featured, followed by 20-25 pages of maps, in separate state by state sections. Glossary p.12-13. Index to properties p.273-278. Index (*i.e.* gazetteer) p.279-302. *Class No:* 919.4

[5714]

The Cambridge dictionary of Australian places. Appleton, R. *and* Appleton, A., *comps.* Cambridge, Cambridge Univ. Press, 1992. xii,356p. maps. £40; $65. ISBN: 0521395062.

National gazetteer listing 'virtually every population centre in the country with pronunciation guide and etymological, geographical, and historical and economic information. 26 maps. *Class No:* 919.4

[5715]

Explore Australia the complete touring companion. 10th anniversary ed. London, Robert Hale, 1992. x,462p. col.illus., col.maps. index. £21.95. ISBN: 0709046251.

First published by George Philip and O'Neil 1980.

Introductory material for the motorist then A-Z touring guide, 750 towns and including places of historic interest, state by state with detailed maps for every State and Territory. Gazetteer of 10000 place names p.481-514. Frequently reissued. *Class No:* 919.4

[5716]

The Heritage of Australia the illustrated register of the national estate. Melbourne, Macmillan Company of Australia in association with Australian Heritage Commission, 1981. various pagination. illus., (some col.), maps, bibliogs., index. £40. ISBN: 0333337506.

6,600 places of historical interest (buildings and structures, national parks, Aboriginal sites, etc.) expertly described. Arranged State by State in 40 regional sections. Glossary p.86-89. Analytical index. Over 7,500 photographs. Monumental work. *Class No:* 919.4

Papua—New Guinea

[5717]

Papua New Guinea handbook: Business and travel guide. 11th ed. Sydney, Pacific Publications, 1985. 280p. illus., maps, plans.

First published as *The Handbook of Papua and New Guinea* in 1954. Revised at intervals.

Geography - History - The People - Land use - Finance - Commerce - Industry - Transport and communications - Social services - Religion. Pt.2: Provincial directory. *Class No:* 919.54

Polynesia

[5718]

STANLEY, D. South Pacific handbook New ed. Chico, California, Moon Publications, 1992. 588p. illus., maps, charts, bibliog., index. $13.95. ISBN: 0918373999.

Comprehensive guide to the history, geogoraphy, climate, cultures and customs of the 19 territories in the South Pacific. 138 maps. 12 col.pages. Generously illustrated. 'Of particular value are the maps and information on how to get to remote outer islands of the various Pacific nations; (G.W. Fry and R. Mauricio. *The Pacific Basin and Oceania,* 1987. Entry 166). *Class No:* 919.6

[5719]

Tourist guide to Tahiti and her islands. Papeete, Tahiti Tourist Promotion Board, 1989. 28p. illus., maps, tables, sd. US$5.00; Aust$6.00; NZ$7.00; FFr330; CFP550.

Basic information *e.g.* airport services, accommodation, ferry services covering not only Tahiti and Moorea but also other islands and island groups within French Polynesia: Leeward Society Islands (Bora Bora, Raiatea); the Tuamotu Archipelago (Rangiroa, Maahi, Huahune); Marquesas Islands; Gambier Islands; and Austral Islands. Also available *gratis* within French Polynesia as an insert to *Tahiti Sun Press* (Papeete. ISSN 07596774). *Class No:* 919.6

Fiji

[5720]

Fiji handbook business and travel guide. Douglas, N. *and* Douglas, N. Sydney and New York, Pacific Publications, 1987. 264p. illus. (some col.), maps, tables, bibliog., index, softcover. ISBN: 085807060x.

Previously published as *Fiji handbook and travel guide.*

1. The place, the past and the people - 2. Parliament, the public sector and productivity - 3. The traveller in Fiji. Chronology of Fiji p.21-24. Bibliography p.258-9. 9 maps and 16p. of coloured plates. *Class No:* 919.611

[5721]

STANLEY, D. Finding Fiji. Chico, California, Moon Publications, 1992. 127p. col. illus., maps, charts, bibliog., index, pbk. $6.95. ISBN: 0918373921.

Practical travel guide with Fijiian vocabulary. 26 maps. Subject and place-name index. Extracted from the author's *South Pacific handbook* (q.v.). *Class No:* 919.611

Micronesia

[5722]

STANLEY, D. Micronesia handbook guide to the Caroline, Gilbert, Mariana and Marshall Islands. 2nd ed. Chico, California, Moon Publications, 1989. col. illus., maps, charts, bibliog., index, pbk. $9.95. £8.95. ISBN: 0918373247.

Detailed travel guide to the seven island groups lying between Hawaii and the Philippines including the Republic of Belau, Territory of Guam, Nauru and Kiribati. Bibliography p.273-79. Glossary p.281-82. 69 maps. Subject and place-name index. *Class No:* 919.65

Hawaii

[5723]

BISIGNANI, J.D. Hawaii handbook. Chico, California, Moon Publications, 1992. 788p. col.illus., maps, bibliog., index, pbk. $15.95. ISBN: 0918373484.

Detailed introduction to the island's geography, history culture and tourist attractions. Hawaiian and pidgin glossaries. 74 maps. Subject and place-name index. Note also the author's *Maui handbook* (2nd ed. 1989. 235p. ISBN 0918373603); *Oahu handbook* 0918373492; *Kauai* 0918373301' and *Big Island* 0918373476. *Class No:* 919.69

Greenland

[5724]

YDEGAARD, T. Greenland. Leicester, Cordee, 1990. 184p. £9.95. ISBN: 1871890004.

Complete trekking and travel guide. *Class No:* 919.88

92 Biography

Biography

Worldwide

[5725]

Almanac of famous people a comprehensive reference guide to more than 25,000 famous and infamous newsmakers from Biblical times to the present. Stetler, S.L., *ed.* 4th ed. Detroit, Gale Research Co., 3v., 1989. 3083p. $103.50. ISBN: 0810327848. ISSN: 1040127x.

First published as *Biography almanac* (1981); 3rd ed. 1987.

V.1-2 Over 25000 Biographies including subject's name, nicknames, dates of birth and death (where appropriate), nationality, occupation or best-known activity, with citations to biographical sketches or articles appearing in over 300 readily available sources. V.3. Chronological, geographical and occupational indexes. 'It is basically a biographical dictionary ... contemporary popular singers, television stars, stage personalities, and cinema actors are covered more completely than in other biographical dictionaries' (*Choice*, v,.24,no.10, June 1987, p.1528). *Class No:* 929(100)

[5726]

The Annual obituary. Chicago and London, St. James Press, 1980-. Annual. bibliogs., indexes.

1980 and 1981 edition published by St. Martins Press (New York) and Macmillan (London).

1993 volume edited by Deborah Andrews 1994. 900p. ISBN 1558623205, £62.50. Contains 350 obituaries consisting of a 500-2000 word essay, a detailed bio-bibliographical section and, where relevant, a reading list. All volumes are kept in print with consolidated alphabetical and professional indexes. 'Although focussing on elite personalities, provides well-written analytical essays that supplement major biographical publications' (*Choice*, v.27,no.5, January 1990, p.761). *Class No:* 929(100)

[5727]

The Cambridge biographical encyclopedia. Crystal, D., *ed.* Cambridge University Press, 1994. 1280p. illus., maps, diagrs. £179. ISBN: 0521469562.

1. 15,000 short biographies A-Z with emphasis on 20th century - 2. Ready reference (details of further 10,000 people) including monarchs, heads of state, famous family trees, prize winners in science, literature and sport - 3. Connections (*i.e.* visual account of 50 topics in key areas of exploration, history, the arts, science and technology) - 4. Chronology. *Class No:* 929(100)

[5728]

CHALMERS, A. The General biographical dictionary containing an historical and critical account of the lives and writings of the most eminent persons in every nation, particularly the British and Irish; from the earliest times. New ed. London, Nichols, 32v., 1812-17.

Several earlier eds. First published 1761-1767. Reprint, Nendeln, Liechtenstein, Kraus Reprint, 1976.

An account of persons of all nations, eminent for genius, learning, public spirit and virtue, with a preference, as to extent of narrative, to those of our own country. Discursive entries. *Class No:* 929(100)

[5729]

Chambers biographical dictionary. Magnusson, M. *and* Goring, R., *eds.* 5th ed. Edinburgh, Chambers, 1990. xii,1604p. £30. ISBN: 055016040x, UK.

1st ed. 1897; 4th ed. 1961. In North America published as *Cambridge biographical dictionary* (Cambridge Univ. Press, $34.50. 0521395186).

80 contributors. Contains 20,000 profiles of famous persons from earliest times to the present day (1/3 larger than the previous edition). Now gives greater prominence to 20th century figures, especially women, and focusses more attention on areas such as art, business, films, the media, politics, sport, and theatre, with a broader international overview, particularly United States and Australia (R. Benaud 10 lines, R.B. Simpson 12 lines but no entry for A.R. Border). Entries give an essential outline of life and achievements. 'As a single-volume, worldwide, all-period biographical dictionary, this has no peers' (*Library Journal*, v.116,no.1, January 1991, p.88). *Class No:* 929(100)

[5730]

Current biography. New York, H.W. Wilson, 1940-. Monthly except December. ports. $58.00 US and Canada; $68.00 elsewhere. ISSN: 00113344.

Each monthly issue now contains 16-18 profiles, some 2500-3000 words in length, of people 'who make today's headlines and tomorrow's history. Biographies are rewritten and updated when necessary. In December the monthly biographies are revised and cumulated into a single A-Z sequence in the *Current biography yearbook*. *Class No:* 929(100)

[5731]

—Current biography yearbook. New York, H.W. Wilson, 1940-. Annual. 1940-1985 $40.00 US and Canada, $50.00 in other countries. 1986-1989 $58.00 US and Canada, $68.00 in other countries. ISSN: 00849499.

A cumulation, published in December, of all biographies printed in the previous 11 months issues of *Current biography* to which are added a list of sources consulted, a classification of the subjects profiled by their professions, and a cumulative index to the articles from all previous *Yearbooks* of the decade. *Class No:* 929(100)

[5732]

Current Biography cumulated index 1940-1990. New York, H.W. Wilson, 1991. 135p. $25 US. and Canada; $29. elsewhere. ISBN: 0824208196.

Provides access to almost 20,000 biographies. Lists subjects of all the articles and revisions and obituaries in *Current biography*. Entries include changes in title and cross-references to variants and pseudonyms. *Class No:* 929(100)

[5733]

A Dictionary of twentieth-century world biography. Briggs, A., *ed.* Oxford, Oxford Univ. Press, 1992. 615p. £19.95. ISBN: 0192116797.

Originally published as *Longman dictionary of 20th century biography* (1985).

1750 A-Z biographies of those who have made their mark on the 20th century. Data: family background, education, achievements and/or misdemeanours, and the events they influenced. *Class No:* 929(100)

[5734]

Great lives from history series. Magill, F.N., *ed.* Englewood Cliffs, New Jersey and Pasadena, California, Salem Press, 1987-.

1. *American series.* 5v., 1987,2606p. bibliogs., index. $325.00 £207.25. ISBN 0893565296. 456 biographies both living and dead. 2. *British and Commonwealth series.* 5v., 1988. xix,2683p. bibliogs., index. $325.00 £244.25. ISBN 0893565350. 475 biographies covering the period from 7th to 20th centuries. Non-European Commonwealth figures will be included in future sets. 3. *Ancient and medieval series.* 5v., 1988.2420p. bibliogs., index. $325.00 £202.00. ISBN 0893565458. 470 biographies of non-British individuals from all continents except Australia ranging in time from Ancient Egypt to the Italian Renaissance. 4. *Renaissance to 1900 series.* 5v., 1990.2500p. £304.95. ISBN 0893565512. *Twentieth century series.* 5v. 1990. 2527p. index. 0893565652. $325.

This major project focusses unevenly on famous individuals in all fields of endeavour. Brief (2-3000 word) signed biographies include vital statistics, area of distinction, early life, career, place in history, and an annotated bibliography. Critical appraisal and comparisons are mixed *Reference Books Bulletin 1987-1988* remarked of the *American series,* its 'emphasis on the subject's contributions and achievements makes most of the articles more celebratory hagiography than balanced, critical analysis and evaluation such as that found in the *Dictionary of American Biography,* for instance' (p.148-9). *Library Journal,* v.112,no.10, 1 June 1987, p.103 observed 'One can quibble about selection, but the articles are more literary and scholarly than those in the *McGraw-Hill Encyclopedia of World Biography'. Class No:* 929(100)

[5735]

Historic world leaders. Commire, A., *ed.* Detroit, Gale research Co., 5v., 1993. 1500p. illus., ports., maps. ISBN: 0810384086, set.

1. *Western Europe.* ISBN 0810384094. 2. *Eastern Europe.* 0810384108. 3. *Asia and Australia.* 0810384116. 4. *Africa/Middle East.* 0810384124. 5. *United States. Canada and South and Latin America.* 0810384132. Profiles of and descriptive essays on social, political, and religious leaders from the earliest times. Each volume is arranged geographically and then A-Z by name. All entries end with a list of sources for further study. *Class No:* 929(100)

[5736]

The Hutchinson dictionary of biography. 2nd ed. Oxford, Helicon, 1993. 760p. index, ports. £20. ISBN: 0091776392.

Originally published as *The Hutchinson paperback dictionary of biography* (Arrow Books, 1990).

8000 entries (500 new to this ed.) on the 'most important topical or noteworthy people of our own times and previous eras'. *Reference Reviews,* 7(5), 1993: 40-41 goes overboard. 'This work approaches close to being the perfect reference book. Its subject matter is of high topicality and enduring interest'. *Class No:* 929(100)

[5737]

The International who's who 1994-95. 58th ed. London, Europa Publications, 1989. Distributed in North America by Gale Research Co. 1808p. £140. ISBN: 0946653984. ISSN: 00749613.

1st ed. 1935.

20,000 biographies (700 new to this edition). Data: date of birth, nationality, education, career, honours, personal details. Includes a section on reigning royal families. 'Each new edition of this authoritative work of reference is the result of a thorough revision of its predecessor' (*International Affairs,* v.61, no.4, August 1985, p.736-7). *Class No:* 929(100)

[5738]

The Macmillan dictionary of biography. Jones, B. *and* Dixon, M.V. 3rd ed. London, Macmillan, 1989. 917p. pbk. £12.99. ISBN: 0333514262.

First published by Macmillan Press in 1981.

7500 brief biographies, 400 new to this edition, with some minor figures dropped. Longest entries, *e.g.* Jesus, Lenin, Mozart run to 500-1000 words. Most end with references to other sources. First edition published under a cloud - see letter from Barry Jones in *TLS,* no.4135, 2 February 1982, p.719. 'As one of the ostensible co-authors I wish to dissociate myself from the book in every way as I think it lacks the fundamental prerequisite of any reference book, viz, accuracy. In a careful re-reading of the published text I have picked up at least 3000 factual errors, quite apart from absurdities in the text and gross omissions'. *Class No:* 929(100)

[5739]

MICHAUD, J.F. Biographie universelle, ancienne et moderne. New ed. Paris, Desplaces, 45v., 1843-65.

First published 1811-1862. 85v. (Initially 1811-1828, 52v., but two major supplements, in 3v. (mythology) and 30v., were added.). Reprint of 1843-65 ed. Graz, Akademische Druk-und Verlagsanstalt, 1964).

Although it is in some respects dated, the work is still useful because of the high standard of scholarship of the contributors. (300 writers collaborated in the compilation of the work.) Lengthy, signed articles, with adequate bibliographical information. One serious defect of the first edition was that many of the entries had strong royalist and Catholic bias. This was to a large degree corrected in the second edition, although it still occurs in some of the earlier volumes. The English articles are not entirely satisfactory, for there are many errors of fact and some 'inadequacy of treatment', but with all its shortcomings 'there is no book where [the] errors are so few in proportion to the great extent of the work'. For a detailed account of the history and development of *Michaud,* particularly its law suit with Firmin Didot on the question of literary copyright and the

....(contd.)

publication of *Hoefer,* see p.204-210 of an article by R.C. Christie in the *Quarterly Review,* v.157, January 1884. *Class No:* 929(100)

[5740]

—HOEFER, J. Ch. F. Nouvelle biographie générale depuis les temps les plus reculés jusqu' à nos jours, avec les renseignements bibliographiques et l'indication des sources à consulter. Paris, Didot, 46v., 1852-66.

Originally *Nouvelle biographie universelle,* but, as the result of a legal action taken by the owners of Michaud (*qv*), the title was changed. Published in weekly parts, 10 to a volume.

Concise articles for 52,420 eminent living men as well as for important deceased persons omitted from Michaud. A popular work; for scholarship does not compare with the older work. No original work was involved in the compilation of Hoefer, for many of the articles were condensations of entries contained in other bibliographical works published by Firmin Didot, while others are taken in their entirety or were extracts or abridgements of articles taken from Michaud. *Class No:* 929(100)

[5741]

Newsmakers. Gareffa, P.M., *ed.* Detroit, Gale Research Co., 1989-. Quarterly. £64.00.

Published 1985-87 as *Contemporary newsmakers.*

Newsmakers 92. 0810322455. 3 quarterly softbound issues *pa.* each containing approximately 50 'lively, informative biographical profiles of the people making today's headlines'. A hardbound annual cumulation is enhanced by four indexes (subject, person, occupation, keyword) allowing immediate access to all entries included in the series since 1985. Also available online, on disk, and magetape. *Class No:* 929(100)

[5742]

Newsworthies people in the news. Biggleswade, Beds., Clover Publications, 1987-. 2pa., annual cumulation. £21.95pa.

1990 v. covers September 1988 to August 1989. Its mimeographed, single-line entries record obituaries, interviews and profiles drawn from *The Times, Sunday Times, Observer, The Independent, Daily Telegraph, Guardian, Financial Times* and as listed in the weekly *Clover Newspaper Index* or *Clover Information Index.* *Class No:* 929(100)

[5743]

OETTINGER, E.M. Moniteur des dates. Biographisch-genealogisch-historisches Welt-Register enthaltend die Personal-Akten der Menschheit von mehr als 100,000 geschichtlichen Persönlichkeiten aller Zeiten und Nationen von Erschaffung des Welt bis auf den heutigen Tag. Graz, Akademische Druk-und Verlagsanstalt, 9v., 1964. 1718p. ISBN: 3201000175.

Originally published Leipzig. Denicke, 1866-73; Hermann 1873-82.

More than 100,000 very brief biographical entries for historical persons of all times and nations. *Class No:* 929(100)

[5744]

Webster's new biographical dictionary. Springfield, Massachusetts, Merriam-Webster, 1983. xviii,1130p. $21.95. ISBN: 0877795436.

Webster's biographical dictionary first published 1943. This was updated 21 times.

Based firmly upon its predecessor but 'wholly revised and reedited'. One major change: living persons are not now included. 30,000 biographies 'present in a single volume biographical information on important, celebrated, or notorious figures from the last five thousand years, beginning with Menes, King of Egypt, *c.*3100 B.C. This new work has increased coverage of Asia, Africa and Third World countries but main emphasis remains on American, Canadian and British subjects. Biographies p.1-1090. Pronouncing lists of name elements, titles, and prenames p.1091-1130. Thumb index. *Class No:* 929(100)

[5745]

Who was when: a dictionary of contemporaries. De Ford, M.A. *and* Jackson, J.S. 3rd ed. New York, H.W. Wilson, 1976. 184p. index. $47.00 (US and Canada) $52.00 (other countries). ISBN: 0824205324.

Chronological list of birth and death dates of 10,000 influential figures from 500B.C. to 1974. *Class No:* 929(100)

[5746]

Who's who in international affairs. London, Europa, 1990. Distributed in North America by Gale Research Co. 640p. indexes. £150. $295. ISBN: 0946653631.

Over 7,000 biographical entries for principal figures in the spheres of international politics and economics, cultural, and scientific affairs. Data: date and place of birth; family details; education; positions held and years appointed; current position; publications *etc.* Nationality and organization indexes. 'Provides biographical information on many people who are difficult to locate elsewhere' (*Booklist,* v.87,no.18, 15 May 1991, p.1836). *Class No:* 929(100)

[5747]

Who's who in the world 1993-1994. 11th ed. Wilmette, Illinois, Marquis Who's Who Macmillan Directory Division, 1993. 1240p. £220; $319. ISBN: 0837911117.

First published 1970.

31000 sketches of world statesmen, major businessmen; high ranking military officers; heads of education, religious, professional and scientific organizations determined on position of responsibility held or level of achievement obtained. *Class No:* 929(100)

[5748]

The World Almanac biographical dictionary. New York, World Almanac, 1990. Distributed by Pharos Books. 390p. index. $19.95. ISBN: 0886875641.

8000 brief biographical sketches (mostly less than 75 words) of leading personalities in all fields but with heavy emphasis on 'showbiz' and sport. Data: name, date and place of birth, date of death, and an indication of major works and achievements. May be used to supplement *Webster's new biographical dictionary (q.v.).* *Class No:* 929(100)

Bibliographies

[5749]
ARBA guide to biographical dictionaries. Wynar, B.S., *ed.*
Littleton, Colorado, Libraries Unlimited, 1986. xxiii,445p.
indexes. $60.00; £60.00. ISBN: 0872874923.

Compendium of 700+ signed reviews, published in
American Reference Books Annual since its inception of
sources considered to be the most useful published in the
previous 20 years. Pt.1. Universal and national biographies.
Pt.2. Biographies in 21 subject chapters each with
introductory note detailing the most interesting titles, plus
additional sources of information. Appropriate indexing and
abstracting services and existing subject bibliographical
guides are also noted. Author-title and subject indexes. 'A
useful retrospective look at a major body of reference
sources' (*Reference Books Bulletin 1986-1987*, p.151).
Class No: 929(100)(01)

[5750]
**ARNIM, M. Internationale Personalbibliographie 1800-
1943.** 2nd ed. Leipzig (later Stuttgart), Hiersemann, 2v.,
1944-1952. xvi,706p.+834p.

First published 1936 covering the period 1550-1935
(25,000 entries).

Continued by: 2. *1944-1959 und nachträge zur 2. Auflage
von Band 1-11.* Fortgeführt von D. Bock und F. Hodes.
1963. xi,659p. 3. *1944-1975 Fortgefüjrte Auflage von Band
III (1944-1959) mit Nachträgen zur zweiten Auflage von
Band I/II (1800-1943)* Lieferung 1-9: A. Hyppä. 1978-1981.
4. *Zweite völlig neubearbeitete Auflage von Band III
(Berichtszeit 1944-1959) in drei bis zum Jeweiligen
Erschneinungsjahr Ergänztenn Bänden III-V.* Lieferung 10-
18: Jakob-Ryzmkowski. 1981-1984. 5. Lieferung 19-24:
Sad-Zywczynski. Schluslieferung mit Titelbogen zu Band
V..1985-1987. International in scope although with marked
German emphasis, this is an index to bibliographies of
individual authors. Valuable for singling out 'hidden'
bibliographies contained in books, biographical dictionaries
(*e.g.* Kürschner) bio-bibliographies (*e.g.* Poggendorff;
Goedeke), periodical articles, festschriften *etc.* Because these
bibliographies are often appended to biographical material,
this work serves as a key of sorts to biographical data.
Because of entries omitted from the 2nd ed., the 1st ed.
should still be used. *Class No:* 929(100)(01)

[5751]
Bibliography of biography 1970-84. London, The British
Library, Bibliographic Services, 1985. 40 x 1.8 reduction
negative microfiche+binder for permanent storage.
£85.+½AT(UK). £100 (overseas).

95,000 titles (autobiographies, biographies, letters and
diaries of historical and contemporary figures) published
worldwide in 2 alphabetical sequences: by name of
individual concerned and an author-title index. Compiled
from catalogue of records created by The British Library
and The Library of Congress. *Class No:* 929(100)(01)

[5752]
—Bibliography of biography 1988. London, The British
Library. Bibliographic Services, 1988. 454p. £50. (UK).
£60.(Overseas). ISBN: 0712310460. ISSN: 09554629.

List of biographical works published & worldwide
extracted from MARC records created in 1988 by British
Library Bibliographic Services and Library of Congress in 2
sequences *viz.* Name sequence (names as subjects) with
detailed bibliographical information and Author-Title index.
Entries conform to AACR2. for librarians, researchers and

....(contd.)
booksellers. *Bibliography of biography 1989.* 1990. 571p.
softback. £60. (UK), £70. (overseas). ISBN 0712310517
contains information on over 7,000 titles.
Class No: 929(100)(01)

[5753]
—Bibliography of biography on CD-ROM. Boston Spa,
National Bibliographic Service, British Library, 1992.
Annual. Annual subscription £250 + VAT.

Single disc updated annually. First issue contains over
220,000 entries selected from national and international
databases. 14 search indexes covering personal authors,
personal and corporate names as subjects, titles, keywords,
control numbers, languages, country of issues, date of
publication *etc.* '*BoB* is certainly more appealing in this form
than on microfiche! Libraries with sufficient demand for
bibliographic details of a wide range of bibliographical
material could find this a most useful and affordable
acquisition' (*Library Association Record*, v.95, no.3, March
1993, p.174). *Class No:* 929(100)(01)

[5754]
Biographical dictionaries and related works an international
bibliography of more than 16,000 collective biographies,
bio-bibliographies, collections of epitaphs, selected
genealogical works, dictionaries of acronyms and
pseudonyms, historical and specialized dictionaries,
biographical materials in government manuals,
bibliographies of biography, biographical indexes, and
selected portrait catalogues. Slocum, R.B., *ed.* 2nd ed.
Detroit, Gale Research Co., 2v., 1986. 1319p. bibliog.,
indexes. $150.00. ISBN: 0810302348.

First published 1967. Supplements 1972 and 1978.

In 3 sections: universal biography; foreign and U.S.
biography by area; and foreign and U.S. biography by
vocation. Some entries are annotated. Author, title and
subject indexes. Bibliography p.17-23. 4000 items are new
to this edition. *Class No:* 929(100)(01)

[5755]
Biography index: a cumulative index to biographical material
in books and magazines. New York, H.W. Wilson, 1946-,
v.1-. Quarterly paperbound issues and an annual cumulation.
Annual subscription $120.00 US and Canada $130.00
elsewhere. ISSN: 00063053.

Based on more than 2600 periodicals regularly scanned in
the Wilson indexes plus works of individual and collective
(auto)biographies, and obituaries. The main section is A-Z
by biographees (full name, dates, nationality, profession, and
full bibliographic citation). The 2nd section is an index to
professions and occupations. There are 17 biennial or
triennial retrospective volumes 1946-August 1992 each
$160.00 US and Canada, $190.00 elsewhere. Available on
the Wilsondisc database. Wilson Tape, Wilsonline, and on
Wilsearch. *Class No:* 929(100)(01)

[5756]
CIMBALA, D.J., *and others*. Biographical sources: a guide
to dictionaries and reference works. Phoenix, Arizona, Oryx
Press, 1986. x,146p. index. $36.00; £24.75. ISBN:
0897741366.

689 briefly annotated entries arranged under 15 broad
subject headings. The emphasis is on English language
material published or distributed in US and Canada. Faces
stiff competition from *Bibliographical dictionaries and*

.... *(contd.)*
related works and *ARBA guide to biographical dictionaries* reports *Choice*, v.24,no.6, February 1987, p.862.
Class No: 929(100)(01)

[5757]

Dictionary of biographical reference. containing over one hundred thousand names; together with a classed index to the biographical literature of Europe and America. Phillips, L.B. 3rd ed. Detroit, Gale Research Co., 1982. xiv, 1038p. bibliog. $90.00. ISBN: 081033996x.

1st ed. published in 1871. 2nd ed. 1881 as *Great index of biographical reference* 3rd ed. first published by Sampson, Low, Marston & Co. (1889). This edition incorporated Frank Weitenkampf's supplement covering prominent people 1871-1888. Reprinted by Akademische Druk-und Verlagsanstalt of Graz in 1964.

Indexes 42 general and specialized biographical dictionaries. Includes an additional bibliography of *c.*1600 principal works of collective biography in 3 divisions: general biographies, national biographies, and class (*i.e.*, professional) biographies. *Class No:* 929(100)(01)

[5758]

Dictionary of universal biography of all ages and all peoples. Hyamson, A.M., *ed.* 2nd ed. (reprint). Detroit, Gale Research Co., 1981. xii,680p. $45.00. ISBN: 0810341506.

1st ed. 1916. 2nd ed. London, Routledge; New York, E.P. Dutton, 1951.

A finding list of *c.*110,000 biographies contained in the 23 most comprehensive biographical dictionaries and encyclopaedias. Does not include living persons. Entries, usually single-line, include name, nationality, profession, dates (where known) and a coded reference to original dictionary. *Class No:* 929(100)(01)

[5759]

HAVLICE, P.P. And so to bed: a bibliography of diaries published in English. Metuchen, New Jersey, Scarecrow Press, 1987. 706p. £44.60; $59.50. ISBN: 0810819236.

Updates and expands on W. Matthews' *American diaries* (1959), *British diaries* (1950), and *Canadian diaries and autobiographies* (1950).

Lists and annotates diaries by more than 2,500 people published in books and journals. *Class No:* 929(100)(01)

[5760]

International bibliography of biography 1970-1987. London, K.G. Saur, 12v. 1988. £1320.00. ISBN: 0862917506.

Compiled from MARC records created by The British Library and The Library of Congress.

In 2 sequences: Subject sequence (*i.e.* alphabetical listing of individuals covered) and Author/title index. Both autobiographical and biographical titles included. *Class No:* 929(100)(01)

[5761]

JARBOE, B.M. Obituaries: a guide to sources. 2nd ed. Boston, Massachusetts, G.K. Hall, 1989. 400p. indexes, $75. ISBN: 0816104832.

First published 1982.

Encyclopedic handbook encompassing books and articles which index newspapers, obituaries, annuals and yearbooks, and the proceedings of professional organizations. Entries are arranged on a geographical pattern with separate sections for US sources (A-Z by state) and for foreign countries. Author, title and subject indexes. *Class No:* 929(100)(01)

[5762]

LOBIES, J.P. Index bio-bibliographicus notorum hominum. Osnabrück, Biblio Verlag, 1972-. ISBN: 3764807261, complete work.

A. *Allgemeine Einführung.* 1972. B. List of bibliographical works 1972-73. C. *Corpus alphabeticum.* 1976-. v.1-. A (general introduction) has 3 sections: 1. Universal biographies; 2. Biographical works arranged on geographical, historical and linguistic principles (2,000 items); 3. Biographical reference works by vocations (subjects and activities). B. enumerates 5145 bibliographies cited in Part A; author and subject indexes. C. has entries under biographies A-Z. V.52 to Demetrios Demopoulos. V.23 has supplements to B. (entries 5146-5500); v.24 (entries 5501-5750; v.25 (entries 5751-6000); v.40 (entries 6001-6148); v.47 (entries 6149-6215) 1990. V.45/47. Supplement III. *Sectio Sinica cum supplemento Coreano* (v.1 1976) includes a foreword on How to use Index bibliographies for Chinese names. V.2. *Ban yong - Bo Zong* (1979). *Sectio Ameniaca.* V.1A-D (1982); *E-M* (1985); *N-V and Supplement A-V* (1987). 'The aim of this work is a world wide brief biographical presentation of all personalities - including those of the second or third rank - who have been significant in one or the other way for the history of mankind' 3-5 million entries will be listed eventually in this massive and tortuous index.
Class No: 929(100)(01)

[5763]

Obituary index. Wasserman, E.S., *ed.* New York and London, Meckler, Annual, 1989-. 555p. $97.50. £55.00. ISBN: 0887363350. ISSN: 16448659.

Comprises 8 comprehensive indexes: 1. Name index *i.e.* A-Z list of all obituaries published during the course of the year in *The Times, New York Times, Los Angeles Times, Washington Post, Chicago Tribune, Boston Globe* and *The Atlanta Constitution*. Each name cites the newspaper, month, day, section and page of original obituary - 2-7. Separate listings for each newspaper. *Class No:* 929(100)(01)

[5764]

St. James guide to biography. Schellinger, P.E., *ed.* Chicago and London, St. James Press, 1991. x,870p. bibliogs. £90. ISBN: 1558621466.

Not a biographical dictionary but a bibliographic guide with signed critical essays on the biographies of over 700 major figures in world history. 313 contributors.
Class No: 929(100)(01)

Awards & Prizes

[5765]

Nobel Prize winners: an H.W. Wilson biographical dictionary. Wesson, T., *ed.* New York, H.W. Wilson, 1987. xxxiv,1165p. illus., bibliogs. $90.00 US and Canada. $100 other countries. ISBN: 0824207564.

566 x 1500 word profiles of Nobel Prize winners 1901-1986 offering 'a narrative overview of a laureate's life and career, while focussing on the individual's prizewinning work and attempting to assess its significance'. List of winners p.vii-xii. Winners by prize category p.xiii-xix. Alfred Nobel p.xxiii-xxviii. The Nobel Prizes and Nobel Institutions p.xxix-xxxiii. Quinquennial supplements will be published beginning in 1992. 'The work has more depth than *Who's Who of Nobel Prize Winners* ed. by Bernard S. and June H. Schlessinger (1986)' (*Choice* v.25,no.8, April 1988,

....(contd.)
p.1224).

Nobel prize winners supplement 1987-1991 edited by P. Maguire. 1992. 144p. $35. (US and Canada); $40 (elsewhere). Biographical sketches of 49 Nobel Prize winners. *Class No:* 929(100)(079.2)

[5766]
WALTER, C. Winners the blue ribbon encyclopedia of awards. New York, Facts on File, 1982. ix,916p. index. ISBN: 0871963868.

Awards tabulated in 25 categories *e.g.* General achievement, Librarianship and information science, with lists of recipients on an annalistic pattern.
Class No: 929(100)(079.2)

[5767]
The Who's who of Nobel Prize winners. Schlessinger, B.S. *and* Schlessinger, J.H., *eds.* 2nd ed. Phoenix, Arizona, Oryx Press, 1991. 256p. indexes. $39.50; £31.50. ISBN: 089774599x.

1st ed. 1986.

177 contributors. 541 entries arranged by prize category on an annalistic basis 1901-1990. Data: family and personal, selected publications by and about, sources, and a commentary which quotes from the prize citation. Name, education, nationality and religion indexes. 'The first tool that provides biographical information on Nobel Prize winners in all categories ... a useful quick reference source' (*Reference Books Bulletin 1986-7* p.25).
Class No: 929(100)(079.2)

[5768]
World of winners: a current and historical perspective on awards and their winners. Siegman, G., *ed.* 2nd ed. Detroit, Gale Research Co., 1991. 1200p. indexes. $60.00. ISBN: 0810369818. ISSN: 10413529.

First published 1989.

Complete historical record of 75,000 winners and over 1,800 awards arranged alphabetically within 12 subject sections: Arts and letters; Business management, and marketing; Design and architecture, Health and medicine; Humanities, education and library science; Lifestyle; Live performance; Mass media; Music; Public affairs; Science; engineering, and technology; Sports and hobbies. Organization, winner, and award names indexes. Companion volume to *Awards, honors and prizes*.
Class No: 929(100)(079.2)

[5769]
—**SIEGMAN, G.,** *ed.* Awards, honors, and prizes an international directory of awards and their donors. 10th ed. Detroit, Gale Research Co., 2v., 1992. $408.25 set. ISBN: 0810376415.

First published 1969.

1. *United States and Canada.* 2100p. $189.75. ISBN 0810376393 A-Z directory of 5216 organizations sponsoring over 15,500 awards *etc.* in virtually every field of human endeavour. 2. *International and foreign.* 2100p. $217.35. ISBN 0810376407. More than 9300 awards and prizes given in 100 countries other than US and Canada arranged A-Z by sponsoring organization within country sections. Data: purpose of award and elegibility factors; character (monetary, medal, plaque); frequency (year established). Organization, award name, and subject indexes. 'Recognized as the standard work in its field' (*Booklist*, v.84,no.22,

....(contd.)
August 1988, p.1896). *Supplement* 1989. $101.20. ISBN 0810350882 furnishes information on additional awards not covered in main set. *Class No:* 929(100)(079.2)

Jews

[5770]
International biographical dictionary of Central European emigrés 1933-1945. Straus, H.A. *and* Roeder, W., *eds.* München, New York. London, Paris, K.G. Saur, 3v. in 4, 1980-1983. Distributed in the Western Hemisphere by Gale Research Co. £425.00 set. ISBN: 3598100876, set.

1. *Biographisches handbuch der deutschsprachigen emigration nach 1933. Band 1. Politik, Wirtschaft, Öffenliches Leben* 1980. lviii,875p. £149.00. 3598100876 (Ger). 0896641015 (US). 014044818 (UK). 2. *International biographical dictionary of Central European emigrés 1933-1945. Sciences, Arts, Literature. Pt.1. A-K; Pt.2. L-Z* 1983. xciv,1316p. $220.00. £219.00. 359810089. 3. *Gesamtregister/Index.* 1983. xx,277p. $95.00. £99.00. 359810096 Bilingual key to v.1+2. Approximately 8700 biographies mostly of Jews forced to leave Germany, Austria, and Czechoslovakia during the Nazi era. Key for use of Dictionary p.1291-98 (v.2). Glossary p.1299-1301 (v.2). Sponsored by Research Federation for Jewish Immigration (New York) and Institut für Zeitgeschichte (München).

Kurzbiographien zur Geschichte der Juden 1918-1945 (K.G. Saur, 1990. 2598104774) 'Diese Biographie mit nahezu 5000 ergänzt das *Biographisches Handbuch der deutschsprachigen Emigration nach 1993 (dustwrapper).*
Class No: 929(100)(=924)

[5771]
Who's who in world Jewry: a biographical dictionary of outstanding Jews. Rosenblatt, J.T., *ed.* 7th ed. New York, Who's who in World Jewry, 1987. xix,631p. illus. $129.00. ISBN: 0961827203.

First published 1955.

'The personalities included were selected on the basis of their influence, position, and accomplishments, and the data used was supplied by them' (*Introduction*) but 'the list of persons not included is long' (*Booklist*, v.84,no.15, 1 April 1988, p.1327-8). *Class No:* 929(100)(=924)

Black Races

Bibliographies

[5772]
In black and white a guide to magazine articles and books concerning more than 15,000 black individual groups. Spradling, M.M.S., *ed.* 3rd ed. Detroit, Gale Research Co., 2v., 1980. 1282p. $125.00. ISBN: 0810304384.

1st ed. 1971.

A-Z entries by individuals providing information on careers of black people in America, Africa, and elsewhere with bibliographical references to printed sources offering further information. Index of occupations. *Supplement* 1985. xiv,628p. $88.00. Adds 6,700 further individuals and groups. *Class No:* 929(100)(=96)(01)

20th Century

[5773]

VERNOFF, E. *and* **SHORE, R. The International dictionary of 20th century biography.** New York, New American Library; London, Sidgwick & Jackson, 1987. [iii],819p. index. $24.95; £15.00. ISBN: 0453005292, US; 0283995475, UK.

5650 concise biographies of living and dead 'who have made their mark in almost ever field of human endeavor' (*Introduction*). Universal coverage but with marked US emphasis. Entries cite published autobiographies and biographies. 'While many of the figures can also be found in other reference sources, this book brings together entries that would be spread through many other titles' (*Reference Books Bulletin 1986-1987*, p.152). *Class No:* 929(100)"19"

Women

[5774]

The International who's who of women a biographical reference guide to the most eminent and distinguished women in the world today. London, Europa, 1992. xvi,553p. index. £175; $350. ISBN: 0946653852. ISSN: 09653775.

Over 4000 concise profiles of the world's most eminent and distinguished women (Hillary Rodham Clinton 19 lines; Baroness Thatcher 21 lines; Julie Walters 24 lines). Data: name and title; academic degrees and professional qualifications; date and place of birth; nationality; family details; education; career history; major publications, films, plays; honours, awards and prizes; leisure interests. Occupational index. 'There are really no competitors for this publication' (*The Year In Reference 1993*, p.146-8). *Class No:* 929(100)-0055.2

[5775]

The Macmillan dictionary of women's biography. Uglow, J.S., *ed.* 2nd ed. London, Macmillan Reference Books, 1988. xvii,534p. ports, bibliog., index. £29.95; $37.50. ISBN: 0333453034.

1st ed. 1982. Published in US as *The Continuum dictionary of women's biography* (Continuum Publishing Co.).

Essential details of over 2000 women drawn from all periods and cultures with emphasis on British Isles, the Commonwealth, Europe and North America although this edition has an extended treatment of women from 'Third World' countries. 'An excellent reference source. Its scope and compact nature will save users much time. Highly recommended' (*Library Journal*, v.108,no.5, 1 March 1983, p.489). *Class No:* 929(100)-0055.2

[5776]

The World's who's who of women 1990/91. 11th ed. Ely. Cambridgeshire, Melrose Press, 1992. 120p. £75.00.

1st ed. 1973.

Over 7500 entries for the leading women of the world today. Data: birthdates (not always); education; career and appointments; publications. Previous editions carried many more entries and so should not necessarily be discarded. *Class No:* 929(100)-0055.2

Europe

[5777]

Who's who in Europe dictionnaire biographique des personnalités européenes contemporaines. 6th ed. Waterloo, Belgique, Editions SERVI-TECH, 1985,. l,2547p. ISBN: 2870610068.

First published 1965.

Over 40,000 entries (28,000 in 1965 ed.) from 25 countries now including USSR. Entries are *c.*15-25 lines in length and cover politicians, writers, scholars, scientists. *Class No:* 929(4)

[5778]

Who's who in European institutions, organisations and enterprises a biographical encyclopaedia of Sutter's international red series containing some 5000 biographies of top administrators, chairmen, politicians and other leading personalities working with European institutions and organisations and international institutions in Europe, as well as of decision-making executives belonging to leading European enterprises. Dove, J.C., *ed.* 2nd ed. Milano, Who's who in Italy under licence from Who's who A.G. Zurich, 1985. xxiii,1450p. £66.75. ISBN: 8885246001.

Biographies p.3-986. appendix (up-to-date information on the organization and structure of European and international institutions and associations in all fields of economic, scientific, political, intellectual and social life p.991-1043. Register of company, organization and institution profiles p.1405-1450. The aim is a revised edition every 3 years. *Class No:* 929(4)

Europe—Western

[5779]

Biografisch archief van de Benelux/Archives biographiques des Pays du Benelux. [Biographical archive of the Benelux countries.] Van der Meer, E., *ed.* München, K.G. Saur, 12 installments, 1992-94. 700 fiches (24x) Silver or diazo. £8400 (silver); £7730 (diazo) ISBN: 3598326300, Silver; 3598326106, Diazo.

160,000 entries in a single A-Z sequence cumulated from 122 biographical reference works (1598 - beginning of 20th century). Covers former Dutch colonies in Indonesia, the Antilles, and Surinam, and the Belgian Congo. On completion a printed index will be published. *Class No:* 929(400)

Europe—Eastern

[5780]

STROYNOWSKI, J., *ed.* **Who's who in the socialist countries of Europe:** a biographical encyclopaedia of more than 12,600 leading personalities in Albania, Bulgaria, Czechoslovakia, German Democratic Republic, Hungary, Poland, Romania, Yugoslavia. München, New York, London, Paris, K.G. Saur, 3v., 1989. £237.00 $350.00. ISBN: 359810636x, set.

Formerly published as *Who's who in the socialist countries* (1978).

V.1 *A-H. Index*, lx, 461p. ISBN 3598107196. Abbreviations and terms p.ix-xiii. Name index arranged by country p.xv-lx. V.2 *I-O* v, 462-878p. ISBN 359810720x. V.3 *P-Z* v, 879-1367p. ISBN 3598107471.

Biographies of eminent individuals from the spheres of party, government, military, diplomacy, economics, literature, religion, art, and press. Also 350 dissidents. Data:

....(contd.)

full name, nationality, profession, family background, real name, detailed biography (*e.g.* Lech Walesa 55 lines; Nicolae Ceauşescu 52 lines), publications, honours, decorations, prizes. *Class No:* 929(401)

Great Britain

[5781]

Asian directory & who's who international. Sachar, J.S., *comp.* 8th ed. Ilford, Essex, The Asian Observer, 1993. 320p., ports., pbk. £15.95. ISBN: 0905372131. ISSN: 01401076.

First published 1975-76.

Who's who of over 1000 prominent Asians living in UK and also (now) outside UK. Data: birth, marriage, education, arrival date in Britain, position, recreation. Also directory information for organizations involved in race relations, ethnic minority press plus section on Asian history, background, religious groups, festivals, and food. *Class No:* 929(410)

[5782]

British biographical index. Bank, D. *and* Exposito, A., *comps.* London, K.G. Saur, 4v., 1990. xx,2045p. £498. ISBN: 086291390x, set.

1. *A-C.* 08692913918. 2. *D-I.* 0869213926. 3. *J-Q.* 0869213934. 4. *R-Z.* 0869213942. Index to *British biographical archive* which also stands as a biographical dictionary in its own right, listing 170,000 names from 324 biographical reference works published 1601-1929 in a single A-Z sequence. Data: full name; alternative forms of name; dates of birth and death; occupation; sources (original reference work); and exact location in the *Archive* where subject's life is documented. List of sources p.vii-ix in all 4v. Customers who have already purchased the *Archive* automatically receive a copy of this printed index *gratis.* A second index will be published once *British biographical archive Series II* (item 5927) is completed. *Class No:* 929(410)

[5783]

Chambers British biographies the 20th century. Edinburgh, Chambers, 1993. 55p. £10.99. ISBN: 0550160450.

Based on *Chambers biographical dictionary* and *Chambers Scottish biographical dictionary.*

2800 entries including updated information and 295 new entries. *Class No:* 929(410)

[5784]

A Dictionary of Edwardian biography. Edinburgh, Peter Bell, 36v., 1987-.

First published by the Brighton publishers W.T. Pike 1898-1912 in 33 county volumes each of which combined a guide book with an illustrated biographical dictionary. This present series omits the topographical material.

Cheshire 223p. £36.00 ISBN 0946687145; *Dorset* 65p. £20.00. ISBN 0946687005; *Durham* 197p. £25.00. ISBN 0946687061; *Edinburgh and The Lothians* 219p. £25.00. ISBN 0946687102; *Lancashire* 319p. £40.00. ISBN 094668703x; *Leicester & Rutland* 123p. £25.00. ISBN 0946687021; *Liverpool* 183p. £36.00 ISBN 0946687137; *Manchester & Salford* 208p. £36.00 ISBN 0946687129; *Northumberland* 183p. £25.00 ISBN 0946687043; *Sheffield* 139p. £25.00. ISBN 0946687013; *South Wales & Monmouthshire* 155p. £25.00 ISBN 0946687110; *West Riding of Yorkshire* 307p. £40.00 ISBN 0946687080;

....(contd.)

Wiltshire 120p. £25.00 ISBN 0946687056.

Each volume consists on average of about 500 detailed and illustrated biographical sketches of local figures. All are arranged according to such categories as parliamentary, medical, legal, clerical, engineering, landowning and magistracy, business, commerce and insurance, the armed forces, accountants, surveyors, architects, vets & dentists, as well as "art, literature and education". Each volume has been separately indexed.

Master index to whole series and to individual vs. of Pike's New Century Series, 192p. £36.00, ISBN 0946687099. *Class No:* 929(410)

[5785]

The Dictionary of national biography. Oxford, Oxford Univ. Press, 1885-.

1. *The Dictionary of national biography, from the earliest times to 1900.* Edited by Sir Lesley Stephen and Sir Sidney Lee. London, Smith, Elder, 63v., 1885-1900. *First Supplement* in 3v. 1901 for those lives accidentally ommited or who had died after their letter was in print. Using thinner paper the standard edition is now reduced to 22v. incorporating 30,000 lives in 30,500p. retaining the two alphabetical sequences. £795.00. ISBN 0198651015.

2. *The Twentieth Century DNB. The Dictionary of national biography 1901-1911,* edited by Sir Sydney Lee. 1912. 2,088p. £65.00. ISBN 0198652011.

The Dictionary of national biography 1912-1921, edited by H.W.C. Davis and J.R.H. Weaver, 1927. xxvi, 623p. £60.00. ISBN 019865202x.

The Dictionary of National Biography 1922-1930, edited by J.R.H. Weaver, 1937, xiv, 962p. £65.00. ISBN 0198652038.

The Dictionary of National Biography 1931-1940, edited by L.G. Wickham Legg, 1949, xvi, 968p. £65.00. ISBN 0198652046.

The Dictionary of National Biography 1941-1950, edited by L.G. Wickham Legg, and E.T. Williams, 1959. xxi, 1031p. £65.00. ISBN 0198652054.

The Dictionary of National Biography 1951-1960, edited by E.T. Williams and Helen M. Palmer, 1971. xxvi, 1150p. £65.00. ISBN 0198652062.

The Dictionary of National Biography 1961-1970, edited by E.T. Williams and C.S. Nicholls, 1981. 1170p. £65.00. ISBN 0198652070.

The Dictionary of national biography 1971-1980, edited by Lord Blake and C.S. Nicholls, 1986. xix, 1010p. £65.00. ISBN 0198652089. With a cumulative index 1901-1980. 'De mortuis nil nisi bunkum - here was a principle which served the twentieth-century *DNB* for many years. In the latest volume, however, the new chief editor conclusively demonstrates that it has been abandoned' (*English Historical Review,* v.103, no.406, January 1988, p.156-8).

The Dictionary of national biography 1981-1985: with an index covering the years 1901-1985 in one alphabetical series, edited by Lord Blake and C.S. Nicholls, 1990. 608p. £40.00. ISBN 0198652100.

DNB now includes some 35,000 signed entries. Bibliographies are given and the sources of the information are quoted. 'For more than a century it has furnished us with a carefully-written profile of every man or woman who has left a thumb-print on the island story. No other nation can boast a reference work so magisterially exact and yet so hypnotically readable' (*Sunday Times,* 25 March 1990, p.C7).

....(contd.)

Further information: 1. J.L. Kirby's 'The Dictionary of National Biography', *Library Association Record*, v.60, no.6, June 1958, p. 181-91-. 2. A. Bell's Leslie Stephen and DNB', *Times Literary Supplement*, 16 December 1977, p.1478 - 3. R.H. Fritze's 'The Dictionary of National Biography and its early editors and publisher', *Reference Services Review*, v.16, no.4, 1988, p.21-29).
Class No: 929(410)

[5786]

—The Concise dictionary of national biography from earliest times to 1985. Oxford, Oxford Univ. Press, 3v., 1992. 3340p. £125. ISBN: 0198653050.

Details of more than 32,500 men and women who died before 1945 condensed from the 31 volume *DNB* 'Though no substitute for that most readable of all reference books, the Concise DNB is a triumph of compression' (*Times*, 26 Mar 1992, p.5). *Class No:* 929(410)

[5787]

—The Contributor's index to the Dictionary of National Biography 1885-1901. Fenwick, G. Cirencester, Gloucestershire, St. Paul's Bibliographies; Detroit, Omnigraphics, 1989. xli, 413p. index. £50.00. ISBN: 0906795737, UK; 1558888152, US.

Lists 694 contributors and their articles, giving names, dates, *DNB* volume numbers and page references. Unsigned articles are listed separately. *Class No:* 929(410)

[5788]

—Dictionary of national biography. Missing persons. Oxford, Oxford Univ. Press. 1993. 768p. £80. ISBN: 0198652119.

Biographies of 1086 persons who for a variety of reasons were omitted from previous volumes. Compiled from over 100,000 suggestions from the general public and scholars. 12% of entrants in this volume are women compared to 3% in the *DNB* to date. 'This book is not an optional extra; it is an essential part of the main work' (*The Year In Reference 1993*, p.143-5). *Class No:* 929(410)

[5789]

—Dictionary of national biography. Corrections and additions. Boston, G.K. Hall, 1966. iv, 212p.

Cumulated from the *Bulletin of the Institute of Historical Research* covering the year 1923-1963.

1,300 entries, photographically reproduced by offset. A cumulation, A-Z of 'Corrections and additions' to *DNB* appearing in the *Bulletin*, v.1(1923)-36 (1963). A number of corrections and additions are signed; corrections by the staff of the *Bulletin* are in square brackets. The entry 'Sir Robert Howard (1626-1698)' runs to 2½ columns of corrections and additions. An essential supplement to the main work.
Class No: 929(410)

[5790]

—Dictionary of national biography. Errata. London, Smith, Elder & Co., 1904. vi, 300p.

Full use was made of the long list of corrections contributed by W.C. Boulter to *Notes And Queries*.

Issued 'to correct the inevitable misprints and misstatements' found in the substantive work.
Class No: 929(410)

[5791]

—FENWICK, G. Women in the DNB.

According to St. Paul's Bibliographies 'Gillian Fenwick ... is working on *Women in the DNB*. *Class No:* 929(410)

[5792]

—Great Britons Twentieth-century lives. Oxbury, H. Oxford, Oxford University Press, 1985. x, 371p. illus. ISBN: 0192115995.

'Its purpose is to portray the history and character of modern Britain through the lives of those men and women who have left the greatest mark on their time, and to provide a brief, readable, and reliable account of those lives' (*Preface*). 645 entries limited to British subjects who died 1915-1980. Based on information provided by *DNB*. Index of biographies by occupation or sphere of interest p.365-370. *Class No:* 929(410)

[5793]

MILLER, C. Who's really who. 3rd ed. London, Sphere Books, 1987. xiii,337p. ports., pbk. £4.99. ISBN: 0722125402.

First edition published by Blond & Briggs, 1983.

Spotlights 'the 400 or so names that are currently the most gossiped-about in Britain'. The foreword claims 200 new names in this edition (150 according to the back cover) with many old favourites jettisoned. Libraries who see the need to stock this work should therefore not discard earlier editions. Compton Miller's Social Register p.295-337 lists people in 195 different (sometimes contumelious) categories *e.g.* Gracious battleaxes, Mrs. Thatcher's fan club, Flash Arries, Runaway cleavage. The author is senior feature writer on the *Daily Express*. *Class No:* 929(410)

[5794]

PANDE, G.N. and PANDE, G. Indians in Britain - Who's who. 2nd ed. Swansea, Computers and Geotechnics, 1988. 291p. illus., maps. ISBN: 095103801x.

1st ed. 1985.

*c.*400 biographies of business and professional people and academics who 'have achieved a status ... by virtue of which he or she can influence others' published so that the achievements of people of Indian origin can be highlighted. *Class No:* 929(410)

[5795]

People of today. Ellis, P., *ed.* 6th ed. London, Debrett's Peerage, 1993. 80p. +2280p. +[16p.] ISBN: 1870520149.

1st ed. 1988. Previous editions under title of *Debrett's distinguished people of today*. This was a successor to *Debrett's Handbook* the 3rd and last edition of which appeared in 1986.

Over 40,000 entries encompassing top people in business, medicine, publishing, sport, education and academia, art and antiques, politics *etc.* 14% of whom are women (John Major: 18 lines; John Smith: 11 lines; Jeremy John Durham Ashdown: 11 lines). 80 preliminary pages include valuable reference information on The Royal Family and Royal households, Her Majesty's Officers of Arms, general tables of precedence, position of letters after the name, and forms of address of persons of title. Abbreviations include ALA, FLA and FlInfSc. 'Has caused a flap in blue-blood circles because it has seen fit to exclude 400 'superfluous gentry' and instead let in a shower of famous proletarians ... and a shoal of media darlings' (*Sunday Times,* no.8702, 2 June 1991, p.2:5). A detailed look at the selection policy for this edition appears in Geraldine Bedell's 'Bringing the best of the rest to book', *ibid;* 30 September 1990, p.5:2.
Class No: 929(410)

[5796]
Who's who an annual biographical dictionary 1993. 145th ed. London, A & C Black, 1849-. Annual. 63p. + +2093p. £85. ISBN: 0713636637.

Published originally by Bailey Bros, and later by Simpkin, Marshall, Kent, it was in its early days mainly lists of names under various headings, *e.g.* Royal Household, House of Commons, etc, without any individual biographical details. It continued in this style until it was bought by A. & C. Black in 1896. The following year it became *Who's who,* 49th year, 1897 (first year of new issue, edited by Douglas Sladen). Its aim now was 'to include all the most prominent people in the Kingdom, whether their prominence is inherited, or depending upon office, or the result of ability which singles them out from their fellows in occupations open to every educated man and women'. In 1899 the title became *Who's who, 1988, an annual biographical dictionary.* In 1901 it incorporated *Men and women of the time,* adjusted its title and has appeared in this style ever since.

Scope. An authoritative dictionary of contemporary biography, the aim being 'to furnish in as compact a form as possible a series of biographical sketches of eminent living persons of both sexes, in all parts of the civilized world'. The criterion of selection is that of 'personal achievement or prominence, and of a man's or woman's interest to the public at large or to any important section of that public'. Compilation. Initially a questionnaire is sent to a person chosen for inclusion and thereafter a proof of the entry is submitted annually to the biographee for revision. This edition has 29,000 entries (1,000 new): John Major, Neil Kinnock and John Thaw all have 15 lines.
Class No: 929(410)

[5797]
—Who was who ... a companion to Who's who containing the biographies of those who died in the decade... London, A.C. Black, 1929-.
1897-1915. 7th ed., 1987. £40. ISBN 0713626704. *1916-1928.* 5th ed., 1992. £40. 0723601698. *1929-1940.* 2nd ed., 1967. £40. 0713601701. *1941-1950.* 5th ed., 1981. £40. 0713621311. *1951-1960.* 4th ed., 1984. £40. 0713625988. *1961-1970.* 2nd ed., 1979. £40. 0713620080. *1971-1980.* 1981. £40. 0713621761. *1981-1990.* 1992. 845p. 0713633360.

Gives birth and death dates and acts as a key to the appropriate volume. 'The entries are for the most part as they last appeared in Who's who, with the dates of death added and in some cases further additional information to bring them up to date' (*Preface*). *Who was who: a cumulated index 1897-1990.* 1991. 850p. £50. 071363457x.

Who was who. A cumulated index 1897-1990. 1991. 850p. £50. 071363457x. *Class No:* 929(410)

Micromaterials

[5798]
British and Irish biographies 1840-1940. Jones, D.L., *ed.* Cambridge and Alexandria, Virginia, Chadwyck-Healey, 6 parts, 1985-1991. 1400 silver halide microfiche 105mmx148mm, 24xreduction with a cumulated index of names and titles on COM. £30,000 set. £5,500 approx. per part.

Claimed to be the largest British biographical reference work ever compiled, this collection makes available 272 general, professional, and regional biographical dictionaries,

....(contd.)
containing 6½ million entries on 4 million people largely unrepresented in *DNB* or *Who's who.* 1. 382v. on 2218 microfiche with computer output microfiche (COM) index includes 10 general dictionaries: *Burke's handbook to the Most Excellent Order of the British Empire* (1921); *Burke's landed gentry* (1833-1947); *Celebrities of the century* (1890); *Hutchinson women's who's who* (1934); *Ladies who's who 1919-27* (1930); *Men and women of the day (1889-1894); Men of mark 1876-1873* by T. Cooper; *Men of the time 1852-87* continued as *Men and women of the time 1891-1899; People of the period* by A.T. Camden Pratt (1897); and *Women of the day* by F. Hoyt (1885). Plus 14 professional and 31 regional biographical dictionaries. 2. 168v. on 2179 microfiche includes *The biographical quarterly, recording biographical data of noteworthy citizens of the English-speaking countries 1935-36* and *Debrett's Peerage 1900-40* plus 10 professional and 32 regional works. 3. 236v. on 2455 microfiche includes *Debrett's Peerage 1864-1899* and *The Knightage of Great Britain and Ireland 1841* plus 10 professional and 25 regional works. 4. 164v. on *c.*2400 microfiche including *The upper ten thousand: an alphabetical list of all members of noble families, bishops, privy councillors, judges ... 1875-77* continued as *Kelly's handbook to the titled, landed and official classes 1880-1937* continued as *Kelly's handbook of distinguished people 1938-40* plus 10 professional and 21 regional works. 5. Published June 1990. 6. Published June 1991. Many of the works reproduced were originally printed in small editions and access is difficult in any other form.
Class No: 929(410)(003.5)

[5799]
British biographical archive. Baillie, L. *and* Sieveking, P., *eds.* London, K.G. Saur, 1984-1989. 1400x1:24 negative fiches either in Diazo or Silver edition. Diazo £6,000 set or £600 per each of 12 instalments. Silver £6,600 and £660. ISBN: 0862913659, Diazo; 0862913667, Silver.

A single A-Z cumulation of full-text entries from 324 English language biographical reference works originally published 1601-1929 covering every aspect of British biography. *DNB* and *Who was who* are not included. Entries for each individual are arranged together in chronological order. 'British' is interpreted to include inhabitants of colonies born up to a year before independence or home rule and foreign nationals closely associated with Britain. Particularly useful for libraries not holding older standard biographical works. C.A. Toase's 'Micro biography', *Refer,* v.4, no.3, Spring 1987, p.1-5 compares the coverage, arrangement and presentation, and access in the library of *British & Irish biographies 1840-1940* and *British biographical archive*: 'There is hardly any overlap in titles between the two works'. *Class No:* 929(410)(003.5)

[5800]
—The British biographical archive. Series II. Esposito, A., *ed.* London, K.G. Saur, 12 installments, 1991-94. 750 fiche (24x) Silver or Diazo. £6600 (silver); £6000 (diazo).

Continuation of *British Biographical Archive.*

Over 150,000 entries, compiled from 200 biographical sources published 1601-1978, extend the range of occupational groups, increases the sources on women, and includes a greater number of photographic portraits.
Class No: 929(410)(003.25)

Bibliographies

[5801]

HANHAM, H.J. 'Some neglected sources of biographical information: county biographical dictionaries 1890-1937', *Bulletin of the Institute of Historical Research*, v.34, no.89. May 1961, p.55-66.

There are two types of county biographical dictionary, the illustrated volume of local worthies and the county 'Who's who'. Unfortunately the value of all types of such dictionaries is diminished at present by the fact that there is no complete set in existence. The Press-Gaskell series, Pike's New Century series, and county 'Who's who' are briefly described. Appended is a summary of libraries' holdings arranged under English counties A-Z, followed by Wales, Scotland and Ireland. Usually only one major library holding is given per title. *Class No:* 929(410)(01)

[5802]

MATTHEWS, W., *comp.* **British autobiographies:** an annotated bibliography of British autobiographies published or written before 1951. Berkeley, Univ. of California Press, 1955. xiv,376p.

Reprinted Hamden, Conn., Archon Books, 1968.

6,654 very briefly annotated entries for persons 'born in the British Isles' and 'naturalised British subjects'. Arranged A-Z, anonymous works under the first word of the title. Subject and locality index of biographees.

Class No: 929(410)(01)

[5803]

—**MATTHEWS, W.,** *comp.* British diaries: an annotated bibliography of British diaries written between 1442 and 1942. Cambridge, Cambridge Univ. Press, 1950. xxxiv,339p. index.

Diaries arranged chronologically by date of first entry. '... includes diaries written by Englishmen, Scotsmen, Welshmen and Irishmen in the British Isles, in Europe, and on the high seas, and also the diaries of American and other travellers in the British Isles, so far as they have been published in England and in English'. Diaries in manuscript form are recorded with locations. *Class No:* 929(410)(01)

Women

[5804]

BELL, P., *comp.* **Victorian women:** an index to biographies and memoirs. Edinburgh, P. Bell, 1989. [130p.] pbk. ISBN: 1871538017.

2nd of 3 indexes which together will attempt to list all published biographies of British women from the late 18th century to the end of the First World War.

Online A-Z entries (name, status or position, title of biography). Scope: memoirs, autobiographies, journals, diaries, obituaries in book or pamphlet form.

Class No: 929(410)-0055.2

[5805]

CRAWFORD, A., *and others, eds.* **The Europa biographical dictionary of British women:** over 1000 notable women from Britain's past. London, Europa Publications, 1983. Available in North America from G.K. Hall. ix,436p. £27.50; $55.00. ISBN: 0905118774, UK; 0810317893, US.

80 contributors. 'Women whose place in history is recognized' and 'women whose work has had some sort of

....(contd.)

public impact' (*Introduction*). Data: birth and death dates, synopsis of life and career, publications, with additional bibliographical references. *Class No:* 929(410)-0055.2

Scotland

[5806]

BELL, P., *comp.* **Who was who in Edwardian Scotland.** Edinburgh, Peter Bell, 1986. 52 unnumbered pages. sd. ISBN: 0946687080.

Combined index in one A-Z sequence to ten illustrated county biographies published 1896-1912. Single-line entries give names, dates of birth and death, occupation, and reference to original and other biographical volumes. Biographical dictionaries indexed and other reference works cited p.[2-3]. *Class No:* 929(411)

[5807]

A Biographical dictionary of eminent Scotsmen. originally edited by Robert Chambers, New ed. revised under the care of the publishers. With a supplement volume, continuing the biographies to the present time. Thomson, T., *ed.* Edinburgh, Blackie, 5v., 1855.

The original edition (4v.) covered the period up to 1834, but for this edition the stereotypes were revised and reprinted, bringing the information up to 1844. V.5 contains additional entries and is up to 1855. The work contains entries for living persons and dates from the earliest times. *Class No:* 929(411)

[5808]

Chambers Scottish biographical dictionary. Goring, R., *ed.* Edinburgh, Chambers, 1992. xl,468p. index. £25. ISBN: 0550160434.

2400 profiles of 'eminent names from every era and discipline, focussing not just on the well-known, but also on those whose achievement has previously been neglected' (*dustwrapper*). 'Disappointing in its lack of depth and factual information' (*Reference Reviews*, v.7, no.1, 1993, p.42). *Class No:* 929(411)

[5809]

Dictionary of Scottish biography.

In preparation at the University of Stirling. Some 30,000 entries are planned. *Class No:* 929(411)

[5810]

MacGREGOR, F. Famous Scots: the pride of a small nation. Edinburgh, Gordon Wright Publishing, 1984. 328p. ports., index. £9.95. ISBN: 0903065479.

Almost 700 short biographies arranged chronologically within 28 occupation sections. *Class No:* 929(411)

[5811]

Who's who in Scotland. 4th ed. Ayr, Carrick Publishing, 1992. 563p. £24. ISBN: 094672430x.

1st ed. 1986.

5000 entries (4539 in 1st ed.) relating to 'people of achievement and influence from all sections of Scottish society' (Maurice Rifkind 21 lines; Andy Roxburgh 13 lines). Libraries should retain 1st ed. which contains 900 entries deleted from 2nd ed. *Class No:* 929(411)

Ireland

[5812]

BOYLAN, H. Dictionary of Irish biography. 2nd ed. Dublin, Gill & Macmillan; New York, St. Martin's Press, 1988. [xi],420p. bibliog. £30.00; $39.95. ISBN: 0717115747, UK; 0312024975, US.

First published 1978.

About 1300 entries (1100 1st ed.); excludes living persons. Readable accounts of varying length. Bibliography p.413-20. 'This dictionary is very welcome. It has brought into the light many obscure and interesting people as well as the obviously famous' (*British Book News,* 15 January 1979, p.124). *Class No:* 929(415)

[5813]

A Dictionary of Irish biography.

Aidan Duggan's 'A dictionary of Irish biography', *Scholarly Publishing,* v.20,no.1, October 1988,p.39-42 is an account of the 10 year planning towards the launching in 1986 of the Royal Irish Academy's project: 'The Dictionary will contain biographies and assessments of all men and women of note who died on or before 31 December 1989 and who fall into one or other of the following four categories. i Those who were born in Ireland and who in some manner achived a reputation within their native land. ii Those who were born outside Ireland but who came to Ireland and there in some manner achieved an Irish reputation. iii Those who were born in Ireland but who left their native land and in some manner achieved a reputation overseas. iv Those who were neither born in Ireland nor resident in Ireland but who achieved reputations and who clearly liked to think of themselves as essentially Irish. It is hoped that this first volume will be ready for publication in 1992 and that five more volumes will appear at approximately intervals of two to three years'. *Class No:* 929(415)

[5814]

WALLACE, M. Famous Irish lives. 2nd ed. Belfast, Appletree Press, 1991. 96p. pbk. £3.95. ISBN: 0862812755.

First published Newton Abbot, David & Charles, 1983 as *100 Irish Lives.*

Short profiles of the most notable Irish men and women arranged in chronological order of date of birth. Biographies end with things and places to see and suggestions for further reading. Dates in Irish history. *Class No:* 929(415)

[5815]

WEBB, A. Compendium of Irish biography: sketches of distinguished Irishmen and of eminent persons connected with Ireland by office or by their writings. Atlantic Highlands, New Jersey, Humanities Press, 1974. xix,598p.

First published Dublin, Gill, 1878.

Compact sketches of the lives of deceased Irishmen and Irish women. Includes 'those who, though not born in Ireland, took a prominent part in the affairs of the country, or wrote important works respecting it' (*Library of Congress Information bulletin,* v.30,no.37, 16 September 1971). List of 478 authorities consulted. 'Invaluable, never wholly superseded' (Eager, A.R. *A guide to Irish bibliographical material* (1964)). *Class No:* 929(415)

[5816]

Who's who, what's what and where in Ireland. Zimon Publishing Ltd. *and* The Irish Times, *comp.* London, G. Chapman, 1973. vii, 1736p. maps, index.

'Who's who in the Republic of Ireland', p.13-363 (*c.*3,000 entries); 'What's what in the Republic of Ireland' (associations, etc.); 'Where in Ireland' (descriptive gazetteer, p.493-537; more than 350 localities). Section on Northern Ireland, p.539-687. Glossary of Irish words; list of abbreviations; Index of entries in the 'Who's who' section by profession. Subject index. Well printed. 'Remains a useful and convenient compendium' (M.O. Shannon. *Irish Republic.* 1986. Entry 1408). *Class No:* 929(415)

Eire

[5817]

Who's who in Ireland 'the influential 1,000' Cairnduff, M., *comp. and ed.* 2nd ed. Dublin, Hibernian Publishing, 1991. 249p. ports. E£25.50; £22.50. ISBN: 095187280x. ISSN: 07903960.

First published Dun Laoghaire, Vesey Publications, 1984.

Aims 'to shed light on those who play a part in shaping the present and future of the country' (*Foreword*). Data: occupation, education, career. People of tomorrw (*i.e.* under 30) p.239-48. *Class No:* 929(417)

Commonwealth

[5818]

Who's who in the Commonwealth. 2nd ed. Cambridge, International Bibliographical Centre, 1984. xxvi,554p. £52.50. ISBN: 0900332700.

1st ed. 1982.

Upwards of 6000 biographical sketches of living men and women of distinction. Data: place and date of birth, education, career, membership of societies, honours, prizes and awards. *Class No:* 929(41-44)

England

[5819]

BOASE, F. Modern English biography. London, F. Cass, 6v., 1985. £285.00. ISBN: 0714621188.

Originally published Truro, Netherton & Worth, 1892-1921.

A most valuable work, supplementing the *DNB,* particularly for the lesser-known personalities of the 19th century. Each volume contains an analytical index to the entries. About 30,000 short biographical sketches of persons who died between 1851 and 1900. Notes sources of portraits (photographs), lists published works, theatre performances and other facts sometimes omitted in larger works of reference, states the *Times Literary Supplement* leader (no.3,330, 23 December 1965, p.1189-90). Draws on obituaries and notices in *The Times, Illustrated London News* and journals, as well as local newspapers, records, etc., and so has a greater coverage of national and local celebrities who died in the latter part of the 19th century than *DNB* (*qv*). The sub-title of the supplement varies, stating the scope as covering those 'who have died during the years 1851-1900'.

Index to biographies of women in Boase's Modern English Biography, (Edinburgh, Peter Bell, 1986. 30 unnumbered pages, sd. ISBN 0946687072) identifies 1130 women

....(contd.)
entries. Data: birth and death dates and occupation. A number of other subject indexes will be published. *Class No:* 929(420)

Channel Islands
[5820]
LAYZELL, A., *ed.* **Who's who in the Channel Islands 1987.** Jersey, Who's Who in The Channel Islands, 1987. 156p. ports., pbk. £9.95. ISBN: 0951247018.

Biographies listed under individual islands - Jersey; Guernsey; Alderney; Sark; Herm (1); Brecqhou (1); Lihou(1); the other islands (0). *Class No:* 929(423.4)

[5821]
MARR, L.J. Guernsey people. Chichester, Sussex, Phillimore, 1984. xix,245p. index. ISBN: 0850335299.

Sequel to author's *A history of the Bailiwick of Guernsey*. 200 short biographies. Pt.1: Biographical dictionary (p.1-174) with Appendix on Second world War (p.175-8) - 2. Anecdotal jottings (p.181-203) - 3. Family trees (p.206-14) - 4. Early Bailiwick names (p.219-35). *Class No:* 929(423.4)

Wales
[5822]
The Dictionary of Welsh biography down to 1940. London, Honourable Society of Cymmrodorion, 1959. lx,1157p.

Based on the Welsh ed. of 1953.

3,500 signed articles, covering all periods and walks of life. For inclusion the biographee or at least one parent had to be born in Wales. 'The intervening years have enabled the editors to make many corrections' (*Preface*). Appendix of additional biographies. *Class No:* 929(429)

[5823]
EVANS, G. Welsh nation builders. Llandysul, Dyfed, Gomer Press, 1988. 356p. ports. ISBN: 0863834175.

65 biographical essays on 'people who have contributed to building the Welsh nation' (*Preface*), arranged chronologically, from Caradog (fl.30-50 AD) to Saunders Lewis (1893-1985). *Class No:* 929(429)

Germany
[5824]
Allgemeine deutsche Biographie; hrsg. durch die Historische Kommission bei der Königliche Akademie der Wissenschaften. Leipzig, Dunkler & Humblot, 56v., 1875-1912.

1-45: A-Z. 45-55. Nachträge bis 1899, ANDR-Z (A-AD, in v.45). 56: General index to the whole work. The standard German biographical dictionary. Lengthy, authoritative signed articles (about 23,600 in all) containing bibliographies. Includes persons who died before 1899. *Neue deutsche Biographie (qv)* is largely based on this work. *Class No:* 929(430)

[5825]
—Neue deutsche biographie. Hrsg. von der Historischen Kommission bei der Bayerischen Akademie der Wissenschaften. Berlin, Dunker & Humblot, 1953-. v.1-. ISBN: 3428001818, complete set.

Largely based on *Allgemeine deutsche Biographie* (1875-1912) (*qv*).

....(contd.)
v.1-15 (1953-1987): A-Maltzan. Includes all who have had an influence on German history and culture. Signed entries with bibliographies and details of portraits. *Class No:* 929(430)

[5826]
BARTOS-HÖPPNER, B. *and* **BARTOS, B. ...lebt der gross Name noch:** 100 porträts aus Deutschlands Geschichte, Kultur, Politik und Forschung. Wien, Uebrreuter, 1987. 215p. illus., ports. ISBN: 3800014343.

Brief biographies arranged in chronological order of birth date. *Class No:* 929(430)

[5827]
Wer ist wer? Das Deutsche who's who/The German who's who/Le Who's who allemand. Habel, W., *ed.* 31st ed. Lübeck, Schmidt Römhild, 1992. xxxii,1616p. ports. ISBN: 3795020123.

1st ed. *Wer ist's?* 1908. 10th ed. *Degener's wer ist's?* 1938.

About 45000 biographies, of varying length, 2000 included for the first time, with 200 ports. Obituaries since last edition. Government directory p.xxv-xxxii.

Class No: 929(430)

[5828]
Who's who in Germany: a biographical encyclopaedia of Sutter's International Red Series containing about 12,000 biographies of top-ranking personalities in the fields of business, politics, science, the arts, and entertainment. Dove, J.C., *ed.* Essen, Who's Who International Red Series Verlag, 2v., 1992. 3300p. map. $260. ISBN: 3921220653.

First published 1955.

1992 ed. includes for the first time biographies and institutional surveys of reunified Germany. 14000 biographies (3000 new to this ed.) Appendix outlines various aspects of German life and up-to-date statistics of leading enterprises. *Class No:* 929(430)

Micromaterials
[5829]
Deutsches Biographisches archiv. Fabian, B., *ed.* München, K.G. Saur Verlag, 1982-1984. 1447 x 1.24 negative microfiches (by 10 instalments) either in Diazo or Silver film. Diazo £5215.00; $7560. Silver £5740. $8320. ISBN: 3598304102, Diazo; 3598304218, Silver.

A cumulation of 264 German language biographical dictionaries published 1700-1910. Entries number 480,000 covering 280,000 individuals in a single A-Z sequence. A complete listing of the reference works used to compile the *Archiv* is available on request. *Class No:* 929(430)(003.5)

[5830]
—Deutscher Biographischer Index. Gorzny, W., *ed.* München, K.G. Saur Verlag, 4v. 1983-86. xxvi, 2298p. £360.00; $600.00. Free of charge to subscribers of *Deutsches bibliographisches archiv.* ISBN: 3598304323, set.

Printed index to *Deutsches bibliographisches Archiv.* Entries give dates of birth and death, occupation or profession, and location of articles in the *Archiv*. Notes on use (in German and English) p.ix-xi. List of sources (Ger. and Eng.) p.xiii-xxvi. 'The usefulness of the *Index* in drawing together a wide range of information not readily available elsewhere is counterbalanced by the difficulty of using it effectively without the *Archiv*' (*Reference Reviews,*

.... *(contd.)*
v.1, no.2, June 1987, p.77).

Deutscher biographischer index. Neue folge, 7v., 1994.
£1600. 359832486 is a detailed index to *Deutsches
biographisches Archiv. Neue Folge.* Data: basic biographical
information listing sources and fiche reference numbers.
Also a comprehensive biographical dictionary in its own
right. *Class No:* 929(430)(003.5)

[5831]
—Deutsches Biographisches archiv. neue folge bis zur mitte
des 20. Jahrhunderts. [German biographical archive new
sequel up to the mid-20th century.] Gorzny, W., *ed.*
London, Bowker-Saur, 1989-. 1300 fiche in 12 instalments.
£7660. Silver; £6899. Diazo. ISBN: 3598328206, Silver;
3598328346, Diazo.

Entries for c.280,000 individuals from the late 19th
century to the first half of the 20th century collated from 260
biographical dictionaries into one A-Z sequence. Access will
be through the *Deutscher biographischer index* 4v. edition
expanded and revised to include the new material.
Class No: 929(430)(003.5)

Awards & Prizes

[5832]
Deutsche Nobelpreisträger Deutsch Beiträge zur Natur-und
Geistenwissenschaft, dargestellt am Beispiel der
Nobelpreisverleihungen für Frieden, Literatur, Medizin,
Physik und Chemie. Hermann, A., *ed.* München, Verlag
Moos & Partner, 1986. 18p. col.illus., ports., bibliog.,
index. ISBN: 3891640226.

Table of prizewinners in each category p.10-11, 13-15.
Bibliography of prizewinners' writings p.175-182.
Class No: 929(430)(079.2)

German Democratic Republic

[5833]
Namen und daten wichtiger Personen der DDR.
Buch, G., *ed.* 3rd ed. Berlin (West) and Bonn, Verlag
J.H.W. Dietz, 1982. 384p.

1st ed. 1973.

'An invaluable reference book which provides basic facts
on over 2,000 leading figures on GDR life. No comparable
book is published in GDR' (J. Wallace. *East Germany,*
1987. Entry 703). *Class No:* 929(430.2)

Luxembourg

[5834]
MERSCH, J. Biographie nationale du pays de Luxembourg
depuis ses origines jusqu' à nos jours. Luxembourg,
Imprimerie de la Cour Victor Buck, 1947-. fasc. 1-. illus.,
ports., indexes.

fasc. 1-22 (v.1-11). 1947-75. Not arranged A-Z; a series
of lengthy and scholarly contributions on promiment
persons, famous families, etc. Thus, fasc. 9 (1958-60.
280p.) includes 'Les rois du Pays-Bas, grand ducs de
Luxembourg', by Jules Mersch (p.30-280). Footnote
references; quotations from primary sources.
Class No: 929(435.9)

Austria

[5835]
**Neue Österreichische biographie ab 1815. Grosse
Österreicher.** Wien, Amalthea-Verlag, 1923-.

Title has varied: v.1-8 (1923-1935) *Neue Österreichische
biographie 1815-1918*; v.9 (1956) *Neue Österreichische
biographie ab 1815*; v.10 (1956-) *Neue Österreichische
biographie ab 1815 Grosse Österreichischer.* Reprint
volumes 1923-1935 carry the latest version of the title.

18-20 lengthy signed and documented articles (not A-Z) on
19th and 20th century Austrians. Volume indexes, v.8- Band
1. 1977. 3850020754. Band 20. 1979. 3850021068. Band
21. 1982. 3850021572. Band 22. 1982. 3850022536. 18
essays with portraits. Index of biographees v.1-22 in single
A-Z sequence p.167-175. *Class No:* 929(436)

[5836]
Österreiches biographisches Lexikon 1815-1950. Hrsg von
der Österreichischen Akademie der Wissenschaften.
Redigiert von Eva Obermayer-Marnarch. Graz-Köln-Wien,
Böhlaus (v.1-5), Wien, Verlag Österreichischen Akademie
der Wissenschaften (v.6-.).

V.1-9 (1957-1988) A-Savić Žarko. 1988. xxix,448p.
3700114834. Bibliographischer abschnitt p.xix-xxix.
Lieferung 46. *Savinšek-Schou.* 1990. 370011687x.

Each volume contains c.2000 biographies, giving fairly
concise biographical data, with bibliographies. Covers
personalities of the Austro-Hungarian Empire which was
dissolved in 1918. The entry for Count Julius Andrassy runs
to 1½ columns, including bibliography (works by 2½ lines;
material on 10½ lines, including a reference to *Neue
deutsche Biogaphie*). Frequently cited works are listed p.xxi-
xxix.

To some extent continues C. von Wurzbach's
Biographisches Lexikon des Kaiserthums Oesterreich
(Vienna, Zamarski, 60v. 1865-91.) which goes forward
from 1750. *Class No:* 929(436)

[5837]
Who's who in Austria 1982-1983: a biographical
encyclopedia of the international red series containing some
5,500 biographies of prominent living personalities in
Austria. Strute, K. *and* Doelken, T., *eds.* 10th ed. Wörthsee
bei München, Who's Who the International Red Series
Verlag, 1982. xii, 1224p. £66.75. ISBN: 3921220440.
ISSN: 05118913.

First published 1954.

An extensive appendix gives up-to-date information on
political, artistic, intellectual, economic and social life and
internationally renowned enterprises. *Class No:* 929(436)

[5838]
**WURZBACH, c. von. Biographisches Lexicon des
Kaiserthums Osterreich:** enthaltened die Lebensskizzen der
denkwirdigen Personen, welche seit 1750 in den
Österreichischen Kronländern geboren wurden oder darin
gelebt und gewirkt haben. Wien, C. Zamarski, 60v., 1856-
91.

Over 24,000 biographies (with bibliographies) of eminent
persons of the Austro-Hungarian Empire. Standard work of
immense value. *Class No:* 929(436)

Czechoslovakia

Micromaterials

[5839]

Česky biografický archiv a Slovenský biografický archiv. München, K.G. Saur, 12 installments, 1993-. 550 fiches (24x) Silver or Diazzo. £7957. (silver); £7294. (diazzo). ISBN: 3598334311, silver; 3598334303, diazzo.

A single A-Z sequence cumulation of entries for those who influenced the history and culture of the lands now designated the Czech Republic and Slovakia taken from 210 German, Hungarian, Czech, and Slovak language biographical reference works published from 1559 to the mid-20th century. On completion a printed index will be published. *Class No:* 929(437)(003.5)

Slovakia

[5840]

Slovenský biografickík (od roku 833 do roku 1990). [Slovak biographical dictionary.] Zväzok, I., *ed.* Matica Slovenská, Martin, 1986-.

a *A-D*. 1986. 538p. 2. *E-J*. 1987. 587p. 3. *K-L*. 1989. 445p. ISBN 8070900199. 4. *M-Q*. 1990. 562p. 8070900709. When complete will include 15,000 biographical sketches of leading personalities from the time of the Great Moravian Empire to the present. Data: date and place of birth and death; biography (education, occupation, activities); list of published works; books about; monuments. Introduction in Slovak, Russian, English and German.

Class No: 929(437.6)

Hungary

[5841]

FEKETE, M., *ed.* **Prominent Hungarians, home and abroad.** 5th ed. Budapest, HVG Publishing House, 1991. 506p. pbk. ISBN: 9637525025.

Editor regrets that many new government appointments and office holders are held over to the next edition. Information on entrants is sparse. *Class No:* 929(439)

France

[5842]

Dictionnaire de biographie française. Paris, Librarie Letouzey et Ané, 1929-. v.1-. ISBN: 2706301589, complete work.

V.1-16 (1929-1985); A-Guéroult: fasc:97-104 (1986-1990). Lengthy, authoritative, signed articles with good bibliographies and/or sources used. Includes outstanding Frenchmen and women from Metropolitan France and dependent territories, from the earliest times; also foreigners who have played an important part in the life of France. Excludes living persons. *DNB* was one of the models on which the work is based. *Class No:* 929(44)

[5843]

Who's who in France Qui est qui en France Dictionnaire biographique de personalités françaises vivant en France, dans les territoires d'Outre-mer où à l'étranger et de personalités étrangères résident en France 1991-1992. 23rd ed. Paris, Éditions Jacques Lafitte, 1991. 1708p. col. illus. ISSN: 00839531.

First published 1953.

Pt.1 Les Grands Institutions. Souverains et chefs d'État

....(contd.)

depuis l'an 751. Présidents de la République ... Decorations officielles françaises . Régions, départments et villes de France - 2. Le Who's Who des Enterprises - 3. Notices biographiques (p.119-1664) - 4. Vie pratique *i.e.* 9 essays on such topics as Tourisme et voyages, Guide des vins, Guide des médias. *Class No:* 929(44)

Micromaterials

[5844]

Archives biographiques Françaises. Bradley, S., *ed.* Paris, K. G. Saur Editeur S.A.R.L. 1200 fiche (in 12 instalments) either in Diazo or Silver. Prices are volatile, tentative listing is Diazo £6,500, $11,000, Silver £6,900; $11,700. ISBN: 0862914531, Silver; 086291440x, Diazo.

A compilation of 180 original biographical reference works, 18th to 20th century, edited into a single A-Z sequence and providing approximately 150,000 individual lives from the earliest period of French history. Covers Francophone Canada, Switzerland, and French colonies. *Class No:* 929(44)(003.5)

[5845]

—Archives biographiques Françaises. Deuxième Série. München, K.G. Saur, 12 installments, 1993-. 650 fiches (24x) Silver or Diazo. £11,225 (Silver; £10,295 (Diazo) ISBN: 3598335695, Silver; 3598335563, Diazo.

Announced for publication. *Class No:* 929(44)(003.5)

[5846]

—Index biographiqe Français. Dwyer, H., *ed.* K.G. Saur, 4v., 1993. 2400p. £498 (free to subscribers to *Archives biographiques Françaises*). ISBN: 0869218014.

Detailed printed index to *Archives biographiques Françaises*. Data: basic biographical information, listing of biographical citations, and fiche reference numbers. Also a comprehensive biographical dictionary in its own right. *Class No:* 929(44)(003.5)

Italy

[5847]

Dizionario biografico degli Italiani. Roma, Istituto della Enciclopedia Italiana fondata da Giovanni Treccani, 1960-.

V.1-41 (1960-1992). *A-Dugnani. Index v.1-10.* The Italian equivalent to *DNB* but includes living persons. V.32 has 200 contributors and contains long signed articles (*e.g.* Gabriele D'Annunzio has 58 columns of text with 1 col. of bibliography). 'Some exceptional long articles, packed with the results of first-hand research, on comparatively minor characters' (*Times Literary Supplement,* no.3077, 17 February 1961, p.102). *Class No:* 929(450)

[5848]

Who's who in Italy 1992 a biographical encyclopaedia of Sutters international red series containing some 11000 biographies of top-ranking personalities in the fields of business, politics, science, the arts, and entertainment. Milano, Who's who in Italy. 2v., 1992. xx,2272p. map. ISBN: 8885246168. ISSN: 05119006.

First published 1957-1958.

Biographies; Survey of Italy; Sections on political, econommic, cultural, social and religious life (p.1931-2685). Register of company, organization and institution profiles. Over 2000 new entries in this edition. *Class No:* 929(450)

Micromaterials

[5849]

Archivo biografico Italiano. Nappo, T. *and* Furlani, S., *eds.* München, K.G. Saur, 1988-1989. 1400 fiche (24x) by 12 instalments in Silver or Diazo fiche. Silver £8100; Diazo £7290. ISBN: 3598315201, silver; 3598315406, diazo.

Over 200,000 full-text entries, cumulated from 321 Italian-language biographical reference works 1646-1931, in a single A-Z sequence, cover individuals from early Roman times to the 20th century. Coverage extends to the former kingdoms and duchies of Italy, Dalmatia, and Malta.
Class No: 929(450)(003.5)

[5850]

—Archivo biografico Italiano, nuova serie. Nappo, T. *and* Furlani, S., *eds.* München, K.G. Saur, 12 installments, 1992-94. 800 fiches (24x) Silver or Diazo. £9060. (silver); £8320 (diazo). ISBN: 3598331541, Silver; 3598331401, Diazo.

180,000 entries cumulated from 124 Italian language biographical dictionaries. Overlaps with original volume in respect of 19th century material but mainly consists of 20th century biographical source material.
Class No: 929(450)(003.5)

[5851]

—Indico biografico Italiano. München, K.G. Saur, 4v., 1992. 2400p. £810 (free to subscribers of *Archivo biografico Italiano*). ISBN: 35983155504.

Detailed printed index to Archivo biografico Italiano. Data: basic biographical information, listing of biographical citations, and fiche reference numbers. Also a comprehensive biographical dictionary in its own right.
Class No: 929(460)(003.5)

Spain

[5852]

Quien es quien en España 1992. Madrid, Editorial Jose Luis Campillo Alonse, 1992. 1417p. ISBN: 8460426831.

Government and administrative directory p.7-534. Career profiles of prominent persons p.535-1413.
Class No: 929(460)

[5853]

Who's who in Spain. Madrid(?) Who's who in Spain, 1992. 1950p. ISBN: 8885246141.

7500 biographies (1500 new to this edition) of prominent persons in politics, finance, culture, and art. Also information on companies, organizations and institutions.
Class No: 929(460)

Micromaterials

[5854]

Archivo biográfico de España, Portugal e Iberoamérica. Mediavilla, V.H. *and* Nayle, R.A., *eds.* München, K.G. Saur Verlag, 1986-1989. 1500 microfiche (24x in 12 instalments either in Silver or Diazo fiche. Silver edition: £7,950.00. $8,320.00. Diazo: £7,250.00. $7560.00. ISBN: 3598320450, Silver; 3598320302, Diazo.

Single A-Z cumulation of full text entries from 300 biographical reference works published between the 17th and 20th centuries covering the cultural, social, and political history of the Iberian Peninsula and Latin America. *Indice biográfico de España Portugal e Iberoamérica.* 4v., 1990. £325.00. ISBN 3598320604 is a printed index to the *Archivo*

....(contd.)
and also a stand-alone biographical work in its own right. Data: date of birth and death, profession and occupation, office, country and place of origin. Source code and fiche/frame are access points to the main work.
Class No: 929(460)(003.5)

[5855]

—Archivo biográfico de España, Portugal e Iberoamérica. Nueve serie. München, K.G. Saur, 12 installments, 1991-93. 1150 fiches (24x) Silver or Diazzo. £8760 (silver; £8030 (diazzo). ISBN: 3598329644, Silver; 3598329776, diazzo.

180,000 entries cumulated from 333 Spanish and Portuguese language reference works, partly supplementary on persons previously entered in the main work, but including thousands of new entries for personalities from the first half of the 20th century. *Class No:* 929(460)(003.5)

[5856]

—Indice biográfico de España, Portugal e Iberoamérica. Mediavilla, V.H. *and* Nayle, R.A., *eds.* München, K.G. Saur, 4v., 1991. 2400p. £325 *free to subscribers to the *Archivo biográfico*). ISBN: 3598320604.

Detailed printed index to *Archivo biográfico de España, Portugal e Iberoamérica.* Data: basic biographical information, listing of biographical citations, and fiche reference numbers. Also a comprehensive biographical dictionary in its own right. Explanatory notes are in Spanish, Portuguese, English and German.
Class No: 929(460)(003.5)

Portugal

[5857]

O Grande livro dos Portugueses 4000 personalidades em texto e imagem. Nomes, datas, factos com 980 Ilustrações. Lisboa (?), Círculo de Leitores, 1991. 518p. illus. (some col.), ports. (some col.). ISBN: 9724201430.

Brief biographical profiles of celebrated Portuguese men and women from all periods of history. *Class No:* 929(469)

USSR

[5858]

DE BOER, S.P., *and others.* **Biographical dictionary of dissidents in the Soviet Union,** 1956-1985. The Hague, Martinus Nijhoff Publishers, 1982. xviii,679p. bibliog., tables. $165.00. ISBN: 9024725380.

3400 biographies of varying length (Andrej Sakharov, 5 pages; Aleksandr Solženicyn, 3 pages). Glossary p.657-665. Bibliography p.667-679. Comparative table of major articles concerning political offences in the criminal codes of the Union republics and the texts of such articles in the RSFSR Criminal Code p.651-655. Supplementary volumes are a possibility. *Class No:* 929(47)

[5859]

VRONSKAYA, J. *and* **CHUGUEV, V.** **A Biographical dictionary of the former Soviet Union:** *prominent people in all fields from 1917 to the present.* 2nd ed. London, K.G. Saur, 1992. 643p. ports. maps on endpapers, index. £149; $275. ISBN: 0862916216.

First published as *A Biographical dictionary of the Soviet Union* (1989).

Information on more than 7500 personalities (including 200 new to this ed.). Includes 'people who emigrated, defected or moved for any other reason, and even those who

....(contd.)

were born abroad of Russian parentage or their activity involved them closely in Russian life' (*Author's note*). Index by occupations (40 categories) p.495-525. Heavy cultural bias. 'Many kinds of library should find the dictionary well worth the money' (*Reference Reviews*, v.3,no.3, September 1989,p.141). *Class No:* 929(47)

[5860]

Who was who in the Soviet Union: a biographical dictionary of more than 6,400 leading officials from the Central Apparatus and the Republics to 1991. Schulz-Torge, U-J., ed. München, K.G. Saur, 1992. li,412p. £200. ISBN: 3598108109.

Based on 3v. looseleaf *Die Führung der USSR in Partei, Staat, KGB und Militar.*

Career profiles organized according to the Soviet Union's administrative structure: 1. Communist Party - 2. Union Republics - 3. Central government - 4. KGB - 5. The Military. 'Most people included were obscure and minor and it seems unlikely their details would have been much use even when the USSR existed' (*Library Association Record*, v.94, no.11, November 1992, p.736). *Class No:* 929(47)

[5861]

Who's who in the Soviet Union today. Schulz-Torge, U-J. München, K.G. Saur, 2v., 1989-91. 800p. £249.00 (set). £135.00 for each volume. $375.00. ISBN: 3598108108, set; 3598108117, v.1; 3598108125, v.2.

V.1 *Chronological survey of leading officials in the party, the State, the KGB and the armed forces.* V.2 *Biographical entries for 2000 personalities.* Data: full name, nationality, distinctions, party career. Identifies the key political and military figures. *Class No:* 929(47)

Micromaterials

[5862]

Public figures in the Soviet Union: a current biographical index 1984-1987. Bi-annual updates: 1988. Cambridge and Alexandria, Virginia, Chadwyck-Healey in association Radio Free Europe - Radio Liberty Inc. 105x148mm diazo negative reading microfiche at a reduction of 48x. Base file £325. Bi-annual updates £95.

Index commences January 1984 and is updated daily.

A continuously updated cumulated index containing 150,000 entries on 100,000 people in the public eye in the Soviet Union compiled by Radio Liberty published on computer output microfiche (COM) in a storage binder with printed instructions. Entries (in Russian) give surname and patronymic, title, position, organization, place of work, source and notes. Sources include *Pravda, Izvestia,* regional newspapers, party congresses, *etc.* Retrospective material before 1984 is being added selectively to some entries. *Class No:* 929(47)(003.5)

[5863]

The Soviet biographic archive 1954-1985. Cambridge and Alexandria, Virginia, Chadwyck-Healey in association with Radio Free Europe and the Hoover Institution. 2812 silver halide microfiche at 24x reduction. £8000.

Material is added to the Archive at the rate of 100+ items per diem. Annual supplements are expected.

Includes entries for more than 50,000 party and state officials, members of the security organizations, Komsomol personnel, the armed forces, artists, scientists, journalists within the Soviet Union and prominent personalities outside

....(contd.)

the U.S.S.R. but closely involved in Soviet affairs. Compiled from clippings from 35+ newspapers and magazines published centrally or in the constituent republics, Soviet biographical handbooks, international news agencies maintained by Radio Free Europe - Radio Liberty Inc. supplemented by abstracts from biographical works. Clippings and abstracts are arranged in a single Russian alphabet sequence. Intended for government and international organizations, scientific and academic institutions, the mass media of communications, and individual researchers, the Archive is undoubtedly the largest and most easily accessible source of biographical information on Soviet personalities in political and public life in the most recent period. *Class No:* 929(47)(003.5)

RSFSR

[5864]

Who's who in Russia and the new states. Geron, LO. *and* Pravda, A., *eds.* 2nd ed. London I.B. Tauris, 1993. 672p. £95. ISBN: 1850434875.

First published as *The Tauris Soviet Directory the elite of the USSR today* (1989).

Part 1 lists the States alphabetically, with the names of ministries and the addresses of the parliamentary buildings, the state committees and other national bodies, as well as the holders of the most important offices. Part 2 has 4000 career profiles of leading figures in all areas of public life. Data: career history, publications, honours and awards, and personal details.

Covers Armenia, Azerbaijan, Belarus, Estonia, Georgia, Kazakhstan, Kyrgyzstan, Latvia, Lithuania, Moldova, Russian Federation, Tajikistan, Turkmenistan, Ukraine, and Uzbekistan. *Class No:* 929(470)

Poland

[5865]

Polski slownik biograficzny. Cracow, Polska Akademia Nauk, Instytut Historii, 1935-. v.1-. ISBN: 8304001489.

V.1-33 (1935-1992) A-Rzaśniki-Sangusko. Zeszyt 140-142. (1992-1993). The definitive dictionary of Polish biography. V.1-v.7 (A-Frankowski) were published 1935-48 and publication was resumed in 1958. Scholarly, signed articles covering Poles of all historical periods and foreigners who have played an important part in Polish affairs. Articles include references to source material. *Class No:* 929(475)

[5866]

Who's who in Poland a biographical directory comprising about 4000 entries on leading personalities in Poland and information on major state, political, diplomatic, scientific and artistic institutions and organizations. Interpress Publications Warsaw, *ed.* Zurich, Who's Who the International Red Series, 1982. xi,1107p. DM240. £55.00. ISBN: 3921220564.

Following the 4000 biographies is a directory section (p.1058-1107) on *c.*800 institutions. 'A useful if expensive volume' (*International Affairs* v.59,no.3, Summer 1983, p.558-9). *Kto jest kim w Polsce: informator biograficzny* (Warszawa, Wyndawnictwo Interpress, 1984, 1175p. 8322320736) is a translation. *Class No:* 929(475)

[5867]

WISNIEWSKI, J. Who's who in Poland. Toronto, Professional Translators and Publishers, 1981. [iv]239p. £47.00. ISBN: 0919583008.

Exiguous biographies p.1-199. 7 chapters follow: 1. Ruling political parties - 2. Organs of state - 3. Unions, societies and associations - 4. Local government - 5. Church - 6. Trade Unions - 7. Opposition. *Class No:* 929(475)

Micromaterials

[5868]

Polskie archiwum biograficzne. München, K.G. Saur, 12 installments, 1992-95. 550 fiches (24x) Silver or Diazzo. £7294. (silver); £6631. (diazzo). ISBN: 3598327012, silver; 3598327005, diazzo.

A single A-Z sequence cumulation of biographical entries for people who lived and worked within the borders of the Polish state at any time during its history taken from 180 Polish, Russian, German, French, English and Latin language biographical reference works published from the 17th century to 1945. On completion a printed index will be produced. *Class No:* 929(475)(003.5)

Scandinavia

[5869]

Who's who in Scandinavia: a biographical encyclopedia of the international red series containing some 13,000 biographies of living prominent personalities in Denmark, Finland, Iceland, Norway and Sweden. Strute, K. *and* Doelken, T., *eds.* Zurich, Who's who International Red Series, 2v., 1983. viii,614p.+615-1186p. £80.00. ISBN: 3921220262.

'An extensive appendix gives up-to-date information on political, artistic, intellectual, economic and social life and internationally renown (*sic*) enterprises' (*Title page*). *Class No:* 929(48)

Micromaterials

[5870]

Scandinavian biographical archive. Metherell, D., *and others, eds.* London, K.G. Saur, 12 installments, 1989-91 . 828 fiches (24x) Silver or Diazo. £6600 (Silver); £6000 (diazo) ISBN: 0862918146, Silver; 086291809x, Diazo.

Part A. *Denmark. Norway. Iceland.* 383 fiches. £3600 or £3400 (silver or diazo) 0862918421 or 086291843x.

Part B., *Sweden. Finland.* 445 fiches. £3600 or £3400 (silver of diazo) 0862918448 or 0862918456.

150,000 entries in a single A-Z sequence, compiled from 360 biographical reference works, related to people who lived fromn the 8th to the early 20th century. Also includes persons in colonial territories and emigrants worldwide. *Class No:* 929(48)(003.5)

[5871]

—Scandinavian biographical index. London, K.G. Saur, 4v., 1994. £498 (free to subscribers to *Scandinavian biographical archive*) ISBN: 0862918294.

Detailed printed index to Scandinavian biographical archive. Data: basic biographical information, listing of biographical citations, and fiche reference numbers. A comprehensive biographical dictionary in itw own right. *Class No:* 929(48)

Finland

[5872]

Kuka kukin on (aikalaiskirja)/Who's who in Finland. Henkilötietoja nykypolven suomalaisista 1990. 15th ed. Helsinglssä, Kustannusosakeyhtiö Otava, 1990. 1216p. ISBN: 9511084453.

First published 1909; previous edition 1986.

About 4230 entries (750 new to this edition), more detailed than the normal Who's who. Obituary p.1106-1134. In Finnish only but 'English equivalents of some common signs, words and abbreviations used in this book' p.10-11. *Class No:* 929(480)

[5873]

—Kuka kukin oli/Who was who in Finland. Henkilötietoja 1900 - luvulla kuolleista julkisuuden suomalaista. Helsingissä, Kustannusosakeyhtiö Otava, 1961. 543p.

2614 biographies of prominent people who died 1900-1961. *Class No:* 929(480)

[5874]

Vem och vad? biografisk handbok 1992. Ekberg, H., *ed.* Esbo, Holger Schildts Förlag. 572p. ISBN: 9115004950.

First published 1920.

2646 career profiles in a Finnish Who's who in Swedish. Also includes an Obituary. *Class No:* 929(480)

Norway

[5875]

Hvem er hvem 1984. 13th ed. Oslo, Kunnskapsforlaget Aschehoug - Gyldenal, 1984. 626p. ISBN: 8257301868.

First published 1912; 12th ed. 1979. Now published intermittently every 4 or 5 years.

4300 biographies with Obituary p.618-626. Holders of awards and distinctions p.610-617. *Class No:* 929(481)

[5876]

Norge biografisk leksikon. Oslo, H. Aschehoug, 19v., 1923-1983.

Biographical portraits of Norwegians - living and dead - from the earliest times with extensive bibliographical references. A useful feature is the provision of outline family trees when several members of a family have articles devoted to them. *Class No:* 929(481)

Sweden

[5877]

Svenskt biografiskt lexikon. Stockholm, Bonnier (v.1-15); Norstedt & Söner (v.16-19); Norstedt Tryckeri (v.20-.), 1918, v.1-.

v.1-25 (1918-1987): A- Munck; Fasc 136-137to Olsson (1989-1993). Includes prominent Swedish men and women from the earliest times and also those associated with the country over a long period. V.1-10 included living persons but these were excluded from v.11 onwards. Signed, well documented articles, some written by the editorial staff, others by independent experts. The work is under the supervision of Personhistoriska Instituet. *Class No:* 929(485)

[5878]
Vem ärdet: Svensk biografisk handbok 1993. Uddling, H. *and* Paabo, K., *eds.* Stockholm, Norstedt's Förlag, 1992. 1256p. ISBN: 911914072x. ISSN: 03473341.

1st ed. 1912.

The Swedish 'Who's who' containing about 10,000 short factual biographies. Heavy abbreviated entries. Obituary 1989-1990. *Class No:* 929(485)

Denmark
[5879]
Dansk biografisk leksikon. Engelstoft, P. *and* Dahl, S., *eds.* 3rd ed. København, Gyldensal, 16v., 1979-1984. ISBN: 8700055514.

1st ed. 19v. 1887-1905. 2nd ed. 26v. 1933-1934.

Lengthy signed articles with bibliographies. 'Hans Christian Andersen' v.1, p.173-81, including 2 columns of bibliography. Each volume has list of contributors and subject index of biographees. V.16 (1984) includes Supplement p.249-351. *Class No:* 929(489)

[5880]
Kraks blå bog 1993: 8288 biografier over nulevende danske, faerø og grønlandske maend og kvinder. København, Krak, 1993. 1323p. ISBN: 8772254432. ISSN: 09001476.

First published 1910.

Entries include a list of publications where appropriate. Obituaries since previous edition.

Kraks Blå Bog Register over 15229 personer der er biograferet; Kraks Blå Bog 1910-1988. 138p. is an index volume. *Class No:* 929(489)

Iceland
[5881]
Íslenzkir samtídarmenn. [Icelandic contemporaries.] Gudnason, J. *and* Haraldsson, P., *eds.* Reykjavík, Bókaútgáfan Samtídarmenn, 2v., 1965-7.

Who's who of 5000 contemporary Icelanders. *Class No:* 929(491.1)

[5882]
OLASON, P.E. Islenzkar aeviskrár: frá landnámistímum Arsloka 1940. Reykyavík, Birt A Kostnad Hins Islenzka Bókmenntafélags, 6v., 1948-76.

*c.*10,000 biographies of eminent Icelanders from the times of the earliest settlements. *Class No:* 929(491.1)

Netherlands
[5883]
Biographisch woordenboek der Nederlanden bevaltende levensbeschrijvingen van zoodanige personen, die zich op eenigerlei wijze in ons vaderland, hebben vermaard gemaakt. Aa, A.J. van der. Haarlem, Brederode, 12v., 1852-78.

Reprinted Amsterdam,. B.M. Israel, 1972.

14,000 bio-bibliographies. Claimed to be the only available bio-bibliographical dictionary of the Netherlands. *Class No:* 929(492)

[5884]
—Biografisch woordenboek van Nederland. Charité, J., *ed.*

A continuation of *Biographisch woordenboek der Nederlanden* 7v, 1852-78 and *Nieuw Nederlandsch biografisch woordenboek* 10v., 1911-37 (*qqv*).

v.1 s'Gravenhage, Martinus Nijhoff, 1979, xi,680p. ISBN 9024722780. v.2. Amsterdam, Elsevier, 1985. ISBN 9010055019. Separate A-Z sequences: v.1 largely covers only deceased persons since 1910. Over 200 contributors. Extensive bibliogs. appended to entries. *Class No:* 929(492)

[5885]
—Nieuw Nederlandsch biografisch woordenboek. Molhuysen, P.C., *and other, eds.* Leiden, Sijthoff, 10v., 1911-37.

Each volume is a complete A-Z sequence and contains lengthy authoritative articles. Index references are columns, not pages. Each volume contains a cumulative index to the work at that stage and v.10 has an index to the complete work. *Class No:* 929(492)

Belgium
[5886]
Biographie nationale. Académie Royale Des Sciences, Des Lettres et Des Beaux-Arts de Belgique. Bruxelles, Bruylant, 1866-. v.1-.

v.1-28 (1866-1944); v.29-44 (*i.e.,* Supplément 1-16) (1957-1985). The Belgian *DNB*. Long, signed obituaries by specialists (*e.g.* Cardinal Mercier by A. Simon: 21½ columns, including 1 col. of bibliography; Henri Pirenne by F.L. Ganshof: 522/3cols, with sub-headings and 1 col. of bibliography). Each of the supplementary volumes has a separate A-Z sequence and list of contributors. *Class No:* 929(493)

[5887]
DHONDT, J. *and* **VERVAECK, S. Instruments biographiques pour l'histoire contemporaine de Belgique.** 2nd ed. Louvain, Nauwelaarts, 1964. 88p. (*Centre Interuniversitaire d'Histoire Contemporaine. Cahiers 13.*)

A survey for sources for Belgian biography. 5 chapters, on universal and Belgian biographical dictionaries and collections, sources confined to a particular period, province, region or town, and biographical sources of a professional nature (*e.g.* clergy, artists). 294 numbered items, the more important being annotated. Indexes of places, persons and catchwords. *Class No:* 929(493)

[5888]
Le Dictionnaire des belges. Bruxelles, Paul Legrain, 1981. 570p.

90,000 short biographies 1830 to 1980. *Class No:* 929(493)

[5889]
National biografisch woordenboek. Koninklijke Vlaamse Academiën Van Belgë. Brussel, Paleis Der Academiën, 1964-.

V.11. 1985. vii,870p. ISBN 9065690115. V.12. 1987. vii,847p. ISBN 9065690123. Flemish biographical dictionary which includes many people omitted from French-language *Biographie nationale* (*qv*). Also includes biographies of prominent Dutch personalities. Successive volumes have own A-Z sequence with a cumulative index. Well-documented with each entry ending with bibliographical citations. 'There emerges an impressive picture of the

....(contd.)
number of biographies which have been brought up-to-date'
(*Acta Historiae Neerlandica,* v.8,1975,p.160).
Class No: 929(493)

[5890]
Qui est qui en Belgique francophone 1985-1989.
Deccan, R., *ed.* 2nd ed. Bruxelles, Éditions BRD, 1985.
1099p. ISBN: 9065980180. ISSN: 07713792.
First edition 1980.
12584 biographies (10109 in 1980 ed.) of leading
personalities in public life, social organizations, liberal
professions, science, the arts, the mass media *etc.* Royal
Family p.13-14. A third edition is announced for 1990.
Class No: 929(493)

[5891]
Wie is wie in Vlaanderen 1985-1989. Deccan, R., *ed.* 2nd
ed. Brussel, Uitgeverij BRD, 1985. 1455p. ISBN:
9065980172. ISSN: 07717822.
1st ed. 1980.
15219 biographies compared to 12014 in 1ast ed. 'Het
Koninklijk Huis (Royal family) p.13-14. A 3rd ed. is
expected in 1990. *Class No:* 929(493)

Switzerland

[5892]
Who's who in Switzerland including the Principality of
Liechtenstein 1990-1991: a biographical dictionary
containing about 3500 biographies of prominent people in
and of Switzerland (including the Principality of
Liechtenstein. 16th ed. Geneva, Nagel, 1990. 555p. ISBN:
2826308289.
First published 1952.
Significant input of 200 new biographies in this edition.
Glossary p.11-13. *Class No:* 929(494)

Yugoslavia

[5893]
RAJOVIÉ, R., *ed.* **Jugoslovenski sauremenici ko je ko u
Jugoslaviji.** Beograd, Hronometar, 1970. xvi,1207p.
Who's who in Yugoslavia with over 10,000 entries. 'A
new edition is long overdue but this one can still be usefully
referred to for earlier careers of contemporary notables'
(Horton, J.J. *Yugoslavia,* 2nd ed., 1990. Entry 893).
Lengthier entries are signed. *Class No:* 929(497.1)

Asia—Far East

[5894]
Who's who in Australasia and the Far East. Timothy, J., *ed.*
2nd ed. Cambridge, Melrose Press, 1991. 766p. £75.
ISBN: 0948875550.
1st ed. 1989.
*c.*5,500 brief biographies of prominent people from 32
countries and territories including Australia, New Zealand,
China, Hong Kong, Japan, North and South Korea, the
Philippines, Singapore, Malaysia, Vietnam and smaller states
like Tonga, Tuvalu and Vanuatu. 'Some devastating
inconsistencies in inclusion and exclusion' (*Reference
Reviews,* v.6,no.1, 1992, p.45)/ *Class No:* 929(51/52+57)

China

[5895]
BOORMAN, H.L. *and* **HOWARD, A.C.,** *eds.* **Biographical
dictionary of Republican China.** New York, Columbia
Univ. Press, 5v., 1967-79. 1853p. $60.00 each volume.
ISBN: 0231089554, v.1; 0231089562, v.2; 0231089570,
v.3; 0231089589, v.4; 0231045581, v.5.
About 600 essay-biographies of persons, living or dead,
who were prominent during the Republican period, 1911-49.
'Chang Kai-shek': v.1, p.319-43; 1p. of bibliography. V.1
has appended 'General bibliographical reference works'
(p.481-2). The bulk of v.4 is a valuable bibliography (p.97-
418) by Joseph K.H. Cheng, following text order (A-Z,
biographies). Most of the personalities are drawn from
political, military, economic and academic spheres. Chinese
characters follow romanised form of entry name. V.5: *A
personal name index* (1979,[xiii],75p.) has 16 contributors.
Entries are in romanised form, plus Chinese characters.
Names are in bold type if the subject of a biographical essay
in the dictionary. Non-analytical index ('Yuan Shih-k'ai': 1
column). *Class No:* 929(510)

[5896]
GOODRICH, L.C. *and* **FANG, C.,** *eds.* **Dictionary of Ming
biography** 1368-1644. New York, The Ming Biographical
History Project of the Association for Asian Studies;
London, Columbia Univ. Press, 2v., 1976. 1050p. 830p.
illus., maps. $170.00. ISBN: 0231030811, v.1; 023103833x,
v.2; 0685620344, set.
Nearly 650 documented entries; 125 specialist
contributors. Indexes of names, books and subjects. 'An
indispensable acquisition for college and other specialized
libraries;' (*Library Journal,* 1 June 1976, p.1275).
Class No: 929(510)

[5897]
KLEIN, D.W. *and* **CLARK, A.B. Biographic dictionary of
Chinese Communism 1921-1965.** Cambridge, Mass.,
Harvard Univ. Press, 2v., 1971. xvi,641p. 642p. maps.
$81.00. ISBN: 0674074106.
433 biographies, plus 96 appendices on key events and
organizations in the party's history. Well documented (*e.g.*
Chou En-lai: v.1, p.204-19, including 1½ columns of
bibliographical references). Selected bibliography, p.1031-8.
Glossary - name index (p.1170-94): Chinese characters for
*c.*1,750 names. Like Boorman (*qv*), bears 'the stamp of
extensive research and scholarly analysis from the limited
sources of information currently available ... Both Klein and
Boorman adopt Wade's standard form of Romanization,
thereby greatly facilitating comparative study' (*Asian Affairs,*
v.60, pt.2, June 1973, p.196). Boorman is more readable;
Klein, more informative (*The China Quarterly,* October/
December 1971, p.741-8). *Class No:* 929(510)

[5898]
LI XIN *and* **SUN SIBAI. The Biographies of eminent
Chinese in the Republic of China.** Peking, Chung Hwa
Publications, 1978. 408p.
'One of three projected works prepared by the Institute of
Modern History in the Chinese Academy of Social Sciences,
as a foundation programme intended for the eventual writing
of an official history of the Republic of China' (P. Cheng.
China, 1983. Entry 394). *Class No:* 929(510)

[5899]
Who's who in China 1918-1950. With an index compiled by Jerome Cavenaugh. Hong Kong, Chinese Materials Center, 3v., 1983.

Material in these 3 reprint volumes was collected originally from *The China Weekly Review,* previously *Millard's Review,* printed in Shanghai. 'Although the publishers never managed to live up to their initial plan to publish a yearly volume, this was the first important attempt to collect biographical information on Chinese leaders in English. The *Who's who* was a direct offshoot of the weekly's practice of introducing important Chinese in the news through biographical sketches' (*Preface*).
Reprint v.1: Index p.1-198. *Who's who in China 1918-1920 containing the pictures and biographies of some of China's political, financial, business and professional leaders.* Also 2nd ed. (1920). Reprint v.2: 3rd ed. (1925) including Directory of American Returned Students. 972+25p. Supplement to 3rd ed. (1928) 168p. Reprint v.3: 4th ed. (1931) 512p.; Supplement to 4th ed. (1933) 136p. 5th ed. (1936) 300p.; Supplement to 5th ed. (1940) 83p. and 6th ed. (1950) 253p. *Class No:* 929(510)

20th Century

[5900]
BARTKE, W. A Biographical dictionary and analysis of China's Party leadership 1922-1988. München, K.G. Saur, 1990. xi,482p. ports, tables. £127.50. ISBN: 3598108761.

In 3 parts: 1. Biographies of 1049 members of the Central Committee 2nd-13th Central Committees. Data: name in Roman and Chinese script; career profile; visits abroad, A-Z by Western form - 2. Analyses of Central Committee cadres including the Politburo and Central committees - 3. Tables *i.e.,* information on all 13 Central Committees 1922-1988. *Class No:* 929(510)"19"

[5901]
BARTKE, W. Who's who in the People's Republic of China. 3rd ed. London, K.G. Saur, 2v., 1990. 900p. ports., index. £145.00. ISBN: 3598107714.

First published in New York by M.E. Sharpe Inc. and in Brighton, Sussex, by Harvester Press 1981. 2nd ed. published by K.G. Saur in 1987.
'Entries cover a whole range of living Chinese personalities: politicians, soldiers, academics, scientists, diplomats, religious and cultural leaders. Each biography lists posts held, thus enabling the user to assess at a glance the present importance of a party cadre, and includes a photograph where available. Names are also translated into Pinyin, together with Chinese characters... Also contains an occupation index and an appendix on the organisation of the People's Republic of China, with charts and tables detailing the composition and structure of the active leadership of todays China' (*K.G. Saur catalogue*).
Class No: 929(510)"19"

[5902]
Who's who in China: current leaders. Beijing, Foreign Languages Press, 1990. Distributed by China Books & Periodicals. xx,1126p. illus., index. $90. ISBN: 0835123529.

Biographical sketches of 2,100 current senior officials at central and provincial levels. Parallel Chinese/English text. Appendix: Table of major organizations and their leading officials p.1037-78. *Class No:* 929(510)"19"

Hong Kong

[5903]
Who's who in Hong Kong 1984. Hong Kong, Database 1984. xxxii,461p. ports. ISBN: 9620900243.
1st ed. 1979.

Leaders of the community distinguished by their careers, achievements, social or voluntary work of benefit to the community, or honoured by the Crown or the government. Also catalogues major government departments. Governors of Hong Kong p.xvii-xviii. 'A near definitive list of local movers and shakers' (*Foreword*). *Class No:* 929(512.317)

Japan

[5904]
Who's who in Japan 1991-92. 3rd ed. Hong Kong, International Culture Institute, 1992. Distributed in North America by Gale Research Co. and in UK by K.G. Saur. [iv],1281p. £225. ISBN: 3598075804.
First ed. 1984-85.

About 51,000 brief biographies on leading figures in contemporary Japanese society arranged A-Z by family name. Data: name, degree or license, position, education, birthdate, career, honours, membership, hobbies, address and telephone numbers. The Directory of Public and Private Institutions also provides the official names, addresses and telephone numbers of Diet organs, ministries and government agencies, local government offices, companies listed in the First and Second Sections of the Tokyo Stock Exchange, public and private universities, non-profit foundations and organizations, libraries and museums. Biennial revisions are promised. 'Those who can justify purchase will find it to be money well spent' (*Reference Reviews,* v.3,no.1, March 1989, p.42-3). *Class No:* 929(52)

Asia—South & South East

[5905]
RAZI WESTI, S. Biographical dictionary of South Asia. Lahore, Publishers United Ltd., 1980. 511p.

2000 entries of persons who played a prominent role in the history of India, Pakistan and Bangladesh. Not restricted to natives of the sub-continent. *Class No:* 929(54+59)

India

[5906]
BUCKLAND, C.E. Dictionary of Indian biography. New York, Haskell House Publishers, 1968. xii, 494p. bibliog. $85.00; £76.50. ISBN: 0838302777.
First published London, Sonnenschein, 1906.

'The main facts of the lives of about 2,600 persons - English, Indian, foreign, men or women, living or dead - who have been conspicuous in the history of India, or distinguished in the administration of the country, in one or other of its branches, or have contributed to its welfare service and advancement by their studies and literary products, or have gained some special notoriety. The entries date from 1750 'when the English power in India was being established'. It is still useful for the period covered and is not entirely superseded by any other work. Bibliography is appended, together with a list of the reference works consulted by the compiler of the *Dictionary.*
Class No: 929(540)

[5907]

Eminent Indians who was who 1900-1980 also Annual diary of events. New Delhi, published under the auspices of Durga Das Pvt. Ltd., 1985. Rs.250. *Class No:* 929(540)

[5908]

India Who's who 1991-92. Inder Jit, *ed*. 22nd ed. New Delhi, INFA Publications 1992. xliv,182,168a,196bp. index. Rs350. $70.

1st published 1969.

5,000 concise biographies (500 new to this edition) of India's leading personalities in government, the armed services; state government, business, arts, crafts, education, literature, medicine, and the sciences. *Class No:* 929(540)

[5909]

SEN, S.P., *ed*. Dictionary of national biography. Calcutta, Institute of Historical Studies, 4v., 1972-74.

A-D, E-L, M-R, S-Z. Biographies of *c*.1400 Indians (and also foreigners who made India their home). Covers period 1800-1947 and includes living personalities. All entries are signed. Data: personal and family details; early life; career history; personality; general estimate. 'Tagore, Rabindranath' (1861-1941): 13 columns, including 2 cols. of bibliography. *Dictionary of National Biography (Supplement)* v.1. A-D (1986). edited by N.R. Ray. Covers 1947-1972. 'It is expected that the complete set of 4 volumes will be ready for release within 2 years of the appearance of the first volume' (*Preface*). *Class No:* 929(540)

[5910]

SHARMA, J.S. The National bibliographical dictionary of India. New Delhi, Sterling Publishers, 1972. xiii,302p. index.

About 1500 concise entries covering deceased persons only. Cross-references. Excludes non-Indians. Valuable subject index. *Class No:* 929(540)

Iran

[5911]

Who's who in Iran. Meckenheim, Medien & Bücher Verlags, 1990. 352p. ISBN: 392707024.

Concise career biographies of Iranian officials and personalities. Profiles of leaders of Islamic Republic p.17-31. Government agencies p.323-50. Glossary p.13-14. *Class No:* 929(55)

Turkey

[5912]

Günümüz Türkiyesinde kim kindir/Who's who in Turkey 1985-1986. Istanbul, Profesyonel, 1986. 703p.

About 6200 brief biographical sketches. *Class No:* 929(560)

Lebanon

[5913]

Who's who in Lebanon 1993-1994. Bustros, G., *ed*. 11th ed. Beirut, Lebanon, Publitec Publications; London, K.G. Saur, 1992. Distributed worldwide by Gale Research Inc. 505p. £76.00. ISBN: 3598076002. ISSN: 00839612.

First published 1977. Now published biennially.

Concise biographies of 2000 prominent personalities including some foreign residents plus a geographic,

....(contd.)

economic, political, legal, and cultural survey of Lebanon. Lists National Assembly members, ministers, official Lebanese decorations, diplomatic and consular missions. *Class No:* 929(569.3)

Israel

[5914]

Who's who in Israel and Jewish personalities from all the world 1992-93. 25th Biennial English ed. Tel-Aviv, Who's Who in Israel, 1992.

'The Presidency of Israel', 'Members of the 11th Knesset' and 'Members of the Government' precede Pt.1. Personalia, (*c*.3000 biographies). Pt.2. Government, official institutions, public institutions and corporations, public and private enterprises (*e.g.* World Zionist Organization and El-Al Israeli Airlines). *Class No:* 929(569.4)

Afghanistan

[5915]

ADAMEC, L.W. Historical and political who's who of Afghanistan. Graz, Akademische Druk-u. Verlagsanstalt, 1975. ix,385p.

Brief biographies of *c*.1500 persons in 2 sequences: 1945-1974 and 1747-1945. Also Afghan Government members for 20th century. 92 genealogical tables of prominent families. Glossary p.379.85. *First supplement to the Who's who of Afghanistan: Democratic Republic of Afghanistan.* 1979. 53p. Includes corrections to the base volume. *Class No:* 929(581)

[5916]

—**ADAMEC, L.W. A Biographical dictionary of contemporary Afghanistan.** Graz, Akademische Druck-u. Verlagsanstalt, 1987. vi,252p.+24p. of photographs. ISBN: 3201013390.

Biographies of 1600 high government officials, political leaders, military officers, religious leaders *etc.* since 1945. Who's who p.1-209. Government 1919-1978 and 1978-1986 p.213-231. Diplomatic list p.232-242. PDPA leadership p.243-245. Glossary p.246-252. *Class No:* 929(581)

Malaysia

[5917]

New Malaysian who's who. Kuala Lumpur, Kasuya Publishing, 3v. in 2, 1989. $700.

Part 1. Sabah and Sarawak. cdlix,744p. illus., ports, map. ISBN 9839624008. Biographical information on King and Queen, Malay rulers, government ministers *etc.* p.i-xlii. Brief chapters on general business information, Malay business law, economy, taxation, political parties, honours and awards, and 13 Malay states. p.xliv-cdlix. Personalities from East Malaysia p.1-744.

Part 2. West Malaysia. 2v. cdlix,1,498p. 9839624016. On same pattern as Part 1. Personalities from West Malaysia p.1-1,498p.

Biodata on 7,000 people of distinction: education, professional qualifications, career, affiliations, honours and awards, and foreign visits. *Class No:* 929(595)

[5918]
Who's who in Malaysia & Singapore 1983-4. 15th ed. (1st in 2v.). Petaling Jaya, Selangor, Who's Who Publications Sdn Bhd, 1983. iv,477p.+v,263p. ports., index. ISSN: 02171910.

First published 1955.

Similar pattern in v.1 (Malaysia) and v.2 (Singapore): Rulers and Heads of States, Lord President and Speakers of Parliament, Cabinet ministers preceding Biographies, Obituary, and holders of awards and distinctions. *Class No:* 929(595)

Islamic World

[5919]
Arabian personalities of the early twentieth century. Bidwell, R., *ed.* Cambridge, Oleander Press, 1986. viii,362p. map. index. £29.,75. (*Arabia past and present, v.19.*) ISBN: 0906672392.

First published in a strictly limited and confidential edition in 1917.

Primary sourcebook of British intelligence material containing 3700 biographical sketches arranged in 7 regional sections: Hejaz, Asir, Yemen, Aden and Hadramaut, Gulf Coast, Central Arabia, Syrian Desert and Sinai. *Class No:* 929(5.297)

[5920]
Who's who in the Arab World 1993-1994. Gedeon, C.G., *ed.* 11th ed. Beirut, Publitec in association with K.G. Saur. 1000p. bibliog, index. DM528. ISBN: 3598075995. ISSN: 00839752.

1st ed. 1966. Now issued biennially.

Part 1. Biographical section of *c.*6000 sketches of prominent persons in the Arab World indexed by country and profession - 2. Survey of 20 Arab countries Algeria - Yemen - 3. Outline of Arab World: General survey including The League of Arab States; Mahgreb Permanent Consultative Committee; Arab petroleum; Suez Canal; Development of Arab banks; Palestinian problem; Gulf Cooperation Council. Bibliography. 'Although the information ... has value owing to its Arab point of view, the treatment is often shallow and the editing poor' (*Choice*, v.19,no.5, January 1982,p.612). *Class No:* 929(5.297)

Bibliographies

[5921]
AUCHTERLONIE, P. Arabic biographical dictionaries: a summary guide and bibliography. Durham, Middle East Libraries Committee, 1987. iv,60p. bibliog. pbk. £5.25. ISBN: 0948889012.

Research guide in 4 sections: 1. Brief account of historical development of Arabic biographical dictionaries - 2. List of classical dictionaries - 3. Modern biographical dictionaries in Arabic and Western languages - 4. Brief summary of Western scholarship regarding most complete and well known dictionaries. *Class No:* 929(5.297)(01)

Africa

[5922]
Africa who's who. 2nd ed. London, Africa Books Ltd., 1991. viii,1863p. (*Know Africa.*) ISBN: 0903274175. ISSN: 01611570.

1st ed. 1981. Companion volume of *Africa today* and

....(contd.)
Makers of modern Africa (qqv).

Biographical data on over 12000 eminent personalities: nationality and occupation, date and place of birth, education, career, current occupation, publications, national and international honours. *Class No:* 929(6)

[5923]
RAKE, A. Who's who in Africa leaders for the 1990s. Metuchen, N.J., Scarecrow Press, 1992. 448p. index. $59.50. ISBN: 0810825570.

Career profiles of more than 300 political figures in the 47 countries South of the Sahara A-Z by country. Each country section begins with basic geographical, constitutional, and political information. *Class No:* 929(6)

Micromaterials

[5924]
African biographical archive. München, K.G. Saur, 12 instalments, 1993-. 700 fiches (24x) silver or diazzo. £7294 (silver); £6631 (diazzo). ISBN: 3598331002, silver; 3598331010, diazzo.

A single sequence A-Z cumulation of biographical entries from biographical reference works relating to sub-Sahara Africa. *Class No:* 929(6)(003.5)

Sudan

[5925]
HILL, R.L. A Biographical dictionary of the Sudan. London, Cass, 1967. xvi,409p.

The 2nd ed., of *A biographical dictionary of the Anglo-Egyptian Sudan* (1951).

The 1st ed. contained 'over 1,900 short notices of people who have died before 1948 and who have contributed, each after his fashion, to the story of the Sudan; ... not a dictionary of national biography in the accepted sense [but] a record of the human contribution to Sudan history' (*Preface* to the first edition). The 2nd ed. seems to be a reprint of the original text, plus an addendum: 'Notes and corrections', p.395-409, and a new introduction. Not confined to persons who lived in the Sudan. 'Glossary of ranks, titles and other designations', p.ix-xvi. 'An essential reference work of lasting value' (M.W. Daly. *Sudan*, 1983. Entry 229). *Class No:* 929(624)

Ethiopia

[5926]
The Dictionary of Ethiopian biography. Michael, B., *and others, eds.* Addis Ababa, Institute of Ethiopian Studies, Addis Ababa Univ., 1975-. v.1- xi,218p. illus.

1. *From early times to the end of the Zagwé dynasty c.*1270A.D. 21 contributors. 500 signed or initialled entries. Project planned in several volumes on a chronological basis. Previous attempts at Ethiopian biography discussed in the Preface. *Class No:* 929(63)

Nigeria

[5927]

ORIMOLOYE, S.A. **Biographica Nigeriana** a biographical dictionary of eminent Nigerians. Boston, Mass., G.K. Hall, 1977. 368p.

Who's who information on *c.*1,000 leading and notable Nigerians living in Nigeria and abroad, and also non-Nigerians who have contributed greatly to Nigeria's literature, heritage and history. 'Hans Zell': ½p. Includes some entries for those who have recently died (*e.g.* in the upheavals of 1966) 'Biased to the world of learning and letters' (*Foreword*). Claims to be the first comprehensive alphabetical biography of its kind. *Class No:* 929(669)

[5928]

Who's who in Nigeria. Nyaknno Osso, *ed.* Lagos, Newswatch Communications, 1990. 803p. ISBN: 9782704121.

Brief entries on 2500 Nigerian men and women of outstanding accomplishments in all walks of life. Data: birthdate, education and qualifications, awards, national honours, foreign decorations, published works. *Class No:* 929(669)

Africa—Southern

[5929]

Who's who of Southern Africa 1992-93 including Mauritius: an illustrated biographical record of prominent personalities in the Republic of South Africa, Botswana, Mauritius, Namibia, Swaziland, Zimbabwe, and neighbouring countries in South Africa. 85th ed. Johannesburg, Who's Who of Southern Africa, 1992. Annual. 637p. ports. ISBN: 0620169451. ISSN: 00839876.

First published 1907. Title changed from *South African who's who,* in 1959 (43rd ed.).

Republic of South Africa Official guide. Who's who of South Africa. Sections on Namibia, Botswana, Swaziland, Mauritius, Lesotho, Malawi, and Zimbabwe consisting of official directories and who's who (Lesotho and Malawi directories only). *Class No:* 929(68)

South Africa

[5930]

Dictionary of South African biography. Beyers, C.J., *ed.* Various publishers for Human Sciences Research Council (Pretoria), 1968-. (v.1-5. 1968-1987).

V.4 (Butterworth & Co.,1981). xx,803p.ISBN 0409091839. V.5 (Johannesburg, Chris van Rensburg Publications, 1987). 909p. ISBN 0796904200. Biographies of persons who died before 1982. Signed articles. Each volume has an A-Z sequence. Hendrik Frensch Verwoerd (v.4) p.730-40 with half column of references. The whole is to run to several volumes, each with biographies of persons who died up to 5 years before publication, and each with cumulative indexes. A most important, authoritative source for South African biography. Published in English and Afrikaans. *Class No:* 929(680)

[5931]

PHILIP, P. **British residents at the Cape 1785-1829:** biographical records of 4800 pioneers. Cape Town, David Philip, 1981. Distributed in UK by Global Book Resources and by Bowman and Littlefield in US. xxiii, 484p. ISBN: 0908396465.

British regiments which served at the Cape and British ships of war on the Cape station p.xix-xxiii. Bibliography p.481-484. *Class No:* 929(680)

[5932]

SPENCER, S. O'B. **British settlers in Natal 1824-1857:** a biographical register. Pietermaritzburg, Univ. of Natal Press, 1981-. illus. maps, index.

Abbott-Ayres. 1981. xx, 128p. 0869802674. Babbs-Bolton. 1983. xx, 169p. 0869803514. Bond-Byrne. 1985. xx, 159p. 0869804308. Castle-Coventry. 1987. xx, 246p. 0869805436. Enters heads of families or single men and women who arrived in Natal without their parents. Later volumes include addenda and corrigenda. The complete work will consist of *c.*2600 entries. *Class No:* 929(680)

[5933]

TOFFOLI, H.P. *and* SILBER, G. **Who's really who in South Africa.** Johannesburg, Jonathan Ball, 1989. ii,229p. illus. ISBN: 0947464077.

240 irreverent profiles of 'the buzz people of South Africa' whose 'words, deeds, and personalities are in some way woven into the rich and colourful fabric of South African society'. *Class No:* 929(680)

Mauritius

[5934]

Dictionnaire de biographie Mauricienne/Dictionary of Mauritian biography. Port Louis, Société de l'Histoire de l' Ile Maurice, 1941-.

Issued in fascicules: no.1 February 1941; 17p. no.45. April 1990. 1362p.++ 8p. *Mutanda* and *Addenda*. Documented entries for 'all those who, identified with Mauritius, whether by birth, adoption or temporary connection, played a part worth recording in the history of Mauritius' are in English or French (depending on country of origin). No living persons. *Class No:* 929(698.2)

Canada

[5935]

Biographies Canadiennes - Françaises. Who's who in Quebec 1984-1985. 31st ed. Montréal, Éditions Biographiques Canadiennes-Françaises, 1986. 446p. ports., index. ISBN: 292039717. ISSN: 03800830.

First published 1920.

Double page entries giving single biography in French and English (p.160-411). Data: position, education, career, civil status, office address. A good portrait accompanies each biography. Répertoire des Entreprises p.414-442. *Class No:* 929(71)

[5936]

Canadian who's who 1992. Simpson, K., *ed.* Toronto, Univ. of Toronto Press, 1992. Annual. 1150p. $155. ISBN: 0802046649. ISSN: 00689963.

First published in London by Times Publishing Co. 1910. 2nd ed. 1936, substantially longer, incorporated *Canadian men and women of the time.* Then issued triennially with 5 supplementary booklets (*Canadian biographical service*)

.... *(contd.)*

until University of Toronto acquired the publishing rights 1978. *Canadian who's who 1979* (1976-9).First annual volume 1980.

Essential details of some 11,000 prominent Canadians in all walks of life. Standard reference source of Canadian biography.

Canadian who's who index 1898-1984 (1986) compiled by E. McMann is a complete index of entire backlist of Canadian who's who and 1898 and 1912 editions of *Canadian men and women of the time*. xi, 528p. 0802046339. Lists 33,230 names. History of *Canadian who's who* 1910 onwards p.vii-viii.

Canadian who's who on microfiche 1898-1975.

Class No: 929(71)

[5937]
Debrett's illustrated guide to the Canadian establishment. Newman, P.C., *ed.* Agincourt, Ontario, Methuen, 1983; London, Debrett's Peerage Ltd., 1984. 407p. col.illus. £19.95. ISBN: 0458976904.

Part 1. The power network - 2. The Dynasties (p.167-219) 'being portraits of 21 families that for at least three generations have exemplified prestige and leadership of the Canadian establishment' - 3. The Honours list *i.e.* a listing of Canadians of exceptional achievement in all aspects of contemporary Canadian society. Appendix: The Family Foundations (25 largest charitable funds based on family or personal wealth). *Class No:* 929(71)

[5938]
Dictionary of Canadian biography. Toronto, Univ. of Toronto Press, 20v., 1966-. bibliogs., indexes.

French ed. *Dictionnaire biographique du Canada* (Québec, Les Presses de l'Université Laval).

20 entirely self-contained volumes, each covering a specific number of years. The volume in which a biography is included is determined by the date of death or, if this is unknown, the 'floreat' date. 'Biographers should endeavour to provide a readable and stimulating treatment of their subject. Factual information should come from primary sources if possible' (*DCB's Directive to contributors*). Volumes published to date: 1. *1000 to 1700*. 1966. xxiii, 755p. ISBN 0802031420. 2. *1701 to 1740*. 1969. xli,759p. 0802032400. 3. *1741 to 1770*. 1974. xlii, 782p. 0802033148. 4. *1771 to 1800*. 1979. lvii,913p. 0802033512. 5. *1801 to 1820*. 1983. xxv,1044p. 0802033989. 6. *1821 to 1835*. 1987. xxiv,960p. 0802034365. 7. *1836 to 1850*. 1988. xxix,1088p. 0802034527. 8. *1851 to 1860*. 1985. xxxvii,1129p. 0802034225. 9. *1861 to 1870*. 1976. xiii,967p. 0802033199. 10. *1871 to 1880*. 1972. xxix,823p. 0802032877. 11. *1881 to 1890* 1982. xx,1092p. 0802032679. 12. *1891 to 1900*. 1990. 1200p. Can $75. 0802034608. *Index Vs.1-12. 1000-1900*. 1991. 568p. $60. 0802034640 is in 2 parts: (1) list of subjects of biographies; (2) Cumulative Nominal Index, 'a vast web of references and cross-references which stretches across the volumes'.

V.7 has 326 contributors; 538 well-documented biographies ranging from 600 to 10,000 words in length. General bibliography (Archival sources; printed primary sources, reference works; studies) p.938-76. Index of identifications (29 categories of occupations) p.991-1006. Geographical index p.1009-25. Name index p.1029-1088. 'Characterized by careful scholarship, good writing and remarkable breadth of coverage' (*Choice*, v.9, no.12, February 1973, p.1572). F.G. Halpenny's 'The Dictionary of Canadian Biography/Dictionnaire biographique du

.... *(contd.)*

Canada', *Canadian Studies* (British Library, 1984), p.133-43, has more detail. M. Dowding's 'Dictionary side-swiped by funding cutbacks', *Quill & Quires* v.56, no.4, April 1990, p.6 reports that the future volumes are imperilled through a serious loss of funding. *Class No:* 929(71)

[5939]
Who's who in Canada 1994: an illustrated biographical record of leading Canadians from business, the professions, government and academia. 85th ed. Toronto, Global Press, 1994. xxxiii,794p. ports, index. $130. ISBN: 0771539614.

Cross-reference listing by company position, name p.757-794. *Class No:* 929(71)

Newfoundland

[5940]
Dictionary of Newfoundland and Labrador biography. St. John's, Harry Cuff Publications, 1990. vi,408p. bibliog., indexes. ISBN: 0921191510.

Basic reference information on approximately 1,500 individuals 'who have influenced the development of Newfoundland and Labrador as colony, country and province, since the European re-discovery of America in 1497' (*Foreword*). Bibliographic note p.374-9. Geographic index p.380-92. Index of identifications (*i.e.* occupation or profession) p.393-408. *Class No:* 929(718)

Mexico

[5941]
CAMP, R.A. Who's who in Mexico today. Boulder, Colo., Westview Press, 1988. 183p. $45; £38.95. (*Westview Studies on Latin America and the Caribbean.*) ISBN: 0813373972.

Almost 400 biographies of contemporary leaders in all areas of Mexican life including prominent women, opposition political leaders, and members of the Colegio Nacional. Data: date of birth and birthplace; education; party and elected press; government appointments; family information; military service; national awards; and bibliographical references. Complements the author's *Mexican political biographies 1935-1981 (q.v.)*. 'A concise, accurate, and up-to-date biographical dictionary' (*Choice*, v.26, no.2, October 1988, p.284 +6). *Class No:* 929(72)

[5942]
Diccionario biográfico de Mexico. Monterrey, Editorial Revesa, 2v., 1968-1970. vii,643p. + vii,580p.

V.1 covers colonial and early independent Mexico (A-Z) and v.2 completes coverage to 1970. Includes Who's who information on 5,500 living Mexicans. *Class No:* 929(72)

Bibliographies

[5943]
WOODS, R.D., *comp*. **Mexican autobiography** an annotated bibliography. La autobiografia Mexicana: una bibliografia razonada. Westport, Connecticut, Greenwood Press, 1988. 264p. bibliogs., indexes. $39.95; £30.50. (*Bibliographies and Indexes in World History, no.13.*) ISBN: 0313259453. ISSN: 07426801.

325 essays comprehending autobiographies proper, memoirs, diaries, collections of letters *etc.* Data includes basic bibliographical information, author's dates, narrative

....*(contd.)*

dates, and translation or primary edition in English. Translations indexed by author, title and subject. Other indexes provide access by subject, profession or outstanding characteristics of the author and chronological period. Parallel English and Spanish text. *Class No:* 929(72)(01)

20th Century

[5944]

CAMP, R.A. **Mexican political biographies 1935-1981.** 2nd ed. Tucson, Univ. of Arizona Press, 1982. xxi, 447p. $35.00. ISBN: 0816507430.

First published 1976 (1935-1975 coverage).

1350 entries of living and dead Mexican political figures. Includes a bibliographical essay. 'A most useful volume for the student of the Mexican political elite' (*College & Research Libraries*, v.38,no.4, July 1977, p.324). *Class No:* 929(72)"19"

El Salvador

[5945]

ACADEMIA SALVADOREÑA DE LA HISTORIA. **El Salvador y ses hombres.** 2nd ed. San Salvador, Ministerio de Educaccion, 1967. 424p. maps, ports.

First published 1938.

1. Biographical sketches (up to 10p. in length) of prominent Salvadoran persons from 16th to early-20th century in chronological order of date of birth - 2. More biographies at paragraph length (A-Z) p.311-37 - 3. History of Spanish conquest and Founding of San Salvador. *Class No:* 929(728.4)

Caribbean

[5946]

Personalities Caribbean the international guide to who's who in the West Indies. A compendious guide of selected listings - introducing the peoples of the Caribbean, Bahamas and Bermuda, one to another. Levy, A.L. *and* Jacobs, H.P. 7th ed. Kingston, Jamaica, Personalities Ltd., 1983, Biennial. xvi, 17-1027p. ports.

First published 1962 as *Personalities in the Caribbean*.

About 5000 biographies arranged A-Z by country. General listings (p.943-1005) includes biographees in previous edition but who have subsequently moved outside the region and some personalities never domiciled there but who have important links nevertheless. *Class No:* 929(729)

Dominican Republic

[5947]

MARTINEZ, R. **Diccionario biográphico-histórico dominicano 1831-1930.** Santa Domingo, Editora Universidad Autónoma de Santo Domingo, 1971. 528p.

'An indispensable reference work ... contains analyses of 1,137 important Dominican personages of the period' (Schoenhals, K. *Dominican Republic*, 1990. Entry 903). *Class No:* 929(729.3)

Puerto Rico

[5948]

MELON DE DIAZ, E.M. **Puerto-Rico: figures del presente y del pasado y apuntes historicos.** Rio Piedras, Editorial Edil, 1972. 225p. ports.

Over 400 biographies. *Class No:* 929(729.5)

Bibliographies

[5949]

FOWLIE-FLORES, F. **Index to Puerto Rican collective biography.** New York, Greenwood Press, 1987. xxi,215p. $42.95; £30.50. (*Bibliographies and Indexes in American History, no.5.*) ISBN: 0313251932. ISSN: 07426828.

Includes collective biographies, collections of essays, histories, published before or during 1985. Key to sources p.xv-xxi. Sources indexed p.203-212. Bibliography of related materials p.273-4. Bibliographies consulted p.215. *Class No:* 929(729.5)(01)

Latin America

[5950]

Who's who in Latin America a biographical dictionary of notable living men and women of Latin America. Hilton, R., *ed.* 3rd ed. California, Stanford Univ. Press; Chicago, Marquis, 7v., 1945-1971.

First published 1935 (1,000 entries); 2nd ed. 1940 (1500 entries) The 3rd ed. reprinted in 2v. (Detroit, Ethridge, 1971).

1. *Mexico* 1946. xiii,130p. 2. *Central America (i.e.,* Costa Rica, El Salvador, Guatemala, Honduras, Nicaragua and Panama) 1945. xiii,130p. 3. *Colombia, Ecuador and Venezuela* 1951. xvii,149p. 4. *Bolivia, Chile, Peru* 1947. xviii,209p. 5. *Argentine, Paraguay and Uruguay* 1950. xvii,258p. 6. *Brazil* 1948. xxii,269p. 7. *Cuba, Dominican Republic and Haiti* 1951. xvii,77p. Previously in one sequence, the 3rd ed. (8,000 entries) is arranged on a regional basis, which diminishes ease of reference if the country of the biographee is not known. Includes entries for 20 republics; 'qualification for admission... is residence, not nationality'. Ronald Hilton was Director of Hispanic Area Studies, Stanford Univ. *Class No:* 929(729.99)

Bibliographies

[5951]

Index to Spanish American collective biography. Mundo Lo, S. de. Boston, G.K. Hall, 6v., 1981-.

1. *The Andean countries.* 1981. xxix,466p. $60. ISBN 0816181810. 2. *Mexico.* 1982. xxix,373p. 0816185298. 3. *Central America and the Caribbean.* 1984. xxxiii,360p. 0816186367. 4. *The River Plate countries.* 1985. xxxi,388p. $94. 0816186502. Future volumes: 5. *Brazil.* 6. *General Spanish American sources.*

Provides access to references concerning individuals associated with Spanish America, its culture and institutions, as recorded in a variety of sources. The brief annotation includes bibliographical information, note of general content, and symbols of US and Canadian libraries where copies are located. Author, title, biographee, and geographic indexes. There are plans to issue supplements. *Class No:* 929(729.99)(01)

USA

[5952]
Appleton's cyclopaedia of American biography.
Wilson, J.G. *and* Fiske, J., *eds*. New York, Appleton, 7v., 1888-1900. illus.

Reprinted Gale Research Co., 1968.

1-6: A-Z, supplement, A-Z; analytical index. 1888-1889. 7: Supplement, A-Z; pen-names, nick-names, soubriquets; list of deaths in v.1-6; analytical index. 1900. The aim was to include all noteworthy persons, of the American continent by providing entries for 'above 15,000 prominent native and adopted citizens of the United States, including living persons, from the earliest settlement of the country'. Also included are about 1,000 men of foreign birth closely identified with American history. V.7 includes nearly 2,000 additional persons who had become prominent since the publication of the main work. Long articles, signed; for scholarship and authority the corresponding entries in the *DAB* (*qv*) have superseded Appleton which, however, contains many useful articles for persons not dealt with elsewhere. Illustrated, many facsimiles of signatures, with occasional full-length portraits. 'Basic for persons who died between 1789 and 1901' (*RQ,* v.8, no.2, Winter 1969, p.131). *Class No:* 929(73)

[5953]
BEST, H. Debrett's Texas peerage. New York, Coward-McCann, 1983. 385p.illus., index. ISBN: 0698112444.

Part 1. Today's patrician Texans (26 chapters). Part 2. The peerage in 7 chapters: 1. The first families of the Republic of Texas - 2. Signers of the Declaration of Independence - 3. Heroes of the Alamo - 4. Senior officers at the Battle of San Jacinto - 5. Other notables and heroes - 6. The carriage trade of the Republic - 7. The 'Old Three Hundred'. *Class No:* 929(73)

[5954]
Debrett's Presidents of the United States of America.
Williamson, D. Exeter, Devon, Webb & Bower; New York, Salem House, 1989. 208p. illus. (some col.), geneal. tables, ports. (some col.), index. £19.95; $27.50. ISBN: 0863501907, UK; 0881623660, US.

41 biographies George Washington to George Bush in chronological order. Does not set out to be a history of the US although events and campaign issues preceding their terms of office are examined. Also includes family history of the Presidents. Portraits p.97-128. Appendix 1. List of Vice-Presidents. *Class No:* 929(73)

[5955]
Dictionary of American biography. Sponsored by the American Council of Learned Societies, New York. New York, Charles Scribner's Sons, 17v. set, 1985. 19498p. $1,200.00. £960.00. ISBN: 0684173239.

First published New York, Scribners; London, Oxford Univ. Press, 20v. and Index, 1928-37. Supplements 1-7. 1944-81.

The main work carries 13,633 signed articles by 2,243 contributors. *DAB* includes 'in general only those ... who have made some significant contribution to American life in all its manifold aspects'. Article length is determined by relative importance of the person, amount of available authentic material, the nature of his career, and completeness of biographies already published; and this also applies to the appended bibliographies. The index (1937) has 6 pts.: 1. Biographies, with contributors' names; 2. Contributors, with biographies written by them; 3. Birthplaces, (a) State; (b)

....(contd.)
foreign countries; 4. Schools and colleges attended by biographee; 5. Occupations of biographee; 6. Topics. 'The monumental *D.A.B.*' (*RQ*, v.14, no.2, Winter 1974, p.169). W.K. McCoy's 'Dictionary of American Biography', *Reference Services Review*, v.11, no.3, Fall 1983, p.17-20. refs. is a good history and evaluation.

Dictionary of American biography. Supplement 8 1960-1970. 1989. 624p. £60.00. ISBN 0684186187 adds 454 biographies.

Dictionary of American biography. Comprehensive index. 1989. 800p. $80.00. ISBN 0684191146. Indexes subjects from original base volumes and all 8 supplements A-Z by occupation, by school/college, and by contributor.

This series of volumes is now at an end. 'ACLS has announced a successor series, *American National Biography*, to be published by Oxford. The first volume is to be available in both printed and electronic form in about five years' (*Booklist*, v.85, no.12, 15 February 1989, p.979). *Class No:* 929(73)

[5956]
—Concise dictionary of American biography. 4th ed. New York, Scribner, 1990. 1536p. index. $150.00. ISBN: 0684191881.

1st ed. 1964. 2nd ed. 1977. 3rd ed. 1980 was a reprint of 2nd ed. with an 101p. supplement for those who died 1951-60.

Concise version (at an average reduction of 14:1) of all 18,110 biographies included in the full *Dictionary of American biography* and its eight supplements extending coverage to 1970 in a single A-Z sequence. Occupations index. *Class No:* 929(73)

[5957]
DUNLAP, L.W. Our Vice-Presidents and Second Ladies.
Metuchen, New Jersey, Scarecrow Press, 1988. 397p. $35.00; £26.25. ISBN: 0810821141.

Biographical sketches (4-20 pages in length) of 43 Vice-Presidents to George Bush, and all their wives or hostesses, covering from cradle to the grave, and not just their terms of office. *Class No:* 929(73)

[5958]
Encyclopedia of Frontier biography. Thrapp, D.L. Glendale, California, Arthur H. Clark, 3v., 1988. 1698p. bibliogs., index. $175.00. ISBN: 0870621912.

Approximately 4500 biographies of western pioneers and native Americans each accompanied by a short bibliography. 'A wealth of information about persons who lived on the frontier, whether that was the trans-Appalachian frontier, the wide Missouri frontier, the mining regions of the Rockies, or the gold-mining/ranching frontiers of California, Oregon, or Arizona'. *Class No:* 929(73)

[5959]
LOGAN, R.W. *and* **WINSTON, M.R., *eds*. Dictionary of American Negro biography.** New York, W.W. Norton, 1982. xxi,680p. $50.00. ISBN: 0393015130.

270 contributors. 632 extensive signed biographies of Negroes who attained historical significance (Martin Luther King 443 lines) spanning 300 years of American history. No living persons. Classified list of entries (88 categories) p.ix-xxi. 'The work is quite useful but does not replace *Who's who of the colored race* (1915) or *Colored America* (1928-

....*(contd.)*

50). 'Recommended as an essential purchase for all academic and public libraries' (*Choice* v.20,no.10, June 1983, p.1433-4). *Class No:* 929(73)

[5960]
MEIER, M.S. Mexican American biographies: a historical dictionary 1836-1987. New York and London, Greenwood Press, 1988. ix,270p. index. $45.00; £35.95. ISBN: 0313245215.

270 biographies of historical and contemporary *prominentes* in all fields of the Mexican/American experience. Two appendices list biographees by profession and by State. 'Valuable as a starting point for further research' (*Booklist* v.84,no.18, 15 May 1988, p.1585). *Class No:* 929(73)

[5961]
The National cyclopaedia of American biography being the history of the United States as illustrated in the lives of the founders, builders and defenders of the Republic, and of men and women who are doing the work and moulding the thought of the present time. New York, J.T. White, 1892-1984.

Comprising almost 70,000 biographies the work has a complicated structure. Originally planned to rank with the great European biographical dictionaries in 12v. it now encompasses : 1. *Permanent series* (numbered volumes) v.1-63, 1892-1984. Lengthy entries with portraits and facsimile signatures (the series thereby serves as a national portrait gallery or as an historic picture file). Until 1924 each volume contained biographies of both deceased and living persons. Biographies 'are grouped by occupation or location ... in this way, there appears to be a narrative history running over several pages instead of vignettes of isolated persons and incidents'. Access therefore depends largely on the *Index*. No bibliographies. 2. *Current series* (lettered volumes) A-N, 1924-1978. Covers living persons only, the eminent and not so eminent. It is estimated that 75% of those included in the lettered volumes eventually found a place in the *Permanent series*. 3. *N-63* (1984) reverted to the practice of including entries relating to both living and dead persons in the same volume, seemingly to mark the *Cyclopaedia's* demise: 'it is likely to be the final volume ... issued under the auspices of the present publisher' (*Preface*). In fact, after 111 years, the publisher has gone out of business. 4. *Index* 576p. 1984. Replaces the 1971 and 1979 indexes and covers the entire set as described above. W.K. McCoy's 'The National Cyclopedia of American Biography', *Reference Service Review*, v.9,no.4, October/December 1981, p.5-9, from which much of this information is derived, includes 15 refs. and a bibliography. *Class No:* 929(73)

[5962]
Notable Americans: what they did, from 1620 to the present. Hubbard, L.S., *ed.* 4th ed. Detroit, Gale Research Co., 1988. x,733p. indexes. $178.25. ISBN: 0810325349.

1st ed. as *The conspectus of American biography* (1906). Part of *The National Cyclopaedia of American Biography (qv)*. 2nd ed. *White's conspectus of American biography* (1937). 3rd ed. *Notable names in American history: a tabulated register* (1973).

A compendium of 42,000 US officeholders and award winners in government, the military, business, labour, philanthropy, religion, and national associations, arranged in 19 chapters. No biographical information, simply chronological lists of names. 'Even researchers with access

....*(contd.)*

to the multitude of specialized sources ... will appreciate the convenience of this volume' (*Booklist*, v.84,no.18, 15 May 1988, p.1586-6). *Class No:* 929(73)

[5963]
Who was who in America. Wilmette, Illinois, Marquis Who's who Macmillan Directory Division, 1942-. $560.00 the set.

Historical volume (1607-1896). $69.50. 0837902002. 13,450 biographies from America's early days including Leif Ericsson, Columbus and John Cabot. Colour biographical map, time-line history chart and 'Facts at your finger tips' that puts American history into perspective 950A.D. - 20th century. 1. *1897-1942.* $69.50. 0837902010. 2. *1943-1950.* $69.50. 0837902061. 3. *1951-1960.* $69.50. 0837902037. 4. *1961-1968.* $69.50. 0837902045. 5. *1969-1973.* $69.50. 0837902053. 6. *1974-1976.* $69.50. 083790207x. 7. *1977-1987.* $69.50. 083790210x. 8. *1982-1985.* $69.50. 0837902142. 9. *1985-1989.* 1989. 392p £60. 0837902177. 10. *1989-1993.* 1993. 416p. £60. 0837902207. *Index Volume 1607-1993.* 304p. £24. 0837902215. Almost 111,000 notable figures in American history are included. Except for the *Historical volume* all biographies are taken from *Who's who in America*. *Class No:* 929(73)

[5964]
Who's who among Hispanic Americans 1992-93. Unterburger, J.L., *ed.* 2nd ed. Detroit, Gale Research Co., 1992. 475p. indexes. $89.95. ISBN: 0810376040.

First ed. 1990.

5000 A-Z entries for notable contemporary Hispanic Americans across a broad spectrum of professions and occupations. Geographic location, occupation and country of descent indexes. Data: occupation, education, career information, organization affiliations, honours and achievements, military service, sources of further information. Geographic location, occupation, and country of origin indexes. 'A significant tool about an import ethnic group' (*Booklist*, v.87, no.14, 15 March 1991, p.1525). Available online through NEXIS, on diskette, and magnetic tape. *Class No:* 929(73)

[5965]
Who's who in America 1992-1993. 47th ed. Wilmette, Illinois, Marquis Who's Who Macmillan Directory Division, 2v., 1992. 4032p. bibliogs., index. Biennial. £275; $399. ISBN: 0837901472.

First published 1899.

More than 80,000 biographies (and 14,000 'emerging figures'). Each biennial edition is thoroughly revised and features a retiree index, *i.e.* biographies deleted because of career retirement; obituaries; and regional and topical listings. 'A unique reference source with no close competitor' (A. Ricker's Who's Who in America', *Reference Service Review*, v.8,no.4, October/December 1980, p.7-13). *Who's who in America* geographic/professional index 1992-93. 1992. 486p. £59. 0837915074 facilitates access by country, state, or province (of Canada) or by one of 39 professional categories. Names are listed by location under each professional heading.

Marquis who's who (Dialog File 234) contains detailed biographies of over 77,000 leading figures in business, sports, arts, entertainment, science and technology. *Class No:* 929(73)

[5966]

—The Complete Marquis who's who plus. Wilmette, Illinois, Marquis Who's Who, 1993. CD in 4 formats: standard, custom, detailed, and mailing label. Price on application.

'Integrating the current *Who's Who in America,* 14 regional and professional *Who's Who* directories, and recent volumes of *Who Was Who in America,* The Complete Marquis Who's Who Plus contains profiles of 400,000 living notables and 5,200 figures from American history. Within every field of human endeavour - from art to business to medicine. 80000 records on living North American notables. 5200 profiles of leaders who have passed away since 1985. 88000 biographies on individuals of distinctly regional interest. 230,000 entries reflecting members of specific professions and special interest groups from the Marquis Professional and Topical Libraries of titles in addition to *Who's Who in the World, Who's Who of American Women; Who's Who of Emerging Leaders in America; and the Directory of Medical Specialists.* Personal and professional details on entrants including vital statistics, education, family background, addresses, and more'. *(Advt.).*

Class No: 929(73)

[5967]

—Index to Marquis who's who books 1991. Wilmette, Illinois, Marquis Who's Who, 1991. 350p. $62.00.

Successor to *Marquis who's who publications: index to all books* first published 1978; in 2v. 1984.

Referral tool to more than 280,000 individuals listed in the latest editions of Marquis who's who publications.

Class No: 929(73)

[5968]

—KENNEDY, S. 'First look': the Marquis Who's who database, *Online,* v.8,no.2, March 1984, p.31-35.

Scope and standards; database development; unique capabilities; upcoming enhancements; user participation; database specifications. *Class No:* 929(73)

[5969]

—Who's who in the East 1993-1994. 24th ed. Wilmette, Illinois, Marquis Who's Who Macmillan Directory Division, 1992. 1000p. £164. ISBN: 0837906245.

First published 1943.

Biographies of more than 25,000 prominent men and women living in Connecticut, Delaware, District of Columbia, Maine, Maryland, Massachusetts, New Hampshire, New Jersey, New York, Pennsylvania, Rhode Island, Vermont, and the Canadian provinces of New Brunswick, Newfoundland, Nova Scotia, Prince Edward Island, Quebec and Eastern Ontario. *Class No:* 929(73)

[5970]

—Who's who in the Midwest 1992-1993. 23rd ed. Wilmette, Illinois, Marquis Who's Who Macmillan Directory Division, 1992. 768p. £140. ISBN: 0837907233.

First published 1949.

More than 21,000 biographies of prominent men and women living in Illinois, Indiana, Iowa, Kansas, Michigan, Minnesota, Missouri, Nebraska, North Dakota, Ohio, South Dakota, Wisconsin and the Canadian provinces of Manitoba and Western Ontario. *Class No:* 929(73)

[5971]

—Who's who in the South and Southwest 1993-94. 23rd ed. Wilmette, Illinois, Marquis Who's Who Macmillan Directory Division, 1993. 848p. £134. ISBN: 083790823x.

First published 1950.

22,000 + biographies of notable men and women living in Alabama, Arkansas, Florida, Georgia, Kentucky, Louisiana, Missippy, North Carolina, Oklahoma, South Carolina, Tennessee, Texas, Virginia, West Virginia, Puerto Rico, Virgin Islands and Mexico. *Class No:* 929(73)

[5972]

—Who's who in the West 1992-1993. 23rd ed. Wilmette, Illinois, Marquis Who's Who Macmillan Directory Division, 1992. 832p. £140. ISBN: 0837909236.

First published 1949.

Over 21,000 biographies of men and women prominent in Alaska, Arizona, California, Colorado, Hawaii, Idaho, Montana, Nevada, New Mexico, Oregon, Utah, Washington, Wyoming and the Canadian provinces of Alberta, British Columbia and Saskatchewan.

Class No: 929(73)

[5973]

—Who's who of emerging leaders in America 1993-94. 4th ed. Wilmette, Illinois, Marquis Who's Who, 1992. 736p. £145. ISBN: 0837972035.

Profiles over 20,000 men and women who influence all levels of the American society, from medicine and business to law and religion.

Micromaterials

[5974]

The American biographical archive. Baillie, L., *ed.* New York, K.G. Saur Inc., 1986-1988. 1750 fiche (24x) in Silver or Diazo fiche. By 12 instalments. Silver $7,000.00. £6,600.00. Diazo $6900.00. £6,000.00.

A-Z cumulation of full text entries from 367 biographical works of reference covering 350,000 individuals from the earliest period of North American History to the early 20th century. *Class No:* 929(73)(003.5)

[5975]

—American biographical archive. Series II. München, K.G. Saur, 12 installments, 1993-96. 700 fiche (24x) silver or diazo £9,063 (silver); £8400 (diazo). ISBN: 3598335342, Silver; 3598335202, Diazo.

Single A-Z sequence cumulated from a further 250 biographical dictionaries published in 19th and 20th centuries. *Class No:* 929(73)(003.5)

[5976]

—American biographical index. London, K.G. Saur, 4v., 1992. 600p. (*£498. Free to subscribers to American biographical archive..*) ISBN: 0862913829.

Detailed printed index to all entries in *American biographical archive* together with listings of source works and fiche number in that work. *Class No:* 929(73)

[5977]

Black biographical dictionaries 1790-1950. Burkett, R.K., *and others, eds.* Alexandria, Virginia and Cambridge, Chadwyck-Healey, 1989. 1100 silver halide positive reading 49 frame 24xreduction microfiche. $5400.00.

Over 30,000 biographical references and portraits extracted from 300 volumes containing collective

....(contd.)

biographies detailing the lives of 19th and 20th century Afro-Americans. The complete contents of every volume indexed have been reproduced. Sponsored by the W.E.B. Dubois Institute for Afro-American Research, Harvard University.

Black biography 1790-1950 a cumulative index, 3v., 1991. 716p.++ 684p.++ 684p. $900. 0898870852. V.1-12 lists all entrants A-Z in a single sequence with information on gender, birth and death dates, place of birth, occupation, and religious affiliation. V.3 lists names under several categories. 'The entire index thus clearly stands by itself as an immeasurably valuable reference work, providing biographical information on more people of African descent than any other single source' (*Choice,* v.29, no.2, October 1992, p.952). *Class No:* 929(73)(003.5)

Bibliographies

[5978]
American autobiography 1945-1980: a bibliography. Briscoe, M.L., *and others, eds.* Madison, Univ. of Wisconsin Press, 1982-. xiv,365p. index. $35.00; £32.95. ISBN: 0299090906.

Intended as a supplement to L. Kaplan's *Bibliography of American autobiographies* (*qv*).

5008 descriptive entries compiled mainly from *Biography Index.* 'Because of the book's extensive coverage, coupled with the fact that it is a major work in the area and a supplement to Kaplan, this reference tool is an essential purchase for academic and larger public libraries' (*Choice,* v.20,no.8, April 1983, p.1105). *Class No:* 929(73)(01)

[5979]
American diaries: an annotated bibliography of published American diaries and journals. Arksey, L., *and others, eds.* Detroit, Gale Research Co., 2v., 1983-1987. xviii,311p.+Øviii,501p. indexes. $103.00; £78.00 each. ISBN: 0810318008, v.1; 0810318016, v.2.

Supersedes W. Matthew's *American diaries: an annotated bibliography of American diaries written prior to the year 1861* (Berkeley. University of California Press, 1945).

Chronologically arranged bibliography of printed American diaries and journals written 1492-1844 (v.1) and 1845-1980 (v.2). Annotation includes diary's emphasis, historic events mentioned, and diarist's background. 'A good bibliography covering a category of writing that has been increasing in demand' (*Choice,* v.21,no.9, May 1984, p.1271). *Class No:* 929(73)(01)

[5980]
Biographical books 1950-1980. New York, R.B. Bowker, 1980. xlix, 1557p. $110.00; £110.00. ISBN: 0835213153.

Over 45,000 biographies compiled from the database used to generate *American Book Publishing Record;* lists biographical and autobiographical books printed or distributed in US. Retrospective coverage is extended in *Biographical books 1876-1949,* 1983. lviii,1768p. $135.00. £140.00. ISBN 0835216039. *Class No:* 929(73)(01)

[5981]
Biography and genealogy master index: a consolidated index to more than 3,200,000 listings in over 350 current and retrospective biographical dictionaries. Herbert, M.C. *and* McNeil, B., *eds.* 2nd ed. Detroit, Gale Research Co., 8v., 1980-1981. 6000p. $975. £738. (*Gale Biographical Index Series.*) ISBN: 0810310945. ISSN: 07301316.

First edition published 1975-76 *Biographical dictionaries*

....(contd.)

master index edited by D. Labeau and G.C. Tarbert.

More than 3.2 million citations to biographical articles from more than 350 sources. 'Entries give the individual's name, birth and death dates when provided by the indexed source, and a coded citation locating the indexed material ... However, this is neither a "genealogical" index (*e.g.* passenger and cemetery lists are absent) nor a "master" index (coverage is too narrow and selective, and the emphasis is mainly on the US)' [nevertheless] 'when used with care and an understanding of its limitations, the index serves as an important and valuable aid' (*Choice,* v.19, no.1, September 1981, p.45). English language sources only.

McNeil, B. ed. *Biography and genealogy master index 1981-1985 cumulation,* 5v., 1985. 4177p. £568. 0810315068. A cumulation of the 5 annual supplements that updated the base set. An additional 2.3 million citations are recorded. *Biography and genealogy master index 1986-90 cumulation,* 3v., 1990. 3387p. £602. 0810348039. Adds 1,895,000 citations to biographical articles appearing in more than 500 editions and volumes of over 250 sources. Since 1980 over 4 million citations have been added to the base record.

Biography and genealogy master index 1995 (1994. 0810385996) add a further 1,3500,000 entries.

Biography and Genealogy master index CD-ROM 1994. 0810361973. Comprises 19 printed volumes indexing over 8.5 million biographies. *Class No:* 929(73)(01)

[5982]
—**Abridged biography and genealogy master index.** McNeil, B. *and* Unterburger, A.L., *eds.* Detroit, Gale Research Co., 3v., 1988. 3537p. $431.25. £299. ISBN: 0810321491.

1.6 million citations from 115 current and retrospective dictionaries, subject encyclopaedias *etc.* An updated edition is expected after 5 years. 'Libraries unable to afford the full Biography and Genealogy Master Index should consider purchasing the abridged version. Highly recommended' (*Choice,* v.25, no.11/12, July/August 1988, p.1671). *Class No:* 929(73)(01)

[5983]
—**Bio-Base 1990 Master Cumulation.** McNeil, B., *ed.* Detroit, Gale Research Co., 1990. 300 microfiches. £753. ISBN: 0810348284.

B. Bonta and F. Cable's 'The Gale biography series', Reference Services Review, v.10, no.1, Spring 1982, p.25-33 is a comparative review of the history, background, coverage and editorial practices of *Biography and genealogy master index, Bio-Base,* and *Biography master index.*

The 1990 Master Cumulation on microfiche of the *Biography and Genealogy Master Index* database furnishes nearly 7.5 million citations to biographical entries appearing in 1,650 editions and volumes of over 600 biographical dictionaries. Each citation provides the subject's full name (as given in the source indexed), birth and/or death dates, and a code indicating the source of biographical data. Printed bibliography of sources indexed accompanies each set.

Bio-Base 1991-1993 (1993. 37 microfiche cards. 0181037642) is the latest edition. Also available on CD-ROM, diskette, magnetic tape, and online through DIALOG file 287. *Bio-Base* is updated annually, then every five years it is cumulated from its inception to the current edition. *Class No:* 929(73)(01)

[5984]

UNITED STATES. Department of the Interior. Office of Indian Affairs Library. **Biographical and historical index of American Indians and persons involved in Indian affairs.** Boston, Mass., G.K. Hall, 8v., 1966. 4853p. $855.00 (Export $1035.00). ISBN: 0816107165.

200,000 catalogue cards photolithographed. Arranged A-Z by subjects *i.e.,* Indian tribes, events *etc.* especially in latter half of the ninteenth century and the first 20 years of the twentieth century.

There are extensive listings of Indian agents, other personnel of the Bureau of Indian Affairs, Indian chiefs, historically prominent Indians, and other information related to tribal affairs. The Index is arranged alphabetically by subject. *Class No:* 929(73)(01)

Jews

[5985]

American Jewish biographies. New York and Oxford, Facts on File, 1982. ix,493p. bibliog., index. $39.95; £26.50. ISBN: 0871964627.

Over 400 (Introduction) 500 (d/w) biographies of living, US citizens who consider themselves Jewish and who have made 'a permanent contribution to life in this country or are identified with a significant event, issue or movement' (*Preface*). Barbra Steisand 96 lines; Barbara Tuchman 109 lines. Although not as comprehensive as *Who's who in American Jewry* (*qv*) *Reference Quarterly,* v.22,no.4, Summer 1983: 419 remarks that it is 'a valuable compendium of achievements by Jewish personalities in the United States today'. *Class No:* 929(73)(=924)

Black Races

[5986]

Who's who among Black Americans 1991-92. Cloyd, I., *ed.* 7th ed. Detroit, Gale Research, 1992. 1500p. indexes. ISBN: 0810354047.

1st ed. 1976. Formerly published by Educational Communications of Lake Forest. Illinois.

Biographical and career details on 19000 notable individuals. An obituary section contains updated entries for those who have died since being listed in the 6th ed. Geographic and occupations indexes. Previous editions should not be discarded because of large number of biographees who are subsequently deleted. 'An important tool because relatively few African Americans are listed in *Who's who in America'* (*Booklist*, v.86, no.21, July 1990, p.2118). *Class No:* 929(73)(=96)

Negro-African

[5987]

Black biography, 1790-1950: a cumulative index. Gates, H.L., *and others, eds.* Alexandria, Virginia, Chadwyck-Healey, 1991. 2084p. indexes. $900. ISBN: 0898870852.

30,000 career profiles: birth and death dates; occupation (over 40 categories), and religious affiliations (over 50 denominations). *Class No:* 929(73)=96

Women

[5988]

American women 1935-1940 a composite biographical dictionary; a consolidation of all material appearing in the 1939-1940 edition of American women, with a supplement of unduplicated entries from the 1935-1936 and 1937-1938 editions. Howes, D., *ed.* Detroit, Gale Research Co., 2v., 1981. clxii,1208p. indexes. $160.00. ISBN: 0810304031.

About 12000 women from education, the arts, the professions, science, club work, business, and governments. Data includes occupation, membership, public offices, political party, books, and honours. Geographical and occupational indexes. 'Might have been a good who's who at the time of its original publication, but its purchase now is questionable when other sources meet reserchers' needs with more thoroughly' (*Choice,* v.19,no.8, April 1982, p.1043). *Class No:* 929(73)-0055.2

[5989]

HERMAN, K. **Women in particular** an index to American women. Phoenix, Arizona, Oryx, 1985. 740p. indexes. $95.00; £72.75. ISBN: 0897740882.

Biographies of *c.*15,000 women who made a significant contribution to American life. Data: Birth and death dates, career information, ethnicity, religion, and list of sources for further information. Despite some reservations *Library Journal* 15 May 1985, p.57 concluded that it is 'a useful tool that can be recommended for most libraries'. *Class No:* 929(73)-0055.2

[5990]

Who's who of American women 1993-1994. 18th ed. Wilmette, Illinois, Marquis Who's Who Macmillan Directory Division, 1993. 1160p. Biennial. £155. ISBN: 0837904188.

First published 1958.

Over 30,000 biographies. Data: personal, present position, education, career path covering a wide range of professions and disciplines including government, business, the arts, and medicine. *Class No:* 929(73)-0055.2

Bibliographies

[5991]

ADDIS, P.K. **Through a women's I.** an annotated bibliography of American women's autobiographical writings 1946-1976. Metuchen, New Jersey, Scarecrow Press, 1983. xiv,607p. indexes. $37.50. ISBN: 0810815885.

Supplements L. Kaplan's *Bibliography of American autobiographies* (Univ. of Wisconsin Press, 1961) and M.L. Brisco's *American autobiography 1945-1980* (*qv*).

2217 descriptive entries A-Z by author. Introduction includes list of sources p.ix-xiv. *Class No:* 929(73)-0055.2(01)

Argentina

[5992]

CUTOLO, V.O. **Nuevo diccionario biográfico argentino (1750-1930).** Buenos Ayres, Editorial Elche, 7v., 1968-1985. 5053p.

V.1 has about 1000 entries relating to wide range of significant figures both native and foreign born. Data: date and place of birth, education, career, and major publications. Some entries carry extensive bibliographies). Covers January 1982 onwards. *Class No:* 929(82)

[5993]

UDAONDO, E. **Diccionario biográfico argentino.** Buenos Ayres, Imprenta y Casa Editoria Coni, 1938. 1151p.
   c.3300 biographies for personalities active in the period 1800-1920. *Class No:* 929(82)

[5994]

UDAONDO, E. **Diccionario biográfico colonial argentino.** Buenos Ayres, Huarpes, 1945. 980p. illus.
   Biographical dictionary from earliest colonial days to 1810. *Class No:* 929(82)

[5995]

UDAONDO, E., *and others*. **Grandes hombres de nuestria patria.** Buenos Ayres, Editorial Pleamar, 3v., 1968. 1160p. illus., ports, facsims.
   c.300 biographies of outstanding figures in Argentine history. *Class No:* 929(82)

[5996]

VITAVER, P.R., *ed*. **Quién es quién en América del Sur** diccionario biogáfico Argentino 1982-1983. Buenos Ayres, Publicaciones Referenciales Latino Americanas, 1982. xv,799p.
   6000 biographies. Publicaciones Referenciales en el Mundo (list of 112 Who's whos) p.14. *Class No:* 929(82)

Bolivia

[5997]

Quién es quién en Bolivia. La Paz, Editores Quién es Quién en Bolivia. x,338p. ports., index.
   First published 1942.
   c.500 biographies. Forenames appear first in entries. *Class No:* 929(84)

Peru

[5998]

MENDIBURU, M. de. **Diccionario histórico-biográfico de Perú.** 2nd ed. Lima, Enrique Palacios, 11v., 1931-35.
   First published 8v. 1874-90. 3rd ed. commenced in 1976.
   Over 2700 biographies. *Appendice al Diccionario histórico-biográfico del Peru* (Lima, Gill, 5v., 1935-38) has about 4000 entries. *Class No:* 929(85)

Colombia

[5999]

Quién es quién en Colombia. 4th ed. Bogota, Editorial Kelly, 1970.
   Published in 3 earlier editions: 1944, 1948, and 1970. *Class No:* 929(86)

Ecuador

[6000]

Diccionario biografico del Ecuador. Pimentel, R.P. Guayaquil, Mayo, 3v., 1987. 511p.++ 469p.++ 538p. pbk.
   Biographies of those who contributed to the progress and civilization of Ecuador. Not arranged A-Z. *Class No:* 929(866)

Guyana

[6001]

SEYMOUR, A. *and* SEYMOUR, E. **Dictionary of Guyanese biography.** Georgetown, A.J. Seymour, 2v., 1985-1986. bibliog., pbk. Mimeographed.
   2 separate compilations: 1. *1985.* 118p. - 2. *1986.* 97p. Introduction to v.2 looks forward to the possibility of combining them into one compilation. *Class No:* 929(88)

Paraguay

[6002]

Quien es quien en el Paraguay. Monte-Domecq, R., *comp*. 9th ed. Asuncion, Editoria MD & Asociados, 1991. 220p. illus., ports, maps, index.
   Historical synthesis p.19-39; Constitution p.41-61; Political divisions of Paraguay p.63-70; List of Governors-General and Presidents p.71-90. Biographies p.91-174. *Class No:* 929(892)

Uruguay

[6003]

FERNÁNDEZ SALDANA, J.M. **Diccionario uruguayo de biografías 1810-1940.** Montevideo, Amerinda, 1945. 1366p.
   About 800 fairly lengthy biographies of significant historical figures. No bibliographies. *Class No:* 929(899)

[6004]

Quién es quién en el Uruguay. Montevideo, Central de Publicaciones, Panamérica Uruguaya, 1980. 688p. ports.
   Biographical section is followed by banking and business information. *Class No:* 929(899)

Australasia & Oceania

[6005]

Who's who in Oceania 1980-1981. Craig, R.D. *and* Clement, R.T. Laie, Hawaii, The Institute for Polynesian Studies, Brigham Young University Hawaii Campus, 1980. [iii],219p. bibliog.
   Personalities in government, education, science, religion. Excludes Australia, New Zeland, Papua New Guinea and Hawaii. Prime source of information is the 13th ed. of *Pacific Islands year book and who's who* (1978). *Class No:* 929(9)

Micromaterials

[6006]

Australasian biographical archive. München, K.G. Saur. 12 instalments, 1990-94. 420 fiches (x24) silver of diazzo. £6200 (silver; £5500 (diazzo). ISBN: 359832930x, silver; 359832944x, diazzo.
   Arranged A-Z by subject's name, this single sequence cumulation of approx. 100,000 entries from 140 biographical works covers Australia, New Zealand, Papua New Guinea, and South Pacific Islands, from the period of discovery and settlement to the post-war era. On completion a printed index will be published to include name variations, and information on sources and archive location. *Class No:* 929(9)(003.5)

Indonesia

[6007]

Who's who in Indonesia biographies of prominent Indonesian personalities in all fields. Roeder, O.G. *and* Mahiddin, Mahmud, *comps.* 2nd ed. Singapore, Gunung Agung, 1980. vi,428p. ports., softcover.

1st ed. 1971.

President and Government p.1-24. Biographies p.26-385. The first 'Who's who' to be published in Indonesia. About 1,000 entries. 'The book's aim is not to stimulate a personality cult but simply to present biographical information on prominent Indonesians in all fields and all parts of the country' (Foreword to 1st ed.). Appendices 1-13 give directory information. *Class No:* 929(910)

Sarawak

[6008]

Who's who Sarawak 1985-86. 2nd ed. Kuching, Sarawak Publishing House, 1985. 406p. ports. ISSN: 01274619.

'Biographies of prominent people who have won recognition for notable achievements in various fields of human endeavour' (*Introduction*). Also directory information on the Government, M.P.s, Departments and Statutory bodies. *Class No:* 929(911.14)

Philippines

[6009]

MANUEL, E.A. Dictionary of Philippine biography. Quezon City, Filipiniana Publications, 1955, 1970, 1986.

V.1 1955. 511p. illus., index. V.2. 1970. 502p. illus., index. V.3. 1986. xv, 566p. illus., index. All 3v. so far published are separate A-Z sequences of biographical sketches some of which, especially in v.3, are becoming encyclopaedic in nature with extensive bibliographies by and about the persons included. V.3 includes a foreword on documentation, general information, bibliographic features and Towards an encyclopaedia goal: national conditions and needs shaping its form and substance. Future volumes are expected: at what intervals is not vouchsafed. *Class No:* 929(914)

[6010]

The Philippine who's who. Soriano, D.L. 2nd ed. Manila, Who's who Publishers, 1981. 400p.

Brief biographies. Many omissions. *Class No:* 929(914)

[6011]

VILLAREL, H.K., *and others.* **Eminent Filippines.** Manila, National Historical Commission, 1965. xxvi,294p. ports. (*National Historical Commission Publication no.1.*)

About 220 brief biographies including many not found in Manuel's *Dictionary of Philippine biography* (qv). *Class No:* 929(914)

New Zealand

[6012]

The Book of New Zealand women Ko Kui ma te kaupapa. Macdonald, C., *and others, eds.* Wellington, Bridget Williams Books, 1992. xiv,772p. ports, indexes. ISBN: 0908912048.

Signed biographical essays of 300 NZ women (with sources). Indexes to names, subjects, and authors. *Class No:* 929(931)

[6013]

The Dictionary of New Zealand biography. Wellington, Allen & Unwin New Zealand and Department of Internal Affairs, 1990-.

V.1: 1769-1869. 1990. xviii,674p. indexes. ISBN 004641052x. 572 biographical essays (20% of women; 30% Maoris). 'As well as for eminence on a national scale, the people in this Dictionary have been chosen for their standing within less extensive milieux, for their representativeness and for the balance their presence will give to the volume as a whole' (*Introduction*). Glossary of Maori words p.xiv-xv. Categories index (*i.e.* professions and occupations) p.615-25. Tribal and Hapu index p.627-9. Name index p.631-74. Next volume will be in the Maori language and will contain those Maori biographies printed in v.1. Further volumes of *DNZB* will be published in the 1990s covering successive chronological periods. *Class No:* 929(931)

[6014]

MILES, S. 50 Famous New Zealanders portraits and biographies of 50 of the most famous New Zealanders. Auckland, Burnham House, 1985. 115p. col.illus., index. ISBN: 0908615272. *Class No:* 929(931)

[6015]

SCHOLFIELD, G.H., *ed.* **A Dictionary of New Zealand biography.** Wellington, Department of Internal Affairs, 2v., 1940.

Sponsored by the National Historical Committee as an official centennial publication. Entries are for persons, not necessarily resident in New Zealand, 'who had significance in the history of the Dominion' from roughly 1840 onwards. 95% of contributions are the work of the editor; the others are signed by the authors. Documented entries. Short glossaries of Maori words. Bibliography, v.1, p.xviii-xix. Modelled on the *DNB. Class No:* 929(931)

[6016]

Who's who in New Zealand. 12th ed. Wellington, Reed, 1991. ISBN: 0790002248.

First published 1908.

The backgrounds and achievements of almost 3000 prominent NZ men and women in all fields of activity, including business, politics, education, medicine, law, science, the arts, and sport. Data: academic achievements, professional qualifications, positions held, published works, awards and honours, recreations, and family details. *Class No:* 929(931)

Melanesia

[6017]

O'REILLY, P. Calédonians: répertoire biobibliographique de la Nouvelle-Calédonie. 2nd ed. Paris, Musée de l'Homme, 1980. 416p. ports. (*Publications de la Société des Océanistes, No.3.*)

First published 1953 (x,308p.).

French language who's who information on about 1000 living and dead prominent figures. *Class No:* 929(932)

[6018]

O'REILLY, P. Hébridais: répertoire bio-bibliographique des Nouvelles-Hébrides. Paris, Musée de l'Homme, 1957. 290p. ports. (*Publications de la Société des Océanistes, no.6.*)

Biographies not only of notable residents but also of historical figures connected with the island. *Class No:* 929(932)

Australia

[6019]

1000 famous Australians. Adelaide, Rigby, 1978. 368p. ports., index. ISBN: 0727008803.

17 A-Z sections *e.g.* 1. The searchers ... 2. The pioneers ... 10. Reformers and revolutionaries. Concise biographies limited to men and women born in Australia compiled by well known Australian writers. *Class No:* 929(94)

[6020]

AustraAsian who's who. Singh, J., *ed*. Adelaide, Oriental Publications, 1987. xxvi,282p., ports., index. ISBN: 0731600738.

Biographical details of almost 500 leaders of various Asian communities arranged in 12 professional categories. Australian immigration policy p.ix-xi. AustralAsian associations and societies p.xv-xxxiv. *Class No:* 929(94)

[6021]

Australian dictionary of biography. Melbourne Univ. Press, 1966-. Distributed in UK by Europa Publications. ISBN: 0522842364.

Period 1. *Convicts and settlers 1788-1850.* 1966-67. V.1-2. 1116 entries. Period 2. *Gold rush & after 1851-1890.* V.3-6. 1969-76. 2053 entries. Period 3. *Federation and after 1891-1939.* V.7-12. 1979-90. *Index: volumes 1-2 1788-1939.* 1991. xv,236p. 0522844596. bibliog. p.xv. Names (p.1-86). Places of birth (p.87-165). Occupations (p.166-285). Consolidated corrigenda (p.287-326). V.13-16 1940-1980 to be published 1993-. A production of high standard. 'It is the great merit of the *Australian Dictionary of Biography* (unlike the *DNB*) that if offers a genuine cross-section of society' (*Times Literary Supplement,* no. 3435, 28 December 1967, p.1263). *Class No:* 929(94)

[6022]

—GIBBNEY, H.J. *and* SMITH, A.G., *comps.* A Biographical register 1788-1939. Notes from the name index of the Australian Dictionary of Biography. Canberra, Australian National University, Australian Dictionary of Biography, 2v., 1987. xviii,403p.+429p. bibliog., index. ISBN: 0731501047, set.

1. *A-K.* 07351500989. 2. *L-Z.* 0731501039.

8100 entries. Data: name; leading occupation; main place associated with; birth, marriage, death details; biographical outline; and bibliographical references. By-product of 1st 12v. of *Australian dictionary of biography.* Based on a card index maintained since late 1950s which 'as an aid to the publication of the *Dictionary,* now extends far beyond this basic function and encompasses material on many thousands more men and women than those deemed appropriate for a *Dictionary* entry' (*Introduction*). Bibliography of collective biographical material p.xiii-xvii. Occupational index. p.361-429. *Class No:* 929(94)

[6023]

—Occupational index to the Australian Dictionary of Biography (1788-1890) Volumes 1-6. Marshall, J.G. *and* Trahair, R.C.S., *comps.* Bundoora, Victoria, Department of Sociology; School of Social Sciences, La Trobe Univ. 1979. 139p. softcover. ISBN: 0858162156.

Based on the occupations that follow names and dates of each entry. Reproduced from typsescript. *Class No:* 929(94)

[6024]

Debrett's handbook of Australia. 3rd (Bicentennial) ed. Sydney, Collins, 1987. 272+1098p. col. frontis., col. illus. ISBN: 0002178044. ISSN: 08193665.

First published as *Debrett's handbook of Australia and New Zealand* 1982; 2nd ed. 1984.

7000 biographical entries for leading men and women (Kerry Packer 20 lines, Rupert Murdoch 24 lines). Introductory features include J.C. Vaughan's 'New flags for Australia' p.95-96. *Class No:* 929(94)

[6025]

GILLEN, M. The Founders of Australia a biographical dictionary of the First Fleet. Sydney, Library of Australian History, 1989. xlviii, 624p. illus., facsims. bibliog. Aust $56.00. ISBN: 0908120699.

Biographical entries of all 1377 people known to have landed in Sydney Cove, January 1788. A series of appendices provide entries for those who embarked in the First Fleet but who never reached Sydney; non-English First Fleeters; Officers, Passengers, Free Women and Children, and ships and crews. Explanatory notes (on tracing First Fleeters) p.xxxix-xliii. Appendix 10. Abstract of biographical data. Appendix 12. Chronology. Bibliography p.537-544. Published to commemorate the Australian Bicentenary. *Class No:* 929(94)

[6026]

—FIDLON, P.G., *and others, eds.* The First Fleeters a comprehensive listing of convicts, marines, seamen, officers, wives, children and ships. Sydney, Australian Documents Library, 1981. ix, 86p. pbk.

Data: name, status, ship. Does not purport to be a complete list. *Class No:* 929(94)

[6027]

—RYAN, R.B., *ed.* The Second Fleet convicts a comprehensive listing of convicts who sailed in HMS Guardian, Lady Juliana, Neptune, Scarborough and Surprise. Sydney, Australian Documents Library, 1982. xv, 95p. pbk. ISBN: 0908219067.

Data: name/place, date, sentence, ship. *Class No:* 929(94)

[6028]

—RYAN, R.J., *ed.* The Third Fleet convicts: an alphabetical listing of names, giving place and date of conviction, length of sentence and ship of transportation. Cammeray, Horwitz Grahame, 1983. xiv, 126p. ISBN: 072551521x.

Data: name/place,. date, sentence, ship. *Class No:* 929(94)

[6029]

Who's who in Australia: an Australian biographical dictionary and register of prominent people with which is incorporated John's Notable Australians. 29th ed. Melbourne, Information Australia, 1993. 1384p. illus., Triennial publication. ISSN: 08108226.

1st ed. *John's notable Australians* 1906. 3rd ed. *Fred John's annual* 1912. 6th ed. *Who's who in Australia* 1992.

About 8200 Biographies. Preliminary features include words and music Adcance Australia fair; Royal style and titles; Order of precedence of honours and awards; Australian decorations (*illus.*); Australian winners of Nobel prizes; Diplomatic Corps in Australia *etc.* *Class No:* 929(94)

Bibliographies

[6030]

BORCHARDT, D.H. *and* MARSHALL, J.G. 'Biography', chapter 20, *Australians: a guide to sources* (v.10 *Australians. A historical library*, 1988).

Introductory essay and annotated bibliography divided into General biographical dictionaries and regional sources for New South Wales, Queensland, Tasmania, Victoria and Western Australia. *Class No:* 929(94)(01)

Women

[6031]

LOFTHOUSE, A., *comp*. Who's who of Australian women. North Ryde, New South Wales, Methuen Australia, 1982. 504p. frontis, index. ISBN: 0454004370.

Celebrates the lives of 1430 Australian women spanning 3 generations. *Class No:* 929(94)-0055.2

Polynesia

[6032]

O'REILLY, P. Tahitiens: répertoire bio-bibliographique de la Polynésie française. 2nd ed. Paris, Musée de l'Homme, 1975. 670p. ports., index.

Replaces 1st ed. 1962 (xvi, 535p.). and *Supplément*, 1966 (iv,104p.).

1875 annotated entries and includes a list of governors and commandants. 'A valuable who's who of French Polynesia' (G.W. Fry and R. Mauricio. *Pacific Basin and Oceania*, 1987. Entry 922). *Class No:* 929(96)

Fiji

[6033]

Who's who in Fiji Fiji's golden book of record. Berwick, S. Suva, Berwicks Publishing House, 1990. 307p. ports, maps. pbk. ISBN: 0091005493.

A second edition is planned for 1995. Until then a supplement will be published every December to update existing entries and for the inclusion of new biographies.

3 parts: 1. Introduction (customs and traditions; historical background; people; constitutional developments) - 2. Who's who (p.89-242) - 3. Who was who (p.248-307). *Class No:* 929(961.1)

Jews

[6034]

WIGODER, G. Dictionary of Jewish biography. New York, Simon & Schuster, 1991. 567p. ports. $55. ISBN: 013210105x.

Over 750 biographical sketches, of varying length, with bibliographic citations, of famous and infamous Jews of all nationalities from biblical to modern times. Excludes living persons. 'This exceedingly useful work ... can answer a great many reference questions' (*Library Journal*, 1 June 1992, p.188). *Class No:* 929(=924)

Bibliographies

[6035]

ZUBATSKY, D.S. Jewish autobiographies and biographies an international bibliography of books and dissertations in English. New York, Garland, 1989. x,370p. $47. ISBN: 0824056434.

1,800 entries, arranged A-Z by biographee. Mostly confined to 20th century. Major sources consulted p.viii-x. Topical index (*i.e.* by profession or occupation). *Class No:* 929(=924)(01)

929.5/.9 Genealogy & Heraldry

Genealogy & Heraldry

Germany

Bibliographies

[6036]
BIRD, J. 'Some sources for German genealogy and heraldry', *Genealogists' Magazine*, v.13, no.5, March 1960, p. 143-144.
Standard works listed in the major bibliographies with annotations. *Class No:* 929.50/.9(430)(01)

Poland

Bibliographies

[6037]
HOSKINS, J.W. **Polish genealogy and heraldry** an introduction to research. Washington, European Division, Library of Congress, 1987. xii, 114p. illus., map, index, softcover.
Pt.1: 1. Armorials and studies in heraldry - 2. Genealogy - 3. English language publications for Americans seeking their Polish heritage - 4. Select periodicals - 5. Bibliography. Pt.2: 6. Encyclopedias - 7. Biographies - 8. Geographical dictionaries, gazetteers and maps - 9. Histories - 10. Archives and printed sources - 11. Miscellaneous reference works. Chronology p.98-104. List of rulers p.105. See also B. Kles-Pilewski's 'Some sources for Polish genealogy', *Genealogist's Magazine*, v.16, no.4, December 1969, p.150-9, a briefly annotated list of 90 items. *Class No:* 929.50/.9(438)(01)

France

Bibliographies

[6038]
BIRD, J. 'Some sources for French genealogy and heraldry', *Genealogists' Magazine*, v.13, no.8, December 1960, p.237-241.
Annotated lists of standard works from the major bibliographies. *Class No:* 929.50/.9(44)(01)

[6039]
SAFFROY, G. Bibliographie généalogique, héraldique et nobiliaire de la France, des origines à nos jours. Imprimés et manuscrits. Paris, Saffroy, 5v., 1968-88. Published with aid of the Centre National de la Recherche Scientifique.
1. *Généralités*. 1974. 2. *Provinces et colonies françaises. orient latin, refugiés.* 3. *Recueils généalogiques généraux, monographies, familiales et études particulières.* 1974. 830p. 4. *Table générale, auteurs, titres anonymes, matières.* 570p. *Supplément 1969-1983*. 1988. xvi, 286p. ISBN 2901541054.

.... *(contd.)*
V.1 contains a subject index. Entries are subdivided in detail. Items 1506-1931: 'Bibliographies héraldiques et généalogiques' subdivided by country). Includes coloured plates. *Class No:* 929.50/.9(44)(01)

Netherlands

Bibliographies

[6040]
LEENAERTS, R.J. Algemeen genealogisch-heraldisch repertorium voor die Zuildelijke Nederlanden / Répertoire général généalogique et héraldique des Pays-Bas/ Méridionaux/General genealogical and heraldic index of the Southern Netherlands. Handszame, Belgium, Familia et Patra (now Torhout, Belgium, Flandria Nostra), 8v., 1969-1985.
38,824 items from books, periodicals and newspapers. *Class No:* 929.50/.9(492)(01)

USA

Bibliographies

[6041]
FILBY, P.W., *comp*. American and British genealogy and heraldry: a selected list of books. 3rd ed. Boston, New England Historic Genealogical Society, 1983. xix, 940p. $49.95. ISBN: 0880820047.
First two editions published by the American Library Association in 1970 and 1975.
Almost 10,000 entries citing books and definitive periodical articles on genealogy, heraldry, and North American local history with a genealogical slant. Scope enlarged to almost double that of the previous edition. Extensive index of 20,000 entries. Treatment of black and ethnic genealogy is greatly expanded and a completely new section appears listing works in English covering non-English speaking countries. Described as 'unmatched in the field' by Evelyn Haynes' 'Encore Filby!' *Reference Services Review*, v.12, no.3, Fall 1984, p.70-72 which reports that compiler and publisher are contemplating annual or biennial supplements. *Class No:* 929.50/.9(73)(01)

Biographies

[6042]
Who's who in genealogy and heraldry. Meyer, M.K. *and* Filby, P.W., *eds*. 2nd ed. Detroit, Gale Research Co., 1982. 232p. $50. ISBN: 096691200.
Personal and career information on more than 800 (mainly US) professional genealogists and experts in heraldry. Data includes education, accreditations, positions held, awards, publications, and special interests. *Class No:* 929.50/.9(73)(092)

Genealogy

Software

[6043]

PRZECHA, D. *and* LOWREY, J. **Guide to genealogy software.** Baltimore, Genealogical Publishing Co., 1993. 195p. illus., index, pbk. $24.95. ISBN: 080631382x.

'A pragmatic buyer's guide for the computer-literate genealogist faced with the wide array of software designed to help organize and access family data. The authors solicited information, demonstration disks, and documentation from a variety of software producers to glean data on more than 100 genealogy-related programs and utilities' (*Booklist,* v.90, no.1, 1 September 1993, p.87-8). *Class No:* 929.50(003.42)

Bibliographies

[6044]

ACKERMANN, K.T., *ed*. **Genealogical periodical annual index:** key to the genealogical literature. Bowie, Maryland, Heritage Books, 1963-, Annual.

v.25: *1986* (1987. 256p. $17.50 ISBN 1556130724). A surname, locality, topical and book review index to genealogical and related periodical literature (over 260 titles in all). Preceded by D.L. Jacobus's *Index to genealogical periodicals* (Baltimore, Genealogical Publishing Co., 1978. 365p. $17.50). which covers the years up to 1952. *Class No:* 929.50(01)

Handbooks & Manuals

[6045]

STOKVIS, A.M.H.J. **Manuel d'histoire, de généalogie et de chronologie de tous les états du globe** depuis les temps les plus reculés jusqu'à nos jours. Leiden, Brill, 3v., 1888-93. (Reprinted Amsterdam, 1966).

1. *Asie. Afrique. Amérique. Polynésie.* 574p. lxxxip. 2-3. *Les états de l'Europe et leurs colonies.* viii, 584p., xxix, 967p. Comprises historical summaries of states, fiefs *etc.* with lists of sovereigns and elected rulers, and hundreds of skeletal genealogies. *Class No:* 929.50(035)

Dictionaries

[6046]

HARRIS, M. *and* HARRIS, G., *comps*. **Ancestry's concise genealogical dictionary.** Salt Lake City, Ancestry, 1989. 259p. bibliog. $10.95. ISBN: 091648906x.

3500 genealogical and historical terms partially defined. 'The reader would profit from more complete explanations or choices'; nevertheless 'this is a convenient little guide which many a genealogist will find useful' (*Choice,* v.27, no.3, April 1990, p.1298). *Class No:* 929.50(038)

Worldwide

[6047]

JOHNSON, K.A. *and* SAINTY, M.R., *eds*. **Genealogical research directory national and international 1993.** North Sydney, Genealogical Research Directory, 1985-. Annual. Available in UK from SPA Books, Stevenage. 896p. maps. ISBN: 0908120842.

.... (contd.)

Originally published by Library of Australian History, 1981, as *Genealogical research directory (Australasian ed.).*

A medium by which family historians may exchange research data with distant relatives and others. 1993 edition is in 5 parts: (1) Directory of surnames (dates; family names; time period; town, county, province or state); (2) Subjects; (3) One-name studies and organizations; (4) Directory of genealogical societies A-Z by country; (5) Professional notices. Research repositories A-Z by country p.19-24. 10 maps. *Class No:* 929.50(100)

Databases

[6048]

International genealogical index.

Over 30 million baptismal entries from parish and non-parochial registers from all parts of England compiled and computerized by the Genealogical Department of the Church of Latter Day Saints, Salt Lake City, Utah. See J.W. Gibson's *Where to find the international Genealogical Index* (1984),. A specimen page is on p.146 of T.V.H. Fitzhughes' *The dictionary of genealogy* (rev.ed. 1985). *Class No:* 929.50(100)(003.4)

Bibliographies

[6049]

KAMINKOW, M.J., *ed*. **Genealogies in the Library of Congress :** a bibliography. Jamestown, Virginia, Magna Carta Book Company, 2v., 1972. Supplement 1972-1976, 1977. Second Supplement 1976-1986, 1987. 1800p.+285p.+850p. $175. $89.50. (2nd Supp'lt). ISBN: 0910946159, 2v; 0910946302, (2nd Supp'lt.).

'This bibliography brings up to date similar printed works published in 1910 and 1919 under the title *American and English genealogies in the Library of Congress*, as well as the microcard edition which appeared in 1954' (*Editor's note*).

19,208 items plus addenda (734). Bibliographical notes; Library of Congress locations; nearly 25,000 cross-references (including references from family names to authors). Includes all entries in the Library of Congress 'Family name index', and lists not only American and English works but also holdings of Canadian, Irish, Welsh, Scottish, Australian, Latin American, Polish, German, Dutch, Scandinavian, French, Spanish, Italian, Portuguese and Asian sources. 'The most comprehensive bibliography available of family histories of America and Great Britain' (*Library Journal,* v.98, no.8, 15 April 1973, p.1243). Kaminkow's *A complement to Genealogies in the Library of Congress* (Magna Carta Books, 1981. 118p. $83.50. 0910946248) adds a further 20,000 items.

Genealogies catalogued by the Library of Congress since 1986: with a list of established forms of family names and a list of genalogies converted to microform since 1983. Washington, Library of Congress, 1992. 1349p. $70. *Class No:* 929.50(100)(01)

[6050]
SCHREINER-YANTIS, N. **Genealogical and local history books in print.** 4th ed. Springfield, Virginia, Genealogical Books in Print, 3v., 1985. 1722p. $35.00 set. ISBN: 0891570349.

First published as *Genealogical books in print* 1975.

A bibliography of over 30,000 books and microforms valuable to genealogists, family and local historians. 1. General reference (71 categories) p.115-292. - 2. Research sources (A-Z x US State) p.293-1300. 3. Localities other than US, (A-Z by country) p.1301-22. 4. Family genealogies p.1322-1722. Name and address of vendors p.11-114. Each publication is keyed to a vendor. Purpose is to provide an inexpensive method of advertising for publishers and the researcher with a knowledge of publications available in his area of interest. 'Recommended for everyone in the genealogical field' (*RQ,* v.15, no.1, Fall 1975, p.81).
Class No: 929.50(100)(01)

Official Records

[6051]
KEMP, T.J. **Vital records handbook.** Baltimore, Genealogical Publishing Co., 1988. ix, 231p. facsims. $19.95. ISBN: 0806312203.

Complete collection of vital records application forms (for photocopying) with essential data such as name and address of record office, 'phone, fees, and explanation of payment methods, for all record offices in 1. United States - 2. U.S. Trust Territories - 3. Canada, Ireland and United Kingdom. Dates of files held, gaps and omissions, and alternative locations are also indicated. *Class No:* 929.50(100)(093.2)

Jews

Bibliographies

[6052]
ZUBATSKY, D.S. *and* BERENT, I.M. **Jewish genealogy** a sourcebook of family histories and genealogies. New York, Garland Publishing Inc., 1984. xx, 422p. $30. ISBN: 0824090284, US.

Supersedes Herman Meyer's *Bibliographica Genealogica Judaica in USA* (1942), Cecil Roth's *Magna Bibliotheca Anglo Judaica in UK* (1957) and Ruth Lehman's *Nova Bibliotheca Anglo Judaica in UK* (1970).

Surveys and locates some 6300 genealogies covering roughly 3500 Jewish names. 'The book is of greatest value in pinpointing American Jewish families but while the USA predominates, due attention is paid to European, Israeli, UK and Australasian sources' (*Genealogists Magazine,* v.21, no.7, September 1984, p.254). V.2. 1989. 326p. $30. 0824020367 continues and expands coverage.
Class No: 929.50(100)(=924)(01)

Europe

Handbooks & Manuals

[6053]
BAXTER, A. **In search of your European roots:** a complete guide to tracing your ancestors in every country in Europe. Baltimore, Genealogical Publishing Co., 1985. xix, 289p. bibliog. index, pbk. $12.95. ISBN: 0806311142.

A-Z guides of 30 European countries (excluding the

....(contd.)
United Kingdom) are designed to guide the reader through the complexities of genealogical research. Up-to-date information on church, state, and provincial archives. European Jewish records p.11-20. Bibliography p.279-83. Genealogical organizations p.284-6.
Class No: 929.50(4)(035)

[6054]
PRYCE, F.R. **A Guide to European genealogies,** exclusive of the British Isles; with an historical survey of the principal genealogical writers. Library Association theses 1965. Published High Wycombe, University Microfilms, 1972.

An index of 11,300 European families contained in 11 major genealogical compilations, from Pére Anselme to Prinz von Isenburg (*qv.*) Gives references from all titles and lists locations of the works indexed, in 196 British libraries. Includes an annotated bibliography of other important compilations. *Class No:* 929.50(4)(035)

Great Britain

[6055]
PEDERSEN, S. **Searching overseas** a guide to family history sources for Australians & New Zealanders. Kenthurst, New South Wales, Kangaroo Press, 1987. 96p. illus., facsims., index, pbk. ISBN: 0864171595.

Where to find records. Concentrates on UK sources.
Class No: 929.50(410)

[6056]
YEO, G., *comp.* **The British overseas:** a guide to records of their births, baptisms, marriages, deaths and burials, available in the United Kingdom. 2nd ed. London, Guildhall Library, 1988. 72p. pbk. ISBN: 0900422262.

First published 1984.

Part 1. Introduction to the sources. 2. List of known registers for individual places overseas. 'A very useful guide' (*Refer,* v.4, no.1, Spring 1986, p.15).
Class No: 929.50(410)

Bibliographies

[6057]
KAMINKOW, M.J. **A New bibliography of British genealogy** with notes. Baltimore, Maryland, Magna Carta Book Co., 1965. xvii,170p.

1,783 numbered entries, the most important being annotated. 8 parts: 1. General works (bibliography; manuals and introductions; indexes to pedigrees; other indexes; guides, calendars, indexes, etc. to manuscript collections; guide to microfilm holdings; library directories) - 2. Periodicals, including newspapers - 3. Particular subjects ('Army' to 'Wills') - 4. English counties, A-Z - 5. Ireland - 6. Scotland - 7. Wales - 8. Islands (including West Indies). Addenda. Index (authors, series, etc.). 'The main aim has been to list books that have not been listed elsewhere, and to indicate where to look for a list of those that have' (*Introduction*). 'One of the most important genealogical bibliographies published during recent years' (*Genealogists' Magazine,* v.15,no.7, Setpember 1966, p.255-7). Largely replaces H.G. Harrison's *Select bibliography of English genealogy* (1937). *Class No:* 929.50(410)(01)

[6058]

RAYMOND, S. British genealogical periodicals a bibliography of their contents. Birmingham, Federation of Family History Societies, 2v., 1991. 83p. + 39p. £5 and £3. ISBN: 1872094201; 1872094236.

Bibliography of the contents of 19th and early 20th century periodicals. V.1 covers *Collectanea topographica et genealogica* (1834-43); *Topographer and genealogist* (1846-58); and *The Ancestor* (1902-5). V.2 includes coverage of *The Genealogist* (1877-1921). *Class No:* 929.50(410)(01)

[6059]

SIMS, R. An Index to the pedigrees and arms contained in the Heralds' visitations and other genealogical manuscripts in the British Museum. London, J.R. Smith, 1849 (Reprinted Baltimore, Maryland, Genealogical Publishing Co., 1970). vi,330p. $18.50. ISBN: 0806304006.

Arranged by counties - 'an important point because most researchers often know their counties of origin' (*RQ*, v.10,no.1, Fall 1970, p.72). *Class No:* 929.50(410)(01)

[6060]

SQUIBB, G.D. Visitation pedigrees and the genealogist. rev. ed. Chichester, Phillimore, 1978. iv, 47p. pbk. £7. ISBN: 0901262196.

An almost exact reprint of the articles in *The Genealogists' magazine*, v.13, 1960-61, p.225-36, 266-74. First published 1965.

By the Norfolk Herald Extraordinary, and an expert evaluation. Appended list of pedigrees in printed visitations which purport to be copies or collations of original visitations, and a bibliography of printed lists of disclaimers. Indexes of visitations and names. *Class No:* 929.50(410)(01)

Handbooks & Manuals

[6061]

BAXTER, A. In search of your British and Irish roots a complete guide to tracing your English, Welsh, Scottish and Irish ancestors. Baltimore, Genealogical Publishing Co., 1987. xiv, 304p. bibliog., index. $12.95. ISBN: 0806311274.

Reprint of 1982 ed.

15 chapters *e.g.* 1. Starting your family tree ... 3. Adoption ... 7. Wills ... 9-13. regional ... 14. Preparing a family history. Bibliography p.295-9. Sound guide to British records for North American researchers. *Class No:* 929.50(410)(035)

[6062]

HAMILTON-EDWARDS, G. In search of ancestry. 2nd rev. ed. Chichester, Sussex, Phillimore, 1983. ix, 212p. illus., geneal. tables on endpapers, bibliog., index. £8.95. ISBN: 0850334942.

First published by Michael Joseph 1966. Rev. eds. 1969 and 1974.

32 chapters (18-19 Scottish records; 20. Irish records; 21 Welsh records; 22. The Dominions, US and other countries; 24. Society of Genealogists; 25. Public Record Office; 26. British Museum and other libraries; 27. Genealogy and heraldry; 28. Genealogy and biography). Appendix C. List of useful addresses p.170-175. Bibliography p.176-205. Regarded by practising family historians as a first-class introduction to the various types of source material. *Class No:* 929.50(410)(035)

[6063]

HAMILTON-EDWARDS, G. In search of army ancestry. Chichester, Sussex, Phillimore, 1978. 106p. illus., bibliog., index. £8.95. ISBN: 0850332877.

Systematic guide to genealogical sources mainly to the War Office records in the Public Record Office. Bibliography p.96-99. *Class No:* 929.50(410)(035)

[6064]

McLAUGHLIN, E. The McLaughlin guides. The author, Varneys, Rudds Lane, Haddenham, nr. Aylesbury, Bucks.

Series of booklets of varying length (12-32p.) offering expert advice on sources, techniques and procedures, useful addresses, and further reading to the family history enthusiast. *Titles: The Censuses 1841-1881. Use and interpretation.* 3rd ed. 1985. 0907099491. *Interviewing elderly relatives.* 2nd ed. 1985. 0907099394. *St. Catherine's House.* 6th ed. 1985. 090709936x. *Wills before 1858.* 2nd ed. 1985. 0907099505. *Somerset House wills from 1858.* 3rd ed. 1985. 0907099378. *Annals of the poor.* 3rd ed. 1986. 0907099556. *Parish registers.* 1986. 0907099564. *Family history from newspapers.* 1987. 090709970x. *Reading old handwriting.* 2nd ed. 1987. 0907099629. Also available from Mrs. Nora Porter, Federation of Family History Societies, 17 Foxlea Road, Hailey Green, Halesowen, West Midlands, B63, 1DX. *Class No:* 929.50(410)(035)

[6065]

RODGER, N.A.M. Naval records for genealogists. London, HMSO, 1988. iv, 220p. tables, bibliog., index. £4.95. (*Public Record Office Handbooks.*) ISBN: 0114402094.

1. Introduction, scope, arrangement. Records elsewhere. Navy list - 2. Ranks and ratings - 3. Types of service record - 4. Musters and pay books. Appendix 1. Analysis of service records (p.67-136) - 2. Service records in series (p.137-187) - 3. Naval reserve and auxiliary forces. Author index. *Class No:* 929.50(410)(035)

Dictionaries

[6066]

FITZHUGH, T.V.H. The Dictionary of genealogy: a guide to ancestry research. 3rd ed. Sherborne, Dorset, Alphabooks, 1988. 320p. illus., map, facsims. £19.95 ISBN: 0713633484.

1st ed. 1985.

Pt.1. The guide to ancestry research outlines recommended procedures and notes the chief sources of information working back from the Victorian era to Tudor and Plantagenet times and beyond. Pt. 2. The Dictionary (p.25-308) contains over 1000 descriptions, definitions, and locations of virtually all the historical records likely to be examined by genealogists. Scholarly, informative, practical. 'Cleary the result of many years of research' (*Reference Reviews,* v.3, no.3, Septem,ber 1989, p.140-1). *Class No:* 929.50(410)(038)

Yearbooks & Directories

[6067]

1988 National genealogical directory. Caley, J.L., *ed.* 9th ed. Stoke St. Michael, Somerset, NGD., 1988. 139p. ISSN: 09519521.

Surname interests (p.23-120) and special interests (p.121-

....(contd.)

7), linked to numbered list of subscribers. Federation of Family History Societies p.128-9.
Class No: 929.50(410)(058)

[6068]
OWEN, D.B. Guide to genealogical resources in the British Isles. Metuchen, New Jersey, Scarecrow Press, 1989. 399p. indexes. $39.50. ISBN: 0810821532.

279 institutions A-Z by locality with their resources and services. 'A valuable, fairly reasonably priced record useful both to special genealogical and historical collections' (*Choice*, v.27, no.5, January 1990, p.774+6).
Class No: 929.50(410)(058)

Manuscripts & Incunabula

[6069]
KAMINKOW, M.J. Genealogical manuscripts in British libraries: a descriptive guide. Baltimore, Maryland, Magna Carta Book Co., 1967. x,140p.

279 entries, arranged by counties and towns under England, Ireland, Scotland, Wales, Orkneys, plus addenda. Indexes of families; places; authors and subjects. 'A courageous first attempt at a survey of a kind which genealogists have long been waiting for' (*Foreword*).
Class No: 929.50(410)(093)

Libraries

[6070]
HARVEY, R. Genealogy for librarians. 2nd ed. London, Clive Bingley, 1992. viii,194p. bibliog., index. £27.50. ISBN: 0851574084.

1st ed. 1982.

Well documented guide to primary and secondary sources of information mainly confined to England but with some mention of Welsh, Scottish and Irish genealogy and a cursory look into Europe. Chapter 1. The Librarian and the genealogist examines the problems faced by librarians when attempting to provide a service for genealogists. New material in this edition includes divorce and adoption sources. Bibliography p.156-83.
Class No: 929.50(410):061:026/027

Scotland

[6071]
COLLINS, E.K., *comp.* **Beginners' guide to Scottish genealogy.** Dundee, Tay Valley Family History Society, 1990. ii,102p. maps, bibliog., index. sd. ISBN: 1873032021.

1. Introduction and Home start - 2. Civil registration - 3. International Genealogical Index and Old Parish Register Index - 4. Census returns - 5. Old Parish Registers of Scotland - 6. Local records (region by region) - 7. Family History societies - 8. Scottish Record Office - 9. Ancestry out of Scotland - 10. More sources. Bibliography p.90-96. Invaluable practical guide. *Class No:* 929.50(411)

Handbooks & Manuals

[6072]
CORY, K.B. Tracing your Scottish ancestry. Edinburgh, Polygon 1990. xii,195p. map, facsim, bibliog., index, limp cover. ISBN: 0748660542.

Comprehensive manual for would-be family historians. Part 1: A guide to genealogy in Scotland (Search records in New Register House and Scottish Record Office ... Names ... Heraldry ... Clans and tartans *etc.*). Part 2: Step by step guide in searching for family records p.163-86. Appendix 1: Glossary of occupations - 2. Useful addresses - 3. List of parishes, counties and commissariots p.108-52 - 4. Book list p.153-6. Neatly complements C. Sinclair's *Tracing your Scottish ancestors (q.v.)*. *Class No:* 929.50(411)(035)

[6073]
HAMILTON-EDWARDS, G. In search of Scottish ancestry. 2nd ed. Chichester, Sussex, Phillimore, 1983. x, 252p. illus., bibliog. £8.95. ISBN: 0850335132.

First published 1972.

22 Chapters (3. Parish and Nonconformist registers; 4. Surnames and Christian names; 9. Registers of deeds; 10. Other Court registers; 12. The clans and Scottish titles; 15. Migration and the Scotsman abroad; 16. The Scottish Record Office; 17. Scots heraldry and the Lyon Office; 18. Societies and libraries). Appendices A-E: C. Glossary of terms found in earlier legal and other documents p.194-200. D. List of pre-1855 parishes showing county and Commissariat p.201-214. Notes and references. Bibliography p.218-233. 'Much of the second edition ... is concerned with various changes in the location of records' (*Foreword*). 'Written primarily for the researcher with access to archives and libraries of Scotland' (*Library Journal*, v.98, no.2, 15 January 1973, p.151). *Class No:* 929.50(411)(035)

[6074]
SINCLAIR, C. Tracing your Scottish ancestors a guide to ancestry research in the Scottish Record Office. Edinburgh, HMSO, 1990. x,153p. illus., map, bibliog., indexes. limp cover. £5.95. ISBN: 0114941181.

Authoritative survey of the range of materials held in the SRO with 28 chapters on the various types of national and local records associated with different professions and occupations (*e.g.* Tenants and crafters ... litigants ... coal miners). Appendix A: Useful addresses - B. Useful books p.145-6. 'A model of its kind ... an excellent, down-to-earth, step-by-step introduction to the whole business of ancestry research in Scotland' (*Reference Reviews*, v.5, no.1, 1991, p.37-8). *Class No:* 929.50(411)(035)

[6075]
STEEL, D.J. *and* **STEEL, A.E.F. Sources for Scottish genealogy and family history.** Chichester, Sussex, Phillimore for the Society of Genealogists, 1970. xiii, 320p. (*National Index of Parish Registers, no.12.*)

Sections: Historical background - Scottish nomenclature (surnames; Christian names, titles and descriptions) - Parish registers - Ancillary sources (*e.g.* Irregular marriages: Court Records) - Nonconformists, Footnote references. Bibliography (bibliographies; genealogy and archives; history; p.249-76). 'A detailed and scholarly guidebook' (E.G. Grant. *Scotland*, 1982. entry 457).
Class No: 929.50(411)(035)

[6076]

Tracing ancestors in Shetland. Sandison, A. 3rd ed. London, A. Sandison, 1985. 48p. bibliog., pbk. £1.50. ISBN: 0950619124.

First published in Lerwick by T. and J. Manson in 1972.

8 chapters on first steps, Scottish traditions, and sources for Lerwick and county parishes. Appendices on surnames, Shetland family historians, local registraries, and searching New Register House, Edinburgh. Bibliography p.40-43. Distributed in Lerwick by the *Shetland Times*.

Class No: 929.50(411)(035)

[6077]

WHYTE, D. **'Source material for the Scottish Highlands and Islands,'** *Genealogists Magazine*, v.20, no.9, March 1982, p.289-291. *Class No:* 929.50(411)(035)

Ireland

[6078]

McCARTHY, T. **The Irish roots guide.** Dublin, Lilliput Press, 1991. ix,116p. illus. facsims., tables, bibliog., pbk. IR£3.99. ISBN: 0946640777.

Guide to 12 most useful sources of genealogical information (*e.g.* census returns ... Catholic parish records ... tithe applotment books ... records of the graveyard) followed by step-by-step instructions on their use. Chapter 7 Future of Irish genealogy. Bibliography p.113-6. 'An invaluable handbook to reconstructing male and female lines' (*Books Ireland*, no.152, September 1991, p.155).

Class No: 929.50(415)

Bibliographies

[6079]

CAMP, A.J., *comp.* **Sources for Irish genealogy in the library of the Society of Genealogists.** London, Society of Genealogists, 1990. 16p. sd. 0.90p. ISBN: 0946789142.

Wills, local items, parish and non-conformist registers, stone inscriptions, censuses, directories *etc.*

Class No: 929.50(415)(01)

Handbooks & Manuals

[6080]

BEGLEY, D.F., *ed.* **Handbook on Irish genealogy:** how to trace your ancestors and relations in Ireland. 6th ed. Dublin, Heraldic Artists Ltd., 1984 160p. illus. maps, tables, index, pbk. £4.95. ISBN: 0950245593.

First published 1970.

6 chapters: 1. Tracing ancestors and relations in Ireland - 2. Records and record repositories - 3. County maps - 4. Parish registers - 5. Preliminary research in home countries - 6. Emmigrant passenger lists to America. Record repositories and their contents p.129-144. Pedigrees in printed books p.145-149. Published family histories p.150-152. Useful addresses p.154. Reproductions of maps printed to accompany Samuel Lewis' *A Topgraphical dictionary of Ireland* p.41-73. *Class No:* 929.50(415)(035)

[6081]

—BEGLEY, D.F., *ed.* Irish genealogy a record finder. Dublin, Heraldic Artists Ltd., 1981. 257p. illus. index. ISBN: 0950245577.

Sequel to *Handbook on Irish genealogy* (6th ed, 1984).

1. The peoples of Ireland - 2. Historical and administrative divisions of Ireland - 3. Irish census returns - 4. Guide to Irish directories - 5. Genealogical matter in the publications of the Irish Manuscript Commission - 6. Newspapers as a genealogical source - 7. The Registry of Deeds for genealogical purposes - 8. Wills and administrations; 9. Early genealogical sources for attornies and barristers. 10. R.E. Matheson's special report on surnames in Ireland. Gravestone inscriptions recorded in printed sources (arranged by parish) p.233-240; Miscellaneous genealogical sources p.241-248; List of libraries, archives and record offices p.249-251. *Class No:* 929.50(415)(035)

[6082]

FALLEY, M.D. **Irish and Scotch-Irish ancestral research** : a guide to the genealogical records, methods and sources in Ireland. Baltimore, Genealogical Publishing, 2v., 1984. $60. ISBN: 0806301964.

Reprint of 1962 ed.

1: *Repositories and records.*

2: *Bibliography and family index.*

Deals comprehensively with every phase of record searching in the US and in Ireland (where research is virtually impossible because of the destruction of records in 1922). Includes sources of Irish material not in Ireland. 'Easily the best Irish genealogical work ever to have been published' (*Library Journal*, v.88, no.114, August 1963, p.2884). *Class No:* 929.50(415)(035)

[6083]

GRENHAM, J. **Tracing your Irish ancestors** the complete guide. Dublin, Gill and Macmillan, 1992. xxxviii,281p. maps, facsims., bibliogs., pbk. £9.99; $18.95. ISBN: 0717118983.

Pt. 1: Major sources: 1. Civil records - 2. Census - 3. Church - 4. Land records. Pt. 2: Other sources: 5. Wills - 6. The Genealogical Office - 7. Emigration - 8. Registry of deeds - 9. Newspapers - 10. Directories. Pt. 3: Reference guide: 11. Occupations - 12. County source lists - 13. Family histories - 14. Church of Ireland public records in Dublin repositories - 15. Research services, societies and repositories. Well-documented authoritative guide.

Class No: 929.50(415)(035)

[6084]

How to trace your family tree. Dublin, Dublin Public libraries, 1989. bibliog. £2.10. ISBN: 094684108x.

A guide to the major sources of genealogical information in Ireland' (*Introduction*) 'Any would-be researcher will surely find this booklet to be value for money' (*Books Ireland*, no.136, November 1989, p.185).

Class No: 929.50(415)(035)

[6085]

O'LAUGHLIN, M.C. **The Complete book for tracing your Irish ancestors.** Kansas City, Irish Genealogical Foundation, 1982. 224p. bibliog.

Guide to types of records, terminology, repositories and societies in England, Ireland, United States and Canada.

Class No: 929.50(415)(035)

Maps & Atlases

[6086]

GARDNER, D.E., *and others*. **Genealogical atlas of Ireland.**
Salt Lake City, Utah, Deseret Book Co., 1964.

Compiled from Philips' *Handy atlas of the counties of Ireland* (1885) and Samuel Lewis's *Atlas of the counties of Ireland*. It lists the various records and their whereabouts, and has an extensive 40-page gazetteer.
Class No: 929.50(415)(084.3)

[6087]

MITCHELL, B. A New genealogical atlas of Ireland.
Baltimore, Genealogical Publishing Co., 1988. 123p. maps, softcover. $18.95. ISBN: 0806311525.

Identifies and precisely locates 6 major administrative divisions: counties, baronies, civil parishes, dioceses, poor law and probate districts. 'To be used in conjunction with *General alphabetical index to the townlands and towns, parishes and baronies of Ireland* (Dublin, 1861 reprinted by Genealogical Publishing Co. 1984). This has data on localities A-Z including OS sheet number, acreage, name of county, baronry and civil parish in which it is situated.
Class No: 929.50(415)(084.3)

Archives

[6088]

RYAN, J.G. Irish records: sources for family and local history. Glenageary, Dublin, Flyleaf Press; Salt Lake City, Ancestry Publishing, 1989. £24.50. $34.95. ISBN: 0916489221.

'For all its shortcomings, this book is still a very worthwhile contribution to the growing corpus of guides to Irish source material' (*Books Ireland*, no.136, November 1989, p.184-5). *Class No:* 929.50(415)(093.20)

Eire

Archives

[6089]

RYAN, J.G. A Guide to tracing your Dublin ancestors.
Glenageary, Co. Dublin, Flyleaf Press, 1988. 96p. illus., index, pbk. £5.95. ISBN: 0950846619.

Complete listing of all the major record sources in county and city of Dublin. *Class No:* 929.50(417)(093.20)

England & Wales

Handbooks & Manuals

[6090]

CAMP, A.J. My ancestor was a migrant: (in England and Wales): how can I trace where he came from? London, Society of Genealogists, 1987. 44p. index. sd. £2. ISBN: 0901878944.

'Attempts to set out the major record sources which may be used prior to 1851 to trace a movement within England and Wales. It assumes that the resources of the General Register Office after 1st July 1837 have been exhausted'.
Class No: 929.50(42)(035)

[6091]

GARDNER, D.E. *and* **SMITH, F. Genealogical research in England and Wales.** Salt Lake City, Utah, Bookcraft Publishers, 3v., 1956-65. illus., facsims., maps.

V.1 (1956). 1. Brief historic and economic background - 2. Family sources ... - 3. Cemeteries, burial grounds and churchyards - 4. Civil registration of births, marriages and deaths - 5. Examples of civil registration - 6. The census records of England and Wales - 7. How to trace place and family in the 1841-1851 census records - 8. Street and local addresses in the 1851 census returns - 9. The parish and its administration - 10. The parish registers - 11. Laws relating to the keeping of parish registers - 12. How to use parish registers - 13. Bishop's transcripts and their value - 14. Marriage licences and the intention to marry - 15. The Nonconformists, their history and records - 16. The Jews in Great Britain and the Commonwealth - 17. The Roman Catholics and their records - 18. Surnames. Given names. Dialect.

V.2 (1959). 1. Planning research and recording research results - 2. An introduction to probate records - 3. Wills, administrations and inventories - 4. Probate calendars or indexes and act books - 5. Miscellaneous probate records - 6. Examples of the value of probate records - 7. Naval and military records. Merchant shipping records. Churches on foreign soil - 8. Historical events related to genealogical research - 9. The counties of England and Wales.

V.3 (1965) includes a discussion of apprentice and freeman records; reading early English script; Chancery proceedings, schools and university registers; poll books; feet of fines; inquisitions, post-mortems, and manor court rolls.

Gathers together a mass of data, simply explained; many footnote references and facsimiles. Each volume has an analytical index. Chapter 9 of v.2, 'The counties of England' (p.195-307) is supported by numerous black-and-white maps, but the lettering on these is far from clear in many cases, and there is no gazetteer. 'Contains the most up-to-date guide to the whereabouts of the genealogist's main series of records that there is' (*Genealogist's Magazine*, v.13, no.11, September 1961, p.345). The same review states that on probate records it is 'undoubtedly the best that has ever appeared in print'. *Class No:* 929.50(42)(035)

[6092]

Gibson's guides for genealogists. Gibson, J.S.W. Birmingham, Federation of Family History Societies, 1986-.
Titles: Gibson, J.S.W. *Bishops Transcripts and marriage licences bonds and allegations. A guide to their location and indexes.* 2nd ed. 1985. 0907099122. £1. Gibson, J.S.W. *Census return 1841-1881 on microfilm. A directory to local holdings.* 4th ed. 1984. 090709919x. £1.50. (A 5th ed. is in preparation). Gibson, J. and Rogers, C.D. *Coroners' records in England and Wales.* 1988. 0907099718. £1.50. Gibson, J. *General Register Office and international genealogical indexes: where to find them.* 1987. 0907099734. £1. Gibson, J.S.W. *The Hearth tax. Other later Stuart tax lists and the Association Oath rolls.* 1985. 0907099343. £1.50. Gibson, J. and Mills, D. *Land tax assessments c.1690-c.1950.* 1984. 090709922x. £1. Gibson, J.S.W. *Local newspapers 1750-1920 England and Wales; Channel Islands; Isle of Man. A select location list.* 1987. 0907099467. £2. Gibson, J. *Marriage, census, and other indexes for family historians.* 3rd ed. 1988. 0907099793. £1.50. Gibson, J.S.W. *Quarter Sessions records for family historians. A select list.* 2nd ed. 1985. 0907099262. £1.

....(contd.)

Gibson, J. and Peskett, P. *Record Offices: how to find them.* 4th ed. 1987. 0907099726. £1.50. Gibson, J.S.W. *A Simplified guide to probate jurisdictions: where to look for wills.* 3rd ed. 1985. 0907099459. £2. Gibson, J.S.W. *Unpublished personal name indexes in record offices and libraries: an interim list.* 1985. 0907099351. £1. A useful series of booklets indicating where particular classes of records may be located. Available either from J.S.W. Gibson, Harts Cottage, Church Hanborough, Oxford, OX7 2AB, or The Federation of Family History Societies, c/o Benson Room, Birmingham & Midland Institute, Margaret Street, Birmingham, B3 3BS. *Class No:* 929.50(42)(035)

[6093]
ROGERS, C.D. The Family tree detective a manual for analysing and solving genealogical problems in England and Wales, 1538 to the present day. 2nd ed. Manchester, Manchester University Press, 1985. xii, 164p. illus. bibliog. £15. ISBN: 0719018455.

First published 1983.

How to proceed when genealogical sources on parents, marriage, and deaths appear to be exhausted. Select bibliography p.156-159. Index p.160-164. Regarded by the author as being in some ways complementary to Cox and Padfield's *Tracing your ancestors in the Public Record Office* (qv). *Class No:* 929.50(42)(035)

[6094]
WUEHLER, A. 'Genealogical sources for England and Wales', *Reference Services Review,* v.17, no.1, Spring 1989, p.65-70, 80.

'How to begin research ... how to find out what others have previously compiled; how to find and use major records; and what reference tools are available'. Bibliography p.69-70, 80. *Class No:* 929.50(42)(035)

England

[6095]
ROGERS, C.D. *and* **SMITH, J.H. Local family history in England 1538-1914.** Manchester, Manchester Univ. Press, 1991. vi,217p. tables, bibliog., index. ISBN: 0719803200.

In 3 parts: 1. History of the family 1538-1914 (marriage, children, widowed and aged in early modern period and in the industrial age) - 2. Exploitation of source material - 3. Family History agenda (organization, what to investigate, making it public). Resource Research List (bibliography) p.201-11. Brings together genealogy, family history, local history and demography. *Class No:* 929.50(420)

[6096]
WAGNER, Sir Anthony. English genealogy. 3rd ed. Chichester, Sussex, Phillimore, 1983. xiii, 475p. tables. £20. ISBN: 085033473x.

First published Oxford, Clarendon Press, 1960.

1. Purpose - 2. The roots - 3. English and Norman - 4. The social framework - 5. The rise and fall of families - 6. Strangers - 7. Settlers - 8. The records (p.324-350) - 9. The study and literature of genealogy (p.351-407) - 10. The practical approach. Index p.439-475. 'It already has an established place in the literature of its subject' (*Archives,* v.11, no.49, Spring 1973, p.61). *Class No:* 929.50(420)

Databases

[6097]
EAKLE, A.H., *and others.* **Descriptive inventory of the English collections.** Salt Lake City, Univ. of Utah Press, 1979. xvi, 168p. (*Finding Aids To The Microfilmed Manuscript Collection of the Genealogical Society of Utah.*) ISBN: 0874801540.

1. Government records - 2. Legal - 3. Church - 4. Corporate - 5. Personal records - 6. Research aids - 7. London. Principal aim is to provide researchers with a guide to unpublished material. *Class No:* 929.50(420)(003.4)

Bibliographies

[6098]
HUMPHERY-SMITH, C.R. A Genealogist's bibliography. 2nd rev. ed. Chichester, Sussex, Phillimore, 1985. viii, 128p. pbk. £7.95. ISBN: 0850334225.

First published 1976, 2nd rev. ed. 1981. Based on H.G. Harrison's *Select bibliography of English genealogy* (1937).

Classified list of books and articles arranged A-Z by historical counties. Glossary p.95-113; Bibliography p.114-128. *Class No:* 929.50(420)(01)

[6099]
RAYMOND, S. *and* **GIBSON, J. English genealogy** an introductory bibliography. 2nd ed. Birmingham, Federation of Family History Societies, 1991-. 40p. £2. ISBN: 1872094198.

First ed. published 1988.

Introductory guide to over 300 important works. First volume in a series intended to include every county not only in England but also Scotland and Wales.

County Volumes. 1. *Cornwall: a genealogical bibliography* over 1000 works listed. 2. *Devon: a genealogical bibliography. V.1: Sources. V.2: Family history.* 3. *Somerset: a genealogical bibliography.* 107p. £6. 1872094228. 4. *Dorset: a genealogical bibliography.* 113p. £6. 187209421x. 5. *Gloucestershire and Bristol: a genealogical bibliography. Class No:* 929.50(420)(01)

Gazetteers

[6100]
SMITH, F. A Genealogical gazetteer of England: an alphabetical dictionary of places, with the location, ecclesiastical jurisdiction, population, and the date of the earliest entry in the registers of every ancient parish in England. Baltimore, Maryland, Genealogical Publishing Co., 1987. xv,590p. $30.00.

Reprint of 1968 ed.

'One of the most outstanding works of its kind in the last decade' (*Library Journal,* v.93,no.15, 1 September 1968, p.2996). *Class No:* 929.50(420)(083.86)

Archives

[6101]
BEVAN, J. *and* **DUNCAN, A. Tracing your ancestors in the Public Record Office.** 4th ed. London, HMSO, 1990. 244p. illus. bibliog., pbk. £7. (*PRO Handbooks, no.19.*) ISBN: 0114402221.

First published by Cox, J. and Padfield, T. in 1981.505.00/00$a1. For the beginner - 2. What to use in the PRO. - 3. Some useful groups of records - 4. Special groups of people - 5. Pre-Parish Register genealogy - 6. Sources of

....*(contd.)*

help - 7. Useful addresses. Appendix: How to find a record of a birth or baptism (series of questions, yes or no answers referal to text). Biography p.23-4. Invaluable practical guide for all researchers and indispensable to the inexperienced visitor to the PRO. Completely revised and expanded for this edition. 'This is a wonderful book that should be in the library of every archive office and serious researcher, not just genealogists. And make sure it replaces any earlier edition. This is effectively a new book ... double the length of the third edition and better in every way' (*Journal of the Society of Archivists*, v.12,no.2, Autumn 1991, p.162-3). *Class No:* 929.50(420)(093.20)

[6102]
COLWELL, S. **Dictionary of genealogical sources in the Public Record Office.** London, Weidenfeld & Nicolson, 1992. xvii,206p. £20. ISBN: 0297831402.

Introduction (p.vii-xv) guides the reader round PRO, explains how documents are organized, and outlines access procedures. Dictionary entries under countries, personal names, and types of record. Glossary p.198-206. *Class No:* 929.50(420)(093.20)

[6103]
MOULTON, J.W. **Genealogical resources in English repositories.** Colombus, Ohio, Hampton House, 1988. xxxiv, 614p. maps. index. $32. ISBN: 0944485006.

175 Greater London, County and London Borough repositories. Data: location map, directory information, holdings, publications, searches and charges. 'Gives a very good superficial overview of English genealogical resources, but it signally fails to provide backup detailed references to make it useful in the way readers should expect' (*Archives*, v.19, no.81, April 1989, p.47-48). *Class No:* 929.50(420)(093.20)

London

Handbooks & Manuals
[6104]
HARVEY, R., *comp.* **A Guide to genealogical sources in the Guildhall Library.** 3rd ed. London, Guildhall Library, 1988. 56p. index, sd. £4.00. (*Research Guide, no.1.*) ISBN: 0900422254.

2nd ed. 1979.

18 chapters *e.g.* 3. Poll books and registers of electors ... 5. Census returns ... 7. Parish registers ... 13. Apprenticeship - 14. Guilds and livery companies. 'A good starting point for the inexperienced researcher' (*Library Association Record*, v.91, no.1, January 1989, p.54). *Class No:* 929.50(421)(035)

Channel Islands

[6105]
BURNESS, L.R. **'Genealogical research in the Channel Islands',** *Genealogists Magazine*, v.19, no.5, March 1978, p.169-172. *Class No:* 929.50(423.4)

Isle of Man

Handbooks & Manuals
[6106]
NARASINHAM, J. **The Manx family tree** a beginner's guide to records in the Isle of Man. Isle of Man, the author, 1986. vi,48p. map,facsims., index. sd.

Vital records; wills; census, property, ecclesiastical court and other records and their whereabouts. Glossary p.43-5. *Class No:* 929.50(428.9)(035)

Wales

[6107]
BARTRUM, P.C., *comp*. **Welsh genealogies AD300-1400.** Cardiff, Univ. of Wales Press, for the Board of Celtic Studies, 8v., 1974. 941p. geneal. tables.

2nd ed. published on microfiche 1981 which incorporated three lists of additions and corrections.

Compiled mainly from manuscripts in the National Library of Wales. Purpose is to reduce Welsh pedigrees into order and to make the results available in convenient form. V.1-4 lists pedigrees A-Z; v.5-8 comprise classified geographical, alphabetical place name, person, and surname indexes.

Welsh genealogies AD1400-1500. 18v., 1983. 1776p. V.1-10 lists pedigrees: v.11-18: indexes. *Class No:* 929.50(429)

Handbooks & Manuals
[6108]
HAMILTON-EDWARDS, G. **In search of Welsh ancestry.** Chichester, Sussex, Phillimore, 1986. xi, 95p. illus. facsims. bibliog, index. £8.95. ISBN: 0850335639.

15 chapters *e.g.* 2. Welsh Christian and surnames - 3. Civil registrations - 4. Census returns - 5. Parish registers - 6. Nonconformists - 7. Wills and administrations - 8. Professional men - 9. Army and Navy records - 10. Merchant service and East India Company - 11. National Library of Wales - 12. Manor Court Chancery and other records. Appendix C. Useful addresses - D. County Record Offices in Wales - E. Family history societies of Wales. Bibliography p.83-87. *Class No:* 929.50(429)(035)

Germany

[6109]
WRIGHT, R.S. **'Tracing German ancestry',** *Reference Services Review*, v.13, no.4, Winter 1985, p.65-70.

Describes sources of information and agencies relating to immigration, research methods, genealogical sources, and finding localities in Germany. *Class No:* 929.50(430)

Handbooks & Manuals
[6110]
ARBEITSGEMEINSCHAFT OSTDEUTSCHER FAMILIENFORSCHER. **Genealogical guide to German ancestors from East Germany and Eastern Europe.** Neustadt/Aisch, West Germany, Verlag Degener, 1984. 158p. maps, index. ISBN: 3768610292.

1st German ed. 1978; 2nd ed. 1982.

Directory of information and compendium of personal and family records. Section A: Supraregional information (1. Research areas - 2. Family research societies - 3. Vital statistics sources - 4. Gazetteers - 5. Bibliographies and

....(contd.)

literature of homeland territories - 6. Archives and libraries - 7. Other research aids - 8. Special hunts). Section B: Regional information (1. Former German territories east of the Oder-Neisse line - 2. German settlements in Central, Eastern and Southeastern Europe). Glossary p.149. Family name and geographical index. *Class No:* 929.50(430)(035)

[6111]
BAXTER, A. In search of your German roots a complete guide to tracing your ancestors in the Germanic areas of Europe. United Germany ed. Baltimore, Genealogical Publishing Co., 1991. xii, 122p. bibliog., softcover. $9.95. ISBN: 0806313110.

1st ed. 1988.

Expansion of chapter printed in *In search of your European roots* (1985).

12 chaps. *e.g.* 4. The records of the Mormon church - 5. Jewish records - 6. Archives - 7. The Lutheran Church - 8. The Germans in the United States - 9. The Germans in Canada - 10. Records in Germany - 12. German genealogical associations in North America p.113-15. Bibliography p.117-9. *Class No:* 929.50(430)(035)

Czechoslovakia

Handbooks & Manuals

[6112]
MILLER, O.K. Genealogical research for Czech and Slovak Americans. Detroit, Gale Research Co., 1978. xiv, tables, index. $68. (*Genealogy and Local History series, no.2.*) ISBN: 0810314045.

11 chapters: 1. The genealogical library of the Church of Jesus Christ of Latter-Day Saints - 2. History - 3. Geography - 4. Czech and Slovak immigration to America - 5. Sources for genealogical research in Czechoslovakia - 6. Archives - 7. Names - 8. The Calendar - 9. Language - 10 Nobility and Heraldry - 11. Conclusions. Appendix 1. Branch genealogical libraries of the Church of Jesus Christ of Latter-Day Saints p.165-179. Each chapter is followed by a comprehensive bibliography of sources. 3 maps. *Class No:* 929.50(437)(035)

Poland

[6113]
CHORZEMPA, R.A. In search of Polish roots. Baltimore, Genealogical Publishing, 1993. 262p. illus., maps, pbk. $17.95. ISBN: 0806313781.

Investigates resources in Poland and North America. Chorzempa is Director of the Polish Genealogical Society of America. 'Highly recommended for research' (*Library Journal*, v.118, no.10, 1 June 1993. p.102). *Class No:* 929.50(438)

France

Handbooks & Manuals

[6114]
BABINO DI BORGOMALE, H.L. 'Genealogical research in France', *Genealogist's Magazine,* v.10, no.15, September, 1946, p.1-7.

Covers the French nobility; the general armorial of France; parish registers and the registers of the *État-Civil*;

....(contd.)

minutes of notaries public; registers of 'insinuations'; Bibliothèque Nationale and the public archives; private archives; printed sources; and The Public Archives of France. *Class No:* 929.50(44)(035)

[6115]
CURRER-BRIGGS, N. *and* **GAMBIER, R. Huguenot ancestry.** Chichester, Sussex, Phillimore, 1985. x,150p., illus., geneal. tables, bibliog., index. £11.95. ISBN: 0850335647.

7 Sections: 1. Introduction - 2. Areas of Huguenot settlement in Britain - 3. Huguenots in North America and South Africa - 4. Planning and organising a research project - 5. British research sources p.82-107 - 6. Research in France, the Netherlands, Germany and Switzerland p.108-21 - 7. Recording the results. Chronology p.128-131; Bibliography p.133-136. 24p. plates. The only book on the subject. *Class No:* 929.50(44)(035)

Dictionaries

[6116]
VILLAIN, J. La France moderne: dictionnaire généalogique, historique et biographique. Marseille, Lafitte Reprints, 3v., 1979-1980.

First published Sainte-Étienne, Société de l'Imp. Théolier, 1906-1908.

1. *Haute Loire* 1906 (1980). 2. *Drome et Ardèche* 1908 (1979). 3. *Haute-Garonne et Ariege* 1908 (1979). Concentrates on *Les familles bourgeoises*. The intention was to cover all the *Départements* but the project collapsed. *Class No:* 929.50(44)(038)

Sweden

Handbooks & Manuals

[6117]
OLSSON, N.W. Tracing your Swedish ancestry. Stockholm, Almquist & Wiksell, 1985. 26p. map.

First published 1963.

'Brief summary of the most useful Swedish documents for genealogical research, difficulties often encountered, and the addresses of Swedish archives and American institutions of greatest assistance in family history' (L.B. Sather and A. Swanson. *Sweden*, 1987. Entry 315). *Class No:* 929.50(485)(035)

Netherlands

[6118]
FAHY, T.G. 'Genealogical research in the Netherlands', *Genealogists' Magazine,* v.13, no.12, December 1961, p.366-371.

Outline of archive offices and types of source material. *Class No:* 929.50(492)

[6119]
VAN RESANDT, W.W. 'Genealogy in the Netherlands', *Genealogists' Magazine,* v.17, no.10, June 1974, p.547-550.

Overview of research facilities and types of records. *Class No:* 929.50(492)

Belgium

[6120]

VAN HILLE, P. 'Genealogy in Belgium', *Genealogists' Magazine*, v.15, no.15, September 1968, p.647-651.

Notes on types of records and genealogical societies and publications. *Class No:* 929.50(493)

Switzerland

Handbooks & Manuals

[6121]

SUESS, J.H. **Handy guide to Swiss genealogical records.** Logan, Utah, The Everton Publishers, 1978. 92p. illus., facsims, maps, tables.

35 sections including Genealogical research in Switzerland; Records of genealogical value; Addresses of Swiss state archives; Bibliography and research aids; Important dates in Swiss history. *Class No:* 929.50(494)(035)

China

Bibliographies

[6122]

TELFORD, T.A., *and others, comps*. **Chinese genealogies at the Genealogical Society of Utah:** an annotated bibliography. Taipei, Ch'eng Wen Publishing Co., 1983. 50+370p. index.

Covers Chinese class and lineage genealogies and other general works. Items arranged in order of country, province and hsien/shih. Introduction (Chinese genealogies as research sources; the problem of reliability; Chinese genealogies at the Genealogical Society of Utah; surnames; localities; progenitors; chronological distribution; overseas Chinese genealogies; access to the microfilm collection; purpose and arrangement of bibliography) p.1-50. Text (p.1-297) and Locality index (p.297-370) in Chinese script. *Class No:* 929.50(510)(01)

South Africa

Handbooks & Manuals

[6123]

LOMBARD, R.T.J. **Handbook for genealogical research in South Africa.** Pretoria, Human Sciences Research Council, 1977. [vi], 147p. illus., bibliog. ISBN: 0869653903.

Authoritative descriptive manual: 1. Genealogy and genealography - 2. Methodology - 3. Repositories of general sources - 4. Compiling a genealogical table. Bibliography p.129-147. See also the author's 'Genealogical research in South Africa', *Genealogists Magazine*, v.19, no.8, December 1978, p.274-6. *Class No:* 929.50(680)(035)

Canada

[6124]

DOUGLAS, A. **'Genealogical research in Canada'** *Genealogists' Magazine*, v.23, no.6, June 1990, p.217-21.

Useful introductory guide. Lists Provincial Archives addresses. *Class No:* 929.50(71)

[6125]

MERRIMAN, B. **'Genealogy in Canada'**, *Genealogists Magazine* v.19, no.9, March 1979, p.306-311, bibliog. *Class No:* 929.50(71)

[6126]

WHYTE, D. **A Dictionary of Scottish emigrants to Canada before Confederation.** Toronto, Ontario Genealogical Society, 1986. xvi, 443p. bibliog., softcover. ISBN: 0920036090.

12501 entries listing name, parentage, place of origin, dates of birth and death, destination, date and ship, occupation, wife/husband parentage, date of marriage, children, sources of information. Bibliography - Guide to the references p.439-43. With dependants not separately listed records over 30000 names. *Class No:* 929.50(71)

Bibliographies

[6127]

MENNIE DE VARENNES, K. **Bibliographie annotée d'ouvrages généalogiques au Canada** / Annotated bibliography of genealogical works in Canada. Markham, Ontario, Fitzhenry & Whiteside in association with the National Library of Canada and the Canadian Government Publishing Centre, Supply and Services Canada, 6v., 1986. xvi, 2080p.

V.1: 0889029113 has author/title index (p.1-327); index of parishes (p.331-49); subject index (p.443-66); list of periodicals (p.467-70); list of genealogical societies in Canada (p.471-3). Monumental work of inestimable value. *Class No:* 929.50(71)(01)

Handbooks & Manuals

[6128]

BAXTER, A. **In search of your roots:** a guide for Canadians seeking their ancestors. Toronto, The Macmillan Company of Canada, 1978. 203p. bibliog., index. ISBN: 0770518559.

19 chapters detail all possible sources of pertinent information for every province in Canada and around the world. Bibliography (by chapter) p.277-291. *Class No:* 929.50(71)(035)

[6129]

'Tracing your ancestors in Canada', *Genealogists' Magazine*, v.15, no.8, December 1966, p.293-303.

Reprinted from Public Archives of Canada booklet of same name.

Census records - Canadian Records (including list of those available from Public Archives of Canada) - Land, military, immigration records - Wills - Loyalist sources - Printed sources - List of inventories published. *Class No:* 929.50(71)(035)

Newfoundland

[6130]

BISHOP, J. **'Newfoundland family records'**, *Genealogists' Magazine*, v.20, no.9, March 1982, p.293-295. *Class No:* 929.50(718)

Jamaica

[6131]

WRIGHT, P. 'Materials for family history in Jamaica', *Genealogist's Magazine*, v.15, no.7, September 1966, p.239-250.

Discursive essay on the surviving records and monument inscriptions. *Class No:* 929.50(729.2)

Bahamas

[6132]

WHITTLETON, E.H. 'Family history in the Bahamas', *Genealogist's Magazine*, v.18, no.4, December 1975, p.187-191.

Indicates whereabouts of extant records.
Class No: 929.50(729.6)

Barbados

[6133]

BRANDOW, J., *comp.* **Genealogies of Barbados families.** Baltimore, Maryland, Genealogical Publishing Co., 1983. 753p. $40. ISBN: 0806310049.

Much material derives from V.L. Oliver: *Caribbeana: being miscellaneous papers relating to the history, genealogy, topography and antiquities of the British West Indies* (London, Mitchell Hughes & Clarke, 6v., 1912) and early issues of the *Journal of the Barbados Museum and Historical Society*.

*c.*100 well known families included. See also C.J. Stanford's 'Genealogical sources in Barbados', *Genealogist's Magazine*, v.17, no.9, March 1974, p.493-8 and no.10, June 1974, p.563-4. *Class No:* 929.50(729.86)

Latin America

Handbooks & Manuals

[6134]

DE PLATT, L. Genealogical historical guide to Latin America. Detroit, Gale Research Co., 1978. xvi, 273p. tables, index. $68. (*Genealogy and Local History Series, no.4.*) ISBN: 0810313898.

29 chapters: 1. Research standards - 2. Civil registration - 3. Ecclesiastical records - 4. Palaeography - 5. Abbreviations used during 15th, 16th, 17th centuries - 5. Research aids - 7. Colonial calendar - 8. Ecclesiastical divisions of Latin America 1492-1912 (bibliog.) - 9. Popular movements - 10. Political divisions - 11-29. Latin America A-Z by country. *Class No:* 929.50(729.99)(035)

USA

[6135]

BOAM, T.L. 'Modern sources for genealogical research in the United States', *Genealogists' Magazine*, v.19, no.1, March 1977, p.5-9.

Review of 20th-century sources relating primarily to migrants from the British Isles. Bibliography of 30 items. *Class No:* 929.50(73)

[6136]

COLDHAM, P.W. The Complete book of emigrants. Baltimore, Genealogical Publishing, 4v., 1987-93.

1. *1607-1660* (1987). 600p. ISBN 0806311924. $34.95. 2. *1661-1699* (1990). 900p. 0806312823. $49.95. 3. *1700-1750* (1992). 752p. 080631334x. $44.95. 4. *1751-1776* (1993). 357p. 0806313765. $29.95. Definitive list of c.100,000 passengers to the New World throughout the colonial period based on English sources. Arranged by year and date of record. Data: name, age, occupation, residence, ship, destination, and precise source citation. Each volume includes indexes to persons and ships. *Class No:* 929.50(73)

[6137]

FILBY, P.W. *and* **MAYER, M.K.,** *eds.* **Passenger and immigration lists index** a guide to published arrival records of about 500,000 passengers who came to the United States and Canada in the seventeenth, eighteenth, and nineteenth centuries. Detroit, Gale Research Company, 1980-. ISSN: 07368267.

Replaced H. Lancour's *A bibliography of ship passenger lists 1538-1828* (3rd ed., 1963).

1. *Preliminary edition*. 1980. xv, 324p. £322. ISBN 0810310996. 75,000 names as an appetiser for potential purchasers of the three volume complete work. How to read a citation p.xi-xii; sources indexed p.xiii-ix. 2. *First edition* in 3 vols: A-G; H-N; O-Z. 1981. xxxv, 2339p. £322. $425. 0810310996. This 3 volume base set indexed 300 published sources encompassing over 480,000 people. Sources indexed p.xiii-xxxv. Key to title codes for locating sources on endpapers. 3. *First edition 1982-1985 Cumulated Supplements* in 4 vols: A-E; F-K; L-R; S-Z. 1985. lxviii, 858p.+lxviii, 859-1698p.+lxviii, 1699-2609p.+lxviii, 2610-3404p. £360. $475. 0810317958. A cumulation of 4 annual supplements augmenting the First edition. 'These are excellent, easy-to-use sources that are highly recommended' (*American Reference Books Annual 1987*, p.170). 4. *1986 Supplement*. 1986. 686p. £117. $140. 0810317990. A further 125,000 citations. 5. *1987 Supplement*. 1987. xx, 645p. £117. $140. 0810325756. 125,000 citations. 6. *1988 Supplement*. 1988. xxx, 644p. £117. 0810325764. 125,000 citations. 7. *1989 Supplement*. 1989. xxv. 722p. £117. 0810325772. 125,000 citations. 8. *1990 Supplement*. 1990. £117. 0810325780. 9. *1986-1990 Cumulated Supplements*. 1990. £370. 0810325799. *1991 Supplement*. 630p. 0810369699. *1992 Supplement*. 630p. 0810376032, and *1993 Supplement*. 0810380412 add another 375000 citations. Enables researchers to locate ancestors who emigrated to North America and the West Indies in 17th-19th centuries. Main entries contain (1) Name and age of passenger as given in the original source; (2) date and place of arrival; (3) code indicating the specific source containing the arrival record; (4) page number on which the name appears in original source; (5) names of all accompanying passengers, their age, and their relationship to the main passenger. An insight into the compiler's aims and intention can be gleaned from P.W. Filby 'Passenger and naturalization lists: the new sources', *Reference Quarterly*, v.23, no.2, Winter 1983, p.193-194. *Class No:* 929.50(73)

[6138]

TEPPER, M., *ed.* **Passengers to America:** a consolidation of ship passenger lists from the New England Historical and Genealogical Register. Baltimore, Genealogical Publishing Co., Inc., 1980. xii, 554p. $20. ISBN: 0806307676. *Class No:* 929.50(73)

[6139]

—TEPPER, M., *ed.* Emigrants to Pennsylvania, 1641-1819: a consolidation of ship passenger lists from the Pennsylvania Magazine of History and Biography. Baltimore, Genealogical Publishing Co., Inc., 1975. x, 292p. $15. ISBN: 0808306823. *Class No:* 929.50(73)

[6140]

—TEPPER, M., *ed.* Immigrants to the middle colonies: a consolidation of ship passenger lists and associated data from the New York Genealogical and Biographical Record. Baltimore, Genealogical Publishing Co., Inc., 1979. xiii, 178p. $12. ISBN: 0808307927. *Class No:* 929.50(73)

[6141]

—TEPPER, M., *ed.* New World immigrants: a consolidation of ship passenger lists and associated data from periodical literature. Baltimore, Genealogical Publishing Co., Inc., 2v. 1980. xxii, 568p.+vii, 602p. index. $40. ISBN: 0806308540.

Index of names and ships. *Class No:* 929.50(73)

Micromaterials

Bibliographies

[6142]

Genealogical and biographical research A select catalog of National Archives microfilm publications. Washington DC, National Archives Trust Fund Board, US General Services Administration, 1983. xii, 77p. pbk. $2. ISBN: 0911333061.

'This catalog is one of a series describing National Archives microfilm publications related to subjects of high research interest ... The catalogs contain both detailed descriptions of the records and roll-by-roll listings for each publication'. Others are *Black studies, American Indians, Diplomatic records, Immigrant and passenger arrivals* and *Military service records. Class No:* 929.50(73)(003.5)(01)

Bibliographies

[6143]

Bibliography of genealogy and local history periodicals with union list of major US collections. Clegg, M.B., *ed.* Fort Wayne, Ind., Allen County Library Foundation, PERSI Project, 1990. unpaged, index. $75.

c.5,500 genealogy and local history periodicals held in 11 libraries are listed A-Z by title under place and family names. The genealogical collections of the Allen County Public Library, Fort Wayne, form the base list. Reproduced from a computer database. *Class No:* 929.50(73)(01)

[6144]

FILBY, P.W., *ed.* **Passenger and immigration lists bibliography. 1538-1900:** being a guide to published lists of arrivals in the United States and Canada. 2nd ed. Detroit, Gale Research Co., 1988. xli, 324p. index. £84. $110. ISBN: 0810327406.

First edition published in 1981. *First Supplement* published 1984. To be used in conjunction with *Passenger and immigration lists index (qv).*

Lists over 2500 published sources incorporating those published in *First Supplement*, and adds more than 750 new sources. Numbered and annotated entries are arranged A-Z by author or title. The index provides access to places of emigration, immigration, ship names, ports of departure and arrival, and places of settlement. 'An essential source for

.... (contd.)

research in immigration history, ethnic studies, and genealogy' (*Booklist*, v.85, no.5, 1 November 1988, p.464). *Class No:* 929.50(73)(01)

[6145]

HOROWITZ, L. A **Bibliography of military name lists** from pre-1675 to 1900: a guide to genealogical sources. Metuchen, N.J., Scarecrow Press, 1990. xxxvii,1080p. £94.95. ISBN: 0810821664.

6656 briefly annotated entries 'designed to help genealogists and researchers identify a person through his military service' (*Introduction*) arranged in 10 chronological periods corresponding to American wars. Data is from payrolls, muster lists, obituaries, pension and bounty land records *etc.* but not from county or city histories. *Class No:* 929.50(73)(01)

[6146]

McCRACKEN, G.E. 'State and Federal sources for American genealogy'. Genealogists Magazine. v.19, no.4, December 1977, p.138-40. *Class No:* 929.50(73)(01)

[6147]

NEWBERRY LIBRARY. Chicago. **The Genealogical index of the Newberry Library.** Boston, Mass., G.K. Hall, 4v., 1960. 3916p.

512,000 cards, photolithographically reproduced. Arranged under surnames A-Z. Includes many analytical entries from town and country histories and registers, as well as published family histories. The outstanding feature of this index is the coverage of Midwest towns and counties and areas of migration thereto. Now available only on Microfilm (8 reels. $345.00 Export $415.00. ISBN 0816113173). *Class No:* 929.50(73)(01)

[6148]

ROSENBERG, J. 'American family history', *Choice*, v.20, no.5, January 1983. p.675-684.

Literature review of general works and works on The European background; The Colonial family; Nineteenth-century families; The Black family; The Twentieth-century. List of works cited p.682-684. *Class No:* 929.50(73)(01)

[6149]

UEBRICK-PACHELI, W. 'Select bibliography of genealogical research aids published by the National Archives and Records Administration', *Reference Services Review*, v.15, no.1, Spring 1987, p.43-45.

Descriptive guide to major NARA publications. *Class No:* 929.50(73)(01)

[6150]

YOUNG, T.M. **Afro-American genealogy sourcebook.** New York, Garland, 1987. ix,199p. illus. $39. ISBN: 0824086848.

Lists and describes the most often used resources in genealogy and family history research of African-Americans. Arranged in 4 parts: 1. Background reading and basic reference sources - 2. Private resources - 3. Public records - 4. Directory of resources. *Class No:* 929.50(73)(01)

Handbooks & Manuals

[6151]

EAKLE, A. *and* **CERNY, J.,** *comps.* **The Source** a guidebook of American genealogy. Salt Lake City, Ancestry Publishing Co., 1984. xii, 786p. illus., facsims., maps., tables. $39.95. ISBN: 0916489000.

16 contributors. 23 chapters arranged in 3 parts: 1. Major record sources - 2. Published general sources - 3. Special records (immigrant, urban, Indian, Spanish, Negro, Asian, Jewish). Appendix A. Regional Federal archives and record centres - B. State historical archives and record depositories - C. Historical societies and agencies in the US - D. Genealogical Society of Utah and branches - E. Selected research libraries - F. Where to write for vital records - G. Genealogical societies of the US - H. Genealogy book publishers. Chapter bibliographies. Glossary p.742-748. Bibliographic index (material not cited in chapter bibliographies) p.750-9. Subject index p.760-86. 'Compact yet wide-ranging, this authoritative work must surely remain the definitive textbook on genealogy in the United States for much time to come' (*Genealogists Magazine,* v.21, no.7, September 1984, p.256). *Class No:* 929.50(73)(035)

[6152]

GREENWOOD, V.D. The Researcher's guide to American genealogy. 2nd ed. Baltimore, Genealogical Publishing Co., Inc., 1990. 623p. illus. facsims. tables, index. $24.95.

24 well-documented chapters *e.g.* 5. An introduction to research tools: reference materials ... 11. Using census returns ... 16. Local land records, identify and evaluate the various types of records. The final chapter is on Canadian research. 'The most comprehensive how-to book on American genealogical and local history research' (*Library Journal,* v.99, no.12, 15 June 1974, p.1692). *Class No:* 929.50(73)(035)

[6153]

LAW, H.T. How to trace your ancestors to Europe: 117 stories of how ancestors were traced to their birthplaces in 20 European countries. Salt Lake City, Cottonwood Books, 1987. 422p. illus. map. indexes. $19. ISBN: 0935775013.

Pt.1. Case studies of 117 successful searches for the home towns of European ancestors. Pt.2. Research methods and outline of 46 United States resource centres. *Class No:* 929.50(73)(035)

[6154]

SMITH, J.C. Ethnic genealogy a research guide. Westport, Conn., Greenwood Press, 1983. xxxix, 440p. $46.95. ISBN: 0313225931.

Part 1. General information on sources, procedures, and genealogical research. Part 2. Utilizing major repositories with chapters on The National Archives and Records Services p.123-173 and The Genealogical Society of Utah Library p.175-205. Part 3. comprises separate chapters on American-Indian, Asian-American, Black American, and Hispanic American records and research. Each chapter is fully documented and equipped with an extended bibliography. Index p.403-435. 'The work is particularly helpful in identifying the location of resources that should be used to support the research' (*Choice,* v.21, no.8, April 1984, p.1110). *Class No:* 929.50(73)(035)

Glossaries

[6155]

BENTLEY, E.P. The Genealogist's address book. Baltimore, Md., Genealogical Publishing Co., 1991. 408p. pbk. $29.95. ISBN: 0806312920.

Directory information and publications of over 7,000 organizations and institutions that can assist with genealogical research: 1. National (including National Archives and its regional centres, government departments and agencies) - 2. State listings of vital records offices, county and regional archives, libraries and societies - 3. Ethnic archives *etc.* - 4. Special resources (hereditary societies, adoption information, immigration research centres *etc.*) - 5. Periodicals and newsletters. 'Essential for institutions or individuals seriously pursuing genealogical research' (*Library Journal,* v.116,no.1, January 1991, p.88). *Class No:* 929.50(73)(038.1)

Yearbooks & Directories

[6156]

EICHHOLZ, A., *ed.* **Ancestry's red book:** American, state, county and town sources. Salt Lake City, Ancestry, 1989. 758p. maps, bibliog., index. $39.95. ISBN: 0916489477.

Comprehensive guide to genealogical research resources arranged A-Z by State. All types of record are within its ambit and it also acts as a location guide for newspapers and periodicals, and private manuscript collections, and as a directory of archives, libraries and genealogical and historical societies. Special attention is given to immigration, naturalization and various ethnic groups. 'It becomes the new standard, quick-reference handbook for American genealogy' (*Library Journal,* v.115, no.7, 15 April 1990, p.80). *Class No:* 929.50(73)(058)

Maps & Atlases

[6157]

MOFFAT, R.M. 'Maps, atlases, & gazetteers for genealogical research' *Western Association of Map Libraries Bulletin,* v.12,no.1, November 1980, p.21-30.

115 items listed A-Z by geographical region. *Class No:* 929.50(73)(084.3)

Archives

[6158]

Guide to genealogical research in the National Archives. Washington, National Archives Trust Fund Board, 1983. xiii, 304p. illus. geneal. tables, maps. $35. ISBN: 0911333002.

Supersedes *Guide to genealogical records in the National Archives* compiled by M.B. Colket and F.E. Bridgers (1964).

20 chapters: 1. Census records ... 2. Passenger arrival lists ... 12 Records of Black Americans ... 20. Cartographical records grouped in 4 sections, population and immigration, military, particular groups, and miscellaneous. Introduction (p.1-38) includes notes on the value and limitations of Federal records, research methods and aims, and the National Archives' resources and research facilities. Selected as an outstanding reference source by the American Library Association. *Class No:* 929.50(73)(093.20)

[6159]
TURNER, F.H. 'Using America's National Archives'
Genealogists Magazine, v.20, no.3, September 1980, p.97-99.
Concentrates on census, service records, and passenger lists. *Class No:* 929.50(73)(093.20)

Libraries

[6160]
'The Challenge of genealogical reference services',
Reference Quarterly, v.23, no.2, Winter 1983.
Contents: M.A. Reinhart and D.R. Brown 'Introduction'; L.D. Bockstruck 'Four centuries of genealogy'; R.E. Bidlack 'The awakening: genealogy as it relates to library service'; J.C. Parker 'Becoming the ideal library for genealogy patrons'; P.W. Filby 'Passengers and naturalization lists'; J.P. Reid 'Searching for genealogies in the Library of Congress computer catalog'; and C. Clement 'Improved genealogical reference services through automation. The L.D.S. Genealogy Library'.
Class No: 929.50(73):061:026/027

[6161]
Directory of American libraries with genealogy or local history collections. Filby, P.W., *comp.* Wilmington, Delaware, Scholarly Resources, 1988. 319p. index. $75. ISBN: 0842022864.
A-Z State by State, town by town directory of US and Canadian libraries and archives. 'Even though admittedly incomplete ... a must purchase for libraries serving genealogists' (*Wilson Library Bulletin*, v.63, no.1, September 1988, p.95). *Class No:* 929.50(73):061:026/027

[6162]
'Genealogy and libraries,' *Library Trends*, v.32, no.1, Summer 1983.
Contents: D.F. Carothers' 'Introduction'; R.E. Bidlack 'Genealogy today'; B.R. Linder 'An overview of genealogical research in the National Archives'; R. Turnbaugh 'The impact of genealogical users on state archives programmes'; S. M. Andrusko 'Genealogical research at the Library of Congress'; D.F. Carothers' 'Resources of a large academic research library'; R.J. Ashton 'A commitment to excellence in genealogy: how the public library became the only tourist attraction in Fort Wayne, Indiana'; P.T. Sinko and S.N. Peters 'A survey of genealogists at the Newberry Library'; D.M. Mayfield 'The genealogical library of the Church of Jesus Christ of Latter Day Saints'; R.J. Crandall 'The New England Genealogical Society'; and J.E. Jelks and J.W. Sikes' 'Approaches to black family history'. All articles end with extensive references. *Class No:* 929.50(73):061:026/027

[6163]
PARKER, J.C. **Library service for genealogists.** Detroit, Gale Research Company, 1981. xii, 362p. $68. ISBN: 0810314894.
24 Chapters: 2. Collection development ... 6. How-to-do-it books - 7. Vital records - 8. Finding family histories - 9. Genealogical name indexes - 10. Genealogical periodicals and periodical indexes ... 12. Census schedules - 13. Finding county and city histories ... 15. Sources listing ancestors as individuals. Index p.311-362.
Class No: 929.50(73):061:026/027

Australia

[6164]
JOSEPH, A. 'Anglo-Australian genealogy', *Genealogists Magazine* v.20, no.5, March 1981, p.152-157 and no.6, June 1981, p.181-188. *Class No:* 929.50(94)

Handbooks & Manuals

[6165]
HAWKINGS, D.T. **Bound for Australia.** Chichester, Sussex, Phillimore, 1987. xvi, 269p. illus., facsims., tables, bibliog., index. £12.85. ISBN: 0850336147.
Guide in 9 chapters 'to enable the descendent of a convict to trace his ancestor and to discover as much as possible about that individual's personal life and crime; his (or her) journey to New South Wales; and his (or her) life in the colony' (*Preface*). Favourably received in *Archives* v.18, no.79, April 1988, p.175-6. *Class No:* 929.50(94)(035)

[6166]
McCLAUGHLIN, T. **From shamrock to wattle** digging up your Irish ancestors. Sydney, Collins, 1985. 162p. illus., facsims., gen. tables, bibliog., index. pbk. ISBN: 0002173301.
Directs Australian family historians to available source material in Australia and Ireland. Bibliography p.145-53.
Class No: 929.50(94)(035)

[6167]
REAKES, J. **The A-Z genealogical handbook.** North Ryde, New South Wales, Methuen, 1986. 268p. ISBN: 0454009534.
Explains in simple terms the contents and availability of records. *Class No:* 929.50(94)(035)

[6168]
REAKES, J. **How to trace your convict ancestors** their lives, times & records. Sydney, Hale & Iremonger, 1987. 71p. illus. ISBN: 086806274x.
17 chapters *e.g.* 2. Trials ... 3. Hulks ... 4. The voyage... 5. Assignment ... 8. Musters ... 9. Pardons ... 16. Books ... 17. Addresses guide the researcher through the key events in a convict's life, discussing the records most useful to family historians. Glossary p.67-69. *Class No:* 929.50(94)(035)

Jews

Bibliographies

[6169]
The Encyclopedia of Jewish genealogy Vol.1. Sources in the United States and Canada. Kurzweil, A. *and* Weiner, M., *eds.* Northvale, N.J., Jason Aronson, 1991. xxii,226p. bibliogs., index. $30; £16.95. ISBN: 0876688350.
1st of 3v. V.2 will cover sources in Europe, Australia and South America; v.3 will be arranged by topic *e.g.* The Holocaust; Sephardic Jewry.
1. Immigration and naturalization - 2. Institution resources in US (A-Z x state and city) - 3. Canadian resources. Extensive appendices include directories of Jewish genealogical and historical societies worldwide; Federal archives and research centres; and French, German, Hungarian, and Polish-Jewish records in the Salt Lake City Family History Library. *Class No:* 929.50(=924)(01)

Family Histories

Databases

[6170]

GOATLY, B. 'A Screenful of forebears' *The Micro User*, v.7, no.4, June 1989, p.20-22.

Review and comparison of 2 computer databases designed for family history records: 1. Exeter, Devon, Minerva Software, *Ancestry*. For use with the Archimedes. 2. Barrhill, South Ayrshire, Micro Aid, *Family history system*. For use with 8 bit BBC Micro or Archimedes. 'If you have an Archimedes and are keenly interested in genealogy you must buy Minerva's Ancestry program. It is powerful, graphic and above all friendly ... In comparison the Archimedes version of the Family History System is something of a disaster, with flaws that render it unreliable and frustrating ... the BBC version is competent'. *Class No:* 929.52(003.4)

[6171]

HAWGOOD, D. **Computers for family history:** an introduction. 3rd ed. London, Hawgood Computing, 1989. 72p. illus., bibliog., index, pbk. £2.50. ISBN: 0948151048. 1st ed. 1985.

1. Computers - 2. Information and its storage - 3. Programming and software - 4. Data handling and database packages - 5. Word processing - 6. Genealogy packages. Appendix 1. Which computer for genealogy? - 2. Further reading, clubs and useful addresses. Glossary p.63-8. Favourably reviewed in *Genealogists Magazine*. v.21, no.10, June 1985, p.372. *Class No:* 929.52(003.4)

Handbooks & Manuals

[6172]

FLETCHER, W. **Recording your family history** a guide to preserving oral history with videotape, audiotape, suggested topics and questions, interview techniques. New York, Dodd Mead, 1986. 313p. index. $18.95. ISBN: 0396088864.

A practical easy to use handbook designed to facilitate a 'life history interview' with elderly relatives. *Class No:* 929.52(035)

[6173]

HEY, D. **The Oxford guide to family history.** Oxford, Oxford Univ. Press, 1993. x,246p. illus. (a few col.), facsims, bibliog., indexes. £19.95. ISBN: 0198691777.

1. Study of family history - 2. Family names - 3. Mobility and stability - 4. Family and society - 5. Guide to the records. Bibliography p.231-6. Both a social history and a practical introductory guide to relevant records and their location. *Class No:* 929.52(035)

Worldwide

Handbooks & Manuals

[6174]

CURRER-BRIGGS, N. **Worldwide family history.** London, Routledge & Kegan Paul, 1982. ix, 230p. maps. ISBN: 0710009348.

Explains how English-speaking people of foreign descent can begin tracing their ancestors. Part 1. describes the history and archives of Europe, Islam, China, and Japan.

....(contd.)

Part 2. deals with colonial shipping in the seventeenth and eighteenth centuries, the settlement of the Americas, including chapters on Anglo-Saxon, Dutch, Scandinavian, German, Polish, French, Spanish, Italian, Greek and Slav emigrants, and a record of the early European settlement of South Africa, Australia, and New Zealand. Appendix 1. Heraldry and genealogical research; 2. Chief sources of information in the form of a combined bibliography and list of addresses for Europe and the United States. *Class No:* 929.52(100)(035)

Europe

[6175]

DE RANDECK, J.H. **Les plus anciennes familles du monde** Répertoire encyclopédique des 1,400 plus anciennes familles du monde, encore existantes, originaires d'Europe. Genève, Éditions Slatkine, 2v., 1984. 1636p. ISBN: 2051005575.

Family history in brief with 'significant' persons enumerated A-Z by family. Strongest criterion for inclusion is longevity and continuity (not, it is claimed, nobility, power, wealth). *Class No:* 929.52(4)

Great Britain

Bibliographies

[6176]

British Family history printed sources in the Department of Printed Books. Hurworth, M.S., *comp.* London, British Library Reference Division, 1981. 15p. sd. *gratis*.

Purpose is 'to help readers to find genealogical sources in the Department of Printed Books' (now English Language, Western and Eastern European Collections). Material listed includes Family histories; Parish Registers; Biographical records; Poll books and electoral registers; Wills; and Guides and reference books. The addresses of libraries, record depositories and societies connected with heraldry and genealogy are also given. *Class No:* 929.52(410)(01)

[6177]

FEDERATION OF FAMILY HISTORY SOCIETIES. **Current publications by member societies.** 2nd ed. Doncaster, FFHS, 1984. 32p. £1.25.

List of publications issued by The Society of Genealogists, The Heraldry Society, Institute of Heraldic and Genealogical Studies, local societies, A-Z, and of FFHS. *Class No:* 929.52(410)(01)

[6178]

THOMSON, T.R., *comp.* **A Catalogue of British family histories.** 3rd ed. with addenda by G. Barrow. London, Research Publishing Co., in conjunction with the Society of Genealogists, 1980. 229p. £6. ISBN: 0705000974. First published 1928.

Nearly 2000 entries Abbot-Yvery. Entries are asterisked if items are privately printed. 'Purports to be a complete list of British Family histories' (*Preface*). 3rd edition includes 'Addenda', Acland-Yeamans (p.185-229). *Class No:* 929.52(410)(01)

Handbooks & Manuals

[6179]

COLE, J.A. *and* **ARMSTRONG, M. Tracing your family tree:** the complete guide to discovering your family history. Wellingborough, Northamptonshire, Equation, 1988. 208p. illus., maps, tables, bibliog., index. pbk. £8.99. ISBN: 185336035x.

1. Where and how to start - 2. Civil registration of births, marriages and deaths - 3. The Census returns - 4. Parish registers - 5. Non-conformists and their records - 6. Wills and administrations - 7. Parish records, civil records, poor law, Quarter Sessions records and records of the Clerk of the Peace - 8. County Record Offices - 9. The Church of Jesus Christ of Later Day Saints and the International Genealogical Index - 10. Manorial records - 11. Directories and newspapers - 12. Miscellaneous sources - 13. The Public Record Office - 14. Genealogical societies. Appendix: Some useful dates for the family historian; some miscellaneous terms, abbreviations and colloquialisms; regnal years; useful addresses etc. p.195-204. Bibliography p.175-190. Glossary p.191-194. 'A complete workbook for the would-be genealogist'. *Class No:* 929.52(410)(035)

[6180]

COLWELL, S. The Family history book a guide to tracing your ancestors. 2nd rev. ed. Oxford, Phaidon, 1989. 192p. illus. genealogical tables, maps, bibliog. £14.95. ISBN: 0714825948.

1. Genealogy in the past and its uses; 2. Tracing your ancestors; 3. Using your sources; 4. How our ancestors lived; 5. Emigration and travel; 6. The study of names; 7. Heraldry. Appendix 1. Calendar of dates; 2. Registration Districts 1837-1851 and 1852-1946; 3. Useful addresses. *Class No:* 929.52(410)(035)

[6181]

Debrett's family historian. A guide to tracing your ancestry. Currer-Briggs, N. *and* Gambier, R. Exeter, Devon, Debrett/Webb & Bower, 1981. 208p. illus. (some col.), geneal tables, maps. ISBN: 0905649516.

More discursive than *Beginning your family history* but covers much the same ground. Chapter 2. Genealogy and genetics. 11. Immigrants. 12. Emigration to Australia and America. Appendix Record Offices, libraries and societies p.193-205. *Class No:* 929.52(410)(035)

[6182]

MARKWELL, F.C. *and* **SAUL, P. Tracing your ancestors:** the A-Z guide. 3rd ed. Newbury, Berkshire, Countryside Books in association with Federation of Family History Societies, 1988. 224p. illus., maps, index. £7.95. ISBN: 1853060283.

1st ed. as *The Family historian's enquire within.*

Invaluable compendium of definitions, explanations, record sources, locations, societies, publications, bibliographies, dates, *etc.* Appendix 1. PRO Records at Kew and Chancery Lane - 2. PRO Information Series pamphlets in numerical order p.194-6 - 3. Units of the British Army - 4. Chapman county codes. 8 maps. 'Both an encylcopaedia and an omnium gatherum of sources and extinct occupations, with many references to publications on specific topics' (*Refer*, v.4, no.1, Spring 1984, p.16). A priority purchase for all libraries and serious family historians. *Class No:* 929.52(410)(035)

[6183]

PELLING, G. Beginning your family history. 5th ed. Newbury, Berkshire, Countryside Books in association with The Federation of Family History Societies, 1990. 80p. illus., facsims, bibliogs., index. £3.50. ISBN: 1853060844.

First published by FFHS 1980.

The aim of the fifth edition remains to provide the beginner with preliminary information on family sources, instructions on how to construct a pedigree chart, and with notes on the various types of source materials, their location, access and usefulness, necessary to research back to the sixteenth century. Chapter bibliographies and a comprehensive list of FFHS publications. *Class No:* 929.52(410)(035)

Scotland

[6184]

FULTON, A. Scotland and her tartans the romantic heritage of the Scottish clans and families. London, Hodder & Stoughton, 1991. 224p. col. illus., index. £14.99. ISBN: 0340572086.

Main section 'Clans and family tartans' (p.46-209) provides descriptive and historical notes on clans A-Z with Branches, Tartans and Motto. Col. illus. of 265 authentic tartan sets. Also The clan tradition - Kinship of the clan - Highland dress - The '45 rebellion - Suppression and dispersal - Wearing the tartan - Tracing your Scottish ancestry. *Class No:* 929.52(411)

[6185]

MacLEAN, C. The Almanac: an account of the origins of the principal tribes of Scotland. Illustrated with examples of the tartans adopted by each. Moffat, Lochar Publishing, 1990. 142p. col. illus., bibliog. £5.95. ISBN: 094840339x.

Definitive A-Z list of the clans and names of Scotland giving origin of names; lands; principal branches; slogan and motto; heraldic badge; leading figures; and tartan. Appendix 1. Clans, septs and dependants - 2. The Chief of clans and names - 3. Clan societies. Bibliography p.144. Pocket book size. *Class No:* 929.52(411)

Bibliographies

[6186]

FERGUSON, J.P., *comp.* **Scottish family histories.** 2nd ed. Edinburgh, National Library of Scotland, 1986. xii, 254p. £14.95. ISBN: 0902220683.

Scottish family histories held in Scottish libraries first published Edinburgh, Scottish Central Library, 1960.

Lists some 3200 works. This edition incorporates periodical articles and the holdings of the National Library of Scotland. Cooperating libraries are included in Key to Library Codes (p.x-xii). *Class No:* 929.52(411)(01)

Handbooks & Manuals

[6187]

ADAM, F. The Clans, septs and regiments of the Scottish Highlands. 8th ed. revised by Sir Thomas Innes of Learney. Edinburgh & London, Johnston & Bacon, 1970. 692p. illus. (pl.), map. £17.50. ISBN: 0717945006.

First published 1908.

6 parts: 1. History of the clan system - 2. Structure of the clan system - 3. Celtic culture - 4. Highland forces - 5. Clan

....*(contd.)*

insignia and heraldry - 6. Clan lists and culture. 17 plates and 56p. of tartans (112). Clan map of Scotland. A standard, well-documented account. *Class No:* 929.52(411)(035)

[6188]
MOODY, D. Scottish family history. London, B.T. Batsford, 1988. 219p. bibliog. index. £14.95. ISBN: 0713477244.

7 chaps: 1. The humble and the mighty: sources of biography - 2. Working lives - 3. Living, dying, moving house: the study of demography - 4. Kin, clan and community - 5. Exploring local society - 6. Culture and beliefs - 7. Family, church and state. Chapter bibliographies p.179-205. References p.206-213. Analytical index.
Class No: 929.52(411)(035)

[6189]
Scottish clans & tartans History of each Clan and full list of Septs. London, New Orchard, 1991. 55p. + 96 double pages print and col. illus. map. ISBN: 0850791635.

First published c.1891.

Concise guide to Gaelic language, highland dress, clan ceremonial, armorial bearings, clan systems *etc.* introduces 96 double pages each giving short history and colour illustration of individual clan tartans.
Class No: 929.52(411)(035)

Ireland

[6190]
Burke's Irish family records. Montgomery-Massingberd, H.J. London, Burke's Peerage, 1976. 1300p.

Previously as *Burke's Genealogical and heraldic history of landed gentry of Ireland*, first published 1899; 4th ed. 1958.

The genealogical histories of 514 Irish families, Acton ... Yeats (*c.*100 of Celtic origin), from their earliest recorded male ancestor down to the present day. Includes biographical entries for each member of the family (living and dead). Full cross-references. Addenda, p.1235-7.
Class No: 929.52(415)

[6191]
GREENHAM, J. Clans and families of Ireland heritage and heraldry. Dublin: Gill & Macmillan, 1993. 184p., col. illus. I£12.99. ISBN: 0717120325.

A-Z listing of 200 family names, with short notes on their derivations, origins, and history, complemented with chapters on immigration, emigration, and Irish heraldry.
Class No: 929.52(415)

[6192]
MACLYSAGHT, E. Irish families their names, arms and origins. 4th ed. Dublin, Hodges Figgis, 1978. 368p.

The main sequence is A-Z by family name ignoring prefixes 'O' and 'Mac'; it deals with names and origins. Coloured plates illustrate almost 250 Irish family arms and crests, with descriptive captions. Bibliography (p.316-38), in 2 parts: 1. Irish family histories: 2. General (including 'Periodicals containing much material for family history'); County, diocesan and local histories. Detailed index. The author was formerly Chief Herald of Ireland.
Class No: 929.52(415)

[6193]
—MACLYSAGHT, E. More Irish families a new revised and enlarged edition ... incoporating Supplement to Irish families, with an essay on Irish chieftainries. Dublin, Irish Academic Press, 1982. 254p. port., maps, bibliog.

More Irish families first published by Gorman in 1960; *Supplement* by Helicon Press in 1964.

Forms single companion volume to *Irish families*. A-Z sequence by family name extending coverage p.21-213. Appendix 1. Additional information for articles in the basic work; 3. The commonest English, Scottish and Welsh surnames in modern Ireland; 4. Explanation of technical terms used in text; and 5. Bibliography of works relating to the Irish abroad p.232-233. Maps and index to maps p.235-243; Index p.244-254. *Class No:* 929.52(415)

[6194]
YURDAN, M. Irish family history. London, B.T. Batsford, 1990. xii,194p. maps, bibliog., index. £14.95. ISBN: 0713462752.

Guidance on where to find relevant archives and on how to interpret the records available in 8 chapters e.g. 2. The leaving of Ireland - 3. Making a start with research - 4. The ancestor abroad. Conclusion: the future of Irish Family History Research p.168-71. Key dates in Irish history p.ix-xi. Glossary p.172-5. Useful addresses p.176-86. Bibliography p.187-91. *Class No:* 929.52(415)

Bibliographies

[6195]
MACLYSAGHT, E. Bibliography of Irish family history. 2nd ed. Shannon, Irish Academic Press, 1982. 71p. pbk. £2. ISBN: 071650507x.

Previously published in the author's *The Surnames of Ireland* (4th edition, revised and corrected 1978) but omitted from the 5th edition (1980). It was first issued as a separate publication in 1981 and is reissued in a 2nd edition revised and expanded.

850 entries A-Z by family. 'The reader is also advised to consult the list of reports in the National Library on manuscript collections in private keeping given in *Analecta Hibernica* v.XXII, p.371-387: these are supplementary to those in print in other numbers of *Analecta Hibernica* which are included in this bibliography' (Foreword).
Class No: 929.52(415)(01)

Handbooks & Manuals

[6196]
Burke's introduction to Irish ancestry. Montgomery-Massingberd, H. London, Burke's Peerage Ltd., 1976. viii, 64p. sd. ISBN: 0850110211.

First printed in the US ed. of *Burke's Irish Family records* (1976).

6 essays: The Irish in America; The High Kings in Ireland; The Irish chieftainries; The Irish Genealogical Office (p.51-55); The Irish Genealogical Research Societies (p.56-58); Tracing your Irish ancestry (p.59-64).
Class No: 929.52(415)(035)

Northern Ireland

Archives

[6197]

NEILL, K. **How to trace family history in Northern Ireland.** Belfast, Irish Heritage Association and Lisburn, Co. Antrim, B.Q. Publications, 1986. 92p. spiral binding. £5. ISBN: 095081931x.

Comprehensive guide to repositories and types of records including an introductory guide to the Public Record Office of Northern Ireland and A-Z list of civil parishes and local registrar district offices. For amateur and overseas researchers. *Class No:* 929.52(416)(093.20)

England

Archives

[6198]

COLWELL, S. **Family roots** discovering the past in the Public Record Office. London, Weidenfeld and Nicolson, 1991. 231p. illus., facsims, geneal., tables, diagrs., bibliog., index. £15.99. ISBN: 0297830260.

Part 1. 'Understanding the sources': 1. The legal system - 2. Holding and transfer of land - 3. Tax and other sources of revenue - 4. Strangers and settlers. Part 2. 'The Sources at work' consists of 9 case studies containing examples of the types of information to be derived from the records in the PRO. Chapter notes p.207-16. Bibliography p.217-22. *Class No:* 929.52(420)(093.20)

London

Archives

[6199]

BOURNE, S. **Ten London repositories:** a practical guide for the family historian. 2nd ed. Northfleet, Kent, S. Bourne, 1987. [20]p. ISBN: 0951067834.

First published 1985.

Provides basic information on facilities and services, outlines the main groups of records held, points out practical problems, and suggests useful advance reading. *Class No:* 929.52(421)(093.20)

Germany

Bibliographies

[6200]

Familiengeschichte Bibliographie hrsg, unter dem Schutze der Arbeitsgemeinschaft der deutschen familien und wappenkundlichen vereine von der Zentralstelle für Deutsche Personen=und Familiengeschichte. Wiesbaden, Martin Sändig, 8v., 1969-.

First published in Leipzig 1900-.

Lists titles of genealogical works published in the German language since 1897. V.6 includes Gesamtregister zur Familiengeschichtelichen 1897-1937. *Class No:* 929.52(430)(01)

USA

[6201]

Burke's Presidential families of the United States of America. Montgomery-Massingberd, H., *ed.* 2nd ed. London, Burke's Peerage Ltd., 1981. xiv, 598p.+94p. Appendix. illus. ISBN: 0850110335.

First published 1975.

A chapter on each of the 39 Presidents from George Washington to Ronald Reagan covering their character, career, writings, ancestry, wives, siblings, and descendants. Information on Jefferson Davis (President of the Confederate States of America); the Vice-Presidents; Presidential ancestral tables; and Presidential elections is appended. Guide to the reader, appendix p.73-75. Index of 3000 surnames. 'Important and invaluable reference work for both historians and genealogists of American pedigree' (*Genealogists Magazine*, v.20, no.6, June 1981, p.190). Older books still of value are R.B. Henry's *Genealogies of the families of the Presidents* and W.L. Zorn's *The Descendants of the Presidents of the US* (2nd ed. 1955). 'Both books are outdated but not superseded and should be retained' (*Genealogists Magazine*, v.18, no.3, September 1975, p.142-3. *Class No:* 929.52(73)

[6202]

WALCH, T., *comp.* **Our family, our town:** essays on family and local history sources in the National Archives. Washington, National Archives, 1987. 223p. illus. $20. ISBN: 0911333509.

Practical advice and encouragement for the use of federal records in family and local history research. Military pension records, census schedules, ship passenger lists, and court documents are among the materials discussed. *Class No:* 929.52(73)

Bibliographies

[6203]

NEW ENGLAND HISTORIC GENEALOGICAL SOCIETY. **The Greenlaw Index of the New England Historic Genealogical Society.** Boston, Mass., G.K. Hall, 1979. 4 reels. $205.00 (Export $245.00). ISBN: 0816113351.

The Index lists over 35,000 surnames, with information from the thousands of historical and genealogical works acquired by the Society's library between 1902 and 1940. Indexed are town and country histories, collateral as well as main lines in family histories, genealogical compendia, and some periodicals. Continues *Index to American genealogies* (Albany, Joel Munsell's Sons, 5th ed., 1900). *Class No:* 929.52(73)(01)

Reviews & Abstracts

[6204]

American family history a historical bibliography. Brown, J.S. *and* Kinnell, S.K. Santa Barbara, California and Oxford, ABC-Clio Information Services, 1984. xii,282p. indexes. £28.70. (*ABC-Clio Research Guides, no.12.*) ISBN: 0874363802.

1167 abstracts and citations of journal articles A-Z by author arranged in 4 chapters - 1. The family in historical perspective - 2. The family and other social institutions - 3. Familial roles and relationships - 4. Individual family histories. Author and subject indexes. Compiled from the

....*(contd.)*

ABC-Clio historical database 1973-1982. 'A very useful source' (*Choice,* v.22,no.7, March 1985, p.959).
Class No: 929.52(73)(048)

New Zealand

[6205]

BROMELL, A. Tracing family history in New Zealand. Wellington, Government Printing Office, 1988. 196p. illus., map, facsims, bibliog., index. ISBN: 0477013767.

Supplements *Family history research in New Zealand: a beginner's guide* (NZ Society of Genealogists, 1984).

Authoritative manual in 19 chapters *e.g.* 4. Maori genealogy or whakapapa ... 5. Arrival in New Zealand ... 7. National archives ... 18. Researching overseas. Bibliography p.184-189. Useful addresses p.189-191.
Class No: 929.52(931)

[6206]

BROMELL, A. Tracing your family outside New Zealand. Petone, G.P. Publications, 1991. 196p.

Emphasis is on copy-records deposited in New Zealand but there is also a basic introduction to records held in Scotland, Ireland, and Australia. *Class No:* 929.52(931)

Archives

[6207]

Family history at National Archives. Wellington, Allen & Unwin and National Archives, 1990. xiv,162p. illus.

Guide to immigration, tax, military, educational, and court records held in New Zealands' National Archives. 'Will surely channel the enthusiasm of New Zealand genealogists in many profitable directions' (*Journal of the Society of Archivists,* v.13, no.2, Autumn 1992, p.156-7).
Class No: 929.52(931)(093.20)

Australia

[6208]

The Bicentennial dictionary of Western Australians pre 1829-1888. Erikson, R., *comp.* Nedlands, Univ. of Western Australia Press, 4v., 1987. xxiv, 3419p. ISBN: 0855642785, set.

Supersedes *Dictionary of Western Australians:* 1. *Early Settlers 1829-1850* (1979) and *Supplement* (1981) - 2. *Bond 1858-1868* (1979) - 3. *Free 1850-1868* (1979) - 4. *The challenging years 1868-1888* (2v., 1984-85) now described as working copies designed to encourage public participation in the collection of family records.

V.5. Atkinson, A. *Asian immigrants to Western Australia 1829-1901* (1988. xvi, 464p. illus.,map,tables. ISBN 0855642874 covers Chinese, Japanese, Indian, Filipino, Afghan and Malay immigration. Of the original set of volumes, *The golden years 1889-1914* (1986. 1006p. 0855642505), retains its value. This work is an official project of the Australian Bicentennial Authority.
Class No: 929.52(94)

[6209]

COFFEY, H.W. *and* **MORGAN, M.J. Irish families in Australia and New Zealand.** Melbourne, P.O. Box 135, 1978-.

Preliminary paperback edition: 1. *1788-1878* (Abbott-Dwyer-Gray). 1978. 140p. 0959595228. 2. *1788-1979* (Eades-Kate). 1979. 141-307p. 0959595236. 3. *1788-1980* (Laffy-Quirke). 1980. 308-505p. 0959595244. 4. *1788-1981* (Rafferty-Young). 1981. 506-639p. 0959595252. A total of 2710 brief biographies.

Revised edition: 1. *1788-1983* (Abbot-Dynan). 1983. 248p. 0959595260. 1353 persons included compared to 580 entries in preliminary edition. *Class No:* 929.52(94)

Bibliographies

[6210]

PEAKE, A.G. Bibliography of Australian family history. Dulwich, South Australia, Tudor Australia Press, 1988. 112p. softcover. ISBN: 0958917728.

2900 entries A-Z by primary surname comprising family histories and pedigrees with Australian connections. Cut off date: end of 1987. *Class No:* 929.52(94)(01)

Handbooks & Manuals

[6211]

HALL, N.V. Tracing your family history in Australia a guide to sources. Adelaide, Rigby, 1985. xvi, 324p. ISBN: 0727019538.

Family history sources, the location of records, record categories, are reviewed State by State. Appendix 1. Published family histories. 2. Record location codes (references to 247 locations where the most important collections of records are kept) p.277-306. Bibliography p.307-324. *Class No:* 929.52(94)(035)

[6212]

RAY, P. *and* **JOHNSTON, K. 'Genealogy',** chapter 19, *Australians: a guide to sources* (v.10 *Australians. A historical Library,* 1988).

Introductory essay plus an annotated bibliography in 4 sections: Tracing your ancestors; Genealogical societies and congresses; Public records and listings; Vital registers and graveyard inscriptions. *Class No:* 929.52(94)(035)

Archives

[6213]

Relations in records a guide to family history sources in the Australian archives. Canberra, Australian Government Publishing Service, 1988. xx, 161p. illus., facsims., softcover. ISBN: 0644068477.

Comprehensive guide to Commonwealth archives of genealogical interest stored in the regional offices arranged in 4 categories: immigration and shipping; defence; population; Commonwealth government employees. Using the guide and Australian Archives control systems and finding aids p.xi-xx. Indispensable reference tool for all Australian genealogists and family historians.
Class No: 929.52(94)(093.20)

Parish Registers

Great Britain

[6214]

National index of parish registers. Chichester, Sussex, Phillimore for the Society of Genealogists, 1966-. v.1-.

1: *General sources of births, marriages and deaths before 1837.* 1966. Rev.ed. 1976. 2: *Sources for Nonconformist genealogy and family history.* 1973. 3. *Sources for Roman Catholic and Jewish genealogy and family history.* 1974. 4: *South-east England* 1980. 5: *South Midlands and Welsh Border,* 1966. New ed. 1977. 11,pt.1: *Durham and Northumberland.* 1979. £4.20. 12: *Sources for Scottish genealogy and family history.* 1970. V.12, by D.J. Steel (1970, xiii,32p.) has sections: Historical background - Catholic nomenclature - Parish registers - Ancillary sources (*e.g.* Monumental inscriptions; Court records) - Nonconformists - Bibliography, p.249-76 (A. Bibliographies; B. Genealogy and archives; C. History). Index.
Class No: 929.53(410)

[6215]

SOCIETY OF GENEALOGISTS. Parish register copies. Part One Society of Genealogists Collection. 6th ed. London, Society of Genealogists, 1983. v,47p. sd. ISBN: 090187857x.

First published in 1937 as *A catalogue of parish register copies in the possession of the Society of Genealogists* (1937). 5th ed. under current title in 1980.

1. England and Wales - 2. Scotland - 3. Ireland - 4. Overseas - 5. Registers of Roman Catholic, Quaker, Jewish and foreign churches in the British Isles. Includes accessions reported in *Genealogists Magazine* to March 1983.
Class No: 929.53(410)

[6216]

—SOCIETY OF GENEALOGISTS. Parish register copies. Part Two other than the Society of Genealogists collection. 2nd ed. 1974. London, Society of Genealogists, 1978. xi,50p. sd. ISBN: 0901878375.

First published 1971.

A-Z list of English and Welsh counties. Key to locations p.v-x. Regarded as a temporary guide until all regional volumes of *National index of parish registers* are printed.
Class No: 929.53(410)

England & Wales

[6217]

Original parish registers in Record Offices and libraries. Matlock, Derbyshire, Local Population Studies, in association with the Cambridge Group for the History of Population and Social Structure, 1974-.

First published 1974. 128p. £3. 1st Supplt. 1976. 60p. £2. 2nd Supplt. 1978. 64p. £2. 3rd. Supplt. 1980. 92p. £3.75. Fourth Supplt. 1982. 96p. £4.50.

Sections: England (by counties); Wales (by counties); Isle of Man. Includes original registers, rough books of register entries, duplicate books made simultaneously, early replacement copies. *Class No:* 929.53(42)

Handbooks & Manuals

[6218]

BURKE, A.M. Key to the ancient parish registers of England and Wales. Baltimore, Maryland, Genealogical Publishing Co., 1981. 163p. facsims. $15. ISBN: 0806304456.

First published by Eyre & Spottiswoode in 1908.

Gives parish, county and date of earliest entry for parishes having registers of an earlier date than 1913. Annotated index to parish registers p.39-163. Still of value until *National index of parish registers* (1966-) is completed.
Class No: 929.53(42)(035)

Maps & Atlases

[6219]

The Phillimore atlas and index of parish registers. Humphery-Smith, C.R., *ed.* Chichester, Sussex, Phillimore, 1984. v, 92p. maps, 91-281p. index. £30.00. ISBN: 0850333989.

'Phillimore & Co. Ltd., had the idea of publishing a consolidated guide to parish records at the same time as the Institute of Heraldic and Genealogical Studies was considering a new edition of its book of parish maps with improved new maps and an index to parishes and research sources. The two ideas have been brought together'.

Atlas contains 42 full page historical county genealogical maps of pre-1832 parishes each accompanied by a reproduction of a topographical map from J. Bell's *A new and comprehensive gazetteer of England and Wales* (1834). 'Each parish map shows the ancient parochial boundaries, the probate court jurisdiction affecting each area by colour coding, the situation of churches and chapels where relevant, and the dates of commencement of the original registers of the parish that have survived'. The index is A-Z by county and is linked to the county maps by grid references and indicates whether parishes are included in the *International Genealogical Index*. A glowing review in *Genealogists Magazine,* v.21,no.7, September 1984, p.255 describes this as 'a genealogist's dream index'.
Class No: 929.53(42)(084.3)

London

[6220]

GUILDHALL LIBRARY, LONDON. A Handlist of parish registers, register transcripts and related records at Guildhall Library. Part One: City of London. 6th rev. ed. London, Guildhall Library, 1990. 130p. pbk. (*Guildhall Library Research Guide, no.4.*) ISBN: 0900422300.

1st ed. 1963.

Arranged A-Z by Church. *Class No:* 929.53(421)

Wales

[6221]

WILLIAMS, C.J. *and* **WATTS-WILLIAMS, J.,** *eds.* **Cofrestri plwyf Cymru/Parish registers of Wales.** Aberystwyth, National Library of Wales & Welsh County Archivists Group in association with the Society of Genealogists, 1986. xliv, 217p. maps, facsims., index. £6.95. (*National Index of Parish Registers, no.13.*) ISBN: 0907158145.

Parish lists of the 13 historical counties of Wales describing the registers of over 1000 parishes and chapelries

....(contd.)

in existence before 1812, and of 200 post-1812 for which records are held by a repository. List of repositories p.xxx. Bilingual introduction. *Class No:* 929.53(429)

Canada

Bibliographies

[6222]
BIRKETT, P. Checklist of parish registers. 4th ed. Ottawa, Canadian Government Publishing Centre, 1986. 205p. C$12.00. ISBN: 0660538636.

Cross-referenced listing of parish registers on microfilm or microfiche at the National Archives that contain records of birth, baptisms, marriages and deaths. A-Z by place name within each province or region. *Class No:* 929.53(71)(01)

Heraldry

Bibliographies

[6223]
ST. LOUIS PUBLIC LIBRARY. Heraldry index of the St. Louis Public Library. Boston, Mass., G.K. Hall, 4v., 1980. 2464p. $495.00 (Export $598.00). ISBN: 0816103119.

81,200 entries listing more than 100,000 coats of arms and other insignia of individuals, families, tribes, cities, countries, provinces, states, nations, dioceses, regiments, ships, squadrons, colleges, universities, fraternities, and similar groupings from around the world. Some 860 books and periodicals in English, French, German, Dutch, Russian, and Danish are indexed. The *Heraldry Index* is a completely new compilation and its entries do not duplicate those found in Burke's *General Armory*. Biestap's *Armorial Général,* and Fairbairn's *Crests*. *Class No:* 929.6(01)

Encyclopaedias

[6224]
ROTHERY, G.C. Concise encyclopedia of heraldry. London, Bracken Books, 1985. xix, 359p. illus. (some col.), glossary. ISBN: 0946495327.

First published as *ABC of heraldry* by Stanley Paul & Co., 1915.

A layman's guide to the language and symbolism of heraldry. Glossary of heraldic terms p.332-340. *Class No:* 929.6(031)

Handbooks & Manuals

[6225]
BOUTELL, C. Boutell's heraldry revised by J.P. Brooke-Little. Rev. ed. London, Warne, 1983. x,368p. illus. (inc.pl.). ISBN: 0723230935.

First published 1950. Based on Boutell's *The manual of heraldry* (1863) and *English heraldry* (1867).

27 chapters (1. The beginning and growth of heraldry - 2. Definitions, heraldic language and blazonry ... 8. Heraldic charges ... 22. Flags ... 26. Recent trends and developments - 27. Heraldic authorities and sources. 28 col.pl. Critical bibliography (p.302-313) 'designed to be read as part of the

....(contd.)

book rather than used simply as a catalogue for reference'. Glossary and index p.314-68. 'A must for all heraldry addicts' (*TLS,* no.3755, 22 February 1974, p.189 on the 1973 ed.). *Class No:* 929.6(035)

[6226]
FRANKLYN, J. Shield and crest: an account of the art and science of heraldry. 3rd ed. London, MacGibbon & Kee, 1967,. xviii,521p. illus. (inc.col.pl.).

First published 1960.

A notable grammar of heraldic practice, with splendid examples in colour of shields and crests current in the 20th century. The blazonry and charges are described in great detail and with particular regard to their original use and meaning. Descriptions of plates are unhelpfully relegated to end of text. A good index of proper names, but some of the charges are given only under general headings, *e.g.* fish, flower. The 3rd ed. has *c.*24 pages of extra information, chiefly enlargements of existing sections; some extra illustrations. Almost every page reset. 'One of the standard textbooks of heraldry in English in the 20th century' (*Times Literary Supplement,* no.3,413, 27 July 1967, p.693). *Class No:* 929.6(035)

[6227]
GAYRE OF GAYRE *and* **NIGG, R. Heraldic standards and their ensigns.** Edinburgh, Oliver & Boyd, 1959. xix,132p. 16 col.pl., index.

The aim is to clarify and illustrate the various types of heraldic ensigns. Claims to be the first book devoted to the heraldic flag. 1. The pennon - 2. The lance pennon - 3. The personal banner - 4. The guidon - 5. The heraldic standard - 6. The streamer - 7. The heraldic household badge - 8. The gonfallon or gonfallion - 9. Heraldic vanes - 10. Banderolles and helm-streamers - 11. The armorial or heraldic flag. Footnote references. *Class No:* 929.6(035)

[6228]
NEUBECKER, O. Heraldry: sources, symbols and meaning. London, Macdonald & Co. (Black Cat imprint), 1988. 288p. illus. (mainly col.). £22.50. ISBN: 0748101985.

First published London, Macdonald & Jane's 1976.

Sections: The herald - Terminology (p.42-55) - The shield - The sign - The helmet - The crown - Heraldic accessories (*e.g.* Badges) - The right of arms - Armorial display. Early armorials (p.268-72). Bibliography, p.273-5 (grouped). Index. Profusely illustrated (2,200 col. illus.). International in scope.

O. Neubecker's *Guide to heraldry* (New York, McGraw-Hill, 1980, 264p.) is an abridgment. *Class No:* 929.6(035)

[6229]
WOODCOCK, T. *and* **ROBINSON, J.M. The Oxford guide to heraldry.** Oxford, Oxford Univ. Press, 1988. xli, 233p. illus. (some col) bibliog. £17.50. ISBN: 0192116584.

1. Origins of heraldry - 2. English heraldry - 3. Grantees of English arms - 4. The shield of arms - 5. Crests - 6. Supporters, badges and mottoes - 7. Marshalling of arms - 8. Heraldic authority in Great Britain - 9. American heraldry - 10. The use of heraldry as decoration. Appendix A. The Royal Arms of Great Britain - B. English and Scottish Kings of Arms. Glossary of heraldic terms in open use p.197-206. Bibliography p.207-210. Analytical index. 'Illustrated guide to the history and uses of heraldic symbols ... intended as a non-specialist introduction ... written with full authority,

....(contd.)

avoiding romantic myths and pseudo-heraldic terms' (d/w). Authors are Somerset Herald and Fitzalan Pursuivant Extraordinary respectively. *Class No:* 929.6(035)

[6230]
WOODWARD, J. *and* **BURNETT, G. A Treatise on heraldry, British and foreign,** with English and French glossaries. Newton Abbot, Devon, David and Charles, 1969. First published 1892. 2nd ed. Edinburgh, Johnston, 2v., 1896.

The best English survey of continental heraldic practice. The illustrations are excellent. It covers the origin, history, and practical application of armory. V.2 contains an index of proper names and subjects. This treatise serves as an introduction to Rietstap's *Armorial général (qv).*
Class No: 929.6(035)

Dictionaries
[6231]
BROOKE-LITTLE, J.P. An Heraldic alphabet. 2nd rev. ed. London, Robson Books, 1985. 226p. illus. (incl.col.pl.) pbk. £8.95.

First published Macdonald. 1973.

Prefatory essay, followed by the alphabet, p.30-224 *c.*1,700 terms; numerous cross-references. 'Partition, lines of: ½p. of text, 1p. of illus. *(qv).* The author is Richmond Herald of Arms. No bibliography or index. 'Aims to explain the jargon as it is today' *(TLS,* no.3757, 25 January 1974, p.72). *Class No:* 929.6(038)

[6232]
FOSTER, J. The Dictionary of heraldry feudal coats of arms and pedigrees. London, Bracken books, 1989. xvi, 240p. illus., col. coats of arms, geneal. tables. ISBN: 1851703098.

First published as *Some feudal coats of arms* (London, James Parker, 1902).

Feudal coats of arms p.1-214 (A-Z by family and individuals); Men of coat armour their bearings and badges with many chart pedigrees and royal descents p.215-240. *Class No:* 929.6(038)

[6233]
FRANKLYN, J. *and* **TANNER, J. An encyclopaedic dictionary of heraldry.** Oxford, Pergamon Books, 1970. xiv,307p. illus. (inc.pl.); facsims.

The glossary, p.1-355, has *c.*8,000 entries and cross-references, 474 illus.; 18p. of colour plates; text facing illus. Appendix 2: Analysis of blazon, p.350-67. 'Even if Gough & Parker's *A Glossary of terms used in heraldry* (1967) is held, this work's illustrations make it indispensable' *(Library Journal,* v.95,no.15, 1 September 1970, p.2788).
Class No: 929.6(038)

[6234]
FRIAR, S., *ed.* **A New dictionary of heraldry.** Sherborne, Dorset, Alphabooks, 1987. 384p. illus. (some col). coats of arms, bibliog. £15.95. $30. ISBN: 0906670446, UK; 0517566656, US.

Published in the United States by Harmony under the title *A dictionary of heraldry.*

34 distinguished contributors define and expand upon more than 1000 terms in heraldry and armory. A list of general books is included under the entry 'Bibliography in the A-Z sequence. 16 col. plates. 'The attention to modern (or vernacular) heraldry ... makes this book unique'

....(contd.)

(Booklist, v.84, no.15, 1 April 1988, p.1321). The editor is Keeper of the Heraldry Society's Register of Armorial Bearings. *Class No:* 929.6(038)

[6235]
PARKER, J. A Glossary of terms used in heraldry. Newton Abbot, Devon, David & Charles, 1970. xxxii, 659p. illus., col. frontis., index. ISBN: 715347640.

First published 1894.

Contents: A synoptical table of the chief terms used in British heraldry p.xv-xxxii; Glossary p.1-634. Index to the names etc., whose coats of arms will be found blazoned in the course of this glossary p.635-639. *Class No:* 929.6(038)

Worldwide
[6236]
The International armorial register. A register of armorial bearings in current use with the names and addresses of the bearers and the authority for their use. Dingli-Attard-Inguanez, M., *ed.* Missouri, Universal Intelligence Data Bank of America, 1984. 380p. $27.50. ISBN: 0961074000. *Class No:* 929.6(100)

Europe
[6237]
RIETSTAP, J.B. Armorial général: précédé d'un dictionnaire des termes du blason. 2nd ed. Gouda, Van Goor, 2v. , 1884-87. Reprinted Paris, Dupont, 1904; Institut Héraldique, 1905-14; The Hague, Nijhoff, 1926-34; New York, Barnes & Noble, 1965. illus.

First published 1861.

The standard encyclopaedia of European arms with entries arranged A-Z by families.

Supplément par V. Rolland and H. Rolland (The Hague, Nijhoff, 7v. in 8, 1926-54; London, Heraldry Today, 1965). *Table du Supplément* par H. Rolland (Lyon, Société Sauvegarde Historique, 1951. 190p.).

Plates illustrating the arms in Riestap's original work were published under the title *Armories des familles contenues dans l'Armorial Général* (Paris, Institut Héraldique Universel, 6v., 1903-26; The Hague, Nijhoff, 1938). A 3rd. ed. of these plates edited by V. Rolland and H. Rolland (with text in English) was published under the title of *General illustrated armorial* (Lyon, Sauvegarde Historique, 6v., 1953). This was reprinted as *Illustrations to the 'Armorial Général' of J.B. Rietstap* (London, Heraldry Today, 3v., 1967). *Class No:* 929.6(4)

[6238]
VOLBORTH, C.A. von. Heraldry customs, rules and styles. Poole, Dorset, Blandford Press, 1981. vii, 1-217 plates (some col). 229p. bibliog. ISBN: 0713709405.

Illustrative guide (1250 illustrations, 150 in colour) to European heraldry. Bibliography (mainly of European publications) p.219-221. Index of names, arms and devices p.223-219. *Class No:* 929.6(4)

[6239]

—VOLBORTH, C.A. von. The Art of heraldry. Poole, Dorset, Blandford Press, 1987. 224p. coats of arms (mostly col.), bibliog. £40. ISBN: 0713713909.

Originally planned as a replacement to the author's *Heraldic customs, rules and styles* (1981).

1. Heraldic design - 2. Heraldic art and craft over the centuries - 3. An international exhibition of heraldic works by artists and artisans from the end of the nineteenth century. Design of new armorial bearings p.218. Index of names p.222-224; general index p.224. *Class No:* 929.6(4)

Dictionaries

[6240]

STALINS, G.F.L., *and others*. Vocabulaire-atlas héraldique en six langues: Francçais - English - Deutsch - Español - Italiano - Nederlandsch. Paris, Société du Grand Armorial de France, 1952.

At head of title-page: Académie Internationale d'Héraldique. Pt.1. tabulates principal terms in heraldry in six languages - 2. A-Z listing of terms for each of the languages - 3. Black and white plates.
Class No: 929.6(4)(038)

Great Britain

[6241]

BROOKE-LITTLE, J.P. Royal heraldry beasts and badges of Britain. 3rd rev. ed. Derby, Pilgrim Press, 1981. 24p. illus. (mostly col.), sd. 75p.

Illustrated guide to the Royal Arms; the royal helms, mantlings, mottoes and insignia; and the King's, Queen's and Windsor beasts. *Class No:* 929.6(410)

[6242]

BURKE, Sir J.B. The General armory of England, Scotland, Ireland and Wales; comprising a registry of armorial bearings from the earliest to the present time with a Supplement. London, Harrison, 1884. lxxix,50,1185p.

First published 1842. This edition reprinted London, Burke's Peerage, 1961 and Baltimore, Md., Genealogical Publishing Co., 1969.

The 1884 ed. contains descriptions of about 60,000 coats-of-arms. The work is in dictionary form, the entries being under the name of the family or corporation. The illustrations are confined to the arms of the English and Welsh dynasties. An index of mottoes includes the names of the families concerned.

Morant, A. *General armory two: additions and corrections to Burke's 'General armory'*, edited by C.R. Humphery-Smith (East Ardsley, Wakefield, West Yorkshire. Tabard Press: Heraldry Today, 1973. 240p.).
Class No: 929.6(410)

[6243]

The Cambridge armorial. Humphery-Smith, C., *ed.* London, Orbis, 1985. 141p. coats of arms (some col.). ISBN: 0856138711.

Descriptive text with profuse illustrations of armorial bearings of the Colleges (in order of foundation), approved foundations, and 2 schools. Notes on their origins, historical associations, and heraldic significance. Glossary p.142-4.
Class No: 929.6(410)

Bibliographies

[6244]

MOULE, T. Biblioteca heraldica Magnae Britanniae: a bibliography of heraldry, genealogy, nobility, knighthood and ceremonies from 1469-1821. London, Heraldry Today, 1966. 692p. illus. £30. ISBN: 0900455144.

First published 1822.

A classic bibliography of 810 items, arranged chronologically. Includes lists of visitations and the principal foreign books on genealogy and heraldry. The reprint is less unwieldy than the original. 'The outstanding bibliography of British heraldry' (*Oxford guide to heraldry*, 1988).
Class No: 929.6(410)(01)

Handbooks & Manuals

[6245]

BRIGGS, G., *comp*. Civic and corporate heraldry: a dictionary of impersonal arms of England, Wales & Northern Ireland. London, Heraldry Today, 1971. 432p. illus.

Armorial bearings A-Z, p.24-428, preceded by an illustrated glossary of 162 heraldic terms. Supplementary list of obsolete civic authorities. Nearly 1,000 clear drawings. 'Impersonal' covers towns, counties and other civic authorities, as well as schools, colleges, univs., insurance companies, banks, industrial corporations and ecclesiastical bodies. *Class No:* 929.6(410)(035)

[6246]

FOX-DAVIES, A.C. A Complete guide to heraldry: revised and annotated by J.P. Brooke-Little. London, Orbis Books, 1985. xii,528p. illus., bibliog., index. £20.00.

First published 1909. Rev. ed. 1949.

A comprehensive, authoritative guide to the rules, practice and art of heraldry, revised by the Richmond Herald of Arms. Arranged in 42 systematic, short chapters, lavishly illustrated (nearly 800 drawings; 26 new coloured pl.). Comprises the history of armory; a detailed description of the treatment of charges used, regalia, seals, badges, cadency, the law of armorial bearings, and the artistic employment of heraldry. Bibliography, updated, p.486-8.
Class No: 929.6(410)(035)

[6247]

SUMMERS, P.G. How to read a coat of arms. Sherborne, Dorset, Alphabooks; San Leandro, California, Interbook, 1986. 40p. illus. bibliog. £3.95. $5.95. ISBN: 0906670438.

First published in 1967 and many times reprinted by the National Council of Social Service for the Standing Conference for Local History (now the British Association for Local History).

1. Reading a coat of arms - 2. Funeral hatchments and armorial panels - 3. Recording a coat of arms - 4. Identifying a coat of arms - 5. Further study - 6. Entitlement to arms. Bibliography p.39-40. 41 figures. "To provide the minimum amount of information to enable anyone ignorant of heraldry to take the first step towards reading a coat of arms".
Class No: 929.6(410)(035)

Dictionaries

[6248]
PAPWORTH, J.W. *and* MORANT, A.W.W. **Papworth's Ordinary of British armorials.** London, Heraldry Today. xxii, 1,125p. £55. ISBN: 090045542x.

Photolithographed reproduction of *An alphabetical dictionary of coats of arms* (1874), with a new introduction.

Enclyclopaedic; not superseded. May be called Burke's 'General armory' in reverse. Arms are listed A-Z, under the heraldic charges. Description of each coat-of-arms is followed by name of family to which it belongs. Index of the charges described. According to *Genealogists' handbook* (4th ed., 1967, p.30), *Papworth's Ordinary'*, like Burke's 'General Armory', is 'both inaccurate and incomplete', despite the fact that it is indispensable for identifying coat of arms. *Class No:* 929.6(410)(038)

Yearbooks & Directories

[6249]
FOX-DAVIES, A.C. **Armorial families;** a directory of gentlemen of coat-armour. 7th ed. London, Hurst & Blackett, 2v., 1929. Reprinted Newton Abbot, Devon, David & Charles, 1970.

First published 1895.

Introductory chapter on the abuse of arms. The entries are in A-Z order, by families. Only those arms which are officially recorded are included. Full heraldic descriptions are given, with accounts of the recent bearers of the arms. Well illustrated. Index of quarterings.

Class No: 929.6(410)(058)

[6250]
FOX-DAVIES, A.C. **The Book of public arms:** a complete encyclopaedia of all royal territorial, municipal, corporate, official and impersonal arms. London, Jack, 1915. xx,877p.

First published 1894.

Arranged in A-Z order of entries, this work is still the current authority. Each entry gives a full description of the arms, crest, and motto borne, together with the date of the grant, where such exists. *Class No:* 929.6(410)(058)

Scotland

Handbooks & Manuals

[6251]
INNES OF LEARNEY, Sir T. **Scots heraldry** a practical handbook of the historical principles and modern application of the art and science. 2nd ed. Edinburgh, Oliver & Boyd, 1934. Reprinted Johnston & Bacon, 1978. xi,131p. illus., bibliog., index. ISBN: 0717942247.

The standard work on the Scottish practice of armory. Guide to further study of Scottish heraldry (a bibliography) p.119-21. Author was Lord Lyon King of Arms 1945-1969. *Class No:* 929.6(411)(035)

[6252]
PAUL, J.B. **An Ordinary of arms contained in the Public Register of all arms and bearings in Scotland.** Baltimore, Maryland, Genealogical Publisdhing Co., 1969. xxiv,428p. index.

First published Edinburgh, Green, 1893.

The Scottish equivalent of Papworth's Dictionary, the entries (over 5,500) being under the heraldic charges. Index of family names. *Class No:* 929.6(411)(035)

[6253]
URQUHART, R.M. **Scottish burgh and county heraldry.** London, Heraldry Today, 1973. xii, 274p. illus., map. £25. ISBN: 0900455241.

The arms of the burghs and county councils are arranged under counties, with *c.*2-3 black-and-white illus. per page. Appendix: 'Chronological table of matriculations of boroughs, counties and county councils'. Bibliography, p.254-6. Reference notes. Index. *Class No:* 929.6(411)(035)

[6254]
URQUHART, R.M. **Scottish civic heraldry:** regional, islands, districts. London, Heraldry Today, 1979. 101p. illus., maps, index. £15. ISBN: 0900455268.

1: The new councils and their heraldry; 2: The arms of the Councils. Bibliography, p.93-4. Reference notes. Black-and-white maps only. *Class No:* 929.6(411)(035)

England

[6255]
FRIAR, S. **Heraldry for the local historian and genealogist.** Gloucester, Alan Sutton, 1992. xi,271p. illus. (inc. col. pl.), bibliog. £16.99. ISBN: 086299893x.

1. Heraldry: an historical perspective - 2. Armigers: nobility and gentry - 3. Documents, seals and manuscripts - 4. Architectural and decorative features - 5. Monuments, effigies, brasses and hatchments - 6. Heraldic artefacts - 7. Blazon: terminology of armory - 8. Marshalling, cadency and augmentations of honour - 9. Liveries, badges - 10. Royal heraldry. Bibliography p.247-52. Glossary p.256-71. Fully illustrated sourcebook for all researchers not just local historians or genealogists. *Class No:* 929.6(420)

[6256]
SUMMERS, P., *ed*. **Hatchments in Britain.** Chichester, Sussex, Phillimore, 1974-.

The series will comprise 10 volumes and a supplementary volume on the history and development of the hatchment. Errors and ommissions will be dealt with in an *addendum* when the series is complete.

1. *Northamptonshire, Warwickshire and Worcestershire.* 1976. xi, 113p. illus. £11.95. 0850330858.

2. *Norfolk and Suffolk.* 1976. xiv, 157p. illus. £11.95. 0850332303.

3. *The Northern Counties. Cumberland, Westmorland, Durham, Northumberland, Lancashire and Yorkshire.* 1980. xiv, 186p. illus. £11.95. 0850333296.

4. *Bedfordshire, Berkshire, Buckinghamshire, Oxfordshire and Wiltshire.* 1983. xv, 167p. illus. £11.95. 0850334519.

5. *Kent, Surrey and Sussex.* 1985. xv, 174p. illus. £11.95. 0850335353.

6. *Cambridgeshire, Essex, Hertfordshire, Huntingdonshire and Middlesex.* 1985. xv, 166p. illus. £11.95. 085335361.

7. *Cornwall, Devon, Dorset, Gloucestershire, Hampshire, Isle of Wight, Somerset.* 1988. 208p. £11.95. 0850336511.

8. *Lincolnshire, Nottinghamshire, Cheshire, Staffordshire, Derbyshire, Leicestershire, Rutland.* 1988. 192p. £11.95. 085033652x.

In preparation: 9. *Herefordshire, Shropshire, Monmouthshire, Wales, Scotland, Ireland, and former British Colonies.* 10. *History and development of the hatchment. Class No:* 929.6(420)

[6257]
WAGNER, A. **Heralds of England:** a history of the office and College of Arms. London, Heraldry Today, 1985. 634p. illus. (of coats of arms), ports. £48. ISBN: 0900455411.

Originally published by H.M. Stationery ffice, 1967.

An authoritative account, sumptuously printed and illustrated. 44p of plates, 13 in colour.
Class No: 929.6(420)

[6258]
—CHESSHYRE, H. *and* AILES, A. Heralds of today: a biographical list of officers of the College of Arms, London, 1963-86. Gerrards Cross, Buckinghamshire, Van Duren, 1986. 71p. photos. index. ISBN: 0905715314.

Primarily intended as a supplement to the London Survey Committee's *The College of Arms London* (1963).

Brief history of the history and jurisdiction of the 13 offices of the College of Arms and of the 8 Officers of Arms Extraordinary together with biographical accounts of the holders. *Class No:* 929.6(420)

Handbooks & Manuals

[6259]
PINCHES, J.H. *and* PINCHES, R.V. **The Royal heraldry of England.** London, Heraldry Today, 1974. xviii,334p. illus. (incl.col.pl.), tables, bibliog., index. £40.00. ISBN: 090045525x.

Sections: The English - The Normans - The Plantagenets - The Lancastrians - The Yorkists - The Tudors - The Stewarts - House of Hanover - House of Saxe-Coburg - House of Windsor... House of Mountbatten - Windsor. 258 black-and-white illus. Bibliography, p.ix-xii. Authoritative. 'Highly recommended' (*RQ*, v.14,no.3, Spring 1975, p.266-7). *Class No:* 929.6(420)(035)

Wales

[6260]
SIDDONS, M.P. **The Development of Welsh heraldry.** Aberystwyth, National Library of Wales, 3v., 1991-1993. £150.; $300.

V.1: 1991. xxvi,433p. illus. (inc. 24 col. pl.), index. £50. $100. ISBN 090715851x. Examines the origins and development of heraldry in Wales to the early 17th century. 1. Origin - 2. Sources other than manuscripts - 3. Heraldic manuscripts - 4. Heraldry in Welsh poetry - 5. Development and characteristics - 6. Advance - 7. Heraldry of the Welsh princes - 8. Influence of the Heralds. 16 Appendices including C. Welsh heraldic vocabulary and P. Dates of appearance of arms in Wales.

Volume 2 contains in Welsh armorial listing coats of arms in alphabetical order of the names of the pesons to whom they were attributed or the families bearing them, with sources.

Volume 3 is an ordinary of Welsh arms according to blazon in order to permit the identification of a given coat of arms. *Class No:* 929.6(429)

Australia

[6261]
LOW, C., *ed*. **A Roll of Australian arms** corporate and personal borne by lawful authority. Adelaide, Rigby, 1971. xxxii, 184p. coats of arms (some col.), bibliog., index.

....(contd.)
Corporate arms (Commonwealth and pan-Australia and then State by State) p.3-62. Personal arms p.65-171. Bibliography p.173. Glossary p.174-7. *Class No:* 929.6(94)

Ecclesiastical

Vatican City

[6262]
MARTIN, J. **Heraldry in the Vatican** / L'Araldica in Vaticano / Heraldik im Vatikan. Gerrards Cross, Buckinghamshire, Van Duren, 1987. 228p. illus. (some col.), coats of arms (some col.), plans, index. £36. ISBN: 090571525x.

Developed from articles first printed in *L'Osservatore della Domenica* (1969).

20 Heraldic tours of the Vatican. Appendix A. Plan of St. Peter's Basilica - B. Plan of Vatican City State. Text in English, Italian and German. Author is Prefect of the Pontifical Household. *Class No:* 929.6:28(456.31)

Crests & Mottoes

Handbooks & Manuals

[6263]
ELVIN, C.N. **A Hand-book of mottoes borne by the nobility, gentry, cities, public companies, etc. ... With Supplement by R. Pinches.** London, Heraldry Today, 1971. £14. ISBN: 0900455047.

First published 1859.

The 1971 ed. is a reprint, with an added index and a supplement. The much-needed index contains 5,000 names. The original (names, A-Z) had annotations, but no details of dates or authorities. Often gives the address as well as name of family associated with each motto. 'This is by far the best edition and is heartily recommended for most libraries' (*RQ*, v.11, no.2, Winter 1971, p.184). *Class No:* 929.624(035)

Great Britain

[6264]
FAIRBAIRN, J. **Fairbairn's book of crests** of the families of Great Britain and Ireland. 4th ed. rev. and enl. by A.C. Fox-Davies. London, Heraldry Today, 1983. £45. ISBN: 0900455387.

First published 1859.

Crests arranged by surnames. *Class No:* 929.624(410)

Badges & Emblems

[6265]
GORMAN, J. **Banners bright** an illustrated history of the banners of the British trade union movement. London, Allen Lane, 1973. viii,184p. illus. (some col.)., index. ISBN: 0713902906.

Study of the rise and decline of trade union banners, especially their history, style, and subject matter. Illustrations p.57-182. *Class No:* 929.628

[6266]
LEESON, R.A. **United we stand** an illustrated account of Trade Union emblems. Bath, Adams & Dart, 1971. 72p. illus. (1 col.), bibliog. ISBN: 239000897.

Illustrated narrative history. *Class No:* 929.628

[6267]
NAOKI MUKODA. **Emblems.** Tokyo, Bijutsu Shuppan-sha, 1987. 127p. col.illus. ISBN: 4568500834.

490 blazer badges grouped in 8 sections: 1. British military emblems - 2. University - 3. Sports - 4. United States uniform patches - 5. Regional emblems - 6. Emblems arranged by motifs - 7. Brand emblems - 8. Emblem variations. The story of emblems (bilingual Japanese and English text) p.113-25. *Class No:* 929.628

[6268]
WILLIAMS, D. *and* MUIRHEAD, G. **Northumberland miners' banners.** Ashington, Mid Northumberland Arts Group, 1987. 36p. illus., bibliog., pbk. £1.95. ISBN: 0904790584.

Description, history and significance of some colliery banners. Bibliography p.36. *Class No:* 929.628

[6269]
WILLIAMSON, D. **Debrett's guide to heraldry and regalia.** London, Headline, 1992. 160p. illus. (mostly col.), bibliog., index. £17.99. ISBN: 0747206090.

Pt.1: Heraldry: 1. Origin and development - 2. Rules - 3. Heralds and the College of Arms - 4. Scottish heraldry - 5. Modern heraldry - 6. Continental heraldry. Pt.2: Regalia: 7. Origins - 8. English regalia and the Coronation ceremony - 9. Non-royal - 10. Royal regalia and Coronations of the World. Appendix 1. Glossary (p.118-34) - 2. Royal regalia England and Scotland - 3. Coronations of British Sovereigns - 4. Royal regalia worldwide. Bibliography p.155-7. *Class No:* 929.628

Nobility

Europe

[6270]
RUVIGNY AND RAINEVAL, 9th Marquis of. **The Titled nobility of Europe:** an international peerage or Who's Who of the sovereigns, princes and nobles of Europe. London, Burke's Peerage, 1980. lxxii, 1605p. coats of arms. £50. ISBN: 0850110289.

Facsimile edition. First published by Harrison in 1914.

Accounts of existing titles and biographies of living members of noble families in 2 A-Z sequences: The Royal and Princely houses (p.1-206) and The mediatized Princely and noble houses (p.207-1598). Coverage is somewhat uneven, many minor titles (especially of barons) being omitted, and some national entries (*e.g.* French, Spanish) being slight. *Class No:* 929.7(4)

Great Britain

[6271]
The **Complete peerage of England, Scotland, Ireland, Great Britain and the United Kingdom** extant, extinct or dormant. Cokayne, G.E. Gloucester, Alan Sutton, 6 vols. 1984. £75. ISBN: 0904387828.

.... (contd.)

First edition published 1887-1898 in 8v.; new edition revised and enlarged in 12v. 1910-59. V.13 *Peers created 1901-1938* (1940). This present edition is reprinted photographically in reduced format enabling the complete work to be published in a 6v. boxed set.

Excellent biographical data giving fully, yet concisely, particulars of parentage, birth, honours, officers, public services, marriage, death and burial of every holder of a peerage; well documented. Throws valuable light on the whole history of the House of Lords.

According to *Genealogists' Magazine* (v.17, no.10, June 1961, p.319), there is progressively less hope of the index volume being printed. *Class No:* 929.7(410)

[6272]
LEESON, F.L. **A Directory of British peerages:** from the earliest times to the present day. 2nd ed. London, Society of Genealogists, 1984. xi, 174p. index. ISBN: 0901878642.

Replaces E. Solly's *An index of hereditary English, Scottish and Irish titles of honour* (1880).

A-Z by title and surname in one sequence giving title, rank, period covered by peerage, its destination, and family name. Introduction p.v-x includes notes on other sources. 'Not intended as a work of expertise but as a ready-reference compilation for those wishing to find out quickly whether or when a certain peerage existed, with its rank(s), nationality, ownership, approximate period and fate' (*Introduction*). *Class No:* 929.7(410)

[6273]
SOLLY, E. **An Index of hereditary English, Scottish, and Irish titles of honour.** London, Longmans Green for the Index Society, 1880. ix, 205p.

Reissued by Genealogical Publishing Co., of Baltimore in 1965.

Index of peerages and baronetages of the United Kingdom showing the date when each separate title was conferred, the changes they underwent and their present condition, whether existent, modified, dormant or extinct. *Class No:* 929.7(410)

Bibliographies

[6274]
Burke's family index. Montgomery-Massingberd, H.J., *ed.* London, Burke's Peerage, 1976. xxxii, 171p. £9.50. ISBN: 085011022x.

Two main features: 'A bibliography of *Burke's*, 1826-1976 (p.xiii-xxx) - 'The family index' (p.1-171). The latter is a comprehensive A-Z listing of the 20,000 families that have appeared in Burke's publications, 1826-1976. *Class No:* 929.7(410)(01)

Handbooks & Manuals

[6275]
Burke's Peerage and Baronetage. Townsend, P., *ed.* 105th ed. London, Burke's Peerage, 1970. lxxxv,3259p. illus. (coats of arms).

First published 1826 as *Burke's Genealogical heraldic history of the peerage and baronetage of the United Kingdom.*

Peerage and baronetage (p.1-2910) - 'the genealogical history of the families holding Peerages and Baronetcies, from their earliest recorded origins down to 1969/70 set out

....(contd.)

in narrative pedigree, accompanied by armorial illustration'. 'Dartmouth': 5½ columns; O'Neill: over 18 columns. Appendix: Lists of peerages and baronetcies in order of precedence; and notes on members of families whose titles are extinct'. Index: 'Family names which differ from that of the title, and guide to subsidiary title'. 2nd impression (1975) omits sections on the Royal Family and Knightage. 3rd impression (1978) has preceding supplement: ' The successions, extinctions and creations of Peerages and Baronetcies ... 1969/70 to April 1978', p.vi-xix. *Class No:* 929.7(410)(035)

[6276]
Debrett's Peerage and Baronetage 1990. Kidd, C. *and* Williamson, D., eds. London, Debretts Peerage and Macmillan; New York, St. Martins Press, 1990. 123+P1336+Œ968p. col.port., illus., coats of arms. £120.00. ISBN: 033338847x, UK; 0312046405, US.

Founded in 1769; renamed Debrett in 1802. 'Modern technology has come to Debrett at last and the complete text of the Peerage and Baronetage has now been computerized. This means we shall be able to produce amended family articles between editions, which we hope will appear every five years (Preface to 1985 ed.).

Comprises information concerning the Royal Family, the Peerage, Privy Councillors, Scottish Lords of Session, Baronets, Chiefs of clans in Scotland. Other information includes H.M. Officers of Arms; tables of general precedence; guide to the wearing of Orders; Foreign and Commonwealth Orders. Entries provide illustration of coat of arms and lists of living relatives, collateral branches and predecessors. This edition includes F.J. French's 'Debrett: Book and Man: A history of the Peerage (p.14-20). 1985 ed. included her 'A bibliographical check list of Debrett's principal publications'. *Class No:* 929.7(410)(035)

Yearbooks & Directories

[6277]
Burke's genealogical and heraldic history of the landed gentry. Townsend, P., *ed.* 18th ed. London, Burke's Peerage, 3v., 1965-72.

1st ed., *Burke's Genealogical ... history of commoners* (1833-38. 4v.); 2nd ed. *Landed gentry of Great Britain and Ireland,* with an index of about 100,000 names (1843-49, 3v.).

Contains biographical sketches of *c.*600 distinguished families of England, Scotland and Wales; 500 armorial illustrations; index of families. Gives brief biographical sketch of present head of family; name of wife and children (if any); lineage; arms (both illustration and description); seat. Perhaps one-half of the families are no longer landowning. American families with British ancestry are included in the 1939 ed., p.2539-3021, published separately in 1948 as *Burke's Distinguished families of America: the lineages of 1,600 families of British origin now resident in the United States of America.* Burke, Sir J.B. *A genealogical and heraldic history of colonial gentry* (London, Harrison, 1891-95. 2v. illus.), with excellent reproductions of 120 coats of arms, was reprinted by Genealogical Publishing Co., Baltimore, Md., in 1970. *Class No:* 929.7(410)(058)

[6278]
—SAYER, M.J. 'The Scope of Burke's Landed Gentry', *Genealogist's Magazine,* v.19,no.4, December 1977, p.120-124 and 'Pedigrees of County Families, *ibid,* v.19,no.10, June 1979, p.354-362; v.20,no.2, June 1980, p.56-59; v.20,no.4, December 1980, p.135; v.20, no.5, March 1981, p.157-160; v.6,no.8, December 1981, p.267-273; v.7,no.9, March 1982,p.304-308.

Lists of landed families not appearing in any edition of *Burke's Landed Gentry. Class No:* 929.7(410)(058)

Scotland

Handbooks & Manuals

[6279]
The Scots peerage founded on Wood's edition of Sir Robert Dougals's Peerage of Scotland; containing an historical and genealogical account of the nobility of that kingdom. Paul J.B., Sir, *ed.* Edinburgh, Douglas, 9v., 1901-14. illus. (coats of arms).

Contains biographies in narrative form not only of title-holders but of all offspring in the male line. A very comprehensive name index is contained in v.9. *Class No:* 929.7(411)(035)

Commonwealth

[6280]
BURKE, Sir J.B. A Genealogical history of the dormant, abeyant, forfeited, and extinct peerages of the British Empire. New ed. London, Harrison, 1883. xii,642p.

Reprinted London, Burke's Peerage and Baltimore, Genealogical Publishing Co., 1978.

Useful for ancestry and descendants of peers; but personal details should be taken from Cokayne (*qv.*).

Previous editions of the *Dictionary of the peerages of England, Scotland and Ireland, extinct, dormant and in abeyance* appeared in 1831, 1840 and 1846, edited by John Burke.

A genealogical and heraldic history of the extinct and dormant baronetcies of England, Ireland and Scotland, by J. and J.B. Burke (2nd ed. London, 1844) has been reprinted (London, Burke's Peerage, 1964. 652p. armorial illus.). *Class No:* 929.7(41-44)

[6281]
—PINE, L.G. The New extinct peerage 1184-1971: containing extinct, abeyant, dormant and suspended peerages with genealogies and arms. London, Heraldry Today, 1972. xxviii,313p. ISBN: 0900455233.

Serves as a supplement to Burke's *Genealogical history ...* Index to surnames and title. *Class No:* 929.7(41-44)

[6282]
HAYDN, J. The Book of dignities: containing lists of the official personages of the British Empire, civil, diplomatic, heraldic, judicial, ecclesiastical, municipal, naval and military ... with the sovereigns and rulers of the world, the orders of knighthood of the United Kingdom and India. Baltimore, Maryland, Genealogical Publishing Co., 1970. xxviii,1170p. $40.00. ISBN: 0806304316.

First published London. W.H. Allen, 1894. Based on R. Beatson's *A political index* (3rd ed. 1806. 3v.), which contains some fuller lists.

An invaluable compilation. Important offices are listed

....(contd.)

from their beginnings, others from 1760. For sovereigns, officers of state and bishops, Haydn is superseded by the Royal Historical Society's *Handbook of British chronology* (1939). *Class No:* 929.7(41-44)

Hungary

Middle Ages

[6283]

BOULTON, D'A.J.D. **Knights of the Crown:** the monarchial orders of knighthood in later medieval Europe 1325-1520. Woodbridge, Suffolk, The Boydell Press, 1987. xxv, 540p. illus. £45. ISBN: 0851154174.

Examines the historical background, foundation, statutes, name and title, members, privileges and obligations, officers, corporate attitudes, insignia and formal costume of 13 orders which attached the presidential office to the crown of the princely founder or made it hereditary in his house. Bibliography p.503-524. *Class No:* 929.7(439)"01/14"

France

[6284]

DE LA CHENAYE-DESBOIS ET BODIER, A. **Dictionnaire de la Noblesse:** contenant les généalogies, l'histoire & la chronologie des familles nobles de la France, l'explication de leurs armes et l'état des grandes terres du Royaume, possédées à titre de Principautés, Duchés, Marquisats, Comptés, Vicomptés, Baronies *etc.* ... 3rd ed. Nendeln, Liechtenstein, Kraus Reprints, 19v., 1969.

Reprint of 3rd ed. (Paris, 1863-78).

'On a jouit à ce dictionnaire Le Tableau Généalogique et Historique des Maisons Souveraines de l'Europe et une notice des familles étrangères, les plus anciennes, les plus nobles et les plus illustrées'. *Class No:* 929.7(44)

Spain

[6285]

Elenco de grandezas y titulos nobiliarios Españoles 1985. 18th ed. Madrid, Hidalguia, 1985. 1026p. bibliogs., index. softcover. ISBN: 840005895x.

Royal Family (including chronology of the Spanish monarchy) p.9-17. Nobility A-Z by title p.13-811. Name index p.815-903. Bibliografia fundamental para consulta relativa a legislacion nobiliaria p.1011-3. List of significant archive offices p.1015-1018. *Class No:* 929.7(460)

Orders & Decorations

[6286]

MĚŘIČKA, V. **The Book of orders and decorations.** London, Hamlyn, 1975. 248p. illus. (some col.), bibliog. ISBN: 0600367312.

An exhaustive analytical survey including general sections on Awards in the Ancient World - Orders and general awards - Collecting Orders and decorations. A Collectors' vade mecum includes General standard terminology for Orders and decorations (p.211-8); Survey of mottoes (p.219-23); List of Orders according to country or place of origin (p.224-38); and Bibliography (p.239-41). 41 col.pl. *Class No:* 929.71

Worldwide

[6287]

DORLING, H. Taprell. **Ribbons and medals.** Ed. and rev. by A.A. Purves. London, Osprey in association with Spink & Son Ltd., 1983. 320p.+20p. col. illus. ISBN: 0850455162.

First published as an 80-page booklet by George Philip and Son in 1916. Eight revised editions 1919-1974 with supplements between editions.

5 chapters: 1. British orders and decorations - 2. Commonwealth awards - 3. United Nations awards - 4. Order of Malta - 5. Foreign countries awards. *Class No:* 929.71(100)

Europe

[6288]

HIERONYMUSSEN, P. **Orders, medals and decorations of Britain and Europe in colour.** London, Blandford Press, 1967. 256p. illus. (inc. col. pl).

Originally as *Europaeiske ordner i farver* [European orders in colour] (Copenhagen, Politikens Forlag, 1966).

The 80 coloured plates (450 photographs) of orders medals and decorations of 28 European nations are preceded by an introductory essay and followed by an encyclopaedia of orders (date of institution; to whom it may be given; classes; whether or not returnable on death of holder). 'An excellent general guide in a comparatively small volume' (*Times Literary Supplement*, no.3,414, 3 August 1967, p.713). *Class No:* 929.71(4)

Great Britain

Bibliographies

[6289]

LITHERLAND, A.R. *and* SIMPKIN, B.T. **Spinks standard catalogue of British and associated orders decorations & medals** with valuations. London, Spink, 1990. 222p. col. illus., bibliog. £25. ISBN: 090760532x.

Historical and numismatic descriptions and illustrations to 336 orders, decorations and medals. Guide to order of wearing p.11-12. Bibliography p.202-3. *Class No:* 929.71(410)(01)

Commonwealth

[6290]

BATE, C.K. *and* SMITH, M.G. **For bravery in the field** recipients of the Military Medal 1919-1939: 1939-1945: 1945-1991. London, Bayonet Publications, 1991. vii,542p. illus., index. £55. ISBN: 1873996004.

A roll of Military Medal recipients marshalled in 3 distinct chronological sections. An introduction (p.1-16) covers all aspects of the award: naming, verification, citations, recommendations, posthumous awards, investitures, forfeitures and restorations, gratuities, precedence *etc.* *Class No:* 929.71(41-44)

[6291]
HENDERSON, D.V. **Dragons can be defeated** a complete record of the George Medal's progress 1940-1983. London, Spink, 1984. 120p. tables, bibliog. £12. ISBN: 0907605141.

The creation of the G.M. - 2. The first few years - 3. The period since the war - 4. Honorary awards. Table 1. A-Z list of award winners: Name, rank, position, organization, action, place, date, London Gazette citation. Table 2. Alphabetical list of honorary awards to foreign nations. Bibliography p.117-8. *Class No:* 929.71(41-44)

[6292]
JOCELYN, A. **Awards of honour:** the orders, decorations, medals and awards of Great Britain and the Commonwealth, from Edward III to Elizabeth II. London, A & C Black, 1956. xx, 276p. illus. (20 col. pl). index.

17 chapters: Introduction and definitions; Orders; Ribands of orders; Decorations and campaign medals; Long service and good conduct medals; Dominion and colonial decorations and medals; Miscellaneous decorations and medals; etc. The 20 colour-plates consist of mounted reproductions of medals and ribbons. Detailed index, p.265-76. Page size 31 x 25cm. *Class No:* 929.71(41-44)

[6293]
The Register of the George Cross. 2nd ed. Cheltenham, This England Books, 1992. 151p. ports., bibliog. £14.95. ISBN: 0906324173.

A-Z by recipient. Data: name, vital statistics, and short narrative of award and deed. Short history of the George Cross p.6-7. Town and county connections p.147-9. Bibliography p.150. *Class No:* 929.71(41-44)

[6294]
The Register of the Victoria Cross. 2nd rev. ed. Cheltenham, This England Books, 1988. 308p. ports., bibliog. £19.50. ISBN: 0906324076.

A-Z by name of recipient. Data: rank, unit, other decorations, place and date of deed, place of date of birth and death, place of memorial, town or county connection, and portrait. Short history of the V.C. p.6-7. Dates on which awards were published in *The London Gazette* p.284-289. Bibliography p.322. *Class No:* 929.71(41-44)

Rank & Precedence

[6295]
CARLISLE, N. **A Concise account of the several foreign orders of knighthood** and other marks of honourable distinction especially of such as have been conferred upon British subjects together with the names and achievements of those gallant men who have been presented with honorary sword, or plate, by The Patriotic Fund Institution. London, John Hearne, 1839. Reprinted by London Stamp Exchange, 1988. xxix, 582p. index. £38. ISBN: 094813027x.

1. Descriptive history of Foreign orders with annotated lists of British recipients A-Z by country: The Empire of Austria to Wurtemburg p.1-485. 2. Patriotic Fund awards p.486-539. *Class No:* 929.73

Great Britain

[6296]
PARRY, C.J. **'British knighthoods',** *Genealogist's Magazine,* v.19, no.6, June 1978, p.203-204.

Brief outline of the degree and honour of knighthood. *Class No:* 929.73(410)

England & Wales

[6297]
SQUIBB, G.D. **Precedence in England and Wales.** Oxford, Clarendon Press, 1981. xviii,139p. bibliog. £40. ISBN: 0198253893.

Examines the manner in which laws of precedence have developed and presents tables of precedence 'which differ in some respects from those set out in current works of reference'. Appendix 4: Modern tables of precedence p.119-125. Bibliography p.126-130; index p.131-139. *Class No:* 929.73(42)

Vatican City

[6298]
CARDINALE, H.E. **Orders of knighthood, awards and the Holy See:** a historical, juridical and practical compendium. 3rd ed. Gerrards Cross, Bucks, Van Duren, 1985. 336p. illus. (many col.), bibliog. £29.50. ISBN: 0905715268.

1st ed. 1983; 2nd ed. 1984.

'Contains all the historical, juridical and practical information about each pontifical Order and Award and other Catholic or originally Catholic Orders of Knighthood' (*Preface to 1st ed.*). Bibliography p.317-8. *Class No:* 929.73(456.31)

China

[6299]
GARRETT, V.M. **Mandarin squares** mandarins and their insignia. Hong Kong, Oxford Univ. Press, 1990. vii,66p. illus. (some col.), bibliog., index. £6.95. (*Images of Asia.*) ISBN: 0195852397.

Mandarin squares are the embroidered insignia sewn on to the robes of the ruling mandarin classes in China's Qing dynasty (1644-1911). This short book provides an account of the Chinese system of government and traces the origin, development and symbolism of mandarin squares. Glossary p.60. Bibliography p.62-3. *Class No:* 929.73(510)

Royalty

[6300]
Burke's Royal Families of the world. London, Burke's Peerage, 2v., 1977-80.

1: *Europe & Latin America,* 1977. xxv,594p. 2: *Africa & the Middle East.* 1980. xvi.320p. V.1 is arranged under 48 countries (Albania ... Yugoslavia). Includes princely and ducal houses. Introductory historical essays; biographies; pedigrees. Appendices: A. The mediatized sovereign states of the Holy Roman Empire - B. Principal order of knighthood - C. Ancestral tables - D. Select bibliography, p.569-70. Index of names in the pedigrees, p.571-88. Addendum. 'Comprehensive and definitive ... will become an indispensable reference book' (*The Times,* 4 July 1977, p.14). *Class No:* 929.731

[6301]
McNAUGHTON, A., *comp.* **The Book of Kings: a royal genealogy.** New York, Quadrangle, New York Times Book Co., 3v., 1974. 1480p. illus.

1. *The Royal Houses.* 2. *The families.* 3. *Plates, indexes.* 'This very comprehensive catalog of all the legitimate descendants of George I (*Choice,* v.12,no.9, November, 1144). V.3 has over 100 plates and an extensive index. 'A

....(contd.)

clearly arranged and important reference source on European royalty' (*Library Journal*, 1 May 1975, p.836). *Class No:* 929.731

[6302]
OPFELL, O.S. Queens, Empresses, Grand Duchesses and Regents women rulers of Europe, A.D.1328-1989. Jefferson, McFarland, 1989. xiii,282p., ports., bibliog., index. $25.95. ISBN: 0899503853.

39 biographical chapters including material on their subjects' impact upon history. Bibliography (by ruler) p.161-70. For the general reader. *Class No:* 929.731

Encyclopaedias

[6303]
GURNEY, G. Kingdoms of Asia the Middle East and Africa: an illustrated encyclopedia of ruling monarchs from ancient times to the present. New York, Crown Publishers, 1986. viii, 438p. illus., maps, tables, index. $24.95. ISBN: 0517552566.

Historical record of 4000 royal sovereigns. 845 photographs. *Class No:* 929.731(031)

Chronologies

[6304]
CARPENTER, C. The Guinness book of kings, rulers & statesmen. Enfield, Middlesex, Guinness Superlatives, 1978. vii,312p. index. ISBN: 090042446x.

Chronological lists of Heads of State and Government A-Z by State 3000BC to present day. *Class No:* 929.731(090)

Worldwide

Chronologies

[6305]
MORBY, J.E. Dynasties of the world a chronological and genealogical handbook. Oxford, Oxford Univ. Press, 1989. xv, 254p. tables, bibliogs., index. £29.95. ISBN: 0192158724.

1. Ancient Near East - 2. Hellenistic World - 3. Roman and Byzantine worlds - 4. Barbarian West - 5. Europe - 6. Islamic dynasties - 7. India - 8. Far East - 9. Africa - 10. New World. Chronological tables giving years of rule, family relationships of major world dynasties. Notes contain supplementary information regarding chronological problems, calendars, dating systems and royal styles. *Class No:* 929.731(100)(090)

Europe

[6306]
KROLL, M. *and* **LINDSEY, J. The Country Life book of Europe's royal families.** London, Country Life Books, distributed by Hamlyn, 1979. 208p. illus. (some col.), maps, coats of arms, geneal. tables.

Section 1. Reigning families gives recent history whilst Section 2. Non-reigning families relates their fortunes in exile. Map section showing Europe's changing boundaries 1360-1919 p.8-15. Index p.204-208. *Class No:* 929.731(4)

[6307]
LOUDA, J. *and* **MacLAGEN, M. Lines of succession** heraldry of the royal families of Europe. Rev. ed. London, Macdonald, 1992. 308p. illus., col. heraldic and genealogical tables, maps. £15. ISBN: 0356203352.

Detailed treatment of all the present and former kingdoms of Europe and all German and Italian grand-duchies from the eleventh century onwards. Heraldry is presented as an indispensable adjunct to royal genealogy, coats of arms in full colour are employed to illustrate 'the various matrimonial alliances and territorial acquisitions or losses, or rises in rank.' Chap. 14. Dynastic relations is illustrated by Tables 59-60 Relationship of European monarchs before and at the time of the First World War and 61-62 Common descent of the present European sovereigns since William the Conqueror. The text describes the historical background to each royal family tree. Index p.300-306. List of tables p.306-308. *Class No:* 929.731(4)

[6308]
WILLIAMSON, D. Debrett's Kings and Queens of Europe. Exeter, Webb & Bower, 1988. 208p. illus. (some col.), maps, geneal. tables, bibliog., index. £19.95. ISBN: 086350194x.

Concise factual information on every monarch who has reigned over parts of Europe over the last thousand years, supported by outline historical text on each royal house, arranged in 8 regional chapters: The Iberian Peninsula to the Balkans. Appendix: 29 Genealogical tables. Bibliography p.204-205. The Monarchs of Europe and some claimants *i.e.* dynastic tables on endpapers. Omits Holy Roman Emperors and the Imperial German, Austrian and Russian dynasties and minor sovereigns, Grand Dukes, Electors *etc.* *Class No:* 929.731(4)

Encyclopaedias

[6309]
GURNEY, G. Kingdoms of Europe an illustrated encyclopaedia of ruling monarchs from ancient times to the present. New York, Crown Publishers Inc., 1982. x,627p., map, illus., index. $24.95. ISBN: 0517543958.

Records the reigns of monarchs from the Roman Empire to Queen Elizabeth II in 20 geographical chapters plus six appendices for other independent grand duchies and principalities. 1700 illustrations. *Class No:* 929.731(4)(031)

Great Britain

[6310]
Burke's guide to the Royal Family. Montgomery-Massingberd, H.J., *ed.* London, Burke's Peerage, 1973. xvi,358p. illus., diagrs. £21.85.

The monarchy in Britain, p.3-115; the Royal family (biographies of members (p.118-84); the Royal lineage (narrative pedigrees, p.185-333). Appendices (A-F; F: The list of Royal Warrant holders, p.342-56). 27 plates; 15 coloured drawings of royal heraldry; 24 portraits; Abbreviations, p.xiii-xvi. *Class No:* 929.731(410)

[6311]

Debrett's Kings and Queens of Britain. Williamson, D. Exeter, Webb & Bower/Michael Joseph, 1986. 240p. illus. (some col.), geneal. tables, bibliog. ISBN: 086350101x.

12 Sections: 1. Kingship in ancient Britain - 2. Roman Britain and the English settlements - 3. The Kings of Wessex and All England - 4-12. Sucessive Royal houses. Appendix B. Genealogical tables p.212-234. Index p.237-240.
Class No: 929.731(410)

[6312]

WEIR, A. Britain's Royal Families the complete genealogy. London, The Bodley Head, 1989. 4b iv,386p. bibliog., index. £15.00. ISBN: 0370313100.

9 chronological chapters (1. The Saxon and Danish Kings of England... 9. The House of Saxe-Coburg-Gotha becomes the House of Windsor). Brief biographical data on all monarchs and their parents, siblings, issue (legitimate and bastard). Bibliography p.334-44. *Class No:* 929.731(410)

[6313]

Who's who in the Royal Family: the first one hundred and fifty in line of succession to the British throne. Reynolds, D. London, Proteus Books, 1982. 110p. illus., geneal. tables. £3.95. $7.95.

Short individual biographies for the first 65 in line of succession. The remainder listed with full titles.
Class No: 929.731(410)

England

[6314]

DYER, R. Royal tombs of England. Leeds, Pocket Booklets, 1985. 24p. illus., pbk. £1. $1.50. (*Britain's Heritage Series.*) ISBN: 0950978760.

Chronological list burial/tomb sites.
Class No: 929.731(420)

Women

[6315]

JACKSON, G.M. Women who ruled. Santa Barbara. Calif., and Oxford, ABC Clio, 1990. xii,190p. ports., bibliog. $39.50; £33.50. ISBN: 0874365600.

Over 270 women rules from Dido, legendary founder of Carthage, to Violeta Chamorro, President of Nicaragua from 1990. Data: title, years of reign or office, region of the world ruled, alternative name(s) with biographical sketch. Chronology p.9-13. Notes (of source material) p.171-84. Bibliography p.185-90. *Class No:* 929.731-0055.2

Flags & Banners

[6316]

BARRACLOUGH, E.M.C. *and* **CRAMPTON, W.G.,** *eds.* **Flags of the world.** 3rd ed. 1981 reprint. London, Warne, 1981. 264p. illus. (mostly col.). £16.95. ISBN: 0723227977.

First published 1897. 3rd ed. 1978.

14 chapters: 2. The UK and N. Ireland; 3. The Commonwealth and Dependencies of the UK; 4. North America; 5. Latin America and the Caribbean; 6. Europe; 7. Africa; 8. The Middle East; 9. Asia; 10. Oceania and Australasia; 11. International organizations; 12. Signal flags;

....(contd.)

13. Flags worn by merchant ships; 14. Yacht flags. Supplement *i.e.* updating with page references to main text p.241-252. Bibliography p.253-254; Index p.255-262. 'No other book comes forward as a serious rival' (*Library Review* v.30, Winter 1981, p.258-259). *Class No:* 929.9

[6317]

CRAMPTON, N. New Observer's book of flags. rev. ed. London, Warne, 1984. 191p. illus. (inc. col. pl). index. £3.95. ISBN: 0723216673.

First published 1959 as *The Observer's book of flags.*

Aims 'not only to help the observer to recognise the most important of the world's flags but to increase his knowledge of flag-lore' (*Preface*). Sections: International flags - Great Britain - North America; Canada; The United States of America - Mexico and Central and South America - The Western powers - Europe - Asia - Africa - Australia, etc. Analytical index. 74 plates in colour; *c.*60 line-drawings. Pocket-sized. *Class No:* 929.9

[6318]

CRAMPTON, W. The Complete guide to flags. London, Kingfisher Books, 1989. 136p. col. illus., col. maps, index. £9.95. ISBN: 086272466x.

Flags of all nations and states (including US states and British colonies) unusually grouped according to their common features *e.g.* heraldic devices, coloured crosses, and those related by political ideologies. Each flag is illustrated in colour with an explanation of its history and main features. Glossary p.132. *Class No:* 929.9

[6319]

DEVEREUX, E. Book of world flags. London, Apple Press, 1992. 112p. col. illus., col. maps. £9.95. ISBN: 1850763968.

Flags of all independent nations and their dependencies including geographical divisions of United Kingdom, Australian states and Territories, Canadian provinces, and constituent states of US. A-Z by country. Additional data: history and symbolism of flags. New States up to 1992 *e.g.* Kazakhstan, Kirgizstan geographical data but no flag information. *Class No:* 929.9

[6320]

GREAT BRITAIN Ministry of Defence. Director General of Supplies & Transport (Navy). **Flags of all nations.** 2nd ed. London, H.M. Stationery Office, 1989. Variously paginated, col. illus., diagrs. £49. ISBN: 0117725676.

First published for The Admiralty in 1956.

Authoritative illustrated description of national flags and ensigns with sections on British Royal Standards; international organizations; the Commonwealth, European countries and NATO; and the rest of the World. Flag terminology p.xi-xiii. Loose leaf in substantial ring-binder to allow the insertion of new and revised information.
Class No: 929.9

[6321]

KANNIK, P. A Handbook of flags. London, Methuen, 1958. 203p. illus. (col. pl).

Originally published in Denmark, 1956. Colour reproduction of 861 official flags of the present time, including those of individual states of Germany, Russia and the United States; also some 80 national coats of arms. Historical and descriptive notes, but limited to recent years.

....(contd.)

The Great Britain section includes several rarely depicted departmental badges, *e.g.* British Ocean Weather Ships, Northern Lights Commissioner's flag. *Class No:* 929.9

[6322]

PREBBLE, G.H. **The Symbols, standards, flags and banners of ancient and modern nations.** Boston, Massachusetts, G.K. Hall, 1980. 156p. illus.

A reprint of *History of flags of US and other nations.* Boston, Osgood, 1893.

Traces in detail the meanings, symbolism and uses of bannerets, banderoles, guidons, pennons, ensigns, gonfalons, standards and flags. *Class No:* 929.9

[6323]

SMITH, W. **Flags and arms across the world.** London, Cassell, 1980. 256p. col. illus. index. ISBN: 0304306592.

A field guide to the flags of 174 nations: national flags, coats of arms, state and provincial flags, presidential and ministerial banners, - nearly 1,000 full-colour illus. States dates when flags, arms, etc., were officially adopted. International flags, signals and pennants. Histories of some of the major national flags. Flag index. Pocket-sized. *Class No:* 929.9

[6324]

SMITH, W. **Flags through the ages and across the world.** New York, McGraw-Hill, 1975. 357p. illus. (some col.).

A guide to flags and coats of arms of 157 countries and dependencies, plus non-national flags (*e.g.* ethnic groups). Illustrated glossary of flag terms; flag symbols; flag etiquette and customs. Bibliography, p.350-1. Over 3,000 illus. (2,257 in colour). Well documented. 'Designed for quick reference or a leisurely survey' (*Library Journal,* v.101,no.8, 15 April 1976, p.967). *Class No:* 929.9

[6325]

TALOCCI, M. **Guide to the flags of the world.** Revised and updated by Whitney Smith. London, Sidgwick & Jackson, 1989. 271p. col. illus., maps, bibliog., index, pbk. £7.99. ISBN: 0283988703.

First published as *Guida alle bandiere di tutto il mondo* (Milano, Arnoldo Mondadori Editore, 1977). English edition first published 1982.

Vividly illustrated flags and arms A-Z by country within continents with final section on International flags. Glossary p.260-3. Bibliography p.271. *Class No:* 929.9

Bibliographies

[6326]

SMITH, S., *comp. and ed.* **The Bibliography of flags of foreign nations.** Boston, Massachusetts, G.K. Hall, 1965. viii, 169p.

3,053 numbered entries (plus interpolations), with brief notes. Two parts: 1. Topical entries (*e.g.* heraldic flags; naval flags; religious flags; legal aspects of flags) - 2. Countries (Afghanistan ... Zanzibar, p.44-163; UK: nos.2844-3011K). Cross-references. 3 appendices (2. Chronological list of general flag items through 1960; 3. Items on flag etiquette and ceremony. *Class No:* 929.9(01)

Encyclopaedias

[6327]

The Orbis encyclopedia of flags and coats of arms. Mucha, L. London, Orbis, 1985. 220p. illus. (many col.), col. maps, bibliog., index. £4.95. ISBN: 085613645x.

Pocket sized handbook introducing the basic history and rules of vexillology, describing and illustrating in colour the flags and coats of arms of all independent nations. Arranged in 8 sections: Europe, Asia, Africa; North and Central America; South America; Australia and Oceania; Antarctic; United Nations. Glossary p.211-215. Over 400 colour illustrations. 6 maps. *Class No:* 929.9(031)

Maps & Atlases

[6328]

World of flags. Pottinger, D., *comp.* Edinburgh, John Bartholomew, nd. col. illus., map. 305 x 225mm (folded). ISBN: 0702805912.

Pictorial map illustrating 524 flags of the world arranged in columns in alphabetical order and indicating their geographical location. *Class No:* 929.9(084.3)

Great Britain

[6329]

PERRIN, W.G. **British flags:** their early history and their development at sea; with an account of the origin of the flag as a national device. Cambridge, Cambridge Univ. Press, 1922. xii, 207p. illus.

Chapters: 1. The origin of the flag and its development up to the end of the 13th century - 2. Early English, Scottish and Irish flags - 3. The union flags and jacks - 4. Flags of command - 5. Colours of distinction - 6. Flag signals - 7. Ceremonial and other usages. 13 coloured illus.; analytical index. *Class No:* 929.9(410)

[6330]

SWINSCOE, A. **The British flag** how? when? why? Glasgow, Brown, Son, & Ferguson, 1978. 20p., col. illus., sd. £2. ISBN: 0851743277.

First published 1954.

The patron Saints - Growth of the Union flag - Heraldic notes - Flying the flag - Story of the ensigns - Notes on the Commonwealth period. *Class No:* 929.9(410)

Scotland

[6331]

HARRIS, P., *ed.* **Story of Scotland's flag.** Glasgow, Lang Syne Publishers, 1992. 48p. illus. £4.95. ISBN: 1852171731.

Condensed, partly rewritten edition of McMillan, W. and Stewart, A. *The Story of the Scottish Flag* (1925).

The history of the St. Andrew's Cross from the Middle Ages to the 20th century. *Class No:* 929.9(411)

Ireland

[6332]

HAYES-MCCOY, G.A. **A History of Irish flags from earliest times.** Dublin, Academy Press; Boston, G.K. Hall, 1979. 240p. col. illus.

Comprehensive illustrated survey. *Class No:* 929.9(415)

Canada

[6333]

'The Canadian flag/Le drapau canadien', *The Archivist,*
v.17,no.1, January-February 1990.

Complete issue devoted to the Canadian flag with articles
on Birth of a flag, Choosing a national flag, The Royal Mark
in New France, Conserving the Proclamation of the
Canadian flag, The Governor-General's flag, and others.
Class No: 929.9(71)

USA

[6334]

CANNON, D.D. The Flags of the Confederacy : an
illustrated history. Wilmington, North Carolina, Broadfoot,
Publishing, 1988. 128p. col. illus. $29.95. ISBN:
0918518628.

72 col. illus. *Class No:* 929.9(73)

[6335]

GUENTER, S.M. The American flag cultural shifts from
creation to codification. Cranbury, N.J., Associated Univ.
Presses, 1990. 254p. illus., bibliog., index. $34.50. ISBN:
0838633846.

A study of the 'evolving relationship between the symbol
of the American flag and the development of the nation'
(Preface). Chapter notes p.213-37. Bibliography p.238-47.

A complete history of 'Old Glory' is available in C.M.
Debarr's and J.A. Bonkowske's *Saga of the American flag:
an illustrated history* (Harbinger House, 1990. 91p. col.
illus., bibliog.). *Class No:* 929.9(73)

[6336]

**RICHARDSON, E.W. Standards and colors of the
American Revolution.** Philadelphia, Univ. of Pennsylvania
Press and the Pennsylvania Society of the Revolution and its
Color Guard, 1982. xvii, 341p. col. illus. ISBN:
0812278399.

Sumptuously illustrated (64 col. plates) encyclopaedic
work on the design, emblems, and unit descriptions of
revolutionary flags. 22. chapters: 1. Flag design and
symbols - 2. Liberty flags - 3. Continental and Union
colours - 4. Continental army - 5. Navy privateers - 6-18.
State flags A-Z - 19. French forces - 20. British and Loyalist
colours - 21. German colours - 22. Post-war colours.
Appendix 1. Chronological summary of George Washington
correspondence, orders and events and other documentation
relating to Continental Army standards and colours - 2.
Philadelphia flagmakers and flagpainters. Glossary p.275-83.
References and notes p.285-323. Bibliography p.325-333.
Class No: 929.9(73)

[6337]

SHEARER, B.F. *and* **SHEARER, B.S. State names, seals,
flags and symbols** a historical guide. Westport, Connecticut,
Greenwood Press, 1987. viii, 239p. col. illus. bibliog.,
index. $39.95; £32.95. ISBN: 0313245592.

Replaces G.E. Shankle's *State names, flags, seals, songs,
birds, flowers, and other symbols* (1938).

9 well-documented chapters: 1. State names and
nicknames - 2. Mottoes - 3. Seals - 4. Flags - 5. Capitals - 6.
Flowers - 7. Trees - 8. Birds - 9. Songs. Bibliography of
State histories p.205-218. 'Should be part of the basic
reference collection of every academic, public, or school
library'. (*Choice*, v.25, no.9, May 1988, p.1386).
Class No: 929.9(73)

[6338]

SMITH, W. The Flag book of the United States. New York,
Morrow, 1970. xiii,306p. illus.

Historical survey, chapters 2-4; chapter 5, Flags of the
states and territories (Alabama ... Wyoming, p.89-227);
chapter 6, Other American flags. Bibliography, p.279-92;
short glossary; index; p.299-306. 209 flags in good colour;
64 line-drawings. *Class No:* 929.9(73)

Australia

[6339]

The Australian national flag. 2nd ed. Canberra, Australian
Government Publishing Service, 1985. 28p. illus. (some
col.), diagrs., sd. ISBN: 0644040467.

1st ed. 1982.

Includes international rules for flying flags.
Class No: 929.9(94)

93/99 History

History

[6340]
BARNES, H.E. **A History of historical writing.** 2nd ed. New York, Dover Publications, 1962; London, Constable, 1963. xiii, 440p. pbk. $5.60. ISBN: 048620104x.

First published 1937.

A running commentary in 15 chapters, each with updated 'Selected references' appended. Detailed index of authors and titles p.407-40. The succeeding period is dealt with in *Historiography, method, history teaching: a bibliography of books and articles in English 1965-1973* by A.S. Birkos and L.A. Tambs (Hamden, Connecticut, Shoe String Press, 1975. xi, 130p. $19.50. ISBN 0208014209).
Class No: 930.0

[6341]
BOIA, L., *ed.* **Great historians from antiquity to 1800:** an international dictionary. Westport, Connecticut, Greenwood Press, 1989. 432p. $65.00; £58.50. ISBN: 0313245177.

Sponsored by the Commission on the History of Historiography of the International Committee of the Historical Sciences.

Brief articles on the life and work of 600 historians.
Class No: 930.0

[6342]
—Great historians of the modern age: an international dictionary. Boia, L., *and other, eds.* Westport, Conn., Greenwood Press, 1990. 841p. indexes. $95; £75.85. ISBN: 0313273286.

Essays on 900 19th and 20th century historians arranged in 38 country or region chapters. 'Far more comprehensive coverage than *The Blackwell Dictionary of Historians* ... an excellent biographical dictionary' (*Choice,* v.29, no.3, November 1991, p.416). *Class No:* 930.0

[6343]
BREISACH, E. **Historiography** ancient, medieval & modern. Chicago, Univ. of Chicago Press, 1983. xii, 487p., bibliog., index. $35. ISBN: 0226072746.

Detailed chronological text of the historiography of the western world from the early Greeks to the 20th century. Bibliography p.429-464. *Class No:* 930.0

[6344]
GOOCH, G.P. **History and historians in the nineteenth century.** 2nd ed. London, Longmans, 1952. 547p.

First published 1913.

2nd ed. has additional footnotes and an introduction on recent historical studies. A detailed and scholarly survey by a specialist in the period. *Class No:* 930.0

[6345]
HAY, D. **Annalists and historians:** Western historiography from the eighth to the eighteenth century. London, Methuen, 1977. viii, 215p. pbk. £8.95. ISBN: 0416811906.

Due emphasis on the importance of the Bible and the Lives of the Saints in the earlier period and on the Enlightenment historians in the later period. References; index. 'Fills a long-felt gap in the literature ... Ideally suited to that undergraduate audience for whom it is clearly intended' (*British Book News*, January, 1978, p.17).
Class No: 930.0

[6346]
Historiography: an annotated bibliography of journal articles, books and dissertations. Kinnell, S., *ed.* Santa Barbara, California, ABC-Clio, 2v., 1987. 376p,482p., indexes. $137.50. £110. set. (*ABC-Clio Bibliography Series.*) ISBN: 0874364906, v.1; 0874364914, v.2.

8000 entries published 1970 onwards extracted from *America History and Life* and *Historical Abstracts.* V.1 treats broad topics *e.g.* individual historians whilst v.2 is arranged on a geographical basis. Author and subject indexes. *Class No:* 930.0

Databases
[6347]
'A Sampler of databases for searches in history,' *RQ,*, v.21no.4, Summer 1982, p.360-363.

Short reviews of 8 databases - *American history and life - Comprehensive dissertation index - ERIC - Historical abstracts - Magazine index - The Philosophy index - Soc Seisearch - Smithsonian Science Information Exchange,* plus 7 additional files, considering their subject coverage, indexing, currency of information, and the type of source document. *Class No:* 930.0(003.4)

[6348]
SCHÜRER, K. *and* ANDERSON, S.J. A Guide to historical datafiles held in machine-readable form. London, Association for History and Computing, 1992. v,339p. indexes. ISBN: 0951535218.

Part 1: Introduction (nature and scope) - 2. Inventory of historical datafiles - 3. Datafiles overseas - 4. Index. Information on 650 files. Data: study, purpose, content, period, place, reference. *Class No:* 930.0(003.4)

Bibliographies
[6349]
Bibliographie internationale des sciences historiques/ International bibliography of historical sciences. Paris, Colin (now München, K.G. Saur), 1930-. Annual. Edited for the International Committee of Historical Sciences, Lausanne, Published with Unesco aid and under the patronage of the International Council for Philosophy and Humanistic Sciences. Available in North America from G.K. Hall. ISSN: 00742015.

....(contd.)
V.58 *1989* xxiv,472p. ISBN 3598204132. £118. has 8329 unannotated entries arranged in Classes A-U, subdivided by countries, subjects and periods (*e.g.* A. Auxiliary historical sciences; C. Prehistory and protohistory; D. Ancient East; I. Middle Ages; K. Modern times; general works; L. Modern religious history; N. Modern economic and social history; P. International relations; modern history). Index of authors and persons; geographical index. Tardy appearance, but valuable for coverage of Africa, Asia, Eastern and Southern Europe. *Class No:* 930.0(01)

[6350]
Bibliographies in history: an index to bibliographies in history journals and dissertations ... Kinnell, S., *ed.* Santa Barbara, California, ABC-Clio, 2v., 1988. $144.50. £130. set. ISBN: 087436521x, set.
1. *Covering the US and Canada.* 137p. index. $85. £51. ISBN 0874365228. About 5100 entries. 2. *Covering all countries in the world except the US and Canada.* 322p. index. $85. £51. ISBN 0874365236. About 3000 entries. Entries relate to articles or dissertations published 1971-1987 extracted from *America History and Life* and *Historical Abstracts* with author and subject indexes. 'Students will be able to avoid the tedium of extensive searching in the print indexes' (*Choice*, v.26, no.10, June 1989, p.1652).
Class No: 930.0(01)

[6351]
DAY, A.E. History a reference handbook. London, Clive Bingley; Hamden, Connecticut, 1977. 354p. index. £25.00. ISBN: 0851572251, UK; 0208015361, US.
787 entries of varying length covering bibliographies, dictionaries, atlases and encyclopedias, research, the nature of historical writings *etc.* in a single A-Z sequence.
Class No: 930.0(01)

[6352]
FRICK, E. Library research guide to history: illustrated research strategy and sources. Ann Arbour, Michigan, Pierian Press, 1980. x, 81p. facsims, pbk. $15. ISBN: 0876501234.
12 chapters (*e.g.* 3. Where to find books on your topic; 7. Collecting current information; 10. Using guides to historical literature. Appendix 3: 'Basic reference sources for courses in history' (p.53-79; 21 classes, subdivided). Aimed at American students writing term papers or taking history courses. *Class No:* 930.0(01)

[6353]
FRITZE, R.H., *and others, eds.* Reference sources in history an introductory guide. Santa Barbara, Calif. and Oxford, ABC-Clio, 1990. 319p. index. $49.50. £45.95. ISBN: 0874361648.
685 cross-referenced entries for major reference works listed in 14 form chapters *e.g.* book review indexes, core journals, dissertations and theses, archives and manuscripts. Entries consist of full bibliographical citations and evaluative annotations. Author and title index. Coverage is for all historical periods and for all geographical areas although the emphasis is on English-language items relating to Anglo-American and European history. 'An accurate, current and reliable work that supersedes Helen J. Poulton's classic but dated *The Historian's Handbook*' (*Library Journal*, v.116,no.7, 15 April 1991, p.84). *Class No:* 930.0(01)

[6354]
Historische bibliographie. Herausgegeben von der Arbeitsgemeinschaft ausseruniversitärer historische Forschungseinrichtungen in der Bundesrepublik Deutschland. München, R. Oldenbourg Verlag, 1986-. Annual. ISSN: 09335420.
Berichtsjahr 1989 (1990). 379p. ISBN 3846644653 has 5569 unannotated entries arranged in 2 sections: 1. Allgemeiner (Gegeschichte als Wissenschaft; Quellenkunde; Allgemeines) - 2. Chronologisch - systematischer (Vor-und Frühgeschichte; Frühe Hochkulturen; Die antike Welt; Die europäische Welt; Asien; Afrika; Amerika; Australien und Oceanien; Die Welt im 20. Jahrhunderts).
Class No: 930.0(01)

[6355]
Recently published articles. Washington, American Historical Association, 1976-. 3 *pa.* $20.00. members. $28.00. non-members and institutions. ISSN: 01455311.
Formerly (1895-1975) a section of *The American Historical Review*.
Lists more than 15,000 references *pa.* in all fields of history. Draws on over 3,000 periodicals, a fair proportion being in foreign languages. Systematically arranged (20 sections) by periods, continents and countries. Claims to be 'the most current and comprehensive bibliography of periodical literature about history available'.
Class No: 930.0(01)

[6356]
RICHARDSON, R.C. The Study of history: a bibliographical guide. Manchester, Manchester Univ. Press, 1988. Distributed in North America by St. Martins Press. xiv,98p. index. £29.95; $55.00. (*History and Related Disciplines Selected Bibliographies*.) ISBN: 0719018811.
Approximately 2,100 entries arranged in 9 chronological and thematic divisions: 1. General works *i.e.,* bibliographies, philosophy of history, methods and purposes, quantification, historiographical surveys - 2-9. Ancient History to Twentieth Century. 'Although the emphasis is heavily toward British historiography this book should prove very useful to undergraduates, beginning graduate students, and their instructors' (*Choice,* v.26,no.2, October 1988, p.295-6). *Class No:* 930.0(01)

Encyclopaedias

[6357]
Chronicle of the world. Burne, J., *ed.* Rev ed. Farnborough, Chronicle Communications, 1993. (UK ed.). 1296p. illus., (mostly col.), maps, index. £39.95. ISBN: 1872031005, UK.
Follows *Chronik der Menscheit* and *Chronique de l'Humanité.*
The history of the last 3.5 million years to 1945 in double-page spreads (the earliest covering long periods of time; the latest devoted to two years, or even one year) as if being reported by a modern journalist. 50 essays give overview summaries *e.g.* The dating of Egyptian history ... The Crusades ... The end of Imperial China. A last section, 'The nations of the world', A-Z by present day names, gives broad geographical and political details and a summary of their history. 'Commendably non-Eurocentric and despite its inbuilt deficiencies is an attractive, user-friendly and innovative encyclopedia' (*Sunday Times*, no.8631, 14 January 1990, p.H14). *Class No:* 930.0(031)

[6358]
The Guinness encyclopedia of world history. Anderson, M., *and others, eds*. Enfield, Guinness Publishing, 1992. 306p. illus (mostly col.), col. maps, tables. £21.95. ISBN: 0851129943.

40 contributors. 94 chapters arranged in 6 sections: 1. Ancient World (4000 BC-AD 400) - 2. Other worlds (Prehistory - 1900) - 3. Medieval world (400-1500) - 4. Broadening horizons (1500-1789) - 5. Revolution, industry and empire (1789-1914) - 6. Modern world (1914-), each preceded by a time chart banded into geographical and thematic columns. A-Z Factfinder (p.235-306) contains 3000++ entries on individual rulers, statesmen, wars, treaties, ideologies *etc*. 'Best single-volume work of this type, especially valuable for its non-Eurocentric approach' (*Archives*, v.20, no.89, April 1993, p.121).
Class No: 930.0(031)

[6359]
History of humanity. London, Routledge in association with Unesco, 7v., 1994-.

V.1: S.J. De Laet. ed. *From the origins of humanity to the third millennium*. 1994. 1440p. illus., maps, bibliog., index. £85. 0415093058. Over 40 contributors. Divided into 2 main sections: 1. From anthropogenesis to the beginnings of food production - 2. From the beginnings of food production to the first states. 74 maps.

Further volumes: 2. *Third millennium to the seventh century BC*. 1994. 0415093066. 3. *Seventh century BC to seventh century AD*. 1995. 0415093074. 4. *Seventh to the sixteenth century*. 1996. 0415093082. 5. *Sixteenth to the eighteenth century*. 1997. 0415093090. 6. *Nineteenth century*. 1998. 0415093104. 7. *Twentieth century*. 1999. 0415093112.

'Provides readers with as broad a picture as possible of the different cultures of the world and of their development and does not impose one particular philosophy of history but gives all philosophies their rightful place. It includes chapters on all cultures encompassing Chinese, African and Indian as well as Western perceptions of history and the philosophy of history. It includes the most recent findings of historical research and the latest developments in historical methodology, covering both our cultural and scientific heritage'. *Class No:* 930.0(031)

[6360]
JUDGE, H., ed. **World history from earliest times to 1800.** Oxford, Oxford University Press, 1988. 391p. col.illus., col.maps, geneal. tables, col.chron.charts on end papers. £19.50; $39.95. (*Oxford Illustrated Encyclopedia Vol.3.*)

45 contributors. More than 2300 A-Z cross-referenced entries covering human evolution, archaeological discoveries, early civilizations and empires, rulers, statesmen, military and naval campaigns, treaties, histories of individual countries. For home and school use. 350 illustrations. *Class No:* 930.0(031)

[6361]
—BLAKE, R., ed. World history from 1800 to the present day. Oxford, Oxford Univ. Press, 1988. [iv],391p. col.illus., col.maps, geneal. tables, col.chron.charts on end papers. £19.50; $39.95. (*Oxford Illustrated Encyclopaedia Vol.4.*) ISBN: 01986936x.

35 contributors. Over 2300 A-Z entries covering 19th and 20th century social and political changes, two world wars, the Industrial Revolution and other disasters. 350 illustrations. 'For school,, general reference and most other

....(contd.)
quick reference libraries it will prove an essential item' (*Library Review*, v.38,no.2, 1989,p.49).
Class No: 930.0(031)

[6362]
LANGER, W.L., *comp. and ed*. An Encyclopedia of world history ancient, medieval and modern chronologically arranged. London, Harrap/Galley Press, 1987. viii,1609p. geneal.tables. ISBN: 0861366476.

First published 1940. This edition is text of *The new illustrated encyclopedia of world history* (Boston, Houghton Mifflin, 5th ed. 1972) with a new section covering the period 1971-1986, p.1359-1403.

7 major periods covering Palaeolithic period to the present time, subdivided by countries and areas. Appendix (p.1405-1417) lists Roman and Byzantine emperors, Caliphs, Roman Popes, Holy Roman Emperors, Kings of England and France, US Presidents, European and New World universities formed prior to 1900. *Class No:* 930.0(031)

[6363]
Larousse encyclopedia of ancient and medieval history. Dunan, M., *ed*. London, Hamlyn, 1981. 413p. illus. (some col.), maps, bibliog., index. 0600023710.

Translated from *Histoire universelle Larousse v.1* (1964).

Continous narrative in 6 sections: 1. Eastern peoples and empires - 2. The supremacy of the Eastern Mediterranean - 3. The great empires of antiquity - 4. Middle Ages - 5. The barbarian invasion - 6. The rise of Europe in the 14th and 15th centuries. Bibliography p.248. *Class No:* 930.0(031)

[6364]
Longman illustrated encyclopedia of world history. London, Ivyleaf, 1989. 1039p. illus., diagrs., maps, index. ISBN: 0863630006.

First published London, Longman, 1976 in 2v. as *Longman illustrated companion to world history*.

Over 2000 entries relating to major events and personalities that have influenced world development from ancient times to the present. 900 black and white illustrations. Analytical index. For home and school use.
Class No: 930.0(031)

[6365]
STEWART, R. The Illustrated encyclopedia of historical facts from the dawn of the Christian era to the new world order. London, Simon & Schuster, 1992. 320p. illus. (some col.), col. maps, index. £17.50. ISBN: 0671711105.

Concentrates on 480 major world events with 5 pictorial introductory essays on successive historical periods. Micropedia of people p.280-95; of places p.296-300. Historical charts p.301-13. For family and school use.
Class No: 930.0(031)

Dictionaries

[6366]
The Blackwell dictionary of historians. Cannon, J., *and others eds*. Oxford, Blackwell Reference, 1988. xiv,480p. bibliogs., index. £50. $75. ISBN: 063114708x.

200 contributors. Over 450 biographical entries including 50 living historians, 60 French, 40 Germans and 20 Italians. In addition there are 25 national historiographical surveys and 40 thematic entries. 'No reference library of reasonable size that lays claim to having any worthwhile coverage of

....*(contd.)*

British or overseas history should be without it' (*Library Association Record*, v.91, no.5, May 1989, p.291).
Class No: 930.0(038)

[6367]
BURGUIÈRE, A. Dictionnaire des sciences historiques. Sous la direction d'André Burguière. Paris, Presses Universitaires De France, 1986. ix,693p. ISBN: 2130393616.

95 contributors. Entries on schools of history, concepts, historians *etc.*, with bibliographies appended. 'Un inventaire suffisament large et approfondi des ressources intellectuelles d'une discipline qui est arrivée à un stade de maturité ... mais non d'immobilité' (*Avant-Propos*).
Class No: 930.0(038)

[6368]
Chambers dictionary of world history. Boyd, K., *ed.* Edinburgh, Chambers, 1993. viii,996p. maps. £30. ISBN: 0550150056.

35 contributors. 7500 cross-referenced entries relating to political, military, and diplomatic history from the earliest times to the 1990s. 'A single volume of substantial size ... which will be useful for most quick reference purposes for professional and educational users' (*Preface*). 36 maps.
Class No: 930.0(038)

[6369]
COOK, C. Macmillan dictionary of historical terms. 2nd ed. London, Macmillan Press, 1989. 350p. £29.95. ISBN: 033344972x.

First published 1983.

Over 2,000 terms 'frequently encountered by both undergraduates and research students'. Coverage is worldwide with additional material on non-European history in this new edition. Recommended as a supplement to B. Wetterau's *Macmillan's concise dictionary of world history* in *Library Journal*, v.109, no.4, 1 March 1984, p.478.
Class No: 930.0(038)

[6370]
Dictionary of world history. Howat, G.M.D., *ed.* London, Nelson, 1973. xxvii,1720p. index. ISBN: 0171440056.

194 contributors. 20,000 entries of 100 words average length but some extending to 500++ words. 8000 relate to prominent individuals; 5000 to events; 7000 to institutions, cultural movements *etc.*; and a smaller number to particular places. Emphasis is political more than social or economic, with military, diplomatic and scientific affairs represented less fully. Glossary p.xxv-xxvii. This British based work of scholarship is weighted towards the twentieth century.
Class No: 930.0(038)

[6371]
HARBOTTLE, T.B. Dictionary of historical allusions: a guide to names and nicknames, sobriquets and similar appellations ... and terms commonly found in historical writings, but omitted from standard dictionaries and encyclopedias. Detroit, Gale Research Co., 1968. 306p.

First published London, Sonnenschein, 1904.

'A useful source for indentification of fugitive phrases' (*Wilson Library Bulletin*, v.43, no.10, June 1969. p.1022). 'Leans towards English history' (*Choice*, v.6, no.12, February 1970, p.1731). *Class No:* 930.0(038)

[6372]
The Hutchinson dictionary of world history. Oxford, Helicon, 1993. x,699p. maps, tables, geneal. tables. £20. ISBN: 0091771528.

Over 5000 entries including longer feature articles (*e.g.* Age of Discovery, Gandhi and Indian Nationalism) relating to key individuals, events, major movements, and histories of every modern country, from prehistory to post-Communism. 7 Appendices. World Chronology p.676-99 and 100 thematic chronologies. 70 maps.
Class No: 930.0(038)

[6373]
MOURRE, M. Dictionnaire d'histoire universelle. Paris, Éditions Universitaires, 2v., 1981. 2368p.

First published 1968.

Entries (some with bibliographies) for persons, events, institutions and places. Includes contemporary figures. Small type. Some French slant. Very favourably reviewed in *Bulletin critique du livre français*, May 1969, entry no.76694. *Class No:* 930.0(038)

[6374]
MOURRE, M. Dictionnaire encyclopédique d'histoire. Paris, Bordas, 8v., 1978. x,4894p. illus. col.plates.

Natural emphasis on France and French history does not detract from its authority. V.8 has Répertoire des noms communes (thematic guide) p.4836-48. First great universal historical dictionary to be published in France since C. Dezobry and T. Bachelet's *Dictionnaire général de biographie et d'histoire* (1857). *Class No:* 930.0(038)

[6375]
The Oxford minidictionary of twentieth-century world history. Oxford, Oxford Univ. Press, 1990. 444p. limp cover. £2.25. ISBN: 0198661614.

Covers the important events, individuals, and historical movements in c.1,000 cross-referenced entries. Well suited for examination revision. *Class No:* 930.0(038)

[6376]
WETTERAU, B., *comp.* **World history:** a dictionary of important people, places, and events from ancient times to the present. New York, Henry Holt; London, Robert Hale, 1994. xvi,1173p. $45. ISBN: 080507350x, US; 0709054238, UK.

Revision of *Macmillan's concise dictionary of world history* (1983).

10,000 cross-referenced entries including 100 historical outlines of broad topics (*e.g.* Holy Roman Empire and American Revolution), chronologies, and specific items covering events, important individuals, locations *etc.*
Class No: 930.0(038)

Theses

[6377]
Dissertations in history June 1970-June 1980. Volume III: an index to dissertations completed in history departments of United States and Canadian universities. Kuehl, W.F., *ed.* Santa Barbara, California, and Oxford, ABC-Clio, 1986. 466p. £52.12. ISBN: 087436356x.

Lists approximately 9000 doctoral dissertations. A continuation of v.I+II (Lexington, Univ. of Kentucky Press, 1965-72) which cover the period 1873-1970 and include *c.*13,535 dissertations from 80 universities.
Class No: 930.0(043)

[6378]

Doctoral dissertations in history. Washington, American Historical Association, Institutional Services Program, 1976-. v.1-10, 2 *pa*; v.11-. Annually.

Formerly titled *List of doctoral dissertations in history in progress or recently completed in the United States.*

V.12: 1987 has 212 entries listed by category or theme with brief annotations indicating whether dissertations are completed or in progress. Sections: General - Historiography - Ancient - Medieval - Modern European - Near and Middle East - Africa - Latin America - Canada - United States - United States: regional. Author and subject index. *Class No:* 930.0(043)

Bibliographies

[6379]

Historical research for higher degrees in the United Kingdom. London. Univ. of London Institute of Historical Research, 1967 - . V.1. -. Annual.

List previously published in the journal *History* (1920-29); the Institute's *Bulletin* (1930-32); as a supplement to the *Bulletin* (1933-66). Then as *Historical research for university degrees* (1967-85).

Pt 2. Theses in progress 1989 1989. vii, 183p. ISBN 1871348013. ISSN 02686724. Similar period and area headings. Author index.

No.50 *Pt 1. Theses completed 1988.* 1989. vi, 49p. ISBN 1871348005. ISSN 02686716. Entries under broad chronological and topographical headings: Philosophy of history - Historiography - Ancient history - Medieval Europe - Modern Europe - Modern Britain and Ireland - International history - Africa - America and the West Indies - Asia - Australasia. Index of universities, subjects and authors. *Class No:* 930.0(043)(01)

[6380]

JACOBS, P.M., *comp.* **History theses 1901-1970** historical research for higher degrees in the universities of the United Kingdom. London, Institute of Historical Research, Univ. of London, 1976. viii,456p. £5. ISBN: 0901179345.

7,633 numbered entries, in chronological order under subjects. Main headings: Philosophy of history - Historiography - Ancient history - Historical geography - Britain - Medieval Europe and Byzantium - Medieval England - Medieval Wales - Medieval Scotland - Medieval Ireland - World - Modern Europe - Britain (5 periods) - Middle and Near East - Africa - Asia - America - Australia and New Zealand - Pacific Ocean and Islands. Author and subject (partly analytical) indexes. *Class No:* 930.0(043)(01)

[6381]

—**HORN, J.M.** History theses 1971-80 historical research for higher degrees in the universities of the United Kingdom. London, Univ. of London Institute of Historical Research, 1984. ix, 294p. index. £8. ISBN: 0901179817.

Follows P.M. Jacobs *History theses 1901-1970.*

4416 numbered entries arranged in similar fashion to Jacobs. *Class No:* 930.0(043)(01)

Reviews & Abstracts

[6382]

Historical Abstracts bibliography of the world's historical literature. Santa Barbara, California, ABC-Clio; Oxford, Clio Press, 1955-. Priced on Service Rate Principle depending on library's annual book fund. ISSN: 03632717.

1. Boehm H. ed. *Historical abstracts 1775-1945: bibliography of the world's periodical literature* v.1-16. 1955-1970. Up to 1964 this offered universal coverage but from 1965 US and Canada were removed and included in *America history and life (qv).* 2. V.17-. 1971-. Published in 2 parts: *Part A. Modern history abstracts 1450-1914* and *Part B. Twentieth century abstracts.* Entries relating to the period 1914-1945 appeared in both parts in v.17-20. 3. From 1980 (v.31) coverage was extended to books and dissertations. 4. 5 retrospective volumes were published 1980-1984 to include references that were previously outside *Historical Abstract's* scope and also references not available when the original volumes appeared. These retrospective volumes (26-30) can only be purchased in conjunction with the relevant current volumes *i.e.* 26/31, 27/32, 28/33, 29/34 and 30/35.

Contains abstracts and shorter annotations from over 1900 major historical journals published in 84 countries and in 45 languages. Books are selected from reviews in 13 historical and bibliographical journals whilst dissertations are derived from *Dissertation Abstracts International. Modern history abstracts 1450-1914* and *Twentieth century abstracts* are both published quarterly: nos. 1-3 contain references arranged by subject (vs. 1-2 have indexes) and no.4 contains a cumulative annual index. *Modern History Abstracts* is divided into 3 sub-parts: 1. General (*i.e.* bibliography, methodology, historiography, archive, libraries, societies *etc.*) - 2. Topics (*e.g.* international relations, wars, political history, science and technology) - 3. Area and Country (8 geographical divisions). *Twentieth century abstracts* omits sub-part 1. Bibliographic entries printed in *Historical abstracts* are available online from File 39, DIALOG Information Services covering 1973 to date.

Five year indexes are issued: V. 1-5 (1955-59) £240; vs. 6-10 (1960-64) £240; V.11-15 (1965-69) £240; vs. 16-20 (1970-74) £420; vs. 21-25 (1975-79) £420; vs. 31-35 (1980-84) £420; vs. 36-40 (1985-89) £375. v.26-30 (retrospective) £310.

Historical abstracts on disc. 1991. ISSN 03632717 includes Modern history abstracts 1450-1914 and 20th century abstracts 1914-1991. *Class No:* 930.0(048)

[6383]

—List of periodicals (revised 1987) surveyed for America: history and life and Historical abstracts. Santa Barbara, California, ABC-Clio, 1987. 29p. sd. *gratis.*

A-Z list of titles scrutinised. Each title is followed by years of coverage and a two-lettered code for the country of publication. *Class No:* 930.0(048)

Periodicals

[6384]

HENIGE, D., *comp.* **Serial bibliographies and abstracts in history:** an annotated guide . Westport, Conn., Greenwood Press, 1986. ix,220p. index. $35. £27.95. (*Bibliographies and Indexes in World History, no.2.*) ISBN: 0313250707.

874 annotated items A-Z by title consisting of 'all bibliographies which address in whole or in part any aspect of the past. Data: history and frequency of publication, types

....(contd.)
of indexes, kinds of material included, languages represented and, in some instances, a word of commendation. Subject index. 'Smaller or less well known sources that are nonetheless of enormous value can be identified through this tool' (*Reference Services Review*, v.17, no.4, Winter 1989, p.69-70). *Class No:* 930.0(051)

[6385]
STIEG, M.F. The Origin and development of scholarly historical periodicals. Tuscaloosa, Univ. of Alabama Press, 1986. xi,261p. tables, bibliog. $31.95. ISBN: 0817302735.
Chronological study with emphasis on *Historische Zeitschrift; English Historical Reivew; Deutsche Zeitschrift für Geschichtswissenschaft; Mississippi Valley Historical Review; Zeitschrift für Sozial-und Wirtschaftsgeschichte; Catholic Historical Review* and *Journal of the History of Ideas.* Chap.8. Bibliographic control and use. Chapter notes p.199-266; Bibliography p.227-247. Index p.249-261. *Class No:* 930.0(051)

Bibliographies
[6386]
BOEHM, E.H., *and others.* **Historical periodicals directory.** Santa Barbara, California and Oxford, ABC-Clio, 5v., 1981-1986. £339.50. ISBN: 0874361672, set.
Updates Boehm and Adolphus' *Historical periodicals* (*qv.*).
1. *US and Canada.* 1981. xii,180p. $95. £62.25. 0874360188. 2. *Europe: West, North, Central and South.* 1983. xv,597p. $110. £70.50. 0874360196. 3. *Europe, East and Southeast.* 1984. xv,252p. $95. £66.50. 087436020. 4. *Latin America and the West Indies* 1955. xiv,157p. $95. £67.50. 0874360218. 5. *Australia and New Zealand.* 1986. xiii,227p. $95. £73.50. 0874360226. Includes cumulative title index and subject/geographic index. 63 contributors covers 8900 titles. Lesser known titles deliberately sought to include information not found elsewhere. Aims to be comprehensive, for current periodicals and those that have ceased publication since 1960. Data: title; dates and frequency; address; scope; language; where abstracted; former title (if any). 'While the effort put into this set must be admired, it is really needed only in research libraries' (*Choice*, v.24, no.9, May 1987, p.1380). *Class No:* 930.0(051)(01)

[6387]
CARON, P. *and* **JARYC, M. World list of historical periodicals and bibliographies.** Oxford, etc., International Committee of Historical Sciences, 1939. 391p. indexes.
The original list of 3,103 periodicals is supplemented by annual additions in the *International bibliography of historical sciences*, v.16-, 1947-. A useful selection, but far from exhaustive for British periodicals and publications of societies. *Class No:* 930.0(051)(01)

[6388]
FYFE, J. History journals and serials: an analytical guide. Westport, Connecticut, Greenwood Press, 1986. xxiii,351p. index. $46.95. (*Annotated bibliographies of serials: a subject approach No.8.*) ISBN: 0313239991. ISSN: 07485190.
689 entries in 35 geographical and topical sections (1. Universal history ... 7. Genealogy and family history ... 22-34. Geographical regions ... 35. Indexes and abstracts) forming a comprehensive and detailed annotated

....(contd.)
bibliography of major journals of international reputation in the English language. Aimed primarily at helping the librarian to select journals and the historian for personal reading and the submission of manuscripts. Table of abstracts, indexes and databases p.xvii-xx. Directory of microform and reprint publishers p.xxi-xxiii. 'The compiler has done a good job' (*Choice*, v.24, no.3, November 1986, p.454). *Class No:* 930.0(051)(01)

[6389]
KIRBY, J.L. A Guide to historical periodicals in the English language. London, Historical Association, 1970. 48p. (*Helps for Students of History, no.80.*)
A helpful, very briefly annotated list of *c*.286 periodicals in 6 sections (1. Bibliographical guide and indexes - 2. General historical periodicals - 3. Periodicals devoted to a limited period (medieval; modern) - 4. Periodicals with subject specialization - 5. Periodicals limited to a special area - 6. British local periodicals (no annotations). Annotations indicate coverage and presence of reviews. Index of titles. *Class No:* 930.0(051)(01)

[6390]
STEINER, D.R. *and* **PHILLIPS, C.R. Historical journals** a handbook for writers and reviewers. 2nd ed. Jefferson, N.C., McFarland, 1993. 274p. index. $39.95. ISBN: 0899508014.
1st ed. 1981.
Arranged A-Z by title of journal the purpose of this handbook is to help authors and reviewers place their work. Lists nearly 700 journals. Data: subject area; address; names of editor/book review editor; subscription details; circulation and readership; where journal is indexed or abstracted *etc.* Subject index. *Class No:* 930.0(051)(01)

Quotations
[6391]
Chronological dictionary of quotations. Wright, E., *ed.* rev. ed. London, Bloomsbury, 1993. ix,445p. indexes. £17.99. ISBN: 0747514755.
First published as *Who said what when* (1988).
Over 7000 quotations largely selected for their historical interest (*i.e.* for the light they throw on an important event or figure). Arranged in 13 sections: 1. The Old Testament .... 13. The Post-War World. Keyword and name indexes. *Class No:* 930.0(082.2)

[6392]
PALMER, A. *and* **PALMER, V. A Dictionary of historical quotations.** 2nd ed. London, Granada Publishing, 1985. xi,404p. pbk. £3.95. ISBN: 0586085076.
First edition published by Harvester Press in 1976 under the title of *Quotations in history.*
Over 2000 quotations ranging in time from the crowning of Charlemagne (AD800) to present day. Arranged A-Z by speakers. Key word indexes. A note on the circumstances of each remark would have been helpful; also a chronological index. 'Decidedly Western in orientation' (*sic!*) 'but it serves a vital need' (*Library Journal*, 15 December 1976, p.2259). *Class No:* 930.0(082.2)

Maps & Atlases

[6393]
Atlas historique l'histoire du monde en 317 cartes. Sous la direction de Georges Duby. Paris, Larousse, 1988. 315p. col.maps, index. ISBN: 2035030099.

Updated ed. of *Atlas historique Larousse*.

A global, political, economic, cultural, artistic and religious history from prehistoric times to the present accompanied by a detailed chronology.
Class No: 930.0(084.3)

[6394]
Atlas of modern world history. Middleton, H. *and* Heater, D., *eds*. Oxford, Oxford Univ. Press, 1989. 64p. illus. (some col.), facsims, col. maps, pbk. £7.95. ISBN: 0198316771.

119 maps in 29 chronological units (1. Europe c.1900 ... 29. The Middle East since 1945) depict the course of 20th century history for the student and general reader. Unit 30 is a Time-chart p.62-3. *Class No:* 930.0(084.3)

[6395]
The Collins atlas of world history. Vidal-Naquet, P., *and others*. London, Collins, 1988. xi,340p. col.illus., col.maps,. geneal, table, index. £20.00. ISBN: 0002177765.

First published as *Le grand livre de l'histoire du Monde* (Hachette Paris, 1986).

'The atlas charts the parallel and diverging developments of different continents through a series of double-page spreads, each consisting of an authoritative, yet accessible, text complemented by specially prepared maps and high quality illustrations' (*d/w*). Conspicuously lacks either a contents page or an introduction on purpose, scope, or arrangement. *Class No:* 930.0(084.3)

[6396]
Grosser historische Weltatlas. München, Bayerischer Schulbuch-Verlag, 3v., 1978-81.

First published 1953.

1. *Vorgeschichte und Altertum* edited by H. Bengston and V. Milojčič. 6th ed., 1978. xiii, A-D, IA-IB, 56p. 19p. index. ISBN 3762760055. 2. *Mittelalter* edited by J. Engel. 2nd ed., 1979. xxii, 88p. 62p. index. 372761124. 3. *Neuzeit* edited by J. Engel and E.W. Zeeden. 4th ed., 1981. xxvi, 110p. 36p. index. 3762760217. Well-coloured, clearly lettered maps with transparent overlays. Unequalled as detailed historical atlases for their respective periods.
Class No: 930.0(084.3)

[6397]
MOORE, R.R., *ed.* **Rand McNally atlas of world history.** New ed. Chicago, Rand McNally, 1992. 192p. illus., col.maps, tables, bibliogs., indexes. pbk. $45. ISBN: 0528832883.

World section of 87 political, economic, social and cultural maps under 4 periods: 1. The Ancient World - 2. Heirs to the Ancient World - 3. Age of European supremacy - 4. Emergence of the Modern World. Special section of 8 maps on US history. Continuous narrative text but little changed from 1981 and 1983 editions. Criticized for sloppy use of terms, garish presentation, and for too much detail. 'However, it covers the major events in history ... recommended for a student looking for an inexpensive study aid' (*Cartographica*, v.26,no.2, Summer 1989, p.103-4).
Class No: 930.0(084.3)

[6398]
Philip's atlas of world history. Moore, R.I., *ed.* Rev. ed. London, Philip, 1992. 176p. illus., col. maps, bibliogs., index. £17.99. ISBN: 0540056774.

First published 1987.

24 historical essays integrated with 87 map features (including further readings) capture major historical events in 5 period divisions: 1. Ancient World - 2. Heirs to the ancient world - 3. Age of European supremacy - 4. Europe divided - 5. Emergence of the modern world. Current to end of 1990. *Class No:* 930.0(084.3)

[6399]
SHEPHERD, W.R. Shepherd's historical atlas. 9th rev. ed. New York, Barnes & Noble, 1980. xii, 226p. 115p. maps. $35.95. ISBN: 0060138467.

First published 1911. Modelled on F.W. Putzger's *Historicher Weltatlas* (1877). This edition includes a feature 'Maps since 1929' prepared by C.S. Hammond & Co., p.218-26.

226 pages of well-coloured, clear maps and plans, with instructive comments covering the period 1450BC-1965AD. About 15% of the maps concern the US Index-gazetteer (*c.*28,000 entries). The 1973 'revised' ed. merely updates and re-titles 2 maps in the 'Maps since 1929' supplement.

One of the best historical atlases in English. 'Suitable for senior forms of secondary schools and for colleges and universities' (Treharne, R.F. *Bibliography of historical atlases* (1939), p.9). Page size, 25 x15.5cm.
Class No: 930.0(084.3)

[6400]
The Times atlas of world history. Parker, G., *ed.* 4th rev. ed. London, Times Books; 1993. 358p. illus., col.maps, index. £40. ISBN: 0723005346.

1st ed. 1978; 3rd ed. 1989.

126 succinct essays on major themes from 91 expert contributors, illustrated by over 600 maps, arranged in 7 sections (1. The world of early man - 2. The first civilizations - 3. The Classical civilizations of Eurasia - 4. The world of divided regions - 5. The work of the emerging West - 6. The age of European dominance - 7. The age of global civilization). World chronology to 1984, p.15-27. Glossary of 100,000 entries with supplementary information on individuals, peoples, events, treaties *etc.* p.297-334. Bibliography p.296. Index gazetteer p.335-360. The background to its publication is explained in Ambrose Ways's 'The visible shape of history', *Sunday Times Magazine,* 3 September 1978, p.63-6. 'Any library without this volume cannot claim a basic collection ... In a class by itself' (*Choice*, v.16,no.1, March 1979, p.62). 'A superb atlas has been meticulously updated and improved' (*Booklist*, v.86,no.113, 1 March 1990, p.1378).
Class No: 930.0(084.3)

[6401]
—**The Times concise atlas of world history.** Barraclough, G., *ed.* 4th ed. London, Time Books, 1992. viii,184p. col.maps, bibliog. ISBN: 0723003866.

1st ed. 1982.

In 4 sections: 1. Early man and the civilizations of the ancient world; 2. Decline and recovery the emergence of a new world; 3. The rise of the West; 4. The modern world. Although modelled on *The Times atlas of world history* it is not simply a condensed version but stands on its own merits as a compact historical atlas. 'No fewer than 70 of the 320 maps ... are entirely new or radically changed'

....(contd.)

(*Introduction*). Bibliography p.152. Index gazetteer p.153-154. This edition is substantially revised principally because of recent advances in archaeological knowledge and because of the collapse of Communist regimes in Eastern Europe. 'A superb work, not least because of its determined avoidance of an eurocentric perspective' (*Archives*, v.20, no.89, April 1993. p.122). *Class No:* 930.0(084.3)

[6402]
TOYNBEE, A.J. *and* **MYERS, E.D. Historical atlas and gazetteer.** London, Oxford Univ. Press, 1959. Under the auspices of the Royal Institute of International Affairs. x, 257p. maps.

Forms v.11 of *A Study of history*.

Consists of (i) a gazetteer of all place-names mentioned in v.1-10 and in the appendix to v.11 of *A study of history*, consisting of brief locations with occasional notes; (ii) an atlas (p.88-202) of 103 black-and-white maps, some of them double-paged; (iii) an index to the place-names in the atlas. The maps are in five groups, the first giving synoptic views of civilizations and higher religions, the others illustrating primary, secondary and tertiary civilizations (up to 1955) in the Old World, and civilizations in the New World. Tends to concentrate on the Mediterranean and Southern Asian axes of civilization. Some of the mechanical tints used as shading patterns are confusing on the smaller-scale maps but usually the lettering and presentation are admirable. Page size, 24 x 17.5cm. *Class No:* 930.0(084.3)

Biographies

[6403]
Das Grosse Personen Lexicon zur Weltgeschichte in Farbe Band 1. A-L; Band 2. L-Z. Braunschweig, Chronik Verlag, 2v., 1983. 1511p., illus. (some col.), ports., tables. ISBN: 3883790184.

'3000 Biographien aus Geschichte und Politik, Kunst und Literatur, Wirtschaft und Technik' (front cover). Geburts-und-Todestage in chronologischer Folge p.1457-1511.
Class No: 930.0(092)

[6404]
People in world history an index to biographies in history journals and dissertations covering all countries of the world except Canada and the U.S. Kinnell, S., *ed.* Santa Barbara, California, and Oxford, ABC-Clio, 2v., 1988. 800p. £113.95 set. ISBN: 0874365503, set; 0874365511, v.1; 087436552x, v.2.

A-Z reference guide to biographical material extracted from the ABC-Clio database with an introductory chapter consisting of article abstracts on biographical writing. A detailed subject index in v.2 allows access by career, politics, religion, ethnic group, place of residence, country of origin, or by the source of the biographical material.
Class No: 930.0(092)

Ancient Greece & Rome

[6405]
MOMIGLIANO, A. The Classical foundations of modern historiography. Berkely, Univ. of California Press, 1990. xiv,162p. bibliog., index. ISBN: 0520068904.

6 university lectures: 1. Persian, Greek, Jewish historiography - 2. Herodotean and Thucididean traditions - 3. Rise of antiquarian research - 4. Fabius Pictor and the

....(contd.)

origins of national history - 5. Tacitus and the Tacitist tradition - 6. Origins of ecclesiastical historiography. Bibliographical note p.xiii-xiv. *Class No:* 930.0(37/38)

Europe

[6406]
A Selected bibliography of modern historiography. Attila, Pók, *ed.* Westport, Conn., Greenwood Press, 1992. xv,284p. indexes. £52.79. (*Bibliographies and Indexes in World History, no.24.*) ISBN: 031327231x. ISSN: 07426941.

Expands L.D. Stephens' *Historiography: a bibliography* (Metuchen, N.J., Scarecrow Press, 1975).

Listing of 2454 mostly unannotated entries relating to books and journal articles arranged in 6 geographically subdivided national chapters. Strong Central European presence. Prepared under the auspices of the Institute of History of the Hungarian Academy of Sciences. *Class No:* 930.0(4)

Great Britain

[6407]
ARNSTEIN, W.L., *ed.* **Recent historians of Great Britain** essays on the post-1945 generation. Ames, Iowa State University Press, 1990. x,207p. bibliogs., index. ISBN: 0813805929.

Assessments of the published works and achievements of 8 modern British historians. *Class No:* 930.0(410)

[6408]
BOND, B., *ed.* **The First World War and British military history.** Oxford, Clarendon Press, 1991. xiv,330p. bibliog., index. ISBN: 0198222998.

11 essays by separate hands in 4 sections: 1. Establishing the historical foundation (*i.e.* preoccupations and limitations of authors in the field) - 2. Battle of the memoirs (bitter controversies of reputations of political and military leader) - 3. Indirect approaches (Middle East campaigns) - 4, Great War rediscovered (history in the wake of 1960's media saturation). Chronology of publications on First World War military histories p.vii-x. Concentrates heavily on Western Front. *Class No:* 930.0(410)

Bibliographies

[6409]
ELTON, G.R. Modern historians on British history 1485-1945: a critical bibliography. London, Methuen, 1970. viii,239p.

Based on English version of 'Literaturbericht' (to May 1967), appearing in *Sonderheft 3* (1969) of *Historische Zeitschrift*. Essays, in 13 sections: 1. Introduction - 2. Works of reference - 3. Sources - 4. General - 5. The sixteenth century - 6. The seventeenth century - 7. The eighteenth century 8. The nineteenth century - 9. The twentieth century - 10. Social history - 11. History of ideas - 12. Scotland - 13. Ireland. Indexes: authors and editors; subjects. 'A valuable element of the work is the references to reviews in scholarly journals of many of the works cited' (*Library Journal*, v.97, no.18, 15 April 1973, p.1384). *Class No:* 930.0(410)(01)

[6410]

WATSON, C.A. **The Writing of history in Britain:** a bibliography of post-1945 writings about British historians and biographers. New York, Garland Publishing, 1982. xvi,726p. index. $75.00. ISBN: 0824093305.

3862 annotated entries arranged by topic in 6 chronological chapters (The Middle Ages - The Twentieth Century) plus a final chapter on multiperiod works. Favourably reviewed in *Choice,* v.20,no.4, December 1982, p.864. *Class No:* 930.0(410)(01)

Ireland

[6411]

Irish historiography.

1. *Irish historiography 1936-70* edited by T.W. Moody. Dublin, Irish Committee of Historical Sciences, 1971. viii,155p. 'Not a bibliography but an assessment and interpretation' (*Introductory*). 7 papers, arranged chronologically (1. Ireland before the Norman invasion ... 7. Twentieth-century Ireland, 1914-70), with an additional chapter on 'Thirty-five years of Irish historiography'. Appendix: 'A new History of Ireland under the auspices of the Royal Irish Academy (Stage I) conspectus'.

2. *Irish historiography 1970-79* edited by J. Lee. Cork Univ. Press, 1981, viii,238p. pbk. ISBN 0902561200. 9 papers: 1. Gaelic Ireland to 1603 - 2. Medieval Ireland 1169-1534 - 3. Ireland 1534-1660 - 4. 1660-1800 - 5. 1800-1921 - 6. Ireland since 1921-7. Irish ecclesiastical history since 1500 - 8. Irish economic history since 1500 - 9. Index to Bulletin of the Irish Committee of Historical Sciences 1939-1974. *Class No:* 930.0(415)

England

[6412]

GRANSDEN, A. **Historical writing in England.** London, Routledge & Kegan Paul; Ithaca, New York, Cornell Univ. Press, 2v., 1974-82. illus., facsims., bibliog., indexes.

1. *c.550-c.1307.* 1974. xxiv,610p. 071007476x. 21 chapters: 1. Gildas and Nennius - 2. Bede... 5. Anglo-Saxon chroniclers - 6. History of Norman Conquest ... 21. The chronicle of London. Appendix B. Local history in the thirteenth century (p.519-21) - D. Chronological index of the principal literary sources for English history to *c.*1307 (p.524-9).

2. *c. 1307 to the early sixteenth century.* 1982. xxiv,644p. 071000480x. 14 chapters: 1. Chroniclers of the reign of Edward II ... 7. The biographies of Henry V... 9. Chronicles of the Wars of the Roses: English. Epilogue (p.454-79) assesses the historiographical achievments of medieval England. Appendix H. Chronological Indices (The principal literary sources for English history ... 1307-1485; Annals; Local histories; Antiquarian works of the 15th century) p.499-503. Bibliography p.504-15. Extremely well-documented survey of medieval chronicles, annals, local history *etc. Class No:* 930.0(420)

Netherlands

[6413]

DE VRIES, P. 'The Writing and study of history in the Netherlands in the nineteenth century', *Acta Historiae Neerlandica,* v.3, 1968, p.247-265. *Class No:* 930.0(492)

Asia—Middle & Near East

[6414]

LEWIS, B. *and* HOLT, P.M., *eds.* **Historians of the Middle East.** London, Oxford Univ. Press, 1962. xi,519p. index.

41 contributions, - papers presented at conferences held at the School of Oriental and African Studies, London University, 1956-58. Parts: 1. Arabic, Persian and Turkish historiography to the 12th/19th century (1-22) - 2. European (including Russian) historical writing on the Near and Middle East, from the Middle Ages to the present day (23-32) - 3. Modern Middle Eastern historical writing (33-38) - 4. General theories (39-41). Footnote references. *Class No:* 930.0(53+56)

Asia—South & South East

[6415]

PHILIPS, C.H., *ed.* **Historians of India, Pakistan and Ceylon.** London, Oxford Univ. Press, 1961. x, 504p. index. (*Historical Writing On The People of Asia, no.1.*)

Papers presented at conferences held at the school of Oriental and African Studies, London University, 1956-58. Pt.1 deals with historiography current in the early empires; Pt.2 covers historical writings in the periods of European dominance and nationalist movements. Footnote references (for chapter 26, 115 such references). *Class No:* 930.0(54+59)

India

[6416]

DE SOUZA, J.P. *and* KULKARNI, C.M. **Historiography in Indian languages.** Delhi, Oriental, 1972. 275p. bibliogs.

21 essays on Bengali, Gujarati, Kannada, Malayalam, Marathi, Punjabi, Tamil and Telugu writings. *Class No:* 930.0(540)

[6417]

PATHAK, V.S. **Ancient historians of India:** a study in historical biographies. London, Asia Publishing House, 1966. xi, 184p.

Running commentary on historical works; many footnotes. Chapters: 1. The beginnings of historical traditions - 2. The *Harshacharita* - 3. The *Vikramanikadeva-charita* - 4. The *Vikramakabhyutlaya* - 5. The *Prithraraja-vijava* - 6. History in historical narrative. Bibliography (p.173-7); index. *Class No:* 930.0(540)

Asia—South East

[6418]

HALL, D.G.E., *ed.* **Historians of South-East Asia.** London, Oxford Univ. Press, 1961. viii,342p. index. (*Historical writing on the people of Asia.*)

25 chapters, by various contributors, - papers presented at conferences held at the School of Oriental and African Studies. London University 1956-58. Pt.1: Indigenous writings (9 chapters; p.13-104); pt.2: Western writings (chapters, 10-25; p.107-335) (*e.g.* 'Some aspects of Spanish historical writing on the Philippines', by C.R. Boxer, p.200-12). Covers Malaya, Burma, Indonesia, Vietnam. Numerous footnote references.

The same editor has written a brief general survey, 'On the study of Southeast Asian history', in *Pacific Affairs,* v.33,no.3, September 1960, p.268-81. *Class No:* 930.0(59)

Islamic World

[6419]

CHOUEIRI, Y.M. Arab history and the nation state a study in modern Arab historiography' 1820-1980. London, Routledge, 1989. xix, 238p. bibliog., index. £30. ISBN: 0415031133.

6 well-annotated chapters separated into 2 parts: 1. Pioneers and amateurs 1820-1920 (a general development of Arab historiography with emphasis on Egypt, Syria and North Africa) - 2. The professional historians: managers of legitimation (a critical analysis and assessment of 3 modern Arab historians). Glossary p.220-2. List of dynasties p.223. Bibliography p.224-31. *Class No:* 930.0(5.297)

Africa

[6420]

JEWSIEWICKI, B. *and* **NEWBURY, D. African historiographies:** what history for which Africa? Beverley Hills, and London, Sage Publications, 1986. 320p. bibliog., index. $29.95. (*Sage series on African modernization and development.*) ISBN: 0803924984.

23 essays grouped in 5 categories: 1. The epistemology of African studies - 2. The historiography of oral discourse - 3. Africa from the outside - 4. Africa from within - 5. Which way out? Trends in the developing historiography of Africa. Bibliography p.279-316. 'Bound to make a significant contribution to the study and general understanding of African history' (*Choice*, v.24, no.4, December 1986, p.671). *Class No:* 930.0(6)

Latin America

[6421]

THOMAS, J.R. Biographical dictionary of Latin American historians and historiography. Westport, Connecticut, Greenwood Press, 1984. xiv, 420p. bibliog., index. $50.95. £38.50. ISBN: 0313230048.

Introduction (p.3-77): 'The men who wrote history'; 'The meaning of history'; 'Historic truth and the way to find it'; 'Literary style and type of history produced'; 'Historiographic polemics.' 250 Bio-bibliographical sketches p.81-361. Appendix 1. Listing by birth place. 2. By year of birth. 3. Careers. 4. Subjects researched by major historians. *Class No:* 930.0(729.99)

[6422]

WILGUS, A.C. The Historiography of Latin America: a guide to historical writing 1500-1800. Metuchen, New Jersey, Scarecrow Press, 1976. xvi,33p. tables. $32.50; £27.50. ISBN: 0810808595.

Biobibliographical data on European and American born historical writers of the period, writing in eight languages. Each century is treated as a unit. Bibliography of *c*.450 references. *Class No:* 930.0(729.99)

USA

[6423]

BELLOT, H.H. American history and historians a review of recent contributions to the interpretation of the history of the United States. Westport, Connecticut, Greenwood Press, 1974. xi,336p., maps. $22.50. ISBN: 0837173256.

Reprint of the original edition published by Univ. of Oklahoma Press and Athlone Press 1952.

.... (contd.)

Historiography of America in the US 1890-1940, with valuable bibliographical notes attached to each chapter. *Class No:* 930.0(73)

[6424]

Twentieth-century American historians. Wilson, C.N., *ed.* Detroit, Gale Research Co., 1983. xi,519p. ports. $76.00. (*Dictionary of Literary Biography v.17.*) ISBN: 0810311445.

54 contributors. Literary biographies of 59 historians whose most important work, published during the 20th-century, concentrates chiefly on US history. Bibliography p.489-492. *Class No:* 930.0(73)

[6425]

—American historians 1866-1912. Wilson, C.N., *ed.* Detroit, Gale Research Co., 1986. xiv,428p. ports., bibliog., index. $88.00. (*Dictionary of Literary Biography, v.47.*) ISBN: 0810317257.

Bio-critical essays on 46 historians. Appendix 'Recording the Civil War'. *Class No:* 930.0(73)

[6426]

—American historians 1607-1865. Wilson, C.N., *ed.* Detroit, Gale Research Co., 1984. xv,382p. ports. $82.00. (*Dictionary of Literary Biography v.30.*) ISBN: 0810317087.

35 contributors. Literary biographies of 46 historians - chroniclers of the Colonial and Revolutionary periods; the literary historians of the early - 19th century; and other popular and specialized historians of the same period. Bibliography p.347-351. *Class No:* 930.0(73)

Middle Ages

Encyclopaedias

[6427]

GRABOIS, A. The Illustrated encyclopedia of medieval civilization. Jerusalem, The Jerusalem Publishing House Ltd.; London, Octopus, 1980. Distributed in North America by Mayflower. 751p., illus., (inc. col. pl.), maps, bibliog., tables, index. $25. ISBN: 070640856x.

Intended for the general public this impressive book has 4,000 entries (with 1-3 references appended) covering all aspects of Christendom, Islam, and the oriental civilizations of India, China and Japan from the 4th to the 15th century. Many cross references. Select bibliography p.9-11. Chronological table (AD395-1429) p.741-745. 'Index of persons, terms and symbols which are not title of entries in the encyclopedia'. 'Highly and enthusiastically recommended for all libraries' (*Choice*, v.18, no.6, February 1983, p.776). *Class No:* 930.0"01/14"(031)

Maps & Atlases

[6428]

PLATT, C. The Atlas of medieval man. London, Macmillan London Ltd., 1979. 256p. illus. (many col.), maps. ISBN: 0333270797.

Profusely illustrated century by century overview of medieval politics, religion, warfare, exploration, technology and culture A.D.1000-1500 with the world divided into 8 major areas: Western and Eastern Europe; Near and Far East; South East Asia; India; Africa; and the Americas. Particularly valuable for this comparative approach. *Class No:* 930.0"01/14"(084.3)

Chronologies

[6429]

MAS-LATRIE, L. **Trésor de chronologie, d'histoire, et de géographie** pour l'étude et l'emploi des documents du moyen âge. Paris, Palme, 1859. 2300 col.

Reprinted Torino, Bottego d'Erasmo, 1962.

This massive work provides for the world (excluding America) a basic chronological structure. Chapters on and tables of the various eras are followed by lists of saints and Fathers of the Church (the latter being a table of contents and index to Migne's *Patrologia*, of popes, cardinals, councils and emperors. Lists of rulers, and ecclesiastics for the countries of Europe, Asia and Africa). With natural emphasis on France. *Class No:* 930.0"01/14"(090)

19th Century

Dictionaries

[6430]

BELCHAM, J. *and* PRICE, R. **A Dictionary of nineteenth-century world history** Oxford, Blackwell, 1994. 400p. ISBN: 0631183523.

First point of reference on political, diplomatic, social, economic, and military history with due emphasis on the role of women, African-American and native American figures, and on non-European themes. *Class No:* 930.0"18"(038)

20th Century

Encyclopaedias

[6431]

The Facts on File encyclopedia of the 20th century. Drexel, J., *ed.* New York and Oxford, Facts On File, 1991. ix,1046p. illus., maps, index. $79.95; £39.95. ISBN: 0816024618.

26 contributors. Over 8,000 A-Z entries, 3 columns to the page, covering all fields of human endeavour: art, literature, entertainment, exploration, science, politics, and warfare, providing a guide to the most significant events, people, places, and movements in 20th century history (Mikhail Sergeyevich Gorbachev, 90 lines; Popeye, the sailor man, 20 lines; Boris Nikolayevich Yeltsin, 40 lines). Country entries have boxed chronologies. 750 illus. 150 maps. *Class No:* 930.0"19"(031)

Handbooks & Manuals

[6432]

COOK, C. *and* STEVENSON, J. **The Longman handbook of world history since 1914.** London, Longman, 1991. ix,539p. maps, bibliog., index. £22. ISBN: 0582485886.

Essential facts and figures on major aspects of world twentieth-century history from the outbreak of the First World War organized in 6 sections: 1. Political history in 6 regions + lists of Heads of State and selected ministers/rulers A-Z by country (p.182-244) - 2. Wars and international affairs - 3. Economic and social - 4. Biographies (p.371-409) - 5. Glossary of terms (p.413-62) - 6. Bibliography (p.465-506). 10 maps. A key one-stop compendium. *Class No:* 930.0"19"(035)

Dictionaries

[6433]

TEED, P. **Dictionary of twentieth-century history (1914-1990).** Oxford, Oxford University Press, 1992. 630p. £14.95. ISBN: 0192116762.

Dictionary of nearly 2000 entries relating to major countries, figures, movements, and events that have shaped the century from the First World War to the Iraqi invasion of Kuwait in 1990. Also covers social, cultural, and technological developments. *Class No:* 930.0"19"(038)

Maps & Atlases

[6434]

DOCKRILL, M.L. **The Collins atlas of twentieth century world history.** Glasgow, Harper Collins, 1991. 160p. illus., col. maps, bibliog., index. £14.99; $29.95. ISBN: 0004350618, UK; 0060160098, US.

Published in US as *Atlas of twentieth century world history.*

53 double-page map and text spreads under 5 chronological period divisions 1900-1990, each ending with a chronology of political, social, scientific, and cultural events since 1945. Also 10 essays on periods of strong significance in world history. Glossary p.154-5. Bibliography p.155. *Class No:* 930.0"19"(084.3)

Philosophy of History

Dictionaries

[6435]

RITTER, H. **Dictionary of concepts in history.** Westport, Connecticut, Greenwood Press, 1986. xix,490p. index. $55.00; £49.50. ISBN: 0313227004. ISSN: 07303335.

Attempts 'to identify and discuss some of the key concepts of contemporary historical analysis'. Entries consist of a concise definition of the idea in question, a discussion of the history of the idea, an annotated list of references cited, and suggestions for follow-up reading. 'A phenomenal volume that deserves a place in every reference library' (*Libraries and Culture,* v.24,no.3, Summer 1989. p.396-7). *Class No:* 930.1(038)

Chronology

[6436]

ASIMOV, I. **Asimov's chronology of the world.** New York and London, Harper Collins, 1991. 674p. index. £19.99; $35. ISBN: 0062700367, US; 0002550040, UK.

Combined chronology of world history from 15 billion years ago to 1945. Narrative chapters divided into geographic sections. 'History at a glance' (12 unnumbered preliminary pages). For the general reader rather than the serious student. *Class No:* 930.24

[6437]

BEAL, G. **The Independent book of anniversaries.** London, Headline, 1992. viii,503p. indexes. £20. ISBN: 0747206848.

A page for every day of the year includes a list of the notable people who were born or died on that day and the significant events in history which occurred on that day. Sources discussed p.vii-viii. Indexes of people and events. *Class No:* 930.24

[6438]
Book of days: an encyclopedia of information sources on historical figures and events, keyed to calendar dates. Ann Arbor, Michigan, Pierian Press. Annual 1987-.

1987. 730p. $98. 0876502249. 08910146. 1988. 776p. $98. ISBN 0876502486. ISSN 08910146. Each annual volume contains hundreds of 'resource guides' (or, pathfinders) covering a broad range of subjects that can be precisely dated. Dates selected commemorate anniversaries of important historical events and well-known people. The research guides consist of an introductory essay; reference sources; adult, young adult and children's works on the subject; recordings; feature films; other A/V resources; discussion and project suggestions; sources of further information; cross-reference dates; background information on the contributor; and other events on the day in question. Subject, chronological and contributor indexes. *Reference Books Bulletin 1986-1987*, p.153-4 notes a 'wide variation in the quality of the guides' and recommends 'a more consistent and rigorously applied editorial standard for the bibliographies'. *Class No:* 930.24

[6439]
Encyclopedia of dates and events. Pascoe, L.S., ed. 3rd ed. London, Headway/Hodder & Stoughton, 1991. iv,827p., index. pbk. £16.99. ISBN: 0340539909.

1st ed. 1968. This edition revised by B.A. Phythian.

Chronology from 5000BC to 1988 (with short section on prehistory) arranged in 4 columns across the double page: History - Literature - Arts - Science. Record of man's achievements in brief factual entries. Detailed index p.714-827. *Class No:* 930.24

[6440]
Everyman's dictionary of dates. Butler, A., ed. 7th ed. London, J.M. Dent, 1986. Distributed in the United States by Biblio Distribution Centre of Totowa, New Jersey. viii,631p. £15. $29.95. ISBN: 0460030337.

First published 1911. 6th ed. last reprinted in 1974.

Basic purpose remains 'to make useful dates accessible to the general reader'. Calendars p.1-20. Over 8000 entries A-Z p.21-555. New to this edition is a chronological timebanding section (p.558-631) relating events in the main section to events in other fields of endeavour. No index but 'likely to be the most useful for answering miscellaneous reference questions' (*RQ*, v.11, no.2, Winter 1971, p.164-165). *Class No:* 930.24

[6441]
FREEMAN-GRENVILLE, G.S.P. Chronology of world history: a calendar of principal events from 3000 BC to AD 1976. 2nd ed. London, Rex Collings, 1978. 746p. tables. £15. ISBN: 0860361039.

First published 1975.

Columns have 6 headings: Western Europe - Central & Eastern Europe - Egypt & Africa - The Near East & India - The Far East - Religion & culture. Records chiefly political and military events, whereas B. Grun's *The timetables of history* (*qv*) 'stresses cultural, scientific and other nonpolitical events and trends' (*Library Journal* 1 March 1979, p.618). Index (*c.*20,000 entries). The 2nd ed. updates the chronology by 3 years, as well as making additions to the original. *Class No:* 930.24

[6442]
GRUN, B. The Timetables of history: a chronology of world events based on Werner Stein's *Kulturfahrplan*. Rev. ed. New York, Simon & Schuster, 1987. 688p. $17.95. ISBN: 0317634356.

Kulturfahrplan first compiled 1946. This ed. first published 1975.

Information presented in 7 columns across the double page: 1. History and politics - 2. Literature, theater - 3. Religion, philosophy, learning - 4. Visual arts - 5. Music - 6. Science, technology, growth - 7. Daily life. Timetables start at 5000BC; annual from AD501. Preferred to C. McEvedy's *The Macmillan world history fact finder* by *Library Journal* 1st September 1985, p.190, largely because of its superior 82 page index. *Class No:* 930.24

[6443]
HAYDN, J. Dictionary of dates and universal information relating to all ages and nations. By the late Benjamin Vincent, rev. and brought up to date ... continuing the history of the world to midsummer 1910. 25th ed. New York, Dover, 1969. xii,1614p.

First published 1841.

A dictionary of miscellaneous subjects, arranged A-Z. Each subject is treated chronologically (*e.g.* 'Coroner', in which some statutes relating to coroners are mentioned; 'Mexico', in which *c.*200 events from 1503 onwards are recorded; and 'Telephone', a list of events in the history of the telephone. 'Useful in large libraries for older topics' (*RQ*, v.12, no.2, Winter 1971, p.164). *Class No:* 930.24

[6444]
HOUGH, G.L. Chambers dates. 2nd ed. Edinburgh, Chambers, 1989. 373p., index, pbk. £5.99. ISBN: 0550118314.

1st ed. 1983 under title of *Chamber's dictionary of dates*.

6000 important (?) events throughout history summarized for every day of the year in calendar order. *Class No:* 930.24

[6445]
JOHNSON, D.E. From day to day; a calendar of notable birthdays and events. Metuchen, N.J., Scarecrow Press, 1990. ix,850p. index. $72.50. ISBN: 0810823543.

15000 entries arranged in monthly chapters each beginning with its history and special days. An introductory chapter on the calendar (p.1-8) covers its evolution, the moon cycle, the change from the Julian to the Gregorian calendar etc. A comprehensive index of proper names p.736-850. *Class No:* 930.24

[6446]
JUNG, K.M. Weltgeschichte in Stickworten. Berlin, Safari-Verlag, 1965. 1190p;. illus., ports., maps.

Chronology up to 1965; 6 synoptic columns. German and European slant. *Class No:* 930.24

[6447]
McEVEDY, C. The Century world history factfinder. London, Century Publishing. 1984. 207p. illus. (some col.), col.maps, tables, index. £12.95. ISBN: 0712601937.

Historic highlights 3000B.C.-1954A.D. adduced by 2p. spreads of text, maps and illustrations grouped in 8 chronological sections. Concentrates on political, military and diplomatic history. *Class No:* 930.24

[6448]

Ribbons of time world history year by year since 1492. London, Mitchell Beazeley, 1988. 128p. col. illus., maps. bibliog. index. £8.95. ISBN: 0855337206.

Divided into 6 colour coded categories of human achievement: 1. World events - 2. Literature, religion and philosophy - 3. Art and architecture - 4. Music and other performing arts - 5. Science and technology - 6. National events (British Is.). Bibliography p.122. 50 time panoramas. Over 600 four-colour images. Family reference work. *Class No:* 930.24

[6449]

STEINBERG, S.H. **Historical tables 58BC-AD1990.** 12th ed. updated by J. Paxton. London, Macmillan Reference Books, 1991. ix,324p. £25.00. ISBN: 0333566610.

First published 1939; 11th ed. 1986.

Double-page spread. 6 columns with headings: 1. Western Europe - 2. Central, Northern and Eastern Europe - 3. Countries overseas - 4-6 vary at different periods *e.g.* 4. Constitutional history - 5. Economic history and Natural science - 6. Cultural life. Exact day is given, if available. Progressively fuller entries. This edition reassesses some entries for the early 1980s and adds an index of major events since 55BC (p.291-324). *Class No:* 930.24

[6450]

TRAGER, J. **The People's chronology** a year-by-year record of human events from prehistory to the present. Rev. ed. New York, Harry Holt; London, Aurum Press, 1992. ix,1237p. illus., index. $45; £30. ISBN: 0805017860, US; 1854102346, UK.

First published 1979.

Single sequence of 35000+ descriptive entries covers 30 different fields of human activity (*e.g.* politics, exploration, technology, sport, environment). Analytical index p.1127-1237. *Class No:* 930.24

[6451]

WETTERAU, B., *comp*. **The New York Public Library book of chronologies.** New York, Prentice Hall, 1990. 634p. bibliog., index. $29.95. ISBN: 0136204511.

Timelines arranged in 14 topical chapters *e.g.* Technology, Arts, Sports, War and military history, Politics and law, Education. Bibliography p.622-4. *Class No:* 930.24

[6452]

The World Almanac directory of dates. New York, Longman, 1982. Published in cooperation with World Almanac Publications. 318p. illus. ISBN: 0911818251.

A-Z chronology of major events and phenomena throughout history. Concise entries with basic information. *Class No:* 930.24

Reviews & Abstracts

[6453]

ROGERS, S.W. **'Selected historical chronologies',** *Reference Services Review,* v.11,no.2, Summer 1983, p.15-19.

Comparative review of 12 well-known chronological works that focus on more than one country, examining their scope, format, strengths, special features, and any recognizable bias. *Class No:* 930.24(048)

Archives

Dictionaries

[6454]

Dictionary of archival terminology. Dictionnaire de terminologie archivistique English and French with equivalents in Dutch, German, Italian, Russian and Spanish. Walne, P., *ed.* 2nd ed. München, K.G. Saur, 1988. 212p. indexes. £35. (*ICA Handbook Series, no.7.*) ISBN: 3598202792.

First published 1984 when it superseded *Lexicon of archival terminology* (Elsevier, 1964).

Lists *c.*500 specialist terms of archival science in 7 languages arranged A-Z with definitions in English language order followed by French equivalents and definitions and then by equivalent terms only for the other languages. *Class No:* 930.25(038)

[6455]

WILLIAMS, A.E. **Termau archifau/Archive terms.** Caernarfon, Gwaanaeth Archifau Gwynedd, 1986. iv, 55p. pbk. £4. ISBN: 0901337366.

A vocabulary of archive terms with Welsh-English, English-Welsh sections. Based primarily on the type of material found in local record offices. 'Will be a most useful and valuable reference work in those record offices where documents are catalogued in Welsh and where a large number of scholars are Welsh speaking' (*Journal of the Society of Archivists,* v.8, no.3, April 1987, p.171). *Class No:* 930.25(038)

Yearbooks & Directories

[6456]

VANRIE, V., *ed.* **International directory of archives.** München & London, K.G. Saur, 1988. 397p. £39.00. ISBN: 359821233x.

A new and revised ed. of *Internationale Jahrbuch der Archive.*

Lists archives of historical interest open to the public organized A-Z by country. Data: name of director; name of archive; address with telephone and telex; bibliographic details; hours; user facilities. *Class No:* 930.25(058)

Worldwide

[6457]

INTERNATIONAL COUNCIL OF ARCHIVES, *ed.* **Guides to the sources for the history of the nations/Guides des sources de l'histoire des nations. 3rd series North Africa, Asia and Oceania.** München, K.G. Saur, 1972-.

1. *Guide des sources de l'histoire d'Afrique du Nord, d'Asie et d'Océanie conservées en Belgique* compiled by E. Vandevoude and A. Vanrie. 1972. 622p. Edited by Archives Générales du Royaume.

2. *Sources de l'histoire d'Asie et de l'Océanie dans les archives et bibliothèques françaises* 2v., 1981. *Pt.1 Archives,* xxiii, 539p. £110.00 ISBN 3598214723. *Pt.2 Bibliothèque Nationale* xi, 315p. £65.00. 3598214731. Edited by the Commission Française du Guide des Sources de l'Histoire des Nations. There is a mention of Pt.3 *Aux sources existant dans les autres bibliothèques de Paris et de province.*

3. *Sources on the history of North Africa, Asia and Oceania in Scandinavia. Pt.1 Denmark* compiled by R.C. Hansen. 1980. 842p. £110.00. 359821474x. *Pt. 2 Finland,*

....*(contd.)*

Norway, Sweden, compiled by B. Federly and others. 1981. 224p. £65.00. 3598214758. Edited by the National Archives of Denmark, Finland, Norway and Sweden.

4. *Sources on the history of Asia and Oceania in the Netherlands Pt.1 Up to 1796* compiled by P.H. Roessingh, 1982. 337p. £65.00. 3598214766. *Pt.2 Sources 1796-1940* compiled by F.P. Jacquet. 1983. 547p. £95.00. 3598214774. Edited by the Netherlands State Archive Service.

5. *Sources de l'histoire du Proche-Orient et de l'Afrique dans les archives et bibliothèques françaises Pt.1 Archives* in preparation. 3598214782. *Pt.2 Bibliothèque Nationale*, 1984. ix, 480p. £85.00. 3598214790. Edited by the Commission Française du Guide des Sources de l'Histoire des Nations.

6. *Quellen zur Geschichte Nordafrikas, Asiens und Ozeaniens in der Bundesrepublik Deutschland bis 1945* compiled by E. Ritter, 1984. xlvi, 386p. £65.00. 3598214804.

7. *Guia de fuentes para la historia de Asia en España*, compiled by L.S. Belda, 1987. 284p. £90.00. 3598214820.

8. *Quellen zur Geschichte Afrikas, Asians und Ozeaniens im Österreichischen Staatsarchiv* 1986. xii, 273p. £75.00. 3598214847. Edited by the International Council on Archives.

9. *Sources on the history of Latin America, Africa, Asia, Australia and Oceania in Hungary*, 1990. 520p. £69.00. 359821455. Edited by the National Archives of Hungary.

10. *Sources on the history of Africa, Asia and Oceania in Yugoslavia* 1990. 250p. £65.00. 3598214863. Edited by the Union of the Societies of Archivists in Yugoslavia.

Invaluable for historical research this series also serves as a guide to the organization of European national archives. *Class No:* 930.25(100)

[6458]
O'NEILL, J.E. *and* KRAUSKOPF, R.W., *eds*. **World War II: an account of its documents.** Washington, Howard Univ. Press, 1976. xix,269p. illus. $15.00. ISBN: 0822580531.

Comprises the 18 papers presented at the 8th Conference of the UN National Archives and Records Service, devoted to historical research on World War II. 'The papers cover wartime diplomacy, military biography, access to archival sources, the roles of science and technology and of wartime emergency agencies, and official history programmes' (*Unesco Bulletin for Libraries*, v.31,no.2, March/April 1977, entry 87). *Class No:* 930.25(100)

Pacific Ocean

[6459]
MANDER-JONES, P., *ed*. **Manuscripts in the British Isles relating to Australia, New Zealand and the Pacific.** Canberra, Australian National Univ. Press, 1973. Distributed by Angus & Robertson. xxiii, 697p.

Sponsored by the National Library of Australia and the Australian National Univ. Library.

Inventory of source material in nearly 100 public and private collections, societies (London: p.3-376), firms - arranged geographically 'British Isles' includes Eire. Area covered extends as far as Galápagos. Juan Fernandez, the Marianas, Hawaiian Is., Antarctica. Very detailed index of 90p. 'Sets an even higher standard than its predecessors in this field' (*Commonwealth*, v.17, no.3, June 1973, p.82). *Class No:* 930.25(265)

[6460]
Pacific history a list of primary sources held in University of Queensland libraries. St. Lucia, Univ. of Queensland Library, 1989. 42p. sd. *gratis.*

Briefly annotated list of government reports, consular despatches, Colonial Office correspondence relating to the Pacific as a whole and specifically to Fiji, Hawaii, Kiribati, Nauru, New Caledonia, Norfolk Islands, Papua New Guinea, Samoa, Solomon Is., Tahiti, Tonga, and Vanuatu. *Class No:* 930.25(265)

Europe

[6461]
'Libraries and archives for historians', *History*, v.53,no.179, October 1968 - v.58,no.194, October 1973.

1. Germany, October 1969, p.385-8. 2. Spain. June 1969, p.226-8. 3. France. February 1970, p.65-8. 4. Russia. June 1970, p.21-3. 5. Italy and the Vatican. February 1971, p.50-54. 6. Belgium. June 1971. p.231-3. 7. Poland. October 1971, p.408-10. 8. The Netherlands. June 1972, p.217-20. 9. Austria. October 1972, p.383-6. 10. Ireland. October 1973,. p.392-6. Very brief surveys of archival collections, citing guides and noting facilities for consultation. *Class No:* 930.25(4)

Great Britain

[6462]
'Archives and manuscript collections in the United Kingdom: a supplementary list,' *Archives* v.14, no.63, Spring 1980, p.163-177. Offprints may be obtained from British Records Association, The Charterhouse, Charterhouse Square, London, EC1M 6AU.

Directory of 92 archive and manuscript collections, arranged A-Z by first significant word in title, prepared to admit *bona fide* students, researchers and historians. Data: name, address and telephone number, responsible officer, and material held. First of a series planned by British Records Association to assemble details of archive and manuscript collections not listed in *Record repositories of Great Britain*. *Class No:* 930.25(410)

[6463]
Calendars of charters and rolls in the manuscript collections of the British Library. Cambridge, Chadwyck-Healey, 1989. 18 reels of positive silver halide 35mm microfilm. £950.

Entries for over 75,000 documents including 6000 European documents mostly from France. These include deeds, royal letters, papal bulls, monastic charters, manorial documents, farm accounts, wills, treaties, diplomatic papers, royal household accounts, maps, chronicles, heraldic and illustrated material. 'The calendars of charters are the only fully descriptive catalogue of the contents of these collections. They contain short summaries of the contents of charters acquired by the Department of Manuscripts up to 1911 ... For other types of records such as manorial documents a detailed listing is provided' (*Publisher's brochure*). *Class No:* 930.25(410)

[6464]

CHURCH, R. *and* COLE, J., *comps*. **In and around record repositories in Great Britain and Ireland.** 2nd ed. Huntingdon, Family Tree Magazine, 1990. 102p. bibliog., index. limp cover. £4.95. ISBN: 0951146548.

First published as *In and around record offices in Great Britain and Ireland* by Wiltshire Family History Society in 1987.

Detailed guide to the procedures and facilities of over 200 repositories which hold archives and local history collections. A-Z by 'new counties'. Data: Car parks, facilities for children and disabled, document ordering, postal research, publications, places of interest nearby, nearest Tourist Information Centre. *Class No:* 930.25(410)

[6465]

COX, J. **The Nation's memory: a pictorial guide to the Public Record Office.** London, HMSO, 1988. 64p. illus. (some col). location maps on endpapers. pbk. £3.50. ISBN: 0114402167.

4 contributors. A popular guide to the buildings and to the P.R.O's services. Attempts to convey something of the range of records available for consultation. Of particular value is 'Division of record groups between Chancery Lane and Kew' p.28-29. *Class No:* 930.25(410)

[6466]

FOSTER, J. *and* SHEPPARD, J. **British archives:** a guide to archive resources in the United Kingdom. 2nd ed. London, Macmillan; New York, Stockton Press, 1989. lviii, 834p. bibliog., index. £65. ISBN: 0333443470.

1st ed. 1982.

1048 entries (340 more than 1st ed.). Data: address; telephone; enquiries to (*i.e.* named officer), hours, access, historical background, acquisition policy, major collections, significant non-manuscript material, finding aids, facilities, and publications. Index to collections p.797-828. Guide to key subjects p.829-34. Useful addresses p.xlvii-lii. Useful publications p.liii-lvii. 'Aims to consolidate information for the historian and archivist and provide a starting point for the first-time user of archives' (*Introduction*). Definitive work much improved in this edition. The authors' 'British Archives and archives in Britain', *Journal of the Society of Archivists*, v.11, no.4, October 1990, p.151-5 is an illuminating commentary. *Class No:* 930.25(410)

[6467]

GREAT BRITAIN. HM Stationery Office. **Government Publications Sectional List 17, revised 1 January 1985: Publications of the Royal Commission on Historical Manuscripts.** London, HMSO., 1985. 28p., index. *gratis.*

Sections: Reports and calendar series - Guides to sources for British history - Prime Ministers' papers series - Joint publications series (prepared by local and other record societies) - Other publications. *Class No:* 930.25(410)

[6468]

GREAT BRITAIN. HM Stationery Office. **Government Publications Sectional List 24, revised 1 January 1984: British National Archives.** London, HMSO., 1984. 87p. *gratis.*

Publications of the Public Record Offices in London and Belfast, the Scottish Record Office and the House of Lords Record Office. Sections: 1. PRO: Calendars, guides *etc.* - 2. PRO lists and indexes - 2A. PRO lists and indexes. Supplementary series - 3. PRO Privy Council registers - 4. Rerum Britannica Medii Aevi scriptores - 5. Publications of

.... *(contd.)*

the Record Commissioners - 6. Works in facsimile - 8. House of Lords Record Office publications - 9. Miscellaneous publications - 10. Ireland - 11. Northern Ireland - 12. Scotland. Analytical index. Some entries are annotated. This admirable Section List is regrettably now discontinued. *Class No:* 930.25(410)

[6469]

GREAT BRITAIN. Public Record Office. **Guide to the contents of the Public Record Office.** London, HMSO, 3v., 1963-69.

Supersedes M.S. Guiseppi's *Guide to the manuscripts preserved in the Public Record Office* (1923-24. 2v.), of which it is largely a revision.

The Records transferred to the PRO between 1923 and 1960 'have not only lengthened previously existing series but have added upwards of two thousand classes not known to Giuseppi's *Guide* (*Preface*). Arrangement is by administrative provenance. General classes (*e.g.* Records of the High Court of Admiralty) are allotted separate sections, with introductions. Each type of record (*e.g.* Prize Appeal Records) is briefly annotated. Each volume has a key to regnal numbers; chronological index to statutes cited in text; index of persons and places; index of subject. V.1 has a glossary. V.3 has corrigenda and addenda to v.102. *Class No:* 930.25(410)

[6470]

GREAT BRITAIN. Public Record Office. **Handbooks.** London, HMSO, 1954-. 1-.

1. *Guide to seals in the Public Record Office.* 2nd ed. ISBN 0114401454. 2. *Domesday rebound. Notes on the physical features and history of the Record.* 1954. 3. *List of papers of the Committee of Imperial Defence to 1914.* 1964. 0114401470. 4. *List of Cabinet papers 1880-1914.* 1964. 5. *Shakespeare in the Public Records.* 1964. 7. *List of documents relating to the Household and Wardrobe, John to Edward I.* 1964. 8. *List of Colonial Office Confidential Prints, to 1916.* 1965. 9. *List of Cabinet papers 1915 and 1916.* 1966. 10. *Classes of Departmental papers for 1906-1938.* 1966. 11. *The Records of the Cabinet Office to 1922.* 1966. 0114401500. 12. *The Records of the Forfeited Estates Commission.* 1968. 0114401519. 13. *The Records of the Foreign Office 1782-1939.* 1969. 14. *Records of interest to social scientists 1919 to 1939.* 1971. 011440027x. 15. *The Second World War: a guide to documents in the P.R.O.* 1972. 16. *Records of interest to social scientists. Unemployment insurance, 1911 to 1939.* 1975. 0114400636. 17. *The Cabinet Office to 1945.* 1975. 0114400342. 18. *Records of interest to social scientists 1919-1939: Employment and unemployment.* 1978. 0114400911. 20. *The Records of General Eyre.* 1980. 0114401233. 21. The court of Star Chamber and its records. 1985. x,112p. £7.95. 0114401918. 23. Making sense of the Census: the manuscript returns for England and Wales 1801-1901. 1989. x,146p. £9.95. 0114402191.

No.11(viii,52p.) 'aims to give some guidance in the use of a group of records which has been described as "the most valuable single collection of modern material for historical purposes that can be obtained from official sources"' (*Introduction*). Pt.2 gives 'Summary of Cabinet Office Records to 1922'. 4 plates. *Class No:* 930.25(410)

[6471]
GREAT BRITAIN. Public Record Office. **Information for readers.** London, Public Record Office. 7p. sd. *gratis.*

Basic information: 1. Introduction - 2. How to get there (Chancery Lane and Kew) - 3. Readers' tickets - 4. Hours of opening - 5. The reading rooms - 6. The records and their means of reference - 7. Photocopying services - 8. Other facilites - 9. Copyright - 10. Official records not in the PRO - 11. General rules - 12. Division of records between the buildings. Indispensable for the first-time researcher.
Class No: 930.25(410)

[6472]
GREAT BRITAIN. Royal Commission on Historical Manuscripts. **Accessions to repositories and records added to the National Register of Archives.** London, HMSO. Annual. ISSN: 03080986.

1958-1971 as *List of accessions to repositories.*

1991 ed. (1992) vi,99p. £13.50 ISBN 0114402299. With contributions from over 200 repositories, this publication sets out to provide historians with a concise report of the more important or unusual accessions in the British Isles during the past year. Accessions are listed within sections relating to national, special and local repositories in England, Wales, Scotland and the Isle of Man. Also listed are reports added to the National Register of Archives in 1991. Lists of accessions to archives were published in the *Bulletin of the Institute of Historical Research* from 1923 to 1953. From 1954 to 1956 this was covered by the *Bulletin* of the National Register of Archives (London, NRA. Limited circulation), and from 1957 they were published separately as 'List of accessions to repositories'. *Class No:* 930.25(410)

[6473]
GREAT BRITAIN. Royal Commission on Historical Manuscripts. **Guide to the location of collections described in the Reports and Calendars series 1870-1980.** London, HMSO., 1982. [x], 80p. £3.95. (*Guides to sources for British history No.3.*) ISBN: 0114401446.

Locates major groups of papers and the more important single documents recorded in the 236 volumes of Records and Calendars published by RCHMss since it was established. Arranged A-Z by owner. 'Each volume or group of volumes in the Reports and Calendar series is separately indexed. But these indexes are also amalgamated in the *Guide to the reports of the Royal Commission on Historical Manuscripts Pt.1. Topographical Reports issued 1870-1911*(1914); *1911-1957* (1973). Pt.2. *Index of persons: reports issued 1870-1911* (2v, 1935-1938); *1911-1957* (3v, 1966)' (*Bibliographical note*). *Class No:* 930.25(410)

[6474]
GREAT BRITAIN. Royal Commission on Historical Manuscripts. **Guide to the reports on collections of manuscripts** of private families, corporations and institutions in Great Britain and Ireland issued by the Royal Commission on Historical Manuscripts. London, HMSO, 1914-73.

Pt.1. *Topographical guide.* Reports issued *1870-1911.* 1914. *1911-1957* 1973. xi,536p. ISBN 0114400377.

Pt.2: *Index of persons.* Reports issued *1870-1911.* 2v., 1935-38. *1911-1957.* 3v., 1966. xviii,xvi,xvi,1861p. A cumulated index of all persons mentioned in the individual volumes. *Class No:* 930.25(410)

[6475]
GREAT BRITAIN. Royal Commission on Historical Manuscripts. **Record repositories in Great Britain.** 9th ed. London, HMSO, 1991. vi,46p. index. £3.50. ISBN: 0114402434.

First published 1964.

A geographical directory of 258 repositories which systematically collect and preserve written records. Data: addresses etc.; names and custodians; hours of opening; facilities; and published guides. 'There are three essential tools for the historian choosing to search the vast collections held by local record offices in Great Britain. This is one of them' (*Journal of the Society of Archivists,* v.29, no.9, May 1992, p.90). *Class No:* 930.25(410)

[6476]
GREAT BRITAIN. Royal Commission on Historical Manuscripts. **Surveys of historical manuscripts in the United Kingdom** a select bibliography. London, HMSO, 1989. iv, 20p. indexes. sd. £1.50. ISBN: 0118875299.

Details of nationwide surveys of historical records. Covers 150 completed surveys and 40 in progress in business, economic, ecclesiastical, genealogical, legal, literary and artistic scientific and medical fields. *Class No:* 930.25(410)

[6477]
Guides to sources for British history based on the National Register of Archives. London, HMSO, 1982-.

1. *Papers of British cabinet ministers 1782-1900.* 1982. xi, 75p. £3.95. ISBN 0114401217. 2. *The manuscript papers of British scientists 1600-1940.* 1982. vii, 109p. £3.95. ISBN 0114401225. 3. *Guide to the location of collections described in the Reports and Calendar Series 1870-1980.* 1982. viii, 71p. £3.95. ISBN 0114401446. 4. *Private papers of British diplomats 1782-1900.* 1986. v, 80p. index. £5.95. ISBN 014401888. 5. *Private papers of British colonial governors 1782-1900.* 1986. vii, 66p. ISBN 011440206x. 6. *Papers of British churchmen 1780-1940* 1987, x, 96p. £7.95. ISBN 0114402124. 7. *Papers of British politicians 1782-1900.* 1989. 100p. £8. ISBN 011440223x. 8. *Records of British business and industry 1760-1914.* 1990. 146p. 0114402264. Royal Commission on Historical Manuscripts series of digests of privately owned collections of papers in 'the areas of historical study for which the information itself is most comprehensive and most obviously in scholarly demand.' *Class No:* 930.25(410)

[6478]
MACFARLANE, A. A Guide to English historical records. Cambridge, Cambridge Univ. Press, 1983. ix, 134p. bibliog. ISBN: 0521252253.

Describes the nature of historical records of the period 1200-1800 in five chapters: 1. Rediscovering the English past - 2. Some problems and limitations - 3. Records of the State - 4. Records of estates - 5. Ecclesiastical jurisdiction. Not to be regarded as a systematic guide. Bibliography p.127-134. No index. 'Gives helpful direction on how and where searches might be conducted' (*Choice,* v.21, no.10, June 1984, p.1448). *Class No:* 930.25(410)

[6479]
MACFARLANE, L.J. 'The Vatican archives, with special reference to sources for British and Irish medieval history' *Archives,* v.4, no.21, Lady Day 1959, p. 29-44 and v.4, no.22, Michaelmas 1959, p.84-101.

101 references. The second article has two appendices: 1. 'Transcripts and microfilms of British and Irish material

.... *(contd.)*

extracted from the Vatican archives already available in Great Britain and Ireland'; 2. 'Sources in Rome other than the Vatican which contain British and Irish material'.

Supplemented by L.J. Macfarlane's 'The Vatican archives, with special reference to sources for British medieval history (*Archives*, v.4, no.21, 1959, p.29-44; 92 references) and 'The Vatican archives, with special reference to British and Irish medieval history' (*Archives*, v.4, no.22, 1959, p. 84-101; 101 references). *Class No:* 930.25(410)

[6480]
The National inventory of documentary sources in the United Kingdom and Ireland. Cambridge and Alexandria, Virginia, Chadwyck-Healey, 1985-. Silver halide positive microfiche at 24 x reduction. Two subscription plans. Large order discount.

NIDS is an open-ended series published in units (each containing several hundred finding aids) at the rate of 8 *per annum*. Units 25 x 32 are published 1988/89.

Provides immediate access to over 12000 archives and manuscript collections in national and local government records offices, government academic and public libraries, museums, specialist research institutions, and private collections, by reproducing their finding aids on microfiche. The indexing apparatus offers 3 possible access routes; a list of finding aids; a names and subjects index; and also by titles. A free handbook, *How to use the National Inventory of Documentary Sources in the United Kingdom and Ireland in your research*, is available to prospective users and purchasers. G. Palmer's 'The National Inventory and local history', *Local History*, no.6, May 1985, p.10-11 stresses its usefulness in that area. *Class No:* 930.25(410)

[6481]
Public Record Office current guide 1992. London, Public Record Office, 1992. 24p. 16 fiche in end pocket. ISBN: 1873162030.

Introduction (1. Records in PRO - 2. Access - 3. Arrangement - 4. Scope of Guide - 5. Use - 6/8. Contents and arrangement - 9. Appendices: Table of reigns and Glossary p.19-24). Part 1. Fiches Administrative histories (6) - 2. Class descriptions (8) - 3. Index (2). *Class No:* 930.25(410)

[6482]
The Records of the nation The Public Record Office 1838-1988. The British Record Society 1888-1988. Martin, G.H. *and* Spufford, P., *eds*. Woodbridge, Suffolk, Boydell Press/ The British Record Society, 1990. viii,312p. tables, index. £35. $73. ISBN: 0851155383.

21 chapters by different hands in 4 sections: 1. The history and development of the PRO- - 2. Calendars and indexes - 3. Contrasting consumers - 4. The probate records of the nation: new approaches to wills, inventories and accounts. Includes chapter 8. The thirty-year rule and freedom of access ... 11. National Register of Archives and other nationwide finding aids ... 14. A genealogist's view of the Public Records. Edited texts of papers given at the historical conference in London to mark the PRO's 150th anniversary and the British Record Society's centenary. *Class No:* 930.25(410)

Scotland

[6483]
FERGUSSON, J. 'The Public Records of Scotland', *Archives*, no.8, 1952, p.30-8 and v.2, no.9, 1953, p.4-10. *Class No:* 930.25(411)

[6484]
LIVINGSTONE, M. A Guide to the public records of Scotland deposited in H.M. General Register House, Edinburgh. Edinburgh, H.M. General Register House, 1905,. xxvii,233p.

Descriptive lists in four classes: 1. Crown, Parliament, Revenue and Administration - 2. Judicial records - 3. Titles to land, dignities and offices - 4. Ecclesiastical and miscellaneous records. 4 appendices (*e.g.* 3. Records of Chancery). Index. *Class No:* 930.25(411)

[6485]
STEVENSON, D. *and* **STEVENSON, W.R. Scottish texts and calendars** an analytical guide to serial publications. London, Royal Historical Society; Edinburgh, Scottish Historical Society, 1987. xli, 233p. ISBN: 0861931114, RHS; 0906245087, SHS.

Designed as a companion volume to E.L.C. Mullins' *Text and calendars (qv.)* and is therefore limited to private society publications. Updates, and to a certain extent, replaces C.S. Terry's *A catalogue of the publications of Scottish historical and kindred clubs and societies, and of the volumes relevant to Scottish history issued by His Majesty's Stationery Office 1780-1908* (1909) and C. Matheson's *A catalogue of the publications of Scottish historical and kindred clubs and societies 1908-1927* (1928). Also includes appendix: Royal Commission On The Ancient and Historical Monuments of Scotland Inventories p.189-191. Index p.193-233. *Class No:* 930.25(411)

Ireland

[6486]
HELFERTY, S. *and* **REFAUSSÉ, R., eds. Directory of Irish archives.** 2nd ed. Blackrock, Co. Dublin, Irish Academic Press, 1993. 154p. indexes. softcover. £24.95. ISBN: 0716525070.

First published in 1988.

224 organizations and repositories holding educational, religious and cultural archival material or records of historical significance. A-Z by name of institution. Appendix: Institutions and organizations believed to hold archives but which did not respond to the questionnaires. County and subject indexes. 'The Directory makes no pretence to be a totally comprehensive guide to Irish archives. It is rather an introduction to the many scattered locations where primary source material for the study of Irish history can be found' (*Introduction*) 'The most useful work of reference of its kind to have appeared in this country in recent years' (*Irish Genealogist*, v.7, no.3, 1988, p.482). *Class No:* 930.25(415)

[6487]
LESTER, D., comp. Irish research a guide to collections in North America, Ireland, and Great Britain. Westport, Conn., Greenwood Press, 1987. xvii,348p. index. £47.50. (*Bibliographies And Indexes In World History, no.9.*) ISBN: 0313246645.

792 entries listing libraries and repositories in US (A-Z by State); Canada (A-Z by Province); Ireland and Northern Ireland; and England and Wales (A-Z by County). Appendix

....(contd.)

A: Bookstores and bookdealers - B. Irish local newspapers. Data: A. Purpose of the organization - B. General (Irish) collections - C. Special collections - D. Special services - E. Special rules (use of collections, hours, fees *etc.* - F. Special tips for researchers from the librarians. 'A research tool ... for any area of Irish research' (*Introduction*). but predominently for historical researchers. *Class No:* 930.25(415)

[6488]
NATIONAL LIBRARY OF IRELAND Dublin. **Manuscript sources for the history of Irish civilisation.**
Hayes, R.J., *ed.* Boston, Massachusetts, G.K. Hall, 11v., 1965. First Supplement, 3v., 1979.

A union index (310,000 card entries photolithographically reproduced) to manuscripts relating to Ireland and the activities of Irishmen at home and abroad, 5th-20th century. Assembled from the collections of 678 libraries and archives in 395 places in 30 countries, and from more than 600 private collections. Four main divisions: persons and institutions; subjects; places; dates. The fifth division consists of lists of manuscripts by location. (G.K. Hall & Co., *Catalog, 1979-1980, p.39*). Now available only on microfilm (22 reels). £869. ISBN 0816113831. *First Supplement 1965-1975.* 1979. £310. 0816102481. A further 73,400 cards. *Class No:* 930.25(415)

[6489]
PROCHASKA, A. Irish history from 1700: a guide to sources in the Public Record Office. London, British Records Association, 1986. 96p. bibliog., index. pbk. £6.75. (*Archives and the user, 6.*) ISBN: 0900222077.

Introduction (location and availability of records in P.R.O. and an outline of British administration in Ireland) - Summary of classes of public records which contain material of relevance p.13-87. 'The documents in the PRO. in London constitute one of the largest collections within one institution of primary source material for the study of Ireland before 1900' (*Introduction*). *Class No:* 930.25(415)

Northern Ireland

[6490]
DARWIN, K. 'The Public Record Office of Northern Ireland' *Archives,* v.6, no.30, 1963. p.108-116.
Class No: 930.25(416)

Commonwealth

[6491]
COMMONWEALTH ARCHIVISTS ASSOCIATION.
Colonial related archive and manuscript collections in the UK summary guide to the archive and manuscript collections relevant to the former British Colonial territories in the UK. Burdett, A., *comp.* London, Commonwealth Archivists Association, 1988. 97p.

Lists almost 200 collections A-Z by repository in London, rest of England, Scotland, Wales and Northern Ireland. Omits Public Record Office collections, business archives, and regimental museums. *Class No:* 930.25(41-44)

[6492]
COMMONWEALTH ARCHIVISTS ASSOCIATION.
Commonwealth sources in British official records. Colonial and Dominion Offices. London, Commonwealth Archivists Association, 1985. 93p. typescript, sd.

A catalogue produced by the Public Record Office and the Institute for Commonwealth Studies listing A-Z by country and subject the main Colonial and Dominion Offices record classes relating to Commonwealth countries. Also indicates records now on microfilm. *Class No:* 930.25(41-44)

[6493]
GIPSON, L.H. A Guide to manuscripts relating to the history of the British Empire 1748-1776. New York, Knopf, 1970. xxii,490, xxvip. (*The British Empire before the American Revolution, v.15.*)

A detailed guide to depositories and manuscript sources, official and also belonging to private societies, business firms and church organizations. 11 parts: 1. London depositories of manuscripts (p.3-324) - 2. The English counties (A-Z) - 3. Wales - 4. Scotland - 5. Northern Ireland - 6. Republic of Ireland - 7. France - 8. Spain - 9. Canada - 10. Atlantic and West Indies islands - 11. The United States (p.437-90). Index. *Class No:* 930.25(41-44)

Germany

[6494]
HAASE, C. The Records of German history in Germany and certain other record offices: with short notes on libraries and other collections. Boppard am Rhein, Harald Boldt, 1975. [vii], 194p.

A. Archivie: 1. Literatur - 2. Die zentralen deutschen archivalien - 3. Regionale und lokal Archivverwaltungen und Archivie der Bundesrepublik Deutschland - 4. Archivie in der Deutschen Demokratischen Republik - 5. Oesterreich - 6. Sonstige Hinweise auf Archivalien zur deutschen Geschichte. B. Bibliotheken: 1. Bundesrepublik - 2. DDR - 3. Oesterreich. C. Museen. D. Sonstige wichtige Forschungemöglichkeiten und Forschungschilfen. Glossary p.180-182. *Class No:* 930.25(430)

[6495]
LENZ, W. Archivalische Quellen zur deutschen Geschichten seit 1500/Manuscript sources for the history of Germany since 1500 in Great Britain. Boppard am Rhein, Harald Boldt Verlag, 1975. xxviii,372p. (*Publications of the German Historical Institute, no.1.*) ISBN: 3764616326.

Detailed list of holdings of British national and local archives in the field of modern German history: 1. England (London, p.1-200, then countries A-Z) - 2. Wales - 3. Scotland - 4. N. Ireland, Isle of Man, Guernsey, Jersey. Name index; subject index (11 main headings). *Class No:* 930.25(430)

Hungary

[6496]
KURUCZ, G. Guide to documents and manuscripts in Great Britain relating to the Kingdom of Hungary from the earliest times to 1800. London, Mansell, 1992. xiv,708p. index. £85; $170. ISBN: 0720121469.

Archives and manuscripts (inc. diaries, travelogues, personal and institution papers) relating to Hungary, Austria,

....*(contd.)*

Turkey, and Transylvania, in 36 UK repositories arranged A-Z by location. 'This guide is the result of a painstaking piece of research, and will be of enormous value to historians' *(Reference Reviews,* v.7, no.2, 1993, p.46). *Class No:* 930.25(439)

France

[6497]
Les Inventaires des Archives Nationales de Paris. Paris, Chadwyck-Healey France in association with La Direction des Archives de France, 1991. Fr.215,000. £20,475. ISBN: 2869760116.

740 finding aids (95% not previously published) to the most important collections, and a 132p. printed catalogue and index with a bibliography of research guides and an introduction to the history and use of the Archives. Available either as a complete set or in discrete sections: Complete edition: *Les inventaires des Archives Nationales de Paris.* *Separate sections:* 1. *Section Ancienne* (Middle Ages and Ancien Regime (up to 1789)). Fr.117,600. £11,200. 2869760124. 2. *Section Moderne et Contemporaine* (1789-1940 and 1940-). Fr.62,500. £5,950. 2869760132. 3. *Archives Privées* Fr.44,100. 2869760140. £4,200. 4. *Plans* Fr.14,700. £1,400. 2869760159. *Subject sub-sections:* 1. *La révolution Francaise* Fr.36,700. £3,500. 2869760175. 2. *Les Beaux-Arts* Fr.11,000. £1,050. 2869760153.

Guide de l'utilisateur des Archives Nationales. pbk. 2869760167 is an extremely useful guide even for experienced users.

Les Archives nationales. La Memoire de la France, a glossay A4 brochure, is available from Chadwyck-Healey France, 3 rue de Marivaux, 75002 Paris.
Class No: 930.25(44)

[6498]
—Les Archives Nationales. Etat général des fonds. Paris, Archives Nationales, 5v. 1978-88.

1. *L'ancien régime* edited by E. Taillemite. 1978. 820p. 2860000208. 2. *1789-1940* edited by R. Mathieu. 1978. 656p. 2860000216. 3. *Marine et outre-mer* edited by J. Favier. 1980. 713p. 2860000259. 4. *Fonds divers et additions et corrections aux tomes I, II et III..* edited by R. Marquant. 1986. 432p. 2860000267. 5. *1940-1958 Fondes conservés à Paris.* 1988. Fr220. 2680001425. 'On y trouvera, en revanche, en cinq volumes l'ensemble des ressources documentaires offertes par les Archives Nationales à la date du ler juillet 1976'. This detailed inventory is arranged in broad categories each of which is given an introduction to guide users. 'L'État général des fonds ne dispense pas du recours aux inventaires, il y conduit'. L.L. Frader's 'A guide to the Archives Nationales', *French Historical Studies,* v.15, no.1, Spring 1987, p.170-2 is useful.

A detailed survey of the Archives Nationales collection. L.L. Frader's 'A guide to the Archives Nationales', *French Historical Studies,* v.15, no.1, Spring 1987, p.170-2 is a useful introduction.

The two series, L'état général des fonds and *L'état des inventaires,* follow the same organization: major chronological divisions and then "série". There is no general index to the set, but the table of the standard classification system used in the French archives and detailed tables of

....*(contd.)*

contents in each volume provide access to the section containing relevant material' *(College & Research Libraries,* v.52, no.2, March 1991, p.188-9. *Class No:* 930.25(44)

[6499]
—LES ARCHIVES NATIONALES. L'état des inventaires. Paris, Archives Nationales, 6v., 1985-. Distributed by La Documentation Française.

1. *Ancien régime.* 1985. Fr150. ISBN 28600000674. 2. *1789-1940.* 3. *Marine et Outre-Mer.* 4. *Fonds divers.* 1986. Fr160. 28600001034.

Together with *L'état des inventaires archives départementales, communales et hospitalières* (Paris, Archives Nationales, 2v., 1984. Fr390. set) the completed set of 6v. describe all inventories for regional and national archives, and constitute a major revision of H. Courteault's *État des inventaires des archives nationales, départementales, communales et hospitalières au ier. Janvier 1937* (Paris, Didier, 1938) and its *Supplement 1937-1954* (1955). This information is derived from 'France-Archives', *College & Research Libraries,* v.52, no.2, March 1991, p.188-191). *Class No:* 930.25(44)

[6500]
LANGLOIS, C.V. and STEIN, H. Les Archives de l'histoire de France. Paris, Picard, 1891-93. xviii, 1000p.

Reprinted Nendeln, Liechtenstein, Krauss, 1966.

Fundamental guide to the archive sources for French history in France and elsewhere, including a note on the repository concerned and a description of the classes of documents contained therein. Information on inventories is brought up to date in Courteault *(qv).*

Pt. 1: Archives Nationales, des ministères, départmentales, municipales, et hospitalières; pt.2: Archives relating to French in foreign archive repositories; pt.3: Archives relating to France in French and other libraries.
Class No: 930.25(44)

[6501]
La Révolution française à travers les archives des états généraux au 18 brumaire. Paris, Archives Nationales - La Documentation Française, 1988. 438p. facsims. ISBN: 2860001433, Archives Nationales; 2110019964, La Documentation Française.

251 manuscript and printed documents arranged in 15 chronological and thematic chapters with historical commentary. Un mot sur la provenance des documents et sur les textes de présentation p.437. 'Cet ouvrage n'est ni un manual d'histoire, ni une catalogue d'exposition: il tient un peu des deux *(Avant-propos). Class No:* 930.25(44)

Italy

[6502]
Guida generale degli archivi di stato Italiani. Roma, Ministero Per I Beni Culturali E Ambientali. Ufficio Centrale Per I Beni Archivistici, 5v., 1981-1990.

1. *A-E* 1981. xviii, 1040p. 2. *F-M* 1983. xvi, 1088p. 3. *N-R* 1986. xiv, 1301p. 'Archivo centrale dello Stata' with index v.1, p.33-295 then arrangement is A-Z by state archive. Descriptive entries, many with bibliographical references. To be completed in 5v. including an index volume. 'This will make available in print a summary description of what are probably the most extensive archival records, in terms of

....(contd.)

both chronological range and type of material preserved in a single country' (*Archives*, v.18, no.79, April 1988, p.167-168). *Class No:* 930.25(450)

Vatican City

[6503]

BOYLE, L.E. A Survey of the Vatican archives and of its medieval holdings. Toronto, Pontifical Institute of Medieval Studies, 1972. 250p. bibliog., index. ISBN: 0888443501.

General introduction. Bibliography p.173-221.

Class No: 930.25(456.31)

[6504]

FINE, K.A. Des Vatikanische Archiv Einführung in die Bestände und ihre Erforschung. 2nd ed. Rome, Regensburg, 1951. xii, 185p.

First published 1943.

Necessary tool for anyone proposing to work on the Vatican Archives. Introduction on the organization and history of the Archives; List of the archive groups, with brief descriptions and notes on inventories and bibliography; List of published registers, accounts, and reports of papal nuncios. *Class No:* 930.25(456.31)

Malta

[6505]

DONALDSON, G. A Handlist of manuscripts in the British Isles relating to Malta. Valletta Government Printing Press, 1950. 85p. (*Institute of Historical Research publication no.7.*)

Entries are arranged topographically *i.e.* name of town of county where they are located. *Class No:* 930.25(458.2)

Spain

[6506]

Guia de les archivos estatales Españoles. 2nd ed. Madrid, Ministerio De Cultura Direccion General De Bellas Artes Y Archivos. Subdireccion General De Archivos Inspeccion Tecnica De Archivos, 1984. 244p. illus. map, tables, index, pbk. ISBN: 8450506522.

First published 1977.

Directory arranged in 4 sections: Archives historicos Generales; Regionales; De Distrito; Provinciales. *Class No:* 930.25(460)

USSR

[6507]

GRIMSTED, P.K. Archives and manuscript repositories in the USSR. Princeton, Princeton Univ. Press, 3v., 1972-1988.

1. *Moscow and Leningrad.* 1972. xxx, 436p. $64.50. ISBN 0691051496. Parts A-G (A. General archival bibliography and research aids - B. Central State archives of the USSR - C. Archives and manuscript collections of the Academy of Sciences of the USSR - D. Special archives - E. Manuscript divisions of libraries and museums in Leningrad - G. Republic and local archives in Moscow and Leningrad.) Appendix 2: Reference aids for paleography and ancillary history disciplines. Glossary of archival terms. Author-title index; subject index (p.415-36). 'Provides firm guidelines

....(contd.)

for those working with regional sources in the USSR today' *Library journal*, v.98, no.13, July 1973, p.2056).

—Supplement 1: Bibliographical addenda. Zug, Inter Documentation Co. AG, 1976, 217p.

425 annotated entries (*e.g.* for *c.*150 selected catalogues, etc. of medieval Slavic manuscript collections).

2. *Estonia, Latvia, Lithuania, and Belorussia.*. 1981. xliii, 929p. $81.50. ISBN 0691052794. Parts H-L (H. General archival bibliography and research aids - I. Estonia - J. Latvia - K. Lithuania - L. Belorussia). Appendix 1. Procedural information: archival organization, access and working conditions - 2. Geographic name tables - 3. Charts and maps of administrative territorial divisions - 4. Glossary of archival terms (p.689-715). Pt. M. A preliminary bibliography of descriptions of archival materials ... now in collections outside the USSR. p.717-830. Author/title and subject indexes.

3. *Ukraine and Moldavia. Book 1. General bibliography and institutional directory.* 1988. liii,1107p. $125.00. ISBN 069105391x. In 3 parts: 1. Bibliographical list of reference literature relevant to historians, archivists *etc.* - 2. Specific archival and manuscript repositories (short description of institution; published lists of collection's holdings) - Appendix: Procedural information for research in Soviet archives. Book 2 will recount the historical development of these institutions. *Class No:* 930.25(47)

[6508]

—GRIMSTEAD, P.K. A Handbook for archival research in the USSR. International Research and Exchanges Board, Kennan Institute for Advanced Russian Studies, 1989. Distributed by IREX of Princeton, New Jersey. 430p. index, pbk. $19.95.

Definitive and well-documented work on Soviet archive administration and its terminology. Access to archival material is explicated and the major bibliographies and reference works listed. 3 appendices focus on the more important repositories in Leningrad and Moscow; the state archives of the Russian Soviet Republic; and the state archives of the non-Russian republic. 'This impressive, thorough, and well-organized reference tool will prove indispensable to anyone contemplating archival research in the Soviet Union' (*Choice*, v.27, no.2, October 1989, p.288). *Class No:* 930.25(47)

[6509]

—GRIMSTED, P.K. 'Recent publications on archives and manuscript collections in the Soviet Union' : a selective survey. *Slavic Review*, v.41, no.3, Fall 1982, p.511-533. Also distributed as an offprint. *Class No:* 930.25(47))

[6510]

—GRIMSTED, P.K. Recent Soviet archival literature: a review and preliminary bibliography of selected reference aids. Washington, DC., Kennan Institute for Advanced Russian Studies, 1987. 122p. sd. (*Occasional paper No.7.*)

Some material previously appeared as 'A new Soviet Directory of Archives and Manuscript Repositories: a major contribution,' *Slavic Review*, v.45, no.3, Fall 1986, p.534-544.

In 3 parts: 1. General archival bibliographies and reference aids - 2. Literature relating to individual repositories or systems - 3. Bibliography of selected recent Soviet archival literature. 'The present study is in origin ... an overgrown review article of a major new Soviet archival reference publication. At the same time and in a broader

....*(contd.)*

context, it is a hasty update of my earlier coverage and review of recent general Soviet archival reference literature, with emphasis on repositories in Moscow and Leningrad' (*Preface*). *Class No:* 930.25(47)

RSFSR

[6511]
GRANT, S.A. *and* BROWN, J.H. **The Russian Empire and the Soviet Union** : a guide to manuscript and archival materials in the United States. Boston, Massachusetts, G.K. Hall for the Kennan Institute for Advanced Russian Studies, The Wilson Center, 1981. xi, 632p. indexes. ISBN: 0816113009.

Arrangement is A-Z by state, city and thereunder by repository, institution or individual. *Class No:* 930.25(470)

[6512]
Guide to the collections in the Hoover Institution archives relating to Imperial Russia, the Russian revolutions and civil war, and the first emigration. Leadenham, C.A., *comp.* Stanford, Calif., Stanford Univ., Hoover Institution Press, 1986. xx,208p. index. £16.60; $18.95. (*Hoover Bibliographic Series, no.68.*) ISBN: 081792681x.

Descriptive list of 676 archival collections arranged under 13 broad chronological, geographical and subject headings. List of collection titles A-Z p.1-14. Index p.147-208. The Hooverian Institution holds the largest archive pertaining to 20th century Russian affairs outside the Soviet Union. *Class No:* 930.25(470)

[6513]
HARTLEY, J.M., *ed.* **The Study of Russian history from British archival sources.** London, Mansell Publishing Ltd., 1986. lx, 184p. £26.00. ISBN: 0720117844.

11 papers read at a conference organized by the London School of Slavonic and East European Studies in 1984 as part of a project to prepare a comprehensive guide to sources in the British Isles. P.H. Grimsted's 'Foreign collections and Soviet archives' comments on the need to be aware of the corresponding papers in the Soviet Union. 'The hope she expresses, that other western countries will follow the British example and draw up a guide along the lines promised here will be widely shared' (*Archives*, v.18, no.78, 1987, p.115-116). *Class No:* 930.25(470)

[6514]
—HARTLEY, J.M. **Guide to documents and manuscripts in the United Kingdom relating to Russia and the Soviet Union.** London, Mansell Publishing Ltd., 1987. xxiii, 526p. bibliog., index. £50.00 $110.00. ISBN: 0720118050.

The product of a three-year project undertaken at the School of Slavonic and East European Studies 'to record systematically for the first time the location of documentary material relating to Russia and the Soviet Union in the United Kingdom' 331 repositories and their collections are listed A-Z by town. Bibliography p.xxiii. Does not cover material in the Public Record Office, the House of Lords, or the India Office Library and Records, whose collections were judged to be generally known. Unfortunately questionnaires to almost 400 institutions reasonably expected to hold important material either failed to elicit a reply or else resulted in a nil return. But Appendix 1. Privately held papers described in the printed reports of The Royal Commission on Historical Manuscripts, or listed in the

....*(contd.)*

National Register of Archives and the National Register of Archives of Scotland p.409-418. Appendix 2. Unrecorded papers in private ownership p.418-421. 'Of crucial value to historians, particularly as so much material in Russia is inaccessible' (*Archives*, v.18, no.78, 1987, p.124-125). *Class No:* 930.25(47)

[6515]
LESURE, M. **Les Sources de l'histoire de Russie aux Archives Nationales.** Paris, École des Hautes Études en Sciences-Sociales, 1970. 502p. index. (*Études sur l'Histoire, l'Économie et la Sociologie des Pays Slaves, no.15.*) ISBN: 2713204941.

Encompasses public, private and business firm sources. Detailed index of persons, subjects and places. *Class No:* 930.25(470)

Poland

[6516]
MILEWSKI, W., *and others.* **Guide to the archives of the Polish Institute and Sikorski Museum.** London, Orbis Books, 1985. xxiv, 25-375p. index. ISBN: 0901149284.

323 entries relating to Records of the Civil Service; Private collections; and Subject collections. An outline history of the Archives, p.xi-xviii. The Institute's archives contain the largest collection of primary sources ouside Poland, with special emphasis on the Second World War period. 3 further volumes are planned, the next to appear is expected to be *The Polish armed forces 1939-1947*. *Class No:* 930.25(475)

Netherlands

[6517]
PIRENNE, L.P.L., *ed.* **De Rijksarchieven in Nederland.** S'Gravenhage, Staatsuitgeverij, 2v., 1973.

Official guide to the Dutch archives which summarises the contents of the State collections and indicates the extent of different categories of records. 'This is the most up-to-date guide available ... but it should be noted that it does not deal with municipal archives or with those of private firms or families unless they have found their way into the keeping of the state' (*Acta Historiae Neerlandica*, v.8, 1975, p.159). *Class No:* 930.25(492)

Belgium

[6518]
Het Rijkarchief in de provinciën Overzicht van de fondsen en verzamelingen 1. De Vlaamse provinciën. Brussel, Algemeen Rijksarchief, 1975. 405p.

Survey of material in the archive depositories of the provinces of Antwerp, Beveren-Waas, Bruges, Ghent, Hasselt, Kortrijk and Ronse. Data includes history, contents, and survey of printed and manuscript inventories. *Class No:* 930.25(493)

Asia

[6519]

NUNN, G.R. **Asia and Oceania** a guide to archival and manuscript sources in the United States. London and New York, Mansell Publishing Ltd., 5v., 1985. 2550p. £280.00; $415.00. ISBN: 0720117135.

V.1 Alabama - District of Columbia. [xxvi], 495p. Sources p.xvi-xxvi. V.2 District of Columbia. 496-1036p. V.3. Florida - Minnesota. 1037-1489p. V.4. Mississippi-Wyoming. 1491-1904p. V.5. Index. 1905-2456p. Annotated descriptive entries encompassing all unpublished materials, notably archives and manuscripts in 100 major and 360 smaller repositories, but excluding doctoral dissertations. Geographical coverage is Afghanistan eastwards *i.e.,* excluding Israel, Arab Middle East, Soviet Asia and also Hawaii and Australia. 'An indispensable research tool with which academic libraries will need to equip themselves' (*British Book News,* October 1985, p.588). *Class No:* 930.25(5)

[6520]

NUNN, G.R. **Canada and Asia: a guide to archives and manuscripts.** London, Mansell, 1993. 800p. £120; $240. ISBN: 0720121108.

Definitive listing of archival holdings listed by province, city or town, and name of repository. Exhaustive subject index. Complementary volume to the author's *Asia and Oceania: a guide to archival and manuscript sources in the United States (q.v.). Class No:* 930.25(5)

Asia—Far East

[6521]

MATTHEWS, N *and* WAINWRIGHT, M.D., *comps*. **A Guide to manuscripts and documents in the British Isles relating to the Far East.** London, Oxford Univ. Press, 1977. xiv, 182p. ISBN: 0197135919.

'Far East' embraces China, Japan, Korea, Mongolia, Tibet and Soviet Asia. The inventory covers such repositories as the Public Records Office, county record offices, missionary society archives and material still in private custody. *Class No:* 930.25(51/52+57)

Tibet

[6522]

SINGH, A.K.J. **A Guide to source materials in the India Office Library and Records for the history of Tibet, Sikkim and Bhutan** 1765-1950. London, The British Library, 1988. viii, 187p. £30. ISBN: 071230634x.

'The main emphasis of the guide is upon the archives held in India Office Records both official and private, which uniquely document the development of British India's political relations with the Himalayan region'. Appendix: Brief notes on other archival sources in Britain, India, Sikkim, Bhutan and China p.171-2. *Class No:* 930.25(515)

Asia—Middle & Near East

[6523]

GREAT BRITAIN. India Office Library and Records. **Sources for Middle East studies.** Tuson, P. 2nd ed. London, India Office Library And Records, 1984. 21p. bibliog. sd. *gratis.*

Originally as *A brief guide to sources for Middle East studies in India Office Records* (1982).

....(contd.)

Introduction (Britain, India and the Middle East; India Office Records) p.1-4. Descriptive list of IOR sources, p.5-14. Index of Middle East countries covered by the Records, p.15-21. Bibliography, p.21. *Class No:* 930.25(53+56)

[6524]

MATTHEWS, N. *and* WAINWRIGHT, M.D. **A Guide to manuscripts and documents in the British Isles relating to the Middle East and North Africa.** Oxford, Oxford Univ. Press, 1980. 482p.

One of a series of 4v. (the others concern the Far East, Africa south of the Sahara, and South and south-east Asia) recognised by the International Council on Archives and Unesco as the UK contribution to the 'Sources of history of the nations: Asia and North Africa' series.

Coverage: the Arab countries of Middle East and North Africa, Israel, Cyprus, Turkey, Iran and certain regions of the Caucasus, Central Asia and the Crimea. Sections: England (London, p.1-221); Rest of England (locations A-Z), Wales, Scotland, Northern Ireland, Eire. 'Papers in private custody', p.387-419. Some detail in inventories. Inclusion of material does not necessarily mean that is is available for study. Detailed index, p.421-82. An essential reference source 'until at least the end of the century' (*British book news*, July 1980, p.401). *Class No:* 930.25(53+56)

Asia—South & South East

[6525]

LOW, D.A., *and others eds*. **Government archives in South Asia:** a guide to national and state archives in Ceylon, India and Pakistan. Cambridge, Cambridge Univ. Press, 1969. xii, 355p. chart. ISBN: 521075076.

Contents: Ceylon (introduction; holdings; publications) - India (introduction; national archives of India; records of Residencies and Agencies, Andra Pradesh ... West Bengal) - Pakistan (East Pakistan; West Pakistan). An inventory, with emphasis on the national archives of India. No index. 'The most comprehensive and up-to-date account of the historical material available in the national and state archives of India, Pakistan and Ceylon. It does not, however, cover district records' (*Asian Affairs*, v.57, N.S. no.1, pt.2, June 1970, p.236-7). *Class No:* 930.25(54+59)

[6526]

WAINWRIGHT, M.D. *and* MATTHEWS, N., *comps*. **A Guide to Western manuscripts and documents in the British Isles relating to South and South East Asia.** London, Oxford Univ. Press, 1965. xix,532p.

Lists of 80 manuscript depositories in London (p.1-258); England (excluding London (p.259-357); Wales and Monmouthshire; Scotland; Northern Ireland; Eire; Papers in private ownership (not deposited); Addenda. Omits the India Office Library collections; 'to have included these would at least have doubled the size of the work' (*Preface*). Detailed index, p.475-532. Well produced. 'An indispensable source of reference' (*Times Literary Supplement,* no.3,297, 6 May 1965, p.357). *Class No:* 930.25(54+59)

[6527]
—PEARSON, J.D. A Guide to manuscripts and documents in the British Isles relating to South and South-East Asia. London, Mansell, 2v., 1989-1990. ISBN: 0720119618.

Supplement to *A guide to Western manuscripts and documents in the British Isles relating to South and South East Asia* (1965).

1. *London*. 1989. vii,319p. index. £60.00. ISBN 0720119618. 2. *British Isles*. 1990. xvi,384p. index. £70.00. ISBN 072012011x. J.D. Pearson writes on 'The supplement to Wainwright and Matthews', *South Asian Studies* (British Library, 1986), p.106-8. *Class No:* 930.25(54+59)

India

[6528]
INTERNATIONAL COUNCIL OF ARCHIVES. Guide to the sources of Asian history 3. India. New Delhi, National Archives of India, 6v., 1987-.

1. National Archives. 1987. xi,165p. Guide to 11 A-Z ministry archives of Government of India. Each chapter gives genesis of the current structure of the Ministry concerned, its organizational history, access regulations, and photographic services. 'A useful source of information on the rich collections of the National Archives' (*Bulletin of the School of Oriental and African Studies, Univ. of London*, v.54, no.1, 1991, p.241-2). Projected volumes. 2. National Archives - 3/5. State/Union/Territory archives - 6. Directory of custodial institutions in India. *Class No:* 930.25(540)

[6529]
MOIR, M. A General guide to the India Office Records. London, The British Library, 1988. xvl, 331p. frontis., bibliog., index. £35.00. ISBN: 0712306293.

Extends W. Foster's *A guide to the India Office Records 1600-1858* (Eyre & Spottiswoode for The India Office, 1919).

1. The administrative background (p.3-124) - 2. The India Office Records (Summary list of 50 lettered classes p.129-30; Descriptive inventory A-Z p.131-275). Appendix 2. Notes on archival sources ... for areas outside British India or on its frontiers. Bibliography p.292-300. Analytical index. Authoritative, comprehensive and well-documented account of IOR holdings. IOR is 'the most important accumulation of historical source material in Britain for the study of politics, administration and commerce in South Asia and related areas from the early seventeenth to the mid-twentieth century' (*Preface*). *Class No:* 930.25(540)

[6530]
SETON, R. The Indian Mutiny 1857-58 a guide to source material in the India Office Library and Records. London, The British Library, 1986. xvi, 99p.+8p.pl. illus., bibliog., index. £12.95. ISBN: 0712300414.

Indispensable guide to the wealth of archival material dispersed in the IOLR's vast collections. Grouped in 4 main sections: 1. Records of the East India Company, the Board of Control, and the India Office - 2. Proceedings of the Government of India and of the Presidencies and Provinces - 3. Records of Residents and Agents in the Princely States - 4. Private papers. Bibliography p.89-94. Intended 'to facilitate access to the more rewarding sources' (*Introduction*). *Class No:* 930.25(540)

[6531]
SHAFAAT AHMAD KHAN. Sources for the history of British India in the seventeenth century. London, Curzon Press; Totowa, New Jersey, Rowman and Littlefield, 1975. ix, 395p. index. ISBN: 0700700471, UK; 0874715628, US.

First published in 1926.

Assembles and annotates manuscript material physically scattered in the British Museum Library, the Public Record Office, Bodleian Library, All Souls College Oxford, India Office Library and Records, Guildhall Library, and Lambeth Palace Library, with a final chapter on archives in Indian record offices. *Class No:* 930.25(540)

[6532]
SUTTON, S.C. A Guide to the India Office Library with a note on the India Office records. 2nd ed. London, HMSO, 1967. Reprinted with correction 1971. xii, 122p. illus., facsims.

First published 1952.

The India Office Library is one of the largest Orientalist libraries in the world. Resources comprise printed books; MSS; drawings and prints; photographs. The account of India Office records, a new feature 'will be useful until the full guide to the Records, now being prepared, is completed ... Indispensable for all serious orientalists' (*Times literary supplement*, no.3,442, 15 February 1968, p.166). *Class No:* 930.25(540)

Sri Lanka

[6533]
WIMALARATNE, K.D.G. An Introduction to the national archives - Sri Lanka. Colombo, National Science Council of Sri Lanka, 1978. 32p. bibliog.

'A survey of the development, functions and organization of Sri Lanka's national archives (V. Samaraweera. *Sri Lanka*, 1987. Entry 551). *Class No:* 930.25(548.7)

Pakistan

[6534]
ATIQUE ZAFAR SHEIKH. 'The National Archives of Pakistan' p.210-215, *South Asian studies* (British Library, 1986).

Includes a list of important holdings. *Class No:* 930.25(549)

[6535]
A Handbook of archives and material on Pakistan's freedom struggle. 3rd ed. Karachi, Archives of Freedom Movement, University of Karachi, 1988. xxxii,417p. col. illus. Rs300; $30. ISBN: 9698069003.

Detailed guide to All-India Muslim League (1906-47) and the Pakistan Muslim League (1947-69) archives. *Class No:* 930.25(549)

Israel

[6536]
ALSBERG, P.A., *ed*. Guide to the archives of Israel. Jerusalem, Israel Archives Association, 1973. 257p.

Original ed. published in Hebrew 1966.

Inventories archives, and major collections of documents, papers and monographs dealing with Zionist, Jewish or Israeli history, sciences, politics, etc. Comprehensive and informative. B. Wassersteins 'Libraries and archives 12:

....*(contd.)*

Israel', *Archives*, v.60, 1975, p.56-61 gives a brief history of the collections in the Jewish National Library, the Hebrew University Library, and other archives in Jerusalem. *Class No:* 930.25(569.4)

[6537]

SEGALL, A., *ed*. **Guide to Jewish archives.** Jerusalem. World Council on Jewish Archives, 1981. 90p.

Lists repositories in Israel and elsewhere with details of history and scope of their collections. *Class No:* 930.25(569.4)

Myanmar

[6538]

GREAT BRITAIN. India Office Library and Records. **A Brief guide to the sources for the study of Burma** in the India Office Records. Griffin, A.A. London, India Office Library and Records, 1979. 25p., map.

Introduction (*c.* 1600-1795; 1795-1897; 1897-1948) - Sources (1. Correspondence; 2. Proceedings; 3. Minutes; 4. Departmental records; 5. Non-archival collections and special groups; 6. Official publications; 7. Maps; 8. European manuscripts; 9. Biographical sources). Appendices: 1. Summary list of main classes and series of official archives; 2. List of European manuscript collections (17). *Class No:* 930.25(591)

Africa

[6539]

'Archival resources for African studies in the United Kingdom, p.190-213, *African studies* (The British Library, 1986).

In government departments; societies and other organizations; local record and archives offices; and in private archives. *Class No:* 930.25(6)

[6540]

HANNAM, H. 'The Documentation of colonial rule in Africa', *African Research and Documentation*, no.27, 1981, p.8-14.

A description of the various classes of documents produced in connection with British colonies. Useful table of Publications of British African colonies deposited in the Public Record Office, A-Z by colony, p.13-14. *Class No:* 930.25(6)

[6541]

MWIYERIWA, S.S. 'Developments in African archives', p.246-257, *African studies* (The British Library, 1986).

'The nature of the archival landscape in Africa' with specific reference to Uganda; Ghana; Senegal; Sudan; Nigeria; Kenya; Zanzibar; Zimbabwe, Zambia, Malawi; and elsewhere. 11 refs. *Class No:* 930.25(6)

[6542]

PEARSON, J.D. **Guide to documents and mansucrips in the British Isles relating to Africa.** London, Mansell, 2v., 1993. 300p.++ 300p. £200. ISBN: 0720120888, (1); 072012090x, (2).

Much extended and revised edition of N. Matthews and M.D. Wainwrights *A Guide to manuscripts and documents in the British Isles relating to Africa* (OUP, 1971).

1. London. 2. British Isles outside London. Lists and describes manuscripts in African and Western languages

....*(contd.)*

relating to Africa south of the Sahara. Pearson is Emeritus Professor of Bibliography with special reference to Asia and Africa in the University of London. *Class No:* 930.25(6)

[6543]

SOUTH, A., *comp*. **Guide to non-Federal archives and manuscripts in the United States relating to Africa.** London, Hans Zell for the National Archives and Records Administration, Washington, D.C., 2v., 1989. ix,1250p. £140.00. ISBN: 0905450566, v.1; 0905450574, v.2; 0905450558, set.

V.1: Alabama - New Mexico. V.2: New York - Wisconsin. Index. Describes material located in US A-Z by state, city and by series or collection. Entries include name of series or collection title, dates, amount of material, subjects, and areas of Africa concerned. Bibliography p.1106-9. Alphabetical list of repositories p.1110-21. *Class No:* 930.25(6)

Sudan

[6544]

HOLT, P.M. 'The Archives of the Mahdia', *Sudan Notes and Records*, v.36, no.1, 1955, p.71-80.

The Archive is now held at the Central Record Office in Khartoum. *Class No:* 930.25(624)

Africa—West

[6545]

COMMONWEALTH ARCHIVISTS ASSOCIATION. **West African sources in British Colonial Office records.** London, Commonwealth Archivists Association, 1987. 26p. A4 size typescript. sd.

Records relating to The Gambia, Sierra Leone, Ghana, Nigeria and Fernando Po. *Class No:* 930.25(66)

[6546]

Guide to materials for West African history in European archives. London, Athlone Press, 5v., 1962-73.

1. *Materials for West African history in the archives of Belgium and Holland*, by P. Carson. 1962. 86p. 2: *Materials for West African history in Portuguese archives*, by A.F.C. Ryder. 1965. vi,92p. 3: *Materials for West African history in Italian archives*, by J.R. Gray and D.S. Chambers. 1965. viii,104p. 4: *Materials for West African history in French archives*, by P. Carson. 1968. viii,170p. 5: *Materials for West African history in the archives of the United Kingdom*, by N. Matthews. 1973. 225p. V.2 deals with the main sources, in Lisbon, Coimbra, Evora and Porto. Individual volumes and documents are singled out for special mention. Detailed abstract of manuscript catalogues, indexes, etc., with an indication of inadequacies. Index. Most of the items in v.3 are in Rome, notably the Vatican archives. V.5 includes not only major collections, *e.g.* British Library and Rhodes House, but papers held in, for example, the Municipal Library, Warrington or the Companies Registration Office, Edinburgh. *Class No:* 930.25(66)

Africa—East & Equatorial

[6547]

CHAPMAN, D. *and* COOK, M. 'The Archive services of East Africa' *Archives*, v.8, no.38, 1967, p.70-80.

Surveys holdings in Kenya, Tanzania and Uganda. *Class No:* 930.25(67)

Kenya

[6548]

GREGORY, R.G., *and others*. **A Guide to the Kenya national archives.** Syracuse, New York, Program of Eastern African Studies, Syracuse Univ., 1968. vi,452p. (*Syracuse Univ. Eastern African Bibliographical Studies, no.3.*)

Guide to the microfilms of the provincial and district annual reports, record books, and handing-over reports; miscellaneous correspondence; and intelligence reports. *Class No:* 930.25(676.2)

[6549]

THURSTON, A. **Guide to archives and manuscripts relating to Kenya** and East Africa in the United Kingdom. Oxford, Hans Zell, 2v., 1991. xvii,1196p. index. £120; $222. ISBN: 0905450477.

A guide to official and non-official records, the bulk of which date from 1945, concerning the pre-independence period in more than 250 British archival repositories including the Public Record Office and Rhodes House Library. Oxford.

V.1: *Official Records.* xvii,617p. 0905450477. In 2 pts: 1. Official records (Public Record Office; Crown Agents for overseas governments; Foreign & Commonwealth Office; India Office Library & Records *etc.*) - 2. Non-official archives and manuscripts. Administrative chronology of Kenya and East Africa p.xiii. List of principal office holders in Kenya Colony and its predecessors p.xii.

V.2: *Non-official Archives and Mansucripts.* 618-1196p. index 090545099x. Private papers of organizations and individuals held in university libraries, local repositories, museums etc. Regionally arranged guide to records mostly dating from 1945 concerning the pre-independence period held in more than 150 repositories. 'A work of amazing diligence, which collates and integrates a vast body of scattered information' (*Library Association Record,* v.83, no.8, August 1991, p.543). *Class No:* 930.25(676.2)

Africa—Southern

[6550]

Directory of manuscript collections in Southern Africa. Cape Town, South African Library, 1986. viii, 89p. pbk. £4. ISBN: 0869680587.

102 of the more significant repositories in Malawi, South Africa, Zambia and Zimbabwe listed A-Z by institution. Information includes history of their collections, acquisition policy, area of specialization, and publications. 'A useful basic guide' (*African Research and Documentation,* no.42, 1986, p.50-51). *Class No:* 930.25(68)

South Africa

[6551]

Archives year book for South African history. Pretoria, Government Printer, 1938-. Annual.

'This important series consists of original contributions in Afrikaans, English and Nederlands, based on the South African archival sources. The series deals with numerous aspects of South African history and is regarded as a mirror of the activities of history students at South African universities' (Musiker, R. *Guide to South African reference books* (4th ed.). 1965.p.73). *Class No:* 930.25(680)

Zimbabwe

[6552]

JOHNSTONE, I.J. **A Guide to Zimbabwe-related documentation in Britain.** Harare, National Archives of Zimbabwe, 1985. 503p. index.

A thorough guide to archives in London (A-Z by institution) and outside London (A-Z by town or city). Poorly reproduced from typescript. *Class No:* 930.25(689.1)

[6553]

KAMBA, A.S. 'National archives of Zimbabwe' *African Research and Documentation*, no.28, 1982, p.10-12.

Outline description of its organization, functions, and publications. *Class No:* 930.25(689.1)

Canada

[6554]

CANADA. Public Archives of Canada. **Catalogue of the Public Archives/Catalogue de la Bibliothèque des Archives Publiques.** Boston, Mass., G.K. Hall, 12v., 1979. $1250. Export $1510.00. ISBN: 081610316x.

Main author-catalogue of *c.*40,000 publications; chronological catalogue of pamphlets published between 1495 and 1950; list of catalogued periodicals. Covers all aspects of Canadian history and culture. *Class No:* 930.25(71)

[6555]

Guide des sources de l'histoire du Canada conservées en France. Ottawa, Archives Publiques Canada, 1982. xix, 157p. ISBN: 0660908867.

9 contributors. The results of a survey undertaken in the Archives Nationales (Paris), the archival repositories of the Départements, in government ministries, and the Bibliothèque Nationale. Chronological limits: from the origins of French Canada to 1940. Preliminaries also in English translation. *Class No:* 930.25(71)

America — Central

[6556]

Research guide to Central America and the Caribbean. Grieb, K., *ed.* Madison, Univ. of Wisconsin Press, 1985. xv,431p. $35.00; £42. ISBN: 0299100502.

75 contributors. Divided between essays on the current state of research and surveys of specific US library and archive resources. In 3 sections: Central America, the Caribbean, and English-speaking Caribbean nations. 'A reference work of exceptional value' (*Bulletin of Latin American Research,* v.6, no.1, 1987, p.116-7). *Class No:* 930.25(728)

Belize

[6557]

BURDAN, J.A. **Archives of British Honduras.** London, Sifton Praed, 3v., 1931-35.

V.1. 1587-1800; v.2 1801-1840; v.3 1841-1884. Each contains a detailed chronology. 'A very important source for Belizean history' (R.L. Woodward. *Belize.* 1980. Entry 234). *Class No:* 930.25(728.2)

Caribbean

[6558]

INGRAM, K.E. **Manuscripts relating to Commonwealth Caribbean countries** in United States and Canadian repositories. St. Lawrence, Barbados, Caribbean Univs. Press in association with Bowker, New York, 1975. xxix, 422p. ISBN: 0854740295.

1,038 numbered entries (with interpolations). 91 repositories (including map collections), those visited being indicated. Geographical order of repositories; entries arranged chronologically. Data include extended descriptions, provenance notes, bibliographical references, and details of the existence of reproductions. Supplement: Chronological short list of entries, 1498-1959. 'List of works to which reference has been made', p.xii-xx. Index, p.345-422. *Class No:* 930.25(729)

[6559]

TYSON, G.F. **A Guide to manuscript sources in United States and West Indian depositories relating to the British West Indies during the era of the American Revolution.** Wilmington, Delaware, Scholarly Resources,1979. xvii,96p. bibliog. index. $25.00. ISBN: 0842021310.

Focuses specifically on manuscript materials relating to Antigua, Bahamas, Barbados, Bermuda, British Virgin Islands, Dominica, Grenada, Jamaica, Montserrat, Nevis, St. Kitts, St. Lucia, St. Vincent, and Tobago for the period 1763-1783. U.S. Depositories A-Z by State; West Indian depositories A-Z by island. Bibliography p.90. *Class No:* 930.25(729)

Jamaica

[6560]

INGRAM, K.E. **Sources of Jamaican history 1655-1838** : a bibliographical survey with particular reference to manuscript sources. Zug, Switzerland, Inter Documentation Co., 2v., 1976. xvii+Øiii, 1310p. ISBN: 3857500174.

Part 1 (1-8 *e.g.* 2. British and Irish repositories and sources 3. Jamaican repositories and sources; 7. Some printed sources; 8. Maps and pictorial records) - Part 2: Descriptive lists, A-K (A. Descriptive list of manuscripts in British, Irish and Jamaican repositories, p.189-947, C. Bibliographies, catalogues and guides ... H. Newspapers and periodicals ... J. Law of Jamaica; K. Parliamentary papers). Supplement, p.1123-1200. Detailed index, p.1200-1310. A descriptive inventory, by the Librarian, Univ. of West Indies. 'Will ... remain for many years to come the most valuable guide to documentary material on Jamaican history for the pre-1838 period' (*Archives*, v.14, no.62, Autumn 1979, p.114-15). *Class No:* 930.25(729.2)

[6561]

—INGRAM, K.E. Sources for West Indian studies a supplementary listing with particular reference to manuscript sources. Zug, Switzerland, Inter Documentation Co., 1983. 412p.

1169 entries describe historical and literary source materials in West Indian depositories. Supplements his *Sources of Jamaican history* (1976). *Class No:* 930.25(729)

Leeward & Windward Islands

[6562]

BAKER, E.C. **A Guide to records in the Leeward Islands.** Oxford, Blackwell for the Univ. of the West Indies, 1965. x, 102p. map, index.

Based on a survey made in 1962. An inventory of records in Antigua, Montserrat, Nevis, St. Christopher and the British Virgin Islands, with some descriptive notes. Includes newspapers; one of the appendices covers maps, plans and drawings. *Class No:* 930.25(729.7)

[6563]

BAKER, E.C. **A Guide to records in the Windward Islands.** Oxford, Blackwell for the Univ. of the West Indies, 1968. xii, 95p., map, index.

An inventory of records in Grenada, St. Vincent, St. Lucia, and Dominica. 'An invaluable source' (R.A. Myers *Dominica*, 1987. Entry 455). *Class No:* 930.25(729.7)

Barbados

[6564]

CHANDLER, M.J. **A Guide to records in Barbados.** Oxford, Blackwell for the Univ. of West Indies, 1965. xi, 204p. map, index.

Based on a survey made in 1960, and the first of a series of volumes that are to cover the records of all the territories in the West Indies. The full inventory (p.1-164) is followed by appendices on special types of material (*e.g.* acts and laws, newspapers, maps and plans). Detailed index. *Class No:* 930.25(729.86)

Latin America

[6565]

Guide des sources de l'histoire de l'Amérique Latine et des Antilles dans les archives françaises. Paris, Archives Nationales, 1984. 711p. ISBN: 2860001042.

Research guide arranged by institution in 3 categories: Archives Nationales; Départemenales et communales; Privées. *Class No:* 930.25(729.99)

[6566]

INTERNATIONAL COUNCIL OF ARCHIVES. **Guides to the sources for the history of the nations: A. Latin America.**

1. *A guide to manuscript sources for the history of Latin America and the Caribbean in the British Isles* by P. Walne. London, Oxford Univ. Press, 1973. 2. *Führer durch die Quellen zur Lateinamerikas in der Bundesrepublik Deutschlands* by R. Hauschild-Thiessen and E. Bachman. Bremen, Schüneman, 1973. 3. *Übersicht über die Quellen zur Geschichte Lateinamerikas in Archiven der Deutschen Demokratischen Republik.* Potsdam, Staatliche Archivverwaltung, 1971. 4. *Guide du chercheur dans les archives françaises: les sources de l'histoire de l'Amérique*

....(contd.)

latine by D. Ozanam. Paris, Institute des Hautes Études de l'Amérique latine, 1963. 5. *Guida delle fonti per la storia dell'America latina esistenti in Italia* by E. Lodolini. Rome, Direzione Generale degli Archivi di Stato, 1976. 6. *Guida della fonti per la storia dell'America latina negli archivi della Santa Sede e negli archivi ecclesiastici d'Italia* by L. Pásztor. Vatican City, Archivo Vaticano, 1970. 7. *Guia di fuentes para la historia de Ibero-América conservados en España* Madrid, Dirección General de Archivos y Bibliotecas, 2v., 1966-69. 8. *Fuentes para la historia de Ibero-América: Escandinavia* by M. Mörner. Stockholm, Riksarkivet, 1968. 9. *Guide to the sources in the Netherlands for the history of Latin America* by M.P.H. Roessingh. The Hague, Algemeen Rijkarchief, 1968. 10. *Guide des sources de l'histoire d'Amérique latine conservées en Belgique* by L. Liagre & J. Barten, Bruxelles, Archives Généraux, 1967. *Class No:* 930.25(729.99)

[6567]
NAUMAN, A.K. A Handbook of Latin American and Caribbean national archives/Guia de los archivos nacionales de America Latino y el Caribe. Detroit, Blaine Ethridge, 1983. ix, 127p. bibliog.

Introduction to resources for potential first-time users. Collections, services, access A-Z by country omitting Cuba, Haiti, Trinidad & Tobago. English and Spanish text. *Class No:* 930.25(729.99)

[6568]
ULIBARRI, G.S. *and* **HARRISON, J.P. Guide to materials on Latin America in the National Archives of the United States.** Washington, National Archives and Records Service, 1974. 489p. $25.00. ISBN: 0911333223.

Supersedes J.P. Harrison's *Guide to materials on Latin America in the National Archives* (1961).

A detailed inventory, with notes on representative documents. Index of issuing bodies, geographic names and selected subjects. Appendices provide lists of National Archives files and of US diplomatic and consular posts with archival records. 'Materials' includes maps, photographs and films. 'An indispensable aid for the researcher' (*Library of Congress information bulletin*, 4 July 1975, p.280-1). *Class No:* 930.25(729.99)

[6569]
WALNE, P., *ed*. **A Guide to manuscript sources for the history of Latin America and the Caribbean in the British Isles.** London, Oxford Univ. Press in collaboration with the Institute of Latin American Studies, Univ. of London, 1973. xx,580p.

A detailed inventory of public repositories. Appendix: 'The British in South America - an archive report'. Addenda. Index, p.521-80 (Ship's names: over 4 columns). A first-rate research tool in its field. 'This is a basic reference work' (*Library Journal*, v.98, no.14, August 1973, p.2266). *Class No:* 930.25(729.99)

USA

[6570]
Archives accessions annual 1988. Joyce, W.L., *ed*. Westport, Conn., Meckler, 1990. 129p. £87.50. ISBN: 0887364209.

Records the holdings of 227 libraries, local history societies, state archival agencies, and special collection repositories. It is the first of an anticipated series, listing

....(contd.)

archive accessions in the US, whose aim is to provide researchers with up-to-date information on acquisitions of genuine research interest. Although dependent on voluntary cooperation it may be compared to the Royal Commission on Historical Manuscript's annual. *Accession to Repositories and Reports added to the National Register of Archives*. *Class No:* 930.25(73)

[6571]
Guide to the National Archives of the United States. New ed. Washington, National Archives Publications, 1987; London, Smithsonian Institution Press, 1988. xxxii, 806p. $25.00 £19.95. ISBN: 0911333231.

Updates 1974 edition.

Comprehensive guide to the records of the Federal Government within the context of the agencies that created or received them. *Class No:* 930.25(73)

[6572]
Guide to the study of United States history outside the US 1945-1980. Hanke, L., *ed*. New York, Kraus International Publications, 5v., 1984-. $418.00. ISBN: 0527368172.

1. *Introductory material. Perspectives. Essays and Reports: Africa through China* lxix, 614p. 2. *Essays and reports: Colombia through India* xi, 627p. 3. *Essays and reports: Israel through Venezuela. Author index v.1-3* 4. *Bibliography: items 1 through 1663* 5. *Bibliography: items 1664 through 3148. Author index. v.4-5.* Compiled by 500 scholars worldwide. Bibliography in 5 sections with several subdivisions: Comprehensive works; Colonial period; The new nation 1789-1876; Growth and development 1876-1945; Post World War II 1945-1980. 'Aims to report on teaching and research ... and to describe archival materials relating to any period of US history in foreign collections' (*Introduction*). *Class No:* 930.25(73)

[6573]
KOENIG, W.J. *and* **MAYER, S.L. European manuscript sources of the American Revolution.** New York & London, R.B. Bowker, 1974. xxiv, 328p. ISBN: 0859350010.

Lists more than 250 repositories in over 100 cities. 3 parts: 1. The British Isles (p.3-141; London, p.23-100) - 2. The Netherlands, France; Spain (p.147-269) - 3. Austria, Germany, Italy, Russia, Sweden (p.273-319). General index. Introductions on continental countries. 'An essential key to diaries, diplomatic correspondence, journals, letters, newspapers, and ships' logs ... It is a monumental achievement' (*RQ*, v.14, no.4, Summer 1975, p.357). *Class No:* 930.25(73)

[6574]
LARSEN, J.C., *ed*. **Researcher's guide to archives and regional history sources.** Hamden, Connecticut, Shoe String Press, 1988. xiv, 167p. $27.50. £19.95. ISBN: 0208012442.

14 contributors. Basic information on skills needed for researching and on location of specific sources. *Class No:* 930.25(73)

[6575]
MUNDEN, K.W. *and* BEERS, H.P. **The Union: a guide to Federal archives relating to the Civil War.** Washington, National Archives & Records Service, 1986. x, 721p. $25.00. ISBN: 0911333460.

Reprint of 1962 edition.

Arranged by departments with detailed notes; analytical index p.505-721. H.P. Beers *The Confederacy a guide to the archives of the government of the Confederate States of America*. 1986. $25.00. ISBN 0911333185 is a companion volume. *Class No:* 930.25(73)

[6576]
NATIONAL HISTORICAL PUBLICATIONS AND RECORDS COMMISSION. **Directory of archives and manuscript repositories in the United States.** 2nd ed. Phoenix, Arizona, Oryx, 1988. 853p. index. $55.00. £36.70. ISBN: 0897744756.

1st ed. 1978. This was a revised ed. of P.M. Hanser's *A Guide to archives and manuscripts in the United States* (1961).

Data on 4560 repositories (an increase of 1400 on the 1978 ed.), museums, galleries, archives and libraries in all 50 states. Arranged A-Z by state/territory, subdivided by locality. Index of repositories in alphabetical order. 'Historians, graduate students, and genealogists will find it indispensable in planning research trips' (*Choice*, v.26, no.2, October 1988, p.286). *Class No:* 930.25(73)

[6577]
The National inventory of documentary sources in the United States. Alexandria, Virginia, and Cambridge, Chadwyck-Healey Inc., 1983-. Silver Halide (archivally permanent) 24 x microfiche in envelopes.

Part 1. *Federal records.* 1985. 1911 microfiche. £3,750. 0898870267. 428 current finding aids in the National Archives and Record Service and a single-indexed finding aids to 7 Presidential Libraries. Separate printed index. Part 2. *Manuscript Division, Library of Congress.* 1983. 889 microfiche. £1,950. 0898870283. Registers to almost 800 of the most important collections. Separate printed index. Part 3. *State Archives, Libraries and Historical Societies.* Academic Libraries and other repositories. Published in 10 units per annum accompanied by COM indexes, 1984-. £6,000 annual subscription. Alternative subscription plans per unit are available. There is an annual updating service to parts 1 and 2. It is anticipated that Part 3 will continue for at least five years before the backlog of existing finding aids is exhausted.

An awesome reference work providing an immediate access to thousands of finding aids to collections the length and breadth of the United States. Potential subscribers are advised to apply for *Handbook for the researcher* and a booklet *NUCMC RLIN and NIDS* advertized as being available *gratis* from the publishers at 1021 Prince Street, VA 22314 or Cambridge Place, Cambridge, CB2 1 NR. *Class No:* 930.25(73)

[6578]
RAIMO, J.W., *ed.* **A Guide to manuscripts relating to America in Great Britain and Ireland.** Westport, Connecticut and London, Meckler Books, 1979. 494p. $150.00. £85.00. ISBN: 0930466063.

A revision of the *Guide* edited by R. Crick and M. Alman (1961), and published on behalf of the British Association for American Studies.

Locates and describes over 300,000 documents on the

....(contd.)
history and literature of the American colonies and the US, held in *c.*325 repositories. Includes political, economic, social and intellectual history as well as American domestic and international affairs, and direct US influence in Great Britain and Ireland. 100 new entries, p.357-467. 'An excellent revision' (*College & research libraries*, January 1980, p.61, noting the very detailed indexing of personal and geographical names, subjects and depositories). *Class No:* 930.25(73)

[6579]
SZUCS, L. *and* LUEBKING, S.H. **The Archives: a guide to the National Archives Field Branches.** Salt Lake City, Ancestry, 1985. 340p. $35.95. ISBN: 091648923x.

Guide to the holdings of the National Archives' 11 regional archives. *Class No:* 930.25(73)

[6580]
UNITED STATES. National Archives. **Guide to cartographic records in the National Archives.** Washington, National Archives, 1971. 444p. index. $25. ISBN: 0911333193.

The National Archives has among its holdings more than 1.6 million maps and approximately 9 million aerial photographs. This guide describes those materials that are maintained in the Cartographic and Architectural Branch, as well as other maps filed with closely related textual records held by other custodial units of the National Archives. Entries arranged under Government departments, agencies, *etc*. *Class No:* 930.25(73)

Amerindians, North

[6581]
HILL, E., *ed.* **Guide to records in the National Archives relating to American Indians.** Washington, National Archives, 1984. 467p. illus. $25.00. ISBN: 0911333134.

First published 1981.

Includes concise information about records that trace the evolution of federal Indian policy, the effects of national policies on traditional Indian culture, Indian wars and their results, and the role of Native Americans in the development of U.S. society. *Class No:* 930.25(73)(=97)

Paraguay

[6582]
WHIGHAM, T.L. *and* COONEY, J.W. 'Paraguayan history: manuscript sources in the United States', *Latin American Research Review*, v.18, no.1, 1983, p.104-17.

Guide to the major collections. *Class No:* 930.25(892)

Australasia & Oceania

[6583]
Catalogue of manuscripts of Australasia and the Pacific in the Mitchell Library Sydney. Sydney. Trustees of the Public Library of New South Wales. 1967 and 1969.

1. *Series A.* 1967. 293p. Primary and secondary source material catalogues 1945-1963. Subject and author indexes.
2. *Series B.* 1969. 500p. Material added 1963-1967. *Class No:* 930.25(9)

Brunei

[6584]

CHUA SUI GIM. 'Guide to modern archives and manuscripts found in the UK relating to Brunei, Sabah and Sarawak,' *Brunei Museum Journal*, v.5, no.1, 1981, p.56-77.

Covers the pre-1963 period. *Class No:* 930.25(911.13)

New Zealand

[6585]

Archives New Zealand a directory of archives and manuscript repositories in New Zealand, the Cook Islands, Fiji, Niue, Tokelau, Tonga, and Western Samoa. Rogers, F., *comp.* Auckland, Archives Press, 1984. vii, 65p. maps, index.

Directory information (inc. hours, fees, acquisition policy, access restriction, published guides) to 155 repositories. Bibliography p.v. 2 maps. Complements *National Register of Archives and Manuscripts in New Zealand.*

Class No: 930.25(931)

[6586]

Directory of archives and manuscript repositories in New Zealand, the Cook Islands, Fiji, Niue, Tokelau, Tonga, and Western Samoa. 2nd ed. Plimmerton, Archives Press, Archives New Zealand. vi,73p. NZ$30. ISBN: 0959777741.

194 entries arranged geographically then A-Z by institution. Data: Name and address, access, guides and other publications, charges *etc. Class No:* 930.25(931)

Australia

[6587]

Directory of archives in Australia. Burnstein, S., *and others, comps.* Granville, NSW, Ambassador Press for the Australian Society of Archivists, 1992. x,527p. index. A$30. ISBN: 0947219064.

458 entries arranged by jurisdiction and geographical area, then A-Z by name of institution. Data: name and address; access details, published guides *etc. Class No:* 930.25(94)

[6588]

Guide to collections of manuscripts relating to Australia a selective union list. Canberra, National Library of Australia, 1986. 21 microfiche set. 42 x reduction. $Aust.20.00. ISSN: 07259107.

First published 1965.

Lists collections of private papers, business records, certain restricted collections and 'fugitive' official collections (*i.e.* hard to find official records held outside the national or State archives offices). Includes some entries relating to other geographic regions notably the Pacific Islands and areas neighbouring Australia. Arranged in 2 pts: entries in numerical order and a consolidated name index of collections and sub-groups within collections. An invaluable tool for all those engaged in historical prime source material.

Class No: 930.25(94)

[6589]

NATHAN, E. 'Archives', chapter 2, Australians: a guide to sources (v.10. *Australians. A historical library*, 1988).

Public records - Archives legislation - Official publications - Access to government archives - Guides and finding aids - Non-government archives. *Class No:* 930.25(94)

[6590]

WHITE, O., *and others, comps*. **Our heritage** a directory of archives and manuscript repositories in Australia. Sydney, Australian Society of Archivists, 1983. 301p. index, softcover. ISBN: 0959556559.

State by state guide. Includes repositories holding film and sound archives and machine readable records.

Class No: 930.25(94)

Palaeography & Epigraphy

[6591]

BISCHOFF, B. Latin palaeography Antiquity and the Middle Ages. Cambridge Univ. Press in association with The Medieval Academy of Ireland, 1990. xi,291p. facsims., bibliog., indexes. £12.95. ISBN: 0521364736.

First published as *Paläographie des romischen Altertums und des abendländischen Mittelalters,* Berlin, Erich Schmidt Verlag, 1979. 2nd ed. 1986.

Authoritative and comprehensive account of the history of the Latin script: A. Codicology - B. History of the Latin script - C. Manuscripts in cultural history. *Class No:* 930.27

[6592]

BROWN, M.P. A Guide to Western historical scripts: from antiquity to 1600. London, The British Library, 1990. Published in North America by Univ. of Toronto Press. 138p. Facsims., bibliogs. £17.95. ISBN: 0712301771.

1. Roman system of scripts - 2. National hands - 3. The insular system of scripts - 4. Anglo-Saxon - 5. Caroline minuscule - 6. Protogothic - 7. Gothic - 8. Italic - 9. Humanistic system of scripts. Appendix: Some common abbreviations p.136. Glossary p.8. Bibliography p.9-12. Index of scripts p.137. Index of manuscripts p.138. 55 plates. A survey of the evolution of scripts with examples in broad chronological sequence. The author is a Curator in the Department of Manuscripts, the British Library.

Class No: 930.27

[6593]

DENHOLM-YOUNG, N. Handwriting in England and Wales. Cardiff, Univ. of Wales Press, 1954. xi, 102p. [33p]. illus., maps.

An introduction to the study of palaeography, with bibliography and annotated plates for students beginning their research on some aspect of English or Welsh history or literature. Emphasis is on the period from the coming of the Caroline minuscule to the 17th century. Sections on types of hands are supplemented by valuable guidance on particular problems and on the use of palaeography in the criticism of texts. *Class No:* 930.27

[6594]

HECTOR, L.C. The Handwriting of English documents. 2nd ed. Dorking, Surrey, Kohler & Coombes, 1980. 136p. illus. (pl.), bibliog., index. £15.00. ISBN: 0903967162.

First published 1958. 2nd ed. London, E. Arnold, 1966.

Six chapters: 1. The equipment of the writers - 2. The equipment of the reader - 3. Abbreviations - 4. Scribal conventions and expedients - 5. English handwriting from the Conquest to 1500-6. English handwriting since 1500. Transcripts of passages represented in plates; bibliography, p.132-3 (works asterisked contain transcribed facsimiles); index. *Class No:* 930.27

[6595]
JENKINSON, H. **The Later court hands in England,** from the 15th to the 17th century, illustrated from the Common Papers of the Scriveners' Company of London, the English Writing Masters and the Public Records. Cambridge, Cambridge Univ., 2v., 1927.

Pt.1: Text; pt.2: plates.

Standard work on English hands of the 15th, 16th and 17th centuries, containing (pt.1) valuable study on various aspects, bibliography, and transcripts and notes for the plates in pt.2. Alphabets in pt.2. *Class No:* 930.27

[6596]
JOHNSON, C. *and* JENKINSON, H. **English court hands AD1066-1500** illustrated chiefly from the Public Records. Oxford, Clarendon Press, 2v., 1915.

Pt.1: Text; pt.2: Plates.

Standard work on English medieval chancery, exchequer and legal hands, containing (pt.1) valuable study on various aspects and bibliography of development of individual letters, abbreviations, and transcripts (where necessary), with detailed notes for the plates in pt.2. *Class No:* 930.27

[6597]
PARKES, M.B. **English cursive book hands 1250-1500.** 2nd ed. London, Scholar Press, 1979. xxxii, 24p. facsims., bibliog. £15. ISBN: 0859675351.

First published Oxford, Clarendon Press, 1969.

Basically, 24 pages of examples of book hands, with notes and transcriptions facing. Preliminaries include notes on Anglicana book hands, the handwriting of university scribes, the handwriting of individual scribes, etc.' also a valuable introduction (footnoted), 'a note on palaeographic terms' (p.xxvi) and a select bibliography. *Class No:* 930.27

[6598]
WRIGHT, C.E. **English vernacular hands** from the twelfth to the fifteenth centuries. Oxford, Clarendon Press, 1960. xx,25p. facsims, bibliog.

24 facsimiles and transcriptions. The introduction (p.1-xx) discusses The Vernacular Manuscript Tradition and Handwriting. *Class No:* 930.27

Bibliographies

[6599]
JONES, L.E. **Medieval Latin palaeography:** a bibliographical introduction. Toronto, Univ. of Toronto Press, 1984. xvi, 399p. index. $35. £26. ISBN: 0802056121.

2207 briefly annotated entries constitute an 'outstanding bibliography' which 'provides a clear, thorough, and reliable introduction to the rich and complicated literature of medieval Latin palaeography' (*Choice*, v.22, no.10, June 1985, p.1467). Index locorum, nominum, rerum p.334-391. Index codicum p.392-399. *Class No:* 930.27(01)

[6600]
LONDON UNIVERSITY. Library. **The Palaeography Collection in the University of London Library:** an author and subject catalogue. Boston, Mass., G.K. Hall, 2v., 1968.

A collection primarily concerned with material for the study of the manuscript book in Greek, Latin and Western European languages. The author catalogue comprises *c.*10,800 cards; the subject catalogue *c.*13,100 cards. *Class No:* 930.27(01)

[6601]
THORP, J. **Books on palaeography:** sixteenth to eighteenth century handwriting, *Local Historian,* v.16, no.6, May 1985, p.327-334. *Class No:* 930.27(01)

Ancient Greece

[6602]
SCHUBART, W. **Griechische paläographie.** München, Verlag C.H. Beck, 1966. vii,184p.illus. ISBN: 3406013376.

Abteilung 1:4, 1 of the *Handbuch der Altertumswissenschaft. Class No:* 930.27(37)

Ancient Rome

[6603]
GORDON, A.E. **Illustrated introduction to Latin epigraphy.** Berkeley, Univ. of California Press, 1983. xxv, 264p.+64p. plates. bibliog. index. $50. ISBN: 0520038983.

2 Parts: Introduction - Latin epigraphy defined; provenience of Latin inscriptions; sources and collections; technical details; subject matter; problems of inscriptions; contents of this selection; miscellaneous information; bibliography p.54-65. The Inscriptions p.69-185. Concordances p.237-242. *Class No:* 930.27(38)

[6604]
LOWE, E.A., *ed.* **Codices Latini antiquiores:** a palaeographical guide to Latin manuscripts prior to the ninth century. Oxford, Clarendon Press, 1934-. illus., (pl.), maps.

Country locations:

1: *Vatican City.*

2: *Great Britain, Ireland*, 2nd ed. 1972. 84p. £17.50. Suppt. 1971. £17.50.

3/4: *Italy.*

5: *Paris.*

6: *France.*

7: *Switzerland.*

8/9: *Germany.*

10: *Austria, Belgium, Czechoslovakia, Denmark, Egypt and Holland.*

11: *Hungary, Luxembourg, Poland, Russia, Spain, Sweden, United States and Yugoslavia.*

Supplement. 1972. £55. ISBN 019818218x.

Class No: 930.27(38)

[6605]
STEFFENS, F. **Paléographie latine:** 125 facsimilés en phototypie, accompagnés de transcriptions et d'explications avec un exposé systématique de l'histoire de l'écriture latine. Éd. française d'après la nouvelle éd allemande par R. Coulon. Paris, Champion, 1910. xl, 125p. 125pl.

Standard work for the study of Latin palaeography and diplomatic. Examples of papal, imperial and private documents; book hand and court hand. Transcript and detailed notes for each plate. *Class No:* 930.27(38)

USA

[6606]
STRYKER-RODDA, A. **Understanding Colonial handwriting.** Baltimore, Genealogical Publishing Co., 1981. 26p. sd. ISBN: 0806311533.

First published in Spring-Summer 1980 issue of *New*

....(contd.)

Jersey History.

For family historians unskilled in palaeography.

Class No: 930.27(73)

Ancient History & Ancient Peoples

[6607]

BENGSTON, H. Introduction to ancient history. 6th ed. Berkeley, Univ. of California Press., 1970. viii, 213p. bibliogs. index. $35.00. ISBN: 0520031504.

Translated from *Einführung in die alte Geschichte* first published in 1949; 6th ed. 1969.

Authoritative standard work reorganized in this English language edition to conform to the plan of the *Cambridge ancient history*. 9 sections all with their own bibliographies: 1. Scope of ancient history - 2. History of the study of Antiquity from the Renaissance to the present - 3. Fundamentals of the study of ancient history - 4. The sources (Literature and documents; Historiography; Myths, saga, folktales) - 5. The monuments - 6. Basic disciplines: epigraphy, papyrology, numismatics - 7. Allied disciplines - 8. Reference works - 9. Bibliography. 'Historians will probably not want to discard the substantive articles on ancient history topics provided by Sandys' *Companion to Latin studies* ... but the beginner and the librarian will find the bibliographies in this work of far greater value' (*Library Journal*, v.97, no.18, 15 April 1972, p.1385).

Class No: 931

[6608]

The Cambridge ancient history. Cambridge, Cambridge Univ. Press.

Originally published in 12v. and 5v. of plates (1923-1929). Revised volumes are in process of replacing original volumes.

The present edition is planned to reflect the advances in scholarship since the 1920s. 1. Pt.1: *Prolegomena and prehistory.* 3rd ed., 1970. £55. ISBN 0521070511. Pt.2: *Early history of the Middle East.* 3rd ed., 1971. £70. 0521077915. 2. Pt.1: *History of the Middle East and the Aegean region c.1800-1380 BC. New ed; 1973. £65. 0521082307. 2. Pt.2: c.1830-1000 BC* 3rd ed., 1975. £70. 0521086914. *Plates to volumes 1 and 2.* 1977. £32.50. 0521205719. 3. Pt.1: *The prehistory of the Balkans, the Middle East and the Aegean world 10th to 8th centuries BC.* 2nd ed., 1982. £70. 0521224969 3. Pt.2 *Assyrian and Babylonian Empires and other states of the Near East from the eighth to the sixth centures.* 2nd ed. 1992. 0521227178. Pt.3 *The expansion of the Greek world, 8th to 6th centuries BC.* 2nd ed., 1982. £45. 0521234476. *Plates to v.3.* 1984. £35. 0521242894. 4. *Persia, Greece and the Western Mediterranean c.525-479 BC.* 2nd ed. 1988. £60. 0521228042. *Plates to volume 4* 1988. 0521305802. 5. *The Fifth Century* 1992. 618p. £60. 052123347x. 6. *Macedon 401-301 BC.* £50. 052104488x. 7. Pt.1: *The Hellenistic World.* 2nd ed., 1984. £50. 052123445x. 7. Pt.2: *The rise of Rome to 220 BC. 1990. £60. 0521234468. Plates to v.7, pt:1.* 1984. £30. 0521243548. 8. *Rome and the Mediterranean to 133 BC.* 2nd ed. 1989. £50. 0521234484. 9. *The last age of The Roman Republic 133-44 BC.* £70. 0521204491x. 10. *The Augustan Empire 44 BC-AD70.* £70.

....(contd.)

05212044928. 11. *The Imperial Peace AD 70-192.* 052120449936. 12. *Imperial crisis and recovery AD 193-324.* £65. 05212044944. *Class No:* 931

[6609]

CLAYTON, P. *and* PRICE, M.J. The Seven wonders of the Ancient World. London and New York, Routledge, 1988. 192p. illus., map, bibliog., index. £17.95. $29.95. ISBN: 0415002796.

6 contributors. 8 chapters: 1. Great pyramid at Giza - 2. Hanging gardens of Babylon - 3. Statues of Zeus at Olympia - 4. Temple of Artemis at Ephesos - Mausoleum at Halicarnassus - 6. Colossus of Rhodes - 7. Pharos of Alexandria - 8. Epilogue: some forgotten wonders. Bibliography p.169-172. 89 illustrations. *Class No:* 931

[6610]

CRAWFORD, M. Sources for ancient history. Cambridge, Cambridge Univ. Press, 1983. xi, 238p. illus. bibliog., index. £30.00. (*Studies in the Uses of Historical Evidence.*) ISBN: 0521247829.

4 essays examining the historical use and interpretation of ancient literature, classical epigraphy and archaeology, and numismatic evidence from the ancient Mediterranean. 'Spankingly up-to-date in their concepts, examples and bibliographies' (*Antiquity*, v.58, no.223, July 1984, p.149). *Class No:* 931

Encyclopaedias

[6611]

COTTERELL, A., *ed*. The Encyclopedia of ancient civilizations. London, Viking, 1988. 367p. illus. (some col.), maps, plans, geneal tables, bibliog., index. £16.95. ISBN: 0670825956.

Originally published Leicester, Windward, 1980.

38 contributors. 58 essays: Prehistory - The emergence of civilization - then geographically Egypt; West Asia; India; Europe; China; America. Bibliography p.356-361. 28 maps. Analytical index. 'Useful but not indispensable. Recommended for all general libraries'. (*Choice*, v.18, no.8, April 1981, p.1070). *Class No:* 931(031)

Dictionaries

[6612]

SPEAKE, G., *ed*. Dictionary of ancient history. Oxford, Blackwell, 1993. 400p. maps, tables, charts. ISBN: 0631180699.

Compendium of current knowledge about Graeco-Roman world in 2000 A-Z entries relating to the years 776BC-AD476 and covering major events, institutions, prominent individuals *etc.* *Class No:* 931(038)

Maps & Atlases

[6613]

Atlas of the Greek and Roman world in antiquity. Hammond, N.G.L., *ed.* Park Ridge, New Jersey, Noyes Press, 1981. viii, 56p. maps. £44.24; $48.00. ISBN: 081555060x.

35 contributors. 46 maps (various scales) divided into 3 sections: 1. Greek prehistory and history - 2. Topographical maps - 3. Roman history. 10,000 sites are located although many identifications are no more than probables. Appendix

....*(contd.)*

1. Founding dates of Greek colonies - 2. Modern names for sites in Roman Britain - 3. In Gaul, Germany and the Alps. *Class No:* 931(084.3)

[6614]

LLORIS, F.B. and SIMÓN, F.M. Atlas de historia antigua. Zaragoza, Diputación General de Aragón. Departamento de Cultura y Educación and Libros Portico, 1987. 127p. col. maps, indexes. ISBN: 8485264789.

72 single or double-page maps: 1. Principales lenguas y escrituras del Oriente Proximo - 2. Sumer: el periodo protodinastico (*c*.2900 - *c*.2340) ... 72. El mundo Mediterraneo en epoca de Justiniano (*c*.565). Refreshing lack of text. *Class No:* 931(084.3)

[6615]

OLIPHANT, M. The Atlas of the Ancient World. Charting the great civilizations of the past. London, Ebury Press, 1992. 220p. illus. (many col.), col. maps, bibliog., index. £19.99. ISBN: 0091770408.

Popular illustrated atlas in 9 sub-divided sections: 1. Mesopotamia and Near East - 2. Egypt - 3. Persia - 4. Prehistoric Europe - 5. Greece and the Aegean - 6. Roman world - 7. India - 8. China - 9. The Americas. Chronology of the Ancient World p.202-11. Bibliography p.212-13. Analytical index. *Class No:* 931(084.3)

[6616]

Peoples and places of the past The National Geographic illustrated cultural atlas of the ancient world. 5th ed. Washington, National Geographic Society, 1983. 424p. col. illus., col. maps. $69.95. £49.95. ISBN: 087044462x.

16 textual, pictorial and cartographic chapters with chronologies and bibliographies provide a sumptuous folio volume for the well-heeled general reader. *Class No:* 931(084.3)

[6617]

The Times atlas of ancient civilizations. Scarre, C., *ed.* London, The Times. 1989. Each issue 12p. col.illus., col.maps, col.diagrs., sd.

Published in 7 weekly parts, 16 October - 27 November 1989, as a supplement to *The Times* newspaper. Illustrations and maps are adapted from *The Times atlas of world history* and *Past worlds* (*qqv*).

1. The Near East - 2. Egypt - 3. Greece - 4. China - 5. Rome - 6. South Asia - 7. The Americas (Introduction and 9 full page pictorial features: Early Andean cultures; The Americas 8500-2000BC; First cities of Central America; Central America 3000-500BC; The Maya and the Moche; Central and South America 500BC - AD1000; North American cultures; North America 1000BC - AD1000; Central America - a modern traveller's guide). *Class No:* 931(084.3)

Chronologies

[6618]

BICKERMAN, E.J. Chronology of the Ancient World. Rev. ed. London, Thames & Hudson, Ithaca, New York, Cornell Univ. Press, 1980. 223p. illus., tables, index. $32.50. (*Aspects of Greek and Roman life*.) ISBN: 0500400393, UK; 080141282x, US.

First published in English 1968. Adopted from *Chronologie* published in Leipzig (2nd ed., 1963).

Elucidates the basic problems of ancient chronology ... 1.

....*(contd.)*

The Calendar - 2. Chronography (the principles of antiquity in computing the years) - 3. Applied chronology (rules derived from these principles to relate ancient dates to modern time reckoning - 4. Notes (p.96-108) - 5. The tables (p.109-218) including astronomical canon, Olympian years, Roman consuls and emperors, and ending with chronological tables of Greek and Roman history 776 BC and AD 476. Analytical index.

Note James, P. and others: *Centuries of darkness: a challenge to the conventional chronology of Old World archaeology* (London, Cape, 1991) argues for a radical shift in the currently accepted chronology of the ancient Near East and Mediterranean world. *Class No:* 931(090)

[6619]

JAMES, P., and others. Centuries of darkness a challenge to the conventional chronology of Old World archaeology. London, Jonathan Cape, 1991. xxii,434p. illus., maps, bibliog., index. £15.95. ISBN: 022402647x.

Argues' for a radical shift in the currently accepted chronology of the ancient Near East and Mediterranean world to repair 'a gigantic academic blunder, perpetuated by the convenience of a seemingly reliable time-scale as well as the sheer complexity of the issues involved' (*p.320*). Appendix 1. Dendochronology and radiocarbon dating - 2. Greek and Roman theories on ancient chronology. Chapter notes and references p.345-94. Bibliography p.395-426. *Class No:* 931(090)

[6620]

MELLERSH, H.E.L. Chronology of the Ancient World: 10,000BC to AD799. London, Barrie & Jenkins, 1976. x, 500p. Reprinted Oxford, Helicon, 1994.

Double-page spreads, usually. 10-year periods for 600BC-AD350. Under each period (as appropriate): General events - A. Politics, law and economics - B. Science and discovery - C. Religion and philosophy - D. The arts - E. Literature - F. Births and deaths. Analytical index, p.467-500. *Class No:* 931(090)

Asia—Near East

[6621]

NISSEN, H.J. The Early history of the ancient Near East 9000-2000 BC. Univ. of Chicago Press, 1988. xiv,215p. illus., drawings, maps, bibliog., index. £23.95. ISBN: 0226586561.

Translated with new material from *Grundzüge einer Geschichte der Frühzeit des Vordern Orients* (Darmstadt, Wissenschaftliche Buchgesellschaft, 1983).

Single-volume overview of 7,000 years development in the ancient Near East from the beginnings of settled life to the formation of the first regional states. Bibliography (by chapter) p.203-10. *Class No:* 931(56)

Ancient China

[6622]

WALDRON, A.,. The Great Wall of China from history to myth. Cambridge, Cambridge Univ. Press, 1990. xvi,296p. illus., maps, bibliog., index. £30. (*Cambridge Studies in Chinese History, Literature and Institutions.*) ISBN: 052136518x.

Historical narrative in 11 chapters: 1. Introduction: what is the Great Wall of China? - 2. Early Chinese walls - 3.

....*(contd.)*

Strategic origins ... 5. Security without walls: early Ming strategy and its collapse ... 7. Politics and military policy at the turn of the 16th century ... 11. The Wall acquires new meanings. Chapter notes p.227-55. Bibliography (Chinese and Japanese and Western materials) p.256-78. Glossary p.279-85. See also the author's 'The problem of the Great Wall of China', *Harvard Journal of Asiatic Studies,* v.43, no.2, 1983. *Class No:* 931.5

Ancient Egypt

[6623]

ADAMS, W.Y. Nubia, corridor to Africa. London, Allen Lane, 1977. xxv,797p. illus. (incl.pl.), tables, maps, plans, index. £35.00. ISBN: 0713905794.

'Nubia'- now Southern Egypt and Northern Sudan. 20 chapters. Prologue - Pt.1: Tribal beginning - Pt.2: Dynasties and empires - Pt.3: Medieval civilizations - Epilogue. Chapter notes, (p.681-772) including 'Principal sources'. Analytical index, p.773-97. 87 illus., plans and maps; 24 plates. *Class No:* 932

[6624]

DAVIES, W.V. Egypt and Africa. Nubia from prehistory to Islam. London, British Museum Press in association with the Egypt Exploration Society, 1991. x,320p. + + 16p. pl. maps, plans, bibliogs. ISBN: 0714109622.

30 essays by different hands on various aspects of the archaeology and early history of Nubia including Jean Vercoutter's L'Archéologie Nubrienne et Soudainaise: passé présent et futur'. Celebrates the opening of The Raymond and Sackler Gallery of Egypt and Africa, British Museum, July 1991. *Class No:* 932

[6625]

HARRIS, J.R., *ed.* **The Legend of Egypt.** 2nd ed. Oxford, Clarendon Press, 1971. xi, 511p., 25p. illus.

1st ed. by S.R.K. Glanville 1942.

14 contributors. 16 chapters (1. The calendars and chronology - 2. Mathematics and astronomy ... 4. Technology and materials - 5. Medicine - 6. Mystery, myth and magic ... 9. Literature ... 16. The contribution to Islam). Chapter bibliographies; footnote references. General, Egyptian, Coptic and Greek indexes, 24 plates. *Class No:* 932

[6626]

HART, G. Pharaohs and pyramids: a guide through Old Kingdom. Egypt. London, The Herbert Press, 1991. 240p. col. illus., map, bibliog., index. £17.95. ISBN: 1871569362.

A chronological history and guide to the principal pyramids and other surviving monuments constructed after the unification of Upper and Lower Egypt. King list p.9. Time chart p.10-11. Bibliography p.235-6. *Class No:* 932

[6627]

HOBSON, C. Exploring the world of the Pharaohs. London, Thames & Hudson, 1987. 192p. col. illus., map, bibliog., index. £12.95.

6 chapters with full scholarly apparatus: 1. Discovering the past - 2. Egyptian origins - 3. Pyramids - 4. The shifting sands - 5. Temples - 6. Egypt's legacy. Chronology p.8-9. Bibliography p.178-9. Gazetteer p.180-187. Glossary p.186-187. 'Designed specifically with the modern visitor in mind ... it is first and foremost a general handbook to ancient Egypt ... it is also a vade-mecum to the country; it contains

....*(contd.)*

much background information not easily accessible in standard works (*Foreword* by T.G.H. James).
Class No: 932

[6628]

MURNANE, W.J. The Penguin guide to Ancient Egypt. London, Allen Lane, Penguin Books, 1983. 367p. maps, bibliog.

6 chapters on ancient Egyptian civilization precede a descriptive architectural and historical guide to significant museums and sites. *Class No:* 932

[6629]

QUIRKE, S. Who were the Pharaohs? a history of their names with a list of cartouches. London, British Museum Publications, 1990. 80p. illus., bibliog., index. £4.95. ISBN: 071410955x.

Traces the evolution of royal names from the dawn of Egyptian writing, c.3000 BC., to the Roman period. Section 5: The principal names of the kings of Egypt gives their cartouches. Bibliography p.79. *Class No:* 932

[6630]

WEST, J.A. The Traveller's key to ancient Egypt: a guide to the sacred places of ancient Egypt. New York, Knopf, 1985. London, Harrap Columbus, 1987. xiv,480p. illus., pbk. $18.45; £8.95. ISBN: 074710011x, UK; 0394514416, US.

Detailed and practical guidebook in 23 thematic and topographical chapters *e.g.* 1. Historical overview ... 2. Development of Egyptology ... 4-6. Giza ... 12. Cairo Museum. Appendix 1. Dynasties and kings - 2. Further reading (p.448-9) - 3. Egyptological, architectural, technical glossary p.450-4 - 4. Travelling tips. *Class No:* 932

Encyclopaedias

[6631]

BUNSON, M. The Encyclopedia of ancient Egypt. New York and Oxford, Facts On File, 1991. xv,291p. illus., maps, bibliog., index. £21.95. ISBN: 0816020930.

1500 A-Z entries covering all aspects of ancient Egypt from the prehistoric period (c.3200 BC) to the fall of the New Kingdom (1070 BC). Time-lines p.x-xiii. Queens of Egypt consolidated list p.217-8. Bibliography p.284-6. Subject index p.287-91. *Class No:* 932(031)

Dictionaries

[6632]

POSENER, G. A Dictionary of Egyptian civilization. New York, Tudor Publishing Co., 1959; London, Methuen, 1962. x, 324p. illus., maps, indexes.

Originally as *Dictionnaire de la civlization égyptienne* (Paris, Hazan, 1959).

A small dictionary with signed articles, ranging from brief entries to essays (*e.g.* on hieroglyphics; mummifying). Profusely illustrated - 315 clear illus., of which 145 are in colour. Many cross-references. *Class No:* 932(038)

Maps & Atlases

[6633]

BAINES, J. *and* **MÁLEK, J. Atlas of Ancient Egypt.** Oxford, Phaidon, 1980. 240p. illus. (mostly col.), col. maps, bibliog., index. £22.50. ISBN: 0714819581.

'A systematic survey of the most important sites with ancient Egyptian monuments, an assessment of their historical and cultural importance and a brief description of their salient features' (*Introduction*). 3 parts: 1. The cultural setting - 2. A journey down the Nile - 3. Aspects of Egyptian society. Museums with Egyptian collections p.224-5. Glossary p.226-7. Bibliography p.231-2. Gazetteer p.233-5. Analytical index. 36 maps. 530 illustrations (380 in colour). *Class No:* 932(084.3)

Biographies

[6634]

DAVID, R. *and* **DAVID, A.E. A Biographical dictionary of ancient Egypt.** London, Seaby, 1992. 179p. maps, bibliog., indexes. £18.50. ISBN: 1852640324.

More than 200 entries cover important historical and cultural figures of ancient Egypt during the period 3100BC to AD600. This scholarly work of reference also includes an outline history, a glossary, chronologies and 4 maps. *Class No:* 932(092)

Jewish History

[6635]

BRIGHT, J. A History of Israel. 3rd ed. London, SCM Press, 1984; New York, Westminster, 1980. 501p. index, limp cover. £10.50; $18.95. ISBN: 0334020468, UK; 0664213812, US.

1st UK ed. 1960. 3rd ed. 1981. 1st US ed. 1959.

12 chronological chapters organized in 6 parts: 1. Antecedents and beginnings: the age of the Patriarchs - 2. The formative period - 3. Israel under the Monarchy - 4. The Monarchy: crisis and downfall - 5. Tragedy and beyond: the exile and post-exile periods - The formative period: Judaism. 8 Chronological charts p.466-474. Scriptural references p.486-501. *Class No:* 933

[6636]

DOTHAN, T. The Philistines and their material culture. New Haven, Connecticut, Yale University Press, 1983. xxii, 310p. illus., tables, maps, index. $55.00. £58.75. ISBN: 0300022581.

Revised and expanded edition of the author's book of the same title published in Hebrew (Jerusalem, Bialik Institute and Israel Exploration Society, 1967).

6 chapters (1. The historical sources ... 6. Absolute chronology and conclusions). Copiously illustrated and heavily annotated account of the archaeological evidence set against the background known from textual sources of the period between the late Bronze and Early Iron Ages. *Class No:* 933

[6637]

GRANT, M. The History of ancient Israel. London, Weidenfeld and Nicolson; New York, Scribner, 1984. ix, 317p., bibliog., maps, index. ISBN: 0297783661, UK; 0684180812, US.

Definitive study in 20 chapters ordered in 7 pts: 1. Land of Canaan - 2. From Abraham to the Judges - 3. The United Kingdom - 4. The Divided Kingdoms - 5. Babylonian and

....(contd.)

Persian rule - 6. Greek rule and liberation - 7. Roman dependency. Tables of dates in 4 geographical columns p.286-91. Notes p.293-8. Bibliography p.299-302. 'An excellent introduction to a fascinating subject ... highly recommended for general and college libraries' (*Choice*, v.22, no.4, December 1984, p.601). *Class No:* 933

[6638]

NOTH, M. The History of Israel. 2nd ed. in rev. and corr.translation. London, SCM, 1983. vii,487p. bibliog., index, pbk. £9.50. ISBN: 0334020441.

Originally published as *Geschichte Israels* Göttingen, Vandenboek & Ruprecht, 1983. Previous ed. London, A.C. Black 1960.

Chronological narrative in 10 chapters. Bibliography p.455-8. Index of Biblical references p.459-69. *Class No:* 933

[6639]

SOGGIN, J.A. A History of ancient Israel from the beginnings to the Bar Kochba revolt AD 135. London, SCM Press, 1984; New York, Westminster, 1985. 436p. illus., bibliogs., index. £10.50. $29.95. ISBN: 0334020433, UK; 0664212581, US.

Tanslated from *Storia d'Israele, dalle origine alla rivolta di Bar- Kochba 135 d.C.* (Brescia, Case Editrice Paideia, 1985).

14 chronological and thematic chapters in 4 parts: 1. Introductory problems - 2. Traditions about the Proto-history of the people - 3. A house divided - 4. Under the empires of East and West. Chapter 2 Methodology, bibliography and sources p.18-40 is useful as are the extensive bibliographies included in all chapters. Appendix 1. An introduction to the archaeology of Syria and Palestine p.357-367 - 2. Chronology of the First Temple Period: a presentation and evaluation of the sources. *Class No:* 933

Bibliographies

[6640]

CUTTER, C. *and* **OPPENHEIM, M.F. Jewish reference sources:** a selective, annotated bibliographic guide. New York, Garland Publishing Inc., 1982. xiii,180p. $24.00. ISBN: 082409347x.

Critical evaluations of 391 books on Jewish history, culture, religion, and contemporary issues, with the emphasis on 1970-1982 publications, arranged in 19 (subdivided) sections. Author and title index. *Class No:* 933(01)

[6641]

EDELHEIT, A.J. *and* **EDELHEIT, H. The Jewish world in modern times:** a selected, annotated bibliography. Boulder, Colorado, Westview Press; London, Mansell Publishing Ltd., 1988. xix,569p. £37.50. $65.00. ISBN: 0813305721, US; 072011988x, UK.

2170 descriptive and critically annotated entries limited to books, articles and pamphlets available to the American Jewish reading public. *Part 1. The Jewish World:* 1. Surveys of Jewish history - 2. Social History - 3. Emancipation and transformation of European Jewry - 4. Religious trends - 5. Cultural trends - 6. Antisemitism - 7. Public affairs - 8. The Holocaust - 9. Zionism and Jewish nationalism. *Part 2. The Jewish Community:* 10. Central Europe and Scandinavia - 11. Eastern Europe and the Balkans - 12. U.S.S.R. - 13. Western Europe - 14. The Americas - 15. US and Canada -

....(contd.)

16. The Middle East - 17. Land of Israel - 18. Africa, Asia and the Pacific - 19. Bibliographies and guides (p.458-459). Introduction: The outline of modern Jewish history p.1-8. *Class No:* 933(01)

[6642]
KAPLAN, J., *ed*. **International bibliography of Jewish history and thought.** München, K.G. Saur, 1984. xviii, 462p. index. ISBN: 3598075030.

First published in Jerusalem by Magnes Press in 1983 under the title of *2000 Books and more: an annotated and selected bibliography of Jewish history and thought.*

2190 citations mainly in English but with others also in Hebrew, German, French, Spanish and Portuguese grouped in 6 sections: 1. General works - 2. The Biblical period - 3. The Period of the Second Temple - 4. Medieval - 5. Modern - 6. Jewish communities. Brief descriptive and critical annotations. 'A very useful reference work' (*Choice*, v.21, no.5, January 1984, p.692). *Class No:* 933(01)

[6643]
MOR, M *and* RAPPAPORT, U. **Bibliography of works on Jewish history** in the Hellenistic and Roman periods 1976-1980. Jerusalem, The Zalman Shazar Center, 1982. xvii, 95p. index. ISSN: 03335119.

Continues Rappaport's 'Bibliography of works on Jewish history in the Hellenistic and Roman periods 1946-1970', *Studies in the history of the Jewish people and the land of Israel*, no.2, 1972, p.247-321 and Rappaport and Mors' *Bibliography of works on Jewish history in the Hellenistic and Roman periods 1971-1975* published by The Institute of Advanced Studies in Jerusalem in 1976.

770 items in Western languages arranged in 34 sections covering the period from the Second Temple to the Herods. Compiled with the aid of Haifa On-line Bibliographical Text System (HOBITS) which is being used to keep current bibliographical database. *Class No:* 933(01)

[6644]
PURVIS, J.D. **Jerusalem, the Holy City:** a bibliography. Metuchen, New Jersey, Scarecrow Press, 1988. xii, 499p. index. $42.50. (*American Theological Library Association Bibliography No.20*.) ISBN: 0810819996.

5827 unannotated entries in 40 chapters grouped in 8 Parts: 1. General studies - 2. The Biblical period to 587BC - 3. Second Temple period - 4. Roman Jerusalem - 5. Judaism - 6. Christian Jerusalem - 7. A Muslim city - 8. Jerusalem in modern times. Author and subject indexes p.432-499. *Class No:* 933(01)

[6645]
SCHWAB, M. **Index of articles relative to Jewish history and literature** published in periodicals from 1665 to 1900. New York, Ktav, 1972. 613p.

Originally published as *Répertoire des articles relatifs à l'histoire et la littérature juives ...* (Paris, Geuthner, 1914-23).

An author index of articles in 90 periodicals (7 only in English; the majority are in French, German and Hebrew). Subject index. 'This index is a very important research tool for scholars of Judaica in all fields' (*Choice*, v.9,no.5-6, July/August 1972, p.628). Text in English and Hebrew. *Class No:* 933(01)

Encyclopaedias

[6646]
Encyclopedia of Jewish history: events and eras of the Jewish people. Shamir, I. *and* Shavit, S., *eds*. Jerusalem, Massada Publishers; New York, Facts On File, 1986. 288p. col. illus., maps, diagrs., index. £17.95. ISBN: 0816012202.

30 contributors. Concise information on events and key figures in the annals of the Jewish people, from the beginnings to modern times, arranged in over 100 historical entries with 12 appendices on Jewish culture and ethnology. Each entry comprises a central article of *c*.800 words accompanied by maps, photographs and diagrams. 'Connections', appearing on each pair of facing pages, direct the reader to related chapters. Major themes p.13-19. Chronological chart of Jewish and World history p.247-263. Glossary p.265-274. *Class No:* 933(031)

Maps & Atlases

[6647]
BACON, J. **The Illustrated atlas of Jewish civilization.** London, Deutsch; New York, Macmillan, 1990. 224p. illus (some col.), col. maps, index. £19.95. $35. ISBN: 0233985697, UK; 0025434152, US.

Introduction: Mapping Jewish history (by Martin Gilbert) - 1. From Abraham to the destruction of the Second Temple - 2. Age of prayer and thought C.E. 70 to the Spanish Inquisition - 3. High Middle Ages to Moses Mendelssohn - 4. Jewish enlightenment to the eve of Holocaust - 5. The dark side: anti-Semitism - 6. The Holocaust - 7. Israel and world Jewry following World War 2. No bibliography. 'A successful blend of beautiful cartography, arresting illustrations, and informative text covering the entire range of the Jewish historical experience from patriarchal times to the present' (*Library Journal*, v.116,no.4, 1 March 1991, p.84). *Class No:* 933(084.3)

[6648]
BEINART, H., *ed*. **Atlas of medieval Jewish history.** New York, Simon & Schuster, 1992. 144p. illus., maps, bibliog., indexes. £29.95. ISBN: 0130506915.

116 maps stretching for 1000 years from the barbarian invasions to the Crusades, Black Death, expulsion of the Jews from Spain, and to Chmielnicki massacres in the 17th century. *Class No:* 933(084.3)

[6649]
COHN-SHERBOCK, D. **Atlas of Jewish history.** London, Routledge, 1993. 224p. illus. maps. £35. ISBN: 0415086841.

Atlas and guide in 15 sections: 1. Ancient Near East and the Israelites ... 3. Captivity and return ... 6. Judaism under Islam in the Middle Ages - 7. Jews in medieval Christian Europe - 13. Jewry in 19th and early 20th centuries - 14. The Holocaust - 15. Israel. 113 maps. *Class No:* 933(084.3)

[6650]
DE LANGE, N. **Atlas of the Jewish world.** Oxford, Phaidon, 1984. 240p. illus. (many col.), col.maps, geneal tables, bibliog., index. £22.50. ISBN: 0714823244.

Text covers historical and cultural background and a survey of the Jewish world today which with 48 maps successfully endeavours 'to give an account, as plainly as possible, of the Jews: who they are, and how they have come to be where they are today', 15 special features *e.g.* The kingdom of Herod; The Jewish year; Jerusalem the holy city. Chronology p.8-9. Glossary p.226-227. Bibliography

....(contd.)

p.230-23'. Gazetteer p.233-238. 'This comprehensive survey makes a notable contribution that has much to offer to all who wish to be informed with scholarly balance about the Jewish people'. (*Geographical Journal*, v.152, no.2, July 1986, p.283-284). *Class No:* 933(084.3)

[6651]
FRIESEL, E. Atlas of modern Jewish history. New York, Oxford Univ. Press, 1990. 159p. illus., col. maps, diagrs., tables, bibliog., index. $49.95; £25. ISBN: 0195053931.

Revised from the 1983 Hebrew edition published by Carta, The Israel Map and Publishing Co.

185 three colour maps and dozens of charts and line drawings arranged in 7 main sections: 1. Jewish demography - 2. European countries 17th century to World War I - 3. Major themes in Jewish history - 4. Muslim countries - 5. European Jewry in the interwar years - 6. European Jewry 1940 to 1980s - 7. New centers of Jewry. Bibliography p.145-7. Greatly surpasses M. Gilbert's *Jewish history atlas*. 'Offers a unique perspective on the development of the Jewish people' (*Booklist*, v,87, no.1, 1 September 1990, p.79-80). *Class No:* 933(084.3)

Chronologies

[6652]
BLOCH, A.P. Day by day in Jewish history: a chronology and calendar of historic events. New York, KTAV Publishing House, 1983. xii,336p. bibliog., index. $20.00. ISBN: 0870687360.

List of anniversaries (with emphasis mainly on personalities and events closely involved in Jewish life) according to the Jewish calendar with cross references to civil dates based on the calendrical tables in E. Mahler's *Handbuch der Jüdischen Chronologie*. Names of Hebrew months p.ix. Chronological entries p.1-279. Civil dates p.281-291. Table of years p.293-312. Bibliography p.313-314. 'The very detailed general index makes this a very practical guide to a variety of historical data' (*Choice*, v.21,no.1, September 1983, p.58). *Class No:* 933(090)

[6653]
BLOCH, A.P. Once a day an anthology of Jewish historical anniversaries for every day of the year. Hoboken, New Jersey, Ktav Publishing House, 1987. xv,376p. index. ISBN: 0881251089.

Summaries of events or capsule biographies of prominent figures in Jewish history noted for each day of the year (arranged according to the Christian calendar). *Class No:* 933(090)

[6654]
GRIBETZ, J., *and others*. **The Timelines of Jewish history:** a chronology of the most important people and events in Jewish history. New York, Simon & Schuster, 1993. 752p. illus., maps. $35. ISBN: 067140070.

Although over half the contents relate to 20th century, the chronology ranges from prehistoric times. Entries are tabulated under 3 headings: General history, Jewish history, Jewish culture. *Class No:* 933(090)

Biographies

[6655]
COMAY, J. Who's who in Jewish history after the period of the Old Testament. London, Weidenfeld & Nicolson, 1974. 448p. illus. (some col.), facsims., maps, chron.table, indexes. ISBN: 0297765728.

Continues same author's *Who's who in the Old Testament, together with the Apocrypha* (Weidenfeld & Nicolson, 1971).

Over 1000 A-Z entries covering period from Hasmonean Dynasty to modern Israel. With limited exceptions restricted to dead persons who have contributed significantly to Jewish history and thought. Glossay p.10-11. Chronological (13 sections) p.12-33. Thematic index p.439-448. No bibliographies. *Class No:* 933(092)

Ancient India & Ancient Indo-China

[6656]
BHATTACHARJEE, A. A History of ancient India. 2nd ed. Liverpool, Lucas Publications, 1988. 480p. maps, geneal tables, bibliog., index. £15.95. ISBN: 1851800255.

1st ed. 1979.

17 chapters including 2. Sources of ancient Indian history - 3. Prehistory ... 16. The Deccan - 17. The distant South. Bibliography p.469-72. 'Purports to present within a single ambit and a convenient compass a critical approach to the history of ancient India' (*Preface to 1st ed.*). *Class No:* 934

North, West & East European Peoples

[6657]
BURNS, T.S. A History of the Ostrogoths. Bloomington, Indiana Univ. Press, 1984. xvii, 299p., illus., tables, maps, bibliog. $29.95. ISBN: 0253328314.

Well documented study based on primary Roman sources and modern archaeological research. Chapter notes p.221-257. Bibliography p.259-289. Index p.291-299. *Class No:* 936

[6658]
CHISTIE, N. The Lombards. Oxford, Blackwell, 1994. 320p. illus. (*Peoples of Europe.*) ISBN: 0631182381.

5th-6th century Longobard history primarily based on archaeological sources. *Class No:* 936

[6659]
COLLINS, R. The Basques. Oxford & New York, Basil Blackwell, 1986. xiv,272p., illus. maps, geneal. tables, index. £25. (*The Peoples of Europe*.) ISBN: 0631174786.

7 chapters (*e.g.* 1. An ancient people ... 2. The Basques and Rome ... 3. Gascony and Pamplona) forming 'a study in detail of the history of the Basques and of the western Pyrenees in the period between the Roman conquest ... and the late twelfth century'. No bibliography but reference is made to C. Cuerpo's and J. Bilbao's *Eusko-Bibliografia* (San Sebastian, 10v, 1960-75). 15 maps. *Class No:* 936

[6660]
CUNLIFFE, B. *and* **CAMPBELL, J.,** *eds*. **The Peoples of Europe.** Oxford, Basil Blackwell, 1986-. illus., maps.

European tribes and peoples from their origins in prehistory to the present day based on archaeological and historical evidence.

Forthcoming titles: Abulafia, D. *The Sicilians*. 1995; G and Rasmussen, T. *The Etruscans*. 1994. 0631177159; Byrne, J. and Herity. *The Irish*. 1994. 0631167374; Chibnall, M. *The Normans*. 1994. 0631186719; Collins, R.

....*(contd.)*

The Spanish. 1995. 0631159223; Dumville, D. *The Celts.* 1996. 0631160841; Hawkes, S.C. *The Early English.* 1994. 063116801x; Heather, P. *The Goths.* 1994. 0631165363; Heywood, C. *The Turks.* 1994. 0631158979; Hurst, M. *The Hungarians.* 1994. 0631180494; Redgate, E. *The Armenians.* 1993. 0631143726; Thomas, C. *The Picts.* 1994. 0631140298; and Thompson, E.A. *The Huns.* 1995. 0631159995. *Class No:* 936

[6661]
GALLIOU, P. and JONES, M. The Bretons. Oxford, Blackwell, 1991. xviii,334p. illus., maps, geneal. tables, bibliog., index. (*The Peoples of Europe.*) ISBN: 0631164065.

Chronological account of Breton archaeology and medieval history: 1. Early Armorica ... 7. Carolingian Brittany ... 13. Breton society at the end of the Middle Ages - 14. Britanny and the Bretons since 1491. Bibliography p.288-311. *Class No:* 936

[6662]
JAMES, E. The Franks. Oxford and New York, Basil Blackwell, 1988. xii,265p., illus. maps, bibliog., index. £25. (*The Peoples of Europe.*) ISBN: 0631148728.

Introduction 'Who were the Franks?' and 6 chapters: 1. The Sources (historical sources, archaeological and linguistic evidence) - 2. The Franks before Clovis - 3. Conquests - 4. Conversion to Christianity - 5. Frankish kings and their subjects - 6. Economy and society. Bibliography p.246-250. 'The story of how the Franks became the French and why they became so important in European history'. *Class No:* 936

[6663]
POL, A. The Thracians. Oxford, Blackwell, 1991. 256p. (*Peoples of Europe.*) ISBN: 0631135626.

Describes the formation of a Thracian culture in Bronze Age Southeastern Europe and Asia Minor and traces its development. Early Greek historical sources and the archaeological evidence are explored. *Class No:* 936

[6664]
TODD, M. The Early Germans. Oxford, Blackwell, 1992. xiii,285p. illus., maps, bibliog., index. (*The Peoples of Europe.*) ISBN: 0631163972.

Part 1. Germania: 1. Land and people - 2. Social fabric - 3. Advance of Rome ... 5. Trade and diplomacy - 6. Cult, art and technology. Part 2. Germans in Europe. 7. Gothic kingdoms - 8. Suebi and Vandals - 9. Franks, Alamanni, Burgundians - 10. Northern peoples (Saxons, Frisians) - 11. Gepids and Lombards - 12. Thuringians and Bavarians. Bibliography p.272-5. 6 maps. Both archaeological and literary sources are tapped to advantage in this history. *Class No:* 936

[6665]
WILKES, J. The Illyrians. Oxford, Blackwell, 1992. xxiii,351p. illus., maps, bibliog., index. (*The Peoples of Europe.*) ISBN: 0631146717.

Pt.1 Search for Illyrians: 1. Rediscovery. 2. Prehistoric Illyrians - 3. Naming Illyrians.

Pt.2 Greek Illyrians: 4. Neighbouring the Greeks - 5. Enemies of Macedonia - 6. Kingdom of Illyrians.

Pt.3 Roman Illyrians: 7. Illyricum - 8. Life and death among Illyrians - 9. Imperial Illyrians. Bibliography p.281-325. 4 maps. *Class No:* 936

[6666]
WOLFRAM, W. History of the Goths. New and completely revised from 2nd German ed. Berkeley and London, Univ. of California Press, 1988. xii,613p. and 7p. maps. bibliog., index. $39.95. ISBN: 0520052595.

First published as *Geschichte der Goten: von den Anfängen bis zur Mitte des sechsten Jahrhunderts.* (München, Verlag C.H. Beck, 2nd ed. 1980)

Authoritative and comprehensive academic treatise arranged in 5 sections: 1. The names - 2. Formation of the Gothic tribes before the invasion of the Huns - 3. Forty-year migration and the formation of the Visigoths 376/378 to 416/418 - 4. Kingdom of Toulouse 418 to 507 - 5. The 'new' Ostrogoths. 3 Appendices: 1. Roman Experors - 2. Survey of Gothic history p.367-71 - 3. Genealogical charts. Chapter notes p.377-534. Bibliography p.537-73. Formidable and extremely well-documented work. *Class No:* 936

Ancient Greece & Rome

[6667]
CARY, M. The Geographical background of Greek and Roman history. Westport, Connecticut, Greenwood Press, 1982. vi,331p. maps. £37.50. ISBN: 0313231877.

First published Oxford, Clarendon Press, 1949.

The opening chapter gives a concise account of the Mediterranean environment as a whole; succeeding chapters deal regionally with the various parts of the ancient world, including the Near East. Footnotes carry copious and exact references. *Class No:* 937/938

[6668]
GREEN, P. Alexander to Actium: the historical evolution of the Hellenistic Age. Berkeley/Los Angeles, Univ. of California Press; London, Thames & Hudson, 1990. xxiii,970p. illus., maps, geneal., tables, bibliog., index. £36. ISBN: 0520056116, US.

An extremely well-documented historical survey in 37 chapters divided into 5 parts: 1. Alexander's funeral games 323-276 BC. - 2. The zenith century 276-222 BC. - 3. Phalanx and legion 221-168 BC. - 4. The breaking of nations 167-116 BC. - 5. Rome triumphant 116-30 BC. Chronological table p.683-727. Genealogical tables (Macedonian and Thracian dynasties; Seleucids; Ptolemies; Attalids; Greek Indo-Bactrian kings) p.732-9. Chapter notes p.741-908. Bibliography p.909-28. 'Green's encyclopedic zest for the classics is spiced by wide knowledge of other fields, literary and political. His masterpiece is crammed with generous allusion' (*Sunday Times,* no.8655, 3 February 1991, Section 6, p.1-2). *Class No:* 937/938

[6669]
Oxford history of the classical world. Boardman, J., *and others.* Oxford, Oxford University Press, 1986. x, 882p., illus., maps, tables. £27.50. ISBN: 0198721129.

Subsequently published in 2v. - 1. *Greece and the Hellenistic World.* 1988. 448p. illus., maps, bibliog., index, pbk. £9.95. ISBN 0192821652 - 2. *Rome.* 1988. 448p. illus (some col.), maps, ports., bibliog., index. pbk. £9.95. ISBN 0192821660.

32 chapters divided into three sections: Greece (8th-4th century BC); Greece and Rome; and Rome. Within each section political and social history chapters are interspersed

....(contd.)

with others relating to literature, philosophy and the arts. Chapter bibiliographies. Tables of events p.830-860. Index p.873-882. 16 col. plates. *Class No:* 937/938

[6670]
PFEIFFER, R. History of Classical scholarship. Oxford, Clarendon Press, 2v., 1968-76.

1: *From the beginnings to the end of the Hellenistic age.* 1968. xviii, 311p. £35. ISBN 0198143427. 2. *From 1300-1850.* 1976. 213p. £35. 0198143648.

V.1 (pt.1: Prehistory of Greek scholarship; pt.2: The Hellenistic age) is concerned with foundations laid by the Greek scholar poets in the last 3 centuries BC. Numerous footnotes; analytical general index. V.2 reaches its climax in the rebirth of Hellenism in 18th-century Germany. V.3 is to trace the continuity of Classical scholarship up to modern times. *Class No:* 937/938

Bibliographies

[6671]
DONLAN, W., ed. 'The Classical world' bibliography of Greek and Roman history. New York, Garland, 1978. 234p.

Reprints 14 articles from *The Classical World*, 1954/71, - bibliographies of recent work on Herodotus (1954-63), Thucydides (1942-67), Livy (1940-58), Tacitus (1948-68), Julius Caesar (1935-61), Philo and Josephus (1937-59), Alexander the Great (1948-67), and Julian the Apostate (1945-64). Aimed at 'scholars beginning a new piece of research and teachers preparing fresh courses' (*The Classical world*, v.73, no.4, December 1979/January 1980, p.256). *Class No:* 937/938(01)

Encyclopaedias

[6672]
GRANT, M. and KITZINGER, R. Civilization of the Ancient Mediterranean. Greece and Rome. New York, Charles Scribner's Sons, 3v., 1988. xxvii, xiv, xiv, 1980p. $225.00. £160.00. ISBN: 0684188643, v.1; 0684188651, v.2; 068418866x, v.3; 0684175940, set.

88 contributors. Historical summary of Greece (p.3-44); of Rome (p.45-85). 97 essays under broad subject headings: Land and Sea - Population - Agriculture and food - Technology - Government and society - Economics - Religion - Private and social life - Women and family life - Literary and performing arts - Philosophy - Visual arts. Each essay concludes with a bibliography. Epilogue: progress of classical scholarship p.1819-32. Chronological table p.xvii-xxiv. 'A comprehensive overview of current thinking about the classical world ... this set really stands alone as a unique source' (*Booklist*, v.84, no.20, 15 June 1988, p.1716). *Class No:* 937/938(031)

[6673]
GRANT, M. A Guide to the Ancient World : a dictionary of classical place-names. New York, H.W. Wilson, 1986. 14p., maps+728p. $65.00. US $75.00. other countries. £54.00. ISBN: 0824207424.

900 historical, geographical, archaeological essays (150 to 1500 words in length) on significant place-names of historical importance, ranging from the Atlantic Ocean to Pakistan, and from the Sahara to southern Russia, from the first millenium BC to the late 5th century AD, encompassing

....(contd.)

references to contemporary writers, modern names, and precise geographical locations. Bibliography p.711-28. 'For information on towns and cities the dated Princeton encyclopedia of classical sites ... covers similar ground with greater accuracy and completeness' (*Choice*, v.24, no.5, January 1987, p.742). *Class No:* 937/938(031)

[6674]
PAULY, A.F. von and WISSOWA, G. Pauly's Real-Encyclopädie der classichen Altertumswissenschaft. Stuttgart, Metzler (later München, Druckenmüller, 1894-.1967. Supplement - Bänden 1-. 1903-. (Supplt. 15. 1978).

Published in 2 parallel series. 1. Reihe A-Q (24v. in 32 pts.) completed 1963; 2. Reihe R-Z (110v. in 19 pts.) completed 1967.

Comprehensive signed articles, with adequate bibliographies, cover every aspect of classical literature, history, geography, antiquities and civilization. The article 'Ptolemain als Geograph', in Suppt. 10: p.679-834; bibliography, p.819-34. 'P. Cornelius Tacitus', in Suppt. 11: adds cols. 347-511 (in 13 sections) to the original entry in v.4. An indispensable work of scholarship for any library. Gärtner H. and Wünsch A. *Pauly's Real-Encyclopädie der classicher Altertumswissenschaft Register der Nachträge Und Supplemente* (1980). xxii, 250p. *Der Kleine Pauly. Lexikon der Antike auf der Grundlage von Pauly's Real-Encyclopädie der classichen Altertumswissenschaft ...* bearb. und hrsg. von K. Ziegler und W. Sontheimer, 5v., 1964-75 is the work of 99 contributors, mostly German. The article on Aristophanes: nearly 5 columns (against 23 in the original), with 10 lines of references. Well produced. 'Indispensable supplement to the original and much easier to use' (*Papers of the Bibliographical Society of America*, v.70, no.2, 1976, p.303). *Class No:* 937/938(031)

[6675]
YONAH, M.A. and SHATZMAN, I. Illustrated encyclopedia of the Classical World. London, Sampson Low, 1976. 509p. illus. (inc. col. pl.), tables, maps, bibliog., index. ISBN: 0562000372.

2300 short and long entries (some with brief bibliographies) relating to people, places, concepts and institutions in the fields of art, history, law, literature, mythology, philosophy, religion and science. Lists of Greek, Macedonian, Egyptian, Roman, *etc.* rulers. Classified bibliography p.501-3. Index of names, terms and subjects not included as entry titles p.504-9. 6 maps. *Class No:* 937/938(031)

Dictionaries

[6676]
A Dictionary of ancient history. Speake, G., ed. Oxford, Blackwell, 1994. x,758p. maps, geneal tables, bibliog. £35. ISBN: 0631180699.

11 academic contributors. 2000 cross-referenced A-Z entries relating to major events, institutions, individuals, periods, places *etc.* in the Ancient World from 776BC to AD476 linked by references to bibliography (p.685-734). Appendix includes 3 genealogical tables and list of Roman Emperors. 10 maps. *Class No:* 937/938(038)

[6677]
WARRINGTON, J. Everyman's classical dictionary 800BC-AD337. London, J.M. Dent, 1961. xxxvii, 537p. £11.50. ISBN: 0460030043.

Claims to supplant Sir William Smith's *Smaller classical dictionary* (revised by H.E. Blakeney and J. Warrington, London, Dent, 1956. xxiv, 352p.). 'Hundreds of articles are supplied on persons and subjects ignored by the old volume' (*Preface*). Articles vary in length from about 8 words to 2 pages (*e.g.* on Heracles). On writers, the articles cite the 'best' editions and translations. According to the *Times literary supplement* no. 3106, 8 September 1961, p.592, it is conspicuously less well planned and somewhat less reliable than the *Oxford companion to Classical literature*.
Class No: 937/938(038)

[6678]
The Oxford classical dictionary. Hammond, N.G.L. *and* Scullard, H.H. 2nd ed. Oxford, Oxford University Press, 1970. xxii, 1176p. £37.50. ISBN: 0198691173.

First published 1948. Modelled on Lübker's *Reallexicon* (8th ed. 1914).

About 350 contributors. All articles are signed; appended bibliographies ('Spain': 1¾ cols. in 3 sections, 24 lines of bibliography; 'Sparta': 3 cols., including lists of Agiads and Eurypontids; 'Origen': 1½ cols., 16 lines of bibliography). Designed to cover the same ground as the older dictionaries by Sir William Smith. 'The editors have introduced only a few changes. They have allowed a little more space for the achaeological background ... They have included more people, places and persons (for example, lesser rulers ...). They have paid more attention to the later Roman Empire' (*Preface*). Sources, p.ix-xxii. 'Index of names which are not titles of entries in the dictionary', p.1154-73. The essential one-volume reference work in this field, although Sir P. Harvey's *Oxford companion to Classical literature* has proved more practical for quick reference.
Class No: 937/938(038)

Maps & Atlases

[6679]
TALBERT, R.J.A. Atlas of Classical History. London, Croom Helm; New York, Macmillan, 1985. 217p. maps, bibliog., tables. £19.95. $50.00. ISBN: 0709924216, UK; 0029331102, US.

134 maps arranged chronologically: 'The Aegean in the Bronze Age' - 'Dioceses and provinces of the Roman Empire in AD 314. Bibliography p.179-189. Gazetteer p.190-217. Primarily intended for A level and undergraduate level students. Concern about the clarity of its small scale maps is expressed in *Choice*, v.23, no.5, January 1986, p.723. *Class No:* 937/938(084.3)

Biographies

[6680]
RADICE, B. Who's who in the Ancient World a handbook to the survival of the Greek and Roman classics. rev. ed. Harmondsworth, Middlesex, Penguin Books, 1973. xlvi, 225p. illus., pbk. £5.95. ISBN: 0140510559.

First published London, Blond, 1971.

An encyclopaedia of *c.1,00 historical and mythical persons and places ('Helen': 2+T columns; 'Seneca': 11/3 cols.; 'Odysseus': 4 cols.). References to paintings, sculpture, music and literature. Select bibliography, p.xlvi.*

.... (contd.)
*Table of main dates (Greece; Rome; Near East). Detailed index, p.165-225. 'An extremely useful reference work for the average reader' (*Choice*, v.9, no.1, March 1972, p.46).*
Class No: 937/938(092)

[6681]
SMITH, W. Dictionary of Greek and Roman biography and mythology. New York, AMS Press. $245.00. ISBN: 0404061303.

First published London, John Murray, 3v., 1880.

The period covered is from the earliest times to the fall of the Western Empire in A.D. 746. Short entries; no authorities cited in situ. An appendix cites the most important works consulted. Also *Dictionary of Greek and Roman geography*. $140.00. (3v., 1880) and *Dictionary of Greek and Roman antiquities*. $65.00. (2v., 1890-91). These 3 works, though much dated and partly at least superseded by Pauly and others, still retain their value.
Class No: 937/938(092)

Ancient Greece

[6682]
BURY, J.B. *and* MEIGGS, R. A History of Greece to the death of Alexander the Great. 4th ed. London, Macmillan, 1975. 577p. illus., maps, bibliog., index.

18 chapters (1. The beginnings of Greece and the heroic age ... 18. The conquest of the Far East). Chronological table. Bibliographies, p.509-16. Notes to text, illus., and maps, p.517-55. Glossary. Analytical index, p.561-77. 92 black-and-white illus., 36 good clear maps. 'The future of Bury's history as a major reference work seems assured' (*New History*, July 1975, p.1). *Class No:* 937

Dictionaries

[6683]
TRAVLOS, J. Pictorial dictionary of ancient Athens. London, Thames & Hudson, 1971. xvi, 590p. illus. (inc. pl.), maps. £85. ISBN: 087817267x.

Originally published by the German Archaeological Institute 1970.

A monumental work on the typography and architecture of Athens, 3000BC-AD300, arranged A-Z (Agora ... Zeus Phratios). Admirably illustrated and well documented (*e.g.* 'Agora': p.1-29; 37 figures; 20 references. 'Stadium': p.498-504; 8 illus.; 13 references. 722 references, ground plans and photographs. Sources p.xi-xii. Also references in text.
Class No: 937(038)

Maps & Atlases

[6684]
Atlas of the Greek world. Levi, P. Oxford, Phaidon, 1980. 239p. illus., tables, maps, plans. £22.50. ISBN: 071482044x.

87 maps, mostly diagrammatic; *c.* 500 illus. (350 in colour) - Well-written text, in 6 parts (1. The land in context - 2. The Age of Bronze - 3. The age of tyranny - 4. The age of Pericles - 5. The age of Alexander - 6. The fate of Hellenism. Glossary. Bibliography, p.227-8. Index and gazetteer (in tiny print). Not an atlas in the conventional sense, maps being ancillary to illus. Criticised in *British Book News* (March 1980, p.186) for paucity of physical

.... *(contd.)*

maps, - 'so important to the understanding of ancient Greece ... Nevertheless, it will be useful for schools where classical studies are taught.' *Class No:* 937(084.3)

Chronologies

[6685]

WARREN, P. *and* HANKEY, V. **Aegean Bronze Age chronology.** Bristol, Bristol Classical Press, 1989. x,230p. illus., tables. £24. ISBN: 090651567x.

3 main chapters: 1. Introduction (inc. evidence that has become available in recent years) - 2. Relative (pottery based) chronology - 3. Absolute chronology recorded by radiocarbon dating and ceramic synchronisms.
Class No: 937(090)

Biographies

[6686]

BOWDER, D., *ed*. **Who was who in the Greek World** 776BC-30BC. Oxford, Phaidon; Ithaca, New York, Cornell Univ. Press, 1982. 239p. illus., maps, geneal tables, bibliog., index. £18.00; $35.00. ISBN: 0714822078, UK; 0801415381, US.

12 contributors. Over 750 entries 'to provide a scholarly and readable account of the lives, achievements, and works of all the more notable personages' (*Introduction*). Entries end with bibliographical source references. A brief essay on the Mycenean and Minoan periods, 'The Homeric heroes', carries entries for legendary leaders. Chronology p.6-9. Glossary p.217-23. Bibliography p.224-7. 'Its major virtue is to bring together in short compass the most recent biographical and historical information on a large number of ancient Greek (and a few non-Greek) personages' (*Choice,* v.20,no.8, April 1983, p.116). *Class No:* 937(092)

[6687]

DEVELIN, R. **Athenian officials 684-321 BC.** Cambridge, Cambridge Univ. Press, 1989. xix,556p. bibliog., indexes. £55. ISBN: 0521328802.

A year-by-year list of officials from archaic and classical Athens with a short notice of their activities and the evidence relating to an individual's office in a particular year. Also contains all state decrees datable to any year or which include relevant information. Chronology p.xi-xii. References and bibliography p.xiii-xix. Modelled on T.R.S. Broughton's *The Magistrates of the Roman Republic.*
Class No: 937(092)

Ancient Rome

[6688]

AUFSTIEG UND NIEDERGANG DER RÖMISCHEN WELT. Geschichte und Kultur Roms im Spiegel der neueren Forschung. **Rise and decline of the Roman world.** Temporini, H. *and* Haase, W., *eds.* Berlin & New York, Walter de Gruyter, 1972-.

Teil 1: *Von den Aufängen Roms bis zum Ausgang der Republik,* 4v. in 1 and *Tafeln* (1972-73). Teil 2: *Principat. Politische Geschichte,* 15v. in 10 (1974-88) *Künste,* 3v. in 1 (1981-85); *Recht,* 3v. (1976-82); *Religion,* 27v. in 11 (1978-93); *Sprache und Literatur,* 21v. in 6 (1980-92); *Philosophie, Wissenschaften, Technik,* 6v. in 1 (1987-92). V.18.2 *Religion (Heidentum: Die Religiösen Verhältnisse In Den Provinzen)* edited by W. Haase. 1989. xi, 875-1655p.

.... *(contd.)*

ISBN 3110103664 has 15 chapters by various hands in 3 languages. Most have bibliographies and/or lists of illustration sources. A truly remarkable and impressive work of scholarship. *Class No:* 938

[6689]

BRAUND, D. **Augustus to Nero** a sourcebook on Roman history 31BC-AD68. London, Croom Helm, 1985. xiii, 334p. bibliog., index. £17.95. $28.95. ISBN: 0709906595.

849 sources - inscriptions, coins, papyri, literary texts - arranged in 8 sections and translated: 1. Imperial family - 2. Imperial household - 3. Senators - 4. Equites - 5. Armed forces - 6. Imperial administration - 7. Kings, cities, and towns - 8. Society and economy. Bibliographical note p.v-xi.
Class No: 938

[6690]

CARY, M. *and* SCULLARD, H.H. **A History of Rome** down to the reign of Constantine. 3rd ed. London, Macmillan; New York, St. James Press, 1975. xxvii,694p. bibliog., index.

First published 1935.

Aims to provide 'a comprehensive survey of Roman history down to the dawn of the Middle Ages' (*Preface* to 2nd ed.). 6 parts: 1. Pre-Roman Italy - 2. The Roman conquest of Italy - 3. The conquest of the Mediterranean - 4. The fall of the Republic - 5. Consolidation of the Roman Empire - 6. The decline of the Roman Empire. Chronological table, List of emperors. Genealogical tables. 'Brief list of books', p.575. Notes and references (by chapters), p.577-658. Glossary. Analytical index, p.667-94. Favourably reviewed in TLS, no.3863, 26 March 1976, p.350. *Class No:* 938

Bibliographies

[6691]

ROLLINS, A. **Rome in the fourth century** an annotated bibliography with historical overview. Jefferson, N. Carolina, McFarland, 1991. xxxiii,324p. index. $48.50; £36. ISBN: 0899506240.

1432 entries restricted to 20th century material in the English language arranged in 12 thematic sections: 1. General works - 2. Politics and government - 3. Military matters - 4. Literature and education - 5. Monetary matters - 6. Economy, technology, science and medicine - 7. Society and art -`8. Foreign affairs and barbarians - 9. Religion and philosophy - 10. Christianity - 11. Church and state. The period covered is AD 284 - AD 395. *Class No:* 938(01)

[6692]

ROLLINS, A.M., *comp.* **The Fall of Rome** a reference guide. Jefferson, North Carolina, McFarland, 1983. xiv, 130p. index. $19.95. £14.35. ISBN: 089950034x.

260 items forming 'a select and selectively annotated guide to twentieth century literature in English on the fall of Rome' (*Introduction*). Chronology p. xiii-xiv. *Class No:* 938(01)

Encyclopaedias

[6693]

WACHER, J., *ed.* **The Roman world.** London, Routledge & Kegan Paul, 2v., 1987. 1,478+Øiv,479-872p. maps, plans, diagrs., bibliog., index. £120.00. ISBN: 0710208944, v.1; 0710208952, v.2; 0710099754, set.

Encyclopaedic survey by 33 archaeologists and historians

....(contd.)

on all aspects of the Roman world organized in 11 parts each ending with an extensive bibliography: 1. Introduction - 2. The rise of the Empire - 3. The Army - 4. The Frontiers - 5. Cities, towns and villages - 6. Government and law - 7. Rural life - 8. Economy - 9. Society - 10. Religion and burial - 11. Postscript. General Bibliography p.xxv-xxx. Chronological table p.xxiv-xliii. Glossary p.xliv-l. *Class No:* 938(031)

Dictionaries

[6694]
NASH, E. **Pictorial dictionary of ancient Rome.** Rev. ed. London, Thames & Hudson, 2v., 1968. 544p. 535p. illus. (pl.), plans. £127. ISBN: 0878172653.

First published 1961-62. Sponsored by the Deutsches Archäologisches Institut.

1: *Amphitheatrum Castrense-Lacus Curtius.*

2: *Lacus Inturnae-Volcanal.*

Essentially a pictorial record (v.1: 674 half-tones; v.2: 664) of the city of Rome's ancient monuments and buildings, with brief descriptions and bibliographies. 'Fornix Fabianus': v.1, p.398-400; 4 illus.; 6 lines of description; bibliography of 26 items. Scholarly (v.1 has general bibliography, p.9-12; pictorial sources, p.12-13).

Class No: 938(038)

[6695]
RICHARDSON, L. **A New topographical dictionary of Ancient Rome.** Baltimore, John Hopkins Univ. Press, 1992. 458p., illus., plans. $65; £49. ISBN: 0810843006.

Updates S.B. Platner's *Topographical dictionary of Ancient Rome* (1929).

Description and concise history, geographical and topographical features, of the known buildings and monuments of ancient Rome, with measurements, dates and references to significant ancient and modern sources. Entries extend from a few lines to 2000 word essays. 'No book for beginners. A basic knowledge of Latin and Roman civilization is required' (*Choice*, v.30, no.8, April 1993, p.1299). *Class No:* 938(038)

Portraits

[6696]
TOYNBEE, J.M.C. **Roman historical portraits.** London, Thames & Hudson, 1978. 409p. ports. £18.00. ISBN: 0500232776.

Covers the late Republic and Augustan period. A catalogue of portraits of identifiable notables of the age precedes entries on the individuals concerned, with commentary on the portraiture. Largely devoted, despite the title, 'to portraits of foreign (*i.e.*, non-Roman) rulers from the third century B.C. to the fifth century A.D. who were in one way or another involved in the history of Rome as allies, client princes or antagonists' (*Annual Bulletin of Historical Literature*, v.64, 1980, p.18). *Class No:* 938(084.10)

Maps & Atlases

[6697]
CORNELL, T. and MATTHEWS, J. **Atlas of the Roman world.** Oxford, Phaidon; New York, Facts on File, 1982. 240p. col. illus., col., maps, bibliog., index. £18.50. $40.00. ISBN: 0714821527, UK; 0871966522, US.

....(contd.)

Pt.1. Early history and the Republic - 2. From Republic to Empire - 3. Provinces of the Empire - 4. The Empire in Decline. 21 special features *e.g.* Roman patriotism, The city of Constantine, The Roman legacy. Chronological table p.6-7. Bibliography p.228-230. Gazetteer p.231-236. Analytical index. 62 maps. 470 illustrations (257 in colour). 'Superior to most other introductory surveys of Rome' (*Choice*, v.20, no.3, November 1982, p.406). *Class No:* 938(084.3)

Chronologies

[6698]
BAGNALL, R.S., *and others*. **Consuls of the Later Roman Empire.** Atlanta, Georgia, Scholars Press for The American Philological Association, 1987. viii,759p. tables, bibliog., indexes. (*Philological Monographs no.36.*) ISBN: 155540099x.

1. History of the Consulate - 2. The Evidence (p.97-617) - 3. Critical appraisal - 4. Bibliography (p.700-8) - 5. Indices. 'This book is not so much concerned with these men as figures in the society of late antiquity as it is devoted to their utility for identifying years: consulates as a means of reckoning time' (*Preface*). *Class No:* 938(090)

Biographies

[6699]
BOWDER, D., *ed*. **Who was who in the Roman world.** Oxford, Phaidon; New York, Cornell Univ. Press, 1980. 256p. 282 illus., maps, bibliog., geneal tables, index. £15.00. ISBN: 0714820490, UK; 0801413583, US.

More than 900 biographies, arranged A-Z according to whichever is best known, praenomen, nomen, or cognomen, covering the period 753BC-AD476, *i.e.* from the legendary date of the foundation of Rome to the collapse of the Roman Empire in the West. Entries end with a bibliographical reference either to an ancient source or to a modern book. Index to persons mentioned but without an entry p.232-235. Glossary p.236-242. Bibliography p.243-245. Maps and Stemmata p.246-252. Its greatest strength, reports *Choice*, v.18 no.8 April 1981: p.1078+1080, 'is the large number of entries on very minor figures'. *Class No:* 938(092)

[6700]
BROUGHTON, T.R.S. **Magistrates of the Roman Republic.** Atlanta, Ga., Scholars Press, 3v., 1986.

Originally published New York, American Philological Association (1951-52) and *Supplement* (1960).

1. *509BC-100BC.* xix,578p. ISBN 0891308121. Abbreviations (p.xvi-xix). Annual lists of magistrates and other officials (p.1-578). Data: ancient evidence regarding the name, office, date, and summary of activities in office. 2. *99BC-31BC.* ix,647p. 0891308113. Annual lists as in v.1 (p.1-428). Appendices: 1, Monetales - 2. Magistrates *etc.* of uncertain date (p.462-86) - 3. Supplementary list of Senators (p.487-98). Bibliography (p.499-523). Index of careers *i.e.* name and chronological list of offices (p.524-636). Note on chronology (p.637-9). 3. *Supplement.* vii,294p. Additions and corrections (p.1-225). Errata (p.227-35). Abbreviations (p.236-88). Bibliography (p.239-83). Concordance of names in the Index (v.2) and the relevant articles published in Pauly-Wissowa's *Reallexikon* since 1952 (p.284-94). This Supplement incorporates additional matter first printed in *Supplement of the magistrates of the Roman Republic* (1960). *Class No:* 938(092)

[6701]

GRANT, M.J. The Roman emperors: a biographical guide to the rulers of Imperial Rome. 31BC-AD476. London, Weidenfeld & Nicolson; New York, Scribners, 1985. xv, 367p. illus., maps, geneal. tables, indexes. £14.95. $25.00. ISBN: 0297785559, UK; 0684183889, US.

92 essays arranged in 9 dynastic sections outline the political and military events of each reign and provide a physical description of each emperor taken from contemporary coins and sculptures. Key to Latin terms p.335-43. Index of Latin and Greek authors p.345-51. Index to maps and plans (with modern equivalents of place-names) p.353-67. 'An absolute must for every library' (*Choice*, v.23, no.5, January 1986, p.726). *Class No:* 938(092)

[6702]

JONES, A.H.M., *and others.* **The Prosopography of the Later Roman Empire.** Cambridge, Cambridge Univ. Press, 3v., 1971-92.
AD 260-395. 1971. xxii, 1152p. £100.00. ISBN 0521072336. 2. *AD 395-527. 1980. 1324p. £100.00. 0521201594.* 3. *AD 527-641.* 2v. 1992. 1626p. £200. 0521201608.

Detailed information on the officials who ruled the later Roman Empire. The prosopography (A-Z, names), in v.1, p.1-994, gives brief biographies and cites sources (Flavius Stilicho, p.853-8). Fragmentary names and anonymi, p.997-1040; Fasti consulares, p.1041-1127; Stemmata (family trees); p.1128-47. Index to Fasti; index to consulares. Sources, p.xi-xx. A monumental specialized compilation, continuing *Prosopographia Imperii Romani* (1897-98) and complementing H. Marrou's *Prosopographie Chretienne*, and providing a complete secular biography of the Roman Empire. *Class No:* 938(092)

Ancient Africa

[6703]

PHILLIPSON, D., *ed.* **The Peoples of Africa.** Oxford, Basil Blackwell.

Series announced 1989. To be on same pattern as *The peoples of Europe* (*qv*). Titles planned: Beach, D. *The Shona and their neighbours.* 1993. 256p. 0631176780. 15 maps; Brett, M. and Fentress, E. *The Berbers.* 1994. 0631168524; Horton. *The Swahili.* 1993. 063118919x; Le May, G.H. *The Afrikaners.* 1994. 0631182047; McIntosh, R.J. and McIntosh, S.K. *The People of the Middle Niger.* 1994. 0631173617; Pankhurst, R. *The Ethiopians.* 1994. 0631184686; and Robertshaw, P. and Sobania, N. *The Maasai, the Dinka and the East African pastoralists.* 1995. 0631183833. *Class No:* 939.7

[6704]

PICARD, C.G. *and* **PICARD, C. Carthage:** a survey of Punic history and culture from its birth to the final tragedy. 4th rev. ed. London, Sidgwick and Jackson, 1987. vi,362p. illus. (pl.), maps,. bibliog., index. £17.95. ISBN: 0283995327.

First published as *Le monde de Carthage* (Paris, 1956) and in English as *Carthage* (1964).

1. Carthage before the Magonids - 2. The Magonids - 3. Carthage under the oligarchy - 4. The first war against Rome - 5. The Barcid Revolution - 6. Hannibal - 7. The death throes of Carthage. Chronology p.5-14. Bibliography p.347-53. 52 plates. *Class No:* 939.7

[6705]

RAVEN, S. Rome in Africa. 3rd ed. London, Routledge, 1993. xxxiii,254p. illus., maps, bibliog., index. ISBN: 0415082617.

First published by Evans Brothers 1969; 2nd ed. Longman 1984.

Narrative history in 14 chapters with strong archaeological content. Chronology p.xix-xxv. Bibliography p.241-3. *Class No:* 939.7

Ancient North America

[6706]

BRAY, W. *and* **FEEST, C., eds. The Peoples of America.** Oxford, Basil Blackwell.

On same pattern as *The peoples of Europe* (*qv*). Forthcoming titles include Browne, D.M. and Silverman, H. *The Nascas.* 1994. 1557862249; D'Altroy , T.N. *The Incas.* 1995. 0631176772; Kolata, A.L. *The Tiwanaku.* 1993. 1557861838; and Snow, D. *The Iroquois.* 1993. 1557862257. *Class No:* 939.71-.73

[6707]

JENNINGS, J.D., *ed.* **Ancient North Americans.** San Francisco, W.H. Freeman, 1983. xii,642p. $29.95. ISBN: 0716714280.

12 chapters by different hands: 1. Changing directions in archaeological thought - 2. Origins - 3. Alaska and the Northwest Coast - 4. Pioneers. *Class No:* 939.71-.73

Ancient Central America

[6708]

DAVIES, N. The Ancient kingdoms of Mexico. London, Allen Lane, 1982. 272p. illus., maps, bibliog., index. £12.50. ISBN: 0713912456.

Covers the period 1500BC-AD1500 focussing on the Olmec, Teotihuacan, Toltec and Aztec civilizations. Popular work but useful for its Comparative chronology p.11; Principal Archaeological Sites of Mexico p.255-6; and Bibliography p.257-64. *Class No:* 939.728

Ancient South America

[6709]

JENNINGS, J.D., *ed.* **Ancient South Americans.** San Francisco, W.H. Freeman, 1983. xi,414p. $29.95. ISBN: 0716714299.

1. Changing directions in archeological thought - 2. Mesoamerica - 2. The Palao-Indians - 4. The Northern Andes - 5. Central Andean civilization - 6. The Southern Andes - 7. Lowland South America and the Antilles - 8. Pre-Columbian transoceanic contacts. Glossary p.395-8. *Class No:* 939.8

Ancient Australasian Peoples

[6710]

BELLWOOD, P. *and* **GLOVER, I., eds. The Peoples of Southeast Asia and the Pacific.** Oxford, Basil Blackwell.

On same pattern as *The peoples of Europe* (*qv*). Forthcoming titles include Anderson, A. *The Maoris;* Davidson, J. *The Vietnamese.* 1996. 0631170383; Fox, J.J. *People of the Lesser Sundas.* 1995. 063117463x; Hobart, A. and others. *The Balinese.* 1995. 063117687x; Kirch, P. *The*

....(contd.)

Polynesians. 1994. 1557861129; Milner, A.C. and
Matheson, V. *The Malays*. 1995. 063117222x; Pelras, C.
The Bugis. 1994. 0631172319; Spriggs, M. *The Island
Polynesians*. 1994. 0631167277; and Thomas, N. *The
Fijians*. 1994. 0631173269. *Class No:* 939.9

[6711]
BELLWOOD, P. The Polynesians: prehistory of an island
people. Rev. ed. London, Thames and Hudson, 1987. 175p.
illus., maps, bibliog., index, pbk. (*Ancient People and
Places, no.92..*) ISBN: 0500274509.
First published 1978.
6 chapters: 1. Introduction (geography of Polynesia;
European navigators; the influence of the Polynesians,
theories before 1952) - 2. Culture - 3. Archaeological origins
- 4. Tropical chiefdoms A.D.1200-1800 - 5. Into Southern
Waters - 6. Achievements. Bibliography p.166-171. 107
illus. Analytical index. 'An excellent introduction to a
fascinating theme' (*Geographical Journal*, v.146, no.1,
March 1990, p.122-3). *Class No:* 939.9

[6712]
MABBETT, I.W. *and* **CHANDLER, D.P. The Khmers.**
Oxford, Blackwell, 1993. 288p. illus., maps. (*Peoples of
South-East Asia and the Pacific*.) ISBN: 0631175822.
Story of the early civilization of the Khmers (or
Cambodains), the development of states within Indian
culture, the Empire of Angkor (8th to 14 century), its decline
and subsequent changes. 10 maps. *Class No:* 939.9

Mediaeval & Modern History

[6713]
The New Cambridge modern history. Cambridge,
Cambridge Univ. Press, 14v., 1957-79.
Reappraisal of the period covered by *Cambridge modern
history* (13v. and atlas, 1902-26) omitting chapter
bibliographies. These were eventually published
subsequently: J. Roach, *A Bibliography of modern history*
(1968) (*qv*.).
1. *The Renaissance 1483-1520* edited by G.R. Potter.
1957. xxxvi, 532p. £55.00. ISBN 0521045414. 2nd ed.
planned for 1991. 2. *The Reformation 1520-1559* edited by
G.R. Elton. 2nd ed., 1990. 750p. £35.00. 0521345367. 3.
The Counter-Reformation and price revolution 1559-1610
edited by W.B. Wenham. 1968. xvi, 599p. £55.00.
0521045436. 4. *The Decline of Spain and the Thirty Years'
War 1609-48/59* edited by J.P. Cooper. 1970. xxi, 832p.
£75.00. 0521076188. 5. *The Ascendancy of France 1648-88*
edited by F.L. Carsten. 1961. £65.00. 0521045444. 6. *The
Rise of Great Britain and Russia 1685-1715/25* edited by
J.S. Bromley. 1970. xxxiv, 947p. £75.00. 0521075246. 7.
The Old Régime 1713-63 edited by J.O. Lindsay. 1957. xx,
625p. £65.00. 0521045452. 8. *The American and French
Revolutions 1763-93* edited by A. Goodwin. 1965. xxiii,
747p. £65.00. ISBN 0521045460. 9. *War and peace in an
age of upheaval 1793-1830* edited by C.W. Crawley. 1965.
xiv, 748p. £75.00. 0521045479. 10. *The Zenith of European
power 1830-70* edited by J.P.T. Bury. 1960. xxii, 765p.
£75.00. 0521045487. 11. *Material progress and world-wide
problems 1870-1898* edited by F.H. Hinsley. 1962. xi, 743p.
£75.00. 0521045495. 12. *The Shifting balance of world
forces 1898-1945* edited by C.L. Mowat. 2nd ed. 1968.

....(contd.)

xxvii, 845p. £75.00. 0521045517. 13. *Companion volume*
edited by P. Burke. 1979. vi, 378p. £45.00. 0521221285. 14
contributors. 12 overview essays on specific themes to
complement v.6-12. *e.g.* 2. The environment and the
economy ... 9. The scientific revolution ... 12. On the last
2,500 years in Western history, and some remarks on the
coming 500. 14. *The Atlas* edited by H.C. Darby and H.
Fullard. 1970. 319p. £65.00. 0521077087. *Class No:* 94

Bibliographies

[6714]
ROACH, J., ed. A Bibliography of modern history.
Cambridge, Cambridge Univ. Press, 1968. xxiv,388p.
Bibliographical companion to *The New Cambridge modern
history*.
The 6,040 entries (usually unannotated) are very largely
the work of the *c*.200 contributors to the NCMH. 3 main
sections: A. 1493-1648 (to be used with v.12-4 of NCMH) -
B. 1648-1793 (with v.5-8) - C. 1793-1945 (with v.9-12). 195
sections and many itemised cross-references. Cites many
published series 'and those books are noted which contain
useful bibliographies' (*Introduction*). Main emphasis is on
books in English mostly published prior to 1961; over 80%
of them concern Europe, and 75%, Western Europe.
Analytical subject-index. *Class No:* 94(01)

Handbooks & Manuals

[6715]
GIBBONS, S. A Handbook of modern history. London and
New York, Longman, 1986. 271p. illus., index. £12.50.
ISBN: 0582204992, UK; 0582224527, US.
450 A-Z cross-referenced articles on events, personalities,
organizations, political ideas and concepts, important
scientific and cultural influences. 30 photographs.
Class No: 94(035)

Dictionaries

[6716]
HABERKERN, E. *and* **WALLACH, J.F. Hilfswörterbuch
für Historiker, Mittelalter und Neizeit.** Bern, Francke,
2v., 1980-7. Tübingen, 2v., 1980-87.
1. *Erster Teil A-K.* 7th ed., 1987, 367p. 22.80. ISBN
3772012914. 2. *L-Z.* 6th ed., 1980. 311p. 19.80.
3772012930.
About 20,000 terms in many languages connnected with
medieval and modern history are briefly defined. In A-Z
order, with numerous cross-references, particularly from a
term in one language to its equivalent in German. Many
entries for Latin terms; also for such English terms as
'District Councils', 'Boroughs', 'Town Councils',
'Overseers', 'Parliament' (1½cols.), 'Vestry' (¼col.). Gives
country of origin. No bibliographies. *Class No:* 94(038)

[6717]
PALMER, A. Penguin dictionary of modern history 1789-
1945. 2nd ed. Harmondsworth, Middlesex, Penguin Books,
1983. 315p.
First published by Cresset Books 1962.
International in scope although British affairs predominate.
History of individual states is summarised 'only where there
are not many topics or biographies from that country
included elsewhere' (Preface to 1st ed.). Over 100 fresh

....(contd.)

entries in this ed. mainly concerned with American, Asian and Australasian affairs. Useful for the small library and for school use. *Class No:* 94(038)

Yearbooks & Directories

[6718]

The Annual register a record of world events, 1992. Day, A.J. *and* Hoffman, V., eds. Harlow, Essex, Longman, 1992. xvi, 612p., illus. (pl), tables, map, index. £89. ISBN: 0582079268.

First edited in 1758 by Edmund Burke as *The Annual register: a review of public events at home and abroad for the year ...*

Running commentary in 19 subdivided sections: 1. United Kingdom - 2. Western Central and Southern Europe - 3. Eastern Europe - 4. Americas and Caribbean - 5. Middle East and North Africa - 6. Equatorial Africa - 7. Central and Southern Africa - 8. South Asia and Indian Ocean - 9. South-East and East Asia - 10. Australasia and South Pacific - 11. International organizations - 12. Security, arms control and disarmament - 13. Religion - 14. The Sciences - 15. The Law - 16. The Arts - 17. Sport - 18. Economic and social affairs - 19. Documents and reference - 20. Obituary - 21. Chronicle of principal events in 1989. p.595-609. Analytical index. *Class No:* 94(058)

Almanacs

[6719]

The Statesman's year-book historical companion. Paxton, J., ed. London, Macmillan Reference Books, 1988. xi, 356p. index. £19.95. ISBN: 0333436598.

Celebrates the 125th anniversary of *The stateman's yearbook (qv)*.

Records the salient constitutional and political events of each country (extracted from various editons of *The Statesman's year-book)*. 'Particular attention has been given to the turbulent political histories of countries becoming independent in this century' *(Preface)*. Arrangement is A-Z by country. Further readings. *Class No:* 94(059)

Maps & Atlases

[6720]

The New Cambridge modern history. v.14. The Atlas. Darby, H.C. *and* Fullard, H. Cambridge, Cambridge Univ. Press, 1970. xxiv,319p. maps (some col.). £65.00. ISBN: 0521077087.

Supersedes *The Cambridge modern history atlas* (2nd ed., 1924).

288 pages of coloured maps; no text. Three groups: the first depicts exploration and political acquisition of parts of the world, plus achievement of independence, 1945-68; the second group covers wars and treaty settlements, from the Peasants' War of 1524-6 to World War II. The third group is of regional maps, each sub-group in chronological order. Well balanced: 15 areas are covered. 'Although it is designed to serve the need of readers of the *New Cambridge modern history,* the atlas is also intended to illustrate school or university courses on modern history' *(Geo Abstracts,* 1972/1, entry 72D/0321). 'One of the most informative and best historical atlases, but also one of the most compact and easiest to handle' *(Library Journal,* v.97, no.18, 15 April

....(contd.)

1972, p.1386), giving fuller coverage than does Shepherd's *Historical atlas (qv)*. Page size, 20x28.5cm. *Class No:* 94(084.3)

[6721]

The Times atlas of medieval civilizations. Scarre, C., ed. London, The Times, 1990. 16p. col. illus., col. maps. Binder £5.50.

Illustrations and maps adapted from *The Times atlas of world history* and *Past worlds. The Times atlas of archaeology (qvv)* and from *The Times. The world: an illustrated history.*

Five parts issued with *The Times* at weekly intervals, 22 September - 20 October 1990. 1. *Dawn of a new age* - 2. *Western Christendom* - 3. *The Empires of Asia* - 4. *New worlds* - 5. Europe ascendant. Each issue contains 8 double-page pictorial features. The period covered ranges from the Germanic invasions and the collapse of the Classical World to the Age of Discovery 1475-1600. *Class No:* 94(084.3)

Sound Recordings & Tapes

[6722]

Oral history index: an international directory of oral history interviews. Wasserman, E.S., ed. Westport, Conn., Meckler, 1990. 434p. £90; $145. ISBN: 0887363490.

Over 30,000 oral historal transcripts from 400 institutions in US, Canada, UK and Israel principally arranged A-Z by name of person(s) interviewed. Data: interview date; subject content; and a coded reference to a second sequence of entries for institutions and collections. Compiled from questionnaires sent to 1,300 institutions. 'An immensely thorough basic guide which is primarily geared to the needs of biographers and family historians' *(Reference Reviews,* v,5, no.1, 1991, p.39-40). Supplements A. Smith's *Directory of oral history collections. Class No:* 94(086.7)

Bibliographies

[6723]

HAVLICE, P.P. Oral history a reference guide and annotated bibliography. Jefferson, North Carolina, McFarland, 1985. 144p. indexes. softcover. $29.95; £29.95. ISBN: 0899501389.

773 entries (abstracts, indexes, catalogues, journals, colloquia *etc.*) range over entire field. Main emphasis is on North American material but European and African items are included. Subject and title indexes allow easy access. 'An important reference tool, superior to the less comprehensive and less up-to-date bibliographies currently available' *(Choice,* v.23,no.2, October 1985,p.171). *Class No:* 94(086.7)(01)

[6724]

HENIGE, D. Oral historiography. London, Longman, 1982. 150p. bibliog., index. £12.50. ISBN: 0582643643.

7 sections: 1. Putting oral historiography in its place - 2. Before the field: approaching oral data - 3. In the field: collecting oral data - 4. After the field: the context of interpretation - 5. The content of interpretation - 6. Oral history: testimony of the recent past - 7. Sharing primary resources. Bibliography p.131-46. *Class No:* 94(086.7)(01)

[6725]

PERKS, R., *comp.* **Oral history:** an annotated bibliography. London, British Library National Sound Archive, 1990. xv,183p. index. pbk. £12.95. ISBN: 071230505x.

23132 numbered entries A-Z by author relating to books, pamphlets, periodicals, articles, catalogues, and published recordings. Coverage is comprehensive for UK and selective for elsewhere. *Class No:* 94(086.7)(01)

Yearbooks & Directories

[6726]

SMITH, A. **Directory of oral history collections.** Phoenix, Arizona, Oryx Press, 1988. 142p. indexes. $49.50; £33.65. ISBN: 0897743229.

Lists 476 repositories in 49 states and District of Columbia with entries arranged by state and city. Data: postal address, telephone, staff, size of collection, hours and access, finding aids, general and significant holdings. Described as a 'preliminary' edition, coverage is inevitably incomplete. An 'expanded and more comprehensive version is promised. *Class No:* 94(086.7)(058)

Modern Times

Chronologies

[6727]

WILLIAMS, N. **Chronology of the modern world 1763-1992.** Oxford, Helicon, 1994.

First published London, Barrie & Jenkins, 1966.

Left-hand page: One or more of the chief events of the year, selected to form head-lines. Right-hand page: The most significant of the year under headings: A. Politics, economics, law and education - B. Science, technology, discovery - C. Scholarship - D. Philosophy and religion - E. Art, sculpture, fine arts and architecture - F. Music - G. Literature - H. The press - J. Drama and entertainment - K. Sport - L. Statistics - M. Births and deaths of notabilities. Detailed index (713-1020) of *c.*24,000 entries (subjects subdivided by countries; 'Political parties'; nearly 13 columns. A chronology, with progressively fuller entries, that strikes a balance between political and cultural events. *Class No:* 94"15/19"(090)

18th Century

Dictionaries

[6728]

BLACK, J. *and* PORTER, R. **A Dictionary of eighteenth century world history.** Oxford, Blackwell, 1993. 512p. £35. ISBN: 0631180680.

Combines short entries, compendia of biographical facts, wars and events, and longer interpretative essays and up-to-date reports on current thinking and research. *Class No:* 94"17"(038)

19th Century

Encyclopaedias

[6729]

Chronik des 19. Jahrhunderts. Dortmund, Chronik Verlag. Announced for publication. *Class No:* 94"18"(031)

20th Century

[6730]

VADNEY, T. **The World since 1945.** New York & Oxford, Facts On File, 1987. 570p. maps, bibliog., index. £18.95; $29.95. ISBN: 0816018154.

Part 1. From the Second World War to decolonization. Chapter 1. Origins of the post-1945 world - 2. The United States as a global power - 3. The Third World: Colonialism, neo-colonialism, and revolution - 4. Asia in crisis - 5. The alliances - 6. Decolonization in Africa. Part 2. The Post-missile crisis era. 7. A neo-colonial world: Latin America - 8. The wars in Indo-China - 9. Asia's great powers - 10. The developed centres - 11. The superpowers and the Third World: the Middle East and Latin America - 12. Trends. Bibliographical note (in narrative form) p.528-35. Chronology p.536-43. Covers political, economic, diplomatic, and military events shaping global history. 'The strategy has been to select particular cases as examples of more general trends, and to explore them in some detail' (*Preface*). *Class No:* 94"19"

Bibliographies

[6731]

Bibliographie zur Zeitgeschichte. Beilage der Vierteljahrshefte für Zeitgeschichte. München (subsequently Stuttgart), Deutsche Verlagsanstalt, 1953-. 2*Pa.*

Jahrgang 38 (1990) 127p. has 1838 entries in 14 sections: 1. Hilfsmittel - 2. Geschichtewissenschaft - 3. Biographien ... 8. Deutsche Geschichte des 20 Jahrhunderts ... 10. Geschichte der Weimarer Republik ... 14. Geschichte der Deutschen Demokratischen Republik. *Class No:* 94"19"(01)

[6732]

—Bibliographie zur Zeitgeschichte 1953-1980: Kumulation der Zeitschrift Jahrgang 1-28. München, K.G. Saur, 3v., 1982-83. ISBN: 3598104200, set.

1. *Allegemeiner Teil* (Hilfsmittel - Geschichtwissenschaft - Gesellschaft und Politik - Biographien). 1982. xxvi,1505p. ISBN 3598104219. 2. *Geschichte des 20. Jahrhunderts bis 1945* (Allgemeine Geschichte - Europäische Gegeschichte - Geschichte des 1. Weltkrieges - Deutsche Geschichte - Geschichte einzelner Staaten - Geschichte des II Weltkrieges) 1982. viii,559p. 3598104227. 3. *Geschichte seit 1945* (Allgemeine Geschichte - Europäische Geschichte - Geschichte einzelner Staaten) 1983. 501p. 3598104235. *Class No:* 94"19"(01)

[6733]

HARCOURT, P. *and* ROBINSON, F. **Twentieth-century world history:** a select bibliography. London, Croom Helm; New York, Barnes & Noble, 1979. 154p. ISBN: 0709900201, UK; 006492680x, US.

Annotated bibliography in 27 thematic and regional areas of study. 'Based on the experience of University of London which pioneered a course in 20th-century world history ... Highly recommended' (*Choice*, v.17, no.3, May 1980, p.363); but critically reviewed in *History*, v.65, 1980, p.90-91. *Class No:* 94"19"(01)

Encyclopaedias

[6734]

Chronicle of the 20th century. Mercer, D., *editor in chief.*
Rev. ed. Farnborough, Chronicle Communications, 1993.
1456p. illus. (some col.), col. maps, ports, index. £39.95.
ISBN: 1872031455.

1st ed. 1988. Published in 13 language editions and in 15
countries, the editorial content being adapted to suit each
national readership. Belgium: Éditions Chronique; Denmark:
Ladewman Forlageaktieslskab; Finland: Gummerus
Kustannus OY; France: Librairie Larousse Éditions
Chronique; Federal Republic of Germany: Harenberg
Kommunikation; Iceland: Swart a huitu Bokaforlag; Japan:
Kodansha Ltd.; Netherlands: Elsevier Boeken B.V./Agon;
Norway: J.W. Cappelens Forlag A/S; Spain: Plaza & Janes;
Sweden: Bonnier Fakla Bokförlag AB; Switzerland: Ex
Libris; Taiwan: Chin Show Cultural Enterprises; USA:
Chronicle Publications Inc.

16 contributors are listed: all well-known journalists.
Concerns itself entirely with events, devoting 1-3 pages
(each 11 in. x 9 in.) to each month from January 1900 - June
1993, presenting a monthly calendar, a diary of events, and
illustrated 'news reports'. Cross-references point forward in
time, linked previous events are traced by means of the
detailed analytical index (p.1296-1356). 'The best new
reference book of the year ... reduces the history of the last
88 years to monthly news summaries as they might have
appeared in a middle brow tabloid ... It is a brilliant book for
finding out when things happened and what exactly
happened, almost as good as an entire newspaper cuttings
library' (*The Independent*, no.665, 26 November 1988,
p.32). *Class No:* 94"19"(031)

Dictionaries

[6735]

BROWNSTONE, D.M. *and* **FRANCK, I.M. Dictionary of
20th Century history.** New York, Prentice Hall, 1990.
444p. $24.95; £17.95. ISBN: 0132098830.

Almost 4,000 cross-referenced entries relating to key
events (wars, revolutions, crimes and scandals *etc.*), world
leaders, political and social movements and ideas, and
scientific discoveries (BBC 12 lines; Prague Spring 91.;
Watergate 62). 2 cols. x page. Pronounced US bias.
Class No: 94"19"(038)

[6736]

**The Penguin dictionary of twentieth-century history 1900-
1991.** 4th ed. London, Penguin, 1992. ii,437p. pbk. £6.99.
ISBN: 014052640.

1st ed. 1979; 3rd ed. 1990. Published in US as *Facts On
File dictionary of twentieth-century history.*

Cross referenced guide to political, diplomatic, military,
economic, and social and religious affairs. Entries of varying
length (100-2000 words). 120 expanded and revised entries
in this edition and 7 new entries (De Klerk, 2nd Gulf War,
Intifada, Kohl, John Major, Saddam Hussein, Yeltsin).
Class No: 94"19"(038)

Glossaries

[6737]

BBC World Service glossary of current affairs.
Williams, T.G., *ed.* Harlow, Essex, Longman Current
Affairs; Chicago, St. James Press, 1991. 813p. index. £95.
ISBN: 0582068479, UK; 1558621083, US.

.... (contd.)

Explanations and meanings of over 7,000 legal, political,
financial, administrative, media, constitutional, judicial,
measurement, religious, terms etc., including abbreviations
and acronyms, particular to individual countries listed A-Z
with an international section. Index p.775-813.
Class No: 94"19"(038.1)

Yearbooks & Directories

[6738]

**Facts on File - Weekly world news digest with cumulative
index.** New York and Oxford, Facts On File, October/
November 1940-. $525. £175. *per annum.* ISSN: 00146641.

News reports from government press releases and 50 US
and foreign newspapers with cumulative twice-monthly and
quarterly indexes. A 32p. coloured *World Atlas* is supplied
to insert into the annual slide-binder. *Facts on File news
digest CD-ROM* 1988. £465. 'delivers the full text and maps
of any news item appearing in the 1980-1987 volumes of the
News digest. That's 9000 pages of text, over 12 million
words and more than 500 maps on one disc that's updated
annual (*advt*). Annual update disc (1980-1989, 1980-1990)
£125. *Facts on File world news digest yearbooks.* Individual
Yearbooks 1941-1987. £72. per volume. Decennial sets:
1940s, 9v., £425; 1950s, 10v., £475; 1960s, 10v., £475;
1960s, 10v., £475; 1970s, 10v., £475; 1980s, 8v., £432.
Complete set of 47 yearbooks £2050. Also available on
microfiche. *Facts on File world news digest 5 year indexes:
1946-1950; 1951-1955; 1956-60; 1961-1965; 1966-1970;
1971-75; 1976-80; 1981-85.* £72. each or £425. the set. Also
available on microfiche. *Class No:* 94"19"(058)

Maps & Atlases

[6739]

CHALIAND, G. *and* **RAGEAU, J-P. Atlas politique du XXe
siècle.** Paris, Seuil, 1988. 215p. col. maps, tables. ISBN:
202009875x.

More than 300 maps clarify the changing frontiers of the
modern world in 45 geographic and thematic sections.
Chronology p.209-11. *Class No:* 94"19"(084.3)

[6740]

GILBERT, M. Recent history atlas, 1860 to 1960. 3rd rev
ed. London, Weidenfeld & Nicolson, 1977. ix, 121p. tables,
maps, pbk. £4.50. ISBN: 0297773313.

1st ed. 1966.

121 black-and-white maps (1. The European Empires in
1870 ... 21. South America since 1800 ... 80. Siege of
Leningrad ... 121. American preparedness in 1960). Clear
mapping; statistical data. No index-gazetteer. Page size, 13 x
21cm. *Class No:* 94"19"(084.3)

[6741]

NATKIEL, R. Atlas of 20th century history. London,
Hamlyn Bison, 1982. 256p. illus.maps. ISBN: 0600384667.

200 maps charting the progress of war and diplomacy
complemented by explanatory text by Sommerville and J.N.
Westwood. *Class No:* 94"19"(084.3)

Chronologies

[6742]

FERRELL, R.H., *ed.* **The Twentieth century: an almanac.** London, Harrap, 1986. 512p., illus., maps, index. £12.95. ISBN: 0245543937.

Chronological arrangement of events in 8 major sections. *Class No:* 94"19"(090)

Contemporary

[6743]

Chronicle of the year 1993. Farnborough, JL International Publishing, 1993. 120p. illus. (some col.), maps, tables, index. £14.95. ISBN: 1872031323; 0582077400.

Chronicle of the year came to the UK in 1988. In France *Chronique de l'année* (Paris Larousse) started in 1985 whilst earlier English language editions were published in the US.

Month by month summary of important events. The World's Nations section gives brief updates on each nation's geographical location, population, membership of international organizations, capital, official language, religion, political status, Head of state and government, Gross National Product, currency and coloured illustration of the National flag. *Class No:* 94"312"

Chronologies

[6744]

L'Histoire au jour le jour (1944-1985). Paris, Editions La Découverte/Le Monde, 1985. 864p., illus., maps (some col.). 360F. ISBN: 2707117293.

Divided in 4 parts: 1. 1944-54 Les années froides - 2. 1955-62 Le temps des ruptures - 3. 1963-73 Les printemps éphémères - 4. 1974-85. Une aussi longue crise. Each part consists of 3 sections (Les relations internationales; Les aires géopolitiques; La France). Signed and dated extracts from *Le Monde* newspaper with tabulated diaries of events. Very fragile case. *Class No:* 94"312"(090)

Modern History—Developing Countries

Encyclopaedias

[6745]

The Current history encyclopedia of developing nations. Thompson, C.L., *and others.* New York, McGraw-Hill, 1982. ix,395p. illus., maps, index. ISBN: 0070643873.

63 contributors. Evaluates 93 developing nations 'in terms of the ways in which they satisfy the basic human needs of their citizens. The focus is on people under pressure of economic development' (*Preface*). *Class No:* 94-773(031)

Mediaeval & Modern History—Europe

[6746]

DUROSELLE, J-B. **Europe: a history of its peoples.** Mayne, R., *trans.* London, Viking, 1990. 423p. illus. (mostly col.), col. maps, tables, index. £25. ISBN: 0670829226.

Published simultaneously by Bertelsmann Lexikon Verlag;

....(contd.)

Librairie Academique Perrin (Fr); Aquilar El Pais (Sp); Lademann (Dk); Kosmos (Neths); Fabbri Bompiani (It); and Circulo de Leitores/Dom Quixote (Port).

1. What is Europe - 2. Prehistory - 3. The Celts - 4. Classical antiquity - 5. The first four centuries A.D. in the West - 6. The Germanic age - 7. Charlemagne: King of Europe? - 8. Europe under siege - 9. The heyday of Western Christianity (12th and 13th centuries) - 10. Towards a Europe of the States (14th and 15th centuries) - 11. Renaissance, Reformation and expansion - 12. Absolutism, liberties and cosmopolitanism - 13. Revolution and disillusion - 14. Napoleon: Europe by force - 15. Industrial Revolution - 16. Romanticism and the nations - 17. Road to European disaster (1871-1914) - 18. Europe destroys itself (1914-1945) - 19. Recovery and resurgent hopes. A single-volume history of Europe 'seen in overall European as opposed to national perspective' intended for students and general readers. The absence of a scholarly apparatus, apart from chapter chronologies, reduces its reference value. *Class No:* 940

[6747]

PEDERSEN, R.N. **One Europe 100 nations.** Clevedon, Avon, Channel View Books, 1992. 144p. col. illus., col. maps, bibliog. £14.95. ISBN: 1853591238.

Brief description of origins, history, minorities, linguistic struggle, political status for each of Europe's potential and *de facto* governing nations including Pomerania, Thuringia, Galicia, Castille, Normandy, Brittany, Cornwall, Shetland Is. *etc.* Col. illus. of flag and arms. Useful only for identifying current and historical 'minority' nations subsumed within nation-state borders. *Class No:* 940

[6748]

SCAMMELL, G.V. **The World encompassed:** the first European maritime empires.*c.*800-1650. London, Methuen; Berkeley, Univ. of California Press, 1982. xiv,538p. illus., maps, index. $47.50. ISBN: 0416762808, UK; 0520044223, US.

Covers an unfamiliar period: 800-1650, focussing in turn on the Norse, Hanse, Venetian, Genoese, Portuguese, Spanish, Dutch, French and English maritime ventures. Extensive bibliographical notes to each chapter further enhance a scholarly and well-researched book. *Class No:* 940

Mediaeval History—Europe

[6749]

BARBER, R. **The Penguin guide to medieval Europe.** Harmondsworth, Penguin Books, 1984. 379p., illus., maps. pbk. £8.99. ISBN: 0140466339.

4 Parts: 1. Christendom; 2. Empire and nations; 3. Lords, princes and vassals; 4. The world of learning. Appendix: Libraries and museums p.353-358. 'A guide to the intellectual and political history of Europe in the Middle Ages as much as a handbook to some of its surviving relics'. *Class No:* 940.1

[6750]
The Cambridge medieval history. Gwatkin, H.M., *and others, eds.* Cambridge, Cambridge Univ. Press, 8v., 1911-36. illus., tables, maps, bibliogs, indexes.

1. *The Christian Roman Empire and the foundation of the Teutonic Kingdoms.* 1911. xxiii,754p. ISBN 0521045320. 2. *The Rise of the Saracens and the foundation of the Western Empire.* 813. xxiii,889p. 0521045339. 3. *Germany and the Western Empire.* 1922. xxxviii,700p. 0521045347. 4. *The Eastern Roman Empire (717-1453).* 1923. 2nd ed. as *The Byzantine Empire. Pt.1. Byzantium and its neighbours.* 1966. xl,1168p. £90. 0521045355. *Pt.2. Government, church and civilisation.* 1967. xlii,517p. £60. 0521045363. 5. *Contest of Empire and Papacy.* 1926. xliv,1005p. 0521045371. 6. *Victory of the Papacy.* 1929. xli,1047p. £90. 052104538x. 7. *Decline of Empire and Papacy.* 1932. xxxviii,1073p. 0521045398. 8. *The Close of the Middle Ages.* 1936. xxviii,1079p.

A closely-packed survey, each chapter being an authoritative statement by a scholar of repute. An important feature of each volume is the very full bibliography. The 2nd ed. of v.4(2v.xl,1168p.; xlii,517p.) shows a considerable expansion, with 42 plates, 18 maps, numerous tables; general and chapter bibliographies, p.808-1041 p.377-476); analytical indexes.
'By far the most useful and comprehensive work in English' (Davis, R.H.C. *Medieval European history*, p.5). *Class No:* 940.1

[6751]
FOSSIER, R., *ed.* **The Cambridge illustrated history of the Middle Ages.** Cambridge, Cambridge Univ. Press, 3v., 1986-. illus. (inc. col. pl.), geneal. tables, maps, bibliog., index.

First published Paris, Colin Armand, 1983 as *Les mondes nouveaux 350-950* and *Le temps des crises 1250-1520.* An English translation of v.2 *L'Eveil de l'Europe 950-1250* is in hand.
1. *350-950.* 1989. xxiii,556p. £30. ISBN 0521266440. 3. *1250-1520.* 1986. xviii,554p. £49.50. 0521266467. 10 chapters arranged in 3 sections: 1. Crisis of growth in Europe - 2. A new deal in the East and South - 3. Towards the modern age in the West. Glossary p.x-xviii. Bibliography p.524-534. Index p.535-554. A synthesis of the latest scholarly research on the medieval period. Lavishly illustrated. 'New insights, new angles, new perspectives are to be found here' (*Journal of Medieval History,* v.9, no.2, June 1983, p.145). *Class No:* 940.1

Bibliographies

[6752]
BAK, J.M. Medieval narrative sources : a chronological guide: (with a list of major letter collections). New York, Garland, 1987. xviii,117p., bibliog., index. $20. (*Garland reference library of the humanities, no.734.*) ISBN: 0824084403.

1001 collections deployed in 3 major chronological divisions: Early Middle Ages (to 900AD); Central Middle Ages (900-1300AD); Late Middle Ages (1300-1500AD). Data: Author/title; Date; Editions; Translations. Only sources for which there are printed editions are included. Major bibliography of medieval narrative sources p.xv-xviii. Author, regions and places indexes. *Class No:* 940.1(01)

[6753]
CHEVALIER, C.V. Répertoire des sources historiques du moyen âge. Nouv. éd. refondue, corr. et augm. Paris, Picard, 4v., 1897-1907 (reprinted 1959-60).

First published 1877-1903. Two parts: *Bio-bibliographie* (1877-86); nouv.éd., 1905-07. 2v. *Topobibliographie* (1894-1903 (1959 reprint). 2v. F390).
'One of the most important bibliographical monuments ever devoted to the study of medieval history,' containing 'an enormous mass of useful information' (*Encyclopaedia Britannica*, 11th ed. (1910-11), v.6, p.114), but without evaluation. The *Bio-bibliographie* has entries under the 'names of all the historical personages alive between the years 1 and 1500 who are mentioned in printed books', etc. *Topobibliographie*, arranged by place and topic, endeavours to do the same for places, institutions and the like. 'Though very useful, this is by no means so complete as the *Bio-bibliographie*' (*op.cit.*). *Class No:* 940.1(01)

[6754]
CROSBY, E.U., *and others.* **Medieval studies:** a bibliographical guide. New York, Garland Publishing, 1983. xxv,1131p., frontis. $109. ISBN: 0824091078.

9000 annotated entries relating to the history and culture of the Western European Middle Ages, Byzantium, and medieval Islamic civilization listed in 138 chapters - 1. History and historical method; 2. Historiography; 3. Historiography of the Middle Ages; 4. Modern historical writing; 7. Encyclopaedias and dictionaries; 10. Biography; 13. Guides to archives and libraries; 19. General medieval history; 22-37 geographical chapters; 46. Maritime history; 47. Travel and exploration; 123. Archaeology; 124. Chronology; 127. Geography; 129. Cartography; 130. Maps and atlases; 136. Genealogy; 177. Heraldry; 138. Serials. All entries are furnished with brief descriptions of subject matter and its importance in the field. Index of authors and editors p.1058-1127. Index of topics p.1129-1131. *Class No:* 940.1(01)

[6755]
International medieval bibliography. Leeds, School of History, Univ. of Leeds, 1967- Annual, then 2pa.

V.26. Pt.1. Jan-June 1992. xlviii,399p. has 4987 entries covering *c*1000 journals and festschriften *etc.* on medieval topics AD450-1500 with some extensions to certain topics and areas. Arrangement: general bibliography, general culture and history then by 61 A-Z topics *e.g.* Archaeology (general artifacts, sites), Genealogy, Heraldry, Historiography, Local history, subdivided by geographical areas. Works on Africa, the Near East and Oriental topics are only included when they bear directly on the study of medieval Europe. Author and general indexes. *Class No:* 940.1(01)

[6756]
PAETOW, L.J. A Guide to the study of medieval history. Rev. ed. prepared under the auspices of the Medieval Academy of America. London, Kegan Paul, 1931. (Reprinted New York, Klaus, 1964). xix,643p.

First published 1917 (552p).
Valuable guide to bibliographies, printed sources and secondary works for the history of medieval Europe and its Eastern neighbours. Pt.1. Numbered list of books arranged by subject under the headings Bibliography - Reference - Auxiliary Studies - Modern works - Collections of sources. Pts.2 & 3 arranged by topic, each containing an introduction, recommendations for reading, and a

772

....*(contd.)*

bibliography referring to pt.1. This edition adds material published 1917-1928. Revised and corrected edition (New York, Kraus Reprints, 1980. cxii,643p. 0527253456) has Errata (p.xxi-li) and an Addendum (p.liii-cxii) of *c.* 1100 titles published before 1930 but not in 1917 or 1931 editions. *Literature of medieval history 1930-1975: a supplement to Louis John Paetow's 'A guide to the study of medieval history* edited by G.C. Boyce (New York, Kraus International Publications, 5v., 1981. 2630p. $595.00 0527104620) follows the same format but with 55,000 references is some four times larger. 'A very valuable bibliography on medieval European history from 500 to 1500' (*Choice,* v.19,no.1, September 1981, p.45-6). *Class No:* 940.1(01)

[6757]
Repertorium fontium historiae Medii Aevi: primum ab A. Potthast, nunc cura collegii historicorum e pluribus nationibus emendatum et auctum. Rome, Istituto Storico Italiano per il Medio Evo, 1962-. v.1-. (v.1-5, 1962-1984).
  1. *Series collectionum* 2-5. *Fontes A-H.*
  Sponsored by Istituto Storico per il Medio Aevo, Istituti di Archeologia, Storia e Storia dell'Arte in Roma, Medieval Academy of America, etc. V.1 gives contents of all the collections of narrative sources. V.2 is the first part of a detailed description of sources, A-Z (*c.*15,000 entries). The entry 'Abaelardus' (3 columns) has subheadings for manuscripts, medieval translations, editions, modern translations and commentaries. V.2 also includes a general list of sources (p.3-46) and list of journals cited (p.49-87). Designed to supersede A. Potthast's *Bibliotheca historica Medii Aevi/Wegweiser durch die Geschichtswerke des europäischen Mittelalters bis 1500* (2. verb. u. verm. Aufl. Berlin, Weber 1896. 2v. Reprinted 1955) - at present the fullest guide to printed sources (excluding records) for the history of medieval Europe, A.D.400-*c.*1500. *Class No:* 940.1(01)

Encyclopaedias

[6758]
Lexicon des Mittelalters. München and Zurich, Artemis Verlag.
  Printed in fascicules later collected in bound volumes. The work was originally planned to be completed in 5v. plus an index volume but this number seems likely to be exceeded.
  1. *Aachen-Bettelordenskirchen.* 1980. lxiii,2107p. 370889018. 2. *Bettlerwesen - Codex von Valemura.* 1983. viii,2222p. 3760889026. 3. *Codex Wintoniensis - Erziehungs-und Bildungsweren.* 1986. viii,2218p. 3760889034.
  Signed and documented articles on the history and culture of the Middle Ages (*i.e.,*A.D.300-1500). 'Series and scholarly rather than popular and not lavishly illustrated ... Coverage of subjects, persons and places is extremely full' (*Journal of Medieval History,* v.5,no.2, June 1979, p.154). *Class No:* 940.1(031)

[6759]
LOYN, H.R., *ed.* **The Middle Ages:** a concise encyclopaedia. London, Thames & Hudson, 1989. Distributed in US by Norton. 352p. illus., maps, bibliog. £24.00; $39.95. ISBN: 0500251037.
  40 contributors. Nearly 100 cross-referenced A-Z entries including biographies (John of Gaunt: 17 lines and 2 refs.);

....*(contd.)*

broad themes *e.g.* chivalry (83 lines and 4 refs.), feudalism, heresy; wars and battles, artistic highlights, covering the period AD. 400-1500. Bibliographical note p.352. 250 illus. 'An accessible and valuable tool' (*Booklist,* v.86,no.2, 15 September 1989, p.207). *Class No:* 940.1(031)

Dictionaries

[6760]
DAHLMUS, J. Dictionary of medieval civilization. New York, Macmillan Publishing Co., London, Collier Macmillan, 1984. viii, 700p. £52. ISBN: 0029078709.
  6600 plus entries defining medieval terms and concepts. Topics covered include people, events, institutions etc., spanning the period AD300-1500. There is no bibliographical apparatus. 'An excellent source of brief, accurate information on things medieval' (*Wilson Library Bulletin,* v.59, no.2, October 1984, p.145). *Class No:* 940.1(038)

[6761]
STRAYER, J.R., ed. Dictionary of the Middle Ages. New York, Charles Scribner's Sons, 13v., 1982-1989. Distributed in UK by Macmillan. illus., maps. £780.00.
  v.13 *Index.* 1989. 0684182793. Over 5000 commissioned articles, mostly from US and Canadian academics, cover all aspects of medieval life in Christendom and Islam. Entries range from 500 word definitions to critical essays of 10,000 words on major figures and topics. All are signed and end with bibliogs., and cross-references. More than 1000 illustrations, charts, and maps. Published under the auspices of the American Council of Learned Societies. The Dictionary receives a grant from the National Endowment for the Humanities. *Class No:* 940.1(038)

[6762]
ZOPHY, J.W., ed. The Holy Roman Empire: a dictionary handbook. Westport, Connecticut, Greenwood Press, 1980. xxvii,551p. maps,bibliog., index. £40.00; $50.95. ISBN: 0313214573.
  Short signed essays with bibliographies appended on notable persons, places, terms, and important events, as well as significant topics in social, urban, economic, military, and women's history, from the time of Charlemagne to the Napoleonic dissolution in 1806. 32 contributors. 8 maps. Appendix A. The Holy Roman Emperors and their predecessor Kings p.501-502. B. Chronology p.503-504. Bibliography p.507-512. Indifferent review in *Choice,* v.18,no.8, April 1981, p.1080. *Class No:* 940.1(038)

[6763]
—**ZOPHY, J., ed.** An Annotated bibliography of the Holy Roman Empire. Westport, Connecticut, Greenwood Press, 1986. 398p. index. $65.00; £65.00. (*Bibliographies and Indexes in World History, no.3.*)
  Over 3000 briefly annotated entries in 11 categories: 1. General historical surveys - 2. Constitutional and institutional history - 3. Emperors - 4. The Church - 5. The nobility - 6. Peasantry - 7. Economic and social history - 8. Towns and territories - 9. War and diplomacy - 10. Culture - 11. Reformation. 'Should serve as a valuable reference source for locating the most important scholarly works on any subject of German history during the period of the thousand-year Reich' (*German Studies Review,* v.10,no.1, February 1987, p.159-60). *Class No:* 940.1(01)

Yearbooks & Directories

[6764]

Répertoire international des médiévistes. 6th ed. Paris, London, München, New York, K.G. Saur, 2v., 1987. x,1259,ixp. index. £95.00. ISBN: 3598106831.

First published 1953.

The 6th ed. of 'RIM' has almost 5000 entries (A-K,L-Z) in more than 25 languages for medievalists (historians, academics, conservators, archivists, archaeologists) in 43 countries. Data cites books and articles published and forthcoming. New to this edition is a subject index.
Class No: 940.1(058)

Maps & Atlases

[6765]

MATTHEW, D. Atlas of medieval Europe. Oxford, Phaidon; New York, Facts on File, 1986. 240p. illus. (some col.), col.maps, bibliog., index. £18.50; $40.00. ISBN: 0714823023, UK; 0871961334, US.

First published 1983.

26 topics presented in map form and arranged in 4 parts: 1. Disintegration of the Ancient World - 2. Breaking new ground - 3. The fruits of civilization - 4. Consolidation of the land. 9 Special features including 'The invention pf printing' and 'Medieval mapmaking'. Chronology p.8-9. Glossary p.226-7. Bibliography p.229-231. Gazetteer p.231-7. 224 maps. 'Makes a misunderstood period intelligible to a popular audience' (*Wilson Library Bulletin,* v.58,no.3, November 1983, p.224). *Class No:* 940.1(084.3)

Chronologies

[6766]

STOREY, R.L. Chronology of the medieval world 800 to 1491. London, Barrie & Jenkins, 1973. xii, 705p. tables.

Worldwide coverage. Double-page spread. The left-hand page is divided A-E by year, month or precise day; right-hand page, F-L (F. Law and politics - G. Economics, science, technology and discovery - H. Religion and education - J. Art, architecture and music - K. Literature, philosophy and scholarship - L. Births and deaths). Detailed, analytical index. 'a valuable acquisition for reference collections' (*Library Journal,* v.98, no.13, July 1973, p.2070). *Class No:* 940.1(090)

Atlantic Ocean

[6767]

FERNÁNDEZ-ARMESTO, F. Before Columbus exploration and colonisation from the Mediterranean to the Atlantic 1229-1492. London, Macmillan Education; Univ. of Pennsylvania Press, 1987. x,283p. maps, bibliog., index. £30.00. (*New Studies in Medieval History*.) ISBN: 0333403827, UK; 0812280830, US.

9 chapters: 1. The island conquests of the House of Barcelona - 2. The first 'Atlantic' Empire: Andalusia and its environs - 3. A Mediterranean land empire - 4. The Genose Mediterranean - 5. The rim of Africa - 6. Mapping the Eastern Atlantic - 7. The Atlantic crucible - 8. From the Canaries to the New World - 9. The mental horizon. References p.253-66. Bibliography p.267-75. A valuable work of research and synthesis in a somewhat neglected period. *Class No:* 940.1(261)

Crusades

[6768]

AMIN MAALOUF. The Crusades through Arab eyes. London, Al Saqi Books, 1984. iv,295p. maps, bibliog., index. £20. $30. ISBN: 0863561136.

First published as *Les croisades vues par les Arabes* (Paris, Éditions J-C Lattès, 1983).

16 chronological chapters. Notes and sources p.267-276. Chronology p.277-280. Glossary p.281-281. 'Based almost exclusively on the testimony of contemporary Arab historians and chroniclers' (*Foreword*).
Class No: 940.1"1095-13"

[6769]

RUNCIMAN, S. A History of the Crusades. Cambridge, Cambridge Univ. Press, 3v., 1962-68. illus. (pl.), tables, maps, bibliogs., index. £27.50 each vol.

1. *The First Crusade and the foundation of the Kingdom of Jersualem.* 1968. xiv,377. ISBN 052106161x. 2. *The Kingdom of Jerusalem and the Frankish East 1100-1187.* 1962. xii,523p. 0521961628. 3. *The Kingdom of Acre and the later Crusades.* 1966. xii,503p. 0521961636.

Detailed coverage, well footnoted, of the Crusades from the 11th to the 14th century and the states it created in the Holy Land and in neighbouring countries. V.1 has Appendix 1: 'Principal sources for the history of the First Crusade'. Bibliography (1. Original sources, p.342-50); 2. Modern works (authors, A-Z), p.350-60. Index p.361-77.
Class No: 940.1"1095-13"

[6770]

SETTON, K.M., *ed.* **A History of the Crusades.** Madison, Univ. of Wisconsin Press, 6v., 1969-1990. $40. each volume.

V.1-2 first published by Univ. of Pennsylvania Press 1955-1962.

1. *The first hundred years* edited by M.W. Baldwin, 1969. xxxi,707p. ISBN 0299048314. 2. *The later Crusades 1189-1311* edited by R.L. Wooff and H.W. Hazard. 2nd ed. 1969, xxii,859p. 0299048411. 3. *The fourteenth and fifteenth centuries* edited by H.W. Hazard. 1975. xxi,819p. 0299066703. 4. *The art and architecture of the Crusader states* edited by H.W. Hazard. 1977. xxvii,414+10p. 029906820x. 5. *The impact of the Crusades on the Near East* edited by N.P. Zacour and H.W. Hazard. 1985. xxii,599p. 0299091406. 6. *The impact of the Crusades on Europe* edited by N.P. Zacour and H.W. Hazard. 1990. xxiii,703p. 029910740x. V.5 has 10 chapters (*e.g.* 1. Arab culture in the twelfth century ... 2. Impact of the Crusades on Moslem lands ... 8. The Teutonic Knights in the Crusader states); gazetteer and notes on maps, p.519-552; and 13 maps V.4 carries 'Addenda and corrigenda' to v.1-4. V.6 has H.E. Mayer and J. McLellans' Select bibliography of the Crusades (p.511-644). This immense compilation includes A. General works, research aids, historiography - B. Narrative sources in many Western and Near Eastern languages - C. Secondary Works. Also Gazetteer and note on maps p.483-510. *Class No:* 940.1"1095-13"

Bibliographies

[6771]

MAYER, H.E. Bibliographie zur Geschichte der Kreuzzüge. Hannover, Hansche Buchhandlung, 1960. 270p. DM36.

5362 entries covering every aspect of the Crusades.

....(contd.)

'Future historians of the Crusades will have their work greatly simplified by the publication of this vast and remarkably complete bibliography' (*English Historical Review*, v.77, no.303, April 1962, p.346).
Class No: 940.1"1095-13"(01)

Maps & Atlases

[6772]

The Atlas of the Crusades. Riley-Smith, J., *ed.* London, Times Books, 1990; New York, Facts on File, 1991. 192p. col. illus., col. maps, bibliog., index. £19.95, $40. ISBN: 0723003610, UK; 0816021864, US.

19 contributors. 22 narrative chapters arranged in 4 parts: 1. The way of God - 2. Defence of Christendom - 3. Crusading and the world of Chivalry - 4. The last crusaders. Chronology (in 3 cols: The East; Europe and North Africa; Background events) p.10-19. Glossary p.176-9. Bibliography p.173. History ranges from Urban II's. First crusade 1095 AD to the late eighteenth century.
Class No: 940.1"1095-13"(084.3)

Renaissance

Bibliographies

[6773]

Bibliographie internationale de l'Humanisme et de la Renaissance: ouvrage publié sur la recommendation du Conseil International de la Philosophie et des Sciences Humaines avec le concours de l'UNESCO. Genève, Droz, 1966-. v.1-. Annual.

V.20 Travaux parus en 1984. 1988. cxi, 835p. has *c.*5000 unannotated entries organized in 2 parts: 1. Personnages et oeuvres anonymes - 2. Subjects divided by countries (Histoire - Religion et vie religieuse, doctrines philosophiques, politiques et juridiques - Littérature, enseignement et pédagogie, grammaire et linguistique, théâtre, technique du livre, bibliothèques - Arts - Sciences et techniques. About 2000 periodicals are now scanned. Author index. A valuable research tool, even if slow to appear.
Class No: 940.1"1095-1300"(01)

Encyclopaedias

[6774]

BERGIN, T.G. *and* **SPEAKE, J.,** *eds.* **Encyclopedia of the Renaissance.** New York, Facts on File, 1987. London, B.T. Batsford Ltd. 1988. 454p., illus., geneal. tables, bibliog. £40. $45. ISBN: 0816013152, US; 0713459670, UK.

28 contributors. 2500 A-Z cross-referenced entries relating to individuals, issues and events in all fields of human endeavour in 14th-16th century Europe. Bibliography (in subject categories) p.433-440. Sparse chronological table p.441-454. 32 col. plates. 'Easily the best one-volume reference available' (*Choice*, v.25, no.8, April 1988, p.1219). *Class No:* 940.1"1095-1300"(031)

Dictionaries

[6775]

Dictionary of the Renaissance. Schweitzer, F.M. *and* Wedeck, E., *eds.* New York, Philosophical Library; London, Vision, 1967. xxii,646p.

Over 4000 entries: biographical sketches; political and military matters; social evolution; town and city histories *etc.,*. No bibliography. *Class No:* 940.1"1095-1300"(038)

Maps & Atlases

[6776]

BLACK, C., *and others.* **Atlas of the Renaissance.** London, Cassell, 1993. 240p. col. illus., col. maps, bibliog., index. £20. ISBN: 0304343188.

11 contributors. Pt.1: The Heartland of the Renaissance (*i.e.* medieval Italy) - Renaissance and the wider world (Italy and Venice, Germany and the Low Countries. France, Spain and Portugal, England and Scotland). 38 special features (*e.g.* The Discovery of antiquity ... the printer-publisher ... New learning). Chronology p.8-9. Gazetteer p.230-33. Bibliography p.229. 42 maps. Authoritative, lavishly produced compendium. *Class No:* 940.1"1095-1300"(084.3)

Modern History—Europe (1492-)

[6777]

European political facts. London, Macmillan, 4v, 1978-86. tables.

1. *European political facts 1648-1789* by J. Babuscio and R.M. Dunn. 1984. 400p. £35. ISBN 033321111. 2. *European political facts 1789-1848* by C. Cook and J. Paxton. 1981. 195p. £38. 0333216970. 3. *European political facts 1848-1918* by C. Cook and J. Paxton. 1978. viii, 342p. £38. 0333151003. 4. *European political facts 1918-1990* by C. Cook and J. Paxton. 1992. 310p. 0333547764. V.3 has 15 sections: 1. The making of modern Europe - 2. Heads of state - 3. Parliament - 4. Ministers - 5. Elections - 6. Political issues ... 10. Population and urbanization - 11. Economic development ... 14. The labour movement and the trade unions - 15. The Revolutionary movement (chronologies), including biographical notes on major revolutionaries. Subjects subdivided into countries. Select bibliography, p.337-8. Index. 'Throughout the aim has been to provide comparable material' (*Preface*). *Class No:* 940.2

[6778]

MAYER, A. Annals of European civilization 1501-1900. London, Cassell, 1949. xxiii, 457p. indexes.

'Annals' (p.43-305) - arranged chronologically; under each year countries or areas (British Isles; Low Countries; Northern Europe; Central Europe, Latin Europe; Slavonic Europe) are subdivided by subjects A-Z and then into events.

'Summaries' (p.309-457) - arranged A-Z by subjects (*e.g.* Literature) which are subdivided chronologically. The 41 subjects (with country division in the case of Literature and Painting) include Academies, Chemistry, Libraries, Newspapers, Periodicals, Physics, etc.

An index of names and an index of places precede (p.1-42). *Class No:* 940.2

Bibliographies

[6779]

BROMLEY, J.S. *and* GOODWIN, A., *eds*. **A Select list of works on Europe and Europe overseas 1715-1815.** Edited for the Oxford Eighteenth-Century Group. Oxford, Clarendon Press, 1956. xii, 132p.

Mainly books, with some periodical titles. Ten of the 27 chapters deal with general aspects; chapters 11-25, with specific countries; chapters 26-27, with geographical aspects and biographical dictionaries. No index of annotations, but items of 'specific usefulness as introductions to some larger subject' (*Preface*) are asterisked. Includes material in German, French, Italian, etc. *Class No:* 940.2(01)

[6780]

DUNTHORN, H. *and* SCOTT, H.M. **Early modern European History *c.* 1492-1788: a select bibliograpy.** London, The Historical Association, 1983. 107p. index. (*Help for Students of History No.90.*) ISBN: 0852782594.

Replaces A. Davies *Modern European History 1494-1788; a select bibliography* (London, The Historical Association 1966).

Descriptive list of books and articles including a few in French, German, Spanish and Italian intended for sixth-formers and undergraduates. 14 sections, 5 on general aspects (European expansion, economic and social history, religion, political history) and 9 on national histories. 'Aims to include the last recent publications without neglecting older material that remains valuable' (*Preface*).
Class No: 940.2(01)

Handbooks & Manuals

[6781]

COOK, C. *and* STEVENSON, J. **The Longman handbook of modern European History 1763-1985.** 2nd rev. ed. London and New York, Longman, 1992. viii, 488p. maps, bibliog., geneal tables, index. £28. $39.95. ISBN: 0582072913.

Quick reference guide organized in 7 sections: 1. Principal rulers and ministers - 2. Political events (chronology in 27 topics *e.g.* 19. Italian Fascism ... 23. Spain 1909-1939 ... 27. The movement for European unity) - 3. War, diplomacy and imperialism - 4. Economic and Social - 5. Biographies - 6. Glossary (p.301-330) - 7. Topic Bibliography (p.335-394). Maps p.396-412. Analytical index. Companion volume to *The Longman handbook of modern British history 1714-1987* (*q.v.*). 'An outstanding reference work, containing much information not available elsewhere in a single volume' (*Reference Reviews*, v.2, no.4, December 1988, p.224-5). *Class No:* 940.2(035)

Dictionaries

[6782]

WILLIAMS, E.N. **The Penguin dictionary of English and European history, 1485-1789.** London, Allen Lane, 1980. 509p. index. £5.99. ISBN: 0140510842.

Published in New York as *The Facts on File dictionary of European history 1485-1789* at $22.50.

'Follows the mainstream of political history without diverging too far into economics, the arts or science'. One third of the scholarly and substantial entries relate to English history. Extensive cross-references but no references to other sources. No bibliography. Analytical index p.469-509. *Class No:* 940.2(038)

Maps & Atlases

[6783]

MAGOCSI, P.R. **Historical atlas of East Central Europe.** University of Toronto Press, 1994. $85. ISBN: 0802006078.

89 political and thematic maps with accompanying text covering from the early 5th century to January 1993. The atlas encompasses Poland, the Czech Republic, Slovakia, Hungary, Romania, Slovenia, Crotia, Bosnia-Herzegovina, Yugoslavia, Macedonia, Albania, Bulgaria, and Greece. Also included are the eastern parts of Germany (historic Mecklenburg, Brandenburg, Prussia, Saxony, and Lusatia), Bavaria, Austria, north-eastern Italy (historic Venetia), the lands of historic Poland-Lithuania (present-day Lithuania, Belarus, and Ukraine up to the Dnieper River), Moldova, and western Turkey. *Class No:* 940.2(084.3)

[6784]

POOLE, R.A. **Historical atlas of modern Europe,** from the decline of the Roman Empire; comprising also maps of parts of Asia, Africa and the New World connected with European history. Oxford, Clarendon Press, 1902. vii,328p. 90pl. of maps.

Based on Menke's ed. of Spruner's *Hand-Atlas* (1880), with additional material from Longnon's *Atlas historique de la France* (1885-89) and new maps for the British Isles, Byzantine, Asian and Colonial history. Each plate is accompanied by a note by an authority. Period dealt with: A.D. 285-1897, with a supplementary map on South Africa just previous to 1900. No index. *Class No:* 940.2(084.3)

Chronologies

[6785]

WILLIAMS, N. **Chronology of the expanding world 1492 to 1762.** London, Barrie and Jenkins, 1969. x,700p.

Left-hand pages record political and military events by calendar dates (categories A-M, giving actual day, if required); right-hand pages, under subjects, deal with politics, law, economics, science, arts ... birth and deaths of celebrities. Detailed, analytical index, p.553-700.
Class No: 940.2(090)

16th & 17th Centuries

Bibliographies

[6786]

CARTER, C.H. **The Western European powers 1500-1700.** London, Hodder & Stoughton, 1971. 347p. index. ISBN: 0340126965.

1. The subject and the sources - 2. Archival materials - 3. Archives and archival collections: central repositories - 4. Public documents - 5. Contemporary publications - 6. Code, cypher and security - 7. Research in the diplomatic sources. England, France, Spain and Spanish Netherlands most closely studied. *Class No:* 940.2"15/16"(01)

16th Century

Biographies

[6787]

Contemporaries of Erasmus: a biographical register of the Renaissance and Reformation. Bietenholz, P. *and* Deutscher, T.B., *eds.* Toronto/Buffalo/London, Univ. of Toronto Press, 3v., 1985-.

....*(contd.)*

Companion volumes to the publisher's *Collected works of Erasmus* (1974-).

1: *A-E.* 1985. xii,462p. illus. $90. ISBN 0802025072. 2: *F-M.* 1986. xii,490p. illus. $90. 0802025714. 3. *N-Z.* 1987. $90. 0802025757. A biographical dictionary of identifiable persons from the second half of the 15th and the first half of the 16th century mentioned in the writings of Erasmus - political leaders, religious figures, scholars *etc.*, in effect forming a biographical reference source for most human endeavours for the entire period. Entries are signed or initialled (v.2 has 122 contributors) and vary in length *e.g.* Emperor Charles V: 4p; Martin Luther; 3½p.; Thomas Green, Vice Chancellor, Cambridge University, 1523-24,: 21 lines. Short or extended bibliographies are appended to entries as appropriate. *Class No:* 940.2"15"(092)

18th Century

Encyclopaedias

[6788]
The Blackwell companion to the Enlightenment. Yolton, J.W., *and others, eds.* Oxford, Blackwell, 1991. x,581p. illus., bibliogs., index. £60; $74. ISBN: 0631154035.

Over 100 academic contributors. Main focus is the period 1720-80. All facets of the period covered A-Z. Signed articles of varying length, most with a select bibliography. An authoritative and comprehensive reference work. *Class No:* 940.2"17"(031)

19th Century

Bibliographies

[6789]
MEYER, J.A. An Annotated bibliography of the Napoleonic era: recent publications, 1945-1985. Westport, Connecticut, Greenwood Press, 1987. xvii,288p.index. $39.95; £45.00. (*Bibliographies and Indexes in World History.*)

1754 entries with indicative rather than critical annotations in 10 chapters: 1. Research aids - 2. Printed primary sources - 3. General histories - 4. Napoleon - 5. Napoleon's family - 6. Personal lives - 7. France and the world - 8. The art of war on land - 9. Naval affairs - 10. Supplement (1736-1754). Excludes journal articles. Intended as a companion volume to O'Connelly's *Historical dictionary of Napoleonic France 17990-1815.* 'A valuable current source for history in the early 19th Century' (*Choice,* v.25,no.4, December 1987, p.602). *Class No:* 940.2"18"(01)

World Wars 1 & 2

[6790]
British vessels lost at sea 1914-18 and 1939-45. Cambridge Patrick Stephen, 1988. 304p. index. £14.95. ISBN: 1852601345.

Reprint of *Navy losses* and *Merchant shipping losses* (HMSO, 1919) and *Ships of the Royal Navy: statement of losses during the Second World War* and *British merchant vessels lost or damaged by enemy action during Second World War* (HMSO, 1947). Under this title first published in

....*(contd.)*

2v., 1976-77.

Data: class, name, tonnage, date of completion, date of loss, how lost and where. *Class No:* 940.3+940.53

Bibliographies

[6791]
BAYLISS, G.M. Bibliographic guide to the two World Wars: an annotated survey of English-language reference materials. London & New York, R.B. Bowker, 1977. xv,578p. ISBN: 0859350134.

Over 2,500 concisely annotated entries. Sections A-G (A. General guides - B. Bibliographies - C. Libraries, museums, archives, societies and associations - D. Dictionaries and encyclopedias - E. Periodicals, directories, union lists, indexes and abstracts - F. Biographies - G. Other reference works (1-14, *e.g.* audiovisual aids; documentary collections and treaties; maps, atlases and gazetteers; statistics; theses and dissertations). Author, title, regional and country, subject (subdivided by country) indexes. Indexes are lacking in precision, and range of items included in sections is too wide (*e.g.* 'D. Dictionaries and encyclopedias' occupies p.183-242 and includes general dictionaries *ad lib.*). *Class No:* 940.3+940.53(01)

[6792]
BIBLIOTHEK FÜR ZEITGESCHICHTE - WELTSKRIEGBÜCHEREI Stuttgart. **Katalog der Bibliothek...** Boston, Mass., G.K. Hall, 2v., 1968.

Alphabetischer Katalog, 11v. 8159p. $1090.00 (Export $1320.00) ISBN 081610798x. *Systematischer Katalog,* 20v. 11332p. $1980.00 ($2395.00). ISBN 0816101752. 408,000 photolithographed catalogue cards.

The scope of the collection, similar to that of the Hoover Library, now encompasses political history, foreign relations, military affairs, and wars of the twentieth century, including coverage of the Korean and Vietnamese conflicts. *Class No:* 940.3+940.53(01)

[6793]
GREAT BRITAIN. HM Stationery Office. **Government Publications Sectional List 60, 1990. History in print.** London, HMSO., 1990. vii,28p.

Expanded version of old *Sectional List 60 Histories of the First and Second World Wars;* 24. *British National Archives;* 27. *Ancient Monuments;* and 59. *Royal Commissions,* which although discontinued are worth retaining for reference use.

Priced list of HMSO historical publications including those emanating from English Heritage; Royal Commission on Ancient and Historical Monuments in Wales; Royal Commission on Historical Monuments (England); and Royal Commission on the Ancient and Historical Momuments of Scotland. *Class No:* 940.3+940.53(01)

[6794]
HIGHAM, R., ed. Official histories essays and bibliographies from around the world. Kansas State Univ. Press, 1970. xi, 644p. bibliogs. $12.00. ISBN: 0686208161.

Essays on American, British, Dutch, French, German, Indian, Italian, New Zealand, Norwegian, Polish, Russian and South African war histories and historical offices are all included. *Class No:* 940.3+940.53(01)

Archives

[6795]

MAYER, S.L. *and* **KOENIG, W.J. The Two World Wars** a guide to manuscript collections in the United Kingdom. London & New York, R.B. Bowker, 1976. xii,317p. index. ISBN: 0859350142.

Limits the scope of material covered 'to the area of military history, and to the political and diplomatic history of the World wars only insofar as they impinged on the military domain' (*Introduction*). Arranged under towns A-Z and then by name of collection, further subdivided into 'World War I' and 'World War II'. A valuable inventory of resources, although the great resources of the Public Record Office are considered only in general terms (the PRO having its own guide, *The Second World War (qv)*).
Class No: 940.3+940.53(093.20)

World War 1

[6796]

FAYLE, C.E. Seaborne trade. London, John Murray, 3v. 1820-1924.

v.1 *The Cruiser period.* 1920. xvii, 442p. 2. *From the opening of the submarine campaign to the appointment of the shipping controller.* 1923. xv, 424p. 3. *The Period of unrestricted submarine warfare.* 1924. xx, 501p. Based on official documents. *Class No:* 940.3

[6797]

FRANKS, N.L.R. Over the front a complete record of the fighter aces and units of the United States and French Air Services 1914-1918. London, Grub Street, 1992. 230p. illus., maps, tables, bibliog. £27.50. ISBN: 0948817542.

Biographies of American and French fighter pilots on the Western Front. Data: place and date of birth; previous military service; decorations; post-war career; citations received; full list of all claimed victims. Bibliography p.128. *Class No:* 940.3

[6798]

History of the Great War : based on official documents by direction of the Historical Section of The Committee of Imperial Defence. London, HMSO, 1922-1987.

Military Operations. East Africa August 1914 - September 1916 by C. Hordern. *Egypt and Palestine* (2v.). 1. *From the outbreak of war with Germany to June 1917* by G. Macmunn and C. Falls. 1928. xvii, 445p. 2. *From June 1917 to the end of war* by C. Falls. 1930. 395-748p. *(sic). France and Belgium* compiled by J.E. Edmonds (13v). *1914.* 1925. xxv, 548p. *1914* October to November, xxviii, 548p. *1915.* 1927. xliii, 433p. *1915.* 1928. xliv, 488p. *1916* 1932. xxxvi, 523p. *Appendices.* 1932. 232p. *1916 2nd July 1916 to the end of the Battle of the Somme* by W. Miles. 1938. xlv, 601p. *Maps and appendices.* 1935. x, 119p. *1917 The German retreat to the Hindenburg line and the Battle of Arras* by C. Falls. 1940. xxxix, 586p. *Appendices.* 1940. xi, 158p. *1917 The Battle of Cambrai* by W. Miles. 1948. xvi, 399p. *1918* v1. *The German offensive and its preliminaries.* 1935. xxx, 569p. *Appendices.* 1935. viii, 148p. 2.*The Continuation of the German offensive.* 1937. xxviii, 550p. 3. *May-July. The German offensives and the first Allied counter-offensive.* 1939. xxxii, 385p. 4. *26th September - 11th November. The Advance to victory.* 1947. xxix, 675p. 5. *September 26 - November 11. The Advance to victory.* 1947. xxix, 675p.

Italy, 1915-1919 by J. Edmonds and others. 1949. xxix, 450p. *Macedonia* (2v) by C. Falls. V.1. *From the outbreak*

....(contd.)

of war to the Spring of 1917. 1933. xvi, 409p. V.2. *From the Spring of 1917 to the end of the war.* 1935. xvi, 365p. *The Campaign in Mesopotamia 1914-1918* (4v). by F. Moberly. 1924-1927. vii, 402p.+Øiv, 581p.+Øiii, 460p.+Øiii, 447p. *Togoland and the Cameroons 1914-1916* by F. Moberly. 1931. xxv, 469p. *Gallipoli* (2v). by C.F. Aspinall-Oglander. V.1 *Inception of the campaign to May 1915.* 1929. xvii, 380p. 2. *May 1915 to the evacuation* 1932. xv, 517p. *Operations in Persia 1914-1919* by F.J. Moberly. 1987. xxii, 490p. ISBN 011290453x. *Transportation on the Western Front 1914-1918* by A.M. Henniker. 1937. xxxiv, 531p. *The Occupation of the Rhineland 1918-1939.* by J.E. Edmonds. 1987. xxv, 444p. ISBN 0112904548. *A history of the blockade of Germany and of the countries associated with her in the great war Austria-Hungary, Bulgaria, and Turkey 1914-1918* by A.C. Bell. xvi, 845p. *Class No:* 940.3

[6799]

HURD, A. The Merchant Navy. London, John Murray, 3v. 1921-1929. xiv, 473p.+Øviip., 464p.+Øix, 400p.

Based on official documents. *Class No:* 940.3

[6800]

Lloyd's war losses. The First World War Casualties to shipping through enemy causes 1914-1918. London, Lloyd's of London Press, 1990. viii,381 double pages, 383-404p. index. £75. ISBN: 1850443149.

A facsimile reprint of the original manuscript record held at the Guildhall Library, City of London.

Chronological listing of 6,927 British, allied and neutral merchant vessels destroyed, detained or captured by the Central Powers. Data: date, name of vessel, flag, tons gross, how sunk, voyage and cargo, summary (gross tonnage and how sunk). *Class No:* 940.3

[6801]

Naval Operations. Corbett, J.S. *and* Newbolt, H. London, Longmans Green, 4v., 1920-1931.

V.1. To the Battle of the Falklands December 1914 by J.S. Corbett. 1920. xiv, 470p. V.2. by J.S. Corbett. 1921. xi, 382p. V.3 by J.S. Corbett. 1923. xiv, 417p. V.4 by H. Newbolt. 1928. xiii, 412p. V.5. by H. Newbolt. 1931. xx, 452p. All 5 vs. supplemented with independent boxes of maps. *Class No:* 940.3

[6802]

SHORES, C., *and others.* **Above the trenches** a complete record of the fighter aces and units of the British Empire Air Forces 1915-1920. London, Grub Street, 1990. 397p. maps, tables, ports. £35. ISBN: 0948817194.

Over 800 biographies of individual fighter scout pilots (place & date of birth, previous military service, and postwar career) and a full list of downed aircraft with date, time, type of aircraft flown, and source of information. Also brief squadron histories (p.30-43). Covers British, Canadian, Australian, New Zealand, South African and American fighter aces. *Class No:* 940.3

[6803]

The War in the air: being the story of the part played in the Great War by the Royal Air Force. Raleigh, W., *ed. v.1* and Jones, H.A., *ed. v.2-6.* Oxford, The Clarendon Press, 6v. and Appendices, 1922-1937.

V.4-5 have associated boxed maps. Appendix volume (1937) includes 46 documents *e.g.* List of squadrons Royal Flying Corps and Royal Air Force which served on the

....(contd.)

Western Front 1914-16 (p.130-141) and List of naval squadrons which served with the RFC and RAF ... (p.142-144). Based chiefly on the records of the Air Ministry. *Class No:* 940.3

Bibliographies

[6804]
ENSER, A.G.S. A Subject bibliography for the First World War. Books in English 1914-1987. 2nd ed. Aldershot, Hampshire, Gower, 1990. xi,412p. indexes. £45. ISBN: 0566056194.

First published by Andre Deutsch in 1979.

6800 entries drawn from standard bibliographical sources listed under 350 A-Z subject headings. Omits works of less than 40p., poetry, fiction, juvenile books, humour, Rolls of Honour, and publications of the War Graves Commission. Author, subject and titled books indexes.
Class No: 940.3(01)

[6805]
FALLS, C. War books an annotated bibliography of the books about the Great War. London, Greenhill Books; Novato, California, Presidio Press, 1989. xx, 328p. index. £19.95. ISBN: 1853670405.

First published as *War books: a critical guide.* (Peter Davies, 1930).

Arranged in 7 categories :1. History; general - 2. History; formations and units - 3. History; foreign - 4. Reminiscences - 5. Reminiscences; foreign - 6. Fiction - 7. Fiction; foreign. This edition adds only 40 books. 'Will find an important place on the reference shelves of all students of Great War literature' *Antiquarian Book Monthly Review,* v.16, no.11, November 1989 p.430).

New introduction by R.J. Wyatt. *Class No:* 940.3(01)

[6806]
NEW YORK PUBLIC LIBRARY. RESEARCH LIBRARIES. Subject catalog of the World War I. Collection. Boston, Mass., G.K. Hall, 4v., 1961. 4 reels. $280.00 (Export $340.00). ISBN: 0816114242.

61,300 photolithographed entries including works in many languages, analytical entries for scholarly journal articles, and thousands of pamphlets. No longer available in printed book form. *Class No:* 940.3(01)

[6807]
SMITH, M.J. World War I in the air a bibliography and chronology. Metuchen, N.J., Scarecrow Press, 1977. xix,271p. illus., index. $27.50. ISBN: 0810809907.

2035 virtually unannotated items in a single A-Z by author or title sequence restricted to English language material. Chronology p.207-49. Appendix 1. List of WWI 'aces'. Subject index. *Class No:* 940.3(01)

[6808]
TAYLOR, L., *and others, comps.* **Subject index of the books relating to the European War, 1914-1918,** acquired by the British Museum, 1914-1920. London, H. Pordes, 1970. viii,196p.

First published London, British Museum, 1922.

In 5 parts (heavily sub-divided as witnessed by Index to sub-headings p.194-6): 1. Bibliography - 2. Military and naval history - 3. Political and social history - 4. General and miscellaneous works - 5. Peace and reconstruction.
Class No: 940.3(01)

Encyclopaedias

[6809]
Encyclopaedia Britannica v.29-31. 13th ed. London and New York, The Encyclopaedia Britannica Co. Ltd., 1926.

These 3v. are supplements to the 13th ed. covering the period 1910-1926.

V.31 World War (p.1072-1094): Introduction - Early operations - The events of 1915 - From Verdun to the entry of America - The penultimate year - The Allied victory by B. H. Liddell Hart. World War Naval (p.1094-1111): The opening of hostilities - Cruiser warfare - The Dardanelles - The North Sea. Bibliog. By A.C. Dewar. World War Bibliography (p.1112-1115) designed to give the general reader the best information available in book form. Includes citations of French, German and Italian material. Still of value. *Class No:* 940.3(031)

[6810]
HAYTHORNTHWAITE, P.J. The World War One sourcebook. London, Arms and Armour, 1992. 412p. illus., maps, tables, bibliog., index. £25. ISBN: 1854091026.

Encyclopedic work in 7 sections: 1. History of the war (*i.e.* a brief chronology) - 2. Weapons and tactics - 3. Review of all combatant states (nature of government and brief accounts of their armed forces) - 4. Biographies of important military and naval leaders - 5. Sources - 6. Miscellanea - 7. Glossary (of contemporary military terms and colloquialisms) p.387-402. *Class No:* 940.3(031)

Maps & Atlases

[6811]
BANKS, A. A Military atlas of the First World War. London, Leo Cooper, 1989. xii,338p. illus., maps, plans, indexes. £14.95. ISBN: 0850521459.

First published Heinemann Educational Books 1974.

13 sections, each with brief introduction; commentary by Alan Palmer: The pre-war situation - War on the Western Front in 1914 ... The War in 1918 - The peripheral campaigns (*e.g.* Middle East) - Weapons - The war at sea - The war in the air. Clear maps and drawings. Detailed plans. *Class No:* 940.3(084.3)

[6812]
GILBERT, M. First World War atlas. Cartography by Arthur Banks and Terry Bicknell. 2nd ed. London, Weidenfeld and Nicolson, 1985. xvl, 159, xxxviip. maps, bibliog., index. £10.95. ISBN: 0297786172.

First published 1970.

Over 150 annotated black-and-white maps, covering military, naval, aerial, diplomatic, technical and economic aspects in 9 sections. Excellent classified bibliography p.xvii-xxvii. *Class No:* 940.3(084.3)

Chronologies

[6813]
Chronology of the Great War: three volumes in one 1914-1915, 1916-1917, 1918-1919. London, Greenhill Books, 1988. xiii, 211, 220, 275p. tables, indexes. ISBN: 185367012x.

Facsimile of *Chronology of the war* (Constable, 3v., 1918-20). issued under the auspices of the Ministry of Information.

1. Day by day record of events in 6 cols. (Western, Eastern, Southern Fronts, Asiatic and Egypt theatres, Naval

....(contd.)

and overseas operations, Political) - 2. Appendices explaining and enlarging on important events - 3. Index incorporating items not represented in daily record. In 3 sequences. *Class No:* 940.3(090)

[6814]
GRAY, R. *and* **ARGYLE, C. Chronicle of the First World War.** New York and Oxford, Facts On File, 2v., 1990-91. £39.95 (set). ISBN: 0816025975, set.

1. *1914-1916.* 1990. 352p. maps, bibliog., tables, index. £21.95. ISBN 0816021392. Preliminary sections, 'Prelude to Sarajevo' p.8-9; 'Sarajevo to the Outbreak of War', p.9-10. Glossary (of abbreviations and First World War terminology) p.314-35. Bibliography p.309-13. 19 maps.

1917-1921. 1990. 383p. maps, bibliog., tables, index. £21.95. 0816025959. Supplementary material: Armistice Terms 11 Nov. 1918, p.264. Chronology: towards peace 1919-1921, p.265-78. The Peace process 1918-1923, p.279-80. Who's who in the First World War p.298-318. Glossary p.339-60. Bibliography p.334-38. 15 maps.

Definitive day-by-day outline of events, 28 July 1914 - 31 December 1916 and 1 January 1917 - 31 December 1918, presented in 9 vertical columns: 1. Western Front - 2. Eastern Front - 3. Southern Fronts - 4. Turkish Fronts - 5. African operations - 6. Sea war - 7. Air war - 8. International events - 9. Home Fronts. 'A minutely researched and definitive historical resource ... it will not easily be superseded' (*Reference Reviews,* v.6, no.1, 1992, p.47). *Class No:* 940.3(090)

[6815]
HERMAN, G. The Pivotal conflict a comprehensive chronology of the First World War, 1914-1919. Westport, Conn., Greenwood Press, 1992. xv,800p. ISBN: 0313227934.

Detailed chronology 28 June 1914 - 28 June 1919 in 3 subdivided columns: Military (Western, Eastern, Southern fronts and Colonial/Sea/Air); International-Diplomatic (Formal agreements, Conferences, Other contacts, Declarations); Domestic (Politics, Economic/Social, Cultural/Technological). Reproduced from typescript. *Class No:* 940.3(090)

Biographies

[6816]
HERWIG, H.H. *and* **HEYMAN, N.M. Biographical dictionary of World War I.** Westport, Connecticut, Greenwood Press, 1982. xiv, 624p. bibliog. £55.00. $67.95. ISBN: 0313213569.

Introduction (p.1-59) covers the origins of war, the Western front, the war in the East, the war at sea, the home front, and the Peace. Dictionary of biographical sketches p.61-365. Chronology p.367-376. Bibliography (p.395-406) lists works in 6 languages. Index. p.407-424. 'A model of its genre in both form and content and will likely become for all large libraries the standard reference work on the subject' (*RQ,* v.22, no.2, Winter 1982, p.196-197). *Class No:* 940.3(092)

[6817]
Officers died in the Great War 1914-19. Polstead, Suffolk, J.B. Hayward, 1988. 294p. £18.00. ISBN: 0903754401.

First published by HMSO 1919. Reprinted by J.L.R. Samson 1975.

34,000 casualties listed with rank, date of death, nature of casualty. Pt.1 Old and New Armies. Pt.2 Territorial Force. Pt.3 (new to this edition) Indian Army 1914-1920 listing a further 1400 officers killed in combat. Appendix 1. Regimental rolls - 2. List of deceased Territorial officers. *Class No:* 940.3(092)

[6818]
Soldiers died in the Great War 1914-19. Polstead, Suffolk, J.B. Hayward, 80v. 1988-89.

Originally published 1920.

Commemorates 635,000 soldiers listed A-Z by regiment or corps. Data: rank, place of birth, theatre of war, date and nature of casualty. *Class No:* 940.3(092)

USA

Bibliographies

[6819]
WOODWARD, D.R. *and* **MADDOX, R.F. America and World War I** : a selected annotated bibliography of English-language sources. New York, Garland Publishing Inc., 1985. xvii, 368p. index. $49.00. (*Wars of the United States,* 6.)

2041 briefly annotated entries arranged in 8 sections: Reference works; Manuscripts, repositories and libraries; Origins and outbreak of war; Military aspects; Home front; Social and intellectual impact; Diplomacy; and The Peace Settlements. Chronology p.335-342. *Class No:* 940.3(73)(01)

Europe (From 1919)

Dictionaries

[6820]
STEVENSON, J., *ed.* **Macmillan dictionary of British and European history since 1914.** London, Macmillan, 1991. ix,437p. £35; $69.50. ISBN: 0333456254.

Published in US as *The Columbia Dictionary of European political history* (Columbia University Press, 1992. ISBN 0231078803).

1500 A-Z cross-referenced entries on the major events, individuals, topics, political groupings, and issues of the 20th century. Extra-European events are only recorded in terms of their significance to European affairs. Most entries have bibliographical references. *Class No:* 940.5(038)

Europe—Eastern

[6821]
The Times guide to Eastern Europe inside the other Europe. A comprehensive handbook. Sword, K., *ed.* 2nd ed. London, Times Books, 1990. 270p. maps, index. £7.95. ISBN: 0723004382.

10 contributors. Part 1. (8 chapters on each of Eastern bloc countries plus Albania and Yugoslavia). Part 2. The Soviet Union (9. An overview: from dogmatism to uncertainty - 10. Russia - 11. The Baltic States - 12. Byelorussia - 13. Ukraine - 14. Moldavia). 12 Appendices:

....(contd.)

1. Warsaw Pact 1955 - 2. Helsinki Conference 1973-75 ... 6. Eastern Europe after the First World War ... 8. Languages and Nations of Eastern Europe - 9. Nationalities in the USSR ... 11. 1990 Election results. Attempts to present a considered assessment of the history and development of Eastern Europe from the end of World War 2. *Class No:* 940.5(401)

Bibliographies

[6822]

PHILIPP, W. Bibliographie zur Osteuropäischen Geschichte: Verzeichnis der zwischen 1965 und 1974 veröffentlichen Literatur in westeuropäischen Sprachen zur Osteuropäischen Geschichte. [Bibliography of Russian and East European history: list of modern works published between 1965 and 1974 in Western languages on Russian and East European history to 1945.] Wiesbaden., Otto Harrassowitz, 1983. lxix,1059p. (*Bibliographische Mitteilungen des Osteuropa-Instituts an der Freien Universität Berlin.*) ISBN: 3447022329.

A continuation of Klaus Meyer's bibliography with the same title covering 1939-1964 published in 1972.

17,839 unannotated items selected for their scholarly value divided geographically with thematic sub-divisions. *Class No:* 940.5(401)(01)

World War 2

[6823]

BOOKMAN, J.T. *and* **POWERS, S.T. The March to victory** a guide to World War II battles and battlefields from London to the Rhine. New York, Harper & Row, 1986. xi, 340p. illus., maps, ports, bibliog., index. $18.95. ISBN: 006015506x.

7 sections (The Battle of Britain and the bomber offensive; Normandy; The breakout from Normandy; Pursuit across France; Operation Market Garden (*i.e.* Arnhem); Battle of the Bulge; and Through the West Wall to the Rhine) describe the battlefields, the exploits of individuals and particular units, identify relics in the field, and locate museums and monuments. Appendix A. Museums (A-Z by country) p.312-320. Select bibliography p.321-326. Narrative and illustrations betray US origin. *Class No:* 940.53

[6824]

BROWN, D. Warship losses of World War Two. London, Arms And Armour, 1990. 256p. maps, indexes. ISBN: 0853688028.

A detailed record of over 1600 ships sunk or scuttled. Part 1. Chronology of warship losses (p.25-127) - 2. Summary of warship classes and particulars (A-Z by country); warship armament; theatres of war; statistical analysis. Indexes of principal battles and actions and ship losses p.238-9. *Class No:* 940.53

[6825]

CRAVEN, W.F. *and* **CATE, J.L.,** *eds.* **The Army Air Forces in World War II.** Chicago, The University of Chicago Press, 7v. 1948-1958. illus., maps.

1. *Plans and early operations from January 1939 to August 1942.* 1948. xxxi, 788p. 2. *Europe: Torch to Pointblank. August 1942 to December 1943.* 1949. xxi, 897p. 3. *Europe: Argument to V-E Day. January 1944 to May 1945.* 1951. xxxix, 948p. 4. *The Pacific: Guadalcanal*

....(contd.)

to Saipan. August 1942 to July 1944. 1950. xxxii, 825p. 5. *The Pacific. Matterhorn to Nagasaki. June 1944 to August 1945.* 1953. xxxviii, 878p. 6. *Men and planes.* 1955. xlvii, 808p. 7. *Services around the world* 1958. lii, 667p. Extensive chapter notes and analytical indexes. *Class No:* 940.53

[6826]

DETWILER, D.S., *ed.* **World War II German military studies** : a collection of 213 special reports on the Second World War prepared by Former officers of the Wehrmacht for the United States Army. New York, Garland Publishing Inc., 24v. 1980.

In 10 parts: Introduction and guide (Contents, German military historiography before 1945. Complete listing of German military studies held at the US National Archives in Washington). (v.1.); 2. European theater historical interrogations (v.2-3); 3. Command structure (v.4-6); 4. The OKW war diary (v.7-11); 5. The Western theater (v.12); 6. The Mediterrenan theater (v.13-14); 7. The Eastern theater (v.15-19); 8. Diplomacy, strategy and military theory (v.20-21); 9. German military government (v.22); 10. Special topics (v.23). *Class No:* 940.53

[6827]

History of the Second World War. London, HMSO, 1949-. tables, charts, maps.

Certain volumes have been reprinted by Kraus-Thomson Organization Ltd.

United Kingdom. Military histories edited by Sir J.R.M. Butler. Grand strategy (6v.). Campaigns: The campaign in Norway - France and Flanders, 1939-40 - The Mediterranean and Middle East (6v.) - The war against Japan (5v.) - Victory in the West (2v.) - The defence of the United Kingdom - The war at sea (3v.) - The strategic air offensive against Germany 1939-1945 (4v.) - Civil affairs and military government (4v.).

United Kingdom. Civil series, edited by Sir K. Hancock. Introductory (4v., including Statistical digest of the war) - General series (16v.) - War production series (8v.).

United Kingdom. Medical series, Editor-in-chief, Sir A.S. McNalty Clinical volumes (3v.) - Fighting services: Royal Navy (2v.); Army (7v.); Royal Air Force (4v.) - Medical services in wars - Civilian services (4v.).

British Foreign Policy in the Second World War by L. Woodward (5v.).

British intelligence in the Second World War by F.H. Hinsley and others (5v. in 6, 1979-1990). V.1 ISBN 0116309334; v.2 0116309342; v.3 0116309350; v.4 *Security and counter-intelligence.* 1990. xii,408p. 0116309520; v.5 *Strategic deception.* 1990. 288p. 0116309547.

S.O.E. in France: an account of the work of the British Special Operations Executive in France 1940-1944 by M.R.D. Foot.

Sir J.R.M. Butler's 'The British Military Histories of the War of 1939-45' and Sir K. Hancock's 'British Civil Histories of the Second World War', p.511-14 and p.518-25, Robin Higham's *Official histories* (Kansas State University Library, 1970) offer interesting insights. *Class No:* 940.53

[6828]
Lloyd's war losses. The Second World War. London, Lloyd's, 2v., 1989-1991.

Facsimile reprint of the original typescript held at the Guildhall Library, City of London.

1. *British allied and neutral merchant vessels sunk or destroyed by war causes.* 1989. x,1053p. index. ISBN 1850442177. Chronological listing of 5411 vessels lost due to enemy action in 2 sequences: 1. Sunk or destroyed - 2. Captured. Data: date, name, tons gross, voyage, cargo, position, how sunk, personnel, remarks.

2. *Statistics showing monthly losses - Vessels posted at Lloyd's as missing or untraced - British allied and neutral merchant vessels seriously damaged by war causes - Naval craft lost - Vessels lost by mines or underwater explosions since the cessation of hostilities.* ... 1991. ix,1925p. indexes. 1850444129.

'An enormous research tool for maritime libraries and those with significant collections devoted to the two world wars' (*Reference Reviews*, v.6, no.6, 1992, p.42).
Class No: 940.53

[6829]
MASON, F.K. Battle over Britain a history of the German air assaults on Great Britain, 1917-18 and July-December 1940, and of the development of Britain's air defences between the World Wars. Bourne End, Bucks, Aston Publications, 1990-. 539p. illus., maps, tables, bibliog., index. £39.95. ISBN: 0946627150.

First published by McWhirter Twins Ltd. in 1969.

A monumental study of the Battle of Britain in 2 parts: 1. Preparation for battle (p.13-88) which includes an account of the German raids over Britain in the First World War and the history of the Royal Air Force and the Luftwaffe in the interwar years and 2. The Battle (p.89-398), the central narrative, which includes accurate day-by-day tables of Fighter Command and Luftwaffe losses. 13 Appendices: A. Fighter Command pilots and aircrew - B. Luftwaffe ditto - C. The fighting aircraft - D. Luftwaffe order of battle - E. British aircraft production and availability - F. Representative bomb damage - G. Victoria Cross and George Cross awards - H. German intelligence of the R.A.F. - I. Royal Navy losses in home waters 1 July-31 Oct 1940 - J. Bombing of British towns and cities - K. Ground defences - L. Air/Sea rescue services - M. Contemporary examination of German aircraft crashes. Bibliography p.524-6. Analytical index. *Class No:* 940.53

[6830]
MIDDLEBROOK, M. *and* **EVERITT, C. The Bomber Command war diaries** an operational reference book. Harmondsworth, Middlesex, Viking, 1985. 804p. illus., map, facsim., bibliog., index. ISBN: 0670801372.

Based on official Air Ministry documentation, and strictly limited to units flying under the operational control of RAF Bomber Command, these diaries record every single operation mounted. Pt.1 The Diaries are divided into 21 strategic, tactical or technical time-periods (*e.g.* 1. The Phoney War, 3 Sep 1939 to 8/9 April 1940 ... 21. Victory, 1 Jan 1945 - 7/8 May 1945). Data for each day/night: forces engaged, losses, actual damage, and descriptive notes. Pt.2 Operational Statistics (sorties and casualties) p.705-12. Pt.3 Squadrons' Second World War service, raids, sorties, losses, p.715-86. Sources and bibliography p.787-90.
Class No: 940.53

[6831]
MITCHELL, W.H. *and* **SAWYER, L.A. The Empire ships** a record of British-built and acquired Merchant Ships during the Second World War. 2nd ed. London, Lloyd's of London Press, 1990. viii,504p. illus., bibliog., indexes. £38. ISBN: 1850442754.

First published 1965.

In 1939 a standard naming system was adopted by the Ministry of Shipping: all merchant ships built in Britain or acquired on government account would be given the prefix Empire to their name. These ships are listed here within general ship types and sublisted to every building yard. Data: yard number; gross tonnage; overall length, engine details; historical details (change of name and/or ownership); and launching/completion dates. Special section on Operation Overlord (Normandy landings). Bibliography p.487. *Class No:* 940.53

[6832]
Orders of battle: United Kingdom and colonial formations and units in the Second World War 1939-1945. Joslen, H.F., *comp.* London, HMSO, 2v. 1960. xii, 404p. + Ø, 405-628p. index.

9 Parts: 1. Divisions (with Appendix on composition and war establishment) - 2. Armoured, cavalry, tank, motor machine gun brigades - 3. Infantry brigades - 4. Parachute and air/landing brigades - 5. Colonial brigades - 6. Miscellaneous brigades - 7. GHQ, Army Group, Army and Corps troops - 8. British units ... in Indian formations - 9. British units in the colonies and Faroe Islands. Supplement: Formations and units engaged in The Battle of El Alamein 23 Oct. 1942 and The assault landings in Normandy 6-7 June 1944. Analytical index. No reference to the forces deployed by Commonwealth countries. Prepared for the Historical Section of the Cabinet Office. *Class No:* 940.53

[6833]
OVERY, R.J. The Air war 1939-1945. London, Europa Publications, 1980. xii, 263p. bibliog., tables index. £13.50. ISBN: 0905118537.

9 chapters: 1. Preparing for war - 2-3. The European air war September 1939-41; 1941-45 - 4. The air war in the Far East - 5. Strategic bombing offences - 6. Leadership, organization and training - 7. The aircraft economies - 8. Science, research and intelligence - 9. Conclusions. Notes p.212-239. Bibliography p.240-256. Analytical index. *Class No:* 940.53

[6834]
PLUMMER, R. The Ships that saved an army: a comprehensive record of the 1300 'little ships' of Dunkirk. Wellingborough, Northamptonshire, Patrick, Stephens, 1990. 240p. illus., bibliog., index. £17.99. ISBN: 1852602104.

Descriptive catalogue of all ships known to have been involved in Operation Dynamo, the evacuation of the British Expeditionary Force, and allied troops, from the beaches of Dunkirk, 26 May - 3rd June 1940. Bibliography p.235. *Class No:* 940.53

[6835]
POLMAR, N. *and* **ALLEN, T.B. America at war 1941-1945.** New York, Random, 1991. 940p. illus., maps, bibliog., index. $35. ISBN: 0394585305.

Encyclopedia in 2 parts: 1. Chronology 1 January 1941 - 19 December 1945 (48p.) - 2. A-Z War Guide consisting of 2400 cross-referenced entries (a few sentences to several

....(contd.)

pages) relating to political and military personalities, events, campaigns, battles, equipment, and social issues. 'Its currency and emphasis upon the American viewpoint make it a unique and useful work; (*Booklist*, v.88, no.10, 15 May 1992, p.980). *Class No:* 940.53

[6836]
SMITH, G. **The War at sea** Royal & Dominion Navy actions in World War 2. London, Ian Allan, 1989. 192p. illus., maps, bibliog., index. £19.95. ISBN: 0711017395.

Records details of all ship losses - when, where, and in what circumstances. Enemy ships sunk by R.N. and Dominion navies are also included. Background events and major warship losses indicated monthly in 4 war theatres: Atlantic; European waters, the Mediterranean, and Indian and Pacific Oceans. Maps p.180-7. Bibliography p.176. Analytical index. *Class No:* 940.53

[6837]
WHITTAKER, L.B., *comp*. **Stand down:** orders of battle for the units of the Home Guard of the United Kingdom, November 1944. Newport, R. Westlake, 1990. 153p. ISBN: 1871167140.

Home guard units deployed in 7 formations: 1. General service battalions - 2. Sector organizations - 3. Anti-Aircraft regiments - 4. Light AA troops - 5. Transport columns - 6. Regimental affiliations - 7. HG. identity parade. Data: Battalion; Company; date mustered. *Class No:* 940.53

[6838]
YOUNG, J.M. **Britain's sea war:** a diary of ship losses 1939-1945. Wellingborough, Northamptonshire, Patrick Stephens, 1989. 288p. illus., index. £14.95. ISBN: 185260042x.

A day-by-day account of the Merchant Navy's losses 3 September 1939 to 14 September 1945 with details of each vessel's size,' ownership, route and cargo, and loss of life. Index of ships p.246-88. *Class No:* 940.53

Bibliographies

[6839]
BLOOMBERG, M. *and* WEBER, H. **World War II and its origins** : a selected annotated bibliography of books in English. Littleton, Colorado, Libraries Unlimited, 1975. 311p., index.

Annotated entries for 1,603 English-language titles, arranged in chapters (chapter 1 covers relevant reference books; chapter 2: 'Pre-War years, 1919-1939'. Later chapters concern military, political, social, cultural and technological aspects of the War). Final selection of items for inclusion was based on citation frequency as well as on personal choice. Author-title-biographee index, but no subject index. 'A valuable guide' (*RQ*, v.15, no.1, Fall 1975, p.71). *Class No:* 940.53(01)

[6840]
CONTROVICH, J.T. **The Central Pacific campaign,** 1943-1944: a bibliography. Westport, Conn., Meckler, 1990. 152p. index. $45.; £28. (*Meckler's Bibliographies of Battles and Leaders, no.2.*) ISBN: 0887363253.

1128 briefly annotated items arranged in 11 sub-divided sections: 1. Campaign narratives - 2. Reference works (atlases, bibliographies, research aids, newspaper indices) - 3. General histories - 4. Memoirs and biographies - 5/7.

....(contd.)

Gilbert Islands, Marshall Islands, Marianas operations - 8/11. Army Air Force, Army, Marine Corps and Naval unit histories. *Class No:* 940.53(01)

[6841]
ENSER, A.G.S. **A Subject bibliography of the Second World War** books in English 1939-1974. London, Deutsch, 1977. 592p. £29.50. ISBN: 0233967427.

Approximately 7000 unannotated entries Abyssinia-Zhukov. 'Omits, in general, works of less than 30 pages, poetry, fiction, juvenile literature, humour, cartoons and the publications of the War Graves Commission' (*Preface*). Cross-references. Author index; subject index (simply a list of the subject headings used). Decided British orientation; no annotations - in contrast to Bloomberg and Weber - unhelpful in selection. Compiled mainly from *British National Bibliography, Cumulative Book Index* and 'Whitaker' (*sic*). *Class No:* 940.53(01)

[6842]
—ENSER, A.G.S. A Subject bibliography of the Second World War and aftermath books in English 1975-1987. 2nd ed. Aldershot, Gower, 1990. 304p. index. £45. ISBN: 0566057360.

Supersedes *A subject bibliography of the Second World War: books in English 1975-1983* (1985). Incorporates more than 1500 new entries which are arranged under subject headings A-Z *e.g.* Aircraft carriers ... Hungary ... Stalin. *Class No:* 940.53(01)

[6843]
FUNK, A.L. **The Second World War** a select bibliography of books in English published since 1975. Claremont, Calif., Regina Books, 1985. xi, 210p. £22.30. ISBN: 0941690156.

2132 items closely classified in 5 sections: 1. General (*i.e.* bibliographies, research aids, collections of documents) - 2. International situation prior to the war - 3. The War - 4. Consequences of the war - 5. Nations at war. Prepared for the American Committee on the History of the Second World War on the occasion of the 16th International Congress of Historical Sciences, Stuttgart, August 1985. *Class No:* 940.53(01)

[6844]
NEW YORK PUBLIC LIBRARY. RESEARCH LIBRARIES. **Subject catalog of the World War II Collections.** Boston, Mass., G.K. Hall, 3v., 1977. 2184p. $300.00 (Export $365. 00). ISBN: 0816100748.

45,800 photolithographed catalogue cards. *Class No:* 940.53(01)

[6845]
PUFFER, R.L. **'The Day of infamy in print',** *Library Journal*, v.116, no.14, 1 September 1991, p.206-7.

New titles provoked by 50th anniversary of Pearl Harbour listed and briefly annotated in 5 categories: Pearl Harbour - Pacific battles and campaigns - Eyewitness accounts - Biographies - Reference. *Class No:* 940.53(01)

[6846]
SBREGA, J.J. **The War against Japan, 1941-1945** an annotated bibliography. New York, Garland, 1989. xxv,1050p. indexes. $95. (*Wars Of The United States, no.10.*) ISBN: 0842089405.

5259 annotated entries arranged in 6 main subdivided sections: 1. General works ('A. Reference works *i.e.* atlases; dictionaries; encyclopedias, almanacs, statistics;

.... *(contd.)*

bibliographies; historiographies; chronologies; uniforms. B. General accounts. C. Documents and records. D. Military histories. E. East Asian histories) - 2. Diplomatic and political aspects - 3. Economic and legal - 4. Military aspects - 5. Religious - 6. Social and cultural. Appendix D: Chronology p.979-91. Author and subject indexes. 'Careful, often lengthy, occasionally brilliant annotations accompany each title ... thereby dramatically increasing the value of the work' (*Choice*, v.27,no.9, May 1990, p.1484).

Class No: 940.53(01)

[6847]

SMITH, M.J. World War II: a bibliography of sources in English. Metuchen, New Jersey, Scarecrow Press, 4v. in 3, 1976. $72.50.

1. *The European theater.* 337p. $25.00. ISBN 0810808846. 2. *The Pacific theater.* 427p. $30.00. 0810809699. 3(1) *General works. Naval hardware and the All hands chronology (1941-1945).* 3(2) *Home fronts and special studies.* $40. 0810809702. 586p. 1976. Briefly annotated entries for books, monographs, periodical articles, government documents and dissertations, up to December 1973. Author and name index per volume and cumulated indexes in the final volume. 'Should be consulted widely in future' (*Library Journal,* 15 November 1976, p.2360).

V.3 Pt.1. *General works. Naval hardware ... and chronology* (1941-1945). *Class No:* 940.53(01)

[6848]

SMITH, M.J. World War II at sea: a bibliography of sources in English 1974-1989. Metuchen, N.J., Scarecrow Press, 1990. ix,304p. index. £24.35. ISBN: 0810822601.

3465 unannotated entries deployed in 4 heavily subdivided parts: 1. Reference/General works and Biography - 2. The European Theater (A. General Works, B-E. Regional and campaign subdivisions) - 3. The Pacific Theater (A. General Works; B. Japanese triumphant - C. Tide slowly turns - D. Island hopping - E. Allies triumphant) - 4. Home fronts and special studies. *Class No:* 940.53(01)

[6849]

SMITH, M.J. World War II The European and Mediterranean theaters : an annotated bibliography. New York, Garland Publishing Inc., 1984. xxiii, 450p. index. (*Wars of the United States.*) ISBN: 0824090136.

2827 entries arranged in 6 sections: Reference works; Special studies; The War in the air; The War on land; The War at sea; 16mm. documentary film guide, with extensive cross references. List of journals cited p.411-412. Preponderantly US sources. Favourably reviewed in *Choice*, v.22, no.6, February 1985, p.800. *Class No:* 940.53(01)

[6850]

ZIEGLER, J., *comp*. **World War II** books in English 1945-1956. Stanford, California, Hoover Institution Press, Stanford Univ., 1971. xvii,223p. ISBN: 0817924515.

4,519 unannotated entries for non-fiction items (of 50 or more pages), arranged in 8 subject groups (1. General works - 2. Prelude to the War - 3. Military aspects of the War - 4. Political aspects ... 8. War crimes trials). Introduction: 'A survey of the existing bibliographical coverage' (p.xiii-xvii). No index. 'Scholarly and clear set out' (*International Affairs,* v.48,no.2, April 1972, p.371). *Class No:* 940.53(01)

Encyclopaedias

[6851]

BAUDOT, M., *and others*. **The Historical encyclopedia of World War II.** New York, Facts on File, 1980; London, Macmillan, 1981. xxii, 548p. maps, tables, bibliog. $24.95. ISBN: 0871964015, US; 0333282116, UK.

First published in Paris 1977, by Éditions Castermann under the title of *Encyclopédie de la guerre 1939-1945*.

Introduction: Origins of the second world war p.vii-xxii; ABC Plans - Zitadelle p.1-507; Conclusion: Immediate and long-range consequences of the war p.509-526. Chronology p.527-544. Bibliography p.545-548. Castigated in *Choice*, v.18, no.7, March 1981, p.924 for its unbalanced coverage and compared unfavourably with *The Simon and Schuster Encyclopaedia of World War II*. *Class No:* 940.53(031)

[6852]

CHANDLER, D. and **COLLINS, J.L.,** *eds*. **The D-Day encyclopedia.** New York, Simon & Schuster; Oxford, Helicon, 1994. li,665p. illus., maps, bibliogs., index. £40. ISBN: 0091782651, UK.

141 academic and military contributors. 437 cross-referenced, profusely illustrated articles, all ending with short further readings, cover the period 6-18 June 1994. Guide to German military units p.605. Table of comparative ranks p.607. Glossary of acronyms, code names and special terms p.609-13. Analytical index. Authoritative and definitive reference work published to mark the 50th anniversary of Operation Overlord. *Class No:* 940.53(031)

[6853]

CHANT, C. The Encyclopedia of code names of World War II. London, Routledge & Kegan Paul, 1987. viii, 344p. £40.00. ISBN: 0710207182.

'Not so much as a complete listing ... but a summary of the more important strategic and operational codenames' (*Introduction*). Even so the 3000 entries arranged alphabetically include many given to some of the more obscure military operations. *Class No:* 940.53(031)

[6854]

PERRETT, B. and **HOGG, I. Encyclopedia of the Second World War.** Harlow, Essex, Longman, 1989. 447p. illus., maps, bibliog., index. £19.95. ISBN: 0582893283.

Over 3000 A-Z entries relating to battles and campaigns, personalities, arms and equipment, codenames *etc.* Bibliography p.445-46. Over 400 contemporary photographs and 60 maps. The dustwrapper claim to be 'the ultimate reference book of the war' verges on hyperbole. *Class No:* 940.53(031)

[6855]

The Simon and Schuster encyclopedia of World War II. Parrish, T., *ed*. New York, Simon & Schuster, 1978. 767p. illus., maps, bibliog., index. softcover. ISBN: 0671242776.

47 contributors. 4000 A-Z cross referenced articles. Lengthier entries are signed. Glossary of terms and abbreviations p.703-07. Chronology: the war in synopsis p.708-15. Bibliography p.716-21. 'For browsing general readers and war buffs; scholars will need more depth' (*Choice*, v.'6, no.4, June 1979. p.512). *Class No:* 940.53(031)

[6856]
SNYDER, L.L. **Historical guide to World War II**. Westport, Connecticut, Greenwood Press, 1982. xii, 838p. $50.95. ISBN: 0313232164.

Almost 900 entries (mostly) relating to non-military aspects (unlike Marcel Baudot's *Historical encyclopaedia of World War II*) with emphasis on economic, political, social, cultural and psychological aspects. Dunkirk: 49 lines+3 refs; Pearl Harbour 114+6; Dieppe 113+3; Stalingrad 90+5. Gracie Fields 15+0; Vera Lynn 0; Marlene Dietrich 11+2; Tokyo Rose 39+0. Abbreviations WW II acronyms p.ix-xii. Appendix 1 Chronology p.785-789; 2. Ten basic books (5 UK, 5 US) p.790. Index p.791-838. 'For the professional historian, the amateur scholar, the WW II buff, and especially for the student essayist' (*Preface*).
Class No: 940.53(031)

Dictionaries

[6857]
WHEAL, E-A., *and others*. **A Dictionary of the Second World War**. London, Grafton Books, 1989. xv, 514p.+24p. of plates, illus., maps, ports. £25.00. ISBN: 0246133910.

Analytical entries of the men and machines, battles and campaigns, politics, events, the plans and accidents of global warfare in a single sequence (Aachen-Zuiho). 7 Appendices, each a campaign chronology, p.524-41. Basically an Anglo-Saxon interpretation of events justified on the grounds that only Great Britain and the United States fought a world war.
Class No: 940.53(038)

Almanacs

[6858]
The World Almanac Book of World War II. Young, P., *ed.* Englewood Cliffs, New Jersey, Prentice-Hall, 1981. 514p. illus. maps, tables, index. $16.95. ISBN: 0139678514.

A paperback 'revised' edition was issued by Ballantine Books in 1986 but the revisions were minimal.

4 sections: 1. Chronology June 1919 Treaty of Versailles to June 1950 Korea - 2. Weapons and equipment - 3. Biographies - 4. Casualties: a summing up. 16p. maps. Principal aim to be 'a detailed day by day analysis and commentary about what took place on every front'. *Reference Quarterly*, v.21, no.2, Winter 1981, p.205-6 commends it as 'easy access to basic facts on the events, people and machines involved in the conflict'.
Class No: 940.53(059)

Maps & Atlases

[6859]
GOODENOUGH, S. **War maps: World War II** from September 1939 to August 1945, air, sea and land battle by battle. London, Peerage, 1988. 192p., illus., (some col.), maps (some col.), bibliog., index. ISBN: 1850521093.

First published London, Macdonald, 1982.

Arranged according to war theatres: Europe; North Africa; Italy; Russian front; Allied invasion of North-West Europe; War in the Orient. Bibliography p.186.
Class No: 940.53(084.3)

[6860]
MANN, J. **The Atlas of D-Day and the Normandy landings**. London, Viking, 1994. 144p. illus. (some col.), col. maps. £16. ISBN: 0670856177.

Over 60 maps chart the progress of Allied and German units. The accompanying text explores the tactics, equipment and operations of both sides. *Class No:* 940.53(084.3)

[6861]
MESSENGER, C. **World War Two Chronological atlas** when, where, how and why. London, Bloomsbury; New York, Macmillan, 1989. 255p. £19.95. $32.50. ISBN: 0747502293, UK; 0025843915, US.

US title: *The chronological atlas of World War Two*.

13 chronological sections: 1. The legacy of the First World War ... 13. The Legacy (1945 to the present). Each double-page describes and maps a particular phase of the conflict in a continuous diary form. Over 200 col. maps. 'An excellent reference work for those who want a vivid and immediate grasp of the war' (*Booklist*, v.86, no.5, 1 November 1989, p.522). *Class No:* 940.53(084.3)

[6862]
PITT, B. and PITT, F. **Chronological atlas of World War II**. London, Macmillan, 1989. xi,178p. col. maps, bibliog., index.

Published in US by Summit Books as *The Month-by-month atlas of World War II*.

Double-page map and text spreads for each month of the war showing areas held by the original aggressors, Germany and Japan, with larger-scale detailed maps of current areas of conflict. Bibliography p.167. 'Both *The Times Atlas of the Second World War* and C. Messenger's *Chronological Atlas of World War Two* are preferable' (*Choice*, v.27, no.9, May 1990, p.1484). *Class No:* 940.53(084.3)

[6863]
SOMMER, R.L. and NATKIEL, R. **War maps** campaigns & battles of World War II. London, Tiger Books International, 1985 (1988 reprint). 192p. illus. (some col.), maps, indexes. £12.95. ISBN: 187046110x.

Closely integrated maps, text and illustrations arranged in 11 theatre of war sections: Blitzkrieg - The war in Northern waters ... Fortress Europe overthrown.
Class No: 940.53(084.3)

[6864]
The Times atlas of the Second World War. Keegan, J., *ed.* London, Times Books, 1989. 254p. col. illus., col. maps, col. diagrs., bibliog., index. £27.50. ISBN: 0723003173.

13 contributors. 90 double-page geographic, thematic and chronological features (maps, text, illustrations) delineating every theatre of war. Military formations and units and key to map symbols p.13. Chronology (6 colour coded geographic bands) p.14-27. Bibliography p.208. Glossary p.209-19. 450 full-colour maps and major battle reconstructions. 150 photographic illustrations and diagrams. 'Conceived as a means of conveying to its users both the totality and complexity of the Second World War ... its coverage is not exclusively military' (*Introduction*).
Class No: 940.53(084.3)

Audio-Visual Materials

Great Britain

[6865]

THORP, F. *and* PRONAY, N. **British official films in the second world war** a descriptive catalogue. Oxford and Santa Barbara, Calif., Clio Press, 1980. x, 321p. illus. $45.00. ISBN: 0903450275.

An annalistic record of 1887 films officially produced and distributed by a British government agency 1939-1946. Entries give length, summary, the name of a holding archive, review source, and credits, and are broadly according to the film's purpose. Introduction (p.1-56) expands on The Ministry of Information's propaganda policy and notes the sources used in compiling the catalogue. Index of titles p.271-290; index of credits p.291-321. 'A rich source of information' (*Choice*, v.18, no.10, June 1981, p.1399). *Class No:* 940.53(086)(410)

Chronologies

[6866]

ARGYLE, C. **Chronology of World War II.** New York, Exeter Books, London, Marshall Cavendish, 1980. 200p. illus., maps. ISBN: 0896730719, US; 0856858641, UK.

6300 entries relating to land campaigns, war at sea and in the air, the Home Front, the occupied countries, the secret war of intelligence, and diplomacy in a day-by-day record: Sep 1939 - 30 Sep 1945. Countdown to war: from Versailles to Poland 1929-39 p.4-7. Glossary p. 185-186. *Class No:* 940.53(090)

[6867]

Chronicle of the Second World War. Mercer, D., *ed.* London, Longman/Chronicle Communications, 1992. 791p. illus. (some col.), maps, diagrs., index. £29.95. ISBN: 0582075734.

Chronicle of events from the German invasion of Poland, 1 Sep 1939 to the Japanese surrender 2 Sep 1945 reported as if in a contemporary newspaper. On average 2 pages for each week of the war. Glossary p.670-1. 175 maps. Analytical index. 'Compares very favourably with other popular encyclopedic and chronological works of the 1939-45 war' (*Reference Reviews*, v.5, no.3, 1991, p.39-40). *Class No:* 940.53(090)

[6868]

Chronology and index of the Second World War 1938-1945. Royal Institute of International Affairs, *comp.* Westport, Connecticut and London, Meckler, 1990. 448p. index. £50.00. ISBN: 088736568x.

First published 1947 as *Chronology of the Second World War.* Under current title published Reading, Newspaper Archive Developments 1975.

Period: 29 September 1938-24 October 1945. A day to day account of events. Analytical index. 'Of all the works published on the war, none has proved to be more useful' (*Preface to 1975 ed.*). *Class No:* 940.53(090)

[6869]

GORALSKI, R. **World War II almanac 1931-1945** a political and military record. New York, Putnam, London, Hamish Hamilton, 1981. xii, 486p. illus., maps, bibliog. £9.95. $17.95. ISBN: 0399125485, US; 0241105730, UK.

A day by day chronology of military, political and diplomatic events beginning with the Japanese invasion of Manchuria in 1931 and ending with their surrender in

....(contd.)

September 1945. Men and arms (p.421-455) tabulates comparative ranks of all the major belligerents, their peak strengths, casualities, shipping losses, weaponry, military formations etc. Bibliography p.456-466. 'A fine reference source' (*Choice*, v. no. October 1981, p.220). *Class No:* 940.53(090)

[6870]

ROHWER, J. *and* HÜMMELCHEN, G. **Chronology of the war at sea 1939-1945** v.1 1939-1942: v.2 1943-1945. 2nd ed. London, Greenhill Books, 1992. xv, 288+Ø, 289-650p. illus. index. ISBN: 1853671177.

First published as *Chronik des Seekrieges 1939-1945* by Gerhard Stelling A.G. English edition substantially amplified and revised the orginal German language text.

A detailed chronology of World War II at sea. For a given date, subdivision into North Atlantic, South Atlantic, Baltic Sea, for each theatre of operations. Includes naval actions, fleet movements, convoys, naval air actions, and periodical assessments of overall situation. Preface (p.vii-xi) gives detail of German, British, Commonwealth, United States, Italy, USSR, Japanese and French documentary source material. Abbreviations and glossary p.xiii-xiv. Indexes of naval actions, convoys, personalities and ships' names. *Class No:* 940.53(090)

[6871]

SOMERVILLE, D. **World War II day by day.** Leicester, Magna Books, 1989. 320p. illus., maps, index. £22.95. ISBN: 1854220810.

Lavishly illustrated chronolgy and record of events. Begins June 1919 and ends June 1950 to cover events leading up to the war and the immediate post-war world. 400 illus. 50 maps. *Class No:* 940.53(090)

Biographies

[6872]

MASON, D. **Who's who in World War II.** London, Weidenfeld & Nicolson, 1978. 363p. illus., ports., maps. ISBN: 0297773763.

About 175 biographies, with 154 good illus. and portraits. (General Alexander ... General Zhukov). 'Rommel': p.255-62; 5 illus. Glossary, p.351-63. 4p. of maps appended. British, American and German biographies predominate. 'A very interesting and well produced work of reference on the War' (*Library Review*, Autumn 1979, p.186). *Class No:* 940.53(092)

[6873]

WYNN, K.G. **Men of the Battle of Britain** a who was who of the pilots and aircrew, British, Commonwealth and Allied, who flew with Royal Air Force Fighter Command July 10 to October 31 1940. Norwich, Gliddon Books, 1989. x,470p. ports., bibliog. £35. ISBN: 0947893156.

Short service biographies of 2,927 men awarded the Battle of Britain clasp to the 1939-1945 Star having flown at least one authorized operational sortie during the period stated. Data: Service number; rank; category; nationality; squadron(s). Squadron rolls p.453-66. Bibliography p.467-9. Glossary p.470. *Class No:* 940.53(092)

Archives

[6874]

CANTWELL, J.D. The Second World War a guide to documents in the Public Record Office. 2nd ed. London, HMSO, 1992. 233p. £10.95. (*Public Record Office Handbooks, no.15.*) ISBN: 011440254x.

First published 1972.

Revised edition of a guide issued to accompany the release of 2WW documents. 62 A-Z sections relating to government ministries or departments, indicating offices held by leading civil and military figures, describing the committee structure, and listing their records by registered file numbers. *Class No:* 940.53(093.20)

USA

[6875]

Federal records of World War II. Detroit, Gale Research Co., 2v., 1982. 2134p. $75.00. ISBN: 081030998x.

First published by US National Archives (1950).

V.1 *Civilian agencies* covers activities and records of over 100 agencies. V.2 *Military agencies* is a guide to the records of the departments of Interallied and Interservice Military Agencies, the War Department and the Army, the Naval Establishment and the Theatres of Operations. Name, acronym and analytical indexes. Official guide. *Class No:* 940.53(093.20)(73)

Europe

[6876]

HAESTRUP, J. European resistance movements 1939-1945 a complete history. Westport, Connecticut and London, Meckler Books, 1981. 566p., bibliog., index. $65. £34. ISBN: 0930466365.

Comprehensive account of the development of resistance movements in Europe 1939-1945 in 7 chapters: 1. Survey of problems - 2. Emergence and background - 3. Forms of civil disobedience - 4. Intelligence service - 5. The Home Front and fronts abroad - 6. Paramilitary forms of action - 7. Conclusion. *Class No:* 940.53(4)

Germany

[6877]

Das Deutsche Reich und der Zweite Weltkrieg. Hrsg. vom Militärgeschichtliches Forschungsamt. Stuttgart, Deutsche Verlags-Anstalt, 10v., 1979-.

1. Deist, W. and others *Ursachen und Voraussetzungen der deutschen Kriegspolitik.* 1979. 764p. ISBN 3421019347. 2. Maier, K.A. and others *Die Errichtung der Hegemonie auf dem europäischen Kontinent.* 1979. 439p. ISBN 3421019355. 3. Schreiber, G. and others *Der Mittelmeeraum und Südosteuropa. Von der non belligeranza Italians bis zum Kriegseintritt der Vereinigten Staaten.* 1984. xii, 733p. ISBN 3421060975. 4. Boog, H. and others *Der angriff auf die Sowjetunion.* 1983. xix, 1170p. ISBN 3421060983. *Beiheft* 1983. 27 col. maps in spiral binding.

5/1. Kroener, B. and others *Organization und Mobilisierung des deutschen Machtberiches. Kriegsverwaltung, Wirtschaft und Personelle Ressourcen 1932-1941.* 1988, xvii, 1061p. col. maps, bibliog., tables, graphs, index. ISBN 3421062323. 20 heavily documented ch. in 3 parts: 1. Auf dem Weg zur Kontinentalherrschaft - 2. Die Mobilisierung deutscher Wirtschaft für Hitlers

....(contd.)

Kriegführung - 3. Die Personellen Ressourcen den Dritten Reiches in Spannungsfeld zwischen Wehrmacht, Bürokratie und Kriegswirtschaft 1939-42. Bibliography p.1033-52. *Titles in preparation.* 5/2. *Organization und Mobilisierung* ... *1942-1944/45.* 6. *Die Ausweitung zum Weltkrieg 1941/42-1943.* 1990. xix,1181p. 3421062331. 7. *Das Deutsche Reich in der Defensive. Der Krieg im Western und in Mittelmeerraumsee 1943/44.* 8a. *Das Deutsche Reich in der Defensive. Der Krieg im Osten und Südosten 1943/44.* 9/1. *Staat und Gesellschaft im Kriege. Innenpolitik und Volksgemeinschaft 1939-1944/45.* 9/2. *Staat und Gesellschaft im Kriege. Die Entwicklung des militärischen Instruments im Kriege.* 10.*Das Ende des Dritten Reiches.* *Class No:* 940.53(430)

[6878]

—**Germany and the Second World War.** Militärgeschictliches Forschungsamt, Freiburg im Breisgau, *ed.* Oxford, Clarendon Press, 10v., 1990-.

1. Deist, W. and others. *The Build-up of German aggression.* 1990. xxviii,799p. tables, maps on endpapers, bibliog., index. £80. ISBN 019822866x. Glossary of German terms p.xxvii-xxviii. Bibliography p.733-88 (for the English edition has been supplemented by works published 1979-86). 2. Maier, K.A., and others *Germany's initial conquests in Europe,* 1991. xiv,444p. illus. bibliog., index. £65. 0198228856. Bibliography p.421-39. An intensively researched and well-documented cooperative but not necessary unanimous history by the staff of the German Research Institute for Military History examining the Second World War from the German point of view. *Class No:* 940.53(43)

USSR

Bibliographies

[6879]

PARRISH, M. The USSR in World War II : an annotated bibliography of books published in the Soviet Union, 1945-1975. With an addenda for the years 1975-1980. New York, Garland Publishing Inc., 2v., 1981. xxi, 308p.+vii, 309-906p. ISBN: 0824094859.

1521 entries in 5 parts: The military campaigns; the Soviet armed forces; Geographic areas of the USSR during the war; Subject divisions; Economic divisions. 'An attempt to organize, classify, and annotate the Soviet books, pamphlets, theses, pictorial collections etc., written since 1945 about the Great Patriotic War ... Not only books published in major cities but also from numerous provincial presses as well as dissertations are included' (*Preface*). Coverage does not extend from 1941 because of the disruption of publishing in the confusion of war and the unavailability of all but a fraction of wartime publications. 'Scholars interested in in-depth research will have to reach beyond this work' (*RQ,* v.21, no.1, Fall 1981, p.105). *Class No:* 940.53(47)(01)

Asia

[6880]

War in Asia and the Pacific. Detwiler, D.S. New York, Garland Publishing Inc., 15v. 1980.

1. *Introduction and guide.* Chapter 7 is Chronology of the Pacific War from Japanese point of view. 2. *Political background of the war.* 3. *Command, administration, and*

.... *(contd.)*

special operations. 4-5. *The Naval armament program and naval operations.* 6-7. *The Southern Area.* 8-9. *China, Manchuria, and Korea.* 10-11. *Japan and the Soviet Union* 12. *Defense of the Homeland and end of the war.* 13-15. *The Sino-Japanese and Chinese civil wars.* Based on surviving documentation, supplemented by personal records, of investigation undertaken by the Japanese government after the surrender in 1945, translated into English, and now on file in the Department of the Army's Center of Military History in Washington. *Class No:* 940.53(5)

USA

[6881]

GREENFIELD, K.R., *ed.* **United States Army in World War 2.** Washington, Historical Division, Department of The Army, 58v., 1947-77.

Published in 11 series *viz* 1. The War Department - 2. Army ground forces- 3. Army service forces - 4. Western Hemisphere - 5. War in the Pacific - 6. China, Burma, India theater - 7. European theater of operations - 8. Mediterranean theater - 9. Middle East theater - 10. Technical services - 11. Special studies. Scholarly and extensive bibliographies, glossaries of abbreviations and code names, and analytical indexes enhance the reference value of this mammoth series.

K.R. Greenfield's 'Scholarship and the U.S. Army in World War II' p.551-552 and S. Conn's 'The Army's World War II history and related publications', p.553-564, Robin Higham's *Official histories* (Kansas State University Library, 1970) contain much useful information not easily available elsewhere. *Class No:* 940.53(73)

Bibliographies

[6882]

World War II from an American perspective : an annotated bibliography. Santa Barabara (California) and Oxford, ABC-Clio Inc., 1983. vi, 277p. index. £23.10. ISBN: 0874360358.

1107 citations of scholarly articles from historical and related journals published 1971-1981 extracted from the American Bibliographical Center's data base. *Class No:* 940.53(73)(01)

Commonwealth

[6883]

BELOFF, M. Imperial sunset. London, Macmillan, 2v., 1988-89. maps, tables, index.

Britain's Liberal empire first published 1963.

1. *Britain's Liberal Empire, 1897-1921.* 408p. £33. ISBN 0333444906. - Diamond Jubilee - The weary titan - The Empire and the Ententes - War and war aims - The Empire and the peace - Apogee of Empire - Chronology 1897-1921.

2. *Dream of Commonwealth, 1921-42.* 352p. £37.50. 0333404394. Pt.1: The attempt at consolidation 1921-1932. Britain as a Middle Eastern Power - Palestine - Empire into Commonwealth - The economic argument - Imperial defence and arms control - Singapore - The Indian Ambiguity. Pt.2: The quickening pace, 1932-1939. The Empire and the world depression - Trusteeship, indirect rule and colonial development - The Empire and rearmament - Clearing the decks: Ireland, India, The Middle East - The Empire and

.... *(contd.)*

appeasement. Pt.3: The Accounting. The Empire goes to war - Defeat and the shadow of dissolution - Signposts to the future - Notes - Chronology - Biographical Notes.

Marks Britain's decline as an imperial power. The author is Emeritus Professor of Government and Public Administration in Oxford University. *Class No:* 941-44

[6884]

BUTLER, D. *and* **LOW, D.A., eds.** **Sovereigns and surrogates** constitutional Heads of State in the Commonwealth. London, Macmillan, 1991. 365p. bibliog., index. (*Cambridge Commonwealth Series.*) ISBN: 0333524438.

11 contributors. Primarily focuses on the constitutional powers and functions of the Governor-Generals or Presidents in 'those independent countries in the Commonwealth which have in large measure preserved the Westminster form of government, with executive power exercised by a Prime Minister and Cabinet answerable to the legislature, but with a Governor-General or President broadly carrying out the ceremonial and constitutional functions expected of the British sovereign'. Appendix 1. Constitutional Heads in the Commonwealth 1945-1990 p.331-54. Bibliography p.355-7. *Class No:* 941-44

[6885]

The Cambridge history of the British Empire. Cambridge, Cambridge Univ. Press, 8v., 1929-1988.

1: *The old Empire, from the beginnings to 1783.* 1929. 2: *Growth of the new Empire, 1783-1870.* 1940. 3: *The Empire-Commonwealth, 1870-1919;* edited by E.A. Benians. 1959. 4: *British India, 1497-1858;* edited by H.H. Dodwell. 1929. 5: *Indian Empire, 1858-1918, with chapters on the development of administration, 1818-1858;* edited by H.H. Dodwell, 1932. 6: *Canada and Newfoundland.* 1930. 7: pt.1: *Australia;* edited by E. Scott. Reissued 1988. xxv,759p. £35.00. ISBN 0521356210. 7: pt.2: *New Zealand* 1933. 8: *South Africa, Rhodesia and the Protectorates.* 2nd ed. 1963. Each volume carries some 20-30 chapters by specialists. The lengthy, valuable bibliography appended to each volume is divided into pt.1, Collections of MSS in public and private archives and official papers and publications, and pt.2, Other works. *Class No:* 941-44

[6886]

DOXEY, M.P. The Commonwealth Secretariat and the contemporary Commonwealth. Basingstoke, Hampshire, Macmillan, 1989. ix,172p. bibliog., index. £33. (*Cambridge Commonwealth series.*) ISBN: 0333457285.

A 'down-to-earth' description of the activities conducted by the Secretariat itself or under its auspices: 1. The shape and character of the modern Commonwealth - 2. The Secretariat - 3. The office of Commonwealth Secretary-General - 4. Secretariat at work - 5. Cooperation in social and professional fields - 6. International affairs: the political dimensions - 7. Southern African problems - 8. Assessment. Appendix A: Commonwealth membership 1988. Chapter notes and references p.152-65. *Class No:* 941-44

[6887]

DROWER, G. Britain's dependent territories a fistful of islands. Aldershot, Dartmouth, 1992. 276p. maps, tables, bibliog., index. £32.50. ISBN: 1885212420.

Britain still retains the world's largest overseas empire, consisting mainly of islands in the Atlantic and Caribbean.

....*(contd.)*

This is an overview of recent political history in the various territories and their views regarding the imperial links. Bibliography p.241-71. 7 maps. *Class No:* 941-44

[6888]
LLOYD, T.O. The British Empire 1558-1983. Oxford, Oxford Univ. Press, 1984. xvii,430p. maps, tables, bibliog., index. (*Shorter Oxford History of the Modern World.*) ISBN: 0198730241.

13 chronological chapters forming a single-volume complete history of the British Empire. Bibliographical essay p.387-398. 'Will certainly become the standard text on imperial history' (*Choice,* v.22,no.7, March 1985, p.1058-1059). *Class No:* 941-44

[6889]
McINTYRE, W.D. The Significance of the Commonwealth 1965-90. London, Macmillan, 1990. ix,305p. tables, index. £35. ISBN: 0333553160.

Review of the Commonwealth's structural and functional development and the main issues confronting it since the Secretariat was established in 1964. Not confined to political and constitutional issues, it extends to popular aspects of its activities like youth programmes, arts festivals and sport. Chapter notes p.270-91. *Class No:* 941-44

[6890]
MANSERGH, N. The Commonwealth experience. 2nd ed. London, Macmillan, 2v., 1982. ISBN: 0333331680, set.

First published as a single volume by Weidenfeld & Nicolson (1969).

V.1 *The Durham Report to Anglo-Irish Treaty* xii,275p. ISBN 0333331583. 7 chapters in 2 pts.: 1. The foundation members - 2. The British Commonwealth of Nations 1914-21. Notes p.244-61. V.2. *From British to multiracial Commonwealth.* ix,299p. maps. ISBN 0333331605. 7 chapters in 2 pts.: 1. The British Commonwealth of Nations 1921-1947 - 2. The Commonwealth since 1947 - 3. Retrospect 1838-1981. Notes p.258-73. Bibliography p.274-85. Definitive account of origins, development, pattern and concept of inter-state relations, and the Commonwealth's experience in peace and war. *Class No:* 941-44

Bibliographies

[6891]
CATTERALL, P. 'The Empire, the Commonwealth and the Mandated Territories' *British history 1945-1987: an annotated bibliography (q.v.).*

'External relations', chapter 3 of *British history 1945-1987: an annotated bibliography* (1980) includes 1080 items listed in the following sub-divided sections: B. The Empire ... General - C. Empire and Commonwealth in Asia - D. Middle East - E. Sub-Saharan Africa - F. Caribbean - G. Australasia and the Pacific - H. Canada - I. Gibraltar and Malta - J. Atlantic and Antarctic (p.102-95). The aim of these sections 'has been to provide an extensive guide to the nature of the literature on the demission of power, both generally and area by area, and, where appropriate, on the continuation of Commonwealth relations' (*Preface*). *Class No:* 941-44(01)

[6892]
GIPSON, L.H. A Bibliographical guide to the history of the British Empire 1784-1776. New York, Knopf, 1969. 478p. (*The British Empire before the American Revolution, v.14.*)

Covers the constitutional, political, economic and some social aspects of British imperialism. Some entries are annotated; periodical articles are included. Overall arrangement is by geographical area, followed by bibliographical tools, printed source materials, secondary work, maps and cartographical aids. Index of authors and selected topics. More up-to-date and much more comprehensive than the bibliography in the *Cambridge history of the British Empire,* 'Probably the most ample bibliography on the topic at the present time' (*College and Research Libraries,* v.30, July 1969, p.379). V.1-13 comprise an encyclopaedic survey of the Empire during the period. *Class No:* 941-44(01)

[6893]
PALMEGIANO, E. The British Empire in the Victorian press 1832-1867. New York, Garland Publishing, 1986. 256p. indexes. $40.00. (*Themes in European Expansion.*) ISBN: 0824098021.

1. List of magazines published in London that dealt exclusively or extensively with imperial concerns - 2. Inventory of over 2000 articles from 50 general journals. *Class No:* 941-44(01)

Micromaterials

[6894]
Rhodes House Library Subject Catalogue. Cambridge and Alexandria, New York, Chadwyck-Healey, 1989. 105x148mm, 49 frame silver halide microfiche at a 24x reduction. Approx 540 microfiche with 132p. printed guide to the subject headings. £1600.00.

Entries for about 175,000 printed works 1760-1988, with references to archive material, arranged under 24 regional or country headings sub-divided where appropriate. A detailed subject arrangement (fully outlined in the printed guide) plus cross-references facilitate immediate access. A major reference guide and research tool for the study of Africa south of the Sahara, The Commonwealth (excluding South Asia), and the United States in history, politics, and government. Rhodes House Library, Oxford, is a dependent library of the Bodleian. *Class No:* 941-44(01)(003.5)

Maps & Atlases

[6895]
Atlas of the British Empire. Bayly, C.H., *ed.* London, Hamlyn, 1989. 256p. illus. (mostly col.), col.maps, index. £25.00. ISBN: 0600568318.

13 academic contributors. 41 chapters arranged in 4 sections: 1. Voyages and plantations 1500-1763 - 2. Age of free enterprise 1763-1860 - 3. Heydey of Empire 1860-1914 - 4. The World Wars 1914-1945 - 5. Retreat from Empire 1945 - the present. 39 col.maps. Lack of bibliography detracts from reference value. Condemned as a 'Coffee-table Book of the British Empire' in Royal Commonwealth Society *Library Notes,* new series, no.295, February 1990, p.7. *Class No:* 941-44(084.3)

Biographies

[6896]

ROYAL COMMONWEALTH SOCIETY. Biography catalogue of the Library of the Royal Commonwealth Society. Simpson, D.H. London, Royal Commonwealth Society, 1961. xxiii,511p. £7.50. ISBN: 0905067355.

'The aim has been to list all the Library's biographical material. Books published up to the autumn of 1960 and periodicals to the close of 1959 have been included' (*Preface*). Some 12,000 entries for over 6,500 individuals, embracing periodical articles and analytical entries from volumes of collective biography, as well as books and pamphlets. The main sequence, 'Individual biographies' (p.-388) is followed by 'Collective biography and country indexes' (p.388-431), 'Addenda' (p.433-5) and 'Supplementary list of authors' (p.441-511). 'The men and women included are in the main, those born in, or actively connected with, countries of the Commonwealth, and persons in the United Kingdom who have been of significance in Imperial affairs' (*Preface*). There are also numerous entries for explorers and travellers of many countries. Items asterisked represent books or periodicals destroyed by enemy action but inserted for their bibliographical value. Entries include full name, dates of birth and death and a brief description of the biographee; they indicate the presence of portraits and illustrations. Supplemented in v.7 of the RCS *Subject catalogue of the Royal Commonwealth Society* (Boston, Mass., G.K. Hall, 1971). *Class No:* 941-44(092)

Government State Papers

[6897]

GREAT BRITAIN. Public Record Office. The Records of the Colonial and Dominion Offices. Pugh, R.M. London, H.M. Stationery Office, 1964. vi,119p., facsims.

Designed to introduce the searcher to a large mass of public records, - the Colonial Office and Commonwealth Relations Office (previously Dominions Office) groups. 3 sections; the first describes administrative arrangements for handling Commonwealth relations; the second describes records that these administrations have created, particularly during the last century or so; the third has brief notes in the classes that make up this complex. Annotated list of record classes, p.57-119. *Class No:* 941-44(093.200)

Great Britain

[6898]

English historical documents. Douglas, D.C., *ed.* London, Eyre Methuen; New York, Oxford Univ. Press, 1953-. v.1-. diagrs. maps.

1. *c.500-1042* edited by D. Whitelock. 2nd ed., 1979. xxxii,960p. ISBN 0413324907. 2. *1042-1189* edited by D.C. Douglas and G.W. Greenaway. 2nd rev. ed., 1980. xxiv,1064p. £65. 0413325008. 3. *1189-1327* edited by H. Rothwell. 1975. xxiv,1032p. £65. 0413233006. 4. *1327-1485* edited by A.R. Myers. 1969. lxviii,1236p. £65. 0413233103. 5. *1485-1558* edited by C.H. Williams. 1967, xviii,1082p. £65. 0413233200. 6. *1558-1603* In preparation. 7. (1) *1603-1640*; (2) *1640-1660* In preparation. 8. *1660-1714* edited by A. Browning. 1953. xxxii, 966p. £65. 0413206505. 9. *American colonial documents to 1776* edited by Jensen. 1955. xxiv, 888p. £65. 0413206602. 10. *1714-1783* edited by D.B. Horn and M. Ransome. 1957. xxviii,

....(contd.)

972p. £65. 0413233502. 11. *1783-1832* edited by A. Aspinall and E.A. Smith. 1959. xxx,992p. £65. 041323360x. 12. (1) *1833-1874* edited by G.M. Young and W.D. Handcock. 1956. xxiv,1018p. 12. (2) *1874-1914* edited by W.D. Handcock. 1977. xxiv,726p. £65. 0413233707.

Aims 'to make generally accessible a wide selection of the fundamental sources of English history' (*General preface*, v.12, pt.1). Each volume has a lengthy general introduction and a select bibliography; each of its parts has its own introduction and select bibliography. All documents (or selections from documents) are translated into English (as necessary), the text being well footnoted. V.12, pt.1 (12 parts has 269 items, including departmental and Royal Commission reports, *Times* leaders, legislation and statistical data. V.12, pt.2 (12 parts) covers such subjects as economic structure and development; religion and the churches; imperialism and foreign affairs; law penal system and courts; central and local government; education; poor law and problem of poverty; factories, health and housing; trade unions and socialism. *Class No:* 941.0

[6899]

The Oxford history of England. Oxford, Clarendon Press, 1936-1981. £25.00 each volume.

1A: *Roman Britain* by P. Salway. 1981. ISBN 019821717x. This replaced the first part of *Roman Britain and the English settlements* by R.G. Collingwood and J.N.L. Myres, 2nd ed., 1937. 1B: *The English settlements* by J.N.L. Myers. £17.50. 2. *Anglo-Saxon England* by F.M. Stenton, 3rd ed. 1971. 0198217161. 3. *From Domesday Book to Magna Carta 1087-1216* by A.L. Poole, 2nd ed. 1955. 0198217072. 4. *The thirteenth century 1216-1307* by M. Powicke, 2nd ed. 1962. 0198217080. 5. *The fourteenth century 1307-1399* by M. McKisack. 1964. 0198217129. 6. *The fifteenth century 1399-1485* by E.F. Jacob. 1964. 0198217145. 7. *The earlier Tudors 1485-1558* by J.D. Mackie. 1964. 0198217064. 8. *The reign of Elizabeth 1558-1603* by J.B. Black. 2nd ed. 1959. 0198217013. 9. *The early Stuarts 1603-1660* by G. Davies. 2nd ed. 1959. 0198217048. 10. *The later Stuarts 1660-1714* by G. Clark. 2nd ed. 1956. 0198217021. 11. *The Whig supremacy 1714-1760* by B. Williams. 2nd ed. revised by C.H. Stuart 1962. 0198217102. 12. *The reign of George III 1760-1815* by J.S. Watson. 1964. 0198217137. 13. *The age of reform 1815-1870* by L. Woodward. 2nd ed. 1962. 0198217110. 14. *England 1870-1914* by R.C.K. Ensor. 1964. 0198217056. 15. *English history 1914-1945* by A.J.P. Taylor. 1965. 0198217153. *Consolidated index* edited by R. Raper 1991. vi,622p. 0198217862. Raper's 'Making the consolidated index of Oxford History of England', *The Indexer*, v.18, no.1, April 1992. p.1-2 is of interest.

Standard introduction to the periods concerned with valuable critical bibliographies. V.15, brilliantly and occasionally controversially written (see *Times Literary Supplement*, no.3329, 16 December 1965, p.1169-70, 'History Taylor-made'), has a lengthy bibliography in the form of a running commentary (p.602-39). *Class No:* 941.0

[6900]

—The New Oxford history of England. Oxford, Clarendon Press, 1989-.

Successor to the *Oxford history of England.* 'Each volume will set out an authoritative view of the present state of scholarship, presenting a distillation of the new knowledge built up by a half-century's research and publication of new sources...'

1st volume published: Langford, P. *A Polite and commercial people England 1727-1783.* 1989. xix,803p. illus. (incl.pl.), tables, bibliog., index. £25.00. ISBN 0198228287. 14 chapters. Chronology p.727-739. Bibliography (p.741-766) is in continuous narrative form and is subdivided into 20 thematic sections. Analytical index. *Class No:* 941.0

Bibliographies

[6901]

Bibliographical handbooks. Hecht, J.J., *general editor.* Cambridge, Cambridge Univ. Press, for the Conference on British Studies, 1968-.

Anglo-Norman England 1066-1154 by M. Altschul. 1969. *The High Middle Ages in England 1154-1377* by B. Wilkinson. 1978. *Late-medieval England 1377-1485* by D.J. Guth. 1976. *Tudor England 1485-1603 by M. Levine. 1968. Restoration England 1660-1689* by W.L. Sachse. 1971. *Late Georgian and Regency England 1760-1837* by R.A. Smith. 1984. 0521255384. *Victorian England 1837-1901* by J.L. Altholz. 1970. *Modern England 1901-1984* by A.F. Havighurst. 1987. £25. 0521309743. First published as *Modern England 1901-1970* (1976). This volume has 2670 briefly annotated entries, some with references to further material. Numerous cross-refrences. 16 sections: 1. Bibliographies - 2. Catalogues, guides and handbooks - 3. General surveys - 4. Constitutional history - 5. Political history - 6. Foreign relations - 7. Social history - 8. Economic - 9. Labour - 10. Urban - 11. Agricultural - 12. Science and technology - 13. Military and naval - 14. Religious - 15. Fine arts - 16. Intellectual history. Index of authors, editors and translators. Subject range does not include literature *per se.* Many entries for periodical articles, as well as for biographies and other printed sources. Provides scholars and advanced students with handy guides to writings on each period, and also serves as a basis for research. *Class No:* 941.0(01)

[6902]

Bibliography of British history. Oxford, Clarendon Press, 1928-. Issued under the direction of the American Historical Association and the Royal Historical Society of Great Britain.

1. *A bibliography of English history to 1485* edited by E.B. Graves. 1975, xxiv,1103p. £60.00. ISBN 0198223919 (7,221 entries). Basically a revision of C. Gross' *Sources and literature of English history from the earliest times to about 1485* (London, Longmans, 2nd ed. 1915).

2. *Tudor period 1485-1603* edited by C. Read. 2nd ed. 1959. xxviii,624p. Reprinted Hassocks, Sussex, Harvester Press; Totowa, New Jersey, Rowan & Littlefield. 0855276843 (UK). 0847660745 (US) (6,543 entries). First published 1933.

3. *Stuart Period 1603-1714* edited by G. Davies and M.F. Keeler. 2nd ed., 1970. xxxv,734p. £60.00. 0198213719. (4,350 entries). First published 1928.

4. *The Eighteenth Century 1714-1789* edited by S.

....(contd.)

Pargellis and J.D. Medley. Harvester Press and Rowan and Littlefield. 1971. xxvi,642p. 0855271361 (UK) (4,558 entries).

5. *1789-1851* edited by L.M. Brown and I.R. Christie. 1977, xxxi,759p. £55.00. 0198223900. (4,782 entries).

6. *1851-1914* edited by H.J. Hanham. 1978. xxvii,1606p. £70.00. 019823897. (10,829 entries).

Each volume has entries (mostly annotated) in sections, and usually with section introductions. *Stuart period, 1603-1714* is invaluable for its references to MS sources. The *1789-1851* volume has 15 sections: 1. General reference works - 2. Political history - 3. Constitutional history - 4. Legal history - 5. Ecclesiastical history - 6. Military history - 7. Naval history - 8. Economic history - 9. Social history - 10. Cultural history - 11. Local history - 12. Wales - 13. Scotland - 14. Ireland - 15. The British Empire. Index, p.603-759. The 1851-1914 volume, with its massive index (p.1239-1606), lacks section introductions. Alan Day's 'Birthpangs of a bibliography', *New Library World,* v.79, no.938, August 1978, p.154-7, is a brief account of this monumental and invaluable series. *Class No:* 941.0(01)

[6903]

CHRISTIE, J.R. British history since 1760: a select bibliography. London, Historical Association, 1970. 56p. index, sd. *(Helps For Students of History, no.H81.)*

'With a few exceptions, excludes collections of private source material and periodical articles' *(Preface).* 5 sections: 1. Bibliography and periodicals - 2. General series and general works - 3. Later Hanoverian Age - 4. Victorian Britain - 5. The nineteenth century. Some brief annotations. *Class No:* 941.0(01)

[6904]

HARDY, T.D. Descriptive catalogue of materials relating to the history of Great Britain and Ireland to the end of the reign of Henry VII. London, Longmans, 3v. in 4, 1862-71. *(The Rolls Series.)*

Vol. 1: *From the Roman period to the Norman invasion,* 2v. 1862. cxxxic,918p. Vol.2: *From AD1066 to AD1200.* 1865. civ,601p. Vol.3: *From AD1200 to AD1327.* 1871. cxxii,482p.

The documentary sources of early British history arranged chronologically by the year in which the latest event is recorded. 'If even major libraries understandably jib at the full cost of a full reprint edition of The Rolls Series they would be well advised to consider the purchase of these particular volumes ' (Day. A.E. *History: a reference handbook,* 1977,. Entry 210). *Class No:* 941.0(01)

[6905]

MILLER, H. *and* NEWMAN, A. Early modern British history 1485-1760: a select bibliography. London, Historical Association, 1970. 42p. sd. *(Helps For Students of History, no.H79.)*

About 600 entries, with occasional annotations. 12 sections: 1. Bibliographies - 2. General surveys - 3. Government and politics - 4. Civil War and Interregnum - 5. Religion - 6. Structure and society - 7. Economic changes - 8. Thought - 9. The arts - 10. Military and naval - 11. British and Europe - 12. Overseas expansion. All titles are published in London, unless otherwise stated. Index. *Class No:* 941.0(01)

[6906]

Rerum Britannicarum medii aevi scriptores or Chronicles and memorials of Great Britain and Ireland during the Middle Ages. London, Longmans Green, 253v., 1858-1911. (*The Rolls Series.*)

Reprinted by Kraus Reprints 1965.

Published under the direction of the Master of the Rolls these erudite volumes contain the primary sources of the history of Great Britain from the Roman invasion to the reign of Henry VIII. Editors were instructed to give the most correct text from a collation of the extant manuscripts, to introduce the text by describing their age and peculiarities, and to give a brief account of the life and time of the author. M.D. Knowles' presidential address to the Royal Historical Society (*Transactions of the RHS,* 5th series, v.11, 1961 p.137-59) reviews the preliminary moves leading to this monumental enterprise, the various editorial mishaps, and criticism of the series. *Class No:* 941.0(01)

[6907]

Royal Historical Society. Annual bibliography of British and Irish history. London, Harvester Wheatsheaf; since 1990 Oxford Univ. Press, 1976-. Annual.

Published for Royal Historical Society.

Comprehensive and authoritative survey of books and articles published in a calendar year. Arranged in 14 sub-divided sections: A. Auxiliary (Archives, Bibliography, Works of reference) - B. General - C/I. by historical period - J. Medieval Wales - K. Scotland before the Union - L/M. Ireland - N. Empire & Commonwealth post-1783. Each section is edited by a specialist in the period. Separate author, personal name, place, and subject indexes. *1991* volume (1992. ISBN 0198204612 lists over 4000 books and articles. *Class No:* 941.0(01)

[6908]

Writings on British History. London, Institute of Historical Research, annual.

1901-1933 (1968-70). 5v. in 7 (Williams Dawson): 1. *The auxiliary sciences and general works* - 2. *The Middle Ages* - 3. *The Tudor and Stuart periods* - 4. *The eighteenth century* - 5. *1815-1914. 1934-1945* (1937-60). 8v. (William Dawson). *1946-1948* (1973). (Inst. Hist. Res). *1949-1951* (1975). *1952-1954* (1975). *1955-1957* (1977). *1958-1959* (1977). *1960-1961* (1978). *1962-1964* (1979). *1965-1966* (1981). *1967-1968* (1982). *1969-1970* (1984). *1971-1972* (1985). *1973-1974* (1986).

The 1973-74 v. has sub-title: 'a bibliography of books and articles on the history of Great Britain from *c.*450AD to 1939 published during the year 1973-74 inclusive with appendix containing a select list of publications in these years on British history since 1939' (xix, 283p.). It has 5193 numbered entries, unannotated, but references to reviews are included. Over 400 journals scanned. Part 1. General works (Auxiliary sciences; Bibliographies and indexes; Archives and collections; Historiography, study and teaching; British history in general; English local history and topography; Wales and Monmouthshire; Scotland; Ireland; British Empire and Commonwealth; Genealogy and family history; Collected biography) - 2. Period histories (7 periods: Pre-conquest: Medieval; Tudor; Stuart; 18th century; 19th century; 20th century). Appendix: Select list of works published in the years 1973-74 on British history since 1939. Analytical index p.207-283. Slow progress is being made on the time-lag in publication. 'The *Writings* should be available, not only in every academic library, but also in

....(contd.)

every city and county reference library that claims to cater for serious historical study' (*History*, v.41, Feb-June-October 1956, p.361-363). *Class No:* 941.0(01)

Encyclopaedias

[6909]

The Cambridge historical encyclopedia of Great Britain and Ireland. Haigh, C. Cambridge, Cambridge Univ. Press, 1985. 392p. illus. (some col.), maps (some col.), bibliog. £30. ISBN: 0521255597.

60 chapters contributed by academic historians arranged in 7 chronological sections: 1. Britons and Romans *c.*100 BC-AD 409 - 2. Saxons, Danes and Normans 409-1154 - 3. Medieval empire: England and her neighbours 1154-1450 - 4. Reformation and inflation 1450-1625 - 5. Disorder to stability: Britain and Ireland 1625-1783 - 6. Political reform and economic revolution 1783-1901 - 7. From imperial power to European partner 1901-1975. An overview of each chapter and marginal notes on events and personalities throughout justify the title. Who's Who (800 very brief biographical entries) p.338-373. Further readings (by chapter) p.374-376. Index p.377-391. 'As a work of ready reference it is not easy to find the limited information it contains, yet it is an indigestible read from cover to cover ... it essentially attempts too much in too small a space' (*British Book News*, December 1985, p.759-760).
Class No: 941.0(031)

[6910]

Chronicle of Britain incorporating a chronicle of Ireland. Heald, H., *ed.* Farnborough, JL International Publishing 1296p. illus. (mostly col.), col. maps, geneal., tables, index. £29.95. ISBN: 1872031358.

25 academic chief consultants and 23 journalist contributors. Sumptuously illustrated double-page spreads, each with a chronology, relate the events of British history (c.6500BC - 1991) as if reported in a newspaper of the age. By the 16th century each double-page relates to a single year. An appendix contains illustrated features on the UK parliamentary system, Britian and the Commonwealth, and the monarchy. British ministries 1721-1992 (giving principal Secretaries of State) p.1218-9. Analytical index p.1236-96. *Class No:* 941.0(031)

[6911]

Chronicle of the Royal Family. Mercer, D., *ed.* London, Chronicle Communications, 1991. 624p. £29.95. ISBN: 0582090067, UK; 187203120x, Can.

Intended to complement *Chronicle of Britain and Ireland.* (*q.v.*).

15 contributors. *Contents:* 1. From tribes to kingdoms (the story to 850 AD) - Chronicle from 850 to 1991 p.12-587. Appendix: A-Z gazetteer of palaces and royal residences p.588-611. Over 1750 illustrations. Accompanied by 55cm x 75cm wallchart, *Kings and Queens of England and Scotland,* displaying main lines of succession of royal houses. Follows Chronicle pattern of reporting historical events as though they had just happened. Book of descriptive reportage rather critical analysis. *Class No:* 941.0(031)

Handbooks & Manuals

[6912]

COOK, C. *and* STEVENSON, J. **The Longman handbook of modern British history 1714-1987.** 2nd ed. London, Longman, 1988. xi,418p., tables, geneal. tables, bibliog., index. £18.95. ISBN: 0582013283.

First published 1983.

Essential facts and figures arranged in 7 sections: 1. Political history (political chronology, lists of principal ministers, British monarchs, *etc.*) - 2. Social - 3. Economic - 4. Foreign affairs and defence - 5. Biographies - 6. Glossary (p.308-325) - 7. Topic bibliographies (p.331-397). Intended for teachers, sixth form and undergraduate students. 'A remarkably compendious handbook' (*British Book News*, November 1983, p.715). *Class No:* 941.0(035)

Dictionaries

[6913]

The Illustrated dictionary of British history. Marwick, A., *ed.* London, Thames and Hudson; New York, W.W. Norton, 1980. 319p. illus. £8.95. £19.95. ISBN: 0500250723, UK.

2000 mostly brief A-Z entries but including 20 longer, signed 'interpretative essays' (*e.g.* Prehistoric Britain, Monarchy, and The economy since 1870) primarily intended for the lay reader. 372 illustrations but a dearth of maps and with no bibliographical support. Unfavourably compared to *Steinberg's Dictionary of British history* in *Choice*, v.19, no.1, September 1981, p.50 but 'many teachers will find it a useful work of reference in classroom or library' it is reported in *School Librarian*, v.29, no.1, March 1981, p.73. *Class No:* 941.0(038)

[6914]

KENYON, J., *ed.* **A Dictionary of British history.** London, Secker & Warburg, 1987; New York, Stein and Day, 1983. viii, 415p. maps. geneal. tables. £15. ISBN: 0436233088.

27 contributors. 3000 short A-Z entries relating to social and political events, foreign affairs, major cultural and scientific development, and prominent men and women of Britain and its overseas possessions, 55BC to AD1970. Chronology p.373-410. Genealogy of British monarchs p.411-415. *Class No:* 941.0(038)

Maps & Atlases

[6915]

COOK, C. *and* STEVENSON, J. **Longman atlas of modern British history:** a visual guide to British society and politics 1700-1970. London, Longman, 1978. 208p. diagrs., charts, maps.

3 parts (38 sections, each with introduction): 1. Economic history - 2. Social history - 3. Political history. Black-and-white maps; many bar diagrams; statistical data. 'Riots and public order' (p.158-61); 9. maps; 6 diagrams. Bibliography (by sections), p.192-8; sources, p.199-201. Index of names. Index, p.204-8. 'The Longman atlas, while displaying a number of problems, should still prove to be a good general introduction to British history, and will also be of interest to students of modern studies' (*Library Review*, Autumn 1979, p.198). *Class No:* 941.0(084.3)

[6916]

FALKUS, M. *and* GILLINGHAM, J., *eds.* **Historical atlas of Britain.** Rev. ed. London, Kingfisher Books, 1987. 223p. col. illus., col. maps. £19.95. ISBN: 0862722950.

First published London, Granada, 1981.

21 academic contributors. Arranged in 6 chronological chapters 4000 BC to the present day dealing with political changes and 2 chapters on social and economic developments. Chronology of world history p.216-217. Index p.218-223. 'Although much more expensive and ambitious than G.S.P. Freeman-Grenville's *Atlas of British History* (London 1879), it is a much superior work' (*Choice*, v.19, no.9, May 1982, p.1216). *Class No:* 941.0(084.3)

[6917]

GILBERT, M. **The Dent atlas of British history.** 2nd ed. London, J.M. Dent, 1993. 144p. maps. ISBN: 0460861794.

First published by Weidenfeld & Nicolson 1968.

144 black and white outline political, war and conflict, trade and industry, religious, and social and economic maps (26 new to this edition) from The Celts in Britain by 50 BC to Public spending 1993-1994. *Class No:* 941.0(084.3)

[6918]

GREAT BRITAIN. Ordnance Survey. **Historical maps and guides.** Southampton, Ordnance Survey, 1924-.

Archaeological and historical maps: *Ancient Britain.* 1 inch to 10 miles. North and South sheets printed back to back. £5.00 - *Roman Britain* 1 inch to 10 miles. £5.00 - *Hadrian's Wall.* Scale 1:50,000. £3.25 - *Londinium.* 25 inches to 1 mile (1:2500). £2.20 - *Roman and Anglian York* (1:2500). £3.25 - *Viking and Medieval York* (1:2500). £3.25 - *Roman and Medieval Bath.* 50 inches to 1 mile (1:1250). £3.25 - *Georgian Bath* (1:2500). £3.25. Also *Britian before the Norman Conquest.* North or South sheets. 1 inch to 10 miles (1:625.000). £3.40 each flat or £9.00 both folded with text and cover. Out of print titles: *Neolithic Wessex; Trent Basin (Neolithic); Neolithic South Wales; Celtic earthworks of Salisbury Plain; Antonine Wall; Britain in the Dark Ages;* and *Monastic Britain. Class No:* 941.0(084.3)

Bibliographies

[6919]

FORDHAM, H.G. **The Road-books and itineraries of Great Britain 1570-1850:** a catalogue. Cambridge, Cambridge Univ. Press, 1924. xiv,72p.

A chronological survey, without annotations. There is an index of names of authors, publishers and printers.

The author has also compiled a *Hand-list of catalogues and works of reference relating to carto-bibliography and kindred subjects for Great Britain and Ireland, 1720 to 1927* (Cambridge Univ. Press, 1928. 25p.) and *Studies in carto-bibliography, British and French, and in the bibliography of itineraries and road-books.* 1914. x, 180p. (Reprinted London, Dawsons Pall Mall, 1969, x, 180p. £15. ISBN 0712903925. *Class No:* 941.0(084.3)(01)

Chronologies

[6920]

CASTLEDEN, R. **Harrap's book of British dates** a comprehensive chronological dictionary of British dates from prehistoric times to the present day. London, Harrap, 1991. 446p. index. £14.95. ISBN: 0245603514.

Year by year entries with background information provide

....(contd.)

the dates for important political, dynastic, religious, and scientific events, which have shaped and influenced British traditions and culture. *Class No:* 941.0(090)

[6921]

FRYDE, E.B., *and others.* **Handbook of British chronology.** 3rd ed. London, Royal Historical Society 1986. xxxix, 605p. £25. (*R.H.S. Guides And Handbooks.*) ISBN: 0861931068. ISSN: 00804398.

First published in 1939 edited by F.M. Powicke; second edition in 1961 edited by Powicke and E.B. Fryde.

Lists of rulers, with style and significant dates, of officers of state, bishops, dukes, marquesses and earls; tables of parliament and councils. The 3rd ed. adds the names of Chancellors and Under-Treasurers of the Exchequer 1559-1713, First Secretaries of State 1962-1968, and Commanders-in-chief of land forces 1642-1904. Bibliographical guide to the lists of English office-holders p.xxiii-xxxix. 'Clearly the editors have produced a most co-ordinated work of reference' (*Archives*, v.18, no.78).
Class No: 941.0(090)

[6922]

Handbook of dates for students of English history. Cheney, C.R. 2nd ed. London, Royal Historical Society, 1961. xviii,164p. tables, bibliog., index. (*Royal Society Guides And Handbooks, no.4.*)

1. Reckonings of time (inc. Julian and Gregorian calendars) - 2. Rulers of England ... 4. Saint's Days and Festivals used in dating - 5. Legal chronology ... 7. English calendar for AD1752 *etc.* Bibliography p.xi-xviii.
Class No: 941.0(090)

[6923]

PALMER, A. *and* **PALMER, V. The Chronology of British history** from 250,000BC to the present day. London, Century, 1992. 569p. maps, tables, index. £20. ISBN: 0712621733.

Entries under various units of time (annually since 1855) of significant dates and events and key landmarks in arts and sciences, scholarship, literature and drama, music, popular entertainment, and fashion. 50 lists (*e.g.* English and Scottish monarchs, prime ministers). 19 maps.
Class No: 941.0(090)

Biographies

[6924]

Who's who in British history. Treasure, G.R., *ed.* London, Shepheard-Walwyn; New York, St. James Press, 8v., 1988-. maps, bibliog., index.

Replaces 'Who's who in history' series published by Basil Blackwell (5v. 1960-1975).

1. Fletcher R. *Roman Britain and Anglo-Saxon England.* 1989. xxv,245p. ISBN 0856830895 - 2. Tyerman, C. *Early medieval England - 3.* Hicks, M. *Late medieval England.* 1991. 400p. 0856830925 - 4. Routh, C.R.N. *Tudor England.* 1990. 476p. 0856830933 - 5. Hill. C.P. *Stuart Britain.* 1988. xiv,466p. 0856830755 - 6. Treasure, G.R. *Early Hanoverian Britain.* 1991. 0856830763 - 7. Treasure, G.R. *Late Hanoverian Britain.* 1991. 480p. 0856830941 - 8. *Victorian Britain.* (to be announced) 1992. 'Each volume paints a portrait of an age. The persons selected are not confined to those who made their mark on church or state, but extended to a wider cross-section of society, including artists, explorers, scientists, entrepreneurs and eccentrics.

....(contd.)

The series differs from the conventional *Who's Who* in two major respects: 1. entries are arranged in a broadly chronological rather than alphabetical sequence to facilitate reading about contemporaries; 2. each essay conveys more than the bare facts of the subject's life; it places him in the context of his age and evokes what was distinctive and interesting in his personality and achievement' (*Publisher's announcement*). *Class No:* 941.0(092)

Government State Papers

[6925]

ELTON, G.R. England 1200-1640. Cambridge, Cambridge Univ. Press, 1976. 225p., index. (*The Sources Of History: Studies in The Use of Historical Evidence.*)

First published London, Hodder & Stoughton 1969.

Examines the range of material and sources available under 8 heads: 1. Narratives - 2. Official records; The State - 3. Official records; The church - 4. Official records; Lesser authorities - 5. Private materials - 6. The law - 7. Books and writings - 8. Non-documentary sources.
Class No: 941.0(093.200)

Jews

[6926]

JONES, P.F. The Jews of Britain a thousand years of history. Moreton-In-Marsh, Gloucestershire, Windrush Press, 1990. 208p. illus. £15.95. ISBN: 090007566x.

Traces the history of Britain's Jewish community from Roman times to the present. Marks the 700th anniversary of the expulsion of the Jews by Edward I.
Class No: 941.0(=924)

Middle Ages

Bibliographies

[6927]

DAVIS, G.R.C. Medieval cartularies of Great Britain: a short catalogue. London, Longmans Green, 1958. xxi, 182p.

Pt.1. Cartularies of religious houses (p.2.-137); pt.2. Secular cartularies. 1,344 entries, with a bibliographical description of each; if an item is asterisked, it has been deposited on loan. Arrangement in pt.1, under England and Wales, and Scotland, is A-Z by locations. Effective use of bold type. Indexes: 1. Present owners etc., of MSS (corporate; private); 2. Former owners, etc., of MSS. Described in *Annual bulletin of historical literature* (no.44 (1960), p.15) as 'indispensable guide to the location of monastic and other cartularies', in public or private ownership. *Class No:* 941.0"01/14"(01)

[6928]

GRAVES, E.B., *ed.* **A Bibliography of English history to 1485.** Based on *The Sources and literature of English history from the earliest times to about 1485* by Charles Gross. Issued under the sponsorship of the Royal Historical Society, the American Historical Association and the Medieval Academy of America. Oxford, Clarendon Press, 1975. xxiv, 1103p. £60. $135. ISBN: 0198223919.

C. Gross's *Sources and literature of English history, from the earliest times to about 1485* (2nd ed. London, Longmans Green, 1915, xxiv, 820p. (Reprinted Gloucester, Mass., Smith, 1952) was first published in 1900.

....(contd.)

7,225 annotated entries. 'Basically a revision' of Gross (first published 1900; 2nd ed. 1915). Part 1: General works and auxiliary sciences - 2. Archives, source collections and modern narratives (section 7. Local history) - 3. From pre-history to Anglo-Saxon Conquest - 4. The Anglo-Saxon period - 5. From Normans to Tudors (section 13-23); 13. Chronicles and Royal biographies; 14. Law tracts; 15. Public administrative records; 16. Modern political narratives; 17. Military and naval history; 18. Land tenure and estates; 19. Agrarian society; 20. Urban society; 21. The church, 1066-1485; 22. Modern studies of the medieval English church; 23. Intellectual interests, 1066-1485). Index, p.937-1103. Section introductions. 'Like previous editions, it includes for the pre-Norman periods some fundamental studies on Welsh and Irish history' (*Preface*). The basic bibliography of the period. *Class No:* 941.0"01/14"(01)

[6929]
MACRAY, W.D. A Manual of British historians to AD1600: containing a chronological account of the early chroniclers and monkish writers, their printed works and unpublished manuscripts. London, Pickering, 1845. Reprinted Naarden, Van Bekhoven, 1967. xxii, 110p. bibliog., indexes.

Recent research has corrected some of Macray's dates and ascriptions, but the *Manual* remains the only basic list of medieval British chroniclers and historians. Short biographical sketch, list of MS texts and bibliography of printed editions are provided for each author. Arrangement, chronological. *Class No:* 941.0"01/14"(01)

Institutions & Associations

[6930]
PINHORN, M., *comp.* **Historical, archaeological and kindred societies in the United Kingdom:** a list. Hulverstone Manor, Isle of Wight, Pinhorn, 1986. 105p. £10.00. ISBN: 901262226.

First published by Univ. of London Institute of Historical Research in 1965 (rev. ed. 1968) with S.E. Harcup as compiler.

An A-Z list giving date of foundation, number of members, permanent address or name and address of the Secretary, is indexed by a topographical list p.76-100. National Societies p.101-102. A 'Pinhorn history addresses - update service' has appeared in *Local History* (*qv*) from issue no.13, November/December 1986 onwards. *Class No:* 941.0:061:061.2

Roman & Anglo Saxon Period

[6931]
Anglo-Saxon England. Cambridge Univ. Press, 1972-. v.1-. Annual. illus. ISSN: 02636751.

No.17. *1988.* ix, 335p. 0521365716. contains 13 articles and a Bibliography for 1987 (p.283-335) of all significant books, articles and reviews in any branch of Anglo-Saxon studies, arranged in 9 sections *e.g.* Palaeography, History ... Archaeology. V.5 (1976), v.10 (1982) and v.15 (1986) contain detailed quinquennial indexes. No. 21 *1992* is given over to the proceedings of the International Society of Anglo-Saxonists, at Stony Brook, New York, 22-26 July 1991. *Class No:* 941.01

[6932]
ARNOLD, C.J. An Archaeology of the early Anglo-Saxon kingdoms. London, Routledge, 1988. xv,224p. illus., tables, maps, bibliog., index. ISBN: 0415003490.

Definitive study of the evolving social and political structure of Anglo-Saxon England 500-700 A.D. in the light of archaeological evidence including chapter 1. A history of early Anglo-Saxon archaeology. Bibliography p.203-17. *Class No:* 941.01

[6933]
CLAYTON, P.A., *ed.* **A Companion to Roman Britain.** Oxford, Phaidon, 1980. 208p. illus., (some col.), plans, maps, index.

6 contributions by 6 specialists: 1. Introduction: Setting the scene - 2. Social organization - 3. The people - 4. Christianity in Roman Britain - 5. The economy - 6. The end of Roman Britain. Gazetteer, p.165-97. Appendices: A. Some museums with Romano-British collections; B. The governors of Roman Britain and the emperors of Rome. Chapter bibliographies, p.202-3. Analytical index. 350 illus. of villas, towns, fortifications, temples, theatres, sculptures, coins. 'This well-presented and richly illustrated work' (*British Book News*, October 1980, p.637). *Class No:* 941.01

[6934]
FRERE, S. Britannia a history of Roman Britain. 3rd ed. extensively revised. London, Routledge & Kegan Paul, 1987. xvi, 423p.+32p. plates., illus., maps, bibliog., index. £25.00. ISBN: 0710212151.

1st ed. 1967; 2nd ed. 1978.

16 chapters *e.g.* 1. The background: the British Iron Age ... 6. The retreat from Scotland ... 14. Romanization of Britain ... 16. End of Roman Britain. Bibliography p.380-402. *Class No:* 941.01

[6935]
FRY, L.P.S. Roman Britain history and sites. Newton Abbot, Devon, David & Charles; Totowa, New Jersey, Barnes & Noble 1984. 560p. illus., maps, bibliog. £16. ISBN: 0715382675, UK; 0389204390, US.

17 chronological chapters (p.9-269) summarizing Roman involvement with Britain are followed by a gazetteer (p.274-520) of more than 1000 entries representing 'the great bulk (though not all) of the Roman sites in England, Wales and Scotland' arranged alphabetically by county and by region in Scotland. A large number of sites that are no longer visible are included. Notes (*i.e.* list of selected references relating to individual sites) p.527-543; glossary p.544-545; bibliography p.546-552; index of people and places p.553-558; subject index p.559-560. 'The gazetteer contains more entries than any similar compendium' (*Choice*, v.22, no.1, September 1984, p.166). *Class No:* 941.01

[6936]
SALWAY, P. Roman Britain. Oxford, Clarendon Press, 1981. xx+[xivp. maps], 824p. bibliog., index. £25.00. ISBN: 019821717x.

21 chapters in 5 parts: 1. The first Roman contacts - 2. The Roman conquest - 3. Imperial crisis and recovery - 4. Roman Britain and the fifth century world - 5. Britain under Roman rule. Appendices: 1. Note on Roman names - 2. Roman Emperors from Augustus to Justinian - 3. Governors of the British provinces. Bibliography p.753-75, 'a review of sources in general, not a collection of references for individual statements in the text', is divided into the

....*(contd.)*

following sections: Ancient authors; The Roman Empire; Roman Britain: bibliographies and abstracts; Finds and excavations; Topography, regional and local surveys; Inscriptions; General works; Periodicals; Monuments and special subjects. *Class No:* 941.01

[6937]
WHITTOCK, M.J. The Origins of England 410-600. London, Croom Helm, 1986. xi,273p. index. £35.00. ISBN: 0709936796.

Presents the latest thinking on the literary sources, archaeology, and place name study in 4 heavily annotated chapters: 1. The coming of the English - 2. Romans and the English - 3. English Society - 4. The founding of the kingdoms. Appendix 1. King Lists/Genealogies (*i.e.*, a comparison of 2-3 sources for Bernicia, Deira, East Anglia, Essex, Kent, Lindsay, Mercia and Wessex (p.253-259). 2. The tribal heritage. 3. Early English Personal Names. *Class No:* 941.01

Bibliographies

[6938]
BONSER, W. An Anglo-Saxon and Celtic bibliography (450-1087). Oxford, Blackwell, 1957. xxvii,574p.

11,975 items, from 422 periodicals, collected works, etc. Closely classified. 1. General topics and historical source material - 2. Political history - 3. Local history - 4. Constitutional history and law - 5. Social and economic history - 6. Ecclesiastical history and religion - 7. Geography and place-names - 8. General culture - 9. Archaeology - 10. Numismatics and seals - 11. Epigraphy - 12. Art. A separate *Indices* volume provides author, subject, and topographical indexes. *Class No:* 941.01(01)

[6939]
BONSER, W. A Romano-British bibliography (55BC - AD449). Oxford, Blackwell, 2v., 1964.

9,370 items, closely classified; 15 classes and 666 subdivisions. Classes: 1. General topics - 2. History - 3. Army, fleet and defence - 4. Social and economic - 5. Religion - 6. Geography - 7. General archaeology - 8. Numismatics - 9. Art - 10-15. Regions of England, Scotland and Wales. 'Periodicals and collective works abstracted': 253 items. No annotations, but brief explanatory notes sometimes follow title, and presence of maps and plates is indicated. V.2 consists of indexes: author; subject; personal names; place-names (a) England, (b) Scotland (c) Wales and Monmouthshire. A valuable compilation for the period. *Class No:* 941.01(01)

[6940]
IRELAND, S. Roman Britain a sourcebook. London, Croom Helm, 1986. 266p. illus. maps. bibliog. ISBN: 070991315x.

Greek and Roman references to Britain translated into English and listed in 3 sequences: 1. The geography and people of Britain - 2. The political and military history - 3. Religion, commerce and society. Introduction (p.1-9) considers literary, epigraphic and numismatic evidence. Bibliography p.247-249. Index of literary sources p.250-253. Index of inscriptions P.254-256. General index. p.257-266. *Class No:* 941.01(01)

[6941]
Research on Roman Britain 1960-89. Todd, M., *ed.* London, Society for the Promotion of Roman Studies, 1989. xi,271p. illus., maps, plans, bibliog., index. A4 pbk. £19.50. (*Britannia Monograph Series, no.1.*) ISBN: 0907764134.

16 thematic bibliographical essays by different hands: 1. The later Iron Age in Southern Britain and beyond ... 4. The northern frontiers ... 6. The early cities ... Constantine I to Constantine III - 16. A prospect of Roman Britain. Bibliography (1960-88) p.251-65. *Class No:* 941.01(01)

Maps & Atlases

[6942]
HILL, D. An Atlas of Anglo-Saxon England. Oxford, Blackwell, 1981. xi,180p. maps, chron. tables, bibliog. ISBN: 0631111816.

244 maps cover the physical, political, and economic geography of Anglo-Saxon England within the context of Viking Scandinavia, Iceland, and Western Europe. Bibliography p.167. Index locorum p.168-180. Favourably reviewed in *Antiquity*, v.57, no.219, March 1983, p.66-67. *Class No:* 941.01(01)(084.3)

Handbooks & Manuals

[6943]
MAXFIELD, V.A., *ed*. The Saxon shore a handbook. University of Exeter, 1989. vi,178p. illus., maps, plans, bibliog. (*Exeter Studies in History, no.25.*) ISBN: 0859893308. ISSN: 02608626.

8 essays by independent hands present an up-to-date survey of the Saxon shore, its geographical setting, its forts and fleet. Gazetteer of sites p.113-64. Bibliography p.165-78. *Class No:* 941.01(035)

Maps & Atlases

[6944]
JONES, B. *and* MATTINGLY, D. An Atlas of Roman Britain. Oxford, Blackwell Reference, 1990. x,341p. illus., maps, bibliog., index. £22.50. $49.94. ISBN: 0631137912.

Presents in cartographic form the whole corpus of knowledge of Romano - British studies: 1. Physical context - 2. Britain and the Roman geographers - 3. Britain before the conquest - 4. Conquest and garrisoning of Britain - 5. Development of the Provinces - 6. Economy - 7. Countryside - 8. Religion - 9. Devolution. Bibliography (by chapter) p.321-32. 273 maps. 'Perceptively abreast of the latest archaeological and literary discoveries' (*Choice*, v.28,no.9, May 1991, p.1546). *Class No:* 941.01(084.3)

Biographies

[6945]
BIRLEY, A.R. The Fasti of Roman Britain. Oxford, Clarendon Press, 1981. xii,476p. bibliog., index. ISBN: 0198148216.

Records the careers of almost 200 Romans who served in Britain either as governor or as a senior civil or military officer. Bibliography p.436-43. *Class No:* 941.01(092)

[6946]
WILLIAMS, A., *and others*. **A Biographical dictionary of Dark Age Britain** England, Scotland and Wales c.500-c.1050. London, Seaby, 1991. Distributed by Batsford. xlii,253p. geneal. tables, bibliog. ISBN: 1852640472.

Biographical sketches of varying length accompanied by a short list of references. Glossary p.viii-ix. Chronological tables p.x-xxiii. Genealogical and regnal tables p.xxiv-xlii. Consolidated list of references p.244-53.

Class No: 941.01(092)

Government State Papers

Bibliographies

[6947]
SAWYER, P.H. **Anglo-Saxon charters:** an unannotated list and bibliography. London, Royal Historical Society, 1968. xiii,538p. £8.00. (*RHS Guides and Handbooks, no.8.*) ISBN: 0901050180.

Lists 1875 charters 'granting land or secular rights over land that purport to have been issued in England before the Norman Conquest (*Preface*). The first section lists chronologically the charters of which reasonably full texts have been preserved; the second lists charters lost or only partly preserved. Data on each charter include MS source, printed (with or without translation) form, plus comments. Bibliography, p.1-25; list of manuscripts, (A-Z by locality or name), p.44-67. Detailed index of persons and places. A valuable tool for the researcher in this field.

Class No: 941.01(093.200)(01)

Plantaganets

Encyclopaedias

[6948]
HALLAM, E. **The Plantagenet encyclopedia** an alphabetical guide to 400 years of English history. London, Weidenfeld and Nicolson, 1990. 224p. col.illus., maps, geneal tables, bibliog., index. £14.95. ISBN: 0297830031.

Over 1200 A-Z entries relating to prominent people, places and events from the origins of the House of Anjou to the Battle of Bosworth Field. Sumptuously illustated. Bibliography p.216-8. *Class No:* 941.03(031)

Tudors

[6949]
POWELL, K. *and* COOK, C. **English historical facts 1485-1603.** London, Macmillan, 1977. vii,228p. £35.00. ISBN: 0333148886.

First published 1977.

Sourcebook of facts, figures and dates presented in 11 sections: 1. Crown and central government - 2. Parliament - 3. The judicature and the courts - 4. Local government - 5. The Church - 6. Education - 7. War, rebellion and diplomacy - 8. Scotland and Ireland - 9. Tudor economic legislation - 10. Population and growth of towns - 11. Tudor biographies. Bibliography p.221-8. No index.

Class No: 941.05

Bibliographies

[6950]
RASOR, E.L. **The Spanish Armada of 1588** historiography and annotated bibliography. Westport, Conn., Greenwood Press, 1993. xviii,277p. index. (*Bibliographies of Battles and Leaders, no.10.*) ISBN: 0313283036.

1. Historiographical section (*i.e.* a series of thematic bibliographical essays - 2. Annotated bibliography (p.87-257) of 1114 entries. Chronology p.259-61.

Class No: 941.05(01)

Dictionaries

[6951]
FRITZE, R., *ed*. **Historical dictionary of Tudor England** 1485-1603. Westport, Conn, Greenwood Press, 1991. xvii,594p. bibliog., index. $86. ISBN: 0313265984.

66 contributors. 295 signed cross-referenced entries (250-2,000 words in length) relating to the leading figures, events, laws, institutions, and specific topics (*e.g.* exploration) of the whole Tudor period. Entries end with lists of further readings. Chronology p.557-70. Bibliography p.571-80. One of *Library Journal's* 'Best reference books' 1991.

Class No: 941.05(038)

Biographies

[6952]
PALMER, A. *and* PALMER, V. **Who's who in Shakespeare's England.** New York, St. Martin's Press, 1981; Brighton, Harvester Press, 1983. xxvi,280p. illus. map. ISBN: 0855277181.

More than 700 concise biographies of Shakespeare's contemporaries 1590-1623. Glossary p.276-280. 'Inaccurate statements are numerous ... its usefulness is restricted mainly to those who have no access to basic reference sources on the topic' (*Choice*, v.19,no.6, February 1982, p.746+748). *Class No:* 941.05(092)

Stuarts

[6953]
COOK, C. *and* WROUGHTON, J. **English historical facts 1603-1688.** London, Macmillan, 1980. viii,231p., bibliog. £35. ISBN: 0333186346.

11 sections: 1. The monarchy - 2. Selected holders of major public offices - 3. Glossary of central government - 4. Biographies - 5. Parliament - 6. Local government - 7. The Church - 8. The armed forces - 9. Overseas trade and the colonies - 10. Education and learning - 11. Population and the towns. Bibliographical note p.230-1. Slated in *Choice*, v.18, no.10, May 1981, p.1232, for 'some extraordinary gaps' (*e.g.* nothing on Royal Navy, important buildings, agriculture, Scotland, Wales or Ireland). No index.

Class No: 941.06

Bibliographies

[6954]
MORRILL, J.S. **Seventeenth century Britain 1603-1714.** Folkestone, Dawson-Archon; Hamden, Connecticut, Shoe String Press, 1980. 189p. index. £12. (*Critical bibliographies in modern history.*) ISBN: 0712908390, UK; 0208017852, US.

1263 annotated entries in 11 sections (sub-divided): 1.

....(contd.)

General - 2. Government - 3. Political - 4. Political and constitutional thought - 5. Military and naval - 6. Ecclesiastical - 7. Economic and Social - 9. Local studies - 10. Cultural - 11. Scotland, Ireland and Wales. *Class No:* 941.06(01)

Dictionaries

[6955]
NEWMAN, P.R. Companion to the English Civil Wars. New York & Oxford, Facts on File, 1990. xxiv,192p. bibliog., maps. $29.95; £13.95. ISBN: 0816022372.

Over 1,000 A-Z cross-referenced entries (50-200 words) define and describe the events, persons, places, issues, and military terminology of the period 1642-1651. Chronology p.167-76. Bibliography p.177-80. 'The entries ... seek to stress the 'British' aspect of the wars, and to lay stress upon the Irish dimension' (*Preface*). *Class No:* 941.06(038)

Maps & Atlases

[6956]
BAKER, A. A Battlefield atlas of the English Civil War. London, Ian Allan Ltd., 1987. 128p., illus., maps, index. ISBN: 0711016542.

56 double-page map and text features on battles, actions and engagements, in date order, with 'enough detail to make the background to the battles and their effect on the war understandable'. *Class No:* 941.06(084.3)

Manuscripts & Incunabula

[6957]
UPTON, E.S. Guide to sources of English history from 1603 to 1660 in early reports of the Royal Commission on Historical Manuscripts. 2nd ed. New York, Scarecrow Press, 1964. 258p.

1st ed. 1952.

The main part is virtually a reprint: 'Subject index to materials on English history, 1603-1660 in the first nine reports' (p.35-248). Appendix A: 'Parliamentary proceedings, 1621 to 10 February 1642, in print'; B: 'List of collections within the scope of this Guide' (*c*.125 collections). Analytical index; asterisked entry indicates that the Report gives the contents of the manuscript item with a fair degree of detail. *Class No:* 941.06(093)

Georgian & Regency Period

[6958]
COOK, C. *and* **STEVENSON, J. British historical facts 1688-1760.** London, Macmillan Press, 1988. x,252p. £38. ISBN: 0333172329.

14 sections: 1. The Monarchy - 2. Chronology - 3. Administration and political biographies - 4. Selected holders of public offices - 5. Parliament - 6. Elections - 7. Religion - 8. Treaties and diplomacy - 9. Armed forces - 10. Colonies - 11. Law and order - 12. Social developments - 13. The Economy and finance - 14. Local government. *Class No:* 941.07

[6959]
COOK, C. *and* **STEVENSON, J. British historical facts 1760-1830.** London, Macmillan, 1980. ix,197p. £35. ISBN: 0333215125.

15 sections: The monarchy - Ministries and administrations - Selected holders of public office - The peerage and Order of Knighthood - Parliaments and elections - Foreign affairs - The armed forces - The Empire and India - Radicalism, trade unions and political reform - Law and order - The press - Religion - Selected holders of local government office - The economy - Social developments. Sources stated; bibliographies appended to most sections. Appended bibliographical note, p.196-7. 'Seems destined to become the essential reference work for its period' (*British Book News*, July 1980, p.406-7). But no index. *Class No:* 941.07

Victorian Age

[6960]
COOK, C. *and* **KEITH, B. British historical facts 1830-1900.** London, Macmillan, 1975. xi, 279p. bibliog. £38. ISBN: 333132203.

17 chapters: 1. Ministries - 2. Political parties - 3. Parliament ... 5. Parliamentary reform ... 10. Armed services - 11. Education - 12. The Press - 13. Religion - 14. Population - 15. The economy - 16. Trade unions and the co-operative movement - 17. The British Empire. 'Bibliographical note', p.277-9. 'It lists almost all who held high political, judicial, military or administrative office in Britain between 1830 and 1900; and provides basic information about their institutions and the world in which they lived' (*Preface*). *Class No:* 941.08

Bibliographies

[6961]
Annual bibliography of Victorian studies. Brahma Chauduri, *ed.* Edmonton, LITIR Database, Department of English, University of Alberta, 1977-.

1987 volume (1989) is in 5 parts: Pt.1 (3062 entries): General reference works; Fine arts; Social sciences; Science and technology; Language and literature - 2. Subject index - 3. Author index - 4. Title index - 5. Reviewer index. Master list of journals p.xv-xxii. A computer generated reference tool covering British Victorian period 1830-1914.

Cumulative volumes: A *comprehensive bibliography of Victorian studies* is now available *V.1 1970-1974* (1984). 0919237118. *V.2 1975-1979* (1985). 0919237126. *V.3 1980-1984* (1985). 0919237134. Also *Cumulative bibliography of Victorian studies 1970-1984.* 2v., 1988. $795. 1. Classified listings, 924p. (2 cols. per page); 2. Subject, author, and title indexes. 812p. ISBN 0919237177. *Class No:* 941.08(01)

[6962]
NICHOLLS, D. Nineteenth-century Britain 1815-1914. Folkestone, Kent, Dawson-Archon Books, 1978. 170p.

960 annotated entries in 9 sections (subdivided): 1. General - 2. Political and constitutional - 3. Foreign, imperial and defence - 4. Economic - 5. Social - 6. Education - 7. Religion - 8. Wales, Scotland and Ireland - 9. Literary and cultural (very thin). Appendix A: Addenda; B. A guide to periodical literature. *Class No:* 941.08(01)

[6963]

PROPAS, S.W. **Victorian studies** a research guide. New York, Garland, 1992. xxi,334p. index. $30. ISBN: 0824058402.

678 annotated entries relating to English-language reference works (books, microforms, periodicals, and databases) relating to all aspects of the Victorian period in Great Britain, Ireland, and the British Empire. Arranged under form and discipline headings. *Class No:* 941.08(01)

Encyclopaedias

[6964]

MITCHELL, S., *ed*. **Victorian Britain:** an encyclopedia. New York, Garland, 1988; London, St. James Press, 1991. xxi,986p. illus., bibliog., index. $125. ISBN: 0824015134, US; 1558621059, UK.

More than 400 signed articles cross-referenced covering persons, events, institutions, groups, and artifacts in Great Britain 1837-1901 are enhanced with individual authoritative bibliographies. Chronology p.xi-xxi. Research Materials for Victorian Studies p.887-93. Analytical index. 'Intended to serve as an overview and point of entry into the complex interdisciplinary field of Victorian studies' (*Preface*).
Class No: 941.08(031)

20th Century

[6965]

Keesing's United Kingdom record. London, Longman, 1988-. 6 issues a year. £60 per annum (UK); £70.00 or $122.00 elsewhere. ISSN: 0952195x.

v.1. *1988* v.2. *1989* A detailed, factual, up-to-date account of events in the United Kingdom and of its external affairs based on the press, official sources and other services. Each issue contains reports of major events, obituaries, a diary of parliamentary business, and a summary of current economic data. Cumulative subject/name indexes. *Class No:* 941.082

[6966]

MORGAN, K.O. **The People's peace:** British history 1945-1989. Oxford, Oxford Univ. Press, 1990. xiii,558p. illus., bibliog., index. £20. ISBN: 0198227647.

14 chapters assessing the course of recent British history arranged in 3 sections: 1. The era of advance 1945-1961 - 2. The years of retreat 1961-1979 - 3. Storm and stress 1979-1989. Bibliography p.517-32. 'The first major assessment of what can now be seen as a clearly definable area. It is an outstanding work: comprehensive, lucid and judicious' (*Sunday Times,* no.8,681, 6 January 1991. p.8.10).
Class No: 941.082

Bibliographies

[6967]

CATTERALL, P. **British history 1945-1987** an annotated bibliography. Oxford, Basil Blackwell for the Institute of Contemporary British History, 1990. xxxii,843p. indexes. £100. ISBN: 0631170499.

8644 entries record the significant literature on events between the 1945 and 1987 general elections. They are marshalled into 15 heavily sub-divided chapters: 1. General - 2. Political and constitutional history - 3. External relations - 4. Defence - 5. Legal system - 6. Religion - 7. Economic history - 8. Environmental history - 9. Social history - 10. Education - 11. Intellectual and cultural history - 12. Local

.... (contd.)

history - 13. Wales - 14. Scotland - 15. Northern Ireland. Chapter 2 has 10 sub-categories (General; Histories of Post-war administrations; Constitution; Monarchy; Administration and central government; Parliament; Party history and political biography; Political thought; Electoral history; Pressure groups). Official publications, specialist articles from academic journals, bibliographies and databases are included. 'There can hardly be a research library in the country, or further afield for that matter, that will not need to order it despite its ton-up price' (*Reference Reviews,* v.5,no.3, 1991, p.41). *Reference Reviews* Best Generalist Reference Work 1991. *Class No:* 941.082(01)

Yearbooks & Directories

[6968]

Contemporary Britain an annual review. Catterall, P., *ed.* Oxford, Blackwell Reference for the Institute of Contemporary British History, 1990-. ISSN: 09575960.

1992 ed. 1992. 484p. £45. 0631184945/ 41 x 3000 word essays ending with chronologies covering different aspects of contemporary development, interpreting and reviewing legislation, reports, initiatives, speeches and events to act 'both as an analysis of contemporary Britain and as a record of events'. Grouped in 12 areas: 1. The year in perspective - 2. Politics - 3. The media - 4. Law and order - 5. External relations - 6. The economy - 7. Social policy - 8. Society - 9. Environment - 10. Religion - 11. Culture - 12. Regions. The yearbook of the Institute of Contemporary British History. *Class No:* 941.082(058)

Archives

[6969]

COOK, C. **Sources in British political history 1900-1951.** London, Macmillan, 6v., 1975-1985. £175. set. ISBN: 0333387899.

1. *A Guide to the archives of selected organizations and societies,* 1976. xiii, 330p. £33. ISBN 0333150368. 2. *A Guide to the papers of selected public servants,* 1976. xiii, 297p. £35. ISBN 0333150376. 3/4. *A Guide to the private papers of Members of Parliament,* 1977. xiv, 369p. £35. each. ISBNs 0333150384 and 0333191609. 5. *A Guide to the private papers of selected writers, intellectuals and publicists,* 1978. xiii, 221p. £35. ISBN 0333221249. 6. *First consolidated supplement,* 1985. x, 271p. £35. ISBN 0333265688. In 2 pts: 1. A Guide to the papers of organizations, societies, and pressure groups - 2. A Guide to the personal papers of private individuals. Appendix 1. A note on archival sources since 1931. 'A towering achievement of scholarship and a supremely useful bibliographical tool' (*TLS,* no.3821, 30 May 1975, p.809) on v.1. *Class No:* 941.082(093.20)

[6970]

MOWAT, C.L. **Great Britain since 1914.** Cambridge, Cambridge Univ. Press, 1976. 224p. index.

First published Hodder & Stoughton 1971.

8 sections: 1. Since 1914; recent or contemporary? - 2. Standard and official [sources] - 3. Cabinet and other papers - 4. Memoirs, diaries and biographies - 5. Contemporary writing - 6. Images, sounds and objects (film; photographs, pictures; sound records; interviews; museums; history on the ground) - 7. Some varieties of history (economic history; official history; the history of science) - 8. The Zinoviev

....(contd.)

letter: a case study. Detailed, non-analytical index.

C.L. Mowat's *British history since 1926: a select bibliography* (London, Historical Association, 1960, 32p. (Helps for students of history, no.61). has 4 sections: 1. Bibliographies and general references. 2. Before the war, 1926-39 - 3. The War years, 1939-45 - 4. Since 1945. Deliberately excludes military and diplomatic history of World War II. Some annotations and occasional running commentary. *Class No:* 941.082(093.20)

Scotland

[6971]

CAIRNEY, C.T. Clans and families of Ireland and Scotland: an ethnography of the Gael AD500-1750. Jefferson, North Carolina, McFarland & Co., 1989. xii, 210p. illustration, map, bibliog., index. £19.45. $25.95. ISBN: 0899503624.

1. The identity of the Gaels - 2. Gael society - 3. The coming of Gaeldom - 4. Kingdom of the Picts: Christianity, paganism and the making of Gaelic Scotland - 5. Tribal nomenclature - 6. The Cruithne - 7. The Ereinn - 8. The Laigin - 9. The Gaels - 10. The Vikings and Normans. Appendix 1. The Coats of arms (p.157-169) - 2. List of surnames (p.171-96). Bibliography p.197-203. Purpose: 'to provide in one volume an authoritative and comprehensive account of the Gaelic tribes and clans' (*Introduction*). *Class No:* 941.1

[6972]

CRAWFORD, B.C. Scandinavian Scotland. Leicester, Leicester Univ. Press; Atlantic Highlands, New Jersey, Humanities Press, 1987. xiv,274p. illus., maps, diagrs., bibliog., index. £30.00. ISBN: 0718511972, UK.

Introduction: Sources and evidence - 1. The geographical framework - 2/3. Chronological *c.*800-954; 975-1065 - 4. Linguistic - 5. Archaeological framework Pt.1: Settlement and economy - 6. Pt.2: Conversion and the organization of Christianity - 7. Literary framework: Norse society in the settlements. Chapter notes p.226-51. Bibliography p.252-63. *Class No:* 941.1

[6973]

Debrett's Royal Scotland. Goodman, J. *and* Moncreiffe, Sir Ian. Exeter, Webb & Bower in association with Debrett's Peerage Ltd., 1983. 224p. illus. (many col.), map. bibliog. index. £12.95. ISBN: 0905649591.

Pt.1. Royal castles, palaces and houses - 2. Pageantry and ceremony (*e.g.* The Honours of Scotland; Royal Company of Archers; Order of the Thistle) - 3. Royal visits to Scotland (George IV to Prince Charles). Bibliography p.218-220. Monarchs of Scotland since AD 1005 p.218. The Royal Family of Scotland on endpapers. *Class No:* 941.1

[6974]

GRANT, I.F. *and* **CHEAPE, H. Periods in Highland history.** London, Shepheard-Walwyn, 1987. xiii, 306p. illus. maps, index. £14.95. ISBN: 0856830577.

A structured history in 7 chronological periods. References p.289-99. *Class No:* 941.1

[6975]

MOODY, D. Scottish towns a guide for local historians. London, Batsford, 1992. 190p. illus., map, bibliog., index. £14.99. (*Batsford Local History Series.*) ISBN: 0713464976.

Outline history and topography of Scottish towns and a guide to source materials for local research. 5 chapters: 1. Introduction (visual and standard sources, mapping, and typology of towns) - 2. Story of a house - 3. Homes and suburbs - 4. Business - 5. The public town (civic facilities and services). Chapter notes p.135-56. Bibliography p.168-73. *Class No:* 941.1

[6976]

The New history of Scotland. Wormald, J., *ed.* London, Edward Arnold, later Edinburgh Univ. Press. maps, geneal tables, bibliogs., indexes.

1. *Warlords and holy men AD800-1000* by A.P. Smyth. 2. *Kingship and unity 1000-1306* by G.W.S. Barrow. 3. *Independence and nationhood 1306-1469* by A. Grant. 4. *Court, Kirk and community 1470-1625* by J. Wormald. 5. *Lordship to patronage 1603-1745* by R. Mitchison. 6. *Integration, enlightenment, and industrialization 1746-1832* by B. Lenman (rev. ed. 1992. 200p.pbk. £9.50. ISBN 0748603859). 7. *Industry and ethos 1832-1914* by S. Checkland and O. Checkland. 8. *No gods and precious few heroes 1914-1980* by C. Harvie (rev. ed. 1992. 192p. pbk. £9.50. 0748603875). Presents the latest research on Scottish history from the earliest period to the present day. *Class No:* 941.1

[6977]

ROSS, S. The Monarchs of Scotland. Moffat, Dumfries & Galloway, Lochar Publishing, 1990. 192p. illus. (some col.), col. maps, facsims., geneal. tables, bibliog. £14.95. ISBN: 0948403225.

Their vital records, personalities, achievements, and role in the creation and presentation of the Kingdom of Scotland from Kenneth MacAlpin to Queen Anne. Bibliography p.6-7. Chronology p.185-8. *Class No.* 941.1

[6978]

THOMSON, D.S., *ed.* **The Companion to Gaelic Scotland.** New ed. Oxford, Blackwell, 1987. xx, 363p. illus., maps, bibliog., pbk. ISBN: 0631155783.

A-Z entries encompassing archaeology, history, geography, language and place names, literature and music by 70 named contributors, p.1-307. Chronology 55BC to 1975 p.309-311; bibliography p.313-335; index p.337-363. 'A lasting source book for students of Gaelic and Scotland' (*British Book News* March, 1984, p.187-188). *Class No:* 941.1

[6979]

WEBSTER, B. Scotland from the eleventh century to 1603. Cambridge, Cambridge Univ. Press, 1976. 240p. index. (*The Sources of History.*)

9 footnoted chapters - 1. The nation and its history - 2. Narrative sources - 3. Charter evidence - 4. Unwritten evidence - 5. Government records - 6. The records of medieval Scots law - 7. Foreign sources - 8. The sixteenth century - 9. Conclusion. Detailed, analytical index, p.235-40. *Class No:* 941.1

Bibliographies

[6980]

OSBORNE, B.D., *ed*. **Scottish local studies resources** a directory of publications from Scottish public libraries. 2nd ed. Motherwell, Scottish Library Association, 1988. 63p. index. £3. ISBN: 0900649674.

First published 1986.

Details of 340 books and pamphlets in print issued by 35 libraries arranged A-Z by local authority name. 'This publication promises more than it achieves, but within its limits it contains much valuable information' (*Reference Reviews*, v.2, no.3, September 1988, p.161).

Class No: 941.1(01)

Encyclopaedias & Dictionaries

[6981]

DONNACHIE, J. *and* HEWITT, G. **Companion to Scottish history:** from the Reformation to the present. London, B.T. Batsford, 1989. 268p. illus., maps. £17.95; $27.50. ISBN: 0713457392.

Major events and personalities in essays ranging from less than 100 to more than 3000 words arranged A-Z but is 'neither a dictionary nor an encyclopedia' (*Preface*). Selection of topics 'governed partly by the relative historical importance of each entry and partly by the findings of recent research.' 13 Appendices including 1. Chronological table (p.217-23) ... 11. Principal surnames and territorial titles. 17 maps. 'Very well done and will be useful to laypeople and students interested in modern Scottish history' (*Booklist*, v.86, no.22, August 1990, p.2198 + +2200).

Class No: 941.1(03)

Handbooks & Manuals

[6982]

MOODY, D. **Scottish local history:** an introductory guide. London, B.T. Batsford, 1986. 178p. illus., bibliog., index. £17.95. ISBN: 071345220x.

1. Introduction (study and techniques) - 2. The Public Library and its collections - 3. Archive offices and their records - 4. The individual and the community - 5. Buildings - 6. Settlements (history of villages, towns, and parishes) - 7. Writing and publishing results. Appendix. Table of local government functions 1832-1975: a selective list p.146-153. Bibliography p.154-169. Useful handbook filling a gap.

Class No: 941.1(035)

Dictionaries

[6983]

DONALDSON, G. *and* MORPETH, R.S. **A Dictionary of Scottish history.** Edinburgh, John Donald Publishers, 1977. v, 234p. £5.50. ISBN: 0859760189.

About 5,000 very brief entries. 'Mary, Queen of Scotland': nearly ½column. 'We have tried to be comprehensive with events, with institutions (both civil and ecclesiastical) and with titles and offices' (*Preface*). As to biographical notices, - hardly any limits at all.

Class No: 941.1(038)

Yearbooks & Directories

[6984]

COX, M. **Exploring Scottish history:** a directory of resource centres for local history. Aberdeen Univ. Press, 1991. 120p. pbk. £5.95. ISBN: 0080412149.

Guide to the collections and services of over 250 archive and record offices. Data: hours, facilities, and other directory information. *Class No:* 941.1(058)

Maps & Atlases

[6985]

Historical map of Scotland. Edinburgh, John Bartholomew, nd. 250 x 170 mm (folded). ISBN: 0851525687.

Illustrates prominent figures in Scottish history, places and the areas and names of the Scottish clans. Coats of arms of the main towns and cities are displayed.

Class No: 941.1(084.3)

[6986]

McNEILL, P. *and* NICHOLSON, R., *eds*. **An Historical atlas of Scotland** *c*.400-*c*.1600. St. Andrews, The Univ. Atlas Committee of the Conference of Scottish Medievalists, 1975. x, 213p.

129 black-and-white maps, p.104-213, in 63 sections. Text, by various hands, on each sections (1. The geographical setting ... 16. The evolution of the frontier, *c*.400-1018AD ... 33. The Western Isles, *c*.1085-1286AD ... 55. The coming of the Reformation). Section references; bibliographies. Includes aspects of place names, monuments, ecclesiastical sites, etc. 'The unsophisticated appearance ... belies the high standard of its contents' (*British Book News*, August 1977, p.588). *Class No:* 941.1(084.3)

Chronologies

[6987]

DUNBAR, A.H. **Scottish Kings** a revised chronology of Scottish history 1005 - 1625. With notices of the principal events, tables of regnal years, pedigrees, calendars, etc. Edinburgh, David Douglas, 1899. xv,420p. col. maps, tables, geneal., tables, bibliog., index.

The main part of this comprehensive handbook, 'Reigns of the Scottish Kings' (p.1-279) contains particulars of the parentage, vital records of each Sovereign with short notices of the principal events during their reign followed by the names of contemporary Sovereigns in England and France. 'An endeavour to settle the exact date of every noteworthy event in Scottish history' (Preface). *Class No:* 941.1(090)

[6988]

HORAN, M. **Scottish dates.** Edinburgh, Chambers, 1990. iii,91p. illus. £2.50. (*Chambers Mini Guides*.) ISBN: 0550200576.

Informative chronological pocket size guide to over 250 momentous events on a wide diversity of topics (political, constitutional, literary, sporting *etc*.) from the Roman invasion in AD 80 to the Lockerbie bomb in 1988.

Class No: 941.1(090)

Biographies

[6989]

DONALDSON, G. *and* **MORPETH, R.S. Who's who in Scottish history.** Oxford, Blackwell, 1973. xx, 254p. ports., index.

About 250 'Biographies of those who have figured prominently in political and ecclesiastical history, but special attention has been given to writers, scientists and others who contributed to the cultural development of Scotland' (E.G. Grant, Scotland, 1982. Entry 426). Glossary p.242-6. *Class No:* 941.1(092)

Orkney & Shetland

[6990]

SCHLEI, L.K. The Shetland story. London, B.H. Batsford, 1988. 273p. illus. (some col.), map, bibliog., index. £14.95. ISBN: 0713455128.

26 chapters *e.g.* 3. Early history ... 4. Norse times ... 5. In Scotland ... 6. In Britain ... 11. Place names ... 20. Scalloway - 21. Mainland - 22. The North Isles - 23. North Sea islands - 24. Atlantic Islands - 25. Fair Isle. Bibliography p.265-269. 16 col,. & 75 b/w plates. *Class No:* 941.12

[6991]

THOMSON, W.P.L. History of Orkney. Edinburgh, Mercat Press, 1987. xvi,321p. 16p. pl. illus., maps, geneal tables, bibliog., index. £14.95. ISBN: 0901824828.

28 chronological chapters *e.g.* 1. Pictish Orkney ... 14. Under Scottish rule ... 27. Twentieth century: a second farming revolution - 28. Twentieth century: war and peace. Glossary p.260-2. Chapter references p.263-90. Bibliography p.291-303. A scholarly and well-documented work. *Class No:* 941.12

Clackmannanshire

Bibliographies

[6992]

BROWN, W.C. Clackmannanshire a guide to historical sources. Forth Naturalist and Historian, Univ. of Stirling and Central Regional Council in association with the Clackmannanshire Field Studies Society and Clackmannanshire District Council, 1980. 390p. maps, flexible cover. ISBN: 095069620x.

Based on a thesis to The Library Association, 'A Bibliography of Clackmannan District'.

1659 briefly annotated items, ranging from the scholarly to the ephemeral, relating to life in Clackmannanshire from earliest times until 1977, in 3 sections: 1. The county (35 subdivisions) - 2. Towns and villages - 3. Bibliography of family history. Exhaustive list of sources of information. *Class No:* 941.35(01)

Ireland

[6993]

HARTIGAN, M. The History of the Irish in Britain. London, Irish in Britain History Centre, 1986. 85p. index. sd. £2.50. ISBN: 0951094505.

Over 750 entries relating to history, sociology, demography, economic, politics and historical geography. Includes some unpublished theses and conference papers. *Class No:* 941.5

[6994]

New Gill History of Ireland. Dublin, Gill & Macmillan, 6v, 1988-1994.

Gill History of Ireland first published in 11 paperback volumes 1972-1975.

1. *Medieval Ireland: the enduring tradition* by M. Richter. 1988. £25. 0717116069 2. *Sixteenth-century Ireland: the incomplete conquest* by C. Lennon. 1991. 0717116220. 3. *Seventeenth-century Ireland: the war of religion* by B. Fitzpatrick. 1988. £25. 0717115763. 4. *Eighteenth-century Ireland: the long peace* by E.M. Johnston. 1989. 0717108961. 5. *Nineteenth-century Ireland: the search for stability* by D.G. Boyce. 1990. 0717116204. 6. *Twentieth-century Ireland: nation and state* by D. Keogh 1994. 0717116255. Intended to offer the reader 'an accessible and up-to-date survey of Irish history'. *Class No:* 941.5

[6995]

A New history of Ireland. Moody, T.W., *and others.* Oxford, Clarendon Press, 10v., 1976-.

1. *Prehistoric and early Ireland* 2. *Medieval Ireland 1169-1534* edited by A. Cosgrove. 1987. xlviii, 982p.+42p. plates. £75.00. 0198217412. 3. *Early modern Ireland 1534-1691* edited by T.W. Moody and others. 1976. lxiii, 736p. £55.00. 0198217390. 4. *Eighteenth-century Ireland 1691-1800* edited by T.W. Moody and W.E. Vaughan. 1985. 914p. £70.00. ISBN 0198217420. 5. *Ireland under the Union 1. 1801-70* edited by W.E. Vaughan. 1988. lxv, 850p. £75.00. ISBN 0198217439. 6. *Ireland under the Union 2. 1870-1921* 7. *Ireland 1921-1984* And 3 Companion volumes: 8. *A chronology of Irish history to 1976* edited by T.W. Moody and others. 1987. xii, 591p. £60.00. ISBN 0198217447. 9. *Maps, genealogies, lists: a comprehensive guide to Irish history* edited by T.W. Moody and others. 1982. xii, 59'p. £95.00. ISBN 0198217455. 10. *Irish Historical Documents.* Authoritative large-scale, cooperative history to be completed in 10v. with some 70 contributors, published under the auspices of the Royal Irish Academy. T.W. Moody's 'A New History of Ireland' *Irish Historical Studies*, v.XVI, no.63, March 1969, p.1-17 outlines its genesis and planning. *Class No:* 941.5

[6996]

NEWMAN, P.R. Companion to Irish history 1603-1921 from the submission of Tyrone to Partition. Oxford & New York, Facts On File, 1991. xi,244p. maps, bibliog. £13.95. ISBN: 081602572x.

Compendium of cross-referenced A-Z entries relating to the personalities, organizations, policies, legislation, battles, philosophies, and beliefs which shaped Irish history. Appendices gives names of Viceroys of Ireland 1603-1921; Deputies in Ireland 1603-1880; and Chief Secretaries in Ireland 1603-1921. Chronology p.230-3. Bibliography p.234-6. 6 maps. *Class No:* 941.5

Bibliographies

[6997]

CARTY, J. Bibliography of Irish history 1870-1921. Dublin, National Library of Ireland, 2v., 1936-40.

The first 2v. in a proposed series of bibliographies of Irish history. Entries are confined to publications in the collections of the National Library of Ireland, but they include books, rare pamphlets, parliamentary papers and other official publications, and articles in periodicals.

V.2, covering 1912-21, arranged by period, deals almost

....(contd.)

exclusively with political history; v.1, covering 1870-1911 (2,727 items), arranged by subject embraces political, economic, social, literary and ecclesiastical history, and as such serves as an excellent bibliography of Ireland for the period. *Class No:* 941.5(01)

[6998]

CULLEN, C. *and* HENCHY, M., *comps*. **Writings on Irish history 1987** incorporating addenda from previous years. Dublin, The Irish Committee of Historical Sciences and A New History of Ireland. 1991. x,73p. index. pbk. ISBN: 0950209740.

Printed in *Irish Historical Studies* 1936-1978. Published on microfiche 1979-83. Issued as a separate publication 1984 onwards.

Arranged in 9 sections: 1. General - 2. Prehistoric - 3. Fifth Century to 1169 - 4/8. Chronological periods - 9. Northern Ireland 1921-. Author index. *Class No:* 941.5(01)

[6999]

EDWARDS, R.W.D. *and* O'DOWD, M. **Sources for early modern Irish history 1534-1641.** Cambridge, Cambridge University Press, 1985. x, 222p. index. £30. (*The Sources of History.*) ISBN: 052125020x.

A critical guide to the written sources of Irish history in 8 chapters: 1. Irish civil central administration; 2. Irish civil local administration; 3. English and other central administrations and Ireland; 4. Irish ecclesiastical administration; 5. Contemporary accounts; 6. Maps and drawings; 7. Archival collections; and 8. Historiography. 'One of the main aims ... is to emphasise the need for historians to understand the administrative machinery which produced the documents they use'. Favourably received in *Irish Historical Studies*, v. xxv, no.99, May 1987, p.322-323. *Class No:* 941.5(01)

[7000]

JOHNSTON, E.M. **Irish history** a select bibliography. 2nd ed. London, Historical Association, 1972. 76p.

1st ed. 1968.

Over 700 very briefly annotated entries. Section A: Reference and general books - B: Selected works on special periods (each with short historical introduction). 'A guide to much of the modern research in that field, both general and for successive periods' (*TLS* no.3674, 28 July 1972, p.900). *Class No:* 941.5(01)

[7001]

NATIONAL LIBRARY OF IRELAND. **Sources for the history of Irish civilization** articles in Irish periodicals. Boston, Mass., G.K. Hall, 9v., 1970.

271,000 photolithographed catalogue cards for all the articles published in Irish historical, literary and scientific periodicals from about 1800 to the end of 1969; includes most of the book reviews. Entries are under persons, subjects, places in Ireland and, where appropriate, under dates, arrangement being similar to that in *Manuscript sources for the history of Irish civilization (qv).* Now available only on microfilm (18 reels). $990.00 (Export $1198.00). ISBN 0816113491. *Class No:* 941.5(01)

Dictionaries

[7002]

HICKEY, D. J. *and* DOHERTY, J.E. **A Dictionary of Irish history 1800 - 1980.** Dublin. Gill & Macmillan, 1987. 615p. pbk. £12.95. ISBN: 0717115674.

First published in 1980 as *A Dictionary of Irish history since 1800*.

c. 2000 entries (100 - 3,000 words) covering all aspects of Irish history, not simply political topics. No bibliographies, but works are cited in text. Cross-references. 'An invaluable work of reference' (*British Book News.* April 1981, p.253). *Class No:* 941.5(038)

Theses

[7003]

'**Theses on Irish history**' completed in Irish universities, *Irish Historical Studies,* v.26,no.4, November 1989, p.406-7.

Annual feature. Data: title; author; degree and institution; supervisor. *Class No:* 941.5(043)

Maps & Atlases

[7004]

EDWARDS, R.D. **An Atlas of Irish history.** 2nd ed. London, Methuen, 1981. 286p. maps, bibliog., index. ISBN: 0416748201.

First published in 1973.

Almost 100 black and white maps, charts and graphs illustrate all aspects of Irish social and political history. Bibliography p.272-278. 'An excellent general reference work.' (*Choice*, v.19, no.5, January 1982, p.604). *Class No:* 941.5(084.3)

[7005]

Historical map of Ireland. Edinburgh, John Bartholomew, nd. 250 x 175 mm (folded). ISBN: 0851525512.

Illustrates places and characters in Irish history, the areas and names of the Irish clans, and the coats of arms of the principal towns and cities. *Class No:* 941.5(084.3)

[7006]

An Illustrated historical map of Ireland. Edinburgh, John Bartholomew, nd. 239 x 156 mm (folded). ISBN: 0717942775.

Lists the important places and the principal dates of Irish history. *Class No:* 941.5(084.3)

[7007]

Irish historic towns atlas. Andrews, J.H. *and* Simms, A., *eds*. Dublin, Royal Irish Academy, 1986-.

Published in fascicules.

1. *Kildare* by J.H. Andrews. 1986. 16p. text+9 maps+2 plates. IR£15. 0901714518. 2. *Carrickfergus* by P. Robinson. 1988. 12p. text+6 maps+2 plates. IR£15. 0901714526. 3. *Bandon* by P. O'Flanaghan. 1988. 16p. text+5 maps+2 plates. IR£18. 0901714747. Each fascicule includes an extensive essay explaining the history of the town's development and a topographical information section. 'When complete the Atlas will make available a series of carefully researched historical town plans for a substantial selection of Irish towns, representing various size categories, various regions of the country (both North and South), and various periods of origin and growth, with some bias in favour of the medieval period, but not excluding the estate towns, industrial towns, and resort towns characteristic of more modern times' (*Irish Geography* v.21, no.1, 1988,

....(contd.)
p.48-49). K.M. Davies' 'The Irish Historic Towns Atlas - a recentcomer to the European Towns Atlas scene', *Bulletin of Society of University Cartographers* v.21, no.2, 1988, p.61-5 is informative. *Class No:* 941.5(084.3)

Chronologies

[7008]
A Chronology of Irish history to 1976. Moody, T.W., *and others.* Oxford, Clarendon Press, 1982. xii, 591p. index. £60. (*A New History of Ireland.*) ISBN: 0198217447.

All dateable important events in the text of the *New history* are included along with others which do not find a place there, allowing the *Chronology* to stand as an independent reference work. Arranged in periods (each furnished with an introduction and glossary) corresponding with the primary divisions of the *New history* (*qv*). Analytical index p.473-591. *Class No:* 941.5(090)

[7009]
CREALEY, A.H. An Irish almanac notable events in Ireland from 1014 to the present. Mercier, 1993. 196p. pbk. ISBN: 1856350355.

A daily calendar with notes on events up to June 1992 that happened on that day with the relevant year. Mainly political events are listed but social, literary, academic, artistic, and legal events are also covered. List of centenaries falling due 1994-2003 are listed. *Class No:* 941.5(090)

[7010]
DOHERTY, J.E. *and* **HICKEY, D.J. A Chronology of Irish history since 1500.** Dublin, Gill and Macmillan, 1989. xiv,395p. index. ISBN: 0717116344.

Annalistic pattern: within each year the significant events of Irish life listed by date. In the case of particularly dramatic years (*e.g.* 1798 or 1919) there is an extended day by day account. For students and general readers. *Class No:* 941.5(090)

[7011]
GRIFFIN, W.D. Ireland 6000 BC-1972: a chronology and fact book. Dobbs Ferry, New York, Oceana, 1973. 154p. bibliog. $8.50. ISBN: 0379163020.

Consists of a 30p. chronology (ancient-modern times) plus the text of important documents in Irish history. *Class No:* 941.5(090)

Middle Ages

Bibliographies

[7012]
ASPLIN, P.W.A. Medieval Ireland *c.*1170-1495 : a bibliography of secondary works. Dublin, Royal Irish Academy, 1971. xv, 139p.

721 entries, with brief, critical annotations; includes many periodical articles. 18 sections (1. Bibliographies, and guides - 2. Serials - 3. Essays, Festschiften - 4. Historical geography - 5. General history ... 10. History of literature - 11. History of science and technology ... 14. Archaeology - 15. Numismatics - 16. Seals - 17. Genealogy - 18. Heraldry.) Index. of authors, subjects, etc., p.17-39.

The first in a series of publications associated with the nine-volume *New history of Ireland* (*qv*). *Class No:* 941.5"01/14"(01)

[7013]
HUGHES, K. Early Christian Ireland introduction to the sources. Cambridge, Cambridge Univ. Press, 1976. 320p. (*The Sources of History.*)

First published London, The Sources of History Ltd; Ithaca, New York, Cornell Univ. Press, 1972.

9 footnoted chapters: 1. Archaeology - 2. Secular laws - 3. Ecclesiastical legislation - 4. The annals - 5. Secular literature - 6. Ecclesiastical learning - 7. Hagiography - 8. Art and architecture - 9. 11th and 12th century histories and compilations. Bibliography, p.302-15 (by chapters), brief index. *Class No:* 941.5"01/14"(01)

20th Century

Chronologies

[7014]
O'DONNELL, J., *ed.* **Ireland the past twenty years: an illustrated chronology.** Dublin, Institute of Public Administration, 1986. 135p. illus. pbk. £4.95. ISBN: 0906980674.

Day by day record of events 1 June 1967 - 26 September 1986. 'Gives an impression of what has been going on in Irish society ... it lists events the media have seized on as important, as well as the many of the organizational changes the yearbook has recorded since it first appeared' (*Introduction*). Time-span: 1 January 1967 - 26 September 1986. *Class No:* 941.5"19"(090)

Irish Civil War

[7015]
HOPKINSON, M. Green against green the Irish Civil War. Dublin, Gill and Macmillan; New York, St. Martin's Press, 1988. xvi, 336p., illus. maps, bibliog., index. £30. $39.95. ISBN: 0717112020, UK; 0312024487, US.

37 chapters arranged in 6 periods: 1. 1912-1921 - 2. From the Treaty to the attack on the Four Courts - 3. The opening of the war - 4. The early civil war - 5. The War's end Jan-Apr. 1923 - 6. The post war period. Ch. notes p.277-316. Bibliography p.317-22. Analytical index. Definitive, scholarly, well-documented, and 'the best account yet and should be in all libraries' (*Choice*, v.26, no.9, May 1989, p.1576). *Class No:* 941.509

Biographies

[7016]
O'FARRELL, P. Who's who in the Irish War of Independence 1916-1921. Dublin & Cork, The Mercier Press, 1980. 189p. ISBN: 0853426046.

Over 1000 sketches of personalities involved in both sides of the conflict (Eamonn de Valera 31 lines; Michael Collins 30 lines; Winston Churchill 3 lines). Appendix A. Chronology p.158-9 - C. The Irish dead p.162-75 - D. Crown Forces casualties p.176-86. 'Some entries are from reliable verbal sources' (*Introduction*). *Class No:* 941.509(092)

Northern Ireland

[7017]
BARDON, J. Belfast: an illustrated history. Belfast, The Blackstaff Press, 1982. 322p. illus., bibliog., index. £16.95. ISBN: 0856402729.

11 Chronological chapters: 1-6 pre-twentieth century. Bibliography p.314-6. *Class No:* 941.6

[7018]
BARDON, J. A History of Ulster. Belfast, Blackstaff Press, 1992. x,914p. maps, bibliog., index. £29.95. ISBN: 0856404667.

Comprehensive political, social and economic history in 15 chronological chapters (*e.g.* 1. Early Ulster c.7000 BC - AD 800 - 2. Viking raids and Norman invasion c.800-1300 ... 12. Wartime Ulster 1939-1945 ... 15. Direct rule 1972-1992). Chapter notes p.837-63. Bibliography p.865-78. 5 maps. Analytical index. 'A long awaited, definitive history of the Province' (*Books Ireland,* no.161, September 1992, p.162). *Class No:* 941.6

[7019]
QUEENS UNIVERSITY BELFAST. The Institute of Irish Studies. **Ordnance Survey memoirs.** Belfast, Institute of Irish Studies, Queens Univ. Belfast in association with The Royal Irish Academy, 1990-. 140p. illus., maps. £15.

1. *Parishes of County Armagh* (1990). 2. *Parishes of County Antrim: 1. South East Antrim covering present day Newtonabbey* (1990). 3. *Parishes of Co. Down: 1. South Down* (1990). 4. *Parishes of Co. Fermanagh: 1. Enniskillen* (1990).

'In the 1830s a major series of parish accounts or memoirs was commissioned to accompany the new Ordnance Survey maps. However, only the northern part of Ireland was covered before the scheme was dropped, and only one parish Memoir was published at the time. Now, 150 years later, it is planned that the Memoirs will be published in full' (*Publisher's advt.*). 'No other country in Europe has source material to equal the scope and detail of this most important series of texts' ('The publication of the O.S. Memoirs', *The Linen Hall Review,* v.7, no.1/2. Summer 1990, p.4-6). *Class No:* 941.6

[7020]
WICHERT, S. Northern Ireland since 1945. London, Longman, 1991. xiv,229p. maps, tables, bibliog., index. £21. (*The Postwar World.*) ISBN: 0582023912.

Narrative history in 8 chapters divided into 3 parts: 1,. 1921-1939: the roots of the problem - 2,. 1940-1968: the limits of modernization - 3. 1969-1989: the problems exposed. 4 maps. Bibliography p.204-10. *Class No:* 941.6

Chronologies

[7021]
DEUTSCH, R. and MAGOWEN, V. Northern Ireland 1968-1974 a chronology of events. Belfast, The Blackstaff Press, 3v., 1973-75.

1. *1968-1971* (1973. x, 280p. bibliog. index. 856400270). 2. *1972-1973* (1974. viii, 147-408p. bibliog. index. 856400505). 3. *1974-1975* (1975. v, 209p. bibliog. index. 856400807).

'A major work of reference, consisting of a day-to-day account of events compiled from press and radio reports, official statistics and announcements, *etc.* It also contains a number of valuable statistical tables and appendices of

....(contd.)
election results' (Elliot, J.D. *Northern Ireland*, Library Association, Public Libraries Group, 1980, p.14). *Class No:* 941.6(090)

[7022]
HALL, M. 20 years: a concise chronology of events in Northern Ireland from 1968-1988. Newtonabbey, Northern Ireland, Island Publications, 1988. 11,121p. maps, bibliog., pbk. £4.95. ISBN: 0951419404.

Despite dating in title, charts events from 26 February 1962. Bibliography p.120-1. 3 maps. *Class No:* 941.6(090)

[7023]
LAUFER, D. 'Chronology of main events in Northern Ireland since 1969', p.393-401, *RUSI and Brassey's Defence Yearbook 1987* (London, Brassey's Defence Publishers, 1988. ISBN 0080336078).

From 21 April 1969 to 12 June 1986. *Class No:* 941.6(090)

Eire

[7024]
SOMERVILLE-LARGE, P. Dublin: the first thousand years. Belfast, Appletree Pess, 1988. 330p. bibliog., index. £14.95. ISBN: 0862812062.

14 chronological chapters (1. The Vikings AD837-1170 ... 12. Post 1916). Bibliography p.299-304. 'A well-integrated body of historical research' (*Sunday Times*, no. 8575, 11 December 1988, p.G1.). *Class No:* 941.7

Bibliographies

[7025]
BOYLAN, H. This arrogant city. Dublin, A.A. Farmer, 1984. 75p.

Selective bibliography of books about Dublin and its history intended for the general reader. *Class No:* 941.7(01)

[7026]
NOLAN, W. Tracing the past: sources for local studies in the Republic of Ireland. Dublin, Geography Publications, 1982. x, 149p. illus., maps, bibliog., pbk. £4.50. ISBN: 0906602017.

Englarged and rewritten version of *Sources for local studies* (1977).

8 chapters - 1. The administrative framework - 2. Traces and sources before 1550 - 3/7. Sources: 1550-1650; 1650-1700; 1700-1800; 1800-1850; 1850-1900 - 9. Writing a local study - our national repositories. Extremely useful bibiliographical section (bibiliographies, journals, articles on sources; chapter references; selective county bibliographies) p.123-146. Maps for local studies p.147-149. *Class No:* 941.7(01)

Encyclopaedias

[7027]
BENNETT, D. Encyclopaedia of Dublin. Dublin, Gill and Macmillan, 1991. xiii,277p. illus., bibliog., index. £30. ISBN: 0717115992.

A-Z entries providing a complete portrait of the city, its origins and institutions, industry and commerce, streets and

....(contd.)

buildings, libraries and theatres, and eminent personalities. Celebrates Dublin as the European City of Culture. Bibliography p.275-7. *Class No:* 941.7(031)

Chronologies

[7028]

O'DONNELL, E.E. The Annals of Dublin. Dublin, Wolfhound Press, 1987. 237p. illus., maps, charts, bibliog., index. £15.95. ISBN: 0863271489.

An annotated and illustrated chronology celebrating Dublin's millenium in 29 chronological chapters: 1. Geological preamble ... 29. Modern Dublin. 13 appendices *e.g.* 1. Roll of the Honorary freedom of the city - 2. Some literary connections... 4. Dublin architects ... 6. Easter rising 1916. Bibliography p.224-8. *Class No:* 941.7(090)

England & Wales—Local History

[7029]

The Darwen County Histories. Chichester, Sussex, Phillimore.

Bristol and Gloucestershire by B. Smith and E. Ralph. - *Buckinghamshire* by K. Tiller - *Cambridgeshire* by B. Galloway - *Cheshire* by D. Sylvester - *Cornwall* by I. Soulsby. 1986. - *Cumberland and Westmorland* by W. Rollinson - *Derbyshire* by J. Childs. 1987. - *Devon* by R. Stanes - *Dorset* by C. Cullingford - *County Durham* by D. Pocock and R. Norris - *Essex* by A.C. Edwards - *Gwynedd* by D. Sylvester - *Hampshire* by B. Carpenter-Turner - *Herefordshire* by J. and M. West - *Hertfordshire* by T. Rook - *Huntingdonshire* by M. Wickes - *Kent* by F. Jessup - *Lancashire* by J.J. Bagley - *Leicestershire and Rutland* by R. Millward - *Lincolnshire* by A. Rogers - *Norfolk* by S.W. Martins - *Northamptonshire* by R.L. Greenall - *Northumberland and Newcastle* by L. Hepple - *Nottinghamshire* by D. Kaye - *Oxfordshire* by M. Jessup - *Shropshire* by B. Trinder - *Somerset* by R. Dunning - *Staffordshire* by M.W. Greenslade - *Suffolk* by D. Dymond and P. Northeast - *Surrey* by P. Brandon - *Sussex* by J.R. Armstrong - *Warwickshire and Birmingham* by T. Slater - *Wiltshire* by B. Watkin - *Worcestershire* by D. Lloyd and *Buckinghamshire* by M. Reed.

'In contrast to *The Victoria history of the counties of England* the objective is to produce a concise and readable synopsis of the history of each county from prehistory to the present day'. Each volume has about 40,000 words of text and between 16 and 20 maps. 'All the authors show their ability to absorb local detail and recent research into a general narrative' (*Local Historian,* v.17, no.5, Febuary 1987, p.299). *Class No:* 942.1/.9

[7030]

Dictionary of land surveyors and local cartographers of Great Britain and Ireland *c.*1540-1850. Bendall, S., *ed.* 2nd ed. London, British Library, 1992. 700p. illus. £85. ISBN: 0712302473.

12,000 entries relating to all persons likely to have measured land or made maps of land in areas smaller than a complete county, including local military surveyors. All entries are complete with bibliographical references. *Class No:* 942.1/.9

[7031]

Domesday Book. Morris, J., *ed.* Chichester, Sussex, Phillimore, 40v., 1975-86. maps, indexes. £500. With index volumes £600. All volumes priced individually. ISBN: 0850331285, set.

'The only uniform English translation ever made, in parallel text with the original Latin' (*Phillimore catalogue*). Only previous edition was printed in 1733 and then only of 1250 copies.

34 county volumes (5 counties in 2v.) and Boldon Book, a 12th century survey of Northumberland and Durham. Each volume has an introduction, glossary, maps, indexes and notes. Fundamental source material for local historians. *Class No:* 942.1/.9

[7032]

—BATES, D. A Bibliography of Domesday Book. Woodbridge, Suffolk, The Boydell Press, 1987. xi, 166p. index. £25. $35. ISBN: 0851154336.

4684 briefly annotated items identifying place-names, interpreting terminology and statistics, and assessing how the record was made and its administrative and legal significance. In 3 pts: 1. General studies - 2. Local studies A-Z by historical counties - 3. Name and analytical subject index. Comprehensive in coverage 1886-1984; selective prior to 1856. *Class No:* 942.1/.9

[7033]

—Great Domesday. Williams, A., *Editor-in-chief.* Library ed. London & New York, Alecto Historical Editions (at the invitation of the Public Record Office), 1986-87. £3,000. ISBN: 094845900x.

1. Two linen bound cases containing the 413 folios of the manuscripts sewn into booklets. ISBN 0948459018 ISBN 0948459026. 2. Two linen bound cases containing translations divided into County booklets. ISBN 0948419034 ISBN 0948459042. 3. One linen bound case containing 33 loose leaf County maps to a scale of 3" to 1 mile and one complete map of Domesday England. ISBN 0948419050. 4. Two linen bound volumes of indices prepared by the University of California at Santa Barbara. ISBN 0948459069 ISBN 0948459077. Index v.1: *Index Nominum* contains 2 separate indices of persons: List of English landholders recorded in *DB* as owning property before the Conquest in 1066; and landholders at the time of the Domesday Survey in 1086. V.2 includes *Index Locorum* (all places mentioned in the manuscript) and *Index Rerum* (references to social, fiscal and judicial matters). 5. Optional: The UCSB Domesday data base on magnetic tape for those purchasers with access to a mainframe computer.

The County Edition, published in association with *The Daily Telegraph,* 1987-88, consists of 31 separately available county volumes. The *Telegraph Sunday Magazine,* no.468, 13 October 1985 carried 4 features and 3 boxed special items. *Class No:* 942.1/.9

[7034]

—HALLAM, E.M. Domesday Book through nine centuries. London, Thames and Hudson, 1986. 224p. illus., maps, index. £12.50. ISBN: 0500250979.

1. The making of D.B. - 2. The representation and uses of D.B. 1087-1272 - 3. D.B. as a working record 1672-1700 - 4. The ancient demesne and D.B. to 1833 - 5. D.B. in antiquarian and historical writing 1570-1800 - 6. D.B. since 1800. Some facts and figures p.8-9. Ch. notes p.177-98. Glossary p.218-9. Author is Assistant Keeper, Public Record Office. *Class No:* 942.1/.9

[7035]
—HINDE, T. **The Domesday Book: England's heritage then and now.** London, Hutchinson in association with the English Tourist Board, 1985. 351p. col. illus., col. maps, facsims., bibliog., index. £16.95. ISBN: 0091618304.

Introduction: The story of Domesday Book p.10-18. Descriptive gazetteer of 12000 places listed A-Z by their modern names under 37 historical (pre-1974) counties. Key to Domesday entries p.20-21. Glossary p.336-7. Major Domesday landholders p.338-42. Bibliography p.343-6. 143 colour and 62 black/white photographs. 322 drawings. Translations used are from Phillimore & Co.'s Domesday Book Series (*qv*). *Class No:* 942.1/.9

[7036]
—Index to Domesday Book. Dodgson, J. McN., *ed.* Chichester, Sussex, Phillimore, 3v., 1990.

Companion volumes to Phillimore's edition of Domesday Book.

Part 1. *Places* by J.McN. Dodgson and J.J.N. Palmer. £30. ISBN 085033702x. Includes more than 16,000 place-names. Part 2. *Persons* by J.McN. Dodgson and J.J.N. Palmer. £35. 0850337038. More than 21,000 persons, personal names, surnames and titles. Part 3. *Subjects* by J.D. Foy. £35. 0850337046. Nearly 5,000 substantive items and many thousands of references. 'It will serve as a guide to historians at all levels, covering as it does every aspect of Domesday'.

'This great three-part index will indeed, *for the first time ever*, provide a comprehensive apparatus to meet the needs of serious study and historical research. It will be a guide to the new work made possible on local, manorial, county and national history; on agrarian, urban, ecclesiastical and legal history; on geography, topography and economics; on demography, ethnology and genealogy; and not least, on the origins and meanings of the place names and personal names in the Domesday Book.' *(Phillimore catalogue).*
Class No: 942.1/.9

[7037]
EDWARDS, P. **Rural life guide to local records.** London, Batsford, 1993. 176p. illus. facsims., bibliog., index. £19.99. ISBN: 0713467878.

1. Government of rural England - 2. Village society - 3. Population trends - 4. Earning a living - 5. Peasant world - 6. Family and neighbourhood - 7. Rural housing. Chapter notes p.156-69. Bibliography p.170-2. Examination of types of records available to local historian. *Class No:* 942.1/.9

[7038]
GOODER, E.A. **Latin for local history** an introduction. 2nd ed. London, Longman, 1978. iv, 173p. pbk. £6.95. ISBN: 0582487285.

1st ed. 1961. This edition substantially revised.

A self-teaching manual and guide to the kind of Latin encountered in historical records. Select word list for the reading of local historical records p.121-71. 'Indispensable for every neophyte beginning work on medieval record sources' (*Antiquaries Journal,* v.59, pt.1, 1979, p.163). *Class No:* 942.1/.9

[7039]
GREEN, J.A. **English sheriffs to 1154.** London, HMSO, 1990. 106p. pbk. £17.50. ISBN: 0114402361.

Detailed critical list identifying and dating of sheriffs of all English counties before 1154. An introduction outlines the difficulties of using the original source material.
Class No: 942.1/.9

[7040]
GUY, S., *comp.* **English local studies handbook** a guide to resources for each county including libraries, record offices, societies, journals and museums. University of Exeter Press, 1992. xiv,343p. maps. pbk. £6.95. ISBN: 0859893693.

Addresses and telephone numbers arranged by county together with location maps of the 'old' and 'new' counties. National societies and journals covering local history topics listed p.ix-xii. Useful directories and handbooks p.xiii-xiv. *Class No:* 942.1/.9

[7041]
LEWIS, C. **Particular places** an introduction to English local history. London, The British Library, 1989. 84p. illus. (6 col.) pbk. £8.95. ISBN: 0712301755.

Publication coincided with the British Library exhibition to mark the 200th volume of the *Victoria County History.*

Coordinated overview of family, parish, urban and regional history and the interdependence of local and national history. Final section on the scope of *VCH* and its changes over the last 90 years. 'An extraordinarily rich piece of work. No local historian should be without it' (*Library Review,* v.39, no.1, 1990, p.63-64).
Class No: 942.1/.9

[7042]
Local history. Nottingham, Sherwood Press, Quarterly, 1984-. ISSN: 02662698.

Carries a regular 'Listings' review feature of about 50 titles arranged under thematic headings (*e.g.* sources, family history) and also A-Z by historical county. No.24 December 1989 has 'Sources' (p.31-33), an index of the 'Listings' entries to date. *Class No:* 942.1/.9

[7043]
A **Regional history of England.** Cunliffe, B. *and* Hey, D., *eds.* London, Longman, 1986-. illus.

10 regions each covered by two linked but independent volumes written by authors who have been actively involved in local research. The first relying on archaeological data covering the period up to 1000 AD; and the second extending the coverage to the present day. Higham, N. *The northern counties to AD 1000.* 1986. 404p. £25.00. ISBN 0582492750. McCord, N. and Thompson, R. *The northern counties from AD 1000.* Jones, G.D.B. *The Lancashire/ Cheshire region to AD 1000.* Smith, J. *The Lancashire/ Cheshire region from AD 1000.* Manby, T.G. *Yorkshire to AD 1000.* Hey, D. *Yorkshire from AD 1000.* 1986. 360p. pbk. £11.50. 0582492122. Rowley, R.T. *The Severn Valley and West Midlands to AD 1000.* Rowlands, M.B. *The West Midlands from AD 1000* 1987. 464p. £26.00. 0582492157. Rowley, R.T. *The Welsh borders from AD 1000.* May, J. *The East Midlands to AD 1000.* Beckett, J.V. *The East Midlands from AD 1000.* 1988. 448p. £25.00. 0582492696. Miles, D. *The South Midlands and upper Thames to AD 1000.* Broad, J. *The South Midlands and upper Thames from AD 1000.* Rodwell, W.J. *The Eastern counties to AD 1000.* Holderness, B.A. *The Eastern counties from AD 1000.* Todd, M. *The South West to AD 1000.* 1987. 360p. £25.00.

....(contd.)

0582492734. Coleman, B. and Higham, R.A. *The South West from AD 1000*. Cunliffe, B. *Wessex to AD 1000*, 0582492793. Bettey J.H. *Wessex from AD 1000*. 1986. 336p. £25.00. 0582492076. Drewett, P. *The South East to AD 1000*. 1988. 394p. £25.00. 0582492718. Brandon, P. and Short, B. *The South East from AD 1000*. 1989. 0582492467. 'The new Longman series ... is ambitious and deserves to succeed' (*Antiquity*, v.62, no.234, March 1988, p.194). *Class No: 942.1/.9*

[7044]

STUART, D. Manorial records. Chichester, Sussex, Phillimore, 1992. 160p. illus., facsims. £12.95. ISBN: 0850338212.

Structured manual and guide to the use of manorial records in the study of genealogy or local history. Explains the nature and Latin vocabulary in manorial court rolls, rentals and extents, accounts and custumals. *Class No: 942.1/.9*

[7045]

TATE, W.E. The Parish chest: a study of the records of parochial administration in England. 3rd rev. ed. Chichester, Sussex, Phillimore, 1983. xvii,369p. illus. £14.95. ISBN: 0850335078.

First published 1946.

A well-illustrated guide to ecclesiastical and civil parish institutions. Includes a glossary, references, cumulated chapter bibliographies, and appendices (2: 'County and other major Local Record offices in England'), 15 plates. Invaluable and almost indispensable for the study of parish history. *Class No: 942.1/.9*

[7046]

The Victoria history of the counties of England. London, Constable and St. Catherine Press; subsequently London, Oxford Univ. Press, for the Institute of Historical Research, 1901-. (Many volumes reprinted by Dawson (Folkestone, Kent).

General introduction (1970). xi,281p. ISBN 0197227163. Contains a history of the project founded in 1899 and a bibliographical excursus *i.e.* a list of volumes published to date together with the names of their editors; year of publication; and contents lists for all volumes augmented with author and title indexes.

General introduction: supplement 1970 - 1990 (1990). 67p. 0197227775. Includes The *VCH* 1970-90 (p.1-8); State of *VCH* as at December 1990; Counties completed, in progress, dormant or unstarted (p.9-14); Contents lists of volumes published 1971-90 (p.15-56); Indexes of titles and authors; Corrigenda to *General Introduction*.

An indispensable series. Only Northumberland and Westmorland have still to be attempted. Each volume is by various hands and is heavily footnoted. General articles on each county usually occupy v.1-2 or v.1-3, with topography or history of parishes, boroughs and hundreds in later volumes. 'The history of each county will be complete in itself, beginning with the natural features and the flora and fauna, followed by the antiquities, pre-Roman and post-Roman; a translation and critical study of the Domesday Survey; and articles upon political, ecclesiastical, social and economic history; architecture, arts, industries, biography, folklore and sport' (*Introduction*). The evolution of VCH 'from antiquarianism to professionalism' is traced in *Times literary supplement,* 13 November 1970, p.1327. Other useful commentaries include W.R. Powell's 'The Victoria

....(contd.)

History of the Counties of England', *Library Association Record,* v.59,no.8 August 1957, p.259-262; R.B. Pugh's 'The Victoria County Histories', *History Today* v.20,no.12, December 1970, p.885-887; and C.R.J. Currie's 'Victoria County History'. *The Historian,* no.8, Autumn 1985, p.16-18. C. Elrington's 'The Victoria County History' (*Local Historian* v.22,no.3, August 1992, p.128-37. map) looks at progress in recent years, at counties completed, ongoing, dormant, and not yet started. *Class No: 942.1/.9*

[7047]

WEST, J. Town Records. Chichester, Sussex, Phillimore, 1983. xviii,366p. illus., maps, tables, bibliogs., index. £20.00. ISBN: 0850334721.

Essentially a gazetteer to local sources of information. 12 chapters: 1. The present state of the towns 1971-1981. (Includes tables with headings: Name of town; 1971 county; status; date incorporated; population; location of archives; 1981 county; district; status; population; location of archives) - 2. Origins of the towns A.D.60 - 1066 - 3. Boroughs in the Domesday Survey - 4. Medieval Borough charters - 5. Gild and Borough ordnances *c.*1066-1600 - 6. Town maps and plans - 7. The municipal Boroughs before 1835 - 8. Improvements and other Acts 1720-1835 - 9. Commercial directories 1763-1900 - 10. Provincial newspapers from 1690 - 11. The national censuses - 12. Photographs as evidence. Bibliography p.350. Chapter notes p.352-54. 23 plates. 'This book will endeavour to help the searcher, however unskilled, to find and use the essential records of his own town' (*Introduction*). *Class No: 942.1/.9*

[7048]

WHYBRA, J. A Lost English county Winchcombeshire in the tenth and eleventh centuries. Woodbridge, Suffolk, Boydell Press, 1990. ix,136p. maps, geneal. tables, bibliog., index. £35; $67. (*Studies in Anglo-Saxon History, no.1.*) ISBN: 0851155006.

The creation, development and demise of a vanished English shire. 11 chapters: 1. The English shire system - 2. Liber Wigorniensis: References to Winchcombeshire ... 10. England in the early eleventh century and the demise of W. - 11. W. lost and found. Bibliography p.134-6. *Class No: 942.1/.9*

Bibliographies of Bibliographies
[7049]

HUMPHREYS, A.L. A Handbook of county bibliography: being a bibliography of bibliographies relating to the counties and towns of Great Britain and Ireland. London, Dawson Pall Mall, 1974. x,501p.

First published London, Humphreys, 1917.

6,000 bibliographies, under counties A-Z; general works are followed by those on individual towns and villages. Includes manuscript and periodical sources. Full bibliographical details, with occasional brief annotations. Index (p.399-500) of authors, personal names, places and subjects, with full data under each entry as well as page references. *Class No: 942.1/.9(009)*

[7050]

LISTER, A. 'Bibliographies of the County Histories', *Antiquarian Book Monthly Review,* v.19, no.12, issue 224, December 1992, p.546-50.

Bibliographical history and survey. *Class No: 942.1/.9(009)*

Bibliographies

[7051]

ANDERSON, J.P. The Book of British topography: a classified catalogue of the topographical works in the library of the British Museum relating to Great Britain and Ireland. London, Satchell, 1881. xvi,472p.

Reprinted E.P. Publishing Ltd., 1976.

Nearly 14,000 entries, with full titles of works, but no annotations or pagination. Contents: Catalogues - General topography (including England and English counties A-Z) - Wales (general; regional; counties, A-Z) - Scotland (general; counties, A-Z) - Ireland (general; counties A-Z) - Addenda - Index of places and subjects. The 'General topography' section includes such topics as antiquities, directories, islands, railways and views. *Class No:* 942.1/.9(01)

[7052]

BARLEY, M.W. A Guide to British topographical collections. Harvey, P.D.A. *and* Poole, J.E. London, Council for British Archaeology, 1974. 159p. £6. ISBN: 0900312246.

'Describes briefly those collections of topographical illustrations - that is, drawings, prints, photographs - to be found in public repositories and also in a few private collections in Britain' *Introduction.* Arranged under counties (traditional names), then towns, holding institutions, and the collections themselves. Some sources cited, p.8-9. Data: name of collection; size; types of material; subjects. 'An indispensable guide alike to the topographer and to the art and architectural historian' (*British Book News,* April 1978, p.286-7). *Class No:* 942.1/.9(01)

[7053]

CHAPLIN, R. A Buyer's guide to local history pamphlets 1978-80 *Local Historian* v.14, no.4, November 1980, p.211-221 and v.14, no.7, August 1981, p.419-427.

Literature review of oral history; diaries and memoirs; guides to sources and methods; family history; houses and families; people; portraits of the artist; and industrial history publications. Consolidated lists p.218-221 and p.427. *Class No:* 942.1/.9(01)

[7054]

'Local history bookshop' *Local History Magazine,* no.24, November 1989, p.19-21.

'A basic collection of books likely to be of use to the relative newcomer to the subject - although none of them would be out of place on the shelves of the more experienced researcher'. In 7 categories: 1. Research and fieldwork for beginners - 2. Guides to particular sources - 3. Reference - 4. Handwriting and palaeography - 5. Place-names and maps - 6. Buildings - 7. Genealogy and family history. *Class No:* 942.1/.9(01)

[7055]

MAKEPEACE, C.E. Local history, p.230-65, *Printed reference material* edited by P.W. Lea and A.E. Day (London, Library Association, 1990. xxv,589p. refs., index. £39. ISBN 1856040186).

A critical running commentary on the various forms and types of local history material including bibliographies, records, archival sources, newspapers and periodicals, parliamentary papers, directories, genealogical research, census reports, place-names, biographical information, maps, and ephemera. *Class No:* 942.1/.9(01)

[7056]

MULLINS, E.L.C., *comp.* **A Guide to the historical and archaeological publications of societies in England and Wales. 1901-1933.** Compiled for the Institute of Historical Research. London, Athlone Press, 1968. xiii, 850p.

6,560 entries for books and periodical articles issued by more than 400 local and national societies in England and Wales, Isle of Man and Channel Islands. Listed A-Z (ranging from the Society of Glass Technology to the Friends Historical Society). Excellent detailed, analytical index, p.491-788; index of authors. Complements *Writings on British history,* which excludes publications of societies. *Class No:* 942.1/.9(01)

[7057]

PORTER, S. Exploring urban history sources for local historians. London, Batsford, 1990. 160p. bibliog., index. £14.95. ISBN: 0713451378.

A comprehensive guide to finding and using the primary and secondary documentation resources available to local historians: 1. Antiquarian and historical background - 2. Site and layout - 3. Buildings - 4. Pre-modern population and society - 5. Population and society from 1800 - 6. Civic administration - 7. Government, Parliament and the Courts - 8. Culture and leisure. Chapter notes p.141-51. Bibliography p.152-3. *Class No:* 942.1/.9(01)

[7058]

STEPHENS, W.B. Sources for English local history studies in the use of historical evidence. 2nd ed. Cambridge, Cambridge Univ. Press, 1981. xv, 342p. facsims., tables, index. £40. (*Sources of History.*) ISBN: 0521237637.

Revised and expanded edition of book of same title published by Manchester Univ. Press, in 1973.

9 chapters: 1. Introduction (146 footnotes, citing many of the sources) - 2. Population and social structure - 3. Local government and politics - 4. Poor relief, charities, prices and wages - 5. Industry, trade and communications - 6. Agriculture - 7. Education - 8. Religion - 9. Houses, housing, and health. Analytical index p.326-342. 'An indispensable research tool, both for beginners and scholars' (*British Book News,* January 1982, p.62). *Class No:* 942.1/.9(01)

[7059]

UPCOTT, W. A Bibliographical account of the principal works relating to English topography. East Ardsley, Wakefield, E.P. Publishing, 1978. ix,1576p.

First published R. & A. Taylor, 3v., 1818.

Section on general topographic works, followed by that on county histories, alphabetically arranged. Analyses rather less than 1500 works (J. Nichols' *The history and antiquities of the county of Leicester* (1795-1811. 4v. in 8) is allotted 43p., whereas J.P. Anderson's *The book of British topography* (1881) gives Nichols only 6 lines). 'Still an indispensable work of reference' (*British Book News,* July 1979, p.564). *Class No:* 942.1/.9(01)

Encyclopaedias

[7060]

RICHARDSON, J. The Local historian's encyclopaedia. 2nd ed. New Barnet, Herts., Historical Publications, 1986. 263p. illus., bibliogs., index. £13.95. ISBN: 095036567x.

First published 1974.

20 self contained sections covering all aspects of local history: Archives, documents and printed records p.54-99;

....(contd.)

Museums, libraries and county record offices p.108-114; Organizations and societies p.115-134; Genealogy p.135-140; Heraldry p.213-219;p Archaeology p.234-249. All sections end with a bibliography. *Class No:* 942.1/.9(031)

Handbooks & Manuals

[7061]

CAMPBELL-KEASE, J. A Companion to local history research. London, A & C Black, 1989. 384p. maps, illus., index. £15.95. ISBN: 0713631457.

33 chapters in 5 sections: 1. Outline history and sources for the local historians - 2. Basic record sources - 3. More detailed records by period - 4. Specialist topics, archives and collections (16 chapters) - 5. Writing a local history. Appendix 1. Publications of the Royal Commission on the Historical Monuments in England - 2. Status of the Victoria County History programme. Major study which 'identifies and describes the principal material available for the study of local history, indicates where it may be found, and set it against the broader framework of national, as well as regional events'. The author writes at length of his book in *Local History*, no.26, November 1989, p.11-13. *Class No:* 942.1/.9(035)

[7062]

FRIAR, S. The Batsford companion to local history. London, Batsford, 1991. 432p. maps, bibliog., index. £19.95. ISBN: 0713461810.

Over 2,000 cross-referenced A-Z entries ranging from brief definitions to short essays on major subjects covering such topics as architecture, education, genealogy, legal and ecclesiastical terms, place-names *etc. Class No:* 942.1/.9(035)

[7063]

IREDALE, D. Local history research and writing. Chichester, Sussex, Phillimore, 1980. 244p. £5.95. ISBN: 0850333997.

First published Leeds, Elmfield Press, 1974.

Includes hints on research techniques and problems (*e.g.* linguistic and palaeographical), use and drafting of maps. Also discusses types of archives and physical objects (*e.g.* monuments) for study. Helpful bibliography of standard works. Appended lists of useful addresses and of British record repositories. 'It will save them [aspiring local historians] many wasted hours' (*British Book News*, March 1875,p.207). *Class No:* 942.1/.9(035)

[7064]

RIDEN, P. Local history a handbook for beginners. London, Batsford Academic and Educational Ltd., 1983. 175p. illus., bibliog., index. ISBN: 0713438703.

7 chapters: 1. Local history today - 2. At the library - 3. At the Record Office - 4. Maps - 5. Landscapes and buildings - 6. The Public Record Office and other national collections - 7. Writing and publication. Bibliography p.162-9 'of material which should be available in any public library with a local studies section' For the part-time amateur enthusiast. *Class No:* 942.1/.9(035)

Dictionaries

[7065]

MORRIS, J. A Latin glossary for family and local historians. Birmingham, Federation of Family History Societies, 1989. 39p. £1.75. ISBN: 0907099890.

'Not intended to be a comprehensive dictionary of all the Latin words likely to be found in records of interest to family historians. It does, however, aim to include most of the commoner words which occur in parish registers, wills, and the simpler types of title deeds and manorial records' (*Foreword*). *Class No:* 942.1/.9(038)

Yearbooks & Directories

[7066]

MAXTED, I., *comp.* **British national directories 1781-1819:** an index to places in the British Isles included in trade directories with general provincial coverage. Exeter, J. Maxted, 1989. vii,34p. map. A4 pbk. (*Exeter Working Papers in British Book Trade History. Special series, no.2.*) ISBN: 0951275216.

Listing by place p.1-23 (data: county, place, date code to one of 13 county based directories). County index p.24-31. 'Before the series of county based directories introduced by Pigot in 1820 there was a series of national directories, normally issued as supplements to London directories, which covered over one thousand places throughout the British Isles, the majority of which had no directory of their own. This index records the coverage in two tables, one in a single alphabetical sequence of places and the other arranged by county' (*Introduction*). *Class No:* 942.1/.9(058)

[7067]

NORTON, J.E. Guide to the national and provincial directories of England and Wales excluding London, published before 1856. London, Royal Historical Society, 1984. vii,241p. £12.00. (*RHS guides and handbooks, no.5.*) ISBN: 0861931025.

First published 1950. Complements *The London directories, 1677-1855,* by C.W.F. Goss (London, Archer, 1932, xi, 147p.).

878 numbered entries (English, national-chronologically arranged; English, local - by counties A-Z, then chronologically; Welsh chronologically; addenda). Locations are given for each directory. Excludes directories of particular trades or professions, but includes 'a number of histories and guide books to which directories have been added'. Index of authors, printers and publishers. General index. A valuable introduction deals with the origin and development of directories, authorship, methods of compilation and tests of reliability. *Class No:* 942.1/.9(058)

Bibliographies

[7068]

ENSING, R.J. Directories. London, Wandsworth Historical Society, 1985. 32p. bibliog., sd. 0.75p. (*Guides to Local History Sources no.1.*) ISBN: 0905121015.

Of wide interest because of its historical examination of the *P.O. London Directory* and Kelly's Directories. *Class No:* 942.1/.9(058)(01)

[7069]
SHAW, G. *and* TIPPER, A. **British directories:** a bibliography and guide to directories published in England and Wales (1850-1950) and Scotland (1773-1950). Leicester, Leicester Univ. Press, 1988. ix,440p. illus., bibliog., index. £45.00. ISBN: 0718512928.

Extends coverage and complements (1) Goss, C.W.F. *The London directories 1677-1855* (1932) and Norton, J.E. *Guide to the national and provincial directories of England and Wales, excluding London* (1950).

1. Introduction and guide (previous works and guides) - 2. Bibliography (English, Welsh, Scottish directories and British directories of commerce, industry and trades) - 3. Library holdings and index. 2,200 titles arranged by county and then chronologically. Publishers, place, and subject indexes. 'To be revered for years to come by local, family and industrial historians, librarians, archivists and many others. An essential purchase for every large reference collection or historical research centre' (*Reference Reviews*, v.3,no.3, September 1989, p.139-40). *Class No:* 942.1/.9(058)(01)

Maps & Atlases

[7070]
HINDLE, B.P. **Maps for local history.** London, Batsford, 1988. 160p. maps. bibliog. index. £17.95. (*Batsford Local History Series*.) ISBN: 0713455545.

Introduction. 6 chapters: 1. Early maps of Britain - 2. County maps - 3. Estate, enclosure and tithe maps - 4. Town plans - 5. Transport maps - 6. Ordnance Survey maps. Appendix 1. Scales - 2. County maps (*i.e.* large scale county maps of England) 1699 - 1839 - 3. Local map collections. *Class No:* 942.1/.9(084.3)

[7071]
LOBEL, M.D., *ed*. **The British atlas of historic towns** to c.1520.

1. *Banbury, Caernarvon, Glasgow, Hereford, Nottingham, Reading, Salisbury* (London, Lovell-Johns, Cook, Hammond & Kell, 1969). 2. *Bristol, Cambridge, Coventry, Norwich* (London, Scolar Press, 1975). 3. *The City of London from prehistoric times to c.1520* (Oxford Univ. Press, 1989, 99p. £75. 0198229798). Published for the Historic Towns Trust these large format atlases present meticulously detailed colour maps, a textual commentary setting the towns in their historical context, and a gazetteer providing indispensable source material for known streets and buildings in the medieval period. *Class No:* 942.1/.9(084.3)

[7072]
OLIVER, R. **Ordnance Survey maps** a concise guide to historians. London, Charles Close Society, 1993. 192p. bibliog. £12.95. ISBN: 087059813x.

Includes a list of towns for which plans exist and an A-Z county by county checklist with dates. *Class No:* 942.1/.9(084.3)

[7073]
Ordnance Survey County Street Atlases. Southampton, Ordnance Survey; London, Philip.

Berkshire, 1990. viii,176p. ISBN 0319002276; *Buckinghamshire*, 1990. viii,237p. 0319002268; *East Essex*, 1990. viii,228p. 0319002179. *West Essex*. 1990. viii,218p. 0319002187; *North Hampshire*, 1991. viii,228p. 031900241; *South Hampshire*, 1991. viii,253p.; *Hertfordshire*, new ed. 1990. viii,203p. 0319002292; *East Kent*, 2nd ed. 1992.

....(contd.)
viii,239p. 0319003000; *West Kent*, rev. ed. 1992. viii,226p.; *Oxfordshire*, 1992. vii,279p. 0319003027; *Surrey*, 14th ed. 1991. 160p.++ 65p. 054005612x; *East Sussex*, 2nd ed. 1992. 031922187; *West Sussex*, 3rd ed., 1992. viii,233p. 0319003051; and *Warwickshire*, 1992. viii,246p. 0319003027.

All streets, roads and lanes, parks, woods, farms, bridleways and footpaths, Post Offices, schools and libraries, hospitals, police and fire stations, ferry ports and harbours are clearly marked on a scale of 3 1/2 inches to the mile. Stacey, M. 'Current UK street maps for libraries' *Refer* v.8,no.1, Winter 1992, p.1-4, 6-7 lists 12 major series. *Class No:* 942.1/.9(084.3)

[7074]
SMITH, D. **Maps and plans for the local historian and collector:** a guide to types of maps of the British Isles produced before 1914 valuable to local and other historians. London, B.T. Batsford, 1988. 240p. illus. (inc. 6 col. plates), facsims., bibliog., index. £19.95. ISBN: 0713451912.

Introduction and 20 chapters each with its own (sometimes extensive) bibliography: 1. Sources - 2. Documentation - 3. Parliamentary deposited plans and associated documents - 4. Estate plans - 5. Enclosure - 6. Title - 7. Regional maps - 8. Drainage - 9. County - 10. County divisions - 11. Military - 12. Ordnance Survey - 13. Transport and communications - 14. Marine charts - 15. Settlement plans - 16. Specialized urban plans - 17. Other parish plans - 18. London - 19. Industrial maps - 20. Themes and thematic maps. Notes p.211-220. Bibliography p.221. County bibliography p.223-5. Analytical index. *Class No:* 942.1/.9(084.3)

[7075]
Street maps of British towns. London, British Telecommunications, 1987. 304p. col. illus., col. maps. £16.50. (*Yellow Pages Guide*.) ISBN: 0948257326.

250 A-Z Town plans with street indexes and Amenities Directory (Emergency services, places of interest, entertainment, sport and leisure). Route planning atlas 1":10 miles p.283-303. Motorway service stations p.282. *Class No:* 942.1/.9(084.3)

Bibliographies

[7076]
ARMITAGE, G. **'County cartobibliographies of England and Wales: a select list'.** *Map Collector*, no.52, Autumn 1990, p.16-24.

1. General cartobibliography of British Isles. 2. English and Welsh counties A-Z. *Class No:* 942.1/.9(084.3)(01)

[7077]
HARLEY, J.B. **Maps for the local historian** : a guide to the British sources.. London, National Council of Social Service for Standing Conference for Local History, 1972. 86p. facsims. bibliog. ISBN: 0719908345.

Reprinted from *The Amateur Historian* and *The Local Historian*.

Deals in turn with town plans; estate enclosure and communication maps; maritime charts; and county maps. Bibliographical postscript (p.77-86). *Class No:* 942.1/.9(084.3)(01)

[7078]

SKELTON, R.A. County atlases of the British Isles 1579-1859: a bibliography. London, Carta Press, 1970. Reprinted by Dawsons, 1978. £20.00. ISBN: 0712908730.

124 county atlases, from Saxton to the Ordnance Survey, p.7-206; brief bibliographical descriptions and notes. Appendix B: 'Maps of parts of the British Isles in general atlases before 1650: a select list'; C: 'The London map-trade before 1700; with a biographical list of London map-publishers'. Indexes: Persons; Titles of atlases; Subjects. Page size, 25.5 x 18.6cm. Supersedes most of the first hundred pages of Chubb's *The printed maps in the atlases of Great Britain and Ireland, 1579-1870* (1927).
Class No: 942.1/.9(084.3)(01)

[7079]

—HODSON, D., *comp.* County atlases of the British Isles: a bibliography. Welwyn, Hertfordshire, Tewin Press, 1984-.

1. *Atlases published 1704 to 1742 and their subsequent editions.* 1984. xvi,200p. £20. ISBN 0950914908. 2. *Atlases published 1743 to 1763 and their subsequent editions.* 1989. xvi,193p. £30. 0950914916. Continues R.A. Skelton's *County atlases of the British Isles 1579-1850* which records works published 1579-1703. 'No reference library should be without these two volumes' (*Library Association Record,* v.92, no.9, September 1990, p.685). *Class No:* 942.1/.9(084.3)

Official Records

Bibliographies

[7080]

EMMISON, F.G. *and* **GRAY, I. County records** (Quarter Sessions, Petty Sessions, Clerk of the Peace and Lieutenancy). 4th rev. ed. London, Historical Association, 1973. £3.20. (*Helps for Students of History, no.H62.*) ISBN: 0852781822.

First published 1948.

Confined to England and Wales. Sections: 1. Introduction - 2. Records of the Courts of Quarter Sessions and of Petty Sessions - 3. Other county records - 4. Topography and genealogy in county records - 5. Local and national history in county records. Appendix 1: Printed catalogues and transcripts of county records; 2. The County Record Office and the student (with addresses of repositories). Facilities. Selected records (types), p.29-32. *Class No:* 942.1/.9(093.2)(01)

Archives

[7081]

EMMISON, F.G. *and* **SMITH, W.J.,** *comps.* **Materials for theses in local record offices.** 2nd ed. London, The Historical Association, 1980. 48p. index, sd. £1.60. (*Helps for Students of History, no.87.*) ISBN: 0852782063.

1st ed. 1973.

Covers England, Wales and Scotland, under counties. Briefly annotated entries, mainly for local record offices. Data: name and address; list of publications; descriptive comment on major holdings. (Certain classes of archives are generally omitted because 'they are well represented in most Local Repositories'. 'Corporation of London Records

....(contd.)

Office, Guildhall': over 1p. Detailed index of subjects, bodies, persons (families and certain locations).
Class No: 942.1/.9(093.20)

[7082]

GIBSON, J. *and* **PESKETT, P. Record offices** how to find them. 5th ed. Birmingham, Federation of Family History Societies, 1991. 60p. maps. index. sd. £2.50. ISBN: 1872094244.

70 street maps indicating location of county and diocesan record offices. Routes from 'bus and railway stations and nearby carparks are indicated. *Class No:* 942.1/.9(093.20)

[7083]

'Local archives of Great Britain', *Archives,* 1948-71. illus., facsims.

A series of articles featuring the holdings of record offices in Great Britain. 1. 'The County Record Office at Bedford', no.1, 1949, p.10-20. 2. 'The Essex Record Office', no.2, 1949, p.8-16. 3. 'The Glamorgan County Record Office', no.3, 1950, p.7-16. 4. 'The County Record Office of Hertford', no.4, 1950, p.16-24. 5. 'The Birmingham Reference Library', no.5, 1951, p.11-21. 6. 'The Lincolnshire Archives Committee', no.6, 1951, p.5-16. 7. 'The Lancashire Record Office', no.7, 1952. p.45-51. 8. 'Norwich City Libraries', v.2, no.10, 1953, p.86-93. 9. 'The records of the City of London', v.2, no.11, 1954, p.123-30. 10. 'The Warwickshire County Record Office and the preservation of records in Warwickshire', v.2, no.12, 1954, p.192-204. 11. 'The Kent Archives Office', v.2, no.13, 1955, p.237-52. 12. 'The Guildhall Library', v.2, no.14, 1955, p.312-23. 13. The L.C.C. Record Office', v.2, no.16, 1956, p.477-86. 14. The City of Bristol Record Office', v.3, no.17, 1957, p.88-96. 17. 'The Ipswich and East Suffolk Record Office', v.4, no.21, 1959, p.18-28. 18. 'The Berkshire Record Office', v.4, no.22, 1959. p.65-74. 19. 'Record Office work in Staffordshire', v.4, no.24, 1960, p.204-13. 10. 'Shakespeare's birthplace library, Stratford-on-Avon', v.5, no.26. 1961, p.90-99. 21. 'The Plymouth Archives Department', v.5, no.26, 1961, p.100-05. 22. 'The Worcestershire Record Office', v.5, no.27, 1962, p.151-9. 23. 'Newcastle-upon-Tyne City Archives Office', v.5, no.28, 1962, p.226-33. 24. 'The Middlesex County Record Office', v.6, no.29, 1963, p.30-9. 25. 'The Gloucestershire County Record Office', v.6, no.31, 1964, p.178-185. 26. 'Archives in the Gloucester City Library', v.6, no.32, 1964, p.225-8. 27. 'The Caernarvonshire Record Office', v.7, no.33, 1965, p.34-9. 28. 'Cumberland, Westmorland and Carlisle Record Office 1960-1965', v.7, no.34, 1965, p.80-86. 29. 'The Dorset Record Office', v.7, no.36, 1966, p.207-14. 30. 'The Norfolk and Norwich Record Offices', v.8, no.38, 1967, p.63-69. 31. 'The London Borough of Hammersmith Record Office', v.9, no.44, 1970, p.192-6. 31. 'The Flintshire Record Office', v.10, no.45, 1971, p.38-46. *Class No:* 942.1/.9(093.20)

[7084]

MORTON, A. *and* **DONALDSON, G. British national archives and the local historian:** a guide to official record publications. London, The Historical Association, 1980. 52p. £1.60. (*Help for students of history, no.88.*) ISBN: 0852782365.

Descriptive guide in 2 parts: 1. Public Record Office publications (Chancery, Exchequer and Judicial records,

....*(contd.)*

state papers, and Treasury, Privy Council and Parliamentary archives) - 2. Scottish Record Office publications. *Class No:* 942.1/.9(093.20)

[7085]
RIDEN, P. Record sources for local history. London, B.T. Batsford, 1987. 253p. bibliog., index. £14.95. (*Batsford Local History Series.*) ISBN: 0713447265.

A guide to the main archival sources available to the local historian in 6 sections: 1. Records and Record Offices - 2. The Middle Ages - 3. Early modern central government and the local communities - 4. Modern local government - 5. The modern local government system - 6. Local material amongst the modern records of Central Government. Appendix 2: 'The division of records at the P.R.O.' (p.190-93), outlining the distribution of record groups between Kew and Chancery Lane is particularly useful. Chapter notes p.196-219. Bibliography p.220-243. *Class No:* 942.1/.9(093.20)

Bibliographies

[7086]
MULLINS, E.L.C. Texts and calendars : an analytical guide to serial publications. London, Royal Historical Society, 1958. xi, 674p. index. £8. (*RHS Guides and Handbooks, no.7.*) ISBN: 0901050148.

Covers texts and calendars for English and Welsh history issued by the various Record Commissions, the Public Record Office and local authorities and record societies. Parts: 1. Official bodies - 2. National bodies - 3. English local societies - 4. Welsh societies - 5. Addenda. Index. Invaluable in supplying complete lists of the publications of such bodies as the Camden Society, Harleian Society, English Place-Name Society, Rolls series, etc., with full subject index.

Texts and calendars: an analytical guide to serial publications 1957-1982. (1983). xi, 323p. ISBN 0861931009. More than 20 new series, notably the publications of the London and Suffolk Record Societies, along with *corrigenda* to the original work. *Class No:* 942.1/.9(093.20)(01)

Libraries

[7087]
HOBBS, J.L. *and* **CARTER, G.A. Local history and the library.** 2nd ed. London, Grafton Books, 1973. 344p. illus. £25. ISBN: 0233956158.

1st ed. 1962.

17 chapters (1. Local history: its value and use ... 4. Manuscript records ... 8. Exhibitions, publicity and display ... 11. The use of local research materials ... 13. Accommodation ... 17. A local classification scheme). Bibliography, p.313-22 (by subjects). Detailed and partly analytical index, p.325-38; Index of special collections mentioned in the text, p.341-4. A standard text in its field. *Class No:* 942.1/.9:061:026/027

[7088]
—NICHOLS, H. Local studies librarianship. London, Bingley, 1979. 128p. £7.95. ISBN: 0851572723.

A concentrated introduction that includes a chapter on 'Assistance to readers' (ommissions are noted in *Library Association Record*, v.81, no.8, 1979, p.389). 'A worthy successor to J.L. Hobbs' *Local history in the library* (*British Book News*, August 1979, p.635). *Class No:* 942.1/.9:061:026/027

London

[7089]
ATKINS, P.J. The Directories of London 1677-1977. London, Mansell, 1990. xii,732p. illus., bibliog., indexes. £60. ISBN: 0720120632.

Not so much a revision or update of C.W.F. Goss's *The London directories 1677-1855: a bibliography with notes on their origin and development* (1932) as a replacement work.

A magisterial guide to the history and development of printed London directories (directory types; history; compilation; and uses) together with a comprehensive bibliography (5800 items) and a list of the holdings of 65 libraries. Appendix: Bibliography of Directory titles (entries carry coded location guide) p.1-3. Title, publisher, and topographical indexes. 'Scholars, researchers and librarians - all will be grateful ... a fine example for future bibliographers to follow' (*Library Association Record*, v.92, no.8, August 1980. p.599). Library Association McColvin Medal commendation 1991. *Class No:* 942.1

[7090]
GREATER LONDON COUNCIL. The Survey of London. London, London County Council (then Athlone Press), 1900-.

Out of print volumes are being reprinted by AMS Press (New York).

1. *Bromley-by-Bow* (1900); 2, 4, 7, 11. *Chelsea* (1909-1927) v.7. £27.50. ISBN 048548027x; 3, 5. *St. Giles in the Fields* (1912-14); 6. *Hammersmith* (1915); 8. *St. Leonard, Shoreditch* (1922); 9. *St. Helen, Bishopgate* (1924); 10, 13, 14. *St. Margaret, Westminster* (1926-30); 12, 15. *All Hallows, Barking* (1929-34) v.15. £45. 0485482150; 16, 18, 20. *St. Martins-in-the-Fields* (1935-40); 17, 19, 21, 24. *St Pancras* (1936-52); 22. *St. Saviour and Christchurch, Southwark* (1950); 23, 26. *St. Mary, Lambeth* (1951-56); 25. *St. George the Martyr, Southwark* (1955) £35. 0485482258; 27. *Spitalfields and Mile End New Town* (1957); *Hackney,* pt.1 (1960) £35. 0485482282; 29-32. *St. James, Westminster* (5v., 1960-63) v.31-32 £65. 0485482312; 33-34. *St. Anne, Soho* (1966) £75. 0485482339; 35. *Theatre Royal, Drury Lane and the Royal Opera House, Covent Garden* (1970) £50. 0485482355; 36. *St. Paul, Covent Garden* (1970) £55. 0485482363; 37. *Northern Kensington* (1973) £55. 0485482371; 38. *The Museums area of South Kensington and Westminster* (1975) £60. 048548238x; 39-40. *The Grosvenor Estate* (1977-80) £55 and £70. 0485482398 and 0485482401; *Southern Kensington-Brompton* (1983) £55. 0485482241x; 42. *Southern Kensington-Kensington Square to Earls Court* (1986) £65. 0485482428. An historical survey of the administrative county of London. Each volume gives a detailed history of a parish, or part of a parish, with descriptions and illus. of historically important buildings. V.42 has 152p. plates, chapter references p.414-59, index p.461-502. *Class No:* 942.1

[7091]

KIEK, J. Everybody's historic London a history and guide. London, Quiller Press, 1984. 248p. illus., maps, bibliog., index. pbk. £4.95. ISBN: 0907621392.

Convenient concise history and guide to the capital in 14 well-illustrated chapters including 1. Landmarks in the history of London - 2. Roman London ... 4. Medieval London ... 11. London names - 12. The lost rivers. Also 20 day tours p.208-41. Reading lists to every chapter.
Class No: 942.1

[7092]

The Shell guide to the history of London. Dalzell, W.R. London, Michael Joseph, 1981. 496p. illus., maps, bibliog., index. ISBN: 0718120159.

9 chronological chapters (1. Roman London; 2. The London of William the Conqueror; 3. Chaucer's London ... 9. Twentieth-century London). Appendix 1. Historical maps p.475-480. 2. The Origins of some street names p.481-484. Bibliography p.485. Generously illustrated. *Class No:* 942.1

[7093]

The Victoria history of London including London without the Bars, Westminster and Southwark. London, Constable, 1909. £70.00. ISBN: 0712906053.

Reprinted by Dawsons Pall Mall 1974.

V.1 (all published) deals with pre-conquest London, and with ecclesiastical history down to modern times.
Class No: 942.1

Bibliographies

[7094]

ADAMS, B. London illustrated 1604-1951 a survey and index of topographical books and their plates. London, Library Association, 1983. xxxiii, 586p.+24p. plates. bibliog. £75. ISBN: 0853657343.

Catalogue (p.3-521) describes 238 books and sets of prints containing over 8000 plates illustrating London by means of line-engraving, etching or lithography. Detail includes notes on the volume's publishing history and its illustrations; transcription of the title page, its collation; and a checklist of its London plates. Chronological numbered list of books p.xxv-xxvii; list of illustrations p.xxix-xxx, topographical index p.523-556; index to artists, engravers, architects, authors, book titles, and select publishers p.557-562. Bibliography p.583-586. Absence of maps a surprising feature. 'A monumental task ... accomplished triumphantly' (*British Book News*, September 1983, p.541).
Class No: 942.1(01)

[7095]

COHEN, B. The Thames 1580-1980: a general bibliography. London, Ben Cohen, 1985. [v], 335p. ISBN: 0951039105.

19 sections *e.g.* 1. Barrage, barrier, floods, drainage ... 2-3. Bridges ... 4. Docks, wharves, employment ... 5. Embankments ... 13. Navigation, tides, canals ... 15. River craft, transport, boat yards. No index on the advice of booksellers and librarians! Fills an undoubted gap.
Class No: 942.1(01)

[7096]

CREATON, H., *ed*. Bibliography of printed works on London history to 1939. London, Library Association, 1994. 896p. £80. ISBN: 1856040747.

22000++ items recording books and articles on the history of London from the Dark Ages to the beginning of the Second World War. Area covered is the City of London and the former GLC. A supplement is planned to cover new material on the period. *Class No:* 942.1(01)

[7097]

MARCAN, P., comp. Greater London local history directory and bibliography: a borough by borough guide to local history organisations, their activities, and publications, 1983-1987. High Wycombe, Buckinghamshire, Peter Marcan Publications, 1988. iv, 83p. £15. ISBN: 0951028987.

Updates *London's local history* (1985).

Over 300 entries arranged within each borough in 8 categories: municipal collections and museums; historical and archaeological societies; community publishing projects and oral history groups; and amenity conservation societies, with separate sections on family history societies, of organizations spanning more than 1 borough and 'umbrella' organizations and record offices in adjacent counties. 'A valuable resource in local history libraries both in London and in other parts of the country. It will show researchers what is available and what work is being done in this popular and little-recorded field' (*Reference Reviews*, v.2, no.3, September 1988, p.162). *Class No:* 942.1(01)

[7098]

MARCAN, P., *and others, comps*. London's local history: an annotated catalogue of publications and resources issued by Greater London local authorities, local historical and archaeological societies, amenity societies and community publishing projects during the 1960s, 1970s and early 1980s with listings of local history collections, museums, societies, and notes on London wide historical societies and library collections. 2nd impression with corrections and amendments. High Wycombe, Buckinghamshire, Peter Marcan Publications, 1985. vi, 58p. pbk. £9.50. (*Public Library Resources Series.*) ISBN: 0950421162.

First published 1983. Supplemented by *Greater London local history directory and bibliography* (1988).
Class No: 942.1(01)

Encyclopaedias

[7099]

The Book of London. Leapman, M., *ed*. London, Weidenfeld & Nicolson, 1989. 320p. illus. (many col.), maps, bibliog., index. £18. ISBN: 0297796240.

27 contributors. Every aspect of London's past and present is covered in this encyclopedic work arranged in 5 main parts and divided into 37 distinct sections: 1. The Growth of London (Londinium, Medieval London ... From the Great Fire to the Regency ... Twentieth-Century London, Chronology p.42) - 2. The Areas of London (*e.g.* The Thames, The City of London) - 3. A Place to live (*e.g.* Georgian terraces and Regency villas, Victorian houses for the masses, The growth of the suburbs) - 4. A Place to work - 5. A Place to enjoy (Theatre, Music ... A London Calendar). The Makers of London (architects and builders) p.302-6. Glossary of place names p.307. Bibliography p.308-10. *Class No:* 942.1(031)

[7100]
WEINREB, B. *and* HIBBERT, C. **The London encyclopaedia.** Rev. ed. London, Macmillan, 1993. xii,1060p. illus., indexes. £45. ISBN: 0333560280.

First published 1983.

164 contributors. Approximately 5000 cross-referenced entries form a complete portrait of the whole of Greater London: history, tradition, streets and buildings, people and events. 'An attractive and fascinating compilation' (*Reference Reviews*, v.2, no.2, June 1988, p.93-4). *Class No:* 942.1(031)

Maps & Atlases

[7101]
The A to Z of ... London. maps, facsims., bibliog., indexes.

1. *A to Z of Elizabethan London* by A. Prockter and R. Taylor. London Topographical Society, 1979. 0902087150. Maps p.1-32. Place name index p.33-62. Bibliography p.xii. 2. *A to Z of Georgian London.* 1982. viii,88p. £16.00. 0902087169. Maps and atlas p.1-49. Place name index p.51-85. Bibliography p.viii. 3. *A to Z of Regency London.* Lympne Castle, Kent, Harry Margary, in association with Guildhall Library London, 1985. xvi,116p. £17.50. 090345136x. Atlas p.1-81. Index p.82-116. 4. *A to Z of Victorian London.* 1987. viii,140p. £19.50. 0903451394. Atlas p.1-120. Index p.121-140. Imaginative presentation of the street plans of London. *Class No:* 942.1(084.3)

[7102]
BARKER, F. *and* JACKSON, P. **The History of London in maps.** London, Barrie & Jenkins, 1990. 192p. illus. (some col.), maps (some col.). £19.95. ISBN: 0712636501.

A cartographical survey of 400 years of London's history with over 150 maps, paintings, engravings and photographs *etc.* *Class No:* 942.1(084.3)

[7103]
The Times London history atlas. Clout, H., *ed.* London, Times Books, 1991. 190p. col. illus., col. maps, bibliog., index. £19.99. ISBN: 0723003424.

Traces growth of London from Roman period to present day: 1. Land under London (geology; River Thames) - 2/7. Roman, Anglo-Saxon and Norman, medieval, Tudor and Stuart, Georgian, and Victorian London - 8. Between the wars - 9. Post-war London - 10. London themes - 11. Places in London. 5 band thematic chronology p.12-17. Etymology of London place names p.172-7. Bibliography p.178-9. Magnificently produced. *Class No:* 942.1(084.3)

Bibliographies

[7104]
HOWGEGO, J. **Printed maps of London circa 1553-1850.** 2nd ed. Folkestone, Dawson, 1978. xv, 295p. illus. ports., maps (facsims.). £35.00. ISBN: 0712908218.

First published, 1964 (I.Dartington and J Howgego).

422 items with bibliographical notes. 40 locations, including Paris (Bibliothèque Nationale), Dublin, Leiden and Royal Library, Copenhagen. Valuable general introduction, p.1-34 (10 sections; *e.g.* 4. Pre-Fire map - names of London); 63 references. The catalogue (p.43-284) notes different editions. 'A select bibliography', p.35-36. Well produced. 'Every serious student of the history of the capital

....(contd.)
will consider the new edition an essential possession' (*Library Association Record*, v.81, no.5. May 1979, p.243). *Class No:* 942.1(084.3)(01)

Biographies

[7105]
GIBSON, P. **The Capital companion:** a street by street guide to London and its inhabitants. Exeter, Webb & Bower, 1985. 446p. illus. £12.95. ISBN: 0863500420.

1200 entries (780 biographies in a single A-Z sequence with 400 streets) relating to Central London *i.e.* a rectangle 4½miles x 3 miles centred on Leicester Square. A 'must' for tourists arriving at Heathrow or Gatwick intending to do London at the double. *Class No:* 942.1(092)

Archives

Micromaterials

[7106]
Historical gazetteer of London before the Great Fire. Keene, D., *ed.* Cambridge and Alexandria, Virginia, Chadwyck-Healey.

Part 1. *Cheapside* by D. Keene and V. Harding. £195. 57 microfiche in a binder with printed introduction and 4 printed maps. A new series based on surviving documents recording London's development from 12th century onwards including deeds, rentals, accounts, surveys, livery company records, parish and monastic houses records. *Class No:* 942.1(093.20)(003.5)

Roman Times

[7107]
MERRIFIELD, R. **The Roman city of London.** London, Benn, 1965. 344p. illus. (inc.pl.), maps, plans, bibliog., index.

4 chapters: 1. Archaeology in the city of London - 2. Historical outline - 3. The topography of Roman London (p.81-154; 68 references) - 4. Visiting Roman London. Gazetteer (p.189-325: General; Wall; Gates; Bastions; including references to illus. and sources). Bibliography, p.327-32 (most important sources are asterisked). 140 plates; 'Intended for the general reader, including a guide for the visitor' (*Foreword*). 'The definitive work' (Dawe, D. *The city of London* (1972), p.25). His *Roman London* (London, Cassell, 1969, [12],212p. illus., maps, records finds in the 4 years subsequent to *The Roman city of London*. Bibliography, p.[11-12]. *Class No:* 942.1"0055-0449"

19th Century

Maps & Atlases

[7108]
HYDE, R. **Printed maps of Victorian London 1851-1900.** Folkestone, Kent, Dawson, 1975. xv,271p., illus., facsims., plans, maps, indexes. £25. ISBN: 0712906401.

General introduction (16 sections: 1. Maps of London in the year of the Great Exhibition ... 7. Thematic maps ... 13. 19th century atlases of London ... 16. Select bibliography, p.52-53) - 313 numbered entries (author; title; publisher; page size; scale; coverage; series or other features). 3

....(contd.)

appendices (3. Aids to dating). Title and general indexes. Awarded the LA Besterman Medal for an outstanding bibliography/guide to the literature in 1975. *Class No:* 942.1"18"(084.3)

Middlesex

[7109]

The Victoria history of the county of Middlesex. London, Constable, (subsequently Oxford Univ. Press for the Institute of Historical Research), 1911-. v.1-9 (1911-1989). illus., maps. £40, £50, £50, £40, £40, £50, £60, £60, £60. ISBN: 0197227139, v.1; 0712904484, v.2; 0712910344, v.3; 0197227279, v.4; 0197227422, v.5; 0197227503, v.6; 0197227562, v.7; 0197227627, v.8; 0197227724, v.9.

V.1-3 deal with the general history of Middlesex. V.1 contains articles on its physiography and prehistory, religious houses, etc., with a translation of the Middlesex Domesday. V.2 covers the history, industries and sport of the county and begins the topographical account continued in v.4-9. *Class No:* 942.19

Surrey

[7110]

AUBREY, J. The Natural history and antiquities of the County of Surrey. Dorking, Kohler & Coombes, 5v., 1975. ISBN: 0903967251, set.

First published London, E. Curll, 1718-19.

'Consists basically of the topographical notes of a Perambulation of the County carried out ... in the summer of 1673 ... partly rewritten ... in 1717 by the Oxford bibliophile Richard Rawlinson' (*Introduction* by J.L. Nevison). *Class No:* 942.21

[7111]

MANNING, O. and BRAY, W. The History and antiquities of the county of Surrey. Simmons, J., *ed.* East Ardsley, Yorkshire, EP Publishing Ltd., 3v. 1974. ISBN: 0854096035, set; 0854098585, v.1; 0854096035, v.2; 0854098607, v.3.

First published London, J. Nichols, 1804-1814.

Standard county history published in collaboration with Surrey County Library. *Class No:* 942.21

[7112]

The Victoria history of the county of Surrey. London, Constable, 1902-14, 4v. and Index. Reprinted Dawsons 1968. illus., maps. £50, £70, £70, £50. ISBN: 0712902368, v.1; 0712902376, v.2; 0712902384, v.3; 0712902392, v.4.

V.1 comprises the archaeology, Domesday survey, and natural history of Surrey. The various aspects of economic and social history are contained in v.2, and the topographical survey initiated. The last is completed in v.4 which has additional ch. on antiquities and civil history. *Class No:* 942.21

Kent

[7113]

HASTED, E. The History and topographical survey of the county of Kent containing the ancient and present state of it. Simmons, J., *ed.* East Ardsley, Yorkshire, EP Publishing Ltd., 12v. and atlas, 1972. ISBN: 0854097988.

First published Canterbury, W. Bristow, 1797-1801.

....(contd.)

The classic history of Kent. It is the 2nd ed., the first being published between 1778-99. The first volume comprises the general history of the county. The individual places are arranged under Hundreds. Each volume has its own index. Reprinted with the collaboration of Kent County Library. *Class No:* 942.23

[7114]

The Victoria history of the county of Kent. London, Constable and St. Catherine's Press, 1908-32, v. 1-3 only. Reprinted Dawsons. illus., maps. £60, £50, £50. ISBN: 0712906061, v.1; 071290607x, v.2; 0712906088, v.3.

No topographical volumes for this county have been issued. The general introductory matter has been extended to more than the usual volumes to allow for the detailed survey of the county's maritime history and Roman remains. *Class No:* 942.23

Bibliographies

[7115]

BENNETT, G., comp. The Kent bibliography a finding list of Kent material in the public libraries of the County and of the adjoining London Boroughs. London, The Library Association, London & Home Counties Branch, 1977. ix, 452p. £11. ISBN: 0902119206.

About 10,000 entries, with 21 locations of repositories. One A-Z sequence of places, subjects, persons (*e.g.* Sir Winston Churchill). Data: author, title, date of publication, location. Includes much local government material. 'Should prove to be of major importance to scholars, researchers and librarians in the field of local studies' (*Library Review, v.28, Summer 1979, p.132*). Bergess, W. *The Kent bibliography: supplement.* 1981, vii, 368p. pbk. £9.50. ISBN 0902119303. Updates material to 31 December 1978 as reported by contributing libraries. List of repositories p.vii. *Class No:* 942.23(01)

[7116]

—BERGESS, W. Kent maps and plans in the libraries of Kent and the adjoining London Boroughs: a finding list. London, Library Association London and Home Counties Branch, 1992. viii,386p. indexes. £30. ISBN: 0902119346.

'Inevitably it suffers from the shortcomings of the catalogues from which information was abstracted [but] ... a very welcome addition to the field of local studies aids' (*Library Association Record*). *Class No:* 942.23(01)

[7117]

Bibliotheca Cantiana or antiquarian Kentish books. Volume 1. Being an account of the published material, books, acts of parliament, maps and ephemera, relating to the County of Kent up to the year 1836. Chatham, Kent, John Hallewell Publications, 1980. 360p. index. ISBN: 0905540220.

Reprinted from the original edition of John Russell-Smith 1836.

Volumes covering the years 1836-1900 were reported to be in preparation. *Class No:* 942.23(01)

Archives

[7118]

KENT COUNTY COUNCIL. County Archives Committee. **Guide to the Kent County Archives Office** by Felix Hull. Maidstone, Kent County Council, 1958. First Supplement 1957-1968, 1971. Second Supplement 1969-1980, 1983. xvi,

....(contd.)

290p. viii, 236p. vii, 232p. illus. ISBN: 0905155467, Second Supplement.

The 1958 Guide is a detailed calendar of official and private (deposited) archives received up to 1956. The Second Supplement has 7 parts: 1. Designated public records - 2. Nationalized industries - 3. Official county and other official deposited records - 4. Parish records - 5. Ecclesiastical and other society archives - 6. Unofficial deposited archives - 7. South East Kent Branch in Folkestone Central Library. *Class No:* 942.23(093.20)

Sussex

[7119]

HORSFIELD, T.W. The History, antiquities and topography of the county of Sussex. Lewes, Sussex Press, 2v., 1835. (Reprinted Dorking, Kohler & Coombes, 1974). £50. ISBN: 0903967200. *Class No:* 942.25

[7120]

The Victoria history of the county of Sussex. London, Constable and Oxford Univ. Press for the Institute of Historical Research, 1905-. V.1-4, 6 (pts.1-3), 7, 9 and Index v.1-4, 7 and 9 (1905-1987). £60, £60, £25, £30, £50, £50, £50, £40, £40, £25. ISBN: 0712905855, v.1; 0712905863, v.2; 0712905871, v.3; 071290588x, v.4; 0197227538, v.6 pt.2; 0197227678, v.6 pt.2; 0197227686, v.6 pt.3; 0712905898, v.7; 0712905901, v.9; 019722766x, Index.

The various aspects of the county's history and antiquities are surveyed in v.1-3. The topographical survey is commenced in v.3 and continues in the subsequent volumes. *Class No:* 942.25

Bibliographies

[7121]

HOLLINGDALE, E.A., *comp.* **Sussex bibliography.** Lewes, East Sussex County Library, 1970-. pbk.

1975-76 (1978) £0.50. ISBN 0861470273. *1977* (1978) £0.40. 0900348623. *1978* (1979) £0.50. 0900348801. *1979* (1980) £0.60. 0900348879. Very useful bibliography. A sad loss if deceased. *Class No:* 942.25(01)

[7122]

LESLIE, K.C. *and* **McCANN, T.J. Local history in West Sussex** a guide to sources. 2nd rev. ed. Chichester, West Sussex County Council, 1975. v, 61p. illus. ISBN: 0900801379.

1st ed. 1971.

3 main parts: 1. Printed sources - 2. Pictorial and oral sources - 3. Documentary sources. *Class No:* 942.25(01)

Maps & Atlases

[7123]

STEER, F.W., *ed.* **A Catalogue of Sussex maps.** Lewes, Sussex Record Society, 2v., 1962-68. indexes.

1. *Estate and title award maps.* zxvi,240p. £5.00. ISBN 0900801077. 2. *Private estate maps.* vi,228p. About 2000 briefly annotated entries. *Class No:* 942.25(084.3)

Hampshire

[7124]

TURLEY, R.V., *ed.* **Hampshire and Isle of Wight bibliographies** selected nineteenth century sources. Winchester, Barry Sherlock, 1975. xxviii, 432p. illus., facsims., maps. ISBN: 0903330180.

A selection of important sources - Cope (1879), Gilbert & Godwin (1891), with Wilson suppt. (1896/97) and Davis suppt, (1904/5); Smith (1878), plus Hampshire sections of Upcott (1818); Holton (1863) and Anderson (1881). Detailed, partly analytical index, p.391-427. Provenance of reprinted bibliography, p.428. Map of place-names. *Class No:* 942.27

[7125]

The Victoria history of Hampshire and the Isle of Wight. London, Constable, 1900-14. 5v. and index. Reprinted Dawsons. illus., maps. £60, £60, £60, £70, £70, £15. ISBN: 071290591x, v.1; 0712905928, v.2; 071290593, v.3; 071290594, v.4; 071290595, v.5; 0712905960, Index.

V.1 covers the county's archaeology, natural history, and Domesday survey. Religious history, education, and forestry are in v.2 which also commences the topography, concluded in v.5, along with the economic and general history of the region. Complete. *Class No:* 942.27

Isle of Wight

[7126]

WORSLEY, R. The History of the Isle of Wight. Simmons, J., *ed.* Ardsley, East Yorkshire, EP Publications Ltd., 1975. xviii, 274, 19, clxiiip. illus. (pl.), coats of arms, geneal. tables, maps. ISBN: 0715810936.

First published London, A. Hamilton, 1781.

Standard antiquarian county history and topography. *Class No:* 942.28

Bibliographies

[7127]

PARKER, A.G. Isle of Wight a guide to sources. Newport, Isle of Wight Teachers' Centre, 1975. ix,235p. Mimeographed.

About 3,000 entries,some annotated. Sections: Local history. General works - General sources of information (national; local) - Geology and geography - Topography ... Sociology and economics - Technology. Industry Communications - Local administration - Biography. Personal names. Genealogy. Heraldry- Isle of Wight local history - Customs. Folklore. Arts and architecture - Language and books - Ecclesiastical history. Index to Isle of Wight place-names. *Class No:* 942.28(01)

Berkshire

[7128]

The Victoria history of Berkshire. London, Constable and St. Catherine's Press, 1906-1927. 4v. and index. Reprinted London, Dawsons Pall Mall, 1972. illus., maps. £50, £40, £60, £60, £15. ISBN: 0712905278, v.1; 0712905286, v.2; 0712905294, v.3; 0712905308, v.4; 0712905316, Index.

V.1-2 are devoted to the introductory chapters on history and economic and social history. V.3-4 comprise the topographical survey. Complete. *Class No:* 942.29

Wiltshire

[7129]

The Victoria history of the county of Wiltshire. London, Oxford Univ. Press for the Institute of Historical Research, 1953-. Some volumes reprinted by Dawson. illus., maps. V.1(pt.2) £40; v.6 £50; v.7 £50; v.8 £40; v.9 £40; v.10 £40; v.11 £60; v.12 £60; v.13 £60.v.14 £60. ISBN: 019722735x, v.1 pt.2; 0712910328, v.6; 0712910360, v.7; 0197227104, v.8; 0197227368, v.9; 0197227406, v.10; 0197227511, v.11; 0197227597, v.12; 0197227694, v.13; 0197227791, v.14.

V.1 (pt.1) is largely an archaeological gazetteer; pt.2 covers archaeology and prehistory. V.2 is devoted to the Anglo-Saxon period and the Wiltshire Domesday which is treated in detail. V.3 covers ecclesiastical history. V.4 includes agriculture, industries, transport, forests, and sport. V.5-6 cover political history (*i.e.* city government from 1066 onwards and parliamentary representation) whilst v.7-14 are topographical. *Class No:* 942.31

Dorset

[7130]

HUTCHINS, J. The History and antiquities of the county of Dorset. Simmons, J., *ed.* 3rd ed. by W. Shipp and J. W. Hodson. East Ardsley, Yorkshire. EP Publishing Ltd., 4v. 1973. ISBN: 0854099743, set 0854098542, v.1. 0854098550, v.2. 0854098569, v.3.

1st ed. 1774. 3rd ed. first published Westminster, J.B.Nichols, 1861-74.

The classic history of Dorset. The 3rd. ed. is a fine example of detailed topography. The introductory chapters cover the history, natural history and general topography of the county. The description of individual places follows, by Hundreds. The fourth volume has indexes of persons and places. Published in collaboration with Dorset County Library. *Class No:* 942.33

[7131]

The Victoria history of the county of Dorset. London, Constable, 1908-. Reprinted Dawsons. illus., maps. £50, £25. ISBN: 0712906703, v.2; 019722718x, v.3.

V.2 covers the economic, political, religious and social history whilst v.3 contains a translation of the Dorset Domesday and Geld Rolls, plus commentary articles. *Class No:* 942.33

Channel Islands

[7132]

HOCART, R. 'Guernsey: local history in an insular context', *Local Historian,* v.21, no.2, February 1991, p.20-3.

Running narrative review of sources for local history including the holdings of the Priaulx Library, the Island's Archive Service and the Société Guernesiaise. Major standard histories of Guernsey are also noted. *Class No:* 942.34

[7133]

MARR, L.J. A History of the Bailiwick of Guernsey the islanders' story. Chichester, Sussex, Phillimore, 1982. xvi,301p. illus. (pl.+col.pl.), maps on endpapers, bibliog., index. £15.00. ISBN: 0850334594.

67 short chapters deal with the religious, feudal, political, naval and military, and the social and economic aspects of

....(contd.)

Guernsey history. 18 appendices including lists of Lords of the Isles, Wardens and sub-wardens, Governors and Lieutenant Governors. Chronological table p.285-93. Bibliography p.xv-xvi. *Class No:* 942.34

[7134]

SYVRET, M. *and* **STEVENS, J. Balleine's history of Jersey.** Rev. & enl. ed. Chichester, Sussex, Phillimore for La Société Jersiaise, 1981. xiv,306p. maps on endpapers. bibliog., index. £25.00. ISBN: 0850334136.

G.R. Balleine's *History of Jersey* first published 1950.

33 chronological chapters. Bibliography p.xiii-xiv. Sources (*i.e.,* chapter notes) p.279-295. 34 plates (12 col.). 2 maps. *Class No:* 942.34

Devonshire

[7135]

POLWHELE, R. The History of Devonshire. Dorking, Surrey, Kohler & Coombes, 3v., 1977. ISBN: 0903967049.

First published Exeter, Cadell, 1797-1806.

Standard history of the antiquarian type. *Class No:* 942.35

[7136]

The Victoria history of the County of Devon. London, Constable, 1906. v.1 only. Reprinted Dawson. illus., map. £65.00. ISBN: 0712906711.

This single volume comprises the archaeology, natural history, and feudal survey of the county. *Class No:* 942.35

Bibliographies

[7137]

HAMILTON-LEGGATT, P. The Dartmoor bibliography 1534-1991 including a 1992 supplement. Non fiction. Tiverton and Exeter, Devon Books in association with The Dartmoor National Park Authority, 1992. xii,367p. index. £25. ISBN: 0861148738.

Unannotated entries arranged by form: 1. Books, pamphlets & leaflets - 2. Articles. Appendix 1. Directories - 2. Theses - 3. Maps - 4. Local journals and magazines - 5. Local newspapers. Alphabetico-classified index p.277-359. Previous bibliographies p.viii. *Class No:* 942.35(01)

Cornwall

[7138]

POLSUE, J. Lake's parochial history of the County of Cornwall. Wakefield, West Yorkshire, E.P. Publishing Ltd. in collaboration with Cornwall County Library, 4v., 1974. illus., geneal tables. (*Classical County Histories.*) ISBN: 085409539x, set.

First published Truro, W. Lake, 4v., 1867-73.

1. xix,x,412p. ISBN 0715810332 2. ix,411p. ISBN 0715810340. 3. vi,416p., ISBN 0715810359. 4. vii,352+167, xip. A-Z parochial histories with emphasis on genealogy, heraldry, manors, and antiquities. V.4 has supplementary papers. *Class No:* 942.37

[7139]

POLWHELE, R. History of Cornwall civil, military, religious, architectural, agricultural, commercial, biographical and miscellaneous. Simmons, J., *ed*. Dorking, Surrey, Kohler & Coombes, 3v., 1978. ISBN: 0903967111, set.

First published Falmouth, Cadell & Davies, 5v., 1803-06. *Class No:* 942.37

[7140]

The Victoria history of the county of Cornwall. London, Constable and St. Catherine's Press, 1902-24, v.1 and 2 (pts. 5 and 8) only. £75.00. ISBN: 071290672x.

V.1 Zoology and archaeology; pts. 5 and 8 of v.2 cover Romano-British antiquities and the Domesday survey respectively. *Class No:* 942.37

Scilly Isles

[7141]

BOWLEY, R.L. The Fortunate islands the story of the Isles of Scilly. 8th ed. rev. and enl. St. Mary's, Bowley Publications, 1990. 224p. illus., map, bibliog., index. ISBN: 0900184280.

1st ed. by E.L. Bowley 1945; 7th ed. 1980.

Chronological and thematic history in 12 chapters: 1. Antiquity - 2. Lyonesse and King Arthur - 3. Romans, Saxons, and Vikings ... 9. Wrecks, lighthouses and lifeboats. Appendix 1. Place names and dialect - 2. Population and area - 3. Isles of Scilly (list) - 4. Governors - 5. Chronological survey p.194-9. Bibliography p.200-22. *Class No:* 942.371

Somerset

[7142]

COLLINSON, J. *and* RACK, E. The History and antiquities of the county of Somerset ... Gloucester, Alan Sutton, 1983. illus., map. ISBN: 0862990033.

First published Bath, Cruttwell, 3v., 1791.

The standard survey of this county. V.1 has a general introduction which is followed by descriptions of the individual places, by Hundreds. Each volume has a place index. A brief, general index is included in v.3. A complete index, by F.W. Weaver and E.H. Bates, was published, by Barnicott and Pearce of Taunton in 1898. A *Supplement* was added in 1939 by Barnicotts, The Wessex Press. *Class No:* 942.38

[7143]

DUNNING, R.W. A History of Somerset. 2nd ed. Bridgewater, Somerset County Library, 1987. viii,108p. 24p.pl. illus.(some col.), maps, plan, bibliog., index. pbk. ISBN: 0861831284.

1st ed. 1978.

1. The Saxon founders - 2. Middle Ages - 3. Medieval church, the Reformation and a new order - 4. Expanding economy 1540-1700 - 5. Civil War and rebellion - 6. The revolutionary era 1700-1850 - 7. The county in the modern world. Epilogue. Bibliography p.99. *Class No:* 942.38

[7144]

The Victoria history of the county of Somerset. London, Constable and Oxford Univ. Press for the Institute of Historical Research, 5v., 1906-1985. V.1-3 reprinted by Dawsons Pall Mall. . £60, v.2 out of print; £40, £50, £50, £60. ISBN: 0197227805, v.6; 0712903755, v.1; 0197227392, v.3; 0197227473, v.4; 0197227643, v.5; 0197227805, v.6.

V.1-2 cover the archaeology, economic, natural and social history of Somerset. V.3-6 are topographical. *Class No:* 942.38

Gloucestershire

[7145]

ATKYNS, R. The Ancient and present state of Glostershire. Simmons, J., *ed*. 2nd ed. East Ardsley, Yorkshire, EP Publishing Ltd., 2v., 1974. ISBN: 0854098615.

2nd ed. first published London, W. Bowyer, 1712.

Well illustrated (v.1 *Plates*) county history and topography reprinted in collaboration with Gloucester County Library. *Class No:* 942.41

[7146]

BIGLAND, R. Historical, monumental and genealogical collections, relative to the county of Gloucester; printed from the original papers of the late Ralph Bigland, Esq., Garter Principal King of Arms. Frith, B., *ed*. Gloucester, Gloucester Record Society, 4v., 1989-1994. c 400p. each volume, illus., indexes. ISBN: 0900197285.

First published 1791-1899.

1. *Abbenhall-Cromhall*. County history arranged by parish. Material includes manorial descents, names of incumbents, tables of marriages, births and burials, and comments on markets and other features of the local economy. For some parishes there are geological and botanical essays. *Class No:* 942.41

[7147]

RUDDER, S. A New history of Gloucestershire. Dursley, Gloucestershire, Alan Sutton, 1977. ISBN: 0904387135. *Class No:* 942.41

[7148]

The Victoria history of the county of Gloucester. London, Constable and Oxford Univ. Press for the Institute of Historical Research. 1907-. v.2, 4, 6-8, 10-11. illus., maps. £50, £60, v.6 out of print; £50, £40, £40, £40. ISBN: 0712905553, v.2; 0197227716, v.4; 0197227554, v.7; 0197227244, v.8; 0197227252, v.10; 0197227457, v.11.

V.2 covers the ecclesiastical, economic, industrial and sporting history of the county. V.4 recounts the history of the city of Gloucester whilst v. 6-8, 10-11, are topographical surveys. V.1 is in active preparation. *Class No:* 942.41

Handbooks & Manuals

[7149]

Avon local history handbook. Moore, J.S., *ed*. Chichester, Sussex, Phillimore for Avon Local History Association, 1979. xi, 188p. bibliogs., index. ISBN: 0850333180.

13 contributors. 12 chapters on approach, methodology and use of sources *e.g.* 6. Industry ... 8. Local administration and politics. Bibliography: Books and articles p.102-142; Primary sources p.143-75. *Class No:* 942.41(035)

Maps & Atlases

[7150]

AVON COUNTY COUNCIL. A Catalogue of historic maps in Avon. Bristol, County of Avon Public Relations and Publicity Department, nd. 98p. ISBN: 08603632261.

Entries arranged first by district, then modern parish, and finally in chronological order. *Class No:* 942.41(084.3)

Monmouthshire

[7151]

BRADNEY, J.A. A History of Monmouthshire from the coming of the Normans down to the present time. London, Mitchell, Hughes and Clarke, 4v. in 12, 1906-1933.

Arranged according to Hundreds. *Class No:* 942.43

Maps & Atlases

Bibliographies

[7152]

Mapping of Monmouthshire: a descriptive catalogue of pre-Victorian maps of the county (now Gwent) from Saxton in 1577, with details of British atlases published during that period. Bristol, Regional Publications, 1985. £10.95. ISBN: 0906570182. *Class No:* 942.43(084.3)(01)

Herefordshire

[7153]

DUNCUMB, J. Collections towards the history and antiquities of the county of Hereford. Hereford, Wright; London, John Murray; Hereford, Jakeman & Carver, 7v., 1804-1915. illus. (pl.) map.

Duncumb's first volume gives a general description and history of the county. He then commenced a survey, by Hundreds. This series was added to by his successors. *Class No:* 942.44

[7154]

The Victoria history of the county of Hereford. London, Constable, 1908. v.1 only. Reprinted Dawson. illus., map. £50. ISBN: 071290669x.

This single volume covers natural history, archaeology, the Domesday survey, political history and agriculture. Complete. *Class No:* 942.44

Shropshire

[7155]

ANDERSON, J.C. Shropshire: its early history and antiquities ... Didsbury, Manchester, E.J. Morten, 1972. viii, 491p. ISBN: 0901598461.

First published London, Wills and Sotheran, 1864. Arranged A-Z by Hundreds. *Class No:* 942.45

[7156]

The Victoria history of Shropshire. London, Constable and Oxford Univ. Press for the Institute of Historical Research, 1908-. v.1-4, 8, 11. illus., maps. £40, £40, £50, £60, £40, £50. ISBN: 0712903070, v.1; 0197227295, v.2; 0197227309, v.3; 0197227759, v.4; 0197227317, v.8; 0197227635, v.11.

V.1 embraces the archaeology, Domesday survey, industries and natural history of the county. V.2 includes an index of the Shropshire Domesday in v.1 plus a general

.... (contd.)

index to v.1-2. V.3 encompasses county government, parliamentary representation; officers, seals and arms. V.4 is taken up with agriculture and v.8-11 are topographical. *Class No:* 942.45

Staffordshire

[7157]

PLOT, R. The Natural history of Stafford-Shire. Didsbury, Manchester, E.J. Morten, 1973. ISBN: 0901598658.

First published at The Theatre, Oxford, 1686.

One of the earliest county histories. *Class No:* 942.46

[7158]

The Victoria history of the County of Stafford. London, Constable and Oxford Univ. Press for the Institute of Historical Research, 1908-. v.1-6, 8, 17 and 20. illus., maps. £50, £40, £40, £50, £50, £50, v.8 out of print, £40, £60. ISBN: 0712903089, v.1; 0197227155, v.2; 0197227325, v.3; 0712910387, v.4; 0712910395, v.5; 0197227333, v.6; 0197227783, v.14; 0197227430, v.17; 0197227651, v.20.

V.1 covers the county's natural history, archaeology and history. V.2 is mainly concerned with industrial history and v.3 with religious aspects. V.6 is devoted to agriculture and school histories and v.8 to the city of Stoke on Trent and the Borough of Newcastle under Lyme. V.4-5 and 20 are topographical. *Class No:* 942.46

Biographies

[7159]

STUART, D., *ed.* **People of the Potteries** a dictionary of local biography. Keele, Staffordshire, Department of Adult Education, Univ. of Keele, v.1., 1985. viii,9-250p. ISBN: 0903160234.

600 brief biographies of persons living in the 6 towns now comprising Stoke upon Trent 1760-1910 (Arnold Bennett 50 lines and 3 references). Appendix: The people of the Potteries and the struggle for Federation p.239-50. *Class No:* 942.46(092)

Worcestershire

[7160]

The Victoria history of the county of Worcester. London, Constable and St. Catherine's Press, 1901-1926, 4v. and index. Reprinted Dawsons Pall Mall. illus., maps. £40, £50, v.3 out of print, £70, £15. ISBN: 0712904794, v.1; 0712904808, v.2; 0712904824, v.4; 0712904840, Index.

The county's archaeology, Domesday survey and natural history are covered in v.1. V.2 deals with ecclesiastical and political history and begins the topography. V.4 concludes this last and also has chapters on economic and social history. *Class No:* 942.47

Warwickshire

[7161]

The Victoria history of the county of Warwick. London, Constable and Oxford Univ. Press for the Institute of Historical Research, 1904-69. 8v. and index. illus., maps. v.7 £40, v.8 £40. ISBN: 0197227082, v.7; 0197227341, v.8.

....(contd.)

Archaeology, natural history and the Domesday survey are in v.1. V.2 comprises the economic, political, religious and social history of the county. The remaining volumes are topographical. V.7 deals with the growth of Birmingham and v.8 with the story of Coventry and Warwick. Complete. *Class No:* 942.48

Bibliographies

[7162]

LANE, J., *comp.* **Warwickshire local history sources.** Leamington Spa, History Sources, 1988. 112p. illus., maps, facsims., plans. pbk. ISBN: 095130500x.

1. Records and record offices in Warwickshire - 2. Apprenticeship and child labour - 3. Education - 4. Enclosure of Butlers Marston - 5. Friendly societies - 6. Medicine - 7. Old and new Poor Law - 8. Prisons - 9. Transport - 10. Urban and rural unrest - 11. Newspapers and directories - 12. Research notes. Poorly reproduced from typescript. *Class No:* 942.48(01)

Handbooks & Manuals

[7163]

BLIZZARD, A. *and* BAIRD, P. **Five ways into Birmingham's past.** Birmingham, Citypack Ltd., 1989. 60p. illus., facsims., bibliog., index. sd. ISBN: 1871837006.

5 sections each showing a different approach to Birmingham's local history. Reading; Visual; House; Family; and Oral plus methods of research, resources, and lists of Birmingham branch libraries, museums, and county record offices. Glossary p.5-9. *Class No:* 942.48(035)

Derbyshire

[7164]

The Victoria history of the county of Derby. London, Constable, 1905-07. 2v. Reprinted Dawson. illus., maps. £50, £50. ISBN: 0712904468, v.1; 0712904476, v.2.

These 2v. contain the natural history, archaeology, the Domesday survey, economic and political history, and ecclesiastical foundations of Derbyshire. There are no topographical volumes. *Class No:* 942.51

Maps & Atlases

Bibliographies

[7165]

NICHOLS, H. **Local maps of Derbyshire to 1770:** an inventory and introduction. Matlock, Derbyshire Library Service, 1980. xxi, 183p. bibliog., index. pbk. ISBN: 0903463091.

379 descriptive entries arranged A-Z by parish, urban district council or borough. Glossary p.172-5. Bibliography p.180-3. Index of surveyors p.176-9. *Class No:* 942.51(084.3)(01)

Nottinghamshire

[7166]

THOROTON, R. **History of Nottinghamshire.** Simmons, J., *ed.* 3rd ed. enlarged by J. Throsby. East Ardsley, Yorkshire, EP Publishing Ltd., 3v., 1972. ISBN: 0854097457, v.1; 0854097554, v.2; 0854097562, v.3. 3rd ed. published London, J. Throsby, 1797.

The standard account of Nottinghamshire. Thoroton's work was originally published in 1677. V.3 contains an index to the earlier volumes. Published in collaboration with Nottinghamshire County Library. *Class No:* 942.52

[7167]

The Victoria history of the county of Nottingham. London, Constable, 1906-10. v.1-2 only: Reprinted Dawson. illus., maps. £50, £50. ISBN: 0712904530, v.1; 0712904549, v.2.

These 2v. contain the introductory chapters on the various aspects of the county's economy and history. *Class No:* 942.52

Bibliographies

[7168]

DOBBIN, M., *comp.* **Nottinghamshire history and topography:** a select descriptive bibliography to 1980. 21 Mapperley Hall Drive, Nottingham, the compiler, 1983. ISBN: 0950862908.

533 items arranged chronologically for Nottinghamshire then for individual places A-Z. Literature, periodicals, poll books, biography and family history excluded. Author and subject indexes. No pagination. *Class No:* 942.52(01)

Maps & Atlases

[7169]

NICHOLS, H. **Local maps of Nottinghamshire to 1800:** an inventory. Nottingham, Nottinghamshire County Council Leisure Services. xii,162p. ISBN: 0900943068.

Data: date; scale; O.S. coordinates; brief description; and location. 'A very useful research tool for local historians' (*The Cartographical Journal,* v.25,no.2, December 1988, p.182). *Class No:* 942.52(084.3)

Archives

[7170]

KENNEDY, P.A. **Guide to the Nottinghamshire County Records Office.** Nottingham, Nottinghamshire County Council, 1960. xii, 180p. illus., facsims, maps, indexes.

A detailed list of the public and private records in the custody of the Nottinghamshire County Council and Diocesan Record Office. Three sections: 1. Official records of the County Council (p.1-39) - 2. Ecclesiastical records (p.40-92) - 3. Private deposits (p.93-152). *Class No:* 942.52(093.20)

Lincolnshire

[7171]

History of Lincolnshire. Thirsk, J., *(later Barley, M.),* eds. Lincoln, Society for Lincolnshire History and Archaeology. 1970-. illus., maps, bibliog., index.

1. *Prehistoric Lincolnshire* by J. May. 1977. xix, 251p. ISBN 0902668005. 2. *Roman Lincolnshire* by J.B. Whitwell. 1970. xxv, 155p. 0902668013. 3. *Anglo-Saxon Lincolnshire*

.... *(contd.)*

by D.A. Bullough. 4. *Land and people in medieval Lincolnshire* by G. Platts. 1985. xx, 340p. 090266803x. 5. *Church and society in medieval Lincolnshire* by D.M. Owen. 1971. xxii, 170p. 0902668048. 6. *Tudor Lincolnshire* by G.A.J. Hodgett. 1975. xvii, 212p. 0902668056. 7. *Seventeenth-century Lincolnshire* by C. Holmes. 1980. xv, 279p. 0902668064. 8. *The agricultural revolution in Lincolnshire* by T. H. Beastall. 1978. xii, 256p. 0902668072. 9. *The church and dissent in Lincolnshire* by M.R. Watts. 10. *Rural society and county government in nineteenth-century Lincolnshire* by R.J. Olney. 1979. xiv, 202p. 0902668099. 11. *Lincolnshire towns and industries 1700-1914.* 1982. xvi, 300p. 0902668102. 12. *Twentieth-century Lincolnshire* ed. by D.R. Mills. 1989. xvi, 401p. 0902669145 has 12-footnoted chapters, a bibliography (p.373-401) and an index. *Class No:* 942.53

[7172]

The Victoria history of the county of Lincoln. London, Constable, 1906. illus., maps. £65. ISBN: 071291045x.

Only v.2 has appeared. It concerns the ecclesiastical, economic, social and political history of the county. *Class No:* 942.53

Bibliographies

[7173]

SHORT, D.M., *comp*. **A Bibliography of printed items relating to the city of Lincoln.** Woodbridge, Suffolk, The Boydell Press for The Lincoln Record Society, 1990. xx, 540p. port. index. £19.95. (*The Lincoln Record Society, vol. 79.*) ISBN: 0901503525. ISSN: 02672634.

Based on Com's *Bibliotheca Lincolniensis* (1904).

4931 entries in 27 major (subdivided) sections: 1. Bibliography - 2. Natural history - 3. History - 4. Topography ... 15. Libraries - 16. Archives ... 23. Biographical - 24. Directories - 25. Almanacs. *Class No:* 942.53(01)

Leicestershire

[7174]

NICHOLS, J. **The History and antiquities of the county of Leicester.** Simmons, J., *ed.* East Ardsley, Yorkshire, EP Publishing, 4v. in 8, 1972. ISBN: 0854096868, v.1(1); 0854096876, v.1(2); 0854096884, v.2(1); 0854096892, v.2(2); 0854096906, v.3(1); 0854096914, v.3(2); 0854096922, v.4(1); 0854096930, v.4(2).

First published London, J. Nichols, 1795-1811.

The standard, and most detailed work on Leicestershire. The county's general history and topography are contained in v.1. In the other volumes the individual places are described under their respective Hundreds. Reprinted in collaboration with Leicestershire County Library. *Class No:* 942.542

[7175]

The Victoria history of the county of Leicester. London, Constable, St. Catherine's Press, and Oxford Univ. Press for the Institute of Historical Research, 1907-. 5v. V.1-3 reprinted by Dawsons. illus., maps. V.1 out of print, £40, £40, £70, v.5 out of print. ISBN: 0712903682, v.2; 0712903690, v.3; 0712910441, v.4.

V.1 comprises natural history, archaeology, ecclesiastical history, and the Domesday survey. Religious, political, and

.... *(contd.)*

agrarian history are covered in v.2 whilst v.3 deals with industries, transport, population, education, and sport. V.4 is devoted to the city of Leicester and v.5 begins the county topographical sequence. *Class No:* 942.542

Maps & Atlases

[7176]

STRACHAN, A.J. **Atlas of Leicestershire.** 2nd ed. Leicester, Univ. of Leicester Community and Employment Research Unit, 1986. 71p. maps, diagr. ringbinder. £3.50.

1st ed. 1985.

71 maps showing administrative boundaries, historical setting, population, agriculture, contemporary statistics, nature reserves, Leicester, and county towns. For home, school and college use. *Class No:* 942.542(084.3)

Rutland

[7177]

The Victoria history of the county of Rutland. London, Constable, St. Catherine's Press and Oxford Univ. Press for the Institute of Historical Research, 1908-36, 2v. and index. illus., maps. £40, £40, £5.00. ISBN: 0712906614, v.1; 0712906622, v.2; 0197226612, Index.

Complete. V.1 covers natural history, archaeology, the Domesday survey, and various aspects of economic and social history. V.2 is purely topographical. *Class No:* 942.545

[7178]

WRIGHT, J. **The History and antiquities of the county of Rutland.** Simmons, J., *ed.* East Ardsley, Yorkshire, EP Publishing Ltd., 1973. ISBN: 0854098534.

First published 1684.

Includes James Wright's additions of 1687 and 1714 and Harrods additions 1785-90. *Class No:* 942.545

Northamptonshire

[7179]

The Victoria history of the county of Northampton. London, Constable, St. Catherine's Press, and Oxford Univ. Press for the Institute of Historical Research, 1902-37, v.1-4 only. Reprinted Dawson. illus., maps. £50, £70, £40, £40. ISBN: 0712904492, v.1; 0712904506, v.2; 0712904514, v.3; 0712904522, v.4.

The general chapters on antiquities, natural and social history are contained in v.1-2. The topographical survey commences in v.2. A genealogical volume was issued in 1906. *Class No:* 942.55

Huntingdonshire

[7180]

The Victoria history of the county of Huntingdonshire. London, St. Catherine Press and Institute of Historical Research, 3v. and index, 1926-1938.

The natural history, antiquities and religious history comprise v.1 whilst v.2 surveys the general and economic history of the county. The topographical chapters begin in v.2 and are concluded in v.3. *Class No:* 942.562

Maps & Atlases

[7181]

DICKINSON, P.G.M., *comp*. **Maps in the County Record Office, Huntingdon.** St. Ives, Imray, Lawrie, Norrie & Wilson, 1968. viii, 72p. map.

Maps of Huntingdonshire (county maps; parish maps - Miscellaneous maps) provincial; county; naval charts and plans; transport and communications maps; drainage; foreign; etc. Appendix A & B (B: list of Huntingdonshire maps in the Nottinghamshire Record Office). Index of cartographers. *Class No:* 942.562(084.3)

Bedfordshire

[7182]

The Victoria history of the county of Bedford. London, Constable, 1904-14. 3v. and index. Reprinted by Dawsons Pall Mall. illus., maps. £50, £50, £50, £15. ISBN: 0712905324, v.1; 9712905332, v.2; 0712905340, v.3; 0712905359, Index.

Complete. V.1 comprises natural history, archaeology, the Domesday survey, and ecclesiastical history and foundations. In v.2 is a review of the political, economic and agrarian history, and accounts of schools and sport. The topographical chapters, with emphasis on churches and manors, begin in v.2 and conclude in v.3.
Class No: 942.565

Bibliographies

[7183]

CONISBEE, L.R. **A Bedfordshire bibliography** with some comments and biographical notes. Luton, Bedfordshire Historical Record Society, 1962. 333p.

About 6,000 items with locations in 17 libraries.

Three main sections: A. The county (subjects, A-Z) - B. Places (Bedford; Dunstable; Luton; other towns and villages) - C. Persons. Omits all manuscripts, since the *Guide to the Bedfordshire Record Office* contains a catalogue of its documents, official and unofficial archives, and a list of its local manuscript map collections.
Supplements 1967. 128p. £3.50. ISBN 0851550274. *1971.* 85p. £3.50. 0851550282. *1977.* 86p. 0851550398.
Class No: 942.565(01)

Maps & Atlases

[7184]

CHAMBERS, B. **Printed maps and town plans of Bedfordshire** 1576-1900. Bedford, Bedford Historical Record Society, 1983. 250p. illus., bibliog., index. (*Bedford Historical Record Society Publications, no.62.*) ISBN: 0851550444.

1. The mapping of Bedfordshire. Locations are given for most of the maps recorded. 2. Catalogue of county maps (p.27-206) and town plans (p.207-23). Bibliography p.25.
Class No: 942.565(084.3)

Oxfordshire

[7185]

The Victoria history of the county of Oxford. London, Constable and Oxford Univ. Press for the Institute of Historical Research, 1899-. V.1-. V.1, 9-10 reprinted by Dawsons. illus., maps. £60, £60, v.3 out of print, £50, £60,

....(contd.)
v.6-8 out of print, £40, £40, £60. ISBN: 0712904565, v.1; 0712910417, v.2; 0197227147, v.4; 0712910425, v.5; 0197227260, v.9; 0197227287, v.10; 0197227589, v.11; 0197227740, v.12.

Natural history, archaeology, the Domesday survey, political history, and education fill v.1. V.2 is devoted to religious history, industries and sport. The University takes up the whole of v.3 and v.4 is devoted to the city of Oxford. V.5-12 are occupied with the topographical survey. V.13 is in active preparation. *Class No:* 942.572

Bibliographies

[7186]

CORDEAUX, E.H. *and* MERRY, D.H. **A Bibliography of printed works relating to Oxfordshire** (excluding the University and City of Oxford). Oxford, Clarendon Press, 1955. xv,411p.

Also issued by the Oxford Historical Society (new series, v.11. 1977. £18). Considered a model of its kind. Locations of books not in the Bodleian Library are indicated. *Supplementary volume.* 1981. xxvii,289p. includes *addenda, corrigenda* and other relevant items.

A Bibliography of printed works relating to the City of Oxford. 1976,. xiv, 377p. is arranged under 17 main headings *e.g.* History and topography; Heraldry; Biography; Directories, surveys, handbooks and almanacs.
Class No: 942.572(01)

Encyclopaedias

[7187]

HIBBERT, C., *ed*. **The Encyclopaedia of Oxford.** London, Macmillan, 1988. xiii, 562p. illus., maps, bibliog., indexes. £30. ISBN: 033339917x.

100 contributors. 1020 unattributed, documented, cross-referenced entries on personages, places, buildings, institutions. 7 Appendices (Bishops; Mayors and Lord Mayors; MPs; Burgesses; Vice Chancellors; Chancellors; Presidents of the Union since 1900). Glossary p.533. Bibliography p.534-6. 250 drawings, prints and photographs. 'This book is the ideal point of reference for any information about Oxford' (*Reference Reviews*, v.3, no.2, June 1989, p.92). *Class No:* 942.572(031)

Buckinghamshire

[7188]

The Victoria history of the county of Buckingham. London, Constable and St. Catherine Press, 1905-28. 4v. and index. Reprinted Dawsons Pall Mall. illus., maps. £50, v.2 is out of print, £60, £60, £15. ISBN: 0712903704, v.1; 0712903720, v.3; 0712903739, v.4; 0712903747, Index.

V.1 covers the natural history, archaeology, ecclesiastical history, and the Domesday survey. V.2 deals with the economic and social history and initiates the topographical survey concluded in v.3-4. Complete. *Class No:* 942.575

Hertfordshire

[7189]

CHAUNCEY, H. The Historical antiquities of Hertfordshire ... Dorking, Surrey, Kohler & Coombes, 2v., 1975. xviii, xv, 592p.+613p. illus., map. ISBN: 0903967014.

First published London, Griffin, 1700. 2nd ed. Bishops Stortford, Griffin 1826.

Standard antiquarian account of history and topography of towns and villages. *Class No:* 942.58

[7190]

CUSSANS, J.E. History of Hertfordshire. Simmons, J., *ed.* East Ardsley, Yorkshire, EP Publishing, 3v., 1972. ISBN: 085409833x, v.1; 0854098348, v.2; 0854098356, v.3.

First published London, Stephen Austin 1870-1881.

Reprinted in collaboration with Hertfordshire County Library. *Class No:* 942.58

[7191]

The Victoria history of the county of Hertford. London, Constable and Oxford Univ. Press for the Institute of Historical Research, 1902-37. 4v. and index. Reprinted Dawsons Pall Mall. illus., maps. £50, £60, £60, £60, £15. ISBN: 0712904571, v.1; 0712904476x, v.2; 0712904778, v.3; 0712904786, v.4; 0712904832, Index.

The topographical survey is contained in v.2-4. Antiquities, history and natural history spread over v.1, 2 and 4. A genealogical volume was published in 1907. Complete. *Class No:* 942.58

Maps & Atlases

[7192]

HODSON, D. Printed maps of Hertfordshire. Folkestone, Dawson, 1975. 251 p. maps, index. ISBN: 0712906215.

First published London, Map Collectors Circle, 5 pts., 1969-72.

Parts: 1. 1577-1784(1969) - 2. 1785-1820 - 3. 1821-1860(1970) - 4. 1861 - 1885 (1971) - 5. 1886 - 1900, and supplement (1972). Detailed bibliographical descriptions; major locations (*e.g.* British Museum; RGS). Pt.5 concludes with a section on Ordnance Survey maps. 'This is as complete a catalogue as possible of the county maps of Hertfordshire printed before 1901' (*Introduction.* pt.1). *Class No:* 942.58(084.3)

Cambridgeshire

[7193]

The Victoria history of the county of Cambridgeshire and the Isle of Ely. London, Oxford, Univ. Press for the Institute of Historical Research, 1938-. V.1-9 and index v. 1-4. illus., maps. £50. £50, £60, £40, £40, £40, £25, £60, £69, £10. ISBN: 0712902414, v.1; 071290242, v.2; 0712902430, v.3; 0712802449, v.4; 0197227171, v.5; 0197227465, v.6; 0197227481, v.7; 0197227570, v.8; 0197227732, v.9; 0197226973 Index.

V.1 comprises natural history and the Domesday survey. Archaeology is completed in v.2 which also covers ecclesiastical, economic, political and social history. V.3 is devoted to the city, colleges and university and V.7 to Roman Cambridgeshire. V.4-6, 7-9 are topographical. *Class No:* 942.59

Norfolk

[7194]

The Victoria history of the county of Norfolk. London, Constable, 1901-06. v.1-2 only. Reprinted Dawson. illus., maps. £40, £70. ISBN: 0712906452, v.1; 0712906460, v.2.

This series has never been completed. V.1 covers the natural history and archaeology of the county. The Domesday survey, art, political and religious history are in v.2. *Class No:* 942.61

Bibliographies

[7195]

COLMAN, J.J. Bibliotheca Norfolciensis a catalogue of writings of Norfolk men and of works relating to the county of Norfolk, in the library of Mr. J.J. Colman, at Carrow Abbey, Norwich. Norwich, privately printed, 1896. viii, 592p. *Class No:* 942.61(01)

[7196]

DARROCH, E. *and* TAYLOR, B. A Bibliography of Norfolk history. Norwich, Univ. of East Anglia, 1975. xviii, 447p. £7.20. ISBN: 0902171097.

At head of title-page: 'Centre of East Anglian Studies'. 7,304 entries, unannotated. Sections (closely classified): Directories - Almanacks, annuals, handbooks - Newspapers - Geography - Guide books and descriptive works - History and archaeology - Politics and administration - Economic history - Religion - Culture and recreation - Art, architecture, monuments - Biography - Individual locations (including King's Lynn, Norwich, Yarmouth), p.196-422. *Class No:* 942.61(01)

Maps & Atlases

[7197]

CHUBB, T. Descriptive list of the printed maps of Norfolk, 1874-1916 with biographical notes and tabular index; and, A descriptive list of Norwich plans, 1541-1914, by G.P. Stephens. Norwich, Jarrold, 1928. xvi, 289p. *Class No:* 942.61(084.3)

Suffolk

[7198]

The Victoria history of the county of Suffolk. London, Constable, 1907-11. v.1-2 only. Reprinted Dawson. illus., maps. £70, £50. ISBN: 0712906479, v.1; 0712906487, v.2.

General review of the county's antiquities, economy, and general history. No topographical chapters. *Class No:* 942.64

Bibliographies

[7199]

STEWARD, A.V., *comp.* A Suffolk bibliography. Ipswich, Suffolk Records Society, v.20, 1979 (distributed by Boydell Press). xxiii,453p. ISBN: 0851151159.

8,123 numbered entries. Directories, almanacs, annuals, handbooks, newspapers and periodicals - Geography, landscape and climate - Guide books and descriptive works - General and political history - Economic history and communications - Local government, social services, and justice - Religion - Social history, culture and recreation - Architecture - Biography, genealogy, and heraldry -

....(contd.)

Individual and family biography, A-Z (nos.2057-3511) - Localities, Action ... Yoxford (nos.3512-3812), with subject subdivisions. Index of authors, editors, publishers, sponsors and titles (for anonyma). *Class No:* 942.64(01)

Maps & Atlases

[7200]

DYMOND, D. *and* **MARTIN, E.,** *eds*. **An Historical atlas of Suffolk.** 2nd ed. Ipswich, Suffolk County Council Planning Department and Suffolk Institute of Archaeology and History, 1989. 160p. illus., maps (some col.), bibliog., index. ISBN: 0860551539.

1st ed. 1988.

27 contributors. 62 double-page text and map features in 8 sections: 1. Physical setting - 2. Administrative units - 3. Early settlement - 4. Medieval Suffolk - 5. Suffolk since 1550 - 6. Industries - 7. Urban growth - 8. Vernacular architecture. Further information (*i.e.* sources and bibliography) p.136-54. *Class No:* 942.64(084.3)

Essex

[7201]

MORANT, P. History and antiquities of the county of Essex. Simmons, J., *ed.* East Ardsley, Yorkshire, EP Publishing Ltd., 2v., 1978. ISBN: 0715813013, set; 0715613021, v.1; 071581303x, v.2.

First published London, Osborne, 1768.

Reprinted in collaboration with Essex County Library. *Class No:* 942.67

[7202]

The Victoria history of the county of Essex. London, Constable and Oxford Univ. Press for the Institute of Historical Research, 1903-. v.1-8. *Bibliography* and *Bibliography: Supplement.* illus., maps. £75, £75, £60, £60, £40, £40, £50, £60, £40, £40. ISBN: 0712907742, v.1; 0712907750, v.2; 0712907769, v.3; 0712907777, v.4; 0197227120, v.5; 0197227198, v.6; 0197227201, v.7; 019727721x, v.8; 0197227708, Bibliog. Supplt.

V.1-2 contain natural history, archaeology, and general history. V.3 is limited to Roman Essex. V.4-8 are topographical. The *Bibliography* volume and *Supplement* have 3 pts: 1. The county (subdivided) - 2. Biography and family history - 3. Places and regions. *Class No:* 942.67

Cheshire

[7203]

A History of Cheshire. Bagley, J.J., *ed.* Chester, Cheshire Community Publications Trust, 1964-. v.1-. illus.

1. Cheshire before the Romans, by W.J. Varley. 1964 - 2. Roman Cheshire, by F.H. Thompson. 1965 - 3. Pre-conquest Cheshire 383-1066, by J.D. Bulock. 1972 - 4. Cheshire under the Norman earls, by B.M.C. Husain. 1973 - 5. Cheshire under the three Edwards, by H.J. Hewitt. 1967 - 6. Cheshire in the later Middle Ages, by J.T. Driver. 1971 - 7. Tudor Cheshire, by J. Beck, 1969 - 8. The Civil Wars in Cheshire, by R.N. Dore. 1966 - 9. Cheshire 1660-1780: Restoration to Industrial Revolution, by H. Hodson. 1978 - 10. Squire and tenant: rural life in Cheshire 1760-1900. *Class No:* 942.71

[7204]

ORMEROD, G. The History of the county palatine and city of Chester... 2nd ed. by T. Helsby. London, Routlege, 3v., 1882. illus. (pl.), maps.

The standard work on this county. V.1 deals with Chester and the Hundred of Buclow. The other volumes complete the survey, all places being arranged under the Hundreds. Most of the plates are engraved views. There are many pedigrees and tables of charities, clergy, and populations. V.3 contains an index of families and places. *Index and appendix.* Didsbury, Manchester, E.J. Morten, 1980, 350p. illus. ISBN 0859720438. *Class No:* 942.71

[7205]

The Victoria history of the county of Chester. London, Oxford Univ. Press for the Institute of Historical Research, 1979-. v.1-. v.1-3. illus., maps. £60, £50, £50. ISBN: 0197227619, v.1; 019722749x, v.2; 0197227546, v.3.

V.1 includes physique, prehistory, Romans, Anglo-Saxons and Domesday. Administrative history, parliamentary representation, forests and population are in v.2 and v.3 covers the general ecclesiastical history of the county (including Chester Cathedral and medieval religious houses). V.5 is in active preparation. *Class No:* 942.71

Bibliographies

[7206]

The History of the County Palatine of Chester a short bibliography and guide to sources. Walsh, A.C. *and* Allan, A.R., *comps.* Chester, Cheshire Community Council Publications Trust, 1983. 72p. sd.

3 sections: 1. Cheshire *i.e.* 29 A-Z categories (*e.g.* Archaeology - Bibliography - Chester histories) - 2. City of Chester - 3. Individual places in Cheshire A-Z. A few items are very briefly annotated. *Class No:* 942.71(01)

Archives

[7207]

KENNETT, A.M., *ed*. **Archives and records of the City of Chester.** Council of the City of Chester, 1985. 144p. index. ISBN: 0950833223.

1. Official records - 2. Public records - 3. Private records - 4. Access and facilities. *Class No:* 942.71(093.20)

Lancashire

[7208]

The Victoria history of the county of Lancaster. London, Constable, 1906-14. 8v. Reprinted Dawsons. illus., maps, indexes. out of print.

V.1 covers archaeology, the feudal survey, and natural history. Economic, political, religious and social history are in v.2. The remaining volumes are topographical. Complete. V.2: ISBN 0712910549 and V.5 ISBN 0712910557 reprinted 1991. £75 each. *Class No:* 942.72

Bibliographies

[7209]

FISHWICK, H. The Lancashire Library: a bibliographical account of books on topography, biography, history, science and miscellaneous literature relating to the County Palatine; including an account of Lancashire tracts, pamphlets and

....*(contd.)*

sermons printed before 1720 ... London, George Routledge; Warrington, Percival Pearse, 1875. xi, 443p.

Reprinted London, S.R. Publishers, 1969.

Class No: 942.72(01)

[7210]
HORROCKS, S., *ed.* **Contributions towards a Lancashire bibliography.** Manchester Joint Committee of the Lancashire Bibliography, 1968-.

1. *Lancashire directories 1684-1957.* 1968. vii, 78p. £1.50. 2. *Lancashire Acts of Parliament 1266-1957.* 1969. x, 350p. 3. *Lancashire business histories.* 1971. xii, 116p. 4. *Lancashire family histories pedigrees heraldry.* 1972. xi, 201p. 5. *Registers ... monumental inscriptions, names, wills.* 1973. xi, 162p. 6. *Lancashire history and topography. Historical periods Pre-Roman, Roman, Pre-Norman.* 1973. x, 130p. £1.50. 7. *Lancashire history. Historical periods; Norman, Plantagenet, Lancaster & York, Tudor.* 1974. x, 99p. £6.00. 8. *Lancashire history. Historical period: Stuart.* 1976. x, 122p. £1.50. 9. *Lancashire history. Historical period: Hanover.* 1978. xiv, 242p. £1.50. 10. Turner, P.R. comp. *Transport history. Railways.* 1981, xiv, 321p. £6.00. ISBN 0902217135. 11. *Manchester Ship Canal: a guide to historical sources,* edited by P. Hodson. 1985. £10.95. 0902217143. *Class No:* 942.72(01)

Yorkshire

[7211]
DRAKE, F. Eboracum or the history and antiquities of the City of York ... Simmons, J., *ed.* East Ardsley, Yorkshire, EP Publishing, 1978. ISBN: 0715813048.

First published, London, W. Bowyer, 1736.

Class No: 942.74

[7212]
HUNTER, J. South Yorkshire the history and topography of the Deanery of Doncaster in the Diocese and County of York. Simmons, J., *ed.* East Ardsley, Yorkshire, EP Publishing, 2v. 1974. ISBN: 0854095993, set; 0554095292, v.1; 0554095306, v.2.

First published London, J. B. Nichols, 1828.

Reprinted in collaboration with Sheffield City Library.

Class No: 942.74

[7213]
The Victoria history of the county of York. London, Constable, St. Catherine's Press, and Oxford Univ. Press for the Institute of Historical Research,1907-. illus., maps.

General series: 1. £60. ISBN 071296096; 2. £60. ISBN 071290610x; 3. £60. ISBN 0712906118; Index. 1925. £15. ISBN 0712906126. Complete. Introductory surveys for the whole county of the type normally to be found in the 1st two volumes of the Victoria histories.

East Riding: 1. *The city of Kingston-upon-Hull*, out of print; v.2-6 are topographical volumes. 2. £40. ISBN 0197227384; 3. £40. ISBN 0197227449; v.4 £50. 019722752x; v.5 £60. ISBN 0197227600; v.6 £60. ISBN 0197227767. V.7 is in active preparation. *North Riding* A complete topographical survey in 2v. Out of print. *Index* £70. ISBN 0712903119.

The city of York covers the history from Roman times to 1959 as well as particular institutions and aspects of the city. £70. ISBN 0712910298. *Class No:* 942.74

[7214]
Who's who 1992. The 1992 directory of senior figures across our circulation area. 2nd ed. York, York & County Press, 1992. 160p. ports. £2.50.

1350 thumbnail biographical sketches of those who 'through their careers, public service or voluntary work, affect the political, economic, scientific and artistic life of' North and East Yorkshire. *Class No:* 942.74

Bibliographies

[7215]
BOYNE, W. The Yorkshire library a bibliographical account of books on topography, tracts of the seventeenth century, biography, spaws, geology, botany, maps, views, portraits, and miscellaneous literature relating to the county ... Hull, N.T. Leslie, 1974. 304p. £6. ISBN: 085963020x.

Originally published London, Taylor, 1869.

Class No: 942.74(01)

Maps & Atlases

Bibliographies

[7216]
WHITAKER, H., *ed.* **A Descriptive list of the printed maps of Yorkshire and its Ridings, 1577-1900.** Leeds, Yorkshire Archaeological Society, 1971. 261p. illus.(pl.). £8.00. ISBN: 0902122088.

First published 1933.

This bibliography forms v.86, for 1933, of the Yorkshire Archaeological Society 'Record series'. The introduction gives a concise survey of the development of English cartography. The 706 items are chronologically arranged; detailed descriptive notes. Tabular index (name; date; title; dimensions; work in which map was issued; number); supplementary index of authors, engravers, printers and publishers. *Class No:* 942.74(084.3)(01)

Durham County

[7217]
SURTEES, R. The History and antiquities of the county palatine of Durham. Simmons, J., *ed.* East Ardsley, Yorkshire, EP Publishing Ltd., 4v., 1972. ISBN: 0854098143, v.1; 0854098151, v.2; 085409816x, v.3; 0854098178, V.4.

First published London, Nichols and Bentley, 1816-40.

The standard work on this county. A view of the general history of Durham precedes the excellent topographical survey to which the majority of the volumes are devoted. Pedigrees are given and the engraved plates are fine. Reprinted in collaboration with Durham County Library. *Class No:* 942.81

[7218]
The Victoria history of the county of Durham. London, Constable and St. Catherine's Press, 1905-28. v.1-3 only. Reprinted Dawson. illus., maps. £50 each volume. ISBN: 0712903046, v.1; 0712903054, v.2; 0712903062, v.3.

The general chapters on the various aspects of the county's history are in the first 2 volumes. V.3 is a topographical survey of the city of Durham. *Class No:* 942.81

Northumberland

[7219]
MARSDEN, J. **Northanhymbre saga** the history of the Anglo-Saxon kings of Northumbria. London, Kyle Cathie, 1992. 259p. illus., maps, geneal. table, bibliog. £18.99. ISBN: 1856260550.

History of Anglo-Saxon kingdom extending from the Humber to Firth of Forth c.547-764 based on Old English, Old Irish, Britonic-Welsh, and Latin documentary sources. Genealogies p.237-40. Chronology p.241-4. Bibliography p.245-50. 4 maps. *Class No: 942.82*

Bibliographies

[7220]
NORTHUMBERLAND LOCAL HISTORY SOCIETY. **Northumberland handlist of sources.** Newcastle, Northumberland Record Office, 1972.

1. *General* iv, 21p. 2. *Topography* vi, 21p. *Class No: 942.82(01)*

Cumberland

[7221]
HODGSON, H.W., *comp*. **A Bibliography of the history and topography of Cumberland.** Carlisle, Joint Archives Committee for Cumberland, Westmorland and Carlisle, Record Office, 1968. 301p. ISBN: 0950037109.

About 8-9,000 entries for authors, subjects A-Z. For 'Political, Social and Economic Historians. Geographers, Architectural Historians. Postgraduates, Students at Colleges of Education and even Schoolchildren' (*Foreword*). *Class No: 942.85*

[7222]
HUTCHINSON, W. **The History and antiquities of Cumberland and some places adjacent.** Simmons, J., *ed.* East Ardsley, Yorkshire, EP Publications Ltd, 2v., 1974. ISBN: 0854095403, set; 0715810650, v.1. 0715810669, v.2.

First published Carlisle, F. Jollie, 1794-97.

Reprinted with the collaboration of Cumberland County Library. *Class No: 942.85*

[7223]
The Victoria history of the county of Cumberland. London, Constable, 1901-05, V.1-2 only. Reprinted Dawson. illus., maps. £50, £60. ISBN: 071290302x, v.1; 0712903038, v.2.

V.1 contains archaeology, natural history, and Domesday survey. Ecclesiastical, economic, political, and sporting history are in v.2. There are no topographical chapters. *Class No: 942.85*

[7224]
Who's who in Cumbria 1986. 4th ed. Carlisle, Border Press, 1986. 59p. sd.

4th ed. of an annual publication.

Biographies of prominent people in the community or in a particular business or profession. Date: name, address, tel. no., education, career, offices, birth date, family, leisure interests. *Class No: 942.85*

Westmoreland

[7225]
NICOLSON, J. *and* BURN, R. **The History and antiquities of the counties of Westmorland and Cumberland.** Simmons, J., *ed.* East Ardsley, Yorkshire, EP Publications Ltd., 2v., 1976. ISBN: 0854096256, set; 0854096809, v.1; 0854096825, v.2.

First published London, L.W. Strachan and T. Cadell, 1777.

The most complete of the antiquarian histories of the two counties. Reprinted in cooperation with Cumbria County Library. *Class No: 942.88*

Isle of Man

[7226]
KINVIG, R.H. **The Isle of Man:** a social, cultural and political history. 3rd ed. Liverpool, Liverpool Univ. Press, 1975. xv,198p.

First published as *A history of the Isle of Man* (1944).

13 chapters 1. The physical and human background - 2. The prehistory of man - 3. The early Christian period, 450-800 ... 11. Fiscal and political reform in the nineteenth century - 12. The structure of the Manx economy - 13. Modern times. Glossary of words found in Manx place-names, p.177-82. Bibliography, p.183-90 (by chapters). Detailed index. 50 plates. *Class No: 942.89*

Bibliographies

[7227]
CUBBON, W., *comp*. **A Bibliographical account of works relating to the Isle of Man,** with biographical memoranda and copious literary references. London, Oxford Univ. Press for the Manx Museum and Ancient Monuments Trustees, 2v., 1933-39. illus. index.

Systematically arranged. V.2 includes annotated lists of Manx periodicals, newspapers, directories, *etc. Class No: 942.89(01)*

Wales

[7228]
DAVIES, J. **Hanes Cymru.** London, Allen Lane The Penguin Press, 1990. xiii,710p. maps, diagrs., bibliog., index. £30. ISBN: 0713990112.

Single-volume Welsh-language history of Wales. Comprehensive in scope and coverage. Bibliography p.xiii. *Class No: 942.9*

[7229]
The History of Wales. Oxford, Clarendon Press; Univ. of Wales Press, 6v., 1981-.

2. *Conquest, coexistence, and change: Wales 1063-1415* by R.R. Davies. 1987. £40.00. ISBN 0198217323. 3. *Recovery, reorientation, and reformation: Wales 1415-1642* by G. Williams. 1987. £40.00. 019888217331. 4. *The foundation of modern Wales 1642-1780* by G.H. Jenkins. 1988. £40.00. 0198217734x. 6. *Rebirth of a nation: Wales 1880-1980* by K.O. Morgan. 1981. £27.50. 0198217366. Major history of the Principality. *Class No: 942.9*

[7230]

HOWELL, R. **A History of Gwent.** Llandysul, Dyfed, Gomer, 1988. 226p. illus., map, index. £5.95. ISBN: 0863833381.

Concise overview history in 32 chronological and thematic chapters (*e.g.* Earliest inhabitants ... Roman Gwent ... Early industrialization ... Myth of Monmouthshire ... Modern Gwent) and 3 Appendices (Arthurian Gwent - Castles - Seasonal traditions). Chapter notes. *Class No:* 942.9

Bibliographies

[7231]

DAVIES, J. **'What to read on the history of Wales before 1536,'** *Local Historian*, v.17, no.5, February 1987, p.265-268 and 'What to read on the history of Wales since 1536', ibid, v.17, no.6, May 1987.

Literature surveys with consolidated lists of works mentioned A-Z by author. *Class No:* 942.9(01)

[7232]

JONES, P.H. **A Bibliography of the history of Wales.** Cardiff, University of Wales Press, 1989. Compiled for the History and Law Committee of the University of Wales Board of Celtic Studies. 75p. pbk. + 21 microfiche with a holder. £37.00. ISBN: 0708310370.

1st ed. 1931; 2nd ed. 1962 and 4 supplements 1962-1972.

Includes 22,000 items (5,400 in previous ed. and supplements). Now computerized so that it consists of 3 sets of microfiche (48 x reduction): main classified sequence, author-title index, and KWIC index to titles of records in the classified sequence. 'Without the help of the accompanying printed handbook both historians and librarians would have difficulty in getting to grips with the layout of various indexes. Indeed the handbook is essential, and provides a comprehensive and thorough guide to using the Bibliography and also, for those who are unacquainted with indexing methods, a good description of a Key Word in Context index... The editor has to be praised on the scope, accuracy detail and amount of material included'. (*Reference Reviews*, v.3, no.3, September 1989, p.137-8). *Class No:* 942.9(01)

[7233]

Welsh history and its sources. Herbert, T. *and* Jones, G.E., *eds.* Cardiff, Univ. of Wales Press, 6v., 1988. illus., maps, bibliog., index.

Publication of an Open University in Wales project funded by a Welsh Office Research Development grant 1985-1988. Each volume contains 5-7 topics of crucial importance comprising an essay cross-referenced in detail to the sources on which that essay is based, and a discussion of the strengths and weaknesses of the documentary material. Titles: 1. *Edward I and Wales.* xxxvi, 158p. £7.95. ISBN 0708310125. 2. *Tudor Wales.* xxvi, 177p. £7.95. ISBN 0708309712. 3. *The remaking of Wales in the eighteenth century.* xxvi, 192p. £7.95. ISBN 0708310133. 4. *People and protest: Wales 1815-1880.* xxx, 215p. £7.95. ISBN 0708309887. 5. *Wales 1880-1914.* xxiv, 193p. £7.95. ISBN 0708309674. 6. *Wales between the wars.* xxiv, 296p. £9.95. ISBN 0708309895. *Class No:* 942.9(01)

[7234]

Welsh history review Cylchgrawn Hanes Cymru. Cardiff, University of Wales Press for History and Law Committee of Board of Celtic Studies, 1960-.

Carries regular feature 'Articles relating to the history of Wales' published during a calendar year *e.g.* 1989 in v.15, no.4, December 1991, p.633-50. *Class No:* 942.9(01)

Maps & Atlases

[7235]

REES, W. **An Historical atlas of Wales** from early to modern times. 3rd. ed. London, Faber, 1977. vii,73p. 71pl. of maps.

First published Cardiff, the author, 1951.

71 line-maps illustrating various aspects of Welsh history (geological, political, ecclesiastical, social, economic, industrial and educational) from its origins to approximately the end of the 19th century, with adequate textual description. Various scales. Page size, 18.5x25cm. *Class No:* 942.9(084.3)

Middle Ages

[7236]

DAVIES, W. **Wales in the early Middle Ages.** Leicester, Leicester Univ. Press, 1982. xiv, 263p. illus., map, bibliog., index. (*Studies in the early history of Britain.*) ISBN: 0718511638.

A scholarly and well-documented account of Welsh history from the end of the Roman occupation to the beginning of the Norman Conquest in 7 chapters: 1. Land, landscape and environment - 2. Economy - 3. Social ties and social strata - 4. Secular politics - 5. Kings, law and order - 6. The Church - 7. Christianity and spirituality. An appendix on Source Material (p.198-218) examines records, laws, narrative sources, poems and stories, scholarly and liturgical writings, non-Welsh sources, place names, and the physical evidence. Chapter notes p.222-246. Bibliography p.247-254. *Class No:* 942.9"01/14"

[7237]

JACK, R.I. **Medieval Wales.** Cambridge, Cambridge Univ. Press, 1976. 255p. index. £19.50. (*Sources of History.*) ISBN: 0521214556.

9 chapters: 1. Literary sources - 2. The official records of Wales and their preservation - 3. The records of the English government - 4. Archives of individuals and corporations - 5. Ecclesiastical records - 6. The antiquaries - 7. Archaeology and numismatics - 8. Cartography and place-names - 9. Conclusions. Running commentary. Adequate cross-references. *Class No:* 942.9"01/14"

Caernarvonshire

[7238]

DODD, A.H. **A History of Caernarvonshire 1284-1900.** Wrexham, Bridge Books, 1990. 438p. illus., bibliogs., index. £14.95. ISBN: 1872424074.

First published Caernarvon, Caernarvonshire Historical Society, 1948.

15 chapters: 1. Making of the shire - 2. Tudor Caernarvonshire ... 13. Politics and religion (1780-1900) ... 15. Local government in the 19th century. Chapter bibliographies. *Class No:* 942.92

Denbighshire

Bibliographies

[7239]
DENBIGHSHIRE COUNTY LIBRARY. **Bibliography of the county.** Ruthin, Denbighshire County Library, 3v., 1935-7.

1: *Biographical sources.* 2: *Historical and topographical sources.* 3: *Denbighshire authors and their works.* A rev.ed. of pt.2 appeared in 1951 and a supplement, 1955-57 (56p.), in 1959 (Sections: list of periodicals; Denbighshire in general; towns, A-Z, with subdivisions). The three parts are easily the most comprehensive printed bibliography for any Welsh county and together constitute a remarkable tool for the study of Denbighshire local history.
Class No: 942.932(01)

Cardiganshire

[7240]
MEYRICK, S.R. **The History and antiquities of the county of Cardigan ...** Brecon, Davies & Co., 1907.
Class No: 942.95

Radnor

[7241]
WILLIAMS, J. **A General history of the county of Radnor...** Brecknock, Davies & Co., 1905. xviii,441p. illus., index.

19 chapters. Some notes on the County families p.379-415. *Class No:* 942.962

Brecknock

[7242]
JONES, T. **A History of the county of Brecknock...** Brecknock, Blisset, Davies & Co., 3v., 1909-11. V.4 published by Brecknock Society, 1930. plates, maps.
Class No: 942.965

Glamorgan

[7243]
Glamorgan county history. Williams, G., *ed.* Cardiff, Glamorgan County History Trust, 1936-. v.1-. illus., maps.

1. *Natural history* edited by W.M. Tattersall. 1936. (1971 reprint). xix, 444p. £15.00. ISBN 0904730026. 2. *Early Glamorgan prehistory and early history* edited by H.N. Savory. 1984. xx, 522p. £39.95. 0904730042. 3. *The Middle Ages* edited by T.B. Pugh. 1971. xix, 704p. £15.00. 090473000x. 4. *Early modern Glamorgan from the Act of Union of 1536 to the Industrial Revolution* edited by G. Williams. 1974. xviii, 717p. £15.00. 0904730018. 5. *Industrial Glamorgan from 1700-1970* edited by A.H. John and G. Williams. 1980. xiv, 671p. £35.00. 0904730034. *Glamorgan society 1780-1980* 1988. xv, 448p. £39.95. 0904730050. *Class No:* 942.97

Carmarthenshire

[7244]
LLOYD, J.E. **A History of Carmarthenshire.** Cardiff, London, 2v., 1937-39.

1. *From prehistoric times to the Act of Union (1536).* xix, 374p. 2. *From the Act of Union (1536) to 1900.* xv, 548p. *Class No:* 942.98

Europe—Eastern

[7245]
HELD, J., *ed.* **The Columbia history of Eastern Europe in the twentieth century.** New York, Columbia Univ. Press, 1992. lxxii,435p. maps, bibliog., index. ISBN: 0231076967.

10 papers present overviews of the 20th century history of Eastern Europe and of Albania, Bulgaria, Czechoslovakia, East Germany, Hungary, Poland, Romania, and Yugoslavia. Chronology p.xi-lxix. Bibliography (p.405-16) includes non-English language material. 3 maps. *Class No:* 943/

Handbooks & Manuals

[7246]
Handbook of reconstruction in Eastern Europe and the Soviet Union. White, S., *ed.* Harlow, Essex, Longman Current Affairs, 1991. viii,407p. maps, tables, index. £75. ISBN: 0582085020.

11 contributors. Country profiles A-Z. Data: Detailed chronology of events 1989-1990; political and economic overviews; key economic factors; foreign economic relations; who's who of prominent personalities; and media. Key documents and election results are also included. *Class No:* 943/(035)

Germany

[7247]
WEHLER, H-U. **The German Empire 1871-1918.** Leamington Spa, Warwickshire, Berg Publishers, 1985. [iii].293p. bibliog., index. £29.50. ISBN: 0907582222.

Translated from *Das Deutsche Kaiserreich 1871-1918* (Göttingen, Vandenhoeck u. Ruprecht, 6th ed., 1985).
Outstanding modern study. Chapter notes p.248-264 and an important bibliography p.264-290. *Class No:* 943.0

Bibliographies of Bibliographies

[7248]
OBERSCHELD, R. **Die Bibliographien zur deutschen Landesgeschichte und Landeskunde im 19. und 20. Jahrhundert.** Frankfurt am Main, Klostermann, 1967. 102p. index.

A bibliography of bibliographies of German regional history. 249 numbered items, with brief annotations. 1. Allgemeine Teil - 2. Bibliographic der Bibliographien (general section, the localities A-Z, Baden ... Württemberg). *Class No:* 943.0(009)

Bibliographies

[7249]
BAUMGART, W. **Bücherverzeichnis zur deutschen Geschichte.** Hilfsmittel, Handbücher, Quellen. München, Deutscher Taschenbuch Verlag, 1982. 14.80. ISBN: 3423032472.

....*(contd.)*

Based on his *Bibliographie zum Studium des neueren Geschichte* (1969).

A selective bibliography of German history, covering all aspects and periods. Includes more general reference works. *Class No:* 943.0(01)

[7250]
DAHLMANN, F.C. Dahlmann-Waitz. Quellenkunde der deutschen Geschichte. Bibliographie der Quellen und der Literatur zur deutschen Geschichte. 10. Aufl. hrsg. in Max Planck-Institut. Stuttgart, Hiersemann, 7v., 1965-. ISBN: 377726511x.

First published 1830. 9th ed. 2v., 1931-32.

1. *Einleitung. Verzeichnis der Abkürzungen und der Siegel. Abschnitt 1 bis 38* (1969). 771p. ISBN 3777269018. 2. *Abschnitt 39-57* (1971). 764p. 3777271098. *Register zu Bände l und z (1985).* 480p. 3777285196. 3. *Abschnitt 58-120* (1984). 766p. 3777284386. 4. *Abschnitt 121-136* (1987). 452p. 3777287156. 5. *Abschnitt 158-236* (1980). 852p. 3777280062. 6. *Abschnitt 237 bis 279* (1987). 776p. 3777287253.

Follows the general plan of the 9th ed.; a general section, including auxiliary subjects such as methodology, palaeography, diplomatic; sections on aspects of German history (*e.g.* legal, military, economic, ecclesiastical, literary, art and music); and the major part, a chronologically arranged bibliography of German history. Lfg.6 (1967), items 45-176, deals with libraries, museums, palaeography, epigraphy, handwriting, diplomatic, etc. A list of *c.*1,200 journals appear in Lfg.1. A substantial revision of what is the basic bibliography for German history. *Class No:* 943.0(01)

[7251]
FONT, J.C. German history and civilization 1806-1914: a bibliography of scholarly periodical literature. Metuchen, New Jersey, The Scarecrow Press, 1974. xix,342p. ISBN: 0810807424.

5701 entries culled from 150 journals arranged in 11 sections: 1. Church history - 2. Constitutional, legal, administrative - 3. Diplomacy - 4. Economics and social - 5. Historiography - 6. Intellectual and cultural - 7. Judaism and anti-semitism - 8. Military - 9. Nationalism - 10. Political history, political thought, political parties - 11. Science, medicine. *Class No:* 943.0(01)

[7252]
Jahresberichte für deutsche Geschichte. Jahrgang 1-9/10, 11-14, 15/16. 1925-40. Leipzig, Koehler, 14v., 1927-42. Neue folge, Jahrgang 1-. 1949-. Berlin, Akademie Verlag, 1952-.

Neue Folge. 35 Jahrgang 1986 (1988. 842p. ISBN 3050005513. ISSN 0075286x) has 8239 entries in 5 sections: A Geschichtswissenschaft - B. Zeitlich umfassend - C/F. 3 chronological periods 500-1945. Register der Verfasser-und Sachtitelschriften p.580-753. Sachregister p.754-842. Updates *Dahlmann-Waitz* (*qv*). *Class No:* 943.0(01)

[7253]
KEYSER, E., *ed*. Bibliographie zur Städtgeschichte Deutschlands. Köln, Böhlau, 1969. ix,404p. indexes. (*Acta Collegii historiae urbanae Societatis historicorum internationalis.*)

One of a series sponsored by the International Committee for the History of Towns. Arranged by regions, then by towns A-Z. *Class No:* 943.0(01)

Encyclopaedias

[7254]
Die Chronik Berlins. Dortmund, Chronik Verlag, 1986. 608p. col. illus., col. maps, index. DM89. (*Die Chronik Städtebände.*)

History of Berlin retold with chronologies, narrative text, maps and illustrations as if in a contemporary newspaper. 1690 individual articles and 71 summary articles. *Class No:* 943.0(031)

[7255]
Chronik der Deutschen. New ed. Dortmund, Chronik Verlag, 1987. 1216p. illus. (some col.), maps, (some col.). DM98.

Illustrated annals arranged in 24 historical divisions (*e.g.* 1. Ur-und Frühgeschicte 800 v. Chr.-100 v. Chr ... 4. Das Reich der Karolinger 750-919 ... 18. Das Zeitalter Bismarcks 1870-1890 ... 24. Rezession und politische Wende 1966-1987) centennially 800BC to AD1; decennially AD1-1789; yearly 1789-1983. Each century, decade, or year comprises a calendar, and 'news reports' presented with integrated text, photographs and maps. *Class No:* 943.0(031)

[7256]
GEBHARDT, B. Handbuch der deutschen Geschichte. 9. neu bearb. Auf. hrsg. von H. Grundmann. Stuttgart, Ernst Klett Verlag., 1970-, v.1.

First published 1891-92. 1954-68. 5v.

1. *Frühzeit und Mittelatter.* 1970. xxiv,898p. ISBN 3129025103. 2. *Von der Reformation bis zum Ende der Absolutismus.* 1970. xvii,905p. 3129025200. 3. *Von der Französischen Revolution bis zum Ersten Weltkrieg.* 1973. x,583p. 3129025308. 4/1. *Die Zeit der Weltkriege. Der erste Weltkriege. Die Weimaren Republik.* 1973. xii,329p. 3129025405. 4/2. *Die Zeit der Weltkriege. Deutschland unter der Herrschaft des Nationalsozialismus 1933-1939. Der Zweite Weltkrieg. Das Ende des Reiches und die Entstehung der Republik Österreich, der Bundesrepublik Deutschland und der Deutschen Demokratischen Republik.*

To be completed in 5v. Arranged by period and subject, the contributions by specialists in this massive compendium 'provide an invaluable bibliography and framework of facts for German history from prehistoric times ...' (White, C.M., and others. *Sources of information in the social sciences* (2nd ed., 1973, entry B473, on the 8th ed.). *Class No:* 943.0(031)

Handbooks & Manuals

[7257]
Deutschland - Ploetz Deutsche Geschichte zum Nachschlagen. Conze, W., *ed*. Freiburg, Verlag Ploetz, 1986. 319p., illus., bibliog., index. ISBN: 3876403073.

Previously as *Ploetz Deutsche Geschichte Epochen und Daten* (1979).

Ereignisse und Entwicklungen (Events and Developments) *i.e.* introductory essays and chronologies in 9 sections: 1. Das Hochmittelalter 911-1254 - 2. Das Spätmittelhalter 1254-1493 - 3. Reformation. Gegen reformation. Dreissigjähriger Krieg 1493-1648 - 4. Absolutismus und Aufklärung 1649-1792 - 5. Das Ende des Reichs und der Deutsche Bund 1792-1851 - 6. Im Zeitalter der bürglichen Nationalstaaten 1851-1890 - 7. In der Epoche des Imperialismus 1890-1918 - 8. Republik und NS- Diktatur 1919-1945. 9. Deutschland seit 1945. Literaturauswahl p.286-9. *Class No:* 943.0(035)

[7258]
Handbuch der historischen Stätten Deutschland. Stuttgart, Kröner, 1958-. Alfred Kröner. maps, plans.

   1. *Schlesvig-Holstein.* 3rd ed., 1976. 313p. ISBN 3520271036. 2. *Niedersachsen und Bremen.* 5th ed., 1986. xci,608p. 3520272059. 3. *Nordrhein-Westfalen.* 2nd ed., 1970. clx,838p. 3520273020. 4. *Hessen.* 3rd ed., 1976. 540p. 3520274035. 5. *Rheinland-Pfalz und Saarland.* 3rd ed., 1976. xliii,523p. 3520275031. *Baden-Württemburg.* 1980. 1093p. 352027602x. 7. *Bayern.* 3rd ed., 1981. lxxii,962p. 3520277034. 8. *Sachsen.* 1965. 9. *Thüringen.* 2nd ed., 1989. lxxxi,580p. 3520313022. 10 *Berlin und Brandenberg.* 2nd ed., 1985. 677p. 352031102x. 11. *Provinz Sachsen-Anhalt.* 2nd ed., 1987. 738p. 3520314029. 12. *Schliesen.* 1977. 13. *Ost-und Westpreussen.* 1981. lxix, 284p. 352031701x. 14. *Schlesien.* 1977. xcii,699p. 3520316013. A series of German regional histories. Descriptive entries. *Class No:* 943.0(035)

Dictionaries

[7259]
FEST, W. Dictionary of German history 1806-1945. London, George Prior, 1978. 189p. ISBN: 0860431088.

   Entries A-Z for *c.*700 topics, with emphasis on the political angle and 20th century. Most articles have short bibliographical notes, covering writings published 1950-77. Cross-references. Intended as 'an aid to study, not as a substitute for it' (*Preface*). 'This is the first dictionary of modern German history in the English language' (*Library review*, Autumn 1979, p.193). 'A valuable reference book that should be in every undergraduate library' (*Choice*, v.16, no.4, June 1979, p.508). *Class No:* 943.0(038)

[7260]
RÖSSLER, H. *and* **FRANZ, G.,** *and others*. **Sachwörterbuch zur deutschen Geschichte.** München, Oldenbourg, 1958. xl,iv,1472p. (Kraus Reprint, 2v., 1970).

   A companion volume to *Biographisches Wörterbuch zur deutschen Geschichte* (Munich, Oldenbourg, 1952, xlviii,968p.). A dictionary of German history. Entries cover political and economic events (*e.g.* Weltkrieg II), institutions, countries (*e.g.* Austria, Switzerland), places, battles (with plans) and cultural subjects (*e.g.* Music, Literature). Compact, signed articles,' with short bibliographies (*e.g.* 'Hanse': 6 columns, with a 6-line bibliography). Many cross-references. An excellent work of its kind. *Class No:* 943.0(038)

[7261]
TADDEY, G., *ed*. **Lexikon der deutschen Geschichte.** Personen, Ereignisse, Institutionen der Zeitwende bis zum Ausgang des 2. Weltkrieges. 2nd ed. Stuttgart, Alfred Kröner, 1983. xii,1391p. ISBN: 3520813025.

   Brief signed and documented entries, A-Z, for persons, events and institutions, from the origins of the Germanic peoples and barbarian invasions up to the fall of the Third Reich. 1945. 'Clear and practical; (*Bulletin des Bibliotheques de France*, v.25,no.7, July 1980, entry 1092). *Class No:* 943.0(038)

Reviews & Abstracts

[7262]
BERGAHN, V.R. '**Germany 1860-1918**', *The Historian*, no. 15, Summer 1987, p.10-12.

   Review of recent publications. *Class No:* 943.0(048)

Maps & Atlases

[7263]
Der grosse Bildatlas zur Deutschen Geschichte von Karl Dem Grossen biz zur Wiedervereinigung. München, Bertelsmann Lexicon Verlag, 1991. 296p.++ 32 col. pl. illus. (many col.), col. maps, bibliogs., index. ISBN: 3570065472.

   16 contributors. Illustrated atlas in 21 chapters (*e.g.* 1. Germanen, Franken, Karolinger ... 10. Der Dreissigjährige Krieg ... 17. Nationalsozialismus in Deutschland ... 21. Die Bundesrepublik von den sechziger Jahren zur Wiedereinigung. *Class No:* 943.0(084.3)

Chronologies

[7264]
HELLVIG, G. Daten der deutschen Geschichte. Politik und Kultur in Deutschland, Österreich und in der Schweiz. Gütersloh & Berlin, Bertelsmann, 1976. 384p., tables.

   A chronology divided in 11 periods, from the Old Stone Age to 1976. 2-column tables, headed 'Politics' and 'Culture'. Appended data on treaties, organizations, history museums, etc. Summaries of Austrian and Swiss history. Detailed, non-analytical index. *Class No:* 943.0(090)

Biographies

[7265]
BOSL, K., *and others, eds*. **Biographisches Wörterbuch zur deutschen Geschichte.** München & Bern, Francke, 3v., 1973-75. 3330 cols., 4-105p. ISBN: 3317015128.

   First published 1952. Companion volume to *Sachwörterbuch zur deutschen Geschichte* (1958).

   1. *A-H*; 2. *I-R*; 3. *S-Z*, and *Namenregister für das Gesamtwerk*.

   Signed and documented articles on deceased persons. 'Friedrich I. Barbarossa': v.1, cols. 740-51; ½col. of bibliography. 'Wallenstein'; v.1, cols. 3024-31; 17 lines of bibliography. 'Hitler'; v.1, cols. 1174-91; 1 col. of bibliography. Cross-references; genealogical tables. Index appended to v.3, p.4-105. A valuable source. *Class No:* 943.0(092)

16th & 17th Centuries

Bibliographies

[7266]
STOKES, L.D. Medieval and Reformation Germany (to 1648). London, Historical Association, 1972. 67p. (*Helps for Students of History, no.84.*)

   About 1,400 references to books and periodical articles, in running commentary form. Directed 'towards university students and others interested in the subject who are unable to read materials in a language other than English' (*Preface*). Sections: Bibliographies (including the major German works)

....(contd.)
- Geography - General surveys - Origins to 800AD - The Middle Ages 800-1500 (12 divisions) - The Reformation era. 1500-1648 (25 divisions). *Class No:* 943.0"15/16"(01)

16th Century

Bibliographies

[7267]
SCHOTTENLOHER, K. **Bibliographie zur deutschen Geschichte im Zeitalter der Glaubensspaltung** 1517-1585. Im Auftrag der Kommission zur Erforschung der Geschichte der Reformation und Gegenreformation. Leipzig, Hiersemann, 6v., 1933-60 (1956-58 reprint). V.7 (Supplement), 1962-66. 4700p. ISBN: 3777256056.
  1. *Personen A-L.* xii,631p. ISBN 3777256664. 2. *Personen M-Z. Orte und Landschaften.* xii,760p. 3777256145. 3. *Reich und Kaiser; Territorien und Landesherren.* viii,569p. 3777255708. 4. *Gesamtdarstellung, Stoffe.* viii,762p. 3777257141. 5. *Ergänzungen, Berichtigungen, Zeittafel.* viii,546p. 3777258040. 6. *Verfasser-und Titelverzeichnis zu Band 1-5.* viii,677p. 377725813x. 7. *Das Schrifttum von 1938-1960 nebst Nachträgen zu Band 1-6.* viii,691p. 3777266019.
  The most comprehensive bibliographies of the German Reformation. V.1 contains 14,652 numbered entries; v.5, 52,199 entries (books and periodical articles). Subdivision is minute; many cross-references. V.7 covers items 52,200-65,621 in 5 sections, plus supplement.
  Class No: 943.0"15"(01)

19th Century

Bibliographies

[7268]
BORN, K.E., *ed.* **Bismarck-Bibliographie.** Quellen and Literatur zur Geschichte Bismarcks und seiner Zeit. Köln & Berlin, G. Grotesche, 1966. 259p. ISBN: 3774500029.
  About 4,000 entries in 18 sections: (5. Der Staatsmann (1862-1890), p.44-143 ... 1. Bismarck in der Kunst ... 17. Zeitungen und Zeitschriften Jahrbücher, Kalender, Mitteilungsblätter - 18. Literaturberichte, Bibliographen). Author index. *Class No:* 943.0"18"(01)

20th Century

Micromaterials

[7269]
US Military intelligence reports: Germany 1919-1941. Frederick, Maryland, University Microfilms of America Inc., 1983. 28 reels x 35mm microfilm with printed guide. $1700.00. ISBN: 0890934266.
  Over 25,000 pages of previously uncollected and unpublished contemporary reports on all aspects of German history from the end of the Great War to the entry of the United States into World War II.
  Class No: 943.0"19"(003.5)

Bibliographies

[7270]
HAUPT, M. **Die Berliner Mauer** : Vorgeschichte, Bau, Folgen, Literaturbericht und Bibliographie zum 20. Jahrestag des 13. August 1961. [The Berlin Wall, its historical background, construction and consequences.] München, Bernard & Graefe, 1981. 230p., map on endpapers, index. (*Schriften der Bibliothek für Zeitgeschichte, no.21.*)
  Books and periodical articles 1945-1961.
  Class No: 943.0"19"(01)

[7271]
INSTITUT FÜR ZEITGESCHICHTE München. **Kataloge der Bibliothek des Instituts für Zeitgeschichte.** Boston, Mass., G.K. Hall, 1977.
  Alphabetischer Katalog. 5v., 3458p. $420.00 (Export $510.00). ISBN 0816107246. *Sachkatalog.* 6v., 4501p. $540.00 ($655.00). ISBN 0816101760. *Länderkatalog* 2v., 1144p. $145.00 ($175.00). ISBN 0816101779. *Biographischer Katalog,* 764p. $100.00 ($120.00). ISBN 0816101787.
  Erster Nachtragsband, 1973: *Alphabetischer Katalog.* 2 reels $140.00 ($170.00). ISBN 0816114048. *Sachkatalog.* 2v., 1165p. $255.00 ($310.00). ISBN 0816101795. *Biographischer Katalog und Länderkatalog.* 588p. $120.00 ($145.00). ISBN 0816110751.
  Photolithographic reproduction of the author, subject, regional and biographical catalogues (248,600 cards) of the Library of the Institute which specialises in the history of the Weimar Republic, National Socialism and the Third Reich (*i.e.,* post-1918 Germany). *Class No:* 943.0"19"(01)

[7272]
KEHR, H. **After Hitler: Germany 1945-1963.** London. Vallentine Mitchell for the Wiener Library, 1963. 261p.
  Bibliography of more than 2700 entries (based on holdings of the Wiener Library) encompassing the Allied wartime plans for Germany, the occupation, Berlin, the Federal Republic, the German Democratic Republic etc.
  Class No: 943.0"19"(01)

[7273]
MEYER, G.P. **Bibliographie zur deutschen Revolution 1918/19.** Göttingen, Vandenhoeck & Ruprecht, 1977. 188p. pbk. ISBN: 3525354819.
  1850 entries arranged under 37 thematic and regional headings. *Class No:* 943.0"19"(01)

[7274]
STACHURA, P.D. **The Weimar era and Hitler 1918-1933:** a criticial bibliography. Oxford, Clio Press; Santa Barbara, California, ABC-Clio Press, 1977. xvii,276p. £34.50.
  3000+ citations, drawn from secondary literature (monographs, document collections, festschriften, pamphlets, dissertations and theses, and articles) published 1945-1975, arranged in 2 parts: The Weimar Republic (19 chapters) and The rise of national socialism (11 chaps.) *e.g.* 1. General studies ... 4. Political events ... 7. Political movements ... 8. Paramilitary formations ... 22. The National Socialist movement ... 23. Biographies and studies of National Socialist leaders. *Class No:* 943.0"19"(01)

[7275]

The Weimar Republic: a historical bibliography. Santa Barbara, California, and Oxford, ABC-Clio Information Services, 1984. xii,285p. indexes. (ABC-Clio Research Guide). £26.35. ISBN: 0874363780.

1035 abstracts of periodical articles published 1973-1982, culled from the *American History & Life* and *Historical Abstracts* databases, arranged in 9 sections: The Weimar Republic in historical context - The Beginnings of the Republic - Government, politics, and the economy - Weimar culture and society - The Jews of Weimar - Christianity in transition - The Growth of German communism - The Road to Nazi hegemony - The End of the Republic. A Subject Profile Index carries generic and specific index terms. 'Students of this very active field of scholarship will welcome the convenient repackaging of a decade's *Historical Abstracts*' (*Choice*, v.22,no.2, October 1984, p.255).
Class No: 943.0"19"(01)

Maps & Atlases

[7276]

HILGEMANN, W. Atlas zur deutsche Zeitgeschichte 1918-1968. München, Piper, 1984. 208p. col. maps, tables, bibliog. ISBN: 3492024602.

103 geographical/historical features in 5 sections: 1. Ende des Kaiserreichs 1918 - 2. Weimarer Republik (1919-1933) - 3. Das Drittes Reich (1933-1945) - 4. Deutschland unter den Besatzungsmächten (1945-1949) - 5. Bundesrepublik Deutschland und Sowjetische Besatzungszone - DDR (1949-1968). Chronology p.194-208. Bibliography p.193.
Class No: 943.0"19"(084.3)

Biographies

[7277]

BENZ, W. and GRAML, H., eds. Biographisches lexikon zur Weimarer Republik. München, Verlag, C.H. Beck, 1988. 392p. 49.80. ISBN: 3406329888.

59 contributors. Over 500 biographical sketches of prominent people 1918-1933 (Konrad Adenauer: 80 lines; Rosa Luxemburg: 61 lines). Die Regierungen der Weimarer Republik p.382-386. Politische Chronik p.387-392.
Class No: 943.0"19"(092)

Nazi Germany

[7278]

HILDEBRAND, K. The Third Reich. London, George Allen and Unwin, 1984. xii, 184p. maps., bibliog., index. £32. ISBN: 0049430335.

Translated from *Das Dritte Reich* (München, R. Oldenbourg Verlag, 1979).

Part 1. Historical survey *i.e.* 4 chronological chapters 1933-1945. Part 2. Basic problems and trends of research, in effect an academic literature survey in 7 thematic chapters. Chronology p.164-171. Bibliography p.172-177. Analytical index. Primary attention is devoted 'to those elements and problems ... which have been identified as important by a research tradition of over thirty years standing'.
Class No: 943.0"1933-1945"

Bibliographies

[7279]

KEHR, H. and LANGMAID, J. The Nazi era 1919-1945: a select bibliography of published works from the early roots to 1980. London, Mansell Publishing Ltd., 1982. xvi,621p. index. £40.00. ISBN: 070211618x.

6523 works are listed, some with brief annotations, encompassing some 20 languages although preponderantly in English and German. Arrangement is in 9 parts each minutely divided and sub-divided to the point of confusion: 1. Reference books - 2. Nationalsozialistische Deutsche Arbeiterpartei - 3. From struggle to consolidation of power - 4. The Third Reich - 5. The criminal state - 6. Road to war - 7. World War II - 8. War crimes - 9. After the fall of the Third Reich. Analytical index p.529-561. 'Compiled with great scholarly care ... comprehensively covers the varied phenomena of Nazism ... this is a magnificent work' (*Choice*, v.20,no.4, December 1982, p.561).
Class No: 943.0"1933-1945"(01)

[7280]

ROBBINS, K. 'Nazi Germany', *The Historian*, no.1, Autumn 1983, p.20-3.

Review of the most significant publications of the last decade. *Class No:* 943.0"1933-1945"(01)

[7281]

SNYDER, L.L., ed. The Third Reich 1933-1945: a bibliographical guide to German national socialism. New York, Garland Publishing Inc., 1987. 284p. index. $42.00. ISBN: 0824084632.

850 annotated entries grouped in 13 sections: 1. Documentary materials - 2. General - 3. Biography - 4. Politics and government - 5. Economics - 6. Social structure - 7. National Socialist culture - 8. Religion - 9. Psychological motivations - 10. Foreign policy - 11. Resistance movement - 12. Anti-semitism and the holocaust - 13. World War II. Cannot compare in coverage with H. Kehr's *The Nazi era* but 'recommended for undergraduate students beginning a research project' (*Choice*, v.25,no.5, January 1985, p.752).
Class No: 943.0"1933-1945"(01)

[7282]

The Third Reich, 1933-1939: a historical bibliography. Santa Barbara, California and Oxford, ABC-Clio Information Services, 1984. xii,239p. indexes. £27.30. ISBN: 6874363799.

932 abstracts of journal articles printed 1973-1982 drawn from the publisher's renowned database. Arranged A-Z by author in 7 chapters: 1. Nazi Germany in historical context - 2. Domestic policies and politics - 3. Nazi foreign policy - 4. Culture and society in Hitler's Germany - 5. The crushing of German Jewry - 6. Christianity in crisis - 7. The Left under siege. The Subject Profile Index incorporates both generic and specific terms. *Class No:* 943.0"1933-1945"(01)

[7283]

—The Third Reich at war: a historical bibliography. Santa Barbara, California and Oxford, ABC-Clio Information Services. xii,270p. index. £27.30. ISBN: 0874363934.

Abstracts of 1061 journal articles, published 1973-1982, selected from the publisher's vast historical information database, assembled in 7 chapters: 1. Wartime Germany - 2. Trade and diplomacy - 3. Invasion and occupation of Poland - 4. At war with Western Europe - 5. Eastern and Southeastern Europe - 6. Russia - 7. The Holocaust. Author and subject indexes. *Class No:* 943.0"1933-1945"(01)

[7284]
WIENER LIBRARY. London. **Persecution and resistance under the Nazis.** 2nd ed. London, Vallentine Mitchell, 1960. 208p. (*Catalogue series, no.1.*)

1043 entries. Includes number of illegal pamphlets. From holdings of Wiener Library. *Class No:* 943.0"1933-1945"(01)

Encyclopaedias

[7285]
The Encyclopedia of the Third Reich. Zentner, C. *and* Bedürftig, F., *eds.* New York, Macmillan, 2v., 1991. 1120p. illus., bibliog., index. $175. ISBN: 0028975006.

Translated from *Das grosse Lexikon des Dritten Reiches* (1985).

40 contributors to this scholarly compendium of over 3,000 entries for events, people, culture, ideology, and almost every facet of Nazi Germany. 1,200 illustrations. 'The currently definitive reference source' (*Library Journal,* v.116,no.7, 15 April 1991, p.82). *Class No:* 943.0"1933-1945"(031)

[7286]
SNYDER, L.L. **Encyclopedia of the Third Reich.** Blandford Press, 1989. [xx],410p. illus., ports., tables, bibliog. £14.95. ISBN: 0713721677.

First published London, Hale, 1976.

Entries A-Z on the events, institutions and personalities of Nazi Germany. 'Hitler':p.150-160, 5 ports. and illus., 5 references. 'See' references from English to German. Bibliography p.389-410. Calendar of significant dates p.iii-xx. 'A sound reference work' (*Library Journal,* v.102,no.8, 15 April 1977, p.177). *Class No:* 943.0"1933-1945"(031)

Dictionaries

[7287]
TAYLOR, J. *and* SHAW, W. **A Dictionary of the Third Reich.** London, Grafton Books, 1987. Distributed in North America by St. Martin's Press. 401p. illus., maps, bibliog. £12.95. ISBN: 0246131780, UK; 0886873630, US.

Chronology p.11-20. A-Z of the Third Reich p.21-312. Military campaigns p.367-382. Selected quotations p.383-390. Bibliography p.391-392. For students and general readers. Cross-references. Notwithstanding some idiosyncratic entries noticed *Reference Reviews* v,2,no.1, March 1988, p.35 reports that it is 'clearly based on a wealth of knowledge of the Third Reich'. *Class No:* 943.0"1933-1945"(038)

Maps & Atlases

[7288]
FREEMAN, M. **Atlas of Nazi Germany.** London, Croom Helm; New York, Macmillan, 1987. 205p. illus., maps, bibliog., index. £35. ISBN: 0709910738, UK; 029106818, US.

In 6 parts: 1. Rise of the Nazi party; 2. Adminstrative and political studies; 3. Society; 4. Population and economics; 5. The search for living space; the Third Reich at war; 6. The war machine. References p.191-192. Bibliographical guide p.195-196. Glossary p.193. 'This visual history will be very helpful to students up to the graduate level' (*Choice,* v.25, no.8, April, 1988, p.1222). *Class No:* 943.0"1933-1945"(084.3)

Chronologies

[7289]
EDELHEIT, H. *and* EDELHEIT, A.J. **A World in turmoil** an integrated chronology of the Holocaust and World War II. Westport, Conn., Greenwood Press, 1991. xiii,450p. bibliog., indexes. £67.50. (*Bibliographies and Indexes in World History, no. 22.*) ISBN: 0313282188.

Concentrates on the most important political and diplomatic events primarily in Europe and the Middle East affecting world and Jewish history 30 January 1933 to 14 May 1958 (the date of the establishment of the State of Israel). Glossary p.385-403. Bibliography p.405-14. Name, place and subject indexes. *Class No:* 943.0"1933-1945"(090)

[7290]
HAUNER, M. **Hitler: a chronology of his life and time.** London, Macmillan Press, 1983. xi,221p., bibliog., index. £22.50. ISBN: 0333309839.

Traces every known detail of Hitler's career with an itinerary of his movements on a daily basis and a chronological guide to his speeches and writings. Glossary p.ix. Bibliography p.204-5. *Class No:* 943.0"1933-1945"(090)

Biographies

[7291]
STOCKHORST, E. **Fünftausend Köpfe:** ver war was im Dritten Reich. 2nd ed. Kiel, Arndt-Verlag, 1985. 464p. charts. ISBN: 3887411261.

First published Velbert, Blick u. Bild Verlag, 1967.

About 5,000 biographies of personalities prominent in the Third Reich (1933-45). Concise career information ('Goebbels': ½ col.; Hitler: ¾ col). Organizational lists and charts precede. *Class No:* 943.0"1933-1945"(092)

[7292]
WISTRICH, R. **Who's who in Nazi Germany.** London, Weidenfeld and Nicolson, 1982. 359p. ISBN: 029778109x.

Nearly 350 biographies of individuals prominent or significant in Nazi Germany based on personal files, documentary material, press cuttings and historical works held in the Wiener Library. Glossary of major German terms in the text p.348-351. Bibliography p.353-359. 'Highly recommended for all institutions where history is taught' (*Choice,* v.20,no.8, April 1983, p.1116). *Class No:* 943.0"1933-1945"(092)

Jews

[7293]
GILBERT, M. **The Holocaust** : the Jewish tragedy. London, Collins, 1986. 959p. illus., maps, bibliog., index. £25. ISBN: 0002163055.

Definitive history in 41 chapters. Notes and sources p.831-96. 25 maps. Analytical index. *Class No:* 943.0"1933-1945"(=924)

[7294]
GUTMAN, I., *ed.* **Encyclopedia of the Holocaust.** New York, Maxwell Macmillan, 4v., 1989. 1,1905p. illus., maps, bibliog., index. $335. ISBN: 0028960904, set; 0028971639, v.1; 0028971647, v.2; 0028971655, v.3; 0028971663, v.4.

950 signed and well-documented A-Z cross-referenced articles (most have reading lists of 2-12 items), contributed by 207 leading international scholars, cover all aspects of the

....*(contd.)*

Holocaust, including the history, politics and major figures of the Third Reich; the ideological roots of racism and anti-Semitism; Nazi medical practices and experiments; and the organization of genocide. Appendices include a glossary (p.1751); a detailed chronology 1920-1945 (p.1759); a list of major Jewish organizations in Germany 1893-1943; the structure of the Einsatzgruppen from June 1941; a summary of the Nuremburg Trial and subsequent trials with lists of defendants, and a country by country analysis of estimated Jewish losses in the Holocaust. V.4 has a detailed index. 'This wealth of information about one of the major events in the history of western civilization belongs in all public and academic libraries' (*Booklist*, v.86,no.13, 1 March 1990, p.1375 + 8). *Class No:* 943.0"1933-1945"(=924)

[7295]
MENDELSOHN, J., *ed*. **The Holocaust** selected documents in eighteen volumes. New York Garland Publishing Inc., 1982. ISBN: 082404875x, to 082404892x.

A documentary history of the persecution of the Jews 1933-1945 arranged in rough chronological order. All facsimiles are taken from the National Archives in Washington.

Planning and Preparation: V.1-2 Legalizing the holocaust; 3. The Crystal Night pogrom; 4. Propaganda and Aryanization 1938-1944; 5. Jewish emigration 1933 to the Evian Conference 1938; 6. Jewish emigration 1938-1940; 7. Jewish emigration: The S.S. St. Louis affair.

The Killing of the Jews: v.8 Deportation of the Jews to the East; 9. Medical experiments on Jewish inmates of concentration camps; 10. The Einsatzgruppen or Murder Commandos; 11 The Wannsee protocol and a 1944 report on Auschwitz by the Office of Strategic Services; 12. The final solution in the extermination camps and the aftermath; 13. The judicial system and the Jews in Nazi Germany.

Rescue attempts: v.14 Relief and rescue of Jews from Nazi oppression 1943-45; 15. Relief and rescue in Hungary and the failure of the Joel Brand mission; 16. Rescue to Switzerland. The Musy and Saly Mayer affairs.

Punishment: v.17 Punishing the perpetrators of the Holocaust. The Brandt, Pohl, and Ohlendorf cases; 18. The Ohlendorf and Von Weizsaecker cases.

Introduction to the series v.1, p. vii-xii. Each of the 18v. begins with an introduction outlining the historical context. Of the documents produced slightly more than 2/3 are in English translation, the remainder are mostly in German. *Class No:* 943.0"1933-1945"(=924)

Bibliographies

[7296]
EDELHEIT, A.J. *and* EDELHEIT, H. **Bibliography on holocaust literature.** Boulder, Colorado, Westview Press, 1986. xxxvi,842p. index. $80. ISBN: 081337233x.

More than 9000 items relating to English language books, pamphlets, periodical articles and dissertations arranged in 20 minutely subdivided chapters organized in 4 major sections: 1. Before the storm - 2. The perpetrators - 3. The crucible - 4. Aftermath. Author index. Absence of a subject index leads to difficulties with a subject approach although there is a detailed table of contents. 'The most comprehensive list of materials on the Holocaust yet published' (*Reference Books Bulletin 1986-87*, p.154). *Supplement* published 1990. *Class No:* 943.0"1933-1945"(=924)(01)

[7297]
LASKA, V. **Nazism, resistance & holocaust in World War II.** Metuchen, New Jersey, Scarecrow Press, 1985. xxii, 205p. £18.00. ISBN: 0810817713.

1907 numbered entries, some briefly annotated arranged in 13 chapters: 1. Jews and anti-Semitism - 2. Nazism - 3. Resistance - Women - 4. Jewish resistance - 5. Holocaust - 6. Holocaust - Women - 7. Women in hiding - 8. Pre-1945 knowledge of the Holocaust - 9. War crimes - 10. Art and photographs - 11. Philosophy and interpretation - 12. Literature - 13. Addenda. Not confined to Jews. *Class No:* 943.0"1933-1945"(=924)(01)

[7298]
'**Remembering the Holocaust**', *Booklist,* v.85, no. 19, 1 June 1989, p.1742-1752.

'A representative multimedia list of what is available to the general public'. Citations to original *Booklist* and *Reference Books Bulletin* entries are provided. *Class No:* 943.0"1933-1945"(=924)(01)

Maps & Atlases

[7299]
GILBERT, M. **Atlas of the Holocaust.** 2nd rev. ed. Oxford, Pergamon Press, 1988. 256p. illus., maps, index, pbk. £10.95. ISBN: 0080367615.

316 maps and accompanying text charting the destruction of the major Jewish communities in Europe from the anti-semitism of pre-war Germany onwards. *Class No:* 943.0"1933-1945"(=924)(084.3)

Federal Republic of Germany

[7300]
BARK, D.L. *and* GRESS, D.R. **A History of West Germany.** 2nd ed. Oxford, Blackwell, 2v., 1993. ISBN: 1557863237.

1st ed. 1989.

1. *From shadow to substance 1945-1963.* lvi,591p. illus., maps, bibliog., index. Bibliographic essay p.527-36. Documents and sources p.537-40. Bibliography p.541-66. Analytical index.

2. *Democracy and its discontents 1963-1991.* xvii,862p. Bibliographic essay p.798-808. Documents and sources p.809-12. Bibliography p.813-38. Analytical index. Exhaustive, scholarly and thoroughly researched history of post-World War 2 social, political and economic developments in West Germany. *Class No:* 943.01

[7301]
BRACHER, K.D., *eds*. **Geschichte der Bundesrepublik Deutschland.** Mannheim, F.A. Brockhaus, 5v., in 6, 1981-87. ISBN: 3765307408.

1. *Jahre der Besatzung 1945-1949* (1981) ed. by T. Eschenburg. ISBN 3765307416. 2. *Die Ära Adenauer 1949-1957* (1981) ed. by H.P. Schwarz. 3765307424. 3. *Die Ära Adenauer 1957-1963* (1983) ed. by H.P Schwarz. 3765307432. 4. *Von Erhard zur Grossen Koalition 1963-1969* (1984) ed. by K. Hildebrandt. 376530440. 5/1. *Republik in Wandel 1969-1974. Die Ära Brandt.* (1985) ed. by K.D. Bracher. 3765307459. 5/2. *Republik im Wandel 1974-1982. Die Ära Schmidt* (1987) ed. by W. Jäger and W. Link. Text is abundantly supported by statistics, tables, maps, chronologies and bibliographies to form 'a coherent,

....(contd.)
well-written, informative and balanced account of recent German history' (*TLS*, no.4246, 17 August 1984, p.921).
Class No: 943.01

Encyclopaedias

[7302]
Die Chronik Bayerns. Nöhbauer, H.F., *ed.* 2nd ed. Dortmund, Chronik Verlag, 1987. 640p. illus. (mostly col.), col. maps, col. coats of arms, index. DM89. ISBN: 3883790885.

Covers Bavarian history 400BC-1987 in journalistic format; each single or double page spread anchored to a specific period. 12 period overviews *e.g.* Von Steinzeithöhlen zu Keltenstädten ... Bayern unter der ersten Wittelsbachern ... 1933 Bayerns auf dem Weg in die Diktatur. Anhang: Bayern in Daten und Zahlen p.597-625.
Class No: 943.01(031)

[7303]
Die Chronik der Stadt Bonn. Dortmund, Chronik Verlag, 1988. 320p. col. illus., col maps, index. DM68. (*Die Chronik Stätebände.*)

History of the city of Bonn presented as if in a contemporary newspaper: chronologies, news reports *etc.* 662 individual and 17 summary articles.
Class No: 943.01(031)

[7304]
Chronik des Ruhrgebiets. Havenberg, B., *ed.* Dortmund, Chronik Verlag, 1987. 671p. illus. (mostly col.), col. maps, col. coats of arms, index. DM89. ISBN: 3883790893.

19 chronological and thematic overviews *e.g.* Germanen, Römer, Sachsen und Franken ... Das Ruhrgebiet im Nationsozialismus ... Sport in Ruhrgebiet ... Schreiben in Ruhrgebiet link journalistic text on annalistic pattern. Anhang: Das Ruhrgebiet in Daten und Zahlen p.631-56.
Class No: 943.01(031)

German Democratic Republic

[7305]
McCAULEY, M. The German Democratic Republic since 1945. London, Macmillan Press in association with the School of Slavonic and East European Studies, Univ. of London, 1983. xiv,282p. maps, bibliog., tables, index. £38.00. (*Studies in Russia and East Europe.*)

Outline study with impressive bibliography mainly consisting of German items (p.265-273) and a useful Chronology (p.195-264). *Class No:* 943.02

[7306]
OSMOND, J. German reunification a reference guide and commentary. Harlow, Essex, Longman, 1992. xviii,311p. tables, bibliog., maps, index. £45. ISBN: 0582096502.

Part 1: Revolution and reunification (including chronology of events 1989-92, p.3-14) - 2. Politics, economy and society - 3. Reference section (directory of German reunification *i.e.* political parties and movements, key figures and institutions; election results; economic indicators; texts of significant treaties). Bibliography p.197-302. Analytical index. Emphasis throughout is on the former East Germany.
Class No: 943.02

Luxembourg

[7307]
NEWCOMER, J. The Grand Duchy of Luxembourg: the evolution of nationhood 963A.D. to 1983. Lanham, Maryland and London, Univ. Press of America in arrangement with Texas Christian Univ., 1984. xiii,343p. maps, bibliog., index. $25.50; £26.85. ISBN: 0819138452.

23 chapters. Despite dismissive appraisal in *Choice*, v.22,no.4 December 12984, p.605 this general history retains some value for its Bibliographic Essay p.319-327.
Class No: 943.59

Austria

[7308]
CARSTEN, F.L. The First Austrian republic 1918-1938 a study based on British and Austrian documents. Aldershot, Hampshire, Gower/Maurice Temple Smith, 1986. 309p. map, bibliog., index. £28.00. ISBN: 0566051621.

10 chapters (5. last years of democratic government 1930-32 ... 7. Austria under Schuschnigg ... 9. The end of independence). Bibliography p.294-296. To a large extent based on reports from the British legation in Vienna.
Class No: 943.6

[7309]
JELAVICH, B. Modern Austria empire and republic 1915-1986. Cambridge, Cambridge Univ. Press, 1986. xvii, 346p. illus. maps., bibliog. index. £39.50. ISBN: 0521316251.

7 chronological chapters concerned mainly with political history. Bibliography p.331-337. 'Her judgements of a host of complex and controversial issues are sensible and balanced' (*Choice* v.25, no.8, April 1988, p.1296).
Class No: 943.6

[7310]
KANN, R.A. A History of the Hapsburg Empire 1526-1918. Los Angeles, Univ. of California Press, 1974. xiv, 646p. maps, index. $77.50. ISBN: 0520024087.

11 chapters (1. Towards the union of the Hapsburg lands ... 10. New beginnings; cultural trends from 1860 to 1918 - 11. Bibliographical essay, p.565-606: 1. The Hapsburg Empire: general works; 2. Literature on the history of the national groups: some running commentary). 4. appendices: 1. Population and nationality statistics - 2. The Austrian Hapsburg and Hapsburg-Lorraine rulers, from the middle of the 15th century to 1918 - 3. Chronology - 4. Maps. Analytical index, p.623-46. *Class No:* 943.6

[7311]
MACARTNEY, C.A. The Hapsburg Empire 1790-1918. London, Weidenfeld & Nicolson, 1971. xiv, 908p. maps, bibliog., index.

18 chapters (1. The monarchy in 1780 ... 5. The system at its zenith (1815-30)... 9. 1848 ... 15. Hungary under Dualism (p.687-731:1867-1903; 104 footnotes ... 18. The end of the monarchy). Many footnotes. 3 appendices (3. Place names). Bibliography (running commentary, by chapters), p.838-63. Analytical index. p.864-908. 6 maps. 'Has remained one of the best general works on the subject. A revised and shorter version is *The House of Austria; the later phase, 1790-1918* (Edinburgh, U.P., £10;£5). This contains much new material and 2 helpful maps' (*Annual bulletin of historical literature*, v.64; 1978. 1980. p.105).
Class No: 943.6

Bibliographies

[7312]
BRIDGE, F.R. **The Hapsburg monarchy 1804-1918** : books and pamphlets published in the United Kingdom between 1818 and 1967. A critical bibliography. London, Univ. of London, School of Slavonic and East European Studies, 1967. 82p. index. sd.

649 briefly annotated entries in 3 sections: General history, diplomatic and military history, biography and memoirs. *Class No:* 943.6(01)

[7313]
Österreichische historische bibliographie/Austrian historical bibliography. Salzburg, Verlag Wolfgang Neugebauer; Santa Barbara, California, Clio Press, 1965-. Annual.

Lists the historical literature in Austrian periodicals or by Austrian publishers. The 1991v. (1993. 395p. 3853761275 has 3523 numbered entries. Sections: Bibliographies - Collections of essays - Auxiliary sciences - Austria (nos. 817-2476) - General and European history - Europe: nations - Non-European areas (by continent). Includes dissertations and festschriften. Author index. Five year indexes *1965-1969* (1974); *1970-1974* (1979); *1975-1979* (1983) 566p. 385376097x; 1980-1984 (1989. 793p. 3853760961); and 1985-1989 (1993. 3853760953). *Class No:* 943.6(01)

[7314]
—Österreichische historische bibliographie. Ergänzungsheft 1. Liste der Zeitschriften/Austrian historical bibliography. Supplement 1. List of periodicals 1949-1979. (1980). Paulhart, H. *and* Paulhart, H., *eds.* 32p. sd. ISBN: 3853761003.

300 numbered entries. *Class No:* 943.6(01)

[7315]
—Österreichische historische bibliographie. Supplement 2. Information und Dokumentation auf dem Gebiet der Geschichte. (1985). Hödl, G., *and others.* 55p. ISBN: 3853760937. *Class No:* 943.6(01)

Encyclopaedias

[7316]
Die Chronik Österreichs. Dortmund, Chronik Verlag, 1984. 648p. col. illus., col. maps, index. DM89.

Notable political, social, economic, cultural and military events in Austrian history presented in a contemporary newspaper style by means of chronologies, narrative maps and illustrations, mingled together. Includes 1,604 individual self-contained articles. *Class No:* 943.6(031)

[7317]
Die Chronik Wiens. Dortmund, Chronik Verlag, 1988. 528p. col. illus., col. maps, index. (*Die Chronik Städtebände.*)

Political, social, economic, cultural and military events presented as if in a contemporary newspaper. 1,240 individual and 9 summary articles. *Class No:* 943.6(031)

Chronologies

[7318]
KLEINDEL, W. **Österreich: Daten zur Geschichte und Kultur.** Wien, Überreuter, 1978. 570p.

10,000 dates from prehistory to 1977. Includes abridged versions of treaties and other historical documents and a

....(contd.)
complete list of rulers. 'An unusual but extremely useful reference aid' (D. Salt and A.F. Radley. *Austria*. 1986. Entry 752). *Class No:* 943.6(090)

[7319]
VEXLER, R. **Austria: a chronology and fact book** 1437-1973. Dobbs Ferry, New York, Oceana Publications, 1977. 154p. bibliog. $8.50. (*World Chronology Series.*) ISBN: 037916311x.

'A useful reference tool for the student of history and the general reader wishing to find his bearings amidst the entanglements of the Hapsburg dynasty' (D. Salt and A.F. Radley. *Austria*, 1986. Entry 757). *Class No:* 943.6(090)

20th Century

Bibliographies

[7320]
MALINA, P. *and* SPANN, G. **Bibliographie zur Österreichischen Zeitgeschichte 1918-1980.** Wien, Verlag für Geschichte und Politik, 3v., 1980.

Handbooks, bibliographical references and general works on political, social and economic history are listed. *Class No:* 943.6"19"(01)

Czechoslovakia

[7321]
SKILLING, H.G., *ed.* **Czechoslovakia 1918-88.** London, Macmillan in association with St. Anthony's College, Oxford, 1991. xv,232p. ISBN: 0333510828.

12 chapters by separate hands in 6 sections: 1. Triumph and tragedy of Czechoslovak leadership - 2. Independence achieved 3. Czechoslovakia in Europe - 4. The nationalities - 5. Political culture and economic change - 6. Literature: free, official and independent. 6 Appendices. Proceedings of a University of Toronto conference held 28-30 October 1988 to mark 70th anniversary of Czechoslovakia's independence. *Class No:* 943.7

Biographies

[7322]
STURM, H., *ed.* **Biographisches lexikon zur Geschichte der Böhmischen Länder.** München, R. Oldenbourg Verlag, 2v. 1979-1984.

1. *A-H* 1979. [xiv], 715p. 3486494910. 2. *I-M* 1984. 724p. 3486525514. Lieferung 1985-89. 3. *N-Z.* *Class No:* 943.7(092)

20th Century

[7323]
RENNER, H. **A History of Czechoslovakia since 1945.** London and New York, Routledge, 1989. xi, 200p. bibliog., index. £25.00. ISBN: 0415003636.

9 well-documented chronological chapters. Ch. notes p.162-92. Bibliogaphy p.193-6. *Class No:* 943.7"19"

Bibliographies

[7324]

HEJZLAR, Z. *and* **KUSIN, V.V. Czechoslovakia 1968-1969** chronology, bibliography, annotation. New York, Garland, 1975. 316p. ISBN: 0824010558.

Contents include Framework and lessons of the Prague Spring p.5-10; Chronicle p.13-148; Main documents in English translation p.151-154; Alexander Dubček in 1968-69 (a bibliography of speeches, articles and interviews) p.157-163; Bibliography of Czech and Slovak articles 1968-1970 p.182-257; Bibliography of books 1968-1974 p.261-316. *Class No:* 943.7"19"(01)

[7325]

PARRISH, M. The 1968 Czechoslovak crisis a bibliography 1968-1970. Santa Barbara, ABC Clio Press, 1971. v, 41p. index. softcover. ISBN: 0874360757.

781 unannotated entries relating to books, pamphlets, journal articles, newspapers *etc. Class No:* 943.7"19"(01)

Poland

[7326]

The Cambridge history of Poland. Reddaway, W.F., *ed.* Cambridge, Cambridge Univ. Press, 2v., 1941-50.

1: *From the origins to Sobieski (to 1696).* 1950.

2: *From Augustus II to Pilsudski (1696-1935).* 1941.

The standard work in English; a co-operative effort still awaiting the volume of bibliography. *Class No:* 943.8

[7327]

DAVIES, N. A History of Poland : God's playground. v.1. The origins to 1795. v.2 1795 to the present. Oxford, Clarendon Press; New York, Columbia Univ. Press, 1982. xxxiii, 605p.+Øxvii, 725p. illus. maps, diagrs., index. £27.50 $30.00 each. $120.00. ISBN: 0198225555, v.1; 019822592x, v.2, UK; 0231053509, v.1; 0231053525, v.2, US.

V.1. - 18 chronological and thematic chapters in 2 sections: The Origins to 1572 and The Life and death of the Polish - Lithuanian republic 1569-1795. Chapter 1. 'Millenium: a thousand years of history' is a superb review of Polish historiography. V.2. - 23 chapters in further 2 sections: Poland destroyed and reconstructed and Contemporary Poland since 1944. Bibliography v.2, p.680-684. *Class No:* 943.8

[7328]

GIEYSZTOR, A., *and others.* **A History of Poland.** 2nd ed. Warsaw, PWN-Polish Scientific Publishers, 1980. Distributed by Hippocrene Books of New York. 668p. illus. maps, bibliog., index. $76.25. ISBN: 8301003928.

5 contributors. 4 parts (25 chapters, plus 'Conclusion'): Medieval Poland - The Commonwealth of gentry - Poland under foreign rule - Poland 1918-1939. Bibliography, p.727-40 (A. Bibliographical works; B. More important textbooks and synthetic works - C. Textbooks covering longer periods; D. History of various regions and towns). Chronological tables. Well illustrated. Non-analytical index, 42 maps. 'A reference work deserving a place alongside the *Cambridge history of Poland* (*Choice*, v.18, no.1, September 1980, p.148+150). *Class No:* 943.8

Bibliographies

[7329]

DAVIES, N. Poland past and present a selected bibliography of works in English. Newtonville, Massachusetts, Oriental Research Partners, 1977. xxi, 187p. maps on endpapers, index. $26.00. ISBN: 0892500107.

1822 unannotated items dealing with all aspects of Polish history, culture, politics, and ethnic groups. Appendix 1. Handlist of over 200 periodicals related to study of Polish history - 2. Glossary (50 terms frequently encountered) - 3. Gazetteer. *Class No:* 943.8(01)

Maps & Atlases

[7330]

POGONOWSKI, I.C. Poland a historical atlas. New York, Hippocrene Books, 1987. 322p. maps, col.coats of arms on endpapers, bibliog., index. $27.50. ISBN: 0870522825.

4 introductory historical essays. The main Atlas section (p.47-219) is arranged in 8 chronological periods: 1. Poland in western civilization 966-1986. 2. Hereditary monarchy *c.*840-1370. 3. Transition to constitutional monarchy 1370-1493. 4. Constitutional monarchy 1493-1569. 5. The first Polish Republic 1569-1795. 6. The century of partition 1795-1918. 7. The Second Polish Republic 1918-1945. 8. The Third Polish Republic 1944-present. Appendix (text, maps and charts) on Prehistory and language evolution p.227-60. Bibliography p.261. Multilingual glossary of place names p.265-7. Outline of Polish history p.269-95. Comprehensive and detailed maps supported by authoritative text. *Class No:* 943.8(084.3)

Chronologies

[7331]

WLODARSKI, B. Chronologia polska. 492p.

'A valuable reference work' (R.C. Lewanski. *Poland.* 1984. Entry 85) containing *inter alia* Polish medieval calendars, comparative tables of various calendars, and tables of the monarchs and princes of Poland. *Class No:* 943.8(090)

Hungary

[7332]

A History of Hungary. Sugar, P.F., *and others, eds.* Bloomington and Indianapolis, Indiana Univ. Press; London, I.B. Tauris, 1990. xv,432p. illus., maps, bibliog., index. $35; £24.95. ISBN: 0253355788, US; 1850432864, UK.

Single-volume cooperative history (20 US, Canadian and Hungarian scholars) arranged in 21 chronological chapters e.g. 1. Hungary before the Hungarian conquest - 2. Prehistory ... 9. Principality of Transylvania ... 14. Dual Monarchy 1867-1890 ... 21. Contemporary Hungary 1956-1984 - Epilogue 1985-1990. Bibliography p.405-15. Analytical index. 'An outstanding collection that is due to become a standard work' (*Choice,* v,28, no.9, May 1991, p.1546). *Class No:* 943.9

[7333]
HOENSCH, J.K. **A History of modern Hungary 1867-1986** translated by Kim Traynor. London & New York, Longman, 1988. xiii, 320p. illus. maps, bibliog. index. £18.50. ISBN: 0582014840.

First published as *Geschichte Ungarns 1867-1983* by Verlag W. Kohlhammer of Stuttgart.

Political, social and economic history in 6 chronological chapters. Chronology (5th century AD to 1983) p.285-293. Bibliography p.294-307. Author is Professor of Eastern European History in the University of the Saarland Saarbrucken. *Class No:* 943.9

Bibliographies

[7334]
TELEK, J. **History of Hungary and the Hungarians 1848-1971** : a select bibliography. Toronto, Hungarian History Studies, 2v., 1980-1981. vii, 395p.+Øvi, 963p. index. ISBN: 0920984045, v.1; 0920984061, v.2.

V.1. first published in 1972 and reprinted with additons in 1980; v.2 first published in 1978.

4177 annotated entries in v.1; 9374 in v.2 arranged in 12 chapters (*e.g.* 4. Hungarian civilization and culture ... 10. After World War II ... 11. Foreign relations ... 12. Geography). Based on mongraphs held in the Univ. of Toronto library. *Class No:* 943.9(01)

[7335]
VÖLGYES, I. **The Hungarian Soviet Republic 1919** an evaluation and a bibliography. Stanford, Calif., Hoover Institution Press, Stanford Univ., 1970. ix, 90p. ISBN: 817924310.

2 introductory chapters: A capsule history of the Hungarian Soviet Republic and The historiography of the HSR. Bibliography in 5 sections: 1. Bibliographies, documents, reference works - 2. General works - 3. Hungarian Soviet Republic - 4. Works of special scope - 5. Autobiographies etc. *Class No:* 943.9(01)

France

[7336]
The Cambridge history of modern France. Cambridge, Cambridge Univ. Press; Paris Éditions de la Maison des Sciences de l'Homme, 8v. 1983-.

Each volume is a translation of a title or titles from the series *Nouvelle histoire de la France contemporaine* published by Éditions de Seuil of Paris 1972-.

1. *Restoration and reaction 1815-1848* by A. Jardin and A-J. Tudesq. 1983. xviii, 409p. £42.50. 0521252415 (UK). 2735100383 (Fr). 2. *The Republican experiment 1848-1852* by M. Agulhon. 1983. xiv, 211p. £27.50. 0521248299 (UK). 2735100286 (Fr). 3. *The Rise and Fall of the Second Empire 1852-1871* by A. Plessis. 1985. xvii, 193p. £27.50. 0521252423 (UK). 2735100758 (Fr). 4. *The Third Republic from its origins to the Great War 1871-1914* by J-M. Mayeur and M. Reberioux. 1984. xxi, 392p. £40.00. 0521249317 (UK). 2735100677 (Fr). 5. *The Decline of the Third Republic 1914-1938* by P. Bernard and H. Dubief 1985. xviii, 358p. £35.00. 0521252407 (UK). 2735100766 (Fr). 6. *From Munich to the Liberation 1938-1944* by J-P. Azema. 1984. xxxix, 294p. £30.00. 0521252377 (UK). 2735100782 (Fr). 7. *The Fourth Republic 1944-1958* by J-P. Rioux. 1987. xv, 531p. £40.00. 0521252385 (UK). 2735101665

....(contd.)
(Fr).

Authors are either established historians or young scholars currently involved in the field. *Class No:* 944

[7337]
DUBY, G., *ed.* **Histoire de la France.** Paris, Références Larousse, 1986-1987. illus., diagrs., plans, tables, maps, bibliogs. ISBN: 2037200110.

First published 1970-72.

1. *naissance d'une nation des origines à 1348.* 1986. 483p. 2037200102. Chronology p.445-461. Chapter bibliographies p.473-483. 2. *dynasties et révolutions de 1348 à 1852.* 1986. 543p. 2037200129. Chronology p.485-507. Bibliography p.521-543. 3. *Les temps nouveaux de 1852 à nos jours.* 1987. 2037200137. Chronology p.583-621. Bibliography p.633-652. An attractive production, including cultural, social and economic aspects of French history. *Class No:* 944

[7338]
DUBY, G. *and* WALLON, A., *eds.* **Histoire de la France rurale.** Paris, Éditions du Seuil, 4v., 1975-76. illus., facsims., diagrs., tables, maps, indexes.

1. *La formation des campagnes françaises, des origines au XIVe seècle* 1975. 620p. Bibliographie p.604-11 - 2. *L'âge classique des paysans 1340-1789.* 1975. 620p. Notes p.592-9. Bibliographie p.602-11 - 3. *Apogée et crise de la civilization paysanne 1789-1914.* 1976. 569p. Bibliographie p.548-57. ISBN 2020044137 - 4. *La fin de la France paysanne, de 1914 à nos jours.* 1977. 667p. Notes p.632-47. Bibliographie p.650-7. 2020046377. *Class No:* 944

[7339]
DUBY, G. **Histoire de la France urbaine.** Paris Éditions du Seuil, 5v., 1980-85. illus., maps, diagrs., indexes. ISBN: 2020055910, set.

1. *La ville antique, des origines au IXe siècle.* 1980. 600p. *Principaux auteurs anciens et documents cités* p.576-7. Bibliographie p.576-7. ISBN 2020055902 - 2. *La ville médiévale des Carolingiens à la Renaissance.* 1980. 653p. Bibliographie p.616-39. 2020056666 - 3. *La ville classique de la Renaissance au Révolutions.* 1981. 651p. Notes p.624-7. Bibliographie p.630-7. 2020059789 - 4.*La ville de l'âge industrial* - 5. *La ville d'aujourd'hui croissance urbaine et crise du citadin.* 1985. 668p. Notes p.651-8. Bibliographie p.659-663. 2020089165. *Class No:* 944

[7340]
LAVISSE, E., *ed.* **Histoire de France depuis les origines jusqu' à la Révolution.** Paris, Hachette, 9v. in 18, 1900-11.

Volumes in print (Tallendier): 1. *Le Christianisme, les Barbares, Mérovingiens et Carolingiens.* 1961. 400p. ISBN 2235011268. 6. *Charles VII, Louis XI et la minorité de Charles VIII 1422-1492.* 1981. 490p. 2235011853. 7. *Charles VIII, Louis XII et François 1er. Les guerres 1492-1547.* 1982. 432p. 2235013430. 8. *Henri II, la lutte contre la maison d'Autriche 1519-1559.* 1983. 448p. 2235013651.

No series for French history on a comparable scale has since appeared. Based on firsthand use of documents. The political attitude of the various contributors is moderately 'left of centre'. Despite its age, Lavisse is still a standard work for its many sound chapters and critical bibliographies.

Lavisse H. *Histoire de France, de la Révolution à la paix de 1919.* Paris, Hachette, 10v., 1920-22. V.10 of the second set: *Tables générales des origines à la paix de 1919.* *Class No:* 944

[7341]
L'Almanach de Paris. Paris, Encyclopaedia Universalis, 2v., 1990. 336p. illus. 630F.
   1. *Des origines à 1788.* ed. M. Fleury.
   2. *De 1789 à nos jours* ed. J. Tulard.
'Une chronologie illustré par des documents d'époque. Toute d'histoire de Paris, tous les événements, tous les personnages et tous les lieux se trouvent rassemblés dans ces deux volumes' (*Livres de France*, n.122, Septembre 1990, p.56). *Class No:* 944

[7342]
Nouvelle histoire de Paris. Paris, Association pour la publication d'une histoire de Paris, Bibliothèque historique de la ville de Paris. Distributed by Hachette.
   1. Boussard, J. *De la fin du siège de 885-886 à la mort de Philippe Auguste* -2. Cazelles, R. *De la fin du régime de Philippe Auguste à la mort de Charles V (1223-1380)* - 3. Favier, J. *Paris au XVe siècle (1380-1500)* - 4. Babelon, J.P. *Paris au XVIe siècle* - 5. Reinard, M. *La Révolution (1789-1799)* - 6. Tulard, J. *Le Consultat et l'Empire (1800-1815)* - 7. De Sauvigny, Gr. de B. *La Restauration (1815-1830)* - 8. Girard, L. *La Deuxième République et le Second Empire (1848-1870)* - 9. Rials, S. *De Trochu à Thiers (1870-1873)* - 10. Lavedan, P. *Histoire de l'urbanisme à Paris* - 11. De Villefosse, R.H. *Solennités, fêtes et Réjouissances parisiennes.*
   Pillorget, R. *Paris sous les premiers Bourbons 1594-1661.* 1988. 741p. has 15 chapters. Sources et bibliographie p.641-700. Index des Personnages. Index des lieux et monuments. *Class No:* 944

[7343]
Peuples et pays de France. Plasseraud, Y., *ed.* Paris, les Éditions d'Organisation, 1981-. illus., map, bibliog.
   L'Alsace edited by P. Klein. 1981. 2708104136. *Le Comté de Nice* edited by R. Debrie. 1981. 2708104225. *La Picardie* edited by A. Compan. 1981. 2708103830. Substantial cooperative regional histories each typically consisting of 17-18 chapters. Extremely useful and detailed bibliographies (up to 12 pages in length). *Class No:* 944

Bibliographies

[7344]
BARBIER, F. Bibliographie de l'histoire de France. Paris, Masson, 1987. 283p. Fr.160. ISBN: 2225808287.
   Part 1. Bibliographie Générale: Chap 1. Notions (i.e. La recherche bibliographique and La recherche documentaire). Chap 2. L'historien et le travail en biblothèque. Part 2. Bibliographie de l'histoire générale: 3. Histoire générale. 4. Histoire des Religions.
   Part 3. Bibliographie générale de l'histoire de France: 7. Manuels généraux et bibliographies d'ensemble. 8. L'accès au documents. 9. Sources legislatives et réglementaires. 10. L'accès aux documents: sources manuscrites. Part 4. Quelques domaines spécialisés. All entries are very briefly annotated. *Class No:* 944(01)

[7345]
CARON, P. and STEIN, H. Répertoire bibliographique de l'histoire de France, années 1920/21-1930/31. Aalen, Scientia Verlag und Antiquariat Karl Schilling, 6v., 1972. 500 First published Paris, Picard, 1923-38.
   A biennial bibliography of the history of France from the beginning to 1914, omitting the history of literature, art, science. Books and articles in periodicals published during

.... (contd.)
the two years under review are listed, with explanations where necessary and notes of reviews, by subject. Indexes of persons and places. *Class No:* 944(01)

[7346]
CENTRE NATIONAL DE LA RECHERCHE SCIENTIFIQUE. INSTITUT D'HISTOIRE MODERNE ET CONTEMPORAINE. Bibliographie annuelle de l'histoire de France du cinquième siècle à 1958. Paris, Éditions du CNRS, 1956-. Annual. ISSN: 00676918.
   Continues *Répertoire de l'histoire de France*, by P. Caron and H. Stein (années 1920/21-1930-31. Paris, Picard, 1923-38, 6v.), itself preceded by Répertoire méthodique de l'histoire moderne et contemporaine de la France pour l'année 1898-1912/12.
   Année 1989 (1990. xciv,1231p. ISBN 2222044561) has 13657 entries. Systematic arrangement in 9 broad groups: 1. Manuels généraux et sciences auxiliaires de l'histoire - 2. Histoire politique de la France - 3. Histoire des institutions - 4. Histoire économique - 5. Sociale - 6. Histoire religieuse - 7. La France outre-mer 8. Histoire de la civilization - 9. Histoire locale. Liste des périodiques dépouillés et des leurs abbréviations p.xv-xciv. Subject and author indexes. *Class No:* 944(01)

[7347]
GANDILHON, R. and SAMARAN, C.M.D. Bibliographie générale des travaux historiques et archéologiques, publiés par les sociétés savantes de la France: Période 1910-40. Paris, Imprimerie Nationale, 1944-. v.1-. (v.1-5, 1944-61).
   List of books and articles on historical and archaeological subjects published by French learned societies between 1910 and 1940; arranged A-Z by Département, then by place of publication, then by society; a note on each society and its publications is followed by an analysis of the contents of each volume of its publications. V.5: *Seine-et-Marne-Yonne, France d'Outre-mer et étranger* (1961, 583p. F80) records 9,138 publications from 104 societies. No indication whether subject and author indexes are planned.
   For earlier publications, see *Bibliographie générale des travaux historiques et archéologiques publiés par les sociétés de la France [-1885 and 1886-1900]*, compiled by Robert de Lasteyrie (c.1888-1918), 6v. and its annual continuation; *Bibliographie annuelle des travaux historiques et archéologiques* under the same compiler, covering the years 1901-10 (1906-14, 3v., reprinted New York, 1965). *Class No:* 944(01)

[7348]
MOLINIER, A., and others. Les Sources de l'histoire de France depuis les origines jusqu'en 1815. Paris, Picard, 18v., 1901-35.
   Pt.1. *Des origines aux guerres d'Italie.* 1. *Époque primitive Mérovingiens et Carolingiens.* 2. *Époque féodale, les Capétiens jusqu'en 1180.* 3. *Les Capétiens 1180-1328.* 4. *Les Valois 1328-1461.* 5. *Introduction générale, Les Valois (suite), Louis XI et Charles VIII (1461-94).* 6. *Table générale.* Pt.1. in print from New York, Lennox Hill.
   Pt.2. *Le XVIe siècle (1494-1610)* by H. Hauser. 1. *Les premières guerres d'Italie, Charles VIII et Louis XII (1494-1515).* 2. *François I et Henri II (1515-59).* 3. *Les guerres de religion (1559-89).* 4. *Henri IV (1589-1610).*
   Pt.3. *Le XVIIe siècle (1610-1715)* by E. Bourgeois and L. André. 1. *Géographie et histoire générale.* 2. *Mémoires et lettres.* 3. *Biographies.* 4. *Journaux et pamphlets.* 5. *Histoire*

.... *(contd.)*

politique et militaire. 6. *Histoire maritime et coloniale, histoire religieuse.* 7. *Histoire économique, histoire administrative.* 8. *Histoire provinciale et locale. Additions et corrections. Table générale.* Pt.4. *Le XVIIIe siècle* was never published.

A critical bibliography, arranged by subject, of the printed narrative sources for the history of France. *Class No:* 944(01)

[7349]
'Recent books and dissertations on French history', *French Historical Studies*, 1958-. Quarterly. ISSN: 00161071.

A regular feature since the first issue. Listed under 8 headings: 1. Bibliographical, reference and archival publications - 2. General and miscellaneous - 3. Ancient and medieval - 4. 1500 to 1774 - 5. the Revolutionary period and Napoleon - 6. 1815 to 1870 - 7. The Third Republic - 8. 1940 to the present. Since Fall 1987 the Bibliography has been available on 5.25 inch floppy disk prepared on IBM compatible computer (Wordperfect system). *Class No:* 944(01)

Micromaterials

[7350]
Bibliothèque Nationale Catalogue de l'histoire de France. Paris, Cambridge and Alexandria, Virginia, Chadwyck-Healey, 1988. 1500 positive silver halide 105 x 148 mm fiche at 24x reduction with printed guide subject index. £3500. ISBN: 2869760051.

Contents: Catalogue de l'histoire de France 1855-1895 (200,000 records) and unpublished card catalogues 1895-1987 (550,000 records) in 16 main sections: miscellaneous; historical periods; reigns; journals and publications; religion; constitutional; administrative; diplomatic; military history; manners and customs; archaeology; local; social; family history; biography; economic history. Printed subject index includes A-Z list of 500 subject terms with cross-references to the *Catalogue. Class No:* 944(01)(003.5)

Encyclopaedias

[7351]
Chronique de la France et des Français. Paris, Librarie Larousse. 1300p. col.illus., col.maps.

A history of France from the earliest period to contemporary times reported year by year in newspaper style. 'Pour découvir comment les Français ont fait la France' (*Larousse Catalogue Général 1990*). *c.*3000 illustrations. *Class No:* 944(031)

Dictionaries

[7352]
Dictionnaire d'histoire de France Perrin. De Caux, A. *and* Castelot, A., *eds.* Paris, Librairie Académique Perrin, 1981. 1076p. illus. (some col.), maps. ISBN: 2262002282.

Massive A-Z encyclopedia of events, prominent figures, places, institutions. *etc.* with countless illustrations including full colour plates. 'Compiègne' p.223-4. 2 illus. 'Diên Biên Phu' p.299-305. 16 illus. 2 maps. No bibliographical apparatus. *Class No:* 944(038)

[7353]
Historical dictionaries of French history. Westport, Connecticut, Greenwood Press; London, Aldwych Press, 1985-1987. bibliogs., indexes.

1. Scott, S.F. and Rothaus, B. *eds. Historical dictionary of the French Revolution 1789-1799.* 2v. 1985. xvii, 1143p. $95.00. ISBN 0313211418, US. 0861720431, UK. 2. Connelly, O. *ed. Historical dictionary of Napoleonic France 1799-1815.* 1985. xiii, 586p. $65.00. £53.50. 0313213216, US. 0867120423, UK. 3. Newman, E.L. *ed. Historical dictionary of France from the 1815 Restoration to the Second Empire.* 2v., 1987. xvii, 1241p. $135.00. £115.00. 0313227519, US. 0861720474, UK. 4. Echard, W.E. *ed. Historical dictionary of the French Second Empire 1952-1870.* 1985. xvi, 829p. $87.50. £68.50. 0313211361, US. 086172044x, UK. 5. Hutton, P.H. *ed. Historical dictionary of the Third French Republic 1870-1940.* 2v., 1986. xvi, 1206p. $125.00. £115.00. 0313220880, US. 0861720466, UK. 6. *Historical dictionary of the French Fourth and Fifth Republics 1946-1991* edited by W. Northcutt. 1992. xv,527p. £68.; $85. 0313263566.

A multitude of contributors. Well-documented signed entries relating to leading personalities, events, constitutional developments, chronologies *etc.* R.A. Jonces and D.A. Pinkney's 'The Greenwood Press' historical dictionaries of French history', *French Historical Studies*, v.15, no.2, Fall 1987, p.345-57 subjects them to a detailed scrutiny. *Class No:* 944(038)

Maps & Atlases

[7354]
Atlas historique de la France. Paris, Plon, 1985. 150p. col. maps, tables. 185.00 F. £20.50. ISBN: 2259013171.

10 chapters: 1. Chronologie de l'histoire de France (p.8-39) - 2. La France avant la France - 3. Des Mérovingiens aux Capétiens - 4. Le royaume de France - 5. La monarchie absolue et la fin de l'ancien régime - 6. Le xix siècle - 7. La France contemporaine - 8. La France en Europe - 9. Faits et chiffres - 10. Souverains, chefs d'État et régimes. Closely integrated maps and text although mixture of specially drawn maps for this publication and many maps from *Atlas géneral Vidal-Lablache* is unsettling. *Class No:* 944(084.3)

[7355]
SINCLAIR, S. Atlas de géographie historique de la France et de la Gaulle de la conquête césarienne à nos jours. Paris, Sedes, 1985. 260p. maps, geneal. tables, bibliog., index. softcover. ISBN: 2718122107.

13 chapters assembled in 3 parts: 1. Histoire - 2. Géographie administative et judiciare - 3. Géographie réligieuse. Bibliographie critique p.211-230. 'L'ouvrage couvre la quasi totalité de l'histoire nationale, dans tous ses aspects' (*Introduction*). *Class No:* 944(084.3)

Middle Ages

Bibliographies

[7356]
SOCIÉTÉ DES HISTORIENS MÉDIÉVISTES DE L'ENSEIGNEMENT SUPÉRIEUR. Bibliographie de l'histoire médiévale en France (1965-1990). Paris, Publications de la Sorbonne, 1992. ii,486p. index. 190F. ISBN: 2859442146. ISSN: 02904500.

21 sections *e.g.* 1. Histoire des campagns médiévales en

....*(contd.)*

France - 2. Histoire urbaine en France Xe-XVe siècle ... 9. L'Archéologie médiévale ... 21. Vingt ans d'informatique en histoire médiévale. 'C'est un guide bibliographique commode, à l'usage des chercheurs, des bibliothèques et des amateurs d'histoire du Moyen-Age'.
Class No: 944"01/14"(01)

Dictionaries

[7357]
FAVIER, J. Dictionnaire de la France Médiévale. Paris, Fayard, 1993. 1016p. illus. (51 col.), maps, geneal. tables. F750.

5835 A-Z entries relating to people, events, movements, *etc.* of the period 600AD to 1500. 27 maps and plans.
Class No: 944"01/14"(038)

Modern Times

Bibliographies

[7358]
SAULNIER, E. *and* MARTIN, E. Bibliographie des travaux publiés de 1866 à 1897 sur l'histoire de la France, de 1500 à 1789. Paris, Presses Universitaires de France, 2v., 1932-38.

A list of books and articles, with references to reviews, relating to the history of France during the period 1500 to 1789, published in the years 1866 to 1897. Arranged by subject. *Class No:* 944"15/19"(01)

17th Century

Dictionaries

[7359]
Dictionnaire du Grand Siècle. Bluche, F., *ed.* Paris, Fayard, 1990. 1640p. illus. (inc. 24 col. pl.), index. ISBN: 2213024251.

250 contributors. Short and long signed articles on the personalities, military, political, religious, and commercial history of the period from the accession of Henry IV to the death of his grandson Louis XIV *i.e.* 1589-1715.
Class No: 944"16"(038)

18th & 19th Centuries

Dictionaries

[7360]
Dictionnaire Napoléon. Tulard, J., *ed.* Paris, Fayard, 1987. 1767p. illus., maps. Fr950. ISBN: 2213020353.

Authoritative and comprehensive dictionary of 'tous les personnages marquants de la période 1800-1815' with the battles and grand themes (*e.g.* Armée; Musique militaire; Presse) of the Napoleonic era. 204 contributors.
Class No: 944"17/18"(038)

French Revolution

[7361]
DOYLE, W. The Oxford history of the French Revolution. Oxford, Clarendon Press, 1989. xi, 466p. + 16p. of plates., illus., maps, ports., bibliog., index. £17.50. $29.95. ISBN: 0198227817.

Authoritative and reliable narrative covering the period from the accession of Louis XVI (1774) to Napoleon's triumph (1802). Notes p.426-33. Appendix 1. Chronology p.434-41. 2. The Revolutionary Calendar p.442-3. Bibliography p.444-8. Analytical index.
Class No: 944"1789-1799"

[7362]
HAYTHORNTHWAITE, P.J. The Napoleonic source book. London, Arms And Armour, 1990; New York, Facts on File, 1991. 414p. illus., maps, bibliog., index. £19.95; $40. ISBN: 0853689695, UK; 0816025479, US.

1. The Campaigns (a brief chronological account of the Revolutionary and Napoleonic Wars with a list of battles and treaties) - 2. Weapons and the practice of war - 3. Nations involved in the Napoleonic Wars (a review of each state's participation and of their military and naval forces) - 4. Biographies (40 of the leading military officers) - 5. Sources (review of the development of Napoleonic literature and a list of references for further reading) p.365-84 - 6. Miscellanea - 7. Glossary (contemporary military terms) p.397-405. 'Each section and most entries are accompanied by a reference list' (*Introduction*). Over 200 illustrations. 18 maps. *Class No:* 944"1789-1799"

[7363]
LEFEBVRE, G. The French Revolution. London, Routledge & Kegan Paul; New York, Columbia Univ. Press. 2v., 1962-64.

Originally as *La Révolution Française* (Paris, Presses Universitaires de France, 1957).

1: *From its origins to 1793.* Translated by E.M. Evanson. 1962. xviii, 366p. $36.00. ISBN 0231023421 US. 2: *From 1793 to 1799.* Translated by J.H. Stewart and J. Friguglietti. 1964. xiv, 430p. $36.00. ISBN 023102519x US. V.2 has 3 parts (17 chapters): 1. The Coalition and the Revolution, to the treaties of 1795 - 2. The victorious offensive of the Revolution - The world at the advent of Napoleon. Conclusion. Bibliography, p.361-95 (by chapters and sections). Analytical index. Balanced and thorough. 'Lefebvre may very well be the greatest historian of the Revolution' (F. Chamber. *France,* 1980. Entry 86).
Class No: 944"1789-1799"

Bibliographies

[7364]
CALDWELL, R.J. The Era of the French Revolution a bibliography of the history of western civilization, 1789-1799. New York, Garland Publishing Inc., 2v, 1985. xvi, 609p. + 611-1299p. $200.00. ISBN: 0824087941.

A monumental work containing 42,240 citations (many annotated) in 6 large sections: 1. General history in the French Revolutionary era - 2. The French Revolution 1787-1799 - 3. Biography - 4. Local history - 5. National history of Europe - 6. National history of the Americas. 'The present bibliography fulfills the need for a thorough catalogue of French Revolution history even though such a work cannot be absolutely comrprehensive.' (*Preface*).
Class No: 944"1789-1799"(01)

[7365]
DOYLE, W. The French Revolution : a bibliography of works in English. London, The Historical Association, 1988. 35p. pbk. ISBN: 0852783043.

A-Z by author list of scholarly titles. Excludes material dealing exclusively with Ancien Régime or Napoleonic period. 'To guide those unable to read French to whatever is available in English, irrespective of its original authorship' (*Foreword*). *Class No:* 944"1789-1799"(01)

[7366]
French Revolutionary collections in the British Library : list of the contents of the three special collections of pamphlets, journals and other works in the British Library, relating chiefly to the French Revolution. Fortescue, G.K., *comp. Revised and augmented by A.C. Brodhurst.* 2nd ed. London, The British Library, 1979. 87p. index. ISBN: 0904654214.

First published 1899.

Key to 48,000 books, pamphlets and sets of periodical volumes. See also Brodhurst's 'The French Revolution collections in the British Library', *British Library Journal*, v.2, no.2, Autumn 1976. *Class No:* 944"1789-1799"(01)

[7367]
HAMPSON, N. 'The French Revolution', *The Historian*, no.21, Winter 1988/89, p.10-11.

Surveys publications commemorating the Revolution's bicentenary. *Class No:* 944"1789-1799"(01)

[7368]
HARDY, J.D., *and others.* The Maclure collection of French Revolutionary materials. Philadelphia, Univ. of Pennsylvania Press, 1964. xxix, 456p.

About 12,000 entries, catalogued by volumes; v.1-643 contain legislative proceedings, private journals and other serials; v.644-1460, private works, topical series, miscellaneous works, etc. Meticulously arranged; no annotations. Indexes of deputies, authors (excluding deputies), committees and commissions. The Maclure Collection compares in variety with those at Cornell, Harvard, Chicago and Columbia Universities and New York Public Library. 'An intelligent use of the collection, with the catalogue as a supervisor, might save the research student a year's work in French libraries' (*Times literary Supplement*, no.3411, 13 July 1967, p.628). *Class No:* 944"1789-1799"(01)

[7369]
Les Livres de la Révolution française. Paris, Éditions Professionnelles Du Livre, 1989. 150p. 90F.

A special issue of *Préfaces.*

Contains 150 reviews of the most significant works published since 1985 and a bibliography of *c.*1500 titles in print. *Class No:* 944"1789-1799"(01)

[7370]
MONGLOND, A. La France révolutionnaire et impériale: annales de bibliographie méthodique et description des livres illustrés. Genève, Statkines Reprints, 9v., 1976. 6115p.

First published Paris, Imprimerie Nationale 1930-63.

V.1-9: 1789-1812. An exhaustive bibliography of books, pamphlets and articles on various aspects of life in France, 1789-1815. Arranged chronologically by years; under each year: La vie française - La tradition littéraire - Les relations littéraires avec l'étranger - La littérature nouvelle. *Class No:* 944"1789-1799"(01)

[7371]
STEVANOVIC, B. 'French books', *Booklist,* v.86,no.11, 1 February 1990, p.1073-4.

62 briefly annotated titles A-Z by author of books published or reprinted in France to commemorate the bicentennial of the French Revolution. *Class No:* 944"1789-1799"(01)

Micromaterials

[7372]
Images of the French Revolution a comprehensive archive of 38,000 images. Paris, Bibliothèque Nationale; London, Pergamon Press, 1989. Videodisk (12"/30 cm. optical disk) compatible with all Laservision PAL or NTSC disk drives. £250.00. ISBN: 0080374174.

Images, drawn principally from the holdings of the Department of Engravings, are arranged in 7 sections: 1. Events of the Revolution - 2. Themes in culture & art - 3. Archives and documents - 4. The Revolution commemorated and celebrated - 5. The Revolution & 19th century polemic - 6. France at the end of the 18th century - 7. Revolution collections in the BN; The Videodisk. Supplied with a booklet comprising a general introduction; text of the summaries, and additonal information. Printed catalogue: v.1. contains an historical background to the BN's collections; subject listing; classsification guide; and bilingual (French/English) index. V.2-3 includes over 15,000 bibliographical notes. A software version is available £265.00. ISBN 0080374182. Videodisk and booklet + database with user manual and interface cable £565.00. ISBN 0080374190. Complete package: videodisk and booklet; 3v. printed catalogue; database and user mannual £655.00. ISBN 0080372473. *Class No:* 944"1789-1799"(01)(003.5)

[7373]
—The French Revolution research collection & videodisk. Lucas, C., *editor-in-chief.* Oxford, Pergamon Press, in cooperation with the Bibliothèque Nationale, Paris, 1989-92. 1,000,000p. on 105 x 148mm microfiche with a videodisk. £43,000.

Reproduces over 1 million pages of primary documentary material, mostly printed documents, but where necessary for a balance of coverage, a number of import manuscripts are included. 12 sections are organized in 2 parts. Part 1. Common core sections: 1. Newspapers edited by H. Gough (100,000p.) - 2. Memoirs & autobiographies ed. by C. Lucas (100,000p.) - 3. Basic printed collections ed. by C. Lucas (150,000p.) - 4. Bibliographical & research tools (20,000p). Part 2. Thematic sections: 5. Pre-revolutionary debate edited by J. Popkin and D. Van Kley (30,000p.) - 6. Political themes (Local government; Extra-parliamentary politics; Political authors) (160,000p.) - 7. Resistance to the Revolution ed. by R. Dupuy (100,000p.) - 8. Religion ed. by T. Tackett (100,000p.) - 9. The reorganization of society (The abolition of the corporate society and feudalism; The countryside; Towns and townspeople; Women & the family; Public Assistance) (125,000p.) - 10. The Economy (Policy, trade and finance; Agriculture; Industry & Technology) (100,000p.) - 11. War & the colonies (The Army and the Navy, The colonies) (65,000p.) - 12. Culture ed. by J. Leith (95,000p.). *Images of the French Revolution* (*qv*). *Class No:* 944"1789-1799"(01)(003.5)

Encyclopaedias

[7374]

Chronicle of the French Revolution. London, Longman, 1989. 700p. illus. (mostly col.), indexes. £29.95. ISBN: 0582051940.

Chronologies (8 days - 1 month) and 'news reports' present an 'as it happened' account of the Revolution from the Declaration of the Rights of Man to the rise of Napoleon Bonaparte. 3000 major and minor social and political events are chronicled. There is a list of the composition of French governments 1788-1799. Over 1700 illustrations. *Class No:* 944"1789-1799"(031)

[7375]

JONES, C. The Longman companion to the French Revolution. London and New York, Longman, 1988. xiii, 473p. maps, geneal. table, bibliog., index. £40.00 $79.95. ISBN: 0582494184.

Compendious reference work organized in 13 sub-divided sections covering the period 1787-1799: 1. Political chronology - 2. Framework of government - 3. The Executive - 4. Structure of the Terror: the institutions of revolutionary government 1792-1795 - 5. International relations and war - 6. Politics - 7. Administration, justice and finance - 8. Religion and ideas - 9. Society and the economy - 10. Biographies (over 500 *dramatis personae* highlighting minor figures) - 11. Glossary of over 400 terms (p.401-424) - 12. The Revolutionary Calendar - 13. Bibliography (p.432-5). For all scholars, students and general readers requiring detailed factural data. *Class No:* 944"1789-1799"(031)

Dictionaries

[7376]

FURET, F. *and* **OZOUF, M.,** *eds.* **A Critical dictionary of the French Revolution.** Cambridge, Massachusetts, Harvard Univ. Press, 1989. 1168p. illus., (some col.). $101.95. £67.95. ISBN: 0674177282.

99 essays A-Z by key words and themes under 5 major headings: Events - Actors - Institutions and creations - Ideas - Historians and commentators. François Furet is Professor of History and Social Thought in the Univ. of Chicago; Mona Ozouf is Director of Research at the Centre Nationale de la Recherche Scientifique. *Class No:* 944"1789-1799"(038)

[7377]

PAXTON, J. Companion to the French Revolution. New York and Oxford, Facts On File, 1988. x,231p. + 4p. maps. diagrs., bibliog. $24.95; £11.95. ISBN: 0816011168.

Over 1000 A-Z entries (25 to 600 words in length) relating to facts, figures, dates, defintions, people and places of significance in the period 1769-1804. Chronology p.211-225. Bibliography p.227-231. 'A wide array of useful information on the epoch, will be useful in public libraries' (*Booklist,* v.84, no.16, 15 April 1988, p.1404). *Class No:* 944"1789-1799"(038)

[7378]

SOBOUL, A. Dictionnaire historique de la Révolution Française. Suratteau, J-R. *and* Gendron, F., *eds.* Paris, Presses Universitaires De France, 1989. xlvii,1132p. maps, bibliog., index. Fr495.00. ISBN: 2130425224.

English ed. *The French Revolution 1787-1799 from the storming of the Bastille to Napoleon.* London, Unwin Hyman, 1989. £30. ISBN 0044456107.

64 contributors offer over 1000 authoritative, well-

.... *(contd.)*

documented and signed essays of varying length on the principal persons, places, events, and political ideologies of the Revolution (États-Généraux: 3p. 3refs.; Jean-Paul Marat: 4p., 8 refs.). Aperçu historiographique p.xv-xxxi. Bibliographie générale p.xxxiii-xxxvi. Tableau chronolgique synoptique p.xxxviii-xlvii. *Class No:* 944"1789-1799"(038)

Maps & Atlases

[7379]

Atlas de la Révolution Française. Paris, Éditions de l'École des Hautes Études en Sciences Sociales, 5v., 1987-89.

1. *Routes et communications* by G. Arbellot and others. 1987. 91p. FFr90. 2713208947. 2. *L'Enseignement 1760-1815* by D. Julia and others. 1987. 105p. FFr90. 2713208939. 3. *L'Armée et la guerre* edited by J.P. Bertrand and D. Reichel, 1989. 79p. 2713209277. 4. *Le Territoire (1): réalités et représentations* by D. Nordman and M.V. Ozouf-Marignier. 1989. 106p. FFr120. 2713209293. 5. *Le Territoire (2): les limites administratives.* 1989. 125p. FFr150. 2713209420. National, regional and provincial maps supported by an explanatory text. 'A judicious blending of large-scale maps and 'close-ups' revealing the situation in this or that town, portion of territory, or sector of the national frontier' (*French History,* v.5, no.1, March 1991, p.118-9). *Class No:* 944"1789-1799"(084.3)

Chronologies

[7380]

GODECHOT, J. La Révolution française commentée, 1787-1799. Paris, Perrin, 1988. 392p. bibliog., index. F125. ISBN: 2262005087.

11 sections forming a day by day chronology which in effect becomes an outline history. A biographical dictionary includes 401 profiles. A bibliographical essay summarizes the historiography of the period. 'A most convenient handbook to the Revolutionary era, one that students can consult with confidence' (*French Historical Studies,* v.16, no.1, Spring 1989, p.217-21). *Class No:* 944"1789-1799"(090)

Biographies

[7381]

CARATINI, R. Dictionnaire des personages de la Révolution. Paris, LePré aux Clercs, 1988. xiv, 577p. illus. £23.85. ISBN: 2714422322.

3000 entries of French and foreign personalities of note and secondary importance caught up in the Revolution 1789-1795. Bibliography p.543-46. Chronology p.547-77. *Class No:* 944"1789-1799"(092)

[7382]

La Révolution Française Dictionnaire biographique. Manceron, C. *and* Manceron, A. Paris, Renaudot, 1989. 571p. Fr180. ISBN: 2877420086.

Definitive biographical details of all leading personalities and lesser known participants in all aspects of the Revolution. *Class No:* 944"1789-1799"(092)

19th & 20th Centuries

Bibliographies

[7383]
Bibliothèque Nationale Catalogue de la Troisième République 1870-1940. Amalvi, C., *comp.* Paris, Chadwyck-Healey France, 3v., 1990-91. 1800p. index. £240. ISBN: 2869760043.

V.1: *1871-1876;* v.2: *1877-1899;* v.3: *1900-1940* (includes a cumulated index of authors). 30,000 catalogue records relating to contemporary and retrospective works on French political, constitutional, colonial, religious and social history extracted from BN's *Catalogue de l'Histoire de France (q.v.).* A Four-page descriptive brochure is available. *Class No:* 944"18/19"(01)

19th Century

[7384]
CALDWELL, R.J. The Era of Napoleon a bibliography of the history of Western civilization 1799-1815. New York, Garland, 2v., 1991. xxi,1447p. $210. ISBN: 0824056442.

48,000 entries, some annotated, relating to books, periodicals, and dissertations. More than 50% cover France (French biography and local history account for some 14,000 entries). The majority of the items cited are non-English language works. Many of the chronological and thematic sections have introductions signalling the most valuable items. *Class No:* 944"18"

20th Century

Bibliographies

[7385]
COMITÉ FRANÇAIS DE SCIENCES HISTORIQUES. La Recherche historique en France de 1940 à 1965. Paris, Centre National de la Recherche Scientifique, 1965. lxiv, 519p.

A classified list of French writings during the period on all areas and aspects. 6,460 entries, indicating presence of portraits, maps, etc. in classes A-U, with subdivisions (p.207-477). Preceded by sections, 1. 'L'enseignement et recherche' - 2. 'Les publications (Les inventaires et d'archives; Thèses; Revues)'. Author index. *La Recherche historique en France depuis 1965.* 1980. 154p. ISBN 2222026423. *Class No:* 944"19"(01)

[7386]
EVLETH, D., *comp.* **France under the German occupation, 1940-1944** an annotated bibliography. Westport, Conn., Greenwood Press, 1991. xii,220p. indexes. £56.80. (*Bibliographies and Indexes in World History, no. 20.*) ISBN: 0313274746.

Selective annotated bibliography of printed works available in libraries, mainly related to metropolitan France, arranged in 7 heavily subdivided major sections: 1. The Vichy regime - 2. Daily life - 3. Collaboration - 4. The Resistance - 5. Position of the Communists - 6. Liberation - 7. The Purge. Guide to the Press under the Occupation p.193-4. Brief guide to the principal archives and libraries p.195-9. *Class No:* 944"19"(01)

[7387]
HEINZ, G. *and* **PETERSON, A.F. The French Fifth Republic** establishment and consolidation (1958-1965) an annotated bibliography of the holdings of the Hoover Institution. Stanford, California, Hoover Institution Press, 1970. xiii, 170p. indexes. $11.95. ISBN: 0817924418.

2134 items listed 'Not an exhaustive bibliography of the works relating to the Fifth Republic published in France or elsewhere but it is hoped that no serious omissions will be discovered as far as scholarly reference works, memoirs, biographies, government documents and periodicals are concerned' (*Introduction*). Followed by *The French Fifth Republic: continuity and change 1966-1970: a bibliography.* 1974. 125. $11.95. ISBN 0817925414. *Class No:* 944"19"(01)

Maps & Atlases

[7388]
BOUJU, P.M., *and others.* **Atlas historique de la France contemporaine** 1800-1965. Paris, Armand Colin, 1966. 234p., graphs, maps.

461 clearly-drawn maps and graphs (2-4 per page) in 8 chapters: 1. Le territoire national et l'administration - 2. La population - 3. Economique et financiére - 4. Forces politiques et opinions publiques - 5. Forces et croyances religieuses - 6. L'enseignement et l'instruction - 7. Information, culture et loisirs - 8. Le français hors de France. 'Orientation bibliographique', p.218-21. No index, but full contents-list. 'An extremely useful visual presentation of many aspects of French political, social, economic, religious and cultural life during the past 150 years' (*International Affairs*, v.43, no.4, October 1967, p.811). *Class No:* 944"19"(084.3)

Libraries

[7389]
McCRANK, L.J., *ed.* **Bibliographical foundations of French historical studies.** New York, Haworth Press, 1992. xii,243p. index. $29.95. (*Primary Sources and Original Works v.1, nos.1/2.*) ISBN: 1560241500. ISSN: 10428216.

Detailed information on bibliographic sources and institutions. 1. Bibliographic methods and French historical studies - 2. French archives and libraries - 3. Post-Revolution French bibliographic connections with the New World - 4. French Revolution of archives and libraries: from royal to national and from private to public institutions. Derived from selected papers presented at the annual conference of the Association of the Bibliography of History in conjunction with the American Historical Association, San Francisco, 1992. *Class No:* 944:061:026/027

Italy

[7390]
Longman history of Italy. Hay, D., *ed.* Harlow, Essex, Longman, 1980-. illus., tables, maps.

1. *Italy in the early Middle Ages 600-1216* by T.S. Brown. 2. *Italy in the age of Dante and Petrarch 1216-1380* by J. Larner. 1980. 3. *Italy in the age of the Renaissance 1380-1530* by D. Hay and J. Law. £19.95. ISBN 0582483581. 4. *Italy 1530-1630* by E. Cochrane. 1988. £19.95. ISBN 0582483646. 5. *Italy in the Age of Reason 1685-1789* by D. Carpanetto and G. Ricuperati. 1987. £19.95. ISBN

....(contd.)
0582483387. 6. *Italy in the seventeenth century* by D. Sella -
7. *Italy in the age of the Risorgimento 1790-1870* by H.
Hearder. ISBN 0582491460. 8. *Modern Italy 1871-1982* by
M. Clark. 1985. ISBN 058248362x.

V.2 has 12 chapters, each with chapter notes (*e.g.* 8. The
countryside, p.153-227, has 1¾p. of running bibliographical
commentary, with 6 references. Scholarly. 'To appreciate
this book fully, at least a basic knowledge of medieval
history is required ... Maps and illustrations need to be used
more imaginatively' (*British Book News*, January 1981,
p.61-62, on v.2). *Class No:* 945.0

[7391]
Storia d'Italia. Galasso, G., *ed.*   Torino, UTET, 1978-.
bibliog., index.

Introduzione: L'Italia come problema storigraphico. 1979.
ISBN 8802034311. 1. Delogu, P. and others. *Longobardi e
Bizantini.* 1980. 8802035105. 2. Fumagelli, P. *Il regno
Italico.* 1978. 8802025538x. 3. Guillou, A. and others. *Il
mezzogiorno dai Bizantini a Federico II.* 1983. 8802038716.
4. Capitani, P. and others. *Comuni e signorie: instituzioni,
società e lotte per l'egemonia.* 1981. 8802035687. 5.
Patrone, A.M.N. and Airaldi, G. *Comuni e signorie:
nell'Italia settentrionale.* 1986. 8802040362. 7(1) Cracco, G.
and others. *Comuni e signorie: nell'Italia nordori éntale e
centrale: Veneto, Emilia Romagna, Toscana.* 1987.
880204397. (2) Arnaldi, G. and others. *Lazio, Umbria e
Marche, Luca.* 1987. 8802040389. 8. Notario,P. and Nada,
N. *Il Piemonte sabaudo.* 1993. 8802047219. 9. Constantini,
C. *La Repubblica di Genova: nell'et à moderna.* 1986.
8802025398. 10. Day, J. and others. *La Sardegna
medioevale e moderna.* 1984. 8802039062. 11. Sella, D. and
Capra, C. *Il Ducato di Milano 1535-1796.* 1984.
8802038295. 12(1) Cozzi, G. and Knapton, M. *La
Repubblica di Venezia nell'et à moderna: dalla guerra di
Chiggia al 1517.* 1986. 8802040265. (2) Cozzi, G. and
others *Dal 1517 alla fine della Repubblica.* 1992.
8802044988. 13(1) Diaz, F. *Il granducato di Toscana;
Medici.* 1982. 8802024510. (3) Coppini, R.P. *Dagli 'anni
francesci' all' Unità.* 8802047200. 14. Caravale, M. and
Caracciolo, A. *Lo stato pontificio de Martino V a Pio IX.*
1986. 8802025193. 15. Galasso, G. *Il regno di Napoli 1266-
1494.* 1992. 8802044996. 16. *La Sicilia dal Vespro all'Unit
à d'Italia.* 1989. 8802042357. 17. Marini, L. and others.
Ducati Padani Trento e Trieste. 1979. 8802034737. 18.
Zaghi, C. *L'Italia di Napoleone dalla Cisalpina al Regno.*
1986. 8802039550. 20. Capone, A. *Destra e sinistra da
Cavour a Crispi.* 1982. 8802036578. 21. Gaeta, F. *La crisi
di fine e l'età giolittiana.* 19822. 8802037582. 23. Colarizzi,
S. *La seconda guerra mondiale e la Repubblica.* 1984.
8802037957. *Class No:* 945.0

Bibliographies
[7392]
Bibliografia storica nazionale. Roma and Bari, Laterza and
Figli, 1942-. (Giunta Centrale Per Gli Studi Storici). Annual.
L60,000. ISSN: 00852317.

Anni 45-46. 1983-1984. (xxxv,528p.) has 7711 numbered
entries in 8 sections: A. Scienze ausiliare ... C. Preistoria e
protohistoria ... G. Storia moderna 1871-1945 - H. Storia
contemporanea 1946-1984. Annual bibliography of books
and articles published in Italy and outstanding foreign
publications, relating mainly to Italian history and related
historical subjects. *Class No:* 945.0(01)

[7393]
COPPA, F.J. *and* **ROBERTS, W. Modern Italian history** an
annotated bibliography. Westport, Conn., Greenwood Press,
1990. ix,226p. indexes. $45. £39.95. (*Bibliographies and
Indexes in World History, no. 18.*) ISBN: 0313248125.
ISSN: 07426852.

865 entries deployed in 7 sections: 1. General and
reference works - 2. Monographic studies - 3. 18th century
Italy - 4. The Risorgimento 1796 to 1861 - 5. Liberal Italy
1861 to 1922 - 6. Facist Italy 1922 to 1945 - 7. Italian
Republic, 1945 to present. Author and subject indexes. 'A
judiciously framed guide to recent Italian history' (*RQ*, Fall
1991, p.32). *Class No:* 945.0(01)

Dictionaries
[7394]
COPPA, F.J., *ed.* **Dictionary of modern Italian history.**
Westport, Connecticut, Greenwood Press, 1985. xxvi, 496p.
bibliogs., index. £62.25. $56.95. ISBN: 031322983x.

58 contributors survey 'the chief events, personalities,
institutions, systems and problems of Italy from the
eighteenth century to the present' in dictionary form. Longer
entries end with bibliogaphical references. Appendix A.
Chronology p.459-468. 'An excellent and much needed
book' (*Choice*, v.23, no.4, December 1985, p.580).
Class No: 945.0(038)

19th Century

Bibliographies
[7395]
Bibliografia della'et à del Risorgimento: in onore di Alberto
M. Ghisalberti. Firenze, Leo S. Olschki, 4v., 1971-77.
(*Biblioteca di Bibliografia Italiana, no.63.*)

V.1 (xxxvi, 758p.) covers the Risorgimento (1815-70) in
14 sections, plus a prefatory bibliography of A-M
Ghisalberti (Opere generale - II settecento ... L'Italia nel
sistema napoleonico ... Trieste). Each section consists of a
lengthy bibliograpy including periodical articles, with an
introduction (*e.g.* 'II regno lombardo-veneto', p.615-742,
has bibliography, with running commentary, p.637-742).
V.4 is an index volume. *Class No:* 945.0"18"(01)

20th Century

Dictionaries
[7396]
CANNISTARO, P.V., *ed.* **Historical dictionary of Fascist
Italy.** Westport, Connecticut, Greenwood Press, 1982. xxix,
657p. maps, index. £63.75. $76.95. ISBN: 0313213278.

56 contributing scholars provide mini-essays on political,
military, diplomatic, economic, cultural, intellectual history.
Biographical entries feature prominently and each entry ends
with bibliographical references. Appendix A. Chronology
p.579-582. J. Italian place-names altered during the Fascist
regime p.607-630. 'The most comprehensive reference work
on Italian fascism and a most welcome one' (*Choice*, v.20,
no.5, January 1983. p.690). *Class No:* 945.0"19"(038)

Sicily

[7397]

FINLEY, M.I., *and others*. **History of Sicily**. London, Chatto & Windus, 1986. x,246p. 16p.plates, maps, bibliog., index. ISBN: 0701131551.

A much abridged and revised edition of M.I. Finley's *History of Sicily: ancient Sicily to the Arab conquest;* D. Mack Smith's *History of Sicily: medieval Sicily 800-1713*, and Smith's *History of Sicily: modern Sicily after 1973* (1968).

Bibliography p.234-38. 'It is no reflection on the scholarly excellence of the original three volumes to say that this edition is likely to prove much more attractive and valuable to the more general reader' (*Geographical Journal*, v.154, no.1., March 1988, p.127). *Class No:* 945.082

Malta

[7398]

GERADA-AZZOPARDI, E. **Malta: an island republic.** Boulogne. Editions Delroisse, 1980. 270p. col. illus., map, bibliog.

Sections: At the crossroads of destiny - History - Neolithic Malta - The temple builders of the Copper Age - The Bronze Age - The entrance of Malta into history - Medieval Malta - The Knights of St. John - The golden era of the Knights of Malta - The uprising against the French - The British period - Malta after the war. Sources and selected bibliography, p.266-7 (6 sections). Map of the Maltese Islands. *Class No:* 945.82

Bibliographies

[7399]

CUSCHIERI, C. **Index historicus**. Valetta, Malta Univ. Press, 1979. 151p.

A classified index of articles from selected journals and collections. Author and subject index. *Class No:* 945.82(01)

[7400]

GALEA, J. **Bibliography of the Great Siege of Malta 1565-1965**. Mdina, Malta Univ. Press, 1965. 135p. *Class No:* 945.82(01)

Spain

[7401]

BARD, R. **Navarra: the durable kingdom**. Reno, Univ. of Nevada Press, 1982. xiii,254p. geneal. table, bibliog., index. $22.95. (*The Basque Series*.) ISBN: 0874170737.

Outline history in 17 annotated chapters: 1. Prehistory: the mystery of the Basques ... 2. From Celts to Romans ... 8. Dynastic decline 1349 to 1517 ... 16. Into the twentieth century ... 17. The durable province. Appendix A. Rulers of the Kingdom of Navarra 818-1512. B. The Carlist succession to 1936. Bibliography p.230-240. Analytical index. 'A useful contribution ... but need continues for a longer, more thoroughly researched, and more thorough examination of Navarrese history in English' (*Choice*, v.20, no.7, March 1983, p.1044). *Class No:* 946.0

[7402]

LYNCH, J., *ed*. **A History of Spain.** Oxford, Basil Blackwell, 14v., 1989-.

Castro, M.C.F.: *Prehistory of Spain*. Richardson, J.S. *Roman Spain*. Collins, R. *Visigothic Spain*. Collins, R. *Arab conquest of Spain 710-797*. 1989. 208p. £29.50. 0631159231. Collins, R. *Caliphs and Kings 798-1033*. Reilly, B. *Contest of Christian and Muslim Spain 1031-1157*. 1992. 272p. £40. 063116913x. Linehan, P. *Spain 1157-1300*. McKay, A. *Spain: centuries of crisis 1300-1474*. Edwards, J. *Spain of the Catholic monarchs 1474-1520*. Lynch, J. *Spain 1516-1598 From nation state to world empire*. 1991. £45. 0631176969. Lynch, J. *Hispanic world in crisis and change 1598-1700*. 1992. 464p. £45. 0631176977. Lynch, J. *Bourbon Spain 1700- 1808*. 1989. xiv,450p. £45. 0631145761. Blinkhorn, M. *Emergence of modern Spain*. Robinson, R. *Spain since 1939*.

Scholarly and well-documented multi-volume history 'designed to advance research and thinking on the subject as well as to represent its current state'. *Class No:* 946.0

[7403]

MENÉNDEZ PIDAL, R., *ed*. **Historia de España.** Madrid, Espasa-Calpe, 1935-. illus., ports., facsims, maps, bibliogs. ISBN: 8423948005, set.

1. *España Primitiva* 3v., 1952-1963: *España Prehistórica, Protohistórica, Preromana* - 2. *España Romana 218 A de JC - 414 de JC* 2v., 1982 - 3. *España Visigoda* 2v., 1991. 8423949958 and 8423949966 - 4/5. *España Musulmana (711-1031)* 2v. 1950-57.

6. *Los Comienzos de la Reconquista (711-1038)*. 1956 - 7. *La España Christiana de los siglos VIII al XI*. 1980 - 10. *Los Reinos Christianos en los sigles XIX y XII*. 1992. 8423948129 - 13. *La Expansión Peninsular y Mediterránea (c.1212 - c.1350)*. 2v. 1990. 8423948153 and 8423948242. 14. *España Christiana de la reconquista. Luchas civiles (c.1350-1410)*. 1966. *Los trastámaras de Castilla y Aragón en el Siglo XV*. 1965-. - 17. *La España de los reyes católicos* 2v., 1968.

19. *El siglo XVI*.1989. 8423944827 - 20. *La España del Emperador Carlos V*. 3e. 1982. 8423948285 - 22. *Felipe II, El hombre y la politica*. 2v. 1955. 23. *La Crisis del siglo XVII*. 1989. 842394994x.

24. *La España de Felipe III*. 1979 - 25. *La España de Felipe IV. El Gobierno de la Monarquía, la crisis de 1640 y el fracaso de la hegemonía europea*. 1982. - 26. *El siglo del Quijote (1580-1650)* 2v., 1986.

29. *La Época de los primeros Borbones*. 2v. 1985 - 31. *La Época de la ilustración*. 2v. 1987-88 - 32. *La España de Fernando VII*, 2nd ed. 1978 - 34. *La era Isabelina y el sexenio democrático (1834-1874)*. 1981 - 35. *Época del Romanticismo (1808-1874)*. 2v. 1989.

37. *Los comienzos del siglo XX (1898-1931)*. 1984. 39. *La Edad de plata de la cultura Española*. 1993. 8423949974.

A monumental history, planned to encompass 40 titles (many in 2v.), by various authorities. Some titles are reported to be 'in prepraration'; others are 'projected'. Critical chapter bibliographies and notes emphasise the scholarly value of this immense work. *Class No:* 946.0

[7404]
PAYNE, S.G. The Franco regime 1936-1975. Madison, Univ. of Wisconsin Press, 1987. xvii,677p. illus., maps, biblilg., index. ISBN: 0229110702.

A chronological political history in 23 chapters ordered in 4 parts: 1. Origins - 2. The Civil War 1936-1939 - 2. The Dictadura 1939-1959 - 4. Developmentalism and decay 1959-1975. Chronology p.xv-xvii. Bibliography p.645-54. 5 maps. Analytical index. *Class No:* 946.0

[7405]
VALDEAVELLANO, L.G. de. Historia de España antigua y medieval. Madrid, Alianza Editoria, 3v., 1988. maps, bibliog., index. ISBN: 8420691003, set.

1. *De los orígenes al siglo X* viii,514p.+9p. maps. ISBN 842069097x. 2. *Del siglo X a las Navas de Tolosa.* 693p.+6p. maps. 8420690988. 3. *Castilla y Aragón en el siglo XIII.* 204p.+6p. geneal. tables. 8420690996. A work of considerable scholarship. V.1: has Bibliografia General p.29-41 and Fuentes p.43-104. *Class No:* 946.0

Bibliographies

[7406]
THOMPSON, I.A.A. 'Spain: the centuries of greatness and decline' *The Historian* no.18, Spring 1988, p.14-17.

Review of English-language publications of the 1970s and 1980s regarding the history of early modern Spain.
Class No: 946.0(01)

Encyclopaedias

[7407]
Enciclopedia de historia de España. Artola, M., *ed.* Madrid, Alianza Editorial, 1988-. maps, bibliog. ISBN: 8420652253.

1. *Economía. Sociedad.* 1988. vi,7-715p. ISBN 8420652253. 2. *Instituciones. Políticas. Imperio.* 798p. 8420652261. 2. *Iglesia. Pensamiento. Cultura.* 552p. 842065227x. *Class No:* 946.0(031)

[7408]
Gran enciclopedia de España. Zaragoza, Enciclopedia de España, 20v., 1990-. In progress. col. illus., col. maps. ISBN: 8487544010.

Historical perspective on the culture and people of Spain more suited to academic than to home use because of its 'small-size print, extensive use of abbreviations, and lack of subheadings that makes longer entries difficult to read' (*Booklist*, v.89, no.7, 1 Dec 1992, p.693).
Class No: 946.0(031)

Handbooks & Manuals

[7409]
BLEYE, P.A. Manual de historia de España. Novena edición, revisada por C.A. Molina. Madrid, Espasa-Calpe, 3v., 1963-1964. illus. bibligs.

First published 1914; 6th ed. 1947.
Prehistoria. Edades antigua y media 1963. 1071p. 2. *Reyes católicos - Casa de Austria (1474-1700)* 1964. 1200p. 3. *Casa de Borbón (1700-1808). España contemporánea (1808-1955)* 1964. 1057p. V.1 has 45, v.2 has 38, and v.3 has 38 chapters, each with its own bibliography, and each divided into numbered topics. *Class No:* 946.0(035)

Dictionaries

[7410]
BLEIBERG, G. Diccionario de historia de España. 2nd ed. corregida y aumentada. Madrid, Alianza, 3v., 1986. viii, 1358p.; 1179p.; v, 1207p. ISBN: 8420652989.

1st published. Ediciones de la Revista de Occident, 1952.
Signed articles A-Z. About 76 contributors. 'Arabismo (en España)'; p.289-93; numerous references in the text. Includes articles on Latin America and its Spanish connections ('Historiadores de América': v.2, p.373-9). Excludes living persons. V.3 includes as appendices a bibliography (p.1083-1111), plus a further bibliography for 1931-1968 (p.1113); chronology p.1115-92, and 24p. of outline maps.

'This is an excellent encyclopaedic dictionary, which also includes coverage of Spain's expansion in Europe and overseas' (G.J. Shields. *Spain*, 1985. Entry 131).
Class No: 946.0(038)

[7411]
KERN, R.W. and DODGE, M.D., eds. Historical dictionary of modern Spain 1700-1988. Westport, Connecticut, Greenwood Press, 1990. 697p. maps, bibliog., index. £85.00; $76. ISBN: 0313259712.

70 contributors. Entries cover important personalities and events in 6 major areas: politics, government, diplomacy; institutions, culture; society and the armed forces. 'This new reference work on Spain could serve as a model for other historical dictionaries. Among its winning features are the fact that it treats a topic on which there has not been a single general reference work in this century and that it has an experienced editor who is a noted scholar in his own right, a first-rate cast of international contributors, a judicious choice of entries, a consistent style, a superior bibliography, and a good index'. (*Booklist*, v.86, no.20, 15 Jan 1990, p.2030-1).
Class No: 946.0(038)

[7412]
OLSON, J.S., ed. Historical dictionary of the Spanish Empire. Westport, Conn., Greenwood Press, 1992. x,705p. bibliog., index. $89.50. ISBN: 0313264139.

1,300 brief descriptive essays on people, places, events, institutions, and historical developments in the Spanish Empire from the Castilians' first landing in the Canary Islands to the loss of Spanish Sahara in 1975.
Class No: 946.0(038)

Reviews & Abstracts

[7413]
Indice histórico español: bibliografia histórica de España. Barcelona, Teide,1953-. v.1-. Publicación cuatrimestral del Centro de Estudios Históricos Internacionales, Universidad de Barcelona. ISSN: 05373522.

V.29 (1983-1991). 2078 abstracts from 135 contributors on many aspects of Spain and, more selectively, Hispanic America and elsewhere ordered in 7 regional sections: 1. Obras generales - 2. Historia de España - 3-5. Edad antigua, media, moderna - 6. América - 7. Otros territorios (Marruecos, Filipinas, Océania). *Class No:* 946.0(048)

Maps & Atlases

[7414]
PIDAL, G.M. **Atlas historica Español.** Barcelona, Editora Nacional, 1941.

36 double pages of facing text and maps.
Class No: 946.0(084.3)

Canary Islands

[7415]
TORRES, A.M. **Historia general de las Islas Canarias.** Las Palmas, Editora Regional Canaria, 6v., 1977-81. col.illus., maps, indexes.

'A definitive history of the Canary Islands first published 1893-1895 revised with numerous coloured plates, a volume of biographies, and indexes' (H.G.R. King. *Atlantic Ocean,* 1985. Entry 708). *Class No:* 946.0(649)

Middle Ages

Bibliographies

[7416]
FAULHABER, C.B. **Libros y bibliotecas en la España medieval: una bibliografia de fuentes impresas.** London, Grant & Culier, 1987. 213p. indexes, pbk. £18,00. (*Research Bibliographies and Checklists No.47.*) ISBN: 0729302660.

666 annotated entries: España; Corona de Aragon; Navarra; Corona de Castilla; Francia; Italia with geographical sub-divisions. Separate subject, chronological, toponymic, persons and modern scholarship indexes p.185-213. *Class No:* 946.0"01/14"(01)

[7417]
FERREIRO, A. **The Visigoths in Gaul and Spain AD 488-711** a bibliography. Leiden, E.J. Brill, 1988. lxii, 822p. indexes. ISBN: 9004087931.

9096 unannotated entries in 17 sections: 1. Reference - 2. General studies - 3. Invasions - 4. Social - 5. Law - 6. Culture - 7. Palaeography - 8. Ecclesiastical - 9. Liturgy - 10. Patristics - 11. Isodore of Seville - 12. Archaeology - 13. Sueves - 14. Toulouse - 15. Other peoples - 16. Collected essays and Studia Honoraria - 17. Congresses. Abbvreviations (periodicals) p.xv-lxii. Author and subject indexes. *Class No:* 946.0"01/14"(01)

16th Century

[7418]
LOVETT, A.W. **Early Hapsburg Spain 1517-1598.** Oxford, Oxford Univ. Press, 1986. maps, geneal table, bibliogs., index. £25.00. ISBN: 0198221398.

Is especially valuable for its extensive bibliography p.305-340. *Class No:* 946.0"15"

18th Century

Bibliographies

[7419]
AGUILAR PINAL, F. **Bibliografia de Estudios sobre Carlos III y su epoca.** Madrid. Consejo Superior De Investigacions Cientificas, 1988. xxiii,428p. index. ISBN: 8400069064.

....(contd.)
8176 unannotated entries organized in 3 subdivided parts: 1. Historia politica y militar - 2. Historia economica y social - 3. Historia cultural y Cientifica (inc 4 exploraciones y viejes). *Class No:* 946.0"17"(01)

19th Century

Bibliographies

[7420]
DEL BURGO, J. **Bibliografia del Siglo XIX** Guerras Carlistas luchas politicas. 2nd ed. Pamplona, 1978. xxix,1072p. ISBN: 8423503429.

First published in 5v. 1953-1960.

Entries of books and articles relating to political history from the reign of Fernando VII to Alfonso Carlos de Bourbón y Austria-Este (1931-36) arranged A-Z by author and title. Subject guide to reigns, wars and other events covered p.xxvii-xxix. *Class No:* 946.0"18"(01)

20th Century

[7421]
The Spanish Civil War revolution and counter revolution. London, Harvester Wheatsheaf, 1991. xxxii,1074p. £50. ISBN: 074500763.

Massively researched and documented narrative history and analysis of Republican politics 1936-39. Acronyms p.xxiii-xxiv. Leading participants p.xxv-xxxii. Chapter notes p.745-935. Bibliography p.937-1018. 5 maps. Analytical index. *Class No:* 946.0"19"

Bibliographies

[7422]
GARCIA DURAN, J. **Bibliography of the Spanish Civil War.** Montevideo, El Siglo Ilustrada, 1964. 559p.

6248 items arranged A-Z under subject or form headings. 'Intended to serve as a main source of research of the Spanish civil war and its political, social, economic, and ideological background, as well as its aftermath'. Index of subject matters p.555-559. *Class No:* 946.0"19"(01)

Dictionaries

[7423]
CORTADA, J.W., *ed.* **Historical dictionary of the Spanish Civil War** 1936-1939. Westport, Connecticut, Greenwood Press, 1982. xxviii, 571p. maps, bibligo. $76.95. ISBN: 0313220549.

800 signed entries of varying length by 40 contributors on all aspects of the Civil War. Appendix A. Chronology 1930-1939; B. Military History; C. Civil War governments; D. Compendium of archives and libraries (A-Z by country) p.537-543; Selected bibliography of bibliographies p.544-546; Analytical index p.547-571. 'The long entries written by various experts and the inclusion of some rather unusual topics enhance the value of this reference tool' (*Choice* v.21, no.1, September 1983, p.62). *Class No:* 946.0"19"(038)

[7424]

RUBIO CABEZA, M. **Diccionario de la Guerra Civil Espanola.** Barcelona, Editorial Planeta, 2v., 1987. 819p. illus., ports., bibliog. ISBN: 8432058602, set; 8432058572, v.1; 8432058580, v.2.

Political, military, diplomatic events, organizations, institutions, individuals *etc.* in a single A-Z sequence. *Class No:* 946.0"19"(038)

Gibraltar

[7425]

DENNIS, P. **Gibraltar and its people.** Newton Abbot, Devon, David & Charles, 1990. 176p. illus., map, bibliog., index. £13.95. ISBN: 0715394932.

A narrative history with thematic chapters on Gibraltar's status as a British colony and a comparative scrutiny of other colonial enclaves. Appendix 1. Some notable dates (p.163-5) - 2. Article X of the Treaty of Utrecht. Bibliography p.169-71. *Class No:* 946.82

[7426]

JACKSON, W.G.F. **The Rock of the Gibraltarians:** a history of Gibraltar. London & Toronto, Associated Univ. Presses, 1987. 379p. illus., maps, bibliog., index. £30. ISBN: 0838632378.

17 well-documented chronological chapters setting Gibraltar's history in the context of world events. Notes p.339-357. Bibliography p.358-363. *Class No:* 946.82

[7427]

MORRIS, D.S. *and* **HAIGH, R.H.** **Britain, Spain and Gibraltar 1945-90** the eternal triangle. London, Routledge, 1992. xii,180p. map, index. £35. ISBN: 0415071453.

Account of Gibraltar's post-war constitutional and political history and of its relations and negotiations with Spain. Chapter notes p.153-75. *Class No:* 946.82

Portugal

[7428]

BOXER, C.R. **The Portuguese seaborne empire 1415-1825.** 2nd ed. London, Carcanet in association with The Calouste Gulbenkian Foundation, 1991. xiv,426p. illus., maps, bibliog., index. ISBN: 0856359629.

First published Hutchinson, 1969.

A well-documented survey in 16 chapters. 6 appendices (*e.g.* 1: Outward-bound Portuguese East Indiamen. 1501-1800). Glossary p.386-91. Chapter bibliographies, p.392-413, with some annotations. Analytical index, p.415-26. 16 illus.; 7 maps. *Class No:* 946.9

[7429]

OLIVEIRA MARQUES, A.H. de. **History of Portugal.** 2nd ed. New York and London, Columbia Univ. Press, 2v., 1976. illus., ports., maps, bibliog..

1. From Lusitania to Empire. 2. From Empire to Corporate State. 'The most important book on Portuguese history in English ... it concludes with a good and partially annotated bibliography' (P.T.H. Unwin. *Portugal*, 1987. Entry 174). *Class No:* 946.9

[7430]

SERRÃO, J. *and* **OLIVEIRA MARQUES, A.D. de,** *eds.* **Nova história de Portugal.** Lisboa, Editorial Presenca, 13v., 1986?-.

1. *Des origens a Romanização.* 2. *Islam e reconquista Christa.* 3. *Do condado Portucalense à crise do século XIV.* 4. *Portugal na crise dos séculos XIV e XV.* 5. *Descobrimentos e renascimento.* 6. *Da contra-reforma à restauração.* 7. *Da restaração ao auro do Brasil.* 8. *A crise do antigo regime.* 9. *A instauração do liberalismo.* 10. *A restauração.* 11. *Da monarquia para à républica.* 12. *O estado novo.*

V.11 (1991) 839p. tables. ISBN 9722314203 is in 16 thematic chapters. Fontes e bibliografia p.747-75. Indice dos mapas, gráficos e quadros p.777-81. Indice analitico p.783-827. *Class No:* 946.9

Bibliographies

[7431]

ACADEMIA PORTUGUESA DA HISTORIA. Guía de bibliografia histórica portuguesa. Lisboa, 1959-. v.1.

Aims to cover Portugal from the 9th century to 1910 and meet the need for a comprehensive bibliography of Portuguese history. *Class No:* 946.9(01)

[7432]

DE SILVA, D. **The Portuguese in Asia** an annotated bibliography on studies on Portuguese colonial history in Asia, 1498-*c*.1800. Zug, Switzerland, IDC AG, 1987. xxiv,313p. index. (*Bibliotheca Asiatic no.22.*) ISBN: 3300000068.

2773 entries in 9 main divisions: 1. Reference works - 2. Historiography - 3. Cartography - 4. Navigation - 5. Travel & Description - 6. Conquest, expansion and decline - 7. Religion - 8. Economic foundations - 9. Impact on Asian society. For the researcher. 1000 scarce titles from the *Bibliography* will be made available on microfiche - p.313. Correlation table of microfiche editions. 'An excellent and innovative work, admirably indexed and cross-referenced' (*Portuguese Studies*, No.4, 1988, p.238). *Class No:* 946.9(01)

[7433]

WELSH, D.V., *comp.* **A Catalog of the William B. Greenlee collection** of Portuguese history and literature and the Portuguese materials in the Newberry Library. vii, 342p. indexes.

Sections on general reference works and political, ecclesiastical, economic, military, naval, social and cultural history. *Class No:* 946.9(01)

Dictionaries

[7434]

SERRÃO, J., *ed.* **Dicionário de historia de Portugal.** 2nd ed. Porto, Livraria Figueirinhas, 6v. 1981. illus. maps, tables, bibliogs., index.

First published in 4v. by Iniciativas Editoriais of Lisbon 1963-71.

Subjects covered include political, legal and economic institutions; economic, social and technical history; cultural, ideological and religious movements; biographies; and articles on Portuguese literature, language, science and

....(contd.)

philosophy, archaeology, numismatics, palaeography and diplomatic. Longer signed entries include extensive bibliographies. *Class No:* 946.9(038)

[7435]
—SERRÃO, J. Pequeno dicionário de historia de Portugal. Porto, Figueirinhas, 1987. 654p. illus. maps. softcover.
First published by Iniciativas Editoriais 1976.
Class No: 946.9(038)

Chronologies
[7436]
SERRÃO, J. Cronologia geral da historia de Portugal. 5th ed. Lisboa, Livros Horizonte, 1956. 247p. index. pbk.
1st ed. 1971.
Descends from section bearing same title printed in v.4 *Dicionário de historia de Portugal* (1971). Stops at 1930.
Class No: 946.9(090)

Middle Ages

Bibliographies
[7437]
OLIVEIRA MARQUES, A.H. de. Guia do estudante de historia medieval portuguesa. 3rd ed. Lisboa, Editoria Estampa, 1988. 291p.
First published by Ediçes Cosmos 1964.
A running commentary in 8 chapters, covering bibliographies, atlases and dictionaries, handbooks, history auxiliaries, printed sources, archives and collections of manuscripts. *Class No:* 946.9"01/14"(01)

Contemporary

Bibliographies
[7438]
CHILCOTE, R.H., *comp.* The Portuguese revolution of 25 April 1974: annotated bibliography on the antecedents and aftermath/Revolução Portuguesa de 25 de Abril de 1974: bibliografia anotada sombre os antecedentes e evolução posterior. Coimbra, Centro de Documentação 25 de Abril, Universidade de Coimbra, 1987. xv, 329p. indexes.
In 2 separate A-Z sequences: 1. Monographs and pamphlets (1116 entries) - 2. Periodical articles (1047 entries). Author and acronyms indexes. 'A later volume will include the listings for the third part, an annotated list of periodical titles, and part 4, a list of relevant organizations'. *Class No:* 946.9"312"(01)

[7439]
GALLAGHER, T. Dictatorial Portugal a bibliographical essay *Iberian Studies* v.9, no.1, Spring 1980, p.11-21.
Limited mainly to post-1974 writings. 106 references.
Class No: 946.9"312"(01)

Russia
[7440]
Longman history of Russia. Shukman, H., *general ed.* Harlow, Essex, Longman, 7v., 1981-.
1. *Kievan Russia 850-1240* by D. Obolensky. 2. *The Crisis of medieval Russia 1200-1304* by J. Fennell. 1987.

....(contd.)

296p. 3. *The Formation of Muscovy 1304-1613* by R.O. Crummey. 1987. xv, 275p. £22.00. 0582491525. 4. *The Making of Russian absolutism 1613-1801* by P. Dukes. 1982. viii, 197p. £22.00. 05824864x. 5. *Russia in the age of reaction and reform 1801-1881* by D. Saunders. 1983. 6. *Russia in the age of modernization and revolution 1881-1917* by Hans Rogger. 1983. viii, 323p. 7. *The Russian revolution 1917* by S. Smith. 8. *The Soviet Union since 1917* by M. McCauley, 1981. iv, 290p. 0582489792. For student and non-specialist readership. Extensive bibliographies in all volumes. *Class No:* 947/

[7441]
McKEAN, R.B. 'Russia 1855-1917'. *The Historian*, no 5, Winter 1984/85, p.12-15.
A guide to recent publications on Tsarist Russia.
Class No: 947/

[7442]
PAXTON, J. Encyclopedia of Russian history: from the Christianization of Kiev to the breakup of the Soviet Union. Santa Barbara, Calif., and Oxford, ABC-Clio, 1993. 484p. maps, bibliog. $65. ISBN: 0874366909.
Much revised version of Paxton's *Companion to Russian history* (Batsford, 1983).
A-Z encyclopedia on post-Soviet Russia and the new sovereign states that were once republics of the Soviet Union. 2500 entries comprise this encyclopedia, gazetteer, atlas and chronology covering 100 years of history. 'This first-rate reference monograph will prove an invaluable asset for scholars' (*Library Journal,* v.118, no.21, December 1993. p.116). *Class No:* 947/

[7443]
PIPES, R. The Russian Revolution 1899-1919. London, Collins Harvill, 1990. xxvii,946p. £20. ISBN: 0679400745.
Continues the author's *Russia under the old regime.*
Comprehensive overview of the Revolution and of the events that preceded it in 18 chapters divided into 2 parts: 1. Agony of the Old Regime - 2. Bolsheviks conquer Russia. Chronology p.847-56. Chapter notes p.857-914. 100 works on the Russian Revolution (bibliographical essay) p.915-9. 4 maps. Widely acclaimed for its scholarly analysis.
Class No: 947/

[7444]
VERNADSKY, G., *and others, eds*. A Source book for Russian history from early times to 1917. New Haven, Connecticut, Yale Univ. Press, 3v., 1973.
1: *Early times to the late seventeenth century.* 352p.
2: *Peter the Great to Nicholas I.* 322p.
3: *Alexander II to the February Revolution.* 344p.
Praised in *TLS* (no.3705, 9 March 1973, p.260) for the careful translations of texts, informal notes and thoroughness of references. *Class No:* 947/

Bibliographies
[7445]
CROWTHER, P.A., *ed*. A Bibliography of works in English on early Russian history to 1800. Oxford, Blackwell, 1969. xvii, 263p. indexes.
2,081 + 83 entries, in 20 sections (1. Bibliography - 2. Historiography - 3. General works - 4. The Slavs, Early Panslavism - 5. General history - 6. Diplomatic and foreign relations ... 19. Local and regional history - 20. Travel and

....(contd.)

description, contemporary accounts). Introductory sectional notes single out important items. Occasional annotations; references to reviews. Cross-references. Name and subject index.

A companion to David Shapiro's *A select bibliography of works in English on Russian history, 1801-1917* (Oxford, Blackwell, 1962. xii, [i], 106p.), which lists 1,070 books and articles in 21 sections, with evaluative sectional annotations and references to reviews. Covers all aspects of Russian history up to 1961, deliberately omitting more inclusive bibliographies and histories. Author index. *Class No:* 947/ (01)

[7446]
EGAN, D.R. *and* **EGAN, M.A. Russian autocrats from Ivan the Great to the fall of the Romanov dynasty** : an annotated bibliography of English language sources to 1985. Metuchen, New Jersey, Scarecrow Press, 1987. xxxv, 512p. $49.50. ISBN: 0810819589.

2082 descriptively annotated items, including popular and journalistic sources, on the 26 Czars who ruled Russia 1492-1917 arranged in 14 chronological sections for single or successive rulers. Chronology p.xxxv. Author and subject indexes. *Class No:* 947/(01)

[7447]
MAGOCSI, P.R. Galicia: a historical survey and bibliographic guide. Toronto, Univ. of Toronto Press in association with the Canadian Institute of Ukrainian Studies and the Harvard Ukrainian Research Institute, 1983. xix,299p. maps, index. ISBN: 0802024823.

1. Bibliographical and archival aids - 2. General studies - 3. Early history to 1340 - 4-9. Chronological periods to the present - 10. Minorities. An introduction to the basic historical problems of Galicia and a guide to the major published primary and secondary sources. More than 1000 notes and 3000 references. 'It is a meticulously researched, highly scholarly guide, prepared in the best tradition of bibliography' (*Choice*, v.21, no.6, February 1984, p.806). *Class No:* 947/(01)

Handbooks & Manuals

[7448]
Handbuch der Geschichte Russlands. Hellman, M., *and others, eds.* Stuttgart, Anton Hiersemann, 1976-. ISBN: 377276219.

Band 1. *Von der Kiewer Reichsbildung bis zum Moskauer Zartum (Anfänge bis 1613).* Lieferung 1-12 (1976-1988). Band 2. *Vom Randstaat zur Hegemonialmacht (1613-1856).* Lieferung 1-8 (1981-1988). Band 3. *Von dem autokratischen Reformen zum Sowjetstaat (1856-1945).* Lieferung 1-18 (1981-1987). Long articles by various hands. Extremely thorough and well-documented cooperative history issued in fascicules. *Class No:* 947/(035)

Dictionaries

[7449]
PUSHKAREV, S.G. Dictionary of Russian historical terms from the eleventh century to 1917. New Haven, Connecticut, Yale Univ. Press, 1970. xi, 199p.

A companion to *A source book for Russian history*. It aims 'to assist English-speaking readers to understand the specialized works on Russia' (*Preface*). The most important

....(contd.)

terms referring to social categories and political, military, educational and other institutions are supplied with brief historical sketches. 'A comprehensive reference work; more restricted but more scholarly than Paxton' (R. Pearson. *Russia and Eastern Europe.* 1989, Entry 1.128). *Class No:* 947/(038)

Maps & Atlases

[7450]
CHEW, A.F. An Atlas of Russian history : eleven centuries of changing borders. Rev. ed. New Haven, Connecticut, Yale Univ. Press, 1970. xii, 127p. maps, pbk. $13.95. ISBN: 0300014457.

First published 1947.

Ranges from ninth century to end of Second World War. *Class No:* 947/(084.3)

[7451]
GILBERT, M. Dent atlas of Russian history. 2nd ed. London, J.M. Dent, 1993. v,197p. maps, bibliog., index. £14.99. ISBN: 0460861751.

First published as *Russian history atlas* (Weidenfeld & Nicolson, 1972).

161 pages of black and white outline maps arranged in 4 sections: 1. Ancient and early modern Russia (beginning with the Slavs 800BC) - 2. Imperial Russia - 3. Soviet Union - 4. End of Soviet Union. Bibliography (atlases, maps, reference works) p.162-6. Analytical index. *Class No:* 947/ (084.3)

18th Century

Bibliographies

[7452]
CLENDENNING, P. *and* **BARTLETT, R. Eighteenth century Russia** : a select bibliography of works published since 1955. Newtonville, Massachusetts, Oriental Research Partners, 1981. x, 262p. $30.00. (*Russian Bibliography Series; no.3.*) ISBN: 0892501103.

270 entries, English, Russian, French and German material grouped in 14 sections: 1. Bibliography and reference - 2. Historiography and source studies - 3. General works - 4. Selections and collections of documents - 5. General history (by period) - 6. Political history - 7. Social and economic - 8. Diplomacy and international relations - 9. Military and naval - 10. Geography, demography, ethnology - 11. Individuals, biographies, memoirs - 12. Intellectual and cultural - 13. Religion - 14. Local and regional, national and ethnic minorities. For undergraduates and graduates embarking on research. *Class No:* 947/"17"(01)

USSR

[7453]
BOHDAN NAHAYLO *and* **SWOBODA, V. Soviet disunion** a history of the Nationalities Problem in the USSR. London, Hamish Hamilton, 1990. xvi,432p. illus., maps, bibliog., index. £20. ISBN: 0241125405.

History of the non-Russian nationalities in the Soviet Union since the Russian Revolution. 18 chaps: 1. Nations of the Russian Empire ... 3. 1919: Sovereign Soviet Republics - 4. Moslem nations ... 17. Crisis in the Empire - 18. Waiting for Gorbachev. Appendix (National structure of the USSR in

....*(contd.)*
early 1990 and The Union Republics) p.360-8. Chapter notes p.369-411. Bibliography p.412-7. 6 maps. *Class No:* 947

[7454]
CARR, E.H. A History of Soviet Russia. London, Macmillan, 10v. in 15, 1917-1958. £395.00. ISBN: 0333242165.
1. *The Bolshevik Revolution 1971-1923.* 1. *1917-1923* 1978. 430p. £35.00 ISBN 0333085663 - 2. *The economic order.* 1951. 400p. £35.00. ISBN 0333022858 - 3. *Soviet Russia and the World.* 1978. £35.00. ISBN 0333060040.
2. *The Interregnum 1923-1924* 1978. 392p. £35.00 ISBN 0333097238. First published 1954.
3. *Socialism in one country 1924-1926.* 3v. in 4. 1. 1978. 588p. £35.00. ISBN 0333034422. First published 1958. 2. 1978. 494p. £35.00. ISBN 0333071611. First published 1959. 3. Pt.1. 1978. £35.00. ISBN 0333245687. First published 1964. 3. Pt.2. 1978. £35.00. ISBN 0333245695. First published 1964.
4. *Foundations of a planned economy 1926-1929* 3v. in 6. 1. Pt.1. 1978. £35.00. ISBN 0333245709. First published 1969. 1. Pt.2. 1978. £35.00. ISBN 0333245717. First published 1969. 2. 1978. 530p. £35.00. ISBN 0333111338. First published 1971. 3. Pt.1. 1979. £35.00. ISBN 0333132041. First published 1976. 3. Pt.2. 1979. £35.00. ISBN 0333192702. First published 1976. 3. Pt.3. 1978. £35.00. ISBN 0333194934. These volumes written jointly by E.H. Carr and R.W.Davies.
A monumental study of Soviet Russian history during the period; footnotes and bibliographies. 'A work of the greatest value for its masterly ordering and analysis of official documentation, and its unfailing clarity and readability' (Auty, R. and Obolensky, D., eds. *Companion to Russian studies.* 1: *An introduction to Russian history* (1976), p.308-9). *Class No:* 947

[7455]
DE MOWBRAY, S.A. Key facts in Soviet history. Volume 1. 1917 to 22 June 1941. Boston, Massachusetts, G.K. Hall; London, Pinter Publishers in association with John Spiers, 1990. xiii,386p. maps, bibliog., index. $40. £45. ISBN: 0816118205, US; 0861870131, UK.
Short accounts of the main events in Soviet history month by month emphasising internal developments in political, economic, military, and social affairs but also including cultural, scientific and technological fields. List of sources p.361-75. To be completed by a second volume continuing the course of Soviet history to the present and an index volume. Based largely on English-language sources. *Class No:* 947

[7456]
SMITH, F., ed. The Nationalities question in the Soviet Union. London, Longman, 1990. ix,389p. map, tables, bibliog., index. £28. ISBN: 0582039533.
20 academic and professional contributors. 19 'national' chapters grouped in 6 regions: 1. Baltic republics - 2. South-Western borderlands - 3. Transcaucasia - 4. Muslim Central Asia - 5. Non-Russians of the Russian republics - 6. The Diaspora nationalities (Crimean Tatars and the Jews). Extensive chapter notes. Bibliography p.373-8. Analytical index. A straight forward guide to 20 of the former Soviet Union's 140 different nationalities. *Class No:* 947

[7457]
The USSR in 1991 a record of events. Tolz, V. *and* Newton, M., eds. Boulder, Colo., Westview Press, 1993. Published in cooperation with Radio Free Europe and Radio Liberty. ix,997p. ISBN: 0813387175.
3rd and last of series of chronological record of events 1989-1991.
Headlined daily record of events in USSR arranged in monthly chapters. Name and subject indexes. Vivid description of the last days of the USSR. *Class No:* 947

Bibliographies

[7458]
HORAK, S.M., comp. Russia, the USSR and Eastern Europe. A bibliographic guide to English language publications 1981-1985. Littleton, Colo., Libraries Unlimited, 1987. 273p. indexes. ISBN: 087287561x.
Follows the compiler's *Russia, The USSR ... 1964-1974.* (1978. 488p.) and *Russia, The USSR ... 1975-1980* (1982. 279p.) Updates P.L. Horecky's *Russia and Eastern Europe. A bibliographic guide to Western language publications* (Univ. of Chicago Press, 1965. 473p.).
Annotated entries (a total of 3673 in this and previous volumes) for the Russian Empire prior to 1917; the individual Soviet republics; and other Eastern *bloc* countries. *Class No:* 947(01)

[7459]
PEARSON, R., comp. Russia and Eastern Europe 1789-1985 a bibliographical guide. Manchester, Manchester Univ. Press, 1989. Distributed in North America by St. Martin's Press. xiii,210p. indexes. £40.00. (*History And Related Disciplines Select Bibliographies.*) ISBN: 0719017343.
5144 briefly annotated entries in 3 main sections: General; Nineteenth-century Russia and Eastern Europe; Twentieth-century Soviet Union... Subdivided A-Z by state and 16 subject headings *e.g.* Historiography ... National minorities ... War... Economy ... Tourist. Author index. Bibliographical details incomplete but a useful work nevertheless. *Class No:* 947(01)

[7460]
The Rise and fall of the Soviet Union a selected bibliography of sources in English. Edelheit, A.J. *and* Edelheit, H., eds. Westport, Conn., Greenwood Press, 1992. xviii,430p. indexes. $65. (*Bibliographies and Indexes in World History, no.27.*) ISBN: 0313286256. ISSN: 07426852.
2016 cross-referenced entries (some annotated) arranged in 12 chapters sub-divided into large thematic or chronological sections: 1. Reference works (Research guides; bibliographies; collections of primary sources) ... 3. Overviews of Soviet history (Historical overviews; Soviet political system; Social issues) ... 6. Stalinist Russia (Domestic policy; Foreign Policy to 1939; Terror) ... 12. Biographies and memoirs. Glossary p.345-52. Author/title and subject indexes. *Class No:* 947(01)

Encyclopaedias

[7461]
The Blackwell encyclopaedia of the Russian Revolution. Shukman, H., ed. Oxford, Blackwell Reference, 1988. xiv,418p., maps on endpapers, bibliogs., index. £45.00; $65.00. ISBN: 0631152385.
Part 1 consists of 128 cross-referenced, initialled articles,

....(contd.)

from 45 contributors, arranged in an approximate chronological sequence 1860-1921. Part 2 comprises 174 biographies, long enough to be useful, including Sir Robert Bruce Lockhart, Josef Pilsudski, John Reed, and Sidney Reilly. Short reading lists are appended to all Pt.1 articles and to many of the biographies. Designed as a reference source for students and teachers and for general readers interested in 20th century history. The editor is Director of the Russian and East European Centre, St. Anthony's College, Oxford. 'Unique as a reference source devoted to this topic' (*Booklist*,v.88,no.5, 1 November 1988, p.460). *Class No:* 947(031)

[7462]
The Modern encyclopaedia of Russian and Soviet history. Wieczynski, J., *ed.* Gulf Breeze, Florida, Academic International Press, 1976-1993.

55v. so far published: v. 1-46 (1976-1987) comprise the base set. A series of supplementary volumes starting with the second half of v.46 is in process of publication. V.55. *Supplement Witchcraft in Russia - Zvenigord.* 1993. 274p. 0875690645 has signed articles, essays and bibliographes. Articles in English include translations from Russian sources (*e.g. Sovetskaya istoricheskaya entsiklopediya* as well as contributions by Western scholars. Coverage: persons, places, events and concepts relative to Russian/Soviet history. *Class No:* 947(031)

[7463]
SHAW, W. *and* **PRYCE, D. Encyclopedia of the USSR** 1905 to the present. Lenin to Gorbachev. London, Cassell, 1990. 351p. illus., maps, bibliog., index. £20. ISBN: 0304318183.

In 3 main parts: 1. Chronology of important dates and events, January 1905 to July 1990 (p.12-98) - 2. Encyclopedia *i.e.* political and economic background information arranged A-Z by topic (p.100-227) - 3. Biographies (p.230-318). Gazetteer of changed or alternative place-names p.329-30. Bibliography p.331-4. 8 maps. Useful compact guide for students and general readers. *Class No:* 947(031)

Dictionaries

[7464]
JACKSON, G. *and* **DEVLIN, R.,** *eds.* **Dictionary of the Russian Revolution.** Westport, Connecticut, Greenwood Press, 1989. xviii,704p., maps, bibliog., indexes. $75. ISBN: 0313211310.

100 or so contributors. *c.*300 signed A-Z cross-referenced entries, 1/3 2000-4000 word essays, remainder shorter articles on the institutions, personalities and events of the Revolution. 'There is excellent coverage of the myriad committees, parties, interest groups, and other organizations that had a role in shaping the events of the period' (*Booklist*, v.86, no.4, 15 December 1989, p.422). *Class No:* 947(038)

[7465]
WILSON, A. *and* **BACHKATOV, N. Russia revised** an alphabetical key to the Soviet collapse and the new republics. London, Deutsch, 1992. xii,258p. bibliog., index. £9.99. ISBN: 0233987673.

First published as *Les nouveaux Soviétiques de l'A à Z* (Paris, Cahmann-Lévy).

Pinpoints major developments up to the first months of 1992. A-Z sequence of persons, organizations, concepts and

....(contd.)

statistics, geographical entities, and political terminology *etc.* Bibliography p.248. Thematic index p.49-55. Both authors were newspaper correspondents in Moscow as the Soviet Union disintegrated. *Class No:* 947(038)

Reviews & Abstracts

[7466]
The Current digest of the post-Soviet press. Columbus, Ohio, Current Digest of the Soviet Press, 1949-. Weekly. ISSN: 00113425.

Founded by the American Council of Learned Societies and the Social Sciences Research Council in 1949.

Quarterly indexed weekly extracts and abstracts in English from the Soviet press offered as documentary material without editorial comment for use in teaching and research. Annual indexes from v.28 (1976). Online version (DIALOG File 645. $84./hr. $0.25. per offline print. *Class No:* 947(048)

Maps & Atlases

[7467]
MILNER-GULLAND, R. *and* **DEJEVSKY, N. Atlas of Russia and the Soviet Union.** Oxford, Phaidon, 1989. 240p. illus. (some col.), col. maps, bibliog., index. £19.50. ISBN: 0714825492.

Narrative history in 3 major parts: 1. The geographical background - 2. The historical period - 3. Regions and republics of the Soviet Union (Belorussia; Moldavia and the Ukraine; The Baltic Republics; Transcaucasia; RSFSR; Central Asia). 24 special features *e.g.* Novgorod the Great ... Tolstoy the revolutionary ... Religion in the Soviet Union. Chronological table p. 8-9. The rulers of Russia and the Soviet Union p.10-11. Bibliography p.225-27. Glossary p.228-29. Gazetter p.232-34. *Class No:* 947(084.3)

Armenia

[7468]
CHAHIN, M. The Kingdom of Armenia. London, Croom Helm, 1987. 332p. 16p. plates, illus. maps, index. £40. $49.95. ISBN: 070994800x.

28 chapters (2 parts). 1. Uhartu - 2. Armenia. Main emphasis (2/3) is on Uhartu. Chronology of the ancient Near East p.iv-vii. Maps p.viii-xi. No bibliography. *Class No:* 947(479.25)

Maps & Atlases

[7469]
ARMEN, G. Hayasdanee badmagan adias. New York (?), Armenian National Education Committee, 1987. 51p. $29.

Historical maps of Armenia to the present day. *Class No:* 947(479.25)(084.3)

20th Century

Bibliographies

[7470]
Russia in the twentieth century : the catalogue of the Bakhmeteff Archive of Russian and East European history and culture. Boston, Mass., G.K. Hall, 1987. xi, 187p. ISBN: 081610462x.

The archive is held in The Rare Books and Manuscript Library, Columbia University. Catalogues 900 collections and 1.2 million letters, manuscripts and documents. Entries, listed under the name of an individual, describes each collection's contents and significance. Complements S.A. Grant and J.H. Brown's *The Russian Empire and the Soviet Union* (1981) (*qv*). 'The publication of this guide marks a significant advance in our knowledge of resources outside the homeland available for the study of Russian and East European culture' (*Slavic Review*. v.47, no.2, Summer 1988, p.332-3). *Class No:* 947"19"(01)

Baltic States

[7471]
HIDEN, J. *and* **SALMON, P. The Baltic nations and Europe** Estonia, Latvia and Lithuania in the twentieth century. London, Longman, 1991. x,224p. maps, tables, bibliog., index. £19.99. ISBN: 0582082463.

Part 1 of this comprehensive account of the three Baltic Republics in the 20th century is a summary of their history from the Middle Ages to the First World War. Bibliographical essay (by chapter) p.193-9. 3 maps. *Class No:* 947.4

[7472]
KIRBY, D. Northern Europe in the early modern period The Baltic World 1492-1772. London, Longman, 1990. xii,443p. maps, bibliog., index. $43.25. ISBN: 0582004101.

14 chapters in 4 parts: 1. The Baltic at the end of the Middle Ages - 2. The Livonian Wars - 3. Sweden as a great power - 4. Rise of Russia. Table of contemporary rulers in the Baltic lands 1500-1772 p.426-9. Glossary p.430-1. Bibliography p.405-15. 4 maps. Primarily conceived ... as a general introduction to the history and historical controversies of the Baltic region' (*Preface*). The first volume to appear in a sequence ... that explores the history of the Baltic World, and Northern Europe more generally. *Class No:* 947.4

Estonia

[7473]
RAUN, T.V. Estonia and the Estonians. Stanford, Calif., Hoover Institution, 1987. 313p. bibliog. index. $31.95. ISBN: 0817985115.

Thorough and extremely well documented history of Estonia. Extensive bibliography and glossary. 'In terms of scope, completeness of coverage, accuracy of scholarship, and readability, there are no other works in English that compare with this study' (*Choice*, v.25, no.4, December 1987, p.675). *Class No:* 947.42

Ukraine

[7474]
SUBTELNY, O. Ukraine: a history. Toronto, Univ. of Toronto Press in association with the Canadian Institute of Ukrainian Studies, 1988. xii, 666p.+58p. plates, illus., maps, bibliog., index. $49.95. £35.00. ISBN: 0802058086.

28 ch. organized in 5 pts: 1. Kievian Rus' - 2. The Polish-Lithuanian period - 3. The Cossack era - 4. Ukraine under Imperial rule - 5. Twentieth-century Ukraine. Notes p.573-87. Glossary p.589-90. Bibliography p.591-620. 29 maps. Massive work of scholarship covering from the earliest period. 'No other one-volume English-language work can surpass this well-balanced survey' (*Choice*, v.26, no.11-12, July/August 1989. p.1890). *Class No:* 947.7

Maps & Atlases

[7475]
MAGOCSI, P.R. *and* **MATTHEWS, G.J.,** *cartographer.* **Ukraine: a historical atlas.** Toronto, Univ. of Toronto Press, 1985. [64]p. maps. $40.00. ISBN: 0802032484.

24 maps and commentary with emphasis on politics and administrative changes but with geographical, military and cultural developments also represented *e.g.* 1. Geography of the Ukrainian lands ... 2. Ethnolinguistic setting ... 3. Greek colonies and the Steppe hinterland ... 24. The Ukrainian Soviet Socialist Republic since World War 2. 'An excellent supplement to historical textbooks illustrating complicated periods of Ukrainian history (*Choice*, v.24, no.5, January 1987, p.744). *Class No:* 947.7(084.3)

Georgia

[7476]
CHIROVSKY, N.L. An Introduction to Ukrainian history. New York, Philosophical Library, 3v., 1981-86.

1. *Ancient and Kievan-Galician Ukraine-Rus'* 1981. 347p. 2. *The Lithuanian-Rus' Commonwealth, the Polish domination and the Cossack-Hetman state.* 1984. 400p. 3. *Nineteenth and Twentieth century Ukraine.* 1986. 517p. Ukrainian culture, economy, social structure, religion, literature music, theatre, as well as its political history is dealt with in this 3v. work. 'The most comprehensive coverage of Ukrainian history' (Wynar, B.S. *Ukraine,* 1990. Entry no.29). *Class No:* 947.922

[7477]
SUNG, R.G. The Making of the Georgian nation. London, I.B. Tauris, 1989. xviii,395p. maps, bibliog., index. ISBN: 1850431205.

14 chapters ordered in 3 parts: 1. The rise and fall of the Georgian monarchies - 2. Georgia in the Russian Empire - 3. Revolutionary and Soviet Georgia. Chapter notes p.325-80. Bibliography p.381-5. Glossary p.319-24. *Class No:* 947.922

Scandinavia

[7478]
SAWYER, P.H. Kings and Vikings Scandinavia and Europe AD700-1100. London and New York, Methuen, 1982. x,182p.+16p. plates. illus., map, bibliog., index. ISBN: 0416741800.

10 well-annotated chapters including 1. The age of the

....(contd.)

Vikings: an introductory outline and 3. Contemporary sources. Bibliography p.155-177. Analytical index. *Class No:* 948

Bibliographies

[7479]

Guide to Nordic bibliography. Munch-Petersen, E., *ed.* Kobenhavn, Nord, 1984. 235p. maps, index. ISBN: 8773030805.

A collaborative publication of the 5 Nordic library schools to present the various national bibliographies and essential subject bibliographies of Denmark, Iceland, Norway, Sweden and Finland to an international audience. History, Local history, Geography, Travel, Maps, Biography and biobibliographical dictionaries, Genealogy, Heraldry, Archives and Classical antiquity are all encompassed p.194-215. *Class No:* 948(01)

[7480]

OAKLEY, S.P., *comp.* **Scandinavian history 1520-1970** : a list of books and articles in English. London, Historical Association, 1984. 232p. (*Helps for Students of History, no.91.*) ISBN: 0852782683.

Arranged in chronological sections divided geographically and then by subject. 'A very userful partially annotated bibliography of works published from 1880-1980' (L.B. Sather. *Norway.* 1986. Entry 939). *Class No:* 948(01)

Dictionaries

[7481]

NORDSTROM, B.J. Dictionary of Scandinavian history. Westport, Connecticut, Greenwood Press, 1986. xix, 703p. bibliog. index. $75.00; £73.50. ISBN: 0313228876.

400 initialled entries contributed by 77 scholars cover the major events and personalities in the history of Denmark, Finland, Iceberg, Norway and Sweden, with some information on Greenland and the Faroe Islands from A.D. 1000 to the present day. Entries on major topics open with a general introduction followed by a detailed study in some or all of the Nordic countries. 5 Appendices. Bibliography (p.661-663); Monarchs; Presidents; Prime ministers and governments; and a chronology. Index p.685-703. 'Fills a serious gap in English-language reference sources on the Scandinavian countries' (*Choice,* v.23, no. 10, June 1986, p.1519). *Class No:* 948(038)

Chronologies

[7482]

VEXLER, R., *ed.* **Scandinavia: a chronology and fact book** 1319-1974. Dobbs Ferry, New York, Oceana Publications, 1977. 185p. $8.50. ISBN: 0379163144.

Key dates in Scandinavian history. *Class No:* 948(090)

Middle Ages

[7483]

PULSIANO, P., *ed.* **Medieval Scandinavia** an encyclopedia. New York, Garland, 1993. xix,768p. illus., maps, diagrs., bibliogs., index. $95. ISBN: 0824047877.

Over 250 scholars contribute cross-referenced articles

....(contd.)

varying in length from 150-5000 words on all aspects of medieval Norden (*i.e.* Denmark, Finland, Iceland, Norway, and Sweden). *Class No:* 948"01/14"

Finland

[7484]

JUTIKKALA, E. *and* **PIRINEN, K. A History of Finland.** Translated by P. Sjöblom. New and rev. ed. London, Heinemann, 1974. 253p. +3p. maps, bibliog., index.

First published 1968 by Praeger.

12 chapters: 1. The settlement of Finland begins - 2. Finland is drawn into the Western cultural sphere - 3. Finland in the Scandinavian Union - 4. From the Middle Ages to the modern era - 5. Finland as part of a great power ... 10. Independent Finland. *Class No:* 948.0

Bibliographies

[7485]

RANTANEN, T. *and* **PÄRSSINEN, L. Suomen historiallinen bibliografia 1961-1970.** Helsinki, Finsk historisk bibliografi/Finnish historical bibliography, 1983. xxvii, 647p. (*Suomen Historiallinen Seura. Käsekirjoga 9.*) ISBN: 9519254463.

26 chapters: 1. General publications - 2. Historical research - 3. Archives and museums - 4. Auxiliary sciences - 5. Population - 6. General works covering several periods - 7. Prehistory - 8. Middle Ages - 9. Modern times - 10. Legal and consitutional history - 11. History of the Diet parties - 12. Administration - 13. Military - 14. Ecclesiastical - 15. History of learning - 16. History of Literature - 17. Folklore - 18. Art -19. Economic - 20. Social - 21. Language and nationality questions - 22. Cultural - 23. Genealogy - 24. Biography - 25. Local - 26. Finns abroad. Total of 13275 entries. Index p.533-647. *Class No:* 948.0(01)

[7486]

Suomen historiallinen bibliografia. Helsinki, 1940-. (Suomen Historiallinen Seura). (*Finsk Historisk Bibliografi/Finnish Historical Bibliography/Bibliogaphie Historique Finlandaise.*)

1544-1900 by J. Vallinkoski and H. Schauman. 1961. xix,571p. *1901-1925* by A.H. Maliniemi and E. Kivikoski. 1940. xx,525,108p. *1926-1950* by J. Vallinkoski and H. Schauman. 2v., 1955-56. *1951-1960* by P. Lamminen. 1968. xxiv,836p. *1961-1970* by T. Rantanen and L. Pärssinen. 1983. A systematically arranged series of retrospective bibliographies of writings (books and periodical articles) on Finnish history. Includes items in other languages. Russian-language publications are included in the volumes for 1544-1900 and 1926-50, but omitted for 1901-25. Includes history of special subjects. Does not entirely displace the earlier annual bibliographies published in, or as appendices to, *Historiallinen aikakauskirja,* 1905-15, 1917, and covering 1905-16 (these also include research on Scandinavian and General history). *Class No:* 948.0(01)

Maps & Atlases

[7487]
Suomen historian Kartasto/Atlas of Finnish history.
Jutikkala, E., *ed.* 2nd ed. Porvoo, Werner Söderström, 1959.
83 thematic maps with captions in Finnish and English.
Class No: 948.0(084.3)

Vikings

[7488]
JONES, G. A History of the Vikings. 2nd ed. Oxford, Oxford Univ. Press, 1982. xvi,504p. illus. (inc.plates), maps. ISBN: 0192158821.
4 parts (14 chapters) 1. The Northern people to A.D.700 - 2. The Viking kingdom to the close of the tenth century - 3. The Viking movement overseas - 4. The Viking age ends (to 1066). Select bibliography p.431-444. Supplementary booklist in English 1984 p.430. *Class No:* 948.01

Norway

[7489]
BULL, E., *and others.* **Det Norske folks liv og historie gjennem tidene.** Oslo, llv., 1929-38. illus., ports., maps, facsims.
A general and social history of Norway from the beginnings up to present times. 'The accepted authority' (Roach, J.; ed. *A bibliography of modern history* (1968), p.212). *Class No:* 948.1

[7490]
DERRY, T.K. A History of modern Norway 1814-1972.
Rev. ed. London, Greenwood Press. 1979. xii, 503p. illus., maps, index. £24.75. ISBN: 0313214670.
13 chapters (1. Introductory; Norway in 1814 ... 5. The separation from Sweden, 1884-1905 ... 7. Norwegians abroad ... 12. War and recovery, 1939-1949 - 13. The latest age. Epilogue 1965-1972. Reference notes. Partly analytical index. Comprehensive. *Class No:* 948.1

Bibliographies

[7491]
Bibliografi til Norges historie. Oslo, Grøndahl, 1927-. Annual (later biennial).
Originally issued by Norske Historiske Forening as part of *Historisk Tidsskrift* (1916-) and subsequently as a supplement.
Prepared by Oslo Univ. Library the bibliography covers books, pamphlets and periodical articles. Decennial volumes with author indexes for 1916-1925; 1926-1935; 1936-1945; 1946-1955; 1956-1965; 1966-1975. *Class No:* 948.1(01)

[7492]
Norwegian local history: a bibliography of material in the collections of the Memorial Library, University of Wisconsin - Madison. Hill, D.A., *ed.* Jefferson, North Carolina, McFarland, 1989. 144p. index. £26.25. ISBN: 0899503772.
c.1300 items including settlement books of individual places, directories, anniversary volumes *etc.*
Class No: 948.1(01)

Maps & Atlases

[7493]
HAGEN, R.M., *with others.* **Norsk historisk atlas.** Oslo, J.W. Cappelens Forlag, 1980. 386p. maps. (*Norges Historie, no.15.*)
96p. of historical maps precede outlines of important topics in Norwegian history. *Class No:* 948.1(084.3)

Sweden

[7494]
SCOTT, F.D. Sweden the nations history. 2nd ed. Edwardsville, Southern Illinois Univ. Press, 1988. 688p. maps, bibliog. $45.00. ISBN: 0809315130.
'The most recent, complete and authoritative survey in English of Sweden's history' (L.B. Sather and A. Swanson. *Sweden*, 1987. Entry 147). *Class No:* 948.5

[7495]
Den Svenska historien. Stockholm, S. Bonniers, 10v., 1966-68. illus., diagrs., maps.
1. *Forntild, vikingtild och tidig medeltid till 1319* - 2. *Medeltid 1319-1520* 3. *Vasatiden 1520-1611* - 4. *Gustav Adolfs och Kristina tid 1611-1654* - 5. *Karolinska tiden 1654-1718* - 6. *Frihetstiden 1719-1722* - 7. *Gustavianska tiden 1772-1809* - 8. *Karl Johanstiden och den liberalismen 1809-1865* - 9. *Industri och fochrörelser 1866-1920* - 10. *Vår egen från 1920 till 1960 - talet.* *Class No:* 948.5

Bibliographies

[7496]
BRING, S.E. Bibliografisk handbok till Sveriges historia.
Stockholm, Norstedt, 1934. xx,780p.
Bibliographical guide to Swedish history. Chapters on historical method, bibliographical aids in general, archives and libraries, publishing societies, historiography, etc.; then chapters on periods of Swedish history. The index occupies the last 110 pages. *Class No:* 948.5(01)

[7497]
Svensk historisk bibliografi systematisk förteckning över skrifter och uppsatser som röra Sveriges historia.
Setterwall, K. *Svensk historisk bibliografi 1771-1874* Uppsala, Appelberg, 1937. *1875-1900* (Stockholm, Norstedt, 1907). *1901-1920.* (Uppsala, Appelberg, 1923). 2. Sjogren, P. *Svensk historisk bibliografi 1921-1925* (Stockholm, Norstedt, 1956). 3. Bohrn, H. and Elfstrand, P. *Svensk historisk bibliografi 1936-1950* (Stockholm, Norstedt, 1964). Rydbeck, J. *Svensk historisk bibliografi 1951-1960* 1968. 5. Bachman, M.L. *Svensk historisk bibliografi 1961-1970* 1984.
Issued under the auspices of the Svenska Historiska Föreningen. Bibliographies of sources and secondary works (books and periodical articles) arranged by period and by subject. Cumulated from the annual *Svensk historisk bibliografi*, supplement to *Historisk Tidskrift* (Stockholm). 'An essential source for the study of Swedish history' (L.B. Sather and A. Swanson. *Sweden*, 1987. Entry 995).
Class No: 948.5(01)

Denmark

[7498]

Danmarks historie. København, Politiken, 14v. & Index, 1977-78.

De oeldste tider indtil ar 600 [Earliest times to 600A.D.]. 14: *Besoeltelse og atomtid, 1939-1978* [Occupation and the nuclear age, 1939-78]. Each volume covers a particular period and an appended bibliography. The index (*Register*) includes a survey of books concerning, or largely concerning, the history of Denmark. *Class No:* 948.9

[7499]

JONES, W.G. **Denmark** : a modern history. Rev. ed. London, Croom Helm, 1986. 248p. map. bibliog., index. £35.00. ISBN: 0709914687.

Previously published by Benn in 1970.

Chapter 1. Early history in brief (*c*.850-1814); remaining 8 chapters concerned with nineteenth and twentieth centuries. Appendix 1. The Faroe Islands (p.218-227). Appendix 2. Greenland (p.228-237). Bibliography p.238-240. This edition omits Appendix on Danish West Indies. *Class No:* 948.9

Bibliographies

[7500]

ERICHSEN, B. *and* KRARUP, A. **Dansk historisk bibliografi** Systematisk fortegnelse over bidrag til Danmarks historie til udgangen af 1912. København, Gad, 3v., 1917-1927.

1. *Danmarks historie. Danmarks stats-og kulturforhold.* 2. *Danmarks topografi.* 3. *Personalhistorie* [biography]. V.1-2 list more than 20,000 references to sources and secondary works (books, articles, etc.);. name and title indexes in v.2. History of the arts included. *Class No:* 948.9(01)

[7501]

—Dansk historisk bibliografi. Udgivet af den Danske Historiske Forening ved H. Bruun. København, Hagerup, 1956-.

1913-1942 - 6v., 1966-77. *1943-1947.* 1956. 18,594p. Similar systematic arrangement to Erichsen and Krarup's bibliography. Subject and title index. *Class No:* 948.9(01)

Middle Ages

[7502]

YOUNG, G.V.C. **From the Vikings to the Reformation** a chronicle of the Faroe Islands up to 1538. Douglas, Isle of Man, Shearwater Press, 1979. 184p. illus. £5.50. ISBN: 0904980200. *Class No:* 948.9"01/14"

Iceland

Faeroe Islands

[7503]

JACKSON, A. **The Faroes** the faraway islands. London, Robert Hale, 1991. 223p. illus., maps, bibliog., index. ISBN: 070904304x.

19 chapters in 5 sections comprise this handbook for visitors: 1. Ancient past (556-1856) - 2. Traditional and recent past (1848-1948) - 3. Current political and social setting - 4. A tour through the islands - 5. Basic facts

....(contd.)

(Transport and accommodation; Chronology p.207-12; Glossary p.213-6; Bibliography p.217-8). This is by far the most comprehensive work in English. *Class No:* 949.12

Netherlands

[7504]

Algemeine geschiedenis der Nederlanden. Haarlem, Fibula-Van Dischoek, 15v., 1979-.

1. *Nederland en België 1840-1914.* 1979. 453p. IBSN 9022838137. 'In almost every respect superior to the corresponding volume in the old AGN' (*Low Countries History Yearbook,* v.12, 1979, p.148). 4. 1300-1520. 1980. 5. *Sociaal-economische geschiedenis; Geografie en demografie 1500-1800; Instellingen 1480-1780; Politieke en religiegeschiedenis na 1480.* 1980. 552p. ISBN 9022838064. 6. *Nieuw tijd: Sociaal-economische geschiedenis 1490-1580; Politieke geschiedenis 1558-1648; Religiegeschiedenis 1517-1648.* 1979. 457p. ISBN 9022838072. 7. *Nieuw tijd: Sociaal-economische geschiedenis 1590-1650; Overzee geschiedenis circa 1590-1680' Socio-culturele geschiedenis 1500-1800* 1980. 418p. ISBN 902283808. 8. *Nieuw tijd: Sociaal-economische geschiedenis 1650-1800; Politieke geschiedenis 1648-1700; Religiegeschiedenis tweede helft 17de eeuw.* 1979. 474p. ISBN 902283809. 14. *Nieuwste tijd. Nederland en België 1914-1940.*1979. 434p. ISBN 9022838153. 'A truly monumental lavishly illustrated and beautifully produced work in quarto ... It deals with the history of the area now occupied by modern Belgium and the Netherlands from prehistoric times until the present day. (*Journal of Medieval History,* v.7, no.3, September 1981. p.301). *Class No:* 949.2

Bibliographies

[7505]

BUCK, H. de. **Bibliografie der geschiedenis van Nederland.** Leiden, E.J. Brill, 1968. xx, 712p. indexes.

'The standard bibliographical work on Dutch history and the initial point of departure for most research projects' (P. King and M. Wintle, *The Netherlands,* 1988. Entry 989). Cut off date is 1963. Arranged by subject with author, personal name, and place name indexes. *Class No:* 949.2(01)

[7506]

COOLHAAS, W. P. **A Critical study of studies on Dutch colonial history.** 2nd ed. rev. by G.J. Schutte. The Hague, Martinus Nijhoff, 1980. 264p. indexes. (*Koninklijk Instituut voor Taal, Land-en Volkenkunde Bibligoraphical Series, no.4.*) ISBN: 9024723078.

1st ed. 1960. Enlarged from the author's 'Chronique de l'Histoire coloniale outre-mer neérlandaise' (*Revue d'histoire des colonies,* v.44, 1957, p.311-448).

6 main sections: 1. Archives - 2. Journals, institutes, university chairs - 3. Books of travel - 4. The area covered by the charter of the VOC (United East Indies Company) - 5. The Netherlands East Indies after 1795 - 6. The area covered by the charter of the Westindische Compagnie ... to the present day. Covers general works; sources; monographs; biographies, regional studies. 3 Indexes: by year, personal names, and placenames. 'An extremely useful and full bibliography covering all aspects of Dutch colonial history' (*Low Countries History Yearbook,* no.15, 1982, p.203). *Class No:* 949.2(01)

[7507]

HERVIJNEN, G., *and others*. **Bibliografie van de stedengeschiedenis van Nederland.** [Bibliography of the urban history of the Netherlands.] Leiden, E.J. Brill, 1978. 355p. map, indexes.

3,331 entries for books, articles and dissertations. Arranged in provincial sections. Sponsored by the Commission Internationale pour l'Histoire des Villes. *Class No:* 949.2(01)

[7508]

The Low Countries History Yearbook. The Hague, Martinus Nijhoff, v.11-15, 1979-1982.

Formerly *Acta Historiae Neerlandica* v.1-10, 1966-1978 published in Leiden by E.J. Brill (v.1-5, 1966-1971) and subsequently at The Hague (v.6-10, 1973-1978) by Martinus Nijhoff.

Founded to end the isolation of Dutch historians imposed by their language and to enable them 'to participate to a greater extent in international discussion' (*Introduction to v.1*). Extremely valuable bibliographical surveys were a regular feature 1973 onwards *viz.* v.6 (1973): A.C. Carter: 'Survey of recent Dutch historiography' p.175-199; J. Dhondt: 'Belgian historiography written in Dutch 1969-1971', p.201-19. V.7 (1974): W. Blockmans and others: 'Belgian historiography written in Dutch 1971-1973', p.253-65.

'Survey of Recent Historical Works on Belgium and the Netherlands Published in Dutch', with various editors, in v.8 (1975) p.159-200; v.10 (1978) p.195-254; v.11 (1979) p.181-215; v.12 (1979) p.126-64; v.13 (1980) p.133-191; v.14 (1981) p.182-220; v.15 (1982) p.137-204. All these surveys, 1973-1982, ended with a section 'Recent Works on the History of the Low Countries published in English' (slightly variant titles). A.C. Carter and others *Historical research in the Low Countries 1970-1975: a critical survey* (The Hague, Martinus Nijhoff, 1981. 275p. bibliog., indexes). is a collection of bibliographical surveys first printed in *Acta Historiae Neerlandica,* 1973-77 and is continued by J. Kossman-Putto and E. White's *Historical research in the Low Countries 1981-83: a critical survey* (Leiden, E.J. Brill, 1985. 117p. bibliog). *Class No:* 949.2(01)

[7509]

Repertorium der verhandelingen en bijdragen betreffende de geschiedenis des vaderslands in tijdschriften en mengelwerken tot op 1939. Petit, L.D. Leiden, E.J. Brill, 5v., 1907-53.

'Repertory of treatises, and contributions concerning the history of the Netherlands, in periodicals and collected works.'

V.1: up to 1900; v.2: 1901-10; v.3: 1911-20; v.4: 1921-29; v.5: 1930-39. *Class No:* 949.2(01)

[7510]

—Repertorium van boeken en tijdschriftartikelen betreffende de geschiedenis van Nederland ... 1940-. Bos, Th. S.H., *ed.* Leiden, E.J. Brill (later The Hague, Martinus Nijhoff), 1943-. Initially triennial, now annual.

A classified listing of Dutch history publications. 'An indispensable research tool' (P. King and M. Wintle. *The Netherlands*, 1988. Entry 1019). *Class No:* 949.2(01)

Encyclopaedias

[7511]

Kroniek van Nederland. Rotterdam, Elsevier (later Agon), 1987.

Dutch history reported on a chronological basis as if in a contemporary newspaper with news reports, summary articles, and closely interwoven illustrations. *Class No:* 949.2(031)

Dictionaries

[7512]

Nijhoffs Geschiedenis-lexicon Nederlanden België. Volmuller, H.W.J., *comp.* 's Gravenhage-Antwerpen, Martinus Nijhoff, 1981. 655p. illus., maps. ISBN: 9024790786. *Class No:* 949.2(038)

[7513]

REINSMA, R.,. Van Goor's woordenboek der Vaderlandse geschiedenis. Den Haag, Van Goor Zonen, 1973. 464p. ISBN: 9000019087.

Brief notes on people, events, publications, historical terms *etc.* in single A-Z sequence. *Class No:* 949.2(038)

Chronologies

[7514]

JANSEN, H.P.H. Kalendarium geschiedenis van de Lage Landen in jaartallen. [A History of the Low Countries year by year.] Utrecht and Antwerp, Het Spectrum, 1974. 264p.

First published 1971.

Chronological factbook from prehistory to 1974. *Class No:* 949.2(090)

Biographies

[7515]

TAMSE, C.A., *ed*. Nassau en Oranje in de Nederlandse geschiedenis. Alphen a.d. Rijn, Sijthoff, 1979. 424p. ISBN: 9021824477.

Biographical sketches of Princes of the House of Orange prominent in Dutch history either as stadholders or monarchs. No bibliographical footnotes. *Class No:* 949.2(092)

Belgium

[7516]

PIRENNE, H. Histoire de Belgique. Bruxelles, Lamertin, 7v., 1900-32.

1. *Des orignes au commencement du XIVe siècle.* 5.éd. 1929. 2. *Du commencement du XIVe siècle à la mort de Charles le Téméraire.* 3.éd. 1922. 3. *De la mort de Charles le Téméraire à l'arrivée du duc d'Albe dans le Pays-Bas (1567).* 3.éd. 1923. 4. *La révolution-politique et religieuse...* 3.éd. 1927. 5. *La fin du régime espagnol. Le régime autrichien. La révolution brabançonne et la révolution liégeoise.* 2.éd. 1926. 6. *La conquête française. Le royaume du Pays-Bas La révolution belge.* 1926. 7. *De la révolution de 1830 à la guerre de 1914,* 1932. Footnotes. Full contents lists; volume indexes. 'This is an indispensable and standard work' (Mallinson, V. *Belgium* (1966),p.232). *Class No:* 949.3

Bibliographies

[7517]

BELDER, J. de and **HANNES, J. Bibliographie de l'histoire de Belgique 1865-1914.** Louvain, Nauwelaarts, 1965. 301p. indexes. *(Centre Interuniversitaire d'Histoire Contemporaine. Cahiers, 38.)*

The second in a series of bibiliographies on the history of Belgium since 1789. (See also entries for P. Gérin and S. Vervaeck.).

The Belder-Hannes volume has 2,442 numbered, unannotated entries covering all aspects of history, - general; law and institutions; internal politics and ideology; international relations of Belgium; military history; economic and social history; history of Belgian expansion (Congo, p.159-211); intellectual and scientific life; education; religious history; press; local history - Author and subject indexes. *Class No:* 949.3(01)

[7518]

'Bulletin d'histoire de Belgique', *Revue du Nord,* v.37-. 1955-. Annual.

Stems from J. Dhondt and M.A. Arnoulds' 'Le Travail historique en Belgique (1944-1947), *Revue du Nord,* v.29, 1947, p.301-21 and v.30, 1948, p.77-96. Continued as 'Bibliographie de l'Histoire de Belgique' in the same quarterly journal, v.33-34 and as 'Chronique et Bulletin De l'Histoire De Belgique pour 1952,' *ibid.,* v.35, 1953, p.151-83. (un bulletin crique des ouvrages les plus importants parus dans l'année en Belgique).

1988-1989, *Revue du Nord,* v.73, no.289, Janvier-Mars 1991, p.103-167 is in 5 sections: 1. Généralités - 2. Sciences auxiliaires - archives - 3. Moyen Age - 4. Du XVe siècle á 1830 - 5. Époque contemporaine. Author index. 146 extensively annotated items. *Class No:* 949.3(01)

[7519]

GÉRIN, P. Bibliographie de l'histoire de Belgique 1789-21 juillet 1831. Louvain, Nauwelaerts, 1960. 430p. Centre Interuniversitaire d'Histoire Contemporaine. Cahiers, no.15.

3,385 numbered, unannotated entries, sytematically arranged. Covers all aspects of history. Basic works are asterisked; locations in 7 libraries, including the Bibliothèque Nationale, Paris. Author index; subject index (non-analytical, more than 200 unspecified entries under 'Révolution de 1830').

Continued in S. Vervaeck's *Bibliografie van de geschiedenis van België, ... 1831-1865* (Louvain, Nauwelaerts, 1965, 303p.), followed by Belder and Hannes' *Bibliographie ... 1865-1914. Class No:* 949.3(01)

[7520]

PIRENNE, H. Bibliographie de l'histoire de Belgique : catalogue méthodique et chronologique des sources et des ouvrages principaux relatifs à l'histoire de tous les Pays-Bas jusqu'en 1598 et à l'histoire de Belgique jusqu'en 1914. 3rd ed. Bruxelles, Lamertin, 1931. viii, 440p.

First published Gand, H. Engelcke, 1893. 2nd ed. 1902.

Essential guide to the sources and secondary works for the history of Belgium (Low Countries before 1598). *Class No:* 949.3(01)

Encyclopaedias

[7521]

Chronique de la Belgique. Bruxelles, Éditions Chronique, 1987.

A Flemish edition. *Kroniek van België* is also published by Elsevier (subsequently Agon).

Belgian history reported on a chronological basis as if in a contemporary newspaper with chronologies, summary articles, and closely interwoven illustrations. *Class No:* 949.3(031)

Switzerland

[7522]

LUCK, J.M. A History of Switzerland the first 100,000 years. Before the beginnings to the days of the present. Palo Alto, California, The Society for the Promotion of Science and Scholarship, 1985. xiv, 887p. illus., maps, tables, bibliog., index. $36.00. ISBN: 093066406x.

11 chronological heavily sub-divided chapters. Glossary p.846-7. Bibliography (425 items) p.849-59. 80p. plates. Analytical index. *Class No:* 949.4

[7523]

Nouvelle histoire de la Suisse et des Suisses. Lausanne, Editions Payot Lausanne, 3v., 1982-83. 368+304+328p. illus.

V.1: Introduction - L'Empreinte des anciennes civilisations - Les Racines de l'indépendance - L'Heure de la puissance. 1982. FS58. ISBN 2601003014. 2. Réformes, ruptures et croissances - Vie et mort de l'Ancient Régime - La Quête d'un état national 1983. FS58. 2601003022. 3. La Suisse des radicaux - Menace et repliement - Une course accélérée vers l'avenir. 1983. FS58. 2601003030. An authoritative cooperative history. A new single volume edition appeared in 1986 (1008p. illus. (some col.), indexes). FS98. 2601030178. *Class No:* 949.4

Bibliographies

[7524]

BARTH, H. Bibliographie der Schweizergeschichte, enthaltend die selbstandig erschienen Druckwerke zur Geschichte der Schweiz bis Ende 1912. Basle, Basler Buch- und Antiquariatshandlung, 3v., 1914-15. (Reprinted New York, Kraus).

A very full bibliography (35,000 items) of sources and secondary works (books and periodical articles, by period (v.1) and by subject (v.2-3). Includes history of the arts and a lengthy section, 'Personengeschichte'. *Class No:* 949.4(01)

[7525]

Bibliographies et ouvrages de reference Suisse et particulièrement suisses romandes. Essai de bibliographie analytique. Courten, R. de. Neuchâtel, Groupe romand de formation professionelle de l'Association des bibliothècaires suisses, 1982. 60 leaves reproduced from typescript. pbk. Swiss Fr.20.

Over 200 mostly annotated titles presented in 4 sections: 1. Bibliographies Nationales - 2. Bibliographies Spéciales - 3. Bibliographies Spécialisées (Histoire Suisse; Biographie; Généalogie Héraldique; Histoire cantonale; Géographie) 4. Livres d'Adresse; Annuaires; Guides; Enclopédies. *Class No:* 949.4(01)

Encyclopaedias

[7526]

Chronik der Schweiz. Dortmund, Chronik Verlag, 1987. 640p. coll. illus., col. maps, index. DM89.

Swiss history presented as if in a contemporary newspaper. Political, social, economic, cultural amd military events all loom large. 1,639 individual, self contained articles. *Class No:* 949.4(031)

Handbooks & Manuals

[7527]

Handbuch der schweizer Geschichte. 2 Aufl. Zurich, Verlag Berichthaus, 2v., 1980. xx, 672p; xii, 648p.

First published 1972-77.

Considered the best guide to the history of Switzerland. 'This is not a work which will afford pleasure to the literary reader, but it is an excellent guide to the books and journals.' (Hughes, C. *Switzerland*, 1975. p.278). *Class No:* 949.4(035)

Dictionaries

[7528]

Dictionnaire historique et biographique de la Suisse publié avec la recommendation de la Socété Générale Suisse d'Histoire. Neuchâtel, Administration du Dictionnaire, 7v. & supplts. 102, 1921-1934.

German edition as *Historisch-biographisches Lexikon der Schweitz.*

A major Swiss reference tool, covering all aspects of history; particularly rich on biographies, with genealogical data, Signed articles, with bibliographies; well illustrated. *Class No:* 949.4(038)

Greece

[7529]

CLOGG, R. A Short history of modern Greece. 2nd ed. Cambridge, Cambridge Univ., Press, 1986. viii, 242p. map. bibliog., index. £25.00. ISBN: 0521328373.

8 chapters (1. 'Waiting for the barbarians': the downfall of Byzantium, 1204-1453 ... 8. From authoritarianism to democracy, 1974-. Bibliography, 8. Cyprus). Analytical index. 'Greatly to be recommended ... An honest and authoritative attempt to be fair-minded' (TLS, No.4001, 23 November 1979, p.5). *Class No:* 949.5

[7530]

WOODHOUSE, C.M. Modern Greece : a short history. 4th ed. London, Faber, 1986. 344p. maps. bibliog., index. pbk. £4.95. ISBN: 0571138276.

First published in 1968 as *Story history of modern Greece.* 2nd edition under present title 1977.

12 chapters including 12. Trial of democracy 1977 - added for this edition. Bibliography (by chapters) p.325-329. 4 maps. *Class No:* 949.5

Middle Ages

[7531]

CHEETHAM, N. Medieval Greece. New Haven and London, Yale Univ. Press, 1981. x, 341p. maps, general tables, bibliog., index. $40.00. £35.50. ISBN: 0300024215.

14 chronological chaps: 1. Death of ancient Hellas ... 14.

.... (contd.)

Crete (1204-1669) cover an unfamiliar period for the general educated public. Note on sources p.302-305. Appendix: List of rulers p. Bibliography p.328-332. The author was a member of the Diplomatic Service in Greece for many years. *Class No:* 949.5"01/14"

Albania

[7532]

POLLO, S. *and* PUTO, A. The History of Albania from its origins to the present day. London, Routledge & Kegan Paul, 1981. xiii, 322p. ports., index. ISBN: 071000365x.

First published as *L'histoire de l'Albanie*, and written 'with the kind co-operation of the Historical Institute of the Science Academy of the People's Republic of Albania'.

12 chapters (1. Prehistoric and ancient times: the Illyrians ... 4. The age of Skanderkeg ... 6. The rebirth of the Albanian nation (1844-1912) ... 9. Albania under Zogu's regime - 10. The struggle against Fascism for national liberation (1939-) ... 12. Albania today. Bibliography, p.294-304 (Sources and documents; 2. Collected refeences; 3. Authors and studies), with occasional explanatory notes, 87 illus. The narrative goes up to 1970. A pioneer history, on Marxist orthodox lines. *The Times* review (18 July 1981, p.9) finds that 'the translation, plainly from a French version, is deplorably inept'. *Class No:* 949.65

Bibliographies

[7533]

DANIEL, O. Albanie une bibliographie historique. Paris, Éditions du Centre National de la Recherche Scientifique, 1985. 616p. Fr.335.00. ISBN: 2222032369.

Introduction (p.9-15) includes Une Albanie mythique; Le problème des sources d'étude; Les bibliographies de l'Albanie; and Nécessité d'une nouvelle bibliographie. 4380 unannotated entries in 4 large, subdivided sections: 1. Sources documentaires - 2. Études générales - 3. Sources historiques générales - 4. Histoire de l'Albanie. *Class No:* 949.65(01)

Balkans

[7534]

FINE, J.V.A. The Early medieval Balkans a critical survey from the sixth to the late twelfth century. Ann Arbor, Univ. of Michigan Press, 1983. xxvi, 336p. maps, bibliog., index. $34.50. ISBN: 0472100254.

Introduction - Balkan geography and society - 1. Historical background - 2. Slavic invasions - 3. Balkans in the eighth century - 4. Bulgaria in the ninth century - 5. Bulgaria under Symeon 893-927 - 6. Bulgaria after Symeon 927-1018 - 7. Dukla and the Central and Eastern Balkans from the death of Basil II 1025 to the 1180s - 8. Croatia and Dalmatia. Appendix: Medieval rulers. Glossaries (terms and peoples) p.299-308. Sources referred to in the text p.309-313. Bibliography p.315-18. Analytical index. *Class No:* 949.7

[7535]
—FINE, J.V.A. **The Late medieval Balkans** a critical survey from the late twelfth century to the Ottoman Conquest. Ann Arbor, Univ. of Michigan Press, 1987. xvi, 683p. bibliog., index. $39.95. ISBN: 0472100793.

10 chronological chapters covering 12th to early 15th centuries. Appendix: Medieval rulers. Glossary p.621-7. Sources referred to in text p.629-31. Bibliography p.633-43. Analytical index. *Class No:* 949.7

[7536]
JELAVICH, B. **History of the Balkans. v.1. Eighteenth and nineteenth centuries. v.2. Twentieth century.** Cambridge, Cambridge University Press, 1983. xiv, 407p.+Øi, 476p. illus., maps, bibliog., index. £42.00 each. ISBN: 0521252490, V.1; 0521254485, V.2.

Considers the history of the major Balkan nationalities - the Albanians, Bulgars, Croats, Greeks, Romanians, Serbs and Slovenes. An introdcution to v.1 presents the historical background up the beginning of the 18th century. Bibliography p.457-460 (v.2). 'This set can be highly recommended to undergraduate and graduate students, faculty, government experts, information services, and the general public' (*Choice*), v.21, no.6, February 1984, p.873). *Class No:* 949.7

[7537]
POULTON, H. **The Balkans** minorities and states in conflict. London, Minority Rights, 1991. x,243p. maps, bibliog., index. ISBN: 1873194250.

Historical and current studies of ethnic conflicts in Yugoslavia, Bulgaria, Greece, and Albania. *Class No:* 949.7

Biographies

[7538]
BERNATH, M. *and* SCHROEDER, F.V., *eds*. **Biographisches lexikon zur Geschichte Südesteuropas.** München, R. Oldenbourg Verlag, 4v., 1974-1981.

1. *A-F* 1974. xvi, 557p. 348647961. 2. *G-K* 1976. [iii], 542p. 3486494211. 3. *L-P* 1979. 500p. 3486489917. 4. *R-Z* 1981. 596p. index. 3486424211. Personenregister p.509-596.

1500 signed biographical sketches of varying length (Metternich: 4p; Admiral Horthy: 2p.) with accompanying bibliographies covering the history of Hungary, Rumania, Yugoslavia, Bulgaria, Albania, Greece, Ottoman Empire, Hapsburg monarchy, Slovakia to 1945. *Class No:* 949.7(092)

Yugoslavia

[7539]
MAGAŠ, B. **The Destruction of Yugoslavia** tracking the break-up 1980-92. London, Verso 1993. xxv,366p. map, table. ISBN: 0860913767.

5 parts: 1. The Kosovo watershed and its aftermath (1981-87) - 2. Interregnum (1980-88) - 3. Milošević assails the federal order (1988-89) - 4. Systemic Collapse (1990-91) - 5. War (Jun-Dec 1991). Political analysis, reportage, and personal reflection in chronological narrative. *Class No:* 949.71

[7540]
PRIBICHEVICH, S. **Macedonia** : its people and history. Philadelphia, Pennsylvania State Univ. Press, 1982. 270p. col. illus, maps, bibliog., index. $24.95 £19.05. ISBN: 0271003154.

Bibliography p.261-266. 'A lucid, brief account from antiquity to the present ... For the person who is not familiar with Macedonia, this is a very good introduction' (*Choice*, v.20, no.3, November 1982, p.487). *Class No:* 949.71

[7541]
SINGLETON, F. **A Short history of the Yugoslav peoples.** Cambridge, Cambridge Univ. Press, 1985. xiv, 309p. maps, tables, bibliog. index. £22.50 $39.50. ISBN: 0521254787.

14 chapters (1. The lands of the South Slavs ... 3. The early Slav Kingdoms ... 4. The South Slavs under foreign rule ... 9. Yugoslavia and the Second World War ... 12. The 1960s - a decade of reform ... 14. Yugoslavia after Tito). Bibliography p.286-297. 8 tables, 4 maps, 'This book should be in every university, college, secondary school, and public library' (*Choice* v.23, no.4, December 1985, p.655). *Class No:* 949.71

Bibliographies

[7542]
MATULIC, R. **Bibliography of sources on Yugoslavia.** Palo Alto, California, Ragusan, 1981. viii, 252p. indexes. $18. ISBN: 0918660130.

Unannotated entries for 3000 books and *c.* 1500 periodical articles mainly in the English language. 'A very useful reference tool, particularly for historians' (Horton, J.J. *Yugoslavia*, 2nd ed., 1990. Entry 908). *Class No:* 949.71(01)

[7543]
TERRY, G.M. **Yugoslav history:** a bibliographic index to English language articles. 2nd ed. Nottingham, Astra, 1990. xxxiii,168p. £17.50. ISBN: 0946134235.

Nearly 3000 entries covering all articles contained in English-language journals, *festschriften,* conference proceedings and collected papers. 1945 to the present, on the historical, diplomatic, political, social, economic, legal, intellectual, and religious development of Yugoslavia and its people. There are separate sections on each of the constituent republics. *Class No:* 949.71(01)

Rumania

[7544]
OTETEA, A., *ed*. **A Concise history of Romania.** London, Robert Hale, 1985. 591p. illus., bibliog., index. £15.95. ISBN: 0709018657.

17 chapters based on *The history of the Romanian people* (1970). Bibliog. p.559-566. *Class No:* 949.81

[7545]
PASCU, S. **A History of Transylvania.** Detroit, Wayne State Univ. Press, 1982. xxiv,318p. illus., maps, bibliog., index. $89.70. ISBN: 0814317227.

Basis of the present work first published as *Voieodatul Transilvaniei* (Cluj, Editura Dacia, 2v., 1972-79).

14 chapters *e.g.* 1. Pre-Roman Transylvania ... 2. Roman rule and Daco-Roman civilization ... 5. The Transylvania Voivodate ... 7. Turkish suzerainty ... 8. Under the Hapsburgs ... 14. Great Romania. Bibliography p.298-311. *Class No:* 949.81

Asia

[7546]

The Cambridge history of early Inner Asia. Sinor, D., *ed.* Cambridge, Cambridge Univ. Press, 1990. x,518p. maps, bibliog., index. £45. ISBN: 0521243041.

1. The concept of Inner Asia - 2. Geographic setting - 3. Inner Asia at the dawn of history - 4. Scythians and Sarmatians - 5. The Hsiung-nu - 6. Indo-Europeans - 7. Hun period - 8. The Avars - 9. Peoples of the Russian forest belt - 10. Peoples of the South Russian steppes - 11. Establishment and dissolution of the Türk empire - 12. The Uighurs - 13. The Karakhanids and early Islam - 14. Early medieval Tibet - 15. Forest people of Manchuria: Kitans and Jurchens. Bibliography p.424-94. 'This volume is a splendid synthesis of narrative and analytical history, and a definitive work of reference' (*Choice*, v.28,no.1, September 1990, p.190). *Class No:* 95

[7547]

History of civilizations of Central Asia. London, HMSO for Unesco, 6v., 1993-.

V.1: *The Dawn of civilization: earliest times to 700BC* edited by A.H. Dani and V.M. Masson. 1993. 535p. illus., maps, £27. ISBN 9231027190. *Class No:* 95

[7548]

MORGAN, D. The Mongols. Oxford & New York, Basil Blackwell, 1986. xv, 238p. illus., maps, geneal tables, bibliog. index. £15. (*The Peoples of Europe.*) ISBN: 0631135561.

8 chapters: 1. The study of Mongol history - 2. Nomads of the Steppe: Asia before Chingiz Khan - 3. Chingis Khan and the founding of the Mongol empire - 4. Nature and institutions - 5. The Mongols in China - 6. Expansion to the West - 7. The Mongols and Europe - 8. What became of the Mongols? Bibliography p.207-218. Chronology p.219-221. The author is Lecturer in the History of the Near and Middle East at the School of Oriental and African Studies in the University of London. *Class No:* 95

[7549]

ROGERS, M. *and* **KNOX, R.J.,** *eds.* **The Peoples of Asia.** Oxford, Basil Blackwell.

Series announced 1989. On same pattern as *The Peoples of Europe* (qv). *Class No:* 95

Encyclopaedias

[7550]

Encyclopedia of Asian history. Embree, A.T., *editor in chief.* New York, Charles Scribner's Sons; London, Collier Macmillan, 4v., 1988. xiii, 528+538+516+478p. $325.00. £275.00. ISBN: 0684186195.

The history of the project is well told in D.C. Smith's 'The Encyclopedia of Asian history'. *Scholarly Publishing*, v.19, no.4, July 1988, p.202-209.

Covers all aspects of Asian civilization from the earliest period to the present. Excludes the Arabian peninsula, the Middle East and the Soviet Union except for the Central Asian republics. 1200 biographies of living and dead including Europeans closely involved with Asia. All entries are signed and most carry a bibliography. V4. includes list of entries p.319-356; Directory of (over 430) contributors p.357-371; synoptic outline; and an analytical index. Prepared under the auspices of the The Asia Society and intended 'to make available the highest level of contemporary scholarship on Asia to a nonspecialist

....(contd.)

audience'. 'An excellent overview of the subject ... large academic libraries will find it a must purchase, and others should consider it for its valuable scholarship and broad coverage' (*Booklist*, v.85, no.1, 1 September 1988, p.45). *Class No:* 95(031)

Handbooks & Manuals

[7551]

PHILIPS, C.H. Handbook of Oriental history. London, Dawsons Pall Mall, 1963. viii,265p. £5.00. (*Royal Historical Society Guides and Handbooks, no.6.*) ISBN: 0901050164.

First published London, Royal Historical Society, 1951.

5 sections (on the Near and Middle East, India and Pakistan, South-East Asia and the Archipelago, China and Japan, each by a specialist on the area). Each section gives guidance on: romanization of words; personal names; place-names; glossary of basic words; systems of dating; dynasties and rulers. A basic handbook for westerners embarking on studies relating to Oriental history. *Class No:* 95(035)

20th Century

[7552]

Asian recorder a weekly digest of Asian events with index. New Delhi, M.S.R. Khemchand, 1955-. weekly. continuous pagination.

Events by country A-Z (including Near East but not Soviet Asia) as well as Asian events generally. Source of entries acknowledged. Quarterly and annual indexes. *Class No:* 95"19"

Asia—Far East

[7553]

BORTHWICK, M. Pacific century the emergence of modern Pacific Asia. Boulder, Colo., Westview Press; North Sydney, Allen & Unwin, 1992. xvii,590p. illus., maps, tables, bibliog., index. ISBN: 0813313724, US; 1863732802, Aust.

13 subdivided chapters *e.g.* 1. Dynasties, empires, and ages of commerce: Pacific Asia to the 19th century - 2. Seaborne barbarians: incursions by the West ... 10. China's long march to modernization - 11. Beyond the revolution: Indonesia and Vietnam - 12. Siberian salient - 13. Regional perspective. Bibliography p.547-54. Interdisciplinary study of Southeast and East Asian history. *Class No:* 95.1/.2

Islamic World

[7554]

The Cambridge history of Islam. Holt, P.M., *and others,* *eds.* Cambridge, Cambridge Univ. Press, 2v. in 4, 1970. illus.

1A: *The Central Islamic lands from pre-Islamic times to the First World War.* 1B: *The Central Islamic lands since 1918.* 2A: *The Indian sub-continent, South-East Asia, Africa and the Muslim West.* 2B: *Islam society and civilisation.* Aims 'to present the history of Islam as a whole cultural whole' (*Preface*). V.1 includes dynastic lists, a bibliography (p.737-50), glossary and detailed index (p.755-815). V.2 has a bibliography (p.891-905), glossary and equally lengthy index (p.911-66). 'Not at all conducive to continuous reading

....(contd.)

and yet not quite reference articles ... But ... will remain a standard work for many years to come' (*International Affairs*, v.47,no.4, October 1971, p.838-9).
Class No: 95.297

[7555]
HITTI, P.K. **History of the Arabs** from earliest times to the present. 10th rev. ed. London, Macmillan, 1970. xxiv,822p. illus., maps, index.

6 parts (52 charts): 1. The pre-Islamic age - 2. The rise of Islam and the Caliphal State - 3. The Umayyad and the Abbasid Empires - 4. The Arabs in Europe; Spain and Sicily - 5. The last of the medieval Moslem states - 6. Ottoman rule and independence. No bibliography, but heavily footnoted. 21 maps. A standard text. *Class No:* 95.297

[7556]
HOURANI, A. **A History of the Arab peoples.** London, Faber; Cambridge, Mass., Harvard Univ. Press, 1991. xviii,551p. maps, geneal. tables, bibliog., indexes. £25; $24.95. ISBN: 0571133789, UK.

Full-scale narrative history of the Arabic-speaking parts of the Islamic world, from the rise of Islam to the present day, in 26 chapters arrayed in 5 sections: 1. The making of a world (7th-10th century) - 2. Arab Muslim societies (11-15th century) - 3. The Ottoman Age (16th-18th century) - 4. Age of European empires (1800-1939) - 5. Age of nation-states (1939). Chapter notes p.494-9. Bibliography p.500-29. 12 maps. 'In a masterly summational work, the whole story of the Arab peoples is laid out before us' (*Independent on Sunday,* 24 February 1991, Sunday Review section, p.22). *Class No:* 95.297

[7557]
HUMPHREYS, R.S. **Islamic history** a framework for enquiry. Rev. ed. London, Tauris, 1991. xiv,401p. bibliog., index. £14.95. ISBN: 1850433607.

First published Minneapolis, Bibliotheca Islamica, 1988.

12 chapters in 2 parts: 1. Sources and research tools (1. Reference works - 2. Sources: an analytical survey) - 2. Problems in Islamic history (3. Early historical tradition - 4. Modern historians ...). Bibliographic index p.311-94. 'A practical guide to the bibliography and research skills required for productive work in this area ... a useful overview of the current state of Islamic historiographical studies' (*Preface*) Concerned with Central Islamic Lands (*i.e.* Nile to Oxus region), North Africa and Spain. *Class No:* 95.297

[7558]
The **Middle East Journal.** Washington, D.C., Middle East Institute, 1967-. Quarterly.

Each issue includes a chronology of events in thematic sections (*e.g.* Arab-Israeli conflict, Petroleum affairs, Regional affairs) and A-Z by country sections. Chronology 16 Apr - 15 Jul 1993 in v.47, no.4, Autumn 1993, p.667-93. Also a Bibliography of Periodical Literature, an unannotated selective listing of periodical material dealing with the Middle East since the beginning of Islam including documents, geography, history, economic conditions, biography, bibliography, and book review sections. Autumn 1993 issue has 725 items. *Class No:* 95.297

[7559]
The **Muslim World: a historical survey.** Translated from the German by F.R.C. Bagley. New York, Humanities Press; Leiden, E.J. Brill, 4v., 1960-81. bibliogs., indexes.

1. *The Age of the Caliphs* by B. Spuler. 1960. viii, 138p. 2. *The Mongol period* by B. Spuler. 1960. viii, 126p. 3. *The Last great Muslim empires.* 1969. x, 303p. 4. *Modern times.* 1981. x, 370p. V.4 has 7 chapters by various hands: 1. The Ottoman Empire 1774-1918 - 2. Turkey since the Armistice of Mudros - 3. Iran in the 19th and 20th centuries - 4. Central Asia under Russian rule - 5. Modern Afghanistan - 6. Arabian peninsula in the 19th century - 7. Short history of Indonesia. Chapter bibliographies. Indexes of personal names, geographical names and technical terms. *Class No:* 95.297

[7560]
NIZAMI, F.A., *ed.* **History of the Islamic world.** London, Macmillan in association with the Oxford Centre of Islamic Studies.

A new multi-volume history in 12v. is announced for publication over the next 5 years. Expected titles include 1. *The rise and spread of Islam 570AD to 661AD* - 2. *Umayyads and the early Abbasids* - 3. *The central lands to 1850* (to include the Mediterranean littoral and Southern Europe) - 4. *Africa* (excluding Egypt) - 5. *Central Asia* - 6. *The Ottomans* - 7. *Iran* - 8. *South Asia* - 9. *South-east Asia* - 10. *The modern Middle East* - 11. *Modern Europe and the Americas.* *Class No:* 95.297

[7561]
SAUVAGET, J. **Introduction to the history of the Muslim East** a bibliographical guide. 2nd ed. Berkeley and Los Angeles, Univ. of California Press, 1982. xxi, 252p. $35. ISBN: 0313234884.

Originally as *Introduction à l'histoire de l'Orient musulman* (1943; éd refondue. 1961).First published in English 1965.

Running commentary in 3pts: 1. The sources of Muslim history (chapters 1-9) - 2. Tools of research and general works (chapter 10: General information; 11: Special disciplines; 12. Dynastic series and tribal genealogies; 13: The main outlines of Muslim history) - 3. Historical bibliography (chapters 15-24). Index of names. Many references to periodical articles. *Class No:* 95.297

Dictionaries

[7562]
SHIMONI, Y., *ed.* **Political dictionary of the Arab World.** Jerusalem, The Jerusalem Publishing House; New York, Macmillan; London, Collier-Macmillan, 1987. 520p. maps. $50. £40. ISBN: 0029164222.

A revised and updated version of *Political dictionary of the Middle East in the twentieth century* (2nd ed., 1974).

About 500 A-Z informative essays and articles (up to 2000 words long) on the leading personalities, institutions, general issues, and political movements of the 20th century up to the mid-1980s. Excludes Cyprus, Turkey and Iran. *Class No:* 95.297(038)

Maps & Atlases

[7563]

HAZARD, H.W., *comp.* **Atlas of Islamic history.** 3rd ed. Princeton, New Jersey, Princeton Univ. Press, 1954. 49p. maps. (*Princeton Oriental Studies, no.12.*)

1st ed. 1951; 2nd ed. 1952.

Maps cover the Islamic world from the seventh century; also the Near East, the Crusades, the Ottoman Empire, the Middle East and the Far East. 20 maps on the right hand page and historical data facing. Appendices: coversion table of dates, index of place names. *Class No:* 95.297(084.3)

[7564]

An Historical atlas of Islam. Leiden, E.J. Brill, 1981. viii, 71p. maps, index. ISBN: 9004061169.

Forms part of *The Encyclopaedia of Islam*, new edition (*qv*).

73 coloured maps grouped in 9 sections: 1. The Early Muslim earth and sky - 2. The extension of the Muslim world - 3. Early Arabia - 4. The Near and Middle East - 5. Anatolia and the Balkans - 6. Muslim Spain - 7. North Africa - 8. India and the Indian seas - 9. The Far East. Index of place names p.58-70. Introduction carries bibliographical references. *Class No:* 95.297(084.3)

[7565]

HUSSAIN MENES. Atlas of the history of Islam. Cairo, Al-Zahraa for Arab Mass Media, 1987. 523p. col. maps, geneal tables, index. £40.50.

A comprehensive atlas of Islamic history in 213 full colour pages of maps, complemented by a history of all Muslim nations: 1. Introduction to Islamic geography and cartography - 2. Expansion of Islam - 3. Historical charts of Islam to 1985 - 4. The World before the rise of Islam - 5. The life and times of Prophet Mohammad - 6. Conquests of the first century of Islam - 7. Umayyad and Abbasid Caliphates - 8. North Africa and Al-Andalus (Moslem Iberia) - 9. Historical development of Arabia - 10. The eastern wing of the Islamic world - 11. Muslim India - 12. The Crusades - 13. Muslim activity in the Mediterranean - 14. The development of Egypt and Syria - 15. Egypt - 16. Islamic State of the Nile Valley (Egypt and Sudan) - 17. The Ottoman Empire - 18. The later development of Islam in Africa - 19. The economy. Routes of communication by earth and sea and pilgrimage - 20. Islam in modern times (including The Palestinian question). Apart from the Contents page the atlas is in Arabic throughout. The author is Professor of Islamic History in the University of Cairo. *Class No:* 95.297(084.3)

Chronologies

[7566]

Les Grandes dates de l'Islam. Mantran, R., *comp.* Paris, Larousse, 1990. 288p. col. maps, geneal. tables, index. ISBN: 2037400063.

6 contributors. 11 chapters.: 1. Le monde arabe préislamique et les débuts de l'Islam ... 5. Dynasties non arabes (1055-1258) ... 9. Hégémonies française et britannique (1920-1945) ... 14. L'affirmation musulmane (1963-1989). Bibliographies for every chapter. Glossaire p.255-64. Tableaux dynastiques p.265-80. *Class No:* 95.297(090)

[7567]

RAHMAN, H.U. **A Chronology of Islamic history** 570-1000CE. London, Mansell, 1989. ix, 181p. maps, geneal. tables, index. £30. (*East-West Islamic Studies.*) ISBN: 0702119820.

Concise reference guide to the chief events of Islamic history from the birth of Muhammed to the year 1000 in the Christian era. Genealogy of the Umayyads 661-750CE; the Abbasids 750-1258CE; the Shi'ite Imams. *Class No:* 95.297(090)

Asia—Middle & Near East

[7568]

GRESH, A. *and* VIDAL, D. **An A-Z of the Middle East.** Rev. ed. London, Zed Books, 1990. xxi,261p. maps, bibliog., index. £29.95; $49.95. ISBN: 0862328802.

1st English ed. 1987. Translation of *Les cent portes du Proche-Orient* (Paris, 1986).

Brief guide to people, countries, events, and movements, prominent in the political and economic development of the Middle East. Entries average two pages and contain description and analysis. Chronology of events 1947-1990 (updated for this English edition). 'Something rather more serious than a bluffer's guide while falling just short of being an encyclopaedia' (*The Independent*, no.1336, 26 January 1991, p.26). *Class No:* 95.3/.6

[7569]

A History of the Near East. Holt, P.M., *ed.* London, Longman, 7v., 1986-. maps, bibliogs., tables, index.

A history of the region from the coming of Islam to the present day. Noteworthy for the excellent bibliographical surveys in each volume. *Titles* 1. *The Prophet and the age of Caliphates: the Islamic Near East from the sixth to the eleventh century* by Hugh Kennedy. 1986. 440p. £24.00. 0582493129. 2. *The Age of the Crusades: the Near East from the eleventh century to 1517* by P.M. Holt. 1986. xiii, 250p. £15.95. 058249303x. 3. *The Rise of the Ottoman Empire 1300-1574* by Colin Imber. 4. *The Decline of the Ottoman Empire 1574-1792* by R.C. Ropp. 5. *The Making of the modern Near East 1792-1923* by M.E. Yapp. 1987. xii, 404p. £25.00. 0582013666. 6. *The Near East since the First World War* by M.E. Yapp. 1990. £32. 0582495008. 7. *Medieval Persia 1040-1797* by David Morgan. 1988. x, 197. £17.95. 0582014832. *Class No:* 95.3/.6

[7570]

KREYENBROEK, P.G. *and* SPER, S., *eds.* **The Kurds** a contemporary overview. London, Routledge, 1992. xii,250p. tables, bibliog., index. ISBN: 0415072654.

10 papers by different hands on the life and recent history of the Kurds in Iraq, Turkey, Iran, the Soviet Union, Syria, and Lebanon, and on Kurdish ethnicity, nationalism, and language. Chapter notes p.219-33. Bibliography p.234-41. *Class No:* 95.3/.6

[7571]

OVENDALE, R. **The Longman companion to the Middle East since 1914.** London, Longman, 1992. x,378p. maps, bibliogs., index. £13.99. (*Longman Companions to History no.1.*) ISBN: 0582063051.

Comprehensive guide in 9 sections: 1. Annotated chronologies - 2. Biographies - 3. Treaties and alliances - 4. Religion & sects - 5. Rulers, political parties and movements (country by country) - 6. Glossary - 7. Economic & social data - 8. Maps - 9. Bibliographies. *Class No:* 95.3/.6

Bibliographies

[7572]
ATIYEH, G.N., *comp*. **The Contemporary Middle East 1948-1973** a selective and annotated bibliography. Boston G.K. Hall, 1975. xxvi,664p. ISBN: 0816110859.

6,500 annotated entries, primarily for material in the social sciences. Arranged geographically, subdivided by subject. Author and subject indexes. Compiler is head of the Near East section at Library of Congress. 'This indispensable guide' (*Choice*, v.11,no.12, February 1975, p.1547, p.1547). *Class No:* 95.3/.6(01)

[7573]
OLSON, W.J. **Britain's elusive empire in the Middle East, 1900-1921:** an annotated bibliography. New York, Garland Publishing Inc., 1982. xxvii, 404p. index. $61. (*Themes in European Expansion*.) ISBN: 0824092732.

Part 1 (p.1-68) is a magisterial survey of the international political and diplomatic background to 20th century British foreign policy in the Middle East. Part 2 comprises 664 extensively annotated entries (offering a critical analysis of their subject content) concerned with Empire and imperialism; international rivalry; Britain in the Middle East; Nationalism, westernization, Pan-Islam; and recent doctoral theses on the Middle East. 'There is probably no better introduction now available to the literature of the topics with which it deals' (*Choice*, v.20, no.1, September 1982, p.56). *Class No:* 95.3/.6(01)

Reviews & Abstracts

[7574]
The Middle East in conflict a historical bibliography. Santa Barbara, California and Oxford, ABC Clio Information Services, 1985. ix, 302p. indexes. $75. £58.05. (*Clio Bibliography Series, no.19*.) ISBN: 0874363810.

3,258 abstracts of articles published 1973-1982 drawn from the publisher's renowned historical database arranged in 9 sub-divided geographical and topical chapters: 1. General - 2. Political integration and cooperation - 3. International relations, aid, and trade - 4. The Middle East in the World Wars - 5. Intra-regional wars and conflicts - 6. North Africa - 7. The Fertile Crescent - 8. The Arabian Peninsula - 9. The Northern tier (Iran. Afghanistan. Pakistan). Subject Profile Index (SPIndex) and author index (p.213-97) offer generous access points. Some material could have been omitted without loss to overall subject coverage. *Class No:* 95.3/.6(048)

Maps & Atlases

[7575]
FREEMAN-GRENVILLE, G.S. **Historical atlas of the Middle East.** New York, Simon & Schuster, 1993. 144p. maps, bibliog., index. $65.

113 black and white and tinted maps and accompanying text cover the period 2500BC to date. The whole Islamic world is encompassed from Western Europe to Indonesia. *Class No:* 95.3/.6(084.3)

20th Century

Bibliographies

[7576]
GARDNER, J.A. **The Iraq-Iran War:** a bibliography. London, Mansell Publishing Ltd; Boston, G.K. Hall, 1988. xvi, 124p. index. £24.00. $56.00. ISBN: 0720118794, UK; 0816189978, US.

509 numbered and annotated entries in 7 chapters: 1. Introductory sources - 2. Background - 3. Iraq at war 1980-87 - 4. Domestic impact - 5. Foreign impact - 6. The conflict in the gulf - 7. The literature and films of war. Material in Arabic and Persian as well as Western and European languages is included. Author and title indexes. 'Highly recommended for larger political science collections and all Middle East collections' (*Choice*, v.26, no.10, June 1989, p.1661). *Class No:* 95.3/.6"19"(01)

Asia—South & South-East

[7577]
The Cambridge history of Southeast Asia. Tarling, N., *ed.* Cambridge, Cambridge Univ. Press, 2 vols., 1992.

1. *From early times to c.1800.* xv,655p. maps, bibliog. £55. ISBN 0521355052. 2. *The Nineteenth and twentieth centuries.* 704p. maps, bibliog., £55. 0521355052. Cooperative history covering whole of mainland and island Southeast Asia from Burma to Indondesia. Thematic and regional rather than strictly national and chronological approach. Extensive bibliographical essays appended to all chapters. *Class No:* 95.4/.0

[7578]
HALL, D.G.E. **A History of South-East Asia.** 4th ed. London, Macmillan, 1981. xxx, 1070p. illus. maps, bibliog., index. ISBN: 0333241630.

First published 1955.

4 Parts: 1. To the beginning of the sixteenth century - 2. South-East Asia from the beginning of the sixteenth century to the end of the eighteenth - 3. The period of European territorial expansion - 4. Nationalism and the challenge to European domination. Appendix of dynastic lists with governors and governors-general p.954-986. Bibliography (12 sections) p.989-1039. 11 maps. *Class No:* 95.4/.0

Bibliographies

[7579]
CASE, M.H. **South Asian history 1750-1950** a guide to periodicals, dissertations and newspapers. Princeton, New Jersey, Princeton Univ. Press; London, Oxford Univ. Press, 1968. viii,561p.

About 17,000 entries, some annotated, covering the Indian sub-continent. Part 1: Articles (p.11-386) covers political, economic, social and cultural history, Part 2: Dissertations. Part 3: Newspapers. Author, dissertation (by university) and subject indexes. *Class No:* 95.4/.0(01)

[7580]
DALBY, A. **South-East Asia:** a guide to reference material. Oxford, Hans Zell, 1993. 320p. £55. (*Regional Reference Guides, no.2*.) ISBN: 1873836007.

Evaluates and analyses the contents of books and non-reference materials in politics, religion, society, history, language, geography, economics, and development. *Class No:* 95.4/.0(01)

Maps & Atlases

[7581]

SCHWARTZBERG, J.E., *with others eds*. **A Historical atlas of South Asia**. 2nd ed. New York, Oxford Univ. Press, 1992. xxxix, 369p. illus., maps, tables. £200. ISBN: 0195068696.

First published by Univ. of Chicago Press 1978.

149p. of maps (mostly coloured); 117p. of historical narrative, 'South Asia' extends from Afghanistan through the Indian sub-continent, to Burma. 14 sections of maps, including geopolitical, economic, social and cultural themes. (section 14; 'A geopolitical synopsis'; 60 small-scale maps). Bibliography of 38p. 48p. of index, photographs and diagrams. This edition includes 20p. of addenda and corrections. 'One of the very best atlases for any region of the world ... providing a distinctly *geographical* view of history' (*Bulletin*, Special Libraries Association, Geography and Map Division, no.118, December 1979, p.60, 61).
Class No: 95.4/.0(084.3)

China

[7582]

Essays on the sources for Chinese history. Leslie, D.D., *and others, eds*. Canberra, Australian National Univ. Press, 1973. xii, 378p. bibliog., index. ISBN: 0708103987.

24 Western and Oriental academic contributors. *Contents* Archaeological studies in China; oracle bones; pre-Han literature; wooden documents; standard histories; comments on later standard histories; universal histories; local gazetteers; unofficial regional records; genealogical registers; legal sources; compilation and historical value of the Tao-tsang; Tun-huang manuscripts; Tibetan, Manchu, Arabic, Western, Jesuit and Russian sources; archives on modern China; Chinese newspapers; sources on Kuomintang and republican China, the history of the Chinese Communist Party, and the Chinese Peoples Republic; overseas Chinese; and lexicology as a primary source of material for the history of modern China. All except the last of these are accompanied by bibliographies. *Class No:* 951

[7583]

FAIRBANK, J.K. *and* TWITCHETT, D., *eds*. **The Cambridge history of China**. Cambridge, Cambridge Univ. Press, 1978-.

The Ch'in and Han Empires 221BC-AD20. 1986 xli,981p. £85. 0521243270. 2. *Sui and t'ang china 589-906 pt.1*. 1979, xx,850p. 052124467., 6. *Alien regimes and border states 710-1368*. 816p. £75. 0521243319. 7. *The ming dynasty 1368-1644 pt.1*. 1988. xxv,976p. £50. 0521243327. 8. Will be a topical volume of Ming history. 10. *Late ch'ing 1800-1911. pt.1*. 1978. xvi,313p. £80. 0521214475. 11. *Late ch'ing 1800-1911 pt.2*. 1980. 754p. £80. 0521220297. 12. *Republican China 1912-1949 pt.1*. 1983. xviii,1002p. £90. 0521235413. 13. *Republican China 1912-1949 pt.2*. 1986. xix,1092p. £70. 0521243386. 14. *The people's republic pt.1. The emergence of revolutionary China 1949-1965*. xvii,722p. £70. 052124336x. 15. *The people's republic pt.2: revolutionaries within the Chinese revolution 1966-1982*. £75. 0521243378. All volumes have extensive bibliographies, most have bibliographical essays and all have a glossary. The maps have been prepared on the basis of the historical reconstruction of the most up-to-date historical atlas of China, the *Chung-kuo li-shih ti-t'u-chi (Shanghai 1975)*. 'When the CHofC was first planned in 1966, the aim was to provide a substantial account of the history of China

....(contd.)
as a benchmark for the western history - reading public: an account of the current state of knowledge in six volumes. Since then the outpouring of current research, the application of new methods, and the extension of scholarship into new fields have further stimulated Chinese historical studies. This growth is indicated by the fact that the history has now become a planned 15 vols., but will still leave out such topics as the history of art and of literature, many aspects of economics and technology, and all the riches of local history' (*General Editor's Preface*). *Note* Eastman, L.E. and others. *The Nationalist era in China 1927-1949* (1991, x,406p. index. £35. 052139273x) was originally published as v.13 of *Cambridge history of China Class No:* 951

[7584]

FRANCK, I.M. *and* BROWNSTONE, D.M. **The Silk Road:** a history. New York and Oxford, Facts On File Publications, 1987. 294p. maps,. bibliog., index. $24.95; £17.95. ISBN: 0816011222, UK.

Well documented popular history from primary and secondary sources of the 5000 mile route linking East and West from pre-classical times to the present. 5 maps including two on endpapers depicting the main and connecting routes in Roman-Han and Early T'ang and Muslim times. Bibliography p.281-291. *Class No:* 951

[7585]

GERNET, J. **A History of Chinese civilization**. Cambridge, Cambridge Univ. Press, 1982. xxvii,772p. illus., maps, bibliog., index. £45.00; $37.50. ISBN: 0521241308.

Translation of *Le Monde Chinois* published by Librarie Armand Colin of Paris in 1972.

Comprehensive single-volume handbook to Chinese history. Chronological tables p.680-735. Bibliography p.736-757. Analytical index. *Class No:* 951

[7586]

O'NEIL, H.B. **Companion to Chinese history**. New York and Oxford, Facts on File Publications, 1987. x, 397p. maps. £13.95. (*Companions to History Series*.) ISBN: 087196841x.

Almost 1000 brief A-Z entries range from prehistory to 1985 with geographical and personal names well to the fore. Chronology (1506-1985) p.379-83. 14 b/w outline maps p.384-97. Brief bibliographies are appended to many of the entries. 'Useful to the western non-specialist who needs a guide to an unfamiliar civilization' (*Reference Reviews*, v.3, no.1, March 1989, p.42). *Class No:* 951

[7587]

WEI, B.P.T. **Shanghai:** crucible of modern China. Hong Kong, London, New York, Oxford Univ. Press, 1987. xvi, 299p. illus. (21 plates). maps on endpapers, bibliog. index. ISBN: 0195838319, UK; 0195838311, US.

14 chapters - 1. Shanghai before the coming of the foreigner - 2. The Opium War ... 5. The cosmopolitan city ... 13. The Nationalist era ... 14. Epilogue: Shanghai after 1945. Bibliography (inc. Sources in Chinese and Japanese) p.269-283. Glossary p.284-291. Analytical index. The author is an honorary lecturer in history and a research associate at the Centre of Asian Studies in the University of Hong Kong. *Class No:* 951

Bibliographies

[7588]

CHESNEAUX, J. *and* LUST, J. **Introduction aux études d'histoire contemporaine de Chine 1898-1949.** Paris, Mouton, 1964. 148p. (*Maison Sciences de l'Homme. Matériaux pour l'Étude de l'Extrême-Orient moderne et contemporain. Travaux 2.*)

About 600 briefly annotated entries. Author's name in romanised form precedes name in Chinese characters. 7 sections: 1. Introduction - 2. Quelques points de repère - 3. Bibliographie générale (including doctoral theses and research periodicals, ceased and current, p.31-43- 4. Sources de caractère général (archives, etc,) - 5. État des questions, par périod - 6. État des questions, par publications (*e.g.* economic, history; military history; biography) - 7. Appendices (1. Transcriptions - 2. Noms de personnes). Index (romanised); index (Chinese characters). *Class No:* 951(01)

[7589]

FRANKE, W. **An Introduction to the sources of Ming History.** Kuala Lumpur and Singapore, Univ. of Malaya Press, 1962. Distributed overseas by Oxford Univ. Press.

Enlarged and completely revised edition of *Preliminary notes on the important Chinese literary sources for the history of the Ming Dynasty (1365-1644)* published in the Studia Serica Monographs series by The Chinese Cultural Studies Research Institute, West China Union University, Chengtu (1948).

Introduction (the present state of research, some aspects of Ming historiography. The Veritable Records, transmission of works written by Ming authors). 9. Sections: 1. Works on the annalistic pattern - 2. Official and private historical compilations - 3. Biographical - 4. Notes dealing with historical subjects - 5. Memorials - 6. Political institutions - 7. Foreign affairs and military organizations - 8. Geography and local histories - 9. Economy and technology, encyclopaedias, collectanea. Author and title indexes. 'Not a bibliography of works which have been written, but an introduction to the available sources of Ming history' (*Foreword*). *Class No:* 951(01)

[7590]

HERVOUET, Y., *ed*. **A Sung bibliography** /Bibliographie des Sung. Hong Kong, Chinese Univ. Press, 1979. Distributed by Columbia Univ. Press. 598p.

The Sung dynasty: A.D.960-1279. 'A valuable research tool and as such belongs in all libraries equipped for research in traditional Chinese history and civilization' (*Choice*, v.16, no.8, October 1979, p.1000). *Class No:* 951(01)

[7591]

NATHAN, A.J. **Modern China 1840-1972;** : an introduction to sources and research aids. Ann Arbor, Univ. of Michigan Press, 1973. vi, 95p.

About 400 entries. Part 1: Research aids and libraries (1. Bibliographies ... 6. Biography and Elites). Part 2: Major types of primary sources (*e.g.* Chinese newspapers, radio and periodicals; government publications; diplomatic archives; Russian-language materials; materials on Taiwan). Includes many Chinese items. Author and title indexes. 'An inexpensive and valuable item for Asian studies collections' (*Library journal*, v.98, no.20, 15 November 1973, p.3365). *Class No:* 951(01)

Dictionaries

[7592]

DILLON, M. **Dictionary of Chinese history.** London, Cass, 1979. ix,240p. chron. table, map. £19.50. ISBN: 0714631078.

Aims 'to provide a quick and easy reference to the names and terms which occur most frequently in English-language works on China and which can be usefully explained in a few hundred words' (*Preface*). Entries cover the period from pre-history to the end of 1977. 'Mao Tse-tung': over 1p.; 'Congress of the Chinese Communist Party': nearly 2p. Cross-references. *Class No:* 951(038)

[7593]

LEUNG, E. P-w., *ed*. **Historical dictionary of revolutionary China 1839-1976.** Westport, Conn., Greenwood Press, 1992. xvii,566p. map, bibliog., index. $85; £76.50. ISBN: 0313264570.

73 academic contributors. Dictionary consists of (c.270) short signed essays on events, ideas, personalities, battles, organizations *etc.* each with a list of references attached. Chronology p.495-519. Bibliography p.521-43. Glossary (of names in Roman and Chinese scripts) p.546-52. 'A major contribution to the meager collection of English-language reference materials' (*Choice,* v.30, no.2, October 1992, p.274). *Class No:* 951(038)

Maps & Atlases

[7594]

CHEN CHEN-SIANG. **An Historical and cultural atlas of China.** Tokyo, Hara Shobo, 1982. xx,190p. folded maps (some col.). Y29,600. ISBN: 4562012331.

First published in a single-sheet format by International House for China Studies 1975-79.

118 folded map sheets covering almost every aspect of Chinese life and culture. Each map is supplemented by an explanatory essay which may run into several pages. This is a Japanese-Chinese bilingual edition but there is a detailed English preface explaining the process of compiling the atlas and English legends to all the maps. *Class No:* 951(084.3)

Chronologies

[7595]

CHENG, J. **A Chronology of the People's Republic of China 1949-1984.** Beijing, Foreign Languages Press, 1986. 99p. sd. ISBN: 0835115666.

Briefly records most important political, economic, and cultural events. *Class No:* 951(090)

[7596]

CHENG, P.P. **Chronology of the People's Republic of China 1970-1979.** Metuchen, New Jersey, Scarecrow Press, 1986. vii,621p. bibliog., indexes. $55.00. ISBN: 0810817519.

10 annual chapters chronicling events on a daily basis as recorded in Chinese, Japanese, British, French and United States newspapers. Appendix A. Bibliographical sources p.569-570. Further reading p.571-572. 'Excellent for use as quick reference, to refresh reader memory, or to introduce the novice to the major events of the period' (*Choice,*v.24, no.10, June 1987, p.1599). Continues the same writer's *A Chronology of the People's Republic of China from October 1, 1949* (Totowa, New Jersey, Littlefield Adams, 1972). *Class No:* 951(090)

[7597]
DOLBY, W. **Chronological tables of Chinese history.**
Edinburgh, Univ. of Edinburgh Department of Chinese,
1985. [59] leaves reproduced from typescript. pbk.
'This present work does not go into the finer points of
cyclical locations or the pinpointing of months or days, but
merely provides a broad run-through of the principal
dynasties, rulers, by title and by personal names and
surnames, and ruler's reign-periods' (*Preface*). Ranges
645BC-1911A.D. English and Chinese text.
Class No: 951(090)

[7598]
MACKERRAS, C. **Modern China:** a chronology from 1842
to the present. London, Thames & Hudson, 1982. 703p.
maps, index. £22.50. ISBN: 0500250847.
Left hand pages chronicles major political or general
incidents, military or civilian, domestic or foreign relations.
Right hand pages divided into 6 categories: economy;
official appointments, dismissals, resignations; cultural and
social; publications; natural disasters; births and deaths.
Introduction (p.7-20) describes the sources, lists general
works, and specific topic chronologies. Glossary of titles and
technical terms p.644-646. General index p.647-694.
Geographical index p.695-703. 'Aims to present a classified
and factually detailed chronology of modern China'.
Class No: 951(090)

20th Century

[7599]
CHESNEAUX, J., *with others*. **China: the People's Republic
1949-1976.** Hassocks, West Sussex, Harvester Press, New
York, Pantheon, 1979. xii,255p. tables, maps.
Originally as *La Chine: un nouveau Communisme 1949-
1976.*
8 chapters. Chapters 1-7, chronological; 8: 'The Chinese
way'. Chapter 4: 'The Great Leap Forward, 1958-1962':
p.83-112. Chapter bibliographies and documents ('coming
directly/indirectly from the Chinese authorities and include
information from the national press, the local press when
possible, official publications and materials, as well as the
accounts of visitors who have been allowed to enter China'
(*Preface*). Glossary of Chinese terms and names
(transliterated and in Chinese characters). Analytical index.
'A valuable introductory textbook' (*TLS*, no.4003, 7
December 1979, p.101). 'The historical presentation stops
short of the major economic and international problems'
(*International Affairs*, January 1980, p.193).
Class No: 951"19"

[7600]
—CHESNEAUX, J., *and others*. **China from the 1911
Revolution to Liberation.** New York, Pantheon, 1978. 469p.
Covers political, economic, social and cultural changes
and foreign affairs. *Class No:* 951"19"

Bibliographies

[7601]
Sino-Soviet conflict: a historical bibliography. Santa Barbara,
California, and Oxford, ABC-Clio Information Services,
1985. xii, 190p. index. $40. £32.25. ISBN: 0317697544.
842 annotated entries covering the period 1914 onwards
abstracted from the publisher's history database 1965-1982.
Class No: 951"19"(01)

Hong Kong

[7602]
CAMERON, N. **An Illustrated history of Hong Kong.** Hong
Kong, Oxford Univ. Press, 1991. iv,362p. illus (inc. col.
pl.), maps, bibliog., index. £25; $39.95. ISBN: 0195849973.
Narrative history of 'British' Hong Kong in 24 chapters
(*e.g.* 3. Treaty of Nanjing ... 10. Growth of Chinese
institutions ... 20. Invasion and occupation (by Japan) ... 23.
Growth on industrial giant). Chapter notes p.327-32.
Bibliography p.342-5. Glossary p.346. 7 maps and on
endpapers. 'The best overall history to date of the British
Colony' (*Choice*, v.29, no.3, November 1991).
Class No: 951.2317

[7603]
WELSH, F. **A History of Hong Kong.** London, Harper
Collins, 1993. xv,624p.++ 12p. pl. illus., maps, bibliog.,
index. ISBN: 0002158523.
Narrative history in 17 chapters. Appendix A: British
governments and prominent Chinese (1830-1992) p.542-7 -
B. Governors (1841-1992) p.548. Chapter notes p.549-75.
Bibliography p.576-91. *Class No:* 951.2317

Macau

[7604]
MONTALTO DE JESUS, C.A. **Macau histórico.** Macau,
Livros Do Oriente, 1990. 352p. illus. ISBN: 9729418012.
Previously published in English as *Historic Macao:
international traits in China old and new* (Hong Kong, Kelly
and Walsh, 1902; Macao, Salesian Printing Press and
Tipografia Mercantil, 2nd ed. 1926).
Narrative history in 29 chronological chapters. Chapter
notes. p.335-50. *Class No:* 951.2318

Chronologies

[7605]
GOMES, L.G. **Efemérides da história de Macau.** [An
Almanac of the history of Macau.] Macau, Noticias de
Macau, 1954. 267p. (*Colecção Notícias de Macau, no.12.*)
'This chronological register of past events relating to the
Portuguese in Asia is arranged by days of the month. Events
included range from the late 16th century to 1950' (R.L.
Edmonds. *Macau*, 1989. Entry 99).
Class No: 951.2318(090)

Tibet

[7606]
GOLDSTEIN, M.C. **A History of modern Tibet** 1913-1951:
the demise of the Lamaist state. Berkely, Univ. of California
Press, 1989. xxxvi,898p. illus., maps, bibliog., index.
ISBN: 0520061403.
A detailed history (21 chapters) in 2 parts: 1. Era of the
13th Dalai Lama and Reting 1913-1940 and 2. Era of the
Taktra and the 14th Dalai Lama. Appendix A. Anglo-
Chinese Convention of 1906 - B. Anglo-Russian Convention
of 1907 - C. The Simla Agreements of 1914. Glossary of
Tibetan terms p.843. Bibliography p.845-54. 11 maps.
'Examines what happended and why, and balances the
traditional focus on international relations with an emphasis
on the intricate web of internal affairs and events' (*Preface*).
'This book deserves high praise as the first attempt at an

....(contd.)
unbiased comprehensive account of Tibetan politics from 1913-1951', (*Journal of Asian studies,* v.49,no.4, November 1990, p.901). *Class No:* 951.5

Bibliographies

[7607]
CHAND, A. **Tibet past and present** a select bibliography with chronology of historical events 1660-1981. New Delhi, Sterling Publishers Pvt Ltd., 1982. Distributed in North America by Humanities Press. 257p. index. $24.50.

1. Introduction (to Tibetan history) p.1-67 - 2. Chronology p.68-108 - 3. Bibliography p.109-248. Arranged by subject with author index. 'This publication should not be inflicted upon anyone' (*Choice,* v.20,no.8, April 1983, p.1106). *Class No:* 951.5(01)

Mongolia

[7608]
BAWDEN, C.R. **The Modern history of Mongolia.** 2nd rev. ed. London, Kegan Paul International, 1989. xiv,476p. 24p. pl. illus., maps, bibliog., index. pbk. ISBN: 0710303262.

First published London, Weidenfeld & Nicolson, 1968. In fact this 'revised' edition has the text of the 1st ed. reprinted without alteration. Only revision is the incoporation of a Supplementary bibliography p.455!.

Narrative in 9 chapters from loss of Mongol independence to post-Second World War achievements. Chapter notes p.439-47. Bibliographical note. p.451-4. *Class No:* 951.7

Korea

[7609]
HAN, Woo-Keun. **The History of Korea.** 14th printing. Seoul, The Eul-Koo Publishing Co., 1983. xii, 551p. illus. (some col.) maps, geneal.tables, bibliog., index.

Authoritative history in 37 chapters covering the primitive, ancient, medieval, modern and contemporary periods. Bibliography (books and articles in Japanese, Korean and Western languages) p.516-527. Author is Professor of Korean History in Seoul National University. *Class No:* 951.9

[7610]
LEE, Ki-baik. **A New history of Korea.** Cambridge, Massachussetts, Harvard Univ. Press, 1984. xxii, 474p. illus. (some col.) maps, tables, bibliog., index. $25. ISBN: 0674615751.

First published in Korea as *Kuksa Sillon* (*A new history of our nation*) in 1961. Revised as *Han'guksa Sillon* (*A new history of Korea*) in 1967 and 1976.

Authoritative standard history in 16 chronological chapters subdivided into 73 sections: 1. The communal societies of prehistoric times ... 2. Walled-town states and confederated kingdoms ... 14. Nationalist stirrings and imperialist aggression ... 16. The beginnings of democracy. Bibliography p.395-413. Index-Glossary p.415-474. 'Supplements but by no means supersedes Woo-Keun Han's *The History of Korea*' (*Choice,* v.22, no.11-12, July-August 1985, p.1681). *Class No:* 951.9

20th Century

[7611]
FARRAR-HOCKLEY, A. **The British part in the Korean War.** London, HMSO, 2v., 1990.

An official history consisting of chronological treatment of political and military events. 1. *A Distant obligation.* 1990. xxii,512p. illus., col. maps, bibliog. index. £35. ISBN 0116309539. Concerned with decision of the British government to commit military forces to the Korean War. Bibliography p.469-79. *Class No:* 951.9"19"

Bibliographies

[7612]
BLANCHARD, C.H. **Korean War bibliography and maps of Korea.** New York (?), Korean Conflict Research Foundation, 1964. iv,181p.+25 maps.

Comprehensive listing of sources of reference - books, periodicals, US and foreign. 25 black-and-white maps. *Class No:* 951.9"19"(01)

[7613]
McFARLAND, K.D. **The Korean War** an annotated bibliography. New York, Garland, 1986. xxxiii, 463p. $70. £69. (*Wars of the United States, no.8.*) ISBN: 0824090683.

2311 English language entries paraded in 23 chapters *e.g.* 1. Reference works ... 7. US Army in Korea ... 12. The United Nations and the war ... 17. Peace negotiations and the armistice ... 19. Post-war Korea. Author and subject indexes. 'Because of its intelligent chapter arrangement, it may be used as an overview of any one of a score of war-related topics' (*Reference Books Bulletin 1986-1987*), p.155). *Class No:* 951.9"19"(01)

Dictionaries

[7614]
MATRAY, J.I., *ed.* **Historical dictionary of the Korean War.** xxiii,626p. Westport, Conn., Greenwood Press, 1991. xxiii,626p. bibliogs. $85; £66.30. ISBN: 0313259240.

Series of signed mini-essays with their primary emphasis on political and diplomatic developments but with a substantial military element, each with brief biographies, describing the significant personalities, controversies, policy announcements, and combat operations. Appendix A. Statistical information - B. Summary of personnel changes - C. Chronology (p.559-74). Bibliography p.575-90. Analytical index. 20 maps. *Class No:* 951.9"19"(038)

Almanacs

[7615]
SUMMERS, H.G. **Korean War almanac.** New York and Oxford, Facts On File, 1990. xv,330p. illus., maps, bibliog., index. $24.95; £20. ISBN: 0816017379.

3 parts: 1. The setting (historical and geographical overviews) - 2. Chronology of events 25 Jun 1950 - 6 Sept 1953 - 3. The Korean War A-Z (375 entries of varying length relating to the people, battles, weapons, military units and key concepts of the war, some with cross-references and most with suggestions for further reading. 10 maps. Bibliography p.312-20. 'No rival in its chosen field' (*Reference Reviews,* v.4, no.3, 1990, p.31). *Class No:* 951.9"19"(059)

South Korea

Dictionaries

[7616]

NAHM, A.C. **Historical dictionary of the Republic of Korea.** Metuchen, N.J., Scarecrow Press, 1993. 272p. bibliog., maps. $39.50. (*Asian Historical Dictionaries, no.11.*) ISBN: 0810826308.

Over 250 entries relating to political and historical figures, important social and political events, leading organizations, international agreements *etc.* that contributed to the development of South Korea is supplemented by 53p. chronology, 55p. introductory essay on Korean history, and 57p. bibliography. Nevertheless 'only marginally useful to Korean history scholars (*Library Journal,* 15 June 1993. p.64). *Class No:* 951.95(038)

Japan

[7617]

The Cambridge history of Japan. Cambridge, Cambridge Univ. Press, 6v., 1989-1991.

1. Brown, D.M. *ed. Ancient Japan.* 1992. 650p. £60. 0521223520. 2. McCullough, W. and Shively D.H. *eds. Heian Japan.* forthcoming. 0521223539. 3. Kozo Yamamura *ed. Medieval Japan.* 1990. 734p. £70. 0521223547. 4. Hall, J.W. *ed. Sengoku and Edo.* 1991. 976p. £65. 0521223555. 5. Jansen, M.B. *ed. The Nineteenth century.* 1989. 886p. £70. 0521223563. 6. Duus, P. *ed. The Twentieth century.* 1989. 836p. £70. 0521223571. Last volume has 14 chapters arranged in 4 pts: 1. Domestic politics - 2. External relations - 3. Economic development - 4. Social and intellectual change. Multi-volume cooperative history on the familiar Cambridge pattern providing a summary of the state of present knowledge of Japanese history for students and scholars. Supported by The Japan Foundation. *Class No:* 952

[7618]

CORTAZZI, H. **The Japanese achievement.** London, Sidgwick and Jackson; New York, St. Martin's Press, 1990. xviii,350p. illus., maps, bibliog., index. £20. (*Great Civilizations series.*) ISBN: 0283996471, UK; 031204237x, US.

Narrative history in 11 chapters (1. Origins - 2. Beginnings of Japanese civilization ... 11. From defeat to riches 1945-89). Chapter notes p.307-17. Glossary p.318-32. Bibliography p.333-40. *Class No:* 952

[7619]

LEHMANN, J.P. **The Roots of modern Japan.** London, Macmillan; New York, St. Martin's Press, 1982. xv, 352p. bibliog., index. £16. (*Macmillan Asian Histories.*) ISBN: 0333266048.

9 chronological chapters mainly concerned to address the causes and consequences of Japan's rapid transformation into a modern state in 19th and 20th centuries. Glossary of Japanese terms p.316-331. Bibliographical note p.332-342. *Class No:* 952

[7620]

NOUËT, N. **The Shogun's city** a history of Tokyo. Folkestone, Paul Norbury, 1990. nn 252p. illus., maps, index. £12.95. ISBN: 0904404617.

First published as *Histoire de Tokyo* (Paris, Presses, Universitaires de France, 1961).

Narrative history from Tokyo's earliest beginnings to the modern city surveying political, social and cultural developments. No bibliography in this English language edition. *Class No:* 952

[7621]

SANSOM, G.A. **A History of Japan.** Folkestone, Kent, Dawson, 3v., 1979.

First published London, Cresset Press, 1958-63.

1. A history of Japan to 1334. 500p. £12.00. ISBN 0712908080. 2. 1334-1615. xix,442p. £12.00. 0712908099. 3. 1615-1687. xii,255p. £9.00. 0712908202. A standard work. Each volume carries a bibliographical note (*e.g.* v.2: p.419-26) and a detailed index. *Class No:* 952

Bibliographies

[7622]

BUNN, J.M. *and* ROBERTS, A.D.S., *comps.* **A Union list of Japanese local histories in British libraries.** Oxford, Bodleian Library, 1981. xvii,406p. pbk. £12.00. ISBN: 0900177837.

Resources of 6 libraries in 2 parts: 1. Histories referring to large geographical areas embracing more than 1 prefecture - 2. A-Z listing by single prefectures. Index of places and of obsolete place-names with their nearest modern equivalent. *Class No:* 952(01)

[7623]

DOWER, J.W. **Japanese history and culture from ancient to modern times: seven basic bibliographies.** Manchester, Manchester Univ. Press, 1986. vi,232p. £27.50; $34.50. ISBN: 0719019141, UK; 0910129207, US.

1. Ancient and medieval Japan - 2. Early modern and modern Japan 1600-1945 - 3. Japan abroad - 4. Japan and the crisis in Asia 1931-1945: primary materials in English - 5. Occupied Japan and the cold war in Asia - 6. Bibliographies and research guides - 7. Journals and other serial publications. Compiler holds the Joseph Naiman Endowed Chair in Japanese Studies, University of California. 'Dower's selection of English-language primary sources ... includes many unusual, elusive, but valuable sources' (*Choice,* v.24, no.11-12, July/August 1987,p.1674). *Class No:* 952(01)

[7624]

FUKUDA, N., *ed.* **Japanese history:** a guide to survey histories by period. Ann Arbor, Center for Japanese Studies, Univ. of Michigan, 1984. xix,120p. index. $12.00. ISBN: 093951219x.

Updates J.W. Hall's *Japanese history: a guide to Japanese reference and research materials* issued by the same publishers in 1954.

Almost 1000 annotated entries relating to books published 1955-1980 arranged by historical period with subject subdivisions: A. General history - B. Prehistory. Ancient history - C. Medieval - D. Early modern - E. Modern and Contemporary - F. Local history. Title index. *Class No:* 952(01)

[7625]
NAGAO, P.M., *comp*. **Japanese local histories** in the Library of Congress. Washington, Library of Congress, 1987. vii,324p. maps, bibliog., index. $29. ISBN: 0844405434.

2,848 entries including many works published under the auspices of prefectural, city, and village administrations. Arranged A-Z by romanized title (modified Hepburn system) and within 47 prefectures each preceded by a map. *Class No:* 952(01)

Dictionaries

[7626]
HUNTER, J. **Concise dictionary of modern Japanese history.** Berkeley, Univ. of California Press, 1984. xvi, 347p. map, index. $47.50. ISBN: 0520043901.

Information on the individuals and political, diplomatic and socioeconomic events, and institutions that have played a significant role in Japan's modern history 1853-1980. Aimed primarily at non-Japanese speakers, non-specialists, and undergraduate students. Japanese - English glossary of historical terms. 'The special virtue of Hunter ... is the reliable citation of additional accessible sources in English' (*Choice*, v.22, no.6, February 1985, p.795).
Class No: 952(038)

Maps & Atlases

[7627]
COLLCUT, M., *and others*. **Cultural atlas of Japan.** Oxford, Phaidon; New York, Facts On File, 1988. 240p. col. illus., col. maps, bibliog., index. $40. ISBN: 0714825263, UK; 0816019274, US.

9 chapters (*i.e.* map, illustrations and text) in 3 divisions: 1. Origins - 2. Historical period - 3. Modern Japan with 19 special features (*e.g.* Ainu of Hokkaido, Samurai society in the medieval age, Japan and the West) and 12 site features. The rulers of Japan p.228-9. Chronology p.8-9. Glossary p.230-1. Gazetteer p.233-6. Bibliography p.225-7. 46 maps. *Class No:* 952(084.3)

Chronologies

[7628]
TARO SAKAMOTO AND SHIGEMI KESADO. **Japanese chronology.** Tokyo, International Society for Educational Information, 1974. 73p. sd. (*Understanding Japan, no.32*.)

An extensive listing of events in Japanese history from the Jomon period to 1972. *Class No:* 952(090)

Biographies

[7629]
IWAO, S., *ed.* **Biographical dictionary of Japanese history.** Tokyo, Kodansha International Ltd. in collaboration with the International Society of Educational Information, 1978. Distributed in North America by Harper & Row and by Phaidon in UK. 655p. maps, geneal tables, index. $39.50; £19.95. ISBN: 0870112740.

521 biographies. 4 Periods: Ancient; Medieval; Early Modern; Modern. Japanese characters follow transliterated form of name. 19 appendices (Imperial family lineage; regents; shoguns; institutions and terms). Bibliography

....(contd.)
p.580-618. 'Its utility for the reader who cannot use Japanese is limited' (*Journal of Asian Studies,* v.39,no.1, November 1979, p.183). *Class No:* 952(092)

Archives

[7630]
BORSA, I. 'Archives in Japan,' *Journal of the Society of Archivists*, v.7,no.5, April 1984, p.287-298.

A brief examination of the National Archives of Japan; Imperial Household, Agency, Archives and Mausoleum Division; National Defence College; Diplomatic Record Office; and Yomei Library, Kyoto. *Class No:* 952(093.20)

Saudi Arabia

[7631]
AL-FARSY, F. **Saudi Arabia** a case study in development. 4th ed. London, Routledge & Kegan Paul, 1986. 264p. illus., maps, tables, bibliog., index.

1st ed. 1978.

'An extremely valuable work providing an informative, fact-filled description of the structure of the Saudi government' (F.A. Clements. *Saudi Arabia,* 1988. Entry 669). *Class No:* 953.2

Dictionaries

[7632]
RILEY, C.L. **Historical and cultural dictionary of Saudi Arabia.** Metuchen, N.J., Scarecrow Press, 1972. vi,133p. bibliog. (*Historical and Cultural Dictionaries of Asia, no.1.*) ISBN: 0810805340.

Dictionary p.1-121. Bibliography p.123-133.
Class No: 953.2(038)

Yemen

[7633]
BIDWELL, R. **The Two Yemens.** London, Longman; Boulder, Colorado, Westview Press, 1983. xviii, 350p. map, bibliog., index. £31.50. ISBN: 0582783216, UK; 0865312958, US.

9 chronological chapters and postscript with a brief survey of pre-Islamic Yemen and subsequent emphasis on the post-war period. Bibliography p.338-342. 'A lucid and absorbing account' (*Geographical Journal*, v.153, no.1, March 1987, p.124). *Class No:* 953.3

Oman

[7634]
ALLEN, C.H. **Oman** the modernization of the Sultanate. Boulder, Colorado, Westview Press; London, Croom Helm, 1987. xiii, 154p. maps, bibliog., index. £30. (*Profiles: nations of the contemporary world.*) ISBN: 0813301254, US; 070995106x, UK.

9 chapters: 1. Land and people - 2. Ancient and medieval history - 3. Oman's imperial age - 4. Imamate and Sultanate - 5. Challenges to unity - 6. Political development - 7. Economic and social development - 8. Oman and the world - 9. Oman to 2000. Bibliographic essay p.131-139. Glossary p.141-142. *Class No:* 953.5

[7635]
HAWLEY, D. **Oman and its renaissance.** Rev. ed. London, Stacey International, 1987. 256p. illus. (some col.), maps (some col.), 1 geneal. table, bibliog., index. £30. ISBN: 0905743512.

8 sections: History, Terrain, People, Habitat, Cultural heritage, Religion, Commerce, Oman's renaissance. Rulers of Omen AD 751-1970 p.9. Chronology p.246-247. Glossary p.248-249. Bibliography p.250-251. 30 maps. *Class No:* 953.5

Dictionaries

[7636]
ANTHONY, J.D., *and others.* **Historical and cultural dictionary of the Sultanate of Oman and the Emirates of Eastern Arabia.** Metuchen, N.J., Scarecrow Press, 1976. viii,136p. bibliog. (*Historical and Cultural Dictionaries of Asia, no.9.*)

Dictionary p.1-128. Bibliography p.129-36. Covers the area of al-Bahrayn, Qatar, United Arab Emirates, and Oman. *Class No:* 953.5(038)

Persian Gulf

[7637]
Bahrain through the ages. Abdullah bin Khalid al Khalifa *and* Rice, M., *eds.* London, Kegan Paul International, 1993. xiii,621p. index. ISBN: 071030272x.

37 papers presented originally at the historical sessions of the conference 'Bahrain Through the Ages' organized to mark the 200th anniversary of the arrival in the Bahrain islands of the Al-Khalifa family in 1783. Extensive chapter notes. Reference works on Bahrain p.78-97. *Class No:* 953.6

[7638]
GRAZ, L. **The Turbulent Gulf.** London, I.B. Tauris in association with The Gulf Centre for Strategic Studies, 1990. xi,312p. bibliog., index. ISBN: 185043199x.

Focuses on 'one or two salient aspects' of each of the Gulf States in turn. Chapter notes p.263-88. Bibliography p.299-302. The book was in the press when Iraq invaded Kuwait, 2 August 1990. *Class No:* 953.6

[7639]
POTTS, D.T. **The Arabian Gulf in antiquity.** Oxford, Clarendon Press, 2v., 1990. illus., map, tables, indexes. £45. each volume.

1. *From prehistory to the fall of the Achaemenid Empire.* xxviii,419p. ISBN 0198143907. 2. *From Alexander the Great to the coming of Islam.* xxii,369p. 0198143915. Comparative study of the archaeology and ancient history of the region. Heavily footnoted but lacks a consolidated bibliography. *Class No:* 953.6

[7640]
ZAHLAN, R.S. **The Creation of Qatar.** London & New York, Routledge, 1989. 160p. maps., bibliog., index. ISBN: 0415039363.

First published 1979.

11 chronological chapters (1. Bahrein and the Al-Khalifah 1766-1820 - 11. Prospects for the future: year 2000). 3 Appendices. Bibliography p.148-55. *Class No:* 953.6

[7641]
ZAHLAN, R.S. **The Making of the modern Gulf states:** Kuwait, Bahrain, Qatar, The United Arab Emirates and Oman. London, Unwin Hyman, 1989. ix,180p. illus., maps, index. pbk. ISBN: 0044452934.

Story of the formation, evolution from colonial dependency, and economic transformation. 10 chapters: 1. The Gulf in history - 2. Emergence of the Gulf states ... 10. International setting. *Class No:* 953.6

Chronologies

[7642]
Gulf Crisis chronology. BBC World Service, *comp.* London, Longman Current Affairs, 1991. ix,454p. indexes. £65; $115. ISBN: 0582090059.

Day-to-day coverage of events in the Gulf conflict from the 2 August 1990 invasion of Kuwait by Iraq to the 3 March 1991 ceasefire. Name and subject indexes p.289-454. 'An invaluable tool for the study of the Gulf War which helps place closely spaced events in context' (*Choice*, v.29, no.11-12, July/August 1992, p.1656). *Class No:* 953.6(090)

United Arab Emirates

[7643]
PECK, M.C. **The United Arab Emirates** a venture in unity. Boulder, Colo., Westview Press; London, Croom Helm, 1986. xv,176p. illus., maps, tables, bibliog., index. (*Profiles/Nations of the Contemporary Middle East.*) ISBN: 0865311889, US; 0709940386, UK.

1. Land and people - 2. Historical background - 3. Society and culture - 4. Economy - 5. Domestic politics - 6. Regional and international arenas. Bibliography p.161-4. *Class No:* 953.62

[7644]
TARYAM, A.O. **The Establishment of the United Arab Emirates 1950-1985.** London, Croom Helm, 1987. [vi], 290p. maps, index. £30. ISBN: 070994330x.

7 well-documented chapters: 1. Internal and External influences and their impact on the Arab Emirates 1950-60 - 2. Oil and the Change in British Policy - 3. The British Withdrawal Decision and Local, Regional and International Reactions - 4. The Dubai Agreement and Talks over the Proposed Nine-member Union - 5. Failure of Talks about the Nine-member Union and the Success of the Seven-member Union - 6. The Federation of the Emirates and the Conflict between the Constitutional Structure and Regional Authorities - 7. Evaluation of the Economic and Social Development in the United Arab Emirates. The Introduction (p.1-8) is a literature review of recent books and a list of sources. *Class No:* 953.62

Kuwait

[7645]
SCHOFIELD, R. **Kuwait and Iraq:** historical claims and territorial disputes. London: Royal Institute of International Affairs, 1991. 137p. maps. £9.75. ISBN: 0905031350.

A report compiled for the Middle East Programme of the Royal Institute of International Affairs.

Historical outline of Iraqi claims on Kuwaiti territory and of the international status of Kuwait since the 18th century. No bibliography but profuse footnotes and references. 10 maps. *Class No:* 953.68

India

[7646]

BASHAM, A.L., *ed*. **A Cultural history of India.** Oxford, Clarendon Press, 1984. xx,585p.+Øp. illus., tables, maps. £19.95. ISBN: 0195615204.

A new ed. of *Legacy of India* edited by G.T. Garratt (1937). First published under this title 1975.

28 contributors. 4 main parts (34 chapters): 1. The ancient heritage - 2. Age of Muslim dominance - 3. Challenge and response: the coming of the West - 4. India and the world outside. Footnotes. 'Books for further reading', p.507-17. Detailed, analytical index. Scholarly. *Class No:* 954.0

[7647]

BASHAM, A.L. The Wonder that was India a survey of the history and culture of the Indian sub-continent before the coming of the Muslims. 3rd rev. ed. London, Sidgwick & Jackson, 1967. xxi,568p. illus. (some col.), maps on endpapers, bibliog., index. ISBN: 0283354577.

10 chapters *e.g.* 2. Prehistory - 3. History of ancient and medieval empires - 4. Political life and thought. 10 Appendices including Cosmology and geography, the calendar, the alphabet and its pronunciation. Bibliography and references p.516-39. For the general reader. *Class No:* 954.0

[7648]

BENCE-JONES, M. The Viceroys of India. London, Constable, 1982. xv,343p. illus., ports., bibliog., index. ISBN: 0094638101.

15 chapters: 1. The office and the men before it ... 15. Wavell and Mountbatten. Source references p.317-33. Analytical index. Covers affairs of state, ceremonial, and social life. *Class No:* 954.0

[7649]

BHATTARCHARJEE, A. A History of modern India. Liverpool, Lucas Publications, 1988. 439p. 3p.plates. maps, geneal table, bibliog., index. ISBN: 1851800263.

Narrative history in 25 chapters *e.g.* 2. The later Mughals ... 14. The Sepoy mutiny of 1857 ... 19. The age of Mahatma Gandhi - 20. Final strides to freedom ... 25. Indo-Pak relations from independence to Tashkent. 5 Appendices: C. Important dates and events (p.416-22). Bibliography p.428-33. *Class No:* 954.0

[7650]

The Cambridge history of India. Rapson, E.J., *and others*. Cambridge, Cambridge Univ. Press, v.1, 3-6 and Supplementary volume, 1922-1953 (reprinted 1957-64). illus., maps, bibliogs., indexes.

1. *Ancient India.* 1922. xxii,684p. 2. Never published 'because the mansucript was allegedly destroyed upon the intervention of the British Government' (B.K. Gupta and D.S. Kharbas. *India, 1984*). 3. *Turks and Afghans.* 1928. xxxiii, 752p. 4. *Mughal period.* 1937. xxvii, 693p. 5. *British India 1497-1858.* 1929. xxii, 683p. 6. *The Indian Empire 1859-1918.* New ed. (Delhi, S. Chand & Co.), 1964. xxix, 759p. Supplementary volume: *The Indus civilization* by Sir Mortimer Wheeler (3rd ed. 1968. xi, 144p.) first published 1953. The new ed. of v.6 comprises 'The Indian Empire, with chapters on the development of administration, 1818-1858', edited by H.H. Dodwell, and 'The last phase, 1919-1947', by R.R. Sethi (19 chapters added to the original volume). V.5 contains 32 chapters by specialists; chapter

....(contd.)

bibliographies, p.609-53; chronological tables, p.613-8. Footnote references; no maps or illustrations. *Class No:* 954.0

[7651]

CORREIA-AFONSO, J. Indo-Portuguese history: sources and problems. Bombay, Oxford University Press, 1981. xii,201p. maps on endpapers, index. ISBN: 195612612.

Selected papers from the International Seminar on Indo-Portuguese history, Goa, 1978. These include Source material from the Goa archives; Indian history in the Cartorio des Jesuitas; The Portuguese Empire in India *c.*1550-1650; and some possible fields of research in the history of Portuguese India. *Class No:* 954.0

[7652]

MAJUMDAR, R.C., *and others*. **The History and culture of the Indian people.** Bombay, Bharatiya Vidya Bhavan, 11v., 1951-1978. maps, bibliogs.

1. *The Vedic age* (1951). 2. *The age of imperial unity* (1951). 3. *The classical age* (1954). 4. *The age of Imperial Kanauj* (1955). 5. *The struggle for Empire* (1957). 6. *The Delhi Sultanate* (1960). 7. *The Mughal Empire* (1974). 8. *The Maratha supremacy* (1977). 9-10. *British paramountcy and Indian Renaissance* (1963). 11. *Struggle for freedom* (2nd ed. 1978). Helps to bridge the gap in coverage of *The Cambridge history of India*. 75 contributors in all. Up-to-date bibliographies are appended to each volume. 'One of the most comprehensive studies of Indian history' (A.J. Mukherjee. *Guide to selected reference tools*, 1979. p.237). *Class No:* 954.0

[7653]

MOON, P. The British conquest and dominion of India. London, Duckworth, 1989. xi,1235p. illus., maps, bibliog., index. ISBN: 0715621696.

Outstanding narrative history in 77 chapters. Maps p.1199-1213. Glossary p.1214-15. Bibliography p.1216-18. Analytical index. *Class No:* 954.0

[7654]

The New Cambridge history of India. Johnson, G., *ed*. Cambridge Univ. Press, 30v., 1988-. Available in India through Orient Longman of Bombay. bibliogs., maps.

The original *Cambridge history of India* (1922-1953) (*q.v.*) formulated a chronology for Indian history and described the administrative structures of government. This new series consists of 30 self-contained thematic volumes in 4 distinct parts: 1. The Mughals and their contemporaries - 2. Indian States and their transition to colonialism - 3. The Indian Empire and the beginnings of modern society - 4. The evolution of contemporary South Asia.

Volumes published to date: Part 1: 1. Pearson, N.M. *The Portuguese in India*, 1988. 178p. xiv,244p. 0521266939. 3. Beach, M.C. *Mughal and Rajput painting*. 1993. 300p. £40. 0521400279. 4. Asher, C.B. *Architecture of Mughal India*. 1993. 350p. £40. 0521267285. 5. Richards, J.F. *The Mughal Empire*. 1993. 1521251192. Part 2: 1. Bayly, C.A. *Indian society and the making of the British Empire*. 1988. xi,230p. 0521250927 - 2. Marshall, P.J. *Bengal: the British bridgehead. Eastern India 1740-1828*. 1988 xv,195p. 0521253306 - 3. Grewal, J.S. *The Sikhs of the Punjab*. 1991. 272p. 0521268842. Part 3: 1. Jones, K.W. *Socio-religious reform movements in British India*. 1990. xi,243p. 0521249864. 3. Tomlinson, B.R. *Economy of modern India 1860-1970*. 1993. £24.95. 052136230x. Part 4: 1. Brass, P.

....(contd.)

The politics of India since independence. 1990. 368p. 0521266130.

'We do not expect the *New Cambridge History of India* to be the last word on the subject but an essential voice in a continuing discourse about it' (Johnson, G. The New Cambridge History of India', p.113-116, *South Asian Studies,* The British Library, 1986. *Class No:* 954.0

[7655]
SARKAR, S. **Modern India:** 1885-1947. London, Macmillan, 1989. xxv, 489p. bibliog., index. £38.50. (*Cambridge Commonwealth Series.*) ISBN: 0333438051.

First published in Madras 1983.

8 chronological chapters forming 'the single most helpful volume now available on the modern history of India, not least for students in schools, colleges and universities' (*Foreword* by D.A. Low). *Class No:* 954.0

[7656]
WINK, A. **Al-Hind The Making of the Indo-Islamic world.** Leiden & Kinderhook (NY), E.J. Brill, 5v., 1990-1998. maps,bibliogs.

1. *Early medieval India and the expansion of Islam 7th-11th centuries.* 1990. viii,396p. Gld.165. US$82.50. ISBN 9004092498. 2. *The Slave Kings and the Islamic conquest of India 11th-13th centuries.* c.1991. 3. *Indo-Muslin society 14th-15th centuries.* c.1994. 4. *Imperial formations 16th-17th centuries.* c.1996. 5. *State and society in the eighteenth century.* c.1998. Encyclopedic work 'which aims to analyze the process of momentous and long-term change which came with the Islamization of the regions which the Arabs called AL-HIND, that is India and large parts of its Indianized hinterland' (*Publisher's brochure*). *Class No:* 954.0

[7657]
WOLPERT, S. **A New history of India.** 4th ed. New York, Oxford Univ. Press, 1993. 518p. maps, bibliog., index. £32.50. ISBN: 0195076591.

1st ed. 1977.

Narrative history for the student or interested general reader in 26 chapters. *e.g.* The Ecological setting - Aryan Age (1500-1000BC) - Impact of Islam (711-1556) - Indian nationalism (1885-1905) - From Janata Raj to Rajiv Raj - India today. *Class No:* 954.0

Bibliographies

[7658]
BROWN, J.M. **'Modern India'** imperialism and nationalism *c.*1880-1947' *The Historian,* no.23, Summer 1989, p.10-12.

Surveys the principal publications of the 1980s. *Class No:* 954.0(01)

[7659]
KHARBAS, D.S. **Maharashtra and the Marathas** their history and culture: a bibliographic guide to western language material. Boston, Mass., G.K. Hall, 1975. xxi, 642p. bibliog., index. ISBN: 0816111863.

5809 catalogue cards photolithographed. Arranged in 18 main sections. *Class No:* 954.0(01)

[7660]
SCHOLBERG, H. *and* DIVIEN, E. **Bibliographie des Français dans l'Inde.** Pondicherry, The Historical Society of Pondicherry, 1973. lxiv, 216p. maps, index.

1130 items organized in 32 lettered sections in 4 parts: 1. L'Exploration - 2. Le Commerce - 3. L'Histoire - 4. Les Français aux Indes. Historical writings on the French in India (Eng.) p.xxviii-xxxvi. Bibliographic research for a study of the French in India (Eng.) p.li-lxiv. Author, subject and title index. *Class No:* 954.0(01)

[7661]
SCHOLBERG, H. **Bibliography of Goa and the Portuguese in India.** New Delhi, Promilla & Co., 1982. xix,413p. illus. index. Rs300.

10 sections: 1. General works - 2. Bibliography and other sources - 3 History - 4. Biography - 5. Early historical accounts - 6. The people - 7. Government and politics - 8. Humanities - 9. Journals - 10. Religious life. Includes a supplement of 5 special papers on the sources for Indo-Portuguese history. Entries indicate location of copies in Indian or US academic libraries. *Class No:* 954.0(01)

[7662]
SEN, S.P., *ed.* **Sources of the history of India.** Calcutta, Institute of Historical Studies, 3v., 1978-80.

1. *Karnataka. Andhra Pradesh. Maharashtra. Goa* 2. *Rajasthan. Haryana. Meghalaya. Uttar Pradesh. Jammu and Kashmir.* 3. *Assam. Sikkim. Tamil Nadu.* 'A thorough description and analysis of archaeological, epigraphic, numismatic and written records covering ancient, medieval, and modern periods of regional and national history' (B.K. Gupta and D.S. Kharbas. *India* 1984. Entry 139). *Class No:* 954.0(01)

[7663]
SHARMA, S.R. **A Bibliography of Mughal India (1526-1707AD).** Bombay, Karnatka Publishing House, 1938. ix, 206p. index.

Reprinted by Porcupine Press (Philadelphia, 1977).

Survey organized in 12 categories: 1. Original authorities - 2. Official records - 3. Official histories - 4. Royal autobiographies - 5. Non-official histories - 6. Provincial histories - 7. Biographies and memoirs - 8. Gazetteers - 9. Private letter books - 10. Administrative manuals - 11. Literary works - 12. Foreign works. Appendix 1. European travellers and their accounts ... 4. Original sources of Mughal India. *Class No:* 954.0(01)

Dictionaries

[7664]
BHATTACHARYA, S. **Dictionary of Indian history.** Westport, Connecticut, Greenwood Press, 1977. 963p. $58.50. ISBN: 0837195152.

First published 1972.

*c.*3000 entries relating to events, places, persons and institutions. *Class No:* 954.0(038)

[7665]
KURIAN, G.T. **Historical and cultural dictionary of India.** Metuchen, N.J., Scarecrow Press, 1976. xxii,307p. map, bibliog. (*Historical and Cultural Dictionaries of Asia, no.8.*) ISBN: 0810809516.

Chronology of Indian History p.xi-xxii. Dictionary p.1-262. Bibliography p.263-306. *Class No:* 954.0(038)

[7666]
MEHRA, P. **A Dictionary of Modern Indian history 1707-1947.** Delhi, Oxford Univ. Press, 1985. xv, 823p. maps, bibliogs., index. Rs 250. £25. ISBN: 195615522.

400 compact essays, each concluding with a short bibliography, forming a succinct guide to men and affairs from the reign of Bhadur Shah I (1707-12), last of the Great Mughals, to independence. Glossary p.767-768. Select chronology, p.769-803. Governors-General and Viceroys of India. 1774-1947 p.805-807. 'The standard reference work in its field for many years to come' (*Reference Reviews* v.2, no.3, September 1988, p.163. *Class No:* 954.0(038)

Maps & Atlases

[7667]
IRFAN HABIB. **An Atlas of the Mughal Empire** political and economic maps with detailed notes, bibliography and index. Delhi, Oxford Univ. Press for Centre of Advanced Study in History, Aligarh Muslim University, 1982. 60p. maps, xvii, 102p.

32 political and 32 economic regional maps complemented by Notes (p.1-72) offering references to sources for every place, feature, or piece of information exhibited on the maps. Bibliography chronologically arranged within broad subdivisions p.73-77. 'A landmark in research into the pre-British period' (*Choice*, v.20, no.7, March 1983, p.956). *Class No:* 954.0(084.3)

Chronologies

[7668]
BHATTACHERJE, S.B. **Encyclopaedia of Indian events and dates.** New Delhi, Sterling Publishers Private Ltd., 1986. vi,456p.

A. Events by dates p.1-79. B. Events by years p.82-317. C. Dynasties of India p.319-357 (only relatively important rulers find a place). D. Analytical index p.358-456. Period covered is 4241 BC-AD1985. *Class No:* 954.0(090)

[7669]
BURGESS, J. **The Chronology of Indian history** medieval & modern. Delhi, Cosmo Publications, 1972. vi,483p. index.

Reprint of *The chronology of modern India, for four hundred years from the close of the fifteenth century, A.D. 1494-1894* (Edinburgh, Grant, 1913).

Detailed enumeration of events 1492-1894.
Class No: 954.0(090)

[7670]
Directory of British-Indian dates: (legal historical and biographical) being a compendium of all the dates essential to the study of British rule in India upto 1860. New Delhi, Deep Publications, n.d. 177p.

First published in Edinburgh by William Blackwood in 1866.

3 Parts: 1. Legislation (On annalistic pattern) to 1860 - 2. Persons and places A-Z - 3. Regulations for the year 1793-1832. *Class No:* 954.0(090)

[7671]
KAUL, V. **India since independence** chronology of events. New Delhi, Sagar Publications, 1978-. Now annually. Continuous pagination. ISBN: 8170820006, set.

Two foundation volumes: *1947-1966* and *1967-1977* (1978). 845p. Continued by annual volumes to *1984* (1988) (2003-3104p) ISBN 817082009x. Day by day record of political, social, economic, scientific and sporting events. *Class No:* 954.0(090)

[7672]
SHARMA, J.S. **India since the advent of the British** a descriptive chronology from 1600 to Oct.2, 1969. New Delhi, Chand, 1970. xxx,817p.

In 6 parts (1: 1600-1895 ... 6: 15 August 1947 to 2nd October 1969, by days, under months and years). Index (p.783-817) 'includes names of places, events, newspapers, some important books, subjects and other related information appearing in the text' (*Introduction*). *Class No:* 954.0(090)

20th Century

[7673]
The Indian Annual Register: an annual digest of public affairs of India recording the nation's achievements each year in matters political, economic, industrial, educational, social etc. New Delhi, Gian Publishing House, 1990 -. tables, index. ISBN: 8121202132, set.

Reprint set covering 1919 - 47.

Slightly confused volume numbering system with each year being covered by 2v. *1923 v.1 Supplement* is in fact supplement to v.2. with index for v.1 and v.2. and *Supplement.* 1928 v.2. 516p. ISBN 8121202981 includes Chronicle of events, July-December 1928, p.1-8. *Class No:* 954.0"19"

Himalayan States

[7674]
SINGH, A.K.J. **Himalayan triangle** a historical survey of British India's relations with Tibet, Sikkim and Bhutan 1765-1950. London, The British Library, 1988. xii, 408p. bibliog., maps, index. £35. ISBN: 0712306307.

Well-documented examination of the complex diplomatic history of India's Himalayan frontier. Bibliography p.383-396 includes notes on archival sources in Bhutan, India, Sikkim and China. *Class No:* 954.13

[7675]
SUKHDEV SINGH CHARAK. **History and culture of Himalayan states.** New Delhi, Light and Life Publications, 1978-.

1-2. *Himachal Pradesh.* 1978-1979. 4-7. *Jamma Kingdom.* 1980-. Projected 15v. series on all facets of the history of Jamma and Kashmir, Himachal Pradash, Assam, Sikkim, Bhutan, and possibly Nepal. *Class No:* 954.13

Nepal

[7676]
RISHIKESH SHAHA. **Modern Nepal:** a political history 1769-1955. New Delhi. Manohar, 2v., 1990. ISBN: 8185425027, set.

1. *1769-1885.* ix,318p. map. bibliog., index. ISBN 8185425035. Chronology p.293-300. Bibliography p.301-10. 2. *1885-1955.* x,364p. bibliog., index. 8185425043.

....*(contd.)*

Chronology p.332-43. Bibliography p.344-53. Running account of political trends and developments in 17 well-documented chapters. Bibliographies include material in Western and Nepali languages. *Class No:* 954.135

Dictionaries

[7677]
HEDRICK, B.C. *and* HEDRICK, A.K. **Historical and cultural dictionary of Nepal.** Metuchen, New Jersey, Scarecrow Press, 1972. viii,198p. £24.00. (*Historical And Cultural Dictionaries of Asia, no.2.*) ISBN: 0810806495.

Entries, A-Z, on various aspects of Nepal's history, religion, art, administration, literature and society. Bibliography p.181-98. 'A curious combination of tourist-guide material and brief excursuses in more substantial and important subjects (*Library Journal*, v.98,no.5, 1 March 1973, p.728). *Class No:* 954.135(038)

Sri Lanka

[7678]
DE SILVA, C.R. *and* DE SILVA, D. **The History of Ceylon (*c.*1500-1658)** a historiographical and bibliographical survey, *Ceylon Journal of Historical and Social Studies*, ns. v.3, no.1, January-June 1973, p.52-77.

340 entries, some annotated. "Surveys the historical sources and writings related to the period of Portuguese rule in Sri Lanka' (V. Samaraweera. *Sri Lanka*, 1987. Entry 620). *Class No:* 954.87

[7679]
DE SILVA, K.M. **A History of Sri Lanka.** London, C. Hurst; Berkeley Univ. of California Press, 1981. xx,603p. illus., maps, bibliog., index. $49.50. ISBN: 0905838505, UK; 0520043200, US.

38 chronological chapters in 6 parts: 1. Ancient Sri Lanka - 2. The decline of the Sinhalese kingdom - 3. Sri Lanka and the Western powers - 4. Under British rule - 5. Sri Lanka in the twentieth century - 6. Independence and after. Sri Lanka's rulers: a chronological list p.565-573. Glossary p.574-6. Bibliography p.577-580. *Class No:* 954.87

Pakistan

[7680]
OMAR NORMAN. **Pakistan: a political and economic history** since 1947. Rev. ed. London, Kegan Paul International, 1990. xvii,238p. maps, tables, bibliog., index. pbk. £7.95. ISBN: 0710303890.

First published as *The Political economy of Pakistan* in 1988.

Chronological and thematic narrative in 11 chapters divided into 3 parts: From partition to civil war 1947 to 1971 - 2. Authoritarian populism under Bhutto 1971 to 1977 - 3. Military rule under Zia 1977 to 1988. Chronology of major political events p.xiii-xv. Bibliography p.204-33. Analytical index. *Class No:* 954.9

Dictionaries

[7681]
BURKI, S.J. **Historical dictionary of Pakistan.** Metuchen, N.J., Scarecrow Press, 1991. xxxvi,254p. maps, bibliog. $35; £26.25. (*Asian Historical Dictionaries, no.3.*) ISBN: 0810824116.

Chronology (712-1991) p.xlii-xxxvi. Dictionary (political parties, historical events, principal personalities, economic plans, diplomatic relations, *etc.*) p.17-228. Bibliography (in 5 thematic sections) p.229-51. 2 maps. Introduction (p.1-15) is valuable essay on the background to Pakistan's separation from India in 1947. 'A very authoritative and readable source' (Choice, v.29, no.2, October 1992). *Class No:* 954.9(038)

Bangladesh

Dictionaries

[7682]
BAXTER, C. *and* RAHMAN, S. **Historical dictionary of Bangladesh.** Metuchen, New Jersey, Scarecrow Press, 1989. 144p. bibliog. $22.50. £21.40. (*Historical Dictionaries of Asia, no.2.*) ISBN: 081082177x.

Chronology of important events (1500BC - 1986) p.vii-x. Dictionary p.27-97. Bibliography (17 sub-headings) p.99-123. 'Will be on the shelves and bed tables of every foreigner who travels or works in Bangladesh, and will also be a great help to scholars' (*Pacific Affairs,* v.64, no.1, Spring 1991, p.124-5). *Class No:* 954.93(038)

Iran

[7683]
The Cambridge history of Iran. Cambridge, Cambridge Univ. Press, 7v., 1986-1991. illus., diagrs., tables, maps. ISBN: 0521451485, set.

1. *The Land of Iran* edited by W.B. Fisher. 1968. 804p. £85. ISBN 0521069351. 2. *The Median and Archaemenian periods* edited by I. Gershevitch. 1985. £90. 0521200911. 3. *The Seleucid, Parthian and Sasanid periods*, 2pts., edited by E. Yar-Shater. 1983. £80++£85. 0521246938 and 0521246998. 4. *From the Arab invasion to the Saljuqs* edited by R.N. Frye. 1975. 747p. £80. 0521200938. 5. *The Saljuq and Mongol periods* by J.A. Boyle. 1968. 778p. £80. 052106936x. 6. *The Timurid and Sefavid periods* edited by P. Jackson and L. Lockhart. 1986. 1120p. £95. 0521200946. 7. *From Nadir Shah to the Islamic Republic* edited by P. Avery and G.R.G. Hambly. 1989. £85. 0521200954. 8. Bibliography. All aspects of the religious, philosophical, political, economic, scientific and artistic elements in Iranian civilization are studied, with some emphasis on the geographical and ecological factors which have contributed to that civilization's special character. *Class No:* 955

Bibliographies

[7684]
HAMBLY, G.R.G. 'Continuities in the Iranian past since the 7th century C.E.', *Choice*, v.27, no.5, January 1990, p.744-52.

Bibliographical essay which considers *inter alia*, Historical

....*(contd.)*

writing; Turks and Mongols; Timurids and Safavids; Social history; and Journals and reference works.
Class No: 955(01)

Gazetteers

[7685]
Historical gazetteer of Iran. Adamec, L.W., *ed.* Graz, Akademische Druck-u. Verlagsanstalt, 1976-.

1. *Teharan and Northwestern Iran.* 1976. xvii, 734p.+200 unnumbered pages of maps. 2. *Meshad and Northeastern Iran.* 1981. xix, 708p.+188p. maps. 3201011592 ... 4. *Zahidan and Southern Iran.* x, 480p.+156p. maps. 3201014281. Each volume is arranged in 5 parts: Geographical and historical dictionary; glossary of geographical, historical and political terms; index of subtribes; map section. Based on formerly secret archival material compiled by the General Staff of British India during the 19th and early 20th centuries and updated from contemporary Iranian and western sources. 'Geographers will be pleased to have available the comprehensive map section ... they will equally regret that there is no adequate reference to the sources of these maps and that vital detail such as scale and date is omitted also. It would appear that the map section is a collection of sheets gathered from a variety of sources ... at an approximatel scale of 1:300,000' (*Geographical Journal*, v.144, no.1, March 1978, p.160-161). *Class No:* 955(083.86)

Byzantium

Bibliographies

[7686]
HARVARD UNIVERSITY. DUMBARTON OAKS RESEARCH LIBRARY. Dictionary catalogue of the Byzantine Collection of the Dumbarton Oaks Research Library. Boston, Mass., G.K. Hall, 1975. 12 reels (microfilm). $1390.00 (Export $1680.00). ISBN: 0816115028.

174,000 photolithographed catalogue cards. This collection of over 82,000 volumes covers all aspects of Byzantine history and culture, with particular strengths in art, architecture, archaeology, and published literary and historical texts and documents. It also provides extensive coverage of the late Graeco-Roman world, early and medieval Islam, and the world of the Orthodox Slavs.
Class No: 956+949.61(01)

Handbooks & Manuals

[7687]
MAZAL, O. Handbuch der Byzantinistik. Graz, Akademische Druck-u. Verlagsanstalt, 1989. 279p. bibliog., index. ISBN: 320101432x.

14 chapters: 1. Gegenstand und Aufgaben der Byzantinistik - 2. Die Geschichte der byzantinischen Studien ... 9. Die Geschichte der byzantinischen literatur ... 11. Die byzantinische Kunst. Liste der Kaiser p.209. Liste der Patriarchen p.210. Bibliography p.21-245.
Class No: 956+949.61(035)

Dictionaries

[7688]
The Oxford dictionary of Byzantium. Kazhdan, A.P., *ed.* New York, Oxford Univ. Press, 3v., 1991. li,2232p. illus., geneal. tables, maps. $245. £200. ISBN: 0195046528.

Over 5,500 initialled entries from 128 contributors relating to all aspects of Byzantine history and civilization from the 4th to the 15th century and covering all regions that at any time formed part of the Byzantine Empire or had significant connections with Byzantium. Average length of entries is 200 words although major thematic entries go up to 1,000 words. Most end with a list of bibliographic references. 24 maps. 'For its coverage and authority it will last for many years as the most significant reference item covering the whole vast field of Byzantine studies' (*Reference Reviews*, v.5,no.4, 1991, p.34-5). *Reference Reviews* Best Specialist Reference Work 1991. *Class No:* 956+949.61(038)

Biographies

[7689]
NICOL, D.M. A Biographical dictionary of the Byzantine Empire. London, Seaby, 1991. xxviii,156p. geneal., tables, bibliog., index. £18.50. ISBN: 1852640480.

Brief biographies of 'most persons of note and influence in the East Roman or Byzantine Empire from the establishment of its capital at Constantinople in AD 330 to its conquest by the Ottoman Turks in 1453'. Chronology p.xiii-xv. Genealogical tables p.xvii-xxvii. References p.149-56.
Class No: 956+949.61(092)

Turkey

[7690]
SHAW, S.J. *and* **SHAW E.K. History of the Ottoman Empire and modern Turkey.** Cambridge, Cambridge Univ. Press, 2v., 1977.

1: *Empire of the Gazis: the rise and decline of the Ottoman Empire,* 1280-1808. xiii, 351p.

2: *Reform, revolution and republic: the rise of modern Turkey,* V.1 has 2 parts: 1. Rise of the Ottoman Empire, 1280-1566; 2. Decentralisation and traditional reform in response to challenge. Bibliography: 'Ottoman history to 1808', p.302-24 (1. General histories - 2. Bibliographies - 3. General reference works - 4/11. Periods), with brief running commentary. Non-analytical index. V.2 is based on both Ottoman and European sources. 'Will remain an outstanding reference work ... excellent bibliographies at the end of each volume list all major works both in Turkish and English' (M. Güçlü. *Turkey*, 1981, Entry 674). *Class No:* 956

Bibliographies

[7691]
BODURGIL, A. Atatürk and Turkey a bibliography 1919-1938. Washington, Library of Congress, 1974. 74p.

1338 entries for books and periodicals in Western languages on Kemal Atatürk (1881-1938).
Class No: 956(01)

[7692]

—BODURGIL, A. Turkey, politics and government a bibliography 1938-1975. Washington, Library of Congress, 1976. vii,176p. indexes.

2020 entries for books and articles. Sections: Reference sources - Bibliographies ... Relations with the Arab world and the Middle East - The Straights question. Periodical sources p.123-35. *Class No:* 956(01)

Cyprus

[7693]

HILL, G. A History of Cyprus. Cambridge, Cambridge Univ. Press, 4v., 1972.

1. To the conquest by Richard Lion Heart. xviii, 352p. 2. The Frankish period 1192-1432. xl, 496p. 3. The Frankish period 1432-1571. vi, 497-1198p. 4. The Ottoman period, the British colony. xxxi, 640p. 'With its footnote documentation and bibliographies in several languages, the work constitutes one of the most comprehensive and judicious bibliographical guides to Cyprus studies' (P.M. Kitromilides and M.L. Evriviades. *Cyprus*, 1982. Entry 135). *Class No:* 956.43

[7694]

PANTELI, S. A New history of Cyprus. London and The Hague, East-West Publications, 1984. x, 437p. £12.95. ISBN: 0856921270.

14 chronological chapters 1. Cyprus through the centuries ... 4. 1914-1925 Cyprus becomes a British crown colony ... 14. Cyprus since 1960. 6 Appendices inc. a chronology, lists of British administrators, Ottoman sultans, Greek monarchs, Orthodox Archbishops of Cyprus. Bibliography p.423-430. Concentrates on 'the unexplored years between 1877 and 1950' (*Preface*). *Class No:* 956.43

Iraq

[7695]

MARR, P. The Modern history of Iraq. Boulder, Colorado, Westview Press; London, Longman, 1985. xviii, 382p. illus., maps, bibliog., index. £39. $49. ISBN: 0865311196, US; 0582782445, UK.

10 chronological and thematic chapters: 1. Legacy of the past ... 2. British mandate 1926-1932 ... 10. The Iran-Iraq war. Notes p.313-344. Bibliography p.343-353. Glossary p.355-359. 'A timely, comprehensive, and much-needed modern history of Iraq' (*Choice*, v.23, no.2, October 1985, p.349). *Class No:* 956.7

[7696]

ROUX, G. Ancient Iraq. 3rd ed. London, Penguin, 1992. xxii,547p. illus., maps, tables, index. £7.99. ISBN: 014012523x.

First published by George Allen & Unwin 1964.

Political, cultural, and socio-economic history of Mesopotamia to the Christian era. 25 chapters (*e.g.* 1. Geographical setting ... 9. Akkadians - 10. Great Kingdom of Ur... 19. Assyrian Empire ... 24. Splendour of Babylon). Bibliography and chapter notes p.433-97. Chronological tables p.500-15. 4 maps. *Class No:* 956.7

Lebanon

[7697]

COBBAN, H. The Making of modern Lebanon. London, Hutchinson, 1985; Boulder, Colorado, Westview Press, 1986. 248p. illus., bibliog. index. (*The Making of the Middle East.*) ISBN: 0091607914, UK; 0813303079, US.

8 chronological chapters, the last 6 of which focus on events since 1920. Bibliography p.237-241. Analytical index. 'Cobban's well researched and clearly written history records with sensitivity and precision the stages of the development of the Lebanese entity, from the coming of the Ottoman Turks to the present' (*Choice*, v.23, no.6, February 1986, p.916). *Class No:* 956.93

Israel & Palestine

[7698]

ASALI, K.J., *ed.* Jerusalem in history. Buckhurst Hill, Essex, Scorpion Publishing, 1989. 295p. illus., map, bibliog., index.

9 contributors from 7 countries present an outline history 3000BC - 1987 A.D. 1. Bronze Age - 2. Jerusalem from 1000-63BC - 3. Rome and Byzantium - 4. Early Islamic period - 5. Crusader Jerusalem - 6. Ayyubids and Mamluks - 7. Ottomans - 8. Jerusalem in the 19th century - 9. The transformation of Jerusalem 1917-1987 A.D. Bibliography (by chapter) p.279-91. *Class No:* 956.94

[7699]

GIL, M. A History of Palestine 634-1099. Rev. ed. Cambridge, Cambridge Univ. Press, 1992. xxvi,968p. bibliog., index. ISBN: 0521404371.

First published in Hebrew by Tel Aviv University in 1983.

1. The Conquest - 2. Islam strikes roots - 3. Local population and the Muslims - 4. Economy - 5. Palestine from the beginning of Abbasid rule to the Fatimids - 6. Fatimid conquest - 7. The Christians - 8. Jewish population and its leadership - 9. Karaites and Samaritans - 10. Crusaders' conquest and the fate of Palestinian Jewry. Glossary of Hebrew and Arabic terms p.xxv-xxvi. Chronology p.893-61. Bibliographical index p.862-911. Based on extant sources of the period which are discussed in *Preface* (p.xii-xx). *Class No:* 956.94

[7700]

SACHAR, H.M. A History of Israel.

1. *From the rise of Zionism to our time* Oxford, Basil Blackwell, 1977. xix, 883, xlix p. bibliog., maps, index. 0613117870. 2. *From the aftermath of the Yom Kippur War* New York and Oxford, Oxford Univ. Press, 1987. xv, 319p. bibliog. maps, index. $19.95. £19.50. 0195043863. Extremely well-documented standard history with extensive bibliographies. *Class No:* 956.94

Bibliographies

[7701]

SHERMAN, J., *ed*. The Arab-Israeli conflict 1945-1971 a bibliography. New York, Garland Publishing Inc., 1978. xvii, 419p. illus., maps, index. $63. ISBN: 0824098293.

3694 English-language citations arranged on an annalistic pattern supported by bibliographical and supplementary notes. Author and subject indexes. *Class No:* 956.94(01)

Maps & Atlases

[7702]

GILBERT, M. The Dent atlas of the Arab-Israeli conflict.
6th ed. London, J.M. Dent, 1993. 152p. £14.99. ISBN:
0460861778.

First published as *The Arab-Israeli conflict: its history in
maps* by Weidenfeld & Nicolson 1974.

147 clear maps with descriptive insets. In various periods:
Prelude to conflict - The Jewish national home [1917-47] -
The conflict intensifies - The State of Israel [1948-67] - After
the Six Day War - The Yom Kippur War - Camp David and
after. Covers before the Christian period to the 19890s.
Class No: 956.94(084.3)

[7703]

GILBERT, M. Jerusalem illustrated history atlas.
Jerusalem, Steimatzky's Agency Ltd; London, the author
with the Board of Deputies of British Jews; New York,
Macmillan Publishing Inc., 1977(?). 128p. maps. illus.,
bibliog.

66 maps trace the city's history from Biblical times to the
present day with special emphasis on developments over the
last 150 years. Bibliography p.124-128.
Class No: 956.94(084.3)

Jordan

[7704]

**MA'AN ABU NOWAR. The History of the Hashemite
Kingdom of Jordan.** Vol.1 The creation and development
of Transjordan: 1920-1929. Oxford, Ithaca Press for The
Middle East Centre of St. Anthony's College Oxford, 1989.
xiii,313p. illus., maps, bibliog., index. £24. (*St. Anthony's
Middle East Monographs, no.21.*) ISBN: 0863721192.

Social, economic, political and legal history of Jordan in 9
chapters *e.g.* 2. Creation of Trans-Jordan - 3. From
statelessness to mandate state ... 7. Independence under
mandate. Bibliography p.252-9. *Class No:* 956.95

Dictionaries

[7705]

**GUBSER, P. Historical dictionary of the Hashemite
Kingdom of Jordan.** Metuchen, N.J., Scarecrow Press,
1991. xxi,140p. maps, bibliog. £16.90. (*Asian Historical
Dictionaries, no.4.*) ISBN: 0810824493.

Chronology p.xiii-xxi. Introduction (overview, geography
and climate, people, history) p.1-14. Dictionary p.15-87.
Bibliography p.89-140. 2 maps. *Class No:* 956.95(038)

Siberia

[7706]

FORSYTH, J. A History of the peoples of Siberia Russia's
North Asian colony 1581-1990. Cambridge, Cambridge
Univ. Press, 1992. xx,455p. illus., maps, bibliog., index.
ISBN: 0521403111.

Ethnohistory narrating and interpreting the gradual
conquest and exploitation of Siberia and tracing the history
of the Buryat Mongols, Yakuts, Tatars, Samoyeds,
Tunguses, Chukchi, and other Siberian tribes. 17
Chronological chapters *e.g.* 1. Siberia discovered ... 5.
Russia's North Asian colony ... 7. Expansion in the North
Pacific ... 12. Native peoples ... 15. Soviet Siberia after
1941. 17. Siberia in the 1980s. *Class No:* 957.1

[7707]

WOOD, A., *ed*. **The History of Siberia** from Russian
conquest to Revolution. London, Routledge, 1991. xiv,192p.
£35. ISBN: 0415058732.

9 essays by separate hands *e.g.* 1. Siberia's role in
Russian history ... 5. The Siberian native peoples before and
after the Russian conquest - 6. Tsarist Russia in colonial
America ... 9. Siberia in revolution and civil war. Glossary
p.xi-xiv. No bibliography but extensive chapter notes and
references. *Class No:* 957.1

Kazakhstan

[7708]

OLCOTT, M.B. The Kazakhs. Stanford, Calif., Hoover
Institution Press, 1987. xxv,341p. maps, tables, bibliog.,
index. £25.75. (*Studies of Nationalities in the USSR.*) ISBN:
0817983813.

Historical narrative of The Kazakh Soviet Socialist
Republic (now Kazakhstan) from the 15th century but
highlighting contemporary political and economic problems.
11 chapters arranged in 3 parts: 1. Rise and fall of the
Kazakh Khanate - 2. Kazakhs in Imperial Russia - 3.
Revolutionary and Soviet Kazakhstan. 12 Appendices.
Glossary p.277-82. Chapter notes p.283-308. Bibliography
(inc. Russian language sources) p.309-34. *Class No:* 957.4

Uzbekistan

[7709]

ALLWORTH, E.A. The Modern Uzbeks from the fourteenth
century to the present: a cultural history. Stanford, Calif.,
Hoover Institution Press, 1990. xiv,410p. illus., map,
geneal., table, bibliog., index. (*Studies Of Nationalities In
The USSR.*) ISBN: 0817987312.

18 chapters in 2 main divisions: 1. Bases of Uzbek group
identity - 2. Conflict between old and new modernity (7.
History ... 10. Politics - 11. Homeland ... 14. Genealogy).
Chapter notes p.331-74. Bibliography p.375-94. Analytical
index. Allworth is Professor of Turko-Soviet Studies in
Columbia University. *Class No:* 957.51

[7710]

CRITCHLOW, J. Nationalism in Uzbekistan a Soviet
Republic's road to sovereignty. Boulder, Colo., Westview
Press, 1991. xviii,231p. map, tables, bibliog., index. pbk.
ISBN: 0813384036.

11 well-documented chapters in 3 sections: 1. Rise of
Uzbek nationalism - 2. Uzbek nationalism today - 3.
Problems of sovereignty. Bibliography p.215-8. Analytical
index. Critchlow is a fellow at the Russian Research Center,
Harvard University. *Class No:* 957.51

Afghanistan

Dictionaries

[7711]

**M. JAMIL HANIFI. Historical and cultural dictionary of
Afghanistan.** Metuchen, N.J., Scarecrow Press, 1976.
viii,141p. bibliog. (*Historical and Cultural Dictionaries of
Asia, no.5.*) ISBN: 0810808927.

Dictionary p.1-126. Bibliography p.127-41.
Class No: 958.1(038)

Myanmar

[7712]
TAYLOR, R.H. **The State in Burma.** London, C. Hurst; Honolulu, Hawaii Univ. Press, 1987. xvi,395p. maps, tables, bibliog., index. $32. ISBN: 1850650284.

The nature of the Burmese state at five different periods: 1. The pre-colonial state - 2. Rationalization of the state 1825-1942 - 3. Politics 1886 to 1942 - 4. Displacement of the state 1942 to 1962 - 5. Reasserting the state 1962 to 1987. Glossary p.xii-xiv. Bibliography p.373-86. 'Will become the unquestioned standard history of nineteenth and twentieth century Burmese history' (*Annual Bulletin of Historical Literature*, v.74, 1990, p.181). *Class No:* 959.1

Dictionaries

[7713]
MARING, J.M. *and* MARING, E.G. **Historical and cultural dictionary of Burma.** Metuchen, N.J., Scarecrow Press, 1973. vi,290p. (*Historical and Cultural Dictionaries of Asia, no.4.*) ISBN: 0810805960.

1600 entries relating to Burmese history, culture, physical geography, natural history, economics, politics and demography. Dictionary p.1-281. Bibliography p.283-90. *Class No:* 959.1(038)

Thailand

[7714]
TERWIEL, B.J. **A History of modern Thailand.** St. Lucia, Univ. of Queensland Press, 1983. xiv,379p. maps, bibliog., index. $29.95. (*History of Southeast Asia.*) ISBN: 0702218928.

10 chronological chapters. Glossary p.350-353. Bibliography p.354-369. Analytical index. 'A good contemporary introduction' (*Choice*, v.21,no.10, June 1984, p.1520). *Class No:* 959.3

[7715]
WYATT, D.K. **Thailand a short history.** New Haven, Connecticut, Yale Univ. Press 1983. xviii, 351p. illus., maps, bibliog., index. $35. ISBN: 0300030541.

10 chapters: 1. Beginnings of Tai history - 2. The Tai and the Classical Empires AD1000-1200 - 3. A Tai century 1200-1351 - 4. Ayudhya and its neighbors 1351-1569 - 5. The Empire of Ayudhya 1569-1767 - 6. The early Bangkok Empire 1767-1851 - 7. Mongkut and Chulalongkorn 1851-1910 - 8. Rise of elite nationalism 1910-1932 - 9. The military ascendant 1932-1957 - 10. Development and revolution 1957-1982. Appendix A. Kings of Sukhothai - B. Kings of Lan Na - C. Kings of Ayudhya, Thonburi and Bangkok - D. Prime Ministers of Thailand. Chapter notes p.315-19. Bibliography p.321-32. Analytical index. 'The discursive bibliography is the best available introduction to the historiography of Thailand in English and some other Western languages, and includes a guide to primary sources' (M. Watts. *Thailand*, 1986. Entry 229). *Class No:* 959.3

Dictionaries

[7716]
SMITH, H.E. **Historical and cultural dictionary of Thailand.** Metuchen, N.J., Scarecrow Press, 1976. vi,213p. bibliog. (*Historical and Cultural Dictionaries of Asia, no.6.*) ISBN: 0810809265.

A-Z entries relating to Thai history, Buddhism,

....(contd.)
ethnolinguistic groupings, economy, geography, government etc. Dictionary p.1-207. Bibliography p.209-13. *Class No:* 959.3(038)

Malaysia

[7717]
ANDAYA, B.W. *and* ANDAYA, L.Y. **A History of Malaysia.** London, The Macmillan Press; New York, St. Martin's Press, 1982. xx,350p. maps,bibliog., index. £18.00; $30.00. (*Macmillan's Asian Histories.*) ISBN: 0333276728, UK; 0213381204, US.

Contents: Introduction: Environment and peoples - 1. Heritage of the past - 2. Melaka and its heirs - 3. Demise of the Malay entrepot state 1699-1819 - 4. A new world is created 1819-74 - 5. The making of British Malaya 1874-1919 - 6. The functioning of colonial society 1919-57 - 7. The forging of a nation 1957-80 - Conclusion: some themes in Malaysian history. Notes and further readings p.305-329. Glossary p.330-336. Analytical index. 'Beyond question the best general history of Malysia in print' (*Choice*, v.20,nol.7, March 1983, p.1042). *Class No:* 959.5

Bibliographies

[7718]
HEUSSLER, R. **British Malaya.** a bibliographical and biographical compendium. New York, Garland Publishing Inc., 1981. xvii, 193p. $40. (*Themes in European Expansion.*) ISBN: 0824093690.

Part 1. Bibliographies (in 8 sections): 1. Bibliographies and directories - 2. History and social science - 3. British policy and administration - 4. Biography and autobiography - 5. Malay studies - 6. Immigrant peoples - 7. War, insurrection and terrorism - 8. Miscellaneous. Pt. 2. Biographies *i.e.* brief career details of family background and education of the personnel of the Malayan Civil Service from the assumption of Colonial Office responsibility in 1867 to the Japanese conquest in 1942. Author and subject indexes. 'An indispensable reference work for the historical collections of Southeast Asia' (*English Historical Review*, v.99, no.392, July 1984, p.657). *Class No:* 959.5(01)

Dictionaries

[7719]
KAUR, A. **Historical dictionary of Malaysia.** Metuchen, N.J., Scarecrow Press, 1993. xxvi,300p. maps, tables, bibliog. £37.50. (*Asian Historical Dictionaries, no.13.*) ISBN: 0810826291.

Political parties, historical events, legislative measures, leading political figures, economic affairs *etc.* in single A-Z sequence. Chronology p.xv-xxi. Dictionary p.23-157. Bibliography (form and subject divisions) p.158-262. Appendix 1-2. Rulers and Prime Ministers. Glossary p.299-300. 5 maps. *Class No:* 959.5(038)

Singapore

[7720]
CHEW, E.T. *and* LEE, E., *eds.* **A History of Singapore.** Singapore, Oxford Univ. Press, 1991. xx,442p. illus., maps, tables, bibliog., index. £27; $59. ISBN: 0195889177.

Issued under the auspices of the Southeast Asian Studies

....(contd.)

Program, Institute of Southest Asian Studies, Singapore. It virtually supersedes C.M. Turnbull's *A History of Singapore 1829-1975.* (Kuala Lumpur, OUP., 2nd ed. 1977).

Cooperative history. 18 well-documented chapters arranged in 7 sections: 1. Geography and early history - 2. Polity and economy under British rule to 1942 - 3. Under Japanese rule - 4. Transition to independence - 5. Securing of independence - 6. Social transformation - 7. Foreign policy and domestic issues. Bibliography p.401-27. 'A significant addition to Singapore's historiography' (*Journal of Southeast Asian Studies,* v.23, no.1, March 1992, p.203-5). *Class No:* 959.513

Dictionaries

[7721]

MULLINER, K. *and* **MULLINER, L.T. Historical dictionary of Singapore.** Metuchen, N.J., Scarecrow Press, 1991. xxxii,251p. maps, bibliog., index. (*Asian Historical Dictionaries, no.7.*) ISBN: 081082504x.

Chronology p.xxi-xxxii. Overview (*i.e.* Geography - The People - Economy - History) p.1-21. Dictionary (persons, localities, events, ideologies *etc.*) p.23-164. Appendices (Heads of Government, Cabinets, General Elections, Population, Distribution of Chinese) p.165-77. Bibliography p.179-238. 4 maps. *Class No:* 959.513(038)

Cambodia

[7722]

CHANDLER, D.P. A History of Cambodia. 2nd ed. Boulder, Colorado, Westview Press, 1992. xvi, 237p. illus., map, bibliog., index. £31.25. $35. ISBN: 0813309263.

First published 1983.

10 chronological chapters *e.g.* 2. The beginnings of Cambodian history - 3. Kingship and society at Angkor ... 8. Early stages of the French protectorate ... 10. Roads to independence and revolution. A note on the names 'Cambodia' and 'Kampuchea' p.xv-xvi. Chapter notes p.197-218. Bibliographical essay p.219-222. Analytical index. 'The first scholarly general history of the country and its people to appear for more than half a century' (*Choice,* v.21, no.5, January 1984, p.748). *Class No:* 959.6

[7723]

CHANDLER, D.P. The Tragedy of Cambodian history politics, war, and revolution since 1945. New Haven, Yale Univ. Press, 1991. xiii,306p. illus., maps, bibliog., index. ISBN: 0300049196.

Sequel to *A History of Cambodia* (2nd ed. 1992) (*q.v.*).

8 chronological chapters cover the period 1945-79. Chapter notes p.319-80. Bibliography p.381-7. 3 maps. Some overlap for 1945-53 with *A History of Cambodia* because of newly opened archival sources. 'A major contribution to Cambodian studies' (*Choice,* v.29, no.11-12, July-August 1992, p.1734). *Class No:* 959.6

Vietnam

Dictionaries

[7724]

DUICKER, W.J. Historical dictionary of Vietnam. Metuchen, New Jersey, Scarecrow Press, 1989. xiv, 269p. maps, tables, bibliog. £30.90. $32.50. (*Historical Dictionaries of Asia, no.1.*) ISBN: 0810821648.

Dictionary of cross-referenced entries relating to prominent and important organizations, broad themes of current and historical significance p.11-203. Bibliography (bibliographical essay on key books in English and books listed under 8 major subject-headings) p.203-9. Appendix 1. Outline history of Vietnam (p.247-8) - 2. Chronology of events p.249-64. 'Valuable reference tool for students and nonspecialists' (*Choice,* v.27, no.2, October 1989, p.284). *Class No:* 959.7(038)

[7725]

WHITFIELD, D.J. Historical and cultural dictionary of Vietnam. Metuchen, N.J., Scarecrow Press, 1976. viii,369p. maps, bibliog. (*Historical and Cultural Dictionaries of Asia, no.7.*) ISBN: 0810808870.

Dictionary p.1-337. Appendix 1. Outline history of Vietnam p.339-40. 2. Dynastic chronology p.341-6. Bibliography p.359-69. 12 maps. *Class No:* 959.7(038)

Vietnam War

[7726]

DAVIDSON, P.B. Vietnam at war: the history 1946-1975. Novato, California, Presidio Press; London, Sidgwick & Jackson, 1988. cxii, 838p. illus., maps, bibliog., index. $27.50. £16.95. ISBN: 0283997125, UK; 0891413065, US.

27 well-documented chapters: 2. The French campaign 1946-47 ... 11. Dien Bien Phu: a critique ... 18. The Tet offensive ... 26. Defeat - 27. Why we lost the war. Glossary p.795-818. Bibliography p.819-27. Analytical index. 'This fascinating book is the finest military history of the Vietnam War now available' (*Choice,* v.26 no.1 September 1988, p.217). *Class No:* 959.70

[7727]

SMITH, R.B. An International history of the Vietnam war. London, Macmillan, 4v., 1983-.

1. *Revolution versus containment, 1955-61.* 1983. xiii, 301p. £38. 0333242467. 2. *The struggle for South-East Asia, 1961-65.* 1985. xii, 492p. £38. 0333339576. 3. *The making of a limited war, 1965-66* 1991. xiv,490p. £38. 033339584. V.2 has 19 chapters organized in 5 chronological sections with a bibliography, notes, and index. The author is Reader in the History of South-East Asia, School of Oriental and African studies, University of London. 'Examples of modern historical writing at its best and inspire the confident expectation that the five volume work, when complete, will constitute a standard and indispensable historical record of the Vietnam War' (*International Affairs,* v.67,no.4, October 1991, p.803).

Forthcoming volumes: 4. *The Crippled giant 1967-70;* 5. *The Dénouement* 1970-75. *Class No:* 959.70

[7728]
STANTON, S.L. **Vietnam order of battle.** Washington, US News Books, 1981. xvii, 396p. illus., maps, tables, index. ISBN: 0891937005.

Brief but authoritative war accounts of all major units involved. 34 chapters deployed in 9 sections: 1. US Army organizations in Vietnam - 2. Major commands - 3. Divisions and separate infantry brigades - 4. Combat units - 5. Combat support units - 6. Service units - 7. Special warfare units - 8. Other US services - 9. Allies. 6 Appendices including US Army Medal of Honor recipients; Sources p.387-91; and Army badges and insignia in Vietnam. 31p. col. plates. *Class No:* 959.70

Micromaterials

[7729]
The History of the Vietnam War. Godstone, Surrey, UMI, 9 units, 1989 - 1991. Microfiche.

1. *Grand Strategy and general assessment of the Vietnam War.* 1989. 1,132 fiche (75,000p. documentary material). $3,415.00. In 3 major sections: General materials - Chronological materials - Insurgency warfare. Included is the US Department of Defense *United States - Vietnam relations 1945 - 1967,* better known as the 'Pentagon Papers'.

2. *General history of the Vietnam War.* 1989. 1,034 fiche. $3,715.00. Chronicles day-to-day routine military activity.

3. *Topical history of the Vietnam War.* 1989 1,500 fiche. $3,450.00. 15 chronologically arranged sections *e.g.* 1. Allied war participants - 2. Anti-war activity ... 4. Legal and legislative ... 14. War atrocities.

4. *Political settlement efforts.* 1990. 14 sections *e.g.* 3 - 12. Political settlement - 13. Ceasefire period - 14. Postwar.

5. *The National Liberation Front (Viet Cong).* 1990. 11 sections: 1. General studies . . . 7. Military activities - 8. Political struggle ... 11. Documentation.

6. *The Democratic Republic of Vietnam (North Vietnam).* 1990. 10 sections: 2. Government and politics/Communist Party ... 9. Communications and motivation.

7. *Republic of Vietnam (South Vietnam).*1991 Government and society 1956 - 1975 including a historical file with French colonial materials in 5 sections: 1. General - 2. History - 3. Chronological - 4. Education/intellectual - 5. Economic.

8. *Indochina (Cambodia and Laos)* 1991. 4 sections: 1. War in Cambodia - 2. War in Laos - 3. Ho Chi Min trail - 4. Indochinese Communist relations.

9. *The Asian Region during the Vietnam War.* 1991.

From the Indochina Archives at the Univ. of California, Berkeley. Includes 15,500 books, pamphlets and monographs; 6,000 newspaper and periodical articles. *Class No:* 959.70(003.5)

Bibliographies

[7730]
BURNS, R.D. *and* LEITENBERG, M. **The Wars in Vietnam, Cambodia and Laos, 1945-1982:** a bibliographic guide. Santa Barbara, California and Oxford, ABC-Clio Information Services, 1984. xxxii, 290p. maps, tables. (*War/ Peace Bibliography Series.*) ISBN: 0874363101.

6200 entries in 9 chapters: 1. General reference aids - 2. Southeast Asia - 3. Vietnam: from the first to the third Indochina wars - 4. United States and the politics of

.... *(contd.)*
intervention - 5. Congress, international law and negotiation - 6. Strategy, tactics and support efforts - 7. Combat operations - 8. The costs of war - 9. The war at home. Chronology p.xxix-xxxii. Glossary p.265-267. 'The most complete general bibliography on this topic currently available' (*Choice*, v.21, no.10, June 1984, p.1438). *Class No:* 959.70(01)

[7731]
PEAKE, L.A. **The United States in the Vietnam War 1954-1975:** a selected, annotated bibliography. New York, Garland Publishing Inc., 1986. xx, 406p. index. $49. (*Wars of the United States.*) ISBN: 0824089464.

1549 briefly annotated entries (some evaluative) grouped into 10 broad categories each divided into more specific topics: 1. General reference - 2. Southeast Asia - 3. Vietnam - 4. Vietnam and the US government - 5. The war - 6. American military experience in Vietnam - 7. The media war - 8. Literature, film, music and art - 9. Domestic impact - 10. Consequences. Chronology p.345-364. List of principal characters p.365-366. Glossary p.367-375. Intended for a broad audience: general readers, military buffs, collectors of militaria *etc. Class No:* 959.70(01)

[7732]
RUSCIO, A. **La Première guerre d'Indochine (1945-1954).** Bibliographie. Paris, Éditions L'Harmaltan, 1987. 286p. indexes. ISBN: 2858028311.

2356 unannotated entries relating to French, English, Vietnamese, Russian, Chinese and Japanese material. *Class No:* 959.70(01)

[7733]
SUGNET, C.L., *and others.* **Vietnam War bibliography** selected from Cornell University's John M. Echols Collection of Southeast Asia. Lexington, Massachusetts, D.C. Heath & Co., 1983. xiii,572p. $45.00. ISBN: 066906680x.

3 sections: 1. 3000 entries covering US involvement in Vietnam from the mid-1940s to 1975 listed alphabetically by title - 2. Name, subject and alternative title index p.461-563 - 3. Acronyms and cross-references p.565-572. The Echols Collection (1953-) is a national resource for Southeast Asian studies. 'The most comprehensive annotated guide to the literature of the vietnam War currently available' (*Choice,* v.21,no.6, February 1984, p.807-808). *Class No:* 959.70(01)

Dictionaries

[7734]
OLSON, J.S. **Dictionary of the Vietnam War.** Westport, Connecticut, Greenwood Press, 1988. viii, 584p. £53.25. $65. ISBN: 0313249431.

Brief descriptive entries on the personalities, legislation, military operations relating to US participation in the Vietnam War. Appendix D. Select bibliography p.525-46 - E. Chronology 1945-1975 p.547-60 - F. Maps p.561. Analytical index. *Class No:* 959.70(038)

Almanacs

[7735]
SUMMERS, H.G. **Vietnam War almanac.** New York and Oxford, Facts On File Publications, 1985. x, 414p. illus., maps, bibliog., index. £16.94. $24.95. ISBN: 081601017x.

3 pts: 1. The setting (introductory history from ancient times to 1959) - 2. Chronology of events in Vietnam and the United States - 3. The Vietnam War A-Z (500 entries relating to people, battles, weapons, controversial issues etc., some with cross-references and suggestions for further reading). Bibliography p.367-382. 21 maps. 'A thorough guide to the war' (*Reference Reviews*, v.2, no.3, September 1988, p.163). *Class No:* 959.70(059)

Africa

[7736]
Unesco general history of Africa. Paris, UNESCO; London, Heinemann Educational Books Ltd.; Berkeley, Univ. of California Press, 1981-. illus., maps, tables, bibliog. index.

1. *Methodology and African prehistory* edited by J. Ki-Zerbo. 1981. xxvii, 819p. 28 chaps. Bibliography p.753-800. 0435948075 (UK); 05200039122 (US) 9231017071 (Fr). 2. *Ancient civilizations of Africa* edited by G. Mokhtar. 1981. xvii, 804p. 29 chapters. Bibliography p.742-785. 0435948059 (UK); 0520039130 (US); 9231017084 (Fr). 3. *Africa from the seventh to the eleventh century* edited by M. El Fasi and I. Hrbek. 1988. 869p. $45. ISBN 9231017098 (US). 4. *Africa from the twelfth century to the sixteenth century* edited by D.T. Niane. 1984. xxvii, 751p. 27 chaps. Bibliography p.692-733. 0435948105 (UK); 0520039157 (US); 9231017101 (Fr). 5. *Africa from the sixteenth to the eighteenth century* edited by B.A. Ogot. 6. *Africa in the nineteenth century until the 1880s* edited by J.F.A. Ajayi. 1989. 29 chapters. £18.00. ISBN 0435948121 (UK); 0520039173 (US); 9231017128 (Fr). 7. *Africa under colonial domination 1880-1935* edited by A.A. Boahen 1985. xxvii, 865p. 30 chapters. Bibliography p.815-844. ISBN 043594813x (UK); 0520039181 (US); 9231017136 (Fr). 8. *Africa since 1935* edited by A.A. Mazrui. 15 years in the planning this is a cooperative history on the grand scale. It reacts against what is seen as Euro-centred, warped ethno-history. Essential issues are the slave trade, colonisation, relations between sub-Sahara Africa and the Arab world, and decolonisation and nation building in an endeavour to highlight historical data allowing 'a clear picture of the evolution of the different peoples of Africa and their specific socio-cultural setting.' Each volume is edited by a native specialist, stressing cultural aspects and oral tradition and contains an important and extensive bibliographical essay. *Class No:* 96

Bibliographies

[7737]
HARGREAVES, J.D. **'Notes on French sources for African history in the later nineteenth century'**, *African Research and Documentation*', no.36, 1984, p.1-6, refs.

'Essentially user's notes and comparisons with British sources' (*abstract*). *Class No:* 96(01)

Encyclopaedias

[7738]
STEWART, J. **African states and rulers:** an encyclopaedia of native, colonial and independent states and rulers past and present. Jefferson, N.C., McFarland, 1989. xx,395p. bibliog., index. $45. ISBN: 089950390x.

1139 A-Z name entries. Data: official name of country; dates for that name; location; capital(s); other names known by; lists of rulers and their dates. Bibliography p.303-5. Index of 10500 rulers p.307-95. According to preface based on author's 1970's notes now lost! Less than ecstatic review in *Choice*, v.27, no.2, October 1989, p.294. *Class No:* 96(031)

Dictionaries

[7739]
African historical dictionaries. Metuchen, New Jersey, Scarecrow Press, 1974-.

Series now comprises over 40v. Each 'treats an individual country, providing in dictionary form basic information about its geography, history, economic and social aspects, major persons, events and institutions. With bibliographies'. A critical overview of the series' accuracy, balance, accessibility, with a final section headed 'A miscellany of defects',. can be found in D. Henige's 'African historical dictionaries through the looking glass' (*African Journal*, v.10,no.2,1979, p.120-128). *Class No:* 96(038)

[7740]
GRACE, J. *and* LAFFIN, J. **Fontana dictionary of Africa since 1960.** London, Fontana Press, 1991. xix,395p. map, bibliog. £7.99. ISBN: 0006862144.

Over 1,000 A-Z entries recording events, movements, and personalities significant in African history and politics. Chronology p.x-xiv. Bibliography p.vii-ix. *Class No:* 96(038)

[7741]
NUNEZ, B. **Dictionary of Portuguese-African civilization.** Oxford, Hans Zell, 2v. 1992. £48 for each vol. ISBN: 0873836708, set.

1. *From discovery to independence.* 432p. bibliog. 0837836104. 2. *Biographies - from ancient kings to presidents.* 08373836651. Over 3000 entries in v.1 identify historical and political events, social life and customs, geographical names, flora and fauna, organizations, literature, and culture in Portuguese Africa - Angola, Cape Verde, Guinea-Bissau, Mozambique, Sao Tome and Principe. *Class No:* 96(038)

Theses

[7742]
JOYNES, S. **'Theses on Anglophone Africa recently completed in British universities'**, *African Research and Documentation*, no.35, 1984, p.76-82.

Continued in New theses on Anglophone Africa notified in the United Kingdom during 1984, *ibid*, no.37, 1985, p.84-90; Theses ... recently completed ... *ibid*, no.38, 1985, p.74-82 and no.40, 1986, p.42-48; Theses on Anglophone Africa notified as in progress in British universities during 1985, *ibid*, no.41, 1986, p.48-54; Theses ... as in progress ... during 1986, *ibid*, no.43, 1987, p.44-51; Theses ... recently completed ... *ibid*, no.44, 1987, p.52-59. Arranged by region subdivided by country. *Class No:* 96(043)

Maps & Atlases

[7743]
ADE AJAYI, J.F. *and* CROWDER, M., *eds*. **Historical atlas of Africa.** Harlow, Essex, Longman, 1985. 72p. maps + 72p. 22 plates. £66.00. ISBN: 058264335x.

72 maps of 3 types: event maps concerning historical events and locations of towns, battles, trade routes; process maps forming a visual interpretation of historical processes; and quantitative maps consisting of numerical data characterizing historical relationships. Ten years in the planning this is a more ambitious atlas than Fage and Verity's *The atlas of African history.* 'An invaluable and accurate source for ... the development of the continent during the last three thousand years' (*African Affairs* v.85,no.339, June 1986, p.301-302). *Class No:* 96(084.3)

[7744]
FREEMAN-GRENVILLE, G.S.P. **The New atlas of African history.** London, Macmillan; New York, Simon & Schuster, 1991. 144p. col. maps, index. £35; $65. ISBN: 0333559002, UK; 0136121519, US.

103 x two colour maps with commentaries provide an illustrated history of the African continent from prehistory to 1990 (e.g. 1. Africa-physical ... 4. Early Stone Age ... 9. Movements in Northern Africa between c.3500BC and c.500BC ... 67. European exploration ... 101. Principal languages ... 103. Vegetation). 'Suffers in comparison with Historical Atlas of Africa' (*Library Journal*). *Class No:* 96(084.3)

[7745]
KWAMENA-POH, M., *and others*. **African history in maps.** London, Longman, 1982. 76p. index, softcover. £6.35. ISBN: 0582603315.

36 two-colour maps faced by concise text covering the period from AD 1000 to the present. For student use. *Class No:* 96(084.3)

Bibliographies

[7746]
FERRO, D.P. **'The Mapping of Africa: a guide to sources',** *African Research and Documentation*, no.28,1982,p.13-16.
Survey of 26 general sources. *Class No:* 96(084.3)(01)

Chronologies

[7747]
FREEMAN-GRENVILLE, G.S.P. **Chronology of African history.** Oxford, Oxford University Press, 1973. xxii,312p.

Tabulates the principal events and dates in African history 1000BC-1971. 6 columns across the double page record the migration of peoples, dynasties, wars and treaties, and the emergence of modern states. *Class No:* 96(090)

Biographies

[7748]
LIPSCHUTZ, M.R. *and* RASMUSSEN, R.K. **Dictionary of African historical biography.** 2nd ed. Berkeley, Calif, University of California Press, 1986. xiii, 328p. maps, bibliog., index. $40. ISBN: 0520051793.

First published by Aldine in 1978.

900 entries (57 new to this edition) mainly of political

....(contd.)
leaders from academically popular regions. Bibliography p.291-316. 'Essential for all academic libraries' (*Choice*, v.24, no.8, April 1987, p.1201-2). *Class No:* 96(092)

[7749]
Makers of modern Africa profiles in history. Bing, A., *ed.* London, Africa Books Ltd. 1991. xvii,797p. ports., maps. (*Know Africa*.) ISBN: 0903274183. ISSN: 02611570.

Companion volume to *Africa today* and *Africa who's who* (*qqv*).

650 biographical sketches of eminent Africans now dead but who shaped the destiny of modern Africa. Includes Africans of European descent. *Class No:* 96(092)

[7750]
Political leaders of contemporary Africa south of the Sahara a biographical dictionary. Glickman, H., *ed.* Westport, Conn., Greenwood Press, 1992. xxii,361p. bibliog., index. ISBN: 0313267812.

54 A-Z signed, expertly-written, essay-length biographies, each with a short bibliography, which collectively outline the history of black Africa in the post-colonial period. Country list of subjects p.311-3. Chronology (1892-1991) p.315-36. Bibliographical note p.337-8. *Class No:* 96(092)

[7751]
SIMPSON, D.H. **'Biographical sources for colonial history in Africa',** *African Research and Documentation*, no.29, 1982, p.19-21.

Assessment of general biographical reference works. *Class No:* 96(092)

19th Century

[7752]
GRIFFITHS, I. **'The Scramble for Africa: inherited political boundaries',** *Geographical Journal*, v.152, no.2, July 1986, p.204-216. maps, bibliog.

Historical account of the problems resulting from the European partition of Africa following the Berlin Conference 1884-1885. *Class No:* 96"18"

20th Century

[7753]
COOK, C. *and* KILLINGRAY, D. **African political facts since 1945.** London, The Macmillan Press Ltd., 1983. vii,263p. bibliog. £45. ISBN: 033256824.

11 chapters: 1. Chronology of major events; 2. Governors and Heads of State; 3. Major ministerial appointments; 4. Constitutions and parliaments; 5. Political parties; 6. Trade Unions; 7. Conflicts, armed forces and coups; 8. Foreign affairs and treaties; 9. Population and ethnic groups; 10. Basic economic statistics; 11. Biographies. Bibliography p.257. Index p.258-263. *Class No:* 96"19"

Africa—North

[7754]
ABUN-NASR, J.M. **A History of the Magrib in the Islamic period.** 3rd ed. Cambridge, Cambridge Univ. Press, 1987. xvi,455p. maps,bibliog., index. £40.00; $65.00. ISBN: 0521331846.

Supersedes the author's *A History of the Maghrib* (1971, 2e. 1975).

....*(contd.)*

8 chronological chapters: 1. Introduction (land and people) - 2. Call of the minaret: the establishment of Islam in the Maghrib and Spain - 3. Under Berber dynasties - 4. Ottoman rule - 5. Morocco consolidates her national identity - 6. Age of aggressive European colonisation - 7. 1919 to independence - 8. Epilogue: after independence. Glossary p.xiii-xvi. Bibliography p.429-439. Analytical index. The history of the region now comprising Morocco, Tunisia, Algeria and Libya. 'There is not a better history of the Maghrib available in English' (*Choice,* v.25,no.8, April 1988, p.1299). *Class No: 960/965*

Tunisia

[7755]

PERKINS, K.J. **Tunisia** crossroads of the Islamic and European worlds. Boulder, Colorado, Westview Press; London, Croom Helm. 1986. xii,192p. illus., map, bibliog., index. $29.50. (*Profiles: Nations of the Contemporary Middle East.*) ISBN: 0865315914, US; 0709940505, UK.

12 chapters: 1. Land and people - 2. Pre-Islamic Tunisia - 3. Introduction of Islam and Arab rule - 4. Berber dynasties - 5. Ottoman and Husainid Tunisia ... 8. Tunisian Nationalist Movement ... 12. Foreign relations. Glossary of foreign words p.179-80. Bibliography p.181-3. *Class No:* 961.1

Dictionaries

[7756]

PERKINS, K.J. **Historical dictionary of Tunisia.** Metuchen, New Jersey, Scarecrow Press, 1989. xxvi,234p. map, bibliog. £28.05. (*African Historical Dictionaries, no.45.*) ISBN: 0810822261.

Chronology p.ix-xix. Rulers of Tunisia (800-1988) p.xxi-xxiii. Introduction: Tunisia: an overview p.1-10. Dictionary p.11-148. Bibliography (under 10 headings) p.149-234. 'A useful, valuable and needed addition to works about Tunisia' (*Choice,* v.27, no.8, April 1990, p.1303-4). *Class No:* 961.1(038)

Libya

[7757]

WRIGHT, J. **Libya:** a modern history. London, Croom Helm, 1981. 288p.

12 chapters forming 'a good basic history of Libya' (R.I. Lawless. *Libya* 1987. Entry 149). *Class No:* 961.2

Dictionaries

[7758]

HAHN, L. **Historical dictionary of Libya.** Metuchen, New Jersey, Scarecrow Press, 1981. xiv,116p. map, bibliog. £21.00; $20.00. (*African Historical Dictionaries, no.33.*) ISBN: 0810814420.

Recent political chronology p.xi-xiii. Dictionary p.11-84. Bibliography p.85-108. *Class No:* 961.2(038)

Egypt

[7759]

VATIKIOTIS, P.J. **The History of Egypt.** 4th ed. London, Weidenfeld & Nicolson. 1991. xvi,572p. maps. bibliog. index. ISBN: 0297820346.

First published 1969 as *The modern history of Egypt.* 2nd ed. with present title 1980.

Introduction: 'Background to modern Egypt.' 5 parts (18 chapters): 1. Social and political foundations of modern Egypt, 1805-82 - 2. Conservative and liberal response to Europe, 1882-1914 - 3. Society, government and politics, 1919-39 - 4. From the old order to the new, 1930-84 - 5. The search for a modern culture and society. Chapter notes. Bibliography. This edition is revised and updated to 1990. *Class No:* 962.0

Dictionaries

[7760]

KING, J.W. **Historical dictionary of Egypt.** Metuchen, New Jersey, Scarecrow Press, 1984. xiii, 719p. map, bibliog. £57. $49.50. (*African Historical Dictionaries, no.36.*) ISBN: 0810816709.

Chronology p.26-88. Dictionary p.89-650. Bibliography p.651-719. 'A work of considerable value for all students of Egypt' (*International Affairs,* v.61, no.3, Summer 1985, p.368). *Class No:* 962.0(038)

Sudan

[7761]

DALY, M.W. **Imperial Sudan** The Anglo-Egyptian condominium 1934-1956. Cambridge, Cambridge Univ. Press, 1991. xvi,471p. illus., map, bibliog., index. £55; $79.50. ISBN: 0521391636.

Follows Daly's *Empire on the Nile: The Anglo-Egyptian Sudan 1898-1934* (CUP, 1986).

12 chapters *e.g.* 3. Sudan in Anglo-Egyptian relations - 4. Development of Sudanese nationalist politics 1934-90 ... 9. Path to self-government. Glossary p.xv-xvi. Chapter notes p.402-49. Bibliography p.450-7. 'Together, these two volumes provide a comprehensive history of the Anglo-Egyptian condominium and should represent the standard work on the subject for many years ... this book is unmatched in studies of modern Sudan' (*The Middle East Journal,* v.46, no.1, Winter 1992, p.98-9). *Class No:* 962.4

[7762]

HOLT, P.M. **A History of the Sudan:** from the coming of Islam to the present day. 4th ed. London, Longman, 1988. x, 262p. maps, bibliog., index, pbk. £7.95. ISBN: 0582004063.

First published 1961. 3rd ed. 1979.

16 chronological chapters arranged in 5 parts: 1. Before the Turko-Egyptian conquest - 2. The Turko-Egyptian period - 3. The Mahdist state 1881-98 - 4. The Anglo-Egyptian condominium 1899-1955 - 5. The independent state. This edition extends coverage to 1986. Chapter notes p.227-233. Bibliography p.243-250. 5 maps. Author is Professor of Near and Middle East History in the University of London. *Class No:* 962.4

[7763]
Sudan state and society in crisis. Voll, J.O., *ed.* Bloomington, Indiana Univ. Press in association with the Middle East Institute, Washington D.C., 1991. xi,170p. map, index. ISBN: 0253362709.

8 well-documented chapters by independent hands on recent Sudanese history and the country's current problems (*e.g.* Islamization in Sudan: a critical assessment and a missed opportunity? Sudans stabilization program 1979-1982). Anlaytical index. *Class No: 962.4*

[7764]
WOODWARD, P. Sudan 1898-1989 the unstable state. Boulder, Colo., Lynne Rienner; London, Lester Crook Academic Publishing, 1990. xiv,271p. map, bibliog., index. $35.

A political history in 6 chronological chapters: 1, Establishment of the Condominium - 2. Condominium under pressure - 3. Condominium to independence - 4. Nationalist generation in power 1956 to 1969 - 5. The Numeiri years - 6. A new beginning? 1985 to 1989. Glossary p.vii-viii. Chronology p.ix-xii. Chapter notes p.241-59. Bibliography p.261-4. *Class No: 962.4*

Dictionaries

[7765]
FLUEHR-LOBBAN, C, and others. Historical dictionary of The Sudan. 2nd ed. Metuchen, New Jersey, Scarecrow Press, 1992. cvii,409p. illus., maps, bibliog. (*African Historical Dictionaries, no.53.*) ISBN: 0810825473.

Substantially revised and expanded update of J.O. Voll's *Historical dictionary of the Sudan* (1978).

Entries of varying length for historical events; social, religious, and ethnic groups; political and cultural institutions, and geographical locations and regions. Detailed chronology p.xix-lxx. Introduction (geography, population and migration, history, present government and economics) p.lxxi-xvii. Dictionary p.1-247. Bibliography (7 subject divisions) p.249-396. Appendix 1-4 rulers of Sudan. *Class No: 962.4(038)*

Ethiopia

[7766]
BAHRU ZEWDE. A History of modern Ethiopia 1855-1974. London, James Currey; Athens, Ohio Univ. Press, Addis Ababa Univ. Press, 1991. x,244p. illus., maps, bibliogs., index. £25. (*Eastern African Studies.*) ISBN: 0852550677, UK; 0821409719, US.

Narrative history in 5 parts: 1. Background - 2. Unification and independence 1855-1896 - 3. From Adwa to Maychaw 1896-1935 - 4. Italian occupation 1936-1941 - 5. From liberation to revolution 1941-1974. Glossary p.232-4. Chapter bibliographies. 8 maps. *Class No: 963*

Bibliographies

[7767]
MARCUS, G. The Modern history of Ethiopia and the Horn of Africa a selected and annotated bibliography. Stanford, California, Hoover Institution Press, Stanford Univ., 1972. xxii, 641p.

2,042 entries, drawn from 151 periodicals (mostly Western European geographical journals). Wide coverage (ethnology, ethnobotany, ethnozoology, geology,

....(contd.)
climatology, social anthropology, cultural history, contemporary affairs, material culture, economics, sociology, history, linguistics, etc.). Four indexes: authors, geographical names, other proper nouns, subjects. 'A most practical guide' (*The Geographical Journal*, v.139, pt.1, February 1973, p.154). *Class No: 963(01)*

Dictionaries

[7768]
PROUTY, C. and ROSENFELD, E. Historical dictionary of Ethiopia. Metuchen, NJ., Scarecrow Press, 1981. xv, 436p. bibliog., index. £39. $36. (*African Historical Dictionaries, no.32.*)

Dictionary p.1-191. Bibliography p.192-407. *Class No: 963(038)*

Morocco

Dictionaries

[7769]
SPENCER, W. Historical dictionary of Morocco. Metuchen, New Jersey, Scarecrow Press, 1980. xliv, 152p. map, bibliog. £21. $20. (*African Historical Dictionaries, no.24.*) ISBN: 0810813629.

Dynasties of Morocco p. ix-xiii. High Commissioners of the Spanish protectorate p. xiv-xv. Resident-Generals of the French protectorate p.xv. Glossary p. xviii-xxiv. Chronology p.xxv-xxxix. Dictionary p.13-112. Bibliography p.113-52. *Class No: 964(038)*

Western Sahara

[7770]
DAMIS, J. Conflict in Northwest Africa: the Western Sahara dispute. Stanford, California, Hoover Institution Press, Stanford Univ., 1983. xviii, 196p. maps, tables, bibliog., index. (*Hoover International Studies.*) ISBN: 0817977813.

5 chapters: 1. The land and the people - 2. Parties to the conflict - 3. Evolution of the conflict - 4. Role of third parties - 5. Towards a resolution. Bibliography p.180-7. 'Aims to present a balanced and concise analysis of the major factors and developments ... since 1975' (*Introduction*). *Class No: 964.8*

Dictionaries

[7771]
HODGES, T. Historical dictionary of Western Sahara. Metuchen, New Jersey, Scarecrow Press, 1982. xxxix,431 p. map. bibliog. £39. $37.50. (*African Historical Dictionaries, no.35..*) ISBN: 0810814978.

Chronology p.xv - xxxix. Dictionary p. 13 - 369. Bibliography p.371-431. *Class No: 964.8(038)*

Algeria

[7772]
AGERON, G.R. Modern Algeria: a history from 1830 to the present. London, Hurst, 1991. x,166p. maps, bibliog., index. £16.50. ISBN: 1850650276.

First published as *Histoire de l'Algérie contemporaine*, 1964. 9th ed. 1990.

887

....(contd.)

9 chapters arranged in 5 main sections: 1. Under the military 1830 to 1870 - 2. Colonial Algeria 1870 to 1930 - 3. Will Algeria survive? (1930-1954) - 4. Algerian War - 5. Independent Algeria. Bibliography p.145-60 is useful for French language sources. 'No other work in English - or French for that matter - covers the period of French rule in Algeria so satisfactorily' (*Journal of Imperial and Commonwealth History*, v.20, no.3, September 1992, p.493-4). *Class No:* 965

[7773]
ENTELIS, J.P. Algeria the revolution institutionalized. Boulder, Colo., Westview Press; London, Croom Helm, 1986. xii,239p. illus., map, tables, bibliog., index. (*Profiles Nations Of The Contemporary East.*) ISBN: 0865314705, US; 070990973x, UK.

1. Introduction (geographical features; population) - 2. Imprint of history: antiquity to 1919 - 3. 1919 to the present - 4. Culture and society in transition - 5. Political economy of development - 6. Dynamics of political life - 7. Worldview. Bibliography p.217-23. *Class No:* 965

Dictionaries

[7774]
HEGGOY, A.A. Historical dictionary of Algeria. Metuchen, New Jersey, Scarecrow Press, 1981. x, 237p. maps, bibliog., index. £24. $24. (*African Historical Dictionaries, no.28.*) ISBN: 0810813769.

Glossary of Arabic, French and Turkish terms p.37-44. Chronology p.45-9. Dictionary p.51-183. Bibliography p.185-205. Appendix 1. French Governors in colonial Algeria. 'A useful and important tool for the researcher and student' (*Africana Journal*, v.13, no.1-4, 1982, p.234-5). *Class No:* 965(038)

Africa—West

[7775]
AJAYI, J.F.A. *and* **CROWDER, M. History of West Africa.** London, Longman. 568p.+764p.

1st ed. 1971-74 (1v.).

V.1. 3rd ed. 1985. pbk. £16.95. ISBN 0582646839 deals with prehistory up to 1800. V.2 2nd ed., 1987. pbk. £16.95. 0582016045. 'Somewhat patchy treatment of regions outside the Islamic sphere' (*African Affairs*, v.73,no.291, April 1974, p.235). *Class No:* 966

Maps & Atlases

[7776]
CATCHPOLE, B. *and* **AKINJOGBIN, I.A. A History of West Africa in maps and diagrams.** London, Collins Education, 1989. ix,150p. illus., maps, diagrs., index. ISBN: 00326520x.

100 double page features (map, illus., notes) arranged in 3 chronological sections: 1000-1800; 1800-1918; 1918 to the present day for students of the West African Examination Council's syllabus. *Class No:* 966(084.3)

Mauritania

Dictionaries

[7777]
GERTEINY, A.G. Historical dictionary of Mauritania. Metuchen, New Jersey, Scarecrow Press, 1981. xvi, 98p. maps, tables, bibliog. £21. $17.50. (*African Historical Dictionaries, no.31.*) ISBN: 0810814331.

Recent political chronology p.ix-xi. Dictionary p.19-82. Bibliography p.83-96. *Class No:* 966.12(038)

Mali

Dictionaries

[7778]
IMPERATO, P. J. Historical dictionary of Mali. 2nd ed. Metuchen, New Jersey. Scarecrow Press, 1956. xvii, 379p. maps. bibliog. £32.50 $35.00. (*African Historical Dictionaries, no.11.*) ISBN: 081081885x.

1st ed. 1977.

Chronology p.1-24. Dictionary p.77-255. Bibliography p.256-359. 5 maps. *Class No:* 966.21(038)

Upper Volta

Dictionaries

[7779]
McFARLAND, D.M. Historical dictionary of Upper Volta (Haute Volta). Metuchen, New Jersey, Scarecrow Press, 1978. xxi, 217p. maps, bibliog. £24. $24. (*African Historical Dictionaries, no.14.*) ISBN: 0810810883.

Chronology p.1-52. Dictionary p.53-161. Bibliography p.163-217. List of major ethnic groups p.xvii-xviii. 4 maps. *Class No:* 966.25(038)

Niger

[7780]
FUGELSTAD, F. A History of Niger. Cambridge, Cambridge Univ. Press, 1984. viii, 275p. £20. $39.50. (*African Studies series.*) ISBN: 0521252687.

A descriptive and analytical account concentrating on the colonial period. 7 chapters: 1. Peoples and societies of Niger: early history to 1850 - 2. The revolutionary years 1850-1908 - 3. The decisive years 1908-22 - 4. Summing up and looking ahead - 5. The great silence: the classic period of colonial rule 1922-45 - 6. Towards a new order 1945-60 - 7. Conclusion. Notes p.193-241. Glossary p.242-243. Bibliography p.244-265. 'A significant piece of scholarship that ... raises important questions about the study of the colonial period' *Choice*, v.22, no.2, October 1984, p.325-326). *Class No:* 966.26

Dictionaries

[7781]
DECALO, S. Historical dictionary of Niger. 2nd ed. Metuchen, New Jersey, Scarecrow Press, 1989. xxxvi,408p. maps, tables, bibliog. £33.25. (*African Historical Dictionaries, no.20.*) ISBN: 0810822237.

1st ed. 1979.

Recent political chronology p.xiii-xvi. Dictionary p.11-236. Bibliography p.237-408. *Class No:* 966.26(038)

Senegal

Bibliographies

[7782]
PORGÈS, L., *ed*. **Bibliographie des régions du Sénégal:** complément pour la periode des origines à 1965 et mise à jour 1966-1973. Berlin, Mouton-De Gruyter, 1977. 686p. maps. F186. *Class No:* 966.3(01)

Dictionaries

[7783]
COLVIN, L.G. **Historical dictionary of Senegal.** Metuchen, NJ, Scarecrow Press, 1981. xiv, 399p. maps, bibliog. tables. £27. $26.50. (*African Historical Dictionaries, no.23.*) ISBN: 0810813696.
Chronology of important events p.17-41. Dictionary p.121-293. Bibliography p.297-339. *Class No:* 966.3(038)

Sierra Leone

[7784]
ALIE, J.A.D. **A New history of Sierra Leone.** London, Macmillan, 1990. xvii,300p. illus., maps, index. pbk. £6.95. ISBN: 0333519841.
Narrative survey of Sierra Leone's political, socio-cultural, and economic development in 12 chapters (*e.g.* 1. Land and people ... 3. Establishment and development of Sierra Leone colony ... 10. Transfer of power). Appendix 1. Governors of Sierra Leone ... 4. National anthem - 5. Flag - 6. Coat of arms - 7. Honours and awards. Chapter bibliographies. 16 maps. *Class No:* 966.4

Dictionaries

[7785]
FORAY, C.P. **Historical dictionary of Sierra Leone.** Metuchen, New Jersey, Scarecrow Press, 1977. lvii, 279p. maps, bibliog. £30. $28.50. (*African Historical Dictionaries, no.12.*) ISBN: 0810810352.
Chronology p.xiii-xxv. Dictionary p.1-236. Bibliography p.237-279. 4 maps. *Class No:* 966.4(038)

Gambia

Dictionaries

[7786]
GAILEY, H.A. **Historical dictionary of The Gambia.** 2nd ed. Metuchen, New Jersey, Scarecrow Press, 1987. viii, 172p. map, bibliog. £16.90. $22.50. (*African Historical Dictionaries, no.4.*) ISBN: 0810820013.
1st ed. 1975.
Chronology p.xiii-xviii. Chief executives 1829- p.xxi-xxii. Dictionary p.25-145. Bibliography p.146-176.
Class No: 966.51(038)

Guinea

Dictionaries

[7787]
O'TOOLE, T.E. **Historical dictionary of Guinea (Republic of Guinea/Conakry).** 2nd ed. Metuchen, New Jersey, Scarecrow Press, 1987. xxv, 204p. map, bibliog., tables. £16.90. $22.50. (*African historical dictionaries, no.16.*) ISBN: 0810820005.
1st ed. 1978.
Chronological list of major events p.xii-xv. Dictionary p.13-124. Bibliography p.125-204. *Class No:* 966.52(038)

Guinea-Bissau

Dictionaries

[7788]
LOBBAN, R. *and* FORREST, J. **Historical dictionary of the Republic of Guinea-Bissau.** 2nd ed. Metuchen, New Jersey, Scarecrow Press, 1988. xx, 211p. maps, bibliog. £18.75. $25. (*African Historical Dictionaries; no.22.*) ISBN: 0810820862.
1st ed. under the title of *Historical dictionary of the Republics of Guinea-Bissau and Cape Verde* (1979).
Chronology p.xv-xx. Dictionary p.17-135. Bibliography p.136-203. Appendix C. The peoples of Guinea-Bissau. *Class No:* 966.57(038)

Cape Verde Islands

Dictionaries

[7789]
LOBBAN, R. *and* HALTER, M. **Historical dictionary of The Republic of Cape Verde.** 2nd ed. Metuchen, New Jersey, Scarecrow Press, 1988. xix, 171p. maps, bibliog. £16.90. $22.50. (*African Historical Dictionaries, no.42.*) ISBN: 0810820870.
First published as *Historical dictionary of the Republics of Guinea-Bissau and Cape Verde* in 1979.
Chronology p.xiii-xix. Dictionary p.13-119. Bibliography p.120-65. *Class No:* 966.58(038)

Liberia

Dictionaries

[7790]
DUNN, D.E. *and* HOLSOE, S.E. **Historical dictionary of Liberia.** Metuchen, New Jersey, Scarecrow Press, 1985. xx, 274p. maps, bibliog., index. £22.50. $27.50. (*African Historical Dictionaries, no.38.*) ISBN: 0810817675.
Chronology p.xiii-xx. Dictionary p.15-192. Bibliography p.193-240. 7 maps. 'Far more scholarly than most of the Scarecrow volumes' (*Journal of African History*, 1982, no.3, p.468-9). *Class No:* 966.62(038)

Ivory Coast

Dictionaries

[7791]

MUNDT, R.J. **Historical dictionary of the Ivory Coast.** Metuchen, New Jersey, Scarecrow Press, 1987. xxvii, 246p. map, tables, bibliog. £29.50. $29.50. (*African Historical Dictionaries, no.41.*) ISBN: 0810820293.

Chronology p.xv-xviii. Dictionary p.15-139. Bibliography p.140-246. *Class No:* 966.68(038)

Ghana

Dictionaries

[7792]

McFARLAND, D.M. **Historical dictionary of Ghana.** Metuchen, New Jersey, Scarecrow Press, 1985. lxxx, 296p. maps, bibliog. £33. $32.50. (*African Historical Dictionaries, no.39.*) ISBN: 0810817616.

Chronology p.xix-lxxx. Dictionary p.13-198. Bibliography p.199-289 (19 sections). 5 Appendices: 1. List of Ghanaian people - 2. Rules of Asante - 3. British administrators of the Gold Coast - 4. Ghanaian leaders from 1951 - 5. European posts on the Gold Coast. 4 maps. 'Contains a wide and well-arranged array of information' (*Choice*, v.23, no.2, October 1985, p.274). *Class No:* 966.7(038)

Togo

Dictionaries

[7793]

DECALO, S. **Historical dictionary of Togo.** 2nd ed. Metuchen, New Jersey, Scarecrow Press, 1987. xxvi,331p. maps, tables, bibliog. £24.50; $32.50. (*African Historical Dictionaries, no.9.*) ISBN: 0810819546.

1st ed. 1976.
Political chronology p.xxv-xxvi. Dictionary p.11-212. Bibliography p.216-331. 'An essential reference tool' (*Booklist*, v.74, no.22, 15 July 1988, p.1758-1759). 4 maps. *Class No:* 966.8(038)

Benin

Dictionaries

[7794]

DECALO, S. **Historical dictionary of Benin.** 2nd ed. Metuchen, New Jersey, Scarecrow Press, 1987. xxvii, 349p. maps, tables, bibliog. £26.25. $35. (*African Historical Dictionaries, no.7.*) ISBN: 0810819244.

1st ed. 1976 as *Historical dictionary of Dahomey (People's Republic of Benin).*
Recent political chronology p.xv-xvii. Dictionary p.13-227. Bibliography p.229-349. 6 maps. *Class No:* 966.82(038)

Maps & Atlases

[7795]

ROESE, P.M. *and* ROSE, A.C. **Ein Atlas zur Geschichte Benins** von den Anfängen bis 1897, *Ethnographisch-Archäologische Zeitschrift*, v.29,no.2, 1988, p.301-337.

14 maps. *Class No:* 966.82(084.3)

Nigeria

[7796]

IKIME, O., *ed.* **Groundwork of Nigerian history.** Ibadan, Heinemann for the Historical Society of Nigeria, 1980. 615p. maps. bibliog.

28 essays grouped in 4 sections: 1. Geographical and archaeological backgrounds - 2. Nigeria before 1800 - 3. 19th Century - 4. 20th Century. 18 maps. 'This essential volume intended ... as a comprehensive history of the nation for university students' (R. A. Myers. *Nigeria*, 1989. Entry 162). *Class No:* 966.9

[7797]

ISICHEI, E. **A History of Nigeria.** London, Longman, 1983. xix,517p. illus, maps. bibliog. index. £19.95. ISBN: 0582643317.

20 meticulously documented thematic chapters with an emphasis on the pre-colonial period. Bibliography p.488-503. The author is Professor of History at the University of Jos. 'A highly original, extensively researched and breathtakingly labor-intensive insight into the many millenia of Nigerian history' (*Africana Journal*, v.14, no.4, 1987, p.338-40). *Class No:* 966.9

Dictionaries

[7798]

OYEWOLE, A. **Historical dictionary of Nigeria.** Metuchen, New Jersey, Scarecrow Press, 1987. vii, 391p. maps, bibliog. £37.50. $37.50. (*African Historical Dictionaries, no.40.*) ISBN: 081081787x.

Selected chronology p.viii-xii. Dictionary p.11-345. Bibliography p.347-381. *Class No:* 966.9(038)

Africa—East & Equatorial

[7799]

BIRMINGHAM, D. *and* MARTIN, P.M. **History of Central Africa.** London, Longman, 2v., 1983. xii, 315p.+Ø, 432p. illus. maps. bibliog., index. ISBN: 0582646731, v.1; 0582646758, v.2.

V1. concentrates on the culture and accomplishments of the native peoples of Central Africa before the European arrival. 7 chapters: 1. Society and economy before AD 1400 ... 3. The peoples of the forest ... 6. The Indian Ocean zone. Bibliographical essay p.278-296. V2. focusses on the colonial and post-colonial periods. 9. chapters: 1. The violence of Empire ... 2. Equatorial Africa under colonial rule ... 8. The Northern republics 1960-1980 ... 9. Settlers and liberators in the South. Bibliographical essay p.383-400. Analytical indexes. Devised for undergraduate students. *Class No:* 967

[7800]

CASADA, J. **'British exploration in East Africa':** a bibliography with commentary, *Africana Journal*, v.5, no.3, Fall 1974, p.195-239.

Books and articles by and on 10 British nineteenth-century explorers. *Class No:* 967

[7801]
LINIGER-GOUMAZ, M. **Small is not always beautiful:** the story of Equatorial Africa. London, C. Hurst, 1988. xx, 198p. maps, bibliog., index. £19.50. ISBN: 1850650233.

First published Rouen, Editions des Peuples Noir, 1986 under the title *Connaître la Guinée Équatoriale.*

7 Chapters: 1. Physical and human geography - 2. The colonial period - 3. Independence miscarried - 4. Demographic and cultural aspects of the Nguema era - 5. The Economy - 6. Present and future - 7. Conclusions. Bibliographical note p.170-174. Bibliography of post-independence publications p.175-9. *Class No:* 967

[7802]
LOW, D.A. *and* SMITH, A., *eds.* **History of East Africa.** Oxford, Clarendon Press, 3v., 1963-76. xiii,500p. li,766p. xii,691p. tables, maps, bibliogs.

1 [to 1898], edited by R. Oliver and G. Matthew. 1963. 2 [from 1890s to close of world War II], edited by V. Harlow and E.M. Chilver. 1965. 3 [1945-1963], edited by D.A. Low and Alison Smith. 1976. V.1 (12 chapters; 10 contributors) 'directly surveys results of original research' (*Prefatory note*). Bibliographies, p.457-80; analytical index. While conceding that it is an indispensable work of reference, the reviewer in *Commonwealth Journal* (v.6,no.5, October 1963, p.218) complains of uneveness of treatment and lack of general maps. V.3 (14 chapters, footnoted) has 40p. of statistical tables and a select bibliography in 4 sections. Analytical index, p.665-91). Studied from an African as well as a European standpoint. *Class No:* 967

[7803]
WILLS, A.J. **An Introduction to the history of Central Africa** Zambia, Malawi, Zimbabwe. 4th ed. Oxford, Oxford Univ. Press, 1985. xix, 556p. maps, tables, bibliog., index. £22.50. ISBN: 0198730756.

First published 1964.

12 chapters covering the area's pre-colonial history; the period of settlement and colonization; white-colonial rule; with substantial treatment of the two decades since Zambia's independence and Rhodesia's Unilateral Declaration of Independence. This latest edition adds chapters on the struggle for the liberation of Zimbabwe. Notes p.500-520. Bibliography p.521-533. Analytical index. *Class No:* 967

Bibliographies

[7804]
OFCANSKY, T.P. **British East Africa 1850-1963:** an annotated bibliography. New York, Garland Publishing, 1985. xxiii, 474p. index. $66. ISBN: 0824091647.

3089 annotated entries divided under 19 headings - East Africa, Kenya, Uganda, Tanganyika, Zanzibar and subject headings *e.g.* East African campaign (1914-18); Agriculture; Indian community; Mau-Mau revolt. *Journal of African History*, v.29, no.1, 1988, p.142-3, is not favourably impessed: ' a sad example of what can happen when bibliography is not taken seriously.' *Class No:* 967(01)

Cameroon

[7805]
TAMBI EYONGETAH MBUAGBAW. **A History of the Cameroon.** 2nd ed. Harlow, Essex, Longman, 1987. vii,151p. maps, index. pbk. ISBN: 0582585260.

First published 1974.

....(contd.)

31 chronological chapters: 1. Geography and peoples - 2. The Carthaginian 'discovery' of Cameroon... 30. Cameroon under Ahidjo - 31. Cameroon and the 'New Deal'. 11 maps. Student textbook. *Class No:* 967.11

Dictionaries

[7806]
DE LANCEY, M.W. *and* MOKEBA, H.B. **Historical dictionary of the Republic of Cameroon.** 2nd ed. Metuchen, New Jersey, Scarecrow Press, 1990. xxii,297p. maps, bibliog. £28.15. (*African Historical Dictionaries, no.48.*) ISBN: 0810823705.

Replaces V.T. Le Vine and R.P. Nye's *Historical dictionary of Cameroon* (1974) the 1st volume in the African Historical Dictionaries series.

Chronology p.xv-xxii. Dictionary p.13-212. Bibliography p.213-97. *Class No:* 967.11(038)

Equatorial Guinea

Dictionaries

[7807]
LINIGER-GOUMAZ, M. **Historical dictionary of Equatorial Guinea.** 2nd ed. Metuchen, New Jersey, Scarecrow Press, 1988. xxx, 238p. bibliog. £24. $24. (*African Historical Dictionaries, no.21.*) ISBN: 0810821206.

1st ed. 1979.

Note on place-names p.ix-x. Chronology p.xiii-xxvi. Dictionary p.1-192. Bibliography p.193-238. 'Essential for African studies programs and recommended for university, college, and larger public libraries' *Choice*, v.26, no.9, May 1989, p.1496). *Class No:* 967.18(038)

Gabon

Dictionaries

[7808]
GARDINIER, D.E. **Historical dictionary of Gabon.** Metuchen, New Jersey, Scarecrow Press, 1981. xxvii, 254p. maps, tables, bibliography. £24. $24. (*African Historical Dictionaries, no.30.*) ISBN: 0810814358.

Chronology p.xiv-xx. Dictionary p.22-197. Bibliography p.198-254. 'Particularly useful are references following the dictionary entries to citations in the bibliography for further information' (*Choice*, v.19, no.9, May 1982, p.1215). *Class No:* 967.21(038)

Congo

Dictionaries

[7809]
THOMPSON, V. *and* ADLOFF, R. **Historical dictionary of the People's Republic of The Congo.** 2nd ed. Metuchen, New Jersey, Scarecrow Press, 1984. xxi, 239p. maps, bibliog. £22. $22.50. (*African Historical Dictionaries, no.2.*) ISBN: 0810817160.

1st ed. 1974.

Recent chronology p.xv. Dictionary p.33-228. Bibliography p.229-39. *Class No:* 967.24(038)

Angola

Dictionaries

[7810]
MARTIN, P.M. *and* BROADHEAD, S.H., *reviser*.
Historical dictionary of Angola. 2nd ed. Metuchen, New
Jersey, Scarecrow Press, 1980. 344p. maps, bibliog., tables,
index. £29.65. (*African Historical Dictionaries, no.26.*)
ISBN: 0810825325.
Chronology. Dictionary. Bibliography. 'A useful little
book ... the select unannotated bibliography is most welcome
as there had not been a general bibliography of Angola since
1912' (*Journal of African History*, v.22, no.4, 1981, p.578).
Class No: 967.3(038)

Central African Republic

[7811]
KALCK, P. **Historical dictionary of The Central African
Republic.** Metuchen, New Jersey, Scarecrow Press, 1980.
xlii, 152p. map. bibliog. $19.50. (*African Historical
Dictionaries, no.27.*) ISBN: 0810813602.
Heads of government p.xxi-xxiii. Chronology p.xxiv-xli.
Dictionary p.1-135. Bibliography p.137-152. 5 maps.
Class No: 967.41

Chad

Dictionaries

[7812]
DECALO, S. **Historical dictionary of Chad.** 2nd ed.
Metuchen, New Jersey, Scarecrow Press, 1987. xxxvi,
532p. maps, tables, bibliog. £35.60. $47.50. (*African
Historical Dictionaries, no.13.*) ISBN: 0810819376.
1st ed. 1976.
Chronology p.xvi-xxii. Dictionary p.21-338. Bibliography
p.339-532. 12 tables. 7 maps. 'A major new edition ...
essential for African studies programs' (*Choice*, v.25,
no.11/12, July/August 1988, p.1672).
Class No: 967.43(038)

Zaire

Dictionaries

[7813]
BOBB, F.S. **Historical dictionary of Zaire.** Metuchen, New
Jersey, Scarecrow Press, 1988. xxxiv, 349p., map, tables,
bibliog. £28.15. $37.50. (*African Historical Dictionaries,
no.43.*) ISBN: 0810821095.
Chronology p.xiii-xix. Guide to format and current names
p.xxi. Dictionary p.13-232. Bibliography p.233-349. 'Not
nearly so comprehensive as it should be' (*Choice*, v.26,
no.11/12, July/August 1989, p.1808). *Class No:* 967.5(038)

Burundi

Dictionaries

[7814]
WEINSTEIN, W. **Historical dictionary of Burundi.**
Metuchen, New Jersey, Scarecrow Press, 1976. xvii, 368p.
£30. (*African Historical Dictionaries, no.8.*) ISBN:

.... (contd.)
0810809621.
Chronology p.1-62. Dictionary p.63-287. Bibliography
p.289-368. *Class No:* 967.597(038)

Uganda

Bibliographies

[7815]
GERTZEL, C. **Uganda:** an annotated bibliography of source
materials (with particular reference to the period since 1971
and up to 1988). London, Hans Zell, 1991. x,288p. index.
£39; $90. ISBN: 0905450833.
2062 entries muster under 11 form and subject headings to
provide a comprehensive guide to recent Ugandan history
and politics. An extensive bibliographical essay (p.1-24)
outlines how to use the Bibliography and introduces the
sources available for research. *Class No:* 967.61(01)

Kenya

[7816]
OCHIENG, W.R., *ed.* **A Modern history of Kenya 1895-
1980.** London, Evans, 1989. v,259p. tables, bibliog., index.
ISBN: 0237510820.
8 essays by independent hands each dealing with
consecutive discrete periods: 1. Conquest state - 2.
Establishment of colonial rule 1905-1920 ... 7. Independent
Kenya 1963-1986. Published to coincide with 60th birthday
of B.A. Ogot, Kenya's senior historian. *Class No:* 967.62

[7817]
OCHIENG', W.R., *ed*. **Themes in Kenyan history.** Nairobi,
Heinemann Kenya; London, James Currey; Athens, Ohio
Univ. Press, 1990. vii,261p. map, bibliogs., index. pbk.
£9.95. ISBN: 0852550731, UK; 0821409778, US.
16 contributors. Interdisciplinary exposition in 20 well-
documented chapters *e.g.* Migrations and emergence of
societies ... Urbanization ... Government ... Trade since
early times ... Nationalism and decolonization ... Diplomacy
and international relations. *Class No:* 967.62

Dictionaries

[7818]
OGOT, B.A. **Historical dictionary of Kenya.** Metuchen,
New Jersey, Scarecrow Press, 1987. xviii, 279p. map,
bibliog. £24. (*African Historical Dictionaries, no.29.*) ISBN:
0810814196.
Chronology p.iv-xvi. Dictionary p.9-218. Bibliography
p.219-76. Appendix A. Commissioners and Governors
1895-1963. 'Of especial interest are the short biographies of
leading personalities in post-independence Kenya' (*Journal
of African History*, v.23, no.3, 1982, p.431).
Class No: 967.62(038)

Somalia

[7819]
LEWIS, J.M. **A Modern history of Somalia** nation and state
in the Horn of Africa. London, Longman, 1980. ix, 279p.
maps, index, pbk. £4.50. ISBN: 058264657x.
1st 8 chapters first published as *The modern history of
Somaliland from nation to state* (Weidenfeld & Nicolson,

....*(contd.)*
1965).

2 new chapters: 9. The Somali revolution 1969-76 - 10. Nationalism, ethnicity and revolution in the Horn of Africa, take the story up to 1978. Chapter notes p.256-272. 3 maps. Analytical index. *Class No:* 967.7

Dictionaries

[7820]

CASTAGNO, M. Historical dictionary of Somalia. Metuchen, New Jersey, Scarecrow Press, 1975. xxviii, 213p. map. bibliog. £24. $24. (*African Historical Dictionaries, no.6.*) ISBN: 0810808307.

Chronology, p.xxiv-xxviii. Dictionary p.1-164. Bibliography p.165-213. *Class No:* 967.7(038)

Tanzania (Tanganyika)

[7821]

YEAGER, R. Tanzania: an African experiment. Boulder, Colorado, Westview Press; Aldershot, Hampshire, Gower, 1982. xii, 136p. illus., map, tables, bibliog., index. £18.50 $31.50. (*Profiles: Nations of Contemporary Africa.*) ISBN: 0891589236, US; 0566005549, UK.

7 chapters: 1. The origins of Tanzania - 2. The ecology of change - 3. The ambiguities of independence - 4. Towards Socialism and democracy - 5. Towards socialism and self-reliance - 6. International leadership and dependence - 7. Assessing the Tanzanian experiment. Bibliography p.127-130. 'Essential reading for all those interested in understanding the recent African past' (*Choice*, v.20, no.3, November 1982, p.483). *Class No:* 967.8

Bibliographies

[7822]

ROBERTS, A. 'A Bibliography of primary sources for Tanzania 1799-1899', *Tanzania Notes and Records*, v.73, 1974, p.65-92.

424 items recorded-mostly 19th century travellers' accounts. 'A very useful and important compilation' (C. Darch. *Tanzania*, 1985. Entry 670). *Class No:* 967.8(01)

Dictionaries

[7823]

KURTZ, L.S. Historical dictionary of Tanzania. Metuchen, New Jersey, Scarecrow Press, 1978. xxxi, 331p. maps, bibliog. £30. (*African Historical Dictionaries, no.15.*) ISBN: 0810811014.

Rulers of Tanganyika, Zanzibar and Tanzania p.x-xiii. Chronology p.xiv-xxiii. Dictionary p.1-254. Bibliography p.255-331. 'Written so crudely and naively and with so little regard for modern scholarship, as to defy mere tinkering' (*Journal of African History*, v.23, no.1, 1982, p.139. *Class No:* 967.8(038)

Mozambique

[7824]

HENRIKSEN, T.H. Mozambique: a history. London, Rex Collings; Cape Town, David Philip, 1978. xi, 276p. maps, index. £13.50. ISBN: 0860360172.

....*(contd.)*

2 Parts (10 chapters): 1. Invasions and empires - 2. Colonialism and nationalism. Chapter notes p.233-246. Emphasis on period after 1900. *Class No:* 967.9

[7825]

História de Moçambique. Maputo, Departmento de História, Univ. Eduardo Mondlane, 4v., 1982 - .

1. 159p. 2. 336p. Imperialist aggression 1886-1930. 3. (Covers period 1930-1962) 4. História da luta Armada de Libertação Nacional. 'The first consistent attempt at a Marxist interpretation of Mozambiqan history, and highly recommended' (C. Darch. *Mozambique*, 1987. Entry 140). *Class No:* 967.9

Dictionaries

[7826]

AZEVEDO, M. Historical dictionary of Mozambique. Metuchen, NJ., Scarecrow Press, 1991. xxx,250p. map, tables, bibliog., index. £22.15. (*African Historical Dictionaries, no. 47.*) ISBN: 0810824132.

Brief essays on significant people, events, institutions, and places *etc.* in Mozambique's history. Introduction (location, climate, physical features, population, history) p.1-28. Dictionary p.19-131. Bibliography (in 12 sections) p.132-230. Chronology p.xiii-xxiii. *Class No:* 967.9(038)

Africa—Southern

[7827]

OMER-COOPER, J.D. History of Southern Africa. London, James Currey; Portsmouth, New Hampshire, Heinemann Educational Books Inc., 1987. xiii, 298p. illus., maps, bibliog., index. £25. $20. ISBN: 0852550103, UK; 0435080105, US.

9 chapters: 1. The Khoisan people and Bantu-speaking settlement ... 4. The mass migration of the mfecane & the Great Trek ... 9. The three phases of apartheid. Appendix 1. The enclave states Lesotho, Swaziland and Botswana. 2. Namibia. Bibliography (by chapter) p.278-285. Analytical index. 'The most important theme is the historical explanation of that peculiar system of systematic racial discrimination, repression and exploitation known as apartheid'. *Class No:* 968

Bibliographies

[7828]

KALLEY, J.A. The Transkei region of Southern Africa 1877-1978: an annotated bibliography. Boston, G.K. Hall, 1980. xxii, 218p. maps on endpapers. index.

Expanded, updated, and annotated version of the compiler's *Transkei bibliography 1945 to independence* published by the South African Institute of International Affairs (1976).

1439 items arranged in 22 broad subject sections: B. Bibliographers ... C. Biographies ... 17. History and archaeology ... R. Official publications of the Cape of Good Hope colony (reproduced from Reuben Musiker's *Guide to Cape of Good Hope publications 1854-1910* published in 1976). Author and subject indexes. *Class No:* 968(01)

[7829]
THOMPSON, L., *and others*. **Southern African history before 1900** a select bibliography of articles. Stanford, California, Hoover Institution Press, Stanford Univ., 1971. xii, 102p. ISBN: 817924914.

1,136 unannotated items, in 26 main sections (1. Historiography and methodology - 2. Archives, bibliographies and other sources ... 4. Archaeology ... 10. The Bantu-speaking peoples of Southern Africa ... 20. The Transvaal, 1852-1899 ... 23. Rhodesia ... 24. The Indians - 25. British imperial policy in Southern Africa (nos. 1093-1133) - 26. German imperial policy in Southern Africa). Draws on 31 journals. 'This is a select bibliography, designed by historians for historians' (*Preface*). *Class No:* 968(01)

South Africa

[7830]
DAVENPORT, T.R.H. **South Africa** a modern history. 4th ed. London, Macmillan, 1991. xxv, 662p. illus., maps, tables, bibliog., index. £35. ISBN: 0333550331.

1st ed. 1977; 3rd ed. 1987.

20 subdivided chapters in 3 parts: 1. Prelude to white dominion - 2. Consolidation of a White state - 3. Political economy of South Africa. This edition incorporates revised material on South African prehistory and focuses 'on the rapidly changing socio-economic and political scene since the mid-term crisis of P.W. Botha's Government'. Appendix: Heads of State 1652-1990 p.558-63. Bibliographical Notes (by chapter) p.568-613. *Class No:* 968.0

[7831]
FEBRUARY, V. **The Afrikaners of South Africa.** London, Kegan Paul International, 1991. x, 296p. illus., maps, tables, bibliog., index. £35. (*Monographs from the African Studies Centre Leiden.*) ISBN: 071030353x.

Narrative political and cultural history in 6 chapters: 1. From 'Dietsman' to 'Duusman' ... 5. The Herren (Volk) and the 'Volkies' ... Postscript: The monolith under pressure. Chapter notes p.249-73. Bibliography p.274-8. 4 maps. *Class No:* 968.0

[7832]
Reader's Digest illustrated history of South Africa. Oakes, D., *ed.* 2nd ed. Cape Town, Reader's Digest, 1989. 485p. illus., maps, tables, bibliog., index.

1st ed. 1988.

Reliable history of South Africa. L.Witz and C. Hamiltons' 'Reaping the whirlwind'. *South African Historical Journal,* no.24, May 1991, p.185-202 explores some of the issues raised by the public demand for non-apartheid history, traces the circumstances which created the market for this particular title, and why it hs proved more successful than similar ventures. *Class No:* 968.0

[7833]
THEAL, G.M. **History of South Africa south of Zambesi** from earliest times to 1884. London, F. Cass, 11v., 1969. £45.00. ISBN: 0714625647.

Published in 5v. by Swan and Sonnenschein 1888-93; in 8v. 1907-10; and in 11v. by Allen and Unwin 1919-1926.

1: *Ethnography and conditions of South Africa before 1505.*

2-4: *History of South Africa before 1795.*

5-9: *History of South Africa since 1795.*

10-11: *History of South Africa, 1873-1884.*

....(contd.)

'By far the most comprehensive and minute history of South Africa, with pro-Boer bias. A monumental work based on wide research among original documents, etc.' (Sonnenschein, W.S. *Best books,* v.3., p.1505). 'A pioneering work of the chronicle type' (Musiker, R. *Guide to South Africa reference books* (4th ed., 1971), entry no.553). *Class No:* 968.0

Bibliographies

[7834]
COETZER, P.W. *and* LE ROUX, J.H., *comps.* **General sources on South African political history since 1902.** Boston, G.K. Hall, 1979. xi, 763p. $75.00. ISBN: 0816182450.

Articles in periodical publications grouped in 20 sections *e.g.* 16. History ... 18. South West Africa/Namibia... 19. World Wars I & II ... 17. Race relations/United Nations Organization/Policy of separate development. *Class No:* 968.0(01)

[7835]
—COETZER, P.W. *and* LE ROUX, J.H., *eds.* **Index to periodical articles on South African political and social history since 1902.** Boston, G.K. Hall, 1982. xx, 616p. $69.96.

Index by subjects of 19,000 articles in 850 international journals. *Class No:* 968.0(01)

[7836]
—GEYSER, O., *and others.* Register of private document collections on the political history of South Africa since 1902. Boston, G.K. Hall, 1979. xx, 150p. index. ISBN: 0816182442.

Description, location and access details A-Z by owner of collection. Development of archive services in South Africa in the twentieth century p.xv-xvi. *Class No:* 968.0(01)

[7837]
MULLER, C.F.J., *and others eds.* **A Select bibliography of South African history** a guide for historical research. Pretoria, Univ. of South Africa, 1966. Supplement 1974. xi, 215p.

Main work has 2,521 numbered entries, sometimes annotated, for books only. 31 sections in 3 parts: 1. General (section 1: Aids to research - bibliographies; guides to archival and other sources; historiography; etc.) - 2. Periods (sections 4-16) - 3. Subjects (sections 17-31, including biographies and autobiographies). Authors' index; index to persons mentioned in titles, biographies and autobiographies. *Supplement* adds 1,400 entries. 'The edition of 1966 and its supplements remain of value' (*Introduction to South African history and historians,* 1979). *Class No:* 968.0(01)

[7838]
—MULLER, C.F.J., *and others eds.* South African history and historians : a bibliography. Pretoria, Univ. of South Africa, 1979. xv, 411p. indexes. ISBN: 0869811584.

Preceded by *A select bibliography of South African history* (1966); its *Supplement* (1974); and updated material in *Kleio* (1974-76).

4518 unannotated entries organized in 3 parts (31 sections): 1. General (Aids to research; Historiography; General histories) - 2. Periods (*e.g.* Prehistory ... Exploration ... The Great Trek) - 3. Subjects (*e.g.* South Africa in Southern Africa ... The Blacks, Coloured and

....(contd.)

Asian peoples of South Africa ... Local history - Biographies and autobiographies). 'Not merely a compilation brought up to date ... some material, earlier rejected, now finds a place; much that was previously included has for various reasons been omitted from this selection' (*Introduction*).
Class No: 968.0(01)

[7839]
MUSIKER, N. **South African history:** a bibliographical guide with special reference to territorial expansion and colonization. New York, Garland Publishing Inc., 1984. xxix, 297p. index. $84. (*Themes in European Expansion.*) ISBN: 0824091744.

1028 items, focussing on 'the fabric of South African history as the term is generally understood', with descriptive and evaluative annotations, drawn up in 18 chronological and geographical sections: 2. Travel and exploration ... 4. Cape general history ... 6. Zululand ... 12. South Africa 1910-1980. Author-title and subject-topographical indexes.
Class No: 968.0(01)

[7840]
SCHOEMAN, K., *comp*. **Bibliography of the Orange Free State until 31 May 1910.** Cape Town, South African Library, 1984. xvi, 227p.

2500 titles covering historical, political, economic and cultural developments grouped in 17 sections (sub-divided) 1. Reference works ... 2A. Early history and archaeology ... 11. Local history. 'A thoroughly researched and valuable compilation' (*African Research and Documentation*, no.39, 1985, p.28). *Class No:* 968.0(01)

Dictionaries

[7841]
SAUNDERS, C. **Historical dictionary of South Africa.** Metuchen, New Jersey, Scarecrow Press, 1983. xxviii, 241p. map, bibliog., indexes. £22.80. $25. (*African Historical Dictionaries, no.37.*) ISBN: 0810816296.

Chronology p.xiii-xxvi. Dictionary p.5-196. Bibliography p.197-234. 'One of the most interesting and well-organized titles in the series' (*Choice*, v.21, no.7, March 1984, p.958). *Class No:* 968.0(038)

Botswana

Dictionaries

[7842]
MORTON, F., *and others*. **Historical dictionary of Botswana.** Metuchen, New Jersey, Scarecrow Press, 1990. xx, 216p. bibliog. maps. £28.05. (*African Historical Dictionaries, no.40.*) ISBN: 0810822245.

Replaces R.P. Stephens *Historical dictionary of the Republic of Botswana* (African Historical Dictionaries, no.5).

Dictionary of persons and institutions, geographical and historical features and events *etc*. Chronology p.xiii-xvi. Note on African languages and glossary p.xvii-xviii. Dictionary p.1-141. Bibliography p.143-216. 5 maps.
Class No: 968.1(038)

Swaziland

Dictionaries

[7843]
GROTPETER, J.J. **Historical dictionary of Swaziland.** Metuchen, New Jersey, 1975. xiv, 251p. map. bibliog. £24. (*African Historical Dictionaries, no.3.*) ISBN: 0810808056.

Dictionary p.1-194. Bibliography p.195-243. Appendix A. A chronology of some important dates for Swaziland p.244-249 - B. Kings of Swaziland p.250. *Class No:* 968.34(038)

Lesotho

Dictionaries

[7844]
HALIBURTON, G. **Historical dictionary of Lesotho.** Metuchen, New Jersey, Scarecrow Press, 1977. xxxv, 223p. maps, geneal. tables, bibliog. £24. $24. (*African Historical Dicitonaries, no.10.*) ISBN: 0810809931.

Chronology p.xii-xvii. Dictionary p.1-184. Bibliography p.185-223. 3 maps. *Class No:* 968.61(038)

Namibia

[7845]
'**Namibia: the making of a new nation'**, *United Nations Chronicle*, v.26, no.1, March 1989, p.34-48.
Class No: 968.8

Bibliographies

[7846]
SCHOEMAN, E. **The Namibian issue 1920-1930:** a select and annotated bibliography. Boston, Mass., G.K. Hall, 1982. xxix,247p. index. $38.

1489 items in many European languages and Afrikaans including 175 United Nations General Assembly and Security Council resolutions, and a very useful Chronology of Namibian events. 'Any university or research library needs this superb reference work, which has few, if any equals' (*Africana Journal*, v.14, no.4, 1987, p.360-1).
Class No: 968.8(01)

Zimbabwe

Bibliographies

[7847]
DORO, M.E. **Rhodesia/Zimbabwe:** a bibliographic guide to the nationalist period. Boston, G.K. Hall & Co., 1984. xvi,247p. index. $55.00. (*A Reference Publication in African Studies.*) ISBN: 0816182752.

A guide to the research resources relating to Zimbabwe's history 1960-1980 divided into 4 major units: Reference sources; Socioeconomic and political context; the U.D.I. era; and United States foreign policy. 'An extremely thorough examination of the subject ... useful as a contribution to historiography as well as bibliography' (*African Research Documentation*, no.40, 1984, p.27).
Class No: 968.91(01)

Dictionaries

[7848]

RASMUSSEN, R.K. *and* RUBERT, S.C. **Historical dictionary of Zimbabwe.** 2nd ed. Metuchen, New Jersey, Scarecrow Press, 1990. xxxv,502p. maps, bibliog. $55; £41.25 (*African Historical Dictionaries no.18.*) ISBN: 0810823373.

First published as *Historical dictionary of Rhodesia/ Zimbabwe* (1979).

Chronology. Dictionary. Bibliography. A major revision with a large number of new entries reflecting independence from colonial rule. A systematic and generally reliable work of reference' (*Journal of African History*, v.,23, no.1, 1982, p.140). *Class No:* 968.91(038)

Zambia

[7849]

ROBERTS, A. **A History of Zambia.** London, Heinemann Educational, 1977. xx,288, viip. illus., ports., maps. ISBN: 043594245x.

Ranges from the pre-colonial period up to the end of the first decade of independence (1974). 12 chapters: 1. The natural setting ... 3/4. The Iron Age - 5. The peoples of Zambia, *c.* 1500-*c.*1700 ... 8. African intruders, *c.*1840-*c.*1890 - 9. The British take over, *c.*1800-1900 ... 10. Ten years of independence, 1964-1974. Bibliography, p.256-79. Index. 'As a survey of Zambian history this scholarly work has no serious rival' (*British Book News*, July 1977, p.574). *Class No:* 968.94

Dictionaries

[7850]

GROTPETER, J.J. **Historical dictionary of Zambia.** Metuchen, New Jersey, Scarecrow Press, 1979. xviii,410p. map, bibliog. £36.00. (*African Historical Dictionaries, no.19.*)

Chronology p.x-xviii. Dictionary p.1-341. Bibliography p.344-410. *Class No:* 968.94(038)

Malawi

Dictionaries

[7851]

CROSBY, C.A. **Historical dictionary of Malawi.** Metuchen, New Jersey, Scarecrow Press, 1980. xxxvi, 169p. map. bibliog. £24. $24. (*African Historical Dictionaries, no.25.*) ISBN: 0810812878.

Chronology p.xi-xvii. Dictionary p.1-118. Bibliography p.119-169. *Class No:* 968.97(038)

Comoro Islands

[7852]

NEWITT, M. **The Comoro Islands** struggle against dependency in the Indian Ocean. Boulder, Colorado, Westview Press; London, Gower, 1984. x, 144p. illus., map, bibliog, index. £19.50. $31.50. (*Profiles: nations of contemporary Africa.*) ISBN: 0865312923, US; 056600545x, UK.

Well documented overview of geography, history, politics, society, economy, and foreign relations. Bibliographical essay p.131-4. Analytical index. *Class No:* 969.41

Seychelles

[7853]

FRANDA, M. **The Seychelles:** unquiet islands. Boulder, Colorado, Westview Press; Aldershot, Hampshire, Gower, 1982. 140p. illus., maps, bibliog., index. £19.50. $28.50. (*Profiles. Nations of Contemporary Africa.*) ISBN: 0865312664, US; 90566005522, UK.

5 chapters (History, People, Politics, Economy, Change). Extensive chapter notes and Bibliography p.129. Despite some weaknesses, a limited bibliography, and an inadequate index, *Choice*, v.20, no.6, February 1983, p.873-874 concludes that 'there is no better modern introduction to the Seychelles'. *Class No:* 969.6

Mauritius

Dictionaries

[7854]

SELVON, S. **Historical dictionary of Mauritius.** 2nd ed. Metuchen, New Jersey, Scarecrow Press, 1992. xl,253p. map, tables, bibliog. £26.25; $20.00. (*African Historical Dictionaries, no.49.*) ISBN: 0810824809.

First published (L. Riviere as author) 1982.

Chronology of major events. Dictionary. Bibliography. *Class No:* 969.82(038)

America

[7855]

FAGAN, B.F. **Kingdoms of gold, Kingdoms of jade** The Americas before Columbus. London, Thames and Hudson, 1991. 240p. illus. (some col.) maps, bibliog., index. £16.95. ISBN: 050005062.

Splendidly illustrated chronological narrative of rise and fall of American pre-Columbian civilizations. 14 chapters grouped in 5 parts: 1. Civilizations of 1492 - 2. First Americans - 3. Civilizations of ancient Mesoamerica - 4. Civilizations of the Andes - 5. Chiefdoms of North America. Bibliography (by chapter) p.230-4. *Class No:* 97

[7856]

FINGERHUT, E.R. **Who first discovered America?** a critique of writings on pre-Columbian voyages. Claremont, California, Regina Books 1984. viii,147p. maps, bibliogs., index. $17.95. (*Guides to Historical Issues, no.1.*) ISBN: 0941690105.

Historiographic study in 9 chapters: Pt.1. The travelers: 1. Prehistoric and ancient Atlantic travelers - 2. Transatlantic contacts between medieval Europe and North America - 3. Norse expeditions to North America - 4/5. Transpacific contacts with America - 6. Sub-Sahara Africa connection with the New World. Pt.2 Transocean cultural diffusion vs. independent development. 7. Basic issues - 8. Biological evidence and claims of Pre-Columbian contact across the oceans - 9. Summary. Bibliographical sections list nearly 450 modern references. *Class No:* 97

Bibliographies

[7857]

Columbus literature guides.

1. Metz, A. 'Christopher Columbus: a selection guide to literature 1970-1989', *Reference Services Review*, v.19, no.4, 1991, p.21-44. 91 annotated entries arranged in 5 sub-divided parts: 1. European intellectual background - 2.

....(contd.)

Exploration - 3. Christopher Columbus - 4. Conquest and colonization - 5. Miscellaneous (Heraldry; Quincentennial).

2. Fialkoff, F. and De Candido, K. 'Rediscovering Columbus', *Library Journal*, v.116, no.13, August 1991, p.120-2. Literature review of books to be published in 1991 Fall season.

3. 'Dealing with Columbus', *Booklist*, v.88, no.4, 15 Oct 1991. p.369-80. 'A valid overview of how Columbus and his voyages have been read and misread over several centuries.

2. Shreve, J. 'Christopher Columbus: a bibliographic voyage', *Choice*, v.29, no.5, January 1992, p.703-11. Bibliographical essay assessing the books 'felt to have worth as potential additions to American collections arranged in 9 sections. Biographies - Language of Columbus - Family - Columbus' log and other writings - Toscanelli Letter - Landfall and other murky waters - Reference works - Other books - Poetry and fiction. Consolidated list of works cited p.709-11.

3. French and Spanish language material is considered in 'Les éditeurs sur les pas de Christophe Colomb', *Livres hebdo*, v.13, no.20, 17 Mai 1991, p.57-60.
Class No: 97(01)

[7858]
NEW YORK PUBLIC LIBRARY. Reference Department. **Dictionary catalog of the History of the Americas Collection.** Boston, Mass., G.K. Hall, 28v., 1960-61. First Supplement 9v., 1974. 26398p.+6871p. $2290.00 (Export $2770) and $985.00 ($1190.00). ISBN: 081610540, 28v. set.

A photolitho reproduction of the original dictionary catalogue cards, including Library of Congress printed cards, handwritten entries, etc. Headings are only legible with difficulty. Entries cover many articles in learned periodicals. Entries under some headings are very extensive (*e.g.* 'Folklore', p.7255-7336). 'Essentially a series of bibliographies', states the *Introduction*, which notes the material brought together under 'American languages', 'Indians, North America', 'Indians, South America', 'Pioneer life', 'US-Foreign relations', 'Irish in the US', 'Germans in the US', 'Cuba', 'Mexico', etc. There are 144 entries under 'Dwight Eisenhower', entries under 'Brazil' occupy p.2658-2821; entries under 'Cuba', p.5516-5617.
Class No: 97(01)

[7859]
NEWBERRY LIBRARY. Chicago. **Dictionary catalog of the Edward E. Ayer Collection of America and American Indians.** Boston, Mass., G.K. Hall, 16v., 1961. First Supplement, 3v., 1970. Second Supplement, 4v., 1980.

Catalog (1961) available on microfilm by request. $1165.00 (Export $1281.00). *First Supplement.* 2017p. $330.00 ($400.00). ISBN 0816108102. *Second Supplement.* 2705p. $365.00 ($440.00). ISBN 0816103259. A total of 267,700 catalogue cards photolithographed. The main fields are: 1) the Indian of the Americas from prehistory and archaeology to modern studies in ethnology and anthropology; 2) the contact of the white man with native tribes, including eighteenth and nineteenth-century books of travel and description which mention Indians; 3) voyages and travels during the period of exploration and early settlement; 4) cartography, especially from the fifteenth century through the eighteenth century; and 5) Hawaii, the Philippines, and adjacent Oceania. *Class No:* 97(01)

[7860]
PROVOST, F. Columbus an annotated guide to the scholarship on his life and writings 1750-1988. Detroit, Omnigraphics, 1991. xxxii,225p. indexes. $48.

Continues Columbus references in *European America: a chronological guide to works printed in Europe relating to the Americas 1493-1750* (6v., 1980-).

780 items in 7 sections: 1. Collections of sources, texts and studies - 2/3. Primary documents - 4. Life - 5. Columbiana - 6. Bibliographies - 7. Columbus scholarship. 'Gives easy access to nearly every aspect of Columbus and his enterprise in a usable format with every entry annotated' (*William and Mary Quarterly*, 3rd ser, v.49, no.2, April 1992, p.254).

Supplementing this Guide, Provost's *Columbus dictionary* (Omnigraphics, 1991. 142p. bibliog refs. $75. ISBN 1558881581) includes entries for persons, places, and events associated with Columbus' voyages. *Class No:* 97(01)

Encyclopaedias
[7861]
The Christopher Columbus encyclopedia. Bedini, S.A., ed. New York, Simon & Schuster, 1991; London, Macmillan, 2v., 1992. xxii,787p. illus., maps, ports. $175. £95. ISBN: 0131426621, US; 033358995, UK.

About 350 signed A-Z articles (350-10,000 words) from over 150 contributors on Columbus' life; the contemporary world (social, political, economic and cultural institutions of Europe, biographies of reigning monarchs); Pre-Columbian exploration and discovery; Science and technology of discovery; The New World (archaeology, settlements, natural history); and Post-Columbian exploration and discovery. Issues raised are discussed both from the indigenous and European viewpoint. Published to mark the quincentenary of Columbus' first voyage to America in 1492. 'Will remain a useful reference source long after the quincentenary is over' (*Booklist*, v.88, no.4, 15 Oct 1991, p.379). *Class No:* 97(031)

Maps & Atlases
[7862]
GREAT BRITAIN. Public Record Office. **Maps and plans in the Public Record Office. America and West Indies.** Penfold, P.A. London H.M. Stationery Office, 1975. xv,835p. £18.00. ISBN: 0114400539.

Inventory of 4,493 items, plus interpolations. 6 sections: 1. America, North America, Atlantic Ocean, Greenland - 2. Canada (nos. 143-1986) - 3. United States of America (nos.1987-2952) - 4. West Indies - 5. Mexico, Central America - 6. South America (nos.4081-446). Data: Title; date; description; nature (*e.g.* manuscript; slightly coloured); scale; compass indicator; location in PRO). Range is from large area maps to plans of buildings. Index of persons, 'but not of place-names and subjects of major interest' (*British Book News*, October 1975.p.698). *Class No:* 97(084.3)

America—North & Central
[7863]
New American world a documentary history of North America to 1612. Quinn, D.B., *ed.* London, Macmillan, 5v., 1979. maps, bibliog., index. £295.00 boxed set. ISBN: 0333263839, set.

....(contd.)

1. *America from concept to discovery. Early exploration of North America.* xxxvii,486p.+[70]p. ISBN 0333263847. 68 maps.

2. *Major Spanish searches in Eastern North America. The Franco-Spanish clash in Florida. The beginnings of Spanish Florida.* xxiv,594p.+[19]p. ISBN 0333263855. 19 maps.

3. *English plans for North America. The Roanoke voyages. New England ventures.* xxvi,494p.+[22]p. ISBN 0333263863. 25 maps.

4. *Newfoundlands from fishery to colony. Northwest Passage searches.* xxvi,454p.+[14]p. ISBN 03332638781. 16 maps.

5. *The extension of settlement in Florida, Virginia, and the Spanish southwest.* xxvi,490p.+[22]p. ISBN 0333263898. Bibliography p.513-28. Index p.531-72. 20 maps.

In all 851 documents in English or in English translation are printed with 148 maps. 'Must immediately become an indispensable tool for most libraries' (*TLS*, 2 May 1980).
Class No: 971/973

Maps & Atlases

[7864]
From sea charts to satellite images interpreting North American history through maps. Buisseret, D., *ed.* Chicago, Univ. of Chicago Press 1990. xvi,324p. illus. (some col.), maps, index. ISBN: 0226079929.

A collection of 12 essays, by 10 different hands: 1. European antecedents of New World maps - 2. Maps of the age of European exploration ... 7. City maps and plans - 8. North American county maps and atlases ... 10. Topographical surveys of the United States - 11. Twentieth-century highway maps. Glossary p.317-8. 'Each chapter begins with a general survey of the nature and history of the type of map in question, goes on to give eight or ten commentated examples ... of the way such maps can be used by historians, and concludes with a section on how to find this material' (*Preface*). *Class No: 971/973(084.3)*

Biographies

Bibliographies

[7865]
People in history an index to US and Canadian biographies in history journals and dissertations. Kinnell, S., *ed.* Santa Barbara, California, and Oxford, ABC-Clio, 2v., 1988. $137.00; £103.75. ISBN: 0874364930, set.

Guide to biographical material relating to 6,000 individuals prominent in American history extracted from 737 journals on the ABC-Clio database. An extensive subject index allows access by a number of descriptors.
Class No: 971/973(092)(01)

Canada

[7866]
Chronicle of Canada. Montreal, Chronicle Publications, 1990. 980p. col. illus., col. maps. £29.95. ISBN: 0920417176.

Concise popular newspaper style articles and datelines on Canadian history in 6 chronological sections: 1. New World BC 4.6 million to 1607 - 2. Foundations 1608 to 1763 - 3.

....(contd.)

Conquest and change 1764 to 1867 - 4. Nation building 1867 to 1913 -5. War and peace 1914 to 1945 - 6. Canada comes of age 1945 to 1989. *Class No: 971*

[7867]
Generations: A history of Canada's peoples. Toronto, McClelland & Stewart in association with the Multiculturalism Directorate, Department of the Secretary of State and the Canadian Government Publishing Centre, Supply and Services Canada, 1980-.

1. *An olive branch on the family tree. The Arabs in Canada.* by B. Abu-Laban. 1980. vii,259p. 2. *The Canadian odyssey, the Greek experience in Canada* by P.D. Chimbos. 1980. ix,176p. 3. *From fjord to frontier. A history of the Norwegians in Canada.* by G. Loken. 1980. viii,264p. 4. *Struggle and hope: the Hungarian-Canadian experience.* by N.F. Dreisziger and others. 1982. viii,247p. 5. *A heritage in transition. Essays in the history of Ukranians in Canada.* by M.R. Lupul. 1982. viii,344p. 6. *For a better world: a history of the Croatians in Canada* by A.W. Rasporich. 1982. xiii,279p. 7. *From China to Canada. A history of the Chinese communities in Canada.* 1982. viii,369p. Readable histories of some of the many ethnic groups in contemporary Canada. *Class No: 971*

Bibliographies

[7868]
BEAULIEU, A., *and others*. Guide d'Histoire du Canada. Québec. Presses de l'Université Laval, 1969. xvi, 540p. (*Les Cahiers de l'Institut d'Histoire, no.13.*)

Based on A. Beaulieu's *Guide de l'etudiant en histoire du Canada.* Well-annotated entries for general reference works, MS and printed sources, maps and atlases, general, regional and specialised histories of Canada; historical auxiliary subjects; and relevant periodicals. *Class No: 971(01)*

[7869]
A Bibliography of Canadiana being items in the Metropolitan Toronto Library relating to the early history and development of Canada. Toronto, Metropolitan Toronto Library Board, 1934-.

V1. Staton, F.M. and Tremaine, M. eds., 1934. 828p. illus. 4646 numbered and annotated entries encompassing books, pamphlets and broadsides on Canada published 1534-1867. Author and selected subject indexes.

First supplement. Boyle, G.M. ed. 1959. 333p. A further 1640 entries.

Second supplement. Alston, S. ed. 1. *To 1800.* 2. *1801-1849.* 1985. 839p. 0887730299. Items 6800-8040 with Name, title, place of publication, printers, publishers, maps and plans, illustrations, and subject indexes. 3. *1850-1867.* 1985. 910p. 0887730299 Items 8041-9655. Bibliography p.27-34. Key to bibliographical sources p.19-25. *Second supplement* orders titles by imprint date, previously arrangement was by date of content significance. A bibliographical catalogue *par excellence* for researchers.
Class No: 971(01)

[7870]

GAGNON, P. **Essai de bibliographie Canadienne** inventaire d'une bibliothèque comprenant imprimés manuscrits, estampes etc. rélatifs à l'histoire du Canada et des pays adjacents avec des notes bibliographiques. New York, Irvington, 2v. vii, 711+462p. facsims. $90.00. ISBN: 0891977511, set; 0697000044, v.1; 0697000052, v.2.

V.1. originally published by the author 1895; v.2. by City of Montreal in 1913.

Definitive bibliography of Canadian history. V1. has 5018 items V2. *Collection Gagnon depuis 1895 à 1900 inclusivement, d'après les notes bibliographiques et le catalogue de l'auteur* is a supplement. *Class No:* 971(01)

[7871]

GLENBOW-ALBERTA INSTITUTE. Library, Calgary, Alberta. **Catalogue of the Glenbow Historical Library.** Boston, Mass., G.K. Hall, 4v., 1973. 3144p. $400.00 (Export $485.00). ISBN: 081610994x.

67000 photlithographed catalogue cards, classified by the Dewey Decimal Scheme. The Library concentrates mainly on the Canadian West, from Hudson's Bay to the Pacific. *Class No:* 971(01)

[7872]

A Reader's guide to Canadian history. Toronto, University of Toronto Press, 2v., 1982.

V2, is a revision of Granatstein's *Canada since 1867: a bibliographic guide* (2nd ed., 1977).

1. *Beginnings to Confederation* edited by D.A. Muise. 1982. xv, 253p. index. $12.95. 0802064426. 2. *Confederation to the present* edited by J.L. Granatstein and P. Stevens. xiv, 329p. index. $13.95. 0802064906. A literature survey composed of 19 chronological, thematic and geographical chapters each beginning with a bibliographic essay followed by annotated lists of significant titles. 'An essential purchase for any library whose patrons have an interest in Canada' (*Choice*, v.20, no.5, January 1983, p.692). *Class No:* 971(01)

[7873]

SCHULTZ, J., *ed*. **Writing about Canada** a handbook for modern Canadian history. Scarborough, Ontario, Prentice-Hall Canada, 1990. xiii,282p. bibliogs., index. ISBN: 0139709304.

10 bibliographical essays by separate hands: 1. Writing about politics - 2. Economics - 3. Ideas - 4. Regions - 5. Rural life and agriculture - 6. Business - 7. Labour - 8. Women - 9. Ethnicity - 10. War. Each essay concludes with 'Endnotes' (*i.e.* bibliographical references). Appendix: Historiographical chronology p.251-61. Analytical index. *Class No:* 971(01)

[7874]

SMITH, D.L., *ed*. **The History of Canada** an annotated bibliography. Santa Barbara, Calif, and Oxford, ABC-Clio Information Services, 1983. xi, 325p. index. $55.00. £45.00. (*Clio Bibliography Series no.10.*) ISBN: 0874360471.

3362 abstracts of periodical literature 1973-1978 drawn from the *America History and Life* database grouped in 10 sections: 1. General Canadian history - 2. The natural setting - 3. The native peoples - 4. Pre-Columbian exploration and exploitation - 5. New France - 6. British North America 1763-1867 - 7. Emergent nationalism 1867-1914 - 8. Achievement of nationhood 1914-1945 - 9. The

....(contd.)

contemporary scene since 1945 - 10. Canada: regions. Subject and author indexes. Index to periodicals. *Class No:* 971(01)

[7875]

THIBAULT, C., *comp*. **Bibliographia Canadiana.** Don Mills, Ontario, Longmans Canada, 1973. lxiv,795p.

25,568 unannotated entries, many for articles. 4 parts, with subdivisions: 1. Tools of research - 2. The French colonial régime - 3. British North America, 1713-1867 - 4. The Dominion of Canada, 1867-1967 (nos.12, 427-23, 485). Subject, name and locality index, in English and French. Sources, p.xiii-lxiv. 'Attempts to produce for scholars & students of Canadian history what the *Harvard Guide to American history* achieved for American studies' (*RQ*, v.14,no.1, Fall 1974, p.71). *Class No:* 971(01)

[7876]

WATERSTON, E., *and others, eds*. **The Travellers: Canada to 1900** an annotated bibliography of works published in English from 1577. Guelph, Ontario, Univ. of Guelph, 1989. 321p. illus. indexes. Can$49.00. ISBN: 0889551707.

Historical introduction. Over 700 items arranged in chronological order with author/title and subject indexes. *Class No:* 971(01)

Encyclopaedias

[7877]

STORY, N. **The Oxford companion to Canadian history and literature.** Toronto, Oxford Univ. Press, 1967. xx, 935p. maps, bibliog.

Parent volume contains *c.*1,900 articles (1,500 on Canadian history). Extensive bibliographies (*e.g.* 'Arcadia: bibliography': p.5-6; 'Rebellion of 1837: bibliography': p.699-700). 5 appendices (2. Governors General, etc.). List of titles referred to (title-date-author), p.866-935, *c.*6,000 entries. Important for entries on people, places, periodicals and societies of Canada. 'A very valuable reference tool' (*RQ*, v.7, no.4, Summer 1968, p.191).

W. Toye's *Supplement to the Oxford companion to Canadian history and literature* (1973) ISBN 0195402057 adds nearly 200 entries covering the period 1967-72. *Class No:* 971(031)

Dictionaries

[7878]

BERCUSON, D.J. and GRANATSTEIN, J.L. **The Collins dictionary of Canadian history** 1867 to the present. Toronto, Collins, 1988. xviii, 270p. illus. $24.95. ISBN: 0002177587.

Guide to the people, institutions, and events that have shaped Canada since Confederation in 1867. Timelines (political, social and economic, scientific and technical, artistic and cultural, and sport) p.x-xii. Long list of appendices *e.g.* Canada's Governors General, federal election results, *etc.* Sources p.269-70. 5 maps. *Class No:* 971(038)

Maps & Atlases

[7879]

Canada then and now maps of the nation's growth 1867-1982. Ottawa, Energy Mines and Resources Canada, nd. $5.95. (Canada). $7.15 (US and international).

3 maps showing Canada at the time of Confederation, the progressive evolution of provincial boundaries, and a modern map of Canada. Published to commemorate the repatriation of the constitution. There is also a French version: *Le Canada d'hier à aujourd'hui.*
Class No: 971(084.3)

[7880]

Historical atlas of Canada. maps, bibliog. Univ. of Toronto Press, 3v., 1987-.

V.1: *From the beginning to 1800.* edited by R.C. Harris. 1987. xviii,198p. ISBN 0862024955. 69 two-page cartographic presentations, *i.e.* maps and closely integrated text, arranged in 6 sections: 1. Prehistory; 2. The Atlantic realm; 3. Inland expansion; 4. The St. Lawrence settlements; 5. The Northwest; 6. Canada in 1800, each introduced by a scholarly essay. Notes (including primary and secondary sources) p.179-198. 'A magisterial work of value to all interested in Canada, general and learned readers alike, and it is difficult to imagine that it could be even remotely paralleled in the future' (*Geographical Journal;* v.154,no.2, July 1988, p.295-296. V.2: *The Land transformed 1800-1891* edited by R.L. Gentilcore. 1994. V.3: *Addressing the twentieth century 1891-1961* edited by D. Kerr and D.W. Holdsworth, 1990. [xx],197p. $95. 0802034489. 66 map and text features: Canada 1891-1961: an overview (1. Canada in 1891 - 2. Territorial evolution - 3. Economic growth - 4. Population distribution) - Part 1. The great transformation 1891-1929 and Part 2. Crisis and response 1929-1961. 'The initiators and engineers of this project should be justly proud of their efforts: we should be most appreciative of their version' (*Cartographica,* v.28,no.2, Summer 1991, p.91-4). *Class No:* 971(084.3)

Chronologies

[7881]

COOKE, A. *and* **HOLLAND, C.** **The Exploration of Northern Canada** 500 to 1920 a chronology. Toronto, The Arctic History Press, 1978. 549p.+25p., maps. ISBN: 0771022654.

First printed in *Polar Record,* May 1970-September 1973.

1. Chronology (p.11-348) with details of each voyage or expedition date, its nature, leader, and frequently other senior names, and its ship or sledge, the expedition's point of departure, dates of its duration, a succinct account, and references. 2. Roster of names (5000 entries). 3. Bibliography (p.449-505). Index. *Class No:* 971(090)

[7882]

The Fitzhenry and Whiteside book of Canadian facts and dates. Myers, J., *ed.* Markham, Ontario, Fitzhenry & Whiteside, 1986. 354p. indexes. ISBN: 0889025843.

Detailed chronology of Canadian history including both established and little known facts about people, places and events. Annual sections since 1600 but earliest date is 20,000,000 BC. Index of names p.295-310. General index p.310-354. *Class No:* 971(090)

[7883]

HILL, B.H.W., *comp.* **Canada 875-1973** a chronology and fact book. Dobbs Ferry, New York Oceana, 1973. v, 152p. bibliog. $8.50. (*World Chronology Series.*) ISBN: 0379163071.

Bibliography p.135-50. *Class No:* 971(090)

[7884]

MYERS, J. Canadian facts and dates. Toronto, Fitzhenry and Whiteside, 1991. 404p. indexes. £24.95. ISBN: 1550410733.

7000 entry chronology of Canada from prehistoric beginnings to contemporary political, social and cultural events. Detailed general index and index of names. *Class No:* 971(090)

Official Records

[7885]

COOK, T. *and* **WRIGHT, G.T. Historical records of the Government of Canada** Documents historiques du governement du Canada. 2nd ed. Ottawa, Federal Archives Division, Public Archives of Canada, 1981. 84+88p. indexes, softcover. ISBN: 0662509935.

128 record groups (*e.g.* Governor-General's office; Royal Commissions; Public Archives of Canada) in numerical sequence p.9-76. New to this ed. are brief outlines of the principal functions and administrative background of each record group. Subject classification, p.77-80. Alphabetical index. Separate English and French sequences. 'This guide has been prepared to provide researchers and government officials with a concise description of the holdings of the Division' (*Preface*). *Class No:* 971(093.2)

Amerindians, North

Dictionaries

[7886]

'Glossary of Indian tribal names', *Dictionnary of Canadian biography,* v.1, 1966, p.12-16; v.2, 1969, p.xxvi-xxxix; v.3, 1974, p.xxxi-xliii and 'Glossary of native peoples', v.4, 1979, p.l-lvii.

'To assist the reader in identifying and locating geographically those tribes encountered by Europeans in the early exploration and development of Canada, but makes no claim to be a detailed and complete summary' (*v.1*).
Class No: 971(=97)(038)

Contemporary

[7887]

Canadian news facts the indexed digest of Canadian current events. Toronto, Marpep Publishing Ltd., twice-monthly, 1967-. Continuous pagination, cumulative indexes.

Comprehensive news reference system providing fully indexed reports of current events as gleaned from 19 provincial newspapers and the *New York Times.* V.24, no.10, 16th May-31st May 1989, p.4006-4013, has paragraphs on Parliament, The Provinces, Politics, Across Canada, Canadian-US relations, Business, Labor, Human rights, Environment, Energy, Economy, Agriculture, Sports. *Class No:* 971"312"

Canadian Provinces (History)

[7888]
COATES, K.S. *and* MORRISON, W.R. **Land of the midnight sun** a history of the Yukon. Edmonton, Alberta, Hurtig, 1988. vii,336p. illus., map, bibliog., index. $29.95. ISBN: 0888303319.

9 chronological chapters: 1,. The natives' Yukon - 2. The fur trade ... 8. War and upheaval 1939-1946 - 9. The new Yukon 1946-1987. Chapter notes p.300-19. Bibliography p.320-7. *Class No:* 971.1

[7889]
PECK, M. **The Bitter with the sweet: New Brunswick 1604-1984.** Tantallon, Nova Scotia, Four East Publications, 1983. x, 174p. illus., maps. ISBN: 0969004184.

20 chapters arranged in 3 sections: Founders of the province; A developing society; and The second century. Chapter notes p.165-168. Bibliography p.169-172. 'Written for New Brunswick's Bicentennial year, this book tells the story of individuals and institutions that exemplify important aspects of the province's history' (*Acknowledgements*). *Class No:* 971.1

Bibliographies

[7890]
BISHOP, G.B. **Bibliography of Ontario history 1867-1976** cultural, economic, political, social. Toronto, Univ. of Toronto Press, 2v., 1980. A project of the Ontario Historical Studies Series for the Government of Ontario. xviii, 1760p. index. ISBN: 0802023592, set. ISSN: 03809188.

2nd ed. of *Ontario since 1867: a bibliography* (1974).

Lists 15,000 books, manuscripts, pamphlets, periodical articles with library locations.

Gervais, G. and others, eds. *The Bibliography of Ontario 1976-1986.* Toronto, Dundurn Press, 1989. xxxiv,605p. index. ISBN 1550020315. In 8 parts: 1. General - 2. Ontario before 1783 - 3. Economic history - 4. Social - 5. Political - 6. Military - 7. Culture and civilization - 8. Regional and local. Produced by the Institute of Northern Ontario Research and Development. *Class No:* 971.1(01)

[7891]
BRITISH COLUMBIA Library of the Provincial Archives. **Dictionary catalogue of the Library.** Boston, Mass., G.K. Hall, 8v., 1971. $790.00 Export 955.00.

176,00 photolithographed catalogue cards, representing material on Western Canada, Alaska and Northwestern US. Classified under the Dewey Decimal System with Library of Congress subject headings. *Class No:* 971.1(01)

[7892]
Canadian local histories to 1950: a bibliography. Morley, W.F.E., *ed.* Toronto, Univ. of Toronto Press, 3v., 1967-78. illus., facsims., maps.

Sponsored by the Centennial Commission as a Centennial of Canadian Confederation Project under the Publications Assistance Programme.

1. *The Atlantic Provinces:* Newfoundland, Nova Scotia, New Brunswick, Prince Edward Island, by W.F.E. Morley. 1967. xx, [1], 137p. 2. *La province du Québec,* by A. Beaulieu and W.F.E. Morley. 1971. xxvii,408p. 3. *Ontario and the Canadian North,* by W.F.E. Morley. 1978. xxxii, 322p. V.3 has 2 parts (1. Ontario and regions; counties and districts; cities, towns and townships - 2. Canadian North; Hudson's Bay; Northern Territories; Yukon Territories).

.... (contd.)
Sources, p.xxi-xxvii; locations: *c.*80 Canadian and 21 US libraries. Geographical and general indexes. 12 illus. and maps. *Class No:* 971.1(01)

[7893]
HALE, L.L. **Vancouver centennial bibliography:** a project of the Vancouver Historical Society. Vancouver, Vancouver Historical Society, 4v., 1986. xi, 1791p. ISBN: 0969237804, set; 0969237812, v.1; 0969237820, v.2; 0969237839, v.3; 0969237847, v.4.

1. Books, pamphlets and broadsides. 2. 15 sections based on format *e.g.* theses, articles, film and video productions. 3. Name and title index. 4. Subject and series index. 15090 unannotated entries taken from major libraries and archives in British Columbia, the National Library of Canada, and the Public Archives of Canada. Citations according to AACR2. Locations given. *Class No:* 971.1(01)

Maps & Atlases

[7894]
GENTILCORE, R.L. *and* HEAD, C.G. **Ontario's history in maps.** Toronto, Univ. of Toronto Press for the Ontario Historical Studies Series, 1984. xvii, 284p. maps (some col.), facsims., bibliog. ISBN: 0802034004.

268 maps illustrated and accompanied by text and notes. A cartobibliographical essay 'Sources for early maps on Ontario' (p.276-284) includes 106 references. No index but a detailed list of maps p.x-xiii. 'Our guiding principle has been to present maps as valuable documentary sources for the history of Ontario' (*Introduction*). *Class No:* 971.1(084.3)

Quebec

Bibliographies

[7895]
AUBIN, P. *and* CÔTÉ, L-M. **Bibliographie de l'histoire du Québec et du Canada** / Bibliography of the history of Quebec and Canada 1946-1965. Quebec, Institut Québécois De Recherche Sur la Culture. 2v.,1987. lxxvii,1396p. ISBN: 2892240980.

21,845 entries arranged in systematic classification of 6 divisions: General history; Prehistory; Ethnohistory; Exploration; Euro-Canada era; Demographic indexes and genealogies p.1-793. Classification tables p.xii-xiii. French and English indexes of terms used in systematic and analytic classification p.xxii-lxxvii. Analytic classification (subject index) p.797-1337. Classification by author (author index) p.1341-89. List of consulted periodicals (over 400) p.1393-6. Admirably controlled bibliography. Modelled on *Bibliographie annuelle de l'histoire de France.* This volume follows 2 previous volumes *1966-1975* and *1976-1980* (2nd ed. 1985. ISBN 2892240557) which contains 20,224 entries. *1981-1985* is in preparation. *Class No:* 971.4(01)

[7896]
Guide de l'histoire du Québec. Rouillard, J., *ed.* Montréal, Éditions du Méridien, 1991. 200p. Can$14.95. ISBN: 2894150520.

'Cette bibliographie est en fait un essai bibliographique dans lequel un groupe d'universitaires, d'historiens et de spécialistes des sciences humaines font un choix des

....(contd.)

meilleurs travaux ... Divisé selon les périodes traditionnelles entre le Régime français, le Régime brittanique et le Québec contemporain'. *Class No:* 971.4(01)

Chronologies

[7897]
PROVENCHER, J. **Chronologie du Québec.** Montréal, Les Éditions du Boréal, 1991. 240p. Can$22.95. ISBN: 2890524159.

Stretches from prehistory to 1980. Later political, social, and cultural events are set in North American and global context. *Class No:* 971.4(090)

Mexico

[7898]
COSIO VILLEGAS, D., *ed.* **Historia moderna de Mexico. 9v. in 10.** Mexico City, 1955-72.

1-3. *La republica restaurada.* 1. *La vida politica* (1955); 2. *La vida economica* (1955); 3. *La vida social* (1957). 4-9. *El porfiriato.* 4. *La vida social* (1957); 5-6. *La vida exterior* (1960-1963); 7. *La vida economica* (1965); 8-9. *La vida politica* (1970-1972). Review article of entire work: C.A. Hale's 'The Liberal impulse: Daniel Cosio Villegas and the Historia moderna de Mexico', *Hispanic American Historical Review*, v.54, no.3, August 1974, p.479-498. *See also* S.R. Ross' 'Cosio Villegas Historia moderna de Mexico', *ibid.*, v.46, no.3, August 1966, p.274-282. 'The most extensive and significant undertaking in Modern Mexican historiography' (Griffin, C.C. *Latin America*, Entry no.4160). *Class No:* 972

[7899]
MEYER, M.C. *and* SHERMAN, W.L. **The Course of Mexican history.** 4th ed. New York, Oxford Univ. Press, 1991. xii,718,xxxviip. illus., maps, bibliog., index. ISBN: 0195065999.

First published 1979; 3rd ed. 1987.

45 chapters in 10 sections: 1. Pre-Columbian Mexico - 2. Spanish conquest ... 7. Modernization of Mexico 1876-1910 ... 10. The Revolution shifts gear: Mexico since 1940. Appendix: Mexican heads of state 1349-1988 p.i-iv. Chapter bibliographies. Select bibliography for those who read Spanish p.v-xix. Over 30 maps and charts. New to this edition: new section on US/Mexico border relations; a re-evalutation of classic Maya civilization; introduction to administration of Carlos Salinas de Gortari). 'As a summary reference volume for the general reader it is superior to all others' (*Hispanic American Historical Review*, v.60,no.1, February 1980, p.99-101). *Class No:* 972

Bibliographies

[7900]
GONZÁLEZ, L., *and others eds.* **Fuentes de la historia contemporáneo de México. Libros y folletos.** Mexico City, El Colégio de México, 3v., 1961-62.

24,078 annotated entries for books and pamphlets. 9 parts (1. Generalidades - 2. Territorio - 3. Sociedad - 4. Economia - 5. Politica - 6. Religión - 7. Educación - 8. Filosofiá y ciencias - 9. Letras y artes. *Class No:* 972(01)

Dictionaries

[7901]
BRIGGS, D.C. *and* ALISKY, M. **Historical dictionary of Mexico.** Metuchen, New Jersey, Scarecrow Press, 1981. xiv,259,bibliog. $24.00; £22.50. (*Latin American Historical Dictionaries, no.21.*) ISBN: 0810813912.

Dictionary p.1-235. Bibliography p.237-259. 'A major disappointment. Although it does contain much helpful material, especially recent politics in Mexico, the book is weak on historical data' (*Choice*, v.19,no.2, October 1981, p.218). *Class No:* 972(038)

[7902]
NELSON, G.E. *and* NELSON, M.B. **Mexico A-Z** an encyclopedic dictionary of Mexico. Cuernevaca, Centro Para Retirados, 1975. maps, bibliog.

Comprehensive historical and cultural dictionary from the earliest times to the present. *Class No:* 972(038)

20th Century

Bibliographies

[7903]
ROSS, S.R. **'Bibliography of sources for contemporary Mexican history'**, *Hispanic American Historical Review*, v.39, no.2, May 1959, p.234-238. *Class No:* 972"19"(01)

[7904]
ROSS, S.R., *comp.* **Fuentes de la historia contemporáneo de México. Periodicas y revistas.** Mexico City, El Colégio de Mexico, 2v., 1965-67.

Over 27,000 briefly annotated entries for articles in periodicals and newspapers published in Mexico and southwest USA. Chronologically arranged. Chiefly on 20th century Mexico. *Class No:* 972"19"(01)

Guatemala

Dictionaries

[7905]
MOORE, R.C. **Historical dictionary of Guatemala.** Rev. ed. Metuchen, New Jersey, Scarecrow Press, 1973. viii, 9-285p. bibliog., index. (*Latin American Historical Dictionaries, no.1.*) ISBN: 0810806045.

Dictionary p.9-242. Bibliography p.243-280. 'Many of the entries on historical figures constitute the only information to be found on them' (*Library Journal*, v.93, no.8, 15 April 1968, p.1618). *Class No:* 972.81(038)

Honduras

Encyclopaedias

[7906]
ORTEGA, R.C. **Enciclopedia histórica de Honduras** obra fundamental de información y consulta e imprescindible auxiliar pedagógico para maestros ... [Historical encyclopedia of Honduras: a fundamental work of information and reference and an indispensable teaching aid for teachers...] Tegucigalpa, Graficentro Editores, 1988-. In process.

Fundamental information on the history and culture of Honduras intended for student use. V.1 of this multi-volume work deals with the pre-Columbian and Colonial periods.

....*(contd.)*

'This is not really an encyclopaedia and access to its contents is difficult for lack of an index' (Howard-Reguindin, P.F. *Honduras*, 1992, Entry no.187). *Class No:* 972.83(031)

Dictionaries

[7907]
MEYER, H.K. Historical dictionary of Honduras. Metuchen, New Jersey, Scarecrow Press, 1976. xiv, 399p. illus., maps, bibliog. (*Latin American Historical Dictionaries, no.13.*) ISBN: 0810809214.
   Dictionary p.1-383. Bibliography and maps p.384-99.
Class No: 972.83(038)

El Salvador

Dictionaries

[7908]
FLEMION, P.F. Historical dictionary of El Salvador. Metuchen, New Jersey, Scarecrow Press, 1972. vi,7-157p. bibliog. (*Latin American Historical Dictionaries, no.5.*) ISBN: 0810804719.
   Dictionary p.7-147. Bibliography p.149-57.
Class No: 972.84(038)

[7909]
GARCÍA, M.A. Diccionario histórico-enciclopédico de la Républica de El Salvador. San Salvador, Tipografiá del Diario Latino, 13v., 1927-55.
   V.1-13 A-Col. Largely a biographical dictionary although 'they contain an enormous amount of information on Salvadoran and Central American history' (R.L. Woodward. *El Salvador* 1990. Entry 636). *Class No:* 972.84(038)

Nicaragua

Bibliographies

[7910]
ARGÜELLO, C.M. 'Bibliografía de Nicaragua' *Inter-American Review of Bibliography*, v.4, 1954, p.9-22.
   'A basic guide to the principal historical literature of Nicaragua in Spanish' (R.L. Woodward. *Nicaragua*, 1983. Entry 148). *Class No:* 972.85(01)

Dictionaries

[7911]
MEYER, H.K. Historical dictionary of Nicaragua. Metuchen, New Jersey, Scarecrow Press, 1972. xiii,503p. illus., maps, bibliog. (*Latin American Historical Dictionaries, no.6.*) ISBN: 0810804883.
   Dictionary p.1-482. Bibliography p.483-99. List of maps p.500-3. *Class No:* 972.85(038)

Costa Rica

[7912]
Historia general de Costa Rica. De la Cruz, V., *ed.* San José, Euroamericana de Ediciones Costa Rica, 4v., 1988. illus., maps, bibliog.
   V.1: 459p. Geography of Costa Rica. V.2: 489p. Spanish exploration and conquest in colonial period. Also

....*(contd.)*

archaeology. V.3: 623p. History: independence, federation (1821-38), to 1870. V.4: 663p. History : Liberal Republic (1870-1949). Supplement (65p.) of Documents referring to independence. V.1-3 include biographical inserts. A narrative rather than an interpretative history.
Class No: 972.86

Bibliographies

[7913]
JUNKINS, R.J. 'Historical sources in Costa Rica', *Latin American Research Review*, v.23, no.3, 1988, p.117-27.
   Well-documented 'summary of the main domestic sources of material for studying the history of Costa Rica.'
Class No: 972.86(01)

Dictionaries

[7914]
CREEDMAN, T.S. Historical dictionary of Costa Rica. 2nd ed. Metuchen, New Jersey, Scarecrow Press, 1991. xxii,338p. maps, bibliog. £31.90; *m42.50. (*Latin American Historical Dictionaries, no.16.*) ISBN: 0810822156.
   1st ed. 1977.
   Chronology (1502-1990) p.xv-xxii. Dictionary (events, persons, cultural developments *etc.*) p.1-300. Bibliography p.301-38. 2 maps. *Class No:* 972.86(038)

Panama

Dictionaries

[7915]
HEDRICK, B.C. *and* HEDRICK, A.K. Historical dictionary of Panama. Metuchen, New Jersey, Scarecrow Press, 1970. vi,7-105p. bibliog. (*Latin American Historical Dictionaries, no.2.*) ISBN: 081080347x.
   Dictionary p.7-100. Bibliography p.101-5.
Class No: 972.87(038)

Caribbean

[7916]
WILLIAMS, E. From Columbus to Castro the history of the Caribbean 1492-1949. London, Andre Deutsch, 1970; New York, Harper & Row, 1973. 576p. illus., tables, bibliog., index.
   29 chapters: 26. Twentieth-century colonialism - 27. The colonial nationalist movement - 28. Castroism - 29. The future of the Caribbean. 'One of the most comprehensive studies' (R.A. Myers, *Dominica*, 1987. Entry 188).
Class No: 972.9

Dictionaries

[7917]
LUX, W. Historical dictionary of the British Caribbean. Metuchen, New Jersey, Scarecrow Press, 1975. x,11-226p. bibliog. (*Latin American Historical Dictionaries, no.12.*) ISBN: 0810808471.
   Dictionary in separate sections for Barbados, British Honduras (Belize), Guyana, Jamaica, Leeward Islands, Trinidad & Tobago, and Windward Islands. Bibliography p.251-66. *Class No:* 972.9(038)

Maps & Atlases

[7918]
ASHDOWN, P. **Caribbean history in maps.** London and New York, Longman, 1979. iv, 84p. maps, plans, index, pbk. $10.95. ISBN: 0582765412.

77 black-and-white maps, with commentary in margins. Covers the Caribbean region up to 1978. 15 sections: 1. General - 2. The Amerindian peoples - 3. European exploration and settlement - 4. Slavery and the plantation society - 5. European rivalry and changes of ownership - 6. Revolt and revolution - 7. Emancipation - 8. The decline of sugar - 9. Problems, 1834-1900 - 10. The USA in the Caribbean - 11. Economic distress and the rise of nationalism - 12. Regional co-operation; failure and success - 13. The West Indies in the 1970s - 14. West Indian heroes (p.53-58: *c.*100) - 15. The history of individual states (maps 68-77: Cuba; Hispànola; Puerto Rico; Jamaica; the Lesser Antilles; the Bahamas; Barbados, Trinidad; Belize; Guyana). For schools. *Class No:* 972.9(084.3)

18th Century

Biographies

[7919]
BURKHOLDER, M.A. **Biographical dictionary of Councilors of the Indies.** Westport, Connecticut, Greenwood Press, 1986. 224p. bibliog., index. $67.95. £59.95. ISBN: 0313240248.

172 biographies of men who served on the Council 1717-1808. Ancillary material includes archival abbreviations; a chronology of Spain and her colonies in the 18th century; and a glossary. The Council was the supreme judicial tribunal for Spain's colonial empire.
Class No: 972.9"17"(092)

Cuba

[7920]
PÉREZ, L.A. **Cuba between reform and revolution.** New York, Oxford Univ. Press, 1988. xiv,504p. map, tables, bibliog., index. £20. (*Latin American Histories.*) ISBN: 0195045866.

Continuous narrative history in 12 chapters: 1. Geography and pre-Columbian peoples ... 10. Eclipse of old Cuba ... 12. Socialist Cuba. Political chronology p.382-99. The outstanding feature of this work is the extensive (22 sections) selective guide to the literature p.400-93. *Class No:* 972.91

Dictionaries

[7921]
SUCHLICKI, J. **Historical dictionary of Cuba.** Metuchen, New Jersey, Scarecrow Press, 1988. xxxvi, 368p. bibliog. $39.50; £29.65. (*Latin American Historical Dictionaries, no.22.*) ISBN: 0810820714.

Chronology p.xvii-xxxvi. Dictionary p.1-305. Bibliography p.306-59. 4. Appendices: 1. Country brief (geographical, economic and political data) - 2. Diplomatic relations - 4. Presidents of Cuba. 'The entries are informative, readable, and generally impartial ... particularly useful are the biographical entries for political leaders, painters, musicians, and writers' (*Booklist,* v.85,no.3, 1 October 1988, p.240-1). *Class No:* 972.91(038)

20th Century

Micromaterials

[7922]
The Cuban missile crisis 1962. Cambridge, Alexandria, Virginia and Paris, Chadwyck-Healey in cooperation with The National Security Archive, Washington D.C., 1990. 15,000p. government documentation on silver halide microfiche plus 2v. printed Guide. bibliogs, index. £2200.00. (*The Making of US Policy series no.4; Nuclear History series, no.1.*) ISBN: 0898870704.

Full history including Bay of Pigs episode; US secret war against the Castro regime; the Soviet deployment of Cuban based missiles; the US naval blockade; and US-USSR diplomacy. Documents are arranged in chronological order. Printed Guide in 2v.: 1. Name, organization and subject index - 2. Events chronology; glossaries of key individuals and organizations; chronological document bibliography; and a bibliography of secondary sources. Invaluable collection of primary source material. *Class No:* 972.91"19"(003.5)

Bibliographies

[7923]
PEREZ, L.A. **Historiography in the Revolution** a bibliography of Cuban Scholarship 1959-1979. New York, Garland Publishing, 1982. xxiv, 318p. indexes. $48.00. ISBN: 0824093291.

3,783 unannotated entries in 3 sub-divided parts: 1. General and 12 chronological sub-divisions ending with 1940-1952. - 2. 12 thematic classes *.e.g.* Women ... Communism in Cuba ... Bibliography ... Historiography and method - 3. Biographies. Almost entirely Spanish language material. 'An invaluable source' (*Library Journal,* 15 November 1982, p.2,164). *Class No:* 972.91"19"(01)

[7924]
PEREZ, L.A. **In the service of the Revolution** two decades of Cuban historiography 1959-1979, *Hispanic American Historical Review,* v.60, no.1, February 1980, p.78-89.

The politics of Republican historiography - Revisionists and revolutionaries - History at the barricades - The Past as solidarity. *Class No:* 972.91"19"(01)

Jamaica

[7925]
BLACK, C.V. **The History of Jamaica.** Harlow, Essex, Longman Caribbean, 1988. 176p. illus., maps, index. pbk. £4.10. ISBN: 0582038987.

First published Collins Educational 1958.
21 chronological chapters: 1. The first Jamaicans - 2. The discovery - 3. Jamaica under the Spaniards ... 21. Independent Jamaica. Important dates in the islands history p.7-8. *Class No:* 972.92

Dominican Republic

Dictionaries

[7926]
DOMINGUEZ, U.R. *and* LÉON, M.D. de, *comps.* **Diccionario hisórico dominicano.** Santo Domingo, Editora Universitara - USAD, 1986. 365p. illus., maps.

'A useful compilation of 2800 terms pertaining to the

....*(contd.)*
political and economic history of the Dominican Republic
(K. Schoenhals: *Dominican Republic*, 1990. Entry 898).
Class No: 972.93(038)

[7927]
DOMINGUEZ, U.R. *and* **DE LÉON, M.D. Diccionario histórico dominicano.** Santo Domingo, Editora Universitaria - USAD, 1986. 365p. illus., maps.
2800 entries relating to political and economic history.
Class No: 972.93(038)

Haiti

Bibliographies

[7928]
LAWLESS, R. Haiti a research handbook. New York, Garland, 1990. ix,354p. indexes. $48. ISBN: 0824065433.
4 other contributors. 2040 unannotated items in 33 topical divisions each beginning with a short introductory essay: 1. Bibliographies - 2. General history - 3. Pre-history - 4. Colonial history - 5. Independence - 6. Post-independence (1820-1915) - 7. Occupation (1915-1934) - 8. Post-occupation (1934-1957) - 9. Duvalier era (1957-1986) - 10. Post-Duvalier (1986-.) ... 27. Migration.
Class No: 972.94(01)

Dictionaries

[7929]
PERUSSE, R. Historical dictionary of Haiti. Metuchen, New Jersey, Scarecrow Press, 1977. xiv,124p. map, bibliog. (*Latin American Historical Dictionaries, no.15.*) ISBN: 0810810069.
Chronology p.xi-xiv. Dictionary p.1-106. Appendix: Haitian Chiefs of State p.107-8. Bibliographical Essay p.109-15. Bibliography p.116-24. *Class No:* 972.94(038)

Puerto Rico

[7930]
TOVAR, F.B. A Chronological history of Puerto Rico. New York, Plus Ultra Educational Publishers, 1973. 589p.
Over 5,000 names and events recorded from prehistory to 1972. For school and home use. *Class No:* 972.95

Bibliographies

[7931]
SILVESTRINI-PACHECO, B. *and* **ARROYO, M.** 'Sources for the study of Puerto Rican history' a challenge to the historian's imagination, *Latin American Research Review*, v.16, no.2, 1981. p.156-71.
Reviews archival sources in Spain, Puerto Rico, and the United States. 'An excellent article' (F.E. Cevallos. *Puerto Rico*. 1985. Entry 81). *Class No:* 972.95(01)

Dictionaries

[7932]
FARR, K.R. Historical dictionary of Puerto Rico and US Virgin Islands. Metuchen, New Jersey, Scarecrow Press, 1973. vii, 148p. bibliog. $13.00. (*Latin American Historical*

....*(contd.)*
Dictionaries, no.9.) ISBN: 0810806703.
Dictionary p.126. Bibliography p.127-48.
Class No: 972.95(038)

Chronologies

[7933]
CORDASCO, F., *comp.* **The Puerto Ricans 1493-1973** : a chronology-factbook. Dobbs Ferry, New York, Oceana Publications, 1973. 137p. bibliog. (*Ethnic Chronology Series, no.1.*)
Heavy emphasis on Puerto Ricans in New York.
Class No: 972.95(090)

Bahamas

[7934]
CRATON, M. A History of the Bahamas. 3rd ed. Waterloo, Ontario, San Salvador Press, 1986. 332p. maps, bibliog.
1st ed. 1962.
'The most authoritative general political history of the Bahamas' (P.G. Boultbee. *The Bahamas.*, 1989. Entry 255).
Class No: 972.96

Bibliographies

[7935]
CASH, P., *and others.* **Sources of Bahamian history.** London, Macmillan Caribbean, 1991. xiii,374p. illus., drawings, map, bibliog., index. £5.95. ISBN: 0333437467.
32 chronological and thematic sections exploring contemporary written, pictorial and archaeological material in 6 divisions: 1. Peoples of the Bahamas - 2. American connection - 3. British connection - 4. African connection - 6. Colony of free people - 6. Decolonisation. List of references in text order p.343-65. Question and answer approach for use in schools and colleges.
Class No: 972.96(01)

Bermuda

[7936]
ZUILL, W.S. The Story of Bermuda and her people. 2nd rev. ed. London, Macmillan Caribbean, 1987. xvi, 240p. illus. (inc. 4 col. plates), maps, bibliog., index. pbk. £5.95. ISBN: 0333341562.
First published 1973; 2nd ed. 1983.
4 Parts (23 chapters): 1. Pre-settlement Bermuda - 2. The Archipelago - 3. Story of the Bermuda people - 4. Modern Bermuda. Bibliography p.231-232. For students and the general reader. *Class No:* 972.98

Archives

[7937]
ROWE, H. A Guide to the records of Bermuda. Hamilton, Bermuda, 1984. 132p. $12.00.
'The result of painstaking and accurate research, it contains among other merits valuable historical notes about every agency and activity on which records are held' (*Library Association Record*, v.86,no.4, April 1984, p.179).
Class No: 972.98(093.20)

Barbados

[7938]
BECKLES, H. McD. **A History of Barbados:** from Amerindian settlement to nation-state. Cambridge, Cambridge Univ. Press, 1990. xv,224p. illus., maps, tables, bibliog., index. £22.50; $37.50. ISBN: 0521353742.

Authoritative chronological narrative in 9 chapters: 1. The first Barbadians c.650-c.1540 - 2. English colonization 1625-1644 ... 9. Some post-independence trends. Chapter notes p.211-3. Bibliography p.214-9. 'A clear, competent, and comprehensive social history' (*Hispanic American Historical Review*, v.72, no.4, November 1992, p.601).
Class No: 972.986

Bibliographies

[7939]
BOSTON PUBLIC LIBRARY. **Bibliotheca Barbadiensis** a catalog of materials relating to Barbados 1650-1860. Boston, Mass., Boston Public Library, 1968. 27p. indexes.

Printed books, pamphlets and manuscripts listed chronologically. Many rare items cited.
Class No: 972.986(01)

[7940]
HANDLER, J.S. **A Guide to source material for the study of Barbados history 1627-1834.** Carbondale & Edwardsville, Southern Illinois Univ. Press; London and Amsterdam, Feffer & Simons, 1971. xvi, 205p. $12.50. ISBN: 0809304368.

5 sections (1. Printed books, pamphlets, broadsheets (5 periods) - 2. Parliamentary papers - 3. Newspapers - 4. Prints - 5. Manuscripts (p.121-82). 18 library locations for section 1.) A detailed inventory, with introductory note. Analytical index, p.183-205. An extremely useful bibliography ... by a leading Caribbean scholar' (R.B. Potter and G.M.S. Dunn. *Barbados*, 1987. Entry 940).
Class No: 972.986(01)

Trinidad & Tobago

[7941]
BRERETON, B. **A History of modern Trinidad 1783-1962.** Kingston, Jamaica, Heinemann, 1982. x, 262p. illus., maps, bibliog., index, pbk. $15.00. £10.25. ISBN: 0435981161.

12 chronological chapters covering the period 1498-1962. Chronology of major events p.250-253. Bibliography p.255-258. For A-level and undergraduate use. The author is Senior Lecturer in History, University of the West Indies.
Class No: 972.987

Netherlands Antilles

Dictionaries

[7942]
GASTMANN, A. **Historical dictionary of the French and Netherlands Antilles.** Metuchen, New Jersey, Scarecrow Press, 1978. viii,162p. bibliog. $19.00; £19.00. (*Latin American Historical Dictionaries, no.18.*) ISBN: 0810811537.

Dictionary in 3 sections: General, French, Netherlands Antilles p.1-47. Bibliography (3 sections) p.149-62.
Class No: 972.988(038)

Latin America

[7943]
The Cambridge history of Latin America. Bethell, L., *ed.* Cambridge, Cambridge Univ. Press, 1984-.

1-2. *Colonial Latin America* v.1: 1984. xx,645p. £65. ISBN 0521232236. V.2: 1984. xx,912p. £70. 0521245168. 3. *From independence to 1870.* 1985. xx,945p. £80. 0521232244. 4-5. *1870-1930* v.1: 1986. xiii,676p. £65. 0521232252. V.2: 1986. xviii,951p. £80. 0521245176. 7. *Latin America since 1830: Mexico, Central America and the Caribbean since 1930* 1990. 656p. 05212451848. *Latin America since 1930. Spanish South America.* 1992. xiv,775p. 0521266521. £70. Volume 6 will bring together general essays on major themes in the economic, social and political history of Latin America from the crisis of the 1930s to the crisis of the 1980s. Volume 8 is a history of the nine republics of Spanish South America (From Argentina to Venezuela). Volume 9 will have two distinct parts: a history of Brazil since 1930, and general essays on the intellectual and cultural history of Latin America in the twentieth century. V.10 is planned to be a bibliographical essay. All volumes are equipped with long bibliographic essays for each chapter with special emphasis on books and articles published in the last 20 years. 'This work measures up to the standards of solid scholarship that characterize other multi-volume Cambridge histories. The international contributors are all reputable specialists and present competent, up-to-date surveys' (*Choice*, v.23, no.9, May 1986, p.1446).
Class No: 972.99 (53424/0). Class No: 972.99

[7944]
Historia de España. Tuñón de Lara, M., *general editor.* Barcelona, Editorial Labor, 1983 and 1986. maps, tables, bibliog., indexes.

v.6 *América Hispánica (1492-1898)* by G. Céspedes del Castillo. 1983. 526p. 8433594265. 15 chapters in 4 parts: 1. La nueva frontera (1450-1550) - 2. Los reinos de las Indas (1550-1750) - 3. Las provincias de Ultramar (1750-1808) - 4. La desintegración de la Monarquia (1808-1898).

v.13. *Textos y documentos de la América Hispánica (1492-1898)* 1986. lxxxvi, 478p. 8433594478. Arranged according to v.6. *Class No:* 972.99

[7945]
PARRY, J.H., *ed.* **New Iberian world** a documentary history of the discovery and settlement of Latin America to the early seventeenth century. New York, Times Books and Hector & Rose, Toronto, Fitzhenry and Whiteside Ltd., 1984. 5v. 2912p. maps, bibliog., index. $500.00 the set. ISBN: 0812910702 (set).

1. *The Conquerors and the conquered* (Native societies, Iberian precedents. The formal structure of empire). xlix, 442p.+17p. maps. 081290710. General Introduction p.xxxix-xlviii. 2. *The Caribbean* (The Discovery of the New World, The Settlement of the West Indies, The Spanish Main). xxi, 552p.+16p. maps. 0812910729. 3. *Central America and Mexico* (The Isthmus, The Gulf of Honduras and the Gulf of Mexico 1503-1518, The invasion of central Mexico, Expansion from Mexico). xix, 582p.+18p. maps. 0812910737. 4. *The Andes* (The Discovery and conquest of Peru, Spanish Peru, The Northern Andes). xvii, 549p.+19p. maps. 0812910745. 5. *Coastlines, rivers and forests.* xvii, 572p. 0812910753. Maps p.461-498. Bibliography p.499-506. Index p.509-572. 494 documents 2/3 of them available in English for the first time. 110 plates and maps. Comprehensive name and subject index. The policy of the editors is to include 'small samples of all principal types of

....*(contd.)*

document that occur in the colonial archives and within each type to select documents for their significance.' Comments on the *Archivo de Indias* at Seville, and other notable collections, may be found in the General Introduction. All 5 v. include a useful glossary. 'Given its quality, this collection immediately becomes the standard source of translated documents for students, scholars, and general readers interested in the Americas in the 16th century' (*Choice*, v.22, no.5, January 1985, p.734-735). *Class No:* 972.99

[7946]
SKIDMORE, T.E. *and* SMITH, P.H. **Modern Latin America.** 3rd ed. New York, Oxford Univ. Press, 1992. xii,449p. illus., maps, tables, bibliog., index. ISBN: 0195076486.

1st ed. 1984; 2nd ed. 1989.

Authoritative survey of Latin American history with emphasis on 19th and 20th centuries. Chapter 1. The colonial foundations 1492-1880s - 2. Transformation of modern Latin America 1880s - 1990s, then individual chapters on Argentina, Chile, Brazil, Peru, Mexico, Cuba, The Caribbean, Central America, 11. Latin America, the United States and the World. and 12. What future for Latin America. Heads of State A-Z by country p.411-8. Further reading p.419-35 in narrative form by chapter. Analytical index. *Class No:* 972.99

Bibliographies

[7947]
COVINGTON, P.H., *and others eds*. **Latin America and the Caribbean** a critical guide to research sources. Westport, Conn., Greenwood Press, 1992. xvi,924p. bibliogs., indexes. $115; £103.50. (*Bibliographies and Indexes in Latin American and Caribbean Studies, no.2.*) ISBN: 0313264031.

49 US contributors. 5924 evaluative annotated entries arranged in 15 chapters (*e.g.* General - Anthropology - Art and Architecture - Data Bases ... Womens Studies) each comprising Essay and Bibliography (subdivided by country). Indispensable compendium of reference sources in US research libraries. *Class No:* 972.99(01)

[7948]
GRIFFIN, C.C. *and* WARREN, J.B., *eds*. **Latin America:** a guide to the historical literature. Madison Univ. of Wisconsin Press, 1979. xxx, 700p. index. $35.00. ISBN: 0299082202.

First published Austin, Univ. of Texas Press, 1972.

7,087 annotated entries. 37 contributors. Includes material in Spanish and Portuguese. Some of the critical annotations are signed. 7 parts: 1. Reference - 2. General (including individual countries, A-Z) - 3. Background - 4. Colonial Latin America - 5. Independence - 6. Latin America since independence - 7. International relations since 1830. *Class No:* 972.99(01)

[7949]
HUMPHREYS, R. **Latin American history** a guide to literature in English. London, Oxford Univ. Press, 1958. xiii, 197p.

First published 1941.

2,089 items, surveyed mostly in running commentary form. Covers books and 69 periodicals. Scope excludes British, French, Dutch and US possessions. 14 sections: 1.

....*(contd.)*

General reference works - 2. Bibliographies and guides - 3. Periodicals - 4. General histories and comprehensive works - 5. The land and the environment - 6. Ancient people and cultures - 7. The Spanish Empire in America ... 12. The republics of South America since 1830 ... 14. Mexico since 1830. Biographical index; index of authors, editors and translators. *Class No:* 972.99(01)

Encyclopaedias

[7950]
MARTIN, M.R. *and* LOVETT, G.H. **An Encyclopedia of Latin-American history.** Westport, Connecticut, Greenwood Press, 1981. vi, 384p. $35.00. £32.50. ISBN: 0313228817.

First published by Abelard-Schuman in 1956.

Political, economic and cultural development, including relations with Europe and North America, of all Latin American nations, from the earliest times, in dictionary form. Entries cover geographical features, government institutions, major wars and battles, and biographies of important figures. *Class No:* 972.99(031)

Dictionaries

Amerindians, South

[7951]
OLSON, J.S. **The Indians of Central and South America** an ethnohistorical dictionary. Westport, Conn., Greenwood Press, 1991. xiii,515p. bibliog., index. $76. ISBN: 0313263876.

Cross-referenced entries provide social, demographic, and historical data on c.500 extant Amerindian tribes located south of Mexico with bibliographical citations. Appendix A. Tribal list by country (p.427-34) - B. Chronology of the conquest of Central and South America (p.435-50). Bibliography (by tribe) p.451-504. 'It has incorporated and updated information from a myriad of sources, filling a major void in Latin American research materials' (*Library Journal*, v.116, no.10, 1 June 1991, p.128). *Class No:* 972.99(038)(=98)

Theses

Great Britain

[7952]
ZUBATSKY, D.S., *comp*. **Doctoral dissertations in history and the social sciences on Latin America and the Caribbean accepted by universities in the United Kingdom 1920-72.** London, Institute of Latin American Studies, Univ. of London, 1973. 16p. sd. *Class No:* 972.99(043)(410)

Maps & Atlases

[7953]
LOMBARDI, C.L., *and others*. **Latin American history** a teaching atlas. Madison and London, Univ. of Wisconsin Press, 1984. xvi, 104+39p. maps, bibliog., index. $22.50. £27.00. ISBN: 0299097102.

Maps are grouped in 3 sections: 1. Environment - 2. Colonial period (Iberian background; Amerindians;

....(contd.)

Discovery and conquest; Colonial governments; Trade; Independence of Spanish America) - 3. Modern period (Boundaries; International relations; Population; Economics and society). Bibliography p.xiv-xvi. 'A highly useful instrument of reference recommended to teachers and students alike' (*Bulletin of Latin American Research*, v.4, 1985, p.89-90). *Class No: 972.99(084.3)*

USA

[7954]

DE GREGORIO, W.A. The Complete book of US Presidents. New York, Dembner Books, 1984. xi,691p. ports., index. $25.00. ISBN: 0934878366.

40 chapters *i.e.*, 1 for each President. Information on physical description; personality; ancestry; father, mother, siblings; collateral relatives; children, subsequent descendants, living descendants; birth, childhood, education; early romance, marriage, extra-marital affairs; military service; career before President; Party nomination, opponents, campaign and issues; election, inaugural address; Vice-President(s), cabinet, administration, Supreme Court appointments; Retirement, death; President praised, criticized; President quotes; Books by and about President. Appendix: Political composition of Congress 1789-1985. 'Should be purchased for all reference collections' (*Choice*, v.22,no.1, September 1984, p.60). *Class No: 973*

[7955]

DENVER PUBLIC LIBRARY. Catalog of the Western History Department. Boston, Mass., G.K. Hall, 7v., 1970. First supplement 1975. 5731p. $695.00. Export $840.00. ISBN: 0816108641.

First supplement. 3 reels. $130.00. Export $155.00. ISBN 0816113955. Total of 138.00 catalogue cards photolithographed. The Library contains material on the social, economic, political, cultural, and historical development of the United States west of the Mississippi River. *Class No: 973*

[7956]

MEINIG, D.W. The Shaping of America: a geographical perspective on 500 years of history. New Haven and London, Yale Univ. Press, 3v., 1986-.

1: *Atlantic America 1492-1800*. 1986. xxii,500p. illus., maps, tables, bibliog., index. 2: *Continental America 1800-1867*. 1993. 0300056583. Views the United States 'as a gigantic geographic growth with a continually changing geographic character, structure, and system'. *Class No: 973*

Bibliographies

[7957]

American history a bibliographic review. Fitzgerald, C.B., *ed.* Westport, Connecticut and London, Meckler Books, 1985-. V.1-. Annual. £34.00.

V.4. 1989. 300p. $59.50. ISBN 0887363628. Regular features include articles on the state of the art in historical bibliography, a bibliographic essay, an authorized bibliography of a contemporary historian, a listing of bibliographies in progress, book reviews, research notes and prize announcements. *Class No: 973(01)*

[7958]

BARBER, G.D. and HAMMOND, C.B. 'American history reference sources, 1986-1987' *Reference Services Review,* v.17,no.4,. Winter 1989, p.59-72.

Previous current survey printed in *RSR*, Summer 1987. Evaluative reviews of 28 in print titles. *Class No: 973(01)*

[7959]

BEERS, H.B. Bibliographies in American history 1942-1978 a guide to materials for research. Woodbridge, Connecticut, Research Publications Inc., 2v., 1982. xviii, 512p.+Øii, 513-946p. index. $260.00. ISBN: 0892350385.

Continues *Bibliographies in American history* (1942).

11,784 entries grouped in 12 chapters, forming a comprehensive guide to bibliographic listings from the end of World War II to the late 1970s and covering the major areas of North and South American history - politics, economics, military, genealogy, and local history etc. V.2 is taken up with Chap.12. States, territories, possessions and dependencies listing archives and manuscripts, maps, newspapers etc. A-Z by state. *Class No: 973(01)*

[7960]

Bibliographic guide to North American history 1988. Boston, Mass., G.K. Hall, 1978-. Annual. v, 691p. $250.00. ISBN: 0816171076. ISSN: 01476491.

Lists material catalogued by The Research Libraries of New York Public Library and the Library of Congress in a single A-Z sequence. 'Entries cover all aspects of United States and Canadian history, including Indians, the discovery of America and early exploration, Colonial history, the American Revolution, the War of 1812, the War with Mexico, slavery, Civil War, Spanish-American War, US local history, Canadian political and constitutional history, history of Canadian nationalities and races, Canadian provincial history, and the British and French periods' (G.K. Hall & Co. *Catalog of publications, 1979-1980*, p.127). Serves as an annual supplement to *United States Local History Catalog* (G.K. Hall, 1974). *Class No: 973(01)*

[7961]

Harvard guide to American history. Freidel, F., *ed.* Cambridge, Mass., Harvard Univ. Press, 2v., 1974. xxx, 605p.+Øxvi, 609-1290p. ISBN: 0674375602.

1st ed. 1954 succeeded E. Channing and others' *Guide to the study and reading of American history* (Boston, Ginn, 1912).

V.1 has 4 parts (29 sections): 1. Research methods and materials (including unpublished primary sources; microform materials; reference works) - 2. Biographies and personal records. 3. Comprehensive and area histories - 4. Histories of special subjects (*e.g.* physical environment; economic history; intellectual history; the arts; pure and applied sciences), about 20,000 entries. No annotations, but each section has an introduction.

V.2 has 5 parts, arranged chronologically: 5. America, to 1789 - 6. United States, 1789-1860 - 7. Civil War and reconstruction - 8. Rise of industry and empire - 9. Twentieth century (p.927-1067). Cumulated index of names (p.107-1274) and subject index (p.1275-90; in small type). 'Remains the best single source for those studying the history of the US' (*RQ*, Spring 1975, v.14, no.3, p.261). *Class No: 973(01)*

[7962]
MAKOWER, J., *ed*. **The American history sourcebook.**
Prentice Hall Press, 1988. 548p. illus., bibliog., indexes.
$40.00. ISBN: 0130274917.

More than 3000 entries relating to museums, libraries,
archives, photocollections, historical societies, and other
sources of information on US history, politics, and culture.
Data: location, telephone, hours, charges, areas of
specialization, important holdings, and services. Key dates in
American history p.403-427. An American history
bibliography p.428-38. Organization and subject indexes. 'A
worthwhile addition to reference collections in public, high
school and academic libraries' (*Choice*, v.26, no.5, May
1989, p.1483). *Class No:* 973(01)

[7963]
MARTIN, F.S. *and* GOEHLERT, R.U. **American
Presidents** a bibliography. Washington, Congressional
Quarterly, 1987. xviii, 756p. indexes. $135.00. ISBN:
0871874164.

13150 unannotated entries citing English-language books,
articles, dissertations, essays and research reports
concerning all US presidents, George Washington to Ronald
Reagan, in chronological order. For each president entries
are arranged in 5 categories: biographies; private life; public
career; Presidential years; and writings. Emphasis
throughout is on scholarly rather than popular material.
Author and subject indexes. 'A well-constructed finding tool'
(*Choice*, v.25, no.4, December 1987, p.602).
Class No: 973(01)

[7964]
**Meckler's bibliographies of the Presidents of the United
States 1789-1989.** Fitzgerald, C.B., *ed*. Westport,
Connecticut and London, Meckler Books, 50v., 1988-. v.1-.

Provides comprehensive annotated bibliographies,
President by President, covering manuscripts and archives,
biographies and monographs, articles and dissertations,
government documents and oral histories, libraries,
museums and iconographic resources.

Each text will also contain an introductory historical essay,
a chronology of significant events in the subjects life,
comprehensive indexing by author and subject, and a list of
serial publications cited. A cumulated index is planned upon
completion of the project in December 1992.
Class No: 973(01)

[7965]
MEIER, M.S., *comp*. **Bibliography of Mexican American
history.** Westport, Connecticut, Greenwood Press, 1984.
xiii, 500p. indexes. $40.95. ISBN: 031323776x.

A major work marshalling 4372 briefly annotated entries
in 12 chronological, subject and bibliographical form
chapters 'providing access to information necessary for a
more sophisticated understanding of the Mexican American
experience and its contribution to contemporary America'
(*Preface*). 'A particular strength ... is the extensive list of
obscure master theses and dissertations' (*Choice*, v.22, no.2,
October 1984, p.250). *Class No:* 973(01)

[7966]
UNIVERSITY OF MICHIGAN. William L. Clements
Library. **Author/title and chronological card catalogs of
Americana 1493-1860.** Boston, Mass., G.K. Hall, 7v.,
1970. 4752p.

95,500 photolithographed catalogue cards for books,

....(contd.)
pamphlets and broadsides pertaining to early America, and
written and published contemporaneously.
Class No: 973(01)

[7967]
UNIVERSITY OF WASHINGTON. Seattle. **The Dictionary
catalog of the Pacific Northwest Collection of the
University of Washington Libraries.** Boston, Mass., G.K.
Hall, 6v., 1972. 5010p. $665.00 (Export $805.00). ISBN:
0816109850.

105,000 photolithographed catalogue cards. The collection
documents the history of early exploration, the fur trade, the
missionary movement, immigration mining, lumbering, and
other industries, and the growth of political and social
institutions. Geographical focus is on the states of
Washington, Oregon, Idaho, Montana, and Alaska with
references to adjacent states and provinces.
Class No: 973(01)

[7968]
Writings on American history : a subject bibliography of
articles 1962-1983/84. Washington and White Plains, New
York, Kraus International Publications and the American
Historical Association, 15v., 1974-1985. $685.00.

Succeeds the annual *Writings on American history* 1902-
1960 (1930-72; various publishers). *Writings on American
history 1961* filling the gap in 2v. 1979. $60.00. ISBN
0527982520. *Class No:* 973(01)

[7969]
—Writings on American history, 1962-73 a subject
bibliography of books and monographs. White Plains, New
York, Kraus International Publications and the American
Historical Association, 10v., 1985. 6530p. index. $1300.
ISBN: 0527982687.

Cites more than 50,000 books and monographs and is
compiled from Library of Congress catalogue cards. V.1
includes sections on history and historians and a
chronological classification. V.7(pt), v.8 and v.9(pt)
comprise a geographical classification. The added emphasis
on biography and genealogy in this set is reflected in the rest
of v.9. V.10 is the index. *Class No:* 973(01)

Encyclopaedias
[7970]
Chronicle of America. Kirschon, J., *ed*. Mount Kisko, New
York Chronicle Publications, 1990. Distributed in North
America by Prentice Hall and by Raincoast Books of
Vancouver, and by Longman in the UK. 956p. col. illus.,
col. maps, index. £29.95. ISBN: 0131337459, US;
0582066891, UK.

A lavishly illustrated annalistic history of the US from
prehistoric times to the 1980s recounted in a vivid (purported
contemporaneous) journalese style. *Class No:* 973(031)

[7971]
GARRATY, J.A. **1001 things everyone should know about
American history.** New York, Doubleday, 1989. 256p.
illus. $19.95.

Divided into 8 parts relating to politics, ideas, people,
presidents, literature and music, military affairs, and
'what'ses' (*i.e., what's new, what's old, what's great etc.*).
'Enough information is given to make this a useful reference
source or simply a place to turn for diversion' (*Booklist*,
v.85, no.16, 15 april 1989, p.1427). *Class No:* 973(031)

[7972]

MORRIS, R.B., *ed*. **Encyclopedia of American history.** 6th ed. New York, Harper & Row, 1981. 1328p. $29.45. ISBN: 0061816051.

First published 1953; 5th Bicentennial ed. 1976.

3 parts: 1. Basic chronology, to 1975 - 2. Topical chronology (The expansion of the nation - Population, immigration and ethnic stock - Leading Supreme Court decisions - The American economy - Science, invention and technology - Thought and culture - Mass media) - 3. Five hundred notable Americans, p.961-1191 (George Washington; 1½ columns). 42 maps and charts. Analytical index. p.1193-1245. In this ed. more space is devoted to minorities, ethnic groups and women. *Class No:* 973(031)

[7973]

The Oxford companion to American history. Johnson, T.H. *and* Wish, H. Oxford, Oxford Univ. Press, 1966. vi, 906p. tables. £35.00. $49.95. ISBN: 019500597x.

4,710 cross-referenced entries (including 1,835 biographies). mostly 'summaries of lives, events and places significant in the founding and growth of the nation' (*Preface*). Lengthier articles have references. Tables give names and dates of persons who held high office. Appended text of Constitution and amendments. A useful 1v. reference work to all aspects of American history and thought from colonial times onwards. *Class No:* 973(031)

[7974]

The Reader's companion to American history. Foner, E. *and* Garraty, J., *eds*. Boston, Houghton Mifflin, 1991. xxii,1226p. tables, maps, index. $35; £24.95. ISBN: 0395513723.

400 contributors. Over 1000 A-Z, cross-referenced and signed entries, either giving essential information on specific topics, longer interpretative essays on broad issues, or biographies, relating to the political, economic, social and culture US history. Sponsored by the Society of American Historians. 'Informative and readable, an excellent combination of political, and social history' (*Booklist*, v.88, no.9, 1 January 1992, p.851-2). *Class No:* 973(031)

[7975]

The Reader's encyclopedia of the American West. Lamar, H.R. New York, Harper & Row, 1988. ix, 1306p. illus., ports., facsim. $29.50. £18.95. ISBN: 0060157267.

First published by Thomas Y. Crowell 1977.

2400 A-Z entries from *c*. 200 contributors cover the people and places, lore and legend, and the history of the US trans-Mississippi states plus Alaska and Hawaii (*e.g* 'California': p.149-54, 2 maps; 'Custer' 1½ columns, port., and 17 lines of references). Comprehensive and well produced although more maps could have been provided. *Class No:* 973(031)

[7976]

ROLLER D.C. *and* **TWYMAN, R.W.,** *eds*. **The Encyclopedia of Southern history.** Baton Rouge, Louisiana, Louisiana State Univ. Press, 1979. 1421p. tables, maps, bibliogs., index. $90. ISBN: 0807105759.

1,100 contributors: *c*.2,900 signed articles. Encyclopedic, including biographies and detailed history of each state. ('South' is defined as 'all the states and the District of Columbia where slavery was legal in 1860' (p.1125).) Bibliographies are appended to most entries. 35 maps; 75

....(contd.)

tables. 'The best and most accessible single reference to the American South' (*Library Journal*, v.105, no.7, 1 April 1980, p.842). *Class No:* 973(031)

Handbooks & Manuals

[7977]

PRUCHA, F.P. Handbook for research in American history a guide to bibliographies and other reference works. Lincoln, Nebraska and London, Univ. of Nebraska Press, 1987. xiii, 289p. index. $21.95. £20.85. ISBN: 0803236824.

Over 1500 items listed or described in 32 chapters arranged in 2 parts: 1. Categories of material including printed documents of the Federal government; national archives; State and local materials; and databases - 2. 15 special subjects *e.g.* Political history; American Indians; chronological periods. 'There are few similar guides to bibliographic sources of American history that present so much information for both beginners and researchers in such a manageable compass' (*Reference Reviews*, v.2, no.2, June 1988, p.89). *Class No:* 973(035)

[7978]

Webster's guide to American history a chronological, geographical and biographical survey and compendium. Van Doren, C. *and* McHenry, R. Springfield, Massachusetts, Merriam, 1971. 1428p. illus., maps, index.

Part 1 (p.1-636): an illustrated chronology of events, 1492-1969, supported by *c*.1,000 quotations from primary sources. Part 2 (p.637-792) is a series of coloured and black-and-white maps, and statistical tables and charts, arranged by broad topics. Part 3 contains over 1,000 biographies of notable Americans. Index. 'Recommends itself for the home library or the student's personal reference shelf' (*College & Research Libraries*, v.32,no.4, July 1971, p.314). *Class No:* 973(035)

Dictionaries

[7979]

Dictionary of American history. New York, Scribner, 7v. & Index, 1976-77. 3344p. £500.00. ISBN: 0684138565.

First published 1940 (5v. & Index).

800 contributions; 7,200 signed entries, A-Z (Aachen ... Zwaanendael colony). Brief bibliographies (*e.g.* 'Alaska' (4 sections): 12 columns; 4 references; 'Mexican War (1846-1848)': 3½ columns. 3 references; 'Afro Americans': over 12 columns, 8 references; 'Antitrust laws ': 2½ cols., 5 references). Coverage of science and technology has been improved; lack of treatment of the arts is corrected (*e.g.* 'Theater': 9½ columns, 10 references); and coverage of native American Indians and Afro-Americans made more adequate, according to the *Preface*. No biographies. Index v. (xviii, 503p.) - *c*.90,000 entries. A standard, basic work. 'Most highly recommended' (*Library Journal*, v.102,no.13, July 1977, p.1480).

Concise dictionary of American history. Rev. ed. 1983, 1140p. $60.00. ISBN 0684173212. Adds new articles and revises others. 'A handy addition at reference desks far from the main set (*Choice*, v.20,no.11-12, July-August 1983, p.1572). *Class No:* 973(038)

[7980]

HYUNG-CHAN KIM, *ed*. **Dictionary of Asian American history.** Westport, Connecticut, Greenwood Press, 1986. xv, 627p. bibliog., index. $65. ISBN: 0313237603.

13 contributors. Divided into 2 main sections: 1. 15 essays on the historical development of ethnic groups from Asian countries and Pacific Islands and their place in the American social order - 2. More than 800 dictionary entries encompassing all aspects of the history of Asian Americans in the US. Appendix A. Bibliography p.565-577. B. Chronology (1820-1985) p.580-602. 'An excellent one-volume dictionary' (*Reference Books Bulletin 1986-1987*, p.157). *Class No:* 973(038)

[7981]

MEIER, M.S. *and* RIVERA, F. **Dictionary of Mexican American history.** Westport, Connecticut, Greenwood Press, 1981. xiii, 498p. maps, bibliog., index. $46.95. £34.50. ISBN: 0313212031.

28 contributors. All aspects of Mexican American history from the early 16th century are covered in entries of varying length some of which include suggestions for further reading. Appendix A. Bibliography p.377-383. B. Chronology (50,000 BC to 1980) p.385-395. C. Complete text of the Treaty of Guadalupe Hidalgo. D. Mexican American journals. 5 maps. Intended as a basic guide for undergraduates, librarians and scholars. *Class No:* 973(038)

Reviews & Abstracts

[7982]

America history and life article abstracts and citations of reviews and dissertations covering the United States and Canada. Santa Barbara, California, ABC Clio; Oxford, Clio Press, 1964-.

1954-1963 Abstracts of the world's periodical literature relating to the history of the United States and Canada included in *Historical Abstracts*. These were subsequently published as Vol.0 of *America history and life*. V. 1-10 (1964-1978) limited to abstracts. V. 11-25 (1979-1988) published in 4 parts: A. Articles, abstracts and citations (3 issues) - B. Index to book reviews (2 issues) - C. American history index (books, articles and dissertations) - D. Annual index. V.26-. (1989-) 5 issues a year: issues 1-4 carry abstracts, reviews and dissertations, issue 5 is a cumulative annual index.

V.29. 1992 has 14,869 entries arranged in 6 parts subdivided under subject classification headings: 1. North America - 2. Canada - 3. United States national history to 1945 - 4. United States national history 1945 to present - 5. United States regional, state and local history (in 7 regional sub-divisions) - 6. History. The Humanities and Social Sciences (*e.g.* Archives, libraries, museums; General bibliography; Historiography; Methodology; Teaching and study of history). Subject, author, book and film title and reviewer indexes. Comprehensive worldwide coverage drawing upon more than 2000 journals in 45 languages. Cumulative quinquennial indexes are available: V.1-5 (1964-1968) £197.00; v.6-10 (1969-1973) £197.00; v.11-15 (1974-1978) £340.00; v.16-20 (1979-1983) £388.00. v.21-25 (1984-1988). Falk, J.D. and Kinnell, S. *Searching America history and life and Historical abstracts on DIALOG*, rev. ed., 1987. 116p. (ABC-Clio Guides to Online Searching), £27.05. ISBN 0874360919. See also Bucknall, T. 'Searching

....(contd.)

Historical Abstracts and America: History And Life Online And On CD-ROM'. *Database*, v.15, no.4, August 1992, p.36-9. *Class No:* 973(048)

Almanacs

[7983]

The Almanac of American history. Schlesinger, A.M., *ed*. New York, G.P. Putnam, 1983. 623p. illus., maps, index. $24.95. ISBN: 0399128530.

5 sections each consisting of an introductory essay and an illustrated and annotated chronology: 1. Founding a nation 986-1787 - 2 Testing a union 1788-1865 - 3. Forging a nation 1866-1900 - 4. Expanding resources 1901-1945 - 5. Emerging as a world power 1946-. *Class No:* 973(059)

Quotations

[7984]

CONLIN, J.R. **The Morrow book of quotations in American history.** New York, Morrow, 1984. 346p. $15.95. ISBN: 0688020682.

Highly selective list. 'Because of the subject matter's broad appeal this will be more useful than many other specialized quotation books' (*Wilson Library Bulletin*, v.59, no.4, December 1984, p.292-3). *Class No:* 973(082.2)

Illustrations

[7985]

American historical images on file. Smith, C., *ed*. New York and Oxford, Facts on File, 1988.

1. *The American Civil War* 1988. 300p. £55.00. $125.00. 0816016097. 2. *Key issues in American constitutional history* 1988. 300p. £55.00. $125.00. 0816016100. 3. *The faces of America* 1988. 366p. £55.00. $125.00. 0816016089. Prints, drawings, painting, photographs, maps, charts and documents with descriptive cross-referenced text, on looseleaf pages in ring binders. For school use. *Class No:* 973(084.1)

Maps & Atlases

[7986]

Atlas of American frontiers. Stokie, Il., Rand McNally, 1992. 192p. col. illus., col. maps. $49.95.

Photographic and cartographic history of the development of the United States from the early exploration to the opening of the West. Contents include 10 pages of historical maps drawn 1650-1930; maps illustrating significant historical concepts; and contemporary reference maps of present-day USA. *Class No:* 973(084.3)

[7987]

Atlas of American history. Jackson, K.T. 2nd ed. New York, Scribners, 1985. xv, 294p. maps. $55.00. ISBN: 0684184117.

First published 1943 edited by J.T. Adam.

The 1st ed. designed to accompany the *Dictionary of American history*, (1940 ed.), had 147 carefully drawn outline, black-and-white maps, arranged chronologically in 10 sections. The 1978 ed. adds 51 maps, mostly concerned with 20th-century developments. Index-gazetter (c.7,500

....(contd.)

entries). The maps are lacking in detail, - 'uninspired and unimaginative' (*Choice*, v.15, no.7, September 1978, p.842). *Class No:* 973(084.3)

[7988]
Atlas of American history. Ferrell, R.H. *and* Natkiel, R. Rev. ed. New York and Oxford, Facts on File Publications, 1990. 192p. illus., (some col.), col. maps, facsims., col. plans. index. $24.95. £18.95. ISBN: 0816010285.

First published 1987.

A useful single volume atlas of *c.*200 x 2 or 4 colour maps drawn in 1986-7 not too happily married to a superfluous illustrated history arranged in 6 chronological sections *e.g.* 1. The colonial era ... 5. The two World Wars ... 6. America in a divided world. 3 Map essays: Territorial expansion of the USA, Population; Presidential elections. 143 historical paintings, drawings and photographs. 'For the modern period the Facts on File atlas has much broader and more up-to-date coverage than its predecessors' (*Booklist*, v.84, no.13, 1 March 1988, p.1102). This edition merely adds one map, 1988 election figures, and the name of George Bush to the list of US presidents.
Class No: 973(084.3)

[7989]
Atlas of United States history. Maplewood, New Jersey, Hammond. 64p. maps, index. $10.95. ISBN: 0843711426.

More than 100 maps, diagrams and inset chronological and thematic maps: exploration; expansion; wars, growth and the economy; urban problems. For home and school use. *Class No:* 973(084.3)

[7990]
GILBERT, M. Dent atlas of American history. 3rd ed. London, J.M. Dent, 1993. 138p. maps. ISBN: 0460861735.

First published as *American history atlas* by Weidenfeld & Nicolson (1968).

138 black and white outline political, military, social history, transport, and economic maps (26 new to this edition) from Origins of settlement in America 50,000-1000 BC to Defence preparedness in space 1992-1993.
Class No: 973(084.3)

[7991]
Historical atlas of the United States. Garrett, W., *ed.* Centennial ed. Washington, National Geographic Society, 1988. 288p. illus. (some col.), maps, diagrs., tables, facsims. $59.95. ISBN: 0870447475.

5 thematic chapters: 1. People - 2. Boundaries - 3. Economy - 4. Networks - 5. Communities alternate with 5 chronological chapters 1400-1988. A heavy preponderance of text, 450 photographs, and 80 graphs over its 380 maps make this volume not so much an atlas as 'a pleasant, illustrated, popularized, brief US history' (*Choice*, v.26, no.9, May 1989, p.1496). Bibliography p.260-73.
Class No: 973(084.3)

[7992]
Historical atlas series. Norman, Univ. of Oklahoma Press, 1976-. maps, bibliog., index.

Historical atlas of Arizona by H.P. Walker and D. Bufkin. 2nd ed., 1986. 137p. £19.95. ISBN 0806120231 *Arkansas* by G.T. Hanson and C.H. Moneyhon. 1989. 142,xxp. £27.95. 080611844x. *Kansas* by H.E. Socolofsky and H. Self. 2nd ed., 1989. 192p. 19.75. 0806121572. *Massachusetts* by R.W. Wilkie and J. Tager. 1990.160p. £42.95. 0870236970. *Oklahoma* by J.W. Morris and others,

....(contd.)

3rd ed., 1987. 208p. £23.95. 0806119918. *Washington* by J. Scott and R. de Lorme. 1988. 200p. £27.95. 0806121084. *Texas* by A.R. Stephens and W. Homes. 1989. 160p. £19.75. 0806121580. *The American West* by W.A. Beck and Y.D. Haase. 1989. £23.75. 0806121939.

'Each atlas includes a physical description of the state, its exploration by Europeans, the history of its native population, its political history, and such other topics as economic development, transportation, agriculture, and education. With good reason, the earlier atlases have been favorably reviewed. They offer, in one volume, a concise historical, geographical, ethnographical, political, and economic overview and thus are handy reference books'. (*Choice,* v.27,no.5, January 1990, p.762+4).
Class No: 973(084.3)

[7993]
McEVEDY, C. The Penguin atlas of North American history. Harmondsworth, Middlesex, Penguin, 1988. 112p. col.maps, index. pbk. £4.95; $6.95. ISBN: 0140511288.

Mixture of base map, used in 47 of the 57 maps depicted, and text commentary on left hand page to cover the period 20,000 BC to 1870 with a 1987 postscript. First fifth of the atlas is allocated to the pre-Columbian period. 'What this book demonstrates is that a good historical atlas of North America cannot be squeezed into an 8½-by-7 inch format' (*Booklist*, v.85,no.11, 1 February 1989, p.927).
Class No: 973(084.3)

[7994]
UNIVERSITY OF MICHIGAN. William L. Clements Library. **Research catalog of maps of America to 1860** in the William L. Clements Library. Boston, Mass., G.K. Hall, 1972. 4 reels (microfilm). $270.00 (Export $350.00). ISBN: 0816112274.

43,800 photolithographed catalogue cards relevant to discovery and exploration, American colonial history, the Revolution, the War of 1812, and the opening of the American West. *Class No:* 973(084.3)

Bibliographies

[7995]
WHEAT, J.C. *and* **BRUN, C.F. Maps and charts published in America before 1800** a bibliography. rev. ed. London, Holland Press, 1979. 215p. maps. $125.00. ISBN: 0900470895.

915 maps, plus list of 552 books referred to. Arranged by region, then chronologically. Entries gives descriptions, map size and scale. Emphasis on USA. Very favourably reviewed in *RQ* (v.9, no.2, Winter 1969, p.181-2).
Class No: 973(084.3)(01)

Chronologies

[7996]
CARRUTH, G., *ed*. **The Encyclopedia of American facts and dates.** 8th ed. New York, Harper & Row, 1987. 1008p. index. $29.95. £26.95. ISBN: 0061811432.

7th ed. New York, Crowell, 1979.

Chronologically arranged, columns across the double page: Politics and government; war; disasters; vital statistics - Books; painting; drama; architecture, sculpture - Science; industry; economics; education; religion; philosophy - Sports; fashions; popular entertainment; folklore; society.

....(contd.)

Detailed, analytical index. 'This new edition is superior to the sixth and seventh editions. First, page size is larger, and this makes it easier to locate entries. Second, the new material is not added as a supplement' (*Reference Books Bulletin* 1986-1987, p.157).

What happened when: a chronology of lives and events in America. 1989. viii, 599p. $12.95. £8.95. 0060963182 is an abridged version. *Class No:* 973(090)

[7997]
CLEMENTS, J. Chronology of the United States. New York, McGraw Hill, 1975. 247p. illus., maps, index. ISBN: 0070113289.

Facing pages present events of every year 1789-1974. For popular use. *Class No:* 973(090)

[7998]
HORNSBY, A. Chronology of African-American history significant events and people from 1619 to the present. Detroit, Gale Research, 1991. xlvii,526p. bibliog., index. $49.95. ISBN: 081037093x.

Entries are arranged chronologically by year, month and day and include important births and deaths, thumbnail biographies, rebellions and demonstrations, elections, and awards. A substantial introduction covers the African historical background and period reviews of Black history and progress. Excerpts from relevant legislation and court decisions are contained in an appendix (p.439-88). Bibliography p.489-506. 'This well-written and highly readable chronology is enthusiastically recommended to all public and academic libraries as a basic outline guide' (*Choice*, v.29, no.5, January 1992, p.722). *Class No:* 973(090)

[7999]
URDANG, L., *ed.* The Timetables of American history. New York, Simon and Schuster, 1981. vi,470p. illus., index. ISBN: 0671252453.

Inspired by B. Grun's *The Timetables of history (qv).*

Chronology starting 1000A.D.; 1010A.D.; and yearly 1492-1980, in 4 columns across the double page: History and politics; The arts; Science and technology; Miscellaneous each sub-divided America and elsewhere. Index of 16,000 subjects and proper names. *Class No:* 973(090)

[8000]
The World almanac of the American West. Bowman, J.S., *ed.* New York, World Almanac, 1986. Distributed by Ballantine. 368p. illus. (some col.), index. $29.95. ISBN: 0886872731.

A descriptive chronology of events 1492-1985 recording the American movement westwards of the Appalachian Mountains, each year covered in 2-3 pages, with boxed biographies and short thematic essays. *Class No:* 973(090)

Biographies

[8001]
Biographical directories of American and United States Governors. Westport, Connecticut and London, Meckler Books, 1978-1989. ports., bibliogs., indexes.

1. Raimo, J.W. *Biographical directory of American colonial and revolutionary governors 1607-1789.* 1980. xii, 521p. $125.00. £72.00. ISBN 09300466071. 2. McMullin, T.A. and Walker, D.A. *Biographical directory of American*

....(contd.)

territorial governors. 1984. 353p. £58.00. 093046611x. 3. Sobel, R. and Raimo J.W. *Biographical directory of the governors of the United States 1789-1978.* 1989. 1816p. £195.00. 0887363377. Originally published in 4 v. 1978. £265.00. 0930466004. 4. Raimo, J.W. *Biographical directory of the governors of the United States 1978-1983.* 1985. 352p. £42.00. 0930466624. 5. Mullaney, M.M. *Biographical directory of the governors of the United States 1983-1988.* 1989. 398p. $55.00. £32.00. 0887361773. Biographical and career information including campaign issues and main achievements in office on all men and women who have served as governors arranged A-Z by state in chronological order. Individual bibliographies indicate location of the governor's papers. In many instances information in these volumes updates entries in *Dictionary of American biography* or *Dictionary of national biography*. *Class No:* 973(092)

[8002]
Directory of American scholars Vol.1 History. Jaques Cattell Press. 8th ed. New York, R.R. Bowker, 1982. xi,924p. index. $90.00. ISBN: 0835214788.

Profiles approximately 11,000 scholars in all fields of historical study including art history, musicology, and archaeology. Data: primary discipline, education, honorary degrees, professional experience, membership of learned societies, honours and awards, research interest, publications. Geographic index p.859-924. *Class No:* 973(092)

[8003]
KANE, J.N. Facts about the Presidents a compilation of biographical and historical information. 5th ed. New York, H.W. Wilson, 1989. 428p. ports., index. $45.00 US and Canada; $50.00 other countries. ISBN: 0824207742.

1st ed. 1959.

Pt.1: Biographical data George Washington - George Bush. A chapter for each President in chronological order of office. Genealogical compilation - elections - Congressional sessions - Cabinet and Supreme Court appointments - Vice-Presidents - highlights of life and administration. Pt.2: Comparative data: chronology - family history and background. Compendium of facts, anecdotes and statistics. *Class No:* 973(092)

[8004]
Presidential election campaign biographies 1824-1976. Godstone, Surrey, UMI, 1990. 1,367 105 x 148 mm microfiche plus a printed author, title and subject index.

Biographies describe candidates' family background, education, occupation, and political career. Information on those who failed to gain their party's nomination is also included. *Class No:* 973(092)

Jews

Bibliographies

[8005]
GUROCK, J.S. American Jewish history: a bibliographical guide. New York, Anti-Reformation League of B'nai B'rith, 1983. xxi,195p., bibliog., index, pbk. $6.95. ISBN: 088464037x.

Valuable introduction on the growth of American Jewish historiography p.xv-xxi. Pt.1. Bibliographical reviews of the Colonial and early national periods (1654-1850); the eras of

....(contd.)

German and East European immigration (1840-1924); the modern period; and on special topics. Pt.2. Future directions includes suggestions for further research. Bibliography p.121-171. Author and subject indexes.

Class No: 973(=924)(01)

Amerindians, North

Bibliographies

[8006]

HIRSCHFELDER, A.B. Annotated bibliography of the literature on American Indians published in State Historical Society publications. New York, Kraus International Publications, 1982. xv, 356p. illus., index. $60.00. ISBN: 0527408891.

1182 entries from 13 state historical society publications. 3 access routes are provided by a subject, a persons, places and titles; and an Indian Nation index. 'Highly recommended' (*Choice* v.21, no.2, October 1983, p.252).

Class No: 973(=97)(01)

[8007]

HOXIE, F.E. *and* **MARKOWITZ, H. Native Americans** an annotated bibliography. Pasadena, Calif.; Englewood Cliffs, N.J., Salem Press, 1991. xiii,325p. index. $40. ISBN: 0893566705.

Over 1000 descriptive summaries of books mostly published in last 30 years relating to North American Indian history and anthropology. 4 Major sections: 1. General studies and reference works (by 8 culture areas) - 2. History (colonial America, US. and Canada 1776-1990) - 3. Culture areas subdivided by topic - 4. Contemporary life (family, religion, economic development, health/alcoholism, Indian law and government *etc.*). Author index. 'An excellent reference for both introductory and advanced students ... highly recommended for all academic libraries' (Choice, v.29, no.2). *Class No:* 973(=97)(01)

Encyclopaedias

[8008]

BRAUN, M. *and* **WALDMAN, C. Encyclopedia of native American tribes.** New York and Oxford, Facts on File Publications, 1988. xiii, 293p. col. illus., col. maps, bibliog., index. $35.00 £18.95. ISBN: 0816014213.

The cultural and social historic record of more than 150 Indian tribes of North and Central America, arranged A-Z by tribe, covering location, migration, contact with Europeans, wars, and contemporary tribal affairs. Glossary p.265-273. Bibliography, grouped in 11 broad categories, p.275-278, lacks publication dates. 11 maps. 250 illustrations. 'As a work of reference this book should prove both useful and entertaining' (*Bulletin of Society of University Cartographers*, v.22, no.1, 1988, p.46-47).

Class No: 973(=97)(031)

[8009]

Handbook of North American Indians. Washington, Smithsonian Institution, 1978-. illus., maps, bibliogs., index.

A planned 20v. 'encyclopedic summary of what is known about the prehistory, history, and cultures of the aboriginal peoples of North America who lived north of the urban civilizations of central Mexico' (*Preface*). 5. *Arctic*. 1984. 845p. $29.00 - 6. *Subarctic*. 1981. 853p. $25.00 - 7.

....(contd.)

Northwest coast. 1990. 777p. illus., maps, bibliog., index. $38. - 8. *California.* 1981. 800p. $25.00. 9. *Southwest.* 1979. 701p. $23.00 - 10. *Southwest.* 1983. 884p. $25.00 - 11. *Great Basin.* 1986. 868p. $27.00 - 15. *Northeast.* 1978. 924p. $27.00. V.9. *Southwest* has 50 contributors and 59 chapters including 1. Introduction - 2. History of archaeological research - 3. History of Ethnological research. Key to tribal territories map p.ix. Bibliography p.625-78. Volumes yet to be published: 1. *Introduction* - 2. *Indians in contemporary society* - 3. *Environment, origins, and population* - 4. *History of Indian-White relations* - 12. *Plateau* - 13. *Plains* - 14. *Southeast* - 16. *Technology and visual arts* - 17. *Languages* - 18/19. *Biographical dictionary* - 20. *Index.* *Class No:* 973(=97)(031)

Handbooks & Manuals

[8010]

HEARD, J.N. Handbook of the American frontier: four centuries of Indian-White relationships. Metuchen, NJ., Scarecrow Press, 5v., 1987-. Distributed in UK by Shelwing Ltd. of Folkestone, Kent. (*Native American Resources Series, no.1.*)

1. *Southeastern Woodlands.* 1987. 2. *Northeastern Woodlands.* 1990. xi,403p. £31.90. 0810823241. Future volumes: will cover the Great Plains (v.3) and the Rocky Mountains, southwestern districts and the Pacific coast (v.4). V.5 will be a general index, choronology and bibliography.

Series of brief articles (up to 2p. in length with a few slightly longer), ending with source attributions, concerning American Indian tribes and leaders, explorers, traders, frontier settlers, soldiers, missionaries, mountain men, battles, massacres, forts, treaties, and other topics of interest in the history of the first 48 United States from the arrival of the earliest seafarers to the end of the Indian wars four hundred years later, arranged in 4 A-Z sequences.

Class No: 973(=97)(035)

Maps & Atlases

[8011]

TANNER, H.H., *ed.* **Atlas of Great Lakes Indian history.** Norman, Univ. of Oklahoma Press for the Newberry Library, 1986. xv,224p. illus., maps, bibliog., index. $75.00; £62.00. ISBN: 0806115157.

33 newly researched colour maps of the Great Lakes region of the US and Canada, particularly of the Ohio Valley, depicting the movement of Indian communities 1640-1871. *e.g.* 6. The Iroquois Wars 1641-1701... 12. Distribution of Indian and white settlements *c.*1830. Bibliographic essay p.183-5. Bibliography p.187-208.

Class No: 973(=97)(084.3)

[8012]

WALDMAN, C. Atlas of the North American Indian. New York and Oxford, Facts on File Publications, 1985. xi, 276p. illus., maps (mostly col.), bibliog., index. $29,95. £18.95. ISBN: 0871968509.

Over 100 two-colour maps, together with complementary text cover the history, culture and location of the Indian people of Canada, the United States, and Central America. An appendix includes Chronology p.212-222; Indian tribes of US and Canada with historical and contemporary locations p.222-233; Federal and State Indian reservations, trust areas and native villages p.233-239; Indian bands in

....(contd.)

Canada p.239-244; Major Indian place-names in US and Canada p.244-260; Museums, historical societies and archaeological sites p.260-265; and Bibliography p.266-267. *Class No:* 973(=97)(084.3)

Chronologies

[8013]

DENNIS, H.C., *comp*. **The American Indian 1492-1970** a chronology and fact book. 2nd ed. Dobbs Ferry, New York, Oceana, 1977. 177p. tables. $8.50. (*Ethnic Chronology Series.*) ISBN: 0379005263.

Chronology, p.1-78, 'Some prominent Indian figures of the past'; 'A random sampling of contemporary Indians and their actitivies'. 9 appendices (*e.g.* Indian wars and local disturbances; Indian museums; Some Indian publications; A reading and research bibliography, p.128-33 (authors, A/Z). Index to Indian tribes and prominent leaders. *Class No:* 973(=97)(090)

Biographies

[8014]

WALDMAN, C. **Who was who in Native American history:** Indians and non-Indians from early contacts through 1900. New York and Oxford, Facts On File, 1990. vi,410p. illus., ports. £30. ISBN: 0816017972.

Over 1000 cross-referenced entries relating to Indian tribal leaders, medicine men, warrior chiefs, and army scouts and also to European explorers, statesmen, army officers, traders, artists and photographers, scholars and educators whose influence and policies affected native American history. Entry content: birth and death dates and concise biographies (John Cabot 29 lines ... Cochise 75 lines ... Buffalo Bill Cody 93 lines ... George Custer 112 lines ... Geronimo 132 lines). Appendix: Native Americans listed by tribe and non-Indians listed by occupation p.400-10. Restricted to North America. *Class No:* 973(=97)(092)

18th Century

Maps & Atlases

[8015]

CAPPON, L.J., *and others*. **Atlas of early American history** the Revolutionary era 1760-1790. Princeton, New Jersey, Princeton Univ. Press for Newberry Library & Institute of Early American History & Culture, 1976. 157p. maps. $235.00. ISBN: 0691046344.

268 maps, mostly in colour, covering political, religious, cultural, economic, demographic and military aspects of the period, with explanatory text. Full index. Very favourably reviewed in *Library journal*, 15 November 1976, p.2357-8. *Class No:* 973"17"(084.3)

Colonial Period

Bibliographies

[8016]

LYDON, J.G. **Struggle for empire** a bibliography of the French and Indian War. New York, Garland, 1986. xxi,272p. indexes. $42. (*Wars Of The United States, no.7.*) ISBN: 0824090691.

....(contd.)

1508 annotated English, French, and Spanish language items relating to the extension of the Europeon Seven Years War (1756-1763) to North America. 22 chapters in Topical (*e.g.* Military and Naval ... Indian relations ... Forts and topography) and Geographical divisions. Bibliographical references (items 1458-1508) p.245-53. *Class No:* 973.02(01)

Encyclopaedias

[8017]

FARAGHER, J.M., *ed*. **The Encyclopedia of Colonial and Revolutionary America.** New York and Oxford, Facts on File, 1989. 448p. illus., maps, bibliogs., index. $50.00; £45.00. ISBN: 0816017441.

*c.*1500 entries of varying length cover political, military, social, economic and cultural aspects of the period (including French, Spanish and Russian America). About half the entries are biographical. Some longer entries are signed and carry bibliographies. 'A superb ready reference tool for all levels' (*Choice*, v.27,no.11-12, July-August 1990, p.1804). *Class No:* 973.02(031)

War of Independence

Bibliographies

[8018]

BLANCO, R.L. **The War of the American Revolution** a selected annotated bibliography of published sources. New York, Garland, 1984 xxvii,654p. indexes. $56. (*Wars of the United States, no.1.*) ISBN: 082409171x.

3740 items in 14 sections: 1. Causes of the war - 2. Campaigns and battles - 3. American army ... 6. British army - 7. German troops ... 10. Diplomacy ... 14. Bibliographies. Periodicals cited p.xv-xxvii *Class No:* 973.03(01)

[8019]

GEPHART, R.M. **Revolutionary America 1763-1789: a bibliography.** Washington, Library of Congress, 2v., 1984. (Distributed by Government Printing Office). xl,1672p. illus. on endpapers, index. $38. ISBN: 0844403598, v.1; 0844403792, v.2.

14110 annotated entries (encompassing over 20,000 titles) arranged in 12 chronological and thematic chapters (*e.g.* 1. Research aids ... 2. General studies: regional, state and local ... 10. The making of the Constitution ... 12. Biographies and personal primary sources) followed by an extensive essay, The Presentation and Publication of Documentary Sources on the American Revolution, p.1469-1671. 'This monumental work is absolutely essential' (*Choice*, v.22, no.1, September 1984, p.62). *Class No:* 973.03(01)

[8020]

SMITH, D.L., *ed*. **Era of the American Revolution:** a bibliography. Santa Barbara, California and Oxford, Clio Press, 1975. xiv,381p. (*Clio Bibliographical Series, no.4.*) ISBN: 0874361788.

1401 signed abstracts of articles published worldwide in 11 sections: 1. Interpreting the Revolution: the historical view - 2. General history: Lexington - Concord - 3. Participants - 4. Decade of controversy 1763-1775 - 5. The war for Rights: before the Declaration of Independence - 6. The war for independence - 7. The Revolution and the West

....(contd.)

- 8. The Loyalists - 9. The Confederation - 10. The Constitution - 11. Revolutionary society. Coverage is continued in *America: history and life*.
Class No: 973.03(01)

[8021]
ZINK, S.D. 'Location and analysis of the historical publications produced by agencies of the United States Government during the era of the American Revolution Bicentennial 1974-1976', *Publishing History*, v.27, 1990, p.77-100.

489 publications are recorded: scholarly monographs; brief popular historical sketches; historical bibliographies; essays; lectures; memoirs; collections of documents; historical reference works and guides. Agencies covered include the Departments of the Interior, Defense, and Agriculture, Congress, and the Smithsonian Institution.
Class No: 973.03(01)

Encyclopaedias

[8022]
The American Revolution an encyclopedia. Blanco, R.L., *ed.* New York, Garland, 2v., 1992. 1800p. maps, bibliogs. $175. (*Military History of the United States, no. 1.*) ISBN: 082405623x.

Over 130 specialist contributors. 700 entries consisting of short essays each with bibliographical references on the battles, campaigns and naval engagements, along with more than 400 biographical sketches of the leading American, British, French, German and Spanish commanders and prominent American and British statesmen. Coverage extends to Canada, the West Indies, and the waters of the Indian Ocean. A glossary explains contemporary terms.
Class No: 973.03(031)

[8023]
The Blackwell encyclopedia of the American Revolution. Greene, J.P. *and* Pole, J.R., *eds.* Oxford, Blackwell, 1991. xvi,845p. illus., maps, bibliogs., index. £60; $49.95. ISBN: 1557862443.

75 full length articles by different hands exploring all aspects of the Revolution: 1. Context - 2/3. Themes and events - 4. External effects - 5. Internal effects - 6. Concepts - 7. Biographies. Chronology in 3 columns: 1. Political and legal events - 2. Military campaigns - 3. Scientific, cultural, educational, scientific and religious developments (p.794-827). Guides to further reading after every article. Analytical index. 'A very thorough compendium of recent scholarly thinking on this critical period' (*Booklist*, v.88, no.6, 15 November 1991, p.640). *Class No:* 973.03(031)

Maps & Atlases

[8024]
HARLEY, J.B., *and others.* **Mapping the American Revolutionary War.** Chicago and London, Univ. of Chicago Press, 1978. vii,187p., illus. maps, bibliog., index. $39.95. ISBN: 0226316319.

3 contemporary and 2 retrospective essays. Notes p.148-172. Bibliography p.173-182. 'Provides the final word on the subject' (*Geographical journal*, v.145, no.1, March 1979, p.146-147). *Class No:* 973.03(084.3)

[8025]
SYMONDS, C.L. **A Battlefield atlas of the American Revolution.** Annapolis, Maryland, The Nautical and Aviation Publishing Company of America. 1986. 110p. illus. maps. ISBN: 0933852533.

Part 1. Early campaignes - 2. The turning point - 3. A global war - 4. The war moves south. Epilogue: The world turned upside down. 41 double-page map/text features. Bibliography p.109-10. *Class No:* 973.03(084.3)

Biographies

[8026]
BOATNER, M.M. Cassell's biographical dictionary of the American War of Independence 1763-1783. London, Cassell, 1973. xviii,1287p., maps, diagrs., bibliog., index. ISBN: 0304292966.

Published in US as *Encyclopedia of the American Revolution.*

Nearly 2,000 cross-referenced entries providing the background and origins of the war; biographies (1/3 of total); and political issues and events. Bibliography p.1253-73. Index to maps p.1257-87. *Class No:* 973.03(092)

[8027]
PURCELL, L.E. Who was who in the American Revolution. New York and Oxford, Facts On File, 1993. 576p. illus., bibliog., index. $60; £39.95. ISBN: 0816021074.

Biographical sketches of 1500 British, loyalist, patriot, French, German, Polish and African Americans prominent in the war. *Class No:* 973.03(092)

Early Nineteenth Century, 1809-1845

Bibliographies

[8028]
SMITH, D.W. The War of 1812 an annotated bibliography. New York, Garland, 1985. xxiv,340p. indexes. $61. (*Wars of the United States, no.3.*) ISBN: 0824089456.

1393 annotated entries in 9 sub-divided sections: 1. Bibliographies - 2. General histories - 3. Coming of the war - 4. Canadian-American theater - 5. War in the South - 6. British offensive 1814 - 7. War at sea - 8. Internal scene - 9. Peace. Chronology p.xix-xxiii. Author and subject indexes. *Class No:* 973.05(01)

American Civil War

[8029]
Battle chronicles of the Civil War. McPherson, J.M., *ed.* New York, Macmillan, 6v., 1989. illus., maps, bibliog., index. $299. ISBN: 0029206618.

40 contributors. A chronological military history: v.1-5 are each devoted to one year of the war 1861-65, with over 100 essays reprinted from the periodical, *Civil War Times Illustrated;* v.6 consists of essays on the Presidents of the Confederate and United States and their most renowned military leaders, a bibliography, and an index to the complete set. A 35-minute videotape is included.
Class No: 973.07

[8030]
KATCHER, P. **The American Civil War source book.**
London, Arms and Armour Press, 1992. 318p. illus., maps,
bibliog., index. £24.95. ISBN: 1854091042.

Single-volume reference source in 10 sections: 1.
Campaigns - 2. Weapons and the practice of war - 3.
Military life - 4. Forces of the United States - 5. Forces of
the Confederate States - 6. Militia of the individual states - 7.
Biographies - 8. Sources (published, graphic arts,
photography, videos) p.294-300 - 9. Miscellanea - 10.
Glossary (p.309-11). Bibliography p.295-6. 10 maps.
Class No: 973.07

Bibliographies

[8031]
MURDOCK, E.C., *comp*. **The Civil War in the North** a
selective annotated bibliography. New York, Garland, 1987.
xx,761p. $58.00. (*Wars of the United States, no.9.*) ISBN:
0824089413.

5608 briefly annotated entries divided into 11 chapters: 1.
Introduction (reference and general works) - 2. Government
- 3. Army - 4. Navy - 5. Lincoln - 6. Biographies and
personal accounts - 7. Soldier life - 8. The written word - 9.
The Arts - 10. Minorities - 11. Special topics. Author and
subject indexes. *Class No:* 973.07(01)

[8032]
NEVINS, A., *and others, eds*. **Civil War books** a critical
bibliography. Wilmington, North Carolina, Broadfoot, 2v.,
1984. ix, 278p.; ix, 326p. $50.00. ISBN: 0916107094.

First published Baton Rouge, Louisiana Univ. Press,
1967-69.

V.1: *c.*2,500 entries, with *c.*20-word evaluative
annotations. 7 'categories': 1. Military aspects: Mobilization;
organization; administration and supply - 2. Military aspects:
Campaigns - 3. Military aspects: Soldier life - 4. Prisons and
prisoners of war - 5. The negro - 6. The navies - 7.
Diplomacy. Arranged by authors, A-Z, under categories.
V.2 has entries for *c.*2,400 general works, biographies, and
the government, politics, social and economic studies, state
and local studies covering the Confederacy and the Union.
Brief, evaluative annotations. Excludes periodical articles,
dissertations, masters theses, pure literature. Author, title
and subject index to both volumes, p.249-326.
Class No: 973.07(01)

Encyclopaedias

[8033]
CURRENT, R.N., *ed*. **Encyclopedia of the Confederacy.**
New York, Simon & Schuster, 4v., 1993. illus., maps,
bibliogs., index. $355. ISBN: 0132759918.

331 US academic contributors. 1368 articles (all 250
words or more in length) on every aspect of the Confederacy
including 843 biographies, 51 on the Civil War battles, and
major articles on 'Bibliography and Historiography' and
'Diaries, Letters and Memoirs'. 67 maps.
Class No: 973.07(031)

[8034]
NEELY, M.E. **The Abraham Lincoln encyclopedia.** New
York, McGraw Hill, 1982. xii, 356p. illus., bibliogs. index.
ISBN: 00700461457.

Entries for Lincoln's career, family, friends and enemies,
the places he lived, events, his leading biographers, libraries
with major Lincoln collections, societies *etc.* but not
intended as a Civil War encyclopedia. 'Will become an
indispensable reference source in every library' (*Choice*,
v.19, no.7, March 1982, p.893-4). *Class No:* 973.07(031)

Maps & Atlases

[8035]
Civil War maps: an annotated list of maps and atlases in The
Library of Congress. Stephenson, R.W., *comp*. 2nd ed.
Washington, Library of Congress, 1989. 410p. maps (some
col.), indexes. $46. ISBN: 0844405981.

Descriptive but not analytical guide to 2200 maps and
70++ atlases and sketch books. Data: author; title;
publisher/printer; scale; and size. Indexes of (1) map title
and (2) personal names (*i.e.* cartographers, engravers,
lithographers, printers, publishers, surveyors). An
introduction includes sections on pre-war, Union,
Confederate maps *etc.* and gives information on the Union
Army's Corps of Topographical Engineers and the
Confederate Topographical Department. 'A unique and
commendable reference work' (*Geographical Journal*,
v.157., no.1, March 1991, p.96). *Class No:* 973.07(084.3)

[8036]
SYMONDS, C.L. **A Battlefield atlas of the Civil War.** 2nd
ed. Baltimore, Maryland, The Nautical And Aviation
Publishing Company of America, 1987. xv,106p. illus.,
maps, bibliog. ISBN: 0933852495.

43 double-page map features of the major engagements
'but does not supersede Vincent J. Esposito's *The West Point
atlas of the Civil War* (1962)'. (*Choice*, v.21,no.17, March
1984, p.1047). *Class No:* 973.07(084.3)

Bibliographies

[8037]
A Guide to Civil War maps in the National Archives. Rev.
ed. Washington, National Archives Publications, 1986.
140p. illus. $30.00. ISBN: 0911333363.

First published 1964.

Arranged in 2 parts: 1. a general guide to the 8000 maps
in the Cartographic and Architectural Branch of the Archives
- 2. a description of selected maps in greater detail.
Class No: 973.07(084.3)(01)

Chronologies

[8038]
BOWMAN, J.S., *ed*. **American Civil War day by day.** New
York, Facts On File, 1989. 224p., illus. (some col.), maps.
£18.95. ISBN: 0816021813.

Pictorial chronology covering military history and also
political, social and economic aspects of the war. 350
photographs. 13 maps. *Class No:* 973.07(090)

Biographies

[8039]

BOATNER, M.M. Cassell's biographical dictionary of the American Civil War 1861-1865. London, Cassell, 1973. xvi, 974p. maps, bibliog.

First published New York, David McKay, 1959, as *The Civil War dictionary* (rev. ed. 1988) ISBN 081291726x.

Over 400 cross-referenced articles on campaigns, leading personnel, and political, social and economic events. Emphasis is on 'briefly covering the maximum number of important subjects rather than attempting a more detailed treatment of a smaller number of selected highspots' (*Introduction*). Sectional maps p.955-69. Bibliography p.970-74. *Class No:* 973.07(092)

[8040]

SIFAKIS, S. Who was who in the Civil War. New York and Oxford, Facts On File, 1988. ix,766p. illus., bibliog., index. $45.00; £25.00. ISBN: 0816010552.

Compendium of over 2500 concise biographies of the major military leaders (all 583 Union and 425 Confederate general officers) and leading political figures. Appendix A. Chronology p.742-46 - B. Officers receiving thanks of US Congress p.747. Bibliography p.748-49. 'An outstanding reference work' (*Booklist,*v.85,no.3, 1 October 1988, p.245.

Who was who in the Confederacy (1989. xi,324p. 0816022046) and *Who was who in the Union* (1989, ix,479p. 0816022038) were published in softcovers.
Class No: 973.07(092)

Manuscripts & Incunabula

Bibliographies

[8041]

SELLERS, J.R., *comp*. **Civil War manscuripts** a guide to the collections in the Manuscript Division of the Library of Congress. Washington, Library of Congress, 1986. xvii,391p. ports., index. $20.00. ISBN: 0844403814.

Evolved from L.W. Dunlap's checklist *Civil War manuscripts* (1967).

1064 collections arranged A-Z by collection title. Data given: brief statement of identification; nature of collection; type of materials; content description; and finding aids. Analytical index. *Class No:* 973.07(093)(01)

Later Nineteenth Century, 1865-1901

Bibliographies

[8042]

VENZON, A.C. The Spanish-American War an annotated bibliography. New York, Garland, 1990. xi,255p., indexes. $40. (*Wars Of The United States, no.11.*) ISBN: 0824079744.

Select bibliography consisting of 1180 (mostly) annotated items written in English language and arranged in 17 subdivided sections e.g. 1. General works ... 3. Biographies - 4. US Army - 5. US Navy ... 7. Cuba - 8. Philippines - 9. Puerto Rico. Also includes works on the Philippine-American War 1899-1902. Subject and author indexes.
Class No: 973.08(01)

Dictionaries

[8043]

TREFOUSSE, H.L. Historical dictionary of reconstruction. Westport, Conn., Greenwood Press, 1991. xii,284p. bibliog., index. $65. ISBN: 0313258627.

Nearly 250 A-Z cross-referenced articles (many over 1000 words) dealing with current research on major personalities, concepts and issues, relating to the period 1863-1877. At the end of each article there is a listing of the latest available literature. Chronology p.ix-xii. Bibliography p.263-6. 'A valuable addition to the historical reference literature of the US' (*Booklist,* v.88, no.7, 1 December 1991, p.721).
Class No: 973.08(038)

20th Century

Bibliographies

[8044]

KYVIG, D.E. and BLASIO, M.A. New day/New deal a bibliography of the great American depression 1929-1941. Westport, Connecticut, and London, Greenwood Press 1988. ix, 306p. index. $45.00. £40.50. (*Bibliographies and Indexes in American History.*) ISBN: 0313260273. ISSN: 07426828.

4600 unannotated English language items (1300 books, 2500 articles/essays, 800 discs) grouped in 44 subject categories arranged in 13 chapters *e.g.* 1. Overviews and general histories ... 2. Bibliography and historiography ... 5. The Hoover administration ... 6. The Roosevelt administration ... 13. After effects. *Class No:* 973.09(01)

Dictionaries

[8045]

Historical dictionary of the Progressive Era 1890-1920. Buenker, J.D. *and* Kantowicz, E.R., *eds*. Westport, Conn., Greenwood Press, 1988. ix,599p. bibliogs., indexes. $85; £73.10. ISBN: 0313243093.

197 contributors. Over 800 signed A-Z entries describing the most important people, events, organizations, legislation, and concepts of the period of study. Each entry ends with a brief bibliography. Chronology p.537-48. Name, title and subject indexes. 'An excellent, handy reference guide to one of the most important and certainly one of the most written-about eras of American history' (*Choice,* v.26, no.7, March 1990, p.1122+ +4). *Class No:* 973.09(038)

[8046]

OLSON, J.S. Historical dictionary of the 1920s from World War I to the New Deal, 1919-1933. Westport, Connecticut, Greenwood Press, 1988. Distributed in UK by Eurospan. xii, 420p. bibliog., index. $55.00. £49.50. ISBN: 0313256837.

Over 700 cross-referenced entries of varying length relating to personalities and political and social issues with suggestions for further reading. 'An asset for all reference collections and a useful handbook for students of twentieth-century American history' (*Booklist,* v.85, no.6, 15 November 1988, p.554). *Class No:* 973.09(038)

[8047]
OLSON, J.S., *ed*. **Historical dictionary of the New Deal** From inauguration to preparation for war. Westport, Connecticut, Greenwood Press, 1985. viii, 611p. Bibliog. index. $67.95. ISBN: 0313238731.

50 contributors. Approximately 700 cross-referenced brief descriptive essays on the personalities, agencies, and legislation important to the New Deal 1933-1940. Appendix A. A New Deal chronology, 1933-1941 (p.553-561) - B. Bibliography (p.563-575) - C. New Deal Personnel (p.577-586) - D. Acronyms (p.587-588). 'The most comprehensive work of its kind yet published' (*Choice*, v.23, no.9, May 1986, p.1370). *Class No:* 973.09(038)

Local Histories

[8048]
RUSSO, D.J. **Keepers of our past** local historical writing in the United States 1820s-1930s. Westport, Conn., Greenwood Press, 1988. xiii,281p. bibliog., index. $39.95l £29.95. ISBN: 0313262365. ISSN: 00849219.

Traces the transition of local history from a favourite pursuit of local antiquarians to the province of academic historians in 4 stages: 1/2. Early, later antiquarians - 3. Formulaic local history (as a publishing venture, as an editorial project, as literature) - 4. Coming of the academics. Chapter notes p.215-54. Bibliography p.255-74. 'Recommended to Ph.D. candidates and professional historians researching and writing local history' (*Choice*, v.26, no.7, March 1989, p.1237). *Class No:* 974/979

Bibliographies

[8049]
FILBY, P.W. **A Bibliography of American county histories.** Baltimore, Genealogical Publishing Co. Inc., 1985. xiv, 449p. $24.95. ISBN: 0806311266.

Replaces Clarence S. Peterson's *Consolidated bibliography of county histories in fifty states* (1961).

Identifies all county histories of any consequence published before December 1984. Arranged alphabetically by state and then by county. No index. 'Libraries serving genealogists no longer can provide adequate reference service without it' (*RQ*, v.25, no.2, Winter 1985, p.252-253). *Class No:* 974/979(01)

[8050]
KAMINKOW, M.J., *ed*. **United States local histories in the Library of Congress** a bibliography. Randallstown, Maryland, Magna Carta Book Co., 5v., 1975. 4500p. $225.00. ISBN: 0910946175.

1: *Atlantic States, Maine to New York.*
2: *Atlantic States, New Jersey to Florida.*
3: *Middle West. Alaska, Hawaii.*
4: *The West.*
Supplement and Index.
Entries for the 50 states are arranged by Library of Congress call numbers in class F(DU, in the case of Hawaii). 'Material cannot be traced by author or title' (*RQ*, v.16, no.2, Winter 1976, p.188). *Class No:* 974/979(01)

[8051]
NEW YORK LIBRARY. The Research Libraries. Local History and Genealogy divison. **United States Local History Catalog.** Boston, Mass., G.K. Hall, 2v., 1974. (981p.) 2 reels. $165.00 (Export $200.00). ISBN: 0816112851.

Lists the separate bound monographs and serials cataloged in the Research Libraries' United States local history classification scheme. It is included in the *Dictionary Catalog of the Local History and Genealogy Division* of the New York Public Library but it may also be purchased and used independently by readers with particular interests in United States local history.

Supplemented annually by the *Bibliographic Guide to North American History. Class No:* 974/979(01)

[8052]
NEW YORK PUBLIC LIBRARY. Research Libraries. **Dictionary catalog of the Local History and Genealogy Division.** Boston, Mass., G.K. Hall, 20v., 1974.

325,000 photolithographically reproduced catalogue cards, - a key to information about people and places, especially those usually unmentioned in more general histories. Now available only on microfilm (16 reels. $1600. Export $1935.00. ISBN 0816114684). *Class No:* 974/979(01)

[8053]
STEPHENS, W.B. **Sources for U.S. history** nineteenth-century communities. Cambridge, Cambridge Univ. Press, 1991. xviii,558p. £55. (*The Sources of History.*) ISBN: 0521353157.

1. Introduction (published, unpublished, and cartographic sources) - 2. Demography - 3. Ethnicity and race - 4/5. Land, settlement and farming - 6. Religion - 7. Local government, politics and organized labor - 8. Manufacturing, mining and business - 9. Maritime, communications, fur trade - 10. Education - 11. Poverty, health and crime. Series of detailed bibliographic essays on contemporary sources for research. *Class No:* 974/979(01)

Yearbooks & Directories

[8054]
AMERICAN ASSOCIATION FOR STATE AND LOCAL HISTORY. **Directory of historical agencies in North America.** Smith, B.P., *ed*. 13th ed. Nashville, Tennessee, the Association, 1986, Biennial since 1959. vi,686p. illus., pbk. $64.95. ISBN: 0910050775.

First published 1956 as *Directory of historical societies and agencies in United States and Canada.* Updates *Historical societies in the United States and Canada: a handbook* (Washington, the Association, 2nd ed., 1944).

9375 entries A-Z by state or province, then by city or town. Also includes list of Historical and Archaeological Areas Administered by the National Park Service. General data: name and address; date founded; president/secretary; number of members and staff; publication; 'major programs' (*e.g.* library; museums; sites; oral history). Entries for organisations are included even if 'questionnaire not received'. *Class No:* 974/979(058)

Bibliographies

[8055]

City & State directories in print An annotated guide to over 4,500 State, City, and Local directories, rosters, guides, and lists of all kinds, covering: Arts and entertainments; Business & industry; Computers & telecommunications; Education; Government; Health and medicine; Law; Real Estate; Recreation; Science & technology; Social services; Travel; and many other topics. First Edition 1990-91. Towell, J.E. *and* Montney, C.B., *eds.* Detroit, Gale Research Inc. 1989. xix,966p. indexes. $145. ISBN: 0810318482. ISSN: 10438939.

Scope: 'general commercial and manufacturing directories; general and specialized lists of cultural institutions; directories of individual industries, trades and professions; rosters of professional and scientific societies; guides to events, accommodations, restaurants, and entertainments; and lists of community services. It also includes membership lists of special-interest groups of all kinds - political, recreational, cultural *etc.*; publications of government agencies listing their own activities or the programs supported by them; and a wide variety of lists and guides on other subjects' (*Introduction*). Arranged A-Z by State and US Territories. Subject, and title and keyword indexes. *Class No:* 974/979(058)(01)

Maps & Atlases

[8056]

LONG, J.H. Historical atlas and chronology of county boundaries 1788-1980. Boston, G.K. Hall, 4v., 1984. maps, plans, bibliogs.

1. *Delaware, Maryland, New Jersey, Pennsylvania.* 251p. Bibliography p.247-51. 2. *Illinois. Indiana. Ohio.* 321p. Bibliography p.317-21. 4. *Iowa, Missouri.* 375p. Bibliography p.371-5. 5. *Minnesota. North Dakota. South Dakota.* 479p. Bibliography p.475-9. Data: boundaries at international level down to counties; seats of government at each level; relevant coastlines; names of states. With boundary and regional maps and county chronologies. *Class No:* 974/979(084.3)

[8057]

NEWBERRY LIBRARY HISTORICAL BOUNDARY DATA FILE. Historical atlas and chronology of county boundaries 1788-1980. Boston, Mass, G.K. Hall, 5v., 1984. 1920p. maps, bibliogs. $475.00 (Export $720.00). ISBN: 081610431x, set.

1. *Delaware, Maryland, New Jersey, Pennsylvania.* ISBN 0816104492. 2. *Illinois, Indiana, Ohio.* ISBN 0816104506. 3. *Michigan and Wisconsin* ISBN 0816104514. 4. *Iowa and Missouri.* ISBN 0816104522. 5. *Minnesota, North Dakota, South Dakota.* ISBN 0816104530. Each is available separately at $99.00 (Export $108.00).

A compilation of maps and texts describing country and state boundary changes. Each volume includes a detailed history emphasizing major events and disputes affecting boundaries, a chronology of changes, and select bibliographies. *Class No:* 974/979(084.3)

Alaska

[8058]

NASKE, C-M. *and* **SLOTNIK, H.E. Alaska** a history of the 49th state. 2nd ed. Norman, Univ. of Oklahoma Press, 1987. xiv,349p. illus., maps, tables, bibliog., index. ISBN: 0806120991.

1st ed. Grand Rapids, Mich., W.B. Eerdman, 1979.

A well-documented historical narrative from early times with an emphasis on major developments in the 20th century. 15 chapters: 1. The Great Land and its peoples - 2. The early Russian period - 3. Russian naval rule and the sale of Alaska - 4. American purchase and settlement ... 8. Alaska's rocky road to Statehood - 9. Transition to statehood - 10. The State of Alaska ... 14. The oil boom. 8 Appendices: A. The Governors of Alaska ... D. Delegates to Congress. Chapter notes p.305-20. Bibliographical essay: the sources of Alaska's history p.321-35. Analytical index. *Class No:* 979.8

America—South

Bibliographies

[8059]

GOODMAN, E.J. The Exploration of South America: an annotated bibliography. New York, Garland Publishing, 1983. xx,174p. bibliog., index. $43.00. (*Themes in European expansion, no.4.*) ISBN: 0824091809.

915 briefly annotated items (some relating to Spanish and Portuguese language material) in 11 form, thematic, and chronological period sections. 'A strong recommendation to have the book any any library even if only slightly concerned with South America' (*Geographical Journal,* v.150, no.3, November 1984, p.383-4). *Class No:* 980(01)

Brazil

[8060]

BURNS, E.B. A History of Brazil. 2nd ed. New York, Columbia Univ. Press, 1880. x, 579p. illus., maps, bibliog., index. $32.50. ISBN: 0231047487.

First published 1970.

Standard single volume economic, social, cultural and political history. Chronology p.541-546. Glossary of Portuguese words used in text p.547-550. Bibliographical essay p.551-556. 6 maps. Analytical index. *Class No:* 981

[8061]

História geral da civilização Brasiliera. São Paulo, Diffel, 10v., 1960-83.

A Época Colonial. 1. *Do descobrimento à expansão territorial.* 1960. 2. *Administraçao, economia, sociedade.* 1977. *O Brasil Monárquico.* 1. *O processo de emancipação.* 1976. 2. *Dispersâo e unidade.* 1978. 3. *Reações e transações.* 1976. 4. *Declínio e queda do império.* 1982. 5. *Do império à República,* 3rd ed., 1983. *O Brasil Republicano.* 1. *Estrutura de poder e economica (1889-1930).* 1977. 2. *Sociedade e instituições (1889-1930).* 2nd ed., 1978. 3. *Sociedade e política (1930-1964).* 1981. Large scale cooperative history. *Class No:* 981

[8062]
Order and progress a political history of Brazil. Schneider, R.M. Boulder, Colo., Westview Press, 1991. xvii,486p. map, index. $55. ISBN: 0813310776.

10 chapters: 2. Monarchical Brazil ... 5. Quest for development and democracy 1946 to 1960 ... 7. The Military as ruler ... 10. Brazil faces the 1990s. Chapter notes p.388-466. List of Chief Executives of Republican Brazil p.467-8. 'A cogently written narrative that students of modern Brazil will find indispensable' (*Choice*, v.29, no.4, December 1991, p.652). *Class No:* 981

Bibliographies

[8063]
DUTRA, F.A. **A Guide to the history of Brazil 1500-1822.** Santa Barabara, California and Oxford, ABC-Clio, 1980. xxviii, 625p.

939 numbered entries in 26 sections (1. Bibliographies - 2. The Portuguese background - 3. The history of Brazil ... 26. The historiography of colonial Brazil, 1500-1822). Lengthy annotations. Entries include analyticals, periodical articles and dissertations. Glossary, p.591-601. Index of authors, editors, translators and illustrators. Index of 19th and 20th century authors cited in the text but not abstracted. Biographical index. 'Highly recommended for colleges and universities ... and for larger public libraries' (*Choice*, v.18, no.5, January 1981, p.634). *Class No:* 981(01)

[8064]
LEVINE, R.M. **Brazil since 1930** an annotated bibliography for social historians. New York, Garland, 1980. 336p. $48.00. ISBN: 082409543x.

Topical divisions: reference; urban, rural, society, cultural and educational aspects. Author and subject indexes. 'There is no comparable work available for the American scholar' (*Choice*, v.17, no.5/6, July/August 1980, p.654). *Class No:* 981(01)

[8065]
—LEVINE, R.M. Brazil 1822-1930 an annotated bibliography for social historians. New York, Garland, 1983. 504p. $66.00. ISBN: 0824092120. *Class No:* 981(01)

[8066]
SKIDMORE, T.E. **The Historiography of Brazil 1889-1964;** *Hispanic American Historical Review*, v.55, no.4, November 1975 p.716-748 and v.56, no.1, February 1976, p.81-109.

Ideologies and assumptions - From Empire to Republic - The Old Republic 1889-1930 - 1930-1945 - 1945-1964 - State and local politics - Labor and the left - Economic history - Foreign relations. *Class No:* 981(01)

Dictionaries

[8067]
Dicionário histórico-biográfico Brasileiro 1930-1983. Beloch, I. *and* Alves de Abreu, A., *eds.* Rio de Janeiro, Editora Forense - Universitária, 4v., 1984. xxxi, 3634p. bibliog.

Huge work (3 columns to the page) with 4,493 entries (3,741 biographies). Over 750 thematic articles deal with institutions; events; political concepts; constitutions; notorious laws and degrees. '*The* authoritative reference work on recent Brazilian history' (*Hispanic American Historical Review*, v.67, no.3, August 1987, p.545-546). *Class No:* 981(038)

[8068]
LEVINE, R.M. **Historical dictionary of Brazil.** Metuchen, New Jersey, Scarecrow Press, 1979. xi,297p. $24.00; £22.50. (*Latin American Historical Dictionaries no.19.*) ISBN: 0810811782.

Dictionary p.1-228. Bibliography p.229-97. Definitions 'treat not only people and events but Brazilian civilization in several dimensions'. 'A most helpful reference work' (S.V. Bryant. *Brazil.* 1985. Entry 145). *Class No:* 981(038)

Chronologies

[8069]
FITZGIBBON, R.H. **Brazil** a chronology and fact book 1488-1973. Dobbs Ferry, New York, Oceana Publications, 1974. 150p. bibliog. $8.50. ISBN: 0379163098.

Of major political, social, and economic events. Includes list of rulers 1808-1974. *Class No:* 981(090)

Argentina

[8070]
ROCK, D. **Argentina 1516-1982: from Spanish colonization to the Falklands War and Alphonsin.** Los Angeles, Univ. of California Press, 1985. London, I.B. Tauris, 1986. xxix, 478p. illus., maps, bibliog., index. $40.00 £29.50. ISBN: 0520051890, US; 1850430861, UK.

'A standard work: undramatic but judicious and convincing' (*International Affairs*, v.62, no.4, Autumn 1986, p.717). *Class No:* 982

Falkland Islands

[8071]
AZPIRI, J.L.M. **Historia completa de las Malvinas** Tomos I-III. Buenos Aires, Editorial Oriente, 3v., 1966. maps, bibliog.

'A very thoroughly documented history of the Falkland Islands (Malvinas), though biased towards Argentina's territorial claims' (H.G.R. King, *Atlantic Ocean.* 1985. Entry 781). *Class No:* 982.91

[8072]
BECK, P. **The Falkland Islands as an international problem.** London, Routledge, 1988. xii,211p. maps, tables, bibliog., index. £35. ISBN: 041500909x.

Extremely well-documented historical survey of the nature and development of the 170 year old dispute between Argentina and the United Kingdom. Extensive chapter notes. Bibliography p.197-205. 4 maps. 'Although the conflict itself is not covered in detail, subsequent developments are, and this is a useful compendium of events ... presented in a balanced way' (*British Bulletin of Latin America, the Caribbean, Portugal and Spain*, no.81, October 1989, p.34). *Class No:* 982.91

[8073]
HOFFMAN, F.L. *and* HOFFMAN, O.M. **Sovereignty in dispute: the Falklands/Malvinas 1493-1982.** Boulder, Colorado, Westview Press, 1984. xiv, 194p. illus., maps, bibliog., index. $20.00 £22.00. (*Special studies on Latin America and the Caribbean.*)

An outline of the European discovery of the Falklands and a survey of the longstanding dispute between the United Kingdom and the Republic of Argentina in 12 chapters, 6 of

....*(contd.)*

which are devoted to events leading up to the war in the South Atlantic. Chronology, p.179-181. Bibliography p.182-185. *Class No:* 982.91

[8074]

KING, H.G.R. 'Falklands War 1982' and 'Contemporary relations between Great Britain and Argentina: Sovereignty issues' *The Atlantic Ocean*, 1985, p.181-95.

Entries 810-875. British official and unofficial sources, Argentine and other sources. Sound coverage. *Class No:* 982.91

Bibliographies

[8075]

MUNDO LO, S. de. The Falkland/Malvinas Islands a bibliography of books 1619-1982. Urbana, Illinois, Albatross, 1983. 65p. index. $9.00.

Items, some briefly annotated, arranged A-Z by author with select subject index. 'Very useful for academic libraries with an interest in Latin American history or politics' (*Choice*, v.21, no.3, November 1983, p.404). *Class No:* 982.91(01)

[8076]

ORGILL, A. The Falklands War background, conflict, aftermath: an annotated bibliography. London, Mansell, 1993. xii,132p. £35. ISBN: 0720121302.

822 entries relating to mainly English and Spanish language books, document collections and journal articles in 6 sub-divided sections: Bibliographies; Sovereignty dispute; 1982 Crisis; Diplomatic and political aspects; 1982 War; Aftermath. *Class No:* 982.91(01)

[8077]

RASOR, E.L. The Falklands/Malvinas campaign a bibliography. Westport, Conn., Greenwood Press, 1992. xiii,196p. index. $45; £36.40. (*Bibliographies of Battles and Leaders, no.6.*) ISBN: 0313281513.

Part 1: Narrative and historiographical survey. 11 bibliographical essays (2. Sources - 3. Geography ... 5. Diplomacy - 6. The forces - 7. Operations ... 11. Research). Part 2: 554 annotated items, mostly English language material, including oral histories, official histories, pertinent journal and periodical articles, conference papers *etc.* but generally excluding popular magazines and newspapers. *Class No:* 982.91(01)

[8078]

REVELLO, J.T. Bibliografía de las Islas Malvinas, obras, mapas y documentos. Buenos Aires, Imprenta de la Universidad, 1953. 260p. maps. (*Universidad de Buenos Aires Facultad de Filosofía y Letras, Publicaciones del Instituto de Investigaciónes Historicas No.99.*)

'A comprehensive annotated bibliography ... with special reference to historical and geographical works before 1900. It includes a list of early maps including those in the Ministerio de Marina, Madrid' (H.G.R. King. *Atlantic Ocean*. 1985. Entry 768). *Class No:* 982.91(01)

Chile

[8079]

ENCINA, F.A. *and* **CASTEDO, L. Resumen de la historia de Chile 1535-1925.** Santiago, Empresa Editora Zig-Zag, 4v., 1954-1982.

Encina's 20v. *Historia de Chile 1535-1891* completed in early 1950s. A 3v. abridgement was added to by Castedo who took the story up to 1935.

'The volume by Castedo is a major contribution to twentieth-century Chilean history' (H. Blakemore. *Chile.* 1988. Entry 102). *Class No:* 983

[8080]

GALDAMES, L. A History of Chile. Chapel Hill, Univ. of North Carolina Press, 1941. xii, 565p.

Originally published as *Estudio de la historia de Chile.*

Biographical notes p.441-535 *i.e.* biographical dictionary of celebrated figures in the development and history of Chile. *Class No:* 983

Bibliographies

[8081]

BLAKEMORE, H. 'The Chilean Revolution of 1891 and its historiography'. *Hispanic American Historical Review*, v.45, no.3, August 1965, p.393-421.

'A seminal article' (H. Blakemore. *Chile.* 1988. Entry 620). *Class No:* 983(01)

[8082]

SATER, W.F. 'A Survey of recent Chilean historiography 1965-1976' *Latin American Research Review*, v.14, no.2, 1979, p.55-88.

'An excellent and comprehensive survey ... omits no article or book' (H. Blakemore. *Chile.* 1988. Entry 618). *Class No:* 983(01)

Dictionaries

[8083]

BIZZARO, S. Historical dictionary of Chile. 2nd ed. Metuchen, New Jersey, Scarecrow Press, 1987. xv,583p. maps, bibliog. £41.25; $55.00. (*Latin American Historical Dictionaries, no.7.*) ISBN: 0810819643.

1st ed. 1972.

Dictionary p.1-534. Bibliography p.535-83. 'A global view of the history and politics of Chile emphasizing the contemporary period' (Introduction). 'A welcome version, updated and much enlarged' (H. Blakemore, *Chile,* 1988, Entry no.614). *Class No:* 983(038)

19th Century

Bibliographies

[8084]

COLLIER, S. 'Historiography of the Portalion period (1830-1891) in Chile', *Hispanic American Historical Review*, v.57, no.4, November 1977, p.660-690.

Traditional interpretations - The Revisionists - Social and economic approaches - Recent research and writing. *Class No:* 983"18"(01)

Bolivia

[8085]
KLEIN, H.S. Bolivia the evolution of a multi-ethnic society. New York, Oxford Univ. Press, 1982. xvii, 318p. maps, tables, bibliog., index. $29.95. (*Latin American Histories*.) ISBN: 0195030117.

9 chronological/thematic chapters: 1. Geography and pre-Columbian civilization ... 8. The National Revolution 1959-1964 ... 9. The emergence of a New Order 1964-1980. Political chronology p.270-274. Bolivian bibliographical essay p.275-293. 7 maps. Analytical index. 'Bolivia ... has lacked a modern historical survey in English. This excellent little volume takes care of the problem' (*Choice*, v.20, no.1, September 1982, p.164). *Class No:* 984

Dictionaries

[8086]
HEATH, D.B. Historical dictionary of Bolivia. Metuchen, New Jersey, Scarecrow Press, 1972. vi,324p. $15.00. (*Latin American Historical Dictionaries no.4.*)

About 2,000 very brief entries, covering people, places, events, institutions, etc. that have been important in the history of Bolivia and its antecedent, Alto Peru.'Towards understanding Bolivia: a biblio essay', p.255-324.
Class No: 984(038)

Peru

[8087]
Historia general de los Peruanos. 11th ed. Lima, Ediciones Peisa, 3v., 1988. illus., maps. ISBN: 9459968847, set.

1. Doig, F.K. *El Perú antiguo.* 783p. 38 chapters organized in 7 parts: 1. Conceptos preliminares - 2. Los primeros Peruanos - 3. Formacion de la alta cultura (2000BC-AD300) - 4. El apogeo cultural/Artesanal (300-800) - 5. El fenomeno Tiahuanaco y Tiahuanaco-Huari (800-1200) - 6. Principales culturas tardias (1200-1438) - 7. El incanato (1220-1522). Bibliografia de arqueologia Peruana p.759-778.

2. Barrencha, R.P. and others. *El Perú virreinal.* 691p. Short studies in 6 parts: 1. Vision introductoria - 2. Los Incas de Vilcabamba - 3. Virreinato Peruano - 3/4. Aspectos sociologicos y costumbristas - 5. Indagaciones sombres - 6. Iconografia biografia de los Virreyos y Gobernadores 1535-1824 p.603-691.

3. Valárel, C.D. and others. *El Perú Republicano.* 722p.+[8]p. col. maps, 723-773p. 1. Tupac Amaru (Precursor de la Independencia) - 2. Emancipacion y republica hasta 1899-3. El Perú de 1900 a 1985 - 4. Indagaciones sombre El Perú Republicano - 5. Inconografia y biografia de los Presidentes del Perú. Apéndice: Mapas e información de los Departamentos del Peru p.723-73.
Class No: 985

Bibliographies

[8088]
BARRENECHEA, R.P. Fuentes historicas peruanas. Lima, Instituto Raúl Porras Barrenechea, 1963. 601p.

'This classic bibliography of Peruvian history ... remains a standard work of reference for researchers' (J.R. Fisher, *Peru*, 1989. Entry 692). *Class No:* 985(01)

[8089]
BASADRE, J. Introduccíon a las bases documentales para la historia de la república del Perú, con algunas reflexiones. Lima, Villanueva, 3v., 1971. 1076p; 177p.

Follows compilers *Historia de la república de Perú 1822-1933.*

More than 170,000 items cited in v.1-2 with v.3 index. 'A monumental and indispensable work of reference' (J.R. Fisher. *Peru*, 1989. Entry 696). *Class No:* 985(01)

[8090]
TAURO, A. Bibliografia peruana de historia 1940-1953. Lima, 1953. 196p.

1214 annotated entries. 'It is indicative of the historiographical emphasis then in vogue that over 400 deal with the pre-hispanic and conquest period, 300 with the colonial era and only 150 with post independence; there is a separate section on local history' (J.R. Fisher. *Peru*, 1989, Entry 688). *Class No:* 985(01)

Dictionaries

[8091]
ALISKY, M. Historical dictionary of Peru. Metuchen, New Jersey, Scarecrow Press, 1979. vi,157p. bibliog. $18.50. (*Latin American Historical Dictionaries, no.20.*) ISBN: 0810812355.

Dictionary p.9-116. Appendix A: Chronology of rulers of the Inca Empire p.119-20 - B. Departments of the Republic of Peru p.121-2. Bibliography p.132-57.
Class No: 985(038)

Colombia

Dictionaries

[8092]
DAVIS, R.H. Historical dictionary of Colombia. Metuchen, New Jersey, Scarecrow Press, 1977. viii,280p. (*Latin American Historical Dictionaries, no.14.*) ISBN: 0810809990.

Chronology p.1-41. Dictionary p.43-1231. Bibliographical guide to Colombian history (7 sections) p.233-280.
Class No: 986(038)

Ecuador

Bibliographies

[8093]
NORRIS, R.E. Guía bibliogáfia para el estudio de la historia ecuatoriana. Austin, Institute of Latin American Studies, Univ. of Texas, 1978. 295p. (*Guides and Bibliographies Series no.11.*)

4000 entries. 'The work is valuable ... for articles printed in Ecuadorian periodicals' (D. Corkhill. *Ecuador*. 1989. Entry 542). *Class No:* 986.6(01)

Dictionaries

[8094]
BORK, A.W. *and* **MAIER, G. Historical dictionary of Ecuador.** Metuchen, New Jersey, Scarecrow Press, 1973. x, 11-192p. bibliog. (*Latin American Historical Dictionaries,*

....(contd.)
no.10.) ISBN: 081080638x.
Dictionary p.11-160. 8 appendices. Bibliography p.175-92.
Class No: 986.6(038)

Venezuela
[8095]
EWELL, J. **Venezuela** a century of change. Stanford, California, Stanford Univ. Press; London, C. Hurst & Co., 1984. xiii, 258p. maps, tables, bibliog., index. $27.50. £12.50. ISBN: 0804712131, US; 090583836x, UK.
7 chronological/thematic chapters covering the period 1890s to date. List of Presidents since 1871 p.228. Bibliography p.236-244. Glossary of Spanish terms p.245-247. Analytical index. 'A good general introduction to modern Venezuelan history' (*Bulletin of Latin American Research*, v.4, no.2, 1985, p.168-169). *Class No:* 987

[8096]
LOMBARDI, J.V. **Venezuela** the search for order, the dream of progress. New York, Oxford Univ. Press, 1982. xii, 348p. maps, tables. $29.95. ISBN: 0195030133.
Comprehensive political and economic history. Chronology 1498-1979 p.269-287. Excellent bibliographical essay p.288-314. *Class No:* 987

Bibliographies
[8097]
Guia para el estudio de la historia de Venezuela. Caracus, Academia Nacional De La Historia, 1982. 217p. pbk.
Bibliography of about 700 annotated entries arranged A-Z by author. *Class No:* 987(01)

Dictionaries
[8098]
RUDOLPH, D.K. *and* RUDOLPH, G.A. **Historical dictionary of Venezuela.** Metuchen, New Jersey, Scarecrow Press, 1971. vi,7-142p. bibliog. (*Latin American Historical Dictionaries, no.3.*) ISBN: 0810804239.
Dictionary p.7-123. Bibliography p.124-42.
Class No: 987(038)

Guyana

20th Century
[8099]
MANLEY, R.H. **Guyana emergent** the post independence struggle for nondependent development. 2nd ed. Cambridge, Mass., Schenkman, 1982. ix, 176p. bibliog., index.
First published 1979.
8 chapters (1. The slave colony ... 8. Beyond the first post-independence decade). Chapter notes. This edition adds Epilogue, taking the story up to 1980, and adds a bibliography. *Class No:* 988.1"19"

Paraguay
[8100]
WARREN, H.G. **Paraguay an informal history.** Westport, Connecticut, Greenwood Press, 1982. xii, 393p. maps. bibliog. index. $48.50. ISBN: 0313236518.
Reprint of 1st ed. 1949 published by Univ. of Oklahoma Press.
Standard history in 20 chapters. Appendix: Governors, dictators, and presidents of Paraguay 1536-1941, p.355-8. Bibliographical essay p.359-68. 8 maps. 'Remains one of the best introductions to the history of Paraguay' (R.A. Nickson, *Paraguay*, 1987. Entry 81). *Class No:* 989.2

Dictionaries
[8101]
NICKSON, R.A. **Historical dictionary of Paraguay.** 2nd ed. Metuchen, New Jersey, Scarecrow Press, 1993. xxi,685p. maps, bibliog. $69.50; £69.50. (*Latin American Historical Dictionaries, no.24.*) ISBN: 0810826437.
Replaces C.J. Kolinski's *Historical Dictionary of Paraguay* (1973).
Over 1600 cross-referenced entries, 'an impressive range of persons, places, institutions, events, cultural topics, politics, administrations and geographical facts' (*Reference Reviews*, no.7, 1993, p.45-6). Chronology 1515-1989. Bibliography of 540 entries. 5 maps. *Class No:* 989.2(038)

Uruguay
[8102]
BLANCA PARÍS DE ODDONE, M. **Cronología comparada de la historia del Uruguay (1830-1945).** Montevideo, Universidad de la República, 1968. 189p. map, bibliog.
Entries in 3 divisions: 1. Politics and administration - 2. Technology, economy, society - 3. Culture. Indexes to place-names, personal names and institutions. *Class No:* 989.9

Dictionaries
[8103]
WILLIS, J.L. **Historical dictionary of Uruguay.** Metuchen, New Jersey, Scarecrow Press, 19. vii,275p. bibliog. $24.00. (*Latin American Historical Dictionaries, no.11.*) ISBN: 0810807661.
Dictionary p.1-260. Bibliography p.261-75.
Class No: 989.9(038)

Australasia

Indonesia
[8104]
ABEYASKERE, S. **Jakarta: a history.** Rev. ed. Singapore, Oxford Univ. Press, 1987. xviii,298p.+16p. plates, illus., maps, index. softcover. ISBN: 0195889479.
General history of the city in 6 well-documented chapters (1. Company town: early origins to 1800... 4. Japanese occupation and the struggle for independence 1942-9... 6. Java under Sadikin and his successors 1966-1985). Glossary p.264-6. Bibliography p.267-84. 9 maps. This revised edition includes a new bibliography. *Class No:* 991

[8105]
RIKLEFS, M.C. A History of modern Indonesia: *c.*1300 to present. 2nd ed. London, The Macmillan Press, 1991. 340p. maps, bibliog., index. $18. (*Macmillan's Asian Histories.*) ISBN: 0333576896.

1st ed. 1981.

Comprehensive introductory text in 6 parts: 1. Emergence of the modern era (1300-1650) - 2. Struggles for hegemony (1630-1800) - 3. Creation of a colonial state (1800-1910) - 4. Emergence of the idea of Indonesia (1900-1942) - 5. Destruction of the colonial state (1942-50) - 6. Independent Indonesia. Bibliography p.292-307. Maps p.310-318. *Class No:* 991

[8106]
WESSELING, H.L. 'Dutch historiography on European Expansion since 1945', p.122-39, P.C. Emmer and H.L. Wesseling eds: *Reappraisals in Overseas History. Essays on post-war historiography about European expansion.* The Hague, Leiden Univ. Press-Nijhoff, 1979. 248p. ISBN: 906021447.

Historiographical survey on the history of Indonesia and Dutch colonial policies. *Class No:* 991

Dictionaries

[8107]
CRIBB, R. Historical dictionary of Indonesia. Metuchen, N.J., Scarecrow Press, 1992. lxxiv,663p. maps, bibliog. $72.50. (*Asian Historical Dictionnaires, no.9.*) ISBN: 0810825422.

Covers the entire area of the Republic of Indonesia *i.e.* Irian Jaya (Western New Guinea) and East Timor. Chronology p.xxxvii-lx. Maps p.lxii-lxxiv. Dictionary p.1-502. Bibliography p.549-661. Appendices list Governors-General Netherland East Indies, rulers of early states, Indonesian cabinets, Presidents *etc.* *Class No:* 991(038)

Chronologies

[8108]
TAYLOR, J.G. The Indonesian occupation of East Timor 1974-1989 a chronology. London, Catholic Institute for International Relations in association with the Refugee Studies Programme, Univ. of Oxford, 1990. iv,102p. illus., map, index. £14.99. ISBN: 1852870516.

An essential reference tool for events (727 listed) in this former Portuguese colony beginning 18 months before the Indonesian invasion, occupation, and annexation. From 1977 onwards events recorded include a source reference, usually an English-language publication, although some articles in translation from the Portuguese or Bahasa Indonesian are also to be found. *Class No:* 991(090)

Borneo

[8109]
KING, V.T. The Peoples of Borneo. Oxford, Blackwell, 1993. xii,339p. illus., maps, bibliog., index. (*The Peoples of South-East Asia and The Pacific.*) ISBN: 0631172211.

1. Island of Borneo: general perspectives - 2. People - 3. Prehistory - 4. India, China and Islam - 5. Europeans and Borneo: from early trade to independence - 6. Economic systems - 7. Socio-political organization - 8. Worldview and

....(contd.)
religion - 9. Material culture - 10. Modernization and development. Bibliography p.305-24. 10 maps. Analytical index. *Class No:* 991.1

Bibliographies

[8110]
Borneo in history a catalogue of books in the Borneo collection of the University Library describing Borneo before 1960. Francis, S., *comp.* Brunei Darussalam, Universiti Brunei Darussalam, 1990. 70p. illus. typescript.

Annotated A-Z by author listing of all bound books and reports in the University Library's Borneo collection. *Class No:* 991.1(01)

Philippines

Bibliographies

[8111]
RETANA Y GAMBOA, W.E. Aparato bibliográfico de la historia general de Filipinas deducido de la collección que posee en Barcelona la Compañia General de Tabacos de dichas Islas. Manila, Pedro B. Ayuda, 3v., 1964.

First published Madrid; Minuesa de los Rios, 1906.

4623 items. Arranged chronologically. V.1: 1524-1800; v.2: 1801-1886; v.3: 1887-1905. 'These three stately volumes remain the best bibliography of the Spanish period' (Richardson, J. *Philippines*, 1989. Entry 947). *Class No:* 991.4(01)

Dictionaries

[8112]
MARING, E.G. *and* MARING, J.M. Historical and cultural dictionary of The Philippines. Metuchen, N.J., Scarecrow Press, 1973. vii,240p. bibliog. (*Historical and Cultural Dictionaries of Asia, no.3.*) ISBN: 0810805634.

1800 entries relating to Philippine history, culture, physical geography, natural history, economics, politics and demography. Dictionary p.1-231. Bibliography p.233-40. *Class No:* 991.4(038)

Oceania

[8113]
CAMPBELL, I.C. A History of the Pacific Islands. St. Lucia, Univ. of Queensland Press, 1990. 239p. maps, tables, bibliog., index. pbk. ISBN: 0702222917.

First published Christchurch, Univ. of Canterbury Press, 1989.

Narrative history in 17 chapters of Polynesian, Melanesian, Micronesian and European cultures and activities in the Pacific Ocean *e.g.* 1. The original inhabitants - 2. Austronesian colonization - 3. Polynesia: the age of European discovery ... 15. Attaining independence. Glossary p.229-31. Bibliography p.232-5. 8 maps. *Class No:* 993

[8114]

HOWE, K.R. **Where the waves fall** a new South Sea Islands history from first settlement to colonial rule. Sydney, Allen and Unwin; Honolulu, Hawaii Univ. Press, 1984. xix,403p. illus., maps, bibliog., index. ISBN: 0868613436, Aust; 0824809211, US.

A thematic overview of the history of Polynesia and Island Melanesia from c.50,000BC to colonial rule in the 19th century. Chapter 16: Considering the new historiography. Chapter notes and references p.353-74. Bibliography p.375-92. *Class No:* 993

[8115]

SCARR, D. **The History of the Pacific Islands** kingdoms of the reefs. South Melbourne, Macmillan, 1990. xi,426p. illus., maps, bibliog., index. $59.95. ISBN: 073290210x.

Narrative history in 20 chapters encompassing native cultural societies, local responses to European voyagers, the colonial experience, and postwar independence movements, 'from Micronesia to glimpses of New Zealand, and from Hawaii to Papua New Guinea'. Chapter notes p.363-88. Bibliography p.389-415. 'No doubt that this is an ambitious and important work ... it will make a permanent scholarly mark' (*Pacific Affairs*, v.65, no.1, Spring 1992, p.137-8). *Class No:* 993

[8116]

SPATE, O.H.K. **The Pacific since Magellan.** Canberra, Australian National Univ. Press; London, Croom Helm, 3v. 1979-1988.

1. *The Spanish Lake.* 1979, xxiv,372p. £40.00. Chapter notes p.293-354. illus. 25 maps. ISBN 0708107272 Aust. 070990049x UK. 2. *Monopolists and freebooters.* 1983. xxi,426p. £35.00. Notes p.337-412. illus. 28 maps. 0708118445 Aust. 0709923716 UK. 3. *Paradise found and lost.* 1988. xxi,410p. £40.00. Notes p.325-95. illus. 28 maps. 0080344003 Aust. 0415025656 UK. Aim is 'to seek to explicate the process by which the greatest blank on the map became a nexus of global commercial and strategic relations' (*Preface to v.1*). 'An excellent survey of the scholarship about this area ... but the work suffers seriously from lack of a bibliography' (*Choice*, v.27,no.1, September 1989, p.198). *Class No:* 993

Bibliographies

[8117]

KRAUSS, N.L.H. **Bibliography of the Banks Islands, Western Pacific.** Honolulu, the author, 1971. 10p. sd.

152 annotated entries. *Class No:* 993(01)

[8118]

KRAUSS, N.L.H. **Bibliography of the Line Islands, Central Pacific.** Honolulu, the author, 1970. 18p. index, sd.

317 entries A-Z by author with note on history of discovery and constitutional and administrative status. *Class No:* 993(01)

[8119]

KRAUSS, N.L.H. **Bibliography of the Tokelau or Union Islands. Central Pacific.** Honolulu, the author, 1969. 11p. sd.

135 entries A-Z by author. With note on history of discovery and administrative and constitutional status. *Class No:* 993(01)

[8120]

KRAUSS, N.L.H. **Niué, South Pacific.** Honolulu, the author, 1970. 16p. sd.

206 entries A-Z by author with note on history of discovery and administrative and constitutional status. *Class No:* 993(01)

Dictionaries

[8121]

CRAIG, R.D. *and* KING, F.P., *eds.* **Historical dictionary of Oceania.** Westport, Connecticut, Greenwood Press, 1981. xxxv, 392p. maps, bibliog., index. $67.95. ISBN: 0313210608.

106 contributors and almost 500 entries cover the exploration, European settlement, and government of the islands of Melanesia, Micronesia and Polynesia. 7 Appendices (2. Historical chronology ... 3. Prehistoric settlements ... 4. European explorers). Bibliography p.373-375. 19 maps. *Class No:* 993(038)

New Zealand

[8122]

OLSSEN, E. **A History of Otago.** Dunedin, John McIndoe Ltd., 1984. xvi, 270p. illus. (some col.), maps. ISBN: 0868680583.

Bibliographical note p.245. Index p.259-270. 'Attempts to explain the distinctive character of Otago's past'. *Class No:* 993.1

[8123]

RICE, G., *ed.* **Oxford history of New Zealand.** 2nd ed. Wellington, Oxford Univ. Press (NZ), 1993. xviii,755p. maps, tables, bibliog., index. Pbk. ISBN: 0195582578.

First published 1981 edited by W.H. Oliver and B.R. Williams.

Single volume cooperative history (by 22 scholars) whose structure 'combines a broad chronological shape with a detailed thematic analysis' (*Introduction*). Chapter references p.607-64. Chapter bibliographies p.665-735. Glossary of Maori terms p.586-7. Analytical index. *Class No:* 993.1

Bibliographies

[8124]

WOOD, G.A. **Studying New Zealand history.** Dunedin, Univ. of Otago Press, 1992. 145p. index.

Research guide to reference works and bibliographies, periodicals and theses, national, regional and local sources, and newspapers, pamphlets and photographs. 'The organization of material is clear, the sections are well signposted and the information is comprehensive and detailed' (*New Zealand Geographer*, v.48, no.2, October 1992, p.92). *Class No:* 993.1(01)

Chronologies

[8125]

The New Zealand book of events. Auckland, Reed Methuen, 1986. 448p. index. ISBN: 0474001237.

49 contributors. General reference source organized in 14 chapters: 1. The Maori - 2. European settlement - 3. Transport - 4. Communications - 5. Industries - 6. Trade, taxes and the economy - 7. The work force - 8. Government

....(contd.)
- 9. Law - 10. Defence - 11. Social development - 12. Science and environment - 13. Arts - 14. Disasters. Glossary of Maori words p.11. *Class No:* 993.1(090)

[8126]
REED, A.W., *comp.* It happened in New Zealand: a day-by-day illustrated chronology of famous and interesting events in New Zealand history from 1640 to 1971. Wellington, A.H. and A.W. Reed, 1973. 114p. illus., map, index. ISBN: 0589007602.
Factual unannotated chronology. Analytical index.
Class No: 993.1(090)

Melanesia
[8127]
HOARE, M. Norfolk Islands an outline of its history 1774 - 1987. 4th ed. St. Lucia, Univ. of Queensland Press, 1988. xv11, 206p. illus. map. bibliog.., index. pbk.
1st ed. 1969.
Authoritative account in 4 pts; 1. European discovery, prehistory and 1st penal settlement (1774 - 1814) - 2. 2nd penal settlement (1825 - 1856) - 3. The Pitcairn Islanders and their descendants (1856 - 1945) - 4. The post war years. Chronology p. xiii - xvii. Bibliography p.175-93.
Class No: 993.2/.7

Bibliographies
[8128]
KRAUSS, N.L.H. Bibliography of the Santa Cruz Islands, Western Pacific. Honolulu, the author, 1969. 8p. sd.
97 entries A-Z by author. Note on history of discovery and administrative and constitutional status.
Class No: 993.2/.7(01)

[8129]
KRAUSS, N.L.H. Bibliography of the Torres Islands, Southwest Pacific. Honolulu, the author, 1971. 4p. sd.
47 unannotated entries. *Class No:* 993.2/.7(01)

Chronologies
[8130]
O'REILLY, P. 'Chronologique de Wallis et Futuna' *Journal de la Société des Océanistes*, v.19, 1963, p.12-45.
Summary of major political and economic events.
Class No: 993.2/.7(090)

Australia
[8131]
Australian Ethnic Heritage Series. Gigler, M., *ed.* Melbourne, Australian Ethnic Press, 1983-.
A multi-volume series highlighting the background of the various national groups represented in Australia's population and their individual contributions to its history *e.g.* Prentis, M.D. *The Scottish in Australia.* 1987. 173p. illus., bibliog., index. A$16.00. 11 chapters. 3 Appendixes: 1. Governors and Governors General of Scottish birth or ancestry - 2. Premiers and Prime Ministers of Scottish birth or ancestry - 3. Scottish Christian names in Australia. Bibliography p.167-9.
Other titles: *The Afghans in Australia; The Americans; The Baltic peoples Lithuanians, Latvians, Estonians; The Czechs;*

....(contd.)
The Cornish; The Dutch; The Germans; The Hungarians; The Italians; The Jews; The Lebanese; The Maltese; The Poles; The Scandinavians; The Spanish. Class No: 994

[8132]
CANNON, M. The Exploration of Australia. Sydney, Reader's Digest, 1987. 304p. illus. (some col.), col.maps, bibliog., index. ISBN: 0864380364.
8 chronological and thematic chapters *e.g.* 1. Who really discovered the Great South Land? ... 8. The age of scientific expeditions ... 9. New technology revolutionises exploration. Chronology p.294-7. Bibliography p.298-299. Popular reference work at a high level of accomplishment.
Class No: 994

[8133]
Chronicle of Australia. Farnborough, Chronicle Communications, 1993. 768p. illus. (some col.), col. maps, ports., index. £39.95. ISBN: 1872031889.
History of Australia in familiar 'Chronicle' format *i.e.* historical events reported as if contemporary newspapers.
Class No: 994

[8134]
CLARK, C.M.H. A History of Australia. Melbourne, Melbourne Univ. Press, 6v., 1962-87. illus., tables, maps, indexes.
1. *From the earliest times to the age of Macquarie.* 1962. (new ed. 1977). xii, 422p. £25.00. ISBN 0522840056. 2. *New South Wales and Van Diemen's Land 1822-38.* 1968. xiii, 364p. £25.00. 0522838219. 3. *The Beginning of an Australian civilization 1824-51.* 1973. 491p. £25.00. 0522840544. 4. *The Earth abideth for ever 1851-88.* 1978. 427p. 0522841473. 5. *The People make laws 1888-1915.* 1981. 964p. 0522842232. 'The most comprehensive survey of our past' (Borchardt, D.H. *Australian bibliography* (1974), p.58). C.M.H. Clark is considered by many to be Australia's leading historian, though his strong and avowed bias against authoritarianism, the bourgeoisie, the church, the cult of heroes, and his fight against empty traditions have aroused much criticism' (*RSR*, v.7, no.2, April/June 1979, p.9). *Class No:* 994

[8135]
'The Cocos (Keeling) Islands', p.171-175, *Debrett's handbook of Australia and New Zealand* (2nd ed., 1984).
Outline history from early 19th century onwards.
Class No: 994

[8136]
Debrett's bicentennial Australia. Jarman, R., *ed.* South Perth, Western Australia, Debrett's Peerage (Australasia) in association with the Australian Bicentennial Authority, 1987. 208p. col. illus., col. ports., softcover. Aust. $15.95. ISBN: 0949137049.
28 contributors. 'The primary purpose of this book is to provide a fully illustrated look at some of the most interesting aspects of Australia during its Bicentenary, and to provide a guide to all major national events' (*Introduction*).
Class No: 994

[8137]

FITZGERALD, R. From 1915 to the early 1980s: a history of Queensland. St. Lucia (Queensland), Univ. of Queensland Press, 1984. xvii,653p. illus., maps. ISBN: 0702217344.

Part 1. From 1945 to 1957 Labor dominance. Part 2. 1957 to the early 1980s Conservative monopoly. Appendix. Queensland premiers 1859 to 1982 p.635-636. Index p.637-653. All chapters extensively footnoted and documented. *Class No:* 994

[8138]

—FITZGERALD, R. From the Dreaming to 1915: a history of Queensland. St. Lucia, Queensland, Univ. of Queensland Press, 1982. xviii,m354p. illus., maps. ISBN: 0702216348.

The theme is 'the effect of a particularly European idea of progress upon the land, the flora and fauna, the institutions, and the peoples of Queensland'. Part 1. The Dreamtime to 1859 investigates aboriginal culture and the European voyages of exploration and discovery. Part 2. 1859 to 1915 examines Queensland's development, and explores the growth of regionalism, and concludes with the politics of the period. Each chapter is heavily annotated. Index p.343-354. *Class No:* 994

[8139]

MILLAR, T.B. Recent Australian historiography. London, University of London, Institute of Commonwealth Studies, 1987. 18p. sd. £1.50. (*Working papers in Australian studies.*) ISBN: 0902499653.

1. What is history?; 2. Large histories; 3. Aborigines in Australian history; 4. Women; 5. The growing diversity; 6. Documents. *Class No:* 994

[8140]

The Oxford history of Australia. Bolton, G., *ed.* Melbourne, Oxford University Press, 5v., 1986-90. maps, bibliogs., tables, indexes.

1. Murray, T. *Aboriginal Australia.* 2. Kociumbras, J. *Colonial Australia 1770-1860. possessions.* 1992. xv,397p. £25. 0195546105. 3. Kingston, B. *Time of hope 1880-1900.* 4. MacIntyre, S. *The succeeding age 1901-1942.* 5. Bolton, G. *1942-1988 The Middle Way.* 1990. xiv,334p. 019554613x. Chapter notes p.293-317. Bibliographic note p.320-1. 'A very solid contribution to the understanding of Australia's historical development' (*Choice,* v.27,no.2, October 1989, p.366+8). *Class No:* 994

[8141]

POWELL, A. Far country a short history of the Northern Territory. Melbourne, Melbourne Univ. Press, 1982. xii, 301p. illus., maps, bibliog., index. ISBN: 0522842569.

10 chronological chapters focussing on political and economic themes. Chapter notes p.245-269. Bibliography p.270-287. 'Should be extremely useful to both scholars and students' (*Choice,* v.20, no.11-12, July-August 1983, p.1644). *Class No:* 994

[8142]

ROBSON, L. A History of Tasmania. Melbourne, Oxford Univ. Press, 2v., 1983-91. $A.50. £38.

V.1 *Van Diemen's Land from the earliest times to 1855.* 1983. viii,632p. maps on endpapers, bibliog., index. $A50; £38. ISBN 0915543645. 24 chronological chapters. 3 Appendices: 1. Bibliography p.559-569 - B. Reference notes - C. Convicts on board the first and last transportation ships to Van Diemen's Land. 2. *Colony and state from 1856 to the 1980s.* 1991. 663p. bibliog., index. $A98. 0195530314. 'An

....(contd.)

essential acquisition for any collection supporting courses on Australia' (*Choice,* v.29, nos. 11-12, July/August 1992, p.1735). *Class No:* 994

[8143]

SCHILDER, G. Australia unveiled the share of the Dutch navigators in the discovery of Australia. Amsterdam, Theatrum Orbis Terrarum, 1976. xi, 419p. illus., maps, bibliog., indexes.

Survey with distinct cartographical emphasis of the Dutch discoveries of the Northern, Western and Southern coasts of Australia 1606-1644 in 26 chapters of text *e.g.* 3. Terra Australis: the development of geographical concept ... 7. The Dutch discovery of the fifth continent ... 26. Retrospect: a summary of Dutch discoveries in Australia to the time of Tasman. 3 chapters of maps p.239-419. Bibliography p.211-233. Name, ship and localities indexes. *Class No:* 994

[8144]

WILLIAMS, G. *and* **FROST, A.,** *eds.* **Terra Australis to Australia.** Melbourne, Oxford Univ. Press in association with the Australian Academy of the Humanities, 1988. xviii, 242p. illus. (some col.), facsims., maps, index. $A95. £50. ISBN: 0195549082.

How European concepts of a southern continent emerged. In 6 chapters: 1. Terra Australis: theory and speculation - 2. Java la Grande: the enigma of the Dutch maps - 3. New Holland: the Dutch discoveries - 4. New Holland to New South Wales: the English approaches - 5. New South Wales: expectations and reality - 6. Australia: the emergence of a continent. Well documented. The Academy's contribution to the Bicentenary. *Class No:* 994

Bibliographies

[8145]

FEATHERSTONE, G.A. A Bibliography of Victorian history. Ascot Vale, Victoria, Red Rooster Press, 1986. xv,202p. *Class No:* 994(01)

[8146]

FERGUSON, J.A. Bibliography of Australia. Sydney and London, Angus and Robertson, 1941-1969. Canberra, National Library of Australia; Winchester, St. Paul's Bibliographies, 1986-. v.1-7 £32.00 each; v.8 £45.00. Set of 8v. £230.00.

1. *1784-1830* 1941. 2. *1831-1838* 1945. 3. *1839-1845* 1951. 4. *1846-1850* 1955. 5. *1851-1900 A-G* 1963. 6. *1851-1900 H-P* 1965. 7. *1851-1900 Q-Z* 1969. 8. Addenda *1784-1850 (v.1-4)* 1986. x, 705p. index. 0642993076. A second *Addenda* volume will cover v.5-7.

Covers all printed matter relating to Australia, wherever published, in the period concerned. Arranged chronologically under year of publication, with author and anonymous title index. Covers books, pamphlets, broadsides, newspapers, periodicals and government publications. V.4 includes addenda to v.1-3 and it own index. Locations of items in ten Australian libraries and also the British Museum. 'Painstakingly compiled and spaciously and clearly set out' (*Times Literary Supplement* no.3333, 13 January 1966, p.29). *Class No:* 994(01)

[8147]
Index to journal articles on Australian history. Hogan, T., *and others eds*. Armidale, New South Wales, Univ. of New England Publishing Unit, 1981-. vii, 203p. ISBN: 0858341379.

3 sections: 1. List of journals indexed - 2. A-Z subject index - 3. 4,019 entries from 50 journals A-Z by author. Coverage to the end of 1973. The intention was to issue a supplement every 5 years.

Continued by Crittenden, V. and Thawley, J: *Index to journal articles on Australian history for 1979*. Kensington, Univ. of New South Wales, 1981. 90p. softcover. $A4.50. 0949776017. At this point it was decided to prepare an annual compilation for the years 1980-1988 and finally to cumulate them into a single Bicentennial volume.

Crittenden, V. and Thawley, J.: *Index to journal articles on Australian history 1974-1978*. 1981. 238p. $A6.75. 0949776033. Over 2000 entries including book reviews appearing in the indexed journals. 'This listing in effect constitutes a bibliography of the vast majority of Australian monographs which were received during those years' (*Introduction*). Crittenden, V. and others: *Index to journal articles on Australian history for 1980*. 1981. 161p. $A9.25. 0949776157.

Crittenden, V. and Thawley: *Index to journal articles on Australian history for 1981*. 1982. 110 0949776068.

Crittenden, V. and others: *Index to journal articles on Australian history for 1982*, North Balwyn, Victoria, Austalian Reference Publications History Project, 1987. 186p. $A16.00. 0958787603. *Class No:* 994(01)

[8148]
JOHNSTON, W.R. *and* **ZERNER, M. A Guide to the history of Queensland** a bibliographic survey of related resources in Queensland history. Brisbane, Library Board of Queensland, 1985. 241p. index. ISBN: 0724214917.

Reworked from W.R. Johnston's *A Bibliography of Queensland history* (1981).

6 sections: reference and general; Aborigines and early settlement; economic history; political and social; local. Author-title and subject indexes. For the general reader not the thesis writer. *Class No:* 994(01)

Encyclopaedias

[8149]
Australians a historical library. Broadway, New South Wales, Fairfax, Syme and Weldon; Cambridge, Cambridge Univ. Press, 11v., 1988. illus. tables, bibliog., index. A$695.00. £400.00 the set $495.00. ISBN: 0949288098, Australia; 052134073x, UK.

Cooperative history, 10 years in the making, involving 400 scholars and researchers, consisting of 5 history books, 5 reference works and a Guide and Index volume. *Titles:* 1. *Australians to 1788*; 2. *Australians 1838*; 3. *Australians 1888*; 4. *Australians 1938*; 5. *Australians from 1939*. Volumes 2-4 are instances of the distinctive 'slicing' method of writing history whereby single years are examined to explore every aspect of national life. Graeme Davison, an editor and contributor, expands on this in 'Slicing History. Nationhood And The Bicentennial', *History Today*, v.38. January 1988, p.25-32.

Reference Works: 6. *Australians: A historical atlas* (the first large-scale historical atlas of Australia). 7. *Australians: A historical dictionary*. xx, 462p. illus. index. A succinct overview of Australian history in 1233 entries encompassing

....(contd.)
historical episodes, concepts, institutions, industries, movements, achievements and failures and biography. 8. *Australians: Events and places*. xvi, 476p. col. illus. col. maps, index. 1. A chronology 1788-1984 accompanied by 2 'timeline' special features: Aboriginal Australia and European exploration to 1788. 2. A historical gazetteer and descriptive account of places that centres on their historical significance grouped in 32 regions. 9. *Australians: Historical statistics*. 17 chapters each with a brief introductory essay. 10. *Australians: A guide to sources*. xviii, 473p. 55 chapters in 10 sections: 1. The writing of Australian history ... 2. Archives ... 19. Genealogy ... 20. Biography. 11. *Australians. The Guide and Index*. 112p. Links the individual volume indexes and connects the more detailed information in individual volumes with the broader themes of Australian history. 'Prepared with great scholarly care from original sources ... can be recommended for public and academic libraries' (*Booklist*, v.85, no.2, 15 September 1988, p.128-130). *Class No:* 994(031)

[8150]
Australia's yesterdays a look at our recent past. 3rd ed. Sydney, Reader's Digest, 1986. 360p. illus. (some col.), col. maps, index. £17.95. ISBN: 0949819980.

Pictorial encyclopedia. Part 1. Australia in the 20th century - 2. The passing years 1901-85 (historic events year by year) - 3. Makers of modern Australia (biographies of the Australians who made the news). Analytical index. *Class No:* 994(031)

Dictionaries

[8151]
BASSETT, J. The Concise Oxford dictionary of Australian history. Melbourne, Oxford Univ. Press, 1986. 276p. £8.95. ISBN: 0195544226.

About 550 entries relating to the principal people, institutions, places, ideas, movements, events, documents and artefacts generally considered to be historically significant. But 'more suited to browsing or the pursuit of trivia' (*Choice*, v.25, no.5, January 1988, p.741).

Bassett's *The Oxford illustrated dictionary of Australian history* (1993. 304p. £27.50; *m49.95. 0195532430) is for general readers interested in Australian history. *Class No:* 994(038)

[8152]
DOCHERTY, J.C. Historial dictionary of Australia. Metuchen, N.J., Scarecrow Press, 1992. xvi,284p. maps, bibliog. £35. (*Oceanian Historical Dictionaries, no.1.*) ISBN: 0810826135.

Entries for all States and Territories and urban centres with more than 100,000 people, major export commodities, biographies, political parties, historical events. 30p. chronology. List of Governors, list of prime ministers. 10p. bibliog. essay and sixty-page bibliography arranged in 35 sections. *Class No:* 994(038)

[8153]
MURPHY, B. Dictionary of Australian history. Sydney, McGraw-Hill, 1982. 304p. illus., maps on endpapers, bibliog., index. ISBN: 0070729468.

350 cross-referenced entries describe significant events, issues and personalities. 'Designed primarily as a companion to a broader treatment of Australia's historical experience' (*Preface*). Bibliography p.291. 40 illus. *Class No:* 994(038)

Theses

Bibliographies

[8154]

FRY, E.C. Theses on Australian history accepted for higher degrees of universities in the United Kingdom 1901-1976: a bibliography. Canberra, National Library of Australia, 1980. vi, 55p. pbk. ISBN: 0642898030.

Descriptive and analytical bibliography of 82 theses from 11 universities. Data: author, title, degree, university, year accepted, subject, period and geographical area covered. *Class No:* 994(043)(01)

Maps & Atlases

[8155]

Australians: a historical atlas. Camm, J.C.R. *and* McQuilton, J., *eds.* Broadway, NSW., Fairfax, Syme and Weldon, 1987. xiii,290p. illus. (mostly col.), col. maps, col. graphs, col. tables, index. ISBN: 0949288187.

Forms part of *Australians a historical library (q.v.).*
15 chapters with text, illustrations and maps closely integrated. *I. Place:* 1. Environment - 2. Aboriginal landscapes - 3. European discovery and exploration - 4. Rural landscapes - 5. Urban - 6. Mining, manufacturing and transport. *II. People:* 7. Immigrant nations - 8. Life and death - 9. Religion and education - 10. Convicts, bushrangers, larrikins - 11. Australians and war - 12. Great Depression - 13. Government. *III. Landscapes:* 14. City - 15. Country. 'The atlas in its design, lay-out, cartography, photography and quality of reproduction, diagrams, printing and binding, is as nearly perfect as it is possible to imagine' (*Geographical Journal,* v.155,no.2, July 1989, p.290-1). *Class No:* 994(084.3)

[8156]

TERRY, T.M. The Discovery of Australia the charts and maps of the navigators and explorers. London, Hamish Hamilton, 1982. 159p. maps, facsims, bibliog., index. ISBN: 0241108632.

'The story of the discovery and exploration of Australia and the way in which the navigators' and explorers' knowledge and speculations were made available to the public through published maps' in 15 chapters of text and accompanying maps *e.g* 1. Terra incognita ... 3. First discoveries ... 9. The great expeditions ... 14. Across the desert ... 15. The changing map of Australia. Bibliography p.156. 85 plates. *Class No:* 994(084.3)

Chronologies

[8157]

BARKER, A. When was that? chronology of Australia. Sydney, John Ferguson, 1988. xii,562p. index. ISBN: 0949118184.

Guide to events in Australia's history from the beginnings of European settlement to its bicentenary in 1988. A mainline chronology of political and general events against precise dates is followed by separate lists dealing with architecture and building; science, technology, and discovery; arts and entertainment; books and writing; sport and recreation; statistics, social change and environment. Analytical index p.423-562. *Class No:* 994(090)

[8158]

Collins milestones in Australian history. Brown, R., *comp and* Appleton, R., *ed..* Sydney, Collins, 1986. x, 835p. ISBN: 0002165813.

An annalistic guide to significant events and achievements described as 'a kind of ready reckoner of Australian heritage, carefully arranged to provide quick accurate answers to those who, what, when and where questions.' 20,000 entries (60,000 facts) are listed under six headings: A. History, Politics, Economics, Law; B. Science, Technology, Transport, Discovery; C. Arts; D. Religion, Learning; E. Sport; F. *Historia dignum.* Each of these headings is allocated 1-2 columns for every year 1788-1984, two columns to the page. A comprehensive index p.743-835 is almost half as long as the 300,000 word text. Map of Australia on endpapers. *Class No:* 994(090)

[8159]

FRASER, B., *ed*. The Macquarie book of events. Dee Why, New South Wales, Macquarie Library, 1983. 608p. illus. ISBN: 0949757071.

36 contributors. 10,000 events that shaped Australia divided into 63 chapters arranged in 17 'ordered chronologies'. Entries contain background information and end with short reading lists. For students, teachers, journalists, businessmen *etc. Class No:* 994(090)

[8160]

Great events in Australia's history from discovery to the present. French's Forest, New South Wales, Child & Associates, 1988. 462p. illus., index. ISBN: 0867771410.

Detailed and comprehensive chronology of Australia's 200 years of European settlement. Over 300 entries, 500 illus. *Class No:* 994(090)

Biographies

[8161]

ELDER, B., *ed*. The A to Z of who's who in Australia's history. Brookevale, New South Wales, Child & Associates, 1987. 513p., illus., bibliog. ISBN: 0867773707.

Over 1000 brief biographies encompassing not only the country's major political, judicial and bureaucratic figures but also revolutionaries, movie stars, gold fossickers, and sporting heroes *etc.* (Sir Donald Bradman 42 lines, 2 illus.; Dame Nellie Melba 44 lines). Chronology of Australian history p.506-508. Bibliography p.513. *Class No:* 994(092)

Institutions & Associations

[8162]

REID, R. *and* REID, A. Into history: a guide to historical, genealogical, family history and heritage societies, groups and organisations in Australia. North Ryde, New South Wales, R.S. and A.F. Reid, 1988. various pagination (325p). index. softcover with spiral binding. ISBN: 0731627725.

Descriptive listings A-Z by State. Data: date established, aims and interests, activities, specific projects, memberships, meetings, publications, and research facilities. *Class No:* 994:061:061.2

Fiji

[8163]

SCARR, D. **Fiji a short history.** Sydney and London, George Allen & Unwin, 1984. xvi, 202p. illus., maps, bibliog., index. ISBN: 0868613118.

4 sections: 1. In the islands of Degai - 2. Search for stability 1865-1875 - 3. The multi-racial community 1875-1914 - 4. The makings of a nation. References p.178-188. Bibliography p. 189-195. Glossary p. xii, xiii.
Class No: 996.11

Encyclopaedias

[8164]

The Cyclopedia of Fiji (illustrated); a complete historical and commercial review of Fiji.../a compendium of statistics and data concerning the Group never yet compiled or brought together in a single publication/descriptive and biographical facts, figures, and illustrations. Papakura, Central Auckland, R. McMillan, 1984. 332+4p.

Facsimile reprint of work first published in Sydney by McCarron Stewart in 1907.

Index to portraits of Fiji colonists p.330-332.
Class No: 996.11(031)

Samoa

[8165]

MASTERMAN, S. **An Outline of Samoan history.** Apia, Western Samoa, Commercial Printers Ltd., 1980. 79+23p.

17 chronological chapters *e.g.* 3. Samoa before 1830 ... 6. Growth of trade: the Germans in Samoa ... 7. US and Samoa ... 8. Great Britain, Australia and New Zealand in Samoa ... 16. Towards self-government. 7. Appendices *e.g.* 6. Chronological history of Western Samoa p.13-23. Reproduced from author's typescript. *Class No:* 996.13

Encyclopaedias

[8166]

Cyclopedia of Samoa, Tonga, Tahiti, and the Cook Islands (illustrated). A complete review of the history and traditions and the commercial development of the islands with statistics and data never before compiled in a single publication. Descriptive and biographical facts, figures and illustrations. Papakura, Central Auckland, R. McMillan, 1983. Various paginations, illus., maps.

Facsimile reprint of a work first published in Sydney by McCarron Stewart in 1907. *Class No:* 996.13(031)

Tuvalu

[8167]

LARACY, H., *ed*. **Tuvalu** a history. Institute of Pacific Studies and Extension Services, Univ. of South Pacific and Ministry of Social Services, Government of Tuvalu, 1983. 208p. illus., maps, bibliog. index.

17 contributors. 21 chapters in 4 parts: 1. Origin and culture - 2. Island traditions - 3. Fresh winds - 4. From Ellice to Tuvalu. Appendix A. Some important dates p.185-186. B. Some important facts p.187-189. Bibliography p.200-204. *Class No:* 996.14

Micronesia

Bibliographies

[8168]

KRAUSS, N.L.H. **Bibliography of Nauru, Western Pacific.** Honolulu, the author, 1970. 14p. sd.

280 entries A-Z by author. Note on history of discovery and constitutional and administrative status.
Class No: 996.5(01)

[8169]

KRAUSS, N.L.H. **Bibliography of the Ocean Islands (Banaba), Western Pacific.** Honolulu, the author, 1969. 7p. sd.

78 unannotated entries. *Class No:* 996.5(01)

[8170]

KRAUSS, N.L.H. **Bibliography of The Phoenix Islands,** Central Pacific. Honolulu, the author, 1970. 15p. sd. index.

230 entries A-Z by author. Also information on history of discovery and administrative and constitutional status.
Class No: 996.5(01)

Kiribati

[8171]

MACDONALD, B. **Cindarellas of empire** towards a history of Kiribati and Tuvalu. Canberra, Australian National Univ. Press, 1982. xx, 335p. maps, bibliog., index. ISBN: 0708116167.

14 chapters *e.g.* 1. The islands and their people ... 8. Rigidity and reforms: the Gilbert and Ellice Islands 1909-1941 ... Epilogue: From separation to independence. Notes p.227-296. Bibliography p.297-314. Traces history from early 19th century to late 1970s. *Class No:* 996.82

Hawaii

[8172]

TABRAH, R. **Hawaii a bicentennial history.** New York, W.W. Norton; Nashville, American Association for State and Local History, 1980. xi, 233p.+18p. plates. maps, bibliog., index. $14.95. (*The States And The Nation Series.*) ISBN: 0393056805.

A popular history in 17 chronological chapters. Descriptive reading list p.225-6. 'One of the better histories in the series and one of the best about Hawaii in a long time' (*Choice*, v.18, no.5, January 1981, p.718). *Class No:* 996.9

Biographies

[8173]

DAY, A.G. **A Biographical dictionary: historical makers of Hawaii.** Honolulu, Mutual Publishers, 1984. 174p.

Biographies of key figures in history of Hawaii.
Class No: 996.9(092)

Polar Regions

[8174]

KIRWAN, L.P. **The White road** a survey of Polar exploration. London, Hollis & Carter., 1959. x,374p. illus., maps, bibliog., index.

Published in US by W.W. Norton under title of *A history of Polar exploration.*

24 chapters organized in 5 parts: 1. Age of discovery - 2.

....(contd.)

Age of exploration - 3. Age of adventure and research - 4. Heroic age - 5. Postscript to polar history. Bibliography p.355-64. Complete survey of Arctic and Antarctic exploration. *Class No:* 998/999

[8175]

MICKLEBURGH, E. Beyond the frozen sea visions of Antarctica. London, Bodley Head, 1987. 256p. illus., (some col.), maps, bibliog., index. £15.00. ISBN: 0370310276.

4 chronological sections: 18th to late 20th century. Sources p.241-5. Further reading p.247-8. Analytical index. *Class No:* 998/999

Bibliographies

[8176]

Antarctic miscellany books, periodicals & maps relating to the discovery and exploration of Antarctica. Spence, S.A., *comp.* Mitcham, Surrey, J.J.H. Simper and J.I. Simper, 1980. xi,220p. illus. £20.00. ISBN: 095072708.

First published 1966. *Class No:* 998/999(01)

[8177]

DAY, A.E. Search for the Northwest Passage an annotated bibliography. New York, Garland, 1986. xiv,632p. index. $78.00. (*Garland Reference Library Of Social Science, no.186.*) ISBN: 0824092880.

5160 entries arranged in 11 chapters: 1. Encyclopaedic works, maps and atlases *etc.* - 2. The search begins (1497-1553) - 3. Strait of Anian (1542-1677) - 4. Elizabethan/Stuart trading ventures (1566-1634) - 5. Hudson's Bay Company (1668-1791) - 6. Pacific search resumed (1761-1795) - 7. Royal Navy by land and sea (1815-1839) - 8. Sir John Franklin (1845-1848) - 9. Search for Franklin (1847-1880) - 10. The Passage navigated (1903-1984) - 11. Reference works. 'An excellent bibliographic source and a valuable addition to any reference collection' (*Association of Canadian Map Libraries And Archives Bulletin,* no.68, September 1988, p.25-26). *Class No:* 998/999(01)

[8178]

The North West Passage 1534-1859 a catalogue of an exhibition of books and manuscripts in the Toronto Public Library. Firth, E.G. Toronto, Baxter Publishing Co. in cooperation with the Toronto Public Library, 1963. [28]p. illus., maps on endpapers, facsims., index, pbk.

90 annotated entries in approximate chronological order of expedition or voyage. *Class No:* 998/999(01)

Encyclopaedias

[8179]

HOLLAND, C. Arctic exploration and development c.500b.c. to 1915 an encyclopedia. New York, Garland, 1994. xvi,704p. maps, bibliog., indexes. $95. ISBN: 0824076486.

Many entries relating to expeditions to Canada are rewritten from *The Exploration of Northern Canada* (1978) (*q.v.*).

Nearly 1900 entries of varying length constitute a comprehensive chronological record of expeditions, voyages, and historical events from the earliest times. Data: year, general and specific areas of activity; leader(s), captain(s) and name(s) of ships; nationality and main purpose of expedition; place and date of departure and return; names of financial supporters and other sponsors; and an itinerary

....(contd.)

of the expedition, charting its progress, events, discoveries, dates and place-names. Glossary p.xv-xvi. Bibliography p.527-73. Appendix (list of main expedition members) p.575-624. Maps p.626-55. General and ship indexes. *Class No:* 998/999(031)

[8180]

STEWART, J. Antarctica an encyclopedia. Jefferson, N.C., McFarland, 2v., 1990. xxii,v,1193p. bibliog. $135. ISBN: 0899504701, set; 0899505597x, v.1; 0899505988, v.2.

A-Z encyclopedia, with 15,000 cross-referenced entries on geographical features, expeditions, people, scientific subjects, and general interest items, with distinct historical and geographical bias. A Capsule history p.xv-xviii. Chronology (1502 to 1990) p.1133-60. Expeditions p.1161-70. Bibliography p.1173-93. A major work. *Class No:* 998/999(031)

Chronologies

[8181]

HEADLAND, R.K., *comp.* Chronological list of Antarctic expeditions and related historical events. Cambridge, Cambridge Univ. Press, 1989. vii, 730p. illus., maps, bibliog., index. £65; $125. (*Studies in Polar Research.*) ISBN: 0521309034.

Based on B. Roberts' 'Chronological list of Antarctic expeditions', *Polar Record,* v.59, no.8, May 1958, p.97-134 and v.9, no.60, September 1958, p.191-239. Material in these lists had already appeared in the *Antarctic Pilot* (London, Hydrographic Department, 2nd ed., 1948).

Over 3,200 entries covering the period 700BC-1988 provide brief descriptions of events, names of individuals, ships, and source citations for each expedition. The region covered is the far south in general and Antarctica in particular. Bibliography p.604-21. 'An invaluable reference book for any investigation of Antarctic history' (*Choice,* v.28, no.1, September 1990, p.76++78). *Class No:* 998/999(090)

Manuscripts & Incunabula

Bibliographies

[8182]

HOLLAND, C., *ed.* Manuscripts in the Scott Polar Research Institute Cambridge, England a catalogue. New York, Garland, 1982. xii,815p. $121.00. ISBN: 0824093941.

Introduction gives details of the scope of SPRI's collection, a history of the catalogue, and of its organization and use. 6 indexes of Arctic and Antarctic exploration, whaling and sealing voyages p.742-815. *Class No:* 998/999(093)(01)

Greenland

[8183]

GAD, F. The History of Greenland. London, C. Hurst, 2v. 1970-1973.

V.3 published in København by Nyt Nordisk Forlag (1982).

1. *Earliest times to 1700.* 1970. xiii, 350p. £30.00. ISBN 0900966238. 2. *1700-1782.* 1973. xviii, 446p. £35.00. 0900966572.

....(contd.)

3. *1782-1808* V.1 ranges over 4,000 years in 9 chapters. Notes and references p.319-33; literature p.334-9; glossary p.340. V.2 deals with Greenland's connection with the Danes in 23 chapters. Note on source material p.430-2; glossary p.433-5. A third volume was to have covered Greenland until the end of the first decade of the 20th century but this has not so far appeared in English translation. 'This comprehensive, detailed and solidly documented history of Greenland from the first inhabitants to 1808' (K.E. Miller. *Denmark*, 1987. Entry 717).
Class No: 998.8

Author / Title Index

The index reference is to the running number given to each item. The running numbers are in one sequence throughout the volume and can be found at the top right-hand corner of the entry for each item.

This index is of authors and titles in one sequence. The names of the authors are printed in bold type. Where works are jointly authored, only the first name is indexed. All books and periodicals listed or mentioned in the text, except where cited as the source of review quotations or for purposes of comparison, are entered under the headings given. All entries in *Walford* have title entries in the index; where the main heading in *Walford* is under title, added entries to the index have usually been made for an editor or compiler.

Filing is word by word, with groups of initials counted as single words. Since *Walford* uses only initials and not forenames it may occasionally happen that titles by different authors with the same surname and initials are found grouped together.

The arrangement of entries under an author is alphabetically by title. To save space, most sub-titles have been omitted, and many lengthy titles have been shortened.

ABSEES (Abstracts: Soviet and East European series) **2227**

Abstracts in social gerontology **1050**

Abstracts of folklore studies **4082**

Abstracts of military biography **3351**

The Abu-Ghazaleh English-Arabic dictionary of accountancy **2520**

Abu-Ghazaleh, T.
The Abu-Ghazaleh English-Arabic dictionary of accountancy **2520**

Abun-Nasr, J.M.
A History of the Magrib in the Islamic period **7754**

Aby, S.H.
Sociology **983**

Academia Portuguesa Da Historia
Guía de bibliografia histórica portuguesa **7431**

Academia Salvadoreña de la Historia
El Salvador y ses hombres **5945**

Academic dress and insignia of the world **3862**

Academic year abroad, l991/92 **3859**

Academical dress **3860**

Academical dress of British universities **3864**

Académie Royale Des Sciences, Des Lettres et Des Beaux-Arts de Belgique
Biographie nationale **5886**

The Access resource guide **2975**

Access to information in local government **3244**

Accessions to repositories and records added to the National Register of Archives **6472**

Accounting and finance abstracts **2521**

Accounting and tax index **2522**

Accounting in Scotland **2511**

Achterberg, E. and Lanz, K.
Enzyklapädisches Lexikon für das Geld- Bank- und Borsenwesen **2030**

Achtermeier, P.J. and Society of Biblical Literature
Harper's Bible dictionary **428**

Ackermann, A.S.E.
Popular fallacies **4127**

Ackermann, K.T.
Genealogical periodical annual index **6044**

ACP-basic statistics, 1988 **1171**

Acres, W.M.
The Bank of England from within, 1694-1900 **2147**

Acronyms relating to international development/Liste de sigles en développement international/Sigles relacionadas con desarrollo internacional **2939**

Actanna an Oireachtais/The Acts of the Oireachtais passed in the year … consisting of the Public General Acts and the Private Acts, with tables and index **2765**

The Acts of the Parliaments of Scotland, 1424-1707 **2760**

Adam, F.
The Clans, septs and regiments of the Scottish Highlands **6187**

Adam, J.H.
Longman dictionary of business English **2461**

Adamec, L.W.
A Biographical dictionary of contemporary Afghanistan **5916**
Historical and political gazetteer of Afghanistan **5672**
Historical and political who's who of Afghanistan **5915**
Historical gazetteer of Iran **7685**

Adams, B.
London illustrated 1604-1951 **7094**
'London in print' **4478**

Adams, C.J.
A Reader's guide to the great religions **348**

Adams, J. and Averley, G.
A Bibliography of eighteenth century legal literature **2824**

Adams, M.
Libraries and open learning **3825**
The Middle East **4646**

Adams, W.Y.
Nubia, corridor to Africa **6623**

Adamson, P. and Adamson, L.
State of the world's children, 1992 **3638**

Aday, R.H.
Crime and the elderly **1037**

Addis, P.K.
Through a women's I **5991**

Ade Ajayi, J.F. and Crowder, M.
Historical atlas of Africa **7743**

Adelmann, F.J.
Contemporary Chinese philosophy **119**

Adels, J.H.
The Wisdom of the saints **560**

Adkins, L and Adkins, R.A.
The Handbook of British archaeology **4221**

Adler, J.A.
Elsevier's dictionary of criminal science in eight languages **3117**

Adler, M.J. and Van Doran, C.
Great treasury of Western thought **80**

Adult education **3815**

Adult education in continental Europe **3819**

Adult literacy **3813**

Advances in experimental social psychology **1024**

Adventuring in the Pacific **5705**

Advertiser's annual **2629**

Advertising in Britain: a history **2640**

Aegean Bronze Age chronology **6685**

Afghanistan **4728**

Africa **4772, 4780**

Africa: a guide to reference material **4784**

Africa bibliography **4777**

Africa contemporary record **4787**

Africa since 1914 **4778**

Africa south of the Sahara **4873**

Africa south of the Sahara 1994 **4788**

Africa today **4769**

Africa who's who **5922**

African archaeology **4283**

African biographical archive **5924**

African boundaries **2911**

African dress **3947**

African economic handbook **2295**

African historical dictionaries **7739**

African historiographies **6420**

African history in maps **7745**

African international relations **1591**

The African political dictionary **1416**

African political facts since 1945 **1418, 7753**

African population census reports **1330**

The African slave trade and its suppression **1534**

African states and rulers **7738**

African studies **4770**

The African studies companion **4774**

African studies information resources directory **4789**

African trade **1992**

African urbanization **1100**

Africana catalogue of the Ibadan University Library **4811**

Africa's three religions **892**

The Afrikaners of South Africa **7831**

Afro-American genealogy sourcebook **6150**

Afro-American reference **1080**

After Hitler: Germany 1945-1963 **7272**

The Age of battles **3433**

Age of ideologies **1385**

Ageron, G.R.
Modern Algeria **7772**

Aging **1038**

Agrawal, D.P.
The Archaeology of India **4267**

Aguilar Pinal, F.
Bibliografia de Estudios sobre Carlos III y su epoca **7419**

Aharoni, Y.
The Archaeology of the land of Israel **4276**

Aicardi de Saint-Paul, M.
Gabon **4845**

Aikens, C.M. and Takayasu Higuchi
Prehistory of Japan **4263**

Air Force badges and insignia of World War 2 **3399**

The Air Force List, 1994 **3484**

Air University Library index to military periodicals **3324**

The Air war 1939-1945 **6833**

Air wars and aircraft **3480**

Aitchison, J.
Unesco thesaurus **968**

Ajaegbu, H.I.
African urbanization **1100**

Ajayi, J.F.A. and Crowder, M.
History of West Africa **7775**

Akai, A. and Matadeen, J.
Atlas for Guyana and Trinidad and Tobago **5424**

Al-Ani, K.A.M.
The Encyclopaedia of modern Iraq **4711**

Al-Farsy, F.
Saudi Arabia **7631**

Al Faruqi, I.R.
The Cultural atlas of Islam **4759**

Al-Hind The Making of the Indo-Islamic world **7656**

Al-Tabarī, Abu Ja'far Muhammad bin Jarir
The commentary on the Qur'ān **859**

Alaska **5017, 8058**

The Alaska handbook **5018**

Alaska-Yukon handbook **5700**

Alaskan maps **5435**

Alawar, Mohamed A.
A Concise bibliography of Northern Chad and Fezzan in Southern Libya **4852**

Albania **4563-4564**

The Albanian encyclopaedic dictionary **4565**

Albanie **7533**

Albery, N. and Yale, V.
Encyclopedia of social inventions **1112**

Albion, R.G.
Naval and maritime history **3505**

Alchemy **169-170**

Aldcroft, D.H. and Rodger, R.
Bibliography of European economic and social history **1785**

Aldcroft, H.
The British economy **2230**

Alderson, M.
International mortality statistics **1341**

Alderton, D.
The industrial archaeology of regions in the British Isles. No.1. East Anglia **4399**

Alderton, D. and Booker, J.
The Batsford guide to the industrial archaeology of East Anglia **4398**

Aldous, J. and Hill, R.
International bibliography of research in marriage and the family, 1900-1964 **1343**

Alexander, M.
British folklore, myths and legends **4085**

Alexander, R.J.
Biographical dictionary of Latin American and Caribbean leaders **1677**
Political parties of the Americas **1672**

Alexander to Actium **6668**

Alexander, Y
A Bibliography of Israel & Zionism **4717**

Alfabetische catalogus van de boeken en brochures. Alphabetical catalog of the books and pamphlets of the International Institute of Social History **951**

Alfrey, J. and Putnam, T.
The Industrial heritage **4386**

Algarin, J.P.
Japanese folk literature **4104**

Algemeen genealogisch-heraldisch repertorium voor die Zuildelijke Nederlanden **6040**

Algemeine geschiedenis der Nederlanden **7504**

Algeria **4808, 7773**

Algerian bibliography **4809**

Alie, J.A.D.
A New history of Sierra Leone **7784**

Alisky, M.
Historical dictionary of Peru **8091**

All England law reports **2743**

All the men of the Bible **456**

All the monies of the world **2160**

All the women of the Bible **457**

All you need to know about exchange rates **2164**

Allard, D.C.
US naval history sources in the United States **3535**

Allchin, B. and Allchin, R.
The rise of civilization in India and Pakistan **4268**

Allen, C.H.
Oman **7634**

Allen, J.P. and Turner, E.J.
We the people **1083**

Allen, M. and Hodgkinson, R.
Buying a business **2438**

Allen, W.R.
Black American families, 1965-1984 **1078**

Allgemeine deutsche Biographie **5824**

Allied Dunbar investment and savings guide, 1993 **2192**

Allison, B.
'Map acquisitions: the major sources' **5222**

Allworth, E.
Soviet Asia: bibliographies **4725**

Allworth, E.A.
The Modern Uzbeks **7709**

The Almanac **6185**

The Almanac of American history **7983**

The Almanac of American politics, 1990 **3050**

The Almanac of British politics **1397, 3012**

The Almanac of Cyprus 1992 **4706**

Almanac of famous people **5725**

An Almanac of the history of Macau **7605**

An Almanack for the year of Our Lord ... 1868- **948**

Alphabetischer Katalog der Bibliothek **4444**

Alsberg, P.A.
Guide to the archives of Israel **6536**

Altaner, B.
Patrology **643**

Altbach, P.G.
Comparative higher education abroad **3839**
Comparative higher education: research trends and bibliography **3840**
Higher education in developing nations **3849**
International bibliography of comparative education **3685**
International higher education **3845**
Research on foreign students and international study **3686**

Altbach, P.G. and Kelly, D.H.
Higher education in international perspective **3841**

Altengarten, J.S. and Molyneaux, G.A.
The History, philosophy and methodology of geography **5189**

Alter, R. and Kermode, F.
The Literary guide to the Bible **423**

Alternatives in print **984**

Amalvi, C.
Bibliothèque Nationale Catalogue de la Troisième République 1870-1940 **7383**

The Amateur archaeologist's handbook **4291**

AMBA guide to business schools **2437**

Ambert, A.N. and Melendez, S.E.
Bilingual education **3687**

America and World War I **6819**

America at war 1941-1945 **6835**

America history and life **7982**

American and British genealogy and heraldry **6041**

American archaeology past and future **4293**

Andrea, Zh.
'Archaeology in Albania' **4258**
Andreucci, F. and Detti, T.
Il movimento operaio italiano:
dizionario biografico, 1853-1943
1905
Andrews, J.A. and Hines, W.D.
Keyguide to information sources on
the international protection of
human rights **3053**
'The Literature of human rights'
3054
'Recent periodicals and source
materials in law' **2664**
Andrews, J.H. and Simms, A.
Irish historic towns atlas **7007**
Andrews, L.
The Royal Mail direct mail handbook
2628
Andriot, D.
Guide to US government statistics
1275
Andriott, D.
Place guide **5689**
Angel, W.D.
Youth movements of the world **3645**
Angeles, P.A.
Dictionary of Christian theology **537**
A Dictionary of philosophy **68**
Angerer, M.
Harrap's five-language business
dictionary **1958**
Anglo-American legal bibliographies
2662
'Anglo-Australian genealogy' **6164**
Anglo-Jewish bibliography, 1937-1970
832
Anglo-russkii ekonomicheskii slovar …/
English-Russian economics dictionary
1756
Anglo-russkii i russko-angliiskii slovar
po morskomu pravu/English-Russian
and Russian-English law of the sea
dictionary **2917**
An Anglo-Saxon and Celtic bibliography
6938
Anglo-Saxon charters **6947**
Anglo-Saxon England **6931**
Anglo-Scandinavian law dictionary
2708
Angola **4848**
The Angus & Robertson concise
Australian encyclopedia **5085**
Anikin, A.V.
Anglo-russkii ekonomicheskii slovar
…/ English-Russian economics
dictionary **1756**
Ankarloo, B. and Henningsen, G.
Early modern European witchcraft
165
Annalists and historians **6345**
The Annals of Dublin **7028**

Annals of European civilization 1501-
1900 **6778**
Année africaine, 1963- **1590**
L'Année psychologique. 1894- **260**
L'Année sociologique **1010**
Anniversaries and holidays **3983**
Annotated bibliography of Afghanistan
4727
Annotated bibliography of corporate
finance **2097**
An Annotated bibliography of
exploration in Africa **5133**
An Annotated bibliography of selected
works about Republic of China **4638**
An Annotated bibliography of the Holy
Roman Empire **6763**
Annotated bibliography of the literature
on American Indians **8006**
An Annotated bibliography of the
Napoleonic era **6789**
Annotated bibliography on clandestine
employment **1812**
Annotated bibliography on the economic
history of India **2290**
An Annotated critical bibliography of
feminist criticism **4013**
Annotated handbook of biblical
quotations, verses and parables **444**
Annotated list of publications, 1947-
1987 **233**
Annotated world list of selected current
geographical serials **5178**
Annuaire administratif et judiciaire de
Belgique **3305**
Annuaire de l'Afrique du Nord **4795**
Annuaire statistique … 1992 **1208**
Annuaire statistique de la Belgique,
1990 **1233**
Annuaire statistique de la France, 1993
1214
Annual abstract of statistics, 1990 **1216**
Annual abstract of statistics, 1994 **1193**
Annual bibliography of Indian
archaeology **4271**
Annual bibliography of Victorian studies
6961
Annual bulletin of housing and building
statistics for Europe … 1991 **3219**
Annual census of production reports …
1970 - **2337**
Annual economic report, 1991 **2291**
Annual Egyptological bibliography/
Bibliographie **4187**
The Annual obituary **5726**
The Annual register **6718**
Annual review of European Community
affairs, 1992 **2876**
The Annual review of psychology **261**
Annual review of sociology **1011**
Annual survey of Commonwealth law,
1965-1977, v.1-13 **2769**
Annuario bibliografico di archaeologia
4154

Annuario statistico italiano, 1993 **1215**
Anson, P.F. The religious orders and
congregations of Great Britain and
Ireland **638**
Anstruther, G.
The Seminary priests **696**
Antarctic miscellany **8176**
The Antarctic Treaty regime **5110**
Antarctica **5464, 8180**
Antheume, B. and Bonnemaison, J.
Atlas des îles et états du Pacifique Sud
5445
Anthony, J.D.
Historical and cultural dictionary of
the Sultanate of Oman and the
Emirates of Eastern Arabia **7636**
Anthony, P. and Arnold, J.
Costume: a general bibliography
3910
Anti-evolution **415**
Anti-semitic propaganda **1453**
Anti-semitism **1060**
The Antonine Wall **4353**
Anuario estadístico de Cuba, 1987
1268
Anuario estadístico de España, 1990
1217
Anuario estadístico para América Latina
y el Caribe … Statistical year-book
for Latin America and the Caribbean,
1992 **1271**
Anuário estatístico, 1991 **1218**
Anuário estatístico do Brasil, 1992
1280
Anuarul statistic al Republicii Socialiste
România. Romania statistical
yearbook, 1992 **1239**
APAIS: Australian public affairs
information service **902**
Aparato bibliográfico de la historia
general de Filipinas **8111**
The Apartheid handbook **1069**
The Apocrypha and Pseudepigrapha of
the Old Testament in English … **505**
Appleby, B.L.
Elsevier's dictionary of commercial
terms and phrases in five languages
1957
Appleby, R.C.
Modern business administration **2540**
Appleton, G.
The Oxford book of prayer **605**
Appleton, R. and Appleton, A.
The Cambridge dictionary of
Australian places **5714**
Appleton's cyclopaedia of American
biography **5952**
Applied behavioural economics **217**
'Approaches to the Japanese economic
"miracle"' **1794**
The Aquarian dictionary of festivals
3968

Bancroft Library University of California, Berkeley
Catalog of printed books **4996**
Index to printed maps **5227**
Bander, E.J. and Wallach, J.
Medical legal dictionary **2842**
Bangla Desh **4698**
Bangladesh **4697**
Bangladesh. Bureau of Statistics
Statistical yearbook of Bangladesh, 1991 **1251**
Bank, D. and Exposito, A.
British biographical index **5782**
Bank Negara Malaysia
Quarterly bulletin, 1968- **2292**
The Bank of England **2146**
The Bank of England, 1891-1944 **2148**
The Bank of England from within, 1694-1900 **2147**
The Bank of England note **2163**
Bank of England quarterly bulletin **1790**
Bank of Japan
Economic statistics annual **2282**
Bank of Thailand
Annual economic report, 1991 **2291**
Quarterly bulletin **1255**
Banker's almanac 3000 world ranking, 1994 **2140**
The Bankers' almanac and year book ... 1993 **2137**
Banking dictionary **2134-2135**
Banking in the EC **2120**
Banking terminology **2126**
Banks, A.
A Military atlas of the First World War **6811**
A World atlas of military history, 1861-1945 **3456**
A World atlas of military history to 1500 **3455**
Banks, A.S.
Political handbook of the world **4421**
Political handbook of the world, 1990. Annual **1367**
Banks, O.
The Biographical dictionary of British feminists **4040-4041**
Bankwörterbuch/Banking dictionary **2132**
Banners bright **6265**
Bannock, G.
Dictionary of economics **1732**
Bannock, G. and Manser, W.
International dictionary of finance **2044**
Banuazizi, A. and Prouchestia, G.
Social stratification in the Middle East and North Africa **1143**
A Baptist bibliography **716**
Baptist bibliography **717**
Baptist Missionary Society: directory **718**

The Baptist Union directory for 1992-93. 131st year **719**
The Baptists **715**
Bar-On, R.
Travel and tourism data **2342**
Barbados **4963**
Barber, C. and Williams, J.G.
The Ancient stones of Wales **4370**
Barber, G.D. and Hammond, C.B.
'American history reference sources, 1986-1987' **7958**
Barber, R.
The Penguin guide to medieval Europe **6749**
Pilgrimages **583**
Barber, R. and Barker, J.
Tournaments, jousts, chivalry and pageants in the Middle Ages **3987**
Barber, R. and Riches, A.
A Dictionary of fabulous beasts **4131**
Barbier, F.
Bibliographie de l'histoire de France **7344**
Barbour, K.M.
Nigeria in maps **4840**
Barca, M.
Explore historic Australia **5713**
Barcomb, D.
Office automation **2490**
Bard, R.
Navarra **7401**
Bardenhewer, O.
Geschichte der altkirchlichen Literatur **627**
Bardill and Cobbe, J.H.
Lesotho **4880**
Bardis, P.D.
Dictionary of quotations in sociology **1015**
Bardon, J.
Belfast: an illustrated history **7017**
A History of Ulster **7018**
Bare ruined choirs: the dissolution of the English monasteries **641**
Bark, D.L. and Gress, D.R.
A History of West Germany **7300**
Barker, A.
When was that? **8157**
Barker, F. and Jackson, P.
The History of London in maps **7102**
Barker, R.L.
The Social work dictionary **3561**
Barker, W.P.
Who's who in Church history **623**
Barley, M.W.
European towns **3258**
A Guide to British topographical collections **7052**
Barnard, H.C. and Lauwerys, J.A.
A Handbook of British educational terms **3714**
Barnes, H.E.
A History of historical writing **6340**

Barnes, J.
Aristotle: a bibliography **18**
Barnes, R.M.
The Uniforms and history of the Scottish regiments **3472**
Baron, J.L.
A Treasury of Jewish quotations **844**
Baron, S. and Jones, P.
Macmillan dictionary of retailing **2617**
Baron, S.W.
A Social and religious history of the Jews **845**
Barraclough, E.M.C. and Crampton, W.G.
Flags of the world **6316**
Barraclough, G.
The Times concise atlas of world history **6401**
Barrenechea, R.P.
Fuentes historicas peruanas **8088**
Barret, J.
Géographie et cartographie du Gabon **5385**
Barrett, D.B.
World Christian encyclopedia **512**
Barrett, J.K. and Malonis, J.A.
Encyclopedia of women's associations worldwide **4060**
Barron's finance and investment handbook **2100**
Barron's real estate handbook **1937**
Barrow, C. and Golzen, G.
Taking up a franchise **2622**
Barrow, L.
Independent spirits **158**
Barrow, M.
Women, 1870-1928 **4005**
Barrow, R. and Milburn, G.
A Critical dictionary of educational concepts **3715**
Bartel, H.
Sachwörterbuch der Geschischte Deutschlands und der deutscher Arbeiterbewegung **1917**
Barth, H.
Bibliographie der Schweizergeschichte **7524**
The Bartholomew/Warne atlas of Europe **5251**
Bartholomew world atlas **5469**
Barthorp, M.
The Armies of Britain, 1485-1980 **3458**
Bartke, W.
A Biographical dictionary and analysis of China's Party leadership 1922-1988 **5900**
Who's who in the People's Republic of China **5901**
Bartos-Höppner, B. and Bartos, B.
...lebt der gross Name noch **5826**

Bartrum, P.C.
  Welsh genealogies AD300-1400 **6107**
Barucci, P. *and* Carpenter, K.
  Italian economic literature in the
    Kress Library, 1475-1850 **1792**
Barzelatto, F.
  Country profiles **5040**
Basadre, J.
  Introducción a las bases documentales
    para la historia de la república del
    Perú **8089**
Basch, R.
  Finding foreign firms **2365**
Basham, A.L.
  A Cultural history of India **7646**
  The Wonder that was India **7647**
The Basic business library **2459**
A Basic dictionary of geography **5175**
Basic documents of African regional
  organizations **2906**
Basic documents of Asian regional
  organizations **2905**
Basic documents on human rights **3062**
Basic facts about the United Nations
  2867
Basic map library **5399**
Basic statistics of the Community, 1993
  1180
'A Basic stock of religious books' **349**
Basic terms of business and finance
  1750
The Basques **6659**
Bass, D.C. *and* Boyd, S.H.
  Women in American religious history
    4048
Bass, G.F.
  Ships and shipwrecks of the Americas
    4313
Basseches, B.
  A Bibliography of Brazilian
    bibliographies/Uma bibliographia
    das bibliografias brasileiras **5019**
Bassett, J.
  The Concise Oxford dictionary of
    Australian history **8151**
Bassett, R.
  A Guide to Central Europe **5536**
Bastable, P.K.
  Logic: depth grammar of rationality
    323
Batalden, S.K. *and* Batalden, S.L.
  The Newly independent states of
    Eurasia **4724**
Batchelor, S.
  The Tibet guide **5659**
Bate, C.K. *and* Smith, M.G.
  For bravery in the field **6290**
Bate, J. St. J.
  Management guide to office
    automation **2491**
The Bateman concise encyclopaedia of
  Australia **5088**

Bater, P. *and* Parkinson, H.
  Business and company databases,
    1988 **1980**
Bates, D.
  A Bibliography of Domesday Book
    7032
The Batsford companion to local history
  7062
The Batsford guide to the industrial
  archaeology of East Anglia **4398**
The Batsford guide to the industrial
  archaeology of South-East England
  4404
Batson, H.E.
  A Select bibliography of modern
    economic theory, 1870-1929 **1805**
Batten, D. *and* Dresser, P.
  Encyclopedia of governmental
    advisory organizations **3313**
Battle chronicles of the Civil War **8029**
The Battle honours of the British and
  Indian armies, 1695-1914 **3397**
Battle honours of the Royal Navy **3520**
Battle over Britain **6829**
A Battlefield atlas of the American
  Revolution **8025**
A Battlefield atlas of the Civil War
  8036
A Battlefield atlas of the English Civil
  War **6956**
Battles and battlescenes of World War
  Two **3429**
Battles in Britain **3434**
Battley, N.
  McGraw-Hill world futures and
    options directory, 1991-92 **2171**
Baudot, M.
  The Historical encyclopedia of World
    War II **6851**
Baudry, G.-H.
  Pierre Teilhard de Chardin **54**
Bauer, J.B.
  Encyclopedia of Biblical theology
    419
Bauer, K.J. *and* Roberts, S.S.
  Register of ships of the U.S. Navy,
    1775-1990: major combatants **3531**
Baumgart, W.
  Bücherverzeichnis zur deutschen
    Geschichte **7249**
Bäuml, B.J. *and* Bäuml, F.H.
  A Dictionary of gestures **3997**
Bavei, T.J. van **19**
Bawden, C.R.
  The Modern history of Mongolia
    7608
Baxter, A.
  In search of your British and Irish
    roots **6061**
  In search of your European roots
    6053
  In search of your German roots **6111**
  In search of your roots **6128**

Baxter, C.
  Bangladesh **4697**
Baxter, C. *and* Rahman, S.
  Historical dictionary of Bangladesh
    7682
Baxter, P.M.
  Psychology **3**
Baylen, J.O. *and* Gossman, N.J.
  Biographical dictionary of modern
    British radicals **1685**
Bayliss, G.M.
  Bibliographic guide to the two World
    Wars **6791**
Bayly, C.H.
  Atlas of the British Empire **6895**
BBC World Service
  Gulf Crisis chronology **7642**
BBC World Service glossary of current
  affairs **6737**
Beach, M.
  A Subject bibliography of the history
    of American higher education **3856**
Beacham, W.
  Beacham's guide to key lobbyists
    1634
Beacham's guide to key lobbyists **1634**
Beal, G.
  The Independent book of
    anniversaries **6437**
Bean, R.
  International labour statistics **1829**
Beattie, D.
  Company administration handbook
    2542
Beauchamp, E.R. *and* Rubinger, R.
  Education in Japan **3755**
Beaulieu, A.
  Guide d'Histoire du Canada **7868**
Beaver, P.
  Encyclopaedia of the modern Royal
    Navy **3509**
Beazley, C.R.
  The Dawn of modern geography
    5127
Bechtle, T.C. *and* Riley, M.F.
  Dissertations in philosophy accepted
    at American Universities, 1861-
    1975 **74**
Beck, C.
  Political science thesaurus **1429**
Beck, P.
  The Falkland Islands as an
    international problem **8072**
Becker, L. *and* Becker, C.
  Encyclopedia of ethics **333**
Becker, U. von
  Rechtswörterbuch für die gewerbliche
    Wirtschaft **3125**
Becket, H.
  The Dictionary of espionage **1611**
Beckles, H. McD.
  A History of Barbados **7938**
A Bedfordshire bibliography **7183**

Bernal, I.
Bibliografía arqueología y etnografía: Mesoamérica **4295**
Bernal, J.
A History of Mexican archaeology **4294**
Bernal, M.-L.H.
'Reference sources in international law' **2843**
Bernard, Y *and* **Colli, J.-C.**
Dictionnaire économique et financier **1721**
Vocabulaire économique et financier **1722**
Wörterbuch der Wirtschaft und Finanzen.. **1723**
Bernath, M. *and* **Schroeder, F.V.**
Biographisches lexikon zur Geschichte Südesteuropas **7538**
Berndt, J.
Rural sociology **1101**
Bernhardt, R.
Encyclopedia of public international law **2850**
Bernice P. Bishop Museum. Honolulu
Dictionary catalog of the Library of the Bernice P. Bishop Museum **5102**
Bernot, D.
Bibliographie Birmane **4740**
Bernstein, E.
Peace resource book **2963**
Berry, D.M.
A Bibliographic guide to educational research **3689**
Berry, L.
Tanzania in maps **4871**
Bertrand Russell **45**
Berwick, S.
Who's who in Fiji **6033**
Beschorner, N.
Bibliography of Libya 1970-1990 **4797**
Beseler, D. von *and* **Jacobs-Wüstefeld, B.**
Englisch-deutsches und deutsch-englisches Wörterbuch der Rechts und Geschäftssprache. Law dictionary: technical dictionery of the Anglo-American legal terminology, including commercial and statistical terms **2707**
Best, H.
Debrett's Texas peerage **5953**
Best, R.A. *and* **Picquet, D.C.**
Computer crime, abuse, liability and security: a comprehensive bibliography, 1970-1984 **3077**
'Best reference works for the study of minority and third world women' **4017**

Besterman, T.
Education - a bibliography of bibliographies **3682**
Besterman, T.A.
A World bibliography of African bibliographies **4775**
Bethell, L.
The Cambridge history of Latin America **7943**
Better said and clearly written **2500**
Bevan, J. *and* **Duncan, A.**
Tracing your ancestors in the Public Record Office **6101**
Beverly, E.
Public international law **2844**
Beyers, C.J.
Dictionary of South African biography **5930**
Beyond the frozen sea **8175**
Bhattacharjee, A.
A History of ancient India **6656**
Bhattacharya, S.
Dictionary of Indian history **7664**
Bhattacherje, S.B.
Encyclopaedia of Indian events and dates **7668**
Bhattarcharjee, A.
A History of modern India **7649**
Bhuckory, C.K.
Mauritius guide **5679**
Bhutan **4687**
The Bible on-line **417**
Biblical quotations **443**
Bibliofem **4007**
Bibliografi til Norges historie **7491**
Bibliografía arqueología y etnografía: Mesoamérica **4295**
Bibliografia de Estudios sobre Carlos III y su epoca **7419**
'Bibliografía de Nicaragua' **7910**
Bibliografia del Siglo XIX **7420**
Bibliografia della'et à del Risorgimento **7395**
Bibliografia macaense **4606**
Bibliografia peruana de historia 1940-1953 **8090**
Bibliografía Puertorriqueña (1493-1930) **4951**
Bibliografia Somalia **4864**
Bibliografia storica nazionale **7392**
Bibliografie der geschiedenis van Nederland **7505**
Bibliografie van de stedengeschiedenis van Nederland **7507**
Bibliografisk handbok till Sveriges historia **7496**
Bibliographia **3238**
Bibliographia Canadiana **7875**
Bibliographia Cartesiana **23**
Bibliographia logica **321**
Bibliographia patristica **644**
Bibliographic and information services in education **3683**

'A Bibliographic essay of selected secondary sources on the common law and customary law of English speaking Sub-Saharan Africa' **2809**
Bibliographic guide to black studies, 1975- **1089**
Bibliographic guide to business and economics **2445**
A Bibliographic guide to educational research **3689**
Bibliographic guide to law. 1975-Annual **2665**
Bibliographic guide to maps and atlases **5228**
Bibliographic guide to North American history 1988 **7960**
Bibliographic guide to psychology **221**
Bibliographic guide to Soviet and East European studies **4443**
A Bibliographic guide to Spanish diplomatic history, 1460-1977 **1584**
A Bibliographic guide to studies on the status of women **4008**
A Bibliographic guide to the comparative study of ethics **331**
Bibliographic guide to the legal aspects of international finance **2104**
Bibliographic guide to the two World Wars **6791**
Bibliographic services in education **3681**
A Bibliographical account of the principal works relating to English topography **7059**
A Bibliographical account of works relating to the Isle of Man **7227**
Bibliographical aids and reference tools for the literature of education **3690**
'Bibliographical aids for studies on Namibia' **4884**
'Bibliographical aids for studies on South West Africa' **4883**
A Bibliographical dictionary of the British Colonial Service, 1939-1966 **1529**
Bibliographical foundations of French historical studies **7389**
'Bibliographical guide to early British law books' **2785**
Bibliographical guide to Iran **4700**
A Bibliographical guide to New Testament research **488**
A Bibliographical guide to the history of the British Empire 1784-1776 **6892**
A Bibliographical guide to the Indian-White relations in the United States **1061**
Bibliographical guide to the law of the United Kingdom, the Channel Islands and the Isle of Man **2742**
Bibliographical handbooks **6901**
Bibliographie annotée d'ouvrages généalogiques au Canada **6127**

Blombach-Schäfer, U.
The New Europe **5249**
Blondel, J.
Government ministers in the
contemporary world **3284**
The Organization of governments
3280
World leaders **3285**
Blondel, J. *and* **Walker, C.**
Directory of European political
scientists **1387**
Blond's encyclopedia of education **3708**
Bloomberg, M. *and* **Weber, H.**
World War II and its origins **6839**
Bloomfield, G.T.
New Zealand **1284**
Bloomfield, V.
Commonwealth elections, 1945-1970
1509
Research for Canadian studies in
Britain **4914**
Resources for Australian and New
Zealand studies **5072**
'Resources for Australian and New
Zealand studies in the United
Kingdom', p. 67-75 **5073**
Bloor, S.G.
Reference guide to management
techniques and activities **2552**
Bluche, F.
Dictionnaire du Grand Siècle **7359**
Blue Guide Wales **5627**
Blue guides **5508**
The Blue Plaque guide **5617**
Blum, A.A.
International handbook of industrial
relations **1860**
Blunden, C. *and* **Elvin, M.**
Cultural atlas of China **4601**
Boam, T.L.
'Modern sources for genealogical
research in the United States' **6135**
Boardman, J.
Oxford history of the classical world
6669
Boase, F.
Modern English biography **5819**
Boatner, M.M.
Cassell's biographical dictionary of
the American War of Independence
1763-1783 **8026**
Cassell's biographical dictionary of
the American Civil War **8039**
Bobb, F.S.
Historical dictionary of Zaire **7813**
Bochénski, I.M.
Contemporary European philosophy
112
Bodensieck, J.H.
The Encyclopedia of the Lutheran
Church **706**
Bodurgil, A.
Atatürk and Turkey **7691**

Bodurgil, A. *(contd.)*
Turkey, politics and government
7692
Boeder, R.B.
Malawi **4896**
Boehm, E.H.
Historical periodicals directory **6386**
Boehm, K. *and* **Wellings, N.**
The Student book, 1994 **3890**
Boehn, M. von *and* **Fischel, O.**
Modes and manners of the nineteenth
century **3928**
Boehn, M.von
Modes and manners from the Middle
Ages to the end of the eighteenth
century **3927**
Boff, K.R.
Handbook of perception and human
performance **291**
Bogdanor, V.
The Blackwell encyclopedia of
political institutions **1430**
Boggs, R.S.
Bibliography of Latin American
folklore **4107**
Bogle, J.
Who lies where? **5550**
Bogue, D.J.
The Population of the United States
1332
Bohdan Nahaylo *and* **Swoboda, V.**
Soviet disunion **7453**
Boia, L.
Great historians from antiquity to
1800 **6341**
Great historians of the modern age
6342
Bolivia **5028, 8085**
Bollier, J.A.
The Literature of theology **532**
Bolton, G.
The Oxford history of Australia **8140**
Bolton, J.L.
The Medieval English economy,
1150-1500 **2241**
The Bomber Command war diaries
6830
Bond, B.
The First World War and British
military history **6408**
Bond, D.
The Guinness guide to 20th-century
fashion **3950**
Bond, M.F.
Guide to the records of Parliament
3022
Bonkowske, J.A.
The American flag **6335**
Bonser, W.
An Anglo-Saxon and Celtic
bibliography **6938**

Bonser, W. *(contd.)*
A Bibliography of folklore, as
contained in the first eighty years of
the publications of the Folklore
Society **4072**
A Prehistoric bibliography **4217**
A Romano-British bibliography **6939**
**Book Marketing Council The
Publishers Association.**
Catalogue of maps and guides 1990
5229
Book of Biblical quotations **440**
The Book of British topography **7051**
The Book of Catholic quotations **676**
Book of days **6438**
The Book of dignities **6282**
The Book of Druidry **881**
The Book of festivals **3970**
The Book of goddesses and heroines
758
The Book of Jewish books **827**
The Book of Kings: a royal genealogy
6301
The Book of London **7099**
The Book of New Zealand women
6012
The Book of orders and decorations
6286
The Book of public arms **6250**
The Book of saints **559**
The Book of the States, 1992-93 **3276**
Book of world city rankings **3254**
Book of world flags **6319**
Book review index to social science
periodicals **943**
Bookman, J.T. *and* **Powers, S.T.**
The March to victory **6823**
Books and periodicals on line **1946,
2660**
'Books Hadrians Wall 1979-89' **4342**
Books in English on the Soviet Union,
1917-73 **4523**
Books of Welsh interest **4480**
Books on Buddhism **808**
'Books on disability' **3627**
Books on palaeography **6601**
Books on Sweden in English **4548**
Boorman, H.L. *and* **Howard, A.C.**
Biographical dictionary of Republican
China **5895**
Booth, D. *and* **Perrott, D.**
The Shell book of the islands of
Britain **5585**
Bootle, R.
Directory of world stock exchanges
2172
Booz, E.B.
A Guide to Tibet **5660**
Borchardt, C.F.A. *and* **Vorster, W.S.**
South African theological
bibliography.. **548**
Borchardt, D.H. *and* **Francis, R.D.**
How to find out in psychology **215**

Brandow, J.
Genealogies of Barbados families **6133**
Brand's popular antiquities of Great Britain **4092**
Branigan, K.
The Atlas of archaeology **4175**
Branson, M.L.
The Reader's guide to the best evangelical books **509**
Brasseur, P.
Bibliographie générale du Mali **4814**
Brassey's armed services careers yearbook, 1987/88 **3371**
Brassey's battles **3427**
Brassey's multilingual military dictionary **3335**
Brassey's Soviet and communist quotations **209**
Brauer, J.C.
The Westminster dictionary of church history **621**
Braund, D.
Augustus to Nero **6689**
Braunthal, J.
History of the International **1638**
Brawer, M.
Atlas of South America **5436**
Atlas of the Middle East **5351**
"Yavneh" comprehensive atlas **5499**
Brawer, M. and Machlis, G.
Israel touring and road atlas **5364**
Bray, J. and Nawang Tsering Shakspo
A Bibliography of Ladakh **4678**
Bray, W. and Feest, C.
The Peoples of America **6706**
Bray, W. and Trump, D.
Penguin dictionary of archaeology **4168**
Brazil **5020, 8069**
Brazil 1822-1930 **8065**
Brazil in reference books 1965-1989 **5021**
Brazil. Instituto Brasileiro de Geografia e Estatística
Anuário estatístico do Brasil, 1992 **1280**
Brazil since 1930 **8064**
Brealey, R.A and Edwards, H.
A Bibliography of finance **2026**
Bréhier, É.
The History of philosophy **82**
Breisach, E.
Historiography **6343**
Breithart, B.R.
Who's who in the behavioral sciences **274**
Bremond, J. and Geledan, A.
Dictionnaire économique et social **1748**
Brennan, E.
Heritage: a visitors guide **5600**

Brereton, B.
A History of modern Trinidad 1783-1962 **7941**
Brereton, J.M.
A Guide to the regiments and corps of the British Army **3466**
The Brethren encyclopedia **725**
The Bretons **6661**
Brett, D.T.
The Police of England and Wales **3213**
Breu, J.
Atlas der Donauländer **5252**
A Breviate of British diplomatic blue books, 1919-1939 **1570**
A Breviate of Parliamentary Papers, 1900-1916 **3031**
A Breviate of Parliamentary Papers, 1917-1939 **3032**
A Breviate of Parliamentary Papers, 1940-1954 **3033**
Brewer, E.C.
A Dictionary of miracles, imitative, realistic and dogmatic **549**
Bridge, F.R.
The Hapsburg monarchy 1804-1918 **7312**
Bridges **1135**
Bridgman, J. and Clarke, D.
German Africa **4779**
A Brief guide to the industrial heritage of West Yorkshire **4401**
A Brief guide to the sources for the study of Burma **6538**
A Brief history of psychology **272**
Briggs, A.
A Dictionary of twentieth-century world biography **5733**
Briggs, D.C. and Alisky, M.
Historical dictionary of Mexico **7901**
Briggs, G.
Civic and corporate heraldry **6245**
Briggs, K.M.
A Dictionary of British folk-tales in the English language **4093**
A Dictionary of fairies **4132**
Bright, J.
A History of Israel **6635**
Bring, S.E.
Bibliografisk handbok till Sveriges historia **7496**
Briscoe, M.L.
American autobiography 1945-1980 **5978**
Britain 1994 **4456**
Britain and the world, 1815-1986 **1556**
Britain, Spain and Gibraltar 1945-90 **7427**
Britain speaks out, 1937-87 **1034**
Britain votes. 5: British Parliamentary election results, 1988-1992 **1504**
Britain's dependent territories **6887**

Britain's elusive empire in the Middle East, 1900-1921 **7573**
'Britain's national parks' **5551**
Britain's privately owned companies **2391**
Britain's Royal Families **6312**
Britain's sea war **6838**
Britannia **6934**
British and American utopian literature, 1516-1985 **328**
British and foreign state papers **2929**
British and Irish biographies 1840-1940 **5798**
British archaeological abstracts **4222**
British archaeological bibliography **4218**
British archaeology **4219**
British archives **6466**
'The British Army, 1815-1856: recent writing reviewed' **3461**
'The British Army, 1856-1914: recent writing reviewed' **3462**
British army cloth insignia **3409**
British army uniforms and insignia of World War II **3415**
The British atlas of historic towns **7071**
British autobiographies **5802**
British banking, 1960-85 **2143**
British battles and medals **3368**
British biographical archive **5799**
The British biographical archive. Series II **5800**
British biographical index **5782**
The British budgetary system **2074**
British bulletin of publications on Latin America **4974**
British business history **1791**
British calendar customs **4088**
British Chamber of Commerce
Six language business dictionary **1961**
British Columbia Library of the Provincial Archives
Dictionary catalogue of the Library **7891**
The British conquest and dominion of India **7653**
British Consultants Bureau
Directory **2646**
British Council
Scholarships abroad **3871**
Studying and living in Britain 1991 **4451**
British defence directory **3372**
British diaries **5803**
British directories **7069**
British directories as sources in historical geography **5209**
British directory of legal services, 1990/91 **2745**
British East Africa 1850-1963 **7804**
The British economy **2230**

Canney, M.
Catalogue of the Goldsmiths' Library of economic literature **1707**

Cannistaro, P.V.
Historical dictionary of Fascist Italy **7396**

Cannon, D.D.
The Flags of the Confederacy **6334**

Cannon, J.
The Blackwell dictionary of historians **6366**

Cannon, M.
The Exploration of Australia **8132**

Canon law abstracts **3173**

CANS (Citizens Advice Notes) **3574**

Cantor, G.
Historic landmarks of Black America **5690**

Cantwell, J.D.
The Second World War a guide to documents in the Public Record Office **6874**

Cape Verde **4829**

Capek, M.E.S.
A Women's thesaurus **4058**

Capie, F.
Directory of economic institutions **1770**

Capie, F. *and* Collins, M.
The Inter-war British economy **2234**

Capie, F. *and* Webber, A.
A Monetary history of the United Kingdom, 1870-1982 **2122**

The Capital companion **7105**

Cappelens bilatlas Norden **5321**

Cappelen's car atlas of the Nordic states **5321**

Cappon, L.J.
Atlas of early American history **8015**

Capps, D.
Psychology of religion **407**

Caprenter, C.
The Guinness UK data book **4452**

Caratini, R.
Dictionnaire des personages de la Révolution **7381**

Carbani, F.
Bibliografia Somalia **4864**

Card catalog of the Peace Palace Library, The Hague. Microfiche edition **2955**

Cardinale, H.E.
Orders of knighthood, awards and the Holy See **6298**

Career discovering encyclopedia **1894**

Careers encyclopedia **1890**

Careless, G.C. *and* Morris, P.
Bibliographies of books printed before 1800 **350**

Carey, P.
Maritime Southeast Asian studies in the United Kingdom **4730**

Caribbean
Research guide to Central America and the Caribbean **6556**

The Caribbean **4931**

Caribbean book list **4932**

Caribbean economic handbook **2305**

The Caribbean handbook 1992/93 **4937**

Caribbean history in maps **7918**

Caribbean studies **4934**

Caribbean travel resource guide **5685**

Carlisle, N.
A Concise account of the several foreign orders of knighthood **6295**

Carlson, A.R.
German foreign policy, 1890-1914, and colonial policy to 1914 **1578**

Carman, J. *and* Juergensmeyer, M.
A Bibliographic guide to the comparative study of ethics **331**

Carman, W.Y.
British military uniforms from contemporary pictures: Henry VII to the present day **3417**

Carnes, P.
Fable scholarship **4073**

Caron, F.
An Economic history of modern France **2259**

Caron, P. *and* Jaryc, M.
World list of historical periodicals and bibliographies **6387**

Caron, P. *and* Stein, H.
Répertoire bibliographique de l'histoire de France **7345**

Carpatho-Rusyn studies **4445**

Carpenter, A. *and* Provorse, C.
World Almanac of the USA **4994**

Carpenter, C.
The Guinness book of kings, rulers & statesmen **6304**

Carr, E.H.
A History of Soviet Russia **7454**

Carr-Saunders, A.M.
A Survey of social conditions in England and Wales **1133**

Carroll, B.A.
Peace and war **2952**

Carroll, M.
Acronyms relating to international development/Liste de sigles en développement international/Sigles relacionadas con desarrollo internacional **2939**

Carruth, G.
The Encyclopedia of American facts and dates **7996**

Carskadon, M.A.
Encyclopedia of sleep and dreaming **295**

Carson, A.
Feminist spirituality and the feminine divine **578**

Carstairs, A. McL.
A Short history of electoral systems in Western Europe **1496**

Carsten, F.L.
The First Austrian republic 1918-1938 **7308**

Carte archéologique de la Gaulle **4252**

Carte archéologique de la Gaulle Romaine **4253**

Carter, C.H.
The Western European powers 1500-1700 **6786**

Carter, H.
Atlas cenedlaethol Cymru/National atlas of Wales **5285**

Carter, P.
The Social work and social welfare yearbook, 1991 **3573**

Carter, S. *and* Ritchie, M.
Women's studies **4000**

Carthage **6704**

Cartobibliography of the Cameroon **5384**

Carty, J.
Bibliography of Irish history 1870-1921 **6997**

Carus-Wilson, E.M.
Essays in economic history **1774**

Carver, Field Marshall Lord
Twentieth century warriors **3393**

Carver, T.
The Cambridge companion to Marx **40**

Cary, M.
The Geographical background of Greek and Roman history **6667**

Cary, M. *and* Scullard, H.H.
A History of Rome **6690**

Casada, J.
'British exploration in East Africa' **7800**

Casada, J.A.
An Annotated bibliography of exploration in Africa **5133**

Case, M.H.
South Asian history 1750-1950 **7579**

Casey, J.
The History of the family **1119**

Cash, P.
Sources of Bahamian history **7935**

Cashin, J.A.
Cashin's handbook for auditors **2531**

Cashin's handbook for auditors **2531**

Cashmore, E.E.
Dictionary of race and ethnic relations **1065**

Cassell's biographical dictionary of the American War of Independence 1763-1783 **8026**

Cassels, A.
Italian foreign policy, 1918-1945 **1583**

Christensen, D. *and* Fieguth, M.
Historic Saskatchewan **5682**
Christensen, D.E.
Contemporary German philosophy,
v.1-6, 1982-87 **115**
Christian England **589**
Christian periodical index **691**
Christian pilgrimage in modern Western
Europe **515**
Christian symbols, ancient and modern
573
The Christian tradition **544**
The Christian year **554**
Christianity in a revolutionary age **522**
Christianity in tropical Africa **530**
Christie, J.R.
British history since 1760 **6903**
Christienne, C.
French military aviation **3487**
Christodoulou, A.
The Almanac of Cyprus 1992 **4706**
The Christopher Columbus
encyclopedia **7861**
Christophers, A.
An Index to nineteenth-century British
educational biography **3752**
**Chronicle and memorials of Great
Britain and Ireland**
Rerum Britannicarum medii aevi
scriptores **6906**
Chronicle of America **7970**
Chronicle of Australia **8133**
Chronicle of Britain **6910**
Chronicle of Canada **7866**
Chronicle of parliamentary elections and
development; 1 July 1986/30 June
1987 **1491**
Chronicle of the 20th century **6734**
Chronicle of the First World War **6814**
Chronicle of the French Revolution
7374
Chronicle of the Royal Family **6911**
Chronicle of the Second World War
6867
Chronicle of the world **6357**
Chronicle of the year 1993 **6743**
The Chronicle of Western fashion **3943**
Die Chronik Bayerns **7302**
Die Chronik Berlins **7254**
Chronik der Deutschen **7255**
Chronik der Schweiz **7526**
Die Chronik der Stadt Bonn **7303**
Chronik des 19. Jahrhunderts **6729**
Chronik des Ruhrgebiets **7304**
Die Chronik Österreichs **7316**
Die Chronik Wiens **7317**
Chronique de la Belgique **7521**
Chronique de la France et des Français
7351
Chronologia polska **7331**
Chronological atlas of World War II
6862

Chronological dictionary of quotations
6391
A Chronological history of Puerto Rico
7930
Chronological history of United States
foreign relations, 1776-January 20
1981 **1599**
Chronological list of Antarctic
expeditions **8181**
Chronological table of the Statutes,
covering the legislation from 1235 to
the end of 1990 **2751**
Chronological tables of Chinese history
7597
Chronologie du Québec **7897**
Chronologies in New World
archaeology **4289**
'Chronologique de Wallis et Futuna'
8130
A Chronology and fact book of the
United Nations, 1941-1991 **2868**
Chronology and index of the Second
World War 1938-1945 **6868**
Chronology of African-American
history **7998**
Chronology of African history **7747**
The Chronology of British history **6923**
Chronology of British Parliamentary by-
elections, 1983-1987 **1501**
'The Chronology of colonization in New
Zealand' **4300**
A Chronology of conflict and
revolution, 1945-1985 **1464**
The Chronology of Indian history **7669**
A Chronology of Irish history since
1500 **7010**
A Chronology of Irish history to 1976
7008
A Chronology of Islamic history **7567**
A Chronology of Islamic history, 570-
1000 C.E **873**
'Chronology of main events in Northern
Ireland since 1969' **7023**
A Chronology of post war British
politics **1399**
Chronology of the Ancient World **6618,
6620**
Chronology of the expanding world
1492 to 1762 **6785**
Chronology of the Great War **6813**
Chronology of the medieval world 800
to 1491 **6766**
Chronology of the modern world 1763-
1992 **6727**
A Chronology of the People's Republic
of China 1949-1984 **7595**
Chronology of the People's Republic of
China 1970-1979 **7596**
Chronology of the United States **7997**
Chronology of the war at sea 1939-1945
6870
Chronology of world history **6441**
Chronology of World War II **6866**

Chua Sui Gim
'Guide to modern archives and
manuscripts found in the UK
relating to Brunei, Sabah and
Sarawak,' **6584**
Chubb, T.
Descriptive list of the printed maps of
Norfolk, 1874-1916 **7197**
Chun Moon, K.
Korea Annual 1992 **4617**
The Church explorer's guide to symbols
and their meaning **576**
A Church history of Scotland **651**
The Church of England year book, 1993
690
The Church of God, Seventh Day **720**
The Church of Scotland year-book,
1992 **709**
Church, R. *and* Cole, J.
In and around record repositories in
Great Britain and Ireland **6464**
Church vestments **597**
Cimbala, D.J.
Biographical sources **5756**
Cindarellas of empire **8171**
Cipolla, C.M.
The Fontana economic history of
Europe **2223**
CIS/Index **3049**
Cities of the United States **4991**
Cities of the world **4419**
City & State directories in print **8055**
The City directory, 1992 **2062**
City map library **5401**
City University. Business School
Working paper series, 1977- **2199**
Civic and corporate heraldry **6245**
Civic ceremonial **3985**
Civil liberty **3073**
The Civil Service today **3201**
The Civil Service year book, 1993
3204
Civil War books **8032**
The Civil War in the North **8031**
Civil War manuscripts **8041**
Civil War maps **8035**
Civilization of the Ancient
Mediterranean. Greece and Rome
6672
Clackmannanshire **6992**
Clans and families of Ireland **6191**
Clans and families of Ireland and
Scotland **6971**
The Clans, septs and regiments of the
Scottish Highlands **6187**
Clapham, J.
The Bank of England **2146**
Clapp, B.W.
Documents in English economic
history: England from 1000 to 1760
2249
Documents in English economic
history: England since 1760 **2250**

Clarie, T.C.
  Occult/paranormal bibliography **137**
Clark, C.M.H.
  A History of Australia **8134**
Clark, I.F.
  The Tale of the future **195**
Clark, J.
  History of the International **1638**
Clark, J.D.
  Atlas of African prehistory **4285**
Clarke, B.R. *and* Neave, G.R.
  The Encyclopedia of higher education **3877**
Clarke, C.G.
  Jamaica in maps **5421**
Clarke, H.
  The Archaeology of medieval England **4242**
Clarke, J.L.
  Sierra Leone in maps **5380**
Clarke, P.B.
  Find out in education **3694**
  Finding out in education **3696**
Clarke, R.A. *and* Matko, D.J.I.
  Soviet economic facts, 1917-80 **2266**
Clarke, S.
  The Complete fundraising handbook **3538**
Clason, W.E.
  Elsevier's lexicon of international and national units **3228**
The Classical foundations of modern historiography **6405**
Classical mythology **781**
Classical political economy **1713**
'The Classical world' bibliography of Greek and Roman history **6671**
'The Classical world' bibliography of philosophy, religion and rhetoric **16, 747**
A Classified bibliography of literature on the Acts of the Apostles **504**
Classified catalog of the ecumenical movement **591**
The Classified catalogue of the Royal Institute of International Affairs for international relations, defence, diplomacy, international law, politics and economics.. **1548**
Clay, K.
  The School administrator's resource guide **3801**
Clay, R.M.
  The Mediaeval hospitals of England **3622**
Clayton, D. *and* Jameson, E.
  Bibliography of policy related education documents in selected countries in Africa, Asia, the Caribbean and the Pacific **3736**
Clayton, P.
  Guide to the archaeological sites of Britain **4332**

Clayton, P. *and* Price, M.J.
  The Seven wonders of the Ancient World **6609**
Clayton, P.A.
  A Companion to Roman Britain **6933**
Cleere, H.F.
  Archaeological heritage management in the modern world **4320**
Clegg, H.A.
  A History of British trade unions since 1889 **1911**
Clegg, J.
  Dictionary of social services **3562**
Clegg, M.B.
  Bibliography of genealogy and local history periodicals with union list of major US collections **6143**
Clements, F.A.
  Kuwait **4668**
  Oman **4659**
  Saudi Arabia **4655**
  United Arab Emirates **4663**
Clements, J.
  Chronology of the United States **7997**
Clements, M.N.
  The Marketing glossary **2598**
Clendenning, P. *and* Bartlett, R.
  Eighteenth century Russia **7452**
The Clerks of the Counties, 1360-1960 **3274**
Cleveland Public Library. John G. White Department
  Catalog of folklore, folklife and folk songs **4074**
Clews, B.H.A.
  Malta year book 1989 **4512**
Clifton, C.S.
  Encyclopedia of heresies and heretics **672**
Clinch, M.A.
  Guide to Northern Territory research resources in Northern Territory collections **5081**
Clinch, P.
  Business law **3130**
Cline, M.W.
  Scholar's guide to intelligence literature **1607**
Clogg, M.J. *and* Clogg, R.
  Greece **4562**
Clogg, R.
  A Short history of modern Greece **7529**
Close, A.C.
  Washington's representatives .. **1635**
Clout, H.
  The Times London history atlas **7103**
Clowes, W.L.
  The Royal Navy **3512**
Cloyd, I.
  Who's who among Black Americans 1991-92 **5986**

Clwyd Library Service catalogue of the collection of Arthurian literature **4118**
CMG Information Services
  Faculty white pages, 1991 **3907**
Coarelli, F.
  Guida archeologica di Roma **4378**
Coastal and maritime archaeology **4308**
Coates, K.S. *and* Morrison, W.R.
  Land of the midnight sun **7888**
Cobban, H.
  The Making of modern Lebanon **7697**
Cobo, B.
  Inca religion and customs **895**
Cochrane, P.
  Scottish military dress **3419**
Cockerell, H.
  Dictionary of insurance **3657**
Cockerell, H.A.L. *and* Green, E.
  The British insurance business, 1547-1970 **3671**
Cockle, M.J.D.
  A Bibliography of English military books up to 1642 **3325**
Cocks, B.
  The European Parliament **2993**
Cockton, P.
  Subject catalogue of the House of Commons Parliamentary papers, 1801-1900 **3007**
'The Cocos (Keeling) Islands', p.171-175, *Debrett's handbook of Australia and New Zealand* (2nd ed., 1984) **8135**
The Code of canon law **3175**
The Code of canon law in English translation **3174**
Codices Latini antiquiores **6604**
Codlin, E.M.
  Aslib directory **971**
Coe, A. *and* Furlong, P.
  A Modern companion to the European Community **2889**
Coe, M.
  Atlas of ancient America **4288**
Coetzer, P.W. *and* Le Roux, J.H.
  General sources on South African political history since 1902 **7834**
  Index to periodical articles on South African political and social history since 1902 **7835**
Coffey, H.W. *and* Morgan, M.J.
  Irish families in Australia and New Zealand **6209**
Cofrestri plwyf Cymru/Parish registers of Wales **6221**
Coggins, R.J.
  A Dictionary of Biblical interpretation **462**
Cohen, A.
  Soncino books of the Bible **856**

Cohen, B.
The Thames 1580-1980 **7095**
Cohen, D.
Psychology exposed **222**
Cohen, H. *and* Coffin, T.P.
The Folklore of American holidays
3976
Cohen, J.
Special bibliography in monetary
economics and finance **2027**
Cohen, S.S.
Anti-semitism **1060**
Cohn, E.J.
Manual of German law **2788**
Cohn-Sherbock, D.
Atlas of Jewish history **6649**
Cohn-Sherbok, D.
The Dictionary of Judaica **841**
A Dictionary of Judaism and
Christianity **842**
Cokayne, G.E.
The Complete peerage of England,
Scotland, Ireland, Great Britain and
the United Kingdom **6271**
Coldham, P.W.
The Complete book of emigrants
6136
Cole, A. *and* Campbell, P.
French electoral systems and elections
since 1789 **1510**
Cole, G.D.H.
A History of Socialist thought **190**
Cole, J.A. *and* Armstrong, M.
Tracing your family tree **6179**
Cole, W.O. *and* Sambhi, P.S.
A Popular dictionary of Sikhism **816**
The Sikhs: their religious beliefs and
practices **817**
Coleman, E.A.
The Opulent era: fashions of Worth,
Doucet and Pingat **3960**
Coleman, K.
Legal reference work in non-law
libraries **2667**
Coleman, P.G.
'Social gerontology' **1039**
Coletta, P.E.
A Bibliography of American naval
history **3533**
A Selected and annotated bibliography
of American naval history **3534**
Collcut, M.
Cultural atlas of Japan **7627**
A Collection of Chinese proverbs **4148**
Collections in British libraries on
Middle Eastern and Islamic studies
4652
The Collections of the British Museum
4323
Collections towards the history and
antiquities of the county of Hereford
7153

A Collector's guide to the history and
uniform of Das Heer **3420**
Colledge, J.J.
Ships of the Royal Navy **3513-3514**
College administration **3852**
Collett, P.
Foreign bodies **3991**
Collett, R.J.
Northern Ireland statistics **1199**
Collier, S.
The Cambridge encyclopaedia of
Latin America and the Caribbean
4936
'Historiography of the Portalion
period (1830-1891) in Chile' **8084**
Collin, P.H.
Dictionary of banking and finance
2127
Dictionary of business, English/
French, French/English **1965**
Dictionary of government and politics
3181
English business dictionary **2462**
English law dictionary **2700**
Collinge, J.M.
Officials of Royal Commissions of
Inquiry, 1815-70 **3293**
Collingwood, R.G. *and* Richmond, I.
The Archaeology of Roman Britain
4226
Collingwood, R.G. *and* Wright, R.P.
The Roman inscriptions of Britain
4338-4339
Collins atlas of the world **5470**
The Collins atlas of twentieth century
world history **6434**
The Collins atlas of world history **6395**
Collins business German **2466**
Collins China guides and Collins
illustrated guides **5656**
Collins dictionary of archaeology **4167**
Collins dictionary of business **1955**
The Collins dictionary of Canadian
history **7878**
Collins dictionary of sociology **1014**
Collins, D.O.
Siberia and the Soviet Far East **4726**
Collins, E.K.
Beginners' guide to Scottish
genealogy **6071**
Collins field guide to archaeology in
Britain **4318**
The Collins guide to France **5635**
Collins, K.T.
Key words in education **3716**
Collins, M.
Money and banking in the U.K.: a
history **2061**
Collins, M.E.
Education journals and serials **3730**
Collins milestones in Australian history
8158

Collins, R.
The Basques **6659**
Collins road atlas Europe 1990 **5245**
Collins road atlas France 1990 **5304**
Collins road atlas Italy 1990 **5309**
Collinson, D.
Fifty major philosophers **104**
Collinson, J. *and* Rack, E.
The History and antiquities of the
county of Somerset .. **7142**
Collis, J.
The European Iron Age **4202**
Collison, J.
Directory of domiciliary and hospital
patients' library services in the
United Kingdom **3621**
Collison, R.L.
Kenya **4861**
Uganda **4860**
Colman, J.J.
Bibliotheca Norfolciensis **7195**
Colombo, J.R.
Colombo's Canadian references **4908**
Colombo's Canadian references **4908**
'Colonial America, 1607-1776' **964**
Colonial governors **1523**
Colonial related archive and manuscript
collections in the UK **6491**
Colonialism in Africa, 1870-1960 **1522**
Columbia **5031**
The Columbia history of Eastern Europe
in the twentieth century **7245**
**Columbia University. Center for the
Study of Human Rights**
Human rights **3055**
Columbus **7860**
Columbus dictionary
Columbus **7860**
Columbus literature guides **7857**
Colvin, H.M.
The History of the King's Works
4364
Colvin, L.G.
Historical dictionary of Senegal **7783**
Colwell, S.
Dictionary of genealogical sources in
the Public Record Office **6102**
The Family history book **6180**
Family roots **6198**
Comay, J.
Who's who in Jewish history after the
period of the Old Testament **6655**
Who's Who in the Old Testament **486**
Combe, D.A.
'French legal bibliographies' **2793**
Combined retrospective index to
journals in sociology, 1894-1974 **987**
Combroux, J.
Atlas de la Nouvelle - Calédonie et
Dépendences **5460**
COMECON data, 1990 **1183**
COMECON foreign trade data, 1986
2426

A dictionary of saints
See
The lives of the saints$zThe Lives of the saints
Dictionary of Scandinavian history **7481**
Dictionary of Scottish biography **5809**
Dictionary of Scottish business biography, 1860-1960 **2475**
Dictionary of Scottish church history and theology **624**
A Dictionary of Scottish emigrants to Canada before Confederation **6126**
A Dictionary of Scottish history **6983**
The Dictionary of SDI **3445**
A Dictionary of ships of the Royal Navy of the Second World War **3516**
A Dictionary of social science methods **967**
A Dictionary of social sciences **930**
Dictionary of social services **3562**
Dictionary of social welfare **3591**
Dictionary of South African biography **5930**
A Dictionary of special education terms **3835**
A Dictionary of statistical terms **1149**
The Dictionary of statistics **1150**
A Dictionary of superstitions **4126**
Dictionary of taxation **2092**
A Dictionary of terms and techniques in archaeology **4169**
A Dictionary of the Bible **429**
Dictionary of the Ecumenical movement **590**
A Dictionary of the European Communities **2894-2895**
Dictionary of the history of ideas **58, 65**
Dictionary of the language of financial reports **2051**
Dictionary of the Middle Ages **6761**
Dictionary of the Napoleonic wars **3437**
A Dictionary of the proverbs in England in the sixteenth and seventeenth centuries **4143**
Dictionary of the Renaissance **6775**
Dictionary of the Russian Revolution **7464**
A Dictionary of the Second World War **6857**
A Dictionary of the social sciences **929**
Dictionary of the Targumin, the Talmud Babli and Yerushalmi, and the Midrashic literature **858**
A Dictionary of the Third Reich **7287**
Dictionary of the Vietnam War **7734**
Dictionary of Third World terms **4436**
Dictionary of twentieth-century history (1914-1990) **6433**
A Dictionary of twentieth-century world biography **5733**

Dictionary of United States economic history **2313**
Dictionary of universal biography **5758**
The Dictionary of Welsh biography down to 1940 **5822**
Dictionary of world history **6370**
A Dictionary of world mythology **759**
The Dictionary of world politics **1348**
Dictionnaire anglais-français et lexique français-anglais des termes politiques, juridiques et économiques **1373**
Dictionnaire bilingue de la publicité et de la communication **2643**
Dictionnaire biographique du mouvement ouvrier français de 1789-1939 **1918**
Dictionnaire canadien des relations du travail **1865**
Dictionnaire critique de sociologie **1007**
Dictionnaire critique du Marxisme **206**
Dictionnaire de biographie française **5842**
Dictionnaire de biographie Mauricienne/ Dictionary of Mauritian biography **5934**
Dictionnaire de la France Médiévale **7357**
Dictionnaire de la Noblesse **6284**
Dictionnaire de Paris **5636**
Dictionnaire de préhistoire **4170**
Dictionnaire de spiritualité, ascétique et mystique, doctrine et histoire **579**
Dictionnaire de termes juridiques en quatre langues ... Legal dictionary in four languages **2699**
Dictionnaire des antiquités grecques et romaines **4324**
Le Dictionnaire des belges **5888**
Dictionnaire des personages de la Révolution **7381**
Dictionnaire des philosophies antiques **95**
Dictionnaire des sciences historiques **6367**
Dictionnaire d'histoire de France Perrin **7352**
Dictionnaire d'histoire universelle **6373**
Dictionnaire du Grand Siècle **7359**
Dictionnaire économique et financier **1721**
Dictionnaire économique et social **1748**
Dictionnaire économique et social: dictionnaire Thomas Suavet **935**
Dictionnaire encyclopédique de psychologie **237**
Dictionnaire encyclopédique d'histoire **6374**
Le Dictionnaire encyclopédique militaire soviétique **3332**
Dictionnaire français-anglais de l'économie monétaire **2050**
Dictionnaire géographique de la France **5641**

Dictionnaire géographique et administratif universel d'Haïti **4949**
Dictionnaire historique de la Révolution Française **7378**
Dictionnaire historique et biographique de la Suisse **7528**
Dictionnaire juridique **2710**
Dictionnaire juridique et économique. Wörterbuch der Rechts .. **2695**
Dictionnaire Napoléon **7360**
Dictionnaire politique et diplomatique **1374**
Dictionnaire universel des poids et mesures anciens et modernes **3229**
Didik, F.X.
East European business directory **2390**
Diehl, K.S.
Hymns and tunes - an index **599**
Diercke Weltatlas **5472**
Dietl, E.-E.
Wirtschaftswörterbuch: Wörterbuch für den Wirtschafts-, Handels- und Rechtsverkehr .../Commercial dictionary: dictionary of commercial, business and legal terms - including the terminology of the European Communities **932**
Wörterbuch für Recht, Wirtschaft und Politik. Dictionary of legal, commercial and political terms **931**
Dietz, P.
The Last of the regiments **3469**
Dietz, W.
World directory of national parliamentary libraries **3052**
A Digest and index of tax cases .. **2094**
Digest of commercial laws of the world **3128**
Digest of statistics, Northern Ireland **1201**
Digest of Welsh historical statistics **1205**
Digest of Welsh statistics, 1992 **1204**
Diggs, E.L.
Black chronology **1085**
Dilling, C. and Claster, B.L.
Female psychology **224**
Dillon, M.
Dictionary of Chinese history **7592**
Dimitrov, T. D.
World bibliography of international documentation **2860**
Dinan, D.
Historical dictionary of the European Community **2893**
Diner, H.R.
Women and urban society **1093**
Ding Choo Ming
A Bibliography of bibliographies on Malaysia **4746**

Dingli-Attard-Inguanez, M.
The International armorial register **6236**

Dinsdale, W. A. *and* Pearce, E A.
French for insurance officials **3661**

Dion, G.
Dictionnaire canadien des relations du travail **1865**
Diosbóireachtai pairliminte/ Parliamentary debates **3038**
Diplomatic handbook **3316**
The Diplomatic Service list, 1993 **3318**

Dippold, M.F.
Une bibliographie du Cameroun **4844**
Direct-line distances **5511**
Directories **7068**
The Directories of London 1677-1977 **7089**
Directory, 1985/86 **726**
Directory for older people **1053**
Directory for the disabled **3631**
Directory of adult education documentation and information services **3823**
Directory of African universities **3903**
Directory of alternative communities in the British Isles **947**
Directory of American libraries with genealogy or local history collections **6161**
Directory of American philosophers, 1994-95 **129**
Directory of American scholars Vol.1 History **8002**
Directory of archives and manuscript repositories in New Zealand **6586**
Directory of archives and manuscript repositories in the United States **6576**
Directory of archives in Australia **6587**
The Directory of British importers **2430**
Directory of British-Indian dates **7670**
A Directory of British peerages **6272**
Directory of Christian Councils **588**
Directory of Christian groups, communities and networks **611**
Directory of Community legislation in force **2904**
Directory of demographic research centers **1338**
The Directory of directors **2398**
Directory of domiciliary and hospital patients' library services in the United Kingdom **3621**
Directory of economic institutions **1770**
Directory of educational documentation and information services **3772**
Directory of employers; associations, trade unions, joint organisations, etc **1854**
Directory of European banking and financial associations **2138**
Directory of European business **2382**

Directory of European Communities trade and professional associations **2361**
Directory of European Cummunity and related databases **2881**
Directory of European political scientists **1387**
The Directory of export buyers in the UK **2434**
Directory of federal and state business assistance **2017**
Directory of financial futures exchanges **2173**
Directory of financial information sources **2022**
Directory of firms **2526**
Directory of foreign document collections **1594**
Directory of foreign trade organizations in Eastern Europe **2425**
Directory of grant-making trusts, 1991 **3540**
Directory of health centres, 1986 **3608**
Directory of higher education institutions in the European Community **3885**
Directory of historical agencies in North America **8054**
Directory of hospitals **3620**
Directory of independent hospitals and health services, 1994 **3609**
The Directory of international sources of business information **1949**
The Directory of international terrorism **1486**
Directory of Irish archives **6486**
Directory of Irish company names, 1988 **2400**
A Directory of Islamic financial institutions **2067**
The Directory of jobs and careers abroad **1883**
Directory of law libraries in the British Isles **2828**
Directory of management consultants in the UK **2648**
Directory of manuscript collections in Southern Africa **6550**
Directory of medical and health care libraries in the United Kingdom and Republic of Ireland, 1990 **3616**
Directory of mental health libraries and information centers **279**
Directory of multinationals **2005**
Directory of national voluntary organisations in Scotland **3575**
Directory of non-medical research on disability.
Directory of non-medical research relating to handicapped people, 1987 **3633**

Directory of non-medical research relating to handicapped people, 1987 **3633**
Directory of nursing homes **3614**
Directory of officials and organisations in China, 1963-1983 **3306**
Directory of oral history collections **6726**
Directory of orthodox parishes and clergy in the British Isles **695**
Directory of post-graduate and post-experience courses, 1988-89 **3874**
Directory of pressure groups in the European Community **1629**
Directory of published proceedings. Series SSH: Social sciences/ humanities **974**
Directory of research grants, 1994 **3876**
Directory of resources for aging, gerontology, and retirement **1054**
Directory of services for elderly people in the UK **1055**
Directory of social research organisations in the United Kingdom **977**
Directory of social science information courses **982**
Directory of solicitors and barristers, 1992 **3160**
Directory of South Asian library resources in the UK and the Republic of Ireland **4675**
Directory of South-East Asian library collections in the United Kingdom and Western Europe **4739**
Directory of special education **3837**
Directory of statistics in Canada, 1985- **1266**
Directory of technical and further education, 1993 **3847**
Directory of the American Psychological Association **281**
Directory of the British Consultants Bureau **2646**
Directory of the Commission of the European Communities (September 1988) **2900**
Directory of the world's capital ships **3500**
Directory of theatre resources **3956**
Directory of town plans in Britain **5260**
Directory of world stock exchanges **2172**
Directory of youth services and child care in the UK **3644**
Disarmament terminology **2964**
Disasters at sea **5161**
Discover Britain **5564**
The Discoverers **5119**
Discovery and exploration **5120, 5122**
Discovery & Exploration in scotland **4231**

Eisler, R.
Kant-Lexikon. Nachschlagewerk zu Kants sämlichen Schriften, Briefen und handschriftlichen Nachlass **31**

Eitner, K
Nigeria: Auswahlbibliographie **4838**

Eitzen, K.H.
German-English, English-German military dictionary **3343**

Ekberg, A.
Uppslagsverket Finland **4543**

Ekberg, H.
Vem och vad? biografisk handbok 1992 **5874**

El-Hi textbooks and serials in print **3790**

El Nasri, A.R.
A Bibliography of the Sudan 1938-1958 **4802**

El Salvador **4922**

El Salvador y ses hombres **5945**

El-Sherbini, M.
Terrorism: current readings **1474**

El'Adah, S.F.
A Dictionary of diplomacy and international affairs **1557**

Elazar, D.J.
Federal systems of the world **1445**

Elder, B.
The A to Z of who's who in Australia's history **8161**

Eldridge, J. Recent British sociology **1016**

Elections since 1945 **1490**

An Electoral atlas of Europe, 1968-1981 **1495**

The Electoral politics dictionary **1512**

Elenchus of biblica **418**

Elenco de grandezas y titulos nobiliarios Españoles 1985 **6285**

The Eliade guide to world religions **369**

Eliade, M.
The Encyclopedia of religion **373**
A History of religious ideas **343**
Yoga **819**

Eliade, M. *and* Coullardo, A.P.
The Eliade guide to world religions **369**

Eliot, J.
Indonesia, Malaysia & Singapore handbook 1993 **5673**
Thailand, Indochina & Burma handbook 1993 **5674**

Elkins, D. *and* Elkins, T.H.
France **5203**

Elkins, T.H.
'Atlases and maps of Berlin,' **5289**

Elling, R.H.
Cross-national study of health systems - countries, world regions, and special problems **3584**

Ellington, H. *and* Harris, D.
Dictionary of instructional technology **3795**

Elliot, J.M. *and* Elliot, R.R.
The Arms control, disarmament and military security dictionary **2965**
The Arms control, disarmament, and military security dictionary **3340**

Elliott, J.K.
A Bibliography of Greek New Testament manuscripts **487**

Elliott, J.M. *and* Ali, S.R.
The State and local government political dictionary **3275**

Elliott, S.P.
A Reference guide to the United States Supreme Court **3164**

Ellis, A.
Philosophical books **11**

Ellis, C.
A Collector's guide to the history and uniform of Das Heer **3420**

Ellis, J.
The Russian Orthodox Church **663**

Ellis, J.T. *and* Trisco, R.
A Guide to American Catholic history **685**

Ellis, P.
People of today **5795**

Ellis, P. B.
A Dictionary of Celtic mythology **882**
A Dictionary of Irish mythology **766**

Ellis, P.B.
A Guide to early Celtic remains in Britain **4333**
History of the Irish working class **1846**

Ellis, S.
The ANC in exile **1075**

Cassell's biographical dictionary of the American Civil War **8039**

Elsevier's banking dictionary **2128**

Elsevier's dictionary of commercial terms and phrases in five languages **1957**

Elsevier's dictionary of criminal science in eight languages **3117**

Elsevier's dictionary of export financing **2432**

Elsevier's dictionary of financial terms in English, German, Spanish, French, Italian and Dutch **2042**

Elsevier's dictionary of insurance and risk prevention in English, French, Spanish, German and Portuguese **3651**

Elsevier's dictionary of office automation in four languages **2489**

Elsevier's dictionary of police and criminal law **3119, 3210**

Elsevier's dictionary of the labour market **1819**

Elsevier's fiscal and customs dictionary in five languages **2038**

Elsevier's lexicon of international and national units **3228**

Elsevier's lexicon of stock-market terms **2169**

Elton, G.R.
England 1200-1640 **6925**
Modern historians on British history 1485-1945 **6409**

Elvin, C.N.
A Hand-book of mottoes borne by the nobility, gentry, cities, public companies, etc. ... With Supplement by R. Pinches **6263**

Elwell-Sutton, L.P.
Bibliographical guide to Iran **4700**

Elwell, W.A.
Evangelical dictionary of theology **538**

Emblems **6267**

Embree, A.T.
Encyclopedia of Asian history **7550**

Emerson, W.K.
Chevrons **3423**

Emigrants to Pennsylvania, 1641-1819 **6139**

Emily Post's etiquette **3994**

Eminent Filippines **6011**

Eminent Indians who was who 1900-1980 **5907**

Emmison, F.G. *and* Gray, I.
County records **7080**

Emmison, F.G. *and* Smith, W.J.
Materials for theses in local record offices **7081**

The Empire ships **6831**

'The Empire, the Commonwealth and the Mandated Territories' **6891**

Employee relations bibliography and abstracts **1866**

Employee relations bibliography and abstracts. 1989-. v.1-. Quarterly **1867**

Employers' organizations of the world **1851**

Employment gazette **1836**

Employment relations in the United Kingdom **1870**

Enayat, H.
Modern Islamic political thought **1442**

Enciclopedia de historia de España **7407**

Enciclopedia filosofica **57**

Enciclopedia histórica de Honduras **7906**

Encina, F.A. *and* Castedo, L.
Resumen de la historia de Chile 1535-1925 **8079**

Encyclopaedia Britannica v.29-31 **6809**

Encyclopaedia Indica **4683**

Encyclopaedia Iranica **4703**

'Gaelic law in early and medieval Ireland; a bibliography' **2762**

Gagnon, P.
Essai de bibliographie Canadienne **7870**

Gailey, H.A.
Historical dictionary of The Gambia **7786**

Gaister, T.H.
The New golden bough **745**

Galang, Z.M.
Encyclopedia of the Philippines **5059**

Galasso, G.
Storia d'Italia **7391**

Galdames, L.
A History of Chile **8080**

Galea, J.
Bibliography of the Great Siege of Malta 1565-1965 **7400**

Galicia **7447**

Gallagher, T.
Dictatorial Portugal **7439**

Gallaudet encyclopedia of deaf people and deafness **3636**

Galli, R.E.
Guinea-Bissau **4828**

Gallia informations **4251**

Galliou, P. *and* Jones, M.
The Bretons **6661**

The Gallup survey of Britain **1033**

The Gambia **4822**

Gamble, C.
The Palaeolithic settlement of Europe **4203**

Gamble, D.P.
The Gambia **4822**

Gamble, D.P. *and* Sperling, L.
A General bibliography of The Gambia **4823**

Gander, T.
Encyclopaedia of the modern Royal Air Force **3483**
Encyclopedia of the modern British army **3468**

Gandilhon, R. *and* Samaran, C.M.D.
Bibliographie générale des travaux historiques et archéologiques **7347**

Garcia Duran, J.
Bibliography of the Spanish Civil War **7422**

García, I.R.
Diccionario de términos juridicos **2698**

Garcia, J.
The Gibraltar Year Book and Finance Centre handbook **4519**

García, M.A.
Diccionario histórico-enciclopédico de la República de El Salvador **7909**

Gardinier, D.E.
Gabon **4846**
Historical dictionary of Gabon **7808**

Gardner, D.E.
Genealogical atlas of Ireland **6086**

Gardner, D.E. *and* Smith, F.
Genealogical research in England and Wales **6091**

Gardner, F.L.
Bibliotheca astrologica **175**

Gardner, J.A.
The Iraq-Iran War **7576**

Gardner, J.L.
Reader's Digest atlas of the Bible **449**

Gareffa, P.M.
Newsmakers **5741**

Garland, C.E.
A Digest and index of tax cases .. **2094**

Garlick, K.B.
Garlick's Methodist registry, 1983 **721**

Garlick's Methodist registry, 1983 **721**

Garner, B.A.
A Dictionary of modern legal usage **2701**

Garner, J.F.
Civic ceremonial **3985**

Garner, P.
Financial management handbook **2034**

Garraty, J.A.
1001 things everyone should know about American history **7971**

Garrett, V.M.
Mandarin squares **6299**

Garrett, W.
Historical atlas of the United States **7991**

Gartside, L.
Modern business correspondence **2486**

Garvin, B.
Italy **4504**

Gascoigne, B.
Encyclopaedia of Britain **4454**

Gaskell, G.A.
Dictionary of all Scriptures and myths **379**

Gastmann, A.
Historical dictionary of the French and Netherlands Antilles **7942**

Gates, H.L.
Black biography, 1790-1950: a cumulative index **5987**

Gauld, A.
A History of hypnotism **270**

Gaunt, P.
The Cromwellian gazetteer **5554**

Gaur, A.
South Asian studies **4677**

Gaute, J.H.H. *and* Odell, R.
New Murderer's who's who **3099**

Gavet-Imbert, M.
Guinness book of explorers and exploration **5116**

Gay, W. *and* Pearson, M.
The Nuclear arms race **2950**

Gayre of Gayre *and* Nigg, R.
Heraldic standards and their ensigns **6227**

A Gazetteer of early burial sites **4223**

The Gazetteer of India **4686**

Gazetteer of Scotland **5590**

Gazetteer of the Falkland Islands Dependencies **5704**

Gazetteers **5524**

Gazetteers and glossaries of geographical names of the member-countries of the United Nations **5528**

Gazetteers of Canada **5681**

Geahigan, P.C. *and* Rose, R.F.
Business serials of the US government **1995**

Gebhardt, B.
Handbuch der deutschen Geschichte **7256**

Geddes, C.L.
Guide to reference books for Islamic studies **863**

Gedeon, C.G.
Who's who in the Arab World 1993-1994 **5920**

Gee, P.
Spicer and Pegler's book-keeping and accounts **2527**

Gehman, H.S.
The New Westminster dictionary of the Bible **427**

Geisst, C.R.
A Guide to financial institutions **2101**
A Guide to the financial markets **2167**

Geldsetzer, L.
Bibliography of the international congresses of philosophy/ Bibliographie der internationalen Philosophie Kongress, 1900-1978.. **131**

Genealogical and biographical research **6142**

Genealogical and local history books in print **6050**

Genealogical atlas of Ireland **6086**

A Genealogical gazetteer of England **6100**

Genealogical guide to German ancestors from East Germany and Eastern Europe **6110**

Genealogical historical guide to Latin America **6134**

A Genealogical history of the dormant, abeyant, forfeited, and extinct peerages of the British Empire **6280**

The Genealogical index of the Newberry Library **6147**

Genealogical manuscripts in British libraries **6069**

The Government of Northern Ireland, 1922-72 **3037**

Government publications. Sectional list 2. Revised May 1988: Education and science **3738**

Government publications. Sectional list 3, revised June 1988: Energy, trade and industry **2231**

Government publications. Sectional list 5, revised August 1991: Environment **3241**

Government publications. sectional list 11, revised December 1988: Department of Health and Social Security **3602**

Government Publications Sectional List 17, revised 1 January 1985: Publications of the Royal Commission on Historical Manuscripts **6467**

Government publications: Sectional list 21: Employment, health and safety. **1834**

Government Publications Sectional List 24, revised 1 January 1984: British National Archives **6468**

Government publications. Sectional list 26, (revised September 1987): Home Office **3295**

Government Publications: Sectional List 27, revised 1 April 1982: Ancient monuments and historic buildings in the care of the state **4337**

Government publications. Sectional list 29, revised January 1992. Inland Revenue **2084**

Government publications. Sectional list 43, revised February 1992 **1925**

Government publications. Sectional list 44, revised January 1991: Treasury and Civil Service **3203**

Government publications. Sectional list 56: Office of Population Censuses and Surveys **1313**

Government Publications Sectional List 60, 1990. History in print **6793**

Government publications: Sectional list 69, revised April 1987. Overseas affairs **1545**

Government publications. Sectional list 71: revised 1 June 1989. Scotland **3611**

Government Publications Sectional List 71, revised June 1989: Scotland **4458**

Government Publications Sectional list 72, revised 1 November 1987: Northern Ireland **4464**

The Government Social Survey **1131**

Government statistics **1186**

Government support for British business **1977**

Gowan, S.J.
Portugese-speaking Africa 1900-1979 **4849**

Gower handbook of quality management **2585**

Goyer, D.S. and Draaijer, G.E.
The Handbook of national population censuses [v.3]: Europe **1296**

Grabois, A.
The Illustrated encyclopedia of medieval civilization **6427**

Grace, J. and Laffin, J.
Fontana dictionary of Africa since 1960 **7740**

Graduate careers services directory, 1991-92 **1891**

Graduate studies, 1993/94 **3888**

Grady, J. and Weale, M.
British banking, 1960-85 **2143**

Graesse, J.G.T.
Orbinus Latinus **5512**

Graham, B.J. and Proudfoot, L.J.
Historical geography of Ireland **5198**

Graham, I.
Encyclopedia of advertising **2630**

Graham, J
Macmillan directory of global financial markets **2102**

Gran atlas de Carreteras España Portugal **5312**

Gran enciclopedia de España **7408**

La Gran enciclopedia de Puerto Rico **4952**

Granberry, J.A.
Bibliography of Bahaman prehistory **4296**

The Grand Duchy of Luxembourg **7307**

O Grande livro dos Portugueses **5857**

Les Grandes dates de l'Islam **7566**

Grandes hombres de nuestria patria **5995**

Grandin, A.
Bibliographie générale des sciences juridiques, politiques, économiques et sociales de 1800 à 1925/6 **909**

Gransden, A.
Historical writing in England **6412**

Grant, D.
Business histories and biographies **2372**

Grant, E.G.
Scotland **4457**

Grant, I.F. and Cheape, H.
Periods in Highland history **6974**

Grant, L.
Civil liberty **3073**

Grant, M.
A Guide to the Ancient World **6673**
The History of ancient Israel **6637**
The Visible past **4194**

Grant, M, and Hazel, J.
Who's who in classical mythology **789**

Grant, M. and Kitzinger, R.
Civilization of the Ancient Mediterranean. Greece and Rome **6672**

Grant, M.J.
The Roman emperors **6701**

Grant, P.
Literature of mysticism in Western tradition **188**

Grant, S.A. and Brown, J.H.
The Russian Empire and the Soviet Union **6511**

The Grants register, 1993-95 **3872**

Granville, W.
A Dictionary of sailors' slang **3495**

Graphis design **2637**

Graslund, B.
The Birth of prehistoric chronology **4181**

Grassl, W.
Dictionary of conservative thought **67**

Grattan-Guinness, I.
Psychical research **216**

Graulich, D. and Graulich, C.
Guide to foreign legal materials: Belgium, Luxembourg, Netherlands **2734**

Graves, E.B.
A Bibliography of English history to 1485 **6928**

Gravette, A.G.
Cuba official guide **4939**

Gray, I.H.
Mythology of all races **753**

Gray, R. A.
Serial bibliographies in the humanities and sciences **901**

Gray, R. and Argyle, C.
Chronicle of the First World War **6814**

Grayson, L.
Library and information services for local government in Great Britain **3253**
The Social and economic impact of new technology, 1978-84 **1023**

Graz, L.
The Turbulent Gulf **7638**

Great battles of the American Civil War **3438**

Great Britain
Chronological table of the Statutes, covering the legislation from 1235 to the end of 1990 **2751**
Index to local and personal Acts **2786**
Statutory Instruments. 1890- **2739**

Great Britain. Cabinet Office
British foreign policy in the Second World War **1572**
Public bodies, 1993 **3193**

Greek religion in the archaic and classical periods **779**

Green against green **7015**

Green, H.
Guide to the battlefields of Great Britain and Ireland **3435**

Green, J.
Maritime archaeology **4310**

Green, J.A.
English sheriffs to 1154 **7039**

Green, M.
The Gods of the Celts **878**

Green, M.L.
Dictionary of Celtic myth and legend **883**

Green, M.M.
A Gibraltar bibliography **4517**

Green, P.
Alexander to Actium **6668**

Green, W.C. and Reeves, W.R.
The Soviet military encyclopedia **3380**

Greenaway, D.
Companion to contemporary economic thought **1802**

Greenbert, B.
How to find out in psychiatry **311**

Greene, J.P.
Medieval monasteries **632**

Greene, J.P. and Pole, J.R.
The Blackwell encyclopedia of the American Revolution **8023**

Greener, M.
The Penguin business dictionary **2463**

Greenfield, G.M. and Maram, S.L.
Latin American labor organizations **1847**

Greenfield, K.R.
United States Army in World War 2 **6881**

Greenham, J.
Clans and families of Ireland **6191**

Greenland **5109, 5724**

Greenland past and present **5107**

The Greenlaw Index of the New England Historic Genealogical Society **6203**

Greenlaw, M.J. and McIntosh, M.E.
Educating the gifted **3827**

Greenstein, C.H.
Dictionary of logical terms and symbols **319**

Greenwald, D.
The Concise McGraw-Hill dictionary of modern economics **1736**
Encyclopedia of economics **1714**
The McGraw-Hill dictionary of modern economics **1735**

Greenwood, D.
Who's buried where in England **5606**

Greenwood, J.
Industrial archaeology and industrial history series **4397**
Industrial archaeology in Western Europe: a bibliography **4390**

Greenwood, V.D.
The Researcher's guide to American genealogy **6152**

Gregg, J.R.
Gregg shorthand dictionary **2508**

Gregg shorthand dictionary **2508**

Gregory, D.
Wales before 1066 **4373**

Gregory, R.G.
A Guide to the Kenya national archives **6548**

Gregory, R.L. and Zangwill, O.L.
The Oxford companion to the mind **245**

Gregory, R.W.
Anniversaries and holidays **3983**

Grenada **4962**

Grenville, J.A.S.
The Major international treaties, 1914-1945 **2935**

Grenville, J.A.S. and Wasserstein, B.
The Major international treaties since 1945 **2936**

Gresh, A. and Vidal, D.
An A-Z of the Middle East **7568**

Grey, I.
The Parliamentarians **1623**

Greyerz, K. von
Religion and society in early modern Europe, 1500-1800 **526**

Gribetz, J.
The Timelines of Jewish history **6654**

Grieb, K.
Research guide to Central America and the Caribbean **6556**

Griechische paläographie **6602**

Griffin, A.A.
A Brief guide to the sources for the study of Burma **6538**

Griffin, C.C.
Latin American **2308**

Griffin, C.C. and Warren, J.B.
Latin America **7948**

Griffin, D.
Encyclopaedia of modern British army regiments **3463**

Griffin, T. and McCaskill, M.
Atlas of South Australia **5453**

Griffin, W.D.
Ireland 6000 BC-1972: a chronology and fact book **7011**

Griffith, J.A.G. and Ryle, M.
Parliament: functions, practice and procedures **1619**

Griffiths, I.
'The Scramble for Africa: inherited political boundaries' **7752**

Griffiths, J.L.
An Atlas of African affairs **4792**

Grim, R.E.
Historical geography of the United States **5215**

Grimal, P.
A Concise dictionary of classical mythology **786**
The Dictionary of classical mythology **785**
Larousse world mythology **755**

Grimes, J.
A Concise dictionary of Indian philosophy **124**

Grimes, R.L.
Research in ritual studies **594**

Grimstead, P.K.
A Handbook for archival research in the USSR **6508**

Grimsted, P.K.
Archives and manuscript repositories in the USSR **6507**
'Recent publications on archives and manuscript collections in the Soviet Union' **6509**
Recent Soviet archival literature: a review and preliminary bibliography of selected reference aids **6510**

Grinstein, A.
The Index of psychoanalytic writings **302**
Sigmund Freud's writings: a comprehensive bibliography **303**

Grisoli, A.
Guide to foreign legal materials: Italian **2797**

Groenlandica. Catalogue of Groenlandica collection in the National Library of Greenland **5108**

Grollenberg, L.H.
Atlas of the Bible **446**
Penguin shorter atlas of the Bible **447**

Gropp, A.E.
A Bibliography of Latin American bibliographies **4967**
A Bibliography of Latin American bibliographies published in periodicals **4970**

Gross, C.
A Bibliography of British municipal history **3262**

Gross, E.
This day in religion **3980**

Gross, J.S.
Webster's new world illustrated encyclopedic dictionary of real estate **1931**

Der Grosse ADAC General Atlas **5291**

Der Grosse Bertelsmann Weltatlas **5477**

Der grosse Bildatlas zur Deutschen Geschichte **7263**

Hieronymussen, P.
Orders, medals and decorations of Britain and Europe in colour **6288**
Higgs, E.
Making sense of the census **1321**
Higham, C.
The Archaeology of mainland Southeast Asia **4281**
Higham, R.
A Guide to sources of US military history **3479**
A Guide to the sources of British military history **3373**
Official histories **6794**
'Higher education', 1980-85 **3843**
Higher education in developing nations **3849**
Higher education in international perspective **3841**
Higher education in the European Community **3851**
Higher education in the United Kingdom, 1992-93 **3886**
Higson, C.W.J.
Sources for the history of education **3732**
Hildebrand, K.
The Third Reich **7278**
Hildenbrand, S.
Women's collections **4049**
Hildreth, S.S.
The A to Z of Wall Street: 2500 terms for the street smart investor **2187**
Hiler, H. and Hiler, M.
Bibliography of costume **3912**
Hilfswörterbuch für Historiker, Mittelalter und Neizeit **6716**
Hilgard, E.R. and Bower, G.H.
Theories of learning **3779**
Hilgemann, W.
Atlas zur deutschen Zeitgeschichte **7276**
Hill, B.H.W.
Canada 875-1973 **7883**
Hill, B.W.
British parliamentary parties, 1742-1832, from the fall of Walpole to the first Reform Act **1655**
The Growth of British parliamentary parties, 1689-1742 **1654**
Hill, D.
An Atlas of Anglo-Saxon England **6942**
Hill, D.A.
Norwegian local history **7492**
Hill, D.M.
'Local government' **3237**
Hill, E.
Guide to records in the National Archives relating to American Indians **6581**
Hill-forts of Britain **4336**

Hill, G.
A History of Cyprus **7693**
Hill, K.T.
Festivals USA **3978**
Hill, R.J.
The Soviet Union **2270**
Hill, R.L.
A Bibliography of the Anglo-Egyptian Sudan **4801**
A Biographical dictionary of the Sudan **5925**
Hillebrandt, W.
'Bibliographical aids for studies on Namibia' **4884**
Hills, P.J.
A Dictionary of education **3719**
Hillyer, N.
The New Bible dictionary **430**
Hilton, R.
Who's who in Latin America **5950**
Himalayan triangle **7674**
Himmelstrup, J. and Birket-Smith, K.
Søren Kierkegaard **33**
Hinde, T.
The Domesday Book **7035**
Hinding, A.
Women's history sources **4051**
Hindle, B.P.
Maps for local history **7070**
Hindu mythology **799**
The Hindu world **798**
Hindustan yearbook and who's who 1988 **4685**
Hines, W.
'Bibliography on British and Irish legal history (works published after 1985)' **2750**
Hinnells, J.R.
Facts on File dictionary of religions **381**
The Penguin dictionary of religions **381**
Who's who of religions **402**
Hinrichsen, A.
Baedeker's Reisenhandbücher 1832-1944 **5506**
Hinshelwood, R.D.
A Dictionary of Kleinian thought **300**
Hintauer, S.
Canadian legal directory, 1987 **2811**
Hinton, J.
Labour and Socialism **1658**
Hints to exporters visiting.. **2209**
Hirschberger, J.
A Short history of Western philosophy **109**
Hirschfelder, A.B.
Annotated bibliography of the literature on American Indians **8006**
Hirschfolder, A. and Morin, P.
The Encyclopedia of native American religions **741**

Hispanic American information directory **5013**
Hispanic Council and Luso-Brazilian Council. Canning House Library
Author and subject catalogues of the Canning House Library **4976**
Hispanic Society of America New York
Catalogue of the Library of the Hispanic Society of America **4977**
L'Histoire au jour le jour (1944-1985) **6744**
Histoire de Belgique **7516**
Histoire de France depuis les origines jusqu' à la Révolution **7340**
Histoire de la France **7337**
Histoire de la France rurale **7338**
Histoire de la France urbaine **7339**
Histoire de la philosophie. Périod chrétienne **98**
Histoire de la population française **1139**
Histoire des relations internationales **1561**
Histoire générale du socialisme **191**
Histoire monetaire de la France, 1800-1980 **2063**
Historia completa de las Malvinas **8071**
Historia de España **7403, 7944**
Historia de España antigua y medieval **7405**
História de Moçambique **7825**
Historia general de Costa Rica **7912**
Historia general de las Islas Canarias **7415**
Historia general de los Peruanos **8087**
História geral da civilização Brasiliera **8061**
Historia moderna de Mexico. 9v. in 10 **7898**
Historia religionum **399**
Historial dictionary of Australia **8152**
Historians of India, Pakistan and Ceylon **6415**
Historians of South-East Asia **6418**
Historians of the Middle East **6414**
Historic costuming **3955**
Historic landmarks of Black America **5690**
Historic monuments of Northern Ireland **4360**
Historic Saskatchewan **5682**
Historic warships **3499**
Historic world leaders **5735**
Historical Abstracts **6382**
An Historical and cultural atlas of China **7594**
Historical and cultural dictionary of Afghanistan **7711**
Historical and cultural dictionary of Burma **7713**
Historical and cultural dictionary of India **7665**

Hsüeh, C.-T.
The Chinese Communist movement, 1937-1949 **1670**

Hubbard, L.S.
Notable Americans **5962**

Huber, K.R.
Women in Japanese society **4046**

Hubert, H.
The Greatness and decline of the Celts **879**
The Rise of the Celts **880**

Hübscher, A.
Schopenhauer-Bibliographie **50**

Hudland, M.F.
Penguin shorter atlas of the Bible **447**

Hudson, A.H.
Dictionary of commercial law **3123**

Hudson, G.L.
Monaco **4503**

Hudson, K.
World industrial archaeology **4387**

Hudson, K. and Nicholls, A.
The Cambridge guide to the historic places of Britain and Ireland **5559**

Hudson, R.
An Atlas of EEC affairs **2903**

Huellmantel, M.B.
European business services directory **2383**

Hughes, K.
Early Christian Ireland **7013**

Hughes, M.M.
The Sexual barrier **4012**

Hughes, R.
The Caribbean **4931**
Caribbean book list **4932**

Hughes, S. and Reynolds, P.
Industrial archaeology of the Swansea region **4407**

Huguenot ancestry **6115**

Hultgren, A.J.
New Testament Christology **489**

Human resources abstracts **1801**
The Human resources glossary **2576**
The Human resources management yearbook, 1993 **2572**
Human rights **3055-3056, 3060**
Human rights bibliography **3057**
Human rights directory **3067**
Human rights directory: Latin America **3068**
Human rights organizations and periodicals directory, 1993 **3065**
Human rights reports **3059**
Human rights sourcebook **3058**
Human rights terminology in international law **3071**
Human services in postrevolutionary Cuba **1144**

Humana, C.
World human rights guide **3063**

Humby, M.
A Guide to the literature of education **3701**

Hume, D.
A Bibliography of David Hume, and of Scottish philosophy **28**

Humm, M.
An Annotated critical bibliography of feminist criticism **4013**
The Dictionary of feminist theory **4001**

Humphery-Smith, C.
The Cambridge armorial **6243**

Humphery-Smith, C.R.
A Genealogist's bibliography **6098**
The Phillimore atlas and index of parish registers **6219**

Humphreys, A.L.
A Handbook of county bibliography **7049**

Humphreys, C.A.
A Popular dictionary of Buddhism **809**

Humphreys, R.
Latin American history **7949**

Humphreys, R.S.
Islamic history **7557**

A Hundred and fifty years of archaeology **4182**
A Hundred years of international relations **1560**
A Hundred years of philosophy **90**
A Hundred years of sociology **1016**
Hungarian economic reforms **2257**
The Hungarian Soviet Republic 1919 **7335**
Hungary **4498-4499**

Hungary. Központi Statisztikai Hivatal
Magyar statisztikai evkönyv. Statistical yearbook ... 1992 **1212**

Hunger in history **1105**

Hunt, E.H.
British labour history, 1815-1914 **1838**

Hunt, T.C. and Carper, J.C.
Religious colleges and universities in America **3781**

Hunter, B.
The Statesman's year-book **4425**

Hunter, J.
Concise dictionary of modern Japanese history **7626**
South Yorkshire **7212**

Hunter, N.R.
Index to business reports **1970**

Huntington Free Library and Reading Room, New York
Dictionary catalog of the American Indian collections **1090**

Hupper, W.G.
An Index to English periodical literature on the Old Testament and ancient Near Eastern studies. V.I **439**

Hurd, A.
The Merchant Navy **6799**

Hurst, M.
Key treaties for the Great Powers, 1814-1914 **2934**

Hurworth, M.S.
British Family history **6176**

Hury, C. and Christophory, J.
Luxembourg **4491**

Huson, T. and Postlethwaite, T.N.
The International encyclopedia of education **3678**

Hussain Menes
Atlas of the history of Islam **7565**

Hustwit, J. and Webley, M.
Information in social welfare **3604**

Hutchins, J.
The History and antiquities of the county of Dorset **7130**
The Hutchinson dictionary of biography **5736**
The Hutchinson dictionary of world history **6372**
The Hutchinson guide to the world **5513**

Hutchinson, L.
Standard handbook for secretaries **2494**

Hutchinson, T.P. and Ke, Y.
An Index to corrections, addenda, and comments that were published in statistical journals, 1970-1991 **1146**

Hutchinson, W.
The History and antiquities of Cumberland and some places adjacent **7222**

Hutchinson, W.K.
American economic history **2315**
History of economic analysis **1809**

Hutton, R.
The Pagan religions **740**

Huws, G. and Roberts, D.H.E.
Wales **4479**

Hvem er hvem 1984 **5875**
Hvem, Hva, hvor **4546**

Hyamson, A.M.
Dictionary of universal biography **5758**

Hyde, M.
Library and information services to business and industry **1999**

Hyde, R.
Printed maps of Victorian London 1851-1900 **7108**

Hymns and tunes - an index **599**
Hymns and tunes indexed **601**

International dictionary of psychology
Macmillan dictionary of psychology
252

International dictionary of the securities industry **2170**

International directory of archives **6456**

The International directory of business information sources and services **2479**

International directory of company histories **2371**

International directory of executive education **3838**

The International directory of government **3288**

International directory of market research organizations **2611**

International directory of marketing information sources **2592**

International directory of non-official statistical sources, 1990 **1159**

International directory of philosophy and philosophers, 1993-1994 **79**

International directory of private investigators **3084**

International directory of psychologists **268**

International directory of psychology **269**

International directory of research institutions on higher education **3858**

International directory of theatre, dance and folk festivals **3971**

International directory of voluntary work **3565**

International Economic Association
The Organisation and retrieval of economic knowledge **1797**

International economic indicators **2216**

International economic institutions **1799**

International encyclopedia of comparative law **2836**

The International encyclopedia of education **3678**

The International encyclopedia of educational technology **3680**

International encyclopedia of foundations **3542**

The International encyclopedia of higher education **3844**

International encyclopedia of population **1297**

International encyclopedia of psychiatry, psychology, psychoanalysis & neurology **240**

The International encyclopedia of sociology **996**

International encyclopedia of statistics **1148**

The International encyclopedia of teaching and teacher education **3786**

International encyclopedia of the social sciences **926**

International encyclopedia of the social sciences. v.18: Biographical supplement **953**

International financial statistics **2055**

The International foundation directory **3543**

International genealogical index **6048**

International glossary of abbreviations for theology and related subjects **347**

International glossary of social gerontology **1049**

International governmental organizations: constitutional documents **2861**

International guide to accounting journals **2523**

International guide to African studies research/Études africaines, guide international de recherches **4771**

International guide to qualifications in education **3865**

International handbook of aging **1048**

International handbook of contemporary developments in criminology **3115**

International handbook of educational systems **3735**

International handbook of industrial relations **1860**

International handbook of psychology **243**

International handbook of race and race relations **1064**

International handbook of universities **3879**

International handbook on local government reorganization **3239**

International higher education **3845**

International historical statistics **1167**

International historical statistics: Africa and Asia **1168**

International historical statistics: Europe, 1750-1988 **1169**

International history of city development **3259**

An International history of the Vietnam war **7727**

International Institute for Strategic Studies.
Strategic survey, 1992-93 **3364**

International journal of legal information **2721**

International labour conventions and recommendations, 1919-1991, with supplements 1992-1993 **1828**

International labour documentation (New series) **1820**

International Labour Office
Annotated bibliography on clandestine employment **1812**

Bibliography of published research of the World Employment Programme **1813**

Bulletin of labour statistics **1830**

International Labour Office *(contd.)*
Catalogue of publications in print, 1994-95 **1814**

ILO Thesaurus **1850**

International labour conventions and recommendations, 1919-1991, with supplements 1992-1993 **1828**

International standard classification of occupations **1878**

Register of periodicals in the ILO library **1822**

Vocational rehabilitation and the employment of the disabled **3629**

Vocational training **1898**

Yearbook of labour statistics, 1993 **1831**

International Labour Organisation
Bibliography of periodicals on the quality of life **1823**

International labour review **1815**

International labour statistics **1829**

International law dictionary **2851**

The International law dictionary **2853**

International law of the sea and marine affairs **2916**

International legal books in print, 1993-94 **2676**

An International list of articles on the history of education **3733**

International list of geographical serials 1980 **5179**

International marketing data and statistics **2600**

International marketing handbook **2601**

International medieval bibliography **6755**

International meditation bibliography, 1950-1982 **582**

International mergers and acquisitions **2019**

International migrations **1514**

International military and defense encyclopedia **3328**

The International military encyclopaedia **3362**

International Monetary Fund
Balance of payments yearbook, 1938, 1946, 1947- **2362**

A Manual on government finance statistics **2071**

The International Monetary Fund **2154**

The International Monetary Fund, 1944-1992 **2155**

International mortality statistics **1341**

International negotiations: a bibliography **1546**

International Nietzsche bibliography **42**

International organisations, 1918-1945 **2857**

International organizations in education **3816**

International peace directory **2969**

The International peace directory **2974**

Kamba, A.S.
'National archives of Zimbabwe'
6553
Kaminkow, M.J.
Genealogical manuscripts in British
libraries 6069
Genealogies in the Library of
Congress 6049
A New bibliography of British
genealogy 6057
United States local histories in the
Library of Congress 8050
Kane, E.
Doing your own research 966
Kane, J.N.
The American counties 5693
Facts about the Presidents 8003
Facts about the States 4992
Kanka, A.G.
Poland 4496
Kann, R.A.
A History of the Hapsburg Empire
7310
Kanner, B.
Women in English social history,
1800-1914 4044
The Women of England 4029
Kannik, P.
A Handbook of flags 6321
Military uniforms in colour 3404
Kant-Lexikon. Nachschlagewerk zu
Kants sämlichen Schriften, Briefen
und handschriftlichen Nachlass 31
Kantautas, A. and Kantautas, F.
A Lithuanian bibliography 4532
Kaplan, F.M.
Encyclopedia of China today 4597
Kaplan, J.
International bibliography of Jewish
history and thought 6642
Kapsner, O.L.
A Benedictine bibliography 612
Catholic religious orders 633
Karasik, T.W.
Russia & Eurasia facts & figures
annual (formerly USSR facts and
figures annual) 1222
Karkhanis, S.
Jewish heritage in America 4999
Karni, R.S.
Bibliography of Malaysia and
Singapore 4748
Directory of South-East Asian library
collections in the United Kingdom
and Western Europe 4739
Karolle, B. G.
Atlas of Micronesia 5461
Karp, R.S.
Law books for lazy people 2814
Karpinski, L.M.
The Religious life of man 357

Kartographiches Institut Bertelsmann
Der Grosse Bertelsmann Weltatlas
5477
Kaser, M.C.
'Soviet statistical abstracts.. 1221
Kaser, M.C. and Radice, E.A.
The Economic history of Eastern
Europe, 1919-1975 1788
Kassis, H.E.
A Concordance of the Qur'an 861
Kasten, S.
'Religion periodical indexes' 390
Katalog der Bibliothek.. 6792
Katalog der Bibliothek des Deutschen
Archäologisches Instituts 4158
Kataloge der Bibliothek des Instituts für
Zeitgeschichte 7271
Katcher, P.
The American Civil War source book
8030
Katô, G.
Meiji taishô shôwa Shintô shoseki
mokuroku 889
Shintô shoseki mokuroku 890
Katz, K.
Handbook of major Soviet
nationalities 4529
Kauffman, J.W. and Hallahan, D.P.
Handbook of special education 3831
Kaul, V.
India since independence 7671
Kaur, A.
Historical dictionary of Malaysia
7719
Kavass, I.I.
Soviet law in English 2800
Kavass, I.I. and Sprudzs, A.
A Guide to the United States treaties
in force 2933
Kay, E.
International businessmen's who's
who 1976
Kayyali, M.S.
Modern military dictionary 3349
The Kazakhs 7708
Kazhdan, A.P.
The Oxford dictionary of Byzantium
7688
Kazmer, D.R. and Kazmer, Y.
Russian economic history 2269
KBS bibliography of standard reference
books for Japaneses studies 4623
Kearley, T. and Fischer, W.
Charles Szladits' guide 2787
Keatinge, R.W.
Peruvian prehistory 4297
Keay, J.
The Royal Geographical Society
history of world exploration 5151
Keay, W.
Expedition guide 5140

Keegan, J.
The Times atlas of the Second World
War 6864
World armies 3366
Keegan, J. and Wheatcroft, A.
Who's who in military history 3361
Keele, H.M. and Kiger, J.C.
Foundations 3551
Keeler, M.F.
The Long Parliament, 1640-1641
3025
Keene, D.
Historical gazetteer of London before
the Great Fire 7106
Keepers of our past 8048
Keesing's United Kingdom record 6965
Keeves, J.P.
Educational research, methodology,
and measurement 3765
Kehr, H.
After Hitler: Germany 1945-1963
7272
Kehr, H. and Langmaid, J.
The Nazi era 1919-1945 7279
Keightley, D.N.
The Origins of Chinese civilization
4262
Keith-Lucas, B and Richards, P. G.
A History of local government in the
twentieth century 3247
Kellas, J.G.
The Scottish political system 1663
Kelly, D. H.
Women's education in the Third
World - 3777
Kelly, J.N.D.
Early Christian creeds 570
The Oxford dictionary of Popes 686
Kelly, M.A.
Labor and industrial relations 1862
Kelly, T.
A History of adult education 3817
Kelly's business directory, 1994 1943
Kelly's United Kingdom exports
British exports, 1994 2433
Kemp, T.J.
Vital records handbook 6051
Kempner, T.
Penguin management handbook 2539
Kemp's property industry year book,
1987 1938
Kenkyusha's English-Japanese
dictionary of trade and industry 1760
Kennedy, J.R.
Library research guide to education
3702
Library research guide to religion and
theology 359
Kennedy, L. and Ollerenshaw, P.
An Economic history of Ulster, 1820-
1940 2246

Kennedy, P.A.
Guide to the Nottinghamshire County Records Office **7170**
Kennedy, S.
'First look' **5968**
Kennedy, T.F.A.
A Descriptive atlas of the Pacific Islands **5237**
Kennett, A.M.
Archives and records of the City of Chester **7207**
Kenney, J.F.
The Sources for the early history of Ireland **652**
Kennington, D.
Gypsies and travelling people **4066**
The Kent bibliography **7115**
Kent County Council. County Archives Committee
Guide to the Kent County Archives Office **7118**
Kent, G.O.
A Catalog of files and microfilm of the German Foreign Ministry archives, 1920-1945 **1581**
Kent maps and plans **7116**
Kenya **4861**
Kenya. Survey of Kenya
National Atlas of Kenya **5389**
Kenyon, J.
A Dictionary of British history **6914**
Kepars, I.
Australia **5083**
Keppie, L.
Scotland's Roman remains **4355**
Kepple, R.J.
Reference works for theological research **533**
Kerber, J.E.
Coastal and maritime archaeology **4308**
Kern, R.W. and Dodge, M.D.
Historical dictionary of modern Spain 1700-1988 **7411**
Kern-Simirenko, C. and Wawro, W.
'Reference materials in Russian and Soviet area studies, 1987-88' **4524**
Kerr, N. and Kerr, M.
A Guide to Anglo-Saxon sites **5609**
A Guide to medieval sites in Britain **5562**
A Guide to Norman sites in Britain **5563**
Kesler, J.
Theatre costume **3952**
Kettridge, J.O.
French-English and English-French dictionary of commercial and financial terms, phrases and practice **1749**
Key abstracts, business automation, 1989- **2481**
Key British enterprises, 1993 **1983**

Key date **1129**
Key facts in Soviet history **7455**
Key note guides **1975**
Key resources on teaching, learning, curriculum and faculty development **3842**
Key to economic science **1765**
Key to the ancient parish registers of England and Wales **6218**
Key treaties for the Great Powers, 1814-1914 **2934**
Key words in education **3716**
Key words in international trade **2423**
Keyes, C.F.
Thailand **4743**
Keyguide to information sources in archaeology **4160**
Keyguide to information sources in business ethics **339**
Keyguide to information sources on the international protection of human rights **3053**
Keyser, D.J. and Sweetland, R. C.
Test critiques **316**
Keyser, E.
Bibliographie zur Städtgeschichte Deutschlands **7253**
Khan, M.A.
A Glossary of Islamic economics **937**
Kharbas, D.S.
Maharashtra and the Marathas **7659**
The Khmers **6712**
Kibbee, J.
American folklore **4108**
Kidd, C. and Williamson, D.
Debrett's Peerage and Baronetage 1990 **6276**
Kidd, S.
Dictionary of industrial security **3215**
Kidron, M. and Segal, R.
The New state of the world atlas **5480**
Kiek, J.
Everybody's historic England **5610**
Everybody's historic London **7091**
Kiell, N.
Psychoanalysis, psychology and literature **227**
Kies, C.
The Occult in the Western world **138**
Kiger, J.C.
International encyclopedia of foundations **3542**
Kightly, C.
The Customs and ceremonies of Britain **3967**
Killanin, Lord and Duignan, M.V.
Shell guide to Ireland **5598**
Killick, A.
The Economies of East Africa **2298-2299**
Kim, E. and Ziring, L.
The Asian political dictionary **1409**

Kimble, G.H.T.
Geography in the Middle Ages **5187**
Kime's international law directory for 1993-94.. **3158**
Kimmich, C.M.
German foreign policy, 1918-1945 **1579**
Kincade, W.H. and Hayner, P.B.
The Access resource guide **2975**
Kindleberger, C.P.
A Financial history of Western Europe **2059**
King, A.A.
The Rites of Eastern Christendom **661**
King, D. and Ranck, S.
Papua New Guinea atlas **5459**
King, Han-Kyo
Studies on Korea **4613**
King, H.G.R.
The Arctic **5106**
Atlantic Ocean **4429**
'Falklands War 1982' and 'Contemporary relations between Great Britain and Argentina: Sovereignty issues' **8074**
King, J.
New Zealand handbook **5709**
King, J.W.
Historical dictionary of Egypt **7760**
King, P. and Wintle, M.
The Netherlands **4556**
King, R.
The New geography of European migrations **1516**
King, V.T.
The Peoples of Borneo **8109**
The Kingdom of Armenia **7468**
The Kingdom of Swaziland **4878**
Kingdoms of Asia the Middle East and Africa **6303**
Kingdoms of Europe **6309**
Kingdoms of gold, Kingdoms of jade **7855**
Kings and Vikings **7478**
The King's England **5611**
Kingston Publishers
Atlas of the Commonwealth of the Bahamas **5423**
Kinloch, G. C.
Social stratification **1108**
Kinnear, M.
The British voter **1505**
Kinnell, S.
Bibliographies in history **6350**
Historiography **6346**
People in history **7865**
People in world history **6404**
Kinnell, S.K.
Communism in the world since 1945 **202**
Military history of the United States **3390**

Lent, J.A. *and* **Mulliner, K.**
Malaysian studies **4745**

Lentz, H. M.
Assassinations and executions **1483**

Lenz, W.
Archivalische Quellen zur deutschen Geschichten seit 1500/Manuscript sources for the history of Germany since 1500 in Great Britain **6495**

Léon-Dufour, K.
Dictionary of Biblical theology **434**

Leonard, D.
Pocket guide to the European Community **2890**

Leonard, D. *and* **Natkiel, R.**
World atlas of elections **1492**

Lerman, A.
The Jewish communities of the world **1084**

Lerner, R.M.
Encyclopedia of adolescence **1035**

Leroi-Gourhan, A.
Dictionnaire de préhistoire **4170**
La Préhistoire **4166**

Les Archives Nationales
L'état des inventaires **6499**

Leskošek, V.
Yugoslavia **4568**

Leslie, A.
The Which? guide to Scotland **5592**

Leslie, D.D.
Essays on the sources for Chinese history **7582**

Leslie, K.C. *and* **McCann, T.J.**
Local history in West Sussex **7122**

Leslie, N.B.
The Battle honours of the British and Indian armies, 1695-1914 **3397**

Lesly's public relations handbook **2654**

Lesobre, J. *and* **Sommer, H.**
Lexique: risque, assurance, réassurance: français - anglais/américain, anglais/américain - français. Lexicon: risk, insurance, reinsurance **3662**

Lesotho **4880-4881**

The Lessons of modern war **3431**

Lester, D.
Irish research **6487**
Suicide **3100**

Lester, R.G. *and* **Cropley, I.**
Information sources in finance and banking **2028**

Lesure, M.
Les Sources de l'histoire de Russie aux Archives Nationales **6515**

L'état des inventaires **6499**

Leung, E. P-w.
Historical dictionary of revolutionary China 1839-1976 **7593**

Levi, P.
Atlas of the Greek world **6684**

Levine, H.M. *and* **Owen, D.B.**
An American guide to British social science resources **972**

Levine, M.L. *and* **Rachlis, E.**
The Complete book of Bible quotations **441**

Levine, R.M.
Brazil 1822-1930 **8065**
Brazil since 1930 **8064**
Historical dictionary of Brazil **8068**
Race and ethnic relations in Latin America and the Caribbean **1077**

Levy, A.L. *and* **Jacobs, H.P.**
Personalities Caribbean **5946**

Levy, L.W.
Encyclopedia of the American Constitution **2987**

Lewin, E.
Subject catalogue of the Library of the Royal Empire Society **4472**

Lewis, A.R. *and* **Runyan, T.J.**
European naval and maritime history, 300-1500 **3506**

Lewis, B. *and* **Holt, P.M.**
Historians of the Middle East **6414**

Lewis, C.
Particular places **7041**

Lewis, J.M.
A Modern history of Somalia **7819**

Lewis, P.
Squadron histories **3486**

Lewis, R.
Termau cyfraith/Welsh terms .. **2717**

Lewis, S.
A Topographical dictionary of Ireland **5597**

Lewis, T.
Harrap's English-Brazilian Portuguese business dictionary **1755**

Lewytzkyj, B.
The Soviet Union: facts, figures, data **1219**

Lexicon des Mittelalters **6758**

A Lexicon of economics **1734**

Lexikon der Ägyptologie **4188**

Lexikon der christlichen Ikonographie **577**

Lexikon der deutschen Geschichte **7261**

Lexikon der Pädagogik **3712**

Lexikon zur Soziologie **1006**

Lexique du monde arabe moderne **4766**

Lexique: risque, assurance, réassurance: français - anglais/américain, anglais/américain - français. Lexicon: risk, insurance, reinsurance **3662**

Lexique UEC **2519**

LEXIS **2743**

Leydon, M.
Market research: a guide to British Library holdings **2608**

Li, T-ch.
Social science reference sources **911**

Li Xin *and* **Sun Sibai**
The Biographies of eminent Chinese in the Republic of China **5898**

Liberal Party
The History of the Liberal Party, 1895-1970 **1662**

Liberia **4830**

Liberia in maps **5381**

'Libraries and archives for historians' **6461**

Libraries and open learning **3825**

Libraries and special collections on Latin America and the Caribbean **4938**

Library and information services for local government in Great Britain **3253**

Library and information services for the legal profession **2826**

Library and information services to business and industry **1999**

Library Association. Industrial Group
Industrial and commercial libraries **2000**

Library Catalogue **4576**

Library of Congress Staff
Bibliographic guide to law. 1975- Annual **2665**

Library research guide to education **3702**

Library research guide to history **6352**

Library research guide to religion and theology **359**

Library research guide to sociology **986**

Library service for genealogists **6163**

Libros y bibliotecas en la España medieval: una bibliografia de fuentes impresas **7416**

Libya **4798, 7757**

Licensing **2420**

Lieberman, S.
The Contemporary Spanish economy **2260**

Lieberthal, K.G. *and* **Dickson, B.J.**
Research guide to central party and government meetings in China, 1949-1986 **3200**

Liechtenstein **4560**

Liechtenstein. Amt für Volkswirtschaft
Statistisches Jahrbuch, 1992 **1235**

Liesner, T.
One hundred years of economic statistics **2215**

Lillywhite, B.
London signs **2645**

Lim, P.
ASEAN A Bibliography **4735**

Lim Pui Huen, P.
The Malay world of Southeast Asia **4736**

Limb, P.
The ANC and black workers **1072**

Lindberg, G.
International law dictionary **2851**
Lindon, J.
Scandinavian mythology **768**
Lindop, C. *and* Fisher, D.
Discover Britain **5564**
Lindsay, T.F. *and* Harrington, M.
The Conservative Party, 1918-1979
1657
Lindsey, M.P.
Dictionary of mental handicap **3630**
Lindzey, G. *and* Aronson, E.
Handbook of social psychology **244**
Lineage book of British land forces,
1660-1978 **3370**
Lines, C.
Companion to the Industrial
Revolution **4389**
Lines of succession **6307**
Ling, T.O.
A Dictionary of Buddhism **810**
Liniger-Goumaz, M.
Historical dictionary of Equatorial
Guinea **7807**
Small is not always beautiful **7801**
The Lion concise book of Christian
thought **543**
The Lion handbook of Christian belief
514
Liosta a iarbhunscoileanna (List of post-
primary schools). 1987-88 **3812**
Lipinski,, A.
The Directory of jobs and careers
abroad **1883**
Lippy, C.H.
Religious periodicals of the United
States **391**
Twentieth-century shapers of
American popular religion **403**
Lippy, C.H. *and* Williams, P.W.
Encyclopedia of the American
religious experience **654**
**Lipschutz, M.R. *and* Rasmussen,
R.K.**
Dictionary of African historical
biography **7748**
A List of ancient monuments in Scotland
1990 **4345**
List of current journals,1991 **3352**
List of current trade union periodicals
1904
A List of English law officers, King's
Counsel and holders of patents of
procedure **2782**
A List of geographical atlases in the
Library of Congress **5235**
List of periodicals (revised 1987)
surveyed for America: history and life
and Historical abstracts **6383**
Lister, A.
'Bibliographies of the County
Histories' **7050**

Lister, J. *and* Lister, R.E.
Annotated bibliography of corporate
finance **2097**
A Literary and biographical history **679**
The Literary guide to the Bible **423**
'The Literature and sources of
education' **3695**
'The Literature and sources of public
administration' **3179**
'The Literature of human rights' **3054**
Literature of mysticism in Western
tradition **188**
The Literature of political science **1362**
The Literature of social anthropology
991
The Literature of terrorism **1477**
'The Literature of terrorism' **1480**
The Literature of theology **532**
Litherland, A.R. *and* Simpkin, B.T.
Spinks standard catalogue of British
and associated orders decorations &
medals **6289**
Lithuania: an encyclopaedic survey
4534
A Lithuanian bibliography **4532**
Litvinoff, S.
The Illustrated guide to the
supernatural **144**
Liverpool University. Library
A Catalogue of the gypsy books
collected by the late Robert Andrew
Scott Macfie **4065**
Lives and letters in American
parapsychology **164**
The Lives of the Popes in the early
Middle Ages **688**
The Lives of the saints **561**
Living religions **370**
Livingstone, M.
A Guide to the public records of
Scotland **6484**
Les Livres de la Révolution française
7369
Lloris, F.B. *and* Simón, F.M.
Atlas de historia antigua **6614**
Lloyd, C.
Atlas of maritime history **3491**
Lloyd, J.E.
A History of Carmarthenshire **7244**
Lloyd, S.
The Archaeology of Mesopotamia
4192
Lloyd, T.O.
The British Empire 1558-1983 **6888**
Lloyd's Nautical year book, 1993 **3667**
Lloyd's war losses. The First World
War **6800**
Lloyd's war losses. The Second World
War **6828**
L'Almanach de Paris **7341**
Lobban, R. *and* Forrest, J.
Historical dictionary of the Republic
of Guinea-Bissau **7788**

Lobban, R. *and* Halter, M.
Historical dictionary of The Republic
of Cape Verde **7789**
Lobbying **1632**
Lobbying - an insider's guide to the
Parliamentary process **1630**
Lobel, M.D.
The British atlas of historic towns
7071
Lobies, J.P.
Index bio-bibliographicus notorum
hominum **5762**
'Local archives of Great Britain' **7083**
Local family history in England 1538-
1914 **6095**
'Local government' **3237**
Local government handbook, England
and Wales **3250**
Local government in England and Wales
3249
Local heroines **5586**
The Local historian's encyclopaedia
7060
Local history **7042, 7055, 7064**
Local history and the library **7087**
'Local history bookshop' **7054**
Local history in West Sussex **7122**
Local history of education in England
and Wales **3750**
Local history research and writing **7063**
Local maps of Derbyshire to 1770 **7165**
Local maps of Nottinghamshire to 1800
7169
Local studies librarianship **7088**
'Location and analysis of the historical
publications produced by agencies of
the United States Government during
the era of the American Revolution
Bicentennial 1974-1976' **8021**
Lock, C.B.M.
Geography and cartography **5168**
Lock, D.
Gower handbook of quality
management **2585**
Handbook of management **2546**
Locke, M.
College administration **3852**
Locke, T.
The Holiday Which? guide to the
Lake District **5608**
Lockyer, H.
All the men of the Bible **456**
All the women of the Bible **457**
Lodge, K.
Directory of services for elderly
people in the UK **1055**
Loeb, K.
Women's studies **4015**
Lofthouse, A.
Who's who of Australian women
6031
LOGA: local government annotations
service **3242**

McNeil, B.
Bio-Base 1990 Master Cumulation
5983
McNeil, B. *and* Unterberger, A.
Business master biography index
2417
McNeil, B. *and* Unterburger, A.L.
Abridged biography and genealogy
master index **5982**
McNeil, R.A.
Latin American studies **4979**
McNeill, F.M.
The Silver bough **3973**
McNeill, P. *and* Nicholson, R.
An Historical atlas of Scotland **6986**
McNulty, N.G.
International directory of executive
education **3838**
McPherson, J.M.
Battle chronicles of the Civil War
8029
The Macquarie book of events **8159**
The Macquarie illustrated world atlas
5481
Macquarie Islands **5082**
Macquarrie, J.
Twentieth-century religious thoughts
508
Macquarrie, J. *and* Childers, J.F.
A New dictionary of Christian ethics
572
Macray, W.D.
A Manual of British historians to
AD1600 **6929**
McShane, P.
United Kingdom statistical sources
1191
MacSween, A. *and* Sharp, M.
Prehistoric Scotland **4347**
Madagascar **4898**
Maddox, G.L.
The Encyclopedia of aging **1045**
Madura and surrounding islands **5050**
Mafia **3121**
Magaš, B.
The Destruction of Yugoslavia **7539**
Magill, F.N.
Great lives from history series **5734**
Magill, F.N. *and* McGreal, I.P.
World philosophy **77**
Magistrates of the Roman Republic
6700
Magna bibliotheca anglo-judaica **831**
Magnusson, M. *and* Goring, R.
Chambers biographical dictionary
5729
Magocsi, P.R.
Carpatho-Rusyn studies **4445**
Galicia **7447**
Ucrainica at the University of Toronto
Library **4535**
Magocsi, P.R. *and* Matthews, G.J.
Ukraine: a historical atlas **7475**

Magraw, R.
A History of the French working-class
1140
Maguire, M.
Bibliography of published work on
Irish foreign relations, 1921-78
1577
Magyar statisztikai evkönyv. Statistical
yearbook ... 1992 **1212**
Magyarország nemzeti atlasza/National
atlas of Hungary **5298**
Maharashtra and the Marathas **7659**
Mahoney, M.H.
Women in espionage **1613**
Mai, L.H.
Men and ideas in economics **1782**
Main economic indicators, 1965-.
Monthly **2217**
Mair, D. *and* Miller, A.
A Modern guide to economic thought
1803
Maital, S.
Applied behavioural economics **217**
Maitron, J.
Dictionnaire biographique du
mouvement ouvrier français de
1789-1939 **1918**
Majama'al-lughat **938**
Major companies of Europe, 1993/94
2388
Major companies of the Arab world,
1993/94 **2409**
Major companies of the Far East and
Australasia, 1993-94 **2407**
Major companies of the USA, 1989/90
2415
Major financial institutions of Europe,
1994 **2106**
The Major international treaties, 1914-
1945 **2935**
The Major international treaties since
1945 **2936**
Major legal systems of the world today
2837
Major stock markets of Europe **2178**
Majumdar, R.C.
The History and culture of the Indian
people **7652**
Makdisi, J.
'Islamic law bibliography' **2807**
Makepeace, C.E.
Local history **7055**
Maker, R.N.
Egypt **4799**
Makers of modern Africa **7749**
The Makers of modern geography **5185**
The Making of geography **5186**
The Making of modern Lebanon **7697**
The Making of the Georgian nation
7477
The Making of the modern Gulf states
7641
Making sense of the census **1321**

Makower, J.
The American history sourcebook
7962
The Map catalog **5431**
Malawi **4896**
The Malay world of Southeast Asia
4736
Malaysia **4747**
Malaysia 1986 official year book **4749**
Malaysia. Department of Statistics
Yearbook of statistics **1257**
Malaysian studies **4745**
Mali **1261, 4813, 4815**
Malina, P. *and* Spann, G.
Bibliographie zur Österreichischen
Zeitgeschichte 1918-1980 **7320**
Mallan, C.
Guide to the Yucatan peninsula **5683**
Mallory, J.P. *and* McNeill, T.E.
The Archaeology of Ulster **4240**
Malta **4510**
Malta: an island republic **7398**
Malta. Central Office of Statistics
Annual abstract of statistics, 1990
1216
Malta handbook **4511**
Malta year book 1989 **4512**
Maltby, A.
The Government of Northern Ireland,
1922-72 **3037**
Maltby, A. *and* Maltby, J.
Ireland in the nineteenth-century
3039
Mamalakis, M.J.
Historical statistics of Chile **1281**
Man, myth and magic **141**
Management and accounting research
2529
Management and marketing abstracts
2560
Management bibliographies and reviews
2561
Management contents **2562**
Management contents, 1975- **1708**
Management dictionary **2556**
Management for the future: a
bibliography **2535**
Management guide to office automation
2491
Management information systems **2569**
Management media directory **2568**
A Manager's guide to patents, trade
marks & copyright **3138**
Manceron, C. *and* Manceron, A.
La Révolution Française **7382**
Manchester, A.H.
Sources of English legal history **2781**
Mancuso, J.
Mancuso's small business resource
guide **2007**
Mancuso's small business resource
guide **2007**
Mandarin squares **6299**

Mander-Jones, P.
 Manuscripts in the British Isles
  relating to Australia, New Zealand
  and the Pacific **6459**
Manley, J.
 Atlas of prehistoric Britain **4225**
Manley, R.H.
 Guyana emergent **8099**
Mann, H.K.
 The Lives of the Popes in the early
  Middle Ages **688**
Mann, J.
 The Atlas of D-Day and the
  Normandy landings **6860**
Mann, M.
 The International encyclopedia of
  sociology **996**
 Macmillan student encyclopedia of
  sociology **997**
Manning, O. *and* Bray, W.
 The History and antiquities of the
  county of Surrey **7111**
Manning, P.
 Slavery and African life **1535**
Manning, T.D. *and* Walker, C.F.
 British warship names **3515**
Manorial records **7044**
Manpower Services Commission.
 Training Services
 Glossary of training terms **1899**
Man's conquest of the Pacific **4185**
Manschreck, C.L.
 History of Christianity in the world
  524
Manser, M.
 Chambers book of business quotations
  1974
Mansergh, N.
 The Commonwealth experience
  1525, 6890
Mansfield, A.D. *and* Mansfield, V.
 The History of underclothes **3932**
Manson, T.W.
 A Companion to the Bible **461**
Mantran, R.
 Les Grandes dates de l'Islam **7566**
Manual de historia de España **7409**
A Manual of British historians to
 AD1600 **6929**
Manual of business library practice
 2476
Manual of German law **2788**
Manual of law French **2709**
Manual of law librarianship **2691**
Manual of procedure in the public
 business **3000**
Manual of the terminology of public
 international law (peace) and
 international organization: En/Fr/Sp/
 Russ **2852**
A Manual on government finance
 statistics **2071**

A Manual on medical literature for law
 librarians **2839**
Manuale bilingue di corrispondinza e
 comunicazione commerciale. Italiane-
 Inglese **2504**
Manuel d'archéologie égyptienne **4189**
Manuel d'histoire, de généalogie et de
 chronologie de tous les états du globe
  6045
Manuel, E.A.
 Dictionary of Philippine biography
  6009
The Manuscript catalogue of the library
 .. **4476**
Manuscript sources for the history of
 Irish civilisation **6488**
Manuscripts in the British Isles relating
 to Australia, New Zealand and the
 Pacific **6459**
Manuscripts in the Scott Polar Research
 Institute Cambridge, England **8182**
Manuscripts relating to Commonwealth
 Caribbean countries **6558**
The Manx family tree **6106**
Manx Museum And National Trust
 The Ancient and historic monuments
  of the Isle of Man **4369**
'Map acquisitions: the major sources'
  5222
The Map catalog **5431**
Map catalogue **5279**
Map collections in Australia **5226**
Map librarianship **5223-5224**
Map of the New Europe wallchart **5248**
Map of Wales **4376**
'The Mapping of Africa: a guide to
 sources' **7746**
Mapping of Monmouthshire **7152**
Mapping the American Revolutionary
 War **8024**
'Maps and atlases of the Middle East'
  5352
Maps and charts published in America
 before 1800 **7995**
Maps and plans for the local historian
 and collector **7074**
Maps and plans in the Public Record
 Office 3. Africa **5370**
Maps and plans in the Public Record
 Office. America and West Indies
  7862
'Maps, atlases, & gazetteers for
 genealogical research' **6157**
Maps, atlases and guides. Catalogue
 1994 **5271**
Maps for local history **7070**
Maps for the local historian **7077**
Maps in the County Record Office,
 Huntingdon **7181**
Maps of Africa **5371**
The Maps of Canada **5412**
The Map's Road atlas of India **5355**

Marcan, P.
 Greater London local history
  directory and bibliography **7097**
 London's local history **7098**
Marcell, D.W.
 American studies **4995**
The March to victory **6823**
Marcus, G.
 The Modern history of Ethiopia and
  the Horn of Africa **7767**
Marcus, G.J.
 A Naval history of England **3501**
Mardall, B.
 How to find out in politics and
  government **1360**
Marder, J.V.
 British education thesaurus **3766**
Marenbon, J.
 Early medieval philosophy (480-1150)
  89
 Later medieval philosophy (1150-
  1350) **88**
Margolis, S.
 Adventuring in the Pacific **5705**
Marie J.-B.
 Glossaire des droits de l'homme **3066**
Marine archaeology of Indian Ocean
 countries **4312**
Marine badges and insignia of the world
 3398
Marine Conservation Society
 The Heinz good beach guide 1993
  5565
Maring, E.G. *and* Maring, J.M.
 Historical and cultural dictionary of
  The Philippines **8112**
Maring, J.M. *and* Maring, E.G.
 Historical and cultural dictionary of
  Burma **7713**
Maritime affairs **2912**
Maritime archaeology **4306, 4310**
Maritime archaeology in Australia **4314**
Maritime boundaries and ocean
 resources **2909**
The Maritime political boundaries of the
 world **2910**
Maritime Southeast Asian studies in the
 United Kingdom **4730**
Marken, J.W.
 Native American Bibliography Series
  5002
Market economy and planned economy
 934
Market House Books
 A Concise dictionary of business
  1962
Market research: a guide to British
 Library holdings **2608**
Market research abstracts **2612**
Market research: international directory
 of published market research **2613**
Marketing and sales management **2591**
The Marketing dictionary **2594**

Matulic, R.
Bibliography of sources on
Yugoslavia **7542**
Maunder, W.F. (to 1987) *and*
Fleming, M.C. (from 1985)
Reviews of United Kingdom statistical
sources **1190**
Mauretania **4812**
Mauricio, R.
Pacific Basin and Oceania **4430**
Mauritius **4900-4901**
Mauritius guide **5679**
Maxfield, V.A.
The Saxon shore **6943**
Maxted, I.
British national directories 1781-1819
7066
Maxwell-Hyslop, A.R.
A Concise dictionary of classical
mythology **786**
May, H.G.
Oxford Bible atlas **448**
Mayer, A.
Annals of European civilization 1501-
1900 **6778**
Mayer, F.
Diercke Weltatlas **5472**
Mayer, H.E.
Bibliographie zur Geschichte der
Kreuzzüge **6771**
Mayer, S.L. *and* **Koenig, W.J.**
The Two World Wars **6795**
Mayerchak, P.M.
Scholar's guide to Washington DC for
Southeast Asian studies: Brunei.
Burma. Cambodia. Indonesia. Laos.
Malaysia. Philippines. Singapore.
Thailand. Vietnam **4731**
Mayhew, S. *and* **Penny, A.**
The Concise Oxford dictionary of
geography **5172**
Maynard, H.B.
Industrial engineering handbook **2580**
Mayne, R.
Europe: a history of its peoples **6746**
Western Europe **4441**
Mayo, J.
A History of ecclesiastical dress **596**
Mays, J.L.
Harper's Bible commentary **478**
Mazal, O.
Handbuch der Byzantinistik **7687**
Mazúr, E.
Atlas SSR **5297**
Mead, F.S.
Encyclopaedia of religious quotations
393
Mead, W.R.
An Historical geography of
Scandinavia **5213**
Meagher, P.K.
Encyclopedic dictionary of religion
669

Meaney, A.
A Gazetteer of early burial sites **4223**
Meckler's bibliographies of the
Presidents of the United States 1789-
1989 **7964**
The Mediaeval hospitals of England
3622
Mediavilla, V.H. *and* **Nayle, R.A.**
Archivo biográfico de España,
Portugal e Iberoamérica **5854**
Indice biográfico de España, Portugal e
Iberoamérica **5856**
Medical and health information
directory **3615**
Medical, Health and Welfare
Libraries Group of the Library
Association
Directory of medical and health care
libraries in the United Kingdom and
Republic of Ireland, 1990 **3616**
Medical legal dictionary **2842**
Medical risks **1340**
Medieval and Reformation Germany (to
1648) **7266**
Medieval Archaeology **4212**
Medieval cartularies of Great Britain
6927
The Medieval English economy, 1150-
1500 **2241**
Medieval Greece **7531**
Medieval Ireland *c.*1170-1495 **7012**
Medieval Latin palaeography **6599**
Medieval monasteries **632**
Medieval monasticism **631**
Medieval narrative sources **6752**
Medieval religious houses **637**
Medieval religious houses: Ireland **636**
Medieval religious houses: Scotland
635
Medieval Scandinavia **7483**
Medieval studies **6754**
Medieval Wales **7237**
Medium companies of Europe, 1993-94
2389
Mee, A.
The King's England **5611**
The MEED/TAIC Middle East financial
directory, 1986 **2066**
Meerhaeghe, M.S.G., van
International economic institutions
1799
Megalithic mysteries **4326**
Megaw, J.V.S. *and* **Simpson, D.D.A.**
Introduction to British prehistory
4213
Meghdessian, S.R.
The Status of the Arab woman **4057**
Megrah, M. *and* **Ryder, F.R.**
Paget's law of banking **2142**
Mehra, P.
A Dictionary of Modern Indian
history 1707-1947 **7666**

Meier, H.K. *and* **Meier, R.A.**
Switzerland **4559**
Meier, M.S.
Bibliography of Mexican American
history **7965**
Mexican American biographies **5960**
Meier, M.S. *and* **Rivera, F.**
Dictionary of Mexican American
history **7981**
Meier, R.
Liechtenstein **4560**
Meier-Welcker, H.
Handbuch zur deutschen
Militärgeschichte, 1648-1939 **3375**
Meiji taishô shôwa Shintô shoseki
mokuroku **889**
Meinhardt, P.
Company law in Europe **3129**
Meinhardt, P. *and* **Davis, N.**
Company law in Great Britain **3132**
Meinig, D.W.
The Shaping of America **7956**
Melanesia - New Caledonia
Bibliographie méthodique, analytique
et critique de la Nouvelle -
Calédonie **5075**
Melanesia - Vanuatu
Bibliographie méthodique, analytique
et critique des Nouvelles-Hébrides
5078
Mellersh, H.E.L.
Chronology of the Ancient World
6620
Melon de Diaz, E.M.
Puerto-Rico: figures del presente y del
pasado y apuntes historicos **5948**
Melton, J.G.
Biographical dictionary of American
cults and sect leaders **659**
Encyclopedia of American religions
371-372
Encyclopedic handbook of cults in
America **742**
Melton, J.G. *and* **Geisendorfer, J.V.**
Religious bodies in the United States
656
Melton, J.G. *and* **Köszegi, M.A.**
Religious information sources **366**
Meltzer, D.J.
American archaeology past and future
4293
Melvin, P.M.
American community organizations
1092
Member of Parliament **3001**
Members of Parliament, 1734-1832
3027
Men and ideas in economics **1782**
Men of the Battle of Britain **6873**
Mendelsohn, H.N.
A Guide to information sources for
social work and the human services
3560

The Middle East review: economic and
business report, 1989 **2285**

A Middle East studies handbook 570-
1974 **4647**

Middlebrook, M. and Everitt, C.
The Bomber Command war diaries
6830

Middleton, D.
'Guide to the publications of the Royal
Geographical Society 1830-1892'
5118

Middleton, H. and Heater, D.
Atlas of modern world history **6394**

Mieczkowski, B.
'Approaches to the Japanese
economic "miracle"' **1794**

Miesenbock, K.J.
'Small businesses and exporting: a
literature review' **2010**

Miethe, T.L.
Augustinian bibliography, 1970-1980
20

Miethe, T.L. and Bourke, V.J.
Thomastic bibliography, 1940-1978
52

Mihailov, D.
Bulgaria **5654**

Mihailov, D. and Smolenov, P.
Guide to Sofia **5655**

Miles, C.W.N.
Walmsley's rural estate management
1933

Miles, S.
50 Famous New Zealanders **6014**

Miletich, J.J.
Retirement **1044**

Milewski, W.
Guide to the archives of the Polish
Institute and Sikorski Museum
6516

**Militärgeschichtlichen Forschungsant
durch Friedrich Forstmeier ... [et
al]**
Handbuch zur deutschen
Militärgeschichte, 1648-1939 **3375**

**Militärgeschictliches Forschungsamt,
Freiburg im Breisgau**
Germany and the Second World War
6878

A Military atlas of the First World War
6811

The Military balance, 1993-94 **3363**

Military Eitzen.
German-English, English-German
military dictionary **3343**

Military history of the United States
3390

The Military in imperial history **3377**

Military intelligence, 1870-1991 **3439**

The Military-naval encyclopedia of
Russia and the Soviet Union **3382**

Military uniforms in colour **3404**

Milkias, P.
Ethiopia **4804**

Millar, T.B.
Recent Australian historiography
8139

Millard, P.
Trade associations and professional
bodies **2356**

Miller, A.J.
Confrontation, conflict and dissent
1028

Miller, C.
Lobbying **1632**
Who's really who **5793**

Miller, D.
The Blackwell encyclopaedia of
political thought **1431**
The World's navies **3494**

Miller, E.W.
'State atlases' **5432**

Miller, H. and Newman, A.
Early modern British history 1485-
1760 **6905**

Miller, I.M.
Jobfile 89 **1892**

Miller, J.
Dictionary of financial regulations,
1988/89 **2058**

Miller, J.C.
Slavery **1532**

Miller, K.E.
Denmark **4552**
Greenland **5109**

Miller, M.S. and Miller, J.L.
Harper's encyclopedia of Bible life
421

Miller, O.K.
Genealogical research for Czech and
Slovak Americans **6112**

Miller, P.M. and Wilson, M.J.
A Dictionary of social science
methods **967**

Miller, R.
'The Literature of terrorism' **1480**

Miller, R.M. and Smith, J.D.
Dictionary of Afro-American slavery
1537

Miller, T.B.
Current international treaties **2920**

Miller, W.C.
Minorities in America **1459**

Miller, W.C. and Vowell, F.N.
A Comprehensive bibliography for the
study of American minorities **1081**

Mills, C.M.
A Bibliography of the Northern
Territory **5084**

Mills, G.
Modern office management **2487**

Milner-Gulland, R. and Dejevsky, N.
Atlas of Russia and the Soviet Union
7467

Milton, R.
The English ceremonial book **3986**

Minahasa and Bolaangmongondow
5051

Minahaw, A.
Encyclopedia of social work **3578**

Minchinton, W.
Guide to industrial archaeology sites
in Britain **4393**

Mind your own local business **1952**

Ministers of the Crown **3294**

Minnick, W.L.
Spies and provocateurs **1610**

Minorities in America **1459**

Minorities Rights Group
World directory of minorities **1456**

Minority organizations **1462**

Mir, M.
Dictionary of Qur'ānic terms and
concepts **871**

Miskin, C.
Directory of law libraries in the
British Isles **2828**
Library and information services for
the legal profession **2826**

MIT dictionary of modern economics
The Macmillan dictionary of modern
economics **1717**

Mitchell, A.
The New Penguin guide to personal
finance **1124**

Mitchell, A. and Ó Snodaigh, P.
Irish political documents, 1869-1916
1401
Irish political documents, 1916-1949
1400

Mitchell, B.
A New genealogical atlas of Ireland
6087

The Mitchell Beazley world atlas of
exploration **5123**

Mitchell, B.R.
British historical statistics **1196**
International historical statistics **1167**
International historical statistics:
Africa and Asia **1168**
International historical statistics:
Europe, 1750-1988 **1169**

Mitchell, G.D.
A Hundred years of sociology **1016**
A New dictionary of sociology **1003**

Mitchell, J.V.
Tests in print III **318**

Mitchell, R.C. and Turner, H.W.
A Comprehensive bibliography of
modern African religious
movements **893**

Mitchell, S.
Victorian Britain **6964**

Mitchell, W.H. and Sawyer, L.A.
The Empire ships **6831**

Mitros, J.F.
Religions **360**

Mitsubishi Corporation
Japanese business language **1968**
Tatemae and honne **1969**
Mitzel, H.E.
Encyclopedia of educational research **3775**
Modern Algeria **7772**
Modern Austria **7309**
Modern British politics **1650**
Modern British society **1125**
Modern business administration **2540**
Modern business correspondence **2486**
Modern Catholic dictionary **675**
Modern China **7598**
Modern China 1840-1972 **7591**
Modern Chinese society **4593**
A Modern companion to the European Community **2889**
A Modern dictionary of sociology **1005**
The Modern encyclopaedia of Russian and Soviet history **7462**
The Modern encyclopedia of religions in Russia and the Soviet Union **404**
Modern English biography **5819**
Modern European imperialism **1524**
Modern French philosophy **117**
Modern geographers **5184**
Modern geography: an encyclopedic survey **5170**
Modern German philosophy **114**
Modern Greece **7530**
A Modern guide to economic thought **1803**
Modern historians on British history 1485-1945 **6409**
The Modern history of Ethiopia and the Horn of Africa **7767**
The Modern history of Iraq **7695**
A Modern history of Kenya 1895-1980 **7816**
The Modern history of Mongolia **7608**
A Modern history of Somalia **7819**
Modern India **7655**
'Modern India' **7658**
Modern Ireland **4461**
Modern Islamic political thought **1442**
Modern Italian history **7393**
Modern Latin America **7946**
Modern legal systems cyclopedia **3150**
Modern military dictionary **3349**
Modern Nepal **7676**
Modern office management **2487**
Modern political thought **1435**
Modern proverbs and proverbial sayings **4145**
Modern revolutions and revolutionists **1467**
'Modern sources for genealogical research in the United States' **6135**
Modern Syria **4712**
The Modern theologians **546**
The Modern Uzbeks **7709**
Modernity and tradition **4654**

Modes and manners from the Middle Ages to the end of the eighteenth century **3927**
Modes and manners of the nineteenth century **3928**
Moffat, D.
Economics dictionary **1739**
Moffat, R.M.
'Maps, atlases, & gazetteers for genealogical research' **6157**
Mohen, J-P.
The World of megaliths **4322**
Mohr, B.
Higher education in the European Community **3851**
Moir, M.
A General guide to the India Office Records **6529**
Moldenke, H.N. and Moldenke, A.L.
Plants of the Bible **459**
Molhuysen, P.C.
Nieuw Nederlandsch biografisch woordenboek **5885**
Molinier, A.
Les Sources de l'histoire de France depuis les origines jusqu'en 1815 **7348**
Moll, J.
Uniforms of the Royal Navy during the Napoleonic Wars **3413**
Moll, V.P.
Virgin Islands **4956**
Moller-Christensen, V. and Jorgensen, K.E.J.
Encyclopedia of Bible creatures **458**
Mollo, A. and Smith, D.
World army uniforms since 1939 **3405**
Molyneux, P.
Directory of European banking and financial associations **2138**
Momeni, J.A.
Demography of racial and ethnic minorities in the United States **1460**
Housing and racial/ethnic minority status in the United States **1461**
Momigliano, A.
The Classical foundations of modern historiography **6405**
Monaco **4503**
Monaghan, P.
The Book of goddesses and heroines **758**
Monahan, P.
Guide to London docklands **5618**
The Monarchs of Scotland **6977**
Monarchs, rulers, dynasties and kingdoms of the world **3281**
The Monastic order in England **639**
Monasticon Anglicanum **640**
A Monetary history of the United Kingdom, 1870-1982 **2122**
Money **2158**

Money and banking in the U.K.: a history **2061**
Money, banking and macroeconomics: a guide to information sources **2029**
The Money book **2165**
The Money encyclopedia **2033**
Mongeau, S.
Directory of nursing homes **3614**
Monglond, A.
La France révolutionnaire et impériale **7370**
Mongolia **4611**
Mongolia today **4610**
Mongolian-English-Russian dictionary of legal terms and concepts **2694**
Mongolian Peoples Republic national atlas **5345**
The Mongols **7548**
Moniteur des dates **5743**
Monro, I.S. and Cook, D.E.
Costume index **3911**
Monroe, P.
A Cyclopedia of education **3711**
Monroe, W.S.
Bibliography of education **3703**
Montague-Smith, P.
Debrett's correct form **3998**
Montalto de Jesus, C.A.
Macau histórico **7604**
Monte-Domecq, R.
Quien es quien en el Paraguay **6002**
Montgomery, H. and Cambray, P.G.
A Dictionary of political phrases and allusions **1381**
Montgomery-Massingberd, H.
Burke's introduction to Irish ancestry **6196**
Burke's Presidential families of the United States of America **6201**
Montgomery-Massingberd, H.J.
Burke's family index **6274**
Burke's guide to the Royal Family **6310**
Burke's Irish family records **6190**
Monthly bibliography **921-922**
Monthly digest of statistics **1194**
Monthly index to the *Financial times*. **1710**
Montserrat **4957**
Monumenta Britannica **4328**
Monuments of Syria **4382**
Moody, D.
Scottish family history **6188**
Scottish local history **6982**
Scottish towns **6975**
Moody, M.
Property information source book, 1989 **1939**
Moody, T.W.
A Chronology of Irish history to 1976 **7008**
A New history of Ireland **6995**

NATO: a bibliography and resource guide **2945**

NATO glossary of terms and definitions (English and French) **3346**

Natoli, J. and Rusch, F.L.
Psychocriticism **229**

Natural and supernatural **151**

The Natural history and antiquities of the County of Surrey **7110**

The Natural history of Stafford-Shire **7157**

The Nature of women **4018**

Nauman, A.K.
A Handbook of Latin American and Caribbean national archives/Guia de los archivos nacionales de America Latino y el Caribe **6567**

Naumann, St. E.
Dictionary of Asian philosophies **118**

Navabpour, R.
Iran **4702**

Naval and maritime history **3505**

A Naval history of England **3501**

Naval Operations **6801**

Naval records for genealogists **6065**

Naval terms dictionary **3498**

Naval who's who, 1917 **3521**

Navarra **7401**

The Navy list **3511**

The Nazi era 1919-1945 **7279**

'Nazi Germany' **7280**

Nazism, resistance & holocaust in World War II **7297**

L'Encyclopédie de la Polynésie **5099**

Nebenzahl, K.
Atlas of Columbus and the great discoveries **5121**

Neely, M.E.
The Abraham Lincoln encyclopedia **8034**

Negev, A.
Archaeological encyclopedia of the Holy Land **4280**

Negley, G.R.
Utopian literature **197**

The Negro almanac **1087**

Neil, W.
Concise dictionary of religious quotations **394**

Neill, K.
How to trace family history in Northern Ireland **6197**

Neill, S.
Concise dictionary of the Christian world missions **607**

A History of Christianity in India **529**

Neilson, J.
Reports of the European Communities, 1952-1977: an index to authors and chairmen **2897**

Neilson, J., comp.
Reports of the European Communities, 1952 -1977 **2884**

Nelson, G.E. and Nelson, M.B.
Mexico A-Z **7902**

Nelson, T. and Gross, A.
Good books for the curious traveler **5115**

Nemeth, G.
The Complete guide to Hungary **5632**

Nemmer, E.E.
Dictionary of economics and business **1737**

Neolithic Britain **4331**

Neolithic Europe **4206**

Nepal **4689**

Nesbit, R.C.
An Illustrated history of the R.A.F **3482**

Nesbitt, M.
New Zealand **5067**

The Netherlands **4556**

The Netherlands Antilles and Aruba **4965**

Netherlands. Centraal Bureau voor de Statistiek
Statistical yearbook of the Netherlands, 1881- **1232**

The Netherlands in 50 maps **5330**

Nettleship, H. and Sandys, J.E.
A Dictionary of Classical antiquites **4325**

Netton, I.R.
A Popular dictionary of Islam **869**

Neu, J.
The Cambridge companion to Freud **24**

Neubecker, O.
Heraldry: sources, symbols and meaning **6228**

Neuberg, A.
The State of Israel **4718**

Neue deutsche biographie **5825**

Neue Österreichische biographie ab 1815. Grosse Österreicher **5835**

Neue politische Literatur **1377**

Neufeld, M.E. and Leab, D.J.
American working class history **1827**

Neuhaus, K. and Haltern, M.
Euro-business: German **2467**

Neuwirth, P.D.
Cashin's handbook for auditors **2531**

Nevett, T.R.
Advertising in Britain: a history **2640**

Nevins, A.
Civil War books **8032**

New African yearbook 1993-1994 **4790**

New American world **7863**

The New Arthurian encyclopedia **4121**

The New astrology **174**

The New atlas of African history **7744**

The New atlas of the Bible **451**

The New Bible dictionary **430**

A New bibliography of British genealogy **6057**

The New book of Christian quotations **521**

New book of world rankings **1157**

The New Cambridge history of India **7654**

The New Cambridge modern history **6713**

The New Cambridge modern history. v.14. The Atlas **6720**

A New Catholic commentary on Holy Scripture **474**

New Catholic encyclopedia **670**

New China's population **1328**

The New cosmopolitan world atlas **5486**

The New criminals **3079**

New day/New deal **8044**

A New dictionary of Christian ethics **572**

A New dictionary of Christian theology **541**

A New dictionary of heraldry **6234**

A New dictionary of liturgy and worship **595**

A New dictionary of political analysis **1368**

A New dictionary of sociology **1003**

The New dictionary of statistics **1151**

The New dictionary of theology **539**

New earnings survey **1876**

The New encyclopedia of archaeological excavations in the Holy Land **4279**

New England Historic Genealogical Society
The Greenlaw Index of the New England Historic Genealogical Society **6203**

The New Europe **5249**

The New extinct peerage 1184-1971 **6281**

A New genealogical atlas of Ireland **6087**

New geographical literature and maps **5169**

The New geography of European migrations **1516**

New Gill History of Ireland **6994**

The New golden bough **745**

The New guide to the diplomatic archives of Western Europe **1566**

New Guinea
A New Guinea bibliography **5049**

A New Guinea bibliography **5049**

A New history of Cyprus **7694**

A New history of Gloucestershire **7147**

A New history of India **7657**

A New history of Ireland **6995**

A New history of Korea **7610**

The New history of Scotland **6976**

A New history of Sierra Leone **7784**

A New history of the Royal Mint **2161**

New Iberian world **7945**

The New immigration **1520**

The New international atlas **5487**
The New international dictionary of Biblical archaeology **425**
The New international dictionary of New Testament theology **494**
The New international dictionary of the Christian Church **587**
The New Islamic presence in Western Europe **874**
The New Jerome Biblical commentary **475**
The New Jerusalem Bible **463**
New Larousse encyclopedia of mythology **756**
New literature on old age **1041**
New Malaysian who's who **5917**
The New manager's handbook **2548**
New movements in the social sciences and humanities **3778**
New Observer's book of flags **6317**
The New Oxford atlas **5488**
The New Oxford history of England **6900**
The New Palgrave: a dictionary of economics **1715**
The New Palgrave dictionary of money and finance **1716**
The New Penguin guide to personal finance **1124**
The New Penguin guide to the law **2777**
New place names of the world **5522**
The New quotable woman **4026**
The New religions of Japan **887**
The New Shell guide to Britain **5569**
The New Shell guide to the Channel Islands **5625**
The New source book for the disabled **3632**
New sources of grants and aid for businessmen in the UK **1979**
New sources of information, 1973-1989 **162**
New South Wales. The Mitchell Library
Dictionary catalog of printed books **5043**
The New standard Jewish encyclopedia **840**
The New state of the world atlas **5480**
New Testament abstracts **495**
The New Testament Apocrypha and Pseudepigrapha **506**
New Testament Christology **489**
A New topographical dictionary of Ancient Rome **6695**
New Westminster dictionary of liturgy and worship **595**
The New Westminster dictionary of the Bible **427**
The New Whitehall series **3291**
New World immigrants **6141**
New York **5000**

New York Library. The Research Libraries. Local History and Genealogy divison
United States Local History Catalog **8051**
New York Public Library
Dictionary catalog of the Jewish collection **830**
Dictionary catalog of the Schomburg Collection of Negro Literature and History **1088**
The New York Public Library book of chronologies **6451**
New York Public Library. Reference Department
Dictionary catalog of the History of the Americas Collection **7858**
New York Public Library. Research Libraries
Dictionary catalog of the Local History and Genealogy Division **8052**
New York Public Library. Research Libraries
Dictionary catalog of the Slavonic Collection **4446**
Subject catalog of the World War I. Collection **6806**
Subject catalog of the World War II Collections **6844**
New York Public Library. Research Libraries. Map Division
Dictionary catalog of the Map Division **5225**
New York Public Library. The Research Libraries
Dictionary catalog of the Oriental Collection of the New York Public Library, Reference Libraries **4577**
New York University School of Law
Russian-English law dictionary **2714**
New Zealand **1284, 5064, 5067**
'New Zealand at 150' **5066**
New Zealand atlas **5451**
The New Zealand book of events **8125**
New Zealand. Department of Statistics
Official yearbook, 1993 **1283**
New Zealand handbook **5709**
New Zealand in maps **5452**
New Zealand Library Association
A Bibliography of New Zealand bibliographies **5063**
New Zealand official yearbook 1993 **5070**
Newberry Library. Chicago
Dictionary catalog of the Edward E. Ayer Collection of America and American Indians **7859**
The Genealogical index of the Newberry Library **6147**

Newberry Library Historical Boundary Data File
Historical atlas and chronology of county boundaries 1788-1980 **8057**
Newby, E.
The Mitchell Beazley world atlas of exploration **5123**
Newcomer, J.
The Grand Duchy of Luxembourg **7307**
Newell, V.J.
The Folklore of the British Isles **4087**
'Newfoundland family records' **6130**
Newham, G.
'Choosing a business database: the expert approach.' **2443**
Newitt, M.
The Comoro Islands **7852**
The Newly independent states of Eurasia **4724**
Newman, L.
Hunger in history **1105**
Newman, O. *and* Foster, A.
European business rankings **2381**
Newman, P.
The New Palgrave dictionary of money and finance **1716**
Newman, P.C.
Debrett's illustrated guide to the Canadian establishment **5937**
Newman, P.R.
Companion to Irish history 1603-1921 **6996**
Companion to the English Civil Wars **6955**
Newsmakers **5741**
Newson, T.
A Housing bibliography **3220**
Newsworthies **5742**
Newton, M.
Mass murder **3096**
Newton, N.
The Shell guide to the islands of Britain **5584**
Newton, V.
Commonwealth Caribbean legal literature **2767**
Neymeyer, R.J.
Bibliography of the English speaking Caribbean **4929**
Ngo, V.V.
Cartobibliography of the Cameroon **5384**
Penguin dictionary of archaeology **4168**
The NHS handbook **3601**
Nicaragua **4923-4924**
Nicholas, D.
Commodities futures trading **2347**
The Middle East: its oil, economics and investment policies **2065**
Nicholls, D.
Nineteenth-century Britain 1815-1914 **6962**

The Oxford companion to politics of the world **1349**

The Oxford companion to the mind **245**

The Oxford companion to the Supreme Court of the United States **3172**

Oxford dictionary of American legal quotations **2728**

The Oxford dictionary of Byzantium **7688**

The Oxford dictionary of English proverbs **4142**

The Oxford dictionary of nursery rhymes **4135**

The Oxford dictionary of Popes **686**

The Oxford dictionary of saints **567**

The Oxford dictionary of the Christian Church **586**

Oxford economic atlas of the world **2200**

Oxford encyclopaedia of European Community law **2887**

The Oxford guide to family history **6173**

The Oxford guide to heraldry **6229**

The Oxford history of Australia **8140**

The Oxford history of England **6899**

Oxford history of New Zealand **8123**

Oxford history of the Christian Church **618**

Oxford history of the classical world **6669**

The Oxford history of the French Revolution **7361**

The Oxford illustrated history of Christianity **525**

The Oxford minidictionary of twentieth-century world history **6375**

The Oxford movement and its leaders **609**

Oyewole, A.
Historical dictionary of Nigeria **7798**

The Pacific Basin **2277**

Pacific Basin and Oceania **4430**

A Pacific bibliography **5044**

Pacific century **7553**

Pacific history **6460**

Pacific island names **5706**

Pacific islands yearbook **5047**

Pacific mythology **774**

The Pacific since Magellan **8116**

Packer, B. and Sandy, C.
The Touche Ross tax guide for the self-employed **2090**

Packer, J.I.
Marshall's Bible handbook **424**

Paenson, I.
Manual of the terminology of public international law (peace) and international organization: En/Fr/Sp/Russ **2852**

Systematic glossary, English-French-Spanish-Russian, of selected economic and social terms **1718**

Paenson, I. *(contd.)*
Systematic glossary of the terminology of statistical methods **1289**

Paetow, L.J.
A Guide to the study of medieval history **6756**

Paetzel, H.W.
Complete multilingual dictionary of advertising, marketing and communications: English, French, German **2633**

The Pagan religions **740**

Page, G.T. and Thomas, J.B.
International dictionary of education **3721**

Page, R.
Sources of economic information: Ireland **2247**

Paget's law of banking **2142**

PAIS international in print **913**

PAIS subject headings **914**

Paisley, D.
German studies: British resources **4483**

Pakistan **4693-4695**

Pakistan: a political and economic history **7680**

Pakistan. Federal Bureau of Statistics
Statistical pocket book of Pakistan, 1990 **1250**

Pakistan handbook **5669**

Pakistan year book 1990-91 **4696**

The Paladin dictionary of battles **3425**

The Palaeography Collection in the University of London Library **6600**

The Palaeolithic age **4153**

The Palaeolithic settlement of Europe **4203**

Paléographie latine **6605**

Palgrave, R.H.I.
The New Palgrave: a dictionary of economics **1715**

Paliwoda, S.J. and Harrison, A.C.
AMBA guide to business schools **2437**

Palmegiano, E.
The British Empire in the Victorian press 1832-1867 **6893**

Palmer, A.
Penguin dictionary of modern history **6717**

Palmer, A. and Palmer, V.
The Chronology of British history **6923**

A Dictionary of historical quotations **6392**

Who's who in Shakespeare's England **6952**

Palmer, J.
Jane's dictionary of naval terms **3497**

Palmer, K.A.
Index to New Zealand legal writing and cases **2823**

Palmer's company law **3133**

The Palmist's companion **185**

Pan American Union. Columbus Memorial Library
Index to Latin American periodical literature, 1929-1960 **4980**

Panama **4926**

Pande, G.N. and Pande, G.
Indians in Britain - Who's who **5794**

'A Panorama of Polish archaeology', *Antiquity*, v.65, no. 248, September 1991, p.583-721 **4247**

Panteli, S.
A New history of Cyprus **7694**

Pantelidis, V.S.
Arab education, 1956-78: a bibliography **3758**

Pape, C. and Freitag, V.
Topographischer atlas Berlin **5288**

Pappadakis, N. and Glassner, M.
International law of the sea and marine affairs **2916**

Papua New Guinea **5092**

Papua New Guinea atlas **5459**

Papua New Guinea handbook: Business and travel guide **5717**

Papworth, J.W. and Morant, A.W.W.
Papworth's Ordinary of British armorials **6248**

Papworth's Ordinary of British armorials **6248**

Papy, L.
Atlas et géographie de la France moderne **5201**

Para Research Inc
Astrology books in print, 1981 **176**

Paraguay **5036, 5038**

Paraguay: a bibliography **5037**

Paraguay an informal history **8100**

'Paraguayan history: manuscript sources in the United States' **6582**

The Paranormal **136**

Parapsychology **161**

Pardeck, J.T.
Child welfare training and practice **3640**

Parekh, B.
Contemporary political thinkers **1434**

A Parents' guide to education **3713**

The Parents' guide to independent schools, 1989/90 **3811**

Parfitt, T.W.
Zaire **4856**

Paris
L'Almanach de Paris **7341**
Nouvelle histoire de Paris **7342**

Pariser, H.S.
Guide to Jamaica including Haiti **5686**

Pariser, H.S. *(contd.)*
Guide to Puerto Rico and the Virgin Islands including the Dominican Republic **5687**
The Parish chest **7045**
Parish, D.W.
Bibliography of State bibliographies 1970-82 **5014**
Parish register copies. Part One Society of Genealogists Collection **6215**
Parish register copies. Part Two other than the Society of Genealogists collection **6216**
Park, Y.S. *and* Essayyad, M.
International banking and financial centers **2023**
Parker, A.G.
Isle of Wight **7127**
Parker, D. *and* Parker, J.
A History of astrology **182**
Parker's astrology **173**
Parker, F. *and* Parker, B.J.
US higher education **3857**
Parker, F.J.
Togo **4834**
Parker, G.
The Times atlas of world history **6400**
Parker, G. *and* Parker, B.
A Dictionary of the European Communities **2894**
Parker, J.
A Glossary of terms used in heraldry **6235**
Parker, J.C.
Library service for genealogists **6163**
Parker, N.
Charities and broadcasting **3544**
Parker, R.H.
Macmillan dictionary of accounting **2518**
Parker's astrology **173**
Parkes, M.B.
English cursive book hands 1250-1500 **6597**
Parkinson, G.H.R.
An Encyclopaedia of philosophy **60**
The Handbook of Western philosophy **64**
Parks directory of the United States **5697**
Parks, E.D.
Early English hymns **598**
Parliament and government **1618**
Parliament: functions, practice and procedures **1619**
The Parliament of Great Britain **3004**
The Parliamentarians **1623**
The Parliamentary debates. Fifth series. House of Commons: official report 1909- **2997**

The Parliamentary debates. Fifth series. House of Lords: official report, 1909-**2998**
Parliamentary elections results in Ireland, 1801-1922 **1507**
Parliamentary elections results in Ireland, 1918-1992: Irish elections to Parliaments and Parliamentary assemblies at Westminster and Belfast, Dublin, Strasbourg **1508**
The Parliaments of Scotland **3035**
Parliaments of the world **2991**
Parrinder, E.G.
A Dictionary of religious and spiritual quotations **396**
Parrinder, G.
Africa's three religions **892**
Dictionary of non-Christian religions **739**
An Illustrated history of the world's religions **738**
Parrish, M.
The 1968 Czechoslovak crisis **7325**
The USSR in World War II **6879**
Parrish, T.
The Simon and Schuster encyclopedia of World War II **6855**
Parry, C.
The Consolidated treaty series, 1648-1918 **2928**
Encyclopedic dictionary of international law **2854**
Parry, C. *and* Hopkins, C.
An Index of British treaties, 1101-1968 **2931**
Parry, C.J.
'British knighthoods' **6296**
Parry, J.H.
New Iberian world **7945**
Parry, R.
Scottish political facts **1506**
Particular places **7041**
Partington, D.H.
The Middle East annual issues and events **4649**
Partnow, E.
The New quotable woman **4026**
Party systems in Denmark, Austria, Switzerland, the Netherlands and Belgium **1646**
Pascoe, L.S.
Encyclopedia of dates and events **6439**
Pascu, S.
A History of Transylvania **7545**
Paskins, B.
'Peace studies and disarmament.' **2958**
Pasley, M.
Germany **4484**
Pass, C.
Collins dictionary of business **1955**
Dictionary of economics **1740**

Passenger and immigration lists bibliography. 1538-1900 **6144**
Passenger and immigration lists index **6137**
Passengers to America **6138**
Passmore, J.A.
A Hundred years of philosophy **90**
Recent philosophers **91**
Past imperfect **4317**
The Past today **5710**
Past worlds **4178**
Pastor, Freiherr von L.
The History of the Popes, from the close of the Middle Ages **689**
Patai, R.
Encyclopedia of Zionism and Israel **4720**
Paterson, L. *and* McCrone, D.
The Scottish government yearbook, 1992 **3186**
Pates, A.
The Education factbook **3740**
Pathak, V.S.
Ancient historians of India **6417**
Pathfinder maps **5263**
A Patient's guide to the National Health Services **3618**
Patients' rights **3617**
Patmore, E.
International handbook of aging **1048**
A Patristic Greek lexicon **647**
Patrology **643, 645**
Patten, J.
English towns, 1500-1700 **3266**
Patterns of fashion **3918**
Patterson, M.L.P.
South Asian civilizations **4670**
Patterson M.L.P. *and* Inden, R.B.
Introduction to the civilization of India, South Asia **4671**
Patterson, S.C.
'Understanding the British Parliament' **1617**
Pattie, T.S.
Astrology **177**
Paul, J.B.
An Ordinary of arms contained in the Public Register of all arms and bearings in Scotland **6252**
Paul J.B., Sir
The Scots peerage **6279**
Paulhart, H. *and* Paulhart, H.
Österreichische historische bibliographie. Ergänzungsheft 1. Liste der Zeitschriften/Austrian historical bibliography. Supplement 1. List of periodicals 1949-1979. (1980) **7314**
Pauly, A.F. von *and* Wissowa, G.
Pauly's Real-Encyclopädie der classichen Altertumswissenschaft **6674**

Rahner, K. *and* Vorgrimler, H.
Concise theological dictionary **540**
Rai, P.M.
Sikhism and the Sikhs **818**
Raimo, J.W.
Biographical directory of the
governors of the United States,
1978-1983 **3278**
A Guide to manuscripts relating to
America in Great Britain and
Ireland **6578**
Raistrick, D.
Lawyers' law books **2685**
'Recommended holdings for law
libraries' **2686**
Rajović, R.
Jugoslovenski sauremenici ko je ko u
Jugoslaviji **5893**
Rake, A.
Who's who in Africa **5923**
Raleigh, W. *and* Jones, H.A.
The War in the air: being the story of
the part played in the Great War by
the Royal Air Force **6803**
Ramesh Chander Dogra
Jammu and Kashmir **4682**
Ramirez Mitchell, R.A.
Abstracts of military biography **3351**
Ramsay, A.
Eurojargon **2880**
Property development and
management into the nineties **1940**
Ramsay, P.G.
Multicultural education **3704**
Ramsden, R.
The age of Balfour and Baldwin,
1902-1940 **1656**
Ramsey, A.
Eurostat index **1177**
Rana, M.S.
Indian government and politics **3308**
Rand McNally atlas of world history
6397
Rand McNally city map collection **5426**
Rand McNally illustrated atlas of China
5341
Rand McNally road atlas United States.
Mexico, Canada **5404**
Rand McNally state map collection
5427
Rand McNally world atlas of nations
5493
Rand McNally world facts & maps
5518
Randle, P.H.
Atlas del Desarrollo Territorial de La
Argentina **5439**
The Random House guide to business
writing **2496**
Rank, R.
'Criminal law and criminology' **3091**

Rantanen, T. *and* Pärssinen, L.
Suomen historiallinen bibliografia
1961-1970 **7485**
Rao, S.R.
Marine archaeology of Indian Ocean
countries **4312**
Raper, D.
Law databases, 1988 **2661**
Raphael, B.
When disaster strikes **135**
Rapson, E.J.
The Cambridge history of India **7650**
Rashdall, H.
The Universities of Europe in the
Middle Ages **3850**
Rasmussen, R.K. *and* Rubert, S.C.
Historical dictionary of Zimbabwe
7848
Rasor, E.L.
British naval history since 1815 **3507**
The Falklands/Malvinas campaign
8077
The Spanish Armada of 1588 **6950**
Rath V.
Index to Indian economic journals,
1916-1965 **1705**
Rathbone, C. *and* Stephenson, M.
Guide to political quotations **1382**
Rau, W.E.
A Bibliography of pre-independence
Zambia **4895**
Raun, T.V.
Estonia and the Estonians **7473**
Raven, S.
Rome in Africa **6705**
Ravier, E.
Bibliographie des oeuvres de Leibniz
38
Ray, P. *and* Johnston, K.
'Genealogy' **6212**
Raymond, S.
British genealogical periodicals **6058**
Raymond, S. *and* Gibson, J.
English genealogy **6099**
Rayner, C.
Philip's geographical digest 1992-93
5182
Razi Westi, S.
Biographical dictionary of South Asia
5905
Reader, I.
Religion in contemporary Japan **886**
The Reader's companion to American
history **7974**
The Reader's Digest Atlas of Australia,
produced in conjunction with the
Division of National Mapping,
Department of National Resources
5457
Reader's Digest atlas of Southern Africa
5391
Reader's Digest atlas of the Bible **449**
Reader's Digest atlas of the world **5494**

Reader's Digest country Australia **5080**
Reader's Digest driver's atlas of the
British Isles **5270**
Reader's Digest guide to New Zealand
5711
Reader's Digest guide to places of the
world **5519**
Reader's Digest illustrated history of
South Africa **7832**
Reader's Digest touring guide to Britain
5573
Reader's Digest town tours in Britain
5574
Reader's Digest you and your rights
3074
The Reader's encyclopedia of the
American West **7975**
A Reader's guide to Canadian history
7872
The Reader's guide to the best
evangelical books **509**
A Reader's guide to the great religions
348
A Reader's guide to the social sciences
910
Reading, H.F.
A Dictionary of social sciences **930**
A Ready reference to philosophy East
and West **81**
Reakes, J.
The A-Z genealogical handbook **6167**
How to trace your convict ancestors
6168
Real estate/Bienes raíces **1932**
Real estate dictionary **1930**
The Real estate industry **1926**
Reallexikon der Assyriologie und
vorderasiatischen Archäologie **4266**
Reallexikon der germanischen
Altertumskunde **4245**
Reallexikon für Antike und Christentum.
Sachwörterbuch **743**
Reams, B.D.
American legal literature **2816**
Reams, B.D. *and* Yoak, S.D.
The Constitution of the United States
3045
The Constitutions of the States **3046**
Réau, L.
Iconographie de l'art chrétien **574**
Reber, R.S.
The Penguin dictionary of psychology
259
Recent additions to Baker Library **1701**
Recent archaeological discoveries in
India **4269**
Recent archaeological discoveries in
Japan **4265**
Recent Australian historiography **8139**
'Recent books and dissertations on
French history' **7349**
'Recent books on world religions' **354**
Recent British sociology **1016**

Reynolds, R.F.
'Indexing of legal journal literature and the history and development of the *Index to foreign legal periodicals'.* **2687**

Reynolds, S.
An Introduction to the history of English medieval towns **3265**

Rhind, D.
A Census user's handbook **1298**

Rhodes House Library Subject Catalogue **6894**

Rhodesia/Zimbabwe **4889-4890, 7847**

Rhymer, J.
Atlas of the Biblical world **450**

Rhys, J.
Celtic folklore: Welsh and Manx **4100**

Ribbons and medals **6287**

"Ribbons, bells and squeaking fiddles" **4099**

Ribbons of time **6448**

RIC: Répertoire bibliographique des institutions de religions - croyances. Bibliographical repertory of Christian institutions **610**

Ricardian Britain **5558**

Ricci, J.
Elsevier's banking dictionary **2128**

Rice, G.
Oxford history of New Zealand **8123**

Richards, J.H. and Fung, K.I.
Atlas of Saskatchewan **5411**

Richardson, A.
A Theological word book of the Bible **436**

Richardson, A. and Bowden, J.
A New dictionary of Christian theology **541**

Richardson, E.W.
Standards and colors of the American Revolution **6336**

Richardson, J.
The Local historian's encyclopaedia **7060**
Philippines **5058**

Richardson, L.
A New topographical dictionary of Ancient Rome **6695**

Richardson, R.C.
The Study of history **6356**

The Riches of ancient Australia **4385**

The Riches of British archaeology **4215**

Richie, M.
Women's studies **4004**

Richman, J. and Draycott, A.T.
Stone's justice's manual, 1993 **3149**

Richmond, L. and Stockford, B.
Company archives **2399**

Riden, P.
Local history **7064**
Record sources for local history **7085**

The Rider encyclopedia of Eastern philosophy and religion **790**

Ridinger, R.B.M.
The Peace Corps **2959**

Rietstap, J.B.
Armorial général **6237**

Riff, M.
Dictionary of modern political ideologies **1437**

The Rights of women **4033**

Het Rijkarchief in de provinciën **6518**

De Rijksarchieven in Nederland **6517**

Riklefs, M.C.
A History of modern Indonesia **8105**

Riley, C.L.
Historical and cultural dictionary of Saudi Arabia **7632**

Riley, R.C.
Belgium **4558**

Riley-Smith, J.
The Atlas of the Crusades **6772**

Rise and decline of the Roman world **6688**

The Rise and fall of the Soviet Union **7460**

The rise of civilization in India and Pakistan **4268**

The Rise of the Celts **880**

Rishikesh Shaha
Modern Nepal **7676**

Risse, W.
Bibliographia logica **321**

Ritchie, A.
Picts **4351**
Scotland BC **4356**
Viking Scotland **4352**

Ritchie, A. and Breeze, D.J.
Invaders of Scotland **4350**

Ritchie, G. and Ritchie, A.
Scotland: archaeology and early history **4233**

The Rites of Eastern Christendom **661**

Ritter, H.
Dictionary of concepts in history **6435**

Ritter, J.
Historisches Wörterbuch der Philosophie **62**

Roach, J.
A Bibliography of modern history **6714**

Road atlas of the USSR **5319**

The Road-books and itineraries of Great Britain 1570-1850 **6919**

Roaf, M.
Cultural atlas of Mesopotamia and the Ancient Near East **4381**

Robb, L.A.
Diccionario de términos legales. Spanish-English and English-Spanish dictionary of legal terms **2712**

Robbins, K.
The Blackwell biographical dictionary of British political life in the twentieth century **1651**
'Nazi Germany' **7280**

Robbins, M.
The Amateur archaeologist's handbook **4291**

Robbins, N.C.
Mexico **4918**

Roberts, A.
'A Bibliography of primary sources for Tanzania 1799-1899' **7822**
A History of Zambia **7849**

Robert's dictionary of industrial relations **1864**

Roberts, G.
Atlas of discovery **5124**

Roberts, G. and Edwards, A.
A New dictionary of political analysis **1368**

Roberts, H.S.
Robert's dictionary of industrial relations **1864**

Roberts, N.
Use of social science literature **915**

Robertshaw, P.
A History of African archaeology **4284**

Robertson, A.S.
The Antonine Wall **4353**

Robertson, B.
The RAF **3485**

Robertson, D.
A Dictionary of modern defense and strategy **3444**
A Dictionary of modern politics **1369**
Guide to modern defense and strategy **3334**

Robertson, J.A.
Bibliography of the Philippine Islands 1493-1898 **5060**

Robinson, A. and Millward, R.
The Shell book of the British coast **5575**

Robinson, C.P.
Allied Dunbar investment and savings guide, 1993 **2192**

Robinson, D.
Heritage in Wales **4375**

Robinson, F.
Atlas of the Islamic world since 1500 **4767**
The Cambridge encyclopedia of India, Pakistan, Bangladesh, Sri Lanka, Nepal, Bhutan and the Maldives **4674**

Robinson, R.
Business history of the world **2473**

Robson, L.
A History of Tasmania **8142**

Rocca, R.G. *and* **Dziak, J.J.**
Bibliography on Soviet intelligence and security services **1614**

Rock, D.
Argentina 1516-1982: from Spanish colonization to the Falklands War and Alphonsin **8070**

Rock, J.M.
Money, banking and macroeconomics: a guide to information sources **2029**

The Rock of the Gibraltarians **7426**

Rocznik statystyczny, 1990 **1211**

Rodger, F.
Serial publications in the British Parliamentary Papers, 1900-1968 **3013**

Rodger, N.A.M.
Naval records for genealogists **6065**

Rodrigues, L.J. *and* **Bernet Soler, J.**
Harrap's glossary of English and Spanish commercial and industrial terms **2351**

Roeder, H.
Saints and their attributes **555**

Roeder, O.G. *and* **Mahiddin, Mahmud**
Who's who in Indonesia **6007**

Roesdahl, E.
Viking age Denmark **4257**

Roese, P.M. *and* **Rees, A.R.**
A Bibliography of Benin **4836**

Roese, P.M. *and* **Rose, A.C.**
Ein Atlas zur Geschichte Benins **7795**

Roett, R. *and* **Sacks, R.S.**
Paraguay **5036**

Rogers, C.D.
The Family tree detective **6093**

Rogers, C.D. *and* **Smith, J.H.**
Local family history in England 1538-1914 **6095**

Rogers, F.
Archives New Zealand **6585**

Rogers, M. *and* **Knox, R.J.**
The Peoples of Asia **7549**

Rogers, S.W.
'Selected historical chronologies' **6453**

Rogerson, J.
The New atlas of the Bible **451**

Rohn, P.H.
World treaty index **2938**

Rohwer, J. *and* **Hümmelchen, G.**
Chronology of the war at sea 1939-1945 **6870**

Rolef, S.H.
A Political dictionary of the State of Israel **1414**

Roll, E
A History of economic thought **1807**
A Roll of Australian arms **6261**

Roller D.C. *and* **Twyman, R.W.**
The Encyclopedia of Southern history **7976**

Rollins, A.
Rome in the fourth century **6691**

Rollins, A.M.
The Fall of Rome **6692**

Romain, A.
Dictionary of legal and commercial terms **3126**

Roman Britain **4227, 6935-6936, 6940**
The Roman city of London **7107**
The Roman emperors **6701**
Roman Germany **4377**
Roman historical portraits **6696**
The Roman inscriptions of Britain **4338-4339**
The Roman world **6693**
Romania **4571**
România: atlas rutier **5336**

Romania. Direcţia Centrala de Statistica
Anuarul statistic al Republicii Socialiste România. Romania statistical yearbook, 1992 **1239**

A Romano-British bibliography **6939**
The Romans, their gods and their beliefs **780**
Rome in Africa **6705**
Rome in the fourth century **6691**

Romer, J.-C.
Le Dictionnaire encyclopédique militaire soviétique **3332**

Room, A.
Corporate eponymy **2373**
Place-name changes 1900-1991 **5520**
The Roots of modern Japan **7619**

Roper, F.W. *and* **Bourkman, J.A.**
Introduction to reference sources in the health sciences **3588**

Roper, G.
The Bibliography of the Arab Middle East **4763**

Roscher, W.H.
Ausführliches Lexikon der griechischen und römischen Mythologie **777**

Rose, H.J.
A Handbook of Greek mythology **782**

Rose, P.I.
The New immigration **1520**

Rosen, O.
Encyclopedia of Jewish institutions **850**

Rosenberg, J.
'American family history' **6148**

Rosenberg, J.M.
Dictionary of banking and financial services **2047**
Dictionary of business and management **2465, 2553**
Dictionary of investing **2114**

Rosenberg, J.M. *(contd.)*
McGraw-Hill dictionary of business acronyms **2441**
McGraw-Hill dictionary of Wall Street acronyms **2166**

Rosenberg, M.B. *and* **Bergstrom, L.V.**
Women and society **4016**

Rosenberg, P.M. *and* **Durr, W.T.**
The Urban information thesaurus **1095**

Rosenblatt, J.T.
Who's who in world Jewry **5771**

Rosie, G.
The Directory of international terrorism **1486**

Rosignoli, G.
Air Force badges and insignia of World War 2 **3399**
Army badges and insignia of World War 2 **3400-3401**

Ross, A. *and* **Cyprien, M.**
A Traveller's guide to Celtic Britain **5576**

Ross, J.A.
Family planning and child survival **3625**
International encyclopedia of population **1297**

Ross, S.
The Monarchs of Scotland **6977**

Ross, S.R.
'Bibliography of sources for contemporary Mexican history' **7903**
Fuentes de la historia contemporáneo de México. Periodicas y revistas **7904**

Ross, S.T.
French military history, 1661-1799 **3378**

Rossi, E.E. *and* **McCrea, B.P.**
The European political dictionary **1392**

Rossi, E.E. *and* **Plano, J.C.**
Latin America: a political dictionary **1422**

Rossi, J.
The Gulag handbook **3106**

Rössler, H. *and* **Franz, G.**
Sachwörterbuch zur deutschen Geschichte **7260**

Rostow, W.W.
Theorists of economic growth **1804**

Roth, C.
Magna bibliotheca anglo-judaica **831**

Roth, C. *and* **Widoger, G.**
Concise Jewish encyclopedia **839**

Roth, C. *and* **Wigoder, G.**
Encyclopaedia Judaica **834**

Rothermund, D.
An Economic history of India **2289**

Rothery, G.C.
Concise encyclopedia of heraldry **6224**

The Rough guide to Israel and the Occupied Territories **5671**

The Rough guides **5521**

Rouillard, J.
Guide de l'histoire du Québec **7896**

Rouse, R. and Neill, S.C.
A History of the ecumenical movement **592**

The Rousseau dictionary **44**

Routh, G.
Occupations of the people of Great Britain, 1801-1981 **1885**

The Routledge compendium of primary education **3810**

The Routledge dictionary of twentieth-century political thinkers **1438**

Roux, G.
Ancient Iraq **7696**

Rowat, D.C.
International handbook on local government reorganization **3239**

Rowe, D.J.
Northern business histories **2404**

Rowe, H.
A Guide to the records of Bermuda **7937**

Rowe, K.E.
Methodist Union catalog: pre-1976 imprints **722**

Rowland, I.
Timor **5061**

Rowley, E.E.
The Financial system today **2036**

Rowley, H.H.
A Companion to the Bible **461**
Dictionary of Bible place names **445**

Rowntree, D.
A Dictionary of education **3722**

Roy, A.K. and Gidwani, N.N.
A Dictionary of Indology **4684**

Royal Britain **5561**

Royal Commonwealth Society
Biography catalogue of the Library **6896**
The Manuscript catalogue of the library .. **4476**
Subject catalogue of the Library of the Royal Empire Society **4472**

The Royal Geographical Society history of world exploration **5151**

Royal heraldry **6241**

The Royal heraldry of England **6259**

Royal Historical Society. Annual bibliography of British and Irish history **6907**

Royal Institute of International Affairs
Chronology and index of the Second World War 1938-1945 **6868**

Royal Institute of International Affairs *(contd.)*
Documents on international affairs, 1928-1963 **1564**
Survey of international affairs, 1920/23-66 **1562**

Royal Institute of International Affairs. Library
The Classified catalogue of the Royal Institute of International Affairs for international relations, defence, diplomacy, international law, politics and economics.. **1548**
Index to periodical articles, 1950-1964 .. **1549**
Index to periodical articles, 1965-1972 .. **1550**
Index to periodical articles, 1979-1989 **1551**

The Royal Mail direct mail handbook **2628**

The Royal Marines - a pictorial history, 1664-1988 **3519**

Royal National Institute for the Blind. Reference Library
Works on blindness and associated subjects **3635**

The Royal Navy **3512**

The Royal Navy day by day **3518**

Royal Navy language **3496**

Royal Scottish Geographical Society
The Early maps of Scotland to 1850.. **5273**

Royal tombs of England **6314**

Royal United Services Institute for Defence Studies
R.U.S.I. and Brassey's defence yearbook, 1991 **3353**

Royle, T.
A Dictionary of military quotations **3354**

Ruben, D.H.
Philosophy journals and serials **78**

Rubio Cabeza, M.
Diccionario de la Guerra Civil Espanola **7424**

Ruble, B.A. and Teeter, M.J.
A Scholars' guide to humanities and social sciences in the Soviet Union and the Baltic States **959**

Ruck, A.
The Holiday Which? guide to France **5638**

Rudavsky, A.
'Sources for a Judaica reference collection' **829**

Rudder, S.
A New history of Gloucestershire **7147**

Rudolph, D.K. and Rudolph, G.A.
Historical dictionary of Venezuela **8098**

The Rules of the Communist party of the Soviet Union **1668**

Runciman, S.
A History of the Crusades **6769**

Ruokonen, K and Rinne, B.
Economic and business libraries in Scandinavia **1793**

Rural life guide to local records **7037**

Rural sociology **1101**

Ruscio, A.
La Première guerre d'Indochine (1945-1954) **7732**

Rush, M.
Parliament and government **1618**

R.U.S.I. and Brassey's defence yearbook, 1991 **3353**

Russell, B.
History of Western philosophy **92**

Russell, J.B.
A History of witchcraft throughout the ages **167**

Russell, P.E.
Spain **4513**

'Russia 1855-1917' **7441**

Russia and Eastern Europe 1789-1985 **7459**

Russia & Eurasia facts & figures annual (formerly *USSR facts and figures annual*) **1222**

Russia in the twentieth century **7470**

Russia revised **7465**

Russia, the USSR and Eastern Europe **7458**

Russia/USSR **4526**

Russian autocrats from Ivan the Great to the fall of the Romanov dynasty **7446**

Russian economic history **2269**

The Russian Empire and the Soviet Union **6511**

Russian-English/English-Russian glossary of statistical terms **1154**

Russian-English law dictionary **2714**

Russian-English military dictionary **3347**

The Russian Orthodox Church **663**

Russian philosophical terminology **73**

Russian psychology **278**

The Russian Revolution 1899-1919 **7443**

Russo, D.J.
Keepers of our past **8048**

Rust, V.D.
Education in East and West Germany **3753**

Rutherford, D.
Dictionary of economics **1720**

Ruud, I.M.
Women and Judaism **4056**

Ruvigny and Raineval, 9th Marquis of
The Titled nobility of Europe **6270**

Rwanda **4859**

Ryan, C.C.
Small business **2011**

Scholfield, G.H.
A Dictionary of New Zealand biography **6015**

The School administrator's resource guide **3801**

School librarianship **3808**

School organization and management abstracts **3803**

Schooley, H.
Conflicts in Central America **1593**

The Schools' who's who, 1987 **3806**

Schopenhauer-Bibliographie **50**

Schopflin, G.
The Soviet Union and Eastern Europe **4522**

Schottenloher, K.
Bibliographie zur deutschen Geschichte im Zeitalter der Glaubensspaltung **7267**

Schraeder, P.J.
Djibouti **4867**

Schreiner-Yantis, N.
Genealogical and local history books in print **6050**

Schroeder, S.
Cuba: a handbook **1269**

Schubart, W.
Griechische paläographie **6602**

Schultz, D.P. and Schultz, S.E.
History of modern psychology **271**

Schultz, J.
Writing about Canada **7873**

Schultze, S.
Population information in nineteenth-century census volumes **1334**
Population information in twentieth-century census volumes.. **1335**

Schulz, A.
International and regional politics in the Middle East and North Africa **1589**

Schulz-Torge, U-J.
Who was who in the Soviet Union **5860**
Who's who in the Soviet Union today **5861**

Schumacher, S. and Woerner, G.
The Rider encyclopedia of Eastern philosophy and religion **790**

Schürer, K. and Anderson, S.J.
A Guide to historical datafiles held in machine-readable form **6348**

Schutz, H.
The Prehistory of Germanic Europe **4204**

Schwab, M.
Index of articles relative to Jewish history and literature **6645**

Schwartz, B.
China off the beaten track **5657**

Schwartz, C.A.
'Post-Stalin Soviet leadership studies' **3303**

Schwartzberg, J.E.
A Historical atlas of South Asia **7581**

Schwartzkopf, R.B.
'State atlases from the eighties' **5433**

Schwarz, U. and Hadik, L.
Strategic terminology **3446**

Schweitzer, F.M. and Wedeck, E.
Dictionary of the Renaissance **6775**

SCIMP: European index of management periodicals **1711**

SCIMP/SCANP thesaurus **1712**

SCIMP [Selective cooperative index of management periodicals] **2563**

SCOLMA directory of libraries and special collections on Africa in the UK and in Europe **4791**

'The Scope of Burke's Landed Gentry' **6278**

Scotland **4457**

Scotland and her tartans **6184**

Scotland: archaeology and early history **4233**

Scotland BC **4356**

Scotland before history with a gazetteer of ancient monuments **4354**

Scotland from the eleventh century to 1603 **4347**

Scotland. Parliament
The Acts of the Parliaments of Scotland, 1424-1707 **2760**

Scotland through the ages **4346**

Scotland's regions **3248**

Scotland's Roman remains **4355**

Scots heraldry **6251**

The Scots peerage **6279**

Scott, B.K.C.
Dictionary of military abbreviations **3323**

Scott, D.L.
Wall Street words **2188**

Scott, D.L. and Scott, K.
Guide to the National Park areas Eastern States **5699**
Guide to the National Park areas Western States **5698**

Scott, F.D.
Sweden **7494**

Scott, H.F. and Scott, W.F.
Armed forces of the USSR **3379**

Scott, I.
Hong Kong **4604**

Scott, J.W.
A Synoptic index to the 'Proceedings of the Aristotelian Society.. **17**

Scott-Roberts, F.
Macmillan directory of international asset managers **2193**

Scottish abstract of statistics, 1992 **1197**

Scottish archaeology **4232**

Scottish burgh and county heraldry **6253**

Scottish church history **625**

Scottish civic heraldry **6254**

Scottish clans & tartans **6189**

Scottish current law year book ... 1948-**2756**

Scottish dates **6988**

Scottish economic bulletin **2243**

Scottish family histories **6186**

Scottish family history **6188**

The Scottish financial sector **2109**

The Scottish government yearbook, 1992 **3186**

The Scottish jurists **2835**

Scottish Kings **6987**

Scottish labour leaders, 1918-1939 **1664**

The Scottish law directory, 1987 **3162**

The Scottish legal system **2754**

Scottish local history **6982**

Scottish local studies resources **6980**

Scottish military dress **3419**

Scottish Office
Scottish economic bulletin **2243**
Scottish Office statistical publications **1198**

Scottish political facts **1506**

The Scottish political system **1663**

Scottish texts and calendars **6485**

Scottish towns **6975**

'The Scramble for Africa: inherited political boundaries' **7752**

Screen, J.E.O.
Finland **4542**

'A Screenful of forebears' **6170**

Scrivener, D. and Sheehan, M.
Bibliography of arms control verification **3327**

Scrivener, R.S.
USSR economic handbook **2265**

Scruton, R.
From Descartes to Wittgenstein **101**
A Dictionary of political thought **1439**
Thinkers of the new Left **189**

Seaborne trade **6796**

Seager, J. and Olson, A.
Women in the world **4028**

Search for the Northwest Passage **8177**

Searching overseas **6055**

Searing, S.E.
Introduction to library research in women's studies **4059**

Seaton, A.
The German army; 1933-45 **3374**

Sebba, G.
Bibliographia Cartesiana **23**

Seccombe, I.J.
Jordan **4723**
Syria **4713**

The Second Fleet convicts **6027**

The Second World War **6843**

The Second World War a guide to documents in the Public Record Office **6874**

The Secret wars **1608**

Secretarial administration **1954**
Segal, A.
  Careers encyclopedia **1890**
Segal, G.
  Political and economic encyclopedia of the Pacific **1364**
  The World affairs companion **4416**
Segall, A.
  Guide to Jewish archives **6537**
Seide, K.
  A Dictionary of arbitration and its terms **3157**
Seldon, A. *and* Pennance, F.G.
  Everyman's dictionary of economics **1742**
Seldon Society
  A Centenary guide to the publications of the Seldon Society **2749**
Select bibliographies on aging **1040**
A Select bibliography for the study, sources and literature of English mediaeval economic history **2252**
A Select bibliography of adult continuing education in Great Britain, including works published to the end of the year 1981 **3821**
'Select bibliography of genealogical research aids published by the National Archives and Records Administration' **6149**
A Select bibliography of modern economic theory, 1870-1929 **1805**
A Select bibliography of moral philosophy **330**
A Select bibliography of South African history **7837**
Select bibliography of South African native life and problems **1074**
Select list of British Parliamentary Papers, 1833-1899 **3030**
A Select list of reports of enquiries of the Irish Dáil and Senate, 1922-1972 **3040**
A Select list of works on Europe and Europe overseas 1715-1815 **6779**
A Selected and annotated bibliography of American naval history **3534**
Selected and annotated bibliography of youth, youth work and provision for youth **3646**
A Selected bibliography of modern historiography **6406**
'Selected historical chronologies' **6453**
Selected list of UK theses and dissertations in management studies **2558**
Selected references to literature on marine expeditions, 1700-1960 **5146**
A Selected vocabulary of financial terms **2046**
A Selective bibliography of philosophical logic **320**
A Selective bibliography on Kant **30**

Selective cooperative index of management periodicals **2563**
A Selective listing of monographs and government documents on the Falkland/Malvinas Islands in the Library of Congress **5026**
The Self-help guide **3572**
Seligman, E.R.A.
  Encyclopaedia of the social sciences **925**
Selkirk, A.
  The Riches of British archaeology **4215**
Sell, K.D.
  Divorce in the 70s **1346**
Sell, K.D. *and* Sell, B.H.
  Divorce in the United States, Canada and Great Britain **1345**
Sellers, J.R.
  Civil War mansucripts **8041**
Selvon, S.
  Historical dictionary of Mauritius **7854**
Selwyn, N.
  Dictionary of employment law **1844**
The Seminary priests **696**
Sen, S.P.
  Dictionary of national biography **5909**
  Sources of the history of India **7662**
Senegal **4819**
Senior, M.
  The Illustrated who's who in mythology **764**
Serial bibliographies and abstracts in history **6384**
Serial bibliographies in the humanities and sciences **901**
Serial publications in the British Parliamentary Papers, 1900-1968 **3013**
Serials on aging **1051**
Serrão, J.
  Cronologia geral da historia de Portugal **7436**
  Dicionário de historia de Portugal **7434**
  Pequeno dicionário de historia de Portugal **7435**
Serrão, J. *and* Oliveira Marques, A.D. de
  Nova história de Portugal **7430**
Service, A. *and* Bradbery, J.
  The Standing stones of Europe **4327**
Sessional information digest. 1991-92 **1622**
Sessional Papers of the eighteenth century: George I and II **3028**
Sessional Papers of the eighteenth century: George III **3029**
Seton, R.
  The Indian Mutiny 1857-58 **6530**

Setton, K.M.
  A History of the Crusades **6770**
The Seven wonders of the Ancient World **6609**
Seventeenth century Britain 1603-1714 **6954**
The Sexual barrier **4012**
Seychelles **4899**
The Seychelles **7853**
Seyffert, O.
  A Dictionary of Classical antiquites **4325**
Seymour, A. *and* Seymour, E.
  Dictionary of Guyanese biography **6001**
Seymour-Smith, C.
  Macmillan dictionary of anthropology **1004**
Seymour, W.
  Battles in Britain **3434**
  Great sieges of history **3432**
Seymour, W.A.
  Ordnance Survey **5268**
Shackleton on the law and practice of meetings **3197**
Shadbolt, M.
  Reader's Digest guide to New Zealand **5711**
Shafaat Ahmad Khan
  Sources for the history of British India in the seventeenth century **6531**
Shafritz, J.M.
  The Dorsey dictionary of American government and politics **3188**
  The Facts on File dictionary of military science **3342**
  The Facts on File dictionary of public administration **3182**
  The HarperCollins dictionary of American government and politics **3189**
  War on words **3356**
Shaikh, F.
  Islam and Islamic groups **860**
Shamir, I. *and* Shavit, S.
  Encyclopedia of Jewish history **6646**
Shanghai **7587**
Shanks, D.
  Guide to bibliographies on education **3684**
Shannon, G.W.B.
  'Folk literature and children' **4077**
Shannon, M.O.
  Irish Republic **4466**
  Modern Ireland **4461**
  Northern Ireland **4465**
  Oman and Southeastern Arabia **4660**
Shap Working Party on World Religions in Education
  Festivals in world religions **3972**
Shapero, F.R.
  Oxford dictionary of American legal quotations **2728**

Skone James, E.P.
Copinger and Skone James on copyright **3142**

Skyrme, T.
History of the Justices of the Peace **3165**

Slaven, A *and* Checkland, S.
Dictionary of Scottish business biography, 1860-1960 **2475**

Slavens, T.P.
Sources of information for investors in the Commonwealth of Independent States (formerly: The Soviet Union) **2195**

Slavery **1532**

Slavery and African life **1535**

Slavery - the Afro-American experience. **1534**

Slavic studies **4447**

Slocum, R.B.
Biographical dictionaries and related works **5754**

Slovak biographical dictionary **5840**

Slovenský biografickík **5840**

Slownik prawniczy polsko-angielski/ Polish-English dictionary of legal terms **2716**

Small business **2011**

The Small business guide: sources of information for new and small businesses **2013**

The Small business index **2008**

Small business sourcebook **2012**

'Small businesses and exporting: a literature review' **2010**

Small is not always beautiful **7801**

Smallwood, J.R. *and* Pitt, R.D.W.
Encyclopedia of Newfoundland and Labrador **4917**

Smart, N.
Nineteenth-century religious thought in the West **545**
The World's religions **401**

Smelser, N. J.
Handbook of sociology **998**

Smethurst, J.M.
A Bibliography of co-operative societies' histories **1942**

Smith, A.
Directory of oral history collections **6726**

Smith, A.H.
East European economic handbook **2229**

Smith, B.L. *and* Smith, C.M.
International communication and political opinion **1029**

Smith, B.P.
Directory of historical agencies in North America **8054**

Smith, C.
American historical images on file **7985**

Smith, D.
Maps and plans for the local historian and collector **7074**

Smith, D.L.
Era of the American Revolution **8020**
The History of Canada **7874**
Parks directory of the United States **5697**

Smith, D.M.
Guide to bishops' registers of England and Wales **694**

Smith, D.W.
The War of 1812 **8028**

Smith, E.C. *and* Zurcher, A.J.
Dictionary of American politics **2989**

Smith, F.
A Genealogical gazetteer of England **6100**
The Nationalities question in the Soviet Union **7456**

Smith, G.
'How to find US business information' **1994**
Inspiration and information **3937**
The War at sea **6836**

Smith, G.R.
The Yemens **4658**

Smith, H.
The British labour movement to 1970 **1908**

Smith, H. *and* Sheard, W.
Academic dress and insignia of the world **3862**

Smith, H.E.
Historical and cultural dictionary of Thailand **7716**

Smith, H.L.
British feminism in the twentieth century **4038**
British women in the 20th century **4039**

Smith, I.A. *and* Grunts, M.V.
Baltic States **4531**

Smith, J.
A Descriptive catalogue of Friends' books **734**

Smith, J.C.
Ethnic genealogy **6154**

Smith, J.D.
Black slavery in the Americas **1536**

Smith, M.J.
The Secret wars **1608**
The Soviet air and strategic rocket forces, 1939-1980 **3488**
The Soviet army, 1939-1980 **3476**
The Soviet navy, 1941-1978 **3526**
The United States Navy and Coast Guard, 1946-1983 **3530**
World War I in the air **6807**
World War II **6847**
World War II at sea **6848**
World War II The European and Mediterranean theaters **6849**

Smith-Morris, M.
The Economist book of vital world statistics.. **1155**

Smith, N.
Legal research techniques **2688**

Smith, P.
The Babi and Baha'i religions **877**

Smith, P.C. *and* Oakley, D.
The Royal Marines - a pictorial history, 1664-1988 **3519**

Smith, R.
Catastrophes and disasters **5160**
Mythologies of the world **748**
Wildest Britain **5577**

Smith, R.B.
An International history of the Vietnam war **7727**

Smith, S.
The Bibliography of flags of foreign nations **6326**

Smith, W.
Dictionary of Greek and Roman biography and mythology **6681**
The Flag book of the United States **6338**
Flags and arms across the world **6323**
Flags through the ages and across the world **6324**

Smolka-Day, M.I.
Bibliographic guide to the legal aspects of international finance **2104**

Smurthwaite, D.
Ordnance Survey complete guide to the battlefields of Britain **3436**

Smyth, D.
Guide to Irish mythology **767**

Snow, P.
The United States **5015**

Snow, P.A.
A Bibliography of Fiji, Tonga and Rotuma **5100**

Snowdon, J.
European folk dress **3941**
The Folk dress of Europe **3942**

Snyder, E. M.
'Guide to Israel legal bibliography: primary sources' **2806**

Snyder, E.M. *and* Kreiner, E.
Israel **4719**

Snyder, L.L.
Encyclopedia of nationalism **1449**
Encyclopedia of the Third Reich **7286**
Historical guide to World War II **6856**
The Third Reich 1933-1945 **7281**

Snyder, P.
The European women's almanac **4037**

Sobel, L.A.
Political terrorism **1471**

Vancouver centennial bibliography **7893**

Vandalism **3076**

Vande Kemp, H.
Psychology and theology in Western thought, 1672-1965 **234**

Vandier, J.V.
Manuel d'archéologie égyptienne **4189**

Vanrie, V.
International directory of archives **6456**

'The Vatican archives, with special reference to sources for British and Irish medieval history' **6479**

Vatican City State **4507**

Des Vatikanische Archiv **6504**

Vatikiotis, P.J.
The History of Egypt **7759**

Vaughan, H.H.
Welsh proverbs with English translations **4146**

Vedic bibliography **794**

Vekené, E. van der
Bibliographie der Inquisition **642**

Vem ärdet: Svensk biografisk handbok 1993 **5878**

Vem och vad? biografisk handbok 1992 **5874**

Venezuela **5033, 8095-8096**

Vennetier, P.
Atlas de la Côte d'Ivoire **5382**
Atlas de la République Centrafricaine **5387**

Venzon, A.C.
The Spanish-American War **8042**

Vercoutter, J.
Egypt and Africa **6624**

Vernadsky, G.
A Source book for Russian history **7444**

Vernoff, E. and Shore, R.
The International dictionary of 20th century biography **5773**

Vernon, K.D.C.
Information sources in management and business **2456, 2536**

Vernon, K.D.C. and Lang, V.
The London classification of business studies **2477**

Vernon, K.D.C. and Newman, S.J.
SCIMP/SCANP thesaurus **1712**

Verrou-Karakosta, T.H. and Katzopoulos, K.K.
Balkan Bibliography **4566**

Verstappen, B.
Human rights reports **3059**

Verwey, G. and Renooij, D.C.
The Economist's handbook **2219**

Vesey, G.
Philosophers ancient and modern **106**

Vessie, P.A.
Zen Buddhism **806**

Vexler, R.
Austria: a chronology and fact book **7319**
Scandinavia: a chronology and fact book **7482**

VGM's careers encyclopedia **1895**

V.I. Lenin **1408**

The Viceroys of India **7648**

Vichas, B.P.
Annotated handbook of biblical quotations, verses and parables **444**

Victoria Cross, 1856-1920 **3395**

The Victoria history of Berkshire **7128**

The Victoria history of Hampshire and the Isle of Wight **7125**

The Victoria history of London **7093**

The Victoria history of Shropshire **7156**

The Victoria history of the counties of England **7046**

The Victoria history of the county of Bedford **7182**

The Victoria history of the county of Buckingham **7188**

The Victoria history of the county of Cambridgeshire and the Isle of Ely **7193**

The Victoria history of the county of Chester **7205**

The Victoria history of the county of Cornwall **7140**

The Victoria history of the county of Cumberland **7223**

The Victoria history of the county of Derby **7164**

The Victoria history of the County of Devon **7136**

The Victoria history of the county of Dorset **7131**

The Victoria history of the county of Durham **7218**

The Victoria history of the county of Essex **7202**

The Victoria history of the county of Gloucester **7148**

The Victoria history of the county of Hereford **7154**

The Victoria history of the county of Hertford **7191**

The Victoria history of the county of Huntingdonshire **7180**

The Victoria history of the county of Kent **7114**

The Victoria history of the county of Lancaster **7208**

The Victoria history of the county of Leicester **7175**

The Victoria history of the county of Lincoln **7172**

The Victoria history of the county of Middlesex **7109**

The Victoria history of the county of Norfolk **7194**

The Victoria history of the county of Northampton **7179**

The Victoria history of the county of Nottingham **7167**

The Victoria history of the county of Oxford **7185**

The Victoria history of the county of Rutland **7177**

The Victoria history of the county of Somerset **7144**

The Victoria history of the County of Stafford **7158**

The Victoria history of the county of Suffolk **7198**

The Victoria history of the county of Surrey **7112**

The Victoria history of the county of Sussex **7120**

The Victoria history of the county of Warwick **7161**

The Victoria history of the county of Wiltshire **7129**

The Victoria history of the county of Worcester **7160**

The Victoria history of the county of York **7213**

Victorian Britain **6964**

Victorian science and religion **414**

Victorian studies **6963**

Victorian women **5804**

Vidal-Naquet, P.
The Collins atlas of world history **6395**

Vienna Institute for Comparative Economic Studies,
COMECON data, 1990 **1183**
COMECON foreign trade data, 1986 **2426**

Viet, J.
Thesaurus of individual development terms **2331**
Thesaurus of vocational training **3768**

Viet, J. and Slype, G.van
EUDISED; multilingual thesaurus **3767**

Vietnam **4753-4756**

Vietnam at war **7726**

Vietnam order of battle **7728**

Vietnam War almanac **7735**

Vietnam War bibliography **7733**

Viking age Denmark **4257**

Vilar, P.
A History of gold and money, 1450-1920 **2162**

Village studies **1102**

Villain, J.
La France moderne **6116**

Villarel, H.K.
Eminent Filippines **6011**

Viller, M.
Dictionnaire de spiritualité, ascétique et mystique, doctrine et histoire **579**

Wedgewood, J.C.
History of Parliament, 1439-1509
3017
Weekes, R.V.
The World of Islam **868, 4765**
Weekly information bulletin **1621**
Weekly law reports **2771**
Weekly official intelligence **2181**
Weeks, A.L.
Brassey's Soviet and communist
quotations **209**
Weeks, G.
Family directory **1116**
Weeks, J.
Jane's pocket-book: armies of the
world **3454**
Wehler, H-U.
The German Empire 1871-1918 **7247**
Wei, B.P.T.
Shanghai **7587**
Wei-Chin Lee
Taiwan **4636**
Wei, K.T.
Women in China **4045**
Weigall, D.
Britain and the world, 1815-1986
1556
Weightman, A.E.
Heraldry in the Royal Navy **3508**
The Weights and measures of England
3231
Weigley, R.F.
The Age of battles **3433**
The Weimar era and Hitler 1918-1933
7274
The Weimar Republic **7275**
Weinberg, J.R.
A Short history of medieval
philosophy **99**
Weinberg, M.
World racism and related inhumanities
1063
Weinreb, B. and Hibbert, C.
The London encyclopaedia **7100**
Weinstein, W.
Historical dictionary of Burundi **7814**
Weir, A.
Britain's Royal Families **6312**
Early Ireland **4359**
Welch, J.M.
Free bank letters as sources of
economic and financial information
2124
Welch, T.F. and Kato, H.
Japan today! **5664**
Welfare, poverty and development in
Latin America **1145**
Welland, D.
The United States **4993**
Wellner, I.
Budapest **5633**

Wells, R.V.
The Population of the British colonies
in America before 1776 **1333**
Welsby, P.A.
A History of the Church of England,
1945-1980 **692**
Welsh, B.W.W. and Butorin, P.
Dictionary of development **1783**
Welsh, D.V.
A Catalog of the William B. Greenlee
collection **7433**
Welsh economic trends/Tueddiadau'r
economi, 1992 **2253**
Welsh, F.
A History of Hong Kong **7603**
Welsh folk customs **4101**
Welsh genealogies AD300-1400 **6107**
Welsh history and its sources **7233**
Welsh history review **7234**
Welsh nation builders **5823**
Welsh Office
Health and personal social services
statistics for Wales, 1991 **3613**
Welsh economic trends/Tueddiadau'r
economi, 1992 **2253**
Welsh social trends/Tueddiadau
Cymdeithasol, 1991 **1137**
Welsh Office atlas/Atlas y Swyddfa
Cymreig **5286**
Welsh proverbs, in English and Welsh
4147
Welsh proverbs with English
translations **4146**
Welsh social trends/Tueddiadau
Cymdeithasol, 1991 **1137**
Weltgeschichte in Stickworten **6446**
Wenckstern, F. von
A Bibliography of the Japanese
Empire **4627**
Wenner, M.W.
The Yemen Arab Republic **4657**
Wepsiec, J.
Sociology **994**
Wer ist wer? Das Deutsche who's who/
The German who's who/Le Who's
who allemand **5827**
Werner, E.T.C.
Dictionary of Chinese mythology **771**
Werner, J.
'Recent literature on organized crime'
3090
Wertheimer, M.
A Brief history of psychology **272**
Wertheimer, M.L.
'Psychology' **235**
Wesseling, H.L.
'Dutch historiography on European
Expansion since 1945' **8106**
Wesson, T.
Nobel Prize winners **5765**
West African sources in British Colonial
Office records **6545**

West, B. W. and Dickinson, R. L.
Street talk in real estate **1936**
The West Bank and Gaza atlas **5363**
West European economic handbook
2226
West Germany **4487**
West India Reference Library
The Catalogue of the West India
Reference Library **4935**
The West Indies **5214**
West Irian **5054**
West Irian Irian Jaya
West Irian **5054**
West, J.
Town Records **7047**
West, J.A.
The Traveller's key to ancient Egypt
6630
West Kalimantan **5048**
Westergaard, D.J.
Modern British society **1125**
Westermann Lexikon der Geographie
5176
Western Europe **4441**
Western Europe 1993 **2225, 4440**
Western European costume … and its
relation to the theatre **3954**
Western European economic
organizations **2320**
Western European political parties **1647**
The Western European powers 1500-
1700 **6786**
Western European statistics **1176**
Western Sahara **4807**
Westfall, G.
Bibliography of official statistical
yearbooks and bulletins **1166**
French colonial Africa **1531**
Westhorp, C.
The World's armies **3452**
Westminster dictionary of Christian
ethics **572**
Westminster dictionary of Christian
theology **541**
The Westminster dictionary of church
history **621**
Weston, R.
Gold **2153**
Wetterau, B.
The New York Public Library book
of chronologies **6451**
World history **6376**
Whalen L
Human rights **3060**
Whaling, F.
Religion in today's world **346**
What about women? Information
sources for women's studies **4025**
'What to read in English religious
history' **653**
'What to read on the history of Wales
before 1536,' **7231**
What was that dance? **4090**

Wheal, E-A.
A Dictionary of the Second World War **6857**

Wheat, J.C. and Brun, C.F.
Maps and charts published in America before 1800 **7995**

Wheatley, K.
National Maritime Museum guide to maritime Britain **5580**

Wheeler-Bennett, J.W.
Documents on international affairs, 1928-1963 **1564**

Wheeler, Sir M.
The Indus civilization **4270**

Whelan, J.
Qatar **4662**

Whelpton, J.
Nepal **4689**

When disaster strikes **135**

When was that? **8157**

Where the waves fall **8114**

Where to find business information **1689, 2448**

Where to study in the UK **3893**

Which degree? **3868**

The Which? guide to Brittany and Normandy **5642**

The Which? guide to Scotland **5592**

The Which? guide to Spain **5647**

The Which? guide to the West Country **5615**

The Which? guide to Yorkshire and the Peak District **5614**

Which subject? Which career? **1889**

Whigham, T.L. and Cooney, J.W.
'Paraguayan history: manuscript sources in the United States' **6582**

While you're away **5138**

Whistler, L.
The English festivals **3974**

Whitaker, H.
A Descriptive list of the printed maps of Yorkshire and its Ridings, 1577-1900 **7216**

Whitaker, J.
An Almanack for the year of Our Lord ... 1868- **948**

Whitaker, R.E.
The Eerdmans analytical concordance to the Revised Standard Version of the Bible **472**

Whitaker, S.
The Good retreat guide **416**

White, A.S.
A Bibliography of regimental histories of the British Army **3471**

White, A.W.R.
Neolithic Europe **4206**

White, J.P. and O'Connell, J.F.
A Prehistory of Australia, New Guinea and Sahul **4298**

White, O.
Our heritage **6590**

White, P.M.
Soviet urban and regional planning **1097**

White, R.
New sources of information, 1973-1989 **162**

White, R.A. and Dale, L.A.
Parapsychology **161**

The White road **8174**

White, S.
Communist and post-Communist political systems **1642**
Handbook of reconstruction in Eastern Europe and the Soviet Union **7246**
The New astrology **174**
Political and economic encyclopedia of the Soviet Union and Eastern Europe **1648**

White supremacy and its associated groups **1059**

Whitehead, G. and Whitehead, D.H.
Pitman business correspondence **2499**

Whitehouse, D. and Whitehouse, R.
Archaeological atlas of the world **4179**

Whitehouse, J.E.
A Police bibliography **3207**

Whitehouse, R.D.
The Macmillan dictionary of archaeology **4171**

Whiteside, R.M.
Major financial institutions of Europe, 1994 **2106**

Whitfield, D.J.
Historical and cultural dictionary of Vietnam **7725**

Whiting, B.J.
Early American proverbs and proverbial phrases **4150**
Modern proverbs and proverbial sayings **4145**

Whiting, B.J. and Whiting, H.W.
Proverbs, sentences and proverbial phrases, from English writings mainly before 1500 **4144**

Whitly, W.T.
Baptist bibliography **717**

Whitmore, E.C. and Perera, S.B.
Dreams: a portal to the source **294**

Whittaker, L.B.
Stand down **6837**

Whittington, C.
'On the road: an annotated list of travel guides', *Reference Books Bulletin 1987-1988*, p.16-19 **5529**

Whittleton, E.H.
'Family history in the Bahamas' **6132**

Whittock, M.J.
The Origins of England 410-600 **6937**

Who first discovered America? **7856**

Who lies where? **5550**

Who lived where in Europe **5532**

Who lived where in the USA **5691**

Who owns what in world banking **2139**

Who owns whom, 1993 **2364**

Who was when **5745**

Who was who .. **5797**

Who was who in America **5963**

Who was who in American politics **1682**

Who was who in Edwardian Scotland **5806**

Who was who in Egyptology **4190**

Who was who in Native American history **8014**

Who was who in the American Revolution **8027**

Who was who in the Civil War **8040**

Who was who in the Greek World **6686**

Who was who in the Roman world **6699**

Who was who in the Soviet Union **5860**

Who were the Pharaohs? **6629**

Who, what, when **4546**

Who's buried where in England **5606**

Who's for health? Community health in developing countries **3597**

Who's really who **5793**

Who's really who in South Africa **5933**

Who's who **5796**

Who's who 1992. The 1992 directory of senior figures across our circulation area **7214**

Who's who among Black Americans 1991-92 **5986**

Who's who among Hispanic Americans 1992-93 **5964**

Who's who in accountancy **2525**

Who's who in Africa **5923**

Who's who in America 1992-1993 **5965**

Who's who in American politics, 1993-94 **1681**

Who's who in Asian and Australasian politics **1410, 1428**

Who's who in Australasia and the Far East **5894**

Who's who in Australia **6029**

Who's who in Austria 1982-1983 **5837**

Who's who in British economics **1789**

Who's who in British history **6924**

Who's who in Canada 1994 **5939**

Who's who in China 1918-1950. With an index compiled by Jerome Cavenaugh **5899**

Who's who in China: current leaders **5902**

Who's who in Church history **623**

Who's who in classical mythology **789**

Who's who in Cumbria 1986 **7224**

Who's who in Cypriote archaeology **4274**

Who's who in economics **1781**

Wiseberg, L.S. *and* Scoble, H.M. *and* Human Rights Internet staff
Human rights directory 3067
Wiseman, J.A.
Botswana 4877
Political leaders in Black Africa 1419
Wises New Zealand guide 5712
Wisniewski, J.
Who's who in Poland 5867
Wistrich, R.
Who's who in Nazi Germany 7292
Witt, H.
Hong Kong 1993 4605
Wittgenstein: a bibliographic guide 132
Wlodarski, B.
Chronologia polska 7331
Woefel, C.J.
Encyclopedia of banking and finance 2031
Woerner, R.K.
The Alaska handbook 5018
Woito, R.S.
To end war 2960
Wolfram, W.
History of the Goths 6666
Wolman, B.B.
Dictionary of behavioral science 253
Handbook of parapsychology 160
International directory of psychology 269
International encyclopedia of psychiatry, psychology, psychoanalysis & neurology 240
Wolman, J.B.
Handbook of developmental psychology 242
Wolpert, S.
A New history of India 7657
Women 4003
Women, 1870-1928 4005
Women and aging 4050
Women and Judaism 4056
Women and society 4016
Women and urban society 1093
Women in American history 4052
Women in American religious history 4048
Women in China 4045
Women in classical mythology 788
Women in developing countries 4036
Women in English social history, 1800-1914 4044
Women in espionage 1613
Women in Ireland 4043
Women in Japanese society 4046
Women in management review and abstracts 2565
Women in particular 5989
Women in South Asia: A guide to resources 4047
Women in the DNB 5791
Women in the Third World 4034-4035
Women in the world 4028

Women in Western European history 4031-4032
Women into the unknown 5135
The Women of England 4029
Women online 4002
Women remembered 4054
Women studies abstracts 4022
Women studies encyclopedia 4020
Women who ruled 6315
Women's collections 4049
Women's education in the Third World - 3777
Women's history sources 4051
Women's London 5624
The Women's movement in the seventies 4014
Women's organizations 4053
Women's studies 4000, 4004, 4015
Women's studies: a bibliography of dissertations, 1870-1982 4011
Women's studies index. 1989- 4023
A Women's thesaurus 4058
The Wonder that was India 7647
Wong, J.
Asian economic handbook 2276
Wood, A.
The History of Siberia 7707
Wood,, A.
The Times guide to the European Parliament, June 1989 2995
Wood, A.
The Times guide to the House of Commons, June 1992 3002
Wood, E.E.
Yoga dictionary 822
Wood, E.S.
Collins field guide to archaeology in Britain 4318
Wood, F.
Chinese studies 4587
Wood, G.A.
Studying New Zealand history 8124
Woodbury, M.
Childhood information resources 3642
A Guide to sources of educational information 3706
Woodcock, R.
The Hamlyn dictionary of geography 5220
Woodcock, T. *and* Robinson, J.M.
The Oxford guide to heraldry 6229
Woodhead, P.
Keyguide to information sources in archaeology 4160
Woodhouse, C.M.
Modern Greece 7530
Woodhouse, T.
The International peace directory 2974
Woods, L.J.
PAIS subject headings 914

Woods, R.D.
Mexican autobiography 5943
Reference materials on Latin America in English 4985
Woods, R.L.
The World treasury of religious quotations 395
Woodward, D.R. *and* Maddox, R.F.
America and World War I 6819
Woodward, J. *and* Burnett, G.
A Treatise on heraldry, British and foreign 6230
Woodward, P.
Sudan 1898-1989 7764
Woodward, R.L.
Belize 4920
El Salvador 4922
Guatemala 4919
Nicaragua 4924
Woodward, Sir L.
British foreign policy in the Second World War 1572
Woodworth, D.
Summer jobs abroad, 1989 1884
Woolnough, K.
Chambers Scottish guides 5587
Words and phrases legally defined 2702
Work on women 4010
Work related abstracts 1868
Work Research Unit Information Service news and abstracts 2582
The Workhouse system, 1834-1929 3549
Working abroad 1881
Working holidays 1882
Working paper series, 1977- 2199
Works on blindness and associated subjects 3635
World advertising review 2639
The World affairs companion 4416
World agricultural economics and rural sociology abstracts (WAERSA) 1768
The World almanac & book of facts, 1993 949
The World Almanac biographical dictionary 5748
The World Almanac Book of World War II 6858
The World Almanac directory of dates 6452
The World almanac of the American West 8000
World Almanac of the USA 4994
The World almanac of US politics, 1993-1995 1424
World: an excerpt from the British Museum 'Catalogue of printed maps, charts and plans.' 5501
World armies 3366
World army uniforms since 1939 3405
The World atlas of archaeology 4180
World atlas of elections 1492

Subject Index

The index reference is to the running number given to each item. The running numbers are in one sequence throughout the volume and can be found at the top right-hand corner of the entry for each item.

The index is computer generated, thus terms for the index have been largely derived from the headings and sub-headings used throughout *Walford*, but many other entries have been added, including synonyms, inverted headings, and cross-references. Some form headings such as 'Bibliographies', 'Dictionaries', etc., are omitted as leading to too great a bulk.

The arrangement of the index is alphabetical and filing is word by word, with groups of initials counted as single words. Under each main heading printed in bold type in the index will be found a resumé of all the subject terms used under that heading and the numbers of the items to which they refer. Similarly, under each narrower sub-heading there is a list of terms used. Where the term in the index needs to be qualified by the broader term of which it is a sub-division, then the broader term is given in square brackets, *e.g.* **Malta** [Archives] or [Statistics].

Business Organization (Economics)
(contd.)
Africa
  Bibliographies **1992**
America — North **1993**
Asia
  Periodicals & Progress Reports
  1990
  Bibliographies **1948-1953**
  Biographies **1976**
  Databases **1946-1947**
  Dictionaries **1955**
    Arabic **1967**
    English **1962-1964**
    French **1965-1966**
    Japanese **1968-1969**
    Laws **1956**
    Polyglot **1957-1961**
  Great Britain **1977-1979**
    Biographies **1986**
    Databases **1980**
    Histories **1985**
    Periodicals **1982**
    Reports Literature **1981**
    Yearbooks & Directories **1983-**
    1984
Handbooks & Manuals **1954**
Italy
  Bibliographies **1988**
Japan
  Bibliographies **1991**
Libraries **1999-2000**
Mergers **2019-2021**
Monopolies
  Dictionaries **2018**
Multinationals
  Bibliographies **2003**
  Dictionaries **2004**
  Yearbooks & Directories **2005**
Private Firms
  Great Britain **2001**
  USA **2002**
Quotations **1972-1974**
Reports Literature
  Bibliographies **1970**
Scotland
  Bibliographies **1987**
Small Businesses **2006-2007**
  Bibliographies **2008-2013**
  Europe—Western **2016**
  Handbooks & Manuals **2014-2015**
  USA **2017**
Tables & Data Books **1975**
USA
  Bibliographies **1994**
  Histories **1996-1998**
  Periodicals & Progress Reports
  1995
USSR
  Bibliographies **1989**
  Yearbooks & Directories **1971**
Business Relationships (Economics)
  1943-1944

Business Relationships (Economics)
(contd.)
Abbreviations & Symbols **1945**
Africa
  Bibliographies **1992**
America — North **1993**
Asia
  Periodicals & Progress Reports
  1990
  Bibliographies **1948-1953**
  Biographies **1976**
  Databases **1946-1947**
  Dictionaries **1955**
    Arabic **1967**
    English **1962-1964**
    French **1965-1966**
    Japanese **1968-1969**
    Laws **1956**
    Polyglot **1957-1961**
  Great Britain **1977-1979**
    Biographies **1986**
    Databases **1980**
    Histories **1985**
    Periodicals **1982**
    Reports Literature **1981**
    Yearbooks & Directories **1983-**
    1984
Handbooks & Manuals **1954**
Italy
  Bibliographies **1988**
Japan
  Bibliographies **1991**
Libraries **1999-2000**
Mergers **2019-2021**
Monopolies
  Dictionaries **2018**
Multinationals
  Bibliographies **2003**
  Dictionaries **2004**
  Yearbooks & Directories **2005**
Private Firms
  Great Britain **2001**
  USA **2002**
Quotations **1972-1974**
Reports Literature
  Bibliographies **1970**
Scotland
  Bibliographies **1987**
Small Businesses **2006-2007**
  Bibliographies **2008-2013**
  Europe—Western **2016**
  Handbooks & Manuals **2014-2015**
  USA **2017**
Tables & Data Books **1975**
USA
  Bibliographies **1994**
  Histories **1996-1998**
  Periodicals & Progress Reports
  1995
USSR
  Bibliographies **1989**
  Yearbooks & Directories **1971**
Business Schools **2437**

Businesses **2364**
Archives **2375**
Asia—Far East **2407**
Australia
  Biographies **2419**
  Bibliographies **2368-2369**
Canada **2410**
Databases **2365-2367**
Dictionaries
  Polyglot **2370**
Eire
  Yearbooks & Directories **2400**
England
  Histories **2401-2404**
Europe **2381**
Europe—Eastern
  Yearbooks & Directories **2390**
Europe—Western
  Handbooks & Manuals **2385-2386**
  Yearbooks & Directories **2387-**
  2389
Europe
  Biographies **2384**
  Yearbooks & Directories **2382-**
  2383
Germany **2405**
Great Britain
  Archives **2399**
  Biographies **2398**
  Histories **2394-2397**
  Yearbooks & Directories **2391-**
  2393
Histories **2371-2373**
Islamic World **2409**
Japan
  Yearbooks & Directories **2408**
Latin America **2411**
Official Records **2374**
USA
  Bibliographies **2412-2413**
  Biographies **2417-2418**
  Yearbooks & Directories **2414-**
  2416
USSR **2406**
Worldwide
  Yearbooks & Directories **2376-**
  2380
Businesses, Small **2006-2007**
  Bibliographies **2008-2013**
  Europe—Western **2016**
  Handbooks & Manuals **2014-2015**
  USA **2017**
Byzantium (History)
  Bibliographies **7686**
  Biographies **7689**
  Dictionaries **7688**
  Handbooks & Manuals **7687**
Caernarvonshire (History) **7238**
Cambodia (History) **7722-7723**
Cambridgeshire (History) **7193**
Cameroon
  Bibliographies **4842-4844, 5384**
  [Area Studies] **4841-4844**

Online and Database Services Index

The index reference is to the running number given to each item. The running numbers are in one sequence throughout the volume and can be found at the top right hand corner of the entry for each item. This index is of authors and titles in one sequence. The names of authors are printed in bold type. Filing is word by word with groups of initials counted as single words.

The titles appearing in this index have been published as electronic databases. The databases are available on subscription as online database services, or in CD-ROM or disk formats. An indication of the names of some of the hosts from whom the online databases are available is given in the text.